S0-BRR-722

LITERATURE

of the

WESTERN WORLD

LITERATURE
of the
WESTERN WORLD
The Ancient World
Through the Renaissance

fourth edition

volume I

Brian Wilkie   James Hurt
University of Arkansas   *University of Illinois*

PRENTICE HALL, Upper Saddle River, New Jersey 07458

Library of Congress Cataloging-in-Publication Data

Literature of the western world / [compiled by] Brian Wilkie
and James Hurt.—4th ed.
   p.   cm.
Includes bibliographical references and indexes.
Contents: —v. 1. Ancient world through the renaissance.
ISBN 0-13-220872-5 (pbk. : v. 1)
   1. Literature—Collections.   I. Wilkie, Brian.
II. Hurt, James.
PN6014.L615   1997
808.8—dc20   96-20978
                                                    CIP

Production editor: Joan E. Foley
Editorial director: Charlyce Jones Owen
Executive editor: Nancy Perry
Editorial assistant: Joan Polk
Marketing manager: Gina Sluss
Senior managing editor: Bonnie Biller
Copy editor: Mary Louise Byrd
Permissions researcher: Frederick Courtright
Production assistant: Yvonne Thrower
Prepress and manufacturing buyer: Mary Ann Gloriande
Cover design director: Jayne Conte
Cover art: Stilleben Mit Krug und Afrikanischer Schale by Ernst Ludwig Kirchner.
   Christie's, London/Superstock

This book was set in 10/11 Baskerville by Lithokraft II
and was printed and bound by Rand McNally. The cover was printed
by The Lehigh Press, Inc.

For permission to use copyrighted material, grateful acknowledgment
is made to the copyright holders starting on page 2223, which are
hereby made part of this copyright page.

Printed in the United States of America
10 9 8 7 6 5 4 3 2

ISBN 0-13-220872-5
ISBN 0-13-272352-2 (Instructor's
Edition)

Prentice-Hall International (UK) Limited, London
Prentice-Hall of Australia Pty. Limited, Sydney
Prentice-Hall Canada Inc., Toronto
Prentice-Hall Hispanoamericana, S.A., Mexico
Prentice-Hall of India Private Limited, New Delhi
Prentice-Hall of Japan, Inc., Tokyo
Simon & Schuster Asia Pte. Ltd., Singapore
Editora Prentice-Hall do Brasil, Ltda., Rio de Janeiro

Contents

Preface

The first edition of *Literature of the Western World*, which appeared in 1984, was intended to provide the best possible resource for survey courses in world literature. With this goal in mind, the editors committed themselves to several principles. First, no author was to be represented by a mere snippet. Almost all works were to be presented in their entirety, or—for those few works such as *Don Quixote* too long to be included complete—in substantial and readable abridgments, with omitted parts summarized where summaries were feasible and appropriate. Second, the anthology was to offer a wide range of choices. The book was to be capacious enough to include far more in each volume than would be read in any one version of the course. Whenever possible, more than one selection by an author was to be included so as to offer either a choice or an opportunity to compare and trace common themes through two or three works. This inclusiveness would make it possible for teachers to tailor their assignments to their individual needs and tastes, for students to "read around" the assigned texts and follow up special interests, and for students to take away from the course a basic collection of world literature for their personal libraries. Third, the book was to use the best translations available, the ones that best combined accuracy and sensitivity to the original with readability. This did not always mean—though it frequently did—selecting the most recent or the best-known translations; it did mean choosing the translations that best revealed why the originals were great works of art. Fourth, the anthology was to be timely, presenting works that engage the interest of contemporary experts and general readers alike. Every effort was made to bring alive a work's context, through extensive historical, cultural, and biographical information, along with a few avenues for critical interpretation. Fifth, and most important, the anthology was to be as useful as possible to both teachers and students. Period and author introductions were to be not only informative but also clear in content, style, and format. Notes were to be full and strictly pertinent, and such aids as diagrams, chronologies, and suggestions for further reading were to be provided wherever they would be helpful. The book, in short, was to supply everything needed up to the point where instruction begins without usurping the instructor's responsibility for—and delight in—exploration and interpretation.

The enthusiastic reception given *Literature of the Western World* in its first three editions encouraged the editors to believe that their principles were sound and that they had succeeded in providing the sort of textbook needed for world literature courses. The response to the collection from users of the book throughout the United States did not suggest a need for any basic changes in the conception of the book. Therefore, the underlying goals of

xiii

this fourth edition remain the same as those of the first three: complete works, a range of choice, the best translations, a contemporary point of view, and ample support material. Within these boundaries, however, a great many changes, both large and small, have been made to keep the book up to date and to bring it even closer to what teachers tell us they would like to have.

In general, our policy in making changes has been to leave the great masterpieces of each period in place while enriching them with other arresting contemporary works, thereby rendering the period in three-dimensional relief or simply fleshing it out. At the same time, we have been able to streamline the books slightly by trimming works that teachers told us were seldom taught. The result, we hope, is a set of volumes that meet the needs of teachers and students even more precisely. In the section on the Ancient World, we have responded to many requests by including the Mesopotamian epic *Gilgamesh*, dating from two millennia before Christ. In the Middle Ages section, we have added selections from the *Koran*, to parallel our selections from the Hebrew and Christian bibles. We have also restored the popular *Song of Roland* from our second edition. Other additions to the medieval selections include Andreas Capellanus's *Art of Courtly Love*, the Proofs of the Existence of God of Saints Anselm and Aquinas, and the charming English romance, *Sir Gawain and the Green Knight*. Changes in the Renaissance section include an alternative translation of Machiavelli's *The Prince* and the substitution of Shakespeare's *Henry IV, Part 1*, for *King Lear*. In Volume II, we have complied with a number of requests by substituting Goethe's *Faust, Part 1*, for *The Sorrows of Young Werther*. (In an ideal world, perhaps we could have both.) We have added Mary Shelley's haunting *Frankenstein*, a novel which seems to generate more critical interest each year, as technology continues to raise hard questions about people and their machines. We have strengthened our representation of certain Modernist concerns by adding Isak Dinesen's tragicomic novella *Babette's Feast*, about the confrontation of two cultures; Italo Calvino's sophisticated postmodern narrative "Under the Jaguar Sun"; Cynthia Ozick's harrowing tale of the Holocaust, *The Shawl*; and Jamaica Kincaid's tale of growing up female and colonized, *Annie John*.

For the new selections, as for the old, we have devoted a great deal of attention to identifying and obtaining rights to the best translations. *Gilgamesh* appears in the distinguished contemporary treatment by David Ferry. Our new Ovid selections are in engagingly colloquial renderings by Peter Green and Daryl Hine. The *Koran* appears in Arthur J. Arberry's version, by all odds the most honored English interpretation. For *The Song of Roland*, we have retained the Patricia Terry translation, which won approval in our first and second editions, and for *Sir Gawain and the Green Knight*, we have used the translation by Theodore Howard Banks, Jr., which reproduces quite accurately the metrical form of the original. Goethe's *Faust* appears in a version by the distinguished American poet Randall Jarrell, and Italo Calvino has been rendered by his authorized translator, William Weaver.

Besides major changes in selections, innumerable small changes were made in presentation. Introductions have been revised, in some cases heavily, and many annotations have been rewritten for thoroughness and clarity. With help from Mary Comstock, Suzanne McCray, and Matthew Conner, we have revised and updated the suggestions for further reading to take into account recent, in some cases major, work on some of our authors in the last few years. We remain, however, deeply indebted to Nancy K. Barry, Frances Stickney Newman, and Willard J. Rusch for the bibliographies they compiled for the first edition and have continued to signal this debt by using their respective initials where appropriate. As in earlier editions, our aim has been to list works that are reliable and authoritative for non-expert readers; many works indispensable to advanced scholarly study have been consciously omitted.

To attempt to represent five thousand years of literature in a pair of books, even large ones, is a quixotic undertaking. But we believe that our fourth-edition changes have moved the book closer to our goals. In any anthology, the part must stand for the whole. We have tried to represent the great national literatures of the West—French, German, Russian, Spanish, English, American—in a balanced if necessarily noncomprehensive way. We have also been concerned to represent literature by women with an approach to adequacy and to include works by both women and men that explore issues of gender, from Christine de Pizan's *Book of the City of Ladies* and Marguerite de Navarre's *Heptameron* through Mme de La Fayette's *Princesse de Clèves,* Ibsen's *A Doll House* and Chopin's *The Awakening* to Woolf's *A Room of One's Own* and Jamaica Kincaid's *Annie John.* Care has been taken to present a balanced range of genres, from the sweep of epic to the miniature world of the lyric poem. Seventeen plays are included: a sizable drama anthology within the larger one. We are especially proud of our representation of prose fiction. Our decision, taken in the early stages of planning the anthology, not to represent the novel by one massive text but rather to enlarge the area of choice has been vindicated by the users of the book. Our four novels—*The Princesse de Clèves, Frankenstein, The Awakening,* and *Annie John*—supplemented by such substantial novellas and other prose narratives as *Candide, Narrative of the Life of an American Slave, Notes from Underground, The Death of Ivan Ilyitch, Dora, Heart of Darkness, The Metamorphosis, Babette's Feast,* and *The Shawl* represent half a dozen national literatures and a wide range of prose forms. We hope that *Literature of the Western World,* fourth edition, will please its many old friends and win new ones.

Among old friends are a great many who took an active part in planning and advising on this edition. They include: Ruth Albrecht, Lane Community College; Katya Amato, Portland State University; Michael Atkinson, University of Cincinnati; Michael Beard, University of North Dakota; M. Susan Beck, University of Wisconsin—River Falls; Stephen C. Behrendt, University of Nebraska; Rebecca B. Chalmers, University of Maryland—Eastern Shore; John O. Clements, Indiana State University; Konrad A. Czynski, Moorhead State University; Kathy Wantangasa Dickison, Lexington Community College; Joan Digby, C.W. Post Campus, Long Island University; James G. Dixon III, Grove City College; Michael Eckert, Montgomery College; Walter Everett, University of Southern Indiana; Frank Ficarra, California State University—Chico; Adam Fischer, Coastal Carolina Community College; Andrea Glebe, University of Nevada—Las Vegas; Myrna Goldenberg, Montgomery College; John H. Gottcent, University of Southern Indiana; Virginia B. Guilford, Bowie State University; John Hagge, Iowa State University; Karen C. Hatch, California State University—Chico; Dennis R. Hoilman, Ball State University; Bruce W. Hozeski, Ball State University; Michael Johmann, University of Louisville; Anna Joy, Sacramento City College; Elaine B. Kalmar, University of Northern Iowa; Ann Kimbrough, University of Minnesota; Lawrence F. Laban, Virginia

Commonwealth University; Gerald M. Lary, Angelo State University; Joe Lenz, Drake University; Thomas E. Lewis, University of Iowa; Gregory Mason, Gustavus Adolphus College; Jack Miller, Normandale Community College; Joyce M. Miller, Collin County Community College; Deanne G. Minahan, University of Wisconsin—Superior; Rob Modica, Pima Community College—East Campus; Kevin Morris, Greenville Technical College; Ronald D. Morrison, Morehead State University; Alan F. Nagel, University of Iowa; Jeff Nelms, Tarrant County Jr. College, NE; Thomas Parker, California State University—Chico; James D. Pendleton, Virginia Commonwealth University; Sue Pine, Florida Community College at Jacksonville; Mary Sue Ply, Southeastern Louisiana University; Ron Reed, Hazard Community College; Karl C. Sandberg, Macalester College; Judith Saunders, Marist College.

For advice on particular authors and periods we warmly thank Charles Hansford Adams, Lynn Altenbernd, John Bateman, Susan Bazargan, Barbara Bowen, Vincent Bowen, Edward Brandabur, David Bright, Jackson Campbell, Joseph Candido, Robert Cochran, Howard Cole, John Dussinger, Karen Ford, Chester Fontenot, Eva Frayne, John Frayne, John Friedman, Stanley Gray, Achsah Guibbory, Jan Hinely, Bernard Hirsch, Frank Hodgins, Allan Holaday, Anthony Kaufman, David Kay, Keneth Kinnamon, Joan Klein, Dale Kramer, John Locke, James Marchand, Donald Masterson, Linda Mazer, Michael Mullin, Cary Nelson, John K. Newman, Michael Palencia-Roth, William Quinn, Vernon Robbins, Michael Shapiro, Charles Shattuck, Janet Levarie Smarr, Arnold Stein, Dorothy Stephens, Jack Stillinger, Zohreh Sullivan, Benjamin Uroff, Leon Waldoff, Emily Watts, and Richard Wheeler.

For conceiving the idea of this anthology and providing expert guidance throughout the project, we thank D. Anthony English. Our production editor Joan Foley performed intelligently and heroically the immense task of guiding the book through the press. The alertness, sensitivity to style, and literary expertise of our copyeditor, Mary Louise Byrd, and of Ann Wilkie have been of great value. For further help with copyediting and proofreading, we are deeply indebted to Elisabeth Fleshler and Mary Deeg. Technical help in preparing the manuscript was provided by Rhonda Benish Adams, Chad Andrews, Mary Comstock, and Nancy Saunders. Especially helpful in this capacity was Amanda Benish, who performed several demanding tasks under pressure, meticulously and with dispatch.

Brian Wilkie

James Hurt

LITERATURE

of the

WESTERN WORLD

The Ancient World

*T*HE "ancient world," as it is represented in this book, consists mainly of three civilizations that flourished in the millennium before Christ in a comparatively small area around the Mediterranean Sea: those of the ancient Hebrews, the Greeks, and the Romans. One of our selections, the *Gilgamesh* epic, opens a window on the even older Mesopotamian world out of which the Hebrew culture emerged and which was to condition that culture in many ways. To the farsighted anthropologist taking a long view of time, such a sampling of the ancient world would be too limited both chronologically and geographically. By the second millennium B.C., humankind was already old upon the earth and had created many other civilizations, some of them highly developed. Some of them, too, flourished in areas far from the Mediterranean—in the Orient, in Africa, and in the Americas. Nevertheless, it is to the Hebrews, the Greeks, and the Romans that we look for the main literary traditions of Western culture that concern this anthology. These traditions are the riverhead of Western literature, although we can discern other contributions near the source and continuing tributary streams from Africa and the East.

The core of Hebrew culture has always been religion, and it is through religion that it has most strongly influenced the Western world. It would be neither possible nor very useful to review here the course of the development of the Hebrews' culture and conception of God. But much of their view of the world is summed up in the prophet Micah's deceptively simple words: "He has showed you, O man, what is good; and what does the Lord require of you but to do justice, and to love kindness, and to walk humbly with your God?" No Greek or Roman could have written, or even have understood, these words. They imply a cluster of ideas wholly alien to the Greek and Roman worldviews but at the very heart of Hebraism: the existence of a single God, from whom the idea of "the good" derives, and a moral role for human beings in which they, along with everything else, are subordinated to God. (Micah's terms for ethical behavior in this world—"justice" and "kindness"—would not have puzzled either a Greek or a Roman, but both would have defined these words differently.) The Hebrew "Yahveh" came to be the God of all mankind and, at the same time, the God of each individual. The result of this personal relationship was a stress upon individual experience, an emphasis upon conscience (including a social conscience), and a concentration upon introspection and the spiritual life. The Hebrews were continually involved in negotiations, individual and collective, with a father-God.

The course of Greek thought was significantly different. When the people we now know as Greeks began to filter into the Greek peninsula about

1

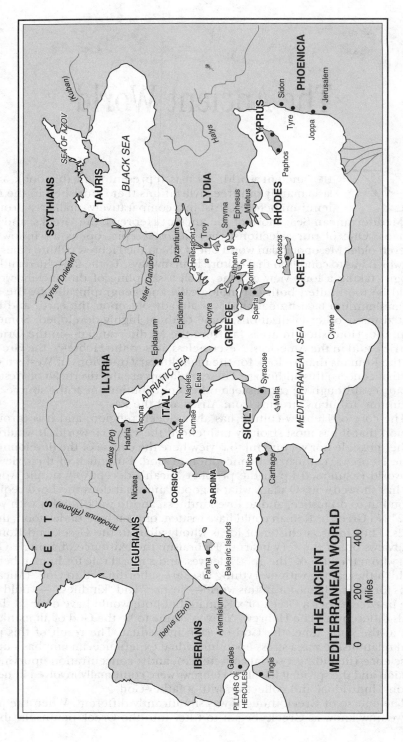

THE ANCIENT MEDITERRANEAN WORLD

2000 B.C., they brought with them a primitive polytheism based on personifications of natural forces, which they humanized and attempted to propitiate by means of prayers, libations, and sacrifices. Greek religion changed and developed, of course, over its long history, but even in its most fully developed form it carried few if any implications for morality or conscience in the Hebrew sense. The Greek gods were superior to humans, in power, beauty, and immortality, but they were not ethically superior, and, unlike Yahveh, they did not demand that people follow an exacting code of morality. The Greeks looked not to their gods for an ethical code, but to their own reason and innate sense of the good. The result was a culture that seems, even to a modern "post-Christian" reader, remarkably serene and guiltfree. The Greeks, it has been said, had a strong sense of crime, but none at all of sin.

The Greeks found the main significance of life not in the relation of human beings with God, but in human beings' relations with themselves and with their fellows. If, for the sake of focus, we simplify the Greek view of the world as we did the Hebrew, we may find it stated best in the mottoes the Greeks inscribed over the gates of the temple to Apollo at Delphi: "Know thyself" and "Nothing too much." An ancient Hebrew would have misunderstood these phrases as badly as an ancient Greek would have misunderstood Micah's words. "Knowing" oneself implied to a Greek none of the spiritual struggles or the wrestling with angels with which the Hebrew was preoccupied. People came to know themselves in Greece through experience, through involvement in the world. The crucial tableau in Hebrew history is one person alone on a mountaintop, learning directly from God "what is good." The Greeks had their mountaintops, too, but the messages they received there from the gods were characteristically riddling and enigmatic; the responsibility for knowledge was thrown squarely back upon the questioner. The Greek tableau corresponding to the person on the mountaintop is a group of people in lively, earnest conversation, exercising the privilege Socrates said was characteristic of free citizens: "They can have their talk out in peace, wandering at will from one subject to another, their only aim to attain the truth."

Or the emblematic tableau might be a group of people at the great Olympic Games, competing in athletics or in horseracing, drama, music, or poetry; or it could be the audience at a production of an Aeschylean tragedy at the City Dionysia in the theater of Dionysus in Athens. For to the Greeks there were no sharp divisions between the intellectual, physical, and spiritual sides of human nature. To "know oneself" was to know one's mind, body, and spirit as a harmonious balanced system. The Greek view of human nature as a seamless unity was so deep and so thoroughgoing that it provides a stumbling block to our understanding of their institutions and their literature. We attend class, or watch the Rose Bowl on television, or go to a play or to church, and all of these are separate activities, each carried on by specialists and directed at different aspects of our personalities. It is hard for us to understand the very different Greek attitude toward, for example, the Great Games, in which the same contestants might compete in the five athletic events of the *pentathlon* and in music and poetry. The Games were a religious festival as well, dedicated to the worship of Zeus or Apollo or Poseidon. And were the great dramatic festivals artistic events or religious ceremonies? The Greeks would not have understood such a question, any more than they would have understood our attempts to distinguish between "sin" and "error" in

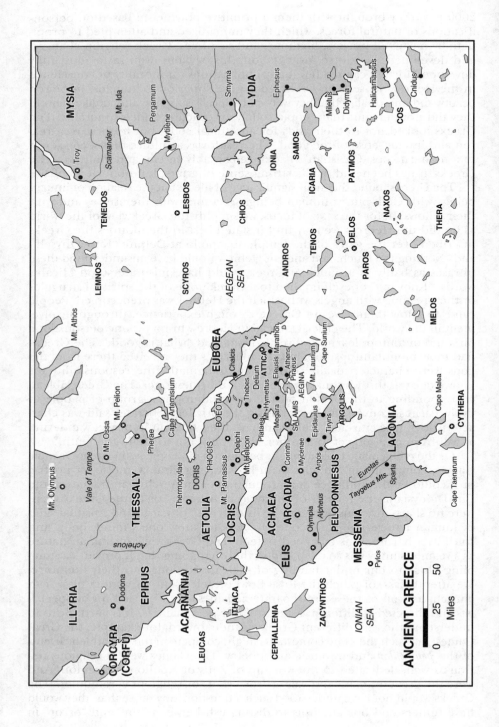

ANCIENT GREECE

0 25 50 Miles

Ancient Greece. NOTE: Some of the names below are spelled in various ways by translators. Asterisks (*) indicate the places described in the list.

ARCADIA. Setting of much ancient pastoral poetry.

ARGOS. In Aeschylus, the city of Agamemnon, Clytemnestra, Orestes, and Electra.

CORCYRA (Corfu). Conjectural home island of the Phaeacians in Homer's *Odyssey*.

CORINTH. Center of wealth, commerce, and shipbuilding; setting of Euripides' *Medea*.

CYTHERA. Island where Aphrodite came to land after being born of the sea foam.

DELOS. Birthplace of Apollo and Artemis.

DELPHI. Site of the great oracle of Apollo; the center of Greek prophetic utterance. The Omphalos (Navelstone), believed to be the center of the earth, was located there.

DODONA. Site of the great oracle of Zeus.

HELICON. Mountain sacred to the Muses; location of the Hippocrene, the fountain of poetic inspiration.

ITHACA. Home island of Odysseus.

LESBOS. Home island of Sappho.

MARATHON. Plain (26 miles from Athens) where the Greeks defeated the Persians in 490 B.C.

MYCENAE. Center of a great ancient culture; in Homer, the city of Agamemnon.

OLYMPIA. With Delphi, one of the two greatest religious centers of Greece; site of the ancient Olympic Games.

OLYMPUS. Mountain home of the gods.

OSSA, PELION. Mountains piled atop one another in an attempt by the Titans to take the gods by storm.

PARNASSUS. Mountain associated with Apollo and the Muses and hence with learning and the arts.

PELION. See Ossa.

PLATAEA. Site of victory by the Greeks, under Pausanias, over the Persians in 479 B.C.

PYLOS. Home of Nestor; visited by Telemachus in Homer's *Odyssey*.

SALAMIS. Site of defeat of Xerxes and the Persian navy by the Greeks in 480 B.C.

SPARTA. Principal enemy of Athens in the Peloponnesian War (431–404 B.C.); home of Menelaus and Helen of Troy in Homer's *Odyssey*.

THEBES. City of Oedipus and Antigone.

THERMOPYLAE. A mountain pass heroically defended in 480 B.C. by the Spartans, under Leonidas, against the Persian invaders.

TROY. Site of the Trojan War, fought by the Greeks to reclaim Helen.

5

such dramatic characters as King Oedipus. In institutions, as in human personalities, the Greeks did not differentiate the spirit, the mind, and the flesh.

The other Delphic inscription, "Nothing too much," is also a deceptively simple statement. The concept does not suggest a timid moderation, "playing it safe," but something almost the opposite. It insists that people confront reality unflinchingly, refusing the temptation to retreat into defensive and self-deluding inflations and exaggerations. This principle is consistent with "knowing oneself," since self-knowledge ends in accepting what it is to be human and avoiding the temptation to be either less or more than human. Morally, exaggeration and excess manifest themselves in *hubris,* which is not just pride but also a self-deluding rejection of human limitations. To the fifth-century Greeks, the luxurious and despotic Persian emperor Xerxes represented the sort of overweening man who closed his eyes to human boundaries and whom the gods delighted in cutting down. Greek tragedy is full of parallel examples of people who fall through their attempts to be something other than human. Artistically, the principle of "nothing too much" was also expressed in a deep dislike of any elaboration or ornamentation that shielded the viewer from a direct view of "the thing itself." Greek art, whether it be the epics of Homer, the architecture of the Parthenon, or a sculpted Apollo, is characterized by a direct, unblinking view of reality and a combination of passion and restraint that is the essence of classicism. This is not to say that Greek art was "realistic" in the modern sense. Idealization— the attempt to capture the essence of a thing—was also fundamental to Greek art. But the ideal originated in the recognizable.

The leisure which made possible the Greeks' passionate but clear-eyed exploration of themselves and the world around them had a price: slavery and the subjugation of women. The Greek male was freed from demanding physical labor by the existence of a sizable slave class, made up mostly of "barbarians" (non-Greeks) captured in war. The institution of slavery was rarely questioned by the Greeks; one of the ironies of history is that its most freedom-loving culture accepted slavery, for the most part, as a matter of course. Nor did women share in the free exploration of the world men enjoyed. Greek women had few rights and were confined to the home. They managed domestic matters, and they bore and raised the children (at least in Athens; customs differed among the city-states). Greek children were almost exclusively in the company of women until the age of seven and then were rigidly segregated by sex; the result, predictably, was a perpetuation of traditional attitudes on the part of Greek women and a deep-seated distrust and even fear of women on the part of Greek men. This fear expressed itself in widespread homosexuality ("Greek love"), a rigid compartmentalization of sexual qualities, a glorification of "male" at the expense of "female" qualities, and a mythology full of female fright-figures, from the shrewish Hera to the Medusa, whose gaze turned men to stone, to the fearsome Furies, goddesses of blood vengeance, to the fierce Medea, who killed her children to avenge herself upon her faithless husband. (There were, of course, idealized women in myth, too: Athena, the patroness of Athens, was the goddess of wisdom.) The tragedian Euripides, in many ways an ironic commentator upon the ways of his contemporaries, questioned his culture's attitudes toward both slaves and women, but his was a rare voice in an intensely male-oriented society.

6

Greek culture reached its peak in the fifth century B.C. and was centered in Athens, which dominated the city-states of the peninsula and its islands for most of the century. But the power of Athens and Greece alike was severely eroded during a series of bitter internecine wars which ended in 338 B.C. when the kingdom of Macedonia conquered Greece. Greek art and learning had a brief Indian summer, the third-century "Hellenistic" (as opposed to the earlier "Hellenic") period, in the city of Alexandria in northern Egypt. Greek culture maintained some of its integrity through the days of the Roman Empire, and it passed on part of its legacy to Christianity. But the deathblow to even nominal Greek political independence came in 146 B.C., when the armies of the rising Republic of Rome marched into Greece and turned it into a mere province for the growing Roman Empire.

If the Hebrews looked to God for the meaning of life and the Greeks looked for it in the world around them, the Romans looked to earthly, human authority. It was a Roman, Horace, who wrote that it is "sweet and seemly to die for one's country," a phrase which encapsulates a number of Roman attitudes, including the subordination of the individual to the state, an obsession with death, and the cultivation of a stoic denial of personal feeling. Many Greeks suffered or risked death for their country, but it is hard to imagine their idealizing their sacrifice in this way. The Roman tableau to match the Hebrew on a mountaintop and the Greek talking with friends might be the uniformed centurion marching in a column behind his commander to triumph or death. The Roman Empire took shape over centuries of constant war; in our first glimpse of Rome at the end of the sixth century B.C., it is at war, attacking neighbor after neighbor until by 133 B.C. the nation was the undisputed ruler of the whole Mediterranean. The Roman virtues were those of the soldier: discipline, control, and obedience to authority.

Authority hedged the Roman around from earliest childhood. The Roman family was a miniature of the state, headed by a stern father whose power was almost absolute. He owned all the property and could, by writing a letter, divorce his wife or even condemn her to death. The Greek family, male-oriented as it was, was never patriarchal in the Roman sense; the Greek grew up thinking of himself as an individual, but the Roman was above all else a member of a family and, later, of a clan and a nation. Roman religion reinforced these feelings of subordination to authority. The earliest Roman religion, which continued to be the domestic religion throughout the years of the empire, rested on a belief in spirits that inhabited particular localities; each household had its own *lares, penates,* and *manes,* which, respectively, watched over its lands and buildings, guarded the family's other possessions, and embodied the spirits of its male ancestors. Romans must have grown up feeling that they were constantly observed by such spirits. When the more generalized gods of the Romans—Jupiter, Juno, Venus, and Mars—were merged, under Greek influence, with the Greek pantheon of Zeus, Hera, Aphrodite, and Ares, the result was a state religion the outward observances of which were enforced with a rigidity totally alien to the Greek mentality. In the late Empire, Stoic philosophy deeply influenced thoughtful Romans; it has been called the true Roman religion. Although Stoicism originated with a Greek—Zeno of Citium—its emphasis on endurance and the repression of feeling made a strong appeal to the Romans' instinct for authority. The version of Stoicism developed in Rome taught the individual to sub-

7

own will to the family, to the state, and to God. He was to do his duty without question, cultivating self-denial and impassive reserve. Altogether, the Stoic view of the world was ideally suited to the Roman temperament.

The great Roman contribution to civilization was the instrument of social organization—law. The Romans were able to extend their sway over so much of the world and maintain it so long because wherever they went they brought with them the concept of authority. In their system, no one was wholly exempt from the rule of an impersonal force. Forbidding as such impersonality may seem, it also left a cherished legacy to posterity. We owe to the Romans the principles that a person must be assumed innocent until proven guilty, that the law must be applied judiciously, with due regard to the particular situation, and that all individuals are equal before the law.

Roman art was largely derivative from the Greeks. After 272 B.C., when the Romans captured the Greek city of Tarentum, Greek artists and scholars poured into Rome, and as Horace expressed it, "Conquered Greece took captive her fierce conqueror." Roman architecture, sculpture, drama, poetry, and painting were all copied from Greek models, often with a considerable distortion through inflation, as in the gigantic Roman temples copied from small Greek originals, or through refinement, as in Seneca's polished imitations of Greek tragedy.

In a survey of ancient literature (even that of the cultures represented in this book), variety is more apparent than unity. But we can follow a few threads related to the development of the major literary genres: narrative, drama, poetry, and expository literary prose.

The characteristic narrative forms of the ancient world are the folktale, the epic, and the history. We may pass over the folktale fairly quickly, since our knowledge of it in the ancient world is indirect and inferential. We know that a large body of folk narrative must have been in oral circulation since earliest times among the Hebrews, the Greeks, and the Romans. But these tales have reached us only as they were incorporated into written narratives. We can detect signs of them in, for example, *Gilgamesh*, the Hebrew Bible, Homer, and Virgil.

In narrative, the greatest achievement of the ancient world was the epic. Long heroic poems seem to be a natural form in most early literatures. There are the Exodus epic in the Bible and the *Iliad* and the *Odyssey* at the dawn of Greek literature. But we can also point to, among others, the Babylonian *Gilgamesh* (c. 2000 B.C.), the Indian *Mahabharata* (A.D. 350–500), the Old English *Beowulf* (eighth century A.D.), and the German *Nibelungenlied* (c. A.D. 1200). These are all "folk epics"—that is, although they may have been put into final form by single authors, they were developed by folk poets, over extended periods of time, from traditional materials that dealt with the legendary histories of their peoples.

The folk epics have a wide variety of forms, but they are linked by certain recurring characteristics. Though not all are regarded as, like the Bible, "sacred books," all hold special places in their cultures as major statements of national or cultural identity. They purport to tell the stories of the formation or the early history of an entire people; thus they are never regarded as mere fictional entertainment but are held in some degree of reverence. All of them, too, center on heroes, drawn from history or legend, who are regarded not merely as individuals but as embodiments of the special values

8

of their cultures. The settings are vast, ranging across nations or the entire world. Even when the action is confined to a limited place, as in Homer's *Iliad,* that place is the scene of great events determining the fate of nations. The action is similarly grand, involving deeds that exemplify extraordinary qualities treasured by the culture, especially military prowess, physical strength, and spiritual force. Often the action takes the hero on a journey which consists of a series of trials testing his heroism. The gods of the culture often involve themselves in the action, as the Lord does in the Exodus story, or as, in a very different way, the Olympian gods enter the plots of the Homeric epics. The style is at once exalted and simple, grand but not highly embellished. And the point of view is objective; the action is seen from an impersonal angle, without authorial intrusion and with the emphasis on external action rather than inner motivations.

The epic form captured the imaginations of a great many poets who attempted to incorporate its qualities in original works, or art epics. In addition to employing the features of folk epics, these poets developed a number of epic conventions, which refine and develop the features inherent in the folk epic, especially the epics of Homer. The art epic opens with a statement of a grand governing theme and an invocation to an appropriate muse to inspire and instruct the poet. The poet plunges *in medias res,* or "into the middle of things," with earlier action recounted at a later point in the epic. There are, characteristically, catalogs of warriors, ships, armies; extended formal speeches by the main characters; and epic similes, extended set-pieces which develop comparisons at length. The greatest ancient art epic is Virgil's *Aeneid;* Ovid's *Metamorphoses* is another, in some ways, though he introduces the epic conventions in a playful and deliberately trivializing way.

The other major narrative form of the ancient world is the history. The dividing line between epic and history is not always precise; the epic finds its roots in legendary history, and history is often seen through epic lenses. About half of the Old Testament is presented as a history of the Hebrews, though a good part of it—the Exodus saga—blends history with folk epic. But we cannot reconstruct from the Old Testament a factual account of early Israel such as a modern historian would write. Hebrew history is history seen through faith; and the purpose of the Hebrew Bible is not to record precise dates and circumstances but, rather, to trace out the underlying design of history as a revelation of religious truth.

History in the modern sense begins in the fifth century B.C. with Herodotus and his Greek history of the Persian Wars. Here, too, fact and fancy are often mingled; Herodotus begins with a lively travelogue of the Persian Empire, reporting everything he has seen and heard, though he is careful to say he does not necessarily believe all of it. The modern critical and scientific treatment of history begins with Herodotus' younger contemporary Thucydides, whose history of the Peloponnesian War makes a quite modern attempt not only at factual accuracy but also at historical interpretation. The Romans carried on the tradition of historical writing. The romantic and patriotic Livy's *History of Rome* is the historical counterpart to Virgil's epic *Aeneid,* while Tacitus' *Histories* and *Annals* chronicle Rome's later degeneracy, in a savage parallel to the contemporary verse satires of Juvenal. The beginning of modern notic of how to organize and develop a sustained narrative lies as much in the of these historians as in that of the more frankly "literary" writers.

9

Of the major literary kinds, drama has had the most sporadic history. Perhaps because a fairly complex set of social and intellectual circumstances are necessary to make theatrical production possible, drama has flourished in only three fairly brief periods in Western history, and the first of these is in the Greece of the fifth century B.C. (the other two ages are the late Renaissance and early neoclassical period, between about 1580 and 1700, and the modern period, since about 1860).

There is some evidence that a dramatic tradition existed in Egypt as early as 3000 B.C., but practically nothing is known of it. The Hebrews had no theater, although the Book of Job shows some evidence of the influence of Greek tragedy, and the Song of Solomon may have some relation to a quasi-dramatic wedding performance. It is to Greece that we look for the beginnings of Western drama.

Greek drama originated in the sixth century B.C., in the worship of Dionysus. Four annual festivals were consecrated to him: the Rural Dionysia (in December), the Lenaia (in January), the Anthesteria (in February), and the City or Great Dionysia (in March). The god was worshipped at these festivals through the performances of dithyrambs, which were hymns of ecstasy narrating an incident in the life of the god and performed by choruses of singers and dancers. The step from narration to drama presumably was taken when a chorus leader moved from telling about the god to impersonating him and acting out his story. The Greeks believed that this revolutionary innovator was a man named Thespis, who is therefore traditionally regarded as the first actor in history. It was Thespis, too, who won the prize for tragedy in 534 B.C., when the City Dionysia was reorganized and a contest for tragedy was established. Dithyrambic performances took place on the circular stone platforms which were used as threshing floors in the center of Greek villages; these platforms seem to have provided the model for the *orchestra,* or circular dancing place, which served as the central acting area of the fully developed Greek theater.

It is in the fifth century that we emerge from theatrical legend into theatrical history. By the time Aeschylus, the oldest of the Greek dramatists whose works survive, began competing in the tragedy contests in 499 B.C., the contests had been held for about thirty-five years and the methods of production had assumed essentially the form they kept throughout the great age of the Greek theater. The festivals were civic and religious rituals, occasions for exploring the fundamental ideas and values that made Athens a unified community. The annual dramatic festivals were organized, and the plays produced, by a cooperative effort of the civic leaders of the city, eminent private sponsors, and the artists themselves, in accordance with rules that by the fifth century had become standard. The audience consisted, in effect, of the whole citizenry, brought together not in a spirit of playgoing whim but of communal solidarity. (Women attended the tragedies but not the comedies.) During the fifth century, the Great Dionysia, the most important of the annual festivals, included four days devoted to plays. On the first day, five comedies, by different authors, were presented. On each of the next three days, plays by a single author were acted: three tragedies, followed by a broadly comic "satyr play" designed to relieve the intensity of the tragedies. Prizes were awarded to the best actor and to the best combination of playwright and producer.

Plan of the theater of Dionysus at Athens. A. Orchestra B. Chorus Entrance C. Altar to Dionysus D. Skene.

At Athens, plays were acted in the Theater of Dionysus, a vast outdoor arena located on sloping ground near the Acropolis. Between the sixth and fourth centuries, the most important era of Greek drama, the theater evolved considerably. At first it was little more than a circular acting space, or *orchestra*, at the foot of a concave hillside where the audience sat on the ground. By the fifth century, permanent seats for the audience had been built and a long building called the *skene* had been constructed behind the *orchestra*. The *skene*, which became increasingly elaborate architecturally as time passed, provided dressing rooms, a backdrop for the action (scenery was apparently minimal), and a place through which the principal actors could make their entrances and exits. The *skene* often represented an edifice, integral to the story, where indoor actions could be imagined to happen, offstage—in Agamemnon's palace, for example. (The direct presentation of indoor scenes is unusual in Greek plays, as are killings and other violent episodes.) It is possible, though not certain, that a raised platform directly in front of the *skene* formed a stage slightly elevated above the *orchestra*. At the extreme left and right of the *skene* were corridors, separating it from the seating area, through which the Chorus usually entered near the beginning of the play and exited near the end.

11

The players—all of them males—consisted of the principal actors and the Chorus. Originally, there was only one principal, but in the course of the fifth century a second actor was added (by Aeschylus) and later a third (by Sophocles), making possible face-to-face confrontations between characters and thus enhancing psychological realism. It must be understood that the number of characters in a play was not limited to the number of actors; one actor often played two or more roles, and conversely the same character could be played by more than one actor. This flexibility was achieved primarily by the use of stylized masks, a device that served several purposes: to maintain elementary verisimilitude (by allowing an adult male to play a young girl or old woman, for example); to help the audience (many of whom sat far from the action) recognize the identity and emotional state of the characters; and to help portray the characters as generalized types rather than simply as individuals.

The Chorus, which probably numbered twelve or fifteen in tragedy and twenty-four in comedy, was a distinctive part of Greek drama. It could represent various groups, from the citizens of Argos in Aeschylus' *Agamemnon,* to the Furies in his *Eumenides,* to the animal grotesques in comedies such as Aristophanes' *The Frogs* or *The Wasps.* Its functions were equally various: it could take part in the play's action, reflect the response the playwright was trying to evoke in the audience, bring out through sympathy or antipathy the salient traits of a principal character, and voice philosophical ideals. Not least, its singing and dancing helped sustain the play's mood and enhance it as spectacle.

Music and dance were important in both tragedy and comedy, helping to create elevated, festive, or ceremonial effects. The choral poems were sung, in a variety of lyric verse forms, to the accompaniment of dance and of musical instruments including the flute. Ordinary dialogue was probably delivered as a quasi-musical chant or in some other way that distinguished it from the tone of ordinary speech. A number of people have pointed out that, in its stylized manner, its spectacle, and its integration of different art media, Greek drama has its closest modern analogue in grand opera. (And indeed, opera originated in a seventeenth-century attempt to reconstruct the staging of Greek drama.)

Only forty-five Greek plays have survived: seven tragedies by Aeschylus, seven tragedies by Sophocles, seventeen tragedies and one satyr play by Euripides, eleven comedies by Aristophanes, and two comedies by Menander (only one of which is intact). Even this small sampling, hardly likely to encompass the full range of Greek drama, is highly varied. Tragedy ranges from the titanic culture-histories of Aeschylus, through the marvelously crafted humanistic dramas of Sophocles, to Euripides' ironic dramas of inner division and self-deception (some of which are more like comedies of manners than like tragedies). Aristophanes' Old Comedy is the Greek dramatic form most remote from modern drama. He strings upon a sketchy, fantastic, often perfunctory plot, scenes of farce, parody, and topical satire, punctuated with choruses of beautiful lyric poetry. It was not Old Comedy but New Comedy—surviving only in the works of the fourth-century Menander—that was to establish the pattern of later comedy. New Comedy turned from fantasy and satire to deal with contemporary middle-class private life. The choruses were subordinated to intrigue-plots, which usually dealt with a young man's attempt to marry against his father's opposition.

The Roman theater, like many aspects of Roman culture, was modeled on that of the Greeks. In Rome, where Greek-inspired plays began to be performed in the third century B.C., plays were performed at festivals honoring the gods or for special occasions, such as a state funeral or a military victory. The theaters were constructed along Greek lines, although by the first century A.D. they had come to be much larger and more elaborate than the Greek theaters, reflecting the Roman love of excess. Thirty-seven Roman plays survive: twenty-one comedies by Plautus (c. 254–184 B.C.); six comedies by Terence (195–159 B.C.); nine tragedies by Seneca (4 B.C.–65 A.D.), the Stoic philosopher and adviser to the Emperor Nero; and one tragedy formerly attributed to Seneca but now agreed to be the work of a later, anonymous author. Roman comedy, like Greek New Comedy, dealt with intrigues arising from middle-class life, while Seneca's stiff, melodramatic dramas, not meant for production, are reworkings of Greek tragedies. (Five of his nine extant plays are adapted from Euripides.)

Greek tragedy expressed the Greek spirit both in its unflinching treatment of basic issues in human life ("Know thyself") and in its strict economy of means ("Nothing too much"). Greek comedy embodied the Greeks' freedom of thought and expression, as well as their involvement in public life. Roman drama carried on the Greek achievement and was to be the version of classical drama that initially influenced the theater when it was reborn during the Renaissance.

Of all the genres, lyric poetry travels least well. Narrative and drama lose a great deal with the passage of time and loss of cultural associations. Subtleties disappear with translation into other languages. But the broad outlines of a story and the power of the stage are rugged—thus epic and drama can survive the passing of time and changes in language better than lyric poetry, which depends so much on nuance and the precise word.

"Lyric" originally meant "sung to the lyre," and perhaps the central fact about lyric poetry in the ancient world is its close connection with music. The lyric poet was literally a "lyricist" in Hebrew and Greek cultures, as we are reminded by stories about David as a harpist and of Sappho's skill upon the lyre.

The Hebrew Bible is full of song, and the lyric portions of it should be read with imaginary, if not real, music in the background. The role of music and poetry in Hebrew worship is suggested by many passages in the Old Testament, among them the description of David's bringing of the ark to Jerusalem (I Chron. 16:7–36) and the descriptions of worship in the Psalms. In Psalm 42, the speaker tells of leading the throng to the House of God "with glad shouts and songs of thanksgiving," while in Psalm 68 another procession is described, "the singers in front, the minstrels last, between them maidens playing timbrels."

Hebrew poetry, like most ancient Near Eastern poetry, did not depend on rhyme or a fixed line length but, rather, on a loose rhythm and parallelism. A unit of Hebrew verse characteristically consists of two lines, each with three or four heavily stressed syllables, the second line parallel to the first in that it either paraphrases, develops, or completes it:

13

What is man, that thou art mindful of him?
and the son of man, that thou visitest him? [PSALMS 8:4]

The simple, exalted power of this form is perceptible even in English translation.

The early Greeks described poetry as either "lyric" or "choric." Lyric poetry was the expression of a single singer accompanied by the lyre, while choric poetry was a group expression, sung by a chorus, usually also with instrumental accompaniment. The greatest school of lyric poets in Greece was centered among the Aeolians, on the eastern coast of the Aegean Sea and on the island of Lesbos, in the sixth century B.C. The great Aeolian lyricists, Sappho and Alcaeus, also inspired an Ionian school of lyricists on the mainland of Greece. The major successor to Sappho and Alcaeus was Anacreon, who was born in Teos in Asia Minor but spent much of his life in Athens. The leader of the Dorian school of the fifth century was the "choric" poet Pindar. Late Greek poetry of the Hellenistic period is best represented by Theocritus, whose *Idylls* established the pattern for centuries to come of pastoral poetry, in which the subject matter, whatever it may be, is cast in terms of rural scenes and characters.

In lyric poetry, as in much else, the Greeks set out on paths we still follow. The very conception of a "lyric" voice, intensely individual and personal, uncovering the subtle movements of thought and emotion and linking them to musicality, was Greek. Perhaps the most direct heir to Greek lyricism among the Romans was the first-century B.C. Catullus, whose most famous poems, those about his mistress "Lesbia," seem to explore all the convolutions of a self in the grip of an ambivalent passion. The other great Latin lyricists seem tame by comparison—they are polished and even elegant but they lack the naked self-revelation of the Greeks and of Catullus. Virgil is almost as well known for his *Eclogues* as for the *Aeneid;* in these poems he follows Theocritus in urbanely surveying many subjects under the cloak of the pastoral idiom. The other great Augustan lyricist was Horace, whose polished style, charm, and tone of detached common sense made him the most imitated classical poet of the European Enlightenment. Ovid was primarily a storyteller rather than a lyricist, but in his *Art of Love, Amores,* and *Metamorphoses,* we see again the Greek lyric inspiration, translated into Roman smartness and a cynical, amusing detachment.

Finally, a narrow definition of literary genres should not rule out such masterpieces of discursive prose as we find in much of the Old Testament and in Plato and Aristotle. Such works have had an incalculable impact upon later literature. The voices of the Hebrew prophets, of Plato's genial and humane Socrates, and of Aristotle, the indefatigable analyst of the nature and meaning of almost everything, must be included among the voices of the ancient world.

FURTHER READING *(prepared by J. H.): The Oxford History of the Classical World,* ed. by John Boardman, Jasper Griffin, and Oswyn Murray, 1986, is a very fine comprehensive treatment of the ancient Greek and Roman world, lavishly illustrated, combining history and sociology with good essays on ancient literature, art, and philosophy. An excellent overview of ancient history is provided by Chester G. Starr, *A History of the Ancient World,* 1965. The transition from ancient agriculture-myth cultures to

14

urban ones is well treated in William Irwin Thompson, *The Time Falling Bodies Take to Light: Mythology, Sexuality, and the Origins of Culture*, 1981. A standard brief introduction to Hebrew history is John Bright, *A History of Israel*, 2nd ed., 1972. Even briefer and very useful are B. K. Rattey, *A Short History of the Hebrews*, 2nd ed., 1964, and Harry Orlinsky, *Ancient Israel*, 2nd ed., 1960. J. B. Bury's *History of Greece*, revised by R. Meiggs, 1951, and Michael Grant's *History of Rome*, 1978, are recommended for what their titles promise. Classical Greece is well treated in S. Hornblower, *The Greek World, 479–323*, 1983, and J. K. Davies, *Democracy and Classical Greece*, 1978. T. Cornell and J. Matthews, *Atlas of the Roman World*, 1982, includes, besides good maps and illustrations, a general history of Rome. Also useful are studies of the history of ideas in the ancient world. For the Hebrews, see James Muilenburg, *The Way of Israel*, 1961, and Norman Snaith, *Distinctive Ideas of the Old Testament*, 1947. Important special topics are treated in Frank M. Cross, *Canaanite Myth and Hebrew Epic*, 1973; Dennis J. McCarthy, *Old Testament Covenant: A Survey of Current Opinions*, 1972; and John H. Otwell, *And Sarah Laughed*, 1977, which examines the role of women in the Old Testament. Of many feminist perspectives on the ancient world, especially noteworthy are Jane E. Burns, *Bodytalk*, 1994 (which addresses the medieval world also); Gerda Lerner, *The Creation of Patriarchy*, 1986; and Eva Cantarella, *Pandora's Daughters*, trans. Maureen B. Fant, 1987. Of special importance in understanding the literary practice of the Hebrews, as well as individual books of the Bible, is Northrop Frye's *The Great Code: The Bible and Literature*, 1982. H. D. F. Kitto's *The Greeks*, 1951, C. M. Bowra's *The Greek Experience*, 1957, A. Andrewes' *The Greeks*, 1967, and K. J. Dover's lavishly illustrated *The Greeks*, 1981, are all clear, accurate introductions to Greek ideas and culture. An important literary history of Greece is Albin Lesky, *A History of Greek Literature*, 1963, trans. James Willis and Cornelis de Heer, 1966. Briefer, but still valuable, overviews are provided by C. M. Bowra, *Ancient Greek Literature*, 1933, and K. J. Dover, ed., *Ancient Greek Literature*, 1980. On Greek drama and the Greek theater, T. B. L. Webster's *Greek Theatre Production*, 1962, Peter Arnott's *Greek Scenic Conventions*, 1962, and Margarete Bieber's *The History of the Greek and Roman Theater*, 2nd ed., 1961, are authoritative. Albin Lesky's *Greek Tragic Poetry*, 1983, is a comprehensive account. H. D. F. Kitto's *Greek Tragedy*, 3rd ed., 1961, is a standard critical survey; Jan Kott's *The Eating of the Gods*, 1973, surveys the plays from a more recent perspective. Hugh Lloyd-Jones, *The Justice of Zeus*, 2nd ed., 1984, puts Greek tragic drama in a broad perspective. M. I. Finley, ed., *The Legacy of Greece*, 1981, collects major essays reappraising the Greek heritage. R. H. Barrow's *The Romans*, 1949, is a useful brief introduction to Roman thought and culture. J. Wight Duff's two-volume history of Roman literature has not been superseded: *A Literary History of Rome from the Origins to the Close of the Golden Age*, 3rd ed., 1953; and *A Literary History of Rome in the Silver Age*, 3rd ed., 1964. Michael Grant's *Roman Literature*, 1954, is also accurate and readable, as is Moses Hadas's *History of Latin Literature*, 1952. Hadas's *Ancilla to Classical Reading*, 1954, is a thoughtful and lively handbook for the student of both Greek and Roman literature. R. M. Ogilvie's *Roman Literature and Society*, 1980, is a good author-by-author introduction and survey. On the forging of the ancient epic tradition and its modern heritage, see John Kevin Newman, *The Classical Epic Tradition*, 1986.

15

Gilgamesh

(C. 2000 B.C.)

Consider this: If we traveled backward in time, twenty centuries would take us to the era of Christ. We would then be only halfway back to the era when the epic *Gilgamesh* was coming into existence, and much less than halfway back in time to the civilization and culture out of which the poem arose. It would seem that we had approached the very border of primitive history.

But consider this too: The poet Herbert Mason published in 1970 an English rendering of *Gilgamesh*, testifying in an autobiographical postscript to a feeling of deep affinity with the poem. His absorption with it, he reveals, dates to his discovery of *Gilgamesh* in a course on oral epic at Harvard in the 1950s. The course, taught by the distinguished scholar Albert Lord, discriminated between primitive and sophisticated epics. *Gilgamesh* was classified among the sophisticated ones.

When we put these two observations together, the inference to be drawn is obvious: It is a mistake to assume that what is historically early must be, as literature, rough-hewn. Of *Gilgamesh* the opposite is emphatically true, as Lord maintained. For well over a thousand years, the poem was familiar, loved, and admired over a wide geographic area, not only in its place of origin but also through much of the Near Eastern world. At the other end of the vast time line we are drawing, the poem has had a special fascination for twentieth-century readers. *Gilgamesh* is a heroic poem, affirming the intensity that human life derives from its very brevity. At the same time, it is almost an antiheroic poem, obsessed with the bitterly agonizing puzzle of inescapable human mortality. Many centuries after *Gilgamesh*, Homer was to examine these same existential themes—when, in the *Odyssey*, Odysseus chooses temporal life in lieu of the goddess Kalypso's offer of immortality; when the dead Akhilleus tells Odysseus in the Underworld that the lowliest station among the living is better than supremacy among the dead; and when, at the end of the *Iliad*, Akhilleus broods over his own mortality in the presence of Priam, who has come to retrieve the corpse of his son from the man who has slain him. It seems safe to say, then, that the enduring appeal of *Gilgamesh*, though its world and atmosphere are in many ways unique and utterly strange, arises largely from the universal interest inherent in its themes and worldview.

In light of what has just been said, it is all the more astonishing that *Gilgamesh* sank into oblivion for two and a half thousand years. The way in which it was rediscovered, in the mid-nineteenth century, constitutes one of the most exciting chapters in the annals of archaeology. The poem originated in the region, corresponding roughly to modern Iraq, called Mesopotamia, a word that means "between the rivers," the rivers being the Tigris and Euphrates. During the three or four millennia before Christ, Mesopotamia was ruled in succession by a number of ancient peoples and dynasties. The written languages of the region, among the earliest in human history, used cuneiform ("wedge-shaped") characters, the meaning of which was lost to the world for more than two thousand years. In 1839, Austen Henry Layard, a young Englishman, happened on the ruins of the ancient Mesopotamian city of Nineveh. Among the things he discovered in excavating the site were thousands of pieces of broken clay tablets, covered with cuneiform characters, which he delivered to the British Museum. In 1853, Layard's colleague Hormuzd Rassam unearthed at Nineveh part of the extensive ancient library amassed by the last great Assyrian king, Assurbanipal, who reigned in the seventh century B.C. This library contained, on its clay tablets, a fragmentary but substantially complete version of the work later recognized as *Gilgamesh*, written in cuneiform in Akkadian, which over a long period had been the main international language of the Near Eastern world. The setting of the poem is the ancient Mesopotamian city of Uruk, much of which was to be excavated in the 1920s and 1930s by German archaeologists. Uruk, which the epic declares was built and ruled by Gilgamesh, is called Erech in the Hebrew Bible and, as part of modern Iraq, is called Warka. Gilgamesh himself may well have been a historical person who lived in the twenty-seventh century B.C. American experts, from the University of Pennsylvania especially, also played a key role, through their Mesopotamian researches late in the nineteenth century, in discovering far more ancient versions, in Sumerian, of the main episodes in *Gilgamesh*.

Discoveries had been made, but they would have meant little if the meaning of cuneiform had remained a mystery. The main breakthrough on this front was made by the English soldier and diplomat Henry Rawlinson, who broke the cuneiform code by analyzing the "Record of Darius," a multilingual Persian inscription in stone. (A similar method had been used earlier in the nineteenth century to decipher ancient Egyptian hieroglyphics, with the aid of the Rosetta Stone, discovered by one of Napoleon's soldiers, which was inscribed in both hieroglyphics and Greek.) The major significance of the unearthed cuneiform tablets was first largely recognized by George Smith, who, in 1872, noted that they recorded a pre-biblical account of the Flood.

The textual study of *Gilgamesh* is enormously complicated. Since the first find at Nineveh (and even there more than one copy was found), many further pertinent fragments have been unearthed. Some passages of the "standard" version from Assurbanipal's excavated library appear in that version only, but many episodes of the poem are found also in the much older Sumerian texts, which go back past 2000 B.C. Still other fragments of the poem, in large numbers, have been found over a wide area of the Near East, written in several different ancient languages. (Some of these fragments represent schoolboy exercises, done with the varying degrees of accuracy one can expect from schoolboys.) The version from Assurbanipal's library is sometimes attributed to a poet named Sin-leqe-unninni, who lived during the Kassite period (about 1650–1150 B.C.), but, as with Homer later, it is unclear just what role he may have played in putting the poem together.

If we could be sure there was an "ideal" text of *Gilgamesh*, the various fragments discovered here and there by archaeologists could be expected to firm up, progressively, an authentic version of the poem. In fact, though, newly discovered pieces of it often do the opposite, introducing new variants and textual bypaths. It seems very possible that there has never been a single authoritative version, the poem having evolved and branched rather than being composed in the ordinary sense of the word. *Gilgamesh* has been transmitted in writing but also orally, after the fashion of other works of folk literature the appeal of which often lies, precisely, in the variety of their retellings.

Because all the versions of *Gilgamesh* are, in one sense or another, fragmentary, one might expect that reading it would be a disjointed experience. That is not the case, however; translations of *Gilgamesh* can differ significantly from one another, but they all relate essentially the same powerfully unified story. The "standard" version is fairly consistent in its style, the verse having a highly fluid and flexible meter. The poem is also framed effectively—for example, by nearly identical passages at beginning and end inviting the reader to take in the glories of the city of Uruk.

The main unifying element, though, is thematic. The heroic motif of comradeship in performing awesome feats blends organically with the motif of coping with death, of achieving—figuratively or more literally—immortality. Much of the existential appeal of *Gilgamesh* lies in its uncompromising, unglamorized presentation of the brute fact of death. Heroic achievement is heroic because it faces unflinchingly the obscenity of death, and the stakes are literally infinite; no gardens of the blessed or Elysian Fields or Valhallas await the slain hero. One can leave great achievements behind— a great city, for example, if one is Gilgamesh—but they *are* left behind. The intimate, recognizably human psychology of *Gilgamesh* is striking: Enkidu comes to see some of his noblest achievements, in bitter retrospect, as follies or disasters. The quest for eternal life undertaken by Gilgamesh in the latter part of the poem is not idle fantasy; at the deepest level it reflects the unthinkableness that almost everyone feels at the prospect of simply ceasing to exist, of leaving behind—in Thomas Gray's words—"the warm precincts of the cheerful day."

Gilgamesh is about what it means to be human. Among other things, that involves being civilized, becoming part of a city, a human community. We catch only brief glimpses of nature in the poem, and then mainly as a mocking mirage such as Gilgamesh finds when he reaches the oceanside paradise over which the female vintner Siduri presides, or as the forbidding territory of the monster Huwawa. The most telling episode in this respect is Enkidu's encounter with the temple harlot sent out to cope with him. The sexual initiation she affords Enkidu is not an indulgence of "nature" but quite the opposite: Thereafter he is alienated from the communion with animals he had hitherto experienced. Sexual union brings him into a human world, a world that, as for Gilgamesh too, makes the career of heroism possible and meaningful but also, by the same token, makes it tragic, in a mode available only to members of a generically human collectivity.

NOTE ON THE TEXT AND TRANSLATION

Because *Gilgamesh* has to be recaptured from fragmentary tablets, scrupulously faithful scholarly translations (for example, Stephanie Dalley's in *Myths from Mesopotamia*, 1989) must use an elaborate system of brackets, blank spaces, and the like. Such renderings are confusing for general readers. Like other translators addressing such readers, David Ferry has used some poetic licenses: occasional conjectures, supplementary readings from versions other than the "standard" one, condensations or omissions of obscure passages, and the like.

FURTHER READING *(prepared by B.W.):* An authoritative and succinct discussion of *Gilgamesh* is included in Stephanie Dalley, *Myths from Mesopotamia*, 1989. As the title indicates, this book also includes several other myths deriving from related languages and cultures. A less recent but fuller and very clearly written account of the poem, including the story of its discovery and the historic deciphering of cuneiform, is the long Introduction to N. K. Sandars's translation, *The Epic of Gilgamesh*, 1960. An even fuller account of the archaeological adventures appears, along with much else, in Lewis Spence, *Myths and Legends: Babylonia and Assyria*, n.d. Provocative critical insights into the poem are among the good points of the Introduction to *Gilgamesh*, trans. John Gardner, John Maier, and Richard A. Henshaw. Valuable treatments of Mesopotamian culture and civilization include A. Leo Oppenheim, *Ancient Mesopotamia*, 1977; Thorkild Jacobsen, *The Treasure of Darkness: A History of Mesopotamian Religion*, 1976; William Irwin Thompson, *The Time Falling Bodies Take to Light: Mythology, Sexuality, and the Origins of Culture*, 1981; and Samuel Noah Kramer, *Sumerian Mythology*, 1944. On *Gilgamesh* and the Bible, see Alexander Heidel, *The Gilgamesh Epic and Old Testament Parallels*, 1963. In *Somewhere I Have Travelled*, 1992, Thomas Van Nortwick discusses *Gilgamesh* (and Virgil) in terms of personal growth and self-realization. Since the standard text is imperfect and translators therefore often have to resort to creative intuition, it is useful and enjoyable to compare different translations; their number continues to grow.

GILGAMESH

Translated by David Ferry

TABLET I

i

THE STORY

of him who knew the most of all men know;
who made the journey; heartbroken; reconciled;

who knew the way things were before the Flood,
the secret things, the mystery; who went

to the end of the earth, and over; who returned,
and wrote the story on a tablet of stone.

He built Uruk,[1] He built the keeping place
of Anu and Ishtar.[2] The outer wall

shines in the sun like brightest copper; the inner
wall is beyond the imagining of kings.   10

---

[1]An ancient royal city in what is now southern Iraq, on the Euphrates River. It was not actually founded by the historical Gilgamesh, but he was one of the city's early rulers.
[2]Anu was father of the gods and ruler of the heavens; Ishtar was goddess of love, war, and fertility.

Study the brickwork, study the fortification;
climb the great ancient staircase to the terrace;

study how it is made; from the terrace see
the planted and fallow fields, the ponds and orchards.

This is Uruk, the city of Gilgamesh
the Wild Ox, son of Lugalbanda,[3] son

of the lady Wildcow Ninsun,[4] Gilgamesh
the vanguard and the rear guard of the army,

Shadow of Darkness over the enemy field,
the Web, the Flood that rises to wash away   20

the walls of alien cities, Gilgamesh
the strongest one of all, the perfect, the terror.

It is he who opened passes through the mountains;
and he who dug deep wells on the mountainsides;

who measured the world; and sought out Utnapishtim[5]
beyond the world; it is he who restored the shrines;

two-thirds a god, one-third a man, the king.
Go to the temple of Anu and Ishtar:

open the copper chest with the iron locks;
the tablet of lapis lazuli[6] tells the story.   30

ii

There was no withstanding the aura or power of the Wild
Ox Gilgamesh. Neither the father's son

nor the wife of the noble; neither the mother's daughter
nor the warrior's bride was safe. The old men said:

"Is this the shepherd of the people? Is this
the wise shepherd, protector of the people?"

The gods of heaven listened to their complaint.
"Aruru[7] is the maker of this king.

Neither the father's son nor the wife of the noble
is safe in Uruk; neither the mother's daughter   40

nor the warrior's bride is safe. The old men say:
'Is this the shepherd of the people? Is this

---

[3]A legendary hero and king, celebrated in Sumerian poems.
[4]Ninsun was a minor goddess, associated with wisdom.
[5]Wise man and priest; his name means "He who saw life."
[6]Opaque, deep blue gemstone.
[7]Goddess of birth and creation.

the wise shepherd, protector of the people?
There is no withstanding the desire of the Wild Ox.'"

They called the goddess Aruru, saying to her:
"You made this man. Now create another.

Create his double and let the two contend.
Let stormy heart contend with stormy heart

that peace may come to Uruk once again."
Aruru listened and heard and then created   50

out of earth clay and divine spittle the double,
the stormy-hearted other, Enkidu,[8]

the hairy-bodied wild man of the grasslands,
powerful as Ninurta the god of war,

the hair of his head like the grain fields of the goddess,[9]
naked as Sumuqan the god of cattle.

He feeds upon the grasslands with gazelles;
visits the watering places with the creatures

whose hearts delight, as his delights, in water.

iii

One day a hunter came to a watering place   60
and *saw* Enkidu; he stood expressionless,

astonished; then with his silent dogs he went
home to his father's house, fear in his belly.

His face was as one estranged from what he knows.
He opened his mouth and said to his father: "Father,

I saw a hairy-bodied man today
at the watering place, powerful as Ninurta

the god of war; he feeds upon the grasslands
with gazelles; he visits the watering places

with the beasts; he has unset my traps and filled   70
my hunting pits; the creatures of the grasslands

get away free. The wild man sets them free.
Because of him I am no longer a hunter."

His father said: "Go to Uruk and there
present yourself to Gilgamesh the king,

---

[8] In this version, the name Enkidu has its heaviest accent on the first syllable and a secondary accent on the third.
[9] The goddess of grain was named Nisaba.

who is the strongest of all, the perfect, the terror,
the wise shepherd, protector of the people.

Tell him about the power of the wild man.
Ask him to send a harlot back with you,

a temple prostitute,[10] to conquer him
with her greater power. When he visits the watering place, 80

let her show him her breasts, her beauty, for his wonder.
He will lie with her in pleasure, and then the creatures,

the gazelles with whom he feeds upon the grasslands,
and the others with whom he visits the watering places,

will flee from him who ranged the hills with them."
So the hunter went to Gilgamesh in Uruk

and told him about the power of the wild man,
and how he had unset the traps and filled

the pits, so that the creatures got away free.
The lord of Uruk said to the hunter then: 90

"When you return, a temple prostitute
will go with you and with her beauty conquer

the wild man. He will lie with her and then
the gazelles with whom he feeds upon the grasslands,

and the others with whom he visits the watering places,
will flee from him who ranged the hills with them."

iv

The harlot and the hunter traveled together
taking three days, back to the watering place.

For three more days they waited, and finally
Enkidu came with the creatures that love the water, 100

the gazelles and the others, so as to drink their fill.
The temple prostitute looked at him, Enkidu,

the hairy-bodied wild man of the grasslands,
the hair of his head like the grain fields of the goddess,

naked as Sumuqan the god of cattle.
"That is Enkidu, Shamhat, show him your breasts,

show him your beauty. Spread out your cloak on the ground.
Lie down on it. The wild man will look at you.

Show him your body. The hairy-bodied man
will come to you and lie down on you; and then 110

---

[10]Ritual prostitution was part of religious worship.

show him the things a woman knows how to do.
The gazelles and with them all the other creatures

will flee from him who ranged the hills with them."
And so the harlot, Shamhat, showed him her breasts,

showed him her body. The hairy-bodied man
came over to her, and lay down on her, and then

she showed him the things a woman knows how to do.
For seven days Enkidu in his wonder

lay with her in pleasure, and then at last   120
went to seek out the company of the creatures

whose hearts delight in feeding upon the grasslands,
and visiting the watering places, and

ranging the hills. But seeing him, they fled.
The creatures were gone, and everything was changed.

His body that loved to range the hills was now
unable to follow; but in the mind of the wild man

there was beginning a new understanding.
Bewildered, he turned, and sought out the company

of the temple prostitute. He sat down beside her,   130
and looked into her face, and listened to her:

"Enkidu, now you are beautiful as a god.
Why do you seek the company of beasts?

Come with me to the city, to Uruk,
to the temple of Anu and the goddess Ishtar.

Gilgamesh is the ruler, the strongest of all,
the terror. The aura and power of his desire

can be withstood by no one." Then Enkidu,
whose heart was beginning to know about itself

and longed for a companion, cried aloud: 140
"Take me to Uruk, the city of Gilgamesh,

whose aura and power cannot be withstood.
I will cry out in Uruk, challenging him:

'It is I, Enkidu. The strength of the wild man
born in the wilderness cannot be withstood.'"

The temple prostitute replied: "Come then
to Uruk, where the processions are, and music,

and let us go together through the dancing
to the palace hall where Gilgamesh presides,

the favorite of the gods, the beautiful,   150
strongest of all, the terror, the most desired.

Look at his radiant face, the favorite
of Shamash and Enlil, Ea,[11] and Anu.

While you were grazing beastlike with gazelles,
before your mind had any understanding,

his mind, a gift to the gifted of the gods,
had a dream of you before you knew of him.

In the early morning Gilgamesh arose
and told his mother his dream: 'I had a dream.

A star fell from the heavens, a meteorite,   160
and lay on the empty plain outside Uruk.

The men and women came and wondered at it.
I strove with it to lift it but could not.

I was drawn to it as if it was a woman.'
All-knowing Rimat-Ninsun spoke to him,

the lord of Uruk, Gilgamesh. His mother,
All-knowing Rimat-Ninsun, spoke and said:

'The star that fell from the heavens, the meteorite
that lay on the empty plain outside Uruk,

the star you could not lift when you strove with it,   170
the star you were drawn to as if drawn to a woman,

is the strong companion, powerful as a star,
the meteorite of the heavens, a gift of the gods.

That you were drawn to it as if drawn to a woman
means that this companion will not forsake you.

He will protect and guard you with his life.
This is the fortunate meaning of your dream.'

Then Gilgamesh the lord of Uruk said:
'May the dream as you interpret come to pass.'"

The temple prostitute thus told the tale.   180

TABLETS II AND III

i

Shamhat took off her robe and divided it
so that the wild man also could be clothed.

---

[11] Shamash, brother and husband of the love goddess Ishtar, was god of the sun. Enlil was god of earth, wind, spirit, and destiny, somewhat analogous to the Greek god Zeus; Enlil later succeeded to Anu's position of supremacy among the deities. Ea was god of waters, dwelling in an abyss and associated with wisdom.

When this was done and both of them were clothed,
she took him by the hand as a goddess might,

leading a worshipper into the temple precinct;
as if he was a child she held his hand

and they began their journey. They came to a camp
where shepherds lived, who gathered about and wondered

at the huge size and strength of Enkidu,
the hairy-bodied wild man of the grasslands. 10

They said to each other: "He is like Gilgamesh,
twice the size of ordinary men,

stronger and taller than a battlement.
He is like a star that has fallen from the heavens."

They cooked food and set it down before him;
they brought out beer they had brewed and set it down.

But Enkidu knew nothing about these things,
so he sat and stared at the cooked food and the beer

for a very long time, not knowing what to do.
Then Shamhat, the harlot, the temple prostitute, 20

said: "Enkidu, this is the food and drink
men eat and drink. Eat and drink your fill."

So Enkidu ate his fill of the cooked food,
and drank the beer. Seven jugs of the beer

and he was suddenly joyful, and sang aloud.
Then he washed his hairy body, anointed himself

with oil, and dressed his body in new clothes,
so that he looked as beautiful as a bridegroom.

He took up a weapon to guard the flocks and shepherds
against the wolves and lions that preyed upon them. 30

Therefore, at night, with Enkidu to guard them,
the shepherds could lie down in peaceful sleep.

ii

One day a stranger came into the camp
bearing a richly decorated platter,

and Enkidu asked Shamhat to question him.
"Where are you going? Where are you hurrying to?"

The young man opened his mouth and said to them:
"I am going to the wedding feast in Uruk,

bearing delicious offerings on the platter,
ceremonial offerings for the feast. 40

Before the husband, Gilgamesh will lie
in pleasure with the bride in the marital chamber.

There is no withstanding the aura or power of the desire
of the Wild Ox Gilgamesh, the strongest of all."

Then Enkidu was full of anger and said:
"Take me to Uruk, the city of Gilgamesh,

whose aura and power cannot be withstood.
I will cry out in Uruk, challenging him:

'It is I, Enkidu. The strength of the wild man
born in the wilderness cannot be withstood.'"   50

So they set out for the wedding feast in Uruk.

iii

Enkidu entered Uruk; then, amazement
crowded the streets at the sight of the size of him,

the strength and beauty, the likeness to Gilgamesh.
"One has appeared worthy of Gilgamesh,

stormy heart to struggle with stormy heart."
"The wedding feast of the goddess of love is ready."[1]

Enkidu stood, guardian on the threshold
of the marital chamber, to block the way of the king,

the aura and power of the Wild Ox Gilgamesh,   60
who was coming to the chamber to take the bride.

Stormy heart struggled with stormy heart
as Gilgamesh met Enkidu in his rage.

At the marital threshold they wrestled, bulls contending;
the doorposts shook and shattered; the wrestling staggered,

wild bulls locked-horned and staggering staggered wrestling
through the city streets; the city walls and lintels

shuddered and swayed, the gates of the city trembled
as Gilgamesh, the strongest of all, the terror,

wrestled the wild man Enkidu to his knees.   70
And then the rage of Gilgamesh subsided.

He turned his chest away. Enkidu said:
"You are the strongest of all, the perfect, the terror.

The Lady Wildcow Ninsun bore no other.
Enlil has made you sovereign over the city."

---

[1] The goddess of love is, naturally, associated with wedding festivities.

Then Enkidu and Gilgamesh embraced,
and kissed, and took each other by the hand.

iv

Enkidu listened as Rimat-Ninsun spoke
to Gilgamesh her son: "Enkidu has neither

father nor mother; there is no one to cut 80
the wild man's hair. He was born on the grasslands and grazed

with gazelles and the other beasts on the grass of the grasslands;
Enkidu, the companion, will not forsake you."

Enkidu listened, and wept, and felt his weakness.
Then Enkidu and Gilgamesh embraced,

and kissed, and took each other by the hand.

v

Enkidu spoke these words to Gilgamesh:
"Huwawa's[2] mouth is fire; his roar the floodwater;

his breath is death. Enlil made him guardian
of the Cedar Forest, to frighten off the mortal 90

who would venture there. But who would venture
there? Huwawa's mouth is fire; his roar

is the floodwater; he breathes and there is death.
He hears the slightest sound somewhere in the Forest.

Enlil made him terrifying guardian,
whose mouth is fire, whose roar the floodwater.

Helpless is he who enters the Cedar Forest."
But Gilgamesh replied: "Who is the mortal

able to enter heaven? Only the gods
can live forever. The life of man is short. 100

What he accomplishes is but the wind.
Where is the courage that you used to have?

Where is the strength? It is Gilgamesh
who will venture first into the Cedar Forest,

and you can follow after, crying out:
'Go on, go forward, go on, embrace the danger!'

You who have fought with lions and with wolves,
you know what danger is. Where is your courage?

---

[2] Huwawa (also known as Humbaba) is a monstrous nature god, dwelling in a forest guarded
by enchantment.

If I should fall, my fame will be secure.
'It was Gilgamesh who fought against Huwawa!'   110

It is Gilgamesh who will venture into the Forest
and cut the Cedar down and win the glory.

My fame will be secure to all my sons."

vi

So the two warriors went to the armor makers,
who made them weapons as they watched them work,

axes, and swords, and adzes,[3] weighty and mighty,
making each of them ready for the adventure.

The people gathered at the Seven-Bolt Gate,
and Gilgamesh, the king of Uruk, said:

"It is Gilgamesh who will venture into the Forest   120
and cut the Cedar down and win the glory.

My fame will be secure to all my sons.
The journey I will undergo has never

been undergone before. Give me your blessing.
I will return to celebrate the feast

of the New Year. Uruk will shout in praise."
The old men of the city said to him:

"Gilgamesh the king is a young man. His valiant
heart is restless and does not know its danger.

Huwawa's mouth is fire, his roar is the roar   130
of the floodwater; he breathes and there is death.

Helpless is he who enters the Cedar Forest."
Gilgamesh, the king of Uruk, said:

"It is Gilgamesh who will venture into the Forest."
The old men said: "Though you are strongest of all,

do not put all your trust in your own strength.
Let Enkidu, who knows the way to the Forest,

who knows the wilderness, let him go first.
Enkidu the companion will not forsake you.

Let him go first to find the way through the passes.   140
Let him whose heart delights in water find

the hidden wilderness places where the cold
pure secret of the earth may be disclosed

---

[3]An adz is an axlike tool with a curved blade, used for working wood.

to quench your thirst. Offer to Shamash water.
May the god Shamash grant you your desire.

Be mindful of your father, Lugalbanda.
Be mindful of his memory. May he protect you."

Then Enkidu spoke and said to Gilgamesh:
"It is your restless heart's desire to venture

into the Cedar Forest. Enkidu   150
the companion will not forsake you. Let Enkidu,

who knows the wilderness, and knows the way
to the Cedar Forest, let Enkidu go first

to find the way through the passes and find the water
to quench your thirst and offer to the god."

vii

Then Gilgamesh and Enkidu together
went to the palace, Egalmah, to Ninsun

the All-knowing, mother of Gilgamesh.
Gilgamesh told his mother about the adventure,

how it is Gilgamesh who would kill Huwawa,   160
and cut the Cedar down and win the glory.

Ninsun listened grieving to what he said,
and then went grieving to her chamber where

she purified herself and put on garments
suitable to her task, and sprinkled ritual

water on the ground. She mounted the stairs
to the palace roof and at the altar burned

and offered offerings of plants, fragrant
and sacred, to propitiate the god:

"Why have you given my son a restless heart?   170
No one has ever undergone the journey

that he will undergo. Huwawa's mouth
is fire. O Shamash, my son Gilgamesh

is going to the Forest on your errand,
to kill the demon hateful to the sun god.

When Shamash sees him setting out on the road,
or in the mountain passes, or entering

the Forest, may Shamash guard and keep him safe.
And may the stars, the watchmen of the night,

watch over Gilgamesh and the companion."   180
Rimat-Ninsun, the mother of Gilgamesh,

in the company of the votaries of the temple,
spoke and said to Enkidu the companion,

placing a sacred pendant about his neck:
"Though not my son, here I adopt you son,

not to forsake my son in the future danger."
Then from the Seven-Bolt Gate the two departed,

hearing the warnings and blessings of the city.

TABLETS IV AND V

i

The two of them traveled fifty leagues[1] a day,
never resting except at night trying

to rest, stopping only once a day to eat;
in three days' walk a hundred and fifty leagues,

a three weeks' walk for an ordinary man.
The third day Enkidu found the hidden water

to quench their thirst and offer to the god.
They dug a well and drank their fill and offered

a libation[2] to the god. Then Gilgamesh
climbed to a high place on the mountainside   10

and offered the god an offering of flour:
"May the mountain bring a fortunate dream from Shamash."

They made camp there that night and Enkidu
prepared a sleeping place, prepared a shelter

against the wind that blew along the mountain.
The two of them sheltered themselves against the wind.

After a time the oblivion of sleep
poured in upon the king, the strongest of all.

He slept, but at midnight suddenly awoke,
and awakened the companion, Enkidu: 20

"Did you call out to me, just now, in the night?
Why did I waken? Was it you that touched me?

---

[1] A league is three miles.
[2] The pouring of a liquid as a religious offering.

Was it a god went through the camp? A dream?
What makes my skin creep? I had a dream.

I dreamed we were going through a mountain gorge
and the huge mountain fell down on the two of us.

We were as little as flies compared to the mountain."
Enkidu, born in the wilderness, replied:

"The dream you dreamed tonight is fortunate.
The mountain that you dreamed about is Huwawa. 30

Huwawa will fall down like a mountain and die.
His dead body will lie on the plain like a mountain."

On the next day they traveled fifty leagues,
and fifty leagues a day for two days more.

Then Enkidu found the water. They dug a well
to quench their thirst and offer to the god,

and Gilgamesh offered his offering of flour:
"May Shamash grant a fortunate dream tonight."

Enkidu, born in the wilderness, made a shelter.
The two of them sheltered themselves against the wind. 40

After a time the oblivion of sleep
poured in upon the king. He fell asleep,

but at midnight suddenly woke up, disturbed,
and said to the companion, Enkidu:

"Did you call out to me in the night? Was it you
that touched me? Was it a god went through the camp?

In the dream I had, a great bull head was thrashing
over my body in glory, and bellowing

over me, me helpless on the ground; the breath
of the bull snout breathed on me; the bellowing 50

bull noise shook the earth and broke it open;
the choking dust rose up and filled the dream.

Then one brought water to me in my dream."
"The dream you dreamed tonight is fortunate.

The bull you dreamed of in your dream is not
the demon enemy guardian of the Forest.

The bull is Shamash. The wrestling is his blessing.
The one who brought you water is your father."

On the next day they traveled fifty leagues,
in three days' time one hundred and fifty leagues, 60

a three weeks' walk for an ordinary man.
Then Enkidu found the place to dig a well

to quench their thirst and offer to the god,
and Gilgamesh made his offering of flour:

"May Shamash grant a fortunate dream tonight."
Enkidu, born in the wilderness, made a shelter.

The two of them sheltered themselves against the wind
and a shower of rain that passed across the mountain.

After a time the oblivion of sleep
poured in upon the king. He slept, but at midnight   70

suddenly awoke, and said to the companion:
"Did you call out to me, just now, in the night?

Why did I waken? Was it you that touched me?
Was it a god went through the camp? A dream?

What makes me fearful? I had a dream.
The earth shook and the sky shook; and a white glare

filled up the sky, and then there was nothing at all
but silence and darkness, and after that the lightning

broke out and the thunder everywhere, and then
the rain was fire that was raining down,   80

and then the rain was ashes raining down.
Let us go back from the mountain, down to the plain.

Let us consider all these things together."
But Enkidu once again told Gilgamesh

that the dream he had dreamed that night was fortunate.
So day after day they journeyed on to the Forest.

There were other dreams that disturbed the sleep of the king,
night after night as they journeyed to the Forest,

and Enkidu always said they were fortunate.
Gilgamesh, weeping, prayed to the god Shamash: 90

"Be mindful of the promise asked in Uruk.
Guard and protect those who go on your errand,

to kill the demon hateful to the god.
Protect us as we pass through fearfulness."

There was a noise in the sky that spoke and said:
"Seven terrors are the garments of Huwawa.

The aura of Huwawa is the terrors.
Helpless is he who enters the Cedar Forest

when the demon wears the seven. Hurry, Huwawa
has not put on the seven. He wears but one."   100

ii

They came to the Cedar Forest that grew upon
the sides of the Cedar Mountain, throne of Irnini,[3]

forbidden dwelling place of immortal gods.
This was the place the guardian demon guarded

to frighten away the daring mortal who
would venture there. But who would venture there?

This was the place Huwawa was; Huwawa's
breath is death. Beautiful is the Forest;

green upon green the cedars; fragrant the air
with the fragrance of cedar trees; the box[4] that grew   110

along the silent walks of the guardian demon,
shadowed and still, utterly still, was fragrant.

Then Gilgamesh was afraid, and Enkidu
was afraid, and they entered into the Forest, afraid,

the two of them together, and felled some cedars.
The guardian of the Cedar Forest roared.

Then followed confusions of voices and also of hearts.
"The life of man is short." "Helpless is he

who enters the Forest." "Protect us as we pass
through fearfulness." "Where is the strength, the courage?"   120

Always the face of Huwawa was somewhere there.
There was the noise of swords, daggers, and axes,

confusions of noises in the Cedar Forest.
Then Gilgamesh saw the face of Huwawa the demon

and fled from the face, hiding himself away,
and Enkidu found him and said: "Two people, companions,

they can prevail together against the terror."
There was the noise of swords, daggers, and axes,

confusions of noises in the Cedar Forest.
Always the face of Huwawa was somewhere there.   130

The guardian of the Forest roared, and then
the companions fought each other in the confusions

of hearts, confusions of noises, swords, and axes.
Then Enkidu saw the face of Huwawa the demon

and fled from the face, hiding himself away,
and Gilgamesh found him and said: "Two people, companions,

[3]Another name for Ishtar, the love goddess.
[4]An evergreen, used for hedges.

they can prevail together against the terror."
Then Gilgamesh said: "The face of Huwawa keeps changing!"

Enkidu said: "You are the strongest of all."
Gilgamesh, weeping, cried out to the god Shamash: 140

"Protect us as we pass through fearfulness."
Then Shamash heard the prayer of Gilgamesh

and raised up thirteen storms against Huwawa;
the Wind of Simurru and the North Wind and the South

Wind and the West Wind and the East Wind and the Bone-
Cold Wind and the Great Storm Wind and the Great Snow Wind

and the Ice Wind and the Sand Wind and the Screaming
Wind and the Devil Wind and the Bad Wind;

he raised up thirteen storms to beat against
the face of the aura of the demon Huwawa,   150

beating their tempest feet upon the earth
and breaking the earth wide open, splitting the mountains,

lightning and thunder revolving everywhere.
Then Gilgamesh was able to get at him.

iii

Huwawa spoke and said to Gilgamesh:
"I will cut down the trees for you. Make me your servant.

Shamash has sent you upon this errand against me.
You are the child of the Lady Wildcow Ninsun.

You are the king in Uruk. I will be guardian
of the wood to build the gates of the city of Uruk."   160

Enkidu spoke and said to Gilgamesh:
"Do not listen to the demon. He must be killed,

obliterated utterly. Listen to me."
Huwawa said: "Do not listen to him who has

neither father nor mother, child of the wilderness.
When Enlil hears of this, the first of gods,

the god of the wilderness, Enkidu knows
that there will be a curse because of this."

Enkidu said: "The demon must be killed
before Enlil and the other gods are told.   170

Huwawa must be killed and you must build
out of the wood of the tallest cedar a gate,

a gate for the city, a great monument telling
how Gilgamesh slew the guardian of the Forest."

Then the two of them together seized the demon
and by the tongue pulled all his insides out,

and so he died. Then Gilgamesh built the gate
made from the cedar taller than all the rest

of the cedar trees that grew in the Cedar Forest.
They built a raft and they floated the gate to the city. 180

Enkidu steered the raft and Gilgamesh carried
the head of Huwawa, the guardian of the Forest.

TABLET VI

i

When Gilgamesh the king came back to the city
after the victory over the demon Huwawa,

he washed the filth of battle from his hair
and washed the filth of battle from his body,

put on new clothes, a clean robe and a cloak
tied with a sash, and cleaned and polished the weapons

that had been bloody with the hateful blood
of the demon Huwawa, guardian of the Forest,

and put a tiara on his shining hair,
so that he looked as beautiful as a bridegroom. 10

The goddess Ishtar saw him and fell in love
with the beauty of Gilgamesh and longed for his body.

"Be my lover, be my husband," she spoke and said.
"Give me the seed of your body, give me your semen;

plant your seed in the body of Ishtar.
Abundance will follow, riches beyond the telling:

a chariot of lapis lazuli
and brass and ivory, with golden wheels,

and pulled, instead of mules, by storm beasts harnessed.
Enter our house: from floor and doorpost breathes 20

the odor of cedar; the floor kisses your feet.
Princes and kings bow down to offer their wealth,

the best of the yield of orchard, garden, and field.
Your doe goats give you triplets, your ewes also;

your chariot steeds and oxen beyond compare."
Gilgamesh answered and said: "What could I offer

the queen of love in return, who lacks nothing at all?
Balm for the body? The food and drink of the gods?

I have nothing to give to her who lacks nothing at all.
You are the door through which the cold gets in.   30

You are the fire that goes out. You are the pitch
that sticks to the hands of the one who carries the bucket.

You are the house that falls down. You are the shoe
that pinches the foot of the wearer. The ill-made wall

that buckles when time has gone by. The leaky
waterskin soaking the waterskin carrier.

Who were your lovers and bridegrooms? Tammuz[1] the slain,
whose festival wailing is heard, year after year,

under your sign. He was the first who suffered.
The lovely shepherd bird whom Ishtar loved,   40

whose wing you broke and now wing-broken cries,
lost in the darkness on the forest floor:

'My wing is broken, broken is my wing.'
The lion whom you loved, strongest of beasts,

the mightiest of the forest, who fell into
the calamity of the pits, the bewildering

contrivances of the goddess, seven times seven.
You broke the great wild horse and snaffled him:

he drinks the water his hobbled hooves have muddied.
The goatherd who brought you cakes and daily for you   50

slaughtered a kid, you turned him into a wolf
chased away by the herdsmen, whose hairy flanks,

smelly and mangy, the guardian dogs snap at.
You loved Ishullanu, your father's gardener,

who brought you figs and dates to adorn your table.
You looked at him and showed yourself to him

and said: 'Now, touch me where you dare not, touch me
here, touch me where you want to, touch me here.'

He said: 'Why should I eat the rotten food,
having been taught to eat the wholesome food?   60

Why should I sin and be cursed and why should I live
where the cold wind blows through the reeds upon the outcast?'

Some say the goddess turned him into a frog
among the reeds, with haunted frog voice chanting,

---

[1]Tammuz, or Thammuz (the Babylonian equivalent of Adonis), was a vegetation god whose death was mourned by devotees; he symbolized the coming of winter.

beseeching what he no longer knows he longs for;
some say into a mole whose blind foot pushes

over and over again against the loam
in the dark of the tunnel, baffled and silent, forever.

And you would do with me as you did with them."

ii

Ishtar was enraged and went to the gods in heaven, 70
to Anu her father and to her mother Antum.

"The king of Uruk has insulted me.
He has found out and told about my foulness."

Anu her father said to the goddess then:
"Why do you rage? Was it not you who longed

for the semen of Gilgamesh? Was it not you
who desired his body? Why then do you rage?

He has found out and told about your foulness."
The goddess said to the god her father thus:

"Give me the Bull of Heaven that I may punish 80
Gilgamesh the king, who has found out

and told about the foulness of the goddess.
Give me the Bull of Heaven with which to kill him.

Give me the Bull of Heaven or I will go
to the Underworld and break its doors and let

the hungry dead come out to eat the living.
How many are the dead compared to the living!"

Then Anu her father god said to the goddess:
"If I should give the Bull of Heaven to you,

then there would follow seven years of husks. 90
Have you prepared for this? Have there been garnered

grasses and grain to help sustain the people?"
Ishtar replied to the god her father thus:

"I have prepared for this, for I have garnered
grasses and grain to help sustain the people

during the time of seven years of husks."

iii

So Anu gave the Bull of Heaven to her,
and it came down from heaven snorting and bellowing.

Euphrates shook. The city of Uruk shook
and the earth broke open under the great bull noise. 100

One hundred men of Uruk fell in the pit
and died in the pit the bellowing broke open.

The Bull of Heaven bellowed and Uruk shook,
Euphrates shook, and the earth broke open again.

One hundred men of Uruk fell in the hole
the great bull noise broke open, and died in the hole.

For the third time the Bull of Heaven bellowed
and Uruk shook; and Enkidu fought the Bull

and took hold of the Bull by the horns and the great bull head
thrashed over him and the reeking bull slobber poured   110

over his face and Enkidu fought the Bull
and the foul tail of the Bull brushed over his face

and Enkidu wrestled and Enkidu cried out
to Gilgamesh: "The life of man is short,

let us contend with the Bull of Heaven, and win,"
and Gilgamesh fought, and fighting the Bull they cried:

"Two people, companions, they can prevail together,"
and Enkidu seized the Bull by the reeking tail

and Gilgamesh thrust his sword with the skill of a butcher
between the shoulders and horns, and they killed the Bull.   120

They tore out the great bull heart and offered the heart
to Shamash, bowing before the god, two brothers.

After the battle the two sat down and rested.

iv

Then Ishtar was enraged and the goddess climbed
the parapet of the city of Uruk

and spoke her curse: "Woe be to Gilgamesh
for insult to Ishtar, for Gilgamesh

found out and told the foulness of the goddess,
and killed the Bull of Heaven which Anu sent

in punishment from heaven to shake the city."   130
Then Enkidu was enraged against the goddess.

He seized a haunch of the slaughtered Bull of Heaven
and tore it loose and flung it toward the wall

on which the goddess stood, and said to her:
"If I could reach you I would do to you

what you have seen me do to the Bull of Heaven.
I would festoon you with the guts of the Bull."

Ishtar went to her temple and with her maidens,
the votaries, and the temple prostitutes,

did ritual mourning over the haunch of the Bull.   140
But Gilgamesh gathered the craftsmen of the city

to show them the wonderful Bull and how it was made:
the great horns of lapis lazuli,

the coating on the horns two fingers thick.
He cut off the horns and filled the horns with oil,

six measures of oil, and then he offered the oil
in homage to his father, Lugalbanda;

he carried the horns to his chamber in the palace
and hung them in the chamber as a trophy.

Then Gilgamesh and Enkidu together   150
went hand in hand, two brothers, to the Euphrates,

and washed their hands in the calm river waters.
The people of the city gathered to bless them

and watch them in their progress through the streets.
Gilgamesh spoke and said: "I am the strongest.

My fame will be secure to all my sons.
The city scorns the goddess and shouts in praise

of Gilgamesh because he has won the glory."
That night there was dancing and singing in the palace

in celebration of the victory.   160
But afterwards, when all had fallen asleep,

Enkidu had a dream and he awakened
to tell the dream to Gilgamesh the king.

"Why is it that the gods are meeting in council?"

TABLET VII

i

"I dreamed that the gods were offended and held a council,
and Anu said: 'They have killed the Bull of Heaven

and killed Huwawa. One of them must die,
the one of them who felled the tallest cedar.'

Then Enlil said that Enkidu must die
but Gilgamesh, the gifted, must not die.

And Shamash said: 'The two of them went together,
companions on my errand into the Forest.

Why then should Enkidu, who went, companion,
into the Cedar Forest on my errand, 10

why should he die?' Angry Enlil said:
'You went with them as if *you* were companion,

day after day as they went upon their journey
to violate the Forest and kill the guardian.'"

ii

And so it was that Enkidu fell sick.
Gilgamesh looked at him and weeping said:

"Why am I left to live while my brother dies?
Why should he die and I be spared to live?"

Enkidu said: "Must I now go to sit
among the dead, in the company of the dead 20

without my brother?" Gilgamesh said: "Must I
now sit outside the door of the house of the dead

while Enkidu sits in the house of the dead among
the shadow companions?" Then Enkidu cursed the portal

made of the cedar tree they had felled in the Forest:
"You stupid wooden door that does not hear.

I searched for twenty leagues to find the cedar,
tallest of all, with which to make a great

monument for the city, suitable
to celebrate the story of the famous 30

victory in the Forest over the guardian.
If I had known that this would happen to me

I would have taken my ax and chopped to bits
the wood of the cedar I helped bring to the city.

Grant that some future king destroy the portal
or that a god obliterate from it

utterly the name of Enkidu.
May the name of the companion be forgotten."

Gilgamesh listened to him and weeping said:
"The stormy heart of Enkidu the companion 40

rages with understanding of the fate
the high gods have established for mankind.

To rage against the gods of heaven is futile.
What Enlil has ordained cannot be changed.

This is the truth told in the frightening dream.
Gilgamesh the brother will pray to the gods,

beseeching the high gods to spare the companion;
Gilgamesh the king will build a statue

to celebrate the fame of Enkidu."

iii

In the early hours of the next morning dawning, 50
Enkidu, sleepless, weeping, cried out to Shamash:

"As for the hunter who saw me in the grasslands,
may the creatures which he hunts, the gazelles and the others,

get away from him free. May the hunter starve
because he saw me at the watering place.

Fill in his hunting pits, unset his traps,
so that he can no longer be a hunter."

With the first light of the early morning dawning,
Enkidu, sleepless, cried out against the harlot:

"As for the harlot who brought me to the city, 60
this is the curse of Enkidu against her:

May the garbage of the city be what you eat.
May you drink what flows along the alley gutters.

May you importune in the alley shadows.
May you have no home. May you sleep on the city doorsteps.

May there be signs of vomit on your clothes.
May all men curse and revile you and turn away.

Because of you the creatures fled from me,
who dwelt with them and ranged the hills with them."

Then Shamash spoke and said to Enkidu: 70
"Why do you curse the temple prostitute?

Because of her you eat the food and drink
the palace affords. Because of her you wear

the garments suitable for a prince to wear;
you sit in the place of honor nearest the king;

the great ones of the earth bow down before you.
Gilgamesh is your friend and your companion.

The grief of Gilgamesh for you will be
the cause of woe and wailing in the city.

Gilgamesh the king will build a statue 80
to celebrate the fame of Enkidu.

When you are gone, then Gilgamesh will wear
the skins of beasts and hairy-bodied wander

grieving in the wilderness for you."
Enkidu heard what Shamash said to him,

and for a time his stormy heart was quiet.
He repented the curse and blessed the harlot, saying:

"This is the blessing of Enkidu on Shamhat:
May no man revile or curse or turn away.

May the old man comb his locks and beard to please you.   90
May the young unbuckle his belt in joy for you.

May your house be full of gifts, crystal and gold,
camelian and lapis lazuli,

earrings and filigree ornaments, fine new clothes.
May the priests invite you with honor into the temple."

                                    iv

In the early hours of the next morning dawning,
Enkidu lay in his bed, fear in his belly.

He told a dream to Gilgamesh who was there.
"I had a dream. There was a noise in the sky

and a noise in the earth in answer. On a dark plain   100
I was alone. But there was one, a man,

with a lion head, and the paws of a lion too,
but the nails were talons, the talons of an eagle.

The face was dark. He took hold of me and seized me,
I fought with him, I hit at him, but he

kept moving about in the dark, too quick for me,
and then with a blow he capsized me like a raft.

I cried out in the dark to Gilgamesh,
'Two people, companions,' but the man overpowered me,

and raged like a wild bull over me in glory,   110
and Gilgamesh was afraid and did not help me.

Then I was changed into something like a bird,
with a bird's arms, as spindly as a bird's,

and feathered like a bird. He seized an arm
and led me to the dwelling of Irkalla,[1]

the House of Darkness, the House of No Return.
No one comes back who ever enters there.

The garments that they wear are made of feathers.
The food they eat is clay, the drink is dirt.

---

[1]Queen of the underworld; also called Ereshkigal.

Stillness and dust are on the door and door bolt. 120
There is no light of any sort at all.

Dead kings were there, and princes of old kingdoms,
dead high priests and acolytes[2] were there,

dead chanters and anointers, bearers of ointments;
Etana[3] was there and Sumuqan[4] was there,

and on her throne Ereshkigal the Queen
of the Underworld, and kneeling before her was

Belit-Seri the Scribe who holds the tablet
on which the fate of everyone is written.

She turned her head and looked at us and said: 130
'Who has led here this latest to arrive?'"

v

Gilgamesh said: "The dream is terrible."
Enkidu said: "We went together through

the dangers of the Forest and we killed
the Bull of Heaven. Do not forget how we,

two people together, prevailed against the terror."
Enkidu lay suffering on the bed of terror

another day and another day and another,
and the long nights between, and day after day

the suffering of Enkidu grew worse. 140
On the twelfth day he raised up in his bed

and spoke these words to Gilgamesh and said:
"Gilgamesh, who encouraged me in the battle,

saying, 'Two people, companions, they can prevail,'
Gilgamesh is afraid and does not help me!"

After that Gilgamesh heard the death rattle.

TABLET VIII

i

With the first light of the early morning dawning,
in the presence of the old men of the city,

---

[2]Assistants to a priest.
[3]A king of earlier times. Seeking a magical plant to make his wife fertile, he was carried
toward heaven but fell back to earth.
[4]God of cattle (referred to earlier, in Tablet I, line 56).

Gilgamesh, weeping, mourned for Enkidu:
"It is Enkidu, the companion, whom I weep for,

weeping for him as if I were a woman.
He was the festal garment of the feast.

On the dangerous errand, in the confusions of noises,
he was the shield that went before in the battle;

he was the weapon at hand to attack and defend.
A demon has come and taken away the companion.   10

He ranged the hills together with the creatures
whose hearts delight to visit the watering places.

A demon has come and taken him away.
He was the first to find the way through the passes

to go to the Cedar Forest to kill Huwawa.
He sought the wilderness places to find the water

with which to quench our thirst on the way to the Forest.
Together we killed Huwawa; together we fought

the bellowing Bull of Heaven, and killed the Bull,
and together the two of us sat down to rest.   20

Then a demon came and took away the companion.
You are asleep. What has taken you into your sleep?

Your face is dark. How was your face made dark?"
Enkidu's eyes were unmoving in their sockets.

Gilgamesh touched the heart of the companion.
There was nothing at all. Gilgamesh covered

Enkidu's face with a veil like the veil of a bride.
He hovered like an eagle over the body,

or as a lioness does over her brood.

ii

With the first light of the early morning dawning,   30
Gilgamesh said to Enkidu the companion:

"May the wild ass in the mountains braying mourn.
May the furtive panthers mourn for Enkidu,

the gazelles and the other grazing creatures mourn
for Enkidu at the wilderness watering places.

May the pathways to the Cedar Forest mourn.
May the passes through the mountains mourn for you.

May the old men of the city mourn, and those
who warned and blessed us on our journey mourn.

May the grasslands wail as if they were your mother. 40
May the gazelle your mother and the wild ass

your father mourn for Enkidu their child.
The milk you were suckled on was the milk of the creatures,

and the creatures taught you to graze in the wild pastures.
May the holy river mourn, the river Ulaja;

Euphrates mourn whose pure river waters
we made libations of, and drank the waters.

May the young men of the city who fought the Bull,
may they mourn for Enkidu who protected them.

May the farmer who sings of you as he works in the field 50
mourn as he works in the field, may the shepherds mourn,

who brought you the beer and the cooked food in their camp,
may they mourn for you because you protected them

so that they slept at night in peaceful sleep.
May the harlot weep for you who showed you her body

and showed you the things a woman knows how to do.
May the priests mourn in the rite of lamentation.

Listen to me, you elders of the city,
it is Enkidu, the companion, whom I weep for."

iii

Gilgamesh called together the makers of statues, 60
lapidaries,[1] forgers, workers in copper and gold,

and commanded that there be made a statue of him,
of Enkidu the companion, to honor his deeds.

And Gilgamesh spoke to Enkidu's memory, saying:
"You wore the garments suitable for a prince.

You sat in the place of honor nearest the king.
The great ones of the earth bowed down before you.

Gilgamesh was your friend and your companion.
Gilgamesh the king has built a statue

to celebrate the fame of Enkidu. 70
The grief of Gilgamesh for you has been

the cause of woe and wailing in the city.
Now you are gone, and Gilgamesh will wear

the skins of beasts and wander hairy-bodied
grieving in the wilderness for you."

---

[1]Cutters and workers of precious stones.

With the first light of the early morning dawning,
he made an altar and on the altar offered,

in a carnelian bowl, an offering
of honey, and in another bowl, of lapis

lazuli made, an offering of butter:
these offerings to propitiate the god.   80

TABLET IX

i

Gilgamesh wandered in the wilderness
grieving over the death of Enkidu

and weeping saying: "Enkidu has died.
Must I die too? Must Gilgamesh be like that?"

Gilgamesh felt the fear of it in his belly.
He said to himself that he would seek the son

of Ubartutu, Utnapishtim,[1] he,
the only one of men by means of whom

he might find out how death could be avoided.
He said to himself that he would hasten to him,

the dangers of the journey notwithstanding.   10

ii

At night in the mountain passes there were lions,
and Gilgamesh was afraid, and entered afraid

into the moonlit mountain passes, praying
to Sin the moon god: "Hear my prayer and save me

as I enter into the passes where there are lions!"
At night when he lay down to sleep there were

confusions of dreams and in the dreams confusions
of noises, confusions of swords, daggers, axes.

An adversary gloried over him
in struggle, and in the dream who knows who won?   20

[1]Utnapishtim (mentioned earlier, in Tablet I, line 25) had been granted immortality by
the gods.

iii

Gilgamesh came to the mountain called Mashu,[2]
whose great twin heads look one way and the other:

the one looks toward the setting of the sun;
the other toward the rising of the sun.

The great twin heads brush up against the Heavens;
the great udders of the mountain hang down into

the shadows of the Cavern of the Earth.
Twin Dragon Scorpion Beings whose look is death

are the guardians of the entrance into the mountain.   30
The aura of the demon guardian Beings

shimmers across the surface of the mountain.
The shimmering of the light is death to look at.

The Male Twin Monster Being said to the Female:
"Who is it dares come here must be a god."

The Female Twin Monster Being said to her husband:
"Two-thirds a god. The third part is mortal."

Terror in the body of Gilgamesh
seized hold of him from within and held him there

in terror. But then, in terror, he went forward.   40
Then the Male Dragon Being said to him:

"Who is it dares come here? Why have you journeyed
through fearful wilderness making your way through dangers

to come to this mountain no mortal has ever come to?"
Gilgamesh answered, his body seized in terror:

"I come to seek the father, Utnapishtim,
who was admitted to the company

of gods, who granted him eternal life.
I come to seek the answer to the question

that I must ask concerning life and death."   50
The Scorpion Monster Being said to him:

"No mortal has ever journeyed through the mountain.
This is the path of the sun's journey by night.

Lightless the sun utterly lightless goes
from the setting to the rising through the mountain.

This is the path of the sun, utterly dark,
twelve leagues of darkness through, utterly lightless.

---

[2] In Akkadian, the name Mashu means "twins."

No mortal would ever be able to go this way."
Gilgamesh said, his body seized in terror:

"This is the way that Gilgamesh must go,   60
weeping and fearful, struggling to keep breathing,

whether in heat or cold, campanionless.
Open the gate to the entrance into the mountain."

Monster Husband and Wife murmured together.
Then the Male Twin Monster said to Gilgamesh:

"The gate to the entrance into the mountain is open.
May Gilgamesh in safety make the journey."

After the Scorpion Dragon Being spoke,
Gilgamesh went to the entrance into the mountain

and entered the darkness alone, without a companion.   70
By the time he reached the end of the first league

the darkness was total, nothing behind or before.
He made his way, companionless, to the end

of the second league. Utterly lightless, black.
There was nothing behind or before, nothing at all.

Only, the blackness pressed in upon his body.
He felt his blind way through the mountain tunnel,

struggling for breath, through the third league, alone,
and companionless through the fourth, making his way,

and struggling for every breath, to the end of the fifth,   80
in the absolute dark, nothing behind or before,

the weight of the blackness pressing in upon him.
Weeping and fearful he journeyed a sixth league,

and, blind, to the end of the seventh league, alone,
without a companion, seeing nothing at all,

weeping and fearful, struggling to keep breathing.
At the end of the eighth league he cried aloud

and tried to cry out something against the pressure
of blackness: "Two people, who are companions, they . . . !"

There was nothing behind or before him in the darkness;   90
utterly lightless, the way of the sun's night journey.

He struggled to breathe, trying to breathe the darkness.
He was weeping and fearful, alone, without a companion.

Just then, at the end of the ninth league, just once
the rough tongue of the North Wind licked at his face.

It was like the tongue of a wild bull or a lion.
He struggled on through darkness, trying to breathe.

The darkness pressed in upon him, both nothing and something.
After he struggled, blind, his companionless way

through eleven leagues of the darkness, nothing at all 100
and something, ahead of him, a league ahead

a little light, a grayness, began to show.
Weeping and fearful, struggling to keep breathing,

he made his way through the last league of the journey,
twelve leagues in the darkness, alone, companionless,

weeping and fearful, struggling to keep breathing,
he made his way and finally struggled out free

into the morning air and the morning sunlight.

iv

He emerged from the mountain into a wonderful garden.
Gilgamesh looked at the garden and wondered at it. 110

The fruit and foliage of the trees were all
the colors of the jewels of the world,

carnelian and lapis lazuli,
jasper, rubies, agate, and hematite,

emerald, and all the other gems the earth
has yielded for the delight and pleasure of kings.

And beyond the garden Gilgamesh saw the sea.

TABLET X

i

Veiled Siduri,[1] a tavern keeper, keeps
a tavern on the shore of the glittering sea.

They have given a golden mixing bowl to her
and an ale flagon. She gazed along the shore;

she gazed and gazed and saw that there was coming
along the shore a hairy-bodied man,

a wanderer, who was wearing an animal skin,
coming toward her tavern along the shore.

---

[1] Siduri, whose name in the Hurrian language means "young woman," is a divine vintner.

It was Gilgamesh approaching, two-thirds a god,
but one-third mortal and grieving in his heart.   10

He looked like one who has undergone a journey,
his face bitten by hunger or by sorrow.

"Who is this man," she said to herself, "who is it,
hairy-bodied, wearing the skin of a beast,

coming toward my tavern along the shore,
looking like one who has undergone a journey,

his face bitten by hunger or by sorrow?"
She was afraid, and shut the door to her tavern,

and slid the door bolt to, and locked the door.
Gilgamesh heard the sound of the door shutting   20

and heard the sound of the door bolt sliding to.
He called to the tavern keeper: "Tavern keeper,

why have you shut the door against me so?
If you do not let me in I will break the lock

and break the door that shuts me out of the tavern.
It is I who killed the lions in the passes.

It is Gilgamesh, who killed the demon guardian,
Huwawa the guardian of the Cedar Forest.

It is I, who wrestled the Bull of Heaven and killed him.
My fame will be secure to all my sons."   30

Siduri spoke to Gilgamesh and said:
"If you are Gilgamesh who killed the demon,

and if you killed the lions in the passes,
and if it is you who wrestled the Bull and killed him,

why do you look like one who has undergone
a terrible journey, why do you look like one

who grieves, why do you wear the skin of a beast,
why is it that you roam the wilderness?"

Gilgamesh spoke to the tavern keeper and said:
"I look like one who has undergone a journey,   40

like one whose grief lives in his heart, and I wander
the wilderness wearing the skin of a beast because

I grieve for the death of Enkidu the companion,
he who has fought with lions and with wolves.

Together we made the journey across the mountains
through the dangerous passes to the Cedar Forest;

he found the secret places where there was water;
together we slew Huwawa the guardian demon;

we fought the Bull of Heaven together and killed him.
Enkidu, the companion, whom I loved, 50

who went together with me on the journey
no one has ever undergone before,

now Enkidu has undergone the fate
the high gods have established for mankind.

Seven days and nights I sat beside the body,
weeping for Enkidu beside the body,

and then I saw a worm fall out of his nose.
Must I die too? Must Gilgamesh be like that?

It was then I felt the fear of it in my belly.
I roam the wilderness because of the fear. 60

Enkidu, the companion, whom I loved,
is dirt, nothing but clay is Enkidu.

Weeping as if I were a woman I roam
the paths and shores of unknown places saying:

'Must I die too? Must Gilgamesh be like that?'"
Then veiled Siduri replied to Gilgamesh:

"Who is the mortal who can live forever?
The life of man is short. Only the gods

can live forever. Therefore put on new clothes,
a clean robe and a cloak tied with a sash, 70

and wash the filth of the journey from your body.
Eat and drink your fill of the food and drink

men eat and drink. Let there be pleasure and dancing."
But Gilgamesh replied to the tavern keeper:

"Tell me the way to find the only one
of men by means of whom I might find out

how death can be avoided. Tell me the way.
What are the signs of the way to Utnapishtim?

If I must cross the sea, I will cross the sea.
If not, I will wander in unknown places, seeking." 80

The tavern keeper replied to Gilgamesh:
"Not from the beginning of time has anyone ever

been able to go across the glittering sea.
Shamash alone, the Sun, crosses the sea.

He is the only one. Nobody else.
The waters are treacherous, crossing the waters is fearful,

and far out in the waters, forbidding the way,
there slide the other waters, the waters of death.

Urshànabi[2] the boatman dwells out there,
on an island out there somewhere in the waters.   90

What will you do if you get as far as his island?
He guards the Stone Things and he searches out,

there in the island forest, the Urnu-Snakes.[3]
What will you do if you get to his far-off island,

far out in the treacherous waters? Let Urshànabi
look at the face of Gilgamesh. Perhaps

he will take you with him across the waters of death;
if not, then Gilgamesh must abandon the crossing."

ii

After he crossed the treacherous glittering waters
as far as the island where Urshànabi was,   100

Gilgamesh raised his ax and drew out his dagger
and entered the island forest. He got to the place

where the Stone Things were, and fell upon them and broke them.
The boatman in the forest heard the noises

of dagger and ax; there was confusion of battle.
Gilgamesh fought a wingèd adversary

that gloried over him in the confusion.
Then Gilgamesh pinioned the wings of the adversary.

He took the broken Stone Things and stowed them away,
together in the boat with the Urnu-Snakes.   110

iii

Urshànabi the boatman said to him:
"Your face is bitten by hunger or by sorrow.

Why do you look like one who has undergone
a terrible journey? Why do you look like one

who grieves? Why do you wear the skin of a beast?
Why is it that you roam the wilderness?"

And Gilgamesh replied then to the boatman:
"I look like one who has undergone a journey,

like one whose grief lives in his heart, and I wander
the wilderness wearing the skin of a beast because   120

---

[2] The ferryman over the waters of death.
[3] Apart from having an apparently sacred status, the Stone Things and the Urnu-Snakes
are obscure in their significance.

I grieve for the death of Enkidu the companion,
he who has fought with lions and with wolves.

Together we made the journey across the mountains
through the dangerous passes to the Cedar Forest;

born in the wilderness, Enkidu made a shelter
against the winds that blew across the mountains;

together we slew Huwawa the guardian demon;
we fought the Bull of Heaven together and killed him.

Enkidu, the companion, whom I loved,
who went together with me on the journey   130

no one has ever undergone before,
now Enkidu has undergone the fate

the high gods have established for mankind.
Seven days and nights I sat beside the body,

weeping for Enkidu beside the body,
and then I saw a worm fall out of his nose.

I roam the wilderness because of the fear.
Enkidu, the companion, whom I loved,

is dirt, the companion Enkidu is clay.
Must I die too? Must Gilgamesh be like that?"   140

Gilgamesh spoke and said then to the boatman:
"Tell me the way to find the only one

of men by means of whom I might find out
how death can be avoided. Tell me the way.

What are the signs of the way to Utnapishtim?
If I must cross the waters of death, I will.

If not, I will wander in unknown places, seeking."
Urshànabi replied to Gilgamesh:

"With your own hands you have made the crossing harder.
You broke the talismans,[4] you broke the Stone Things;   150

you took the Urnu-Snakes, which is forbidden.
Take up your ax, go back into the forest.

Cut sixty poles and then cut sixty more,
each pole of sixty cubits;[5] fit them with rings

to strengthen them for poling; find pitch
to seal the wood against the waters of death.

---

[4] Objects possessing and conferring supernatural powers.
[5] The cubit, a measure based on the length of the forearm, was approximately twenty inches.
Sixty cubits would be about a hundred feet.

When you have finished, bring me back the poles."
So Gilgamesh went back into the forest,

cut sixty poles and then cut sixty more,
banded the poles, and sealed them against the waters,   160

and then brought back to the boatman what he had made.
Then Gilgamesh and Urshànabi embarked

on the little boat and made the perilous journey,
by the third day sailing as far as would have been

a two months' sail for an ordinary boat.
And they arrived at the place of the waters of death.

Urshànabi then said to Gilgamesh:
"Let us make our way using the punting[6] poles.

Be sure your hands touch nothing of the water."
So Gilgamesh took up a punting pole   170

to pole the little boat through the waters of death,
and after a time the wooden pole was broken

because of the might of Gilgamesh the king
poling the little boat through the deadly waters.

And so it was with a second pole, and a third,
a fourth pole, a fifth, and a sixth, and a seventh also;

and so it was with sixty poles, and then
with a sixty-first, and sixty-second, and -third,

and a sixty-fourth, and -fifth, through the death waters,
till all the poles were broken because of his might.   180

Then Gilgamesh stripped himself and as a sail
held up the animal skin he had been wearing,

and so the little boat sailed on the waters.

iv

The old man standing on the faraway shore
gazed at a little boat approaching. He gazed

at a boat approaching across the waters of death,
and wondering said to himself, consulting his heart:

"The Stone Things have been broken, and there is one
other than Urshànabi in the boat.

I gaze and gaze across the waters of death   190
but I cannot tell who sails in the boat approaching."

---

[6] Punting is propelling a boat through water with a pole.

v

The old man spoke and said to Gilgamesh:
"Your face is bitten by hunger or by sorrow.

Why do you look like one who has undergone
a terrible journey? Why do you look like one

who grieves? Why do you wear the skin of a beast?
Why is it that you roam the wilderness?"

And Gilgamesh spoke to the old man and said:
"I look like one whose grief lives in his heart,

because of the death of Enkidu the companion.   200
Together we made the journey across the mountains

through the dangerous passes to the Cedar Forest;
he told me how the dreams were fortunate;

together we made the festal gate of cedar.
We fought the Bull of Heaven together and killed him,

and after we killed the Bull sat down and rested.
Two brothers, we washed our hands in the calm waters.

Enkidu, the companion, whom I loved,
who went together with me on the journey

no one has ever undergone before,   210
now Enkidu has undergone the fate

the high gods have established for mankind.
I saw the worm drop out of Enkidu's nose.

Must I die too? Must I too be like that?
I wandered the desert seeking Utnapishtim,

he who is called by men the Faraway;
I lived on the flesh of beasts I hunted down,

lions, and tigers, the bear, the hyena, the panther;
I wore the skins of beasts I had hunted down.

There was no sleep for me in the deserts or mountains.   220
The tavern keeper shut her door against me.

I lay in the dirt as if I were a beast."
The old man spoke and said to Gilgamesh:

"You who were born the son of a goddess mother,
why do you grieve because of a mortal father?

How long does a building stand before it falls?
How long does a contract last? How long will brothers

share the inheritance before they quarrel?
How long does hatred, for that matter, last?

Time after time the river has risen and flooded.   230
The insect leaves the cocoon to live but a minute.

How long is the eye able to look at the sun?
From the very beginning nothing at all has lasted.

See how the dead and the sleeping resemble each other.
Seen together, they are the image of death.

The simple man and the ruler resemble each other.
The face of the one will darken like that of the other.

The Annunaki gathered in assembly;
Mammetum,[7] Mother Goddess, she was with them.

There they established that there is life and death.   240
The day of death is set, though not made known."

TABLET XI

i

Gilgamesh spoke and said to the old man then:
"When I looked at you I thought that you were not

a man, one made like me; I had resolved
to challenge you as one might challenge a demon,

a stranger-adversary. But now I see
that you are Utnapishtim, made like me,

a man, the one I sought, the one from whom
I might find out how death can be avoided.

Tell me then, father, how it came about
that you were admitted to the company   10

of gods, who granted you eternal life."
The father Utnapishtim spoke and said:

"I will tell Gilgamesh the king the story;
a secret of the gods I will disclose.

There was an ancient city, Shuruppak[1]—
you know of it—most fortunate of cities,

god-favored, on the banks of the Euphrates.
The gods in heaven decided in their council

---

[7]The Annunaki (offspring of Anu) are gods of one's destiny. Mammetum, also a goddess of destiny, is perhaps another name for the birth goddess Aruru.
[1]A primordial city, about twenty miles northwest of Uruk.

to bring the flood down on the fortunate city.
They sat in secret council together, deciding. 20

Anu was there, the councilor Enlil,
Ninurta[2] of the Silence, and there also

was the god Ennugi, monitor of canals.
And there was Ea, cleverest of the gods.

The voice of Ea telling me the secret
came whispering through the reed walls of my house:

'You reed house walls, listen and hear me whisper;
listen and be attentive to what I tell you.

Utnapishtim, son of Ubartutu,
abandon your house, abandon what you possess, 30

abandon your house and build a boat instead.
Seek life instead of riches, save yourself.

Take with you, on the boat you build, an instance
of each thing living so that they may be

safe from obliteration in the flood.
Perform the construction of the boat with care.

Let the length of the boat and the width of the boat be equal.
Roof over the boat as the abyss is roofed.'

The whispering voice spoke through the rustling walls:
'You reed house walls, listen and hear what I say.' 40

I listened and heard and spoke to the whispering voice:
'I hear what you say. What will I tell the others?

What will I tell the old men and the people?'
Ea the god whispered to me, his servant:

'Tell them you can no longer live in the city,
because you are out of favor with Enlil.

The city is the city of Enlil,
and therefore Utnapishtim, whom he hates,

must find another domicile and another
god who will be his patron and protector, 50

and you have therefore decided to depart
from Shuruppak and seek another home.

Tell them Ea the god will be your patron,
whose domicile is Apsu the abyss.[3]

---

[2] God of war and also of wells.
[3] Apsu includes the waters beneath the earth.

Under the roof of Apsu is where you go.
As for the city, fortunate Shuruppak,

in the morning dawning, abundance will then rain down:
there will be plenty, a flood of bounty, the city

teeming with heaven's profusion, game birds falling,
fishes unheard-of before in song or story,   60

tumbling loaves of fresh-baked morning bread;
grain will come showering in from all the grain fields;

a harvest of everything, yes, more than enough.
These are the things to tell the elders and people.'[4]

ii

"In the first hours of the early morning dawning,
all the people came out for the boat-building,

the little children, the weak as well as the strong,
everyone carrying something: asphalt, and oil,

and pitch, the best of timber with which to build.
Day after day I labored building the boat.   70

Ten times a dozen cubits were the walls;
ten times a dozen cubits was each deck.

There were six decks; the cabin was divided
into nine compartments. I made up the plans;

I drew a picture of them for our guidance.
I hammered the boat together, and plugged the holes

with water plugs to keep the water out.
I made the bitumen[5] pitch in the pitch kiln,

three *sar* of bitumen pitch to caulk the hull
and, to be certain, three *sar* to caulk the inside.   80

I counted punting poles and put them aboard;
I had the basket bearers stow the supplies

of oil and foodstuffs, everything I needed.
As for the people who came to help in the work

each day was like a New Year's holiday:
I slaughtered sheep and bullocks for their feasting;

for drinking there was wine and beer, plenty,
as if there was a river overflowing.

---

[4]In lines 57–64 the translator tries to provide substitutes for certain untranslatable puns
in the original language, where, for example, "bread" puns on "darkness" and "wheat" on "misfortune."

[5]A substance derivable from coal or oil.

On the seventh day I finished building the boat.
I opened a bowl of ointment for my hands. 90

I commanded the loading of everything I owned
that could be carried, silver, and gold, and all

the instances of living things to be
saved from obliteration in the flood;

and all my household people I took with me.
At sunset on that day I launched the boat.

The launching was very hard to manage. It took
much shifting and much maneuvering on the ways

to get the unwieldy boat down into the river,
and two-thirds of its weight under the water 100

in order to prevent it from capsizing.
As darkness was coming on I heard the god:

'Abundance will rain down, more than enough!
Get yourself inside, and close the hatch!'

I saw the signs of morning in the sky.
'Abundance will rain down, more than enough!'

I got myself inside, and closed the hatch.
To Puzuramurri the caulker, who, outside,

caulked up the hatch with pitch, I gave my house.

iii

"In the early hours of the next morning dawning 110
there was the noise of Adad[6] in the clouds

that rose and filled the morning sky with blackness.
Shullat the herald of the dread Adad

moved out over the mountains and over the valleys,
bellowing; Hanish[7] the herald of the dread

Adad moved over the plains and over the cities;
everything turned to darkness as to night.

From time to time the Annunaki blazed
terrible light. Then rain came down in floods.

Beneath, the god of the Underworld, Nergal,[8] 120
broke down his own doorposts and opened the earth.

[6] God of storm, thunder, and lightning.
[7] The gods Shullat and Hanish are heralds of storm.
[8] Husband of the aforementioned queen of the underworld, Ereshkigal.

Ninurta god of chaos and of war
opened the dikes, and other floods burst forth.

The South Wind rushed in flooding over the mountains.
Brother could not see brother in the welter;

none of the gods in heaven could see the earth;
the land was shattered like a shattered pot;

confusions of dread Adad were everywhere.
Terrified gods got themselves up as high

as they could go, nearest the highest heaven,   130
cringing against the wall like beaten dogs.

Ishtar cried out like a woman in her birth pangs,
the sweet-voiced lady cried: 'The days that were

have now become as featureless as clay
because of what I said when I went to the gods

in heaven, bringing calamity down on those
whom now the sea engulfs and overwhelms,

my children who are now the children of fish.'
The Annunaki sat and wept with her,

the cowering gods wept, covering their mouths.   140
Six days and nights the storm went on this way,

the South Wind flooding over the mountains and valleys
until the seventh day when the storm birth labor

subsided at last, the flood subsided at last.
I opened the hatch. The daylight touched my face.

I looked outside. Nothing was moving at all.
It looked as flat as a flat clay roof looks flat;

and all the human beings had turned to clay.
I fell to my knees and wept. The tears ran down

the sides of my nose. I wept in the total silence.   150
I looked outside and looked as far as I could,

trying to find, looking across the world,
something. And then, far off, something was there.

What looked like signs of an island could faintly be seen;
and then the boat was caught and held from under

by the peak rock of a mountain under the water.
It was Mount Nisir[9] the boat was grounded on.

A first day it was held, and a second day;
a third day the boat was held from under,

---

[9]Analogous to, but different from, the Mount Ararat of the biblical flood story in Genesis
6–9.

and a fourth day, and a fifth; a sixth day, 160
and then on the seventh day I freed a dove.

The dove flew free and flew away from the boat,
seeking a place for its little feet to alight,

and finding none, flew back to the boat to perch.
I freed a swallow then and it flew free

and flew away from the boat, seeking a place
for its little feet to alight, and finding none,

flew back to the boat to find a place to alight.
I freed a raven then and it flew free

and flew away from the boat, and never returned. 170
It had found a place to alight, and circled about

the place, and alighted, and settled itself, and ate,
and never after that returned to the boat.

Then I set free all the other birds in the boat
and they flew free, scattering to the winds.

iv

"I went ashore and offered a sacrifice.
I poured out a libation; I set out seven

vessels of offerings on a stand, and then
set seven more; I made a fire of wood

of myrtle, wood of cane, and wood of cedar. 180
I lit the fire. The odor touched the nostrils

of the Igigi gods[10] and gave them pleasure.
I slaughtered a sheep to make a sacrifice;

the gods collected like flies about the altar.
The great goddess progenitrix Ishtar

came down from heaven wearing about her neck
the pendant Anu gave her for her adornment,

of lapis lazuli ornately made.
She said: 'Just as this pendant never shall

forgotten be by the goddess, so the goddess 190
never will forget calamitous days.

The gods may come to the ritual but forbidden
is the presence of Enlil, by whose command

---

[10] The gods in heaven.

the flood was peremptorily brought down
on the heads of all my children, engulfing them.'

When the god Enlil came to the sacrifice
he saw the boat, and the sight filled him with rage.

He spoke in anger to the gathered gods:
'How is it that one man has saved himself?

No breath of life was meant to be kept safe   200
from its obliteration in the flood.'

Ninurta opened his mouth and said to the god:
'Ea, the cleverest of the gods, deviser,

let Ea speak and give Enlil his answer.'
Then Ea opened his mouth and said to the god:

'The punishment should always fit the crime.
Let him who has performed an evil act

be punished for that act. Let not the flood
be brought down on the heads of all for what

one man has done; and he who has transgressed,   210
show pity to him, lest he be cut off

from all his fellows. Better that a lion
should come into the village and prey upon it,

taking a few, than that the flood drown all.
Better a wolf should find its ravening way

into the fold, devouring some, much better
than that the flood turn all that breathes to clay.

Better that famine starve a few of them
than that a harvest of waters obliterate all.

Better that Erra the plague god, better that he   220
take hold of some, seize them and bear them away

to the Underworld, than that the flood drown all.
I did not tell the secret to the man.

He listened to the wind and guessed the secret.
Let the gods sitting in council now decide

how to reward the wise man for his wisdom.'
The god Enlil then went on board the boat.

He took me by the hand and made me kneel;
he took my wife by the hand and made her kneel.

The god then touched our foreheads, blessing us,   230
and said: 'You were but human; now you are

admitted into the company of gods.
Your dwelling place shall be the Faraway,

the place which is the source of the outflowing
of all the rivers of the world there are.'

And so they led us to the Faraway,
the place we dwell in now, which is the source

of all the rivers flowing through the world."
Then scornful Utnapishtim said to the king:

"Tell me, who would bring all the gods together   240
so that for *you* they might in council decide

what your deserving is, that you be granted
admittance into the company of gods?

Let there be now a test of Gilgamesh.
Let him but keep himself awake for a week,

six nights and seven days, to show his worth."
So Gilgamesh sat down to begin the test.

v

Almost as soon as Gilgamesh the king
sat down to test himself, a mist of sleep,

as ocean mist comes over the shore from the waters,   250
came over his eyes, and so the strongest slept.

Then Utnapishtim spoke to his wife and said:
"See how this hero sleeps who asks for life.

As ocean mist blows over the land from the waters,
so the mist of sleep comes over the eyes of the king."

The wife of Utnapishtim answered him:
"Touch and awaken him, so that he may

return in safety to his native city,
entering through the gate of his departure."

But Utnapishtim said: "Man is deceitful.   260
Therefore he will deceive us. Every day,

as he lies sleeping, you must bake a wafer
and place the wafer near him, making a mark

upon the nearby wall for every day
this hero sleeps who seeks eternal life."

She baked a wafer every day, of bread,
for every day that Gilgamesh lay sleeping.

The first wafer was dry as dust; the second
only less so than the first; the third

was soggy and rotten; the fourth wafer was white   270
in the crust; there were spots of mold on the fifth;

the sixth wafer looked almost as if it was fresh;
and the seventh—Gilgamesh started and waked up

as Utnapishtim touched him on the forehead.
Gilgamesh said: "I had almost fallen asleep

when you reached out and touched me and kept me awake."
But Utnapishtim said to Gilgamesh:

"Look at the wafers and look at the marks on the wall:
a mark and a wafer for every day you have slept.

The first wafer is dry as dust; the second   280
is only less so than the first; the third

is soggy and rotten; the fourth wafer is white
in the crust; there are spots of mold on the fifth;

the sixth wafer looks almost as if it is fresh;
and the seventh—but it is then that you awoke."

Then Gilgamesh said to him: "What shall I do?
Who takes us away has taken hold of me.

Death is in my chamber when I sleep;
and death is there wherever I set foot."

                                        vi

Utnapishtim said to the boatman then: 290
"Though your delight has been to cross the waters,

the harbor now is closed, the crossing forbidden.
The waters and the shore now shun the boatman.

The hairy-bodied man you brought across
the perilous waters, wearing the skin of a beast

that hides his beauty, let Urshànabi take him
to the washing place. There let him wash his body,

washing away the filth that hides his beauty.
Manifest be the beauty of Gilgamesh.

Take the skin of a beast he wore on the journey   300
and throw it away in the sea. Let Gilgamesh

bind up his shining hair with a new fillet.[11]
Let him put on a spotless festal robe.

Let him return to his native city in honor
in the royal garments appropriate to himself."

The boatman led the king to the washing place.
Gilgamesh washed his body, washing away

---

[11]An ornamental or ceremonial strip of ribbon.

the filth that obscured his beauty; then Urshànabi
took the skin of a beast and threw it away.

Manifest was the beauty of Gilgamesh.   310
He bound up his shining hair with a new fillet;

he put on a festal robe, utterly spotless,
a royal garment appropriate to himself.

Then he and the boatman boarded the little boat
and the boat began to move away from the shore.

But the wife of Utnapishtim said to her husband:
"This man has undergone a terrible journey.

What will you give him for his return to his city?"
Gilgamesh, hearing, took up his punting pole

and brought the little boat back to the shore.   320
Utnapishtim spoke and said to him:

"Gilgamesh, you who have made the terrible journey,
what shall I give you for your return to your city?"

Then Utnapishtim said to Gilgamesh:
"A secret of the gods I will disclose.

There is a plant that grows under the waters,
thorny to seize, as a rose is thorny to seize.

How-the-Old-Man-Once-Again-Becomes-a-Young-Man
is the name of the plant that grows under the waters.

Descend into the waters and seize the plant."   330
So Gilgamesh tied heavy stone weights to his feet

to bring him down through the waters of the abyss
to the place where he could find the magic plant.

He seized the thorny plant that cut his hands;
he cut the stone weights loose from his heavy feet;

and the waters cast him up upon the shore.

vii

Gilgamesh said to Urshànabi the boatman:
"Urshànabi, this plant is a wonderful plant.

New life may be obtained by means of it.
I will carry the thorny plant back to my city.   340

I will give some of the plant to the elders there,
to share among them, telling them it is called

How-the-Old-Man-Once-Again-Becomes-a-Young-Man.
And I will take my share of the magic plant,

once more to become the one who is youngest and strongest."

viii

At twenty leagues they stopped only to eat;
at thirty leagues they stopped to rest for the night.

Gilgamesh found a spring, a pool of pure water.
He entered the water, to refresh himself.

In the reeds nearby a serpent of the place   350
became aware of the fragrance of the plant,

breathed its perfume, desired it, and approached,
and stole away with it among the reeds.

As it disappeared the serpent shed its skin.
When Gilgamesh found out what the serpent had done

he sat down weeping by the pool of water.
He took Urshànabi by the hand and said:

"What shall I do? The journey has gone for nothing.
For whom has my heart's blood been spent? For whom?

For the serpent who has taken away the plant.   360
I descended into the waters to find the plant

and what I found was a sign telling me to
abandon the journey and what it was I sought for."

ix

At twenty leagues they stopped only to eat.
At thirty leagues they stopped to rest for the night.

And so they traveled until they reached Uruk.
There Gilgamesh the king said to the boatman:

"Study the brickwork, study the fortification;
climb the great ancient staircase to the terrace;

study how it is made; from the terrace see   370
the planted and fallow fields, the ponds and orchards.

One league is the inner city, another league
is orchards; still another the fields beyond;

over there is the precinct of the temple.
Three leagues and the temple precinct of Ishtar

measure Uruk, the city of Gilgamesh."

The Old Testament (Hebrew Bible)

(Tenth Century B.C. to Second Century B.C.)

The Old Testament develops a single central theme: the history of the ancient Hebrews' evolving perceptions of God. (The term Old Testament is used in this anthology as being the most familiar term for the pre-Christian part of the Bible. Some people, however, including many Jews and biblical scholars, prefer the more theologically neutral term Hebrew Bible.) The setting is the tiny land of Palestine, the characters are the members of a small group of nomadic, Semitic tribes, and the time is a span of about fourteen centuries, from about 1800 B.C. to about 400 B.C. The story is above all a history, for the Hebrews—the ancient people whose culture has been transmitted by the Jews—were unusual, though not unique, among early peoples in conceiving of their religion not as the product of a single magnificent revelation, but as the result of a long series of experiences with their God. To the Hebrews, history was the story of a series of transactions with a stern but loving deity.

Although the Book of Genesis deals with the earliest events in the history of humankind, it was, in its final form, one of the last written books of the Old Testament. A group of Priestly revisers constructed the book, in about the middle of the fourth century B.C. Their sources were a much earlier version (the "J document") and an undetermined number of intermediate accounts.

The book as we have it divides into two parts. The first section is an account of prehistorical racial beginnings, and the second is a history of the origin of the Hebrews, descendants of the three patriarchs Abraham, Isaac, and Jacob. The account of the Creation that opens the book is a poetic treatment that in concrete narrative embodies certain basic Hebrew beliefs. Some of the matters "explained" in this account are fairly trivial: why snakes crawl on the ground, for example, and why women are afraid of them. But most of the questions raised are of the grandest magnitude: Who rules the world? What is humanity's relationship to God? How can we account for the presence of suffering in the world? Why do people wage war against each other? Genesis provides no final answers to these questions; the rest of the Old Testament, and the New Testament as well, is devoted to exploring the questions more fully, and people today are still engaged in debating some of the issues raised by the Creation story: Should women be subordinate to men, and must there be mistrust between men and women? Is work to be conceived of as a punishment? Are human beings by nature sinful, and is their natural relation to God that of suppliants seeking to atone for their sins?

Such questions do not obscure the major assumptions about the world that the first part of Genesis establishes. The Hebrews maintained that there is a Supreme Being, that He makes certain ethical demands upon human beings, and that their chief duty is to serve God and to carry out His will.

With the eleventh chapter of Genesis, the focus abruptly narrows from the prehistory of humankind as a whole to the Hebrew people in particular and to their origins in the family of Abraham. The stories of Abraham, Isaac, Jacob, Esau, and Joseph, which follow, bear, like the earlier part of

Genesis, the marks of primitive, folktale origins and later, more sophisticated revision. The key episodes, as in the earlier portion, are those in which God reveals Himself to humanity and establishes a series of "covenants," or agreements. These covenants represent a series of unfolding or developing perceptions of God, from the first (broken) covenant in the Garden, through the covenant of the rainbow, to the great covenant made with Abraham, and subsequently repeatedly renewed, that He would "make of thee a great nation."

It is generally agreed that the Book of Job is the literary masterpiece of the Old Testament and one of the great works of all literature. It contains some of the most magnificent poetry in the Bible, and its seemingly simple structure, on rereading, reveals itself as endlessly resonant in its implications. And yet it is somewhat surprising that this book should be in the Bible at all, so sharp is its questioning of traditional Hebrew thought. Its subject is an eternal one—why do the good suffer?—and although of course it arrives at no answer to the unanswerable question, its reasoning is so keen and its emotional power so deep that the careful reader of Job can never again accept easy and shallow answers to the question.

Nothing is known of the author of Job, and its precise date is uncertain, but scholars now generally date it in the fifth century B.C. Such dating would make it roughly contemporary with Aeschylus' *Prometheus Bound* and Sophocles' *Oedipus Rex,* both of which also deal profoundly with the question of human suffering. This common theme and the book's dramatic form have tempted critics to speculate that the author was directly influenced by Greek tragedy, though there is no external evidence of such influence.

Job's debate with his conventional friends Eliphaz, Bildad, and Zophar sharply challenges the traditional Deuteronomic view of human suffering. Job and his "Comforters" agree that his suffering comes from God, but they differ radically on its meaning. The Comforters reconcile God's absolute power and absolute goodness by insisting that Job's suffering is a just punishment for sin. Job insists with equal vehemence that he has not deserved his fate and that no simple equation can be made between sin and suffering. But his lament is directed as much to God Himself as to the Comforters, as he calls into question not only their facile explanations but also the fundamental idea of any sort of justice or "covenant" between limited man and limitless God. "How should man be just with God?" he cries, "If he will contend with Him, he cannot answer Him one of a thousand."

The resolution of the book comes when God speaks "out of the whirlwind" in a theophany that recalls God's other appearances to human beings throughout the Old Testament. God's reply is simultaneously a rebuke to Job and a vindication of his position that God's power is too great to be reckoned in human terms. Ultimately, God approves the tormented questioner more than the complacent moralizers: "My wrath is kindled against thee, and against thy two friends," He tells Eliphaz, "for ye have not spoken of me the thing that is right, as my servant Job hath." The wager won, God restores to Job all that he has lost, and the book ends. The central question is still unanswered, but the issue has been dramatized more vividly than ever before or since.

The Psalms (a word that literally means "Songs") are thoroughly and obviously an expression of Hebrew ideas, expressed in some of the most beautiful lyric poetry in world literature. Martin Luther called these 150 songs "a Bible in miniature," and indeed they do encapsulate much of Hebrew history, psychology, and theology. Written over almost the entire time span of the Old Testament, they were used in ancient times for liturgical purposes (the exact nature of which is a subject of controversy) and continue to be so used in modern Jewish and Christian worship. They include hymns, meditations, exhortations, songs of praise, and commentaries on the significance of historical events for the Hebrew people. In tone they range widely, from quietude to rage, from exultation to deep grief. They are deeply Hebraic in their celebration of nature, not for its own sake but as God's handiwork, in their portrayal of God as transcendently great and powerful but in intimate touch with His people, and in their expression of communal ideals through an intensely personal tone.

NOTE ON THE TEXT

These selections from the Old Testament are from the King James Version of 1611. There are a number of more accurate, modern translations, but none has had comparable influence upon English speech and literature. Genesis has been condensed for the sake of narrative continuity. Omissions of large sections are marked in footnotes.

FURTHER READING *(prepared by F.S.N. and M.C.):* The 1975 revision, by Allen C. Myers et al., of *The Eerdmans Bible Dictionary,* repr. 1987, is an excellent one-volume comprehensive reference work on the Bible, arranged alphabetically. Good introductions to the Bible include Stephen L. Harris, *Understanding the Bible,* 1992; and Bernhard Anderson, *Understanding the Old Testament,* 1986. George A. Buttrick, ed., *The Interpreter's Bible,* 12 vols., 1952, gives, in addition to background material on the Old Testament (vol. 7), introductions, exegesis, and exposition on individual books. John E. Steinmueller and Kathryn Sullivan, eds., *Catholic Biblical Encyclopedia: Old Testament,* 1956, have compiled a valuable work of reference. Dealing with the books as literary types is Georg Fohrer's *Introduction to the Old Testament,* 1965, trans. David E. Green, 1968. The relationship between literary art and biblical strategy and meaning is explored incisively in Meir Sternberg's *The Poetics of Biblical Narrative: Ideological Literature and the Drama of Reading,* 1985, and in two books by Robert Alter: *The Art of Biblical Narrative,* 1981, and *The Art of Biblical Poetry,* 1985. Alter has also edited, with Frank Kermode, *The Literary Guide to the Bible,* 1987, a collection of authoritative essays. John B. Gabel and Charles B. Wheeler, *The Bible as Literature: An Introduction,* 1986, is especially useful for basic background. Kenneth R. R. Gros Louis, ed., *Literary Interpretations of Biblical Narratives,* 1982, is accurately described by its title. General studies, including information on background, canon, literary merits and individual books, are offered by Otto Eissfeldt, *The Old Testament,* 1934, trans. Peter R. Ackroyd, 1965, repr. 1974; and by Aage Bentzen, *Introduction to the Old Testament,* 1948, 7th ed., 1967. Gabriel Josipovici, *The Book of God,* 1988, is a literary-critical study of biblical narrative, including the relationships between books. Jon Douglas Levinson, *The Death and Resurrection of the Beloved Son,* 1994, examines the roles of sons and heirs in the Bible. Harold Bloom, *The Book of J,* 1990, is a startlingly provocative reading of the "J" author's contributions to the Pentateuch, suggesting the possibility that a woman wrote them; the volume includes also a boldly original translation of the passages, by David Rosenberg. Charlotte Mandel, *The Marriage of Jacob,* 1992, is a novella-poem rendering the Jacob story in a way that vividly portrays the culture of the era.

THE OLD TESTAMENT

King James Version (1611)

from GENESIS

THE CREATION OF THE WORLD

(Genesis I:1–2:3)
In the beginning God created the heaven and the earth. And the earth was
without form, and void; and darkness was upon the face of the deep. And
the Spirit of God moved upon the face of the waters. And God said, "Let
there be light": and there was light. And God saw the light, that it was good:
and God divided the light from the darkness. And God called the light Day,
and the darkness he called Night. And the evening and the morning were
the first day.

And God said, "Let there be a firmament in the midst of the waters, and
let it divide the waters from the waters." And God made the firmament, and
divided the waters which were under the firmament from the waters which
were above the firmament: and it was so.[1] And God called the firmament
Heaven. And the evening and the morning were the second day.

And God said, "Let the waters under the heaven be gathered together
unto one place, and let the dry land appear": and it was so. And God called
the dry land Earth; and the gathering together of the waters called he Seas:
and God saw that it was good. And God said, "Let the earth bring forth grass,
the herb yielding seed, and the fruit tree yielding fruit after his kind, whose
seed is in itself, upon the earth": and it was so. And the earth brought forth
grass, and herb yielding seed after his kind, and the tree yielding fruit, whose
seed was in itself, after his kind: and God saw that it was good. And the evening
and the morning were the third day.

And God said: "Let there be lights in the firmament of the heaven to
divide the day from the night; and let them be for signs, and for seasons,
and for days, and years; and let them be for lights in the firmament of the
heaven to give light upon the earth." And it was so. And God made two great
lights; the greater light to rule the day, and the lesser light to rule the night:
he made the stars also. And God set them in the firmament of the heaven
to give light upon the earth. And to rule over the day and over the night,
and to divide the light from the darkness: and God saw that it was good.
And the evening and the morning were the fourth day.

And God said, "Let the waters bring forth abundantly the moving creature that hath life, and fowl that may fly above the earth in the open firmament of heaven." And God created great whales, and every living creature
that moveth, which the waters brought forth abundantly, after their kind,
and every winged fowl after his kind: and God saw that it was good. And
God blessed them, saying, "Be fruitful, and multiply, and fill the waters in

---

[1]These lines rest upon a belief that the world was created out of a watery chaos. The "firmament" was thought of as a solid dome that divided the "waters above" from the "waters below."

the seas, and let fowl multiply in the earth." And the evening and the morning were the fifth day.

And God said, "Let the earth bring forth the living creature after his kind, cattle,[2] and creeping thing, and beast of the earth after his kind": and it was so. And God made the beast of the earth after his kind, and cattle after their kind, and every thing that creepeth upon the earth after his kind: and God saw that it was good.

And God said, "Let us make man in our image, after our likeness: and let them have dominion over the fish of the sea, and over the fowl of the air, and over the cattle, and over all the earth, and over every creeping thing that creepeth upon the earth." So God created man in his own image, in the image of God created he him; male and female created he them. And God blessed them, and God said unto them, "Be fruitful, and multiply, and replenish the earth, and subdue it: and have dominion over the fish of the sea, and over the fowl of the air, and over every living thing that moveth upon the earth." And God said, "Behold, I have given you every herb bearing seed, which is upon the face of all the earth, and every tree, in the which is the fruit of a tree yielding seed; to you it shall be for meat. And to every beast of the earth, and to every fowl of the air, and to every thing that creepeth upon the earth, wherein there is life, I have given every green herb for meat." And it was so. And God saw every thing that he had made, and, behold, it was very good. And the evening and the morning were the sixth day.

Thus the heavens and the earth were finished, and all the host of them. And on the seventh day God ended his work which he had made; and he rested on the seventh day from all his work which he had made. And God blessed the seventh day, and sanctified it: because that in it he had rested from all his work which God created and made. . . .

THE FALL

(Genesis 2:4–3:24)
In the day that the Lord God made the earth and the heavens, and every plant of the field before it was in the earth, and every herb of the field before it grew (for the Lord God had not caused it to rain upon the earth, and there was not a man to till the ground) there went up a mist from the earth, and watered the whole face of the ground. And the Lord God formed man of the dust of the ground, and breathed into his nostrils the breath of life; and man became a living soul. And the Lord God planted a garden eastward in Eden; and there he put the man whom he had formed. And out of the ground made the Lord God to grow every tree that is pleasant to the sight, and good for food; the tree of life also in the midst of the garden, and the tree of knowledge of good and evil. And a river went out of Eden to water the garden; and from thence it was parted, and became into four heads. The name of the first is Pison: that is it which compasseth the whole land of Havilah, where there is gold; and the gold of that land is good: there is bdellium[3] and the onyx stone. And the name of the second river

[2]All domestic animals.
[3]The meaning of this word is obscure. It may be either a fragrant gum resin or a precious stone such as carbuncle, crystal, or pearl.

is Gihon: the same is it that compasseth the whole land of Ethiopia. And the name of the third river is Hiddekel: that is it which goeth toward the east of Assyria. And the fourth river is Euphrates.

And the Lord God took the man, and put him into the garden of Eden to dress[4] it and to keep it. And the Lord God commanded the man, saying, "Of every tree of the garden thou mayest freely eat: but of the tree of the knowledge of good and evil, thou shalt not eat of it: for in the day that thou eatest thereof thou shalt surely die."

And the Lord God said, "It is not good that the man should be alone; I will make him a help meet for him." And out of the ground the Lord God formed every beast of the field, and every fowl of the air; and brought them unto Adam[5] to see what he would call them: and whatsoever Adam called every living creature, that was the name thereof. And Adam gave names to all cattle, and to the fowl of the air, and to every beast of the field; but for Adam there was not found a help meet for him. And the Lord God caused a deep sleep to fall upon Adam, and he slept: and he took one of his ribs, and closed up the flesh instead thereof; and the rib, which the Lord God had taken from man, made he a woman, and brought her unto the man.

And Adam said,

> "This is now bone of my bones,
>   and flesh of my flesh:
> She shall be called Woman,
>   because she was taken out of Man."

Therefore shall a man leave his father and his mother, and shall cleave unto his wife: and they shall be one flesh. And they were both naked, the man and his wife, and were not ashamed.

Now the serpent was more subtil than any beast of the field which the Lord God had made. And he said unto the woman, "Yea, hath God said, 'Ye shall not eat of every tree of the garden'?" And the woman said unto the serpent, "We may eat of the fruit of the trees of the garden: but of the fruit of the tree which is in the midst of the garden, God hath said, 'Ye shall not eat of it, neither shall ye touch it, lest ye die.'" And the serpent said unto the woman, "Ye shall not surely die: for God doth know that in the day ye eat thereof, then your eyes shall be opened, and ye shall be as gods, knowing good and evil."[6]

And when the woman saw that the tree was good for food, and that it was pleasant to the eyes, and a tree to be desired to make one wise, she took of the fruit thereof, and did eat, and gave also unto her husband with her; and he did eat. And the eyes of them both were opened, and they knew that they were naked; and they sewed fig leaves together, and made themselves aprons.

And they heard the voice of the Lord God walking in the garden in the cool of the day: and Adam and his wife hid themselves from the presence of the Lord God amongst the trees of the garden. And the Lord God called

---

[4] Tend or cultivate.   [5] "Adam" means "man."

[6] Only the tree of "the knowledge of good and evil" is mentioned in the temptation story. The previously mentioned "tree of life" does not appear.

unto Adam, and said unto him, "Where art thou?" And he said, "I heard thy voice in the garden, and I was afraid, because I was naked; and I hid myself." And he said, "Who told thee that thou wast naked? Hast thou eaten of the tree, whereof I commanded thee that thou shouldest not eat?" And the man said, "The woman whom thou gavest to be with me, she gave me of the tree, and I did eat." And the Lord God said unto the woman, "What is this that thou hast done?" And the woman said, "The serpent beguiled me, and I did eat." And the Lord God said unto the serpent,

> "Because thou hast done this,
> thou are cursed above all cattle,
> and above every beast of the field.
> Upon thy belly shalt thou go,
> and dust shall thou eat
> all the days of thy life:
> And I will put enmity between thee and the woman,
> and between thy seed[7] and her seed;
> It shall bruise thy head,
> and thou shalt bruise his heel."

Unto the woman he said,

> "I will greatly multiply thy sorrow and thy conception;
> In sorrow thou shalt bring forth children;
> And thy desire shall be to thy husband,
> And he shall rule over thee."

And unto Adam he said, "Because thou hast hearkened unto the voice of thy wife, and hast eaten of the tree, of which I commanded thee, saying, 'Thou shalt not eat of it':

> "Cursed is the ground for thy sake;
> in sorrow shalt thou eat of it all the days of thy life.
> Thorns also and thistles shall it bring forth to thee;
> and thou shalt eat the herb of the field;
> In the sweat of thy face
> shalt thou eat bread,
> Till thou return unto the ground;
> for out of it wast thou taken:
> For dust thou art,
> and unto dust shalt thou return."

And Adam called his wife's name Eve; because she was the mother of all living.[8] Unto Adam also and to his wife did the Lord God make coats of skins, and clothed them.

And the Lord God said, "Behold, the man is become as one of us, to know good and evil: and now, lest he put forth his hand, and take also of

---

[7]Descendants.
[8]"Eve" in Hebrew resembles the word for "living."

the tree of life, and eat, and live for ever—" therefore the Lord God sent him forth from the garden of Eden, to till the ground from whence he was taken. So he drove out the man; and he placed at the east of the garden of Eden Cherubims,[9] and a flaming sword which turned every way, to keep the way of the tree of life.

CAIN AND ABEL

(Genesis 4:1–5:5)
And Adam knew[10] Eve his wife; and she conceived, and bore Cain, and said, "I have gotten a man from the Lord." And she again bore his brother Abel. And Abel was a keeper of sheep, but Cain was a tiller of the ground. And in process of time it came to pass that Cain brought of the fruit of the ground an offering unto the Lord. And Abel, he also brought of the firstlings of his flock and of the fat thereof. And the Lord had respect unto Abel and to his offering: but unto Cain and to his offering he had not respect.[11] And Cain was very wroth, and his countenance fell. And the Lord said unto Cain, "Why are thou wroth? and why is thy countenance fallen? If thou doest well, shalt thou not be accepted? and if thou doest not well, sin lieth at the door. And unto thee shall be his desire, and thou shalt rule over him."

And Cain talked with Abel his brother: and it came to pass, when they were in the field, that Cain rose up against Abel his brother, and slew him. And the Lord said unto Cain, "Where is Abel thy brother?" And he said, "I know not: am I my brother's keeper?" And he said, "What hast thou done? the voice of thy brother's blood crieth unto me from the ground. And now art thou cursed from the earth, which hath opened her mouth to receive thy brother's blood from thy hand. When thou tillest the ground, it shall not henceforth yield unto thee her strength; a fugitive and a vagabond shalt thou be in the earth." And Cain said unto the Lord, "My punishment is greater than I can bear. Behold, thou hast driven me out this day from the face of the earth; and from thy face shall I be hid; and I shall be a fugitive and a vagabond in the earth; and it shall come to pass that every one that findeth me shall slay me." And the Lord said unto him, "Therefore whosoever slayeth Cain, vengeance shall be taken on him sevenfold." And the Lord set a mark upon Cain, lest any finding him should kill him. And Cain went out from the presence of the Lord, and dwelt in the land of Nod, on the east of Eden. . . .

And Adam knew his wife again; and she bore a son, and called his name Seth: "For God," said she, "hath appointed me another seed instead of Abel, whom Cain slew." And to Seth, to him also there was born a son; and he called his name Enos; then began men to call upon the name of the Lord. . . .

---

[9]Guardians of sacred areas, depicted as winged creatures, half human and half lion.
[10]Had sexual intercourse with.
[11]The Cain and Abel story reflects the tensions between nomadic shepherds and farmers. (Compare the tension between hunter and shepherd in the story of Jacob and Esau.) No reason is given for God's refusal of Cain's offering.

And the days of Adam after he had begotten Seth were eight hundred years: and he begot sons and daughters. And all the days that Adam lived were nine hundred and thirty years: and he died. . . .[12]

THE FLOOD

(Genesis 6:1–9:29)
And it came to pass, when men began to multiply on the face of the earth, and daughters were born unto them, that the sons of God saw the daughters of men that they were fair; and they took them wives of all which they chose.[13] And the Lord said, "My spirit shall not always strive with man, for that he also is flesh: yet his days shall be a hundred and twenty years." There were giants in the earth in those days; and also after that, when the sons of God came in unto the daughters of men, and they bore children to them, the same became mighty men which were of old, men of renown. And God saw that the wickedness of man was great in the earth, and that every imagination of the thoughts of his heart was only evil continually. And it repented the Lord that he had made man on the earth, and it grieved him at his heart. And the Lord said, "I will destroy man whom I have created from the face of the earth; both man, and beast, and the creeping thing, and the fowls of the air; for it repenteth me that I have made them." But Noah found grace in the eyes of the Lord. . . .

Noah was a just man and perfect in his generations, and Noah walked with God. And Noah begot three sons, Shem, Ham, and Japheth. . . .

And God said unto Noah, "The end of all flesh is come before me; for the earth is filled with violence through them; and, behold, I will destroy them with the earth.[14] Make thee an ark of gopher wood;[15] rooms shalt thou make in the ark, and shalt pitch it within and without with pitch. And this is the fashion which thou shalt make it of: the length of the ark shall be three hundred cubits,[16] the breadth of it fifty cubits, and the height of it thirty cubits. A window shalt thou make to the ark, and in a cubit shalt thou finish it above; and the door of the ark shalt thou set in the side thereof; with lower, second, and third stories shalt thou make it. And, behold, I, even I, do bring a flood of waters upon the earth, to destroy all flesh, wherein is

---

[12] Various explanations have been offered to account for the extraordinary life spans attributed to figures of the Old Testament. The simplest is that they are exaggerations—such as appear in other national legends—intended to glorify the beginnings of the race.

[13] This account of the mating of "the sons of God" and "the daughters of men" is a good example of the primitive conceptions of divinity that still survive in the Old Testament. The story was perhaps originally intended to account for the existence of the Nephilim, a tribe of men of gigantic size and strength; this narrative may be compared to the stories of the matings of gods and mortal women in Greek mythology.

[14] The biblical account of the Flood has much in common with other accounts of great floods, especially in the Babylonian *Gilgamesh* epic. In this other work, the hero also builds an ark, it comes to rest on a mountain, birds are sent out to see if the flood is subsiding, and the hero makes burnt offerings for his deliverance. The Genesis version differs, however, in that the Flood is not sent capriciously but as a punishment for human wickedness.

[15] An ark is a large ship. The kind of wood used is unidentified; "gopher" simply means "tree" in Hebrew.

[16] A cubit is an ancient unit of measurement based on the length of the forearm, usually about 20 inches.

the breath of life, from under heaven; and everything that is in the earth shall die. But with thee will I establish my covenant;[17] and thou shalt come into the ark, thou, and thy sons, and thy wife, and thy sons' wives with thee. And of every living thing of all flesh, two of every sort shalt thou bring into the ark, to keep them alive with thee; they shall be male and female. Of fowls after their kind, and of cattle after their kind, of every creeping thing of the earth after his kind, two of every sort shall come unto thee, to keep them alive. And take thou unto thee of all food that is eaten, and thou shalt gather it to thee; and it shall be for food for thee, and for them." Thus did Noah; according to all that God commanded him, so did he. And the Lord said unto Noah, "Come thou and all thy house into the ark; for thee have I seen righteous before me in this generation. Of every clean beast thou shalt take to thee by sevens, the male and his female; and of beasts that are not clean by two, the male and his female.[18] Of fowls also of the air by sevens, the male and the female; to keep seed alive upon the face of all the earth. For yet seven days, and I will cause it to rain upon the earth forty days and forty nights; and every living substance that I have made will I destroy from off the face of the earth."

And Noah did according unto all that the Lord commanded him. And Noah went in, and his sons, and his wife, and his sons' wives with him, into the ark, because of the waters of the flood. Of clean beasts, and of beasts that are not clean, and of fowls, and of every thing that creepeth upon the earth, there went in two and two unto Noah into the ark, the male and the female, as God had commanded Noah. And it came to pass after seven days that the waters of the flood were upon the earth. In the six hundredth year of Noah's life in the second month, the seventeenth day of the month, the same day were all the fountains of the great deep broken up, and the windows of heaven were opened.[19] And the waters prevailed, and were increased greatly upon the earth; and the ark went upon the face of the waters. And the waters prevailed exceedingly upon the earth; and all the high hills, that were under the whole heaven, were covered. Fifteen cubits upward did the waters prevail; and the mountains were covered. And all flesh died that moved upon the earth, both of fowl, and of cattle, and of beast, and of every creeping thing that creepeth upon the earth, and every man. All in whose nostrils was the breath of life, of all that was in the dry land, died. And every living substance was destroyed which was upon the face of the ground, both man, and cattle, and the creeping things, and the fowl of the heaven; and they were destroyed from the earth: and Noah only remained alive, and they

[17] This "covenant," or agreement, between God and Noah, which is expanded after the Flood and marked with the sign of the rainbow, is the first of several such covenants in the Old Testament. The agreements culminate in the repeated covenant with Abraham and his descendants, which has become the central idea in Judaism. The conditions under which God allowed Adam and Eve to live in the Garden are an implicit covenant that anticipates these later covenants.

[18] "Clean beasts" include those that have cloven hooves and chew a cud. See Leviticus, Chapter 11. The distinction between clean and unclean here is apparently a later addition, not harmonized with the rest of the text, since Noah takes in two of each animal, regardless of status.

[19] As a result of the blending of different accounts, two explanations are given for the Flood. The first is that it rained for forty days and forty nights, while here it is said that "all the fountains of the great deep [were] broken up, and the windows of heaven were opened." In other words, chaos returned through the opening up of subterranean seas and the opening of the domelike firmament that restrained "the waters above." See the beginning of Genesis.

that were with him in the ark. And the waters prevailed upon the earth a hundred and fifty days.

And God remembered Noah, and every living thing, and all the cattle that was with him in the ark: and God made a wind to pass over the earth, and the waters assuaged. The fountains also of the deep and the windows of heaven were stopped, and the rain from heaven was restrained; and the waters returned from off the earth continually: and after the end of the hundred and fifty days the waters were abated. And the ark rested in the seventh month, on the seventeenth day of the month, upon the mountains of Ararat. And the waters decreased continually until the tenth month: in the tenth month, on the first day of the month, were the tops of the mountains seen.

And it came to pass at the end of forty days that Noah opened the window of the ark which he had made: and he sent forth a raven, which went forth to and fro, until the waters were dried up from off the earth. Also he sent forth a dove from him, to see if the waters were abated from off the face of the ground; but the dove found no rest for the sole of her foot, and she returned unto him into the ark, for the waters were on the face of the whole earth: then he put forth his hand, and took her, and pulled her in unto him into the ark. And he stayed yet other seven days; and again he sent forth the dove out of the ark; and the dove came in to him in the evening; and, lo, in her mouth was an olive leaf plucked off: so Noah knew that the waters were abated from off the earth. And he stayed yet other seven days; and sent forth the dove; which returned not again unto him any more.

And it came to pass in the six hundredth and first year, in the first month, the first day of the month, the waters were dried up from off the earth: and Noah removed the covering of the ark, and looked, and, behold the face of the ground was dry. And in the second month, on the seven and twentieth day of the month, was the earth dried. And God spoke unto Noah, saying, "Go forth of the ark, thou, and thy wife, and thy sons, and thy sons' wives with thee. Bring forth with thee every living thing that is with thee, of all flesh, both of fowl, and of cattle, and of every creeping thing that creepeth upon the earth; that they may breed abundantly in the earth, and be fruitful, and multiply upon the earth." And Noah went forth, and his sons, and his wife, and his sons' wives with him. Every beast, every creeping thing, and every fowl, and whatsoever creepeth upon the earth, after their kinds, went forth out of the ark.

And Noah builded an altar unto the Lord; and took of every clean beast, and of every clean fowl, and offered burnt offerings on the altar. And the Lord smelled a sweet savor; and the Lord said in his heart, "I will not again curse the ground any more for man's sake; for the imagination of man's heart is evil from his youth; neither will I again smite any more every thing living, as I have done. While the earth remaineth, seedtime and harvest, and cold and heat, and summer and winter, and day and night shall not cease."

And God blessed Noah and his sons, and said unto them, "Be fruitful, and multiply, and replenish the earth. And the fear of you and the dread of you shall be upon every beast of the earth, and upon every fowl of the air, upon all that moveth upon the earth, and upon all the fishes of the sea; into your hand are they delivered. Every moving thing that liveth shall be meat for you; even as the green herb have I given you all things. But flesh with the life thereof, which is the blood thereof, shall ye not eat. And surely your blood of your lives will I require; at the hand of every beast will I require it, and at the hand of man; at the hand of every man's brother will I require the life of man. Whoso sheddeth man's blood, by man shall his blood be shed: for in the image of God made he man." . . . And God spoke unto Noah, and to his sons with him, saying, "And I, behold, I establish my covenant with you, and with your seed after you; and with every living creature that is with you, of the fowl, of the cattle, and of every beast of the earth with you; from all that go out of the ark, to every beast of the earth. And I will establish my covenant with you; neither shall all flesh be cut off any more by the waters of a flood; neither shall there any more be a flood to destroy the earth."

And God said, "This is the token of the covenant which I make between me and you and every living creature that is with you, for perpetual generations: I do set my bow in the cloud, and it shall be for a token of a covenant between me and the earth. And it shall come to pass, when I bring a cloud over the earth, that the bow shall be seen in the cloud: and I will remember my covenant, which is between me and you and every living creature of all flesh; and the waters shall no more become a flood to destroy all flesh. And the bow shall be in the cloud; and I will look upon it, that I may remember the everlasting covenant between God and every living creature of all flesh that is upon the earth." [20] And God said unto Noah, "This is the token of the covenant, which I have established between me and all flesh that is upon the earth." . . .

And Noah began to be a husbandman, and he planted a vineyard: and he drank of the wine, and was drunken; and he was uncovered within his tent. And Ham, the father of Canaan, saw the nakedness of his father, and told his two brethren without. And Shem and Japheth took a garment, and laid it upon both their shoulders, and went backward, and covered the nakedness of their father; and their faces were backward, and they saw not their father's nakedness.[21] And Noah awoke from his wine, and knew what his younger son had done unto him. And he said, "Cursed be Canaan; a servant of servants shall he be unto his brethren." And he said, "Blessed be the Lord God of Shem; and Canaan shall be his servant. God shall enlarge Japheth, and he shall dwell in the tents of Shem; and Canaan shall be his servant."

And Noah lived after the flood three hundred and fifty years. And all the days of Noah were nine hundred and fifty years: and he died. . . .

THE TOWER OF BABEL

(Genesis II:I–II:9)
And the whole earth was of one language, and of one speech. And it came to pass, as they journeyed from the east, that they found a plain in the land

[20] The rainbow was often regarded by primitive peoples as God's bow from which he shot arrows of lightning. Here it becomes rather a sign in the heavens that God's anger has abated.
[21] There is some confusion here in names. God places the curse on Canaan rather than on Ham, who is said to have committed the offense. The incident implies that Israel's later subjugation of Canaan was the consequence of the Canaanites' sexual perversions.

of Shinar; and they dwelt there. And they said one to another, "Go to, let us make brick, and burn them thoroughly." And they had brick for stone, and slime had they for mortar. And they said, "Go to, let us build us a city and a tower, whose top may reach unto heaven; and let us make us a name, lest we be scattered abroad upon the face of the whole earth." [22] And the Lord came down to see the city and the tower, which the children of men builded. And the Lord said, "Behold, the people is one, and they have all one language; and this they begin to do: and now nothing will be restrained from them, which they have imagined to do. Go to, let us go down, and there confound their language, that they may not understand one another's speech." So the Lord scattered them abroad from thence upon the face of all the earth: and they left off to build the city. Therefore is the name of it called Babel; because the Lord did there confound the language of all the earth: and from thence did the Lord scatter them abroad upon the face of all the earth. . . .

THE STORY OF ABRAHAM AND ISAAC

(Genesis II:27–25:28)
Now these are the generations of Terah: Terah begot Abram, Nahor and Haran; and Haran begot Lot. And Haran died before his father Terah in the land of his nativity, in Ur of the Chaldees. And Abram and Nahor took them wives: the name of Abram's wife was Sarai; and the name of Nahor's wife, Milcah, the daughter of Haran, the father of Milcah, and the father of Iscah. But Sarai was barren; she had no child.

And Terah took Abram his son, and Lot the son of Haran his son's son, and Sarai his daughter-in-law, his son Abram's wife; and they went forth with them from Ur of the Chaldees, to go into the land of Canaan; and they came unto Haran, and dwelt there. And the days of Terah were two hundred and five years: and Terah died in Haran.

Now the Lord had said unto Abram, "Get thee out of thy country, and from thy kindred, and from thy father's house, unto a land that I will show thee: and I will make of thee a great nation, and I will bless thee, and make thy name great; and thou shalt be a blessing. And I will bless them that bless thee, and curse him that curseth thee: and in thee shall all families of the earth be blessed." [23]

So Abram departed, as the Lord had spoken unto him; and Lot went with him: and Abram was seventy and five years old when he departed out of Haran. And Abram took Sarai his wife, and Lot his brother's son, and all their substance that they had gathered, and the souls that they had gotten in Haran; and they went forth to go into the land of Canaan; and into

---

[22] Mesopotamian cities were marked by ziggurats, pyramidlike towers regarded as the gateways to heaven. The story of the Tower of Babel not only alludes to such structures but also is an etiological story accounting for the origin of languages and the cultural magnificence of Babylon. The episode also emphasizes humanity's continuing pride and sinfulness even after the Flood.

[23] This is the first statement of the often-repeated "covenant" with Israel around which much of Old Testament history revolves.

the land of Canaan they came. And Abram passed through the land unto the place of Sichem, unto the plain of Moreh. And the Canaanite was then in the land. And the Lord appeared unto Abram, and said, "Unto thy seed will I give this land." And there builded he an altar unto the Lord, who appeared unto him. And he removed from thence unto a mountain on the east of Beth-el, and pitched his tent, having Beth-el on the west, and Hai on the east: and there he builded an altar unto the Lord, and called upon the name of the Lord. And Abram journeyed, going on still toward the south. . . .[24]

And it came to pass after these things that God did tempt Abraham, and said unto him, "Abraham": and he said, "Behold, here I am." And he said, "Take now thy son, thine only son Isaac, whom thou lovest, and get thee into the land of Moriah; and offer him there for a burnt offering upon one of the mountains which I will tell thee of." And Abraham rose up early in the morning, and saddled his ass, and took two of his young men with him, and Isaac his son, and cleft the wood for the burnt offering, and rose up, and went unto the place of which God had told him. Then on the third day Abraham lifted up his eyes, and saw the place afar off. And Abraham said unto his young men, "Abide ye here with the ass; and I and the lad will go yonder and worship, and come again to you." And Abraham took the wood of the burnt offering, and laid it upon Isaac his son; and he took the fire in his hand, and a knife; and they went both of them together.

And Isaac spoke unto Abraham his father, and said, "My father": and he said, "Here am I, my son." And he said, "Behold the fire and the wood: but where is the lamb for a burnt offering?" And Abraham said, "My son, God will provide himself a lamb for a burnt offering": so they went both of them together. And they came to the place which God had told him of; and Abraham built an altar there, and laid the wood in order, and bound Isaac his son, and laid him on the altar upon the wood. And Abraham stretched forth his hand, and took the knife to slay his son. And the angel of the Lord called unto him out of heaven, and said, "Abraham, Abraham": and he said, "Here am I." And he said, "Lay not thine hand upon the lad, neither do thou any thing unto him: for now I know that thou fearest God, seeing thou hast not withheld thy son, thine only son from me." And Abraham lifted up his eyes, and looked, and beheld behind him a ram caught in a thicket by his horns: and Abraham went and took the ram, and offered him up for a burnt offering in the stead of his son. And Abraham called the name of that place Jehovah-jireh: as it is said to this day, "In the mount of the Lord it shall be seen. . . .[25]

---

[24] Abram and his family migrate to Egypt and then return to Canaan. His nephew Lot settles in the cities of the fertile plain of Jordan. To mark His covenant with the Hebrews, God changes Abram's name to Abraham and Sarai's to Sarah, requires that all males of Abraham's line be circumcised, and miraculously causes Sarah to bear a son, Isaac, in her very old age. Angered by the practice of sodomy, God sends down fire and brimstone to destroy the cities of the plain, Sodom and Gomorrah, sparing only Lot and some of his kin.

[25] The story of the near-sacrifice of Isaac has many analogues in other religions and literatures, including the story of Agamemnon's sacrifice of his daughter Iphigenia, referred to in the *Iliad* and in Aeschylus' *Agamemnon*. The form the story takes here seems to celebrate perfect faith and to condemn human sacrifice.

So Abraham returned unto his young men, and they rose up and went together to Beer-sheba; and Abraham dwelt at Beer-sheba. . . .[26]

And Isaac was forty years old when he took Rebekah to wife, the daughter of Bethuel the Syrian of Padan-aram, the sister to Laban the Syrian. And Isaac intreated the Lord for his wife, because she was barren: and the Lord was intreated of him, and Rebekah his wife conceived. And the children struggled together within her; and she said, "If it be so, why am I thus?" And she went to enquire of the Lord. And the Lord said unto her,

> "Two nations are in thy womb,
>   and two manner of people shall be separated from thy bowels;
> And the one people shall be stronger than the other people;
>   and the elder shall serve the younger."

And when her days to be delivered were fulfilled, behold, there were twins in her womb. And the first came out red, all over like a hairy garment; and they called his name Esau. And after that came his brother out, and his hand took hold on Esau's heel; and his name was called Jacob:[27] and Isaac was threescore years old when she bore them. And the boys grew: and Esau was a cunning hunter, a man of the field; and Jacob was a plain man, dwelling in tents. And Isaac loved Esau, because he did eat of his venison: but Rebekah loved Jacob.

THE STORY OF JACOB

(Genesis 25:29–35:29)
And Jacob sod pottage:[28] and Esau came from the field, and he was faint: and Esau said to Jacob, "Feed me, I pray thee, with that same red pottage; for I am faint" (therefore was his name called Edom). And Jacob said, "Sell me this day thy birthright." And Esau said, "Behold, I am at the point to die: and what profit shall this birthright do to me?" And Jacob said, "Swear to me this day!" And he swore unto him: and he sold his birthright unto Jacob. Then Jacob gave Esau bread and pottage of lentils; and he did eat and drink, and rose up, and went his way: thus Esau despised his birthright. . . .

And Esau was forty years old when he took to wife Judith the daughter of Beeri the Hittite, and Bashemath the daughter of Elon the Hittite: which were a grief of mind unto Isaac and to Rebekah.

And it came to pass that when Isaac was old, and his eyes were dim, so that he could not see, he called Esau his eldest son, and said unto him, "My

---

[26]After Sarah dies, Abraham seeks a bride for Isaac. Resolved that his son shall marry a woman of his own Mesopotamian people rather than any of the local Canaanite women, Abraham sends his steward to his former homeland. While stopping by a well, the steward providentially encounters Rebekah, Isaac's first cousin. She travels to her new homeland in Canaan and is married to Isaac. Abraham dies and is buried beside Sarah.

[27]The name Jacob can mean either "he takes by the heel" or "he supplants." The second meaning is particularly relevant in the light of Jacob's later history. The character of Jacob is a version of the "trickster hero," and his often rather crudely comic exploits in the sections that follow still betray their origins in folktales.

[28]Cooked food.

son": and he said unto him, "Behold, here am I." And he said, "Behold now, I am old, I know not the day of my death. Now therefore take, I pray thee, thy weapons, thy quiver and thy bow, and go out to the field, and take me some venison; and make me savory meat, such as I love, and bring it to me, that I may eat; that my soul may bless thee before I die."

And Rebekah heard when Isaac spoke to Esau his son. And Esau went to the field to hunt for venison, and to bring it. And Rebekah spoke unto Jacob her son, saying, "Behold, I heard thy father speak unto Esau thy brother, saying, 'Bring me venison, and make me savory meat, that I may eat, and bless thee before the Lord before my death.' Now therefore, my son, obey my voice according to that which I command thee. Go now to the flock, and fetch me from thence two good kids of the goats; and I will make them savory meat for thy father, such as he loveth: and thou shalt bring it to thy father, that he may eat, and that he may bless thee before his death." And Jacob said to Rebekah his mother, "Behold, Esau my brother is a hairy man, and I am a smooth man. My father peradventure will feel me, and I shall seem to him as a deceiver; and I shall bring a curse upon me, and not a blessing." And his mother said unto him, "Upon me be thy curse, my son; only obey my voice, and go fetch me them." And he went, and fetched, and brought them to his mother; and his mother made savory meat, such as his father loved. And Rebekah took goodly raiment of her eldest son Esau, which were with her in the house, and put them upon Jacob her younger son; and she put the skins of the kids of the goats upon his hands, and upon the smooth of his neck; and she gave the savory meat and the bread, which she had prepared, into the hand of her son Jacob.

And he came unto his father, and said, "My father": and he said, "Here am I; who art thou, my son?" And Jacob said unto his father, "I am Esau thy firstborn; I have done according as thou badest me: arise, I pray thee, sit and eat of my venison, that thy soul may bless me." And Isaac said unto his son, "How is it that thou hast found it so quickly, my son?" And he said, "Because the Lord thy God brought it to me." And Isaac said unto Jacob, "Come near, I pray thee, that I may feel thee, my son, whether thou be my very son Esau or not." And Jacob went near unto Isaac his father; and he felt him, and said, "The voice is Jacob's voice, but the hands are the hands of Esau." And he discerned him not, because his hands were hairy, as his brother Esau's hands; so he blessed him. And he said, "Art thou my very son Esau?" And he said, "I am." And he said, "Bring it near to me, and I will eat of my son's venison, that my soul may bless thee." And he brought it near to him, and he did eat: and he brought the wine, and he drank. And his father Isaac said unto him, "Come near now, and kiss me, my son." And he came near, and kissed him: and he smelled the smell of his raiment, and blessed him, and said,

> "See, the smell of my son
> is as the smell of a field which the Lord hath blessed:
> Therefore God give thee of the dew of heaven,
> and the fatness of the earth,
> and plenty of corn and wine:
> Let people serve thee,
> and nations bow down to thee:

Be lord over thy brethren,
and let thy mother's sons bow down to thee:
Cursed be every one that curseth thee,
and blessed be he that blesseth thee."

And it came to pass, as soon as Isaac had made an end of blessing Jacob, and Jacob was yet scarce gone out from the presence of Isaac his father, that Esau his brother came in from his hunting. And he also had made savory meat, and brought it unto his father, and said unto his father, "Let my father arise, and eat of his son's venison, that thy soul may bless me." And Isaac his father said unto him, "Who art thou?" And he said, "I am thy son, thy firstborn Esau." And Isaac trembled very exceedingly, and said, "Who? where is he that hath taken venison, and brought it me, and I have eaten of all before thou camest, and have blessed him? yea, and he shall be blessed." And when Esau heard the words of his father, he cried with a great and exceeding bitter cry, and said unto his father, "Bless me, even me also, O my father." And he said, "Thy brother came with subtilty, and hath taken away thy blessing." And he said, "Is not he rightly named Jacob? for he hath supplanted me these two times: he took away my birthright; and, behold, now he hath taken away my blessing." And he said, "Hast thou not reserved a blessing for me?" And Isaac answered and said unto Esau, "Behold, I have made him thy lord, and all his brethren have I given to him for servants; and with corn and wine have I sustained him: and what shall I do now unto thee, my son?" And Esau said unto his father, "Hast thou but one blessing, my father? bless me, even me also, O my father." And Esau lifted up his voice, and wept. And Isaac his father answered and said unto him,

"Behold, thy dwelling shall be the fatness of the earth,
and of the dew of heaven from above;
And by thy sword shalt thou live,
and shalt serve thy brother;
And it shall come to pass when thou shalt have the dominion,
that thou shalt break his yoke from off thy neck."

And Esau hated Jacob because of the blessing wherewith his father blessed him: and Esau said in his heart, "The days of mourning for my father are at hand; then will I slay my brother Jacob."[29] And these words of Esau her elder son were told to Rebekah: and she sent and called Jacob her younger son, and said unto him, "Behold, thy brother Esau, as touching thee, doth comfort himself, purposing to kill thee. Now therefore, my son, obey my voice; and arise, flee thou to Laban my brother to Haran. And tarry with him a few days, until thy brother's fury turn away; until thy brother's anger turn away from thee, and he forget that which thou hast done to him. Then I will send, and fetch thee from thence: why should I be deprived also of you both in one day?"

---

[29] Jacob's hoodwinking of Isaac reflects the ancient belief in the magical nature of formal blessings and curses; once a blessing had been pronounced, even in error, it could not be withdrawn.

And Rebekah said to Isaac, "I am weary of my life because of the daughters of Heth: if Jacob take a wife of the daughters of Heth, such as these which are of the daughters of the land, what good shall my life do me?" And Isaac called Jacob, and blessed him, and charged him, and said unto him, "Thou shalt not take a wife of the daughters of Canaan. Arise, go to Padan-aram, to the house of Bethuel thy mother's father; and take thee a wife from thence of the daughters of Laban thy mother's brother. And God Almighty bless thee, and make thee fruitful, and multiply thee, that thou mayest be a multitude of people; and give thee the blessing of Abraham, to thee, and to thy seed with thee; that thou mayest inherit the land wherein thou art a stranger, which God gave unto Abraham." . . .

And Jacob went out from Beer-sheba, and went toward Haran. And he lighted upon a certain place, and tarried there all night, because the sun was set; and he took of the stones of that place, and put them for his pillows, and lay down in that place to sleep. And he dreamed, and, behold, a ladder set up on the earth, and the top of it reached to heaven: and, behold, the angels of God ascending and descending on it. And, behold, the Lord stood above it, and said, "I am the Lord God of Abraham thy father, and the God of Isaac: the land whereon thou liest, to thee will I give it, and to thy seed; and thy seed shall be as the dust of the earth, and thou shalt spread abroad to the west, and to the east, and to the north, and to the south: and in thee and in thy seed shall all the families of the earth be blessed. And, behold, I am with thee, and will keep thee in all places whither thou goest, and will bring thee again into this land; for I will not leave thee until I have done that which I have spoken to thee of." And Jacob awaked out of his sleep, and he said, "Surely the Lord is in this place; and I knew it not." And he was afraid, and said, "How dreadful is this place! this is none other but the house of God, and this is the gate of heaven."

And Jacob rose up early in the morning, and took the stone that he had put for his pillows, and set it up for a pillar, and poured oil upon the top of it. And he called the name of that place Beth-el:[30] but the name of that city was called Luz at the first. And Jacob vowed a vow, saying, "If God will be with me, and will keep me in this way that I go, and will give me bread to eat, and raiment to put on, so that I come again to my father's house in peace; then shall the Lord be my God: and this stone, which I have set for a pillar, shall be God's house: and of all that thou shalt give me I will surely give the tenth unto thee."

Then Jacob went on his journey, and came into the land of the people of the east. And he looked, and beheld a well in the field, and, lo, there were three flocks of sheep lying by it; for out of that well they watered the flocks: and a great stone was upon the well's mouth. And thither were all the flocks gathered: and they rolled the stone from the well's mouth, and watered the sheep, and put the stone again upon the well's mouth in his place. And Jacob said unto them, "My brethren, whence be ye?" And they said, "Of Haran are we." And he said unto them, "Know ye Laban the son of Nahor?" And they said, "We know him." And he said unto them, "Is he well?" And they said, "He is well: and, behold, Rachel his daughter cometh with the sheep." And he said, "Lo, it is yet high day, neither is it time that

---

[30] "The House of God."

the cattle should be gathered together: water ye the sheep, and go and feed them." And they said, "We cannot, until all the flocks be gathered together, and till they roll the stone from the well's mouth; then we water the sheep." And while he yet spoke with them, Rachel came with her father's sheep: for she kept them. And it came to pass, when Jacob saw Rachel the daughter of Laban his mother's brother, and the sheep of Laban his mother's brother, that Jacob went near, and rolled the stone from the well's mouth; and watered the flock of Laban his mother's brother. And Jacob kissed Rachel, and lifted up his voice, and wept. And Jacob told Rachel that he was her father's brother, and that he was Rebekah's son: and she ran and told her father.

And it came to pass, when Laban heard the tidings of Jacob his sister's son, that he ran to meet him, and embraced him, and kissed him, and brought him to his house. And he told Laban all these things. And Laban said to him, "Surely thou art my bone and my flesh." And he abode with him the space of a month. And Laban said unto Jacob, "Because thou art my brother, shouldest thou therefore serve me for nought? tell me, what shall thy wages be?" And Laban had two daughters: the name of the elder was Leah, and the name of the younger was Rachel. Leah was tender-eyed;[31] but Rachel was beautiful and well favored. And Jacob loved Rachel; and said, "I will serve thee seven years for Rachel thy younger daughter." And Laban said, "It is better that I give her to thee than that I should give her to another man. Abide with me."

And Jacob served seven years for Rachel; and they seemed unto him but a few days, for the love he had to her. And Jacob said unto Laban, "Give me my wife, for my days are fulfilled, that I may go in unto her." And Laban gathered together all the men of the place, and made a feast. And it came to pass in the evening that he took Leah his daughter, and brought her to him; and he went in unto her. And Laban gave unto his daughter Leah Zilpah his maid for a handmaid. And it came to pass that in the morning, behold, it was Leah: and he said to Laban, "What is this thou hast done unto me? did not I serve with thee for Rachel? wherefore then hast thou beguiled me?" And Laban said, "It must not be so done in our country, to give the younger before the firstborn. Fulfil her week, and we will give thee this also for the service which thou shalt serve with me yet seven other years."[32] And Jacob did so, and fulfilled her week: and he gave him Rachel his daughter to wife also. And Laban gave to Rachel his daughter Bilhah his handmaid to be her maid. And he went in also unto Rachel, and he loved also Rachel more than Leah, and served with him yet seven other years.

And when the Lord saw that Leah was hated, he opened her womb: but Rachel was barren. And Leah conceived, and bore a son, and she called his name Reuben: for she said, "Surely the Lord hath looked upon my affliction; now therefore my husband will love me."[33] And she conceived again, and bore a son; and said, "Because the Lord hath heard that I was hated, he hath therefore given me this son also": and she called his name Simeon. And she conceived again, and bore a son; and said, "Now this time will my

[31] The word here translated "tender-eyed" apparently means, more precisely, "dull-eyed."
[32] Laban's cheating of Jacob, an example of "the trickster out-tricked," succeeds because of the custom of leading the bride to the bridal tent in darkness.
[33] "Reuben" means "See, a son!"

husband be joined unto me, because I have borne him three sons": therefore was his name called Levi. And she conceived again, and bore a son: and she said, "Now will I praise the Lord": therefore she called his name Judah; and left bearing.

And when Rachel saw that she bore Jacob no children, Rachel envied her sister; and said unto Jacob, "Give me children, or else I die." And Jacob's anger was kindled against Rachel: and he said "Am I in God's stead, who hath withheld from thee the fruit of the womb?" And she said, "Behold my maid Bilhah, go in unto her; and she shall bear upon my knees, that I may also have children by her." And she gave him Bilhah her handmaid to wife: and Jacob went in unto her. And Bilhah conceived, and bore Jacob a son. And Rachel said, "God hath judged me, and hath also heard my voice, and hath given me a son": therefore called she his name Dan.[34] And Bilhah Rachel's maid conceived again, and bore Jacob a second son. And Rachel said, "With great wrestlings have I wrestled with my sister, and I have prevailed": and she called his name Naphtali.

When Leah saw that she had left bearing, she took Zilpah her maid, and gave her Jacob to wife. And Zilpah Leah's maid bore Jacob a son. And Leah said, "A troop cometh": and she called his name Gad.[35] And Zilpah Leah's maid bore Jacob a second son. And Leah said, "Happy am I, for the daughters will call me blessed": and she called his name Asher.[36]

And Reuben went in the days of wheat harvest, and found mandrakes in the field, and brought them unto his mother Leah. Then Rachel said to Leah, "Give me, I pray thee, of thy son's mandrakes."[37] And she said unto her, "Is it a small matter that thou hast taken my husband? and wouldest thou take away my son's mandrakes also?" And Rachel said, "Therefore he shall lie with thee to-night for thy son's mandrakes." And Jacob came out of the field in the evening, and Leah went out to meet him, and said, "Thou must come in unto me; for surely I have hired thee with my son's mandrakes." And he lay with her that night. And God hearkened unto Leah, and she conceived, and bore Jacob the fifth son. And Leah said, "God hath given me my hire, because I have given my maiden to my husband": and she called his name Issachar. And Leah conceived again, and bore Jacob the sixth son. And Leah said, "God hath endued me with a good dowry; now will my husband dwell with me, because I have borne him six sons": and she called his name Zebulun. And afterwards she bore a daughter, and called her name Dinah. And God remembered Rachel, and God hearkened to her, and opened her womb. And she conceived, and bore a son; and said, "God hath taken away my reproach": and she called his name Joseph; and said, "The Lord shall add to me another son."[38]

And it came to pass, when Rachel had borne Joseph, that Jacob said unto Laban, "Send me away, that I may go unto mine own place, and to my country. Give me my wives and my children, for whom I have served thee, and let me go: for thou knowest my service which I have done thee." And Laban

---

[34]"Dan" means "He judged."   [35]"Gad" means "Fortune."
[36]"Asher" means "Happy."
[37]Mandrakes are the roots of a potatolike plant that were thought to have aphrodisiac qualities and to stimulate conception.
[38]"Joseph" means "He adds."

said unto him, "I pray thee, if I have found favor in thine eyes, tarry: for I have learned by experience that the Lord hath blessed me for thy sake." And he said, "Appoint me thy wages, and I will give it." And he said unto him, "Thou knowest how I have served thee, and how thy cattle was with me. For it was little which thou hadst before I came, and it is now increased unto a multitude; and the Lord hath blessed thee since my coming: and now when shall I provide for mine own house also?" And he said, "What shall I give thee?" And Jacob said, "Thou shalt not give me any thing: if thou wilt do this thing for me, I will again feed and keep thy flock. I will pass through all thy flock to-day, removing from thence all the speckled and spotted cattle, and all the brown cattle among the sheep, and the spotted and speckled among the goats: and of such shall be my hire. So shall my righteousness answer for me in time to come, when it shall come for my hire before thy face: everyone that is not speckled and spotted among the goats, and brown among the sheep, that shall be counted stolen with me." And Laban said, "Behold, I would it might be according to thy word." And he removed that day the he-goats that were ringstreaked and spotted, and all the she-goats that were speckled and spotted, and every one that had some white in it, and all the brown among the sheep, and gave them into the hand of his sons. And he set three days' journey betwixt himself and Jacob: and Jacob fed the rest of Laban's flocks.

And Jacob took him rods of green poplar, and of the hazel and chestnut tree; and peeled white strakes in them, and made the white appear which was in the rods. And he set the rods which he had peeled before the flocks in the gutters in the watering troughs when the flocks came to drink, that they should conceive when they came to drink. And the flocks conceived before the rods, and brought forth cattle ringstreaked, speckled, and spotted.[39] And Jacob did separate the lambs, and set the faces of the flocks toward the ringstreaked, and all the brown in the flock of Laban; and he put his own flocks by themselves, and put them not unto Laban's cattle. And it came to pass, whensoever the stronger cattle did conceive, that Jacob laid the rods before the eyes of the cattle in the gutters, that they might conceive among the rods. But when the cattle were feeble, he put them not in: so the feebler were Laban's, and the stronger Jacob's. And the man increased exceedingly, and had much cattle, and maidservants, and menservants, and camels, and asses.

And he heard the words of Laban's sons, saying, "Jacob hath taken away all that was our father's; and of that which was our father's hath he gotten all this glory." And Jacob beheld the countenance of Laban and, behold, it was not toward him as before. And the Lord said unto Jacob, "Return unto the land of thy fathers, and to thy kindred; and I will be with thee." And Jacob sent and called Rachel and Leah to the field unto his flock and said unto them, "I see your father's countenance, that it is not toward me as before; but the God of my father hath been with me. And ye know that with all my power I have served your father. And your father hath deceived me, and changed my wages ten times; but God suffered him not to hurt me. If he

---

[39]Jacob's trick depends upon the notion of prenatal influence, the belief that a pregnant animal's experiences influence her offspring. The cows and ewes see spotted rods and give birth to spotted offspring.

said thus, 'The speckled shall be thy wages'; then all the cattle bore speckled: and if he said thus, 'The ringstreaked shall be thy hire'; then bore all the cattle ringstreaked. Thus God hath taken away the cattle of your father, and given them to me. And it came to pass at the time that the cattle conceived, that I lifted up mine eyes, and saw in a dream, and, behold, the rams which leaped upon the cattle were ringstreaked, speckled, and grisled. And the angel of God spoke unto me in a dream, saying, 'Jacob.' And I said, 'Here am I.' And he said, 'Lift up now thine eyes, and see, all the rams which leap upon the cattle are ringstreaked, speckled, and grisled: for I have seen all that Laban doeth unto thee. I am the God of Beth-el, where thou anointedst the pillar, and where thou vowedst a vow unto me: now arise, get thee out from this land, and return unto the land of thy kindred.'" And Rachel and Leah answered and said unto him, "Is there yet any portion or inheritance for us in our father's house? Are we not counted of him strangers? for he hath sold us, and hath quite devoured also our money. For all the riches which God hath taken from our father, that is ours, and our children's: now then, whatsoever God hath said unto thee, do."

Then Jacob rose up, and set his sons and his wives upon camels; and he carried away all his cattle, and all his goods which he had gotten, the cattle of his getting, which he had gotten in Padan-aram, for to go to Isaac his father in the land of Canaan. And Laban went to shear his sheep: and Rachel had stolen the images that were her father's.[40] And Jacob stole away unawares to Laban the Syrian, in that he told him not that he fled. So he fled with all that he had; and he rose up, and passed over the river, and set his face toward the mount Gilead.

And it was told Laban on the third day that Jacob was fled. And he took his brethren with him, and pursued after him seven days' journey; and they overtook him in the mount Gilead. And God came to Laban the Syrian in a dream by night, and said unto him, "Take heed that thou speak not to Jacob either good or bad."

Then Laban overtook Jacob. Now Jacob had pitched his tent in the mount: and Laban with his brethren pitched in the Mount of Gilead. And Laban said to Jacob, "What hast thou done, that thou hast stolen away unawares to me, and carried away my daughters, as captives taken with the sword? Wherefore didst thou flee away secretly, and steal away from me; and didst not tell me, that I might have sent thee away with mirth, and with songs, with tabret, and with harp? And hast not suffered me to kiss my sons and my daughters? thou has now done foolishly in so doing. It is in the power of my hand to do you hurt: but the God of your father spoke unto me yesternight, saying, 'Take thou heed that thou speak not to Jacob either good or bad.' And now, though thou wouldest needs be gone, because thou sore longedst after thy father's house, yet wherefore hast thou stolen my gods?" And Jacob answered and said to Laban, "Because I was afraid: for I said, 'Peradventure thou wouldest take by force thy daughters from me.' With whomsoever thou findest thy gods, let him not live: before our brethren discern thou what is thine with me, and take it to thee." For Jacob knew not that Rachel had stolen them.

---

[40] These "images," later called "gods," are either small statues of household deities (like the Roman Lares and Penates) or images of ancestors.

And Laban went into Jacob's tent, and into Leah's tent, and into the two maidservants' tents; but he found them not. Then went he out of Leah's tent, and entered into Rachel's tent. Now Rachel had taken the images, and put them in the camel's furniture, and sat upon them. And Laban searched all the tent, but found them not. And she said to her father, "Let it not displease my lord that I cannot rise up before thee; for the custom of women is upon me." [41] And he searched, but found not the images.

And Jacob was wroth, and chid with Laban: and Jacob answered and said to Laban, "What is my trespass? what is my sin, that thou hast so hotly pursued after me? Whereas thou hast searched all my stuff, what hast thou found of all thy household stuff? set it here before my brethren and thy brethren, that they may judge betwixt us both. This twenty years have I been with thee; thy ewes and thy she-goats have not cast their young, and the rams of thy flock have I not eaten. That which was torn of beasts I brought not unto thee;[42] I bore the loss of it; of my hand didst thou require it, whether stolen by day, or stolen by night. Thus I was; in the day the drought consumed me, and the frost by night; and my sleep departed from mine eyes. Thus have I been twenty years in thy house; I served thee fourteen years for thy two daughters, and six years for thy cattle: and thou hast changed my wages ten times. Except the God of my father, the God of Abraham, and the fear of Isaac, had been with me, surely thou hadst sent me away now empty. God hath seen mine affliction and the labor of my hands, and rebuked thee yesternight."

And Laban answered and said unto Jacob, "These daughters are my daughters, and these children are my children, and these cattle are my cattle, and all that thou seest is mine: and what can I do this day unto these my daughters, or unto their children which they have borne? Now therefore come thou, let us make a covenant, I and thou; and let it be for a witness between me and thee." And Jacob took a stone, and set it up for a pillar. And Jacob said unto his brethren, "Gather stones"; and they took stones, and made a heap: and they did eat there upon the heap. And Laban called it Jegar-sahadutha: but Jacob called it Galeed.[43] And Laban said, "This heap is a witness between me and thee this day." Therefore was the name of it called Galeed and Mizpah,[44] for he said, "The Lord watch between me and thee, when we are absent one from another. If thou shalt afflict my daughters, or if thou shalt take other wives beside my daughters, no man is with us; see, God is witness betwixt me and thee."

And Laban said to Jacob, "Behold this heap, and behold this pillar, which I have cast betwixt me and thee! This heap be witness, and this pillar be witness, that I will not pass over this heap to thee, and that thou shalt not pass over this heap and this pillar unto me, for harm. The God of Abraham, and the God of Nahor, the God of their father, judge betwixt us." Then Jacob offered sacrifice upon the mount, and called his brethren to eat bread: and

---

[41] That is, she is menstruating.

[42] According to the Code of Hammurabi, then the law in Mesopotamia, a shepherd was not responsible to his employer for animals "torn by beasts." Despite his trickery and sharp dealing, Jacob represents himself as one who goes even beyond the law in his honesty and hard work.

[43] Both these names mean "the heap of witness," in Laban's Aramaic and Jacob's Hebrew.

[44] "Mizpah" means "Watchpost."

they did eat bread, and tarried all night in the mount. And early in the morning Laban rose up, and kissed his sons and his daughters, and blessed them: and Laban departed, and returned unto his place.

And Jacob went on his way, and the angels of God met him. And when Jacob saw them, he said, "This is God's host": and he called the name of that place Mahanaim.[45] And Jacob sent messengers before him to Esau his brother unto the land of Seir, the country of Edom. And he commanded them, saying, "Thus shall ye speak unto my lord Esau: 'Thy servant Jacob saith thus, "I have sojourned with Laban, and stayed there until now; and I have oxen, and asses, flocks, and menservants, and womenservants; and I have sent to tell my lord, that I may find grace in thy sight.""

And the messengers returned to Jacob, saying, "We came to thy brother Esau, and also he cometh to meet thee, and four hundred men with him." Then Jacob was greatly afraid and distressed; and he divided the people that was with him, and the flocks, and herds, and the camels, into two bands; and said, "If Esau come to the one company, and smite it, then the other company which is left shall escape."

And Jacob said, "O God of my father Abraham, and God of my father Isaac, the Lord which saidst unto me, 'Return unto thy country, and to thy kindred, and I will deal well with thee!' I am not worthy of the least of all the mercies, and of all the truth, which thou hast showed unto thy servant; for with my staff I passed over this Jordan; and now I am become two bands. Deliver me, I pray thee, from the hand of my brother, from the hand of Esau: for I fear him, lest he will come and smite me, and the mother with the children. And thou saidst, 'I will surely do thee good, and make thy seed as the sand of the sea, which cannot be numbered for multitude.'"

And he lodged there that same night; and took of that which came to his hand a present for Esau his brother: two hundred she-goats, and twenty he-goats, two hundred ewes, and twenty rams, thirty milch camels with their colts, forty kine, and ten bulls, twenty she-asses, and ten foals. And he delivered them into the hand of his servants, every drove by themselves; and said unto his servants, "Pass over before me, and put a space betwixt drove and drove." And he commanded the foremost, saying, "When Esau my brother meeteth thee, and asketh thee, saying, 'Whose art thou? and whither goest thou? and whose are these before thee?' then thou shalt say, 'They be thy servant Jacob's; it is a present sent unto my lord Esau: and, behold, also he is behind us.'" And so commanded he the second, and the third, and all that followed the droves, saying, "On this manner shall ye speak unto Esau, when ye find him. And say ye moreover, 'Behold, thy servant Jacob is behind us.'" For he said, "I will appease him with the present that goeth before me, and afterward I will see his face; peradventure he will accept of me." So went the present over before him: and himself lodged that night in the company.

And he rose up that night, and took his two wives, and his two womenservants, and his eleven sons, and passed over the ford Jabbok. And he took them, and sent them over the brook, and sent over that he had. And Jacob was left alone; and there wrestled a man with him until the breaking of the day. And when he saw that he prevailed not against him, he touched the hollow of his thigh; and the hollow of Jacob's thigh was out of joint, as

---

[45] "Two armies."

he wrestled with him. And he said, "Let me go, for the day breaketh." And he said, "I will not let thee go, except thou bless me." And he said unto him, "What is thy name?" And he said "Jacob." And he said, "Thy name shall be called no more Jacob, but Israel: for as a prince hast thou power with God and with men, and hast prevailed." And Jacob asked him, and said, "Tell me, I pray thee, thy name." And he said, "Wherefore is it that thou dost ask after my name?" And he blessed him there. And Jacob called the name of the place Peniel: "For I have seen God face to face, and my life is preserved." And as he passed over Peniel the sun rose upon him, and he halted upon his thigh. Therefore the children of Israel eat not of the sinew which shrank, which is upon the hollow of the thigh, unto this day: because he touched the hollow of Jacob's thigh in the sinew that shrank.[46]

And Jacob lifted up his eyes, and looked, and, behold, Esau came, and with him four hundred men. And he divided the children unto Leah, and unto Rachel, and unto the two handmaids. And he put the handmaids and their children foremost, and Leah and her children after, and Rachel and Joseph hindermost. And he passed over before them, and bowed himself to the ground seven times, until he came near to his brother.

And Esau ran to meet him, and embraced him, and fell on his neck, and kissed him: and they wept. And he lifted up his eyes, and saw the women and the children; and said, "Who are those with thee?" And he said, "The children which God hath graciously given thy servant." Then the handmaidens came near, they and their children and they bowed themselves. And Leah also with her children came near, and bowed themselves: and after came Joseph near and Rachel, and they bowed themselves. And he said, "What meanest thou by all this drove which I met?" And he said, "These are to find grace in the sight of my lord."

And Esau said, "I have enough, my brother; keep that thou hast unto thyself." And Jacob said, "Nay, I pray thee, if now I have found grace in thy sight, then receive my present at my hand: for therefore I have seen thy face, as though I had seen the face of God, and thou wast pleased with me. Take, I pray thee, my blessing that is brought to thee; because God hath dealt graciously with me, and because I have enough."

And he said, "Let us take our journey, and let us go, and I will go before thee." And he said unto him, "My lord knoweth that the children are tender, and the flocks and herds with young are with me: and if men should overdrive them one day, all the flock will die. Let my lord, I pray thee, pass over before his servant: and I will lead on softly, according as the cattle that goeth before me and the children be able to endure, until I come unto my lord unto Seir."

And Esau said, "Let me now leave with thee some of the folk that are with me." And he said, "What needeth it? let me find grace in the sight of my lord." So Esau returned that day on his way unto Seir. And Jacob journeyed

---

[46] The meaning of this strange wrestling episode is rather obscure. Jacob's wrestling with God may be intended to represent symbolically his own inner struggle to throw off his rather defective past character and become a worthier man. The reference to the "sinew which shrank" in "the hollow of the thigh" seems to be an attempt to account for the Jewish ritual of removing the sciatic nerves, with the arteries and tendons of the thigh, in meat intended to be eaten.

to Succoth, and built him a house, and made booths for his cattle: therefore the name of the place is called Succoth.[47] And Jacob came to Shalem, a city of Shechem, which is in the land of Canaan, when he came from Padan-aram; and pitched his tent before the city. And he bought a parcel of a field, where he had spread his tent, at the hand of the children of Hamor, Shechem's father, for a hundred pieces of money. And he erected there an altar, and called it El-elohe-Israel. . . .[48]

And God said unto Jacob, "Arise, go up to Beth-el, and dwell there: and make there an altar unto God, that appeared unto thee when thou fleddest from the face of Esau thy brother." Then Jacob said unto his household, and to all that were with him, "Put away the strange gods that are among you, and be clean, and change your garments: and let us arise, and go up to Beth-el; and I will make there an altar unto God, who answered me in the day of my distress, and was with me in the way which I went." And they gave unto Jacob all the strange gods which were in their hand, and all their earrings which were in their ears; and Jacob hid them under the oak which was by Shechem.[49] And they journeyed: and the terror of God[50] was upon the cities that were round about them, and they did not pursue after the sons of Jacob.

So Jacob came to Luz, which is in the land of Canaan, that is, Beth-el, he and all the people that were with him. And he built there an altar, and called the place El-beth-el: because there God appeared unto him, when he fled from the face of his brother. But Deborah Rebekah's nurse died, and she was buried beneath Beth-el under an oak: and the name of it was called Allon-bachuth.

And God appeared unto Jacob again, when he came out of Padan-aram, and blessed him. And God said unto him, "Thy name is Jacob: thy name shall not be called any more Jacob, but Israel shall be thy name": and he called his name Israel. And God said unto him, "I am God Almighty: be fruitful and multiply; a nation and a company of nations shall be of thee, and kings shall come out of thy loins; and the land which I gave Abraham and Isaac, to thee I will give it, and to thy seed after thee will I give the land." And God went up from him in the place where he talked with him. And Jacob set up a pillar in the place where he talked with him, even a pillar of stone: and he poured a drink offering thereon, and he poured oil thereon. And Jacob called the name of the place where God spoke with him, Beth-el.

And they journeyed from Beth-el; and there was but a little way to come to Ephrath: and Rachel travailed, and she had hard labor. And it came to pass, when she was in hard labor, that the midwife said unto her, "Fear not; thou shalt have this son also." And it came to pass, as her soul was in departing (for she died), that she called his name Ben-oni: but his father called

[47]"Booths."

[48]"God, the God of Israel."

[49]The worshipers had to undergo ceremonial purification (washing and changing clothes), and they were required to renounce strange (or foreign) gods. The earrings that they surrendered were magical amulets used in pagan worship.

[50]The "Terror of God" was a mysterious panic said to seize and paralyze the enemy in early accounts of holy wars.

him Benjamin.[51] And Rachel died, and was buried in the way to Ephrath, which is Beth-lehem. And Jacob set a pillar upon her grave: that is the pillar of Rachel's grave unto this day. And Israel journeyed, and spread his tent beyond the tower of Edar.

And it came to pass, when Israel dwelt in that land, that Reuben went and lay with Bilhah his father's concubine: and Israel heard it. . . .[52]

And Jacob came unto Isaac his father unto Mamre, unto the city of Arbah, which is Hebron, where Abraham and Isaac sojourned. And the days of Isaac were a hundred and fourscore years. And Isaac gave up the ghost, and died, and was gathered unto his people, being old and full of days: and his sons Esau and Jacob buried him. . . .[53]

from JOB

CHAPTER 1

There was a man in the land of Uz, whose name was Job; and that man was perfect and upright, and one that feared God, and eschewed evil. And there were born unto him seven sons and three daughters. His substance also was seven thousand sheep, and three thousand camels, and five hundred yoke of oxen, and five hundred she asses, and a very great household; so that this man was the greatest of all the men of the east.

And his sons went and feasted in their houses, every one his day; and sent and called for their three sisters to eat and to drink with them. And it was so, when the days of their feasting were gone about, that Job sent and sanctified them, and rose up early in the morning, and offered burnt offerings according to the number of them all: for Job said, "It may be that my sons have sinned, and cursed God in their hearts." Thus did Job continually.

Now there was a day when the sons of God came to present themselves before the Lord, and Satan[1] came also among them. And the Lord said unto Satan, "Whence comest thou?" Then Satan answered the Lord, and said, "From going to and fro in the earth, and from walking up and down in it." And the Lord said unto Satan, "Hast thou considered my servant Job, that there is none like him in the earth, a perfect and an upright man, one that feareth God, and escheweth evil?" Then Satan answered the Lord, and said, "Doth Job fear God for nought? Hast not thou made an hedge about him, and about his house, and about all that he hath on every side? thou hast blessed the

---

[51]"Ben-oni" means "son of my sorrow," but "Benjamin" means "son of my right hand" or "son of the South."

[52]This mysterious episode apparently accounts for Reuben's loss of prestige as the first-born son.

[53]The last fourteen chapters of Genesis, here omitted, tell the story of Jacob's son Joseph and his rise to power in the land of Egypt.

[1]As the ruler of a band of evil spirits opposed to God, Satan appears by name only three times in the King James Version of the Old Testament, though he appears frequently in the New Testament. In Job, he appears in the Prologue but is never mentioned in the debate with the Comforters.

work of his hands, and his substance is increased in the land. But put forth thine hand now, and touch all that he hath, and he will curse thee to thy face." And the Lord said unto Satan, "Behold, all that he hath is in thy power; only upon himself put not forth thine hand." So Satan went forth from the presence of the Lord.

And there was a day when his sons and his daughters were eating and drinking wine in their eldest brother's house: and there came a messenger unto Job, and said, "The oxen were plowing, and the asses feeding beside them: and the Sabeans fell upon them, and took them away; yea, they have slain the servants with the edge of the sword; and I only am escaped alone to tell thee." While he was yet speaking, there came also another, and said, "The fire of God is fallen from heaven, and hath burned up the sheep, and the servants, and consumed them; and I only am escaped alone to tell thee." While he was yet speaking, there came also another, and said, "The Chaldeans made out three bands, and fell upon the camels, and have carried them away, yea, and slain the servants with the edge of the sword; and I only am escaped alone to tell thee." While he was yet speaking, there came also another, and said, "Thy sons and thy daughters were eating and drinking wine in their eldest brother's house: and, behold, there came a great wind from the wilderness, and smote the four corners of the house, and it fell upon the young men, and they are dead; and I only am escaped alone to tell thee."

Then Job arose, and rent his mantle, and shaved his head, and fell down upon the ground, and worshipped, and said,

> "Naked came I out of my mother's womb,
> And naked shall I return thither:
> The Lord gave, and the Lord hath taken away;
> Blessed be the name of the Lord."

In all this Job sinned not, nor charged God foolishly.

CHAPTER 2

Again there was a day when the sons of God came to present themselves before the Lord, and Satan came also among them to present himself before the Lord. And the Lord said unto Satan, "From whence comest thou?" And Satan answered the Lord, and said, "From going to and fro in the earth, and from walking up and down in it." And the Lord said unto Satan, "Hast thou considered my servant Job, that there is none like him in the earth, a perfect and an upright man, one that feareth God, and escheweth evil? and still he holdeth fast his integrity, although thou movedst me against him, to destroy him without cause." And Satan answered the Lord, and said, "Skin for skin,[2] yea, all that a man hath will he give for his life. But put forth thine hand now, and touch his bone and his flesh, and he will curse thee to thy face." And the Lord said unto Satan, "Behold, he is in thine hand; but save his life."

So went Satan forth from the presence of the Lord, and smote Job with sore boils from the sole of his foot unto his crown. And he took him a

---

[2]"A hide for a hide"—a proverbial expression used by tradesmen.

potsherd[3] to scrape himself withal; and he sat down among the ashes. Then said his wife unto him, "Dost thou still retain thine integrity? curse God, and die." But he said unto her, "Thou speakest as one of the foolish women speaketh. What? shall we receive good at the hand of God, and shall we not receive evil?" In all this did not Job sin with his lips.

Now when Job's three friends heard of all this evil that was come upon him, they came every one from his own place; Eliphaz the Temanite, and Bildad the Shuhite, and Zophar the Naamathite: for they had made an appointment together to come to mourn with him and to comfort him. And when they lifted up their eyes afar off, and knew him not, they lifted up their voice, and wept; and they rent every one his mantle, and sprinkled dust upon their heads toward heaven. So they sat down with him upon the ground seven days and seven nights, and none spake a word unto him: for they saw that his grief was very great.

CHAPTER 3

After this opened Job his mouth, and cursed his day. And Job spake, and said,

"Let the day perish wherein I was born,
    and the night in which it was said, There is a man child conceived.
Let that day be darkness;
    Let not God regard it from above,
    neither let the light shine upon it.
Let darkness and the shadow of death stain it;
    let a cloud dwell upon it;
    let the blackness of the day terrify it.
As for that night, let darkness seize upon it;
    let it not be joined unto the days of the year,
    let it not come into the number of the months.
Lo, let that night be solitary,
    let no joyful voice come therein.
Let them curse it that curse the day,
    who are ready to raise up their mourning.
Let the stars of the twilight thereof be dark;
    let it look for light, but have none;
    neither let it see the dawning of the day:
Because it shut not up the doors of my mother's womb,
    nor hid sorrow from mine eyes.

"Why died I not from the womb?
    why did I not give up the ghost when I came out of the belly?
Why did the knees prevent me?
    or why the breasts that I should suck?
For now should I have lain still and been quiet,
    I should have slept: then had I been at rest,

[3]A piece of broken pottery.

With kings and counsellors of the earth,
      which built desolate places for themselves;
Or with princes that had gold,
      who filled their houses with silver:
Or as an hidden untimely birth I had not been;
      as infants which never saw light.
There the wicked cease from troubling;
      and there the weary be at rest.
There the prisoners rest together;
      they hear not the voice of the oppressor.
The small and great are there;
      And the servant is free from his master.

"Wherefore is light given to him that is in misery,
      and life unto the bitter in soul;
Which long for death, but it cometh not;
      and dig for it more than for hid treasures;
Which rejoice exceedingly,
      and are glad, when they can find the grave?
Why is light given to a man whose way is hid,
      and whom God hath hedged in?
For my sighing cometh before I eat,
      and my roarings are poured out like the waters.
For the thing which I greatly feared is come upon me,
      and that which I was afraid of is come unto me.
I was not in safety, neither had I rest,
      neither was I quiet; yet trouble came."

CHAPTER 4

Then Eliphaz the Temanite answered and said,

"If we assay to commune with thee, wilt thou be grieved?
      but who can withhold himself from speaking?
Behold, thou hast instructed many,
      and thou hast strengthened the weak hands.
Thy words have upholden him that was falling,
      and thou hast strengthened the feeble knees.
But now it is come upon thee, and thou faintest;
      it toucheth thee, and thou art troubled.
Is not this thy fear, thy confidence, thy hope,
      and the uprightness of thy ways?
Remember, I pray thee, who ever perished, being innocent?
      or where were the righteous cut off?[4]
Even as I have seen, they that plow iniquity,
      and sow wickedness, reap the same.

---

[4] Here, as throughout, Eliphaz upholds the doctrine that the good prosper and the wicked are punished in this world. Suffering is thus a proof of sin.

By the blast of God they perish,
>and by the breath of his nostrils are they consumed.
The roaring of the lion, and the voice of the fierce lion,
>and the teeth of the young lions, are broken.
The old lion perisheth for lack of prey,
>and the stout lion's whelps are scattered abroad.

"Now a thing was secretly brought to me,
>and mine ear received a little thereof.
In thoughts from the visions of the night,
>when deep sleep falleth on men,
Fear came upon me, and trembling,
>which made all my bones to shake.
Then a spirit passed before my face;
>the hair of my flesh stood up:
It stood still,
>but I could not discern the form thereof:
An image was before mine eyes,
>there was silence, and I heard a voice, saying,
Shall mortal man be more just than God?
>shall a man be more pure than his maker?
Behold, he put no trust in his servants;
>and his angels he charged with folly:
How much less in them that dwell in houses of clay,
>whose foundation is in the dust,
>which are crushed before the moth?
They are destroyed from morning to evening:
>they perish for ever without any regarding it.
Doth not their excellency which is in them go away?
>they die, even without wisdom."

CHAPTER 5

"Call now, if there be any that will answer thee;
>and to which of the saints wilt thou turn?
For wrath killeth the foolish man,
>and envy slayeth the silly one.
I have seen the foolish taking root:
>but suddenly I cursed his habitation.
His children are far from safety,
>and they are crushed in the gate,
>neither is there any to deliver them.
Whose harvest the hungry eateth up,
>and taketh it even out of the thorns,
>and the robber swalloweth up their substance.
Although affliction cometh not forth of the dust,
>neither doth trouble spring out of the ground;
Yet man is born unto trouble,
>as the sparks fly upward.

"I would seek unto God,
     and unto God would I commit my cause:
Which doeth great things and unsearchable;
     marvellous things without number:
Who giveth rain upon the earth,
     and sendeth waters upon the fields:
To set up on high those that be low;
     that those which mourn may be exalted to safety.
He disappointeth the devices of the crafty,
     so that their hands cannot perform their enterprise.
He taketh the wise in their own craftiness:
     and the counsel of the froward is carried headlong.
They meet with darkness in the daytime,
     and grope in the noonday as in the night.
But he saveth the poor from the sword,
     from their mouth, and from the hand of the mighty.
So the poor hath hope,
     And iniquity stoppeth her mouth.

"Behold, happy is the man whom God correcteth:
     therefore despise not thou the chastening of the Almighty:[5]
For he maketh sore, and bindeth up:
     he woundeth, and his hands make whole.
He shall deliver thee in six troubles:
     yea, in seven there shall no evil touch thee.
In famine he shall redeem thee from death:
     and in war from the power of the sword.
Thou shalt be hid from the scourge of the tongue:
     neither shalt thou be afraid of destruction when it cometh.
At destruction and famine thou shalt laugh:
     neither shalt thou be afraid of the beasts of the earth.
For thou shalt be in league with the stones of the field:
     and the beasts of the field shall be at peace with thee.
And thou shalt know that thy tabernacle shall be in peace;
     and thou shalt visit thy habitation, and shalt not sin.
Thou shalt know also that thy seed shall be great,
     and thine offspring as the grass of the earth.
Thou shalt come to thy grave in a full age,
     like as a shock of corn cometh in in his season.
Lo this, we have searched it, so it is;
     hear it, and know thou it for thy good."

CHAPTER 6

But Job answered and said,

"Oh that my grief were thoroughly weighed,
     and my calamity laid in the balances together!

[5] This is the orthodox Jewish doctrine of *musar;* God imposes suffering to chasten or correct.

For now it would be heavier than the sand of the sea:
    therefore my words are swallowed up.[6]
For the arrows of the Almighty are within me,
    the poison whereof drinketh up my spirit:
    the terrors of God do set themselves in array against me.
Doth the wild ass bray when he hath grass?
    or loweth the ox over his fodder?
Can that which is unsavory be eaten without salt?
    or is there any taste in the white of an egg?
The things that my soul refused to touch
    are as my sorrowful meat.
Oh that I might have my request;
    and that God would grant me the thing that I long for!
Even that it would please God to destroy me;
    that he would let loose his hand, and cut me off!
Then should I yet have comfort;
    yea, I would harden myself in sorrow: let him not spare;
    for I have not concealed the words of the Holy One.
What is my strength, that I should hope?
    and what is mine end, that I should prolong my life?
Is my strength the strength of stones?
    or is my flesh of brass?
Is not my help in me?
    and is wisdom driven quite from me?

"To him that is afflicted pity should be showed from his friend;
    but he forsaketh the fear of the Almighty.
My brethren have dealt deceitfully as a brook,
    and as the stream of brooks they pass away;
Which are blackish by reason of the ice,
    and wherein the snow is hid:
What time they wax warm, they vanish:
    when it is hot, they are consumed out of their place.
The paths of their way are turned aside;
    they go to nothing, and perish.
The troops of Tema looked,
    the companies of Sheba waited for them.
They were confounded because they had hoped;
    they came thither, and were ashamed.
For now ye are nothing;
    ye see my casting down, and are afraid.
Did I say, 'Bring unto me'?
    or, 'Give a reward for me of your substance'?
Or, 'Deliver me from the enemy's hand'?
    or, 'Redeem me from the hand of the mighty'?

---

[6] Job replies to Eliphaz by saying that the orthodox explanation cannot be valid in his case, since his suffering exceeds any possible cause.

"Teach me, and I will hold my tongue:
    and cause me to understand wherein I have erred.
How forcible are right words!
    but what doth your arguing reprove?
Do ye imagine to reprove words,
    and the speeches of one that is desperate, which are as wind?
Yea, ye overwhelm the fatherless,
    and ye dig a pit for your friend.

"Now therefore be content, look upon me;
    for it is evident unto you if I lie.
Return, I pray you, let it not be iniquity;
    yea, return again, my righteousness is in it.[7]
Is there iniquity in my tongue?
    cannot my taste discern perverse things?"

CHAPTER 7

"Is there not an appointed time to man upon earth?
    are not his days also like the days of an hireling?
As a servant earnestly desireth the shadow,
    and as an hireling looketh for the reward of his work:
So am I made to possess months of vanity,
    and wearisome nights are appointed to me.
When I lie down, I say, 'When shall I arise, and the night be gone?'
    and I am full of tossings to and fro unto the dawning of the day.
My flesh is clothed with worms and clods of dust;
    my skin is broken, and become loathsome.
My days are swifter than a weaver's shuttle,
    and are spent without hope.

"O remember that my life is wind:
    mine eye shall no more see good.
The eye of him that hath seen me shall see me no more:
    thine eyes are upon me, and I am not.
As the cloud is consumed and vanisheth away:
    so he that goeth down to the grave shall come up no more.
He shall return no more to his house,
    neither shall his place know him any more.

"Therefore I will not refrain my mouth;
    I will speak in the anguish of my spirit;
    I will complain in the bitterness of my soul.
Am I a sea, or a whale,
    that thou settest a watch over me?

---

[7] This line would be clearer if translated "Let no injustice be done; my cause is righteous."

When I say, 'My bed shall comfort me,
    my couch shall ease my complaint';
Then thou scarest me with dreams,
    and terrifiest me through visions:
So that my soul chooseth strangling,
    and death rather than my life.
I loathe it; I would not live alway:
    let me alone; for my days are vanity.
What is man, that thou shouldest magnify him?
    and that thou shouldest set thine heart upon him?
And that thou shouldest visit him every morning,
    and try him every moment?
How long wilt thou not depart from me,
    nor let me alone till I swallow down my spittle?
I have sinned; what shall I do unto thee, O thou preserver of men?
    why hast thou set me as a mark against thee,
    so that I am a burden to myself?
And why dost thou not pardon my transgression,
    and take away mine iniquity?
For now shall I sleep in the dust;
    and thou shalt seek me in the morning, but I shall not be."

CHAPTER 8

Then answered Bildad the Shuhite, and said,

"How long wilt thou speak these things?
    and how long shall the words of thy mouth be like a strong wind?
Doth God pervert judgment?
    or doth the Almighty pervert justice?
If thy children have sinned against him,
    and he have cast them away for their transgression;
If thou wouldest seek unto God betimes,
    and make thy supplication to the Almighty;
If thou wert pure and upright;
    surely now he would awake for thee,
    and make the habitation of thy righteousness prosperous.
Though thy beginning was small,
    yet thy latter end should greatly increase.

"For enquire, I pray thee, of the former age,
    and prepare thyself to the search of their fathers:[8]
(For we are but of yesterday, and know nothing,
    because our days upon earth are a shadow:)
Shall not they teach thee, and tell thee,
    and utter words out of their heart?

[8]In his eagerness to uphold orthodoxy, Bildad suggests that the cause of Job's suffering may be not in his own sins but in those of his family.

Can the rush grow up without mire?
  can the flag grow without water?
Whilst it is yet in his greenness, and not cut down,
  It withereth before any other herb.
So are the paths of all that forget God;
  and the hypocrite's hope shall perish:
Whose hope shall be cut off,
  and whose trust shall be a spider's web.
He shall lean upon his house, but it shall not stand:
  he shall hold it fast, but it shall not endure.
He is green before the sun,
  and his branch shooteth forth in his garden.
His roots are wrapped about the heap,
  and seeth the place of stones.
If he destroy him from his place,
  then it shall deny him, saying, 'I have not seen thee.'
Behold, this is the joy of his way,
  and out of the earth shall others grow.

"Behold, God will not cast away a perfect man,
  neither will he help the evil doers:
Till he fill thy mouth with laughing,
  and thy lips with rejoicing.
They that hate thee shall be clothed with shame;
  and the dwelling place of the wicked shall come to nought."

CHAPTER 9

Then Job answered and said,

"I know it is so of a truth:
  but how should man be just with God?
If he will contend with him,
  he cannot answer him one of a thousand.
He is wise in heart, and mighty in strength:
  who hath hardened himself against him, and hath prospered?
Which removeth the mountains, and they know not:
  which overturneth them in his anger.
Which shaketh the earth out of her place,
  and the pillars thereof tremble.
Which commandeth the sun, and it riseth not;
  and sealeth up the stars.
Which alone spreadeth out the heavens,
  and treadeth upon the waves of the sea.
Which maketh Arcturus, Orion, and Pleiades,
  and the chambers of the south.
Which doeth great things past finding out;
  yea, and wonders without number.

Lo, he goeth by me, and I see him not:
　　he passeth on also, but I perceive him not.
Behold, he taketh away, who can hinder him?
　　Who will say unto him, 'What doest thou?'

"If God will not withdraw his anger,
　　the proud helpers do stoop under him.
How much less shall I answer him,
　　and choose out my words to reason with him?
Whom, though I were righteous, yet would I not answer,
　　but I would make supplication to my judge.
If I had called, and he had answered me;
　　yet would I not believe that he had hearkened unto my voice.
For he breaketh me with a tempest,
　　and multiplieth my wounds without cause.
He will not suffer me to take my breath,
　　but filleth me with bitterness.
If I speak of strength, lo, he is strong:
　　and if of judgment, who shall set me a time to plead?
If I justify myself, mine own mouth shall condemn me:
　　if I say, I am perfect, it shall also prove me perverse.
Though I were perfect, yet would I not know my soul:
　　I would despise my life.
This is one thing, therefore I said it,
　　he destroyeth the perfect and the wicked.
If the scourge slay suddenly,
　　he will laugh at the trial of the innocent.
The earth is given into the hand of the wicked:
　　he covereth the faces of the judges thereof;
　　if not, where, and who is he?

"Now my days are swifter than a post:[9]
　　they flee away, they see no good.
They are passed away as the swift ships:
　　as the eagle that hasteth to the prey.
If I say, 'I will forget my complaint,
　　I will leave off my heaviness, and comfort myself':
I am afraid of all my sorrows,
　　I know that thou wilt not hold me innocent.
If I be wicked, why then labor I in vain?
If I wash myself with snow water,
　　and make my hands never so clean;
Yet shalt thou plunge me in the ditch,
　　and mine own clothes shall abhor me.
For he is not a man, as I am, that I should answer him,
　　and we should come together in judgment.
Neither is there any daysman[10] betwixt us,
　　that might lay his hand upon us both.

[9]Runner.　　[10]Umpire.

Let him take his rod away from me,
    and let not his fear terrify me:
Then would I speak, and not fear him;
    but it is not so with me.

CHAPTER 10

"My soul is weary of my life; I will leave my complaint upon myself;
    I will speak in the bitterness of my soul.
I will say unto God, 'Do not condemn me;
    show me wherefore thou contendest with me.
Is it good unto thee that thou shouldest oppress,
    that thou shouldest despise the work of thine hands,
    and shine upon the counsel of the wicked?
Hast thou eyes of flesh?
    or seest thou as man seeth?
Are thy days as the days of man?
    are thy years as man's days,
That thou enquirest after mine iniquity,
    and searchest after my sin?
Thou knowest that I am not wicked;
    and there is none that can deliver out of thine hand.
Thine hands have made me and fashioned me together round about;
    yet thou dost destroy me.
Remember, I beseech thee, that thou hast made me as the clay;
    And wilt thou bring me into dust again?
Hast thou not poured me out as milk,
    and curdled me like cheese?
Thou hast clothed me with skin and flesh,
    and hast fenced me with bones and sinews:
Thou hast granted me life and favor,
    and thy visitation hath preserved my spirit.
And these things hast thou hid in thine heart:
    I know that this is with thee.
If I sin, then thou markest me,
    and thou wilt not acquit me from mine iniquity.
If I be wicked, woe unto me;
    and if I be righteous, yet will I not lift up my head.
I am full of confusion;
    therefore see thou mine affliction;
For it increaseth. Thou huntest me as a fierce lion:
    and again thou showest thyself marvellous upon me.
Thou renewest thy witnesses against me,
    and increasest thine indignation upon me;
    changes and war are against me.

"Wherefore then hast thou brought me forth out of the womb?
    Oh that I had given up the ghost, and no eye had seen me!
I should have been as though I had not been;
    I should have been carried from the womb to the grave.

Are not my days few? cease then,
  and let me alone, that I may take comfort a little,
Before I go whence I shall not return,
  even to the land of darkness[11] and the shadow of death;
A land of darkness, as darkness itself;
  and of the shadow of death, without any order,
  and where the light is as darkness."

CHAPTER 11

Then answered Zophar the Naamathite, and said,

"Should not the multitude of words be answered?
  and should a man full of talk be justified?
Should thy lies make men hold their peace?
  and when thou mockest, shall no man make thee ashamed?
For thou hast said, 'My doctrine is pure,
  and I am clean in thine eyes.'
But oh that God would speak,
  and open his lips against thee;
And that he would show thee the secrets of wisdom,
  that they are double to that which is!
Know therefore that God exacteth of thee less than thine iniquity
  deserveth.[12]

"Canst thou by searching find out God?
  canst thou find out the Almighty unto perfection?
It is as high as heaven; what canst thou do?
  deeper than hell; what canst thou know?
The measure thereof is longer than the earth,
  and broader than the sea.
If he cut off, and shut up,
  or gather together, then who can hinder him?
For he knoweth vain men:
  he seeth wickedness also; will he not then consider it?
For vain man would be wise,
  though man be born like a wild ass's colt.

"If thou prepare thine heart,
  and stretch out thine hands toward him;
If iniquity be in thine hand, put it far away,
  and let not wickedness dwell in thy tabernacles.
For then shalt thou lift up thy face without spot;
  yea, thou shalt be steadfast, and shalt not fear:

[11] The concept of hell, like the figure of Satan, is late in developing in the Old Testament period. The "land of darkness" mentioned here is the Hebrew *sheol*, a shadowy place where the dead go, similar to the Greek Hades. It does not imply reward or punishment for one's life on earth.

[12] Zophar, too, insists that Job has deserved his suffering and that God dispenses justice on earth.

Because thou shalt forget thy misery,
    and remember it as waters that pass away:
And thine age shall be clearer than the noonday;
    thou shalt shine forth, thou shalt be as the morning.
And thou shalt be secure, because there is hope;
    yea thou shalt dig about thee, and thou shalt take thy rest in safety.
Also thou shalt lie down, and none shall make thee afraid;
    yea, many shall make suit unto thee.
But the eyes of the wicked shall fail, and they shall not escape,
    and their hope shall be as the giving up of the ghost."

CHAPTER 12

And Job answered and said,

"No doubt but ye are the people,
    and wisdom shall die with you.
But I have understanding as well as you;
    I am not inferior to you:
    yea, who knoweth not such things as these?
I am as one mocked of his neighbor,
    who calleth upon God, and he answereth him:
    the just upright man is laughed to scorn.
He that is ready to slip with his feet
    is as a lamp despised in the thought of him that is at ease.
The tabernacles of robbers prosper,
    and they that provoke God are secure;
    into whose hand God bringeth abundantly.

"But ask now the beasts, and they shall teach thee;
    and the fowls of the air, and they shall tell thee:
Or speak to the earth, and it shall teach thee:
    and the fishes of the sea shall declare unto thee.
Who knoweth not in all these
    that the hand of the Lord hath wrought this?
In whose hand is the soul of every living thing,
    and the breath of all mankind.
Doth not the ear try words?
    and the mouth taste his meat?
With the ancient is wisdom;
    and in length of days understanding.

"With him is wisdom and strength,
    he hath counsel and understanding.
Behold, he breaketh down, and it cannot be built again:
    he shutteth up a man, and there can be no opening.
Behold, he withholdeth the waters, and they dry up:
    also he sendeth them out, and they overturn the earth.
With him is strength and wisdom:
    the deceived and the deceiver are his.

He leadeth counsellors away spoiled,
 and maketh the judges fools.
He looseth the bond of kings,
 and girdeth their loins with a girdle.
He leadeth princes away spoiled,
 and overthroweth the mighty.
He removeth away the speech of the trusty,
 and taketh away the understanding of the aged.
He poureth contempt upon princes,
 and weakeneth the strength of the mighty.
He discovereth deep things out of darkness,
 and bringeth out to light the shadow of death.
He increaseth the nations, and destroyeth them:
 he enlargeth the nations, and straiteneth them again.
He taketh away the heart of the chief of the people of the earth,
 and causeth them to wander in a wilderness where there is no way.
They grope in the dark without light,
 and he maketh them to stagger like a drunken man."

CHAPTER 13

"Lo, mine eye hath seen all this,
 mine ear hath heard and understood it.
What ye know, the same do I know also:
 I am not inferior unto you.
Surely I would speak to the Almighty,
 and I desire to reason with God.
But ye are forgers of lies,
 ye are all physicians of no value.
O that ye would altogether hold your peace!
 and it should be your wisdom.
Hear now my reasoning,
 and hearken to the pleadings of my lips.
Will ye speak wickedly for God?
 and talk deceitfully for him?
Will ye accept his person?
 will ye contend for God?
Is it good that he should search you out?
 or as one man mocketh another, do ye so mock him?
He will surely reprove you,
 if ye do secretly accept persons.
Shall not his excellency make you afraid?
 and his dread fall upon you?
Your remembrances are like unto ashes,
 your bodies to bodies of clay.
Hold your peace, let me alone, that I may speak,
 and let come on me what will.
Wherefore do I take my flesh in my teeth,
 and put my life in mine hand?

Though he slay me, yet will I trust in him:[13]
 but I will maintain mine own ways before him.
He also shall be my salvation:
 for an hypocrite shall not come before him.[14]
Hear diligently my speech,
 and my declaration with your ears.
Behold now, I have ordered my cause;
 I know that I shall be justified.
Who is he that will plead with me?
 for now, if I hold my tongue, I shall give up the ghost.
Only do not two things unto me:
 then will I not hide myself from thee.
Withdraw thine hand far from me:
 and let not thy dread make me afraid.
Then call thou, and I will answer:
 or let me speak, and answer thou me.
How many are mine iniquities and sins?
 make me to know my transgression and my sin.
Wherefore hidest thou thy face,
 and holdest me for thine enemy?
Wilt thou break a leaf driven to and fro?
 and wilt thou pursue the dry stubble?
For thou writest bitter things against me,
 and makest me to possess the iniquities of my youth.
Thou puttest my feet also in the stocks,
 and lookest narrowly unto all my paths;
 thou settest a print upon the heels of my feet.
And he, as a rotten thing, consumeth,
 as a garment that is moth eaten."

CHAPTER 14

"Man that is born of a woman
 is of few days, and full of trouble.
He cometh forth like a flower, and is cut down:
 he fleeth also as a shadow, and continueth not.
And dost thou open thine eyes upon such an one,
 and bringest me into judgment with thee?
Who can bring a clean thing out of an unclean?
 not one.
Seeing his days are determined,
 the number of his months are with thee,
 thou hast appointed his bounds that he cannot pass;

---

[13] The latter part of this line should read "I have no hope," a more defiant and despairing statement.

[14] Job argues that his eagerness to confront God is a proof of his blamelessness, for a guilty man would not dare to come before Him.

Turn from him, that he may rest,
    till he shall accomplish, as an hireling, his day.

"For there is hope of a tree, if it be cut down, that it will sprout again,
    and that the tender branch thereof will not cease.
Though the root thereof wax old in the earth,
    and the stock thereof die in the ground;
Yet through the scent of water it will bud,
    and bring forth boughs like a plant.
But man dieth, and wasteth away:
    yea, man giveth up the ghost, and where is he?
As the waters fail from the sea,
    and the flood decayeth and drieth up:
So man lieth down, and riseth not:
    till the heavens be no more, they shall not awake,
    nor be raised out of their sleep.
O that thou wouldest hide me in the grave,
    that thou wouldest keep me secret, until thy wrath be past,
    that thou wouldest appoint me a set time, and remember me!
If a man die, shall he live again?
    all the days of my appointed time will I wait,
    till my change come.
Thou shalt call, and I will answer thee:
    thou wilt have a desire to the work of thine hands.
For now thou numberest my steps:
    dost thou not watch over my sin?
My transgression is sealed up in a bag,
    and thou sewest up mine iniquity.

"And surely the mountain falling cometh to nought,
    and the rock is removed out of his place.
The waters wear the stones:
    thou washest away the things which grow out of the dust of the earth;
    and thou destroyest the hope of man.
Thou prevailest for ever against him, and he passeth:
    thou changest his countenance, and sendest him away.
His sons come to honor, and he knoweth it not;
    and they are brought low, but he perceiveth it not of them.
But his flesh upon him shall have pain,
    and his soul within him shall mourn."

CHAPTER 19

Then Job answered [the Comforters] and said,

"How long will ye vex my soul,
    and break me in pieces with words?
These ten times have ye reproached me:
    ye are not ashamed that ye make yourselves strange to me.

And be it indeed that I have erred,
    mine error remaineth with myself.
If indeed ye will magnify yourselves against me,
    and plead against me my reproach:
Know now that God hath overthrown me,
    and hath compassed me with his net.
Behold, I cry out of wrong, but I am not heard:
    I cry aloud, but there is no judgment.
He hath fenced up my way that I cannot pass,
    and he hath set darkness in my paths.
He hath stripped me of my glory,
    and taken the crown from my head.
He hath destroyed me on every side, and I am gone:
    and mine hope hath he removed like a tree.
He hath also kindled his wrath against me,
    and he counteth me unto him as one of his enemies.
His troops come together,
    and raise up their way against me,
    and encamp round about my tabernacle.

"He hath put my brethren far from me,
    and mine acquaintance are verily estranged from me.
My kinsfolk have failed,
    and my familiar friends have forgotten me.
They that dwell in mine house, and my maids, count me for a stranger:
    I am an alien in their sight.
I called my servant, and he gave me no answer;
    I intreated him with my mouth.
My breath is strange to my wife,
    though I intreated for the children's sake of mine own body.
Yea, young children despised me;
    I arose, and they spake against me.
All my inward friends abhorred me:
    and they whom I loved are turned against me.
My bone cleaveth to my skin and to my flesh,
    and I am escaped with the skin of my teeth.
Have pity upon me, have pity upon me, O ye my friends;
    for the hand of God hath touched me.
Why do ye persecute me as God,
    and are not satisfied with my flesh?

"Oh that my words were now written!
    Oh that they were printed in a book!
That they were graven with an iron pen
    and lead in the rock for ever!
For I know that my redeemer liveth,
    and that he shall stand at the latter day upon the earth:
And though after my skin worms destroy this body,
    yet in my flesh shall I see God:

Whom I shall see for myself,
>and mine eyes shall behold, and not another;[15]
>though my reins be consumed within me.
But ye should say, 'Why persecute we him,
>seeing the root of the matter is found in me?'
Be ye afraid of the sword:
>for wrath bringeth the punishments of the sword,
>that ye may know there is a judgment."

CHAPTER 29

Moreover Job continued his parable, and said,

"Oh that I were as in months past,
>as in the days when God preserved me;
When his candle shined upon my head,
>and when by his light I walked through darkness;
As I was in the days of my youth,
>when the secret of God was upon my tabernacle;
When the Almighty was yet with me,
>when my children were about me;
When I washed my steps with butter,
>and the rock poured me out rivers of oil;
When I went out to the gate through the city,
>when I prepared my seat in the street!
The young men saw me, and hid themselves:
>and the aged arose, and stood up.
The princes refrained talking,
>and laid their hand on their mouth.
The nobles held their peace,
>and their tongue cleaved to the roof of their mouth.
When the ear heard me, then it blessed me;
>and when the eye saw me, it gave witness to me:
Because I delivered the poor that cried,
>and the fatherless, and him that had none to help him.
The blessing of him that was ready to perish came upon me:
>and I caused the widow's heart to sing for joy.
I put on righteousness, and it clothed me:
>my judgment was as a robe and a diadem.
I was eyes to the blind,
>and feet was I to the lame.
I was a father to the poor:
>and the cause which I knew not I searched out.
And I brake the jaws of the wicked,
>and plucked the spoil out of his teeth.

---

[15] The Hebrew text is unclear at this point. The word translated "Redeemer" here was a legal term meaning "avenger" or "vindicator." Job probably is saying that after his death he will see God, in the role of "avenger," vindicate him posthumously in the eyes of the world.

Then I said, 'I shall die in my nest,
    and I shall multiply my days as the sand.'
My root was spread out by the waters,
    and the dew lay all night upon my branch.
My glory was fresh in me,
    and my bow was renewed in my hand.

"Unto me men gave ear,
    and waited, and kept silence at my counsel.
After my words they spake not again;
    and my speech dropped upon them.
And they waited for me as for the rain;
    and they opened their mouth wide as for the latter rain.
If I laughed on them, they believed it not;
    and the light of my countenance they cast not down.
I chose out their way, and sat chief,
    and dwelt as a king in the army,
    as one that comforteth the mourners."

CHAPTER 30

"But now they that are younger than I
    have me in derision,
Whose fathers I would have disdained
    to have set with the dogs of my flock.
Yea, whereto might the strength of their hands profit me,
    in whom old age was perished?
For want and famine they were solitary;
    fleeing into the wilderness in former time desolate and waste.
Who cut up mallows by the bushes,
    and juniper roots for their meat.
They were driven forth from among men,
    (they cried after them as after a thief;)
To dwell in the cliffs of the valleys,
    in caves of the earth, and in the rocks.
Among the bushes they brayed;
    under the nettles they were gathered together.
They were children of fools, yea, children of base men:
    they were viler than the earth.

"And now am I their song,
    yea, I am their byword.
They abhor me, they flee far from me,
    and spare not to spit in my face.
Because he hath loosed my cord, and afflicted me,
    they have also let loose the bridle before me.
Upon my right hand rise the youth;
    they push away my feet,
And they raise up against me
    the ways of their destruction.

They mar my path,
    they set forward my calamity, they have no helper.
They came upon me as a wide breaking in of waters:
    in the desolation they rolled themselves upon me.
Terrors are turned upon me:
    they pursue my soul as the wind:
    and my welfare passeth away as a cloud.

"And now my soul is poured out upon me;
    the days of affliction have taken hold upon me.
My bones are pierced in me in the night season:
    and my sinews take no rest.
By the great force of my disease is my garment changed:
    it bindeth me about as the collar of my coat.
He hath cast me into the mire,
    and I am become like dust and ashes.
I cry unto thee, and thou dost not hear me:
    I stand up, and thou regards me not.
Thou art become cruel to me:
    with thy strong hand thou opposest thyself against me.
Thou liftest me up to the wind;
    thou causest me to ride upon it,
    and dissolvest my substance.
For I know that thou wilt bring me to death,
    and to the house appointed for all living.

"Howbeit he will not stretch out his hand to the grave,
    though they cry in his destruction.
Did not I weep for him that was in trouble?
    was not my soul grieved for the poor?
When I looked for good, then evil came unto me:
    and when I waited for light, there came darkness.
My bowels boiled, and rested not:
    the days of affliction prevented me.
I went mourning without the sun:
    I stood up, and I cried in the congregation.
I am a brother to dragons,
    and a companion to owls.
My skin is black upon me,
    and my bones are burned with heat.
My harp also is turned to mourning,
    and my organ into the voice of them that weep."

CHAPTER 31

"I made a covenant with mine eyes;
    why then should I think upon a maid?
For what portion of God is there from above?
    and what inheritance of the Almighty from on high?

Is not destruction to the wicked?
    and a strange punishment to the workers of iniquity?
Doth not he see my ways,
    and count all my steps?

If I have walked with vanity,
    or if my foot hath hasted to deceit;
Let me be weighed in an even balance,
    that God may know mine integrity.
If my step hath turned out of the way,
    and mine heart walked after mine eyes,
    and if any blot hath cleaved to mine hands;
Then let me sow, and let another eat;
    yea, let my offspring be rooted out.

"If mine heart have been deceived by a woman,
    or if I have laid wait at my neighbor's door;
Then let my wife grind unto another,[16]
    and let others bow down upon her.
For this is an heinous crime;
    yea, it is an iniquity to be punished by the judges.
For it is a fire that consumeth to destruction,
    and would root out all mine increase.

"If I did despise the cause of my manservant or of my maidservant,
    when they contended with me;
What then shall I do when God riseth up?
    and when he visiteth, what shall I answer him?
Did not he that made me in the womb make him?
    and did not one fashion us in the womb?

"If I have withheld the poor from their desire,
    or have caused the eyes of the widow to fail;
Or have eaten my morsel myself alone,
    and the fatherless hath not eaten thereof;
(For from my youth he was brought up with me, as with a father,
    and I have guided her from my mother's womb;)
If I have seen any perish for want of clothing,
    or any poor without covering;
If his loins have not blessed me,
    and if he were not warmed with the fleece of my sheep;
If I have lifted up my hand against the fatherless,
    when I saw my help in the gate:
Then let mine arm fall from my shoulder blade,
    and mine arm be broken from the bone.
For destruction from God was a terror to me,
    and by reason of his highness I could not endure.

---

[16] That is, grind grain as a servant for someone else.

"If I have made gold my hope,
 or have said to the fine gold, 'Thou art my confidence';
If I rejoiced because my wealth was great,
 and because my hand had gotten much:
If I beheld the sun when it shined,
 or the moon walking in brightness;
And my heart hath been secretly enticed,
 or my mouth hath kissed my hand:
This also were an iniquity to be punished by the judge:
 for I should have denied the God that is above.

"If I rejoiced at the destruction of him that hated me,
 or lifted up myself when evil found him:
Neither have I suffered my mouth to sin
 by wishing a curse to his soul.
If the men of my tabernacle said not,
 'Oh that we had of his flesh! we cannot be satisfied.'
The stranger did not lodge in the street:
 but I opened my doors to the traveller.
If I covered my transgressions as Adam,
 by hiding mine iniquity in my bosom:
Did I fear a great multitude,
 or did the contempt of families terrify me,
 that I kept silence, and went not out of the door?
Oh that one would hear me!
 behold, my desire is, that the Almighty would answer me,
 and that mine adversary had written a book.
Surely I would take it upon my shoulder,
 and bind it as a crown to me.
I would declare unto him the number of my steps;
 as a prince would I go near unto him.

"If my land cry against me,
 or that the furrows likewise thereof complain;
If I have eaten the fruits thereof without money,
 or have caused the owners thereof to lose their life:
Let thistles grow instead of wheat,
 and cockle instead of barley."

The words of Job are ended.

CHAPTER 38

Then the Lord answered Job out of the whirlwind,[17] and said,

"Who is this that darkeneth counsel
 by words without knowledge?

---

[17]God appears in a whirlwind elsewhere in the Old Testament as well, notably in Nahum 1:3 and Psalms 18:7–15.

Gird up now thy loins like a man;
    for I will demand of thee, and answer thou me.

"Where wast thou when I laid the foundations of the earth?
    declare, if thou hast understanding.
Who hath laid the measures thereof, if thou knowest?
    or who hath stretched the line upon it?
Whereupon are the foundations thereof fastened?
    or who laid the corner stone thereof;
When the morning stars sang together,
    and all the sons of God shouted for joy?

"Or who shut up the sea with doors,
    when it brake forth, as if it had issued out of the womb?
When I made the cloud the garment thereof,
    and thick darkness a swaddlingband for it,
And brake up for it my decreed place,
    and set bars and doors,
And said, 'Hitherto shalt thou come, but no further:
    and here shall thy proud waves be stayed'?
Hast thou commanded the morning since thy days;
    and caused the dayspring[18] to know his place;
That it might take hold of the ends of the earth,
    that the wicked might be shaken out of it?
It is turned as clay to the seal;
    and they stand as a garment.
And from the wicked their light is withholden,
    and the high arm shall be broken.

"Hast thou entered into the springs of the sea?
    or hast thou walked in the search of the depth?
Have the gates of death been opened unto thee?
    or hast thou seen the doors of the shadow of death?
Hast thou perceived the breadth of the earth?
    declare if thou knowest it all.

"Where is the way where light dwelleth?
    and as for darkness, where is the place thereof,
That thou shouldest take it to the bound thereof,
    and that thou shouldest know the paths to the house thereof?
Knowest thou it, because thou wast then born?
    or because the number of thy days is great?

"Hast thou entered into the treasures of the snow?
    or hast thou seen the treasures of the hail,
Which I have reserved against the time of trouble,
    against the day of battle and war?

---

[18] Dawn.

By what way is the light parted,
    which scattereth the east wind upon the earth?
Who hath divided a watercourse for the overflowing of waters,
    or a way for the lightning of thunder;
To cause it to rain on the earth, where no man is;
    on the wilderness, wherein there is no man;
To satisfy the desolate and waste ground;
    and to cause the bud of the tender herb to spring forth?

"Hath the rain a father?
    or who hath begotten the drops of dew?
Out of whose womb came the ice?
    and the hoary frost of heaven, who hath gendered it?
The waters are hid as with a stone,
    and the face of the deep is frozen.

"Canst thou bind the sweet influences of Pleiades,
    or loose the bands of Orion?
Canst thou bring forth Mazzaroth in his season?
    or canst thou guide Arcturus with his sons?[19]
Knowest thou the ordinances of heaven?
    canst thou set the dominion thereof in the earth?

"Canst thou lift up thy voice to the clouds,
    that abundance of waters may cover thee?
Canst thou send lightnings, that they may go,
    and say unto thee, 'Here we are'?
Who hath put wisdom in the inward parts?
    or who hath given understanding to the heart?
Who can number the clouds in wisdom?
    or who can stay the bottles of heaven,
When the dust groweth into hardness,
    and the clods cleave fast together?

"Wilt thou hunt the prey for the lion?
    or fill the appetite of the young lions,
When they couch in their dens,
    and abide in the covert to lie in wait?
Who provideth for the raven his food?
    when his young ones cry unto God,
    they wander for lack of meat."

CHAPTER 39

"Knowest thou the time when the wild goats of the rock bring forth?
    or canst thou mark when the hinds do calve?
Canst thou number the months that they fulfil?
    or knowest thou the time when they bring forth?

---

[19] These are all stars or constellations.

They bow themselves, they bring forth their young ones,
  they cast out their sorrows.
Their young ones are in good liking, they grow up with corn;
  they go forth, and return not unto them.

"Who hath sent out the wild ass free?
  or who hath loosed the bands of the wild ass?
Whose house I have made the wilderness,
  and the barren land his dwellings.
He scorneth the multitude of the city,
  neither regardeth he the crying of the driver.
The range of the mountains is his pasture,
  and he searcheth after every green thing.

"Will the unicorn[20] be willing to serve thee,
  or abide by thy crib?
Canst thou bind the unicorn with his band in the furrow?
  or will he harrow the valleys after thee?
Wilt thou trust him, because his strength is great?
  or wilt thou leave thy labor to him?
Wilt thou believe him, that he will bring home thy seed,
  and gather it into thy barn?

"Gavest thou the goodly wings unto the peacocks?
  or wings and feathers unto the ostrich?
Which leaveth her eggs in the earth,
  and warmeth them in dust,
And forgetteth that the foot may crush them,
  or that the wild beast may break them.
She is hardened against her young ones, as though they were not hers:
  her labor is in vain without fear;
Because God hath deprived her of wisdom,
  neither hath he imparted to her understanding.
What time she lifteth up herself on high,
  she scorneth the horse and his rider.

"Hast thou given the horse strength?
  hast thou clothed his neck with thunder?
Canst thou make him afraid as a grasshopper?
  the glory of his nostrils is terrible.
He paweth in the valley, and rejoiceth in his strength:
  he goeth on to meet the armed men.
He mocketh at fear, and is not affrighted;
  neither turneth he back from the sword.
The quiver rattleth against him,
  the glittering spear and the shield.

---

[20] Or wild ox.

He swalloweth the ground with fierceness and rage:
 neither believeth he that it is the sound of the trumpet.
He saith among the trumpets, 'Ha, ha';
 and he smelleth the battle afar off,
 the thunder of the captains, and the shouting.

"Doth the hawk fly by thy wisdom,
 and stretch her wings toward the south?
Doth the eagle mount up at thy command,
 and make her nest on high?
She dwelleth and abideth on the rock,
 upon the crag of the rock, and the strong place.
From thence she seeketh the prey,
 and her eyes behold afar off.
Her young ones also suck up blood:
 and where the slain are, there is she."

CHAPTER 40

Moreover the Lord answered Job, and said,

"Shall he that contendeth with the Almighty instruct him?
He that reproveth God, let him answer it."

Then Job answered the Lord, and said,

"Behold, I am vile; what shall I answer thee?
 I will lay mine hand upon my mouth.
Once have I spoken; but I will not answer:
 yea, twice; but I will proceed no further."

Then answered the Lord unto Job out of the whirlwind, and said,

"Gird up thy loins now like a man:
 I will demand of thee, and declare thou unto me.
Wilt thou also disannul my judgment?
 wilt thou condemn me, that thou mayest be righteous?
Hast thou an arm like God?
 or canst thou thunder with a voice like him?

"Deck thyself now with majesty and excellency;
 and array thyself with glory and beauty.
Cast abroad the rage of thy wrath:
 and behold every one that is proud, and abase him.
Look on every one that is proud, and bring him low;
 and tread down the wicked in their place.
Hide them in the dust together;
 and bind their faces in secret.

Then will I also confess unto thee
    that thine own right hand can save thee.

"Behold now behemoth,[21] which I made with thee;
    he eateth grass as an ox.
Lo now, his strength is in his loins,
    and his force is in the navel of his belly.
He moveth his tail like a cedar:
    the sinews of his stones are wrapped together.
His bones are as strong pieces of brass;
    his bones are like bars of iron.

"He is the chief of the ways of God:
    he that made him can make his sword to approach unto him.
Surely the mountains bring him forth food,
    where all the beasts of the field play.
He lieth under the shady trees,
    in the covert of the reed, and fens.
The shady trees cover him with their shadow;
    the willows of the brook compass him about.
Behold, he drinketh up a river, and hasteth not:
    he trusteth that he can draw up Jordan into his mouth.
He taketh it with his eyes:
    his nose pierceth through snares."

CHAPTER 41

"Canst thou draw out leviathan[22] with an hook?
    or his tongue with a cord which thou lettest down?
Canst thou put an hook into his nose?
    or bore his jaw through with a thorn?
Will he make many supplications unto thee?
    will he speak soft words unto thee?
Will he make a covenant with thee?
    wilt thou take him for a servant for ever?
Wilt thou play with him as with a bird?
    or wilt thou bind him for thy maidens?
Shall the companions make a banquet of him?
    shall they part him among the merchants?
Canst thou fill his skin with barbed irons?
    or his head with fish spears?
Lay thine hand upon him,
    remember the battle, do no more.

[21]Probably the hippopotamus, here presented as a primeval monster.
[22]A mythological version of the crocodile, here presented as a sea monster emblematic of primeval chaos.

Behold, the hope of him is in vain:
    shall not one be cast down even at the sight of him?
None is so fierce that dare stir him up:
    who then is able to stand before me?
Who hath prevented me, that I should repay him?
    whatsoever is under the whole heaven is mine.
"I will not conceal his parts,
    nor his power, nor his comely proportion.
Who can discover the face of his garment?
    or who can come to him with his double bridle?
Who can open the doors of his face?
    his teeth are terrible round about.
His scales are his pride,
    shut up together as with a close seal.
One is so near to another,
    that no air can come between them.
They are joined one to another,
    they stick together, that they cannot be sundered.
By his neesings[23] a light doth shine,
    and his eyes are like the eyelids of the morning.
Out of his mouth go burning lamps,
    and sparks of fire leap out.
Out of his nostrils goeth smoke,
    as out of a seething pot or caldron.
His breath kindleth coals,
    and a flame goeth out of his mouth.
In his neck remaineth strength,
    and sorrow is turned into joy before him.
The flakes of his flesh are joined together:
    they are firm in themselves; they cannot be moved.
His heart is as firm as a stone;
    yea, as hard as a piece of the nether millstone.
When he raiseth up himself, the mighty are afraid:
    by reason of breakings they purify themselves.
The sword of him that layeth at him cannot hold:
    the spear, the dart, nor the habergeon.
He esteemeth iron as straw,
    and brass as rotten wood.
The arrow cannot make him flee:
    slingstones are turned with him into stubble.
Darts are counted as stubble:
    he laugheth at the shaking of a spear.
Sharp stones are under him:
    he spreadeth sharp pointed things upon the mire.
He maketh the deep to boil like a pot:
    he maketh the sea like a pot of ointment.

---

[23] Sneezes (which send out drops of water reflecting the sun).

He maketh a path to shine after him;
>   one would think the deep to be hoary.
Upon earth there is not his like,
>   who is made without fear.
He beholdeth all high things:
>   he is a king over all the children of pride."

CHAPTER 42

Then Job answered the Lord, and said,

"I know that thou canst do every thing,
>   and that no thought can be withholden from thee.
'Who is he that hideth counsel without knowledge?'
Therefore have I uttered that I understood not;
>   things too wonderful for me, which I knew not.
'Hear, I beseech thee, and I will speak:
>   I will demand of thee, and declare thou unto me.'
I have heard of thee by the hearing of the ear:
>   but now mine eye seeth thee.
Wherefore I abhor myself, and repent
>   in dust and ashes."

And it was so, that after the Lord had spoken these words unto Job, the Lord said to Eliphaz the Temanite, "My wrath is kindled against thee, and against thy two friends: for ye have not spoken of me the thing that is right, as my servant Job hath. Therefore take unto you now seven bullocks and seven rams, and go to my servant Job, and offer up for yourselves a burnt offering; and my servant Job shall pray for you: for him will I accept: lest I deal with you after your folly, in that ye have not spoken of me the thing which is right, like my servant Job." So Eliphaz the Temanite and Bildad the Shuhite and Zophar the Naamathite went, and did according as the Lord commanded them: the Lord also accepted Job. And the Lord turned the captivity of Job, when he prayed for his friends: also the Lord gave Job twice as much as he had before. Then came there unto him all his brethren, and all his sisters, and all they that had been of his acquaintance before, and did eat bread with him in his house: and they bemoaned him, and comforted him over all the evil that the Lord had brought upon him: every man also gave him a piece of money, and every one an earring of gold. So the Lord blessed the latter end of Job more than his beginning: for he had fourteen thousand sheep, and six thousand camels, and a thousand yoke of oxen, and a thousand she asses. He had also seven sons and three daughters. And he called the name of the first, Jemima; and the name of the second, Kezia; and the name of the third, Keren-happuch. And in all the land were no women found so fair as the daughters of Job: and their father gave them inheritance among their brethren. After this lived Job an hundred and forty years, and saw his sons, and his sons' sons, even four generations. So Job died, being old and full of days.

from PSALMS

PSALM 8

1   O Lord our Lord,[1]
         how excellent is thy name in all the earth!
         who has set thy glory above the heavens.
2   Out of the mouth of babes and sucklings[2] hast thou ordained
             strength
         because of thine enemies,
         that thou mightest still the enemy and the avenger.

3   When I consider thy heavens, the work of thy fingers,
         the moon and the stars, which thou hast ordained;

4   What is man, that thou art mindful of him?
         and the son of man,[3] that thou visitest him?

5   For thou hast made him a little lower than the angels,
         and hast crowned him with glory and honor.
6   Thou madest him to have dominion over the works of thy hands;
         thou hast put all things under his feet:
7   All sheep and oxen,
         yea, and the beasts of the field;
8   The fowl of the air, and the fish of the sea,
         and whatsoever passeth through the paths of the sea.

9   O Lord our Lord,
         how excellent is thy name in all the earth!

PSALM 23

1   The Lord is my shepherd;
         I shall not want.
2   He maketh me to lie down in green pastures:
         he leadeth me beside the still waters.
3   He restoreth my soul:
         he leadeth me in the paths of righteousness for his name's sake.

4   Yea, though I walk through the valley of the shadow of death,
         I will fear no evil: for thou art with me;
         thy rod and thy staff[4] they comfort me.

---

[1] Numbers in left margin are biblical verse numbers.
[2] Infants at the breast.
[3] "Son of man" means any individual person.
[4] The rod keeps off enemies; the staff is an emblem of protection.

5   Thou preparest a table before me in the presence of mine enemies:
        thou anointest my head with oil;
        my cup runneth over.[5]
6   Surely goodness and mercy shall follow me all the days of my life:
        and I will dwell in the house of the Lord for ever.[6]

PSALM 91

1   He that dwelleth in the secret place of the Most High[7]
        shall abide under the shadow of the Almighty.
2   I will say of the Lord, He is my refuge and my fortress:
        my God; in him will I trust.
3   Surely he shall deliver thee from the snare of the fowler,[8]
        and from the noisome[9] pestilence.
4   He shall cover thee with his feathers,
        and under his wings shalt thou trust:
        his truth shall be thy shield and buckler.[10]
5   Thou shalt not be afraid for the terror by night;
        nor for the arrow that flieth by day;
6   Nor for the pestilence that walketh in darkness;
        nor for the destruction that wasteth at noonday.

7   A thousand shall fall[11] at thy side,
        and ten thousand at thy right hand;
        but it shall not come nigh thee.
8   Only with thine eyes shalt thou behold
        and see the reward of the wicked.

9   Because thou hast made the Lord, which is my refuge,
        even the Most High, thy habitation;
10   There shall no evil befall thee,
        neither shall any plague come nigh thy dwelling.

11   For he shall give his angels charge over thee,
        to keep thee in all thy ways.
12   They shall bear thee up in their hands,
        lest thou dash thy foot against a stone.
13   Thou shalt tread upon the lion and adder:
        the young lion and the dragon shalt thou trample under feet.

14   Because he hath set his love upon me,[12]
        therefore will I deliver him:
        I will set him on high, because he hath known my name.

---

[5]In verse 5, the metaphor shifts; God is a host lavishing attentions on a dinner guest.
[6]One possible meaning is "I will spend my life worshipping in God's temple."
[7]Dwells in God's presence, or perhaps, more specifically, in the Temple.
[8]Hunter of game birds.   [9]Harmful.   [10]Shield; defense.
[11]Shall be stricken by the plague.
[12]Verses 14–16 are thought of as spoken by God.

15   He shall call upon me, and I will answer him:
        I will be with him in trouble;
        I will deliver him, and honor him.
16   With long life will I satisfy him,
        and show him my salvation.

PSALM 103

1   Bless the Lord, O my soul:
        and all that is within me, bless his holy name.
2   Bless the Lord, O my soul,
        and forget not all his benefits:
3   Who forgiveth all thine iniquities;
        Who healeth all thy diseases;
4   Who redeemeth thy life from destruction;
        who crowneth thee with loving-kindness and tender mercies;
5   Who satisfieth thy mouth with good things;
        so that thy youth is renewed like the eagle's.

6   The Lord executeth righteousness
        and judgment for all that are oppressed.
7   He made known his ways unto Moses,
        his acts unto the children of Israel.
8   The Lord is merciful and gracious,
        slow to anger, and plenteous in mercy.
9   He will not always chide:
        neither will he keep his anger for ever.
10   He hath not dealt with us after [13] our sins;
        nor rewarded us according to our iniquities.

11   For as the heaven is high above the earth,
        so great is his mercy toward them that fear him.
12   As far as the east is from the west,
        so far hath he removed our transgressions from us.
13   Like as a father pitieth his children,
        so the Lord pitieth them that fear him.
14   For he knoweth our frame;
        he remembereth that we are dust.

15   As for man, his days are as grass:
        as a flower of the field, so he flourisheth.
16   For the wind passeth over it, and it is gone;
        and the place thereof shall know it no more.
17   But the mercy of the Lord is from everlasting to everlasting
        upon them that fear him,
        and his righteousness unto children's children;
18   To such as keep his covenant,
        and to those that remember his commandments to do them.

[13] In proportion to.

19   The Lord hath prepared his throne[14] in the heavens;
          and his kingdom ruleth over all.
20   Bless the Lord, ye his angels, that excel in strength,
          that do his commandments, hearkening unto the voice of his
          word.
21   Bless ye the Lord, all ye his hosts;
          ye ministers of his, that do his pleasure.
22   Bless the Lord, all his works in all places of his dominion:
          bless the Lord, O my soul.

PSALM 114

1   When Israel went out of Egypt,
          the house of Jacob from a people of strange language;
2   Judah was his sanctuary,
          and Israel[15] his dominion.

3   The sea saw it,[16] and fled:
          Jordan was driven back.
4   The mountains skipped like rams,
          and the little hills like lambs.

5   What ailed thee, O thou sea, that thou fleddest?
          thou Jordan, that thou wast driven back?
6   Ye mountains, that ye skipped like rams;
          and ye little hills, like lambs?

7   Tremble, thou earth, at the presence of the Lord,
          at the presence of the God of Jacob;
8   Which turned the rock into a standing water,[17]
          the flint into a fountain of waters.

PSALM 130

1   Out of the depths have I cried unto thee, O Lord.
2   Lord, hear my voice:
          let thine ears be attentive to the voice of my supplications.

3   If thou, Lord, shouldest mark iniquities,
          O Lord, who shall stand?

[14] Established His (God's own) throne.

[15] Judah was the southern kingdom of Palestine, settled by the tribes of Judah and Benjamin; Israel was the northern kingdom, settled by the tribes descended from Jacob's ten other sons.

[16] Saw God's presence. The reference is to the miraculous dividing of the waters when the Hebrews escaped from Egypt (Exodus 14); Jordan, in the following line, is the river crossed by the Hebrews forty years later, when they entered the Promised Land (Joshua 3). The Jordan too was miraculously dried up to allow a crossing.

[17] A pool. During the Hebrews' forty years of wandering, God empowered Moses to draw water from a rock by striking it with his staff (Exodus 17).

4	But there is forgiveness with thee,
	that thou mayest be feared.
5	I wait for the Lord,
	my soul doth wait, and in his word do I hope.
6	My soul waiteth for the Lord more than they that watch for the
	morning:
	I say, more than they that watch for the morning.
7	Let Israel hope in the Lord:
	for with the Lord there is mercy,
	and with him is plenteous redemption.
8	And he shall redeem Israel from all his iniquities.

PSALM 137

1	By the rivers of Babylon,[18] there we sat down,
	yea, we wept, when we remembered Zion.
2	We hanged our harps upon the willows in the midst thereof.
3	For there they that carried us away captive required of us a song;
	and they that wasted[19] us required of us mirth, saying,
	Sing us one of the songs of Zion.
4	How shall we sing the Lord's song in a strange land?
5	If I forget thee, O Jerusalem,
	let my right hand forget her cunning.
6	If I do not remember thee,
	let my tongue cleave to the roof of my mouth;
	if I prefer not Jerusalem above my chief joy.
7	Remember, O Lord, the children of Edom[20]
	in the day of Jerusalem;
	who said, Rase[21] it, rase it,
	even to the foundation thereof.
8	O daughter of Babylon, who are to be destroyed;
	happy shall he be, that rewardeth thee as thou hast served us.
9	Happy shall he be, that taketh and dasheth
	thy little ones against the stones.

[18] The irrigation canals of the Tigris and Euphrates rivers, in Babylonia. The Babylonians conquered the Hebrews' homeland (Zion) in 597 B.C., inaugurating sixty years of exile and captivity.
[19] Laid waste.
[20] A land south of the Dead Sea; an ally of the Babylonians in the sack of Jerusalem.
[21] Raze; demolish.

PSALM 139

1	O Lord, thou hast searched me, and known me.
2	Thou knowest my downsitting and mine uprising;
	thou understandest my thought afar off.
3	Thou compassest my path and my lying down,
	and art acquainted with all my ways.
4	For there is not a word in my tongue,
	but, lo, O Lord, thou knowest it altogether.
5	Thou hast beset me behind and before,
	and laid thine hand upon me.
6	Such knowledge is too wonderful for me;
	it is high, I cannot attain unto it.
7	Whither shall I go from thy Spirit?
	or whither shall I flee from thy presence?
8	If I ascend up into heaven, thou art there:
	if I make my bed in hell,[22] behold, thou art there.
9	If I take the wings of the morning,[23]
	and dwell in the uttermost parts of the sea;
10	Even there shall thy hand lead me,
	and thy right hand shall hold me.
11	If I say, Surely the darkness shall cover me;
	even the night shall be light about me.
12	Yea, the darkness hideth not from thee;
	but the night shineth as the day:
	the darkness and the light are both alike to thee.
13	For thou hast possessed my reins:[24]
	thou has covered me in my mother's womb.
14	I will praise thee; for I am fearfully and wonderfully made:
	marvelous are thy works; and that my soul knoweth right well.
15	My substance was not hid from thee
	when I was made in secret,
	and curiously wrought in the lowest parts of the earth.[25]
16	Thine eyes did see my substance, yet being unperfect;
	and in thy book all my members were written,
	which in continuance were fashioned,
	when as yet there was none of them.
17	How precious also are thy thoughts unto me, O God!
	How great is the sum of them!
18	If I should count them, they are more in number than the sand:
	when I awake, I am still with thee.
19	Surely thou wilt slay the wicked, O God:
	depart from me therefore, ye bloody men.

[22] Sheol, the place of the dead (roughly equivalent to the Greek Hades).
[23] Travel as fast as the dawn spreads.
[24] "Didst form my inward parts" (Revised Standard Version).
[25] A metaphor for the womb.

20   For they speak against thee wickedly,
           and thine enemies take thy name in vain.
21   Do not I hate them, O Lord, that hate thee?
           And am not I grieved with those that rise up against thee?
22   I hate them with perfect hatred:
           I count them mine enemies.
23   Search me, O God, and know my heart:
           try me, and know my thoughts:
24   And see if there be any wicked way in me,
           and lead me in the way everlasting.

Homer

(Eighth Century B.C.)

Like the Bible, Homer's *Iliad* and *Odyssey* are fundamental sources of the culture and literature of the Western world. These epics have been revered not only as masterpieces of language and narrative but also as expressions of central truths about human beings and their place in the scheme of things. They grow out of a story the elements of which are as follows: While a guest at the palace of Meneláos (*Menelaus* in the more familiar English spelling), who was king of Sparta in southern Greece, the Trojan prince Paris fell in love with Helen, his host's supremely beautiful wife, and carried her off to Troy, apparently with her consent. Under the command of Meneláos' brother Agamémnon, the Greeks organized an army and sailed to Troy in order to recapture Helen, to avenge the dishonor of her husband, and to punish Paris for his violation of the sacred code of hospitality. But, despite outnumbering the Trojans, the Greeks were long frustrated in their attempt to take the city, which was to fall only after ten years of siege. The *Iliad* focuses on one important episode in the war, a quarrel between Agamémnon and Akhilleus (Achilles) over ownership of a prisoner slavegirl. The epic then records the tragic consequences of the quarrel: it describes the death of Akhilleus' beloved companion Patróklos (Patroclus) while Akhilleus was sulking on the sidelines and the subsequent revenge taken by Akhilleus on the Trojan hero Hektor (Hector), who had killed his friend. The action of the *Odyssey* takes place after the war is over. The poem concentrates on one of the foremost Greek warriors against Troy, the resourceful Odysseus, who must overcome many obstacles and tribulations in order to return to his wife and homeland. The actual fall of Troy is not described in either of the two Homeric poems. (One ancient account of the city's fall was written many centuries later by the Roman poet Virgil in his *Aeneid,* Book II.)

Again like the Bible, the two Homeric epics have for centuries caused controversy. Debates continue today as strongly as ever. To say that the *Iliad* and *Odyssey* were written by Homer is in fact almost a nonstatement, since the meaning of its very terms is ambiguous. What exactly *are* the two poems?

Are some parts more authentic than others? Were they composed as wholes or did they evolve? Was Homer a real person or is his name merely a convenient label for a legendary figure or group? Are both poems the work of the same author? If he was an individual, when and where did he live? At what stage of their history were the poems (originally meant to be sung or recited) put into the written form we know? To what extent does the written version preserve the oral version? Were Troy and the Trojan War as described in the *Iliad* historical? Many of these questions, some of which date to early antiquity, still cannot be answered with complete certainty.

Some probabilities have emerged, however. In the later nineteenth century, the great amateur archaeologist Heinrich Schliemann proved by his excavations that Troy did indeed once exist. A war similar to the one Homer describes probably did occur, around the early twelfth century B.C. Most authorities now believe also that Homer was a single person, who lived around the eighth century B.C. and was a professional bard or minstrel like Demódokos and Phêmios in the *Odyssey*. His homeland was probably Ionia, a region south of Troy in Asia Minor (modern Turkey) that faces Greece across the Aegean Sea. Tradition says that he was blind.

His role in composing the *Iliad* and *Odyssey* is harder to define. Undoubtedly he inherited a large store of traditional material that included many prominent incidents and characters of the tale of Troy. He regarded this material as history, and many poems on the subject would have been familiar to him and to his audience. But he probably deserves the main credit at least for shaping and refining this material into the monumental works we know, giving to them the unity, power, and artistry that Aristotle later praised so highly in his *Poetics*. These qualities have caused Homer to be honored as one of the supreme poets of the world. Whether the *Iliad* and *Odyssey* were actually put in written form by him (he lived in an age and place barely emerging from several centuries of illiteracy), were recorded by a scribe to whom he dictated, or were written down only after a considerable period of oral transmission is still much debated.

That the *Iliad* and *Odyssey* were originally intended to be heard rather than read is the first thing new readers need to know about the poems. The fact explains, for example, the frequent repetitions—of single phrases, of whole lines, and sometimes of long passages. Such repetition is characteristic of all forms of oral communication, since—as lecturers, auctioneers, playwrights, and orators know—repetition enhances clarity and helps achieve the desired emphasis. The repetition may even be, as some scholars now believe, a key to the poems' origins, in the oral-formulaic method, a process by which singers improvised by combining traditional phrases with original ones to flesh out a memorized narrative outline. If we ignore the poems' oral manner we put an unnecessary distance between ourselves and their original audience. Moreover, we can misinterpret many of their strategies, especially the "Homeric epithets," the recurrent brief phrases used to describe things or persons. The reader may wonder why Hera, the queen of the gods, is called "white-armed" in some passages and "Goddess of the Golden Chair" in others, where either label (or neither) would seem appropriate, or why Akhilleus is "the great runner" even when he is not running, or why the striking phrase "tamer of horses" should be applied to two different men. The answer is that Homer inserted such phrases in places where they fit the poetic rhythm, even where they are not especially relevant to the narrative context. (The Greek meter, dactyllic hexameter, combines long [—] and short [˘] syllables in the pattern —˘ ˘ —˘ ˘—˘ ˘ — ˘˘— ˘ — —, with certain substitutions permitted.) It is a mistake, then, to read too much into such phrases or to use them to interpret particular passages, even when the phrases do sound appropriate.

An even more serious error is to look down on Homer as a simple, primitive poet, one whose accomplishments, like those of a precocious child, are impressive mainly because of his early age. In fact, there have been few if any greater artists than Homer. The stories he tells are vivid and powerful in their sweep, but they are also subtle and skillfully shaded. For example, all the principal men in the *Iliad*, Greeks and Trojans, are brave in battle, but their styles of bravery are distinctive: Agamémnon is savage, Akhilleus is proud and supremely confident, Hektor is patriotic, Odysseus is pragmatic (as in the *Odyssey* as well). Seemingly fleeting details can be quite significant. When, in Book IV of the *Odyssey*, Telémakhos approaches the palace of Meneláos, one of the king's men hesitates to admit the young man as the code of hospitality would dictate. Meneláos is furious, but we can guess why his man is nervous: years before, another guest named Paris had been welcomed by Meneláos but had gone on to abduct his beautiful wife, Helen, and thus had set off the entire Trojan War. We must be alert to such subtleties, since Homer's objective manner usually leaves connections unstated. Characterizations are fully individualized. Penélopê in the *Odyssey* is not merely the object of the suitors' lust and greed but also a fully imagined, resourceful wife and woman, a fit mate for the crafty Odysseus. The green young man Telémakhos and the inexperienced but enterprising Phaiákian princess Nausikaa (Nausicaä) are richly realized characters in themselves and also effective foils for Odysseus, the seasoned veteran of life and experience. One of the major achievements of the Homeric poems is that they combine richness of detail and nuance with a masterful control of the poems' general movement and pattern.

Homer's control results partly, as Aristotle later pointed out, from his careful limiting of his material; the *Iliad* treats a single episode in the ten-year Trojan War and the *Odyssey* centers on the troubled homecoming of a single warrior. But the poems have also a far more ambitious aim: to describe as fully as possible the heroic world. Heroism is the theme of both poems. Since the *Iliad* is a tragedy and a war poem, it celebrates the heroism that faces and suffers death. The *Odyssey* is a kind of comedy, and the heroism it celebrates is that of survival, the triumph over death. The *Iliad* derives much of its intensity from its almost claustrophobic atmosphere, its setting confined to a few square miles in and around the besieged city of Troy where thousands of men are cramped together. The closeness of atmosphere is relieved only occasionally by scenes involving the Olympian gods and through similes reminding the audience of the world of nature and peacetime. The *Odyssey* is wholly different. Its geographic vistas are almost endless, taking in the far, romantic reaches of the known and fabled Mediterranean world and even the realm of the dead. In intriguing contrast is the second half of the poem, where the setting narrows to that of a domestic drama on Odysseus' home island. Here the arena of heroism is neither the defeat of an army nor the perils of distant travel but a struggle to reassert private rights to home and property. The suspense of Odysseus' plot against the suitors emerges from a context not of the cosmic but of familiar human detail—a world of good and bad servants, favorite beds, kitchen logistics. In different ways, then, the *Odyssey* is both more panoramic and more intimate than the *Iliad.*

The Homeric divinities, similarly, seem both remote and familiar. Their role and relationship to human beings are very difficult to define. In some ways they seem like projections (often in a comic vein) of human activities and the human environment: Poseidon of the sea, Hephaistos of fire and metalworking, Apollo of medicine and archery, Athêna of resourcefulness, Aphrodítê of love and sex, and so forth. They are thoroughly humanized, and in their rivalries, loyalties, plots, and bickerings they sometimes seem to parody the human beings, on a scale actually smaller than life. On the other hand, they are utterly superior to human beings, in power and above all in their exemption from death. (Paradoxically, the strictest limitation of their power is their inability to share their immortality with their human protégés.) They continually intervene, especially at key moments, to shape the course of events on earth. In doing so they would seem to limit human freedom. Yet the poems also make it clear that humans are responsible for their deeds and that they do have choices. The immortals' actions frequently seem to be confirmations rather than causes of what happens; we can say that Odysseus is resourceful because the goddess Athena aids him or that she aids him because, like her, he is resourceful. In any event, the presence of the divinities in the world of the poems emphasizes both the brevity and the urgency of human life and thus enhances our sense of the mystery in the world.

The *Iliad* and *Odyssey* are the definitive epics in the Western tradition. Seven centuries after Homer, Virgil creatively imitated and synthesized the two Homeric epics in the *Aeneid,* a story of the Trojan survivors who, under Ainéias, or Aeneas, journeyed like Odysseus through hardships to lay in Italy the foundations of Roman greatness after a battle resembling that in the *Iliad.* Virgil sophisticated the epic, making it a more strictly literary form and using it for doctrinal purposes, as a vehicle for fostering Roman political and religious values. Seventeen hundred years after Virgil, Milton wrote the definitive English epic, *Paradise Lost,* in an attempt to "justify the ways of God to men" and to preach an essentially Christian heroism. Both Milton and Virgil depict a universe governed by an ultimately just providential force, and each either implies or states that his form of heroism has superseded earlier epic values. Each found a model in Homer, despite the vast differences between their metaphysics and Homer's apparent unconcern with it. That indebtedness testifies that Homer was not only a great poet but also one whose vision has universal application.

FURTHER READING *(prepared by F.S.N. and M.C.):* Oliver Taplin provides an introductory essay on Homer, with a useful bibliography, in *The Oxford History of the Classical World,* ed. John Boardman, Jasper Griffin, and Oswyn Murray, 1986. A description of the life and culture of pre-Homeric civilization is given by John Chadwick, *The Decipherment of Linear B,* 1960. Howard Clarke's *Homer's Readers,* 1981, surveys clearly what is known of the circumstances under which the Homeric epics were composed. Two introductory works on Homer are W. A. Camps, *An Introduction to Homer,* 1980; and Jasper Griffin, *Homer* (in the Past Masters series), 1980. On the Homeric problem, G. S. Kirk, *Homer and the Oral Tradition,* 1976, is useful. A stimulating sampling of essays by artists such as Tolstoy, Pound, and Cavafy has been edited by George

Steiner and Robert Fagles, *Homer: A Collection of Critical Essays,* 1962; while learned studies by classical scholars such as Bowra, Lord, and Blegen have been assembled by Alan J. B. Wace and Frank H. Stubbings, *A Companion to Homer,* 1962. An informative and readable critical commentary on the *Iliad,* based specifically on the Robert Fitzgerald translation and including a foreword by him, is James C. Hogan's *A Guide to the Iliad,* 1979. Martin Mueller, *The Iliad,* 1984, is a fine introduction. Mark W. Edwards, *Homer: Poet of the Iliad,* 1987, is also recommended for its valuable insights. Katherine Callan King discusses the Achilles myth in *Achilles,* 1987. On the *Iliad* as tragedy, see C. W. Macleod's introduction to his edition of and commentary on the *Iliad,* Book XXIV, 1982. For a treatment of human mortality in the poem, along with discussion of the Homeric deities, see J. Griffin's *Homer on Life and Death,* 1980. Analysis of individual scenes in the *Odyssey* as they contribute to the poem's effect appears in B. Fenik, *Studies in the Odyssey,* 1974. The poem's effect is also well captured in N. Austin, *Archery at the Dark of the Moon,* 1975. M. I. Finley, *The World of Odysseus,* 1964, discusses the sociology of the *Odyssey.* Charles Taylor, ed., *Essays on the Odyssey: Selected Modern Criticism,* 1963, provides twentieth-century interpretations of the work. Jasper Griffin, *Homer: The Odyssey,* 1987, is a good introduction to the poem. George E. Dimock, *The Unity of the Odyssey,* 1989, is especially good on the coherence of the poem. On the motif of hospitality in the *Odyssey,* see Steve Reece, *The Stranger's Welcome,* 1993. The multiple roles of Penelope are the subject of Nancy Felson-Rubin, *Regarding Penelope,* 1994. The latter half of the poem is well treated in Sheila Murnagham, *Disguise and Recognition in the Odyssey,* 1987.

THE ILIAD

Translated by Robert Fitzgerald

For the events leading up to the Trojan War, see the first paragraph of the Introduction to Homer. As the *Iliad* opens, Troy is undergoing its tenth year of siege by the Greek coalition (called at different times Akhaians, Danääns, and Argives). Although they outnumber the Trojans, the Greeks have not been able to take Troy and win back Helen—this despite the presence on the Greek side of the great warrior Akhilleus (Achilles) and the Myrmidons, his tough and disciplined army.

The gods take a strong interest in the war and are divided in their allegiances, some supporting the Greeks and some the Trojans. The division is explained in part by a mythological episode that occurred before Paris and Helen eloped. Paris had judged a dispute among Hêra (queen of the gods), the warlike goddess Athêna, and Aphrodítê (goddess of love and beauty) over which of the three was most beautiful. He decided for Aphrodítê, who had promised him as a reward the most beautiful woman in the world and then kept her promise by giving him Helen. As a result, Aphrodítê sides with Paris and his people while Hêra and Athêna oppose them bitterly.

Many persons and places in the *Iliad* are best known to readers by their Latinized names, such as *Achilles* and *Ajax.* The present translator has used forms (*Akhilleus, Aías*) closer to the Greek spelling and pronunciation. An acute accent (´) indicates stress; thus *Aías* is accented on the first syllable, *Agamémnon* on the third one. A circumflex accent (^) indicates that the vowel sound is long; thus *Lêto* is pronounced Laytoe. A dieresis (¨) indicates pronunciation as a separate syllable; thus *Danääns* has three syllables rather than two. [*Editors' headnote.*]

BOOK ONE: QUARREL, OATH, AND PROMISE

Anger be now your song, immortal one,[1]
Akhilleus' anger, doomed and ruinous,
that caused the Akhaians[2] loss on bitter loss
and crowded brave souls into the undergloom,[3]
leaving so many dead men—carrion
for dogs and birds; and the will of Zeus was done.[4]
Begin it when the two men first contending
broke with one another—

                                        the Lord Marshal

Agamémnon, Atreus' son, and Prince Akhilleus.
Among the gods, who brought this quarrel on?   10
The son of Zeus by Lêto.[5] Agamémnon
angered him, so he made a burning wind
of plague rise in the army: rank and file
sickened and died for the ill their chief had done
in despising a man of prayer.
This priest, Khrysês, had come down to the ships[6]
with gifts, no end of ransom for his daughter;
on a golden staff he carried the god's white bands[7]
and sued for grace from the men of all Akhaia,
the two Atreidai[8] most of all:

                                        "O Captains   20

Meneláos and Agamémnon, and you other
Akhaians under arms!
The gods who hold Olympos,[9] may they grant you
plunder of Priam's[10] town and a fair wind home,
but let me have my daughter back for ransom
as you revere Apollo, son of Zeus!"

Then all the soldiers murmured their assent:

"Behave well to the priest. And take the ransom!"

---

[1] The first lines are the model for the "opening formula" used by epic poets after Homer: the invocation of the Muse, or spirit of inspiration; the request that she "sing" the poem; the statement of the main theme, along with a hint at its consequences; the abrupt leap into the story itself. Compare the opening lines of Homer's *Odyssey,* Virgil's *Aeneid,* and Milton's *Paradise Lost.*

[2] The Greek forces.   [3] Aïdês (Hades), the shadowy realm of the dead.

[4] Zeus was the king of the gods. Homer considers all events in the poem and life in general as manifestations of Zeus's will, although human beings do have a limited but significant freedom to choose and are responsible for their actions; the interrelationship of human and divine will is complex and ambiguous. Even Zeus is to some extent limited by fate; in later Greek literature fate is regarded as an even more mysterious and impersonal force.

[5] *son . . . Lêto.* Apollo, god of archery, prophecy, and healing (as well as its opposite, disease).

[6] The Greek fleet is drawn up on the beach bordering the plain of Troy.

[7] The staff and ribbons are symbolic of Apollo, who as god of prophecy is patron of the prophet-priest Khrysês.

[8] Sons of Atreus. For the history of the house of Atreus, see Aeschylus' *Oresteia.*

[9] The mountain where the gods live.   [10] The king of Troy.

But Agamémnon would not. It went against his desire,
and brutally he ordered the man away: 30

"Let me not find you here by the long ships
loitering this time or returning later,
old man; if I do,
the staff and ribbons of the god will fail you.
Give up the girl? I swear she will grow old
at home in Argos,[11] far from her own country,
working my loom and visiting my bed.
Leave me in peace and go, while you can, in safety."

So harsh he was, the old man feared and obeyed him,
in silence trailing away 40
by the shore of the tumbling clamorous whispering sea,
and he prayed and prayed again, as he withdrew,
to the god whom silken-braided Lêto bore:

"O hear me, master of the silver bow,
protector of Ténedos and the holy towns,
Apollo, Sminthian,[12] if to your liking
ever in any grove I roofed a shrine
or burnt thighbones in fat upon your altar—
bullock or goat flesh—let my wish come true:
your arrows on the Danáäns[13] for my tears!" 50

Now when he heard this prayer, Phoibos Apollo
walked with storm in his heart from Olympos' crest,
quiver and bow at his back, and the bundled arrows
clanged on the sky behind as he rocked in his anger,
descending like night itself. Apart from the ships
he halted and let fly, and the bowstring slammed
as the silver bow sprang, rolling in thunder away.
Pack animals were his target first, and dogs,
but soldiers, too, soon felt transfixing pain
from his hard shots, and pyres[14] burned night and day. 60
Nine days the arrows of the god came down
broadside upon the army. On the tenth,
Akhilleus called all ranks to assembly. Hêra,[15]
whose arms are white as ivory, moved him to it,
as she took pity on Danáäns dying.

[11]A region of southern Greece, ruled by Agamémnon.
[12]*Ténedos.* An island nearby. *Sminthian.* A name of Apollo meaning "mouse god," perhaps a reference to the god's ability to bring on plague, rodents being carriers.
[13]Another name for the Greek forces.
[14]Bonfires for cremating the dead.
[15]Queen of the gods who strongly supports the Greeks. See headnote to the *Iliad.* The phrase "whose arms are white as ivory" is one of many repeated verbal formulas; some of them can have a particular, appropriate effect, but most of them are used more automatically, in accordance with the needs of poetic meter in oral poetry.

All being mustered, all in place and quiet,
Akhilleus, fast in battle as a lion,
rose and said:

                                        "Agamémnon, now, I take it,
the siege is broken, we are going to sail,
and even so may not leave death behind:
if war spares anyone, disease will take him . . .   70
We might, though, ask some priest or some diviner,
even some fellow good at dreams—for dreams
come down from Zeus as well—
why all this anger of the god Apollo?

Has he some quarrel with us for a failure
in vows or hekatombs?[16] Would mutton burned
or smoking goat flesh make him lift the plague?"

Putting the question, down he sat. And Kalkhas,
Kalkhas Thestórides,[17] came forward, wisest   80
by far of all who scanned the flight of birds.[18]
He knew what was, what had been, what would be,
Kalkhas, who brought Akhaia's ships to Ilion[19]
by the diviner's gift Apollo gave him.
Now for their benefit he said:

                                                    "Akhilleus,
dear to Zeus, it is on me you call
to tell you why the Archer God is angry.
Well, I can tell you. Are you listening? Swear
by heaven that you will back me and defend me,
because I fear my answer will enrage   90
a man with power in Argos, one whose word
Akhaian troops obey.

                        A great man in his rage is formidable
for underlings: though he may keep it down,
he cherishes the burning in his belly
until a reckoning day. Think well
if you will save me."

Said Akhilleus:

                                                    "Courage.
Tell what you know, what you have light to know.
I swear by Apollo, the lord god to whom
you pray when you uncover truth,   100
never while I draw breath, while I have eyes to see,

---

[16]Lavish sacrifices to the gods.
[17]The suffix *-ides* means "son of."
[18]Prophets, or diviners, discovered the gods' will by observing omens such as the direction of birds in flight.
[19]Troy.

shall any man upon this beachhead dare
lay hands on you—not one of all the army,
not Agamémnon, if it is he you mean,
though he is first in rank of all Akhaians."

The diviner then took heart and said:

"No failure

in hekatombs or vows is held against us.
It is the man of prayer whom Agamémnon
treated with contempt: he kept his daughter,
spurned his gifts: for that man's sake the Archer   110
visited grief upon us and will again.
Relieve the Danááns of this plague he will not
until the girl who turns the eyes of men
shall be restored to her own father—freely,
with no demand for ransom—and until
we offer up a hekatomb at Khrysê.[20]
Then only can we calm him and persuade him."

He finished and sat down. The son of Atreus,
ruler of the great plain, Agamémnon,
rose, furious. Round his heart resentment   120
welled, and his eyes shone out like licking fire.
Then, with a long and boding look at Kalkhas,
he growled at him:

"You visionary of hell,

never have I had fair play in your forecasts.
Calamity is all you care about, or see,
no happy portents; and you bring to pass
nothing agreeable. Here you stand again
before the army, giving it out as oracle
the Archer made them suffer because of me,
because I would not take the gifts   130
and let the girl Khrysêis go; I'd have her
mine, at home. Yes, if you like, I rate her
higher than Klytaimnestra, my own wife!
She loses nothing by comparison
in beauty or womanhood, in mind or skill.

For all of that, I am willing now to yield her
if it is best; I want the army saved
and not destroyed. You must prepare, however,
a prize of honor for me, and at once,
that I may not be left without my portion—   140
I, of all Argives. It is not fitting so.

---

[20]Khrysês' town; the names of priest, town, and daughter (Khrysêis) are virtually the same word.

While every man of you looks on, my girl
goes elsewhere."

Prince Akhilleus answered him:

"Lord Marshall, most insatiate of men,
how can the army make you a new gift?
Where is our store of booty? Can you see it?
Everything plundered from the towns has been
distributed; should troops turn all that in?[21]
Just let the girl go, in the god's name, now;   150
we'll make it up to you, twice over, three
times over, on that day Zeus gives us leave
to plunder Troy behind her rings of stone."

Agamémnon answered:

                                                                         "Not that way

will I be gulled, brave as you are, Akhilleus.
Take me in, would you? Try to get around me?
What do you really ask? That you may keep
your own winnings, I am to give up mine
and sit here wanting her? Oh, no:
the army will award a prize to me   160
and make sure that it measures up, or if
they do not, I will take a girl myself,
your own, or Aías', or Odysseus' prize![22]
Take her, yes, to keep. The man I visit
may choke with rage; well, let him.
But this, I say, we can decide on later.

Look to it now, we launch on the great sea
a well-found ship, and get her manned with oarsmen,
load her with sacrificial beasts and put aboard
Khryseis in her loveliness. My deputy,   170
Aías, Idómeneus,[23] or Prince Odysseus,
or you, Akhilleus, fearsome as you are,
will make the hekatomb and quiet the Archer."

Akhilleus frowned and looked at him, then said:

"You thick-skinned, shameless, greedy fool!
Can any Akhaian care for you, or obey you,
after this on marches or in battle?
As for myself, when I came here to fight,
I had no quarrel with Troy or Trojan spearmen:

---

[21] The Greeks have made several side raids on towns near Troy.
[22] *Aías, Odysseus.* Two of the principal Greek warriors and leaders. There are two Aíases;
the one referred to here is the "greater" Aías, son of Télamôn. Odysseus, noted for his resourcefulness, is the hero of Homer's other epic, the *Odyssey.*
[23] Ruler of Krete (Crete); another prominent leader among the Greeks.

they never stole my cattle or my horses, 180
never in the black farmland of Phthía[24]
ravaged my crops. How many miles there are
of shadowy hills between, and foaming seas!
No, no, we joined for you, you insolent boor,
to please you, fighting for your brother's sake
and yours, to get revenge upon the Trojans.
You overlook this, dogface, or don't care,
and now in the end you threaten to take my girl,
a prize I sweated for, and soldiers gave me!

Never have I had plunder like your own 190
from any Trojan stronghold battered down
by the Akhaians. I have seen more action
hand to hand in those assaults than you have,
but when the time for sharing comes, the greater
share is always yours. Worn out with battle
I carry off some trifle to my ships.
Well, this time I make sail for home.
Better to take now to my ships. Why linger,
cheated of winnings, to make wealth for you?"

To this the high commander made reply: 200

"Desért, if that's the way the wind blows. Will I
beg you to stay on my account? I will not.
Others will honor me, and Zeus who views
the wide world most of all.

                                        No officer

is hateful to my sight as you are, none
given like you to faction,[25] as to battle—
rugged you are, I grant, by some god's favor.
Sail, then, in your ships, and lord it over
your own battalion of Myrmidons.[26] I do not
give a curse for you, or for your anger. 210
But here is warning for you:

                                        Khrysêis

being required of me by Phoibos Apollo,
she will be sent back in a ship of mine,
manned by my people. That done, I myself
will call for Brisêis at your hut, and take her,
flower of young girls that she is, your prize,
to show you here and now who is the stronger
and make the next man sick at heart—if any
think of claiming equal place with me."

---

[24]Akhilleus' homeland, in northern Greece.
[25]Insubordination; subversive dissent.
[26]Akhilleus' troops.

A pain like grief weighed on the son of Pêleus,[27]   220
and in his shaggy chest this way and that
the passion of his heart ran: should he draw
longsword from hip, stand off the rest, and kill
in single combat the great son of Atreus,
or hold his rage in check and give it time?
And as this tumult swayed him, as he slid
the big blade slowly from the sheath, Athêna
came to him from the sky.[28] The white-armed goddess,
Hêra, sent her, being fond of both,
concerned for both men. And Athêna, stepping   230
up behind him, visible to no one
except Akhilleus, gripped his red-gold hair.

Startled, he made a half turn, and he knew her
upon the instant for Athêna: terribly
her grey eyes blazed at him. And speaking softly
but rapidly aside to her he said:

"What now, O daughter of the god of heaven
who bears the stormcloud, why are you here? To see
the wolfishness of Agamémnon?
Well, I give you my word: this time, and soon,   240
he pays for his behavior with his blood."

The grey-eyed goddess Athêna said to him:

"It was to check this killing rage I came
from heaven, if you will listen. Hêra sent me,
being fond of both of you, concerned for both.
Enough: break off this combat, stay your hand
upon the sword hilt. Let him have a lashing
with words, instead: tell him how things will be.
Here is my promise, and it will be kept:
winnings three times as rich, in due season,   250
you shall have in requital for his arrogance.
But hold your hand. Obey."

                                                        The great runner,
Akhilleus, answered:

                                            "Nothing for it, goddess,
but when you two immortals speak, a man
complies, though his heart burst. Just as well.
Honor the gods' will, they may honor ours."

---

[27]Akhilleus' father.
[28]Associated with crafts, resourcefulness, and skill in general, Athêna is a powerful agent
of divine assistance to the Greeks in the *Iliad* and the faithful patron of Odysseus in the *Odyssey*.
For her opposition to Troy and allegiance to the Greeks, see the headnote to the *Iliad*.

On this he stayed his massive hand
upon the silver pommel, and the blade
of his great weapon slid back in the scabbard.
The man had done her bidding. Off to Olympos,   260
gaining the air, she went to join the rest,
the powers of heaven in the home of Zeus.

But now the son of Pêleus turned on Agamémnon
and lashed out at him, letting his anger ride
in execration:

                                                  "Sack of wine,
you with your cur's eyes and your antelope heart!
You've never had the kidney to buckle on
armor among the troops, or make a sortie
with picked men—oh, no; that way death might lie.
Safer, by god, in the middle of the army—   270
is it not?—to commandeer the prize
of any man who stands up to you! Leech!
Commander of trash! If not, I swear,
you never could abuse one soldier more!

But here is what I say: my oath upon it
by this great staff: look: leaf or shoot
it cannot sprout again, once lopped away
from the log it left behind in the timbered hills;
it cannot flower, peeled of bark and leaves;
instead, Akhaian officers in council   280
take it in hand by turns, when they observe
by the will of Zeus due order in debate:[29]
let this be what I swear by then: I swear
a day will come when every Akhaian soldier
will groan to have Akhilleus back. That day
you shall no more prevail on me than this
dry wood shall flourish—driven though you are,
and though a thousand men perish before
the killer, Hektor.[30] You will eat your heart out,
raging with remorse for this dishonor   290
done by you to the bravest of Akhaians."

He hurled the staff, studded with golden nails,
before him on the ground. Then down he sat,
and fury filled Agamémnon, looking across at him.
But for the sake of both men Nestor arose,
the Pylians' orator, eloquent and clear;
argument sweeter than honey rolled from his tongue.
By now he had outlived two generations

---

[29] To hold the staff signifies that one has the floor in the discussion.
[30] Son of Priam and chief warrior on the Trojan side; a central character in the *Iliad.*

of mortal men, his own and the one after,
in Pylos land, and still ruled in the third.   300
In kind reproof he said:

                                            "A black day, this.

Bitter distress comes this way to Akhaia.
How happy Priam and Priam's sons would be,
and all the Trojans—wild with joy—if they
got wind of all these fighting words between you,
foremost in council as you are, foremost
in battle. Give me your attention. Both
are younger men than I, and in my time
men who were even greater have I known
and none of them disdained me. Men like those   310
I have not seen again, nor shall: Peiríthoös,
the Lord Marshal Dryas, Kaineus, Exádios,
Polyphêmos, Theseus—Aigeus' son,
a man like the immortal gods. I speak
of champions among men of earth, who fought
with champions, with wild things of the mountains,
great centaurs[31] whom they broke and overpowered.
Among these men I say I had my place
when I sailed out of Pylos, my far country,
because they called for me. I fought   320
for my own hand among them. Not one man
alive now upon earth could stand against them.
And I repeat: they listened to my reasoning,
took my advice. Well, then, you take it too.
It is far better so.

                              Lord Agamémnon,

do not deprive him of the girl, renounce her.
The army had allotted her to him.
Akhilleus, for your part, do not defy
your King and Captain. No one vies in honor
with him who holds authority from Zeus.   330
You have more prowess, for a goddess bore you;[32]
his power over men surpasses yours.

But, Agamémnon, let your anger cool.
I beg you to relent, knowing Akhilleus
a sea wall for Akhaians in the black waves of war."

Lord Agamémnon answered:

                                   "All you say

is fairly said, sir, but this man's ambition,
remember, is to lead, to lord it over
everyone, hold power over everyone,

---

[31]Mythological beings, shaped like horses but having human torsos and heads.
[32]Thetis, a sea nymph, had been the mate of Akhilleus' father, Pêleus.

give orders to the rest of us! Well, one 340
will never take his orders! If the gods
who live forever made a spearman of him,
have they put insults on his lips as well?"

Akhilleus interrupted:

"What a poltroon,[33]

how lily-livered I should be called, if I
knuckled under to all you do or say!
Give your commands to someone else, not me!
And one more thing I have to tell you: think it
over: this time, for the girl, I will not
wrangle in arms with you or anyone, 350
though I am robbed of what was given me;
but as for any other thing I have
alongside my black ship, you shall not take it
against my will. Try it. Hear this, everyone:
that instant your hot blood blackens my spear!"

They quarreled in this way, face to face, and then
broke off the assembly by the ships. Akhilleus
made his way to his squadron and his quarters,
Patróklos[34] by his side, with his companions.

Agamémnon proceeded to launch a ship, 360
assigned her twenty oarsmen, loaded beasts
for sacrifice to the god, then set aboard
Khrysêis in her loveliness. The versatile
Odysseus took the deck, and, all oars manned,
they pulled out on the drenching ways of sea.
The troops meanwhile were ordered to police camp
and did so, throwing refuse in the water;
then to Apollo by the barren surf
they carried out full-tally hekatombs,
and the savor curled in crooked smoke toward heaven. 370

That was the day's work in the army.

Agamémnon

had kept his threat in mind, and now he acted,
called Eurýbatês and Talthýbios,
his aides and criers:[35]

"Go along," he said,

"both of you, to the quarters of Akhilleus
and take his charming Brisêis by the hand

---

[33] Coward.
[34] Akhilleus' chariot driver and dearest friend; a central character in the *Iliad*.
[35] Heralds.

to bring to me. And if he balks at giving her
I shall be there myself with men-at-arms
in force to take her—all the more gall for him."

So, ominously, he sent them on their way,   380
and they who had no stomach for it went
along the waste sea shingle toward the ships
and shelters of the Myrmidons. Not far
from his black ship and hut they found the prince
in the open, seated. And seeing these two come
was cheerless to Akhilleus. Shamefast, pale
with fear of him, they stood without a word;
but he knew what they felt and called out:

                                               "Peace to you,
criers and couriers of Zeus and men!
Come forward. Not one thing have I against you: 390
Agamémnon is the man who sent you
for Brisêis. Here then, my lord Patróklos,
bring out the girl and give her to these men.
And let them both bear witness before the gods
who live in bliss, as before men who die,
including this harsh king, if ever hereafter
a need for me arises to keep the rest
from black defeat and ruin.

                                              Lost in folly,
the man cannot think back or think ahead
how to come through a battle by the ships."   400

Patróklos did the bidding of his friend,
led from the hut Brisêis in her beauty
and gave her to them. Back along the ships
they took their way, and the girl went, loath to go.

Leaving his friends in haste, Akhilleus wept,
and sat apart by the grey wave, scanning the endless sea.
Often he spread his hands in prayer to his mother:

"As my life came from you, though it is brief,
honor at least from Zeus who storms in heaven
I call my due. He gives me precious little.   410
See how the lord of the great plains, Agamémnon,
humiliated me! He has my prize,
by his own whim, for himself."

                                              Eyes wet with tears,
he spoke, and her ladyship his mother heard him
in green deeps where she lolled near her old father.[36]

---

[36]Nêreus, father of the Nereids (sea nymphs).

Gliding she rose and broke like mist from the inshore
grey sea face, to sit down softly before him,
her son in tears; and fondling him she said:

"Child, why do you weep? What grief is this?
Out with it, tell me, both of us should know."   420
Akhilleus, fast in battle as a lion,
groaned and said:

                        "Why tell you what you know?
We sailed out raiding, and we took by storm
that ancient town of Eëtíôn called Thêbê,
plundered the place, brought slaves and spoils away.[37]
At the division, later,
they chose a young girl, Khrysêis, for the king.
Then Khrysês, priest of the Archer God, Apollo,
came to the beachhead we Akhaians hold,
bringing no end of ransom for his daughter;   430
he had the god's white bands on a golden staff
and sued for grace from the army of Akhaia,
mostly the two Atreidai, corps commanders.
All of our soldiers murmured in assent:
'Behave well to the priest. And take the ransom!'
But Agamémnon would not. It went against his desire,
and brutally he ordered the man away.
So the old man withdrew in grief and anger.
Apollo cared for him: he heard his prayer
and let black bolts of plague fly on the Argives.   440

One by one our men came down with it
and died hard as the god's shots raked the army
broadside. But our priest divined the cause
and told us what the god meant by the plague.

I said, 'Appease the god!' but Agamémnon
could not contain his rage; he threatened me,
and what he threatened is now done—
one girl the Akhaians are embarking now
for Khrysê beach with gifts for Lord Apollo;
the other, just now, from my hut—the criers   450
came and took her, Briseus' girl, my prize,
given by the army.
                    If you can, stand by me:
go to Olympos, pray to Zeus, if ever
by word or deed you served him—
and so you did, I often heard you tell it
in Father's house: that time when you alone
of all the gods shielded the son of Krónos[38]

---

[37] Elaborate, sometimes verbatim, repetitions of earlier material are frequent in Homer.
Eëtíôn is the father of Andrómakhê, wife of the Trojan hero Hektor.
[38] Krónos was father of Zeus and ruler of the gods in the divine generation overthrown by
Zeus and the Olympians.

from peril and disgrace—when other gods,
Pallas Athêna, Hêra, and Poseidon,[39]
wished him in irons, wished to keep him bound,   460
you had the will to free him of that bondage,
and called up to Olympos in all haste
Aigaion, whom the gods call Briareus,
the giant with a hundred arms, more powerful
than the sea-god, his father. Down he sat
by the son of Krónos, glorying in that place.
For fear of him the blissful gods forbore
to manacle Zeus.

                    Remind him of these things,
cling to his knees and tell him your good pleasure
if he will take the Trojan side   470
and roll the Akhaians back to the water's edge,
back on the ships with slaughter! All the troops
may savor what their king has won for them,
and he may know his madness, what he lost
when he dishonored me, peerless among Akhaians."

Her eyes filled, and a tear fell as she answered:

"Alas, my child, why did I rear you, doomed
the day I bore you?[40] Ah, could you only be
serene upon this beachhead through the siege,
your life runs out so soon.   480
Oh early death! Oh broken heart! No destiny
so cruel! And I bore you to this evil!
But what you wish I will propose
To Zeus, lord of the lightning, going up
myself into the snow-glare of Olympos
with hope for his consent.

                        Be quiet now
beside the long ships, keep your anger bright
against the army, quit the war.

                        Last night
Zeus made a journey to the shore of Ocean
to feast among the Sunburned,[41] and the gods   490
accompanied him. In twelve days he will come
back to Olympos. Then I shall be there
to cross his bronze doorsill and take his knees.
I trust I'll move him."

---

[39] God of the ocean, brother of Zeus, and a supporter of the Greeks in the war.

[40] Akhilleus is fated to die young and will in fact be killed in the Trojan War, though his death is not described in the *Iliad*. See also Akhilleus' somewhat different account in Book IX of his "two possible destinies."

[41] The Ethiopians, a people believed to live at the edge of the world, which was envisaged as flat and surrounded by a body of water called Ocean.

Thetis left her son
still burning for the softly belted girl
whom they had wrested from him.

Meanwhile Odysseus
with his shipload of offerings came to Khrysê.
Entering the deep harbor there
they furled the sails and stowed them, and unbent
forestays to ease the mast down quickly aft 500
into its rest; then rowed her to a mooring.
Bow-stones were dropped, and they tied up astern,
and all stepped out into the wash and ebb,
then disembarked their cattle for the Archer,
and Khrysêis, from the deepsea ship. Odysseus,
the great tactician, led her to the altar,
putting her in her father's hands, and said:

"Khrysês, as Agamémnon's emissary
I bring your child to you, and for Apollo
a hekatomb in the Danáäns' name. 510
We trust in this way to appease your lord,
who sent down pain and sorrow on the Argives."

So he delivered her, and the priest received her,
the child so dear to him, in joy. Then hastening
to give the god his hekatomb, they led
bullocks to crowd around the compact altar,
rinsed their hands and delved in barley baskets,
as open-armed to heaven Khrysês prayed:

"Oh hear me, master of the silver bow,
protector of Ténedos and the holy towns, 520
if while I prayed you listened once before
and honored me, and punished the Akhaians,
now let my wish come true again. But turn
your plague away this time from the Danáäns."

And this petition, too, Apollo heard.
When prayers were said and grains of barley strewn,
they held the bullocks for the knife, and flayed them,
cutting out joints and wrapping these in fat,
two layers, folded, with raw strips of flesh,
for the old man to burn on cloven faggots, 530
wetting it all with wine.

Around him stood
young men with five-tined forks in hand, and when
the vitals had been tasted, joints consumed,
they sliced the chines and quarters for the spits,
roasted them evenly and drew them off.
Their meal being now prepared and all work done,

they feasted to their hearts' content and made
desire for meat and drink recede again,
then young men filled their winebowls to the brim,
ladling drops for the god in every cup.   540
Propitiatory songs rose clear and strong
until day's end, to praise the god, Apollo,
as One Who Keeps the Plague Afar; and listening
the god took joy.

                                             After the sun went down
and darkness came, at last Odysseus' men
lay down to rest under the stern hawsers.

When Dawn spread out her finger tips of rose
they put to sea for the main camp of Akhaians,.
and the Archer God sent them a following wind.
Stepping the mast they shook their canvas out,   550
and wind caught, bellying the sail. A foaming
dark blue wave sang backward from the bow
as the running ship made way against the sea,
until they came offshore of the encampment.
Here they put in and hauled the black ship high,
far up the sand, braced her with shoring timbers,
and then disbanded, each to his own hut.

Meanwhile unstirring and with smoldering heart,
the godlike athlete, son of Pêleus, Prince
Akhilleus waited by his racing ships.   560
He would not enter the assembly
of emulous men, nor ever go to war,
but felt his valor staling in his breast
with idleness, and missed the cries of battle.
Now when in fact twelve days had passed, the gods
who live forever turned back to Olympos,
with Zeus in power supreme among them.

                                                            Thetis
had kept in mind her mission for her son,
and rising like a dawn mist from the sea
into a cloud she soared aloft in heaven   570
to high Olympos. Zeus with massive brows
she found apart, on the chief crest enthroned,
and slipping down before him, her left hand
placed on his knees and her right hand held up
to cup his chin, she made her plea to him:[42]

"O Father Zeus, if ever amid immortals
by word or deed I served you, grant my wish

---

[42] This posture—one hand on the knees, the other on the chin—was conventional for seekers of help from the powerful.

and see to my son's honor! Doom for him
of all men comes on quickest.

Now Lord Marshal

Agamémnon has been highhanded with him, 580
has commandeered and holds his prize of war.
But you can make him pay for this, profound
mind of Olympos!

Lend the Trojans power,

until the Akhaians recompense my son
and heap new honor upon him!"

When she finished,

the gatherer of cloud said never a word
but sat unmoving for a long time, silent.
Thetis clung to his knees then spoke again:

"Give your infallible word, and bow your head,
or else reject me. Can you be afraid 590
to let me see how low in your esteem
I am of all the gods?"

Greatly perturbed,

Lord Zeus who masses cloud said:

"Here is trouble,

You drive me into open war with Hêra
sooner or later:
she will be at me, scolding all day long.
Even as matters stand she never rests
from badgering me before the gods: I take
the Trojan side in battle, so she says.

Go home before you are seen. But you can trust me 600
to put my mind on this; I shall arrange it.
Here let me bow my head, then be content
to see me bound by that most solemn act
before the gods. My word is not revocable
nor ineffectual, once I nod upon it."

He bent his ponderous black brows down, and locks
ambrosial[43] of his immortal head
swung over them, as all Olympos trembled.
After this pact they parted: misty Thetis
from glittering Olympos leapt away 610
into the deep sea; Zeus to his hall retired.
There all the gods rose from their seats in deference
before their father; not one dared

---

[43]Celestial; literally, ambrosia is the food of the gods. Their drink is nectar, which is later
served to them.

face him unmoved, but all stood up before him,
and thus he took his throne.

             But Hêra knew

he had new interests; she had seen
the goddess Thetis, silvery-footed daughter
of the Old One of the sea, conferring with him,
and, nagging, she inquired of Zeus Kroníon:

"Who is it this time, schemer? Who has your ear?   620
How fond you are of secret plans, of taking
decisions privately! You could not bring yourself,
could you, to favor me with any word
of your new plot?"

          The father of gods and men
said in reply:

            "Hêra, all my provisions
you must not itch to know.
You'll find them rigorous, consort though you are.
In all appropriate matters no one else,
no god or man, shall be advised before you.
But when I choose to think alone,   630
don't harry me about it with your questions."

The Lady Hêra answered with wide eyes:

"Majesty, what a thing to say. I have not
'harried' you before with questions, surely;
you are quite free to tell what you will tell.
This time I dreadfully fear—I have a feeling—
Thetis, the silvery-footed daughter
of the Old One of the sea, led you astray.
Just now at daybreak, anyway, she came
to sit with you and take your knees; my guess is   640
you bowed your head for her in solemn pact
that you will see to the honor of Akhilleus—
that is, to Akhaian carnage near the ships."

Now Zeus the gatherer of cloud said:

               "Marvelous,
you and your guesses; you are near it, too.
But there is not one thing that you can do about it,
only estrange yourself still more from me—
all the more gall for you. If what you say
is true, you may be sure it pleases me.
And now you just sit down, be still, obey me,   650
or else not all the gods upon Olympos
can help in the least when I approach your chair
to lay my inexorable hands upon you."

At this the wide-eyed Lady Hêra feared him,
and sat quite still, and bent her will to his.
Up through the hall of Zeus now all the lords
of heaven were sullen and looked askance. Hêphaistos,[44]
master artificer, broke the silence,
doing a kindness to the snowy-armed
lady, his mother Hêra.

He began: 660

"Ah, what a miserable day, if you two
raise your voices over mortal creatures!
More than enough already! Must you bring
your noisy bickering among the gods?
What pleasure can we take in a fine dinner
when baser matters gain the upper hand?
To Mother my advice is—what she knows—
better make up to Father, or he'll start
his thundering and shake our feast to bits.
You know how he can shock us if he cares to— 670
out of our seats with lightning bolts!
Supreme power is his. Oh, soothe him, please,
take a soft tone, get back in his good graces.
Then he'll be benign to us again."
He lurched up as he spoke, and held a winecup
out to her, a double-handed one,
and said:

"Dear Mother, patience, hold your tongue,
no matter how upset you are. I would not
see you battered, dearest.

It would hurt me,

and yet I could not help you, not a bit. 680
The Olympian is difficult to oppose.
One other time I took your part he caught me
around one foot and flung me
into the sky from our tremendous terrace.
I soared all day! Just as the sun dropped down
I dropped down, too, on Lemnos—nearly dead.
The island people nursed a fallen god."

He made her smile—and the goddess, white-armed Hêra,
smiling took the winecup from his hand.
Then, dipping from the winebowl, round he went 690
from left to right, serving the other gods
nectar of sweet delight.

---

[44] The lame god of fire and of metal crafts. He had once before been thrown from Olympos for taking Hêra's side against Zeus, landing on the Aegean island of Lemnos.

                                                    And quenchless laughter
broke out among the blissful gods
to see Hêphaistos wheezing down the hall.
So all day long until the sun went down
they spent in feasting, and the measured feast
matched well their hearts' desire.
So did the flawless harp held by Apollo
and heavenly songs in choiring antiphon
that all the Muses sang.

                                                    And when the shining   700
sun of day sank in the west, they turned
homeward each one to rest, each to that home
the bandy-legged wondrous artisan
Hêphaistos fashioned for them with his craft.
The lord of storm and lightning, Zeus, retired
and shut his eyes where sweet sleep ever came to him,
and at his side lay Hêra, Goddess of the Golden Chair.

BOOK II. *Persuaded by Thetis to side with Akhilleus, Zeus sends a deceiving dream to Agamémnon which leads him to believe that the fall of Troy is at hand. As a test of his army's determination, Agamémnon calls the troops together and tells them that they must abandon the siege of Troy and admit defeat despite their superior numbers. The soldiers, all too happy to go home, rush toward the ships; but Odysseus, under the influence of Hêra and Athêna, rallies them. Thersítês, a repulsive common soldier, reviles Agamémnon for his greed, lust, and ill-treatment of Akhilleus. Nestor proposes that, to foster loyalty and discipline, the army should be mustered by nation and clan. A long catalog follows, listing the Greek commanders, giving information about their geographic and family backgrounds, and specifying the number of ships each leader commands. (The total number of ships is over 1,200.) A briefer catalog of the Trojans and of their allies from other regions concludes the Book.*

BOOK III. *As the armies approach each other, Paris offers single combat; he is soon recognized by Menelǻos, the husband whom Paris has cuckolded. At first Paris is cowed, but after Hektor expresses contempt for his softness he agrees to face Menelǻos. (We learn in this Book that Paris is hated or despised by both armies and even by Helen.) A treaty is proposed by which the victor in the duel is to have Helen and the armies are to end the war, without further fighting. Next we see Helen herself in Troy; the aged counselors of Priam, the Trojan king, are awed by Helen's beauty but desire that she should go back to her husband so that the war can end. Priam himself, however, is fond of Helen. From atop the city walls she points out to him, at his request, the chief leaders of the Greeks. Priam goes out onto the plain to ratify the treaty but returns before the duel, which he considers too painful to watch. The single combat begins; Menelǻos is about to triumph when Aphrodítê, goddess of love and protector of Paris, rescues Paris and returns him to the safety of his bedchamber in Troy. The goddess then sends to him the reluctant Helen, who goes to bed with Paris but only after taunting him. Since the mysteriously vanished Paris cannot be found, the Greeks claim victory and demand that Helen and other agreed-upon compensation be delivered up to them.*

BOOK IV. *The gods are feasting on Mount Olympos. Zeus deliberately provokes his wife, Hêra, by suggesting that, since Menelǻos has won the duel, he should be awarded Helen and the war should end now, with Troy spared. Predictably, the fiercely vindictive goddess is angered; she wins from Zeus permission for Athêna to incite some Trojan to break the pledged truce agreement and thus rekindle the hostilities. Athêna, in disguise, tempts the archer Pándaros,*

who is fighting for the Trojans, to launch an arrow at Menéláos; he is slightly wounded by the shot. The truce broken, Agamémnon rouses the Greeks to battle through a combination of flattery and taunts. Fierce fighting breaks out between the two armies.

BOOK V. *The war continues to rage—man against man, man against god, god against god. Athêna and Hêra aid the Greeks; Apollo, Aphrodítê, and Arês aid the Trojans. The central human figure is the great Greek warrior Diomêdês; he kills the truce-breaker Pándaros after being wounded by an arrow from him and puts the Trojan hero Aineías in grave danger before Aineías is assisted by Apollo and his mother Aphrodítê. Aphrodítê and Arês are both wounded by Diomêdês and retire to Olympos; the beautiful goddess is told by Zeus, affectionately, that she is too soft for battle, but Zeus expresses loathing for the universally hated war god. The battle itself is indecisive.*

from BOOK SIX: INTERLUDES IN FIELD AND CITY

The immortals having retired from the field, battle continues; the Trojans begin to retreat. Agamémnon vows to kill the whole Trojan people, including children. Hektor's brother Hélenos, a prophet, urges him to return to Troy and have the women offer propitiatory offerings to Athêna so that the goddess may restrain her protégé Diomêdês. Diomêdês is about to fight a stranger (Glaukos) when they discover that their grandfathers were sworn friends; the two agree not to fight each other. Hektor arrives at Troy. Book VI continues:

Now, when Hektor reached the Skaian Gates[1]
daughters and wives of Trojans rushed to greet him
with questions about friends, sons, husbands, brothers.
"Pray to the gods!" he said to each in turn,
as grief awaited many. He walked on
and into Priam's palace, fair and still,
made all of ashlar,[2] with bright colonnades.
Inside were fifty rooms of polished stone
one by another, where the sons of Priam
slept beside their wives;[3] apart from these   290
across an inner court were twelve rooms more
all in one line, of polished stone, where slept
the sons-in-law of Priam and their wives.
Approaching these, he met his gentle mother
going in with Laódikê, most beautiful
of all her daughters. Both hands clasping his,
she looked at him and said:

                                        "Why have you come
from battle, child? Those fiends, the Akhaians, fighting

---

[1] The main portal of the city.
[2] Rectangular building blocks.
[3] Priam had fifty sons, by his queen, Hékabê, and by other women.

around the town, have worn you out; you come
to climb our Rock[4] and lift your palms to Zeus! 300
Wait, and I'll serve you honeyed wine.
First you may offer up a drop to Zeus,
to the immortal gods, then slake your thirst.
Wine will restore a man when he is weary
as you are, fighting to defend your own."

Hektor answered her, his helmet flashing:

"No, my dear mother, ladle me no wine;
You'd make my nerve go slack: I'd lose my edge.
May I tip wine to Zeus with hands unwashed?
I fear to—a bespattered man, and bloody, 310
may not address the lord of gloomy cloud.
No, it is you I wish would bring together
our older women, with offerings, and go visit
the temple of Athêna, Hope of Soldiers.
Pick out a robe, most lovely and luxurious,
most to your liking in the women's hall;
place it upon Athêna's knees;[5] assure her
a sacrifice of heifers, twelve young ones
ungoaded ever in their lives, if in her mercy
relenting toward our town, our wives and children, 320
she keeps Diomêdês out of holy Troy.
He is a wild beast now in combat and pursuit.
Make your way to her shrine, visit Athêna,
Hope of Soldiers.
                                        As for me, I go
for Paris, to arouse him, if he listens.
If only earth would swallow him here and now!
What an affliction the Olympian
brought up for us in him—a curse for Priam
and Priam's children![6] Could I see that man
dwindle into Death's night, I'd feel my soul 330
relieved of its distress!"

So Hektor spoke, and she walked slowly on
into the mégaron.[7] She called her maids,
who then assembled women from the city.
But Hékabê went down to the low chamber
fragrant with cedar, where her robes were kept,
embroidered work by women of Sidonia

---

[4] The hill on which the city stands.
[5] The knees of her statue.
[6] It is worth remembering that Paris as well as Hektor is a son of Hékabê, the addressee here.
[7] The great hall of the house.

Aléxandros[8] had brought, that time he sailed
and ravished Helen, princess, pearl of kings.
Hékabê lifted out her loveliest robe, 340
most ample, most luxurious in brocade,
and glittering like starlight under all.
This offering she carried to Athêna
with a long line of women in her train.
On the Akrópolis,[9] Athêna's shrine
was opened for them by Theanô, stately
daughter of Kisseus, wife to Antênor,[10]
and chosen priestess of Athêna. Now
all crying loud stretched out their arms in prayer,
while Theanô with grace took up the robe 350
to place it on fair-haired Athêna's knees.
She made petition then to Zeus's daughter:

　　　　　　　　　　　　　　　　　　　　　　　　"Lady,
excellent goddess, towering friend of Troy,
smash Diomêdês' lance-haft! Throw him hard
below the Skaian Gates, before our eyes!
Upon this altar we'll make offering
of twelve young heifers never scarred!
Only show mercy to our town,
mercy to Trojan men, their wives and children."

These were Theanó's prayers, her vain prayers. 360
Pallas Athêna turned away her head.

During the supplication at the shrine,
Hektor approached the beautiful house Aléxandros
himself had made, with men who in that time
were master-builders in the land of Troy.
Bedchamber, hall, and court, in the upper town,
they built for him near Priam's hall and Hektor's.
Now Hektor dear to Zeus went in, his hand
gripping a spear eleven forearms long,
whose bronze head shone before him in the air 370
as shone, around the neck, a golden ring.
He found his brother in the bedchamber
handling a magnificent cuirass[11] and shield
and pulling at his bent-horn bow, while Helen
among her household women sat nearby,
directing needlecraft and splendid weaving.
At sight of him, to shame him, Hektor said:

[8]Another name for Paris. He and Helen had stopped in Sidonia (Phoenicia) on their way
to Troy.
[9]The most elevated part of the city.
[10]A Trojan lord and counselor.
[11]A piece of armor designed to cover the chest and back.

"Unquiet soul, why be aggrieved in private?
Our troops are dying out there where they fight
around our city, under our high walls.   380
The hue and cry of war, because of you,
comes in like surf upon this town.
You'd be at odds with any other man
you might see quitting your accursèd war.
Up; into action, before torches thrown
make the town flare!"

                                            And shining like a god

Aléxandros replied:

                                                  "Ah, Hektor,

this call to order is no more than just.
So let me tell you something: hear me out.
No pettishness, resentment toward the Trojans,   390
kept me in this bedchamber so long,
but rather my desire, on being routed,
to taste grief to the full.

                                        In her sweet way

my lady rouses me to fight again—
and I myself consider it better so.
Victory falls to one man, then another.
Wait, while I put on the wargod's gear,
or else go back; I'll follow, sure to find you."

For answer, Hektor in his shining helm
said not a word, but in low tones   400
enticing Helen murmured:

                                          "Brother dear—

dear to a whore, a nightmare of a woman!
That day my mother gave me to the world
I wish a hurricane blast had torn me away
to wild mountains, or into tumbling sea
to be washed under by a breaking wave,
before these evil days could come!—or, granted
terrible years were in the gods' design,
I wish I had had a good man for a lover
who knew the sharp tongues and just rage of men.   410
This one—his heart's unsound, and always will be,
and he will win what he deserves. Come here
and rest upon this couch with me, dear brother.
You are the one afflicted most
by harlotry in me and by his madness,
our portion, all of misery, given by Zeus
that we may live in song for men to come."

Great Hektor shook his head, his helmet flashing,
and said:

                                          "No, Helen, offer me no rest;
I know you are fond of me. I cannot rest. 420
Time presses, and I grow impatient now
to lend a hand to Trojans in the field
who feel a gap when I am gone. Your part
can be to urge him—let him feel the urgency
to join me in the city. He has time:
I must go home to visit my own people,
my own dear wife and my small son. Who knows
if I shall be reprieved again to see them,
or beaten down under Akhaian blows
as the immortals will."

                                          He turned away 430
and quickly entered his own hall, but found
Princess Andrómakhê was not at home.
With one nursemaid and her small child, she stood
upon the tower of Ilion, in tears,
bemoaning what she saw.

                                   Now Hektor halted
upon his threshold, calling to his maids:

"Tell me at once, and clearly, please,
my lady Andrómakhê, where has she gone?
To see my sisters, or my brothers' wives?
Or to Athêna's temple? Ladies of Troy 440
are there to make petition to the goddess."

The busy mistress of the larder answered:

"Hektor, to put it clearly as you ask,
she did not go to see your sisters, nor
your brothers' wives, nor to Athêna's shrine
where others are petitioning the goddess.
Up to the great square tower of Ilion
she took her way, because she heard our men
were spent in battle by Akhaian power.
In haste, like a madwoman, to the wall 450
she went, and Nurse went too, carrying the child."
At this word Hektor whirled and left his hall,
taking the same path he had come by,
along byways, walled lanes, all through the town
until he reached the Skaian Gates, whereby
before long he would issue on the field.
There his warmhearted lady
came to meet him, running: Andrómakhê,
whose father, Eëtíôn, once had ruled
the land under Mount Plakos, dark with forest, 460
at Thêbê under Plakos—lord and king
of the Kilikians. Hektor was her lord now,

head to foot in bronze; and now she joined him.
Behind her came the maid, who held the child
against her breast, a rosy baby still,
Hektoridês, the world's delight, as fresh
as a pure shining star. Skamándrios[12]
his father named him; other men would say
Astýanax, "Lord of the Lower Town,"
as Hektor singlehandedly guarded Troy.   470
How brilliantly the warrior smiled, in silence,
his eyes upon the child! Andrómakhê
rested against him, shook away a tear,
and pressed his hand in both her own, to say:

"Oh, my wild one, your bravery will be
your own undoing! No pity for our child,
poor little one, or me in my sad lot—
soon to be deprived of you! soon, soon
Akhaians as one man will set upon you
and cut you down! Better for me, without you,   480
to take cold earth for mantle. No more comfort,
no other warmth, after you meet your doom,
but heartbreak only. Father is dead, and Mother.[13]
My father great Akhilleus killed when he
besieged and plundered Thêbê, our high town,
citadel of Kilikians. He killed him,
but, reverent at least in this, did not
despoil him. Body, gear, and weapons forged
so handsomely, he burned, and heaped a barrow
over the ashes. Elms were planted round   490
by mountain-nymphs of him who bears the stormcloud.[14]
Then seven brothers that I had at home
in one day entered Death's dark place. Akhilleus,
prince and powerful runner, killed all seven
amid their shambling cattle and silvery sheep.
Mother, who had been queen of wooded Plakos,
he brought with other winnings home, and freed her,
taking no end of ransom. Artemis
the Huntress shot her in her father's house.[15]
Father and mother—I have none but you,   500
nor brother, Hektor; lover none but you!
Be merciful! Stay here upon the tower!
Do not bereave your child and widow me!
Draw up your troops by the wild figtree; that way
the city lies most open, men most easily

---

[12] Hektor's son is named for Skamánder, a river on the Trojan plain.
[13] Khrysêis, the woman awarded to Agamémnon, was also taken during the raid on Thêbê
that Andrómakhê describes in the following lines; the same expedition included a raid on
another city where Akhilleus captured Brisêis, whom he has given up to Agamémnon.
[14] Nymphs associated with Zeus.
[15] The arrows of Artemis, goddess of the hunt, were a symbol of death for women.

could swarm the wall where it is low:
three times, at least, their best men tried it there
in company of the two called Aías, with
Idómeneus, the Atreidai, Diomêdes—
whether someone who had it from oracles 510
had told them, or their own hearts urged them on."

Great Hektor in his shimmering helmet answered:

"Lady, these many things beset my mind
no less than yours. But I should die of shame
before our Trojan men and noblewomen
if like a coward I avoided battle,
nor am I moved to. Long ago I learned
how to be brave, how to go forward always
and to contend for honor, Father's and mine.
Honor—for in my heart and soul I know 520
a day will come when ancient Ilion falls,
when Priam and the folk of Priam perish.
Not by the Trojans' anguish on that day
am I so overborne in mind—the pain
of Hékabê herself, or Priam king,
or of my brothers, many and valorous,
who will have fallen in dust before our enemies—
as by your own grief, when some armed Akhaian
takes you in tears, your free life stripped away.
Before another woman's loom in Argos 530
it may be you will pass, or at Messêis
or Hypereiê fountain, carrying water,
against your will—iron constraint upon you.
And seeing you in tears, a man may say:
'There is the wife of Hektor, who fought best
of Trojan horsemen when they fought at Troy.'
So he may say—and you will ache again
for one man who could keep you out of bondage.
Let me be hidden dark down in my grave
before I hear you cry or know you captive!" 540

As he said this, Hektor held out his arms
to take his baby. But the child squirmed round
on the nurse's bosom and began to wail,
terrified by his father's great war helm—
the flashing bronze, the crest with horsehair plume
tossed like a living thing at every nod.
His father began laughing, and his mother
laughed as well. Then from his handsome head
Hektor lifted off his helm and bent
to place it, bright with sunlight, on the ground. 550
When he had kissed his child and swung him high
to dandle him, he said this prayer:

"O Zeus
and all immortals, may this child, my son,
become like me a prince among the Trojans.[16]
Let him be strong and brave and rule in power
at Ilion; then someday men will say
'This fellow is far better than his father!'
seeing him home from war, and his arms
the bloodstained gear of some tall warrior slain—
making his mother proud."

After this prayer,   560
into his dear wife's arms he gave his baby,
whom on her fragrant breast
she held and cherished, laughing through her tears.
Hektor pitied her now. Caressing her,
he said:

"Unquiet soul, do not be too distressed
by thoughts of me. You know no man dispatches me
into the undergloom against my fate;
no mortal, either, can escape his fate,
coward or brave man, once he comes to be.
Go home, attend to your own handiwork   570
at loom and spindle, and command the maids
to busy themselves, too. As for the war,
that is for men, all who were born at Ilion,
to put their minds on—most of all for me."

He stooped now to recover his plumed helm
as she, his dear wife, drew away, her head
turned and her eyes upon him, brimming tears.
She made her way in haste then to the ordered
house of Hektor and rejoined her maids,
moving them all to weep at sight of her.   580
In Hektor's home they mourned him, living still
but not, they feared, again to leave the war
or be delivered from Akhaian fury.

Paris in the meantime had not lingered:
after he buckled his bright war-gear on
he ran through Troy, sure-footed with long strides.
Think how a stallion fed on clover and barley,
mettlesome, thundering in a stall, may snap
his picket rope and canter down a field
to bathe as he would daily in the river—   590
glorying in freedom! Head held high
with mane over his shoulders flying,
his dazzling work of finely jointed knees

[16] Hektor's prayer for his son would seem to contradict what he has just said about the
inevitable destruction of the Trojans. His mood changes during this episode.

takes him around the pasture haunts of horses.[17]
That was the way the son of Priam, Paris,
ran from the height of Pergamos,[18] his gear
ablaze like the great sun,
and laughed aloud. He sprinted on, and quickly
met his brother, who was slow to leave
the place where he had discoursed with his lady.   600
Aléxandros was first to speak:

                                        "Dear fellow,"

he said, "have I delayed you, kept you waiting?
Have I not come at the right time, as you asked?"

And Hektor in his shimmering helm replied:

"My strange brother! No man with justice in him
would underrate your handiwork in battle;
you have a powerful arm. But you give way
too easily, and lose interest, lose your will.
My heart aches in me when I hear our men,
who have such toil of battle on your account,   610
talk of you with contempt. Well, come along.
Someday we'll make amends for that, if ever
we drive the Akhaians from the land of Troy—
if ever Zeus permit us, in our hall,
to set before the gods of heaven, undying
and ever young, our winebowl of deliverance."[19]

BOOK VII. *Athêna and Apollo collaborate to arrange a temporary halt in the fighting, by instigating another single combat, this time between Hektor and a Greek opponent. Hektor utters the challenge, stipulating that the corpse of the man defeated is to be given proper rites. After the Greeks hesitate, Meneláos comes forward, but he is then dissuaded and the foremost Greek warriors volunteer. The greater Aías is chosen by lot to face Hektor. Their duel ends indecisively, and the two men exchange gifts. A truce is arranged during which both armies are to recover their dead and give them proper funerals. The Greeks intend also to build a wall around their encampment near the ships. During a council of the Trojans it is proposed that Helen be surrendered; Paris insists that he will keep her, though he is willing to give up the treasure he had brought to Troy with her. When that offer is made to the Greeks, they refuse it and indicate that even the restoration of Helen will not satisfy them. The dead are cremated and the Greeks build their ramparts.*

BOOK VIII. *Asserting his supreme power over the other deities, Zeus commands them not to intervene in the fighting. Led by the exultant Hektor, the Trojans drive the Greeks back to their seaside encampment behind the walls. When Hêra and Athêna prepare to enter the battle on the Greek side, Zeus again asserts his will, forcing them to return reluctantly to Olympos.*

[17] This extended comparison is an example of the "Homeric simile," which typically illustrates an action or state of mind but is also, to some extent, a small, self-contained picture or story. Most of Homer's similes are drawn from nature (storms, the sea, etc.) or from the familiar activities of shepherd, farmer, or hunter.

[18] The citadel of Troy.

[19] Hektor hopes that some day they may celebrate a ritual thanksgiving to the gods for the city's survival.

Zeus decrees that Hektor shall give the Greeks no respite until the time when Akhilleus, roused by the death of his good friend Patróklos, shall return to action. At nightfall the Trojans do not return to the city as usual but encamp on the field, preparing what they hope will be a decisive attack the next day.

BOOK NINE: A VISIT OF EMISSARIES

So Trojans kept their watch that night.

                                                                    To seaward
Panic that attends blood-chilling Rout
now ruled the Akhaians. All their finest men
were shaken by this fear, in bitter throes,
as when a shifting gale
blows up over the cold fish-breeding sea,
north wind and west wind wailing out of Thrace
in squall on squall, and dark waves crest, and shoreward
masses of weed are cast up by the surf:
so were Akhaian hearts torn in their breasts.   10

By that great gloom hard hit, the son of Atreus[1]
made his way amid his criers and told them
to bid each man in person to assembly
but not raise a general cry. He led them,
making the rounds himself, and soon the soldiers
grimly took their places. Then he rose,
with slow tears trickling, as from a hidden spring
dark water runs down, staining a rock wall;
and groaning heavily he addressed the Argives:

"Friends, leaders of Argives, all my captains,   20
Zeus Kronidês entangled me in folly
to my undoing. Wayward god, he promised
solemnly that I should not sail away
before I stormed the inner town of Troy.
Crookedness and duplicity, I see now!
He calls me to return to Argos beaten
after these many losses. That must be
his will and his good pleasure, who knows why?
Many a great town's height has he destroyed
and will destroy, being supreme in power.   30
Enough. Now let us act on what I say:
Board ship for our own fatherland! Retreat!
We cannot hope any longer to take Troy!"

At this a stillness overcame them all,
the Akhaian soldiers. Long they sat in silence,

---

[1]Agamémnon (the higher-ranking son), not Meneláos.

hearing their own hearts beat. Then Diomêdês
rose at last to speak. He said:

"My lord,
I must contend with you for letting go,
for losing balance. I may do so here
in assembly lawfully. Spare me your anger.   40
Before this you have held me up to scorn
for lack of fighting spirit;[2] old and young,
everyone knows the truth of that. In your case,
the son of crooked-minded Krónos gave you
one gift and not both: a staff of kingship
honored by all men, but no staying power—
the greatest gift of all.
What has come over you, to make you think
the Akhaians weak and craven as you say?
If you are in a passion to sail home,   50
sail on: the way is clear, the many ships
that made the voyage from Mykênê[3] with you
stand near the sea's edge. Others here will stay
until we plunder Troy! Or if they, too,
would like to, let them sail for their own country!
Sthênelos[4] and I will fight alone
until we see the destined end of Ilion.
We came here under god."

When Diomêdês
finished, a cry went up from all Akhaians
in wonder at his words. Then Nestor stood   60
and spoke among them:

"Son of Tydeus, formidable
above the rest in war, in council, too,
you have more weight than others of your age.
No one will cry down what you say, no true
Akhaian will, or contradict you. Still,
you did not push on to the end.
I know you are young; in years you might well be
my last-born son, and yet for all of that
you kept your head and said what needed saying
before the Argive captains. My own part,   70
as I am older, is to drive it home.
No one will show contempt for what I say,
surely not Agamémnon, our commander.
Alien to clan and custom and hearth fire

---

[2]Agamémnon made this charge in Book IV; in fact, Diomêdês is one of the bravest warriors among the Greeks.
[3]Agamémnon's chief city (also spelled *Mycenae*).
[4]Diomêdês' comrade and charioteer.

is he who longs for war—heartbreaking war—
with his own people.
                                                    Let us yield to darkness
and make our evening meal. But let the sentries
take their rest on watch outside the rampart
near the moat;[5] those are my orders for them.
Afterward, you direct us, Agamémnon,   80
by right of royal power. Provide a feast
for older men, your counselors. That is duty
and no difficulty: your huts are full of wine
brought over daily in our ships from Thrace
across the wide sea, and all provender
for guests is yours, as you are high commander.
Your counselors being met, pay heed to him
who counsels best. The army of Akhaia
bitterly needs a well-found plan of action.
The enemy is upon us, near the ships,   90
burning his thousand fires. What Akhaian
could be highhearted in that glare? This night
will see the army saved or brought to ruin."

They heeded him and did his will. Well-armed,
the sentries left to take their posts, one company
formed around Thrasymêdês, Nestor's son,
another mustered by Askálaphos
and Iálmenos, others commanded by
Meríonês, Aphareus, Dêípyros,
and Kreion's son, the princely Lykomêdês.   100
Seven lieutenants, each with a hundred men,
carrying long spears, issued from the camp
for outposts chosen between ditch and rampart.
Campfires were kindled, and they took their meal.
The son of Atreus led the elder men
together to his hut, where he served dinner,
and each man's hand went out upon the meal.
When they had driven hunger and thirst away,
Old Nestor opened their deliberations—
Nestor, whose counsel had seemed best before,   110
point by point weaving his argument:

"Lord Marshal of the army, Agamémnon,
as I shall end with you, so I begin,
since you hold power over a great army
and are responsible for it: the Lord Zeus
put in your keeping staff and precedent
that you might gather counsel for your men.
You should be first in discourse, but attentive
to what another may propose, to act on it

---

[5] The defensive ditch outside the walls.

if he speak out for the good of all. Whatever 120
he may initiate, action is yours.
On this rule, let me speak as I think best.
A better view than mine no man can have,
the same view that I've held these many days
since that occasion when, my lord, for all
Akhilleus' rage, you took the girl Brisêis
out of his lodge—but not with our consent.
Far from it; I for one had begged you not to.
Just the same, you gave way to your pride,
and you dishonored a great prince, 130
a hero to whom the gods themselves do honor.
Taking his prize, you kept her and still do.
But even so, and even now, we may
contrive some way of making peace with him
by friendly gifts, and by affectionate words."

Then Agamémnon, the Lord Marshal, answered:

"Sir, there is nothing false in your account
of my blind errors. I committed them;
I will not now deny it. Troops of soldiers
are worth no more than one man cherished by Zeus 140
as he has cherished this man and avenged him,
overpowering the army of Akhaians.
I lost my head, I yielded to black anger,
but now I would retract it and appease him
with all munificence. Here before everyone
I may enumerate the gifts I'll give.
Seven new tripods and ten bars of gold,
then twenty shining caldrons, and twelve horses,
thoroughbreds, who by their wind and legs
have won me prizes: any man who owned 150
what these have brought me could not lack resources,
could not be pinched for precious gold—so many
prizes have these horses carried home.
Then I shall give him seven women, deft
in household handicraft—women of Lesbos
I chose when he himself took Lesbos town,
as they outshone all womankind in beauty.
These I shall give him, and one more, whom I
took away from him then: Briseus' daughter.
Concerning her, I add my solemn oath 160
I never went to bed or coupled with her,
as custom is with men and women.
These will be his at once. If the immortals
grant us the plundering of Priam's town,
let him come forward when the spoils are shared
and load his ship with bars of gold and bronze.
Then he may choose among the Trojan women

twenty that are most lovely, after Helen.
If we return to Argos of Akhaia,
flowing with good things of the earth, he'll be   170
my own adopted son, dear as Orestês,
born long ago and reared in bounteous peace.[6]
I have three daughters now at home, Khrysóthemis,
Laódikê, and Iphiánassa.
He may take whom he will to be his bride
and pay no bridal gift, leading her home
to Pêleus' hall. But I shall add a dowry
such as no man has given to his daughter.
Seven flourishing strongholds I'll give him:
Kardamylê and Enopê and Hirê   180
in the wild grassland; holy Phêrai too,
and the deep meadowland of Ántheia,
Aipeia and the vineyard slope of Pêdasos,
all lying near the sea in the far west
of sandy Pylos. In these lands are men
who own great flocks and herds; now as his liegemen,
they will pay tithes[7] and sumptuous honor to him,
prospering as they carry out his plans.
These are the gifts I shall arrange if he
desists from anger. Let him be subdued!   190
Lord Death indeed is deaf to appeal, implacable;
of all gods therefore he is most abhorrent
to mortal men. So let Akhilleus bow to me,
considering that I hold higher rank
and claim the precedence of age."

                                                                  To this

Lord Nestor of Gerênia replied:

"Lord Marshal of the army, Agamémnon,
this time the gifts you offer Lord Akhilleus
are not to be despised. Come, we'll dispatch
our chosen emissaries to his quarters   200
as quickly as possible. Those men whom I
may designate, let them perform the mission.
Phoinix,[8] dear to Zeus, may lead the way.
Let Aías follow him, and Prince Odysseus.
The criers, Hódios and Eurýbatês,
may go as escorts. Bowls for their hands here!

---

[6] The murder of Agamémnon by his wife, and his son Orestês' later murder of her in revenge, are mentioned in Homer's *Odyssey* and are the central incidents of Aeschylus' *Oresteia*. The following lines fail to mention Agamémnon's best-known daughters, Iphigeneia and Electra. The sacrifice of Iphigeneia by Agamémnon in order to gain favorable winds for the voyage to Troy and Electra's support of her brother in the murder of their mother are important in Aeschylus' plays.

[7] Shares of crops, animals, and so on.

[8] Akhilleus' tutor.

Tell them to keep silence, while we pray
that Zeus the son of Krónos will be merciful."

Nestor's proposal fell on willing ears,
and criers came at once to tip out water   210
over their hands, while young men filled the winebowls
and dipped a measure into every cup.
They spilt their offerings[9] and drank their fill,
then briskly left the hut of Agamémnon.
Nestor accompanied them with final words
and sage looks, especially for Odysseus,
as to the effort they should make to bring
the son of Pêleus round.
                                                    Following Phoinix,
Aías and Odysseus walked together
beside the tumbling clamorous whispering sea,   220
praying hard to the girdler of the islands[10]
that they might easily sway their great friend's heart.
Amid the ships and huts of the Myrmidons
they found him, taking joy in a sweet harp
of rich and delicate make—the crossbar set
to hold the strings being silver. He had won it
when he destroyed the city of Eëtíôn,
and plucking it he took his joy: he sang
old tales of heroes, while across the room
alone and silent sat Patróklos, waiting   230
until Akhilleus should be done with song.
Phoinix had come in unremarked,[11] but when
the two new visitors, Odysseus leading,
entered and stood before him, then Akhilleus
rose in wonderment, and left his chair,
his harp still in his hand. So did Patróklos
rise at sight of the two men. Akhilleus
made both welcome with a gesture, saying:

"Peace! My two great friends, I greet your coming.
How I have needed it! Even in my anger,   240
of all Akhaians, you are closest to me."

And Prince Akhilleus led them in. He seated them
on easy chairs with purple coverlets,
and to Patróklos who stood near he said:

---

[9]That is, as tribute to the gods.
[10]Poseidon, god of the ocean.
[11]*Phoinix . . . unremarked.* Like "Following Phoinix" a few lines earlier, these words are inserted by the translator as a way of coping with a major problem in the Greek text, which does not mention Phoinix as walking from Agamémnon's hut to that of Akhilleus.

"Put out an ampler winebowl, use more wine
for stronger drink,[12] and place a cup for each.
Here are my dearest friends beneath my roof."

Patróklos did as his companion bade him.
Meanwhile the host set down a carving block
within the fire's rays; a chine of mutton   250
and a fat chine of goat he placed upon it,
as well as savory pork chine. Automédôn[13]
steadied the meat for him, Akhilleus carved,
then sliced it well and forked it on the spits.
Meanwhile Patróklos, like a god in firelight,
made the hearth blaze up. When the leaping flame
had ebbed and died away, he raked the coals
and in the glow extended spits of meat,
lifting these at times from the firestones
to season with pure salt. When all was done   260
and the roast meat apportioned into platters,
loaves of bread were passed round by Patróklos
in fine baskets. Akhilleus served the meat.
He took his place then opposite Odysseus,
back to the other wall, and told
Patróklos to make offering to the gods.
This he did with meat tossed in the fire,
then each man's hand went out upon the meal.
When they had put their hunger and thirst away,
Aías nodded silently to Phoinix,   270
but Prince Odysseus caught the nod. He filled
a cup of wine and lifted it to Akhilleus,
saying:

                                "Health, Akhilleus. We've no lack
of generous feasts this evening—in the lodge
of Agamémnon first, and now with you,
good fare and plentiful each time.
It is not feasting that concerns us now,
however, but a ruinous defeat.
Before our very eyes we see it coming
and are afraid. By a blade's turn, our good ships   280
are saved or lost, unless you arm your valor.
Trojans and allies are encamped tonight
in pride before our ramparts, at our sterns,
and through their army burn a thousand fires.
These men are sure they cannot now be stopped
but will get through to our good ships. Lord Zeus
flashes and thunders for them on the right,[14]
and Hektor in his ecstasy of power

---

[12] Wine was usually served mixed, often with water.
[13] Third-ranking man among the Myrmidons, after Akhilleus and Patróklos.
[14] Favorable omens appeared on the observer's right.

is mad for battle, confident in Zeus,
deferring to neither men nor gods. Pure frenzy 290
fills him, and he prays for the bright dawn
when he will shear our stern-post beaks away
and fire all our ships, while in the shipways
amid that holocaust he carries death
among our men, driven out by smoke. All this
I gravely fear; I fear the gods will make
good his threatenings, and our fate will be
to die here, far from the pastureland of Argos.
Rouse yourself, if even at this hour
you'll pitch in for the Akhaians and deliver them 300
from Trojan havoc. In the years to come
this day will be remembered pain for you
if you do not. No remedy, no remedy
will come to hand, once the great ill is done.
While there is time, think how to keep this evil
day from the Danáäns!

                                        My dear lad,

how rightly in your case your father, Pêleus,
put it in his farewell, sending you out
from Phthía to take ship with Agamémnon!
'Now as to fighting power, child,' he said, 310
'if Hêra and Athêna wish, they'll give it.
Control your passion, though, and your proud heart,
for gentle courtesy is a better thing.
Break off insidious quarrels, and young and old,
the Argives will respect you for it more.'
That was your old father's admonition:
you have forgotten. Still, even now, abandon
heart-wounding anger. If you will relent,
Agamémnon will match this change of heart
with gifts. Now listen and let me list for you 320
what just now in his quarters he proposed:
seven new tripods, and ten bars of gold,
then twenty shining caldrons, and twelve horses,
thoroughbreds, that by their wind and legs
have won him prizes: any man who owned
what these have brought him would not lack resources,
could not be pinched for precious gold—so many
prizes have these horses carried home.
Then he will give you seven women, deft
in household handicraft: women of Lesbos 330
chosen when you yourself took Lesbos town,
as they outshone all womankind in beauty.
These he will give you, and one more, whom he
took away from you then: Briseus' daughter,
concerning whom he adds a solemn oath
never to have gone to bed or coupled with her,
as custom is, my lord, with men and women.

These are all yours at once. If the immortals
grant us the pillaging of Priam's town,
you may come forward when the spoils are shared   340
and load your ship with bars of gold and bronze.
Then you may choose among the Trojan women
twenty that are most lovely, after Helen.
And then, if we reach Argos of Akhaia,
flowing with good things of the earth, you'll be
his own adopted son, dear as Orestês,
born long ago and reared in bounteous peace.
He has three daughters now at home, Khrysóthemis,
Laódikê, and Iphiánassa.
You may take whom you will to be your bride   350
and pay no gift when you conduct her home
to your ancestral hall. He'll add a dowry
such as no man has given to his daughter.
Seven flourishing strongholds he'll give to you:
Kardamylê and Enopê and Hirê
in the wild grassland; holy Phêrai too,
and the deep meadowland of Ántheia,
Aipeia and the vineyard slope of Pêdasos,
all lying near the sea in the far west
of sandy Pylos. In these lands are men   360
who own great flocks and herds; now as your liegemen,
they will pay tithes and sumptuous honor to you,
prospering as they carry out your plans.
These are the gifts he will arrange if you
desist from anger.

                              Even if you abhor
the son of Atreus all the more bitterly,
with all his gifts, take pity on the rest,
all the old army, worn to rags in battle.
These will honor you as gods are honored!
And ah, for these, what glory you may win!   370
Think: Hektor is your man this time: being crazed
with ruinous pride, believing there's no fighter
equal to him among those that our ships
brought here by sea, he'll put himself in range!"

Akhilleus the great runner answered him:

"Son of Laërtês and the gods of old,
Odysseus, master soldier and mariner,
I owe you a straight answer, as to how
I see this thing, and how it is to end.
No need to sit with me like mourning doves   380
making your gentle noise by turns. I hate
as I hate Hell's own gate that man who hides
one thought within him while he speaks another.
What I shall say is what I see and think.

Give in to Agamémnon? I think not,
neither to him nor to the rest. I had
small thanks for fighting, fighting without truce
against hard enemies here. The portion's equal
whether a man hangs back or fights his best;
the same respect, or lack of it, is given   390
brave man and coward. One who's active dies
like the do-nothing. What least thing have I
to show for it, for harsh days undergone
and my life gambled, all these years of war?
A bird will give her fledglings every scrap
she comes by, and go hungry, foraging.
That is the case with me.
Many a sleepless night I've spent afield
and many a day in bloodshed, hand to hand
in battle for the wives of other men.   400
In sea raids I plundered a dozen towns,
eleven in expeditions overland
through Trojan country, and the treasure taken
out of them all, great heaps of handsome things,
I carried back each time to Agamémnon.
He sat tight on the beachhead, and shared out
a little treasure; most of it he kept.
He gave prizes of war to his officers;
the rest have theirs, not I; from me alone
of all Akhaians, he pre-empted her.   410
He holds my bride,[15] dear to my heart. Aye, let him
sleep with her and enjoy her!
                               Why must Argives
fight the Trojans? Why did he raise an army
and lead it here? For Helen, was it not?
Are the Atreidai of all mortal men
the only ones who love their wives? I think not.
Every sane decent fellow loves his own
and cares for her, as in my heart I loved
Brisêis, though I won her by the spear.
Now, as he took my prize out of my hands,   420
tricked and defrauded me, he need not tempt me;
I know him, and he cannot change my mind.
Let him take thought, Odysseus, with you
and others how the ships may be defended
against incendiary attack. By god,
he has achieved imposing work without me,
a rampart piled up overnight, a ditch
running beyond it, broad and deep,
with stakes implanted in it! All no use!
He cannot hold against the killer's charge.   430

---

[15]Brisêis; she is not literally his wife, however.

As long as I was in the battle, Hektor
never cared for a fight far from the walls;
his limit was the oak tree by the gate.
When I was alone one day he waited there,
but barely got away when I went after him.
Now it is I who do not care to fight.
Tomorrow at dawn when I have made offering
to Zeus and all the gods, and hauled my ships
for loading in the shallows, if you like
and if it interests you, look out and see   440
my ships on Hellê's waters in the offing,[16]
oarsmen in line making the sea-foam scud!
And if the great Earthshaker[17] gives a breeze,
the third day out I'll make it home to Phthía.
Rich possessions are there I left behind
when I was mad enough to come here; now
I take home gold and ruddy bronze, and women
belted luxuriously, and hoary iron,
all that came to me here. As for my prize,
he who gave her took her outrageously back.   450
Well, you can tell him all this to his face,
and let the other Akhaians burn
if he in his thick hide of shamelessness
picks out another man to cheat. He would not
look me in the eye, dog that he is!
I will not share one word of counsel with him,
nor will I act with him; he robbed me blind,
broke faith with me: he gets no second chance
to play me for a fool. Once is enough.
To hell with him, Zeus took his brains away!   460
His gifts I abominate, and I would give
not one dry shuck for him. I would not change,
not if he multiplied his gifts by ten,
by twenty times what he has now, and more,
no matter where they came from: if he gave
what enters through Orkhómenos' town gate
or Thebes of Egypt, where the treasures lie—
that city where through each of a hundred gates
two hundred men drive out in chariots.[18]
Not if his gifts outnumbered the sea sands   470
or all the dust grains in the world could Agamémnon
ever appease me—not till he pays me back
full measure, pain for pain, dishonor for dishonor.
The daughter of Agamémnon, son of Atreus,
I will not take in marriage. Let her be
as beautiful as pale-gold Aphrodítê,
skilled as Athêna of the sea-grey eyes,

---

[16] *Hellê's waters:* the Hellespont (the modern Dardanelles). *offing:* horizon.
[17] Poseidon.
[18] *Orkhómenos:* an important city northwest of Athens. *Thebes:* an ancient, royal city of Egypt.

I will not have her, at any price. No, let him
find someone else, an eligible Akhaian,
kinglier than I.

                                    Now if the gods   480

preserve me and I make it home, my father
Pêleus will select a bride for me.
In Hellas[19] and in Phthîa there are many
daughters of strong men who defend the towns.
I'll take the one I wish to be my wife.
There in my manhood I have longed, indeed,
to marry someone of congenial mind
and take my ease, enjoying the great estate
my father had acquired.

                                    Now I think

no riches can compare with being alive,   490
not even those they say this well-built Ilion
stored up in peace before the Akhaians came.
Neither could all the Archer's shrine contains
at rocky Pytho,[20] in the crypt of stone.
A man may come by cattle and sheep in raids;
tripods he buys, and tawny-headed horses;
but his life's breath cannot be hunted back
or be recaptured once it pass his lips.
My mother, Thetis of the silvery feet,
tells me of two possible destinies   500
carrying me toward death: two ways:
if on the one hand I remain to fight
around Troy town, I lose all hope of home
but gain unfading glory; on the other,
if I sail back to my own land my glory
fails—but a long life lies ahead for me.
To all the rest of you I say: 'Sail home:
you will not now see Ilion's last hour,'
for Zeus who views the wide world held his sheltering
hand over that city, and her troops   510
have taken heart.

                        Return, then, emissaries,
deliver my answer to the Akhaian peers—
it is the senior officer's privilege—
and let them plan some other way, and better,
to save their ships and save the Akhaian army.
This one cannot be put into effect—
their scheme this evening—while my anger holds.
Phoinix may stay and lodge the night with us,
then take ship and sail homeward at my side
tomorrow, if he wills. I'll not constrain him."   520

---

[19] This word later came to mean all of Greece; here it refers to a region in northern Greece.
[20] Temple of Apollo at Delphi in Greece; visitors seeking the god's oracular guidance made
rich offerings.

After Akhilleus finished, all were silent,
awed, for he spoke with power.
Then the old master-charioteer, Lord Phoinix,
answered at last, and let his tears come shining,
fearing for the Akhaian ships:

                                                                "Akhilleus,

if it is true you set your heart on home
and will not stir a finger to save the ships
from being engulfed by fire—all for this rage
that has swept over you—how, child, could I
be sundered from you, left behind alone?   530
For your sake the old master-charioteer,
Pêleus, made provision that I should come,
that day he gave you godspeed out of Phthía
to go with Agamémnon. Still a boy,
you knew nothing of war that levels men
to the same testing, nothing of assembly
where men become illustrious. That is why
he sent me, to instruct you in these matters,
to be a man of eloquence and action.
After all that, dear child, I should not wish   540
to be left here apart from you—not even
if god himself should undertake to smooth
my wrinkled age and make me fresh and young,
as when for the first time I left the land
of lovely women, Hellas. I went north
to avoid a feud with Father, Amyntor
Orménidês. His anger against me rose
over a fair-haired slave girl whom he fancied,
without respect for his own wife, my mother.
Mother embraced my knees and begged that I   550
make love to this girl, so that afterward
she might be cold to the aging man. I did it.
My father guessed the truth at once, and cursed me,
praying the ghostly Furies[21] that no son
of mine should ever rest upon his knees:
a curse fulfilled by the immortals—Lord
Zeus of undergloom and cold Perséphonê.[22]
I planned to put a sword in him, and would have,
had not some god unstrung my rage, reminding me
of country gossip and the frowns of men;   560
I shrank from being called a parricide
among the Akhaians. But from that time on
I felt no tie with home, no love for lingering
under the rooftree of a raging father.
Our household and our neighbors, it is true,
urged me to stay. They made a handsome feast

[21]Spirits who avenge sins, especially against blood kindred.
[22]*Zeus of undergloom:* Aïdês (Hades), ruler of the dead. *Perséphonê:* his queen.

of shambling cattle butchered, and fat sheep;
young porkers by the litter, crisp with fat,
were singed and spitted in Hêphaistos' fire,
rivers of wine drunk from the old man's store. 570
Nine times they spent the night and slept beside me,
taking the watch by turns, leaving a fire
to flicker under the entrance colonnade,
and one more in the court outside my room.
But when the tenth night came, starless and black,
I cracked the tight bolt on my chamber door,
pushed out, and scaled the courtyard wall, unseen
by household men on watch or women slaves.
Then I escaped from that place, made my way
through Hellas where the dancing floors are wide, 580
until I came to Phthía's fertile plain,
mother of flocks, and Pêleus the king.
He gave me welcome, treated me with love,
as a father would an only son, his heir
to rich possessions. And he made me rich,
appointing me great numbers of retainers
on the frontier of Phthía, where I lived
as lord of Dolopês. Now, it was I
who formed your manhood, handsome as a god's,
Akhilleus: I who loved you from the heart; 590
for never in another's company
would you attend a feast or dine in hall—
never, unless I took you on my knees
and cut your meat, and held your cup of wine.
Many a time you wet my shirt, hiccuping
wine-bubbles in distress, when you were small.
Patient and laborious as a nurse
I had to be for you, bearing in mind
that never would the gods bring into being
any son of mine. Godlike Akhilleus, 600
you were the manchild that I made my own
to save me someday, so I thought, from misery.
Quell your anger, Akhilleus! You must not
be pitiless! The gods themselves relent,
and are they not still greater in bravery,
in honor and in strength? Burnt offerings,
courteous prayer, libation, smoke of sacrifice,
with all of these, men can placate the gods
when someone oversteps and errs. The truth is,
prayers[23] are daughters of almighty Zeus— 610
one may imagine them lame, wrinkled things

---

[23]*prayers:* pleas for forgiveness, uttered by a man who, after harming another while possessed by a kind of madness (Folly), repents of his misdeed. If the injured man accepts the plea or prayer he is rewarded, but if he rejects it he may himself be visited by a fit of Folly that drives him to a ruinous act. The allegory is prophetic of what will happen to Akhilleus.

with eyes cast down, that toil to follow after
passionate Folly. Folly is strong and swift,
outrunning all the prayers, and everywhere
arriving first to injure mortal men;
still they come healing after. If a man
reveres the daughters of Zeus when they come near,
he is rewarded, and his prayers are heard;
but if he spurns them and dismisses them,
they make their way to Zeus again and ask   620
that Folly dog that man till suffering
has taken arrogance out of him.

                                        Relent,

be courteous to the daughters of Zeus, you too,
as courtesy sways others, and the best.
If Agamémnon had no gifts for you,
named none to follow, but inveighed against you
still in fury, then I could never say,
'Discard your anger and defend the Argives—'
never, no matter how they craved your help.
But this is not so: he will give many things   630
at once; he promised others; he has sent
his noblest men to intercede with you,
the flower of the army, and your friends,
dearest among the Argives. Will you turn
their words, their coming, into humiliation?
Until this moment, no one took it ill
that you should suffer anger; we learned this
from the old stories of how towering wrath
could overcome great men; but they were still
amenable to gifts and to persuasion.   640
Here is an instance I myself remember
not from our own time but in ancient days:
I'll tell it to you all, for all are friends.
The Kourêtês were fighting a warlike race,[24]
Aitolians, around the walls of Kálydôn,
with slaughter on both sides: Aitolians
defending their beloved Kálydôn
while the Kourêtês longed to sack the town.
The truth is, Artemis of the Golden Chair
had brought the scourge of war on the Aitolians;   650

[24] The story Phoinix proceeds to tell is a parable, drawn from mythology and adapted here to make it fit Akhilleus' situation. Reordered chronologically, the story is as follows: Artemis, goddess of the hunt and of wild life ("Mistress of Long Arrows"), was offended by the failure of Oineus, king of the Aitolians, to honor her. In revenge, she sent a great boar to ravage his land. The king's son, Meléagros, organized a band of men to kill the boar. After it was killed, the Aitolians quarreled with the Kourêtês, a neighboring people, over the animal's head and hide; in the ensuing war the Kourêtês threatened Kálydôn, Oineus' city. In the fighting Meléagros killed his mother Althaiê's brother, who was fighting on the Kourêtês' side. She cursed her son, who therefore retired from battle, putting his city in peril. His people and family implored him to defend it and offered him gifts, but he resisted their pleas until his wife Kleopátrê persuaded him. He then saved the city, but only after it was too late for him to receive the gifts.

she had been angered because Oineus made
no harvest offering from his vineyard slope.
While other gods enjoyed his hekatombs
he made her none, either forgetful of it
or careless—a great error, either way.
In her anger, the Mistress of Long Arrows
roused against him a boar with gleaming tusks
out of his wild grass bed, a monstrous thing
that ravaged the man's vineyard many times
and felled entire orchards, roots, 660
blooms, apples and all. Now this great boar
Meléagros, the son of Oineus, killed
by gathering men and hounds from far and near.
So huge the boar was, no small band could master him,
and he brought many to the dolorous pyre.[25]
Around the dead beast Artemis set on
a clash with battlecries between Kourêtês
and proud Aitolians over the boar's head
and shaggy hide. As long, then, as Meléagros,
backed by the wargod, fought, the Kourêtês 670
had the worst of it for all their numbers
and could not hold a line outside the walls.
But then a day came when Meléagros
was stung by venomous anger that infects
the coolest thinker's heart: swollen with rage
at his own mother, Althaiê, he languished
in idleness at home beside his lady,
Kleopátrê.
                    This lovely girl was born
to Marpessê of ravishing pale ankles,[26]
Euênos' child, and Idês, who had been 680
most powerful of men on earth. He drew
the bow against the Lord Phoibos Apollo
over his love, Marpessê, whom her father
and gentle mother called Alkýonê,
since for her sake her mother gave that seabird's
forlorn cry when Apollo ravished her.
With Kleopátrê lay Meléagros,
nursing the bitterness his mother stirred,
when in her anguish over a brother slain
she cursed her son. She called upon the gods, 690
beating the grassy earth with both her hands
as she pitched forward on her knees, with cries
to the Lord of Undergloom and cold Perséphonê,
while tears wetted her veils—in her entreaty

---

[25] The fire in which the dead were cremated.
[26] The poem digresses for a few lines to describe the parents of Meléagros' wife, Kleopátrê. Her father Idês and the god Apollo had been rivals for the love of her mother Marpessê (who chose her human lover), also called Alkýonê, a name denoting a seabird with a mournful cry.

that death come to her son. Inexorable
in Érebos[27] a vampire Fury listened.
Soon, then, about the gates of the Aitolians
tumult and din of war grew loud; their towers
rang with blows. And now the elder men
implored Meléagros to leave his room,   700
and sent the high priests of the gods, imploring him
to help defend the town. They promised him
a large reward: in the green countryside
of Kálydôn, wherever it was richest,
there he might choose a beautiful garden plot
of fifty acres, half in vineyard, half
in virgin prairie for the plow to cut.
Oineus, master of horsemen, came with prayers
upon the doorsill of the chamber, often
rattling the locked doors, pleading with his son.   710
His sisters, too, and then his gentle mother
pleaded with him. Only the more fiercely
he turned away. His oldest friends, his dearest,
not even they could move him—not until
his room was shaken by a hail of stones
as Kourêtês began to scale the walls
and fire the city.

                                            Then at last his lady
in her soft-belted gown besought him weeping,
speaking of all the ills that come to men
whose town is taken: soldiers put to the sword;   720
the city razed by fire; alien hands
carrying off the children and the women.
Hearing these fearful things, his heart was stirred
to action: he put on his shining gear
and fought off ruin from the Aitolians.
Mercy prevailed in him. His folk no longer
cared to award him gifts and luxuries,
yet even so he saved that terrible day.
Oh, do not let your mind go so astray!
Let no malignant spirit   730
turn you that way, dear son! It will be worse
to fight for ships already set afire!
Value the gifts; rejoin the war; Akhaians
afterward will give you a god's honor.
If you reject the gifts and then, later,
enter the deadly fight, you will not be
accorded the same honor, even though
you turn the tide of war!"

                                            But the great runner
Akhilleus answered:

[27]Part of the realm of the dead.

"Old uncle Phoinix, bless you,
that is an honor I can live without. 740
Honored I think I am by Zeus's justice,
justice that will sustain me by the ships
as long as breath is in me and I can stand.
Here is another point: ponder it well:
best not confuse my heart with lamentation
for Agamémnon, whom you must not honor;
you would be hateful to me, dear as you are.
Loyalty should array you at my side
in giving pain to him who gives me pain.
Rule with me equally, share half my honor,[28] 750
but do not ask my help for Agamémnon.
My answer will be reported by these two.
Lodge here in a soft bed, and at first light
we can decide whether to sail or stay."

He knit his brows and nodded to Patróklos
to pile up rugs for Phoinix' bed—a sign
for the others to be quick about departing.
Aías, however, noble son of Télamôn
made the last appeal. He said:

"Odysseus,
master soldier and mariner, let us go. 760
I do not see the end of this affair
achieved by this night's visit. Nothing for it
but to report our talk for what it's worth
to the Danáäns, who sit waiting there.
Akhilleus hardened his great heart against us,
wayward and savage as he is, unmoved
by the affections of his friends who made him
honored above all others on the beachhead.
There is no pity in him. A normal man
will take the penalty for a brother slain 770
or a dead son. By paying much, the one
who did the deed may stay unharmed at home.
Fury and pride in the bereaved are curbed
when he accepts the penalty. Not you.
Cruel and unappeasable rage the gods
put in you for one girl alone. We offer
seven beauties, and much more besides!
Be gentler, and respect your own rooftree
whereunder we are guests who speak for all
Danáäns as a body. Our desire 780
is to be closest to you of them all."

---

[28] This is not meant literally; Akhilleus is saying, in effect, "Ask any favor except that I help Agamémnon."

Akhilleus the great runner answered him:

"Scion[29] of Télamôn and gods of old,
Aías, lord of fighting men, you seemed
to echo my own mind in what you said!
And yet my heart grows large and hot with fury
remembering that affair: as though I were
some riffraff or camp follower, he taunted me
before them all!

                                    Go back, report the news:
I will not think of carnage or of war   790
until Prince Hektor, son of Priam, reaches
Myrmidon huts and ships in his attack,
slashing through Argives, burning down their ships.
Around my hut, my black ship, I foresee
for all his fury, Hektor will break off combat."[30]

That was his answer. Each of the emissaries
took up a double-handed cup and poured
libation by the shipways. Then Odysseus
led the way on their return. Patróklos
commanded his retainers and the maids   800
to make at once a deep-piled bed for Phoinix.
Obediently they did so, spreading out
fleeces and coverlet and a linen sheet,
and down the old man lay, awaiting Dawn.
Akhilleus slept in the well-built hut's recess,
and with him lay a woman he had brought
from Lesbos, Phorbas' daughter, Diomêdê.
Patróklos went to bed at the other end,
and with him, too, a woman lay—soft-belted
Iphis, who had been given to him by Akhilleus   810
when he took Skyros, ringed by cliff, the mountain
fastness of Enyéus.

                                    Now the emissaries
arrived at Agamémnon's lodge. With cups
of gold held up, and rising to their feet
on every side, the Akhaians greeted them,
curious for the news. Lord Agamémnon
put the question first:

                                    "Come, tell me, sir,
Odysseus, glory of Akhaia—will Akhilleus
fight off ravenous fire from the ships
or does he still refuse, does anger still   820
hold sway in his great heart?"

---

[29] Offspring.
[30] Akhilleus is apparently modifying his earlier resolve to sail away the next morning.

That patient man,
the Prince Odysseus, made reply:

"Excellency,

Lord Marshal of the army, son of Atreus,
the man has no desire to quench his rage.
On the contrary, he is more than ever
full of anger, spurns you and your gifts,
calls on you to work out your own defense
to save the ships and the Akhaian army.
As for himself, he threatens at daybreak
to drag his well-found ships into the surf,   830
and says he would advise the rest as well
to sail for home. 'You shall not see,' he says,
'the last hour that awaits tall Ilion,
for Zeus who views the wide world held his sheltering
hand over the city, and her troops
have taken heart.' That was Akhilleus' answer.
Those who were with me can confirm all this,
Aías can, and the two clearheaded criers.
As to old Phoinix, he is sleeping there
by invitation, so that he may sail   840
to his own country, homeward with Akhilleus,
tomorrow, if he wills, without constraint."

When he had finished everyone was still,
sitting in silence and in perturbation
for a long time. At last brave Diomêdês,
lord of the warcry, said:

"Excellency,

Lord Marshal of the army, Agamémnon,
you never should have pled with him, or given
so many gifts to him. At the best of times
he is a proud man; now you have pushed him far   850
deeper into his vanity and pride.
By god, let us have done with him—
whether he goes or stays! He'll fight again
when the time comes, whenever his blood is up
or the god rouses him. As for ourselves,
let everyone now do as I advise
and go to rest. Your hearts have been refreshed
with bread and wine, the pith and nerve of men.
When the fair Dawn with finger tips of rose
makes heaven bright, deploy your men and horses   860
before the ships at once, and cheer them on,
and take your place, yourself, in the front line
to join the battle."

All gave their assent
in admiration of Diomêdês,

breaker of horses. When they had spilt their wine
they all dispersed, each man to his own hut,
and lying down they took the gift of sleep.

BOOK X. *The troubled Agamémnon and his brother Meneláos, unable to sleep, assemble
the Greek chieftains in the night. After they inspect the sentries, Nestor proposes that a recon-
naissance patrol try to discover the Trojan plans. Diomêdês volunteers for the dangerous mission, choosing the wily Odysseus as his partner. Meanwhile the Trojans too decide to send
out a scout, a man named Dolôn. Diomêdês and Odysseus capture him, lead him to believe
he will be taken prisoner alive, get information from him, and then kill him. The two Greeks,
acting on what they have learned, raid the camp of King Rhésos of Thrace, a newcomer
to the war, kill him and several of his men, steal his wondrous horses, and then return triumphantly to the ships.*

BOOK XI. *The next day brings fierce general fighting, gods and goddesses remaining out
of action. At first Agamémnon inflicts severe damage on the Trojans, who retreat before him.
Zeus sends his messenger goddess, Iris, to tell Hektor that he should not engage the enemy
himself until Agamémnon shall be wounded. Soon thereafter the Greek commander is in fact
wounded and forced to return to the camp. Hektor leads a counterattack. Diomêdês is wounded,
by an arrow from Paris, and then Odysseus is wounded too. Meneláos and the greater Aías
come to Odysseus' aid. Nestor takes the wounded Greek physician Makháôn back to the camp
as Aías slowly retreats before a swarm of Trojans. At this point almost all the important Greek
leaders have been put out of action. Akhilleus, aboard his ship, exults over the Greeks' plight
but sends his friend Patróklos to Nestor for information about the wounded man he is attending. Nestor reminds Patróklos that the latter's proper mission is to counsel Akhilleus and goes
on to suggest that Akhilleus authorize Patróklos to lead the Myrmidons, Akhilleus' rested troops,
against the Trojans. Patróklos feels sympathy for the desperate Greeks.*

from BOOK TWELVE: THE RAMPART BREACHED

The immortals still inactive, Hektor leads an assault on the palisaded fort that protects the Greek camp and ships. (The main defenders are now the two Aíases and
the archer Teukros.) Poulýdamas, a Trojan, suggests to Hektor that the Trojan forces
should breach the moat on foot rather than with chariots; Hektor accepts the advice.
But a later suggestion by Poulýdamas, that the army should retreat in accordance
with an apparent ill omen, is scornfully rejected by Hektor. Sarpêdôn—king of Lykia,
son of Zeus, and ally of the Trojans—prepares to attack the wall.

But even so, and even now, the Trojans
led by great Hektor could not yet have breached
the wall and gate with massive bar, had not
Lord Zeus impelled Sarpêdôn, his own son,   330
against the Argives like a lion on cattle.
Circular was the shield he held before him,
hammered out of pure bronze: aye, the smith
had hammered it, and riveted the plates
to thick bull's hide on golden rods rigged out
to the full circumference. Now gripping this,
hefting a pair of spears, he joined the battle,
formidable as some hill-bred lion, ravenous

for meat after long abstinence. His valor
summons him to attempt homesteads and flocks— 340
and though he find herdsmen on hand with dogs
and spears to guard the sheep, he will not turn
without a fling at the stockade. One thing
or the other: a mighty leap and a fresh kill,
or he will fall at the spearmen's feet, brought down
by a javelin thrown hard.

                          So valor drove

Sarpêdôn to the wall to make a breakthrough.
Turning to Glaukos, Hippólokhos' son, he said:

"What is the point of being honored so
with precedence at table, choice of meat, 350
and brimming cups, at home in Lykia,
like gods at ease in everyone's regard?
And why have lands been granted you and me
on Xánthos bank: to each his own demesne,
with vines and fields of grain?

                          So that we two

at times like this in the Lykian front line
may face the blaze of battle and fight well,
that Lykian men-at-arms may say:
'They are no common men, our lords who rule
in Lykia. They eat fat lamb at feasts 360
and drink rare vintages, but the main thing is
their fighting power, when they lead in combat!'
Ah, cousin, could we but survive this war
to live forever deathless, without age,
I would not ever go again to battle,
nor would I send you there for honor's sake!
But now a thousand shapes of death surround us,
and no man can escape them, or be safe.
Let us attack—whether to give some fellow
glory or to win it from him." 370

    BOOK XII. (continued). *After this speech to Glaukos, Sarpêdôn assaults the wall and is partially successful. It is Hektor, however, who finally breaks down one of the gates. His troops swarm into the fort after him, the Greeks fleeing toward the ships.*

    BOOK XIII. *Confident that his earlier prohibition will keep the other gods from interfering in the war, Zeus relaxes his vigilance. The sea god, Poseidon, however, takes advantage of the opportunity and comes covertly to the Greeks' aid, inciting them to stiff resistance. Fierce battle continues, reflected in many scattered engagements. Zeus' plan, we learn, is to give the Trojans a limited victory in answer to Thetis' plea in Book I that Akhilleus be vindicated, but the god will not let the Greeks be utterly defeated. Idómeneus the king of Krete (Crete) performs valiant deeds on the Greek side. The Trojans falter, but Hektor rallies them. The Book ends as the Greeks prepare to resist still another Trojan offensive.*

    BOOK XIV. *With Agamémnon, Diomêdês, and Odysseus all wounded, the Greeks are on the point of being routed. Agamémnon proposes to launch the ships, but Odysseus scorns the idea as cowardice and bad strategy. Diomêdês urges that the three return to the fight, at least to encourage their comrades. Poseidon continues to help the Greeks; to support him, Hêra decides to hoodwink Zeus by seducing him and then making him fall asleep—a project in which she wins the help of Aphrodítê by deception and of the god Sleep by bribes. With Zeus asleep, Poseidon is able to help the Greeks even more than before, and the tide of battle is turned. The greater Aías wounds Hektor with a large stone so that he has to be carried out of battle. The Trojans withdraw in panic.*

BOOK XV. *Zeus awakens, sees the Trojans being routed by the Greeks and Poseidon, and is enraged at the trick Hêra has played on him. He predicts the future course of the war: the Greeks will be driven back to the ships again, Akhilleus will send Patróklos into the fight, Hektor will kill Patróklos and then be killed by Akhilleus, the Greeks will take Troy. But for the time being Zeus will continue to humiliate the Greeks as part of his plan to vindicate Akhilleus. He sends Hêra back to Olympos with instructions to summon Iris and Apollo. When they come to him, he sends Iris to order Poseidon out of the action and Apollo to reinvigorate the wounded Hektor. Poseidon angrily and reluctantly obeys, and Apollo leads Hektor and the Trojans back to the ships, leveling the protective walls and making a causeway across the moat. The dismayed Patróklos, who since the end of Book XI has been attending one of the wounded in the Greeks' camp, hurries away to persuade Akhilleus to come to the rescue. Zeus' will is that the Trojans shall set fire to part of the Grecian fleet.*

BOOK SIXTEEN: A SHIP FIRED, A TIDE TURNED

That was the way the fighting went
for one seagoing ship. Meanwhile Patróklos
approached Akhilleus his commander, streaming
warm tears—like a shaded mountain spring
that makes a rockledge run with dusky water.
Akhilleus watched him come, and felt a pang for him.
Then the great prince and runner said:

"Patróklos,

why all the weeping? Like a small girlchild
who runs beside her mother and cries and cries
to be taken up, and catches at her gown,   10
and will not let her go, looking up in tears
until she has her wish: that's how you seem,
Patróklos, winking out your glimmering tears.
Have you something to tell the Myrmidons
or me? Some message you alone have heard
from Phthía? But they say that Aktor's son,
Menoitios, is living still, and Pêleus,
the son of Aíakos, lives on
amid his Myrmidons.[1] If one of these
were dead, we should be grieved.

Or is this weeping   20
over the Argives, seeing how they perish

---

[1] *Menoitios, Pêleus.* The fathers of, respectively, Patróklos and Akhilleus.

at the long ships by their own bloody fault!
Speak out now, don't conceal it, let us share it."

And groaning, Patróklos, you replied:

"Akhilleus, prince and greatest of Akhaians,
be forbearing. They are badly hurt.
All who were the best fighters are now lying
among the ships with spear or arrow wounds.
Diomêdês, Tydeus' rugged son, was shot;
Odysseus and Agamémnon, the great spearman,   30
have spear wounds; Eurýpylos[2]
took an arrow shot deep in his thigh.
Surgeons with medicines are attending them
to ease their wounds.
                                        But you are a hard case,
Akhilleus! God forbid this rage you nurse
should master me. You and your fearsome pride!
What good will come of it to anyone, later,
unless you keep disaster from the Argives?
Have you no pity?
Pêleus, master of horse, was not your father,   40
Thetis was not your mother! Cold grey sea
and sea-cliffs bore you, making a mind so harsh.
If in your heart you fear some oracle,
some word of Zeus, told by your gentle mother,
then send me out at least, and send me quickly,[3]
give me a company of Myrmidons,
and I may be a beacon to Danääns!
Lend me your gear to strap over my shoulders;
Trojans then may take me for yourself
and break off battle, giving our worn-out men   50
a chance to breathe. Respites are brief in war.
We fresh troops with one battlecry might easily
push their tired men back on the town,
away from ships and huts."

                                        So he petitioned,

witless as a child that what he begged for
was his own death, hard death and doom.

                                        Akhilleus

out of his deep anger made reply:

"Hard words, dear prince. There is no oracle
I know of that I must respect, no word

---

[2]A wounded Greek warrior whom Patróklos has been tending since the action of Book XI.
[3]This suggestion, like certain other points in Patróklos' speech, was made first by Nestor
in Book XI.

from Zeus reported by my gentle mother.[4]   60
Only this bitterness eats at my heart
when one man would deprive and shame his equal,
taking back his prize by abuse of power.
The girl whom the Akhaians chose for me
I won by my own spear. A town with walls
I stormed and sacked for her. Then Agamémnon
stole her back, out of my hands, as though
I were some vagabond held cheap.

                                                               All that
we can let pass as being over and done with;
I could not rage forever. And yet, by heaven, I swore   70
I would not rest from anger till the cries
and clangor of battle reached my very ships!
But you, now, you can strap my famous gear
on your own shoulders, and then take command
of Myrmidons on edge and ripe for combat,
now that like a dark stormcloud the Trojans
have poured round the first ships, and Argive troops
have almost no room for maneuver left,
with nothing to their rear but sea. The whole
townful of Trojans joins in, sure of winning,   80
because they cannot see my helmet's brow
aflash in range of them. They'd fill the gullies
with dead men soon, in flight up through the plain,
if Agamémnon were on good terms with me.
As things are, they've outflanked the camp. A mercy
for them that in the hands of Diomêdês
no great spear goes berserk, warding death
from the Danáäns! Not yet have I heard
the voice of Agamémnon, either, shouting
out of his hateful skull. The shout of Hektor,   90
the killer, calling Trojans, makes a roar
like breaking surf, and with long answering cries
they hold the whole plain where they drove the Akhaians.
Even so, defend the ships, Patróklos.
Attack the enemy in force, or they
will set the ships ablaze with whirling fire
and rob Akhaians of their dear return.
Now carry out the purpose I confide,
so that you'll win great honor for me, and glory
among Danáäns; then they'll send me back   100
my lovely girl, with bright new gifts as well.
Once you expel the enemy from the ships,
rejoin me here. If Hêra's lord,
the lord of thunder, grants you the day's honor,

---

[4]These words seem to contradict what Akhilleus has said in Book IX about his "two possible destinies"; possibly the excited Akhilleus means something like "That is not the point right now."

covet no further combat far from me
with Trojan soldiers. That way you'd deny me
recompense of honor. You must not,
for joy of battle, joy of killing Trojans,
carry the fight to Ilion![5] Some power
out of Olympos, one of the immortal gods, 110
might intervene for them. The Lord Apollo
loves the Trojans. Turn back, then, as soon
as you restore the safety of the ships,
and let the rest contend, out on the plain.
Ah, Father Zeus, Athêna, and Apollo!
If not one Trojan of them all
should get away from death, and not one Argive
save ourselves were spared, we two alone
could pull down Troy's old coronet of towers!"

These were the speeches they exchanged. Now Aías 120
could no longer hold:[6] he was dislodged
by spear-throws, beaten by the mind of Zeus
and Trojan shots. His shining helm rang out
around his temples dangerously with hits
as his helmplates were struck and struck again;
he felt his shoulder galled on the left side
hugging the glittering shield—and yet they could not
shake it, putting all their weight in throws.
In painful gasps his breath came, sweat ran down
in rivers off his body everywhere; 130
no rest for him, but trouble upon trouble.

Now tell me, Muses, dwellers on Olympos,
how fire first fell on the Akhaian ships!
Hektor moved in to slash with his long blade
at Aías' ashwood shaft, and near the spearhead
lopped it off. Then Telamônian Aías
wielded a pointless shaft, while far away
the flying bronze head rang upon the ground,
and Aías shivered knowing in his heart
the work of gods: how Zeus, the lord of thunder, 140
cut off his war-craft in that fight, and willed
victory to the Trojans. He gave way
before their missiles as they rushed in throwing
untiring fire into the ship. It caught
at once, a-gush with flame, and fire lapped
about the stern.
                              Akhilleus smote his thighs
and said to Patróklos:

[5] To the city of Troy itself.
[6] Aías is aboard one of the beached ships, using a long spear to ward off attackers.

"Now go into action,
prince and horseman! I see roaring fire
burst at the ships. Action, or they'll destroy them,
leaving no means of getting home. Be quick,   150
strap on my gear, while I alert the troops!"

Patróklos now put on the flashing bronze.
Greaves were the first thing, beautifully fitted
to calf and shin with silver ankle chains,
and next he buckled round his ribs the cuirass,
blazoned with stars, of swift Aiákidês;[7]
then slung the silver-studded blade of bronze
about his shoulders, and the vast solid shield;
then on his noble head he placed the helm,
its plume of terror nodding high above,   160
and took two burly spears with his own handgrip.
He did not take the great spear of Akhilleus,
weighty, long, and tough. No other Akhaian
had the strength to wield it, only Akhilleus.
It was a Pêlian ash, cut on the crest
of Pêlion, given to Akhilleus' father
by Kheirôn[8] to deal death to soldiery.
He then ordered his war-team put in harness
by Automédôn,[9] whom he most admired
after Prince Akhilleus, breaker of men,   170
for waiting steadfast at his call in battle.
Automédôn yoked the fast horses for him—
Xánthos and Balíos, racers in wind.
The stormgust Podargê, who once had grazed
green meadowland by the Ocean stream, conceived
and bore them to the west wind, Zephyros.
In the side-traces Pêdasos, a thoroughbred,
was added to the team; Akhilleus took him
when he destroyed the city of Eëtíôn.
Mortal, he ran beside immortal horses.   180
Akhilleus put the Myrmidons in arms,
the whole detachment near the huts. Like wolves,
carnivorous and fierce and tireless,
who rend a great stag on a mountainside
and feed on him, their jaws reddened with blood,
loping in a pack to drink springwater,
lapping the dark rim up with slender tongues,
their chops a-drip with fresh blood, their hearts
unshaken ever, and their bellies glutted:
such were the Myrmidons and their officers,   190

---

[7]Akhilleus' father, Pêleus (son of Aíakos).
[8]A centaur who had tutored Akhilleus; also spelled *Chiron*.
[9]When Patróklos assumes command, his normal post as charioteer is assumed by
Automédôn, the third-ranking among Akhilleus' Myrmidons.

running to form up round Akhilleus' brave
companion-in-arms.

And like the god of war
among them was Akhilleus: he stood tall
and sped the chariots and shieldmen onward.

Fifty ships there were that Lord Akhilleus,
favored of heaven, led to Troy. In each
were fifty soldiers, shipmates at the rowlocks.
Five he entrusted with command and made
lieutenants, while he ruled them all as king.
One company was headed by Menésthios   200
in his glittering breastplate, son of Spérkheios,
a river fed by heaven. Pêleus' daughter,
beautiful Polydôrê, had conceived him
lying with Spérkheios, untiring stream,
a woman with a god; but the world thought
she bore her child to Periêrês' son,
Bôros, who married her in the eyes of men
and offered countless bridal gifts. A second
company was commanded by Eudôros,
whose mother was unmarried: Polymêlê,   210
Phylas' daughter, a beautiful dancer
with whom the strong god Hermês fell in love,
seeing her among singing girls who moved
in measure for the lady of belling hounds,
Artemis of the golden shaft. And Hermês,
pure Deliverer, ascending soon
to an upper room, lay secretly with her
who was to bear his brilliant son, Eudôros,
a first-rate man at running and in war.
When Eileithyía,[10] sending pangs of labor,   220
brought him forth to see the sun-rays, then
strong-minded Ekheklêos, Aktor's son,
led the girl home with countless bridal gifts;
but Phylas in his age brought up the boy
with all kind care, as though he were a son.
Company three was led by Peísandros
Maimálidês, the best man with a spear,
of all Myrmidons after Patróklos.
Company four the old man, master of horse,
Phoinix, commanded. Alkimédôn, son   230
of Laërkês, commanded company five.
When all were mustered under their officers,
Akhilleus had strict orders to impart:

"Myrmidons, let not one man forget
how menacing you were against the Trojans

[10]Goddess of childbirth.

during my anger and seclusion: how
each one reproached me, saying, 'Ironhearted
son of Pêleus, now we see: your mother
brought you up on rage, merciless man,
the way you keep your men confined to camp   240
against their will! We might as well sail home
in our seagoing ships, now this infernal
anger has come over you!' That way
you often talked, in groups around our fires.
Now the great task of battle is at hand
that you were longing for! Now every soldier
keep a fighting heart and face the Trojans!"

He stirred and braced their spirit; every rank
fell in more sharply when it heard its king.
As when a builder fitting stone on stone   250
lays well a high house wall to buffet back
the might of winds, just so
they fitted helms and studded shields together:
shield-rim on shield-rim, helmet on helmet, men
all pressed on one another, horsehair plumes
brushed on the bright crests as the soldiers nodded,
densely packed as they were.

                                                            Before them all
two captains stood in gear of war: Patróklos
and Automédôn, of one mind, resolved
to open combat in the lead.

                                                            Akhilleus   260

went to his hut. He lifted up the lid
of a seachest, all intricately wrought,
that Thetis of the silver feet had stowed
aboard his ship for him to take to Ilion,
filled to the brim with shirts, wind-breaking cloaks,
and fleecy rugs. His hammered cup was there,
from which no other man drank the bright wine,
and he made offering to no god but Zeus.
Lifting it from the chest, he purified it
first with brimstone,[11] washed it with clear water,   270
and washed his hands, then dipped it full of wine.
Now standing in the forecourt, looking up
toward heaven, he prayed and poured his offering out,
and Zeus who plays in thunder heard his prayer:

"Zeus of Dôdôna,[12] god of Pelasgians,
O god whose home lies far! Ruler of wintry
harsh Dôdôna! Your interpreters,

---

[11]Sulfur.
[12]A shrine of Zeus near Akhilleus' homeland, supervised by the Selloi, primitive people
who interpreted the god's oracles.

the Selloi, live with feet like roots, unwashed,
and sleep on the hard ground. My lord, you heard me
praying before this, and honored me 280
by punishing the Akhaian army. Now,
again, accomplish what I most desire.
I shall stay on the beach, behind the ships,
but send my dear friend with a mass of soldiers,
Myrmidons, into combat. Let your glory,
Zeus who view the wide world, go beside him.
Sir, exalt his heart,
so Hektor too may see whether my friend
can only fight when I am in the field,
or whether singlehanded he can scatter them 290
before his fury! When he has thrown back
their shouting onslaught from the ships, then let him
return unhurt to the shipways and to me,
his gear intact, with all his fighting men."

That was his prayer, and Zeus who views the wide world
heard him. Part he granted, part denied:
he let Patróklos push the heavy fighting
back from the ships, but would not let him come
unscathed from battle.

Now, after Akhilleus

had made his prayer and offering to Zeus, 300
he entered his hut again, restored the cup
to his seachest, and took his place outside—
desiring still to watch the savage combat
of Trojans and Akhaians. Brave Patróklos'
men moved forward with high hearts until
they charged the Trojans—Myrmidons in waves,
like hornets that small boys, as boys will do,
the idiots, poke up with constant teasing
in their daub chambers on the road,
to give everyone trouble. If some traveler 310
who passes unaware should then excite them,
all the swarm comes raging out
to defend their young. So hot, so angrily
the Myrmidons came pouring from the ships
in a quenchless din of shouting. And Patróklos
cried above them all:

"O Myrmidons,

brothers-in-arms of Pêleus' son, Akhilleus,
fight like men, dear friends, remember courage,
let us win honor for the son of Pêleus!
He is the greatest captain on the beach, 320
his officers and soldiers are the bravest!
Let King Agamémnon learn his folly
in holding cheap the best of the Akhaians!"

Shouting so, he stirred their hearts. They fell
as one man on the Trojans, and the ships
around them echoed the onrush and the cries.
On seeing Menoitios' powerful son, and with him
Automédôn, aflash with brazen gear,
the Trojan ranks broke, and they caught their breath,
imagining that Akhilleus the swift fighter   330
had put aside his wrath for friendship's sake.
Now each man kept an eye out for retreat
from sudden death. Patróklos drove ahead
against their center with his shining spear,
into the huddling mass, around the stern
of Prôtesílaos' burning ship. He hit
Pyraikhmês, who had led the Paiônês
from Amydôn, from Áxios' wide river—
hit him in the right shoulder. Backward in dust
he tumbled groaning, and his men at-arms,   340
the Paiônês, fell back around him. Dealing
death to a chief and champion, Patróklos
drove them in confusion from the ship,
and doused the tigerish fire. The hull half-burnt
lay smoking on the shipway. Now the Trojans
wlth a great outcry streamed away; Danáäns
poured along the curved ships, and the din
of war kept on. As when the lightning master,
Zeus, removes a dense cloud from the peak
of some great mountain, and the lookout points   350
and spurs and clearings are distinctly seen
as though pure space had broken through from heaven:
so when the dangerous fire had been repelled
Danáäns took breath for a space. The battle
had not ended, though; not yet were Trojans
put to rout by the Akhaian charge
or out of range of the black ships. They withdrew
but by regrouping tried to make a stand.
                                                                In broken
ranks the captains sought and killed each other,
Menoitios' son making the first kill.   360
As Arêilykos wheeled around to fight,
he caught him with his spearhead in the hip,
and drove the bronze through, shattering the bone.
He sprawled face downward on the ground.
                                                                Now veteran
Meneláos thrusting past the shield
of Thoas to the bare chest brought him down.[13]
Rushed by Ámphiklos, the alert Mégês
got his thrust in first, hitting his thigh

[13] The victors in lines 365–409 are all Greeks.

where a man's muscles bunch. Around the spearhead
tendons were split, and darkness veiled his eyes. 370
Nestor's sons were in action: Antílokhos
with his good spear brought down Atýmnios,
laying open his flank; he fell headfirst.
Now Maris moved in, raging for his brother,
lunging over the dead man with his spear,
but Thrasymêdês had already lunged
and did not miss, but smashed his shoulder squarely,
tearing his upper arm out of the socket,
severing muscles, breaking through the bone.
He thudded down and darkness veiled his eyes. 380
So these two, overcome by the two brothers,[14]
dropped to the underworld of Érebos.
They were Sarpêdôn's true brothers-in-arms
and sons of Amisôdaros, who reared
the fierce Khimaira,[15] nightmare to many men.
Aías,[16] Oïleus' son, drove at Kleóboulos
and took him alive, encumbered in the press,
but killed him on the spot with a sword stroke
across the nape—the whole blade running hot
with blood, as welling death and his harsh destiny 390
possessed him. Now Pênéleos
and Lykôn clashed; as both had cast and missed
and lunged and missed with spears,
they fought again with swords. The stroke of Lykôn
came down on the other's helmet ridge
but his blade broke at the hilt. Pênéleos
thrust at his neck below the ear and drove
the blade clear in and through; his head toppled,
held only by skin, and his knees gave way.
Meríonês on the run overtook Akámas 400
mounting behind his horses and hit his shoulder,
knocking him from the car. Mist swathed his eyes.
Idómeneus thrust hard at Erýmas' mouth
with his hard bronze. The spearhead passed on through
beneath his brain and split the white brain-pan.
His teeth were dashed out, blood filled both his eyes,
and from his mouth and nostrils as he gaped
he spurted blood. Death's cloud enveloped him.
There each Danáän captain killed his man.
As ravenous wolves come down on lambs and kids 410
astray from some flock that in hilly country
splits in two by a shepherd's negligence,
and quickly wolves bear off the defenseless things,

---

[14]Antílokhos and Thrasymêdês, the sons of Nestor.
[15]In fable, the Khimaira (or Chimera) was a monster having a lion's head, a goat's body, and a dragon's tail.
[16]This is the "lesser" Aías.

so when Danáäns fell on Trojans, shrieking
flight was all they thought of, not of combat.
Aías the Tall[17] kept after bronze-helmed Hektor,
casting his lance, but Hektor, skilled in war,
would fit his shoulders under the bull's-hide shield,
and watch for whizzing arrows, thudding spears.
Aye, though he knew the tide of battle turned,   420
he kept his discipline and saved his friends.
As when Lord Zeus would hang the sky with storm,
a cloud may enter heaven from Olympos
out of crystalline space, so terror and cries
increased about the shipways. In disorder
men withdrew. Then Hektor's chariot team
cantering bore him off with all his gear,
leaving the Trojans whom the moat confined;
and many chariot horses in that ditch,
breaking their poles off at the tip, abandoned   430
war-cars and masters. Hard on their heels
Patróklos kept on calling all Danáäns
onward with slaughter in his heart. The Trojans,
yelling and clattering, filled all the ways,
their companies cut in pieces. High in air
a blast of wind swept on, under the clouds,
as chariot horses raced back toward the town
away from the encampment. And Patróklos
rode shouting where he saw the enemy mass
in uproar: men fell from their chariots   440
under the wheels and cars jounced over them,
and running horses leapt over the ditch—
immortal horses, whom the gods gave Pêleus,
galloping as their mettle called them onward
after Hektor, target of Patróklos.
But Hektor's battle-team bore him away.

As under a great storm black earth is drenched
on an autumn day, when Zeus pours down the rain
in scudding gusts to punish men, annoyed
because they will enforce their crooked judgments   450
and banish justice from the market place,
thoughtless of the gods' vengeance; all their streams
run high and full, and torrents cut their way
down dry declivities into the swollen sea
with a hoarse clamor, headlong out of hills,
while cultivated fields erode away—
such was the gasping flight of the Trojan horses.

---

[17] The "greater" Aías.

When he had cut their first wave off, Patróklos
forced it back again upon the ships
as the men fought toward the city. In between   460
the ships and river and the parapet[18]
he swept among them killing, taking toll
for many dead Akhaians. First,
thrusting past Prónoös' shield, he hit him
on the bare chest, and made him crumple: down
he tumbled with a crash. Then he rushed Thestôr,
Enop's son, who sat all doubled up
in a polished war-car, shocked out of his wits,
the reins flown from his hands—and the Akhaian
got home his thrust on the right jawbone, driving   470
through his teeth. He hooked him by the spearhead
over the chariot rail, as a fisherman
on a point of rock will hook a splendid fish
with line and dazzling bronze out of the ocean:
so from his chariot on the shining spear
he hooked him gaping and face downward threw him,
life going out of him as he fell.
                                                        Patróklos
now met Erýlaos' rush and hit him square
mid-skull with a big stone. Within his helm
the skull was cleft asunder, and down he went   480
headfirst to earth; heartbreaking death engulfed him.
Next Erýmas, Amphóteros, Epaltês,
Tlêpolemos Damastoridês, Ekhíos,
Pyris, Ipheus, Euíppos, Polymêlos,
all in quick succession he brought down
to the once peaceful pastureland.
                                                        Sarpêdôn,
seeing his brothers-in-arms in their unbelted
battle jackets downed at Patróklos' hands,
called in bitterness to the Lykians:[19]

"Shame, O Lykians, where are you running?   490
Now you show your speed!
                            I'll take on this one,
and learn what man he is that has the power
to do such havoc as he has done among us,
cutting down so many, and such good men."

He vaulted from his car with all his gear,
and on his side Patróklos, when he saw him,
leapt from his car. Like two great birds of prey
with hooked talons and angled beaks, who screech
and clash on a high ridge of rock, these two

---

[18] The wall of Troy. The river Skamánder, also called Xánthos, flows by the plain.
[19] Lykia, of which Sarpêdôn is king, is a region about two hundred miles southeast of Troy.

rushed one another with hoarse cries. But Zeus,   500
the son of crooked-minded Krónos, watched,
and pitied them. He said to Hêra:

                                                                        "Ai!
Sorrow for me, that in the scheme of things
the dearest of men to me must lie in dust
before the son of Menoitios, Patróklos.
My heart goes two ways as I ponder this:
shall I catch up Sarpêdôn
out of the mortal fight with all its woe
and put him down alive in Lykia,
in that rich land? Or shall I make him fall   510
beneath Patróklos' hard-thrown spear?"
                                                        Then Hêra
of the wide eyes answered him:

                                                "O fearsome power,
my Lord Zeus, what a curious thing to say.
A man who is born to die, long destined for it,
would you set free from that unspeakable end?
Do so; but not all of us will praise you.
And this, too, I may tell you: ponder this:
should you dispatch Sarpêdôn home alive,
anticipate some other god's desire
to pluck a man he loves out of the battle.   520
Many who fight around the town of Priam
sprang from immortals; you'll infuriate these.
No, dear to you though he is, and though you mourn him,
let him fall, even so, in the rough battle,
killed by the son of Menoitios, Patróklos.
Afterward, when his soul is gone, his lifetime
ended, Death and sweetest Sleep can bear him
homeward to the broad domain of Lykia.
There friends and kin may give him funeral
with tomb and stone, the trophies of the dead."   530

To this the father of gods and men agreed,
but showered bloody drops upon the earth
for the dear son Patróklos would destroy
in fertile Ilion, far from his home.
When the two men had come in range, Patróklos
turned like lightning against Thrasydêmos,
a tough man ever at Sarpêdôn's side,
and gave him a death-wound in the underbelly.
Sarpêdôn's counterthrust went wide, but hit
the trace horse, Pêdasos, in the right shoulder.[20]   540
Screaming harshly, panting his life away,

[20] Pêdasos is the third, auxiliary horse harnessed with Akhilleus' two immortal horses.

he crashed and whinnied in the dust; the spirit
left him with a wingbeat. The team shied
and strained apart with a great creak of the yoke
as reins were tangled over the dead weight
of their outrider fallen. Automédôn,
the good soldier, found a way to end it:
pulling his long blade from his hip
he jumped in fast and cut the trace horse free.
The team then ranged themselves beside the pole, 550
drawing the reins taut, and once more,
devoured by fighting madness, the two men clashed.
Sarpêdôn missed again. He drove his spearhead
over the left shoulder of Patróklos,
not even grazing him. Patróklos then
made his last throw, and the weapon left his hand
with flawless aim. He hit his enemy
just where the muscles of the diaphragm
encased his throbbing heart. Sarpêdôn fell
the way an oak or poplar or tall pine 560
goes down, when shipwrights in the wooded hills
with whetted axes chop it down for timber.
So, full length, before his war-car lay
Sarpêdôn raging, clutching the bloody dust.
Imagine a greathearted sultry bull
a lion kills amid a shambling herd:
with choking groans he dies under the claws.
So, mortally wounded by Patróklos
the chief of Lykian shieldsmen lay in agony
and called his friend by name:

                                              "Glaukos, old man, 570
old war-dog, now's the time to be a spearman!
Put your heart in combat! Let grim war
be all your longing! Quickly, if you can,
arouse the Lykian captains, round them up
to fight over Sarpêdôn. You, too, fight
to keep my body, else in later days
this day will be your shame.[21] You'll hang your head
all your life long, if these Akhaians take
my armor here, where I have gone down fighting
before the ships. Hold hard; cheer on the troops!" 580

The end of life came on him as he spoke,
closing his eyes and nostrils. And Patróklos
with one foot on his chest drew from his belly
spearhead and spear; the diaphragm came out,
so he extracted life and blade together.

---

[21] Proper funeral rites were essential for the honor of the dead man and for his well-being
after death—an important theme in the poem.

Myrmidons clung to the panting Lykian horses,
rearing to turn the car left by their lords.

But bitter anguish at Sarpêdôn's voice
had come to Glaukos, and his heart despaired
because he had not helped his friend. He gripped   590
his own right arm and squeezed it, being numb
where Teukros with a bowshot from the rampart
had hit him while he fought for his own men,[22]
and he spoke out in prayer to Lord Apollo:

"Hear me, O lord, somewhere in Lykian farmland
or else in Troy: for you have power to listen
the whole world round to a man hard pressed as I!
I have my sore wound, all my length of arm
a-throb with lancing pain; the flow of blood
cannot be stanched; my shoulder's heavy with it.   600
I cannot hold my spear right or do battle,
cannot attack them. Here's a great man destroyed,
Sarpêdôn, son of Zeus. Zeus let his own son
die undefended. O my lord, heal this wound,
lull me my pains, put vigor in me! Let me
shout to my Lykians, move them into combat!
Let me give battle for the dead man here!"

This way he prayed, and Phoibos Apollo heard him,
cutting his pain and making the dark blood dry
on his deep wound, then filled his heart with valor.   610
Glaukos felt the change, and knew with joy
how swiftly the great god had heard his prayer.
First he appealed to the Lykian captains, going
right and left, to defend Sarpêdôn's body,
then on the run he followed other Trojans,
Poulýdamas, Pánthoös' son, Agênor,
and caught up with Aineías and with Hektor,
shoulder to shoulder, urgently appealing:

"Hektor, you've put your allies out of mind,
those men who give their lives here for your sake   620
so distant from their friends and lands: you will not
come to their aid! Sarpêdôn lies there dead,
commander of the Lykians, who kept
his country safe by his firm hand, in justice!
Arês in bronze has brought him down: the spear
belonged to Patróklos. Come, stand with me, friends,
and count it shame if they strip off his gear
or bring dishonor on his body—these

---

[22] Teukros had wounded Glaukos in Book XII.

fresh Myrmidons enraged for the Danääns
cut down at the shipways by our spears!"   630

At this, grief and remorse possessed the Trojans,
grief not to be borne, because Sarpêdôn
had been a bastion of the town of Troy,
foreigner though he was. A host came with him,
but he had fought most gallantly of all.
They made straight for the Danääns, and Hektor
led them, hot with anger for Sarpêdôn.
Patróklos in his savagery cheered on
the Akhaians, first the two named Aías, both
already aflame for war:

                                        "Aías and Aías,   640
let it be sweet to you to stand and fight!
You always do; be lionhearted, now.
The man who crossed the rampart of Akhaians
first of all lies dead: Sarpêdôn.[23] May we
take him, dishonor him, and strip his arms,
and hurl any friend who would defend him
into the dust with our hard bronze!"

At this they burned to throw the Trojans back.
And both sides reinforced their battle lines,
Trojans and Lykians, Myrmidons and Akhaians,   650
moving up to fight around the dead
with fierce cries and clanging of men's armor.
Zeus unfurled a deathly gloom of night
over the combat, making battle toil
about his dear son's body a fearsome thing.
At first, the Trojans drove back the Akhaians,
fiery-eyed as they were; one Myrmidon,
and not the least, was killed: noble Epeigeus,
a son of Agaklês. In Boudeion,
a flourishing town, he ruled before the war.   660
but slew a kinsman. So he came as suppliant
to Pêleus and to Thetis, who enlisted him
along with Lord Akhilleus, breaker of men,
to make war in the wild-horse country of Ilion
against the Trojans. Even as he touched the dead man,
Hektor hit him square upon the crest
with a great stone: his skull split in the helmet,
and he fell prone upon the corpse. Death's cloud
poured round him, heart-corroding. Grief and pain
for this friend dying came to Lord Patróklos,   670
who pounced through spear-play like a diving hawk

---

[23] The reference is to Book XII; it was actually Hektor who first broke through the defensive wall around the ships, though Sarpêdôn had threatened and damaged it.

that puts jackdaws and starlings wildly to flight:
straight through Lykians, through Trojans, too,
you drove, Patróklos, master of horse,
in fury for your friend. Sthenélaos
the son of Ithaiménês was the victim:
Patróklos with a great stone broke his nape-cord.

Backward the line bent, Hektor too gave way,
as far as a hunting spear may hurtle, thrown
by a man in practice or in competition   680
or matched with deadly foes in war. So far
the Trojans ebbed, as the Akhaians drove them.
Glaukos, commander of Lykians, turned first,
to bring down valorous Báthyklês, the son
of Khalkôn, one who had his home in Hellas,
fortunate and rich among the Myrmidons.
Whirling as this man caught him, Glaukos hit him
full in the breastbone with his spear, and down
he thudded on his face. The Akhaians grieved
to see their champion fallen, but great joy   690
came to the Trojans, and they thronged about him.
Not that Akhaians now forgot their courage,
no, for their momentum carried them on.
Meríonês brought down a Trojan soldier,
Laógonos, Onêtor's rugged son,
a priest of Zeus on Ida, honored there
as gods are. Gashed now under jaw and ear
his life ran out, and hateful darkness took him.
Then at Meríonês Aineías cast
his bronze-shod spear, thinking to reach his body   700
under the shield as he came on. But he
looked out for it and swerved, slipping the spear-throw,
bowing forward, so the long shaft stuck
in earth behind him and the butt quivered;
the god Arês deprived it of its power.
Aineías raged and sneered:

                                                        "Meríonês,
fast dodger that you are, if I had hit you
my spearhead would have stopped your dance for good!"

Meríonês, good spearman, answered him:

"For all your power, Aineías, you could hardly   710
quench the fighting spirit of every man
defending himself against you. You are made
of mortal stuff like me. I, too, can say,
if I could hit you square, then tough and sure
as you may be, you would concede the game
and give your soul to the lord of nightmare, Death."

Patróklos said to him sharply:

"Meríonês,
you have your skill, why make a speech about it?
No, old friend, rough words will make no Trojans
back away from the body. Many a one 720
will be embraced by earth before they do.
War is the use of arms, words are for council.
More talk's pointless now; we need more fighting!"

He pushed on, and godlike Meríonês
fought at his side. Think of the sound of strokes
woodcutters make in mountain glens, the echoes
ringing for listeners far away: just so
the battering din of these in combat rose
from earth where the living go their ways—the clang
of bronze, hard blows on leather, on bull's hide, 730
as longsword blades and spearheads met their marks.
And an observer could not by now have seen
the Prince Sarpêdôn, since from head to foot
he lay enwrapped in weapons, dust, and blood.
Men kept crowding around the corpse. Like flies
that swarm and drone in farmyards round the milkpails
on spring days, when the pails are splashed with milk:
just so they thronged around the corpse. And Zeus
would never turn his shining eyes away
from this mêlée, but watched them all and pondered 740
long over the slaughter of Patróklos—
whether in that place, on Sarpêdôn's body,
Hektor should kill the man and take his gear,
or whether he, Zeus, should augment the moil[24]
of battle for still other men. He weighed it
and thought this best: that for a while Akhilleus'
shining brother-in-arms should drive his foes
and Hektor in the bronze helm toward the city,
taking the lives of many. First of all
he weakened Hektor, made him mount his car 750
and turn away, retreating, crying out
to others to retreat: for he perceived
the dipping scales of Zeus.[25] At this the Lykians
themselves could not stand fast, but all turned back,
once they had seen their king struck to the heart,
lying amid swales of dead—for many
fell to earth beside him when Lord Zeus
had drawn the savage battle line. So now

[24] Turmoil.
[25] Zeus uses a balance scale to weigh alternative results of a conflict. The loser's side of the scale tips down, the winner's up.

Akhaians lifted from Sarpêdôn's shoulders
gleaming arms of bronze, and these Patróklos   760
gave to his soldiers to be carried back
to the decked ships. At this point, to Apollo
Zeus who gathers cloud said:

                                        "Come, dear Phoibos,
wipe away the blood mantling Sarpêdôn;
take him up, out of the play of spears,
a long way off, and wash him in the river,
anoint him with ambrosia, put ambrosial
clothing on him. Then have him conveyed
by those escorting spirits quick as wind,
sweet Sleep and Death, who are twin brothers. These   770
will set him down in the rich broad land of Lykia,
and there his kin and friends may bury him
with tomb and stone, the trophies of the dead."

Attentive to his father, Lord Apollo
went down the foothills of Ida[26] to the field
and lifted Prince Sarpêdôn clear of it.
He bore him far and bathed him in the river,
scented him with ambrosia, put ambrosial
clothing on him, then had him conveyed
by those escorting spirits quick as wind,   780
sweet Sleep and Death, who are twin brothers. These
returned him to the rich broad land of Lykia.

Patróklos, calling to his team, commanding
Automédôn, rode on after the Trojans
and Lykians—all this to his undoing,
the blunderer. By keeping Akhilleus' mandate,
he might have fled black fate and cruel death.
But overpowering is the mind of Zeus
forever, matched with man's. He turns in fright
the powerful man and robs him of his victory   790
easily, though he drove him on himself.
So now he stirred Patróklos' heart to fury.

Whom first, whom later did you kill in battle,
Patróklos, when the gods were calling deathward?
First it was Adrêstos, Autônoös,
and Ekheklos; then Périmos Megadês,
Eristôr, Melánippos; afterward,
Elasos, Moulios, Pylartês. These
he cut down, while the rest looked to their flight.
Troy of the towering gates was on the verge   800
of being taken by the Akhaians, under

---

[26]A mountain near Troy from whieh Zeus often observes the war.

Patróklos' drive: he raced with blooded spear
ahead and around it. On the massive tower
Phoibos Apollo stood as Troy's defender,
deadly toward him. Now three times Patróklos
assaulted the high wall at the tower joint,
and three times Lord Apollo threw him back
with counterblows of his immortal hands
against the resplendent shield. The Akhaian then
a fourth time flung himself against the wall,   810
more than human in fury. But Apollo
thundered:

                "Back, Patróklos, lordly man!
Destiny will not let this fortress town
of Trojans fall to you! Not to Akhilleus,
either, greater far though he is in war!"[27]

Patróklos now retired, a long way off
and out of range of Lord Apollo's anger.
Hektor had held his team at the Skaian Gates,
being of two minds: should he re-engage,
or call his troops to shelter behind the wall?   820
While he debated this, Phoibos Apollo
stood at his shoulder in a strong man's guise:
Ásïos, his maternal uncle, brother
of Hékabê and son of Dymas, dweller
in Phrygia on Sangaríos river.
Taking his semblance now, Apollo said:

"Why break off battle, Hektor? You need not.
Were I superior to you in the measure
that I am now inferior, you'd suffer
from turning back so wretchedly from battle.   830
Action! Lash your team against Patróklos,
and see if you can take him. May Apollo
grant you the glory!"

                And at this, once more
he joined the mêlée, entering it as a god.
Hektor in splendor called Kebríonês
to whip the horses toward the fight. Apollo,
disappearing into the ranks, aroused
confusion in the Argives, but on Hektor
and on the Trojans he conferred his glory.
Letting the rest go, Hektor drove his team   840
straight at Patróklos; and Patróklos faced him
vaulting from his war-car, with his spear
gripped in his left hand; in his right

[27]Akhilleus will be slain before the city is finally taken.

he held enfolded a sparkling jagged stone.
Not for long in awe of the other man,
he aimed and braced himself and threw the stone
and scored a direct hit on Hektor's driver,
Kebríonês, a bastard son of Priam,
smashing his forehead with the jagged stone.
Both brows were hit at once, the frontal bone   850
gave way, and both his eyes burst from their sockets
dropping into the dust before his feet,
as like a diver from the handsome car
he plummeted, and life ebbed from his bones.
You jeered at him then, master of horse, Patróklos:

"God, what a nimble fellow, somersaulting!
If he were out at sea in the fishing grounds
this man could feed a crew, diving for oysters,
going overboard even in rough water,
the way he took that earth-dive from his car.   860
The Trojans have their acrobats, I see."

With this, he went for the dead man with a spring
like a lion, one that has taken a chest wound
while ravaging a cattle pen—his valor
his undoing. So you sprang, Patróklos,
on Kebríonês. Then Hektor, too, leapt down
out of his chariot, and the two men fought
over the body like two mountain lions
over the carcass of a buck, both famished,
both in pride of combat. So these two   870
fought now for Kebríonês, two champions,
Patróklos son of Menoitios, and Hektor,
hurling their bronze to tear each other's flesh.
Hektor caught hold of the dead man's head and held,
while his antagonist clung to a single foot,
as Trojans and Danääns pressed the fight.
As south wind and the southeast wind, contending
in mountain groves, make all the forest thrash,
beech trees and ash trees and the slender cornel
swaying their pointed boughs toward one another   880
in roaring wind, and snapping branches crack:
so Trojans and Akhaians made a din
as lunging they destroyed each other. Neither
considered ruinous flight. Many sharp spears
and arrows trued by feathers from the strings
were fixed in flesh around Kebríonês,
and boulders crashed on shields, as they fought on
around him. And a dustcloud wrought
by a whirlwind hid the greatness of him slain,
minding no more the mastery of horses.   800
Until the sun stood at high noon in heaven

spears bit on both sides, and the soldiers fell;
but when the sun passed toward unyoking time,
the Akhaians outfought destiny to prevail.
Now they dragged off gallant Kebríonês
out of range, away from the shouting Trojans,
to strip his shoulders of his gear. And fierce
Patróklos hurled himself upon the Trojans
in onslaughts fast as Arês, three times, wild
yells in his throat. Each time he killed nine men.   900
But on the fourth demonic foray, then
the end of life loomed up for you, Patróklos.
Into the combat dangerous Phoibos came
against him, but Patróklos could not see
the god, enwrapped in cloud as he came near.
He stood behind and struck with open hand
the man's back and broad shoulders, and the eyes
of the fighting man were dizzied by the blow.
Then Phoibos sent the captain's helmet rolling
under the horses' hooves, making the ridge   910
ring out, and dirtying all the horsehair plume
with blood and dust. Never in time before
had this plumed helmet been befouled with dust,
the helmet that had kept a hero's brow
unmarred, shielding Akhilleus' head. Now Zeus
bestowed it upon Hektor, let him wear it,
though his destruction waited. For Patróklos
felt his great spearshaft shattered in his hands,
long, tough, well-shod, and seasoned though it was;
his shield and strap fell to the ground; the Lord   920
Apollo, son of Zeus, broke off his cuirass.
Shock ran through him, and his good legs failed,
so that he stood agape. Then from behind
at close quarters, between the shoulder blades,
a Dardan fighter speared him: Pánthoös' son,
Euphórbos, the best Trojan of his age
at handling spears, in horsemanship and running:
he had brought twenty chariot fighters down
since entering combat in his chariot,
already skilled in the craft of war. This man   930
was first to wound you with a spear, Patróklos,
but did not bring you down. Instead, he ran back
into the mêlée, pulling from the flesh
his ashen spear, and would not face his enemy,
even disarmed, in battle. Then Patróklos,
disabled by the god's blow and the spear wound,
moved back to save himself amid his men.
But Hektor, seeing that his brave adversary
tried to retire, hurt by the spear wound, charged
straight at him through the ranks and lunged for him   940
low in the flank, driving the spearhead through.

He crashed, and all Akhaian troops turned pale.
Think how a lion in his pride brings down
a tireless boar; magnificently they fight
on a mountain crest for a small gushing spring—
both in desire to drink—and by sheer power
the lion conquers the great panting boar:
that was the way the son of Priam, Hektor,
closed with Patróklos, son of Menoitios,
killer of many, and took his life away.   950
Then glorying above him he addressed him:

"Easy to guess, Patróklos, how you swore
to ravage Troy, to take the sweet daylight
of liberty from our women, and to drag them
off in ships to your own land—you fool!
Between you and those women there is Hektor's
war-team, thundering out to fight! My spear
has pride of place among the Trojan warriors,
keeping their evil hour at bay.
The kites[28] will feed on you, here on this field.   960
Poor devil, what has that great prince, Akhilleus,
done for you? He must have told you often
as you were leaving and he stayed behind,
'Never come back to me, to the deepsea ships,
Patróklos, till you cut to rags
the bloody tunic on the chest of Hektor!'
That must have been the way he talked, and won
your mind to mindlessness."

                                              In a low faint voice,
Patróklos, master of horse, you answered him:

"This is your hour to glory over me,   970
Hektor. The Lord Zeus and Apollo gave you
the upper hand and put me down with ease.
They stripped me of my arms. No one else did.
Say twenty men like you had come against me,
all would have died before my spear.
No, Lêto's son and fatal destiny
have killed me; if we speak of men, Euphórbos.
You were in third place, only in at the death.
I'll tell you one thing more; take it to heart.
No long life is ahead for you. This day   980
your death stands near, and your immutable end,
at Prince Akhilleus' hands."

                                              His own death
came on him as he spoke, and soul from body,
bemoaning severance from youth and manhood,

---

[28] Birds of prey.

slipped to be wafted to the underworld.
Even in death Prince Hektor still addressed him:

"Why prophesy my sudden death, Patróklos?
Who knows, Akhilleus, son of bright-haired Thetis,
might be hit first; he might be killed by me."

At this he pulled his spearhead from the wound,   990
setting his heel upon him; then he pushed him
over on his back, clear of the spear,
and lifting it at once sought Automédôn,
companion of the great runner, Akhilleus,
longing to strike him. But the immortal horses,
gift of the gods to Pêleus, bore him away.

from BOOK SEVENTEEN: CONTENDING FOR A SOLDIER FALLEN

Hektor has seized the armor of Akhilleus that the dead Patróklos had worn. A long
and bitter struggle ensues for possession of his body. The Greeks want to return it
to Akhilleus, the Trojans to desecrate it; moreover, Glaukos, mistakenly believing
that the Greeks now have the corpse of his dead comrade Sarpêdôn, hopes they
may trade it for the corpse of Patróklos. Meneláos defends Patróklos' body with the
help of the greater Aías and other warriors. Glaukos charges Hektor with cowardice;
Hektor, aroused, puts on the armor of Akhilleus/Patróklos (as Zeus predicts Hektor's
death) and leads his followers into the fight for the body. Aineías joins in. This part
of the battlefield has been shrouded in near-darkness by Zeus, though in other places
the sky is clear. Akhilleus is still unaware of his friend's death.

At the end of Book XVI Automédôn, charioteer for Patróklos, withdrew from
the battle along with Akhilleus' immortal horses. We see them again:

Out of range,
the horses of Akhilleus, from the time
they sensed their charioteer[1] downed in the dust   480
at the hands of deadly Hektor, had been weeping.
Automédôn, the son of Diorês,
laid often on their backs his flickering whip,
pled often in a low tone—or he swore at them—
but neither toward the shipways and the beach
by Hellê's waters would they budge, nor follow
Akhaians into battle. No: stock-still
as a gravestone, fixed above the tomb
of a dead man or woman, they stood fast,
holding the beautiful war-car still: their heads   490
curved over to the ground, and warm tears flowed

---

[1]Patróklos, who normally serves as charioteer (that is, when Akhilleus is in action).

from under eyelids earthward as they mourned
their longed-for driver. Manes along the yoke
were soiled as they hung forward under yokepads.
Seeing their tears flow, pitying them, Lord Zeus
bent his head and murmured in his heart:

"Poor things, why did I give you to King Pêleus,
a mortal, you who never age nor die,
to let you ache with men in their hard lot?
For of all creatures that breathe and move on earth   500
none is more to be pitied than a man.
Never at least shall Hektor, son of Priam,
ride behind you in your painted car.
That I will not allow. Is it not enough
that he both has the gear and brags about it?
I shall put fire in your knees and hearts
to rescue Automédôn, bear him away
from battle to the decked ships. Glory of killing,
even so, I reserve to his enemies
until they reach the ships, until sundown,   510
until the dusk comes, full of stars."

BOOK XVII (continued). *Hektor and Aineías try to capture Akhilleus' horses but are driven back by the two Aíases. Zeus allows Athêna to encourage Meneláos; Apollo encourages Hektor once more. Zeus now gives victory to the Trojans. The greater Aías and Meneláos send a runner to Akhilleus with the news of Patróklos' death. With immense difficulty, and sustained by the two Aíases, the Greeks carry Patróklos' body to the rear as the triumphant Trojans advance again, led by Hektor and Aineías.*

BOOK EIGHTEEN: THE IMMORTAL SHIELD

While they were still in combat, fighting seaward
raggedly as fire, Antílokhos[1]
ran far ahead with tidings for Akhilleus.
In shelter of the curled, high prows he found him
envisioning what had come to pass,
in gloom and anger saying to himself:

"Ai! why are they turning tail once more,
unmanned, outfought, and driven from the field
back on the beach and ships? I pray the gods
this may not be the last twist of the knife!   10
My mother warned me once that, while I lived,
the most admirable of Myrmidons
would quit the sunlight under Trojan blows.
It could indeed be so. He has gone down,
my dear and wayward friend!

[1]Son of Nestor, sent in Book XVII to inform Akhilleus of Patróklos' death.

Push their deadly fire away, I told him,
then return! You must not fight with Hektor!"

And while he called it all to mind,
the son of gallant Nestor came up weeping
to give his cruel news:

                       "Here's desolation,   20
son of Pêleus, the worst news for you—
would god it had not happened!—Lord Patróklos
fell, and they are fighting over his body,
stripped of armor. Hektor has your gear."

A black stormcloud of pain shrouded Akhilleus.
On his bowed head he scattered dust and ash
in handfuls and befouled his beautiful face,
letting black ash sift on his fragrant khiton.[2]
Then in the dust he stretched his giant length
and tore his hair with both hands.

                          From the hut   30
the women who had been spoils of war to him
and to Patróklos flocked in haste around him,
crying loud in grief. All beat their breasts,
and trembling came upon their knees.

                          Antílokhos
wept where he stood, bending to hold the hero's
hands when groaning shook his heart: he feared
the man might use sharp iron to slash his throat.
And now Akhilleus gave a dreadful cry.

                          Her ladyship
his mother heard him, in the depths offshore
lolling near her ancient father.[3] Nymphs   40
were gathered round her: all Nêrêïdês
who haunted the green chambers of the sea.
Glaukê, Thaleia, and Kymodokê,
Nesaiê, Speiô, Thoê, Haliê
with her wide eyes; Kymothoê, Aktaiê,
Limnôreia, Melitê, and Iaira,
Amphitoê, Agauê, Dôtô, Prôtô,
Pherousa, Dynaménê, Dexaménê,
Amphinomê, Kallianeira, Dôris,
Panopê, and storied Galateia,   50
Nêmertês and Apseudês, Kallianassa,
Klyméne, Ianeira, Ianassa,
Maira, Oreithyia, Amathyia,
and other Nêrêïdês of the deep sea,

---

[2]A loose, knee-length garment.
[3]Nêreus, a sea-god.

filling her glimmering silvery cave. All these
now beat their breasts as Thetis cried in sorrow:

"Sisters, daughters of Nêreus, hear and know
how sore my heart is! Now my life is pain
for my great son's dark destiny! I bore
a child flawless and strong beyond all men. 60
He flourished like a green shoot, and I brought him
to manhood like a blossoming orchard tree,
only to send him in the ships to Ilion
to war with Trojans. Now I shall never see him
entering Pêleus' hall, his home, again.
But even while he lives, beholding sunlight,
suffering is his lot. I have no power
to help him, though I go to him. Even so,
I'll visit my dear child and learn what sorrow
came to him while he held aloof from war." 70

On this she left the cave, and all in tears
her company swam aloft with her. Around them
a billow broke and foamed on the open sea.
As they made land at the fertile plain of Troy,
they went up one by one in line to where,
in close order, Myrmidon ships were beached
to right and left of Akhilleus. Bending near
her groaning son, the gentle goddess wailed
and took his head between her hands in pity,
saying softly:

       "Child, why are you weeping? 80
What great sorrow came to you? Speak out,
do not conceal it. Zeus
did all you asked: Akhaian troops,
for want of you, were all forced back again
upon the ship sterns, taking heavy losses
none of them could wish."

        The great runner
groaned and answered:

       "Mother, yes, the master
of high Olympos brought it all about,
but how have I benefited? My greatest friend
is gone: Patróklos, comrade in arms, whom I 90
held dear above all others—dear as myself—
now gone, lost; Hektor cut him down, despoiled him
of my own arms, massive and fine, a wonder
in all men's eyes. The gods gave them to Pêleus
that day they put you in a mortal's bed—
how I wish the immortals of the sea
had been your only consorts! How I wish
Pêleus had taken a mortal queen! Sorrow

immeasurable is in store for you as well,
when your own child is lost: never again 100
on his homecoming day will you embrace him!
I must reject this life, my heart tells me,
reject the world of men,
if Hektor does not feel my battering spear
tear the life out of him, making him pay
in his own blood for the slaughter of Patróklos!"

Letting a tear fall, Thetis said:

"You'll be
swift to meet your end, child, as you say:
your doom comes close on the heels of Hektor's own."

Akhilleus the great runner ground his teeth 110
and said:

"May it come quickly. As things were,
I could not help my friend in his extremity.
Far from his home he died; he needed me
to shield him or to parry the death stroke.
For me there's no return to my own country.
Not the slightest gleam of hope did I
afford Patróklos or the other men
whom Hektor overpowered. Here I sat,
my weight a useless burden to the earth,
and I am one who has no peer in war 120
among Akhaian captains—

though in council
there are wiser. Ai! let strife and rancor
perish from the lives of gods and men,
with anger that envenoms even the wise
and is far sweeter than slow-dripping honey,
clouding the hearts of men like smoke: just so
the marshal of the army, Agamémnon,
moved me to anger. But we'll let that go,
though I'm still sore at heart; it is all past,
and I have quelled my passion as I must. 130

Now I must go to look for the destroyer
of my great friend. I shall confront the dark
drear spirit of death at any hour Zeus
and the other gods may wish to make an end.
Not even Hêraklês[4] escaped that terror
though cherished by the Lord Zeus. Destiny
and Hêra's bitter anger mastered him.
Likewise with me, if destiny like his
awaits me, I shall rest when I have fallen!

[4]In myth, Hêraklês (Hercules) was a great Greek hero, a kind of superman. In some versions he was deified at the end of his life.

Now, though, may I win my perfect glory   140
and make some wife of Troy break down,
or some deep-breasted Dardan[5] woman sob
and wipe tears from her soft cheeks. They'll know then
how long they had been spared the deaths of men,
while I abstained from war!
Do not attempt to keep me from the fight,
though you love me; you cannot make me listen."

Thetis, goddess of the silvery feet,
answered:

                                        "Yes, of course, child: very true.
You do no wrong to fight for tired soldiers   150
and keep them from defeat. But still, your gear,
all shining bronze, remains in Trojan hands.
Hektor himself is armed with it in pride!—
Not that he'll glory in it long, I know,
for violent death is near him.

                                        Patience, then.
Better not plunge into the moil of Arês
until you see me here once more. At dawn,
at sunrise, I shall come
with splendid arms for you from Lord Hêphaistos."

She rose at this and, turning from her son,   160
told her sister Nêrêïdês:

                                                          "Go down

into the cool broad body of the sea
to the sea's Ancient; visit Father's hall,
and make all known to him. Meanwhile, I'll visit
Olympos' great height and the lord of crafts,
Hêphaistos, hoping he will give me
new and shining armor for my son."

At this they vanished in the offshore swell,
and to Olympos Thetis the silvery-footed
went once more, to fetch for her dear son   170
new-forged and finer arms.
                                        Meanwhile, Akhaians,
wildly crying, pressed by deadly Hektor,
reached the ships, beached above Hellê's water.
None had been able to pull Patróklos clear
of spear- and swordplay: troops and chariots
and Hektor, son of Priam, strong as fire,
once more gained upon the body. Hektor
three times had the feet within his grasp

---

[5]From the vicinity of Troy.

and strove to wrest Patróklos backward, shouting
to all the Trojans—but three times the pair 180
named Aías in their valor shook him off.
Still he pushed on, sure of his own power,
sometimes lunging through the battle-din,
or holding fast with a great shout: not one step
would he give way. As from a fresh carcass
herdsmen in the wilds cannot dislodge
a tawny lion, famished: so those two
with fearsome crests could not affright the son
of Priam or repel him from the body.
He might have won it, might have won unending 190
glory, but Iris running on the wind
came from Olympos to the son of Pêleus,
bidding him gird for battle. All unknown
to Zeus and the other gods she came, for Hêra
sent her down. And at his side she said:

"Up with you, Pêleidês, who strike cold fear
into men's blood! Protect your friend Patróklos,
for whom, beyond the ships, desperate combat
rages now. They are killing one another
on both sides: the Akhaians to defend him, 200
Trojans fighting for that prize
to drag to windy Ilion. And Hektor
burns to take it more than anyone—
to sever and impale Patróklos' head
on Trojan battlements. Lie here no longer.
It would be shameful if wild dogs of Troy
made him their plaything! If that body suffers
mutilation, you will be infamous!"

Prince Akhilleus answered:

                                        "Iris of heaven,
what immortal sent you to tell me this?" 210

And she who runs upon the wind replied:

"Hêra, illustrious wife of Zeus,
but he on his high throne knows nothing of it.
Neither does any one of the gods undying
who haunt Olympos of eternal snows."

Akhilleus asked:

                              "And now how shall I go
into the fighting? Those men have my gear.
My dear mother allows me no rearming
until I see her again here.
She promises fine arms from Lord Hêphaistos. 220
I don't know whose armor I can wear,

unless I take Aías' big shield.
But I feel sure he's in the thick of it,
contending with his spear over Patróklos."

Then she who runs upon the wind replied:

"We know they have your arms, and know it well.
Just as you are, then, stand at the moat; let Trojans
take that in; they will be so dismayed
they may break off the battle, and Akhaians
in their fatigue may win a breathing spell,   230
however brief, a respite from the war."

                                                                              At this,
Iris left him, running downwind. Akhilleus,
whom Zeus loved, now rose. Around his shoulders
Athêna hung her shield,[6] like a thunderhead
with trailing fringe. Goddess of goddesses,
she bound his head with golden cloud, and made
his very body blaze with fiery light.
Imagine how the pyre of a burning town
will tower to heaven and be seen for miles
from the island under attack, while all day long   240
outside their town, in brutal combat, pikemen
suffer the wargod's winnowing; at sundown
flare on flare is lit, the signal fires
shoot up for other islanders to see,
that some relieving force in ships may come:
just so the baleful radiance from Akhilleus
lit the sky. Moving from parapet
to moat, without a nod for the Akhaians,
keeping clear, in deference to his mother,
he halted and gave tongue. Not far from him   250
Athêna shrieked. The great sound shocked the Trojans
into tumult, as a trumpet blown
by a savage foe shocks an encircled town,
so harsh and clarion was Akhilleus' cry.
The hearts of men quailed, hearing that brazen voice.
Teams, foreknowing danger, turned their cars
and charioteers blanched, seeing unearthly fire,
kindled by the grey-eyed goddess Athêna,
brilliant over Akhilleus. Three great cries
he gave above the moat. Three times they shuddered,   260
whirling backward, Trojans and allies,
and twelve good men took mortal hurt
from cars and weapons in the rank behind.
Now the Akhaians leapt at the chance

---

[6] The aegis, a terror-inspiring shield given by Hêphaistos to Zeus and often used by Athêna.

to bear Patróklos' body out of range.
They placed it on his bed,
and old companions there with brimming eyes
surrounded him. Into their midst Akhilleus
came then, and he wept hot tears to see
his faithful friend, torn by the sharp spearhead, 270
lying cold upon his cot. Alas,
the man he sent to war with team and chariot
he could not welcome back alive.

                                             Her majesty,

wide-eyed Hêra, made the reluctant sun,
unwearied still, sink in the streams of Ocean.
Down he dropped, and the Akhaian soldiers
broke off combat, resting from the war.[7]
The Trojans, too, retired. Unharnessing
teams from war-cars, before making supper,
they came together on the assembly ground, 280
every man on his feet; not one could sit,
each being still in a tremor—for Akhilleus,
absent so long, had once again appeared.
Clearheaded Poulýdamas, son of Pánthoös,
spoke up first, as he alone could see
what lay ahead and all that lay behind.
He and Hektor were companions-in-arms,
born, as it happened, on the same night; but one
excelled in handling weapons, one with words.
Now for the good of all he spoke among them: 290

"Think well of our alternatives, my friends.
What I say is, retire upon the town,
instead of camping on the field till dawn
here by the ships. We are a long way
from our stone wall. As long as that man raged
at royal Agamémnon, we could fight
the Akhaians with advantage. I was happy
to spend last night so near the beach and think
of capturing ships today. Now, though, I fear
the son of Pêleus to my very marrow! 300
There are no bounds to the passion of that man.
He will not be contained by the flat ground
where Trojans and Akhaians share between them
raging war: he will strive on to fight
to win our town, our women. Back to Troy!
Believe me, this is what we face!
Now, starry night has made Akhilleus pause,
but when day comes, when he sorties in arms
to find us lingering here, there will be men
who learn too well what he is made of. Aye, 310

---

[7] This day's fighting had begun in Book XI.

I daresay those who get away will reach
walled Ilion thankfully, but dogs and kites
of Troy will feed on many. May that story
never reach my ears! If we can follow
my battle plan, though galled by it, tonight
we'll husband strength, at rest in the market place.
Towers, high gates, great doors of fitted planking,
bolted tight, will keep the town secure.
Early tomorrow we shall arm ourselves
and man the walls. Worse luck then for Akhilleus,   320
if he comes looking for a head-on fight
on the field around the wall! He can do nothing
but trot back, after all, to the encampment,
his proud team in a lather from their run,
from scouring every quarter below the town.
Rage as he will, he cannot force an entrance,
cannot take all Troy by storm. Wild dogs
will eat him first!"

                                    Under his shimmering helmet
Hektor glared at the speaker. Then he said:

"Poulýdamas, what you propose no longer   330
serves my turn. To go on the defensive
inside the town again? Is anyone
not sick of being huddled in those towers?
In past days men told tales of Priam's city,
rich in gold and rich in bronze, but now
those beautiful treasures of our home are lost.[8]
Many have gone for sale to Phrygia
and fair Mêïoniê, since Lord Zeus
grew hostile toward us.
                                    Now when the son of Krónos
Crooked Wit has given me a chance   340
of winning glory, pinning the Akhaians
back on the sea—now is no time to publish
notions like these to troops, you fool! No Trojan
goes along with you, I will not have it!
Come, let each man act as I propose.
Take your evening meal by companies;
remember sentries; keep good watch; and any
Trojan tired of his wealth, who wants
to lose everything, let him turn it over
to the army stores to be consumed in common!   350
Better our men enjoy it than Akhaians.
At first light we shall buckle armor on
and bring the ships under attack. Suppose
the man who stood astern there was indeed

---

[8] *treasures . . . are lost.* That is, sold to pay the expenses of the war.

Akhilleus, then worse luck for him,
if he will have it so. Shall I retreat
from him, from clash of combat? No, I will not.
Here I'll stand, though he should win; I might
just win, myself: the battle-god's impartial,
dealing death to the death-dealing man." 360

This was Hektor's speech. The Trojans roared
approval of it—fools, for Pallas Athêna
took away their wits. They all applauded
Hektor's poor tactics, but Poulýdamas
with his good judgment got not one assent.
They took their evening meal now, through the army,
while all night long Akhaians mourned Patróklos.

Akhilleus led them in their lamentation,
laying those hands deadly to enemies
upon the breast of his old friend, with groans 370
at every breath, bereft as a lioness
whose whelps a hunter seized out of a thicket;
late in returning, she will grieve, and roam
through many meandering valleys on his track
in hope of finding him; heart-stinging anger
carries her away. Now with a groan
he cried out to the Myrmidons:

                                 "Ah, god,
what empty prophecy I made that day
to cheer Menoitios in his mégaron!
I promised him his honored son, brought back 380
to Opoeis,[9] as pillager of Ilion
bearing his share of spoils,
But Zeus will not fulfill what men design,
not all of it. Both he and I were destined
to stain the same earth dark red here at Troy.
No going home for me; no welcome there
from Pêleus, master of horse, or from my mother,
Thetis. Here the earth will hold me under.
Therefore, as I must follow you into the grave,
I will not give you burial, Patróklos, 390
until I carry back the gear and head
of him who killed you, noble friend.
Before your funeral pyre I'll cut the throats
of twelve resplendent children of the Trojans—
that is my murdering fury at your death.
But while you lie here by the swanlike ships,
night and day, close by, deep-breasted women
of Troy, and Dardan women, must lament

---

[9] The home of Menoitios, Patróklos' father.

and weep hot tears, all those whom we acquired
by labor in assault, by the long spear,   400
pillaging the fat market towns of men."

With this Akhilleus called the company
to place over the campfire a big tripod
and bathe Patróklos of his clotted blood.
Setting tripod and caldron on the blaze
they poured it full, and fed the fire beneath,
and flames licked round the belly of the vessel
until the water warmed and bubbled up
in the bright bronze. They bathed him then, and took
sweet oil for his anointing, laying nard[10]   410
in the open wounds; and on his bed they placed him,
covering him with fine linen, head to foot,
and a white shroud over it.

                                               So all that night
beside Akhilleus the great runner,
the Myrmidons held mourning for Patróklos.
Now Zeus observed to Hêra, wife and sister:

"You had your way; my lady, after all,
my wide-eyed one! You brought him to his feet,
the great runner! One would say the Akhaian
gentlemen were progeny of yours."   420

And Hêra with wide eyes replied:

                                               "Dread majesty,
Lord Zeus, why do you take this tone? May not
an ordinary mortal have his way,
though death awaits him, and his mind is dim?
Would anyone suppose that I, who rank
in two respects highest of goddesses—
by birth[11] and by my station, queen to thee,
lord of all gods—that I should not devise
ill fortune for the Trojans whom I loathe?"

So ran their brief exchange. Meanwhile   430
the silvery-footed Thetis reached Hêphaistos'
lodging, indestructible and starry,
framed in bronze by the bandy-legged god.
She found him sweating, as from side to side
he plied his bellows; on his forge were twenty
tripods to be finished, then to stand
around his mégaron. And he wrought wheels
of gold for the base of each, that each might roll
as of itself into the gods' assembly,

---

[10] Balm made from the aromatic spikenard plant.
[11] Hêra and Zeus are both children of the former supreme deity, Krónos.

then roll home, a marvel to the eyes.   440
The caldrons were all shaped but had no handles.
These he applied now, hammering rivets in;
and as he toiled surehandedly at this,
Thetis arrived.

                          Grace in her shining veil
just going out encountered her—that Grace
the bowlegged god had taken to wife.[12] She greeted
Thetis with a warm handclasp and said:

"My lady Thetis, gracious goddess, what
has brought you here? You almost never honor us!
Please come in, and let me give you welcome."   450

Loveliest of goddesses, she led the way,
to seat her guest on a silver-studded chair,
elaborately fashioned, with a footrest.
Then she called to Hêphaistos:

                               "Come and see!
Thetis is here, in need of something from you!"

To this the Great Gamelegs replied:

"Ah, then we have a visitor I honor.
She was my savior, after the long fall
and fractures that I had to bear, when Mother,[13]
bitch that she is, wanted to hide her cripple.   460
That would have been a dangerous time, had not
Thetis and Eurýnomê[14] taken me in—
Eurýnomê, daughter of the tidal Ocean.
Nine years I stayed, and fashioned works of art,
brooches and spiral bracelets, necklaces,
in their smooth cave, round which the stream of Ocean
flows with a foaming roar: and no one else
knew of it, gods or mortals. Only Thetis
knew, and Eurýnomê, the two who saved me.
Now she has come to us. Well, what I owe   470
for life to her ladyship in her soft braids
I must repay. Serve her our choicest fare
while I put up my bellows and my tools."

At this he left the anvil block, and hobbled
with monstrous bulk on skinny legs to take
his bellows from the fire. Then all the tools
he had been toiling with he stowed
in a silver chest.

---

[12] Hêphaistos' wife is generally identified as Aphrodítê. Here she is identified as Grace, perhaps to indicate that metalworking entails not just strength but also elegant beauty.
[13] Hêra.   [14] Thetis' aunt.

That done, he sponged himself,
his face, both arms, bull-neck and hairy chest,
put on a tunic, took a weighty staff, 480
and limped out of his workshop. Round their lord
came fluttering maids of gold, like living girls:
intelligences, voices, power of motion
these maids have, and skills learnt from immortals.
Now they came rustling to support their lord,
and he moved on toward Thetis, where she sat
upon the silvery chair. He took her hand
and warmly said:

"My Lady Thetis, gracious
goddess, why have you come? You almost never honor us.
Tell me the favor that you have in mind, 490
for I desire to do it if I can,
and if it is a thing that one may do."

Thetis answered, tear on cheek:

"Hêphaístos,
who among all Olympian goddesses
endured anxiety and pain like mine?
Zeus chose me, from all of them, for this!
Of sea-nymphs I alone was given in thrall
to a mortal warrior, Pêleus Aiákidês,
and I endured a mortal warrior's bed
many a time, without desire. Now Pêleus 500
lies far gone in age in his great hall,
and I have other pain. Our son, bestowed
on me and nursed by me, became a hero
unsurpassed. He grew like a green shoot;
I cherished him like a flowering orchard tree,
only to send him in the ships to Ilion
to war with Trojans. Now I shall never see him
entering Pêleus' hall, his home, again.
But even while he lives, beholding sunlight,
suffering is his lot. I have no power 510
to help him, though I go to him. A girl,
his prize from the Akhaians, Agamémnon
took out of his hands to make his own,
and ah, he pined with burning heart! The Trojans
rolled the Akhaians back on the ship sterns,
and left them no escape. Then Argive officers
begged my son's help, offering every gift,
but he would not defend them from disaster.
Arming Patróklos in his own war-gear,
he sent him with his people into battle. 520
All day long, around the Skaian Gates,
they fought, and would have won the city, too,
had not Apollo, seeing the brave son

of Menoitios wreaking havoc on the Trojans,
killed him in action, and then given Hektor
the honor of that deed.

On this account

I am here to beg you: if you will, provide
for my doomed son a shield and crested helm,
good legging-greaves, fitted with ankle clasps,
a cuirass, too. His own armor was lost   530
when his great friend went down before the Trojans.
Now my son lies prone on the hard ground in grief."

The illustrious lame god replied:

"Take heart.

No trouble about the arms. I only wish
that I could hide him from the power of death
in his black hour—wish I were sure of that
as of the splendid gear he'll get, a wonder
to any one of the many men there are!"

He left her there, returning to his bellows,
training them on the fire, crying, "To work!"   540
In crucibles the twenty bellows breathed
every degree of fiery air: to serve him
a great blast when he labored might and main,
or a faint puff, according to his wish
and what the work demanded.

Durable

fine bronze and tin he threw into the blaze
with silver and with honorable gold,
then mounted a big anvil in his block
and in his right hand took a powerful hammer,
managing with his tongs in his left hand.   550

His first job was a shield, a broad one, thick,
well-fashioned everywhere.[15] A shining rim
he gave it, triple-ply, and hung from this
a silver shoulder strap. Five welded layers
composed the body of the shield. The maker
used all his art adorning this expanse.
He pictured on it earth, heaven, and sea,
unwearied sun, moon waxing, all the stars
that heaven bears for garland: Plêïadês,
Hyadês, Oriôn in his might,   560
the Great Bear, too, that some have called the Wain,

---

[15] The pictures on the shield are an attempt to describe comprehensively life in Homer's time and the cosmos as then conceived. Though in its physical structure the shield is modeled on man-made shields as described elsewhere in the *Iliad,* both the craftsmanship and the content clearly go beyond what a human artisan could achieve.

pivoting there, attentive to Oriôn,
and unbathed ever in the Ocean stream.[16]

He pictured, then, two cities, noble scenes:
weddings in one, and wedding feasts, and brides
led out through town by torchlight from their chambers
amid chorales, amid the young men turning
round and round in dances: flutes and harps
among them, keeping up a tune, and women
coming outdoors to stare as they went by.   570
A crowd, then, in a market place, and there
two men at odds over satisfaction owed
for a murder done:[17] one claimed that all was paid,
and publicly declared it; his opponent
turned the reparation down, and both
demanded a verdict from an arbiter,
as people clamored in support of each,
and criers restrained the crowd. The town elders
sat in a ring, on chairs of polished stone,
the staves of clarion criers in their hands,   580
with which they sprang up, each to speak in turn,
and in the middle were two golden measures
to be awarded him whose argument
would be the most straightforward.

                                                        Wartime then;
around the other city were emplaced
two columns of besiegers, bright in arms,
as yet divided on which plan they liked:
whether to sack the town, or treat for half
of all the treasure stored in the citadel.
The townsmen would not bow to either: secretly   590
they armed to break the siege-line. Women and children
stationed on the walls kept watch, with men
whom age disabled. All the rest filed out,
as Arês led the way, and Pallas Athêna,
figured in gold, with golden trappings, both
magnificent in arms, as the gods are,
in high relief, while men were small beside them.
When these had come to a likely place for ambush,
a river with a watering place for flocks,
they there disposed themselves, compact in bronze.   600
Two lookouts at a distance from the troops
took their posts, awaiting sight of sheep

---

[16] The Great Bear (Ursa Major), also called the Wain and the Big Dipper, is close to the
North Star, or Polaris, and therefore seems to rotate around it; for people in the northern
latitudes, then, the constellation is always above the northern horizon, regardless of season
or time of day.

[17] The penalty for a killing could be paid by a gift of money to the dead man's kin. Here
the elders and arbiter argue and judge the case, two measures of gold being awarded for the
best argument or solution.

and shambling cattle. Both now came in view,
trailed by two herdsmen playing pipes, no hidden
danger in their minds. The ambush party
took them by surprise in a sudden rush;
swiftly they cut off herds and beautiful flocks
of silvery grey sheep, then killed the herdsmen.
When the besiegers from their parleying ground
heard sounds of cattle in stampede, they mounted   610
behind mettlesome teams, following the sound,
and came up quickly. Battle lines were drawn,
and on the riverbanks the fight began
as each side rifled javelins at the other.
Here then Strife and Uproar joined the fray,
and ghastly Fate, that kept a man with wounds
alive, and one unwounded, and another
dragged by the heels through battle-din in death.
This figure wore a mantle dyed with blood,
and all the figures clashed and fought   620
like living men, and pulled their dead away.

Upon the shield, soft terrain, freshly plowed,
he pictured: a broad field, and many plowmen
here and there upon it. Some were turning
ox teams at the plowland's edge, and there
as one arrived and turned, a man came forward
putting a cup of sweet wine in his hands.
They made their turns-around, then up the furrows
drove again, eager to reach the deep field's
limit; and the earth looked black behind them,   630
as though turned up by plows. But it was gold,
all gold—a wonder of the artist's craft.

He put there, too, a king's field. Harvest hands
were swinging whetted scythes to mow the grain,
and stalks were falling along the swath
while binders girded others up in sheaves
with bands of straw—three binders, and behind them
children came as gleaners, proffering
their eager armfuls. And amid them all
the king stood quietly with staff in hand,   640
happy at heart, upon a new-mown swath.
To one side, under an oak tree his attendants
worked at a harvest banquet. They had killed
a great ox, and were dressing it; their wives
made supper for the hands, with barley strewn.

A vineyard then he pictured, weighted down
with grapes: this all in gold; and yet the clusters
hung dark purple, while the spreading vines
were propped on silver vine-poles. Blue enamel

he made the enclosing ditch, and tin the fence,   650
and one path only led into the vineyard
on which the loaded vintagers took their way
at vintage time. Lighthearted boys and girls
were harvesting the grapes in woven baskets,
while on a resonant harp a boy among them
played a tune of longing, singing low
with delicate voice a summer dirge. The others,
breaking out in song for the joy of it,
kept time together as they skipped along.

The artisan made next a herd of longhorns,   660
fashioned in gold and tin: away they shambled,
lowing, from byre[18] to pasture by a stream
that sang and rippled in a reedy bed.
Four cowherds all of gold were plodding after
with nine lithe dogs beside them.
                                           On the assault,
in two tremendous bounds, a pair of lions
caught in the van a bellowing bull, and off
they dragged him, followed by the dogs and men.
Rending the belly of the bull, the two
gulped down his blood and guts, even as the herdsmen   670
tried to set on their hunting dogs, but failed:
no trading bites with lions for those dogs,
who halted close up, barking, then ran back.

And on the shield the great bowlegged god
designed a pasture in a lovely valley,
wide, with silvery sheep, and huts and sheds
and sheepfolds there.
                                      A dancing floor as well
he fashioned, like that one in royal Knossos[19]
Daidalos made for the Princess Ariadnê.
Here young men and the most desired young girls   680
were dancing, linked, touching each other's wrists,
the girls in linen, in soft gowns, the men
in well-knit khitons given a gloss with oil;
the girls wore garlands, and the men had daggers
golden-hilted, hung on silver lanyards.
Trained and adept, they circled there with ease
the way a potter sitting at his wheel
will give it a practice twirl between his palms
to see it run; or else, again, in lines
as though in ranks, they moved on one another: 690

---

[18] Barn.

[19] A city in Krete, ruled by the legendary king Minos and renowned for, among other things, dancing. Daidalos (Daedalus) was a master craftsman best known for constructing a labyrinth to contain the Minotaur, a monster half man and half bull.

magical dancing! All around, a crowd
stood spellbound as two tumblers led the beat
with spins and handsprings through the company.

Then, running round the shield-rim, triple-ply,
he pictured all the might of the Ocean stream.

Besides the densely plated shield, he made
a cuirass, brighter far than fire light,
a massive helmet, measured for his temples,
handsomely figured, with a crest of gold;
then greaves[20] of pliant tin.

Now when the crippled god   700
had done his work, he picked up all the arms
and laid them down before Akhilleus' mother,
and swift as a hawk from snowy Olympos' height
she bore the brilliant gear made by Hêphaistos.

BOOK NINETEEN: THE AVENGER FASTS AND ARMS

Dawn in her yellow robe rose in the east
out of the flowing Ocean, bearing light
for deathless gods and mortal men. And Thetis
brought to the beach her gifts from the god of fire.
She found her dear son lying beside Patróklos,
wailing, while his men stood by
in tears around him. Now amid that throng
the lovely goddess bent to touch his shoulder
and said to him:

"Ah, child, let him lie dead,
for all our grief and pain, we must allow it;   10
he fell by the gods' will.
But you, now—take the war-gear from Hêphaistos.
No man ever bore upon his shoulders
gear so magnificent."

And she laid the armor
down before Akhilleus, clanging loud
in all its various glory. Myrmidons
began to tremble at the sound, and dared not
look straight at the armor; their knees shook.
But anger entered Akhilleus as he gazed,
his eyes grown wide and bright as blazing fire,   20
with fierce joy as he handled the god's gifts.

---

[20]Armor for the lower legs.

After appraising them in his delight
he spoke out to his mother swiftly:

                                                                "Mother,

these the god gave are miraculous arms,
handiwork of immortals, plainly—far
beyond the craft of men. By heaven, I'll wear them!
Only, I feel the dread that while I fight
black carrion flies may settle on Patróklos'
wounds, where the spearheads marked him, and I fear
they may breed maggots to defile the corpse,   30
now life is torn from it. His flesh may rot."

But silvery-footed Thetis answered:

                                                                "Child,

you must not let that prey on you. I'll find
a way to shield him from the black fly hordes
that eat the bodies of men killed in battle.
Though he should lie unburied a long year,
his flesh will be intact and firm. Now, though,
for your part, call the Akhaians to assembly.
Tell them your anger against Agamémnon
is over and done with!   40
After that, at once
put on your gear, prepare your heart, for war!"

Her promise gave her son wholehearted valor.
Then, turning to Patróklos, she instilled
red nectar and ambrosia[1] in his nostrils
to keep his body whole.

                                        And Prince Akhilleus

passed along the surf-line with a shout
that split the air and roused men of Akhaia,
even those who, up to now, had stayed
amid the massed ships—navigators, helmsmen,   50
men in charge of rations and ship stores.
Aye, even these now headed for assembly,
since he who for so long had shunned the battle,
Akhilleus, now appeared upon the field.
Resolute Diomêdês and Odysseus,
familiars[2] of the wargod, limped along,
leaning on spears, for both had painful wounds.
They made their way to the forefront and sat down,
and last behind them entered the Lord Marshal
Agamémnon, favoring his wound: he too   60
had taken a slash, from Antênor's son, Koôn.

---

[1]Literally, the drink and food of the gods.
[2]Attendants.

When everyone had crowded in, Akhilleus,
the great battlefield runner, rose and said:

"Agamémnon, was it better for us
in any way, when we were sore at heart,
to waste ourselves in strife over a girl?
If only Artemis had shot her down[3]
among the ships on the day I made her mine,
after I took Lyrnessos!
Fewer Akhaians would have died hard   70
at enemy hands, while I abstained in anger—
Hektor's gain, the Trojans' gain. Akhaians
years hence will remember our high words,
mine and yours. But now we can forget them,
and, as we must, forego our passion. Aye,
by heaven, I drop my anger now!
No need to smolder in my heart forever! Come,
send your long-haired Akhaians into combat,
and let me see how Trojans will hold out,
if camping near the beachhead's their desire!   80
I rather think some will be glad to rest,
provided they get home, away from danger,
out of my spear's range!"

                                        These were his words,
and all the Akhaians gave a roar of joy
to hear the prince abjure his rage.
Lord Marshal Agamémnon then addressed them,
standing up, not in the midst of them,
but where he had been sitting:

                                        "Friends, fighters,
Danááns, companions of Arês: it is fair
to listen to a man when he has risen   90
and not to interrupt him. That's vexation
to any speaker, able though he may be.
In a great hubbub how can any man
attend or speak? A fine voice will be muffled.
While I open my mind to the son of Pêleus,
Argives, attention! Each man weigh my words!
The Akhaians often brought this up against me,
and chided me. But I am not to blame.[4]
Zeus and Fate and a nightmare Fury are,
for putting savage Folly in my mind   100
in the assembly that day, when I wrested

---

[3] Had brought death to her.
[4] *I am not to blame.* Despite these words and his accusation of Folly, Agamémnon does to
some extent admit his fault. His account is roughly analogous to modern expressions like "What
possessed me to do that?"

Akhilleus' prize of war from him. In truth,
what could I do? Divine will shapes these things.
Ruinous Folly, eldest daughter of Zeus,
beguiles us all. Her feet are soft, from walking
not on earth but over the heads of men
to do them hurt. She traps one man or another.
Once indeed she deluded Zeus, most noble
of gods and men, they say. But feminine
Hêra with her underhanded ways   110
tricked him, the day Alkmênê, in high Thebes,
was to have given birth to Hêraklês.[5]
Then glorying Zeus remarked to all the gods:
"Hear me, all gods and goddesses, I'll tell you
of something my heart dwells upon. This day
the childbirth goddess, Eileithyía, brings
into the light a man who will command
all those around him, being of the race of men
who come of my own blood!' But in her guile
the Lady Hêra said: 'You may be wrong,   120
unable to seal your word with truth hereafter.
Come, Olympian, swear me a great oath
he will indeed be lord of all his neighbors,
the child of your own stock in the race of men
who drops between a woman's legs today!'

Zeus failed to see her crookedness: he swore
a mighty oath, and mightily went astray,
for flashing downward from Olympos crest
Hêra visited Argos of Akhaia,
aware that the strong wife of Perseus' son,   130
Sthénelos, was big with child,
just entering her seventh month. But Hêra
brought this child into the world's daylight
beforehand by two months, and checked Alkmênê's
labor, to delay the birth of hers.
To Zeus the son of Krónos then she said:
'Zeus of the bright bolt, father, let me add
a new event to your deliberations.
Even now a superior man is born
to be a lord of Argives: Eurýstheus,   140
a son of Sthénelos, the son of Perseus,
of your own stock. And it is not unfitting
for him to rule the Argives.' This report
sharply wounded the deep heart of Zeus.
He picked up Folly by her shining braids

---

[5]Alkmênê was a mortal woman who, after being seduced by Zeus in the guise of her husband, gave birth to the hero Hêraklês, whom Hêra hated out of jealousy of his mother. During one period of his life he was required to serve Eurýstheus (grandson of Perseus, another son of Zeus) by performing twelve superhumanly difficult labors.

in sudden anger—swearing a great oath
that never to starred heaven or Olympos
Folly, who tricks us all, should come again.
With this he whirled her with one hand and flung her
out of the sky. So to men's earth she came, 150
but ever thereafter made Zeus groan to see
his dear son toil at labors for Eurýstheus.

So, too, with me: when in his shimmering helm
great Hektor slaughtered Argives near the ships,
could I ignore my folly, my delusion?
Zeus had stolen my wits, my act was blind.
But now I wish to make amends, to give
all possible satisfaction. Rouse for war,
send in your troops! I here repeat my offer
of all that Odysseus promised yesterday![6] 160
Stay if you will, though the wargod presses you.
Men in my service will unload the gifts
from my own ship, that you may see how richly
I reward you!"

                              Akhilleus answered:

                                   "Excellency,

Lord Marshal Agamémnon, make the gifts
if you are keen to—gifts are due; or keep them.
It is for you to say. Let us recover
joy of battle soon, that's all!
No need to dither here and lose our time,
our great work still undone. When each man sees 170
Akhilleus in a charge, crumpling the ranks
of Trojans with his bronze-shod spear, let each
remember that is the way to fight his man!"

Replied Odysseus, the shrewd field commander:

"Brave as you are, and like a god in looks,
Akhilleus, do not send Akhaian soldiers
into the fight unfed! Today's mêlée
will not be brief, when rank meets rank, and heaven
breathes fighting spirit into both contenders.
No, tell all troops who are near the ships to take 180
roast meat and wine, for heart and staying power.
No soldier can fight hand to hand, in hunger,
all day long until the sun goes down!
Though in his heart he yearns for war, his legs
go slack before he knows it: thirst and famine
search him out, and his knees fail as he moves.
But that man stayed with victualing and wine

[6]Agamémnon refers to the offer he made in Book IX.

can fight his enemies all day: his heart
is bold and happy in his chest, his legs
hold out until both sides break off the battle!   190
Come, then, dismiss the ranks to make their breakfast.
Let the Lord Marshal Agamémnon
bring his gifts to the assembly ground
where all may see them; may your heart be warmed.
Then let him swear to you, before the Argives,
never to have made love to her, my lord,
as men and women by their nature do.
So may your heart be peaceable toward him!
And let him sate your hunger with rich fare
in his own shelter, that you may lack nothing   200
due you in justice. Afterward, Agamémnon,
you'll be more just to others, too. There is
no fault in a king's wish to conciliate
a man with whom he has been quick to anger!"

And the Lord Marshal Agamémnon answered:

"Glad I am to hear you, son of Laërtês,
finding the right word at the right time
for all these matters. And the oath you speak of
I'll take willingly, with all my heart,
and will not, before heaven, be forsworn.   210
Now let Akhilleus wait here, though the wargod
tug his arm; and all the rest of you
wait here assembled till the gifts have come
down from our quarters, and our peace is made.
For you, Odysseus, here is my command:
choose the finest young peers of all Akhaia
to fetch out of my ship those gifts we pledged
Akhilleus yesterday; and bring the women.
Let Talthýbios[7] prepare for sacrifice,
in the army's name, a boar to Zeus and Hêlios."[8]   220

Replied Akhilleus:

                              "Excellency, Lord Marshal,
another time were better for these ceremonies,
some interval in the war, and when I feel
less passion in me. Look, those men lie dead
whom Hektor killed when Zeus allowed him glory,
and yet you two propose a meal! By god,
I'd send our soldiers into action now
unfed and hungry. Have a feast, I'd say,
at sundown, when our shame has been avenged!

---

[7] Agamémnon's crier, or herald.
[8] The sun or sun god.

Before that, for my part, I will not swallow 230
food or drink—my dear friend being dead,
lying before my eyes, bled white by spear-cuts,
feet turned to his hut's door, his friends in mourning
around him. Your concerns are none of mine.
Slaughter and blood are what I crave, and groans
of anguished men!"

But the shrewd field commander
Odysseus answered:

"Akhilleus, flower and pride
of the Akhaians, you are more powerful
than I am—and a better spearman, too—
only in sizing matters up I'd say 240
I'm just as far beyond you, being older,
knowing more of the world. So bear with me.
Men quickly reach satiety with battle
in which the reaping bronze will bring to earth
big harvests, but a scanty yield, when Zeus,
war's overseer for mankind, tips the scales.
How can a fasting belly mourn our dead?
So many die, so often, every day,
when would soldiers come to an end of fasting?
No, we must dispose of him who dies 250
and keep hard hearts, and weep that day alone.
And those whom the foul war has left unhurt
will do well to remember food and drink,
so that we may again close with our enemies,
our dangerous enemies, and be tough soldiers,
hardened in mail of bronze. Let no one, now,
be held back waiting for another summons:
here is your summons! Woe to the man who lingers
beside the Argive ships! No, all together,
let us take up the fight against the Trojans!" 260

He took as escort sons of illustrious Nestor:
Phyleus' son Mégês, Thoas, and Meríonês,
and the son of Kreion, Lykomêdês, and
Melánippos, to Agamémnon's quarters.
No sooner was the work assigned than done:
they brought the seven tripods Agamémnon
promised Akhilleus, and the twenty caldrons
shining, and the horses, a full dozen;
then they conducted seven women, skilled
in housecraft, with Brisêis in her beauty. 270
Odysseus weighed ten bars of purest gold
and turned back, followed by his young Akhaians,
bearing the gifts to place in mid-assembly.

Now Agamémnon rose. Talthýbios
the crier, with his wondrous voice, stood near him,
holding the boar. The son of Atreus drew
the sheath knife that he carried, hung
beside the big sheath of his sword, and cut
first bristles from the boar. Arms wide to heaven
he prayed to Zeus, as all the troops kept still,   280
all sitting in due order in their places,
hearing their king. In prayer he raised his eyes
to the broad sky and said:

                                        "May Zeus, all-highest
and first of gods, be witness first, then Earth
and Hêlios and the Furies underground
who punish men for having broken oaths,
I never laid a hand on your Brisêis,
proposing bed or any other pleasure;
in my quarters the girl has been untouched.
If one word that I swear is false,   290
may the gods plague me for a perjured liar!"

He slit the boar's throat with his blade of bronze.
Then Talthýbios, wheeling, flung the victim
into the offshore water, bait for fish.
Akhilleus rose amid the Argive warriors,
saying:

                                        "Father Zeus, you send mankind
prodigious follies. Never otherwise
had Agamémnon stung me through and through;
never would he have been so empty-headed
as to defy my will and take the girl!   300
No, for some reason Zeus had death at heart
for the Akhaians, and for many.

                                                          Well:
go to your meat, then we'll resume the fighting."

Thus he dismissed the assembly. All the men
were quick to scatter, each to his own ship.
As for the gifts, the Myrmidons took over
and bore them all to Akhilleus' ship, to stow
within his shelter. There they left the women
and drove the horses to the herd.

                                                   The girl
Brisêis, in her grace like Aphrodíte,   310
on entering saw Patróklos lying dead
of spear wounds, and she sank down to embrace him
with a sharp sobbing cry, lifting her hands
to tear her breast, soft throat, and lovely face,
this girl, shaped like the goddesses of heaven.

Weeping, she said:

"Patróklos, very dear,
most dear to me, cursed as I am, you were
alive still when I left you, left this place!
Now I come back to find you dead, my captain!
Evil follows evil so, for me. 320
The husband to whom father and mother gave me
I saw brought down by spears before our town,
with my three brothers, whom my mother bore.
Dear brothers, all three met their day of wrath.
But when Akhilleus killed my lord, and sacked
the city of royal Mynês, not a tear
would you permit me: no, you undertook
to see me married to the Prince Akhilleus,[9]
conveyed by ship to Phthía, given a wedding
among the Myrmidons. Now must I mourn 330
your death forever, who were ever gentle."

She wailed again, and women sobbed about her,
first for Patróklos, then for each one's grief.
Meanwhile Akhaian counselors were gathered
begging Akhilleus to take food. He spurned it,
groaning:

"No, I pray you, my dear friends,
if anyone will listen!—do not nag me
to glut and dull my heart with food and drink!
A burning pain is in me. I'll hold out
till sundown without food. I say I'll bear it." 340

With this he sent the peers away, except
the two Atreidai[10] and the great Odysseus,
Nestor, Idómeneus, and old Lord Phoinix.
These would have comforted him, but none
could quiet or comfort him until he entered
the bloody jaws of war. Now pierced by memory,
he sighed and sighed again, and said:

"Ah, once
you, too, poor fated friend, and best of friends,
would set a savory meal deftly before us
in our field shelter, when the Akhaians wished 350
no time lost between onsets against Trojans.
Now there you lie, broken in battle. Ah,
lacking you, my heart will fast this day

---

[9] Patróklos was presumably trying to console Brisêis; for Akhilleus to marry a woman taken captive would be unlikely.
[10] Sons of Atreus—that is, Agamémnon and Meneláos.

from meat and drink as well. No greater ill
could come to me, not news of Father's death—
my father, weeping soft tears now in Phthía
for want of that son in a distant land
who wars on Troy for Helen's sake—that woman
who makes the blood run cold. No greater ill,
even should my son die, who is being reared   360
on Skyros, Neoptólemos, if indeed
he's living still.[11] My heart's desire had been
that I alone should perish far from Argos
here at Troy; that you should sail to Phthía,
taking my son aboard your swift black ship
at Skyros, to introduce him to his heritage,
my wide lands, my servants, my great hall.
In this late year Pêleus may well be dead
and buried, or have few days yet to live,
beset by racking age, always awaiting   370
dire news of me, of my own death."

As he said this he wept. The counselors groaned,
remembering each what he had left at home;
and seeing them sorrow, Zeus took pity on them,
saying quickly to Athêna:

                                                     "Daughter,
you seem to have left your fighting man alone.
Should one suppose you care no more for Akhilleus?
There he sits, before the curving prows,
and grieves for his dear friend. The other soldiers
flock to meat; he thirsts and hungers. Come,   380
infuse in him sweet nectar and ambrosia,
that an empty belly may not weaken him."

He urged Athêna to her own desire,
and like a gliding sea hawk, shrilling high,
she soared from heaven through the upper air,
while the Akhaians armed throughout the ranks.
Nectar and ambrosia she instilled
within Akhilleus, that his knees be not
assailed by hollow famine; then she withdrew
to her mighty father's house. Meanwhile the troops   390
were pouring from the shipways to the field.
As when cold snowflakes fly from Zeus in heaven,
thick and fast under the blowing north wind,
just so, that multitude of gleaming helms

---

[11] Skyros was an island east of Greece, in the Aegean Sea. According to some versions of
the legend, the mother of Neoptólemos was a princess of Skyros whom Akhilleus had loved
while hiding out there to avoid the Trojan War. Neoptólemos (also called Pyrrhus) joined the
Greek forces after his father's death and killed Priam when Troy was finally taken (compare
the account in Virgil's *Aeneid,* Book II).

and bossed shields issued from the ships, with plated
cuirasses and ashwood spears. Reflected
glintings flashed to heaven, as the plain
in all directions shone with glare of bronze
and shook with trampling feet of men. Among them
Prince Akhilleus armed. One heard his teeth   400
grind hard together, and his eyes blazed out
like licking fire, for unbearable pain
had fixed upon his heart. Raging at Trojans,
he buckled on the arms Hêphaistos forged.
The beautiful greaves, fitted with silver anklets
first he put upon his legs, and next
the cuirass on his ribs; then over his shoulder
he slung the sword of bronze with silver scabbard;
finally he took up the massive shield
whence came a radiance like the round full moon.   410
As when at sea to men on shipboard comes
the shining of a campfire on a mountain
in a lone sheepfold, while the gusts of nightwind
take them, loath to go, far from their friends
over the teeming sea: just so
Akhilleus' finely modeled shield sent light
into the heavens: Lifting his great helm
he placed it on his brows, and like a star
the helm shone with its horsetail blowing free,
all golden, that Hêphaistos had set in   420
upon the crest. Akhilleus tried his armor,
shrugging and flexing, making sure it fitted,
sure that his gleaming legs had play. Indeed
the gear sat on him light as wings: it buoyed him!
Now from a spear-case he withdrew a spear—
his father's—weighty, long, and tough. No other
Akhaian had the strength to handle it,
this great Pêlian shaft
of ashwood, given his father by the centaur
Kheirôn from the crest of Pêlion   430
to be the death of heroes.

                                                    Automédôn

and Álkimos with swift hands yoked his team,
making firm the collars on the horses,
placing the bits between their teeth, and pulling
reins to the war-car. Automédôn then
took in hand the shining whip and mounted
the chariot, and at his back Akhilleus
mounted in full armor, shining bright
as the blinding Lord of Noon.[12] In a clarion voice
he shouted to the horses of his father: 440

---

[12] The sun.

"Xánthos and Balíos! Known to the world
as foals of great Podargê! In this charge
care for your driver in another way!
Pull him back, I mean, to the Danáäns,
back to the main body of the army,
once we are through with battle; this time,
no leaving him there dead, like Lord Patróklos!"

To this, from under the yoke, the nimble Xánthos
answered, and hung his head, so that his mane
dropped forward from the yokepad to the ground—   450
Hêra whose arms are white as ivory
gave him a voice to say:

                                                  "Yes, we shall save you,
this time, too, Akhilleus in your strength!
And yet the day of your destruction comes,
and it is nearer. We are not the cause,
but rather a great god is, and mighty Fate.
Nor was it by our sloth or sluggishness
the Trojans stripped Patróklos of his armor.
No, the magnificent god[13] that Lêto bore
killed him in action and gave Hektor glory.   460
We might run swiftly as the west wind blows,
most rapid of all winds, they say; but still
it is your destiny to be brought low
by force, a god's force and a man's!"[14]

                                                              On this,
the Furies put a stop to Xánthos' voice.[15]
In anger and gloom Akhilleus said to him:

"Xánthos, why prophesy my death? No need.
What is in store for me I know, know well:
to die here, far away from my dear father,
my mother, too. No matter. All that matters   470
is that I shall not call a halt today
till I have made the Trojans sick of war!"

And with a shout he drove his team
of trim-hooved horses into the front line.

        BOOK XX. *Zeus assembles the gods and tells them that they now have a free hand to inter-*
vene in the war. A brief catalog of the gods follows: on the Greek side Hêra, Athêna, Poseidon,
Hermês, and Hêphaistos; on the Trojan side Arês, Apollo, Artemis (Apollo's sister and god-
dess of the hunt), Lêto (mother of Apollo and Artemis), the river god Xánthos, and Aphrodítê.

        [13]Apollo.
        [14]Akhilleus will one day be slain by the bow of Paris with the help of Apollo, god of archers.
        [15]That a horse should speak violates natural law, of which the Furies are guardians. (Xánthos
is also the name of a river god who appears in Books XX and XXI.)

(For the time being, however, most of the gods stay out of action.) Aineías, incited by Apollo, engages Akhilleus; Poseidon (though he favors the Greeks) saves the Trojan hero by spiriting him away, since Aineías is fated to live and rule over the Trojan survivors of the war. Akhilleus and Hektor exhort their respective armies to fight. At Apollo's suggestion, Hektor stays out of Akhilleus' range, but when one of Hektor's brothers is slain he attacks Akhilleus. Hektor is saved when Apollo hides him in a cloud. Cheated of his prey a second time, Akhilleus rages, killing many Trojans.

   BOOK XXI. *Akhilleus divides the Trojan forces, driving half of them toward the city, half into the river Xánthos (also called Skamánder), which flows by the plain. In the river he kills many men and takes twelve alive who are to pay later for the death of Patróklos. Xánthos, the god and personification of the river, angered by the pollution of his waters and by Akhilleus' slaughter of Trojans, attacks him and puts him in sore danger of drowning. Poseidon, Athêna, and Hêra come to Akhilleus' aid, and the fire god Hêphaistos uses his flames to overcome the raging river, which bubbles with the heat. Now the gods begin a general battle with one another: Athêna against Arês, Athêna against Aphrodítê, Hêra against Artemis. Challenged halfheartedly by Poseidon, Apollo declines to fight, remarking that it is foolish for gods to fight one another for the sake of mere mortals. The deities who favor the Greeks having emerged as victors, all the gods return to Olympos except Apollo, who helps the fleeing Trojans to withdraw safely within the city walls, by impersonating a Trojan and leading Akhilleus on a wild-goose chase. But Hektor remains outside the walls, stranded.*

BOOK TWENTY-TWO: DESOLATION BEFORE TROY

Once in the town, those who had fled like deer
wiped off their sweat and drank their thirst away,
leaning against the cool stone of the ramparts.
Meanwhile Akhaians with bright shields aslant
came up the plain and nearer. As for Hektor,
fatal destiny pinned him where he stood
before the Skaian Gates, outside the city.

Now Akhilleus heard Apollo calling
back to him:

                              "Why run so hard, Akhilleus,
mortal as you are, after a god?   10
Can you not comprehend it? I am immortal.
You are so hot to catch me, you no longer
think of finishing off the men you routed.
They are all in the town by now, packed in
while you were being diverted here. And yet
you cannot kill me; I am no man's quarry."

Akhilleus bit his lip and said:

"Archer of heaven, deadliest
of immortal gods, you put me off the track,
turning me from the wall this way. A hundred   20
might have sunk their teeth into the dust
before one man took cover in Ilion!

You saved my enemies with ease and stole
my glory, having no punishment to fear.
I'd take it out of you, if I had the power."
Then toward the town with might and main he ran,
magnificent, like a racing chariot horse
that holds its form at full stretch on the plain.
So light-footed Akhilleus held the pace.
And aging Priam was the first to see him   30
sparkling on the plain, bright as that star
in autumn rising, whose unclouded rays
shine out amid a throng of stars at dusk—
the one they call Oríôn's dog, most brilliant,
yes, but baleful as a sign: it brings
great fever to frail men.[1] So pure and bright
the bronze gear blazed upon him as he ran.
The old man gave a cry. With both his hands
thrown up on high he struck his head, then shouted,
groaning, appealing to his dear son. Unmoved,   40
Lord Hektor stood in the gateway, resolute
to fight Akhilleus.

                                        Stretching out his hands,
old Priam said, imploring him:

                                                       "No, Hector!

Cut off as you are, alone, dear son,
don't try to hold your ground against this man,
or soon you'll meet the shock of doom, borne down
by the son of Pêleus. He is more powerful
by far than you, and pitiless. Ah, were he
but dear to the gods as he is dear to me!
Wild dogs and kites would eat him where he lay   50
within the hour, and ease me of my torment.
Many tall sons he killed, bereaving me,
or sold them to far islands. Even now
I cannot see two sons of mine, Lykáôn
and Polydôros,[2] among the Trojans massed
inside the town. A queen, Laóthoé,
conceived and bore them. If they are alive
amid the Akhaian host, I'll ransom them
with bronze and gold: both I have, piled at home,
rich treasures that old Altês, the renowned,   60
gave for his daughter's dowry. If they died,
if they went under to the homes of Death,
sorrow has come to me and to their mother.
But to our townsmen all this pain is brief,

---

[1] Sirius, the brightest of the stars, reappears in the eastern skies in the "dog days" of August,
a time associated with disease.
[2] They were slain by Akhilleus in, respectively, Books XXI and XX. Laóthoê, daughter of
Altês, is one of Priam's concubines. (Hektor's mother, Hékabê, is Priam's principal wife and
queen of Troy.)

unless you too go down before Akhilleus.
Come inside the wall, child; here you may
fight on to save our Trojan men and women.
Do not resign the glory to Akhilleus,
losing your own dear life! Take pity, too,
on me and my hard fate, while I live still. 70
Upon the threshold of my age, in misery,
the son[3] of Krónos will destroy my life
after the evil days I shall have seen—
my sons brought down, my daughters dragged away,
bedchambers ravaged, and small children hurled
to earth in the atrocity of war,
as my sons' wives are taken by Akhaians'
ruinous hands. And at the end, I too—
when someone with a sword-cut or a spear
has had my life—I shall be torn apart 80
on my own doorstep by the hounds
I trained as watchdogs, fed from my own table.
These will lap my blood with ravenous hearts
and lie in the entranceway.
                                    Everything done
to a young man killed in war becomes his glory,
once he is riven by the whetted bronze:
dead though he be, it is all fair, whatever
happens then. But when an old man falls,
and dogs disfigure his grey head and cheek
and genitals, that is most harrowing 90
of all that men in their hard lives endure."

The old man wrenched at his grey hair and pulled out
hanks of it in both hands, but moved
Lord Hektor not at all. The young man's mother
wailed from the tower across, above the portal,
streaming tears, and loosening her robe
with one hand, held her breast out in the other,
saying:
                    "Hektor, my child, be moved by this,
and pity me, if ever I unbound
a quieting breast for you. Think of these things, 100
dear child; defend yourself against the killer
this side of the wall, not hand to hand.
He has no pity. If he brings you down,
I shall no longer be allowed to mourn you
laid out on your bed, dear branch in flower,
born of me! And neither will your lady,
so endowed with gifts. Far from us both,
dogs will devour you by the Argive ships."

[3] Zeus.

With tears and cries the two implored their son,
and made their prayers again, but could not shake him.   110
Hektor stood firm, as huge Akhilleus neared.
The way a serpent, fed on poisonous herbs,
coiled at his lair upon a mountainside,
with all his length of hate awaits a man
and eyes him evilly: so Hektor, grim
and narrow-eyed, refused to yield. He leaned
his brilliant shield against a spur of wall
and in his brave heart bitterly reflected:
"Here I am badly caught. If I take cover,
slipping inside the gate and wall, the first   120
to accuse me for it will be Poulýdamas,
he who told me I should lead the Trojans
back to the city on that cursed night
Akhilleus joined the battle. No, I would not,
would not, wiser though it would have been.
Now troops have perished for my foolish pride,
I am ashamed to face townsmen and women.
Someone inferior to me may say:
'He kept his pride and lost his men, this Hektor!'
So it will go. Better, when that time comes,   130
that I appear as he who killed Akhilleus
man to man, or else that I went down
fighting him to the end before the city.
Suppose, though, that I lay my shield and helm
aside, and prop my spear against the wall,
and go meet the noble Prince Akhilleus,
promising Helen, promising with her
all treasures that Aléxandros[4] brought home
by ship to Troy—the first cause of our quarrel—
that he may give these things to the Atreidai?   140
Then I might add, apart from these, a portion
of all the secret wealth the city owns.
Yes, later I might take our counselors' oath
to hide no stores, but share and share alike
to halve all wealth our lovely city holds,
all that is here within the walls. Ah, no,
why even put the question to myself?
I must not go before him and receive
no quarter, no respect! Aye, then and there
he'll kill me, unprotected as I am,   150
my gear laid by, defenseless as a woman.
No chance, now, for charms[5] from oak or stone
in parley with him—charms a girl and boy
might use when they enchant each other talking!

[4]Paris.
[5]Pleasing words. The meaning of the phrase "from oak or stone" is uncertain.

Better we duel, now at once, and see
to whom the Olympian awards the glory."

These were his shifts of mood. Now close at hand
Akhilleus like the implacable god of war
came on with blowing crest, hefting the dreaded
beam of Pêlian ash on his right shoulder. 160
Bronze light played around him, like the glare
of a great fire or the great sun rising,
and Hektor, as he watched, began to tremble.
Then he could hold his ground no more. He ran,
leaving the gate behind him, with Akhilleus
hard on his heels, sure of his own speed.
When that most lightning-like of birds, a hawk
bred on a mountain, swoops upon a dove,
the quarry dips in terror, but the hunter,
screaming, dips behind and gains upon it, 170
passionate for prey. Just so, Akhilleus
murderously cleft the air, as Hektor
ran with flashing knees along the wall.
They passed the lookout point, the wild figtree
with wind in all its leaves, then veered away
along the curving wagon road, and came
to where the double fountains well, the source
of eddying Skamánder. One hot spring
flows out, and from the water fumes arise
as though from fire burning; but the other 180
even in summer gushes chill as hail
or snow or crystal ice frozen on water.
Near these fountains are wide washing pools
of smooth-laid stone, where Trojan wives and daughters
laundered their smooth linen in the days
of peace before the Akhaians came. Past these
the two men ran, pursuer and pursued,
and he who fled was noble, he behind
a greater man by far. They ran full speed,
and not for bull's hide or a ritual beast 190
or any prize that men compete for: no,
but for the life of Hektor, tamer of horses.
Just as when chariot-teams around a course
go wheeling swiftly, for the prize is great,
a tripod or a woman,[6] in the games
held for a dead man, so three times these two
at full speed made their course round Priam's town,
as all the gods looked on. And now the father
of gods and men turned to the rest and said:

[6]In Book XXIII these prizes are offered to the winner of the chariot race in the ceremonial funeral games honoring Patróklos.

"How sad that this beloved man is hunted   200
around the wall before my eyes! My heart
is touched for Hektor; he has burned thigh flesh
of oxen for me often, high on Ida,
at other times on the high point of Troy.
Now Prince Akhilleus with devouring stride
is pressing him around the town of Priam.
Come, gods, put your minds on it, consider
whether we may deliver him from death
or see him, noble as he is, brought down
by Pêleus' son, Akhilleus."

                                               Grey-eyed Athêna   210
said to him:

                              "Father of the blinding bolt,
the dark stormcloud, what words are these? The man
is mortal, and his doom fixed, long ago.
Would you release him from his painful death?
Then do so, but not all of us will praise you."

Zeus who gathers cloud replied:

                                              "Take heart,
my dear and honored child. I am not bent
on my suggestion, and I would indulge you.
Act as your thought inclines, refrain no longer."

So he encouraged her in her desire,   220
and down she swept from ridges of Olympos.
Great Akhilleus, hard on Hektor's heels,
kept after him, the way a hound will harry
a deer's fawn he has startled from its bed
to chase through gorge and open glade, and when
the quarry goes to earth under a bush
he holds the scent and quarters till he finds it;
so with Hektor: he could not shake off
the great runner, Akhilleus. Every time
he tried to spring hard for the Dardan gates   230
under the towers, hoping men could help him,
sending missiles down, Akhilleus loomed
to cut him off and turn him toward the plain,
as he himself ran always near the city.
As in a dream a man chasing another
cannot catch him, nor can he in flight
escape from his pursuer, so Akhilleus
could not by his swiftness overtake him,
nor could Hektor pull away. How could he
run so long from death, had not Apollo   240
for the last time, the very last, come near
to give him stamina and speed?

Akhilleus
shook his head at the rest of the Akhaians,
allowing none to shoot or cast at Hektor—
none to forestall him, and to win the honor.
But when, for the fourth time, they reached the springs,
the Father poised his golden scales.

He placed
two shapes of death, death prone and cold, upon them,
one of Akhilleus, one of the horseman, Hektor,
and held the midpoint, pulling upward. Down   250
sank Hektor's fatal day, the pan went down
toward undergloom, and Phoibos Apollo left him.
Then came Athêna, grey-eyed, to the son
of Pêleus, falling in with him, and near him,
saying swiftly:

"Now at last I think
the two of us, Akhilleus loved by Zeus,
shall bring Akhaians triumph at the ships
by killing Hektor—unappeased
though he was ever in his thirst for war.
There is no way he may escape us now,   260
not though Apollo, lord of distances,
should suffer all indignity for him
before his father Zeus who bears the stormcloud,
rolling back and forth and begging for him.
Now you can halt and take your breath, while I
persuade him into combat face to face."

These were Athêna's orders. He complied,
relieved, and leaning hard upon the spearshaft
armed with its head of bronze. She left him there
and overtook Lord Hektor—but she seemed   270
Dêíphobos in form and resonant voice,
appearing at his shoulder, saying swiftly:

"Ai! Dear brother, how he runs, Akhilleus,
harrying you around the town of Priam!
Come, we'll stand and take him on."

To this,
great Hektor in his shimmering helm replied:

"Dêíphobos, you were the closest to me
in the old days, of all my brothers, sons
of Hékabê and Priam. Now I can say
I honor you still more   280
because you dared this foray for my sake,
seeing me run. The rest stay under cover."

Again the grey-eyed goddess spoke:

"Dear brother, how your father and gentle mother
begged and begged me to remain! So did
the soldiers round me, all undone by fear.
But in my heart I ached for you.
Now let us fight him, and fight hard.
No holding back. We'll see if this Akhilleus
conquers both, to take our armor seaward,   290
or if he can be brought down by your spear."

This way, by guile, Athêna led him on.
And when at last the two men faced each other,
Hektor was the first to speak. He said:

"I will no longer fear you as before,
son of Pêleus, though I ran from you
round Priam's town three times and could not face you.
Now my soul would have me stand and fight,
whether I kill you or am killed. So come,
we'll summon gods here as our witnesses,   300
none higher, arbiters of a pact: I swear
that, terrible as you are,
I'll not insult your corpse should Zeus allow me
victory in the end, your life as prize.
Once I have your gear, I'll give your body
back to Akhaians. Grant me, too, this grace."

But swift Akhilleus frowned at him and said:

"Hektor, I'll have no talk of pacts with you,
forever unforgiven as you are.
As between men and lions there are none,   310
no concord between wolves and sheep, but all
hold one another hateful through and through,
so there can be no courtesy between us,
no sworn truce, till one of us is down
and glutting with his blood the wargod Arês.
Summon up what skills you have. By god,
you'd better be a spearman and a fighter!
Now there is no way out. Pallas Athêna
will have the upper hand of you. The weapon
belongs to me. You'll pay the reckoning   320
in full for all the pain my men have borne,
who met death by your spear."

                                              He twirled and cast
his shaft with its long shadow. Splendid Hektor,
keeping his eye upon the point, eluded it
by ducking at the instant of the cast,
so shaft and bronze shank passed him overhead
and punched into the earth. But unperceived
by Hektor, Pallas Athêna plucked it out

and gave it back to Akhilleus. Hektor said:

"A clean miss. Godlike as you are,   330
you have not yet known doom for me from Zeus.
You thought you had, by heaven. Then you turned
into a word-thrower, hoping to make me lose
my fighting heart and head in fear of you.
You cannot plant your spear between my shoulders
while I am running. If you have the gift,
just put it through my chest as I come forward.
Now it's for you to dodge my own. Would god
you'd give the whole shaft lodging in your body!
War for the Trojans would be eased   340
if you were blotted out, bane that you are."

With this he twirled his long spearshaft and cast it,
hitting his enemy mid-shield, but off
and away the spear rebounded. Furious
that he had lost it, made his throw for nothing,
Hektor stood bemused. He had no other.
Then he gave a great shout to Dêíphobos
to ask for a long spear. But there was no one
near him, not a soul. Now in his heart
the Trojan realized the truth and said: 350

"This is the end. The gods are calling deathward.
I had thought
a good soldier, Dêíphobos, was with me.
He is inside the walls. Athêna tricked me.
Death is near, and black, not at a distance,
not to be evaded. Long ago
this hour must have been to Zeus's liking
and to the liking of his archer son.
They have been well disposed before, but now
the appointed time's upon me. Still, I would not   360
die without delivering a stroke,
or die ingloriously, but in some action
memorable to men in days to come."

With this he drew the whetted blade that hung
upon his left flank, ponderous and long,
collecting all his might the way an eagle
narrows himself to dive through shady cloud
and strike a lamb or cowering hare: so Hektor
lanced ahead and swung his whetted blade.
Akhilleus with wild fury in his heart   370
pulled in upon his chest his beautiful shield—
his helmet with four burnished metal ridges
nodding above it, and the golden crest
Hêphaistos locked there tossing in the wind.
Conspicuous as the evening star that comes,

amid the first in heaven, at fall of night,
and stands most lovely in the west, so shone
in sunlight the fine-pointed spear
Akhilleus poised in his right hand, with deadly
aim at Hektor, at the skin where most   380
it lay exposed. But nearly all was covered
by the bronze gear he took from slain Patróklos,
showing only, where his collarbones
divided neck and shoulders, the bare throat
where the destruction of a life is quickest.
Here, then, as the Trojan charged, Akhilleus
drove his point straight through the tender neck,
but did not cut the windpipe, leaving Hektor
able to speak and to respond. He fell
aside into the dust. And Prince Akhilleus   390
now exulted:

                                                 "Hektor, had you thought
that you could kill Patróklos and be safe?
Nothing to dread from me; I was not there.
All childishness. Though distant then, Patróklos'
comrade in arms was greater far than he—
and it is I who had been left behind
that day beside the deepsea ships who now
have made your knees give way. The dogs and kites
will rip your body. His will lie in honor
when the Akhaians give him funeral."   400

Hektor, barely whispering, replied:

"I beg you by your soul and by your parents,
do not let the dogs feed on me
in your encampment by the ships. Accept
the bronze and gold my father will provide
as gifts, my father and her ladyship
my mother. Let them have my body back,
so that our men and women may accord me
decency of fire when I am dead."

Akhilleus the great runner scowled and said: 410

"Beg me no beggary by soul or parents,
whining dog! Would god my passion drove me
to slaughter you and eat you raw, you've caused
such agony to me! No man exists
who could defend you from the carrion pack—
not if they spread for me ten times your ransom,
twenty times, and promise more as well;
aye, not if Priam, son of Dárdanos,
tells them to buy you for your weight in gold!
You'll have no bed of death, nor will you be   420

laid out and mourned by her who gave you birth.
Dogs and birds will have you, every scrap."

Then at the point of death Lord Hektor said:

"I see you now for what you are. No chance
to win you over. Iron in your breast
your heart is. Think a bit, though: this may be
a thing the gods in anger hold against you
on that day when Paris and Apollo
destroy you at the Gates,[7] great as you are."

Even as he spoke, the end came, and death hid him;   430
spirit from body fluttered to undergloom,
bewailing fate that made him leave his youth
and manhood in the world. And as he died
Akhilleus spoke again. He said:

"Die, make an end. I shall accept my own
whenever Zeus and the other gods desire."

At this he pulled his spearhead from the body,
laying it aside, and stripped
the bloodstained shield and cuirass from his shoulders.
Other Akhaians hastened round to see   440
Hektor's fine body and his comely face,
and no one came who did not stab the body.
Glancing at one another they would say:

"Now Hektor has turned vulnerable, softer
than when he put the torches to the ships!"

And he who said this would inflict a wound.
When the great master of pursuit, Akhilleus,
had the body stripped, he stood among them,
saying swiftly:

                    "Friends, my lords and captains
of Argives, now that the gods at last have let me   450
bring to earth this man who wrought
havoc among us—more than all the rest—
come, we'll offer battle around the city,
to learn the intentions of the Trojans now.
Will they give up their strongpoint at this loss?
Can they fight on, though Hektor's dead?

                                    But wait:

why do I ponder, why take up these questions?
Down by the ships Patróklos' body lies

---

[7] The gates of Troy.

unwept, unburied. I shall not forget him
while I can keep my feet among the living.   460
If in the dead world they forget the dead,
I say there, too, I shall remember him,
my friend. Men of Akhaia, lift a song!
Down to the ships we go, and take this body,
our glory. We have beaten Hektor down,
to whom as to a god the Trojans prayed."

Indeed, he had in mind for Hektor's body
outrage and shame. Behind both feet he pierced
the tendons, heel to ankle. Rawhide cords
he drew through both and lashed them to his chariot,   470
letting the man's head trail. Stepping aboard,
bearing the great trophy of the arms,
he shook the reins, and whipped the team ahead
into a willing run. A dustcloud rose
above the furrowing body; the dark tresses
flowed behind, and the head so princely once
lay back in dust. Zeus gave him to his enemies
to be defiled in his own fatherland.
So his whole head was blackened. Looking down,
his mother tore her braids, threw off her veil,   480
and wailed, heartbroken to behold her son.
Piteously his father groaned, and round him
lamentation spread throughout the town,
most like the clamor to be heard if Ilion's
towers, top to bottom, seethed in flames.
They barely stayed the old man, mad with grief,
from passing through the gates. Then in the mire
he rolled, and begged them all, each man by name:

"Relent, friends. It is hard; but let me go
out of the city to the Akhaian ships.   490
I'll make my plea to that demonic heart.
He may feel shame before his peers, or pity
my old age. His father, too, is old,
Pêleus, who brought him up to be a scourge
to Trojans, cruel to all, but most to me,
so many of my sons in flower of youth
he cut away. And, though I grieve, I cannot
mourn them all as much as I do one,
for whom my grief will take me to the grave—
and that is Hektor. Why could he not have died   500
where I might hold him? In our weeping, then,
his mother, now so destitute, and I
might have had surfeit and relief of tears."

These were the words of Priam as he wept,
and all his people groaned. Then in her turn
Hékabê led the women in lamentation:

"Child, I am lost now. Can I bear my life
after the death of suffering your death?
You were my pride in all my nights and days,
pride of the city, pillar to the Trojans 510
and Trojan women. Everyone looked to you
as though you were a god, and rightly so.
You were their greatest glory while you lived.
Now your doom and death have come upon you."

These were her mournful words. But Hektor's lady
still knew nothing; no one came to tell her
of Hektor's stand outside the gates. She wove
upon her loom, deep in the lofty house,
a double purple web with rose design.
Calling her maids in waiting, 520
she ordered a big caldron on a tripod
set on the hearthfire, to provide a bath
for Hektor when he came home from the fight.
Poor wife, how far removed from baths he was
she could not know, as at Akhilleus' hands
Athêna brought him down.

                                  Then from the tower
she heard a wailing and a distant moan.
Her knees shook, and she let her shuttle fall,
and called out to her maids again:

                                              "Come here.
Two must follow me, to see this action. 530
I heard my husband's queenly mother cry.
I feel my heart rise, throbbing in my throat.
My knees are like stone under me. Some blow
is coming home to Priam's sons and daughters.
Ah, could it never reach my ears! I die
of dread that Akhilleus may have cut off Hektor,
blocked my bold husband from the city wall,
to drive him down the plain alone! By now
he may have ended Hektor's deathly pride.
He never kept his place amid the chariots 540
but drove ahead. He would not be outdone
by anyone in courage."

                                  Saying this, she ran
like a madwoman through the mégaron,
her heart convulsed. Her maids kept at her side.
On reaching the great tower and the soldiers,
Andrómakhê stood gazing from the wall
and saw him being dragged before the city.
Chariot horses at a brutal gallop
pulled the torn body toward the decked ships.
Blackness of night covered her eyes; she fell 550
backward swooning, sighing out her life,

and let her shining headdress fall, her hood
and diadem, her plaited band and veil
that Aphrodítê once had given her,
on that day when, from Eëtíôn's house,
for a thousand bridal gifts, Lord Hektor led her.
Now, at her side, kinswomen of her lord
supported her among them, dazed and faint
to the point of death. But when she breathed again
and her stunned heart recovered, in a burst   560
of sobbing she called out among the women:

"Hektor! Here is my desolation. Both
had this in store from birth—from yours in Troy
in Priam's palace, mine by wooded Plakos
at Thêbê in the home of Eëtíôn,
my father, who took care of me in childhood,
a man cursed by fate, a fated daughter.
How I could wish I never had been born!
Now under earth's roof to the house of Death
you go your way and leave me here, bereft,   570
lonely, in anguish without end. The child
we wretches had is still in infancy;
you cannot be a pillar to him, Hektor,
now you are dead, nor he to you. And should
this boy escape the misery of the war,
there will be toil and sorrow for him later,
as when strangers move his boundary stones.[8]
The day that orphans him will leave him lonely,
downcast in everything, cheeks wet with tears,
in hunger going to his father's friends   580
to tug at one man's cloak, another's khiton.
Some will be kindly: one may lift a cup
to wet his lips at least, though not his throat;
but from the board some child with living parents
gives him a push, a slap, with biting words:
'Outside, you there! Your father is not with us
here at our feast!' And the boy Astýanax
will run to his forlorn mother. Once he fed
on marrow only and the fat of lamb,
high on his father's knees. And when sleep came   590
to end his play, he slept in a nurse's arms,
brimful of happiness, in a soft bed.
But now he'll know sad days and many of them,
missing his father. 'Lord of the lower town'[9]
the Trojans call him. They know, you alone,
Lord Hektor, kept their gates and their long walls.

---

[8] Encroach on his land.
[9] The meaning of the child's nickname, Astýanax.

Beside the beaked ships now, far from your kin,
the blowflies' maggots in a swarm will eat you
naked, after the dogs have had their fill.
Ah, there are folded garments in your chambers, 600
delicate and fine, of women's weaving.
These, by heaven, I'll burn to the last thread
in blazing fire! They are no good to you,
they cannot cover you in death. So let them
go, let them be burnt as an offering
from Trojans and their women in your honor."

Thus she mourned, and the women wailed in answer.

BOOK XXIII. *Led by Akhilleus and his Myrmidons, the Greeks mourn Patróklos. Akhilleus continues to dishonor Hektor's corpse. Patróklos' ghost appears to Akhilleus, asks for speedy burial so that he may be accepted among the dead, and reminds Akhilleus of his own approaching death in the Trojan War. The Greeks conduct Patróklos' funeral rites, which include the slaying by Akhilleus of the twelve Trojans he earlier captured for that purpose. (Hektor's body, meanwhile, is being preserved by Aphrodîté and Apollo from defacement and corruption.) Akhilleus presides over ceremonial athletic contests (the gods still intervening on occasion): chariot racing, boxing, wrestling, foot racing, armed combat, weight throwing, archery, javelin throwing. But the last of these contests is not actually held; Akhilleus awards the victory to Agamémnon in advance.*

BOOK TWENTY-FOUR: A GRACE GIVEN IN SORROW

The funeral games were over. Men dispersed
and turned their thoughts to supper in their quarters,
then to the boon of slumber. But Akhilleus
thought of his friend, and sleep that quiets all things
would not take hold of him. He tossed and turned
remembering with pain Patróklos' courage,
his buoyant heart; how in his company
he fought out many a rough day full of danger,
cutting through ranks in war and the bitter sea.
With memory his eyes grew wet. He lay 10
on his right side, then on his back, and then
face downward—but at last he rose, to wander
distractedly along the line of surf.
This for eleven nights. The first dawn, brightening
sea and shore, became familiar to him,
as at that hour he yoked his team, with Hektor
tied behind, to drag him out, three times
around Patróklos' tomb. By day he rested
in his own hut, abandoning Hektor's body
to lie full-length in dust—though Lord Apollo, 20
pitying the man, even in death,
kept his flesh free of disfigurement.

He wrapped him in his great shield's[1] flap of gold
to save him from laceration. But Akhilleus
in rage visited indignity on Hektor
day after day, and, looking on,
the blessed gods were moved. Day after day
they urged the Wayfinder[2] to steal the body—
a thought agreeable to all but Hêra,
Poseidon, and the grey-eyed one, Athêna.   30
These opposed it, and held out, since Ilion
and Priam and his people had incurred
their hatred first, the day Aléxandros
made his mad choice and piqued two goddesses,
visitors in his sheepfold: he praised
a third, who offered ruinous lust.[3]
Now when Dawn grew bright for the twelfth day,
Phoibos Apollo spoke among the gods:

"How heartless and how malevolent you are!
Did Hektor never make burnt offering   40
of bulls' thighbones to you, and unflawed goats?
Even in death you would not stir to save him
for his dear wife to see, and for his mother,
his child, his father, Priam, and his men:
they'd burn the corpse at once and give him burial.
Murderous Akhilleus has your willing help—
a man who shows no decency, implacable,
barbarous in his ways as a wild lion
whose power and intrepid heart
sway him to raid the flocks of men for meat.   50
The man has lost all mercy;
he has no shame—that gift that hinders mortals
but helps them, too. A sane one may endure
an even dearer loss: a blood brother,
a son; and yet, by heaven, having grieved
and passed through mourning, he will let it go.
The Fates have given patient hearts to men.
Not this one: first he took Prince Hektor's life
and now he drags the body, lashed to his car,
around the barrow[4] of his friend, performing   60
something neither nobler in report
nor better in itself. Let him take care,
or, brave as he is, we gods will turn against him,
seeing him outrage the insensate earth!"

---

[1] The aegis, or shield of Zeus, sometimes lent by him to other immortals.
[2] Hermês, messenger of the gods and also the patron of tricksters and thieves.
[3] For the decision by Paris (Aléxandros) that had offended Hêra and Athêna, see the head-note to the *Iliad*. Paris had been a shepherd at the time of the incident. Poseidon's hatred of the Trojans originated when he was forced to serve as a laborer under Priam's father, Laomédôn, who added insult to injury by withholding the god's wages.
[4] A large mound covering a grave.

Hêra whose arms are white as ivory
grew angry at Apollo. She retorted:

"Lord of the silver bow, your words would be
acceptable if one had a mind to honor
Hektor and Akhilleus equally.
But Hektor suckled at a woman's breast,   70
Akhilleus is the first-born of a goddess—
one I nursed myself. I reared her, gave her
to Pêleus, a strong man whom the gods loved.
All of you were present at their wedding—
you too—friend of the base, forever slippery!—
came with your harp and dined there!

                                        Zeus the stormking
answered her:

                            "Hêra, don't lose your temper
altogether. Clearly the same high honor
cannot be due both men. And yet Lord Hektor
of all the mortal men in Ilion,   80
was dearest to the gods, or was to me.
He never failed in the right gift; my altar
never lacked a feast
of wine poured out and smoke of sacrifice—
the share assigned as ours. We shall renounce
the theft of Hektor's body; there is no way;
there would be no eluding Akhilleus' eye,
as night and day his mother comes to him.
Will one of you now call her to my presence?
I have a solemn message to impart: 90
Akhilleus is to take fine gifts from Priam,
and in return give back Prince Hektor's body."

At this, Iris who runs on the rainy wind
with word from Zeus departed. Midway between
Samos and rocky Imbros,[5] down she plunged
into the dark grey sea, and the brimming tide
roared over her as she sank into the depth—
as rapidly as a leaden sinker, fixed
on a lure of wild bull's horn, that glimmers down
with a fatal hook among the ravening fish.   100
Soon Iris came on Thetis in a cave,
surrounded by a company of Nereids
lolling there, while she bewailed the fate
of her magnificent son, now soon to perish
on Troy's rich earth, far from his fatherland.
Halting before her, Iris said:

---

[5]Islands in the Aegean Sea, northwest of Troy.

"Come, Thetis,
Zeus of eternal forethought summons you."

Silvery-footed Thetis answered:

"Why?
Why does the great one call me to him now,
when I am shy of mingling with immortals,   110
being so heavyhearted? But I'll go.
Whatever he may say will have its weight."

That loveliest of goddesses now put on
a veil so black no garment could be blacker,
and swam where windswift Iris led. Before them
on either hand the ground swell fell away.
They rose to a beach, then soared into the sky
and found the viewer of the wide world, Zeus,
with all the blissful gods who live forever
around him seated. Athêna yielded place,   120
and Thetis sat down by her father, Zeus,
while Hêra handed her a cup of gold
and spoke a comforting word. When she had drunk,
Thetis held out the cup again to Hêra.
The father of gods and men began:

"You've come
to Olympos, Thetis, though your mind is troubled
and insatiable pain preys on your heart.
I know, I too. But let me, even so,
explain why I have called you here. Nine days
of quarreling we've had among the gods   130
concerning Hektor's body and Akhilleus.
They wish the Wayfinder to make off with it.
I, however, accord Akhilleus honor
as I now tell you—in respect for you
whose love I hope to keep hereafter. Go, now,
down to the army, tell this to your son:
the gods are sullen toward him, and I, too,
more than the rest, am angered at his madness,
holding the body by the beaked ships
and not releasing it. In fear of me   140
let him relent and give back Hektor's body!
At the same time I'll send Iris to Priam,
directing him to go down to the beachhead
and ransom his dear son. He must bring gifts
to melt Akhilleus' rage."

Thetis obeyed,
leaving Olympos' ridge and flashing down
to her son's hut. She found him groaning there,

inconsolable, while men-at-arms
went to and fro, making their breakfast ready—
having just put to the knife a fleecy sheep.   150
His gentle mother sat down at his side,
caressed him, and said tenderly:

                                        "My child,
will you forever feed on your own heart
in grief and pain, and take no thought of sleep
or sustenance? It would be comforting
to make love with a woman. No long time
will you live on for me: Death even now
stands near you, appointed and all-powerful.
But be alert and listen: I am a messenger
from Zeus, who tells me the gods are sullen toward you   160
and he himself most angered at your madness,
holding the body by the beaked ships
and not releasing it. Give Hektor back.
Take ransom for the body."

                                        Said Akhilleus:

"Let it be so. Let someone bring the ransom
and take the dead away, if the Olympian
commands this in his wisdom."

                                        So, that morning,
in camp, amid the ships, mother and son
conversed together, and their talk was long.
Lord Zeus meanwhile sent Iris to Ilion.   170

"Off with you, lightfoot, leave Olympos, take
my message to the majesty of Priam
at Ilion. He is to journey down
and ransom his dear son upon the beachhead.
He shall take gifts to melt Akhilleus' rage,
and let him go alone, no soldier with him,
only some crier, some old man, to drive
his wagon team and guide the nimble wagon,
and afterward to carry home the body
of him that Prince Akhilleus overcame.   180
Let him not think of death, or suffer dread,
as I'll provide him with a wondrous guide,
the Wayfinder, to bring him across the lines
into the very presence of Akhilleus.
And he, when he sees Priam within his hut,
will neither take his life nor let another
enemy come near. He is no madman,
no blind brute, nor one to flout the gods,
but dutiful toward men who beg his mercy."

Then Iris at his bidding ran   190
on the rainy winds to bear the word of Zeus,
until she came to Priam's house and heard
voices in lamentation. In the court
she found the princes huddled around their father,
faces and clothing wet with tears. The old man,
fiercely wrapped and hooded in his mantle,
sat like a figure graven—caked in filth
his own hands had swept over head and neck
when he lay rolling on the ground. Indoors
his daughters and his sons' wives were weeping,   200
remembering how many and how brave
the young men were who had gone down to death
before the Argive spearmen.
                                                    Zeus's courier,

appearing now to Priam's eyes alone,
alighted whispering, so the old man trembled:

"Priam, heir of Dárdanos,[6] take heart,
and have no fear of me; I bode no evil,
but bring you friendly word from Zeus,
who is distressed for you and pities you
though distant far upon Olympos. He   210
commands that you shall ransom the Prince Hektor,
taking fine gifts to melt Akhilleus' rage.
And go alone: no soldier may go with you,
only some crier, some old man, to drive
your wagon team and guide the nimble wagon,
and afterward to carry home the body
of him that Prince Akhilleus overcame.
Put away thoughts of death, shake off your dread,
for you shall have a wondrous guide,
the Wayfinder, to bring you across the lines   220
into the very presence of Akhilleus.
He, for his part, seeing you in his quarters,
will neither take your life nor let another
enemy come near. He is no madman,
no blind brute, nor one to flout the gods,
but dutiful toward men who beg his mercy."

Iris left him, swift as a veering wind.
Then Priam spoke, telling the men to rig
a four-wheeled wagon with a wicker box,
while he withdrew to his chamber roofed in cedar,   230
high and fragrant, rich in precious things.
He called to Hékabê, his lady:

---

[6]A son of Zeus and ancestor of Priam (five generations earlier).

"Princess,

word from Olympian Zeus has come to me
to go down to the ships of the Akhaians
and ransom our dead son. I am to take
gifts that will melt Akhilleus' anger. Tell me
how this appears to you, tell me your mind,
for I am torn with longing, now, to pass
inside the great encampment by the ships."

The woman's voice broke as she answered:

"Sorrow, 240

sorrow. Where is the wisdom now that made you
famous in the old days, near and far?
How can you ever face the Akhaian ships
or wish to go alone before those eyes,
the eyes of one who stripped your sons in battle,
how many, and how brave? Iron[7] must be
the heart within you. If he sees you, takes you,
savage and wayward as the man is,
he'll have no mercy and no shame. Better
that we should mourn together in our hall. 250
Almighty fate spun this thing for our son
the day I bore him: destined him to feed
the wild dogs after death, being far from us
when he went down before the stronger man.
I could devour the vitals of that man,
leeching into his living flesh! He'd know
pain then—pain like mine for my dead son.
It was no coward the Akhaian killed;
he stood and fought for the sweet wives of Troy,
with no more thought of flight or taking cover." 260

In majesty old Priam said:

"My heart

is fixed on going. Do not hold me back,
and do not make yourself a raven[8] crying
calamity at home. You will not move me.
If any man on earth had urged this on me—
reader of altar smoke,[9] prophet or priest—
we'd say it was a lie, and hold aloof.
But no: with my own ears I heard the voice,
I saw the god before me. Go I shall,
and no more words. If I must die alongside 270
the ships of the Akhaians in their bronze,

[7]Courageous.
[8]Traditionally, the bird forebodes evil.
[9]Interpreter of omens.

I die gladly. May I but hold my son
and spend my grief; then let Akhilleus kill me."

Throwing open the lids of treasure boxes
he picked out twelve great robes of state, and twelve
light cloaks for men, and rugs, an equal number,
and just as many capes of snowy linen,
adding a dozen khitons to the lot;
then set in order ten pure bars of gold,
a pair of shining tripods, four great caldrons,   280
and finally one splendid cup, a gift
Thracians had made him on an embassy.
He would not keep this, either—as he cared
for nothing now but ransoming his son.

And now, from the colonnade,
he made his Trojan people keep their distance,
berating and abusing them:

                                                                                   "Away,
you craven fools and rubbish! In your own homes
have you no one to mourn, that you crowd here,
to make more trouble for me? Is this a show,   290
that Zeus has crushed me, that he took the life
of my most noble son? You'll soon know what it means,
as you become child's play for the Akhaians
to kill in battle, now that Hektor's gone.
As for myself, before I see my city
taken and ravaged, let me go down blind
to Death's cold kingdom!"

                                                                      Staff in hand,
he herded them, until they turned away
and left the furious old man. He lashed out
now at his sons, at Hélenos and Paris,   300
Agathôn, Pammôn, Antíphonos,
Polítês, Dêíphobos, Hippóthoös,
and Dios—to these nine the old man cried:

"Bestir yourselves, you misbegotten whelps,
shame of my house! Would god you had been killed
instead of Hektor at the line of ships.
How curst I am in everything! I fathered
first-rate men, in our great Troy; but now
I swear not one is left: Mêstôr, Trôïlos,
laughing amid the war-cars; and then Hektor—   310
a god to soldiers, and a god among them,
seeming not a man's child, but a god's.
Arês[10] killed them. These poltroons are left,

[10] Here, as often, the word is not so much the name of a god as a synonym for war itself.

hollow men, dancers, heroes of the dance,
light-fingered pillagers of lambs and kids
from the town pens!
                                        Now will you get a wagon
ready for me, and quickly? Load these gifts
aboard it, so that we can take the road."

Dreading the rough edge of their father's tongue,
they lifted out a cart, a cargo wagon,   320
neat and maneuverable, and newly made,
and fixed upon it a wicker box; then took
a mule yoke from a peg, a yoke of boxwood
knobbed in front, with rings to hold the reins.
They brought out, too, the band nine forearms long
called the yoke-fastener, and placed the yoke
forward at the shank of the polished pole,
shoving the yoke-pin firmly in. They looped
three turns of the yoke-fastener round the knob
and wound it over and over down the pole,   330
tucking the tab end under. Next, the ransom:
bearing the weight of gifts for Hektor's person
out of the inner room, they piled them up
on the polished wagon. It was time to yoke
the mule-team, strong in harness, with hard hooves,
a team the Mysians had given Priam.
Then for the king's own chariot they harnessed
a team of horses of the line of Tros,[11]
reared by the old king in his royal stable.
So the impatient king and his sage crier   340
had their animals yoked in the palace yard
when Hékabê in her agitation joined them,
carrying in her right hand a golden cup
of honeyed wine, with which, before they left,
they might make offering. At the horses' heads
she stood to tell them:

                                        "Here, tip wine to Zeus,
the father of gods. Pray for a safe return
from the enemy army, seeing your heart is set
on venturing to the camp against my will.
Pray in the second place to Zeus the stormking,   350
gloomy over Ida, who looks down
on all Troy country. Beg for an omen-bird,
the courier dearest of all birds to Zeus
and sovereign in power of flight,[12]
that he appear upon our right in heaven.

---

[11] Great-grandfather of Priam. The horses of Trôs, which he received from Zeus, were the
best in the world.
[12] The eagle. Good omens appeared on the right side.

When you have seen him with your own eyes, then,
under that sign, you may approach the ships.
If Zeus who views the wide world will not give you
vision of his bird, then I at least
cannot bid godspeed to your journey,   360
bent on it though you are."

                                              In majesty,
Priam replied:

                                    "My lady, in this matter
I am disposed to trust you and agree.
It is an excellent thing and salutary
to lift our hands to Zeus, invoking mercy."

The old king motioned to his housekeeper,
who stood nearby with a basin and a jug,
to pour clear water on his hands. He washed them,
took the cup his lady held, and prayed
while standing there, midway in the walled court.   370
Then he tipped out the wine, looking toward heaven,
saying:

                          "Zeus, our Father, reigning from Ida,
god of glory and power, grant I come
to Akhilleus' door as one to be received
with kindliness and mercy. And dispatch
your courier bird, the nearest to your heart
of all birds, and the first in power of flight.
Let him appear upon our right in heaven
that I may see him with my own eyes
and under that sign journey to the ships."   380

Zeus all-foreseeing listened to this prayer
and put an eagle, king
of winged creatures, instantly in flight:
a swamp eagle, a hunter, one they call
the duskwing. Wide as a doorway in a chamber
spacious and high, built for a man of wealth,
a door with long bars fitted well, so wide
spread out each pinion. The great bird appeared
winging through the town on their right hand,
and all their hearts lifted with joy to see him.   390
In haste the old king boarded his bright car
and clattered out of the echoing colonnade.
Ahead, the mule-team drew the four-wheeled wagon,
driven by Idaíos,[13] and behind
the chariot rolled, with horses that the old man
whipped into a fast trot through the town.

[13] Priam's crier, or herald.

Family and friends all followed weeping
as though for Priam's last and deathward ride.
Into the lower town they passed, and reached
the plain of Troy. Here those who followed after 400
turned back, sons and sons-in-law. And Zeus
who views the wide world saw the car and wagon
brave the plain. He felt a pang for Priam
and quickly said to Hermês, his own son:

"Hermês, as you go most happily
of all the gods with mortals,[14] and give heed
to whom you will, be on your way this time
as guide for Priam to the deepsea ships.
Guide him so that not one of the Danáäns
may know or see him till he reach Akhilleus." 410

Argeiphontês[15] the Wayfinder obeyed.
He bent to tie his beautiful sandals on,
ambrosial, golden, that carry him over water
and over endless land on a puff of wind,
and took the wand with which he charms asleep—
or, when he wills, awake—the eyes of men.
So, wand in hand, the strong god glittering
paced into the air. Quick as a thought
he came to Hellê's waters and to Troy,
appearing as a boy whose lip was downy 420
in the first bloom of manhood, a young prince,
all graciousness.

After the travelers
drove past the mound of Ilos,[16] at the ford
they let the mules and horses pause to drink
the running stream. Now darkness had come on
when, looking round, the crier
saw Hermês near at hand. He said to Priam:

"You must think hard and fast, your grace;
there is new danger; we need care and prudence.
I see a man-at-arms there—ready, I think, 430
to prey on us. Come, shall we whip the team
and make a run for it? Or take his knees
and beg for mercy?"

Now the old man's mind
gave way to confusion and to terror.
On his gnarled arms and legs the hair stood up,

---

[14]Hermês often acts as a guide, and one of his functions is to conduct the spirits of the dead to the Underworld.

[15]A name for Hermês; see Homer's *Odyssey*, I.53 and note.

[16]Ilos' burial mound. He was grandfather of Priam and founder of Troy (which is therefore sometimes called Ilion).

and he stared, breathless. But the affable god
came over and took his hand and asked:

"Old father,
where do you journey, with your cart and car,
while others rest, below the evening star?
Do you not fear the Akhaians where they lie   440
encamped, hard, hostile outlanders, nearby?
Should someone see you, bearing stores like these
by night, how would you deal with enemies?
You are not young, your escort's ancient, too.
Could you beat off an attacker, either of you?
I'll do no hurt to you but defend you here.
You remind me of my father, whom I hold dear."

Old Priam answered him:

"Indeed, dear boy,
the case is as you say. And yet some god
stretched out his hand above me, he who sent   450
before me here—and just at the right time—
a traveler like yourself, well-made, well-spoken,
clearheaded, too. You come of some good family."

The Wayfinder rejoined:

"You speak with courtesy,
dear sir. But on this point enlighten me:
are you removing treasure here amassed
for safety abroad, until the war is past?
Or can you be abandoning Ilion
in fear, after he perished, that great one
who never shirked a battle, your own princely son?"   460

Old Priam replied:

"My brave young friend, who are you?
Born of whom? How nobly you acknowledge
the dreadful end of my unfortunate son."

To this the Wayfinder replied:

"Dear sir,
you question me about him? Never surmise
I have not seen him with my very eyes,
and often, on the field. I saw him chase
Argives with carnage to their own shipways,
while we stood wondering, forbidden war
by the great anger that Akhilleus bore   470
Lord Agamémnon. I am of that company
Akhilleus led. His own ship carried me

as one of the Myrmidons. My father is old,
as you are, and his name's Polyktôr;[17] gold
and other wealth he owns;
and I am seventh and last of all his sons.
When I cast lots among them, my lot fell
to join the siege against Troy citadel.
Tonight I've left the camp to scout this way
where, circling Troy, we'll fight at break of day;   480
our men are tired of waiting and will not stand
for any postponement by the high command."

Responded royal Priam:

                                          "If you belong

to the company of Akhilleus, son of Pêleus,
tell me this, and tell me the whole truth:
is my son even now beside the ships?
Or has Akhilleus by this time dismembered him
and thrown him to the wild dogs?"

                                          The Wayfinder
made reply again:

                                          "Dear sir,

no dogs or birds have yet devoured your son.   490
Beside Akhilleus' ship, out of the sun,
he lies in a place of shelter. Now twelve days
the man has lain there, yet no part decays,
nor have the blowfly's maggots, that devour
dead men in war, fed on him to this hour.
True that around his dear friend's barrow tomb
Akhilleus drags him when dawn-shadows come,
driving pitilessly; but he mars him not.
You might yourself be witness, on the spot,
how fresh with dew he lies, washed of his gore,   500
unstained, for the deep gashes that he bore
have all closed up—and many thrust their bronze
into his body. The blest immortal ones
favor your prince, and care for every limb
even in death, as they so cherished him."

The old king's heart exulted, and he said:

"Child, it was well to honor the immortals.
He never forgot, at home in Ilion—
ah, did my son exist? was he a dream?—
the gods who own Olympos. They in turn   510
were mindful of him when he met his end.

[17] The name means "having wealth."

Here is a goblet as a gift from me.
Protect me, give me escort, if the gods
attend us, till I reach Akhilleus' hut."

And in response Hermês the Wayfinder
said:

                              "You are putting a young man to the test,
dear sir, but I may not, as you request,
accept a gift behind Akhilleus' back.
Fearing, honoring him, I could not lack
discretion to that point. The consequence, too,   520
could be unwelcome. As for escorting you,
even to Argos' famous land I'd ride
a deck with you, or journey at your side.
No cutthroat ever will disdain your guide."

With this, Hermês who lights the way for mortals
leapt into the driver's place. He caught up
reins and whip, and breathed a second wind
into the mule-team and the team of horses.
Onward they ran toward parapet and ships,
and pulled up to the moat.

                              Now night had fallen,   530
bringing the sentries to their supper fire,
but the glimmering god Hermês, the Wayfinder,
showered a mist of slumber on them all.
As quick as thought, he had the gates unbarred
and open to let the wagon enter, bearing
the old king and the ransom.

                              Going seaward
they came to the lofty quarters of Akhilleus,
a lodge the Myrmidons built for their lord
of pine trees cut and trimmed, and shaggy thatch
from mowings in deep meadows. Posts were driven   540
round the wide courtyard in a palisade,
whose gate one crossbar held, one beam of pine.
It took three men to slam this home, and three
to draw the bolt again—but great Akhilleus
worked his entryway alone with ease.
And now Hermês, who lights the way for mortals,
opened for Priam, took him safely in
with all his rich gifts for the son of Pêleus.
Then the god dropped the reins, and stepping down
he said:

                              "I am no mortal wagoner,   550
but Hermês, sir. My father sent me here
to be your guide amid the Akhaian men.
Now that is done, I'm off to heaven again

and will not visit Akhilleus. That would be
to compromise an immortal's dignity—
to be received with guests of mortal station.
Go take his knees, and make your supplication:
invoke his father, his mother, and his child;
pray that his heart be touched, that he be reconciled."

Now Hermês turned, departing for Olympos, 560
and Priam vaulted down. He left Idaíos
to hold the teams in check, while he went forward
into the lodge. He found Akhilleus, dear
to Zeus, there in his chair, with officers
at ease across the room. Only Automédôn
and Álkimos were busy near Akhilleus,
for he had just now made an end of dinner,
eating and drinking, and the laden boards
lay near him still upon the trestles.

                                       Priam,

the great king of Troy, passed by the others, 570
knelt down, took in his arms Akhilleus' knees,
and kissed the hands of wrath that killed his sons.

When, taken with mad Folly in his own land,
a man does murder and in exile finds
refuge in some rich house, then all who see him
stand in awe.
So these men stood.

                                       Akhilleus

gazed in wonder at the splendid king,
and his companions marveled too, all silent,
with glances to and fro. Now Priam prayed 580
to the man before him:

                        "Remember your own father,
Akhilleus, in your godlike youth: his years
like mine are many, and he stands upon
the fearful doorstep of old age.[18] He, too,
is hard pressed, it may be, by those around him,
there being no one able to defend him
from bane of war and ruin. Ah, but he
may nonetheless hear news of you alive,
and so with glad heart hope through all his days
for sight of his dear son, come back from Troy, 590
while I have deathly fortune.

                                Noble sons

I fathered here, but scarce one man is left me.
Fifty I had when the Akhaians came,

[18] Upon the threshold of death.

nineteen out of a single belly, others
born of attendant women. Most are gone.
Raging Arês cut their knees from under them.
And he who stood alone among them all,
their champion, and Troy's, ten days ago
you killed him, fighting for his land, my prince,
Hektor.

                                    It is for him that I have come   600
among these ships, to beg him back from you,
and I bring ransom without stint.

                                                        Akhilleus,
be reverent toward the great gods! And take
pity on me, remember your own father.
Think me more pitiful by far, since I
have brought myself to do what no man else
has done before—to lift to my lips the hand
of one who killed my son."

                                            Now in Akhilleus
the evocation of his father stirred
new longing, and an ache of grief. He lifted   610
the old man's hand and gently put him by.
Then both were overborne as they remembered:
the old king huddled at Akhilleus' feet
wept, and wept for Hektor, killer of men,
while great Akhilleus wept for his own father
as for Patróklos once again; and sobbing
filled the room.

                            But when Akhilleus' heart
had known the luxury of tears, and pain
within his breast and bones had passed away,
he stood then, raised the old king up, in pity   620
for his grey head and greybeard cheek, and spoke
in a warm rush of words:

                                        "Ah, sad and old!
Trouble and pain you've borne, and bear, aplenty.
Only a great will could have brought you here
among the Akhaian ships, and here alone
before the eyes of one who stripped your sons,
your many sons, in battle. Iron must be
the heart within you. Come, then, and sit down.
We'll probe our wounds no more but let them rest,
though grief lies heavy on us. Tears heal nothing, 630
drying so stiff and cold. This is the way
the gods ordained the destiny of men,
to bear such burdens in our lives, while they
feel no affliction. At the door of Zeus
are those two urns of good and evil gifts

that he may choose for us; and one for whom
the lightning's joyous king dips in both urns
will have by turns bad luck and good. But one
to whom he sends all evil[19]—that man goes
contemptible by the will of Zeus; ravenous 640
hunger drives him over the wondrous earth,
unresting, without honor from gods or men.
Mixed fortune came to Pêleus. Shining gifts
at the gods' hands he had from birth: felicity,
wealth overflowing, rule of the Myrmidons,
a bride immortal at his mortal side.
But then Zeus gave afflictions too—no family
of powerful sons grew up for him at home,
but one child, of all seasons and of none.
Can I stand by him in his age? Far from my country 650
I sit at Troy to grieve you and your children.
You, too, sir, in time past were fortunate,
we hear men say. From Makar's isle of Lesbos
northward, and south of Phrygia and the Straits,
no one had wealth like yours, or sons like yours.[20]
Then gods out of the sky sent you this bitterness:
the years of siege, the battles and the losses.
Endure it, then. And do not mourn forever
for your dead son. There is no remedy.
You will not make him stand again. Rather 660
await some new misfortune to be suffered."

The old king in his majesty replied:

"Never give me a chair, my lord, while Hektor
lies in your camp uncared for. Yield him to me
now. Allow me sight of him. Accept
the many gifts I bring. May they reward you,
and may you see your home again.
You spared my life at once and let me live."

Akhilleus, the great runner, frowned and eyed him
under his brows:

                     "Do not vex me, sir," he said. 670
"I have intended, in my own good time,
to yield up Hektor to you. She who bore me,
the daughter of the Ancient of the sea,
has come with word to me from Zeus. I know
in your case, too—though you say nothing, Priam—
that some god guided you to the shipways here.

---

[19] Misfortune.
[20] Lesbos (of which Makar was a legendary king) is an island off the coastline, south of
Troy; Phrygia lies inland, to the east; the Straits (the Hellespont, or modern Dardanelles) lie
to the north.

No strong man in his best days could make entry
into this camp. How could he pass the guard,
or force our gateway?

                                        Therefore, *let me be.*

Sting my sore heart again, and even here,   680
under my own roof, suppliant though you are,
I may not spare you, sir, but trample on
the express command of Zeus!"

                                        When he heard this,
the old man feared him and obeyed with silence.
Now like a lion at one bound Akhilleus
left the room. Close at his back the officers
Automédôn and Álkimos went out—
comrades in arms whom he esteemed the most
after the dead Patróklos. They unharnessed
mules and horses, led the old king's crier   690
to a low bench and sat him down.
Then from the polished wagon
they took the piled-up price of Hektor's body.
One khiton and two capes they left aside
as dress and shrouding for the homeward journey.
Then, calling to the women slaves, Akhilleus
ordered the body bathed and rubbed with oil—
but lifted, too, and placed apart, where Priam
could not see his son—for seeing Hektor
he might in his great pain give way to rage,   700
and fury then might rise up in Akhilleus
to slay the old king, flouting Zeus's word.
So after bathing and anointing Hektor
they drew the shirt and beautiful shrouding over him.
Then with his own hands lifting him, Akhilleus
laid him upon a couch, and with his two
companions aiding, placed him in the wagon.
Now a bitter groan burst from Akhilleus,
who stood and prayed to his own dead friend:

                                        "Patróklos,
do not be angry with me, if somehow   710
even in the world of Death you learn of this—
that I released Prince Hektor to his father.[21]
The gifts he gave were not unworthy. Aye,
and you shall have your share, this time as well."[22]

---

[21] When Patróklos' funeral was held, in Book XXIII, Akhilleus had promised his dead friend
that he would not return Hektor's body to Priam or allow it to be burned or buried.

[22] The gifts are more than a bribe given to Akhilleus; they are valued not only in themselves but also—as in many primitive heroic cultures—as an outward symbol of the recipient's
honor. Moreover, Akhilleus promises to give Patróklos his share—by burning it as he had burned
other treasures at the funeral.

The Prince Akhilleus turned back to his quarters.
He took again the splendid chair that stood
against the farther wall, then looked at Priam
and made his declaration:

                                  "As you wished, sir,
the body of your son is now set free.
He lies in state. At the first sight of Dawn   720
you shall take charge of him yourself and see him.
Now let us think of supper. We are told
that even Niobê in her extremity
took thought for bread—though all her brood had perished,
her six young girls and six tall sons.[23] Apollo,
making his silver longbow whip and sing,
shot the lads down, and Artemis with raining
arrows killed the daughters—all this after
Niobê had compared herself with Lêto,
the smooth-cheeked goddess.

                        She has borne two children,   730
Niobê said, How many have I borne!
But soon those two destroyed the twelve.

                                    Besides,
nine days the dead lay stark, no one could bury them,
for Zeus had turned all folk of theirs to stone.
The gods made graves for them on the tenth day,
and then at last, being weak and spent with weeping,
Niobê thought of food. Among the rocks
of Sipylos' lonely mountainside, where nymphs
who race Akhelôios river go to rest,
she, too, long turned to stone, somewhere broods on   740
the gall immortal gods gave her to drink.

Like her we'll think of supper, noble sir.
Weep for your son again when you have borne him
back to Troy; there he'll be mourned indeed."

In one swift movement now Akhilleus caught
and slaughtered a white lamb. His officers
flayed it, skillful in their butchering
to dress the flesh; they cut bits for the skewers,
roasted, and drew them off, done to a turn.
Automédôn dealt loaves into the baskets   750
on the great board; Akhilleus served the meat.
Then all their hands went out upon the supper.
When thirst and appetite were turned away,

---

[23]Niobê's presumptuous boast of superiority to Lêto (mother of Artemis and Apollo) and the transformation of the grieving mother to stone are traditional elements of the myth, but much of the story as given here was invented by Homer in order to create a parallel with Priam and Hektor. The poet does something similar with the Meléagros story in Book IX.

Priam, the heir of Dárdanos, gazed long
in wonder at Akhilleus' form and scale—
so like the gods in aspect. And Akhilleus
in his turn gazed in wonder upon Priam,
royal in visage as in speech. Both men
in contemplation found rest for their eyes,
till the old hero, Priam, broke the silence: 760

"Make a bed ready for me, son of Thetis,
and let us know the luxury of sleep.
From that hour when my son died at your hands
till now, my eyelids have not closed in slumber
over my eyes, but groaning where I sat
I tasted pain and grief a thousandfold,
or lay down rolling in my courtyard mire.
Here for the first time I have swallowed bread
and made myself drink wine.

                                                    Before, I could not."

Akhilleus ordered men and serving women   770
to make a bed outside, in the covered forecourt,
with purple rugs piled up and sheets outspread
and coverings of fleeces laid on top.
The girls went out with torches in their hands
and soon deftly made up a double bed.
Then Akhilleus, defiant of Agamémnon,
told his guest:

                                                    "Dear venerable sir,
you'll sleep outside tonight, in case an Akhaian
officer turns up, one of those men
who are forever taking counsel with me—   780
as well they may. If one should see you here
as the dark night runs on, he would report it
to the Lord Marshal Agamémnon. Then
return of the body would only be delayed.
Now tell me this, and give me a straight answer:
How many days do you require
for the funeral of Prince Hektor?—I should know
how long to wait, and hold the Akhaian army."

Old Priam in his majesty replied:

"If you would have me carry out the burial,   790
Akhilleus, here is the way to do me grace.
As we are penned in the town, but must bring wood
from the distant hills, the Trojans are afraid.
We should have mourning for nine days in hall,
then on the tenth conduct his funeral
and feast the troops and commons;
on the eleventh we should make his tomb,

and on the twelfth give battle, if we must."

Akhilleus said:

                                    "As you command, old Priam,
the thing is done. I shall suspend the war   800
for those eleven days that you require."

He took the old man's right hand by the wrist
and held it, to allay his fear.

                                                        Now crier
and king with hearts brimful retired to rest
in the sheltered forecourt, while Akhilleus slept
deep in his palisaded lodge. Beside him,
lovely in her youth, Brisêis lay.
And other gods and soldiers all night long,
by slumber quieted, slept on. But slumber
would not come to Hermês the Good Companion,   810
as he considered how to ease the way
for Priam from the camp, to send him through
unseen by the formidable gatekeepers.
Then Hermês came to Priam's pillow, saying:

"Sir, no thought of danger shakes your rest,
as you sleep on, being great Akhilleus' guest,
amid men fierce as hunters in a ring.
You triumphed in a costly ransoming,
but three times costlier your own would be
to your surviving sons—a monarch's fee—   820
if this should come to Agamémnon's ear
and all the Akhaian host should learn that you are here."

The old king started up in fright, and woke
his herald. Hermês yoked the mules and horses,
took the reins, then inland like the wind
he drove through all the encampment, seen by no one.
When they reached Xánthos, eddying and running
god-begotten river, at the ford,
Hermês departed for Olympos. Dawn
spread out her yellow robe on all the earth,   830
as they drove on toward Troy, with groans and sighs,
and the mule-team pulled the wagon and the body.
And no one saw them, not a man or woman,
before Kassandra.[24] Tall as the pale-gold
goddess Aphrodítê, she had climbed

---

[24]A daughter of Priam and Hékabê. She is prominent in later Greek literature as a prophetess doomed to have her prophecies disbelieved. See, for example, Aeschylus' *Agamémnon,* which shows her as a captive taken from Troy by Agamémnon.

the citadel of Pergamos at dawn.
Now looking down she saw her father come
in his war-car, and saw the crier there,
and saw Lord Hektor on his bed of death
upon the mulecart. The girl wailed and cried   840
to all the city:

                                        "Oh, look down, look down,
go to your windows, men of Troy, and women,
see Lord Hektor now! Remember joy
at seeing him return alive from battle,
exalting all our city and our land!"

Now, at the sight of Hektor, all gave way
to loss and longing, and all crowded down
to meet the escort and body near the gates,
till no one in the town was left at home.
There Hektor's lady and his gentle mother   850
tore their hair for him, flinging themselves
upon the wagon to embrace his person
while the crowd groaned. All that long day
until the sun went down they might have mourned
in tears before the gateway. But old Priam
spoke to them from his chariot:

                                                            "Make way,
let the mules pass. You'll have your fill of weeping
later, when I've brought the body home."

They parted then, and made way for the wagon,
allowing Priam to reach the famous hall.   860
They laid the body of Hektor in his bed,
and brought in minstrels, men to lead the dirge.
While these wailed out, the women answered, moaning.
Andrómakhê of the ivory-white arms
held in her lap between her hands
the head of Hektor who had killed so many.
Now she lamented:

                                        "You've been torn from life,
my husband, in young manhood, and you leave me
empty in our hall. The boy's a child
whom you and I, poor souls, conceived; I doubt   870
he'll come to manhood. Long before, great Troy
will go down plundered, citadel and all,
now that you are lost, who guarded it
and kept it, and preserved its wives and children.
They will be shipped off in the murmuring hulls
one day, and I along with all the rest.
You, my little one, either you come with me
to do some grinding labor, some base toil

for a harsh master, or an Akhaian soldier
will grip you by the arm and hurl you down 880
from a tower here to a miserable death—
out of his anger for a brother, a father,
or even a son that Hektor killed. Akhaians
in hundreds mouthed black dust under his blows.
He was no moderate man in war, your father,
and that is why they mourn him through the city.
Hektor, you gave your parents grief and pain
but left me loneliest, and heartbroken.
You could not open your strong arms to me
from your deathbed, or say a thoughtful word, 890
for me to cherish all my life long
as I weep for you night and day."

                                     Her voice broke,

and a wail came from the women. Hékabê
lifted her lamenting voice among them:

"Hektor, dearest of sons to me, in life
you had the favor of the immortal gods,
and they have cared for you in death as well.
Akhilleus captured other sons of mine
in other years, and sold them overseas
to Samos, Imbros, and the smoky island, 900
Lemnos. That was not his way with you.
After he took your life, cutting you down
with his sharp-bladed spear, he trussed and dragged you
many times round the barrow of his friend,
Patróklos, whom you killed—though not by this
could that friend live again. But now I find you
fresh as pale dew, seeming newly dead,
like one to whom Apollo of the silver bow
had given easy death with his mild arrows."[25]

Hékabê sobbed again, and the wails redoubled. 910
Then it was Helen's turn to make lament:

"Dear Hektor, dearest brother to me by far!
My husband is Aléxandros,
who brought me here to Troy—God, that I might
have died sooner! This is the twentieth year
since I left home, and left my fatherland.[26]
But never did I have an evil word
or gesture from you. No—and when some other
brother-in-law or sister would revile me,
or if my mother-in-law spoke to me bitterly— 920

---

[25] The arrows of Apollo bring death to men as those of his sister, Artemis, do to women.
[26] This statement is puzzling, since the war lasted only ten years. Perhaps we are to understand that the Greeks spent ten years in preparation or that the expedition was delayed ten years en route.

but Priam never did, being as mild
as my own father—you would bring her round
with your kind heart and gentle speech. Therefore
I weep for you and for myself as well,
given this fate, this grief. In all wide Troy
no one is left who will befriend me, none;
they all shudder at me."

                                                                    Helen wept,
and a moan came from the people, hearing her.
Then Priam, the old king, commanded them:

"Trojans, bring firewood to the edge of town.   930
No need to fear an ambush of the Argives.
When he dismissed me from the camp, Akhilleus
told me clearly they will not harass us,
not until dawn comes for the twelfth day."

Then yoking mules and oxen to their wagons
the people thronged before the city gates.
Nine days they labored, bringing countless loads
of firewood to the town. When Dawn that lights
the world of mortals came for the tenth day,
they carried greathearted Hektor out at last,   940
and all in tears placed his dead body high
upon its pyre, then cast a torch below.
When the young Dawn with finger tips of rose
made heaven bright, the Trojan people massed
about Prince Hektor's ritual fire.
All being gathered and assembled, first
they quenched the smoking pyre with tawny wine
wherever flames had licked their way, then friends
and brothers picked his white bones from the char
in sorrow, while the tears rolled down their cheeks.   950
In a golden urn they put the bones,
shrouding the urn with veiling of soft purple.
Then in a grave dug deep they placed it
and heaped it with great stones. The men were quick
to raise the death-mound, while in every quarter
lookouts were posted to ensure against
an Akhaian surprise attack. When they had finished
raising the barrow, they returned to Ilion,
where all sat down to banquet in his honor
in the hall of Priam king. So they performed   960
the funeral rites of Hektor, tamer of horses.

THE ODYSSEY

Translated by Robert Fitzgerald

The ten-year war waged by the Greeks against Troy, culminating in the overthrow of the city, is now itself ten years in the past. Helen, whose flight to Troy with the Trojan prince Paris had prompted the Greek expedition to seek revenge and reclaim her, is now home in Sparta, living harmoniously once more with her husband Meneláos (Menelaus). His brother Agamémnon, commander in chief of the Greek forces, was murdered on his return from the war by his wife and her paramour. Of the Greek chieftains who have survived both the war and the perilous homeward voyage, all have returned except Odysseus, the crafty and astute ruler of Ithaka (Ithaca), an island in the Ionian Sea off western Greece. Since he is presumed dead, suitors from Ithaka and other regions have overrun his house, paying court to his attractive wife Penélopê, endangering the position of his son, Telémakhos (Telemachus), corrupting many of the servants, and literally eating up Odysseus' estate. Penélopê has stalled for time but is finding it increasingly difficult to deny the suitors' demands that she marry one of them; Telémakhos, who is just approaching young manhood, is becoming actively resentful of the indignities suffered by his household.

Many persons and places in the *Odyssey* are best known to readers by their Latinized names, such as *Telemachus*. The present translator has used forms (*Telémakhos*) closer to the Greek spelling and pronunciation. A slanted accent mark (´) indicates stress; thus *Agamémnon* is accented on the third syllable. A circumflex accent (ˆ) indicates that the vowel sound is long; thus *Kêrês* is pronounced "Care-ace." A dieresis (¨) indicates pronunciation as a separate syllable; thus, *Thoösa* has three syllables rather than two. [*Editors' headnote.*]

BOOK ONE: A GODDESS INTERVENES

Sing in me, Muse, and through me tell the story
of that man skilled in all ways of contending,
the wanderer, harried for years on end,
after he plundered the stronghold
on the proud height of Troy.[1]
                                  He saw the townlands
and learned the minds of many distant men,
and weathered many bitter nights and days
in his deep heart at sea, while he fought only
to save his life, to bring his shipmates home.
But not by will nor valor could he save them,   10
for their own recklessness destroyed them all—

---

[1] These lines contain the traditional epic "opening formula" that includes the invocation of the inspiring Muse, the statement of the theme, the identification of the hero (in this case Odysseus), and a glance at the significance of the story.

children and fools, they killed and feasted on
the cattle of Lord Hêlios,[2] the Sun,
and he who moves all day through heaven
took from their eyes the dawn of their return.

Of these adventures, Muse, daughter of Zeus,
tell us in our time, lift the great song again.
Begin when all the rest who left behind them
headlong death in battle or at sea
had long ago returned, while he alone still hungered   20
for home and wife. Her ladyship Kalypso
clung to him in her sea-hollowed caves—
a nymph, immortal and most beautiful,
who craved him for her own.
                                    And when long years and seasons
wheeling brought around that point of time
ordained for him to make his passage homeward,
trials and dangers, even so, attended him
even in Ithaka,[3] near those he loved.
Yet all the gods had pitied Lord Odysseus,
all but Poseidon,[4] raging cold and rough   30
against the brave king till he came ashore
at last on his own land.
                                    But now that god
had gone far off among the sunburnt races,
most remote of men, at earth's two verges,
in sunset lands and lands of the rising sun,
to be regaled by smoke of thighbones burning,
haunches of rams and bulls, a hundred fold.
He lingered delighted at the banquet side.

In the bright hall of Zeus upon Olympos
the other gods were all at home, and Zeus,   40
the father of gods and men, made conversation.
For he had meditated on Aigísthos,[5] dead
by the hand of Agamémnon's son, Orestês,
and spoke his thought aloud before them all:

"My word, how mortals take the gods to task!
All their afflictions come from us, we hear.

---

[2] The offense against Hêlios is described in Book XII.

[3] Odysseus' island homeland, in the Ionian Sea off western Greece (sometimes the spelling
is *Ithaca*).

[4] God of the ocean and brother of the chief of the gods who dwelled on Mount Olympos
(Olympus), Zeus.

[5] While the Greek commander Agamémnon was away fighting against Troy, Aigísthos
(Aegisthus) entered into an adulterous union with Klytaimnéstra (Clytaemnestra), Agamémnon's
wife; they murdered Agamémnon upon his return. The murder was later avenged by Orestês,
son of Agamémnon and Klytaimnéstra, as is related in Aeschylus' trilogy of plays known as
the *Oresteia*.

And what of their own failings? Greed and folly
double the suffering in the lot of man.
See how Aigísthos, for his double portion,
stole Agamémnon's wife and killed the soldier   50
on his homecoming day. And yet Aigísthos
knew that his own doom lay in this. We gods
had warned him, sent down Hermês Argeiphontês,[6]
our most observant courier, to say:
'Don't kill the man, don't touch his wife,
or face a reckoning with Orestês
the day he comes of age and wants his patrimony.'
Friendly advice—but would Aigísthos take it?
Now he has paid the reckoning in full."

The grey-eyed goddess Athena replied to Zeus: 60

"O Majesty, O Father of us all,
that man is in the dust indeed, and justly.
So perish all who do what he had done.
But my own heart is broken for Odysseus,
the master mind of war, so long a castaway
upon an island in the running sea;
a wooded island, in the sea's middle,
and there's a goddess in the place, the daughter
of one whose baleful mind knows all the deeps
of the blue sea—Atlas,[7] who holds the columns   70
that bear from land the great thrust of the sky.
His daughter will not let Odysseus go,
poor mournful man; she keeps on coaxing him
with her beguiling talk, to turn his mind
from Ithaka. But such desire is in him
merely to see the hearthsmoke leaping upward
from his own island, that he longs to die.
Are you not moved by this, Lord of Olympos?
Had you no pleasure from Odysseus' offerings
beside the Argive[8] ships, on Troy's wide seaboard?   80
O Zeus, what do you hold against him now?"

To this the summoner of cloud replied:

"My child, what strange remarks you let escape you.
Could I forget that kingly man, Odysseus?
There is no mortal half so wise; no mortal
gave so much to the lords of open sky.
Only the god who laps the land in water,

---

[6] God of messengers and messenger of the gods; he was also associated sometimes with the wind. "Argeiphontês" connotes brightness or the ability to clear the sky of clouds.

[7] In myth, Atlas is the titanic being who supports the sky. Here he is described as father of the nymph Kalypso, who is holding Odysseus prisoner on her island, Ogýgia.

[8] The collective name for the Greek forces who fought under Agamémnon against Troy.

Poseidon, bears the fighter an old grudge
since he poked out the eye of Polyphêmos,
brawniest of the Kyklopês.[9] Who bore   90
that giant lout? Thoösa, daughter of Phorkys,
an offshore sea lord: for this nymph had lain
with Lord Poseidon in her hollow caves.
Naturally, the god, after the blinding—
mind you, he does not kill the man;
he only buffets him away from home.
But come now, we are all at leisure here,
let us take up this matter of his return,
that he may sail. Poseidon must relent
for being quarrelsome will get him nowhere,   100
one god, flouting the will of all the gods."

The grey-eyed goddess Athena answered him:

"O Majesty, O Father of us all,
if it now please the blissful gods
that wise Odysseus reach his home again,
let the Wayfinder, Hermês, cross the sea
to the island of Ogýgia; let him tell
our fixed intent to the nymph with pretty braids,
and let the steadfast man depart for home.
For my part, I shall visit Ithaka   110
to put more courage in the son, and rouse him
to call an assembly of the islanders,
Akhaian[10] gentlemen with flowing hair.
He must warn off that wolf pack of the suitors
who prey upon his flocks and dusky cattle.
I'll send him to the mainland then, to Sparta
by the sand beach of Pylos;[11] let him find
news of his dear father where he may
and win his own renown about the world."

She bent to tie her beautiful sandals on,   120
ambrosial, golden, that carry her over water
or over endless land on the wings of the wind,
and took the great haft of her spear in hand—
that bronzeshod spear this child of Power can use
to break in wrath long battle lines of fighters.

Flashing down from Olympos' height she went
to stand in Ithaka, before the Manor,

---

[9] The encounter with these one-eyed giants (also spelled *Polyphemus* and *Cyclops*) is described in Book IX.

[10] In a general sense, "Greek"; more especially, descriptive of men living in a region not far from Ithaka.

[11] A city and region of southern Greece ruled by Nestor, an aged king and counselor.

just at the doorsill of the court. She seemed
a family friend, the Taphian captain, Mentês,
waiting, with a light hand on her spear. 130
Before her eyes she found the lusty suitors
casting dice inside the gate, at ease
on hides of oxen—oxen they had killed.
Their own retainers made a busy sight
with houseboys, mixing bowls of water and wine,
or sopping water up in sponges, wiping
tables to be placed about in hall,
or butchering whole carcasses for roasting.

Long before anyone else, the prince Telémakhos
now caught sight of Athena—for he, too, 140
was sitting there, unhappy among the suitors,
a boy, daydreaming. What if his great father
came from the unknown world and drove these men
like dead leaves through the place, recovering
honor and lordship in his own domains?
Then he who dreamed in the crowd gazed out at Athena.
Straight to the door he came, irked with himself
to think a visitor had been kept there waiting,
and took her right hand, grasping with his left
her tall bronze-bladed spear. Then he said warmly: 150

"Greetings, stranger! Welcome to our feast.
There will be time to tell your errand later."

He led the way, and Pallas Athena followed
into the lofty hall. The boy reached up
and thrust her spear high in a polished rack
against a pillar, where tough spear on spear
of the old soldier, his father, stood in order.
Then, shaking out a splendid coverlet,
he seated her on a throne with footrest—all
finely carved—and drew his painted armchair 160
near her, at a distance from the rest.
To be amid the din, the suitors' riot,
would ruin his guest's appetite, he thought,
and he wished privacy to ask for news
about his father, gone for years.

                                              A maid

brought them a silver finger bowl and filled it
out of a beautiful spouting golden jug,
then drew a polished table to their side.
The larder mistress with her tray came by
and served them generously. A carver lifted 170
cuts of each roast meat to put on trenchers[12]
before the two. He gave them cups of gold,

---

[12] Plates.

and these the steward as he went his rounds
filled and filled again.

                                        Now came the suitors,
young bloods trooping in to their own seats
on thrones or easy chairs. Attendants poured
water over their fingers, while the maids
piled baskets full of brown loaves near at hand,
and houseboys brimmed the bowls with wine.
Now they laid hands upon the ready feast   180
and thought of nothing more. Not till desire
for food and drink had left them were they mindful
of dance and song, that are the grace of feasting.
A herald gave a shapely cithern harp
to Phêmios,[13] whom they compelled to sing—
and what a storm he plucked upon the strings
for prelude! High and clear the song arose.

Telémakhos now spoke to grey-eyed Athena,
his head bent close, so no one else might hear:

"Dear guest, will this offend you, if I speak?   190
It is easy for these men to like these things,
harping and song; they have an easy life,
scot free, eating the livestock of another—
a man whose bones are rotting somewhere now,
white in the rain on dark earth where they lie,
or tumbling in the groundswell of the sea.
If he returned, if these men ever saw him,
faster legs they'd pray for, to a man,
and not more wealth in handsome robes or gold.
But he is lost; he came to grief and perished,   200
and there's no help for us in someone's hoping
he still may come; that sun has long gone down.
But tell me now, and put it for me clearly—
who are you? Where do you come from? Where's your home
and family? What kind of ship is yours,
and what course brought you here? Who are your sailors?
I don't suppose you walked here on the sea.
Another thing—this too I ought to know—
is Ithaka new to you, or were you ever
a guest here in the old days? Far and near   210
friends knew this house; for he whose home it was
had much acquaintance in the world."

                                                    To this
the grey-eyed goddess answered:

[13] The house bard, or minstrel.

"As you ask,

I can account most clearly for myself.
Mentês I'm called, son of the veteran
Ankhíalos; I rule seafaring Taphos.
I came by ship, with a ship's company,
sailing the winedark[14] sea for ports of call
on alien shores—to Témesê, for copper,
bringing bright bars of iron in exchange.   220
My ship is moored on a wild strip of coast
in Reithron Bight, under the wooded mountain.
Years back, my family and yours were friends,
as Lord Laërtês[15] knows; ask when you see him.
I hear the old man comes to town no longer,
stays up country, ailing, with only one
old woman to prepare his meat and drink
when pain and stiffness take him in the legs
from working on his terraced plot, his vineyard.
As for my sailing here—   230
the tale was that your father had come home,
therefore I came. I see the gods delay him.
But never in this world is Odysseus dead—
only detained somewhere on the wide sea,
upon some island, with wild islanders;
savages, they must be, to hold him captive.
Well, I will forecast for you, as the gods
put the strong feeling in me—I see it all,
and I'm no prophet, no adept in bird-signs.
He will not, now, be long away from Ithaka,   240
his father's dear land; though he be in chains
he'll scheme a way to come; he can do anything.

But tell me this now, make it clear to me:
You must be, by your looks, Odysseus' boy?
The way your head is shaped, the fine eyes—yes,
how like him! We took meals like this together
many a time, before he sailed for Troy
with all the lords of Argos in the ships.
I have not seen him since, nor has he seen me."

And thoughtfully Telémakhos replied: 250

"Friend, let me put it in the plainest way.
My mother says I am his son; I know not
surely. Who has known his own engendering?
I wish at least I had some happy man
as father, growing old in his own house—

---

[14] This adjective is repeatedly used by Homer to describe the sea. Such "Homeric epithets"
are taken as one sign that the *Iliad* and *Odyssey* were designed for oral delivery.
[15] Father of Odysseus. At this point Laërtês is living in retirement on a farm.

but unknown death and silence are the fate
of him that, since you ask, they call my father."

Then grey-eyed Athena said:

                                 "The gods decreed
no lack of honor in this generation:
such is the son Penélopê bore in you.   260
But tell me now, and make this clear to me:
what gathering, what feast is this? Why here?
A wedding? Revel? At the expense of all?
Not that, I think. How arrogant they seem,
these gluttons, making free here in your house!
A sensible man would blush to be among them."

To this Telémakhos answered:

"Friend, now that you ask about these matters,
our house was always princely, a great house,
as long as he of whom we speak remained here.   270
But evil days the gods have brought upon it,
making him vanish, as they have, so strangely.
Were his death known, I could not feel such pain—
if he had died of wounds in Trojan country
or in the arms of friends, after the war.
They would have made a tomb for him, the Akhaians,
and I should have all honor as his son.
Instead, the whirlwinds got him, and no glory.
He's gone, no sign, no word of him; and I inherit
trouble and tears—and not for him alone,   280
the gods have laid such other burdens on me.
For now the lords of the islands,
Doulíkhion and Samê, wooded Zakynthos,
and rocky Ithaka's young lords as well,
are here courting my mother; and they use
our house as if it were a house to plunder.
Spurn them she dare not, though she hates that marriage,
nor can she bring herself to choose among them.
Meanwhile they eat their way through all we have,
and when they will, they can demolish me."   290

Pallas Athena was disturbed, and said:

"Ah, bitterly you need Odysseus, then!
High time he came back to engage these upstarts.
I wish we saw him standing helmeted
there in the doorway, holding shield and spear,
looking the way he did when I first knew him.
That was at our house, where he drank and feasted
after he left Ephyra, homeward bound
from a visit to the son of Mérmeris, Ilos.

He took his fast ship down the gulf that time 300
for a fatal drug to dip his arrows in
and poison the bronze points; but young Ilos
turned him away, fearing the gods' wrath.
My father gave it, for he loved him well.
I wish these men could meet the man of those days!
They'd know their fortune quickly: a cold bed.
Aye! but it lies upon the gods' great knees
whether he can return and force a reckoning
in his own house, or not.

                                        If I were you,
I should take steps to make these men disperse. 310
Listen, now, and attend to what I say:
at daybreak call the islanders to assembly,
and speak your will, and call the gods to witness:
the suitors must go scattering to their homes.
Then here's a course for you, if you agree:
get a sound craft afloat with twenty oars
and go abroad for news of your lost father—
perhaps a traveller's tale, or rumored fame
issued from Zeus abroad in the world of men.
Talk to that noble sage at Pylos, Nestor, 320
then go to Meneláos,[16] the red-haired king
at Sparta, last man home of all the Akhaians.
If you should learn your father is alive
and coming home, you could hold out a year.
Or if you learn that he is dead and gone,
then you can come back to your own dear country
and raise a mound for him, and burn his gear,
with all the funeral honors due the man,
and give your mother to another husband.

When you have done all this, or seen it done 330
it will be time to ponder
concerning these contenders[17] in your house—
how you should kill them, outright or by guile.
You need not bear this insolence of theirs,
you are a child no longer. Have you heard
what glory young Orestês won
when he cut down that two-faced man, Aigísthos,
for killing his illustrious father?
Dear friend, you are tall and well set up, I see;
be brave—you, too—and men in times to come 340
will speak of you respectfully.

[16]Brother of Agamémnon and husband of Helen of Troy. Also spelled *Menelaus*. Helen's elopement with their Trojan guest, Paris, precipitated the Trojan War.
[17]Suitors for the hand in marriage of the presumably widowed Penélopê, wife of Odysseus.

                                        Now I must join my ship;
my crew will grumble if I keep them waiting.
Look to yourself; remember what I told you."

Telémakhos replied:

                                        "Friend, you have done me
kindness, like a father to his son,
and I shall not forget your counsel ever.
You must get back to sea, I know, but come
take a hot bath, and rest; accept a gift
to make your heart lift up when you embark—
some precious thing, and beautiful, from me,   350
a keepsake, such as dear friends give their friends."

But the grey-eyed goddess Athena answered him:

"Do not delay me, for I love the sea ways.
As for the gift your heart is set on giving,
let me accept it on my passage home,
and you shall have a choice gift in exchange."

With this Athena left him
as a bird rustles upward, off and gone.
But as she went she put new spirit in him,
a new dream of his father, clearer now,   360
so that he marvelled to himself
divining that a god had been his guest.
Then godlike in his turn he joined the suitors.

The famous minstrel still sang on before them,
and they sat still and listened, while he sang
that bitter song, the Homecoming of Akhaians—
how by Athena's will they fared from Troy;
and in her high room careful Penélopê,
Ikários' daughter, heeded the holy song.
She came, then, down the long stairs of her house,   370
this beautiful lady, with two maids in train
attending her as she approached the suitors;
and near a pillar of the roof she paused,
her shining veil drawn over across her cheeks,
the two girls close to her and still,
and through her tears spoke to the noble minstrel:

"Phêmios, other spells you know, high deeds
of gods and heroes, as the poets tell them;
let these men hear some other; let them sit
silent and drink their wine. But sing no more   380
this bitter tale that wears my heart away.
It opens in me again the wound of longing

for one incomparable, ever in my mind—
his fame all Hellas[18] knows, and midland Argos."

But Telémakhos intervened and said to her:

"Mother, why do you grudge our own dear minstrel
joy of song, wherever his thought may lead?
Poets are not to blame, but Zeus who gives
what fate he pleases to adventurous men.
Here is no reason for reproof: to sing   390
the news of the Danaans![19] Men like best
a song that rings like morning on the ear.
But you must nerve yourself and try to listen.
Odysseus was not the only one at Troy
never to know the day of his homecoming.
Others, how many others, lost their lives!"

The lady gazed in wonder and withdrew,
her son's clear wisdom echoing in her mind.
But when she had mounted to her rooms again
with her two handmaids, then she fell to weeping   400
for Odysseus, her husband. Grey-eyed Athena
presently cast a sweet sleep on her eyes.

Meanwhile the din grew loud in the shadowy hall
as every suitor swore to lie beside her,
but Telémakhos turned now and spoke to them:

"You suitors of my mother! Insolent men,
now we have dined, let us have entertainment
and no more shouting. There can be no pleasure
so fair as giving heed to a great minstrel
like ours, whose voice itself is pure delight.   410
At daybreak we shall sit down in assembly
and I shall tell you—take it as you will—
you are to leave this hall. Go feasting elsewhere,
consume your own stores. Turn and turn about,
use one another's houses. If you choose
to slaughter one man's livestock and pay nothing,
this is rapine; and by the eternal gods
I beg Zeus you shall get what you deserve:
a slaughter here, and nothing paid for it!"

By now their teeth seemed fixed in their under-lips,   420
Telémakhos' bold speaking stunned them so.
Antínoös, Eupeithês' son, made answer:

[18] Greece.
[19] The Greeks who fought against the Trojans.

"Telémakhos, no doubt the gods themselves
are teaching you this high and mighty manner.
Zeus forbid you should be king in Ithaka,[20]
though you are eligible as your father's son."

Telémakhos kept his head and answered him:

"Antínoös, you may not like my answer,
but I would happily be king, if Zeus
conferred the prize. Or do you think it wretched?   430
I shouldn't call it bad at all. A king
will be respected, and his house will flourish.
But there are eligible men enough,
heaven knows, on the island, young and old,
and one of them perhaps may come to power
after the death of King Odysseus.
All I insist on is that I rule our house
and rule the slaves my father won for me."

Eurýmakhos, Pólybos' son, replied:

"Telémakhos, it is on the gods' great knees   440
who will be king in sea-girt Ithaka.
But keep your property, and rule your house,
and let no man, against your will, make havoc
of your possessions, while there's life on Ithaka.
But now, my brave young friend,
a question or two about the stranger.
Where did your guest come from? Of what country?
Where does he say his home is, and his family?
Has he some message of your father's coming,
or business of his own, asking a favor?   450
He left so quickly that one hadn't time
to meet him, but he seemed a gentleman."

Telémakhos made answer, cool enough:

"Eurýmakhos, there's no hope for my father.
I would not trust a message, if one came,
nor any forecaster my mother invites
to tell by divination of time to come.
My guest, however, was a family friend,
Mentês, son of Ankhíalos.
He rules the Taphian people of the sea."   460

So said Telémakhos, though in his heart
he knew his visitor had been immortal.

---

[20]At the time of the poem's action, the rulership of most Greek city-states was not automatically passed from father to son.

But now the suitors turned to play again
with dance and haunting song. They stayed till nightfall,
indeed black night came on them at their pleasure,
and half asleep they left, each for his home.

Telémakhos' bedroom was above the court,
a kind of tower, with a view all round;
here he retired to ponder in the silence,
while carrying brands of pine alight beside him   470
Eurýkleia went padding, sage and old.
Her father had been Ops, Peisênor's son,
and she had been a purchase of Laërtês
when she was still a blossoming girl. He gave
the price of twenty oxen[21] for her, kept her
as kindly in his house as his own wife,
though, for the sake of peace, he never touched her.
No servant loved Telémakhos as she did,
she who had nursed him in his infancy.
So now she held the light, as he swung open   480
the door of his neat freshly painted chamber.
There he sat down, pulling his tunic off,
and tossed it into the wise old woman's hands.
She folded it and smoothed it, and then hung it
beside the inlaid bed upon a bar;
then, drawing the door shut by its silver handle
she slid the catch in place and went away.
And all night long, wrapped in the finest fleece,
he took in thought the course Athena gave him.

BOOK TWO: A HERO'S SON AWAKENS

When primal Dawn spread on the eastern sky
her fingers of pink light, Odysseus' true son
stood up, drew on his tunic and his mantle,
slung on a sword-belt and a new-edged sword,
tied his smooth feet into good rawhide sandals,
and left his room, a god's brilliance upon him.
He found the criers with clarion voices and told them
to muster the unshorn[1] Akhaians in full assembly.
The call sang out, and the men came streaming in;
and when they filled the assembly ground, he entered,   10
spear in hand, with two quick hounds at heel;
Athena lavished on him a sunlit grace

---

[21] In the Greek civilization of Homeric times, the ox was a common standard of value. Articles of clothing, weapons, women taken as war prizes, and servants were evaluated in terms of how many oxen they were worth.
[1] Having long or flowing hair.

that held the eye of the multitude. Old men
made way for him as he took his father's chair.

Now Lord Aigýptios, bent down and sage with years,
opened the assembly. This man's son
had served under the great Odysseus, gone
in the decked ships with him to the wild horse country
of Troy—a spearman, Ántiphos by name.
The ravenous Kyklops in the cave destroyed him[2]   20
last in his feast of men. Three other sons
the old man had, and one, Eurýnomos,
went with the suitors; two farmed for their father;
but even so the old man pined, remembering
the absent one, and a tear welled up as he spoke:

"Hear me, Ithakans! Hear what I have to say.
No meeting has been held here since our king,
Odysseus, left port in the decked ships.
Who finds occasion for assembly, now?
one of the young men? one of the older lot?   30
Has he had word our fighters are returning[3]—
news to report if he got wind of it—
or is it something else, touching the realm?
The man has vigor, I should say; more power to him.
Whatever he desires, may Zeus fulfill it."

The old man's words delighted the son of Odysseus,
who kept his chair no longer but stood up,
eager to speak, in the midst of all the men.
The crier, Peisênor, master of debate,
brought him the staff[4] and placed it in his hand;   40
then the boy touched the old man's shoulder, and said:

"No need to wonder any more, Sir,
who called this session. The distress is mine.
As to our troops returning, I have no news—
news to report if I got wind of it—
nor have I public business to propose;
only my need, and the trouble of my house—
the troubles.

                          My distinguished father is lost,
who ruled among you once, mild as a father,
and there is now this greater evil still: 50
my home and all I have are being ruined.

---

[2] This incident is described in Book IX.
[3] Except for Odysseus and his Ithakans, all the Greek warriors against Troy had by this time
returned home or were known to be dead.
[4] The emblem that, placed by the herald in the speaker's hand, gave him the right to speak
as a public official.

Mother wanted no suitors, but like a pack
they came—sons of the best men here among them—
lads with no stomach for an introduction
to Ikários, her father across the sea;
he would require a wedding gift, and give her
to someone who found favor in her eyes.
No; these men spend their days around our house
killing our beeves and sheep and fatted goats,
carousing, soaking up our good dark wine,   60
not caring what they do. They squander everything.
We have no strong Odysseus to defend us,
and as to putting up a fight ourselves—
we'd only show our incompetence in arms.
Expel them, yes, if I only had the power;
the whole thing's out of hand, insufferable.
My house is being plundered: is this courtesy?
Where is your indignation? Where is your shame?
Think of the talk in the islands all around us,
and fear the wrath of the gods,   70
or they may turn, and send you some devilry.
Friends, by Olympian Zeus and holy Justice
that holds men in assembly and sets them free,
make an end of this! Let me lament in peace
my private loss. Or did my father, Odysseus,
ever do injury to the armed Akhaians?
Is this your way of taking it out on me,
giving free rein to these young men?
I might as well—might better—see my treasure
and livestock taken over by you all;   80
then, if you fed on them, I'd have some remedy,
and when we met, in public, in the town,
I'd press my claim; you might make restitution.
This way you hurt me when my hands are tied."

And in hot anger now he threw the staff to the ground,
his eyes grown bright with tears. A wave of sympathy
ran through the crowd, all hushed; and no one there
had the audacity to answer harshly
except Antínoös, who said:

                                        "What high and mighty
talk, Telémakhos! No holding you!   90
You want to shame us, and humiliate us,
but you should know the suitors are not to blame—
it is your own dear, incomparably cunning mother.
For three years now—and it will soon be four—
she has been breaking the hearts of the Akhaians,
holding out hope to all, and sending promises
to each man privately—but thinking otherwise.

Here is an instance of her trickery:
she had her great loom standing in the hall
and the fine warp of some vast fabric on it; 100
we were attending her, and she said to us:
'Young men, my suitors, now my lord is dead,
let me finish my weaving before I marry,
or else my thread will have been spun in vain.
It is a shroud I weave for Lord Laërtês,
when cold death comes to lay him on his bier.
The country wives would hold me in dishonor
if he, with all his fortune, lay unshrouded.'
We have men's hearts; she touched them; we agreed.
So every day she wove on the great loom— 110
but every night by torchlight she unwove it;
and so for three years she deceived the Akhaians.
But when the seasons brought the fourth around,
one of her maids, who knew the secret, told us;
we found her unraveling the splendid shroud.
She had to finish then, although she hated it.

Now here is the suitors' answer—
you and all the Akhaians, mark it well:
dismiss your mother from the house, or make her marry
the man her father names and she prefers. 120
Does she intend to keep us dangling forever?
She may rely too long on Athena's gifts—
talent in handicraft and a clever mind;
so cunning—history cannot show the like
among the ringleted ladies of Akhaia,
Mykênê with her coronet, Alkmênê, Tyro.
Wits like Penélopê's never were before,
but this time—well, she made poor use of them.
For here are suitors eating up your property
as long as she holds out—a plan some god 130
put in her mind. She makes a name for herself,
but you can feel the loss it means for you.
Our own affairs can wait; we'll never go anywhere else,
until she takes an Akhaian to her liking."

But clear-headed Telémakhos replied:

"Antínoös, can I banish against her will
the mother who bore me and took care of me?
My father is either dead or far away,
but dearly I should pay for this
at Ikários' hands, if ever I sent her back. 140
The powers of darkness would requite it, too,
my mother's parting curse would call hell's furies[5]

---

[5] In mythology, the primitive female agents of retribution for evil, especially for evil committed against blood kindred.

to punish me, along with the scorn of men.
No: I can never give the word for this.
But if your hearts are capable of shame,
leave my great hall, and take your dinner elsewhere,
consume your own stores. Turn and turn about,
use one another's houses. If you choose
to slaughter one man's livestock and pay nothing,
this is rapine; and by the eternal gods   150
I beg Zeus you shall get what you deserve:
a slaughter here, and nothing paid for it!"

Now Zeus who views the wide world sent a sign to him,
launching a pair of eagles from a mountain crest
in gliding flight down the soft blowing wind,
wing-tip to wing-tip quivering taut, companions,
till high above the assembly of many voices
they wheeled, their dense wings beating, and in havoc
dropped on the heads of the crowd—a deathly omen—
wielding their talons, tearing cheeks and throats;   160
then veered away on the right hand through the city.
Astonished, gaping after the birds, the men
felt their hearts flood, foreboding things to come.
And now they heard the old lord Halithersês,
son of Mastor, keenest among the old
at reading birdflight into accurate speech;
in his anxiety for them, he rose and said:

"Hear me, Ithakans! Hear what I have to say,
and may I hope to open the suitors' eyes
to the black wave towering over them. Odysseus   170
will not be absent from his family long:
he is already near, carrying in him
a bloody doom for all these men, and sorrow
for many more on our high seamark, Ithaka.
Let us think how to stop it; let the suitors
drop their suit; they had better, without delay.
I am old enough to know a sign when I see one,
and I say all has come to pass for Odysseus
as I foretold when the Argives massed on Troy,
and he, the great tactician, joined the rest.   180
My forecast was that after nineteen years,[6]
many blows weathered, all his shipmates lost,
himself unrecognized by anyone,
he would come home. I see this all fulfilled."

---

[6] These include the ten years of war against Troy.

But Pólybos' son, Eurýmakhos, retorted:

"Old man, go tell the omens for your children
at home, and try to keep them out of trouble.
I am more fit to interpret this than you are.
Bird life aplenty is found in the sunny air,
not all of it significant. As for Odysseus,   190
he perished far from home. You should have perished with him—
then we'd be spared this nonsense in assembly,
as good as telling Telémakhos to rage on;
do you think you can gamble on a gift from him?
Here is what I foretell, and it's quite certain:
if you, with what you know of ancient lore,
encourage bitterness in this young man,
it means, for him, only the more frustration—
he can do nothing whatever with two eagles—
and as for you, old man, we'll fix a penalty   200
that you will groan to pay.
Before the whole assembly I advise Telémakhos
to send his mother to her father's house;
let them arrange her wedding there, and fix
a portion suitable for a valued daughter.
Until he does this, courtship is our business,
vexing though it may be; we fear no one,
certainly not Telémakhos, with his talk;
and we care nothing for your divining, uncle,
useless talk; you win more hatred by it.   210
We'll share his meat, no thanks or fee to him,
as long as she delays and maddens us.
It is a long, long time we have been waiting
in rivalry for this beauty. We could have gone
elsewhere and found ourselves very decent wives."

Clear-headed Telémakhos replied to this:

"Eurýmakhos, and noble suitors all,
I am finished with appeals and argument.
The gods know, and the Akhaians know, these things.
But give me a fast ship and a crew of twenty   220
who will see me through a voyage, out and back.
I'll go to sandy Pylos, then to Sparta,
for news of Father since he sailed from Troy—
some traveller's tale, perhaps, or rumored fame
issued from Zeus himself into the world.
If he's alive, and beating his way home,
I might hold out for another weary year;
but if they tell me that he's dead and gone,
then I can come back to my own dear country
and raise a mound for him, and burn his gear,   230
with all the funeral honors that befit him,
and give my mother to another husband."

The boy sat down in silence. Next to stand
was Mentor, comrade in arms of the prince Odysseus,
an old man now. Odysseus left him authority
over his house and slaves, to guard them well.
In his concern, he spoke to the assembly:

"Hear me, Ithakans! Hear what I have to say.
Let no man holding scepter as a king
be thoughtful, mild, kindly, or virtuous; 240
let him be cruel, and practice evil ways;
it is so clear that no one here remembers
how like a gentle father Odysseus ruled you.
I find it less revolting that the suitors
carry their malice into violent acts;
at least they stake their lives
when they go pillaging the house of Odysseus—
their lives upon it, he will not come again.
What sickens me is to see the whole community
sitting still, and never a voice or a hand raised 250
against them—a mere handful compared with you."

Leókritos, Euênor's son, replied to him:

"Mentor, what mischief are you raking up?
Will this crowd risk the sword's edge over a dinner?
Suppose Odysseus himself indeed
came in and found the suitors at his table:
he might be hot to drive them out. What then?
Never would he enjoy his wife again—
the wife who loves him well; he'd only bring down
abject death on himself against those odds. 260
Madness, to talk of fighting in either case.
Now let all present go about their business!
Halithersês and Mentor will speed the traveller;
they can help him: they were his father's friends.
I rather think he will be sitting here
a long time yet, waiting for news on Ithaka;
that seafaring he spoke of is beyond him."

On this note they were quick to end their parley.
The assembly broke up; everyone went home—
the suitors home to Odysseus' house again. 270
But Telémakhos walked down along the shore
and washed his hands in the foam of the grey sea,
then said this prayer:

                         "O god of yesterday,
guest in our house, who told me to take ship
on the hazy sea for news of my lost father,
listen to me, be near me:
The Akhaians only wait, or hope to hinder me,
the damned insolent suitors most of all."

Athena was nearby and came to him,
putting on Mentor's figure and his tone, 280
the warm voice in a lucid flight of words:

"You'll never be fainthearted or a fool,
Telémakhos, if you have your father's spirit;
he finished what he cared to say,
and what he took in hand he brought to pass.
The sea routes will yield their distances
to his true son, Penélopê's true son,—
I doubt another's luck would hold so far.
The son is rare who measures with his father,
and one in a thousand is a better man, 290
but you will have the sap and wit
and prudence—for you get that from Odysseus—
to give you a fair chance of winning through.
So never mind the suitors and their ways,
there is no judgment in them, neither do they
know anything of death and the black terror
close upon them—doom's day on them all.
You need not linger over going to sea.
I sailed beside your father in the old days,
I'll find a ship for you, and help you sail her. 300
So go on home, as if to join the suitors,
but get provisions ready in containers—
wine in two-handled jugs and barley meal,
the staying power of oarsmen,
in skin bags, watertight. I'll go the rounds
and call a crew of volunteers together.
Hundreds of ships are beached on sea-girt Ithaka;
let me but choose the soundest, old or new,
we'll rig her and take her out on the broad sea."

This was the divine speech Telémakhos heard 310
from Athena, Zeus's daughter. He stayed no longer,
but took his heartache home,
and found the robust suitors there at work,
skinning goats and roasting pigs in the courtyard.
Antínoös came straight over, laughing at him,
and took him by the hand with a bold greeting:

"High-handed Telémakhos, control your temper!
Come on, get over it, no more grim thoughts,
but feast and drink with me, the way you used to.
The Akhaians will attend to all you ask for— 320
ship, crew, and crossing to the holy land
of Pylos, for the news about your father."

Telémakhos replied with no confusion:

"Antínoös, I cannot see myself again
taking a quiet dinner in this company.

Isn't it enough that you could strip my house
under my very nose when I was young?
Now that I know, being grown, what others say,
I understand it all, and my heart is full.
I'll bring black doom upon you if I can— 330
either in Pylos, if I go, or in this country.
And I will go, go all the way, if only
as someone's passenger. I have no ship,
no oarsmen: and it suits you that I have none."

Calmly he drew his hand from Antínoös' hand.
At this the suitors, while they dressed their meat,
began to exchange loud mocking talk about him.
One young toplofty gallant set the tone:

"Well, think of that!
Telémakhos has a mind to murder us.
He's going to lead avengers out of Pylos, 340
or Sparta, maybe; oh, he's wild to do it.
Or else he'll try the fat land of Ephyra—
he can get poison there, and bring it home,
doctor the wine jar and dispatch us all."

Another took the cue:

"Well now, who knows?
He might be lost at sea, just like Odysseus,
knocking around in a ship, far from his friends.
And what a lot of trouble that would give us,
making the right division of his things!
We'd keep his house as dowry for his mother— 350
his mother and the man who marries her."

That was the drift of it. Telémakhos
went on through to the storeroom of his father,
a great vault where gold and bronze lay piled
along with chests of clothes, and fragrant oil.
And there were jars of earthenware in rows
holding an old wine,
mellow, unmixed, and rare; cool stood the jars
against the wall, kept for whatever day
Odysseus, worn by hardships, might come home. 360
The double folding doors were tightly locked
and guarded, night and day, by the serving woman,
Eurýkleia, grand-daughter of Peisênor,
in all her duty vigilant and shrewd.
Telémakhos called her to the storeroom, saying:

"Nurse, get a few two-handled travelling jugs
filled up with wine—the second best, not that
you keep for your unlucky lord and king,

hoping he may have slipped away from death
and may yet come again—royal Odysseus.   370
Twelve amphorai[7] will do; seal them up tight.
And pour out barley into leather bags—
twenty bushels of barley meal ground fine.
Now keep this to yourself! Collect these things,
and after dark, when mother has retired
and gone upstairs to bed, I'll come for them.
I sail to sandy Pylos, then to Sparta,
to see what news there is of Father's voyage."

His loving nurse Eurýkleia gave a cry,
and tears sprang to her eyes as she wailed softly: 380

"Dear child, whatever put this in your head?
Why do you want to go so far in the world—
and you our only darling? Lord Odysseus
died in some strange place, far from his homeland.
Think how, when you have turned your back, these men
will plot to kill you and share all your things!
Stay with your own, dear, do. Why should you suffer
hardship and homelessness on the wild sea?"

But seeing all clear, Telémakhos replied:

"Take heart, Nurse, there's a god behind this plan.   390
And you must swear to keep it from my mother,
until the eleventh day, or twelfth, or till
she misses me, or hears that I am gone.
She must not tear her lovely skin lamenting."

So the old woman vowed by all the gods,
and vowed again, to carry out his wishes;
then she filled up the amphorai with wine
and sifted barley meal into leather bags.
Telémakhos rejoined the suitors.

                                                                 Meanwhile
the goddess with grey eyes had other business: 400
disguised as Telémakhos, she roamed the town
taking each likely man aside and telling him:
"Meet us at nightfall at the ship!" Indeed,
she asked Noêmon, Phronios' wealthy son,
to lend her a fast ship, and he complied.
Now when at sundown shadows crossed the lanes
she dragged the cutter to the sea and launched it,
fitted out with tough seagoing gear,
and tied it up, away at the harbor's edge.

---

[7] Plural form of "amphora," a jar with two handles and a thin neck.

The crewmen gathered, sent there by the goddess.　　　　410
Then it occurred to the grey-eyed goddess Athena
to pass inside the house of the hero Odysseus,
showering a sweet drowsiness on the suitors,
whom she had presently wandering in their wine;
and soon, as they could hold their cups no longer,
they straggled off to find their beds in town,
eyes heavy-lidded, laden down with sleep.
Then to Telémakhos the grey-eyed goddess
appeared again with Mentor's form and voice,
calling him out of the lofty emptied hall:　　　　420

"Telémakhos, your crew of fighting men
is ready at the oars, and waiting for you;
come on, no point in holding up the sailing."

And Pallas Athena turned like the wind, running
ahead of him. He followed in her footsteps
down to the seaside, where they found the ship,
and oarsmen with flowing hair at the water's edge.
Telémakhos, now strong in the magic, cried:

"Come with me, friends, and ger our rations down!
They are all packed at home, and my own mother　　　430
knows nothing!—only one maid was told."

He turned and led the way, and they came after,
carried and stowed all in the well-trimmed ship
as the dear son of Odysseus commanded.
Telémakhos then stepped aboard; Athena
took her position aft, and he sat by her.
The two stroke oars cast off the stern hawsers
and vaulted over the gunnels to their benches.
Grey-eyed Athena stirred them a following wind,
soughing from the north-west on the winedark sea,　　　440
and as he felt the wind, Telémakhos
called to all hands to break out mast and sail.
They pushed the fir mast high and stepped it firm
amidships in the box, made fast the forestays,
then hoisted up the white sail on its halyards
until the wind caught, booming in the sail;
and a flushing wave sang backward from the bow
on either side, as the ship got way upon her,
holding her steady course.
Now they made all secure in the fast black ship,　　　450
and, setting out the winebowls all a-brim,
they made libation to the gods,
　　　　　　　　　　　　　　the undying, the ever-new,
most of all to the grey-eyed daughter of Zeus.
And the prow sheared through the night into the dawn.

BOOK THREE: THE LORD OF THE
WESTERN APPROACHES

The sun rose on the flawless brimming sea
into a sky all brazen–all one brightening
for gods immortal and for mortal men
on plowlands kind with grain.

                                    And facing sunrise
the voyagers now lay off Pylos town,
compact stronghold of Neleus.[1] On the shore
black bulls were being offered by the people
to the blue-maned god who makes the islands tremble:
nine congregations, each five hundred strong,
led out nine bulls apiece to sacrifice,   10
taking the tripes to eat, while on their altars
thighbones in fat lay burning for the god.
Here they put in, furled sail, and beached the ship;
but Telémakhos hung back in disembarking,
so that Athena turned and said:

"Not the least shyness, now, Telémakhos.
You came across the open sea for this—
to find out where the great earth hides your father
and what the doom was that he came upon.
Go to old Nestor, master charioteer,   20
so we may broach the storehouse of his mind.
Ask him with courtesy, and in his wisdom
he will tell you history and no lies."

But clear-headed Telémakhos replied:

"Mentor, how can I do it, how approach him?
I have no practice in elaborate speeches, and
for a young man to interrogate an old man
seems disrespectful—"

                                  But the grey-eyed goddess said:

"Reason and heart will give you words, Telémakhos;
and a spirit will counsel others. I should say   30
the gods were never indifferent to your life."

She went on quickly, and he followed her
to where the men of Pylos had their altars.
Nestor appeared enthroned among his sons,

---

[1]Son of the sea god Poseidon (the "blue-maned god"), he was the founder of Pylos and
the father of Nestor.

while friends around them skewered the red beef
or held it scorching. When they saw the strangers
a hail went up, and all that crowd came forward
calling out invitations to the feast.
Peisístratos in the lead, the young prince,
caught up their hands in his and gave them places 40
on curly lambskins flat on the sea sand
near Thrasymêdês, his brother, and his father;
he passed them bits of the food of sacrifice,
and, pouring wine in a golden cup,
he said to Pallas Athena, daughter of Zeus:

"Friend, I must ask you to invoke Poseidon:
you find us at this feast, kept in his honor.
Make the appointed offering then, and pray,
and give the honeyed winecup to your friend
so he may do the same. He, too, 50
must pray to the gods on whom all men depend,
but he is just my age, you are the senior,
so here, I give the goblet first to you."

And he put the cup of sweet wine in her hand.
Athena liked his manners, and the equity
that gave her precedence with the cup of gold,
so she besought Poseidon at some length:

"Earthshaker, listen and be well disposed.
Grant your petitioners everything they ask:
above all, honor to Nestor and his sons; 60
second, to every man of Pylos town
a fair gift in exchange for this hekatomb;[2]
third, may Telémakhos and I perform
the errand on which last night we put to sea."

This was the prayer of Athena—
granted in every particular by herself.
She passed the beautiful wine cup to Telémakhos,
who tipped the wine and prayed as she had done.
Meanwhile the spits were taken off the fire,
portions of crisp meat for all. They feasted, 70
and when they had eaten and drunk their fill, at last
they heard from Nestor, prince of charioteers:

"Now is the time,"[3] he said, "for a few questions,
now that our young guests have enjoyed their dinner.
Who are you, strangers? Where are you sailing from,
and where to, down the highways of sea water?

---

[2] A grand public sacrifice and offering to the gods.
[3] Hospitality required that no such questions be asked of guests until they had been welcomed and fed.

Have you some business here? or are you, now,
reckless wanderers of the sea, like those corsairs
who risk their lives to prey on other men?"

Clear-headed Telémakhos responded cheerfully,   80
for Athena gave him heart. By her design
his quest for news about his father's wandering
would bring him fame in the world's eyes. So he said:

"Nestor, pride of Akhaians, Neleus' son,
you ask where we are from, and I can tell you:
our home port is under Mount Neion, Ithaka.
We are not here on Ithakan business, though,
but on my own. I want news of my father,
Odysseus, known for his great heart, and I
will comb the wide world for it. People say   90
he fought along with you when Troy was taken.
As to the other men who fought that war,
we know where each one died, and how he died;
but Zeus allotted my father death and mystery.
No one can say for sure where he was killed,
whether some hostile landsmen or the sea,
the stormwaves on the deep sea, got the best of him.
And this is why I come to you for help.
Tell me of his death, sir, if perhaps
you witnessed it, or have heard some wanderer   100
tell the tale. The man was born for trouble.
Spare me no part of it for kindness' sake,
but put the scene before me as you saw it.
If ever Odysseus my noble father
served you by promise kept or work accomplished
in the land of Troy, where you Akhaians suffered,
recall those things for me the way they were."

Then Nestor, prince of charioteers, made answer:

"Dear friend, you take me back to all the trouble
we went through in that country, we Akhaians: 110
rough days aboard ship on the cloudy sea
cruising away for pillage after Akhilleus;[4]
rough days of battle around Priam's[5] town.
Our losses, then—so many good men gone:
Arês' great Aias[6] lies there, Akhilleus lies there,
Patróklos,[7] too, the wondrous counselor,
and my own strong and princely son, Antílokhos—

---

[4] The foremost Greek warrior, central figure of the *Iliad*.
[5] King of Troy.
[6] Another great Greek warrior (also spelled *Ajax*), associated here with Arês, the god of war.
[7] The closest friend of Akhilleus; it was to avenge his death at the hand of the Trojan leader Hektor that Akhilleus—as is narrated in the *Iliad*—re-entered the battle and killed Hektor.

fastest man of them all, and a born fighter.
Other miseries, and many, we endured there.
Could any mortal man tell the whole story? 120
Not if you stayed five years or six to hear
how hard it was for the flower of the Akhaians;
you'd go home weary, and the tale untold.
Think: we were there nine years, and we tried everything,
all stratagems against them,
up to the bitter end that Zeus begrudged us.
And as to stratagems, no man would claim
Odysseus' gift for those. He had no rivals,
your father, at the tricks of war.

                                                    Your father?

Well, I must say I marvel at the sight of you: 130
your manner of speech couldn't be more like his;
one would say No; no boy could speak so well.
And all that time at Ilion,[8] he and I
were never at odds in council or assembly—
saw things the same way, had one mind between us
in all the good advice we gave the Argives.
But when we plundered Priam's town and tower
and took to the ships, God scattered the Akhaians.
He had a mind to make homecoming hard for them,
seeing they would not think straight nor behave, 140
or some would not. So evil days came on them,
and she who had been angered,
Zeus's dangerous grey-eyed daughter, did it,
starting a fight between the sons of Atreus.[9]
First they were fools enough to call assembly
at sundown, unheard of hour;
the Akhaian soldiers turned out, soaked with wine,
to hear talk, talk about it from their commanders:
Meneláos harangued them to get organized—
time to ride home on the sea's broad back, he said; 150
but Agamémnon wouldn't hear of it. He wanted
to hold the troops, make sacrifice, a hekatomb,
something to pacify Athena's rage.
Folly again, to think that he could move her.
Will you change the will of the everlasting gods
in a night or a day's time?
The two men stood there hammering at each other
until the army got to its feet with a roar,
and no decision, wanting it both ways.

---

[8] Troy.

[9] Atreus was father of Agamémnon and Meneláos, the brothers who commanded the Greek
forces. Athena's hostility to the Greeks (whom she generally favored and aided) was occasioned
by outrages committed against the Trojan princess and prophetess Kassandra, who during the
sack of Troy had tried to take refuge at Athena's shrine.

That night no one slept well, everyone cursing   160
someone else. Here was the bane[10] from Zeus.
At dawn we dragged our ships to the lordly water,
stowed aboard all our plunder
and the slave women in their low hip girdles.
But half the army elected to stay behind
with Agamémnon as their corps commander;
the other half embarked and pulled away.
We made good time, the huge sea smoothed before us,
and held our rites when we reached Ténedos,[11]
being wild for home. But Zeus, not willing yet,   170
now cruelly set us at odds a second time,
and one lot turned, put back in the rolling ships,
under command of the subtle captain, Odysseus;
their notion was to please Lord Agamémnon.
Not I. I fled, with every ship I had;
I knew fate had some devilment brewing there.
Diomêdês roused his company and fled, too,
and later Meneláos, the red-haired captain,
caught up with us at Lesbos,
while we mulled over the long sea route, unsure   180
whether to lay our course northward of Khios,
keeping the Isle of Psyria off to port,
or inside Khios, coasting by windy Mimas.
We asked for a sign from heaven, and the sign came
to cut across the open sea to Euboia,
and lose no time putting our ills behind us.
The wind freshened astern, and the ships ran
before the wind on paths of the deep sea fish,
making Geraistos before dawn. We thanked Poseidon
with many a charred thighbone for that crossing.   190
On the fourth day, Diomêdês' company
under full sail put in at Argos port,
and I held on for Pylos. The fair wind,
once heaven set it blowing, never failed.

So this, dear child, was how I came from Troy,
and saw no more of the others, lost or saved.
But you are welcome to all I've heard since then
at home; I have no reason to keep it from you.
The Myrmidon spearfighters returned, they say,
under the son of lionhearted Akhilleus;   200
and so did Poias' great son, Philoktêtês.

---

[10] Ruin; poison

[11] The problem described by Nestor in the following lines is whether the part of the Greek fleet that decided to sail immediately should follow a circuitous course homeward among the islands of the Aegean Sea or head straight across it, by a course that was shorter but farther removed from ports.

Idómeneus brought his company back to Krete;[12]
the sea took not a man from him, of all
who lived through the long war.
And even as far away as Ithaka
you've heard of Agamémnon—how he came
home, how Aigísthos waited to destroy him
but paid a bitter price for it in the end.
That is a good thing, now, for a man to leave
a son behind him, like the son who punished   210
Aigísthos for the murder of his great father.
You, too, are tall and well set-up, I see;
be brave, you too, so men in times to come
will speak well of you."

                                        Then Telémakhos said:

"Nestor, pride of Akhaians, Neleus' son,
that was revenge, and far and wide the Akhaians
will tell the tale in song for generations.
I wish the gods would buckle his arms on me!
I'd be revenged for outrage
on my insidious and brazen enemies.   220
But no such happy lot was given to me
or to my father. Still, I must hold fast."

To this Lord Nestor of Gerênia said:

"My dear young friend, now that you speak of it,
I hear a crowd of suitors for your mother
lives with you, uninvited, making trouble.
Now tell me how you take this. Do the people
side against you, hearkening to some oracle?
Who knows, your father might come home someday
alone or backed by troops, and have it out with them.   230
If grey-eyed Athena loved you
the way she did Odysseus in the old days,
in Troy country, where we all went through so much—
never have I seen the gods help any man
as openly as Athena did your father—
well, as I say, if she cared for you that way,
there would be those to quit this marriage game."

But prudently Telémakhos replied:

"I can't think what you say will ever happen, sir.
It is a dazzling hope. But not for me.   240

---

[12] The Myrmidons were Akhilleus' troops; his son was Pyrrhus, also called Neoptólemus.
Philoktêtês was a Greek warrior who, after having been abandoned on the way to Troy because
of a malodorous wound, later rejoined the Greek forces and was crucial to their success in
the war. Idómeneus, an ally of the Greeks against the Trojans, was king of Krete (Crete).

It could not be—even if the gods willed it."

At this grey-eyed Athena broke in, saying:

"What strange talk you permit yourself, Telémakhos.
A god could save the man by simply wishing it—
from the farthest shore in the world.
If I were he, I should prefer to suffer
years at sea, and then be safe at home;
better that than a knife at my hearthside
where Agamémnon found it—killed by adulterers.
Though as for death, of course all men must suffer it: 250
the gods may love a man, but they can't help him
when cold death comes to lay him on his bier." [13]

Telémakhos replied:

"Mentor, grievously though we miss my father, why
go on as if that homecoming could happen?
You know the gods had settled it already,
years ago, when dark death came for him.
But there is something else I imagine Nestor
can tell us, knowing as he does the ways of men.
They say his rule goes back over three generations,   260
so long, so old, it seems death cannot touch him.
Nestor, Neleus' son, true sage, say how
did the Lord of the Great Plains, Agamémnon, die?
What was the trick Aigísthos used
to kill the better man? And Meneláos,
where was he? Not at Argos [14] in Akhaia,
but blown off course, held up in some far country,
is that what gave the killer nerve to strike?"

Lord Nestor of Gerênia made answer:

"Well, now, my son, I'll tell you the whole story.   270
You know, yourself, what would have come to pass
if red-haired Meneláos, back from Troy,
had caught Aigísthos in that house alive.
There would have been no burial mound for him,
but dogs and carrion birds to huddle on him

---

[13] This final sentence is a definitive expression of the ancient Greek understanding of the difference between human beings and deities. Though gods may be champions and even comrades of mortals, the latter are doomed to die and the gods are not. The distinction has little to do with morality or metaphysics. The gods belong to a different order of beings, though not necessarily to a superior order.

[14] The region ruled by Agamémnon, brother to Meneláos, whose wife Helen had run off with the Trojan prince Paris. Homer's account of the slaying of Agamémnon at his homecoming is at this point a fairly simple justification of Agamémnon and his avenging son Orestês; Aeschylus' account in the *Oresteia* is more psychologically complex. For other accounts of the story, by the Ancient of the Salt Sea and by Agamémnon himself, see Books IV and XI of the *Odyssey*.

in the fields beyond the wall, and not a soul
bewailing him, for the great wrong he committed.
While we were hard-pressed in the war at Troy
he stayed safe inland in the grazing country,
making light talk to win Agamémnon's queen. 280
But the Lady Klytaimnéstra, in the first days,
rebuffed him, being faithful still;
then, too, she had at hand as her companion
a minstrel Agamémnon left attending her,
charged with her care, when he took ship for Troy.
Then came the fated hour when she gave in.[15]
Her lover tricked the poet and marooned him
on a bare island for the seabirds' picking,
and took her home, as he and she desired.
Many thighbones he burned on the gods' altars 290
and many a woven and golden ornament
hung to bedeck them, in his satisfaction;
he had not thought life held such glory for him.

Now Meneláos and I sailed home together
on friendly terms, from Troy,
but when we came off Sunion Point[16] in Attika,
the ships still running free, Onêtor's son
Phrontis, the steersman of Meneláos' ship,
fell over with a death grip on the tiller:
some unseen arrow from Apollo hit him. 300
No man handled a ship better than he did
in a high wind and sea, so Meneláos
put down his longing to get on, and landed
to give this man full honor in funeral.
His own luck turned then. Out on the winedark sea
in the murmuring hulls again, he made Cape Malea,[17]
but Zeus who views the wide world sent a gloom
over the ocean, and a howling gale
came on with seas increasing, mountainous,
parting the ships and driving half toward Krete 310
where the Kydonians live by Iardanos river,
Off Gortyn's coastline in the misty sea there
a reef, a razorback, cuts through the water,
and every westerly piles up a pounding
surf along the left side, going toward Phaistos—
big seas buffeted back by the narrow stone.

---

[15] This passage presents both Klytaimnéstra and her paramour Aigísthos as frivolous and irresponsible dalliers; in other versions of the story, notably in Aeschylus' *Oresteia*, both these adulterers are given an understandable, if not necessarily justifiable, motive for revenge against Agamémnon.

[16] The tip of a promontory, near Athens, in southeastern Greece. The fleet is trying to sail westward around the southern coast.

[17] Located at the extreme southern point of the Greek mainland, directly north of the western end of the island of Krete.

They were blown here, and fought in vain for sea room;
the ships kept going in to their destruction,
slammed on the reef. The crews were saved. But now
those five that weathered it got off to southward,   320
taken by wind and current on to Egypt;
and there Meneláos stayed. He made a fortune
in sea traffic among those distant races,
but while he did so, the foul crime was planned
and carried out in Argos by Aigísthos,
who ruled over golden Mykênai[18] seven years.
Seven long years, with Agamémnon dead,
he held the people down, before the vengeance.
But in the eighth year, back from exile in Attika,
Orestês killed the snake who killed his father.   330
He gave his hateful mother and her soft man
a tomb together, and proclaimed the funeral day
a festal day for all the Argive people.
That day Lord Meneláos of the great war cry
made port with all the gold his ships could carry.
And this should give you pause, my son:
don't stay too long away from home, leaving
your treasure there, and brazen suitors near;
they'll squander all you have or take it from you,
and then how will your journey serve?   340
I urge you, though, to call on Meneláos,
he being but lately home from distant parts
in the wide world. A man could well despair
of getting home at all, if the winds blew him
over the Great South Sea—that weary waste,
even the wintering birds delay
one winter more before the northward crossing.
Well, take your ship and crew and go by water,
or if you'd rather go by land, here are
horses, a car, and my own sons for company   350
as far as the ancient land of Lakedaimon[19]
and Meneláos, the red-haired captain there.
Ask him with courtesy, and in his wisdom
he will tell you history and no lies."

While Nestor talked, the sun went down the sky
and gloom came on the land,
and now the grey-eyed goddess Athena said:

"Sir, this is all most welcome and to the point,
but why not slice the bulls' tongues now, and mix
libations for Poseidon and the gods?   360

---

[18] The capital city of the plain of Argos, ruled over by Agamémnon. Also spelled *Mycenae.*
[19] Sparta; in the far south of Greece. Also spelled *Lacedaemon.*

Then we can all retire; high time we did;
the light is going under the dark world's rim,
better not linger at the sacred feast."

When Zeus's daughter spoke, they turned to listen
and soon the squires brought water for their hands,
while stewards filled the winebowls and poured out
a fresh cup full for every man. The company
stood up to fling the tongues and a shower of wine
over the flames, then drank their thirst away.
Now finally Telémakhos and Athena   370
bestirred themselves, turning away to the ship,
but Nestor put a hand on each, and said:

"Now Zeus forbid, and the other gods as well,
that you should spend the night on board, and leave me
as though I were some pauper without a stitch,
no blankets in his house, no piles of rugs,
no sleeping soft for host or guest! Far from it!
I have all these, blankets and deep-piled rugs,
and while I live the only son of Odysseus
will never make his bed on a ship's deck—   380
no, not while sons of mine are left at home
to welcome any guest who comes to us."

The grey-eyed goddess Athena answered him:

"You are very kind, sir, and Telémakhos
should do as you ask. That is the best thing.
He will go with you, and will spend the night
under your roof. But I must join our ship
and talk to the crew, to keep their spirits up,
since I'm the only senior in the company.
The rest are boys who shipped for friendship's sake,   390
no older than Telémakhos, any of them.
Let me sleep out, then, by the black hull's side,
this night at least. At daybreak I'll be off
to see the Kaukonians[20] about a debt they owe me,
an old one and no trifle. As for your guest,
send him off in a car, with one of your sons,
and give him thoroughbreds, a racing team."

Even as she spoke, Athena left them—seeming
a seahawk, in a clap of wings,—and all
the Akhaians of Pylos town looked up astounded.   400
Awed then by what his eyes had seen, the old man
took Telémakhos' hand and said warmly:

[20]A people who lived near Pylos.

"My dear child, I can have no fears for you,
no doubt about your conduct or your heart,
if, at your age, the gods are your companions.
Here we had someone from Olympos—clearly
the glorious daughter of Zeus, his third child,
who held your father dear among the Argives.
O, Lady, hear me! Grant an illustrious name
to me and to my children and my dear wife!   410
A noble heifer shall be yours in sacrifice,
one that no man has ever yoked or driven;
my gift to you—her horns all sheathed in gold."

So he ended, praying; and Athena heard him.
Then Nestor of Gerênia led them all,
his sons and sons-in-law, to his great house;
and in they went to the famous hall of Nestor,
taking their seats on thrones and easy chairs,
while the old man mixed water in a wine bowl
with sweet red wine, mellowed eleven years   420
before his housekeeper uncapped the jar.
He mixed and poured his offering, repeating
prayers to Athena, daughter of royal Zeus.
The others made libation, and drank deep,
then all the company went to their quarters,
and Nestor of Gerênia showed Telémakhos
under the echoing eastern entrance hall
to a fine bed near the bed of Peisístratos,
captain of spearmen, his unmarried son.
Then he lay down in his own inner chamber   430
where his dear faithful wife had smoothed his bed.

When Dawn spread out her finger tips of rose,
Lord Nestor of Gerênia, charioteer,
left his room for a throne of polished stone,
white and gleaming as though with oil, that stood
before the main gate of the palace; Neleus here
had sat before him—masterful in kingship,
Neleus, long ago a prey to death, gone down
to the night of the underworld.
So Nestor held his throne and scepter now,   440
lord of the western approaches to Akhaia.
And presently his sons came out to join him,
leaving the palace: Ekhéphron and Stratíos,
Perseus and Arêtós and Thrasymêdês,
and after them the prince Peisístratos,
bringing Telémakhos along with him.
Seeing all present, the old lord Nestor said:

"Dear sons, here is my wish, and do it briskly
to please the gods, Athena first of all,

my guest in daylight at our holy feast. 450
One of you must go for a young heifer
and have the cowherd lead her from the pasture.
Another call on Lord Telémakhos' ship
to invite his crewmen, leaving two behind;
and someone else again send for the goldsmith,
Laerkês, to gild the horns.
The rest stay here together. Tell the servants
a ritual feast will be prepared in hall.
Tell them to bring seats, firewood and fresh water."

Before he finished, they were about these errands. 460
The heifer came from pasture,
the crewmen of Telémakhos from the ship,
the smith arrived, bearing the tools of his trade—
hammer and anvil, and the precision tongs
he handled fiery gold with,—and Athena
came as a god comes, numinous, to the rites.

The smith now gloved each horn in a pure foil
beaten out of the gold that Nestor gave him—
a glory and delight for the goddess' eyes—
while Ekhéphron and Stratíos held the horns. 470
Arêtós brought clear lustral water
in a bowl quivering with fresh-cut flowers,
a basket of barley in his other hand.
Thrasymêdês, who could stand his ground in war,
stood ready, with a sharp two-bladed axe,
for the stroke of sacrifice, and Perseus
held a bowl for the blood. And now Nestor,
strewing the barley grains, and water drops,
pronounced his invocation to Athena
and burned a pinch of bristles from the victim. 480
When prayers were said and all the grain was scattered
great-hearted Thrasymêdês in a flash
swung the axe, at one blow cutting through
the neck tendons. The heifer's spirit failed.
Then all the women gave a wail of joy—
daughters, daughters-in-law, and the Lady Eurydíkê,
Klyménos' eldest daughter. But the men
still held the heifer, shored her up
from the wide earth where the living go their ways,
until Peisístratos cut her throat across, 490
the black blood ran, and life ebbed from her marrow.
The carcass now sank down, and they disjointed
shoulder and thigh bone, wrapping them in fat,
two layers, folded, with raw strips of flesh.
These offerings Nestor burned on the split-wood fire
and moistened with red wine. His sons took up
five-tined forks in their hands, while the altar flame

ate through the bones, and bits of tripe went round.
Then came the carving of the quarters, and they spitted
morsels of lean meat on the long sharp tines   500
and broiled them at arm's length upon the fire.

Polykástê, a fair girl, Nestor's youngest,
had meanwhile given a bath to Telémakhos—
bathing him first, then rubbing him with oil.
She held fine clothes and a cloak to put around him
when he came godlike from the bathing place;
then out he went to take his place with Nestor.
When the best cuts were broiled and off the spits,
they all sat down to banquet. Gentle squires
kept every golden wine cup brimming full.   510
And so they feasted to their heart's content,
until the prince of charioteers commanded:

"Sons, harness the blood mares for Telémakhos;
hitch up the car, and let him take the road."

They swung out smartly to do the work, and hooked
the handsome horses to a chariot shaft.
The mistress of the stores brought up provisions
of bread and wine, with victuals fit for kings,
and Telémakhos stepped up on the painted car.
Just at his elbow stood Peisístratos,   520
captain of spearmen, reins in hand. He gave
a flick to the horses, and with streaming manes
they ran for the open country. The tall town
of Pylos sank behind them in the distance,
as all day long they kept the harness shaking.

The sun was low and shadows crossed the lanes
when they arrived at Phêrai.[21] There Dióklês,
son of Ortílokhos whom Alpheios fathered,
welcomed the young men, and they slept the night.
But up when the young Dawn's finger tips of rose   530
opened in the east, they hitched the team
once more to the painted car,
and steered out eastward through the echoing gate,
whipping their fresh horses into a run.
That day they made the grainlands of Lakedaimon,
where, as the horses held to a fast clip,
they kept on to their journey's end. Behind them
the sun went down and all the roads grew dark.

_____

[21] A stopping place on the eastward route from Pylos to Lakedaimon.

BOOK FOUR: THE RED-HAIRED
KING AND HIS LADY

By vales and sharp ravines in Lakedaimon
the travellers drove to Meneláos' mansion,
and found him at a double wedding feast
for son and daughter.

                                        Long ago at Troy
he pledged her to the heir of great Akhilleus,
breaker of men—a match the gods had ripened;
so he must send her with a chariot train
to the town and glory of the Myrmidons.
And that day, too, he brought Alektor's daughter
to marry his tall scion,[1] Megapénthês,   10
born of a slave girl during the long war—
for the gods had never after granted Helen
a child to bring into the sunlit world
after the first, rose-lipped Hermionê,
a girl like the pale-gold goddess Aphroditê.[2]

Down the great hall in happiness they feasted,
neighbors of Meneláos, and his kin,
for whom a holy minstrel harped and sang;
and two lithe tumblers moved out on the song
with spins and handsprings through the company.   20
Now when Telémakhos and Nestor's son
pulled up their horses at the main gate,
one of the king's companions in arms, Eteóneus,
going outside, caught sight of them. He turned
and passed through court and hall to tell the master,
stepping up close to get his ear. Said he:

"Two men are here—two strangers,[3] Meneláos,
but nobly born Akhaians, they appear.
What do you say, shall we unhitch their team,
or send them on to someone free to receive them?"   30

The red-haired captain answered him in anger:

"You were no idiot before, Eteóneus,
but here you are talking like a child of ten.
Could we have made it home again—and Zeus
give us no more hard roving!—if other men
had never fed us, given us lodging?

---

[1] Descendant; son.
[2] Goddess of love and beauty.
[3] The near-breach of hospitality by Eteóneus, which angers Meneláos, is probably explained
by wariness; another guest, Paris, had once abducted Helen and thus set off the war.

                                                                    Bring
these men to be our guests: unhitch their team!"

Eteóneus left the long room like an arrow,
calling equerries[4] after him, on the run.
Outside, they freed the sweating team from harness,   40
stabled the horses, tied them up, and showered
bushels of wheat and barley in the feed box;
then leaned the chariot pole
against the gleaming entry wall of stone
and took the guests in. What a brilliant place
that mansion of the great prince seemed to them!
A-glitter everywhere, as though with fiery
points of sunlight, lusters of the moon.
The young men gazed in joy before they entered
into a room of polished tubs to bathe.   50
Maidservants gave them baths, anointed them,
held out fresh tunics, cloaked them warm; and soon
they took tall thrones beside the son of Atreus.
Here a maid tipped out water for their hands
from a golden pitcher into a silver bowl,
and set a polished table near at hand;
the larder mistress with her tray of loaves
and savories came, dispensing all her best,
and then a carver heaped their platters high
with various meats, and put down cups of gold.   60
Now said the red-haired captain, Meneláos,
gesturing:

                    "Welcome; and fall to; in time,
when you have supped, we hope to hear your names,
forbears and families—in your case, it seems,
no anonymities, but lordly men.
Lads like yourselves are not base born."

                                                                 At this,

he lifted in his own hands the king's portion,
a chine of beef, and set it down before them.
Seeing all ready then, they took their dinner;
but when they had feasted well,   70
Telémakhos could not keep still, but whispered,
his head bent close, so the others might not hear:

"My dear friend, can you believe your eyes?—
the murmuring hall, how luminous it is
with bronze, gold, amber, silver, and ivory!
This is the way the court of Zeus must be,
inside, upon Olympos. What a wonder!"

---

[4] Men who tended to the horses.

But splendid Meneláos had overheard him
and spoke out on the instant to them both:

"Young friends, no mortal man can vie with Zeus.   80
His home and all his treasures are for ever.
But as for men, it may well be that few
have more than I. How painfully I wandered
before I brought it home! Seven years at sea,
Kypros, Phoinikia, Egypt, and still farther
among the sun-burnt races.
I saw the men of Sidon[5] and Arabia
and Libya, too, where lambs are horned at birth.
In every year they have three lambing seasons,
so no man, chief or shepherd, ever goes   90
hungry for want of mutton, cheese, or milk—
all year at milking time there are fresh ewes.
But while I made my fortune on those travels
a stranger killed my brother, in cold blood,—
tricked blind, caught in the web of his deadly queen.
What pleasure can I take, then, being lord
over these costly things?
You must have heard your fathers tell my story,
whoever your fathers are; you must know of my life,
the anguish I once had, and the great house   100
full of my treasure, left in desolation.
How gladly I should live one third as rich
to have my friends back safe at home!—my friends
who died on Troy's wide seaboard, far
from the grazing lands of Argos.
But as things are, nothing but grief is left me
for those companions. While I sit at home
sometimes hot tears come, and I revel in them,
or stop before the surfeit makes me shiver.
And there is one I miss more than the other   110
dead I mourn for; sleep and food alike
grow hateful when I think of him. No soldier
took on so much, went through so much, as Odysseus.
That seems to have been his destiny, and this mine—
to feel each day the emptiness of his absence,
ignorant, even, whether he lived or died.
How his old father and his quiet wife,
Penélopê, must miss him still!
And Telémakhos, whom he left as a new-born child."

Now hearing these things said, the boy's heart rose   120
in a long pang for his father, and he wept,

---

[5] An important city in Phoinikia (Phoenicia), an area along the Syrian coast noted for commerce and craftsmanship.

holding his purple mantle with both hands
before his eyes. Meneláos knew him now,
and so fell silent with uncertainty
whether to let him speak and name his father
in his own time, or to inquire, and prompt him.
And while he pondered, Helen came
out of her scented chamber, a moving grace
like Artemis,[6] straight as a shaft of gold.
Beside her came Adrastê, to place her armchair,   130
Alkippê, with a rug of downy wool,
and Phylo, bringing a silver basket, once
given by Alkandrê, the wife of Pólybos,
in the treasure city, Thebes of distant Egypt.
He gave two silver bathtubs to Meneláos
and a pair of tripods, with ten pure gold bars,
and she, then, made these beautiful gifts to Helen:
a golden distaff,[7] and the silver basket
rimmed in hammered gold, with wheels to run on.
So Phylo rolled it in to stand beside her,   140
heaped with fine spun stuff, and cradled on it
the distaff swathed in dusky violet wool.
Reclining in her light chair with its footrest,
Helen gazed at her husband and demanded:

"Meneláos, my lord, have we yet heard
our new guests introduce themselves? Shall I
dissemble what I feel? No, I must say it.
Never, anywhere, have I seen so great a likeness
in man or woman—but it is truly strange!
This boy must be the son of Odysseus,   150
Telémakhos, the child he left at home
that year the Akhaian host made war on Troy—
daring all for the wanton that I was."

And the red-haired captain, Meneláos, answered:

"My dear, I see the likeness as well as you do.
Odysseus' hands and feet were like this boy's;
his head, and hair, and the glinting of his eyes.
Not only that, but when I spoke, just now,
of Odysseus' years of toil on my behalf
and all he had to endure—the boy broke down   160
and wept into his cloak."

                                        Now Nestor's son,
Peisístratos, spoke up in answer to him:

"My lord marshal, Meneláos, son of Atreus,
this is that hero's son as you surmise,

---

[6] Goddess of the hunt.
[7] A staff used in spinning thread.

but he is gentle, and would be ashamed
to clamor for attention before your grace
whose words have been so moving to us both.
Nestor, Lord of Gerênia, sent me with him
as guide and escort; he had wished to see you,
to be advised by you or assisted somehow. 170
A father far from home means difficulty
for an only son, with no one else to help him;
so with Telémakhos:
his father left the house without defenders."

The king with flaming hair now spoke again:

"His son, in my house! How I loved the man,
And how he fought through hardship for my sake!
I swore I'd cherish him above all others
if Zeus, who views the wide world, gave us passage
homeward across the sea in the fast ships. 180
I would have settled him in Argos, brought him
over with herds and household out of Ithaka,
his child and all his people. I could have cleaned out
one of my towns to be his new domain.
And so we might have been together often
in feasts and entertainments, never parted
till the dark mist of death lapped over one of us.
But God himself must have been envious,
to batter the bruised man so that he alone
should fail in his return." 190

A twinging ache of grief rose up in everyone,
and Helen of Argos wept, the daughter of Zeus,[8]
Telémakhos and Meneláos wept,
and tears came to the eyes of Nestor's son—
remembering, for his part, Antílokhos,
whom the son of shining Dawn[9] had killed in battle.
But thinking of that brother, he broke out:

"O son of Atreus, when we spoke of you
at home, and asked about you, my old father
would say you have the clearest mind of all. 200
If it is not too much to ask, then, let us not
weep away these hours after supper;
I feel we should not: Dawn will soon be here!
You understand, I would not grudge a man
right mourning when he comes to death and doom:
what else can one bestow on the poor dead?—

---

[8] Helen was daughter of Zeus by the mortal woman Lêda. (Lêda was ravished by the god, who took the form of a swan.)
[9] Memnon, an Ethiopian king, was the son of Eos, the goddess of the dawn.

a lock of hair sheared,[10] and a tear let fall.
For that matter, I, too,
lost someone in the war at Troy—my brother,
and no mean soldier, whom you must have known,   210
although I never did,—Antílokhos.
He ranked high as a runner and fighting man."

The red-haired captain Meneláos answered:

"My lad, what you have said is only sensible,
and you did well to speak. Yes, that was worthy
a wise man and an older man than you are:
you speak for all the world like Nestor's son.
How easily one can tell the man whose father
had true felicity, marrying and begetting!
And that was true of Nestor, all his days,   220
down to his sleek old age in peace at home,
with clever sons, good spearmen into the bargain.
Come, we'll shake off this mourning mood of ours
and think of supper. Let the men at arms
rinse our hands again! There will be time
for a long talk with Telémakhos in the morning."

The hero Meneláos' companion in arms,
Asphalion, poured water for their hands,
and once again they touched the food before them.
But now it entered Helen's mind   230
to drop into the wine that they were drinking
an anodyne, mild magic of forgetfulness.
Whoever drank this mixture in the wine bowl
would be incapable of tears that day—
though he should lose mother and father both,
or see, with his own eyes, a son or brother
mauled by weapons of bronze at his own gate.
The opiate of Zeus's daughter bore
this canny power. It had been supplied her
by Polydamna, mistress of Lord Thôn,   240
in Egypt, where the rich plantations grow
herbs of all kinds, maleficent and healthful;
and no one else knows medicine as they do,
Egyptian heirs of Paian,[11] the healing god.
She drugged the wine, then, had it served, and said—
taking again her part in the conversation—

"O Meneláos, Atreus' royal son,
and you that are great heroes' sons, you know
how Zeus gives all of us in turn
good luck and bad luck, being all powerful.   250

---

[10] To strew a lock of one's hair on the dead was a customary part of funeral ritual.
[11] An epithet for Apollo in his role as god of physicians.

So take refreshment, take your ease in hall,
and cheer the time with stories. I'll begin.
Not that I think of naming, far less telling,
every feat of that rugged man, Odysseus,
but here is something that he dared to do
at Troy, where you Akhaians endured the war.
He had, first, given himself an outrageous beating
and thrown some rags on—like a household slave—
then slipped into that city of wide lanes
among his enemies. So changed, he looked   260
as never before upon the Akhaian beachhead,
but like a beggar, merged in the townspeople;
and no one there remarked him. But I knew him—
even as he was, I knew him,
and questioned him. How shrewdly he put me off!
But in the end I bathed him and anointed him,
put a fresh cloak around him, and swore an oath
not to give him away as Odysseus to the Trojans,
till he got back to camp where the long ships lay.
He spoke up then, and told me   270
all about the Akhaians, and their plans—
then sworded many Trojans through the body
on his way out with what he learned of theirs.
The Trojan women raised a cry—but my heart
sang—for I had come round, long before,
to dreams of sailing home, and I repented
the mad day Aphroditê
drew me away from my dear fatherland,
forsaking all—child, bridal bed, and husband—
a man without defect in form or mind."   280

Replied the red-haired captain, Meneláos:

"An excellent tale, my dear, and most becoming.
In my life I have met, in many countries,
foresight and wit in many first rate men,
but never have I seen one like Odysseus
for steadiness and a stout heart. Here, for instance,
is what he did—had the cold nerve to do—
inside the hollow horse,[12] where we were waiting,
picked men all of us, for the Trojan slaughter,
when all of a sudden, you came by—I dare say   290
drawn by some superhuman
power that planned an exploit for the Trojans;
and Deïphobos,[13] that handsome man, came with you.
Three times you walked around it, patting it everywhere,

---

[12] The Greeks had hidden some of their best warriors inside a huge wooden horse, which the Trojans hauled into their city, thus precipitating its overthrow. For a detailed version of the incident, see Virgil's *Aeneid*, Book II.
[13] By the time of the fall of Troy, Helen had been married to this Trojan prince.

and called by name the flower of our fighters,
making your voice sound like their wives, calling.
Diomêdês and I crouched in the center
along with Odysseus; we could hear you plainly;
and listening, we two were swept
by waves of longing—to reply, or go.   300
Odysseus fought us down, despite our craving,
and all the Akhaians kept their lips shut tight,
all but Antiklos. Desire moved his throat
to hail you, but Odysseus' great hands clamped
over his jaws, and held. So he saved us all,
till Pallas Athena led you away at last."

Then clear-headed Telémakhos addressed him:

"My lord marshal, Meneláos, son of Atreus,
all the more pity, since these valors
could not defend him from annihilation—   310
not if his heart were iron in his breast.
But will you not dismiss us for the night now?
Sweet sleep will be a pleasure, drifting over us."

He said no more, but Helen called the maids
and sent them to make beds, with purple rugs
piled up, and sheets outspread, and fleecy
coverlets, in the porch inside the gate.
The girls went out with torches in their hands,
and presently a squire led the guests—
Telémakhos and Nestor's radiant son—   320
under the entrance colonnade, to bed.
Then deep in the great mansion, in his chamber,
Meneláos went to rest, and Helen,
queenly in her long gown, lay beside him.

When the young Dawn with finger tips of rose
made heaven bright, the deep-lunged man of battle
stood up, pulled on his tunic and his mantle,
slung on a swordbelt and a new edged sword,
tied his smooth feet into fine rawhide sandals
and left his room, a god's brilliance upon him.   330
He sat down by Telémakhos, asking gently:

"Telémakhos, why did you come, sir, riding
the sea's broad back to reach old Lakedaimon?
A public errand or private? Why, precisely?"

Telémakhos replied:

"My lord marshal Meneláos, son of Atreus,
I came to hear what news you had of Father.
My house, my good estates are being ruined.

Each day my mother's bullying suitors come
to slaughter flocks of mine and my black cattle;   340
enemies crowd our home. And this is why
I come to you for news of him who owned it.
Tell me of his death, sir, if perhaps
you witnessed it, or have heard some wanderer
tell the tale. The man was born for trouble.
Spare me no part for kindness' sake; be harsh;
but put the scene before me as you saw it.
If ever Odysseus my noble father
served you by promise kept or work accomplished
in the land of Troy, where you Akhaians suffered,   350
recall those things for me the way they were."

Stirred now to anger, Meneláos said:

"Intolerable—that soft men, as those are,
should think to lie in that great captain's bed.
Fawns in a lion's lair! As if a doe
put down her litter of sucklings there, while she
quested a glen or cropped some grassy hollow.
Ha! Then the lord returns to his own bed
and deals out wretched doom on both alike.
So will Odysseus deal out doom on these.   360
O Father Zeus, Athena, and Apollo!
I pray he comes as once he was, in Lesbos,
when he stood up to wrestle Philomeleidês—
champion and Island King—
and smashed him down. How the Akhaians cheered!
If only that Odysseus met the suitors,
they'd have their consummation, a cold bed!
Now for your questions, let me come to the point.
I would not misreport it for you; let me
tell you what the Ancient of the Sea,[14]   370
who is infallible, said to me—every word.

During my first try at a passage homeward
the gods detained me, tied me down to Egypt—
for I had been too scant in hekatombs,
and gods will have the rules each time remembered.
There is an island washed by the open sea
lying off Nile mouth—seamen call it Pharos—
distant a day's sail in a clean hull
with a brisk land breeze behind. It has a harbor,
a sheltered bay, where shipmasters   380
take on dark water for the outward voyage.
Here the gods held me twenty days becalmed.

[14]Proteus, who is described in the following passage.

No winds came up, seaward escorting winds
for ships that ride the sea's broad back, and so
my stores and men were used up; we were failing
had not one goddess intervened in pity—
Eidothea, daughter of Proteus,
the Ancient of the Sea. How I distressed her!
I had been walking out alone that day—
my sailors, thin-bellied from the long fast,   390
were off with fish hooks, angling on the shore—
then she appeared to me, and her voice sang:

'What fool is here, what drooping dunce of dreams?
Or can it be, friend, that you love to suffer?
How can you linger on this island, aimless
and shiftless, while your people waste away?'

To this I quickly answered:

                                                        'Let me tell you,
goddess, whatever goddess you may be,
these doldrums are no will of mine. I take it
the gods who own broad heaven are offended.   400
Why don't you tell me—since the gods know everything—
who has me pinned down here?
How am I going to make my voyage home?'

Now she replied in her immortal beauty:

'I'll put it for you clearly as may be, friend.
The Ancient of the Salt Sea haunts this place,
immortal Proteus of Egypt; all the deeps
are known to him; he serves under Poseidon,
and is, they say, my father.
If you could take him by surprise and hold him,   410
he'd give you course and distance for your sailing
homeward across the cold fish-breeding sea.
And should you wish it, noble friend, he'd tell you
all that occurred at home, both good and evil,
while you were gone so long and hard a journey.'

To this I said:

                                        'But you, now—you must tell me
how I can trap this venerable sea-god.
He will elude me if he takes alarm;
no man—god knows—can quell a god with ease.'

That fairest of unearthly nymphs replied: 420

'I'll tell you this, too, clearly as may be.
When the sun hangs at high noon in heaven,
the Ancient glides ashore under the Westwind,

hidden by shivering glooms on the clear water,
and rests in caverns hollowed by the sea.
There flippered seals, brine children, shining come
from silvery foam in crowds to lie around him,
exhaling rankness from the deep sea floor.
Tomorrow dawn I'll take you to those caves
and bed you down there. Choose three officers 430
for company—brave men they had better be—
the old one has strange powers, I must tell you.
He goes amid the seals to check their number,
and when he sees them all, and counts them all,
he lies down like a shepherd with his flock.
Here is your opportunity: at this point
gather yourselves, with all your heart and strength,
and tackle him before he bursts away.
He'll make you fight—for he can take the forms
of all the beasts, and water, and blinding fire; 440
but you must hold on, even so, and crush him
until he breaks the silence. When he does,
he will be in that shape you saw asleep.
Relax your grip, then, set the Ancient free,
and put your questions, hero:
Who is the god so hostile to you,
and how will you go home on the fish-cold sea.'

At this she dove under a swell and left me.
Back to the ships in the sandy cove I went,
my heart within me like a high surf running; 450
but there I joined my men once more
at supper, as the sacred Night came on,
and slept at last beside the lapping water.
When Dawn spread out her finger tips of rose
I started, by the sea's wide level ways,
praying the gods for help, and took along
three lads I counted on in any fight.
Meanwhile the nereid[15] swam from the lap of Ocean
laden with four sealskins, new flayed
for the hoax she thought of playing on her father. 460
In the sand she scooped out hollows for our bodies
and sat down, waiting. We came close to touch her,
and, bedding us, she threw the sealskins over us—
a strong disguise; oh, yes, terribly strong
as I recall the stench of those damned seals.
Would any man lie snug with a sea monster?
But here the nymph, again, came to our rescue,
dabbing ambrosia under each man's nose—
a perfume drowning out the bestial odor.

[15]A sea nymph.

So there we lay with beating hearts all morning   470
while seals came shoreward out of ripples, jostling
to take their places, flopping on the sand.
At noon the Ancient issued from the sea
and held inspection, counting off the sea-beasts.
We were the first he numbered; he went by,
detecting nothing. When at last he slept
we gave a battlecry and plunged for him,
locking our hands behind him. But the old one's
tricks were not knocked out of him; far from it.
First he took on a whiskered lion's shape,   480
a serpent then; a leopard; a great boar;
then sousing water; then a tall green tree.
Still we hung on, by hook or crook, through everything,
until the Ancient saw defeat, and grimly
opened his lips to ask me:

                                                      'Son of Atreus,
who counselled you to this? A god: what god?
Set a trap for me, overpower me—why?'

He bit it off, then, and I answered:

                                                         'Old one,
you know the reason—why feign not to know?
High and dry so long upon this island   490
I'm at my wits' end, and my heart is sore.
You gods know everything; now you can tell me:
which of the immortals chained me here?
And how will I get home on the fish-cold sea?'

He made reply at once:

                                            'You should have paid
honor to Zeus and the other gods, performing
a proper sacrifice before embarking:
that was your short way home on the winedark sea.
You may not see your friends, your own fine house,
or enter your own land again,   500
unless you first remount the Nile in flood
and pay your hekatomb to the gods of heaven.
Then, and then only,
the gods will grant the passage you desire.'

Ah, how my heart sank, hearing this—
hearing him send me back on the cloudy sea
in my own track, the long hard way of Egypt.
Nevertheless, I answered him and said:

'Ancient, I shall do all as you command.
But tell me, now, the others—   510
had they a safe return, all those Akhaians

who stayed behind when Nestor and I left Troy?
Or were there any lost at sea—what bitterness!—
any who died in camp, after the war?'

To this he said:

'For you to know these things
goes beyond all necessity, Meneláos.
Why must you ask?—you should not know my mind,
and you will grieve to learn it, I can tell you.
Many there were who died, many remain,
but two high officers alone were lost—   520
on the passage home, I mean; you saw the war.
One is alive, a castaway at sea;
the other, Aîas, perished with all hands—
though first Poseidon landed him on Gyrai[16]
promontory, and saved him from the ocean.
Despite Athena's hate, he had lived on,
but the great sinner in his insolence
yelled that the gods' will and the sea were beaten,
and this loud brag came to Poseidon's ears.
He swung the trident[17] in his massive hands   530
and in one shock from top to bottom split
that promontory, toppling into the sea
the fragment where the great fool sat.
So the vast ocean had its will with Aîas,
drunk in the end on salt spume as he drowned.
Meanwhile your brother left that doom astern
in his decked ships—the Lady Hera[18] saved him;
but as he came round Malea
a fresh squall caught him, bearing him away
over the cold sea, groaning in disgust,   540
to the Land's End of Argos, where Thyestês[19]
lived in the days of old, and then his son,
Aigísthos. Now, again, return seemed easy:
the high gods wound the wind into the east,
and back he sailed, this time to his own coast.
He went ashore and kissed the earth in joy,
hot tears blinding his eyes at sight of home.

---

[16]An island in the Aegean. Aîas, who in the following lines is described as punished for his insolent and sacrilegious boasting, is the "lesser," "Locrian" Aîas (Ajax), the son of Oileus; he is not the "greater" Aîas, who was the son of Télamon.

[17]The three-pronged spear wielded by the sea god Poseidon.

[18]Consort of Zeus; queen of the gods. She consistently sided with the Greeks against the Trojans.

[19]Brother of Atreus (the father of Agamémnon and Meneláos). See the headnote to Aeschylus' *Oresteia*. Homer's account here of the murder of Agamémnon differs considerably from the version in Aeschylus; in the *Oresteia*, Agamémnon's wife Klytaimnéstra plays a more significant role than does Aigísthos in the murder.

But there were eyes that watched him from a height—
a lookout, paid two bars of gold to keep
vigil the year round for Aigísthos' sake,   550
that he should be forewarned, and Agamémnon's
furious valor sleep unroused.
Now this man with his news ran to the tyrant,
who made his crooked arrangements in a flash,
stationed picked men at arms, a score of men
in hiding; set a feast in the next room;
then he went out with chariots and horses
to hail the king and welcome him to evil.
He led him in to banquet, all serene,
and killed him, like an ox felled at the trough;   560
and not a man of either company
survived that ambush in Aigísthos' house.'

Before the end my heart was broken down.
I slumped on the trampled sand and cried aloud,
caring no more for life or the light of day,
and rolled there weeping, till my tears were spent.
Then the unerring Ancient said at last:

'No more, no more; how long must you persist?
Nothing is gained by grieving so. How soon
can you return to Argos? You may take him   570
alive there still—or else meanwhile Orestês
will have despatched him. You'll attend the feast.'

At this my heart revived, and I recovered
the self command to question him once more:

'Of two companions now I know. The third?
Tell me his name, the one marooned at sea;
living, you say, or dead? Even in pain
I wish to hear.'

                                        And this is all he answered:

'Laërtês' son, whose home is Ithaka.
I saw him weeping, weeping on an island.   580
The nymph Kalypso has him, in her hall.
No means of faring home are left him now;
no ship with oars, and no ship's company
to pull him on the broad back of the sea.
As to your own destiny, prince Meneláos,
you shall not die in the bluegrass land of Argos;
rather the gods intend you for Elysion[20]

---

[20]As presented here in Homer, this realm (also called *Elysium*) is not part of the underground Hades which Odysseus visits later in the *Odyssey*. It is, rather, a happy land on the extreme western surface of the earth.

with golden Rhadamanthos[21] at the world's end,
where all existence is a dream of ease.
Snowfall is never known there, neither long   590
frost of winter, nor torrential rain,
but only mild and lulling airs from Ocean
bearing refreshment for the souls of men—
the West Wind always blowing.

                                        For the gods

hold you, as Helen's lord, a son of Zeus.'

At this he dove under a swell and left me,
and I went back to the ship with my companions,
feeling my heart's blood in me running high;
but in the long hull's shadow, near the sea,
we supped again as sacred Night came on   600
and slept at last beside the lapping water.

When Dawn spread out her finger tips of rose,
in first light we launched on the courtly breakers,
setting up masts and yards in the well-found ships;
went all on board, and braced on planks athwart
oarsmen in line dipped oars in the grey sea.
Soon I drew in to the great stream[22] fed by heaven
and, laying by, slew bulls in the proper number,
until the immortal gods were thus appeased;
then heaped a death mound on that shore against   610
all-quenching time for Agamémnon's honor,
and put to sea once more. The gods sent down
a sternwind for a racing passage homeward.

So ends the story. Now you must stay with me
and be my guest eleven or twelve days more.
I'll send you on your way with gifts, and fine ones:
three chariot horses, and a polished car;
a hammered cup, too, so that all your days,
tipping the red wine for the deathless gods,
you will remember me."

                                Telémakhos answered: 620

"Lord, son of Atreus, no, you must not keep me.
Not that a year with you would be too long:
I never could be homesick here—I find
your tales and all you say so marvellous.
But time hangs heavy on my shipmates' hands
at holy Pylos, if you make me stay.

---

[21] Ruler of Elysion (sometimes portrayed in ancient literature as a judge of the dead in Hades).

[22] The Nile, believed to have a divine source in the sky.

As for your gift, now, let it be some keepsake.
Horses I cannot take to Ithaka;
let me bestow them back on you, to serve
your glory here. My lord, you rule wide country,   630
rolling and rich with clover, galingale
and all the grains: red wheat and hoary barley.
home we have no level runs or meadows,
but highland, goat land—prettier than plains, though.
Grasses, and pasture land, are hard to come by
upon the islands tilted in the sea,
and Ithaka is the island of them all."

At this the deep-lunged man of battle smiled.
Then he said kindly, patting the boy's hand:

"You come of good stock, lad. That was well spoken.   640
I'll change the gift, then—as indeed I can.
Let me see what is costliest and most beautiful
of all the precious things my house contains:
a wine bowl, mixing bowl, all wrought of silver,
but rimmed with hammered gold. Let this be yours.
It is Hephaistos'[23] work, given me by Phaidimos,
captain and king of Sidon. He received me
during my travels. Let it be yours, I say."

This was their discourse on that morning. Meanwhile
guests were arriving at the great lord's house,   650
bringing their sheep, and wine, the ease of men,
with loaves their comely kerchiefed women sent,
to make a feast in hall.

                                        At that same hour,
before the distant manor of Odysseus,
the suitors were competing at the discus throw
and javelin, on a measured field they used,
arrogant lords at play. The two best men,
Antínoös and Eurýmakhos, presided.
Now Phronios' son, Noêmon, came to see them
with a question for Antínoös. He said: 660

"Do any of us know, or not, Antínoös,
what day Telémakhos will be home from Pylos?
He took my ship, but now I need it back
to make a cruise to Elis, where the plains are.
I have a dozen mares at pasture there
with mule colts yet unweaned. My notion is
to bring one home and break him in for labor."

---

[23] The god of fire and of metalworking. Also spelled *Hephaestus.*

His first words made them stare—for they knew well
Telémakhos could not have gone to Pylos,
but inland with his flocks, or to the swineherd.   670
Eupeithês' son, Antínoös, quickly answered:

"Tell the story straight. He sailed? Who joined him—
a crew he picked up here in Ithaka,
or his own slaves? He might have done it that way.
And will you make it clear
whether he took the ship against your will?
Did he ask for it, did you lend it to him?"

Now said the son of Phronios in reply:

"Lent it to him, and freely. Who would not,
when a prince of that house asked for it, in trouble?   680
Hard to refuse the favor, it seems to me.
As for his crew, the best men on the island,
after ourselves, went with him. Mentor I noted
going aboard—or a god who looked like Mentor.
The strange thing is, I saw Lord Mentor here
in the first light yesterday—although he sailed
five days ago for Pylos."

                                                        Turning away,
Noêmon took the path to his father's house,
leaving the two men there, baffled and hostile.
They called the rest in from the playing field   690
and made them all sit down, so that Antínoös
could speak out from the stormcloud of his heart,
swollen with anger; and his eyes blazed:

"A bad business. Telémakhos had the gall
to make that crossing, though we said he could not.
So the young cub rounds up a first rate crew
in spite of all our crowd, and puts to sea.
What devilment will he be up to next time?—
Zeus blast the life out of him before he's grown!
Just give me a fast ship and twenty men;   700
I'll intercept him, board him in the strait
between the crags of Samê[24] and this island.
He'll fnd his sea adventure after his father
swamping work in the end!"

                                            They all cried "Aye!"
and "After him!" and trailed back to the manor.

---

[24]An island, modern Cephalonia, south and west of Ithaka; also called Kephallênia in this
poem.

Now not much time went by before Penélopê
learned what was afoot among the suitors.
Medôn the crier told her. He had been
outside the wall, and heard them in the court
conspiring. Into the house and up the stairs   710
he ran to her with his news upon his tongue—
but at the door Penélopê met him, crying:

"Why have they sent you up here now? To tell
the maids of King Odysseus—'Leave your spinning:
Time to go down and slave to feed those men?'
I wish this were the last time they came feasting,
courting me or consorting here! The last!
Each day you crowd this house like wolves
to eat away my brave son's patrimony.
When you were boys, did your own fathers tell you   720
nothing of what Odysseus was for them?
In word and act impeccable, disinterested
toward all the realm—though it is king's justice
to hold one man abhorred and love another;
no man alive could say Odysseus wronged him.
But your own hearts—how different!—and your deeds!
How soon are benefactions all forgotten!"

Now Medôn, the alert and cool man, answered:

"I wish that were the worst of it, my Lady,
but they intend something more terrible—   730
may Zeus forfend and spare us!
They plan to drive the keen bronze through Telémakhos
when he comes home. He sailed away, you know,
to hallowed Pylos and old Lakedaimon
for news about his father."

                                                    Her knees failed,
and her heart failed as she listened to the words,
and all her power of speech went out of her.
Tears came; but the rich voice could not come.
Only after a long while she made answer:

"Why has my child left me? He had no need   740
of those long ships on which men shake out sail
to tug like horses, breasting miles of sea.
Why did he go? Must he, too, be forgotten?"

Then Medôn, the perceptive man, replied:

"A god moved him—who knows?—or his own heart
sent him to learn, at Pylos, if his father
roams the wide world still, or what befell him."

He left her then, and went down through the house.
And now the pain around her heart benumbed her;
chairs were a step away, but far beyond her; 750
she sank down on the door sill of the chamber,
wailing, and all her women young and old
made a low murmur of lament around her,
until at last she broke out through her tears:

"Dearest companions, what has Zeus given me?
Pain—more pain than any living woman.
My lord, my lion heart, gone, long ago—
the bravest man, and best, of the Danaans,
famous through Hellas and the Argive midlands—
and now the squalls have blown my son, my dear one, 760
an unknown boy, southward. No one told me.
O brute creatures, not one soul would dare
to wake me from my sleep; you knew
the hour he took the black ship out to sea!
If I had seen that sailing in his eyes
he should have stayed with me, for all his longing,
stayed—or left me dead in the great hall.
Go, someone, now, and call old Dólios,
the slave my father gave me before I came,
my orchard keeper—tell him to make haste 770
and put these things before Laërtês; he
may plan some kind of action; let him come
to cry shame on these ruffians who would murder
Odysseus' son and heir, and end his line!"

The dear old nurse, Eurýkleia, answered her:

"Sweet mistress, have my throat cut without mercy
or what you will; it's true, I won't conceal it,
I knew the whole thing; gave him his provisions;
grain and sweet wine I gave, and a great oath
to tell you nothing till twelve days went by, 780
or till you heard of it yourself, or missed him;
he hoped you would not tear your skin lamenting.
Come, bathe and dress your loveliness afresh,
and go to the upper rooms with all your maids
to ask help from Athena, Zeus's daughter.
She it will be who saves this boy from death.
Spare the old man this further suffering;
the blissful gods cannot so hate his line,
heirs of Arkêsios; one will yet again
be lord of the tall house and the far fields." 790

She hushed her weeping in this way, and soothed her.
The Lady Penélopê arose and bathed,
dressing her body in her freshest linen,

filled a basket with barley, and led her maids
to the upper rooms, where she besought Athena:

"Tireless child of Zeus, graciously hear me!
If ever Odysseus burned at our altar fire
thighbones of beef or mutton in sacrifice,
remember it for my sake! Save my son!
Shield him, and make the killers go astray!"   800

She ended with a cry, and the goddess heard her.
Now voices rose from the shadowy hall below
where the suitors were assuring one another:

"Our so-long-courted Queen is even now
of a mind to marry one of us, and knows
nothing of what is destined for her son."

Of what was destined they in fact knew nothing,
But Antínoös addressed them in a whisper:

"No boasting—are you mad?—and no loud talk:
someone might hear it and alarm the house.   810
Come along now, be quiet, this way; come,
we'll carry out the plan our hearts are set on."

Picking out twenty of the strongest seamen,
he led them to a ship at the sea's edge,
and down they dragged her into deeper water,
stepping a mast in her, with furled sails,
and oars a-trail from thongs looped over thole pins,
ready all; then tried the white sail, hoisting,
while men at arms carried their gear aboard.
They moored the ship some way off shore, and left her   820
to take their evening meal there, waiting for night to come.

Penélopê at that hour in her high chamber
lay silent, tasting neither food nor drink,
and thought of nothing but her princely son—
could he escape, or would they find and kill him?—
her mind turning at bay, like a cornered lion
in whom fear comes as hunters close the ring.
But in her sick thought sweet sleep overtook her,
and she dozed off, her body slack and still.

Now it occurred to the grey-eyed goddess Athena   830
to make a figure of dream in a woman's form—
Iphthimê, great Ikários' other daughter,
whom Eumêlos of Phêrai took as bride.
The goddess sent this dream to Odysseus' house
to quiet Penélopê and end her grieving.

So, passing by the strap-slit[25] through the door,
the image came a-gliding down the room
to stand at her bedside and murmur to her:

"Sleepest thou, sorrowing Penélopê?
The gods whose life is ease no longer suffer thee 840
to pine and weep, then; he returns unharmed,
thy little one; no way hath he offended."

Then pensive Penélopê made this reply,
slumbering sweetly in the gates of dream:

"Sister, hast thou come hither? Why? Aforetime
never wouldst come, so far away thy dwelling.
And am I bid be done with all my grieving?
But see what anguish hath my heart and soul!
My lord, my lion heart, gone, long ago—
the bravest man, and best, of the Danaans, 850
famous through Hellas and the Argive midlands—
and now my son, my dear one, gone seafaring,
a child, untrained in hardship or in council.
Aye, 'tis for him I weep, more than his father!
Aye, how I tremble for him, lest some blow
befall him at men's hands or on the sea!
Cruel are they and many who plot against him,
to take his life before he can return."

Now the dim phantom spoke to her once more:

"Lift up thy heart, and fear not overmuch. 860
For by his side one goes whom all men else
invoke as their defender, one so powerful—
Pallas Athena; in thy tears she pitied thee
and now hath sent me that I so assure thee."

Then said Penélopê the wise:

                                        "If thou art
numinous[26] and hast ears for divine speech,
O tell me, what of Odysseus, man of woe?
Is he alive still somewhere, seeth he day light still?
Or gone in death to the sunless underworld?"

The dim phantom said only this in answer: 870

"Of him I may not tell thee in this discourse,
alive or dead. And empty words are evil."

---

[25]A hole in a door through which a strap was passed. It allowed a person outside to bolt the door on the inside.
[26]Gifted with uncanny spiritual powers.

The wavering form withdrew along the doorbolt
into a draft of wind, and out of sleep
Penélopê awoke, in better heart
for that clear dream in the twilight of the night.

Meanwhile the suitors had got under way,
planning the death plunge for Telémakhos.
Between the Isles of Ithaka and Samê
the sea is broken by an islet, Asteris,   880
with access to both channels from a cove.
In ambush here that night the Akhaians lay.

BOOK FIVE: SWEET NYMPH AND OPEN SEA

Dawn came up from the couch of her reclining,
leaving her lord Tithonos'[1] brilliant side
with fresh light in her arms for gods and men.
And the master of heaven and high thunder, Zeus,
went to his place among the gods assembled
hearing Athena tell Odysseus' woe.
For she, being vexed that he was still sojourning
in the sea chambers of Kalypso,[2] said:

"O Father Zeus and gods in bliss forever,
let no man holding scepter as a king   10
think to be mild, or kind, or virtuous;
let him be cruel, and practice evil ways,
for those Odysseus ruled cannot remember
the fatherhood and mercy of his reign.
Meanwhile he lives and grieves upon that island
in thralldom to the nymph; he cannot stir,
cannot fare homeward, for no ship is left him,
fitted with oars—no crewmen or companions
to pull him on the broad back of the sea.
And now murder is hatched on the high sea   20
against his son, who sought news of his father
in the holy lands of Pylos and Lakedaimon."

To this the summoner of cloud replied:

"My child, what odd complaints you let escape you.
Have you not, you yourself, arranged this matter—
as we all know—so that Odysseus
will bring these men to book, on his return?

[1] The lover of Eos, goddess of the dawn. No mention is made here of the most famous version of his myth, in which Eos wins for him the gift of immortality but forgets, fatefully, to ensure that Tithonos will never grow older. See Tennyson's poem "Tithonus."
[2] The nymph's island, Ogýgia, is located in a western region of the Mediterranean. The geography of Odysseus' wanderings west of Greece is uncertain.

And are you not the one to give Telémakhos
a safe route for sailing? Let his enemies
encounter no one and row home again." 30

He turned then to his favorite son and said:

"Hermês, you have much practice on our missions,
go make it known to the softly-braided nymph
that we, whose will is not subject to error,
order Odysseus home; let him depart.
But let him have no company, gods or men,
only a raft that he must lash together,
and after twenty days, worn out at sea,
he shall make land upon the garden isle,
Skhería,[3] of our kinsmen, the Phaiákians. 40
Let these men take him to their hearts in honor
and berth him in a ship, and send him home,
with gifts of garments, gold, and bronze—
so much he had not counted on from Troy
could he have carried home his share of plunder.
His destiny is to see his friends again
under his own roof, in his father's country."

No words were lost on Hermês the Wayfinder,
who bent to tie his beautiful sandals on,
ambrosial, golden, that carry him over water 50
or over endless land in a swish of the wind,
and took the wand with which he charms asleep—
or when he wills, awake—the eyes of men.
So wand in hand he paced into the air,
shot from Pieria[4] down, down to sea level,
and veered to skim the swell. A gull patrolling
between the wave crests of the desolate sea
will dip to catch a fish, and douse his wings;
no higher above the whitecaps Hermês flew
until the distant island lay ahead, 60
then rising shoreward from the violet ocean
he stepped up to the cave. Divine Kalypso,
the mistress of the isle, was now at home.
Upon her hearthstone a great fire blazing
scented the farthest shores with cedar smoke
and smoke of thyme, and singing high and low
in her sweet voice, before her loom a-weaving,
she passed her golden shuttle to and fro.
A deep wood grew outside, with summer leaves
of alder and black poplar, pungent cypress. 70

---

[3] The land (also spelled *Scheria*) of the Phaiákians (Phaeacians), possibly located on the
southern shore of the Mediterranean, opposite Ithaka, more probably Corfu, an island northwest of Ithaka off the west coast of Greece.
[4] An area on the slopes of Mount Olympos.

Ornate birds here rested their stretched wings—
horned owls, falcons, cormorants—long-tongued
beachcombing birds, and followers of the sea.
Around the smoothwalled cave a crooking vine
held purple clusters under ply of green;
and four springs, bubbling up near one another
shallow and clear, took channels here and there
through beds of violets and tender parsley.
Even a god who found this place
would gaze, and feel his heart beat with delight: 80
so Hermês did; but when he had gazed his fill
he entered the wide cave. Now face to face
the magical Kalypso recognized him,
as all immortal gods know one another
on sight—though seeming strangers, far from home.
but he saw nothing of the great Odysseus,
who sat apart, as a thousand times before,
and racked his own heart groaning, with eyes wet
scanning the bare horizon of the sea.
Kalypso, lovely nymph, seated her guest   90
in a bright chair all shimmering, and asked:

"O Hermês, ever with your golden wand,
what brings you to my island?
Your awesome visits in the past were few.
Now tell me what request you have in mind;
for I desire to do it, if I can,
and if it is a proper thing to do.
But wait a while, and let me serve my friend."

She drew a table of ambrosia near him
and stirred a cup of ruby-colored nectar[5]—   100
food and drink for the luminous Wayfinder,
who took both at his leisure, and replied:

"Goddess to god, you greet me, questioning me?
Well, here is truth for you in courtesy.
Zeus made me come, and not my inclination;
who cares to cross that tract of desolation,
the bitter sea, all mortal towns behind
where gods have beef and honors from mankind?
But it is not to be thought of—and no use—
for any god to elude the will of Zeus.   110

He notes your friend, most ill-starred by renown
of all the peers who fought for Priam's town—
nine years of war they had, before great Troy was down.
Homing, they wronged the goddess[6] with grey eyes,

---

[5] Ambrosia and nectar were the food and drink of the gods.
[6] Compare the passage in Book IV alluding to the insolence of the lesser Aîas, or Ajax.

who made a black wind blow and the seas rise,
in which his troops were lost, and all his gear,
while easterlies and current washed him here.
Now the command is: send him back in haste.
His life may not in exile go to waste.
His destiny, his homecoming, is at hand, 120
when he shall see his dearest, and walk on his own land."

That goddess most divinely made
shuddered before him, and her warm voice rose:

"Oh you vile gods, in jealousy supernal!
You hate it when we choose to lie with men—
immortal flesh by some dear mortal side.
So radiant Dawn once took to bed Orion[7]
until you easeful gods grew peevish at it,
and holy Artemis, Artemis throned in gold,
hunted him down in Delos with her arrows. 130
Then Dêmêtêr of the tasseled tresses yielded
to Iasion,[8] mingling and making love
in a furrow three times plowed; but Zeus found out
and killed him with a white-hot thunderbolt.
So now you grudge me, too, my mortal friend.
But it was I who saved him—saw him straddle
his own keel board, the one man left afloat
when Zeus rent wide his ship with chain lightning
and overturned him in the winedark sea.
Then all his troops were lost, his good companions, 140
but wind and current washed him here to me.
I fed him, loved him, sang that he should not die
nor grow old, ever, in all the days to come.
But now there's no eluding Zeus's will.
If this thing be ordained by him, I say
so be it, let the man strike out alone
on the vast water. Surely I cannot 'send' him.
I have no long-oared ships, no company
to pull him on the broad back of the sea.
My counsel he shall have, and nothing hidden, 150
to help him homeward without harm."

To this the Wayfinder made answer briefly:

"Thus you shall send him, then. And show more grace
in your obedience, or be chastised by Zeus."

---

[7]A gigantic hunter, loved by Eos.
[8]Probably symbolic of harvest wealth, since the offspring of his union with Dêmêtêr, goddess of the fields, was Plutus, who symbolized wealth.

The strong god glittering left her as he spoke,
and now her ladyship, having given heed
to Zeus's mandate, went to find Odysseus
in his stone seat to seaward—tear on tear
brimming his eyes. The sweet days of his life time
were running out in anguish over his exile,   160
for long ago the nymph had ceased to please.
Though he fought shy of her and her desire,
he lay with her each night, for she compelled him.
But when day came he sat on the rocky shore
and broke his own heart groaning, with eyes wet
scanning the bare horizon of the sea.
Now she stood near him in her beauty, saying:

"O forlorn man, be still.
Here you need grieve no more; you need not feel
your life consumed here; I have pondered it,   170
and I shall help you go.
Come and cut down high timber for a raft
or flatboat; make her broad-beamed, and decked over,
so you can ride her on the misty sea.
Stores I shall put aboard for you—bread, water,
and ruby-colored wine, to stay your hunger—
give you a seacloak and a following wind
to help you homeward without harm—provided
the gods who rule wide heaven wish it so.
Stronger than I they are, in mind and power."   180

For all he had endured, Odysseus shuddered.
But when he spoke, his words went to the mark:

"After these years, a helping hand? O goddess,
what guile is hidden here?
A raft, you say, to cross the Western Ocean,[9]
rough water, and unknown? Seaworthy ships
that glory in god's wind will never cross it.
I take no raft you grudge me out to sea.
Or yield me first a great oath, if I do,
to work no more enchantment to my harm."   190

At this the beautiful nymph Kalypso smiled
and answered sweetly, laying her hand upon him:

"What a dog you are! And not for nothing learned,
having the wit to ask this thing of me!
My witness then be earth and sky
and dripping Styx[10] that I swear by—

---

[9] The western Mediterranean.
[10] A river in Hades, the realm of the dead. To swear by Styx was the most solemn oath a
deity could utter.

the gay gods cannot swear more seriously—
I have no further spells to work against you.
But what I shall devise, and what I tell you,
will be the same as if your need were mine.   200
Fairness is all I think of. There are hearts
made of cold iron—but my heart is kind."

Swiftly she turned and led him to her cave,
and they went in, the mortal and immortal.
He took the chair left empty now by Hermês,
where the divine Kalypso placed before him
victuals and drink of men; then she sat down
facing Odysseus, while her serving maids
brought nectar and ambrosia to her side.
Then each one's hands went out on each one's feast   210
until they had had their pleasure; and she said:

"Son of Laërtês, versatile Odysseus,
after these years with me, you still desire
your old home? Even so, I wish you well.
If you could see it all, before you go—
all the adversity you face at sea—
you would stay here, and guard this house, and be
immortal—though you wanted her forever,
that bride for whom you pine each day.
Can I be less desirable than she is?   220
Less interesting? Less beautiful? Can mortals
compare with goddesses in grace and form?"

To this the strategist Odysseus answered:

"My lady goddess, here is no cause for anger.
My quiet Penélopê—how well I know—
would seem a shade before your majesty,
death and old age being unknown to you,
while she must die. Yet, it is true, each day
I long for home, long for the sight of home.
If any god has marked me out again   230
for shipwreck, my tough heart can undergo it.
What hardship have I not long since endured
at sea, in battle! Let the trial come."

Now as he spoke the sun set, dusk drew on,
and they retired, this pair, to the inner cave
to revel and rest softly, side by side.

When Dawn spread out her finger tips of rose
Odysseus pulled his tunic and his cloak on,
while the sea nymph dressed in a silvery gown
of subtle tissue, drew about her waist   240
a golden belt, and veiled her head, and then

took thought for the great-hearted hero's voyage.
A brazen axehead first she had to give him,
two-bladed, and agreeable to the palm
with a smooth-fitting haft of olive wood;
next a well-polished adze; and then she led him
to the island's tip where bigger timber grew—
besides the alder and poplar, tall pine trees,
long dead and seasoned, that would float him high.
Showing him in that place her stand of timber   250
the loveliest of nymphs took her way home.
Now the man fell to chopping; when he paused
twenty tall trees were down. He lopped the branches,
split the trunks, and trimmed his puncheons true.
Meanwhile Kalypso brought him an auger tool
with which he drilled through all his planks, then drove.
stout pins to bolt them, fitted side by side.
A master shipwright, building a cargo vessel,
lays down a broad and shallow hull; just so
Odysseus shaped the bottom of his craft.   260
He made his decking fast to close-set ribs
before he closed the side with longer planking,
then cut a mast pole, and proper yard,
and shaped a steering oar to hold her steady.
He drove long strands of willow in all the seams
to keep out waves, and ballasted with logs.
As for a sail, the lovely nymph Kalypso
brought him a cloth so he could make that, too.
Then he ran up his rigging—halyards, braces—
and hauled the boat on rollers to the water.   270

This was the fourth day, when he had all ready;
on the fifth day, she sent him out to sea.
But first she bathed him, gave him a scented cloak,
and put on board a skin of dusky wine
with water in a bigger skin, and stores—
boiled meats and other victuals—in a bag.
Then she conjured a warm landbreeze to blowing—
joy for Odysseus when he shook out sail!
Now the great seaman, leaning on his oar,
steered all the night unsleeping, and his eyes   280
picked out the Pleiadês, the laggard Ploughman,
and the Great Bear, that some have called the Wain,
pivoting in the sky before Orion;
of all the night's pure figures, she alone
would never bathe or dip in the Ocean stream.[11]

---

[11] In northern latitudes, the Big Dipper (the Great Bear, or Wain) never sets but rather circles around Polaris, the North Star. For Odysseus to keep the constellation on his left would require him to sail eastward.

These stars the beautiful Kalypso bade him
hold on his left hand as he crossed the main.
Seventeen nights and days in the open water
he sailed, before a dark shoreline appeared;
Skhería then came slowly into view 290
like a rough shield of bull's hide on the sea.

But now the god of earthquake, storming home
over the mountains of Asia from the Sunburned land,
sighted him far away. The god grew sullen
and tossed his great head, muttering to himself:

"Here is a pretty cruise! While I was gone
the gods have changed their minds about Odysseus.
Look at him now, just offshore of that island
that frees him from the bondage of his exile!
Still I can give him a rough ride in, and will." 300

Brewing high thunderheads, he churned the deep
with both hands on his trident—called up wind
from every quarter, and sent a wall of rain
to blot out land and sea in torrential night.
Hurricane winds now struck from the South and East
shifting North West in a great spume of seas,
on which Odysseus' knees grew slack, his heart
sickened, and he said within himself:

"Rag of man that I am, is this the end of me?
I fear the goddess told it all too well— 310
predicting great adversity at sea
and far from home. Now all things bear her out:
the whole rondure[12] of heaven hooded so
by Zeus in woeful cloud, and the sea raging
under such winds. I am going down, that's sure.
How lucky those Danaans were who perished
on Troy's wide seaboard, serving the Atreidai![13]
Would God I, too, had died there—met my end
that time the Trojans made so many casts at me
when I stood by Akhilleus after death. 320
I should have had a soldier's burial
and praise from the Akhaians—not this choking
waiting for me at sea, unmarked and lonely."

A great wave drove at him with toppling crest
spinning him round, in one tremendous blow,
and he went plunging overboard, the oar-haft
wrenched from his grip. A gust that came on howling
at the same instant broke his mast in two,

[12] Circle or sphere.
[13] Sons of Atreus—Agamémnon and Meneláos.

hurling his yard and sail far out to leeward.
Now the big wave a long time kept him under,   330
helpless to surface, held by tons of water,
tangled, too, by the seacloak of Kalypso.
Long, long, until he came up spouting brine,
with streamlets gushing from his head and beard;
but still bethought him, half-drowned as he was,
to flounder for the boat and get a handhold
into the bilge—to crouch there, foiling death.
Across the foaming water, to and fro,
the boat careered like a ball of tumbleweed
blown on the autumn plains, but intact still.   340
So the winds drove this wreck over the deep,
East Wind and North Wind, then South Wind and West,
coursing each in turn to the brutal harry.

But Ino[14] saw him—Ino, Kadmos' daughter,
slim-legged, lovely, once an earthling girl,
now in the seas a nereid, Leukothea.
Touched by Odysseus' painful buffeting
she broke the surface, like a diving bird,
to rest upon the tossing raft and say:

"O forlorn man, I wonder   350
why the Earthshaker, Lord Poseidon, holds
this fearful grudge—father of all your woes.
He will not drown you, though, despite his rage.
You seem clear-headed still; do what I tell you.
Shed that cloak, let the gale take your craft,
and swim for it—swim hard to get ashore
upon Skhería, yonder,
where it is fated that you find a shelter.
Here: make my veil your sash; it is not mortal;
you cannot, now, be drowned or suffer harm.   360
Only, the instant you lay hold of earth,
discard it, cast it far, far out from shore
in the winedark sea again, and turn away."

After she had bestowed her veil, the nereid
dove like a gull to windward
where a dark waveside closed over her whiteness.
But in perplexity Odysseus
said to himself, his great heart laboring:

"O damned confusion! Can this be a ruse
to trick me from the boat for some god's pleasure?   370
No I'll not swim; with my own eyes I saw
how far the land lies that she called my shelter.

[14] Maddened by Hera, who was jealous of her for helping to rear the young god Dionysos,
Ino leaped into the sea and was transformed into a nereid, or sea nymph.

Better to do the wise thing, as I see it.
While this poor planking holds, I stay aboard;
I may ride out the pounding of the storm,
or if she cracks up, take to the water then;
I cannot think it through a better way."

But even while he pondered and decided,
the god of earthquake heaved a wave against him
high as a rooftree and of awful gloom. 380
A gust of wind, hitting a pile of chaff,
will scatter all the parched stuff far and wide;
just so, when this gigantic billow struck
the boat's big timbers flew apart. Odysseus
clung to a single beam, like a jockey riding,
meanwhile stripping Kalypso's cloak away;
then he slung round his chest the veil of Ino
and plunged headfirst into the sea. His hands
went out to stroke, and he gave a swimmer's kick.
But the strong Earthshaker had him under his eye, 390
and nodded as he said:

                                "Go on, go on;
wander the high seas this way, take your blows,
before you join that race the gods have nurtured.[15]
Nor will you grumble, even then, I think,
for want of trouble."

                                  Whipping his glossy team
he rode off to his glorious home at Aigai.[16]
But Zeus's daughter Athena countered him:
she checked the course of all the winds but one,
commanding them, "Be quiet and go to sleep."
Then sent a long swell running under a norther 400
to bear the prince Odysseus, back from danger,
to join the Phaiákians, people of the sea.

Two nights, two days, in the solid deep-sea swell
he drifted, many times awaiting death,
until with shining ringlets in the East
the dawn confirmed a third day, breaking clear
over a high and windless sea; and mounting
a rolling wave he caught a glimpse of land.
What a dear welcome thing life seems to children
whose father, in the extremity, recovers 410
after some weakening and malignant illness:
his pangs are gone, the gods have delivered him.
So dear and welcome to Odysseus
the sight of land, of woodland, on that morning.

---

[15] The Phaiákians, or Phaeacians.   [16] An Akhaian city.

It made him swim again, to get a foothold
on solid ground. But when he came in earshot
he heard the trampling roar of sea on rock,
where combers, rising shoreward, thudded down
on the sucking ebb—all sheeted with salt foam.
Here were no coves or harborage or shelter,   420
only steep headlands, rockfallen reefs and crags.
Odysseus' knees grew slack, his heart faint,
a heaviness came over him, and he said:

"A cruel turn, this. Never had I thought
to see this land, but Zeus has let me see it—
and let me, too, traverse the Western Ocean—
only to find no exit from these breakers.
Here are sharp rocks off shore, and the sea a smother
rushing around them; rock face rising sheer
from deep water; nowhere could I stand up   430
on my two feet and fight free of the welter.
No matter how I try it, the surf may throw me
against the cliffside; no good fighting there.
If I swim down the coast, outside the breakers,
I may find shelving shore and quiet water—
but what if another gale comes on to blow?
Then I go cursing out to sea once more.
Or then again, some shark of Amphitritê's[17]
may hunt me, sent by the genius of the deep.
I know how he who makes earth tremble hates me."   440

During this meditation a heavy surge
was taking him, in fact, straight on the rocks.
He had been flayed there, and his bones broken,
had not grey-eyed Athena instructed him:
he gripped a rock-ledge with both hands in passing
and held on, groaning, as the surge went by,
to keep clear of its breaking. Then the backwash
hit him, ripping him under and far out.
An octopus, when you drag one from his chamber,
comes up with suckers full of tiny stones: 450
Odysseus left the skin of his great hands
torn on that rock-ledge as the wave submerged him.
And now at last Odysseus would have perished,
battered inhumanly, but he had the gift
of self-possession from grey-eyed Athena.
So, when the backwash spewed him up again,
he swam out and along, and scanned the coast
for some landspit that made a breakwater.

---

[17]A sea nymph, consort of Poseidon and thus queen of the ocean.

Lo and behold, the mouth of a calm river
at length came into view, with level shores 460
unbroken, free from rock, shielded from wind—
by far the best place he had found.
But as he felt the current flowing seaward
he prayed in his heart:

                "O hear me, lord of the stream:
how sorely I depend upon your mercy!
derelict as I am by the sea's anger.
Is he not sacred, even to the gods,
the wandering man who comes, as I have come,
in weariness before your knees, your waters?
Here is your servant; lord, have mercy on me." 470

Now even as he prayed the tide at ebb
had turned, and the river god made quiet water,
drawing him in to safety in the shallows.
His knees buckled, his arms gave way beneath him,
all vital force now conquered by the sea.
Swollen from head to foot he was, and seawater
gushed from his mouth and nostrils. There he lay,
scarce drawing breath, unstirring, deathly spent.
In time, as air came back into his lungs
and warmth around his heart, he loosed the veil, 480
letting it drift away on the estuary
downstream to where a white wave took it under
and Ino's hands received it. Then the man
crawled to the river bank among the reeds
where, face down, he could kiss the soil of earth,
in his exhaustion murmuring to himself:

"What more can this hulk suffer? What comes now?
In vigil through the night here by the river
how can I not succumb, being weak and sick,
to the night's damp and hoarfrost of the morning? 490
The air comes cold from rivers before dawn.
But if I climb the slope and fall asleep
in the dark forest's undergrowth—supposing
cold and fatigue will go, and sweet sleep come—
I fear I make the wild beasts easy prey."

But this seemed best to him, as he thought it over.
He made his way to a grove above the water
on open ground, and crept under twin bushes
grown from the same spot—olive and wild olive—
a thicket proof against the stinging wind 500
or Sun's blaze, fine soever the needling sunlight;
nor could a downpour wet it through, so dense
those plants were interwoven. Here Odysseus
tunnelled, and raked together with his hands

a wide bed—for a fall of leaves was there,
enough to save two men or maybe three
on a winter night, a night of bitter cold.
Odysseus' heart laughed when he saw his leaf-bed,
and down he lay, heaping more leaves above him.

A man in a distant field, no hearthfires near,   510
will hide a fresh brand in his bed of embers
to keep a spark alive for the next day;
so in the leaves Odysseus hid himself,
while over him Athena showered sleep
that his distress should end, and soon, soon.
In quiet sleep she sealed his cherished eyes.

BOOK SIX: THE PRINCESS AT THE RIVER

Far gone in weariness, in oblivion,
the noble and enduring man slept on;
but Athena in the night went down the land
of the Phaiákians, entering their city.
In days gone by, these men held Hypereia,
a country of wide dancing grounds, but near them
were overbearing Kyklopês,[1] whose power
could not be turned from pillage. So the Phaiákians
migrated thence under Nausíthoös
to settle a New World across the sea,   10
Skhería Island. That first captain walled
their promontory, built their homes and shrines,
and parcelled out the black land for the plow.
But he had gone down long ago to Death.
Alkínoös ruled, and Heaven gave him wisdom,
so on this night the goddess, grey-eyed Athena,
entered the palace of Alkínoös
to make sure of Odysseus' voyage home.
She took her way to a painted bedchamber
where a young girl lay fast asleep—so fine   20
in mould and feature that she seemed a goddess—
the daughter of Alkínoös, Nausikaa.
On either side, as Graces[2] might have slept,
her maids were sleeping. The bright doors were shut,
but like a sudden stir of wind, Athena
moved to the bedside of the girl, and grew

---

[1] These monstrous giants of Sicily are described in Book IX. *Hypereia* means "highlands"; their location is uncertain.
[2] Three goddesses who personify grace and beauty.

visible as the shipman Dymas' daughter,
a girl the princess' age, and her dear friend.
In this form grey-eyed Athena said to her:

"How so remiss, and yet thy mother's daughter? 30
leaving thy clothes uncared for, Nausikaa,
when soon thou must have store of marriage linen,
and put thy minstrelsy in wedding dress!
Beauty, in these, will make folk admire,
and bring thy father and gentle mother joy.
Let us go washing in the shine of morning!
Beside thee will I drub, so wedding chests
will brim by evening. Maidenhood must end!
Have not the noblest born Phaiákians
paid court to thee, whose birth none can excel? 40
Go beg thy sovereign father, even at dawn,
to have the mule cart and the mules brought round
to take thy body-linen, gowns and mantles.
Thou shouldst ride, for it becomes thee more,
the washing pools are found so far from home."

On this word she departed, grey-eyed Athena,
to where the gods have their eternal dwelling—
as men say—in the fastness of Olympos.
Never a tremor of wind, or a splash of rain,
no errant snowflake comes to stain that heaven, 50
so calm, so vaporless, the world of light.
Here, where the gay gods live their days of pleasure,
the grey-eyed one withdrew, leaving the princess.

And now Dawn took her own fair throne, awaking
the girl in the sweet gown, still charmed by dream.
Down through the rooms she went to tell her parents,
whom she found still at home: her mother seated
near the great hearth among her maids—and twirling
out of her distaff yarn dyed like the sea—;
her father at the door, bound for a council 60
of princes on petition of the gentry.
She went up close to him and softly said:

"My dear Papà, could you not send the mule cart
around for me—the gig with pretty wheels?
I must take all our things and get them washed
at the river pools; our linen is all soiled.
And you should wear fresh clothing, going to council
with counselors and first men of the realm.
Remember your five sons at home: though two
are married, we have still three bachelor sprigs; 70
they will have none but laundered clothes each time
they go to the dancing. See what I must think of!"

She had no word to say of her own wedding,
though her keen father saw her blush. Said he:

"No mules would I deny you, child, nor anything.
Go along, now; the grooms will bring your gig
with pretty wheels and the cargo box upon it."

He spoke to the stableman, who soon brought round
the cart, low-wheeled and nimble;
harnessed the mules, and backed them in their traces.   80
Meanwhile the girl fetched all her soiled apparel
to bundle in the polished wagon box.
Her mother, for their luncheon, packed a hamper
with picnic fare, and filled a skin of wine,
and, when the princess had been handed up,
gave her a golden bottle of olive oil
for softening girls' bodies, after bathing.
Nausikaa took the reins and raised her whip,
lashing the mules. What jingling! What a clatter!
But off they went in a ground-covering trot,   90
with princess, maids, and laundry drawn behind.
By the lower river where the wagon came
were washing pools, with water all year flowing
in limpid spillways that no grime withstood.
The girls unhitched the mules, and sent them down
along the eddying stream to crop sweet grass.
Then sliding out the cart's tail board, they took
armloads of clothing to the dusky water,
and trod them in the pits, making a race of it.
All being drubbed, all blemish rinsed away,   100
they spread them, piece by piece, along the beach
whose pebbles had been laundered by the sea;
then took a dip themselves, and, all anointed
with golden oil, ate lunch beside the river
while the bright burning sun dried out their linen.
Princess and maids delighted in that feast;
then, putting off their veils,
they ran and passed a ball to a rhythmic beat,
Nausikaa flashing first with her white arms.

So Artemis goes flying after her arrows flown   110
down some tremendous valley-side—
                                      Taÿgetos, Erymanthos—
chasing the mountain goats or ghosting deer,
with nymphs of the wild places flanking her;
and Lêto's[3] heart delights to see them running,
for, taller by a head than nymphs can be,

---

[3] Mother of Artemis, goddess of the hunt. Taÿgetos and Erymanthos are mountainous places
in Greece.

the goddess shows more stately, all being beautiful.
So one could tell the princess from the maids.

Soon it was time, she knew, for riding homeward—
mules to be harnessed, linen folded smooth—
but the grey-eyed goddess Athena made her tarry,   120
so that Odysseus might behold her beauty
and win her guidance to the town.

                              It happened
when the king's daughter threw her ball off line
and missed, and put it in the whirling stream,—
at which they all gave such a shout, Odysseus
awoke and sat up, saying to himself:

"Now, by my life, mankind again! But who?
Savages, are they, strangers to courtesy?
Or gentle folk, who know and fear the gods?
That was a lust cry of tall young girls—   130
most like the cry of nymphs, who haunt the peaks,
and springs of brooks, and inland grassy places.
Or am I amid people of human speech?
Up again, man; and let me see for myself."

He pushed aside the bushes, breaking off
with his great hand a single branch of olive,
whose leaves might shield him in his nakedness;
so came out rustling, like a mountain lion,
rain-drenched, wind-buffeted, but in his might at ease,
with burning eyes—who prowls among the herds   140
or flocks, or after game, his hungry belly
taking him near stout homesteads for his prey.
Odysseus had this look, in his rough skin
advancing on the girls with pretty braids;
and he was driven on by hunger, too.
Streaked with brine, and swollen, he terrified them,
so that they fled, this way and that. Only
Alkínoös' daughter stood her ground, being given
a bold heart by Athena, and steady knees.

She faced him, waiting. And Odysseus came,   150
debating inwardly what he should do:
embrace this beauty's knees in supplication?
or stand apart, and, using honeyed speech,
inquire the way to town, and beg some clothing?
In his swift reckoning, he thought it best
to trust in words to please her—and keep away;
he might anger the girl, touching her knees.
So he began, and let the soft words fall:

"Mistress: please: are you divine, or mortal?
If one of those who dwell in the wide heaven,   160

you are most near to Artemis, I should say—
great Zeus's daughter—in your grace and presence.
If you are one of earth's inhabitants,
how blest your father, and your gentle mother,
blest all your kin. I know what happiness
must send the warm tears to their eyes, each time
they see their wondrous child go to the dancing!
But one man's destiny is more than blest—
he who prevails, and takes you as his bride.
Never have I laid eyes on equal beauty   170
in man or woman. I am hushed indeed.
So fair, one time, I thought a young palm tree
at Delos[4] near the altar of Apollo—
I had troops under me when I was there
on the sea route that later brought me grief—
but that slim palm tree filled my heart with wonder:
never came shoot from earth so beautiful.
So now, my lady, I stand in awe so great
I cannot take your knees. And yet my case is desperate:
twenty days, yesterday, in the winedark sea,   180
on the ever-lunging swell, under gale winds,
getting away from the Island of Ogýgia.
And now the terror of Storm has left me stranded
upon this shore—with more blows yet to suffer,
I must believe, before the gods relent.
Mistress, do me a kindness!
After much weary toil, I come to you,
and you are the first soul I have seen—I know
no others here. Direct me to the town,
give me a rag that I can throw around me,   190
some cloth or wrapping that you brought along.
And may the gods accomplish your desire:
a home, a husband, and harmonious
converse with him—the best thing in the world
being a strong house held in serenity
where man and wife agree. Woe to their enemies,
joy to their friends! But all this they know best."

Then she of the white arms, Nausikaa, replied:

"Stranger, there is no quirk or evil in you
that I can see. You know Zeus metes out fortune   200
to good and bad men as it pleases him.
Hardship he sent to you, and you must bear it.
But now that you have taken refuge here
you shall not lack for clothing, or any other
comfort due to a poor man in distress.

---

[4] An island in the Aegean Sea, birthplace of Apollo and sacred to him.

The town lies this way, and the men are called
Phaiákians, who own the land and city.
I am daughter to the Prince Alkínoös,
by whom the power of our people stands."
Turning, she called out to her maids-in-waiting: 210

"Stay with me! Does the sight of a man scare you?
Or do you take this one for an enemy?
Why, there's no fool so brash, and never will be,
as to bring war or pillage to this coast,
for we are dear to the immortal gods,
living here, in the sea that rolls forever,
distant from other lands and other men.
No: this man is a castaway, poor fellow;
we must take care of him. Strangers and beggars
come from Zeus: a small gift, then, is friendly.   220
Give our new guest some food and drink, and take him
into the river, out of the wind, to bathe."

They stood up now, and called to one another
to go on back. Quite soon they led Odysseus
under the river bank, as they were bidden;
and there laid out a tunic, and a cloak,
and gave him olive oil in the golden flask.
"Here," they said, "go bathe in the flowing water."
But heard now from that kingly man, Odysseus:

"Maids," he said, "keep away a little; let me   230
wash the brine from my own back, and rub on
plenty of oil. It is long since my anointing.
I take no bath, however, where you can see me—
naked before young girls with pretty braids."

They left him, then, and went to tell the princess.
And now Odysseus, dousing in the river,
scrubbed the coat of brine from back and shoulders
and rinsed the clot of sea-spume from his hair;
got himself all rubbed down, from head to foot,
then he put on the clothes the princess gave him.   240
Athena lent a hand, making him seem
taller, and massive too, with crisping hair
in curls like petals of wild hyacinth,
but all red-golden. Think of gold infused
on silver by a craftsman, whose fine art
Hephaistos taught him, or Athena: one
whose work moves to delight: just so she lavished
beauty over Odysseus' head and shoulders.
Then he went down to sit on the sea beach
in his new splendor. There the girl regarded him,   250
and after a time she said to the maids beside her:

"My gentlewomen, I have a thing to tell you.
The Olympian gods cannot be all averse
to this man's coming here among our islanders.
Uncouth he seemed, I thought so, too, before;
but now he looks like one of heaven's people.
I wish my husband could be fine as he
and glad to stay forever on Skhería!
But have you given refreshment to our guest?"

At this the maids, all gravely listening, hastened   260
to set out bread and wine before Odysseus,
and ah! how ravenously that patient man
took food and drink, his long fast at an end.

The princess Nausikaa now turned aside
to fold her linens; in the pretty cart
she stowed them, put the mule team under harness,
mounted the driver's seat, and then looked down
to say with cheerful prompting to Odysseus:

"Up with you now, friend; back to town we go;
and I shall send you in before my father   270
who is wondrous wise; there in our house with him
you'll meet the noblest of the Phaiákians.
You have good sense, I think; here's how to do it:
while we go through the countryside and farmland
stay with my maids, behind the wagon, walking
briskly enough to follow where I lead.
But near the town—well, there's a wall with towers
around the Isle, and beautiful ship basins
right and left of the causeway of approach;
seagoing craft are beached beside the road   280
each on its launching ways. The agora,[5]
with fieldstone benches bedded in the earth,
lies either side Poseidon's shrine—for there
men are at work on pitch-black hulls and rigging,
cables and sails, and tapering of oars.
The archer's craft is not for the Phaiákians,
but ship designing, modes of oaring cutters
in which they love to cross the foaming sea.
From these fellows I will have no salty talk,
no gossip later. Plenty are insolent.   290
And some seadog might say, after we passed:
'Who is this handsome stranger trailing Nausikaa?
Where did she find him? Will he be her husband?
Or is she being hospitable to some rover
come off his ship from lands across the sea—
there being no lands nearer. A god, maybe?

---

[5] Public meeting place.

a god from heaven, the answer to her prayer,
descending now—to make her his forever?
Better, if she's roamed and found a husband
somewhere else: none of our own will suit her, 300
though many come to court her, and those the best.'
This is the way they might make light of me.
And I myself should hold it shame
for any girl to flout her own dear parents,
taking up with a man, before her marriage.

Note well, now, what I say, friend, and your chances
are excellent for safe conduct from my father.
You'll find black poplars in a roadside park
around a meadow and fountain—all Athena's—
but Father has a garden in the place— 310
this within earshot of the city wall.
Go in there and sit down, giving us time
to pass through town and reach my father's house.
And when you can imagine we're at home,
then take the road into the city, asking
directions to the palace of Alkínoös.
You'll find it easily: any small boy
can take you there; no family has a mansion
half so grand as he does, being king.
As soon as you are safe inside, cross over 320
and go straight through into the mégaron[6]
to find my mother. She'll be there in firelight
before a column, with her maids in shadow,
spinning a wool dyed richly as the sea.
My father's great chair faces the fire, too;
there like a god he sits and takes his wine.
Go past him; cast yourself before my mother,
embrace her knees—and you may wake up soon
at home rejoicing, though your home be far.
On Mother's feeling much depends; if she 330
looks on you kindly, you shall see your friends
under your own roof in your father's country."

At this she raised her glistening whip, lashing
the team into a run; they left the river
cantering beautifully, then trotted smartly.
But then she reined them in, and spared the whip,
so that her maids could follow with Odysseus.
The sun was going down when they went by
Athena's grove. Here, then, Odysseus rested,
and lifted up his prayer to Zeus's daughter: 340

---

[6] The great hall of the house.

"Hear me, unwearied child of royal Zeus!
O listen to me now—thou so aloof
while the Earthshaker wrecked and battered me.
May I find love and mercy among these people."

He prayed for that, and Pallas Athena heard him—
although in deference to her father's brother[7]
she would not show her true form to Odysseus,
at whom Poseidon smoldered on
until the kingly man came home to his own shore.

BOOK SEVEN: GARDENS AND FIRELIGHT

As Lord Odysseus prayed there in the grove
the girl rode on, behind her strapping team,
and came late to the mansion of her father,
where she reined in at the courtyard gate. Her brothers
awaited her like tall gods in the court,
circling to lead the mules away and carry
the laundered things inside. But she withdrew
to her own bedroom, where a fire soon shone,
kindled by her old nurse, Eurymedousa.
Years ago, from a raid on the continent,   10
the rolling ships had brought this woman over
to be Alkínoös' share—fit spoil for him
whose realm hung on his word as on a god's.
And she had schooled the princess, Nausikaa,
whose fire she tended now, making her supper.

Odysseus, when the time had passed, arose
and turned into the city. But Athena
poured a sea fog around him as he went—
her love's expedient, that no jeering sailor
should halt the man or challenge him for luck.   20
Instead, as he set foot in the pleasant city,
the grey-eyed goddess came to him, in figure
a small girl child, hugging a water jug.

Confronted by her, Lord Odysseus asked:

"Little one, could you take me to the house
of that Alkínoös, king among these people?
You see, I am a poor old stranger here;
my home is far away; here there is no one
known to me, in countryside or city."

[7] Poseidon, brother of Athena's father, Zeus.

The grey-eyed goddess Athena replied to him: 30

"Oh, yes, good grandfer, sir, I know, I'll show you
the house you mean; it is quite near my father's.
But come now, hush, like this, and follow me.
You must not stare at people, or be inquisitive.
They do not care for strangers in this neighborhood;
a foreign man will get no welcome here.
The only things they trust are the racing ships
Poseidon gave, to sail the deep blue sea
like white wings in the sky, or a flashing thought."

Pallas Athena turned like the wind, running 40
ahead of him, and he followed in her footsteps.
And no seafaring men of Phaiákia
perceived Odysseus passing through their town:
the awesome one in pigtails barred their sight
with folds of sacred mist. And yet Odysseus
gazed out marvelling at the ships and harbors,
public squares, and ramparts towering up
with pointed palisades along the top.
When they were near the mansion of the king,
grey-eyed Athena in the child cried out: 50

"Here it is, grandfer, sir—that mansion house
you asked to see. You'll find our king and queen
at supper, but you must not be dismayed;
go in to them. A cheerful man does best
in every enterprise—even a stranger.
You'll see our lady just inside the hall—
her name is Arêtê; her grandfather
was our good king Alkínoös's father—
Nausithoös by name, son of Poseidon
and Periboia. That was a great beauty, 60
the daughter of Eurymedon, commander
of the Gigantês[1] in the olden days,
who led those wild things to their doom and his.
Poseidon then made love to Periboia,
and she bore Nausíthoös, Phaiákia's lord,
whose sons in turn were Rhêxênor and Alkínoös.
Rhêxênor had no sons; even as a bridegroom
he fell before the silver bow of Apollo,
his only child a daughter, Arêtê.
When she grew up, Alkínoös married her 70
and holds her dear. No lady in the world,
no other mistress of a man's household,
is honored as our mistress is, and loved,
by her own children, by Alkínoös,

---

[1]The Giants, enormous semihuman beings, offspring of Ge, an ancient earth goddess.

and by the people. When she walks the town
they murmur and gaze, as though she were a goddess.
No grace or wisdom fails in her; indeed
just men in quarrels come to her for equity.
Supposing, then, she looks upon you kindly,
the chances are that you shall see your friends   80
under your own roof, in your father's country."

At this the grey-eyed goddess Athena left him
and left that comely land, going over sea
to Marathon, to the wide roadways of Athens
and her retreat in the stronghold of Erekhtheus.[2]
Odysseus, now alone before the palace,
meditated a long time before crossing
the brazen threshold of the great courtyard.
High rooms he saw ahead, airy and luminous
as though with lusters of the sun and moon,   90
bronze-paneled walls, at several distances,
making a vista, with an azure molding
of lapis lazuli.[3] The doors were golden
guardians of the great room. Shining bronze
plated the wide door sill; the posts and lintel
were silver upon silver; golden handles
curved on the doors, and golden, too, and silver
were sculptured hounds, flanking the entrance way,
cast by the skill and ardor of Hephaistos
to guard the prince Alkínoös's house—   100
undying dogs that never could grow old.
Through all the rooms, as far as he could see,
tall chairs were placed around the walls, and strewn
with fine embroidered stuff made by the women.
Here were enthroned the leaders of Phaiákia
drinking and dining, with abundant fare.
Here, too, were boys of gold on pedestals
holding aloft bright torches of pitch pine
to light the great rooms, and the night-time feasting.
And fifty maids-in-waiting of the household   110
sat by the round mill, grinding yellow corn,
or wove upon their looms, or twirled their distaffs,
flickering like the leaves of a poplar tree;
while drops of oil glistened on linen weft.
Skillful as were the men of Phaiákia
in ship handling at sea, so were these women
skilled at the loom, having this lovely craft
and artistry as talents from Athena.

---

[2]Legendary ruler of Athens, Athena's city. Marathon (several centuries after Homer's time
the site of a great Greek victory over the Persians) was a plain near Athens, cherished by Athena.
[3]Fine blue stone.

To left and right, outside, he saw an orchard
closed by a pale—four spacious acres planted 120
with trees in bloom or weighted down for picking:
pear trees, pomegranates, brilliant apples,
luscious figs, and olives ripe and dark.
Fruit never failed upon these trees: winter
and summer time they bore, for through the year
the breathing Westwind ripened all in turn—
so one pear came to prime, and then another,
and so with apples, figs, and the vine's fruit
empurpled in the royal vineyard there.
Currants were dried at one end, on a platform 130
bare to the sun, beyond the vintage arbors
and vats the vintners trod; while near at hand
were new grapes barely formed as the green bloom fell,
or half-ripe clusters, faintly coloring.
After the vines came rows of vegetables
of all the kinds that flourish in every season,
and through the garden plots and orchard ran
channels from one clear fountain, while another
gushed through a pipe under the courtyard entrance
to serve the house and all who came for water. 140
These were the gifts of heaven to Alkínoös.

Odysseus, who had borne the barren sea,
stood in the gateway and surveyed this bounty.
He gazed his fill, then swiftly he went in.
The lords and nobles of Phaiákia
were tipping wine to the wakeful god, to Hermês—
a last libation before going to bed—
but down the hall Odysseus went unseen,
still in the cloud Athena cloaked him in,
until he reached Arêtê, and the king. 150
He threw his great hands round Arêtê's knees,
whereon the sacred mist curled back;
they saw him; and the diners hushed amazed
to see an unknown man inside the palace.
Under their eyes Odysseus made his plea:

"Arêtê, admirable Rhêxênor's daughter,
here is a man bruised by adversity, thrown
upon your mercy and the king your husband's,
begging indulgence of this company—
may the gods' blessing rest on them! May life 160
be kind to all! Let each one leave his children
every good thing this realm confers upon him!
But grant me passage to my father land.
My home and friends lie far. My life is pain."

He moved, then, toward the fire, and sat him down
amid the ashes. No one stirred or spoke
until Ekhenêos broke the spell—an old man,
eldest of the Phaiákians, an oracle,
versed in the laws and manners of old time.
He rose among them now and spoke out kindly: 170

"Alkínoös, this will not pass for courtesy:
a guest abased in ashes at our hearth?
Everyone here awaits your word; so come, then,
lift the man up; give him a seat of honor,
a silver-studded chair. Then tell the stewards
we'll have another wine bowl for libation
to Zeus, lord of the lightning—advocate
of honorable petitioners. And supper
may be supplied our friend by the larder mistress."

Alkínoös, calm in power, heard him out,   180
then took the great adventurer by the hand
and led him from the fire. Nearest his throne
the son whom he loved best, Laódamas,
had long held place; now the king bade him rise
and gave his shining chair to Lord Odysseus.
A serving maid poured water for his hands
from a gold pitcher into a silver bowl,
and spead a polished table at his side;
the mistress of provisions came with bread
and other victuals, generous with her store.   190
So Lord Odysseus drank, and tasted supper.
Seeing this done, the king in majesty
said to his squire:

                                    "A fresh bowl, Pontónoös;
we make libation to the lord of lightning,
who seconds honorable petitioners."

Mixing the honey-hearted wine, Pontónoös
went on his rounds and poured fresh cups for all,
whereof when all had spilt they drank their fill.
Alkínoös then spoke to the company:

"My lords and leaders of Phaiákia: 200
hear now, all that my heart would have me say.
Our banquet's ended, so you may retire;
but let our seniors gather in the morning
to give this guest a festal day, and make
fair offerings to the gods. In due course we
shall put our minds upon the means at hand
to take him safely, comfortably, well
and happily, with speed, to his own country,

distant though it may lie. And may no trouble
come to him here or on the way; his fate 210
he shall pay out at home, even as the Spinners[4]
spun for him on the day his mother bore him.
If, as may be, he is some god, come down
from heaven's height, the gods are working strangely:
until now, they have shown themselves in glory
only after great hekatombs—those figures
banqueting at our side, throned like ourselves.
Or if some traveller met them when alone
they bore no least disguise; we are their kin; Gigantês,
Kyklopês, rank no nearer gods than we." 220

Odysseus' wits were ready, and he replied:

"Alkínoös, you may set your mind at rest.
Body and birth, a most unlikely god
am I, being all of earth and mortal nature.
I should say, rather, I am like those men
who suffer the worst trials that you know,
and miseries greater yet, as I might tell you—
hundreds; indeed the gods could send no more.
You will indulge me if I finish dinner—?
grieved though I am to say it. There's no part 230
of man more like a dog than brazen Belly,
crying to be remembered—and it must be—
when we are mortal weary and sick at heart;
and that is my condition. Yet my hunger
drives me to take this food, and think no more
of my afflictions. Belly must be filled.
Be equally impelled, my lords, tomorrow
to berth me in a ship and send me home!
Rough years I've had; now may I see once more
my hall, my lands, my people before I die!" 240

Now all who heard cried out assent to this:
the guest had spoken well; he must have passage.
Then tipping wine they drank their thirst away,
and one by one went homeward for the night.
So Lord Odysseus kept his place alone
with Arêtê and the king Alkínoös
beside him, while the maids went to and fro
clearing away the wine cups and the tables.
Presently the ivory-skinned lady
turned to him—for she knew his cloak and tunic 250
to be her own fine work, done with her maids—
and arrowy came her words upon the air:

[4]The Fates, mythological women who determined the span of a human life by spinning, measuring, and cutting the thread symbolic of it.

"Friend, I, for one, have certain questions for you.
Who are you, and who has given you this clothing?
Did you not say you wandered here by sea?"

The great tactician carefully replied:

"Ah, majesty, what labor it would be
to go through the whole story! All my years
of misadventures, given by those on high!
But this you ask about is quickly told: 260
in mid-ocean lies Ogýgia, the island
haunt of Kalypso, Atlas' guileful daughter,
a lovely goddess and a dangerous one.
No one, no god or man, consorts with her;
but supernatural power brought me there
to be her solitary guest: for Zeus
let fly with his bright bolt and split my ship,
rolling me over in the winedark sea.
There all my shipmates, friends were drowned, while I
hung on the keelboard of the wreck and drifted   270
nine full days. Then in the dead of night
the gods brought me ashore upon Ogýgia
into her hands. The enchantress in her beauty
fed and caressed me, promised me I should be
immortal, youthful, all the days to come;
but in my heart I never gave consent
though seven years detained. Immortal clothing
I had from her, and kept it wet with tears.
Then came the eighth year on the wheel of heaven
and word to her from Zeus, or a change of heart,   280
so that she now commanded me to sail,
sending me out to sea on a craft I made
with timber and tools of hers. She gave me stores,
victuals and wine, a cloak divinely woven,
and made a warm land breeze come up astern.
Seventeen days I sailed in the open water
before I saw your country's shore, a shadow
upon the sea rim. Then my heart rejoiced—
pitiable as I am! For blows aplenty
awaited me from the god who shakes the earth.   290
Cross gales he blew, making me lose my bearings,
and heaved up seas beyond imagination—
huge and foundering seas. All I could do
was hold hard, groaning under every shock,
until my craft broke up in the hurricane.
I kept afloat and swam your sea, or drifted,
taken by wind and current to this coast
where I went in on big swells running landward.
But cliffs and rock shoals made that place forbidding,

so I turned back, swimming off shore, and came 300
in the end to a river, to auspicious water,
with smooth beach and a rise that broke the wind.
I lay there where I fell till strength returned.
Then sacred night came on, and I went inland
to high ground and a leaf bed in a thicket.
Heaven sent slumber in an endless tide
submerging my sad heart among the leaves.
That night and next day's dawn and noon I slept;
the sun went west; and then sweet sleep unbound me,
when I became aware of maids—your daughter's— 310
playing along the beach; the princess, too,
most beautiful. I prayed her to assist me,
and her good sense was perfect; one could hope
for no behavior like it from the young,
thoughtless as they most often are. But she
gave me good provender and good red wine,
a river bath, and finally this clothing.
There is the bitter tale. These are the facts."

But in reply Alkínoös observed:

"Friend, my child's good judgment failed in this— 320
not to have brought you in her company home.
Once you approached her, you became her charge."

To this Odysseus tactfully replied:

"Sir, as to that, you should not blame the princess.
She did tell me to follow with her maids,
but I would not. I felt abashed, and feared
the sight would somehow ruffle or offend you.
All of us on this earth are plagued by jealousy."

Alkínoös' answer was a declaration:

"Friend, I am not a man for trivial anger: 330
better a sense of measure in everything.
No anger here. I say that if it should please
our father Zeus, Athena, and Apollo—
seeing the man you are, seeing your thoughts
are my own thoughts—my daughter should be yours
and you my son-in-law, if you remained.
A home, lands, riches you should have from me
if you could be contented here. If not,
by Father Zeus, let none of our men hold you!
On the contrary, I can assure you now 340
of passage late tomorrow: while you sleep
my men will row you through the tranquil night
to your own land and home or where you please.

It may be, even, far beyond Euboia—
called most remote by seamen of our isle
who landed there, conveying Rhadamanthos
when he sought Títyos, the son of Gaia.[5]
They put about, with neither pause nor rest,
and entered their home port the selfsame day.
But this you, too, will see: what ships I have,   350
how my young oarsmen send the foam a-scudding!"

Now joy welled up in the patient Lord Odysseus
who said devoutly in the warmest tones:

"O Father Zeus, let all this be fulfilled
as spoken by Alkínoös! Earth of harvests
remember him! Return me to my homeland!"

In this manner they conversed with one another;
but the great lady called her maids, and sent them
to make a kingly bed, with purple rugs
piled up, and sheets outspread, and fleecy   360
coverlets, in an eastern colonnade.
The girls went out with torches in their hands,
swift at their work of bedmaking; returning
they whispered at the lord Odysseus' shoulder:

"Sir, you may come; your bed has been prepared."

How welcome the word "bed" came to his ears!
Now, then, Odysseus laid him down and slept
in luxury under the Porch of Morning,
while in his inner chamber Alkínoös
retired to rest where his dear consort lay.   370

BOOK EIGHT: THE SONGS OF THE HARPER

Under the opening fingers of the dawn
Alkínoös, the sacred prince, arose,
and then arose Odysseus, raider of cities.
As the king willed, they went down by the shipways
to the assembly ground of the Phaiákians.
Side by side the two men took their ease there
on smooth stone benches. Meanwhile Pallas Athena
roamed through the byways of the town, contriving
Odysseus' voyage home—in voice and feature

---

[5] The lines "It may be . . . Gaia" are somewhat obscure, since Rhadamanthos is pictured in
Book IV as dwelling in Elysion, and Títyos, in Book XI, is punished in Hades. The main point
is clear, though: Alkínoös is boasting of the nautical range and speed of his seafaring people.
Euboia is an island east of Greece. Gaia is another name for Ge, the earth deity.

the crier of the king Alkínoös   10
who stopped and passed the word to every man:

"Phaiákian lords and counselors, this way!
Come to assembly: learn about the stranger,
the new guest at the palace of Alkínoös—
a man the sea drove, but a comely man;
the gods' own light is on him."

                                                    She aroused them,
and soon the assembly ground and seats were filled
with curious men, a throng who peered and saw
the master mind of war, Laërtês' son.
Athena now poured out her grace upon him,   20
head and shoulders, height and mass—a splendor
awesome to the eyes of the Phaiákians;
she put him in a fettle to win the day,
mastering every trial they set to test him.
When all the crowd sat marshalled, quieted,
Alkínoös addressed the full assembly:

"Hear me, lords and captains of the Phaiákians!
Hear what my heart would have me say!
Our guest and new friend—nameless to me still—
comes to my house after long wandering   30
in Dawn lands, or among the Sunset races.
Now he appeals to me for conveyance home.
As in the past, therefore, let us provide
passage, and quickly, for no guest of mine
languishes here for lack of it. Look to it:
get a black ship afloat on the noble sea,
and pick our fastest sailer; draft a crew
of two and fifty from our younger townsmen—
men who have made their names at sea. Loop oars
well to your tholepins,[1] lads, then leave the ship,   40
come to our house, fall to, and take your supper:
we'll furnish out a feast for every crewman.
These are your orders. As for my older peers
and princes of the realm, let them foregather
in festival for our friend in my great hall;
and let no man refuse. Call in our minstrel,
Demódokos, whom God made lord of song,
heart-easing, sing upon what theme he will."

He turned, led the procession, and those princes
followed, while his herald sought the minstrel.   50
Young oarsmen from the assembly chose a crew
of two and fifty, as the king commanded,

---

[1] Pegs on the side of a boat, used as oarlocks.

and these filed off along the waterside
to where the ship lay, poised above open water.
They hauled the black hull down to ride the sea,
rigging a mast and spar in the black ship,
with oars at trail from corded rawhide, all
seamanly; then tried the white sail, hoisting,
and moored her off the beach. Then going ashore
the crew went up to the great house of Alkínoös.   60

Here the enclosures, entrance ways, and rooms
were filled with men, young men and old, for whom
Alkínoös had put twelve sheep to sacrifice,
eight tuskers[2] and a pair of shambling oxen.
These, now, they flayed and dressed to make their banquet.

The crier soon came, leading that man of song
whom the Muse cherished; by her gift he knew
the good of life, and evil—
for she who lent him sweetness made him blind.[3]
Pontónoös fixed a studded chair for him   70
hard by a pillar amid the banqueters,
hanging the taut harp from a peg above him,
and guided up his hands upon the strings;
placed a bread basket at his side, and poured
wine in a cup, that he might drink his fill.
Now each man's hand went out upon the banquet.

In time, when hunger and thirst were turned away,
the Muse brought to the minstrel's mind a song
of heroes whose great fame rang under heaven:
the clash between Odysseus and Akhilleus,   80
how one time they contended[4] at the godfeast
raging, and the marshal, Agamémnon,
felt inward joy over his captains' quarrel;
for such had been foretold him by Apollo
at Pytho[5]—hallowed height—when the Akhaian
crossed that portal of rock to ask a sign—
in the old days when grim war lay ahead
for Trojans and Danaans, by God's will.
So ran the tale the minstrel sang. Odysseus
with massive hand drew his rich mantle down   90
over his brow, cloaking his face with it,
to make the Phaiákians miss the secret tears
that started to his eyes. How skillfully
he dried them when the song came to a pause!

---

[2]Animals with tusks, such as boars.
[3]According to tradition, Homer himself was blind.
[4]This incident probably took place before the action of the *Iliad*.
[5]The shrine of Apollo at Delphi, on Mount Parnassos (Parnassus); the god uttered oracular pronouncements there.

threw back his mantle, spilt his gout of wine!
But soon the minstrel plucked his note once more
to please the Phaiákian lords, who loved the song;
then in his cloak Odysseus wept again.
His tears flowed in the mantle unperceived:
only Alkínoös, at his elbow, saw them,   100
and caught the low groan in the man's breathing.
At once he spoke to all the seafolk round him:

"Hear me, lords and captains of the Phaiákians.
Our meat is shared, our hearts are full of pleasure
from the clear harp tone that accords with feasting;
now for the field and track; we shall have trials
in the pentathlon.[6] Let our guest go home
and tell his friends what champions we are
at boxing, wrestling, broadjump and foot racing."

On this he led the way and all went after.   110
The crier unslung and pegged the shining harp
and, taking Demódokos's hand,
led him along with all the rest—Phaiákian
peers, gay amateurs of the great games.
They gained the common, where a crowd was forming,
and many a young athlete now came forward
with seaside names like Tipmast, Tiderace, Sparwood,
Hullman, Sternman, Beacher and Pullerman,
Bluewater, Shearwater, Runningwake, Boardalee,
Seabelt, son of Grandfleet Shipwrightson;   120
Seareach stepped up, son of the Launching Master,
rugged as Arês,[7] bane of men; his build
excelled all but the Prince Laódamas;
and Laódamas made entry with his brothers,
Halios and Klytóneus, sons of the king.
The runners, first, must have their quarter mile.
All lined up tense; then Go! and down the track
they raised the dust in a flying bunch, strung out
longer and longer behind Prince Klytóneus.
By just so far as a mule team, breaking ground,   130
will distance oxen, he left all behind
and came up to the crowd, an easy winner.
Then they made room for wrestling—grinding bouts
that Seareach won, pinning the strongest men;
then the broadjump; first place went to Seabelt;
Sparwood gave the discus the mightiest fling,
and Prince Laódamas outboxed them all.

Now it was he, the son of Alkínoös,
who said when they had run through these diversions:

[6]An athletic contest consisting of five events.
[7]God of war.

"Look here, friends, we ought to ask the stranger   140
if he competes in something. He's no cripple;
look at his leg muscles and his forearms.
Neck like a bollard;[8] strong as a bull, he seems;
and not old, though he may have gone stale under
the rough times he had. Nothing like the sea
for wearing out the toughest man alive."

Then Seareach took him up at once, and said:

"Laódamas, you're right, by all the powers.
Go up to him, yourself, and put the question."

At this, Alkínoös' tall son advanced   150
to the center ground, and there addressed Odysseus:

"Friend, Excellency, come join our competition,
if you are practiced, as you seem to be.
While a man lives he wins no greater honor
than footwork and the skill of hands can bring him.
Enter our games, then; ease your heart of trouble.
Your journey home is not far off, remember;
the ship is launched, the crew all primed for sea."

Odysseus, canniest of men, replied:

"Laódamas, why do you young chaps challenge me?   160
I have more on my mind than track and field—
hard days, and many, have I seen, and suffered.
I sit here at your field meet, yes; but only
as one who begs your king to send him home."

Now Seareach put his word in, and contentiously:

"The reason being, as I see it, friend,
you never learned a sport, and have no skill
in any of the contests of fighting men.
You must have been the skipper of some tramp
that crawled from one port to the next, jam full   170
of chaffering hands: a tallier of cargoes,
itching for gold—not, by your looks, an athlete."

Odysseus frowned, and eyed him coldly, saying:

"That was uncalled for, friend, you talk like a fool.
The gods deal out no gift, this one or any—
birth, brains, or speech—to every man alike.
In looks a man may be a shade, a specter,
and yet be master of speech so crowned with beauty
that people gaze at him with pleasure. Courteous,

---

[8]A sturdy post to which a ship's ropes were tied.

sure of himself, he can command assemblies, 180
and when he comes to town, the crowds gather.
A handsome man, contrariwise, may lack
grace and good sense in everything he says.
You now, for instance, with your fine physique—
a god's, indeed—you have an empty noddle.[9]
I find my heart inside my ribs aroused
by your impertinence. I am no stranger
to contests, as you fancy. I rated well
when I could count on youth and my two hands.
Now pain has cramped me, and my years of combat 190
hacking through ranks in war, and the bitter sea.
Aye. Even so I'll give your games a trial.
You spoke heart-wounding words. You shall be answered."

He leapt out, cloaked as he was, and picked a discus,
a rounded stone, more ponderous than those
already used by the Phaiákian throwers,
and, whirling, let it fly from his great hand
with a low hum. The crowd went flat on the ground—
all those oar-pulling, seafaring Phaiákians—
under the rushing noise. The spinning disk 200
soared out, light as a bird, beyond all others.
Disguised now as a Phaiákian, Athena
staked it and called out:

                    "Even a blind man,
friend, could judge this, finding with his fingers
one discus, quite alone, beyond the cluster.
Congratulations; this event is yours;
not a man here can beat you or come near you."

That was a cheering hail, Odysseus thought,
seeing one friend there on the emulous field,
so, in relief, he turned among the Phaiákians 210
and said:

            "Now come alongside that one, lads.
The next I'll send as far, I think, or farther.
Anyone else on edge for competition
try me now. By heaven, you angered me.
Racing, wrestling, boxing—I bar nothing
with any man except Laódamas,
for he's my host. Who quarrels with his host?
Only a madman—or no man at all—
would challenge his protector among strangers,
cutting the ground away under his feet. 220
Here are no others I will not engage,
none but I hope to know what he is made of.

[9] Head.

Inept at combat, am I? Not entirely.
Give me a smooth bow; I can handle it,
and I might well be first to hit my man
amid a swarm of enemies, though archers
in company around me drew together.
Philoktêtês[10] alone, at Troy, when we
Akhaians took the bow, used to outshoot me.
Of men who now eat bread upon the earth   230
I hold myself the best hand with a bow—
conceding mastery to the men of old,
Heraklês, or Eurýtos[11] of Oikhalía,
heroes who vied with gods in bowmanship.
Eurýtos came to grief, it's true; old age
never crept over him in his long hall;
Apollo took his challenge ill, and killed him.
What then, the spear? I'll plant it like an arrow.
Only in sprinting, I'm afraid, I may
be passed by someone. Roll of the sea waves   240
wearied me, and the victuals in my ship
ran low; my legs are flabby."

                                                    When he finished,
the rest were silent, but Alkínoös answered:

"Friend, we take your challenge in good part,
for this man angered and affronted you
here at our peaceful games. You'd have us note
the prowess that is in you, and so clearly,
no man of sense would ever cry it down!
Come, turn your mind, now, on a thing to tell
among your peers when you are home again,   250
dining in hall, beside your wife and children:
I mean our prowess, as you may remember it,
for we, too, have our skills, given by Zeus,
and practiced from our father's time to this—
not in the boxing ring nor the palestra[12]
conspicuous, but in racing, land or sea;
and all our days we set great store by feasting,
harpers, and the grace of dancing choirs,
changes of dress, warm baths, and downy beds.
O master dancers of the Phaiákians!   260
Perform now: let our guest on his return
tell his companions we excel the world
in dance and song, as in our ships and running.

---

[10] Philoktêtês had inherited the magical bow of the fabled hero Heraklês (Hercules); a version of his story is dramatized in Sophocles' *Philoctetes*.

[11] Grandson of Apollo, and Heraklês' instructor in bowmanship. He was killed in a competition with Apollo, god of archery. Eurýtos' bow descended to Odysseus.

[12] A public athletics ground.

Someone go find the gittern harp in hall
and bring it quickly to Demódokos!"

At the serene king's word, a squire ran
to bring the polished harp out of the palace,
and place was given to nine referees—
peers of the realm, masters of ceremony—
who cleared a space and smoothed a dancing floor.   270
The squire brought down, and gave Demódokos,
the clear-toned harp; and centering on the minstrel
magical young dancers formed a circle
with a light beat, and stamp of feet. Beholding,
Odysseus marvelled at the flashing ring.

Now to his harp the blinded minstrel sang
of Arês' dalliance with Aphroditê:
how hidden in Hephaistos'[13] house they played
at love together, and the gifts of Arês,
dishonoring Hephaistos' bed—and how   280
the word that wounds the heart came to the master
from Hêlios,[14] who had seen the two embrace;
and when he learned it, Lord Hephaistos went
with baleful calculation to his forge.
There mightily he armed his anvil block
and hammered out a chain, whose tempered links
could not be sprung or bent; he meant that they should hold.
Those shackles fashioned, hot in wrath Hephaistos
climbed to the bower and the bed of love,
pooled all his net of chain around the bed posts   290
and swung it from the rafters overhead—
light as a cobweb even gods in bliss
could not perceive, so wonderful his cunning.
Seeing his bed now made a snare, he feigned
a journey to the trim stronghold of Lemnos,[15]
the dearest of earth's towns to him. And Arês?
Ah, golden Arês' watch had its reward
when he beheld the great smith leaving home.
How promptly to the famous door he came,
intent on pleasure with sweet Kythereia![16]   300
She, who had left her father's side but now,
sat in her chamber when her lover entered;
and tenderly he pressed her hand and said:

---

[13] The lame god of fire and metalworking, husband of Aphroditê.
[14] The sun god.
[15] An island in the Aegean, center of the worship of Hephaistos; it was there that he fell after Zeus, during a fit of anger, threw him out of heaven.
[16] Aphroditê. Also spelled *Cytherea*.

"Come and lie down, my darling, and be happy!
Hephaistos is no longer here, but gone
to see his grunting Sintian[17] friends on Lemnos."

As she, too, thought repose would be most welcome,
the pair went in to bed—into a shower
of clever chains, the netting of Hephaistos.
So trussed, they could not move apart, nor rise,   310
at last they knew there could be no escape,
they were to see the glorious cripple now—
for Hêlios had spied for him, and told him;
so he turned back, this side of Lemnos Isle,
sick at heart, making his way homeward.
Now in the doorway of the room he stood
while deadly rage took hold of him; his voice,
hoarse and terrible, reached all the gods:

"O Father Zeus, O gods in bliss forever,
 here is indecorous entertainment for you,   320
Aphroditê, Zeus's daughter,
caught in the act, cheating me, her cripple,
with Arês—devastating Arês.
Cleanlimbed beauty is her joy, not these
bandylegs I came into the world with:
no one to blame but the two gods[18] who bred me!
Come see this pair entwining here
in my own bed! How hot it makes me burn!
I think they may not care to lie much longer,
pressing on one another, passionate lovers;   330
they'll have enough of bed together soon.
And yet the chain that bagged them holds them down
till Father sends me back my wedding gifts—
all that I poured out for his damned pigeon,
so lovely, and so wanton."

                                                                        All the others
were crowding in, now, to the brazen house—
Poseidon who embraces earth, and Hermês
the runner, and Apollo, lord of Distance.
The goddesses stayed home for shame; but these
munificences ranged there in the doorway,   340
and irrepressible among them all
arose the laughter of the happy gods.
Gazing hard at Hephaistos' handiwork
the gods in turn remarked among themselves:

"No dash in adultery now."

[17] The Sintians, of Lemnos, had a reputation for crudity.
[18] Zeus and Hera.

"The tortoise tags the hare—
Hephaistos catches Arês—and Arês outran the wind."

"The lame god's craft has pinned him. Now shall he
pay what is due from gods taken in cuckoldry."

They made these improving remarks to one another,
but Apollo leaned aside to say to Hermês: 350

"Son of Zeus, beneficent Wayfinder,
would you accept a coverlet of chain, if only
you lay by Aphroditê's golden side?"

To this the Wayfinder replied, shining:

"Would I not, though, Apollo of distances!
Wrap me in chains three times the weight of these,
come goddesses and gods to see the fun;
only let me lie beside the pale-golden one!"

The gods gave way again to peals of laughter,
all but Poseidon, and he never smiled,   360
but urged Hephaistos to unpinion Arês,
saying emphatically, in a loud voice:

                                        "Free him:

you will be paid, I swear; ask what you will;
he pays up every jot the gods decree."

To this the Great Gamelegs replied:

                                        "Poseidon,

lord of the earth-surrounding sea, I should not
swear to a scoundrel's honor. What have I
as surety from you, if Arês leaves me
empty-handed, with my empty chain?"

The Earth-shaker for answer urged again: 370

"Hephaistos, let us grant he goes, and leaves
the fine unpaid; I swear, then, I shall pay it."

Then said the Great Gamelegs at last:

                                        "No more:

you offer terms I cannot well refuse."

And down the strong god bent to set them free,
till disencumbered of their bond, the chain,
the lovers leapt away—he into Thrace,
while Aphroditê, laughter's darling, fled

to Kypros Isle and Paphos,[19] to her meadow
and altar dim with incense. There the Graces   380
bathed and anointed her with golden oil—
a bloom that clings upon immortal flesh alone—
and let her folds of mantle fall in glory.

So ran the song the minstrel sang.

                                                          Odysseus
listening, found sweet pleasure in the tale,
among the Phaiákian mariners and oarsmen.
And next Alkínoös called upon his sons,
Halios and Laódamas, to show
the dance no one could do as well as they—
handling a purple ball carven by Pólybos.   390
One made it shoot up under the shadowing clouds
as he leaned backward; bounding high in air
the other cut its flight far off the ground—
and neither missed a step as the ball soared.

The next turn was to keep it low, and shuttling
hard between them, while the ring of boys
gave them a steady stamping beat.
Odysseus now addressed Alkínoös:

"O majesty, model of all your folk,
your promise was to show me peerless dancers;   400
here is the promise kept. I am all wonder."

At this Alkínoös in his might rejoicing
said to the seafarers of Phaiákia:

"Attend me now, Phaiákian lords and captains:
our guest appears a clear-eyed man and wise.
Come, let him feel our bounty as he should.
Here are twelve princes of the kingdom—lords
paramount, and I who make thirteen;
let each one bring a laundered cloak and tunic,
and add one bar of honorable gold.   410
Heap all our gifts together; load his arms;
let him go joyous to our evening feast!
As for Seareach—why, man to man
he'll make amends, and handsomely; he blundered."

Now all as one acclaimed the king's good pleasure,
and each one sent a squire to bring his gifts.
Meanwhile Seareach found speech again, saying:

---

[19]A city in ancient Cyprus (Kypros), an island south of Turkey where Aphroditê had a cult.

"My lord and model of us all, Alkínoös,
as you require of me, in satisfaction,
this broadsword of clear bronze goes to our guest.   420
Its hilt is silver, and the ringed sheath
of new-sawn ivory—a costly weapon."

He turned to give the broadsword to Odysseus,
facing him, saying blithely:

                                        "Sir, my best
wishes, my respects; if I offended,
I hope the seawinds blow it out of mind.
God send you see your lady and your homeland
soon again, after the pain of exile."

Odysseus, the great tactician, answered:

"My hand, friend; may the gods award you fortune.   430
I hope no pressing need comes on you ever
for this fine blade you give me in amends."

He slung it, glinting silver, from his shoulder,
as the light shone from sundown. Messengers
were bearing gifts and treasure to the palace,
where the king's sons received them all, and made
a glittering pile at their grave mother's side;
then, as Alkínoös took his throne of power,
each went to his own high-backed chair in turn,
and said Alkínoös to Arêtê: 440

"Lady, bring here a chest, the finest one;
a clean cloak and tunic; stow these things;
and warm a cauldron for him. Let him bathe,
when he has seen the gifts of the Phaiákians,
and so dine happily to a running song.
My own wine-cup of gold intaglio[20]
I'll give him, too; through all the days to come,
tipping his wine to Zeus or other gods
in his great hall, he shall remember me."

Then said Arêtê to her maids:

                                        "The tripod: 450
stand the great tripod legs about the fire."

They swung the cauldron on the fire's heart,
poured water in, and fed the blaze beneath
until the basin simmered, cupped in flame.

---

[20]A design cut into the surface.

The queen set out a rich chest from her chamber
and folded in the gifts—clothing and gold
given Odysseus by the Phaiákians;
then she put in the royal cloak and tunic,
briskly saying to her guest:

                                                    "Now here, sir,
look to the lid yourself, and tie it down   460
against light fingers, if there be any,
on the black ship tonight while you are sleeping."

Noble Odysseus, expert in adversity,
battened the lid down with a lightning knot
learned, once, long ago, from the Lady Kirkê.[21]
And soon a call came from the Bathing Mistress
who led him to a hip-bath, warm and clear—
a happy sight, and rare in his immersions
after he left Kalypso's home—where, surely,
the luxuries of a god were ever his.   470
When the bath maids had washed him, rubbed him down,
put a fresh tunic and a cloak around him,
he left the bathing place to join the men
at wine in hall.

                                    The princess Nausikaa,
exquisite figure, as of heaven's shaping,
waited beside a pillar as he passed
and said swiftly, with wonder in her look:

"Fare well, stranger; in your land remember me
who met and saved you. It is worth your thought."

The man of all occasions now met this: 480

"Daughter of great Alkínoös, Nausikaa,
may Zeus the lord of thunder, Hera's consort,
grant me daybreak again in my own country!
But there and all my days until I die
may I invoke you as I would a goddess,
princess, to whom I owe my life."

                                                    He left her
and went to take his place beside the king.

Now when the roasts were cut, the winebowls full,
a herald led the minstrel down the room
amid the deference of the crowd, and paused   490
to seat him near a pillar in the center—
whereupon that resourceful man, Odysseus,

[21]A sorceress; Odysseus' encounter with her is described in Book X. Also spelled *Circe*.

carved out a quarter from his chine of pork,
crisp with fat, and called the blind man's guide:

"Herald! here, take this to Demódokos:
let him feast and be merry, with my compliments.
All men owe honor to the poets—honor
and awe, for they are dearest to the Muse
who puts upon their lips the ways of life."

Gentle Demódokos took the proffered gift 500
and inwardly rejoiced. When all were served,
every man's hand went out upon the banquet,
repelling hunger and thirst, until at length
Odysseus spoke again to the blind minstrel:

"Demódokos, accept my utmost praise.
The Muse, daughter of Zeus in radiance,
or else Apollo[22] gave you skill to shape
with such great style your songs of the Akhaians—
their hard lot, how they fought and suffered war.
You shared it, one would say, or heard it all. 510
Now shift your theme, and sing that wooden horse
Epeios built, inspired by Athena—
the ambuscade Odysseus filled with fighters
and sent to take the inner town of Troy.
Sing only this for me, sing me this well,
and I shall say at once before the world
the grace of heaven has given us a song."

The minstrel stirred, murmuring to the god, and soon
clear words and notes came one by one, a vision
of the Akhaians in their graceful ships 520
drawing away from shore: the torches flung
and shelters flaring: Argive soldiers crouched
in the close dark around Odysseus: and
the horse, tall on the assembly ground of Troy.
For when the Trojans pulled it in, themselves,
up to the citadel, they sat nearby
with long-drawn-out and hapless argument—
favoring, in the end, one course of three:
either to stave the vault with brazen axes,
or haul it to a cliff and pitch it down, 530
or else to save it for the gods, a votive glory—
the plan that could not but prevail.
For Troy must perish, as ordained, that day
she harbored the great horse of timber; hidden
the flower of Akhaia lay, and bore
slaughter and death upon the men of Troy.

---

[22] God of music and prophecy. He would naturally have an affinity with bards.

He sang, then, of the town sacked by Akhaians
pouring down from the horse's hollow cave,
this way and that way raping the steep city,
and how Odysseus came like Arês to   540
the door of Deïphobos,[23] with Meneláos,
and braved the desperate fight there—
conquering once more by Athena's power.

The splendid minstrel sang it.

                                  And Odysseus

let the bright molten tears run down his cheeks,
weeping the way a wife mourns for her lord
on the lost field where he has gone down fighting
the day of wrath that came upon his children.
At sight of the man panting and dying there,
she slips down to enfold him, crying out;   550
then feels the spears, prodding her back and shoulders,
and goes bound into slavery and grief.
Piteous weeping wears away her cheeks:
but no more piteous than Odysseus' tears,
cloaked as they were, now, from the company.
Only Alkínoös, at his elbow, knew—
hearing the low sob in the man's breathing—
and when he knew, he spoke:

"Hear me, lords and captains of Phaiákia!
And let Demódokos touch his harp no more.   560
His theme has not been pleasing to all here.
During the feast, since our fine poet sang,
our guest has never left off weeping. Grief
seems fixed upon his heart. Break off the song!
Let everyone be easy, host and guest;
there's more decorum in a smiling banquet!
We had prepared here, on our friend's behalf,
safe conduct in a ship, and gifts to cheer him,
holding that any man with a grain of wit
will treat a decent suppliant like a brother.   570
Now by the same rule, friend, you must not be
secretive any longer! Come, in fairness,
tell me the name you bore in that far country;
how were you known to family, and neighbors?
No man is nameless—no man, good or bad,
but gets a name in his first infancy,
none being born, unless a mother bears him!
Tell me your native land, your coast and city—
sailing directions for the ships, you know—
for those Phaiákian ships of ours   580
that have no steersman, and no steering oar,

---

[23]Meneláos' wife, Helen, had in Troy been given in marriage to Deïphobos.

divining the crew's wishes, as they do,
and knowing, as they do, the ports of call
about the world. Hidden in mist or cloud
they scud the open sea, with never a thought
of being in distress or going down.
There is, however, something I once heard
Nausíthoös, my father, say: Poseidon
holds it against us that our deep sea ships
are sure conveyance for all passengers. 590
My father said, some day one of our cutters
homeward bound over the cloudy sea
would be wrecked by the god, and a range of hills
thrown round our city. So, in his age, he said,
and let it be, or not, as the god please.
But come, now, put it for me clearly, tell me
the sea ways that you wandered, and the shores
you touched; the cities, and the men therein,
uncivilized, if such there were, and hostile,
and those godfearing who had kindly manners. 600
Tell me why you should grieve so terribly
over the Argives and the fall of Troy.
That was all gods' work, weaving ruin there
so it should make a song for men to come!
Some kin of yours, then, died at Ilion,
some first rate man, by marriage near to you,
next your own blood most dear?
Or some companion of congenial mind
and valor? True it is, a wise friend
can take a brother's place in our affection." 610

BOOK NINE: NEW COASTS AND POSEIDON'S SON

Now this was the reply Odysseus made:

"Alkínoös, king and admiration of men,
how beautiful this is, to hear a minstrel
gifted as yours: a god he might be, singing!
There is no boon in life more sweet, I say,
than when a summer joy holds all the realm,
and banqueters sit listening to a harper
in a great hall, by rows of tables heaped
with bread and roast meat, while a steward goes
to dip up wine and brim your cups again. 10
Here is the flower of life, it seems to me!
But now you wish to know my cause for sorrow—
and thereby give me cause for more.

What shall I
say first? What shall I keep until the end?

The gods have tried me in a thousand ways.
But first my name: let that be known to you,
and if I pull away from pitiless death,
friendship will bind us, though my land lies far.

I am Laërtês' son, Odysseus.
         Men hold me
formidable for guile in peace and war: 20
this fame has gone abroad to the sky's rim.
My home is on the peaked sea-mark of Ithaka
under Mount Neion's wind-blown robe of leaves,
in sight of other islands—Doulíkhion,
Samê, wooded Zakynthos—Ithaka
being most lofty in that coastal sea,
and northwest, while the rest lie east and south.
A rocky isle, but good for a boy's training;
I shall not see on earth a place more dear,
though I have been detained long by Kalypso,   30
loveliest among goddesses, who held me
in her smooth caves, to be her heart's delight,
as Kirkê of Aiaia, the enchantress,
desired me, and detained me in her hall.
But in my heart I never gave consent.
Where shall a man find sweetness to surpass
his own home and his parents? In far lands
he shall not, though he find a house of gold.

What of my sailing, then, from Troy?
        What of those years
of rough adventure, weathered under Zeus?   40
The wind that carried west from Ilion
brought me to Ísmaros,[1] on the far shore,
a strongpoint on the coast of the Kikonês.
I stormed that place and killed the men who fought.
Plunder we took, and we enslaved the women,
to make division, equal shares to all—
but on the spot I told them: 'Back, and quickly!
Out to sea again!' My men were mutinous,
fools, on stores of wine. Sheep after sheep
they butchered by the surf, and shambling cattle,   50
feasting,—while fugitives went inland, running
to call to arms the main force of Kikonês.
This was an army, trained to fight on horseback
or, where the ground required, on foot. They came
with dawn over that terrain like the leaves
and blades of spring. So doom appeared to us,
dark word of Zeus for us, our evil days.

---

[1] The land of the Kikonês, in Thrace (on the northern coast of the Aegean Sea).

My men stood up and made a fight of it—
backed on the ships, with lances kept in play,
from bright morning through the blaze of noon 60
holding our beach, although so far outnumbered;
but when the sun passed toward unyoking time,
then the Akhaians, one by one, gave way.
Six benches were left empty in every ship
that evening when we pulled away from death.
And this new grief we bore with us to sea:
our precious lives we had, but not our friends.
No ship made sail next day until some shipmate
had raised a cry, three times, for each poor ghost
unfleshed by the Kikonês on that field. 70

Now Zeus the lord of cloud roused in the north
a storm against the ships, and driving veils
of squall moved down like night on land and sea.
The bows went plunging at the gust; sails
cracked and lashed out strips in the big wind.
We saw death in that fury, dropped the yards,
unshipped the oars, and pulled for the nearest lee:
then two long days and nights we lay offshore
worn out and sick at heart, tasting our grief,
until a third Dawn came with ringlets shining. 80
Then we put up our masts, hauled sail, and rested,
letting the steersmen and the breeze take over.

I might have made it safely home, that time,
but as I came round Malea[2] the current
took me out to sea, and from the north
a fresh gale drove me on, past Kythera.
Nine days I drifted on the teeming sea
before dangerous high winds. Upon the tenth
we came to the coastline of the Lotos Eaters,
who live upon that flower. We landed there 90
to take on water. All ships' companies
mustered alongside for the mid-day meal.
Then I sent out two picked men and a runner
to learn what race of men that land sustained.
They fell in, soon enough, with Lotos Eaters,
who showed no will to do us harm, only
offering the sweet Lotos to our friends—
but those who ate this honeyed plant, the Lotos,
never cared to report, nor to return:
they longed to stay forever, browsing on 100
the native bloom, forgetful of their homeland.
I drove them, all three wailing, to the ships,

[2] The cape at the southernmost end of Greece; Kythera, mentioned two lines below, is a
sizable island just southwest of Malea.

tied them down under their rowing benches,
and called the rest: 'All hands aboard;
come, clear the beach and no one taste
the Lotos, or you lose your hope of home.'
Filing in to their places by the rowlocks
my oarsmen dipped their long oars in the surf,
and we moved out again on our sea faring.

In the next land we found were Kyklopês,[3]   110
giants, louts, without a law to bless them.
In ignorance leaving the fruitage of the earth in mystery
to the immortal gods, they neither plow
nor sow by hand, nor till the ground, though grain—
wild wheat and barley—grows untended, and
wine-grapes, in clusters, ripen in heaven's rain.
Kyklopês have no muster and no meeting,
no consultation or old tribal ways,
but each one dwells in his own mountain cave
dealing out rough justice to wife and child,   120
indifferent to what the others do.

                                                        Well, then:
across the wide bay from the mainland
there lies a desert island, not far out,
but still not close inshore. Wild goats in hundreds
breed there; and no human being comes
upon the isle to startle them—no hunter
of all who ever tracked with hounds through forests
or had rough going over mountain trails.
The isle, unplanted and untilled, a wilderness,
pastures goats alone. And this is why: 130
good ships like ours with cheekpaint at the bows
are far beyond the Kyklopês. No shipwright
toils among them, shaping and building up
symmetrical trim hulls to cross the sea
and visit all the seaboard towns, as men do
who go and come in commerce over water.
This isle—seagoing folk would have annexed it
and built their homesteads on it: all good land,
fertile for every crop in season: lush
well-watered meads along the shore, vines in profusion,   140
prairie, clear for the plow, where grain would grow
chin high by harvest time, and rich sub-soil.
The island cove is landlocked, so you need
no hawsers out astern, bow-stones or mooring:
run in and ride there till the day your crews
chafe to be under sail, and a fair wind blows.
You'll find good water flowing from a cavern
through dusky poplars into the upper bay.

[3] One-eyed giants, inhabitants of Sicily. Also spelled *Cyclops*.

Here we made harbor. Some god guided us
that night, for we could barely see our bows 150
in the dense fog around us, and no moonlight
filtered through the overcast. No look-out,
nobody saw the island dead ahead,
nor even the great landward rolling billow
that took us in: we found ourselves in shallows,
keels grazing shore: so furled our sails
and disembarked where the low ripples broke.
There on the beach we lay, and slept till morning.

When Dawn spread out her finger tips of rose
we turned out marvelling, to tour the isle, 160
while Zeus's shy nymph daughters flushed wild goats
down from the heights—a breakfast for my men.
We ran to fetch our hunting bows and long-shanked
lances from the ships, and in three companies
we took our shots. Heaven gave us game a-plenty:
for every one of twelve ships in my squadron
nine goats fell to be shared; my lot was ten.
So there all day, until the sun went down,
we made our feast on meat galore, and wine—
wine from the ship, for our supply held out, 170
so many jars were filled at Ísmaros
from stores of the Kikonês that we plundered.
We gazed, too, at Kyklopês Land, so near,
we saw their smoke, heard bleating from their flocks.
But after sundown, in the gathering dusk,
we slept again above the wash of ripples.

When the young Dawn with finger tips of rose
came in the east, I called my men together
and made a speech to them:

                                    'Old shipmates, friends,
the rest of you stand by; I'll make the crossing 180
in my own ship, with my own company,
and find out what the mainland natives are—
for they may be wild savages, and lawless,
or hospitable and god fearing men.'

At this I went aboard, and gave the word
to cast off by the stern. My oarsmen followed,
filing in to their benches by the rowlocks,
and all in line dipped oars in the grey sea.

As we rowed on, and nearer to the mainland,
at one end of the bay, we saw a cavern 190
yawning above the water, screened with laurel,
and many rams and goats about the place

inside a sheepfold—made from slabs of stone
earthfast between tall trunks of pine and rugged
towering oak trees.

                                  A prodigious man

slept in this cave alone, and took his flocks
to graze afield—remote from all companions,
knowing none but savage ways, a brute
so huge, he seemed no man at all of those
who eat good wheaten bread; but he seemed rather   200
a shaggy mountain reared in solitude.
We beached there, and I told the crew
to stand by and keep watch over the ship;
as for myself I took my twelve best fighters
and went ahead. I had a goatskin full
of that sweet liquor that Euanthês' son,
Maron, had given me. He kept Apollo's
holy grove at Ísmaros; for kindness
we showed him there, and showed his wife and child,
he gave me seven shining golden talents   210
perfectly formed, a solid silver winebowl,
and then this liquor—twelve two-handled jars
of brandy, pure and fiery. Not a slave
in Maron's household knew this drink; only
he, his wife and the storeroom mistress knew;
and they would put one cupful—ruby-colored,
honey-smooth—in twenty more of water,
but still the sweet scent hovered like a fume
over the winebowl. No man turned away
when cups of this came round.

                                 A wineskin full   220

I brought along, and victuals in a bag,
for in my bones I knew some towering brute
would be upon us soon—all outward power,
a wild man, ignorant of civility.

We climbed, then, briskly to the cave. But Kyklops
had gone afield, to pasture his fat sheep,
so we looked round at everything inside:
a drying rack that sagged with cheeses, pens
crowded with lambs and kids, each in its class:
firstlings apart from middlings, and the 'dewdrops,'   230
or newborn lambkins, penned apart from both.
And vessels full of whey were brimming there—
bowls of earthenware and pails for milking.
My men came pressing round me, pleading:

                                       'Why not

take these cheeses, get them stowed, come back,
throw open all the pens, and make a run for it?
We'll drive the kids and lambs aboard. We say
put out again on good salt water!'

Ah,
how sound that was! Yet I refused. I wished
to see the caveman, what he had to offer— 240
no pretty sight, it turned out, for my friends.
We lit a fire, burnt an offering,
and took some cheese to eat; then sat in silence
around the embers, waiting. When he came
he had a load of dry boughs on his shoulder
to stoke his fire at suppertime. He dumped it
with a great crash into that hollow cave,
and we all scattered fast to the far wall.
Then over the broad cavern floor he ushered
the ewes he meant to milk. He left his rams 250
and he-goats in the yard outside, and swung
high overhead a slab of solid rock
to close the cave. Two dozen four-wheeled wagons,
with heaving wagon teams, could not have stirred
the tonnage of that rock from where he wedged it
over the doorsill. Next he took his seat
and milked his bleating ewes. A practiced job
he made of it, giving each ewe her suckling;
thickened his milk, then, into curds and whey,[4]
sieved out the curds to drip in withy baskets, 260
and poured the whey to stand in bowls
cooling until he drank it for his supper.
When all these chores were done, he poked the fire,
heaping on brushwood. In the glare he saw us.

'Strangers,' he said, 'who are you? And where from?
What brings you here by sea ways—a fair traffic?
Or are you wandering rogues, who cast your lives
like dice, and ravage other folk by sea?'

We felt a pressure on our hearts, in dread
of that deep rumble and that mighty man. 270
But all the same I spoke up in reply:

'We are from Troy, Akhaians, blown off course
by shifting gales on the Great South Sea;
homeward bound, but taking routes and ways
uncommon; so the will of Zeus would have it.
We served under Agamémnon, son of Atreus—
the whole world knows what city
he laid waste, what armies he destroyed.
It was our luck to come here; here we stand,
beholden for your help, or any gifts 280
you give—as custom is to honor strangers.
We would entreat you, great Sir, have a care

---

[4]The liquid part of separated milk, as distinguished from the lumpy curds.

for the gods' courtesy; Zeus will avenge
the unoffending guest.'[5]

                                                    He answered this
from his brute chest, unmoved:

                                                    'You are a ninny,
or else you come from the other end of nowhere,
telling me, mind the gods! We Kyklopês
care not a whistle for your thundering Zeus
or all the gods in bliss; we have more force by far.
I would not let you go for fear of Zeus—   290
you or your friends—unless I had a whim to.
Tell me, where was it, now, you left your ship—
around the point, or down the shore, I wonder?'

He thought he'd find out, but I saw through this,
and answered with a ready lie:

                                                    'My ship?
Poseidon Lord, who sets the earth a-tremble,
broke it up on the rocks at your land's end.
A wind from seaward served him, drove us there.
We are survivors, these good men and I.'

Neither reply nor pity came from him,   300
but in one stride he clutched at my companions
and caught two in his hands like squirming puppies
to beat their brains out, spattering the floor.
Then he dismembered them and made his meal,
gaping and crunching like a mountain lion—
everything: innards, flesh, and marrow bones.
We cried aloud, lifting our hands to Zeus,
powerless, looking on at this, appalled;
but Kyklops[6] went on filling up his belly
with manflesh and great gulps of whey,   310
then lay down like a mast among his sheep.
My heart beat high now at the chance of action,
and drawing the sharp sword from my hip I went
along his flank to stab him where the midriff
holds the liver. I had touched the spot
when sudden fear stayed me: if I killed him
we perished there as well, for we could never
move his ponderous doorway slab aside.
So we were left to groan and wait for morning.

---

[5] Zeus was the protector and guarantor of the laws of hospitality.
[6] Here used as a singular; his name, we learn later, is Polyphêmos.

When the young Dawn with finger tips of rose 320
lit up the world, the Kyklops built a fire
and milked his handsome ewes, all in due order,
putting the sucklings to the mothers. Then,
his chores being all dispatched, he caught
another brace of men to make his breakfast,
and whisked away his great door slab
to let his sheep go through—but he, behind,
reset the stone as one would cap a quiver.
There was a din of whistling as the Kyklops
rounded his flock to higher ground, then stillness. 330
And now I pondered how to hurt him worst,
if but Athena granted what I prayed for.
Here are the means I thought would serve my turn:

a club, or staff, lay there along the fold—
an olive tree, felled green and left to season
for Kyklops' hand. And it was like a mast
a lugger of twenty oars, broad in the beam—
a deep-sea-going craft—might carry:
so long, so big around, it seemed. Now I
chopped out a six foot section of this pole 340
and set it down before my men, who scraped it;
and when they had it smooth, I hewed again
to make a stake with pointed end. I held this
in the fire's heart and turned it, toughening it,
then hid it, well back in the cavern, under
one of the dung piles in profusion there.
Now came the time to toss for it: who ventured
along with me? whose hand could bear to thrust
and grind that spike in Kyklops' eye, when mild
sleep had mastered him? As luck would have it, 350
the men I would have chosen won the toss—
four strong men, and I made five as captain.

At evening came the shepherd with his flock,
his woolly flock. The rams as well, this time,
entered the cave: by some sheep-herding whim—
or a god's bidding—none were left outside.
He hefted his great boulder into place
and sat him down to milk the bleating ewes
in proper order, put the lambs to suck,
and swiftly ran through all his evening chores. 360
Then he caught two more men and feasted on them.
My moment was at hand, and I went forward
holding an ivy bowl of my dark drink,
looking up, saying:

                                    'Kyklops, try some wine.
Here's liquor to wash down your scraps of men.
Taste it, and see the kind of drink we carried

under our planks. I meant it for an offering
if you would help us home. But you are mad,
unbearable, a bloody monster! After this,
will any other traveller come to see you?'   370

He seized and drained the bowl, and it went down
so fiery and smooth he called for more:

'Give me another, thank you kindly. Tell me,
how are you called? I'll make a gift will please you.
Even Kyklopês know the wine-grapes grow
out of grassland and loam in heaven's rain,
but here's a bit of nectar and ambrosia!'

Three bowls I brought him, and he poured them down.
I saw the fuddle and flush come over him,
then I sang out in cordial tones:

                                                    'Kyklops,   380
you ask my honorable name? Remember
the gift you promised me, and I shall tell you.
My name is Nohbdy: mother, father, and friends,
everyone calls me Nohbdy.'

                                                    And he said:

'Nohbdy's my meat, then, after I eat his friends.
Others come first. There's a noble gift, now.'

Even as he spoke, he reeled and tumbled backward,
his great head lolling to one side; and sleep
took him like any creature. Drunk, hiccuping,
he dribbled streams of liquor and bits of men.   390

Now, by the gods, I drove my big hand spike
deep in the embers, charring it again,
and cheered my men along with battle talk
to keep their courage up: no quitting now.
The pike of olive, green though it had been,
reddened and glowed as if about to catch.
I drew it from the coals and my four fellows
gave me a hand, lugging it near the Kyklops
as more than natural force nerved them; straight
forward they sprinted, lifted it, and rammed it   400
deep in his crater eye, and I leaned on it
turning it as a shipwright turns a drill
in planking, having men below to swing
the two-handled strap that spins it in the groove.
So with our brand we bored that great eye socket
while blood ran out around the red hot bar.
Eyelid and lash were seared; the pierced ball
hissed broiling, and the roots popped.

In a smithy
one sees a white-hot axehead or an adze
plunged and wrung in a cold tub, screeching steam— 410
the way they make soft iron hale and hard—:
just so that eyeball hissed around the spike.
The Kyklops bellowed and the rock roared round him,
and we fell back in fear. Clawing his face
he tugged the bloody spike out of his eye,
threw it away, and his wild hands went groping;
then he set up a howl for Kyklopês
who lived in caves on windy peaks nearby.
Some heard him; and they came by divers ways
to clump around outside and call:

'What ails you, 420
Polyphêmos? Why do you cry so sore
in the starry night? You will not let us sleep.
Sure no man's driving off your flock? No man
has tricked you, ruined you?'

Out of the cave
the mammoth Polyphêmos roared in answer:

'Nohbdy, Nohbdy's tricked me, Nohbdy's ruined me!'

To this rough shout they made a sage reply:

'Ah well, if nobody has played you foul
there in your lonely bed, we are no use in pain
given by great Zeus. Let it be your father, 430
Poseidon Lord, to whom you pray.'

So saying
they trailed away. And I was filled with laughter
to see how like a charm the name deceived them.
Now Kyklops, wheezing as the pain came on him,
fumbled to wrench away the great doorstone
and squatted in the breach with arms thrown wide
for any silly beast or man who bolted—
hoping somehow I might be such a fool.
But I kept thinking how to win the game:
death sat there huge; how could we slip away? 440
I drew on all my wits, and ran through tactics,
reasoning as a man will for dear life,
until a trick came—and it pleased me well.
The Kyklops' rams were handsome, fat, with heavy
fleeces, a dark violet.

Three abreast
I tied them silently together, twining
cords of willow from the ogre's bed;
then slung a man under each middle one

to ride there safely, shielded left and right.
So three sheep could convey each man. I took   450
the woolliest ram, the choicest of the flock,
and hung myself under his kinky belly,
pulled up tight, with fingers twisted deep
in sheepskin ringlets for an iron grip.
So, breathing hard, we waited until morning.

When Dawn spread out her finger tips of rose
the rams began to stir, moving for pasture,
and peals of bleating echoed round the pens
where dams with udders full called for a milking.
Blinded, and sick with pain from his head wound,   460
the master stroked each ram, then let it pass,
but my men riding on the pectoral fleece
the giant's blind hands blundering never found.
Last of them all my ram, the leader, came,
weighted by wool and me with my meditations.
The Kyklops patted him, and then he said:

'Sweet cousin ram, why lag behind the rest
in the night cave? You never linger so,
but graze before them all, and go afar
to crop sweet grass, and take your stately way   470
leading along the streams, until at evening
you run to be the first one in the fold.
Why, now, so far behind? Can you be grieving
over your Master's eye? That carrion rogue
and his accurst companions burnt it out
when he had conquered all my wits with wine.
Nohbdy will not get out alive, I swear.
Oh, had you brain and voice to tell
where he may be now, dodging all my fury!
Bashed by this hand and bashed on this rock wall   480
his brains would strew the floor, and I should have
rest from the outrage Nohbdy worked upon me.'

He sent us into the open, then. Close by,
I dropped and rolled clear of the ram's belly,
going this way and that to untie the men.
With many glances back, we rounded up
his fat, stiff-legged sheep to take aboard,
and drove them down to where the good ship lay.
We saw, as we came near, our fellows' faces
shining; then we saw them turn to grief   490
tallying those who had not fled from death.
I hushed them, jerking head and eyebrows up,
and in a low voice told them: 'Load this herd;
move fast, and put the ship's head toward the breakers.'
They all pitched in at loading, then embarked

and struck their oars into the sea. Far out,
as far off shore as shouted words would carry,
I sent a few back to the adversary:

'O Kyklops! Would you feast on my companions?
Puny, am I, in a Caveman's hands? 500
How do you like the beating that we gave you,
you damned cannibal? Eater of guests
under your roof! Zeus and the gods have paid you!'

The blind thing in his doubled fury broke
a hilltop in his hands and heaved it after us.
Ahead of our black prow it struck and sank
whelmed in a spuming geyser, a giant wave
that washed the ship stern foremost back to shore.
I got the longest boathook out and stood
fending us off, with furious nods to all 510
to put their backs into a racing stroke—
row, row, or perish. So the long oars bent
kicking the foam sternward, making head
until we drew away, and twice as far.
Now when I cupped my hands I heard the crew
in low voices protesting:

                                            'Godsake, Captain!
Why bait the beast again? Let him alone!'

'That tidal wave he made on the first throw
all but beached us.'

                                            'All but stove us in!'

'Give him our bearing with your trumpeting, 520
he'll get the range and lob a boulder.'

                                                              'Aye
He'll smash our timbers and our heads together!'

I would not heed them in my glorying spirit,
but let my anger flare and yelled:

                                            'Kyklops,
if ever mortal man inquire
how you were put to shame and blinded, tell him
Odysseus, raider of cities, took your eye:
Laërtês' son, whose home's on Ithaka!'

At this he gave a mighty sob and rumbled:

'Now comes the weird[7] upon me, spoken of old. 530
A wizard, grand and wondrous, lived here—Télemos,

---

[7] Inescapable destiny.

a son of Eurymos; great length of days
he had in wizardry among the Kyklopês,
and these things he foretold for time to come:
my great eye lost, and at Odysseus' hands.
Always I had in mind some giant, armed
in giant force, would come against me here.
But this, but you—small, pitiful and twiggy—
you put me down with wine, you blinded me.
Come back, Odysseus, and I'll treat you well,   540
praying the god of earthquake to befriend you—
his son I am, for he by his avowal
fathered me, and, if he will, he may
heal me of this black wound—he and no other
of all the happy gods or mortal men.'

Few words I shouted in reply to him:

'If I could take your life I would and take
your time away, and hurl you down to hell!
The god of earthquake could not heal you there!'

At this he stretched his hands out in his darkness   550
toward the sky of stars, and prayed Poseidon:

'O hear me, lord, blue girdler of the islands,
if I am thine indeed, and thou art father:
grant that Odysseus, raider of cities, never
see his home: Laërtês' son, I mean,
who kept his hall on Ithaka. Should destiny
intend that he shall see his roof again
among his family in his father land,
far be that day, and dark the years between.
Let him lose all companions, and return   560
under strange sail to bitter days at home.'

In these words he prayed, and the god heard him.
Now he laid hands upon a bigger stone
and wheeled around, titanic for the cast,
to let it fly in the black-prowed vessel's track.
But it fell short, just aft the steering oar,
and whelming seas rose giant above the stone
to bear us onward toward the island.

                                                      There

as we ran in we saw the squadron waiting,
the trim ships drawn up side by side, and all   570
our troubled friends who waited, looking seaward.
We beached her, grinding keel in the soft sand,
and waded in, ourselves, on the sandy beach.
Then we unloaded all the Kyklops' flock
to make division, share and share alike,
only my fighters voted that my ram,

the prize of all, should go to me. I slew him
by the sea side and burnt his long thighbones
to Zeus beyond the stormcloud, Kronos'[8] son,
who rules the world. But Zeus disdained my offering;   580
destruction for my ships he had in store
and death for those who sailed them, my companions.
Now all day long until the sun went down
we made our feast on mutton and sweet wine,
till after sunset in the gathering dark
we went to sleep above the wash of ripples.

When the young Dawn with finger tips of rose
touched the world, I roused the men, gave orders
to man the ships, cast off the mooring lines;
and filing in to sit beside the rowlocks   590
oarsmen in line dipped oars in the grey sea.
So we moved out, sad in the vast offing,
having our precious lives, but not our friends.

BOOK TEN: THE GRACE OF THE WITCH

We made our landfall on Aiolia Island,
domain of Aiolos[1] Hippotadês,
the wind king, dear to the gods who never die—
an isle adrift upon the sea, ringed round
with brazen ramparts on a sheer cliffside.
Twelve children had old Aiolos at home—
six daughters and six lusty sons—and he
gave girls to boys to be their gentle brides;
now those lords, in their parents' company,
sup every day in hall—a royal feast   10
with fumes of sacrifice and winds that pipe
'round hollow courts; and all the night they sleep
on beds of filigree beside their ladies.
Here we put in, lodged in the town and palace,
while Aiolos played host to me. He kept me
one full month to hear the tale of Troy,
the ships and the return of the Akhaians,
all which I told him point by point in order.
When in return I asked his leave to sail
and asked provisioning, he stinted nothing,   20
adding a bull's hide sewn from neck to tail
into a mighty bag, bottling storm winds;

---

[8] Equivalent of the Roman Saturn. Chief of the gods in the divine generation preceding Zeus and the Olympian dynasty; dethroned by his son Zeus.

[1] God of the winds, son of Hippotês. Commonly spelled *Aeolus*. A tradition locates his island off the north coast of Sicily.

for Zeus had long ago made Aiolos
warden of winds, to rouse or calm at will.
He wedged this bag under my afterdeck,
lashing the neck with shining silver wire
so not a breath go through; only the west wind
he lofted for me in a quartering breeze
to take my squadron spanking home.

No luck:

the fair wind failed us when our prudence failed. 30

Nine days and nights we sailed without event,
till on the tenth we raised our land. We neared it,
and saw men building fires along the shore;
but now, being weary to the bone, I fell
into deep slumber; I had worked the sheet
nine days alone, and given it to no one,
wishing to spill no wind on the homeward run.
But while I slept, the crew began to parley:
silver and gold, they guessed, were in that bag
bestowed on me by Aiolos' great heart; 40
and one would glance at his benchmate and say:
'It never fails. He's welcome everywhere:
hail to the captain when he goes ashore!
He brought along so many presents, plunder
out of Troy, that's it. How about ourselves—
his shipmates all the way? Nigh home we are
with empty hands. And who has gifts from Aiolos?
He has. I say we ought to crack that bag,
there's gold and silver, plenty, in that bag!'

Temptation had its way with my companions, 50
and they untied the bag.

Then every wind

roared into hurricane; the ships went pitching
west with many cries; our land was lost.
Roused up, despairing in that gloom, I thought:
'Should I go overside for a quick finish
or clench my teeth and stay among the living?'
Down in the bilge I lay, pulling my sea cloak
over my head, while the rough gale blew the ships
and rueful crews clear back to Aiolia.

We put ashore for water; then all hands 60
gathered alongside for a mid-day meal.
When we had taken bread and drink, I picked
one soldier, and one herald, to go with me
and called again on Aiolos. I found him
at meat with his young princes and his lady,
but there beside the pillars, in his portico,

we sat down silent at the open door.
The sight amazed them, and they all exclaimed:

'Why back again, Odysseus?'

'What sea fiend

rose in your path?'

'Did we not launch you well   70

for home, or for whatever land you chose?'

Out of my melancholy I replied:

'Mischief aboard and nodding at the tiller—
a damned drowse—did for me. Make good my loss,
dear friends! You have the power!'

Gently I pleaded,

but they turned cold and still. Said Father Aiolos:

'Take yourself out of this island, creeping thing—
no law, no wisdom, lays it on me now
to help a man the blessed gods detest—
out! Your voyage here was cursed by heaven!'   80

He drove me from the place, groan as I would,
and comfortless we went again to sea,
days of it, till the men flagged at the oars—
no breeze, no help in sight, by our own folly—
six indistinguishable nights and days
before we raised the Laistrygonian height
and far stronghold of Lamos.[2] In that land
the daybreak follows dusk, and so the shepherd
homing calls to the cowherd setting out;
and he who never slept could earn two wages,   90
tending oxen, pasturing silvery flocks,
where the low night path of the sun is near
the sun's path by day. Here, then, we found
a curious bay with mountain walls of stone
to left and right, and reaching far inland,—
a narrow entrance opening from the sea
where cliffs converged as though to touch and close.
All of my squadron sheltered here, inside
the cavern of this bay.

Black prow by prow

those hulls were made fast in a limpid calm   100
without a ripple, stillness all around them.

---

[2] Son of Poseidon and king of the Laistrygonians. Traditions place their land in southwest
Italy or in Sicily. The following lines describe the almost continuous daylight of summer in
the far north, but it would have been impossible for Odysseus and his men to reach such latitudes. Traditionally, the shepherd grazes his flock during the night.

My own black ship I chose to moor alone
on the sea side, using a rock for bollard;
and climbed a rocky point to get my bearings.
No farms, no cultivated land appeared,
but puffs of smoke rose in the wilderness;
so I sent out two picked men and a herald
to learn what race of men this land sustained.

My party found a track—a wagon road
for bringing wood down from the heights to town;   110
and near the settlement they met a daughter
of Antiphatês the Laistrygon—a stalwart
young girl taking her pail to Artakía,
the fountain where these people go for water.
My fellows hailed her, put their questions to her:
who might the king be? ruling over whom?
She waved her hand, showing her father's lodge,
so they approached it. In its gloom they saw
a woman like a mountain crag, the queen—
and loathed the sight of her. But she, for greeting,   120
called from the meeting ground her lord and master,
Antiphatês, who came to drink their blood.
He seized one man and tore him on the spot,
making a meal of him; the other two
leaped out of doors and ran to join the ships.
Behind, he raised the whole tribe howling, countless
Laistrygonês—and more than men they seemed,
gigantic when they gathered on the sky line
to shoot great boulders down from slings; and hell's own
crashing rose, and crying from the ships,   130
as planks and men were smashed to bits—poor gobbets[3]
the wildmen speared like fish and bore away.
But long before it ended in the anchorage—
havoc and slaughter—I had drawn my sword
and cut my own ship's cable. 'Men,' I shouted,
'man the oars and pull till your hearts break
if you would put this butchery behind!'
The oarsmen rent the sea in mortal fear
and my ship spurted out of range, far out
from that deep canyon where the rest were lost.   140
So we fared onward, and death fell behind,
and we took breath to grieve for our companions.

Our next landfall was on Aiaia,[4] island
of Kirkê, dire beauty and divine,

[3] Lumps of raw meat.
[4] Later legend placed this island, home of Kirkê (Circe), near the west coast of Italy, near
Rome. Aiêtês was the king of Colchis who lost the magical Golden Fleece to Iêson (Jason)
and the Argonauts; see the headnote to Euripides' *Medea*. Medea, Aiêtês' daughter, was also
a sorceress; witchcraft ran in the family.

sister of baleful Aiêtês, like him
fathered by Hêlios the light of mortals
on Persê, child of the Ocean stream.

We came

washed in our silent ship upon her shore,
and found a cove, a haven for the ship—
some god, invisible, conned us in. We landed,   150
to lie down in that place two days and nights,
worn out and sick at heart, tasting our grief.
But when Dawn set another day a-shining
I took my spear and broadsword, and I climbed
a rocky point above the ship, for sight
or sound of human labor. Gazing out
from that high place over a land of thicket,
oaks and wide watercourses, I could see
a smoke wisp from the woodland hall of Kirkê.
So I took counsel with myself: should I   160
go inland scouting out that reddish smoke?
No: better not, I thought, but first return
to waterside and ship, and give the men
breakfast before I sent them to explore.
Now as I went down quite alone, and came
a bowshot from the ship, some god's compassion
set a big buck in motion to cross my path—
a stag with noble antlers, pacing down
from pasture in the woods to the riverside,
as long thirst and the power of sun constrained him.   170
He started from the bush and wheeled: I hit him
square in the spine midway along his back
and the bronze point broke through it. In the dust
he fell and whinnied as life bled away.
I set one foot against him, pulling hard
to wrench my weapon from the wound, then left it,
butt-end on the ground. I plucked some withies
and twined a double strand into a rope—
enough to tie the hocks of my huge trophy;
then pickaback I lugged him to the ship,   180
leaning on my long spearshaft; I could not
haul that mighty carcass on one shoulder.
Beside the ship I let him drop, and spoke
gently and low to each man standing near:

'Come, friends, though hard beset, we'll not go down
into the House of Death before our time.
As long as food and drink remain aboard
let us rely on it, not die of hunger.'

At this those faces, cloaked in desolation
upon the waste sea beach, were bared;   190
their eyes turned toward me and the mighty trophy,

lighting, foreseeing pleasure, one by one.
So hands were washed to take what heaven sent us.
And all that day until the sun went down
we had our fill of venison and wine,
till after sunset in the gathering dusk
we slept at last above the line of breakers.
When the young Dawn with finger tips of rose
made heaven bright, I called them round and said:

'Shipmates, companions in disastrous time,   200
O my dear friends, where Dawn lies, and the West,
and where the great Sun, light of men, may go
under the earth by night, and where he rises—
of these things we know nothing. Do we know
any least thing to serve us now? I wonder.
All that I saw when I went up the rock
was one more island in the boundless main,
a low landscape, covered with woods and scrub,
and puffs of smoke ascending in mid-forest.'

They were all silent, but their hearts contracted,   210
remembering Antiphatês the Laistrygon
and that prodigious cannibal, the Kyklops.
They cried out, and the salt tears wet their eyes.
But seeing our time for action lost in weeping,
I mustered those Akhaians under arms,
counting them off in two platoons, myself
and my godlike Eurýlokhos commanding.
We shook lots in a soldier's dogskin cap
and his came bounding out—valiant Eurýlokhos!—
So off he went, with twenty-two companions   220
weeping, as mine wept, too, who stayed behind.

In the wild wood they found an open glade,
around a smooth stone house—the hall of Kirkê—
and wolves and mountain lions lay there, mild
in her soft spell, fed on her drug of evil.
None would attack—oh, it was strange, I tell you—
but switching their long tails they faced our men
like hounds, who look up when their master comes
with tidbits for them—as he will—from table.
Humbly those wolves and lions with mighty paws   230
fawned on our men—who met their yellow eyes
and feared them.

                              In the entrance way they stayed
to listen there: inside her quiet house
they heard the goddess Kirkê.

                                      Low she sang
in her beguiling voice, while on her loom
she wove ambrosial fabric sheer and bright,

by that craft known to the goddesses of heaven.
No one would speak, until Politês—most
faithful and likable of my officers, said:

'Dear friends, no need for stealth: here's a young weaver   240
singing a pretty song to set the air
a-tingle on these lawns and paven courts.
Goddess she is, or lady. Shall we greet her?'

So reassured, they all cried out together,
and she came swiftly to the shining doors
to call them in. All but Eurýlokhos—
who feared a snare—the innocents went after her.
On thrones she seated them, and lounging chairs,
while she prepared a meal of cheese and barley
and amber honey mixed with Pramnian wine,   250
adding her own vile pinch, to make them lose
desire or thought of our dear father land.
Scarce had they drunk when she flew after them
with her long stick and shut them in a pigsty—
bodies, voices, heads, and bristles, all
swinish now, though minds were still unchanged.
So, squealing, in they went. And Kirkê tossed them
acorns, mast, and cornel berries—fodder
for hogs who rut and slumber on the earth.

Down to the ship Eurýlokhos came running.   260
to cry alarm, foul magic doomed his men!
But working with dry lips to speak a word
he could not, being so shaken; blinding tears
welled in his eyes; foreboding filled his heart.
When we were frantic questioning him, at last
we heard the tale: our friends were gone. Said he:

"We went up through the oak scrub where you sent us,
Odysseus, glory of commanders,
until we found a palace in a glade,
a marble house on open ground, and someone   270
singing before her loom a chill, sweet song—
goddess or girl, we could not tell. They hailed her,
and then she stepped through shining doors and said,
"Come, come in!" Like sheep they followed her,
but I saw cruel deceit, and stayed behind.
Then all our fellows vanished. Not a sound,
and nothing stirred, although I watched for hours.'

When I heard this I slung my silver-hilted
broadsword on, and shouldered my long bow,
and said, "Come, take me back the way you came.'   280
But he put both his hands around my knees
in desperate woe, and said in supplication:

"Not back there, O my lord! Oh, leave me here!
You, even you, cannot return, I know it,
I know you cannot bring away our shipmates;
better make sail with these men, quickly too,
and save ourselves from horror while we may.'

But I replied:

                                                      'By heaven, Eurýlokhos,
rest here then; take food and wine;
stay in the black hull's shelter. Let me go,   290
as I see nothing for it but to go.'

I turned and left him, left the shore and ship,
and went up through the woodland hushed and shady
to find the subtle witch in her long hall.
But Hermês met me, with his golden wand,
barring the way—a boy whose lip was downy
in the first bloom of manhood, so he seemed.
He took my hand and spoke as though he knew me:

          'Why take the inland path alone,
          poor seafarer, by hill and dale   300
          upon this island all unknown?
          Your friends are locked in Kirkê's pale;[5]
          all are become like swine to see;
          and if you go to set them free
          you go to stay, and never more make sail
          for your old home upon Thaki.[6]

          But I can tell you what to do
          to come unchanged from Kirkê's power
          and disenthrall your fighting crew:
          take with you to her bower   310
          as amulet, this plant I know—
          it will defeat her horrid show,
          so pure and potent is the flower;
          no mortal herb was ever so.

          Your cup with numbing drops of night
          and evil, stilled of all remorse,
          she will infuse to charm your sight;
          but this great herb with holy force
          will keep your mind and senses clear:
          when she turns cruel, coming near   320
          with her long stick to whip you out of doors,
          then let your cutting blade appear,

[5] An enclosed area.   [6] Ithaka.

Let instant death upon it shine,
and she will cower and yield her bed—
a pleasure you must not decline,
so may her lust and fear bestead
you and your friends, and break her spell;
but make her swear by heaven and hell
no witches' tricks, or else, your harness shed,
you'll be unmanned by her as well.'   330

He bent down glittering for the magic plant
and pulled it up, black root and milky flower—
a *molü* [7] in the language of the gods—
fatigue and pain for mortals to uproot;
but gods do this, and everything, with ease.

Then toward Olympos through the island trees
Hermês departed, and I sought out Kirkê,
my heart high with excitement, beating hard.
Before her mansion in the porch I stood
to call her, all being still. Quick as a cat   340
she opened her bright doors and sighed a welcome;
then I strode after her with heavy heart
down the long hall, and took the chair she gave me,
silver-studded, intricately carved,
made with a low footrest. The lady Kirkê
mixed me a golden cup of honeyed wine,
adding in mischief her unholy drug.
I drank, and the drink failed. But she came forward
aiming a stroke with her long stick, and whispered:

'Down in the sty and snore among the rest!'   350

Without a word, I drew my sharpened sword
and in one bound held it against her throat.
She cried out, then slid under to take my knees,
catching her breath to say, in her distress:

'What champion, of what country, can you be?
Where are your kinsmen and your city?
Are you not sluggish with my wine? Ah, wonder!
Never a mortal man that drank this cup
but when it passed his lips he had succumbed.
Hale must your heart be and your tempered will.   360
Odysseus then you are, O great contender,
of whom the glittering god with golden wand
spoke to me ever, and foretold
the black swift ship would carry you from Troy.
Put up your weapon in the sheath. We two

---

[7] Usually spelled *moly.*

shall mingle and make love upon our bed.
So mutual trust may come of play and love.'

To this I said:

                                 'Kirkê, am I a boy,
that you should make me soft and doting now?
Here in this house you turned my men to swine;   370
now it is I myself you hold, enticing
into your chamber, to your dangerous bed,
to take my manhood when you have me stripped.
I mount no bed of love with you upon it.
Or swear me first a great oath, if I do,
you'll work no more enchantment to my harm.'

She swore at once, outright, as I demanded,
and after she had sworn, and bound herself,
I entered Kirkê's flawless bed of love.

Presently in the hall her maids were busy,   380
the nymphs who waited upon Kirkê: four,
whose cradles were in fountains, under boughs,
or in the glassy seaward-gliding streams.
One came with richly colored rugs to throw
on seat and chairback, over linen covers;
a second pulled the tables out, all silver,
and loaded them with baskets all of gold;
a third mixed wine as tawny-mild as honey
in a bright bowl, and set out golden cups.
The fourth came bearing water, and lit a blaze   390
under a cauldron. By and by it bubbled,
and when the dazzling brazen vessel seethed
she filled a bathtub to my waist, and bathed me,
pouring a soothing blend on head and shoulders,
warming the soreness of my joints away.
When she had done, and smoothed me with sweet oil,
she put a tunic and a cloak around me
and took me to a silver-studded chair
with footrest, all elaborately carven.
Now came a maid to tip a golden jug   400
of water into a silver finger bowl,
and draw a polished table to my side.
The larder mistress brought her tray of loaves
with many savory slices, and she gave
the best, to tempt me. But no pleasure came;
I huddled with my mind elsewhere, oppressed.

Kirkê regarded me, as there I sat
disconsolate, and never touched a crust.
Then she stood over me and chided me:

'Why sit at table mute, Odysseus? 410
Are you mistrustful of my bread and drink?
Can it be treachery that you fear again,
after the gods' great oath I swore for you?'

I turned to her at once, and said:

'Kirkê,

where is the captain who could bear to touch
this banquet, in my place? A decent man
would see his company before him first.
Put heart in me to eat and drink—you may,
by freeing my companions. I must see them.'

But Kirkê had already turned away. 420
Her long staff in her hand, she left the hall
and opened up the sty. I saw her enter,
driving those men turned swine to stand before me.
She stroked them, each in turn, with some new chrism;[8]
and then, behold! their bristles fell away,
the course pelt grown upon them by her drug
melted away, and they were men again,
younger, more handsome, taller than before.
Their eyes upon me, each one took my hands,
and wild regret and longing pierced them through, 430
so the room rang with sobs, and even Kirkê
pitied that transformation. Exquisite
the goddess looked as she stood near me, saying:

'Son of Laërtês and the gods of old,
Odysseus, master mariner and soldier,
go to the sea beach and sea-breasting ship;
drag it ashore, full length upon the land;
stow gear and stores in rock-holes under cover;
return; be quick; bring all your dear companions.'

Now, being a man, I could not help consenting. 440
So I went down to the sea beach and the ship,
where I found all my other men on board,
weeping, in despair along the benches.
Sometimes in farmyards when the cows return
well fed from pasture to the barn, one sees
the pens give way before the calves in tumult,
breaking through to cluster about their mothers,
bumping together, bawling. Just that way
my crew poured round me when they saw me come—
their faces wet with tears as if they saw 450
their homeland, and the crags of Ithaka,

---

[8]An oil, usually having sacred or supernatural properties.

even the very town where they were born.
And weeping still they all cried out in greeting:

'Prince, what joy this is, your safe return!
Now Ithaka seems here, and we in Ithaka!
But tell us now, what death befell our friends?'

And, speaking gently, I replied:

'First we must get the ship high on the shingle,
and stow our gear and stores in clefts of rock
for cover. Then come follow me, to see   460
your shipmates in the magic house of Kirkê
eating and drinking, endlessly regaled.'

They turned back, as commanded, to this work;
only one lagged, and tried to hold the others:
Eurýlokhos it was, who blurted out:

'Where now, poor remnants? is it devil's work
you long for? Will you go to Kirkê's hall?
Swine, wolves, and lions she will make us all,
beasts of her courtyard, bound by her enchantment.
Remember those the Kyklops held, remember   470
shipmates who made that visit with Odysseus!
The daring man! They died for his foolishness!'

When I heard this I had a mind to draw
the blade that swung against my side and chop him,
bowling his head upon the ground—kinsman
or no kinsman, close to me though he was.
But others came between, saying, to stop me,

'Prince, we can leave him, if you say the word;
let him stay here on guard. As for ourselves,
show us the way to Kirkê's magic hall.'   480

So all turned inland, leaving shore and ship,
and Eurýlokhos—he, too, came on behind,
fearing the rough edge of my tongue. Meanwhile
at Kirkê's hands the rest were gently bathed,
anointed with sweet oil, and dressed afresh
in tunics and new cloaks with fleecy linings.
We found them all at supper when we came.
But greeting their old friends once more, the crew
could not hold back their tears; and now again
the rooms rang with sobs. Then Kirkê, loveliest   490
of all immortals, came to counsel me:

'Son of Laërtês and the gods of old,
Odysseus, master mariner and soldier,

enough of weeping fits. I know—I, too—
what you endured upon the inhuman sea,
what odds you met on land from hostile men.
Remain with me, and share my meat and wine;
restore behind your ribs those gallant hearts
that served you in the old days, when you sailed
from stony Ithaka. Now parched and spent, 500
your cruel wandering is all you think of,
never of joy, after so many blows.'

As we were men we could not help consenting.
So day by day we lingered, feasting long
on roasts and wine, until a year grew fat.
But when the passing months and wheeling seasons
brought the long summery days, the pause of summer,
my shipmates one day summoned me and said:

'Captain, shake off this trance, and think of home—
if home indeed awaits us,

if we shall ever see 510
your own well-timbered hall on Ithaka.'

They made me feel a pang, and I agreed.
That day, and all day long, from dawn to sundown,
we feasted on roast meat and ruddy wine,
and after sunset when the dusk came on
my men slept in the shadowy hall, but I
went through the dark to Kirkê's flawless bed
and took the goddess' knees in supplication,
urging, as she bent to hear:

'O Kirkê,
now you must keep your promise; it is time. 520
Help me make sail for home. Day after day
my longing quickens, and my company
give me no peace, but wear my heart away
pleading when you are not at hand to hear.'

The loveliest of goddesses replied:

'Son of Laërtês and the gods of old,
Odysseus, master mariner and soldier,
you shall not stay here longer against your will;
but home you may not go
unless you take a strange way round and come 530
to the cold homes of Death and pale Perséphonê.[9]
You shall hear prophecy from the rapt shade

---

[9] *Death* refers to Hades, ruler of the land of the dead. *Perséphonê* was his consort.

of blind Teirêsias[10] of Thebes, forever
charged with reason even among the dead;
to him alone, of all the flitting ghosts,
Perséphonê has given a mind undarkened.'

At this I felt a weight like stone within me,
and, moaning, pressed my length against the bed,
with no desire to see the daylight more.
But when I had wept and tossed and had my fill   540
of this despair, at last I answered her:

'Kirkê, who pilots me upon this journey?
No man has ever sailed to the land of Death.'

That loveliest of goddesses replied:

'Son of Laërtês and the gods of old,
Odysseus, master of land ways and sea ways,
feel no dismay because you lack a pilot;
only set up your mast and haul your canvas
to the fresh blowing North; sit down and steer,
and hold that wind, even to the bourne of Ocean,   550
Perséphonê's deserted strand and grove,
dusky with poplars and the drooping willow.
Run through the tide-rip, bring your ship to shore,
land there, and find the crumbling homes of Death.
Here, toward the Sorrowing Water, run the streams
of Wailing, out of Styx, and quenchless Burning—
torrents[11] that join in thunder at the Rock.
Here then, great soldier, setting foot obey me:
dig a well shaft a forearm square; pour out
libations round it to the unnumbered dead: 560
sweet milk and honey, then sweet wine, and last
clear water, scattering handfulls of white barley.
Pray now, with all your heart, to the faint dead;
swear you will sacrifice your finest heifer,
at home in Ithaka, and burn for them
her tenderest parts in sacrifice; and vow
to the lord Teirêsias, apart from all,
a black lamb, handsomest of all your flock—
thus to appease the nations of the dead.
Then slash a black ewe's throat, and a black ram,   570
facing the gloom of Erebos;[12] but turn
your head away toward Ocean. You shall see, now

[10] A famous soothsayer who figures in many Greek myths and legends; see, for example,
Sophocles' *Oedipus the King.*
[11] The rivers of Hades. The Sorrowing Water is Acheron; the river of Wailing is Cocytus;
the Burning river is Phlegethon.
[12] Part of the realm of Hades; the equivalent of primitive darkness. Also spelled *Erebus.*

souls of the buried dead in shadowy hosts,
and now you must call out to your companions
to flay those sheep the bronze knife has cut down,
for offerings, burnt flesh to those below,
to sovereign Death and pale Perséphonê.
Meanwhile draw sword from hip, crouch down, ward off
the surging phantoms from the bloody pit
until you know the presence of Teirêsias. 580
He will come soon, great captain; be it he
who gives you course and distance for your sailing
homeward across the cold fish-breeding sea.'

As the goddess ended, Dawn came stitched in gold.
Now Kirkê dressed me in my shirt and cloak,
put on a gown of subtle tissue, silvery,
then wound a golden belt about her waist
and veiled her head in linen,
while I went through the hall to rouse my crew.
I bent above each one, and gently said: 590

'Wake from your sleep: no more sweet slumber. Come,
we sail: the Lady Kirkê so ordains it.'

They were soon up, and ready at that word;
but I was not to take my men unharmed
from this place, even from this. Among them all
the youngest was Elpênor—
no mainstay in a fight nor very clever—
and this one, having climbed on Kirkê's roof
to taste the cool night, fell asleep with wine.
Waked by our morning voices, and the tramp 600
of men below, he started up, but missed
his footing on the long steep backward ladder
and fell that height headlong. The blow smashed
the nape cord, and his ghost fled to the dark.
But I was outside, walking with the rest,
saying:

　　　　　　　'Homeward you think we must be sailing
to our own land; no, elsewhere is the voyage
Kirkê has laid upon me. We must go
to the cold homes of Death and pale Perséphonê
to hear Teirêsias tell of time to come.' 610

They felt so stricken, upon hearing this,
they sat down wailing loud, and tore their hair.
But nothing came of giving way to grief.
Down to the shore and ship at last we went,
bowed with anguish, cheeks all wet with tears,
to find that Kirkê had been there before us

and tied nearby a black ewe and a ram:
she had gone by like air.
For who could see the passage of a goddess
unless she wished his mortal eyes aware?   620

BOOK ELEVEN: A GATHERING OF SHADES

We bore down on the ship at the sea's edge
and launched her on the salt immortal sea,
stepping our mast and spar in the black ship;
embarked the ram and ewe and went aboard
in tears, with bitter and sore dread upon us.
But now a breeze came up for us astern—
a canvas-bellying landbreeze, hale shipmate
sent by the singing nymph with sun-bright hair;
so we made fast the braces, took our thwarts,
and let the wind and steersman work the ship   10
with full sail spread all day above our coursing,
till the sun dipped, and all the ways grew dark
upon the fathomless unresting sea.

                                                          By night
our ship ran onward toward the Ocean's[1] bourne,
the realm and region of the Men of Winter,
hidden in mist and cloud. Never the flaming
eye of Hêlios lights on those men
at morning, when he climbs the sky of stars,
nor in descending earthward out of heaven;
ruinous night being rove[2] over those wretches.   20
We made the land, put ram and ewe ashore,
and took our way along the Ocean stream
to find the place foretold for us by Kirkê.
There Perimêdês and Eurýlokhos
pinioned the sacred beasts. With my drawn blade
I spaded up the votive pit, and poured
libations round it to the unnumbered dead:
sweet milk and honey, then sweet wine, and last
clear water; and I scattered barley down.
Then I addressed the blurred and breathless dead,   30
vowing to slaughter my best heifer for them
before she calved, at home in Ithaka,
and burn the choice bits on the altar fire;
as for Teirêsias, I swore to sacrifice
a black lamb, handsomest of all our flock.

---

[1] The great river believed to encompass the entire (flat) world. In the present passage, Homer
locates Hades in the north and not, as is more usual, beneath the surface of the earth.
[2] Fastened; a nautical term. Hêlios is the sun god.

Thus to assuage the nations of the dead
I pledged these rites, then slashed the lamb and ewe,
letting their black blood stream into the wellpit.
Now the souls gathered, stirring out of Erebos,
brides and young men, and men grown old in pain,   40
and tender girls whose hearts were new to grief;
many were there, too, torn by brazen lanceheads,
battle-slain, bearing still their bloody gear.
From every side they came and sought the pit
with rustling cries; and I grew sick with fear.
But presently I gave command to my officers
to flay those sheep the bronze cut down, and make
burnt offerings of flesh to the gods below—
to sovereign Death, to pale Perséphonê.
Meanwhile I crouched with my drawn sword to keep   50
the surging phantoms from the bloody pit
till I should know the presence of Teirêsias.

One shade came first—Elpênor, of our company,
who lay unburied still on the wide earth
as we had left him—dead in Kirkê's hall,
untouched, unmourned, when other cares compelled us.
Now when I saw him there I wept for pity
and called out to him:

                  'How is this, Elpênor,
how could you journey to the western gloom
swifter afoot than I in the black lugger?'   60

He sighed, and answered:

                'Son of great Laërtês,
Odysseus, master mariner and soldier,
bad luck shadowed me, and no kindly power;
ignoble death I drank with so much wine.
I slept on Kirkê's roof, then could not see
the long steep backward ladder, coming down,
and fell that height. My neck bone, buckled under,
snapped, and my spirit found this well of dark.
Now hear the grace I pray for, in the name
of those back in the world, not here—your wife   70
and father, he who gave you bread in childhood,
and your own child, your only son, Telémakhos,
long ago left at home.

                  When you make sail
and put these lodgings of dim Death behind,
you will moor ship, I know, upon Aiaia Island;
there, O my lord, remember me, I pray,
do not abandon me unwept, unburied,

to tempt the gods' wrath,[3] while you sail for home;
but fire my corpse, and all the gear I had,
and build a cairn for me above the breakers—   80
an unknown sailor's mark for men to come.
Heap up the mound there, and implant upon it
the oar I pulled in life with my companions.'

He ceased, and I replied:

                                                             'Unhappy spirit,
I promise you the barrow and the burial.'

So we conversed, and grimly, at a distance,
with my long sword between, guarding the blood,
while the faint image of the lad spoke on.

Now came the soul of Antikleía, dead,
my mother, daughter of Autólykos,   90
dead now, though living still when I took ship
for holy Troy. Seeing this ghost I grieved,
but held her off, through pang on pang of tears,
till I should know the presence of Teirêsias.
Soon from the dark that prince of Thebes came forward
bearing a golden staff; and he addressed me:

'Son of Laërtês and the gods of old,
Odysseus, master of land ways and sea ways,
why leave the blazing sun, O man of woe,
to see the cold dead and the joyless region?   100
Stand clear, put up your sword;
let me but taste of blood, I shall speak true.'

At this I stepped aside, and in the scabbard
let my long sword ring home to the pommel silver,
as he bent down to the sombre blood. Then spoke
the prince of those with gift of speech:

                                                             'Great captain,
a fair wind and the honey lights of home
are all you seek. But anguish lies ahead;
the god who thunders on the land prepares it,
not to be shaken from your track, implacable,   110
in rancor for the son whose eye you blinded.
One narrow strait may take you through his blows:
denial of yourself, restraint of shipmates.
When you make landfall on Thrinákia[4] first
and quit the violet sea, dark on the land

---

[3] The wrath of the gods would be provoked if a body on earth was left unburied and visible.

[4] Sicily. For the outcome of this prophetic warning about molesting the sun god's cattle, see Book XII.

you'll find the grazing herds of Hêlios
by whom all things are seen, all speech is known.
Avoid those kine, hold fast to your intent,
and hard seafaring brings you all to Ithaka.
But if you raid the beeves, I see destruction 120
for ship and crew. Though you survive alone,
bereft of all companions, lost for years,
under strange sail shall you come home, to find
your own house filled with trouble: insolent men
eating your livestock as they court your lady.
Aye, you shall make those men atone in blood!
But after you have dealt out death—in open
combat or by stealth—to all the suitors,
go overland on foot, and take an oar,
until one day you come where men have lived 130
with meat unsalted, never known the sea,
nor seen seagoing ships, with crimson bows
and oars that fledge light hulls for dipping flight.
The spot will soon be plain to you, and I
can tell you how: some passerby will say,
"What winnowing fan[5] is that upon your shoulder?"
Halt, and implant your smooth oar in the turf
and make fair sacrifice to Lord Poseidon:
a ram, a bull, a great buck boar; turn back,
and carry out pure hekatombs at home 140
to all wide heaven's lords, the undying gods,
to each in order. Then a seaborne death
soft as this hand of mist will come upon you
when you are wearied out with rich old age,
your country folk in blessed peace around you.
And all this shall be just as I foretell.'

When he had done, I said at once,

                                        'Teirêsias,

my life runs on then as the gods have spun it.
But come, now, tell me this; make this thing clear:
I see my mother's ghost among the dead 150
sitting in silence near the blood. Not once
has she glanced this way toward her son, nor spoken.
Tell me, my lord,
may she in some way come to know my presence?'

To this he answered:

                                'I shall make it clear
in a few words and simply. Any dead man
whom you allow to enter where the blood is

---

[5] A tool used to separate grain from chaff.

will speak to you, and speak the truth; but those
deprived will grow remote again and fade.'

When he had prophesied, Teirêsias' shade   160
retired lordly to the halls of Death;
but I stood fast until my mother stirred,
moving to sip the black blood; then she knew me
and called out sorrowfully to me:

                                                              'Child,
how could you cross alive into this gloom
at the world's end?—No sight for living eyes;
great currents run between, desolate waters,
the Ocean first, where no man goes a journey
without ship's timber under him.

                                                         Say, now,
is it from Troy, still wandering, after years,   170
that you come here with ship and company?
Have you not gone at all to Ithaka?
Have you not seen your lady in your hall?'

She put these questions, and I answered her:

'Mother, I came here, driven to the land of death
in want of prophecy from Teirêsias' shade;
nor have I yet coasted Akhaia's hills
nor touched my own land, but have had hard roving
since first I joined Lord Agamémnon's host
by sea for Ilion, the wild horse country,   180
to fight the men of Troy.
But come now, tell me this, and tell me clearly,
what was the bane that pinned you down in Death?
Some ravaging long illness, or mild arrows
a-flying down one day from Artemis?[6]
Tell me of Father, tell me of the son
I left behind me; have they still my place,
my honors, or have other men assumed them?
Do they not say that I shall come no more?
And tell me of my wife: how runs her thought,   190
still with her child, still keeping our domains,
or bride again to the best of the Akhaians?'

To this my noble mother quickly answered:

'Still with her child indeed she is, poor heart,
still in your palace hall. Forlorn her nights
and days go by, her life used up in weeping.
But no man takes your honored place. Telémakhos
has care of all your garden plots and fields,

[6] As archer goddess, Artemis provided the gift of painless death. Among other things, she
was protectress of the weak.

and holds the public honor of a magistrate,
feasting and being feasted. But your father 200
is country bound and comes to town no more.
He owns no bedding, rugs, or fleecy mantles,
but lies down, winter nights, among the slaves,
rolled in old cloaks for cover, near the embers.
Or when the heat comes at the end of summer,
the fallen leaves, all round his vineyard plot,
heaped into windrows,[7] make his lowly bed.
He lies now even so, with aching heart,
and longs for your return, while age comes on him.
So I, too, pined away, so doom befell me, 210
not that the keen-eyed huntress with her shafts
had marked me down and shot to kill me; not
that illness overtook me—no true illness
wasting the body to undo the spirit;
only my loneliness for you, Odysseus,
for your kind heart and counsel, gentle Odysseus,
took my own life away.'

                                                    I bit my lip,
rising perplexed, with longing to embrace her,
and tried three times, putting my arms around her,
but she went sifting through my hands, impalpable 220
as shadows are, and wavering like a dream.
Now this embittered all the pain I bore,
and I cried in the darkness:

                                        'O my mother,
will you not stay, be still, here in my arms,
may we not, in this place of Death, as well,
hold one another, touch with love, and taste
salt tears' relief, the twinge of welling tears?
Or is this all hallucination, sent
against me by the iron queen, Perséphonê,
to make me groan again?'

                                        My noble mother 230
answered quickly:

                                        'O my child—alas,
most sorely tried of men—great Zeus's daughter,
Perséphonê, knits no illusion for you.
All mortals meet this judgment when they die.
No flesh and bone are here, none bound by sinew,
since the bright-hearted pyre consumed them down—
the white bones long exanimate[8]—to ash;
dreamlike the soul flies, insubstantial.
You must crave sunlight soon.

[7]Drifted heaps, as of leaves or snow.
[8]Separated from the vital spirit, or "soul."

                                                        Note all things strange
seen here, to tell your lady in after days.'   240

So went our talk; then other shadows came,
ladies in company, sent by Perséphonê—
consorts or daughters of illustrious men—
crowding about the black blood.
                                                        I took thought
how best to separate and question them,
and saw no help for it, but drew once more
the long bright edge of broadsword from my hip,
that none should sip the blood in company
but one by one, in order; so it fell
that each declared her lineage and name.   250

Here was great loveliness of ghosts! I saw
before them all, that princess of great ladies,
Tyro,[9] Salmoneus' daughter, as she told me,
and queen to Krêtheus, a son of Aiolos.
She had gone daft for the river Enipeus,
most graceful of all running streams, and ranged
all day by Enipeus' limpid side,
whose form the foaming girdler of the islands,
the god who makes earth tremble, took and so
lay down with her where he went flooding seaward,   260
their bower a purple billow, arching round
to hide them in a sea-vale, god and lady.
Now when his pleasure was complete, the god
spoke to her softly, holding fast her hand:

'Dear mortal, go in joy! At the turn of seasons,
winter to summer, you shall bear me sons;
no lovemaking of gods can be in vain.
Nurse our sweet children tenderly, and rear them.
Home with you now, and hold your tongue, and tell
no one your lover's name—though I am yours,   270
Poseidon, lord of surf that makes earth tremble.'

He plunged away into the deep sea swell,
and she grew big with Pelias and Neleus,
powerful vassals, in their time, of Zeus.
Pelias lived on broad Iolkos seaboard
rich in flocks, and Neleus at Pylos.
As for the sons borne by that queen of women
to Krêtheus, their names were Aison, Pherês,
and Amytháon, expert charioteer.

---

[9] A queen of Thessaly, enamored of the river god Enipeus, in whose guise Poseidon made
love to her. She bore him two sons: Pelias, the usurper-king of Iolkos (see headnote to Euripides'
Medea), and Neleus (the father of Nestor, who appears earlier in the *Odyssey*).

Next after her I saw Antiopê,   280
daughter of Ásopos. She too could boast
a god for lover, having lain with Zeus
and borne two sons to him: Amphion and
Zêthos, who founded Thebes, the upper city,
and built the ancient citadel. They sheltered
no life upon that plain, for all their power,
without a fortress wall.

                                  And next I saw
Amphitrion's true wife, Alkmênê,[10] mother,
as all men know, of lionish Heraklês,
conceived when she lay close in Zeus's arms;   290
and Megarê, high-hearted Kreon's daughter,
wife of Amphitrion's unwearying son.

I saw the mother of Oidipous, Epikastê,[11]
whose great unwitting deed it was
to marry her own son. He took that prize
from a slain father; presently the gods
brought all to light that made the famous story.
But by their fearsome wills he kept his throne
in dearest Thebes, all through his evil days,
while she descended to the place of Death,   300
god of the locked and iron door. Steep down
from a high rafter, throttled in her noose,
she swung, carried away by pain, and left him
endless agony from a mother's Furies.

And I saw Khloris, that most lovely lady,
whom for her beauty in the olden time
Neleus wooed with countless gifts, and married.
She was the youngest daughter of Amphion,
son of Iasos. In those days he held
power at Orkhómenos, over the Minyai.   310
At Pylos then as queen she bore her children—
Nestor, Khromios, Periklýmenos,
and Pêro, too, who turned the heads of men
with her magnificence. A host of princes
from nearby lands came courting her; but Neleus
would hear of no one, not unless the suitor
could drive the steers of giant Íphiklos
from Phylakê—longhorns, broad in the brow,

---

[10] She is a "true wife" because Zeus had adopted the disguise of her husband, Amphitrion, in order to lie with her; the offspring of this union was Heraklês (Hercules).

[11] More commonly known as *Jocasta*. She was mother and wife of the Theban ruler Oidipous (Oedipus). The story, in which he unwittingly kills his father and marries his mother, is best known through Sophocles' drama *Oedipus the King*. Jocasta committed suicide after learning that she had been guilty of incest.

so fierce that one man only, a diviner,[12]
offered to round them up. But bitter fate   320
saw him bound hand and foot by savage herdsmen.
Then days and months grew full and waned, the year
went wheeling round, the seasons came again,
before at last the power of Íphiklos,
relenting, freed the prisoner, who foretold
all things to him. So Zeus's will was done.

And I saw Lêda,[13] wife of Tyndareus,
upon whom Tyndareus had sired twins
indomitable: Kastor, tamer of horses,
and Polydeukês, best in the boxing ring.   330
Those two live still, though life-creating earth
embraces them: even in the underworld
honored as gods by Zeus, each day in turn
one comes alive, the other dies again.

Then after Lêda to my vision came
the wife of Aloeus, Iphimedeia,
proud that she once had held the flowing sea
and borne him sons, thunderers for a day,
the world-renowned Otos and Ephialtês.
Never were men on such a scale   340
bred on the plowlands and the grainlands, never
so magnificent any, after Orion.
At nine years old they towered nine fathoms tall,
nine cubits in the shoulders, and they promised
furor upon Olympos, heaven broken by battle cries,
the day they met the gods in arms.

                                                                      With Ossa's

mountain peak they meant to crown Olympos
and over Ossa Pelion's[14] forest pile
for footholds up the sky. As giants grown
they might have done it, but the bright son[15] of Zeus   350
by Lêto of the smooth braid shot them down
while they were boys unbearded; no dark curls
clustered yet from temples to the chin.

---

[12] Melampous, who was gifted with prophetic power; the giant released him in return for
his services as a prophet. In some versions of the myth, Melampous performs the described
feats as a service to his brother Bias, who courts and eventually marries Pêro.

[13] Mother, by Zeus, of Helen of Troy. By her mortal husband, Tyndareus, she is also mother
of Agamémnon's wife, Klytaimnéstra, and of the twins named Kastor and Polydeukês (better
known in later myth and in astronomy as the "Gemini," Castor and Pollux). The twins are
granted life after death but can never be both alive at the same time. In some versions of the
myth the twins' father is Zeus.

[14] The mountains Ossa and Pelion are near Olympos, where Zeus and his generation of
deities dwell.

[15] Apollo.

Then I saw Phaidra, Prokris; and Ariadnê,
daughter of Minos,[16] the grim king. Theseus took her
aboard with him from Krete for the terraced land
of ancient Athens; but he had no joy of her.
Artemis killed her on the Isle of Dia
at a word from Dionysos.

                              Maira, then,
and Klymênê, and that detested queen,   360
Eríphylê,[17] who betrayed her lord for gold . . .
but how name all the women I beheld there,
daughters and wives of kings? The starry night
wanes long before I close.

                     Here, or aboard ship,
amid the crew, the hour for sleep has come.
Our sailing is the gods' affair and yours."

Then he fell silent. Down the shadowy hall
the enchanted banqueters were still. Only
the queen with ivory pale arms, Arêtê, spoke,
saying to all the silent men:

                        "Phaiákians,   370
how does he stand, now, in your eyes, this captain,
the look and bulk of him, the inward poise?
He is my guest, but each one shares that honor.
Be in no haste to send him on his way
or scant your bounty in his need. Remember
how rich, by heaven's will, your possessions are."

Then Ekhenêos, the old soldier, eldest
of all Phaiákians, added his word:

"Friends, here was nothing but our own thought spoken,
the mark hit square. Our duties to her majesty.   380
For what is to be said and done,
we wait upon Alkínoös' command."

At this the king's voice rang:

                    "I so command—
as sure as it is I who, while I live,

---

[16] King of Krete (Crete), in some myths regarded as a just man who posthumously became a judge of the dead. In other myths he is a savage ruler who demanded that Athens provide victims for human sacrifice to the monstrous bull called the Minotaur. The Athenian ruler Theseus, husband of Phaidra (Phaedra), killed the Minotaur with the aid of Ariadnê, her sister. After eloping with Ariadnê, Theseus abandoned her on the island of Dia (Naxos). Ariadnê then incurred the anger of the god Dionysos, though in most versions of the myth she wedded him.

[17] Corrupted by Polyneices (son of Oidipous of Thebes) with the gift of a gold necklace, Eríphylê treacherously persuaded her husband, Amphiaraos, to take part in an ill-fated assault on Thebes in which he was killed.

rule the sea rovers of Phaiákia. Our friend
longs to put out for home, but let him be
content to rest here one more day, until
I see all gifts bestowed. And every man
will take thought for his launching and his voyage,
I most of all, for I am master here."   390

Odysseus, the great tactician, answered:

"Alkínoös, king and admiration of men,
even a year's delay, if you should urge it,
in loading gifts and furnishing for sea—
I too could wish it; better far that I
return with some largesse of wealth about me—
I shall be thought more worthy of love and courtesy
by every man who greets me home in Ithaka."

The king said:

                                    "As to that, one word, Odysseus:
from all we see, we take you for no swindler—   400
though the dark earth be patient of so many,
scattered everywhere, baiting their traps with lies
of old times and of places no one knows.
You speak with art, but your intent is honest.
The Argive troubles, and your own troubles,
you told as a poet would, a man who knows the world.
But now come tell me this: among the dead
did you meet any of your peers, companions
who sailed with you and met their doom at Troy?
Here's a long night—an endless night—before us,   410
and no time yet for sleep, not in this hall.
Recall the past deeds and the strange adventures.
I could stay up until the sacred Dawn
as long as you might wish to tell your story."

Odysseus the great tactician answered:

"Alkínoös, king and admiration of men,
there is a time for story telling; there is
also a time for sleep. But even so,
if, indeed, listening be still your pleasure,
I must not grudge my part. Other and sadder   420
tales there are to tell, of my companions,
of some who came through all the Trojan spears,
clangor and groan of war,
only to find a brutal death at home—
and a bad wife behind it.

                                                      After Perséphonê,
icy and pale, dispersed the shades of women,
the soul of Agamémnon, son of Atreus,

came before me, sombre in the gloom,
and others gathered round, all who were with him
when death and doom struck in Aegísthos' hall. 430
Sipping the black blood, the tall shade perceived me,
and cried out sharply, breaking into tears;
then tried to stretch his hands toward me, but could not,
being bereft of all the reach and power
he once felt in the great torque of his arms.
Gazing at him, and stirred, I wept for pity,
and spoke across to him:

                    'O son of Atreus,
illustrious Lord Marshal, Agamémnon,
what was the doom that brought you low in death?
Were you at sea, aboard ship, and Poseidon 440
blew up a wicked squall to send you under,
or were you cattle-raiding on the mainland
or in a fight for some strongpoint, or women,
when the foe hit you to your mortal hurt?'

But he replied at once:

                    'Son of Laërtês,
Odysseus, master of land ways and sea ways,
neither did I go down with some good ship
in any gale Poseidon blew, nor die
upon the mainland, hurt by foes in battle.
It was Aigísthos who designed my death, 450
he and my heartless wife,[18] and killed me, after
feeding me, like an ox felled at the trough.
That was my miserable end—and with me
my fellows butchered, like so many swine
killed for some troop, or feast, or wedding banquet
in a great landholder's household. In your day
you have seen men, and hundreds, die in war,
in the bloody press, or downed in single combat,
but these were murders you would catch your breath at:
think of us fallen, all our throats cut, winebowl 460
brimming, tables laden on every side,
while blood ran smoking over the whole floor.
In my extremity I heard Kassandra,[19]
Priam's daughter, piteously crying
as the traitress Klytaimnéstra made to kill her
along with me. I heaved up from the ground
and got my hands around the blade, but she

---

[18] In Agamémnon's version here, his wife (as in Aeschylus' *Oresteia*) bears a greater responsibility for the murder than in the version outlined in Book IV.

[19] A Trojan princess and prophetess. Agamémnon brought her home from Troy as a slave. Also spelled *Cassandra*.

eluded me, that whore. Nor would she close
my two eyes^{20} as my soul swam to the underworld
or shut my lips. There is no being more fell,   470
more bestial than a wife in such an action,
and what an action that one planned!
The murder of her husband and her lord.
Great god, I thought my children and my slaves
at least would give me welcome. But that woman,
plotting a thing so low, defiled herself
and all her sex, all women yet to come,
even those few who may be virtuous.'

He paused then, and I answered:

                                                                'Foul and dreadful.

That was the way that Zeus who views the wide world   480
vented his hatred on the sons of Atreus—
intrigues of women, even from the start.

                                                                        Myriads

died by Helen's fault, and Klytaimnéstra
plotted against you half the world away.'

And he at once said:

                                                                'Let it be a warning

even to you. Indulge a woman never,
and never tell her all you know. Some things
a man may tell, some he should cover up.
Not that I see a risk for you, Odysseus,
of death at your wife's hands. She is too wise,   490
too clear-eyed, sees alternatives too well,
Penélopê, Ikários' daughter—
that young bride whom we left behind—think of it!—
when we sailed off to war. The baby boy
still cradled at her breast—now he must be
a grown man, and a lucky one. By heaven,
you'll see him yet, and he'll embrace his father
with old fashioned respect, and rightly.

                                                                        My own

lady never let me glut my eyes
on my own son, but bled me to death first.   500
One thing I will advise, on second thought;
stow it away and ponder it.

                                                                Land your ship

in secret on your island; give no warning.
The day of faithful wives is gone forever.

---

^{20} That is, she would not perform the customary funeral rites.

But tell me, have you any word at all
about my son's[21] life? Gone to Orkhómenos
or sandy Pylos, can he be? Or waiting
with Meneláos in the plain of Sparta?
Death on earth has not yet taken Orestês.'

But I could only answer:

'Son of Atreus   510
why do you ask these questions of me? Neither
news of home have I, nor news of him,
alive or dead. And empty words are evil.'

So we exchanged our speech, in bitterness,
weighed down by grief, and tears welled in our eyes,
when there appeared the spirit of Akhilleus,
son of Peleus; then Patróklos' shade,
and then Antílokhos, and then Aias,
first among all the Danaans in strength
and bodily beauty, next to prince Akhilleus.   520
Now that great runner, grandson of Aíakhos,
recognized me and called across to me:

'Son of Laërtês and the gods of old,
Odysseus, master mariner and soldier,
old knife, what next? What greater feat remains
for you to put your mind on, after this?
How did you find your way down to the dark
where these dimwitted dead are camped forever,
the after images of used-up men?'

I answered:

'Akhilleus, Peleus' son, strongest of all   530
among the Akhaians, I had need of foresight
such as Teirêsias alone could give
to help me, homeward bound for the crags of Ithaka.
I have not yet coasted Akhaia, not yet
touched my land; my life is all adversity.
But was there ever a man more blest by fortune
than you, Akhilleus? Can there ever be?
We ranked you with immortals in your lifetime,
we Argives did, and here your power is royal
among the dead men's shades. Think, then, Akhilleus: 540
you need not be so pained by death.'

To this
he answered swiftly:

---

[21]Agamémnon asks about Orestês, who avenged his father's murder.

'Let me hear no smooth talk
of death from you, Odysseus, light of councils.
Better, I say, to break sod as a farm hand
for some poor country man, on iron rations,
than lord it over all the exhausted dead.
Tell me, what news of the prince my son:[22] did he
come after me to make a name in battle
or could it be he did not? Do you know
if rank and honor still belong to Peleus[23]   550
in the towns of the Myrmidons? Or now, may be,
Hellas and Phthia[24] spurn him, seeing old age
fetters him, hand and foot. I cannot help him
under the sun's rays, cannot be that man
I was on Troy's wide seaboard, in those days
when I made bastion for the Argives
and put an army's best men in the dust.
Were I but whole again, could I go now
to my father's house, one hour would do to make
my passion and my hands no man could hold   560
hateful to any who shoulder him aside.'

Now when he paused I answered:

                                            'Of all that—
of Peleus' life, that is—I know nothing;
but happily I can tell you the whole story
of Neoptólemos, as you require.
In my own ship I brought him out from Skyros
to join the Akhaians under arms.

                                    And I can tell you,

in every council before Troy thereafter
your son spoke first and always to the point;
no one but Nestor and I could out-debate him.   570
And when we formed against the Trojan line
he never hung back in the mass, but ranged
far forward of his troops—no man could touch him
for gallantry. Aye, scores went down before him
in hard fights man to man. I shall not tell
all about each, or name them all—the long
roster of enemies he put out of action,
taking the shock of charges on the Argives.
But what a champion his lance ran through
in Eurýpulos[25] the son of Télephos! Keteians   580
in throngs around that captain also died—

---

[22] Neoptólemos, or Pyrrhus, who was brought to the Trojan War after his father's death
and killed Priam, the Trojan king.
[23] Akhilleus' father.
[24] Greece and Peleus' kingdom.
[25] Leader of a force persuaded to join the war in support of the Trojans.

all because Priam's gifts had won his mother
to send the lad to battle; and I thought
Memnon alone in splendor ever outshone him.

But one fact more: while our picked Argive crew
still rode that hollow horse Epeios built,
and when the whole thing lay with me, to open
the trapdoor of the ambuscade or not,
at that point our Danaan lords and soldiers
wiped their eyes, and their knees began to quake, 590
all but Neoptólemos. I never saw
his tanned cheek change color or his hand
brush one tear away. Rather he prayed me,
hand on hilt, to sortie, and he gripped
his tough spear, bent on havoc for the Trojans.
And when we had pierced and sacked Priam's tall city
he loaded his choice plunder and embarked
with no scar on him; not a spear had grazed him
nor the sword's edge in close work—common wounds
one gets in war. Arês in his mad fits 600
knows no favorites.'

                                        But I said no more,
for he had gone off striding the field of asphodel,[26]
the ghost of our great runner, Akhilleus Aiákidês,
glorying in what I told him of his son.

Now other souls of mournful dead stood by,
each with his troubled questioning, but one
remained alone, apart: the son of Télamon,
Aîas, it was—the great shade burning still[27]
because I had won favor on the beachhead
in rivalry over Akhilleus' arms. 610
The Lady Thetis, mother of Akhilleus,
laid out for us the dead man's battle gear,
and Trojan children, with Athena,
named the Danaan fittest to own them. Would
god I had not borne the palm that day!
For earth took Aîas then to hold forever,
the handsomest and, in all feats of war,
noblest of the Danaans after Akhilleus.
Gently therefore I called across to him:

'Aîas, dear son of royal Télamon, 620
you would not then forget, even in death,

---

[26] A flower, possibly a variety of narcissus.
[27] After the death of Akhilleus, the "greater" Aîas (Ajax) and Odysseus had been rival claimants for Akhilleus' weapons; when the arms were awarded to Odysseus, Aîas killed himself.

your fury with me over those accurst
calamitous arms?—and so they were, a bane
sent by the gods upon the Argive host.
For when you died by your own hand we lost
a tower, formidable in war. All we Akhaians
mourn you forever, as we do Akhilleus;
and no one bears the blame but Zeus.
He fixed that doom for you because he frowned
on the whole expedition of our spearmen.   630
My lord, come nearer, listen to our story!
Conquer your indignation and your pride.'

But he gave no reply, and turned away,
following other ghosts toward Erebos.
Who knows if in that darkness he might still
have spoken, and I answered?
                                                        But my heart
longed, after this, to see the dead elsewhere.

And now there came before my eyes Minos,
the son of Zeus, enthroned, holding a golden staff,
dealing out justice among ghostly pleaders   640
arrayed about the broad doorways of Death.

And then I glimpsed Orion, the huge hunter,
gripping his club, studded with bronze, unbreakable,
with wild beasts he had overpowered in life
on lonely mountainsides, now brought to bay
on fields of asphodel.
                                                        And I saw Títyos,
the son of Gaia, lying
abandoned over nine square rods of plain.
Vultures, hunched above him, left and right,
rifling his belly, stabbed into the liver,   650
and he could never push them off.
                                                        This hulk
had once committed rape of Zeus's mistress,
Lêto, in her glory, when she crossed
the open grass of Panopeus toward Pytho.

Then I saw Tántalos[28] put to the torture:
in a cool pond he stood, lapped round by water
clear to the chin, and being athirst he burned
to slake his dry weasand[29] with drink, though drink
he would not ever again. For when the old man

---

[28] The sin for which Tántalos (Tantalus) is being punished here is uncertain—possibly it
is for revealing the gods' secrets, possibly for his serving his son's flesh to the gods (see the
headnote to Aeschylus' *Oresteia*).
[29] Throat.

put his lips down to the sheet of water 660
it vanished round his feet, gulped underground,
and black mud baked there in a wind from hell.
Boughs, too, drooped low above him, big with fruit,
pear trees, pomegranates, brilliant apples,
luscious figs, and olives ripe and dark;
but if he stretched his hand for one, the wind
under the dark sky tossed the bough beyond him.

Then Sísyphos[30] in torment I beheld
being roustabout to a tremendous boulder.
Leaning with both arms braced and legs driving, 670
he heaved it toward a height, and almost over,
but then a Power spun him round and sent
the cruel boulder bounding again to the plain.
Whereon the man bent down again to toil,
dripping sweat, and the dust rose overhead.
Next I saw manifest the power of Heraklês—
a phantom,[31] this, for he himself has gone
feasting amid the gods, reclining soft
with Hêbê of the ravishing pale ankles,
daughter of Zeus and Hêra, shod in gold. 680
But, in my vision, all the dead around him
cried like affrighted birds; like Night itself
he loomed with naked bow and nocked arrow
and glances terrible as continual archery.
My hackles rose at the gold swordbelt he wore
sweeping across him: gorgeous intaglio
of savage bears, boars, lions with wildfire eyes,
swordfights, battle, slaughter, and sudden death—
the smith who had that belt in him, I hope
he never made, and never will make, another. 690
The eyes of the vast figure rested on me,
and of a sudden he said in kindly tones:

'Son of Laërtês and the gods of old,
Odysseus, master mariner and soldier,
under a cloud, you too? Destined to grinding
labors like my own in the sunny world?
Son of Kroníon Zeus or not, how many
days I sweated out, being bound in servitude
to a man far worse than I, a rough master![32]
He made me hunt this place one time 700
to get the watchdog of the dead: no more

---

[30]A Corinthian ruler, noted during his lifetime for cunning treachery. More commonly spelled
Sisyphus.
[31]Heraklês, or Hercules, was taken to heaven after his death. He was thereafter wedded
to the goddess Hêbê.
[32]Eurystheus, in whose service Heraklês was forced to perform many superhumanly difficult feats, including the capture of Cerberus, the dog who guarded the realm of the dead.

perilous task, he thought, could be; but I
brought back that beast, up from the underworld;
Hermês and grey-eyed Athena showed the way.'

And Heraklês, down the vistas of the dead,
faded from sight; but I stood fast, awaiting
other great souls who perished in times past.
I should have met, then, god-begotten Theseus
and Peirithoös,[33] whom both I longed to see,
but first came shades in thousands, rustling   710
in a pandemonium of whispers, blown together,
and the horror took me that Perséphonê
had brought from darker hell some saurian death's head.[34]
I whirled then, made for the ship, shouted to crewmen
to get aboard and cast off the stern hawsers,
an order soon obeyed. They took their thwarts,
and the ship went leaping toward the stream of Ocean
first under oars, then with a following wind.

BOOK TWELVE: SEA PERILS AND DEFEAT

The ship sailed on, out of the Ocean Stream,
riding a long swell on the open sea
for the Island of Aiaia.

                                                      Summering Dawn
has dancing grounds there, and the Sun his rising;[1]
but still by night we beached on a sand shelf
and waded in beyond the line of breakers
to fall asleep, awaiting the Day Star.

When the young Dawn with finger tips of rose
made heaven bright, I sent shipmates to bring
Elpênor's body from the house of Kirkê.   10
We others cut down timber on the foreland,
on a high point, and built his pyre of logs,
then stood by weeping while the flame burnt through
corse and equipment.

                              Then we heaped his barrow,
lifting a gravestone on the mound, and fixed
his light but unwarped oar against the sky.
These were our rites in memory of him. Soon, then,
knowing us back from the Dark Land, Kirkê came
freshly adorned for us, with handmaids bearing
loaves, roast meats, and ruby-colored wine.   20

---

[33] A friend of Theseus.
[34] Reptilian specter.
[1] Aiaia is distinguished from the sunless land of the dead which they have just left behind.

She stood among us in immortal beauty
jesting:

'Hearts of oak, did you go down
alive into the homes of Death? One visit
finishes all men but yourselves, twice mortal!
Come, here is meat and wine, enjoy your feasting
for one whole day; and in the dawn tomorrow
you shall put out to sea. Sailing directions,
landmarks, perils, I shall sketch for you, to keep you
from being caught by land or water
in some black sack of trouble.'

In high humor   30
and ready for carousal, we agreed;
so all that day until the sun went down
we feasted on roast meat and good red wine,
till after sunset, at the fall of night,
the men dropped off to sleep by the stern hawsers.
She took my hand then, silent in the hush,
drew me apart, made me sit down, and lay
beside me, softly questioning, as I told
all I had seen, from first to last.

Then said the Lady Kirkê:

'So: all those trials are over.

Listen with care   40
to this, now, and a god will arm your mind.
Square in your ship's path are Seirênês,[2] crying
beauty to bewitch men coasting by;
woe to the innocent who hears that sound!
He will not see his lady nor his children
in joy, crowding about him, home from sea;
the Seirênês will sing his mind away
on their sweet meadow lolling. There are bones
of dead men rotting in a pile beside them
and flayed skins shrivel around the spot.

Steer wide;   50
keep well to seaward; plug your oarsmen's ears
with beeswax kneaded soft; none of the rest
should hear that song.

But if you wish to listen,
let the men tie you in the lugger,[3] hand
and foot, back to the mast, lashed to the mast,
so you may hear those harpies'[4] thrilling voices;
shout as you will, begging to be untied,

---

[2] In Grecian fable, women who could lure men to their destruction through their entrancing song. Also spelled *Sirens*.

[3] A small boat.

[4] In this passage, the word "harpies" means "temptresses." They are not the obscene and filthy females who appear in Virgil's *Aeneid*, Book III.

your crew must only twist more line around you
and keep their stroke up, till the singers fade.
What then? One of two courses you may take,   60
and you yourself must weigh them. I shall not
plan the whole action for you now, but only
tell you of both.

                                                    Ahead are beetling rocks
and dark blue glancing Amphitritê,[5] surging,
roars around them. Prowling Rocks,[6] or Drifters,
the gods in bliss have named them—named them well.
Not even birds can pass them by, not even
the timorous doves that bear ambrosia
to Father Zeus; caught by downdrafts, they die
on rockwall smooth as ice.

                                                    Each time, the Father   70
wafts a new courier to make up his crew.
Still less can ships get searoom of these Drifters,
whose boiling surf, under high fiery winds,
carries tossing wreckage of ships and men.
Only one ocean-going craft, the far-famed
Argo,[7] made it, sailing from Aiêta;
but she, too, would have crashed on the big rocks
if Hêra had not pulled her through, for love
of Iêson, her captain.

                                                    A second course[8]
lies between headlands. One is a sharp mountain   80
piercing the sky, with stormcloud round the peak
dissolving never, not in the brightest summer,
to show heaven's azure there, nor in the fall.
No mortal man could scale it, nor so much
as land there, not with twenty hands and feet,
so sheer the cliffs are—as of polished stone.
Midway that height, a cavern full of mist
opens toward Erebos and evening. Skirting
this in the lugger, great Odysseus,
your master bowman, shooting from the deck,   90
would come short of the cavemouth with his shaft;
but that is the den of Skylla, where she yaps
abominably, a newborn whelp's cry,

---

[5] Sea nymph; consort of Poseidon. She is the female personification of the ocean.

[6] Possibly the Planctae, islands at the north end of what is now called the Strait of Messina, which divides Sicily from the Italian mainland.

[7] The fabled ship, manned by great heroes and captained by Iêson (Jason), that sailed to capture the Golden Fleece.

[8] The following lines describe the two fabled monsters Skylla (Scylla) and Kharybdis (Charybdis), who presumably personify the dangers of the Strait of Messina. Skylla is a treacherous reef, Kharybdis a whirlpool. The proverbial phrase "between Scylla and Charybdis" has come to mean a situation in which one has to choose between equally dreadful alternatives.

though she is huge and monstrous. God or man,
no one could look on her in joy. Her legs—
and there are twelve—are like great tentacles,
unjointed, and upon her serpent necks
are borne six heads like nightmares of ferocity,
with triple serried rows of fangs and deep
gullets of black death. Half her length, she sways   100
her heads in air, outside her horrid cleft,
hunting the sea around that promontory
for dolphins, dogfish, or what bigger game
thundering Amphitritê feeds in thousands.
And no ship's company can claim
to have passed her without loss and grief; she takes,
from every ship, one man for every gullet.

The opposite point seems more a tongue of land
you'd touch with a good bowshot, at the narrows.
A great wild fig, a shaggy mass of leaves,   110
grows on it, and Kharybdis lurks below
to swallow down the dark sea tide. Three times
from dawn to dusk she spews it up
and sucks it down again three times, a whirling
maelstrom; if you come upon her then
the god who makes earth tremble could not save you.
No, hug the cliff of Skylla, take your ship
through on a racing stroke. Better to mourn
six men than lose them all, and the ship, too.'

So her advice ran; but I faced her, saying: 120

'Only instruct me, goddess, if you will,
how, if possible, can I pass Kharybdis,
or fight off Skylla when she raids my crew?'

Swiftly that loveliest goddess answered me:

'Must you have battle in your heart forever?
The bloody toil of combat? Old contender,
will you not yield to the immortal gods?
That nightmare cannot die, being eternal
evil itself—horror, and pain, and chaos;
there is no fighting her, no power can fight her,   130
all that avails is flight.
                                        Lose headway there
along that rockface while you break out arms,
and she'll swoop over you, I fear, once more,
taking one man again for every gullet.
No, no, put all your backs into it, row on;
invoke Blind Force, that bore this scourge of men,
to keep her from a second strike against you.

Then you will coast Thrinákia,[9] the island
where Hêlios' cattle graze, fine herds, and flocks
of goodly sheep. The herds and flocks are seven,   140
with fifty beasts in each.

                                        No lambs are dropped,
or calves, and these fat cattle never die.
Immortal, too, their cowherds are—their shepherds—
Phaëthousa and Lampetía, sweetly braided
nymphs that divine Neaira bore
to the overlord of high noon, Hêlios.
These nymphs their gentle mother bred and placed
upon Thrinákia, the distant land,
in care of flocks and cattle for their father.

Now give those kine a wide berth, keep your thoughts   150
intent upon your course for home,
and hard seafaring brings you all to Ithaka.
But if you raid the beeves, I see destruction
for ship and crew.

                                        Rough years then lie between
you and your homecoming, alone and old,
the one survivor, all companions lost.'

As Kirkê spoke, Dawn mounted her golden throne,
and on the first rays Kirkê left me, taking
her way like a great goddess up the island.
I made straight for the ship, roused up the men   160
to get aboard and cast off at the stern.
They scrambled to their places by the rowlocks
and all in line dipped oars in the grey sea.
But soon an off-shore breeze blew to our liking—
a canvas-bellying breeze, a lusty shipmate
sent by the singing nymph with sunbright hair.
So we made fast the braces, and we rested,
letting the wind and steersman work the ship.
The crew being now silent before me, I
addressed them, sore at heart:

                                        'Dear friends,   170
more than one man, or two, should know those things
Kirkê foresaw for us and shared with me,
so let me tell her forecast: then we die
with our eyes open, if we are going to die,
or know what death we baffle if we can. Seirênês
weaving a haunting song over the sea
we are to shun, she said, and their green shore

---

[9] Sicily.

all sweet with clover; yet she urged that I
alone should listen to their song. Therefore
you are to tie me up, tight as a splint,   180
erect along the mast, lashed to the mast,
and if I shout and beg to be untied,
take more turns of the rope to muffle me.'

I rather dwelt on this part of the forecast,[10]
while our good ship made time, bound outward down
the wind for the strange island of Seirênês.
Then all at once the wind fell, and a calm
came over all the sea, as though some power
lulled the swell.
                                    The crew were on their feet
briskly, to furl the sail, and stow it; then,   190
each in place, they poised the smooth oar blades
and sent the white foam scudding by. I carved
a massive cake of beeswax into bits
and rolled them in my hands until they softened—
no long task, for a burning heat came down
from Hêlios, lord of high noon. Going forward
I carried wax along the line, and laid it
thick on their ears. They tied me up, then, plumb
amidships, back to the mast, lashed to the mast,
and took themselves again to rowing. Soon,   200
as we came smartly within hailing distance,
the two Seirênês, noting our fast ship
off their point, made ready, and they sang:

> *This way, oh turn your bows,*
>   *Akhaia's glory,*
> *As all the world allows—*
>   *Moor and be merry.*
>
> *Sweet coupled airs we sing.*
>   *No lonely seafarer*
> *Holds clear of entering*   210
>   *Our green mirror.*
>
> *Pleased by each purling note*
>   *Like honey twining*
> *From her throat and my throat,*
>   *Who lies a-pining?*

---

[10]Odysseus shrewdly failed to mention the inevitable devouring of some of his men by Skylla.

Sea rovers here take joy
    Voyaging onward,
As from our song of Troy
Greybeard and rower-boy
    Goeth more learnèd.   220

All feats on that great field
    In the long warfare,
Dark days the bright gods willed,
    Wounds you bore there,

Argos' old soldiery
    On Troy beach teeming,
Charmed out of time we see.
No life on earth can be
    Hid from our dreaming.

The lovely voices in ardor appealing over the water   230
made me crave to listen, and I tried to say
'Untie me!' to the crew, jerking my brows;
but they bent steady to the oars. Then Perimêdês
got to his feet, he and Eurýlokhos,
and passed more line about, to hold me still.
So all rowed on, until the Seirênês
dropped under the sea rim, and their singing
dwindled away.

                                        My faithful company
rested on their oars now, peeling off
the wax that I had laid thick on their ears;   240
then set me free.

                                        But scarcely had that island
faded in blue air than I saw smoke
and white water, with sound of waves in tumult—
a sound the men heard, and it terrified them.
Oars flew from their hands; the blades went knocking
wild alongside till the ship lost way,
with no oarblades to drive her through the water.

Well, I walked up and down from bow to stern,
trying to put heart into them, standing over
every oarsman, saying gently,

                                                'Friends,   250
have we never been in danger before this?
More fearsome, is it now, than when the Kyklops
penned us in his cave? What power he had!
Did I not keep my nerve, and use my wits
to find a way out for us?

Now I say
by hook or crook this peril too shall be
something that we remember.

Heads up, lads!

We must obey the orders as I give them.
Get the oarshafts in your hands, and lay back
hard on your benches; hit these breaking seas.   260
Zeus help us pull away before we founder.
You at the tiller, listen, and take in
all that I say—the rudders are your duty;
keep her out of the combers and the smoke;
steer for that headland; watch the drift, or we
fetch up in the smother, and you drown us.'

That was all, and it brought them round to action.
But as I sent them on toward Skylla, I
told them nothing, as they could do nothing.
They would have dropped their oars again, in panic,   270
to roll for cover under the decking. Kirkê's
bidding against arms had slipped my mind,
so I tied on my cuirass and took up
two heavy spears, then made my way along
to the foredeck—thinking to see her first from there,
the monster of the grey rock, harboring
torment for my friends. I strained my eyes
upon that cliffside veiled in cloud, but nowhere
could I catch sight of her.

And all this time,

in travail, sobbing, gaining on the current,   280
we rowed into the strait—Skylla to port
and on our starboard beam Kharybdis, dire
gorge of the salt sea tide. By heaven! when she
vomited, all the sea was like a cauldron
seething over intense fire, when the mixture
suddenly heaves and rises.

The shot spume

soared to the landside heights, and fell like rain.

But when she swallowed the sea water down
we saw the funnel of the maelstrom, heard
the rock bellowing all around, and dark   290
sand raged on the bottom far below.
My men all blanched against the gloom, our eyes
were fixed upon that yawning mouth in fear
of being devoured.

Then Skylla made her strike,

whisking six of my best men from the ship.
I happened to glance aft at ship and oarsmen
and caught sight of their arms and legs, dangling

high overhead. Voices came down to me
in anguish, calling my name for the last time.

A man surfcasting on a point of rock   300
for bass or mackerel, whipping his long rod
to drop the sinker and the bait far out,
will hook a fish and rip it from the surface
to dangle wriggling through the air:

                                                        so these
were borne aloft in spasms toward the cliff.

She ate them as they shrieked there, in her den,
in the dire grapple, reaching still for me—
and deathly pity ran me through
at that sight—far the worst I ever suffered,
questing the passes of the strange sea.

                                        We rowed on. 310
The Rocks were now behind; Kharybdis, too,
and Skylla dropped astern.

                                Then we were coasting
the noble island of the god, where grazed
those cattle with wide brows, and bounteous flocks
of Hêlios, lord of noon, who rides high heaven.

From the black ship, far still at sea, I heard
the lowing of the cattle winding home
and sheep bleating; and heard, too, in my heart
the words of blind Teirêsias of Thebes
and Kirkê of Aiaia: both forbade me   320
the island of the world's delight, the Sun.
So I spoke out in gloom to my companions:

'Shipmates, grieving and weary though you are,
listen: I had forewarning from Teirêsias
and Kirkê, too; both told me I must shun
this island of the Sun, the world's delight.
Nothing but fatal trouble shall we find here.
Pull away, then, and put the land astern.'

That strained them to the breaking point, and, cursing,
Eurýlokhos cried out in bitterness: 330

'Are you flesh and blood, Odysseus, to endure
more than a man can? Do you never tire?
God, look at you, iron is what you're made of.
Here we all are, half dead with weariness,
falling asleep over the oars, and you
say "No landing"—no firm island earth
where we could make a quiet supper. No:
pull out to sea, you say, with night upon us—

just as before, but wandering now, and lost.
Sudden storms can rise at night and swamp   340
ships without a trace.

                              Where is your shelter
if some stiff gale blows up from south or west—
the winds that break up shipping every time
when seamen flout the lord gods' will? I say
do as the hour demands and go ashore
before black night comes down.

                              We'll make our supper
alongside, and at dawn put out to sea.'

Now when the rest said 'Aye' to this, I saw
the power of destiny devising ill.
Sharply I answered, without hesitation: 350

'Eurýlokhos, they are with you to a man.
I am alone, outmatched.

                              Let this whole company
swear me a great oath: Any herd of cattle
or flock of sheep here found shall go unharmed;
no one shall slaughter out of wantonness
ram or heifer; all shall be content
with what the goddess Kirkê put aboard.'

They fell at once to swearing as I ordered,
and when the round of oaths had ceased, we found
a halfmoon bay to beach and moor the ship in,   360
with a fresh spring nearby. All hands ashore
went about skillfully getting up a meal.
Then, after thirst and hunger, those besiegers,
were turned away, they mourned for their companions
plucked from the ship by Skylla and devoured,
and sleep came soft upon them as they mourned.

In the small hours of the third watch, when stars
that shone out in the first dusk of evening
had gone down to their setting, a giant wind
blew from heaven, and clouds driven by Zeus   370
shrouded land and sea in a night of storm;
so, just as Dawn with finger tips of rose
touched the windy world, we dragged our ship
to cover in a grotto, a sea cave
where nymphs had chairs of rock and sanded floors.
I mustered all the crew and said:

                              'Old shipmates,
our stores are in the ship's hold, food and drink;
the cattle here are not for our provision,
or we pay dearly for it.

                                                Fierce the god is
who cherishes these heifers and these sheep: 380
Hêlios; and no man avoids his eye.'

To this my fighters nodded. Yes. But now
we had a month of onshore gales, blowing
day in, day out—south winds, or south by east.
As long as bread and good red wine remained
to keep the men up, and appease their craving,
they would not touch the cattle. But in the end,
when all the barley in the ship was gone,
hunger drove them to scour the wild shore
with angling hooks, for fishes and sea fowl,   390
whatever fell into their hands; and lean days
wore their bellies thin.

                                        The storms continued.
So one day I withdrew to the interior
to pray the gods in solitude, for hope
that one might show me some way of salvation.
Slipping away, I struck across the island
to a sheltered spot, out of the driving gale.
I washed my hands there, and made supplication
to the gods who own Olympos, all the gods—
but they, for answer, only closed my eyes   400
under slow drops of sleep.

                                Now on the shore Eurýlokhos
made his insidious plea:

                                        'Comrades,' he said,
'You've gone through everything; listen to what I say.
All deaths are hateful to us, mortal wretches,
but famine is the most pitiful, the worst
end that a man can come to.

                                        Will you fight it?
Come, we'll cut out the noblest of these cattle
for sacrifice to the gods who own the sky;
and once at home, in the old country of Ithaka,
if ever that day comes—   410
we'll build a costly temple and adorn it
with every beauty for the Lord of Noon.
But if he flares up over his heifers lost,
wishing our ship destroyed, and if the gods
make cause with him, why, then I say: Better
open your lungs to a big sea once for all
than waste to skin and bones on a lonely island!'

Thus Eurýlokhos; and they murmured 'Aye!'
trooping away at once to round up heifers.
Now, that day tranquil cattle with broad brows   420

were grazing near, and soon the men drew up
around their chosen beasts in ceremony.
They plucked the leaves that shone on a tall oak—
having no barley meal—to strew the victims,
performed the prayers and ritual, knifed the kine
and flayed each carcass, cutting thighbones free
to wrap in double folds of fat. These offerings,
with strips of meat, were laid upon the fire.
Then, as they had no wine, they made libation
with clear spring water, broiling the entrails first; 430
and when the bones were burnt and tripes shared,
they spitted the carved meat.

                                        Just then my slumber
left me in a rush, my eyes opened,
and I went down the seaward path. No sooner
had I caught sight of our black hull, than savory
odors of burnt fat eddied around me;
grief took hold of me, and I cried aloud:

'O Father Zeus and gods in bliss forever,
you made me sleep away this day of mischief!
O cruel drowsing, in the evil hour! 440
Here they sat, and a great work they contrived.'

Lampetía[11] in her long gown meanwhile
had borne swift word to the Overlord of Noon:

'They have killed your kine.'

                                        And the Lord Hêlios
burst into angry speech amid the immortals:

'O Father Zeus and gods in bliss forever,
punish Odysseus' men! So overweening,
now they have killed my peaceful kine, my joy
at morning when I climbed the sky of stars,
and evening, when I bore westward from heaven. 450
Restitution or penalty they shall pay—
and pay in full—or I go down forever
to light the dead men in the underworld.'

Then Zeus who drives the stormcloud made reply:

'Peace, Hêlios: shine on among the gods,
shine over mortals in the fields of grain.
Let me throw down one white-hot bolt, and make
splinters of their ship in the winedark sea.'

---

[11]One of the nymphs who tended her father Hêlios' cattle.

—Kalypso later told me of this exchange,
as she declared that Hermês had told her.   460
Well, when I reached the sea cave and the ship,
I faced each man, and had it out; but where
could any remedy be found? There was none.
The silken beeves of Hêlios were dead.
The gods, moreover, made queer signs appear:
cowhides began to crawl, and beef, both raw
and roasted, lowed like kine upon the spits.

Now six full days my gallant crew could feast
upon the prime beef they had marked for slaughter
from Hêlios' herd; and Zeus, the son of Kronos,   470
added one fine morning.

                                        All the gales
had ceased, blown out, and with an offshore breeze
we launched again, stepping the mast and sail,
to make for the open sea. Astern of us
the island coastline faded, and no land
showed anywhere, but only sea and heaven,
when Zeus Kroníon piled a thunderhead
above the ship, while gloom spread on the ocean.
We held our course, but briefly. Then the squall
struck whining from the west, with gale force, breaking   480
both forestays, and the mast came toppling aft
along the ship's length, so the running rigging
showered into the bilge.

                                        On the after deck
the mast had hit the steersman a slant blow
bashing the skull in, knocking him overside,
as the brave soul fled the body, like a diver.
With crack on crack of thunder, Zeus let fly
a bolt against the ship, a direct hit,
so that she bucked, in reeking fumes of sulphur,
and all the men were flung into the sea.   490
They came up 'round the wreck, bobbing a while
like petrels[12] on the waves.

                                        No more seafaring
homeward for these, no sweet day of return;
the god had turned his face from them.

                                        I clambered
fore and aft my hulk until a comber
split her, keel from ribs, and the big timber
floated free; the mast, too, broke away.
A backstay floated dangling from it, stout
rawhide rope, and I used this for lashing
mast and keel together. These I straddled,   500
riding the frightful storm.

[12] Seabirds.

                                                    Nor had I yet
seen the worst of it: for now the west wind
dropped, and a southeast gale came on—one more
twist of the knife—taking me north again,
straight for Kharybdis. All that night I drifted,
and in the sunrise, sure enough, I lay
off Skylla mountain and Kharybdis deep.
There, as the whirlpool drank the tide, a billow
tossed me, and I sprang for the great fig tree,
catching on like a bat under a bough.   510
Nowhere had I to stand, no way of climbing,
the root and bole being far below, and far
above my head the branches and their leaves,
massed, overshadowing Kharybdis pool.
But I clung grimly, thinking my mast and keel
would come back to the surface when she spouted.
And ah! how long, with what desire, I waited!
till, at the twilight hour, when one who hears
and judges pleas in the marketplace all day
between contentious men, goes home to supper,   520
the long poles at last reared from the sea.

Now I let go with hands and feet, plunging
straight into the foam beside the timbers,
pulled astride, and rowed hard with my hands
to pass by Skylla. Never could I have passed her
had not the Father of gods and men, this time,
kept me from her eyes. Once through the strait,
nine days I drifted in the open sea
before I made shore, buoyed up by the gods,
upon Ogýgia Isle. The dangerous nymph   530
Kalypso lives and sings there, in her beauty,
and she received me, loved me.

                                      But why tell
the same tale that I told last night in hall
to you and to your lady? Those adventures
made a long evening, and I do not hold
with tiresome repetition of a story."

BOOK THIRTEEN: ONE MORE STRANGE ISLAND

He ended it, and no one stirred or sighed
in the shadowy hall, spellbound as they all were,
until Alkínoös answered:

                                      "When you came
here to my strong home, Odysseus, under
my tall roof, headwinds were left behind you.

Clear sailing shall you have now, homeward now,
however painful all the past.

My lords,

ever my company, sharing the wine of Council,
the songs of the blind harper, hear me further:
garments are folded for our guest and friend   10
in the smooth chest, and gold
in various shaping of adornment lies
with other gifts, and many, brought by our peers;
let each man add his tripod and deep-bellied
cauldron: we'll make levy upon the realm
to pay us for the loss each bears in this."

Alkínoös had voiced their own hearts' wish.
All gave assent, then home they went to rest;
but young Dawn's finger tips of rose, touching
the world, roused them to make haste to the ship,   20
each with his gift of noble bronze. Alkínoös,
their ardent king, stepping aboard himself,
directed the stowing under the cross planks,
not to cramp the long pull of the oarsmen.
Going then to the great hall, lords and crew
prepared for feasting.

As the gods' anointed,

Alkínoös made offering on their behalf—an ox
to Zeus beyond the stormcloud, Kronos' son,
who rules the world. They burnt the great thighbones
and feasted at their ease on fresh roast meat,   30
as in their midst the godlike harper sang—
Demódokos, honored by all that realm.

Only Odysseus

time and again turned craning toward the sun,
impatient for day's end, for the open sea.
Just as a farmer's hunger grows, behind
the bolted plow and share, all day afield,
drawn by his team of winedark oxen: sundown
is benison for him, sending him homeward
stiff in the knees from weariness, to dine;
just so, the light on the sea rim gladdened Odysseus,   40
and as it dipped he stood among the Phaiákians,
turned to Alkínoös, and said:

"O king and admiration of your people,
give me fare well, and stain the ground with wine;
my blessings on you all! This hour brings
fulfillment to the longing of my heart:
a ship for home, and gifts the gods of heaven
make so precious and so bountiful.

After this voyage

god grant I find my own wife in my hall
with everyone I love best, safe and sound!   50

And may you, settled in your land, give joy
to wives and children; may the gods reward you
every way, and your realm be free of woe."

Then all the voices rang out, "Be it so!"
and "Well spoken!" and "Let our friend make sail!"

Whereon Alkínoös gave command to his crier:

"Fill the winebowl, Pontónoös: mix and serve:
go the whole round, so may this company
invoke our Father Zeus, and bless our friend,
seaborne tonight and bound for his own country."   60

Pontónoös mixed the honey-hearted wine
and went from chair to chair, filling the cups;
then each man where he sat poured out his offering
to the gods in bliss who own the sweep of heaven.
With gentle bearing Odysseus rose, and placed
his double goblet in Arêtê's hands,
saying:

                    "Great Queen, farewell;
be blest through all your days till age comes on you,
and death, last end for mortals, after age.
Now I must go my way. Live in felicity,   70
and make this palace lovely for your children,
your countrymen, and your king, Alkínoös."

Royal Odysseus turned and crossed the door sill,
a herald at his right hand, sent by Alkínoös
to lead him to the sea beach and the ship.
Arêtê, too, sent maids in waiting after him,
one with a laundered great cloak and a tunic,
a second balancing the crammed sea chest,
a third one bearing loaves and good red wine.
As soon as they arrived alongside, crewmen   80
took these things for stowage under the planks,
their victualling and drink; then spread a rug
and linen cover on the after deck,
where Lord Odysseus might sleep in peace.
Now he himself embarked, lay down, lay still,
while oarsmen took their places at the rowlocks
all in order. They untied their hawser,
passing it through a drilled stone ring; then bent
forward at the oars and caught the sea
as one man, stroking.

                    Slumber, soft and deep   90
like the still sleep of death, weighed on his eyes
as the ship hove seaward.

                    How a four horse team

whipped into a run on a straightaway
consumes the road, surging and surging over it!
So ran that craft and showed her heels to the swell,
her bow wave riding after, and her wake
on the purple night-sea foaming.

                                                    Hour by hour

she held her pace; not even a falcon wheeling
downwind, swiftest bird, could stay abreast of her
in that most arrowy flight through open water,   100
with her great passenger—godlike in counsel,
he that in twenty years had borne such blows
in his deep heart, breaking through ranks in war
and waves on the bitter sea.

                                                    This night at last

he slept serene, his long-tried mind at rest.

When on the East the sheer bright star arose
that tells of coming Dawn, the ship made landfall
and came up islandward in the dim of night.
Phorkys, the old sea baron, has a cove
here in the realm of Ithaka; two points   110
of high rock, breaking sharply, hunch around it,
making a haven from the plunging surf
that gales at sea roll shoreward. Deep inside,
at mooring range, good ships can ride unmoored.
There, on the inmost shore, an olive tree
throws wide its boughs over the bay; nearby
a cave of dusky light is hidden
for those immortal girls, the Naiadês.[1]
Within are winebowls hollowed in the rock
and amphorai; bees bring their honey here;   120
and there are looms of stone, great looms, whereon
the weaving nymphs make tissues, richly dyed
as the deep sea is; and clear springs in the cavern
flow forever. Of two entrances,
one on the north allows descent of mortals,
but beings out of light alone, the undying,
can pass by the south slit; no men come there.

This cove the sailors knew. Here they drew in,
and the ship ran half her keel's length up the shore,
she had such way on her from those great oarsmen.   130
Then from their benches forward on dry ground
they disembarked. They hoisted up Odysseus
unruffled on his bed, under his cover,
handing him overside still fast asleep,

---

[1] Sea nymphs.

to lay him on the sand; and they unloaded
all those gifts the princes of Phaiákia
gave him, when by Athena's heart and will
he won his passage home. They bore this treasure
off the beach, and piled it close around
the roots of the olive tree, that no one passing   140
should steal Odysseus' gear before he woke.
That done, they pulled away on the homeward track.

But now the god that shakes the islands, brooding
over old threats of his against Odysseus,
approached Lord Zeus to learn his will. Said he:

"Father of gods, will the bright immortals ever
pay me respect again, if mortals do not?—
Phaiákians, too, my own blood kin?

                                                I thought
Odysseus should in time regain his homeland;
I had no mind to rob him of that day—   150
no, no; you promised it, being so inclined;
only I thought he should be made to suffer
all the way.

                         But now these islanders
have shipped him homeward, sleeping soft, and put him
On Ithaka, with gifts untold
of bronze and gold, and fine cloth to his shoulder.
Never from Troy had he borne off such booty
if he had got home safe with all his share."

Then Zeus who drives the stormcloud answered, sighing:

"God of horizons, making earth's underbeam   160
tremble, why do you grumble so?
The immortal gods show you no less esteem,
and the rough consequence would make them slow
to let barbs fly at their eldest and most noble.
But if some mortal captain, overcome
by his own pride of strength, cuts or defies you,
are you not always free to take reprisal?
Act as your wrath requires and as you will."

Now said Poseidon, god of earthquake:

                                          "Aye,
god of the stormy sky, I should have taken   170
vengeance, as you say, and on my own;
but I respect, and would avoid, your anger.
The sleek Phaiákian cutter, even now,
has carried out her mission and glides home
over the misty sea. Let me impale her,

end her voyage, and end all ocean-crossing
with passengers, then heave a mass of mountain
in a ring around the city."

Now Zeus who drives the stormcloud said benignly:

"Here is how I should do it, little brother: 180
when all who watch upon the wall have caught
sight of the ship, let her be turned to stone—
an island like a ship, just off the bay.
Mortals may gape at that for generations!
But throw no mountain round the sea port city."

When he heard this, Poseidon, god of earthquake,
departed for Skhería, where the Phaiákians
are born and dwell. Their ocean-going ship
he saw already near, heading for harbor;
so up behind her swam the island-shaker   190
and struck her into stone, rooted in stone, at one
blow of his palm,

        then took to the open sea.
Those famous ship handlers, the Phaiákians,
gazed at each other, murmuring in wonder;
you could have heard one say:

         "Now who in thunder
has anchored, moored that ship in the seaway,
when everyone could see her making harbor?"

The god had wrought a charm beyond their thought.
But soon Alkínoös made them hush, and told them:

"This present doom upon the ship—on me—   200
my father prophesied in the olden time.
If we gave safe conveyance to all passengers
we should incur Poseidon's wrath, he said,
whereby one day a fair ship, manned by Phaiákians,
would come to grief at the god's hands; and great
mountains would hide our city from the sea.
So my old father forecast.

          Use your eyes:
these things are even now being brought to pass.
Let all here abide by my decree:

          We make
an end henceforth of taking, in our ships,   210
castaways who may land upon Skhería;
and twelve choice bulls we dedicate at once
to Lord Poseidon, praying him of his mercy
not to heave up a mountain round our city."

In fearful awe they led the bulls to sacrifice

and stood about the altar stone, those captains,
peers of Phaiákia, led by their king in prayer
to Lord Poseidon.

               Meanwhile, on his island,
his father's shore, that kingly man, Odysseus,
awoke, but could not tell what land it was   220
after so many years away; moreover,
Pallas Athena, Zeus's daughter, poured
a grey mist all around him, hiding him
from common sight—for she had things to tell him
and wished no one to know him, wife or townsmen,
before the suitors paid up for their crimes.

The landscape then looked strange, unearthly strange
to the Lord Odysseus: paths by hill and shore,
glimpses of harbors, cliffs, and summer trees.
He stood up, rubbed his eyes, gazed at his homeland,   230
and swore, slapping his thighs with both his palms,
then cried aloud:

               "What am I in for now?
Whose country have I come to this time? Rough
savages and outlaws, are they, or
godfearing people, friendly to castaways?
Where shall I take these things? Where take myself,
with no guide, no directions? These should be
still in Phaiákian hands, and I uncumbered,
free to find some other openhearted
prince who might be kind and give me passage.   240
I have no notion where to store this treasure;
first-comer's trove it is, if I leave it here.
My lords and captains of Phaiákia
were not those decent men they seemed, not honorable,
landing me in this unknown country—no,
by god, they swore to take me home to Ithaka
and did not! Zeus attend to their reward,
Zeus, patron of petitioners, who holds
all other mortals under his eye; he takes
payment from betrayers!

                  I'll be busy.   250
I can look through my gear. I shouldn't wonder
if they pulled out with part of it on board."

He made a tally of his shining pile—
tripods, cauldrons, cloaks, and gold—and found
he lacked nothing at all.

             And then he wept,
despairing, for his own land, trudging down
beside the endless wash of the wide, wide sea,

weary and desolate as the sea. But soon
Athena came to him from the nearby air,
putting a young man's figure on—a shepherd, 260
like a king's son, all delicately made.
She wore a cloak, in two folds off her shoulders,
and sandals bound upon her shining feet.
A hunting lance lay in her hands.

                                  At sight of her

Odysseus took heart, and he went forward
to greet the lad, speaking out fair and clear:

"Friend, you are the first man I've laid eyes on
here in this cove. Greetings. Do not feel
alarmed or hostile, coming across me; only
receive me into safety with my stores. 270
Touching your knees I ask it, as I might
ask grace of a god.

                              O sir, advise me,

what is this land and realm, who are the people?
Is it an island all distinct, or part
of the fertile mainland, sloping to the sea?"

To this grey-eyed Athena answered:

                                 "Stranger,

you must come from the other end of nowhere,
else you are a great booby, having to ask
what place this is. It is no nameless country.
Why, everyone has heard of it, the nations 280
over on the dawn side, toward the sun,
and westerners in cloudy lands of evening.
No one would use this ground for training horses,
it is too broken, has no breadth of meadow;
but there is nothing meager about the soil,
the yield of grain is wondrous, and wine, too,
with drenching rains and dewfall.

                              There's good pasture

for oxen and for goats, all kinds of timber,
and water all year long in the cattle ponds.
For these blessings, friend, the name of Ithaka 290
has made its way even as far as Troy—
and they say Troy lies far beyond Akhaia."

Now Lord Odysseus, the long-enduring,
laughed in his heart, hearing his land described
by Pallas Athena, daughter of Zeus who rules
the veering stormwind; and he answered her
with ready speech—not that he told the truth,
but, just as she did, held back what he knew,
weighing within himself at every step
what he made up to serve his turn.

Said he: 300

"Far away in Krete I learned of Ithaka—
in that broad island over the great ocean.
And here I am now, come myself to Ithaka!
Here is my fortune with me. I left my sons
an equal part, when I shipped out. I killed
Orsílokhos, the courier, son of Idómeneus.[2]
This man could beat the best cross country runners
in Krete, but he desired to take away
my Trojan plunder, all I had fought and bled for,
cutting through ranks in war and the cruel sea. 310
Confiscation is what he planned; he knew
I had not cared to win his father's favor
as a staff officer in the field at Troy,
but led my own command.

I acted: I

hit him with a spearcast from a roadside
as he came down from the open country. Murky
night shrouded all heaven and the stars.
I made that ambush with one man at arms.
We were unseen. I took his life in secret,
finished him off with my sharp sword. That night 320
I found asylum on a ship off shore
skippered by gentlemen of Phoinikia;[3] I gave
all they could wish, out of my store of plunder,
for passage, and for landing me at Pylos
or Elis Town, where the Epeioi are in power.
Contrary winds carried them willy-nilly
past that coast; they had no wish to cheat me,
but we were blown off course.

Here, then, by night

we came, and made this haven by hard rowing.
All famished, but too tired to think of food, 330
each man dropped in his tracks after the landing,
and I slept hard, being wearied out. Before
I woke today, they put my things ashore
on the sand here beside me where I lay,
then reimbarked for Sidon, that great city.
Now they are far at sea, while I am left
forsaken here."

At this the grey-eyed goddess
Athena smiled, and gave him a caress,
her looks being changed now, so she seemed a woman,
tall and beautiful and no doubt skilled 340
at weaving splendid things. She answered briskly:

[2] The king of Krete (Crete).
[3] Phoenicia; an area of the Syrian coast noted for commerce. Sidon was one of its principal cities.

"Whoever gets around you must be sharp
and guileful as a snake; even a god
might bow to you in ways of dissimulation.
You! You chameleon!
Bottomless bag of tricks! Here in your own country
would you not give your stratagems a rest
or stop spellbinding for an instant?
You play a part as if it were your own tough skin.

No more of this, though. Two of a kind, we are,   350
contrivers, both. Of all men now alive
you are the best in plots and story telling.
My own fame is for wisdom among the gods—
deceptions, too.

                              Would even you have guessed
that I am Pallas Athena, daughter of Zeus,
I that am always with you in times of trial,
a shield to you in battle, I who made
the Phaiákians befriend you, to a man?
Now I am here again to counsel with you—
but first to put away those gifts the Phaiákians   360
gave you at departure—I planned it so.
Then I can tell you of the gall and wormwood
it is your lot to drink in your own hall.
Patience, iron patience, you must show;
so give it out to neither man nor woman
that you are back from wandering. Be silent
under all injuries, even blows from men."

His mind ranging far, Odysseus answered:

"Can mortal man be sure of you on sight,
even a sage, O mistress of disguises?   370
Once you were fond of me—I am sure of that—
years ago, when we Akhaians made
war, in our generation, upon Troy.
But after we had sacked the shrines of Priam
and put to sea, God scattered the Akhaians;
I never saw you after that, never
knew you aboard with me, to act as shield
in grievous times—not till you gave me comfort
in the rich hinterland of the Phaiákians
and were yourself my guide into that city.   380

Hear me now in your father's name, for I
cannot believe that I have come to Ithaka.
It is some other land. You made that speech
only to mock me, and to take me in.
Have I come back in truth to my home island?"

To this the grey-eyed goddess Athena answered:

"Always the same detachment! That is why
I cannot fail you, in your evil fortune,
coolheaded, quick, well-spoken as you are!
Would not another wandering man, in joy, 390
make haste home to his wife and children? Not
you, not yet. Before you hear their story
you will have proof about your wife.

I tell you,

she still sits where you left her, and her days
and nights go by forlorn, in lonely weeping.
For my part, never had I despaired; I felt
sure or your coming home, though all your men
should perish; but I never cared to fight
Poseidon, Father's brother, in his baleful
rage with you for taking his son's eye. 400

Now I shall make you see the shape of Ithaka.
Here is the cove the sea lord Phorkys owns,
there is the olive spreading out her leaves
over the inner bay, and there the cavern
dusky and lovely, hallowed by the feet
of those immortal girls, the Naiadês—
the same wide cave under whose vault you came
to honor them with hekatombs—and there
Mount Neion, with his forest on his back!"

She had dispelled the mist, so all the island 410
stood out clearly. Then indeed Odysseus'
heart stirred with joy. He kissed the earth,
and lifting up his hands prayed to the nymphs:

"O slim shy Naiadês, young maids of Zeus,
I had not thought to see you ever again!

O listen smiling

to my gentle prayers, and we'll make offering
plentiful as in the old time, granted I
live, granted my son grows tall, by favor
of great Athena, Zeus's daughter,
who gives the winning fighter his reward!" 420

The grey-eyed goddess said directly:

"Courage;

and let the future trouble you no more.
We go to make a cache now, in the cave,
to keep your treasure hid. Then we'll consider
how best the present action may unfold."

The goddess turned and entered the dim cave,
exploring it for crannies, while Odysseus
carried up all the gold, the fire-hard bronze,
and well-made clothing the Phaiákians gave him.
Pallas Athena, daughter of Zeus the storm king,   430
placed them, and shut the cave mouth with a stone,
and under the old grey olive tree those two
sat down to work the suitors death and woe.
Grey-eyed Athena was the first to speak, saying:

"Son of Laërtês and the gods of old,
Odysseus, master of land ways and sea ways,
put your mind on a way to reach and strike
a crowd of brazen upstarts.

                                               Three long years
they have played master in your house: three years
trying to win your lovely lady, making   440
gifts as though betrothed. And she? Forever
grieving for you, missing your return,
she has allowed them all to hope, and sent
messengers with promises to each—
though her true thoughts are fixed elsewhere."

                                                       At this
the man of ranging mind, Odysseus, cried:

"So hard beset! An end like Agamémnon's
might very likely have been mine, a bad end,
bleeding to death in my own hall. You forestalled it,
goddess, by telling me how the land lies.   450
Weave me a way to pay them back! And you, too,
take your place with me, breathe valor in me
the way you did that night when we Akhaians
unbound the bright veil from the brow of Troy!
O grey-eyed one, fire my heart and brace me!
I'll take on fighting men three hundred strong
if you fight at my back, immortal lady!"

The grey-eyed goddess Athena answered him:

"No fear but I shall be there; you'll go forward
under my arm when the crux comes at last.   460
And I foresee your vast floor stained with blood,
spattered with brains of this or that tall suitor
who fed upon your cattle.

                                            Now, for a while,
I shall transform you; not a soul will know you,
the clear skin of your arms and legs shriveled,
your chestnut hair all gone, your body dressed
in sacking that a man would gag to see,
and the two eyes, that were so brilliant, dirtied—

contemptible, you shall seem to your enemies,
as to the wife and son you left behind.   470

But join the swineherd first—the overseer
of all your swine, a good soul now as ever,
devoted to Penélopê and your son.
He will be found near Raven's Rock and the well
of Arethousa,[4] where the swine are pastured,
rooting for acorns to their hearts' content,
drinking the dark still water. Boarflesh grows
pink and fat on that fresh diet. There
stay with him, and question him, while I
am off to the great beauty's land of Sparta,   480
to call your son Telémakhos home again—
for you should know, he went to the wide land
of Lakedaimon, Meneláos' country,
to learn if there were news of you abroad."

Odysseus answered:

                              "Why not tell him, knowing
my whole history, as you do? Must he
traverse the barren sea, he too, and live
in pain, while others feed on what is his?"

At this the grey-eyed goddess Athena said:

"No need for anguish on that lad's account.   490
I sent him off myself, to make his name
in foreign parts—no hardship in the bargain,
taking his ease in Meneláos' mansion,
lapped in gold.
                    The young bucks here, I know,
lie in wait for him in a cutter, bent
on murdering him before he reaches home.
I rather doubt they will. Cold earth instead
will take in her embrace a man or two
of those who fed so long on what is his."

Speaking no more, she touched him with her wand,   500
shriveled the clear skin of his arms and legs,
made all his hair fall out, cast over him
the wrinkled hide of an old man, and bleared
both his eyes, that were so bright. Then she
clapped an old tunic, a foul cloak, upon him,
tattered, filthy, stained by greasy smoke,
and over that a mangy big buck skin.

---

[4] The fountain identified with the water nymph Arethousa (Arethusa) is more often
located in Sicily.

A staff she gave him, and a leaky knapsack
with no strap but a loop of string.

Now then,

their colloquy at an end, they went their ways— 510
Athena toward illustrious Lakedaimon
Far over sea, to join Odysseus' son.

BOOK FOURTEEN: HOSPITALITY IN THE FOREST

He went up from the cove through wooded ground,
taking a stony trail into the high hills, where
the swineherd lived, according to Athena.
Of all Odysseus' field hands in the old days
this forester cared most for the estate;
and now Odysseus found him
in a remote clearing, sitting inside the gate
of a stockade he built to keep the swine
while his great lord was gone.

Working alone,

far from Penélopê and old Laërtês, 10
he had put up a fieldstone hut and timbered it
with wild pear wood. Dark hearts of oak he split
and trimmed for a high palisade around it,
and built twelve sties adjoining in this yard
to hold the livestock. Fifty sows with farrows
were penned in each, bedded upon the earth,
while the boars lay outside—fewer by far,
as those well-fatted were for the suitors' table,
fine pork, sent by the swineherd every day.
Three hundred sixty now lay there at night, 20
guarded by dogs—four dogs like wolves, one each
for the four lads the swineherd reared and kept
as under-herdsmen.

When Odysseus came,

the good servant sat shaping to his feet
oxhide for sandals, cutting the well-cured leather.
Three of his young men were afield, pasturing
herds in other woods; one he had sent
with a fat boar for tribute into town,
the boy to serve while the suitors got their fill.

The watch dogs, when they caught sight of Odysseus, 30
faced him, a snarling troop, and pelted out
viciously after him. Like a tricky beggar
he sat down plump, and dropped his stick. No use.
They would have rolled him in the dust and torn him

there by his own steading[1] if the swineherd
had not sprung up and flung his leather down,
making a beeline for the open. Shouting,
throwing stone after stone,
he made them scatter; then turned to his lord
and said:

                    "You might have got a ripping, man!   40
Two shakes more and a pretty mess for me
you could have called it, if you had the breath.
As though I had not trouble enough already,
given me by the gods, my master gone,
true king that he was. I hang on here,
still mourning for him, raising pigs of his
to feed foreigners, and who knows where the man is,
in some far country among strangers! Aye—
if he is living still, if he still sees the light of day.

Come to the cabin. You're a wanderer too.   50
You must eat something, drink some wine, and tell me
where you are from and the hard times you've seen."

The forester now led him to his hut
and made a couch for him, with tips of fir
piled for a mattress under a wild goat skin,
shaggy and thick, his own bed covering.

                                        Odysseus,
in pleasure at this courtesy, gently said:

"May Zeus and all the gods give you your heart's desire
for taking me in so kindly, friend."

                                   Eumaios—
O my swineherd![2]—answered him:

                              "Tush, friend,   60
rudeness to a stranger is not decency,
poor though he may be, poorer than you.

                              All wanderers
and beggars come from Zeus. What we can give
is slight but well-meant—all we dare. You know
that is the way of slaves,[3] who live in dread
of masters—new ones like our own.

---

[1] Farmhouse or farm.

[2] This kind of direct address by the poet, expressing affection, is used in the *Odyssey* only
for Eumaios.

[3] Though owned by masters as in modern forms of slavery, and often obtained by forced
capture, "slaves" in the aristocratic Homeric times were often more like trusted and responsible servants than like maltreated property. Eumaios and Telémakhos' old nurse Eurýkleia,
described elsewhere in the *Odyssey*, are representative examples.

I told you

the gods, long ago, hindered our lord's return.
He had a fondness for me, would have pensioned me
with acres of my own, a house, a wife
that other men admired and courted; all   70
gifts good-hearted kings bestow for service,
for a life work the bounty of god has prospered—
for it does prosper here, this work I do.
Had he grown old in his own house, my master
would have rewarded me. But the man's gone.
God curse the race of Helen and cut it down,
that wrung the strength out of the knees of many!
And he went, too—for the honor of Agamémnon
he took ship overseas for the wild horse country
of Troy, to fight the Trojans."

This being told,   80

he tucked his long shirt up inside his belt
and strode into the pens for two young porkers.
He slaughtered them and singed them at the fire,
flayed and quartered them, and skewered the meat
to broil it all; then gave it to Odysseus
hot on the spits. He shook out barley meal,
took a winebowl of ivy wood and filled it,
and sat down facing him, with a gesture, saying:

"There is your dinner, friend, the pork of slaves.
Our fat shoats are all eaten by the suitors,   90
cold-hearted men, who never spare a thought
for how they stand in the sight of Zeus. The gods
living in bliss are fond of no wrongdoing,
but honor discipline and right behavior.
Even the outcasts of the earth, who bring
piracy from the sea, and bear off plunder
given by Zeus in shiploads—even those men
deep in their hearts tremble for heaven's eye.
But the suitors, now, have heard some word, some oracle
of my lord's death, being so unconcerned   100
to pay court properly or to go about their business.
All they want is to prey on his estate,
proud dogs; they stop at nothing. Not a day
goes by, and not a night comes under Zeus,
but they make butchery of our beeves and swine—
not one or two beasts at a time, either.
As for swilling down wine, they drink us dry.
Only a great domain like his could stand it—
greater than any on the dusky mainland
or here in Ithaka. Not twenty heroes   110
in the whole world were as rich as he. I know:
I could count it all up; twelve herds in Elis,

as many flocks, as many herds of swine,
and twelve wide-ranging herds of goats, as well,
attended by his own men or by others—
out at the end of the island, eleven herds
are scattered now, with good men looking after them,
and every herdsman, every day, picks out
a prize ram to hand over to those fellows.
I too as overseer, keeper of swine,   120
must go through all my boars and send the best."

While he ran on, Odysseus with zeal
applied himself to the meat and wine, but inwardly
his thought shaped woe and ruin for the suitors.
When he had eaten all that he desired
and the cup he drank from had been filled again
with wine—a welcome sight—,
he spoke, and the words came light upon the air:

"Who is this lord who once acquired you,
so rich, so powerful, as you describe him?   130
You think he died for Agamémnon's honor.
Tell me his name: I may have met someone
of that description in my time. Who knows?
Perhaps only the immortal gods could say
if I should claim to have seen him: I have roamed
about the world so long."

                                         The swineherd answered
as one who held a place of trust:

                                             "Well, man,
his lady and his son will put no stock
in any news of him brought by a rover.
Wandering men tell lies for a night's lodging,   140
for fresh clothing; truth doesn't interest them.
Every time some traveller comes ashore
he has to tell my mistress his pretty tale,
and she receives him kindly, questions him,
remembering her prince, while the tears run
down her cheeks—and that is as it should be
when a woman's husband has been lost abroad.
I suppose you, too, can work your story up
at a moment's notice, given a shirt or cloak.
No: long ago wild dogs and carrion   150
birds, most like, laid bare his ribs on land
where life had left him. Or it may be, quick fishes
picked him clean in the deep sea, and his bones
lie mounded over in sand upon some shore.
One way or another, far from home he died,
a bitter loss, and pain, for everyone,
certainly for me. Never again shall I

have for my lot a master mild as he was
anywhere—not even with my parents
at home, where I was born and bred. I miss them   160
less than I do him—though a longing comes
to set my eyes on them in the old country.
No, it is the lost man I ache to think of—
Odysseus. And I speak the name respectfully,
even if he is not here. He loved me, cared for me.
I call him dear my lord, far though he be."

Now royal Odysseus, who had borne the long war,
spoke again:

                                        "Friend, as you are so dead sure
he will not come—and so mistrustful, too—
let me not merely talk, as others talk,   170
but swear to it: your lord is now at hand.
And I expect a gift for this good news
when he enters his own hall. Till then I would not
take a rag, no matter what my need.
I hate as I hate Hell's own gate that weakness
that makes a poor man into a flatterer.
Zeus be my witness, and the table garnished
for true friends, and Odysseus' own hearth—
by heaven, all I say will come to pass!
He will return, and he will be avenged   180
on any who dishonor his wife and son."

Eumaios—O my swineherd!—answered him:

"I take you at your word, then: you shall have
no good news gift from me. Nor will Odysseus
enter his hall. But peace! drink up your wine.
Let us talk now of other things. No more
imaginings. It makes me heavy-hearted
when someone brings my master back to mind—
my own true master.

                                                 No, by heaven,
let us have no oaths! But if Odysseus   190
can come again god send he may! My wish
is that of Penélopê and old Laërtês
and Prince Telémakhos.

                                                 Ah, he's another
to be distressed about—Odysseus' child,
Telémakhos! By the gods' grace he grew
like a tough sapling, and I thought he'd be
no less a man than his great father—strong
and admirably made; but then someone,
god or man, upset him, made him rash,
so that he sailed away to sandy Pylos   200
to hear news of his father. Now the suitors

lie in ambush on his homeward track,
ready to cut away the last shoot of Arkêsios'[4]
line, the royal stock of Ithaka.

No good

dwelling on it. Either he'll be caught
or else Kroníon's[5] hand will take him through.

Tell me, now, of your own trials and troubles.
And tell me truly first, for I should know,
who are you, where do you hail from, where's your home
and family? What kind of ship was yours,   210
and what course brought you here? Who are your sailors?
I don't suppose you walked here on the sea."

To this the master of improvisation answered:

"I'll tell you all that, clearly as I may.
If we could sit here long enough, with meat
and good sweet wine, warm here, in peace and quiet
within doors, while the work of the world goes on—
I might take all this year to tell my story
and never end the tale of misadventures
that wore my heart out, by the gods' will.   220

My native land is the wide seaboard of Krete
where I grew up. I had a wealthy father,
and many other sons were born to him
of his true lady. My mother was a slave,
his concubine; but Kastor Hylákidês,
my father, treated me as a true born son.
High honor came to him in that part of Krete
for wealth and ease, and sons born for renown,
before the death-bearing Kêrês[6] drew him down
to the underworld. His avid sons thereafter   230
dividing up the property by lot
gave me a wretched portion, a poor house.
But my ability won me a wife
of rich family. Fool I was never called,
nor turn-tail in a fight.

My strength's all gone,

but from the husk you may divine the ear
that stood tall in the old days. Misery owns me
now, but then great Arês and Athena
gave me valor and man-breaking power,
whenever I made choice of men-at-arms   240
to set a trap with me for my enemies.

[4] Odysseus' paternal grandfather.
[5] Zeus, son of Kronos.
[6] That is, the forces of death.

Never, as I am a man, did I fear Death
ahead, but went in foremost in the charge,
putting a spear through any man whose legs
were not as fast as mine. That was my element,
war and battle. Farming I never cared for,
nor life at home, nor fathering fair children.
I reveled in long ships with oars; I loved
polished lances, arrows in the skirmish,
the shapes of doom that others shake to see.   250
Carnage suited me; heaven put those things
in me somehow. Each to his own pleasure!
Before we young Akhaians shipped for Troy
I led men on nine cruises in corsairs
to raid strange coasts, and had great luck, taking
rich spoils on the spot, and even more
in the division. So my house grew prosperous,
my standing therefore high among the Kretans.
Then came the day when Zeus who views the wide world
drew men's eyes upon that way accurst   260
that wrung the manhood from the knees of many!
Everyone pressed me, pressed King Idómeneus
to take command of ships for Ilion.
No way out; the country rang with talk of it.
So we Akhaians had nine years of war.
In the tenth year we sacked the inner city,
Priam's town, and sailed for home; but heaven
dispersed the Akhaians. Evil days for me
were stored up in the hidden mind of Zeus.
One month, no more, I stayed at home in joy   270
with children, wife, and treasure. Lust for action
drove me to go to sea then, in command
of ships and gallant seamen bound for Egypt.
Nine ships I fitted out; my men signed on
and came to feast with me, as good shipmates,
for six full days. Many a beast I slaughtered
in the gods' honor, for my friends to eat.
Embarking on the seventh, we hauled sail
and filled away from Krete on a fresh north wind
effortlessly, as boats will glide down stream.   280
All rigging whole and all hands well, we rested,
letting the wind and steersmen work the ships,
for five days; on the fifth we made the delta.[7]
I brought my squadron in to the river bank
with one turn of the sweeps. There, heaven knows,
I told the men to wait and guard the ships
while I sent out patrols to rising ground.

---

[7] The estuary of the Nile River. Though the entire present account by Odysseus of his past
life is meant to deceive, many of his invented stories correspond to what in fact did happen
to him.

But reckless greed carried them all away
to plunder the rich bottomlands; they bore off
wives and children, killed what men they found. 290

When this news reached the city, all who heard it
came at dawn. On foot they came, and horsemen,
filling the river plain with dazzle of bronze;
and Zeus lord of lightning
threw my men into blind panic: no one dared
stand against that host closing around us.
Their scything weapons left our dead in piles,
but some they took alive, into forced labor.
And I—ah, how I wish that I had died
in Egypt, on that field! So many blows 300
awaited me!—Well, Zeus himself inspired me;
I wrenched my dogskin helmet off my head,
dropped my spear, dodged out of my long shield,
ran for the king's chariot and swung on
to embrace and kiss his knees. He pulled me up,
took pity on me, placed me on the footboards,
and drove home with me crouching there in tears.
Aye—for the troops, in battle fury still,
made one pass at me after another, pricking me
with spears, hoping to kill me. But he saved me, 310
for fear of the great wrath of Zeus that comes
when men who ask asylum are given death.

Seven years, then, my sojourn lasted there,
and I amassed a fortune, going about
among the openhanded Egyptians.
But when the eighth came round, a certain
Phoinikian adventurer came too,
a plausible rat, who had already done
plenty of devilry in the world.

                                        This fellow
took me in completely with his schemes, 320
and led me with him to Phoinikia,
where he had land and houses. One full year
I stayed there with him, to the month and day,
and when fair weather came around again
he took me in a deepsea ship for Libya,
pretending I could help in the cargo trade;
he meant, in fact, to trade me off, and get
a high price for me. I could guess the game
but had to follow him aboard. One day
on course due west, off central Krete, the ship 330
caught a fresh norther, and we ran southward
before the wind while Zeus piled ruin ahead.
When Krete was out of sight astern, no land

anywhere to be seen, but sky and ocean,
Kroníon put a dark cloud in the zenith
over the ship, and gloom spread on the sea.
With crack on crack of thunder, he let fly
a bolt against the ship, a direct hit,
so that she bucked, in sacred fumes of sulphur,
and all the men were flung into the water.   340
They came up round the wreck, bobbing a while
like petrels on the waves. No homecoming
for these, from whom the god had turned his face!
Stunned in the smother as I was, yet Zeus
put into my hands the great mast of the ship—
a way to keep from drowning. So I twined
my arms and legs around it in the gale
and stayed afloat nine days. On the tenth night,
a big surf cast me up in Thesprotia.[8]
Pheidon the king there gave me refuge, nobly,   350
with no talk of reward. His son discovered me
exhausted and half dead with cold, and gave me
a hand to bear me up till he reached home
where he could clothe me in a shirt and cloak.
In that king's house I heard news of Odysseus,
who lately was a guest there, passing by
on his way home, the king said; and he showed me
the treasure that Odysseus had brought:
bronze, gold, and iron wrought with heavy labor—
in that great room I saw enough to last   360
Odysseus' heirs for ten long generations.
The man himself had gone up to Dodona[9]
to ask the spelling leaves of the old oak
the will of God: how to return, that is,
to the rich realm of Ithaka, after so long
an absence—openly, or on the quiet.
And, tipping wine out, Pheidon swore to me
the ship was launched, the seamen standing by
to take Odysseus to his land at last.
But he had passage first for me: Thesprotians   370
were sailing, as luck had it, for Doulíkhion,[10]
the grain-growing island; there, he said,
they were to bring me to the king, Akastos.
Instead, that company saw fit to plot
foul play against me; in my wretched life
there was to be more suffering.

---

[8] In Epirus, on the northwest shore of Greece, somewhat north of Ithaka along the mainland coast.

[9] Site of the oldest oracle of Zeus, where the god's utterances were interpreted from the rustling of oak leaves.

[10] An island near Ithaka.

                                        At sea, then,
when land lay far astern, they sprang their trap.
They'd make a slave of me that day, stripping
cloak and tunic off me, throwing around me
the dirty rags you see before you now.   380
At evening, off the fields of Ithaka,
they bound me, lashed me down under the decking
with stout ship's rope, while they all went ashore
in haste to make their supper on the beach.
The gods helped me to pry the lashing loose
until it fell away. I wound my rags
in a bundle round my head and eased myself
down the smooth lading plank into the water,
up to the chin, then swam an easy breast stroke
out and around, putting that crew behind,   390
and went ashore in underbrush, a thicket,
where I lay still, making myself small.
They raised a bitter yelling, and passed by
several times. When further groping seemed
useless to them, back to the ship they went
and out to sea again. The gods were with me,
keeping me hid; and with me when they brought me
here to the door of one who knows the world.
My destiny is yet to live awhile."

The swineherd bowed and said:

                              "Ah well, poor drifter,   400
you've made me sad for you, going back over it,
all your hard life and wandering. That tale
about Odysseus, though, you might have spared me;
you will not make me believe that.
Why must you lie, being the man you are,
and all for nothing?

                              I can see so well
what happened to my master, sailing home!
Surely the gods turned on him, to refuse him
death in the field, or in his friends' arms
after he wound up the great war at Troy.   410
They would have made a tomb for him, the Akhaians,
and paid all honor to his son thereafter. No,
stormwinds made off with him. No glory came to him.

I moved here to the mountain with my swine.
Never, now, do I go down to town
unless I am sent for by Penélopê
when news of some sort comes. But those who sit
around her go on asking the old questions—
a few who miss their master still,
and those who eat his house up, and go free.   420

For my part, I have had no heart for inquiry
since one year an Aitolian[11] made a fool of me.
Exiled from land to land after some killing,
he turned up at my door; I took him in.
My master he had seen in Krete, he said,
lodged with Idómeneus, while the long ships,
leaky from gales, were laid up for repairs.
But they were all to sail, he said, that summer,
or the first days of fall—hulls laden deep
with treasure, manned by crews of heroes.

This time   430

you are the derelict the Powers bring.
Well, give up trying to win me with false news
or flattery. If I receive and shelter you,
it is not for your tales but for your trouble,
and with an eye to Zeus, who guards a guest."

Then said that sly and guileful man, Odysseus:

"A black suspicious heart beats in you surely;
the man you are, not even an oath could change you.
Come then, we'll make a compact; let the gods
witness it from Olympos, where they dwell.   440
Upon your lord's homecoming, if he comes
here to this very hut, and soon—
then give me a new outfit, shirt and cloak,
and ship me to Doulíkhion—I thought it
a pleasant island. But if Odysseus
fails to appear as I predict, then Swish!
let the slaves pitch me down from some high rock,
so the next poor man who comes will watch his tongue."

The forester gave a snort and answered:

"Friend,   450

if I agreed to that, a great name
I should acquire in the world for goodness—
at one stroke and forever: your kind host
who gave you shelter and the hand of friendship,
only to take your life next day!
How confidently, after that, should I
address my prayers to Zeus, the son of Kronos!

It is time now for supper. My young herdsmen
should be arriving soon to set about it.
We'll make a quiet feast here at our hearth."

At this point in their talk the swine had come   460
up to the clearing, and the drovers followed
to pen them for the night—the porkers squealing

[11]Aitolia (or Aetolia) was part of the western Greek mainland, east of Ithaka.

to high heaven, milling around the yard.
The swineherd then gave orders to his men:

"Bring in our best pig for a stranger's dinner.
A feast will do our hearts good, too; we know
grief and pain, hard scrabbling with our swine,
while the outsiders live on our labor."

                                            Bronze
axe in hand, he turned to split up kindling,
while they drove in a tall boar, prime and fat,   470
planting him square before the fire. The gods,
as ever, had their due in the swineherd's thought,
for he it was who tossed the forehead bristles
as a first offering on the flames, calling
upon the immortal gods to let Odysseus
reach his home once more.
                                    Then he stood up
and brained the boar with split oak from the woodpile.
Life ebbed from the beast; they slaughtered him,
singed the carcass, and cut out the joints.
Eumaios, taking flesh from every quarter,   480
put lean strips on the fat of sacrifice,
floured each one with barley meal, and cast it
into the blaze. The rest they sliced and skewered,
roasted with care, then took it off the fire
and heaped it up on platters. Now their chief,
who knew best the amenities, rose to serve,
dividing all that meat in seven portions—
one to be set aside, with proper prayers,
for the wood nymphs and Hermês, Maia's son;
the others for the company. Odysseus   490
he honored with long slices from the chine—
warming the master's heart. Odysseus looked at him
and said:
                        "May you be dear to Zeus
as you are dear to me for this, Eumaios,
favoring with choice cuts a man like me."

And—O my swineherd!—you replied, Eumaios:

"Bless you, stranger, fall to and enjoy it
for what it is. Zeus grants us this or that,
or else refrains from granting, as he wills;
all things are in his power."

                                He cut and burnt   500
a morsel for the gods who are young forever,
tipped out some wine, then put it in the hands
of Odysseus, the old soldier, raider of cities,

who sat at ease now with his meat before him.
As for the loaves, Mesaúlios dealt them out,
a yard boy, bought by the swineherd on his own,
unaided by his mistress or Laërtês,
from Taphians,[12] while Odysseus was away.
Now all hands reached for that array of supper,
until, when hunger and thirst were turned away   510
Mesaúlios removed the bread and, heavy
with food and drink, they settled back to rest.

Now night had come on, rough, with no moon,
but a nightlong downpour setting in, the rainwind
blowing hard from the west. Odysseus
began to talk, to test the swineherd, trying
to put it in his head to take his cloak off
and lend it, or else urge the others to.
He knew the man's compassion.

                                        "Listen," he said,
"Eumaios, and you others, here's a wishful   520
tale that I shall tell. The wine's behind it,
vaporing wine, that makes a serious man
break down and sing, kick up his heels and clown,
or tell some story that were best untold.
But now I'm launched, I can't stop now.

                                        Would god I felt
the hot blood in me that I had at Troy!
Laying an ambush near the walls one time,
Odysseus and Meneláos were commanders
and I ranked third. I went at their request.
We worked in toward the bluffs and battlements   530
and, circling the town, got into canebrakes,[13]
thick and high, a marsh where we took cover,
hunched under arms.

                        The northwind dropped, and night
came black and wintry. A fine sleet descending
whitened the cane like hoarfrost, and clear ice
grew dense upon our shields. The other men,
all wrapt in blanket cloaks as well as tunics,
rested well, in shields up to their shoulders,
but I had left my cloak with friends in camp,
foolhardy as I was. No chance of freezing hard,   540
I thought, so I wore kilts and a shield only.
But in the small hours of the third watch, when stars
that rise at evening go down to their setting,
I nudged Odysseus, who lay close beside me;
he was alert then, listening, and I said:

---

[12] Inhabitants of western Greece. That Eumaios the slave himself acquired a servant is another
sign that in Homeric times slavery was not always degrading serfdom.
[13] Thick growths of cane.

'Son of Laërtês and the gods of old,
Odysseus, master mariner and soldier,
I cannot hold on long among the living.
The cold is making a corpse of me. Some god
inveigled me to come without a cloak.   550
No help for it now; too late.'

                                                 Next thing I knew

he had a scheme all ready in his mind—
and what a man he was for schemes and battles!
Speaking under his breath to me, he murmured:

'Quiet; none of the rest should hear you.'

                                                       Then,

propping his head on his forearm, he said:

'Listen, lads, I had an ominous dream,
the point being how far forward from our ships
and lines we've come. Someone should volunteer
to tell the corps commander, Agamémnon;   560
he may reinforce us from the base.'

                                                       At this,

Thoas jumped up, the young son of Andraimon,
put down his crimson cloak and headed off,
running shoreward.
                              Wrapped in that man's cloak
how gratefully I lay in the bitter dark
until the dawn came stitched in gold! I wish
I had that sap and fiber in me now!"

Then—O my swineherd!—you replied, Eumaios:

"That was a fine story, and well told,
not a word out of place, not a pointless word.   570
No, you'll not sleep cold for lack of cover,
or any other comfort one should give
to a needy guest. However, in the morning,
you must go flapping in the same old clothes.
Shirts and cloaks are few here; every man
has one change only. When our prince arrives,
the son of Odysseus, he will make you gifts—
cloak, tunic, everything—and grant you passage
wherever you care to go."

                                              On this he rose

and placed the bed of balsam near the fire,   580
strewing sheepskins on top, and skins of goats.
Odysseus lay down. His host threw over him
a heavy blanket cloak, his own reserve
against the winter wind when it came wild.

So there Odysseus dropped off to sleep,
while herdsmen slept nearby. But not the swineherd:
not in the hut could he lie down in peace,
but now equipped himself for the night outside;
and this rejoiced Odysseus' heart, to see him
care for the herd so, while his lord was gone.   590
He hung a sharp sword from his shoulder, gathered
a great cloak round him, close, to break the wind,
and pulled a shaggy goatskin on his head.
Then, to keep at a distance dogs or men,
he took a sharpened lance, and went to rest
under a hollow rock where swine were sleeping
out of the wind and rain.

BOOK FIFTEEN: HOW THEY CAME TO ITHAKA

                                                South into Lakedaimon[1]
into the land where greens are wide for dancing
Athena went, to put in mind of home
her great-hearted hero's honored son,
rousing him to return.

                                        And there she found him
with Nestor's lad in the late night at rest
under the portico of Meneláos,
the famous king. Stilled by the power of slumber
the son of Nestor lay, but honeyed sleep
had not yet taken in her arms Telémakhos.   10
All through the starlit night, with open eyes,
he pondered what he had heard about his father,
until at his bedside grey-eyed Athena
towered and said:

                                "The brave thing now, Telémakhos,
would be to end this journey far from home.
All that you own you left behind
with men so lost to honor in your house
they may devour it all, shared out among them.
How will your journey save you then?

                                                Go quickly
to the lord of the great war cry, Meneláos;   20
press him to send you back. You may yet find
the queen your mother in her rooms alone.
It seems her father and her kinsmen say
Eurýmakhos is the man for her to marry.
He has outdone the suitors, all the rest,
in gifts to her, and made her pledges double.

---

[1] The story of Telémakhos, broken off after Book IV, is here resumed.

Check him, or he will have your lands and chattels
in spite of you.

                             You know a woman's pride
at bringing riches to the man she marries.
As to her girlhood husband, her first children,   30
he is forgotten, being dead—and they
no longer worry her. [2]

                                  So act alone.

Go back; entrust your riches to the servant
worthiest in your eyes, until the gods
make known what beauty you yourself shall marry.

This too I have to tell you: now take heed:
the suitors' ringleaders are hot for murder,
waiting in the channel between Ithaka
and Samê's rocky side; they mean to kill you
before you can set foot ashore. I doubt   40
they'll bring it off. Dark earth instead
may take to her cold bed a few brave suitors
who preyed upon your cattle.

                                Bear well out

in your good ship, to eastward of the islands,
and sail again by night. Someone immortal
who cares for you will make a fair wind blow.
Touch at the first beach, go ashore, and send
your ship and crew around to port by sea,
while you go inland to the forester,
your old friend, loyal keeper of the swine.   50
Remain that night with him; send him to town
to tell your watchful mother Penélopê
that you are back from Pylos safe and sound."

With this Athena left him for Olympos.
He swung his foot across and gave a kick
and said to the son of Nestor:

                             "Open your eyes,

Peisístratos. Get our team into harness.
We have a long day's journey."

                                Nestor's son

turned over and answered him:

                                "It is still night,

and no moon. Can we drive now? We can not,   60
itch as we may for the road home. Dawn is near.
Allow the captain of spearmen, Meneláos,

---

[2] These last three lines are a comment on widows in general, not on Penélopê in particular.
Athena assumes this cynical view in order to hasten Telémakhos' return.

time to pack our car with gifts and time
to speak a gracious word, sending us off.
A guest remembers all his days
that host who makes provision for him kindly."

The Dawn soon took her throne of gold, and Lord
Meneláos, clarion in battle,
rose from where he lay beside the beauty   70
of Helen with her shining hair. He strode
into the hall nearby.

                                        Hearing him come,
Odysseus' son pulled on his snowy tunic
over the skin, gathered his long cape
about his breadth of shoulder like a captain,
the heir of King Odysseus. At the door
he stood and said:

                                        "Lord Marshal, Meneláos,
send me home now to my own dear country:
longing has come upon me to go home."

The lord of the great war cry said at once: 80

"If you are longing to go home, Telémakhos,
I would not keep you for the world, not I.
I'd think myself or any other host
as ill-mannered for over-friendliness
as for hostility.

                        Measure is best in everything
To send a guest packing, or cling to him
when he's in haste—one sin equals the other.
'Good entertaining ends with no detaining.'
Only let me load your car with gifts
and fine ones, you shall see.

                                        I'll bid the women   90
set out breakfast from the larder stores;
honor and appetite—we'll attend to both
before a long day's journey overland.
Or would you care to try the Argive midlands
and Hellas, in my company? I'll harness
my own team, and take you through the towns.
Guests like ourselves no lord will turn away;
each one will make one gift, at least,
to carry home with us: tripod or cauldron
wrought in bronze, mule team, or golden cup."   100

Clearheaded Telémakhos replied:

                                        "Lord Marshal

Meneláos, royal son of Atreus,
I must return to my own hearth. I left
no one behind as guardian of my property.

This going abroad for news of a great father—
heaven forbid it be my own undoing,
or any precious thing be lost at home."

At this the tall king, clarion in battle,
called to his lady and her waiting women
to give them breakfast from the larder stores. 110
Eteóneus, the son of Boethoös, came
straight from bed, from where he lodged nearby,
and Meneláos ordered a fire lit
for broiling mutton. The king's man obeyed.
Then down to the cedar chamber Meneláos
walked with Helen and Prince Megapénthês.
Amid the gold he had in that place lying
the son of Atreus picked a wine cup, wrought
with handles left and right, and told his son
to take a silver winebowl.

        Helen lingered 120
near the deep coffers filled with gowns, her own
handiwork.

      Tall goddess among women,
she lifted out one robe of state so royal,
adorned and brilliant with embroidery,
deep in the chest it shimmered like a star.
Now all three turned back to the door to greet
Telémakhos. And red-haired Meneláos
cried out to him:

        "O prince Telémakhos,
may Hêra's Lord of Thunder see you home
and bring you to the welcome you desire! 130
Here are your gifts—perfect and precious things
I wish to make your own, out of my treasure."

And gently the great captain, son of Atreus,
handed him the goblet. Megapénthês
carried the winebowl glinting silvery
to set before him, and the Lady Helen
drew near, so that he saw her cheek's pure line.
She held the gown and murmured:

"I, too,
bring you a gift, dear child, and here it is; 140
remember Helen's hands by this; keep it
for your own bride, your joyful wedding day;
let your dear mother guard it in her chamber.
My blessing: may you come soon to your island,
home to your timbered hall."

       So she bestowed it,
and happily he took it. These fine things

Peisístratos packed well in the wicker carrier,
admiring every one. Then Meneláos
led the two guests in to take their seats
on thrones and easy chairs in the great hall.   150
Now came a maid to tip a golden jug
of water over a silver finger bowl,
and draw the polished tables up beside them;
the larder mistress brought her tray of loaves,
with many savories to lavish on them;
viands were served by Eteóneus, and wine
by Meneláos' son. Then every hand
reached out upon good meat and drink to take them,
driving away hunger and thirst. At last,
Telémakhos and Nestor's son led out   160
their team to harness, mounted their bright car,
and drove down under the echoing entrance way,
while red-haired Meneláos, Atreus' son,
walked alongside with a golden cup—
wine for the wayfarers to spill at parting.
Then by the tugging team he stood, and spoke
over the horses' heads:

                                                   "Farewell, my lads.
Homage to Nestor, the benevolent king;
in my time he was fatherly to me,
when the flower of Akhaia warred on Troy."   170

Telémakhos made this reply:

"No fear
but we shall bear at least as far as Nestor
your messages, great king. How I could wish
to bring them home to Ithaka! If only
Odysseus were there, if he could hear me tell
of all the courtesy I have had from you,
returning with your finery and your treasure."

Even as he spoke, a beat of wings went skyward
off to the right—a mountain eagle, grappling   180
a white goose in his talons, heavy prey
hooked from a farmyard. Women and men-at-arms
made hubbub, running up, as he flew over,
but then he wheeled hard right before the horses—
a sight that made the whole crowd cheer, with hearts
lifting in joy. Peisístratos called out:

"Read us the sign, O Meneláos, Lord
Marshal of armies! Was the god revealing
something thus to you, or to ourselves?"

At this the old friend of the god of battle   190

groped in his mind for the right thing to say,
but regal Helen put in quickly:

"Listen:
I can tell you—tell what the omen means,
as light is given me, and as I see it
point by point fulfilled. The beaked eagle
flew from the wild mountain of his fathers
to take for prey the tame house bird. Just so,
Odysseus, back from his hard trials and wandering,
will soon come down in fury on his house. 200
He may be there today, and a black hour
he brings upon the suitors."

Telémakhos
gazed and said:

"May Zeus, the lord of Hêra,
make it so! In far-off Ithaka, all my life,
I shall invoke you as a goddess, lady."

He let the whip fall, and the restive mares
broke forward at a canter through the town
into the open country.

All that day
they kept their harness shaking, side by side,
until at sundown when the roads grew dim 210
they made a halt at Pherai. There Dióklês
son of Ortílokhos whom Alpheios fathered,
welcomed the young men, and they slept the night.
Up when the young Dawn's finger tips of rose
opened in the east, they hitched the team
once more to the painted car
and steered out westward through the echoing gate,
whipping their fresh horses into a run.
Approaching Pylos Height at the day's end,
Telémakhos appealed to the son of Nestor: 220

"Could you, I wonder, do a thing I'll tell you,
supposing you agree?
We take ourselves to be true friends—in age
alike, and bound by ties between our fathers,
and now by partnership in this adventure.
Prince, do not take me roundabout,
but leave me at the ship, else the old king
your father will detain me overnight
for love of guests, when I should be at sea."

The son of Nestor nodded, thinking swiftly 230
how best he could oblige his friend.
Here was his choice: to pull the team hard over

along the beach till he could rein them in
beside the ship. Unloading Meneláos'
royal keepsakes into the stern sheets,
he sang out:

                           "Now for action! Get aboard,
and call your men, before I break the news
at home in hall to father. Who knows better
the old man's heart than I? If you delay,
he will not let you go, but he'll descend on you   240
in person and imperious; no turning
back with empty hands for him, believe me,
once his blood is up."

                                   He shook the reins
to the lovely mares with long manes in the wind,
guiding them full tilt toward his father's hall.
Telémakhos called in the crew, and told them:

"Get everything shipshape aboard this craft;
we pull out now, and put sea miles behind us."

The listening men obeyed him, climbing in
to settle on their benches by the rowlocks,   250
while he stood watchful by the stern. He poured out
offerings there, and prayers to Athena.

Now a strange man came up to him, an easterner
fresh from spilling blood in distant Argos,
a hunted man. Gifted in prophecy,
he had as forebear that Melampous,[3] wizard
who lived of old in Pylos, mother city
of western flocks.

                         Melampous, a rich lord,
had owned a house unmatched among the Pylians,
until the day came when king Neleus, noblest   260
in that age, drove him from his native land.
And Neleus for a year's term sequestered
Melampous' fields and flocks, while he lay bound
hand and foot in the keep of Phylakos.
Beauty of Neleus' daughter put him there
and sombre folly the inbreaking Fury
thrust upon him. But he gave the slip
to death, and drove the bellowing herd of Iphiklos
from Phylakê to Pylos, there to claim
the bride that ordeal won him from the king.   270
He led her to his brother's house, and went on
eastward into another land, the bluegrass

---

[3] For the stories of Melampous and Amphiaraos, see Book XI and the notes to it.

plain of Argos. Destiny held for him
rule over many Argives. Here he married,
built a great manor house, fathered Antíphatês
and Mantios, commanders both, of whom
Antíphatês begot Oikleiês
and Oikleiês the firebrand Amphiaraos.
This champion the lord of stormcloud, Zeus,
and strong Apollo loved; nor had he ever   280
to cross the doorsill into dim old age.
A woman, bought by trinkets, gave him over
to be cut down in the assault on Thebes.
His sons were Alkmáon and Amphílokhos.
In the meantime Lord Mantios begot
Polypheidês, the prophet, and
Kleitos—famous name! For Dawn[4] in silks
of gold carried off Kleitos for his beauty
to live among the gods. But Polypheidês,
high-hearted and exalted by Apollo   290
above all men for prophecy, withdrew
to Hyperesia[5] when his father angered him.
He lived on there, foretelling to the world
the shape of things to come.

$\qquad\qquad\qquad\qquad\qquad\qquad$ His son it was,

Theoklýmenos, who came upon Telémakhos
as he poured out the red wine in the sand
near his trim ship, with prayer to Athena;
and he called out, approaching:

$\qquad\qquad\qquad\qquad\qquad\qquad$ "Friend, well met

here at libation before going to sea.
I pray you by the wine you spend, and by   300
your god, your own life, and your company;
enlighten me, and let the truth be known.
Who are you? Of what city and what parents?"

Telémakhos turned to him and replied:

"Stranger, as truly as may be, I'll tell you.
I am from Ithaka, where I was born;
my father is, or he once was, Odysseus.
But he's a long time gone, and dead, may be;
and that is what I took ship with my friends
to find out—for he left long years ago."   310

Said Theoklýmenos in reply:

"I too
have had to leave my home. I killed a cousin.

---

[4] Eos, goddess of the dawn.
[5] A town on the Corinthian bay; part of Agamémnon's kingdom.

In the wide grazing lands of Argos live
many kinsmen of his and friends in power,
great among the Akhaians. These I fled.
Death and vengeance at my back, as Fate
has turned now, I came wandering overland.
Give me a plank aboard your ship, I beg,
or they will kill me. They are on my track."   320

Telémakhos made answer:

                                                            "No two ways
about it. Will I pry you from our gunnel[6]
when you are desperate to get to sea?
Come aboard; share what we have, and welcome."

He took the bronze-shod lance from the man's hand
and laid it down full-length on deck; then swung
his own weight after it aboard the cutter,
taking position aft, making a place
for Theoklýmenos near him. The stern lines
were slacked off, and Telémakhos commanded: 330

"Rig the mast; make sail!" Nimbly they ran
to push the fir pole high and step it firm
amidships in the box, make fast the forestays,
and hoist aloft the white sail on its halyards.
A following wind came down from grey-eyed Athena,
blowing brisk through heaven, and so steady
the cutter lapped up miles of salt blue sea,
passing Krounoi[7] abeam and Khalkis estuary
at sundown when the sea ways all grew dark.
Then, by Athena's wind borne on, the ship   340
rounded Pheai by night and coasted Elis,
the green domain of the Epeioi; thence
he put her head north toward the running pack
of islets, wondering if by sailing wide
he sheered off Death, or would be caught.

                                                            That night
Odysseus and the swineherd supped again
with herdsmen in their mountain hut. At ease
when appetite and thirst were turned away,
Odysseus, while he talked, observed the swineherd
to see if he were hospitable still—   350
if yet again the man would make him stay
under his roof, or send him off to town.

---

[6] Gunwale; the top edge of the ship's side.
[7] The following lines describe the ship's northwest course along the southwest coast of Greece.

"Listen," he said, "Eumaios; listen, lads.
At daybreak I must go and try my luck
around the port. I burden you too long.
Direct me, put me on the road with someone.
Nothing else for it but to play the beggar
in populous parts. I'll get a cup or loaf,
maybe, from some householder. If I go
as far as the great hall of King Odysseus 360
I might tell Queen Penélopê my news.
Or I can drift inside among the suitors
to see what alms they give, rich as they are.
If they have whims, I'm deft in ways of service—
that I can say, and you may know for sure.
By grace of Hermês the Wayfinder, patron
of mortal tasks, the god who honors toil,
no man can do a chore better than I can.
Set me to build a fire, or chop wood,
cook or carve, mix wine and serve—or anything 370
inferior men attend to for the gentry."

Now you were furious at this, Eumaios,
and answered—O my swineherd!—

                                          "Friend, friend,
how could this fantasy take hold of you?
You dally with your life, and nothing less,
if you feel drawn to mingle in that company—
reckless, violent, and famous for it
out to the rim of heaven. Slaves
they have, but not like you. No—theirs are boys
in fresh cloaks and tunics, with pomade 380
ever on their sleek heads, and pretty faces.
These are their minions, while their tables gleam
and groan under big roasts, with loaves and wine.
Stay with us here. No one is burdened by you,
neither myself nor any of my hands.
Wait here until Odysseus' son returns.
You shall have clothing from him, cloak and tunic,
and passage where your heart desires to go."

The noble and enduring man replied:

"May you be dear to Zeus for this, Eumaios, 390
even as you are to me. Respite from pain
you give me—and from homelessness. In life
there's nothing worse than knocking about the world,
no bitterness we vagabonds are spared
when the curst belly rages! Well, you master it
and me, making me wait for the king's son.
But now, come, tell me:

what of Odysseus' mother, and his father
whom he took leave of on the sill of age?
Are they under the sun's rays, living still,   400
or gone down long ago to lodge with Death?"

To this the rugged herdsman answered:

"Aye,
that I can tell you; it is briefly told.
Laërtês lives, but daily in his hall
prays for the end of life and soul's delivery,
heartbroken as he is for a son long gone
and for his lady. Sorrow, when she died,
aged and enfeebled him like a green tree stricken;
but pining for her son, her brilliant son,   410
wore out her life.
                               Would god no death so sad
might come to benefactors dear as she!
I loved always to ask and hear about her
while she lived, although she lived in sorrow.
For she had brought me up with her own daughter,
Princess Ktimenê, her youngest child.
We were alike in age and nursed as equals
nearly, till in the flower of our years
they gave her, married her, to a Samian prince,
taking his many gifts. For my own portion   420
her mother gave new clothing, cloak and sandals,
and sent me to the woodland. Well she loved me.
Ah, how I miss that family! It is true
the blissful gods prosper my work; I have
meat and drink to spare for those I prize;
but so removed I am, I have no speech
with my sweet mistress, now that evil days
and overbearing men darken her house.
Tenants all hanker for good talk and gossip
around their lady, and a snack in hall,   430
a cup or two before they take the road
to their home acres, each one bearing home
some gift to cheer his heart."

                               The great tactician
answered:

                               "You were still a child, I see,
when exiled somehow from your parents' land.
Tell me, had it been sacked in war, the city
of spacious ways in which they made their home,
your father and your gentle mother? Or
were you kidnapped alone, brought here by sea
huddled with sheep in some foul pirate squadron,   440
to this landowner's hall? He paid your ransom?"

The master of the woodland answered:

"Friend,

now that you show an interest in that matter,
attend me quietly, be at your ease,
and drink your wine. These autumn nights are long,
ample for story-telling and for sleep.
You need not go to bed before the hour;
sleeping from dusk to dawn's a dull affair.
Let any other here who wishes, though,
retire to rest. At daybreak let him breakfast   450
and take the king's own swine into the wilderness.
Here's a tight roof; we'll drink on, you and I,
and ease our hearts of hardships we remember,
sharing old times. In later days a man
can find a charm in old adversity,
exile and pain. As to your question, now:

A certain island, Syriê by name—
you may have heard the name—lies off Ortýgia[8]
due west, and holds the sunsets of the year.
Not very populous, but good for grazing   460
sheep and kine; rich too in wine and grain.
No dearth is ever known there, no disease
wars on the folk, of ills that plague mankind;
but when the townsmen reach old age, Apollo
with his longbow of silver comes, and Artemis,
showering arrows of mild death.

Two towns

divide the farmlands of that whole domain,
and both were ruled by Ktêsios, my father,
Orménos' heir, and a great godlike man.

Now one day some of those renowned seafaring   470
men, sea-dogs, Phoinikians, came ashore
with bags of gauds for trading. Father had
in our household a woman of Phoinikia,
a handsome one, and highly skilled. Well, she
gave in to the seductions of those rovers.
One of them found her washing near the mooring
and lay with her, making such love to her
as women in their frailty are confused by,
even the best of them.

In due course, then,

he asked her who she was and where she hailed from: 480
and nodding toward my father's roof, she said:

---

[8] Though there were actual places bearing the names of Syriê and Ortýgia, in the present context they refer vaguely to unidentifiable localities, probably in northwestern Greece, and possibly invented by the poet.

'I am of Sidon town, smithy of bronze
for all the East. Arubas Pasha's daughter.
Taphian pirates caught me in a byway
and sold me into slavery overseas
in this man's home. He could afford my ransom.'

The sailor who had lain with her replied:

'Why not ship out with us on the run homeward,
and see your father's high-roofed hall again,
your father and your mother? Still in Sidon   490
and still rich, they are said to be.'

                                                      She answered:

'It could be done, that, if you sailors take
oath I'll be given passage home unharmed.'

Well, soon she had them swearing it all pat
as she desired, repeating every syllable,
whereupon she warned them:

                                                      'Not a word

about our meeting here! Never call out to me
when any of you see me in the lane
or at the well. Some visitor might bear
tales to the old man. If he guessed the truth,   500
I'd be chained up, your lives would be in peril.
No: keep it secret. Hurry with your peddling,
and when your hold is filled with livestock, send
a message to me at the manor hall.
Gold I'll bring, whatever comes to hand,
and something else, too, as my passage fee—
the master's child, my charge: a boy so high,
bright for his age; he runs with me on errands.
I'd take him with me happily; his price
would be I know not what in sale abroad.'   510

Her bargain made, she went back to the manor.
But they were on the island all that year,
getting by trade a cargo of our cattle;
until, the ship at length being laden full,
ready for sea, they sent a messenger
to the Phoinikian woman. Shrewd he was,
this fellow who came round my father's hall,
showing a golden chain all strung with amber,
a necklace. Maids in waiting and my mother
passed it from hand to hand, admiring it,   520
engaging they would buy it. But that dodger,
as soon as he had caught the woman's eye
and nodded, slipped away to join the ship.

She took my hand and led me through the court
into the portico. There by luck she found
winecups and tables still in place—for Father's
attendant counselors had dined just now
before they went to the assembly. Quickly
she hid three goblets in her bellying dress
to carry with her, while I tagged along   530
in my bewilderment. The sun went down
and all the lanes grew dark as we descended,
skirting the harbor in our haste to where
those traders of Phoinikia held their ship.
All went aboard at once and put to sea,
taking the two of us. A favoring wind
blew from the power of heaven. We sailed on
six nights and days without event. Then Zeus
the son of Kronos added one more noon—and sudden
arrows from Artemis pierced the woman's heart.   540
Stone-dead she dropped
into the sloshing bilge the way a tern
plummets; and the sailors heaved her over
as tender pickings for the seals and fish.
Now I was left in dread, alone, while wind
and current bore them on to Ithaka.
Laërtês purchased me. That was the way
I first laid eyes upon this land."

                                        Odysseus,
the kingly man, replied:

                            "You rouse my pity,
telling what you endured when you were young.   550
But surely Zeus put good alongside ill:
torn from your own far home, you had the luck
to come into a kind man's service, generous
with food and drink. And a good life you lead,
unlike my own, all spent in barren roaming
from one country to the next, till now."

So the two men talked on, into the night,
leaving few hours for sleep before the Dawn
stepped up to her bright chair.

                            The ship now drifting
under the island lee, Telémakhos'   560
companions took in sail and mast, unshipped
the oars and rowed ashore. They moored her stern
by the stout hawser lines, tossed out the bow stones,
and waded in beyond the wash of ripples
to mix their wine and cook their morning meal.
When they had turned back hunger and thirst, Telémakhos
arose to give the order of the day.

"Pull for the town," he said, "and berth our ship,
while I go inland across country. Later,
this evening, after looking at my farms,   570
I'll join you in the city. When day comes
I hope to celebrate our crossing, feasting
everyone on good red meat and wine."

His noble passenger, Theoklýmenos,
now asked:

                              "What as to me, my dear young fellow,
where shall I go? Will I find lodging here
with some one of the lords of stony Ithaka?
Or go straight to your mother's hall and yours?"

Telémakhos turned round to him and said:

"I should myself invite you to our hall   580
if things were otherwise; there'd be no lack
of entertainment for you. As it stands,
no place could be more wretched for a guest
while I'm away. Mother will never see you;
she almost never shows herself at home
to the suitors there, but stays in her high chamber
weaving upon her loom. No, let me name
another man for you to go to visit:
Eurýmakhos,[9] the honored son of Pólybos.
In Ithaka they are dazzled by him now—   590
the strongest of their princes, bent on making
mother and all Odysseus' wealth his own.
Zeus on Olympos only knows
if some dark hour for them will intervene."

The words were barely spoken, when a hawk,
Apollo's courier, flew up on the right,
clutching a dove and plucking her—so feathers
floated down to the ground between Telémakhos
and the moored cutter. Theoklýmenos
called him apart and gripped his hand, whispering: 600

"A god spoke in this bird-sign on the right.
I knew it when I saw the hawk fly over us.
There is no kinglier house than yours, Telémakhos,
here in the realm of Ithaka. Your family
will be in power forever."

---

[9] *Eurýmakhos.* Since he is one of Penélopê's principal suitors, it is odd that Eurýmakhos should
be recommended by Telémakhos as a host for his passenger. Indeed, Telémakhos soon changes
his mind and asks the trusted crewman Peiraios to house Theoklýmenos. Possibly Telémakhos,
with something of his father's wariness, hesitates until he has some evidence of Theoklýmenos'
goodwill.

The young prince,

clear in spirit, answered:

"Be it so,

friend, as you say. And may you know as well
the friendship of my house, and many gifts
from me, so everyone may call you fortunate."

He called a trusted crewman named Peiraios,   610
and said to him:

"Peiraios, son of Klýtios,

can I rely on you again as ever, most
of all the friends who sailed with me to Pylos?
Take this man home with you, take care of him,
treat him with honor, till I come."

To this

Peiraios the good spearman answered:
"Aÿe,
stay in the wild country while you will,
I shall be looking after him, Telémakhos.
He will not lack good lodging."

Down to the ship   620

he turned, and boarded her, and called the others
to cast off the stern lines and come aboard.
So men climbed in to sit beside the rowlocks.
Telémakhos now tied his sandals on
and lifted his tough spear from the ship's deck;
hawsers were taken in, and they shoved off
to reach the town by way of the open sea
as he commanded them—royal Odysseus'
own dear son, Telémakhos.

On foot

and swiftly he went up toward the stockade   630
where swine were penned in hundreds, and at night
the guardian of the swine, the forester,
slept under arms on duty for his masters.

BOOK SIXTEEN: FATHER AND SON

But there were two men in the mountain hut—
Odysseus and the swineherd. At first light
blowing their fire up, they cooked their breakfast
and sent their lads out, driving herds to root
in the tall timber.

                                        When Telémakhos came,
the wolvish troop of watchdogs only fawned on him
as he advanced. Odysseus heard them go
and heard the light crunch of a man's footfall—
at which he turned quickly to say:

                                                          "Eumaios,
here is one of your crew come back, or maybe   10
another friend: the dogs are out there snuffling
belly down; not one has even growled.
I can hear footsteps—"

                                        But before he finished
his tall son stood at the door.

                                        The swineherd
rose in surprise, letting a bowl and jug
tumble from his fingers. Going forward,
he kissed the young man's head, his shining eyes
and both hands, while his own tears brimmed and fell.
Think of a man whose dear and only son,
born to him in exile, reared with labor,   20
has lived ten years abroad and now returns:
how would that man embrace his son! Just so
the herdsman clapped his arms around Telémakhos
and covered him with kisses—for he knew
the lad had got away from death. He said:

"Light of my days, Telémakhos,
you made it back! When you took ship for Pylos
I never thought to see you here again.
Come in, dear child, and let me feast my eyes;
here you are, home from the distant places!   30
How rarely, anyway, you visit us,
your own men, and your own woods and pastures!
Always in the town, a man would think
you loved the suitors' company, those dogs!"

Telémakhos with his clear candor said:

"I am with you, Uncle. See now, I have come
because I wanted to see you first, to hear from you
if Mother stayed at home—or is she married
off to someone, and Odysseus' bed
left empty for some gloomy spider's weaving?"   40

Gently the forester replied to this:

"At home indeed your mother is, poor lady,
still in the women's hall. Her nights and days
are wearied out with grieving."

Stepping back
he took the bronze-shod lance, and the young prince
entered the cabin over the worn door stone.
Odysseus moved aside, yielding his couch,
but from across the room Telémakhos checked him:

"Friend, sit down; we'll find another chair
in our own hut. Here is the man to make one!" 50

The swineherd, when the quiet man sank down,
built a new pile of evergreens and fleeces—
a couch for the dear son of great Odysseus—
then gave them trenchers of good meat, left over
from the roast pork of yesterday, and heaped up
willow baskets full of bread, and mixed
an ivy bowl of honey-hearted wine.
Then he in turn sat down, facing Odysseus,
their hands went out upon the meat and drink
as they fell to, ridding themselves of hunger, 60
until Telémakhos paused and said:

"Oh, Uncle,
what's your friend's home port? How did he come?
Who were the sailors brought him here to Ithaka?
I doubt if he came walking on the sea."

And you replied, Eumaios—O my swineherd—

"Son, the truth about him is soon told.
His home land, and a broad land, too, is Krete,
but he has knocked about the world, he says,
for years, as the Powers wove his life. Just now
he broke away from a shipload of Thesprotians 70
to reach my hut. I place him in your hands.
Act as you will. He wishes your protection."

The young man said:

"Eumaios, my protection!
The notion cuts me to the heart. How can I
receive your friend at home? I am not old enough
or trained in arms. Could I defend myself
if someone picked a fight with me?

Besides,
mother is in a quandary, whether to stay with me
as mistress of our household, honoring
her lord's bed, and opinion in the town, 80
or take the best Akhaian who comes her way—
the one who offers most.

I'll undertake,
at all events, to clothe your friend for winter,

now he is with you. Tunic and cloak of wool,
a good broadsword, and sandals—these are his.
I can arrange to send him where he likes
or you may keep him in your cabin here.
I shall have bread and wine sent up; you need not
feel any pinch on his behalf.

                                                  Impossible
to let him stay in hall, among the suitors.   90
They are drunk, drunk on impudence, they might
injure my guest—and how could I bear that?
How could a single man take on those odds?
Not even a hero could.

                              The suitors are too strong."

At this the noble and enduring man, Odysseus,
addressed his son:

                              "Kind prince, it may be fitting
for me to speak a word. All that you say
gives me an inward wound as I sit listening.
I mean this wanton game they play, these fellows,
riding roughshod over you in your own house,   100
admirable as you are. But tell me,
are you resigned to being bled? The townsmen,
stirred up against you, are they, by some oracle?
Your brothers—can you say your brothers fail you?
A man should feel his kin, at least, behind him
in any clash, when a real fight is coming.
If my heart were as young as yours, if I were
son to Odysseus, or the man himself,
I'd rather have my head cut from my shoulders
by some slashing adversary, if I   110
brought no hurt upon that crew! Suppose
I went down, being alone, before the lot,
better, I say, to die at home in battle
than see these insupportable things, day after
day the stranger cuffed, the women slaves
dragged here and there, shame in the lovely rooms,
the wine drunk up in rivers, sheer waste
of pointless feasting, never at an end!"

Telémakhos replied:

                              "Friend, I'll explain to you.
There is no rancor in the town against me,   120
no fault of brothers, whom a man should feel
behind him when a fight is in the making;
no, no—in our family the First Born
of Heaven, Zeus, made single sons the rule.
Arkeísios had but one, Laërtês; he
in turn fathered only one, Odysseus,

who left me in his hall alone, too young
to be of any use to him.
And so you see why enemies fill our house
in these days: all the princes of the islands,   130
Doulíkhion, Samê, wooded Zakýnthos,
Ithaka, too—lords of our island rock—
eating our house up as they court my mother.
She cannot put an end to it; she dare not
bar the marriage that she hates; and they
devour all my substance and my cattle,
and who knows when they'll slaughter me as well?
It rests upon the gods' great knees.

                                   Uncle,
go down at once and tell the Lady Penélopê
that I am back from Pylos, safe and sound.   140
I stay here meanwhile. You will give your message
and then return. Let none of the Akhaians
hear it; they have a mind to do me harm."

To this, Eumaios, you replied:

                                       "I know.
But make this clear, now—should I not likewise
call on Laërtês with your news? Hard hit
by sorrow though he was, mourning Odysseus,
he used to keep an eye upon his farm.
He had what meals he pleased, with his own folk.
But now no more, not since you sailed for Pylos;   150
he has not taken food or drink, I hear,
sitting all day, blind to the work of harvest,
groaning, while the skin shrinks on his bones."

Telémakhos answered:

                                  "One more misery,
but we had better leave it so.
If men choose, and have their choice, in everything,
we'd have my father home.

                                  Turn back
when you have done your errand, as you must,
not to be caught alone in the countryside.
But wait—you may tell Mother   160
to send our old housekeeper on the quiet
and quickly; she can tell the news to Grandfather."

The swineherd, roused, reached out to get his sandals,
tied them on, and took the road.

                                  Who else
beheld this but Athena? From the air
she walked, taking the form of a tall woman,

handsome and clever at her craft, and stood
beyond the gate in plain sight of Odysseus,
unseen, though, by Telémakhos, unguessed,
for not to everyone will gods appear.   170
Odysseus noticed her; so did the dogs,
who cowered whimpering away from her. She only
nodded, signing to him with her brows,
a sign he recognized. Crossing the yard,
he passed out through the gate in the stockade
to face the goddess. There she said to him:

"Son of Laërtês and the gods of old,
Odysseus, master of land ways and sea ways,
dissemble to your son no longer now.
The time has come: tell him how you together   180
will bring doom on the suitors in the town.
I shall not be far distant then, for I
myself desire battle."

                                                  Saying no more,
she tipped her golden wand upon the man,
making his cloak pure white, and the knit tunic
fresh around him. Lithe and young she made him,
ruddy with sun, his jawline clean, the beard
no longer grey upon his chin. And she
withdrew when she had done.
                                        Then Lord Odysseus
reappeared—and his son was thunderstruck.   190
Fear in his eyes, he looked down and away
as though it were a god, and whispered:

                                                  "Stranger,
you are no longer what you were just now!
Your cloak is new; even your skin! You are
one of the gods who rule the sweep of heaven!
Be kind to us, we'll make you fair oblation
and gifts of hammered gold. Have mercy on us!"

The noble and enduring man replied:

"No god. Why take me for a god? No, no.
I am that father whom your boyhood lacked   200
and suffered pain for lack of. I am he."

Held back too long, the tears ran down his cheeks
as he embraced his son.
                                        Only Telémakhos,
uncomprehending, wild
with incredulity, cried out:

"You cannot
be my father Odysseus! Meddling spirits
conceived this trick to twist the knife in me!
No man of woman born could work these wonders
by his own craft, unless a god came into it
with ease to turn him young or old at will.   210
I swear you were in rags and old,
and here you stand like one of the immortals!"

Odysseus brought his ranging mind to bear
and said:

"This is not princely, to be swept
away by wonder at your father's presence.
No other Odysseus will ever come,
for he and I are one, the same; his bitter
fortune and his wanderings are mine.
Twenty years gone, and I am back again
on my own island.

As for my change of skin,   220
that is a charm Athena, Hope of Soldiers,
uses as she will; she has the knack
to make me seem a beggar man sometimes
and sometimes young, with finer clothes about me.
It is no hard thing for the gods of heaven
to glorify a man or bring him low."

When he had spoken, down he sat.

Then, throwing
his arms around this marvel of a father
Telémakhos began to weep. Salt tears
rose from the wells of longing in both men,   230
and cries burst from both as keen and fluttering
as those of the great taloned hawk,
whose nestlings farmers take before they fly.
So helplessly they cried, pouring out tears,
and might have gone on weeping so till sundown,
had not Telémakhos said:

"Dear father! Tell me
what kind of vessel put you here ashore
on Ithaka? Your sailors, who were they?
I doubt you made it, walking on the sea!"

Then said Odysseus, who had borne the barren sea: 240

"Only plain truth shall I tell you, child.
Great seafarers, the Phaiákians, gave me passage
as they give other wanderers. By night
over the open ocean, while I slept,

they brought me in their cutter, set me down
on Ithaka, with gifts of bronze and gold
and stores of woven things. By the gods' will
these lie all hidden in a cave. I came
to this wild place, directed by Athena,
so that we might lay plans to kill our enemies.   250
Count up the suitors for me, let me know
what men at arms are there, how many men.
I must put all my mind to it, to see
if we two by ourselves can take them on
or if we should look round for help."

                                          Telémakhos
replied:

                         "O Father, all my life your fame
as a fighting man has echoed in my ears—
your skills with weapons and the tricks of war—
but what you speak of is a staggering thing,
beyond imagining, for me. How can two men   260
do battle with a houseful in their prime?
For I must tell you this is no affair
of ten or even twice ten men, but scores,
throngs of them. You shall see, here and now.
The number from Doulíkhion alone
is fifty-two, picked men, with armorers,
a half dozen; twenty-four came from Samê,
twenty from Zakýnthos; our own island
accounts for twelve, high-ranked, and their retainers,
Medôn the crier, and the Master Harper   270
besides a pair of handymen at feasts.
If we go in against all these
I fear we pay in salt blood for your vengeance.
You must think hard if you would conjure up
the fighting strength to take us through."

                                           Odysseus
who had endured the long war and the sea
answered:

                                 "I'll tell you now.
Suppose Athena's arm is over us, and Zeus
her father's, must I rack my brains for more?"

Clearheaded Telémakhos looked hard and said: 280

"Those two are great defenders, no one doubts it,
but throned in the serene clouds overhead;
other affairs of men and gods they have
to rule over."

And the hero answered:

"Before long they will stand to right and left of us
in combat, in the shouting, when the test comes—
our nerve against the suitors' in my hall.
Here is your part: at break of day tomorrow
home with you, go mingle with our princes.
The swineherd later on will take me down   290
the port-side trail—a beggar, by my looks,
hangdog and old. If they make fun of me
in my own courtyard, let your ribs cage up
your springing heart, no matter what I suffer,
no matter if they pull me by the heels
or practice shots at me, to drive me out.
Look on, hold down your anger. You may even
plead with them, by heaven! in gentle terms
to quit their horseplay—not that they will heed you,
rash as they are, facing their day of wrath.   300
Now fix the next step in your mind.

                                                        Athena,
counseling me, will give me word, and I
shall signal to you, nodding: at that point
round up all armor, lances, gear of war
left in our hall, and stow the lot away
back in the vaulted store room. When the suitors
miss those arms and question you, be soft
in what you say: answer:

                                        'I thought I'd move them
out of the smoke. They seemed no longer those
bright arms Odysseus left us years ago   310
when he went off to Troy. Here where the fire's
hot breath came, they had grown black and drear.
One better reason, too, I had from Zeus:
suppose a brawl starts up when you are drunk,
you might be crazed and bloody one another,
and that would stain your feast, your courtship. Tempered
iron can magnetize a man.'

                                                        Say that.
But put aside two broadswords and two spears
for our own use, two oxhide shields nearby
when we go into action. Pallas Athena   320
and Zeus All Provident will see you through,
bemusing our young friends.

                                        Now one thing more.
If son of mine you are and blood of mine,
let no one hear Odysseus is about.
Neither Laërtês, nor the swineherd here,
nor any slave, nor even Penélopê.
But you and I alone must learn how far

the women are corrupted; we should know
how to locate good men among our hands,
the loyal and respectful, and the shirkers   330
who take you lightly, as alone and young."

His admirable son replied:

                                                                   "Ah, Father,
even when danger comes I think you'll find
courage in me. I am not scatterbrained.
But as to checking on the field hands now,
I see no gain for us in that. Reflect,
you make a long toil, that way, if you care
to look men in the eye at every farm,
while these gay devils in our hall at ease
eat up our flocks and herds, leaving us nothing.   340

As for the maids I say, Yes: make distinction
between good girls and those who shame your house;
all that I shy away from is a scrutiny
of cottagers just now. The time for that
comes later—if in truth you have a sign
from Zeus the Stormking."

                                                          So their talk ran on,
while down the coast, and round toward Ithaka,
hove the good ship that had gone out to Pylos
bearing Telémakhos and his companions.
Into the wide bay waters, on to the dark land,   350
they drove her, hauled her up, took out the oars
and the canvas for light-hearted squires to carry
homeward—as they carried, too, the gifts
of Meneláos round to Klýtios'[1] house.
But first they sped a runner to Penélopê.
They knew that quiet lady must be told
the prince her son had come ashore, and sent
his good ship round to port; not one soft tear
should their sweet queen let fall.

                                                              Both messengers,
crewman and swineherd—reached the outer gate   360
in the same instant, bearing the same news,
and went in side by side to the king's hall.
He of the ship burst out among the maids:

"Your son's ashore this morning, O my Queen!"

---

[1] Father of the trusty Peiraios; see the end of Book XV.

But the swineherd calmly stood near Penélopê
whispering what her son had bade him tell
and what he had enjoined on her. No more.
When he had done, he left the place and turned
back to his steading in the hills.

By now,
sullen confusion weighed upon the suitors.   370
Out of the house, out of the court they went,
beyond the wall and gate, to sit in council.
Eurýmakhos, the son of Pólybos,
opened discussion:

"Friends, face up to it;
that young pup, Telémakhos, has done it;
he made the round trip, though we said he could not.
Well—now to get the best craft we can find
afloat, with oarsmen who can drench her bows,
and tell those on the island to come home."

He was yet speaking when Amphínomos,   380
craning seaward, spotted the picket ship
already in the roadstead under oars
with canvas brailed up; and this fresh arrival
made him chuckle. Then he told his friends:

"Too late for messages. Look, here they come
along the bay. Some god has brought them news,
or else they saw the cutter pass—and could not
overtake her."

On their feet at once,
the suitors took the road to the sea beach,
where, meeting the black ship, they hauled her in.   390
Oars and gear they left for their light-hearted
squires to carry, and all in company
made off for the assembly ground. All others,
young and old alike, they barred from sitting.
Eupeithês' son, Antínoös, made the speech:

"How the gods let our man escape a boarding,
that is the wonder.

We had lookouts posted
up on the heights all day in the sea wind,
and every hour a fresh pair of eyes;
at night we never slept ashore   400
but after sundown cruised the open water
to the southeast, patrolling until Dawn.
We were prepared to cut him off and catch him,
squelch him for good and all. The power of heaven
steered him the long way home.

Well, let this company plan his destruction,
and leave him no way out, this time. I see
our business here unfinished while he lives.
He knows, now, and he's no fool. Besides,
his people are all tired of playing up to us.   410
I say, act now, before he brings the whole
body of Akhaians to assembly—
and he would leave no word unsaid, in righteous
anger speaking out before them all
of how we plotted murder, and then missed him.
Will they commend us for that pretty work?
Take action now, or we are in for trouble;
we might be exiled, driven off our lands.
Let the first blow be ours.
If we move first, and get our hands on him   420
far from the city's eye, on path or field,
then stores and livestock will be ours to share;
the house we may confer upon his mother—
and on the man who marries her. Decide
otherwise you may—but if, my friends,
you want that boy to live and have his patrimony,
then we should eat no more of his good mutton,
come to this place no more.

        Let each from his own hall
court her with dower gifts. And let her marry
the destined one, the one who offers most."   430

He ended, and no sound was heard among them,
sitting all hushed, until at last the son
of Nísos Aretíadês arose—
Amphínomos.

       He led the group of suitors
who came from grainlands on Doulíkhion,
and he had lightness in his talk that pleased
Penélopê, for he meant no ill.
Now, in concern for them, he spoke:

           "O Friends
I should not like to kill Telémakhos.
It is a shivery thing to kill a prince   440
of royal blood.

      We should consult the gods.
If Zeus hands down a ruling for that act,
then I shall say, 'Come one, come all,' and go
cut him down with my own hand—
but I say Halt, if gods are contrary."

Now this proposal won them, and it carried.
Breaking their session up, away they went
to take their smooth chairs in Odysseus' house.

Meanwhile Penélopê the Wise,
decided, for her part, to make appearance   450
before the valiant young men.

                                                    She knew now
they plotted her child's death in her own hall,
for once more Medôn, who had heard them, told her.
Into the hall that lovely lady came,
with maids attending, and approached the suitors,
till near a pillar of the well-wrought roof
she paused, her shining veil across her cheeks,
and spoke directly to Antínoös:

                                                    "Infatuate,
steeped in evil! Yet in Ithaka they say
you were the best one of your generation   460
in mind and speech. Not so, you never were.
Madman, why do you keep forever knitting
death for Telémakhos? Have you no piety
toward men dependent on another's mercy?
Before Lord Zeus, no sanction can be found
for one such man to plot against another!
Or are you not aware that your own father
fled to us when the realm was up in arms
against him? He had joined the Taphian pirates
in ravaging Thesprotian folk, our friends.   470
Our people would have raided *him*, then—breached
his heart, butchered his herds to feast upon—
only Odysseus took him in, and held
the furious townsmen off. It is Odysseus'
house you now consume, his wife you court,
his son you kill, or try to kill. And me
you ravage now, and grieve. I call upon you
to make an end of it!—and your friends too!"

The son of Pólybos it was, Eurýmakhos,
who answered her with ready speech:

                                                    "My lady   480
Penélopê, wise daughter of Ikários,
you must shake off these ugly thoughts. I say
that man does not exist, nor will, who dares
lay hands upon your son Telémakhos,
while I live, walk the earth, and use my eyes.
The man's life blood, I swear,
will spurt and run out black around my lancehead!
For it is true of me, too, that Odysseus,
raiders of cities, took me on his knees
and fed me often—tidbits and red wine.
Should not Telémakhos, therefore, be dear to me   490
above the rest of men? I tell the lad
he must not tremble for his life, at least

alone in the suitors' company. Heaven
deals death no man avoids."

                                                    Blasphemous lies
in earnest tones he told—the one who planned
the lad's destruction!

                                                    Silently the lady
made her way to her glowing upper chamber,
there to weep for her dear lord, Odysseus,
until grey-eyed Athena   500
cast sweet sleep upon her eyes.

                                              At fall of dusk
Odysseus and his son heard the approach
of the good forester. They had been standing
over the fire with a spitted pig,
a yearling. And Athena coming near
with one rap of her wand made of Odysseus
an old old man again, with rags about him—
for if the swineherd knew his lord were there
he could not hold the news; Penélopê
would hear it from him.

                                                    Now Telémakhos   510
greeted him first:

                                              "Eumaios, back again!
What was the talk in town? Are the tall suitors
home again, by this time, from their ambush,
or are they still on watch for my return?"

And you replied, Eumaios—O my swineherd:

"There was no time to ask or talk of that;
I hurried through the town. Even while I spoke
my message, I felt driven to return.
A runner from your friends turned up, a crier,
who gave the news first to your mother. Ah!   520
One thing I do know; with my own two eyes
I saw it. As I climbed above the town
to where the sky is cut by Hermês' ridge,
I saw a ship bound in for our own bay
with many oarsmen in it, laden down
with sea provisioning and two-edged spears,
and I surmised those were the men.

                                              Who knows?"

Telémakhos, now strong with magic, smiled
across at his own father—but avoided
the swineherd's eye.

                                              So when the pig was done,   530
the spit no longer to be turned, the table
garnished, everyone sat down to feast

on all the savory flesh he craved. And when
they had put off desire for meat and drink,
they turned to bed and took the gift of sleep.

BOOK SEVENTEEN: THE BEGGAR AT THE MANOR

When the young Dawn came bright into the East
spreading her finger tips of rose, Telémakhos
the king's son, tied on his rawhide sandals
and took the lance that bore his handgrip. Burning
to be away, and on the path to town,
he told the swineherd:

        "Uncle, the truth is
I must go down myself into the city.
Mother must see me there, with her own eyes,
or she will weep and feel forsaken still,
and will not set her mind at rest. Your job   10
will be to lead this poor man down to beg.
Some householder may want to dole him out
a loaf and pint. I have my own troubles.
Am I to care for every last man who comes?
And if he takes it badly—well, so much
the worse for him. Plain truth is what I favor."

At once Odysseus the great tactician
spoke up briskly:

       "Neither would I myself
care to be kept here, lad. A beggar man
fares better in the town. Let it be said   20
I am not yet so old I must lay up
indoors and mumble, 'Aye, Aye' to a master.[1]
Go on, then. As you say, my friend can lead me
as soon as I have had a bit of fire
and when the sun grows warmer. These old rags
could be my death, outside on a frosty morning,
and the town is distant, so they say."

          Telémakhos
with no more words went out, and through the fence,
and down hill, going fast on the steep footing,
nursing woe for the suitors in his heart.   30

---

[1] Odysseus means that he is not yet so old that he must remain in one place, subject to a single master.

Before the manor hall, he leaned his lance
against a great porch pillar and stepped in
across the door stone.

                                                                          Old Eurýkleia

saw him first, for that day she was covering
handsome chairs nearby with clean fleeces.
She ran to him at once, tears in her eyes;
and other maidservants of the old soldier
Odysseus gathered round to greet their prince,
kissing his head and shoulders.

                                                                          Quickly, then,

Penélopê the Wise, tall in her beauty   40
as Artemis or pale-gold Aphroditê,
appeared from her high chamber and came down
to throw her arms around her son. In tears
she kissed his head, kissed both his shining eyes,
then cried out, and her words flew:

                                                                          "Back with me!

Telémakhos, more sweet to me than sunlight!
I thought I should not see you again, ever,
after you took the ship that night to Pylos—
against my will, with not a word! you went
for news of your dear father. Tell me now   50
of everything you saw!"

                                                                          But he made answer:

"Mother, not now. You make me weep. My heart
already aches—I came near death at sea.
You must bathe, first of all, and change your dress,
and take your maids to the highest room to pray.
Pray, and burn offerings to the gods of heaven,
that Zeus may put his hand to our revenge.

I am off now to bring home from the square
a guest, a passenger I had. I sent him
yesterday with all my crew to town.   60
Peiraios was to care for him, I said,
and keep him well, with honor, till I came."

She caught back the swift words upon her tongue.
Then softly she withdrew
to bathe and dress her body in fresh linen,
and make her offerings to the gods of heaven,
praying Almighty Zeus
to put his hand to their revenge.

                                                                          Telémakhos

had left the hall, taken his lance, and gone
with two quick hounds at heel into the town,   70

Athena's grace in his long stride
making the people gaze as he came near.
And suitors gathered, primed with friendly words,
despite the deadly plotting in their hearts—
but these, and all their crowd, he kept away from.
Next he saw sitting some way off, apart,
Mentor, with Antiphos and Halithersês,
friends of his father's house in years gone by.
Near these men he sat down, and told his tale
under their questioning.

His crewman, young Peiraios,   80
guided through town, meanwhile, into the Square,
the Argive exile, Theoklýmenos.
Telémakhos lost no time in moving toward him;
but first Peiraios had his say:

Telémakhos,
you must send maids to me, at once, and let me
turn over to you those gifts from Meneláos!"

The prince had pondered it, and said:

"Peiraios,
none of us knows how this affair will end.
Say one day our fine suitors, without warning,
draw upon me, kill me in our hall,   90
and parcel out my patrimony—I wish
you, and no one of them, to have those things.
But if my hour comes, if I can bring down
bloody death on all that crew,
you will rejoice to send my gifts to me—
and so will I rejoice!"

Then he departed,
leading his guest, the lonely stranger, home.

Over chair-backs in hall they dropped their mantles
and passed in to the polished tubs, where maids
poured out warm baths for them, anointed them,   100
and pulled fresh tunics, fleecy cloaks around them.
Soon they were seated at their ease in hall.
A maid came by to tip a golden jug
over their fingers into a silver bowl
and draw a gleaming table up beside them.
The larder mistress brought her tray of loaves
and savories, dispensing each.

In silence
across the hall, beside a pillar, propped
in a long chair, Telémakhos' mother
spun a fine wool yarn.

The young men's hands   110
went out upon the good things placed before them,
and only when their hunger and thirst were gone
did she look up and say:

"Telémakhos,

what am I to do now? Return alone
and lie again on my forsaken bed—
sodden how often with my weeping
since that day when Odysseus put to sea
to join the Atreidai[2] before Troy?

Could you not

tell me, before the suitors fill our house,
what news you have of his return?"

He answered: 120

"Now that you ask a second time, dear Mother,
here is the truth.

We went ashore at Pylos

to Nestor, lord and guardian of the West,
who gave me welcome in his towering hall.
So kind he was, he might have been my father
and I his long-lost son—so truly kind,
taking me in with his own honored sons.
But as to Odysseus' bitter fate,
living or dead, he had no news at all
from anyone on earth, he said. He sent me   130
overland in a strong chariot
to Atreus' son, the captain, Meneláos.
And I saw Helen there, for whom the Argives
fought, and the Trojans fought, as the gods willed.
Then Meneláos of the great war cry
asked me my errand in that ancient land
of Lakedaimon. So I told our story,
and in reply he burst out:[3]

'Intolerable!

That feeble men, unfit as those men are,
should think to lie in that great captain's bed,   140
fawns in the lion's lair! As if a doe
put down her litter of sucklings there, while she
sniffed at the glen or grazed a grassy hollow.
Ha! Then the lord returns to his own bed
and deals out wretched doom on both alike.

So will Odysseus deal out doom on these.
O Father Zeus, Athena, and Apollo!
I pray he comes as once he was, in Lesbos,

[2] Sons of Atreus—Agamémnon and Meneláos.
[3] The following quotation of Meneláos' words summarizes his narrative in Book IV.

when he stood up to wrestle Philomeleidês—
champion and Island King—   150
and smashed him down. How the Akhaians cheered!
If that Odysseus could meet the suitors,
they'd have a quick reply, a stunning dowry!
Now for your questions, let me come to the point.
I would not misreport it for you; let me
tell you what the Ancient of the Sea,
that infallible seer, told me.

                                         On an island

your father lies and grieves. The Ancient saw him
held by a nymph, Kalypso, in her hall;
no means of sailing home remained to him,   160
no ship with oars, and no ship's company
to pull him on the broad back of the sea.'

I had this from the lord marshal, Meneláos,
and when my errand in that place was done
I left for home. A fair breeze from the gods
brought me swiftly back to our dear island."

The boy's tale made her heart stir in her breast,
but this was not all. Mother and son now heard
Theoklýmenos, the diviner, say:

"He does not see it clear—

                                         O gentle lady,   170

wife of Odysseus Laërtiadês,
listen to me, I can reveal this thing.
Zeus be my witness, and the table set
for strangers and the hearth to which I've come—
the lord Odysseus, I tell you
is present now, already, on this island!
Quartered somewhere, or going about, he knows
what evil is afoot. He has it in him
to bring a black hour on the suitors. Yesterday,
still at the ship, I saw this in a portent.   180
I read the sign aloud, I told Telémakhos!"

The prudent queen, for her part, said:

                                                "Stranger,

if only this came true—
our love would go to you, with many gifts;
aye, every man who passed would call you happy!"

So ran the talk between these three.

                                         Meanwhile,

swaggering before Odysseus' hall,
the suitors were competing at the discus throw
and javelin, on the level measured field.

But when the dinner hour drew on, and beasts   190
were being driven from the fields to slaughter—
as beasts were, every day—Medôn spoke out:
Medôn, the crier, whom the suitors liked;
he took his meat beside them.

                                                  "Men," he said,

"each one has had his work-out and his pleasure,
come in to Hall now; time to make our feast.
Are discus throws more admirable than a roast
when the proper hour comes?"

                                                  At this reminder

they all broke up their games, and trailed away
into the gracious, timbered hall. There, first,   200
they dropped their cloaks on chairs; then came their ritual:
putting great rams and fat goats to the knife—
pigs and a cow, too.

                                        So they made their feast.

During these hours, Odysseus and the swineherd
were on their way out of the hills to town.
The forester had got them started, saying:

"Friend, you have hopes, I know, of your adventure
into the heart of town today. My lord
wishes it so, not I. No, I should rather
you stood by here as guardian of our steading.   210
But I owe reverence to my prince, and fear
he'll make my ears burn later if I fail.
A master's tongue has a rough edge. Off we go.
Part of the day is past; nightfall will be
early, and colder, too."

                                                        Odysseus,

who had it all timed in his head, replied:

"I know, as well as you do. Let's move on.
You lead the way—the whole way. Have you got
a staff, a lopped stick, you could let me use
to put my weight on when I slip? This path   220
is hard going, they said."

                                                Over his shoulders

he slung his patched-up knapsack, an old bundle
tied with twine. Eumaios found a stick for him,
the kind he wanted, and the two set out,
leaving the boys and dogs to guard the place.
In this way good Eumaios led his lord
down to the city.

                                            And it seemed to him
he led an old outcast, a beggar man,
leaning most painfully upon a stick,
his poor cloak, all in tatters, looped about him.   230

Down by the stony trail they made their way
as far as Clearwater, not far from town—
a spring house where the people filled their jars.
Ithakos, Nêritos, and Polýktor[4] built it,
and round it on the humid ground a grove,
a circular wood of poplars grew. Ice cold
in runnels from a high rock ran the spring,
and over it there stood an altar stone
to the cool nymphs, where all men going by
laid offerings.
                            Well, here the son of Dólios   240
crossed their path—Melánthios.[5]
                                            He was driving
a string of choice goats for the evening meal,
with two goatherds beside him; and no sooner
had he laid eyes upon the wayfarers
than he began to growl and taunt them both
so grossly that Odysseus' heart grew hot:

"Here comes one scurvy type leading another!
God pairs them off together, every time.
Swineherd, where are you taking your new pig,
that stinking beggar there, licker of pots?   250
How many doorposts has he rubbed his back on
whining for garbage, where a noble guest
would rate a cauldron or a sword?
                                            Hand him
over to me, I'll make a farmhand of him,
a stall scraper, a fodder carrier! Whey
for drink will put good muscle on his shank!
No chance: he learned his dodges long ago—
no honest sweat. He'd rather tramp the country
begging, to keep his hoggish belly full.
Well, I can tell you this for sure: 260
in King Odysseus' hall, if he goes there,
footstools will fly around his head—good shots
from strong hands. Back and side, his ribs will catch it
on the way out!"

---

[4] These three were the founding fathers of the island; Ithakos' name represents the island itself, Nêritos' name an important mountain on the island.

[5] Dólios was a trusty steward of Odysseus' father, Laërtês. As we learn later, Melánthios' sister Melántho, maid to Penélopê, is a mistress of the suitor Eurýmakhos, a fact that probably accounts for the intimacy of her goatherd brother with the suitors.

                                        And like a drunken fool
he kicked at Odysseus' hip as he passed by.
Not even jogged off stride, or off the trail,
the Lord Odysseus walked along, debating
inwardly whether to whirl and beat
the life out of this fellow with his stick,
or toss him, brain him on the stony ground.   270
Then he controlled himself, and bore it quietly.
Not so the swineherd.

                            Seeing the man before him,
he raised his arms and cried:

                                    "Nymphs of the spring,
daughters of Zeus, if ever Odysseus
burnt you a thighbone in rich fat—a ram's
or kid's thighbone, hear me, grant my prayer:
let our true lord come back, let heaven bring him
to rid the earth of these fine courtly ways
Melánthios picks up around the town—
all wine and wind! Bad shepherds ruin flocks!"   280

Melánthios the goatherd answered:

                                          "Bless me!
The dog can snap: how he goes on! Some day
I'll take him in a slave ship overseas
and trade him for a herd!

                                        Old Silverbow
Apollo, if he shot clean through Telémakhos[6]
in hall today, what luck! Or let the suitors
cut him down!

                            Odysseus died at sea;
no coming home for him."

                                        He flung this out
and left the two behind to come on slowly,
while he went hurrying to the king's hall.   290
There he slipped in, and sat among the suitors,
beside the one he doted on—Eurýmakhos.
Then working servants helped him to his meat
and the mistress of the larder gave him bread.

Reaching the gate, Odysseus and the forester
halted and stood outside, for harp notes came
around them rippling on the air
as Phêmios picked out a song. Odysseus
caught his companion's arm and said:

---

[6] That is, if Telémakhos should drop dead.

          "My friend,
here is the beautiful place—who could mistake it?   300
Here is Odysseus' hall: no hall like this!
See how one chamber grows out of another;
see how the court is tight with wall and coping;
no man at arms could break this gateway down!
Your banqueting young lords are here in force,
I gather, from the fumes of mutton roasting
and strum of harping—harping, which the gods
appoint sweet friend of feasts!"

          And—O my swineherd!
you replied:

         "That was quick recognition;
but you are no numbskull—in this or anything.   310
Now we must plan this action. Will you take
leave of me here, and go ahead alone
to make your entrance now among the suitors?
Or do you choose to wait?—Let me go forward
and go in first.

          Do not delay too long;
someone might find you skulking here outside
and take a club to you, or heave a lance.
Bear this in mind, I say."

          The patient hero
Odysseus answered:

        "Just what I was thinking.
You go in first, and leave me here a little.   320
But as for blows and missiles,
I am no tyro[7] at these things. I learned
to keep my head in hardship—years of war
and years at sea. Let this new trial come.
The cruel belly, can you hide its ache?
How many bitter days it brings! Long ships
with good stout planks athwart—would fighters rig them
to ride the barren sea, except for hunger?
Seawolves—woe to their enemies!"

         While he spoke
an old hound, lying near, pricked up his ears   330
and lifted up his muzzle. This was Argos,
trained as a puppy by Odysseus,
but never taken on a hunt before
his master sailed for Troy. The young men, afterward,

---

[7] Inexperienced beginner.

hunted wild goats with him, and hare, and deer,
but he had grown old in his master's absence.
Treated as rubbish now, he lay at last
upon a mass of dung before the gates—
manure of mules and cows, piled there until
fieldhands could spread it on the king's estate.   340
Abandoned there, and half destroyed with flies,
old Argos lay.

                                    But when he knew he heard
Odysseus' voice nearby, he did his best
to wag his tail, nose down, with flattened ears,
having no strength to move nearer his master.
And the man looked away,
wiping a salt tear from his cheek; but he
hid this from Eumaios. Then he said:

"I marvel that they leave this hound to lie
here on the dung pile;   350
he would have been a fine dog, from the look of him,
though I can't say as to his power and speed
when he was young. You find the same good build
in house dogs, table dogs landowners keep
all for style."

                                    And you replied, Eumaios:

"A hunter owned him—but the man is dead
in some far place. If this old hound could show
the form he had when Lord Odysseus left him,
going to Troy, you'd see him swift and strong.
He never shrank from any savage thing   360
he'd brought to bay in the deep woods; on the scent
no other dog kept up with him. Now misery
has him in leash. His owner died abroad,
and here the women slaves will take no care of him.
You know how servants are: without a master
they have no will to labor, or excel.
For Zeus who views the wide world takes away
half the manhood of a man, that day
he goes into captivity and slavery."

Eumaios crossed the court and went straight forward   370
into the mégaron[8] among the suitors;
but death and darkness in that instant closed
the eyes of Argos, who had seen his master,
Odysseus, after twenty years.

---

[8] The great hall of the house.

Long before anyone else
Telémakhos caught sight of the grey woodsman
coming from the door, and called him over
with a quick jerk of his head. Eumaios'
narrowed eyes made out an empty bench
beside the one the carver used—that servant
who had no respite, carving for the suitors. 380
This bench he took possession of, and placed it
across the table from Telémakhos
for his own use. Then the two men were served
cuts from a roast and bread from a bread basket.

At no long interval, Odysseus came
through his own doorway as a mendicant,
humped like a bundle of rags over his stick.
He settled on the inner ash wood sill,
leaning against the door jamb—cypress timber
the skilled carpenter planed years ago 390
and set up with a plumbline.

Now Telémakhos
took an entire loaf and a double handful
of roast meat; then he said to the forester:

"Give these to the stranger there. But tell him
to go among the suitors, on his own;
he may beg all he wants. This hanging back
is no asset to a hungry man."

The swineherd rose at once, crossed to the door,
and halted by Odysseus.

"Friend," he said,
"Telémakhos is pleased to give you these, 400
but he commands you to approach the suitors;
you may ask all you want from them. He adds,
your shyness is no asset to a beggar."

The great tactician, lifting up his eyes,
cried:

"Zeus aloft! A blessing on Telémakhos!
Let all things come to pass as he desires!"

Palms held out, in the beggar's gesture, he
received the bread and meat and put it down
before him on his knapsack—lowly table!—
then he fell to, devouring it. Meanwhile 410
the harper in the great room sang a song.
Not till the man was fed did the sweet harper

end his singing—whereupon the company
made the walls ring again with talk.

                                                            Unseen,
Athena took her place beside Odysseus
whispering in his ear:

                                                    "Yes, try the suitors.
You may collect a few more loaves, and learn
who are the decent lads, and who are vicious—
although not one can be excused from death!"

So he appealed to them, one after another,   420
going from left to right, with open palm,
as though his life time had been spent in beggary.
And they gave bread, for pity—wondering, though,
at the strange man. Who could this beggar be,
where did he come from? each would ask his neighbor;
till in their midst the goatherd, Melánthios,
raised his voice:

                                        "Hear just a word from me,
my lords who court our illustrious queen!

                                                            This man,
this foreigner, I saw him on the road;
the swineherd here was leading him this way;   430
who, what, or whence he claims to be, I could not
say for sure."

                                                At this, Antínoös
turned on the swineherd brutally, saying:

                                                    "You famous
breeder of pigs, why bring this fellow here?
Are we not plagued enough with beggars,
foragers and such rats?

                                        You find the company
too slow at eating up your lord's estate—
is that it? So you call this scarecrow in?"

The forester replied:

                                                        "Antínoös,
well born you are, but that was not well said.   440
Who would call in a foreigner?—unless
an artisan with skill to serve the realm,
a healer, or a prophet, or a builder,
or one whose harp and song might give us joy.
All these are sought for on the endless earth,
but when have beggars come by invitation?

Who puts a field mouse in his granary? My lord,
you are a hard man, and you always were,
more so than others of this company—hard
on all Odysseus' people and on me. 450
But this I can forget
as long as Penélopê lives on, the wise and tender
mistress of this hall; as long
as Prince Telémakhos—"

                             But he broke off
at a look from Telémakhos, who said:

                                     "Be still.
Spare me a long-drawn answer to this gentleman.
With his unpleasantness, he will forever make
strife where he can—and goad the others on."

He turned and spoke out clearly to Antínoös:

"What fatherly concern you show me! Frighten 460
this unknown fellow, would you, from my hall
with words that promise blows—may God forbid it!
Give him a loaf. Am I a niggard? No,
I call on you to give. And spare your qualms
as to my mother's loss, or anyone's—
not that in truth you have such care at heart:
your heart is all in feeding, not in giving."

Antínoös replied:

                             "What high and mighty
talk, Telémakhos! No holding you!
If every suitor gave what I may give him, 470
he could be kept for months—kept out of sight!"

He reached under the table for the footstool
his shining feet had rested on—and this
he held up so that all could see his gift.

But all the rest gave alms,
enough to fill the beggar's pack with bread
and roast meat.
                          So it looked as though Odysseus
had had his taste of what these men were like
and could return scot free to his own doorway—
but halting now before Antínoös 480
he made a little speech to him. Said he:

"Give a mite, friend. I would not say, myself,
you are the worst man of the young Akhaians.
The noblest, rather; kingly, by your look;

therefore you'll give more bread than others do.
Let me speak well of you as I pass on
over the boundless earth!

                                                         I, too, you know,

had fortune once, lived well, stood well with men,
and gave alms, often, to poor wanderers
like this one that you see—aye, to all sorts,   490
no matter in what dire want. I owned
servants—many, god knows—and all the rest
that goes with being prosperous, as they say.
But Zeus the son of Kronos brought me down.

No telling
why he would have it, but he made me go
to Egypt with a company of rovers—
a long sail to the south—for my undoing.
Up the broad Nile and in to the river bank
I brought my dipping squadron. There, indeed,   500
I told the men to stand guard at the ships;
I sent patrols out—out to rising ground;
but reckless greed carried my crews away
to plunder the Egyptian farms; they bore off
wives and children, killed what men they found.
The news ran on the wind to the city, a night cry,
and sunrise brought both infantry and horsemen,
filling the river plain with dazzle of bronze;
then Zeus lord of lightning
threw my men into a blind panic; no one dared   510
stand against that host closing around us.
Their scything weapons left our dead in piles,
but some they took alive, into forced labor,
myself among them. And they gave me, then,
to one Dmêtor, a traveller, son of Iasos,
who ruled at Kypros.[9] He conveyed me there.
From that place, working northward, miserably—"

But here Antínoös broke in, shouting:

                                                              "God!

What evil wind blew in this pest?

                                                         Get over,

stand in the passage! Nudge my table, will you?   520
Egyptian whips are sweet
to what you'll come to here, you nosing rat,
making your pitch to everyone!
These men have bread to throw away on you
because it is not theirs. Who cares? Who spares
another's food, when he has more than plenty?"

---

[9] Cyprus, a large island off the Syrian coast.

With guile Odysseus drew away, then said:

"A pity that you have more looks than heart.
You'd grudge a pinch of salt from your own larder
to your own handy man. You sit here, fat   530
on others' meat, and cannot bring yourself
to rummage out a crust of bread for me!"

Then anger made Antínoös' heart beat hard,
and, glowering under his brows, he answered:

                                        "Now!
You think you'll shuffle off and get away
after that impudence? Oh, no you don't!"

The stool he let fly hit the man's right shoulder
on the packed muscle under the shoulder blade—
like solid rock, for all the effect one saw.
Odysseus only shook his head, containing   540
thoughts of bloody work, as he walked on,
then sat, and dropped his loaded bag again
upon the door sill. Facing the whole crowd
he said, and eyed them all:

                                "One word only,
my lords, and suitors of the famous queen.
One thing I have to say.
There is no pain, no burden for the heart
when blows come to a man, and he defending
his own cattle—his own cows and lambs.
Here it was otherwise. Antínoös   550
hit me for being driven on by hunger—
how many bitter seas men cross for hunger!
If beggars interest the gods, if there are Furies
pent in the dark to avenge a poor man's wrong, then may
Antínoös meet his death before his wedding day!"

Then said Eupeithês' son, Antínoös :

                                        "Enough.
Eat and be quiet where you are, or shamble elsewhere,
unless you want these lads to stop your mouth
pulling you by the heels, or hands and feet,
over the whole floor, till your back is peeled!"   560

But now the rest were mortified, and someone
spoke from the crowd of young bucks to rebuke him:

"A poor show, that—hitting this famished tramp—
bad business, if he happened to be a god.
You know they go in foreign guise, the gods do,
looking like strangers, turning up

in towns and settlements to keep an eye
on manners, good or bad."

But at this notion

Antínoös only shrugged.

Telémakhos, 570

after the blow his father bore, sat still
without a tear, though his heart felt the blow.
Slowly he shook his head from side to side,
containing murderous thoughts.

Penélopê

on the higher level of her room had heard
the blow, and knew who gave it. Now she murmured:

"Would god you could be hit yourself, Antínoös —
hit by Apollo's bowshot!"

And Eurýnomê

her housekeeper, put in:

"He and no other?

If all we pray for came to pass, not one
would live till dawn!"

Her gentle mistress said: 580

"Oh, Nan,[10] they are a bad lot; they intend
ruin for all of us; but Antínoös
appears a blacker-hearted hound than any.
Here is a poor man come, a wanderer,
driven by want to beg his bread, and everyone
in hall gave bits, to cram his bag—only
Antínoös threw a stool, and banged his shoulder!"

So she described it, sitting in her chamber
among her maids—while her true lord was eating.
Then she called in the forester and said: 590

"Go to that man on my behalf, Eumaios,
and send him here, so I can greet and question him.
Abroad in the great world, he may have heard
rumors about Odysseus—may have known him!"

Then you replied—O swineherd!

"Ah, my queen,

if these Akhaian sprigs would hush their babble
the man could tell you tales to charm your heart.
Three days and nights I kept him in my hut;
he came straight off a ship, you know, to me.

---

[10]Affectionate diminutive for an old woman.

There was no end to what he made me hear 600
of his hard roving; and I listened, eyes
upon him, as a man drinks in a tale
a minstrel sings—a minstrel taught by heaven
to touch the hearts of men. At such a song
the listener becomes rapt and still. Just so
I found myself enchanted by this man.
He claims an old tie with Odysseus, too—
in his home country, the Minoan[11] land
of Krete. From Krete he came, a rolling stone
washed by the gales of life this way and that 610
to our own beach.

                        If he can be believed
he has news of Odysseus near at hand
alive, in the rich country of Thesprotia,
bringing a mass of treasure home."

Then wise Penélopê said again:

"Go call him, let him come here, let him tell
that tale again for my own ears.

                           Our friends
can drink their cups outside or stay in hall,
being so carefree. And why not? Their stores
lie intact in their homes, both food and drink, 620
with only servants left to take a little.
But these men spend their days around our house
killing our beeves, our fat goats and our sheep,
carousing, drinking up our good dark wine;
sparing nothing, squandering everything.
No champion like Odysseus takes our part.
Ah, if he comes again, no falcon ever
struck more suddenly than he will, with his son,
to avenge this outrage!"

                        The great hall below
at this point rang with a tremendous sneeze[12]— 630
"kchaou!" from Telémakhos—like an acclamation.
And laughter seized Penélopê.

                        Then quickly,
lucidly she went on:

                        "Go call the stranger
straight to me. Did you hear that, Eumaios?
My son's thundering sneeze at what I said!
May death come of a sudden so; may death
relieve us, clean as that, of all the suitors!

---

[11] Minos, to whom the adjective *Minoan* refers, had been king of Krete (Crete).
[12] A sneeze was regarded as a sign of good luck.

Let me add one thing—do not overlook it—
if I can see this man has told the truth,
I promise him a warm new cloak and tunic."   640

With all this in his head, the forester
went down the hall, and halted near the beggar,
saying aloud:

                    "Good father, you are called
by the wise mother of Telémakhos,
Penélopê. The queen, despite her troubles,
is moved by a desire to hear your tales
about her lord—and if she finds them true,
she'll see you clothed in what you need, a cloak
and a fresh tunic.

                       You may have your belly
full each day you go about this realm   650
begging. For all may give, and all they wish."

Now said Odysseus, the old soldier:

"Friend,
I wish this instant I could tell my facts
to the wise daughter of Ikários, Penélopê—
and I have much to tell about her husband;
we went through much together.

                          But just now
this hard crowd worries me. They are, you said
infamous to the very rim of heaven
for violent acts: and here, just now, this fellow   660
gave me a bruise. What had I done to him?
But who would lift a hand for me? Telémakhos?
Anyone else?

                  No; bid the queen be patient,
Let her remain till sundown in her room,
and then—if she will seat me near the fire—
inquire tonight about her lord's return.
My rags are sorry cover; you know that;
I showed my sad condition first to you."

The woodsman heard him out, and then returned;
but the queen met him on her threshold, crying: 670
"Have you not brought him? Why? What is he thinking?
Has he some fear of overstepping? Shy
about these inner rooms? A hangdog beggar?"

To this you answered, friend Eumaios:

"No:
he reasons as another might, and well,

not to tempt any swordplay from these drunkards.
Be patient, wait—he says—till darkness falls.
And, O my queen, for you too that is better:
better to be alone with him, and question him,   680
and hear him out."

                                        Penélopê replied:

"He is no fool; he sees how it could be.
Never were mortal men like these
for bullying and brainless arrogance!"

Thus she accepted what had been proposed,
so he went back into the crowd. He joined
Telémakhos, and said at once in whispers—
his head bent, so that no one else might hear:

"Dear prince, I must go home to keep good watch
on hut and swine, and look to my own affairs.   690
Everything here is in your hands. Consider
your own safety before the rest; take care
not to get hurt. Many are dangerous here.
May Zeus destroy them first, before we suffer!"

Telémakhos said:

                              "Your wish is mine, Uncle.
Go when your meal is finished. Then come back
at dawn, and bring good victims for a slaughter.
Everything here is in my hands indeed—
and in the disposition of the gods."

Taking his seat on the smooth bench again,   700
Eumaios ate and drank his fill, then rose
to climb the mountain trail back to his swine,
leaving the mégaron and court behind him
crowded with banqueters.

                              These had their joy
of dance and song, as day waned into evening.

BOOK EIGHTEEN: BLOWS AND A QUEEN'S BEAUTY

Now a true scavenger came in—a public tramp
who begged around the town of Ithaka,
a by-word for his insatiable swag-belly,
feeding and drinking, dawn to dark. No pith
was in him, and no nerve, huge as he looked.
Arnaios, as his gentle mother called him,

he had been nicknamed "Iros"[1] by the young
for being ready to take messages.

                                                                This fellow
thought he would rout Odysseus from his doorway,
growling at him:

                                        "Clear out, grandfather,   10
or else be hauled out by the ankle bone.
See them all giving me the wink? That means,
'Go on and drag him out!' I hate to do it.
Up with you! Or would you like a fist fight?"

Odysseus only frowned and looked him over,
taking account of everything, then said:

"Master, I am no trouble to you here.
I offer no remarks. I grudge you nothing.
Take all you get, and welcome. Here is room
for two on this doorslab—or do you own it?   20
You are a tramp, I think, like me. Patience:
a windfall from the gods will come. But drop
that talk of using fists; it could annoy me.
Old as I am, I might just crack a rib
or split a lip for you. My life would go
even more peacefully, after tomorrow,
looking for no more visits here from you."

Iros the tramp grew red and hooted:

"Ho,
listen to him! The swine can talk your arm off,   30
like an old oven woman! With two punches
I'd knock him snoring, if I had a mind to—
and not a tooth left in his head, the same
as an old sow caught in the corn! Belt up!
And let this company see the way I do it
when we square off. Can you fight a fresher man?"

Under the lofty doorway, on the door sill
of wide smooth ash, they held this rough exchange.
And the tall full-blooded suitor, Antínoös,
overhearing, broke into happy laughter.   40
Then he said to the others:

                                        "Oh, my friends,
no luck like this ever turned up before!
What a farce heaven has brought this house!

                                        The stranger
and Iros have had words, they brag of boxing!
Into the ring they go, and no more talk!"

[1]A pun on Iris, goddess of the rainbow and a messenger of the gods.

All the young men got on their feet now, laughing,
to crowd around the ragged pair. Antínoös
called out:

                    "Gentlemen, quiet! One more thing:
here are goat stomachs ready on the fire
to stuff with blood and fat, good supper pudding.   50
The man who wins this gallant bout
may step up here and take the one he likes.
And let him feast with us from this day on:
no other beggar will be admitted here
when we are at our wine."

                                   This pleased them all.
But now that wily man, Odysseus, muttered:

"An old man, an old hulk, has no business
fighting a young man, but my belly nags me;
nothing will do but I must take a beating.
Well, then, let every man here swear an oath   60
not to step in for Iros. No one throw
a punch for luck. I could be whipped that way."

So much the suitors were content to swear,
but after they reeled off their oaths, Telémakhos
put in a word to clinch it, saying:

                                   "Friend,
if you will stand and fight, as pride requires,
don't worry about a foul blow from behind.
Whoever hits you will take on the crowd.
You have my word as host; you have the word
of these two kings, Antínoös and Eurýmakhos—   70
a pair of thinking men."

                         All shouted, "Aye!"
So now Odysseus made his shirt a belt
and roped his rags around his loins, baring
his hurdler's thighs and boxer's breadth of shoulder,
the dense rib-sheath and upper arms. Athena
stood nearby to give him bulk and power,
while the young suitors watched with narrowed eyes—
and comments went around:

"By god, old Iros now retiros."

                                  "Aye,
he asked for it, he'll get it—bloody, too."   80

"The build this fellow had, under his rags!"

Panic made Iros' heart jump, but the yard-boys
hustled and got him belted by main force,

though all his blubber quivered now with dread.
Antínoös' angry voice rang in his ears:

"You sack of guts, you might as well be dead,
might as well never have seen the light of day,
if this man makes you tremble! Chicken-heart,
afraid of an old wreck, far gone in misery!
Well, here is what I say—and what I'll do.   90
If this ragpicker can outfight you, whip you,
I'll ship you out to that king in Epeíros,
Ékhetos[2]—he skins everyone alive.
Let him just cut your nose off and your ears
and pull your privy parts out by the roots
to feed raw to his hunting dogs!"

                                                                     Poor Iros
felt a new fit of shaking take his knees.
But the yard-boys pushed him out. Now both contenders
put their hands up. Royal Odysseus
pondered if he should hit him with all he had   100
and drop the man dead on the spot, or only
spar, with force enough to knock him down.
Better that way, he thought—a gentle blow,
else he might give himself away.

                                                                      The two
were at close quarters now, and Iros lunged
hitting the shoulder. Then Odysseus hooked him
under the ear and shattered his jaw bone,
so bright red blood came bubbling from his mouth,
as down he pitched into the dust, bleating,
kicking against the ground, his teeth stove in.   110
The suitors whooped and swung their arms, half dead
with pangs of laughter.
                                    Then, by the ankle bone,
Odysseus hauled the fallen one outside,
crossing the courtyard to the gate, and piled him
against the wall. In his right hand he stuck
his begging staff, and said:

                                        "Here, take your post.
Sit here to keep the dogs and pigs away.
You can give up your habit of command
over poor waifs and beggarmen—you swab.
Another time you may not know what hit you."   120

When he had slung his rucksack by the string
over his shoulder, like a wad of rags,
he sat down on the broad door sill again,

---

[2] Probably a nonhistorical tyrannical ruler whose name was a byword for cruelty. Epeíros
(Epirus), in the preceding line, is the Grecian mainland north of Ithaka.

as laughing suitors came to flock inside;
and each young buck in passing gave him greeting,
saying, maybe,

                "Zeus fill your pouch for this!
May the gods grant your heart's desire!"

                    "Well done
to put that walking famine out of business."

"We'll ship him out to that king in Epeíros,
Ékhetos—he skins everyone alive."   130

Odysseus found grim cheer in their good wishes—
his work had started well.

                Now from the fire
his fat blood pudding came, deposited
before him by Antínoös—then, to boot,
two brown loaves from the basket, and some wine
in a fine cup of gold. These gifts Amphínomos
gave him. Then he said:

             "Here's luck, grandfather;
a new day; may the worst be over now."

Odysseus answered, and his mind ranged far:

"Amphínomos, your head is clear, I'd say;   140
so was your father's—or at least I've heard
good things of Nísos the Doulíkhion,
whose son you are, they tell me—an easy man.
And you seem gently bred.

                In view of that,
I have a word to say to you, so listen.

Of mortal creatures, all that breathe and move,
earth bears none frailer than mankind. What man
believes in woe to come, so long as valor
and tough knees are supplied him by the gods?
But when the gods in bliss bring miseries on,   150
then willy-nilly, blindly, he endures.
Our minds are as the days are, dark or bright,
blown over by the father of gods and men.

So I, too, in my time thought to be happy;
but far and rash I ventured, counting on
my own right arm, my father, and my kin;
behold me now.

             No man should flout the law,
but keep in peace what gifts the gods may give.

I see you young blades living dangerously,
a household eaten up, a wife dishonored—   160

and yet the master will return, I tell you,
to his own place, and soon; for he is near.
So may some power take you out of this,
homeward, and softly, not to face that man
the hour he sets foot on his native ground.
Between him and the suitors I foretell
no quittance,[3] no way out, unless by blood,
once he shall stand beneath his own roof-beam."

Gravely, when he had done, he made libation
and took a sip of honey-hearted wine,   170
giving the cup, then, back into the hands
of the young nobleman. Amphínomos, for his part,
shaking his head, with chill and burdened breast,
turned in the great hall.
                                        Now his heart foreknew
the wrath to come, but he could not take flight,
being by Athena bound there.
                                        Death would have him
broken by a spear thrown by Telémakhos.
So he sat down where he had sat before.

And now heart-prompting from the grey-eyed goddess
came to the quiet queen, Penélopê: 180
a wish to show herself before the suitors;
for thus by fanning their desire again
Athena meant to set her beauty high
before her husband's eyes, before her son.
Knowing no reason, laughing confusedly,
she said:

                                   "Eurýnomê, I have a craving
I never had at all—I would be seen
among those ruffians, hateful as they are.
I might well say a word, then, to my son,
for his own good—tell him to shun that crowd;   190
for all their gay talk, they are bent on evil."

Mistress Eurýnomê replied:

                                        "Well said, child,
now is the time. Go down, and make it clear,
hold nothing back from him.
                                        But you must bathe
and put a shine upon your cheeks—not this way,
streaked under your eyes and stained with tears.
You make it worse, being forever sad,
and now your boy's a bearded man! Remember
you prayed the gods to let you see him so."

[3] Repayment.

Penélopê replied:

"Eurýnomê, 200
it is a kind thought, but I will not hear it—
to bathe and sleek with perfumed oil. No, no,
the gods forever took my sheen away
when my lord sailed for Troy in the decked ships.
Only tell my Autonoë to come,
and Hippodameía; they should be attending me
in hall, if I appear there. I could not
enter alone into that crowd of men."

At this the good old woman left the chamber
to tell the maids her bidding. But now too 210
the grey-eyed goddess had her own designs.
Upon the quiet daughter of Ikários
she let clear drops of slumber fall, until
the queen lay back asleep, her limbs unstrung,
in her long chair. And while she slept the goddess
endowed her with immortal grace to hold
the eyes of the Akhaians. With ambrosia
she bathed her cheeks and throat and smoothed her brow—
ambrosia, used by flower-crowned Kythereia[4]
when she would join the rose-lipped Graces dancing. 220
Grandeur she gave her, too, in height and form,
and made her whiter than carved ivory.
Touching her so, the perfect one was gone.
Now came the maids, bare-armed and lovely, voices
breaking into the room. The queen awoke
and as she rubbed her cheek she sighed:

"Ah, soft
that drowse I lay embraced in, pain forgot!
If only Artemis the Pure would give me
death as mild, and soon! No heart-ache more,
no wearing out my lifetime with desire 230
and sorrow, mindful of my lord, good man
in all ways that he was, best of the Akhaians!"

She rose and left her glowing upper room,
and down the stairs, with her two maids in train,
this beautiful lady went before the suitors.
Then by a pillar of the solid roof
she paused, her shining veil across her cheek,
the two girls close to her and still;
and in that instant weakness took those men
in the knee joints, their hearts grew faint with lust; 240
not one but swore to god to lie beside her.

[4] Aphroditê, goddess of love.

But speaking for her dear son's ears alone
she said:

                      "Telémakhos, what has come over you?
Lightminded you were not, in all your boyhood.
Now you are full grown, come of age; a man
from foreign parts might take you for the son
of royalty, to go by your good looks;
and have you no more thoughtfulness or manners?
How could it happen in our hall that you
permit the stranger to be so abused?   250
Here, in our house, a guest, can any man
suffer indignity, come by such injury?
What can this be for you but public shame?"

Telémakhos looked in her eyes and answered,
with his clear head and his discretion:

"Mother,
I cannot take it ill that you are angry.
I know the meaning of these actions now,
both good and bad. I had been young and blind.
How can I always keep to what is fair   260
while these sit here to put fear in me?—princes
from near and far whose interest is my ruin;
are any on my side?

                           But you should know
the suitors did not have their way, matching
the stranger here and Iros—for the stranger
beat him to the ground.

                            O Father Zeus!

Athena and Apollo! could I see
the suitors whipped like that! Courtyard and hall
strewn with our friends, too weak-kneed to get up,
chapfallen to their collarbones, the way   270
old Iros rolls his head there by the gate
as though he were pig-drunk! No energy
to stagger on his homeward path; no fight
left in his numb legs!"

                         Thus Penélopê
reproached her son, and he replied. Now, interrupting,
Eurýmakhos called out to her:

                            "Penélopê,
deep-minded queen, daughter of Ikários,
if all Akhaians in the land of Argos
only saw you now! What hundreds more
would join your suitors here to feast tomorrow!   280
Beauty like yours no woman had before,
or majesty, or mastery."

She answered:

"Eurýmakhos, my qualities—I know—
my face, my figure, all were lost or blighted
when the Akhaians crossed the sea to Troy,
Odysseus my lord among the rest.
If he returned, if he were here to care for me,
I might be happily renowned!
But grief instead heaven sent me—years of pain.
Can I forget?—the day he left this island, 290
enfolding my right hand and wrist in his,
he said:

'My lady, the Akhaian troops
will not easily make it home again
full strength, unhurt, from Troy. They say the Trojans
are fighters too; good lances and good bowmen,
horsemen, charioteers—and those can be
decisive when a battle hangs in doubt.
So whether God will send me back, or whether
I'll be a captive there, I cannot tell.
Here, then, you must attend to everything. 300
My parents in our house will be a care for you
as they are now, or more, while I am gone.
Wait for the beard to darken our boy's cheek;
then marry whom you will, and move away.'

The years he spoke of are now past; the night
comes when a bitter marriage overtakes me,
desolate as I am, deprived by Zeus
of all the sweets of life.

How galling, too,
to see newfangled manners in my suitors!
Others who go to court a gentlewoman, 310
daughter of a rich house, if they are rivals,
bring their own beeves and sheep along; her friends
ought to be feasted, gifts are due to her;
would any dare to live at her expense?"

Odysseus' heart laughed when he heard all this—
her sweet tones charming gifts out of the suitors
with talk of marriage, though she intended none.
Eupeithês' son, Antínoös, now addressed her:

"Ikários' daughter, O deep-minded queen!
If someone cares to make you gifts, accept them! 320
It is no courtesy to turn gifts away.
But we go neither to our homes nor elsewhere
until of all Akhaians here you take
the best man for your lord."

                                        Pleased at this answer,
every man sent a squire to fetch a gift—
Antínoös, a wide resplendent robe,
embroidered fine, and fastened with twelve brooches,
pins pressed into sheathing tubes of gold;
Eurýmakhos, a necklace, wrought in gold,
with sunray pieces of clear glinting amber.   330
Eurýdamas's men came back with pendants,
ear-drops in triple clusters of warm lights;
and from the hoard of Lord Polýktor's son,
Peisándros, came a band for her white throat,
jewelled adornment. Other wondrous things
were brought as gifts from the Akhaian princes.
Penélopê then mounted the stair again,
her maids behind, with treasure in their arms.

And now the suitors gave themselves to dancing,
to harp and haunting song, as night drew on;   340
black night indeed came on them at their pleasure.
But three torch fires were placed in the long hall
to give them light. On hand were stores of fuel,
dry seasoned chips of resinous wood, split up
by the bronze hatchet blade—these were mixed in
among the flames to keep them flaring bright;
each housemaid of Odysseus took her turn.

Now he himself, the shrewd and kingly man,
approached and told them:

                                        "Housemaids of Odysseus,
your master so long absent in the world,   350
go to the women's chambers, to your queen.
Attend her, make the distaff whirl, divert her,
stay in her room, comb wool for her.

                                        I stand here
ready to tend these flares and offer light
to everyone. They cannot tire me out,
even if they wish to drink till Dawn.
I am a patient man."

                                        But the women giggled,
glancing back and forth—laughed in his face;
and one smooth girl, Melántho, spoke to him
most impudently. She was Dólios' daughter,   360
taken as ward in childhood by Penélopê
who gave her playthings to her heart's content
and raised her as her own. Yet the girl felt
nothing for her mistress, no compunction,
but slept and made love with Eurýmakhos.
Her bold voice rang now in Odysseus' ears:

"You must be crazy, punch drunk, you old goat.
Instead of going out to find a smithy
to sleep warm in—or a tavern bench—you stay
putting your oar in, amid all our men. 370
Numbskull, not to be scared! The wine you drank
has clogged your brain, or are you always this way,
boasting like a fool? Or have you lost
your mind because you beat that tramp, that Iros?
Look out, or someone better may get up
and give you a good knocking about the ears
to send you out all bloody."

But Odysseus
glared at her under his brows and said:

"One minute:
let me tell Telémakhos how you talk
in hall, you slut; he'll cut your arms and legs off!" 380

This hard shot took the women's breath away
and drove them quaking to their rooms, as though
knives were behind: they felt he spoke the truth.
So there he stood and kept the firelight high
and looked the suitors over, while his mind
roamed far ahead to what must be accomplished.

They, for their part, could not now be still
or drop their mockery—for Athena wished
Odysseus mortified still more.

Eurýmakhos,
the son of Pôlybos, took up the baiting, 390
angling for a laugh among his friends.

"Suitors of our distinguished queen," he said,
"hear what my heart would have me say.

This man
comes with a certain aura of divinity
into Odysseus' hall. He shines.

He shines
around the noggin, like a flashing light,
having no hair at all to dim his lustre."

Then turning to Odysseus, raider of cities,
he went on:

"Friend, you have a mind to work,
do you? Could I hire you to clear stones 400
from wasteland for me—you'll be paid enough—
collecting boundary walls and planting trees?
I'd give you a bread ration every day,
a cloak to wrap in, sandals for your feet.

Oh no: you learned your dodges long ago—
no honest sweat. You'd rather tramp the country
begging, to keep your hoggish belly full."

The master of many crafts replied:

"Eurýmakhos,
we two might try our hands against each other
in early summer when the days are long,   410
in meadow grass, with one good scythe for me
and one as good for you: we'd cut our way
down a deep hayfield, fasting to late evening.
Or we could try our hands behind a plow,
driving the best of oxen—fat, well-fed,
well-matched for age and pulling power, and say
four strips apiece of loam the share could break:
you'd see then if I cleft you a straight furrow.
Competition in arms? If Zeus Kroníon
roused up a scuffle now, give me a shield,   420
two spears, a dogskin cap with plates of bronze
to fit my temples, and you'd see me go
where the first rank of fighters lock in battle.
There would be no more jeers about my belly.
You thick-skinned menace to all courtesy!
You think you are a great man and a champion,
but up against few men, poor stuff, at that.
Just let Odysseus return, those doors
wide open as they are, you'd find too narrow
to suit you on your sudden journey out."   430

Now fury mounted in Eurýmakhos,
who scowled and shot back:

"Bundle of rags and lice!
By god, I'll make you suffer for your gall,
your insolent gabble before all our men."

He had his foot-stool out: but now Odysseus
took to his haunches by Amphínomos' knees,
fearing Eurýmakhos' missile, as it flew.
It clipped a wine steward on the serving hand,
so that his pitcher dropped with a loud clang
while he fell backward, cursing, in the dust.   440
In the shadowy hall a low sound rose—of suitors
murmuring to one another.

"Ai!" they said,
"This vagabond would have done well to perish
somewhere else, and make us no such rumpus.
Here we are, quarreling over tramps; good meat
and wine forgotten; good sense gone by the board."

Telémakhos, his young heart high, put in:

"Bright souls, alight with wine, you can no longer
hide the cups you've taken.[5] Aye, some god
is goading you. Why not go home to bed?—   450
I mean when you are moved to. No one jumps
at my command."

                                        Struck by his blithe manner,
the young men's teeth grew fixed in their under lips,
but now the son of Nísos, Lord Amphínomos
of Aretíadês, addressed them all:

"O friends, no ruffling replies are called for;
that was fair counsel.
                        Hands off the stranger, now,
and hands off any other servant here
in the great house of King Odysseus. Come,
let my own herald wet our cups once more,   460
we'll make an offering, and then to bed.
The stranger can be left behind in hall;
Telémakhos may care for him; he came
to Telémakhos' door, not ours."

                                        This won them over.
The soldier Moulios, Doulíkhion herald,
comrade in arms of Lord Amphínomos,
mixed the wine and served them all. They tipped out
drops for the blissful gods, and drank the rest,
and when they had drunk their thirst away
they trailed off homeward drowsily to bed.   470

BOOK NINETEEN: RECOGNITIONS AND A DREAM

Now by Athena's side in the quiet hall
studying the ground for slaughter, Lord Odysseus
turned to Telémakhos.

                                        "The arms," he said.
"Harness and weapons must be out of sight
in the inner room. And if the suitors miss them,
be mild; just say 'I had a mind to move them
out of the smoke. They seemed no longer

---

[5] That is, they cannot hide the fact that they have drunk so much.

the bright arms that Odysseus left at home
when he went off to Troy. Here where the fire's
hot breath came, they had grown black and drear.   10
One better reason struck me, too:
suppose a brawl starts up when you've been drinking—
you might in madness let each other's blood,
and that would stain your feast, your courtship.

                                                        Iron
itself can draw men's hands.'"

                                         Then he fell silent,
and Telémakhos obeyed his father's word.
He called Eurýkleia, the nurse, and told her:

"Nurse, go shut the women in their quarters
while I shift Father's armor back
to the inner rooms—these beautiful arms unburnished,   20
caked with black soot in his years abroad.
I was a child then. Well, I am not now.
I want them shielded from the draught and smoke."

And the old woman answered:

                                       "It is time, child,
you took an interest in such things. I wish
you'd put your mind on all your house and chattels.[1]
But who will go along to hold a light?[2]
You said no maids, no torch-bearers."

                                            Telémakhos
looked at her and replied:

                                       "Our friend here.
A man who shares my meat can bear a hand,   30
no matter how far he is from home."

                                       He spoke so soldierly
her own speech halted on her tongue. Straight back
she went to lock the doors of the women's hall.
And now the two men sprang to work—father
and princely son, loaded with round helms
and studded bucklers, lifting the long spears,
while in their path Pallas Athena
held up a golden lamp of purest light.
Telémakhos at last burst out:

[1] Possessions other than house and lands.
[2] Maids would normally have been the torchbearers.

"Oh, Father,
here is a marvel! All around I see 40
the walls and roof beams, pedestals and pillars,
lighted as though by white fire blazing near.
One of the gods of heaven is in this place!"

Then said Odysseus, the great tactician,

"Be still: keep still about it: just remember it.
The gods who rule Olympos make this light.
You may go off to bed now. Here I stay
to test your mother and her maids again.
Out of her long grief she will question me."

Telémakhos went across the hall and out 50
under the light of torches—crossed the court
to the tower chamber where he had always slept.
Here now again he lay, waiting for dawn,
while in the great hall by Athena's side
Odysseus waited with his mind on slaughter.

Presently Penélopê from her chamber
stepped in her thoughtful beauty.

So might Artemis
or golden Aphroditê have descended;
and maids drew to the hearth her own smooth chair
inlaid with silver whorls and ivory. The artisan 60
Ikmálios had made it, long before,
with a footrest in a single piece, and soft
upon the seat a heavy fleece was thrown.
Here by the fire the queen sat down. Her maids,
leaving their quarters, came with white arms bare
to clear the wine cups and the bread, and move
the trestle boards where men had lingered drinking.
Fiery ashes out of the pine-chip flares
they tossed, and piled on fuel for light and heat.
And now a second time Melántho's voice 70
rang brazen in Odysseus' ears:

"Ah, stranger,
are you still here, so creepy, late at night
hanging about, looking the women over?
You old goat, go outside, cuddle your supper;
get out, or a torch may kindle you behind!"

At this Odysseus glared under his brows
and said:

"Little devil, why pitch into me again?
Because I go unwashed and wear these rags,

and make the rounds? But so I must, being needy;
that is the way a vagabond must live.   80
And do not overlook this: in my time
I too had luck, lived well, stood well with men,
and gave alms, often, to poor wanderers
like him you see before you—aye, to all sorts,
no matter in what dire want. I owned
servants—many, I say—and all the rest
that goes with what men call prosperity.
But Zeus the son of Kronos brought me down.
Mistress, mend your ways, or you may lose
all this vivacity of yours. What if her ladyship   90
were stirred to anger? What if Odysseus came?—
and I can tell you, there is hope of that—
or if the man is done for, still his son
lives to be reckoned with, by Apollo's will.
None of you can go wantoning on the sly
and fool him now. He is too old for that."

Penélopê, being near enough to hear him,
spoke out sharply to her maid:

                                                      "Oh, shameless,

through and through! And do you think me blind,
blind to your conquest?[3] It will cost your life.   100
You knew I waited—for you heard me say it—
waited to see this man in hall and question him
about my lord; I am so hard beset."

She turned away and said to the housekeeper:

"Eurýnomê, a bench, a spread of sheepskin,
to put my guest at ease. Now he shall talk
and listen, and be questioned."

                                                      Willing hands
brought a smooth bench, and dropped a fleece upon it.
Here the adventurer and king sat down;
then carefully Penélopê began: 110

"Friend, let me ask you first of all:
who are you, where do you come from, of what nation
and parents were you born?"

                                                  And he replied:

"My lady, never a man in the wide world
should have a fault to find with you. Your name

[3] The reference is to Melántho's sexual dalliance with Eurýmakhos. The following words are probably less a threat than a warning that Melántho will have brought on her own punishment.

has gone out under heaven like the sweet
honor of some god-fearing king, who rules
in equity over the strong: his black lands bear
both wheat and barley, fruit trees laden bright,
new lambs at lambing time—and the deep sea   120
gives great hauls of fish by his good strategy,
so that his folk fare well.

                                     O my dear lady,

this being so, let it suffice to ask me
of other matters—not my blood, my homeland.
Do not enforce me to recall my pain.
My heart is sore; but I must not be found
sitting in tears here, in another's house:
it is not well forever to be grieving.
One of the maids might say—or you might think—
I had got maudlin over cups of wine."   130

And Penélopê replied:

                                  "Stranger, my looks,
my face, my carriage, were soon lost or faded
when the Akhaians crossed the sea to Troy,
Odysseus my lord among the rest.
If he returned, if he were here to care for me,
I might be happily renowned!
But grief instead heaven sent me—years of pain.
Sons of the noblest families on the islands,
Doulíkhion, Samê, wooded Zakýnthos,
with native Ithakans, are here to court me,   140
against my wish; and they consume this house.
Can I give proper heed to guest or suppliant
or herald on the realm's affairs?

                                   How could I?

wasted with longing for Odysseus, while here
they press for marriage.

                                 Ruses served my turn
to draw the time out—first a close-grained web
I had the happy thought to set up weaving
on my big loom in hall. I said, that day:
'Young men—my suitors, now my lord is dead,
let me finish my weaving before I marry,   150
or else my thread will have been spun in vain.
It is a shroud I weave for Lord Laërtês
when cold Death comes to lay him on his bier.
The country wives would hold me in dishonor
if he, with all his fortune, lay unshrouded.'
I reached their hearts that way, and they agreed.
So every day I wove on the great loom,
but every night by torchlight I unwove it;
and so for three years I deceived the Akhaians.

But when the seasons brought a fourth year on,   160
as long months waned, and the long days were spent,
through impudent folly in the slinking maids
they caught me—clamored up to me at night;
I had no choice then but to finish it.
And now, as matters stand at last,
I have no strength left to evade a marriage,
cannot find any further way; my parents
urge it upon me, and my son
will not stand by while they eat up his property.
He comprehends it, being a man full grown,   170
able to oversee the kind of house
Zeus would endow with honor.

                                                                     But you too

confide in me, tell me your ancestry.
You were not born of mythic oak or stone."

And the great master of invention answered:

"O honorable wife of Lord Odysseus,
must you go on asking about my family?
Then I will tell you, though my pain
be doubled by it: and whose pain would not
if he had been away as long as I have   180
and had hard roving in the world of men?
But I will tell you even so, my lady.

One of the great islands of the world
in midsea, in the winedark sea, is Krete:
spacious and rich and populous, with ninety
cities and a mingling of tongues.
Akhaians there are found, along with Kretan
hillmen of the old stock, and Kydonians,
Dorians in three blood-lines, Pelasgians [4]—
and one among their ninety towns is Knossos.
Here lived King Minos [5] whom great Zeus received   190
every ninth year in private council—Minos,
the father of my father, Deukálion.
Two sons Deukálion had: Idómeneus,
who went to join the Atreidai before Troy
in the beaked ships of war; and then myself,
Aithôn by name—a stripling next my brother.
But I saw with my own eyes at Knossos once
Odysseus.

---

[4] Kydonians, Dorians, Pelasgians were various ethnic groups, natives of Krete or immigrants.
[5] Minos, sometimes represented as a cruel king (as in Book XI), is here represented as supremely honored. Knossos is on the north shore of Krete. In this version of his autobiography, Odysseus obviously departs from what he had told Eumaios (Book XIV) and Antínoös (Book XVII).

Gales had caught him off Cape Malea,
driven him southward on the coast of Krete, 200
when he was bound for Troy. At Ámnisos,
hard by the holy cave of Eileithuía,[6]
he lay to, and dropped anchor, in that open
and rough roadstead riding out the blow.
Meanwhile he came ashore, came inland, asking
after Idómeneus: dear friends he said they were;
but now ten mornings had already passed,
ten or eleven, since my brother sailed.
So I played host and took Odysseus home,
saw him well lodged and fed, for we had plenty; 210
then I made requisitions—barley, wine,
and beeves for sacrifice—to give his company
abundant fare along with him.

Twelve days

they stayed with us, the Akhaians, while that wind
out of the north shut everyone inside—
even on land you could not keep your feet,
such fury was abroad. On the thirteenth,
when the gale dropped, they put to sea."

Now all these lies he made appear so truthful
she wept as she sat listening. The skin 220
of her pale face grew moist the way pure snow
softens and glistens on the mountains, thawed
by Southwind after powdering from the West,
and, as the snow melts, mountain streams run full:
so her white cheeks were wetted by these tears
shed for her lord—and he close by her side.
Imagine how his heart ached for his lady,
his wife in tears; and yet he never blinked;
his eyes might have been made of horn or iron
for all that she could see. He had this trick— 230
wept, if he willed to, inwardly.

Well, then,

as soon as her relieving tears were shed
she spoke once more:

"I think that I shall say, friend,
give me some proof, if it is really true
that you were host in that place to my husband
with his brave men, as you declare. Come, tell me
the quality of his clothing, how he looked,
and some particular of his company."

---

[6] Ámnisos is an anchorage off Krete. Eileithuía was a goddess, daughter of Hêra, who controlled maternal labor and childbirth.

Odysseus answered, and his mind ranged far:

"Lady, so long a time now lies between,   240
it is hard to speak of it. Here is the twentieth year
since that man left the island of my father.
But I shall tell what memory calls to mind.
A purple cloak, and fleecy, he had on—
a double thick one. Then, he wore a brooch
made of pure gold with twin tubes for the prongs,
and on the face a work of art: a hunting dog
pinning a spotted fawn in agony
between his forepaws—wonderful to see
how being gold, and nothing more, he bit   250
the golden deer convulsed, with wild hooves flying.
Odysseus' shirt I noticed, too—a fine
closefitting tunic like dry onion skin,
so soft it was, and shiny.

                                                                              Women there,
many of them, would cast their eyes on it.
But I might add, for your consideration,
whether he brought these things from home, or whether
a shipmate gave them to him, coming aboard,
I have no notion: some regardful host
in another port perhaps it was. Affection   260
followed him—there were few Akhaians like him.
And I too made him gifts: a good bronze blade,
a cloak with lining and a broidered shirt,
and sent him off in his trim ship with honor.
A herald, somewhat older than himself,
he kept beside him; I'll describe this man:
round-shouldered, dusky, woolly-headed;
Eurýbatês, his name was—and Odysseus
gave him preferment over the officers.
He had a shrewd head, like the captain's own."   270

Now hearing these details—minutely true—
she felt more strangely moved, and tears flowed
until she had tasted her salt grief again.
Then she found words to answer:

                                                                              "Before this
you won my sympathy, but now indeed
you shall be our respected guest and friend.
With my own hands I put that cloak and tunic
upon him—took them folded from their place—
and the bright brooch for ornament.

                                                                              Gone now,
I will not meet the man again   280
returning to his own home fields. Unkind
the fate that sent him young in the long ship
to see that misery at Ilion, unspeakable!"

And the master improviser answered:

                                                   "Honorable

wife of Odysseus Laërtiadês,
you need not stain your beauty with these tears,
nor wear yourself out grieving for your husband.
Not that I can blame you. Any wife
grieves for the man she married in her girlhood,
lay with in love, bore children to—though he   290
may be no prince like this Odysseus,
whom they compare even to the gods. But listen:
weep no more, and listen:
I have a thing to tell you, something true.
I heard but lately of your lord's return,
heard that he is alive, not far away,
among Thesprótians in their green land
amassing fortune to bring home. His company
went down in shipwreck in the winedark sea
off the coast of Thrinákia. Zeus and Hêlios   300
held it against him that his men had killed
the kine of Hêlios. The crew drowned for this.
He rode the ship's keel. Big seas cast him up
on the island of Phaiákians, godlike men
who took him to their hearts. They honored him
with many gifts and a safe passage home,
or so they wished. Long since he should have been here,
but he thought better to restore his fortune
playing the vagabond about the world;
and no adventurer could beat Odysseus   310
at living by his wits—no man alive.
I had this from King Phaidôn of Thesprótia;
and, tipping wine out, Phaidôn swore to me
the ship was launched, the seamen standing by
to bring Odysseus to his land at last,
but I got out to sea ahead of him
by the king's order—as it chanced a freighter
left port for the grain bins of Doulíkhion.
Phaidôn, however, showed me Odysseus' treasure.
Ten generations of his heirs or more   320
could live on what lay piled in that great room.
The man himself had gone up to Dodona
to ask the spelling leaves of the old oak
what Zeus would have him do—how to return to Ithaka
after so many years—by stealth or openly.
You see, then, he is alive and well, and headed
homeward now, no more to be abroad
far from his island, his dear wife and son.
Here is my sworn word for it. Witness this,
god of the zenith, noblest of the gods,   330
and Lord Odysseus' hearthfire, now before me:

I swear these things shall turn out as I say.
Between this present dark and one day's ebb,
after the wane, before the crescent moon,[7]
Odysseus will come."

                                                     Penélopê,
the attentive queen, replied to him:

                                                     "Ah, stranger,
if what you say could ever happen!
You would soon know our love! Our bounty, too:
men would turn after you to call you blessed.
But my heart tells me what must be.   340
Odysseus will not come to me; no ship
will be prepared for you. We have no master
quick to receive and furnish out a guest
as Lord Odysseus was.

                                               Or did I dream him?

Maids, maids: come wash him, make a bed for him,
bedstead and colored rugs and coverlets
to let him lie warm into the gold of Dawn.
In morning light you'll bathe him and anoint him
so that he'll take his place beside Telémakhos
feasting in hall. If there be one man there   350
to bully or annoy him, that man wins
no further triumph here, burn though he may.
How will you understand me, friend, how find in me,
more than in common women, any courage
or gentleness, if you are kept in rags
and filthy at our feast? Men's lives are short.
The hard man and his cruelties will be
cursed behind his back, and mocked in death.
But one whose heart and ways are kind—of him
strangers will bear report to the wide world,   360
and distant men will praise him."

                                                      Warily
Odysseus answered:

                                               "Honorable lady,
wife of Odysseus Laërtiadês,
a weight of rugs and cover? Not for me.
I've had none since the day I saw the mountains
of Krete, white with snow, low on the sea line
fading behind me as the long oars drove me north.

---

[7] Between now and the time of the new moon. As it happens, the day specified will be the
morrow.

Let me lie down tonight as I've lain often,
many a night unsleeping, many a time
afield on hard ground waiting for pure Dawn. 370
No: and I have no longing for a footbath
either; none of these maids will touch my feet,
unless there is an old one, old and wise,
one who has lived through suffering as I have:
I would not mind letting my feet be touched
by that old servant."

And Penélopê said:

"Dear guest, no foreign man so sympathetic
ever came to my house, no guest more likeable,
so wry and humble are the things you say.
I have an old maidservant ripe with years, 380
one who in her time nursed my lord. She took him
into her arms the hour his mother bore him.
Let her, then, wash your feet, though she is frail.
Come here, stand by me, faithful Eurýkleia,
and bathe—bathe your master, I almost said,
for they are of an age, and now Odysseus'
feet and hands would be enseamed like his.
Men grow old soon in hardship."

Hearing this,
the old nurse hid her face between her hands
and wept hot tears, and murmured:

"Oh, my child! 390
I can do nothing for you! How Zeus hated you,
no other man so much! No use, great heart,
O faithful heart, the rich thighbones you burnt
to Zeus who plays in lightning—and no man
ever gave more to Zeus—with all your prayers
for a green age, a tall son reared to manhood.
There is no day of homecoming for you.
Stranger, some women in some far off place
perhaps have mocked my lord when he'd be home
as now these strumpets[8] mock you here. No wonder 400
you would keep clear of all their whorishness
and have no bath. But here am I. The queen
Penélopê, Ikários' daughter, bids me;
so let me bathe your feet to serve my lady—
to serve you, too.

My heart within me stirs,
mindful of something. Listen to what I say:
strangers have come here, many through the years,

[8] Whores.

but no one ever came, I swear, who seemed
so like Odysseus—body, voice and limbs—
as you do."

                              Ready for this, Odysseus answered: 410

"Old woman, that is what they say. All who have seen
the two of us remark how like we are,
as you yourself have said, and rightly, too."

Then he kept still, while the old nurse filled up
her basin glittering in firelight; she poured
cold water in, then hot.

                                         But Lord Odysseus
whirled suddenly from the fire to face the dark.
The scar: he had forgotten that. She must not
handle his scarred thigh, or the game was up.
But when she bared her lord's leg, bending near,   420
she knew the groove at once.

                                         An old wound

a boar's white tusk inflicted, on Parnassos[9]
years ago. He had gone hunting there
in company with his uncles and Autólykos,
his mother's father—a great thief and swindler
by Hermês'[10] favor, for Autólykos pleased him
with burnt offerings of sheep and kids. The god
acted as his accomplice. Well, Autólykos
on a trip to Ithaka
arrived just after his daughter's boy was born.   430
In fact, he had no sooner finished supper
than Nurse Eurýkleia put the baby down
in his own lap and said:

                                         "It is for you, now,
to choose a name for him, your child's dear baby;
the answer to her prayers."

                                   Autólykos replied:

"My son-in-law, my daughter, call the boy
by the name I tell you. Well you know, my hand
has been against the world of men and women;
odium and distrust I've won. Odysseus
should be his given name.[11] When he grows up,   440
when he comes visiting his mother's home

---

[9] The famous mountain near Delphi. Also spelled *Parnassus*.
[10] Noted for cleverness, Hermês was the patron god of thieves, though he is not usually
presented in that role by Homer.
[11] *Odysseus* means something like "wrathful."

under Parnassos, where my treasures are,
I'll make him gifts and send him back rejoicing."

Odysseus in due course went for the gifts,
and old Autólykos and his sons embraced him
with welcoming sweet words; and Amphithéa,
his mother's mother, held him tight and kissed him,
kissed his head and his fine eyes.

The father
called on his noble sons to make a feast,
and going about it briskly they led in   450
an ox of five years, whom they killed and flayed
and cut in bits for roasting on the skewers
with skilled hands, with care; then shared it out.
So all the day until the sun went down
they feasted to their hearts' content. At evening,
after the sun was down and dusk had come,
they turned to bed and took the gift of sleep.

When the young Dawn spread in the eastern sky
her finger tips of rose, the men and dogs
went hunting, taking Odysseus. They climbed   460
Parnassos' rugged flank mantled in forest,
entering amid high windy folds at noon
when Hêlios beat upon the valley floor
and on the winding Ocean whence he came.
With hounds questing ahead, in open order,
the sons of Autólykos went down a glen,
Odysseus in the lead, behind the dogs,
pointing his long-shadowing spear.

Before them
a great boar lay hid in undergrowth,
in a green thicket proof against the wind   470
or sun's blaze, fine soever the needling sunlight,
impervious too to any rain, so dense
that cover was, heaped up with fallen leaves.
Patter of hounds' feet, men's feet, woke the boar
as they came up—and from his woody ambush
with razor back bristling and raging eyes
he trotted and stood at bay. Odysseus,
being on top of him, had the first shot,
lunging to stick him; but the boar
had already charged under the long spear.   480
He hooked aslant with one white tusk and ripped out
flesh above the knee, but missed the bone.
Odysseus' second thrust went home by luck,
his bright spear passing through the shoulder joint;
and the beast fell, moaning as life pulsed away.
Autólykos' tall sons took up the wounded,

working skillfully over the Prince Odysseus
to bind his gash, and with a rune[12] they stanched
the dark flow of blood. Then downhill swiftly
they all repaired to the father's house, and there   490
tended him well—so well they soon could send him,
with Grandfather Autólykos' magnificent gifts,
rejoicing, over sea to Ithaka.
His father and the Lady Antikleía
welcomed him, and wanted all the news
of how he got his wound; so he spun out
his tale, recalling how the boar's white tusk
caught him when he was hunting on Parnassos.

This was the scar the old nurse recognized;
she traced it under her spread hands, then let go,   500
and into the basin fell the lower leg
making the bronze clang, sloshing the water out.
Then joy and anguish seized her heart; her eyes
filled up with tears; her throat closed, and she whispered,
with hand held out to touch his chin:

                                                        "Oh yes!

You are Odysseus! Ah, dear child! I could not
see you until now—not till I knew
my master's very body with my hands!"

Her eyes turned to Penélopê with desire
to make her lord, her husband, known—in vain,   510
because Athena had bemused the queen,
so that she took no notice, paid no heed.
At the same time Odysseus' right hand
gripped the old throat; his left hand pulled her near,
and in her ear he said:

                                                "Will you destroy me,
nurse, who gave me milk at your own breast?
Now with a hard lifetime behind I've come
in the twentieth year home to my father's island.
You found me out, as the chance was given you.
Be quiet; keep it from the others, else   520
I warn you, and I mean it, too,
if by my hand god brings the suitors down
I'll kill you, nurse or not, when the time comes—
when the time comes to kill the other women."

Eurýkleia kept her wits and answered him:

"Oh, what mad words are these you let escape you!
Child, you know my blood, my bones are yours;

[12] Magic spell or charm.

no one could whip this out of me. I'll be
a woman turned to stone, iron I'll be.
And let me tell you too—mind now—if god 530
cuts down the arrogant suitors by your hand,
I can report to you on all the maids,
those who dishonor you, and the innocent."

But in response the great tactician said:

"Nurse, no need to tell me tales of these.
I will have seen them, each one, for myself.
Trust in the gods, be quiet, hold your peace."

Silent, the old nurse went to fetch more water,
her basin being all spilt.

                                    When she had washed
and rubbed his feet with golden oil, he turned, 540
dragging his bench again to the fire side
for warmth, and hid the scar under his rags.
Penélopê broke the silence, saying:

                                          "Friend,
allow me one brief question more. You know,
the time for bed, sweet rest, is coming soon,
if only that warm luxury of slumber
would come to enfold us, in our trouble. But for me
my fate at night is anguish and no rest.
By day being busy, seeing to my work,
I find relief sometimes from loss and sorrow; 550
but when night comes and all the world's abed
I lie in mine alone, my heart thudding,
while bitter thoughts and fears crowd on my grief.
Think, how Pandáreos'[13] daughter, pale forever,
sings as the nightingale in the new leaves
through those long quiet hours of night,
on some thick-flowering orchard bough in spring;
how she rills out and tilts her note, high now, now low,
mourning for Itylos whom she killed in madness—
her child, and her lord Zêthos' only child. 560
My forlorn thought flows variable as her song,
wondering: shall I stay beside my son
and guard my own things here, my maids, my hall,
to honor my lord's bed and the common talk?
Or had I best join fortunes with a suitor,
the noblest one, most lavish in his gifts?
Is it now time for that?

---

[13] In this version of the nightingale myth, Aedon (daughter of Pandáreos and wife of Zêthos) was metamorphosed into a nightingale, through the compassion of Zeus, after she had killed her only son, Itylos, by mistake. She had intended to kill the eldest son of Niobe, her sister-in-law, who had aroused her jealousy by having so many children.

My son being still a callow boy forbade
marriage, or absence from my lord's domain;
but now the child is grown, grown up, a man,   570
he, too, begins to pray for my departure,
aghast at all the suitors gorge on.

                                                              Listen:

interpret me this dream: From a water's edge
twenty fat geese have come to feed on grain
beside my house. And I delight to see them.
But now a mountain eagle with great wings
and crooked beak storms in to break their necks
and strew their bodies here. Away he soars
into the bright sky; and I cry aloud—
all this in dream—I wail and round me gather   580
softly braided Akhaian women mourning
because the eagle killed my geese.

                                                          Then down

out of the sky he drops to a cornice beam
with mortal voice telling me not to weep.
'Be glad,' says he, 'renowned Ikários' daughter:
here is no dream but something real as day,
something about to happen. All those geese
were suitors, and the bird was I. See now,
I am no eagle but your lord come back
to bring inglorious death upon them all!'   590
As he said this, my honeyed slumber left me.
Peering through half-shut eyes, I saw the geese
in hall, still feeding at the self-same trough."

The master of subtle ways and straight replied:

"My dear, how can you choose to read the dream
differently? Has not Odysseus himself
shown you what is to come? Death to the suitors,
sure death, too. Not one escapes his doom."

Penélopê shook her head and answered:

                                                          "Friend,

many and many a dream is mere confusion,   600
a cobweb of no consequence at all.
Two gates for ghostly dreams there are: one gateway
of honest horn, and one of ivory.
Issuing by the ivory gate are dreams
of glimmering illusion, fantasies,
but those that come through solid polished horn
may be borne out, if mortals only know them.
I doubt it came by horn, my fearful dream—
too good to be true, that, for my son and me.
But one thing more I wish to tell you: listen   610
carefully. It is a black day, this that comes.

Odysseus' house and I are to be parted.
I shall decree a contest for the day.
We have tweive axe heads. In his time, my lord
could line them up, all twelve, at intervals
like a ship's ribbing; then he'd back away
a long way off and whip an arrow through.
Now I'll impose this trial on the suitors.
The one who easily handles and strings the bow
and shoots through all twelve axes I shall marry,   620
whoever he may be—then look my last
on this my first love's beautiful brimming house.
But I'll remember, though I dream it only."

Odysseus said:

                                        "Dear honorable lady,
wife of Odysseus Laërtiadês,
let there be no postponement of the trial.
Odysseus, who knows the shifts of combat,
will be here: aye, he'll be here long before
one of these lads can stretch or string that bow
or shoot to thread the iron!"

                                        Grave and wise,   630
Penélopê replied:

                                        "If you were willing
to sit with me and comfort me, my friend,
no tide of sleep would ever close my eyes.
But mortals cannot go forever sleepless.
This the undying gods decree for all
who live and die on earth, kind furrowed earth.
Upstairs I go, then, to my single bed,
my sighing bed, wet with so many tears
after my Lord Odysseus took ship
to see that misery at Ilion, unspeakable.   640
Let me rest there, you here. You can stretch out
on the bare floor, or else command a bed."

So she went up to her chamber softly lit,
accompanied by her maids. Once there, she wept
for Odysseus, her husband, till Athena
cast sweet sleep upon her eyes.

BOOK TWENTY: SIGNS AND A VISION

Outside in the entry way he made his bed—
raw oxhide spread on level ground, and heaped up
fleeces, left from sheep the Akhaians killed.

And when he had lain down, Eurýnomê
flung out a robe to cover him. Unsleeping
the Lord Odysseus lay, and roved in thought
to the undoing of his enemies.
                                        Now came a covey of women
laughing as they slipped out, arm in arm,
as many a night before, to the suitors' beds;
and anger took him like a wave to leap   10
into their midst and kill them, every one—
or should he let them all go hot to bed
one final night? His heart cried out within him
the way a brach[1] with whelps between her legs
would howl and bristle at a stranger—so
the hackles of his heart rose at that laughter.
Knocking his breast he muttered to himself:

"Down; be steady. You've seen worse, that time
the Kyklops like a rockslide ate your men
while you looked on. Nobody, only guile,   20
got you out of that cave alive."

                                                              His rage

held hard in leash, submitted to his mind,
while he himself rocked, rolling from side to side,
as a cook turns a sausage, big with blood
and fat, at a scorching blaze, without a pause,
to broil it quick: so he rolled left and right,
casting about to see how he, alone,
against the false outrageous crowd of suitors
could press the fight.
                                        And out of the night sky
Athena came to him; out of the nearby dark   30
in body like a woman; came and stood
over his head to chide him:

                                                "Why so wakeful,

most forlorn of men? Here is your home,
there lies your lady; and your son is here,
as fine as one could wish a son to be."

Odysseus looked up and answered:

"Aye,
goddess, that much is true; but still
I have some cause to fret in this affair.
I am one man; how can I whip those dogs?   40
They are always here in force. Neither
is that the end of it, there's more to come.

---

[1] Female dog; bitch.

If by the will of Zeus and by your will
I killed them all, where could I go for safety?
Tell me that!"

And the grey-eyed goddess said:

"Your touching faith! Another man would trust
some villainous mortal, with no brains—and what
am I? Your goddess-guardian to the end
in all your trials. Let it be plain as day:
if fifty bands of men surrounded us   50
and every sword sang for your blood,
you could make off still with their cows and sheep.
Now you, too, go to sleep. This all night vigil
wearies the flesh. You'll come out soon enough
on the other side of trouble."

Raining soft

sleep on his eyes, the beautiful one was gone
back to Olympos. Now at peace, the man
slumbered and lay still, but not his lady.
Wakeful again with all her cares, reclining
in the soft bed, she wept and cried aloud   60
until she had had her fill of tears, then spoke
in prayer first to Artemis:

"O gracious

divine lady Artemis, daughter of Zeus,
if you could only make an end now quickly,
let the arrow fly, stop my heart,
or if some wind could take me by the hair
up into running cloud, to plunge in tides of Ocean,
as hurricane winds took Pandáreos' daughters[2]
when they were left at home alone. The gods
had sapped their parents' lives. But Aphroditê   70
fed those children honey, cheese, and wine,
and Hêra gave them looks and wit, and Artemis,
pure Artemis, gave lovely height, and wise
Athena made them practised in her arts—
till Aphroditê in glory walked on Olympos,
begging for each a happy wedding day
from Zeus, the lightning's joyous king, who knows
all fate of mortals, fair and foul—
but even at that hour the cyclone winds
had ravished them away   80
to serve the loathsome Furies.

[2] Pandáreos stole a statue from a temple of Zeus; after the death of Pandáreos, his three
daughters (Aedon and two of her sisters), though pitied by the greatest of the goddesses, were
carried away by the Furies, the avengers of the father's wickedness. This story differs from the
one in Book XIX, in which Aedon was changed into a nightingale.

                                                                          Let me be
blown out by the Olympians! Shot by Artemis,
I still might go and see amid the shades
Odysseus in the rot of underworld.
No coward's eye should light by my consenting!
Evil may be endured when our days pass
in mourning, heavy-hearted, hard beset,
if only sleep reign over nighttime, blanketing
the world's good and evil from our eyes.
But not for me: dreams too my demon sends me.   90
Tonight the image of my lord came by
as I remember him with troops. O strange
exultation! I thought him real, and not a dream."

Now as the Dawn appeared all stitched in gold,
the queen's cry reached Odysseus at his waking,
so that he wondered, half asleep: it seemed
she knew him, and stood near him! Then he woke
and picked his bedding up to stow away
on a chair in the mégaron. The oxhide pad
he took outdoors. There, spreading wide his arms,   100
he prayed:

                              "O Father Zeus, if over land and water,
after adversity, you willed to bring me home,
let someone in the waking house give me good augury,
and a sign be shown, too, in the outer world."

He prayed thus, and the mind of Zeus in heaven
heard him. He thundered out of bright Olympos
down from above the cloudlands, in reply—
a rousing peal for Odysseus. Then a token
came to him from a woman grinding flour
in the court nearby. His own handmills were there,   110
and twelve maids had the job of grinding out
whole grain and barley meal, the pith of men.
Now all the rest, their bushels ground, were sleeping;
one only, frail and slow, kept at it still.
She stopped, stayed her hand, and her lord heard
the omen from her lips:

                                                    "Ah, Father Zeus
almighty over gods and men!
A great bang of thunder that was, surely,
out of the starry sky, and not a cloud in sight.
It is your nod to someone. Hear me, then,   120
make what I say come true:
let this day be the last the suitors feed
so dainty in Odysseus' hall!
They've made me work my heart out till I drop,
grinding barley. May they feast no more!"

The servant's prayer, after the cloudless thunder
of Zeus, Odysseus heard with lifting heart,
sure in his bones that vengeance was at hand.
Then other servants, wakening, came down
to build and light a fresh fire at the hearth. 130
Telémakhos, clear-eyed as a god, awoke,
put on his shirt and belted on his sword,
bound rawhide sandals under his smooth feet,
and took his bronze-shod lance. He came and stood
on the broad sill of the doorway, calling Euríkleia:

"Nurse, dear Nurse, how did you treat our guest?
Had he a supper and a good bed? Has he lain
uncared for still? My mother is like that,
perverse for all her cleverness:
she'd entertain some riff-raff, and turn out 140
a solid man."

                    The old nurse answered him:

"I would not be so quick to accuse her, child.
He sat and drank here while he had a mind to;
food he no longer hungered for, he said—
for she did ask him. When he thought of sleeping,
she ordered them to make a bed. Poor soul!
Poor gentleman! So humble and so miserable,
he would accept no bed with rugs to lie on,
but slept on sheepskins and a raw oxhide
in the entry way. We covered him ourselves." 150

Telémakhos left the hall, hefting his lance,
with two swift flickering hounds for company,
to face the island Akhaians in the square;
and gently born Euríkleia, the daughter
of Ops Peisenóridês, called to the maids:

"Bestir yourselves! you have your brooms, go sprinkle
the rooms and sweep them, robe the chairs in red,
sponge off the tables till they shine.
Wash out the winebowls and two-handled cups.
You others go fetch water from the spring; 160
no loitering; come straight back. Our company
will be here soon; morning is sure to bring them;
everyone has a holiday today."[3]

The women ran to obey her—twenty girls
off to the spring with jars for dusky water,
the rest at work inside. Then tall woodcutters
entered to split up logs for the hearth fire,

---

[3] The day is a special festival.

the water carriers returned; and on their heels
arrived the swineherd, driving three fat pigs,
chosen among his pens. In the wide court   170
he let them feed, and said to Odysseus kindly:

"Friend, are they more respectful of you now,
or still insulting you?"

                                                          Replied Odysseus:

"The young men, yes. And may the gods requite
those insolent puppies for the game they play
in a home not their own. They have no decency."

During this talk, Melánthios the goatherd
came in, driving goats for the suitors' feast,
with his two herdsmen. Under the portico
they tied the animals, and Melánthios   180
looked at Odysseus with a sneer. Said he:

                                                             "Stranger,
I see you mean to stay and turn our stomachs
begging in this hall. Clear out, why don't you?
Or will you have to taste a bloody beating
before you see the point? Your begging ways
nauseate everyone. There are feasts elsewhere."

Odysseus answered not a word, but grimly
shook his head over his murderous heart.
A third man came up now: Philoítios
the cattle foreman, with an ox behind him   190
and fat goats for the suitors. Ferrymen
had brought these from the mainland, as they bring
travellers, too—whoever comes along.
Philoítios tied the beasts under the portico
and joined the swineherd.

                                               "Who is this," he said,
"Who is the new arrival at the manor?
Akhaian? or what else does he claim to be?
Where are his family and fields of home?
Down on his luck, all right: carries himself like a captain.
How the immortal gods can change and drag us down   200
once they begin to spin dark days for us!—
Kings and commanders, too."

                                               Then he stepped over
and took Odysseus by the right hand, saying:

"Welcome, Sir. May good luck lie ahead
at the next turn. Hard times you're having, surely.

O Zeus! no god is more berserk in heaven
if gentle folk, whom you yourself begot,[4]
you plunge in grief and hardship without mercy!
Sir, I began to sweat when I first saw you,
and tears came to my eyes, remembering 210
Odysseus: rags like these he may be wearing
somewhere on his wanderings now—
I mean, if he's alive still under the sun.
But if he's dead and in the house of Death,
I mourn Odysseus. He entrusted cows to me
in Kephallênia,[5] when I was knee high,
and now his herds are numberless, no man else
ever had cattle multiply like grain.
But new men tell me I must bring my beeves
to feed them, who care nothing for our prince, 220
fear nothing from the watchful gods. They crave
partition of our lost king's land and wealth.
My own feelings keep going round and round
upon this tether: can I desert the boy
by moving, herds and all, to another country,
a new life among strangers? Yet it's worse
to stay here, in my old post, herding cattle
for upstarts.

                  I'd have gone long since,
gone, taken service with another king; this shame
is no more to be borne; but I keep thinking 230
my own lord, poor devil, still might come
and make a rout of suitors in his hall."

Odysseus, with his mind on action, answered:

"Herdsman, I make you out to be no coward
and no fool: I can see that for myself.
So let me tell you this. I swear by Zeus
all highest, by the table set for friends,
and by your king's hearthstone to which I've come,
Odysseus will return. You'll be on hand
to see, if you care to see it, 240
how those who lord it here will be cut down."

The cowman said:

                   "Would god it all came true!
You'd see the fight that's in me!"

                         Then Eumaios
echoed him, and invoked the gods, and prayed
that his great-minded master should return.

---

[4] To say that Zeus was their father was a way of describing great leaders.
[5] A large island near Ithaka; modern Cephalonia.

While these three talked, the suitors in the field
had come together plotting—what but death
for Telémakhos?—when from the left an eagle
crossed high with a rockdove in his claws.

Amphínomos got up. Said he, cutting them short: 250

"Friends, no luck lies in that plan for us,
no luck,[6] knifing the lad. Let's think of feasting."

A grateful thought, they felt, and walking on
entered the great hall of the hero Odysseus,
where they all dropped their cloaks on chairs or couches
and made a ritual slaughter, knifing sheep,
fat goats and pigs, knifing the grass-fed steer.
Then tripes were broiled and eaten. Mixing bowls
were filled with wine. The swineherd passed out cups,
Philoítios, chief cowherd, dealt the loaves   260
into the panniers, Melánthios poured wine,
and all their hands went out upon the feast.

Telémakhos placed his father to advantage
just at the door sill of the pillared hall,
setting a stool there and a sawed-off table,
gave him a share of tripes, poured out his wine
in a golden cup, and said:

                                                    "Stay here, sit down
to drink with our young friends. I stand between you
and any cutting word or cuffing hand
from any suitor. Here is no public house   270
but the old home of Odysseus, my inheritance.
Hold your tongues then, gentlemen, and your blows,
and let no wrangling start, no scuffle either."

The others, disconcerted, bit their lips
at the ring in the young man's voice. Antínoös,
Eupeithês' son, turned round to them and said:

"It goes against the grain, my lords, but still
I say we take this hectoring by Telémakhos.
You know Zeus balked at it, or else
we might have shut his mouth a long time past,   280
the silvery speaker."

                                                    But Telémakhos
paid no heed to what Antínoös said.

_____

[6] The bird's appearance on the left is an ill omen.

Now public heralds wound through Ithaka
leading a file of beasts for sacrifice, and islanders
gathered under the shade trees of Apollo,
in the precinct of the Archer—while in hall
the suitors roasted mutton and fat beef
on skewers, pulling off the fragrant cuts;
and those who did the roasting served Odysseus
a portion equal to their own, for so   290
Telémakhos commanded.

                                                    But Athena
had no desire now to let the suitors
restrain themselves from wounding words and acts.
Laërtês' son again must be offended.
There was a scapegrace[7] fellow in the crowd
named Ktésippos, a Samian, rich beyond
all measure, arrogant with riches, early
and late a bidder for Odysseus' queen.
Now this one called attention to himself:

"Hear me, my lords, I have a thing to say.   300
Our friend has had his fair share from the start
and that's polite; it would be most improper
if we were cold to guests of Telémakhos—
no matter what tramp turns up. Well then, look here,
let me throw in my own small contribution.
He must have prizes to confer, himself,
on some brave bathman or another slave
here in Odysseus' house."

                                        His hand went backward
and, fishing out a cow's foot from the basket,
he let it fly.

                                        Odysseus rolled his head   310
to one side softly, ducking the blow, and smiled
a crooked smile with teeth clenched. On the wall
the cow's foot struck and fell. Telémakhos
blazed up:

                        "Ktésippos, lucky for you, by heaven,
not to have hit him! He took care of himself,
else you'd have had my lance-head in your belly;
no marriage, but a grave instead on Ithaka
for your father's pains.

                                        You others, let me see
no more contemptible conduct in my house!
I've been awake to it for a long time—by now   320
I know what is honorable and what is not.

---

[7] Unprincipled.

Before, I was a child. I can endure it
while sheep are slaughtered, wine drunk up, and bread—
can one man check the greed of a hundred men?—
but I will suffer no more viciousness.
Granted you mean at last to cut me down:
I welcome that—better to die than have
humiliation always before my eyes,
the stranger buffeted, and the serving women
dragged about, abused in a noble house."   330

They quieted, grew still, under his lashing,
and after a long silence, Ageláos,
Damástor's son, spoke to them all:

                                              "Friends, friends,
I hope no one will answer like a fishwife.
What has been said is true. Hands off this stranger,
he is no target, neither is any servant
here in the hall of King Odysseus.
Let me say a word, though, to Telémakhos
and to his mother, if it please them both:
as long as hope remained in you to see   340
Odysseus, that great gifted man, again,
you could not be reproached for obstinacy,
tying the suitors down here; better so,
if still your father fared the great sea homeward.
How plain it is, though, now, he'll come no more!
Go sit then by your mother, reason with her,
tell her to take the best man, highest bidder,
and you can have and hold your patrimony,
feed on it, drink it all, while she
adorns another's house."

                                        Keeping his head,   350
Telémakhos replied:

                                        "By Zeus Almighty,
Ageláos, and by my father's sufferings,
far from Ithaka, whether he's dead or lost,
I make no impediment to Mother's marriage.
'Take whom you wish,' I say, 'I'll add my dowry.'
But can I pack her off against her will
from her own home? Heaven forbid!"

                                                  At this,
Pallas Athena touched off in the suitors
a fit of laughter, uncontrollable.[8]
She drove them into nightmare, till they wheezed   360

---

[8] The laughter is a sign that the suitors are out of their right minds.

and neighed as though with jaws no longer theirs,
while blood defiled their meat,[9] and blurring tears
flooded their eyes, heart-sore with woe to come.
Then said the visionary, Theoklýmenos:

"O lost sad men, what terror is this you suffer?
Night shrouds you to the knees, your heads, your faces;
dry retch of death runs round like fire in sticks;
your cheeks are streaming; these fair walls and pedestals
are dripping crimson blood. And thick with shades
is the entry way, the courtyard thick with shades   370
passing athirst toward Érebos, into the dark,
the sun is quenched in heaven, foul mist hems us in . . ."

The young men greeted this with shouts of laughter,
and Eurýmakhos, the son of Pólybos, crowed:

"The mind of our new guest has gone astray.
Hustle him out of doors, lads, into the sunlight;
he finds it dark as night inside!"

The man of vision looked at him and said:

"When I need help, I'll ask for it, Eurýmakhos.
I have my eyes and ears, a pair of legs,   380
and a straight mind, still with me. These will do
to take me out. Damnation and black night
I see arriving for yourselves: no shelter,
no defence for any in this crowd—
fools and vipers in the king's own hall."

With this he left that handsome room and went
home to Peiraios, who received him kindly.
The suitors made wide eyes at one another
and set to work provoking Telémakhos
with jokes about his friends. One said, for instance: 390

"Telémakhos, no man is a luckier host
when it comes to what the cat dragged in. What burning
eyes your beggar had for bread and wine!
But not for labor, not for a single heave—
he'd be a deadweight on a field. Then comes
this other, with his mumbo-jumbo. Boy,
for your own good, I tell you, toss them both
into a slave ship for the Sikels.[10] That would pay you."

Telémakhos ignored the suitors' talk.
He kept his eyes in silence on his father,   400

---

[9] That is, in the eyes of Odysseus, Telémakhos, and Theoklýmenos.
[10] Sicilians.

awaiting the first blow. Meanwhile
the daughter of Ikários, Penélopê,
had placed her chair to look across and down
on father and son at bay; she heard the crowd,
and how they laughed as they resumed their dinner,
a fragrant feast, for many beasts were slain—
but as for supper, men supped never colder
than these, on what the goddess and the warrior
were even then preparing for the suitors,
whose treachery had filled that house with pain.   410

BOOK TWENTY-ONE: THE TEST OF THE BOW

Upon Penélopê, most worn in love and thought,
Athena cast a glance like a grey sea
lifting her. Now to bring the tough bow out and bring
the iron blades. Now try those dogs at archery
to usher bloody slaughter in.

                                    So moving stairward
the queen took up a fine doorhook of bronze,
ivory-hafted, smooth in her clenched hand,
and led her maids down to a distant room,
a storeroom where the master's treasure lay:
bronze, bar gold, black iron forged and wrought.   10
In this place hung the double-torsion bow
and arrows in a quiver, a great sheaf—
quills of groaning.

                            In the old time in Lakedaimon[1]
her lord had got these arms from Íphitos,
Eurýtos'[2] son. The two met in Messenia[3]
at Ortílokhos' table, on the day
Odysseus claimed a debt owed by that realm—
sheep stolen by Messenians out of Ithaka
in their long ships, three hundred head, and herdsmen.
Seniors of Ithaka and his father sent him   20
on that far embassy when he was young.
But Íphitos had come there tracking strays,
twelve shy mares, with mule colts yet unweaned.
And a fatal chase they led him over prairies
into the hands of Heraklês. That massive
son of toil and mortal son of Zeus

[1] The region of Sparta, in southern Greece.
[2] A famous archer.
[3] A region down the coast from Ithaka, in southwestern Greece.

murdered his guest at wine[4] in his own house—
inhuman, shameless in the sight of heaven—
to keep the mares and colts in his own grange.
Now Íphitos, when he knew Odysseus, gave him   30
the master bowman's arm; for old Eurýtos
had left it on his deathbed to his son.
In fellowship Odysseus gave a lance
and a sharp sword. But Heraklês killed Íphitos
before one friend could play host to the other.
And Lord Odysseus would not take the bow
in the black ships to the great war at Troy.
As a keepsake he put it by:
it served him well at home in Ithaka.

Now the queen reached the storeroom door and halted.   40
Here was an oaken sill, cut long ago
and sanded clean and bedded true. Foursquare
the doorjambs and the shining doors were set
by the careful builder. Penélopê untied the strap
around the curving handle, pushed her hook
into the slit, aimed at the bolts inside
and shot them back. Then came a rasping sound
as those bright doors the key had sprung gave way—
a bellow like a bull's vaunt in a meadow—
followed by her light footfall entering   50
over the plank floor. Herb-scented robes
lay there in chests, but the lady's milkwhite arms
went up to lift the bow down from a peg
in its own polished bowcase.

                                        Now Penélopê
sank down, holding the weapon on her knees,
and drew her husband's great bow out, and sobbed
and bit her lip and let the salt tears flow.
Then back she went to face the crowded hall
tremendous bow in hand, and on her shoulder hung
the quiver spiked with coughing death. Behind her   60
maids bore a basket full of axeheads, bronze
and iron implements for the master's game.
Thus in her beauty she approached the suitors,
and near a pillar of the solid roof
she paused, her shining veil across her cheeks,
her maids on either hand and still,
then spoke to the banqueters:

---

[4] Íphitos' pursuit of his lost mares brought him to Tiryns, the city of the great hero-adventurer Heraklês, who, according to certain versions of the story, had something to do with the mares' disappearance. By some accounts, Heraklês killed Íphitos by throwing him down from the city walls.

                                                      "My lords, hear me:
suitors indeed, you commandeered this house
to feast and drink in, day and night, my husband
being long gone, long out of mind. You found   70
no justification for yourselves—none
except your lust to marry me. Stand up, then:
we now declare a contest for that prize.
Here is my lord Odysseus' hunting bow.
Bend and string it if you can. Who sends an arrow
through iron axe-helve sockets,[5] twelve in line?
I join my life with his, and leave this place, my home,
my rich and beautiful bridal house, forever
to be remembered, though I dream it only."

Then to Eumaios:

                                         "Carry the bow forward.   80
Carry the blades."

                            Tears came to the swineherd's eyes
as he reached out for the big bow. He laid it
down at the suitors' feet. Across the room
the cowherd sobbed, knowing the master's weapon.
Antínoös growled, with a glance at both:

                                                          "Clods.
They go to pieces over nothing.

                                             You two, there,
why are you sniveling? To upset the woman
even more? Has she not pain enough
over her lost husband? *Sit down.*
Get on with dinner quietly, or cry about it   90
outside, if you must. Leave us the bow.
A clean-cut game, it looks to me.
Nobody bends that bowstave easily
in this company. Is there a man here
made like Odysseus? I remember him
from childhood: I can see him even now."

That was the way he played it, hoping inwardly
to span the great horn bow with corded gut
and drill the iron with his shot—he, Antínoös,
destined to be the first of all to savor   100
blood from a biting arrow at his throat,
a shaft drawn by the fingers of Odysseus
whom he had mocked and plundered, leading on

---

⁵ The details of the feat to be performed have been much discussed and are not entirely
clear; in any case, the archer had to send an arrow through twelve openings—notches, holes,
or other apertures—in the handles or blades of the axes.

the rest, his boon companions. Now they heard
a gay snort of laughter from Telémakhos,
who said then brilliantly:

"A queer thing, that!
Has Zeus almighty made me a half-wit?
For all her spirit, Mother has given in,
promised to go off with someone—and
is that amusing? What am I cackling for?   110
Step up, my lords, contend now for your prize.
There is no woman like her in Akhaia,
not in old Argos, Pylos, or Mykênê,
neither in Ithaka nor on the mainland,
and you all know it without praise of mine.
Come on, no hanging back, no more delay
in getting the bow bent. Who's the winner?
I myself should like to try that bow.
Suppose I bend it and bring off the shot,
my heart will be less heavy, seeing the queen my mother   120
go for the last time from this house and hall,
if I who stay can do my father's feat."

He moved out quickly, dropping his crimson cloak,
and lifted sword and sword belt from his shoulders.
His preparation was to dig a trench,
heaping the earth in a long ridge beside it
to hold the blades half-bedded. A taut cord
aligned the socket rings. And no one there
but looked on wondering at his workmanship,
for the boy had never seen it done.

He took his stand then   130
on the broad door sill to attempt the bow.
Three times he put his back into it and sprang it,
three times he had to slack off. Still he meant
to string that bow and pull for the needle shot.
A fourth try, and he had it all but strung—
when a stiffening in Odysseus made him check.
Abruptly then he stopped and turned and said:

"Blast and damn it, must I be a milksop
all my life? Half-grown, all thumbs,
no strength or knack at arms, to defend myself   140
if someone picks a fight with me.

Take over,
O my elders and betters, try the bow,
run off the contest."

And he stood the weapon
upright against the massy-timbered door
with one arrow across the horn aslant,

then went back to his chair. Antínoös
gave the word:

                                        "Now one man at a time
rise and go forward. Round the room in order;
left to right from where they dip the wine."

As this seemed fair enough, up stood Leódês   150
the son of Oinops. This man used to find
vision for them in the smoke of sacrifice.
He kept his chair well back, retired by the winebowl,
for he alone could not abide their manners
but sat in shame for all the rest. Now it was he
who had first to confront the bow,
standing up on the broad door sill. He failed.
The bow unbending made his thin hands yield,
no muscle in them. He gave up and said:

"Friends, I cannot. Let the next man handle it.   160
Here is a bow to break the heart and spirit
of many strong men. Aye. And death is less
bitter than to live on and never have
the beauty that we came here laying siege to
so many days. Resolute, are you still,
to win Odysseus' lady Penélopê?
Pit yourselves against the bow, and look
among Akhaians for another's daughter.
Gifts will be enough to court and take her.
Let the best offer win."

                                        With this Leódês   170
thrust the bow away from him, and left it
upright against the massy-timbered door,
with one arrow aslant across the horn.
As he went down to his chair he heard Antínoös'
voice rising:

                                        "What is that you say?
It makes me burn. You cannot string the weapon,
so 'Here is a bow to break the heart and spirit
of many strong men.' Crushing thought!
You were not born—you never had it in you—
to pull that bow or let an arrow fly.   180
But here are men who can and will."

He called out to the goatherd, Melánthios:

"Kindle a fire there, be quick about it,
draw up a big bench with a sheepskin on it,
and bring a cake of lard out of the stores.
Contenders from now on will heat and grease the bow.
We'll try it limber, and bring off the shot."

Melánthios darted out to light a blaze,
drew up a bench, threw a big sheepskin over it,
and brought a cake of lard. So one by one   190
the young men warmed and greased the bow for bending,
but not a man could string it. They were whipped.
Antínoös held off; so did Eurýmakhos,
suitors in chief, by far the ablest there.

Two men had meanwhile left the hall:
swineherd and cowherd, in companionship,
one downcast as the other. But Odysseus
followed them outdoors, outside the court,
and coming up said gently:

                                                    "You, herdsman
and you, too, swineherd, I could say a thing to you,   200
or should I keep it dark?

                                          No, no; speak,

my heart tells me. Would you be men enough
to stand by Odysseus if he came back?
Suppose he dropped out of a clear sky, as I did?
Suppose some god should bring him?
Would you bear arms for him, or for the suitors?"

The cowherd said:

                                          "Ah, let the master come!
Father Zeus, grant our old wish! Some courier
guide him back! Then judge what stuff is in me
and how I manage arms!"

                                          Likewise Eumaios   210
fell to praying all heaven for his return,
so that Odysseus, sure at least of these,
told them:

                                          "I am at home, for I am he.
I bore adversities, but in the twentieth year
I am ashore in my own land. I find
the two of you, alone among my people,
longed for my coming. Prayers I never heard
except your own that I might come again.
So now what is in store for you I'll tell you:
If Zeus brings down the suitors by my hand   220
I promise marriages to both, and cattle,
and houses built near mine. And you shall be
brothers-in-arms of my Telémakhos.
Here, let me show you something else, a sign
that I am he, that you can trust me, look:
this old scar from the tusk wound that I got
boar hunting on Parnassos—
Autólykos' sons and I."

                                                        Shifting his rags
he bared the long gash. Both men looked, and knew,
and threw their arms around the old soldier, weeping,   230
kissing his head and shoulders. He as well
took each man's head and hands to kiss, then said—
to cut it short, else they might weep till dark—

"Break off, no more of this.
Anyone at the door could see and tell them.
Drift back in, but separately at intervals
after me.
                                        Now listen to your orders:
when the time comes, those gentlemen, to a man,
will be dead against giving me bow or quiver.
Defy them. Eumaios, bring the bow   240
and put it in my hands there at the door.
Tell the women to lock their own door tight.
Tell them if someone hears the shock of arms
or groans of men, in hall or court, not one
must show her face, but keep still at her weaving.
Philoítios, run to the outer gate and lock it.
Throw the cross bar and lash it."

                                                        He turned back
into the courtyard and the beautiful house
and took the stool he had before. They followed
one by one, the two hands loyal to him.   250

Eurýmakhos had now picked up the bow.
He turned it round, and turned it round
before the licking flame to warm it up,
but could not, even so, put stress upon it
to jam the loop over the tip
                                        though his heart groaned to bursting.
Then he said grimly:

                                                        "Curse this day.
What gloom I feel, not for myself alone,
and not only because we lose that bride.
Women are not lacking in Akhaia,
in other towns, or on Ithaka. No, the worst   260
is humiliation—to be shown up for children
measured against Odysseus—we who cannot
even hitch the string over his bow.
What shame to be repeated of us, after us!"

Antínoös said:

                                        "Come to yourself. You know
that is not the way this business ends.

Today the islanders held holiday, a holy day,[6]
no day to sweat over a bowstring.

                                     Keep your head.

Postpone the bow. I say we leave the axes
planted where they are. No one will take them.   270
No one comes to Odysseus' hall tonight.
Break out good wine and brim our cups again,
we'll keep the crooked bow safe overnight,
order the fattest goats Melánthios has
brought down tomorrow noon, and offer thighbones burning
to Apollo, god of archers,
while we try out the bow and make the shot."

As this appealed to everyone, heralds came
pouring fresh water for their hands, and boys
filled up the winebowls. Joints of meat went round,   280
fresh cuts for all, while each man made his offering,
tilting the red wine to the gods, and drank his fill.
Then spoke Odysseus, all craft and gall:

"My lords, contenders for the queen, permit me:
a passion in me moves me to speak out.
I put it to Eurýmakhos above all
and to that brilliant prince, Antínoös. Just now
how wise his counsel was, to leave the trial
and turn your thoughts to the immortal gods! Apollo
will give power tomorrow to whom he wills.   290
But let me try my hand at the smooth bow!
Let me test my fingers and my pull
to see if any of the oldtime kick is there,
or if thin fare and roving took it out of me."

Now irritation beyond reason swept them all,
since they were nagged by fear that he could string it.
Antínoös answered, coldly and at length:

"You bleary vagabond, no rag of sense is left you.
Are you not coddled here enough, at table
taking meat with gentlemen, your betters,   300
denied nothing, and listening to our talk?
When have we let a tramp hear all our talk?
The sweet goad of wine has made you rave!
Here is the evil wine can do
to those who swig it down. Even the centaur
Eurýtion,[7] in Peiríthoös' hall

---

[6] With ironic appropriateness, a feast day of Apollo, god of archery; Antínoös makes this an excuse for putting off the present challenge.

[7] The centaurs were an uncivilized tribe (often represented in myth as having horses' trunks and legs and human torsos and heads), inhabitants of Thessaly, in northeastern Greece. They were invited to the wedding of Peiríthoös, king of the Lapíthai, a neighboring people, and at the wedding tried to carry off the bride; the present version tells the story in the singular, of Eurýtion. In the ensuing battle the centaurs were defeated.

among the Lapíthai, came to a bloody end
because of wine; wine ruined him: it crazed him,
drove him wild for rape in that great house.
The princes cornered him in fury, leaping on him   310
to drag him out and crop his ears and nose.
Drink had destroyed his mind, and so he ended
in that mutilation—fool that he was.
Centaurs and men made war for this,
but the drunkard first brought hurt upon himself.

The tale applies to you: I promise you
great trouble if you touch that bow. You'll come by
no indulgence in our house; kicked down
into a ship's bilge, out to sea you go,
and nothing saves you. Drink, but hold your tongue.   320
Make no contention here with younger men."

At this the watchful queen Penélopê
interposed:

                                        "Antínoös, discourtesy
to a guest of Telémakhos—whatever guest—
that is not handsome. What are you afraid of?
Suppose this exile put his back into it
and drew the great bow of Odysseus—
could he then take me home to be his bride?
You know he does not imagine that! No one
need let that prospect weigh upon his dinner!   330
How very, very improbable it seems."

It was Eurýmakhos who answered her:

"Penélopê, O daughter of Ikários,
most subtle queen, we are not given to fantasy.
No, but our ears burn at what men might say
and women, too. We hear some jackal whispering:
'How far inferior to the great husband
her suitors are! Can't even budge his bow!
Think of it; and a beggar, out of nowhere,
strung it quick and made the needle shot!'   340
That kind of disrepute we would not care for."

Penélopê replied, steadfast and wary:

"Eurýmakhos, you have no good repute
in this realm, nor the faintest hope of it—
men who abused a prince's house for years,
consumed his wine and cattle. Shame enough.
Why hang your heads over a trifle now?
The stranger is a big man, well-compacted,
and claims to be of noble blood.

Ai! 350
Give him the bow, and let us have it out!
What I can promise him I will:
if by the kindness of Apollo he prevails
he shall be clothed well and equipped.
A fine shirt and a cloak I promise him;
a lance for keeping dogs at bay, or men;
a broadsword; sandals to protect his feet;
escort, and freedom to go where he will."

Telémakhos now faced her and said sharply:

"Mother, as to the bow and who may handle it 360
or not handle it, no man here
has more authority than I do—not one lord
of our own stony Ithaka nor the islands lying
east toward Elis: no one stops me if I choose
to give these weapons outright to my guest.
Return to your own hall. Tend your spindle.
Tend your loom. Direct your maids at work.
This question of the bow will be for men to settle,
most of all for me. I am master here."

She gazed in wonder, turned, and so withdrew, 370
her son's clearheaded bravery in her heart.
But when she had mounted to her rooms again
with all her women, then she fell to weeping
for Odysseus, her husband. Grey-eyed Athena
presently cast a sweet sleep on her eyes.

The swineherd had the horned bow in his hands
moving toward Odysseus, when the crowd
in the banquet hall broke into an ugly din,
shouts rising from the flushed young men:

         "Ho! Where
do you think you are taking that, you smutty slave?" 380

"What is this dithering?"

         "We'll toss you back alone
among the pigs, for your own dogs to eat,
if bright Apollo nods and the gods are kind!"

He faltered, all at once put down the bow, and stood
in panic, buffeted by waves of cries,
hearing Telémakhos from another quarter
shout:

"Go on, take him the bow!

         Do you obey this pack?
You will be stoned back to your hills! Young as I am

my power is over you! I wish to God   390
I had as much the upper hand of these!
There would be suitors pitched like dead rats
through our gate, for the evil plotted here!"

Telémakhos' frenzy struck someone as funny,
and soon the whole room roared with laughter at him,
so that all tension passed. Eumaios picked up
bow and quiver, making for the door,
and there he placed them in Odysseus' hands.
Calling Eurýkleia to his side he said:

                                              "Telémakhos
trusts you to take care of the women's doorway.   400
Lock it tight. If anyone inside
should hear the shock of arms or groans of men
in hall or court, not one must show her face,
but go on with her weaving."

                                              The old woman
nodded and kept still. She disappeared
into the women's hall, bolting the door behind her.
Philoítios left the house now at one bound,
catlike, running to bolt the courtyard gate.
A coil of deck-rope of papyrus fiber
lay in the gateway; this he used for lashing,   410
and ran back to the same stool as before,
fastening his eyes upon Odysseus.

                                        And Odysseus took his time,
turning the bow, tapping it, every inch,
for borings that termites might have made
while the master of the weapon was abroad.
The suitors were now watching him, and some
jested among themselves:

                                              "A bow lover!"
"Dealer in old bows!"

                                  "Maybe he has one like it
at home!"

                      "Or has an itch to make one for himself."
"See how he handles it, the sly old buzzard!"   420

And one disdainful suitor added this:

"May his fortune grow an inch for every inch he bends it!"

But the man skilled in all ways of contending,
satisfied by the great bow's look and heft,

like a musician, like a harper, when
with quiet hand upon his instrument
he draws between his thumb and forefinger
a sweet new string upon a peg: so effortlessly
Odysseus in one motion strung the bow.
Then slid his right hand down the cord and plucked it, 430
so the taut gut vibrating hummed and sang
a swallow's note.
                              In the hushed hall it smote the suitors
and all their faces changed. Then Zeus thundered
overhead, one loud crack for a sign.
And Odysseus laughed within him that the son
of crooked-minded Kronos had flung that omen down.
He picked one ready arrow from his table
where it lay bare: the rest were waiting still
in the quiver for the young men's turn to come.
He nocked it, let it rest across the handgrip, 440
and drew the string and grooved butt of the arrow,
aiming from where he sat upon the stool.
                                                    Now flashed
arrow from twanging bow clean as a whistle
through every socket ring, and grazed not one,
to thud with heavy brazen head beyond.
                                              Then quietly
Odysseus said:
                        "Telémakhos, the stranger
you welcomed in your hall has not disgraced you.
I did not miss, neither did I take all day
stringing the bow. My hand and eye are sound,
not so contemptible as the young men say. 450
The hour has come to cook their lordships' mutton—
supper by daylight. Other amusements later,
with song and harping that adorn a feast."

He dropped his eyes and nodded, and the prince
Telémakhos, true son of King Odysseus,
belted his sword on, clapped hand to his spear,
and with a clink and glitter of keen bronze
stood by his chair, in the forefront near his father.

BOOK TWENTY-TWO: DEATH IN THE GREAT HALL

Now shrugging off his rags the wiliest fighter of the islands
leapt and stood on the broad door sill, his own bow in his hand.
He poured out at his feet a rain of arrows from the quiver
and spoke to the crowd:

"So much for that. Your clean-cut game is over.
Now watch me hit a target that no man has hit before,
if I can make this shot. Help me, Apollo."

He drew to his fist the cruel head of an arrow for Antínoös
just as the young man leaned to lift his beautiful drinking cup,
embossed, two-handled, golden: the cup was in his fingers:
the wine was even at his lips: and did he dream of death?   10
How could he? In that revelry amid his throng of friends
who would imagine a single foe—though a strong foe indeed—
could dare to bring death's pain on him and darkness on his eyes?
Odysseus' arrow hit him under the chin
and punched up to the feathers through his throat.

Backward and down he went, letting the winecup fall
from his shocked hand. Like pipes his nostrils jetted
crimson runnels, a river of mortal red,
and one last kick upset his table
knocking the bread and meat to soak in dusty blood.   20
Now as they craned to see their champion where he lay
the suitors jostled in uproar down the hall,
everyone on his feet. Wildly they turned and scanned
the walls in the long room for arms; but not a shield,
not a good ashen spear was there for a man to take and throw.
All they could do was yell in outrage at Odysseus:

"Foul! to shoot at a man! That was your last shot!"

"Your own throat will be slit for this!"

                                          "Our finest lad is down!
You killed the best on Ithaka."

                                          "Buzzards will tear your eyes out!"

For they imagined as they wished—that it was a wild shot,   30
an unintended killing—fools, not to comprehend
they were already in the grip of death.
But glaring under his brows Odysseus answered:

"You yellow dogs, you thought I'd never make it
home from the land of Troy. You took my house to plunder,
twisted my maids to serve your beds. You dared
bid for my wife while I was still alive.
Contempt was all you had for the gods who rule wide heaven,
contempt for what men say of you hereafter.
Your last hour has come. You die in blood."   40

As they all took this in, sickly green fear
pulled at their entrails, and their eyes flickered
looking for some hatch or hideaway from death.
Eurýmakhos alone could speak. He said:

"If you are Odysseus of Ithaka come back,
all that you say these men have done is true.
Rash actions, many here, more in the countryside.
But here he lies, the man who caused them all.
Antínoös was the ringleader, he whipped us on
to do these things. He cared less for a marriage 50
than for the power Kronion has denied him
as king of Ithaka. For that
he tried to trap your son and would have killed him.
He is dead now and has his portion. Spare
your own people. As for ourselves, we'll make
restitution of wine and meat consumed,
and add, each one, a tithe of twenty oxen
with gifts of bronze and gold to warm your heart.
Meanwhile we cannot blame you for your anger."

Odysseus glowered under his black brows 60
and said:

                      "Not for the whole treasure of your fathers,
all you enjoy, lands, flocks, or any gold
put up by others, would I hold my hand.
There will be killing till the score is paid.
You forced yourselves upon this house. Fight your way out,
or run for it, if you think you'll escape death.
I doubt one man of you skins by."

They felt their knees fail, and their hearts—but heard
Eurýmakhos for the last time rallying them.

"Friends," he said, "the man is implacable. 70
Now that he's got his hands on bow and quiver
he'll shoot from the big door stone there
until he kills us to the last man.

                                Fight, I say,
let's remember the joy of it. Swords out!
Hold up your tables to deflect his arrows.
After me, everyone: rush him where he stands.
If we can budge him from the door, if we can pass
into the town, we'll call out men to chase him.
This fellow with his bow will shoot no more."

He drew his own sword as he spoke, a broadsword of fine bronze, 80
honed like a razor on either edge. Then crying hoarse and loud
he hurled himself at Odysseus. But the kingly man let fly
an arrow at that instant, and the quivering feathered butt
sprang to the nipple of his breast as the barb stuck in his liver.
The bright broadsword clanged down. He lurched and fell aside,
pitching across his table. His cup, his bread and meat,
were spilt and scattered far and wide, and his head slammed on the
    ground.

Revulsion, anguish in his heart, with both feet kicking out,
he downed his chair, while the shrouding wave of mist closed on his
     eyes.

Amphínomos now came running at Odysseus,   90
broadsword naked in his hand. He thought to make
the great soldier give way at the door.
But with a spear throw from behind Telémakhos hit him
between the shoulders, and the lancehead drove
clear through his chest. He left his feet and fell
forward, thudding, forehead against the ground.
Telémakhos swerved around him, leaving the long dark spear
planted in Amphínomos. If he paused to yank it out
someone might jump him from behind or cut him down with a
     sword
at the moment he bent over. So he ran—ran from the tables   100
to his father's side and halted, panting, saying:

"Father let me bring you a shield and spear,
a pair of spears, a helmet.
I can arm on the run myself; I'll give
outfits to Eumaios and this cowherd.
Better to have equipment."

                                                            Said Odysseus:

"Run then, while I hold them off with arrows
as long as the arrows last. When all are gone
if I'm alone they can dislodge me."

                                                                    Quick
upon his father's word Telémakhos   110
ran to the room where spears and armor lay.
He caught up four light shields, four pairs of spears,
four helms of war high-plumed with flowing manes,
and ran back, loaded down, to his father's side.
He was the first to pull a helmet on
and slide his bare arm in a buckler strap.
The servants armed themselves, and all three took their stand
beside the master of battle.

                                            While he had arrows
he aimed and shot, and every shot brought down
one of his huddling enemies.   120
But when all barbs had flown from the bowman's fist,
he leaned his bow in the bright entry way
beside the door, and armed: a four-ply shield
hard on his shoulder, and a crested helm,
horsetailed, nodding stormy upon his head,
then took his tough and bronze-shod spears.

                                            The suitors
who held their feet, no longer under bowshot,

could see a window high in a recess of the wall,
a vent, lighting the passage to the storeroom.
This passage had one entry, with a door,   130
at the edge of the great hall's threshold, just outside.[1]

Odysseus told the swineherd to stand over
and guard this door and passage. As he did so,
a suitor named Ageláos asked the others:

"Who will get a leg up on that window
and run to alarm the town? One sharp attack
and this fellow will never shoot again."

                                          His answer
came from the goatherd, Melánthios:

                              "No chance, my lord.
The exit into the courtyard is too near them,
too narrow. One good man could hold that portal   140
against a crowd. No: let me scale the wall
and bring you arms out of the storage chamber.
Odysseus and his son put them indoors,
I'm sure of it; not outside."

                              The goatish goatherd
clambered up the wall, toes in the chinks,
and slipped through to the storeroom. Twelve light shields,
twelve spears he took, and twelve thick-crested helms,
and handed all down quickly to the suitors.
Odysseus, when he saw his adversaries
girded and capped and long spears in their hands   150
shaken at him, felt his knees go slack,
his heart sink, for the fight was turning grim.
He spoke rapidly to his son:

"Telémakhos, one of the serving women
is tipping the scales against us in this fight,
or maybe Melánthios."

                                    But sharp and clear
Telémakhos said:

                              "It is my own fault, Father,
mine alone. The storeroom door—I left it
wide open. They were more alert than I.
Eumaios, go and lock that door   160
and bring back word if a woman is doing this
or Melánthios, Dólios' son. More likely he."

---

[1] The window in the *mégaron,* or great hall, connects with an external corridor that runs
to the rear of the house, past the women's chambers, to the storeroom; the only exit from
the corridor to the outdoor courtyard is close to where Odysseus and his three allies have
posted themselves. It is therefore, as Melánthios soon points out, not a safe escape route.

Even as they conferred, Melánthios
entered the storeroom for a second load,
and the swineherd at the passage entry saw him.
He cried out to his lord:

                                        "Son of Laërtês,
Odysseus, master mariner and soldier,
there he goes, the monkey, as we thought,
there he goes into the storeroom.

                            Let me hear your will:
put a spear through him—I hope I am the stronger—   170
or drag him here to pay for his foul tricks
against your house?"

                Odysseus said:

                                    "Telémakhos and I
will keep these gentlemen in hall, for all their urge to leave.
You two go throw him into the storeroom, wrench his arms
and legs behind him, lash his hands and feet
to a plank, and hoist him up to the roof beams.
Let him live on there suffering at his leisure."

The two men heard him with appreciation
and ducked into the passage. Melánthios,
rummaging in the chamber, could not hear them   180
as they came up; nor could he see them freeze
like posts on either side the door.
He turned back with a handsome crested helmet
in one hand, in the other an old shield
coated with dust—a shield Laërtês bore
soldiering in his youth. It had lain there for years,
and the seams on strap and grip had rotted away.
As Melánthios came out the two men sprang,
jerked him backward by the hair, and threw him.
Hands and feet they tied with a cutting cord   190
behind him, so his bones ground in their sockets,
just as Laërtês' royal son commanded.
Then with a whip of rope they hoisted him
in agony up a pillar to the beams,
and—O my swineherd—you were the one to say:

"Watch through the night up there, Melánthios.
An airy bed is what you need.
You'll be awake to see the primrose Dawn
when she goes glowing from the streams of Ocean
to mount her golden throne.

                            No oversleeping   200
the hour for driving goats to feed the suitors."

They stooped for helm and shield and left him there
contorted, in his brutal sling,

and shut the doors, and went to join Odysseus,
whose mind moved through the combat now to come.
Breathing deep, and snorting hard, they stood
four at the entry, facing two score men.
But now into the gracious doorway stepped
Zeus's daughter Athena. She wore the guise of Mentor,
and Odysseus appealed to her in joy: 210

"O Mentor, join me in this fight! Remember
how all my life I've been devoted to you,
friend of my youth!"

                                        For he guessed it was Athena,
Hope of Soldiers. Cries came from the suitors,
and Ageláos, Damástor's son, called out:

"Mentor, don't let Odysseus lead you astray
to fight against us on his side.
Think twice: we are resolved—and we will do it—
after we kill them, father and son,
you too will have your throat slit for your pains   220
if you make trouble for us here. It means your life.
Your life—and cutting throats will not be all.
Whatever wealth you have, at home, or elsewhere,
we'll mingle with Odysseus' wealth. Your sons
will be turned out, your wife and daughters
banished from the town of Ithaka."

Athena's anger grew like a storm wind as he spoke
until she flashed out at Odysseus:

                                    "Ah, what a falling off!
Where is your valor, where is the iron hand
that fought at Troy for Helen, pearl of kings,   230
no respite and nine years of war? How many foes
your hand brought down in bloody play of spears!
What stratagem but yours took Priam's town?
How is it now that on your own door sill,
before the harriers[2] of your wife, you curse your luck
not to be stronger?
                                Come here, cousin, stand by me,
and you'll see action! In the enemies' teeth
learn how Mentor, son of Álkimos,
repays fair dealing!"

                                    For all her fighting words
she gave no overpowering aid—not yet;   240
father and son must prove their mettle still.
Into the smoky air under the roof

---

[2] Predatory dogs or hawks.

the goddess merely darted to perch on a blackened beam—
no figure to be seen now but a swallow.

Command of the suitors had fallen to Ageláos.
With him were Eurýnomos, Amphímedon,
Demoptólemos, Peisándros, Pólybos,
the best of the lot who stood to fight for their lives
after the streaking arrows downed the rest.
Ageláos rallied them with his plan of battle: 250

"Friends, our killer has come to the end of his rope,
and much good Mentor did him, that blowhard, dropping in.
Look, only four are left to fight, in the light there at the door.
No scattering of shots, men, no throwing away good spears;
we six will aim a volley at Odysseus alone,
and may Zeus grant us the glory of a hit.
If he goes down, the others are no problem."

At his command, then, "Ho!" they all let fly
as one man. But Athena spoiled their shots.
One hit the doorpost of the hall, another   260
stuck in the door's thick timbering, still others
rang on the stone wall, shivering hafts[3] of ash.
Seeing his men unscathed, royal Odysseus
gave the word for action.

                               "Now I say, friends,
the time is overdue to let them have it.
Battlespoil they want from our dead bodies
to add to all they plundered here before."

Taking aim over the steadied lanceheads
they all let fly together. Odysseus killed
Demoptólemos; Telémakhos   270
killed Eurýades; the swineherd, Élatos;
and Peisándros went down before the cowherd.
As these lay dying, biting the central floor,
their friends gave way and broke for the inner wall.
The four attackers followed up with a rush
to take spears from the fallen men.

                               Re-forming,
the suitors threw again with all their strength,
but Athena turned their shots, or all but two.
One hit a doorpost in the hall, another
stuck in the door's thick timbering, still others   280
rang on the stone wall, shivering hafts of ash.
Amphímedon's point bloodied Telémakhos'
wrist, a superficial wound, and Ktésippos'
long spear passing over Eumaios' shield

[3] Shafts.

grazed his shoulder, hurtled on and fell.
No matter: with Odysseus the great soldier
the wounded threw again. And Odysseus raider of cities
struck Eurýdamas down. Telémakhos
hit Amphímedon, and the swineherd's shot
killed Pólybos. But Ktésippos, who had last evening thrown   290
a cow's hoof at Odysseus, got the cowherd's heavy cast
full in the chest—and dying heard him say:

"You arrogant joking bastard!
Clown, will you, like a fool, and parade your wit?
Leave jesting to the gods who do it better.
This will repay your cow's-foot courtesy
to a great wanderer come home."

                                          The master
of the black herds had answered Ktésippos.
Odysseus, lunging at close quarters, put a spear
through Ageláos, Damástor's son. Telémakhos   300
hit Leókritos from behind and pierced him,
kidney to diaphragm. Speared off his feet,
he fell face downward on the ground.

At this moment that unmanning thunder cloud,
the aegis,[4] Athena's shield,
took form aloft in the great hall.
                        And the suitors mad with fear
at her great sign stampeded like stung cattle by a river
when the dread shimmering gadfly strikes in summer,
in the flowering season, in the long-drawn days.
After them the attackers wheeled, as terrible as falcons   310
from eyries in the mountains veering over and diving down
with talons wide unsheathed on flights of birds,
who cower down the sky in chutes and bursts along the valley—
but the pouncing falcons grip their prey, no frantic wing avails,
and farmers love to watch those beakèd hunters.
So these now fell upon the suitors in that hall,
turning, turning to strike and strike again,
while torn men moaned at death, and blood ran smoking
over the whole floor.
                            Now there was one
who turned and threw himself at Odysseus' knees—   320
Leódês, begging for his life:

                                    "Mercy,
mercy on a suppliant, Odysseus!
Never by word or act of mine, I swear,
was any woman troubled here. I told the rest
to put an end to it. They would not listen,

---

[4] The shield of Zeus, lent by him to Athena.

would not keep their hands from brutishness,
and now they are all dying like dogs for it.
I had no part in what they did: my part
was visionary—reading the smoke of sacrifice.
Scruples go unrewarded if I die."   330

The shrewd fighter frowned over him and said:

"You were diviner to this crowd? How often
you must have prayed my sweet day of return
would never come, or not for years!—and prayed
to have my dear wife, and beget children on her.
No plea like yours could save you
from this hard bed of death. Death it shall be!"

He picked up Ageláos' broadsword
from where it lay, flung by the slain man,
and gave Leódês' neck a lopping blow   340
so that his head went down to mouth in dust.

One more who had avoided furious death
was the son of Terpis, Phêmios, the minstrel,
singer by compulsion to the suitors.
He stood now with his harp, holy and clear,
in the wall's recess, under the window, wondering
if he should flee that way to the courtyard altar,
sanctuary of Zeus, the Enclosure God.
Thighbones in hundreds had been offered there
by Laërtês and Odysseus. No, he thought;   350
the more direct way would be best—to go
humbly to his lord. But first to save
his murmuring instrument he laid it down
carefully between the winebowl and a chair,
then he betook himself to Lord Odysseus,
clung hard to his knees, and said:

                                                          "Mercy,
mercy on a suppliant, Odysseus!
My gift is song for men and for the gods undying.
My death will be remorse for you hereafter.
No one taught me: deep in my mind a god   360
shaped all the various ways of life in song.
And I am fit to make verse in your company
as in the god's. Put aside lust for blood.
Your own dear son Telémakhos can tell you,
never by my own will or for love
did I feast here or sing amid the suitors.
They were too strong, too many; they compelled me."

Telémakhos in the elation of battle
heard him. He at once called to his father:

"Wait: that one is innocent: don't hurt him. 370
And we should let our herald live—Medôn;
he cared for me from boyhood. Where is *he?*
Has he been killed already by Philoítios
or by the swineherd? Else he got an arrow
in that first gale of bowshots down the room."

Now this came to the ears of prudent Medôn
under the chair where he had gone to earth,
pulling a new-flayed bull's hide over him.
Quiet he lay while blinding death passed by.
Now heaving out from under 380
he scrambled for Telémakhos' knees and said:

"Here I am, dear prince; but rest your spear!
Tell your great father not to see in me
a suitor for the sword's edge—one of those
who laughed at you and ruined his property!"

The lord of all the tricks of war surveyed
this fugitive and smiled. He said:

"Courage: my son has dug you out and saved you.
Take it to heart, and pass the word along:
fair dealing brings more profit in the end. 390
Now leave this room. Go and sit down outdoors
where there's no carnage, in the court,
you and the poet with his many voices,
while I attend to certain chores inside."

At this the two men stirred and picked their way
to the door and out, and sat down at the altar,
looking around with wincing eyes
as though the sword's edge hovered still.
And Odysseus looked around him, narrow-eyed,
for any others who had lain hidden 400
while death's black fury passed.
                                        In blood and dust
he saw that crowd all fallen, many and many slain.

Think of a catch that fishermen haul in to a halfmoon bay
in a fine-meshed net from the white-caps of the sea:
how all are poured out on the sand, in throes for the salt sea,
twitching their cold lives away in Hêlios' fiery air:
so lay the suitors heaped on one another.

Odysseus at length said to his son:

"Go tell old Nurse I'll have a word with her.
What's to be done now weighs on my mind." 410

Telémakhos knocked at the women's door and called:

"Eurýkleia, come out here! Move, old woman.
You kept your eye on all our servant girls.
Jump, my father is here and wants to see you."

His call brought no reply, only the doors
were opened, and she came. Telémakhos
led her forward. In the shadowy hall
full of dead men she found his father
spattered and caked with blood like a mountain lion
when he has gorged upon an ox, his kill—   420
with hot blood glistening over his whole chest,
smeared on his jaws, baleful and terrifying—
even so encrimsoned was Odysseus
up to his thighs and armpits. As she gazed
from all the corpses to the bloody man
she raised her head to cry over his triumph,
but felt his grip upon her, checking her.
Said the great soldier then:

                                                        "Rejoice

inwardly. No crowing aloud, old woman.
To glory over slain men is no piety.   430
Destiny and the gods' will vanquished these,
and their own hardness. They respected no one,
good or bad, who came their way.
For this, and folly, a bad end befell them.
Your part is now to tell me of the women,
those who dishonored me, and the innocent."

His own old nurse Eurýkleia said:

                                                        "I will, then.

Child, you know you'll have the truth from me.
Fifty all told they are, your female slaves,
trained by your lady and myself in service,   440
wool carding and the rest of it, and taught
to be submissive. Twelve went bad,
flouting me, flouting Penélopê, too.
Telémakhos being barely grown, his mother
would never let him rule the serving women—
but you must let me go to her lighted rooms
and tell her. Some god sent her a drift of sleep."

But in reply the great tactician said:

"Not yet. Do not awake her. Tell those women
who were the suitors' harlots to come here."   450

She went back on this mission through his hall.
Then he called Telémakhos to his side
and the two herdsmen. Sharply Odysseus said:

"These dead must be disposed of first of all.
Direct the women. Tables and chairs will be
scrubbed with sponges, rinsed and rinsed again.
When our great room is fresh and put in order,
take them outside, these women,
between the roundhouse[5] and the palisade,
and hack them with your swordblades till you cut   460
the life out of them, and every thought of sweet
Aphroditê under the rutting suitors,
when they lay down in secret."

                                        As he spoke
here came the women in a bunch, all wailing,
soft tears on their cheeks. They fell to work
to lug the corpses out into the courtyard
under the gateway, propping one
against another as Odysseus ordered,
for he himself stood over them. In fear
these women bore the cold weight of the dead.   470
The next thing was to scrub off chairs and tables
and rinse them down. Telémakhos and the herdsman
scraped the packed earth floor with hoes, but made
the women carry out all blood and mire.
When the great room was cleaned up once again,
at swordpoint they forced them out, between
the roundhouse and the palisade, pell-mell
to huddle in that dead end without exit.
Telémakhos, who knew his mind,[6] said curtly:

"I would not give the clean death of a beast   480
to trulls[7] who made a mockery of my mother
and of me too—you sluts, who lay with suitors."

He tied one end of a hawser to a pillar
and passed the other about the roundhouse top,
taking the slack up, so that no one's toes
could touch the ground. They would be hung like doves
or larks in springes[8] triggered in a thicket,
where the birds think to rest—a cruel nesting.
So now in turn each woman thrust her head
into a noose and swung, yanked high in air,   490
to perish there most piteously.
Their feet danced for a little, but not long.

---

[5]A building, with a cone-shaped roof, near the wall surrounding the courtyard; probably
a place for storing implements.
[6]Telémakhos departs from Odysseus' instructions; he gives the offending women a dishonorable death by hanging rather than death by the knife or sword, as in the ritual sacrifice
of an innocent animal.
[7]Harlots.
[8]Nooses, attached to tied branches, used to trap birds and other small animals.

From storeroom to the court they brought Melánthios,
chopped with swords to cut his nose and ears off,
pulled off his genitals to feed the dogs
and raging hacked his hands and feet away.

As their own hands and feet called for a washing,
they went indoors to Odysseus again.
Their work was done. He told Eurýkleia:

                                                            "Bring me

brimstone[9] and a brazier—medicinal   500
fumes to purify my hall. Then tell
Penélopê to come, and bring her maids.
All servants round the house must be called in."

His own old nurse Eurýkleia replied:

"Aye, surely that is well said, child. But let me
find you a good clean shirt and cloak and dress you.
You must not wrap your shoulders' breadth again
in rags in your own hall. That would be shameful."

Odysseus answered:

                                                "Let me have the fire.
The first thing is to purify this place."   510

With no more chat Eurýkleia obeyed
and fetched out fire and brimstone. Cleansing fumes
he sent through court and hall and storage chamber.
Then the old woman hurried off again
to the women's quarters to announce her news,
and all the servants came now, bearing torches
in twilight, crowding to embrace Odysseus,
taking his hands to kiss, his head and shoulders,
while he stood there, nodding to every one,
and overcome by longing and by tears.   520

BOOK TWENTY-THREE: THE TRUNK OF
THE OLIVE TREE

The old nurse went upstairs exulting,
with knees toiling, and patter of slapping feet,
to tell the mistress of her lord's return,
and cried out by the lady's pillow:

---

[9] Sulfur.

"Wake,
wake up, dear child! Penélopê, come down,
see with your own eyes what all these years you longed for!
Odysseus is here! Oh, in the end, he came!
And he has killed your suitors, killed them all
who made his house a bordel[1] and ate his cattle
and raised their hands against his son!"

Penélopê said: 10

"Dear nurse . . . the gods have touched you.
They can put chaos into the clearest head
or bring a lunatic down to earth. Good sense
you always had. They've touched you. What is this
mockery you wake me up to tell me,
breaking in on my sweet spell of sleep?
I had not dozed away so tranquilly
since my lord went to war, on that ill wind
to Ilion.
Oh, leave me! Back down stairs!
If any other of my women came in babbling 20
things like these to startle me, I'd see her
flogged out of the house! Your old age spares you that."

Eurýkleia said:

"Would I play such a trick on you, dear child?
It is true, true, as I tell you, he has come!
That stranger they were baiting was Odysseus.
Telémakhos knew it days ago—
cool head, never to give his father away,
till he paid off those swollen dogs!"

The lady in her heart's joy now sprang up 30
with sudden dazzling tears, and hugged the old one,
crying out:

"But try to make it clear!
If he came home in secret, as you say,
could he engage them singlehanded? How?
They were all down there, still in the same crowd."

To this Eurýkleia said:

"I did not see it,
I knew nothing; only I heard the groans
of men dying. We sat still in the inner rooms
holding our breath, and marvelling, shut in,
until Telémakhos came to the door and called me— 40
your own dear son, sent this time by his father!

---

[1] Bordello; brothel.

So I went out, and found Odysseus
erect, with dead men littering the floor
this way and that. If you had only seen him!
It would have made your heart glow hot!—a lion
splashed with mire and blood.

                                          But now the cold
corpses are all gathered at the gate,
and he has cleansed his hall with fire and brimstone,
a great blaze. Then he sent me here to you.
Come with me: you may both embark this time   50
for happiness together, after pain,
after long years. Here is your prayer, your passion,
granted: your own lord lives, he is at home,
he found you safe, he found his son. The suitors
abused his house, but he has brought them down."

The attentive lady said:

                                          "Do not lose yourself
in this rejoicing: wait: you know
how splendid that return would be for us,
how dear to me, dear to his son and mine;
but no, it is not possible, your notion   60
must be wrong.

                    Some god has killed the suitors,
a god, sick of their arrogance and brutal
malice—for they honored no one living,
good or bad, who ever came their way.
Blind young fools, they've tasted death for it.
But the true person of Odysseus?
He lost his home, he died far from Akhaia."

The old nurse sighed:

                                          "How queer, the way you talk!
Here he is, large as life, by his own fire,
and you deny he ever will get home!   70
Child, you always were mistrustful!
But there is one sure mark that I can tell you:
that scar left by the boar's tusk long ago.
I recognized it when I bathed his feet
and would have told you, but he stopped my mouth,
forbade me, in his craftiness.

                                          Come down,
I stake my life on it, he's here!
Let me die in agony if I lie!"

                                          Penélopê said:

"Nurse dear, though you have your wits about you,
still it is hard not to be taken in   80

by the immortals. Let us join my son, though,
and see the dead and that strange one who killed them."

She turned then to descend the stair, her heart
in tumult. Had she better keep her distance
and question him, her husband? Should she run
up to him, take his hands, kiss him now?
Crossing the door sill she sat down at once
in firelight, against the nearest wall,
across the room from the lord Odysseus.

                                                There

leaning against a pillar, sat the man   90
and never lifted up his eyes, but only waited
for what his wife would say when she had seen him.
And she, for a long time, sat deathly still
in wonderment—for sometimes as she gazed
she found him—yes, clearly—like her husband,
but sometimes blood and rags were all she saw.
Telémakhos' voice came to her ears:

                                           "Mother,
cruel mother, do you feel nothing,
drawing yourself apart this way from Father?
Will you not sit with him and talk and question him?   100
What other woman could remain so cold?
Who shuns her lord, and he come back to her
from wars and wandering, after twenty years?
Your heart is hard as flint and never changes!"

Penélopê answered:

                                "I am stunned, child.
I cannot speak to him. I cannot question him.
I cannot keep my eyes upon his face.
If really he is Odysseus, truly home,
beyond all doubt we two shall know each other
better than you or anyone. There are   110
secret signs we know, we two."

                                       A smile
came now to the lips of the patient hero, Odysseus,
who turned to Telémakhos and said:

"Peace: let your mother test me at her leisure.
Before long she will see and know me best.
These tatters, dirt—all that I'm caked with now—
make her look hard at me and doubt me still.
As to this massacre, we must see the end.
Whoever kills one citizen, you know,
and has no force of armed men at his back,   120
had better take himself abroad by night

and leave his kin. Well, we cut down the flower of Ithaka,
the mainstay of the town. Consider that."

Telémakhos replied respectfully:

"Dear Father,
enough that you yourself study the danger,
foresighted in combat as you are,
they say you have no rival.

We three stand
ready to follow you and fight. I say
for what our strength avails, we have the courage."

And the great tactician, Odysseus, answered:

"Good.   130
Here is our best maneuver, as I see it:
bathe, you three, and put fresh clothing on,
order the women to adorn themselves,   .
and let our admirable harper choose a tune
for dancing, some lighthearted air, and strum it.
Anyone going by, or any neighbor,
will think it is a wedding feast he hears.
These deaths must not be cried about the town
till we can slip away to our own woods. We'll see
what weapon, then, Zeus puts into our hands."   140

They listened attentively, and did his bidding,
bathed and dressed afresh; and all the maids
adorned themselves. Then Phêmios the harper
took his polished shell and plucked the strings,
moving the company to desire
for singing, for the sway and beat of dancing,
until they made the manor hall resound
with gaiety of men and grace of women.
Anyone passing on the road would say:

"Married at last, I see—the queen so many courted.   150
Sly, cattish wife! She would not keep—not she!—
the lord's estate until he came."

So travellers'
thoughts might run—but no one guessed the truth.

Greathearted Odysseus, home at last,
was being bathed now by Eurýnomê
and rubbed with golden oil, and clothed again
in a fresh tunic and a cloak. Athena
lent him beauty, head to foot. She made him
taller, and massive, too, with crisping hair
in curls like petals of wild hyacinth   160

but all red-golden. Think of gold infused
on silver by a craftsman, whose fine art
Hephaistos taught him, or Athena: one
whose work moves to delight: just so she lavished
beauty over Odysseus' head and shoulders.
He sat then in the same chair by the pillar,
facing his silent wife, and said:

                                     "Strange woman,
the immortals of Olympos made you hard,
harder than any. Who else in the world
would keep aloof as you do from her husband   170
if he returned to her from years of trouble,
cast on his own land in the twentieth year?

Nurse, make up a bed for me to sleep on.
Her heart is iron in her breast."

                                          Penélopê
spoke to Odysseus now. She said:

                                     "Strange man,
if man you are . . . This is no pride on my part
nor scorn for you—not even wonder, merely.
I know so well how you—how he—appeared
boarding the ship for Troy. But all the same . . .

Make up his bed for him, Eurýkleia.   180
Place it outside the bedchamber my lord
built with his own hands. Pile the big bed
with fleeces, rugs, and sheets of purest linen."

With this she tried him to the breaking point,
and he turned on her in a flash raging:

"Woman, by heaven you've stung me now!
Who dared to move my bed?
No builder had the skill for that—unless
a god came down to turn the trick. No mortal
in his best days could budge it with a crowbar.   190
There is our pact and pledge, our secret sign,
built into that bed—my handiwork
and no one else's!

                                An old trunk of olive
grew like a pillar on the building plot,
and I laid out our bedroom round that tree,
lined up the stone walls, built the walls and roof,
gave it a doorway and smooth-fitting doors.
Then I lopped off the silvery leaves and branches,
hewed and shaped that stump from the roots up
into a bedpost, drilled it, let it serve   200

as model for the rest. I planed them all,[2]
inlaid them all with silver, gold and ivory,
and stretched a bed between—a pliant web
of oxhide thongs dyed crimson.
                                                There's our sign!
I know no more. Could someone else's hand
have sawn that trunk and dragged the frame away?"

Their secret! as she heard it told, her knees
grew tremulous and weak, her heart failed her.
With eyes brimming tears she ran to him,
throwing her arms around his neck, and kissed him,   210
murmuring:
                                    "Do not rage at me, Odysseus!
No one ever matched your caution! Think
what difficulty the gods gave: they denied us
life together in our prime and flowering years,
kept us from crossing into age together.
Forgive me, don't be angry. I could not
welcome you with love on sight! I armed myself
long ago against the frauds of men,
impostors who might come—and all those many
whose underhanded ways bring evil on!   220
Helen of Argos, daughter of Zeus and Leda,
would she have joined the stranger,[3] lain with him,
if she had known her destiny? known the Akhaians
in arms would bring her back to her own country?
Surely a goddess moved her to adultery,
her blood unchilled by war and evil coming,
the years, the desolation; ours, too.
But here and now, what sign could be so clear
as this of our own bed?
No other man has ever laid eyes on it—   230
only my own slave, Aktoris, that my father
sent with me as a gift—she kept our door.
You make my stiff heart know that I am yours."

Now from his breast into his eyes the ache
of longing mounted, and he wept at last,
his dear wife, clear and faithful, in his arms,
longed for
                        as the sunwarmed earth is longed for by a swimmer
spent in rough water where his ship went down
under Poseidon's blows, gale winds and tons of sea.
Few men can keep alive through a big surf   240

---

[2] That is, planed all the bedposts, of which one was the shaped tree trunk.
[3] Paris, the Trojan guest of Meneláos and Helen, with whom she ran away.

to crawl, clotted with brine, on kindly beaches
in joy, in joy, knowing the abyss behind:
and so she too rejoiced, her gaze upon her husband,
her white arms round him pressed as though forever.

The rose Dawn might have found them weeping still
had not grey-eyed Athena slowed the night
when night was most profound, and held the Dawn
under the Ocean of the East. That glossy team,
Firebright and Daybright, the Dawn's horses
that draw her heavenward for men—Athena   250
stayed their harnessing.

                                        Then said Odysseus:

"My dear, we have not won through to the end.
One trial—I do not know how long—is left for me
to see fulfilled. Teirêsias' ghost forewarned me[4]
the night I stood upon the shore of Death, asking
about my friends' homecoming and my own.
But now the hour grows late, it is bed time,
rest will be sweet for us; let us lie down."

To this Penélopê replied:

                                        "That bed,

that rest is yours whenever desire moves you,   260
now the kind powers have brought you home at last.
But as your thought has dwelt upon it, tell me:
what is the trial you face? I must know soon;
what does it matter if I learn tonight?"

The teller of many stories said:

                                        "My strange one,

must you again, and even now,
urge me to talk? Here is a plodding tale;
no charm in it, no relish in the telling.
Teirêsias told me I must take an oar
and trudge the mainland, going from town to town,   270
until I discover men who have never known
the salt blue sea, nor flavor of salt meat—
strangers to painted prows, to watercraft
and oars like wings, dipping across the water.
The moment of revelation he foretold
was this, for you may share the prophecy:
some traveller falling in with me will say:
'A winnowing fan, that on your shoulder, sir?'

[4] See Book XI.

There I must plant my oar,[5] on the very spot,
with burnt offerings to Poseidon of the Waters: 280
a ram, a bull, a great buck boar. Thereafter
when I come home again, I am to slay
full hekatombs to the gods who own broad heaven,
one by one.
                    Then death will drift upon me
from seaward, mild as air, mild as your hand,
in my well-tended weariness of age,
contented folk around me on our island.
He said all this must come."

                                Penélopê said:

"If by the gods' grace age at least is kind,
we have that promise—trials will end in peace."   290

So he confided in her, and she answered.
Meanwhile Eurýnomê and the nurse together
laid soft coverlets on the master's bed,
working in haste by torchlight. Eurýkleia
retired to her quarters for the night,
and then Eurýnomê, as maid-in-waiting,
lighted her lord and lady to their chamber
with bright brands.

                  She vanished.

                          So they came
into that bed so steadfast, loved of old,
opening glad arms to one another.   300
Telémakhos by now had hushed the dancing,
hushed the women. In the darkened hall
he and the cowherd and the swineherd slept.

The royal pair mingled in love again
and afterward lay revelling in stories:
hers of the siege her beauty stood at home
from arrogant suitors, crowding on her sight,
and how they fed their courtship on his cattle,
oxen and fat sheep, and drank up rivers
of wine out of the vats.

                          Odysseus told   310
of what hard blows he had dealt out to others
and of what blows he had taken—all that story.
She could not close her eyes till all was told.

---

[5] The point of this gesture would be to appease the sea god by spreading his fame even into places where the sea is unknown. This excursion does not, in fact, take place in the *Odyssey*.

His raid on the Kikonês, first of all,
then how he visited the Lotos Eaters,
and what the Kyklops did, and how those shipmates,
pitilessly devoured, were avenged.
Then of his touching Aiolos's isle
and how that king refitted him for sailing
to Ithaka; all vain: gales blew him back   320
groaning over the fishcold sea. Then how
he reached the Laistrygonians' distant bay
and how they smashed his ships and his companions.
Kirkê, then: of her deceits and magic,
then of his voyage to the wide underworld
of dark, the house of Death, and questioning
Teirêsias, Theban spirit.

                      Dead companions,
many, he saw there, and his mother, too.
Of this he told his wife, and told how later
he heard the choir of maddening Seirênês,   330
coasted the Wandering Rocks, Kharybdis' pool
and the fiend Skylla who takes toll of men.
Then how his shipmates killed Lord Hêlios' cattle
and how Zeus thundering in towering heaven
split their fast ship with his fuming bolt,
so all hands perished.

                    He alone survived,
cast away on Kalypso's isle, Ogýgia.
He told, then, how that nymph detained him there
in her smooth caves, craving him for her husband,
and how in her devoted lust she swore   340
he should not die nor grow old, all his days,
but he held out against her.

                      Last of all
what sea-toil brought him to the Phaiákians;
their welcome; how they took him to their hearts
and gave him passage to his own dear island
with gifts of garments, gold and bronze . . .

                    Remembering,
he drowsed over the story's end. Sweet sleep
relaxed his limbs and his care-burdened breast.

Other affairs were in Athena's keeping.
Waiting until Odysseus had his pleasure   350
of love and sleep, the grey-eyed one bestirred
the fresh Dawn from her bed of paling Ocean
to bring up daylight to her golden chair,
and from his fleecy bed Odysseus
arose. He said to Penélopê:

                      "My lady,
what ordeals have we not endured! Here, waiting
you had your grief, while my return dragged out—

my hard adventures, pitting myself against
the gods' will, and Zeus, who pinned me down
far from home. But now our life resumes: 360
we've come together to our longed-for bed.
Take care of what is left me in our house;
as to the flocks that pack of wolves laid waste
they'll be replenished: scores I'll get on raids
and other scores our island friends will give me
till all the folds are full again.

This day
I'm off up country to the orchards. I must see
my noble father, for he missed me sorely.
And here is my command for you—a strict one,
though you may need none, clever as you are. 370
Word will get about as the sun goes higher
of how I killed those lads. Go to your rooms
on the upper floor, and take your women. Stay there
with never a glance outside or a word to anyone."

Fitting cuirass and swordbelt to his shoulders,
he woke his herdsmen, woke Telémakhos,
ordering all in arms. They dressed quickly,
and all in war gear sallied from the gate,
led by Odysseus.

Now it was broad day
but these three men Athena hid in darkness, 380
going before them swiftly from the town.

BOOK TWENTY-FOUR: WARRIORS, FAREWELL

Meanwhile the suitors' ghosts were called away
by Hermês of Kyllênê,[1] bearing the golden wand
with which he charms the eyes of men or wakens
whom he wills.

He waved them on, all squeaking
as bats will in a cavern's underworld,
all flitting, flitting criss-cross in the dark
if one falls and the rock-hung chain is broken.
So with faint cries the shades trailed after Hermês,
pure Deliverer.

He led them down dank ways,
over grey Ocean tides, the Snowy Rock, 10
past shores of Dream and narrows of the sunset,
in swift flight to where the Dead inhabit
wastes of asphodel at the world's end.

---

[1] Birthplace and home of Hermês, in Arcadia.

Crossing the plain they met Akhilleus'[2] ghost,
Patróklos and Antílokhos, then Aías,
noblest of Danaans after Akhilleus
in strength and beauty. Here the newly dead
drifted together, whispering. Then came
the soul of Agamémnon, son of Atreus,
in black pain forever, surrounded by men-at-arms 20
who perished with him in Aigísthos' hall.
Akhilleus greeted him:

          "My lord Atreidês,
we held that Zeus who loves the play of lightning
would give you length of glory, you were king
over so great a host of soldiery
before Troy, where we suffered, we Akhaians.
But in the morning of your life
you met that doom that no man born avoids.
It should have found you in your day of victory,
marshal of the army, in Troy country; 30
then all Akhaia would have heaped your tomb
and saved your honor for your son. Instead
piteous death awaited you at home."

And Atreus' son replied:

          "Fortunate hero,
son of Pêleus, godlike and glorious,
at Troy you died, across the sea from Argos,
and round you Trojan and Akhaian peers
fought for your corpse and died. A dustcloud wrought
by a whirlwind hid the greatness of you slain,
minding no more the mastery of horses. 40
All that day we might have toiled in battle
had not a storm from Zeus broken it off.
We carried you out of the field of war
down to the ships and bathed your comely body
with warm water and scented oil. We laid you
upon your long bed, and our officers
wept hot tears like rain and cropped their hair.
Then hearing of it in the sea, your mother, Thetis,[3]
came with nereids of the grey wave crying
unearthly lamentation over the water, 50
and trembling gripped the Akhaians to the bone.
They would have boarded ship that night and fled
except for one man's wisdom—venerable
Nestor, proven counselor in the past.

---

[2] The following passage mentions several heroes of the Trojan War. Patróklos and Antílokhos were especially close friends of Akhilleus.
[3] A nereid (sea nymph), mother of Akhilleus.

He stood and spoke to allay their fear: 'Hold fast,
sons of the Akhaians, lads of Argos.
His mother it must be, with nymphs her sisters,
come from the sea to mourn her son in death.'

Veteran hearts at this contained their dread
while at your side the daughters of the ancient   60
seagod wailed and wrapped ambrosial shrouding
around you.
                          Then we heard the Muses sing
a threnody[4] in nine immortal voices.
No Argive there but wept, such keening[5] rose
from that one Muse who led the song.
                                    Now seven
days and ten, seven nights and ten, we mourned you,
we mortal men, with nymphs who know no death,
before we gave you to the flame, slaughtering
longhorned steers and fat sheep on your pyre.

Dressed by the nereids and embalmed with honey,   70
honey and unguent in the seething blaze,
you turned to ash. And past the pyre Akhaia's
captains paraded in review, in arms,
clattering chariot teams and infantry.
Like a forest fire the flame roared on, and burned
your flesh away. Next day at dawn, Akhilleus,
we picked your pale bones from the char to keep
in wine and oil. A golden amphora[6]
your mother gave for this—Hephaistos' work,
a gift from Dionysos.[7] In that vase,   80
Akhilleus, hero, lie your pale bones mixed
with mild Patróklos' bones, who died before you,
and nearby lie the bones of Antílokhos,
the one you cared for most of all companions
after Patróklos.
                          We of the Old Army,
we who were spearmen, heaped a tomb for these
upon a foreland over Hellê's waters,[8]
to be a mark against the sky for voyagers
in this generation and those to come.
Your mother sought from the gods magnificent trophies   90
and set them down midfield for our champions. Often

[4] Dirge; lament. The Muses are goddesses of song, literature, and the arts. Homer does not describe them elsewhere as being nine in number; this is one of several anomalies about the present scene in Hades that have caused certain commentators to reject it as unauthentic.
[5] Loud, shrill lamenting for the dead.
[6] A type of jar.
[7] God of wine and revelry.
[8] The Hellespont; the modern Dardanelles, the strait connecting the Aegean Sea with the Sea of Marmara; located just north of Troy.

at funeral games after the death of kings
when you yourself contended, you've seen athletes
cinch their belts when trophies went on view.
But these things would have made you stare—the treasures
Thetis on her silver-slippered feet
brought to your games—for the gods held you dear.
You perished, but your name will never die.
It lives to keep all men in mind of honor
forever, Akhilleus.

As for myself, what joy   100
is this, to have brought off the war? Foul death
Zeus held in store for me at my coming home;
Aigísthos and my vixen cut me down."

While they conversed, the Wayfinder[9] came near,
leading the shades of suitors overthrown
by Lord Odysseus. The two souls of heroes
advanced together, scrutinizing these.
Then Agamémnon recognized Amphímedon,
son of Meláneus—friends of his on Ithaka—
and called out to him:

"Amphímedon,   110
what ruin brought you into this undergloom?
All in a body, picked men, and so young?
One could not better choose the kingdom's pride.
Were you at sea, aboard ship, and Poseidon
blew up a dire wind and foundering waves,
or cattle-raiding, were you, on the mainland,
or in a fight for some stronghold, or women,
when the foe hit you to your mortal hurt?
Tell me, answer my question. Guest and friend
I say I am of yours—or do you not remember   120
I visited your family there? I came
with Prince Meneláos, urging Odysseus
to join us in the great sea raid on Troy.
One solid month we beat our way, breasting
south sea and west, resolved to bring him round,
the wily raider of cities."

The new shade said:

"O glory of commanders, Agamémnon,
all that you bring to mind I remember well.
As for the sudden manner of our death
I'll tell you of it clearly, first to last.   130
After Odysseus had been gone for years
we were all suitors of his queen. She never
quite refused, nor went through with a marriage,

[9] Hermês.

hating it, ever bent on our defeat.
Here is one of her tricks: she placed her loom,
her big loom, out for weaving in her hall,
and the fine warp of some vast fabric on it.
We were attending her, and she said to us:
'Young men, my suitors, now my lord is dead,
let me finish my weaving before I marry, 140
or else my thread will have been spun in vain.
This is a shroud I weave for Lord Laërtês
when cold Death comes to lay him on his bier.
The country wives would hold me in dishonor
if he, with all his fortune, lay unshrouded.'
We had men's hearts; she touched them; we agreed.
So every day she wove on the great loom—
but every night by torchlight she unwove it,
and so for three years she deceived the Akhaians.
But when the seasons brought the fourth around, 150
as long months waned, and the slow days were spent,
one of her maids, who knew the secret, told us.
We found her unraveling the splendid shroud,
and then she had to finish, willy nilly—
finish, and show the big loom woven tight
from beam to beam with cloth. She washed the shrouding
clean as sun or moonlight.
                                      Then, heaven knows
from what quarter of the world, fatality
brought in Odysseus to the swineherd's wood
far up the island. There his son went too 160
when the black ship put him ashore from Pylos.
The two together planned our death-trap. Down
they came to the famous town—Telémakhos
long in advance: we had to wait for Odysseus.
The swineherd led him to the manor later
in rags like a foul beggar, old and broken,
propped on a stick. These tatters that he wore
hid him so well that none of us could know him
when he turned up, not even the older men.
We jeered at him, took potshots at him, cursed him. 170
Daylight and evening in his own great hall
he bore it, patient as a stone. That night
the mind of Zeus beyond the stormcloud stirred him
with Telémakhos at hand to shift his arms
from mégaron to storage room and lock it.
Then he assigned his wife her part: next day
she brought his bow and iron axeheads out
to make a contest. Contest there was none;
that move doomed us to slaughter. Not a man
could bend the stiff bow to his will or string it, 180
until it reached Odysseus. We shouted,
'Keep the royal bow from the beggar's hands

no matter how he begs!' Only Telémakhos
would not be denied.

         So the great soldier
took his bow and bent it for the bowstring
effortlessly. He drilled the axeheads clean,
sprang, and decanted arrows on the door sill,
glared, and drew again. This time he killed
Antínoös.

        There facing us he crouched
and shot his bolts of groaning at us, brought us   190
down like sheep. Then some god, his familiar,[10]
went into action with him round the hall,
after us in a massacre. Men lay groaning,
mortally wounded, and the floor smoked with blood.

That was the way our death came, Agamémnon.
Now in Odysseus' hall untended still
our bodies lie,[11] unknown to friends or kinsmen
who should have laid us out and washed our wounds
free of the clotted blood, and mourned our passing.
So much is due the dead."

           But Agamémnon's 200
tall shade when he heard this cried aloud:

"O fortunate Odysseus, master mariner
and soldier, blessed son of old Laërtês!
The girl you brought home made a valiant wife!
True to her husband's honor and her own,
Penélopê, Ikários' faithful daughter!
The very gods themselves will sing her story
for men on earth—mistress of her own heart,
Penélopê!
Tyndáreus' daughter waited, too—how differently! 210
Klytaimnéstra, the adulteress,
waited to stab her lord and king. That song
will be forever hateful. A bad name
she gave to womankind, even the best."

These were the things they said to one another
under the rim of earth where Death is lord.

Leaving the town, Odysseus and his men
that morning reached Laërtês' garden lands,
long since won by his toil from wilderness—
his homestead, and the row of huts around it   220

---

[10] A friendly attendant spirit.
[11] It is unusual in Homer that the souls of unburied men should be admitted to Hades.

where fieldhands rested, ate and slept. Indoors
he had an old slave woman, a Sikel,[12] keeping
house for him in his secluded age.

Odysseus here took leave of his companions.

"Go make yourselves at home inside," he said.
"Roast the best porker and prepare a meal.
I'll go to try my father. Will he know me?
Can he imagine it, after twenty years?"

He handed spear and shield to the two herdsmen,
and in they went, Telémakhos too. Alone 230
Odysseus walked the orchard rows and vines.
He found no trace of Dólios and his sons
nor the other slaves—all being gone that day
to clear a distant field, and drag the stones
for a boundary wall.

But on a well-banked plot
Odysseus found his father in solitude
spading the earth around a young fruit tree.

He wore a tunic, patched and soiled, and leggings—
oxhide patches, bound below his knees
against the brambles; gauntlets[13] on his hands 240
and on his head a goatskin cowl of sorrow.[14]
This was the figure Prince Odysseus found—
wasted by years, racked, bowed under grief.
The son paused by a tall pear tree and wept,
then inwardly debated: should he run
forward and kiss his father, and pour out
his tale of war, adventure, and return,
or should he first interrogate him, test him?
Better that way, he thought—
first draw him out with sharp words, trouble him. 250
His mind made up, he walked ahead. Laërtês
went on digging, head down, by the sapling,
stamping the spade in. At his elbow then
his son spoke out:

"Old man, the orchard keeper
you work for is no townsman. A good eye
for growing things he has; there's not a nurseling,
fig tree, vine stock, olive tree or pear tree
or garden bed uncared for on this farm.
But I might add—don't take offense—your own
appearance could be tidier. Old age 260
yes—but why the squalor, and rags to boot?

---

[12] Sicilian.   [13] Gloves with protective cuffs.
[14] The goatskin cap is an expression of his mourning.

It would not be for sloth, now, that your master
leaves you in this condition; neither at all
because there's any baseness in your self.
No, by your features, by the frame you have,
a man might call you kingly,
one who should bathe warm, sup well, and rest easy
in age's privilege. But tell me:
who are your masters? whose fruit trees are these
you tend here? Tell me if it's true this island   270
is Ithaka, as that fellow I fell in with
told me on the road just now? He had
a peg loose, that one: couldn't say a word
or listen when I asked about my friend,
my Ithakan friend. I asked if he were alive
or gone long since into the underworld.
I can describe him if you care to hear it:
I entertained the man in my own land
when he turned up there on a journey; never
had I a guest more welcome in my house.   280
He claimed his stock was Ithakan: Laërtês
Arkeísiadês, he said his father was.
I took him home, treated him well, grew fond of him—
though we had many guests—and gave him
gifts in keeping with his quality: seven
bars of measured gold, a silver winebowl
filigreed with flowers, twelve light cloaks,
twelve rugs, robes and tunics—not to mention
his own choice of women trained in service,
the four well-favored ones he wished to take."   290

His father's eyes had filled with tears. He said:

"You've come to that man's island, right enough,
but dangerous men and fools hold power now.
You gave your gifts in vain. If you could find him
here in Ithaka alive, he'd make
return of gifts and hospitality,
as custom is, when someone has been generous.
But tell me accurately—how many years
have now gone by since that man was your guest?
your guest, my son—if he indeed existed—   300
born to ill fortune as he was. Ah, far
from those who loved him, far from his native land,
in some sea-dingle[15] fish have picked his bones,
or else he made the vultures and wild beasts
a trove[16] ashore! His mother at his bier
never bewailed him, nor did I, his father,

---

[15] Dell; valley.
[16] A valuable find.

nor did his admirable wife, Penélopê,
who should have closed her husband's eyes in death
and cried aloud upon him as he lay.
So much is due the dead.

But speak out, tell me further: 310
who are you, of what city and family?
where have you moored the ship that brought you here,
where is your admirable crew? Are you a peddler
put ashore by the foreign ship you came on?"

Again Odysseus had a fable ready.

"Yes," he said, "I can tell you all those things.
I come from Rover's Passage where my home is,
and I'm King Allwoes' only son. My name
is Quarrelman.[17]

Heaven's power in the westwind
drove me this way from Sikania,[18]   320
off my course. My ship lies in a barren
cove beyond the town there. As for Odysseus,
now is the fifth year since he put to sea
and left my homeland—bound for death, you say.
Yet landbirds flying from starboard crossed his bow—
a lucky augury. So we parted joyously,
in hope of friendly days and gifts to come."

A cloud of pain had fallen on Laërtês.
Scooping up handfuls of the sunburnt dust
he sifted it over his grey head, and groaned,   330
and the groan went to the son's heart. A twinge
prickling up through his nostrils warned Odysseus
he could not watch this any longer.
He leaped and threw his arms around his father,
kissed him, and said:

"Oh, Father, I am he!
Twenty years gone, and here I've come again
to my own land!

Hold back your tears! No grieving!
I bring good news—though still we cannot rest.
I killed the suitors to the last man!
Outrage and injury have been avenged!"   340

Laërtês turned and found his voice to murmur:

"If you are Odysseus, my son, come back,
give me some proof, a sign to make me sure."

---

[17] Rover's Passage, Allwoes, and Quarrelman are imaginary assumed (though appropriate)
names.
[18] Sicily, perhaps.

His son replied:

"The scar then, first of all.
Look, here the wild boar's flashing tusk
wounded me on Parnassos; do you see it?
You and my mother made me go, that time,
to visit Lord Autólykos, her father,
for gifts he promised years before on Ithaka.
Again—more proof—let's say the trees you gave me   350
on this revetted[19] plot of orchard once.
I was a small boy at your heels, wheedling
amid the young trees, while you named each one.
You gave me thirteen pear, ten apple trees,
and forty fig trees. Fifty rows of vines
were promised too, each one to bear in turn.
Bunches of every hue would hang there ripening,
weighed down by the god of summer days."

The old man's knees failed him, his heart grew faint,
recalling all that Odysseus calmly told.   360
He clutched his son. Odysseus held him swooning
until he got his breath back and his spirit
and spoke again:

"Zeus, Father! Gods above!—
you still hold pure Olympos, if the suitors
paid for their crimes indeed, and paid in blood!
But now the fear is in me that all Ithaka
will be upon us. They'll send messengers
to stir up every city of the islands."

Odysseus the great tactician answered:

"Courage, and leave the worrying to me.   370
We'll turn back to your homestead by the orchard.
I sent the cowherd, swineherd, and Telémakhos
ahead to make our noonday meal."

Conversing
in this vein they went home, the two together,
into the stone farmhouse. There Telémakhos
and the two herdsmen were already carving
roast young pork, and mixing amber wine.
During these preparations the Sikel woman
bathed Laërtês and anointed him,
and dressed him in a new cloak. Then Athena,   380
standing by, filled out his limbs again,
gave girth and stature to the old field captain
fresh from the bathing place. His son looked on

---

[19] Buttressed by stones.

in wonder at the godlike bloom upon him,
and called out happily:

                                          "Oh, Father,

surely one of the gods who are young forever
has made you magnificent before my eyes!"

Clearheaded Laërtês faced him, saying:

"By Father Zeus, Athena and Apollo,
I wish I could be now as once I was,   390
commander of Kephallenians,[20] when I took
the walled town, Nérikos, on the promontory!
Would god I had been young again last night
with armor on me, standing in our hall
to fight the suitors at your side! How many
knees I could have crumpled, to your joy!"

While son and father spoke, cowherd and swineherd
attended, waiting, for the meal was ready.
Soon they were all seated, and their hands
picked up the meat and bread.

                                    But now old Dólios   400
appeared in the bright doorway with his sons,
work-stained from the field. Laërtês' housekeeper,
who reared the boys and tended Dólios
in his bent age, had gone to fetch them in.
When it came over them who the stranger was
they halted in astonishment. Odysseus
hit an easy tone with them. Said he:

"Sit down and help yourselves. Shake off your wonder.
Here we've been waiting for you all this time,
and our mouths watering for good roast pig!"   410

But Dólios came forward, arms outstretched,
and kissed Odysseus' hand at the wrist bone,
crying out:

                                 "Dear master, you returned!
You came to us again! How we had missed you!
We thought you lost. The gods themselves have brought you!
Welcome, welcome; health and blessings on you!
And tell me, now, just one thing more: Penélopê,
does she know yet that you are on the island?
or should we send a messenger?"

---

[20] Inhabitants of the large island (modern Cephalonia) near Ithaka. Nérikos is on a nearby island.

Odysseus gruffly said,

                                "Old man, she knows.   420
Is it for you to think of her?"

                                        So Dólios

quietly took a smooth bench at the table
and in their turn his sons welcomed Odysseus,
kissing his hands; then each went to his chair
beside his father. Thus our friends
were occupied in Laërtês' house at noon.

Meanwhile to the four quarters of the town
the news ran: bloody death had caught the suitors;
and men and women in a murmuring crowd
gathered before Odysseus' hall. They gave   430
burial to the piteous dead, or bore
the bodies of young men from other islands
down to the port, thence to be ferried home.
Then all the men went grieving to assembly
and being seated, rank by rank, grew still,
as old Eupeithês rose to address them. Pain
lay in him like a brand for Antínoös,
the first man that Odysseus brought down,
and tears flowed for his son as he began:

"Heroic feats that fellow did for us   440
Akhaians, friends! Good spearmen by the shipload
he led to war and lost—lost ships and men,
and once ashore again killed these, who were
the islands' pride.

                         Up with you! After him!—
before he can take flight to Pylos town
or hide at Elis, under Epeian law!
We'd be disgraced forever! Mocked for generations
if we cannot avenge our sons' blood, and our brothers!
Life would turn to ashes—at least for me;
rather be dead and join the dead!

                                     I say   450
we ought to follow now, or they'll gain time
and make the crossing."

                              His appeal, his tears,
moved all the gentry listening there;
but now they saw the crier and the minstrel
come from Odysseus' hall, where they had slept.
The two men stood before the curious crowd,
and Medôn said:

                          "Now hear me, men of Ithaka.
When these hard deeds were done by Lord Odysseus
the immortal gods were not far off. I saw

with my own eyes someone divine who fought   460
beside him, in the shape and dress of Mentor;
it was a god who shone before Odysseus,
a god who swept the suitors down the hall
dying in droves."

                                        At this pale fear assailed them,
and next they heard again the old forecaster,
Halithérsês Mastóridês. Alone
he saw the field of time, past and to come.
In his anxiety for them he said:

"Ithakans, now listen to what I say.
Friends, by your own fault these deaths came to pass.   470
You would not heed me nor the captain, Mentor;
would not put down the riot of your sons.
Heroic feats they did!—all wantonly
raiding a great man's flocks, dishonoring
his queen, because they thought he'd come no more.
Let matters rest; do as I urge; no chase,
or he who wants a bloody end will find it."

The greater number stood up shouting "Aye!"
But many held fast, sitting all together
in no mind to agree with him. Eupeithês   480
had won them to his side. They ran for arms,
clapped on their bronze, and mustered
under Eupeithês at the town gate
for his mad foray.

                                        Vengeance would be his,
he thought, for his son's murder; but that day
held bloody death for him and no return.

At this point, querying Zeus, Athena said:

"O Father of us all and king of kings,
enlighten me. What is your secret will?
War and battle, worse and more of it,   490
or can you not impose a pact on both?"

The summoner of cloud replied:

                                                        "My child,
why this formality of inquiry?
Did you not plan that action by yourself—
see to it that Odysseus, on his homecoming,
should have their blood?

                                        Conclude it as you will.
There is one proper way, if I may say so:
Odysseus' honor being satisfied,

let him be king by a sworn pact forever,
and we, for our part, will blot out the memory 500
of sons and brothers slain. As in the old time
let men of Ithaka henceforth be friends;
prosperity enough, and peace attend them."

Athena needed no command, but down
in one spring she descended from Olympos
just as the company of Odysseus finished
wheat crust and honeyed wine, and heard him say:

"Go out, someone, and see if they are coming."

One of the boys went to the door as ordered
and saw the townsmen in the lane. He turned 510
swiftly to Odysseus.

                                    "Here they come,"

he said, "best arm ourselves, and quickly."

All up at once, the men took helm and shield—
four fighting men, counting Odysseus,
with Dólios' half dozen sons. Laërtês
armed as well, and so did Dólios—
greybeards, they could be fighters in a pinch.
Fitting their plated helmets on their heads
they sallied out, Odysseus in the lead.

Now from the air Athena, Zeus's daughter, 520
appeared in Mentor's guise, with Mentor's voice,
making Odysseus' heart grow light. He said
to put cheer in his son:

                                    "Telémakhos,

you are going into battle against pikemen
where hearts of men are tried. I count on you
to bring no shame upon your forefathers.
In fighting power we have excelled this lot
in every generation."

                                    Said his son:

"If you are curious, Father, watch and see
the stuff that's in me. No more talk of shame." 530

And old Laërtês cried aloud:

"Ah, what a day for me, dear gods!
to see my son and grandson vie in courage!"

Athena halted near him, and her eyes

shone like the sea. She said:

"Arkeísiadês,

dearest of all my old brothers-in-arms,
invoke the grey-eyed one and Zeus her father,
heft your spear and make your throw."

Power flowed into him from Pallas Athena,
whom he invoked as Zeus's virgin child,   540
and he let fly his heavy spear.

It struck

Eupeithês on the cheek plate of his helmet,
and undeflected the bronze head punched through.
He toppled, and his armor clanged upon him.
Odysseus and his son now furiously
closed, laying on with broadswords, hand to hand,
and pikes: they would have cut the enemy down
to the last man, leaving not one survivor,
had not Athena raised a shout
that stopped all fighters in their tracks.

"Now hold!"   550

she cried, "Break off this bitter skirmish;
end your bloodshed, Ithakans, and make peace."

Their faces paled with dread before Athena,
and swords dropped from their hands unnerved, to lie
strewing the ground, at the great voice of the goddess.
Those from the town turned fleeing for their lives.
But with a cry to freeze their hearts
and ruffling like an eagle on the pounce,
the lord Odysseus reared himself to follow—
at which the son of Kronos dropped a thunderbolt   560
smoking at his daughter's feet.

Athena

cast a grey glance at her friend and said:

"Son of Laërtês and the gods of old,
Odysseus, master of land ways and sea ways,
command yourself. Call off this battle now,
or Zeus who views the wide world may be angry."

He yielded to her, and his heart was glad.
Both parties later swore to terms of peace
set by their arbiter, Athena, daughter
of Zeus who bears the stormcloud as a shield—   570
though still she kept the form and voice of Mentor.

Sappho

(Seventh Century B.C. to Sixth Century B.C.)

What we know about Sappho can be briefly stated: She lived in the late seventh and early sixth centuries B.C.; she was born and spent most of her life on the island of Lesbos in the Aegean Sea; her mother's name was Cleis; she had a daughter also named Cleis; her husband's name was Cercolas (probably); she had two brothers named Charaxos and Larichos and possibly a third named Eurygyos; she had a number of young female companions, perhaps her students; and she wrote magnificent poetry. The voice of this earliest woman poet is intensely personal and intensely musical even in the muffled and distorted form in which it has reached us.

Sappho was well known in classical times. She seems to have been prolific, writing perhaps five hundred poems, and she was widely quoted by critics, commentators, and grammarians down through late Roman times. She was one of the poets most parodied on the late Greek comic stage; at least six Greek comedies dealt with her (all are now lost). From these plays sprang a number of legends about Sappho—that she was short, dark, and ugly ("a nightingale with misshapen wings"), that she was a prostitute, and that she died by throwing herself off the Leucadian cliffs when her love for a ferryman named Phaon was not reciprocated. All these legends are now thoroughly discredited.

The earliest surviving manuscript of Sappho's poems dates from the third century B.C., hundreds of years after her death, and its link with what she actually composed is indirect, depending on a long chain of singers who, over that time, transmitted the lyrics orally, at some undetermined point putting them into writing. Sappho was literally a lyric poet, singing or chanting the poems to her own accompaniment on the lyre, and she may never have put them into writing herself at all. The method of transmission, then, was one obstacle to the accurate preservation of her texts.

But Sappho's reputation as a lesbian (in a sexual as well as a geographic sense) was also a major reason why so little of her work survives. Even in classical times, her homosexuality was the source of some disapproval; Ovid wrote that she "taught how to love girls." But this mild disapproval hardened into hatred in the early Middle Ages. About 380 A.D., St. Gregory of Nazianzos, Bishop of Constantinople, ordered all copies of Sappho's works burned wherever they were found, and again in the eleventh century Pope Gregory VII ordered her poems publicly burned in Rome and Constantinople. As a result of such attacks and of the general loss of classical manuscripts during the Middle Ages, not a single collection of Sappho's poems survived the medieval period.

Interest in Sappho reawakened in the Renaissance, however, and scholars attempted to reconstruct her work by assembling all the lines quoted by other Greek and Latin writers. Longinus' *Essay on the Sublime,* for example, contained the complete text of Sappho's "He is more than a hero" (number 39 in this text), and Dionysios of Halikarnassos' *Treatise on Style* contained all of "Prayer to Aphrodite" (number 38). Even so, the results were pitifully small.

And then, incredibly, in 1879, new poems by Sappho were discovered in an ancient rubbish heap in Egypt; further manuscripts came to light during a series of archaeological expeditions in the 1890s. Papyrus scrolls upon which the poems had been copied had been torn, lengthwise, into strips and used as mummy wrappings. Others had been used to stuff mummified crocodiles. As a result of this shredding, the new texts of Sappho, while valuable, include many partial lines; reconstructing what Sappho wrote involves a great deal of guesswork. We now have about seven hundred intelligible lines of Sappho's voluminous verse.

The poet that emerges from this sadly mutilated work is nevertheless powerful and distinctive. Sappho wrote a number of *epithalamia* (wedding songs), to be chanted by a chorus before the bridal chamber. But her favorite poetic form was the short, intensely personal lyric, written to be chanted to the lyre by a solo singer. Most of her poems in this form deal with the passions and relationships within her circle of female companions, and especially with her own feelings about these women. Who these companions were is a matter of some speculation. Earlier critics believed that Sappho was a priestess and the leader of a *thiasos,* an organized group of women devoted to the worship of Aphrodite. More recent scholars have vigorously opposed this view and held that the circle of girls, if it had any formal standing at all, was at most a group of students or apprentices who studied poetry and the lyre with Sappho.

Fortunately, this question does not have to be resolved before we can understand the poems. Whatever her official relationship to the circle of girls, Sappho's emphasis in her poems is almost exclusively personal and passionate. Even the prayers to Aphrodite are full of an aching, human passion, and the pain of longing has seldom been better described than in number 39, where the glimpse of her loved one sitting by a man eclipses the world of perception, leaving only a feeling like death. If Sappho's world has a "hothouse atmosphere," as one critic has said, within its limits it is a psychologically realistic and extraordinarily moving one.

The passion and the intensity in Sappho's poetry are expressed with a limpid simplicity. The English critic C. M. Bowra describes her poetry as "ordinary speech raised to the highest level of expressiveness." The translator of this selection, Mary Barnard, states that her ambition is to capture in English Sappho's "fresh colloquial directness of speech," the quality that, along with her passion and her lyricism, led an anonymous Roman critic to write that "Sappho was not ninth among men but rather tenth among the lovely Muses."

NOTE ON THE TEXT

Because of complex problems of textual reconstruction, the first lines of the poems included here are sometimes to be read as titles, sometimes as integral parts of the poems. Their numbering corresponds to that in the Barnard translation.

FURTHER READING *(prepared by F.S.N.):* Discussion of Sappho's life and work is found in Bruno Snell, *The Discovery of the Mind,* 1948, trans. T. G. Rosenmeyer, 1953, pp. 43–70; Albin Lesky, *A History of Greek Literature,* 1957, 2nd ed. 1963, trans. J. Willis and C. de Heer, 1966, pp. 138–48; and Willis Barnstone, *Sappho: Lyrics in the Original Greek with Translations*, 1965. Denys L. Page, in his *Sappho and Alcaeus: An introduction to the Study of Ancient Lesbian Poetry*, 1955, presents twelve of the longer poems, with translation, commentary, and interpretative material; these analyses are followed by useful general remarks on Sappho's writings. On the form of Sappho's poetry, see Anne Pippin Burnett's lucidly written critical and historical study *Three Archaic Poets: Archilochus, Alcaeus, Sappho*, 1983. Discussions of Sappho in a feminist context are included in *Reflections of Women in Antiquity*, ed. Helene P. Foley, 1981. Other discussions of Sappho from feminist perspectives can be found in Jane Snyder, *The Woman and the Lyre*, 1989, which outlines a female tradition, and in Lawrence Lipking, *Abandoned Women and Poetic Tradition*, 1989. Guidance to writings on Sappho can be found in the apparatus of Richard Jenkyns' *Three Classical Poets: Sappho, Catullus, and Juvenal*, 1982.

POEMS

Translated by Mary Barnard

30

We drink your health

Lucky bridegroom!
Now the wedding you
asked for is over

and your wife is the   5
girl you asked for;
she's a bride who is

charming to look at,
with eyes as soft as
honey, and a face   10

that Love has lighted
with his own beauty.
Aphrodite[1] has surely

outdone herself in
doing honor to you!   15

---

[1] Goddess of love, as well as of the sea and of beauty, flowers, and seasons.

34

Lament for a maidenhead

FIRST
VOICE
    Like a quince-apple
ripening on a top
branch in a tree top

not once noticed by
harvesters or if
not unnoticed, not reached

SECOND
VOICE
    Like a hyacinth in
the mountains, trampled
by shepherds until
only a purple stain
remains on the ground

37

You[1] know the place: then

Leave Crete and come to us
waiting where the grove is
pleasantest, by precincts

sacred to you; incense
smokes on the altar, cold
streams murmur through the

apple branches, a young
rose thicket shades the ground
and quivering leaves pour

down deep sleep; in meadows
where horses have grown sleek
among spring flowers, dill

scents the air. Queen! Cyprian!
Fill our gold cups with love
stirred into clear nectar

[1] The poem is addressed to Aphrodite (the "Cyprian" of line 14).

38

Prayer to my lady of Paphos[1]

Dapple-throned Aphrodite,
eternal daughter of God,
snare-knitter! Don't, I beg you,

cow my heart with grief! Come, 5
as once when you heard my far-
off cry and, listening, stepped

from your father's house to your
gold car, to yoke the pair whose
beautiful thick-feathered wings[2] 10

oaring down mid-air from heaven
carried you to light swiftly
on dark earth; then, blissful one,

smiling your immortal smile
you asked, What ailed me now that 15
made me call you again? What

was it that my distracted
heart most wanted? "Whom has
Persuasion to bring round now

to your love? Who, Sappho, is 20
unfair to you? For, let her
run, she will soon run after;

if she won't accept gifts, she
will one day give them; and if
he won't love you—she soon will 25

love, although unwillingly. . . ."
If ever—come now! Relieve
this intolerable pain!

What my heart most hopes will
happen, make happen; you your- 30
self join forces on my side!

[1] Aphrodite, who was born of the sea foam and washed ashore at Paphos.
[2] The sparrows that drew Aphrodite's chariot.

39

He is more than a hero

He is a god in my eyes—
the man who is allowed
to sit beside you—he

who listens intimately   5
to the sweet murmur of
your voice, the enticing

laughter that makes my own
heart beat fast. If I meet
you suddenly, I can't   10

speak—my tongue is broken;
a thin flame runs under
my skin; seeing nothing,

hearing only my own ears
drumming, I drip with sweat;   15
trembling shakes my body

and I turn paler than
dry grass. At such times
death isn't far from me

40

Yes, Atthis,[1] you may be sure

                                        Even in Sardis
Anactoria will think often of us

of the life we shared here, when you seemed
the Goddess incarnate   5
to her and your singing pleased her best

Now among Lydian women she in her
turn stands first as the red-
fingered moon rising at sunset takes

precedence over stars around her;   10
her light spreads equally
on the salt sea and fields thick with bloom

[1] Atthis and Anactoria were two of the girls in Sappho's circle.

Delicious dew pours down to freshen
roses, delicate thyme
and blossoming sweet clover; she wande

aimlessly, thinking of gentle
Atthis, her heart hanging
heavy with longing in her little breast

She shouts aloud, Come! we know it;
thousand-eared night repeats that cry   20
across the sea shining between us

41

To an army wife, in Sardis:

Some say a cavalry corps,
some infantry, some, again,
will maintain that the swift oars

of our fleet are the finest   5
sight on dark earth; but I say
that whatever one loves, is.

This is easily proved: did
not Helen[1]—she who had scanned
the flower of the world's manhood—   10

choose as first among men one
who laid Troy's honor in ruin?
warped to his will, forgetting

love due her own blood, her own
child, she wandered far with him.   15
So Anactoria, although you

being far away forget us,
the dear sound of your footstep
and light glancing in your eyes

would move me more than glitter   20
of Lydian horse or armored
tread of mainland infantry

[1] Helen of Troy, whose choice of Paris as a lover and subsequent flight with him to Troy
began the Trojan War.

42

I have had not one word from her

Frankly I wish I were dead.
When she left, she wept

a great deal; she said to
me, "This parting must be   5
endured, Sappho. I go unwillingly."

I said, "Go, and be happy
but remember (you know
well) whom you leave shackled by love

"If you forget me, think   10
of our gifts to Aphrodite
and all the loveliness that we shared

"all the violet tiaras,
braided rosebuds, dill and
crocus twined around your young neck   15

"myrrh poured on your head
and on soft mats girls with
all that they most wished for beside them

"while no voices chanted
choruses without ours,   20
no woodlot bloomed in spring without song . . ."

43

It was you, Atthis, who said

"Sappho, if you will not get
up and let us look at you
I shall never love you again!

"Get up, unleash your suppleness,   5
lift off your Chian nightdress[1]
and, like a lily leaning into

---

[1]From the island of Chios, off the coast of Asia Minor.

"a spring, bathe in the water.
Cleis[2] is bringing your best
purple frock and the yellow   10

"tunic down from the clothes chest;
you will have a cloak thrown over
you and flowers crowning your hair . . .

"Praxinoa, my child, will you please
roast nuts for our breakfast? One   15
of the gods is being good to us:

"today we are going at last
into Mitylene, our favorite
city, with Sappho, loveliest

"of its women; she will walk   20
among us like a mother with
all her daughters around her

"when she comes home from exile . . ."

But you forget everything

97

I have often asked you
not to come now
Hermes,[1] Lord, you
who lead the ghosts
home: 5
        But this time
I am not happy; I
want to die, to see
the moist lotus open
along Acheron[2]   10

[2] Sappho's daughter.
[1] The god who guided the dead to the underworld.
[2] The river of Death.

Aeschylus

(C. 525–456 B.C.)

The oldest of the three great Greek tragedians, Aeschylus was born around 525 B.C. in Eleusis, a town near Athens, and died in Sicily in 456. He fought in the Persian wars, taking part in the great Athenian victory at Marathon in 490 and later in other climactic victories over the invading Persians, including the naval battle of Salamis in 480. Earlier that year, the Persians had partially destroyed Athens. Aeschylus' sense of pride in his city's accomplishments and triumphant survival is expressed most directly in his play *The Persians* (472), the only surviving Greek tragedy based on history, but also in the Orestes trilogy, or *Oresteia*. Aeschylus is a definitive spokesman for central Athenian values during the noblest age of ancient Greece. It is probable, in fact, that the eminent political and civic leader Pericles was the "choregus" (roughly equivalent of "producer") for one of Aeschylus' plays.

Today, as was true in antiquity, Aeschylus is called the "Father of Tragedy." He earned the title not only by his achievements as an artist, as typified by the power and loftiness of his stories, themes, and style, but also by his technical innovations. He is said to have introduced the "second actor" (earlier there had been only one and a chorus), thus making possible more complex plots and interactions. (The addition of an actor multiplied the number of possible characters, since parts were regularly doubled and men played female as well as male roles.) At the same time, he preserved the major lyrical and dramatic role of the chorus, which both participates in and comments on the action—this in addition to its musical and choreographic function. His output was impressive: some eighty or ninety plays. Of these, seven have survived: *The Persians, Seven Against Thebes, The Suppliant Maidens, Prometheus Bound,* and the three plays that make up the *Oresteia*.

Greek tragedies were regularly written and performed as cycles of three, each cycle followed by a raucous "satyr play" designed to contrast with the emotional loftiness and intensity of the tragedies. Aeschylus' *Oresteia,* performed in 458 just two years before his death, is the only such cycle of tragedies to have survived in its entirety.

Much of the power of this awesome work lies in the universality of its theme. Like the Book of Job, Virgil's *Aeneid,* and Milton's *Paradise Lost,* the *Oresteia* explores the perennially urgent question of whether suffering and evil can be reconciled with cosmic justice—and, if it can be, how. The literal story, however, focuses on a concrete and practical form of the question: What is the relationship between strict justice and human welfare, individual and communal? Social order, even more obviously than cosmic justice, would seem to demand that evil acts be punished—especially when, as in Aeschylus' trilogy, these acts violate the most fundamental relationships, husband-wife and parent-child. Yet the act of punishment itself frequently seems an obscenity, at odds with our sense of what is noble in humanity and worth loving or emulating in the divine order, however we define it. In our own time the question, independent of theology, underlies the debate about the function of punishment, mercy, rehabilitation, and deterrence in the judicial and penal systems. It is not at all coincidental that the *Oresteia* ends with the establishment of a law court.

Aeschylus explores the question by dramatizing the events growing out of the curse on the lineage of Atreus. The family has been guilty of unspeakable atrocities for generations before the plays' action begins, culminating in Agamemnon's sacrifice of his daughter Iphigeneia and the excesses committed against the innocents of Troy. (See the Headnote to the *Oresteia*.) Within the plays themselves, the chain of violence is extended by two further acts: the murder of Agamemnon by his wife, Clytaemnestra, and the successful conspiracy of their children, Orestes and Electra, to kill their mother in the cause of justice. The main agency and symbol of retaliation are the Furies, repellent primitive beings who in their very unsophistication embody an uncompromising honesty in dealing with elemental evil, especially violations of blood kinship.

"Tragedy" seems hardly the right term for this superdrama, either for the whole or for its separate plays. In Aeschylus' early plays, such as the surviving *Persians* and *Seven Against Thebes*, he placed human affairs in the foreground, with the gods relegated to the background. But in the *Oresteia*, as apparently also in the late Prometheus and Danaid trilogies (now represented only in the surviving *Prometheus Bound* and *The Suppliant Maidens*), he brought the cosmos itself on stage as he dramatized the divisions within the universe and their ultimate reconciliation. The *Oresteia* is not so much a tragedy, in the Aristotelian sense, as it is a Divine Comedy, tracing the emergence of civilization out of darkness into light. This process is presented in terms of sexual conflict and its resolution, conflict which penetrates all levels of existence, from the psychological through the domestic and political to the cosmic. *Agamemnon* presents a world trapped in a net (a crucial image throughout the trilogy) of blood vengeance, a primitive code presided over by the conservative, irrational, female Furies. The nightmare world of *Agamemnon* is shot through with sexual conflict and confusion. The unwifely Clytaemnestra "maneuvers like a man," while Aegisthus is a womanly man, and the heart of Cassandra's premonitory vision (which no one understands) is, "What outrage—the woman kills the man!" Confusion of personal sexual identity is echoed on the domestic level in the marital hatred of Agamemnon and his queen and on the political level in the Trojan War, fought "all for another's woman." The Greek victory has been a rape—"for their mad outrage of a queen we raped their city"—and Agamemnon, who killed his own daughter, has been "the darling of all the golden girls who spread the gates of Troy."

The Libation Bearers introduces the title character of the trilogy, Orestes, who is to become the pivotal figure in the revolution of values the *Oresteia* traces. The law of blood vengeance still reigns, but the vengeance of Orestes and Electra, so reluctant and self-doubting, is very different from the self-confident exultation of Clytaemnestra's bloodletting. Sexual conflict and confusion here are translated into the agonized ambivalence of a son and daughter forced to choose between love for a mother and honor for a father. And by the end of the play, sexual conflicts on the familial and political levels have broadened to a cosmic level in the conflict of the embodied Furies with the male Olympian Apollo, who authorized Orestes' vengeance. This conflict is brought directly on stage as we move from the nightmarish mode of *Agamemnon* and the comparatively realistic and Sophoclean manner of *The Libation Bearers* to the allegorical theomachy of *The Eumenides*. The curiously bisexual Athena, female but motherless, since she sprang straight from the head of Zeus, becomes the instrument for the resolution of sexual conflict, personally for Orestes, politically for Athens, and cosmically, in the reconciliation of the gods. The male Olympians triumph, but the female Furies are honored too, as they are transformed into the Eumenides, the "Kindly Ones," watchers over the rain, sunshine, and fertility of nature. This "Divine Comedy" ends with a distinctly nontragic hymn of triumph to the Athenian balance between the claims of earth and sky, female and male, fertility and control, with an optimism unclouded by the darker visions of Sophocles and Euripides.

Aeschylus' poetic and dramatic style matches the grandeur of his theme. The language, with its daring metaphors and bold dislocations of syntax, mirrors an emotional and intellectual unrest perfectly in keeping with the dramatic excitement and the profundity of theme. Image patterns are used with dazzling skill to heighten effects and to convey nuances of theme and meaning. The patterns are many and omnipresent: of fire, light and darkness, nets, wealth, wind, storm, yokes, animals, hunting, lawsuits, wrestling and other sports, "threeness," and so on. These images are not a code, each image having a static meaning; their significance is always shaped by the immediate context. For example, a yoke can suggest enslavement but also the intimacy of a harmonious bond such as happy marriage. (The word "bond" itself has the same ambiguous meaning.) Moreover, the images evolve in parallel with the evolution of action and values; an example is the ominous torch flame that at the beginning of the *Agamemnon* signals the fall of Troy and the imminent fall of the returning general but at the end of *The Eumenides* symbolizes fertility and deep joy.

As a stage craftsman, Aeschylus is the most daring and flamboyant of the three Greek tragedians. His contemporaries called him the poet of "shock," and a persistent story insisted that he wrote his plays while drunk. He served both as composer and choreographer for his own plays, and the dances he arranged for his choruses were famous for their violence and extravagance: the Persian Lords, for example, in *The Persians,* howl and scrape at the earth to conjure up the ghost of Darius. Shock follows shock in the *Oresteia.* The entrance of Agamemnon and his army is an impressive spectacle, and the dark red carpet running out from the palace door like a stream of blood is one of the most brilliant uses of a stage property in Greek drama. A contemporary testified that the first appearance of the Furies in *The Eumenides,* moaning and dripping blood from their eye sockets, caused children in the audience to faint and women to miscarry. The comment is possibly an exercise of critical license, but it nevertheless captures the shock the scene must have created. And the final great procession of the entire cast out of the theater and up to the hill of the Areopagus, in full view of the audience, is an extraordinary dramatic effect that suddenly moves the timeless, legendary action of the plays into the here and now.

The *Oresteia* is an allusive work that, like Virgil's *Aeneid,* brings together the two wellsprings of Greek literature, the *Iliad* and the *Odyssey,* while also transforming them. The Trojan War is the immediate occasion of the acts that bring on Agamemnon's murder and the ensuing events of the three plays. But the Odyssean themes of the warrior's return to his wife and of the loyal son determined to preserve his father and his house from harm are also reworked by Aeschylus with penetrating irony and insight.

The trilogy makes a political and religious statement, through the medium of great art. But it is more than ideology or theology, and more than art in a narrow sense of the word. It is an emblem of the full range of human nature, one of those rare works—like Dante's *Comedy,* Shakespeare's last plays, Beethoven's last music—that can explore vastness and mystery without losing touch with the human, including the earthy and even the homely. Dante included jokes and personal reminiscences in his account of the cosmos; Beethoven in his last symphony inserted a grunting German-band episode into an Olympian, ecstatic hymn to joy. Aeschylus, in *The Libation Bearers,* reminds us through Orestes' old nurse that the agent and victim of large tragic and providential forces was once a baby who needed to have his diapers changed. The magnificence of the *Oresteia* is ultimately a product of its range, its clear understanding and respect for humanity as many-layered. "Beneath" us lie elemental forces like the Furies; "above" us beckon the Olympian forces of the sky; "around" us lie the familiar facts of our condition in the actual world. All three of these levels, though, are within us, needing to be humanized and synthesized if we are to realize our full potential, individually and communally.

FURTHER READING *(prepared by F.S.N.):* John Herington, *Aeschylus,* 1986, is a clearly written introductory overview of the author's work, expecially valuable for its attention to patterns of diction and theatrical effect. Helen Bacon's essay on Aeschylus in Volume I of *Ancient Writers: Greece and Rome,* ed. T. James Luce, 1982, and Oliver Taplin's *The Stagecraft of Aeschylus,* 1977, are also recommended. Gilbert Murray, in his classic *Aeschylus: The Creator of Tragedy,* 1940, deals not only with the extant works but also with Aeschylus' contribution to tragedy. Anthony J. Podlecki, *The Political Background of Aeschylean Tragedy,* 1966, comments on all seven plays. H. D. F. Kitto in *Form and Meaning in Drama,* 1956, is concerned mainly with the writings of Aeschylus and Sophocles; while Albin Lesky in *Greek Tragedy,* 1938, trans. H. A. Frankfort, 1965, presents material on all three tragedians. Stimulating essays on many aspects of Aeschylean drama are offered by Marsh H. McCall, ed., *Aeschylus: A Collection of Critical Essays,* 1972. Jon Mikalson, *Honor Thy Gods,* 1992, discusses conformity and rebellion in Aeschylus, Euripides, and Sophocles. The Greek text of the three plays, a translation, and general remarks are given by W. Headlam and George Thomson, ed., *The Oresteia of Aeschylus,* 1938, 2nd ed. 1966. Anne Lebeck, in *The Oresteia: A Study in Language and Structure,* 1971, shows how the imagery in the three dramas is interconnected. Hugh Lloyd-Jones's introductions in his translation of the *Oresteia,* 1979, are first-rate.

THE ORESTEIA

Translated by Robert Fagles

Before the action of the first play *(Agamemnon)* begins, a line of evil acts, each inciting an act of terrible retaliation, already extends back several generations. Tantalus, the mythical great-grandfather of Agamemnon, murdered his son Pelops and tried to deceive the gods by serving them his son's flesh at a banquet. The gods saw through his deception, however, restoring Pelops to life and punishing Tantalus in Hades in a manner expressed by the word "tantalize." (The sinner was immersed in water up to his neck, with fruit trees over his head, both the water and the fruit receding when he tried to drink or eat.) Pelops in his turn doublecrossed and then murdered Myrtilus, a conspirator with him in a plot to win a bride for Pelops.

Pelops had two sons, Atreus and Thyestes. Thyestes seduced his brother's wife; in revenge, Atreus first banished Thyestes and then, after luring him home again, served the flesh of Thyestes' children to him at a banquet. Thyestes cursed the house of Atreus and fled. Aegisthus, a surviving son of Thyestes, inherited his father's hatred of the line of Atreus.

The genealogy of Orestes, according to Aeschylus.

Agamemnon and Menelaus are sons of Atreus. Menelaus married the beautiful Helen. She later eloped with Paris (son of King Priam of Troy), whom Menelaus had been entertaining as a guest. Agamemnon and Menelaus then organized a Greek coalition to recapture Helen from Troy and to take revenge on the Trojans. But the Greek fleet was threatened and detained at the port of Aulis by adverse winds and weather. In order to propitiate the gods, especially Artemis, and secure favorable winds, Agamemnon sacrificed the life of his daughter Iphigeneia, thereby extending the line of sacrilegious killings and incurring the hatred of his wife, Clytaemnestra (half-sister to Helen). During Agamemnon's absence at Troy, Clytaemnestra has entered into an adulterous union with Aegisthus, both of whom have a motive for killing Agamemnon. [*Editors' headnote.*]

AGAMEMNON

CHARACTERS

WATCHMAN	CHORUS, THE OLD MEN OF
CLYTAEMNESTRA	ARGOS AND THEIR LEADER
HERALD	*Attendants of Clytaemnestra*
AGAMEMNON	*and of Agamemnon,*
CASSANDRA	*bodyguard of Aegisthus*
AEGISTHUS	

TIME AND SCENE

A night in the tenth and final autumn of the Trojan war. The house of Atreus in Argos.[1] *Before it, an altar stands unlit; a watchman on the high roofs fights to stay awake.*

WATCHMAN.
Dear gods, set me free from all the pain,
the long watch I keep, one whole year awake . . .
propped on my arms, crouched on the roofs of Atreus
like a dog.
    I know the stars by heart,
the armies of the night, and there in the lead   5
the ones that bring us snow or the crops of summer,
bring us all we have—
our great blazing kings of the sky,
I know them, when they rise and when they fall . . .
and now I watch for the light, the signal-fire   10
breaking out of Troy, shouting Troy is taken.
So she commands,[2] full of her high hopes.
That woman—she maneuvers like a man.

And when I keep to my bed, soaked in dew,
and the thoughts go groping through the night   15
and the good dreams that used to guard my sleep . . .
not here, it's the old comrade, terror at my neck.
I mustn't sleep, no—

                    [Shaking himself awake.]

            Look alive, sentry.
And I try to pick out tunes, I hum a little,
a good cure for sleep, and the tears start,   20
I cry for the hard times come to the house,
no longer run like the great place of old.

Oh for a blessed end to all our pain,
some godsend burning through the dark—

               [Light appears slowly in the east;
               he struggles to his feet and scans it.]

                   I salute you!
You dawn of the darkness, you turn night to day—   25
I see the light at last.

---

[1] According to Homer, Agamemnon lived in Mycenae; Aeschylus changes the scene of the tragedy to Argos. Both cities were located in the plain of Argolis, in south-central Greece.

[2] Clytaemnestra, Agamemnon's queen, has established a chain of fire beacons that will relay quickly the news that Troy has fallen.

They'll be dancing in the streets of Argos
thanks to you, thanks to this new stroke of—
                                   Aieeeeee!
There's your signal clear and true, my queen!
Rise up from bed—hurry, lift a cry of triumph   30
through the house, praise the gods for the beacon,
if they've taken Troy . . .
                        But there it burns,
fire all the way. I'm for the morning dances.
Master's luck is mine. A throw of the torch
has brought us triple-sixes[3]—we have won!   35
My move now—

                        [*Beginning to dance, then breaking
                        off, lost in thought.*]

                Just bring him home. My king,
I'll take your loving hand in mine and then . . .
the rest is silence. The ox is on my tongue.[4]
Aye, but the house and these old stones,
give them a voice and what a tale they'd tell.   40
And so would I, gladly . . .
I speak to those who know; to those who don't
my mind's a blank. I never say a word.

                        [*He climbs down from the roof and
                        disappears into the palace through a
                        side entrance. A* CHORUS, *the old men
                        of Argos who have not learned the
                        news, enters and marches around the
                        altar.*]

CHORUS.
    Ten years gone, ten to the day
    our great avenger[5] went for Priam—   45
        Menelaus and lord Agamemnon,
    two kings with the power of Zeus,
    the twin throne, twin scepter,
    Atreus' sturdy yoke of sons
    launched Greece in a thousand ships,   50
    armadas cutting loose from the land,
    armies massed for the cause, the rescue—

                        [*From within the palace* CLYTAEM-
                        NESTRA *raises a cry of triumph.*]

[3]A winning throw of the dice in a game related to backgammon.
    [4]A proverbial phrase, the equivalent of "my lips are sealed." The watchman is probably think-
ing ominously of the guilty affair between Clytaemnestra and Aegisthus.
    [5]Agamemnon and his brother Menelaus (whose wife Helen had run away with Paris, thus
occasioning the war against Troy). Priam was the Trojan king.

the heart within them screamed for all-out war!
Like vultures robbed of their young,
 the agony sends them frenzied, 55
soaring high from the nest, round and
round they wheel, they row their wings,
stroke upon churning thrashing stroke,
but all the labor, the bed of pain,
 the young are lost forever. 60
Yet someone hears on high—Apollo,
Pan or Zeus[6]—the piercing wail
these guests of heaven raise,
and drives at the outlaws, late
but true to revenge, a stabbing Fury![7] 65

[CLYTAEMNESTRA *appears at the
doors and pauses with her entourage.*]

So towering Zeus the god of guests[8]
drives Atreus' sons at Paris,
all for a woman manned by many[9]
the generations wrestle, knees
grinding the dust, the manhood drains, 70
the spear snaps in the first blood rites
 that marry Greece and Troy.
And now it goes as it goes
and where it ends is Fate.
And neither by singeing flesh 75
nor tipping cups of wine[10]
nor shedding burning tears can you
enchant away the rigid Fury.

[CLYTAEMNESTRA *lights the altar-
fires.*]

We are the old, dishonored ones,
the broken husks of men. 80

---

[6]Apollo, Pan, and Zeus are, respectively, the god of prophecy, the god of nature, and the king of the gods.

[7]The Furies are female personifications and agents of vengeance for crime, especially crime against blood kin. In the last play of the trilogy they are redefined as "the Eumenides," or "Kindly Ones."

[8]One of the roles of Zeus. Paris had violated the laws of hospitality by stealing Helen away from the house of his host, Menelaus.

[9]Helen had been courted by innumerable suitors in addition to the man she married (Menelaus) and the man she ran away with (Paris).

[10]Ritual offerings to the gods included sacrificed animals and poured-out wine. The imagery here and the two following lines could refer to any of several persons in the play. Such ambiguity is recurrent in the trilogy.

Even then they cast us off,
the rescue mission[11] left us here
to prop a child's strength upon a stick.
What if the new sap rises in his chest?
He has no soldiery in him,   85
      no more than we,
and we are aged past aging,
gloss of the leaf shriveled,
three legs at a time we falter on.
Old men are children once again,   90
      a dream that sways and wavers
into the hard light of day.
                                        But you,
daughter of Leda, queen Clytaemnestra,
what now, what news, what message
drives you through the citadel   95
      burning victims? Look,
the city gods, the gods of Olympus,
gods of the earth and public markets—
all the altars blazing with your gifts!
      Argos blazes! Torches   100
race the sunrise up her skies—
drugged by the lulling holy oils,
      unadulterated,
run from the dark vaults of kings.
      Tell us the news!   105
What you can, what is right—
Heal us, soothe our fears!
Now the darkness comes to the fore,
now the hope glows through your victims,
beating back this raw, relentless anguish   110
      gnawing at the heart.

                     [CLYTAEMNESTRA *ignores them*
                     and pursues her rituals; they assem-
                     ble for the opening chorus.]

O but I still have power to sound the gods' command at the roads[12]
that launched the kings. The gods breathe power through my
      song,
      my fighting strength, Persuasion grows with the years—

---

[11] The naval and military expedition to bring Helen back from Troy.

[12] In lines 112–258 the chorus recalls fearfully the ominous beginning of the expedition against Troy. The eagles' devouring of the hare was understood by Calchas, the Greek sooth-sayer, to foreshadow the destruction of Troy. But Artemis, goddess of the hunt (and thus protector of pregnant animals) and of childbirth (thus offended by the anticipated slaughter of innocents at Troy) was angered. Unfavorable winds threatened the Greek fleet anchored at Aulis. Ironically, Artemis had to be appeased by the sacrificial killing at Aulis of Agamemnon's daughter Iphigeneia—an example of strict retribution in kind, a central theme in the Orestes trilogy.

I sing how the flight of fury hurled the twin command, 115
         one will that hurled young Greece
and winged the spear of vengeance straight for Troy!
The kings of birds to kings of the beaking prows,[13] one black,
    one with a blaze of silver
           skimmed the palace spearhand right 120
              and swooping lower, all could see,
                  plunged their claws in a hare, a mother
      bursting with unborn young—the babies spilling,
quick spurts of blood—cut off the race just dashing into life!
Cry, cry for death, but good win out in glory in the end. 125

But the loyal seer[14] of the armies studied Atreus' sons,
two sons with warring hearts—he saw two eagle-kings
   devour the hare and spoke the things to come,
"Years pass, and the long hunt nets the city of Priam,
          the flocks beyond the walls, 130
a kingdom's life and soul—Fate stamps them out.
Just let no curse of the gods lour on us first,
    shatter our giant armor
        forged to strangle Troy. I see
           pure Artemis bristle in pity— 135
              yes, the flying hounds of the Father
    slaughter for armies . . . their own victim . . . a woman
trembling young, all born to die—She loathes the eagles' feast!"[15]
Cry, cry for death, but good win out in glory in the end.

    "Artemis, lovely Artemis, so kind 140
to the ravening lion's tender, helpless cubs,
the suckling young of beasts that stalk the wilds—
    bring this sign for all its fortune,
        all its brutal torment home to birth!
I beg you, Healing Apollo,[16] soothe her before 145
her crosswinds hold us down and moor the ships too long,
pressing us on to another victim . . .
      nothing sacred, no
        no feast to be eaten
           the architect of vengeance 150

                [*Turning to the palace.*]

      growing strong in the house
      with no fear of the husband
here she waits

---

[13] The kings of birds are eagles; the kings of the beaking prows are Agamemnon and Menelaus.
[14] Calchas.
[15] We are meant to recall also the abominable meal at which Thyestes was served his children's flesh by Atreus.
[16] Apollo, god of healing, is brother to Artemis.

the terror raging back and back in the future
   the stealth, the law of the hearth, the mother—   155
      Memory womb of Fury child-avenging Fury!"
So as the eagles wheeled at the crossroads,
Calchas clashed out the great good blessings mixed with doom
   for the halls of kings and singing with our fate
we cry, cry for death, but good win out in glory in the end.   160

      Zeus, great nameless all in all,
      if that name will gain his favor,
         I will call him Zeus.
      I have no words to do him justice,
         weighing all in the balance,   165
         all I have is Zeus, Zeus—
Lift this weight, this torment from my spirit,
         cast it once for all.

      He who was so mighty once,[17]
      storming for the wars of heaven,   170
         he has had his day.
And then his son who came to power
      met his match in the third fall
      and he is gone. Zeus, Zeus—
raise your cries and sing him Zeus the Victor!   175
      You will reach the truth:

      Zeus has led us on to know,
      the Helmsman lays it down as law
      that we must suffer, suffer into truth.
We cannot sleep, and drop by drop at the heart   180
      the pain of pain remembered comes again,
      and we resist, but ripeness comes as well.
From the gods enthroned on the awesome rowing-bench
      there comes a violent love.

      So it was that day the king,   185
      the steersman at the helm of Greece,
would never blame a word the prophet said—
swept away by the wrenching winds of fortune
he conspired! Weatherbound we could not sail,
our stores exhausted, fighting strength hard-pressed,   190
      and the squadrons rode in the shallows off Chalkis[18]
      where the riptide crashes, drags,

and winds from the north pinned down our hulls at Aulis,
port of anguish . . . head winds starving,

---

[17] The following lines describe the overthrow of Ouranos (Uranus) by his son Kronos (Saturn) and of the latter by his son Zeus, who now reigns as supreme god.
[18] Chalkis, on the island Euboea, faced the port of Aulis on the mainland.

sheets and the cables snapped 195
　　and the men's minds strayed,
　　the pride, the bloom of Greece
　　was raked as time ground on,
ground down, and then the cure for the storm
and it was harsher—Calchas cried, 200
"My captains, Artemis must have blood!"—
　　as harsh the sons of Atreus
　　　　dashed their scepters on the rocks,
　　could not hold back the tears,

and I still can hear the older warlord saying, 205
"Obey, obey, or a heavy doom will crush me—
Oh but doom *will* crush me
　　once I rend my child,
　　　　the glory of my house—
　　a father's hands are stained, 210
blood of a young girl streaks the altar.
Pain both ways and what is worse?
Desert the fleets, fail the alliance?
　　No, but stop the winds with a virgin's blood,
　　　　feed their lust, their fury?—feed their fury!— 215
　　Law is law!—
　　　　Let all go well."

And once he slipped his neck in the strap of Fate,
his spirit veering black, impure, unholy,
once he turned he stopped at nothing,
　　seized with the frenzy 220
　　　　　　blinding driving to outrage—
wretched frenzy, cause of all our grief!
Yes, he had the heart
　　to sacrifice his daughter!—
　　to bless the war that avenged a woman's loss, 225
　　　　a bridal rite that sped the men-of-war.

"My father, father!"—she might pray to the winds;
no innocence moves her judges mad for war.
Her father called his henchmen on,
　　on with a prayer, 230
　　　　　"Hoist her over the altar
like a yearling, give it all your strength!
She's fainting—lift her,
　　sweep her robes around her,
　　but slip this strap in her gentle curving lips . . . 235
　　　　　here, gag her hard, a sound will curse the house"—
and the bridle chokes her voice . . . her saffron[19] robes

---

[19] Orange-yellow, the traditional color of the bridal garment.

pouring over the sand
                    her glance like arrows showering
wounding every murderer through with pity
                    clear as a picture, live,   240
she strains to call their names . . .
I remember often the days with father's guests
when over the feast her voice unbroken,
     pure as the hymn her loving father
bearing third libations, sang to Saving Zeus—   245
transfixed with joy, Atreus' offspring
          throbbing out their love.

What comes next? I cannot see it, cannot say.
The strong techniques of Calchas do their work.

But Justice turns the balance scales,   250
          sees that we suffer
and we suffer and we learn.
And we will know the future when it comes.
Greet it too early, weep too soon.
          It all comes clear in the light of day.   255
Let all go well today, well as she could want,

                              [*Turning to* CLYTAEMNESTRA.]

our midnight watch, our lone defender,
          single-minded queen.
LEADER.[20]
                              We've come,
Clytaemnestra. We respect your power.
Right it is to honor the warlord's woman   260
once he leaves the throne.
                              But why these fires?
Good news, or more good hopes? We're loyal,
we want to hear, but never blame your silence.
CLYTAEMNESTRA.
Let the new day shine, as the proverb says,
glorious from the womb of Mother Night.[21]   265

                              [*Lost in prayer, then turning to the*
                              CHORUS.]

You will hear a joy beyond your hopes.
Priam's citadel—the Greeks have taken Troy!
LEADER.
No, what do you mean? I can't believe it.

---

[20] The principal spokesman for the chorus.
[21] Ironically, the avenging Furies are also offspring of the primeval Night.

CLYTAEMNESTRA.
Troy is ours. Is that clear enough?
LEADER.
The joy of it,
stealing over me, calling up my tears— 270
CLYTAEMNESTRA.
Yes, your eyes expose your loyal hearts.
LEADER.
And you have proof?
CLYTAEMNESTRA.
I do,
I must. Unless the god is lying.
LEADER.
That,
or a phantom spirit sends you into raptures.
CLYTAEMNESTRA.
No one takes me in with visions—senseless dreams. 275
LEADER.
Or giddy rumor, you haven't indulged yourself—
CLYTAEMNESTRA.
You treat me like a child, you mock me?
LEADER.
Then when did they storm the city?
CLYTAEMNESTRA.
Last night, I say, the mother of this morning.
LEADER.
And who on earth could run the news so fast? 280
CLYTAEMNESTRA.
The god of fire—rushing fire from Ida![22]
And beacon to beacon rushed it on to me,
my couriers riding home the torch.
From Troy
to the bare rock of Lemnos, Hermes' Spur,
and the Escort winged the great light west 285
to the Saving Father's face, Mount Athos hurled it
third in the chain and leaping Ocean's back
the blaze went dancing on to ecstasy—pitch-pine
streaming gold like a newborn sun—and brought
the word in flame to Mount Makistos' brow. 290
No time to waste, straining, fighting sleep,

---

[22]A mountain range near Troy. Clytaemnestra's description of the progress of the flame signal from Troy to Argos is filled with ironic overtones. Mount Athos, here associated with Zeus as "Saving Father," recalls by contrast Agamemnon's slaying of his daughter Iphigeneia; the "murderous" straits of Euripos are the location of her death; the "Black Widow" (Mount Arachnaion, or "Spider Mountain") suggests both Clytaemnestra herself and a web, one of the variants of the net imagery ubiquitous in the play; the "true son" of Ida suggests the causal link between Agamemnon's Trojan adventure and his fate at his homecoming, as well as foreshadowing the avenging role of his son Orestes.

that lookout heaved a torch glowing over
the murderous straits of Euripos to reach
Messapion's watchmen craning for the signal.
Fire for word of fire! tense with the heather   295
withered gray, they stack it, set it ablaze—
the hot force of the beacon never flags,
it springs the Plain of Asôpos, rears
like a harvest moon to hit Kithairon's crest
and drives new men to drive the fire on.   300
That relay pants for the farflung torch,
they swell its strength outstripping my commands
and the light inflames the marsh, the Gorgon's Eye,
it strikes the peak where the wild goats range—
my law, my fire whips that camp!   305
They spare nothing, eager to build its heat,
and a huge beard of flame overcomes the headland
beetling down the Saronic Gulf, and flaring south
it brings the dawn to the Black Widow's face—
the watch that looms above your heads—and now   310
the true son of the burning flanks of Ida
crashes on the roofs of Atreus' sons!

And I ordained it all.
Torch to torch, running for their lives,
one long succession racing home my fire.
                                        One,   315
first in the laps and last,[23] wins out in triumph.
There you have my proof, *my* burning sign, I tell you—
the power my lord passed on from Troy to me.
LEADER.
    We'll thank the gods, my lady—first this story,
    let me lose myself in the wonder of it all!   320
    Tell it start to finish, tell us all.
CLYTAEMNESTRA.
    The city's ours—in our hands this very day!
    I can hear the cries in crossfire rock the walls.
    Pour oil and wine in the same bowl,
    what have you, friendship? A struggle to the end.   325
    So with the victors and the victims—outcries,
    you can hear them clashing like their fates.

    They are kneeling by the bodies of the dead,
    embracing men and brothers, infants over
    the aged loins that gave them life, and sobbing,   330
    as the yoke constricts their last free breath,
    for every dear one lost.

[23]A winning relay team ("first in the laps") achieves the victory when the runner of the anchor leg (the "last") crosses the finish line.

And the others,
there, plunging breakneck through the night—
the labor of battle sets them down, ravenous,
to breakfast on the last remains of Troy. 335
Not by rank but the lots of chance they draw,
they lodge in the houses captured by the spear,
settling in so soon, released from the open sky,
the frost and dew. Lucky men, off guard at last,
they sleep away their first good night in years. 340

If only they are revering the city's gods,
the shrines of the gods who love the conquered land,
no plunderer will be plundered in return.
Just let no lust, no mad desire seize the armies
to ravish what they must not touch— 345
overwhelmed by all they've won!
                                    The run for home
and safety waits, the swerve at the post,[24]
the final lap of the grueling two-lap race.
And even if the men come back with no offense
to the gods, the avenging dead[25] may never rest— 350
Oh let no new disaster strike! And here
you have it, what a woman has to say.
Let the best win out, clear to see.
A small desire but all that I could want.
LEADER.
Spoken like a man, my lady, loyal, 355
full of self-command. I've heard your sign
and now your vision.

[*Reaching toward her as she turns
and re-enters the palace.*]

                    Now to praise the gods.
The joy is worth the labor.
CHORUS.
O Zeus my king and Night, dear Night,[26]
queen of the house who covers us with glories, 360
you slung your net on the towers of Troy,
neither young nor strong could leap
the giant dredge net of slavery,
        all-embracing ruin.

---

[24] The turning-post in a race, where the racers turn and head back for where they started.

[25] The chorus is meant to apply the phrase to the Trojan dead; Clytaemnestra also alludes cryptically to her dead daughter.

[26] The chorus in this passage concentrates on Paris as the evil man whom the gods punish, but much of what they say applies also to Agamemnon and the whole line of Atreus. In the latter part of the song (lines 426 ff.), the chorus begins to sense dimly this more general guilt.

I adore you, iron Zeus of the guests   365
and your revenge—you drew your longbow
year by year to a taut full draw
till one bolt, not falling short
or arching over the stars,
        could split the mark of Paris!   370
The sky stroke of god!—it is all Troy's to tell,
but even I can trace it to its cause:
god does as god decrees.
        And still some say
that heaven would never stoop to punish men   375
who trample the lovely grace of things
untouchable. How wrong they are!
        A curse burns bright on crime—
                full-blown, the father's crimes will blossom,
                burst into the son's.   380
Let there be less suffering . . .
give us the sense to live on what we need.

                Bastions of wealth
                are no defense for the man
                who treads the grand altar of Justice   385
                        down and out of sight.

Persuasion, maddening child of Ruin
overpowers him—Ruin plans it all.
And the wound will smolder on,
        there is no cure,   390
a terrible brilliance kindles on the night.
He is bad bronze scraped on a touchstone:²⁷
put to the test, the man goes black.
        Like the boy who chases
                a bird on the wing,²⁸ brands his city,   395
                brings it down and prays,
but the gods are deaf
to the one who turns to crime, they tear him down.

                So Paris learned:
                he came to Atreus' house   400
                and shamed the tables spread for guests,
                        he stole away the queen.

And she left her land *chaos*, clanging shields,
companions tramping, bronze prows, men in bronze,
        and she came to Troy with a dowry, death,   405
strode through the gates
                defiant in every stride,

²⁷A stone that, rubbed against a metal, shows whether the metal is true or counterfeit.
²⁸To chase a bird on the wing is foolishly to attempt the impossible.

as prophets of the house looked on and wept,
"Oh the halls and the lords of war,
    the bed and the fresh prints of love. 410
I *see* him,[29] unavenging, unavenged,
the stun of his desolation is so clear—
    he longs for the one who lies across the sea
until her phantom seems to sway the house.

            Her curving images, 415
            her beauty hurts her lord,
            the eyes starve and the touch
                of love is gone,

"and radiant dreams are passing in the night,
the memories throb with sorrow, joy with pain . . . 420
    it is pain to dream and see desires
slip through the arms,
            a vision lost forever
winging down the moving drifts of sleep."
So he grieves at the royal hearth 425
    yet others' grief is worse, far worse.
All through Greece for those who flocked to war
they are holding back the anguish now,
    you can feel it rising now in every house;
I tell you there is much to tear the heart. 430

            They knew the men they sent,
            but now in place of men
            ashes and urns come back
                to every hearth.

War, War, the great gold-broker of corpses 435
holds the balance of the battle on his spear!
Home from the pyres he sends them,
    home from Troy to the loved ones,
weighted with tears, the urns brimmed full,
    the heroes return in gold-dust, 440
dear, light ash for men; and they weep,
they praise them, "He had skill in the swordplay,"
        "He went down so tall in the onslaught,"
"All for another's woman." So they mutter
in secret and the rancor steals 445
toward our staunch defenders, Atreus' sons.

            And there they ring the walls, the young,
            the lithe, the handsome hold the graves
            they won in Troy; the enemy earth
                rides over those who conquered. 450

[29] The primary reference is to Menelaus left alone without Helen.

The people's voice is heavy with hatred,
now the curses of the people must be paid,
and now I wait, I listen . . .
    there—there is something breathing
under the night's shroud. God takes aim   455
    at the ones who murder many;
the swarthy Furies stalk the man
gone rich beyond all rights—with a twist
    of fortune grind him down, dissolve him
into the blurring dead—there is no help.   460
The reach for power can recoil,
the bolt of god can strike you at a glance.

          Make me rich with no man's envy,
          neither a raider of cities, no,
          nor slave come face to face with life   465
          overpowered by another.

                  [*Speaking singly.*]

—Fire comes and the news is good,
    it races through the streets
    but is it true? Who knows?
    Or just another lie from heaven?   470

—Show us the man so childish, wonderstruck,
    he's fired up with the first torch,
    then when the message shifts
    he's sick at heart.

              —Just like a woman
to fill with thanks before the truth is clear.   475

—So gullible. Their stories spread like wildfire,
    they fly fast and die faster;
    rumors voiced by women come to nothing.
LEADER.
Soon we'll know her fires for what they are,
her relay race of torches hand-to-hand—   480
know if they're real or just a dream,
the hope of a morning here to take our senses.
I see a herald running from the beach
and a victor's spray of olive shades his eyes
and the dust he kicks, twin to the mud of Troy,   485
shows he has a voice—no kindling timber
on the cliffs, no signal-fires for him.
He can shout the news and give us joy,
or else . . . please, not that.
                Bring it on,
good fuel to build the first good fires.   490

And if anyone calls down the worst on Argos
let him reap the rotten harvest of his mind.

[*The* HERALD *rushes in and kneels
on the ground.*]

HERALD.
Good Greek earth, the soil of my fathers!
Ten years out, and a morning brings me back.
All hopes snapped but one—I'm home at last.   495
Never dreamed I'd die in Greece, assigned
the narrow plot I love the best.
                              And now
I salute the land, the light of the sun,
our high lord Zeus and the king of Pytho[30]—
no more arrows, master, raining on our heads!   500
At Scamander's banks we took our share,
your longbow brought us down like plague.
Now come, deliver us, heal us—lord Apollo!
Gods of the market, here, take my salute.

And you, my Hermes, Escort,   505
loving Herald, the herald's shield and prayer!—
And the shining dead of the land who launched the armies,
warm us home . . . we're all the spear has left.

You halls of the kings, you roofs I cherish,
sacred seats—you gods that catch the sun,   510
if your glances ever shone on him in the old days,
greet him well—so many years are lost.
He comes, he brings us light in the darkness,
free for every comrade, Agamemnon lord of men.

Give him the royal welcome he deserves!   515
He hoisted the pickax of Zeus who brings revenge,
he dug Troy down, he worked her soil down,
the shrines of her gods and the high altars, gone!—
and the seed of her wide earth he ground to bits.
That's the yoke he claps on Troy. The king,   520
the son of Atreus comes. The man is blest,
the one man alive to merit such rewards.

Neither Paris nor Troy, partners to the end,
can say their work outweighs their wages now.
Convicted of rapine, stripped of all his spoils,   525
and his father's house and the land that gave it life—
he's scythed them to the roots. The sons of Priam
pay the price twice over.

---

[30] The archer god Apollo, who had sided with the Trojans and launched the arrows of plague
against the Greeks.

LEADER.
                              Welcome home
  from the wars, herald, long live your joy.
HERALD.
                                        Our joy—
  now I could die gladly. Say the word, dear gods.   530
LEADER.
    Longing for your country left you raw?
HERALD.
    The tears fill my eyes, for joy.
LEADER.
                              You too,
  down the sweet disease that kills a man
  with kindness . . .
HERALD.
                    Go on, I don't see what you—
LEADER.
                                        Love
  for the ones who love you—that's what took you.
HERALD.
                                        You mean   535
  the land and the armies hungered for each other?
LEADER.
    There were times I thought I'd faint with longing.
HERALD.
    So anxious for the armies, why?
LEADER.
                              For years now,
  only my silence kept me free from harm.
HERALD.
                                        What,
  with the kings gone did someone threaten you?
LEADER.
                                        So much . . .   540
  now as you say, it would be good to die.
HERALD.
    True, we *have* done well.
    Think back in the years and what have you?
    A few runs of luck, a lot that's bad.
    Who but a god can go through life unmarked?   545

    A long, hard pull we had, if I would tell it all.
    The iron rations, penned in the gangways
    hock by jowl like sheep. Whatever miseries
    break a man, our quota, every sunstarved day.

    Then on the beaches it was worse. Dug in   550
    under the enemy ramparts—deadly going.
    Out of the sky, out of the marshy flats
    the dews soaked us, turned the ruts we fought from

into gullies, made our gear, our scalps
crawl with lice.
                        And talk of the cold,   555
the sleet to freeze the gulls, and the big snows
come avalanching down from Ida. Oh but the heat,
the sea and the windless noons, the swells asleep,
dropped to a dead calm . . .

But why weep now?   560
It's over for us, over for them.
The dead can rest and never rise again;
no need to call their muster. We're alive,
do we have to go on raking up old wounds?
Good-by to all that. Glad I am to say it.   565

For us, the remains of the Greek contingents,
the good wins out, no pain can tip the scales,
not now. So shout this boast to the bright sun—
fitting it is—wing it over the seas and rolling earth:
"Once when an Argive expedition captured Troy   570
they hauled these spoils back to the gods of Greece,
they bolted them high across the temple doors,
the glory of the past!"
                        And hearing that,
men will applaud our city and our chiefs,
and Zeus will have the hero's share of fame—   575
he did the work.
                        That's all I have to say.
LEADER.
I'm convinced, glad that I was wrong.
Never too old to learn; it keeps me young.

                        [CLYTAEMNESTRA *enters with her*
                        women.]

First the house and the queen, it's their affair,
but I can taste the riches.
CLYTAEMNESTRA.
                        I cried out long ago!—   580
for joy, when the first herald came burning
through the night and told the city's fall.
And there were some who smiled and said,
"A few fires persuade you Troy's in ashes.
Women, women, elated over nothing."   585

You made me seem deranged.
For all that I sacrificed—a woman's way,
you'll say—station to station on the walls
we lifted cries of triumph that resounded

in the temples of the gods. We lulled and blessed   590
the fires with myrrh and they consumed our victims.

[*Turning to the* HERALD.]

But enough. Why prolong the story?
From the king himself I'll gather all I need.
Now for the best way to welcome home
my lord, my good lord . . .
                              No time to lose!   595
What dawn can feast a woman's eyes like this?
I can see the light, the husband plucked from war
by the Saving God and open wide the gates.

Tell him that, and have him come with speed,
the people's darling—how they long for him.   600
And for his wife,
may he return and find her true at hall,
just as the day he left her, faithful to the last.
A watchdog gentle to him alone,

[*Glancing toward the palace.*]

                              savage
to those who cross his path. I have not changed.   605
The strains of time can never break our seal.
In love with a new lord, in ill repute I am
as practiced as I am in dyeing bronze.

That is my boast, teeming with the truth.
I am proud, a woman of my nobility—   610
I'd hurl it from the roofs!

[*She turns sharply, enters the palace.*]

LEADER.
    She speaks well, but it takes no seer to know
    she only says what's right.

[*The* HERALD *attempts to leave; the*
LEADER *takes him by the arm.*]

                    Wait, one thing.
    Menelaus, is he home too, safe with the men?
    The power of the land—dear king.   615
HERALD.
    I doubt that lies will help my friends,
    in the lean months to come.
LEADER.
    Help us somehow, tell the truth as well.

But when the two conflict it's hard to hide—
out with it.
HERALD.
               He's lost, gone from the fleets!   620
He and his ship, it's true.
LEADER.
                   After you watched him
pull away from Troy? Or did some storm
attack you all and tear him off the line?
HERALD.
                       There,
like a marksman, the whole disaster cut to a word.
LEADER.
How do the escorts give him out—dead or alive?   625
HERALD.
No clear report. No one knows . . .
only the wheeling sun that heats the earth to life.
LEADER.
But then the storm—how did it reach the ships?
How did it end? Were the angry gods on hand?
HERALD.
This blessed day, ruin it with *them?*   630
Better to keep their trophies far apart.
When a runner comes, his face in tears,
saddled with what his city dreaded most,
the armies routed, two wounds in one,
one to the city, one to hearth and home . . .   635
our best men, droves of them, victims
herded from every house by the two-barb whip
that Ares[31] likes to crack,
                 that charioteer
who packs destruction shaft by shaft,
careening on with his brace of bloody mares—   640
When he comes in, I tell you, dragging that much pain,
wail your battle-hymn to the Furies, and high time!

But when he brings salvation home to a city
singing out her heart—
how can I mix the good with so much bad   645
and blurt out this?—
             "Storms swept the Greeks,
and not without the anger of the gods!"

Those enemies for ages, fire and water,
sealed a pact and showed it to the world—
they crushed our wretched squadrons.
                 Night looming,   650
breakers lunging in for the kill

---

[31] God of war.

and the black gales come brawling out of the north—
ships ramming, prow into hooking prow, gored
by the rush-and-buck of hurricane pounding rain
by the cloudburst—
                ships stampeding into the darkness,   655
lashed and spun by the savage shepherd's hand!

But when the sun comes up to light the skies
I see the Aegean heaving into a great bloom
of corpses . . . Greeks, the pick of a generation
scattered through the wrecks and broken spars.   660

But not us, not our ship, our hull untouched.
Someone stole us away or begged us off.
No mortal—a god, death grip on the tiller,
or lady luck herself, perched on the helm,
she pulled us through, she saved us. Aye,   665
we'll never battle the heavy surf at anchor,
never shipwreck up some rocky coast.

But once we cleared that sea-hell, not even
trusting luck in the cold light of day,
we battened on our troubles, they were fresh—   670
the armada punished, bludgeoned into nothing.

And now if one of them still has the breath
he's saying *we* are lost. Why not?
We say the same of him. Well,
here's to the best.
                And Menelaus?   675
Look to it, he's come back, and yet . . .
if a shaft of the sun can track him down,
alive, and his eyes full of the old fire—
thanks to the strategies of Zeus, Zeus
would never tear the house out by the roots—   680
then there's hope our man will make it home.

You've heard it all. Now you have the truth.

[*Rushing out.*]

CHORUS.
    Who—what power named the name that drove your fate?—[32]
    what hidden brain could divine your future,

[32] The foregoing inquiries about Menelaus lead naturally to the theme of this choral passage: the significance of Helen, whom Menelaus was bringing home. The chorus, punning on the root meaning of Helen's name in Greek ("destruction," rendered here as "hell"), see her as an agent of ruin inflicted as just punishment for Paris and the Trojans. She is also, however, a scourge to Greece and to the house of Atreus.

steer that word to the mark, 685
to the bride of spears,
    the whirlpool churning armies,
        Oh for all the world a Helen!
Hell at the prows, hell at the gates
hell on the men-of-war, 690
from her lair's sheer veils she drifted
    launched by the giant western wind,
      and the long tall waves of men in armor,
huntsmen trailing the oarblades' dying spoor[33]
slipped into her moorings, 695
    Simois'[34] mouth that chokes with foliage,
        bayed for bloody strife,

for Troy's Blood Wedding Day—she drives her word,
her burning will to the birth, the Fury
late but true to the cause, 700
to the tables shamed
    and Zeus who guards the hearth—
      the Fury makes the Trojans pay!
Shouting their hymns, hymns for the bride
hymns for the kinsmen doomed 705
to the wedding march of Fate,
    Troy changed her tune in her late age,
      and I think I hear the dirges mourning
"Paris, born and groomed for the bed of Fate!"
They mourn with their life breath, 710
    they sing their last, the sons of Priam
        born for bloody slaughter.

So a man[35] once reared
a lion cub at hall, snatched
from the breast, still craving milk 715
    in the first flush of life.
A captivating pet for the young,
and the old men adored it, pampered it
    in their arms, day in, day out,
like an infant just born. 720
Its eyes on fire, little beggar,
fawning for its belly, slave to food.

    But it came of age
and the parent strain broke out
and it paid its breeders back. 725

[33] The track of a wild animal. Having sailed from her home to Troy, Helen is pursued by the Greek fleet ("huntsmen") sailing to recover her.

[34] A river near Troy.

[35] Helen is compared to a lion cub reared as a household pet until, having grown, its latent nature asserts itself in bloodshed. The house can be the Trojans' or that of Agamemnon and Menelaus.

Grateful it was,[36] it went
through the flock to prepare a feast,
an illicit orgy—the house swam with blood,
        none could resist that agony—
                        massacre vast and raw!   730
From god there came a priest of ruin,
adopted by the house to lend it warmth.

And the first sensation Helen brought to Troy . . .
call it a spirit
        shimmer of winds dying   735
                glory light as gold
        shaft of the eyes dissolving, open bloom
    that wounds the heart with love.
But veering wild in mid-flight
she whirled her wedding on to a stabbing end,   740
slashed at the sons of Priam—hearthmate, friend to the death,
        sped by Zeus who speeds the guest,
a bride of tears, a Fury.

There's an ancient saying,[37] old as man himself:
men's prosperity   745
        never will die childless,
                once full-grown it breeds.
        Sprung from the great good fortune in the race
    comes bloom on bloom of pain—
insatiable wealth. But not I,   750
I alone say this. Only the reckless act
can breed impiety, multiplying crime on crime,
        while the house kept straight and just
is blessed with radiant children.

                But ancient Violence longs to breed,   755
                        new Violence comes
            when its fatal hour comes, the demon comes
            to take her toll—no war, no force, no prayer
                can hinder the midnight Fury stamped
            with parent Fury moving through the house.   760

                But Justice shines in sooty hovels,
                        loves the decent life.
        From proud halls crusted with gilt by filthy hands
            she turns her eyes to find the pure in spirit—
        spurning the wealth stamped counterfeit with praise,   765
            she steers all things toward their destined end.

---

[36]Grim humor; the grown lion is like someone thankfully repaying parents for rearing him.
[37]In the following lines the chorus echoes the traditional belief that excess of prosperity in itself brings on punishment by the gods, but the old men go on to insist that the more important cause is evil deeds. Wealth acquired through evil combines both incitements to divine retribution.

[AGAMEMNON *enters in his chariot, his plunder borne before him by his entourage; behind him, half hidden, stands* CASSANDRA.[38] *The old men press toward him.*]

Come, my king, the scourge of Troy,
    the true son of Atreus—
How to salute you, how to praise you
neither too high nor low, but hit   770
the note of praise that suits the hour?
So many prize some brave display,
they prefer some flaunt of honor
    once they break the bounds.
When a man fails they share his grief,   775
but the pain can never cut them to the quick.
When a man succeeds they share his glory,
torturing their faces into smiles.
But the good shepherd[39] knows his flock.
When the eyes seem to brim with love   780
    and it is only unction,
he will know, better than we can know.
That day you marshaled the armies
all for Helen—no hiding it now—
I drew you in my mind in black;   785
you seemed a menace at the helm,
    sending men to the grave
to bring her home, that hell on earth.
But now from the depths of trust and love
I say Well fought, well won—   790
    the end is worth the labor!
Search, my king, and learn at last
who stayed at home and kept their faith
    and who betrayed the city.
AGAMEMNON.
                First,
with justice I salute my Argos and my gods,   795
my accomplices who brought me home and won
my rights from Priam's Troy—the just gods.
No need to hear our pleas. Once for all
they consigned their lots to the urn[40] of blood,
they pitched on death for men, annihilation   800
for the city. Hope's hand, hovering
over the urn of mercy, left it empty.

---

[38]A prophetess, daughter of King Priam of Troy, taken captive by Agamemnon.
[39]Agamemnon, regarded as protector of his subjects.
[40]In deciding law cases, an Athenian juror cast his vote by dropping a pebble into one of two urns signifying conviction and acquittal.

Look for the smoke—it is the city's seamark,
building even now.
                              The storms of ruin live!
Her last dying breath, rising up from the ashes   805
send us gales of incense rich in gold.

For that we must thank the gods with a sacrifice
our sons will long remember. For their mad outrage
of a queen we raped their city—we were right.
The beast of Argos, foals of the wild mare,[41]   810
thousands massed in armor rose on the night
the Pleiades [42] went down, and crashing through
their walls our bloody lion lapped its fill,
gorging on the blood of kings.
                              Our thanks to the gods,
long drawn out, but it is just the prelude.   815

                    [CLYTAEMNESTRA *approaches with her
                    women; they are carrying dark red tapes-
                    tries.* AGAMEMNON *turns to the leader.*]

And your concern, old man, is on my mind.
I hear you and agree, I will support you.
How rare, men with the character to praise
a friend's success without a trace of envy,
poison to the heart—it deals a double blow.   820
Your own losses weigh you down but then,
look at your neighbor's fortune and you weep.
Well I know. I understand society,
the fawning mirror of the proud.
                              My comrades . . .
they're shadows, I tell you, ghosts of men   825
who swore they'd die for me. Only Odysseus:
I dragged that man to the wars but once in harness
he was a trace-horse, he gave his all for me.
Dead or alive, no matter, I can praise him.

And now this cause involving men and gods.   830
We must summon the city for a trial,
found a national tribunal. Whatever's healthy,
shore it up with law and help it flourish.
Wherever something calls for drastic cures
we make our noblest effort: amputate or wield   835
the healing iron, burn the cancer at the roots.

---

[41]Agamemnon refers to the Greek soldiers who, hidden inside the wooden horse, brought
about the fall of Troy. The story is told in Virgil's *Aeneid*, Book II.
    [42] The setting of this constellation is associated in the present context with the approach
of winter and storms.

Now I go to my father's house—
I give the gods my right hand, my first salute.
The ones who sent me forth have brought me home.

> [*He starts down from the chariot,
> looks at* CLYTAEMNESTRA, *stops,
> and offers up a prayer.*]

Victory, you have sped my way before,   840
now speed me to the last.

> [CLYTAEMNESTRA *turns from the
> king to the* CHORUS.]

CLYTAEMNESTRA.
                    Old nobility of Argos
gathered here, I am not ashamed to tell you
how I love the man. I am older,
and the fear dies away . . . I am human.
Nothing I say was learned from others.   845
This is my life, my ordeal, long as the siege
he laid at Troy and more demanding.

                    First,
when a woman sits at home and the man is gone,
the loneliness is terrible,
unconscionable . . .   850
and the rumors spread and fester,
a runner comes with something dreadful,
close on his heels the next and his news worse,
and they shout it out and the whole house can hear;
and wounds—if he took one wound for each report 855
to penetrate these walls, he's gashed like a dragnet,
more, if he had only died . . .
for each death that swelled his record, he could boast
like a triple-bodied Geryon[43] risen from the grave,
"Three shrouds I dug from the earth, one for every body 860
that went down!"
                    The rumors broke like fever,
broke and then rose higher. There were times
they cut me down and eased my throat from the noose.
I wavered between the living and the dead.

> [*Turning to* AGAMEMNON.]

                    And so
our child is gone, not standing by our side,   865

---

[43]A three-headed giant.

the bond of our dearest pledges, mine and yours;
by all rights our child should be here . . .
Orestes.[44] You seem startled.
You needn't be. Our loyal brother-in-arms
will take good care of him, Strophios the Phocian.   870
He warned from the start we court two griefs in one.
You risk all on the wars—and what if the people
rise up howling for the king, and anarchy
should dash our plans?
                                        Men, it is their nature,
trampling on the fighter once he's down.   875
Our child is gone. That is my self-defense
and it is true.
                        For me, the tears that welled
like springs are dry. I have no tears to spare.
I'd watch till late at night, my eyes still burn,
I sobbed by the torch I lit for you alone.   880

                            [*Glancing toward the palace.*]

I never let it die . . . but in my dreams
the high thin wail of a gnat would rouse me,
piercing like a trumpet—I could see you
suffer more than all
the hours that slept with me could ever bear.   885

I endured it all. And now, free of grief,
I would salute that man the watchdog of the fold,
the mainroyal, saving stay[45] of the vessel,
rooted oak that thrusts the roof sky-high,
the father's one true heir.   890
Land at dawn to the shipwrecked past all hope,
light of the morning burning off the night of storm,
the cold clear spring to the parched horseman—
O the ecstasy, to flee the yoke of Fate!

It is right to use the titles he deserves.   895
Let envy keep her distance. We have suffered
long enough.

                                [*Reaching toward* AGAMEMNON.]

---

[44] One of the many ironies in Clytaemnestra's speech; the preceding lines suggest Orestes'
dead sister Iphigeneia. Clytaemnestra has sent Orestes away to the city of Phocis, to clear the
way for Aegisthus and herself, or to protect Orestes against civil mutiny while his father was
away, or perhaps for both reasons.
[45] A cable that supports the mainroyal mast of a ship.

Come to me now, my dearest,
down from the car of war, but never set the foot
that stamped out Troy on earth again, my great one.

Women, why delay? You have your orders. 900
Pave his way with tapestries.

> [*They begin to spread the crimson
> tapestries between the king and the
> palace doors.*]

Quickly.
Let the red stream flow and bear him home
to the home he never hoped to see[46]—Justice,
lead him in!
Leave all the rest to me.
The spirit within me never yields to sleep. 905
We will set things right, with the gods' help.
We will do whatever Fate requires.
AGAMEMNON.
There
is Leda's daughter,[47] the keeper of my house.
And the speech to suit my absence, much too long.
But the praise that does us justice, 910
let it come from others, then we prize it.
This—
You treat me like a woman, groveling, gaping up at me!
What am I, some barbarian peacocking out of Asia?
Never cross my path with robes and draw the lightning.
Never—only the gods deserve the pomps of honor 915
and the stiff brocades of fame. To walk on them . . .
I am human, and it makes my pulses stir
with dread.[48]
Give me the tributes of a man
and not a god, a little earth to walk on,
not this gorgeous work. 920
There is no need to sound my reputation.
I have a sense of right and wrong, what's more—
heaven's proudest gift. Call no man blest
until he ends his life in peace, fulfilled.
If I can live by what I say, I have no fear. 925
CLYTAEMNESTRA.
One thing more. Be true to your ideals and tell me—

---

[46]A grim pun: both "the home in Argos he had lost hope of seeing again" and "the home (death) he hoped never to see."

[47]Clytaemnestra; she and Helen are half-sisters, Leda being mother to both.

[48]Agamemnon feels (or perhaps feigns) reluctance to commit an act of *hubris,* the overweening pride of a man which will bring on angry retribution by the gods.

AGAMEMNON.
  True to my ideals? Once I violate them I am lost.
CLYTAEMNESTRA.
  Would you have sworn this act[49] to god in a time of terror?
AGAMEMNON.
  Yes, if a prophet called for a last, drastic rite.
CLYTAEMNESTRA.
  But Priam—can you see him if he had your success?   930
AGAMEMNON.
  Striding on the tapestries of god, I see him now.
CLYTAEMNESTRA.
  And *you* fear the reproach of common men?
AGAMEMNON.
  The voice of the people—aye, they have enormous power.
CLYTAEMNESTRA.
  Perhaps, but where's the glory without a little gall?[50]
AGAMEMNON.
  And where's the woman in all this lust for glory?   935
CLYTAEMNESTRA.
  But the great victor—it becomes him to give away.
AGAMEMNON.
  Victory in this . . . war of ours, it means so much to you?
CLYTAEMNESTRA.
  O give way! The power is yours[51] if you surrender
  all of your own free will to me.
AGAMEMNON.
                                         Enough.
  If you are so determined—   940

                              [*Turning to the women, pointing to
                                his boots.*]

  Let someone help me off with these at least.
  Old slaves, they've stood me well.
                                         Hurry,
  and while I tread his splendors dyed red in the sea,[52]
  may no god watch and strike me down with envy
  from on high. I feel such shame—   945
  to tread the life of the house, a kingdom's worth
  of silver in the weaving.

---

[49]Clytaemnestra refers to the act of walking on the splendid "red carpet." She also has in mind Agamemnon's willingness in the past to commit an outrage like the killing of his daughter when such an outrage served his purpose.

[50]Clytaemnestra implies that great men must be prepared to endure the "gall" of inferior men's envy.

[51]That is, "If you yield freely and magnanimously to my whim, it is you who will have overcome me" (in their little dispute, what Agamemnon calls "this . . . war of ours").

[52]The red dye of the tapestry-carpet was derived from a kind of sea snail.

[He steps down from the chariot to the tapestries and reveals CASSANDRA, *dressed in the sacred regalia, the fillets,[53] robes, and scepter of* APOLLO.]

Done is done.
Escort this stranger in, be gentle.
Conquer with compassion. Then the gods
shine down upon you, gently. No one chooses   950
the yoke of slavery, not of one's free will—
and she least of all. The gift of the armies,
flower and pride of all the wealth we won,
she follows me from Troy.
                                    And now,
since you have brought me down with your insistence,   955
just this once I enter my father's house,
trampling royal crimson as I go.

[He takes his first steps and pauses.]

CLYTAEMNESTRA.
                              There is the sea
and who will drain it dry? Precious as silver,[54]
inexhaustible, ever-new, it breeds the more we reap it—
tides on tides of crimson dye our robes blood-red.   960
Our lives are based on wealth, my king,
the gods have seen to that.
Destitution, our house has never heard the word.
I would have sworn to tread on legacies of robes,
at one command from an oracle, deplete the house—   965
suffer the worst to bring that dear life back!

[Encouraged, AGAMEMNON *strides to the entrance.]*

When the root lives on, the new leaves come back,
spreading a dense shroud of shade across the house
to thwart the Dog Star's[55] fury. So you return
to the father's hearth, you bring us warmth in winter   970
like the sun—
                    And you are Zeus when Zeus
tramples the bitter virgin grape for new wine[56]
and the welcome chill steals through the halls, at last
the master moves among the shadows of his house, fulfilled.

---

[53] Ribbons. Cassandra had been wooed by Apollo, the god of prophecy, but because she resisted him, she had been cursed with the gift of prophesying to hearers who would always refuse to believe her.

[54] The red fabric had silver woven into it.

[55] The star Sirius, considered as a harbinger of killing heat, disease, and madness.

[56] An allusion to the shedding of the young Iphigeneia's blood.

[AGAMEMNON *goes over the threshold;*
the women gather up the tapestries
while CLYTAEMNESTRA *prays.*]

Zeus, Zeus, master of all fulfillment, now fulfill our prayers—   975
speed our rites to their fulfillment once for all!

[*She enters the palace, the doors close,*
the old men huddle in terror.]

CHORUS.
Why, why does it rock me,[57] never stops,
this terror beating down my heart,
         this seer that sees it all—
it beats its wings, uncalled unpaid   980
thrust on the lungs
the mercenary song beats on and on
singing a prophet's strain—
         and I can't throw it off
like dreams that make no sense,   985
and the strength drains
that filled the mind with trust,
and the years drift by and the driven sand
         has buried the mooring lines
that churned when the armored squadrons cut for Troy . . .   990
and now I believe it, I can prove he's home,
         my own clear eyes for witness—
                       Agamemnon!
Still it's chanting, beating deep so deep in the heart
this dirge of the Furies, oh dear god,
not fit for the lyre,[58] its own master   995
         it kills our spirit
kills our hopes
and it's real, true, no fantasy—
         stark terror whirls the brain
             and the end is coming   1000
                  Justice comes to birth—
I pray my fears prove false and fall
and die and never come to birth!
Even exultant health, well we know,
         exceeds its limits,[59] comes so near disease   1005
it can breach the wall between them.

---

[57] The anguished choral song that follows expresses two levels of awareness by the chorus: (1) its consciousness of the old hereditary curse on the lineage of Atreus and (2) the more immediate suspicion of Clytaemnestra based on the knowledge of her adulterous relationship with Aegisthus.

[58] Not fit for joyous song.

[59] The principle of the golden mean, of steering between too little and too much, applies even to health, according to the Chorus.

Even a man's fate, held true on course,
 in a blinding flash rams some hidden reef;
but if caution only casts the pick of the cargo[60]—
one well-balanced cast— 1010
the house will not go down, not outright;
laboring under its wealth of grief
the ship of state rides on.

Yes, and the great green bounty of god,
sown in the furrows year by year and reaped each fall 1015
can end the plague of famine.

But a man's lifeblood
 is dark and mortal.
Once it wets the earth
what song can sing it back? 1020
Not even the master-healer[61]
 who brought the dead to life—
Zeus stopped the man before he did more harm.

Oh, if only the gods had never forged
the chain that curbs our excess, 1025
 one man's fate curbing the next man's fate,
my heart would outrace my song, I'd pour out all I feel—
 but no, I choke with anguish,
 mutter through the nights.
Never to ravel out a hope in time 1030
and the brain is swarming, burning—

[CLYTAEMNESTRA *emerges from
the palace and goes to* CASSANDRA,
impassive in the chariot.]

CLYTAEMNESTRA.
Won't you come inside? I mean you, Cassandra.
Zeus in all his mercy wants you to share
some victory libations[62] with the house.
The slaves are flocking. Come, lead them 1035
up to the altar of the god who guards
our dearest treasures.
 Down from the chariot,
no time for pride. Why even Heracles,[63]
they say, was sold into bondage long ago,

---

[60] A ship in peril can be saved by jettisoning cargo so as to lighten it; similarly, a man may salvage his happiness and his "house" by forsaking his most prized wealth.

[61] Asclepios, a physician so gifted that he brought a dead man back to life. As punishment for thus violating the natural order, Zeus killed him with a thunderbolt.

[62] Ritual pourings of liquids.

[63] The heroic Heracles (Hercules) had served as a slave to Omphale, queen of Lydia in Asia Minor.

he had to endure the bitter bread of slaves.   1040
But if the yoke descends on you, be grateful
for a master born and reared in ancient wealth.
Those who reap a harvest past their hopes[64]
are merciless to their slaves.
                                        From us
you will receive what custom says is right.   1045

[CASSANDRA *remains impassive.*]

LEADER.
   It's *you* she is speaking to, it's all too clear.
   You're caught in the nets of doom—obey
   if you can obey, unless you cannot bear to.
CLYTAEMNESTRA.
   Unless she's like a swallow, possessed
   of her own barbaric song, strange, dark.   1050
   I speak directly as I can—she must obey.
LEADER.
   Go with her. Make the best of it, she's right.
   Step down from the seat, obey her.
CLYTAEMNESTRA.
                                        Do it *now*—
   I have no time to spend outside. Already
   the victims crowd the hearth, the Navelstone,[65]   1055
   to bless this day of joy I never hoped to see!—
   our victims[66] waiting for the fire and the knife,
   and you,
   if you want to taste our mystic rites, come now.
   If my words can't reach you—

[*Turning to the* LEADER.]

                                        Give her a sign,   1060
   one of her exotic handsigns.
LEADER.
                                        I think
   the stranger needs an interpreter, someone clear.
   She's like a wild creature, fresh caught.
CLYTAEMNESTRA.
                                        She's mad,
   her evil genius murmuring in her ears.
   She comes from a *city* fresh caught.   1065
   She must learn to take the cutting bridle

---

   [64] Men whose wealth ("harvest") is not "ancient" but recent.
   [65] Also the name of a stone at Apollo's shrine in Delphi; Orestes goes to that Navelstone, to be purged of his blood guilt, at the beginning of *The Eumenides*.
   [66] The animals to be sacrificed in the ritual; but Clytaemnestra's statement has also a more sinister private meaning.

before she foams her spirit off in blood—
and that's the last I waste on her contempt!

[*Wheeling, re-entering the palace. The* LEADER *turns to* CASSANDRA, *who remains transfixed.*]

LEADER.
Not I, I pity her. I will be gentle.
Come, poor thing. Leave the empty chariot—   1070
Of your own free will try on the yoke of Fate.
CASSANDRA.
Aieeeeee! Earth—Mother—
                    Curse of the Earth—Apollo Apollo!
LEADER.
Why cry to Apollo?
He's not the god to call with sounds of mourning.
CASSANDRA.
Aieeeeee! Earth—Mother—   1075
                    Rape of the Earth—Apollo Apollo!
LEADER.
Again, it's a bad omen.
She cries for the god who wants no part of grief.[67]

[CASSANDRA *steps from the chariot, looks slowly toward the rooftops of the palace.*]

CASSANDRA.
God of the long road,
                    Apollo *Apollo* my destroyer—
you destroy me once, destroy me twice—   1080
LEADER.
She's about to sense her own ordeal, I think.
Slave that she is, the god lives on inside her.
CASSANDRA.
God of the iron marches,
                    Apollo *Apollo* my destroyer—
where, where have you led me now? what house—   1085
LEADER.
The house of Atreus and his sons. Really—
don't you know? It's true, see for yourself.
CASSANDRA.
No . . . the house that hates god,
          an echoing womb of guilt, kinsmen
                    torturing kinsmen, severed heads,   1090
slaughterhouse of heroes, soil streaming blood—

[67]Apollo is more typically associated with joy.

LEADER.
  A keen hound, this stranger.
  Trailing murder, and murder she will find.
CASSANDRA.
  See, my witnesses—
            I trust to them, to the babies   1095
                      wailing, skewered on the sword,
    their flesh charred, the father gorging on their parts—
LEADER.
  We'd heard your fame as a seer,
  but no one looks for seers in Argos.
CASSANDRA.
    Oh no, what horror, what new plot,   1100
  new agony this?—
  it's growing, massing, deep in the house,
                  a plot, a monstrous—*thing*
                        to crush the loved ones, no,
        there is no cure, and rescue's far away and—   1105
LEADER.
  I can't read these signs; I knew the first,[68]
  the city rings with them.
CASSANDRA.
    You, you godforsaken—you'd do *this*?
  The lord of your bed,
  you bathe him . . . his body glistens, then—   1110
                  how to tell the climax?—
                        comes so quickly, see,
    hand over hand shoots out, hauling ropes—
                                    then lunge!
LEADER.
  Still lost. Her riddles, her dark words of god—
  I'm groping, helpless.
CASSANDRA.
                    No no, look *there!*—   1115
  what's that? some net flung out of hell—
    No, *she* is the snare,
    the bedmate, deathmate, murder's strong right arm!
            Let the insatiate discord in the race
    rear up and shriek "Avenge the victim—stone them dead!"   1120
LEADER.
  What Fury is this? Why rouse it, lift its wailing
  through the house? I hear you and lose hope.
CHORUS.
  Drop by drop at the heart, the gold of life ebbs out.
    We are the old soldiers . . . wounds will come
  with the crushing sunset of our lives.   1125
  Death is close, and quick.

---

[68] The Leader had understood Cassandra's earlier reference to the familiar story of Thyestes'
feast but does not understand her allusion to the imminent murder of Agamemnon.

CASSANDRA.
                              Look out! *look out!*—
        Ai, drag the great bull from the mate!—
              a thrash of robes, she traps him—
        writhing—
                      black horn glints, twists—
                              she gores him through!
                      And now he buckles, look, the bath swirls red—   1130
        There's stealth and murder in that caldron, do you hear?
LEADER.
        I'm no judge, I've little skill with the oracles,
        but even I know danger when I hear it.
CHORUS.
        What good are the oracles to men? Words, more words,
              and the hurt comes on us, endless words   1135
        and a seer's techniques have brought us
        terror and the truth.
CASSANDRA.
        The agony—O I am breaking!—Fate's so hard,
              and the pain that floods my voice is mine alone.
        Why have you brought me here, tormented as I am?   1140
        Why, unless to die with him, why else?
LEADER AND CHORUS.
        Mad with the rapture—god speeds you on
              to the song, the deathsong,
        like the nightingale[69] that broods on sorrow,
              mourns her son, her son,   1145
        her life inspired with grief for him,
        she lilts and shrills, dark bird that lives for night.
CASSANDRA.
        The nightingale—O for a song, a fate like hers!
              The gods gave her a life of ease, swathed her in wings,
        no tears, no wailing. The knife waits for me.   1150
        They'll splay me on the iron's double edge.
LEADER AND CHORUS.
        Why?—what god hurls you on, stroke on stroke
              to the long dying fall?
        Why the horror clashing through your music,
              terror struck to song?—   1155
        why the anguish, the wild dance?
        Where do your words of god and grief begin?
CASSANDRA.
        Ai, the wedding, wedding of Paris,
        death to the loved ones. Oh Scamander,[70]

---

[69] Tereus, husband of Procne, raped his wife's sister Philomela. In revenge, after being informed of the rape by her sister, Procne killed Itys, her son by Tereus, and served the son's flesh as a meal for the father. In some versions of the myth Procne was later metamorphosed into a nightingale, Philomela into a swallow. (In other versions the metamorphoses are reversed, Procne becoming the swallow and Philomela the nightingale.)

[70] A river at Troy.

you nursed my father . . . once at your banks   1160
    I nursed and grew, and now at the banks
of Acheron,[71] the stream that carries sorrow,
it seems I'll chant my prophecies too soon.
LEADER AND CHORUS.
    What are you saying? Wait, it's clear,
a child could see the truth, it wounds within,   1165
                            like a bloody fang it tears—
            I hear your destiny—breaking sobs,
                        cries that stab the ears.
CASSANDRA.
    Oh the grief, the grief of the city
ripped to oblivion. Oh the victims,   1170
the flocks my father burned at the wall,
    rich herds in flames . . . no cure for the doom
that took the city after all, and I,
her last ember, I go down with her.
LEADER AND CHORUS.
    You cannot stop, your song goes on—   1175
some spirit drops from the heights and treads you down
                            and the brutal strain grows—
        your death-throes come and come and
                        I cannot see the end!
CASSANDRA.
    Then off with the veils that hid the fresh young bride—   1180
we will see the truth.
Flare up once more, my oracle! Clear and sharp
as the wind that blows toward the rising sun,
I can feel a deeper swell now, gathering head
to break at last and bring the dawn of grief.   1185
No more riddles. I will teach you.
Come, bear witness, run and hunt with me.
We trail the old barbaric works of slaughter.

These roofs—look up—there is a dancing troupe
that never leaves. And they have their harmony   1190
but it is harsh, their words are harsh, they drink
beyond the limit. Flushed on the blood of men
their spirit grows and none can turn away
their revel breeding in the veins—the Furies!
They cling to the house for life. They sing,   1195
sing of the frenzy that began it all,
strain rising on strain, showering curses
on the man who tramples on his brother's bed.[72]

---

[71]A river in Hades, the underground world of the dead.
[72]Thyestes had provoked Atreus' anger by seducing his wife, thus bringing on Atreus' revenge
and the lineal curse.

There. Have I hit the mark or not? Am I a fraud,
a fortune-teller babbling lies from door to door? 1200
Swear how well I know the ancient crimes
that live within this house.
LEADER.
                                        And if I did?
Would an oath bind the wounds and heal us?
But you amaze me. Bred across the sea,
your language strange and still you sense the truth 1205
as if you had been here.
CASSANDRA.
                            Apollo the Prophet
introduced me to his gift.
LEADER.
    A *god*—and moved with love?
CASSANDRA.
    I was ashamed to tell this once,
    but now . . .
LEADER.
                    We spoil ourselves with scruples, 1210
long as things go well.
CASSANDRA.
                            He came like a wrestler,
magnificent, took me down and breathed his fire
through me and—
LEADER.
                    You bore him a child?
CASSANDRA.
                                        I yielded,
then at the climax I recoiled—I deceived Apollo!
LEADER.
    But the god's skills—they seized you even then? 1215
CASSANDRA.
    Even then I told my people all the grief to come.
LEADER.
    And Apollo's anger never touched you?—is it possible?
CASSANDRA.
    Once I betrayed him I could never be believed.
LEADER.
    We believe you. Your visions seem so true.
CASSANDRA.
                                        Aieeee!—
the pain, the terror! the birth-pang of the seer 1220
who tells the truth—
                        it whirls me, oh,
the storm comes again, the crashing chords!

Look, you see them nestling at the threshold?
Young, young in the darkness like a dream,

like children really, yes, and their loved ones   1225
brought them down . . .
                                       their hands, they fill their hands
with their own flesh, they are serving it like food,
holding out their entrails . . . now it's clear,
I can see the armfuls of compassion, see the father
reach to taste and—
                            For so much suffering,   1230
I tell you, someone plots revenge.
A lion[73] who lacks a lion's heart,
he sprawled at home in the royal lair
and set a trap for the lord on his return.
My lord . . . I must wear his yoke, I am his slave.   1235
The lord of the men-of-war, he obliterated Troy—
he is so blind, so lost to that detestable hellhound[74]
who pricks her ears and fawns and her tongue draws out
her glittering words of welcome—
                             No, he cannot see
the stroke that Fury's hiding, stealth, murder.   1240
What outrage—the woman kills the man!
                                 What to call
that . . . monster of Greece, and bring my quarry down?
Viper coiling back and forth?
                             Some sea-witch?—
Scylla[75] crouched in her rocky nest—nightmare of sailors?
Raging mother of death, storming deathless war against   1245
the ones she loves!
                       And how she howled in triumph,
boundless outrage. Just as the tide of battle
broke her way, she seems to rejoice that he
is safe at home from war, saved for her.

Believe me if you will. What will it matter   1250
if you won't? It comes when it comes,
and soon you'll see it face to face
and say the seer was all too true.
You will be moved with pity.
LEADER.
                           Thyestes' feast,
the children's flesh—that I know,   1255
and the fear shudders through me. It's true,
real, no dark signs about it. I hear the rest
but it throws me off the scent.

---

[73] The "lion" is Aegisthus.
[74] Clytaemnestra.
[75] A female monster, imagined as dwelling in a cave, personifying the dangerous rocks on one side of the strait of Messina, which separates Italy from Sicily. She is described in both Homer's *Odyssey* and Virgil's *Aeneid*.

CASSANDRA.
Agamemnon.
You will see him dead.
LEADER.
Peace, poor girl!
Put those words to sleep.
CASSANDRA.
No use, 1260
the Healer[76] has no hand in this affair.
LEADER.
Not if it's true—but god forbid it is!
CASSANDRA.
You pray, and they close in to kill!
LEADER.
What man prepares this, this dreadful—
CASSANDRA.
Man?
You *are* lost, to every word I've said.[77]
LEADER.
Yes— 1265
I don't see who can bring the evil off.
CASSANDRA.
And yet I know my Greek, too well.
LEADER.
So does the Delphic oracle,
but he's hard to understand.
CASSANDRA.
His *fire!*—
sears me, sweeps me again—the torture! 1270
Apollo Lord of the Light, you burn,
you blind me—
Agony!
She is the lioness,
she rears on her hind legs, she beds with the wolf
when her lion king goes ranging—
she will kill me—
Ai, the torture!
She is mixing her drugs, 1275
adding a measure more of hate for me.
She gloats as she whets the sword for him.
He brought me home and we will pay in carnage.

Why mock yourself with these—trappings, the rod,
the god's wreath, his yoke around my throat? 1280
Before I die I'll tread you—

---

[76]Apollo.
[77]Cassandra means that she has been referring to a woman, not a man.

[*Ripping off her regalia, stamping it
into the ground.*]

Down, out,
die die die!
Now you're down. I've paid you back.
Look for another victim—I am free at last—
make her rich in all your curse and doom.

[*Staggering backward as if wrestling
with a spirit tearing at her robes.*]

See,   1285
Apollo himself, his fiery hands—I feel him again,
he's stripping off my robes, the Seer's robes!
And after he looked down and saw me mocked,
even in these, his glories, mortified by friends[78]
I loved, and they hated me, they were so blind   1290
to their own demise—
                    I went from door to door,
I was wild with the god, I heard them call me
"Beggar! Wretch! Starve for bread in hell!"

And I endured it all, and now he will
extort me as his due. A seer for the Seer.   1295
He brings me here to die like this,
not to serve at my father's altar. No,
the block is waiting. The cleaver steams
with my life blood, the first blood drawn
for the king's last rites.

[*Regaining her composure and moving to the altar.*]

We will die,   1300
but not without some honor from the gods.
There will come another[79] to avenge us,
born to kill his mother, born
his father's champion. A wanderer, a fugitive
driven off his native land, he will come home   1305
to cope the stones of hate that menace all he loves.
The gods have sworn a monumental oath: as his father lies
upon the ground he draws him home with power like a prayer.

Then why so pitiful, why so many tears?
I have seen my city faring as she fared,   1310
and those who took her, judged by the gods,

[78] The Trojans; Cassandra's own people did not heed her.
[79] Orestes, son of Agamemnon and Clytaemnestra.

faring as they fare. I must be brave.
It is my turn to die.

[*Approaching the doors.*]

I address you as the Gates of Death.
I pray it comes with one clean stroke, 1315
no convulsions, the pulses ebbing out
in gentle death. I'll close my eyes and sleep.
LEADER.
So much pain, poor girl, and so much truth,
you've told so much. But if you *see* it coming,
clearly—how can you go to your own death, 1320
like a beast to the altar driven on by god,
and hold your head so high?
CASSANDRA.
No escape, my friends,
not now.
LEADER.
But the last hour should be savored.
CASSANDRA.
My time has come. Little to gain from flight.
LEADER.
You're brave, believe me, full of gallant heart. 1325
CASSANDRA.
Only the wretched go with praise like that.
LEADER.
But to go nobly lends a man some grace.
CASSANDRA.
My noble father—you and your noble children.

[*She nears the threshold and recoils,
groaning in revulsion.*]
LEADER.
What now? what terror flings you back?
Why? Unless some horror in the brain—
CASSANDRA.
Murder. 1330
The house breathes with murder—bloody shambles![80]
LEADER.
No, no, only the victims at the hearth.
CASSANDRA.
I know that odor. I smell the open grave.
LEADER.
But the Syrian myrrh, it fills the halls with splendor,
can't you sense it?

---

[80]A place of bloodshed; a slaughterhouse.

CASSANDRA.
          Well, I must go in now,   1335
mourning Agamemnon's death and mine.
Enough of life!

                      [*Approaching the doors again and
                      crying out.*]

          Friends—I cried out,
not from fear like a bird fresh caught,
but that you will testify to *how* I died.
When the queen, woman for woman, dies for me,   1340
and a man falls for the man who married grief.
That's all I ask, my friends. A stranger's gift
for one about to die.
LEADER.
                 Poor creature, you
and the end you see so clearly. I pity you.
CASSANDRA.
    I'd like a few words more, a kind of dirge,   1345
it is my own. I pray to the sun,
the last light I'll see,
that when the avengers cut the assassins down
they will avenge me too, a slave who died,
an easy conquest.
              Oh men, your destiny.   1350
When all is well a shadow can overturn it.
When trouble comes a stroke of the wet sponge,
and the picture's blotted out. And that,
I think that breaks the heart.

                  [*She goes through the doors.*]

CHORUS.
    But the lust for power never dies—   1355
      men cannot have enough.
No one will lift a hand to send it
from his door, to give it warning,
"Power, never come again!"
Take this man: the gods in glory   1360
gave him Priam's city to plunder,
brought him home in spendor like a god.
But now if he must pay for the blood
his fathers shed, and die for the deaths
he brought to pass, and bring more death   1365
to avenge his dying, show us one
    who boasts himself born free
of the raging angel, once he hears—

              [*Cries break out within the palace.*]

AGAMEMNON.

                                        Aagh!
        Struck deep—the death-blow, deep—
LEADER.

                                        Quiet. Cries,
        but who? Someone's stabbed—
AGAMEMNON.

                                        Aaagh, again . . .   1370
        second blow—struck home.
LEADER.

                                The work is done,
        you can feel it. The king, and the great cries—
        Close ranks now, find the right way out.

                                [*But the old men scatter, each speaks
                                singly.*]

CHORUS.
        —I say send out heralds, muster the guard,
                they'll save the house.

                                —And I say rush in now,   1375
                catch them red-handed—butchery running on their blades.

        —Right with you, do something—now or never!

        —Look at them, beating the drum for insurrection.

                                        —Yes,
                we're wasting time. They rape the name of caution,
                their hands will never sleep.

                                —Not a plan in sight.   1380
        Let men of action do the planning too.

        —I'm helpless. Who can raise the dead with words?

        —What, drag out our lives? bow down to the tyrants,
                the ruin of the house?

                                —Never, better to die
        on your feet than live on your knees.

                                        —Wait,   1385
        do we take the cries for signs, prophesy like seers
        and give him up for dead?

                                —No more suspicions,
        not another word till we have proof.

—Confusion
on all sides—one thing to do. See how it stands
with Agamemnon, once and for all we'll see—   1390

> [*He rushes at the doors. They open
> and reveal a silver caldron that
> holds the body of* AGAMEMNON
> *shrouded in bloody robes, with the
> body of* CASSANDRA *to his left and*
> CLYTAEMNESTRA *standing to his
> right, sword in hand. She strides
> toward the* CHORUS.]

CLYTAEMNESTRA.
Words, endless words I've said to serve the moment!
Now it makes me proud to tell the truth.
How else to prepare a death for deadly men
who seem to love you? How to rig the nets
of pain so high no man can overleap them?   1395

I brooded on this trial, this ancient blood feud
year by year. At last my hour came.
Here I stand and here I struck
and here my work is done.
I did it all. I don't deny it, no.   1400
He had no way to flee or fight his destiny—

> [*Unwinding the robes from* AGA-
> MEMNON's *body, spreading them
> before the altar where the old men clus-
> ter around them, unified as a chorus
> once again.*]

our never-ending, all-embracing net, I cast it
wide for the royal haul, I coil him round and round
in the wealth, the robes of doom, and then I strike him
once, twice, and at each stroke he cries in agony—   1405
he buckles at the knees and crashes here!
And when he's down I add the third, last blow,
to the Zeus who saves the dead beneath the ground
I send that third blow home in homage like a prayer.

So he goes down, and the life is bursting out of him—   1410
great sprays of blood, and the murderous shower
wounds me, dyes me black and I, I revel
like the Earth when the spring rains come down,
the blessed gifts of god, and the new green spear
splits the sheath and rips to birth in glory!   1415

So it stands, elders of Argos gathered here.
Rejoice if you can rejoice—I glory.
And if I'd pour upon his body the libation
it deserves, what wine could match my words?
It is right and more than right. He flooded   1420
the vessel of our proud house with misery,
with the vintage of the curse and now
he drains the dregs. My lord is home at last.

LEADER.
You appall me, you, your brazen words—
exulting over your fallen king.

CLYTAEMNESTRA.
                        And you,   1425
you try me like some desperate woman.
My heart is steel, well you know. Praise me,
blame me as you choose. It's all one.
Here is Agamemnon, my husband made a corpse
by this right hand—a masterpiece of Justice.   1430
Done is done.

CHORUS.
              Woman!—what poison cropped from the soil
or strained from the heaving sea, what nursed you,
drove you insane? You brave the curse of Greece.
      You have cut away and flung away and now
the people cast you off to exile,   1435
broken with our hate.

CLYTAEMNESTRA.
                And now you sentence me?—
you banish *me* from the city, curses breathing
down my neck? But *he*—
name one charge you brought against him then.
He thought no more of it than killing a beast,   1440
and his flocks were rich, teeming in their fleece,
but he sacrificed his own child, our daughter,
the agony I labored into love
to charm away the savage winds of Thrace.

Didn't the law demand you banish him?—   1445
hunt him from the land for all his guilt?
But now you witness what I've done
and you are ruthless judges.
                    Threaten away!
I'll meet you blow for blow. And if I fall
the throne is yours. If god decrees the reverse,   1450
late as it is, old men, you'll learn your place.

CHORUS.
      Mad with ambition,
              shrilling pride!—some Fury
crazed with the carnage rages through your brain—

I can see the flecks of blood inflame your eyes! 1455
But vengeance comes—you'll lose your loved ones,
stroke for painful stroke.

CLYTAEMNESTRA.
Then learn this too, the power of my oaths.
By the child's Rights I brought to birth,
by Ruin, by Fury—the three gods to whom 1460
I sacrificed this man—I swear my hopes
will never walk the halls of fear so long
as Aegisthus lights the fire on my hearth.
Loyal to me as always, no small shield
to buttress my defiance.
                                   Here he lies. 1465
He brutalized me. The darling of all
the golden girls who spread the gates of Troy.
And here his spearprize . . . what wonders she beheld!—
the seer of Apollo shared my husband's bed,
his faithful mate who knelt at the rowing-benches, 1470
worked by every hand.
                          They have their rewards.
He as you know. And she, the swan[81] of the gods
who lived to sing her latest, dying song—
his lover lies beside him.
She brings a fresh, voluptuous relish to my bed! 1475

CHORUS.
Oh quickly, let me die—
no bed of labor, no, no wasting illness . . .
bear me off in the sleep that never ends,
                    now that he has fallen,
now that our dearest shield lies battered— 1480
        Woman made him suffer,
                          woman struck him down.

Helen the wild, maddening Helen,
one for the many, the thousand lives
you murdered under Troy. Now you are crowned 1485
with this consummate wreath, the blood
that lives in memory, glistens age to age.
Once in the halls she walked and she was war,
angel of war, angel of agony, lighting men to death.

CLYTAEMNESTRA.
Pray no more for death, broken 1490
as you are. And never turn
    your wrath on her, call her
the scourge of men, the one alone
who destroyed a myriad Greek lives—
Helen the grief that never heals. 1495

---

[81] In folklore, the swan sings for the first and last time just before its death.

CHORUS.
    The *spirit!*—you who tread
  the house and the twinborn sons[82] of Tantalus—
  you empower the sisters, Fury's twins
                whose power tears the heart!
  Perched on the corpse your carrion raven   1500
          glories in her hymn,
               her screaming hymn of pride.

CLYTAEMNESTRA.
  Now you set your judgment straight,
  you summon *him!* Three generations
      feed the spirit in the race.   1505
  Deep in the veins he feeds our bloodlust—
  aye, before the old wound dies
  it ripens in another flow of blood.
CHORUS.
  The great curse of the house, the spirit,
    dead weight wrath—and you can praise it!   1510
  Praise the insatiate doom that feeds
  relentless on our future and our sons.
  Oh all through the will of Zeus,
  the cause of all, the one who works it all.
    What comes to birth that is not Zeus?   1515
  Our lives are pain, what part not come from god?

  Oh my king, my captain,
  how to salute you, how to mourn you?
  What can I say with all my warmth and love?
  Here in the black widow's web you lie,   1520
  gasping out your life
  in a sacrilegious death, dear god,
  reduced to a slave's bed,
  my king of men, yoked by stealth and Fate,
  by the wife's hand that thrust the two-edged sword. 1525
CLYTAEMNESTRA.
  You claim the work is mine, call me
  Agamemnon's wife—you are so wrong.
  Fleshed in the wife of this dead man,
    the spirit lives within me,
  our savage ancient spirit of revenge.   1530
  In return for Atreus' brutal feast
  he kills his perfect son—for every
  murdered child, a crowning sacrifice.
CHORUS.
  And *you*, innocent of his murder?
  And who could swear to that? and how? . . .   1535

---

[82]"Sons" can refer either to Tantalus' grandsons, Thyestes and Atreus, or to his great-grandsons, Agamemnon and Menelaus, who married the sisters Clytaemnestra and Helen.

and still an avenger could arise,
bred by the fathers' crimes, and lend a hand.
He wades in the blood of brothers,
stream on mounting stream—black war erupts
    and where he strides revenge will stride,   1540
clots will mass for the young who were devoured.

    Oh my king, my captain,
    how to salute you, how to mourn you?
    What can I say with all my warmth and love?
    Here in the black widow's web you lie,   1545
    gasping out your life
    in a sacrilegious death, dear god,
    reduced to a slave's bed,
    my king of men, yoked by stealth and Fate,
    by the wife's hand that thrust the two-edged sword.   1550
CLYTAEMNESTRA.
    No slave's death, I think—
    no stealthier than the death he dealt
    our house and the offspring of our loins,
        Iphigeneia, girl of tears.
    Act for act, wound for wound!   1555
    Never exult in Hades, swordsman,
    here you are repaid. By the sword
    you did your work and by the sword you die.
CHORUS.
                The mind reels—where to turn?
            All plans dashed, all hope! I cannot think . . .   1560
        the roofs are toppling, I dread the drumbeat thunder
        the heavy rains of blood will crush the house
                the first light rains are over—
            Justice brings new acts of agony, yes,
    on new grindstones Fate is grinding sharp the sword of Justice. 1565

    Earth, dear Earth,
    if only you'd drawn me under
    long before I saw him huddled
    in the beaten silver bath.
    Who will bury him, lift his dirge?   1570

                    [*Turning to* CLYTAEMNESTRA.]

    You, can you dare *this?*
    To kill your lord with your own hand
    then mourn his soul with tributes, terrible tributes—
    do his enormous works a great dishonor.
    This godlike man, this hero. Who at the grave   1575
    will sing his praises, pour the wine of tears?
    Who will labor there with truth of heart?

CLYTAEMNESTRA.
    This is no concern of yours.
    The hand that bore and cut him down
    will hand him down to Mother Earth.   1580
    This house will never mourn for him.
        Only our daughter Iphigeneia,
    by all rights, will rush to meet him
    first at the churning straits,
    the ferry[83] over tears—   1585
    she'll fling her arms around her father,
    pierce him with her love.
CHORUS.
          Each charge meets countercharge.
        None can judge between them. Justice.
    The plunderer plundered, the killer pays the price.   1590
The truth still holds while Zeus still holds the throne:
        the one who acts must suffer—
    that is law. Who, who can tear from the veins
   the bad seed, the curse? The race is welded to its ruin.
CLYTAEMNESTRA.
    At last you see the future and the truth!   1595
    But I will swear a pact with the spirit
    born within us. I embrace his works,
    cruel as they are but done at last,
        if he will leave our house[84]
    in the future, bleed another line   1600
    with kinsmen murdering kinsmen.
    Whatever he may ask. A few things
    are all I need, once I have purged
    our fury to destroy each other—
        purged it from our halls.

                    [AEGISTHUS *has emerged from the*
                    palace with his bodyguard and stands
                    triumphant over the body of
                    AGAMEMNON.]

AEGISTHUS.
                  O what a brilliant day   1605
    it is for vengeance! Now I can say once more
    there are gods in heaven avenging men,
    blazing down on all the crimes of earth.
    Now at last I see this man brought down
    in the Furies' tangling robes. It feasts my eyes—   1610
    he pays for the plot his father's hand contrived.

---

[83] The boat in which Charon ferried the dead across the river Styx to Hades.

[84] As the later plays of the triology show, there is sad irony in Clytaemnestra's hope that her deed of revenge will have ended the chain of retributive acts.

Atreus, this man's father, was king of Argos.
My father, Thyestes—let me make this clear—
Atreus' brother challenged him for the crown,
and Atreus drove him out of house and home   1615
then lured him back, and home Thyestes came,
poor man, a suppliant to his own hearth,
to pray that Fate might save him.
                                        So it did.
There was no dying, no staining our native ground
with *his* blood. Thyestes was the guest,   1620
and this man's godless father—

                    [*Pointing to* AGAMEMNON.]

the zeal of the host outstripping a brother's love,
made my father a feast that seemed a feast for gods,
a love feast of his children's flesh.
                                        He cuts
the extremities, feet and delicate hands   1625
into small pieces, scatters them over the dish
and serves it to Thyestes throned on high.
He picks at the flesh he cannot recognize,
the soul of innocence eating the food of ruin—
look,

                    [*Pointing to the bodies at his feet.*]

          that feeds upon the house! And then,   1630
when he sees the monstrous thing he's done, he shrieks,
he reels back head first and vomits up that butchery,
tramples the feast—brings down the curse of Justice:
"Crash to ruin, all the race of Pleisthenes,[85] crash down!"

So you see him, down. And I, the weaver of Justice,   1635
plotted out the kill. Atreus drove us into exile,
my struggling father and I, a babe-in-arms,
his last son, but I became a man
and Justice brought me home. I was abroad
but I reached out and seized my man,   1640
link by link I clamped the fatal scheme
together. Now I could die gladly, even I—
now I see this monster in the nets of Justice.
LEADER.
Aegisthus, you revel in pain—you sicken me.
You say you killed the king in cold blood,   1645
singlehanded planned his pitiful death?
I say there's no escape. In the hour of judgment,

---

[85]Apparently an ancestor of Agamemnon, his exact identity is vague.

trust to this, your head will meet the people's
rocks and curses.
AEGISTHUS.

You say! you slaves at the oars—
while the master on the benches cracks the whip? 1650
You'll learn, in your late age, how much it hurts
to teach old bones their place. We have techniques—
chains and the pangs of hunger,
two effective teachers, excellent healers.
They can even cure old men of pride and gall. 1655
Look—can't you see? The more you kick
against the pricks, the more you suffer.
LEADER.

You, pathetic—
the king had just returned from battle.
You waited out the war and fouled his lair, 1660
you planned my great commander's fall.
AEGISTHUS.

Talk on—
you'll scream for every word, my little Orpheus.[86]
We'll see if the world comes dancing to your song,
your absurd barking—snarl your breath away!
I'll make you dance, I'll bring you all to heel. 1665
LEADER.

You rule Argos? You who schemed his death
but cringed to cut him down with your own hand?
AEGISTHUS.

The treachery was the woman's work, clearly.
I was a marked man, his enemy for ages.
But I will use his riches, stop at nothing 1670
to civilize his people. All but the rebel:
him I'll yoke and break—
no cornfed colt, running free in the traces.
Hunger, ruthless mate of the dark torture-chamber,
trains her eyes upon him till he drops! 1675
LEADER.

Coward, why not kill the man yourself?
Why did the woman, the corruption of Greece
and the gods of Greece, have to bring him down?
Orestes—
If he still sees the light of day,
bring him home, good Fates, home to kill 1680
this pair at last. Our champion in slaughter!
AEGISTHUS.

Bent on insolence? Well, you'll learn, quickly.
At them, men—you have your work at hand!

---

[86] The archetypal poet-musician whose song compelled even nature to listen. See, for example, Ovid's *Metamorphoses*, Book X.

[*His men draw swords; the old men take up their sticks.*]

LEADER.
At them, fist at the hilt, to the last man—
AEGISTHUS.
Fist at the hilt, I'm not afraid to die.   1685
LEADER.
It's death you want and death you'll have—
we'll make that word your last.

[CLYTAEMNESTRA *moves between them, restraining* AEGISTHUS.]

CLYTAEMNESTRA.
No more, my dearest,
no more grief. We have too much to reap
right here, our mighty harvest of despair.
Our lives are based on pain. No bloodshed now.   1690

Fathers of Argos, turn for home before you act
and suffer for it. What we did was destiny.
If we could end the suffering, how we would rejoice.
The spirit's brutal hoof has struck our heart.
And that is what a woman has to say.   1695
Can you accept the truth?

[CLYTAEMNESTRA *turns to leave.*]

AEGISTHUS.
But these . . . mouths
that bloom in filth—spitting insults in my teeth.
You tempt your fates, you insubordinate dogs—
to hurl abuse at me, your master!
LEADER.
No Greek
worth his salt would grovel at your feet.   1700
AEGISTHUS.
I—I'll stalk you all your days!
LEADER.
Not if the spirit brings Orestes home.
AEGISTHUS.
Exiles feed on hope—well I know.
LEADER.
More,
gorge yourself to bursting—soil justice, while you can.
AEGISTHUS.
I promise you, you'll pay, old fools—in good time too!   1705
LEADER.
Strut on your own dunghill, you cock beside your mate.

CLYTAEMNESTRA.
Let them howl—they're impotent. You and I have power now.
We will set the house in order once for all.

> [*They enter the palace; the great doors
> close behind them; the old men dis-
> band and wander off.*]

THE LIBATION BEARERS

CHARACTERS

ORESTES, *son of Agamemnon*   CLYTAEMNESTRA
   and Clytaemnestra   CILISSA, *Orestes' old nurse*
PYLADES, *his companion*   AEGISTHUS
ELECTRA, *his sister*   *A servant of Aegisthus*
CHORUS OF SLAVEWOMEN   *Attendants of Orestes,*
   AND THEIR LEADER   *bodyguard of Aegisthus*

TIME AND SCENE

*Several years have passed since Agamemnon's death. At Argos, before the tomb of
the king and his fathers, stands an altar; behind it looms the house of Atreus.* ORESTES
and PYLADES *enter, dressed as travelers.* ORESTES *kneels and prays.*

ORESTES.
Hermes,[1] lord of the dead, look down and guard
the fathers' power. Be my savior, I beg you,
be my comrade now.
        I have come home
to my own soil, an exile home at last.
Here at the mounded grave I call my father,   5
Hear me—I am crying out to you . . .

> [*He cuts two locks of hair*[2] *and lays
> them on the grave.*]

There is a lock for Inachos[3] who nursed me
into manhood, there is one for death.

---

[1] The messenger of the gods, patron of human messengers and heralds. He also guided
the dead to Hades.
[2] The locks were customary ritual tributes to the dead.
[3] River at Argos; Orestes pays tribute to his original fatherland as well as to his dead father,
Agamemnon.

I was not here to mourn you when you died,
my father, never gave the last salute   10
when they bore your corpse away.

> [ELECTRA *and a chorus of slave-*
> *women enter in procession. They are*
> *dressed in black and bear libations,*
> *moving toward* ORESTES *at the*
> *grave.*]

What's this?
Look, a company moving toward us. Women,
robed in black . . . so clear in the early light.

I wonder what they mean, what turn of fate?—
some new wound to the house?   15
Or perhaps they come to honor you, my father,
bearing cups to soothe and still the dead.
That's right, it must be . . .
Electra, I think I see *her* coming, there,
my own sister, worn, radiant in her grief—   20
Dear god, let me avenge my father's murder—
fight beside me now with all your might!

Out of their way, Pylades.[4] I must know
what they mean, these women turning toward us,
what their prayers call forth.   25

> [*They withdraw behind the tomb.*]

CHORUS.[5]
Rushed from the house we come
    escorting cups for the dead,
in step with the hands' hard beat,
            our cheeks glistening,
flushed where the nails have raked new furrows running blood;   30
and life beats on, and through it all
we nurse our lives with tears,
to the sound of ripping linen beat our robes in sorrow,
    close to the breast the beats throb
and laughter's gone and fortune throbs and throbs.   35

Aie!—bristling Terror[6] struck—
    Terror the seer of the house,

---

[4] Son of Strophios, with whom the exiled Orestes had lived in Phokis after Clytaemnestra
sent him away (see the *Agamemnon*).
[5] The chorus consists of women brought back from Troy as slaves. In the lament that follows they express grief for both the house of Atreus and that of Troy.
[6] Clytaemnestra has been frightened by a nightmare; she has therefore sent the women to
Agamemnon's tomb with propitiatory libations (mixtures of honey and wine).

the nightmare ringing clear
     breathed its wrath in sleep,
in the midnight watch a cry!—the voice of Terror   40
deep in the house, bursting down
on the women's darkened chambers, yes,
and the old ones, skilled at dreams, swore oaths to god and called,
  "The proud dead stir under earth,
they rage against the ones who took their lives."   45

  But the gifts, the empty gifts
     she hopes will ward them off—
good Mother Earth!—that godless woman sends me here . . .
    I dread to say her prayer.
What can redeem the blood that wets the soil?   50
Oh for the hearthfire banked with grief,
  the ramparts down, a fine house down—
dark, dark, and the sun, the life is curst,
  and mist enshrouds the halls
   where the lords of war went down.   55

  And the ancient pride no war,
     no storm, no force could tame,
ringing in all men's ears, in all men's hearts is gone.
    They are afraid. Success,
  they bow to success, more god than god himself.   60
But Justice waits and turns the scales:
  a sudden blow for some at dawn,
for some in the no man's land of dusk
  her torments grow with time,
   and the lethal night takes others.   65

And the blood that Mother Earth consumes
clots hard, it won't seep through, it breeds revenge
     and frenzy goes through the guilty,
seething like infection, swarming through the brain.

For the one who treads a virgin's bed   70
there is no cure. All the streams of the world,
  all channels run into one
to cleanse a man's red hands will swell the bloody tide.

And I . . . Fate and the gods brought down their yoke,
they ringed our city, out of our fathers' halls   75
    they led us here as slaves.
And the will breaks, we kneel at their command—
     our masters right or wrong!
   And we beat the tearing hatred down,
  behind our veils we weep for her,   80

    [*Turning to* ELECTRA.]

her senseless fate.
Sorrow turns the secret heart to ice.
ELECTRA.
                                        Dear women,
you keep the house in order, best you can;
and now you've come to the grave to say a prayer
with me, my escorts. I'll need your help with this.   85
What to say when I pour the cup of sorrow?

                    [*Lifting her libation cup.*]

What kindness, what prayer can touch my father?
Shall I say I bring him love for love, a woman's
love for husband? My mother, love from her?
I've no taste for that, no words to say   90
as I run the honeyed oil on father's tomb.

Or try the salute we often use at graves?
"A wreath for a wreath. Now bring the givers
gifts to match" . . . no, give them pain for pain.[7]

Or silent, dishonored, just as father died,   95
empty it out for the soil to drink and then
retrace my steps, like a slave sent out with scourings
left from the purging of the halls, and throw
the cup behind me, looking straight ahead.

Help me decide, my friends. Join me here.   100
We nurse a common hatred in the house.
Don't hide your feelings—no, fear no one.
Destiny waits us all,

                    [*Looking toward the tomb.*]

                                        born free,
or slaves who labor under another's hand.
Speak to me, please. Perhaps you've had   105
a glimpse of something better.
LEADER.
                                        I revere
your father's death-mound like an altar.
I'll say a word, now that you ask,
that comes from deep within me.
ELECTRA.
                                        Speak on,
with everything you feel for father's grave.   110

---

[7]Electra possibly means "pain for the murderers to match the pain they gave my father."

LEADER.
 Say a blessing as you pour, for those who love you.
ELECTRA.
 And of the loved ones, whom to call my friends?
LEADER.
 First yourself, then all who hate Aegisthus.
ELECTRA.
 I and you. I can say a prayer for us
 and then for—
LEADER.
                     You know, try to say it.   115
ELECTRA.
 There is someone else to rally to our side?
LEADER.
 Remember Orestes, even abroad and gone.
ELECTRA.
 Well said, the best advice I've had.
LEADER.
 Now for the murderers. Remember them and—
ELECTRA.
                                               What?
 I'm so unseasoned, teach me what to say.   120
LEADER.
 Let some god or man come down upon them.
ELECTRA.
 Judge or avenger, which?
LEADER.
 Just say "the one who murders in return!"
ELECTRA.
 How can I ask the gods for that
 and keep my conscience clear?
LEADER.
                            How not,   125
 and pay the enemy back in kind?

                     [ELECTRA *kneels at the grave in prayer.*]

ELECTRA.
                     —Herald king
 of the world above and the quiet world below,
 lord of the dead, my Hermes, help me now.
 Tell the spirits underground to hear my prayers,
 and the high watch hovering over father's roofs,   130
 and have her listen too, the Earth herself
 who brings all things to life and makes them strong,
 then gathers in the rising tide once more.

 And I will tip libations to the dead.
 I call out to my father, Pity me,   135
 dear Orestes too.

Rekindle the light that saves our house!
We're auctioned off, drift like vagrants now.
Mother has pawned us for a husband, Aegisthus,
her partner in her murdering.
            I go like a slave,   140
Orestes driven from his estates while they,
they roll in the fruits of all your labors,
magnificent and sleek. O bring Orestes home,
with a happy twist of fate, my father. Hear me,
make me far more self-possessed than mother,   145
make this hand more pure.

These prayers for us. For our enemies I say,
Raise up your avenger, into the light, my father—
kill the killers in return, with justice!
So in the midst of prayers for good I place   150
this curse for them.
            Bring up your blessings,
up into the air, led by the gods and Earth
and all the rights that bring us triumph.

> [*Pouring libations on the tomb and
> turning to the women.*]

These are my prayers. Over them I pour libations.
Yours to adorn them with laments, to make them bloom, 155
so custom says—sing out and praise the dead.

CHORUS.
Let the tears fall, ring out and die,
        die with the warlord at this bank,
this bulwark of the good, defense against the bad,
the guilt, the curse we ward away   160
with prayer and all we pour. Hear me, majesty, hear me,
    lord of glory, from the darkness of your heart.
                     Ohhhhhh!—

    Dear god, let him come! Some man
with a strong spear, born to free the house,
    with the torsion bow of Scythia[8] bent for slaughter, 165
splattering shafts like a god of war—sword in fist
      for the slash-and-hack of battle!

> [ELECTRA *remains at the grave,
> staring at the ground.*]

ELECTRA.
                 Father,
you have it now, the earth has drunk your wine.
Wait, friends, here's news. Come share it.

---

[8]A region in southwest Asia, noted for its archers and their powerful bows.

LEADER.
                              Speak on,
  my heart's a dance of fear.
ELECTRA.
                              A lock of hair,   170
  here on the grave . . .
LEADER.
                     Whose? A man's?
  A growing girl's?
ELECTRA.
                     And it has the marks,
  and anyone would think—
LEADER.
                              What?
  We're old. You're young, now you teach us.
ELECTRA.
  No one could have cut this lock but I and—   175
LEADER.
  Callous they are, the ones who ought to shear
  the hair and mourn.
ELECTRA.
                  Look at the texture, just like—
LEADER.
  Whose? I want to know.
ELECTRA.
                         Like mine, identical,
  can't you see?
LEADER.
                  Orestes . . . he brought a gift
  in secret?
ELECTRA.
             It's *his*—I can see his curls.   180
LEADER.
  And how could he risk the journey here?
ELECTRA.
  He sent it, true, a lock to honor father.
LEADER.
  All the more cause for tears. You mean
  he'll never set foot on native ground again.
ELECTRA.
                                        Yes!
  It's sweeping over me too—anguish   185
  like a breaker—a sword ripping through my heart!
  Tears come like the winter rains that flood the gates—
  can't hold them back, when I see this strand of hair.

  How could I think another Greek could play
  the prince with this?
                        She'd never cut it,   190

the murderess, my mother. She insults the name,
she and her godless spirit preying on her children.

But how, how can I come right out and say it *is*
the glory of the dearest man I know, Orestes?
Stop, I'm fawning on hope.
                                   Oh, if only   195
it had a herald's voice, kind and human—
I'm so shaken, torn—and told me clearly
to throw it away, they severed it from a head
that I detest. Or it could sorrow with me
like a brother, aye,   200
this splendor come to honor father's grave.

We call on the gods, and the gods well know
what storms torment us, sailors whirled to nothing.
But if we are to live and reach the haven,
one small seed could grow a mighty tree—   205
Look, tracks.
                  A new sign to tell us more.
Footmarks . . . pairs of them, like mine.
Two outlines, two prints, his own, and there,
a fellow traveler's.

                                   [*Putting her foot into* ORESTES'
                                   print.]

                  The heel, the curve of the arch
like twins.

                                   [*While* ORESTES *emerges from behind
                                   the grave, she follows cautiously in
                                   his steps until they come together.*]

                  Step by step, my step in his . . .
                                   we meet—   210
Oh the pain, like pangs of labor—this is madness!
ORESTES.
      Pray for the future. Tell the gods they've brought
      your prayers to birth, and pray that we succeed.

                                   [ELECTRA *draws back, struggling for
                                   composure.*]

ELECTRA.
      The gods—why now? What have I ever won from them?
ORESTES.
      The sight you prayed to see for many years.   215
ELECTRA.
      And you know the one I call?

ORESTES.

                              I know Orestes,
  know he moves you deeply.
ELECTRA.

                              Yes,
  but now what's come to fill my prayers?
ORESTES.

  Here I am. Look no further.
  No one loves you more than I.
ELECTRA.

                              No,   220
  it's a trap, stranger . . . a net you tie around me?
ORESTES.

  Then I tie myself as well.
ELECTRA.

                      But the pain,
  you're laughing at all—
ORESTES.

                      Your pain is mine.
  If I laugh at yours, I only laugh at mine.
ELECTRA.

  Orestes—   225
  can I call you?—are you really—
ORESTES.

                              I am!
  Open your eyes. So slow to learn.
  You saw the lock of hair I cut in mourning.
  You scanned my tracks, you could see my marks,
  your breath leapt, you all but saw me in the flesh—   230
  Look—

                              [*Holding the lock to his temple, then
                              to* ELECTRA'*s.*]

          put it where I cut it.
  It's your brother's. Try, it matches yours.

                              [*Removing a strip of weaving from
                              his clothing.*]

  Work of your own hand, you tamped the loom,
  look, there are wild creatures in the weaving.

                              [*She kneels beside him, weeping; he
                              lifts her to her feet and they embrace.*]

  No, no, control yourself—don't lose yourself in joy!   235
  Our loved ones, well I know, would slit our throats.
LEADER.

  Dearest, the darling of your father's house,

hope of the seed we nursed with tears—you save us.
Trust to your power, win your father's house once more!
ELECTRA.
    You light to my eyes, four loves in one!   240
    I have to call you father, it is fate;
    and I turn to you the love I gave my mother—
    I despise her, she deserves it, yes,
    and the love I gave my sister,[9] sacrificed
    on the cruel sword, I turn to you.   245
    You were my faith, my brother—
    you alone restore my self-respect.

[*Praying.*]

    Power and Justice, Saving Zeus, Third Zeus,[10]
    almighty all in all, be with us now.
ORESTES.
    Zeus, Zeus, watch over all we do,   250
    fledglings reft of the noble eagle father.
    He died in the coils, the viper's dark embrace.
    We are his orphans worn down with hunger,
    weak, too young to haul the father's quarry
    home to shelter.
                    Look down on us!   255
    I and Electra too, I tell you, children
    robbed of our father, both of us bound
    in exile from our house.
                    And what a father—
    a priest at sacrifice, he showered you
    with honors. Put an end to his nestlings now   260
    and who will serve you banquets rich as his?
    Destroy the eagle's brood, you can never
    send a sign that wins all men's belief.
    Rot the stock of a proud dynastic tree—
    it can never shore your altar steaming   265
    with the oxen in the mornings.
                    Tend us—
    we seem in ruins now, I know. Up from nothing
    rear a house to greatness.
LEADER.
                  Softly, children,
    white hopes of your father's hearth. Someone
    might hear you, children, charmed with his own voice   270
    blurt all this out to the masters. Oh, just once
    to see them—live bones crackling in the fire
    spitting pitch!

---

[9]Iphigeneia, sacrificed at Aulis. See headnote to the *Oresteia*.
[10]Zeus in his role as savior. Compare the more material and pragmatic emphasis in the following prayer to Zeus by Orestes.

ORESTES.
                    Apollo will never fail me, no,
his tremendous power, his oracle charges me
to see this trial through.
                    I can still hear the god—   275
a high voice ringing with winters of disaster,
piercing the heart within me, warm and strong,
unless I hunt my father's murderers, cut them down
in their own style—they destroyed my birthright.
"Gore them like a bull!" he called, "or pay their debt   280
with your own life, one long career of grief."

He revealed[11] so much about us,
told how the dead take root beneath the soil,
they grow with hate and plague the lives of men.
He told of the leprous boils that ride the flesh,   285
their wild teeth gnawing the mother tissue, aye,
and a white scurf spreads like cancer over these,
and worse, he told how assaults of Furies spring
to life on the father's blood . . .
                    You can *see* them—
the eyes burning, grim brows working over you in the dark—   290
the dark sword of the dead—your murdered kinsmen
pleading for revenge. And the madness haunts
the midnight watch, the empty terror shakes you,
harries, drives you on—an exile from your city—
a brazen whip will mutilate your back.   295

For such as us, no share in the winebowl,
no libations poured in love. You never see
your father's wrath but it pulls you from the altars.
There is no refuge, none to take you in.
A pariah, reviled, at long last you die,   300
withered in the grip of all this dying.

Such oracles are persuasive,
don't you think? And even if I am not convinced,
the rough work of the world is still to do.
So many yearnings meet and urge me on.   305
The god's commands. Mounting sorrow for father.
Besides, the lack of patrimony[12] presses hard;
and my compatriots, the glory of men
who toppled Troy with nerves of singing steel,
go at the beck and call of a brace of women.   310
Womanhearted he is[13]—if not, we'll soon see.

---

[11]In the following lines Orestes describes the physical, psychological, and social ills that, according to Apollo's oracle, Orestes will have to endure if he does not avenge his father's murder.

[12]What Orestes ought rightfully to inherit.

[13]That is, Aegisthus, who now rules Argos with Clytaemnestra.

[*The* LEADER *lights the altar fires.*
ORESTES, ELECTRA, *and the* CHORUS
*gather for the invocation at the
grave.*]

CHORUS.
Powers of destiny, mighty queens of Fate!—
by the will of Zeus your will be done,
press on to the end now,
  Justice turns the wheel.   315
"Word for word, curse for curse
be born now," Justice thunders,
  hungry for retribution,
"stroke for bloody stroke be paid.
  The one who acts must suffer."   320
Three generations strong the word resounds.
ORESTES.
Dear father, father of dread,
what can I do or say to reach you now?
  What breath can reach from here
to the bank where you lie moored at anchor?[14]   325
What light can match your darkness? None,
but there is a kind of grace that comes
  when the tears revive a proud old house
and Atreus' sons, the warlords lost and gone.
LEADER.
The ruthless jaws of the fire,[15]   330
  my child, can never tame the dead,
                his rage inflames his sons.
Men die and the voices rise, they light the guilty, true—
cries raised for the fathers, clear and just,
  will hunt their killers harried to the end.   335
ELECTRA.
Then hear me now, my father,
it is my turn, my tears are welling now,
  as child by child we come
to the tomb and raise the dirge, my father.
Your grave receives a girl in prayer   340
and a man in flight, and we are one,
  and the pain is equal, whose is worse?
And who outwrestles death—what third last fall?[16]
CHORUS.
But still some god, if he desires,
may work our strains to a song of joy,   345

[14] In the world of the dead; but the phrase calls up also the memory of the Greek fleet at
Aulis, where Agamemnon had committed the outrage on Iphigeneia that ultimately brought
on his murder.
[15] The fire in which the dead are cremated.
[16] The deciding round in a wrestling match.

from the dirges chanted over the grave
may lift a hymn in the kings' halls
and warm the loving cup you stir this morning.
ORESTES.
   If only at Troy
a Lycian[17] cut you down, my father— 350
gone, with an aura left at home behind you,
      children to go their ways
and the eyes look on them bright with awe,
and the tomb you win on headlands seas away
      would buoy up the house . . . 355
LEADER.
   And loved by the men you loved
   who died in glory, there you'd rule
            beneath the earth—lord, prince,
stern aide to the giant kings who judge the shadows there.[18]
You were a king of kings when you drew breath; 360
   the mace you held could make men kneel or die.
ELECTRA.
   No, not under Troy!—
not dead and gone with them, my father,
hordes pierced by the spear Scamander[19] washes down.
   Sooner the killers die 365
as they killed you—at the hands of friends,
and the news of death would come from far away,
      we'd never know this grief.[20]
CHORUS.
   You are dreaming, children,
   dreams dearer than gold, more blest 370
   than the Blest beyond the Northwind's raging.[21]
      Dreams are easy, oh,
   but the double lash is striking home.
   Now our comrades group underground.
   Our masters' reeking hands are doomed— 375
      the children take the day!
ORESTES.
   That thrills his ear,
         that arrow lands!
            Zeus, Zeus, force up from the earth
   destruction, late but true to the mark, 380
   to the reckless heart, the killing hand—
      for parents of revenge revenge be done.

---

[17] The Lycians fought in aid of the Trojans.
[18] The giant kings are Minos, Rhadamanthus, and Aeacus, who were rewarded for their just lives by being made judges of the dead in Hades.
[19] The river Scamander, near Troy.
[20] Electra wishes that Clytaemnestra and Aegisthus had died before they killed Agamemnon.
[21] The chorus refers to the Hyperboreans, a mythical people supposed to live happily in the far north, beyond Boreas (the north wind). They had a special devotion to Apollo.

LEADER.
　And the ripping cries of triumph mine
　to sing when the man is stabbed,
　　　　　　　　　　　　the woman[22] dies—　　　　　　　385
　　why, why hide what's deep inside me,
　　black wings beating, storming the spirit's prow—
　　　　　　　　　　　hurricane, slashing hatred!
ELECTRA.
　Both fists at once
　　　　come down, come down—
　　　　　　　Zeus, *crush* their skulls! Kill! Kill!　　　　390
　Now give the land some faith, I beg you,
　　from these ancient wrongs bring forth our rights.
　　Hear me, Earth, and all you lords of death.
CHORUS.
　It is the law: when the blood of slaughter
　　wets the ground it wants more blood.　　　　　　　395
　　　Slaughter cries for the Fury
　　of those long dead to bring destruction
　　on destruction churning in its wake!
ORESTES.
　Sweet Earth, how long?—great lords of death, look on,
　　you mighty curses of the dead. Look on　　　　　　400
　the last of Atreus' children, here, the remnant
　　helpless, cast from home . . . god, where to turn?
LEADER.
　And again my pulses race and leap,
　　I can feel your sobs, and hope
　　　　　　　　　　　becomes despair　　　　　　　405
　　and the heart goes dark to hear you—
　　then the anguish ebbs, I see you stronger,
　　　　　　　　hope and the light come on me.
ELECTRA.
　What hope?—what force to summon, what can help?
　　What but the pain we suffer, bred by her?　　　　　410
　So let her fawn. She can never soothe her young wolves—
　　Mother dear, you bred our wolves' raw fury.
LEADER AND CHORUS.
　I beat and beat the dirge like a Persian mourner,[23]
　　hands clenched tight and the blows are coming thick and fast,
　　you can see the hands shoot out,　　　　　　　　415
　　　　now hand over hand and down—the head pulsates,
　　　　　　　blood at the temples pounding to explode!

[22]Aegisthus is "the man"; Clytaemnestra is "the woman."
[23]Noted for violent demonstrations of grief.

ELECTRA.
       Reckless, brutal mother—oh dear god!—
          The brutal, cruel cortege,[24]
          the warlord stripped of his honor guard   420
              and stripped of mourning rites—
     you dared entomb your lord unwept, unsung.
ORESTES.
       Shamed for all the world, you mean—
       dear god, my father degraded so!
       Oh she'll pay,   425
       she'll pay, by the gods and these bare hands—
          just let me take her life and *die*!
LEADER AND CHORUS.
       Shamed? *Butchered,* I tell you—hands lopped,
       strung to shackle his neck and arms!
       So she worked,   430
       she buried him, made your life a hell.
          Your father mutilated—do you hear?
ELECTRA.
       You tell him of father's death, but I was an outcast,
       worthless, leashed like a vicious dog in a dark cell.
       I wept—laughter died that day . . .   435
          I wept, pouring out the tears behind my veils.
              Hear *that,* my brother, carve it on your heart!
LEADER AND CHORUS.
       Let it ring in your ears
          but let your heart stand firm.
       The outrage stands as it stands,   440
          you burn to know the end,
     but first be strong, be steel, then down and fight.
ORESTES.
       I am calling you, my father—be with all you love!
ELECTRA.
       I am with you, calling through my tears.
LEADER AND CHORUS.
       We band together now, the call resounds—   445
          hear us now, come back into the light.
       Be with us, battle all you hate.
ORESTES.
       Now force *clash* with force, right with right!
ELECTRA.
       Dear gods, be just—win back our rights.
LEADER AND CHORUS.
       The flesh crawls to hear them pray.   450
          The hour of doom has waited long . . .
       pray for it once, and oh my god, it comes.

---

[24] Followers of or ceremony at a funeral. Agamemnon's mutilated body had received no funeral rites.

CHORUS.
Oh, the torment bred in the race,
            the grinding scream of death
                    and the stroke that hits the vein,   455
      the hemorrhage none can stanch, the grief,
      the curse no man can bear.

But there is a cure in the house
            and not outside it, no,
                    not from others but from *them*,   460
      their bloody strife. We sing to you,
      dark gods beneath the earth.

Now hear, you blissful powers underground—
      answer the call, send help.
Bless the children, give them triumph now.   465

                    [*They withdraw, while* ELECTRA *and*
                    ORESTES *come to the altar.*]

ORESTES.
Father, king, no royal death you died—
give me the power now to rule our house.
ELECTRA.
I need you too, my father.
Help me kill her lover, then go free.
ORESTES.
Then men will extend the sacred feast to you.   470
Or else, when the steam and the rich savor burn
for Mother Earth, you will starve for honor.
ELECTRA.
And I will pour my birthright out to you—
the wine of the fathers' house, my bridal wine,[25]
and first of all the shrines revere your tomb.   475
ORESTES.
O Earth, bring father up to watch me fight.
ELECTRA.
O Persephone,[26] give us power—lovely, gorgeous power!
ORESTES.
Remember the bath—they stripped away your life, my father.
ELECTRA.
Remember the all-embracing net—they made it first for you.
ORESTES.
Chained like a beast—chains of hate, not bronze, my father!   480
ELECTRA.
Shamed in the schemes, the hoods they slung around you!

[25] Electra has been barred from marrying while Clytaemnestra and Aegisthus are alive, lest
she bear a son to avenge Agamemnon.
[26] Queen of the land of the dead.

ORESTES.
Does our taunting wake you, oh my father?
ELECTRA.
Do you lift your beloved head?
ORESTES.
Send us justice, fight for all you love,
or help us pin them grip for grip. They threw you— 485
don't you long to throw them down in turn?
ELECTRA.
One last cry, father. Look at your nestlings
stationed at your tomb—pity
your son and daughter. We are all you have.
ORESTES.
Never blot out the seed of Pelops here. 490
Then in the face of death you cannot die.

[*The* LEADER *comes forward again.*]

LEADER.
The voices of children—salvation to the dead!
Corks[27] to the net, they rescue the linen meshes
from the depths. This line will never drown!
ELECTRA.
Hear us—the long wail we raise is all for you. 495
Honor our call and you will save yourself.
LEADER.
And a fine thing it is to lengthen out the dirge;
you adore a grave and fate they never mourned.
But now for action—now you're set on action,
put your stars to proof.
ORESTES.
　　　　　　　　　So we will. 500
One thing first, I think it's on the track.
Why did she send libations? What possessed her,
so late, to salve a wound past healing?
To the unforgiving dead she sends this sop,
this . . . who am I to appreciate her gifts? 505
They fall so short of all her failings. True,
"pour out your all to atone an act of blood,
you work for nothing." So the saying goes.
I'm ready. Tell me what you know.
LEADER.
　　　　　　　　I know, my boy,
I was there. She had bad dreams. Some terror 510
came groping through the night—it shook her,
and she sent these cups, unholy woman.

---

[27] Floats to keep the net from sinking.

ORESTES.
And you know the dream, you can tell it clearly?
LEADER.
She dreamed she bore a snake, said so herself and . . .
ORESTES.
Come to the point—where does the story end?   515
LEADER.
. . . she swaddled it like a baby, laid it to rest.
ORESTES.
And food, what did the little monster want?
LEADER.
She gave it her breast to suck—she was dreaming.
ORESTES.
And didn't it tear her nipple, the brute inhuman—
LEADER.
Blood curdled the milk with each sharp tug . . .   520
ORESTES.
No empty dream. The vision of a man.
LEADER.
. . . and she woke with a scream, appalled,
and rows of torches, burning out of the blind dark,
flared across the halls to soothe the queen,
and then she sent the libations for the dead,   525
an easy cure she hopes will cut the pain.
ORESTES.
                                No,
I pray to the Earth and father's grave to bring
that dream to life in me. I'll play the seer—
it all fits together, watch!
If the serpent came from the same place as I,   530
and slept in the bands that swaddled me, and its jaws
spread wide for the breast that nursed me into life
and clots stained the milk, mother's milk,
and she cried in fear and agony—so be it.
As she bred this sign, this violent prodigy,   535
so she dies by violence. I turn serpent,
I kill her. So the vision says.
LEADER.
You are the seer for me, I like your reading.
Let it come! But now rehearse your friends.
Say do this, or don't do that—   540
ORESTES.
The plan is simple. My sister goes inside.
And I'd have her keep the bond with me a secret.
They killed an honored man by cunning, so
they die by cunning, caught in the same noose.
So he commands,   545
Apollo the Seer who's never lied before.

And I like a stranger, equipped for all events,
go to the outer gates with this man here,
Pylades, a friend, the house's friend-in-arms.
And we both will speak Parnassian, both try 550
for the native tones of Delphi.[28]
Now, say none
at the doors will give us a royal welcome
(after all the house is ridden by a curse),[29]
well then we wait . . . till a passer-by will stop
and puzzle and make insinuations at the house, 555
"Aegisthus shuts his door on the man who needs him.
Why, I wonder—does he know? Is he home?"
But once through the gates, across the threshold,
once I find that man on *my* father's throne,
or returning late to meet me face to face, 560
and his eyes shift and fall—
I promise you,
before he can ask me, "Stranger, who are you?"—
I drop him dead, a thrust of the sword, and twist!
Our Fury never wants for blood. *His* she drinks unmixed,
our third libation poured to Saving Zeus. 565

[*Turning to* ELECTRA.]

Keep a close watch inside, dear, be careful.
We must work together step by step.

[*To the* CHORUS.]

And you,
better hold your tongues, religiously.
Silence, friends, or speak when it will help.

[*Looking toward* PYLADES *and the
death-mound and beyond.*]

For the rest, watch over me, I need you— 570
guide my sword through struggle, guide me home!

[*As* ORESTES, PYLADES *and* ELEC-
TRA *leave, the women reassemble for
the* CHORUS.]

---

[28] Delphi and Mount Parnassus, both associated with the god Apollo, are in the region (Phokis) where Orestes has lived in exile. He may mean that he will adopt the regional dialect of Delphi or that his words will be delphic (obscure but faithful to the commission given him by Apollo).

[29] The curse would cause the house's inhabitants to sin against the laws of hospitality and also to fear visitors.

CHORUS.
　　Marvels, the Earth breeds many marvels,
　　　　terrible marvels overwhelm us.
　　The heaving arms of the sea embrace and swarm
　　with savage life. And high in the no man's land of night   575
　　torches[30] hang like swords. The hawk on the wing,
　　　　　　the beast astride the fields
　　can tell of the whirlwind's fury roaring strong.

　　　　Oh but a man's high daring spirit,
　　　　　　who can account for that? Or woman's   580
　　desperate passion daring past all bounds?
　　She couples with every form of ruin known to mortals.
　　　　Woman, frenzied, driven wild with lust,
　　　　　　twists the dark warm harness
　　of wedded love—tortures man and beast.   585

　　Well you know, you with a sense of truth
　　　　recall Althaia,[31]
　　the heartless mother
　　who killed her son,
　　ai! what a scheme she had—   590
　　　　　she rushed his destiny,
　　　　　　lit the bloody torch
　　preserved from the day he left her loins with a cry—
　　　　　　the life of the torch paced his,
　　burning on till Fate burned out his life.   595

　　There is one more in the tales of hate:
　　　　remember Scylla,[32]
　　the girl of slaughter
　　seduced by foes
　　to take her father's life.   600
　　　　The gift of Minos,
　　　　　　a choker forged in gold
　　turned her head and Nisos' immortal lock she cut
　　　　　　as he slept away his breath . . .
　　ruthless bitch, now Hermes takes her down.   605

[30] Strange celestial bodies, such as comets.

[31] The chorus in the following passage cites three examples of perverted parental, filial, or conjugal love, all of which in the present context are ironic or double-edged, like the matricide Orestes and Electra are planning. Althaia, in mythology, had been warned at the birth of her son Meleager that his life would end when a certain torch, or brand from the fire, was burnt out. She hid it away, but later her anger with her son, who had killed her brothers, impelled her to burn the torch, bringing on his death.

[32] This Scylla (not to be confused with the monster of the same name who threatened navigators of the straits of Messina) was in myth the daughter of Nisos, king of Megara, whose city was besieged by King Minos of Crete. In Aeschylus' version of her story she succumbed to bribery (in other versions her motive is love for Minos) and cut off a lock of her father's hair on which his life depended.

Now that I call to mind old wounds that never heal—
  Stop, it's time for the wedded love-in-hate,
for the curse of the halls,
      the woman's brazen cunning
            bent on her lord in arms,   610
  her warlord's power—
              Do you respect such things?
I prize the hearthstone warmed by faith,
a woman's temper nothing bends to outrage.

First at the head of legendary crime stands Lemnos.[33]
  People shudder and moan, and can't forget—   615
each new horror that comes
      we call the hells of Lemnos.
            Loathed by the gods for guilt,
  cast off by men, disgraced, their line dies out.
Who could respect what god detests?   620
What of these tales have I not picked with justice?

      The sword's at the lungs!—it stabs deep,
      the edge cuts through and through
    and Justice drives it—Outrage still lives on,
    not trodden to pieces underfoot, not yet,   625
     though the laws lie trampled down,
        the majesty of Zeus.

      The anvil of Justice stands fast
     and Fate beats out her sword.
   Tempered for glory, a child will wipe clean   630
  the inveterate stain of blood shed long ago—
     Fury brings him home at last,
      the brooding mother Fury!

              [*The women leave.* ORESTES *and*
              PYLADES *approach the house of*
              ATREUS.]

ORESTES.
                        Slave, the slave!—
  where is he? Hear me pounding the gates?
  Is there a man inside the house?   635
  For the third time, come out of the halls!
  If Aegisthus has them welcome friendly guests.

             [*A voice from inside.*]

---

[33]An island in the Aegean. It is associated in mythology and legend with atrocities, the most notorious being the attempted slaughter of all husbands and other males by the women of the island, who were jealous of their mistresses.

PORTER.
    All right, I hear you. . . .
    Where do you come from, stranger? Who are you?
ORESTES.
    Announce me to the masters of the house.   640
    I've come for them, I bring them news.
                                                    Hurry,
    the chariot of the night is rushing on the dark!
    The hour falls, the traveler casts his anchor
    in an inn where every stranger feels at home.
                                          Come out!
    Whoever rules the house. The woman in charge.   645
    No, the man, better that way.
    No scruples then. Say what you mean,
    man to man launch in and prove your point,
    make it clear, strong.

                            [CLYTAEMNESTRA *emerges* [34] *from*
                            the palace, attended by ELECTRA.]

CLYTAEMNESTRA.
                            Strangers, please,
    tell me what you would like and it is yours.   650
    We've all you might expect in a house like ours.
    We have warm baths and beds to charm away your pains
    and the eyes of Justice [35] look on all we do.
    But if you come for higher things, affairs
    that touch the state, that is the men's concern   655
    and I will stir them on.
ORESTES.
                            I am a stranger,
    from Daulis, close to Delphi. I'd just set out,
    packing my own burden bound for Argos
    (here I'd put my burden down and rest),
    when I met a perfect stranger, out of the blue,   660
    who asks about my way and tells me his.
                                          Strophios,
    a Phocian, so I gathered in conversation.

---

[34] Orestes had hoped that Aegisthus, about whom he feels "no scruples," would encounter
him first, but (by dramatic logic and the logic of the curse) he is brought immediately face-
to-face with his mother, who is simultaneously his fundamental antagonist, a person whose
intimate relationship to him causes the ambivalent human feelings in both of them, and the
most recent carrier of the self-propagating retaliatory curse that lies on the lineage of Atreus.
    [35] A typical specimen of the irony omnipresent in the trilogy. In extending the expected
hospitable welcome to the guest, Clytaemnestra evokes her murder of her husband
Agamemnon in his bath; the "eyes of Justice" are those that enforce the rites of hospitality
and (for the audience) are the forces that punish an adulterous wife for murdering her husband. The dialogue here between Clytaemnestra and Orestes epitomizes the tragedy of the
entire story: Clytaemnestra had killed her husband because he had murdered their daughter
Iphigeneia at Aulis; now she is engaged in a life-or-death struggle with another of her own
children.

"Well, my friend," he says, "out for Argos
in any case? Remember to tell the parents
he is dead, Orestes . . .
                              promise me please
(it's only right), it will not slip your mind.
Then whatever his people want, to bring him home
or bury him here, an alien, all outcast here
forever, won't you ferry back their wishes?
As it is, a bronze urn is armor to his embers.
The man's been mourned so well . . .."
                                        I only tell you
what I heard. And am I speaking now
with guardians, kinsmen who will care?
It's hard to say. But a parent ought to know.[36]

CLYTAEMNESTRA.
                                            I, I—
your words, you storm us, raze us to the roots,
you curse of the house so hard to wrestle down!
How you range—targets at peace, miles away,
and a shaft from your lookout brings them down.
You strip me bare of all I love, destroy me,
now—Orestes.

And he was trained so well, we'd been so careful,
kept his footsteps clear of the quicksand of death.
Just now, the hope of the halls, the surgeon to cure
our Furies' lovely revel—he seemed so close,
he's written off the rolls.

ORESTES.
                              If only I were . . .
my friends, with hosts as fortunate as you
if only I *could* be known for better news[37]
and welcomed like a brother. The tie between
the host and stranger, what is kinder?
But what an impiety, so it seemed to me,
not to bring this to a head for loved ones.

665
670
675
680
685
690

---

[36] This poignant line has at least three meanings: (a) "Shouldn't a mother know her own son?"; (b) "It is only right that this tragic message be delivered to a parent, not a more distant kinsman or guardian"; (c) "Any mother who killed her son's father should be told what has happened to the son she exiled so that she could commit her crimes." Clytaemnestra's reply, in her lines that follow, shows her mixed feelings as mother of the man she has most to fear.

[37] Messengers were frequently (if illogically) rewarded for bringing good news and were hated or punished for bringing bad news. Clytaemnestra's reply, that the messenger will "receive what you deserve," is another ambiguity; does she mean that he will be rewarded for bringing to Aegisthus (and perhaps to her) the good news that a potentially avenging son is dead, or that the news of this son's death, welcome or not, is a service to the dead son's family, or both? And does Clytaemnestra's reassurance that the messenger will be "as welcome in these halls as one of us" mean that he will be treated kindly or that he will be given the same kind of unnatural treatment that all the house of Atreus has given to its kindred?

I was bound by honor, bound by the rights
of hospitality.
CLYTAEMNESTRA.
                    Nothing has changed.
For all that you receive what you deserve,
as welcome in these halls as one of us.   695
Wouldn't another bear the message just as well?
But you must be worn from the long day's journey—
time for your rewards.

                              [*To* ELECTRA.]

                    Escort him in,
where the men who come are made to feel at home.
He and his retinue, and fellow travelers.   700
Let them taste the bounty of our house.
Do it, as if you depended on his welfare.

And we will rouse the powers in the house
and share the news. We never lack for loved ones,
we will probe this turn of fortune every way.   705

                    [ELECTRA *leads* ORESTES, PYLADES
                    and their retinue into the halls;
                    CLYTAEMNESTRA *follows, while the*
                    CHORUS *reassembles.*]

LEADER.
    Oh dear friends who serve the house,
        when can we speak out, when
    can the vigor of our voices serve Orestes?
CHORUS.
    Queen of the Earth, rich mounded Earth,
    breasting over the lord of ships,   710
    the king's corpse at rest,
    hear us now, now help us,
        now the time is ripe—
    Down to the pit Persuasion goes
    with all her cunning. Hermes of Death,   715
    the great shade patrols the ring
    to guide the struggles, drive the tearing sword.
LEADER.
    And I think our new friend is at his mischief.
    Look, Orestes' nurse in tears.

                              [*Enter* CILISSA.]

Where now, old-timer, padding along the gates?   720
With pain a volunteer to go your way.

NURSE.
"Aegisthus," [38]
your mistress calling, "hurry and meet your guests.
There's news. It's clearer man to man, you'll see."

And she looks at the maids and pulls that long face
and down deep her eyes are laughing over the work   725
that's done. Well and good for her. For the house
it's the curse all over—the strangers make that plain.
But let *him* hear, he'll revel once he knows.
Oh god,
the life is hard. The old griefs, the memories
mixing, cups of pain, so much pain in the halls,   730
the house of Atreus . . . I suffered, the heart within me
always breaking, oh, but I never shouldered
misery like this. So many blows, good slave,
I took my blows.
Now dear Orestes—
the sweetest, dearest plague of all our lives!   735

Red from your mother's womb I took you, reared you . . .
nights, the endless nights I paced, your wailing
kept me moving—led me a life of labor,
all for what?
And such care I gave it . . .
baby can't think for itself, poor creature.   740
You have to nurse it, don't you? Read its mind,
little devil's got no words, it's still swaddled.
Maybe it wants a bite or a sip of something,
or its bladder pinches—a baby's soft insides
have a will of their own. I had to be a prophet.   745
Oh I tried, and missed, believe you me, I missed,
and I'd scrub its pretty things until they sparkled.
Washerwoman and wetnurse shared the shop.
A jack of two trades, that's me,
and an old hand at both . . .
and so I nursed Orestes,   750
yes, from his father's arms I took him once,
and now they say he's dead,
I've suffered it all, and now I'll fetch that man,
the ruination of the house—give him the news,
he'll relish every word.

---

[38] In addition to revealing the nurse Cilissa's hatred for Aegisthus, her words introduce a poignantly human note. Like his mother, Clytaemnestra, Orestes is more, and less, than an instrument in a cosmic system of right and wrong; he was also a human baby who needed feeding and diaper changing. The nurse's comparison of herself to a "prophet" (line 745) in her dealings with a baby joins together the most cosmic, theological implications and the most homely, personal ones.

LEADER.
                              She tells him to come,   755
  but how, prepared?
NURSE.
                         Prepared, how else?
  I don't see . . .
LEADER.
                    With his men, I mean, or all alone?
NURSE.
  Oh, she says to bring his bodyguard, his cutthroats.
LEADER.
  No, not now, not if you hate our master—
  tell him to come alone.   760
  Nothing for him to fear then, when he hears.
  Have him come quickly too, rejoicing all the way!
  The teller sets the crooked message straight.
NURSE.
                                        What,
  you're *glad* for the news that's come?
LEADER.
                                  Why not,
  if Zeus will turn the evil wind to good?   765
NURSE.
  But how? Orestes, the hope of the house is gone.
LEADER.
  Not yet. It's a poor seer who'd say so.
NURSE.
  What are you saying—something I don't know?
LEADER.
  Go in with your message. Do as you're told.
  May the gods take care of cares that come from them.   770
NURSE.
  Well, I'm off. Do as I'm told.
  And here's to the best . . .
  some help, dear gods, some help.

                          [*Exit.*]

CHORUS.
  O now bend to my prayer, Father Zeus,
    lord of the gods astride the sky—   775
  grant them all good fortune,
  the lords of the house who strain to see
                strict discipline return.
  Our cry is the cry of Justice,
                Zeus, safeguard it well.

                              Zeus,   780
  set him against his enemies in the halls!

Do it, rear him to greatness—two, threefold
he will repay you freely, gladly.

Look now—watch the colt of a man you loved,
    yoked to the chariot of pain.   785
Now the orphan needs you—
harness his racing, rein him in,
            preserve his stride so we
can watch him surge in the homestretch,
            storming for the goal.   790

    And you who haunt the vaults
where the gold glows in the darkness,
hear us now, good spirits of the house,
        conspire with us—come,
and wash old works of blood   795
in the fresh-drawn blood of Justice.
Let the gray retainer, murder, breed no more.

And you, Apollo, lord of the glorious masoned cavern,[39]
    grant that this man's house lift up its head,
            that we may see with loving eyes   800
    the light of freedom burst from its dark veil!
    And lend a hand and scheme
for the rights, my Hermes, help us,
sail the action on with all your breath.
        Reveal what's hidden, please,   805
    or say a baffling word
in the night and blind men's eyes—
when the morning comes your word is just as dark.

Soon, at last, in the dawn that frees the house,
    we sea-widows wed to the winds   810
        will beat our mourning looms of song
                and sing, "Our ship's come in!
        Mine, mine is the wealth that swells her holds—
those I love are home and free of death."

But you, when your turn in the action comes, be strong.   815
        When she cries "Son!" cry out "My *father's* son!"
            Go through with the murder—innocent at last.

Raise up the heart of Perseus[40] in your breast!
    And for all you love under earth

---

[39] Apollo's temple at Delphi and the cleft in the earth over which it was built.

[40] The mythical hero Perseus, with the help of Pluto, Hermes, and Athena, killed Medusa, one of the three female monsters (the Gorgons) with snakes in their hair; anyone who looked at her was turned to stone. Athena gave Perseus a mirror so that he would not have to look directly at Medusa.

and all above its rim, now scarf your eyes   820
            against the Gorgon's fury—
    In, go in for the slaughter now!

                              [*Enter* AEGISTHUS, *alone.*]

    The butcher comes. Wipe out death with death.
AEGISTHUS.
    Coming, coming. Yes, I have my summons.
    There's news, I gather, travelers here to tell it.   825
    No joy in the telling though—Orestes dead.
    Saddle the house with a bloody thing like that
    and it might just collapse. It's still raw
    from the last murders, galled and raw.

    But how to take the story, for living truth?   830
    Or work of a woman's panic, gossip starting up
    in the night to flicker out and die?[41]

                              [*Turning to the* LEADER.]

                              Do you know?
    Tell me, clear my mind.
LEADER.
                              We've heard a little.
    But get it from the strangers, go inside.
    Messengers have no power. Nothing like   835
    a face-to-face encounter with the source.
AEGISTHUS.
    —Must see him, test the messenger. Where was he
    when the boy died, standing on the spot?
    Or is he dazed with rumor, mouthing hearsay?
    No, he'll never trap me open-eyed!   840

                              [*Striding through the doors.*]

CHORUS.
    Zeus, Zeus, what can I say?—
    how to begin this prayer, call down
        the gods for help? what words
    can reach the depth of all I feel?
    Now they swing to the work,   845
    the red edge of the cleaver
    hacks at flesh and men go down.
    Agamemnon's house goes down—
        all-out disaster now,
    or a son ignites the torch of freedom,   850

[41]Compare the chorus's skepticism about Clytaemnestra's report of the fall of Troy, in
Agamemnon.

wins the throne, the citadel,
    the fathers' realms of gold.
The last man on the bench,[42] a challenger
must come to grips with two. Up,
like a young god, Orestes, wrestle—   855
    let it be to win.

[*A scream inside the palace.*]

—Listen!
        —What's happening?
                —The house,
what have they done to the house?
LEADER.

                        Back,
till the work is over! Stand back—
they'll count us clean of the dreadful business.   860

[*The women scatter; a wounded
servant of* AEGISTHUS *enters.*]

Look, the die is cast, the battle's done.
SERVANT.

                    Ai,
Ai, all over, master's dead—Aie,
a third, last salute. Aegisthus is no more.

[*Rushing at a side door, struggling
to work it open.*]

Open up, wrench the bolts on the women's doors.
Faster! A strong young arm it takes,   865
but not to save him now, he's finished.
What's the use?
            Look—wake up!
                No good,
I call to the deaf, to sleepers . . . a waste of breath.
Where are you, Clytaemnestra? What are you doing?
LEADER.
Her head is ripe for lopping on the block.   870
She's next, and justice wields the ax.

[*The door opens, and* CLYTAEM-
NESTRA *comes forth.*]

CLYTAEMNESTRA.

                What now?
Why this shouting up and down the halls?

---

[42] The wrestler who must meet the winner of the earlier match or matches.

SERVANT.
    The dead are killing the living,[43] I tell you!
CLYTAEMNESTRA.
    Ah, a riddle. I do well at riddles.
    By cunning we die, precisely as we killed.   875
    Hand me the man-ax, someone, hurry!

                            [*The servant dashes out.*]

    Now we will see. Win all or lose all,
    we have come to this—the crisis of our lives.

                            [*The main doors open;* ORESTES,
                            *sword in hand, is standing over the
                            body of* AEGISTHUS, *with* PYLADES
                            close behind him.]

ORESTES.
    It's you I want. This one's had enough.
CLYTAEMNESTRA.
    Gone, my violent one—Aegisthus, very dear.   880
ORESTES.
    You love your man? Then lie in the same grave.
    You can never be unfaithful to the dead.

                            [*Pulling her toward* AEGISTHUS'
                            body.]

CLYTAEMNESTRA.
    Wait, son—no feeling for this, my child?
    The breast[44] you held, drowsing away the hours,
    soft gums tugging the milk that made you grow?   885

                            [ORESTES *turns to* PYLADES.]

ORESTES.
    What will I do, Pylades—I dread to kill my mother!
PYLADES.
    What of the future? What of the Prophet God Apollo,
    the Delphic voice, the faith and oaths we swear?
    Make all mankind your enemy, not the gods.
ORESTES.
    O you win me over—good advice.

                            [*Wheeling on* CLYTAEMNESTRA,
                            thrusting her toward AEGISTHUS.]

---

[43] The line means (a) the supposedly dead Orestes is killing Aegisthus, and (b) all the dead
victims of the curse on the house are taking revenge.
    [44] Either Clytaemnestra has exposed her breast or Orestes has done so in his violence.

This way— 890
I want to butcher you—right across his body!
In life you thought he dwarfed my father—*Die!*—
go down with him forever!
You love this man,
the man you should have loved you hated.
CLYTAEMNESTRA.
I gave you life. Let me grow old with you. 895
ORESTES.
What—kill my father, then you'd live with me?
CLYTAEMNESTRA.
Destiny had a hand in that, my child.
ORESTES.
This too: destiny is handing you your death.
CLYTAEMNESTRA.
You have no fear of a mother's curse, my son?
ORESTES.
Mother? You flung me to a life of pain. 900
CLYTAEMNESTRA.
Never flung you, placed you in a comrade's house.
ORESTES.
—Disgraced me, sold me, a freeborn father's son.
CLYTAEMNESTRA.
Oh? then name the price I took for you.
ORESTES.
I am ashamed to mention it[45] in public.
CLYTAEMNESTRA.
Please, and tell your father's failings too. 905
ORESTES.
Never judge him—he suffered, you sat here at home.
CLYTAEMNESTRA.
It hurts women, being kept from men, my son.
ORESTES.
Perhaps . . . but the man slaves to keep them safe at home.
CLYTAEMNESTRA.
—I see murder in your eyes, my child—mother's murder!
ORESTES.
You are the murderer, not I—and you will kill yourself.[46] 910
CLYTAEMNESTRA.
Watch out—the hounds of a mother's curse will hunt you down.
ORESTES.
But how to escape a father's if I fail?
CLYTAEMNESTRA.
I must be spilling live tears on a tomb of stone.

---

[45] Orestes probably means both the killing of Agamemnon in the son's absence and his mother's adultery. Her reply in the next line balances these crimes against Agamemnon's killing of Iphigeneia and his adulteries with Trojan women such as his captive, Cassandra.

[46] That is, she will have brought on her own death through her evil acts.

ORESTES.

Yes, my father's destiny—it decrees your death.

CLYTAEMNESTRA.

Ai—you are the snake I bore—I gave you life!

ORESTES.

                                                                    Yes!   915

That was the great seer, that terror in your dreams.

You killed and it was outrage—suffer outrage now.

> [*He draws her over the threshold; the
> doors close behind them, and the
> CHORUS gathers at the altar.*]

LEADER.

I even mourn the victims' double fates.

But Orestes fought, he reached the summit

of bloodshed here—we'd rather have it so.   920

The bright eye of the halls must never die.

CHORUS.

Justice came at last to the sons of Priam,

late but crushing vengeance, yes,

but to Agamemnon's house returned

        the double lion,[47]   925

                        the double onslaught

        drove to the hilt—the exile sped by god,

by Delphi's just command that drove him home.

Lift the cry of triumph O! the master's house

        wins free of grief, free of the ones   930

who bled its wealth, the couple stained with murder,

                        free of Fate's rough path.

He came back with a lust for secret combat,

stealthy, cunning vengeance, yes,

but his hand was steered in open fight   935

        by god's true daughter,

                        Right, Right we call her,

        we and our mortal voices aiming well—

she breathes her fury, shatters all she hates.

Lift the cry of triumph O! the master's house   940

        wins free of grief, free of the ones

who bled its wealth, the couple stained with murder,

                        free of Fate's rough path.

        Apollo wills it so!—

---

[47] Orestes and Pylades. The optimism expressed throughout this choral passage, the belief
that the curse has finally been put to rest and that the chain of acts of revenge has been broken, is shortsighted and premature. Later, the chorus will become aware of this fact.

Apollo, clear from the Earth's deep cleft   945
 his voice came shrill, "Now stealth will master stealth!"
And the pure god came down and healed our ancient wounds,
 the heavens come, somehow, to lift our yoke of grief—
 Now to praise the heavens' just command.

  Look, the light is breaking!   950
The huge chain that curbed the halls gives way.
   Rise up, proud house, long, too long
  your walls lay fallen, strewn along the earth.

  Time brings all to birth—
soon Time will stride through the gates with blessings,   955
 once the hearth burns off corruption, once
the house drives off the Furies. Look, the dice of Fate
 fall well for all to see. We sing how fortune smiles—
 the aliens in the house are routed out at last!

  Look, the light is breaking!   960
The huge chain that curbed the halls gives way.
   Rise up, proud house, long, too long
 your walls lay fallen, strewn along the earth.

> [*The doors open. Torches light*
> PYLADES *and* ORESTES, *sword in*
> *hand, standing over the bodies of*
> CLYTAEMNESTRA *and* AEGISTHUS,
> *as* CLYTAEMNESTRA *stood over*
> *the bodies of* AGAMEMNON *and*
> CASSANDRA.]

ORESTES.
  Behold the double tyranny of our land!
  They killed my father, stormed my fathers' house.   965
  They had their power when they held the throne.
  Great lovers still, as you may read their fate.
  True to their oath, hand in hand they swore
  to kill my father, hand in hand to die.
  Now they keep their word.

> [*Unwinding from the bodies on the*
> *bier the robes that entangled* AGA-
> MEMNON, *he displays them, as* CLY-
> TAEMNESTRA *had displayed them, to*
> *the* CHORUS *at the altar.*]

          Look once more on this,   970
you who gather here to attend our crimes—
the master-plot that bound my wretched father,

shackled his ankles, manacled his hands.
Spread it out! Stand in a ring around it,
a grand shroud for a man.
                              Here, unfurl it   975
so the Father—no, not mine but the One
who watches over all, the Sun can behold
my mother's godless work. So he may come,
my witness when the day of judgment comes,
that I pursued this bloody death with justice,   980
mother's death.
                        Aegisthus, why mention him?
The adulterer dies. An old custom, justice.

But she who plotted this horror against her husband,
she carried his children, growing in her womb
and she—I loved her once   985
and now I loathe, I have to loathe—
                                        what is she?

                        [*Kneeling by the body of his mother.*]

Some moray eel, some viper born to rot her mate
with a single touch, no fang to strike him,
just the wrong, the reckless fury in her heart!

                        [*Glancing back and forth from*
                        CLYTAEMNESTRA *to the robes.*]

This—how can I dignify this . . . snare for a beast?—   990
sheath for a corpse's feet?
                              This winding-sheet,
this tent for the bath of death!
                              No, a hunting net,
a coiling—what to call—?
                              Foot-trap—
woven of robes . . .
why, this is perfect gear for the highwayman   995
who entices guests and robs them blind and plies
the trade of thieves. With a sweet lure like this
he'd hoist a hundred lives and warm his heart,

Live with such a woman, marry *her*? Sooner
the gods destroy me—die without an heir!   1000
CHORUS.
        Oh the dreadful work . . .
        Death calls and she is gone.
            But oh, for you, the survivor,
        suffering is just about to bloom.

ORESTES.
> Did she do the work or not?—Here, come close— 1005
> This shroud's my witness, dyed with Aegisthus' blade[48]—
> Look, the blood ran here, conspired with time to blot
> the swirling dyes, the handsome old brocade.

> [*Clutching* AGAMEMNON*'s robes,
> burying his face in them and
> weeping.*]

> Now I can praise you, now I am here to mourn.
> You were my father's death, great robe, I hail you! 1010
> Even if I must suffer the work and the agony
> and all the race of man—
> I embrace you . . . you,
> my victory, are my guilt, my curse, and still—

CHORUS.
> No man can go through life
> and reach the end unharmed. 1015
> Aye, trouble is now,
> and trouble still to come.

ORESTES.
> But *still,*
> that you may know—
> I see no end in sight,
> I am a charioteer—the reins are flying, look,
> the mares plunge off the track—
> my bolting heart, 1020
> it beats me down and terror beats the drum,
> my dance-and-singing master pitched to fury—

> And still, while I still have some self-control,
> I say to my friends in public: I killed my mother,
> not with a little justice. She was stained 1025
> with father's murder, she was cursed by god.
> And the magic spells that fired up my daring?
> One comes first. The Seer of Delphi who declared,
> "Go through with this and you go free of guilt.
> Fail and—"
> I can't repeat the punishment. 1030
> What bow could hit the crest of so much pain?

> [PYLADES *gives* ORESTES *a branch
> of olive and invests him in the robes
> of Apollo, the wreath and insignia of
> suppliants to Delphi.*][49]

---

[48] Presumably the blade used by Clytaemnestra to kill Agamemnon.

[49] Apollo has promised to purge Orestes from blood guilt after Orestes returns to the god's temple.

Now look on me, armed with the branch and wreath,
a suppliant bound for the Navelstone of Earth,
Apollo's sacred heights
where they say the fire of heaven can never die.   1035

> [*Looking at his hand that still retains
> the sword.*]

I must escape this blood . . . it is my own.
—Must turn toward his hearth,
none but his, the Prophet God decreed.

I ask you, Argos and all my generations,
remember how these brutal things were done.   1040
Be my witness to Menelaus[50] when he comes.
And now I go, an outcast driven off the land,
in life, in death, I leave behind a name for—
LEADER.
But you've done well. Don't burden yourself
with bad omens, lash yourself with guilt.   1045
You've set us free, the whole city of Argos,
lopped the heads of these two serpents once for all.

> [*Staring at the women and beyond,*
> ORESTES *screams in terror.*]

ORESTES.
No, no! Women[51]—look—like Gorgons,
shrouded in black, their heads wreathed,
swarming serpents!
                    —Cannot stay, I must move on.   1050
LEADER.
What dreams can whirl you so? You of all men,
you have your father's love. Steady,
nothing to fear with all you've won.
ORESTES.
                                        No dreams,
these torments, not to me, they're clear, real—the hounds
of mother's hate.
LEADER.
                    The blood's still wet on your hands.   1055
It puts a kind of frenzy in you . . .

---

[50] Brother of Agamemnon and husband of Helen; he has not yet returned to Argos.
[51] The women are the Furies, avengers of blood guilt. In the final play of the trilogy they
will confront Orestes; eventually they will be renamed "the Eumenides" ("Kindly Ones").

ORESTES.

God Apollo!

Here they come, thick and fast,
their eyes dripping hate—
LEADER.

One thing
will purge you. Apollo's touch will set you free
from all your . . . torments.
ORESTES.

You can't see them— 1060
I can, they drive me on! I must move on—

[*He rushes out;* PYLADES *follows close behind.*]

LEADER.
Farewell then. God look down on you with kindness,
guard you, grant you fortune.
CHORUS.
Here once more, for the third time,
the tempest in the race has struck 1065
the house of kings and run its course.
First the children eaten,
the cause of all our pain, the curse.
And next the kingly man's ordeal,
the bath where the proud commander, 1070
lord of Achaea's armies lost his life.
And now a third has come, but who?
A third like Saving Zeus?
Or should we call him death?
Where will it end?— 1075
where will it sink to sleep and rest,
this murderous hate, this Fury?

THE EUMENIDES

CHARACTERS

THE PYTHIA, *the priestess of Apollo*
APOLLO
ORESTES
HERMES
THE GHOST OF CLYTAEMNESTRA

CHORUS OF FURIES AND THEIR
LEADER
ATHENA
Escorting Chorus of Athenian women
Men of the jury, herald, citizens

TIME AND SCENE

The FURIES *have pursued* ORESTES *to the temple of* APOLLO *at Delphi. It is morning. The priestess of the god appears at the great doors and offers up her prayer.*

PYTHIA.[1]
First of the gods I honor in my prayer is Mother Earth,
the first of the gods to prophesy, and next I praise
Tradition, second to hold her Mother's mantic seat,
so legend says, and third by the lots of destiny,
by Tradition's free will—no force to bear her down—   5
another Titan, child of the Earth, took her seat
and Phoebe passed it on as a birthday gift to Phoebus,
Phoebus a name for clear pure light derived from hers.
Leaving the marsh and razorback of Delos,[2] landing
at Pallas' headlands flocked by ships, here he came   10
to make his home Parnassus[3] and the heights.
And an escort filled with reverence brought him on,
the highway-builders, sons of the god of fire who tamed
the savage country, civilized the wilds—on he marched
and the people lined his way to cover him with praise,   15
led by Delphos,[4] lord, helm of the land, and Zeus
inspired his mind with the prophet's skill, with godhead,
made him fourth in the dynasty of seers to mount this throne,
but it is Zeus that Apollo speaks for, Father Zeus.
These I honor in the prelude of my prayers—these gods.   20
But Athena at the Forefront of the Temple[5] crowns our legends.
I revere the nymphs who keep the Corycian rock's[6] deep hollows,
loving haunt of birds where the spirits drift and hover.
And Great Dionysos rules the land. I never forget that day

[1] The name of the priestess derives from the Python, a dragon killed by Apollo when the god assumed power at Delphi. Omitting this incident, the priestess traces the history of the Delphic oracle (the "mantic," or prophetic, center of Greece) in terms of the successive powers or deities who prophesied there. The first was Earth, a primitive maternal being or principle, followed by Themis ("Tradition," associated with justice and custom), followed by Phoebe, a Titaness associated with the moon, followed by her grandson Phoebus, or Apollo, whom the priestess associates in her speech with highway building, the taming of savagery, and generally the advent of the civilized. But in fact, despite the Pythia's natural inclination toward the "Apollonian" values of reason and moderation, the play will be much more even-handed in its treatment of the conflicting claims of the primitive forces represented by the Furies, Mother Night, and Mother Earth, and on the other hand the more "civilized" forces Apollo represents.

[2] The island where Apollo was born.

[3] The mountain at Delphi; generally associated with Apollo, it actually had two peaks, one sacred to him and one to Dionysos, the god of wine who embodies the libidinal energies antithetical to Apollo's moderation. Dionysos rules the temple at Delphi during the winter, when Apollo is absent.

[4] The original king from whom Delphi was supposed to derive its name.

[5] Athena had a shrine near the temple's entrance.

[6] An area of Mount Parnassus; it contained a cave sacred to Pan, god of nature.

he marshaled his wild women in arms—he was all god, 25
he ripped Pentheus[7] down like a hare in the nets of doom.
And the rushing springs of Pleistos, Poseidon's[8] force I call,
and the king of the sky, the king of all fulfillment, Zeus.
Now the prophet goes to take her seat.[9] God speed me—
grant me a vision greater than all my embarkations past! 30

[*Turning to the audience.*]

Where are the Greeks among you? Draw your lots and enter.
It is the custom here. I will tell the future
only as the god will lead the way.

[*She goes through the doors and reappears in a moment, shaken, thrown
to her knees by some terrific force.*]

Terrors—
terrors to tell, terrors all can see!—
they send me reeling back from Apollo's house. 35
The strength drains, it's very hard to stand,
crawling on all fours, no spring in the legs . . .
an old woman,[10] gripped by fear, is nothing,
a child, nothing more.

[*Struggling to her feet, trying to compose herself.*]

I'm on my way to the vault, 40
it's green with wreaths, and there at the Navelstone[11]
I see a man—an abomination to god—
he holds the seat where suppliants sit for purging;[12]
his hands dripping blood, and his sword just drawn,
and he holds a branch (it must have topped an olive) 45
wreathed with a fine tuft of wool, all piety,
fleece gleaming white. So far it's clear, I tell you.

---

[7] The rationalistic Pentheus, opposed to the orgiastic worship of Dionysos, was torn apart
by his mother and other frenzied female worshipers of the god.
[8] God of the ocean.
[9] The seat is a tripod situated over the underground cleft beneath the temple. The Pythia's
role was to relay the utterances of Apollo.
[10] The Pythia was always an elderly woman.
[11] The Omphalos, a cone-shaped rock near or in the temple. It was believed to be the center of the earth.
[12] Because he has taken his mother Clytaemnestra's life, Orestes must be ritually "purged"
of the pollution of blood before he can be tried at law. Here he carries the emblems customary
for those seeking purgation.

But there in a ring around the man, an amazing company—
women,[13] sleeping, nestling against the benches . . .
women? No,   50
Gorgons I'd call them; but then with Gorgons
you'd see the grim, inhuman . . .
                              I saw a picture
years ago, the creatures tearing the feast
away from Phineus—
                    These have no wings,
I looked. But black they are, and so repulsive.   55
Their heavy, rasping breathing makes me cringe.
And their eyes ooze a discharge, sickening,
and what they wear—to flaunt *that* at the gods,
the idols, sacrilege! even in the homes of men.
The tribe that produced that brood I never saw,   60
or a plot of ground to boast it nursed their kind
without some tears, some pain for all its labor.

Now for the outcome. This is his concern,
Apollo the master of this house, the mighty power.
Healer, prophet, diviner of signs, he purges   65
the halls of others—He must purge his own.

                              [*She leaves. The doors of the temple
                              open and reveal* APOLLO *rising over*
                              ORESTES; *he kneels in prayer at the
                              Navelstone, surrounded by the* FURIES
                              who are sleeping. HERMES *waits in
                              the background.*]

APOLLO.
No, I will never fail you, through to the end
your guardian standing by your side or worlds away!
I will show no mercy to your enemies! Now
look at these—

                              [*Pointing to the* FURIES.]

                  these obscenities!—I've caught them,   70
beaten them down with sleep.
                              They disgust me.
These gray, ancient children never touched
by god, man or beast—the eternal virgins.
Born for destruction only, the dark pit,

---

[13] The Furies, who pursue Orestes in revenge for his act of matricide. Appropriately, the priestess of Apollo does not recognize these primitive beings; she guesses that they may be the Gorgons (female monsters the sight of whom turned gazers to stone) or Harpies (hideous bird women sent by Helios the sun god to punish the king Phineus by defiling his food; compare the description of the Harpies in Virgil's *Aeneid,* Book III).

they range the bowels of Earth, the world of death,   75
loathed by men and the gods who hold Olympus.[14]

Nevertheless keep racing on and never yield.
Deep in the endless heartland they will drive you,
striding horizons, feet pounding the earth forever,
on, on over seas and cities swept by tides!   80
Never surrender, never brood on the labor.

And once you reach the citadel of Pallas,[15] kneel
and embrace her ancient idol in your arms and there,
with judges of your case, with a magic spell—
with words—we will devise the master-stroke   85
that sets you free from torment once for all.
I persuaded you to take your mother's life.
ORESTES.
Lord Apollo, you know the rules of justice,
know them well. Now learn compassion too.
No one doubts your power to do great things.   90
APOLLO.
Remember that. No fear will overcome you.

> [*Summoning* HERMES *from the shadows.*]

You, my brother, blood of our common Father,
Hermes, guard him well. Live up to your name,
good Escort. Shepherd him well, he is my suppliant,
and outlaws have their rights that Zeus reveres.   95
Lead him back to the world of men with all good speed.

> [APOLLO *withdraws to his inner sanctuary;* ORESTES *leaves with* HERMES *in the lead.* THE GHOST OF CLYTAEMNESTRA *appears at the Navelstone, hovering over the* FURIES *as they sleep.*]

THE GHOST OF CLYTAEMNESTRA.
You—how can you *sleep?*
Awake, awake—what use are sleepers now?
I go stripped of honor, thanks to you,
alone among the dead. And for those I killed   100
the charges of the dead will never cease, never—

---

[14] There is a natural antipathy between the elemental and ancient force represented by the Furies and the modern, supposedly more advanced Olympian gods, especially Apollo.

[15] Athena; Apollo directs Orestes to her city, Athens. The "ancient idol" was a wooden statue of the goddess located there.

I wander in disgrace, I feel the guilt, I tell you,
withering guilt from all the outraged dead!

But I suffered too, terribly, from dear ones,
and none of my spirits rages to avenge me.   105
I was slaughtered by his matricidal hand.
See these gashes—

> [*Seizing one of the* FURIES *weak with
> sleep.*]

Carve them in your heart!
The sleeping brain has eyes that give us light;
we can never see our destiny by day.

And after all my libations . . . how you lapped   110
the honey, the sober offerings poured to soothe you,
awesome midnight feasts I burned at the hearthfire,
your dread hour never shared with gods.
All those rites, I see them trampled down.
And he springs free like a fawn, one light leap   115
at that—he's through the thick of your nets,
he breaks away!
Mocking laughter twists across his face.
Hear me, I am pleading for my life.
Awake, my Furies, goddesses of the Earth!   120
A dream is calling—Clytaemnestra calls you now.

> [*The* FURIES *mutter in their sleep.*]

Mutter on. Your man is gone, fled far away.
My son has friends to defend him, not like mine.

> [*They mutter again.*]

You sleep too much, no pity for my ordeal.
Orestes murdered his mother—he is gone.   125

> [*They begin to moan.*]

Moaning, sleeping—onto your feet, quickly.
What is your work? What but causing pain?
Sleep and toil, the two strong conspirators,
they sap the mother dragon's deadly fury—

> [*The* FURIES *utter a sharp moan and
> moan again, but they are still asleep.*]

FURIES.
Get him, get him, get him, get him—   130
there he goes.

THE GHOST OF CLYTAEMNESTRA.
                    The prey you hunt is just a dream—
like hounds mad for the sport you bay him on,
you never leave the kill.
                    But what are you *doing?*
Up! don't yield to the labor, limp with sleep.
Never forget my anguish.   135
Let my charges hurt you, they are just;
deep in the righteous heart they prod like spurs.
You, blast him on with your gory breath,
the fire of your vitals—wither him, after him,
one last foray—waste him, burn him out!

                              [*She vanishes. The lead* FURY *urges
                              on the pack.*]

LEADER.
                                        Wake up!   140
I rouse you, you rouse her. Still asleep?
Onto your feet, kick off your stupor.
See if this prelude has some grain of truth.

                              [*The* FURIES *circle, pursuing the scent
                              with hunting calls, and cry out singly
                              when they find* ORESTES *gone.*]

FURIES.
—Aieeeeee—no, no, *no,* they do us wrong, dear sisters.

—The miles of pain, the pain I suffer . . .   145
and all for nothing, all for pain, more pain,
          the anguish, oh, the grief too much to bear.

—The quarry's slipped from the nets, our quarry lost and gone.

          —Sleep defeats me . . . I have lost the prey.

—You—child of Zeus[16]—*you,* a common thief!   150

—Young god, you have ridden down the powers
proud with age. You worship the suppliant,
          the godless man who tears his parent's heart—

—The matricide, you steal him away, and you a god!

          —Guilt both ways, and who can call it justice?   155

—Not I: her charges stalk my dreams,

[16]Apollo.

yes, the charioteer rides hard,
            her spurs digging the vitals,
    under the heart, under the heaving breast—

—I can feel the executioner's lash, it's searing   160
            deeper, sharper, the knives of burning ice—

—Such is your triumph, you young gods,
    world dominion past all rights.
            Your throne is streaming blood,
    blood at the foot, blood at the crowning head—   165

—I can see the Navelstone of the Earth, it's bleeding,
            bristling corruption, oh, the guilt it has to bear—
Stains on the hearth! The Prophet stains the vault,
    he cries it on, drives on the crime himself.
            Breaking the god's first law, he rates men first,   170
                destroys the old dominions of the Fates.

He wounds me too, yet *him* he'll never free,
    plunging under the earth, no freedom then:
            curst as he comes for purging, at his neck
                he feels new murder springing from his blood.   175

                        [APOLLO *strides from his sanctuary*
                        in full armor, brandishing his bow
                        and driving back the FURIES.]

APOLLO.
    Out, I tell you, out of these halls—fast!—
set the Prophet's chamber free!

                        [*Seizing one of the* FURIES, *shaking*
                        an arrow across her face.]

                    Or take
the flash and stab of this, this flying viper
whipped from the golden cord that strings my bow!

Heave in torment, black froth erupting from your lungs,   180
vomit the clots of all the murders you have drained.
But never touch my halls, you have no right.

Go where heads are severed, eyes gouged out,
where Justice and bloody slaughter are the same . . .
castrations, wasted seed, young men's glories butchered,   185
extremities maimed, and huge stones at the chest,
and the victims wail for pity—
spikes inching up the spine, torsos stuck on spikes.

[*The* FURIES *close in on him.*]

So, you hear your love feast, yearn to have it all?
You revolt the gods. Your look, 190
your whole regalia gives you away—your kind
should infest a lion's cavern reeking blood.
But never rub your filth on the Prophet's shrine.
Out, you flock without a herdsman—out!
No god will ever shepherd you with love. 195
LEADER.
 Lord Apollo, now it is your turn to listen.
 You are no mere accomplice in this crime.
 You did it all, and all the guilt is yours.
APOLLO.
 No, how? Enlarge on that, and only that.
LEADER.
 You commanded the guest to kill his mother. 200
APOLLO.
 —Commanded him to avenge his father, what of it?
LEADER.
 And then you dared embrace him, fresh from bloodshed.
APOLLO.
 Yes, I ordered him on, to my house, for purging.
LEADER.
 And we sped him on, and you revile us?
APOLLO.
 Indeed, you are not fit to approach this house. 205
LEADER.
 And yet we have our mission and our—
APOLLO.
 Authority—you? Sound out your splendid power.
LEADER.
 Matricides: we drive them from their houses.
APOLLO.
 And what of the wife who strikes her husband down?
LEADER.
 That murder would not destroy one's flesh and blood. 210
APOLLO.
 Why, you'd disgrace—obliterate the bonds of Zeus
 and Hera queen of brides! And the queen of love
 you'd throw to the winds at a word, disgrace love,
 the source of mankind's nearest, dearest ties.
 Marriage of man and wife is Fate itself, 215
 stronger than oaths, and Justice guards its life.
 But if one destroys the other and you relent—
 no revenge, not a glance in anger—then
 I say your manhunt of Orestes is unjust.
 Some things stir your rage, I see. Others, 220
 atrocious crimes, lull your will to act.

                                              Pallas
will oversee this trial. She is one of us.[17]
LEADER.
    I will never let that man go free, never.
APOLLO.
    Hound him then, and multiply your pains.
LEADER.
    Never try to cut my power with your logic.   225
APOLLO.
    I'd never touch it, not as a gift—your power.
LEADER.
                                              Of course,
great as you are, they say, throned on high with Zeus.
But blood of the mother draws me on—must hunt
the man for Justice. Now I'm on his trail!

                                   [*Rushing out, with the* FURIES *in full
                                   cry.*]

APOLLO.
    And I will defend my suppliant and save him.   230
    A terror to gods and men, the outcast's anger,
    once I fail him, all of my own free will.

                                   [APOLLO *leaves. The scene changes
                                   to the Acropolis in Athens. Escorted
                                   by* HERMES, ORESTES *enters and
                                   kneels, exhausted, before the ancient
                                   shrine and idol of* ATHENA.]

ORESTES.
                                     Queen Athena,
under Apollo's orders I have come.
Receive me kindly. Curst and an outcast,
no suppliant for purging . . . my hands are clean.   235
My murderous edge is blunted now, worn down at last
on the outland homesteads, beaten paths of men.

On and out over seas and dry frontiers,
I kept alive the Prophet's strong commands.
Struggling toward your house, your idol—

                                   [*Taking the knees of* ATHENA'*s idol
                                   in his arms.*]

                                     Goddess,   240
here I keep my watch,
I await the consummation of my trial.

[17]One of the modern Olympian gods, whom the primitive Furies oppose.

[*The* FURIES *enter in pursuit but cannot find* ORESTES, *who is entwined
around* ATHENA'*s idol. The* LEADER
sees the footprints.]

LEADER.

At last!
The clear trail of the man. After it, silent
but it tracks his guilt to light. He's wounded—
go for the fawn, my hounds, the splash of blood,   245
hunt him, rake him down.
Oh, the labor,
the man-killing labor. My lungs are bursting . . .
over the wide rolling earth we've ranged in flock,
hurdling the waves in wingless flight and now we come,
all hot pursuit, outracing ships astern—and now   250
he's here, somewhere, cowering like a hare . . .
the reek of human blood—it's laughter to my heart!

[*Inciting a pair of* FURIES.]

Look, look again, you two,
scour the ground before he escapes—one dodge
and the matricide slips free.

[*Seeing* ORESTES, *one by one they press
around him and* ATHENA'*s idol.*]

FURIES.

—There he is!   255
Clutching the knees of power once again,
  twined in the deathless goddess' idol, look,
he wants to go on trial for his crimes.

—Never . . .
  the mother's blood that wets the ground,
  you can never bring it back, dear god,   260
the Earth drinks, and the running life is gone.

—No,
you'll give me blood for blood, you must!
  Out of your living marrow I will drain
my red libation, out of your veins I suck my food,
    my raw, brutal cups—

—Wither you alive,   265
  drag you down and there you pay, agony
for mother-killing agony!

—And there you will see them all.

Every mortal who outraged god or guest or loving parent:
each receives the pain his pains exact.

—A mighty god is Hades. There   270
   at the last reckoning underneath the earth
      he scans all, he squares all men's accounts
   and graves them on the tablets of his mind.

                              [ORESTES *remains impassive.*]

ORESTES.
   I have suffered into truth. Well I know
   the countless arts of purging, where to speak,   275
   where silence is the rule.[18] In this ordeal
   a compelling master urges me to speak.

                              [*Looking at his hands.*]

The blood sleeps, it is fading on my hands,
the stain of mother's murder washing clean.
It was still fresh at the god's hearth. Apollo   280
killed the swine[19] and the purges drove it off.
Mine is a long story
if I'd start with the many hosts I met,
I lived with, and I left them all unharmed.[20]
Time refines all things that age with time.   285

And now with pure, reverent lips I call
the queen of the land. Athena, help me!
Come without your spear—without a battle
you will win myself, my land, the Argive people[21]
true and just, your friends-in-arms forever.   290
Where are you now? The scorching wilds of Libya,
bathed by the Triton pool[22] where you were born?
Robes shrouding your feet
or shod and on the march to aid allies?
Or striding the Giants' Plain,[23] marshal of armies,   295
hero scanning, flashing through the ranks?
                                                    Come—
you can hear me from afar, you are a god.
Set me free from this!

[18] A person who had not been ritually purged might spread pollution merely by speaking.
[19] The animals normally sacrificed in rites of purgation.
[20] That he has not brought misfortune to his hosts indicates that Orestes has been successfully purged.
[21] Athens had contracted an alliance with Argos (the city where the action of the two earlier plays occurs) a few years before the *Oresteia* was performed.
[22] This lake in Libya, according to one version of the myth, was Athena's birthplace.
[23] The place where the Giants (offspring of Ouranos and Ge, the personification of Earth) unsuccessfully challenged the gods of Olympus. The present passage emphasizes Athena's role as warrior and guardian of her city, Athens.

LEADER.
Never—neither

Apollo's nor Athena's strength can save you.
Down you go, abandoned, 300
searching your soul for joy but joy is gone.
Bled white, gnawed by demons, a husk, a wraith—

[*She breaks off, waiting for reply, but*
ORESTES *prays in silence.*]

No reply? you spit my challenge back?
You'll feast me alive, my fatted calf,
not cut on the altar first. Now hear my spell, 305
the chains of song I sing to bind you tight.
FURIES.
Come, Furies, dance!—

link arms for the dancing hand-to-hand,
now we long to reveal our art,
our terror, now to declare our right
    to steer the lives of men, 310
we all conspire, we dance! we are
the just and upright, we maintain.
Hold out your hands, if they are clean
    no fury of ours will stalk you,
you will go through life unscathed. 315
But show us the guilty—one like this
    who hides his reeking hands,
and up from the outraged dead we rise,
witness bound to avenge their blood
we rise in flames against him to the end! 320

Mother who bore me,
    O dear Mother Night,
to avenge the blinded dead
and those who see by day,
    now hear me! The whelp Apollo 325
spurns my rights, he tears this trembling victim
        from my grasp—the one to bleed,
to atone away the mother-blood at last.

    Over the victim's burning head
this chant this frenzy striking frenzy 330
        lightning crazing the mind
            this hymn of Fury
chaining the senses, ripping cross the lyre,[24]
        withering lives of men!

---

[24] The lyre was associated with Apollo in his role as god of song and of joyful poetry.

This, this is our right,
   spun for us by the Fates,[25]   335
the ones who bind the world,
and none can shake our hold.
   Show us the mortals overcome,
insane to murder kin—we track them down
               till they go beneath the earth,   340
and the dead find little freedom in the end.

    Over the victim's burning head
this chant this frenzy striking frenzy
       lightning crazing the mind
              this hymn of Fury   345
    chaining the senses, ripping cross the lyre,
       withering lives of men!

Even at birth, I say, our rights were so ordained.
   The deathless gods must keep their hands far off—
no god may share our cups, our solemn feasts.   350
We want no part of their pious white robes—
   the Fates who gave us power made us free.

   Mine is the overthrow of houses, yes,
when warlust reared like a tame beast
      seizes near and dear—   355
         down on the man we swoop, aie!
            for all his power black him out!—
for the blood still fresh from slaughter on his hands.

So now, striving to wrench our mandate from the gods,
   we make ourselves exempt from their control,   360
we brook no trial—no god can be our judge.[26]

               [*Reaching toward* ORESTES.]

His breed, worthy of loathing, streaked with blood,
   Zeus slights, unworthy his contempt.

   Mine is the overthrow of houses, yes,
when warlust reared like a tame beast   365
      seizes near and dear—

---

[25] In mythology, the three sisters who control the "thread" of a human life. The first spins the thread, the second measures its length, and the third cuts it off at its destined end, the time of death.

[26] What the Furies are fighting for is not merely the punishment of Orestes as an individual. They also question the basic grounds of justice. How, they protest, can an Olympian—Athena, for example—be legally competent to decide the question of whether the Olympians or the more primeval powers should be the final court of appeal? And, even more fundamentally, should the primitive law of retaliation for crimes against kindred be subordinated to *any* court or technical legal system?

down on the man we swoop, aie!
for all his power black him out!—
for the blood still fresh from slaughter on his hands.

And all men's dreams of grandeur, 370
tempting the heavens,
all melt down, under earth their pride goes down—
lost in our onslaught, black robes swarming,
Furies throbbing, dancing out our rage.

Yes! leaping down from the heights, 375
dead weight in the crashing footfall
down we hurl on the runner
breakneck for the finish—
cut him down, our fury stamps him down!

Down he goes, sensing nothing, 380
blind with defilement . . .
darkness hovers over the man, dark guilt,
and a dense pall overhangs his house,
legend tells the story through her tears.

Yes! leaping down from the heights, 385
dead weight in the crashing footfall
down we hurl on the runner
breakneck for the finish—
cut him down, our fury stamps him down!

So the center holds. 390
We are the skilled, the masterful,
we the great fulfillers,
memories of grief, we awesome spirits
stern, unappeasable to man,
disgraced, degraded, drive our powers through; 395
banished far from god to a sunless, torchlit dusk,[27]
we drive men through their rugged passage,
blinded dead and those who see by day.

---

[27] These two lines, applicable to either the Furies or their victims, are a good gloss on the Furies. Both they and the punished sinners dwell in a dark underground world that is the polar opposite of the heaven and light where the newer gods dwell on Mount Olympus (above, not below, humanity). Since the Furies and the sinners inhabit the same dark place, the Furies can be understood not just as an external force of punishment but also as the internal force of guilty conscience; the sinner is ultimately his or her own avenger. The concept is akin to what Dante intimates in his *Inferno,* that the outer and internal forces that punish sin are not clearly separable. Intriguingly, then, the Furies can be interpreted as either a primitive force superseded by an advance in ethical understanding or—as a modern depth-psychologist might argue—the personification of a timeless fact about human psychology that has been obscured by the illusory progress of "civilization."

Then where is the man
not stirred with awe, not gripped by fear   400
to hear us tell the law that
Fate ordains, the gods concede the Furies,
absolute till the end of time?
And so it holds, our ancient power still holds.
We are not without our pride, though beneath the earth   405
our strict battalions form their lines,
groping through the mist and sunstarved night.

[*Enter* ATHENA, *armed for combat
with her aegis*[28] *and her spear.*]

ATHENA.
From another world I heard a call for help.
I was on the Scamander's banks, just claiming Troy.[29]
The Achaean warlords chose the hero's share   410
of what their spear had won—they decreed that land,
root and branch all mine, for all time to be,
for Theseus' sons a rare, matchless gift.

Home from the wars I come, my pace unflagging,
wingless, flown on the whirring, breasting cape   415
that yokes my racing spirit in her prime.

[*Unfurling the aegis, seeing* ORESTES
and the FURIES *at her shrine.*]

And I see some new companions on the land.
Not fear, a sense of wonder fills my eyes.

Who are you? I address you all as one:
you, the stranger seated at my idol,   420
and you, like no one born of the sown seed,
no goddess watched by the gods, no mortal either,
not to judge by your look at least, your features . . .
Wait, I call my neighbors into question.
They've done nothing wrong. It offends the rights,   425
it violates tradition.
LEADER.
You will learn it all,
young daughter of Zeus, cut to a few words.
We are the everlasting children of the Night.
Deep in the halls of Earth they call us Curses.

[28] Here, a cape worn by Athena.
[29] In Aeschylus' time the Athenians had a colony near Troy that they claimed had been given them by right after the Trojan War. "Theseus' sons" (line 413) are the Athenians; he was the legendary hero of their city.

ATHENA.
Now I know your birth, your rightful name— 430
LEADER.
But not our powers, and you will learn them quickly.
ATHENA.
I can accept the facts, just tell them clearly.
LEADER.
Destroyers of life: we drive them from their houses.
ATHENA.
And the murderer's flight, where does it all end?
LEADER.
Where there is no joy, the word is never used. 435
ATHENA.
Such flight for him? You shriek him on to that?
LEADER.
Yes,
he murdered his mother—called that murder just.
ATHENA.
And nothing forced him on, no fear of someone's anger?
LEADER.
What spur could force a man to kill his mother?
ATHENA.
Two sides are here, and only half is heard. 440
LEADER.
But the oath[30]—he will neither take the oath nor give it,
no, his will is set.
ATHENA.
And you are set
on the name of justice rather than the act.
LEADER.
How? Teach us. You have a genius for refinements.
ATHENA.
Injustice, I mean, should never triumph thanks to oaths. 445
LEADER.
Then examine him yourself, judge him fairly.
ATHENA.
You would turn over responsibility to me,
to reach the final verdict?
LEADER.
Certainly.[31]
We respect you. You show us respect.

[ATHENA *turns to* ORESTES.]

---

[30] The ritual oath of innocence. Orestes refuses it because the fact itself of matricide is for him not the main issue. A few lines later Athena argues that such rituals should not govern in legal contests.
[31] The Furies now agree to be bound by Athena's verdict.

ATHENA.
 Your turn, stranger. What do you say to this?   450
 Tell us your land, your birth, your fortunes.
 Then defend yourself against their charge,
 if trust in your rights has brought you here to guard
 my hearth and idol, a suppliant for purging
 like Ixion,[32] sacred. Speak to all this clearly,   455
 speak to me.
ORESTES.
       Queen Athena, first,
 the misgiving in your final words is strong.
 Let me remove it. I haven't come for purging.
 Look, not a stain on the hands that touch your idol.
 I have proof for all I say, and it is strong.   460

 The law condemns the man of the violent hand
 to silence, till a master trained at purging
 slits the throat of a young suckling victim,
 blood absolves his blood. Long ago
 at the halls of others I was fully cleansed   465
 in the cleansing springs, the blood of many victims.
 Threat of pollution, sweep it from your mind.

 Now for my birth. You will know at once.
 I am from Argos. My father, well you ask,
 was Agamemnon, sea-lord of the men-of-war,   470
 your partisan when you made the city Troy
 a city of the dead.
      What an ignoble death he died
 when he came home—Ai! my blackhearted mother
 cut him down, enveloped him in her handsome net—
 it still attests his murder in the bath.   475
 But I came back, my years of exile weathered—
 killed the one who bore me, I won't deny it,
 killed her in revenge. I loved my father,
 fiercely.
    And Apollo shares the guilt—
 he spurred me on, he warned of the pains I'd feel   480
 unless I acted, brought the guilty down.
 But were we just or not? Judge us now.
 My fate is in your hands. Stand or fall
 I shall accept your verdict.
ATHENA.
      Too large a matter,
 some may think, for mortal men to judge.   485

---

[32]After murdering his father-in-law, Ixion was absolved by Zeus. (Later, after trying to seduce Zeus's consort, Hera, Ixion was punished by being tied in the Underworld to an ever-revolving wheel.)

But by all rights not even I should decide
a case of murder—murder whets the passions.
Above all, the rites have tamed your wildness.
A suppliant, cleansed, you bring my house no harm.
If you are innocent, I'd adopt you for my city. 490

[*Turning to the* FURIES.]

But they have their destiny too, hard to dismiss,
and if they fail to win their day in court—
how it will spread, the venom of their pride,
plague everlasting blights our land, our future . . .

So it stands. A crisis either way. 495

[*Looking back and forth from*
ORESTES *to the* FURIES.]

Embrace the one? expel the other? It defeats me.

But since the matter comes to rest on us,
I will appoint the judges of manslaughter,
swear them in, and found a tribunal here
for all time to come.[33]

[*To* ORESTES *and the* FURIES.]

My contestants, 500
summon your trusted witnesses and proofs,
your defenders under oath to help your cause.
And I will pick the finest men of Athens,
return and decide the issue fairly, truly—
bound to our oaths, our spirits bent on justice. 505

[ATHENA *leaves. The* FURIES *form
their chorus.*]

FURIES.
Here, now,[34] is the overthrow
of every binding law—once his appeal,
his outrage wins the day,
his matricide! One act links all mankind,
hand to desperate hand in bloody license. 510
Over and over deathstrokes

---

[33] The court of the Areopagus, the main forum of the Athenian judicial system.

[34] In the following chorus, the Furies argue that the force they represent, of vengeance and fear of punishment, is the very foundation of social order; if Orestes is acquitted, the whole community will be engulfed by general chaos, since the distinction between good and evil will no longer govern human behavior.

dealt by children wait their parents,
mortal generations still unborn.

We are the Furies still, yes,
but now our rage that patrolled the crimes of men,   515
    that stalked their rage dissolves—
we loose a lethal tide to sweep the world!
Man to man foresees his neighbor's torments,
    groping to cure his own—
        poor wretch, there is no cure, no use,   520
    the drugs that ease him speed the next attack.

Now when the sudden blows come down,
let no one sound the call that once brought help,
"Justice, hear me—Furies throned in power!"
    Oh I can hear the father now   525
    or the mother sob with pain
        at the pain's onset . . . hopeless now,
the house of Justice falls.

There is a time when terror helps,
the watchman must stand guard upon the heart.   530
It helps, at times, to suffer into truth.
    Is there a man who knows no fear
    in the brightness of his heart,
        or a man's city, both are one,
    that still reveres the rights?   535

            Neither the life of anarchy
            nor the life enslaved by tyrants, no,
                worship neither.
Strike the balance all in all and god will give you power;
    the laws of god may veer from north to south—   540
        we Furies plead for Measure.
    Violence is Impiety's child, true to its roots,
but the spirit's great good health breeds all we love
    and all our prayers call down,
        prosperity and peace.   545

            All in all I tell you people,
            bow before the altar of the rights,
                revere it well.
Never trample it underfoot, your eyes set on spoils;
    revenge will hunt the godless day and night—   550
        the destined end awaits.
So honor your parents first with reverence, I say,
and the stranger guest you welcome to your house,
        turn to attend his needs,
            respect his sacred rights.   555

All of your own free will, all uncompelled,
be just and you will never want for joy,
you and your kin can never be uprooted from the earth.
The reckless one—I warn the marauder
dragging plunder, chaotic, rich beyond all rights: 560
he'll strike his sails,
harried at long last,
stunned when the squalls of torment break his spars to bits.

He cries to the deaf, he wrestles walls of sea
sheer whirlpools down, down, with the gods' laughter 565
breaking over the man's hot heart—they see him flailing, crushed.
The one who boasted never to shipwreck
now will never clear the cape and steer for home;
he lived for wealth,
golden his life long— 570
he rams on the reef of law and drowns unwept, unseen.

> [*The scene has shifted to the Areopagus, the tribunal on the Crag of Ares.*[35] ATHENA *enters in procession with a herald and ten citizens she has chosen to be judges.*]

ATHENA.
Call for order, herald, marshal our good people.
Lift the Etruscan battle-trumpet,[36]
strain it to full pitch with human breath,
crash out a stabbing blast along the ranks. 575

> [*The trumpet sounds. The judges take up positions between the audience and the actors.* ATHENA *separates the* FURIES *and* ORESTES, *directing him to the Stone of Outrage and the* LEADER *to the Stone of Unmercifulness, where the* FURIES *form their chorus. Then* ATHENA *takes her stand between two urns that will receive the ballots.*]

And while this court of judgment fills, my city,
silence will be best. So that you can learn
my everlasting laws. And you too,

> [*To* ORESTES *and the* FURIES.]

[35]Ares, the god of war, had according to legend once been tried on the Areopagus (the "Crag of Ares" in Athens), for murder.
[36]Athena's battle trumpet, supposedly made in a region of northern Italy.

that our verdict may be well observed by all.

[APOLLO *enters suddenly and looms*
behind ORESTES.]

Lord Apollo—rule it over your own sphere!   580
What part have you in this? Tell us.
APOLLO.
                                        I come
as a witness. This man, according to custom,
this suppliant sought out my house and hearth.
I am the one who purged his bloody hands.
His champion too, I share responsibility   585
for his mother's execution.
                                        Bring on the trial.
You know the rules, now turn them into justice.

[ATHENA *turns to the* FURIES.]

ATHENA.
The trial begins! Yours is the first word—
the prosecution opens. Start to finish,
set the facts before us, make them clear.   590
LEADER.
Numerous as we are, we will be brief.

[*To* ORESTES.]

Answer count for count, charge for charge.
First, tell us, did you kill your mother?
ORESTES.
I killed her. There's no denying that.
LEADER.
Three falls in the match. One is ours[37] already.   595
ORESTEA.
You exult before your man is on his back.
LEADER.
But *how* did you kill her? You must tell us that.
ORESTES.
I will. I drew my sword—more, I cut her throat.
LEADER.
And who persuaded you? who led you on?
ORESTES.
This god and his command.

[*Indicating* APOLLO.]

---

[37] Three overthrows of the opponent were required to win a wrestling match; the Leader
claims to have won the first.

He bears me witness.   600
LEADER.
The Seer? He drove you on to matricide?
ORESTES.
Yes,
and to this hour I have no regrets.
LEADER.
If the verdict
brings you down, you'll change your story quickly.
ORESTES.
I have my trust; my father will help me from the grave.
LEADER.
Trust to corpses now! You made your mother one.   605
ORESTES.
I do. She had two counts against her, deadly crimes.
LEADER.
How? Explain that to your judges.
ORESTES.
She killed her husband—killed my father too.
LEADER.
But murder set her free, and you live on for trial.
ORESTES.
She lived on. You never drove *her* into exile—why?   610
LEADER.
The blood of the man she killed was not her own.
ORESTES.
And I? Does mother's blood run in my veins?
LEADER.
How could she breed you in her body, murderer?
Disclaim your mother's blood? She gave you life.

[ORESTES *turns to* APOLLO.]

ORESTES.
Bear me witness—show me the way, Apollo!   615
Did I strike her down with justice?
Strike I did, I don't deny it, no.
But how does our bloody work impress you now?—
Just or not? Decide.
I must make my case to them.

[*Looking to the judges.*]

APOLLO.
Just,   620
I say, to you and your high court, Athena.
Seer that I am, I never lie. Not once
from the Prophet's thrones have I declared
a word that bears on man, woman or city
that Zeus did not command, the Olympian Father.   625

This is *his* justice—omnipotent, I warn you.
Bend to the will of Zeus. No oath can match
the power of the Father.
LEADER.
                                                    Zeus, you say,
gave that command to your oracle? He charged
Orestes here to avenge his father's death   630
and spurn his mother's rights?
APOLLO.
                                                    —Not the same
for a noble man to die, covered with praise,
his scepter the gift of god—murdered, at that,
by a woman's hand, no arrows whipping in
from a distance as an Amazon[38] would fight.   635
But as you will hear, Athena, and your people
poised to cast their lots and judge the case.
Home from the long campaign he came, more won
than lost on balance, home to her loyal, waiting arms,
the welcome bath . . .
                                          he was just emerging at the edge,   640
and there she pitched her tent, her circling shroud—
she shackled her man in robes,
in her gorgeous never-ending web she chopped him down!

Such was the outrage of his death, I tell you,
the lord of the squadrons, that magnificent man.   645
Her I draw to the life to lash your people,
marshaled to reach a verdict.
LEADER.
                                                    Zeus, you say,
sets more store by a father's death? He shackled
his own father, Kronos[39] proud with age.
Doesn't that contradict you?   650

[*To the judges.*]

Mark it well. I call you all to witness.
APOLLO.
You grotesque, loathsome—the gods detest you!
Zeus can break chains, we've cures for that,
countless ingenious ways to set us free.
But once the dust drinks down a man's blood,   655
he is gone, once for all. No rising back,
no spell sung over the grave can sing him back—

---

[38] The Amazons were women warriors, noted especially as archers.
[39] Zeus had overcome his father Kronos (the Roman Saturn) and imprisoned him in the
Underworld; Apollo will reply to this charge by arguing that imprisonment is not the same as
irrevocable death.

not even Father can. Though all things else
he can overturn and never strain for breath.
LEADER.
                                             So
you'd force this man's acquittal? Behold, Justice!   660

[*Exhibiting* APOLLO *and* ORESTES.]

Can a son spill his mother's blood on the ground,
then settle into his father's halls in Argos?
Where are the public altars he can use?
Can the kinsmen's holy water touch his hands?
APOLLO.
Here is the truth, I tell you—see how right I am.   665
The woman you call the mother of the child
is not the parent,[40] just a nurse to the seed,
the new-sown seed that grows and swells inside her.
The *man* is the source of life—the one who mounts.
She, like a stranger for a stranger, keeps   670
the shoot alive unless god hurts the roots.
I give you proof that all I say is true.
The father can father forth without a mother.
Here she stands, our living witness. Look—

[*Exhibiting* ATHENA.]

Child sprung full-blown from Olympian Zeus,   675
never bred in the darkness of the womb
but such a stock no goddess could conceive!

And I, Pallas, with all my strong techniques
will rear your host and battlements to glory.
So I dispatched this suppliant to your hearth   680
that he might be your trusted friend forever,
that you might win a new ally,[41] dear goddess.
He and his generations arm-in-arm with yours,
your bonds stand firm for all posterity—
ATHENA.
                                           Now
have we heard enough? May I have them cast   685
their honest lots as conscience may decide?
LEADER.
For us, we have shot our arrows, every one.
I wait to hear how this ordeal will end.

---

[40] This genetic theory is proved, Apollo goes on to argue, by Athena herself, who was born
from Zeus's head.
[41] The people of Argos; at the time of the *Oresteia*, Athens had recently concluded an alliance
with them.

ATHENA.

Of course.

And what can I do to merit your respect?

APOLLO.

You have heard what you have heard.   690

[*To the judges.*]

Cast your lots, my friends,
strict to the oath that you have sworn.

ATHENA.

And now
if you would hear my law, you men of Greece,
you who will judge the first trial of bloodshed.
Now and forever more, for Aegeus' people[42]   695
this will be the court where judges reign.
This is the Crag of Ares, where the Amazons
pitched their tents when they came marching down
on Theseus, full tilt in their fury, erecting
a new city to overarch his city, towers thrust   700
against his towers—they sacrificed to Ares,
named this rock from that day onward Ares' Crag.
Here from the heights, terror and reverence,
my people's kindred powers
will hold them from injustice through the day   705
and through the mild night. Never pollute
our law with innovations. No, my citizens,
foul a clear well and you will suffer thirst.
Neither anarchy nor tyranny, my people.
Worship the Mean, I urge you,   710
shore it up with reverence and never
banish terror from the gates, not outright.[43]
Where is the righteous man who knows no fear?
The stronger your fear, your reverence for the just,
the stronger your country's wall and city's safety,   715
stronger by far than all men else possess
in Scythia's rugged steppes or Pelops' level plain.[44]
Untouched by lust for spoil, this court of law
majestic, swift to fury, rising above you
as you sleep, our night watch always wakeful,   720
guardian of our land—I found it here and now.

So I urge you, Athens. I have drawn this out
to rouse you to your future. You must rise,

[42] The Athenians; Aegeus was a legendary ruler of the city and father of Theseus.
[43] The phrase probably means two things: (a) maintain as part of your conscience a wholesome fear of committing evil, and (b) do not summarily turn away from your city a frightened stranger seeking asylum.
[44] That is, in the wild land of faraway Scythia or in the Grecian land of Pelops that included Argos.

each man must cast his lot and judge the case,
reverent to his oath. Now I have finished. 725

[*The judges come forward, pass
between the urns and cast their lots.*]

LEADER.
Beware. Our united force can break your land.
Never wound our pride, I tell you, never.
APOLLO.
The oracles, not mine alone but Zeus's too—
dread them, I warn you, never spoil their fruit.

[*The* LEADER *turns to* APOLLO.]

LEADER.
You dabble in works of blood beyond your depth. 730
Oracles, your oracles will be stained forever.
APOLLO.
Oh, so the Father's judgment faltered when Ixion,
the first man-slayer came to him for purging?
LEADER.
Talk on, talk on. But if I lose this trial
I will return in force to crush the land. 735
APOLLO.
Never—among the gods, young and old,
you go disgraced. I will triumph over you!
LEADER.
Just as you triumphed in the house of Pheres,[45]
luring the Fates to set men free from death.
APOLLO.
What?—is it a crime to help the pious man, 740
above all, when his hour of need has come?
LEADER.
You brought them down, the oldest realms of order,
seduced the ancient goddesses with wine.
APOLLO.
You will fail this trial—in just a moment
spew your venom and never harm your enemies. 745
LEADER.
You'd ride me down, young god, for all my years?
Well here I stand, waiting to learn the verdict.
Torn with doubt . . . to rage against the city or—

---

[45] Father of Admetus, a favorite of Apollo, who preserved Admetus from destined death
by overcoming "the ancient goddesses"—that is, the Fates—"with wine" (line 743) so that they
agreed to accept an alternative victim. Admetus' wife Alcestis offered her own life instead of
his. The story is told in Euripides' *Alcestis.*

ATHENA.
My work is here, to render the final judgment.
Orestes,

                              [*Raising her arm, her hand clenched
                              as if holding a ballot-stone.*]

          I will cast my lot for you.   750
No mother gave me birth.
I honor the male, in all things but marriage.
Yes, with all my heart I am my Father's child.
I cannot set more store by the woman's death—
she killed her husband, guardian of their house.   755
Even if the vote is equal, Orestes wins.[46]

Shake the lots from the urns. Quickly,
you of the jury charged to make the count.

                         [*Judges come forward, empty the urns,
                         and count the ballot-stones.*]

ORESTES.
O God of the Light, Apollo, how will the verdict go?
LEADER.
O Night, dark mother, are you watching now?   760
ORESTES.
Now for the goal—the noose, or the new day!
LEADER.
Now we go down, or forge ahead in power.
APOLLO.
Shake out the lots and count them fairly, friends.
Honor Justice. An error in judgment now
can mean disaster. The cast of a single lot   765
restores a house to greatness.

                         [*Receiving the judges' count,* ATHENA
                         lifts her arm once more.]

ATHENA.
                    The man goes free,
cleared of the charge of blood. The lots are equal.
ORESTES.
O Pallas Athena—you, you save my house!
I was shorn of the fatherland but you
reclaim it for me. Now any Greek will say,   770

---

[46] In interpreting Athena's decision here, we can accept her own explanation, that she is her father Zeus's child (an Olympian who is biased toward males). But these reasons seem incompatible with her evenhandedness elsewhere in the play. That she has not simply ignored the Furies' side of the case is proved by her later actions and words.

"He lives again, the man of Argos lives
on his fathers' great estates. Thanks to Pallas,
Apollo and Zeus, the lord of all fulfillment,
Third, Saving Zeus." He respected father's death,
looked down on mother's advocates—

[*Indicating the* FURIES.]

he saved me. 775

And now I journey home. But first I swear
to you, your land and assembled host, I swear
by the future years that bring their growing yield
that no man, no helmsman of Argos wars on Athens,
spears in the vanguard moving out for conquest. 780
We ourselves, even if we must rise up from the grave,
will deal with those who break the oath I take—
baffle them with disasters, curse their marches,
send them hawks aloft on the left[47] at every crossing—
make their pains recoil upon their heads. 785
But all who keep our oath, who uphold your rights
and citadel forever, comrade spear to spear,
we bless with all the kindness of our heart.
Now farewell, you and the people of your city.
Good wrestling—a grip no foe can break. 790
A saving hope, a spear to bring you triumph!

[*Exit* ORESTES, *followed by* APOLLO.
The FURIES *reel in wild confusion
around* ATHENA.]

FURIES.
You, you younger gods!—you have ridden down
the ancient laws, wrenched them from my grasp—
and I, robbed of my birthright, suffering, great with wrath,
I loose my poison over the soil, aieee!— 795
poison to match my grief comes pouring out my heart,
cursing the land to burn it sterile and now
rising up from its roots a cancer blasting leaf and child,
now for Justice, Justice!—cross the face of the earth
the bloody tide comes hurling, all mankind destroyed. 800
. . . Moaning, only moaning? What will I do?
The mockery of it, Oh unbearable,
mortified by Athens,
we the daughters of Night,
our power stripped, cast down.

---

[47] The left was the side on which ill omens supposedly appeared. Compare the eagles (mentioned in *Agamemnon,* lines 118 ff.) who appeared on the right before the sacrifice of Iphigeneia at Aulis.

ATHENA.
                                              Yield to me.   805
No more heavy spirits. You were not defeated—
the vote was tied, a verdict fairly reached
with no disgrace to you, no, Zeus brought
luminous proof before us. He who spoke
god's oracle, he bore witness that Orestes   810
did the work but should not suffer harm.

And now you'd vent your anger, hurt the land?
Consider a moment. Calm yourself. Never
render us barren, raining your potent showers
down like spears, consuming every seed.   815
By all my rights I promise you your seat
in the depths of earth,[48] yours by all rights—
stationed at hearths equipped with glistening thrones,
covered with praise! My people will revere you.

FURIES.
You, you younger gods!—you have ridden down   820
        the ancient laws, wrenched them from my grasp—
and I, robbed of my birthright, suffering, great with wrath,
        I loose my poison over the soil, aieee!—
poison to match my grief comes pouring out my heart,
                cursing the land to burn it sterile and now   825
rising up from its roots a cancer blasting leaf and child,
                now for Justice, Justice!—cross the face of the earth
the bloody tide comes hurling, all mankind destroyed.
. . . Moaning, only moaning? What will I do?
        The mockery of it, Oh unbearable,   830
mortified by Athens,
we the daughters of Night,
our power stripped, cast down.

ATHENA.
                                      You have your power,
you are goddesses—but not to turn
on the world of men and ravage it past cure.   835
I put my trust in Zeus and . . . must I add this?
I am the only god who knows the keys
to the armory where his lightning-bolt is sealed.
No need of that, not here.
                              Let me persuade you.
The lethal spell of your voice, never cast it   840
down on the land and blight its harvest home.
Lull asleep that salt black wave of anger—
awesome, proud with reverence, live with me.
The land is rich, and more, when its first fruits,

---

[48]Appropriately, the Furies, who have been all along portrayed as forces of earth and night, will be given cave shrines at the Athenian Acropolis, where they will combine their old role as ministers of avenging justice with a new role as agents of fertility and the blessings symbolized by it.

offered for heirs and the marriage rites, are yours 845
to hold forever, you will praise my words.
FURIES.
    But for me to suffer such disgrace . . . I,
the proud heart of the past, driven under the earth,
condemned, like so much filth,
    and the fury in me breathing hatred— 850
O good Earth,
    what is this stealing under the breast,
what agony racks the spirit? . . . Night, dear Mother Night!
All's lost, our ancient powers torn away by their cunning,
ruthless hands, the gods so hard to wrestle down 855
obliterate us all.
ATHENA.
                I will bear with your anger.
You are older. The years have taught you more,
much more than I can know. But Zeus, I think,
gave me some insight too, that has its merits.
If you leave for an alien land and alien people, 860
you will come to love this land, I promise you.
As time flows on, the honors flow through all
my citizens, and you, throned in honor
before the house of Erechtheus,[49] will harvest
more from men and women moving in solemn file 865
than you can win throughout the mortal world.

Here in our homeland never cast the stones
that whet our bloodlust. Never waste our youth,
inflaming them with the burning wine of strife.
Never pluck the heart of the battle cock 870
and plant it in our people—intestine war
seething against themselves. Let our wars
rage on abroad, with all their force, to satisfy
our powerful lust for fame. But as for the bird
that fights at home—my curse on civil war. 875

This is the life I offer, it is yours to take.
Do great things, feel greatness, greatly honored.
Share this country cherished by the gods.
FURIES.
    But for me to suffer such disgrace . . . I,
the proud heart of the past, driven under the earth, 880
condemned, like so much filth,
    and the fury in me breathing hatred—
O good Earth,
    what is this stealing under the breast,
what agony racks the spirit? . . . Night, dear Mother Night! 885

---

[49]A legendary ruler of Athens; a temple named for him (the Erechtheum) stood on the Acropolis.

All's lost, our ancient powers torn away by their cunning,
ruthless hands, the gods so hard to wrestle down
obliterate us all.
ATHENA.
                              No, I will never tire
of telling you your gifts. So that you,
the older gods, can never say that I,   890
a young god and the mortals of my city
drove you outcast, outlawed from the land.

But if you have any reverence for Persuasion,
the majesty of Persuasion,
the spell of my voice that would appease your fury—   895
Oh please stay . . .
                              and if you refuse to stay,
it would be wrong, unjust to afflict this city
with wrath, hatred, populations routed. Look,
it is all yours, a royal share of our land—
justly entitled, glorified forever.
LEADER.
                                        Queen Athena,   900
where is the home you say is mine to hold?
ATHENA.
Where all the pain and anguish end. Accept it.
LEADER.
And if I do, what honor waits for me?
ATHENA.
No house can thrive without you.
LEADER.
                              You would do that—
grant me that much power?
ATHENA.
                              Whoever reveres us—   905
we will raise the fortunes of their lives.
LEADER.
And you will pledge me that, for all time to come?
ATHENA.
Yes—I must never promise things I cannot do.
LEADER.
Your magic is working . . . I can feel the hate,
the fury slip away.
ATHENA.
                    At last! And now take root   910
in the land and win yourself new friends.
LEADER.
                                        A spell—
what spell to sing? to bind the land forever? Tell us.
ATHENA.
Nothing that strikes a note of brutal conquest. Only peace—
blessings, rising up from the earth and the heaving sea,

and down the vaulting sky let the wind-gods breathe 915
a wash of sunlight streaming through the land,
and the yield of soil and grazing cattle flood
our city's life with power and never flag
with time. Make the seed of men live on,
the more they worship you the more they thrive. 920
I love them as a gardener loves his plants,
these upright men, this breed fought free of grief.
All that is yours to give.
                          And I,
in the trials of war where fighters burn for fame,
will never endure the overthrow of Athens— 925
all will praise her, victor city, pride of man.

> [*The* FURIES *assemble, dancing
> around* ATHENA, *who becomes their
> leader.*]

FURIES.
                    I will embrace
              one home with you, Athena,
                  never fail the city
          you and Zeus almighty, you and Ares 930
      hold as the fortress of the gods, the shield
  of the high Greek altars, glory of the powers.
      Spirit of Athens, hear my words, my prayer
          like a prophet's warm and kind,
            that the rare good things of life 935
              come rising crest on crest,
          sprung from the rich black earth and
          gleaming with the bursting flash of sun.
ATHENA.
  These blessings I bestow on you, my people, gladly.
  I enthrone these strong, implacable spirits here 940
  and root them in our soil.
                          Theirs,
      theirs to rule the lives of men,
        it is their fated power.
  But he who has never felt their weight,
  or known the blows of life and how they fall, 945
  the crimes of his fathers hale him toward their bar,
  and there for all his boasts—destruction,
      silent, majestic in anger,
  crushes him to dust.
FURIES.
                    Yes and I ban
          the winds that rock the olive— 950
            hear my love, my blessing—
    thwart their scorching heat that blinds the buds,
      hold from our shores the killing icy gales,

and I ban the blight that creeps on fruit and withers—
        God of creation, Pan, make flocks increase   955
                and the ewes drop fine twin lambs
                    when the hour of labor falls.
                    And silver, child of Earth,
                    secret treasure of Hermes,
            come to light and praise the gifts of god.   960
ATHENA.
    Blessings—now do you hear, you guards of Athens,
        all that she will do?
    Fury the mighty queen, the dread
    of the deathless gods and those beneath the earth,
    deals with mortals clearly, once for all.   965
    She delivers songs to some, to others
        a blinding life of tears—
    Fury works her will.
FURIES.
                    And the lightning stroke
        that cuts men down before their prime, I curse,
            but the lovely girl who finds a mate's embrace,   970
    the deep joy of wedded life—O grant that gift, that prize,
        you gods of wedlock, grant it, goddesses of Fate!
            Sisters born of the Night our mother,
                    spirits steering law,
                sharing at all our hearths,   975
                at all times bearing down
                to make our lives more just,
        all realms exalt you highest of the gods.
ATHENA.
    Behold, my land, what blessings Fury kindly,
        gladly brings to pass—   980
    I am in my glory! Yes, I love Persuasion;
    she watched my words, she met their wild refusals.
    Thanks to Zeus of the Councils who can turn
    dispute to peace—he won the day.

                    [*To the* FURIES.]

    Thanks to our duel for blessings;   985
        we win through it all.
FURIES.
                    And the brutal strife,
            the civil war devouring men, I pray
        that it never rages through our city, no,
    that the good Greek soil never drinks the blood of Greeks,
        shed in an orgy of reprisal life for life—   990
            that Fury like a beast will never
                rampage through the land.
                Give joy in return for joy,
                one common will for love,

and hate with one strong heart: 995
such union heals a thousand ills of man.
ATHENA.
Do you *hear* how Fury sounds her blessings forth,
how Fury finds the way?
Shining out of the terror of their faces
I can see great gains for you, my people. 1000
Hold them kindly, kind as they are to you.
Exalt them always, you exalt your land,
your city straight and just—
its light goes through the world.
FURIES.
Rejoice,
rejoice in destined wealth, 1005
rejoice, Athena's people—
poised by the side of Zeus,
loved by the loving virgin girl,[50]
achieve humanity at last,
nestling under Pallas' wings 1010
and blessed with Father's love.
ATHENA.
You too rejoice! and I must lead the way
to your chambers by the holy light of these,
your escorts bearing fire.

[*Enter* ATHENA's *entourage of women,
bearing offerings and victims and
torches still unlit.*]

Come, and sped beneath the earth 1015
by our awesome sacrifices,
keep destruction from the country,
bring prosperity home to Athens,
triumph sailing in its wake.
And you,
my people born of the Rock King,[51] 1020
lead on our guests for life, my city—
May they treat you with compassion,
compassionate as you will be to them.
FURIES.
Rejoice!—
rejoice—the joy resounds—
all those who dwell in Athens, 1025
spirits and mortals, come,
govern Athena's city well,

---

[50] The "virgin goddess" Athena; her kinship with the Furies, who are now also kindly
Eumenides, ironically recalls Apollo's sneer at the Furies earlier as "the eternal virgins" (line
73).
[51] The primitive king of the Acropolis.

   revere us well, we are your guests;
   you will learn to praise your Furies,
  you will praise the fortunes of your lives.   1030
ATHENA.
 My thanks! and I will speed your prayers, your blessings—
 lit by the torches breaking into flame
 I send you home, home to the core of Earth,
 escorted by these friends who guard my idol
 duty-bound.
           *[*ATHENA*'s entourage comes forward,*
           bearing crimson robes.[52]*]*

   Bright eye of the land of Theseus,   1035
 come forth, my splendid troupe. Girls and mothers,
 trains of aged women grave in movement,
 dress our Furies now in blood-red robes.
 Praise them—let the torch move on!
 So the love this family bears toward our land   1040
 will bloom in human strength from age to age.

          [The women invest the FURIES *and*
          sing the final chorus. Torches blaze;
          a procession forms, including the
          actors and the judges and the audi-
          ence. ATHENA *leads them from the the-*
          ater and escorts them through the city.]

THE WOMEN OF THE CITY.
 On, on, good spirits born for glory,
 Daughters of Night, her children always young,
      now under loyal escort—
 Blessings, people of Athens, sing your blessings out.   1045

 Deep, deep in the first dark vaults of Earth,
 sped by the praise and victims we will bring,
      reverence will attend you—
 Blessings now, all people, sing your blessings out.

 You great good Furies, bless the land with kindly hearts,   1050
 you Awesome Spirits, come—exult in the blazing torch,
    exultant in our fires, journey on.
 Cry, cry in triumph, carry on the dancing on and on!

 This peace between Athena's people and their guests
 must never end. All-seeing Zeus and Fate embrace,   1055
    down they come to urge our union on—
 Cry, cry in triumph, carry on the dancing on and on!

---

[52] The red robes and torches recall and reverse the ominous symbolism of robes, blood, and torches in the *Agamemnon.*

Sophocles

(496–406 B.C.)

In more than one sense, Sophocles is the central figure among the three great Greek tragedians. He was born in 496 B.C. in Colonus, the suburb of Athens celebrated in his last play, *Oedipus at Colonus;* he died in 406. Much of his life span thus overlapped that of his predecessor, Aeschylus, who died when Sophocles was forty. The third of the great triumvirate, Euripides, was sixteen years younger than Sophocles but died slightly before him. As a dramatist, Sophocles was a consummate artist who combined the high ethical and religious concerns of Aeschylus with the intense interest in individual human psychology characteristic of Euripides. Sophocles' ninety years of life therefore coincided with the entire history—the rise and fall—of the golden age of Greek tragedy. His years also coincided with the rise and fall of the uniquely splendid—and historically tragic—Athenian culture of the fifth century. In 480, when Sophocles was sixteen years old, he took part in a public celebration of the naval victory over the Persians at Salamis, a victory that, coincidentally or not, raised the curtain on the awesome cultural and social achievements of the ensuing age. Sophocles' death occurred only two years before the definitive collapse of Athenian supremacy, when in 404 the city succumbed to Sparta and its allies.

By most accounts, Sophocles was a man comfortably at home in his world and at the center of its public life. He was enormously successful and popular as a man of the theater. His temperament was urbane, gregarious, balanced. He held several important public positions during the years of Athens' primacy—as treasurer, as a diplomatic and military policymaker, as an ambassador, even as a priest. In short, he was what we have come to call a member of the establishment. And yet, intriguingly, he wrote dramas that call into question—though they do not necessarily undermine—the values generally associated with that role. Oedipus, in *Oedipus the King,* is the model of a good ruler, a humanely intelligent and vigorously active leader, a man who earlier saved his adopted city Thebes from disaster. Yet Oedipus is finally driven to self-mutilation and self-imposed exile because he has committed, though unwittingly, the most horrendous crimes against the divine order, the natural order, and the polity: patricide, incest, and the pollution of his city. In *Antigone,* Oedipus' brave, lovable, headstrong daughter confronts her uncle Kreon, the new ruler of Thebes, over an issue—the conflicting demands of civic, familial, and religious principles—that few establishmentarians would press urgently. Probings of these themes, stories, and issues are not what one would normally expect of either a religious pietist or a politically complacent conservative.

That paradox, along with others, makes Sophocles an especially challenging artist and personality. Authorities disagree on how to interpret him, as man or playwright. He wrote more than 120 plays, of which only seven have survived intact: the two included in this volume plus *Ajax, Philoctetes, The Women of Trachis, Electra,* and *Oedipus at Colonus.* His artistic control of plot and other elements of the drama has helped identify Sophocles as the perfect "classicist," and the extravagant praise heaped on him by Aristotle in his *Poetics* has reinforced that image. Yet "classicist" is an inadequate term, and a seriously misleading one if we make the simple-minded but familiar identification of the classical with calm, serene detachment. Sophocles tends to represent in his characters general human types, an approach usually considered classical. Antigone is the archetype of the martyr to principle. Oedipus is the intelligent man brought low by the very intellectual gifts and compulsion to understand that make him admirable (not to mention the universality found in him by Sigmund Freud, who discerned in the "Oedipus complex" a fundamental law of filial and psychic experience). Yet at no time do we lose sight of these characters as individuals racked by conflict, pain, or both. Antigone is indeed a type, but (like Cordelia in Shakespeare's *King Lear,* who has a similar blend of vulnerability and toughness) she embodies that type in a distinct individual personality that includes a waspish streak. Her awareness of the sanctity of the family bond makes her compassionate toward her dead brother Polynices but incongruously contemptuous of her sister Ismene.

One of the pervading themes in Sophocles is the justice of the universe. We are to understand that, in some sense, cosmic justice ultimately prevails. But any cosmic justice that demands the blinding and exile of the essentially just Oedipus and the death of the heroic Antigone would seem ambiguous, indeed very frightening. Few authors of any age have rendered the experience of raw pain—psychological and physical—so compellingly. Significantly, the nineteenth-century poet Matthew Arnold described Sophocles as a man who "saw life steadily and saw it whole" but also as one who heard "the eternal note of sadness" and was preeminently sensitive to "the turbid ebb and flow of human misery."

Sophocles does not treat issues in a vacuum; he is above all a dramatist. The innovations he made in dramatic method and staging have the effect of making conflict more humanly immediate—if not necessarily more powerful—than in Aeschylus. By increasing the number of speaking actors from two to three, Sophocles made possible even more intricate interpersonal relationships than Aeschylus had portrayed; by reducing the lyrical role of the chorus (though he increased its size) Sophocles was able to focus more directly, and in a less stylized way, on complexities of character as conveyed in dialogue. He also expanded the use of stage machinery. The total effect is to intensify our awareness of conflict, both external and within individual characters.

Oedipus the King has a special place in literature; it may well be the most important and influential drama ever written. Aristotle seems to have considered it the definitive tragedy, just as he considered Homer's *Iliad* and *Odyssey* the definitive epics. The play is the best known and most frequently cited example of "dramatic irony," where the audience possesses information of which the main characters in the play are ignorant. The gradual revelation to Oedipus of his past history, an already familiar story the audience would have known from the very beginning of the play, makes for powerful suspense, especially since it is Oedipus himself who relentlessly investigates and puts together the case that—for all the elaborate precautions he has taken not to commit unspeakable crimes—will in the end damn him in his own eyes and in those of other people. The gigantic metaphor of eyes, of seeing and blindness, is worked with virtuoso skill. But the metaphor is not a mere "literary" device; it typifies Sophocles' view of humanity's place in the totality of things. Human beings in his plays are an integral part of a world order that can be only partially understood at best. The cosmic system includes, besides human beings and nature, those darkly inscrutable forces identified—inadequately—as the gods and fate.

Yet Sophocles is not a fatalist either. Despite the sense of inevitability his plays convey, human beings are considered responsible for their acts. But this belief in responsibility raises an even deeper question about necessity and human freedom, for if the lives of men and women are governed by themselves and not by their stars, are not these human beings themselves determined in their behavior by what they "are"? Character may be destiny, but to what extent is character itself an unchangeable given? Even more than such difficult but relatively concrete issues as the conflict between the person and polity, this mind-bending question makes Sophocles' plays touchstones for an appreciation of the human dilemma.

FURTHER READING (*prepared by F.S.N.*): An excellent general introduction to Sophocles and to each of his plays is Ruth Scodel, *Sophocles*, 1984. Now available in English is the classic by Karl Reinhardt, *Sophocles*, 1947, trans. Hazel and David Harvey, 1979, which discusses all the extant plays. Other works dealing with all or some of the Sophoclean dramas are S. M. Adams, *Sophocles the Playwright*, 1957; William Nickerson Bates, *Sophocles: Poet and Dramatist*, 1940, repr. 1961; Bernard M. W. Knox, *The Heroic Temper: Studies in Sophoclean Tragedy*, 1964. Further critical works on the life and thought of Sophocles are T. B. L. Webster, *An Introduction to Sophocles*, 1936, repr. 1969; and H. D. F. Kitto, *Sophocles: Dramatist and Philosopher*, 1958, repr. 1981. A number of modern interpretations of Sophocles are edited by Thomas Marion Woodard, *Sophocles: A Collection of Critical Essays*, 1966. The theatrical production of Sophocles' plays is the subject of David Seale, *Vision and Stagecraft in Sophocles*, 1982; see also the discussion of Sophocles' theater in J. Michael Walton, *The Greek Sense of Theatre: Tragedy Reviewed*, 1985. A close analysis of the word patterns in *Antigone* is given by R. F. Goheen, *The Imagery of Sophocles' Antigone*, 1951. The staging of *Antigone* is discussed in Leo Aylen, *The Greek Theater*, 1985. Charles Segal, *Oedipus Tyrannus*, 1993, presents a succinct but searching analysis of the play. Frederick Ahl, *Sophocles' Oedipus*, 1992, explores the play's cultural complexities. Luci Berkowitz and Theodore F. Brunner, eds., *Sophocles: Oedipus Tyrannus*, 1970, includes both a translation and a number of essays by various scholars on themes such as religion and psychology. See further M. J. O'Brien, ed., *Twentieth Century Interpretations of Oedipus Rex: A Collection of Critical Essays*, 1968.

OEDIPUS THE KING

Translated by Stephen Berg and Diskin Clay

CHARACTERS

OEDIPUS, *king of Thebes*
PRIEST *of Zeus*
KREON, *Oedipus' brother-in-law*
CHORUS OF THEBAN ELDERS
LEADER OF THE CHORUS
TEIRESIAS, *prophet, servant to Apollo*
JOCASTA, *wife of Oedipus*
MESSENGER *from Corinth*

SHEPHERD, *member of Laios' household*
SERVANT, *household slave of Oedipus*
Delegation of Thebans, servants to lead Teiresias and Oedipus; attendants to Oedipus, Kreon, Jocasta; and Antigone and Ismene, the daughters of Oedipus

TIME AND SCENE

Dawn. Silence. The royal palace of Thebes. The altar of Apollo[1] to the left of the central palace. A delegation of Thebans—old men, boys, young children—enters the orchestra[2] by the steps below the altar, assembles, and waits. They carry suppliant boughs—olive branches tied with strips of wool. Some climb the steps between the orchestra and the altar, place their branches on the altar, and return to the orchestra. A PRIEST *stands apart from the suppliants at the foot of one of the two stairs. Silence. Waiting. The central doors open. From inside the palace, limping,[3]* OEDIPUS *comes through the palace doors and stands at the top of the steps leading down into the orchestra. He is dressed in gold and wears a golden crown.*

OEDIPUS. Why children,
   why are you here, why
   are you holding those branches tied with wool,
   begging me for help? Children,
   the whole city smolders with incense.[4]
   Wherever I go I hear sobbing, praying. Groans fill the air.
   Rumors, news from messengers, they are not enough for me.
   Others cannot tell me what you need.
   I am king, I had to come. As king,
   I had to know. Know for myself, know for me.   10
   Everybody everywhere knows who I am: Oedipus. King.
   Priest of Zeus, we respect your age, your high office.
   Speak.
   Why are you kneeling? Are you afraid, old man?
   What can I give you?
   How can I help? Ask.
   Ask me anything. Anything at all.
   My heart would be a stone
   if I felt no pity for these poor shattered people of mine
   kneeling here, at my feet.   20
PRIEST. Oedipus, lord of Thebes, you see us, the people of Thebes,
     your people,
   crowding in prayer around your altar,
   these small children here, old men bent with age, priests, and I,
     the priest of Zeus,
   and our noblest young men, the pride and strength of Thebes.
   And there are more of us, lord Oedipus, more—gathered in the
     city, stunned,
   kneeling, offering their branches, praying before the two great tem-
     ples of Athena[5]

---

[1] The utterances of Apollo, god of prophecy, are central to the play's action. He was also god of healing and, conversely, of plague.

[2] In a Greek theater, the open space in front of the stage.

[3] In Greek, the name Oedipus means "swell-foot." The cause of his lameness is revealed later in the play.

[4] The city has been making religious offerings to appease the angry gods who have visited plague on Thebes.

[5] Goddess of wisdom and knowledge; also, the patron of Athens and of Greek cities in general.

or staring into the ashes of burnt offerings,[6] staring,
waiting, waiting for the god to speak.
Look,
look at it,   30
lord Oedipus—right there,
in front of your eyes—this city—
it reels under a wild storm of blood, wave after wave battering Thebes.
We cannot breathe or stand.
We hunger, our world shivers with hunger. A disease hungers,
nothing grows, wheat, fruit, nothing grows bigger than a seed.
Our women bear
dead things,
all they can do is grieve,
our cattle wither, stumble, drop to the ground,   40
flies simmer on their bloated tongues,
the plague spreads everywhere, a stain seeping through our streets,
    our fields, our houses,
look—god's fire eating everyone, everything,
stroke after stroke of lightning, the god stabbing it alive—
it can't be put out, it can't be stopped,
its heat thickens the air, it glows like smoking metal,
this god of plague guts our city and fills the black world under us
    where the dead go
with the shrieks of women,
living women, wailing.
You are a man, not a god—I know.   50
We all know this, the young kneeling here before you know it, too,
but we know how great you are, Oedipus, greater than any man.
When crisis struck, you saved us[7] here in Thebes,
you faced the mysterious, strange disasters hammered against us
    by the gods.
This is our history—
we paid our own flesh to the Sphinx until you set us free.
You knew no more than anyone, but you knew.
There was a god in it, a god in you.

[*The* PRIEST *kneels.*]

Help us. Oedipus, we beg you, we all turn to you, kneeling to your
    greatness.
Advice from the gods or advice from human beings—you will know
    which is needed.   60

---

[6]Sacrifices to the gods; the inspection of the ashes, it was hoped, would reveal the gods'
will.

[7]Thebes had earlier been ravaged by the Sphinx, a monster with a lion's body and a woman's
head, who proposed a famous riddle, a wrong solution to which was punished by death. The
question was, "What animal moves first on four legs, then on two, then on three, and is weakest when moving on four legs?" Oedipus correctly solved the riddle: Man, who first crawls,
then walks, then goes with a walking stick. The solution of the riddle destroyed the Sphinx
and established Oedipus in power as savior of Thebes.

But help us. Power and experience are yours, all yours.
Between thought and action, between
our plans and their results a distance opens.
Only a man like you, Oedipus, tested by experience,
can make them one. That much I know.
Oedipus, more like a god than any man alive,
deliver us, raise us to our feet. Remember who you are.
Remember your love for Thebes. Your skill was our salvation once
    before.
For this Thebes calls you savior.
Don't let us remember you as the king—godlike in power—   70
who gave us back our life, then let us die.
Steady us forever. You broke the riddle for us then.
It was a sign. A god was in it. Be the man you were—
rule now as you ruled before.
Oh Oedipus,
how much better to rule a city of men than be king of empty earth.
A city is nothing, a ship is nothing
where no men live together, where no men work together.
OEDIPUS. Children, poor helpless children.
I know what brings you here, I know.   80
You suffer, this plague is agony for each of you,
but none of you, not one suffers as I do.
Each of you suffers for himself, only himself.
My whole being wails and breaks
for this city, for myself, for all of you,
old man, all of you.
Everything ends here, with me. I am the man.
You have not wakened me from some kind of sleep.
I have wept, struggled, wandered in this maze of thought,
tried every road, searched hard—   90
finally I found one cure, only one:
I sent my wife's brother, Kreon, to great Apollo's shrine at Delphi;[8]
I sent him to learn what I must say or do to save Thebes.
But his long absence troubles me. Why isn't he here? Where is he?
When he returns, what kind of man would I be
if I failed to do everything the god reveals?

> [*Some of the suppliants by the steps
> to the orchestra stand to announce
> KREON's arrival to the PRIEST.
> KREON comes in by the entrance to
> the audience's left with a garland on
> his head.*]

PRIEST. You speak of Kreon, and Kreon is here.
OEDIPUS. [*turning to the altar of Apollo, then to* KREON]
Lord Apollo, look at him—his head is crowned with laurel, his eyes
    glitter.

---

[8] The most important center of prophecy in Greece; see the description at the beginning
of Aeschylus' *The Eumenides.*

Let his words blaze, blaze like his eyes, and save us.
PRIEST. He looks calm, radiant, like a god. If he brought bad news, 100
would he be wearing that crown of sparkling leaves?
OEDIPUS. At last we will know.
Lord Kreon, what did the god Apollo say?
KREON. His words are hopeful.
Once everything is clear, exposed to the light,
we will see our suffering is blessing. All we need is luck.
OEDIPUS. What do you mean? What did Apollo say? What should we
do?
Speak.
KREON. Here? Now? In front of all these people?
Or inside, privately? 110

[KREON *moves toward the palace.*]

OEDIPUS. Stop. Say it. Say it to the whole city.
I grieve for them, for their sorrow and loss, far more than I grieve
for myself.
KREON. This is what I heard—there was no mistaking the god's
meaning—
Apollo commands us:
Cleanse the city of Thebes, cleanse the plague from that city,
destroy the black stain spreading everywhere, spreading,
poisoning the earth, touching each house, each citizen,
sickening the hearts of the people of Thebes!
Cure this disease that wastes all of you, spreading, spreading,
before it grows so vast nothing can cure it. 120
OEDIPUS. What is this plague?
How can we purify the city?
KREON. A man must be banished. Banished or killed.
Blood for blood. The plague is blood,
blood, breaking over Thebes.
OEDIPUS. *Who* is the man? *Who* is Apollo's victim?
KREON. My lord. before you came to Thebes, before you came to power,
Laios was our king.
OEDIPUS. I know. But I never saw Laios.
KREON. Laios was murdered. Apollo's command was very clear: 130
Avenge the murderers of Laios. Whoever they are.
OEDIPUS. But where *are* his murderers?
The crime is old. How will we find their tracks?
The killers could be anywhere.
KREON. Apollo said the killers are still here, here in Thebes.
Pursue a thing, and you may catch it;
ignored, it slips away.
OEDIPUS. And Laios—where was he murdered?
At home? Or was he away from Thebes?
KREON. He told us before he left—he was on a mission to Delphi, 140
his last trip away from Thebes. He never returned.
OEDIPUS. Wasn't there a witness, someone with Laios who saw what
happened?

KREON. They were all killed, except for one man. He escaped.
    But he was so terrified he remembered only one thing.
OEDIPUS. What was it? One small clue might lead to others.
KREON. This is what he said: bandits ambushed Laios, not one man.
    They attacked him like hail crushing a stalk of wheat.
OEDIPUS. How could a single bandit dare attack a king
    unless he had supporters, people with money, here,
    here in Thebes?   150
KREON. There were suspicions. But after Laios died we had no leader,
    no king.
    Our life was turmoil, uncertainty.
OEDIPUS. But once the throne was empty,
    what threw you off the track, what kept you from searching
    until you uncovered everything, knew every detail?
KREON. The intricate, hard song of the Sphinx
    persuaded us the crime was not important, not then.
    It seemed to say we should focus on what lay at our feet, in front
        of us,
    ignore what we could not see.
OEDIPUS. Now, *I* am here.   160
    I will begin the search again, I
    will reveal the truth, expose everything, let it all be seen.
    Apollo and you were right to make us wonder about the dead man.
    Like Apollo, I am your ally.
    Justice and vengeance are what I want,
    for Thebes, for the god.
    Family, friends—I won't rid myself of this stain, this disease, for
        them—
    they're far from here.[9] I'll do it for myself, for me.
    The man who killed Laios might take revenge on me
    just as violently.   170
    So by avenging Laios' death, I protect myself.
    [*turning to the suppliants*] Rise, children,
    pick up your branches,
    let someone announce my decision to the whole city of Thebes.
    [*to the* PRIEST] I will do everything. Everything.
    And, with the god's help, we will be saved.
    Bright Apollo, let your light help us see.
    Our happiness is yours to give, our failure and ruin yours.
PRIEST. Rise. We have the help we came for, children.
    The king himself has promised.   180
    May Apollo, who gave these oracles, come as our savior now.
    Apollo, heal us, save us from this plague!

                            [OEDIPUS *enters the palace. Its doors
                            close.* KREON *leaves by a door to the*

---

[9]Oedipus means that his wife's first husband, Laios, is now far removed by time and death;
in addition, at this point Oedipus wrongly believes that he is the son of parents who reside
in another city (Corinth).

right on the wing of the stage. The PRIEST *and suppliants go down into the orchestra and leave by the entrance to the left as a chorus of fifteen Theban elders files into the orchestra by the entrance on the right, preceded by a flute player.*]

CHORUS. voice   voice   voice
  voice who knows everything o god
  glorious voice of Zeus[10]
  how have you come from Delphi bathed in gold
  what are you telling our bright city Thebes
  what are you bringing me
  health death fear
  I know nothing   190
  so frightened rooted here
  awed by you
  healer what have you sent
  is it the sudden doom of grief
  or the old curse the darkness
  looming in the turning season

  o holy immortal voice
  hope golden seed of the future
  listen be with me speak
  these cries of mine rise   200
  tell me
  I call to you reach out to you first
  holy Athena god's daughter who lives forever
  and your sister Artemis[11]
  who cradles the earth our earth
  who sits on her great throne at the hub of the market place
  and I call to Apollo who hurls light
  from deep in the sky
  o gods be with us now
  shine on us your three shields[12]   210
  blazing against the darkness
  come in our suffering as you came once before
  to Thebes o bright divinities
  and threw your saving light against the god of grief
  o gods
  be with us now

  pain pain my sorrows have no sound
  no name no word no pain like this

[10] The message or communication from Zeus, king of the gods. More concretely, the "voice" is Apollo, the prophetic spokesman of the supreme god's will and knowledge.

[11] Athena was the daughter of Zeus, born directly without a mother from his head; Artemis, born of Zeus and Leto, is her half-sister and also Apollo's full sister.

[12] The protective power of the three deities invoked (Athena, Artemis, Apollo).

plague sears my people everywhere
everyone army citizens no one escapes   220
no spear of strong anxious thought protects us
great Thebes grows nothing
seeds rot in the ground
our women when they labor
cry Apollo Apollo but their children die
and lives one after another split the air
birds taking off
wingrush hungrier than fire
souls leaping away they fly
to the shore   230
of the cold god of evening[13]
west

the death stain spreads
so many corpses lie in the streets everywhere
nobody grieves for them
the city dies and young wives
and mothers gray-haired mothers wail
sob on the altar steps
they come from the city everywhere mourning their bitter days
prayers blaze to the Healer   240
grief cries a flute mingling
daughter of Zeus[14] o shining daughter show us
the warm bright face of peace of help
of our salvatlon

> [*The doors of the palace open.*
> OEDIPUS *enters.*]

and turn back the huge raging jaws of the death god Ares[15]
drive him back drive him away
his flames lash at me
this is his war these are his shields
shouts pierce us on all sides
turn him back lift him on a strong wind   250
rush him away
to the two seas[16] at the world's edge
the sea where the waters boil
the sea where no traveler can land
because if night leaves anything alive
day destroys it
o Zeus
god beyond all other gods

[13] Hades, god of the Underworld and of the dead.
[14] His daughter Athena.
[15] The god of war, often regarded as the personification of any kind of destruction.
[16] The Atlantic at the western edge of the world, the Black Sea at the eastern.

handler of the fire
father 260
make the god of our sickness
ashes

Apollo
great bowman of light draw back your bow
fire arrow after arrow
make them a wall circling us
shoot into our enemy's eyes
draw the string twined with gold
come goddess[17]
who dances on the mountains 270
sowing light where your feet brush the ground
blind our enemy come
god of golden hair
piled under your golden cap Bacchus
your face blazing like the sea when the sun falls on it
like sunlight on wine
god whose name is our name Bacchus[18]
god of joy god of terror
be with us now your bright face
like a pine torch roaring 280
thrust into the face of the slaughtering war god
blind him
drive him down from Olympos
drive him away from Thebes
forever

OEDIPUS. Every word of your prayers has touched me.
    Listen. Follow me. Join me in fighting this sickness, this plague,
    and all your sufferings may end, like a dark sky,
    clear suddenly, blue, after a week of storms,
    soothing the torn face of the sea, 290
    soothing our fears.
    Your fate looms in my words—
    I heard nothing about Laios' death.
    I know nothing about the murder,
    I was alone, how could I have tracked the killer, without a clue,
    I came to Thebes after the crime was done,
    I was made a Theban after Laios' death. Listen carefully—
    these words come from an innocent man.

[*Addressing the* CHORUS.]

One of *you* knows who killed Laios.
Where is that man? 300

[17]Artemis, goddess of the hunt.
[18] The god of wine, Bacchus or Dionysos, had special associations with Thebes.

Speak.
I command it. Fear is no excuse.
He must clear himself of the dangerous charge.
Who did this thing?
Was it a stranger?
Speak.
I will not harm him. The worst he will suffer is exile.
I will pay him well. He will have a king's thanks.
But if he will not speak because he fears me,
if he fears what I will do to him or to those he loves,   310
if he will not obey me,
I say to him:
My power is absolute in Thebes, my rule reaches everywhere,
my words will drive the guilty man, the man who *knows,*
out of this city, away from Thebes, forever.

Nothing.
My word for him is nothing.
Let him *be* nothing.
Give him nothing.
Let him touch nothing of yours, he is nothing to you.   320
Lock your doors when he approaches.
Say nothing to him, do not speak.
No prayers with him, no offerings with him.
No purifying water.
Nothing.
Drive him from your homes. Let him have no home, nothing.
No words, no food, shelter, warmth of hand, shared worship.
Let him have nothing. Drive him out, let him die.
He is our disease.
                      I know.
                              Apollo has made it clear.
Nothing can stop me, nothing can change my words.   330
I fight for Apollo, I fight for the dead man.
You see me, you hear me, moving against the killer.
My words are his doom.
Whether he did it alone, and escaped unseen,
whether others helped him kill, it makes no difference—
let my hatred burn out his life, hatred, always.
Make him an ember of suffering.
Make all his happiness
ashes.
If he eats at my side, sits at my sacred hearth, and I know these
    things,   340
let every curse I spit out against him find *me,*
come home to *me.*
Carry out my orders. You must,
for me, for Apollo, and for Thebes, Thebes,
this poor wasted city,
deserted by its gods.

I know—the gods have given us this disease.
That makes no difference. You should have acted,
you should have done something long ago to purge our guilt.
The victim was noble, a king— 350
you should have done everything to track his murderer down.
And so,
because I rule now where he ruled;
because I share his bed, his wife;
because the same woman who mothered my children might have
     mothered his;
because fate swooped out of nowhere and cut him down;
because of all these things
I will fight for him as I would fight for my own murdered father.
Nothing will stop me.
No man, no place, nothing will escape my gaze. I will not stop 360
until I know it all, all, until everything is clear.
For every king, every king's son and his sons,
for every royal generation of Thebes, *my* Thebes,
I will expose the killer, I will reveal him
to the light.
Oh gods, gods,
destroy all those who will not listen, will not obey.
Freeze the ground until they starve.
Make their wives barren as stone.
Let this disease that shakes Thebes to its roots— 370
or any worse disease, if there is any worse than this—waste them,
crush everything they have, everything they are.
But you men of Thebes—
you, who know my words are right, who obey me—
may justice and the gods defend you, bless you,
graciously, forever.

LEADER. Your curse forces me to speak, Master.
     I cannot escape it.
     I did not murder the king, I cannot show you the man who did.
     Apollo told us to search for the killer. 380
     Apollo must name him.

OEDIPUS. No man can force the gods to speak.

LEADER. Then I will say the next best thing.

OEDIPUS. If there's a third best thing, say that too.

LEADER. Teiresias sees what the god Apollo sees.
     Truth, truth.
     If you heard the god speaking, heard his voice,
     you might see more, more, and more.

OEDIPUS. Teiresias? I have seen to that already.
     Kreon spoke of Teiresias, and I sent for him. Twice. 390
     I find it strange he still hasn't come.

LEADER. And there's an old story, almost forgotten,
     a dark, faded rumor.

OEDIPUS. What rumor? I must sift each story,
     see it, understand it.

LEADER. Laios was killed by bandits.
OEDIPUS. I have heard that story: but who can show me the man who
      saw the murderer?
      Has anyone seen him?
LEADER. If he knows the meaning of fear,
      if he heard those curses you spoke against him,   400
      those words still scorching the air,
      you won't find him now, not in Thebes.
OEDIPUS. The man *murdered*. Why would words frighten him?

> [TEIRESIAS *has appeared from the
> stage entrance to the right of the
> audience. He walks with a staff and
> is helped by a slave boy and atten-
> dants. He stops at some distance from
> center stage.*]

LEADER. Here is the man who can catch the criminal
      They're bringing him now—
      the godlike prophet who speaks with the voice of god.
      He, only he, knows truth.
      The truth is rooted in his soul.
OEDIPUS. Teiresias, you understand all things,
      what can be taught, what is locked in silence,   410
      the distant things of heaven, and things that crawl the earth.
      You cannot see, yet you know the nature of this plague infesting
          our city.
      Only you, my lord, can save us, only you can defend us.
      Apollo told our messenger—did you hear?—
      that we could be saved only by tracking down Laios' killers,
      only by killing them, or sending them into exile.
      Help us, Teiresias.
      Study the cries of birds, study their wild paths,
      ponder the signs of fire, use all your skills of prophecy.
      Rescue us, preserve us.   420
      Rescue yourself, rescue Thebes, rescue me.
      Cleanse every trace of the growing stain left by the dead man's blood.
      We are in your hands, Teiresias.
      No work is more nobly human than helping others,
      helping with all the strength and skill we possess.
TEIRESIAS. Wisdom is a curse
      when wisdom does nothing for the man who has it.
      Once I knew this well, but I forgot.
      I never should have come.
OEDIPUS. Never should have come? Why this reluctance, prophet?   430
TEIRESIAS. Let me go home.
      That way is best, for you, for me.
      Let me live my life, and you live yours.
OEDIPUS. Strange words. Teiresias, cruel to the city that gave you life.
      Your holy knowledge could save Thebes. How can you keep silent?

TEIRESIAS. What have you said that helps Thebes? Your words are wasted.
　　I would rather be silent than waste my words.
OEDIPUS. Look at us,　　　　　　　　　[OEDIPUS *stands, the* CHORUS *kneel.*]
　　kneeling to you. Teiresias, imploring you.
　　In the name of the gods, if you know—　　　　　　　　　　　　　440
　　help us, tell us what you know.
TEIRESIAS. You kneel because you do not understand.
　　But I will never let you see my grief. Never.
　　My grief is yours.
OEDIPUS. What? You know and won't speak?
　　You'd betray us all, you'd destroy the city of Thebes?
TEIRESIAS. I will do nothing to hurt myself, or you. Why insist?
　　I will not speak.
OEDIPUS. Stubborn old fool, you'd make a rock angry!
　　Tell me what you know! Say it!　　　　　　　　　　　　　　450
　　Where are your feelings? Won't you ever speak?
TEIRESIAS. You call me cold, stubborn, unfeeling, you insult me. But
　　　you,
　　Oedipus, what do you know about yourself,
　　about your real feelings?
　　You don't see how much alike we are.
OEDIPUS. How can *I* restrain my anger when I see how little you care
　　　for Thebes.
TEIRESIAS. The truth will come, by itself,
　　the truth will come
　　no matter how I shroud it in silence.
OEDIPUS. All the more reason why you should speak.　　　　　　　460
TEIRESIAS. Not another word.
　　Rage away. You will never make me speak.
OEDIPUS. I'll rage, prophet, I'll give you all my anger.
　　I'll say it all—
　　Listen: I think you were involved in the murder of Laios,
　　you helped plan it, I think you
　　did everything in your power to kill Laios,
　　everything but strike him with your own hands,
　　and if you weren't blind, if you still had eyes to see with,
　　I'd say you, and *you* alone, did it all.　　　　　　　　　　470
TEIRESIAS. Do you think so? Then obey your own words, obey
　　the curse everyone heard break from your own lips:
　　Never speak again to these men of Thebes,
　　never speak again to me.
　　　　　　　　　　You, it's
　　you.
　　What plagues the city is *you.*
　　The plague is *you.*
OEDIPUS. Do you know what you're saying?
　　Do you think I'll let you get away with these vile accusations?
TEIRESIAS. I am safe.　　　　　　　　　　　　　　　　　480
　　Truth lives in me, and the truth is strong.
OEDIPUS. Who taught you this truth of yours? Not your prophet's craft.

TEIRESIAS. You taught me. You forced me to speak.
OEDIPUS. Speak what? Explain. Teach me.
TEIRESIAS. Didn't you understand?
  Are you trying to make me say the word?
OEDIPUS. What word? Say it. Spit it out.
TEIRESIAS. Murderer.
  I say *you,*
  you are the killer you're searching for.   490
OEDIPUS. You won't say *that* again to me and get away with it.
TEIRESIAS. Do you want more? Shall I make you really angry?
OEDIPUS. Say anything you like. Your words are wasted.
TEIRESIAS. I say you live in shame, and you do not know it,
  do not know that you
  and those you love most
  wallow in shame,
  you do not know
  in what shame you live.
OEDIPUS. You'll pay for these insults, I swear it.   500
TEIRESIAS. Not if the truth is strong.
OEDIPUS. The truth *is* strong, but not your truth.
  You have no truth. You're blind.
  Blind in your eyes. Blind in your ears. Blind in your mind.
TEIRESIAS. And I pity you for mocking my blindness.
  Soon everyone in Thebes will mock you, Oedipus. They'll mock
      you
  as you have mocked me.
OEDIPUS. One endless night swaddles you in its unbroken black sky.
  You can't hurt me, you can't hurt anyone who sees the light of day.
TEIRESIAS. True. Nothing I do will harm you. You, you   510
  and your fate belong to Apollo.
  Apollo will see to *you.*
OEDIPUS. Are these your own lies, prophet—or Kreon's?
TEIRESIAS. Kreon? Your plague is *you,* not Kreon.
OEDIPUS. Money, power, one great skill surpassing another,
  if a man has these things, other men's envy grows and grows,
  their greed and hunger are insatiable.
  Most men would lust for a life like mine—but I did not demand
      my life,
  Thebes gave me my life, and from the beginning, my good friend
      Kreon,
  loyal, trusted Kreon,   520
  was reaching for my power, wanted to ambush me, get rid of me
      by hiring this cheap wizard,
  this crass, conniving priest, who sees nothing but profit,
  whose prophecy is simple profit. *You,*
  what did *you* ever do that proves you a real seer? What did you ever
      see, prophet?
  And when the Sphinx who sang mysteriously
  imprisoned us
  why didn't you speak and set us free?

No ordinary man could have solved her riddle,
it took prophecy, prophecy and skill you clearly never had.
Even the paths of birds, even the gods' voices were useless.   530
But I showed up, I, Oedipus,
stupid, untutored Oedipus,
I silenced her, I destroyed her, I used my wits, not omens,
to sift the meaning of her song.
And this is the man you want to kill so you can get close to King
   Kreon,
weigh his affairs for him, advise him, influence him.
No, I think you and your master, Kreon, who contrived this plot,
will be whipped out of Thebes.
Look at you.
If you weren't so old, and weak, oh   540
I'd make you pay
for this conspiracy of yours.
LEADER. Oedipus, both of you spoke in anger.
Anger is not what we need.
We need all our wits, all our energy to interpret Apollo's words.
Then we will know what to do.
TEIRESIAS. Oedipus, you are king, but you must hear my reply.
My right to speak is just as valid as yours.
I am not your slave. Kreon is not my patron.
My master is Apollo. I can say what I please.   550
You insulted me. You mocked me. You called me blind.
Now hear *me* speak, Oedipus.
You have eyes to see with,
but you do not see yourself, you do not see
the horror shadowing every step of your life,
the blind shame in which you live,
you do not see where you live and who lives with you,
lives always at your side.
Tell me, Oedipus, who are your parents?
Do you know?   560
You do not even know
the shame and grief you have brought your family,
those still alive, those buried beneath the earth.
But the curse of your mother, the curse of your father
will whip you, whip you again and again, wherever you turn,
it will whip you out of Thebes forever,
your clear eyes flooded with darkness.
That day will come.
And then what scoured, homeless plain, what leafless tree,
what place on Kithairon,[19]   570
where no other humans are or ever will be,

---

[19]Also spelled *Cithaeron*. A mountain range near Thebes. Oedipus, as later events will reveal, was abandoned there as a child; it will also be his destination when he goes into exile later. Sophocles' audience knew this detail, and all the other significant elements of the story, at the outset of the play.

where the wind is the only thing that moves,
what raw track of thorns and stones, what rock, gulley,
or blind hill won't echo your screams, your howls of anguish
when you find out that the marriage song,
sung when you came to Thebes, heard in your house,
guided you to *this* shore, this wilderness
you thought was home, *your* home?
And you do not see
all the other awful things 580
that will show you who you really are, show you
to your children, face to face.
Go ahead! Call me quack, abuse Kreon, insult Apollo, the god
who speaks through me, whose words move on my lips.
No man will ever know worse suffering than you,
your life, your flesh, your happiness an ember of pain. Ashes.

OEDIPUS. [*to the* CHORUS] Must I stand here and listen to these attacks?

TEIRESIAS. [*beginning to move away*] I am here, Oedipus, because you
sent for me.

OEDIPUS. You old fool,
I'd have thought twice before asking you to come 590
if I had known you'd spew out such idiocy.

TEIRESIAS. Call me fool, if you like, but your parents,
who gave you life, they respected my judgment.

OEDIPUS. Parents?
What do you mean?
Who are my mother and father?

TEIRESIAS. This day is your mother and father—this day will give you
your birth,
it will destroy you too.

OEDIPUS. How you love mysterious, twisted words.

TEIRESIAS. Aren't you the great solver of riddles?
Aren't you Oedipus?

OEDIPUS. Taunt me for the gift of my brilliant mind. 600
That gift is what makes me great.

TEIRESIAS. That gift is your destiny. It made you everything you are,
and it has ruined you.

OEDIPUS. But if this gift of mine saved Thebes, who cares what
happens to me?

TEIRESIAS. I'm leaving. Boy, take me home.

OEDIPUS. Good. Take him home. Here
I keep stumbling over you, here you're in my way.
Scuttle home, and leave us in peace!

TEIRESIAS. I'm going. I said what I came to say,
and that scowl, darkening your face, doesn't frighten me. How can
you hurt me? 610
I tell you again:
the man you've been trying to expose—
with all your threats, with your inquest into Laios' murder—
that man is here, in Thebes.

Now people think he comes from Corinth, but later
they will see he was born in Thebes.
When they know, he'll have no pleasure in that news.
Now he has eyes to see with, but they will be slashed out;
rich and powerful now, he will be a beggar,
poking his way with a stick, feeling his way to a strange country.   620
And his children—the children he lives with—
will see him at last, see what he is, see who he really is:
their brother and their father; his wife's son, his mother's husband;
the lover who slept with his father's wife; the man who murdered
        his father—
the man whose hands still drip with his father's blood.
These truths will be revealed.

Go inside and ponder *that* riddle, and if you find I've lied,
then call me a prophet who cannot see.

> [OEDIPUS *turns and enters the
> palace.* TEIRESIAS *is led out through
> the stage entrance on the right.*]

CHORUS. who did crimes unnameable things
        things words cringe at   630
        which man did the rock of prophecy at Delphi say
        did these things
        his hands dripping with blood
        he should run now flee
        his strong feet swallowing the air
        stronger than the horses of storm winds
        their hooves slicing the air
        now in his armor
        Apollo lunges at him
        his infinite branching fire reaches out   640
        and the steady dread death-hungry Fates follow and never stop
        their quick scissors[20] seeking the cloth of his life

        just now
        from high snowy Parnassus[21]
        the god's voice exploded its blazing message
        follow his track find the man
        no one knows
        a bull loose under wild bushes and trees
        among caves and gray rocks
        cut from the herd he runs and runs but runs nowhere   650
        zigzagging desperate to get away

---

[20] The three Fates were spinners of the thread of human life; the third, Atropos, cut the thread at a point that determined the moment of death.
[21] The mountain near Apollo's oracle at Delphi.

birds of prophecy birds of death circling his head
forever
voices forged at the white stone core of the earth[22]
they go where he goes always

terror's in me flooding me
how can I judge
what the god Apollo says
trapped hoping confused
I do not see what is here now 660
when I look to the past I see nothing
I know nothing about a feud
wounding the families of Laios or Oedipus
no clue to the truth then or now
nothing to blacken his golden fame in Thebes
and help Laios' family
solve the mystery of his death

Zeus and Apollo know
they understand
only they see 670
the dark threads crossing beneath our life
but no man can say a prophet sees more than I
one man surpasses another
wisdom against wisdom skill against skill
but I will not blame Oedipus
whatever anyone says
until words are as real as things

one thing is clear
years back the Sphinx tested him
his answer was true 680
he was wise and sweet to the city
so he can never be evil
not to me

> [KREON *enters through the stage
> entrance at nght, and addresses the*
> CHORUS.]

KREON. Men of Thebes, I hear Oedipus, our king and master,
has brought terrible charges against me.
I have come to face those charges. I resent them bitterly.
If he imagines I have hurt him, spoken or acted against him
while our city dies, believe me—I have nothing left to live for.
His accusations pierce me, wound me mortally—
nothing they touch is trivial, private— 690

---

[22] The Omphalos, or Navelstone, at Delphi. It was believed to be the center of the earth.

if you, my family and friends,
think I'm a traitor, if all Thebes believes it, says it.
LEADER. Perhaps he spoke in anger, without thinking,
perhaps his anger made him accuse you.
KREON. Did he really say I persuaded Teiresias to lie?
LEADER. I heard him say these things,
but I don't know what they mean.
KREON. Did he look you in the eyes when he accused me?
Was he in his right mind?
LEADER. I do not know or see what great men do. 700

[*turning to* OEDIPUS, *who has
emerged from the palace*]

But here he is—Oedipus.
OEDIPUS. What? *You* here? Murderer!
You dare come here, to my palace, when it's clear
you've been plotting to murder me and seize the throne of Thebes?
You're the bandit, *you're* the killer.
Answer me—
Did you think I was cowardly or stupid?
Is that why you betrayed me?
Did you really think I wouldn't see what you were plotting,
how you crept up on me like a cloud inching across the sun?
Did you think I wouldn't defend myself against you? 710
You thought I was a fool, but the fool was you, Kreon.
Thrones are won with money and men, you fool!
KREON. You have said enough, Oedipus. Now let me reply.
Weigh my words against your charges, then judge for yourself.
OEDIPUS. Eloquent, Kreon. But you won't convince me now.
Now that I know your hatred, your malice.
KREON. Let me explain.
OEDIPUS. Explain?
What could explain your treachery?
KREON. If you think this stubborn anger of yours, this perversity, 720
is something to be proud of, you're mad.
OEDIPUS. And if you think you can injure your sister's husband,
and not pay for it, *you're* mad.
KREON. I would be mad to hurt you. How have I hurt you?
OEDIPUS. Was it you who advised me to send for that great holy prophet?
KREON. Yes, and I'd do it again.
OEDIPUS. How long has it been since Laios disappeared?
KREON. Disappeared?
OEDIPUS. Died. Was murdered . . .
KREON. Many, many years. 730
OEDIPUS. And this prophet of yours—was he practicing his trade at
the time?
KREON. With as much skill, wisdom and honor as ever.
OEDIPUS. Did he ever mention my name?
KREON. Not in my presence.

OEDIPUS. Was there an inquest? A formal inquiry?
KREON. Of course. Nothing was ever discovered.
OEDIPUS. Then why didn't our wonderful prophet, our Theban wizard,
 denounce me as the murderer then?
KREON. I don't know. And when I don't know, I don't speak.
OEDIPUS. But you know this. You know it with perfect certainty. 740
KREON. What do you mean?
OEDIPUS. This: if you and Teiresias were not conspiring against me,
 Teiresias would never have charged *me* with Laios' murder.
KREON. If he said that, you should know.
 But now, Oedipus, it's my right, my turn to question you.
OEDIPUS. Ask anything. You'll never prove I killed Laios.
KREON. Did you marry my sister, Jocasta?
OEDIPUS. I married Jocasta.
KREON. And you gave her an equal share of the power in Thebes?
OEDIPUS. Whatever she wants is hers. 750
KREON. And I share that power equally with you and her?
OEDIPUS. Equally.
 And that's precisely why it's clear you're false, treacherous.
KREON. No, Oedipus.
 Consider it rationally, as I have. Reflect:
 What man, what sane man, would prefer a king's power
 with all its dangers and anxieties,
 when he could enjoy that same power, without its cares,
 and sleep in peace each night? Power?
 I have no instinct for power, no hunger for it either. 760
 It isn't royal power I want, but its advantages.
 And any sensible man would want the same.
 Look at the life I lead. Whatever I want, I get from you,
 with your goodwill and blessing. I have nothing to fear.
 If I were king, my life would be constant duty and constraint.
 Why would I want your power or the throne of Thebes
 more than what I enjoy now—the privilege of power
 without its dangers? I would be a fool to want more
 than what I have—the substance, not the show, of power.
 As matters stand, no man envies me, I am courted 770
 and admired by all. Men wear no smiling masks for Kreon.
 And those who want something from you come to me
 because the way to royal favor lies through me.
 Tell me, Oedipus, why should I give these blessings up
 to seize your throne and all the dangers it confers?
 A man like me, who knows his mortal limits and accepts them,
 cannot be vicious or treacherous by nature.
 The love of power is not my nature, nor is treason
 or the thoughts of treason that go with love of power.
 I would never dare conspire against your life. 780

 Do you want to test the truth of what I say?
 Go to Delphi, put the question to the oracle,
 ask if I have told you exactly what Apollo said.

Then if you find that Teiresias and I have plotted against you,
seize me and put me to death. Convict me
not by one vote alone, but two—yours *and* mine, Oedipus.
But don't convict me on the strength of your suspicions,
don't confuse friends with traitors, traitors with friends.
There's no justice in that.
To throw away a good and loyal friend 790
is to destroy what you love most—
your own life, and what makes life worth living.
Someday you will know the truth:
time, only time reveals the good man;
one day's light reveals the evil man.

LEADER. Good words
for someone careful, afraid he'll fall.
But a mind like lightning
stumbles.

OEDIPUS. When a clever man plots against me and moves swiftly 800
I must move just as swiftly, I must plan.
But if I wait, if I do nothing, he will win, win everything,
and I will lose.

KREON. What do you want? My exile?

OEDIPUS. No. Your death.

KREON. You won't change your mind? You won't believe me?

OEDIPUS. I'll believe you when you teach me the meaning of envy.

KREON. Envy? You talk about envy. You don't even know what sense is.
Can't you listen to me?

OEDIPUS. I *am* listening. To my own good sense. 810

KREON. Listen to *me*. I have sense on my side too.

OEDIPUS. You? You were born devious.

KREON. And if you're wrong?

OEDIPUS. I still must govern.

KREON. Not if you govern badly.

OEDIPUS. Oh Thebes, Thebes . . .

KREON. Thebes is mine too.

LEADER. [*turning to* JOCASTA, *who has entered from the palace, accompanied
by a woman attendant*]
Stop. I see
Jocasta coming from the palace
just in time, my lords, to help you 820
settle this deep, bitter feud raging between you.
Listen to what she says.

JOCASTA. Oedipus! Kreon! Why this insane quarreling?
You should be ashamed, both of you. Forget yourselves.
This is no time for petty personal bickering.
Thebes is sick, dying.
              —Come inside, Oedipus
—And you, Kreon, leave us.
Must you create all this misery over nothing, nothing?

KREON. Jocasta,
Oedipus has given me two impossible choices: 830

    Either I must be banished from Thebes, my city, my home,
    or be arrested and put to death.
OEDIPUS. That's right.
    I caught him plotting against me, Jocasta.
    Viciously, cunningly plotting against the king of Thebes.
KREON. Take every pleasure I have in life, curse me, let me die,
    if I've done what you accuse me of, let the gods
    destroy everything I have, let them do anything to me.
    I stand here, exposed to their infinite power.
JOCASTA. Oedipus, in the name of the gods, believe him.   840
    His prayer has made him holy, naked to the mysterious
    whims of the gods, has taken him beyond what is human.
    Respect his words, respect me, respect these men standing at your
        side.
CHORUS. [*beginning a dirge-like appeal to* OEDIPUS]
    listen to her
    think yield
    we implore you
OEDIPUS. What do you want?
CHORUS. be generous to Kreon give him respect
    he was never foolish before
    now his prayer to the gods has made him great   850
    great and frightening
OEDIPUS. Do you know what you're asking?
CHORUS. I know
OEDIPUS. Then say it.
CHORUS. don't ever cut him off
    without rights or honor
    blood binds you both
    his prayer has made him sacred
    don't accuse him
    because some blind suspicion hounds you   860
OEDIPUS. Understand me:
    when you ask for these things
    you ask for my death or exile.
CHORUS. no
    by the sun
    the god who bathes us in his light
    who sees all
    I will die godless no family no friends
    if what I ask means that
    it is Thebes   870
    Thebes dying wasting away life by life
    this is the misery
    that breaks my heart
    and now this quarrel raging between you and Kreon
    is more more than I can bear
OEDIPUS. Then let him go, if it means I must die
    or be forced out of Thebes forever, stripped of all my rights, all
        my honors.

Your grief, *your* words touch me. Not his.
I pity you. But him,
my hatred will reach him wherever he goes. 880
KREON. It's clear you hate to yield, clear
you yield only under pressure, only
when you've worn out the fierceness of your anger.
Then all you can do is sit, and brood.
Natures like yours are a torment to themselves.
OEDIPUS. Leave. Go!
KREON. I'm going. Now I know
you do not know me.
But these men know I am the man I seem to be, a just man,
not devious, not a traitor. 890

[KREON *leaves.*]

CHORUS. woman why are you waiting
lead him inside comfort him
JOCASTA. Not before I know what has happened here.
CHORUS. blind ignorant words suspicion without proof
the injustice of it
gnaws at us
JOCASTA. From both men?
CHORUS. yes
JOCASTA. What caused it?
CHORUS. enough enough 900
no more words
Thebes is so tormented now
let it rest where it ended
OEDIPUS. Look where cooling my rage,
where all your decent, practical thoughts have led you.
CHORUS. Oedipus I have said this many times
I would be mad helpless to give advice
if I turned against you now
once
you took our city in her storm of pain 910
straightened her course found fair weather
o lead her to safety now
if you can
JOCASTA. If you love the gods, tell me, too, Oedipus—I implore you—
why are you still so angry, why can't you let it go?
OEDIPUS. I will tell you, Jocasta.
You mean more, far more to me than these men here.
Jocasta, it is Kreon—Kreon and his plots against me.
JOCASTA. What started your quarrel?
OEDIPUS. He said I murdered Laios. 920
JOCASTA. Does he know something? Or is it pure hearsay?
OEDIPUS. He sent me a vicious, trouble-making prophet
to avoid implicating himself. He did not say it to my face.
JOCASTA. Oedipus, forget all this. Listen to me:

no mortal can practise the art of prophecy; no man can see the
  future.
One experience of mine will show you why.
Long ago an oracle came to Laios.
It came not from Apollo himself but from his priests.
It said Laios was doomed to be murdered by a son, his son and
  mine.
But Laios, from what we heard, was murdered by bandits from a
  foreign country,   930
cut down at a crossroads. My poor baby
was only three days old when Laios had his feet pierced together
  behind the ankles
and gave orders to abandon our child on a mountain, leave him
  alone to die
in a wilderness of rocks and bare gray trees
where there were no roads, no people.
So you see—Apollo didn't make that child his father's killer,
Laios wasn't murdered by his son. That dreadful act which so terrified Laios—
it never happened.

All those oracular voices meant was nothing, nothing.
Ignore them.   940
Apollo creates. Apollo reveals. He needs no help from men.
OEDIPUS. [*who has been very still*]
  Whlle you were speaking, Jocasta, it flashed through my mind
  like wind suddenly ruffling a stretch of calm sea.
  It stuns me. I can almost see it—some memory, some image.
  My heart races and swells—
JOCASTA. Why are you so strangely excited, Oedipus?
OEDIPUS. You said Laios was cut down *near* a crossroads?
JOCASTA. That was the story. It hasn't changed.
OEDIPUS. Where did it happen? Tell me. Where?
JOCASTA. In Phokis. Where the roads from Delphi and Daulia meet.   950
OEDIPUS. When?
JOCASTA. Just before you came to Thebes and assumed power.
  Just before you were proclaimed King.
OEDIPUS. O Zeus, Zeus,
  what are you doing with my life?
JOCASTA. Why are you so disturbed, Oedipus?
OEDIPUS. Don't ask me. Not yet.
                                        Tell me about Laios.
  How old was he? What did he look like?
JOCASTA. Streaks of gray were beginning to show in his black hair.
  He was tall, strong—built something like you.   960
OEDIPUS. No! O gods, o
  it seems each hard, arrogant curse
  I spit out
  was meant for me, and I

didn't
know it!

JOCASTA. Oedipus, what do you mean? Your face is so strange.
  You frighten me.

OEDIPUS. It *is* frightening—can the blind prophet see, can he really
  see?
  I would know if you told me . . .   970

JOCASTA. I'm afraid to ask, Oedipus.
  Told you what?

OEDIPUS. Was Laios traveling with a small escort
  or with many armed men, like a king?

JOCASTA. There were five, including a herald.
  Laios was riding in his chariot.

OEDIPUS. Light, o light, light
  now everything, everything is clear. All of it.
  Who told you this? Who was it?

JOCASTA. A household slave. The only survivor.   980

OEDIPUS. Is he here, in Thebes?

JOCASTA. No. When he returned and saw that you were king
  and learned Laios was dead, he came to me and clutched my hand,
  begged me to send him to the mountains
  where shepherds graze their flocks, far from the city,
  so he could never see Thebes again.
  I sent him, of course. He deserved that much, for a slave, and more.

OEDIPUS. Can he be called back? Now?

JOCASTA. Easily. But why?

OEDIPUS. I am afraid I may have said too much—   990
  I *must* see him.
  Now.

JOCASTA. Then he will come.
  But surely I have a right to know what disturbs you, Oedipus.

OEDIPUS. Now that I've come this far, Jocasta,
  hope torturing me, each step of mine heavy with fear,
  I won't keep anything from you.
  Wandering through the mazes of a fate like this,
  how could I confide in anyone but you?

  My father was Polybos, of Corinth.   1000
  My mother, Merope, was Dorian.
  Everyone in Corinth saw me as its first citizen,
  but one day something happened,
  something strange, puzzling. Puzzling, but nothing more.
  Still, it worried me.
  One night, I was at a banquet,
  and a man—he was very drunk—said I wasn't my father's son,
  called me "bastard." That stung me, I was shocked.
  I could barely control my anger, I lay awake all night.
  The next day I went to my father and mother,   1010
  I questioned them about the man and what he said.

They were furious with him, outraged by his insult,
and I was reassured. But I kept hearing the word "bastard"
    "bastard"—
I couldn't get it out of my head.
Without my parents' knowledge, I went to Delphi: I wanted the truth,
but Apollo refused to answer me.
And yet he did reveal other things, he did show me
a future dark with torment, evil, horror,
he made me *see*—
see myself, doomed to sleep with my own mother, doomed   1020
to bring children into this world where the sun pours down,
children no one could bear to see, doomed
to murder the man who gave me life, whose blood is *my* blood. My
    father.
And after I heard all this, I fled Corinth,
measuring my progress by the stars, searching for a place
where I would never see those words, those dreadful predictions
come true. And on my way
I came to the place where you say King Laios was murdered.

Jocasta, the story I'm about to tell you is the truth:
I was on the road, near the crossroads you mentioned,   1030
when I met a herald, with an old man, just as you described him.
The man was riding in a chariot
and his driver tried to push me off the road
and when he shoved me I hit him. I hit him.
The old man stood quiet in the chariot until I passed under him,
then he leaned out and caught me on the head with an ugly goad[23]—
its two teeth wounded me—and with this hand of mine,
this hand clenched around my staff,
I struck him back even harder—so hard, so quick he couldn't
    dodge it,
and he toppled out of the chariot and hit the ground, face up.   1040
I killed them. Every one of them. I still see them.

[*to the* CHORUS]

If this stranger and Laios
are somehow linked by blood,
tell me what man's torment equals mine?

Citizens, hear my curse again—
Give this man nothing. Let him touch nothing of yours.
Lock your doors when he approaches.
Say nothing to him when he approaches.
                                    And these, these curses,
with my own mouth I
spoke these monstrous curses against myself.   1050

---

[23]A barbed stick used to prod animals.

[OEDIPUS *turns back to* JOCASTA]

These hands, these bloodstained hands made love to you in your
    dead husband's bed,
these hands murdered him.

If I must be exiled, never to see my family,
never to walk the soil of my country
so I will not sleep with my mother
and kill Polybos, my father, who raised me—his son!—
wasn't I born evil—answer me!—isn't every part of me
unclean? Oh
some unknown god, some savage venomous demon must have done
    this,
raging, swollen with hatred. Hatred   1060
for me.

Holiness, pure, radiant powers, o gods
don't let me see that day,
don't let it come, take me away
from men, men with their eyes, hide me
before I see
the filthy black stain reaching down over me, into me.

[*The* CHORUS *have moved away
from the stage*]

LEADER. Your words make us shudder, Oedipus,
    but hope, hope
    until you hear more from the man who witnessed the murder.   1070
OEDIPUS. That is the only hope I have. Waiting.
    Waiting for that man to come from the pastures.
JOCASTA. And when he finally comes, what do you hope to learn?
OEDIPUS. If his story matches yours, I am saved.
JOCASTA. What makes you say that?
OEDIPUS. Bandits—you said he told you bandits killed Laios.
    So if he still talks about bandits,
    more than one, I couldn't have killed Laios.
    One man is not the same as many men.
    But if he speaks of one man, traveling alone,   1080
    then all the evidence points to me.
JOCASTA. Believe me, Oedipus, those were his words.
    And he can't take them back: the whole city heard him, not only me.
    And if he changes only the smallest detail of his story,
    that still won't prove Laios was murdered as the oracle foretold.
    Apollo was clear—it was Laios' fate to be killed by my son,
    but my poor child died before his father died.
    The future has no shape. The shapes of prophecy lie.
    I see nothing in them, they are all illusions.
OEDIPUS. Even so, I want that shepherd summoned here.   1090
    Now. Do it now.

JOCASTA. I'll send for him immediately. But come inside.
My only wish is to please you.

[JOCASTA *dispatches a servant.*]

CHORUS. fate[24]
be here let what I say be pure
let all my acts be pure
laws forged in the huge clear fields of heaven
rove the sky
shaping my words limiting what I do
Olympos[25] made those laws not men who live and die   1100
nothing lulls those laws to sleep
they cannot die
and the infinite god in them never ages

arrogance insatiable pride
breed the tyrant
feed him on thing after thing blindly
at the wrong time uselessly
and he grows reaches so high
nothing can stop his fall
his feet thrashing the air standing on nothing   1110
and nowhere to stand he plunges down
o god shatter the tyrant
but let men compete let self-perfection grow
let men sharpen their skills
soldiers citizens building the good city
Apollo
protect me always
always the god I will honor

if a man walks through his life arrogant
strutting proud   1120
says anything does anything
does not fear justice
fear the gods bow to their shining presences
let fate make him stumble in his tracks
for all his lecheries and headlong greed
if he takes whatever he wants right or wrong
if he touches forbidden things
what man who acts like this would boast

---

[24] The choral passage that follows seems central to the play, but its application is problematical. The chorus expresses a pious revulsion from the kind of evil acts that bring on divine punishment; it then proceeds to define *hubris*, the state of overweening pride that is especially dangerous in provoking divine wrath. The passage implies that if these ancient moral principles and the gods' oracles no longer can be depended on, all order has been lost. But no character in the play seems to have *deliberately* committed such acts of impiety as the chorus describes.

[25] The mountain home of the gods.

he can escape the anger of the gods
why should I join these sacred public dances 1130
if such acts are honored

no
I will never go to the holy untouchable stone
navel of the earth at Delphi
never again
go to the temples at Olympia at Abai[26]
if all these things are not joined
if past present future are not made one
made clear to mortal eyes
o Zeus if that is your name 1140
power above all immortal king
see these things look
those great prophecies are fading
men say they're nothing
nobody prays to the god of light no one believes
nothing of the gods stays

[JOCASTA *enters from the palace, carrying a branch tied with strands of wool, and a jar of incense. She is accompanied by a servant woman. She addresses the* CHORUS.]

JOCASTA. Lords of Thebes, I come to the temples of the god
with offerings—this incense and this branch.
So many thoughts torture Oedipus. He never rests.
He acts without reason. He is like a man 1150
who has lost everything he knows—the past
is useless to him; strange, new things baffle him.
And if someone talks disaster, it stuns him: he listens, he is afraid.
I have tried to reassure him, but nothing helps.
So I have come to you—
Apollo, close to my life, close to this house,
listen to my prayers: [*she kneels*]
help us purify ourselves of this disease,
help us survive the long night of our suffering,
protect us. We are afraid when we see Oedipus confused
and frightened—Oedipus, the only man who can pilot Thebes 1160
to safety.

[*A* MESSENGER *from Corinth has arrived by the entrance to the orchestra on the audience's left. He sees* JOCASTA *praying, then turns to address the* CHORUS.]

---

[26] Sites of oracles, of Apollo and Zeus respectively.

MESSENGER. Friends,
    can you tell me where King Oedipus lives
    or better still, where I can find him?
LEADER. Here, in this house.
    This lady is his wife and mother
    of his children.
MESSENGER. May you and your family prosper.
    May you be happy always under this great roof.
JOCASTA. Happiness and prosperity to you, too, for your kind words.   1170
    But why are you here? Do you bring news?
MESSENGER. Good news for your house, good news for King Oedipus.
JOCASTA. What is your news? Who sent you?
MESSENGER. I come from Corinth, and what I have to say I know will
        bring you joy.
    And pain perhaps. . . . I do not know.
JOCASTA. Both joy and pain? What news could do that?
MESSENGER. The people of Corinth want Oedipus as their king.
    That's what they're saying.
JOCASTA. But isn't old Polybos still king of Corinth?
MESSENGER. His kingdom is his grave.   1180
JOCASTA. Polybos is *dead?*
MESSENGER. If I'm lying, my lady, let me die for it.
JOCASTA. You. [*to a servant*] Go in and tell Oedipus.
    O oracles of the gods, where are you now!
    This man, the man Oedipus was afraid he would murder,
    the man he feared, the man he fled from has died a natural death.
    Oedipus didn't kill him, it was luck, luck.

                              [*She turns to greet* OEDIPUS *as he
                              comes out of the palace.*]

OEDIPUS. Jocasta, why did you send for me? [*taking her gently by the arm*]
JOCASTA. Oedipus,
    listen to this man, see what those ominous, holy predictions of Apollo
        mean now.   1190
OEDIPUS. Who is this man? What does he say?
JOCASTA. He comes from Corinth.
    Your father is dead. Polybos is dead!
OEDIPUS. What?
    Let me hear those words from your own mouth, stranger.
    Tell me yourself, in your own words.
MESSENGER. If that's what you want to hear first, then I'll say it:
    Polybos is dead.
OEDIPUS. How did he die? Assassination? Illness? How?
MESSENGER. An old man's life hangs by a fragile thread. Anything can
        snap it.   1200
OEDIPUS. That poor old man. It was illness then?
MESSENGER. Illness and old age.
OEDIPUS. Why, Jocasta,
    why should men look to the great hearth at Delphi

or listen to birds shrieking and wheeling overhead—
cries meaning I was doomed to kill my father?
He is dead, gone, covered by the earth.
And here I am—my hands never even touched a spear—
I did not kill him,
unless he died from wanting me to come home. 1210
No. Polybos has bundled up all these oracles
and taken them with him to the world below.
They are only words now, lost in the air.
JOCASTA. Isn't that what I predicted?
OEDIPUS. You were right. My fears confused me.
JOCASTA. You have nothing to fear. Not now. Not ever.
OEDIPUS. But the oracle said I am doomed to sleep with my mother.
How can I live with that and not be afraid?
JOCASTA. Why should men be afraid of anything? Fortune rules our
lives.
Luck is everything. Things happen. The future is darkness. 1220
No human mind can know it.
It's best to live in the moment, live for today, Oedipus.
Why should the thought of marrying your mother make you so afraid?
Many men have slept with their mothers in their dreams.
Why worry? See your dreams for what they are—nothing, nothing
at all.
Be happy, Oedipus.
OEDIPUS. All that you say is right, Jocasta. I know it.
I should be happy,
but my mother is still living. As long as she's alive,
I live in fear. This fear is necessary. 1230
I have no choice.
JOCASTA. But Oedipus, your father's death is a sign, a great sign—
the sky has cleared, the sun's gaze holds us in its warm, hopeful
light.
OEDIPUS. A great sign, I agree. But so long as my mother is alive,
my fear lives too.
MESSENGER. Who is this woman you fear so much?
OEDIPUS. Merope, King Polybos' wife.
MESSENGER. Why does Merope frighten you so much?
OEDIPUS. A harrowing oracle hurled down upon us by some great god.
MESSENGER. Can you tell me? Or did the god seal your lips? 1240
OEDIPUS. I can.
Long ago, Apollo told me I was doomed to sleep with my mother
and spill my father's blood, murder him
with these two hands of mine.
That's why I never returned to Corinth. Luckily, it would seem.
Still, nothing on earth is sweeter to a man's eyes
than the sight of his father and mother.
MESSENGER. And you left Corinth because of this prophecy?
OEDIPUS. Yes. And because of my father. To avoid killing my father.
MESSENGER. But didn't my news prove you have nothing to fear? 1250
I brought good news.

OEDIPUS. And I will reward you for your kindness.

MESSENGER. That's why I came, my lord. I knew you'd remember me
  when you returned to Corinth.

OEDIPUS. I will never return, never live with my parents again.

MESSENGER. Son, it's clear you don't know what you're doing.

OEDIPUS. What do you mean? In the name of the gods, speak.

MESSENGER. If you're afraid to go home because of your parents.

OEDIPUS. I *am* afraid, afraid
  Apollo's prediction will come true, all of it,   1260
  as god's sunlight grows brighter on a man's face at dawn
  when he's in bed, still sleeping,
  and reaches into his eyes and wakes him.

MESSENGER. Afraid of murdering your father, of having his blood
  on your hands?

OEDIPUS. Yes. His blood. The stain of his blood. That terror never leaves
  me.

MESSENGER. But Oedipus, then you have no reason to be afraid.

OEDIPUS. I'm their son, they're my parents, aren't they?

MESSENGER. Polybos is nothing to you.

OEDIPUS. Polybos is not my father?   1270

MESSENGER. No more than I am.

OEDIPUS. But you are nothing to me. Nothing.

MESSENGER. And Polybos is nothing to you either.

OEDIPUS. Then why did he call me his son?

MESSENGER. Because I gave you to him. With these hands
  I gave you to him.

OEDIPUS. How could he have loved me like a father if I am not his
  son?

MESSENGER. He had no children. That opened his heart.

OEDIPUS. And what about you?
  Did you buy me from someone? Or did you find me?   1280

MESSENGER. I found you squawling, left alone to die in the thickets of
  Kithairon.

OEDIPUS. Kithairon? What were you doing on Kithairon?

MESSENGER. Herding sheep in the high summer pastures.

OEDIPUS. You were a shepherd, a drifter looking for work?

MESSENGER. A drifter, yes, but it was I who saved you.

OEDIPUS. Saved me? Was I hurt when you picked me up?

MESSENGER. Ask your feet.

OEDIPUS. Why,
  why did you bring up that childhood pain?

MESSENGER. I cut you free. Your feet were pierced, tied together at the
  ankles   1290
  with leather thongs strung between the tendons and the bone.

OEDIPUS. That mark of my shame—I've worn it from the cradle.

MESSENGER. That mark is the meaning of your name:
  Oedipus, Swollenfoot, Oedipus.

OEDIPUS. Oh gods
  who did this to me?

My mother?
My father?
MESSENGER. I don't know. The man I took you from—he would know.
OEDIPUS. So you didn't find me? Somebody else gave me to you? 1300
MESSENGER. I got you from another shepherd.
OEDIPUS. What shepherd? Who was he? Do you know?
MESSENGER. As I recall, he worked for Laios.
OEDIPUS. The same Laios who was king of Thebes?
MESSENGER. The same Laios. The man was one of Laios' shepherds.
OEDIPUS. Is he still alive? I want to see this man.
MESSENGER. [*pointing to the* CHORUS] These people would know that
    better than I do.
OEDIPUS. Do any of you know this shepherd he's talking about?
    Have you ever noticed him in the fields or in the city?
    Answer, if you have. 1310
    It is time everything came out, time everything was made clear.
    Everything.
LEADER. I think he's the shepherd you sent for.
    But Jocasta, she would know.
OEDIPUS. [*to* JOCASTA]
    Jocasta, do you know this man?
    Is he the man this shepherd here says worked for Laios?
JOCASTA. What man? Forget about him. Forget what was said.
    It's not worth talking about.
OEDIPUS. How can I forget
    with clues like these in my hands? 1320
    With the secret of my birth staring me in the face?
JOCASTA. No, Oedipus!
    No more questions.
    For god's sake, for the sake of your own life!
    Isn't my anguish enough—more than enough?
OEDIPUS. You have nothing to fear,[27] Jocasta.
    Even if my mother
    and her mother before her were both slaves,
    that doesn't make *you* the daughter of slaves.
JOCASTA. Oedipus, you *must* stop.
                    I beg you—stop! 1330
OEDIPUS. Nothing can stop me now. I must know everything.
    Everything!
JOCASTA. I implore you, Oedipus. For your own good.
OEDIPUS. Damn my own good!
JOCASTA. Oh, Oedipus, Oedipus,
    I pray to god you never see who you are!
OEDIPUS. [*to one of the attendants, who hurries off through the exit stage left*]
    You there, go find that shepherd, bring him here.
    Let that woman bask in the glory of her noble birth.

---

[27]Oedipus believes Jocasta's anguish is caused by fears that he is of lowly birth and social station.

JOCASTA. God help you, Oedipus—
   you were born to suffer, born   1340
   to misery and grief.
   These are the last words I will ever speak, ever
   Oedipus.

                           [JOCASTA *rushes offstage into the
                           palace. Long silence.*]

LEADER. Why did Jocasta rush away,
   Oedipus, fleeing in such pain?
   I fear disaster, or worse,
   will break from this silence of hers.
OEDIPUS. Let it break! Let everything break!
   I must discover who I am, know the secret of my birth,
   no matter how humble, how vile.   1350
   Perhaps Jocasta is ashamed of my low birth, ashamed to be my wife.
   Like all women she's proud.
   But Luck, goddess who gives men all that is good, made *me,*
   and I won't be cheated of what is mine, nothing can dishonor me,
      ever.
   I am like the months, my brothers the months—they shaped me
   when I was a baby in the cold hills of Kithairon,
   they guided me, carved out my times of greatness,
   and they still move their hands over my life.
   I am the man I am. I will not stop
   until I discover who my parents are.   1360
CHORUS. if I know if I see
   if the dark force of prophecy is mine
   Kithairon
   when the full moon
   rides over us tomorrow
   listen listen to us sing to you
   dance worship praise you
   mountain where Oedipus was found
   know Oedipus will praise you
   praise his nurse country and mother   1370
   who blessed our king
   I call on you Apollo
   let these visions please you
   god Apollo
   healer
   Oedipus son
   who was your mother
   which of the deathless mountain nymphs who lay
   with the great god Pan[28]
   on the high peaks he runs across   1380
   or with Apollo
   who loves the high green pastures above

_____

[28] God of the forest, of mountains, and of wild nature.

which one bore you
did the god of the bare windy peaks Hermes[29]
or the wild, dervish Dionysos
living in the cool air of the hills
take you
a foundling
from one of the nymphs he plays with
joyously lift you hold you in his arms   1390
OEDIPUS. Old men, I think the man coming toward us now
   must be the shepherd we are looking for.
   I have never seen him, but the years, chalking his face and hair,
      tell me
   he's the man. And my men are with him. But you probably know
      him.
LEADER. I do know him. If Laios ever had a man he trusted,
   this was the man.
OEDIPUS. [*to the* MESSENGER]
   You—is this the man you told me about?
MESSENGER. That's him. You're looking at the man.
OEDIPUS. [*to the* SHEPHERD *who has been waiting, hanging back*]
   You there, come closer.
                              Answer me, old man.
   Did you work for Laios?   1400
SHEPHERD. I was born his slave, and grew up in his household.
OEDIPUS. What was your work?
SHEPHERD. Herding sheep, all my life.
OEDIPUS. Where?
SHEPHERD. Kithairon, mostly. And the country around Kithairon.
OEDIPUS. Do you remember ever seeing this man?
SHEPHERD. Which man?
OEDIPUS. [*pointing to the* MESSENGER]
   This man standing here. Have you ever seen him before?
SHEPHERD. Not that I remember.
MESSENGER. No wonder, master. But I'll make him remember.   1410
   He knows who I am. We used to graze our flocks together
   in the pastures around Kithairon.
   Every year, for six whole months, three years running.
   From March until September, when the Dipper rose, signaling the
      harvest.
   I had one flock, he had two.
   And when the frost came, I drove my sheep back to their winter
      pens
   and he drove his back to Laios' fold.
   Remember, old man? Isn't that how it was?
SHEPHERD. Yes. But it was all so long ago.
MESSENGER. And do you remember giving me a baby boy at the time—   1420
   to raise as my own son?

---

[29] Hermes was born on a mountain (Cyllene); he was also the god of shepherds.

SHEPHERD. What if I do? Why all these questions?
MESSENGER. That boy became King Oedipus, friend.
SHEPHERD. Damn you, can't you keep quiet.
OEDIPUS. Don't scold him, old man.
    It's you who deserve to be punished, not him.
SHEPHERD. What did I say, good master?
OEDIPUS. You haven't answered his question about the boy.
SHEPHERD. He's making trouble, master. He doesn't know a thing.

                                        [OEDIPUS *takes the* SHEPHERD *by the*
                                        cloak]

OEDIPUS. Tell me or you'll be sorry.   1430
SHEPHERD. For god's sake, don't hurt me, I'm an old man.
OEDIPUS. [*to one of his men*] You there, hold him. We'll make him talk.

                                        [*The attendant pins the* SHEPHERD*'s*
                                        arms behind his back]

SHEPHERD. Oedipus, Oedipus,
    god knows I pity you.
    What more do you want to know?
OEDIPUS. Did you give the child to this man?
                                        Speak. Yes or no?
SHEPHERD. Yes.
    And I wish to god I'd died that day.
OEDIPUS. You *will* be dead unless you tell me the whole truth.
SHEPHERD. And worse than dead if I do.   1440
OEDIPUS. It seems our man won't answer.
SHEPHERD. No. I told you already. I gave him the boy.
OEDIPUS. Where did you get him? From Laios' household? Or where?
SHEPHERD. He wasn't *my* child. He was given to me.
OEDIPUS. [*turning to the* CHORUS *and the audience*]
    By whom? Someone here in Thebes?
SHEPHERD. Master, please, in god's name, no more questions.
OEDIPUS. You're a dead man if I have to ask you once more.
SHEPHERD. He was one
    of the children
    from Laios'   1450
    household.
OEDIPUS. A slave child? Or Laios' own?
SHEPHERD. I can't say it . . . it's
    awful, the words
    are awful . . . awful.
OEDIPUS. And I,
    I am afraid to hear them . . .
    but I must.
SHEPHERD. He was Laios' own child.
    Your wife, inside the palace, she can explain it all.   1460
OEDIPUS. *She* gave you the child?
SHEPHERD. My lord . . . yes.

OEDIPUS. Why?
SHEPHERD. She wanted me to abandon the child on a mountain.
OEDIPUS. His own mother?
SHEPHERD. Yes. There were prophecies, horrible oracles. She was afraid.
OEDIPUS. What oracles?
SHEPHERD. Oracles predicting he would murder his own father.
OEDIPUS. But why did you give the boy to this old man?
SHEPHERD. Because I pitied him, master, because I   1470
    thought the man would take the child away, take him to another
        country.
    Instead he saved him. Saved him for—oh gods,
    a fate so horrible, so awful, words can't describe it.
    If you were the baby that man took from me, Oedipus,
    what misery, what grief is yours!
OEDIPUS. [*looking up at the sun*]
    LIGHT   LIGHT   LIGHT
    never again flood these eyes with your white radiance, oh gods,
        my eyes. All, all
    the oracles have proven true. I, Oedipus, I
    am the child
    of parents who should never have been mine—doomed, doomed!   1480
    Now everything is clear—I
    lived with a woman, she was my mother, I slept in my mother's bed,
        and I
    murdered, murdered my father,
    the man whose blood flows in these veins of mine,
    whose blood stains these two hands red.

                                    [OEDIPUS *raises his hands to the*
                                    sun, then turns and walks into the
                                    palace.]

CHORUS. man after man after man
    o mortal generations
    here once
    almost not here
    what are we   1490
    dust ghosts images a rustling of air
    nothing nothing
    we breathe on the abyss
    we are the abyss
    our happiness no more than traces of a dream
    the high noon sun sinking into the sea
    the red spume of its wake raining behind it
    we are you
    we are you Oedipus
    dragging your maimed foot   1500
    in agony
    and now that I see your life finally revealed
    your life fused with the god

blazing out of the black nothingness of all we know
I say
no happiness lasts nothing human lasts

wherever you aimed you hit
no archer had your skill
you grew rich powerful great
everything came falling to your feet   1510
o Zeus
after he killed the Sphinx
whose claws curled under
whose weird song of the future[30] baffled and destroyed
he stood like a tower high above our country
warding off death
and from then on Oedipus we called you
king our king
draped you in gold
our highest honors were yours   1520
and you ruled this shining city
Thebes   Thebes

now
your story is pain pity no story is worse
than yours Oedipus
ruined savage blind
as you struggle with your life
as your life changes
and breaks and shows you who you are
Oedipus   Oedipus   1530
son father you harbored in the selfsame place[31]
the same place sheltered you both
bridegroom
how could the furrow your father plowed
not have cried out all this time
while you lay there unknowing
and saw the truth too late

time like the sun sees all things
and it sees you
you cannot hide from that light   1540
your own life opening itself to you
to all
married unmarried father son
for so long

[30] The Sphinx was a kind of oracle; specifically, her riddle about the three states of man
reflects this play's focus on Oedipus' infancy, prime of manhood, and final weakness when,
blinded, he must use a walking stick.
  [31] Harbored sexually, with Jocasta; geographically, the place alluded to is the mountain
Kithairon, where Laios died and to which Oedipus will flee.

justice comes like the dawn
always
and it shows the world your marriage now

I wish
o child of Laios
I wish I had never seen you   1550
I grieve for you
wail after wail fills me and pours out
because of you my breath came flowing back
but now
the darkness of your life
floods my eyes

> [*The palace doors open. A* SERVANT
> *enters and approaches the* CHORUS
> *and audience.*]

SERVANT. Noble citizens, honored above all others in Thebes,
if you still care for the house of Laios
if you still can feel the spirit of those who ruled before, now
the horrors you will hear, the horrors you will see, will shake   1560
your hearts and shatter you with grief beyond enduring.
Not even the waters of those great rivers Ister and Phasis[32]
could wash away the blood
that now darkens every stone of this shining house,
this house that will reveal, soon, soon
the misery and evil two mortals,
both masters of this house, have brought upon themselves.

The griefs we cause ourselves cut deepest of all.[33]
LEADER. What we already know
has hurt us enough,   1570
has made us cry out in pain.
What more can you say?
SERVANT. This:
Jocasta is dead. The queen is dead.
LEADER. Ah, poor
unhappy Jocasta,
how did she die?
SERVANT. She killed herself. She did it.
But you did not see what happened there,
you were not there, in the palace. You did not see it.   1580
I did.
I will tell you how Queen Jocasta died,
the whole story, all of it. All I can remember.

---

[32]Ister is the Danube River; Phasis is a river flowing into the Black Sea.
[33] The reference may be to the acts of Laios and Oedipus in the distant past or to the recent
suicide and self-blinding of Jocasta and Oedipus. The words "cut deepest of all" can also apply
to the Thebans and to the theatrical audience.

After her last words to Oedipus
she rushed past us through the entrance hall, screaming,
raking her hair with both hands, and flew into the bedroom, *their*
    bedroom,
and slammed the doors shut as she lunged at her bridal bed,
crying "Laios" "Laios"—dead all these years—
remembering Laios—how his own son years ago
grew up and then killed him, leaving her to   1590
sleep with her own son, to have his children, *their* children,
children—not sons, not daughters, something else, monsters. . . .
Then she collapsed, sobbing, cursing the bed where she held both
    men in her arms,
got husband from husband, children from her child.
We heard it all, but suddenly, I couldn't tell what was happening.
Oedipus came crashing in, he was howling,
stalking up and down—we couldn't take our eyes off him—
and we stopped listening to her pitiful cries.
We stood there, watching him move like a bull, lurching, charging,
shouting at each of us to give him a sword, demanding we tell him   1600
where his wife was, that woman whose womb carried him,
him and his children, that wife who gave him birth.
Some god, some demon, led him to her, and he knew—
none of us showed him—
suddenly a mad, inhuman cry burst from his mouth
as if the wind rushed through his tortured body,
and he heaved against those bedroom doors so the hinges whined
and bent from their sockets and the bolts snapped,
and he stood in the room.
There she was—   1610
we could see her—his wife
dangling by her neck from a noose of braided, silken cords
tied to a rafter, still swaying.
And when he saw her he bellowed and stretched up and loosened
    the rope,
cradling her in one arm,
and slowly laid her body on the ground.
That's when it happened—he
ripped off the gold
brooches she was wearing—one on each shoulder of her gown—
and raised them over his head—you could see them flashing—   1620
and tilted his face up and
brought them right down into his eyes
and the long pins sank deep, all the way back into the sockets,
and he shouted at his eyes:
"Now you won't see me, you won't see
my agonies or my crimes,
but in endless darkness, always, there you'll see
those I never should have seen.
And those I should have known were my parents, father and
    mother—

these eyes will never see their faces in the light. 1630
These eyes will never see the light again, never."
Cursing his two blind eyes over and over, he
lifted the brooches again and drove their pins through his eyeballs
    up
to the hilts until they were pulp, until the blood streamed out
soaking his beard and cheeks,
a black storm splashing its hail across his face.

Two mortals acted. Now grief tears their lives apart
as if that pain sprang from a single, sorrowing root
to curse each one, man and wife. For all those years
their happiness was truly happiness, but now, now 1640
wailing, madness, shame and death,
every evil men have given a name,
everything criminal and vile
that mankind suffers they suffer. Not one evil is missing.
LEADER. But now
    does this torn, anguished man
    have any rest from his pain?
SERVANT. No, no—
    then he shouted at us to open the doors and show everyone in Thebes
    his father's killer, his mother's—I cannot say it. 1650
Once we have seen him as he is
he will leave Thebes, lift the curse from his city—
banish himself, cursed by his own curses.
But his strength is gone, his whole life is pain,
more pain than any man can bear.
He needs help, someone to guide him.
He is alone, and blind. Look,
look—the palace doors are opening—now
a thing
so horrible will stand before you 1660
you will shudder with disgust and try to turn away
while your hearts will swell with pity for what you see.

> [*The central doors open.* OEDIPUS
> *enters, led by his household servants.*
> *His mask is covered with blood. The*
> CHORUS *begin a dirge to which*
> OEDIPUS *responds antiphonally.*]

CHORUS. horror horror o what suffering
    men see
    but none is worse than this
    Oedipus o
    how could you have slashed out your eyes
    what god leaped on you
    from beyond that last border of space

what madness entered you   1670
clawing even more misery into you
I cannot look at you

but there are questions
so much I would know
so much that I would see
no   no
the shape of your life makes me shudder
OEDIPUS. I   I
this voice of agony
I am what place am I   1680
where? Not here, nowhere I know!
What force, what tide breaks over my life?
Pain, demon stabbing into me
leaving nothing, nothing, no man I know, not human,
fate howling out of nowhere   what am I
fire   a voice   where   where
is it being taken?
LEADER. Beyond everything to a place
so terrible nothing is seen there, nothing is heard.
OEDIPUS. [*reaching out, groping*]
Thing   thing   darkness   1690
spilling into me, my
black cloud smothering me forever,
nothing can stop you, nothing can escape,
I cannot push you away.

I am
nothing but my own cries breaking
again and again
the agony of those gold pins
the memory of what I did
stab me   1700
again
again.
LEADER. What can you feel but pain.
It all comes back, pain in remorse,
remorse in pain, to tear you apart with grief.
OEDIPUS. Dear, loyal friend
you, only you, are still here with me, still care
for this blind, tortured man.
Oh,
I know you are there, I know you, friend,   1710
even in this darkness, friend, touched by your voice.
 LEADER. What you did was horrible,
but how could you quench the fire of your eyes,
what demon lifted your hands?
OEDIPUS. Apollo   Apollo
it was Apollo, always Apollo,

who brought each of my agonies to birth,
but I,
nobody else, *I*,
I raised these two hands of mine, held them above my head,   1720
and plunged them down,
I stabbed out these eyes.
Why should I have eyes? Why,
when nothing I saw was worth seeing?
Nothing.
LEADER. Nothing. Nothing.
OEDIPUS. Oh friends. Nothing.
  No one to see, no one to love,
  no one to speak to, no one to hear!
               Friends, friends, lead me away now.
  Lead me away from Thebes—Oedipus,   1730
  destroyer and destroyed,
  the man whose life is hell
  for others and for himself, the man
  more hated by the gods than any other man, ever.
LEADER. Oh I pity you,
  I weep for your fate
  and for your mind,
  for what it is to be you, Oedipus.
  I wish you had never seen the man you are.
OEDIPUS. I hate   1740
  the man who found me, cut the thongs from my feet,
  snatched me from death, cared for me—
  I wish he were dead!
  I should have died up there on those wild, desolate slopes of
     Kithairon.
  Then my pain and the pain
  those I love suffer now
  never would have been.
LEADER. These are my wishes too.
OEDIPUS. Then I never would have murdered my father,
  never heard men call me my mother's husband.   1750

  Now
  I am
  Oedipus!
  Oedipus, who lay in that loathsome bed, made love there in that
     bed,
  his father's and mother's bed, the bed
  where he was born.

  No gods anywhere now, not for me,[34] now,
  unholy, broken man.
  What man ever suffered grief like this?

---

[34]Oedipus means that he has been forsaken by the gods.

LEADER. How can I say that what you did was right?   1760
    Better to be dead than live blind.
OEDIPUS. I did what I had to do. No more advice.
    How could *my* eyes,
    when I went down into that black, sightless place beneath the earth,
    the place where the dead go down, how,
    how could I have looked at anything,
    with what human eyes could I have gazed
    on my father, on my mother—
    oh gods, my mother!
    What I did against those two   1770
    not even strangling could punish.

    And my children, how would the sight of them, born as they were
        born,
    be sweet? Not to these eyes of mine, never to these eyes.
    Nothing, nothing is left me now—no city with its high walls,
    no shining statues of the gods. I stripped all these things from
        myself—
    I, Oedipus, fallen lower than any man now, born nobler than the
        best,
    born the king of Thebes! Cursed with my own curses, I
    commanded Thebes to drive out the killer.
    I banished the royal son of Laios, the man the gods revealed
    is stained with the awful stain. The secret stain   1780
    that I myself revealed is *my* stain. And now, revealed at last,
    how could I ever look men in the eyes?
    Never. Never.

    If I could, I would have walled my ears so they heard nothing,
    I would have made this body of mine a wall.
    I would have heard nothing, tasted nothing, smelled nothing, seen
        nothing.
            No thought. No feeling. Nothing. Nothing.
    So pain would never reach me any more.

    O Kithairon,
    why did you shelter me and take me in?   1790
    Why did you let me live? Better to have died on that bare slope of
        yours
    where no man would ever have seen me or known the secret of my
        birth!

    Polybos, Corinth, that house I thought was my father's home,
    how beautiful I was when you sheltered me as a child
    and oh what disease festered beneath that beauty.
    Now everyone knows the secret of my birth, knows
    how vile I am.

    O roads, secret valley, cluster of oaks,

O narrow place where two roads join a third,[35]
roads that drank my blood as it streamed from my hands,   1800
flowing from my dead father's body,
do you remember me now?
Do you remember what I did with my own two hands, there in your
    presence,
and what I did after that, when I came here to Thebes?
O marriage, marriage, you gave me my life, and then
from the same seed, *my* seed, spewed out
fathers, brothers, sisters, children, brides, wives—
nothing, no words can express the shame.
No more words. Men should not name what men should never do.

[*To the* CHORUS]

Gods, oh gods, gods,   1810
hide me, hide me
now
far away from Thebes,
kill me,
cast me into the sea,
drive me where you will never see me—never again.

[*Reaching out to the* CHORUS, *who
back away*]

Touch this poor man, touch me,
don't be afraid to touch me. Believe me, nobody,
nobody but me can bear
this fire of anguish.   1820
It is mine. Mine.
LEADER. Kreon has come.
Now he, not you, is the sole guardian of Thebes,
and only he can grant you what you ask.
OEDIPUS. [*turning toward the palace*]
What can I say to him, how can anything I say
make him listen now?
I wronged him. I accused him, and now everything I said
proves I am vile.
KREON. [*enters from the entrance to the right. He is accompanied by men who
gather around* OEDIPUS]

I have not come to mock you, Oedipus; I have not come to blame
you for the past.

[*To attendants*]

You men, standing there, if you have no respect for human dignity,   1830
at least revere the master of life,

[35]Not only the crossroads where Oedipus killed his father but also the sexual "narrow place"
where Oedipus, his father, and Jocasta conjoined.

the all-seeing sun whose light nourishes
every living thing on earth.
Come, cover this cursed, naked, holy thing,[36] hide him
from the earth and the sacred rain and the light,
you powers who cringe from his touch.
Take him. Do it now. Be reverent.
Only his family should see and hear his grief.
Their grief.

OEDIPUS. I beg you, Kreon, if you love the gods,   1840
grant me what I ask.
I have been vile to you, worse than vile.
I have hurt you, terribly, and yet
you have treated me with kindness, with nobility.
You have calmed my fear, you did not turn away from me.
Do what I ask. Do it for yourself, not for me.

KREON. What do you want from me, Oedipus?

OEDIPUS. Drive me out of Thebes, do it now, now—
drive me someplace where no man can speak to me,
where no man can see me anymore.   1850

KREON. Believe me, Oedipus, I would have done it long ago.
But I refuse to act until I know precisely what the god desires.

OEDIPUS. Apollo has revealed what he desires. Everything is clear.
I killed my father, I am polluted and unclean.
I must die.

KREON. That is what the god commanded, Oedipus.
But there are no precedents for what has happened.
We need to *know* before we act.

OEDIPUS. Do you care so much for me, enough to ask Apollo?
For *me*, Oedipus?   1860

KREON. Now even you will trust the god, I think.

OEDIPUS. I will. And I turn to you, I implore you, Kreon—
the woman lying dead inside, your sister,
give her whatever burial you think best.

                                                        As for me,
never let this city of my fathers see me here in Thebes.
Let me go and live on the mountain, on Kithairon—the mountain
my parents intended for my grave.
Let me die the way they wanted me to die: slowly, alone—
die *their* way.
And yet this much I know—

                                        no sickness,   1870
no ordinary, natural death[37] is mine.

---

[36]Because he bears a burden of guilt that transforms ordinary human nature, Oedipus has, paradoxically, become a kind of sacred being.

[37]In his play *Oedipus at Colonus,* Sophocles continues the story of *Oedipus the King* (though the plays, along with the further continuation, *Antigone,* were written at different periods of Sophocles' life). Since Oedipus died at Colonus, a suburb of Athens that included a place sacred to the Furies, the personified forces of atonement celebrated in the last play of Aeschylus' Orestes trilogy, the present reference to Oedipus' mysterious and sacred death and resting place would have been important to Sophocles' Athenian audience as a sign of the redemptive value of Oedipus' wanderings and sufferings.

I have been saved, preserved, kept alive
for some strange fate, for something far more awful still.
When that thing comes, let it take me
where it will.

[OEDIPUS *turns, looking for something, waiting*]

As for my sons,[38] Kreon,
they are grown men, they can look out for themselves.
But my daughters, those two poor girls of mine,
who have never left their home before, never left their father's side,
who ate at my side every day, who shared whatever was mine,   1880
I beg you, Kreon,
care for them, love them.
But more than anything, Kreon,
I want to touch them,

[*he begins to lift his hands*]

let me touch them with these hands of mine,
let them come to me so we can grieve together.
My noble lord, if only I could touch them with my hands,
they would still be mine just as they were
when I had eyes that could still see.

[OEDIPUS' *two small daughters are brought out of the palace*]

O gods, gods, is it possible? Do I hear   1890
my two daughters crying? Has Kreon pitied me and brought me
what I love more than my life—
my daughters?
KREON. I brought them to you, knowing how much you love them,
    Oedipus,
knowing the joy you would feel if they were here.
OEDIPUS. May the gods who watch over the path of your life, Kreon,
prove kinder to you than they were to me.
Where are you, children?
Come, come to your brother's hands—

[*taking his daughters into his arms*]

his mother was your mother, too,   1900
come to these hands which made these eyes, bright clear eyes once,
sockets seeing nothing, the eyes
of the man who fathered you. Look . . . your father's eyes,
your father—

---

[38] Eteocles and Polyneices. Their enmity in a subsequent war for control of the city of Thebes, and the related ordeals of Oedipus' daughters Antigone and Ismene, are central to Sophocles' *Oedipus at Colonus* and *Antigone*.

who knew nothing until now, saw nothing until now, and became
the husband of the woman who gave him birth.
                                                    I weep for you
when I think how men will treat you, how bitter your lives will be.
What festivals will you attend, whose homes will you visit
and not be assailed by whispers, and people's stares?
Where will you go and not leave in tears?   1910
And when the time comes for you to marry,
what men will take you as their brides, and risk the shame of
    marrying
the daughters of Oedipus?
What sorrow will not be yours?
Your father killed his father, made love
to the woman who gave birth to him. And he fathered you
in the same place where he was fathered.
That is what you will hear; that is what they will say.
Who will marry you then? You will never marry,
but grow hard and dry like wheat so far beyond harvest   1920
that the wind blows its white flakes into the winter sky.
Oh Kreon,
now you are the only father my daughters have.
Jocasta and I, their parents, are lost to them forever.
These poor girls are yours. Your blood.
Don't let them wander all their lives,
begging, alone, unmarried, helpless.
Don't let them suffer as their father has. Pity them, Kreon,
pity these girls, so young and helpless except for you.
Promise me this. Noble Kreon,   1930
touch me with your hand, give me a sign.

                        [KREON *takes his hands*]

                                                    Daughters,
daughters, if you were older, if you could understand,
there is so much more I would say to you.
But for now, I give you this prayer—
                                        Live,
live your lives, live each day as best you can,
may your lives be happier than your father's was.
KREON. No more grief. Come in.
OEDIPUS. I must. But obedience comes hard.
KREON. Everything has its time.
OEDIPUS. First, promise me this.   1940
KREON. Name it.
OEDIPUS. Banish me from Thebes.
KREON. I cannot.   Ask the gods for that.
OEDIPUS. The gods hate me.
KREON. Then you will have your wish.
OEDIPUS. You promise?
KREON. I say only what I mean.
OEDIPUS. Then lead me in.

[OEDIPUS *reaches ou*
his daughters, tryin/
with him]

KREON. Oedipus, come with me. Let your daughters go. Come.
OEDIPUS. No. You will not take my daughters. I forbid it.
KREON. You *forbid* me?
  You have no power any more.
  All the great power you once had is gone,
  gone forever.

[*The* CHORUS *turn to face the audience.* KREON *leads* OEDIPUS *toward
the palace. His daughters follow. He
moves slowly, and disappears into the
palace as the* CHORUS *ends.*]

CHORUS. O citizens of Thebes, this is Oedipus,
  who solved the famous riddle, who held more power than any
      mortal.
  See what he is: all men gazed on his fortunate life,
  all men envied him, but look at him, look.
  All he had, all this man was,
  pulled down and swallowed by the storm of his own life,
  and by the god.
  Keep your eyes on that last day, on your dying.
  Happiness and peace, they were not yours
  unless at death you can look back on your life and say
  I lived, I did not suffer.

1960

ANTIGONE

Translated by Robert Fagles

CHARACTERS

ANTIGONE *daughter of Oedipus and
  Jocasta*
ISMENE *sister of Antigone*
A CHORUS *of old Theban citizens and
  their* LEADER
CREON[1] *king of Thebes, uncle of
  Antigone and Ismene*

A SENTRY
HAEMON *son of Creon and Eurydice*
TIRESIAS *a blind prophet*
A MESSENGER
EURYDICE *wife of Creon*
Guards, attendants, and a boy

---

[1] The Kreon of *Oedipus the King*. The names in this translation sometimes are spelled differently.

TIME AND SCENE

The royal house of Thebes. It is still night, and the invading armies of Argos have just been driven from the city. Fighting on opposite sides, the sons of Oedipus, Eteocles and Polynices, have killed each other in combat. Their uncle, CREON, *is now king of Thebes.*

Enter ANTIGONE, *slipping through the central doors of the palace. She motions to her sister,* ISMENE, *who follows her cautiously toward an altar at the center of the stage.*

ANTIGONE.
My own flesh and blood—dear sister, dear Ismene,
how many griefs our father Oedipus handed down![2]
Do you know one, I ask you, one grief
that Zeus will not perfect for the two of us
while we still live and breathe? There's nothing,
no pain—our lives are pain—no private shame,
no public disgrace, nothing I haven't seen
in your griefs and mine. And now this:
an emergency decree, they say, the Commander
has just now declared for all of Thebes.   10
What, haven't you heard? Don't you see?
The doom reserved for enemies
marches on the ones we love the most.

ISMENE.
Not I, I haven't heard a word, Antigone.
Nothing of loved ones,
no joy or pain has come my way, not since
the two of us were robbed of our two brothers,[3]
both gone in a day, a double blow—
not since the armies of Argos vanished,
just this very night. I know nothing more,   20
whether our luck's improved or ruin's still to come.

ANTIGONE.
I thought so. That's why I brought you out here,
past the gates, so you could hear in private.

---

[2] The two sisters had accompanied their self-blinded father Oedipus in his wanderings and sufferings after his banishment from Thebes. (The banishment is described at the end of *Oedipus the King.*) Possibly we are to regard Oedipus' lineage as afflicted by an inherited curse. Oedipus' crimes, committed unwittingly, had been to kill his father, Laius, the king of Thebes, and to marry his mother.

[3] Oedipus' two sons, Eteocles and Polynices, had been rivals for the rulership of the city. After being exiled by Eteocles, Polynices had recruited a military force in Argos to attack Thebes. In the ensuing battle, the Thebans had defeated the Argives and the brothers Eteocles and Polynices had killed each other, leaving Creon to rule Thebes.

ISMENE.
What's the matter? Trouble, clearly . . .
you sound so dark, so grim.

ANTIGONE.
Why not? Our own brothers' burial![4]
Hasn't Creon graced one with all the rites,
disgraced the other? Eteocles, they say,
has been given full military honors,
rightly so—Creon has laid him in the earth 30
and he goes with glory down among the dead.
But the body of Polynices, who died miserably—
why, a city-wide proclamation, rumor has it,
forbids anyone to bury him, even mourn him.
He's to be left unwept, unburied, a lovely treasure
for birds that scan the field and feast to their heart's content.

Such, I hear, is the martial law our good Creon
lays down for you and me—yes, me, I tell you—
and he's coming here to alert the uninformed
in no uncertain terms, 40
and he won't treat the matter lightly. Whoever
disobeys in the least will die, his doom is sealed:
stoning to death inside the city walls!

There you have it. You'll soon show what you are,
worth your breeding, Ismene, or a coward—
for all your royal blood.

ISMENE.
My poor sister, if things have come to this,
who am I to make or mend them, tell me,
what good am I to you?

ANTIGONE.
                    Decide.
Will you share the labor, share the work? 50

ISMENE.
What work, what's the risk? What do you mean?

ANTIGONE.
                    [*Raising her hands.*]
Will you lift up his body with these bare hands
and lower it with me?

---

[4] It was believed that the unburied were treated with contempt in the underground realm
of the dead. Moreover, to mourn and to prepare bodies for proper burial was the special
duty of the women.

ISMENE.
                              What? You'd bury him—
when a law forbids the city?

ANTIGONE.
                                       Yes!
He is my brother and—deny it as you will—
your brother too.
No one will ever convict me for a traitor.

ISMENE.
So desperate, and Creon has expressly—

ANTIGONE.
                                                    No,
he has no right to keep me from my own.

ISMENE.
Oh my sister, think—   60
think how our own father died,[5] hated,
his reputation in ruins, driven on
by the crimes he brought to light himself
to gouge out his eyes with his own hands—
then mother . . . his mother and wife, both in one,
mutilating her life in the twisted noose—
and last, our two brothers dead in a single day,
both shedding their own blood, poor suffering boys,
battling out their common destiny hand-to-hand.
Now look at the two of us, left so alone . . .   70
think what a death we'll die, the worst of all
if we violate the laws and override
the fixed decree of the throne, its power—
we must be sensible. Remember we are women,
we're not born to contend with men. Then too,
we're underlings, ruled by much stronger hands,
so we must submit in this, and things still worse.

I, for one, I'll beg the dead to forgive me—
I'm forced, I have no choice—I must obey
the ones who stand in power. Why rush to extremes?   80
It's madness, madness.

ANTIGONE.
                              I won't insist,
no, even if you should have a change of heart,

---

[5] The version in *Oedipus at Colonus* is that Oedipus, after long suffering, died a holy and mysterious death. The events Ismene describes here (her mother Jocasta's suicide and Oedipus' self-blinding) take place in *Oedipus the King*.

I'd never welcome you in the labor, not with me.
So, do as you like, whatever suits you best—
I will bury him myself.
And even if I die in the act, that death will be a glory.
I will lie with the one I love and loved by him—
an outrage sacred to the gods! I have longer
to please the dead than please the living here.
In the kingdom down below I'll lie forever.   90
Do as you like, dishonor the laws
the gods hold in honor.

ISMENE.
                          I'd do them no dishonor . . .
but defy the city? I have no strength for that.

ANTIGONE.
You have your excuses. I am on my way,
I will raise a mound for him, for my dear brother.

ISMENE.
Oh Antigone, you're so rash—I'm so afraid for you!

ANTIGONE.
Don't fear for me. Set your own life in order.

ISMENE.
Then don't, at least, blurt this out to anyone.
Keep it a secret. I'll join you in that, I promise.

ANTIGONE.
Dear god, shout it from the rooftops. I'll hate you   100
all the more for silence—tell the world!

ISMENE.
So fiery—and it ought to chill your heart.

ANTIGONE.
I know I please where I must please the most.

ISMENE.
Yes, if you can, but you're in love with impossibility.

ANTIGONE.
Very well, then, once my strength gives out
I will be done at last.

ISMENE.
                          You're wrong from the start,
you're off on a hopeless quest.

ANTIGONE.
    If you say so, you will make me hate you,
    and the hatred of the dead, by all rights,
    will haunt you night and day.   110
    But leave me to my own absurdity, leave me
    to suffer this—dreadful thing. I will suffer
    nothing as great as death without glory.
                                        [*Exit to the side.*]

ISMENE.
    Then go if you must, but rest assured,
    wild, irrational as you are, my sister,
    you are truly dear to the ones who love you.
                            [*Withdrawing to the palace. Enter a*
                            CHORUS, *the old citizens of Thebes,*
                            chanting as the sun begins to rise.]

CHORUS.
    Glory!—great beam of the sun, brightest of all
    that ever rose on the seven gates of Thebes,
        you burn through night at last!
                Great eye of the golden day,   120
    mounting the Dirce's[6] banks you throw him back—
    the enemy out of Argos, the white shield, the man of bronze—
    he's flying headlong now
                the bridle of fate stampeding him with pain!

    And he had driven against our borders,
    launched by the warring claims of Polynices—
    like an eagle screaming, winging havoc
    over the land, wings of armor
    shielded white as snow,
    a huge army massing,   130
    crested helmets bristling for assault.

    He hovered above our roofs, his vast maw gaping
    closing down around our seven gates,
        his spears thirsting for the kill
                but now he's gone, look,
    before he could glut his jaws with Theban blood
    or the god of fire put our crown of towers to the torch.
    He grappled the Dragon[7] none can master—Thebes—
                the clang of our arms like thunder at his back!

        Zeus hates with a vengeance all bravado,   140
        the mighty boasts of men. He watched them

    _____
    [6]A river near Thebes.
    [7]According to myth, the Thebans were descendants of men metamorphosed from the teeth
    of a dragon killed by Cadmus, founder of the city.

coming on in a rising flood, the pride
of their golden armor ringing shrill—
and brandishing his lightning
blasted the fighter just at the goal,
rushing to shout his triumph from our walls.[8]
Down from the heights he crashed, pounding down on the earth!
And a moment ago, blazing torch in hand—
   mad for attack, ecstatic
he breathed his rage, the storm   150
 of his fury hurling at our heads!
But now his high hopes have laid him low
and down the enemy ranks the iron god of war
 deals his rewards, his stunning blows—Ares[9]
rapture of battle, our right arm in the crisis.

Seven captains marshaled at seven gates
seven against their equals, gave
their brazen trophies up to Zeus,
god of the breaking rout of battle,
all but two: those blood brothers,   160
one father, one mother—matched in rage,
spears matched for the twin conquest—
clashed and won the common prize of death.

But now for Victory! Glorious in the morning,
joy in her eyes to meet our joy
 she is winging down to Thebes,
our fleets of chariots wheeling in her wake—
 Now let us win oblivion from the wars,
thronging the temples of the gods
in singing, dancing choirs through the night!   170
 Lord Dionysus,[10] god of the dance
 that shakes the land of Thebes, now lead the way!
       [*Enter* CREON *from the palace,*
       attended by his guard.]

But look, the king of the realm is coming,
Creon, the new man for the new day,
whatever the gods are sending now . . .
what new plan will he launch?
Why this, this special session?
Why this sudden call to the old men
summoned at one command?

---

[8] The fighter is Capaneus. Having scaled the walls of Thebes, he boasted that not even Zeus, king of the gods, could stop him, but Zeus killed him with a thunderbolt.

[9] God of war and of destruction.

[10] God of wine; his mother, Semele, who was ravished by Zeus in the form of lightning, was a Theban.

CREON.   My countrymen
the ship of state is safe. The gods who rocked her,   180
after a long, merciless pounding in the storm,
have righted her once more.
                                        Out of the whole city
I have called you here alone. Well I know,
first, your undeviating respect
for the throne and royal power of King Laius.
Next, while Oedipus steered the land of Thebes,
and even after he died, your loyalty was unshakable,
you still stood by their children. Now then,
since the two sons are dead—two blows of fate
in the same day, cut down by each other's hands,   190
both killers, both brothers stained with blood—
as I am next in kin to the dead,[11]
I now possess the throne and all its powers.

Of course you cannot know a man completely,
his character, his principles, sense of judgment,
not till he's shown his colors, ruling the people,
making laws. Experience, there's the test.
As I see it, whoever assumes the task,
the awesome task of setting the city's course,
and refuses to adopt the soundest policies   200
but fearing someone, keeps his lips locked tight,
he's utterly worthless. So I rate him now,
I always have. And whoever places a friend
above the good of his own country, he is nothing:
I have no use for him.[12] Zeus my witness,
Zeus who sees all things, always—
I could never stand by silent, watching destruction
march against our city, putting safety to rout,
nor could I ever make that man a friend of mine
who menaces our country. Remember this: 210
our country *is* our safety.
Only while she voyages true on course
can we establish friendships, truer than blood itself.
Such are my standards. They make our city great.

Closely akin to them I have proclaimed,
just now, the following decree to our people
concerning the two sons of Oedipus.

_____

[11] Creon is the brother of the dead rivals' mother, Jocasta; he is also a cousin of the former king Laius.
[12] Creon here states his side of the play's central moral and political issue. The word "friend" has also the meaning of "kindred."

Eteocles, who died fighting for Thebes,
excelling all in arms: he shall be buried,
crowned with a hero's honors, the cups we pour   220
to soak the earth and reach the famous dead.

But as for his blood brother, Polynices,
who returned from exile, home to his father-city
and the gods of his race, consumed with one desire—
to burn them roof to roots—who thirsted to drink
his kinsmen's blood and sell the rest to slavery:
that man—a proclamation has forbidden the city
to dignify him with burial, mourn him at all.
No, he must be left unburied, his corpse
carrion for the birds and dogs to tear,   230
an obscenity for the citizens to behold!

These are my principles. Never at my hands
will the traitor be honored above the patriot.
But whoever proves his loyalty to the state—
I'll prize that man in death as well as life.

LEADER.
    If this is your pleasure, Creon, treating
    our city's enemy and our friend this way . . .
    The power is yours, I suppose, to enforce it
    with the laws, both for the dead and all of us,
    the living.

CREON.
                Follow my orders closely then,   240
    be on your guard.

LEADER.
                We are too old.
    Lay that burden on younger shoulders.

CREON.
                        No, no,
    I don't mean the body—I've posted guards already.

LEADER.
    What commands for us then? What other service?

CREON.
    See that you never side with those who break my orders.

LEADER.
    Never. Only a fool could be in love with death.

CREON.
     Death is the price—you're right. But all too often
     the mere hope of money has ruined many men.
                         [*A* SENTRY *enters from the side.*]

SENTRY.
                                                     My lord,
     I can't say I'm winded from running, or set out
     with any spring in my legs either—no sir,   250
     I was lost in thought, and it made me stop, often,
     dead in my tracks, wheeling, turning back,
     and all the time a voice inside me muttering,
     "Idiot, why? You're going straight to your death."
     Then muttering, "Stopped again, poor fool?
     If somebody gets the news to Creon first,
     what's to save your neck?"
                         And so,
     mulling it over, on I trudged, dragging my feet,
     you can make a short road take forever . . .
     but at last, look, common sense won out,   260
     I'm here, and I'm all yours,
     and even though I come empty-handed
     I'll tell my story just the same, because
     I've come with a good grip on one hope,
     what will come will come, whatever fate—

CREON.
     Come to the point!
     What's wrong—why so afraid?

SENTRY.
     First, myself, I've got to tell you,
     I didn't do it, didn't see who did—
     Be fair, don't take it out on me.   270

CREON.
     You're playing it safe, soldier,
     barricading yourself from any trouble.
     It's obvious, you've something strange to tell.

SENTRY.
     Dangerous too, and danger makes you delay
     for all you're worth.

CREON.
     Out with it—then dismiss!

SENTRY.
     All right, here it comes. The body—

someone's just buried it, then run off . . .
sprinkled some dry dust on the flesh,
given it proper rites.

CREON.
                                    What?   280
What man alive would dare—

SENTRY.
                                    I've no idea, I swear it.
There was no mark of a spade, no pickaxe there,
no earth turned up, the ground packed hard and dry,
unbroken, no tracks, no wheelruts, nothing,
the workman left no trace. Just at sunup
the first watch of the day points it out—
it was a wonder! We were stunned . . .
a terrific burden too, for all of us, listen:
you can't see the corpse, not that it's buried,
really, just a light cover of road-dust on it,   290
as if someone meant to lay the dead to rest
and keep from getting cursed.
Not a sign in sight that dogs or wild beasts
had worried the body, even torn the skin.
But what came next! Rough talk flew thick and fast,
guard grilling guard—we'd have come to blows
at last, nothing to stop it; each man for himself
and each the culprit, no one caught red-handed,
all of us pleading ignorance, dodging the charges,
ready to take up red-hot iron in our fists,   300
go through fire, swear oaths to the gods—
"I didn't do it, I had no hand in it either,
not in the plotting, not the work itself!"

Finally, after all this wrangling came to nothing,
one man spoke out and made us stare at the ground,
hanging our heads in fear. No way to counter him,
no way to take his advice and come through
safe and sound. Here's what he said:
"Look, we've got to report the facts to Creon,
we can't keep this hidden." Well, that won out,   310
and the lot fell to me, condemned me,
unlucky as ever, I got the prize. So here I am,
against my will and yours too, well I know—
no one wants the man who brings bad news.

LEADER.
                                    My king,
ever since he began I've been debating in my mind,
could this possibly be the work of the gods?

CREON.
                                             Stop—
before you make me choke with anger—the gods!¹³
You, you're senile, must you be insane?
You say—why it's intolerable—say the gods
could have the slightest concern for that corpse?   320
Tell me, was it for meritorious service
they proceeded to bury him, prized him so? The hero
who came to burn their temples ringed with pillars,
their golden treasures—scorch their hallowed earth
and fling their laws to the winds.
Exactly when did you last see the gods
celebrating traitors? Inconceivable!

No, from the first there were certain citizens
who could hardly stand the spirit of my regime,
grumbling against me in the dark, heads together,   330
tossing wildly, never keeping their necks beneath
the yoke, loyally submitting to their king.
These are the instigators, I'm convinced—
they've perverted my own guard, bribed them
to do their work.
                    Money! Nothing worse
in our lives, so current, rampant, so corrupting.
Money—you demolish cities, root men from their homes,
you train and twist good minds and set them on
to the most atrocious schemes. No limit,
you make them adept at every kind of outrage,   340
every godless crime—money!
                              Everyone—
the whole crew bribed to commit this crime,
they've made one thing sure at least:
sooner or later they will pay the price.
                    [*Wheeling on the* SENTRY.]
                              You—
I swear to Zeus as I still believe in Zeus,
if you don't find the man who buried that corpse,
the very man, and produce him before my eyes,
simple death won't be enough for you,
not till we string you up alive
and wring the immorality out of you.   350
Then you can steal the rest of your days,
better informed about where to make a killing.
You'll have learned, at last, it doesn't pay
to itch for rewards from every hand that beckons.

___

¹³ The chorus's surmise about divine intervention in this first burial is conceivably true;
the play is somewhat ambiguous on the matter.

Filthy profits wreck most men, you'll see—
they'll never save your life.

SENTRY.
                              Please,
may I say a word or two, or just turn and go?

CREON.
Can't you tell? Everything you say offends me.

SENTRY.
Where does it hurt you, in the ears or in the heart?

CREON.
And who are you to pinpoint my displeasure?   360

SENTRY.
The culprit grates on your feelings,
I just annoy your ears.

CREON.
                    Still talking?
You talk too much! A born nuisance—

SENTRY.
                              Maybe so,
but I never did this thing, so help me!

CREON.
                              Yes you did—
what's more, you squandered your life for silver!

SENTRY.
Oh it's terrible when the one who does the judging
judges things all wrong.

CREON.
                    Well now,
you just be clever about your judgments—
if you fail to produce the criminals for me,
you'll swear your dirty money brought you pain.   370
                              [*Turning sharply, reentering the
                              palace.*]

SENTRY.
I hope he's found. Best thing by far.
But caught or not, that's in the lap of fortune:
I'll never come back, you've seen the last of me.
I'm saved, even now, and I never thought,

I never hoped—
dear gods, I owe you all my thanks!
                              [*Rushing out.*]

CHORUS.
                                        Numberless wonders
terrible wonders walk the world but none the match for man—
that great wonder crossing the heaving gray sea,
                    driven on by the blasts of winter
on through breakers crashing left and right,   380
    holds his steady course
and the oldest of the gods he wears away—
the Earth, the immortal, the inexhaustible—
as his plows go back and forth, year in, year out
    with the breed of stallions turning up the furrows.

And the blithe, lightheaded race of birds he snares,
the tribes of savage beasts, the life that swarms the depths—
                    with one fling of his nets
woven and coiled tight, he takes them all,
    man the skilled, the brilliant!   390
He conquers all, taming with his techniques
the prey that roams the cliffs and wild lairs,
training the stallion, clamping the yoke across
    his shaggy neck, and the tireless mountain bull.

And speech and thought, quick as the wind
and the mood and mind for law that rules the city—
    all these he has taught himself
and shelter from the arrows of the frost
when there's rough lodging under the cold clear sky
and the shafts of lashing rain—   400
        ready, resourceful man!
                Never without resources
never an impasse as he marches on the future—
only Death, from Death alone he will find no rescue
but from desperate plagues he has plotted his escapes.

Man the master, ingenious past all measure
past all dreams, the skills within his grasp—
    he forges on, now to destruction
now again to greatness. When he weaves in
the laws of the land, and the justice of the gods
that binds his oaths together   410
        he and his city rise high—
                but the city casts out
that man who weds himself to inhumanity
thanks to reckless daring. Never share my hearth
never think my thoughts, whoever does such things.

[*Enter* ANTIGONE *from the side,
accompanied by the* SENTRY.]

Here is a dark sign from the gods—
what to make of this? I know her,
how can I deny it? That young girl's Antigone!
Wretched, child of a wretched father,   420
Oedipus. Look, is it possible?
They bring you in like a prisoner—
why? did you break the king's laws?
Did they take you in some act of mad defiance?

SENTRY.
She's the one, she did it single-handed—
we caught her burying the body. Where's Creon?
[*Enter* CREON *from the palace.*]

LEADER.
Back again, just in time when you need him.

CREON.
In time for what? What is it?

SENTRY.
                              My king,
there's nothing you can swear you'll never do—
second thoughts make liars of us all.   430
I could have sworn I wouldn't hurry back
(what with your threats, the buffeting I just took),
but a stroke of luck beyond our wildest hopes,
what a joy, there's nothing like it. So,
back I've come, breaking my oath, who cares?
I'm bringing in our prisoner—this young girl—
we took her giving the dead the last rites.
But no casting lots this time; this is *my* luck,
my prize, no one else's.
                         Now, my lord,
here she is. Take her, question her,   440
cross-examine her to your heart's content.
But set me free, it's only right—
I'm rid of this dreadful business once for all.

CREON.
Prisoner! Her? You took her—where, doing what?

SENTRY.
Burying the man. That's the whole story.

CREON.
                                   What?
You mean what you say, you're telling me the truth?

SENTRY.
    She's the one. With my own eyes I saw her
    bury the body, just what you've forbidden.
    There. Is that plain and clear?

CREON.
    What did you see? Did you catch her in the act?   450

SENTRY.
    Here's what happened. We went back to our post,
    those threats of yours breathing down our necks—
    we brushed the corpse clean of the dust that covered it,
    stripped it bare . . . it was slimy, going soft,
    and we took to high ground, backs to the wind
    so the stink of him couldn't hit us;
    jostling, baiting each other to keep awake,
    shouting back and forth—no napping on the job,
    not this time. And so the hours dragged by
    until the sun stood dead above our heads,   460
    a huge white ball in the noon sky, beating,
    blazing down, and then it happened—
    suddenly, a whirlwind!
    Twisting a great dust-storm up from the earth,
    a black plague of the heavens, filling the plain,
    ripping the leaves off every tree in sight,
    choking the air and sky. We squinted hard
    and took our whipping from the gods.

    And after the storm passed—it seemed endless—
    there, we saw the girl!   470
    And she cried out a sharp, piercing cry,
    like a bird come back to an empty nest,
    peering into its bed, and all the babies gone . . .
    Just so, when she sees the corpse bare
    she bursts into a long, shattering wail
    and calls down withering curses on the heads
    of all who did the work. And she scoops up dry dust,
    handfuls, quickly, and lifting a fine bronze urn,
    lifting it high and pouring, she crowns the dead
    with three full libations.[14]
                    Soon as we saw   480
    we rushed her, closed on the kill like hunters,
    and she, she didn't flinch. We interrogated her,
    charging her with offenses past and present—
    she stood up to it all, denied nothing. I tell you,
    it made me ache and laugh in the same breath.
    It's pure joy to escape the worst yourself,

---

[14] Ritual pourings of liquids.

it hurts a man to bring down his friends.
But all that, I'm afraid, means less to me
than my own skin. That's the way I'm made.

CREON.

[*Wheeling on* ANTIGONE]
You,
with your eyes fixed on the ground—speak up. 490
Do you deny you did this, yes or no?

ANTIGONE.
I did it. I don't deny a thing.

CREON.

[*To the* SENTRY.]
You, get out, wherever you please—
you're clear of a very heavy charge.

[*He leaves;* CREON *turns back to*
ANTIGONE]
You, tell me briefly, no long speeches—
were you aware a decree had forbidden this?

ANTIGONE.
Well aware. How could I avoid it? It was public.

CREON.
And still you had the gall to break this law?

ANTIGONE.
Of course I did.[15] It wasn't Zeus, not in the least,
who made this proclamation—not to me. 500
Nor did that Justice, dwelling with the gods
beneath the earth, ordain such laws for men.
Nor did I think your edict had such force
that you, a mere mortal, could override the gods,
the great unwritten, unshakable traditions.
They are alive, not just today or yesterday:
they live forever, from the first of time,
and no one knows when they first saw the light.
These laws—I was not about to break them,
not out of fear of some man's wounded pride, 510
and face the retribution of the gods.
Die I must, I've known it all my life—
how could I keep from knowing?—even without
your death-sentence ringing in my ears.

---

[15] In the following lines Antigone states her creed; compare Creon's maxim in lines 203–205.
Both antagonists can cite religious or political principles. A major question in the play is whether
Antigone and Creon are actually governed by these large principles or by more personal motives
(good or bad).

And if I am to die before my time
I consider that a gain. Who on earth,
alive in the midst of so much grief as I,
could fail to find his death a rich reward?
So for me, at least, to meet this doom of yours
is precious little pain. But if I had allowed   520
my own mother's son to rot, an unburied corpse—
that would have been an agony! This is nothing.
And if my present actions strike you as foolish,
let's just say I've been accused of folly
by a fool.

LEADER.
                    Like father like daughter,
passionate, wild . . .
she hasn't learned to bend before adversity.

CREON.
No? Believe me, the stiffest stubborn wills
fall the hardest; the toughest iron,
tempered strong in the white-hot fire,   530
you'll see it crack and shatter first of all.
And I've known spirited horses you can break
with a light bit—proud, rebellious horses.
There's no room for pride, not in a slave,[16]
not with the lord and master standing by.

This girl was an old hand at insolence
when she overrode the edicts we made public.
But once she had done it—the insolence,
twice over—to glory in it, laughing,
mocking us to our face with what she'd done.   540
I am not the man, not now: she is the man
if this victory goes to her and she goes free.

Never! Sister's child or closer in blood
than all my family clustered at my altar
worshiping Guardian Zeus—she'll never escape,
she and her blood sister, the most barbaric death.
Yes, I accuse her sister of an equal part
in scheming this, this burial.
                                        [*To his attendants.*]
                    Bring her here!
I just saw her inside, hysterical, gone to pieces.
It never fails: the mind convicts itself   550
in advance, when scoundrels are up to no good,
plotting in the dark. Oh but I hate it more

---

[16] This is arrogantly false; Antigone is not in fact a slave.

when a traitor, caught red-handed,
tries to glorify his crimes.

ANTIGONE.
Creon, what more do you want
than my arrest and execution?

CREON.
Nothing. Then I have it all.

ANTIGONE.
Then why delay? Your moralizing repels me,
every word you say—pray god it always will.
So naturally all I say repels you too.
                                        Enough.   560
Give me glory! What greater glory could I win
than to give my own brother decent burial?
These citizens here would all agree,
                    [*To the* CHORUS.]
they would praise me too
if their lips weren't locked in fear.
                    [*Pointing to* CREON.]
Lucky tyrants—the perquisites of power!
Ruthless power to do and say whatever pleases *them.*

CREON.
You alone, of all the people in Thebes,
see things that way.

ANTIGONE.
                    They see it just that way
but defer to you and keep their tongues in leash.   570

CREON.
And you, aren't you ashamed to differ so from them?
So disloyal!

ANTIGONE.
                    Not ashamed for a moment,
not to honor my brother, my own flesh and blood.

CREON.
Wasn't Eteocles a brother too—cut down, facing him?

ANTIGONE.
Brother, yes, by the same mother, the same father.

CREON.
Then how can you render his enemy such honors,
such impieties in his eyes?

ANTIGONE.
   He will never testify to that,
   Eteocles dead and buried.

CREON.
                                   He will—
   if you honor the traitor just as much as him.   580

ANTIGONE.
   But it was his brother, not some slave that died—

CREON.
   Ravaging our country!—
   but Eteocles died fighting in our behalf.

ANTIGONE.
   No matter—Death longs for the same rites for all.

CREON.
   Never the same for the patriot and the traitor.

ANTIGONE.
   Who, Creon, who on earth can say the ones below
   don't find this pure and uncorrupt?

CREON.
   Never. Once an enemy, never a friend,
   not even after death.

ANTIGONE.
   I was born to join in love, not hate—   590
   that is my nature.

CREON.
                          Go down below and love,
   if love you must—love the dead! While I'm alive,
   no woman is going to lord it over me.
                          [*Enter* ISMENE *from the palace, under
                          guard.*]

CHORUS.
                                        Look,
   Ismene's coming, weeping a sister's tears,
   loving sister, under a cloud . . .
   her face is flushed, her cheeks streaming.
   Sorrow puts her lovely radiance in the dark.

CREON.
                                             You—
   in my own house, you viper, slinking undetected,

sucking my life-blood! I never knew
I was breeding twin disasters, the two of you   600
rising up against my throne. Come, tell me,
will you confess your part in the crime or not?
Answer me. Swear to me.

ISMENE.

I did it, yes—
if only she consents—I share the guilt,
the consequences too.

ANTIGONE.

No,
Justice will never suffer that—not you,
you were unwilling. I never brought you in.

ISMENE.

But now you face such dangers . . . I'm not ashamed
to sail through trouble with you,
make your troubles mine.

ANTIGONE.

Who did the work?   610
Let the dead and the god of death bear witness!
I have no love for a friend who loves in words alone.

ISMENE.

Oh no, my sister, don't reject me, please,
let me die beside you, consecrating
the dead together.

ANTIGONE.

Never share my dying,
don't lay claim to what you never touched.
My death will be enough.

ISMENE.

What do I care for life, cut off from you?

ANTIGONE.

Ask Creon. Your concern is all for him.

ISMENE.

Why abuse me so? It doesn't help you now.

ANTIGONE.

You're right—   620
if I mock you, I get no pleasure from it,
only pain.

ISMENE.
            Tell me, dear one,
    what can I do to help you, even now?

ANTIGONE.
    Save yourself. I don't grudge you your survival.

ISMENE.
    Oh no, no, denied my portion in your death?

ANTIGONE.
    You chose to live, I chose to die.

ISMENE.
                            Not, at least,
    without every kind of caution I could voice.

ANTIGONE.
    Your wisdom appealed to one world—mine, another.

ISMENE.
    But look, we're both guilty, both condemned to death.

ANTIGONE.
    Courage! Live your life. I gave myself to death,   630
    long ago, so I might serve the dead.

CREON.
    They're both mad, I tell you, the two of them.
    One's just shown it, the other's been that way
    since she was born.

ISMENE.
                    True, my king,
    the sense we were born with cannot last forever . . .
    commit cruelty on a person long enough
    and the mind begins to go.

CREON.
                        Yours did,
    when you chose to commit your crimes with her.

ISMENE.
    How can I live alone, without her?

CREON.
                            Her?
    Don't even mention her—she no longer exists.   640

ISMENE.
What? You'd kill your own son's bride?

CREON.
Absolutely:
there are other fields for him to plow.

ISMENE.
Perhaps,
but never as true, as close a bond as theirs.

CREON.
A worthless woman for my son? It repels me.

ISMENE.
Dearest Haemon, your father wrongs you so![17]

CREON.
Enough, enough—you and your talk of marriage!

ISMENE.
Creon—you're really going to rob your son of Antigone?

CREON.
Death will do it for me—break their marriage off.

LEADER.
So, it's settled then? Antigone must die?

CREON.
Settled, yes—we both know that.   650
                    [*To the guards.*]
Stop wasting time. Take them in.
From now on they'll act like women.
Tie them up, no more running loose;
even the bravest will cut and run,
once they see Death coming for their lives.
                    [*The guards escort* ANTIGONE *and*
                    ISMENE *into the palace.* CREON
                    *remains while the old citizens form
                    their* CHORUS.]

CHORUS.
Blest, they are the truly blest who all their lives
have never tasted devastation. For others, once
the gods have rocked a house to its foundations
    the ruin will never cease, cresting on and on

---

[17] In some versions, this line is given to Antigone.

from one generation on throughout the race—   660
like a great mounting tide
driven on by savage northern gales,
        surging over the dead black depths
roiling up from the bottom dark heaves of sand
and the headlands, taking the storm's onslaught full-force,
roar, and the low moaning
                            echoes on and on
                                          and now
as in ancient times I see the sorrows of the house,[18]
the living heirs of the old ancestral kings,
piling on the sorrows of the dead
    and one generation cannot free the next—   670
some god will bring them crashing down,
the race finds no release.
And now the light, the hope
        springing up from the late last root
in the house of Oedipus, that hope's cut down in turn
by the long, bloody knife swung by the gods of death
by a senseless word
                    by fury at the heart.
                                    Zeus,
yours is the power, Zeus, what man on earth
can override it, who can hold it back?
Power that neither Sleep, the all-ensnaring   680
    no, nor the tireless months of heaven
can ever overmaster—young through all time,
mighty lord of power, you hold fast
    the dazzling crystal mansions of Olympus.
And throughout the future, late and soon
as through the past, your law prevails:
no towering form of greatness
        enters into the lives of mortals
                        free and clear of ruin.
                                    True,
our dreams, our high hopes voyaging far and wide   690
bring sheer delight to many, to many others
    delusion, blithe, mindless lusts
and the fraud steals on one slowly . . . unaware
till he trips and puts his foot into the fire.
    He was a wise old man who coined
    the famous saying: "Sooner or later
foul is fair, fair is foul
to the man the gods will ruin"—
    He goes his way for a moment only
                    free of blinding ruin.   700

---

[18] The sorrows of the family extend farther into the past than to Oedipus' acts of patricide
and incest; for example, his father, Laius, had been cursed by Pelops (the ancestor of the cursed
family treated in Aeschylus' Orestes trilogy) after Laius had wronged Pelops, his protector during a period of exile, by stealing his son.

[*Enter* HAEMON *from the palace.*]
Here's Haemon now, the last of all your sons.[19]
Does he come in tears for his bride,
his doomed bride, Antigone—
bitter at being cheated of their marriage?

CREON.
We'll soon know, better than seers could tell us.
[*Turning to* HAEMON.]
Son, you've heard the final verdict on your bride?
Are you coming now, raving against your father?
Or do you love me, no matter what I do?

HAEMON.
Father, I'm your *son* . . . you in your wisdom
set my bearings for me—I obey you. 710
No marriage could ever mean more to me than you,
whatever good direction you may offer.

CREON.
Fine, Haemon.
That's how you ought to feel within your heart,
subordinate to your father's will in every way.
That's what a man prays for: to produce good sons—
a household full of them, dutiful and attentive,
so they can pay his enemy back with interest
and match the respect their father shows his friend.
But the man who rears a brood of useless children,
what has he brought into the world, I ask you?
Nothing but trouble for himself, and mockery 720
from his enemies laughing in his face.
Oh Haemon,
never lose your sense of judgment over a woman.
The warmth, the rush of pleasure, it all goes cold
in your arms, I warn you . . . a worthless woman
in your house, a misery in your bed.
What wound cuts deeper than a loved one
turned against you? Spit her out,
like a mortal enemy—let the girl go.
Let her find a husband down among the dead.
Imagine it: I caught her in naked rebellion,
the traitor, the only one in the whole city. 730
I'm not about to prove myself a liar,
not to my people, no, I'm going to kill her!
That's right—so let her cry for mercy, sing her hymns
to Zeus who defends all bonds of kindred blood.
Why, if I bring up my own kin to be rebels,

[19]According to one version of the Thebes saga, Haemon's brother Megareus had committed
suicide in order to propitiate the war god Ares and thus save Thebes.

think what I'd suffer from the world at large.
Show me the man who rules his household well:
I'll show you someone fit to rule the state.   740
That good man, my son,
I have every confidence he and he alone
can give commands and take them too. Staunch
in the storm of spears he'll stand his ground,
a loyal, unflinching comrade at your side.

But whoever steps out of line, violates the laws
or presumes to hand out orders to his superiors,
he'll win no praise from me. But that man
the city places in authority, his orders
must be obeyed, large and small,   750
right and wrong.
                    Anarchy—
show me a greater crime in all the earth!
She, she destroys cities, rips up houses,
breaks the ranks of spearmen into headlong rout.
But the ones who last it out, the great mass of them
owe their lives to discipline. Therefore
we must defend the men who live by law,
never let some woman triumph over us.
Better to fall from power, if fall we must,
at the hands of a man—never be rated   760
inferior to a woman, never.

LEADER.
                            To us,
unless old age has robbed us of our wits,
you seem to say what you have to say with sense.

HAEMON.
Father, only the gods endow a man with reason,
the finest of all their gifts, a treasure.
Far be it from me—I haven't the skill,
and certainly no desire, to tell you when,
if ever, you make a slip in speech . . . though
someone else might have a good suggestion.

Of course it's not for you,   770
in the normal run of things, to watch
whatever men say or do, or find to criticize.
The man in the street, you know, dreads your glance
he'd never say anything displeasing to your face.
But it's for me to catch the murmurs in the dark,
the way the city mourns for this young girl.
"No woman," they say, "ever deserved death less,
and such a brutal death for such a glorious action.

She, with her own dear brother lying in his blood—
she couldn't bear to leave him dead, unburied, 780
food for the wild dogs or wheeling vultures.
Death? She deserves a glowing crown of gold!"
So they say, and the rumor spreads in secret,
darkly . . .
       I rejoice in your success, father—
nothing more precious to me in the world.
What medal of honor brighter to his children
than a father's growing glory? Or a child's
to his proud father? Now don't, please,
be quite so single-minded, self-involved,
or assume the world is wrong and you are right. 790
Whoever thinks that he alone possesses intelligence,
the gift of eloquence, he and no one else,
and character too . . . such men, I tell you,
spread them open—you will find them empty.
                  No,
it's no disgrace for a man, even a wise man,
to learn many things and not to be too rigid.
You've seen trees by a raging winter torrent,
how many sway with the flood and salvage every twig,
but not the stubborn—they're ripped out, roots and all.
Bend or break. The same when a man is sailing: 800
haul your sheets too taut, never give an inch,
you'll capsize, and go the rest of the voyage
keel up and the rowing-benches under.

Oh give way. Relax your anger—change!
I'm young, I know, but let me offer this:
it would be best by far, I admit,
if a man were born infallible, right by nature.
If not—and things don't often go that way,
it's best to learn from those with good advice.

LEADER.
You'd do well, my lord, if he's speaking to the point, 810
to learn from him,
                [*Turning to* HAEMON.]
        and you, my boy, from him.
You both are talking sense.

CREON.
             So,
men our age, we're to be lectured, are we?—
schooled by a boy his age?

HAEMON.
Only in what is right. But if I seem young,
look less to my years and more to what I do.

CREON.
    Do? Is admiring rebels an achievement?

HAEMON.
    I'd never suggest that you admire treason.

CREON.
                                    Oh?—
    isn't that just the sickness that's attacked her?

HAEMON.
    The whole city of Thebes denies it, to a man.   820

CREON.
    And is Thebes about to tell me how to rule?

HAEMON.
    Now, you see? Who's talking like a child?

CREON.
    Am I to rule this land for others—or myself?

HAEMON.
    It's no city at all, owned by one man alone.

CREON.
    What? The city *is* the king's—that's the law!

HAEMON.
    What a splendid king you'd make of a desert island—
    you and you alone.

CREON.
                        [*To the* CHORUS.]
                This boy, I do believe
    is fighting on her side, the woman's side.

HAEMON.
    If you are a woman, yes—
    my concern is all for you.   830

CREON.
    Why, you degenerate—bandying accusations,
    threatening me with justice, your own father!

HAEMON.
    I see my father offending justice—wrong.

CREON.
                                    Wrong?
    To protect my royal rights?

HAEMON.
                        Protect your rights?
When you trample down the honors of the gods?

CREON.
    You, you soul of corruption, rotten through—
    woman's accomplice!

HAEMON.
                        That may be,
    but you will never find me accomplice to a criminal.

CREON.
    That's what *she* is,
    and every word you say is a blatant appeal for her—   840

HAEMON.
    And you, and me, and the gods beneath the earth.

CREON.
    You will never marry her, not while she's alive.

HAEMON.
    Then she will die . . . but her death will kill another.

CREON.
    What, brazen threats? You go too far!

HAEMON.
                            What threat?
    Combating your empty, mindless judgments with a word?

CREON.
    You'll suffer for your sermons, you and your empty wisdom!

HAEMON.
    If you weren't my father, I'd say you were insane.

CREON.
    Don't flatter me with Father—you woman's slave!

HAEMON.
    You really expect to fling abuse at me
    and not receive the same?

CREON.
                        Is that so!   850
    Now, by heaven, I promise you, you'll pay—
    taunting, insulting me! Bring her out,

that hateful—she'll die now, here,
in front of his eyes, beside her groom!

HAEMON.
No, no, she will never die beside me—
don't delude yourself. And you will never
see me, never set eyes on my face again.
Rage your heart out, rage with friends
who can stand the sight of you.

[*Rushing out.*]

LEADER.
Gone, my king, in a burst of anger.   860
A temper young as his . . . hurt him once,
he may do something violent.

CREON.
                              Let him do—
dream up something desperate, past all human limit!
Good riddance. Rest assured,
he'll never save those two young girls from death.

LEADER.
Both of them, you really intend to kill them both?

CREON.
No, not her, the one whose hands are clean—
you're quite right.

LEADER.
                    But Antigone—
what sort of death do you have in mind for her?

CREON.
I will take her down some wild, desolate path   870
never trod by men, and wall her up alive
in a rocky vault, and set out short rations,
just the measure piety demands
to keep the entire city free of defilement.[20]
There let her pray to the one god she worships:
Death[21]—who knows?—may just reprieve her from death.
Or she may learn at last, better late than never,
what a waste of breath it is to worship Death.

---

[20] This method of execution is inconsistent with the earlier passage that decrees death by
stoning (lines 41–43). Creon apparently believes, legalistically, that he can avoid the crime of
shedding kindred blood by merely shutting Antigone up alone and by providing her with food.
Technically no act of execution will have been committed.

[21] Hades, king of the realm of the dead.

[*Exit to the palace.*]

CHORUS.
Love, never conquered in battle
Love the plunderer laying waste the rich!   880
Love standing the night-watch
          guarding a girl's soft cheek,
you range the seas, the shepherds' steadings off in the wilds—
not even the deathless gods can flee your onset,
nothing human born for a day—
whoever feels your grip is driven mad.

          Love!—
you wrench the minds of the righteous into outrage,
swerve them to their ruin—you have ignited this,
this kindred strife, father and son at war
          and Love alone the victor—   890
warm glance of the bride triumphant, burning with desire!
Throned in power, side-by-side with the mighty laws!
Irresistible Aphrodite,[22] never conquered—
Love, you mock us for your sport.

          [ANTIGONE *is brought from the*
          palace under guard.]
But now, even I would rebel against the king,
I would break all bounds when I see this—
I fill with tears, I cannot hold them back,
not any more . . . I see Antigone make her way
to the bridal vault where all are laid to rest.

ANTIGONE.
Look at me, men of my fatherland,   900
     setting out on the last road
looking into the last light of day
the last I will ever see . . .
the god of death who puts us all to bed
takes me down to the banks of Acheron[23] alive—
     denied my part in the wedding-songs,
no wedding-song in the dusk has crowned my marriage—
I go to wed the lord of the dark waters.

CHORUS.
Not crowned with glory or with a dirge,
you leave for the deep pit of the dead.   910
No withering illness laid you low,
no strokes of the sword—a law to yourself,
alone, no mortal like you, ever, you go down
to the halls of Death alive and breathing.

[22] Goddess of love.
[23] A river in the land of the dead.

ANTIGONE.
> But think of Niobe[24]—well I know her story—
>   think what a living death she died,
> Tantalus' daughter, stranger queen from the east:
> there on the mountain heights, growing stone
> binding as ivy, slowly walled her round
> and the rains will never cease, the legends say   920
> the snows will never leave her . . .
>   wasting away, under her brows the tears
> showering down her breasting ridge and slopes—
> a rocky death like hers puts me to sleep.

CHORUS.
> But she was a god, born of gods,[25]
> and we are only mortals born to die.
> And yet, of course, it's a great thing
> for a dying girl to hear, even to hear
> she shares a destiny equal to the gods,
> during life and later, once she's dead.

ANTIGONE.
>   O, you mock me!   930
> Why, in the name of all my fathers' gods
> why can't you wait till I am gone—
>   must you abuse me to my face?[26]
> O my city, all your fine rich sons!
> And you, you springs of the Dirce,
> holy grove of Thebes where the chariots gather,
>   you at least, you'll bear me witness, look,
> unmourned by friends and forced by such crude laws
> I go to my rockbound prison, strange new tomb—
>   always a stranger, O dear god,   940
>   I have no home on earth and none below,
>   not with the living, not with the breathless dead.

CHORUS.
> You went too far, the last limits of daring—
> smashing against the high throne of Justice!
>   Your life's in ruins, child—I wonder . . .
> do you pay for your father's terrible ordeal?

---

[24] Niobe, originally from Phrygia in Asia Minor, was the wife of Amphion, a former ruler of Thebes. Mother of fourteen children, she boasted of her superiority to the goddess Leto, who had only two, Apollo and Artemis. In revenge for her impiety, all of Niobe's children were killed and she was turned into a stone from which flowed a perpetual stream of her tears. There is an irony: Niobe was punished for flouting the gods, while Antigone is being killed for her piety.

[25] Niobe was the daughter of Tantalus, whose father was Zeus.

[26] Antigone's protest probably reflects her bitter reaction to the elders' implication that she is lucky (in sharing the fate of the famed Niobe.)

ANTIGONE.
There—at last you've touched it, the worst pain
the worst anguish! Raking up the grief for father
   three times over, for all the doom
that's struck us down, the brilliant house of Laius. 950
O mother, your marriage-bed
the coiling horrors, the coupling there—
   you with your own son, my father—doomstruck mother!
Such, such were my parents, and I their wretched child.
I go to them now, cursed, unwed, to share their home—
   I am a stranger! O dear brother, doomed
   in your marriage—your marriage murders mine,[27]
      your dying drags me down to death alive!
                           [*Enter* CREON.]

CHORUS.
Reverence asks some reverence in return—
but attacks on power never go unchecked, 960
   not by the man who holds the reins of power.
Your own blind will, your passion has destroyed you.

ANTIGONE.
No one to weep for me, my friends,
no wedding-song—they take me away
in all my pain . . . the road lies open, waiting.
Never again, the law forbids me to see
the sacred eye of day. I am agony!
No tears for the destiny that's mine,
no loved one mourns my death.

CREON.
                           Can't you see?
If a man could wail his own dirge *before* he dies, 970
he'd never finish.
                     [*To the guards.*]
                  Take her away, quickly!
Wall her up in the tomb, you have your orders.
Abandon her there, alone, and let her choose—
death or a buried life with a good roof for shelter.
As for myself, my hands are clean. This young girl—
dead or alive, she will be stripped of her rights,
her stranger's rights, here in the world above.

ANTIGONE.
O tomb, my bridal-bed—my house, my prison
cut in the hollow rock, my everlasting watch!

---

[27]Polynices, as part of his plan to enlist the aid of Argos in attacking Thebes, married a daughter of the Argive king. The war, and Polynices' death, have brought death to Antigone too.

I'll soon be there, soon embrace my own,   980
the great growing family of our dead
Persephone[28] has received among her ghosts.
                                                        I,
the last of them all, the most reviled by far,
go down before my destined time's run out.
But still I go, cherishing one good hope:
my arrival may be dear to father,
dear to you, my mother,
dear to you, my loving brother, Eteocles—
When you died I washed you with my hands,
I dressed you all, I poured the sacred cups   990
across your tombs. But now, Polynices,
because I laid your body out as well,
this, this is my reward. Nevertheless
I honored you—the decent will admit it—
well and wisely too.
                        Never, I tell you,
if I had been the mother of children
or if my husband died, exposed and rotting—
I'd never have taken this ordeal upon myself,
never defied our people's will. What law,
you ask, do I satisfy with what I say?   1000
A husband dead, there might have been another.
A child by another too, if I had lost the first.
But mother and father both lost in the halls of Death,
no brother could ever spring to light again.[29]
For this law alone I held you first in honor.
For this, Creon, the king, judges me a criminal
guilty of dreadful outrage, my dear brother!
And now he leads me off, a captive in his hands,
with no part in the bridal-song, the bridal-bed,
denied all joy of marriage, raising children—   1010
deserted so by loved ones, struck by fate,
I descend alive to the caverns of the dead.

What law of the mighty gods have I transgressed?
Why look to the heavens any more, tormented as I am?
Whom to call, what comrades now? Just think,
my reverence only brands me for irreverence!
Very well: if this is the pleasure of the gods,

---

[28] Consort of Hades, king of the dead.

[29] For various reasons, including the opinion that Antigone's fine distinctions and perhaps
insensitivity here are inconsistent with the rest of the play, some editors and translators reject
lines 995–1004. The appropriateness of the passage has been defended on grounds of dramatic psychology (for example, the marital and maternal roles must be merely imagined by
Antigone, while her role of sister is one she has experienced) and more technical grounds
(for example, the notion that the sibling bond is closer than either the marital one which
involves no blood kinship or the "half-interest" bond of blood kinship that links a child with
one of its two parents).

once I suffer I will know that I was wrong.
But if these men are wrong, let them suffer
nothing worse than they mete out to me— 1020
these masters of injustice!

LEADER.
Still the same rough winds, the wild passion
raging through the girl.

CREON.
[*To the guards.*]
Take her away.
You're wasting time—you'll pay for it too.

ANTIGONE.
Oh god, the voice of death. It's come, it's here.

CREON.
True. Not a word of hope—your doom is sealed.

ANTIGONE.
Land of Thebes, city of all my fathers—
O you gods, the first gods of the race![30]
They drag me away, now, no more delay.
Look on me, you noble sons of Thebes— 1030
the last of a great line of kings,
I alone, see what I suffer now
at the hands of what breed of men—
all for reverence, my reverence for the gods!
[*She leaves under guard: the* CHORUS
gathers.]
CHORUS.
Danaë,[31] Danaë—
even she endured a fate like yours,
in all her lovely strength she traded
the light of day for the bolted brazen vault—
buried within her tomb, her bridal-chamber,
wed to the yoke and broken. 1040
But she was of glorious birth
my child, my child
and treasured the seed of Zeus within her womb,
and cloudburst streaming gold!
The power of fate is a wonder,
dark, terrible wonder—

[30]According to the myths, several of Antigone's forebears in the Theban dynasty were related
to the gods, by blood or marriage.
[31]Danaë's father Acrisius, a king of Argos, had imprisoned her because of a prophecy that
she would bear a son who would kill him. Zeus came to her in a shower of golden rain, begetting Perseus, who did later kill Acrisius.

neither wealth nor armies
towered walls nor ships
black hulls lashed by the salt
can save us from that force.   1050

The yoke tamed him too
    young Lycurgus[32] flaming in anger
king of Edonia, all for his mad taunts
Dionysus clamped him down, encased
in the chain-mail of rock
    and there his rage
            his terrible flowering rage burst—
sobbing, dying away . . . at last that madman
came to know his god—
        the power he mocked, the power   1060
        he taunted in all his frenzy
        trying to stamp out
        the women strong with the god—
        the torch, the raving sacred cries—
        enraging the Muses who adore the flute.
And far north where the Black Rocks[33]
    cut the sea in half
and murderous straits
split the coast of Thrace
    a forbidding city stands   1070
where once, hard by the walls
the savage Ares thrilled to watch
a king's new queen, a Fury rearing in rage
    against his two royal sons—
        her bloody hands, her dagger-shuttle
stabbing out their eyes—cursed, blinding wounds—
their eyes blind sockets screaming for revenge!

They wailed in agony, cries echoing cries
        the princes doomed at birth . . .
and their mother doomed to chains,   1080
walled up in a tomb of stone—
    but she traced her own birth back
to a proud Athenian line and the high gods
and off in caverns half the world away,
born of the wild North Wind
    she sprang on her father's gales,
        racing stallions up the leaping cliffs—

[32] Lycurgus, a legendary Thracian king, had been imprisoned after being driven to madness by the gods for opposing the worship of Bacchus (Dionysus). Maenads (line 1063) were orgiastic female worshipers of the god.

[33] The following lines allude to a third story of imprisonment; most interpreters have found the story itself and its application to Antigone obscure. Phineus, a king of Thrace, divorced his wife Cleopatra (daughter of Boreas, the north wind), who had borne him two sons, and cast her into prison; his second wife blinded the two children and entombed them.

child of the heavens. But even on her the Fates
the gray everlasting Fates rode hard
my child, my child.

> [*Enter* TIRESIAS, *the blind prophet,
> led by a boy.*]

TIRESIAS.
                              Lords of Thebes,   1090
I and the boy have come together,
hand in hand. Two see with the eyes of one . . .
so the blind must go, with a guide to lead the way.

CREON.
What is it, old Tiresias? What news now?

TIRESIAS.
I will teach you. And you obey the seer.

CREON.
                              I will,
I've never wavered from your advice before.

TIRESIAS.
And so you kept the city straight on course.

CREON.
I owe you a great deal, I swear to that.

TIRESIAS.
Then reflect, my son: you are poised,   *could cause*
once more, on the razor-edge of fate. *— retribution*   1100

CREON.
What is it? I shudder to hear you.

TIRESIAS.
                              You will learn
when you listen to the warnings of my craft.
As I sat on the ancient seat of augury,
in the sanctuary where every bird I know
will hover at my hands—suddenly I heard it,
a strange voice in the wingbeats, unintelligible,
barbaric, a mad scream! Talons flashing, ripping,
they were killing each other—that much I knew—
the murderous fury whirring in those wings
made that much clear!
                              I was afraid,   1110
I turned quickly, tested the burnt-sacrifice,
ignited the altar at all points—but no fire,
the god in the fire never blazed.

Not from those offerings . . . over the embers
slid a heavy ooze from the long thighbones,
smoking, sputtering out, and the bladder
puffed and burst—spraying gall into the air—
and the fat wrapping the bones slithered off
and left them glistening white. No fire!
The rites failed that might have blazed the future   1120
with a sign. So I learned from the boy here:
he is my guide, as I am guide to others.
                                        And it is you—
your high resolve that sets this plague on Thebes.
The public altars and sacred hearths are fouled,
one and all, by the birds and dogs with carrion
torn from the corpse, the doomstruck son of Oedipus!
And so the gods are deaf to our prayers, they spurn
the offerings in our hands, the flame of holy flesh.
No birds cry out an omen clear and true—
they're gorged with the murdered victim's blood and fat.   1130
Take these things to heart, my son, I warn you.
All men make mistakes, it is only human.
But once the wrong is done, a man
can turn his back on folly, misfortune too,
if he tries to make amends, however low he's fallen,
and stops his bullnecked ways. Stubbornness
brands you for stupidity—pride is a crime.
No, yield to the dead!
Never stab the fighter when he's down.
Where's the glory, killing the dead twice over?   1140

I mean you well. I give you sound advice.
It's best to learn from a good adviser
when he speaks for your own good:
it's pure gain.

CREON.
                    Old man—all of you! So,
you shoot your arrows at my head like archers at the target—
I even have *him* loosed on me, this fortune-teller.
Oh his ilk has tried to sell me short
and ship me off for years.[34] Well,
drive your bargains, traffic—much as you like—
in the gold of India, silver-gold of Sardis.   1150
You'll never bury that body in the grave,
not even if Zeus's eagles rip the corpse
and wing their rotten pickings off to the throne of god!
Never, not even in fear of such defilement
will I tolerate his burial, that traitor.

---

[34]Ironically, Oedipus (in *Oedipus the King*) had accused Tiresias and Creon himself of a
similar, and equally imaginary, mercenary plot.

Well I know, we can't defile the gods—
no mortal has the power.
                              No,
reverend old Tiresias, all men fall,
it's only human, but the wisest fall obscenely
when they glorify obscene advice with rhetoric—
all for their own gain.   1160

TIRESIAS.
   Oh god, is there a man alive
   who knows, who actually believes . . .

CREON.
                                   What now?
   What earth-shattering truth are you about to utter?

TIRESIAS.
   . . . just how much a sense of judgment, wisdom
   is the greatest gift we have?

CREON.
                           Just as much, I'd say,
   as a twisted mind is the worst affliction known.

TIRESIAS.
   You are the one who's sick, Creon, sick to death.

CREON.
   I am in no mood to trade insults with a seer.

TIRESIAS.
   You have already, calling my prophecies a lie.

CREON.
                                   Why not?   1170
   You and the whole breed of seers are mad for money!

TIRESIAS.
   And the whole race of tyrants lusts for filthy gain.

CREON.
   This slander of yours—
   are you aware you're speaking to the king?

TIRESIAS.
   Well aware. Who helped you save the city?

CREON.
                                   You—
   you have your skills, old seer, but you lust for injustice!

TIRESIAS.
You will drive me to utter the dreadful secret in my heart.

CREON.
Spit it out! Just don't speak it out for profit.

TIRESIAS.
Profit? No, not a bit of profit, not for you.

CREON.
Know full well, you'll never buy off my resolve. 1180

TIRESIAS.
Then know this too, learn this by heart!
The chariot of the sun will not race through
so many circuits more, before you have surrendered
one born of your own loins, your own flesh and blood,
a corpse for corpses given in return, since you have thrust
to the world below a child sprung for the world above,
ruthlessly lodged a living soul within the grave—
then you've robbed the gods below the earth,
keeping a dead body here in the bright air,
unburied, unsung, unhallowed by the rites. 1190

You, you have no business with the dead,
nor do the gods above—this is violence
you have forced upon the heavens.
And so the avengers, the dark destroyers late
but true to the mark, now lie in wait for you,
the Furies[35] sent by the gods and the god of death
to strike you down with the pains that you perfected!

There. Reflect on that, tell me I've been bribed.
The day comes soon, no long test of time, not now,
when the mourning cries for men and women break 1200
throughout your halls. Great hatred rises against you—
cities in tumult,[36] all whose mutilated sons
the dogs have graced with burial, or the wild beasts
or a wheeling crow that wings the ungodly stench of carrion
back to each city, each warrior's hearth and home.

These arrows for your heart! Since you've raked me
I loose them like an archer in my anger,
arrows deadly true. You'll never escape
their burning, searing force.
                              [*Motioning to his escort.*]
Come, boy, take me home. 1210
So he can vent his rage on younger men,

[35] Primitive personifications of vengeance, especially for crimes against kindred.
[36] The cities that organized the army to attack Thebes.

and learn to keep a gentler tongue in his head
and better sense than what he carries now.
                              [*Exit to the side.*]

LEADER.
    The old man's gone, my king—
    terrible prophecies. Well I know,
    since the hair on this old head went gray,
    he's never lied to Thebes.

CREON.
    I know it myself—I'm shaken, torn.
    It's a dreadful thing to yield . . . but resist now?
    Lay my pride bare to the blows of ruin?   1220
    That's dreadful too.

LEADER.
                              But good advice,
    Creon, take it now, you must.

CREON.
    What should I do? Tell me . . . I'll obey.

LEADER.
    Go! Free the girl from the rocky vault
    and raise a mound for the body you exposed.

CREON.
    That's your advice? You think I should give in?

LEADER.
    Yes, my king, quickly. Disasters sent by the gods
    cut short our follies in a flash.

CREON.
                              Oh it's hard,
    giving up the heart's desire . . . but I will do it—
    no more fighting a losing battle with necessity.   1230

LEADER.
    Do it now, go, don't leave it to others.

CREON.
    Now—I'm on my way! Come, each of you,
    take up axes, make for the high ground,
    over there, quickly! I and my better judgment
    have come round to this—I shackled her,
    I'll set her free myself. I am afraid . . .
    it's best to keep the established laws
    to the very day we die.

[*Rushing out, followed by his entourage. The* CHORUS *clusters around the altar.*]

CHORUS.
 God of a hundred names![37]
                              Great Dionysus—
   Son and glory of Semele! Pride of Thebes—   1240
 Child of Zeus whose thunder rocks the clouds—
 Lord of the famous lands of evening—
 King of the Mysteries!
                              King of Eleusis,[38] Demeter's plain
 her breasting hills that welcome in the world—
 Great Dionysus!
                     Bacchus, living in Thebes
 the mother-city of all your frenzied women—
                                                     Bacchus
   living along the Ismenus' rippling waters
 standing over the field sown with the Dragon's teeth!

 You—we have seen you through the flaring smoky fires,
   your torches blazing over the twin peaks[39]   1250
 where nymphs of the hallowed cave climb onward
                       fired with you, your sacred rage—
 we have seen you at Castalia's running spring[40]
 and down from the heights of Nysa[41] crowned with ivy
 the greening shore rioting vines and grapes
        down you come in your storm of wild women
                     ecstatic, mystic cries—
                                          Dionysus—
 down to watch and ward the roads of Thebes!
 First of all cities, Thebes you honor first
 you and your mother, bride of the lightning—   1260
 come, Dionysus! now your people lie
 in the iron grip of plague,
 come in your racing, healing stride
                     down Parnassus' slopes
 or across the moaning straits.
                     Lord of the dancing—
 dance, dance the constellations breathing fire!
 Great master of the voices of the night!

---

[37] The chorus invokes Dionysus as the patron deity of Thebes.
[38] Eleusis, a town near Athens, was the center of the mysterious fertility rites of Demeter, goddess of the fields and harvest.
[39] Parnassus, a mountain near Apollo's shrine at Delphi; one of the peaks was sacred to Apollo, one to Bacchus (Dionysus).
[40] A spring and pool on Mount Parnassus.
[41] A mountain where Dionysus had been reared by nymphs.

Child of Zeus, God's offspring, come, come forth!
Lord, king, dance with your nymphs, swirling, raving
arm-in-arm in frenzy through the night   1270
   they dance you, Iacchus—
                              Dance, Dionysus
giver of all good things!

                              [*Enter a* MESSENGER *from the side.*]

MESSENGER.
                              Neighbors,
friends of the house of Cadmus and the kings,
there's not a thing in this mortal life of ours
I'd praise or blame as settled once for all.
Fortune lifts and Fortune fells the lucky
and unlucky every day. No prophet on earth
can tell a man his fate. Take Creon:
there was a man to rouse your envy once,
as I see it. He saved the realm from enemies,   1280
taking power, he alone, the lord of the fatherland,
he set us true on course—he flourished like a tree
with the noble line of sons he bred and reared . . .
and now it's lost, all gone.
                              Believe me,
when a man has squandered his true joys,
he's good as dead, I tell you, a living corpse.
Pile up riches in your house, as much as you like—
live like a king with a huge show of pomp,
but if real delight is missing from the lot,
I wouldn't give you a wisp of smoke for it,   1290
not compared with joy.

LEADER.
                              What now?
What new grief do you bring the house of kings?

MESSENGER.
Dead, dead—and the living are guilty of their death!

LEADER.
Who's the murderer? Who is dead? Tell us.

MESSENGER.
Haemon's gone, his blood spilled by the very hand—

LEADER.
His father's or his own?

MESSENGER.
                              His own . . .
raging mad with his father for the death—

LEADER.

                                        Oh great seer,
   you saw it all, you brought your word to birth!

MESSENGER.
      Those are the facts. Deal with them as you will.
                              [*As he turns to go,* EURYDICE *enters
                              from the palace.*]

LEADER.
      Look, Eurydice. Poor woman, Creon's wife,   1300
      so close at hand. By chance perhaps,
      unless she's heard the news about her son.

EURYDICE.
                                        My countrymen,
      all of you—I caught the sound of your words
      as I was leaving to do my part,
      to appeal to queen Athena with my prayers.
      I was just loosing the bolts, opening the doors,
      when a voice filled with sorrow, family sorrow,
      struck my ears, and I fell back, terrified,
      into the women's arms—everything went black.
      Tell me the news, again, whatever it is . . .   1310
      sorrow and I are hardly strangers.
      I can bear the worst.

MESSENGER.
                        I—dear lady,
      I'll speak as an eye-witness. I was there.
      And I won't pass over one word of the truth.
      Why should I try to soothe you with a story,
      only to prove a liar in a moment?
      Truth is always best.
                        So,
      I escorted your lord, I guided him
      to the edge of the plain where the body lay,
      Polynices, torn by the dogs and still unmourned.   1320
      And saying a prayer to Hecate of the Crossroads,
      Pluto[42] too, to hold their anger and be kind,
      we washed the dead in a bath of holy water
      and plucking some fresh branches, gathering . . .
      what was left of him, we burned them all together
      and raised a high mound of native earth, and then
      we turned and made for that rocky vault of hers,

[42] Hecate, associated with crossroads, was a goddess of night, magic, and the Underworld;
Pluto is another name for Hades, god of the dead.

the hollow, empty bed of the bride of Death.
And far off, one of us heard a voice,
a long wail rising, echoing 1330
out of that unhallowed wedding-chamber,
he ran to alert the master and Creon pressed on,
closer—the strange, inscrutable cry came sharper,
throbbing around him now, and he let loose
a cry of his own, enough to wrench the heart,
"Oh god, am I the prophet now? going down
the darkest road I've ever gone? My son—
it's *his* dear voice, he greets me! Go, men,
closer, quickly! Go through the gap,
the rocks are dragged back— 1340
right to the tomb's very mouth—and look,
see if it's Haemon's voice I think I hear,
or the gods have robbed me of my senses."

The king was shattered. We took his orders,
went and searched, and there in the deepest,
dark recesses of the tomb we found her . . .
hanged by the neck in a fine linen noose,
strangled in her veils—and the boy,
his arms flung around her waist,
clinging to her, wailing for his bride, 1350
dead and down below, for his father's crimes
and the bed of his marriage blighted by misfortune.
When Creon saw him, he gave a deep sob,
he ran in, shouting, crying out to him,
"Oh my child—what have you done? what seized you,
what insanity? what disaster drove you mad? — Creon
Come out, my son! I beg you on my knees!"
But the boy gave him a wild burning glance,
spat in his face, not a word in reply,
he drew his sword—his father rushed out, 1360
running as Haemon lunged and missed!—
and then, doomed, desperate with himself,
suddenly leaning his full weight on the blade,
he buried it in his body, halfway to the hilt.
And still in his senses, pouring his arms around her,
he embraced the girl and breathing hard,
released a quick rush of blood,
bright red on her cheek glistening white.
And there he lies, body enfolding body . . .
he has won his bride at last, poor boy, 1370
not here but in the houses of the dead.

Creon shows the world that of all the ills
afflicting men the worst is lack of judgment.

　　　　　　　　　　　[EURYDICE *turns and reenters the
　　　　　　　　　　　palace.*]

LEADER.
   What do you make of that? The lady's gone,
   without a word, good or bad.

MESSENGER.
                                    I'm alarmed too
   but here's my hope—faced with her son's death
   she finds it unbecoming to mourn in public.
   Inside, under her roof, she'll set her women
   to the task and wail the sorrow of the house.
   She's too discreet. She won't do something rash.   1380

LEADER.
   I'm not so sure. To me, at least,
   a long heavy silence promises danger,
   just as much as a lot of empty outcries.

MESSENGER.
   We'll see if she's holding something back,
   hiding some passion in her heart.
   I'm going in. You may be right—who knows?
   Even too much silence has its dangers.
                        [*Exit to the palace. Enter* CREON
                        *from the side, escorted by attendants
                        carrying* HAEMON*'s body on a bier.*]

LEADER.
   The king himself! Coming toward us,
   look, holding the boy's head in his hands.
   Clear, damning proof, if it's right to say so—   1390
   proof of his own madness, no one else's,
      no, his own blind wrongs.

CREON.
                        Ohhh,
   so senseless, so insane . . . my crimes,
   my stubborn, deadly—
   Look at us, the killer, the killed,
   father and son, the same blood—the misery!
   My plans, my mad fanatic heart,
   my son, cut off so young!
   Ai, dead, lost to the world,
   not through your stupidity, no, my own.

LEADER.
                                    Too late,   1400
   too late, you see what justice means.

CREON.
                        Oh I've learned

through blood and tears! Then, it was then,
when the god came down and struck me—a great weight
shattering, driving me down that wild savage path,
ruining, trampling down my joy. Oh the agony,
 the heartbreaking agonies of our lives.
                                    [*Enter the* MESSENGER *from the
                                    palace.*]

MESSENGER.
                                                Master,
what a hoard of grief you have, and you'll have more.
The grief that lies to hand you've brought yourself—
                                    [*Pointing to* HAEMON *'s body.*]
the rest, in the house, you'll see it all too soon.

CREON.
What now? What's worse than this?

MESSENGER.
                                The queen is dead.   1410
The mother of this dead boy . . . mother to the end—
poor thing, her wounds are fresh.

CREON.
                                No, no,
harbor of Death, so choked, so hard to cleanse!—
why me? why are you killing me?
Herald of pain, more words, more grief?
I died once, you kill me again and again!
What's the report, boy . . . some news for me?
My wife dead? O dear god!
Slaughter heaped on slaughter?
                                    [*The doors open; the body of*
                                    EURYDICE *is brought out on her bier.*]

MESSENGER.
                                See for yourself:
now they bring her body from the palace.

CREON.
                                Oh no,   1420
another, a second loss to break the heart.
What next, what fate still waits for me?
I just held my son in my arms and now,
look, a new corpse rising before my eyes—
 wretched, helpless mother—O my son!

MESSENGER.
 She stabbed herself at the altar,
 then her eyes went dark, after she'd raised

a cry for the noble fate of Megareus,[43] the hero
killed in the first assault, then for Haemon,
then with her dying breath she called down   1430
torments on your head—you killed her sons.

CREON.

                                                                Oh the dread,
    I shudder with dread! Why not kill me too?—
    run me through with a good sharp sword?
    Oh god, the misery, anguish—
    I, I'm churning with it, going under.

MESSENGER.
    Yes, and the dead, the woman lying there,
    piles the guilt of all their deaths on you.

CREON.
    How did she end her life, what bloody stroke?

MESSENGER.
    She drove home to the heart with her own hand,
    once she learned her son was dead . . . that agony.   1440

CREON.
    And the guilt is all mine—
    can never be fixed on another man,
    no escape for me. I killed you,
    I, god help me, I admit it all!
                                            [*To his attendants.*]
    Take me away, quickly, out of sight.
    I don't even exist—I'm no one. Nothing.

LEADER.
    Good advice, if there's any good in suffering.
    Quickest is best when troubles block the way.

CREON.
                                    [*Kneeling in prayer.*]
    Come, let it come!—that best of fates for me
    that brings the final day, best fate of all.   1450
    Oh quickly, now—
    so I never have to see another sunrise.

LEADER.
    That will come when it comes;
    we must deal with all that lies before us.
    The future rests with the ones who tend the future.

---

[43] The other son of Creon and Eurydice; he had bravely committed suicide to save Thebes.

CREON.
  That prayer—I poured my heart into that prayer!

LEADER.
  No more prayers now. For mortal men
  there is no escape from the doom we must endure.

CREON.
  Take me away, I beg you, out of sight.
  A rash, indiscriminate fool!
  I murdered you, my son, against my will—   1460
  you too, my wife . . .
                        Wailing wreck of a man,
  whom to look to? where to lean for support?
                      [*Desperately turning from* HAEMON
                       to EURYDICE *on their biers.*]
  Whatever I touch goes wrong—once more
  a crushing fate's come down upon my head!
                      [*The* MESSENGER *and attendants
                       lead* CREON *into the palace.*]

CHORUS.
  Wisdom is by far the greatest part of joy,
  and reverence toward the gods must be safeguarded.
  The mighty words of the proud are paid in full
  with mighty blows of fate, and at long last
  those blows will teach us wisdom.   1470
                      [*The old citizens exit to the side.*]

Euripides

(C. 480–406 B.C.)

Aeschylus fought in the momentous Greek naval victory at Salamis in 480
B.C. The adolescent Sophocles helped to celebrate it publicly. Tradition has
it that Euripides was born in Salamis on the very day of the battle. Even if,
or especially if, the tradition is historically inaccurate (he may have been
born a few years earlier), it symbolizes a desire by the ancients to link Euripides
with his two mighty predecessors as the third definitive playwright of the
greatest age of Greece.

Unlike Aeschylus and Sophocles, Euripides seems to have taken little active
part in the official public life of Athens; he was not a social man by temperament. The size of his library indicates that he was extensively learned.
From the year 455 on, he participated regularly in the dramatic contests held
annually in Athens, but he won first prize less often than did Aeschylus or
Sophocles, possibly because of the "irregularities" later alleged, by Aristotle

and other critics, to exist in his work, or possibly because of his nonconformist attitude toward Greek religion and Athenian politics. His political dissidence intensified during the last two decades of his life as the tragic and misguided Peloponnesian War against Sparta and its allies moved inexorably toward a dismal conclusion. His play *The Trojan Women*, for example (produced in 415), exposes the brutality of "heroic" conquerors and, indirectly, shows Euripides' distaste for Athenian imperialism. He spent the last two years of his life in Macedonia, where he died in 406, slightly earlier than Sophocles, who conducted a scene of public mourning for him in the theater. After his death, Euripides' plays were immensely popular; of the ninety he wrote, eighteen have survived, as compared with seven apiece by Aeschylus and Sophocles. Among these is *The Cyclops*, the only extant specimen of the grotesque "satyr play" that in Athenian dramatic practice regularly followed the set of three tragedies performed earlier in the same day. *Medea*, the violent and disturbing play included in this volume, is one of the earlier of Euripides' extant plays. One needs to keep in mind, however, that *Medea* was the work not of a novice but rather of a veteran playwright who, when he wrote the play, had had a quarter-century of experience in composing for the theater.

Euripides' work as a whole illustrates several new departures. The formal structure is looser than in Aeschylus or Sophocles, though perhaps we ought, rather, to call it freer. He made extensive use of the Prologue and, at the end of his plays, was partial to the *deus ex machina* device, whereby a deity intervenes to impose an arbitrary resolution. The endings of his plays are frequently ambiguous or disturbing, as in Medea's escape to Athens. In Euripides, the chorus often sings magnificent lyrics, but they tend to be less integral to the dramatic action than in the plays of Aeschylus or Sophocles. Another recurrent device is the *agon*, a direct and usually hostile confrontation between two characters in which arguments or accusations are exchanged in rapid-fire fashion. Euripides also helped popularize the mode of drama we now call tragicomedy; his *Alcestis*, in which the dead heroine is reclaimed from the grave, is an example. To regard his innovations as regrettable departures from the kind of coherent unity Aristotle called for is unjust to Euripides, who created several powerful forms of drama that are best allowed to operate by their own organically functional rules, without being measured against arbitrary norms of what ancient drama, or tragedy, is supposed to be.

Some of these formal, or antiformal, elements, but more especially the ideas conveyed or implied in his plays, have earned Euripides a reputation as the most "romantic" of the three great tragedians. The alleged untidiness of his dramatic construction often parallels and indeed emphasizes the central Euripidean theme of irrationality, in people and in the cosmos. Throughout *Medea*, the heroine, like many other characters in Euripides, is overcome by passion (sometimes tender, more often violent in the extreme). As an exploration of human values, the play seems to many readers to present an almost maddening stalemate; it is equally impossible either to dismiss Medea's motives or to endorse them, not to mention her hair-raising acts. The same ambivalence informs his last play, *The Bacchae*, which addresses, not incidentally but head-on, the value of the irrational Dionysian drives. This tragedy has been interpreted both as a return by Euripides to religious piety and as profound skepticism, both as an indictment of rationality and as an indictment of irrational fanaticism.

According to the chorus in Aeschylus' *Oresteia,* humanity suffers into truth. In Sophocles much the same thing is true, though the theology is less explicit; for example, in *Oedipus at Colonus* the unspeakable suffering endured by the blinded and exiled king is redeemed at his death, when he is mysteriously transfigured. In the last analysis, both these dramatists are optimists—though by no means facile ones. Euripides is more pessimistic. For him, an intellectual and a skeptic, whatever force governs the world— whether we call that force Fate, the divine will, Necessity, or by any other name—is amoral and entirely indifferent to humanity. As *Medea* shows, human acts of good and evil are thrown into a moral void. Certainly sufferng has meaning for Euripides. But, for him, education through suffering is something humanity has to undergo alone, without much theological comfort. The world, for him, is both utterly unpredictable and also utterly predictable, in the sense that its operation is affected by neither piety nor virtue. Granted that it is dangerous to translate the values of an ancient Athenian into modern terms, it still seems tempting, if not inevitable, to read Euripides as a quintessentially modern man, for better or worse. His view of the world, as in modern scientific determinism, posits a universe (in which laws cannot be changed by human moral acts) almost indistinguishable—from the human point of view—from one that is not governed at all. The universe most metaphysically determined is morally the most chaotic.

Euripides' attitude toward the sexes is another crucial topic. Legend surrounds his birth; at the other end, legend has it that at his death he was torn apart, by dogs or women. Again, the legend may be quaint, but the fact remains that, beginning in his own time, Euripides has been charged with misogyny. Aristophanes, for one, gave weight to the charge, in *Lysistrata* and in other comedies. It is easy to see how, superficially, the creator of a violent and male-threatening witch such as Medea could be regarded as defaming women. It is just as easy, however, and especially from the viewpoint of modern feminism, to see Euripides as a master psychologist and critic of the masculine and feminine mystiques that operate on a powerful thematic and symbolic level in Greek tragedy from Aeschylus' *Oresteia* on. At much the same time that Aristophanes was exploring these mystiques in a comic vein, Euripides was exploring them in a tragic vein, and as more intractable than in Aeschylus.

FURTHER READING *(prepared by F.S.N.):* Gilbert Murray's popular work *Euripides and His Age,* 1913, 2nd ed. 1946, remains an excellent introduction to the historical and cultural context of Euripides' drama. For material on the life and writings of Euripides see D. J. Conacher, *Euripidean Drama: Myth, Theme and Structure,* 1967, and T. B. L. Webster, *The Tragedies of Euripides,* 1967, which also compares the works of Euripides with those of Aeschylus and Sophocles. A challenging modern selection of studies is given by E. Segal, ed., *Euripides: A Collection of Critical Essays,* 1968. Justina Gregory, *Euripides and the Instruction of the Athenians,* 1991, explores Euripides' commitment to social justice and personal responsibility. *Medea* is incisively treated in Emily A. McDermott, *Euripides' Medea: The Incarnation of Disorder,* 1989. Pietro Pucci, in his full-scale discussion of *Medea, The Violence of Pity in Euripides' Medea,* 1980, tackles major problems in interpreting this work. Excellent chapters on *Medea* and *The Bacchae* appear (along with chapters on all the other ancient Greek tragedies) in John Ferguson, *A Companion to Greek Tragedy,* 1972. This book also contains good bibliographies of ancient Greek tragedy in general, of each of the great tragedians in general, and of each separate tragedy. For discussion of the theatrical production of Euripides' plays, see J. Michael Walton, *The Greek Sense of Theatre: Tragedy Reviewed*, 1985.

MEDEA

Translated by Philip Vellacott

The kingship of the city of Iolcus (in Thessaly, the northeastern region of Greece) had been usurped by Pelias. Jason's father, Aeson, was half brother of Pelias and rightful ruler of Iolcus. After a period of protective exile under the tutelage of Chiron the Centaur, Jason returned to Iolcus. His usurper-uncle Pelias then sent Jason off to Colchis (on the Black Sea) to capture the magically potent Golden Fleece of a ram. Jason made the adventurous voyage, in company with some of the most famous and fabled Greek heroes, called the Argonauts after the name of their ship the *Argo*. When Jason reached Colchis, its king Aeetes (Medea's father) agreed to give up the Golden Fleece if Jason performed certain superhumanly difficult tasks. He was able to perform them with the help of Medea, who had fallen in love with him and who possessed magical arts. The heroes then returned with the Golden Fleece to Iolcus, along with Medea, who assisted their return by killing her brother so that her father Aeetes would be delayed in his pursuit. In Iolcus, Medea continued to aid Jason by using her witchcraft to cause the death of Pelias at the hands of his daughters. But Jason was unable to claim his throne, and he and Medea were banished from Iolcus. They settled in Corinth, the setting of the play *Medea*. After some time there, Jason has decided to cast off Medea and to marry Glauce, daughter of Creon, the king of Corinth. This Creon should not be confused with the Creon who, in Sophocles' Oedipus plays, rules Thebes. [*Editors' headnote.*]

CHARACTERS

NURSE	JASON
TUTOR *to Medea's sons*	AEGEUS, *king of Athens*
MEDEA	MESSENGER
CHORUS *of Corinthian women*	MEDEA'S TWO CHILDREN
CREON, *king of Corinth*	

SCENE
Before Jason's house in Corinth

NURSE. If only they had never gone! If the Argo's hull
    Never had winged out through the grey-blue jaws of rock[1]
    And on towards Colchis! If that pine on Pelion's[2] slopes
    Had never felt the axe, and fallen, to put oars
    Into those heroes' hands, who went at Pelias' bidding
    To fetch the golden fleece! Then neither would Medea,

---

[1] The Symplegades, two mythical rocks at the north end of the strait of Bosporus, the entrance to the Black Sea. The rocks were supposed to crush ships that sailed between them.
[2] A mountain in Thessaly.

My mistress, ever have set sail for the walled town
Of Iolcus, mad with love for Jason; nor would she,
When Pelias' daughters, at her instance, killed their father,
Have come with Jason and her children to live here 10
In Corinth; where, coming as an exile, she has earned
The citizens' welcome; while to Jason she is all
Obedience—and in marriage that's the saving thing,
When a wife obediently accepts her husband's will.

But now her world has turned to enmity, and wounds her
Where her affection's deepest. Jason has betrayed
His own sons, and my mistress, for a royal bed,
For alliance with the king of Corinth. He has married
Glauce, Creon's daughter. Poor Medea! Scorned and shamed,
She raves, invoking every vow and solemn pledge 20
That Jason made her, and calls the gods as witnesses
What thanks she has received for her fidelity.
She will not eat; she lies collapsed in agony,
Dissolving the long hours in tears. Since first she heard
Of Jason's wickedness, she has not raised her eyes,
Or moved her cheek from the hard ground; and when her friends
Reason with her, she might be a rock or wave of the sea,
For all she hears—unless, maybe, she turns away
Her lovely head, speaks to herself alone, and wails
Aloud for her dear father, her own land and home, 30
Which she betrayed and left, to come here with this man
Who now spurns and insults her. Poor Medea! Now
She learns through pain what blessings they enjoy who are not
Uprooted from their native land. She hates her sons:
To see them is no pleasure to her. I am afraid
Some dreadful purpose is forming in her mind. She is
A frightening woman; no one who makes an enemy
Of her will carry off an easy victory.

Here come the boys, back from their running. They've no thought
Of this cruel blow that's fallen on their mother. Well, 40
They're young; young heads and painful thoughts don't go together.

[*Enter the* TUTOR *with* MEDEA's
TWO SONS.]

TUTOR. Old nurse and servant of my mistress's house, tell me,
    What are you doing, standing out here by the door,
    All alone, talking to yourself, harping on trouble?
    Eh? What does Medea say to being left alone?
NURSE. Old friend, tutor of Jason's sons, an honest slave
    Suffers in her own heart the blow that strikes her mistress.
    It was too much, I couldn't bear it; I had to come
    Out here and tell my mistress's wrongs to earth and heaven.
TUTOR. Poor woman! Has she not stopped crying yet? 50

NURSE.   Stopped crying?
  I envy you. Her grief's just born—not yet half-grown.
TUTOR. Poor fool—though she's my mistress and I shouldn't say it—
  She had better save her tears. She has not heard the worst.
NURSE. The worst? What now? Don't keep it from me. What has happened?
TUTOR. Why, nothing's happened. I'm sorry I said anything.
NURSE. Look—we're both slaves together: don't keep me in the dark.
  Is it so great a secret? I can hold my tongue.
TUTOR. I'd gone along to the benches where the old men play
  At dice, next to the holy fountain of Peirene;   60
  They thought I was not listening; and I heard one say
  That Creon king of Corinth means to send these boys
  Away from here—to banish them, and their mother too.
  Whether the story's true I don't know. I hope not.
NURSE. But surely Jason won't stand by and see his sons
  Banished, even if he has a quarrel with their mother?
TUTOR. Old love is ousted by new love. Jason's no friend
  To this house.
NURSE.   Then we're lost, if we must add new trouble
  To old, before we're rid of what we had already.
TUTOR. But listen: it's no time to tell Medea this.   70
  Keep quiet, say nothing about it.
NURSE.   Children, do you hear
  What sort of father Jason is to you? My curse
  On—No! No curse; he is my master. All the same,
  He is guilty: he has betrayed those near and dear to him.
TUTOR. What man's not guilty? It's taken you a long time to learn
  That everybody loves himself more than his neighbour.
  These boys are nothing to their father: he's in love.
NURSE. Run into the house, boys. Everything will be all right.

                          [*The children move away a little.*]

  You do your best to keep them by themselves, as long
  As she's in this dark mood; don't let them go to her.   80
  I've watched her watching them, her eye like a wild bull's.
  There's something that she means to do; and I know this:
  She'll not relax her rage till it has found its victim.
  God grant she strike her enemies and not her friends!

                          [MEDEA's *voice is heard from inside*
                            the house.]

MEDEA. Oh, oh! What misery, what wretchedness!
  What shall I do? If only I were dead!
NURSE. There! You can hear; it is your mother
  Racking her heart, racking her anger.
  Quick, now, children, hurry indoors;
  And don't go within sight of her,   90
  Or anywhere near her; keep a safe distance.

Her mood is cruel, her nature dangerous,   *— exposition*
Her will fierce and intractable.
Come on, now, in with you both at once.

> [*The* CHILDREN *go in, and the*
> TUTOR *follows.*]

The dark cloud of her lamentations
Is just beginning. Soon, I know,
It will burst aflame as her anger rises.
Deep in passion and unrelenting,
What will she do now, stung with insult?

MEDEA [*indoors*]. Do I not suffer? Am I not wronged? Should I not weep?   100
   Children, your mother is hated, and you are cursed:
   Death take you, with your father, and perish his whole house!

NURSE. Oh, the pity of it! Poor Medea!
   Your children—why, what have *they* to do
   With their father's wickedness? Why hate *them?*
   I am sick with fear for you, children, terror
   Of what may happen. The mind of a queen
   Is a thing to fear. A queen is used
   To giving commands, not obeying them;
   And her rage once roused is hard to appease.   110

   To have learnt to live on the common level
   Is better. No grand life for me,
   Just peace and quiet as I grow old.
   The middle way, neither great nor mean,
   Is best by far, in name and practice.
   To be rich and powerful brings no blessing;
   Only more utterly
   Is the prosperous house destroyed, when the gods are angry.

> [*Enter the* CHORUS *of Corinthian*
> *women.*]

CHORUS.
   I heard her voice, I heard
   That unhappy woman from Colchis   120
   Still crying, not calm yet.
   Old Nurse, tell us about her.
   As I stood by the door I heard her
   Crying inside the palace.
   And my own heart suffers too
   When Jason's house is suffering;
   For that is where my loyalty lies.

NURSE. Jason's house? It no longer exists; all that is finished.
   Jason is a prisoner in a princess's bed;
   And Medea is in her room   130
   Melting her life away in tears;

No word from any friend can give her comfort.
MEDEA [*still from indoors*].
    Come, flame of the sky,
    Pierce through my head!
    What do I gain from living any longer?
    Oh, how I hate living! I want
    To end my life, leave it behind, and die.
CHORUS.
    O Zeus, and Earth, and Light,
    Do you hear the chanted prayer
    Of a wife in her anguish?   140

                              [*turning to the door and addressing*
                              MEDEA]

    What madness is this? The bed you long for—
    Is it what others shrink from?
    Is it death you demand?
    Do not pray that prayer, Medea!
    If your husband is won to a new love—
    The thing is common; why let it anger you?
    Zeus will plead your cause.
    Check this passionate grief over your husband
    Which wastes you away.
MEDEA. Mighty Themis! Dread Artemis![3]   150
    Do you see how I am used—
    In spite of those great oaths I bound him with—
    By my accursed husband?
    Oh, may I see Jason and his bride
    Ground to pieces in their shattered palace
    For the wrong they have dared to do to me, unprovoked!
    O my father, my city, you I deserted;
    My brother I shamefully murdered!
NURSE. Do you hear what my mistress is saying,
    Clamouring to Themis, hearer of prayer,   160
    And to Zeus, who is named guardian of men's oaths?
    It is no trifling matter
    That can end a rage like hers.
CHORUS. I wish she would come out here and let us see her
    And talk to her; if she would listen
    Perhaps she would drop this fierce resentful spirit,
    This passionate indignation.
    As a friend I am anxious to do whatever I can.
    Go, nurse, persuade her to come out to us.
    Tell her we are all on her side.   170
    Hurry, before she does harm—to those in there;
    This passion of hers is an irresistible flood.

---

[3] Themis is the personification of justice; Artemis is the virgin goddess of the hunt who
protects young creatures and women in childbirth.

NURSE. I will. I fear I shall not persuade her;
Still, I am glad to do my best.
Yet as soon as any of us servants
Goes near to her, or tries to speak,
She glares at us like a mad bull
Or a lioness guarding her cubs.

[*The* NURSE *goes to the door, where
she turns.*]

The men of old times had little sense;
If you called them fools you wouldn't be far wrong.   180
They invented songs, and all the sweetness of music,
To perform at feasts, banquets, and celebrations;
But no one thought of using
Songs and stringed instruments
To banish the bitterness and pain of life.
Sorrow is the real cause
Of deaths and disasters and families destroyed.
If music could cure sorrow it would be precious;
But after a good dinner why sing songs?
When people have fed full they're happy already.   190

[*The* NURSE *goes in.*]

CHORUS.
I heard her sobbing and wailing,
Shouting shrill, pitiful accusations
Against her husband who has betrayed her.
She invokes Themis, daughter of Zeus,
Who witnessed those promises which drew her
Across from Asia to Hellas, setting sail at night,
Threading the salt strait,
Key and barrier to the Pontic Sea.[4]

[MEDEA *comes out. She is not shaken
with weeping, but cool and self-
possessed.*]

MEDEA. Women of Corinth, I would not have you censure me,
So I have come. Many, I know, are proud at heart,   200
Indoors or out; but others are ill spoken of
As supercilious, just because their ways are quiet.
There is no justice in the world's censorious eyes.
They will not wait to learn a man's true character;
Though no wrong has been done them, one look—and they hate.
Of course a stranger must conform; even a Greek

---

[4] The Black Sea.

Should not annoy his fellows by crass stubbornness.
I accept my place; but this blow that has fallen on me
Was not to be expected. It has crushed my heart.
Life has no pleasure left, dear friends. I want to die.   210
Jason was my whole life; he knows that well. Now he
Has proved himself the most contemptible of men.

Surely, of all creatures that have life and will, we women
Are the most wretched. When, for an extravagant sum,
We have bought a husband,[5] we must then accept him as
Possessor of our body. This is to aggravate
Wrong with worse wrong. Then the great question: will the man
We get be bad or good? For women, divorce is not
Respectable; to repel the man, not possible.

Still more, a foreign woman, coming among new laws,   220
New customs, needs the skill of magic, to find out
What her home could not teach her, how to treat the man
Whose bed she shares. And if in this exacting toil
We are successful, and our husband does not struggle
Under the marriage yoke, our life is enviable.
Otherwise, death is better. If a man grows tired
Of the company at home, he can go out, and find
A cure for tediousness. We wives are forced to look
To one man only. And, they tell us, we at home
Live free from danger, they go out to battle: fools!   230
I'd rather stand three times in the front line than bear
One child.
              But the same arguments do not apply
To you and me. You have this city, your father's home,
The enjoyment of your life, and your friends' company.
I am alone; I have no city; now my husband
Insults me. I was taken as plunder from a land
At the earth's edge. I have no mother, brother, nor any
Of my own blood to turn to in this extremity.
So, I make one request. If I can find a way
To work revenge on Jason for his wrongs to me,   240
Say nothing. A woman's weak and timid in most matters;
The noise of war, the look of steel, makes her a coward.
But touch her right in marriage, and there's no bloodier spirit.
CHORUS. I'll do as you ask. To punish Jason will be just.
I do not wonder that you take such wrongs to heart.

                        [CREON *approaches*.]

But look, Medea; I see Creon, King of Corinth;

---

[5] The reference is to the dowry given with the bride in marriage.

He must have come to tell you of some new decision.
CREON. You there, Medea, scowling rage against your husband!
    I order you out of Corinth; take your sons and go
    Into exile. Waste no time; I'm here to see this order   250
    Enforced. And I'm not going back into my palace
    Until I've put you safe outside my boundaries.
MEDEA. Oh! this is the cruel end of my accursed life!
    My enemies have spread full sail; no welcoming shore
    Waits to receive and save me. Ill-treated as I am,
    Creon, I ask: for what offence do you banish me?
CREON. I fear you. Why wrap up the truth? I fear that you
    May do my daughter some irreparable harm.
    A number of things contribute to my anxiety.
    You're a clever woman, skilled in many evil arts;   260
    You're barred from Jason's bed, and that enrages you.
    I learn too from reports, that you have uttered threats
    Of revenge on Jason and his bride and his bride's father.
    I'll act first, then, in self-defence. I'd rather make you
    My enemy now, than weaken, and later pay with tears.
MEDEA. My reputation, yet again! Many times, Creon,
    It has been my curse and ruin. A man of any shrewdness
    Should never have his children taught to use their brains
    More than their fellows. What do you gain by being clever?
    You neglect your own affairs; and all your fellow citizens   270
    Hate you. Those who are fools will call you ignorant
    And useless, when you offer them unfamiliar knowledge.
    As for those thought intelligent, if people rank
    You above *them,* that is a thing they will not stand.
    I know this from experience: because I am clever,
    They are jealous; while the rest dislike me. After all,
    I am not so clever as all that.
                         So you, Creon,
    Are afraid—of what? Some harm that I might do to you?
    Don't let *me* alarm you, Creon. I'm in no position—
    A woman—to wrong a king. You have done me no wrong.   280
    You've given your daughter to the man you chose. I hate
    My husband—true; but you had every right to do
    As you have done. So now I bear no grudge against
    Your happiness: marry your daughter to him, and good luck
    To you both. But let me live in Corinth. I will bear
    My wrongs in silence, yielding to superior strength.
CREON. Your words are gentle: but my blood runs cold to think
    What plots you may be nursing deep within your heart.
    In fact, I trust you so much less now than before.
    A woman of hot temper—and a man the same—   290
    Is a less dangerous enemy than one quiet and clever.
    So out you go, and quickly; no more arguing.
    I've made my mind up; you're my enemy. No craft
    Of yours will find a way of staying in my city.

MEDEA. I kneel to you, I beseech you by the young bride, your child.
CREON. You're wasting words; you'll never make me change my mind.
MEDEA. I beg you! Will you cast off pity, and banish me?
CREON. I will: I have more love for my family than for you.
MEDEA. My home, my country! How my thoughts turn to you now!
CREON. I love my country too—next only to my daughter.   300
MEDEA. Oh, what an evil power love has in people's lives!
CREON. That would depend on circumstances, I imagine.
MEDEA. Great Zeus, remember who caused all this suffering!
CREON. Go, you poor wretch, take all my troubles with you! Go!
MEDEA. I know what trouble is; I have no need of more.
CREON. In a moment you'll be thrown out neck and crop. Here, men!
MEDEA. No, no, not that! But, Creon, I have one thing to ask.
CREON. You seem inclined, Medea, to give me trouble still.
MEDEA. I'll go. [*She still clings to him.*] It was not *that* I begged.
CREON.   Then why resist?
    Why will you not get out?
MEDEA.   This one day let me stay,   310
    To settle some plan for my exile, make provision
    For my two sons, since their own father is not concerned
    To help them. Show some pity: you are a father too,
    You should feel kindly towards them. For myself, exile
    Is nothing. I weep for them; their fate is very hard.
CREON. I'm no tyrant by nature. My soft heart has often
    Betrayed me; and I know it's foolish of me now;
    Yet none the less, Medea, you shall have what you ask.
    But take this warning: if tomorrow's holy sun
    Finds you or them inside my boundaries, you die.   320
    That is my solemn word. Now stay here, if you must,
    This one day. You can hardly in one day accomplish
    What I am afraid of.

                        [*Exit* CREON.]

CHORUS.
    Medea, poor Medea!
    Your grief touches our hearts.
    A wanderer, where can you turn?
    To what welcoming house?
    To what protecting land?
    How wild with dread and danger
    Is the sea where the gods have set your course!   330
MEDEA. A bad predicament all round—yes, true enough;
    But don't imagine things will end as they are now.
    Trials are yet to come for this new-wedded pair;
    Nor shall those nearest to them get off easily.

    Do you think I would ever have fawned so on this man,
    Except to gain my purpose, carry out my schemes?
    Not one touch, not one word: yet he—oh, what a fool!

By banishing me at once he could have thwarted me
Utterly; instead, he allows me to remain one day.
Today three of my enemies I shall strike dead: 340
Father and daughter; and *my* husband.

I have in mind so many paths of death for them,
I don't know which to choose. Should I set fire to the house,
And burn the bridal chamber? Or creep up to their bed
And drive a sharp knife through their guts? There is one fear:
If I am caught entering the house, or in the act,
I die, and the last laugh goes to my enemies.
The best is the direct way, which most suits my bent:
To kill by poison.

So—say they are dead: what city will receive me then? 350
What friend will guarantee my safety, offer land
And home as sanctuary? None. I'll wait a little.
If some strong tower of help appears, I'll carry out
This murder cunningly and quietly. But if Fate
Banishes me without resource, I will myself
Take sword in hand, harden my heart to the uttermost,
And kill them both, even if I am to die for it.

For, by Queen Hecate,[6] whom above all divinities
I venerate, my chosen accomplice, to whose presence
My central hearth is dedicated, no one of them 360
Shall hurt me and not suffer for it! Let me work:
In bitterness and pain they shall repent this marriage,
Repent their houses joined, repent my banishment.

Come! Lay your plan, Medea; scheme with all your skill.
On to the deadly moment that shall test your nerve!
You see now where you stand. Your father was a king,
His father was the Sun-god:[7] you must not invite
Laughter from Jason and his new allies, the tribe
Of Sisyphus.[8] You know what you must do. Besides—

[*She turns to the* CHORUS.]

We were born women—useless for honest purposes, 370
But in all kinds of evil skilled practitioners.
CHORUS. Streams of the sacred rivers flow uphill;
    Tradition, order, all things are reversed:
        Deceit is *men's* device now,
        Men's oaths are gods' dishonour.

---

[6]Goddess of witchcraft, though also in some contexts a protective deity.
[7]Helios, father of Aeetes.
[8]An earlier, legendary king of Corinth, noted for deceitfulness.

Legend will now reverse our reputation;
A time comes when the female sex is honoured;
    That old discordant slander
    Shall no more hold us subject.
Male poets of past ages, with their ballads   380
Of faithless women, shall go out of fashion;
    For Phoebus,[9] Prince of Music,
Never bestowed the lyric inspiration
    Through female understanding—
    Or we'd find themes for poems,
We'd counter with our epics against man.
Oh, Time is old; and in his store of tales
    Men figure no less famous
    Or infamous than women.

So you, Medea, wild with love,   390
Set sail from your father's house,
Threading the Rocky Jaws of the eastern sea;
And here, living in a strange country,
Your marriage lost, your bed solitary,
You are driven beyond the borders,
An exile with no redress.
The grace of sworn oaths is gone;
Honour remains no more
In the wide Greek world, but is flown to the sky.
Where can you turn for shelter?   400
Your father's door is closed against you;
Another is now mistress of your husband's bed;
A new queen rules in your house.

                              [*Enter* JASON.]

JASON. I have noticed—this is not the first occasion—
    What fatal results follow from ungoverned rage.
    You could have stayed in Corinth, still lived in this house,
    If you had quietly accepted the decisions
    Of those in power. Instead, you talked like a fool; and now
    You are banished. Well, your angry words don't upset *me;*
    Go on as long as you like reciting Jason's crimes.   410
    But after your abuse of the King and the princess
    Think yourself lucky to be let off with banishment.
    I have tried all the time to calm them down; but you
    Would not give up your ridiculous tirades against
    The royal family. So, you're banished. However, I
    Will not desert a friend. I have carefully considered
    Your problem, and come now, in spite of everything,
    To see that you and the children are not sent away

[9]Apollo, god of music and poetry.

With an empty purse, or unprovided. Exile brings
With it a train of difficulties. You no doubt 420
Hate me: but I could never bear ill-will to you.
MEDEA. You filthy coward!—if I knew any worse name
For such unmanliness I'd use it—so, you've come!
You, my worst enemy, come to me! Oh, it's not courage,
This looking friends in the face after betraying them.
It is not even audacity; it's a disease,
The worst a man can have, pure shamelessness. However,
It is as well you came; to say what I have to say
Will ease my heart; to hear it said will make you wince.

I will begin at the beginning. When you were sent 430
To master the fire-breathing bulls, yoke them, and sow
The deadly furrow, then I saved your life; and that
Every Greek who sailed with you in the Argo knows.
The serpent that kept watch over the Golden Fleece,
Coiled round it fold on fold, unsleeping—it was I
Who killed it, and so lit the torch of your success.[10]
I willingly deceived my father; left my home;
With you I came to Iolcus by Mount Pelion,
Showing much love and little wisdom. There I put
King Pelias to the most horrible of deaths[11] 440
By his own daughters' hands, and ruined his whole house.
And in return for this you have the wickedness
To turn me out, to get yourself another wife,
Even after I had borne you sons! If you had still
Been childless I could have pardoned you for hankering
After this new marriage. But respect for oaths has gone
To the wind. Do you, I wonder, think that the old gods
No longer rule? Or that new laws are now in force?
You must know you are guilty of perjury to me.

My poor right hand, which you so often clasped! My knees 450
Which you then clung to! How we are besmirched and mocked
By this man's broken vows, and all our hopes deceived!

Come, I'll ask your advice as if you were a friend.
Not that I hope for any help from you; but still,
I'll ask you, and expose your infamy. Where now
Can I turn? Back to my country and my father's house,
Which I betrayed to come with you? Or to Iolcus,
To Pelias's wretched daughters? What a welcome they
Would offer me, who killed their father! Thus it stands:

---

[10] Medea refers in the preceding six lines to the difficult tasks Jason had to accomplish in Colchis to win the Golden Fleece.

[11] Medea had deceitfully persuaded Pelias' daughters that they could magically restore their father's youth by boiling him in a cauldron.

My friends at home now hate me; and in helping you 460
I have earned the enmity of those I had no right
To hurt. For my reward, you have made me the envy
Of Hellene women everywhere! A marvellous
Husband I have, and faithful too, in the name of pity;
When I'm banished, thrown out of the country without a friend,
Alone with my forlorn waifs. Yes, a shining shame
It will be to you, the new-made bridegroom, that your own sons,
And I who saved your life, are begging beside the road!

O Zeus! Why have you given us clear signs to tell
True gold from counterfeit; but when we need to know 470
Bad *men* from good, the flesh bears no revealing mark?
CHORUS. The fiercest anger of all, the most incurable,
Is that which rages in the place of dearest love.
JASON. I have to show myself a clever speaker, it seems.
This hurricane of recrimination and abuse
Calls for good seamanship: I'll furl all but an inch
Of sail, and ride it out. To begin with, since you build
To such a height your services to me, I hold
That credit for my successful voyage was solely due
To Aphrodite,[12] no one else divine or human. 480
I admit, you have intelligence; but, to recount
How helpless passion drove you then to save my life
Would be invidious; and I will not stress the point.
Your services, so far as they went, were well enough;
But in return for saving me you got far more
Than you gave. Allow me, in the first place, to point out
That you left a barbarous land to become a resident
Of Hellas;[13] here you have known justice; you have lived
In a society where force yields place to law.
Moreover, here your gifts are widely recognized, 490
You are famous; if you still lived at the ends of the earth
Your name would never be spoken. Personally, unless
Life brings me fame, I long neither for hoards of gold,
Nor for a voice sweeter than Orpheus![14]—Well, *you* began
The argument about my voyage; and that's my answer.

As for your scurrilous taunts against my marriage with
The royal family, I shall show you that my action
Was wise, not swayed by passion, and directed towards
Your interests and my children's.—No, keep quiet! When I
Came here from Iolcus as a stateless exile, dogged 500
And thwarted by misfortunes—why, what luckier chance
Could I have met, than marriage with the King's daughter?

[12]Goddess of love.
[13]Greece.
[14]A legendary poet and one of the Argonauts; his music was so wonderful that he could enchant nature itself. See the account in Ovid's *Metamorphoses,* Book X.

It was not, as you resentfully assume, that I
Found your attractions wearisome, and was smitten with
Desire for a new wife; nor did I specially want
To raise a numerous family—the sons we have
Are enough, I'm satisfied; but I wanted to ensure
First—and the most important—that we should live well
And not be poor; I know how a poor man is shunned
By all his friends. Next, that I could bring up my sons   510
In a manner worthy of my descent; have other sons,
Perhaps, as brothers to your children; give them all
An equal place, and so build up a closely-knit
And prosperous family. *You* need no more children, do you?
While *I* thought it worth while to ensure advantages
For those I have, by means of those I hope to have.

Was such a plan, then, wicked? Even you would approve
If you could govern your sex-jealousy. But you women
Have reached a state where, if all's well with your sex-life,
You've everything you wish for; but when *that* goes wrong,   520
At once all that is best and noblest turns to gall.
If only children could be got some other way,
Without the female sex! If women didn't exist,
Human life would be rid of all its miseries.
CHORUS. Jason, you have set your case forth very plausibly.
But to my mind—though you may be surprised at this—
You are acting wrongly in thus abandoning your wife.
MEDEA. No doubt I differ from many people in many ways.
To me, a wicked man who is also eloquent
Seems the most guilty of them all. He'll cut your throat   530
As bold as brass, because he knows he can dress up murder
In handsome words. He's not so clever after all.
You dare outface me now with glib high-mindedness!
One word will throw you: if you were honest, you ought first
To have won me over, not got married behind my back.
JASON. No doubt, if I had mentioned it, you would have proved
Most helpful. Why, even now you will not bring yourself
To calm this raging temper.
MEDEA.   That was not the point;
But you're an ageing man, and an Asiatic wife
Was no longer respectable.
JASON.   Understand this: 540
It's not for the sake of any woman that I have made
This royal marriage, but, as I've already said,
To ensure your future, and to give my children brothers
Of royal blood, and build security for us all.
MEDEA. I loathe your prosperous future; I'll have none of it,
Nor none of your security—it galls my heart.
JASON. You know—you'll change your mind and be more sensible.
You'll soon stop thinking good is bad, and striking these
Pathetic poses when in fact you're fortunate.

MEDEA. Go on, insult me: you have a roof over your head.   550
    I am alone, an exile.
JASON.   It was your own choice.
    Blame no one but yourself.
MEDEA.   *My* choice? What did I do?
    Did I make you my wife and then abandon you?
JASON. You called wicked curses on the King and his house.
MEDEA. I did. On your house too Fate sends me as a curse.
JASON. I'll not pursue this further. If there's anything else
    I can provide to meet the children's needs or yours,
    Tell me: I'll gladly give whatever you want, or send
    Letters of introduction, if you like, to friends
    Who will help you.—Listen: to refuse such help is mad.   560
    You've everything to gain if you give up this rage.
MEDEA. Nothing would induce me to have dealings with your friends,
    Nor to take any gift of yours; so offer none.
    A lying traitor's gifts carry no luck.
JASON.   Very well.
    I call the gods to witness that I have done my best
    To help you and the children. You make no response
    To kindness; friendly overtures you obstinately
    Reject. So much the worse for you.
MEDEA.   Go! You have spent
    Too long out here. You are consumed with craving for
    Your newly-won bride. Go, enjoy her.

                          [*Exit* JASON.]

                          It may be—   570
    And God uphold my words—that this your marriage-day
    Will end with marriage lost, loathing and horror left.
CHORUS.
        Visitations of love that come
        Raging and violent on a man
        Bring him neither good repute nor goodness.
        But if Aphrodite descends in gentleness
        No other goddess brings such delight.
        Never, Queen Aphrodite,
        Loose against me from your golden bow,
        Dipped in sweetness of desire,   580
        Your inescapable arrow!

        Let Innocence, the gods' loveliest gift,
        Choose me for her own;
        Never may the dread Cyprian[15]
        Craze my heart to leave old love for new,
        Sending to assault me

---

[15]Aphrodite, goddess of love. Born of the foam of the sea, she made her first appearance
in Cyprus.

Angry disputes and feuds unending;
But let her judge shrewdly the loves of women
And respect the bed where no war rages.

O my country, my home!   590
May the gods save me from becoming
A stateless refugee
Dragging out an intolerable life
In desperate helplessness!
That is the most pitiful of all griefs;
Death is better. Should such a day come to me
I pray for death first.
Of all pains and hardships none is worse
Than to be deprived of your native land.

This is no mere reflection derived from hearsay;   600
It is something we have seen.
You, Medea, have suffered the most shattering of blows;
Yet neither the city of Corinth
Nor any friend has taken pity on you.
May dishonour and ruin fall on the man
Who, having unlocked the secrets
Of a friend's frank heart, can then disown him!
He shall be no friend of mine.

[*Enter* AEGEUS.[16]]

AEGEUS. All happiness to you, Medea! Between old friends
    There is no better greeting.
MEDEA.   All happiness to you,   610
    Aegeus, son of Pandion the wise! Where have you come from?
AEGEUS. From Delphi, from the ancient oracle of Apollo.
MEDEA. The centre of the earth,[17] the home of prophecy:
    Why did you go?
AEGEUS.   To ask for children; that my seed
    May become fertile.
MEDEA.   Why, have you lived so many years
    Childless?
AEGEUS.   Childless I am; so some fate has ordained.
MEDEA. You have a wife, or not?
AEGEUS.   I am married.
MEDEA.   And what answer
    Did Phoebus give you about children?
AEGEUS.   His answer was
    Too subtle for me or any human interpreter.
MEDEA. Is it lawful for me to hear it?

[16] In myth, the father of Theseus, the great Athenian ruler.
[17] The "Navelstone," believed to be the center of the earth, was located at Delphi. Compare
the opening of Aeschylus' *The Eumenides*.

AEGEUS.   Certainly; a brain   620
    Like yours is what is needed.
MEDEA.   Tell me, since you may.
AEGEUS. He commanded me 'not to unstop the wineskin's neck'—
MEDEA. Yes—until when?
AEGEUS.   Until I came safe home again.
MEDEA. I see. And for what purpose have you sailed to Corinth?
AEGEUS. You know the King of Troezen, Pittheus, son of Pelops?
MEDEA. Yes, a most pious man.
AEGEUS.   I want to ask his advice
    About this oracle.
MEDEA.   He is an expert in such matters.
AEGEUS. Yes, and my closest friend. We went to the wars together.
MEDEA. I hope you will get all you long for, and be happy.
AEGEUS. But you are looking pale and wasted: what is the matter?   630
MEDEA. Aegeus, my husband's the most evil man alive.
AEGEUS. Why, what's this? Tell me all about your unhappiness.
MEDEA. Jason has betrayed me, though I never did him wrong.
AEGEUS. What has he done? Explain exactly.
MEDEA.   He has taken
    Another wife, and made her mistress of *my* house.
AEGEUS. But such a thing is shameful! He has never dared—
MEDEA. It is so. Once he loved me; now I am disowned.
AEGEUS. Was he tired of you? Or did he fall in love elsewhere?
MEDEA. Oh, passionately. He's not a man his friends can trust.
AEGEUS. Well, if—as you say—he's a bad lot, let him go.   640
MEDEA. It's royalty and power he's fallen in love with.
AEGEUS.   What?
    Go on. Who's the girl's father?
MEDEA.   Creon, King of Corinth.
AEGEUS. I see. Then you have every reason to be upset.
MEDEA. It is the end of everything! What's more, I'm banished.
AEGEUS. Worse still—extraordinary! Why, who has banished you?
MEDEA. Creon has banished me from Corinth.
AEGEUS.   And does Jason
    Accept this? How disgraceful!
MEDEA.   Oh, no! He protests.
    But he's resolved to bear it bravely.—Aegeus, see,
    I touch your beard as a suppliant, embrace your knees,
    Imploring you to have pity on my wretchedness.   650
    Have pity! I am an exile; let me not be friendless.
    Receive me in Athens;[18] give me a welcome in your house.
    So may the gods grant you fertility, and bring
    Your life to a happy close. You have not realized
    What good luck chance has brought you. I know certain drugs
    Whose power will put an end to your sterility.
    I promise you shall beget children.

---

[18]Athens often boasted of its hospitality to aliens.

AEGEUS.   I am anxious,
    For many reasons, to help you in this way, Medea;
    First, for the gods' sake, then this hope you've given me
    Of children—for I've quite despaired of my own powers.   660
    This then is what I'll do: once you can get to Athens
    I'll keep my promise and protect you all I can.
    But I must make this clear first: I do not intend
    To take you with me away from Corinth. If you come
    Yourself to Athens, you shall have sanctuary there;
    I will not give you up to anyone. But first
    Get clear of Corinth without help; the Corinthians too
    Are friends of mine, and I don't wish to give offence.
MEDEA. So be it. Now confirm your promise with an oath,
    And all is well between us.
AEGEUS.   Why? Do you not trust me?   670
    What troubles you?
MEDEA.   I trust you; but I have enemies—
    Not only Creon, but the house of Pelias.
    Once you are bound by oaths you will not give me up
    If they should try to take me out of your territory.
    But if your promise is verbal, and not sworn to the gods,
    Perhaps you will make friends with them, and agree to do
    What they demand. I've no power on my side, while they
    Have wealth and all the resources of a royal house.
AEGEUS. Your forethought is remarkable; but since you wish it
    I've no objection. In fact, the taking of an oath   680
    Safeguards me; since I can confront your enemies
    With a clear excuse; while *you* have full security.
    So name your gods.
MEDEA.   Swear by the Earth under your feet,
    By the Sun, my father's father, and the whole race of gods.
AEGEUS. Tell me what I shall swear to do or not to do.
MEDEA. Never yourself to expel me from your territory;
    And, if my enemies want to take me away, never
    Willingly, while you live, to give me up to them.
AEGEUS. I swear by Earth, and by the burning light of the Sun,
    And all the gods, to keep the words you have just spoken.   690
MEDEA. I am satisfied. And if you break your oath, what then?
AEGEUS. Then may the gods do to me as to all guilty men.
MEDEA. Go now, and joy be with you. Everything is well.
    I'll reach your city as quickly as I can, when I
    Have carried out my purpose and achieved my wish.

                              [AEGEUS *clasps her hand and hur-
                              ries off.*]

CHORUS. May Hermes, protector of travellers, bring you
    Safe to your home, Aegeus; may you accomplish
    All that you so earnestly desire;
    For your noble heart wins our goodwill.

MEDEA. O Zeus! O Justice, daughter of Zeus! O glorious Sun!   700
    Now I am on the road to victory; now there's hope!
    I shall see my enemies punished as they deserve.
    Just where my plot was weakest, at that very point
    Help has appeared in this man Aegeus; he is a haven
    Where I shall find safe mooring, once I reach the walls
    Of the city of Athens. Now I'll tell you all my plans:
    They'll not make pleasant hearing.

                               [*Medea's* NURSE *has entered; she listens in silence.*]

                                   First I'll send a slave
To Jason, asking him to come to me; and then
I'll give him soft talk; tell him he has acted well,
Tell him I think this royal marriage which he has bought   710
With my betrayal is for the best and wisely planned.
But I shall beg that my children be allowed to stay.
Not that I would think of leaving sons of mine behind
On enemy soil for those who hate me to insult;
But in my plot to kill the princess they must help.
I'll send them to the palace bearing gifts, a dress
Of soft weave and a coronet of beaten gold.
If she takes and puts on this finery, both she
And all who touch her will expire in agony;
With such a deadly poison I'll anoint my gifts.   720

However, enough of that. What makes me cry with pain
Is the next thing I have to do. I will kill my sons.
No one shall take my children from me. When I have made
Jason's whole house a shambles,[19] I will leave Corinth
A murderess, flying from my darling children's blood.
Yes, I can endure guilt, however horrible;
The laughter of my enemies I will not endure.

Now let things take their course. What use is life to me?
I have no land, no home, no refuge from despair.
My folly was committed long ago, when I   730
Was ready to desert my father's house, won over
By eloquence from a Greek, whom with God's help I now
Will punish. He shall never see alive again
The sons he had from me. From his new bride he never
Shall breed a son; she by my poison, wretched girl,
Must die a hideous death. Let no one think of me
As humble or weak or passive; let them understand
I am of a different kind: dangerous to my enemies,
Loyal to my friends. To such a life glory belongs.

---

[19]A slaughterhouse.

CHORUS. Since you have told us everything, and since I want 740
    To be your friend, and also to uphold the laws
    Of human life—I tell you, you must not do this!
MEDEA. No other thing is possible. You have excuse
    For speaking so: you have not been treated as I have.
CHORUS. But—to kill your own children! Can you steel your heart?
MEDEA. This is the way to deal Jason the deepest wound.
CHORUS. This way will bring you too the deepest misery.
MEDEA. Let be. Until it is done words are unnecessary.
    Nurse! You are the one I use for messages of trust.
    Go and bring Jason here. As you're a loyal servant, 750
    And a woman, breathe no word about my purposes.

[*Exit* NURSE.]

CHORUS. The people of Athens, sons of Erechtheus, have enjoyed their
        prosperity
    Since ancient times. Children of blessed gods,
    They grew from holy soil unscorched by invasion.[20]
    Among the glories of knowledge their souls are pastured;
    They walk always with grace under the sparkling sky.
    There long ago, they say, was born golden-haired Harmony,
    Created by the nine virgin Muses[21] of Pieria.

    They say that Aphrodite dips her cup
    In the clear stream of the lovely Cephisus;[22] 760
    It is she who breathes over the land the breath
    Of gentle honey-laden winds; her flowing locks
    She crowns with a diadem of sweet-scented roses,
    And sends the Loves to be enthroned beside Knowledge,
    And with her to create excellence in every art.

    Then how will such a city,
    Watered by sacred rivers,
    A country giving protection to its friends—
    How will Athens welcome
    You, the child-killer 770
    Whose presence is pollution?
    Contemplate the blow struck at a child,
    Weigh the blood you take upon you.
    Medea, by your knees,
    By every pledge or appeal we beseech you,   — Speaking for audience
    Do not slaughter your children!

---

[20]An irony and a significant phrase, for *Medea* was produced in 431, on the eve of the long Peloponnesian War between Athens and the confederacy headed by Sparta. The Athenians ultimately were conquered.
[21]The nine goddesses of the arts, worshiped at Pieria, on the slopes of Mount Olympus.
[22]The main river near Athens.

Where will you find hardness of purpose?
How will you build resolution in hand or heart
To face horror without flinching?
When the moment comes, and you look at them—   780
The moment for you to assume the role of murderess—
How will you do it?
When your sons kneel to you for pity,
Will you stain your fingers with their blood?
Your heart will melt; you will know you cannot.

> [*Enter* JASON *from the palace. Two
> maids come from the house to attend*
> MEDEA.]

JASON. You sent for me: I have come. Although you hate me, I
    Am ready to listen. You have some new request; what is it?
MEDEA. Jason, I ask you to forgive the things I said.
    You must bear with my violent temper; you and I
    Share many memories of love. I have been taking   790
    Myself to task. 'You are a fool,' I've told myself,
    'You're mad, when people try to plan things for the best,
    To be resentful, and pick quarrels with the King
    And with your husband; what he's doing will help us all.
    His wife is royal; her sons will be my sons' brothers.
    Why not throw off your anger? What is the matter, since
    The gods are making kind provision? After all
    I have two children still to care for; and I know
    We came as exiles, and our friends are few enough.'
    When I considered this, I saw my foolishness;   800
    I saw how useless anger was. So now I welcome
    What you have done; I think you are wise to gain for us
    This new alliance, and the folly was all mine.
    I should have helped you in your plans, made it my pleasure
    To get ready your marriage-bed, attend your bride.
    But we women—I won't say we are bad by nature,
    But we are what we are. You, Jason, should not copy
    Our bad example, or match yourself with us, showing
    Folly for folly. I give in; I was wrong just now,
    I admit. But I have thought more wisely of it since.   810
    Children, children! Are you indoors? Come out here.

> [*The* CHILDREN *come out. Their*
> TUTOR *follows.*]

                                  Children,
Greet your father, as I do, and put your arms round him.
Forget our quarrel, and love him as your mother does.
We have made friends; we are not angry any more.
There, children; take his hand.

[*She turns away in a sudden flood of weeping.*]

Forgive me; I recalled
What pain the future hides from us.

[*After embracing* JASON, *the* CHIL-
DREN *go back to* MEDEA.]

Oh children! Will you
All your lives long, stretch out your hands to me like this?
Oh, my tormented heart is full of tears and terrors.
After so long, I have ended my quarrel with your father;
And now, see! I have drenched this young face with my tears.   820
CHORUS. I too feel fresh tears fill my eyes. May the course of evil
  Be checked now, go no further!
JASON.   I am pleased, Medea,
  That you have changed your mind; though indeed I do not blame
  Your first resentment. Only naturally a woman
  Is angry when her husband marries a second wife.
  You have had wiser thoughts; and though it has taken time,
  You have recognized the right decision. This is the act
  Of a sensible woman. As for you, my boys, your father
  Has taken careful thought, and, with the help of the gods,
  Ensured a good life for you. Why, in time, I'm sure,   830
  You with your brothers will be leading men in Corinth.
  Only grow big and strong. Your father, and those gods ⟩ Hubris
  Who are his friends, have all the rest under control.
  I want to see you, when you're strong, full-grown young men, — Irony
  Tread down my enemies.

[*Again* MEDEA *breaks down and weeps.*]

What's this? Why these floods of tears?
  Why are you pale? Did you not like what I was saying?
  Why do you turn away?
MEDEA.   It is nothing. I was thinking
  About these children.
JASON.   I'll provide for them. Cheer up.
MEDEA. I will. It is not that I mean to doubt your word.
  But women—are women; tears come naturally to us.   840
JASON. Why do you grieve so over the children?
MEDEA.   I'm their mother.
  When you just now prayed for them to live long, I wondered
  Whether it would be so; and grief came over me.
  But I've said only part of what I had to say;
  Here is the other thing. Since Creon has resolved
  To send me out of Corinth, I fully recognize

That for me too this course is best. If I lived here
I should become a trouble both to you and him.
People believe I bear a grudge against you all.
So I must go. But the boys—I would like *them* to be   850
Brought up in your care. Beg Creon to let them stay.
JASON. I don't know if I can persuade him; but I'll try.
MEDEA. Then—get your wife to ask her father to let them stay.
JASON. Why, certainly; I'm pretty sure she'll win him over.
MEDEA. She will, if she's like other women. But I too
Can help in this. I'll send a present to your wife—
The loveliest things to be found anywhere on earth.
The boys shall take them.—One of you maids, go quickly, bring
The dress and golden coronet.—They will multiply
Her happiness many times, when she can call her own   860
A royal, noble husband, and these treasures, which
My father's father the Sun bequeathed to his descendants.

> [*A slave has brought a casket, which*
> MEDEA *now hands to her sons.*]

Boys, hold these gifts. Now carry them to the happy bride,
The princess royal; give them into her own hands.
Go! She will find them all that such a gift should be.
JASON. But why deprive yourself of such things, foolish woman?
Do you think a royal palace is in want of dresses?
Or gold, do you suppose? Keep them, don't give them away.
If my wife values me at all she will yield to *me*
More than to costly presents, I am sure of that.   870
MEDEA. Don't stop me. Gifts, they say, persuade even the gods;
With mortals, gold outweighs a thousand arguments.
The day is hers; from now on *her* prosperity
Will rise to new heights. She is royal and young. To buy
My sons from exile I would give life, not just gold.
Come, children, go both of you into this rich palace;
Kneel down and beg your father's new wife, and my mistress,
That you may not be banished. And above all, see
That she receives my present into her own hands.
Go quickly; be successful, and bring good news back,   880
That what your mother longs for has been granted you.

> [*Exit* JASON *followed by the* CHIL-
> DREN *and the* TUTOR.]

CHORUS.
    Now I have no more hope,
    No more hope that the children can live;
    They are walking to murder at this moment.
    The bride will receive the golden coronet,
    Receive her merciless destroyer;

With her own hands she will carefully fit
The adornment of death round her golden hair.

She cannot resist such loveliness, such heavenly gleaming;
She will enfold herself 890
In the dress and the wreath of wrought gold,
Preparing her bridal beauty
To enter a new home—among the dead.
So fatal is the snare she will fall into,
So inevitable the death that awaits her;
From its cruelty there is no escape.

And you, unhappy Jason, ill-starred in marriage,
You, son-in-law of kings:
Little you know that the favour you ask
Will seal your sons' destruction 900
And fasten on your wife a hideous fate. — *foreshadowing*
O wretched Jason!
So sure of destiny, and so ignorant!

Your sorrow next I weep for, pitiable mother;
You, for jealousy of your marriage-bed,
Will slaughter your children;
Since, disregarding right and loyalty,
Your husband has abandoned you
And lives with another wife.

[*The* TUTOR *returns from the palace
with the two* CHILDREN.]

TUTOR. Mistress! These two boys are reprieved from banishment. 910
The princess took your gifts from them with her own hand,
And was delighted. They have no enemies in the palace.

[MEDEA *is silent.*]

Well, bless my soul!
Isn't that good news? Why do you stand there thunderstruck?
MEDEA [*to herself*]. How cruel, how cruel!
TUTOR. That's out of tune with the news I brought.
MEDEA. How cruel life is!
TUTOR.   Have I, without knowing it,
Told something dreadful, then? I thought my news was good.
MEDEA. Your news is what it is. I am not blaming you.
TUTOR. Then why stand staring at the ground, with streaming eyes? 920
MEDEA. Strong reason forces me to weep, old friend. The gods,
And my own evil-hearted plots, have led to this.
TUTOR. Take heart, mistress; in time your sons will bring you home.
MEDEA. Before then, I have others to send home.—Oh, gods!

[*She weeps.*]

TUTOR. You're not the only mother parted from her sons.
   We are all mortal; you must not bear grief so hard.
MEDEA. Yes, friend. I'll follow your advice. Now go indoors
   And get things ready for them, as on other days.

                              [*Exit* TUTOR. *The* CHILDREN *come
                              to* MEDEA.]

O children, children! You have a city, and a home;
And when we have parted, there you both will stay for ever,   930
You motherless, I miserable. And I must go
To exile in another land, before I have had
My joy of you, before I have seen you growing up,
Becoming prosperous. I shall never see your brides,
Adorn your bridal beds, and hold the torches high.
My misery is my own heart, which will not relent.
All was for nothing, then—these years of rearing you,
My care, my aching weariness, and the wild pains
When you were born. Oh, yes, I once built many hopes
On you; imagined, pitifully, that you would care   940
For my old age, and would yourselves wrap my dead body
For burial. How people would envy me my sons!
That sweet, sad thought has faded now. Parted from you,
My life will be all pain and anguish. You will not
Look at your mother any more with these dear eyes.
You will have moved into a different sphere of life.

Dear sons, why are you staring at me so? You smile
At me—your last smile: why?

                              [*She weeps. The* CHILDREN *go from
                              her a little, and she turns to the*
                              CHORUS.]

                   Oh, what am I to do?
Women, my courage is all gone. Their young, bright faces—
I can't do it. I'll think no more of it. I'll take them   950
Away from Corinth. Why should I hurt *them*, to make
Their father suffer, when I shall suffer twice as much
Myself? I won't do it. I won't think of it again.

What is the matter with me? Are my enemies
To laugh at me? Am I to let them off scot free?
I must steel myself to it. What a coward I am,
Even tempting my own resolution with soft talk.
Boys, go indoors.

[*The* CHILDREN *go to the door, but
stay there watching her.*]

If there is any here who finds it
Not lawful to be present at my sacrifice,
Let him see to it. My hand shall not weaken.   960

Oh, my heart, don't, don't do it! Oh, miserable heart,
Let them be! Spare your children! We'll all live together
Safely in Athens; and they will make you happy. . . . No!
No! No! By all the fiends of hate in hell's depths, no!
I'll not leave sons of mine to be the victims of
My enemies' rage. In any case there is no escape,
The thing's done now. Yes, now—the golden coronet
Is on her head, the royal bride is in her dress,
Dying, I know it. So, since I have a sad road
To travel, and send these boys on a still sadder road,   970
I'll speak to them. Come, children; give me your hand, dear son;
Yours too. Now we must say goodbye. Oh, darling hand,
And darling mouth; your noble, childlike face and body!
Dear sons, my blessing on you both—but there, not here!
All blessing here your father has destroyed. How sweet
To hold you! And children's skin is soft, and their breath pure.
Go! Go away! I can't look at you any longer;
My pain is more than I can bear.

[*The* CHILDREN *go indoors.*]

I understand
The horror of what I am going to do; but anger,
The spring of all life's horror, masters my resolve.   980

[MEDEA *goes to stand looking
towards the palace.*]

CHORUS.
    I have often engaged in arguments,
    And become more subtle, and perhaps more heated,
    Than is suitable for women;
    Though in fact women too have intelligence,
    Which forms part of our nature and instructs us—
    Not all of us, I admit; but a certain few
    You might perhaps find, in a large number of women—
    A few not incapable of reflection;

    And this is my opinion: those men or women
    Who never had children of their own at all   990
    Enjoy the advantage in good fortune
    Over those who are parents. Childless people

Have no means of knowing whether children are
A blessing or a burden; but being without them
They live exempt from many troubles.

While those who have growing up in their homes
The sweet gift of children I see always
Burdened and worn with incessant worry,
First, how to rear them in health and safety,
And bequeath them, in time, enough to live on;   1000
And then this further anxiety:
They can never know whether all their toil
Is spent for worthy or worthless children.

And beyond the common ills that attend
All human life there is one still worse:
Suppose at last they are pretty well off,
Their children have grown up, and, what's more,
Are kind and honest: then what happens?
A throw of chance—and there goes Death
Bearing off your child into the unknown.   1010

Then why should mortals thank the gods,
Who add to their load, already grievous,
This one more grief, for their children's sake,
Most grievous of all?
MEDEA. Friends, I have long been waiting for a message from the palace.
      What is to happen next? I see a slave of Jason's
      Coming, gasping for breath. He must bring fearful news.

[*Enter a* MESSENGER.]

MESSENGER. Medea! Get away, escape! Oh, what a thing to do!
      What an unholy, horrible thing! Take ship, or chariot,
      Any means you can, but escape!
MEDEA.   Why should I escape?   1020
MESSENGER. She's dead—the princess, and her father Creon too,
      They're both dead, by your poisons.
MEDEA.   Your news is excellent.
      I count you from today my friend and benefactor.
MESSENGER. What? Are you sane, or raving mad? When you've committed
      This hideous crime against the royal house, you're glad
      At hearing of it? Do you not tremble at such things?
MEDEA. I could make suitable reply to that, my friend.
      But take your time now; tell me, how did they die? You'll give
      Me double pleasure if their death was horrible.
MESSENGER. When your two little boys came hand in hand, and
            entered   1030
      The palace with their father, where the wedding was,
      We servants were delighted. We had all felt sorry
      To hear how you'd been treated; and now the word went round

From one to another, that you and Jason had made it up.
So we were glad to see the boys; one kissed their hand,
Another their fair hair. Myself, I was so pleased,
I followed with them to the princess's room. Our mistress—
The one we now call mistress in your place—before
She saw your pair of boys coming, had eyes only
For Jason; but seeing them she dropped her eyes, and turned   1040
Her lovely cheek away, upset that they should come
Into her room. Your husband then began to soothe
Her sulkiness, her girlish temper. 'You must not,'
He said, 'be unfriendly to our friends. Turn your head round,
And give up feeling angry. Those your husband loves
You must love too. Now take these gifts,' he said, 'and ask
Your father to revoke their exile for my sake.'
So, when she saw those lovely things, she was won over,
And agreed to all that Jason asked. At once, before
He and your sons were well out of the house, she took   1050
The embroidered gown and put it round her. Then she placed
Over her curls the golden coronet, and began
To arrange her hair in a bright mirror, smiling at
Her lifeless form reflected there. Then she stood up,
And to and fro stepped daintily about the room
On white bare feet, and many times she would twist back
To see how the dress fell in clear folds to the heel.

Then suddenly we saw a frightening thing. She changed
Colour; she staggered sideways, shook in every limb.
She was just able to collapse on to a chair,   1060
Or she would have fallen flat. Then one of her attendants,
An old woman, thinking that perhaps the anger of Pan[23]
Or some other god had struck her, chanted the cry of worship.
But then she saw, oozing from the girl's lips, white froth;
The pupils of her eyes were twisted out of sight;
The blood was drained from all her skin. The old woman knew
Her mistake, and changed her chant to a despairing howl.
One maid ran off quickly to fetch the King, another
To look for Jason and tell him what was happening
To his young bride; the whole palace was filled with a clatter   1070
Of people running here and there.
                        All this took place
In a few moments, perhaps while a fast runner might run
A hundred yards; and she lay speechless, with eyes closed.
Then she came to, poor girl, and gave a frightful scream,
As two torments made war on her together: first
The golden coronet round her head discharged a stream
Of unnatural devouring fire: while the fine dress

---

[23] The old woman at first suspects some attack of unreasonable terror such as was associated with the nature god Pan (from whose name the word "panic" derives).

Your children gave her—poor miserable girl!—the stuff
Was eating her clear flesh. She leapt up from her chair,
On fire, and ran, shaking her head and her long hair   1080
This way and that, trying to shake off the coronet.
The ring of gold was fitted close and would not move;
The more she shook her head the fiercer the flame burned.
At last, exhausted by agony, she fell to the ground;
Save to her father, she was unrecognizable.
Her eyes, her face, were one grotesque disfigurement;
Down from her head dripped blood mingled with flame; her flesh,
Attacked by the invisible fangs of poison, melted
From the bare bone, like gum-drops from a pine-tree's bark—
A ghastly sight. Not one among us dared to touch   1090
Her body. What we'd seen was lesson enough for us.

But suddenly her father came into the room.
He did not understand, poor man, what kind of death
Had struck his child. He threw himself down at her side,
And sobbed aloud, and kissed her, and took her in his arms,
And cried, 'Poor darling child, what god destroyed your life
So cruelly? Who robs me of my only child,
Old as I am, and near my grave? Oh, let me die
With you, my daughter!' Soon he ceased his tears and cries,
And tried to lift his aged body upright; and then,   1100
As ivy sticks to laurel-branches, so he stuck
Fast to the dress. A ghastly wrestling then began;
He struggled to raise up his knee, she tugged him down.
If he used force, he tore the old flesh off his bones.
At length the King gave up his pitiful attempts;
Weakened with pain, he yielded, and gasped out his life.
Now, joined in death, daughter and father—such a sight
As tears were made for—they lie there.
                                            To you, Medea,
I have no more to say. You will yourself know best
How to evade reprisal. As for human life,   1110
It is a shadow, as I have long believed. And this
I say without hesitation: those whom most would call
Intelligent, the propounders of wise theories—
Their folly is of all men's the most culpable.
Happiness is a thing no man possesses. Fortune
May come now to one man, now to another, as
Prosperity increases; happiness never.

                        [*Exit* MESSENGER.]

CHORUS. Today we see the will of Heaven, blow after blow, *retribution*
       Bring down on Jason justice and calamity.
MEDEA. Friends, now my course is clear: as quickly as possible   1120
       To kill the children and then fly from Corinth; not
       Delay and so consign them to another hand

To murder with a better will. For they must die,
In any case; and since they must, then I who gave
Them birth will kill them. Arm yourself, my heart: the thing
That you must do is fearful, yet inevitable.
Why wait, then? My accursed hand, come, take the sword;
Take it, and forward to your frontier of despair.
No cowardice, no tender memories; forget
That you once loved them, that of your body they were born. 1130
For one short day forget your children; afterwards
Weep: though you kill them, they were your beloved sons.
Life has been cruel to me.

[MEDEA *goes into the house.*]

CHORUS. Earth, awake! Bright arrows of the Sun,
Look! Look down on the accursed woman
Before she lifts up a murderous hand
To pollute it with her children's blood!
For they are of your own golden race;
And for mortals to spill blood that grew
In the veins of gods is a fearful thing. 1140
Heaven-born brightness, hold her, stop her,
Purge the palace of her, this pitiable
Bloody-handed fiend of vengeance!

All your care for them lost! Your love
For the babes you bore, all wasted, wasted!
Why did you come from the blue Symplegades
That hold the gate of the barbarous sea?
Why must this rage devour your heart
To spend itself in slaughter of children?
Where kindred blood pollutes the ground 1150
A curse hangs over human lives;
And murder measures the doom that falls
By Heaven's law on the guilty house.

[*A child's scream is heard from
inside the house.*]

CHORUS. Do you hear? The children are calling for help.
O cursed, miserable woman!
CHILDREN'S VOICES. Help, help! Mother, let me go!
Mother, don't kill us!
CHORUS. Shall we go in?
I am sure we ought to save the children's lives.
CHILDREN'S VOICES. Help, help, for the gods' sake! She is killing us! 1160
We can't escape from her sword!
CHORUS. O miserable mother, to destroy your own increase,
Murder the babes of your body!
Stone and iron you are, as you resolved to be.

There was but one in time past,
One woman that I have heard of,
Raised hand against her own children.
It was Ino,[24] sent out of her mind by a god,
When Hera, the wife of Zeus,
Drove her from her home to wander over the world.   1170
In her misery she plunged into the sea
Being defiled by the murder of her children;
From the steep cliff's edge she stretched out her foot,
And so ended,
Joined in death with her two sons.

What can be strange or terrible after this?
O bed of women, full of passion and pain,
What wickedness, what sorrow you have caused on the earth!

> [*Enter* JASON, *running and breath-less.*]

JASON. You women standing round the door there! Is Medea
Still in the house?—vile murderess!—or has she gone   1180
And escaped? I swear she must either hide in the deep earth
Or soar on wings into the sky's abyss, to escape
My vengeance for the royal house.—She has killed the King
And the princess! Does she expect to go unpunished?

Well, I am less concerned with her than with the children.
Those who have suffered at her hands will make her suffer;
I've come to save my sons, before Creon's family
Murder them in revenge for this unspeakable
Crime of their mother's.
CHORUS.   Jason, you have yet to learn
How great your trouble is; or you would not have spoken so.   1190
JASON. What trouble? Is Medea trying to kill me too?
CHORUS. Your sons are dead. Their mother has killed both your sons.
JASON. What? Killed my sons? That word kills me.
CHORUS.   They are both dead.
JASON. Where are they? Did she kill them out here, or indoors?
CHORUS. Open that door, and see them lying in their blood.
JASON. Slaves, there! Unbar the doors! Open, and let me see
Two horrors: my dead sons, and the woman I will kill.

> [JASON *batters at the doors.* MEDEA
> *appears above the roof, sitting in a
> chariot drawn by dragons, with the
> bodies of the two children beside her.*]

---

[24]Ino had helped to bring up the god Dionysus, who was born of Zeus and Semele. Hera, Zeus' consort, drove Ino to madness in revenge for Zeus' begetting of Dionysus.

MEDEA. Jason! Why are you battering at these doors, seeking
   The dead children and me who killed them? Stop! Be quiet.
   If you have any business with me, say what you wish.   1200
   Touch us you cannot, in this chariot which the Sun
   Has sent to save us from the hands of enemies.
JASON. You abomination! Of all women most detested
   By every god, by me, by the whole human race!
   You could endure—a mother!—to lift sword against
   Your own little ones; to leave me childless, my life wrecked.
   After such murder do you outface both Sun and Earth—
   Guilty of gross pollution? May the gods blast your life!
   I am sane now; but I was mad before, when I
   Brought you from your palace in a land of savages   1210
   Into a Greek home—you, a living curse, already
   A traitor both to your father and your native land.
   The vengeance due for your sins the gods have cast on me.
   You had already murdered your brother at his own hearth
   When first you stepped on board my lovely Argo's hull.
   That was your beginning. Then you became my wife, and bore
   My children; now, out of mere sexual jealousy,
   You murder them! In all Hellas there is not one woman
   Who could have done it; yet in preference to them
   I married you, chose hatred and murder for my wife—   1220
   No woman, but a tiger; a Tuscan Scylla[25]—but more savage.
   Ah, what's the use? If I cursed you all day, no remorse
   Would touch you, for your heart's proof against feeling. Go!
   Out of my sight, polluted fiend, child-murderer!
   Leave me to mourn over my destiny: I have lost
   My young bride; I have lost the two sons I begot
   And brought up; I shall never see them alive again.
MEDEA. I would if necessary have answered at full length
   Everything you have said; but Zeus the father of all
   Knows well what service I once rendered you, and how   1230
   You have repaid me. You were mistaken if you thought
   You could dishonour my bed and live a pleasant life
   And laugh at me. The princess was wrong too, and so
   Was Creon, when he took you for his son-in-law
   And thought he could exile me with impunity.
   So now, am I a tiger, Scylla?—Hurl at me
   What names you please! I've reached your heart; and that is right.
JASON. You suffer too; my loss is yours no less.
MEDEA.   It is true;
   But my pain's a fair price, to take away your smile.
JASON. O children, what a wicked mother Fate gave you!   1240
MEDEA. O sons, your father's treachery cost you your lives.
JASON. It was not my hand that killed my sons.

---

[25]A monster who attacked mariners sailing between Italy and Sicily through what is now
called the strait of Messina.

MEDEA.   No, not your hand;
  But your insult to me, and your new-wedded wife.
JASON. You thought *that* reason enough to murder them, that I
  No longer slept with you?
MEDEA.   And is that injury
  A slight one, do you imagine, to a woman?
JASON.   Yes,
  To a modest woman; but to you—the whole world lost.
MEDEA. I can stab too: your sons are dead!
JASON.   Dead? No! They live
  To haunt your life with vengeance.
MEDEA.   Who began this feud?
  The gods know.
JASON.   Yes—they know the vileness of your heart.   1250
MEDEA. Loathe on! Your bitter voice—how I abhor the sound!
JASON. As I loathe yours. Let us make terms and part at once.
MEDEA. Most willingly. What terms? What do you bid me do?
JASON. Give me my sons for burial and mourning rites.
MEDEA. Oh, no! I will myself convey them to the temple
  Of Hera[26] Acraea; there in the holy precinct I
  Will bury them with my own hand, to ensure that none
  Of my enemies shall violate or insult their graves.
  And I will ordain an annual feast and sacrifice
  To be solemnized for ever by the people of Corinth,   1260
  To expiate this impious murder. I myself
  Will go to Athens, city of Erechtheus,[27] to make my home
  With Aegeus son of Pandion. You, as you deserve,
  Shall die an unheroic death,[28] your head shattered
  By a timber from the Argo's hull. Thus wretchedly
  Your fate shall end the story of your love for me.
JASON. The curse of children's blood be on you!
  Avenging Justice blast your being!
MEDEA. What god will hear your imprecation,
  Oath-breaker, guest-deceiver, liar?   1270
JASON. Unclean, abhorrent child-destroyer!
MEDEA. Go home: your wife waits to be buried.
JASON. I go—a father once; now childless.
MEDEA. You grieve too soon. Old age is coming.
JASON. Children, how dear you were!
MEDEA. To their mother; not to you.
JASON. Dear—and you murdered them?
MEDEA. Yes, Jason, to break your heart.
JASON. I long to fold them in my arms;
  To kiss their lips would comfort me.   1280

---

[26] The goddess was regarded as defender of wives and marriage.
[27] Legendary Athenian king.
[28] One version of Jason's death is that he died in this way, at Corinth, struck by a falling
beam as he sat near his old ship, the *Argo*.

MEDEA. *Now* you have loving words, now kisses for them:
  Then you disowned them, sent them into exile.
JASON. For God's sake, let me touch their gentle flesh.
MEDEA. You shall not. It is waste of breath to ask.
JASON.
  Zeus, do you hear how I am mocked,
  Rejected, by this savage beast
  Polluted with her children's blood?

  But now, as time and strength permit,
  I will lament this grievous day,
  And call the gods to witness, how   1290
  You killed my sons, and now refuse
  To let me touch or bury them.
  Would God I had not bred them,
  Or ever lived to see
  Them dead, you their destroyer!

                        [*During this speech the chariot has
                        moved out of sight.*]

CHORUS. Many are the Fates which Zeus in Olympus dispenses;
  Many matters the gods bring to surprising ends.
  The things we thought would happen do not happen;
  The unexpected God makes possible;
  And such is the conclusion of this story.[29]   1300

[29] The last five lines are a formulaic ending, used also at the conclusion of several other plays by Euripides, including *Alcestis, Andromache, Helen,* and *The Bacchae.*

Aristophanes

(C. 450–C. 386 B.C.)

Aristophanes was born around 450 B.C., and his death some time during the 380s marks the end of the great century of ancient Greek drama. The chronological sequence of the four preeminent playwrights—the tragedians Aeschylus, Sophocles, and Euripides and the comedian Aristophanes—coincides with two important trends in the theater. In aesthetic form, drama moved from the loftily stylized to the more realistic (as typified in the "New Comedy" of the fourth century, which stressed the individual actors and took away from the chorus its role in the action); in mood and attitude, there was a shift from idealistic optimism to disillusioned cynicism. These trends in the drama parallel trends in Athenian political, religious, and philosophical attitudes. In the epoch ending shortly before 400 B.C., Athens endured military, political, and cultural ordeals that culminated in the overthrow of Athenian democracy and independence. The period when Athens was the moral and political exemplar of what was best in ancient Greece was at an end.

Aristophanes is the only representative of the fifth-century "Old Comedy" whose works have survived. Since biographical information about him is scant, it is difficult to isolate what is distinctive in him from what is characteristic of the Old Comedy; the man and the movement are not clearly separable. If we are thinking about dramaturgy, neither can be called realistic, since the settings, costumes, and freewheeling plots of Aristophanes' plays are often fantastic to the point of surrealism. In *The Wasps* (a play about the Athenian judicial system; 422), in *The Frogs* (a literary satire pitting the deceased tragedians Aeschylus and Euripides against each other; 405), and in *The Birds* (a utopian fantasy-satire; 414), characters or chorus or both are costumed and portrayed grotesquely in the guise of the animals after which the plays are named.

Yet Aristophanes is a realist in his own way—in subject and theme, if not in theatrical style. His plays (of the forty he wrote, eleven have survived) repeatedly present unflattering portraits of actual people—people who may well have been in his audience—disguised thinly or not at all (they include Socrates, Euripides, and the Athenian political leader Cleon, whom Aristophanes despised). His favorite subjects were literary satire, particularly lampoons of Euripides and what Aristophanes chose to see as the other dramatist's hatred of women; intellectual satire of newfangled trends in education, philosophy, and moral values; and above all, political satire, directed mainly against the Athenian effort in the Peloponnesian War. Aristophanes consistently regarded the war as cruelty toward the enemies and allies of Athens and as suicidal folly from the vantage point of Athens itself. In fact, early in his career he was once prosecuted for disloyalty. He got off lightly and immediately resumed his role of political gadfly, which says something about Aristophanes and perhaps about Athenian political tolerance even in its days of militaristic jingoism. Spectators of Aristophanes' plays saw the world pictured not in the long vistas of myth and perennial archetypes about the human condition but in the context of what had happened yesterday and what was likely to happen tomorrow. For all his zany exuberance, Aristophanes was an intellectual, and one concerned intimately with current events.

Lysistrata (411) is one of his masterpieces. A witty specimen of antiwar propaganda, it includes also some of his typical wisecracks about tragedy, literature, and Euripides, though it does not demonstrate much if any of his concern with philosophical issues. The affection and respect Aristophanes felt for women as capable agents and as custodians of ultimate human sanity come across warmly and brilliantly. The same sympathy and admiration emerge in his plays *Thesmophoriazusae,* or *Ladies' Day* (411), in which women plot to avenge themselves on Euripides, and in *Ecclesiazusae,* or *Women in Parliament* (392).

Roman comedy, which established the model for subsequent comedy in Western theater, was modeled on the Greek New Comedy, a form that thrived after the accession of Alexander the Great, when Athens lost its political freedom. New Comedy abandoned the Aristophanic Old Comedy's freedom of structure and political comment in favor of comparatively realistic plots that usually turned around a young man's attempts to marry over his father's objections. But in many ways the spirit of comedy—laughter, irreverence, the celebration of sexuality, and a movement toward liberation from social and personal bonds—was already established in Old Comedy and was transmitted intact to New Comedy and thence to later dramatic history. In Aristophanes, as in comedy ever since, the action begins with a society constricted by authority, proceeds through a series of laughable irreverent events to dissolve that authority, and ends with a new, liberated society, reconstituted around the values of youth, vitality, and sexuality. Many of Aristophanes' plays end with a feast or a dance, forerunners of the boy-gets-girl celebrations of modern comedy. Sexuality triumphs, and as the modern critic Northrop Frye wittily puts it, "the plot usually moves toward an act which, like death in Greek tragedy, takes place offstage, and is symbolized by a closing embrace."

Lysistrata is not far removed from a fertility celebration, and its cheerful, innocent obscenity is basic to its meaning. Underlying its bawdy, topical jokes and its absurd, incredible plot is a serious confrontation of values. Aristophanes, like his epic and tragic predecessors, almost instinctively defines this confrontation along sexual lines. *Lysistrata* begins with a comic Athens in thrall to sterile, destructive "male" values, in pursuit of a war that Aristophanes regards as misguided and hopeless. "War's a man's affair," says Lysistrata; she is quoting Homer, but she gives the line an ironic twist very far from Homer's meaning. To the male thirst for glory and self-destructive competitiveness, Lysistrata opposes not only sexuality but also common sense and a respect for nonheroic ordinary life. In the most famous passage in the play, she compares the state to a ball of tangled yarn, which the housewife must untangle, wash, and weave together into a seamless unity. "It would take a woman," the Commissioner exclaims, "to reduce state questions to a matter of carding and weaving!"

Who "wins" in *Lysistrata?* Just as it is typically Greek to see the world as divided between "male" rationality and abstraction and "female" desire and vitality, so it is typically Greek to see the solution as a balance between the two forces. The women *do* stop the war (a bit of unhistorical wishful thinking on the part of Aristophanes), but the men's claims of honor are satisfied, too, in the peace negotiations. The real winner is "Reconciliation," a concept represented on stage by a statue under whose eyes the resolution is effected and given significance in the form of an enormous naked woman. We seem to be witnessing an earthy, comic echo of the sexual reconciliation and the hymn to Athens at the end of the *Oresteia* when Lysistrata says, "Each man be kind to his woman, and you, women, be equally kind," and the play ends with a joyous hymn to "Athena of the House of Brass."

FURTHER READING *(prepared by F.S.N.):* On the festivals, staging and production of ancient comedy, see F. H. Sandbach, *The Comic Theatre of Greece and Rome,* 1977; Kenneth McLeish, *The Theatre of Aristophanes,* 1980; Leo Aylen, *The Greek Theater,* 1985 (with special attention to *The Frogs*); Katherine Lever, *The Art of Greek Comedy,* 1956; and C. W. Dearden, *The Stage of Aristophanes,* 1976. Useful general material on Aristophanes' life and writings may be found in K. J. Dover, *Aristophanic Comedy,* 1972; and Lois Spatz, *Aristophanes,* 1978. Victor Ehrenberg, *The People of Aristophanes: A Sociology of Old Attic Comedy,* 1943, 3rd ed. 1962, introduces the reader to the farmers, tradesmen, slaves, and family members of the late fifth century B.C. *Yale Classical Studies,* vol. XXVI (1980), is devoted to essays on the interpretation of Aristophanes. Gilbert Murray, in *Aristophanes: A Study,* 1933, in addition to presenting background material on Aristophanes and on comedy in general, devotes a chapter to *Lysistrata.*

LYSISTRATA

Translated by Dudley Fitts

The political and military background of the play is the Peloponnesian war, a series of conflicts between confederacies led by Athens and Sparta. The Peloponnese, of which Sparta was the capital, was a large peninsula that made up southern Greece. The period of the war, from 431 B.C. to 404, was a tragic era, especially for Athens, whose defeat in the latter year marked the end of its greatest political and cultural age. In 413, two years before *Lysistrata* was produced in Athens, the city's naval and military forces had suffered a calamitous defeat in connection with the ill-fated Sicilian expedition that Athenian patriots—or imperialists—had hoped would establish Athenian dominance of the Mediterranean. Through comedy that is sometimes caustic and sometimes good-humored, Aristophanes' play was intended to show the folly of both political power-lust and civil war among Greeks. As art, *Lysistrata* is a triumph; judged in the light of historical consequences, the play was a failure, since the war went on to its disastrous end.

Some of the jokes can be understood only if one keeps in mind that the usual costume in fifth-century Greek comedy included an exaggeratedly prominent leather phallus.

The characters' names are in many instances significant puns: for example, Lysistrata's name means "Dismisser of Armies" and "Myrrhine" puns on the word meaning female genitals. [*Editors' headnote.*]

PERSONS REPRESENTED

LYSISTRATA	COMMISSIONER
KALONIKE	KINESIAS
MYRRHINE	SPARTAN HERALD
LAMPITO	SPARTAN AMBASSADOR
CHORUS	A SENTRY

SCENE: *Athens. First, a public square; later, beneath the walls of the Akropolis; later, a courtyard within the Akropolis.*[1]

Until the *éxodos,* the CHORUS is divided into two hemichori: the first, of Old Men; the second, of Old Women. Each of these has its KORYPHAIOS. In the *éxodos,* the hemichori return as Athenians and Spartans.[2]

The supernumeraries include the BABY SON of Kinêsias; STRATYLLIS, a member of the hemichorus of Old Women; various individual speakers, both Spartan and Athenian.

---

[1] The hill upon which the main civic and religious centers of Athens were located.
[2] The *éxodus* is the last choral song of the play. The *koryphaios* is the principal spokesman for the chorus or, as here, for a division of it.

PROLOGUE

Athens; a public square; early morning; LYSISTRATA *sola.*

LYSISTRATA.
　　If someone had invited them to a festival—
　　of Bacchos, say; or to Pan's shrine, or to Aphroditê's
　　over at Kôlias[3]—, you couldn't get through the streets,
　　what with the drums and the dancing. But now,
　　not a woman in sight!
　　　　　　　　　　　　Except—oh, yes!

　　　　　　　　　　　　[*Enter* KALONIKE]

　　Here's one of my neighbors, at last. Good
　　morning, Kalonikê.
KALONIKE.
　　　　　　　　　　Good morning, Lysistrata.
　　　　　　　　　　　　　　　　　　　Darling,
　　don't frown so! You'll ruin your face!
LYSISTRATA.
　　　　　　　　　　　　Never mind my face.
　　Kalonikê,
　　the way we women behave! Really, I don't blame the men　　　10
　　for what they say about us.
KALONIKE.
　　　　　　　　　No; I imagine they're right.
LYSISTRATA.
　　For example: I call a meeting
　　to think out a most important matter—and what happens?
　　The women all stay in bed!
KALONIKE.
　　　　　　　　　　Oh, they'll be along.
　　It's hard to get away, you know: a husband, a cook,
　　a child . . . Home life can be *so* demanding!
LYSISTRATA.
　　What I have in mind is even more demanding.
KALONIKE.
　　Tell me: what is it?
LYSISTRATA.
　　　　　　　It's big.
KALONIKE.
　　　　　　　　　　Goodness! *How* big?
LYSISTRATA.
　　Big enough for all of us.
KALONIKE.
　　　　　　　　But we're not all here!
LYSISTRATA.
　　We would be, if *that's* what was up!

[3]An area of the Greek coast where Aphroditê, goddess of love, had a temple.

                              No, Kalonikê,   20
this is something I've been turning over for nights,
long sleepless nights.
LYSISTRATA.
                    It must be getting worn down, then,
if you've spent so much time on it.
LYSISTRATA.
                              Worn down or not,
it comes to this: Only we women can save Greece!
KALONIKE.
Only we women? Poor Greece!
LYSISTRATA.
                              Just the same,
it's up to us. First, we must liquidate
the Peloponnesians—
KALONIKE.
                    Fun, fun!
LYSISTRATA.
                    —and then the Boiotians.[4]
KALONIKE.
Oh! But not those heavenly eels!
LYSISTRATA.
                              You needn't worry.
I'm not talking about eels.—But here's the point:
If we can get the women from those places—   30
all those Boiotians and Peloponnesians—
to join us women here, why, we can save
all Greece!
KALONIKE.
          But dearest Lysistrata!
How can women do a thing so austere, so
political? We belong at home. Our only armor's
our perfumes, our saffron dresses and
our pretty little shoes!
LYSISTRATA.
                    Exactly. Those
transparent dresses, the saffron, the
perfume, those pretty shoes—
KALONIKE.
                              Oh?
LYSISTRATA.
                              Not a single man would lift
his spear—
KALONIKE.
          I'll send my dress to the dyer's tomorrow!   40
LYSISTRATA.
     —or grab a shield—

---

[4]Inhabitants of a region opposed to Athens in the war. The area was noted for its succu-
lent eels and other seafood. Athenian sophisticates regarded Boiotia as a crude and backward
place.

KALONIKE.
       The sweetest little negligée—
LYSISTRATA.
 —or haul out his sword.
KALONIKE.
       I know where I can buy
 the dreamiest sandals!
LYSISTRATA.
      Well, so you see. Now, shouldn't
 the women have come?
KALONIKE.
      Come? They should have *flown!*
LYSISTRATA.
 Athenians are always late.
       But imagine!
There's no one here from the South Shore, or from Sálamis.[5]
KALONIKE.
 Things are hard over in Sálamis, I swear.
 They have to get going at dawn.
LYSISTRATA.
       And nobody from Acharnai.[6]
 I thought they'd be here hours ago.
KALONIKE.
      Well, you'll get
 that awful Theagenês woman;[7] she'll be   50
 a sheet or so in the wind.
      But look!
 Someone at last! Can you see who they are?

       [*Enter* MYRRHINE *and other women*]

LYSISTRATA.
 They're from Anagyros.[8]
KALONIKE.
      They certainly are.
 You'd know them anywhere, by the scent.
MYRRHINE.
 Sorry to be late, Lysistrata.
      Oh come,
 don't scowl so. Say something!
LYSISTRATA.
      My dear Myrrhinê,
 what is there to say? After all,
 you've been pretty casual about the whole thing.

[5]An island south of Greece, site of the memorable Greek naval victory over the Persians in 480. Lysistrata (whose name means "dismisser of armies") intends to gather women from Greek cities, both allied with and opposed to Athens.

[6]A town near Athens.

[7]The wife of Theagenês, a notoriously superstitious man. The phrase "a sheet or so in the wind" means drunk.

[8]A malodorous marshland.

MYRRHINE.
$$\text{Couldn't find}$$
my girdle in the dark, that's all.
$$\text{But what } is$$
'the whole thing'?
KALONIKE.
$$\text{No, we've got to wait}$$ 60
for those Boiotians and Peloponnesians.
LYSISTRATA.
That's more like it.—But, look!
Here's Lampitô!

$$[Enter \text{ LAMPITO } with \text{ } women \text{ } from$$
$$Sparta]$$

LYSISTRATA.
$$\text{Darling Lampitô,}$$
how pretty you are today! What a nice color!
Goodness, you look as though you could strangle a bull!
LAMPITO.
Ah think Ah could! It's the work-out
in the gym every day; and, of co'se that dance of ahs
where y' kick yo' own tail.[9]
KALONIKE.
$$\text{What an adorable figure!}$$
LAMPITO.
Lawdy, when y' touch me lahk that,
Ah feel lahk a heifer at the altar!
LYSISTRATA.
$$\text{And this young lady?}$$ 70
Where is she from?
LAMPITO.
$$\text{Boiotia. Social-Register type.}$$
LYSISTRATA.
Ah. 'Boiotia of the fertile plain.'
KALONIKE.
$$\text{And if you look,}$$
you'll find the fertile plain has just been mowed.
LYSISTRATA.
And this lady?
LAMPITO.
$$\text{Hagh, wahd, handsome. She comes from Korinth.}$$
KALONIKE.
High and wide's the word for it.
LAMPITO.
$$\text{Which one of you}$$
called this heah meeting, and why?

[9] The Spartans were proverbially associated with discipline and the more austere virtues. Lampito here refers to a strenuous dance performed as exercise by Spartan females. The translator renders Spartan speech as backwoods southern American because the Athenians condescendingly viewed Spartans as unsophisticated.

LYSISTRATA.

I did.

LAMPITO.

Well, then, tell us:

What's up?

MYRRHINE.

Yes, darling, what *is* on your mind, after all?

LYSISTRATA.

I'll tell you.—But first, one little question.

MYRRHINE.

Well?

LYSISTRATA.

It's your husbands. Fathers of your children. Doesn't it bother you
that they're always off with the Army? I'll stake my life,   80
not one of you has a man in the house this minute!

KALONIKE.

Mine's been in Thrace the last five months, keeping an eye
on that General.[10]

MYRRHINE.

Mine's been in Pylos for seven.

LAMPITO.

And mahn,

whenever he gets a *dis*charge, he goes raht back
with that li'l ole shield of his, and enlists again!

LYSISTRATA.

And not the ghost of a lover to be found!
From the very day the war began—

those Milesians![11]

I could skin them alive!

—I've not seen so much, even,

as one of those leather consolation prizes.—
But there! What's important is: If I've found a way   90
to end the war, are you with me?

MYRRHINE.

I should *say* so!

Even if I have to pawn my best dress and
drink up the proceeds.

KALONIKE.

Me, too! Even if they split me

right up the middle, like a flounder.

LAMPITO.

Ah'm shorely with you.

Ah'd crawl up Taÿgetos[12] on mah knees
if that'd bring peace.

---

[10]Eukrates, an Athenian commander of doubtful loyalty.
[11]Former allies of Athens who had defected shortly before *Lysistrata* was produced. The Milesians reputedly manufactured a kind of dildo, or phallic substitute.
[12]A mountain range near Sparta.

LYSISTRATA.
                    All right, then; here it is:
Women! Sisters!
If we really want our men to make peace,
we must be ready to give up—
MYRRHINE.
                        Give up what!
Quick, tell us!
LYSISTRATA.
               But *will* you?
MYRRHINE.
                   We will, even if it kills us.   100
LYSISTRATA.
Then we must give up going to bed with our men.

                  [*Long silence*]

Oh? So now you're sorry? Won't look at me?
Doubtful? Pale? All teary-eyed?
                  But come: be frank with me.
Will you do it, or not? Well? Will you do it?
MYRRHINE.
                      I couldn't. No.
Let the war go on.
KALONIKE.
             Nor I. Let the war go on.
LYSISTRATA.
You, you little flounder,
ready to be split up the middle?
KALONIKE.
                 Lysistrata, no!
I'd walk through fire for you—you *know* I would!—but don't
ask us to give up *that!* Why, there's nothing like it!
LYSISTRATA.
And you?
BOIOTIAN.
          No. I must say *I'd* rather walk through fire.   110
LYSISTRATA.
What an utterly perverted sex we women are!
No wonder poets write tragedies about us.
There's only one thing we can think of.
                  But you from Sparta:
if you stand by me, we may win yet! Will you?
It means so much!
LAMPITO.
            Ah sweah, it means *too* much!
By the Two Goddesses,[13] it does! Asking a girl
to sleep—Heaven knows how long!—in a great big bed

---

[13] Demeter, goddess of the fields and fertility, and her daughter Persephone, who was associated with both death and fertility.

with nobody there but herself! But Ah'll stay with you!
Peace comes first!

LYSISTRATA.
Spoken like a true Spartan!

KALONIKE.
But if—
oh dear!
—if we give up what you tell us to, 120
will there *be* any peace?

LYSISTRATA.
Why, mercy, of course there will!
We'll just sit snug in our very thinnest gowns,
perfumed and powdered from top to bottom, and those men
simply won't stand still! And when we say No,
they'll go out of their minds! And there's your peace.
You can take my word for it.

LAMPITO.
Ah seem to remember
that Colonel Menelaos threw his sword away
when he saw Helen's breast[14] all bare.

KALONIKE.
But, goodness me!
What if they just get up and leave us?

LYSISTRATA.
In that case
we'll have to fall back on ourselves, I suppose. 130
But they won't.

KALONIKE.
I must say that's not much help. But
what if they drag us into the bedroom?

LYSISTRATA.
Hang on to the door.

KALONIKE.
What if they slap us?

LYSISTRATA.
If they do, you'd better give in.
But be sulky about it. Do I have to teach you how?
You know there's no fun for men when they have to force you.
There are millions of ways of getting them to see reason.
Don't you worry: a man
doesn't like it unless the girl co-operates.

KALONIKE.
I suppose so. Oh, all right. We'll go along.

LAMPITO.
Ah imagine us Spahtans can arrange a peace. But you 140
Athenians! Why, you're just war-mongerers!

---

[14] The reference is to Euripides' play *Andromache;* Menelaos (Menelaus), the cuckolded husband of Helen of Troy, is so struck with Helen's beauty that he abandons his plan to kill her in revenge.

LYSISTRATA.
                                                        Leave that to me.
I know how to make them listen.
LAMPITO.
                                                        Ah don't see how.
After all, they've got their boats; and there's lots of money[15]
piled up in the Akropolis.
LYSISTRATA.
                                        The Akropolis? Darling,
we're taking over the Akropolis today!
That's the older women's job. All the rest of us
are going to the Citadel to sacrifice—you understand me?
And once there, we're in for good!
LAMPITO.
                                                Whee! Up the rebels!
Ah can see you're a good strat*ee*gist.
LYSISTRATA.
                                        Well, then, Lampitô,
what we have to do now is take a solemn oath.[16]   150
LAMPITO.
Say it. We'll sweah.
LYSISTRATA.
                        This is it.
—But where's our Inner Guard?
                                        —Look, Guard: you see this shield?
Put it down here. Now bring me the victim's entrails.
KALONIKE.
But the oath?
LYSISTRATA.
                You remember how in Aischylos' *Seven*
they killed a sheep and swore on a shield? Well, then?
KALONIKE.
But I don't see how you can swear for peace on a shield.
LYSISTRATA.
What else do you suggest?
KALONIKE.
                                Why not a white horse?[17]
We could swear by that.
LYSISTRATA.
                        And where will you get a white horse?
KALONIKE.
I never thought of that. *What* can we do?

---

[15]A fund stored on the Akropolis, designed to finance the war effort.
[16]What follows is a parody of a standard ritual sacrifice and oath of loyalty.
[17]In Aeschylus' tragedy *Seven Against Thebes,* the seven leaders attacking the city take an oath on a shield. (This war provides the background of Sophocles' *Antigone.*) The reference to the white horse is possibly some kind of sexual joke, but commentators are puzzled by the phrase.

LYSISTRATA.

I have it!
Let's set this big black wine-bowl on the ground   160
and pour in a gallon or so of Thasian,[18] and swear
not to add one drop of water.

LAMPITO.

Ah lahk *that* oath!

LYSISTRATA.

Bring the bowl and the wine-jug.

KALONIKE.

Oh, what a simply *huge* one!

LYSISTRATA.

Set it down. Girls, place your hands on the gift-offering.
O Goddess of Persuasion! And thou, O Loving-cup
Look upon this our sacrifice, and
be gracious!

KALONIKE.

See the blood spill out. How red and pretty it is!

LAMPITO.

And Ah must say it smells good.

MYRRHINE.

Let me swear first!

KALONIKE.

No, by Aphroditê, we'll match for it!   170

LYSISTRATA.

Lampitô: all of you women: come, touch the bowl,
and repeat after me—remember, this is an oath—:
I WILL HAVE NOTHING TO DO WITH MY HUSBAND OR MY
    LOVER

KALONIKE.

I will have nothing to do with my husband or my lover

LYSISTRATA.

THOUGH HE COME TO ME IN PITIABLE CONDITION

KALONIKE.

Though he come to me in pitiable condition
(Oh Lysistrata! This is killing me!)

LYSISTRATA.

IN MY HOUSE I WILL BE UNTOUCHABLE

KALONIKE.

In my house I will be untouchable

LYSISTRATA.

IN MY THINNEST SAFFRON SILK   180

KALONIKE.

In my thinnest saffron silk

LYSISTRATA.

AND MAKE HIM LONG FOR ME.

KALONIKE.

And make him long for me.

---

[18]A wine of high quality.

LYSISTRATA.
  I WILL NOT GIVE MYSELF
KALONIKE.
  I will not give myself
LYSISTRATA.
  AND IF HE CONSTRAINS ME
KALONIKE.
  And if he constrains me
LYSISTRATA.
  I WILL BE COLD AS ICE AND NEVER MOVE
KALONIKE.
  I will be cold as ice and never move
LYSISTRATA.
  I WILL NOT LIFT MY SLIPPERS TOWARD THE CEILING   190
KALONIKE.
  I will not lift my slippers toward the ceiling
LYSISTRATA.
  OR CROUCH ON ALL FOURS LIKE THE LIONESS IN THE
     CARVING
KALONIKE.
  Or crouch on all fours like the lioness in the carving
LYSISTRATA.
  AND IF I KEEP THIS OATH LET ME DRINK FROM THIS
     BOWL
KALONIKE.
  And if I keep this oath let me drink from this bowl
LYSISTRATA.
  IF NOT, LET MY OWN BOWL BE FILLED WITH WATER.
KALONIKE.
  If not, let my own bowl be filled with water.
LYSISTRATA.
  You have all sworn?
MYRRHINE.
                    We have.
LYSISTRATA.
                              Then thus
  I sacrifice the victim.

                              [*Drinks largely*]

KALONIKE.
                    Save some for us!
  Here's to you, darling, and to you, and to you!   200

                         [*Loud cries off-stage*]

LAMPITO.
  What's all *that* whoozy-goozy?
LYSISTRATA.
                         Just what I told you.
  The older women have taken the Akropolis.

Now you, Lampitô,
rush back to Sparta. We'll take care of things here. Leave
these girls here for hostages.
                              The rest of you,
up to the Citadel: and mind you push in the bolts.
KALONIKE.
But the men? Won't they be after us?
LYSISTRATA.
                              Just you leave
the men to me. There's not fire enough in the world,
or threats either, to make me open these doors
except on my own terms.
KALONIKE.
                              I hope not, by Aphroditê!   210
After all,
we've got a reputation for bitchiness to live up to.

[*Exeunt*]

PÁRODOS:[19] CHORAL EPISODE

The hillside just under the Akropolis. Enter CHORUS OF OLD MEN *with burning torches and braziers; much puffing and coughing.*

KORYPHAIOS[m].
Forward march, Drakês, old friend: never you mind
that damn big log banging hell down on your back.
CHORUS[m].
There's this to be said for longevity: [STROPHE 1]
You see things you thought that you'd never see.
    Look, Strymodôros, who would have thought it?
    We've caught it—
                  the New Femininity!
The wives of our bosom, our board, our bed—
Now, by the gods, they've gone ahead   220
And taken the Citadel (Heaven knows why!),
Profanèd the sacred statuar-y,[20]
                      And barred the doors,
                      The subversive whores!
KORYPHAIOS[m].
Shake a leg there, Philûrgos, man: the Akropolis or bust!
Put the kindling around here. We'll build one almighty big
bonfire for the whole bunch of bitches, every last one;
and the first we fry will be old Lykôn's woman.[21]

---

[19] The song sung at the first entrance of the chorus. The superscripts m and w indicate division of the chorus into men and women.

[20] An old and revered wooden statue of Athêna in her role as protector of Athens.

[21] A woman noted for lax morality; here, as often elsewhere, Aristophanes refers to actual people of his time.

CHORUS[m].

[ANTISTROPHE 1]

They're not going to give me the old horse-laugh!
No, by Deméter, they won't pull this off!   230
Think of Kleómenés:[22] even he
Didn't go free
               till he brought me his stuff.
A good man he was, all stinking and shaggy,
Bare as an eel except for the bag he
Covered his rear with. God, what a mess!
Never a bath in six years, I'd guess.
               Pure Sparta, man!
               He also ran.

KORYPHAIOS[m].

That was a siege, friends! Seventeen ranks strong
we slept at the Gate. And shall we not do as much   240
against these women, whom God and Euripides[23] hate?
If we don't, I'll turn in my medals from Marathon.

CHORUS[m].

[STROPHE 2]

Onward and upward! A little push,
     And we're there.
Ouch, my shoulders! I could wish
     For a pair
Of good strong oxen. Keep your eye
On the fire there, it mustn't die.
          Akh! Akh!
The smoke would make a cadaver cough!   250

Holy Heraklês, a hot spark   [ANTISTROPHE 2]
     Bit my eye!
Damn this hellfire, damn this work!
     So say I.
Onward and upward just the same.
(Lachês, remember the Goddess: for shame!)
          Akh! Akh!
     The smoke would make a cadaver cough!

KORYPHAIOS[m].

At last (and let us give suitable thanks to God
for his infinite mercies) I have managed to bring   260
my personal flame to the common goal. It breathes, it lives.
Now, gentlemen, let us consider. Shall we insert
the torch, say, into the brazier, and thus extract
a kindling brand? And shall we then, do you think,

---

[22]A Spartan king who, in 508, had occupied the Akropolis in aid of the aristocratic party during a civil conflict in Athens. His occupation was brief, not the six years the senile chorus remembers. The reference to this incident, like the following reminiscence of the great victory at Marathon (490), would make the members of the chorus a hundred or more years old—probably a joke by Aristophanes, designed to emphasize the old men's decrepitude.

[23]Often represented by Aristophanes, perhaps only half-seriously, as a misogynist.

push on to the gate like valiant sheep? On the whole, yes.
But I would have you consider this, too: if they—
I refer to the women—should refuse to open,
what then? Do we set the doors afire
and smoke them out? At ease, men. Meditate.
Akh, the smoke! Woof! What we really need 270
is the loan of a general or two from the Samos[24] Command.
At least we've got this lumber off our backs.
That's something. And now let's look to our fire.

O Pot, brave Brazier, touch my torch with flame!
Victory, Goddess, I invoke thy name!
Strike down these paradigms of female pride,
And we shall hang our trophies up inside.

> [*Enter* CHORUS OF OLD WOMEN *on
> the walls of the Akropolis, carrying
> jars of water*]

KORYPHAIOS[W].
Smoke, girls, smoke! There's smoke all over the place!
Probably fire, too. Hurry, girls! Fire! Fire!
CHORUS[W].
                Nikodikê, run!   [STROPHE 1]   280
            Or Kalyké's done
            To a turn, and poor Kritylla's
            Smoked like a ham.
                        Damn
            These old men! Are we too late?
            I nearly died down at the place
            Where we fill our jars:
                Slaves pushing and jostling—
                Such a hustling
            I never saw in all my days.

            But here's water at last.   [ANTISTROPHE 1]   290
            Haste, sisters, haste!
            Slosh it on them, slosh it down,
            The silly old wrecks!
                        Sex
            Almighty! What they want's
            A hot bath? Good. Send one down.
            Athêna of Athens town,
                Trito-born![25] Helm of Gold!
                Cripple the old
            Firemen! Help us help them drown!

---

[24]An island near Asia Minor. At the time of the play it was the headquarters of Athenian forces.
[25]Athêna, by one account, was born near Tritonis, a lake in Libya.

[*The* OLD MEN *capture a woman,*
STRATYLLIS]

STRATYLLIS.
  Let me go! Let me go!
KORYPHAIOS^W.
                            You walking corpses,   300
  have you no shame?
KORYPHAIOS^m.
                            I wouldn't have believed it!
  An army of women in the Akropolis!
KORYPHAIOS^W.
  So we scare you, do we? Grandpa, you've seen
  only our pickets yet!
KORYPHAIOS^m.
                            Hey, Phaidrias!
  Help me with the necks of these jabbering hens!
KORYPHAIOS^W.
  Down with your pots, girls! We'll need both hands
  if these antiques attack us.
KORYPHAIOS^m.
                            Want your face kicked in?
KORYPHAIOS^W.
  Want your balls chewed off?
KORYPHAIOS^m.
                            Look out! I've got a stick!
KORYPHAIOS^W.
  You lay a half-inch of your stick on Stratyllis,
  and you'll never stick again!   310
KORYPHAIOS^m.
  Fall apart!
KORYPHAIOS^W.
                            I'll spit up your guts!
KORYPHAIOS^m.
                            Euripides! Master!
  How well you knew women!
KORYPHAIOS^W.
                            Listen to him! Rhodippê,
  up with the pots!
KORYPHAIOS^m.
                            Demolition of God,
  what good are your pots?
KORYPHAIOS^W.
                            You refugee from the tomb,
  what good is your fire?
KORYPHAIOS^m.
                            Good enough to make a pyre
  to barbecue you!
KORYPHAIOS^W.
                            We'll squizzle your kindling!

KORYPHAIOS^m.
You think so?
KORYPHAIOS^w.
Yah! Just hang around a while!
KORYPHAIOS^m.
Want a touch of my torch?
KORYPHAIOS^w.
It needs a good soaping.
KORYPHAIOS^m.
How about you?
KORYPHAIOS^w.
Soap for a senile bridegroom!
KORYPHAIOS^m.
Senile? Hold your trap!
KORYPHAIOS^w.
Just *you* try to hold it! 320
KORYPHAIOS^m.
The yammer of women!
KORYPHAIOS^w.
Oh is that so?
You're not in the jury room[26] now, you know.
KORYPHAIOS^m.
Gentlemen, I beg you, burn off that woman's hair!
KORYPHAIOS^w.
Let it come down!

[*They empty their pots on the men*]

KORYPHAIOS^m.
What a way to drown!
KORYPHAIOS^w.
Hot, hey?
KORYPHAIOS^m.
Say,
enough!
KORYPHAIOS^w.
Dandruff
needs watering. I'll make you
nice and fresh.
KORYPHAIOS^m.
For God's sake, you,
hold off!

---

[26]Elderly Athenians frequently served as jurors in law cases.

SCENE I

[*Enter a* COMMISSIONER[27] *accompanied by four constables*]

COMMISSIONER.
These degenerate women! What a racket of little drums,   330
what a yapping for Adonis on every house-top!
It's like the time in the Assembly when I was listening
to a speech—out of order, as usual—by that fool
Demostratos,[28] all about troops for Sicily,
that kind of nonsense—
                                    and there was his wife
trotting around in circles howling
Alas for Adonis!—
                          and Demostratos insisting
we must draft every last Zakynthian[29] that can walk—
and his wife up there on the roof,
drunk as an owl, yowling   340
Oh weep for Adonis!—
                                and that damned ox Demostratos
mooing away through the rumpus. That's what we get
for putting up with this wretched woman-business!
KORYPHAIOS[m].
Sir, you haven't heard the half of it. They laughed at us!
Insulted us! They took pitchers of water
and nearly drowned us! We're still wringing out our clothes,
for all the world like unhousebroken brats.
COMMISSIONER.
Serves you right, by Poseidon![30]
Whose fault is it if these women-folk of ours
get out of hand? We coddle them,   350
we teach them to be wasteful and loose. You'll see a husband
go into a jeweler's. 'Look,' he'll say,
'jeweler,' he'll say, 'you remember that gold choker
'you made for my wife? Well, she went to a dance last night
'and broke the clasp. Now, I've got to go to Sálamis,
'and can't be bothered. Run over to my house tonight,
'will you, and see if you can put it together for her.'
Or another one
goes to a cobbler—a good strong workman, too,
with an awl that was never meant for child's play. 'Here,'   360

[27]One of a group of men appointed to oversee the Athenian legislature after the defeat in Sicily.
[28]One of the most aggressive supporters of the recent disastrous campaign in Sicily. At the time the expedition set forth, the women were celebrating the rituals of Adonis, a god who represented the death-and-resurrection cycle in nature. The women's ritual laments for his death were interpreted as having put a hex on the military expedition.
[29]Dwellers on the island of Zakynthos; they were allies of Athens who, it had been hoped, would strengthen the Athenian forces in the Sicilian campaign.
[30]God of water and ocean.

he'll tell him, 'one of my wife's shoes is pinching
'her little toe. Could you come up about noon
'and stretch it out for her?'
                              Well, what do you expect?
Look at me, for example. I'm a Public Officer,
and it's one of my duties to pay off the sailors.
And where's the money? Up there in the Akropolis!
And those blasted women slam the door in my face!
But what are we waiting for?
                              —Look here, constable,
stop sniffing around for a tavern, and get us
some crowbars. We'll force their gates! As a matter of fact,   370
I'll do a little forcing myself.

> [*Enter* LYSISTRATA, *above, with*
> MYRRHINE, KALONIKE, *and the*
> BOIOTIAN]

LYSISTRATA.
                              No need of forcing.
Here I am, of my own accord. And all this talk
about locked doors—! We don't need locked doors,
but just the least bit of common sense.
COMMISSIONER.
    Is that so, ma'am!
                              —Where's my constable?
                                        —Constable,
arrest that woman, and tie her hands behind her.
LYSISTRATA.
    If he touches me, I swear by Artemis[31]
there'll be one scamp dropped from the public pay-roll tomorrow!
COMMISSIONER.
    Well, constable? You're not afraid, I suppose? Grab her,
two of you, around the middle!
KALONIKE.
                              No, by Pándrosos![32]   380
Lay a hand on her, and I'll jump on you so hard
your guts will come out the back door!
COMMISSIONER.
                              That's what *you* think!
Where's the sergeant?—Here, you: tie up that trollop first,
the one with the pretty talk!
MYRRHINE.
                              By the Moon-Goddess,
just try! They'll have to scoop you up with a spoon!

---

[31] The virgin goddess of the hunt, the moon, and childbirth. In the following lines, she is
referred to as "the Moon-Goddess" and "the Taurian."
[32] Daughter of a legendary ruler of Athens.

COMMISSIONER.
    Another one!
                            Officer, seize that woman!
                                                    I swear
    I'll put an end to this riot!
BOIOTIAN.
                            By the Taurian,
    one inch closer, you'll be one screaming bald-head!
COMMISSIONER.
    Lord, what a mess! And my constables seem ineffective.
    But—women get the best of us? By God, no!
                                            —Skythians![33]   390
    Close ranks and forward march!
LYSISTRATA.
                            'Forward,' indeed!
    By the Two Goddesses, what's the sense in *that*?
    They're up against four companies of women
    armed from top to bottom.
COMMISSIONER.
                            Forward, my Skythians!
LYSISTRATA.
    Forward, yourselves, dear comrades!
    You grainlettucebeanseedmarket girls!
    You garlicandonionbreadbakery girls!
    Give it to 'em! Knock 'em down! Scratch 'em!
    Tell 'em what you think of 'em!

                                    [*General mêlée; the Skythians yield*]

                            —Ah, that's enough!
    Sound a retreat: good soldiers don't rob the dead.   400
COMMISSIONER.
    A nice day *this* has been for the police!
LYSISTRATA.
    Well, there you are.—Did you really think we women
    would be driven like slaves? Maybe now you'll admit
    that a woman knows something about spirit.
COMMISSIONER.
                                    Spirit enough,
    especially spirits in bottles! Dear Lord Apollo!
KORYPHAIOS[m].
    Your Honor, there's no use talking to them. Words
    mean nothing whatever to wild animals like these.
    Think of the sousing they gave us! and the water
    was not, I believe, of the purest.
KORYPHAIOS[w].
    You shouldn't have come after us. And if you try it again,   410
    you'll be one eye short!—Although, as a matter of fact,

---

[33]Archers from the north who made up much of the Athenian police force.

what I like best is just to stay at home and read,
like a sweet little bride: never hurting a soul, no,
never going out. But if you *must* shake hornets' nests,
look out for the hornets.

CHORUS[m].

      Of all the beasts that God hath wrought   [STROPHE 1]
        What monster's worse than woman?
      Who shall encompass with his thought
        Their guile unending? No man.

      They've seized the Heights, the Rock, the Shrine—   420
        But to what end? I wot not.
      Sure there's some clue to their design!
        Have you the key? I thought not.

KORYPHAIOS[m].

We might question them, I suppose. But I warn you, sir,
don't believe anything you hear! It would be un-Athenian
not to get to the bottom of this plot.

COMMISSIONER.

                             Very well.
My first question is this: Why, so help you God,
did you bar the gates of the Akropolis?

LYSISTRATA.

                                Why?
To keep the money, of course. No money, no war.

COMMISSIONER.

You think that money's the cause of war?

LYSISTRATA.

                                I do.   430
Money brought about that Peisandros[34] business
and all the other attacks on the State. Well and good!
They'll not get another cent here!

COMMISSIONER.

                        And what will you do?

LYSISTRATA.

What a question! From now on, we intend
to control the Treasury.

COMMISSIONER.

                        Control the Treasury!

LYSISTRATA.

Why not? Does that seem strange? After all,
we control our household budgets.

COMMISSIONER.

                      But that's different!

LYSISTRATA.

'Different'? What do you mean?

---

[34]A corrupt and venal Athenian politician who plotted to overthrow the city's democratic regime.

COMMISSIONER.
                                    I mean simply this:
   it's the Treasury that pays for National Defense.
LYSISTRATA.
   Unnecessary. We propose to abolish war.   440
COMMISSIONER.
   Good God.—And National Security?
LYSISTRATA.
                                    Leave that to us.
COMMISSIONER.
   You?
LYSISTRATA.
      Us.
COMMISSIONER.
          We're done for, then!
LYSISTRATA.
                                    Never mind.
   We women will save you in spite of yourselves.
COMMISSIONER.
                                    What nonsense!
LYSISTRATA.
   If you like. But you must accept it, like it or not.
COMMISSIONER.
   Why, this is downright subversion!
LYSISTRATA.
                                    Maybe it is.
   But we're going to save you, Judge.
COMMISSIONER.
                                    I don't *want* to be saved.
LYSISTRATA.
   Tut. The death-wish. All the more reason.
COMMISSIONER.
                                    But the idea
   of women bothering themselves about peace and war!
LYSISTRATA.
   Will you listen to me?
COMMISSIONER.
                      Yes. But be brief, or I'll—
LYSISTRATA.
   This is no time for stupid threats.
COMMISSIONER.
                      By the gods,   450
   I can't stand any more!
AN OLD WOMAN.
                      Can't stand? Well, well.
COMMISSIONER.
   That's enough out of you, you old buzzard!
   Now, Lysistrata: tell me what you're thinking.
LYSISTRATA.
   Glad to.
          Ever since this war began

We women have been watching you men, agreeing with you,
keeping our thoughts to ourselves. That doesn't mean
we were happy: we *weren't,* for we saw how things were going;
but we'd listen to you at dinner
arguing this way and that.
                     —Oh you, and your big
Top Secrets!—
               And then we'd grin like little patriots   460
(though goodness knows we didn't feel like grinning) and ask you:
'Dear, did the Armistice come up in Assembly today?'
And you'd say, 'None of your business! Pipe down!' you'd say.
And so we would.

AN OLD WOMAN.
                I wouldn't have by God!

COMMISSIONER.
You'd have taken a beating, then!
                    —Go on.

LYSISTRATA.
Well, we'd be quiet. But then, you know, all at once
you men would think up something worse than ever.
Even *I* could see it was fatal. And, 'Darling,' I'd say,
'have you gone completely mad?' And my husband would look at
    me
and say, 'Wife, you've got your weaving to attend to.   470
'Mind your tongue, if you don't want a slap. "War's
"a man's affair"!'[35]

COMMISSIONER.
           Good words, and well pronounced.

LYSISTRATA.
You're a fool if you think so.
                 It was hard enough
to put up with all this banquet-hall strategy.
But then we'd hear you out in the public square:
'Nobody left for the draft-quota here in Athens?'
you'd say; and, 'No,' someone else would say, 'not a man!'
And so we women decided to rescue Greece.
You might as well listen to us now: you'll have to, later.

COMMISSIONER.
You rescue Greece? Absurd.

LYSISTRATA.
                You're the absurd one.   480

COMMISSIONER.
You expect me to take orders from a woman?
                      I'd die first!

---

[35] Hector addresses these last four words to his wife, Andromache, in Homer's *Iliad,*
Book VI.

LYSISTRATA.
Heavens, if that's what's bothering you, take my veil,
here, and wrap it around your poor head.
KALONIKE.
                                                    Yes,
and you can have my market-basket, too.
Go home, tighten your girdle, do the washing, mind
your beans! 'War's
a woman's affair'!
KORYPHAIOS[W].
                    Ground pitchers! Close ranks!
CHORUS[W].

                                                    [ANTISTROPHE]

                    This is a dance that I know well.
                        My knees shall never yield.
                    Wobble and creak I may, but still   490
                        I'll keep the well-fought field.

                    Valor and grace march on before,
                        Love prods us from behind.
                    Our slogan is EXCELSIOR.[36]
                        Our watchword SAVE MANKIND.
KORYPHAIOS[W].
Women, remember your grandmothers! Remember
that little old mother of yours, what a stinger she was!
On, on, never slacken. There's a strong wind astern!
LYSISTRATA.
O Erôs of delight! O Aphroditê! Kyprian![37]
If ever desire has drenched our breasts or dreamed   500
in our thighs, let it work so now on the men of Hellas
that they shall tail us through the land, slaves, slaves
to Woman, Breaker of Armies!
COMMISSIONER.
                    And if we do?
LYSISTRATA.
Well, for one thing, we shan't have to watch you
going to market, a spear in one hand, and heaven knows
what in the other.
KALONIKE.
                    Nicely said, by Aphroditê!
LYSISTRATA.
As things stand now, you're neither men nor women.
Armor clanking with kitchen pans and pots—
you sound like a pack of Korybantês![38]
COMMISSIONER.
A man must do what a man must do.

---

[36]A Latin motto meaning, roughly, "On to nobler things," or, literally, "higher."
[37]Erôs, Aphroditê, and Kyprian are names for the god and goddess of love.
[38]Devotees of the earth goddess Cybele, whose rites included frenzied dancing and music.

LYSISTRATA.

So I'm told. 510
But to see a General, complete with Gorgon-shield,[39]
jingling along the dock to buy a couple of herrings!

KALONIKE.

I saw a Captain the other day—lovely fellow he was,
nice curly hair—sitting on his horse; and—can you believe it?—
he'd just bought some soup, and was pouring it into his helmet!
And there was a soldier from Thrace
swishing his lance like something out of Euripides,
and the poor fruit-store woman got so scared
that she ran away and let him have his figs free!

COMMISSIONER.

All this is beside the point.

Will you be so kind 520
as to tell me how you mean to save Greece?

LYSISTRATA.

Of course.
Nothing could be simpler.

COMMISSIONER.

I assure you, I'm all ears.

LYSISTRATA.

Do you know anything about weaving?
Say the yarn gets tangled: we thread it
this way and that through the skein, up and down,
until it's free. And it's like that with war.
We'll send our envoys
up and down, this way and that, all over Greece,
until it's finished.

COMMISSIONER.

Yarn? Thread? Skein?
Are you out of your mind? I tell you, 530
war is a serious business.

LYSISTRATA.

So serious
that I'd like to go on talking about weaving.

COMMISSIONER.

All right. Go ahead.

LYSISTRATA.

The first thing we have to do
is to wash our yarn, get the dirt out of it.
You see? Isn't there too much dirt here in Athens?
You must wash those men away.
Then our spoiled wool—
that's like your job-hunters, out for a life
of no work and big pay. Back to the basket,

---

[39] The Gorgon's head, in myth, turned gazers to stone; it was therefore a common design on warriors' shields.

citizens or not, allies or not,
or friendly immigrants.
                            And your colonies?   540
Hanks of wool lost in various places. Pull them
together, weave them into one great whole,
and our voters are clothed for ever.
COMMISSIONER.
                            It would take a woman
to reduce state questions to a matter of carding and weaving.
LYSISTRATA.
You fool! Who were the mothers whose sons sailed off
to fight for Athens in Sicily?
COMMISSIONER.
                            Enough!
I beg you, do not call back those memories.
LYSISTRATA.
                            And then,
instead of the love that every woman needs,
we have only our single beds, where we can dream
of our husbands off with the Army.
                            Bad enough for wives!   550
But what about our girls, getting older every day,
and older, and no kisses?
COMMISSIONER.
                            Men get older, too.
LYSISTRATA.
Not in the same sense.
                            A soldier's discharged,
and he may be bald and toothless, yet he'll find
a pretty young thing to go to bed with.
                                        But a woman!
Her beauty is gone with the first grey hair.
She can spend her time
consulting the oracles and the fortune-tellers,
but they'll never send her a husband.
COMMISSIONER.
Still, if a man can rise to the occasion—   560
LYSISTRATA.
Rise? Rise, yourself!

                            [*Furiously*]

Go invest in a coffin!
                    You've money enough.
                                        I'll bake you
a cake[40] for the Underworld.

---

[40] Part of the customary funeral ritual; a honey cake was the offering with which the dead
person was to propitiate Cerberus, the monster dog who guarded the Underworld, or realm
of the dead.

And here's your funeral
wreath!

[*She pours water upon him*]

MYRRHINE.
And here's another!

[*More water*]

KALONIKE.
And here's
my contribution!

[*More water*]

LYSISTRATA.
What are you waiting for?
All aboard Styx Ferry![41]
Charôn's calling for you!
It's sailing-time: don't disrupt the schedule!
COMMISSIONER.
The insolence of women! And to me!
No, by God, I'll go back to town and show   570
the rest of the Commission what might happen to them.

[*Exit* COMMISSIONER]

LYSISTRATA.
Really, I suppose we should have laid out his corpse
on the doorstep, in the usual way.
But never mind.
We'll give him the rites of the dead tomorrow morning.

[*Exit* LYSISTRATA *with* MYRRHINE
and KALONIKE]

PARÁBASIS:[42] CHORAL EPISODE

KORYPHAIOS[m].

[ODE 1]
Sons of Liberty, awake! The day of glory is at hand.
CHORUS[m].
I smell tyranny afoot, I smell it rising from the land.
I scent a trace of Hippias,[43] I sniff upon the breeze
A dismal Spartan hogo that suggests King Kleisthenês.[44]

---

[41] The dead were ferried by the boatman Charôn across the river Styx to the Underworld.
[42] An address to the audience by the chorus.
[43] The last of the Athenian tyrants; he ruled about a century before the present action.
[44] A notoriously effeminate bisexual.

Strip, strip for action, brothers!
Our wives, aunts, sisters, mothers   580
Have sold us out: the streets are full of godless female rages.
Shall we stand by and let our women confiscate our wages?[45]
KORYPHAIOS[m].

[EPIRRHEMA[46] 1]

Gentlemen, it's a disgrace to Athens, a disgrace
to all that Athens stands for, if we allow these grandmas
to jabber about spears and shields and making friends
with the Spartans. What's a Spartan? Give me a wild wolf
any day. No. They want the Tyranny back, I suppose.
Are we going to take that? No. Let us look like
the innocent serpent, but be the flower under it,
as the poet sings. And just to begin with,   590
I propose to poke a number of teeth
down the gullet of that harridan[47] over there.
KORYPHAIOS[w].

[ANTODE 1]

Oh, is that so? When you get home, your own mammá won't know
    you!
CHORUS[w].
Who do you think we are, you senile bravos? Well, I'll show you.
I bore the sacred vessels[48] in my eighth year, and at ten
I was pounding out the barley for Athêna Goddess; then
    They made me Little Bear
    At the Braunonian Fair;
I'd held the Holy Basket by the time I was of age,
The Blessed Dry Figs had adorned my plump décolletage.   600
KORYPHAIOS[w].

[ANTEPIRRHEMA 1]

A 'disgrace to Athens', am I, just at the moment
I'm giving Athens the best advice she ever had?
Don't I pay taxes to the State? Yes, I pay them
in baby boys. And what do you contribute,
you impotent horrors? Nothing but waste: all
our Treasury,[49] dating back to the Persian Wars,
gone! rifled! And not a penny out of your pockets!
Well, then? Can you cough up an answer to that?
Look out for your own gullet, or you'll get a crack
from this old brogan that'll make your teeth see stars!   610

---

[45] The fund from which the elderly jurors' fees were paid was kept at the Akropolis.

[46] Along with the following "Antode" and "Antepirrhema," this section is a choral song that customarily made a satiric comment on current events.

[47] A sharp-tongued old woman.

[48] In the following lines, the women describe various roles in the rites of Athêna and Artemis. Selected preadolescent Athenian girls of good family were privileged to perform these roles.

[49] A fund originally established in the days of Greek unity to finance the war against Persia; the money had since been misappropriated by unscrupulous politicians.

CHORUS[m].

Oh insolence! [ODE 2]
Am I unmanned?
Incontinence!
Shall my scarred hand
Strike never a blow
To curb this flow-
ing female curse?

Leipsydrion![50]
Shall I betray
The laurels won 620
On that great day?
Come, shake a leg,
Shed old age, beg
The years reverse!

KORYPHAIOS[m.]

[EPIRRHEMA 2]
Give them an inch, and we're done for! We'll have them
launching boats next and planning naval strategy,
sailing down on us like so many Artemisias.[51]
Or maybe they have ideas about the cavalry.
That's fair enough, women are certainly good
in the saddle. Just look at Mikôn's paintings, 630
all those Amazons[52] wrestling with all those men!
On the whole, a straitjacket's their best uniform.

CHORUS[w].

Tangle with me, [ANTODE 2]
And you'll get cramps.
Ferocity
's no use now, Gramps!
By the Two,
I'll get through
To you wrecks yet!

I'll scramble your eggs, 640
I'll burn your beans,
With my two legs.
You'll see such scenes
As never yet
Your two eyes met.
A curse? You bet!

KORYPHAIOS[w].

[ANTEPIRRHEMA 2]
If Lampitô stands by me, and that delicious Theban girl,

---

[50]Another site of patriotic Athenian heroism from the great days (in this instance about a
century earlier) of the city's fight against tyranny.
[51]A queen who had commanded a naval unit in the Persian war against Greece.
[52]Fabled women warriors; Mikôn was a famous contemporary painter.

Ismênia—what good are *you?* You and your seven
Resolutions! Resolutions? Rationing Boiotian eels
and making our girls go without them at Hekatê's Feast!   650
That was statesmanship! And we'll have to put up with it
and all the rest of your decrepit legislation
until some patriot—God give him strength!—
grabs you by the neck and kicks you off the Rock.

SCENE II

[*Re-enter* LYSISTRATA *and her lieutenants*]

KORYPHAIOS[W] [*Tragic tone*].
      Great Queen, fair Architect of our emprise,
      Why lookst thou on us with foreboding eyes?
LYSISTRATA.
      The behavior of these idiotic women!
      There's something about the female temperament
      that I can't bear!
KORYPHAIOS[W].
                        What in the world do you mean?
LYSISTRATA.
      Exactly what I say.
KORYPHAIOS[W].
                        What dreadful thing has happened?   660
      Come, tell us: we're all your friends.
LYSISTRATA.
                                          It isn't easy
      to say it; yet, God knows, we can't hush it up.
KORYPHAIOS[W].
      Well, then? Out with it!
LYSISTRATA.
                        To put it bluntly,
      we're dying to get laid.
KORYPHAIOS[W].
                        Almighty God!
LYSISTRATA.
      Why bring God into it?—No, it's just as I say.
      I can't manage them any longer: they've gone man-crazy,
      they're all trying to get out.
                        Why, look:
      one of them was sneaking out the back door
      over there by Pan's cave; another
      was sliding down the walls with rope and tackle;   670
      another was climbing aboard a sparrow,[53] ready to take off
      for the nearest brothel—I dragged *her* back by the hair!

[53] The bird was associated with Aphroditê, goddess of love.

They're all finding some reason to leave.
                                                 Look there!
There goes another one.
                              —Just a minute, you!
Where are you off to so fast?
FIRST WOMAN.
                                  I've got to get home.
I've a lot of Milesian wool, and the worms are spoiling it.
LYSISTRATA.
    Oh bother you and your worms! Get back inside!
FIRST WOMAN.
    I'll be back right away, I swear I will.
    I just want to get it stretched out on my bed.
LYSISTRATA.
    You'll do no such thing. You'll stay right here.
FIRST WOMAN.
                                          And my wool?   680
You want it ruined?
LYSISTRATA.
                          Yes, for all I care.
SECOND WOMAN.
    Oh dear! My lovely new flax from Amorgos[54]—
    I left it at home, all uncarded!
LYSISTRATA.
                             Another one!
And all she wants is someone to card her flax.
Get back in there!
SECOND WOMAN.
                        But I swear by the Moon-Goddess,
the minute I get it done, I'll be back!
LYSISTRATA.
                                I say No.
If you, why not all the other women as well?
THIRD WOMAN.
    O Lady Eileithyia![55] Radiant goddess! Thou
intercessor for women in childbirth! Stay, I pray thee,
oh stay this parturition. Shall I pollute   690
a sacred spot?
LYSISTRATA.
                      And what's the matter with *you?*
THIRD WOMAN.
    I'm having a baby—any minute now.
LYSISTRATA.
    But you weren't pregnant yesterday.

---

[54]An Aegean island noted for the excellence of its flax.
[55]A goddess of childbirth. To give birth in the precincts of the Akropolis would be sacrl-
legious.

THIRD WOMAN.
                                        Well, I am today.
Let me go home for a midwife, Lysistrata:
there's not much time.
LYSISTRATA.
                        I never heard such nonsense.
What's that bulging under your cloak?
THIRD WOMAN.
                                        A little baby boy.

LYSISTRATA.
    It certainly isn't. But it's something hollow,
    like a basin or—Why, it's the helmet of Athêna!
    And you said you were having a baby.
THIRD WOMAN.
                                        Well, I am! So there!

LYSISTRATA.
    Then why the helmet?
THIRD WOMAN.
                        I was afraid that my pains   700
    might begin here in the Akropolis; and I wanted
    to drop my chick into it, just as the dear doves do.
LYSISTRATA.
    Lies! Evasions!—But at least one thing's clear:
    you can't leave the place before your purification.
THIRD WOMAN.
    But I can't stay here in the Akropolis! Last night I dreamed
    of the Snake.[56]
FIRST WOMAN.
            And those horrible owls,[57] the noise they make!
    I can't get a bit of sleep; I'm just about dead.
LYSISTRATA.
    You useless girls, that's enough: Let's have no more lying.
    Of course you want your men. But don't you imagine
    that they want you just as much? I'll give you my word,   710
    their nights must be pretty hard.
                                Just stick it out!
    A little patience, that's all, and our battle's won.
    I have heard an Oracle. Should you like to hear it?
FIRST WOMAN.
    An Oracle? Yes, tell us!
LYSISTRATA.
                        Here is what it says:
WHEN SWALLOWS SHALL THE HOOPOE[58] SHUN
    AND SPURN HIS HOT DESIRE,
ZEUS WILL PERFECT WHAT THEY'VE BEGUN
    AND SET THE LOWER HIGHER.

---

[56] Though never seen, this mythical snake was considered the guardian of Athêna's temple on the Akropolis.
[57] Birds sacred to Athena.
[58] A bird, here identified with the male sex.

FIRST WOMAN.
Does that mean we'll be on top?
LYSISTRATA.
BUT IF THE SWALLOWS SHALL FALL OUT 720
AND TAKE THE HOOPOE'S BAIT,
A CURSE MUST MARK THEIR HOUR OF DOUBT,
INFAMY SEAL THEIR FATE.
THIRD WOMAN.
I swear, *that* Oracle's all too clear.
FIRST WOMAN.
Oh the dear gods!
LYSISTRATA.
Let's not be downhearted, girls. Back to our places!
The god has spoken. How can we possibly fail him?

[*Exit* LYSISTRATA *with the dissident
women*]

CHORAL EPISODE

CHORUS[m].

[STROPHE]
I know a little story that I learned way back in school
Goes like this:
Once upon a time there was a young man—and no fool—
Named Melanion;[59] and his 730
One aversi-on was marriage. He loathed the very thought.
So he ran off to the hills, and in a special grot
Raised a dog, and spent his days
Hunting rabbits. And it says
That he never never never did come home.
It might be called a refuge *from* the womb.
All right,
all right,
all right!
We're as bright as young Melanion, and we hate the very sight
Of you women!
A MAN.
How about a kiss, old lady? 740
A WOMAN.
Here's an onion for your eye!
A MAN.
A kick in the guts, then?
A WOMAN.
Try, old bristle-tail, just try!

---

[59]An obscure personage; in this context, he is a kind of male equivalent of Artemis, the
determinedly virgin goddess of the hunt.

A MAN.
    Yet they say Myronidês[60]
    On hands and knees
    Looked just as shaggy fore and aft as I!
CHORUS[W].

                                                    [ANTISTROPHE]
    Well, *I* know a little story, and it's just as good as yours.
    Goes like this:
    Once there was a man named Timon[61]—a rough diamond, of
        course,
    And that whiskery face of his   750
    Looked like murder in the shrubbery. By God, he was a son
    Of the Furies, let me tell you! And what did he do but run
    From the world and all its ways,
    Cursing mankind! And it says
    That his choicest execrations as of then
    Were leveled almost wholly at *old* men.
    All right,
            all right,
                    all right!
    But there's one thing about Timon: he could always stand the
        sight
    Of us women.
A WOMAN.
    How about a crack in the jaw, Pop?   760
A MAN.
    I can take it, Ma—no fear!
A WOMAN.
    How about a kick in the face?
A MAN.
    You'd reveal your old caboose?
A WOMAN.
    What I'd show
    I'll have you know,
    Is an instrument you're too far gone to use.

                            SCENE III

[*Re-enter* LYSISTRATA]

LYSISTRATA.
    Oh, quick, girls, quick! Come here!
A WOMAN.
                                    What is it?

___

[60]An Athenian general.
[61]A noted misanthrope (the titular character of one of Shakespeare's plays). The women
choose here to present him as an enemy to males rather than to humankind.

LYSISTRATA.

A man.

A man simply bulging with love.

O Kyprian Queen,[62]

O Paphian, O Kythereian! Hear us and aid us!

A WOMAN.

Where is this enemy?

LYSISTRATA.

Over there, by Demêter's shrine. 770

A WOMAN.

Damned if he isn't. But who *is* he?

MYRRHINE.

My husband.

Kinêsias.

LYSISTRATA.

Oh then, get busy! Tease him! Undermine him!
Wreck him! Give him everything—kissing, tickling, nudging,
whatever you generally torture him with—: give him everything
except what we swore on the wine we would not give.

MYRRHINE.

Trust me.

LYSISTRATA.

I do. But I'll help you get him started.
The rest of you women, stay back.

[*Enter* KINESIAS]

KINESIAS.

Oh God! Oh my God!
I'm stiff from lack of exercise. All I can do to stand up.

LYSISTRATA.

Halt! Who are you, approaching our lines?

KINESIAS.

Me? I.

LYSISTRATA.

A man?

KINESIAS.

You have eyes, haven't you?

LYSISTRATA.

Go away. 780

KINESIAS.

Who says so?

LYSISTRATA.

Officer of the Day.

KINESIAS.

Officer, I beg you,
by all the gods at once, bring Myrrhinê out.

---

[62]*Kyprian* and the names in the following line are epithets for Aphroditê, goddess of love.

LYSISTRATA.
  Myrrhinê? And who, my good sir, are you?
KINESIAS.
  Kinêsias. Last name's Pennison. Her husband.
LYSISTRATA.
  Oh, of course. I beg your pardon. We're glad to see you.
  We've heard so much about you. Dearest Myrrhinê
  is always talking about 'Kinêsias'—never nibbles an egg
  or an apple without saying
  'Here's to Kinêsias!'
KINESIAS.
                      Do you really mean it?
LYSISTRATA.
                                              I do.
  When we're discussing men, she always says   790
  'Well, after all, there's nobody like Kinêsias!'
KINESIAS.
  Good God.—Well, then, please send her down here.
LYSISTRATA.
  And what do *I* get out of it?
KINESIAS.
                      A standing promise.
LYSISTRATA.
  I'll take it up with her.

                                      [*Exit* LYSISTRATA]

KINESIAS.
                      But be quick about it!
  Lord, what's life without a wife? Can't eat. Can't sleep.
  Every time I go home, the place is so empty, so
  insufferably sad. Love's killing me. Oh,
  hurry!

                          [*Enter* MANES, *a slave, with* KINES-
                          IAS' *baby; the voice of* MYRRHINE *is
                          heard off-stage.*]

MYRRHINE.
      But of course I love him! Adore him!—But no,
  he hates love. No. I won't go down.

                          [*Enter* MYRRHINE, *above*]

KINESIAS.
                      Myrrhinê!
  Darlingest Myrrhinette! Come down quick!   800
MYRRHINE.
  Certainly not.
KINESIAS.
              Not? But why, Myrrhinê?

MYRRHINE.
Why? You don't need me.
KINESIAS.
Need you? My God, *look* at me!
MYRRHINE.
So long!

[*Turns to go*]

KINESIAS.
Myrrhinê, Myrrhinê, Myrrhinê!
If not for my sake, for our child!

[*Pinches* BABY]

—All right, you: pipe up!

BABY.
Mummie! Mummie! Mummie!
KINESIAS.
You hear that?
Pitiful, I call it. Six days now
with never a bath; no food; enough to break your heart!
MYRRHINE.
My darlingest child! What a father *you* acquired!
KINESIAS.
At least come down for his sake.
MYRRHINE.
I suppose I must.
Oh, this mother business!

[*Exit*]

KINESIAS.
How pretty she is! And younger!   810
The harder she treats me, the more bothered I get.

[MYRRHINE *enters, below*]

MYRRHINE.
Dearest child,
you're as sweet as your father's horrid. Give me a kiss.
KINESIAS.
Now don't you see how wrong it was to get involved
in this scheming League of women? It's bad
for us both.
MYRRHINE.
Keep your hands to yourself!
KINESIAS.
But our house
going to rack and ruin?
MYRRHINE.
I don't care.

KINESIAS.
                              And your knitting
all torn to pieces by the chickens? Don't you care?
MYRRHINE.
    Not at all.
KINESIAS.
          And our debt to Aphroditê?
    Oh, *won't* you come back?
MYRRHINE.
                         No.—At least, not until you men
    make a treaty and stop this war.
KINESIAS.
                              Why, I suppose   820
    that might be arranged.
MYRRHINE.
                    Oh? Well, I suppose
    I might come down then. But meanwhile,
    I've sworn not to.
KINESIAS.
                Don't worry.—Now, let's have fun.
MYRRHINE.
    No! Stop it! I said no!
                    —Although, of course,
    I *do* love you.
KINESIAS.
              I know you do. Darling Myrrhinê:
    come, shall we?
MYRRHINE.
                Are you out of your mind? In front of the child?
KINESIAS.
    Take him home, Manês.

                    [*Exit* MANES *with* BABY]

          There. He's gone.
                    Come on!
    There's nothing to stop us now.
MYRRHINE.
                         You devil! But where?
KINESIAS.
    In Pan's cave. What could be snugger than that?
MYRRHINE.
    But my purification before I go back to the Citadel?   830
KINESIAS.
    Wash in the Klepsydra.[63]
MYRRHINE.
                And my oath?

---

[63]A spring on the Akropolis.

KINESIAS.
                                        Leave the oath to me.
After all, I'm the man.
MYRRHINE.
                        Well . . . if you say so.
                                        I'll go find a bed.
KINESIAS.
Oh, bother a bed! The ground's good enough for me.
MYRRHINE.
No. You're a bad man, but you deserve something better than dirt.

[*Exit* MYRRHINE]

KINESIAS.
What a love she is! and how thoughtful!

[*Re-enter* MYRRHINE]

MYRRHINE.
                                        Here's your bed.
Now let me get my clothes off.
                                But, good horrors!
We haven't a mattress.
KINESIAS.
                        Oh, forget the mattress!
MYRRHINE.
                                                No.
Just lying on blankets? Too sordid.
KINESIAS.
                                Give me a kiss.
MYRRHINE.
Just a second.

[*Exit* MYRRHINE]

KINESIAS.
                I swear, I'll explode!

[*Re-enter* MYRRHINE]

MYRRHINE.
                                Here's your mattress.
I'll just take my dress off.
                        But look—   840
where's our pillow?
KINESIAS.
                I don't *need* a pillow!
MYRRHINE.
                                        Well, *I* do.

[*Exit* MYRRHINE]

KINESIAS.
I don't suppose even Heraklês[64]
would stand for this!

[*Re-enter* MYRRHINE]

MYRRHINE.
There we are. Ups-a-daisy!
KINESIAS.
So we are. Well, come to bed.
MYRRHINE.
But I wonder:
is everything ready now?
KINESIAS.
I can swear to that. Come, darling!
MYRRHINE.
Just getting out of my girdle.
But remember, now,
what you promised about the treaty.
KINESIAS.
Yes, yes, yes!
MYRRHINE.
But no coverlet!
KINESIAS.
Damn it, I'll be
your coverlet!
MYRRHINE.
Be right back.

[*Exit* MYRRHINE]

KINESIAS.
This girl and her coverlets
will be the death of me.

[*Re-enter* MYRRHINE]

MYRRHINE.
Here we are. Up you go!   850
KINESIAS.
Up? I've been up for ages.
MYRRHINE.
Some perfume?
KINESIAS.
No, by Apollo!
MYRRHINE.
Yes, by Aphroditê!
I don't care whether you want it or not.

[64]A lustful womanizer, Heraklês (Hercules) could also be chivalrous and even self-abasing in his relations with women.

[*Exit* MYRRHINE]

KINESIAS.
For love's sake, hurry!

[*Re-enter* MYRRHINE]

MYRRHINE.
Here, in your hand. Rub it right in.
KINESIAS.
                              Never cared for perfume.
And this is particularly strong. Still, here goes.
MYRRHINE.
What a nitwit I am! I brought you the Rhodian bottle.
KINESIAS.
Forget it.
MYRRHINE.
          No trouble at all. You just wait here.

[*Exit* MYRRHINE]

KINESIAS.
God damn the man who invented perfume!

[*Re-enter* MYRRHINE]

MYRRHINE.
At last! The right bottle!
KINESIAS.
                    I've got the rightest   860
bottle of all, and it's right here waiting for you.
Darling, forget everything else. Do come to bed.
MYRRHINE.
Just let me get my shoes off.
                              —And, by the way,
you'll vote for the treaty?
KINESIAS.
                    I'll think about it.

[MYRRHINE *runs away*]

There! That's done it! The damned woman,
she gets me all bothered, she half kills me,
and she runs! What'll I do? Where
can I get laid?
                —And you, little prodding pal,
who's going to take care of *you?* No, you and I
had better get down to old Foxdog's[65] Nursing Clinic.   870

---

[65]A well-known pimp.

CHORUS^m.
>   Alas for the woes of man, alas
>   Specifically for you.
>   She's brought you to a pretty pass:
>   What are you going to do?
>   Split, heart! Sag, flesh! Proud spirit, crack!
>   Myrrhinê's got you on your back.

KINESIAS.
>   The agony, the protraction!

KORYPHAIOS^m.
>   Friend,
>   What woman's worth a damn?
>   They bitch us all, world without end.

KINESIAS.
>   Yet they're so damned sweet, man!   880

KORYPHAIOS^m.
>   Calamitous, that's what I say.
>   You should have learned that much today.

CHORUS^m.
>   O blessed Zeus, roll womankind
>   Up into one great ball;
>   Blast them aloft on a high wind,
>   And once there, let them fall.
>   Down, down they'll come, the pretty dears,
>   And split themselves on our thick spears.

>   [*Exit* KINESIAS]

SCENE IV

[*Enter a* SPARTAN HERALD]

HERALD.
>   Gentlemen, Ah beg you will be so kind
>   as to direct me to the Central Committee.   890
>   Ah have a communication.

>   [*Re-enter* COMMISSIONER]

COMMISSIONER.
>   Are you a man,
>   or a fertility symbol?

HERALD.
>   Ah refuse to answer that question!
>   Ah'm a certified herald from Spahta, and Ah've come
>   to talk about an ahmistice.

COMMISSIONER.
>   Then why
>   that spear under your cloak?

HERALD.
                    Ah have no speah!
COMMISSIONER.
    You don't walk naturally, with your tunic
    poked out so. You have a tumor, maybe,
    or a hernia?
HERALD.
              You lost yo' mahnd, man?
COMMISSIONER.
                              Well,
    something's up, I can see that. And I don't like it.
HERALD.
    Colonel, Ah resent this.
COMMISSIONER.
                    So I see. But what *is* it?
HERALD.
                              A staff   900
    with a message from Spahta.
COMMISSIONER.
                    Oh. I know about those staffs.[66]
    Well, then, man, speak out: How are things in Sparta?
HERALD.
    Hahd, Colonel, hahd! We're at a standstill.
    Cain't seem to think of anything but women.
COMMISSIONER.
    How curious! Tell me, do you Spartans think
    that maybe Pan's[67] to blame?
HERALD.
    Pan? No. Lampitô and her little naked friends.
    They won't let a man come nigh them.
COMMISSIONER.
    How are you handling it?
HERALD.
                    Losing our mahnds,
    if y' want to know, and walking around hunched over   910
    lahk men carrying candles in a gale.
    The women have swohn they'll have nothing to do with us
    until we get a treaty.
COMMISSIONER.
              Yes, I know.
    It's a general uprising, sir, in all parts of Greece.
    But as for the answer—
              Sir: go back to Sparta
    and have them send us your Armistice Commission.

---

[66] The pun alludes to a Spartan method of cryptography: a message was written on fabric wound around a staff (like an overlapping bandage). It was then unwound, despatched by messenger, and rewound on a staff identical in shape with the sender's. Only then could the scrambled lines of writing be realigned to make sense.
[67] The nature god Pan was held accountable for sudden and inexplicable fits of madness, or "panic." The god could also cause sexual excesses.

I'll arrange things in Athens.
                                            And I may say
that my standing is good enough to make them listen.
HERALD.
A man after mah own haht! Seh, Ah thank you.

[*Exit* HERALD]

CHORAL EPISODE

CHORUS^m.
                    Oh these women! Where will you find   [STROPHE]   920
                    A slavering beast that's more unkind?
                      Where a hotter fire?
                    Give me a panther, any day.
                    He's not so merciless as they,
                      And panthers don't conspire.
CHORUS^w.
                    We may be hard, you silly old ass,   [ANTISTROPHE]
                    But who brought you to this stupid pass?
                      You're the ones to blame.
                    Fighting with us, your oldest friends,
                    Simply to serve your selfish ends—   930
                      Really, you have no shame!
KORYPHAIOS^m.
No, I'm through with women for ever.
KORYPHAIOS^w.
                                            If you say so.
Still, you might put some clothes on. You look too absurd
standing around naked. Come, get into this cloak.
KORYPHAIOS^m.
Thank you; you're right. I merely took it off
because I was in such a temper.
KORYPHAIOS^w.
                                            That's much better.
Now you resemble a man again.
                              Why have you been so horrid?
And look: there's some sort of insect in your eye.
Shall I take it out?
KORYPHAIOS^m.
                    An insect, is it? So that's
what's been bothering me. Lord, yes: take it out!   940
KORYPHAIOS^w.
You might be more polite.
                              —But, heavens!
What an enormous mosquito!
KORYPHAIOS^m.
                              You've saved my life.

That mosquito was drilling an artesian well
In my left eye.
KORYPHAIOS[w].
                    Let me wipe
those tears away.—And now: one little kiss?
KORYPHAIOS[m].
No, no kisses.
KORYPHAIOS[w].
                    You're so difficult.
KORYPHAIOS[m].
You impossible women! How you do get around us!
The poet was right: Can't live with you, or without you.
But let's be friends.
And to celebrate, you might join us in an Ode.   950
CHORUS[m and w].
                    Let it never be said   [STROPHE 1]
                    That my tongue is malicious:
                    Both by word and by deed
I would set an example that's noble and gracious.
                    We've had sorrow and care
                    Till we're sick of the tune.
                    Is there anyone here
                    Who would like a small loan?
                        My purse is crammed,
                        As you'll soon find;   960
And you needn't pay me back if the Peace gets signed.

                    I've invited to lunch   [STROPHE 2]
                    Some Karystian rips[68]—
                    An esurient bunch,
But I've ordered a menu to water their lips.
                    I can still make soup
                    And slaughter a pig.
                    You're all coming, I hope?
                    But a bath first, I beg!
                        Walk right up   970
                        As though you owned the place,
And you'll get the front door slammed to in your face.

                        SCENE V

[*Enter* SPARTAN AMBASSADOR, *with entourage*]

KORYPHAIOS[m].
The Commission has arrived from Sparta.
                                        How oddly
they're walking!

---

[68] People from Karystos, allied with Athens. They were considered uninhibited and morally loose.

                    Gentlemen, welcome to Athens!
How is life in Lakonia?[69]
AMBASSADOR.
                              Need we discuss that?
Simply use your eyes.
CHORUS[m].
                              The poor man's right:
                              What a sight!
AMBASSADOR.
                                        Words fail me.
But come, gentlemen, call in your Commissioners,
and let's get down to a Peace.
CHORAGOS[m].
                                        The state we're in! Can't bear
a stitch below the waist. It's a kind of pelvic   980
paralysis.
COMMISSIONER.
            Won't somebody call Lysistrata?—Gentlemen,
we're no better off than you.
AMBASSADOR.
                              So I see.
A SPARTAN.
Seh, do y'all feel a certain strain
early in the morning?
AN ATHENIAN.
                    I do, sir. It's worse than a strain.
A few more days, and there's nothing for us but Kleisthenês,
that broken blossom.
CHORAGOS[m].
                    But you'd better get dressed again.
You know these people going around Athens with chisels,
looking for statues of Hermês.[70]
ATHENIAN.
                              Sir, you are right.
SPARTAN.
He certainly is! Ah'll put mah own clothes back on.

                              [*Enter* ATHENIAN COMMISSIONERS]

COMMISSIONER.
Gentlemen from Sparta, welcome. This is a sorry business.   990
SPARTAN.   [*To one of his own group*]:
Colonel, we got dressed just in time. Ah sweah,
if they'd seen us the way we were, there'd have been a new wah
between the states.

---

[69] The southern area of Greece. Sparta was its most important city.
[70] Opponents of the expedition to Sicily had mutilated these phallic statues (commonly
located in front of homes) just before the fleet set sail. Some Athenians believed that the van-
dalism had jinxed the Sicilian campaign.

COMMISSIONER.
Shall we call the meeting to order?
                              Now, Lakonians,
what's your proposal?
AMBASSADOR.
                    We propose to consider peace.
COMMISSIONER.
Good. That's on our minds, too.
                              —Summon Lysistrata.
We'll never get anywhere without her.
AMBASSADOR.
                                        Lysistrata?
Summon Lysis-*any*body! Only, summon!
KORYPHAIOS[m].
                              No need to summon:
here she is, herself.

[*Enter* LYSISTRATA]

COMMISSIONER.
                    Lysistrata! Lion of women!
This is your hour to be   1000
hard and yielding, outspoken and shy, austere and
gentle. You see here
the best brains of Hellas (confused, I admit,
by your devious charming) met as one man
to turn the future over to you.
LYSISTRATA.
                              That's fair enough,
unless you men take it into your heads
to turn to each other instead of to us. But I'd know
soon enough if you did.
                    —Where is Reconciliation?
Go, some of you: bring her here.

[*Exeunt two women*]

                    And now, women,
lead the Spartan delegates to me: not roughly   1010
or insultingly, as our men handle them, but gently,
politely, as ladies should. Take them by the hand,
or by anything else if they won't give you their hands.

[*The* SPARTANS *are escorted over*]

There.—The Athenians next, by any convenient handle.

[*The* ATHENIANS *are escorted*]

Stand there, please.—Now, all of you, listen to me.

[*During the following speech the
two women re-enter, carrying an enormous statue of a naked girl; this is*
RECONCILIATION.]

I'm only a woman, I know; but I've a mind,
and, I think, not a bad one: I owe it to my father
and to listening to the local politicians.
So much for that.
                    Now, gentlemen,
since I have you here, I intend to give you a scolding.   1020
We are all Greeks.
Must I remind you of Thermopylai, of Olympia,
of Delphoi?[71] names deep in all our hearts?
Are they not a common heritage?
                              Yet you men
go raiding through the country from both sides,
Greek killing Greek, storming down Greek cities—
and all the time the Barbarian[72] across the sea
is waiting for his chance!
                    —That's my first point.
AN ATHENIAN.
Lord! I can hardly contain myself.
LYSISTRATA.
                         As for you Spartans:
Was it so long ago that Perikleidês[73]   1030
came here to beg our help? I can see him still,
his grey face, his sombre gown. And what did he want?
An army from Athens. All Messênê
was hot at your heels, and the sea-god splitting your land.
Well, Kimôn and his men,
four thousand strong, marched out and saved all Sparta.
And what thanks do we get? You come back to murder us.
AN ATHENIAN.
They're aggressors, Lysistrata!
A SPARTAN.
                         Ah Admit it.
When Ah look at those laigs, Ah sweah Ah'll aggress mahself!
LYSISTRATA.
And you, Athenians: do you think you're blameless?   1040
Remember that bad time when we were helpless,
and an army came from Sparta,

---

[71] The place-names evoke the former days of Greek unity and glory before the tragic civil
war.
[72] Foreign; non-Greek.
[73] An emissary sent from Sparta, earlier in the fifth century, to request help from Athens
in putting down civil war in Sparta and rebellion by Spartan-controlled Messênê. Athens responded
by sending a rescue force led by Kimôn.

and that was the end of the Thessalian menace,
the end of Hippias[74] and his allies.
                              And that was Sparta,
and only Sparta; but for Sparta, we'd be
cringing slaves today, not free Athenians.

> [*From this point, the male responses
> are less to* LYSISTRATA *than to the
> statue*]

A SPARTAN.
  A well shaped speech.
AN ATHENIAN.
                              Certainly it has its points.
LYSISTRATA.
  Why are we fighting each other? With all this history
  of favors given and taken, what stands in the way
  of making peace?
AMBASSADOR.
                              Spahta is ready, ma'am,   1050
  so long as we get that place back.
LYSISTRATA.
                              What place, man?
AMBASSADOR.
  Ah refer to Pylos.[75]
COMMISSIONER.
                  Not a chance, by God!
LYSISTRATA.
  Give it to them, friend.
COMMISSIONER.
                  But—what shall we have to bargain with?
LYSISTRATA.
  Demand something in exchange.
COMMISSIONER.
                              Good idea.—Well, then:
  Cockeville first, and the Happy Hills, and the country
  between the Legs of Mêgara.
AMBASSADOR.
                  Mah government objects.
LYSISTRATA.
  Over-ruled. Why fuss about a pair of legs?

> [*General assent. The statue is
> removed.*]

---

[74] The Spartans had helped Athens to overthrow and expel the tyrant Hippias.

[75] A town; the root meaning of its name is "flank." This and the following lines make a series of puns referring both to control of geographic areas and to portions of the female body as visible in the statue of the nude "Reconciliation." Conventional diplomatic bargaining for territory is thus blended with the sexual diplomacy employed by the women in the play.

AN ATHENIAN.
I want to get out of these clothes and start my plowing.
A SPARTAN.
Ah'll fertilize mahn first, by the Heavenly Twins!
LYSISTRATA.
And so you shall,   1060
once you've made peace. If you are serious,
go, both of you, and talk with your allies.
COMMISSIONER.
Too much talk already. No, we'll stand together.
We've only one end in view. All that we want
is our women; and I speak for our allies.
AMBASSADOR.
Mah government concurs.
AN ATHENIAN.
                                  So does Karystos.
LYSISTRATA.
Good.—But before you come inside
to join your wives at supper, you must perform
the usual lustration.[76] Then we'll open
our baskets for you, and all that we have is yours.   1070
But you must promise upright good behavior
from this day on. Then each man home with his woman!
AN ATHENIAN.
Let's get it over with.
A SPARTAN.
                                  Lead on. Ah follow.
AN ATHENIAN.
Quick as a cat can wink!

                                  [*Exeunt all but the* CHORUSES]

CHORUS[W].
                    Embroideries ánd   [ANTISTROPHE 1]
                    Twinkling ornaments ánd
                    Pretty dresses—I hand
Them all over to you, and with never a qualm.
                    They'll be nice for your daughters
                    On festival days   1080
                    When the girls bring the Goddess
                    The ritual prize.
                          Come in, one and all:
                          Take what you will.
I've nothing here so tightly corked that you can't make it spill.

                    You may search my house,   [ANTISTROPHE 2]
                    But you'll not find
                    The least thing of use,
Unless your two eyes are keener than mine.

---

[76]Ceremonial purification.

Your numberless brats 1090
Are half starved? and your slaves?
Courage, grandpa! I've lots
Of grain left, and big loaves.
I'll fill your guts
I'll go the whole hog;
But if you come too close to me, remember: 'ware the dog!

[*Exeunt* CHORUSES]

ÉXODOS

[*A* DRUNKEN CITIZEN *enters, approaches the gate, and is halted by a* SENTRY]

CITIZEN.
Open. The. Door.
SENTRY.
Now, friend, just shove along!
—So you want to sit down. If it weren't such an old joke,
I'd tickle your tail with this torch. Just the sort of gag
this audience appreciates.
CITIZEN.
I. Stay. Right. Here. 1100
SENTRY.
Get away from there, or I'll scalp you! The gentlemen from Sparta
are just coming back from dinner.

[*Exit* CITIZEN; *the general company
re-enters; the two* CHORUSES *now represent* SPARTANS *and* ATHENIANS.]

A SPARTAN.
Ah must say,
Ah never tasted better grub.
AN ATHENIAN.
And those Lakonians!
They're gentlemen, by the Lord! Just goes to show,
a drink to the wise is sufficient.
COMMISSIONER.
And why not?
A sober man's an ass.
Men of Athens, mark my words: the only efficient
Ambassador's a drunk Ambassador. Is that clear?
Look: we go to Sparta,
and when we get there we're dead sober. The result? 1110
Everyone cackling at everyone else. They make speeches;
and even if we understand, we get it all wrong
when we file our reports in Athens. But today—!

Everybody's happy. Couldn't tell the difference
between *Drink to Me Only* and
The Star-Spangled Athens.
                          What's a few lies,
washed down in good strong drink?

                                  [*Re-enter the* DRUNKEN CITIZEN]

SENTRY.
                                  God almighty,
   he's back again!
CITIZEN.
            I. Resume. My. Place.

                                  [*To an* ATHENIAN]

A SPARTAN.
   Ah beg yo', seh,
   take yo' instrument in yo' hand and play for us.   1120
   Ah'm told
   yo' understand the in*tric*acies of the floot?
   Ah'd lahk to execute a song and dance
   in honor of Athens,
                  and, of cohse, of Spahta.
CITIZEN.
   Toot. On. Your. Flute.

                  [*The following song is a solo—an
                  aria—accompanied by the flute. The*
                  CHORUS OF SPARTANS *begins a slow
                  dance.*]

A SPARTAN.
        O Memory,
        Let the Muse speak once more
        In my young voice. Sing glory.
        Sing Artemision's shore,[77]
        Where Athens fluttered the Persians. *Alalaí,*   1130
        Sing glory, that great
        Victory! Sing also
        Our Leonidas and his men,
        Those wild boars, sweat and blood
        Down in a red drench. Then, then
        The barbarians broke, though they had stood
        Numberless as the sands before!
        O Artemis,
        Virgin Goddess, whose darts
        Flash in our forests: approve   1140

[77]In the former days of Grecian unity, the Athenian fleet had fought against the Persians
near Artemision while the Spartans, led by the hero Leonidas, had bravely fought the Persians
on land, at Thermopylae. *Alalaí* is a battle cry.

This pact of peace and join our hearts,
From this day on, in love.
Huntress, descend!
LYSISTRATA.
All that will come in time.

But now, Lakonians,
take home your wives. Athenians, take yours.
Each man be kind to his woman; and you, women,
be equally kind. Never again, pray God,
shall we lose our way in such madness.
KORYPHAIOS[a].

And now
let's dance our joy.

[*From this point the dance becomes
general*]

CHORUS[a].
Dance, you Graces

Artemis, dance   1150
Dance, Phoibos, Lord of dancing

Dance
In a scurry of Maenads, Lord Dionysos

Dance, Zeus Thunderer
Dance, Lady Hêra
Queen of the Sky

Dance, dance, all you gods
Dance witness everlasting of our pact
Evohí Evohé
Dance for the dearest

the Bringer of Peace
Deathless Aphroditê!
COMMISSIONER.
Now let us have another song from Sparta.   1160
CHORUS[s].

From Taÿgetos, from Taÿgetos,
Lakonian Muse, come down.
Sing to the Lord Apollo
Who rules Amyklai[78] Town.

Sing Athêna of the House of Brass![79]

Sing Lêda's Twins,[80] that chivalry
Respondent on the shore
Of our Eurôtas;[81] sing the girls
That dance along before:

[78]A town, associated with Apollo, in the Spartan region.
[79]The temple of Athêna in Sparta.
[80]The "Heavenly Twins," Castor and Pollux, protectors of their sister, Helen of Troy.
[81]The river of Sparta.

> Sparkling in dust their gleaming feet,   1170
> Their hair a Bacchant[82] fire,
> And Lêda's daughter,[83] thyrsos raised,
> Leads their triumphant choir.
>
> CHORUSES[s and a]
>   Evohé!
>   Evohaí!
>   Evohé!
>   We pass
>   Dancing
>   dancing
>   to greet
> Athêna of the House of Brass.

[82]Associated with the Bacchantes, female worshipers of Bacchus (Dionysus), the god of wine, sex, and revelry.
[83]Helen of Troy, symbol of woman as cause of war but here of woman as reconciler. The thyrsos is a staff carried by worshipers of Dionysus/Bacchus.

Plato

(C.427–C.348 B.C.)

Except for certain great religious teachers, Plato has probably been the most influential thinker in the history of Western culture. Because he believed that dialectic, in the form of oral give-and-take, was a higher form of discourse and a more reliable avenue to wisdom than written treatises, his writings are not necessarily a complete or wholly reliable record of what he believed. But the high reverence in which Plato was held, in his own day and since, has caused his written work to survive more completely than that of virtually any other ancient Greek author. Moreover, the written work itself reflects Plato's dedication to the spoken word, since his most typical literary form is the dialogue. The thirty or more works by Plato that have come down to us concentrate mainly on ethical, political, and metaphysical issues, but they also treat in depth or at least touch on many other important matters that have preoccupied philosophers, including issues in mathematics, logic, and physical science.

Plato was a pioneering thinker, but he was much more than a groundbreaker. Are words merely arbitrary symbols for things and human ideas, or do words have a more absolute relationship to what they signify? Are goodness and beauty realities in themselves—independent of the accidents of our observation and tastes—or are they merely attributes that the human mind generalizes from particular objects it considers good or beautiful? Do we know truth through reason or through some more mysterious or intuitive process?

If love helps us become our best selves and induces ecstatic states of happiness and generosity, why does it also bring out what is most absurd, irrational, and malignant in us? In forming a just political community, should the first task be to perfect individual citizens, in the hope that they will add up to a just polity, or should individuals model their private virtues on a general conception of what the community needs? These questions raised by Plato, and many others like them, have obsessed countless people—practical men and women as well as abstract theoreticians. And—which is most remarkable—in trying to answer such questions, people have again and again gone directly to Plato's works themselves, not merely to later "sophistications" of his thought.

Plato was born around 427 B.C., in Athens, of an aristocratic lineage that claimed descent from preeminent legendary ancestors. He came under the influence of Socrates—the central figure in most of Plato's dialogues—when Plato was about twenty, at which time Socrates was in his early sixties. During the eight or so years before Socrates was tried and condemned to death in 399, Plato was one of many bright and well-born young Athenians who listened and learned in the public places of Athens where Socrates held forth. Plato's family was active in Athenian politics, and he himself was drawn toward public life in the critical last decade of the fifth century (years which witnessed among other dramatic events the final defeat of Athens in its civil war against Sparta). But at this time Plato opted against a political career. Significantly, in the *Apology*, his account of Socrates' trial, he reports Socrates' opinion that to be apolitical is the only way to retain integrity. In Plato's middle and old age, however (he died around 348), he made several journeys to Sicily, partly with the hope of helping the ruling family of Syracuse realize in practical terms the political principles Plato had come to believe in. The effort failed for several reasons, but the fact that Plato did make the attempt to reconcile theoretical principles with actual practice testifies that he was not simply the otherworldly mystic that many people associate with the term "Platonic."

Apart from his own direct teaching, whether or not it was preserved in writing, Plato's most distinctive achievement was to found and lead the Academy (located in an olive grove near Athens, and named after the hero Academus). This assemblage of brilliant original thinkers, brought together under Plato's direction, was the prototype of modern universities and think tanks.

The greatness of Plato, and his incalculable influence, are mainly attributable to the inherent profundity and originality of his thought. Even if it had come down to us in the severely colorless vehicle that in our time is considered normal or even essential for hard thinking in philosophy and science, Plato would occupy a central position among intellectuals. But his appeal has been much broader, and that fact is largely due to the literary forms he used, mainly the dialogue. Plato has often, and rightly, been called a poet (despite the ambiguous view of poetry in works like the *Ion*), because of the high eloquence and supernal beauty he often attains. But Plato is also a master of fiction and, almost literally, of drama. His credentials as a dramatist are revealed on two levels. On one level, ideas themselves are the dramatic characters, and Plato's triumph is to make these competing ideas compelling in themselves, so that we are drawn to one or another of them, our sympathies evoked as if the ideas were our friends or enemies. In addition, though, the human persons who espouse or oppose various ideological positions are drawn with great subtlety and psychological realism. Most of these people were actual historical human beings, so that Plato portrayed from life and not merely from his imagination. But many authors whose explicit aim is biography have not succeeded nearly as well as did Plato in the vivid rendering of personalities. Moreover, the characterization can sometimes color intellectual appraisal. Socrates' argument that poets, their interpreters, and their audiences are governed by inspiration rather than skill or reason might be taken as praise of poetry, or at least as neutral comment on it, except that the portrayal of Ion, poetry's representative in the dialogue, as complacent and fatuous seems to give Socrates' view of poetry a more negative, ironically mocking turn.

Chief among Plato's triumphs of characterization is, of course, Socrates. This multifaceted man—by turns earnest and playful, ironic and unguarded, elevated in mind but physically unprepossessing—emerges as one of the most memorable human beings in history or fiction. To treat him as a mere creature of Plato's art would be absurd, of course, just as it would be absurd to treat Jesus as an invention of the New Testament evangelists. Socrates was a distinct historical individual, in his own right an important personage and an eminent teacher-thinker. But to what extent Plato represented him and his ideas accurately is uncertain. That there was much distortion in Plato's portrait seems unlikely, since Socrates was the most publicly accessible of Athenians, and many of the readers in Plato's audience would have remembered him personally. A much more difficult and important problem is to what extent Plato's ideas coincide with those of his mentor. Plato could hardly have given Socrates so central a place in the dialogues if the pupil had not embraced and retained many of Socrates' ideas. On the other hand, Socrates died a half-century before Plato did, and Plato's ideas must inevitably have developed during that period. Other complications include the fact that the dialogues are not always consistent with one another; in some of them Plato may be dramatizing the clash of ideas for its own sake without trying to propose a solution to which either Socrates or Plato himself would have subscribed. And, on top of these difficulties, there is the question of how nearly Neoplatonism—the occultist developments of his ideas during the two millennia after Plato—is consonant with Plato's thought.

Although such critical, biographical, and historical questions are important, in some ways they are distractions. In one sense Platonism is no more or less than what is contained in Plato's works: a set of ideas and a method for testing and exploring them. Whether or not either Plato or Socrates would have endorsed the ideas, and whether they and their adherents are treated ironically or not, are from the thinker's point of view less important than the truth or falsity of various positions. In the *Symposium,* for example, a fable explaining sexual attraction as the result of a primordial splitting of people into halves is treated facetiously, but the notion of soul mates implied in the fable has survived the ironic context and has become one fundamental model of the nature of love. Part of the power of Plato's works is due to the fact that the concepts expressed in them have a reality that can transcend the human drama through which they are so vividly expressed.

For many people, Platonism has come to suggest otherworldliness, ecstasy, and mysticism. And it is undeniable that the tone and content of the dialogues are sometimes elevated and rhapsodic. The metaphysical doctrine of "Ideas" or "Forms" (introduced in the *Republic* and other dialogues) does indeed seem to suggest that the material world is flawed exactly because it *is* material. But to regard Plato as a mystic—if by that term we mean a devotee of mystery—is misleading, to say the least. Mind, the senses, the mundane, are central in Plato's works; the reasoning is razor-edged, and the frequent analogies are usually to such homely creatures as pack-asses and tanners, even when Socrates is leading the way to sublime insights. One of the challenges Plato poses for the modern reader is that of reconciling the mental states of rationalism and excitement. For most people today, those terms are irreconcilable; for example (the cliché goes), poets and other artists *feel,* while scientists *think.* Plato's works suggest that hard thinking can be a positively sensuous experience. To present it through a literary medium that uses comedy, characterization, local setting, and the like is to imply that thinking is not an alternative to living but one of the best parts of living.

FURTHER READING *(prepared by F.S.N. and M.C.):* A standard treatment of Plato as writer, philosopher, and influential thinker is Paul Friedländer's *Plato,* 1928–1930, 2nd ed. 1953–1957, 3 vols., trans. Hans Meyerhoff, 1958–1969. Other useful works on Plato's life and writings are by Paul Shorey, *What Plato Said,* 1933, repr. 1965; and by G. C. Field, *The Philosophy of Plato,* 1949, 2nd ed. 1969. On the development of Plato's thought see especially I. M. Crombie, *An Examination of Plato's Doctrines,* 2 vols., 1962–1963, and, by the same author, the shortened version *Plato: The Midwife's Apprentice,* 1964. On the role of poetic language and myth in Plato, see Julius A. Elias, *Plato's Defence of Poetry,* 1984. Seth Bernardete, *The Rhetoric of Morality and Philosophy,* 1991, is a rewarding discussion of Plato's rhetoric. His philosophy of punishment, with reference to Greek literature, including Homer, is addressed in Trevor J. Saunders, *Plato's Penal Code,* 1992. C. D. C. Reeve, *Socrates in the Apology,* 1990, is an outstanding analysis of that dialogue, which is also treated helpfully in the introductory materials in R. E. Allen's translation *The Dialogues of Plato,* Vol. I, 1985. Plato's lasting influence is treated in A. H. Armstrong, ed., *The Cambridge History of Later Greek and Early Medieval Philosophy,* 1967. Andrea Nye, *Words of Power,* 1991, is a thoughtful discussion of Plato, Aristotle, and other philosophers from a feminist perspective.

ION

Translated by Benjamin Jowett

Like the *Apology,* the *Ion* is one of the earlier written dialogues of Plato. The incident described takes place, probably, around 405 B.C. We see Socrates engaged in one of his favorite occupations: showing "experts" in various fields that their expertise is founded on ignorance. Ion is both a professional reciter and a professional interpreter of Homer, the greatest of Greek poets, and is therefore part of the Greek educational system. The challenge in reading the *Ion* is to filter its serious message through the dialogue's lightly comic tone and also to judge whether Plato/Socrates is praising poetry or warning us away from it as something dangerous. [*Editors' headnote.*]

SOCRATES. Welcome, Ion. Are you from your native city of Ephesus?

ION. No, Socrates; but from Epidaurus, where I attended the festival of Asclepius.

SOC. And do the Epidaurians have contests of rhapsodes[1] at the festival?

ION. O yes; and of all sorts of musical performers.

SOC. And were you one of the competitors—and did you succeed?

ION. I obtained the first prize of all, Socrates.

SOC. Well done; and I hope that you will do the same for us at the Panathenaea.

ION. And I will, please heaven.

SOC. I often envy the profession of a rhapsode, Ion; for you have always to wear fine clothes, and to look as beautiful as you can is a part of your art. Then, again, you are obliged to be continually in the company of many good poets; and especially of Homer, who is the best and most divine of them; and to understand him, and not merely learn his words by rote, is a thing greatly to be envied.[2] And no man can be a rhapsode who does not understand the meaning of the poet. For the rhapsode ought to interpret the mind of the poet to his hearers, but how can he interpret him well unless he knows what he means? All this is greatly to be envied.

ION. Very true, Socrates; interpretation has certainly been the most laborious part of my art;[3] and I believe myself able to speak about Homer better than any man; and that neither Metrodorus of Lampsacus, nor Stesimbrotus of Thasos, nor Glaucon, nor any one else who ever was, had as good ideas about Homer as I have, or as many.

SOC. I am glad to hear you say so, Ion; I see that you will not refuse to acquaint me with them.

ION. Certainly, Socrates; and you really ought to hear how exquisitely I render Homer. I think that the Homeridae[4] should give me a golden crown.

SOC. I shall take an opportunity of hearing your embellishments of him at some other time. But just now I should like to ask you a question: Does your art extend to Hesiod and Archilochus,[5] or to Homer only?

ION. To Homer only; he is in himself quite enough.

SOC. Are there any things about which Homer and Hesiod agree?

ION. Yes; in my opinion there are a good many.

SOC. And can you interpret better what Homer says, or what Hesiod says, about these matters in which they agree?

ION. I can interpret them equally well, Socrates, where they agree.

---

[1] Professional reciters of poetry, especially Homer's. Ion is fresh from having won the contest among rhapsodes at Epidaurus (site of a festival honoring Asclepius, the legendary physician). He is to compete again in Athens at the annual summer festival (the Panathenaea) honoring the goddess Athene.

[2] At the outset of this dialogue, Socrates, with deceptive offhandedness, compliments Ion on the very skill—understanding as distinguished from rote memory—that the ensuing conversation will show Ion to lack.

[3] The naive Ion uses the word *interpretation* not in Socrates' sense ("understanding") but in the sense of "performing skill."

[4] A group who claimed Homer as an ancestor.

[5] Greek poets of the seventh and eighth centuries B.C.

SOC. But what about matters in which they do not agree?—for example, about divination, of which both Homer and Hesiod have something to say,—

ION. Very true:

SOC. Would you or a good prophet[6] be a better interpreter of what these two poets say about divination, not only when they agree, but when they disagree?

ION. A prophet.

SOC. And if you were a prophet, would you not be able to interpret them when they disagree as well as when they agree?

ION. Clearly.

SOC. But how did you come to have this skill about Homer only, and not about Hesiod or the other poets? Does not Homer speak of the same themes which all other poets handle? Is not war his great argument?[7] and does he not speak of human society and of intercourse of men, good and bad, skilled and unskilled, and of the gods conversing with one another and with mankind, and about what happens in heaven and in the world below, and the generations of gods and heroes? Are not these the themes of which Homer sings?

ION. Very true, Socrates.

SOC. And do not the other poets sing of the same?

ION. Yes, Socrates; but not in the same way as Homer.

SOC. What, in a worse way?

ION. Yes, in a far worse.

SOC. And Homer in a better way?

ION. He is incomparably better.

SOC. And yet surely, my dear friend Ion, in a discussion about arithmetic, where many people are speaking, and one speaks better than the rest, there is somebody who can judge which of them is the good speaker?

ION. Yes.

SOC. And he who judges of the good will be the same as he who judges of the bad speakers?

ION. The same.

SOC. And he will be the arithmetician?

ION. Yes.

SOC. Well, and in discussions about the wholesomeness of food, when many persons are speaking, and one speaks better than the rest, will he who recognizes the better speaker be a different person from him who recognizes the worse, or the same?

ION. Clearly the same.

SOC. And who is he, and what is his name?

ION. The physician.

SOC. And speaking generally, in all discussions in which the subject is the same and many men are speaking, will not he who knows the good know the bad speaker also? For if he does not know the bad, neither will he know the good when the same topic is being discussed.

---

[6]A person able to interpret the gods' will or the future through "divination"—the analysis of dreams, supernatural signs, etc.

[7]Theme; subject.

ION. True.

SOC. Is not the same person skillful in both?

ION. Yes.

SOC. And you say that Homer and the other poets, such as Hesiod and Archilochus, speak of the same things, although not in the same way; but the one speaks well and the other not so well?

ION. Yes; and I am right in saying so.

SOC. And if you knew the good speaker, you would also know the inferior speakers to be inferior?

ION. That is true.

SOC. Then, my dear friend, can I be mistaken in saying that Ion is equally skilled in Homer and in other poets, since he himself acknowledges that the same person will be a good judge of all those who speak of the same things; and that almost all poets do speak of the same things?

ION. Why then, Socrates, do I lose attention and go to sleep and have absolutely no ideas of the least value, when any one speaks of any other poet; but when Homer is mentioned, I wake up at once and am all attention and have plenty to say?

SOC. The reason, my friend, is obvious. No one can fail to see that you speak of Homer without any art or knowledge. If you were able to speak of him by rules of art, you would have been able to speak of all other poets; for poetry is a whole.[8]

ION. Yes.

SOC. And when any one acquires any other art as a whole, the same may be said of them. Would you like me to explain my meaning, Ion?

ION. Yes, indeed, Socrates; I very much wish that you would: for I love to hear you wise men talk.

SOC. O that we were wise, Ion, and that you could truly call us so; but you rhapsodes and actors, and the poets whose verses you sing, are wise; whereas I am a common man, who only speak the truth. For consider what a very commonplace and trivial thing is this which I have said—a thing which any man might say: that when a man has acquired a knowledge of a whole art, the enquiry into good and bad is one and the same. Let us consider this matter; is not the art of painting a whole?

ION. Yes.

SOC. And there are and have been many painters good and bad?

ION. Yes.

SOC. And did you ever know any one who was skillful in pointing out the excellences and defects of Polygnotus[9] the son of Aglaophon, but incapable of criticizing other painters; and when the work of any other painter was produced, went to sleep and was at a loss, and had no ideas; but when he had to give his opinion about Polygnotus, or whoever the painter might be, and about him only, woke up and was attentive and had plenty to say?

ION. No indeed, I have never known such a person.

SOC. Or did you ever know of any one in sculpture, who was skillful in expounding the merits of Daedalus the son of Metion, or of Epeius the

[8] That is, poetry is a single art or craft.

[9] A fifth-century painter famous for murals on a grand scale.

son of Panopeus, or of Theodorus the Samian,[10] or of any individual sculptor; but when the works of sculptors in general were produced, was at a loss and went to sleep and had nothing to say?

ION. No indeed; no more than the other.

SOC. And if I am not mistaken, you never met with any one among flute-players or harp-players or singers to the harp or rhapsodes who was able to discourse of Olympus or Thamyras or Orpheus, or Phemius the rhapsode of Ithaca,[11] but was at a loss when he came to speak of Ion of Ephesus, and had no notion of his merits or defects?

ION. I cannot deny what you say, Socrates. Nevertheless I am conscious in my own self, and the world agrees with me in thinking that I do speak better and have more to say about Homer than any other man. But I do not speak equally well about others—tell me the reason of this.

SOC. I perceive, Ion; and I will proceed to explain to you what I imagine to be the reason of this. The gift which you possess of speaking excellently about Homer is not an art, but, as I was just saying, an inspiration; there is a divinity moving you, like that contained in the stone which Euripides calls a magnet, but which is commonly known as the stone of Heraclea.[12] This stone not only attracts iron rings, but also imparts to them a similar power of attracting other rings; and sometimes you may see a number of pieces of iron and rings suspended from one another so as to form quite a long chain: and all of them derive their power of suspension from the original stone. In like manner the Muse[13] first of all inspires men herself; and from these inspired persons a chain of other persons is suspended, who take the inspiration. For all good poets, epic as well as lyric, compose their beautiful poems not by art, but because they are inspired and possessed. And as the Corybantian revellers[14] when they dance are not in their right mind, so the lyric poets are not in their right mind when they are composing their beautiful strains: but when falling under the power of music and meter they are inspired and possessed; like Bacchic maidens who draw milk and honey from the rivers when they are under the influence of Dionysus but not when they are in their right mind. And the soul of the lyric poet does the same, as they themselves say; for they tell us that they bring songs from honeyed fountains, culling them out of the gardens and dells of the Muses; they, like the bees, winging their way from flower to flower. And this is true. For the poet is a light and winged and holy thing, and there is no invention in him until he has been inspired and is out of his senses, and the mind

---

[10] Daedalus was a legendary sculptor and craftsman, said to be descended from Hephaestus, the god of fire and of metalworking. Epeius was the builder of the gigantic Trojan horse in which Odysseus and other Greeks hid themselves so that they could gain entrance to the city of Troy and conquer it. Theodorus the Samian (sixth century) was a great sculptor in metal, reputedly the co-creator of a famous Apollo at Samos.

[11] Olympus was a legendary inventor of music; Thamyras and Orpheus were other legendary musicians; Phemius is the bard in Homer's *Odyssey* who sings at Odysseus' house in Ithaca.

[12] A town in Asia Minor; the district Magnesia (source of the word *magnet*) is also located there.

[13] The Muses were the nine goddesses of inspiration.

[14] Frenzied, orgiastic female worshipers of the god Dionysus, or Bacchus. The references in the following lines to song, honey, and bees are puns on words spelled nearly alike in Greek, and also clichés of poetic diction.

is no longer in him: when he has not attained to this state, he is power-less and is unable to utter his oracles. Many are the noble words in which poets speak concerning the actions of men; but like yourself when speak-ing about Homer, they do not speak of them by any rules of art: they are simply inspired to utter that to which the Muse impels them, and that only; and when inspired, one of them will make dithyrambs,[15] another hymns of praise, another choral strains, another epic or iambic verses—and he who is good at one is not good at any other kind of verse: for not by art does the poet sing, but by power divine. Had he learned by rules of art, he would have known how to speak not of one theme only, but of all; and therefore God takes away the minds of poets, and uses them as his ministers, as he also uses diviners and holy prophets, in order that we who hear them may know them to be speaking not of themselves who utter these priceless words in a state of unconsciousness, but that God himself is the speaker, and that through them he is conversing with us. And Tynnichus the Chalcidian affords a striking instance of what I am saying: he wrote nothing that any one would care to remember but the famous paean[16] which is in every one's mouth, one of the finest poems ever written, simply an invention of the Muses, as he himself says. For in this way the God would seem to indicate to us and not allow us to doubt that these beautiful poems are not human, or the work of man, but divine and the work of God; and that the poets are only the inter-preters of the Gods by whom they are severally possessed. Was not this the lesson which the God intended to teach when by the mouth of the worst of poets he sang the best of songs? Am I not right, Ion?

ION. Yes, indeed, Socrates, I feel that you are; for your words touch my soul, and I am persuaded that good poets by a divine inspiration interpret the things of the Gods to us.

SOC. And you rhapsodists are the interpreters of the poets?

ION. There again you are right.

SOC. Then you are the interpreters of interpreters?

ION. Precisely.

SOC. I wish you would frankly tell me, Ion, what I am going to ask of you: When you produce the greatest effect upon the audience in the recita-tion of some striking passage, such as the apparition of Odysseus leap-ing forth on the floor, recognized by the suitors and casting his arrows at his feet, or the description of Achilles rushing at Hector, or the sor-rows of Andromache, Hecuba, or Priam,—are you in your right mind?[17] Are you not carried out of yourself, and does not your soul in an ecstasy seem to be among the persons or places of which you are speaking, whether they are in Ithaca or in Troy or whatever may be the scene of the poem?[18]

ION. That proof strikes home to me, Socrates. For I must frankly confess that at the tale of pity my eyes are filled with tears, and when I speak of horrors, my hair stands on end and my heart throbs.

---

[15]Wild choral chants, celebrating Dionysus.

[16]Hymn of joy or praise. Socrates' point is that, since one of the worst of poets wrote one of the greatest of poems, poetry is an irrational, unpredictable phenomenon.

[17]The episode of Odysseus and the suitors is from Homer's *Odyssey*, Book XXII; the other episodes are from Homer's *Iliad*, Books XXII and XXIV.

[18]Ithaca is the setting of the latter half of the *Odyssey*, Troy the setting of the *Iliad*.

SOC. Well, Ion, and what are we to say of a man who at a sacrifice or festival, when he is dressed in holiday attire, and has golden crowns upon his head, of which nobody has robbed him, appears weeping or panic-stricken in the presence of more than twenty thousand friendly faces, when there is no one despoiling or wronging him;—is he in his right mind or is he not?

ION. No indeed, Socrates, I must say that, strictly speaking, he is not in his right mind.

SOC. And are you aware that you produce similar effects on most of the spectators?

ION. Only too well; for I look down upon them from the stage, and behold the various emotions of pity, wonder, sternness, stamped upon their countenances when I am speaking: and I am obliged to give my very best attention to them; for if I make them cry I myself shall laugh, and if I make them laugh I myself shall cry when the time of payment arrives.[19]

SOC. Do you know that the spectator is the last of the rings which, as I am saying, receive the power of the original magnet from one another? The rhapsode like yourself and the actor are intermediate links, and the poet himself is the first of them. Through all these the God sways the souls of men in any direction which he pleases, and makes one man hang down from another. Thus there is a vast chain of dancers and masters and under-masters of choruses, who are suspended, as if from the stone, at the side of the rings which hang down from the Muse. And every poet has some Muse from whom he is suspended, and by whom he is said to be possessed, which is nearly the same thing; for he is taken hold of. And from these first rings, which are the poets, depend others, some deriving their inspiration from Orpheus, others from Musaeus;[20] but the greater number are possessed and held by Homer. Of whom, Ion, you are one, and are possessed by Homer; and when any one repeats the words of another poet you go to sleep, and know not what to say; but when any one recites a strain of Homer you wake up in a moment, and your soul leaps within you, and you have plenty to say; for not by art or knowledge about Homer do you say what you say, but by divine inspiration and by possession; just as the Corybantian revellers too have a quick perception of that strain only which is appropriated to the God by whom they are possessed, and have plenty of dances and words for that, but take no heed of any other. And you, Ion, when the name of Homer is mentioned have plenty to say, and have nothing to say of others. You ask, "Why is this?" The answer is that you praise Homer not by art but by divine inspiration.

ION. That is good, Socrates, and yet I doubt whether you will ever have eloquence enough to persuade me that I praise Homer only when I am mad and possessed; and if you could hear me speak of him I am sure you would never think this to be the case.

SOC. I should like very much to hear you, but not until you have answered a question which I have to ask. On what part of Homer do you speak well?—not surely about every part.

---

[19] Ion means that he will have failed in his competitions (and will therefore "cry") if the audience laughs at his efforts to arouse tearful emotion but that he will be delighted (will "laugh") if he succeeds in arousing such emotion.

[20] Another legendary Greek poet, said to have been a disciple of Orpheus.

ION. There is no part, Socrates, about which I do not speak well: of that I can assure you.

SOC. Surely not about things in Homer of which you have no knowledge?

ION. And what is there in Homer of which I have no knowledge?

SOC. Why, does not Homer speak in many passages about arts? For example, about driving; if I can only remember the lines I will repeat them.

ION. I remember, and will repeat them.

SOC. Tell me then, what Nestor says to Antilochus, his son, where he bids him be careful of the turn at the horserace in honor of Patroclus.

ION.

"Bend gently," he says, "in the polished chariot to the left of them, and urge the horse on the right hand with whip and voice; and slacken the rein. And when you are at the goal, let the left horse draw near, yet so that the nave of the well-wrought wheel may not even seem to touch the extremity; and avoid catching the stone."[21]

SOC. Enough. Now, Ion, will the charioteer or the physician be the better judge of the propriety of these lines?

ION. The charioteer, clearly.

SOC. And will the reason be that this is his art, or will there be any other reason?

ION. No, that will be the reason.

SOC. And every art is appointed by God to have knowledge of a certain work; for that which we know by the art of the pilot we do not know by the art of medicine?

ION. Certainly not.

SOC. Nor do we know by the art of the carpenter that which we know by the art of medicine?

ION. Certainly not.

SOC. And this is true of all the arts;—that which we know with one art we do not know with the other? But let me ask a prior question: You admit that there are differences of arts?

ION. Yes.

SOC. You would argue, as I should, that when one art is of one kind of knowledge and another of another, they are different?

ION. Yes.

SOC. Yes, surely; for if the subject of knowledge were the same, there would be no meaning in saying that the arts were different,—if they both gave the same knowledge. For example, I know that here are five fingers, and you know the same. And if I were to ask whether I and you became acquainted with this fact by the help of the same art of arithmetic, you would acknowledge that we did?

ION. Yes.

SOC. Tell me, then, what I was intending to ask you,—whether this holds universally? Must the same art have the same subject of knowledge, and different arts other subjects of knowledge?

---

[21] The quotation is from Homer's *Iliad*, Book XXIII, which describes the ceremonial funeral athletic games in honor of Patroclus, the slain comrade of Achilles.

ION. That is my opinion, Socrates.

SOC. Then he who has no knowledge of a particular art will have no right judgment of the sayings and doings of that art?

ION. Very true.

SOC. Then which will be a better judge of the lines which you were reciting from Homer, you or the charioteer?

ION. The charioteer.

SOC. Why, yes, because you are a rhapsode and not a charioteer.

ION. Yes.

SOC. And the art of the rhapsode is different from that of the charioteer?

ION. Yes.

SOC. And if a different knowledge, then a knowledge of different matters?

ION. True.

SOC. You know the passage in which Hecamede, the concubine of Nestor, is described as giving to the wounded Machaon a posset,[22] as he says,

"made with Pramnian wine; and she grated cheese of goat's milk with a grater of bronze, and at his side placed an onion which gives a relish to drink."[23]

Now would you say that the art of the rhapsode or the art of medicine was better able to judge of the propriety of these lines?

ION. The art of medicine.

SOC. And when Homer says,

"And she descended into the deep like a leaden plummet, which, set in the horn of ox that ranges in the fields, rushes along carrying death among the ravenous fishes,"—[24]

will the art of the fisherman or of the rhapsode be better able to judge whether these lines are rightly expressed or not?

ION. Clearly, Socrates, the art of the fisherman.

SOC. Come now, suppose that you were to say to me: "Since you, Socrates, are able to assign different passages in Homer to their corresponding arts, I wish that you would tell me what are the passages of which the excellence ought to be judged by the prophet and prophetic art"; and you will see how readily and truly I shall answer you. For there are many such passages, particularly in the Odyssey; as, for example, the passage in which Theoclymenus the prophet of the house of Melampus says to the suitors:—

"Wretched men! what is happening to you? Your heads and your faces and your limbs underneath are shrouded in night; and the voice of lamentation bursts forth, and your cheeks are wet with tears. And the vestibule is full, and the court is full, of ghosts

---

[22] A drink, usually combining milk, spices, and wine.

[23] *Iliad,* Book XI.

[24] *Iliad,* Book XXIV. The lines include a simile, based on the image of a fishing sinker, for the descent of the sea nymph Thetis, Achilles' mother, into the sea.

descending into the darkness of Erebus, and the sun has perished out of heaven, and an evil mist is spread abroad." [25]

And there are many such passages in the Iliad also; as for example in the description of the battle near the rampart, where he says:—

"As they were eager to pass the ditch, there came to them an omen: a soaring eagle, holding back the people on the left, bore a huge bloody dragon in his talons, still living and panting; nor had he yet resigned the strife, for he bent back and smote the bird which carried him on the breast by the neck, and he in pain let him fall from him to the ground into the midst of the multitude. And the eagle, with a cry, was borne afar on the wings of the wind." [26]

These are the sort of things which I should say that the prophet ought to consider and determine.

ION. And you are quite right, Socrates, in saying so.

SOC. Yes, Ion, and you are right also. And as I have selected from the Iliad and Odyssey for you passages which describe the office of the prophet and the physician and the fisherman, do you, who know Homer so much better than I do, Ion, select for me passages which relate to the rhapsode and the rhapsode's art, and which the rhapsode ought to examine and judge of better than other men.

ION. All passages, I should say, Socrates.

SOC. Not all, Ion, surely. Have you already forgotten what you were saying? A rhapsode ought to have a better memory.

ION. Why, what am I forgetting?

SOC. Do you not remember that you declared the art of the rhapsode to be different from the art of the charioteer?

ION. Yes, I remember.

SOC. And you admitted that being different they would have different subjects of knowledge?

ION. Yes.

SOC. Then upon your own showing the rhapsode, and the art of the rhapsode, will not know everything?

ION. I should exclude certain things, Socrates.

SOC. You mean to say that you would exclude pretty much the subjects of the other arts. As he does not know all of them, which of them will he know?

ION. He will know what a man and what a woman ought to say, and what a freeman and what a slave ought to say, and what a ruler and what a subject.

SOC. Do you mean that a rhapsode will know better than the pilot what the ruler of a sea-tossed vessel ought to say?

[25] *Odyssey,* Book XX. The passage quotes the seer Theoclymenus' prediction that the suitors despoiling Odysseus' house will soon be killed by him and descend to Erebus, the realm of darkness in the after-world.

[26] *Iliad,* Book XII. The soaring eagle is a divine sign, or omen, that halts the Trojans as they are about to cross the rampart, or moat, around the Greeks' seaside encampment and burn their ships. A dispute occurs among the Trojan leaders about how a good prophet would interpret the omen.

ION. No; the pilot will know best.

SOC. Or will the rhapsode know better than the physician what the ruler of a sick man ought to say?

ION. He will not.

SOC. But he will know what a slave ought to say?

ION. Yes.

SOC. Suppose the slave to be a cowherd; the rhapsode will know better than the cowherd what he ought to say in order to soothe the infuriated cows?

ION. No, he will not.

SOC. But he will know what a spinning-woman ought to say about the working of wool?

ION. No.

SOC. At any rate he will know what a general ought to say when exhorting his soldiers?

ION. Yes, that is the sort of thing which the rhapsode will be sure to know.

SOC. Well, but is the art of the rhapsode the art of the general?

ION. I am sure that I should know what a general ought to say.

SOC. Why, yes, Ion, because you may possibly have a knowledge of the art of the general as well as of the rhapsode; and you may also have a knowledge of horsemanship as well as of the lyre: and then you would know when horses were well or ill managed. But suppose I were to ask you: By the help of which art, Ion, do you know whether horses are well managed, by your skill as a horseman or as a performer on the lyre—what would you answer?

ION. I should reply, by my skill as a horseman.

SOC. And if you judged of performers on the lyre, you would admit that you judged of them as a performer on the lyre, and not as a horseman?

ION. Yes.

SOC. And in judging of the general's art, do you judge of it as a general or a rhapsode?

ION. To me there appears to be no difference between them.

SOC. What do you mean? Do you mean to say that the art of the rhapsode and of the general is the same?

ION. Yes, one and the same.[27]

SOC. Then he who is a good rhapsode is also a good general?

ION. Certainly, Socrates.

SOC. And he who is a good general is also a good rhapsode?

ION. No; I do not say that.

SOC. But you do say that he who is a good rhapsode is also a good general.

ION. Certainly.

SOC. And you are the best of Hellenic[28] rhapsodes?

ION. Far the best, Socrates.

SOC. And are you the best general, Ion?

ION. To be sure, Socrates; and Homer was my master.

SOC. But then, Ion, what in the name of goodness can be the reason why you, who are the best of generals as well as the best of rhapsodes in all

---

[27] In stubbornly identifying the art of the rhapsode with that of the general, Ion attains his ultimate comic absurdity.

[28] Greek.

Hellas, go about as a rhapsode when you might be a general? Do you think that the Hellenes want a rhapsode with his golden crown, and do not want a general?

ION. Why, Socrates, the reason is, that my countrymen, the Ephesians, are the servants and soldiers of Athens, and do not need a general; and you and Sparta are not likely to have me, for you think that you have enough generals of your own.[29]

SOC. My good Ion, did you never hear of Apollodorus of Cyzicus?

ION. Who may he be?

SOC. One who, though a foreigner, has often been chosen their general by the Athenians: and there is Phanosthenes of Andros, and Heraclides of Clazomenae, whom they have also appointed to the command of their armies and to other offices, although aliens, after they had shown their merit. And will they not choose Ion the Ephesian to be their general, and honor him, if he prove himself worthy? Were not the Ephesians originally Athenians, and Ephesus is no mean city?[30] But, indeed, Ion, if you are correct in saying that by art and knowledge you are able to praise Homer, you do not deal fairly with me, and after all your professions of knowing many glorious things about Homer, and promises that you would exhibit them, you are only a deceiver, and so far from exhibiting the art of which you are a master, will not, even after my repeated entreaties, explain to me the nature of it. You have literally as many forms as Proteus;[31] and now you go all manner of ways, twisting and turning, and, like Proteus, become all manner of people at once, and at last slip away from me in the disguise of a general, in order that you may escape exhibiting your Homeric lore. And if you have art, then, as I was saying, in falsifying your promise that you would exhibit Homer, you are not dealing fairly with me. But if, as I believe, you have no art, but speak all these beautiful words about Homer unconsciously under his inspiring influence, then I acquit you of dishonesty, and shall only say that you are inspired. Which do you prefer to be thought, dishonest or inspired?

ION. There is a great difference, Socrates, between the two alternatives; and inspiration is by far the nobler.

SOC. Then, Ion, I shall assume the nobler alternative; and attribute to you in your praises of Homer inspiration, and not art.

from *THE REPUBLIC*

Translated by Benjamin Jowett

The Republic, the second-longest (after the *Laws*) of Plato's works, is an inquiry into the nature of justice. The inquiry leads, in turn, to an attempt to define the ideal

---

[29] Athens and Sparta were the respective heads of the two confederacies that fought against each other in the great Greek civil ("Peloponnesian") war.

[30] In the Peloponnesian War, Ephesus (Ion's home city in Asia Minor) was first an ally of Athens and then of Sparta.

[31] The Old Man of the Sea described in the *Odyssey*, Book IV, who is able to elude captors and questioners by taking on various forms.

state. The form is that of a dialogue between Socrates and six other ʹ
VII begins with the famous Parable of the Cave (or Den), in which So
ing an older brother of Plato named Glaucon, illustrates the diffe
unenlightened men and enlightened philosophers. The parable al
difficulty philosophers will have in returning to the sphere of practical affairs after
having envisioned the ideal, supra-earthly form of the good. (Nevertheless, in the
just commonwealth such civic service will be the duty of philosopher-rulers.) [*Editors'
headnote.*]

BOOK VII

THE PARABLE OF THE CAVE

And now, I said,[1] let me show in a figure how far our nature is enlightened
or unenlightened:—Behold! human beings living in an underground den,
which has a mouth open towards the light and reaching all along the den;
here they have been from their childhood, and have their legs and necks
chained so that they cannot move, and can only see before them, being prevented by the chains from turning round their heads. Above and behind
them a fire is blazing at a distance, and between the fire and the prisoners
there is a raised way; and you will see, if you look, a low wall built along the
way, like the screen which marionette players have in front of them, over
which they show the puppets.

I see.

And do you see, I said, men passing along the wall carrying all sorts of
vessels, and statues and figures of animals made of wood and stone and various materials, which appear over the wall? Some of them are talking, others silent.

You have shown me a strange image, and they are strange prisoners.

Like ourselves, I replied; and they see only their own shadows, or the shadows of one another, which the fire throws on the opposite wall of
the cave?

True, he said; how could they see anything but the shadows if they were
never allowed to move their heads?

And of the objects which are being carried in like manner they would
only see the shadows?

Yes, he said.

And if they were able to converse with one another, would they not suppose that they were naming what was actually before them?

Very true.

And suppose further that the prison had an echo which came from the
other side, would they not be sure to fancy when one of the passers-by spoke
that the voice which they heard came from the passing shadow?

No question, he replied.

---

[1]The entire dialogue is related, by Socrates, on the day after it is supposed to have occurred.

To them, I said, the truth would be literally nothing but the shadows of the images.

That is certain.

And now look again, and see what will naturally follow if the prisoners are released and disabused of their error. At first, when any of them is liberated and compelled suddenly to stand up and turn his neck round and walk and look towards the light, he will suffer sharp pains; the glare will distress him, and he will be unable to see the realities of which in his former state he had seen the shadows; and then conceive some one saying to him, that what he saw before was an illusion, but that now, when he is approaching nearer to being and his eye is turned towards more real existence, he has a clearer vision,—what will be his reply? And you may further imagine that his instructor is pointing to the objects as they pass and requiring him to name them,—will he not be perplexed? Will he not fancy that the shadows which he formerly saw are truer than the objects which are now shown to him?

Far truer.

And if he is compelled to look straight at the light, will he not have a pain in his eyes which will make him turn away to take refuge in the objects of vision which he can see, and which he will conceive to be in reality clearer than the things which are now being shown to him?

True, he said.

And suppose once more, that he is reluctantly dragged up a steep and rugged ascent, and held fast until he is forced into the presence of the sun himself, is he not likely to be pained and irritated? When he approaches the light his eyes will be dazzled, and he will not be able to see anything at all of what are now called realities.

Not all in a moment, he said.

He will require to grow accustomed to the sight of the upper world. And first he will see the shadows best, next the reflections of men and other objects in the water, and then the objects themselves; then he will gaze upon the light of the moon and the stars and the spangled heaven; and he will see the sky and the stars by night better than the sun or the light of the sun by day?

Certainly.

Last of all he will be able to see the sun, and not mere reflections of him in the water, but he will see him in his own proper place, and not in another; and he will contemplate him as he is.

Certainly.

He will then proceed to argue that this is he who gives the season and the years, and is the guardian of all that is in the visible world, and in a certain way the cause of all things which he and his fellows have been accustomed to behold?

Clearly, he said, he would first see the sun and then reason about him.

And when he remembered his old habitation, and the wisdom of the den and his fellow-prisoners, do you not suppose that he would felicitate himself on the change, and pity them?

Certainly, he would.

And if they were in the habit of conferring honors among themselves on those who were quickest to observe the passing shadows and to remark which of them went before, and which followed after, and which were together;

and who were therefore best able to draw conclusions as to the future, do you think that he would care for such honors and glories, or envy the possessors of them? Would he not say with Homer,

"Better to be the poor servant of a poor master,"[2]

and to endure anything, rather than think as they do and live after their manner?

Yes, he said, I think that he would rather suffer anything than entertain these false notions and live in this miserable manner.

Imagine once more, I said, such a one coming suddenly out of the sun to be replaced in his old situation; would he not be certain to have his eyes full of darkness?

To be sure, he said.

And if there were a contest, and he had to compete in measuring the shadows with the prisoners who had never moved out of the den, while his sight was still weak, and before his eyes had become steady (and the time which would be needed to acquire this new habit of sight might be very considerable), would he not be ridiculous? Men would say of him that up he went and down he came without his eyes; and that it was better not even to think of ascending; and if any one tried to loose another and lead him up to the light, let them only catch the offender, and they would put him to death.

No question, he said.

This entire allegory, I said, you may now append, dear Glaucon, to the previous argument; the prison-house is the world of sight, the light of the fire is the sun, and you will not misapprehend me if you interpret the journey upwards to be the ascent of the soul into the intellectual world according to my poor belief, which, at your desire, I have expressed—whether rightly or wrongly God knows. But, whether true or false, my opinion is that in the world of knowledge the idea of good appears last of all, and is seen only with an effort; and, when seen, is also inferred to be the universal author of all things beautiful and right, parent of light and of the lord of light in this visible world, and the immediate source of reason and truth in the intellectual; and that this is the power upon which he who would act rationally either in public or private life must have his eye fixed.

I agree, he said, as far as I am able to understand you.

Moreover, I said, you must not wonder that those who attain to this beatific vision are unwilling to descend to human affairs; for their souls are ever hastening into the upper world where they desire to dwell; which desire of theirs is very natural, if our allegory may be trusted.

Yes, very natural.

And is there anything surprising in one who passes from divine contemplations to the evil state of man, misbehaving himself in a ridiculous manner; if, while his eyes are blinking and before he has become accustomed to the surrounding darkness, he is compelled to fight in courts of law, or in other

---

[2]In the dim underworld of Hades visited by Odysseus in the *Odyssey,* Book XI, the shade of the great warrior Achilles says that he would rather be alive as the lowliest servant than reign as king of the Underworld.

places, about the images or the shadows of images of justice, and is endeavoring to meet the conceptions of those who have never yet seen absolute justice?

Anything but surprising, he replied.

Any one who has common sense will remember that the bewilderments of the eyes are of two kinds, and arise from two causes, either from coming out of the light or from going into the light, which is true of the mind's eye, quite as much as of the bodily eye; and he who remembers this when he sees any one whose vision is perplexed and weak, will not be too ready to laugh; he will first ask whether that soul of man has come out of the brighter life, and is unable to see because unaccustomed to the dark, or having turned from darkness to the day is dazzled by excess of light. And he will count the one happy in his condition and state of being, and he will pity the other; or, if he have a mind to laugh at the soul which comes from below into the light, there will be more reason in this than in the laugh which greets him who returns from above out of the light into the den.

That, he said, is a very just distinction.

But then, if I am right, certain professors of education must be wrong when they say that they can put a knowledge into the soul which was not there before, like sight into blind eyes.

They undoubtedly say this, he replied.

Whereas, our argument shows that the power and capacity of learning exists in the soul already; and that just as the eye was unable to turn from darkness to light without the whole body, so too the instrument of knowledge can only by the movement of the whole soul be turned from the world of becoming into that of being, and learn by degrees to endure the sight of being, and of the brightest and best of being, or in other words, of the good. . . .

THE APOLOGY

Translated by Benjamin Jowett

In 399 B.C., the seventy-year-old Socrates had made enemies of certain prominent Athenians to the extent that he was brought to trial, on two counts: for atheism and for the corruption of Athenian youth. The *Apology* is Socrates' defense of himself against the charges, both the immediate and specific ones on which he was arraigned and those brought against him during his entire life and career. If the word *apology* is mistakenly understood in its ordinary modern sense, the title of this work will be puzzling, for Socrates' speech is not a confession of guilt or error; it is quite the contrary. Socrates' words are an "apology" in the older sense of *apologia,* meaning an aggressive vindication of himself and of his principles. In keeping with his distinctive style of behavior, Socrates conducts his defense in an utterly personal way, with little regard for expediency or for legal forms and procedures.

Plato himself, then in his late twenties, is mentioned in the *Apology* as among the followers of Socrates present at the trial. If he was indeed present, Plato was in a position to record Socrates' words accurately. To what extent he actually did so, we cannot be sure; as with other Socratic dialogues, we must assume that the *Apology* is a combination of Socrates' ideas and his pupil Plato's own emphases and artistry.

But the image of Socrates that emerges is so compelling that it conveys a strong impression of historical and even reportorial accuracy.

For many centuries readers have been irresistibly drawn to compare Socrates and Jesus. The accounts of their trials and executions are especially worthy of comparison—for both the similarities and the differences. See, for example, Matthew 26–27 and John 18–19. [*Editors' headnote.*]

How you, O Athenians, have been affected by my accusers, I cannot tell; but I know that they almost made me forget who I was—so persuasively did they speak; and yet they have hardly uttered a word of truth. But of the many falsehoods told by them, there was one which quite amazed me;—I mean when they said that you should be upon your guard and not allow yourselves to be deceived by the force of my eloquence. To say this, when they were certain to be detected as soon as I opened my lips and proved myself to be anything but a great speaker, did indeed appear to me most shameless—unless by the force of eloquence they mean the force of truth; for if such is their meaning, I admit that I am eloquent. But in how different a way from theirs! Well, as I was saying, they have scarcely spoken the truth at all; but from me you shall hear the whole truth: not, however, delivered after their manner in a set oration duly ornamented with words and phrases. No, by heaven! but I shall use the words and arguments which occur to me at the moment; for I am confident in the justice of my cause: at my time of life I ought not to be appearing before you, O men of Athens, in the character of a juvenile orator—let no one expect it of me. And I must beg of you to grant me a favor:—If I defend myself in my accustomed manner, and you hear me using the words which I have been in the habit of using in the agora,[1] at the tables of the money-changers, or anywhere else, I would ask you not to be surprised, and not to interrupt me on this account. For I am more than seventy years of age, and appearing now for the first time in a court of law, I am quite a stranger to the language of the place; and therefore I would have you regard me as if I were really a stranger,[2] whom you would excuse if he spoke in his native tongue, and after the fashion of his country:—Am I making an unfair request of you? Never mind the manner, which may or may not be good; but think only of the truth of my words, and give heed to that: let the speaker speak truly and the judge decide justly.

And first, I have to reply to the older charges and to my first accusers, and then I will go on to the later ones. For of old I have had many accusers, who have accused me falsely to you during many years; and I am more afraid of them than of Anytus and his associates,[3] who are dangerous, too, in their own way. But far more dangerous are the others, who began when you were children, and took possession of your minds with their falsehoods, telling

[1] The public marketplace where citizens congregated.

[2] A noncitizen of Athens, whose dialect would have sounded uncouth to Athenians. Socrates' ironic point is that, though he is a genuine and lifelong Athenian, his manner of discourse will sound unconventional, like that of a "stranger" or foreigner.

[3] The three men who pressed charges against Socrates were Anytus, Meletus, and Lycon. Anytus was a wealthy leather merchant who disliked Socrates partly on political grounds and partly because Socrates had tried to persuade Anytus to let his son pursue a career different from his father's. Meletus (cross-examined by Socrates later in the *Apology*) may have been a poet (poets were both adulated and despised by Socrates/Plato). Of Lycon little is known; he may have been a professional orator.

of one Socrates, a wise man, who speculated about the heaven above, and searched into the earth beneath, and made the worse appear the better cause.[4] The disseminators of this tale are the accusers whom I dread; for their hearers are apt to fancy that such enquirers do not believe in the existence of the gods. And they are many, and their charges against me are of ancient date, and they were made by them in the days when you were more impressible than you are now—in childhood, or it may have been in youth—and the cause when heard went by default, for there was none to answer. And hardest of all, I do not know and cannot tell the names of my accusers; unless in the chance case of a Comic poet.[5] All who from envy and malice have persuaded you—some of them having first convinced themselves—all this class of men are most difficult to deal with; for I cannot have them up here, and cross-examine them, and therefore I must simply fight with shadows in my own defense, and argue when there is no one who answers. I will ask you then to assume with me, as I was saying, that my opponents are of two kinds; one recent, the other ancient: and I hope that you will see the propriety of my answering the latter first, for these accusations you heard long before the others, and much oftener.

Well, then, I must make my defense, and endeavor to clear away in a short time, a slander which has lasted a long time. May I succeed, if to succeed be for my good and yours, or likely to avail me in my cause! The task is not an easy one; I quite understand the nature of it. And so leaving the event with God, in obedience to the law I will now make my defense.

I will begin at the beginning, and ask what is the accusation which has given rise to the slander of me, and in fact has encouraged Meletus to prefer this charge against me. Well, what do the slanderers say? They shall be my prosecutors, and I will sum up their words in an affidavit: 'Socrates is an evil-doer, and a curious person, who searches into things under the earth and in heaven, and he makes the worse appear the better cause; and he teaches the aforesaid doctrines to others.' Such is the nature of the accusation: it is just what you have yourselves seen in the comedy of Aristophanes, who has introduced a man whom he calls Socrates, going about and saying that he walks in air, and talking a deal of nonsense concerning matters of which I do not pretend to know either much or little—not that I mean to speak disparagingly of any one who is a student of natural philosophy. I should be very sorry if Meletus could bring so grave a charge against me. But the simple truth is, O Athenians, that I have nothing to do with physical speculations. Very many of those here present are witnesses to the truth of this, and to them I appeal. Speak then, you who have heard me, and tell your neighbors whether any of you have ever known me hold forth in few words or in many upon such matters. . . . You hear their answer. And from what they say of this part of the charge you will be able to judge of the truth of the rest.

---

[4] Socrates was almost entirely concerned with ethical human values, as distinguished from both natural science and the tricks of logic and language associated with the Sophists (professional teachers of rhetoric and logic or pseudo-logic). Nevertheless, his dexterity in discourse and his subtleties of argument caused some people to believe that he was a Sophist.

[5] Aristophanes, who in his play *The Clouds* represented Socrates unfavorably, as a pretender to miraculous powers.

As little foundation is there for the report that I am a teacher, and take money; this accusation has no more truth in it than the other. Although, if a man were really able to instruct mankind, to receive money for giving instruction would, in my opinion, be an honor to him. There is Gorgias of Leontium, and Prodicus of Ceos, and Hippias of Elis,[6] who go the round of the cities, and are able to persuade the young men to leave their own citizens by whom they might be taught for nothing, and come to them whom they not only pay, but are thankful if they may be allowed to pay them. There is at this time a Parian philosopher residing in Athens, of whom I have heard; and I came to hear of him in this way:—I came across a man who has spent a world of money on the Sophists, Callias, the son of Hipponicus, and knowing that he had sons, I asked him: 'Callias,' I said, 'if your two sons were foals or calves, there would be no difficulty in finding some one to put over them; we should hire a trainer of horses, or a farmer probably, who would improve and perfect them in their own proper virtue and excellence; but as they are human beings, whom are you thinking of placing over them? Is there any one who understands human and political virtue? You must have thought about the matter, for you have sons; is there any one?' 'There is,' he said. 'Who is he?' said I, 'and of what country? and what does he charge?' 'Evenus[7] the Parian,' he replied; 'he is the man, and his charge is five minae.' Happy is Evenus, I said to myself, if he really has this wisdom, and teaches at such a moderate charge. Had I the same, I should have been very proud and conceited; but the truth is that I have no knowledge of the kind.

I dare say, Athenians, that some one among you will reply, 'Yes, Socrates, but what is the origin of these accusations which are brought against you; there must have been something strange which you have been doing? All these rumors and this talk about you would never have arisen if you had been like other men: tell us, then, what is the cause of them, for we should be sorry to judge hastily of you.' Now I regard this as a fair challenge, and I will endeavor to explain to you the reason why I am called wise and have such an evil fame. Please to attend then. And although some of you may think that I am joking, I declare that I will tell you the entire truth. Men of Athens, this reputation of mine has come of a certain sort of wisdom which I possess. If you ask me what kind of wisdom, I reply, wisdom such as may perhaps be attained by man, for to that extent I am inclined to believe that I am wise; whereas the persons of whom I was speaking have a superhuman wisdom, which I may fail to describe, because I have it not myself; and he who says that I have, speaks falsely, and is taking away my character. And here, O men of Athens, I must beg you not to interrupt me, even if I seem to say something extravagant. For the word which I will speak is not mine. I will refer you to a witness who is worthy of credit; that witness shall be the God of Delphi[8]—he will tell you about my wisdom, if I have any, and of what sort it is. You must have known Chaerephon; he was early a friend of mine,

---

[6]Noted Sophists and teachers, mainly of rhetoric and logic.

[7]A poet and teacher of oratory, from the island of Paros. The low sum he charged may indicate his low repute as a teacher. A mina was worth about forty dollars.

[8]Site of the most famous temple of Apollo; the god's oracles were pronounced there by the Pythia, his priestess.

and also a friend of yours, for he shared in the recent exile of the people,[9] and returned with you. Well, Chaerephon, as you know, was very impetuous in all his doings, and he went to Delphi and boldly asked the oracle to tell him whether—as I was saying, I must beg you not to interrupt—he asked the oracle to tell him whether any one was wiser than I was, and the Pythian prophetess answered, that there was no man wiser. Chaerephon is dead himself; but his brother, who is in court, will confirm the truth of what I am saying.

Why do I mention this? Because I am going to explain to you why I have such an evil name. When I heard the answer, I said to myself, What can the god mean? and what is the interpretation of his riddle? for I know that I have no wisdom, small or great. What then can he mean when he says that I am the wisest of men? And yet he is a god, and cannot lie; that would be against his nature. After long consideration, I thought of a method of trying the question. I reflected that if I could only find a man wiser than myself, then I might go to the god with a refutation in my hand. I should say to him, 'Here is a man who is wiser than I am; but you said that I was the wisest.' Accordingly I went to one who had the reputation of wisdom, and observed him—his name I need not mention; he was a politician whom I selected for examination—and the result was as follows: When I began to talk with him, I could not help thinking that he was not really wise, although he was thought wise by many, and still wiser by himself; and thereupon I tried to explain to him that he thought himself wise, but was not really wise; and the consequence was that he hated me, and his enmity was shared by several who were present and heard me. So I left him, saying to myself, as I went away: Well, although I do not suppose that either of us knows anything really beautiful and good, I am better off than he is,—for he knows nothing, and thinks that he knows; I neither know nor think that I know. In this latter particular, then, I seem to have slightly the advantage of him. Then I went to another who had still higher pretensions to wisdom, and my conclusion was exactly the same. Whereupon I made another enemy of him, and of many others beside him.

Then I went to one man after another, being not unconscious of the enmity which I provoked, and I lamented and feared this: but necessity was laid upon me,—the word of God, I thought, ought to be considered first. And I said to myself, Go I must to all who appear to know, and find out the meaning of the oracle. And I swear to you, Athenians, by the dog I swear!—for I must tell you the truth—the result of my mission was just this: I found that the men most in repute were all but the most foolish; and that others less esteemed were really wiser and better. I will tell you the tale of my wanderings and of the 'Herculean'[10] labors, as I may call them, which I endured only to find at last the oracle irrefutable. After the politicians, I went to the poets; tragic, dithyrambic, and all sorts. And there, I said to myself, you will be instantly detected; now you will find out that you are more ignorant than they are.

---

[9] Five years earlier, after the defeat of Athens by Sparta in 404, the "Thirty Tyrants" had temporarily ruled and terrorized Athens, driving the democratic leaders (who included Socrates' friend Chaerephon) into temporary exile. The democracy had been reestablished in 403.

[10] The legendary hero Hercules had been forced to undertake a series of superhumanly difficult tasks.

Accordingly, I took them some of the most elaborate passages in their own writings, and asked what was the meaning of them—thinking that they would teach me something. Will you believe me? I am almost ashamed to confess the truth, but I must say that there is hardly a person present who would not have talked better about their poetry than they did themselves. Then I knew that not by wisdom do poets write poetry, but by a sort of genius and inspiration; they are like diviners or soothsayers who also say many fine things, but do not understand the meaning of them.[11] The poets appeared to me to be much in the same case; and I further observed that upon the strength of their poetry they believed themselves to be the wisest of men in other things in which they were not wise. So I departed, conceiving myself to be superior to them for the same reason that I was superior to the politicians.

At last I went to the artisans,[12] for I was conscious that I knew nothing at all, as I may say, and I was sure that they knew many fine things; and here I was not mistaken, for they did know many things of which I was ignorant, and in this they certainly were wiser than I was. But I observed that even the good artisans fell into the same error as the poets;—because they were good workmen they thought that they also knew all sorts of high matters, and this defect in them overshadowed their wisdom; and therefore I asked myself on behalf of the oracle, whether I would like to be as I was, neither having their knowledge nor their ignorance, or like them in both; and I made answer to myself and to the oracle that I was better off as I was.

This inquisition has led to my having many enemies of the worst and most dangerous kind, and has given occasion also to many calumnies. And I am called wise, for my hearers always imagine that I myself possess the wisdom which I find wanting in others: but the truth is, O men of Athens, that God only is wise; and by his answer he intends to show that the wisdom of men is worth little or nothing; he is not speaking of Socrates, he is only using my name by way of illustration, as if he said, He, O men, is the wisest, who, like Socrates, knows that his wisdom is in truth worth nothing. And so I go about the world, obedient to the god, and search and make enquiry into the wisdom of any one, whether citizen or stranger, who appears to be wise; and if he is not wise, then in vindication of the oracle I show him that he is not wise; and my occupation quite absorbs me, and I have no time to give either to any public matter of interest or to any concern of my own, but I am in utter poverty by reason of my devotion to the god.

There is another thing:—young men of the richer classes, who have not much to do, come about me of their own accord; they like to hear the pretenders examined, and they often imitate me, and proceed to examine others; there are plenty of persons, as they quickly discover, who think that they know something, but really know little or nothing; and then those who are examined by them instead of being angry with themselves are angry with me: This confounded Socrates, they say; this villainous misleader of youth!—and then if somebody asks them, Why, what evil does he practice or teach?

---

[11] This view of poets and of their interpreters is elaborated, half-playfully, by Socrates in Plato's *Ion.*

[12] Craftsmen.

they do not know, and cannot tell; but in order that they may not appear to be at a loss, they repeat the ready-made charges which are used against all philosophers about teaching things up in the clouds and under the earth, and having no gods, and making the worse appear the better cause; for they do not like to confess that their pretense of knowledge has been detected—which is the truth; and as they are numerous and ambitious and energetic, and are drawn up in battle array and have persuasive tongues, they have filled your ears with their loud and inveterate calumnies. And this is the reason why my three accusers, Meletus and Anytus and Lycon, have set upon me; Meletus, who has a quarrel with me on behalf of the poets; Anytus, on behalf of the craftsmen and politicians; Lycon, on behalf of the rhetoricians: and as I said at the beginning, I cannot expect to get rid of such a mass of calumny all in a moment. And this, O men of Athens, is the truth and the whole truth; I have concealed nothing, I have dissembled nothing. And yet, I know that my plainness of speech makes them hate me, and what is their hatred but a proof that I am speaking the truth?—Hence has arisen the prejudice against me; and this is the reason of it, as you will find out either in this or in any future enquiry.

I have said enough in my defense against the first class of my accusers; I turn to the second class. They are headed by Meletus, that good man and true lover of his country, as he calls himself. Against these, too, I must try to make a defense:—Let their affidavit be read: it contains something of this kind: It says that Socrates is a doer of evil, who corrupts the youth; and who does not believe in the gods of the state, but has other new divinities of his own. Such is the charge; and now let us examine the particular counts. He says that I am a doer of evil, and corrupt the youth; but I say, O men of Athens, that Meletus is a doer of evil, in that he pretends to be in earnest when he is only in jest, and is so eager to bring men to trial from a pretended zeal and interest about matters in which he really never had the smallest interest. And the truth of this I will endeavor to prove to you.

Come hither, Meletus, and let me ask a question of you. You think a great deal about the improvement of youth?

Yes, I do.

Tell the judges, then, who is their improver; for you must know, as you have taken the pains to discover their corrupter, and are citing and accusing me before them. Speak, then, and tell the judges who their improver is.—Observe, Meletus, that you are silent, and have nothing to say. But is not this rather disgraceful, and a very considerable proof of what I was saying, that you have no interest in the matter? Speak up, friend, and tell us who their improver is.

The laws.

But that, my good sir, is not my meaning. I want to know who the person is, who, in the first place, knows the laws.[13]

---

[13]In the following lines, Socrates calls into play his notorious talent for reducing his opponent's view to foolishness. The half-defiant, half-squirming Meletus is forced to define the non-corrupters of youth first as the "judges" (that is, the men empowered to render the verdict), then the entire audience, then the "senators" (the five hundred select members of the assembly who constituted the Athenian civic council), then the whole "assembly," which in law included the entire adult citizenry of Athens.

The judges, Socrates, who are present in court.

What, do you mean to say, Meletus, that they are able to instruct and improve youth?

Certainly they are.

What, all of them, or some only and not others?

All of them.

By the goddess Herè,[14] that is good news! There are plenty of improvers, then. And what do you say of the audience,—do they improve them?

Yes, they do.

And the senators?

Yes, the senators improve them.

But perhaps the members of the assembly corrupt them?—or do they too improve them?

They improve them.

Then every Athenian improves and elevates them; all with the exception of myself; and I alone am their corrupter? Is that what you affirm?

That is what I stoutly affirm.

I am very unfortunate if you are right. But suppose I ask you a question: How about horses? Does one man do them harm and all the world good? Is not the exact opposite the truth? One man is able to do them good, or at least not many;—the trainer of horses, that is to say, does them good, and others who have to do with them rather injure them? Is not that true, Meletus, of horses, or of any other animals? Most assuredly it is; whether you and Anytus say yes or no. Happy indeed would be the condition of youth if they had one corrupter only, and all the rest of the world were their improvers. But you, Meletus, have sufficiently shown that you never had a thought about the young: your carelessness is seen in your not caring about the very things which you bring against me.

And now, Meletus, I will ask you another question—by Zeus I will: Which is better, to live among bad citizens, or among good ones? Answer, friend, I say; the question is one which may be easily answered. Do not the good do their neighbors good, and the bad do them evil?

Certainly.

And is there any one who would rather be injured than benefited by those who live with him? Answer, my good friend, the law requires you to answer— does any one like to be injured?

Certainly not.

And when you accuse me of corrupting and deteriorating the youth, do you allege that I corrupt them intentionally or unintentionally?

Intentionally, I say.

But you have just admitted that the good do their neighbors good, and the evil do them evil. Now, is that a truth which your superior wisdom has recognized thus early in life, and am I, at my age, in such darkness and ignorance as not to know that if a man with whom I have to live is corrupted by me, I am very likely to be harmed by him; and yet I corrupt him, and intentionally, too—so you say, although neither I nor any other human being is

---

[14]Hera, queen of the gods; this oath is often used by Socrates.

ever likely to be convinced by you. But either I do not corrupt them, or I corrupt them unintentionally; and on either view of the case you lie. If my offense is unintentional, the law has no cognizance of unintentional offenses: you ought to have taken me privately, and warned and admonished me; for if I had been better advised, I should have left off doing what I only did unintentionally—no doubt I should; but you would have nothing to say to me and refused to teach me. And now you bring me up in this court, which is a place not of instruction, but of punishment.

It will be very clear to you, Athenians, as I was saying, that Meletus has no care at all, great or small, about the matter. But still I should like to know, Meletus, in what I am affirmed to corrupt the young. I suppose you mean, as I infer from your indictment, that I teach them not to acknowledge the gods which the state acknowledges, but some other new divinities or spiritual agencies in their stead. These are the lessons by which I corrupt the youth, as you say.

Yes, that I say emphatically.

Then, by the gods, Meletus, of whom we are speaking, tell me and the court, in somewhat plainer terms, what you mean! for I do not as yet understand whether you affirm that I teach other men to acknowledge some gods, and therefore that I do believe in gods, and am not an entire atheist—this you do not lay to my charge,—but only you say that they are not the same gods which the city recognizes—the charge is that they are different gods. Or, do you mean that I am an atheist simply, and a teacher of atheism?

I mean the latter—that you are a complete atheist.

What an extraordinary statement! Why do you think so, Meletus? Do you mean that I do not believe in the godhead of the sun or moon,[15] like other men?

I assure you, judges, that he does not: for he says that the sun is stone, and the moon earth.

Friend Meletus, you think that you are accusing Anaxagoras:[16] and you have but a bad opinion of the judges, if you fancy them illiterate to such a degree as not to know that these doctrines are found in the books of Anaxagoras the Clazomenian, which are full of them. And so, forsooth, the youth are said to be taught them by Socrates, when there are not unfrequently exhibitions of them at the theater (price of admission one drachma at the most); and they might pay their money, and laugh at Socrates if he pretends to father these extraordinary views. And so, Meletus, you really think that I do not believe in any god?

I swear by Zeus that you believe absolutely in none at all.

---

[15]Apollo was the god of the sun, Artemis the goddess of the moon; but, whether the sun and moon were literally identified with these deities or not, reverence for the two great celestial bodies was a hallmark of religious piety for the Greeks. Socrates did, in fact, hold the sun and moon in awe, as is shown in Plato's *Symposium.*

[16]A philosopher-scientist, born around 500 B.C. Socrates, concerned almost entirely with ethics, would have resisted such materialist astrophysical theories. The reference to the theater a few lines later may mean that Anaxagoras' ideas were explored by the playwrights (particularly Euripides and Aristophanes) or that the philosopher's writings could be purchased there (or in some similar public place). In any event, Socrates' point is that such religiously heterodox ideas were freely available to the public apart from anything he might have taught.

Nobody will believe you, Meletus, and I am pretty sure that you do not believe yourself. I cannot help thinking, men of Athens, that Meletus is reckless and impudent, and that he has written this indictment in a spirit of mere wantonness and youthful bravado. Has he not compounded a riddle, thinking to try me? He said to himself:—I shall see whether the wise Socrates will discover my facetious contradiction, or whether I shall be able to deceive him and the rest of them. For he certainly does appear to me to contradict himself in the indictment as much as if he said that Socrates is guilty of not believing in the gods, and yet of believing in them—but this is not like a person who is in earnest.

I should like you, O men of Athens, to join me in examining what I conceive to be his inconsistency; and do you, Meletus, answer. And I must remind the audience of my request that they would not make a disturbance if I speak in my accustomed manner:

Did ever man, Meletus, believe in the existence of human things, and not of human beings? . . . I wish, men of Athens, that he would answer, and not be always trying to get up an interruption. Did ever any man believe in horsemanship, and not in horses? or in flute-playing, and not in flute-players? No, my friend; I will answer to you and to the court, as you refuse to answer for yourself. There is no man who ever did. But now please to answer the next question: Can a man believe in spiritual and divine agencies, and not in spirits or in demigods?[17]

He cannot.

How lucky I am to have extracted that answer, by the assistance of the court! But then you swear in the indictment that I teach and believe in divine or spiritual agencies (new or old, no matter for that); at any rate, I believe in spiritual agencies,—so you say and swear in the affidavit; and yet if I believe in divine beings, how can I help believing in spirits or demigods;—must I not? To be sure I must; and therefore I may assume that your silence gives consent. Now what are spirits or demigods? are they not either gods or the sons of gods?

Certainly they are.

But this is what I call the facetious riddle invented by you: the demigods or spirits are gods, and you say first that I do not believe in gods, and then again that I do believe in gods; that is, if I believe in demigods. For if the demigods are the illegitimate sons of gods, whether by the nymphs or by any other mothers, of whom they are said to be the sons—what human being will ever believe that there are no gods if they are the sons of gods? You might as well affirm the existence of mules,[18] and deny that of horses and asses. Such nonsense, Meletus, could only have been intended by you to make trial of me. You have put this into the indictment because you had nothing real of which to accuse me. But no one who has a particle of understanding will ever be convinced by you that the same men can believe in divine and superhuman things, and yet not believe that there are gods and demigods and heroes.

---

[17] The ensuing cross-examination of Meletus, logically sound or not, should probably be understood as an attempt by Socrates to prove contemptuously that he could easily defeat his opponents at their legalistic game if he did not have more substantial arguments to make (the ones that emerge in the following parts of his speech).

[18] A mule is a sterile animal produced by the union of a jackass with a mare.

I have said enough in answer to the charge of Meletus: any elaborate defense is unnecessary; but I know only too well how many are the enmities which I have incurred, and this is what will be my destruction if I am destroyed;— not Meletus, nor yet Anytus, but the envy and detraction of the world, which has been the death of many good men, and will probably be the death of many more; there is no danger of my being the last of them.

Some one will say: And are you not ashamed, Socrates, of a course of life which is likely to bring you to an untimely end? To him I may fairly answer: There you are mistaken: a man who is good for anything ought not to calculate the chance of living or dying; he ought only to consider whether in doing anything he is doing right or wrong—acting the part of a good man or of a bad. Whereas, upon your view, the heroes who fell at Troy were not good for much, and the son of Thetis[19] above all, who altogether despised danger in comparison with disgrace; and when he was so eager to slay Hector, his goddess mother said to him, that if he avenged his companion Patroclus, and slew Hector, he would die himself—'Fate,' she said, in these or the like words, 'waits for you next after Hector;' he, receiving this warning, utterly despised danger and death, and instead of fearing them, feared rather to live in dishonor, and not to avenge his friend. 'Let me die forthwith,' he replies, 'and be avenged of my enemy, rather than abide here by the beaked ships, a laughing-stock and a burden of the earth.' Had Achilles any thought of death and danger? For wherever a man's place is, whether the place which he has chosen or that in which he has been placed by a commander, there he ought to remain in the hour of danger; he should not think of death or of anything but of disgrace. And this, O men of Athens, is a true saying.

Strange, indeed, would be my conduct, O men of Athens, if I who, when I was ordered by the generals whom you chose to command me at Potidaea and Amphipolis and Delium,[20] remained where they placed me, like any other man, facing death—if now, when, as I conceive and imagine, God orders me to fulfil the philosopher's mission of searching into myself and other men, I were to desert my post through fear of death, or any other fear; that would indeed be strange, and I might justly be arraigned in court for denying the existence of the gods, if I disobeyed the oracle because I was afraid of death, fancying that I was wise when I was not wise. For the fear of death is indeed the pretense of wisdom, and not real wisdom, being a pretense of knowing the unknown; and no one knows whether death, which men in their fear apprehend to be the greatest evil, may not be the greatest good. Is not this ignorance of a disgraceful sort, the ignorance which is the conceit that a man knows what he does not know? And in this respect only I believe myself to differ from men in general, and may perhaps claim to be wiser than they

[19]A sea nymph, mother of Achilles, the hero of Homer's *Iliad*. The Trojan prince and hero Hector had killed Achilles' best friend, Patroclus, an event that brought Achilles back into the battle after a period of sulky neutrality occasioned by his quarrel with the Greek commander Agamemnon. The dialogue cited here, between Achilles and Thetis, occurs in Book XVIII of the *Iliad*.

[20]Sites of battles (fought, respectively, in 432, 422, and 424) in which Socrates had served bravely as a soldier. At Potidaea Socrates had saved the life of the Athenian soldier-playboy Alcibiades; see Plato's *Symposium*.

are:—that whereas I know but little of the world below, I do not suppose that I know: but I do know that injustice and disobedience to a better, whether God or man, is evil and dishonorable, and I will never fear or avoid a possible good rather than a certain evil. And therefore if you let me go now, and are not convinced by Anytus, who said that since I had been prosecuted I must be put to death; (or if not that I ought never to have been prosecuted at all); and that if I escape now, your sons will all be utterly ruined by listening to my words—if you say to me, Socrates, this time we will not mind Anytus, and you shall be let off, but upon one condition, that you are not to enquire and speculate in this way any more, and that if you are caught doing so again you shall die;—if this was the condition on which you let me go, I should reply: Men of Athens, I honor and love you; but I shall obey God rather than you, and while I have life and strength I shall never cease from the practice and teaching of philosophy, exhorting any one whom I meet and saying to him after my manner: You, my friend,—a citizen of the great and mighty and wise city of Athens,—are you not ashamed of heaping up the greatest amount of money and honor and reputation, and caring so little about wisdom and truth and the greatest improvement of the soul, which you never regard or heed at all? And if the person with whom I am arguing, says: Yes, but I do care; then I do not leave him or let him go at once; but I proceed to interrogate and examine and cross-examine him, and if I think that he has no virtue in him, but only says that he has, I reproach him with undervaluing the greater, and overvaluing the less. And I shall repeat the same words to every one whom I meet, young and old, citizen and alien, but especially to the citizens, inasmuch as they are my brethren. For know that this is the command of God; and I believe that no greater good has ever happened in the state than my service to the God. For I do nothing but go about persuading you all, old and young alike, not to take thought for your persons or your properties, but first and chiefly to care about the greatest improvement of the soul. I tell you that virtue is not given by money, but that from virtue comes money and every other good of man, public as well as private. This is my teaching, and if this is the doctrine which corrupts the youth, I am a mischievous person. But if any one says that this is not my teaching, he is speaking an untruth. Wherefore, O men of Athens, I say to you, do as Anytus bids or not as Anytus bids, and either acquit me or not; but whichever you do, understand that I shall never alter my ways, not even if I have to die many times.

Men of Athens, do not interrupt, but hear me; there was an understanding between us that you should hear me to the end: I have something more to say, at which you may be inclined to cry out; but I believe that to hear me will be good for you, and therefore I beg that you will not cry out. I would have you know, that if you kill such an one as I am, you will injure yourselves more than you will injure me. Nothing will injure me, not Meletus nor yet Anytus—they cannot, for a bad man is not permitted to injure a better than himself. I do not deny that Anytus may, perhaps, kill him, or drive him into exile, or deprive him of civil rights; and he may imagine, and others may imagine, that he is inflicting a great injury upon him: but there I do not agree. For the evil of doing as he is doing—the evil of unjustly taking away the life of another—is greater far.

And now, Athenians, I am not going to argue for my own sake, as you may think, but for yours, that you may not sin against the God by condemning me, who am his gift to you. For if you kill me you will not easily find a successor to me, who, if I may use such a ludicrous figure of speech, am a sort of gadfly, given to the state by God; and the state is a great and noble steed who is tardy in his motions owing to his very size, and requires to be stirred into life. I am that gadfly which God has attached to the state, and all day long and in all places am always fastening upon you, arousing and persuading and reproaching you. You will not easily find another like me, and therefore I would advise you to spare me. I dare say that you may feel out of temper (like a person who is suddenly awakened from sleep), and you think that you might easily strike me dead as Anytus advises, and then you would sleep on for the remainder of your lives, unless God in his care of you sent you another gadfly. When I say that I am given to you by God, the proof of my mission is this:—if I had been like other men, I should not have neglected all my own concerns or patiently seen the neglect of them during all these years, and have been doing yours, coming to you individually like a father or elder brother, exhorting you to regard virtue; such conduct, I say, would be unlike human nature. If I had gained anything, or if my exhortations had been paid, there would have been some sense in my doing so; but now, as you will perceive, not even the impudence of my accusers dares to say that I have ever exacted or sought pay of any one; of that they have no witness. And I have a sufficient witness to the truth of what I say—my poverty.

Some one may wonder why I go about in private giving advice and busying myself with the concerns of others, but do not venture to come forward in public and advise the state. I will tell you why. You have heard me speak at sundry times and in divers places of an oracle or sign which comes to me, and is the divinity which Meletus ridicules in the indictment. This sign, which is a kind of voice, first began to come to me when I was a child; it always forbids but never commands me to do anything which I am going to do. This is what deters me from being a politician. And rightly, as I think. For I am certain, O men of Athens, that if I had engaged in politics, I should have perished long ago, and done no good either to you or to myself. And do not be offended at my telling you the truth: for the truth is, that no man who goes to war with you or any other multitude, honestly striving against the many lawless and unrighteous deeds which are done in a state, will save his life; he who will fight for the right, if he would live even for a brief space, must have a private station and not a public one.

I can give you convincing evidence of what I say, not words only, but what you value far more—actions. Let me relate to you a passage of my own life which will prove to you that I should never have yielded to injustice from any fear of death, and that 'as I should have refused to yield' I must have died at once. I will tell you a tale of the courts, not very interesting perhaps, but nevertheless true. The only office of state which I ever held, O men of Athens, was that of senator: the tribe Antiochis, which is my tribe, had the presidency at the trial of the generals who had not taken up the bodies of the slain after the battle of Arginusae; and you proposed to try them in a body, contrary to law, as you all thought afterwards; but at the time I was the only one of the Prytanes who was opposed to the illegality, and I gave my vote against you; and when the orators threatened to impeach and arrest me, and you called and shouted, I made up my mind that I would run the risk, having law and justice with me, rather than take part in your injustice because I feared imprisonment and death. This happened in the days of the democracy.[21] But when the oligarchy of the Thirty was in power, they sent for me and four others into the rotunda, and bade us bring Leon[22] the Salaminian from Salamis, as they wanted to put him to death. This was a specimen of the sort of commands which they were always giving with the view of implicating as many as possible in their crimes; and then I showed, not in word only but in deed, that, if I may be allowed to use such an expression, I cared not a straw for death, and that my great and only care was lest I should do an unrighteous or unholy thing. For the strong arm of that oppressive power did not frighten me into doing wrong; and when we came out of the rotunda the other four went to Salamis and fetched Leon, but I went quietly home. For which I might have lost my life, had not the power of the Thirty shortly afterwards come to an end. And many will witness to my words.

Now do you really imagine that I could have survived all these years, if I had led a public life, supposing that like a good man I had always maintained the right and had made justice, as I ought, the first thing? No indeed, men of Athens, neither I nor any other man. But I have been always the same in all my actions, public as well as private, and never have I yielded any base compliance to those who are slanderously termed my disciples, or to any other. Not that I have any regular disciples. But if anyone likes to come and hear me while I am pursuing my mission, whether he be young or old, he is not excluded. Nor do I converse only with those who pay; but any one, whether he be rich or poor, may ask and answer me and listen to my words; and whether he turns out to be a bad man or a good one, neither result can be justly imputed to me; for I never taught or professed to teach him anything. And if any one says that he has ever learned or heard anything from me in private which all the world has not heard, let me tell you that he is lying.

But I shall be asked, Why do people delight in continually conversing with you? I have told you already, Athenians, the whole truth about this matter: they like to hear the cross-examination of the pretenders to wisdom; there is amusement in it. Now this duty of cross-examining other men has been imposed upon me by God; and has been signified to me by oracles, visions, and in every way in which the will of divine power was ever intimated to any one. This is true, O Athenians; or, if not true, would be soon refuted. If I am or have been corrupting the youth, those of them who are now grown up and have become sensible that I gave them bad advice in the days of their youth should come forward as accusers, and take their revenge; or if they do not like to come themselves, some of their relatives, fathers, brothers, or

---

[21]The Athenian senate consisted of five hundred members, fifty from each of the ten phylae, or "tribes." Socrates belonged to a tribe named for the mythical figure Antiochus. Each tribe served for one-tenth of the year as the executive body of the senate; during that period they were called "Prytanes." While Socrates was serving in that capacity, certain Athenian commanders were indicted for allegedly neglecting the dead after the naval battle of Arginusae in 406. Socrates refused to participate in the trial, which violated due process of Athenian law in a number of ways.

[22]As he had defied the authority of the democratic state, Socrates also defied the tyrannical "Thirty" who ruled in 404, by refusing to extradite Leon from Salamis after he had fled there to escape the despotic regime.

other kinsmen, should say what evil their families have suffered at my hands. Now is their time. Many of them I see in the court. There is Crito, who is of the same age and of the same deme[23] with myself, and there is Critobulus his son, whom I also see. Then again there is Lysanias of Sphettus, who is the father of Aeschines—he is present; and also there is Antiphon of Cephisus, who is the father of Epigenes; and there are the brothers of several who have associated with me. There is Nicostratus the son of Theosdotides, and the brother of Theodotus (now Theodotus himself is dead, and therefore he, at any rate, will not seek to stop him); and there is Paralus the son of Demodocus, who had a brother Theages; and Adeimantus the son of Ariston, whose brother Plato[24] is present; and Aeantodorus, who is the brother of Apollodorus, whom I also see. I might mention a great many others, some of whom Meletus should have produced as witnesses in the course of his speech; and let him still produce them, if he has forgotten—I will make way for him. And let him say, if he has any testimony of the sort which he can produce. Nay, Athenians, the very opposite is the truth. For all these are ready to witness on behalf of the corrupter, of the injurer of their kindred, as Meletus and Anytus call me; not the corrupted youth only—there might have been a motive for that—but their uncorrupted elder relatives. Why should they too support me with their testimony? Why, indeed, except for the sake of truth and justice, and because they know that I am speaking the truth, and that Meletus is a liar.

Well, Athenians, this and the like of this is all the defense which I have to offer. Yet a word more. Perhaps there may be some one who is offended at me, when he calls to mind how he himself on a similar, or even a less serious occasion, prayed and entreated the judges with many tears, and how he produced children in court, which was a moving spectacle, together with a host of relations and friends; whereas I, who am probably in danger of my life, will do none of these things. The contrast may occur to his mind, and he may be set against me, and vote in anger because he is displeased at me on this account. Now if there be such a person among you,—mind, I do not say that there is,—to him I may fairly reply: My friend, I am a man, and like other men, a creature of flesh and blood, and not 'of wood or stone,' as Homer says;[25] and I have a family, yes, and sons, O Athenians, three in number, one almost a man, and two others who are still young; and yet I will not bring any of them hither in order to petition you for an acquittal. And why not? Not from any self-assertion or want of respect for you. Whether I am or am not afraid of death is another question, of which I will not now speak. But, having regard to public opinion, I feel that such conduct would be discreditable to myself, and to you, and to the whole state. One who has reached my years, and who has a name for wisdom, ought not to demean himself. Whether this opinion of me be deserved or not, at any rate the world has decided that Socrates is in some way superior to other men. And if those among you who are said to be superior in wisdom and courage, and any other virtue, demean themselves in this way, how shameful is their conduct! I have seen men of reputation, when they have been condemned, behaving in the

---

[23] District.

[24] The author of the present work. Several of the persons mentioned appear in other works by Plato.

[25] The words are addressed to the disguised Odysseus by his wife, Penelope, in Book XIX of Homer's *Odyssey*.

strangest manner: they seemed to fancy that they were going to suffer something dreadful if they died, and that they could be immortal if you only allowed them to live; and I think that such are a dishonor to the state, and that any stranger coming in would have said of them that the most eminent men of Athens, to whom the Athenians themselves give honor and command, are no better than women. And I say that these things ought not to be done by those of us who have a reputation; and if they are done, you ought not to permit them; you ought rather to show that you are far more disposed to condemn the man who gets up a doleful scene and makes the city ridiculous, than him who holds his peace.

But, setting aside the question of public opinion, there seems to be something wrong in asking a favor of a judge, and thus procuring an acquittal, instead of informing and convincing him. For his duty is, not to make a present of justice, but to give judgment; and he has sworn that he will judge according to the laws, and not according to his own good pleasure; and we ought not to encourage you, nor should you allow yourselves to be encouraged, in this habit of perjury—there can be no piety in that. Do not then require me to do what I consider dishonorable and impious and wrong, especially now, when I am being tried for impiety on the indictment of Meletus. For if, O men of Athens, by force of persuasion and entreaty I could overpower your oaths, then I should be teaching you to believe that there are no gods, and in defending should simply convict myself of the charge of not believing in them. But that is not so—far otherwise. For I do believe that there are gods, and in a sense higher than that in which any of my accusers believe in them. And to you and to God I commit my cause, to be determined by you as is best for you and me.[26]

There are many reasons why I am not grieved, O men of Athens, at the vote of condemnation. I expected it, and am only surprised that the votes are so nearly equal; for I had thought that the majority against me would have been far larger; but now, had thirty votes gone over to the other side, I should have been acquitted. And I may say, I think, that I have escaped Meletus. I may say more, for without the assistance of Anytus and Lycon, any one may see that he would not have had a fifth part of the votes, as the law requires, in which case he would have incurred a fine of a thousand drachmae.[27]

And so he proposes death as the penalty. And what shall I propose on my part, O men of Athens? Clearly that which is my due. And what is my due? What return shall be made to the man who has never had the wit to be idle during his whole life; but has been careless of what the many care for—wealth, and family interests, and military offices, and speaking in the assembly, and magistracies, and plots, and parties. Reflecting that I was really too honest a man to be a politician and live, I did not go where I could do

---

[26]At this point the jurors cast their votes; about 280 vote for conviction, 220 for acquittal. (Plato does not describe these deliberations; there has been no omission from the text.) The next decision is on the sentence.

[27]Socrates ironically intimates that each of his three accusers has captured a third of the vote cast against him—approximately ninety-three apiece, a number lower than the one-fifth (about one hundred) necessary for an accuser to avoid paying a fine. The fine was intended to discourage capricious prosecutions.

no good to you or to myself; but where I could do the greatest good privately to every one of you, thither I went, and sought to persuade every man among you that he must look to himself, and seek virtue and wisdom before he looks to his private interests, and look to the state before he looks to the interests of the state; and that this should be the order which he observes in all his actions. What shall be done to such an one? Doubtless some good thing, O men of Athens, if he has his reward; and the good should be of a kind suitable to him. What would be a reward suitable to a poor man who is your benefactor, and who desires leisure that he may instruct you? There can be no reward so fitting as maintenance in the Prytaneum,[28] O men of Athens, a reward which he deserves far more than the citizen who has won the prize at Olympia in the horse or chariot race, whether the chariots were drawn by two horses or by many. For I am in want, and he has enough; and he only gives you the appearance of happiness, and I give you the reality. And if I am to estimate the penalty fairly, I should say that maintenance in the Prytaneum is the just return.

Perhaps you think that I am braving you in what I am saying now, as in what I said before about the tears and prayers. But this is not so. I speak rather because I am convinced that I never intentionally wronged any one, although I cannot convince you—the time has been too short; if there were a law in Athens, as there is in other cities, that a capital cause should not be decided in one day, then I believe that I should have convinced you. But I cannot in a moment refute great slanders; and, as I am convinced that I never wronged another, I will assuredly not wrong myself. I will not say of myself that I deserve any evil, or propose any penalty. Why should I? Because I am afraid of the penalty of death which Meletus proposes? When I do not know whether death is a good or an evil, why should I propose a penalty which would certainly be an evil? Shall I say imprisonment? And why should I live in prison, and be the slave of the magistrates of the year—of the Eleven?[29] Or shall the penalty be a fine, and imprisonment until the fine is paid? There is the same objection. I should have to lie in prison, for money I have none, and cannot pay. And if I say exile (and this may possibly be the penalty which you will affix), I must indeed be blinded by the love of life, if I am so irrational as to expect that when you, who are my own citizens, cannot endure my discourses and words, and have found them so grievous and odious that you will have no more of them, others are likely to endure me. No indeed, men of Athens, that is not very likely. And what a life should I lead, at my age, wandering from city to city, ever changing my place of exile, and always being driven out! For I am quite sure that wherever I go, there, as here, the young men will flock to me; and if I drive them away, their elders will drive me out at their request; and if I let them come, their fathers and friends will drive me out for their sakes.

Some one will say: Yes, Socrates, but cannot you hold your tongue, and then you may go into a foreign city, and no one will interfere with you? Now I have great difficulty in making you understand my answer to this. For if I

---

[28]A place on the Acropolis where benefactors of Athens were honored. Olympia, in southwestern Greece, was the site of a great festival, held every four years, featuring athletic contests. The modern Olympic Games are named for this festival.

[29]A public committee that enforced and supervised criminal penalties, including executions. It was made up of a representative from each of the ten "tribes," plus a secretary.

tell you that to do as you say would be a disobedience to the God, and therefore that I cannot hold my tongue, you will not believe that I am serious; and if I say again that daily to discourse about virtue, and of those other things about which you hear me examining myself and others, is the greatest good of man, and that the unexamined life is not worth living,[30] you are still less likely to believe me. Yet I say what is true, although a thing of which it is hard for me to persuade you. Also, I have never been accustomed to think that I deserve to suffer any harm. Had I money I might have estimated the offense at what I was able to pay, and not have been much the worse. But I have none, and therefore I must ask you to proportion the fine to my means. Well, perhaps I could afford a mina, and therefore I propose that penalty:[31] Plato, Crito, Critobulus, and Apollodorus, my friends here, bid me say thirty minae, and they will be the sureties. Let thirty minae be the penalty; for which sum they will be ample security to you.[32]

Not much time will be gained, O Athenians, in return for the evil name which you will get from the detractors of the city, who will say that you killed Socrates, a wise man; for they will call me wise, even although I am not wise, when they want to reproach you. If you had waited a little while, your desire would have been fulfilled in the course of nature. For I am far advanced in years, as you may perceive, and not far from death. I am speaking now not to all of you, but only to those who have condemned me to death. And I have another thing to say to them: You think that I was convicted because I had no words of the sort which would have procured my acquittal—I mean, if I had thought fit to leave nothing undone or unsaid. Not so; the deficiency which led to my conviction was not of words—certainly not. But I had not the boldness or impudence or inclination to address you as you would have liked me to do, weeping and wailing and lamenting, and saying and doing many things which you have been accustomed to hear from others, and which, as I maintain, are unworthy of me. I thought at the time that I ought not to do anything common or mean when in danger: nor do I now repent of the style of my defense; I would rather die having spoken after my manner, than speak in your manner and live. For neither in war nor yet at law ought I or any man to use every way of escaping death. Often in battle there can be no doubt that if a man will throw away his arms, and fall on his knees before his pursuers, he may escape death; and in other dangers there are other ways of escaping death, if a man is willing to say and do anything. The difficulty, my friends, is not to avoid death, but to avoid unrighteousness; for that runs faster than death. I am old and move slowly, and the slower runner has overtaken me, and my accusers are keen and quick, and the faster runner, who is unrighteousness, has overtaken them. And now I depart hence condemned by you to suffer the penalty of death,—they too go their ways condemned by the truth to suffer the penalty of villainy and wrong; and I must abide by my award—let them abide by theirs. I suppose that these things may be regarded as fated,—and I think that they are well.

[30] One of Socrates' most memorable axioms.

[31] Socrates' decision to propose a monetary penalty is not mercenary but just the opposite: it is a dramatization of his contempt for money as a measure of life and values.

[32] At this point, the five hundred judges cast another split vote, for the death penalty. (Again, Plato does not describe these deliberations; the text given here is complete.)

And now, O men who have condemned me, I would fain prophesy to you; for I am about to die, and in the hour of death men are gifted with prophetic power. And I prophesy to you who are my murderers, that immediately after my departure punishment far heavier than you have inflicted on me will surely await you. Me you have killed because you wanted to escape the accuser, and not to give an account of your lives. But that will not be as you suppose: far otherwise. For I say that there will be more accusers of you than there are now; accusers whom hitherto I have restrained: and as they are younger they will be more inconsiderate with you, and you will be more offended at them. If you think that by killing men you can prevent some one from censuring your evil lives, you are mistaken; that is not a way of escape which is either possible or honorable; the easiest and the noblest way is not to be disabling others, but to be improving yourselves. This is the prophecy which I utter before my departure to the judges who have condemned me.

Friends, who would have acquitted me, I would like also to talk with you about the thing which has come to pass, while the magistrates are busy, and before I go to the place at which I must die. Stay then a little, for we may as well talk with one another while there is time. You are my friends, and I should like to show you the meaning of this event which has happened to me. O my judges—for you I may truly call judges—I should like to tell you of a wonderful circumstance. Hitherto the divine faculty of which the internal oracle is the source has constantly been in the habit of opposing me even about trifles, if I was going to make a slip or error in any matter; and now as you see there has come upon me that which may be thought, and is generally believed to be, the last and worst evil. But the oracle made no sign of opposition, either when I was leaving my house in the morning, or when I was on my way to the court, or while I was speaking, at anything which I was going to say; and yet I have often been stopped in the middle of a speech, but now in nothing I either said or did touching the matter in hand has the oracle opposed me. What do I take to be the explanation of this silence? I will tell you. It is an intimation that what has happened to me is a good, and that those of us who think that death is an evil are in error. For the customary sign would surely have opposed me had I been going to evil and not to good.

Let us reflect in another way, and we shall see that there is great reason to hope that death is a good; for one of two things—either death is a state of nothingness and utter unconsciousness, or, as men say, there is a change and migration of the soul from this world to another. Now if you suppose that there is no consciousness, but a sleep like the sleep of him who is undisturbed even by dreams, death will be an unspeakable gain. For if a person were to select the night in which his sleep was undisturbed even by dreams, and were to compare with this the other days and nights of his life, and then were to tell us how many days and nights he had passed in the course of his life better and more pleasantly than this one, I think that any man, I will not say a private man, but even the great king will not find many such days or nights, when compared with the others. Now if death be of such a nature, I say that to die is gain; for eternity is then only a single night. But if death is the journey to another place, and there, as men say, all the dead abide, what good, O my friends and judges, can be greater than this? If indeed when the pilgrim arrives in the world below, he is delivered from the professors of justice in this world, and finds the true judges who are said to give judgment there, Minos and Rhadamanthus and Aeacus and Triptolemus,[33] and other sons of God who were righteous in their own life, that pilgrimage will be worth making. What would not a man give if he might converse with Orpheus and Musaeus and Hesiod and Homer?[34] Nay, if this be true, let me die again and again. I myself, too, shall have a wonderful interest in there meeting and conversing with Palamedes, and Ajax[35] the son of Telamon, and any other ancient hero who has suffered death through an unjust judgment; and there will be no small pleasure, as I think, in comparing my own sufferings with theirs. Above all, I shall then be able to continue my search into true and false knowledge; as in this world, so also in the next; and I shall find out who is wise, and who pretends to be wise, and is not. What would not a man give, O judges, to be able to examine the leader of the great Trojan expedition; or Odysseus or Sisyphus,[36] or numberless others, men and women too! What infinite delight would there be in conversing with them and asking them questions! In another world they do not put a man to death for asking questions: assuredly not. For besides being happier than we are, they will be immortal, if what is said is true.

Wherefore, O judges, be of good cheer about death, and know of a certainty, that no evil can happen to a good man, either in life or after death. He and his are not neglected by the gods; nor has my own approaching end happened by mere chance. But I see clearly that the time had arrived when it was better for me to die and be released from trouble; wherefore the oracle gave no sign. For which reason, also, I am not angry with my condemners, or with my accusers; they have done me no harm, although they did not mean to do me any good; and for this I may gently blame them.

Still I have a favor to ask of them. When my sons are grown up, I would ask you, O my friends, to punish them; and I would have you trouble them, as I have troubled you, if they seem to care about riches, or anything, more than about virtue; or if they pretend to be something when they are really nothing,—then reprove them, as I have reproved you, for not caring about that for which they ought to care, and thinking that they are something when they are really nothing. And if you do this, both I and my sons will have received justice at your hands.

The hour of departure has arrived, and we go our ways—I to die, and you to live. Which is better God only knows.[37]

---

[33] The four judges of the dead in the afterlife.

[34] Great poets, legendary and real.

[35] Two victims of unjust or dubious trials or verdicts.

[36] Both were noted for their cunning. In mentioning them here, Socrates is anticipating a meeting not merely with eminent men but with adversaries whose mental agility will put his powers to a real test.

[37] In two other dialogues, the *Crito* and the *Phaedo*, the story of Socrates' last days is concluded. In the former, his friend Crito pleads with Socrates to accept an opportunity to escape from Athens, to which Socrates replies (in his usual style of reasoned argument) that such a course would be wrong, since to defy the Athenian laws that have condemned him is the equivalent of rejecting parents who have nurtured him and whose authority he has implicitly accepted throughout his life. The *Phaedo* includes Socrates' argument for the immortality and inviolability of the soul and narrates his serene death, imposed by his drinking of the poison liquid called hemlock.

Aristotle

(384–322 B.C.)

Probably the most versatile and encyclopedic philosopher who ever lived, Aristotle inherited the Platonic tradition but pointed it in important new directions. He was born in 384 B.C. in Stagira (hence his epithet "the Stagirite"), a town in Macedonia on the far northern border of Greece. Since his father was court physician to the Macedonian king, Aristotle absorbed in his early years a good deal of information about the life sciences—a fact that permanently influenced the tendency of his thought. In 367, at the age of seventeen, he went to Athens and studied there in the Academy directed by Plato. Plato admired his pupil and had a strong influence on him; the young Aristotle seems to have believed even more strongly than Plato that the human soul suffered from the prison house of the body, a view he later changed radically.

When Plato died (in 348 or 347), Aristotle left Athens for twelve years. At Assus, in Asia Minor, he undertook the education of the ruler and wrote part of his *Politics*, arguing that the main purpose of the state was to promote the philosophic life among its best citizens. He also married the ruler's niece and had a daughter by her; after his wife's death he had a son, Nicomachus, by another woman. (It is this son who, because he was believed to have edited the work, gave his name to the *Nicomachean Ethics,* one of two treatises by Aristotle on the subject.) After spending three years at Assus, Aristotle moved to the island of Lesbos, where he resumed his investigation of the life sciences, especially marine biology. Here he combined with his characteristic close observation of objective data an equally characteristic conviction that the various creatures are designed to have distinctive purposes.

Around 342 he returned to his homeland, Macedonia, where the great king Philip now reigned. There he was entrusted with the education of Philip's teenaged son, Alexander. Aristotle's intention was to instill in the prince a combination of the martial and philosophic virtues. When Philip was murdered in 336, Alexander succeeded him, going on to complete the conquest of Greece that his father had begun and thereafter subjugating the Greeks' inveterate Persian enemies and other empires in a vast region stretching as far east as India. In the process, Alexander made obsolete the traditional Greek city-state that Aristotle, anachronistically, continued throughout his life to think of as the political norm.

By 335, Aristotle had returned to Athens (which was now controlled by Macedonia), where he established the Lyceum, a rival institution to the Academy. At the Lyceum, which had an unprecedented library and extensive facilities for scientific work, Aristotle and his colleagues investigated virtually all areas of science, philosophy, and other branches of learning. In 323, at Alexander's death, the Athenians rebelled against Macedonian domination, with which Aristotle (accurately or not) was associated in the public mind. A charge of impiety was brought against him. His life endangered, Aristotle left Athens, apparently in order to prevent the Athenians from repeating the crime they had committed in executing Plato's mentor, Socrates. One year later, in 322, Aristotle died in Chalcis, a town north of Athens.

Most people today find Plato's dialogues more readable than the works of Aristotle, but this difference is misleading. A great deal of Aristotle's writings, especially his earlier ones, has been lost, including many works in a popular vein: letters, poems, and dialogues that in form and content resembled Plato's. Except for fragments, the works of Aristotle known today were not intended by him for written publication; they are, rather, notes for his teaching at the Lyceum. Moreover, ancient editors transformed his work by grouping together under a single title different treatises on the same subject that he wrote at different times. Partly because of such editing, and partly because Aristotle felt obliged to record positions different from his own, he sometimes appears inconsistent or redundant. Ancient testimony indicates that Aristotle's mind, personality, and literary style were warmer than is evident in the matter-of-fact writings that have come down to us.

Aristotle at least touched on virtually all the fields of human knowledge, treating many of them in depth: natural sciences including zoology, embryology, physics, meteorology, astronomy, even chemistry in a rudimentary way; mathematics (most of his work on this subject has been lost); psychology; politics and ethics (which for him were closely related to each other); the language arts including rhetoric and poetics. In many of these disciplines he pioneered and made striking discoveries. Nor was he content to investigate the subjects in isolation; he tried to bring them together, partly by applying consistent principles of systematic method, partly by subsuming them under the axioms of "first philosophy" developed in his *Metaphysics*. This religious-philosophic work is logically prior to the more particular studies, because it treats of the nature of being in itself and delineates the broad principles that govern and differentiate more specific fields of investigation. But both metaphysics and its subsidiary studies depend on a methodology of thinking in general. That methodology, largely developed by Aristotle, is outlined in his *Organon*, a group of tracts dealing with logic and the precise use of language in discourse.

The *Organon* is probably the most permanently valuable of all Aristotle's works; it remains an indispensable sourcebook on how to think straight, both deductively and inductively. The works on natural science have inevitably been superseded by those of researchers who have been able to use modern instruments and modern mathematics, though some of Aristotle's ideas (on the classification of animals, for example) remain roughly valid. His shrewd observations on political science in the *Politics* are still meaningful and provocative, though they are limited somewhat by Aristotle's preoccupation with the peculiar circumstances of the Greek city-state. Much of what he wrote about the humanities, especially ethics and literary theory, is as valuable today as ever; for example, a group of Aristotelian literary critics has been prominent in the twentieth century, and the doctrine of the "tragic flaw" enunciated in the *Poetics* has wide general currency.

Even where Aristotle's ideas have been superseded, they often remain valuable because they constitute so large a part of our intellectual and cultural history. During the Middle Ages and until after the Renaissance, university education was thoroughly grounded in Aristotle, and indeed one of the most fascinating episodes in the emergence of modern science is its efforts, especially in the seventeenth century, to throw off the weight of what had become Aristotelian dogma. (That this struggle had to occur is ironic, since Aristotle himself believed firmly in the inductive method; he taught emphatically that mere theory must yield to observed facts.) Philosophers and theologians like Thomas Aquinas, and poets like Dante, are impossible to understand adequately without an awareness of Aristotle's contributions to their thought. The doctrine of the unmoved first mover of the universe; the idea of a continuous chain of being running up a scale from inanimate matter to God; the tripartite classification of souls into nutritive (animals, plants, human beings), sensitive (animals, humans), and rational (humans, God); the distinction between substance (what a thing really *is*) and accident (nonessential properties); the condemnation of taking interest for money (which in works like Dante's *Inferno* is considered usury); the ethical doctrine of the golden mean between two extremes—these ideas, originated or definitively expressed by Aristotle, are fundamental to Western history, literature, and thought. Perhaps the most frequently recurring intellectual model in his works, and one of the most influential, is his fourfold treatment of causes: the material cause (what a thing is made of); the formal cause (its shape or governing principle); the efficient cause (the process by which it was made); and the final cause (its purpose). His concern with final causes pervades Aristotle's analysis of everything from the parts of animals, to human beings, to the cosmos as a whole.

Plato and Aristotle are sometimes treated as polar opposites—Plato being an idealist and Aristotle a materialist. That is a serious mistake: both were staunchly opposed to any view of humanity or the universe as strictly material in their natures, and both considered the philosophic life the highest of human vocations. (Part of the apparent difference between them arises from the literary vehicles in which their work has survived.) There remains a significant distinction between them, however, in what they say and how they reach their conclusions. Though both are rationalist logicians, Aristotle depends more than Plato on data derived from the visible world; in short, his thought is more empirical. His political and ethical thought is more pragmatic, having less of the visionary emphasis than does Plato's. The two also differ in their views of the relationship between spirit and matter; Plato regards the soul as the true human identity, yoked with an essentially unreal, alien body, while Aristotle teaches that in the human being soul (or form) and body are intimately united and interdependent.

FURTHER READING *(prepared by F.S.N.):* Two excellent general introductions to Aristotle for undergraduates are Jonathan Barnes, *Aristotle,* 1983, and J. L. Ackrill, *Aristotle the Philosopher,* 1981; also valuable is Marjorie Grene, *Portrait of Aristotle,* 1963. Valuable material on the life, thought, and writings of Aristotle may be found in W. D. Ross, *Aristotle,* 1924, 5th ed. repr. 1960; D. J. Allan, *The Philosophy of Aristotle,* 1952; and J. H. Randall, Jr., *Aristotle,* 1960. Werner W. Jaeger, *Aristotle: Fundamentals of the History of His Development,* 1923, trans. Richard Robinson, 1934, 2nd ed. 1948, treats the works in chronological sequence, in order to show Aristotle's intellectual development. On Aristotle's main ethical doctrines, see W. F. R. Hardie, *Aristotle's Ethical Theory,* 1968. Humphry House, *Aristotle's Poetics,* 1956, repr. 1967, and John Jones, *On Aristotle and Greek Tragedy,* 1962, survey what Aristotle has to say about the three great tragedians, and about plot, character, action, catharsis, and imitation. James Hutton, trans., *Aristotle's Poetics,* 1982, is an excellent guide to the work.

from *POETICS*

Translation by Samuel Henry Butcher
as revised by Louise Ropes Loomis;
footnotes by Louise Ropes Loomis

I

I propose to treat of Poetry in itself and of its various kinds, noting the essential quality of each; to inquire into the structure of the plot required for a good poem; into the number and nature of the parts of which a poem is composed; and similarly into whatever else falls within the same inquiry. Following, then, the order of nature, let us begin with the principles which come first.

Epic poetry and tragedy, comedy also and dithyrambic[1] poetry, and the music of the flute and of the lyre in most of their forms, are all in their general conception modes of imitation. They differ, however, from one another in three respects—their mediums, their objects, their manner or mode of imitation being in each case distinct.

For as there are persons who, by conscious art or mere habit, imitate and represent various objects through the medium of color and form, or, again, by the voice; so in the group of arts above mentioned, taken as a whole, the imitation is produced by rhythm, language, or harmony, either singly or combined.

Thus in the music of the flute and of the lyre, harmony and rhythm alone are employed; also in other arts, such as that of the shepherd's pipe, which are essentially similar to these. In dancing, rhythm alone is used without harmony; for even dancing imitates character, emotion, and action, by rhythmical movement. . . .

There are, again, some arts which employ all the means above mentioned—namely, rhythm, tune, and meter. Such are dithyrambic and nomic[2] poetry, and also tragedy and comedy; but between them the difference is that in the first two cases these means are all employed in combination, in the latter, now one means is employed, now another.

Such, then, are the differences of the arts with respect to the medium of imitation.

II

Since the objects of imitation are men in action, and these men must be either of a high or a low type (for moral character mainly answers to this division, goodness and badness being the distinguishing marks of moral differences), it follows that we must represent men either as better than in real

---

[1] For dithyrambic poetry the ordinary English reader may understand what we call lyric poetry. More strictly defined, the dithyramb was a hymn or ode in rapturous style, such as were sung at the festivals of the god Dionysus.

[2] Nomic poetry is instructive poetry, maxims or wise sayings in the form of verse.

life, or as worse, or as they are. It is the same in painting. Polygnotus depicted men as nobler than they are, Pauson as less noble, Dionysius drew them true to life.[3]

Now it is evident that each of the arts of imitation above mentioned will exhibit these differences, and itself become a distinct kind in imitating objects that are thus distinct. Such diversities may be found even in dancing, flute playing, and lyre playing. So again in language, whether prose or verse, unaccompanied by music. Homer, for example, makes men better than they are; Cleophon as they are; Hegemon of Thasos, the inventor of parodies, worse than they are.[4] The same distinction marks off tragedy from comedy; for comedy aims at representing men as worse, tragedy as better than in actual life.

III

There is still a third difference—the manner in which each of these objects may be imitated. For the medium being the same, the objects the same, the poet may imitate by narration—in which case he can either take another personality as Homer does, or speak in his own person, unchanged—or he may present all his characters as living and moving before us.

These, then, as we said at the beginning, are the three differences which distinguish artistic imitation—the medium, the objects, and the manner. So that from one point of view, Sophocles[5] is an imitator of the same kind as Homer—for both imitate higher types of character; from another point of view, he is of the same kind as Aristophanes[6]—for both imitate persons acting and doing. Hence, some say, the name of "drama" is given to such plays, as representing action. . . .

IV

Poetry in general seems to have sprung from two sources, each of them lying deep in our nature. First, the instinct of imitation is implanted in man from childhood, one difference between him and other animals being that he is the most imitative of living creatures, and through imitation learns his earliest lessons. And no less universal is the pleasure he takes in seeing things imitated. We have evidence of this in the facts of experience. Objects which in themselves we view with pain, we delight to contemplate when reproduced with minute fidelity: such as the forms of the most ignoble animals and of dead bodies. The cause of this, again, is that to learn gives the liveliest pleasure, not only to philosophers but to men in general, although their capacity of learning is more limited. Thus the reason why men enjoy seeing a likeness is that in contemplating it they find themselves learning or inferring, and saying perhaps, "Ah, that is he." If they happen not to have seen the original, their pleasure will be due not to the imitation as such, but to the execution, the coloring, or some such other cause.

[3] Unfortunately no work by any of these famous Greek painters has come down to us.

[4] The writings of Cleophon and Hegemon are also lost.

[5] Sophocles was one of the great trio of fifth-century Athenian tragedians, the other two being Aeschylus and Euripides. Seven of Sophocles' tragedies have been preserved.

[6] The famous satirical comedy writer of the end of the fifth century B.C.

Imitation, then, is one instinct of our nature. Next there is the instinct for harmony and rhythm, meters being manifestly sections of rhythm. Persons, therefore, starting with this natural gift developed by degrees their special aptitudes, until their rude improvisations gave birth to poetry.

Poetry now diverged in two directions, according to the individual character of the writers. The graver spirits imitated noble actions and the actions of good men. The more trivial sort imitated the actions of meaner persons, at first composing satires, as the former did hymns to the gods and praises of famous men. A poem of the satirical kind cannot indeed be put down to any author earlier than Homer; though there were probably many such writers. But from Homer onward, instances can be cited—his own *Margites*,[7] for example, and other similar compositions. The appropriate meter was also here introduced; hence the measure is still called the iambic[8] or lampooning measure, being that in which people lampooned one another. Thus the older poets were distinguished as writers either of heroic or of lampooning verse.

As in the serious style Homer is pre-eminent among poets, for he alone combined dramatic form with excellence of imitation, so he too first laid down the main lines of comedy, by dramatizing the ludicrous instead of writing personal satire. His *Margites* bears the same relation to comedy that the *Iliad* and *Odyssey* do to tragedy. And when tragedy and comedy appeared, the two classes of poets still followed their natural bent: the lampooners became writers of comedy, and the epic poets were succeeded by tragedians, since the drama was a larger and higher form of art. . . . Tragedy advanced by slow degrees; each new element that showed itself was in turn developed. Having passed through many changes, it found its natural form, and there it stopped.

Aeschylus first introduced a second actor;[9] he diminished the importance of the chorus, and assigned the leading part to the dialogue. Sophocles raised the number of actors to three, and added scene painting. It was not till late that the short plot was discarded for one of greater compass, and the grotesque diction of the earlier satiric form for the stately manner of tragedy.

V

Comedy is, as we have said, an imitation of characters of a lower type—not, however, in the full sense of the word bad, the ludicrous being merely a subdivision of the ugly. It consists of some defect or ugliness which is not painful

---

[7] The mock battle epic that went by the name of *Margites* has long been lost. Whether it was really the work of the author of the *Iliad*, as Aristotle thought, we cannot judge.

[8] The pattern of the iambic meter was a line composed of a series of pairs of syllables, a short syllable, followed by a long one. We in English still use its equivalent, an unaccented syllable followed by an accented, both in comic verse, such as
> "O oysters, come and walk with us,
> The walrus did beseech,"
and also in grand and serious poetry, such as *Paradise Lost*.

[9] Before Aeschylus' time the embryonic Greek tragedy consisted of speeches by a single actor or narrator telling the chorus what had happened and a series of songs, dances, and responses by the chorus, expressing their wonder, joy, or grief at the news.

or destructive. To take an obvious example, the comic mask is ugly and distorted, but does not imply pain.

The successive changes through which tragedy passed, and the authors of these changes, are well known, whereas comedy has had no history, because it was not at first treated seriously. . . .

Epic poetry agrees with tragedy in so far as it is an imitation in verse of characters of a higher type. They differ in that epic poetry admits but one kind of meter[10] and is narrative in form. They differ, again, in their length: for tragedy endeavors, as far as possible, to confine itself to a single circuit of the sun, or but slightly to exceed this limit; whereas the epic action has no limits of time. This, then, is a second point of difference; though at first the same freedom was admitted in tragedy as in epic poetry. . . .

VI

Tragedy, then, is an imitation of an action that is serious, complete, and of a certain magnitude; in language embellished with every kind of artistic ornament, the several kinds being found in separate parts of the play; in the form of dramatic action, not of narrative; through pity and fear effecting the proper purification of these emotions.[11] By "language embellished," I mean language into which rhythm, harmony, and song enter. By "the several kinds in separate parts," I mean that some parts are rendered through the medium of verse alone, others again with the aid of song.

Now as tragic imitation implies persons acting, it necessarily follows, in the first place, that spectacular equipment will be a part of tragedy. Next, song and diction, for these are the medium of imitation. By diction, I mean the metrical arrangement of the words: as for song, it is a term whose sense everyone understands.

Again, tragedy is the imitation of an action, and an action implies personal actors, who necessarily possess certain distinctive qualities of character and thought; for it is by these that we form our estimate of their actions and these two—thought and character—are the natural causes from which their actions spring, and on their actions all success or failure depends. Now, the imitation of the action is the plot; by plot I here mean the arrangement of the incidents. By character I mean that because of which we ascribe certain qualities to the actors. Thought is needed whenever they speak to prove a statement or declare a general truth. Every tragedy, therefore, must have six parts, which parts determine its quality—namely, plot, character, diction, thought, spectacle, song. . . .

But most important of all is the structure of the incidents. For tragedy is an imitation, not of men, but of action and life, of happiness and misery.

---

[10] To a Greek the only meter admissible in an epic poem was the meter of the *Iliad* and the *Odyssey,* or what was called hexameter verse. Virgil used the same meter for the *Aeneid.* In English a well known example of hexameter verse is Longfellow's *Evangeline:*
"This is the forest primeval: the murmuring pines and the hemlocks"—

[11] Note that an unhappy or what we call a tragic ending was not one of the Greek requirements for a tragedy, though Aristotle thought it the perfect ending. See XIII. Many tragedies ended with a solemn reconciliation after a conflict or quiet after pain, to please the audience, Aristotle says.

And life consists of action, and its end is a mode of activity,[12] not a quality. Now character determines men's qualities, but it is their actions that make them happy or wretched. The purpose of action in the tragedy, therefore, is not the representation of character: character comes in as contributing to the action. Hence the incidents and the plot are the end of the tragedy; and the end is the chief thing of all. So without action there cannot be a tragedy; there may be one without character. . . .

Again, you may string together a set of speeches expressive of character, and well finished in point of diction and thought, and not produce the essential tragic effect nearly so well as with a play which, however deficient in these respects, yet has a plot and artistically constructed incidents. Besides which, the most powerful elements of emotional interest in tragedy—reversal of the situation and recognition scenes[13]—are parts of the plot. A further proof is that novices in the art attain to finish of diction and precision of portraiture before they can construct the plot. It is the same with almost all the early poets.

The plot, then, is the first principle, and, as it were, the soul of a tragedy: character holds the second place. A similar statement is true of painting. The most beautiful colors, laid on confusedly, will not give as much pleasure as a simple chalk outline of a portrait. Thus tragedy is the imitation of an action, and of actors mainly with a view to the action. . . .

The spectacle is, indeed, an attraction in itself, but of all the parts it is the least artistic, and connected least with the art of poetry. For the power of tragedy is felt even apart from representation and actors. Besides, the production of scenic effects is more a matter for the property man than for the poet.

VII

These principles being established, let us now discuss the proper structure of the plot, since this is the first and most important thing in tragedy.

Now, according to our definition, tragedy is an imitation of an action that is complete and whole and of a certain magnitude; for there may be a whole that is wanting in magnitude. A whole is that which has a beginning, a middle, and an end. A beginning is that which does not have to follow anything else, but after which something else naturally takes place. An end, on the contrary, is that which itself naturally follows something else, either by necessity or as a general rule, but has nothing coming after it. A middle is that which follows something else as some other thing follows it. A well-constructed plot must neither begin nor end at haphazard, but conform to these principles.

Again, a beautiful object, whether it be a living organism or any whole composed of parts, must not only have an orderly arrangement of parts, but must also be of a certain magnitude; for beauty depends on magnitude and order. Hence a very tiny creature cannot be beautiful; for the view of it is confused, the object being seen in an almost imperceptible moment of time. Nor, again, can one of vast size be beautiful; for as the eye cannot take it all

---

[12] See the *Ethics,* Book I, Chapter 6.
[13] These two admired features of many old dramatic plots Aristotle explains further on.

in at once, the unity and sense of the whole is lost for the spectator; as it would be if there were a creature a thousand miles long. As, therefore, in the case of living bodies and organisms, a certain magnitude is necessary, and a magnitude which may be easily embraced in one view; so in the plot, a certain length is necessary, and a length which can be easily embraced by the memory. . . . And to state the matter roughly, we may say that the proper length is such as to allow for a sequence of necessary or probable events that will bring about a change from calamity to good fortune, or from good fortune to calamity.

VIII

Unity of plot does not, as some persons think, consist of having a single man as the hero. For infinitely various are the incidents in one man's life which cannot be reduced to unity; and so, too, there are many actions of one man out of which we cannot make one action. Hence the error, as it appears, of all poets who have composed a Heracleid, a Theseid,[14] or other poems of the kind. They imagine that as Heracles was one man, the story of Heracles must also be a unity. But Homer, as in all else he is of surpassing merit, here too—whether from art or natural genius—seems to have happily discerned the truth. In composing the *Odyssey* he did not include all the adventures of Odysseus—such as his wound on Parnassus, or his feigned madness at the mustering of the host[15]—incidents between which there was no necessary or probable connection: but he made the *Odyssey* and likewise the *Iliad* center around an action that in our sense of the word is one. As therefore, in the other imitative arts, the imitation is one when the object imitated is one, so the plot, being an imitation of an action, must imitate one action and that a whole, the structural union of the parts being such that, if any one of them is displaced or removed, the whole will be disjointed and disturbed. For a thing whose presence or absence makes no visible difference is not an organic part of the whole.

IX

It is, moreover, evident from what has been said that it is not the function of the poet to relate what has happened but what may happen—what is possible according to the law of probability or necessity. The poet and the historian differ not by writing in verse or in prose. The work of Herodotus[16] might be put into verse, and it would still be a species of history, with meter no less than without it. The true difference is that one relates what has happened, the other what may happen. Poetry, therefore, is a more philosophical and a higher thing than history: for poetry tends to express the universal, history the particular. . . .

---

[14] That is, a long-drawn narrative of all the exploits of a Heracles or a Theseus.

[15] Incidents said to have occurred before the opening of the *Iliad*.

[16] The first of the great Greek historians, who wrote the story of the world, as he knew it, down through the Persian wars.

But even if a poet chances to take an historical subject, he is nonetheless a poet; for there is no reason why some events that have actually happened should not conform to the law of the probable and the possible, and in virtue of that aspect of them he is their poet or maker.

Of all plots and actions the episodic are the worst. I call a plot "episodic" in which the episodes or acts succeed one another without probable or necessary sequence. Bad poets compose such pieces by their own fault, good poets, to please the players; for, as they write show pieces for competition, they stretch the plot beyond its capacity, and are often forced to break the natural continuity.

But again, tragedy is an imitation not only of a complete action, but of events inspiring fear or pity. Such an effect is best produced when the events come on us by surprise and when, at the same time, they follow as cause and effect. The wonder will then be greater than if they happened of themselves or merely by accident; for coincidences too are most marvelous when they have a look of design. We may instance the statue of Mitys at Argos, which fell upon his murderer while he was watching a festival, and killed him. Such events seem the result of more than chance. Plots, therefore, constructed on these principles are necessarily the best.

X

Plots are either simple or complex, for the actions in real life, of which they are an imitation, are obviously either one or the other. An action which is one and continuous in the sense above defined, I call simple, when the change in the hero's fortune takes place without reversal of the situation and without recognition.

A complex action is one in which the change is accompanied by such a reversal, or by recognition, or by both. These all should arise from the internal structure of the plot, so that what follows should be the necessary or probable result of what went before. It makes a great difference whether the event is caused by or simply happens after the previous action.

XI

Reversal of the situation is a change by which conditions in the play are transformed into their opposite, keeping always to our rule of probability or necessity. Thus in the Oedipus,[17] the messenger comes to cheer Oedipus and free him from his alarms about his mother, but by revealing who Oedipus really is produces the opposite effect. . . .

---

[17] The *Oedipus Tyrannus* [*Oedipus the King*] of Sophocles is a tragedy which Aristotle much admired and which happily has come down to us. At its opening, Oedipus is the prosperous king of Thebes, with a wife, Jocasta, whom he dearly loves. In the course of the play he discovers that . . . he is the child of Jocasta and her former husband, the late King of Thebes, exposed to die in infancy because of an ominous prophecy and rescued by [a shepherd]. He learns also that an arrogant old man he killed in a roadside quarrel was the late king, his father. He is therefore the unwitting murderer of his own father and for years has lived in incest with his own mother. At the news, Jocasta hangs herself and Oedipus puts out his eyes and goes blinded and accursed into banishment.

Recognition, as the name indicates, is a change from ignorance to knowledge, producing love or hate between the persons destined by the poet for good or bad fortune. The best form of recognition is coincident with a reversal of the situation, as in the Oedipus.[18]

Even inanimate things of the most trivial kind may in a sense be objects of recognition. Again, we may recognize or discover whether a person has done a thing or not. But the recognition which is most intimately connected with the plot and action is, as we have said, the recognition of persons. This recognition, combined with a reversal, will produce either pity or fear; and actions producing these effects are those which, by our definition, tragedy represents. Moreover, it is upon such situations that the issue of good or bad fortune will depend. Recognition, then, being between persons, it may happen that one person only is recognized by the other—when the latter is already known—or it may be necessary that the recognition should be on both sides. Thus Iphigenia is revealed to Orestes by the sending of the letter; but another act of recognition is required to make Orestes known to Iphigenia.[19]

Two parts, then, of the plot—reversal of the situation and recognition—turn upon surprises. A third part is the scene of suffering. The scene of suffering is a destructive or painful action, such as a death on the stage, bodily agony, wounds, and the like. . . .

XIII

As a sequel to what has already been said, we must proceed to consider what the poet should aim at, and what he should avoid in constructing his plots; and by what means the specific effect of tragedy will be produced.

A perfect tragedy should, as we have seen, be arranged not on the simple but on the complex plan. It should, moreover, imitate actions which excite pity and fear, this being the distinctive mark of tragic imitation. It follows plainly, in the first place, that the change of fortune presented must not be the spectacle of a virtuous man brought from prosperity to adversity: for this moves neither pity nor fear: it merely shocks us. Nor, again, that of a bad man passing from adversity to prosperity: for nothing can be more alien to the spirit of tragedy; it possesses no single tragic quality; it neither satisfies

---

[18] Shakespeare frequently uses these classical dramatic devices of reversal of situation and recognition. The tragedy of *King Lear* is an outstanding illustration of the first. The themes of disguise, mistaken identity, and revelation or recognition occur again and again, notably in *As You Like It, Twelfth Night, Winter's Tale,* and *The Tempest.*

[19] The reference here is to Euripides' play *Iphigenia in Tauris.* Aristotle summarizes briefly the story of Iphigenia in XVII. As the young daughter of King Agamemnon, she was brought from her home to the port of Aulis to be sacrificed, that her father and his fleet might have a favorable wind to sail to Troy. She was snatched from the altar by the goddess Artemis and disappeared. Years later she is a priestess serving in the savage country of Tauris. Her brother Orestes, whom she left at home, a little child, is now a maddened wanderer, seeking absolution for his crime of killing his mother, Clytemnestra, in revenge for her murder of his father, Agamemnon. When Iphigenia finds Orestes on the shore at Tauris, neither, of course, knows the other. In fact, he has no idea that his long lost sister is alive. Through a letter which she gives him he learns who she is, but meanwhile by a law of the country he is condemned to die as a sacrilegious intruder. Through some words of his at the last moment she discovers that he is Orestes and saves him.

the moral sense nor calls forth pity or fear. Nor, again, should the downfall of an utter villain be exhibited. A plot of this kind would, doubtless, satisfy the moral sense, but it would inspire neither pity nor fear;[20] for pity is aroused by unmerited misfortune, fear by the misfortune of a man like ourselves. Such an event, therefore, will be neither pitiful nor terrible.

There remains, then, the character between these two extremes—that of a man extraordinarily good and just, who yet brings misfortune on himself not by vice or depravity, but by some error or frailty.[21] He must be one who is highly renowned and prosperous, a personage like Oedipus, Thyestes, or other illustrious men of great families.

The best constructed plot should, therefore, be single in its issue, rather than double, as some maintain. The change of fortune should be not from bad to good, but, reversely, from good to bad. It should come about as the result not of vice, but of some great error or frailty, in a character either such as we have described, or better rather than worse. . . . A tragedy, to be perfect according to the rules of art, should be of this construction. Hence they are in error who censure Euripides just because he follows this principle in his plays, many of which end unhappily. It is, as we have said, the right ending. The best proof is that on the stage and in dramatic competition, such plays, if well worked out, are the most tragic in effect; and Euripides, faulty though he may be in the general management of his subject, yet is felt to be the most tragic of the poets.

In the second rank comes the kind of tragedy which some place first. Like the Odyssey, it has a double thread of plot, and also an opposite ending for the good and for the bad actors. It is accounted the best only because of the weakness of the spectators; for the poet is guided in what he writes by the wishes of his audience. The pleasure, however, thence derived is not the true tragic pleasure. It is proper rather to comedy, where those who, in the piece, are the deadliest enemies—like Orestes and Aegisthus[22]—quit the stage as friends at the close, and no one slays or is slain.

XIV

Fear and pity may be aroused by spectacular means; but they may also result from the inner structure of the piece, which is the better way, and indicates a superior poet. For the plot ought to be so constructed that, even without the aid of the eye, he who hears the tale told will thrill with horror and melt to pity at what takes place. This is the impression we should receive from hearing the story of Oedipus. But to produce this effect by the mere spectacle is a less artistic method, and dependent on extraneous aids. Those who

[20] Shakespeare's tragedy of *Richard III* is sometimes cited in disproof of this statement. Richard is an "utter villain" but we take a keen interest in his bold struggle to master fate.

[21] Two notably brave and generous tragic heroes, whose downfall is due to one shortcoming in character or judgment, are, of course, Lear and Othello. Some readers would include Hamlet.

[22] In the tragic story of Agamemnon and his son Orestes, Aegisthus is the paramour of Agamemnon's wife, Clytemnestra, who influences her to murder her husband on his return from Troy. Orestes, her son, kills Aegisthus as well as his mother when he finally avenges his father. [See Aeschylus' *Oresteia—Editors' note.*]

employ spectacular means to create a sense not of the terrible but of the merely monstrous are strangers to the purpose of tragedy; for we must not demand of tragedy any and every kind of pleasure, but only that which is proper to it. And since the pleasure the tragic poet should offer is that which comes from pity and fear through imitation, it is evident that this quality must be impressed on the incidents.

Let us then determine what circumstances strike us as terrible or pitiful.

Actions of this sort must happen between persons who are either friends or enemies or indifferent to one another. If an enemy kills an enemy, there is nothing to excite pity either in the act or the intention—except in so far as the suffering itself is pitiful. So too with indifferent persons. But when the tragic incident occurs between those who are near or dear to one another—if, for example, a brother kills, or intends to kill, a brother, a son his father, a mother her son, a son his mother, or any other deed of the kind is done—these are situations to be looked for by the poet. He may not indeed destroy the framework of the received legends—the fact, for instance, that Clytemnestra was slain by Orestes . . . but he ought to show invention of his own, and skillfully handle the traditional material. . . .

Enough has now been said concerning the structure of the incidents and the right kind of plot.

XV

With regard to the characters there are four things to be aimed at. First, and most important, they must be good. Now any speech or action that manifests some kind of moral purpose will be expressive of character: the character will be good if the purpose is good. The goodness is possible in every class of persons. Even a woman may be good, and also a slave, though the one is liable to be an inferior being, and the other quite worthless. The second thing to aim at is appropriateness. There is a type of manly valor, but manliness in a woman, or unscrupulous cleverness, is inappropriate. Thirdly, a character must be true to life: which is something different from goodness and appropriateness, as here described. The fourth point is consistency: for even though the person being imitated, who suggested the type, is inconsistent, still he must be consistently inconsistent.

As in the structure of the plot, so too in the portraiture of character, the poet should always aim at either the necessary or the probable. Thus a person of a given character should speak or act as it is necessary or probable that he would; just as this event should follow that as a necessary or probable consequence. It is therefore evident that the unraveling of the plot, no less than the complication, must arise out of the plot itself; it must not be brought about by supernatural interference—as in the *Medea*.[23] The supernatural should be employed only for events outside the drama—for past or

---

[23] In Euripides' play *Medea*, the heroine, who out of indignation at her wrongs has killed her two children and brought about the death of her husband's new bride, escapes from his fury into the sky in a magic chariot.

future events, beyond the range of human knowledge, which need to be reported or foretold; for to the gods we ascribe the power of seeing all things. Within the action there must be nothing improbable. If the improbable cannot be excluded, it should be outside the field of the tragedy, as is the improbable element in the *Oedipus* of Sophocles.

Again, since tragedy is an imitation of persons above the common level, the example of good portrait painters should be followed. They, while reproducing the distinctive features of the original, make a likeness true to life and yet more beautiful. So too the poet, in representing men hot tempered or indolent or with other defects of character, should preserve the type and yet ennoble it. In this way Agathon and Homer have portrayed Achilles.[24]

These, then, are rules the poet should observe. Nor should he neglect those appeals to the eye, which, though not among the essentials, are the concomitants of poetry; for here too there is much room for error. But of this enough has been said in our published treatise,...[25]

XVII

In constructing the plot and working it out with the proper diction, the poet should put the scene, as far as possible, before his eyes. In this way, seeing everything with the utmost vividness, as if he were an actual eyewitness, he will discover what is in keeping with it, and be most unlikely to overlook inconsistencies....

Again, the poet should act out his own play to the best of his power, with the gestures that go with it; for those with a sympathetic nature, who themselves feel the emotion, are most convincing; and one who is grieved himself despairs, one who is angry rages with the most lifelike reality. Hence poetry implies either a special gift of nature or a strain of madness. In the one case a man can take the mold of any character; in the other, he is lifted out of his proper self.

As for the story, whether the poet takes it ready-made or constructs it for himself, he should first sketch its general outline and then fill in the episodes and amplify in detail. The general plan may be illustrated by the *Iphigenia*.[26] A young girl is sacrificed; she disappears mysteriously from the eyes of those who sacrificed her; she is transported to another country, where the custom is to offer up all strangers to the goddess. To this ministry she is appointed. Some time later her own brother chances to arrive. The fact that the oracle for some reason ordered him to go there is outside the general plan of the play. The purpose, again, of his coming is outside the action proper. However, he comes, he is seized, and, when on the point of being sacrificed,

---

[24] We have nothing left of any work by Agathon. We know only that he was a playwright who promised to rival Euripides but who left Athens for some reason at the age of forty and died disappointed in a foreign land. At the banquet celebrated in Plato's dialogue of the *Symposium* he was the happy and admired host. For Homer's noble treatment of Achilles, see especially the *Iliad,* Books IX, XIX, XXIV.

[25] Aristotle wrote a dialogue *On Poets,* now lost.

[26] On the story of Iphigenia see XI, note.

reveals who he is. The mode of recognition may be either that of Euripides or of Polyidus,[27] in whose play he exclaims very naturally: "So it was not my sister only, but I too who was doomed to be sacrificed"; and by that remark he is saved.

After this, the names being once given, it remains to fill in the episodes. We must see, however, that they are relevant to the action. In the case of Orestes, for example, there is the madness which led to his capture and his deliverance by means of the purificatory rite. In a play the episodes are short, but in epic poetry they lengthen out the tale. Thus the story of the *Odyssey* can be stated briefly. A certain man is absent from home for many years; he is jealously watched by Poseidon, and quite alone. Meanwhile his home is in a wretched plight—suitors are wasting his substance and plotting against his son. At length, tempest-tossed, he arrives and makes himself known; he attacks the suitors with his own hand, and is himself preserved while he destroys them. This is the essence of the plot; the rest is episode.

XVIII

Every tragedy falls into two parts—complication and unraveling or *dénoue-ment*. Incidents before the play opens and often others within the play itself form the complication; the rest is the unraveling. By the complication I mean all that extends from the beginning of the action to the part which marks the turning point to good or bad fortune. The unraveling is that which extends from the beginning of the change to the end. . . .

Again, the poet should remember what has been often said, and not make an epic structure into a tragedy. By an epic structure I mean one with a mul-tiplicity of plots—as if, for instance, you were to make a tragedy out of the entire story of the *Iliad*. In the epic poem, owing to its length, each part can assume its proper magnitude. In the drama the result is far from answering to the poet's expectation. The proof is that the poets who have dramatized the whole story of the fall of Troy, instead of selecting portions like Euripides; or who have taken the whole tale of Niobe, and not a part of her story, like Aeschylus, either fail utterly or meet with poor success on the stage. . . .

XXIII

As for that poetry which is narrative in form and imitates in meter, the plot manifestly ought, as in a tragedy, to be constructed on dramatic principles. It should have for its subject a single action, whole and complete, with a begin-ning, a middle, and an end. It will thus resemble a living organism in all its unity, and produce the pleasure proper to it. It will differ in structure from historical compositions, which of necessity present not a single action, but a single period, and all that happened within that period to one person or to many, however little connected together the events may be. For as the sea fight at Salamis and the battle with the Carthaginians in Sicily took place

[27] We have no plays of Polyidus.

at the same time but did not tend to any one result, so in the ordinary course of events one thing sometimes follows another, and yet no single end is thereby produced. Such is the way, we may say, most poets write.

Here again, then, as has been already observed, the transcendent excellence of Homer is manifest. He never attempts to make the whole war of Troy the subject of his poem, though that war had a beginning and an end. It would have been too vast a theme, and not easily embraced in a single view. If not that, it would have been overcomplicated by the variety of the incidents in it. As it is, he detaches a single portion, though he admits as episodes many events from the general story of the war—such as the Catalogue of Ships[28] and others—thus diversifying the poem. . . . For this reason the *Iliad* and the *Odyssey* each furnish the subject of but one tragedy, or, at most, of two. . . .

XXIV

Again, epic poetry may have as many kinds as tragedy: it may be simple, or complex, a tale of character or of suffering. The parts also, with the exception of song and spectacle, are the same; for it requires reversals of the situation, recognitions, and scenes of suffering. Moreover, the thought and the diction must be artistic. In all these respects, Homer is our earliest and sufficient model. Indeed each of his poems has a twofold character. The *Iliad* is at once simple and a tale of suffering, and the *Odyssey* complex (for recognition scenes run through it), and at the same time a tale of character. Moreover, in diction and thought they are supreme.

Epic poetry differs from tragedy in the scale on which it is constructed, and in its meter. As regards scale or length, we have already laid down an adequate limit: the beginning and the end must be capable of being brought within a single view. This condition will be satisfied by poems on a smaller scale than the old epics, and answering in length to the group of tragedies presented at a single sitting.[29]

Epic poetry has, however, a great—a special—capacity for enlarging its dimensions, and we can see the reason. In tragedy we cannot imitate several lines of action carried on at one and the same time; we must confine ourselves to the action on the stage and the part taken by the players. But in epic poetry, owing to the narrative form, many events simultaneously transacted can be presented; and these, if relevant to the subject, add mass and dignity to the poem. The epic has here an advantage, and one that conduces to grandeur of effect, to diverting the mind of the hearer, and relieving the story with varying episodes. For sameness of incident soon produces satiety, and makes tragedies fail on the stage. . . .

Homer, admirable in all respects, has the special merit of being the only poet who rightly appreciates the part he should take himself. The poet should

---

[28] In the second half of Book II of the *Iliad*, Homer interrupts the course of his story to insert a catalog of the ships that came to Troy and their leaders.

[29] Greek dramatists of the great period used to produce their plays in groups of four, three more or less connected tragedies followed by a comic or satiric play, all seen by the audience in one sitting.

speak as little as possible in his own person, for it is not this that makes him an imitator. Other poets appear themselves upon the scene throughout, and imitate but little and rarely. Homer, after a few prefatory words, at once brings in a man or woman or other personage, none of them wanting in characteristic qualities, but each with a character of his own.

The element of the wonderful is required in tragedy. But the improbable, on which the wonderful depends for its chief effects, has wider scope in epic poetry, because there the person acting is not seen. Thus, the pursuit of Hector would be ludicrous if placed upon the stage—the Greeks standing still and not joining in the pursuit, and Achilles waving them back.[30] But in the epic poem the absurdity passes unnoticed. Now the wonderful is pleasing, as may be inferred from the fact that everyone tells a story with some addition of his own, knowing that his hearers like it. . . .

But the poet should prefer probable impossibilities to improbable possibilities. The tragic plot must not be composed of improbable parts. Everything improbable should, if possible, be excluded; or, at all events, it should lie outside the action of the play itself. . . .

But once the improbable has been introduced and an air of likelihood imparted to it, we must accept it in spite of the absurdity. Take even the incidents in the *Odyssey* where Odysseus is left upon the shore of Ithaca.[31] How intolerable even these might have been would be apparent if an inferior poet were to treat the subject! As it is, the absurdity is veiled by the poetic charm with which the poet invests it.

The diction should be elaborated in the pauses of the action where there is no expression of character or thought. For, conversely, character and thought are merely obscured by a diction that is over brilliant.

XXV

With respect to problems and their solutions, the number and nature of the sources from which they spring may be thus set forth.

The poet being an imitator, like a painter or any other artist, must of necessity imitate one of three objects: things as they were or are, things as they are said or thought to be, or things as they ought to be. This he does in language—using either current expressions or, it may be, rare words or metaphors. There are also many modifications of language, which we concede to the poets. Add to this, that the standard of correctness is not the same in poetry and in politics, any more than in poetry and in any other art. Within the art of poetry itself there are two kinds of faults—those which touch its essence, and those which are accidental. If the poet intended to describe something right, but described it incorrectly through lack of ability to express himself, his art is faulty. But if his failure was due to a wrong intention—if, for instance, he represented a horse as throwing out both his off legs at once, or introduced technical inaccuracies in medicine, or some other science—the error was not in the essentials of his art. These are the

---

[30]Achilles' pursuit of Hector is described in the *Iliad,* Book XXII.
[31]*Odyssey,* Book XIII.

points of view from which we should consider and answer the questions raised in the problems.

First as to questions which concern the poet's own art. If he describes the impossible, he is guilty of an error; but the error may be justified, if the end of the art be thereby attained (the end being that already mentioned)— if, that is, the effect of this or any other part of the poem is thus rendered more striking. A case in point is the pursuit of Hector. If, however, the end might have been as well or better attained without violating the rules of poetic correctness, the error is not justified; for every kind of error should, if possible, be avoided.

Again, does the error touch the essentials of the poetic art or some accident of it? For example, not to know that a hind has no horns is a less serious matter than to paint it inartistically.

Further, if it be objected that a description is not true to fact, the poet may perhaps reply, "But the objects are as they ought to be"; just as Sophocles said that he drew men as they ought to be, Euripides as they are. In this way the objection may be met. If, however, the description is neither true nor of the thing as it should be, the poet may answer, "This is how men say the thing is." This dictum applies to the tales about the gods. It may well be that these stories are not loftier than the facts nor yet true to fact; they are, very possibly, what Xenophanes[32] says of them. But anyhow, "this is what is said."

XXVI

The question may be raised whether the epic or tragic form of imitation is the higher. If the more refined art is the higher, and the more refined in every case is that which appeals to the better sort of audience, the art which addresses itself to any and everyone is manifestly most unrefined. The audience then is supposed to be too dull to comprehend unless the performers throw in something of their own, who therefore indulge in perpetual movements.

So we are told that epic poetry is addressed to a cultivated audience, who do not need gestures, tragedy to an inferior public. Being then unrefined, it is evidently the lower of the two.

Now, in the first place, this censure attaches not to the poetic but to the actors' art; for gesticulation may be equally overdone in epic recitation. . . . Next, all action is not to be condemned—any more than all dancing—but only that of bad performers. . . . Again, tragedy, like epic poetry, produces its effect even without action; it reveals its power by mere reading. If, then, in all other respects it is superior, this fault, we say, is not inherent in it.

And superior it is, because it has all the epic elements—it may even use the epic meter, with music and spectacular effects as important accessories; and these produce the most lively of pleasures. Further, it creates a vivid impression when read as well as when acted. Moreover, the art in it attains its end

---

[32] Xenophanes of Colophon, who lived almost two hundred years before Aristotle, seems to have been remembered largely for his attacks on and ridicule of the popular polytheism of Greece.

within narrower limits; and the concentrated effect is more pleasurable than one which is spread over a long time and so diluted. What, for example, would be the effect of the *Oedipus* of Sophocles, if it were cast into a form as long as the *Iliad*? Once more, the epic imitation has less unity; as is shown by this, that any epic poem will furnish subjects for several tragedies. . . .

If, then, tragedy is superior to epic poetry in all these respects and, moreover, fulfills its specific function better as an art—for each art ought to produce, not any chance pleasure, but the pleasure proper to it, as already stated—it plainly follows that tragedy is the higher art, as attaining its end more perfectly.

Thus much may suffice concerning tragic and epic poetry in general; their several kinds and parts, with the number of each and their differences; the causes that make a poem good or bad; the objections of the critics and the answer to their objections.

Catullus

(C.84–C.54 B.C.)

Gaius Valerius Catullus, one of the world's great lyric poets and (with Horace) one of the two greatest in Latin literature, was born around 84 B.C. and died young, at about the age of thirty. His birthplace was Verona, in a northern Italian province (Cisalpine Gaul) that was controlled by Rome in Catullus' lifetime but whose inhabitants did not acquire the rights of Roman citizenship until shortly after his death. His father was wealthy and prominent enough to entertain Julius Caesar as a guest. Although Catullus made one long journey in 57–56, to Asia Minor (where he visited the grave of his brother, as is recorded in Poem 101), most of his life was divided between his home province and Rome. He lived during the eventful last days of the Roman republic, but, although his acquaintances included leading political figures like Caesar, Pompey, and Cicero, Catullus apparently had little interest in politics as such. Although he lampooned Caesar and Pompey, for instance, he did so on personal rather than on political grounds. The social set in which he moved seems to have been smart, sophisticated, and for the most part modernist in its insouciantly easygoing morality.

The most intense of his attachments was with a woman whom in his poems Catullus calls Lesbia, in honor of the Greek poet Sappho of Lesbos, whose poetry was in some respects a model for Catullus. It seems virtually certain that Lesbia was in real life a woman named Clodia, seven to ten years older than Catullus, married but scarcely bound to a rather pompous husband. She was an aristocrat, probably, the center of a set of political adventurers, a woman of brilliance and beauty, probably a nymphomaniac, and, if the gossip of the time was accurate, the lover of her brother and the poisoner of her husband. Something is known of her from a hostile portrait in a speech by Cicero defending one of her former lovers against a charge of attempting to poison her. Her husband, Metellus Celer, was governor of Cisalpine Gaul in the year 62, and if Catullus met Clodia then (which is possible though not certain), he would have been twenty-two years old at the time the affair began. The twenty-five poems that depict it can be arranged to form a dramatic sequence (which does not necessarily reflect their order of composition), beginning in idealism and fire (see Poem 51, a close paraphrase of Sappho's "He is more than a hero") and progressing through disillusionment, reconciliation, jealousy, anger, self-pity, and brooding resolution to shake off his passion, to his final dismissal of Lesbia in the elaborately contemptuous Poem 11, where Catullus ironically returns to the verse form named for Sappho. Whether the obloquy heaped on Lesbia-Clodia is entirely just can be questioned; Cicero's attack on her is that of an adversary lawyer in the courtroom, and the resentment felt by rejected lovers is not always reasonable. But she seems to have been wicked enough.

Catullus' personal social set overlapped with a set of poets he was associated with, the Neoterics, or "new poets." Catullus, and the others if they were like him (their work has not survived), broke from the main tradition of Roman poetry and its high-serious epic and tragic concern with public themes like history and war; he preferred more personal and occasional topics. The new poetry has a colloquialism drawn in part from Roman comedy overlaid with the influence of Alexandrianism, the school of the late (fourth and third centuries) Greek poet-scholars. The Alexandrian influence helps account for Catullus' concern with meticulous elegance of form, learned allusion, and taste. There is a good deal of art-for-art's-sake aestheticism in Catullus. Yet, paradoxically, his art is above all one of intensely personal expression, treating subjects drawn from life, and his feelings are expressed with a directness and intimacy that are distinctly romantic. The sound, of Catullus' short lyrics at least, is that of a personal conversational voice easily recognizable as his. The viewpoint is unabashedly subjective. The range is astonishing. The playfully mock-solemn dirge for Lesbia's dead pet sparrow is delicately light of touch, but Catullus can also be grossly obscene (Poem 39 gives a hint, though only a hint, of this side of him). The rapturous first address to Lesbia (51) is in violent contrast with the blistering farewell (11). Each lyric seems a total indulgence of the poet's mood, at least as the poet's art defines it. The control of tones is masterful. Poem 11, for example, has three distinct tones: mock-heroic inflation, scathing hatred, and self-pity.

Catullus' influence on ancient literature was great, extending even to poets very dissimilar to him like Virgil and Horace. All the same, his poetry came precariously close to disappearing as almost all of Sappho's has done. Poem 62 exists in a ninth-century manuscript; Catullus would else be unknown (except for brief fragments) without the discovery around 1300 of a manuscript of the other 115 or so poems of his that we have. Even this manuscript was soon lost again, but fortunately not before it had been copied. To these lucky accidents we owe the survival of a voice expressive of the passion and the dissipation that coexisted with Roman austerity.

FURTHER READING (prepared by F.S.N.): In Catullus, 1992, Charles Martin presents the life of the poet through a reading of his poems, using Martin's own translations. Three good comprehensive introductions to Catullus are Stuart G. P. Small, Catullus: A Reader's Guide to the Poems, 1983; Kenneth Quinn, Catullus: An Interpretation, 1973; and the translation and apparatus in G. P. Goold's Catullus, 1983. Also helpful are the pertinent sections of the volume Latin Literature, ed. E. J. Kenney and W. V. Clausen, 1982, in The Cambridge History of Classical Literature; and Michael Grant, Greek and Latin

Authors, 800 B.C.–A.D. 1000, 1980. C. J. Fordyce, *Catullus: A Commentary*, 1961, offers an excellent commentary, with the Latin text, on most of the poems. T. P. Wiseman, *Catullus and His World: A Reappraisal*, 1985, and Tenney Frank, *Catullus and Horace: Two Poets in Their Environment*, 1928, attempt to place Catullus in his historical setting. Kenneth Quinn, ed., in *Approaches to Catullus*, 1972, assembles a number of respected essays on Catullus which had previously appeared in scholarly journals.

POEMS

Translated by Horace Gregory

1^1

Who shall receive my new-born book,
my poems, elegant and shy,
neatly dressed and polished?^{2}

You, Cornelius,
shall be my single patron,   5
for, long ago, you praised
my slender lines and stanzas;

You, the only man in Italy
whose genius had the vigour
to write the history of the world   10
in three sturdy volumes;

These were books, by Jupiter,
that showed a learned mind and
the strength for heavy labour.

Then, take this little book   15
for what it is, my friend.

Patroness and Muse,
keep these poems green for
a day or so beyond a hundred years,
                                          O Virgin!^{3} 20

---

^{1} This dedicatory poem was written to introduce a collection of Catullus' poems; his surviving work would take up more than one book (that is, scroll), and so it is uncertain which poems the dedication applies to. The addressee is Cornelius Nepos, who had written a history of the world in three scrolls and who, like Catullus, came from Cisalpine Gaul, south of the Alps in northern Italy.

^{2} Polished with pumice (volcanic rock), used to smooth the ends of the papyrus and give the volume elegance.

^{3} *Virgin.* The Muse.

51[1]

He is changed to a god he who looks on her,
godlike he shines when he's seated beside her,
immortal joy to gaze and hear the fall of
      her sweet laughter.

All of my senses are lost and confounded;   5
Lesbia rises before me and trembling
I sink into earth and swift dissolution
      seizes my body.

Limbs are pierced with fire and the heavy tongue fails,
ears resound with noise of distant storms shaking   10
this earth, eyes gaze on stars that fall forever
      into deep midnight.

        *   *   *

This languid madness destroys you Catullus,
long day and night shall be desolate, broken,
as long ago ancient kings and rich cities   15
      fell into ruin.

        *   *   *

3

Dress now in sorrow, O all
you shades of Venus,
and your little cupids weep.

My girl has lost her darling sparrow;
he is dead, her precious toy   5
that she loved more than her two eyes,
O, honeyed sparrow following her
as a girl follows her mother,
never to leave her breast, but tripping

[1] This poem, the first in the "Lesbia" sequence, records the poet's feelings at or near the beginning of his relationship with the woman usually identified as Clodia, a fashionable and emancipated beauty. (The numbering of Catullus' poems does not correspond to the order of their composition or of the events recorded.) The first three stanzas are a near-translation from a poem by Sappho of Lesbos, part of which survives ("He is more than a hero"). Authorities do not agree on whether the last four lines of Catullus's poem are really part of it or represent instead an error in the manuscript. The Latin meter ("sapphics") is also derived from Sappho and, as far as we know, was used only twice by Catullus: once here and once in his bitter farewell to Lesbia (Poem 11). "He" in line one is presumably a rival, possibly Clodia's husband.

now here, now there, and always singing   10
his sweet falsetto
song to her alone.

Now he is gone; poor creature,
lost in darkness,
to a sad place   15
from which no one returns.

O ravenous hell!
My evil hatred rises against your power,
you that devour
all things beautiful;   20
and now this pitiful, broken sparrow,
who is the cause of my girl's grief,
making her eyes weary and red with sorrow.

5

Come, Lesbia, let us live and love,
nor give a damn what sour old men say.
The sun that sets may rise again
but when our light has sunk into the earth,
it is gone forever.   5
          Give me a thousand kisses,
then a hundred, another thousand,
another hundred
          and in one breath
still kiss another thousand,   10
another hundred.
          O then with lips and bodies joined
many deep thousands;
          confuse
their number,   15
          so that poor fools and cuckolds (envious
          even now) shall never
          learn our wealth and curse us
          with their
          evil eyes.   20

85

I hate and love.
          And if you ask me why,
I have no answer, but I discern,
can feel, my senses rooted in eternal torture.

109

My life, my love, you say our love will last forever;
O gods remember
her pledge, convert the words of her avowal into a prophecy.
Now let her blood speak, let sincerity govern each syllable fallen
from her lips, so that the long years of our lives shall be   5
a contract of true love inviolate
against time itself, a symbol of eternity.

39[1]

Egnatius has white teeth and therefore always pleasant, always smiling;
and if a lawyer is telling a sad tale for the defense[2] (a pitiful client),
Egnatius is there with his eternal smile.
If there's a funeral with the mother weeping
over the body of her only son,   5
Egnatius arrives gleaming with his happy smile:
no matter where he is or who he sees or what he does,
he is forever smiling.
                    O what a foul disease,
this smile,   10
            not sweet nor gracious,
nor a sign of social charm.
                        Listen to me, my dear,
good, fine Egnatius,
                if you were Roman, Sabine, Tibertine,   15
or a starved greedy pig from Umbria,
or an Etruscan, short and round, or a dark Lanuvian
with glittering teeth or a man from my own province,[3]
or anybody at all who scrubs his teeth with good clean water daily—
your smile would still offend me; nothing is worse   20
than senseless laughter from a foolish face. But you're a Spaniard,
and we already know the Spanish custom:
                    how Spaniards clean their teeth
and scour their gums with the same water that issues
from their bladders.   25
            So if your teeth are clean, my friend, we know how
you have used your urine.

[1] Egnatius, a Spaniard, was one of Clodia/Lesbia's lovers.
[2] Egnatius is pictured as sitting among the defendant's supporters, where sadness and concern would be fitting.
[3] Six non-Roman peoples who were nevertheless socially accepted. The people of Catullus' own province, in northern Italy south of the Alps, had still not acquired full Roman citizenship in Catullus' lifetime.

8

Poor damned Catullus, here's no time for nonsense,
open your eyes, O idiot, innocent boy, look at what has happened:
once there were sunlit days when you followed after
where ever a girl would go, she loved with greater
love than any woman knew.   5
Then you took your pleasure
and the girl was not unwilling. Those were the bright days, gone;
now she's no longer yielding; you must be, poor idiot,
more like a man! not running after
her your mind all tears; stand firm, insensitive.   10
Say with a smile, voice steady, "Good-bye, my girl," Catullus
strong and manly no longer follows you, nor comes when you are calling
him at night and you shall need him.
You whore! Where's your man to cling to, who will praise your beauty,
where's the man that you love and who will call you his,   15
and when you fall to kissing, whose lips will you devour?
But always, your Catullus will be as firm as rock is.

76

If man can find rich consolation, remembering his good deeds and
    all he has done,
if he remembers his loyalty to others, nor abuses his religion by heart-
    less betrayal
of friends to the anger of powerful gods,[1]
then, my Catullus, the long years before you shall not sink in dark-
    ness with all hope gone,
wandering, dismayed, through the ruins of love.   5
All the devotion that man gives to man, you have given, Catullus,
your heart and your brain flowed into a love that was desolate, wasted,
    nor can it return.
But why, why do you crucify love and yourself through the years?
Take what the gods have to offer and standing serene, rise forth as a
    rock against darkening skies;
and yet you do nothing but grieve, sunken deep in your sorrow, Catullus,   10
for it is hard, hard to throw aside years lived in poisonous love that
    has tainted your brain
and must end.
If this seems impossible now, you must rise
to salvation. O gods of pity and mercy, descend and witness my sor-
    row, if ever
you have looked upon man in his hour of death, see me now in despair.   15

---

[1] That is, does not make dishonest oaths.

Tear this loathsome disease from my brain. Look, a subtle corruption
   has entered my bones,[2]
no longer shall happiness flow through my veins like a river. No longer
   I pray
that she love me again, that her body be chaste, mine forever.
Cleanse my soul of this sickness of love, give me power to rise, resurrected, to thrust love aside,
I have given my heart to the gods, O hear me, omnipotent heaven,   20
and ease me of love and its pain.

11[1]

Furius, Aurelius, bound to Catullus
though he marches piercing farthest India
where echoing waves of the Eastern Oceans
      break upon the shores:

Under Caspian seas, to mild Arabia,   5
east of Parthia,[2] dark with savage bowmen,
or where the Nile, sevenfold and uprising,
      stains its leveled sands,—

Even though he marches over Alps to gaze on
great Caesar's monuments:[3] the Gallic Rhine and   10
Britons who live beyond torn seas, remotest
      men of distant lands—

Friends who defy with me all things, whatever
gods may send us, go now, friends, deliver
these words to my lady, nor sweet—flattering,   15
      nor kind nor gentle:

Live[4] well and sleep with adulterous lovers,
three hundred men between your thighs, embracing
all love turned false, again, again, and breaking
      their strength, now sterile.   20

---

[2] These words echo and contrast with the description of ardent love in Poem 51: "swift dis-
solution/seizes my body./Limbs are pierced with fire."

[1] This poem marks the final contemptuous farewell to Lesbia/Clodia. In the original Latin,
Catullus uses for the second and last time the sapphic verse form used in Poem 51, the over-
ture to the love affair. Furius and Aurelius have apparently been sent as envoys from Lesbia
to seek a reconciliation; since they were not in fact friends of Catullus, his address to them
as fellow comrades-in-arms is perhaps heavily sarcastic. Before getting to the point—his message to Lesbia—the poet surveys the entire known world, from India in the east to Britain in
the west.

[2] A country in what is now northeastern Iran.

[3] Reminders of Julius Caesar's exploits. Caesar crossed the Rhine in the summer of 55 B.C.,
and later in that year he crossed the English Channel to Britain.

[4] The word recalls its use in the first line of the rapturous Poem 5.

She will not find my love (once hers) returning;
she it was who caused love, this lonely flower,[5]
tossed aside, to fall by the plow dividing
    blossoming meadows.

62[1]

BOYS

Twilight and star we hope to see arise, pouring bright rain from Mount
    Olympus[2] down
over the wedding feast, have now arrived, we sing our praise to the
    advancing bride,
rise now to greet her singing:
O Hymen, Hymenaee, come now, O Hymen.[3]

GIRLS

And is it true that Hesperus is here? Witness this company of boys now
    standing   5
facing us and the star of night flames with the fire of Mount Oeta,[4]
O hear them sing and see their ritual, wonder and joy for us to gaze
    upon
O Hymen, Hymenaee, come now, O Hymen.

BOYS

Hear how the girls have set their song in perfect measures, and each
    word recited
sounds from an infallible memory, surely their minds were rooted   10
deep in memorable music while we (our minds and ears distracted)
    wandered, and we shall be outdone;
O victory shall fall to those who sing in perfect rhythm, we must equal
    them and what they say must find
our words a perfect complement.
O Hymen, Hymenaee, come now, O Hymen.

---

[5] The image is another reminiscence of Sappho, who uses a similar image of a damaged flower in "Lament for a maidenhead."

[1] This epithalamium, or wedding song, was not written for any particular wedding. Influenced strongly by Greek poetry, it describes a mixture of Greek and Roman nuptial ceremonies. The setting is the end of an evening feast in the house of the bride's parents; the form is that of a choral competition between the young male and female guests, who are seated apart from each other. The bride makes her appearance in the course of the poem.

[2] That is, the sky; Mount Olympus was the dwelling place of the gods.

[3] A ritual refrain at weddings. (Later, Hymen was personified as the god of marriage.) The refrain is probably an interjection by the poet, not by the singers.

[4] There may have been a cult of Hesperus, the evening star, on Oeta, a mountain in central Greece.

GIRLS

What are these flames that roll against the skies, divorcing mother and
    child, more terrible 15
than earthly fires? These flames of Hesperus that seize a daughter from
    her mother's arms
delivering the girl into the quick embrace of a young husband—here
    is destruction greater
than a tall city given to its enemies.
O Hymen, Hymenaee, come now, O Hymen.

BOYS

What is more beautiful than this rich fire, the crown of heaven rising, 20
the fire that joins the marriage a true contract spoken by husband and
    parents of the bride,
and yet does not disclose its vital power until the marriage bed is made.
    What a gift from heaven
greater than this gift from gods to man in a superlative hour of hap-
    piness?
O Hymen, Hymenaee, come now, O Hymen.

*   *   *

GIRLS

O friends who love us, Hesperus has taken one of us, our sister,
    taken. . . .[5] 25

BOYS

O Hesperus when you rise, our guardian, eyes open the night long,
you come, disguised as dawn star now disclosing thieves hidden under
    night's vast shadow
but virgins cry against you, a false lamentation against him who is desire
coiled in their brains, a secret never spoken.
O Hymen, Hymenaee, come now, O Hymen. 30

GIRLS

We are as flowers[6] in a garden hidden from all men's eyes, no crea-
    ture of the field walks in this place,
no plow divides us; only the gentlest wind, rain from a soft warm cloud
    and the quickening sun to nourish us.

---

[5] Most of the young women's words here and the beginning of the men's reply have been
lost. The women apparently charge Hesperus, herald of night, with being the ally of thieves.
The men answer that, besides alerting the night police to be on guard, Hesperus as morning
star also brings daylight and thus catches thieves (Venus can be either a morning or an evening
star).

[6] The following flower simile, like the one in Catullus's Poem 11, is probably a reminiscence of Sappho's "Lament for a maidenhead."

We are the treasure that many girls and boys desire; but once deflow-
    ered (the flower stained and torn)
the virgin's body rancid, neither boys nor girls will turn to her again
nor can she wake their passion.   35

BOYS

You are as a vine in a barren field that cannot climb by its own strength
nor its fruit prosper (the vine driven downward with its own weight
    neither the ox nor plowman shall teach it how
to grow, but if its body twined round an elm, gives promise of fruit,
    then by this marriage
many a farmer and his beast will wait upon it). So is it with you O
    virgins.
The virgin, perfect, wastes until she ripens in the marriage bed and
    there receives   40
her father's blessing and her husband's love.
Never resist the power of this union made, O virgin; father and mother
    have given you to him, this man, your husband
your maidenhead by this division is not yours alone, you hold one third
    of that which is the treasure
of parents and your husband—this is the lawful contract given to him
    whose hands receive your dowry.
O Hymen, Hymenaee, come now, O Hymen.   45

101^1

Dear brother, I have come these many miles, through strange lands
    to this Eastern Continent
to see your grave, a poor sad monument of what you were, O brother.
And I have come too late; you cannot hear me; alone now I must speak
to these few ashes that were once your body and expect no answer.
I shall perform an ancient ritual over your remains, weeping,   5
(this plate of lentils for dead men to feast upon, wet with my tears)
O brother, here's my greeting: here's my hand forever welcoming you
and I forever saying: good-bye, good-bye.

---

[1] Catullus' brother had died young, in Asia Minor near the site of ancient Troy. In 57 B.C.,
during a term of service abroad, in nearby Bithynia, Catullus visited his brother's grave. He
offers ritual gifts to the dead.

Virgil

(70 B.C.–19 B.C.)

Because of the nobility of his conceptions and his poetic genius, Virgil has had a more continuous and profound impact on European culture, antique and Christian, than any other single classical author. Since his own day his works have been the fare of schoolchildren and of connoisseurs of poetry alike. He has been regarded not only as a prototype of the consummate artist but also as a sage, a religious prophet, and even a sorcerer. Perhaps his most distinctive achievement is to have defined heroism, and its costs, in a context not of primitive social conditions but of a sophisticated, intricately organized civilization and its values.

Like several other great Roman poets, notably Catullus, Horace, and Ovid, Virgil came from the provinces. He was born, like Catullus, in the part of northern Italy called Cisalpine Gaul, in 70 B.C. There he learned the deep love of rural nature that would later shine through his poetry. His father seems to have been a man of humble stock who acquired farmland near Mantua. Virgil nevertheless got a very good education—especially in language and literature, science, and philosophy—at Cremona, Milan, and finally Rome, where he arrived at the age of seventeen. He is said to have contemplated a career in law but to have lacked the quickness and hardihood necessary for success in it. Although he was amiable and made influential friends in the political and cultural circles of Rome, he was a shy, studious person who never married and who took no direct part in public life. A professional poet, he devoted almost all his time to his art and the studies ancillary to it.

His three principal works were the *Eclogues* (written between 42 and 37), the *Georgics* (36–29), and the *Aeneid* (29–19). The *Eclogues* are pastoral poems, in the tradition of the Greek poet Theocritus, depicting the idyllic life of shepherds, but Virgil intriguingly combines with the escapist setting references to actual persons and current topics. Two of the *Eclogues* deal with dispossession from one's land—a poignant, typically Virgilian theme—and are believed to refer to the expropriation of Virgil's family farm for the benefit of soldiers in the army of Mark Antony and Octavian after they defeated the assassins of Julius Caesar at Philippi. (The property was apparently returned to Virgil at a later date.) The *Fourth Eclogue,* which prophesies the birth of a wondrous child who is to restore the Golden Age, was later interpreted by Christians as a prophecy of Jesus; hence its name the "Messianic eclogue." The *Georgics* too has a rural theme and setting; in fact, it is largely a practical handbook for farmers, though the work also has a broad patriotic theme in keeping with Virgil's desire to help restore Italian agriculture and the moral values associated with it. It counterpoints dream and reality, tragedy and comedy, pessimism and optimism. The *Georgics,* composed slowly and carefully, at the rate of less than one line a day, is often praised as the most perfect of all Latin poems. After completing it, Virgil turned to his greatest work, the *Aeneid,* to which he devoted his remaining years. At the time of his death in 19 B.C. he had not quite perfected it and asked that it be burned. Octavian (the emperor Caesar Augustus) is said to have rescued it.

Despite his retiring temperament, Virgil lived at a time when it was not easy for any Roman to avoid the impact of public events. The wars of Roman against Roman had begun decades before Virgil's birth. During his boyhood the republican form of Roman government was proving less and less capable of curbing the ambitions of powerful men. Pompey the Great, one of the two consuls (chief magistrates) in 70, the year Virgil was born, had a meteoric career as general and legislator. In 55, as Virgil reached the traditional age of manhood, Pompey was consul a second time, and in 52 the leader assumed the unprecedented office of sole consul to deal with the gang warfare and street disorders which were racking the life of the capital. Cicero, the eminent Roman thinker and statesman, dreamed that in some such central and autocratic figure as Pompey Rome might find salvation from the ills that were too widespread for its traditional government to control.

In fact, Rome's first autocracy in almost five centuries was to be established not by Pompey but by Julius Caesar, who, at first simply a popular politician from an impoverished noble family, gradually had begun to emerge as an unmatched leader and a strategist of ruthless brilliance. Caesar defeated Pompey in 48 at the Battle of Pharsalus, and during four breathless years he attempted to reshape Roman government as a centralized monarchy on the model of Alexander the Great. But Caesar's audacity went too far. In 44 a group of conspirators led by Brutus assassinated him in Pompey's Theater at Rome. The conspirators had no clear plan of action. It looked as if Rome would collapse under the sheer size of its own problems, when out of the welter of confusion and carnage emerged Caesar's ailing nineteen-year-old grandnephew Octavian. A skilled politician driven by an extraordinary genius, Octavian maneuvered his way through the labyrinth of Roman power politics over the next thirteen years, winning at length the general support of Rome. His most formidable rival, his brother-in-law Mark Antony, had become infatuated with Cleopatra, the queen of Egypt, and even planned to yield her part of the Roman domain. In the climactic naval battle of Actium in 31 (an event foreshadowed in Book III and described in Book VIII of the *Aeneid*), Octavian defeated Antony and Cleopatra. Their subsequent suicide left Octavian supreme in authority, and in 23 he became known as Caesar Augustus. His regime aimed at several goals: the civic renewal of Rome, the revival of traditional religious devotion, and the fostering of a new patriotism. The arts were to be important vehicles for these ideals, all of which are reflected in the *Aeneid*.

For Virgil, as for many other Romans, the restoration of peace was in itself a blessed achievement, an occasion and opportunity for Roman national glory. In Book I of the *Aeneid* Jupiter prophesies a time when

> wars will cease, and a rough age grow gentler,
> White Faith and Vesta, Romulus and Remus,
> Give law to nations. War's grim gates will close,
> Tight-shut with bars of iron, and inside them
> The wickedness of war sit bound and silent,
> The red mouth straining and the hands held tight
> In fastenings of bronze, a hundred hundred.

(I. 305–311)

To "give law to nations"—this, and not mere narrow chauvinism, is the distinctive Roman mission. The shade of Anchises tells his son Aeneas in Book VI:

> Others, no doubt, will better mould the bronze
> To the semblance of soft breathing, draw, from marble,
> The living countenance; and others plead
> With greater eloquence, or learn to measure,
> Better than we, the pathways of the heaven,
> The risings of the stars: remember, Roman,
> To rule the people under law, to establish
> The way of peace, to battle down the haughty,
> To spare the meek. Our fine arts, these, forever.
>
> *(VI. 888–896)*

Although Anchises is historically right in conceding superiority in the fine arts to other nations, specifically Greece, and identifying government as the epitome of Roman greatness, it is somewhat ironic that his exhortation, at once modest and proud, should appear in a poem that is one of the world's aesthetic masterpieces.

The *Aeneid* is, then, a eulogy of Roman values. But it also puts those values in perspective by showing insistently the great cost at which they are achieved and sustained. The poem, particularly in the second half, treats political negotiation and war at length, but war is presented there as a moral tragedy, however necessary, and even admirable, martial prowess and courage may be. Aeneas is no Homeric hero, free to demonstrate valor and prowess for their own sake, with no social obligation beyond himself, his family, and the cohorts banded together under him. The distinctively Virgilian melancholy, combined inextricably with tones of triumph, arises largely from the poet's awareness that public duty requires again and again the sacrifice of personal fulfillment. Aeneas, the mirror of Augustus and of Roman potential, must be educated in suffering before he can perform his mission and become a worthy embodiment of the Roman ideal. His affair with Dido is a personal tragedy on both sides. Since Carthage, the city she rules, was to become an inveterate enemy of Rome in three major wars during the two centuries before Virgil, it would have been easy for him to present this African queen as merely ignoble, a focus for propaganda. That instead he portrays her sympathetically, indeed creating in her the most memorable character in Latin literature, both enhances her own tragic stature and underlines Aeneas' tragic dilemma in having to renounce her in the name of duty.

For the formal vehicle of his story and message, Virgil chose the epic, a literary genre he had aspired to since early in his life. His handling of epic owes something to the Greek Alexandrians, but his primary models are the two Homeric epics. Books I to VI are, like the *Odyssey*, a tale of wandering; Books VII to XII are a war story, like the *Iliad*. But those general correspondences are, in themselves, only the most superficial marks of Homeric influence, and there are ironic differences too. The journey of Homer's Odysseus is a true homecoming; Aeneas' odyssey, despite the ancestral roots the Trojans have in Italy, is a leavetaking, a deracination. Virgil's echoing of Homer is intricate but also intricately varied, so that the echoing is less imitative than expressive. Virgil's synthesizing tour de force overlies a radical originality of the utmost importance in the history of epic. Aristotle, in his *Poetics*, had praised Homer for his objectivity, his effacement of himself, and had identified such self-effacement as the epic poet's proper role. In his own way, of course, Virgil too is objective; that is, he combines with his didacticism flexibility of sympathy with individual human beings, realistic insight into human psychology, and a sense that there is often right on both sides. Yet the *Aeneid* is, after all, a subjective poem—in the sense that the author's presence can be felt everywhere, in the ideas and in the characteristic Virgilian tone of pathos, introspectiveness, and poignancy.

An even more important innovation is Virgil's imaginative redefinition of the role of history in epic. Rather than narrating and directly celebrating modern Roman history, which is ultimately his main concern, he chooses to return to the legendary roots of the Roman experience nearly a millennium earlier, in the wanderings and wars of the Trojans after the fall of their city. In treating the seeds of later Roman history, Roman religious ritual, Roman character traits as having been sown in that era of the dim past, the *Aeneid*, unlike the Homeric models, envisions time and history as a meaningful linear movement toward goals ordained by a mysterious but purposeful providence. Understood in this way, the fall of Troy is ultimately a fortunate fall. In ancient literature the closest thing we have to this is not in pagan literature but in the Bible, especially in the Exodus saga. Both there and in the *Aeneid* we see a guiding providence operating through divinely appointed, half-reluctant heroes, Moses and Aeneas, both of whom must grow into their roles but then rest content not quite to reach the ultimate goal of their people. In both works the journey is out of a disastrous past toward a new promised land that is also an ancestral homeland. Both leaders must mediate between the exigencies of providence and the weariness and backslidings of their followers. It is no wonder that poets in the Judeo-Christian tradition could retrospectively claim Virgil as one of their own.

Except for the Bible, the *Aeneid* may well be the most highly revered book in European literary history, especially before the reemergence of the Greek classics in Europe during the Renaissance. Like the Bible, Virgil's works were used by people seeking supernatural guidance; they opened a copy at random and found wisdom in the first passage their eyes struck. That practice (the *Sortes Vergilianae*) reflects the moral sententiousness of the *Aeneid*, but it also reflects the poem's style. To translate Virgil is especially challenging, for almost every line is dense with meaning, nuance, implication. That is partly owing to the nature of classical Latin, which can produce special effects because the word order is freer than in modern English, and partly to Virgil's painstaking method of composition, which is utterly different from the essentially oral manner of Homer's verse (though Virgil did sometimes read his poetry aloud). The meter is the standard epic meter, dactylic hexameter—each of the six feet made up of a long syllable and two short ones (*dactyl*) or of two long ones (*spondee*). But in addition to this quantitative meter, based on the actual time duration of syllables, Virgil's verse recognizes the stress accents that words possessed in spoken Latin as they do in English, and this stress-accent pattern is played against the quantitative pattern in ways from which Virgil elicits enormously varied expressive effects. It should be noted too that, in the last two feet of Virgil's hexameter line, the stress-accent pattern and the quantitative pattern coincide, so that each line sustains rhythmic tensions that are resolved in the last two feet. The first seven lines of the *Aeneid*, quoted below, are given as a sample; the slash marks indicate the divisions into feet; the long and short syllables are indicated, respectively, by the marks — and ˘; and the normal spoken stress accents are indicated by italics:

Ārmă vĭ/rūm quĕ *că*/nō, Trō/iaē quī / *prī* mŭs ăb / ōrĭs

Ītă lĭ/ām, *fă*/tō *prŏ* fŭ/gŭs, Lā/*vīn* iăquĕ / *vē* nĭt

lī tŏră, / mūl tum ĭl/le ēt *tĕr*/rĭs iăc/*tă* tŭs ĕt / āl tō

vī *sŭ* pĕ/rŭm, *sae*/vae *mĕ* mŏ/rĕm Iū/*nō* nĭs ŏb / *ī* răm,

mūl tă *quŏ*/que ēt bĕl/lō pās/sŭs, dŭm / *cŏn* dĕrĕt / *ŭr* bĕm,

īnfer/*rĕt* quĕ *dĕ*/ōs Lă tĭ/ō, *gĕ* nŭs / ŭn dĕ Lă/*tī* nŭm,

Ālbā/*nī* quĕ *pă*/trēs, *āt*/que āl taē / *moē* nĭă /*Rŏ* maē.

In his poem "To Virgil," composed in 1882 for the 1,900th anniversary of Virgil's death, Tennyson paid tribute to what he called Virgil's "ocean-roll of rhythm":

I salute thee, Mantovano [Mantuan], I that loved thee since my day began, Wielder of the stateliest measure ever molded by the lips of man.

FURTHER READING *(prepared by F.S.N.):* W. F. Jackson Knight, *Roman Vergil,* 1944, 2nd ed. 1966, is especially useful on Virgil's language and style. For a comprehensive treatment of Virgil's work and his debt to Homer and to the Alexandrians, see Brooks Otis, *Virgil: A Study in Civilized Poetry,* 1964. Also valuable on the Alexandrian background to Augustan poetry is J. K. Newman, *Augustus and the New Poetry,* 1967. Lively and stimulating twentieth-century interpretations are presented by Steele Commager, ed., *Virgil: A Collection of Critical Essays,* 1966; by Donald R. Dudley, ed., *Virgil,* 1969; and by John D. Bernard, ed., *Virgil at 2000: Commemorative Essays on the Poet and His Influence,* 1986. A more recent collection, centered on the *Aeneid,* is Harold Bloom, ed., *Modern Critical Interpretations of the Aeneid,* 1987. A useful introduction to the poem is K. W. Grandsen's *Virgil: The Aeneid,* 1990. Viktor Pöschl, *The Art of Vergil: Image and Symbol in the Aeneid,* 1950, trans. Gerda Seligson, 1962, shows how the epic is unified thematically, symbolically, and artistically. Kenneth Quinn, *Virgil's "Aeneid": A Critical Description,* 1968, brings twentieth-century critical methods to bear on traditional material. Also helpful and incisive are W. A. Camps, *An Introduction to Virgil's Aeneid,* 1969, and the Introduction to R. D. Williams's commentary *The Aeneid of Virgil,* 1973. Gordon Williams, *Technique and Ideas in the "Aeneid",* 1983, is excellent, though intellectually demanding. A more accessible recent work, Jasper Griffin's *Virgil,* 1986, can be strongly recommended.

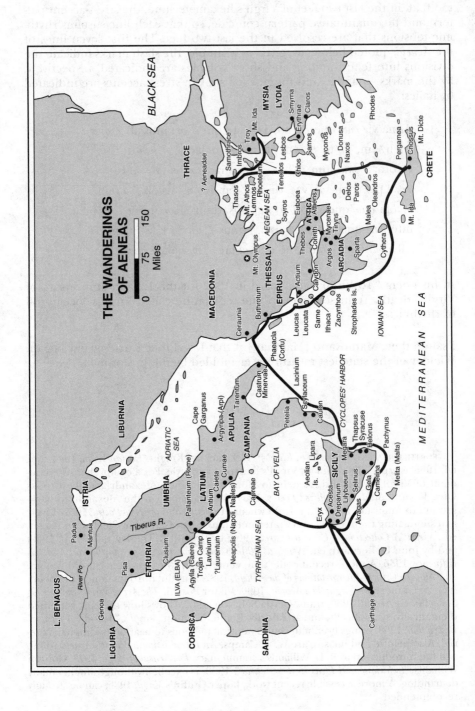

THE WANDERINGS OF AENEAS

from *THE AENEID*

Translated by Rolfe Humphries

BOOK I: THE LANDING NEAR CARTHAGE

Arms and the man I sing,[1] the first who came,
Compelled by fate, an exile out of Troy,
To Italy and the Lavinian coast,[2]
Much buffeted on land and on the deep
By violence of the gods, through that long rage,
That lasting hate, of Juno's. And he suffered
Much, also, in war, till he should build his town
And bring his gods to Latium,[3] whence, in time,
The Latin race, the Alban[4] fathers, rose
And the great walls of everlasting Rome.   10
　Help me, O Muse, recall the reasons: why,
Why did the queen of heaven[5] drive a man
So known for goodness, for devotion, through
So many toils and perils? Was there slight,
Affront, or outrage? Is vindictiveness
An attribute of the celestial mind?
　There was an ancient city, Carthage, once
Founded by Tyrians,[6] facing Italy
And Tiber's[7] mouth, far-off, a wealthy town,
War-loving, and aggressive; and Juno held   20
Even her precious Samos[8] in less regard.
Here were her arms, her chariot, and here,
Should fate at all permit, the goddess burned
To found the empire of the world forever.
But, she had heard, a Trojan race would come,
Some day, to overthrow the Tyrian towers,
A race would come, imperious people,[9] proud
In war, with wide dominion, bringing doom
For Libya. Fate willed it so. And Juno
Feared, and remembered: there was the old war   30

---

[1] Lines 1–16 use the standard epic "opening formula," including the identification of the hero, the proclamation of the theme and of its significance, and the invocation of the inspiring Muse.

[2] The west coast of Italy.

[3] The area of Italy destined to be settled by the Trojans.

[4] The city Alba Longa was founded by Ascanius, Aeneas' son. It produced Romulus, who was, according to legend, the founder of Rome.

[5] Juno, queen of the gods and inveterate enemy of the Trojans.

[6] People from Tyre, a city on the Syrian coast, noted for commerce.

[7] The river of Rome. The epithet *War-loving* refers to the fact that Rome and Carthage fought three wars against each other during the third and second centuries B.C.

[8] An island in the Aegean Sea, site of the great temple of Juno.

[9] The Romans.

She fought at Troy for her dear Greeks; her mind
Still fed on hurt and anger; deep in her heart
Paris' decision[10] rankled, and the wrong
Offered her slighted beauty; and the hatred
Of the whole race; and Ganymede's[11] honors—
All that was fuel to fire; she tossed and harried
All over the seas, wherever she could, those Trojans
Who had survived the Greeks and fierce Achilles,
And so they wandered over many an ocean,
Through many a year, fate-hounded. Such a struggle   40
It was to found the race of Rome!
                                        They were happy
Spreading the sail, rushing the foam with bronze,
And Sicily hardly out of sight, when Juno,
Still nourishing the everlasting wound,
Raged to herself: "I am beaten, I suppose;
It seems I cannot keep this Trojan king
From Italy. The fates, no doubt, forbid me.[12]
Pallas, of course, could burn the Argive ships,
Could drown the sailors, all for one man's guilt,
The crazy acts of Ajax.[13] Her own hand   50
Hurled from the cloud Jove's thunderbolt, and shattered
Their ships all over the sea; she raised up storm
And tempest; she spiked Ajax on the rocks,
Whirled him in wind, blasted his heart with fire.
And I, who walk my way as queen of the gods,
Sister of Jove, and wife of Jove, keep warring
With one tribe through the long, long years. Who cares
For Juno's godhead? Who brings sacrifice
Devoutly to her altars?"
                                        Brooding, burning,
She sought Aeolia, the storm-clouds' dwelling,   60
A land that sweeps and swarms with the winds' fury,
Whose monarch, Aeolus, in his deep cave rules
Imperious, weighing down with bolt and prison
Those boisterous struggling roarers, who go raging
Around their bars, under the moan of the mountain.
High over them their sceptered lord sits watching,
Soothing, restraining, their passionate proud spirit,
Lest, uncontrolled, they seize, in their wild keeping,
The land, the sea, the arch of sky, in ruin
Sweeping through space. This Jupiter feared; he hid them   70

[10] Paris, one of the sons of King Priam of Troy, had been asked to judge which of the three
goddesses Juno, Minerva, and Venus was most beautiful. He chose Venus, who rewarded him
with Helen; Helen's abduction by Paris from her husband, Menelaus, then ignited the Trojan
War.
[11] Promoted over Juno's daughter Hebe as cupbearer to the gods.
[12] Even the gods were considered subject to the superior power of Fate.
[13] Pallas, or Athena (the Greek equivalent of Minerva, goddess of wisdom), had inflicted
the punishment described in revenge for the rape by Ajax of the prophetess Cassandra.

Deep in dark caverns, with a mass of mountain
Piled over above them, and a king to give them
Most certain regulation, with a knowledge
When to hold in, when to let go. Him Juno
Approached in supplication:—"Aeolus,
Given by Jove the power to still the waters,
Or raise them with a gale, a tribe I hate
Is on its way to Italy, and they carry
Troy with them, and their household gods, once beaten.
Shake anger into those winds of yours, turn over   80
Their ships, and drown them; drive them in all directions,
Litter the sea with bodies! For such service
The loveliest nymph I have, Deiopea,
Shall be your bride forever, and you will father
Fair children on her fairness." Aeolus
Made answer: "Yours, O Queen, the task of seeking
Whatever it is you will; and mine the duty
To follow with performance. All my empire,
My sceptre, Jove's indulgence, are beholden
To Juno's favor, by whose blessing I   90
Attend the feasts of the gods and rule this storm-land."
    His spear-butt struck the hollow mountain-side,
And the winds, wherever they could, came sweeping forth,
Whirled over the land, swooped down upon the ocean.
East, South, Southwest, they heave the billows, howl,
Storm, roll the giant combers toward the shore.
Men cry; the rigging creaks and strains; the clouds
Darken, and men see nothing; a weight of darkness
Broods over the deep; the heavy thunder rumbles
From pole to pole; the lightning rips and dazzles;   100
There is no way out but death. Aeneas shudders
In the chill shock, and lifts both hands to heaven:—
"O happy men, thrice happy, four times happy,
Who had the luck to die, with their fathers watching
Below the walls of Troy! Ah, Diomedes,
Bravest of Greeks, why could I not have fallen,
Bleeding my life away on plains of Ilium[14]
In our encounter there, where mighty Hector
Went down before Achilles'[15] spear, and huge
Sarpedon[16] lay in dust, and Simois river   110
Rolled to the sea so many noble heroes,
All drowned in all their armor?" And the gale
Howls from the north, striking the sail, head on;
The waves are lifted to the stars; the oars

[14] Troy.
[15] Hector and Achilles were the chief warriors of the Trojans and Greeks, respectively. The slaying of Hector by Achilles is described in Homer's *Iliad,* Book XXII.
[16] King of Lycia, killed while fighting on the side of the Trojans. The Simois was a river at the battlefield of Troy.

Are broken, and the prow slews round; the ship
Lies broadside on; a wall of water, a mountain,
Looms up, comes pouring down; some ride the crest,
Some, in the trough, can see the boil of the sand.
The South wind hurls three ships on the hidden rocks,
That sea-reef which Italians call the Altars;   120
The West takes three, sweeping them from the deep
On shoal and quicksand; over the stern of one,
Before Aeneas' eyes, a great sea falls,
Washing the helmsman overboard; the ship
Whirls thrice in the suck of the water and goes down
In the devouring gulf; and here and there
A few survivors swim, the Lycian men
Whose captain was Orontes; now their arms,
Their Trojan treasures, float with the broken timbers
On the swing and slide of the waves. The storm, triumphant,   130
Rides down more boats, and more; there goes Achates;
Abas, Aletes, Ilioneus,
Receive the hostile water; the walls are broken;
The enemy pours in.
                        But meanwhile Neptune[17]
Saw ocean in a welter of confusion,
The roar of storm, and deep and surface mingled.
Troublesome business, this; he rose, majestic,
From under the waves, and saw the Trojan vessels
Scattered all over the sea by the might of the waves
And the wreck of sky; he recognized the anger   140
And cunning of his sister, and he summoned
The winds by name:—"What arrogance is this,
What pride of birth, you winds, to meddle here
Without my sanction, raising all this trouble?
I'll—No, the waves come first: but listen to me,
You are going to pay for this! Get out of here!
Go tell your king the lordship of the ocean,
The trident, are not his, but mine. His realm
Reaches no further than the rocks and caverns
You brawlers dwell in; let him rule that palace,   150
Big as he pleases, shut you in, and stay there!"
    This said, he calmed the swollen sea and cloud,
Brought back the sun; Cymothoe and Triton,[18]
Heaving together, pulled the ships from the reef,
As Neptune used his trident for a lever,
Opened the quicksand, made the water smooth,
And the flying chariot skimmed the level surface.
Sometimes, in a great nation, there are riots
With the rabble out of hand, and firebrands fly
And cobblestones; whatever they lay their hands on   160

---

[17] God of the ocean.
[18] Cymothoe and Triton were, respectively, a sea nymph and a sea god.

Is a weapon for their fury, but should they see
One man of noble presence, they fall silent,
Obedient dogs, with ears pricked up, and waiting,
Waiting his word, and he knows how to bring them
Back to good sense again. So ocean, roaring,
Subsided into stillness, as the sea-god
Looked forth upon the waters, and clear weather
Shone over him as he drove his flying horses.
    Aeneas' weary children make for harbor,
Whichever lies most near, and the prows are turned   170
To Libya's coast-line. In a bay's deep curve
They find a haven, where the water lies
With never a ripple. A little island keeps
The sea-swell off, and the waves break on its sides
And slide back harmless. The great cliffs come down
Steep to deep water, and the background shimmers,
Darkens and shines, the tremulous aspen moving
And the dark fir pointing still. And there is a cave
Under the overhanging rocks, alive
With water running fresh, a home of the Nymphs,   180
With benches for them, cut from the living stone.
No anchor is needed here for weary ships,
No mooring-cable. Aeneas brings them in,
Seven weary vessels, and the men are glad
To be ashore again, to feel dry sand
Under the salt-stained limbs. Achates[19] strikes
The spark from the flint, catches the fire on leaves,
Adds chips and kindling, blows and fans the flame,
And they bring out the soaked and salty corn,
The hand-mills, stone and mortar, and make ready,   190
As best they can, for bread.
                        Meanwhile Aeneas
Climbs to a look-out, for a view of the ocean,
Hoping for some good luck; the Phrygian galleys
Might meet his gaze, or Capys' boats, or a pennon
On a far-off mast-head flying. There is nothing,
Nothing to see out yonder, but near the water
Three stags are grazing, with a herd behind them,
A long line browsing through the peaceful valley.
He reaches for the bow and the swift arrows
Borne by Achates, and he shoots the leaders,   200
High-antlered, routs the common herd, and ceases
Only when seven are slain, a number equal
To the ships' tally, and then he seeks the harbor,
Divides the spoil, broaches the wine Acestes
Had stowed for them at Drepanum on their leaving,
A kingly present, and he calms their trouble,

[19] Aeneas' most faithful companion.

Saying: "O comrades, we have been through evil
Together before this; we have been through worse,
Scylla, Charybdis, and the Cyclops' dwelling,[20]
The sounding rocks. This, too, the god will end.   210
Call the nerve back; dismiss the fear, the sadness.
Some day, perhaps, remembering even this
Will be a pleasure. We are going on
Through whatsoever chance and change, until
We come to Latium, where the fates point out
A quiet dwelling-place, and Troy recovered.
Endure, and keep yourself for better days."
He kept to himself the sorrow in the heart,
Wearing, for them, a mask of hopefulness.
They were ready for the feasting. Part lay bare   220
The flesh from the torn hides, part cut the meat
Impaling it, still quivering, on spits,
Setting the kettles, keeping the water boiling,
And strong with food again, sprawling stretched out
On comfortable grass, they take their fill
Of bread and wine and venison, till hunger
Is gone, and the board cleared. And then they talk
For a long time, of where their comrades are,
Are, or may be, hopeful and doubtful both.
Could they believe them living? or would a cry   230
Fall on deaf ears forever? All those captains,
Brave Gyas, brave Cloanthus, Amycus,
Lycus, Orontes—in his secret heart
Aeneas mourns them.
                        Meanwhile, from the heaven
Jupiter watched the lands below, and the seas
With the white points of sails, and far-off people,
Turning his gaze toward Libya. And Venus
Came to him then, a little sadly, tears
Brimming in those bright eyes of hers. "Great father,"
She said, "Great ruler of the world   240
Of men and gods, great wielder of the lightning,
What has my poor Aeneas[21] done? what outrage
Could Trojans perpetrate, so that the world
Rejects them everywhere, and many a death
Inflicted on them over Italy?
There was a promise once, that as the years
Rolled onward, they would father Rome and rulers
Of Roman stock, to hold dominion over
All sea and land. That was a promise, father;
What changed it? Once that promise was my comfort;   250
Troy fell; I weighed one fate against another

---

[20] These perils are described in Book III.
[21] Venus is Aeneas' mother; Anchises, his father, is a mortal.

And found some consolation. But disaster
Keeps on; the same ill-fortune follows after.
What end of it all, great king? One man, Antenor,
Escaped the Greeks, came through Illyrian waters
Safe to Liburnian regions, where Timavus[22]
Roars underground, comes up nine times, and reaches
The floodland near the seas. One man, Antenor,
Founded a city, Padua, a dwelling
For Trojan men, a resting-place from labor, 260
And shares their quietude. But we, your children,
To whom heaven's height is granted, we are betrayed,
We have lost our ships, we are kept from Italy,
Kept far away. One enemy—I tell you
This is a shameful thing! Do we deserve it?
Is this our rise to power?"
                          He smiled, in answer,
The kind of smile that clears the air, and kissed her.
"Fear not, my daughter; fate remains unmoved
For the Roman generations. You will witness
Lavinium's rise, her walls fulfill the promise; 270
You will bring to heaven lofty-souled Aeneas.
There has been no change in me whatever. Listen!
To ease this care, I will prophesy a little,
I will open the book of fate. Your son Aeneas
Will wage a mighty war in Italy,[23]
Beat down proud nations, give his people laws,
Found them a city, a matter of three years
From victory to settlement. His son,
The boy Ascanius, named Ilus once,
When Troy was standing, and now called Iulus, 280
Shall reign for thirty years, and great in power
Forsake Lavinium, transfer the kingdom
To Alba Longa, new-built capital.
Here, for three hundred years, the line of Hector
Shall govern, till a royal priestess bears
Twin sons to Mars, and Romulus, rejoicing
In the brown wolf-skin[24] of his foster-mother,
Takes up the tribe, and builds the martial walls
And calls the people, after himself, the Romans.
To these I set no bounds in space or time; 290
They shall rule forever. Even bitter Juno
Whose fear now harries earth and sea and heaven
Will change to better counsels, and will cherish
The race that wears the toga, Roman masters

---

[22] The river Timavus flows into the Adriatic Sea (east of Italy); Liburnia is part of the Adriatic coast.

[23] The war is described in the second half of the poem, Books VII to XII.

[24] Romulus and his twin, Remus, were supposed to have been suckled by a she-wolf.

Of all the world. It is decreed. The time
Will come, as holy years wheel on, when Troy
Will subjugate Mycenae, vanquish Phthia,
Be lord of Argos.[25] And from this great line
Will come a Trojan, Caesar, to establish
The limit of his empire at the ocean,   300
His glory at the stars, a man called Julius
Whose name recalls Iulus. Welcome waits
For him in heaven; all the spoils of Asia
Will weight him down, and prayer be made before him.
Then wars will cease, and a rough age grow gentler,
White Faith and Vesta,[26] Romulus and Remus,
Give law to nations. War's grim gates will close,
Tight-shut with bars of iron, and inside them
The wickedness of war sit bound and silent,
The red mouth straining and the hands held tight   310
In fastenings of bronze, a hundred hundred."
        With that, he sent down Mercury[27] from heaven
That Carthage might be kindly, and her land
And new-built towers receive them with a welcome,
And their queen, Dido, knowing the will of fate,
Swing wide her doors. On the oarage of his wings
He flies through the wide sweep of air to Libya,
Where, at the will of the god, the folk make ready
In kindliness of heart, and their queen's purpose
Is gracious and gentle.
                                All night long Aeneas   320
Had pondered many a care, and with bright morning
Resolved to reconnoiter; the winds have brought him
To a new country: who lives in it, men
Or only beasts? The fields appear untended.
The fleet lies under a hollow cliff, surrounded
By spikes of shade, and groves arch overhead,
Ample concealment. Aeneas and Achates
Went forth together, armed, down the trail in the forest,
And there his mother met him, a girl, it seemed,
From Thrace or Sparta, trim as any huntress   330
Who rides her horses hard, or outspeeds rivers
In her swift going. A bow hung over her shoulder,
Her hair blew free, her knees were bare, her garments
Tucked at the waist and knotted. As she saw them,
"Ho there, young men," she cried, "have you seen my sister
Around here anywhere? She wears a quiver,
And a spotted lynx-hide; maybe you have heard her
Hunting the boar and shouting?"

---

[25] Cities associated with the Trojans' Greek conquerors: Phthia with Achilles, Mycenae and
Argos with Agamemnon, the Greek commander.
[26] Goddess of the hearth.
[27] Messenger of the gods.

But her son
Responded: "No; we have heard no sounds of hunting,
We have seen no one here. But tell me, maiden, 340
What name to call you by? In voice and feature
You are, I think, no mortal; a goddess, surely,—
Nymph, or Apollo's sister?[28] Whoever you are,
Be kind to us, lighten our trouble, tell us
Under what sky, along what coast of the world,
We wander, knowing neither land nor people,
Driven by gales and billows. Many a victim
We shall make ready for your altar." Venus
Answered: "I have no title to such honor.
The Tyrian girls all wear these crimson leggings 350
Like mine, and carry quivers. Tyrian folk
Live here; their city is Carthage; over the border
Lies Libya, warlike people. Our queen, Dido,
Came here from Tyre; she was fleeing from her brother,—
A long and complicated story; outrage,—
No matter, here it is, in brief. Her husband
Was Sychaeus, wealthiest of all Phoenicians,
At least in land, and Dido loved him dearly
Since first her father gave her to him, virgin,
And then unlucky bride. She had a brother, 360
Pygmalion, king of Tyre, a monster, evil
In wickedness, and madness came between
Those men, the two of them. Pygmalion murdered
Sychaeus at the altar; he was crazy
And blind for gold and crafty; what did he care
About his sister's love? And he kept it quiet
For a long time, kept telling Dido something
To fool her with false comfort, but Sychaeus
Came to her in a dream, a ghost, unburied,
With the wounds in his breast, the story of the altar, 370
The pale lips blurting out the secret horror,
The crime in the dark of the household. *Flee,* he told her,
Forsake this land; and he told her where the treasure
Lay hidden in earth, uncounted gold and silver.
Dido was moved to flight, secured companions,
All those possessed by fear, all those whom hatred
Had made relentless; ships were standing ready,
As it so happened; they put the gold aboard,
And over the sea the greedy tyrant's treasure
Went sailing, with a woman for a captain. 380
They came here; you will see the walls arising
And the great citadel of the town called Carthage.
Here they bought ground; they used to call it Byrsa,
That being a word for bull's hide; they bought only

---

[28] Diana, goddess of the hunt.

What a bull's hide could cover. And now tell me
Who you might be yourselves? what land do you come from,
Bound for what coast?"
                              And he began his answer
With a long sigh: "O goddess, if I told you
All from the first beginning, if you had leisure
To listen to the record of our trouble,   390
It would take me all day long. From ancient Troy,
In case that name means anything, we come
Driven over many seas, and now a storm
Has whipped us on this coast. I am Aeneas,
A good, devoted man; I carry with me
My household gods, saved from the Greeks; I am known
In heaven; it is Italy I seek,
A homeland for me there, and a race descended
From lofty Jove. With a score of ships we started
Over the Phrygian ocean, following fate   400
And the way my mother pointed. Only seven
Are left us now, battered survivors, after
The rage of wind and wave. And here I wander
The wastes of Libya, unknown and needy,
Driven from Europe and Asia." And his mother
Broke in on his complaining:—"Whoever you are,
Some god must care for you, I think, to bring you
Here to the city of Carthage. Follow on,
Go to the royal palace. For, I tell you,
Your comrades have returned, your fleet is safe,   410
Brought to good haven by the turn of the winds,
Unless the augury my parents taught me
Was foolish nonsense. In the heaven yonder
You see twelve swans, rejoicing in long column,
Scattered, a little while ago, and driven
By the swooping eagle, over all the sky,
But now, it seems, they light on land, or watch
Those who came down before them; as they circle
In company, and make a cheerful sound
With whir of wing or song, so, let me tell you,   420
Your ships and men already enter harbor
Or near it under full sail. Keep on, go forward
Where the path leads."
                              And as she turned, her shoulders
Shone with a radiant light; her hair shed fragrance,
Her robes slipped to her feet, and the true goddess
Walked in divinity.[29] He knew his mother,
And his voice pursued her flight: "Cruel again!
Why mock your son so often with false phantoms?

---

[29]A goddess could be distinguished from a mortal by her gait and carriage.

Why may not hand be joined to hand, and words
Exchanged in truthfulness?" So, still reproachful, 430
He went on toward the city, with Achates,
But Venus cast dark air around their going,
A veil of mist, so that no man might see them
Or lay a hand on them, or halt them, asking
The reasons of their coming. She soared upward
To Paphos, happily home to temple and altars
Steaming with incense, redolent with garlands.
  And they went on, where the little pathway led them
To rising ground; below them lay the city,
Majestic buildings now, where once were hovels, 440
A wonder to Aeneas, gates and bustle
And well-paved streets, the busy Tyrians toiling
With stones for walls and citadel, or marking
Foundations for their homes, drainage and furrow,
All under ordered process. They dredge harbors,
Set cornerstones, quarry the rock, where someday
Their theater will tower. They are like bees
In early summer over the country flowers
When the sun is warm, and the young of the hive emerge,
And they pack the molten honey, bulge the cells 450
With the sweet nectar, add new loads, and harry
The drones away from the hive, and the work glows,
And the air is sweet with bergamot and clover.
"Happy the men whose walls already rise!"
Exclaims Aeneas, gazing on the city,
And enters there, still veiled in cloud—a marvel!—
And walks among the people, and no one sees him.
  There was a grove in the middle of the city,
Most happy in its shade; this was the place
Where first the Tyrians, tossed by storm and whirlwind, 460
Dug up the symbol royal Juno showed them,
The skull of a war-horse, a sign the race to come
Would be supreme in war and wealth, for ages,
And Dido here was building a great temple
In Juno's honor, rich in gifts, and blessed
With the presence of the goddess. Lintel and rafter
Were bronze above bronze stairways, and bronze portals
Swung on bronze hinges. Here Aeneas first
Dared hope for safety, find some reassurance
In hope of better days: a strange sight met him, 470
To take his fear away. Waiting the queen,
He stood there watching, under the great temple,
Letting his eyes survey the city's fortune,
The artist's workmanship, the craftsman's labor,
And there, with more than wonder, he sees the battles
Fought around Troy, and the wars whose fame had travelled
The whole world over; there is Agamemnon,

Priam, and Menelaus,[30] and Achilles,
A menace to them all. He is moved to tears.
"What place in all the world," he asks Achates,   480
"Is empty of our sorrow? There is Priam!
Look! even here there are rewards for praise,
There are tears for things, and what men suffer touches
The human heart. Dismiss your fear; this story
Will bring some safety to you." Sighing often,
He could not turn his gaze away; it was only
A picture on a wall, but the sight afforded
Food for the spirit's need. He saw the Greeks,
Hard-pressed, in flight, and Trojans coming after,
Or, on another panel, the scene reversed,   490
Achilles in pursuit, his own men fleeing;
He saw, and tears came into his eyes again,
The tents of Rhesus,[31] snowy-white, betrayed
In their first sleep by bloody Diomedes
With many a death, and the fiery horses driven
Into the camp, before they ever tasted
The grass of Troy, or drank from Xanthus' river.
Another scene showed Troilus, poor youngster,
Running away, his arms flung down; Achilles
Was much too good for him; he had fallen backward   500
Out of his car, but held the reins, and the horses
Dragged him along the ground, his hair and shoulders
Bounding in dust, and the spear making a scribble.
And there were Trojan women, all in mourning,
With streaming hair, on their way to Pallas' temple,
Bearing, as gift, a robe, but the stern goddess[32]
Kept her gaze on the ground. Three times Achilles
Had dragged the body of Hector around the walls,
And was selling it for money. What a groan
Came from Aeneas' heart, seeing that spoil,   510
That chariot, and helpless Priam reaching
His hands, unarmed, across the broken body!
And he saw himself there, too, fighting in battle
Against Greek leaders, he saw the Eastern columns,
And swarthy Memnon's[33] arms. Penthesilea,
The Amazon, blazes in fury, leading
Her crescent-shielded thousands, a golden buckle
Below her naked breast, a soldieress
Fighting with men.

---

[30] Priam was the patriarchal king of Troy, Menelaus was the cuckolded husband of Helen, brother of Agamemnon and co-commander of the Greek forces at Troy.

[31] Rhesus supported the Trojans against the Greeks. Troy could not fall, it was believed, if his horses tasted Troy's grass or drank from its river Xanthus. But before they could do either, Diomedes and Ulysses carried the horses off.

[32] Pallas (the Greek Athena or Roman Minerva) sided with the Greeks against the Trojans.

[33] Ethiopian king who sided with the Trojans.

And as he watched these marvels
In one long fascinated stare of wonder, 520
Dido, the queen, drew near; she came to the temple
With a great train, all majesty, all beauty,
As on Eurotas' riverside, or where
Mount Cynthus[34] towers high, Diana leads
Her bands of dancers, and the Oreads follow
In thousands, right and left, the taller goddess,
The quiver-bearing maiden, and Latona
Is filled with secret happiness, so Dido
Moved in her company, a queen, rejoicing,
Ordering on her kingdom's rising glory. 530
At Juno's portal, under the arch of the temple,
She took her throne, a giver of law and justice,
A fair partitioner of toil and duty,
And suddenly Aeneas, from the crowd,
Saw Trojan men approaching, brave Cloanthus,
Sergestus, Antheus, and all those others
Whom the black storm had driven here and yonder.
This he cannot believe, nor can Achates,
Torn between fear and joy. They burn with ardor
To seek their comrades' handclasp, but confusion 540
Still holds them in the cloud: what can have happened?
They watch from the cover of mist: men still were coming
From all the ships, chosen, it seemed, as pleaders
For graciousness before the temple, calling
Aloud: what fortune had been theirs, he wonders,
Where had they left the ships; why were they coming?
They were given audience; Ilioneus,
Senior to all, began: "O Queen, whom Jove
Has given the founding of a great new city,
Has given to bridle haughty tribes with justice, 550
We, pitiful Trojans, over every ocean
Driven by storm, make our appeal: keep from us
The terrible doom of fire; protect our vessels;
Have mercy on a decent race; consider
Our lot with closer interest. We have not come
To ravish Libyan homes, or carry plunder
Down to the shore. We lack the arrogance
Of conquerors; there is no aggression in us.
There is a place which Greeks have given a name,
The Land in the West; it is powerful in arms, 560
Rich in its soil; Oenotrians used to live there,
And now, the story goes, a younger people
Inhabit it, calling themselves Italians
After their leader's name.[35] We were going there

---

[34] Birthplace of Diana, goddess of the hunt. In the passage following, *Oreads* are mountain nymphs, *the taller goddess* refers to Diana, *Latona* was another name for Leto, mother of Diana.
[35] Italus, a legendary ruler.

When, big with storm and cloud, Orion[36] rising
Drove us on hidden quicksands, and wild winds
Scattered us over the waves, by pathless rocks
And the swell of the surge. A few of us have drifted
Here to your shores. What kind of men are these,
What barbarous land permits such attitudes?   570
We have been denied the welcome of the beach,
Forbidden to set foot on land; they rouse
All kinds of war against us. You despise,
It may be, human brotherhood, and arms
Wielded by men. But there are gods, remember,
Who care for right and wrong. Our king Aeneas
May be alive; no man was ever more just,
More decent ever, or greater in war and arms.
If fate preserves him still, if he still breathes
The welcome air, above the world of shadows,   580
Fear not; to have treated us with kindly service
Need bring you no repentance. We have cities
In Sicily as well, and King Acestes
Is one of us, from Trojan blood. We ask you
To let us beach our battered fleet, make ready
Beams from the forest timber, mend our oarage,
Seek Italy and Latium, glad at knowing
Our king and comrades rescued. But if safety
Is hopeless for him now, and Libyan water
Has been his grave, and if his son Iulus   590
Is desperate, or lost, grant us permission
At least to make for Sicily, whence we came here,
Where king Acestes has a dwelling for us."
The Trojans, as he ended, all were shouting,
And Dido, looking down, made a brief answer:
"I am sorry, Trojans; put aside your care,
Have no more fear. The newness of the kingdom
And our strict need compel me to such measures—
Sentries on every border, far and wide.
But who so ignorant as not to know   600
The nation of Aeneas, manly both
In deeds and people, and the city of Troy?
We are not as dull as that, we folk from Carthage;
The sun shines on us here. Whether you seek
The land in the west, the sometime fields of Saturn,[37]
Or the Sicilian realms and king Acestes,
I will help you to the limit; should you wish
To settle here and share this kingdom with me,
The city I found is yours; draw up your ships;

---

[36] The constellation was believed to presage storms.
[37] Italy, where Saturn dwelt after his dethronement by Jupiter and his new generation of
gods. Saturn's reign is associated with an ancient "golden age" of simplicity.

Trojan and Tyrian I treat alike. 610
Would, also, that your king were here, Aeneas,
Driven by that same wind. I will send good men
Along the coast to seek him, under orders
To scour all Libya; he may be wandering
Somewhere, in woods or town, surviving shipwreck."
    Aeneas and Achates both were eager
To break the cloud; the queen inspired their spirit
With her address. Achates asked Aeneas:—
"What do we do now, goddess-born? You see
They all are safe, our vessels and our comrades, 620
Only one missing, and we saw him drowning,
Ourselves, beneath the waves; all other things
Confirm what Venus told us." And as he finished,
The cloud around them broke, dissolved in air,
Illumining Aeneas, like a god,
Light radiant around his face and shoulders,
And Venus gave him all the bloom of youth,
Its glow, its liveliness, as the artist adds
Luster to ivory, or sets in gold
Silver or marble. No one saw him coming 630
Until he spoke:—"You seek me; here I am,
Trojan Aeneas, saved from the Libyan waves.
Worn out by all the perils of land and sea,
In need of everything, blown over the great world,
A remnant left by the Greeks, Dido, we lack
The means to thank our only pitier
For offer of a city and a home.
If there is justice anywhere, if goodness
Means anything to any power, if gods
At all regard good people, may they give 640
The great rewards you merit. Happy the age,
Happy the parents who have brought you forth!
While rivers run to sea, while shadows move
Over the mountains, while the stars burn on,
Always, your praise, your honor, and your name,
Whatever land I go to, will endure."[38]
His hand went out to greet his men, Serestus,
Gyas, Cloanthus, Ilioneus,
The others in their turn. And Dido marvelled
At his appearance, first, and all that trouble 650
He had borne up under; there was a moment's silence
Before she spoke: "What chance, what violence,
O goddess-born, has driven you through danger,
From grief to grief? Are you indeed that son
Whom Venus bore Anchises? I remember

---

[38] Aeneas' words are ironic in the light of later events in the poem and in history.

When Teucer came to Sidon,[39] as an exile
Seeking new kingdoms, and my father helped him,
My father, Belus, conqueror of Cyprus.
From that time on I have known about your city,
Your name, and the Greek kings, and the fall of Troy.   660
Even their enemies would praise the Trojans,
Or claim descent from Teucer's line. I bid you
Enter my house. I, too, am fortune-driven
Through many sufferings; this land at last
Has brought me rest. Not ignorant of evil,
I know one thing, at least,—to help the wretched."
And so she led Aeneas to the palace,
Proclaiming sacrifice at all the temples
In honor of his welcome, and sent presents
To his comrades at the shore, a score of bullocks,   670
A hundred swine, a hundred ewes and lambs
In honor of the joyous day. The palace,
Within, is made most bright with pomp and splendor,
The halls prepared for feasting. Crimson covers
Are laid, with fine embroidery, and silver
Is heavy on the tables; gold, engraven,
Recalls ancestral prowess, a tale of heroes
From the race's first beginnings.
                              And Aeneas,
Being a thoughtful father, speeds Achates
Back to the ships, with tidings for Iulus,   680
He is to join them; all the father's fondness
Is centered on the son. Orders are given
To bring gifts with him, saved from the Trojan ruins,
A mantle stiff with figures worked in gold;
A veil with gold acanthus running through it,
Once worn by Helen, when she sailed from Sparta
Toward that forbidden marriage, a wondrous gift
Made by her mother Leda; and the sceptre
That Ilione, Priam's eldest daughter,
Had carried once; a necklace hung with pearls;   690
A crown of gold and jewels. Toward the ships
Achates sped the message.
                              Meanwhile Venus
Plotted new stratagems, that Cupid, changed
In form and feature, should appear instead
Of young Ascanius,[40] and by his gifts
Inspire the queen to passion, with his fire
Burning her very bones. She feared the house
Held dubious intentions; men of Tyre

---

[39] Teucer was a Greek exiled by his father; he is not to be confused with the Teucer who was the legendary ancestor of the Trojans (who are therefore sometimes called Teucrians). Sidon was a city near Tyre, Dido's former home.
[40] Aeneas' son is sometimes called Ascanius, sometimes Iulus.

Were always two-faced people, and Juno's anger
Vexed her by night. She spoke to her wingèd son:— 700
"O my one strength and source of power, my son,
Disdainful of Jove's thunderbolt, to you
I come in prayer for help. You know that Juno
Is hateful toward Aeneas, keeping him tossing
All over the seas in bitterness; you have often
Grieved with me for your brother. And now Dido
Holds him with flattering words; I do not trust
Juno's ideas of welcome; she will never
Pause at a point like this. Therefore I purpose
To take the queen by cunning, put around her 710
A wall of flame, so that no power can change her,
So that a blazing passion for Aeneas
Will bind her to us. Listen! I will tell you
How you can manage this. The royal boy,
My greatest care, has heard his father's summons
To come to the city, bringing presents, rescued
From the flames of Troy and the sea; and he is ready.
But I will make him drowsy, carry him off
In slumber over Cythera, or hide him
Deep on Idalium[41] in a secret bower 720
Before he learns the scheme or interrupts it.
You, for one night, no more, assume his features,
The boy's familiar guise, yourself a boy,
So that when Dido takes you to her bosom
During the royal feast, with the wine flowing,
And happiness abounding, you, receiving
The sweetness of her kiss, will overcome her
With secret fire and poison."
                              For his mother
Cupid put off his wings, and went rejoicing
With young Iulus' stride; the real Iulus 730
Venus had lulled in soft repose, and borne him
Warm in her bosom to Idalian groves,
Where the soft marjoram cradled him with blossom
Exhaling shadowy sweetness over his slumber.
And, with Achates leading, Cupid came
Obedient to his mother, bringing gifts.
The queen receives them, on a golden couch
Below the royal tapestries, where spreads
Of crimson wait Aeneas and his Trojans.
Servants bring water for their hands, and bread 740
In baskets, and fine napkins. At the fire
Are fifty serving-maids, to set the feast,
A hundred more, girls, and a hundred boys
To load the tables, and bring the goblets round,

---

[41] Cythera was the island associated with Venus' birth; Idalium was a part of Cyprus associated with worship of her.

As through the happy halls the Tyrians throng,
Admire the Trojan gifts, admire Iulus,
The young god with the glowing countenance,
The charming words, the robe, the saffron veil
Edged with acanthus. More than all the rest,
Disaster-bound, the unhappy queen takes fire,   750
And cannot have enough of looking, moved
Alike by boy and gifts. She watches him
Cling to his father's neck, or come to her
For fondling, and her eyes, her heart, receive him,
Alas, poor queen, not knowing what a god
Is plotting for her sorrow. He remembers
What Venus told him; she forgets a little
About Sychaeus; the heart unused to love
Stirs with a living passion.
When the first quiet settled over the tables,   760
And the boards were cleared, they set the great bowls down,
Crowning the wine with garlands. A great hum
Runs through the halls, the voices reach the rafters,
The burning lamps below the fretted gold,
The torches flaring, put the night to rout.
The queen commands the loving-cup of Belus,
Heavy with gems and gold, and fills it full,
And silence fills the halls before her prayer:—
"Jupiter, giver of laws for host and guest,
Grant this to be a happy day for all,   770
Both Tyrians and travellers from Troy,
And something for our children to remember!
May Bacchus,[42] giver of joy, attend, and Juno
Be kind, and all my Tyrians be friendly!"
She poured libation on the table, touched
The gold rim with her lips, passed on the bowl
To Bitias, who dove deep, and other lords
Took up the challenge. And a minstrel played
A golden lyre, Iopas, taught by Atlas:[43]
Of the sun's labors and the wandering moon   780
He sang, whence came the race of beasts and man,
Whence rain and fire, the stars and constellations,
Why suns in winter hasten to the sea,
Or what delay draws out the dawdling nights.
The Tyrians roar, applauding, and the Trojans
Rejoice no less, and the poor queen prolongs
The night with conversation, drinking deep
Of her long love, and asking many questions
Of Priam, Hector; of the arms of Memnon;
How big Achilles was; and Diomedes,   790

---

[42] God of wine.
[43] The bard Iopas sings of astronomical science, which is associated with Atlas, the gigantic
being who in mythology supports the heavens on his shoulders.

What were his horses like? "Tell us, my guest,"
She pleads, "from the beginning, all the story,
The treachery of the Greeks, the wanderings,
The perils of the seven tiresome years."

BOOK II: THE FALL OF TROY

They all were silent, watching. From his couch
Aeneas spoke: "A terrible grief, O Queen,
You bid me live again, how Troy went down
Before the Greeks, her wealth, her pitiful kingdom,
Sorrowful things I saw myself, wherein
I had my share and more. Even Ulysses,[1]
Even his toughest soldiery might grieve
At such a story. And the hour is late
Already; night is sliding down the sky
And setting stars urge slumber. But if you long   10
To learn our downfall, to hear the final chapter
Of Troy, no matter how I shrink, remembering,
And turn away in grief, let me begin it.[2]

Broken in war, set back by fate, the leaders
Of the Greek host, as years went by, contrived,
With Pallas' help, a horse as big as a mountain.
They wove its sides with planks of fir, pretending
This was an offering for their safe return,
At least, so rumor had it. But inside
They packed, in secret, into the hollow sides   20
The fittest warriors; the belly's cavern,
Huge as it was, was filled with men in armor.
There is an island, Tenedos, well-known,
Rich in the days of Priam; now it is only
A bay, and not too good an anchorage
For any ship to trust. They sailed there, hid
On the deserted shore. We thought they had gone,
Bound for Mycenae,[3] and Troy was very happy,
Shaking off grief, throwing the gates wide open.
It was a pleasure, for a change, to go   30
See the Greek camp, station and shore abandoned;
Why, this was where Achilles camped, his minions,
The Dolopes, were here; and the fleet just yonder,
And that was the plain where we used to meet in battle.
Some of us stared in wonder at the horse,

[1] The Latin name for Odysseus, the Greek hero.
[2] Typically, epic poems begin in the middle of the story, the earlier events being supplied
in a flashback narrative like that of Aeneas in Books II and III.
[3] City in Greece ruled by Agamemnon, the Greek commander.

Astounded by its vastness, Minerva's gift,
Death from the virgin goddess, had we known it.
Thymoetes, whether in treachery, or because
The fates of Troy so ordered, was the first one
To urge us bring it in to the heart of the city,   40
But Capys, and some others, knowing better,
Suspicious of Greek plotting, said to throw it
Into the sea, to burn it up with fire,
To cut it open, see what there was inside it.
The wavering crowd could not make up its mind.

And, at that point, Laocoön came running,
With a great throng at his heels, down from the hilltop
As fast as ever he could, and before he reached us,
Cried in alarm: 'Are you crazy, wretched people?
Do you think they have gone, the foe? Do you think that any   50
Gifts of the Greeks lack treachery? Ulysses,—
What was his reputation? Let me tell you,
Either the Greeks are hiding in this monster,
Or it's some trick of war, a spy, or engine,
To come down on the city. Tricky business
Is hiding in it. Do not trust it, Trojans,
Do not believe this horse. Whatever it may be,
I fear the Greeks, even when bringing presents.'
With that, he hurled the great spear at the side
With all the strength he had. It fastened, trembling,   60
And the struck womb rang hollow, a moaning sound.
He had driven us, almost, to let the light in
With the point of the steel, to probe, to tear, but something
Got in his way, the gods, or fate, or counsel,
Ill-omened, in our hearts; or Troy would be standing
And Priam's lofty citadel unshaken.

Meanwhile, some Trojan shepherds, pulling and hauling,
Had a young fellow, with his hands behind him,
Tied up, and they were dragging him to Priam.
He had let himself be taken so, on purpose,   70
To open Troy to the Greeks, a stranger, ready
For death or shifty cunning, a cool intriguer,
Let come what may. They crowd around to see him,
Take turns in making fun of him, that captive.
Listen, and learn Greek trickiness; learn all
Their crimes from one.
He stopped in the middle, frightened and defenceless,
Looked at the Trojan ranks,—'What land, what waters,
Can take me now?' he cried, 'There is nothing, nothing
Left for me any more, no place with the Greeks,   80
And here are the Trojans howling for my blood!'
Our mood was changed. We pitied him, poor fellow,
Sobbing his heart out. We bade him tell his story,

His lineage, his news: what can he count on,
The captive that he is? His fear had gone
As he began: 'O King, whatever happens,
I will tell the truth, tell all of it; to start with,
I own I am a Greek. Sinon is wretched,
Fortune has made him so, but she will never
Make him a liar. You may perhaps have heard 90
Rumors of Palamedes, son of Belus,[4]
A man of glorious fame. But the Greeks killed him,—
He was against the war, and so they killed him,
An innocent man, by perjury and lying
False witness. Now that he is dead they mourn him.
My father, his poor relative, had sent me
To soldier in his company; I was then
Scarcely beyond my boyhood. Palamedes
Held, for some time, some influence and standing
In royal councils, and we shared his glory, 100
But, and all men know this, Ulysses' hatred,
His cunning malice, pulled him down; thereafter
I lived in darkness, dragging out a lifetime
In sorrow for my innocent lord, and anger,
And in my anger I was very foolish,
I talked; I vowed, if I got home to Argos,
I would have vengeance: so I roused Ulysses
To hate me in his turn, and that began it,
Downfall and evil, Ulysses always trying
To frighten me with hint and accusation, 110
With rumors planted where the crowd would listen;
Oh yes, Ulysses knew what he was doing,
He never stopped, until with Calchas[5] working
Hand in glove with him—why am I telling this,
And what's the use? I am stalling. All the Greeks,
You think, are all alike; what more do you want?
Inflict the punishment. That would be something
Ulysses would rejoice in, and some others
Pay handsome money for!'

But we were all on fire to hear him further. 120
Pelasgian[6] craft meant nothing to our folly.
Trembling and nervous, he resumed his lying:
'The Greeks were tired of the long war; they often
Wanted to sail from Troy for home. Oh, would
That they had only done it! But a storm
Would cut them off, or the wrong wind terrify them.
Especially, just after the horse was finished,

---

[4] Not to be confused with Dido's father Belus, mentioned in Book I.
[5] As a Greek priest and prophet, Calchas' task was to discover and reveal the will of the gods.
[6] Here a synonym for "Greek."

With the joined planks of maple, all the heaven
Roared loud with storm-clouds. In suspense and terror
We sent Eurypylus to ask Apollo   130
What could be done; the oracle was gloomy,
Foreboding: "Blood, O Greeks, and a slain virgin[7]
Appeased the winds when first you came here; blood
Must pay for your return, a life be given,
An Argive life." The word came to our ears
With terror in it, our blood ran cold in our veins,
For whom was fate preparing? who would be
The victim of Apollo? Then Ulysses
Dragged Calchas into our midst, with a great uproar,
Trying his best to make the prophet tell us   140
What the gods wanted. And there were many then
Who told me what was coming, or kept silent
Because they saw, and all too well, the scheme
Ulysses had in mind. For ten days Calchas
Said nothing at all, hid in his tent, refusing
To have a word of his pronounce the sentence,
And all the time Ulysses kept on shouting,
Till Calchas broke, and doomed me to the altar.
And all assented; what each man had feared
In his own case, he bore with great composure   150
When turned another way.
The terrible day was almost on me; fillets
Were ready for my temples, the salted meal
Prepared, the altars standing. But I fled,
I tore myself away from death, I admit it,
I hid all night in sedge and muddy water
At the edge of the lake, hoping, forever hoping,
They might set sail. And now I hope no longer
To see my home, my parents, or my children,
Poor things, whom they will kill because I fled them,   160
Whom they will murder for my sacrilege.
But oh, by the gods above, by any power
That values truth, by any uncorrupted
Remnant of faith in all the world, have pity,
Have pity on a soul that bears such sorrow,
More than I ever deserved.'
He had no need to ask us. Priam said,
Untie him, and we did so with a promise
To spare his life. Our king, with friendly words,
Addressed him, saying, 'Whoever you are, forget   170
The Greeks, from now on. You are ours; but tell me
Why they have built this monstrous horse? who made it,
Who thought of it? What is it, war-machine,

---

[7] Iphigenia, daughter of Agamemnon; her life had been sacrificed to appease the gods and thus gain for the Greeks favorable winds for their expedition against Troy.

Religious offering?' And he, instructed
In every trick and artifice, made answer,
Lifting his hands, now free: 'Eternal fires,
Inviolable godhead, be my witness,
You altars, you accursèd swords, you fillets
Which I as victim wore, I had the right
To break those solemn bonds, I had the right 180
To hate those men, to bring whatever they hide
Into the light and air; I am bound no longer
To any country, any laws, but, Trojans,
Keep to the promise, if I tell the truth,
If I pay back with interest.
All the Greek hope, since first the war began,
Rested in Pallas, always. But Ulysses,
The crime-contriver, and the son of Tydeus[8]
Attacked Minerva's temple, stole her image
Out of the holy shrine, and slew the guards, 190
And laid their bloody hands upon the goddess,
And from that time the Danaan[9] hopes were broken,
Faltered and failed. It was no doubtful anger
Pallas revealed; she gave them signs and portents.
From her image in the camp the upraised eyes
Shot fire, and sweat ran salty down the limbs,
Thrice from the ground she seemed to flash and leap
With vibrant spear and clashing shield. The priest,
Calchas, made prophecy: they must take to flight
Over the sea, and Troy could not be taken 200
Without new omens; they must go to Argos,
Bring back the goddess again, whom they have taken
In curved ships over the sea. And if they have gone,
They are bound for home, Mycenae, for new arms,
New gods, new soldiers; they will be here again
When least expected. Calchas' message warned them,
And so they built this image, to replace
The one they had stolen, a gigantic offering
For a tremendous sacrilege. It was Calchas,
Again, who bade them build a mass so mighty 210
It almost reached the stars, too big to enter
Through any gate, or be brought inside the walls.
For if your hands should damage it, destruction,
(May God avert it) would come upon the city,
But if your hands helped bring it home, then Asia
Would be invading Greece, and doom await
Our children's children.'
                    We believed him, we
Whom neither Diomede nor great Achilles
Had taken, nor ten years, nor that armada,

---

[8] His son was Diomedes, one of the greatest of the Greek warriors.
[9] Greek.

A thousand ships of war. But Sinon did it   220
By perjury and guile.
                              Then something else,
Much greater and more terrible, was forced
Upon us, troubling our unseeing spirits.
Laocoön, allotted priest of Neptune,
Was slaying a great bull beside the altars,
When suddenly, over the tranquil deep
From Tenedos,—I shudder even now,
Recalling it—there came a pair of serpents
With monstrous coils, breasting the sea, and aiming
Together for the shore. Their heads and shoulders   230
Rose over the waves, upright, with bloody crests,
The rest of them trailing along the water,
Looping in giant spirals; the foaming sea
Hissed under their motion. And they reached the land,
Their burning eyes suffused with blood and fire,
Their darting tongues licking the hissing mouths.
Pale at the sight, we fled. But they went on
Straight toward Laocoön, and first each serpent
Seized in its coils his two young sons, and fastened
The fangs in those poor bodies. And the priest   240
Struggled to help them, weapons in his hand.
They seized him, bound him with their mighty coils,
Twice round his waist, twice round his neck, they squeezed
With scaly pressure, and still towered above him.
Straining his hands to tear the knots apart,
His chaplets[10] stained with blood and the black poison,
He uttered horrible cries, not even human,
More like the bellowing of a bull when, wounded,
It flees the altar, shaking from the shoulder
The ill-aimed axe. And on the pair went gliding   250
To the highest shrine, the citadel of Pallas,
And vanished underneath the feet of the goddess
And the circle of her shield.
                              The people trembled
Again; they said Laocoön deserved it,
Having, with spear, profaned the sacred image.
It must be brought to its place, they cried, the goddess
Must be appeased. We broke the walls, exposing
The city's battlements, and all were busy
Helping the work, with rollers underfoot
And ropes around the neck. It climbed our walls,   260
The deadly engine. Boys, unwedded girls
Sang alleluias round it, all rejoicing
To have a hand on the tow-rope. It came nearer,
Threatening, gliding, into the very city.

---

[10] Garlands for the head.

O motherland! O Ilium, home of gods,
O walls of Troy! Four times it stopped, four times
The sound of arms came from it, and we pressed on,
Unheedful, blind in madness, till we set it,
Ill-omened thing, on the citadel we worshipped.
And even when Cassandra[11] gave us warning, 270
We never believed her; so a god had ordered.
That day, our last, poor wretches, we were happy,
Garlanding the temples of the gods
All through the town.
               And the sky turned, and darkness
Came from the ocean, the great shade covering earth
And heaven, and the trickery of the Greeks.
Sprawling along the walls, the Trojans slumbered,
Sleep holding their weary limbs, and the Greek armada,
From Tenedos, under the friendly silence
Of a still moon, came surely on. The flagship 280
Blazed at the masthead with a sudden signal,
And Sinon, guarded by the fates, the hostile
Will of the gods, swung loose the bolts; the Greeks
Came out of the wooden womb. The air received them,
The happy captains, Sthenelus, Ulysses,
Thessandrus, Acamas, Achilles' son
Called Neoptolemus, Thoas, Machaon,
Epeos, who designed the thing,—they all
Came sliding down the rope, and Menelaus
Was with them in the storming of a city 290
Buried in sleep and wine. The watch was murdered,
The open doors welcome the rush of comrades,
They marshal the determined ranks for battle.
    It was the time when the first sleep begins
For weary mortals, heaven's most welcome gift.
In sleep, before my eyes, I seemed to see
Hector, most sorrowful, black with bloody dust,
Torn, as he had been, by Achilles' car,
The thong-marks on his swollen feet. How changed
He was from that great Hector who came, once, 300
Triumphant in Achilles' spoil, from hurling
Fire at the Grecian ships. With ragged beard,
Hair matted with his blood, wearing the wounds
He earned around the walls of Troy, he stood there.
It seemed that I spoke first:—'O light of Troy,
Our surest hope, we have long been waiting for you,
What shores have kept you from us? Many deaths,
Much suffering, have visited our city,
And we are tired. Why do I see these wounds?

---

[11] A daughter of the royal family of Troy; gifted with prophecy, she was nevertheless doomed always to have her true prophecies disbelieved.

What shame has caused them?' Those were foolish questions; 310
He made no answer but a sigh or a groan,
And then: 'Alas, O goddess-born! Take flight,
Escape these flames! The enemy has the walls,
Troy topples from her lofty height; enough
Has been paid out to Priam and to country.
Could any hand have saved them, Hector's would have.
Troy trusts to you her household gods, commending
Her holy things to you; take them, companions
Of destiny; seek walls for them, and a city
To be established, a long sea-wandering over.' 320
From the inner shrine he carried Vesta's chaplets
In his own hands, and her undying fire.

Meanwhile, the city is all confusion and sorrow;
My father Anchises' house, remote and sheltered
Among its trees, was not so far away
But I could hear the noises, always clearer,
The thickening din of war. Breaking from sleep,
I climb to the roof-top, listening and straining
The way a shepherd does on the top of a mountain
When fire goes over the corn, and the winds are roaring, 330
Or the rush of a mountain torrent drowns the fields
And the happy crops and the work of men and oxen
And even drags great trees over. And then I knew
The truth indeed; the craft of the Greeks was hidden
No longer from my sight. The house of a neighbor,
Deiphobus, went up in flames; next door,
Ucalegon was burning. Sigeum's[12] water
Gave back the glow. Men shouted, and the trumpets
Blared loud. I grab my arms, with little purpose,
There was no sense in it, but my heart was burning 340
To mass a band for war, rush to the hilltop
With comrades at my side. Anger and frenzy
Hurry me on. A decent death in battle
Is a helpful thought, sometimes.

And here came Panthus, running from the weapons,
Priest of Apollo, and a son of Othrys,
With holy relics in his hands, and dragging
His little grandson, here came Panthus, running
In madness to my door. 'How goes it, Panthus?
What stronghold still is ours?' I had hardly spoken, 350
When he began, with a groan: 'It has come, this day
Will be our last, and we can not escape it.
Trojans we have been, Troy has been, and glory
Is ours no more. Fierce Jupiter has taken

---

[12] A cape near Troy.

Everything off to Argos, and Greeks lord it
In a town on fire. The horse, high in the city,
Pours out armed men, and Sinon, arrogant victor,
Lights up more fires. The gates are standing open,
And men are there by the thousands, ever as many
As came once from Mycenae; others block 360
The narrow streets, with weapons drawn; the blades
Flash in the dark; the point is set for murder.
A few of the guards are trying, striking blindly,
For all the good it does.'

His words, or the gods' purpose, swept me on
Toward fire and arms, where the grim furies call,
And the clamor and confusion, reaching heaven.
Ripheus joined me, Epytus, mighty in arms,
Came to my side in the moonlight, Hypanis, Dymas,
And young Coroebus, Mygdon's son, poor youngster, 370
Mad with a hopeless passion for Cassandra,
He wanted to help Priam, but never heeded
The warnings of his loved one.
                        As they ranged
Themselves for battle, eager, I addressed them:
'O brave young hearts, it will do no good; no matter.
Even if your will is fixed, to follow a leader
Taking the final risk, you can't help seeing
The fortune of our state. The gods have gone,
They have left their shrines and altars, and the power
They once upheld is fallen. You are helping 380
A town already burnt. So let us die,
Rush into arms. One safety for the vanquished
Is to have hope of none.'
                        They were young, and angry.
Like wolves, marauders in black mist, whom hunger
Drives blindly on, whose whelps, abandoned, wait them
Dry-jawed, so we went on, through foes, through weapons,
To certain death; we made for the heart of the city,
Black night around us with its hollow shadow.
Who could explain that night's destruction, equal
Its agony with tears? The ancient city, 390
A power for many years, comes down, and corpses
Lie littering the streets and homes and altars.
Not only Trojans die. The old-time valor
Returns to the vanquished heart, and the Greek victors
Know what it is to fall. Everywhere sorrow,
Everywhere panic, everywhere the image
Of death, made manifold.

Out of a crowd of Greeks comes one Androgeos,
Thinking us allies, hailing us as friendly:
'Why men, where have you been, you dawdling fellows? 400

Hurry along! Here is plunder for the taking,
Others are busy at it, and you just coming
From the high ships!' And then he knew he had blundered;
He had fallen in with foes, who gave no answer.
He stopped, stepped back, like a man who treads on a serpent
Unseen in the rough brush, and then in panic
Draws back as the purple neck swells out in anger.
Even so, Androgeos pulled away in terror.
We rush them, swarm all over them; they are frightened,
They do not know their ground, and fortune favors   410
Our first endeavor. Coroebus, a little crazy
With nerve and luck, cries out: 'Comrades, where fortune
First shows the way and sides with us, we follow.
Let us change our shields, put on the Grecian emblems!
All's fair in war: we lick them or we trick them,
And what's the odds?' He takes Androgeos' helmet,
Whose plume streams over his head, takes up the shield
With proud device, and fits the sword to his side.
And Ripheus does the same, and so does Dymas,
And all the others, happily being armed   420
With spoil, new-won. We join the Greeks, all going
Under no gods of ours, in the night's darkness
Wade into many a fight, and Greeks by the dozens
We send to hell. And some of them in panic
Speed to the ships; they know that shore, and trust it,
And some of them—these were the abject cowards—
Climb scrambling up the horse's sides, again
Take refuge in the womb.

　　It is not for men to trust unwilling gods.
Cassandra was being dragged from Pallas' temple,   430
Her hair loosed to the wind, her eyes turned upward
To heaven for mercy; they had bound her hands.
Coroebus could not bear that sight; in madness
He threw himself upon them, and he died.
We followed, all of us, into the thick of it,
And were cut down, not only by Greeks; the rooftops,
Held by our friends, rained weapons: we were wearing
Greek crests and armor, and they did not know us.
And the Greeks came on, shouting with anger, burning
To foil that rescue; there was Menelaus,   440
And Agamemnon, and the savage Ajax,
And a whole army of them. Hurricanes
Rage the same way, when winds from different quarters
Clash in the sky, and the forest groans, and Neptune
Storms underneath the ocean. Those we routed
Once in the dark came back again from the byways
And alleys of the town; they mark our shields,
Our lying weapons, and our foreign voices.
Of course we are outnumbered. Peneleus

It was, who slew Coroebus, at the altar 450
Sacred to Pallas. Ripheus fell, a man
Most just of all the Trojans, most fair-minded.
The gods thought otherwise. Hypanis, Dymas,
Were slain by their own men, and Panthus' goodness
Was no protection, nor his priestly office.
I call to witness Troy, her fires, her ashes,
And the last agonies of all our people
That in that hour I ran from no encounter
With any Greek, and if the fates had been
For me to fall in battle, there I earned it. 460
The current swept me off, with two companions,
One, Iphitus, too slow with age, the other,
Pelias, limping from Ulysses' wound.
The noise kept calling us to Priam's palace.

There might have been no fighting and no dying
Through all the city, such a battle raged
Here, from the ground to roof-top. At the threshold
Waves of assault were breaking, and the Greeks
Were climbing, rung by rung, along the ladders,
Using one hand, the right one up and forward 470
Over the battlements, the left one thrust
In the protecting shield. And over their heads
The Trojans pried up towers and planking, wrecking
The building; gilded beams, the spoils of their fathers,
Were ample weapons for the final moment.
Some had the doorways blocked, others, behind them,
Were ready with drawn swords. We had a moment
When help seemed possible; new reinforcement
Might yet relieve the palace.
There was a secret entrance there, a passage 480
All the way through the building, a postern gate,
Where, while the kingdom stood, Andromache[13]
Would go, alone, or bring the little boy,
Astyanax, to Hector's father and mother.
I climbed to the top of the roof, where the poor Trojans
Were hurling down their unavailing darts.
A tower stood on the very edge, a look-out
Over all Troy, the ships and camp of the Greeks.
This we attacked with steel, where the joints were weakest,
And pried it up, and shoved it over. It crashed, 490
A noisy ruin, over the hostile columns;
But more kept coming up; the shower of stones
And darts continued raining.
Before the entrance, at the very threshold

---

[13] Wife of Hector and mother of Astyanax. Hector's parents are Priam and Hecuba, king and queen of Troy.

Stood Pyrrhus,[14] flashing proudly in bronze light,
Sleek as a serpent coming into the open,
Fed on rank herbs, wintering under the ground,
The old slough cast, the new skin shining, rolling
His slippery length, reaching his neck to the sun,
While the forked tongue darts from the mouth. Automedon   500
Was with him, Periphas, Achilles' driver,
A giant of a man, and the host from Scyros,[15]
All closing in on the palace, and hurling flames.
Among the foremost, Pyrrhus, swinging an axe,
Burst through, wrenched the bronze doors out of their hinges,
Smashed through the panelling, turned it into a window.
The long halls came to view, the inner chambers
Of Priam and the older kings; they see
Armed warriors at the threshold.
Within, it is all confusion, women wailing,   510
Pitiful noise, groaning, and blows; the din
Reaches the golden stars. The trembling mothers
Wander, not knowing where, or find a spot
To cling to; they would hold and kiss the doors.
Pyrrhus comes on, aggressive as his father;
No barrier holds him back; the gate is battered
As the ram[16] smashes at it; the doors come down.
Force finds a way; the Greeks pour in, they slaughter
The first one in their path; they fill the courtyard
With soldiery, wilder than any river   520
In flood over the banks and dikes and ploughland.
I saw them, Pyrrhus, going mad with murder,
And Atreus' twin sons,[17] and Hecuba
I saw, and all her daughters, and poor old Priam,
His blood polluting the altars he had hallowed.
The fifty marriage-chambers,[18] the proud hope
Of an everlasting line, are violated,
The doors with the golden spoil are turned to splinters.
Whatever the fire has spared the Greeks take over.
    You would ask, perhaps, about the fate of Priam?   530
When he saw the city fall, and the doors of the palace
Ripped from the hinge, and the enemy pouring in,
Old as he was, he went and found his armor,
Unused so many years, and his old shoulders
Shook as he put it on. He took his sword,
A useless weapon, and, doomed to die, went rushing
Into the midst of the foe. There was an altar
In the open court-yard, shaded by a laurel
Whose shadow darkened the household gods, and here
Hecuba and her daughters had come thronging,   540

---

[14] Achilles' son, fierce like his war-loving father.   [15] Birthplace of Pyrrhus.
[16] The battering ram.   [17] Agamemnon and Menelaus.
[18] The quarters of Priam's fifty sons and their wives; Priam also had fifty daughters.

Like doves by a black storm driven. They were praying
Here at the altar, and clinging to the gods,
Whatever image was left. And the queen saw Priam
In the arms of his youth. 'O my unhappy husband,'
She cried, 'have you gone mad, to dress yourself
For battle, so? It is all no use; the time
Needs better help than yours; not even my Hector
Could help us now. Come to me, come to the altar;
It will protect us, or at least will let us
Die all together.' And she drew him to her.   550
    Just then through darts, through weapons, came Polites,
A son of Priam, fleeing deadly Pyrrhus,
Down the long colonnades and empty hallways,
Wounded, and Pyrrhus after him, vicious, eager
For the last spear-thrust, and he drives it home;
Polites falls, and his life goes out with his blood,
Father and mother watching. And then Priam,
In the very grip of death, cried out in anger:—
'If there is any righteousness in heaven,
To care about such wickedness, the gods   560
Will have the right reward and thanks to offer
A man like this, who has made a father witness
The murder of his son, the worst pollution!
You claim to be Achilles' son. You liar!
Achilles had some reverence, respected
A suppliant's right and trust; he gave me back
My Hector's lifeless body[19] for the tomb,
And let me go to my kingdom.' With the word
He flung a feeble spear, which dropped, deflected
From the rough bronze; it had hung there for a moment.   570
And Pyrrhus sneered: 'So, go and tell my father
The latest news: do not forget to mention,
Old messenger-boy, my villainous behavior,
And what a bastard Pyrrhus is. Now die!'
He dragged the old man, trembling, to the altar,
Slipping in his son's blood; he grabbed his hair
With the left hand, and the right drove home the sword
Deep in the side, to the hilt. And so fell Priam,
Who had seen Troy burn and her walls come down, once monarch,
Proud ruler over the peoples and lands of Asia.   580
He lies, a nameless body, on the shore,
Dismembered, huge, the head torn from the shoulders.
    Grim horror, then, came home to me. I saw
My father when I saw the king, the life
Going out with the cruel wound. I saw Creusa[20]

---

[19]After killing Hector, Achilles agreed to return the corpse to Hector's father, Priam (see Homer's *Iliad,* Book XXIV). Achilles himself has since been slain, struck in the heel (his one vulnerable spot) by an arrow from Paris's bow.
  [20]Aeneas' wife.

Forsaken, my abandoned home, Iulus,
My little son. I looked around. They all
Had gone, exhausted, flung down from the walls,
Or dead in the fire, and I was left alone.
    And I saw Helen, hiding, of all places,   590
At Vesta's shrine, and clinging there in silence,
But the bright flames lit the scene. That hated woman,
Fearing both Trojan anger and Greek vengeance,
A common fury to both lands, was crouching
Beside the altar. Anger flared up in me
For punishment and vengeance. Should she then,
I thought, come home to Sparta safe, uninjured
Walk through Mycenae,[21] a triumphant queen?
See husband, home, parents and children, tended
By Trojan slave-girls? This, with Priam fallen   600
And Troy burnt down, and the shore soaked in blood?
Never! No memorable name, I knew,
Was won by punishing women, yet, for me,
There might be praise for the just abolition
Of this unholiness, and satisfaction
In vengeance for the ashes of my people.
All this I may have said aloud, in frenzy,
As I rushed on, when to my sight there came
A vision of my lovely mother, radiant
In the dark night, a goddess manifest,   610
As tall and fair as when she walks in heaven.
She caught me by the hand and stopped me:[22]—'Son,
What sorrow rouses this relentless anger,
This violence? Do you care for me no longer?
Consider others first, your aged father,
Anchises; is your wife Creusa living?
Where is Iulus? Greeks are all around them,
Only my love between them, fire and sword.
It is not for you to blame the Spartan woman,
Daughter of Tyndareus, or even Paris.   620
The gods are the ones, the high gods are relentless;
It is they who bring this power down, who topple
Troy from the high foundation. Look! Your vision
Is mortal dull, I will take the cloud away,—
Fear not a mother's counsel. Where you see
Rock torn from rock, and smoke and dust in billows,
Neptune is working, plying the trident, prying
The walls from their foundations. And see Juno,
Fiercest of all, holding the Scaean gates,
Girt with the steel, and calling from the ships   630

---

[21] The meaning is "Greece" (from the home city of Agamemnon, the Greek commander).
Helen's actual home city was Sparta.
[22] Though she is Aeneas' mother, Venus as goddess of love naturally protects Helen, the
most beautiful of all women.

Implacable companions. On the towers,—
Turn, and be certain—Pallas takes command
Gleaming with Gorgon and storm-cloud. Even Jove,
Our father, nerves the Greeks with fire and spirit,
And spurs the other gods against the Trojans.
Hasten the flight, my son; no other labor
Waits for accomplishment. I promise safety
Until you reach your father's house.' She had spoken
And vanished in the thickening night of shadows.
Dread shapes come into vision, mighty powers, 640
Great gods at war with Troy, which, so it seemed,
Was sinking as I watched, with the same feeling
As when on mountain-tops you see the loggers
Hacking an ash-tree down, and it always threatens
To topple, nodding a little, and the leaves
Trembling when no wind stirs, and dies of its wounds
With one long loud last groan, and dirt from the ridges
Heaves up as it goes down with roots in air.
Divinity my guide, I leave the roof-top,
I pass unharmed through enemies and blazing, 650
Weapons give place to me, and flames retire.

At last I reached the house, I found my father,
The first one that I looked for. I meant to take him
To the safety of the hills, but he was stubborn,
Refusing longer life or barren exile,
Since Troy was dead. 'You have the strength,' he told me,
'You are young enough, take flight. For me, had heaven
Wanted to save my life, they would have spared
This home for me. We have seen enough destruction,
More than enough, survived a captured city. 660
Speak to me as a corpse laid out for burial,
A quick farewell, and go. Death I shall find
With my own hand; the enemy will pity,
Or look for spoil. The loss of burial[23]
Is nothing at all. I have been living too long
Hated by gods and useless, since the time
Jove blasted me[24] with lightning wind and fire.'
He would not move, however we wept, Creusa,
Ascanius, all the house, insistent, pleading
That he should not bring all to ruin with him. 670
He would not move, he would not listen. Again
I rush to arms, I pray for death; what else
Was left to me? 'Dear father, were you thinking
I could abandon you, and go? what son
Could bear a thought so monstrous? If the gods
Want nothing to be left of so great a city,

[23] Failure to receive proper burial was a grievous misfortune. See Book VI.
[24] The god took revenge because Anchises boasted of Venus' love for him.

If you are bound, or pleased, to add us all
To the wreck of Troy, the way is open for it—
Pyrrhus will soon be here; from the blood of Priam
He comes; he slays the son before the father,   680
The sire at the altar-stone; O my dear mother,
Was it for this you saved me, brought me through
The fire and sword, to see our enemies
Here in the very house, and wife and son
And father murdered in each other's blood?
Bring me my arms; the last light calls the conquered.
Let me go back to the Greeks, renew the battle,
We shall not all of us die unavenged.'
    Sword at my side, I was on the point of going,
Working the left arm into the shield. Creusa   690
Clung to me on the threshold, held my feet,
And made me see my little son:—'Dear husband,
If you are bent on dying, take us with you,
But if you think there is any hope in fighting,
And you should know, stay and defend the house!
To whom are we abandoned, your father and son,
And I, once called your wife?' She filled the house
With moaning outcry. And then something happened,
A wonderful portent. Over Iulus' head,
Between our hands and faces, there appeared   700
A blaze of gentle light; a tongue of flame,
Harmless and innocent, was playing over
The softness of his hair, around his temples.
We were afraid, we did our best to quench it
With our own hands, or water, but my father
Raised joyous eyes to heaven, and prayed aloud:—
'Almighty Jupiter, if any prayer
Of ours has power to move you, look upon us,
Grant only this, if we have ever deserved it,
Grant us a sign, and ratify the omen!'   710
He had hardly spoken, when thunder on the left
Resounded, and a shooting star from heaven
Drew a long trail of light across the shadows.
We saw it cross above the house, and vanish
In the woods of Ida,[25] a wake of gleaming light
Where it had sped, and a trail of sulphurous odor.
This was a victory: my father rose
In worship of the gods and the holy star,
Crying: 'I follow, son, wherever you lead;
There is no delay, not now; Gods of my fathers,   720
Preserve my house, my grandson; yours the omen,
And Troy is in your keeping. O my son,
I yield, I am ready to follow.' But the fire
Came louder over the walls, the flames rolled nearer

[25] A mountain and mountain range near Troy.

Their burning tide. 'Climb to my shoulders, father,
It will be no burden, so we are together,
Meeting a common danger or salvation.
Iulus, take my hand; Creusa, follow
A little way behind. Listen, you servants!
You will find, when you leave the city, an old temple   730
That once belonged to Ceres;[26] it has been tended
For many years with the worship of our fathers.
There's a little hill there, and a cypress tree;
And that's where we shall meet, one way or another.
And one thing more: you, father, are to carry
The holy objects and the gods of the household,
My hands are foul with battle and blood, I could not
Touch them without pollution.'
                                I bent down
And over my neck and shoulders spread the cover
Of a tawny lion-skin, took up my burden;   740
Little Iulus held my hand, and trotted,
As best he could, beside me; Creusa followed.
We went on through the shadows. I had been
Brave, so I thought, before, in the rain of weapons
And the cloud of massing Greeks. But now I trembled
At every breath of air, shook at a whisper,
Fearful for both my burden and companion.
    I was near the gates, and thinking we had made it,
But there was a sound, the tramp of marching feet,
And many of them, it seemed; my father, peering   750
Through the thick gloom, cried out:—'Son, they are coming!
Flee, flee! I see their shields, their gleaming bronze.'
Something or other took my senses from me
In that confusion. I turned aside from the path,
I do not know what happened then. Creusa
Was lost;[27] she had missed the road, or halted, weary,
For a brief rest. I do not know what happened,
She was not seen again; I had not looked back,
Nor even thought about her, till we came
To Ceres' hallowed home. The count was perfect,   760
Only one missing there, the wife and mother.
Whom did I not accuse, of gods and mortals,
Then in my frenzy? What worse thing had happened
In the city overthrown? I left Anchises,
My son, my household gods, to my companions,
In a hiding-place in the valley; and I went back
Into the city again, wearing my armor,
Ready, still one more time, for any danger.

---

[26] Goddess of the fields and harvest.
[27] The loss, literally, of Creusa (exactly what happens to her is not clear) may indicate something about Aeneas' priorities, but it is providentially necessary that Aeneas be free to marry Lavinia as part of the Trojans' later establishment of themselves in Italy.

I found the walls again, the gate's dark portals,
I followed my own footsteps back, but terror,   770
Terror and silence were all I found. I went
On to my house. She might, just might, have gone there.
Only the Greeks were there, and fire devouring
The very pinnacles. I tried Priam's palace;
In the empty courtyards Phoenix and Ulysses
Guarded the spoils piled up at Juno's altar.
They had Trojan treasure there, loot from the altars,
Great drinking-bowls of gold, and stolen garments,
And human beings. A line of boys and women
Stood trembling there.   780
I took the risk of crying through the shadows,
Over and over, 'Creusa!' I kept calling,
'Creusa!' and 'Creusa!' but no answer.
No sense, no limit, to my endless rushing
All through the town; and then at last I saw her,
Or thought I did, her shadow a little taller
Than I remembered. And she spoke to me
Beside myself with terror:—'O dear husband,
What good is all this frantic grief? The gods
Have willed it so, Creusa may not join you   790
Out of this city; Jupiter denies it.
Long exile lies ahead, and vast sea-reaches
The ships must furrow, till you come to land
Far in the West; rich fields are there, and a river
Flowing with gentle current; its name is Tiber.
And happy days await you there, a kingdom,
A royal wife. Banish the tears of sorrow
Over Creusa lost. I shall never see
The arrogant houses of the Myrmidons,[28]
Nor be a slave to any Grecian woman;   800
I am a Dardan woman; I am the wife
Of Venus' son; it is Cybele[29] who keeps me
Here on these shores. And now farewell, and love
Our son.' I wept, there was more to say; she left me,
Vanishing into empty air. Three times
I reached out toward her, and three times her image
Fled like the breath of a wind or a dream on wings.
The night was over; I went back to my comrades.
    I was surprised to find so many more
Had joined us, ready for exile, pitiful people,   810
Mothers, and men, and children, streaming in
From everywhere, looking for me to lead them
Wherever I would. Over the hills of Ida

---

[28] The Greek soldiers who had been led by Achilles.

[29] A goddess identified with Rhea, consort of Saturn during the reign of the older gods. It is possible that Creusa has not died but rather has been mysteriously inducted into the service of Cybele.

The morning-star was rising; in the town
The Danaans held the gates, and help was hopeless.
I gave it up, I lifted up my father,
Together we sought the hills.

BOOK III: THE WANDERINGS OF AENEAS

"After the gods' decision to overthrow
The Asian world, the innocent house of Priam,
And the proud city, built by Neptune, smoked
From the ruined ground, we were driven, different ways,
By heaven's auguries, seeking lands forsaken.
Below Antandros,[1] under Phrygian Ida,
We built a fleet, and gathered men, uncertain
Of either direction or settlement. The summer
Had scarce begun, when at my father's orders,
We spread our sails. I wept as I left the harbor,   10
The fields where Troy had been. I was borne, an exile
Over the deep, with son, companions, household,
And household gods.
                    Far off there lies a land,
Sacred to Mars; the Thracians[2] used to till it,
Whose king was fierce Lycurgus; they were friendly,
Of old, to Troy, when we were prosperous. Hither
I sailed, and on its curving shore established
A city site; Aeneadae, I called it.
This I began, not knowing fate was adverse.

    I was offering my mother proper homage,   20
And other gods, to bless the new beginnings,
I had a white bull ready as a victim
To the king of the gods. There was a mound nearby,
Bristling with myrtle and with cornel-bushes.
I needed greenery to veil the altar,
But as I struggled with the leafy branches,
A fearful portent met my gaze. Black drops
Dripped from the ends of the roots, black blood was falling
On the torn ground, and a cold chill went through me.
I tried again; the shoot resisted; blood   30
Followed again. Troubled, I prayed to the Nymphs,
To the father of the fields, to bless the vision,
Remove the curse; and down on my knees I wrestled
Once more against the stubborn ground, and heard
A groan from under the hillock, and voice crying:

[1] A town near Troy.
[2] Inhabitants of Thrace, an area north of the Aegean Sea, northwest of the Hellespont strait (the modern Dardanelles).

'Why mangle a poor wretch, Aeneas? Spare me,
Here in the tomb, and save your hands pollution.
You know me, I am Trojan-born, no stranger,
This is familiar blood. Alas! Take flight,
Leave this remorseless land; the curse of greed   40
Lies heavy on it. I am Polydorus,
Pierced by an iron harvest; out of my body
Rise javelins and lances.' I was speechless,
Stunned, in my terror.
       Priam, forever unfortunate, had sent
This Polydorus on a secret mission,
Once, to the king of Thrace, with gold for hiding
When the king despaired of the siege and the city's fortune.
And when Troy fell, and Fortune failed, the Thracian
Took Agamemnon's side, broke off his duty,   50
Slew Polydorus, took the gold. There is nothing
To which men are not driven by that hunger.
Once over my fear, I summoned all the leaders,
My father, too; I told them of the portent,
Asked for their counsel. All agreed, a land
So stained with violence and violation
Was not for us to dwell in. Southward ho!
For Polydorus we made restoration
With funeral rites anew; earth rose again
Above his outraged mound; dark fillets made   60
The altar sorrowful, and cypress boughs,
And the Trojan women loosed their hair in mourning.
We offered milk in foaming bowls, and blood
Warm from the victims, so to rest the spirit,
And cry aloud the voice of valediction.
       Then, when we trust the sea again, and the wind
Calls with a gentle whisper, we crowd the shores,
Launch ship again, leave port, the lands and cities
Fade out of sight once more.
                              There is an island[3]
In the middle of the sea; the Nereids' mother[4]   70
And Neptune hold it sacred. It used to wander
By various coasts and shores, until Apollo,
In grateful memory, bound it fast, unmoving,
Unfearful of winds, between two other islands
Called Myconos and Gyaros. I sailed there;
Our band was weary, and the calmest harbor
Gave us safe haven. This was Apollo's city;
We worshipped it on landing. And their king,
Priest of Apollo also, came to meet us,
His temples bound with holy fillets, and laurel.   80

---

[3] Delos, an island in the Aegean, was the birthplace of Apollo.
[4] Doris; Nereids are sea nymphs.

His name was Anius; he knew Anchises
As an old friend, and gave us joyful welcome.
Apollo's temple was built of ancient rock,
And there I prayed: 'Grant us a home, Apollo,
Give walls to weary men, a race, a city
That will abide; preserve Troy's other fortress,
The remnant left by the Greeks and hard Achilles.
Whom do we follow? where are we bidden to go
To find our settlement? An omen, father!'
I had scarcely spoken, when suddenly all things trembled, 90
The doors, and the laurel, and the whole mountain moved,
And the shrine was opened, and a rumbling sound
Was heard. We knelt, most humbly; and a voice
Came to our ears: 'The land which brought you forth,
Men of endurance, will receive you home.
Seek out your ancient mother. There your house
Will rule above all lands, your children's children,
For countless generations.' Apollo spoke,
And we were joyful and confused, together:
What walls were those, calling the wanderers home? 100
My father, pondering history, made answer:
'Hear, leaders; learn your hopes. There is a land
Called Crete, an island in the midst of the sea,
The cradle of our race; it has a mountain,
Ida, like ours, a hundred mighty cities,
Abounding wealth; if I recall correctly,
Teucer, our greatest father, came from there
To the Rhoetean[5] shores to found his kingdom.
Ilium was nothing then, the towers of Troy
Undreamed of; men lived in the lowly valleys. 110
And Cybele, the Great Mother, came from Crete
With her clashing cymbals, and her grove of Ida
Was named from that original; the silence
Of her mysterious rites, the harnessed lions
Before her chariot wheels, all testify
To Cretan legend. Come, then, let us follow
Where the gods lead, and seek the Cretan kingdom.
It is not far; with Jupiter to favor,
Three days will see us there. With prayer, he made
Most solemn sacrifice, a bull to Neptune, 120
One to Apollo, to Winter a black heifer,
A white one for fair winds.
                            The story ran
That no one lived in Crete, Idomeneus[6]
Having left his father's kingdom, that the houses
Were empty now, dwellings vacated for us.

[5] Trojan.
[6] Former king of Crete who fought against Troy. In fulfillment of a vow to kill the first living thing he saw after returning to Crete, he murdered his son. His people thereafter banished him, the gods having visited a plague on Crete as punishment.

We sailed from Delos, flying over the water
Past Naxos, on whose heights the Bacchae revel,
Past green Donysa, snowy Paros,[7] skimming
The passages between the sea-sown islands.
No crew would yield to another; there is shouting,   130
And the cheer goes up, 'To Crete, and the land of our fathers!'
A stern wind follows, and we reach the land.
I am glad to be there; I lay out the walls
For the chosen city, name it Pergamea,[8]
And the people are happy. *Love your hearths,* I told them,
Build high the citadel. The ships were steadied
On the dry beach, the young were busy ploughing,
Or planning marriage, and I was giving laws,
Assigning homes. But the weather turned, the sky
Grew sick, and from the tainted heaven came   140
Pestilence and pollution, a deadly year
For people and harvest. Those who were not dying
Dragged weary bodies around; the Dog-Star[9] scorched
The fields to barrenness; grass withered, corn
Refused to ripen. 'Over the sea again!'
My father said, 'let us return to Delos,
Consult the oracle, implore Apollo
To show us kindliness; what end awaits
Our weary destiny, where does he bid us turn
For help in trouble?'   150
    Sleep held all creatures over the earth at rest;
In my own darkness visions came, the sacred
Images of the household gods I had carried
With me from Troy, out of the burning city.
I saw them plain, in the flood of light, where the moon
Streamed through the dormers. And they eased me, saying:
'Apollo would tell you this, if you went over
The sea again to Delos; from him we come
To you, with willing spirit. We came with you
From the burnt city, we have followed still   160
The swollen sea in the ships; in time to come
We shall raise your sons to heaven, and dominion
Shall crown their city. Prepare to build them walls,
Great homes for greatness; do not flee the labor,
The long, long toil of flight. Crete, says Apollo,
Is not the place. There is a land in the West,
Called by the Greeks, Hesperia:[10] anciency
And might in arms and wealth enrich its soil.
The Oenotrians lived there once; now, rumor has it,

---

[7] Naxos, Donysa, and Paros are islands in the south Aegean, passed during the southward
voyage to Crete.
[8] Named for Pergamus, the citadel of Troy.
[9] Sirius, the brightest star in the sky, first visible in the hot days of late summer.
[10] The western region of the world, associated with Hesperus, the evening star.

A younger race has called it Italy   170
After the name of a leader, Italus.
Dardanus came from there, our ancestor,
As Iasius[11] was. There is our dwelling-place.
Be happy, then, waken, and tell Anchises
Our certain message: seek the land in the West.
Crete is forbidden country.'
    The vision shook me, and the voice of the gods;
(It was not a dream, exactly; I seemed to know them,
Their features, the veiled hair, the living presence.)
I woke in a sweat, held out my hands to heaven,   180
And poured the pure libation for the altar,
Then, gladly, to Anchises. He acknowledged
His own mistake, a natural confusion,
Our stock was double, of course; no need saying
We had more ancestors than one. 'Cassandra,'
Anchises said, 'alone, now I remember,
Foretold this fate; it seemed she was always talking
Of a land in the West, and Italian kingdoms, always.
But who would ever have thought that any Trojans
Would reach the shores in the West? Or, for that matter,   190
Who ever believed Cassandra? Let us yield
To the warning of Apollo, and at his bidding
Seek better fortunes.' So we obeyed him,
Leaving this place, where a few stayed, and sailing
The hollow keels over the mighty ocean.
    We were in deep water, and the land no longer
Was visible, sky and ocean everywhere.
A cloud, black-blue, loomed overhead, with night
And tempest in it, and the water roughened
In shadow; winds piled up the sea, the billows   200
Rose higher; we were scattered in the surges.
Clouds took away the daylight, and the night
Was dark and wet in the sky, with lightning flashing.
We wandered, off our course, in the dark of ocean,
And our pilot, Palinurus, swore he could not
Tell day from night, nor the way among the waters.
For three lost days, three starless nights, we rode it,
Saw land on the fourth, mountains and smoke arising.
The sails came down, we bent to the oars; the sailors
Made the foam fly, sweeping the dark blue water.   210
I was saved from the waves; the Strophades received me,
(The word means Turning-point in the Greek language),[12]

---

[11]Brother of Dardanus.

[12] The Strophades are islands west of Greece, in the Ionian Sea. The Trojans have rounded
the southwest corner of Greece; from this time until shortly after they leave Helenus and
Andromache, their course will be northwest, along the shore and among the islands of Greece
that face Sicily and southern Italy.

Ionian islands where the dire Celaeno
And other Harpies[13] live, since Phineus' house
Was closed to them, and they feared their former tables.
No fiercer plague of the gods' anger ever
Rose out of hell, girls with the look of birds,
Their bellies fouled, incontinent, their hands
Like talons, and their faces pale with hunger.
We sailed into the harbor, happy to see   220
Good herds of cattle grazing over the grass
And goats, unshepherded. We cut them down
And made our prayer and offering to Jove,
Set trestles on the curving shore for feasting.
Down from the mountains with a fearful rush
And a sound of wings like metal came the Harpies,
To seize our banquet, smearing dirtiness
Over it all, with a hideous kind of screaming
And a stinking smell. We found a secret hollow
Enclosed by trees, under a ledge of rock,   230
Where shade played over; there we moved the tables
And lit the fire again; the noisy Harpies
Came out of somewhere, sky, or rock, and harried
The feast again, the filthy talons grabbing,
The taint all through the air. *Take arms,* I ordered,
We have to fight them. And my comrades, hiding
Their shields in the grass, lay with their swords beside them,
And when the birds swooped screaming, and Misenus
Sounded the trumpet-signal, they rose to charge them,
A curious kind of battle, men with sword-blades   240
Against the winged obscenities of ocean.
Their feathers felt no blow, their backs no wound,
They rose to the sky as rapidly as ever,
Leaving the souvenirs of their foul traces
Over the ruined feast. And one, Celaeno,
Perched on a lofty rock, squawked out a warning:—
'Is it war you want, for slaughtered goats and bullocks,
Is it war you bring, you sons of liars, driving
The innocent Harpies from their father's kingdom?
Take notice, then, and let my words forever   250
Stick in your hearts; what Jove has told Apollo,
Apollo told me, and I, the greatest fury,
Shove down your throats; it is Italy you are after,
And the winds will help you, Italy and her harbors
You will reach, all right; but you will not wall the city
Till, for the wrong you have done us, deadly hunger
Will make you gnaw and crunch your very tables!'[14]

---

[13] Foul creatures sent originally by Jove to punish Phineus, king of Thrace, whence the Harpies have emigrated. Celaeno is their leader.

[14] This prophecy will be fulfilled, in an unexpectedly casual way, in Book VII, when the hungry Trojans eat the wheaten platters on which they have placed fruit.

She flew back to the forest. My companions
Were chilled with sudden fear; their spirit wavered,
They call on me, to beg for peace, not now   260
With arms, but vows and praying, filthy birds
Or ill-foreboding goddesses, no matter.
Anchises prayed with outstretched hands, appeasing
The mighty gods with sacrifice:—'Be gracious,
Great gods, ward off the threats, spare the devoted!'
He bade us tear the cable from the shore,
Shake loose the sails. And a wind sprang up behind us,
Driving us northward; we passed many islands,
Zacynthus, wooded, Dulichium, and Same,
The cliffs of Neritus, Laertes' kingdom,   270
With a curse as we went by for Ithaca,
Land of Ulysses. Soon Leucate's headland
Came into view, a dreadful place for sailors,
Where Apollo had a shrine. We were very weary
As we drew near the little town; the anchor
Was thrown from the prow, the sterns pulled up on the beaches.

This was unhoped-for land; we offered Jove
Our purifying rites, and had the altars
Burning with sacrifice. We thronged the shore
With games of Ilium. Naked, oiled for wrestling,   280
The young held bouts, glad that so many islands
Held by the Greeks were safely passed. A year
Went by, and icy winter roughened the waves
With gales from the north. A shield of hollow bronze,
Borne once by Abas,[15] I fastened to the door-posts,
And set a verse below it: *Aeneas won*
These arms from the Greek victors. I gave the order
To man the thwarts and leave this harbor; all
Obeyed, swept oars in rivalry. We left
Phaeacia's airy heights, coasting Epirus,   290
Drawn to Buthrotum, a Chaonian harbor.

And here we met strange news, that Helenus,
The son of Priam, was ruling Grecian cities,
Having won the wife of Pyrrhus and his crown,
And that Andromache once more had married
A lord of her own race. Amazed, I burn
With a strange longing to seek out that hero,
To learn his great adventures. It so happened,
Just as I left the landing, that was the day
Andromache, in a grove before the city,   300
By the waters of a river that resembled
The Simois at home, was offering homage,

---

[15] Not the Trojan mentioned in the storm scene of Book I, but rather a Greek killed at Troy. The present scene takes place at the site of the future naval battle of Actium, where in 31 B.C. Octavian defeated Mark Antony and Cleopatra; see the Introduction to Virgil.

Her annual mourning-gift to Hector's ashes,
Calling his ghost to the place which she had hallowed
With double altars, a green and empty tomb.
I found her weeping there, and she was startled
At the sight of me, and Trojan arms, a shock
Too great to bear: she was rigid for a moment,
And then lost consciousness, and a long time later
Managed to speak: 'Is it real, then, goddess-born?   310
What are you, living messenger or phantom,
Mortal or ghost? If the dear light has left you,
Tell me where Hector is.' I was moved, so deeply
I found it hard to answer to her tears
And through my own, but I did say a little:—
'I am alive; I seem to keep on living
Through all extremes of trouble; do not doubt me,
I am no apparition. And what has happened
To you, dear wife of Hector? Could any gain
Atone for such a loss? Has fortune tried   320
To even matters at all? Does Pyrrhus still
Presume on you as husband?' With lowered gaze
And quiet voice she answered:—'Happy the maiden
Slain at the foeman's tomb, at the foot of the walls;
Happy the daughter of Priam, who never knew
The drawing of the lots,[16] nor came to the bed
Of a conqueror, his captive. After the fire
I travelled different seas, endured the pride
Achilles filled his son with, bore him children
In bondage, till he tired of me and left me   330
For Leda's daughter and a Spartan marriage.
He passed me on to Helenus, fair enough,
Slave-woman to slave-man; but then Orestes,[17]
Inflamed with passion for his stolen bride,
And maddened by the Furies of his vengeance,
Caught Pyrrhus off-guard, and slew him at the altar
In his ancestral home. And Pyrrhus dying,
Part of the kingdom came to Helenus,
Who named the fields Chaonian, the land
Chaonia, after a man from Troy,   340
And filled the heights, as best he could, with buildings
To look like those we knew. But what of yourself?
What winds, what fate, have brought you here, or was it
Some god? did you know you were on our coast? How is
The boy Ascanius, living still, whom Troy
Might have—does he ever think about his mother?

---

[16] For the division of the women among the conquerors.
[17] Pyrrhus married Hermione (daughter of Menelaus and Helen and thus Leda's grand-daughter, not her daughter), to whom Orestes had been betrothed.

Does he want to be a hero, a manly spirit,
Such as his father was, and his uncle Hector?'
She was in tears again, when the son of Priam,
Helenus, with an escort, came from the city, 350
Happy to recognize us, bringing us in
With tears and greeting mingled. I went on,
Seeing a little Troy, low walls that copied
The old majestic ramparts, a tiny river
In a dry bed, trying to be the Xanthus,
I found the Scaean gates, to hold and cling to.
My Trojans, too, were fond of the friendly town,
Whose king received them in wide halls; libations
Were poured to the gods, and feasts set on gold dishes.
Day after day went by, and the winds were calling 360
And the sails filling with a good south-wester.
I put my questions to the king and prophet:
'O son of Troy, the god's interpreter,
Familiar with the tripod and the laurel
Of great Apollo, versed in stars and omens,
Bird-song and flying wing, be gracious to me,
Tell me,—for heaven has prophesied a journey
Without mischance, and all the gods have sent me
The counsel of their oracles, to follow
Italy and a far-off country; one, 370
But one, Celaeno, prophesied misfortune,
Wrath and revolting hunger,—tell me, prophet,
What dangers first to avoid, what presence follow
To overcome disaster?'
                Bullocks slain
With proper covenant, and the chaplets loosened,
He led me to the temple of Apollo,
The very gates, where the god's presence awed me,
And where he spoke, with eloquent inspiration:—
'O goddess-born, the journey over the sea
Holds a clear sanction for you, under Jove, 380
Who draws the lots and turns the wheel of Fate.
I will tell you some few things, not all, that safely
You may go through friendly waters, and in time
Come to Ausonian[18] harborage; the rest
Helenus does not know, or, if he did,
Juno would stop his speaking. First of all,
Italy, which you think is near, too fondly
Ready to enter her nearest port, is distant,
Divided from you by a pathless journey
And longer lands between. The oar must bend 390
In the Sicilian ocean, and the ships

---

[18] Italian.

Sail on a farther coast, beyond the lakes
Of an infernal world, beyond the isles
Where dwells Aeaean Circe,[19] not till then
Can the built city rise on friendly ground.
Keep in the mind the sign I give you now:
One day, when you are anxious and alone
At the wave of a hidden river, you will find
Under the oaks on the shore, a sow, a white one,
Immense, with a new-born litter, thirty young   400
At the old one's udders; that will be the place,
The site of the city, the certain rest from labor.
And do not fear the eating of the tables,
The fates will find a way, Apollo answer.
Avoid this coast of Italy,[20] the lands
Just westward of our own; behind those walls
Dwell evil Greeks, Narycian Locri, soldiers
Of the Cretan king, Idomeneus; the plains
Are full of them; a Meliboean captain
Governs Petelia, a tiny town   410
Relying on her fortress! Philoctetes
Commands her walls. And furthermore, remember,
Even when the ships have crossed the sea and anchored,
When the altars stand on the shore, and the vows are paid,
Keep the hair veiled, and the robe of crimson drawn
Across the eyes, so that no hostile visage
May interfere, to gaze on the holy fire
Or spoil the sacred omens. This rite observe[21]
Through all the generations; keep it holy.
From that first landing, when the wind brings you down   420
To Sicily's coast, and narrow Pelorus widens
The waters of her strait, keep to the left,
Land on the left, and water on the left,
The long way round; the right is dangerous.
Avoid it. There's a story that this land
Once broke apart—(time brings so many changes)—
By some immense convulsion, though the lands
Had been one country once. But now between them
The sea comes in, and now the waters bound
Italian coast, Sicilian coast; the tide   430
Washes on severed shores, their fields, their cities.
Scylla keeps guard on the right; on the left Charybdis,

---

[19] A sorceress who, during Odysseus' wanderings as described in Homer's *Odyssey*, Book X, changed his men into swine. Aeaea is her home island.

[20] In the following lines, Helenus advises Aeneas to avoid the eastern coast of Italy (infested with people hostile to the Trojans) and to sail around Sicily rather than through the narrow passage (the modern straits of Messina) dividing Sicily from the Italian mainland. The straits are guarded on both sides, by a rock and whirlpool mythologized as, respectively, Scylla and Charybdis.

[21] As often in the poem, Virgil ascribes an ancient origin to Roman religious ritual of later times.

The unappeasable; from the deep gulf she sucks
The great waves down, three times; three times she belches
Them high up into the air, and sprays the stars.
Scylla is held in a cave, a den of darkness,
From where she thrusts her huge jaws out, and draws
Ships to her jagged rocks. She looks like a girl
Fair-breasted to the waist, from there, all monster,
Shapeless, with dolphins' tails, and a wolf's belly.   440
Better to go the long way round, make turning
Beyond Pachynus,[22] than to catch one glimpse
Of Scylla the misshapen, in her cavern,
And the rocks resounding with the dark-blue sea-hounds.
And one thing more than any, goddess-born,
I tell you over and over: pray to Juno,
Give Juno vows and gifts and overcome her
With everlasting worship. So you will come
Past Sicily and reach Italian beaches.
You will come to a town called Cumae,[23] haunted lakes,   450
And a forest called Avernus, where the leaves
Rustle and stir in the great woods, and there
You will find a priestess, in her wildness singing
Prophetic verses under the stones, and keeping
Symbols and signs on leaves. She files and stores them
In the depth of the cave; there they remain unmoving,
Keeping their order, but if a light wind stirs
At the turn of a hinge, and the door's draft disturbs them,
The priestess never cares to catch them fluttering
Around the halls of rock, put them in order,   460
Or give them rearrangement. Men who have come there
For guidance leave uncounselled, and they hate
The Sibyl's dwelling. Let no loss of time,
However comrades chide and chafe, however
The wind's voice calls the sail, postpone the visit
To this great priestess; plead with her to tell you
With her own lips the song of the oracles.
She will predict the wars to come, the nations
Of Italy, the toils to face, or flee from;
Meet her with reverence, and she, propitious,   470
Will grant a happy course. My voice can tell you
No more than this. Farewell; raise Troy to heaven.'
      After the friendly counsel, other gifts
Were sent to our ships, carved ivory, and gold,
And heavy silver, cauldrons from Dodona,
A triple breastplate linked with gold, a helmet
Shining with crested plume, the arms of Pyrrhus.

---

[22] The southeastern corner of Sicily, which is triangular.
[23] The meeting with the Sibyl of Cumae, in preparation for Aeneas' descent into the Lower World, occurs in Book VI.

My father, too, has gifts; horses and guides
Are added, and sailing-men, and arms for my comrades.
Anchises bade the fleet prepare; the wind   480
Was rising, why delay? But Helenus
Spoke to Anchises, in compliment and honor:—
'Anchises, worthy of Venus' couch, and the blessing
Of other gods, twice saved from Trojan ruins,
Yonder behold Ausonia! Near, and far,
It lies, Apollo's offering; sail westward.
Farewell, made blest by a son's goodness. I
Am a nuisance with my talking.'
                              And his queen,
Sad at the final parting, was bringing gifts,
Robes woven with a golden thread, a Trojan   490
Scarf for Ascanius, all courteous honor
Given with these:—'Take them, my child; these are
The work of my own hands, memorials
Of Hector's wife Andromache, and her love.
Receive these farewell gifts; they are for one
Who brings my own son back to me; your hands,
Your face, your eyes, remind me of him so,—
He would be just your age.'
                              I, also, wept,
As I spoke my words of parting: 'Now farewell;
Your lot is finished, and your rest is won,   500
No ocean fields to plough, no fleeing fields
To follow, you have your Xanthus and your Troy,
Built by your hands, and blest by happier omens,
Far from the path of the Greeks. But we are called
From fate to fate; if ever I enter Tiber
And Tiber's neighboring lands, if ever I see
The walls vouchsafed my people, I pray these shores,
Italy and Epirus, shall be one,
The life of Troy restored, with friendly towns
And allied people. A common origin,   510
A common fall, was ours. Let us remember,
And our children keep the faith.'
    Over the sea we rode, the shortest run
To Italy, past the Ceraunian rocks.[24]
The sun went down; the hills were dark with shadow.
The oars assigned, we drew in to the land
For a little welcome rest; sleep overcame us,
But it was not yet midnight when our pilot
Sprang from his blanket, studying the winds,
Alert and listening, noting the stars   520
Wheeling the silent heaven, the twin Oxen,

---

[24] After this point, the Trojan fleet changes its course; hereafter, until the storm that beaches
it at Carthage, the fleet will sail southwest past the heel along the sole of the "boot" of southern Italy, then clockwise around Sicily.

Arcturus and the rainy Kids. All calm,
He saw, and roused us; camp was broken; the sail
Spread to the rushing breeze, and as day reddened
And the stars faded, we saw a coast, low-lying,
And made out hills. 'Italy!', cried Achates,
'Italy!' all the happy sailors shouted.
Anchises wreathed a royal wine-bowl, stood
On the high stern, calling:—'Gods of earth and ocean
And wind and storm, help us along, propitious   530
With favoring breath!' And the breeze sprang up, and freshened;
We saw a harbor open, and a temple
Shone on Minerva's headland. The sails came down,
We headed toward the land. Like the curve of a bow
The port turned in from the Eastern waves; its cliffs
Foamed with the salty spray, and towering rocks
Came down to the sea, on both sides, double walls,
And the temple fled the shore. Here, our first omen,
I saw four horses grazing, white as snow,
And father Anchises cried:—'It is war you bring us,   540
Welcoming land, horses are armed for war,
It is war these herds portend. But there is hope
Of peace as well. Horses will bend to the yoke
And bear the bridle tamely.' Then we worshipped
The holy power of Pallas, first to hear us,
Kept our heads veiled before the solemn altar,
And following Helenus' injunction, offered
Our deepest prayer to Juno.
                                    And sailed on,
With some misgiving, past the homes of Greeks;
Saw, next, a bay, Tarentum, and a town   550
That rumor said was Hercules'; against it,
The towers of Caulon rose, and Scylaceum,[25]
Most dangerous to ships, and a temple of Juno.
Far off, Sicilian Etna[26] rose from the waves,
And we heard the loud sea roar, and the rocks resounding,
And voices broken on the coast; the shoals
Leaped at us, and the tide boiled sand. My father
Cried in alarm:—'This must be that Charybdis
Helenus warned us of. Rise to the oars,
O comrades, pull from the danger!' They responded   560
As they did, always, Palinurus swinging
The prow to the waves on the left, and all our effort
Strained to the left, with oars and sail. One moment
We were in the clouds, the next in the gulf of Hell;
Three times the hollow rocks and reefs roared at us,
Three times we saw spray shower the very stars,

---

[25] Tarentum, Caulon, and Scylaceum were cities lying along the sole of the "boot" of Italy.
[26] A volcano.

And the wind went down at sunset; we were weary,
Drifting, in ignorance, to the Cyclops[27] shores.
   There is a harbor, safe enough from wind,
But Etna thunders near it, crashing and roaring,   570
Throwing black clouds up to the sky, and smoking
With swirling pitchy color, and white-hot ashes,
With balls of flame puffed to the stars, and boulders,
The mountain's guts, belched out, or molten rock
Boiling below the ground, roaring above it.
The story goes that Enceladus, a giant,
Struck by a bolt of lightning, lies here buried
Beneath all Etna's weight, with the flames pouring
Through the broken furnace-flues; he shifts his body,
Every so often, to rest his weariness,   580
And then all Sicily seems to moan and tremble
And fill the sky with smoke. We spent the night here,
Hiding in woods, enduring monstrous portents,
Unable to learn the cause. There were no stars,
No light or fire in the sky; the dead of the night,
The thick of the cloud, obscured the moon.
                              And day
Arrived, at last, and the shadows left the heaven,
And a man came out of the woods, a sorry figure,
In hunger's final stages, reaching toward us
His outstretched hands. We looked again. His beard   590
Unshorn, his rags pinned up with thorns, and dirty,
He was, beyond all doubt of it, a Greek,
And one of those who had been at Troy in the fighting.
He saw, far off, the Trojan dress and armor,
Stopped short, for a moment, almost started back
In panic, then, with a wild rush, came on,
Pleading and crying:—'By the stars I beg you,
By the gods above, the air we breathe, ah Trojans,
Take me away from here, carry me off
To any land whatever; that will be plenty.   600
I know I am one of the Greeks, I know I sailed
With them, I warred against the gods of Ilium,
I admit all that; drown me for evil-doing,
Cut me to pieces, scatter me over the waves.
Kill me. If I must die, it will be a pleasure
To perish at the hands of men.' He held
Our knees and clung there, grovelling before us.
We urged him tell his story, his race, his fortune.
My father gave him his hand, a pledge of safety,
And his fear died down a little.

---

[27] One-eyed giants.

'I come,' he said, 610
'From Ithaca, a companion of Ulysses;
My name is Achaemenides;[28] my father,
His name was Adamastus, was a poor man,
And that was why I came to Troy. My comrades
Left me behind here, in their terrible hurry,
To leave these cruel thresholds. The Cyclops live here
In a dark cave, a house of gore, and banquets
Soaking with blood. It is dark inside there, monstrous.
He hits the stars with his head—Dear gods, abolish
This creature from the world!—he is not easy 620
To look at; he is terrible to talk to.
His food is the flesh of men, his drink their blood.
I saw him once myself, with two of our men
In that huge fist of his; he lay on his back
In the midst of the cave, and smashed them on a rock,
And the whole place swam with blood; I watched him chew them
The limbs with black clots dripping, the muscles, warm,
Quivering as he bit them. But we got him!
Ulysses did not stand for this; he kept
His wits about him, never mind the danger. 630
The giant was gorged with food, and drunk, and lolling
With sagging neck, sprawling all over the cavern
Belching and drooling blood-clots, bits of flesh,
And wine all mixed together. And we stood
Around him, praying, and drew lots,—we had found a stake
And sharpened it at the end,—and so we bored
His big eye out; it glowered under his forehead
The size of a shield, or a sun. So we got vengeance
For the souls of our companions. But flee, I tell you,
Get out of here, poor wretches, cut the cables, 640
Forsake this shore. There are a hundred others
As big as he is, and just like him, keeping
Sheep in the caves of the rocks, a hundred others
Wander around this coast and these high mountains.
I have managed for three months, hiding in forests,
In the caves of beasts, on a rocky look-out, watching
The Cyclops, horribly frightened at their cries
And the tramp of their feet. I have lived on plants and berries,
Gnawed roots and bark. I saw this fleet come in,
And I did not care; whatever it was, I gladly 650
Gave myself up. At least, I have escaped them.
Whatever death you give is more than welcome.'
And as he finished, we saw that very giant,
The shepherd Polyphemus, looming huge
Over his tiny flock; he was trying to find

---

[28]One of Ulysses', or Odysseus', sailors. The story he summarizes here is told in Homer's
Odyssey, Book IX.

His way to the shore he knew, a shapeless monster,
Lumbering, clumping, blind in the dark, with a stumble,
And the step held up with trunk of a pine. No comfort
For him, except in the sheep. He reached the sand,
Wading into the sea, and scooped up water   660
To wash the ooze of blood from the socket's hollow,
Grinding his teeth against the pain, and roaring,
And striding into the water, but even so
The waves were hardly up to his sides. We fled
Taking on board our Greek; we cut the cable,
Strained every nerve at the oars. He heard, and struggled
Toward the splash of the wave, but of course he could not catch us,
And then he howled in a rage, and the sea was frightened,
Italy deeply shaken, and all Etna
Rumbled in echoing terror in her caverns.   670
Out of the woods and the thicket of the mountains
The Cyclops came, the others, toward the harbor,
Along the coast-line. We could see them standing
In impotent anger, the wild eye-ball glaring,
A grim assortment, brothers, tall as mountains
Where oak and cypress tower, in the groves
Of Jove or great Diana. In our speed
And terror, we sailed anywhere, forgetting
What Helenus had said: Scylla, Charybdis,
Were nothing to us then. But we remembered   680
In time, and a north wind came from strait Pelorus,
We passed Pantagia,[29] and the harbor-mouth
Set in the living-rock, Thapsus, low-lying,
The bay called Megara: all these were places
That Achaemenides knew well, recalling
The scenes of former wanderings with Ulysses.
    An island faces the Sicanian bay
Against Plemyrium, washed by waves; this island
Has an old name, Ortygia. The story
Tells of a river, Alpheus, come from Elis,[30]   690
By a secret channel undersea, to join
The Arethusan fountains, mingling here
With the Sicilian waters. Here we worshipped
The land's great gods; went on, to pass Helorus,
A rich and marshy land; and then Pachynus
Where the cliffs rose sharp and high; and Camerina,
With firm foundation; the Geloan plains,
And Gela, named for a river; then Acragas,

---

[29] The places named in the following lines are located on the east and south coasts of Sicily;
Drepanum lies directly opposite Carthage, across a narrow part of the Mediterranean, and is
thus approximately where the action of Book I begins.
[30] Part of Greece; thus the river Alpheus must flow under the Ionian and Mediterranean
seas to join the fountain Arethusa. According to the myth, Alpheus was a river god in love
with the nymph Arethusa.

A towering town, high-walled, and sometime famous
For its breed of horses; the city of palms, Selinus;   700
The shoals of Lilybaeum, where the rocks
Are a hidden danger; so at last we came
To Drepanum, a harbor and a shoreline
That I could not rejoice in, a survivor
Of all those storms of the sea. For here I lost
My comforter in all my care and trouble,
My father Anchises. All the storms and perils,
All of the weariness endured, seemed nothing
Compared with this disaster; and I had
No warning of it; neither Helenus,   710
Though he foretold much trouble, nor Celaeno,
That evil harpy, prophesied this sorrow.
There was nothing more to bear; the long roads ended
At that unhappy goal; and when I left there,
Some god or other brought me to your shores.'

And so he told the story, a lonely man
To eager listeners, destiny and voyage,
And made an end of it here, ceased, and was quiet.

BOOK IV: AENEAS AND DIDO

But the queen finds no rest. Deep in her veins
The wound is fed; she burns with hidden fire.
His manhood, and the glory of his race
Are an obsession with her, like his voice,
Gesture and countenance. On the next morning,
After a restless night, she sought her sister:
"I am troubled, Anna, doubtful, terrified,
Or am I dreaming? What new guest is this
Come to our shores? How well he talks, how brave
He seems in heart and action! I suppose   10
It must be true; he does come from the gods.
Fear proves a bastard spirit. He has been
So buffeted by fate. What endless wars
He told of! Sister, I must tell you something:
Were not my mind made up, once and for all,
Never again to marry, having been
So lost when Sychaeus left me for the grave,
Slain by my murderous brother at the altar,
Were I not sick forever of the torch[1]
And bridal bed, here is the only man   20
Who has moved my spirit, shaken my weak will.

[1] Carried in wedding processions; an emblem of marriage.

I might have yielded to him. I recognize
The marks of an old fire. But I pray, rather,
That earth engulf me, lightning strike me down
To the pale shades and everlasting night
Before I break the laws of decency.[2]
My love has gone with Sychaeus; let him keep it,
Keep it with him forever in the grave."
She ended with a burst of tears. "Dear sister,
Dearer than life," Anna replied, "why must you   30
Grieve all your youth away in loneliness,
Not know sweet children, or the joys of love?
Is that what dust demands, and buried shadows?
So be it. You have kept your resolution
From Tyre to Libya, proved it by denying
Iarbas and a thousand other suitors
From Africa's rich kingdoms. Think a little.
Whose lands are these you settle in? Getulians,
Invincible in war, the wild Numidians,
Unfriendly Syrtes, ring us round, and a desert   40
Barren with drought, and the Barcaean rangers.
Why should I mention Tyre, and wars arising
Out of Pygmalion's threats? And you, my sister,
Why should you fight against a pleasing passion?
I think the gods have willed it so, and Juno
Has helped to bring the Trojan ships to Carthage.
What a great city, sister, what a kingdom
This might become, rising on such a marriage!
Carthage and Troy together in arms, what glory
Might not be ours? Only invoke the blessing   50
Of the great gods, make sacrifice, be lavish
In welcome, keep them here while the fierce winter
Rages at sea, and cloud and sky are stormy,
And ships still wrecked and broken."
                                        So she fanned
The flame of the burning heart; the doubtful mind
Was given hope, and the sense of guilt was lessened.
And first of all they go to shrine and altar
Imploring peace; they sacrifice to Ceres,
Giver of law, to Bacchus, to Apollo,
And most of all to Juno, in whose keeping   60
The bonds of marriage rest. In all her beauty
Dido lifts up the goblet, pours libation
Between the horns of a white heifer, slowly,
Or, slowly, moves to the rich altars, noting
The proper gifts to mark the day, or studies
The sacrificial entrails for the omens.
Alas, poor blind interpreters! What woman
In love is helped by offerings or altars?

[2] Dido had sworn to remain faithful to her dead husband.

Soft fire consumes the marrow-bones, the silent
Wound grows, deep in the heart. 70
Unhappy Dido burns, and wanders, burning,
All up and down the city, the way a deer
With a hunter's careless arrow in her flank
Ranges the uplands, with the shaft still clinging
To the hurt side. She takes Aeneas with her
All through the town, displays the wealth of Sidon,
Buildings projected; she starts to speak, and falters,
And at the end of the day renews the banquet,
Is wild to hear the story, over and over,
Hangs on each word, until the late moon, sinking, 80
Sends them all home. The stars die out, but Dido
Lies brooding in the empty hall, alone,
Abandoned on a lonely couch. She hears him,
Sees him, or sees and hears him in Iulus,[3]
Fondles the boy, as if that ruse might fool her,
Deceived by his resemblance to his father.
The towers no longer rise, the youth are slack
In drill for arms, the cranes and derricks rusting,
Walls halt halfway to heaven.

                And Juno saw it,
The queen held fast by this disease, this passion 90
Which made her good name meaningless. In anger
She rushed to Venus:—"Wonderful!—the trophies,
The praise, you and that boy of yours are winning!
Two gods outwit one woman—splendid, splendid!
What glory for Olympus! I know you fear me,
Fear Carthage, and suspect us. To what purpose?
What good does all this do? Is there no limit?
Would we not both be better off, to sanction
A bond of peace forever, a formal marriage?
You have your dearest wish; Dido is burning 100
With love, infected to her very marrow.
Let us—why not?—conspire to rule one people
On equal terms; let her serve a Trojan husband;
Let her yield her Tyrian people as her dowry."

    This, Venus knew, was spoken with a purpose,
A guileful one, to turn Italian empire
To Libyan shores: not without reservation
She spoke in answer: "Who would be so foolish
As to refuse such terms, preferring warfare,
If only fortune follows that proposal? 110
I do not know, I am more than a little troubled
What fate permits: will Jupiter allow it,
One city for the Tyrians and Trojans,
This covenant, this mixture? You can fathom
His mind, and ask him, being his wife. I follow

---

[3] The actual Iulus, not Cupid, who had been substituted for him in Book I.

Wherever you lead." And royal Juno answered:
"That I will tend to. Listen to me, and learn
How to achieve the urgent need. They plan,
Aeneas, and poor Dido, to go hunting
When sunlight floods the world to-morrow morning.   120
While the rush of the hunt is on, and the forest shaken
With beaters and their nets, I will pour down
Dark rain and hail, and make the whole sky rumble
With thunder and threat. The company will scatter,
Hidden or hiding in the night and shadow,
And Dido and the Trojan come for shelter
To the same cave. I will be there and join them
In lasting wedlock; she will be his own,
His bride, forever; this will be their marriage."
Venus assented,[4] smiling, not ungracious—   130
The trick was in the open.
   Dawn, rising, left the ocean, and the youth
Come forth from all the gates, prepared for hunting,
Nets, toils, wide spears, keen-scented coursing hounds.
And Dido keeps them waiting; her own charger
Stands bright in gold and crimson; the bit foams,
The impatient head is tossed. At last she comes,
With a great train attending, gold and crimson,
Quiver of gold, and combs of gold, and mantle
Crimson with golden buckle. A Trojan escort   140
Attends her, with Iulus, and Aeneas
Comes to her side, more lordly than Apollo
Bright along Delos' ridges in the springtime
With laurel in his hair and golden weapons
Shining across his shoulders. Equal radiance
Is all around Aeneas, equal splendor.
   They reach the mountain heights, the hiding-places
Where no trail runs; wild goats from the rocks are started,
Run down the ridges; elsewhere, in the open
Deer cross the dusty plain, away from the mountains.   150
The boy Ascanius, in the midst of the valley,
Is glad he has so good a horse, rides, dashing
Past one group or another: deer are cowards
And wild goats tame; he prays for some excitement,
A tawny lion coming down the mountain
Or a great boar with foaming mouth.
          The heaven
Darkens, and thunder rolls, and rain and hail
Come down in torrents. The hunt is all for shelter,
Trojans and Tyrians and Ascanius dashing
Wherever they can; the streams pour down the mountains.   160
To the same cave go Dido and Aeneas,

---

[4] Having been told by Jove (in Book I) of the destined future of Trojans and Romans, Venus is aware that Juno's plan will fail.

Where Juno, as a bridesmaid, gives the signal,
And mountain nymphs wail high their incantations,
First day of death, first cause of evil. Dido
Is unconcerned with fame, with reputation,
With how it seems to others. This is marriage
For her, not hole-and-corner guilt; she covers
Her folly with this name.
                              Rumor goes flying
At once, through all the Libyan cities, Rumor
Than whom no other evil was ever swifter. 170
She thrives on motion and her own momentum;
Tiny at first in fear, she swells, colossal
In no time, walks on earth, but her head is hidden
Among the clouds. Her mother, Earth, was angry,
Once, at the gods, and out of spite produced her,
The Titans' youngest sister, swift of foot,
Deadly of wing, a huge and terrible monster,
With an eye below each feather in her body,
A tongue, a mouth, for every eye, and ears
Double that number; in the night she flies 180
Above the earth, below the sky, in shadow
Noisy and shrill; her eyes are never closed
In slumber; and by day she perches, watching
From tower or battlement, frightening great cities.
She heralds truth, and clings to lies and falsehood,
It is all the same to her. And now she was going
Happy about her business, filling people
With truth and lies: Aeneas, Trojan-born,
Has come, she says, and Dido, lovely woman,
Sees fit to mate with him, one way or another, 190
And now the couple wanton out the winter,
Heedless of ruling, prisoners of passion.
They were dirty stories, but the goddess gave them
To the common ear, then went to King Iarbas[5]
With words that fired the fuel of his anger.
      This king was Ammon's son, a child of rape
Begotten on a nymph from Garamantia;
He owned wide kingdoms, had a hundred altars
Blazing with fires to Jove, eternal outposts
In the gods' honor; the ground was fat with blood, 200
The temple portals blossoming with garlands.
He heard the bitter stories, and went crazy,
Before the presences of many altars
Beseeching and imploring:—"Jove Almighty,
To whom the Moorish race on colored couches
Pours festive wine, do you see these things, or are we
A pack of idiots, shaking at the lightning

---

[5] A rejected African suitor of Dido, Iarbas is a son of Jove (identified here with Ammon).

We think you brandish, when it is really only
An aimless flash of light, and silly noises?
Do you see these things? A woman, who used to wander   210
Around my lands, who bought a little city,
To whom we gave some ploughland and a contract,
Disdains me as a husband, takes Aeneas
To be her lord and master, in her kingdom,
And now that second Paris, with his lackeys,
Half-men, I call them, his chin tied up with ribbons,
With millinery on his perfumed tresses,
Takes over what he stole, and we keep bringing
Gifts to your temples, we, devout believers
Forsooth, in idle legend."
                And Jove heard him   220
Making his prayer and clinging to the altars,
And turned his eyes to Carthage and the lovers
Forgetful of their better reputation.
He summoned Mercury:—"Go forth, my son,
Descend on wing and wind to Tyrian Carthage,
Speak to the Trojan leader, loitering there
Unheedful of the cities given by fate.
Take him my orders through the rapid winds:
It was not for this his lovely mother saved him
Twice[6] from Greek arms; she promised he would be   230
A ruler, in a country loud with war,
Pregnant with empire; he would sire a race
From Teucer's noble line; he would ordain
Law for the world. If no such glory moves him,
If his own fame and fortune count as nothing,
Does he, a father, grudge his son the towers
Of Rome to be? What is the fellow doing?
With what ambition wasting time in Libya?
Let him set sail. That's all; convey the message."
     Before he ended, Mercury made ready   240
To carry out the orders of his father;
He strapped the golden sandals on, the pinions
To bear him over sea and land, as swift
As the breath of the wind; he took the wand, which summons
Pale ghosts from Hell, or sends them there, denying
Or giving sleep, unsealing dead men's eyes,
Useful in flight through wind and stormy cloud,
And so came flying till he saw the summit
And towering sides of Atlas,[7] rugged giant
With heaven on his neck, whose head and shoulders   250
Are dark with fir, ringed with black cloud, and beaten
With wind and rain, and laden with the whiteness
Of falling snow, with rivers running over

---

[6] First in a combat with Diomede, then during the sack of Troy.
[7] The mountain in Africa, here personified as the giant.

His agèd chin, and the rough beard ice-stiffened.
Here first on level wing the god paused briefly,
Poised, plummeted to ocean, like a bird
That skims the water's surface, flying low
By shore and fishes' rocky breeding-ground,
So Mercury darted between earth and heaven
To Libya's sandy shore, cutting the wind   260
From the home of Maia's [8] father.
Soon as the winged sandals skim the rooftops,
He sees Aeneas founding towers, building
New homes for Tyrians; his sword is studded
With yellow jasper; he wears across his shoulders
A cloak of burning crimson, and golden threads
Run through it, the royal gift of the rich queen.
Mercury wastes no time:—"What are you doing,
Forgetful of your kingdom and your fortunes,
Building for Carthage? Woman-crazy fellow,   270
The ruler of the gods, the great compeller
Of heaven and earth, has sent me from Olympus
With no more word than this: what are you doing,
With what ambition wasting time in Libya?
If your own fame and fortune count as nothing,
Think of Ascanius at least, whose kingdom
In Italy, whose Roman land, are waiting
As promise justly due." He spoke, and vanished
Into thin air. Appalled, amazed, Aeneas
Is stricken dumb; his hair stands up in terror,   280
His voice sticks in his throat. He is more than eager
To flee that pleasant land, awed by the warning
Of the divine command. But how to do it?
How get around that passionate queen? What opening
Try first? His mind runs out in all directions,
Shifting and veering. Finally, he has it,
Or thinks he has: he calls his comrades to him,
The leaders, bids them quietly prepare
The fleet for voyage, meanwhile saying nothing
About the new activity; since Dido   290
Is unaware, has no idea that passion
As strong as theirs is on the verge of breaking,
He will see what he can do, find the right moment
To let her know, all in good time. Rejoicing,
The captains move to carry out the orders.
    Who can deceive a woman in love? The queen
Anticipates each move, is fearful even
While everything is safe, foresees this cunning,
And the same trouble-making goddess, Rumor,
Tells her the fleet is being armed, made ready   300

---

[8] Daughter of Atlas and mother of Mercury.

For voyaging. She rages through the city
Like a woman mad, or drunk, the way the Maenads
Go howling through the night-time on Cithaeron[9]
When Bacchus' cymbals summon with their clashing.
She waits no explanation from Aeneas;
She is the first to speak: "And so, betrayer,
You hoped to hide your wickedness, go sneaking
Out of my land without a word? Our love
Means nothing to you, our exchange of vows,
And even the death of Dido could not hold you.   310
The season is dead of winter, and you labor
Over the fleet; the northern gales are nothing—
You must be cruel, must you not? Why, even,
If ancient Troy remained, and you were seeking
Not unknown homes and lands, but Troy again,
Would you be venturing Troyward in this weather?
I am the one you flee from: true? I beg you
By my own tears, and your right hand—(I have nothing
Else left my wretchedness)—by the beginnings
Of marriage, wedlock, what we had, if ever   320
I served you well, if anything of mine
Was ever sweet to you, I beg you, pity
A falling house; if there is room for pleading
As late as this, I plead, put off that purpose.
You are the reason I am hated; Libyans,
Numidians, Tyrians, hate me; and my honor
Is lost, and the fame I had, that almost brought me
High as the stars, is gone. To whom, O guest—
I must not call you husband any longer—
To whom do you leave me? I am a dying woman;   330
Why do I linger on? Until Pygmalion,
My brother, brings destruction to this city?
Until the prince Iarbas leads me captive?
At least if there had been some hope of children
Before your flight, a little Aeneas playing
Around my courts, to bring you back, in feature
At least, I would seem less taken and deserted."
       There was nothing he could say. Jove bade him keep
Affection from his eyes, and grief in his heart
With never a sign. At last, he managed something:—   340
'Never, O Queen, will I deny you merit
Whatever you have strength to claim; I will not
Regret remembering Dido, while I have
Breath in my body, or consciousness of spirit.
I have a point or two to make. I did not,
Believe me, hope to hide my flight by cunning;
I did not, ever, claim to be a husband,

---

[9]A mountain where the Maenads (female worshipers of Bacchus) conducted their orgiastic rites.

Made no such vows. If I had fate's permission
To live my life my way, to settle my troubles
At my own will, I would be watching over 350
The city of Troy, and caring for my people,
Those whom the Greeks had spared, and Priam's palace
Would still be standing; for the vanquished people
I would have built the town again. But now
It is Italy I must seek, great Italy,
Apollo orders, and his oracles
Call me to Italy. There is my love,
There is my country. If the towers of Carthage,
The Libyan citadels, can please a woman
Who came from Tyre, why must you grudge the Trojans 360
Ausonian land? It is proper for us also
To seek a foreign kingdom. I am warned
Of this in dreams: when the earth is veiled in shadow
And the fiery stars are burning, I see my father,
Anchises, or his ghost, and I am frightened;
I am troubled for the wrong I do my son,
Cheating him out of his kingdom in the west,
And lands that fate assigns him. And a herald,
Jove's messenger—I call them both to witness—
Has brought me, through the rush of air, his orders; 370
I saw the god myself, in the full daylight,
Enter these walls, I heard the words he brought me.
Cease to inflame us both with your complainings;
I follow Italy not because I want to."
    Out of the corner of her eye she watched him
During the first of this, and her gaze was turning
Now here, now there; and then, in bitter silence,
She looked him up and down; then blazed out at him:—
"You treacherous liar! No goddess was your mother,
No Dardanus the founder of your tribe, 380
Son of the stony mountain-crags, begotten
On cruel rocks, with a tigress for a wet-nurse!
Why fool myself, why make pretense? what is there
To save myself for now? When I was weeping
Did he so much as sigh? Did he turn his eyes,
Ever so little, toward me? Did he break at all,
Or weep, or give his lover a word of pity?
What first, what next? Neither Jupiter nor Juno
Looks at these things with any sense of fairness.
Faith has no haven anywhere in the world. 390
He was an outcast on my shore, a beggar,
I took him in, and, like a fool, I gave him
Part of my kingdom; his fleet was lost, I found it,
His comrades dying, I brought them back to life.
I am maddened, burning, burning: now Apollo
The prophesying god, the oracles
Of Lycia, and Jove's herald, sent from heaven,

Come flying through the air with fearful orders,—
Fine business for the gods, the kind of trouble
That keeps them from their sleep. I do not hold you,   400
I do not argue, either. Go. And follow
Italy on the wind, and seek the kingdom
Across the water. But if any gods
Who care for decency have any power,
They will land you on the rocks; I hope for vengeance,
I hope to hear you calling the name of Dido
Over and over, in vain. Oh, I will follow
In blackest fire, and when cold death has taken
Spirit from body, I will be there to haunt you,
A shade, all over the world. I will have vengeance,   410
And hear about it; the news will be my comfort
In the deep world below." She broke it off,
Leaving the words unfinished; even light
Was unendurable; sick at heart, she turned
And left him, stammering, afraid, attempting
To make some kind of answer. And her servants
Support her to her room, that bower of marble,
A marriage-chamber once; here they attend her,
Help her lie down.
                    And good Aeneas, longing
To ease her grief with comfort, to say something   420
To turn her pain and hurt away, sighs often,
His heart being moved by this great love, most deeply,
And still—the gods give orders, he obeys them;
He goes back to the fleet. And then the Trojans
Bend, really, to their work, launching the vessels
All down the shore. The tarred keel swims in the water,
The green wood comes from the forest, the poles are lopped
For oars, with leaves still on them. All are eager
For flight; all over the city you see them streaming,
Bustling about their business, a black line moving   430
The way ants do when they remember winter
And raid a hill of grain, to haul and store it
At home, across the plain, the column moving
In thin black line through grass, part of them shoving
Great seeds on little shoulders, and part bossing
The job, rebuking laggards, and all the pathway
Hot with the stream of work.
                    And Dido saw them
With who knows what emotion: there she stood
On the high citadel, and saw, below her,
The whole beach boiling, and the water littered   440
With one ship after another, and men yelling,
Excited over their work, and there was nothing
For her to do but sob or choke with anguish.
There is nothing to which the hearts of men and women
Cannot be driven by love. Break into tears,

Try prayers again, humble the pride, leave nothing
Untried, and die in vain:—"Anna, you see them
Coming from everywhere; they push and bustle
All up and down the shore: the sails are swelling,
The happy sailors garlanding the vessels. 450
If I could hope for grief like this, my sister,
I shall be able to bear it. But one service
Do for me first, dear Anna, out of pity.
You were the only one that traitor trusted,
Confided in; you know the way to reach him,
The proper time and place. Give him this message,
Our arrogant enemy: tell him I never
Swore with the Greeks at Aulis to abolish
The Trojan race, I never sent a fleet
To Pergamus, I never desecrated 460
The ashes or the spirit of Anchises:
Why does he, then, refuse to listen to me?
What is the hurry? Let him give his lover
The one last favor: only wait a little,
Only a little while, for better weather
And easy flight. He has betrayed the marriage,
I do not ask for that again; I do not
Ask him to give up Latium and his kingdom.
Mere time is all I am asking, a breathing-space,
A brief reprieve, until my luck has taught me 470
To reconcile defeat and sorrow. This
Is all I ask for, sister; pity and help me:
If he grants me this, I will pay it ten times over
After my death." And Anna, most unhappy,
Over and over, told her tears, her pleading;
No tears, no pleading, move him; no man can yield
When a god stops his ears. As northern winds
Sweep over Alpine mountains, in their fury
Fighting each other to uproot an oak-tree
Whose ancient strength endures against their roaring 480
And the trunk shudders and the leaves come down
Strewing the ground, but the old tree clings to the mountain,
Its roots as deep toward hell as its crest toward heaven,
And still holds on—even so, Aeneas, shaken
By storm-blasts of appeal, by voices calling
From every side, is tossed and torn, and steady.
His will stays motionless, and tears are vain.
　　Then Dido prays for death at last; the fates
Are terrible, her luck is out, she is tired
Of gazing at the everlasting heaven. 490
The more to goad her will to die, she sees—
Oh terrible!—the holy water blacken,
Libations turn to blood, on ground and altar,
When she makes offerings. But she tells no one,
Not even her sister. From the marble shrine,

Memorial to her former lord, attended,
Always, by her, with honor, fleece and garland,
She hears his voice, his words, her husband calling
When darkness holds the world, and from the house-top
An owl sends out a long funereal wailing,   500
And she remembers warnings of old seers,
Fearful, foreboding. In her dreams Aeneas
Appears to hunt her down; or she is going
Alone in a lost country, wandering
Trying to find her Tyrians, mad as Pentheus,
Or frenzied as Orestes, when his mother
Is after him with whips of snakes, or firebrands,
While the Avengers menace at the threshold.[10]
  She was beaten, harboring madness, and resolved
On dying; alone, she plotted time and method;   510
Keeping the knowledge from her sorrowing sister,
She spoke with calm composure:—"I have found
A way (wish me good luck) to bring him to me
Or set me free from loving him forever.
Near Ocean[11] and the west there is a country,
The Ethiopian land, far-off, where Atlas
Turns on his shoulders the star-studded world;
I know a priestess there; she guards the temple
Of the daughters of the Evening Star; she feeds
The dragon there, and guards the sacred branches,   520
She sprinkles honey-dew, strews drowsy poppies,
And she knows charms to free the hearts of lovers
When she so wills it, or to trouble others;
She can reverse the wheeling of the planets,
Halt rivers in their flowing; she can summon
The ghosts of night-time; you will see earth shaking
Under her tread, and trees come down from mountains.
Dear sister mine, as heaven is my witness,
I hate to take these arts of magic on me!
Be secret, then; but in the inner courtyard,   530
Raise up a funeral-pyre, to hold the armor
Left hanging in the bower, by that hero,
That good devoted man, and all his raiment,
And add the bridal bed, my doom: the priestess
Said to do this, and it will be a pleasure
To see the end of all of it, every token
Of that unspeakable knave."
                         And so, thought Anna,
Things are no worse than when Sychaeus perished.
She did not know the death these rites portended,
Had no suspicion, and carried out her orders.   540

---

[10] Pentheus was driven to madness by Bacchus for opposing worship of him. Orestes was pursued by the Furies ("Avengers") in revenge for the murder of his mother; see Aeschylus' *Oresteia.*
[11] The waters believed to surround the world.

The pyre is raised in the court; it towers high
With pine and holm-oak, it is hung with garlands
And funeral wreaths, and on the couch she places
Aeneas' sword, his garments, and his image,
Knowing the outcome. Round about are altars,
Where, with her hair unbound, the priestess calls
On thrice a hundred gods, Erebus, Chaos,
Hecate, queen of Hell, triple Diana.
Water is sprinkled, from Avernus[12] fountain,
Or said to be, and herbs are sought, by moonlight 550
Mown with bronze sickles, and the stem-ends running
With a black milk, and the caul of a colt, new-born.
Dido, with holy meal and holy hands,
Stands at the altar, with one sandal loosened
And robes unfastened, calls the gods to witness,
Prays to the stars that know her doom, invoking,
Beyond them, any powers, if there are any,
Who care for lovers in unequal bondage.
    Night: and tired creatures over all the world
Were seeking slumber; the woods and the wild waters 560
Were quiet, and the silent stars were wheeling
Their course half over; every field was still;
The beasts of the field, the brightly colored birds,
Dwellers in lake and pool, in thorn and thicket,
Slept through the tranquil night, their sorrows over,
Their troubles soothed. But no such blessèd darkness
Closes the eyes of Dido; no repose
Comes to her anxious heart. Her pangs redouble,
Her love swells up, surging, a great tide rising 570
Of wrath and doubt and passion. "What do I do?
What now? Go back to my Numidian suitors,
Be scorned by those I scorned? Pursue the Trojans?
Obey their orders? They were grateful to me,
Once, I remember. But who would let them take me?
Suppose I went. They hate me now; they were always
Deceivers: is Laomedon[13] forgotten,
Whose blood runs through their veins? What then? Attend them,
Alone, be their companion, the loud-mouthed sailors? 580
Or with my own armada follow after,
Wear out my sea-worn Tyrians once more
With vengeance and adventure? Better die.
Die; you deserve to; end the hurt with the sword.
It is your fault, Anna; you were sorry for me,
Won over by my tears; you put this load
Of evil on me. It was not permitted,
It seems, for me to live apart from wedlock,
A blameless life. An animal does better.
I vowed Sychaeus faith. I have been faithless." 590

---

[12] *Erebus . . . Avernus* were all associated with death or the Lower World.
[13] King of Troy before Priam; he was noted for deceitfulness.

So, through the night, she tossed in restless torment.
    Meanwhile Aeneas, on the lofty stern,
All things prepared, sure of his going, slumbers
As Mercury comes down once more to warn him,
Familiar blond young god: "O son of Venus,
Is this a time for sleep? The wind blows fair,
And danger rises all around you. Dido,
Certain to die, however else uncertain,
Plots treachery, harbors evil. Seize the moment
While it can still be seized, and hurry, hurry!   600
The sea will swarm with ships, the fiery torches
Blaze, and the shore rankle with fire by morning.
Shove off, be gone! A shifty, fickle object
Is woman, always." He vanished into the night.
And, frightened by that sudden apparition,
Aeneas started from sleep, and urged his comrades:—
"Hurry, men, hurry; get to the sails and benches,
Get the ships under way. A god from heaven
Again has come to speed our flight, to sever
The mooring-ropes. O holy one, we follow,   610
Whoever you are, we are happy in obeying.
Be with us, be propitious; let the stars
Be right in heaven!" He drew his sword; the blade
Flashed, shining, at the hawser; and all the men
Were seized in the same restlessness and rushing.
They have left the shore, they have hidden the sea-water
With the hulls of the ships; the white foam flies, the oars
Dip down in dark-blue water.
                            And Aurora[14]
Came from Tithonus' saffron couch to freshen
The world with rising light, and from her watch-tower   620
The queen saw day grow whiter, and the fleet
Go moving over the sea, keep pace together
To the even spread of the sail; she knew the harbors
Were empty of sailors now; she struck her breast
Three times, four times; she tore her golden hair,
Crying, "God help me, will he go, this stranger,
Treating our kingdom as a joke? Bring arms,
Bring arms, and hurry! follow from all the city,
Haul the ships off the ways, some of you! Others,
Get fire as fast as you can, give out the weapons,   630
Pull oars! What am I saying? O where am I?
I must be going mad. Unhappy Dido,
Is it only now your wickedness strikes home?
The time it should have was when you gave him power.
Well, here it is, look at it now, the honor,
The faith of the hero who, they tell me, carries
With him his household gods, who bore on his shoulders

---

[14] Goddess of the dawn, mate of Tithonus.

His agèd father! Could I not have seized him,
Torn him to pieces, scattered him over the waves?
What was the matter? Could I not have murdered 640
His comrades, and Iulus, and served the son
For a dainty at the table of his father?
But fight would have a doubtful fortune. It might have,
What then? I was going to die; whom did I fear?
I would have, should have, set his camp on fire,
Filled everything with flame, choked off the father,
The son, the accursèd race, and myself with them.
Great Sun, surveyor of all the works of earth,
Juno, to whom my sorrows are committed,
Hecate,[15] whom the cross-roads of the cities 650
Wail to by night, avenging Furies, hear me,
Grant me divine protection, take my prayer.
If he must come to harbor, then he must,
If Jove ordains it, however vile he is,
False, and unspeakable. If Jove ordains,
The goal is fixed. So be it. Take my prayer.[16]
Let him be driven by arms and war, an exile,
Let him be taken from his son Iulus,
Let him beg for aid, let him see his people dying
Unworthy deaths, let him accept surrender 660
On unfair terms, let him never enjoy the kingdom,
The hoped-for light, let him fall and die, untimely,
Let him lie unburied on the sand. Oh, hear me,
Hear the last prayer, poured out with my last blood!
And you, O Tyrians, hate, and hate forever
The Trojan stock. Offer my dust this homage.
No love, no peace, between these nations, ever!
Rise from my bones, O great unknown avenger,
Hunt them with fire and sword, the Dardan settlers,
Now, then, here, there, wherever strength is given. 670
Shore against shore, wave against wave, and war,
War after war, for all the generations."
   She spoke, and turned her purpose to accomplish
The quickest end to the life she hated. Briefly
She spoke to Barce, Sychaeus' nurse; her own
Was dust and ashes in her native country:—
"Dear nurse, bring me my sister, tell her to hurry,
Tell her to sprinkle her body with river water,
To bring the sacrificial beast and offerings,
And both of you cover your temples with holy fillets. 680
I have a vow to keep; I have made beginning
Of rites to Stygian[17] Jove, to end my sorrows,

---

[15] A goddess associated with the Lower World, worshiped at crossways.
[16] Much of the curse that follows is fulfilled (though the poem does not describe the death of Aeneas).
[17] Associated with Styx, a river in the Lower World. The "Stygian Jove" was Hades (also called Dis, Pluto, and Orcus).

To burn the litter of that Trojan leader."
Barce, with an old woman's fuss and bustle,
Went hurrying out of sight; but Dido, trembling,
Wild with her project, the blood-shot eyeballs rolling,
Pale at the death to come, and hectic color
Burning the quivering cheeks, broke into the court,
Mounted the pyre in madness, drew the sword,
The Trojan gift, bestowed for no such purpose,   690
And she saw the Trojan garments, and the bed
She knew so well, and paused a little, weeping,
Weeping, and thinking, and flung herself down on it,
Uttering her last words:—
"Spoils that were sweet while gods and fate permitted,
Receive my spirit, set me free from suffering.
I have lived, I have run the course that fortune gave me,
And now my shade, a great one, will be going
Below the earth. I have built a noble city,
I have seen my walls, I have avenged a husband,   700
Punished a hostile brother. I have been
Happy, I might have been too happy, only
The Trojans made their landing." She broke off,
Pressed her face to the couch, cried:—"So, we shall die,
Die unavenged; but let us die. So, so,—
I am glad to meet the darkness. Let his eyes
Behold this fire across the sea, an omen
Of my death going with him."
                            As she spoke,
Her handmaids saw her, fallen on the sword,
The foam of blood on the blade, and blood on the hands.   710
A scream rings through the house; Rumor goes reeling,
Rioting, through the shaken town; the palace
Is loud with lamentation, women sobbing,
Wailing and howling, and the vaults of heaven
Echo the outcry, as if Tyre or Carthage
Had fallen to invaders, and the fury
Of fire came rolling over homes and temples.
Anna, half lifeless, heard in panic terror,
Came rushing through them all, beating her bosom,
Clawing her face:—"Was it for this, my sister?   720
To trick me so? The funeral pyre, the altars,
Prepared this for me? I have, indeed, a grievance,
Being forsaken; you would not let your sister
Companion you in death? You might have called me
To the same fate; we might have both been taken,
One sword, one hour. I was the one who built it,
This pyre, with my own hands; it was my voice
That called our fathers' gods, for what?—to fail you
When you were lying here. You have killed me, sister,
Not only yourself, you have killed us all, the people,   730
The town. Let me wash the wounds with water,

Let my lips catch what fluttering breath still lingers."
She climbed the lofty steps, and held her sister,
A dying woman, close; she used her robe
To try to stop the bleeding. And Dido tried
In vain to raise her heavy eyes, fell back,
And her wound made a gurgling hissing sound.
Three times she tried to lift herself; three times
Fell back; her rolling eyes went searching heaven
And the light hurt when she found it, and she moaned.   740
    At last all-powerful Juno, taking pity,
Sent Iris[18] from Olympus, in compassion
For the long racking agony, to free her
From the limbs' writhing and the struggle of spirit.
She had not earned this death, she had only sought it
Before her time, driven by sudden madness,
Therefore, the queen of Hades had not taken
The golden lock, consigning her to Orcus.[19]
So Iris, dewy on saffron wings, descending,
Trailing a thousand colors through the brightness   750
Comes down the sky, poises above her, saying,
"This lock I take as bidden, and from the body
Release the soul," and cuts the lock; and cold
Takes over, and the winds receive the spirit.

from BOOK V: THE FUNERAL GAMES FOR ANCHISES

The Trojans return to Sicily, where they solemnize the anniversary of Anchises' death through religious ritual and athletic contests. During the games some of the women, weary of travel and incited by Juno, try to burn the ships, but Jove sends a rainstorm that extinguishes the flames. Aeneas decides to leave the less hardy and zealous of the Trojans behind in Sicily, under the friendly ruler Acestes. The fleet then departs for Italy.

                        The masts are raised, and sail
Stretched from the halyards; right and left they bend
The canvas to fair winds: at the head of the fleet
Rides Palinurus, and the others follow,
As ordered, close behind him; dewy night
Has reached mid-heaven, while the sailors, sleeping,
Relax on the hard benches under the oars,   800
All calm, all quiet. And the god of Sleep
Parting the shadowy air, comes gently down,
Looking for Palinurus, bringing him,
A guiltless man, ill-omened dreams. He settles
On the high stern, a god disguised as a man,
Speaking in Phorbas'[1] guise, "O Palinurus,

---

[18] Goddess of the rainbow, Juno's messenger.
[19] The queen of Hades, or the Lower World, was Proserpina.
[1] A friend of the helmsman Palinurus.

The fleet rides smoothly in the even weather,
The hour is given for rest. Lay down the head,
Rest the tired eyes from toil. I will take over
A little while." But Palinurus, barely   810
Lifting his eyes, made answer: "Trust the waves,
However quiet? trust a peaceful ocean?
Put faith in such a monster? Never! I
Have been too often fooled by the clear stars
To trust Aeneas to their faithless keeping."
And so he clung to the tiller, never loosed
His hand from the wood, his eyes from the fair heaven.
But lo, the god over his temples shook
A bough that dripped with dew from Lethe, steeped
With Stygian magic,[2] so the swimming eyes,   820
Against his effort, close, blink open, close
Again, and slumber takes the drowsy limbs.
Bending above him, leaning over, the god
Shoves him, still clinging to the tiller, calling
His comrades vainly, into the clear waves.
And the god is gone like a bird to the clear air,
And the fleet is going safely over its journey
As Neptune promised.[3] But the rocks were near,
The Siren-cliffs, most perilous of old,
White with the bones of many mariners,   830
Loud with their hoarse eternal warning sound.[4]
Aeneas starts from sleep, aware, somehow,
Of a lost pilot, and a vessel drifting,
Himself takes over guidance, with a sigh
And heartache for a friend's mishap, "Alas,
Too trustful in the calm of sea and sky,
O Palinurus, on an unknown shore,
You will be lying, naked."

BOOK VI: THE LOWER WORLD

Mourning for Palinurus, he drives the fleet
To Cumae's[1] coast-line; the prows are turned, the anchors
Let down, the beach is covered by the vessels.
Young in their eagerness for the land in the west,

[2] Lethe, the river of forgetfulness, and Styx, the river of death, are part of the landscape of the Lower World, described in Book VI.

[3] In response to Venus' pleas, the ocean god Neptune had promised her that the Trojan fleet should reach Italy in safety, but he had also stipulated that one sailor should be drowned.

[4] The Sirens, as described in Homer's *Odyssey*, Book XII, were females who enchanted sailors with their beautiful songs, luring them to destruction. Virgil associates this peril with certain actual rocks in the sea near modern Naples.

[1] A city, near the modern Naples, where Aeneas is to visit the Sybil named Deiphobe, mythical prophet and priestess of Apollo, in preparation for his visit to the Lower World.

They flash ashore; some seek the seeds of flame
Hidden in veins of flint, and others spoil
The woods of tinder, and show where water runs.
Aeneas, in devotion, seeks the heights
Where stands Apollo's temple, and the cave
Where the dread Sibyl dwells, Apollo's priestess,   10
With the great mind and heart, inspired revealer
Of things to come. They enter Diana's grove,
Pass underneath the roof of gold.[2]
                          The story
Has it that Daedalus fled from Minos' kingdom,
Trusting himself to wings he made, and travelled
A course unknown to man, to the cold north,
Descending on this very summit; here,
Earth-bound again, he built a mighty temple,
Paying Apollo homage, the dedication
Of the oarage of his wings. On the temple doors   20
He carved, in bronze, Androgeos' death, and the payment
Enforced on Cecrops' children, seven sons
For sacrifice each year: there stands the urn,
The lots are drawn—facing this, over the sea,
Rises the land of Crete: the scene portrays
Pasiphae in cruel love, the bull
She took to her by cunning, and their offspring,
The mongrel Minotaur, half man, half monster,
The proof of lust unspeakable; and the toil
Of the house is shown, the labyrinthine maze   30
Which no one could have solved, but Daedalus
Pitied a princess' love, loosened the tangle,
Gave her a skein to guide her way. His boy,
Icarus, might have been here, in the picture,
And almost was—his father had made the effort
Once, and once more, and dropped his hands; he could not
Master his grief that much.[3] The story held them;

---

[2] The temple and its environs were sacred to both Apollo and Diana, his sister. In her alter ego as Hecate, she was goddess of the Lower World and was sometimes associated with witchcraft.

[3] Minos was king of Crete. His wife, Pasiphae, in a bovine disguise fabricated by the craftsman Daedalus, made love with a bull and then gave birth to the Minotaur, half bull and half human. Minos then forced Daedalus to construct a labyrinth to contain the Minotaur. After the Athenians killed Androgeos, the son of Minos, the king in revenge forced them (the "children" of Cecrops, an early king of Athens) to sacrifice to the Minotaur, each year, the lives of seven young men and seven young women, chosen by lots drawn from an urn. The Athenian hero Theseus went to Crete and succeeded in killing the monster that was devouring his compatriots. In this enterprise he was helped by Daedalus and the love-smitten Ariadne, Minos' daughter, who gave Theseus a thread to guide him back out of the labyrinth. Imprisoned for his part in this feat, Daedalus with his son Icarus escaped from Crete on wings the father had constructed; Icarus, however, died when he flew too close to the sun, which melted the wax fastenings of his wings. Daedalus, after reaching Italy, built the temple and executed the carvings that Aeneas is examining, though Virgil represents the artist as having been incapable, in his grief, of representing his son's tragic story.

They would have studied it longer, but Achates[4]
Came from his mission; with him the priestess,
Deiphobe, daughter of Glaucus,[5] who tends the temple   40
For Phoebus and Diana; she warned Aeneas:
"It is no such sights the time demands; far better
To offer sacrifice, seven chosen bullocks,
Seven chosen ewes, a herd without corruption."
They were prompt in their obedience, and the priestess
Summoned the Trojans to the lofty temple.
    The rock's vast side is hollowed into a cavern,
With a hundred mouths, a hundred open portals,
Whence voices rush, the answers of the Sibyl.
They had reached the threshold, and the virgin cried: 50
"It is time to seek the fates; the god is here,
The god is here, behold him." And as she spoke
Before the entrance, her countenance and color
Changed, and her hair tossed loose, and her heart was heaving,
Her bosom swollen with frenzy; she seemed taller,
Her voice not human at all, as the god's presence
Drew nearer, and took hold on her. "Aeneas,"
She cried, "Aeneas, are you praying?
Are you being swift in prayer? Until you are,
The house of the gods will not be moved, nor open   60
Its mighty portals." More than her speech, her silence
Made the Trojans cold with terror, and Aeneas
Prayed from the depth of his heart: "Phoebus Apollo,
Compassionate ever, slayer of Achilles
Through aim of Paris' arrow,[6] helper and guide
Over the seas, over the lands, the deserts,
The shoals and quicksands, now at last we have come
To Italy, we hold the lands which fled us:
Grant that thus far, no farther, a Trojan fortune
Attend our wandering. And spare us now,   70
All of you, gods and goddesses, who hated
Troy in the past, and Trojan glory. I beg you,
Most holy prophetess, in whose foreknowing
The future stands revealed, grant that the Trojans—
I ask with fate's permission—rest in Latium
Their wandering storm-tossed gods. I will build a temple,
In honor of Apollo and Diana,
Out of eternal marble, and ordain
Festivals in their honor, and for the Sibyl
A great shrine in our kingdom, and I will place there   80
The lots and mystic oracles for my people

[4] Aeneas' most faithful friend.
[5] Glaucus was a sea god gifted with prophetic powers.
[6] Apollo, patron of archers, helped Paris to slay Achilles by shooting him in the heel, the only part of his body not supernaturally protected.

With chosen priests to tend them.[7] Only, priestess,
This once, I pray you, chant the sacred verses
With your own lips; do not trust them to the leaves,
The mockery of the rushing wind's disorder."[8]
But the priestess, not yet subject to Apollo,
Went reeling through the cavern, wild, and storming
To throw the god, who presses, like a rider,
With bit and bridle and weight, tames her wild spirit,
Shapes her to his control. The doors fly open,   90
The hundred doors, of their own will, fly open,
And through the air the answer comes:—"O Trojans,
At last the dangers of the sea are over;
That course is run, but graver ones are waiting
On land. The sons of Dardanus will reach
The kingdom of Lavinia—be easy
On that account—the sons of Dardanus, also,
Will wish they had not come there. War, I see,
Terrible war, and the river Tiber foaming
With streams of blood. There will be another Xanthus,   100
Another Simois, and Greek encampment,
Even another Achilles, born in Latium,
Himself a goddess' son. And Juno further
Will always be there: you will beg for mercy,
Be poor, turn everywhere for help. A woman
Will be the cause once more of so much evil,
A foreign bride, receptive to the Trojans,
A foreign marriage.[9] Do not yield to evil,
Attack, attack, more boldly even than fortune
Seems to permit. An offering of safety,—   110
Incredible!—will come from a Greek city."[10]
So, through the amplifiers of her cavern,
The hollow vaults, the Sibyl cast her warnings,
Riddles confused with truth; and Apollo rode her,
Reining her rage, and shaking her, and spurring
The fierceness of her heart. The frenzy dwindled,
A little, and her lips were still. Aeneas
Began:—"For me, no form of trouble, maiden,
Is new, or unexpected; all of this
I have known long since, lived in imagination.   120
One thing I ask: this is the gate of the kingdom,

---

[7] The Sibylline books, venerated in Virgil's day, were supposed to contain prophetic oracles important to the guidance of Rome.

[8] See Helenus' instructions to Aeneas in III.455–63, 466–67.

[9] In short, it will be the Trojan War all over again. Xanthus and Simois were rivers at Troy. The second Achilles will be the Italian hero Turnus (son of the nymph Venilia as Achilles had been the son of the nymph Thetis), who will become Aeneas' rival for the princess Lavinia. Thus, according to the prophecy, woman will again be at the root of the troubles, as with Helen and (it may be implied) Dido.

[10] Pallanteum, a city on the site of the future Rome; it had been founded by Evander, king of Arcadia (in Greece), who had emigrated to Italy.

So it is said, where Pluto reigns, the gloomy
Marsh where the water of Acheron[11] runs over.
Teach me the way from here, open the portals
That I may go to my belovèd father,
Stand in his presence, talk with him. I brought him,
Once, on these shoulders, through a thousand weapons
And following fire, and foemen. He shared with me
The road, the sea, the menaces of heaven,
Things that an old man should not bear; he bore them,   130
Tired as he was. And he it was who told me
To come to you in humbleness. I beg you
Pity the son, the father. You have power,
Great priestess, over all; it is not for nothing
Hecate gave you this dominion over
Avernus' groves. If Orpheus could summon
Eurydice from the shadows with his music,
If Pollux could save his brother, coming, going,
Along this path,—why should I mention Theseus,
Why mention Hercules?[12] I, too, descended   140
From the line of Jupiter." He clasped the altar,
Making his prayer, and she made answer to him:
"Son of Anchises, born of godly lineage,
By night, by day, the portals of dark Dis
Stand open: it is easy, the descending
Down to Avernus.[13] But to climb again,
To trace the footsteps back to the air above,
There lies the task, the toil. A few, beloved
By Jupiter, descended from the gods,
A few, in whom exalting virtue burned,   150
Have been permitted. Around the central woods
The black Cocytus glides, a sullen river;
But if such love is in your heart, such longing
For double crossing of the Stygian lake,[14]
For double sight of Tartarus,[15] learn first
What must be done. In a dark tree there hides

[11] One of the rivers of the Lower World.

[12] The legendary musician Orpheus was allowed to lead his dead wife, Eurydice, out of the Lower World (though he lost her after all, being unable to obey the command not to look back as she followed him). Pollux, an immortal who was half-brother to the mortal Castor, wished to die with him but could not; Jupiter, however, agreed to let them exchange places daily, each living alternately in the heavens and in the world of the dead. Theseus and Pirithous had tried to abduct Proserpine, queen of the dead. (She is also called Proserpina and Persephone.) The most difficult of Hercules' famous "labors" was the theft of Cerberus, the three-headed dog guarding the Lower World. (See lines 415–21.)

[13] Dis, like Hades (Greek) and Orcus, is another name for the god Pluto, and also for his realm, the Lower World. Avernus in this passage also means the Lower World, named for a sulfurous volcanic lake near Cumae. See also line 136.

[14] The four rivers of the Lower World (besides Lethe, the river of forgetfulness) were Styx, Acheron, Cocytus, and Phlegethon.

[15] The place in the Lower World where evil was punished. Aeneas actually sees only the walls of Tartarus, but it is described in lines 573–660. *Tartarus* can also mean the Lower World in general.

A bough, all golden, leaf and pliant stem,
Sacred to Proserpine. This all the grove
Protects, and shadows cover it with darkness.
Until this bough, this bloom of light, is found, 160
No one receives his passport to the darkness
Whose queen requires this tribute. In succession,
After the bough is plucked, another grows,
Gold-green with the same metal. Raise the eyes,
Look up, reach up the hand, and it will follow
With ease, if fate is calling; otherwise,
No power, no steel, can loose it. Furthermore,
(Alas, you do not know this!), one of your men
Lies on the shore, unburied, a pollution
To all the fleet, while you have come for counsel 170
Here to our threshold.[16] Bury him with honor;
Black cattle slain in expiation for him
Must fall before you see the Stygian kingdoms,
The groves denied to living men."
                            Aeneas,
With sadness in his eyes, and downcast heart,
Turned from the cave, and at his side Achates
Accompanied his anxious meditations.
They talked together: who could be the comrade
Named by the priestess, lying there unburied?
And they found him on dry sand; it was Misenus, 180
Aeolus' son, none better with the trumpet
To make men burn for warfare. He had been
Great Hector's man-at-arms; he was good in battle
With spear as well as horn, and after Hector
Had fallen to Achilles, he had followed
Aeneas, entering no meaner service.
Some foolishness came over him; he made
The ocean echo to the blare of his trumpet
That day, and challenged the sea-gods to a contest
In martial music, and Triton, jealous, caught him, 190
However unbelievable the story,
And held him down between the rocks, and drowned him
Under the foaming waves.[17] His comrades mourned,
Aeneas most of all, and in their sorrow
They carry out, in haste, the Sibyl's orders,
Construct the funeral altar, high as heaven,
They go to an old wood, and the pine-trees fall
Where wild beasts have their dens, and holm-oak rings
To the stroke of the axe, and oak and ash are riven

---

[16] An unburied corpse was offensive for religious reasons. See the meeting with Palinurus later in Book VI.

[17] Triton was a sea deity, son of Neptune, and was often portrayed as blowing a conch-shell trumpet. The classical gods did not like to be challenged at their own specialties. Appropriately, the father of the trumpeter Misenus (line 181) is the namesake of the god of the winds, Aeolus.

By the splitting wedge, and rowan-trees come rolling   200
Down the steep mountain-side. Aeneas helps them,
And cheers them on; studies the endless forest,
Takes thought, and prays: "If only we might see it,
That golden bough, here in the depth of the forest,
Bright on some tree. She told the truth, our priestess,
Too much, too bitter truth, about Misenus."
No sooner had he spoken than twin doves
Came flying down before him, and alighted
On the green ground. He knew his mother's birds,
And made his prayer, rejoicing,—"Oh, be leaders,   210
Wherever the way, and guide me to the grove
Where the rich bough makes rich the shaded ground.
Help me, O goddess-mother!" And he paused,
Watching what sign they gave, what course they set.
The birds flew on a little, just ahead
Of the pursuing vision; when they came
To the jaws of dank Avernus, evil-smelling,
They rose aloft, then swooped down the bright air,
Perched on the double tree, where the off-color
Of gold was gleaming golden through the branches.   220
As mistletoe, in the cold winter, blossoms
With its strange foliage on an alien tree,
The yellow berry gilding the smooth branches,[18]
Such was the vision of the gold in leaf
On the dark holm-oak, so the foil was rustling,
Rattling, almost, the bract[19] in the soft wind
Stirring like metal. Aeneas broke it off
With eager grasp, and bore it to the Sibyl.
    Meanwhile, along the shore, the Trojans mourned,
Paying Misenus' dust the final honors.   230
A mighty pyre was raised, of pine and oak,
The sides hung with dark leaves, and somber cypress
Along the front, and gleaming arms above.
Some made the water hot, and some made ready
Bronze caldrons, shimmering over fire, and others
Lave and anoint the body, and with weeping
Lay on the bier his limbs, and place above them
Familiar garments, crimson color; and some
Take up the heavy burden, a sad office,
And, as their fathers did, they kept their eyes   240
Averted, as they brought the torches nearer.
They burn gifts with him, bowls of oil, and viands,
And frankincense; and when the flame is quiet
And the ashes settle to earth, they wash the embers
With wine, and slake the thirsty dust. The bones

---

[18] Mistletoe is a parasite with hardly visible roots, so that in winter it contrasts in appearance with the tree it grows on and seems to live a strange, self-sustaining life.

[19] A botanical term translating *brattea,* a thin metallic leaf.

Are placed in a bronze urn by Corynaeus,
Who, with pure water, thrice around his comrades
Made lustral cleansing, shaking gentle dew
From the fruitful branch of olive; and they said
Hail and farewell! And over him Aeneas   250
Erects a mighty tomb, with the hero's arms,
His oar and trumpet, where the mountain rises
Memorial for ever, and named Misenus.[20]
    These rites performed, he hastened to the Sibyl.
There was a cavern, yawning wide and deep,
Jagged, below the darkness of the trees,
Beside the darkness of the lake. No bird
Could fly above it safely, with the vapor
Pouring from the black gulf (the Greeks have named it
Avernus, or A-Ornos, meaning *birdless*),[21]   260
And here the priestess for the slaughter set
Four bullocks, black ones, poured the holy wine
Between the horns, and plucked the topmost bristles
For the first offering to the sacred fire,
Calling on Hecate, a power in heaven,
A power in hell. Knives to the throat were driven,
The warm blood caught in bowls. Aeneas offered
A lamb, black-fleeced, to Night and her great sister,
A sterile heifer for the queen;[22] for Dis
An altar in the night, and on the flames   270
The weight of heavy bulls, the fat oil pouring
Over the burning entrails. And at dawn,
Under their feet, earth seemed to shake and rumble,
The ridges move, and bitches bay in darkness,
As the presence neared. The Sibyl cried a warning,
"Keep off, keep off, whatever is unholy,
Depart from here![23] Courage, Aeneas; enter
The path, unsheathe the sword. The time is ready
For the brave heart." She strode out boldly, leading
Into the open cavern, and he followed.   280
    Gods of the world of spirit, silent shadows,
Chaos and Phlegethon, areas of silence,
Wide realms of dark, may it be right and proper
To tell what I have heard, this revelation
Of matters buried deep in earth and darkness!
    Vague forms in lonely darkness, they were going
Through void and shadow, through the empty realm
Like people in a forest, when the moonlight

---

[20] The promontory at the southwestern end of the Bay of Naples is still called Cape Miseno.

[21] Most authoritative manuscripts of the *Aeneid* omit this parenthetical statement.

[22] The sister of Night (Nox) was Earth (Tellus). The "queen" is Proserpine.

[23] At Roman religious ceremonies, the ritual dismissal of the uninitiated; here applied to Aeneas' companions, who must now leave him. The approaching "presence" (line 275) is that of the goddess Hecate, accompanied by her hounds.

Shifts with a baleful glimmer, and shadow covers
The sky, and all the colors turn to blackness. 290
At the first threshold, on the jaws of Orcus,
Grief and avenging Cares have set their couches,
And pale Diseases dwell, and sad Old Age,
Fear, evil-counselling Hunger, wretched Need,
Forms terrible to see, and Death, and Toil,
And Death's own brother, Sleep, and evil Joys,
Fantasies of the mind, and deadly War,
The Furies' iron chambers, Discord, raving,
Her snaky hair entwined in bloody bands.
An elm-tree loomed there, shadowy and huge, 300
The aged boughs outspread, beneath whose leaves,
Men say, the false dreams cling, thousands on thousands.
And there are monsters in the dooryard, Centaurs,
Scyllas, of double shape, the beast of Lerna,
Hissing most horribly, Briareus,
The hundred-handed giant, a Chimaera
Whose armament is fire, Harpies, and Gorgons,
A triple-bodied giant.[24] In sudden panic
Aeneas drew his sword, the edge held forward,
Ready to rush and flail, however blindly, 310
Save that his wise companion warned him, saying
They had no substance, they were only phantoms
Flitting about, illusions without body.

    From here, the road turns off to Acheron,
River of Hell; here, thick with muddy whirling,
Cocytus boils with sand. Charon is here,
The guardian of these mingling waters, Charon,
Uncouth and filthy, on whose chin the hair
Is a tangled mat, whose eyes protrude, are burning,
Whose dirty cloak is knotted at the shoulder. 320
He poles a boat, tends to the sail, unaided,
Ferrying bodies in his rust-hued vessel.
Old, but a god's senility is awful
In its raw greenness. To the bank come thronging
Mothers and men, bodies of great-souled heroes,
Their life-time over, boys, unwedded maidens,
Young men whose fathers saw their pyres burning,
Thick as the forest leaves that fall in autumn
With early frost, thick as the birds to landfall

---

[24] These lines are a catalog of many of the most famous or fearsome monsters of ancient fable. Centaurs were half man, half horse; Scylla was a six-headed monster (described in III.432–44) who devoured sailors in the straits of Messina; the beast of Lerna was the Hydra, a gigantic many-headed serpent; Briareus, as the text states, was a giant with a hundred hands; the fire-breathing Chimaera was a combination of lion, goat, and serpent; the Harpies were foul bird women (described in III.213–57); the Gorgons (Medusa and her two sisters) were snake-haired female monsters who literally petrified men who gazed on them; the triple-bodied giant was named Geryon.

From over the seas, when the chill of the year compels them 330
To sunlight. There they stand, a host, imploring
To be taken over first. Their hands, in longing,
Reach out for the farther shore. But the gloomy boatman
Makes choice among them, taking some, and keeping
Others far back from the stream's edge. Aeneas,
Wondering, asks the Sibyl, "Why the crowding?
What are the spirits seeking? What distinction
Brings some across the livid stream, while others
Stay on the farther bank?" She answers, briefly:
"Son of Anchises, this is the awful river, 340
The Styx, by which the gods take oath; the boatman
Charon; those he takes with him are the buried,
Those he rejects, whose luck is out, the graveless.
It is not permitted him to take them over
The dreadful banks and hoarse-resounding waters
Till earth is cast upon their bones. They haunt
These shores a hundred restless years of waiting
Before they end postponement of the crossing."
Aeneas paused, in thoughtful mood, with pity
Over their lot's unevenness; and saw there, 350
Wanting the honor given the dead, and grieving,
Leucaspis, and Orontes, the Lycian captain,
Who had sailed from Troy across the stormy waters,
And drowned off Africa, with crew and vessel,
And there was Palinurus, once his pilot,
Who, not so long ago, had been swept over,
Watching the stars on the journey north from Carthage.
The murk was thick; Aeneas hardly knew him,
Sorrowful in that darkness, but made question:
"What god, O Palinurus, took you from us? 360
Who drowned you in the deep? Tell me. Apollo
Never before was false, and yet he told me
You would be safe across the seas, and come
Unharmed to Italy; what kind of promise
Was this, to fool me with?" But Palinurus
Gave him assurance:—"It was no god who drowned me,[25]
No falsehood on Apollo's part, my captain,
But as I clung to the tiller, holding fast
To keep the course, as I should do, I felt it
Wrenched from the ship, and I fell with it, headlong. 370
By those rough seas I swear, I had less fear
On my account than for the ship, with rudder
And helmsman overboard, to drift at the mercy
Of rising seas. Three nights I rode the waters,
Three nights of storm, and from the crest of a wave,

---

[25] Palinurus is ignorant of the role of the god of Sleep in casting him overboard. Apollo's promise is not mentioned elsewhere in the poem.

On the fourth morning, sighted Italy,
I was swimming to land, I had almost reached it, heavy
In soaking garments; my cramped fingers struggled
To grasp the top of the rock, when barbarous people,
Ignorant men, mistaking me for booty,[26]   380
Struck me with swords; waves hold me now, or winds
Roll me along the shore. By the light of heaven,
The lovely air, I beg you, by your father,
Your hope of young Iulus, bring me rescue
Out of these evils, my unconquered leader!
Cast over my body earth—you have the power—
Return to Velia's[27] harbor,—or there may be
Some other way—your mother is a goddess,
Else how would you be crossing this great river,
This Stygian swamp?—help a poor fellow, take me   390
Over the water with you, give a dead man
At least a place to rest in." But the Sibyl
Broke in upon him sternly:—"Palinurus,
Whence comes this mad desire? No man, unburied,
May see the Stygian waters, or Cocytus,
The Furies' dreadful river; no man may come
Unbidden to this bank. Give up the hope
That fate is changed by praying, but hear this,
A little comfort in your harsh misfortune:
Those neighboring people will make expiation,   400
Driven by signs from heaven, through their cities
And through their countryside; they will build a tomb,
Thereto bring offerings yearly, and the place
Shall take its name from you, Cape Palinurus."[28]
So he was comforted a little, finding
Some happiness in the promise.
                                        And they went on,
Nearing the river, and from the stream the boatman
Beheld them cross the silent forest, nearer,
Turning their footsteps toward the bank. He challenged:—
"Whoever you are, O man in armor, coming   410
In this direction, halt where you are, and tell me
The reason why you come. This is the region
Of shadows, and of Sleep and drowsy Night;
I am not allowed to carry living bodies
In the Stygian boat; and I must say I was sorry
I ever accepted Hercules and Theseus
And Pirithous, and rowed them over the lake,
Though they were sons of gods and great in courage.

---

[26] A man carrying valuable goods.
[27] A town near Cumae.
[28] As with Misenus and modern Cape Miseno (line 253), Palinurus' name is still given today to a promontory on the Italian coast (Point Palinuro).

One of them dared to drag the guard of Hell,
Enchained, from Pluto's throne, shaking in terror, 420
The others to snatch our queen from Pluto's chamber."
The Sibyl answered briefly: "No such cunning
Is plotted here; our weapons bring no danger.
Be undisturbed: the hell-hound in his cavern
May bark forever, to keep the bloodless shadows
Frightened away from trespass; Proserpine,
Untouched, in pureness guard her uncle's [29] threshold.
Trojan Aeneas, a man renowned for goodness,
Renowned for nerve in battle, is descending
To the lowest shades; he comes to find his father. 430
If such devotion has no meaning to you,
Look on this branch at least, and recognize it!"
And with the word she drew from under her mantle
The golden bough; his swollen wrath subsided.
No more was said; he saw the bough, and marvelled
At the holy gift, so long unseen; came sculling
The dark-blue boat to the shore, and drove the spirits,
Lining the thwarts, ashore, and cleared the gangway,
And took Aeneas aboard; as that big man
Stepped in, the leaky skiff groaned under the weight, 440
And the strained seams let in the muddy water,
But they made the crossing safely, seer and soldier,
To the far margin, colorless and shapeless,
Grey sedge and dark-brown ooze. They heard the baying
Of Cerberus, that great hound, in his cavern crouching,
Making the shore resound, as all three throats
Belled horribly; and serpents rose and bristled
Along the triple neck. The priestess threw him
A sop with honey and drugged meal; he opened
The ravenous throat, gulped, and subsided, filling 450
The den with his huge bulk. Aeneas, crossing,
Passed on beyond the bank of the dread river
Whence none return.
               A wailing of thin voices
Came to their ears, the souls of infants crying,
Those whom the day of darkness took from the breast
Before their share of living. And there were many
Whom some false sentence brought to death. Here Minos [30]
Judges them once again; a silent jury
Reviews the evidence. And there are others,
Guilty of nothing, but who hated living, 460
The suicides. How gladly, now, they would suffer
Poverty, hardship, in the world of light!

---

[29] Proserpine's father, Jove, was Pluto's brother.
[30] King of Crete, who had ordered the famous labyrinth built; he later was made judge of the dead.

But this is not permitted; they are bound
Nine times around by the black unlovely river;
Styx holds them fast.
                        They came to the Fields of Mourning,
So-called, where those whom cruel love had wasted
Hid in secluded pathways, under myrtle,
And even in death were anxious. Procris, Phaedra,
Eriphyle, displaying wounds her son
Had given her, Caeneus, Laodamia,   470
Caeneus, a young man once, and now again
A young man, after having been a woman.[31]
And here, new come from her own wound, was Dido,
Wandering in the wood. The Trojan hero,
Standing near by, saw her, or thought he saw her,
Dim in the shadows, like the slender crescent
Of moon when cloud drifts over. Weeping, he greets her:—
"Unhappy Dido, so they told me truly
That your own hand had brought you death. Was I—
Alas!—the cause? I swear by all the stars,   480
By the world above, by everything held sacred
Here under the earth, unwillingly, O queen,
I left your kingdom. But the gods' commands,
Driving me now through these forsaken places,
This utter night, compelled me on. I could not
Believe my loss would cause so great a sorrow.
Linger a moment, do not leave me; whither,
Whom, are you fleeing? I am permitted only
This last word with you."
                        But the queen, unmoving
As flint or marble, turned away, her eyes   490
Fixed on the ground: the tears were vain, the words,
Meant to be soothing, foolish; she turned away,
His enemy forever, to the shadows
Where Sychaeus, her former husband, took her
With love for love, and sorrow for her sorrow.
And still Aeneas wept for her, being troubled
By the injustice of her doom; his pity
Followed her going.
                        They went on. They came
To the farthest fields, whose tenants are the warriors,
Illustrious throng. Here Tydeus came to meet him,   500
Parthenopaeus came, and pale Adrastus,[32]
A fighter's ghost, and many, many others,

---

[31] Some of these figures (all women) were evil, some admirable. Procris' jealousy of her
husband led to his killing her by accident; Phaedra nursed a guilty, unrequited love for her
stepson; Eriphyle, having been bribed, sent her husband to his death in war and was then, in
return, killed by her son; Laodamia, on the other hand, was the faithful wife of the first man
to die at Troy and gave up her life to be with him after his death. The sex-changed Caeneus
had been seduced, as a maiden named Caenis, by Neptune.

[32] Three of the seven heroes who led a famous siege of the city of Thebes.

Mourned in the world above, and doomed in battle,
Leaders of Troy, in long array; Aeneas
Sighed as he saw them: Medon; Polyboetes,
The priest of Ceres; Glaucus; and Idaeus
Still keeping arms and chariot;[33] three brothers,
Antenor's sons; Thersilochus; a host
To right and left of him, and when they see him,
One sight is not enough; they crowd around him,   510
Linger, and ask the reasons for his coming.
But Agamemnon's men, the Greek battalions,
Seeing him there, and his arms in shadow gleaming,
Tremble in panic, turn to flee for refuge,
As once they used to, toward their ships, but where
Are the ships now? They try to shout, in terror;
But only a thin and piping treble issues
To mock their mouths, wide-open.
                              One he knew
Was here, Deiphobus, a son of Priam,
With his whole body mangled, and his features   520
Cruelly slashed, and both hands cut, and ears
Torn from his temples, and his nostrils slit
By shameful wounds. Aeneas hardly knew him,
Shivering there, and doing his best to hide
His marks of punishment; unhailed, he hailed him:—
"Deiphobus, great warrior, son of Teucer,
Whose cruel punishment was this? Whose license
Abused you so? I heard, it seems, a story
Of that last night, how you had fallen, weary
With killing Greeks at last; I built a tomb,   530
Although no body lay there, in your honor,
Three times I cried, aloud, over your spirit,
Where now your name and arms keep guard. I could not,
Leaving my country, find my friend, to give him
Proper interment in the earth he came from."
And Priam's son replied:—"Nothing, dear comrade,
Was left undone; the dead man's shade was given
All ceremony due. It was my own fortune
And a Spartan woman's[34] deadliness that sunk me
Under these evils; she it was who left me   540
These souvenirs. You know how falsely happy
We were on that last night; I need not tell you.
When that dread horse came leaping over our walls,
Pregnant with soldiery, she led the dancing,
A solemn rite, she called it, with Trojan women
Screaming their bacchanals;[35] she raised the torches

---

[33] Idaeus had been charioteer to Priam, king of Troy.
[34] Helen, who had left her husband, Menelaus, and run off to Troy with Paris; after Paris's death she had become the wife of Deiphobus.
[35] Wild revels in honor of Bacchus, god of wine. Helen carried one of the torches customary in such revels but used it treacherously, as a signal to the Greeks.

High on the citadel; she called the Greeks.
Then—I was worn with trouble, drugged in slumber,
Resting in our ill-omened bridal chamber,
With sleep as deep and sweet as death upon me—   550
Then she, that paragon of helpmates, deftly
Moved all the weapons from the house; my sword,
Even, she stole from underneath my pillow,
Opened the door, and called in Menelaus,
Hoping, no doubt, to please her loving husband,
To win forgetfulness of her old sinning.
It is quickly told: they broke into the chamber,
The two of them, and with them, as accomplice,
Ulysses came, the crime-contriving bastard.[36]
O gods, pay back the Greeks; grant the petition   560
If goodness asks for vengeance! But you, Aeneas,
A living man—what chance has brought you here?
Vagrant of ocean, god-inspired,—which are you?
What chance has worn you down, to come, in sadness,
To these confusing sunless dwelling-places?"
       While they were talking, Aurora's rosy car
Had halfway crossed the heaven; all their time
Might have been spent in converse, but the Sibyl
Hurried them forward:—"Night comes on, Aeneas;
We waste the hours with tears. We are at the cross-road,   570
Now; here we turn to the right, where the pathway leads
On to Elysium, under Pluto's ramparts.
Leftward is Tartarus, and retribution,
The terminal of the wicked, and their dungeon."
Deiphobus left them, saying, "O great priestess,
Do not be angry with me; I am going;
I shall not fail the roll-call of the shadows.
Pride of our race, go on; may better fortune
Attend you!" and, upon the word, he vanished.
       As he looked back, Aeneas saw, to his left,   580
Wide walls beneath a cliff, a triple rampart,
A river running fire, Phlegethon's torrent,
Rocks roaring in its course, a gate, tremendous,
Pillars of adamant, a tower of iron,
Too strong for men, too strong for even gods
To batter down in warfare, and behind them
A Fury, sentinel in bloody garments,
Always on watch, by day, by night. He heard
Sobbing and groaning there, the crack of the lash,
The clank of iron, the sound of dragging shackles.   590
The noise was terrible; Aeneas halted,
Asking, "What forms of crime are these, O maiden?
What harrying punishment, what horrible outcry?"
She answered:—"O great leader of the Trojans,

---

[36] The insult is meant literally by Deiphobus, suggesting actual infidelity by Ulysses' mother.

I have never crossed that threshold of the wicked;
No pure soul is permitted entrance thither,
But Hecate, by whose order I was given
Charge of Avernus' groves, my guide, my teacher,
Told me how gods exact the toll of vengeance.
The monarch here, merciless Rhadamanthus,[37]   600
Punishes guilt, and hears confession; he forces
Acknowledgment of crime; no man in the world,
No matter how cleverly he hides his evil,
No matter how much he smiles at his own slyness,
Can fend atonement off; the hour of death
Begins his sentence. Tisiphone, the Fury,
Leaps at the guilty with her scourge; her serpents
Are whips of menace as she calls her sisters.
Imagine the gates, on jarring hinge, rasp open,
You would see her in the doorway, a shape, a sentry,   610
Savage, implacable. Beyond, still fiercer,
The monstrous Hydra dwells; her fifty throats
Are black, and open wide, and Tartarus
Is black, and open wide, and it goes down
To darkness, sheer deep down, and twice the distance
That earth is from Olympus.[38] At the bottom
The Titans crawl, Earth's oldest breed, hurled under
By thunderbolts; here lie the giant twins,
Aloeus' sons, who laid their hands on heaven
And tried to pull down Jove; Salmoneus here   620
Atones for high presumption,—it was he
Who aped Jove's noise and fire, wheeling his horses
Triumphant through his city in Elis, cheering
And shaking the torch, and claiming divine homage,
The arrogant fool, to think his brass was lightning,
His horny-footed horses beat out thunder!
Jove showed him what real thunder was, what lightning
Spoke from immortal cloud, what whirlwind fury
Came sweeping from the heaven to overtake him.
Here Tityos, Earth's giant son, lies sprawling   630
Over nine acres, with a monstrous vulture
Gnawing, with crooked beak, vitals and liver
That grow as they are eaten; eternal anguish,
Eternal feast.[39] Over another hangs
A rock, about to fall; and there are tables
Set for a banquet, gold with royal splendor,

[37] Brother of Minos and, like him, a judge in the Lower World.
[38] The dwelling place of the gods.
[39] The Titans, giant offspring of Heaven and Earth, fought alongside Saturn in his unsuccessful struggle against his son Jupiter. The sons of Aloeus, Otus and Ephialtes, were giants who tried to assault the gods by piling the mountains Ossa and Pelion on top of Olympus. Salmoneus imitated Jove's thunder, in a city sacred to Jove, by driving a brass chariot over a brass bridge. Tityos had sexually assaulted the goddess Latona, who was avenged by her children Apollo and Diana.

But if a hand goes out to touch the viands,
The Fury drives it back with fire and yelling.
Why name them all, Pirithous, the Lapiths,
Ixion?[40] The roll of crime would take forever.   640
Whoever, in his lifetime, hated his brother,
Or struck his father down; whoever cheated
A client, or was miserly—how many
Of these there seem to be!—whoever went
To treasonable war, or broke a promise
Made to his lord, whoever perished, slain
Over adultery, all these, walled in,
Wait here their punishment. Seek not to know
Too much about their doom. The stone is rolled,
The wheel keeps turning; Theseus forever   650
Sits in dejection; Phlegyas, accursed,
Cries through the halls forever: *Being warned,*
Learn justice; reverence the gods![41] The man
Who sold his country is here in hell; the man
Who altered laws for money; and a father
Who knew his daughter's bed. All of them dared,
And more than dared, achieved, unspeakable
Ambitions. If I had a hundred tongues,
A hundred iron throats, I could not tell
The fullness of their crime and punishment."   660
And then she added:—"Come: resume the journey,
Fulfill the mission; let us hurry onward.
I see the walls the Cyclops[42] made, the portals
Under the archway, where, the orders tell us,
Our tribute must be set." They went together
Through the way's darkness, came to the doors, and halted,
And at the entrance Aeneas, having sprinkled
His body with fresh water, placed the bough
Golden before the threshold. The will of the goddess
Had been performed, the proper task completed.   670
    They came to happy places, the joyful dwelling,
The lovely greenery of the groves of the blessèd.
Here ampler air invests the fields with light,
Rose-colored, with familiar stars and sun.
Some grapple on the grassy wrestling-ground
In exercise and sport, and some are dancing,
And others singing; in his trailing robe
Orpheus[43] strums the lyre; the seven clear notes
Accompany the dance, the song. And heroes
Are there, great-souled, born in the happier years,   680

---

[40] Ixion, king of the Lapiths, had attempted a sexual assault on Juno; for Pirithous (son of Ixion), see lines 139–40 and note and lines 415–21.

[41] Theseus was punished, perhaps, for his attempt to abduct Proserpina. Phlegyas had burned Apollo's temple at Delphi.

[42] The laborers in the forge of Vulcan, the blacksmith god of fire.

[43] In myth, the prototype of poets and musicians. See note to lines 136–40.

Ilus, Assaracus; the city's founder,
Prince Dardanus.[44] Far off, Aeneas wonders,
Seeing the phantom arms, the chariots,
The spears fixed in the ground, the chargers browsing,
Unharnessed, over the plain. Whatever, living,
The men delighted in, whatever pleasure
Was theirs in horse and chariot, still holds them
Here under the world. To right and left, they banquet
In the green meadows, and a joyful chorus
Rises through groves of laurel, whence the river   690
Runs to the upper world.[45] The band of heroes
Dwell here, all those whose mortal wounds were suffered
In fighting for the fatherland; and poets,
The good, the pure, the worthy of Apollo;
Those who discovered truth and made life nobler;
Those who served others—all, with snowy fillets
Binding their temples, throng the lovely valley.
And these the Sibyl questioned, most of all
Musaeus,[46] for he towered above the center
Of that great throng:—"O happy souls, O poet,   700
Where does Anchises dwell? For him we come here.
For him we have traversed Erebus'[47] great rivers."
And he replied:—"It is all our home, the shady
Groves, and the streaming meadows, and the softness
Along the river-banks. No fixed abode
Is ours at all; but if it is your pleasure,
Cross over the ridge with me; I will guide you there
By easy going." And so Musaeus led them
And from the summit showed them fields, all shining,
And they went on over and down.   710
    Deep in a valley of green, father Anchises
Was watching, with deep earnestness, the spirits
Whose destiny was light, and counting them over,
All of his race to come, his dear descendants,
Their fates and fortunes and their works and ways,
And as he saw Aeneas coming toward him
Over the meadow, his hands reached out with yearning,
He was moved to tears, and called:—"At last, my son,—
Have you really come, at last? and the long road nothing
To a son who loves his father? Do I, truly,   720
See you, and hear your voice? I was thinking so,
I was hoping so, I was counting off the days,
And I was right about it. O my son!
What a long journey, over land and water,
Yours must have been! What buffeting of danger!

---

[44] Three illustrious ancestors of the Trojans.
[45] The river is Eridanus, believed in fable to be the underground source of the river Po.
[46] Legendary poet, taught by Orpheus.
[47] The god of darkness; more generally, the Lower World itself.

I feared, so much, the Libyan realm would hurt you."
And his son answered:—"It was your spirit, father,
Your sorrowful shade, so often met, that led me
To find these portals. The ships ride safe at anchor,
Safe in the Tuscan sea. Embrace me, father;   730
Let hand join hand in love; do not forsake me."
And as he spoke, the tears streamed down. Three times
He reached out toward him, and three times the image
Fled like the breath of the wind or a dream on wings.
    He saw, in a far valley, a separate grove
Where the woods stir and rustle, and a river,
The Lethe,[48] gliding past the peaceful places,
And tribes of people thronging, hovering over,
Innumerable as the bees in summer
Working the bright-hued flowers, and the shining   740
Of the white lilies, murmuring and humming.
Aeneas, filled with wonder, asks the reason
For what he does not know, who are the people
In such a host, and to what river coming?
Anchises answers:—"These are spirits, ready
Once more for life; they drink of Lethe's water
The soothing potion of forgetfulness.
I have longed, for long, to show them to you, name them,
Our children's children; Italy discovered,
So much the greater happiness, my son."   750
"But, O my father, is it thinkable
That souls would leave this blessedness, be willing
A second time to bear the sluggish body,
Trade Paradise for earth? Alas, poor wretches,
Why such a mad desire for light?" Anchises
Gives detailed answer: "First, my son, a spirit
Sustains all matter, heaven and earth and ocean,
The moon, the stars; mind quickens mass, and moves it.
Hence comes the race of man, of beast, of wingèd
Creatures of air, of the strange shapes which ocean   760
Bears down below his mottled marble surface.
All these are blessed with energy from heaven;
The seed of life is a spark of fire, but the body
A clod of earth, a clog, a mortal burden.
Hence humans fear, desire, grieve, and are joyful,
And even when life is over, all the evil
Ingrained so long, the adulterated mixture,
The plagues and pestilences of the body
Remain, persist. So there must be a cleansing,
By penalty, by punishment, by fire,   770
By sweep of wind, by water's absolution,

---

[48] River of forgetfulness.

Before the guilt is gone. Each of us suffers
His own peculiar ghost.[49] But the day comes
When we are sent through wide Elysium,
The Fields of the Blessed, a few of us, to linger
Until the turn of time, the wheel of ages,
Wears off the taint, and leaves the core of spirit
Pure sense, pure flame.[50] A thousand years pass over
And the god calls the countless host to Lethe
Where memory is annulled, and souls are willing   780
Once more to enter into mortal bodies."
    The discourse ended; the father drew his son
And his companion toward the hum, the center
Of the full host; they came to rising ground
Where all the long array was visible,
Anchises watching, noting, every comer.
"Glory to come, my son, illustrious spirits
Of Dardan lineage, Italian offspring,
Heirs of our name, begetters of our future!
These I will name for you and tell our fortunes:[51]   790
First, leaning on a headless spear, and standing
Nearest the light, that youth, the first to rise
To the world above, is Silvius; his name
Is Alban; in his veins Italian blood
Will run with Trojan; he will be the son
Of your late age; Lavinia will bear him,
A king and sire of kings; from him our race
Will rule in Alba Longa. Near him, Procas,
A glory to the Trojan race; and Capys,
And Numitor, and Silvius Aeneas,   800
Resembling you in name, in arms, in goodness,
If ever he wins the Alban kingdom over.
What fine young men they are! What strength, what prowess!
The civic oak already shades their foreheads.
These will found cities, Gabii, Fidenae,
Nomentum; they will crown the hills with towers
Above Collatia, Inuus fortress, Bola,
Cora, all names to be, thus far ungiven.
    "And there will be a son of Mars; his mother

---

[49] This notoriously elusive aphorism, typical of the difficulties in translating Virgil, probably means something like "Each endures his own penance and lives with his own purgatorial
consciousness" (though other meanings have been suggested).
   [50] Certain rare and noble spirits remain in Elysian bliss rather than being reincarnated.
Anchises is one of these.
   [51] In lines 791–808, Anchises describes the Trojan lineage in Italy up to the time of Romulus,
legendary founder (in 753 B.C., several centuries after Aeneas) of Rome proper. Alba Longa,
forerunner of Rome, was the city founded by Ascanius (as we are told in I.278–83). Silvius
was third in the line to rule after Aeneas and Ascanius/Iulus. The persons listed in lines 798–800
were subsequent Alban kings (one of whom, Silvius Aeneas, was denied the throne for a long
time). The aboriginal towns mentioned in lines 805–808 were near Rome.

Is Ilia, and his name is Romulus, 810
Assaracus' descendant. On his helmet
See, even now, twin plumes; his father's honor
Confers distinction on him for the world.
Under his auspices Rome, that glorious city,
Will bound her power by earth, her pride by heaven,
Happy in hero sons, one wall surrounding
Her seven hills, even as Cybele, riding
Through Phrygian cities, wears her crown of towers,
Rejoicing in her offspring, and embracing
A hundred children of the gods, her children, 820
Celestials, all of them, at home in heaven.[52]
Turn the eyes now this way; behold the Romans,
Your very own. These are Iulus' children,[53]
The race to come. One promise you have heard
Over and over: here is its fulfillment,
The son of a god, Augustus Caesar, founder
Of a new age of gold, in lands where Saturn
Ruled long ago;[54] he will extend his empire
Beyond the Indies, beyond the normal measure
Of years and constellations, where high Atlas 830
Turns on his shoulders the star-studded world.[55]
Maeotia[56] and the Caspian seas are trembling
As heaven's oracles predict his coming,
And all the seven mouths of Nile are troubled.
Not even Hercules, in all his travels,
Covered so much of the world, from Erymanthus
To Lerna; nor did Bacchus, driving his tigers
From Nysa's summit.[57] How can hesitation
Keep us from deeds to make our prowess greater?
What fear can block us from Ausonian[58] land? 840
     "And who is that one yonder, wearing the olive,
Holding the sacrifice? I recognize him,
That white-haired king of Rome, who comes from Cures,
A poor land, to a mighty empire, giver
Of law to the young town. His name is Numa.

---

[52] Cybele, a Phrygian (Trojan) deity, considered the mother of the gods, was associated with the building and fortifying of cities.

[53] Iulus, Aeneas' son, was regarded as the progenitor of the Julian clan of Virgil's time, and thus of the line of Caesars.

[54] Augustus was "son of a god" because Julius Caesar, of whom Augustus was the adopted son, was deified at his death. Saturn, after being deposed by his son Jupiter, was supposed to have reigned in Italy during the mythical Age of Gold.

[55] The giant Atlas (sometimes identified with the north African mountain) was imagined as supporting the heavens on his shoulders.

[56] Region north of the Black Sea.

[57] Erymanthus, a mountain range, and Lerna, a lake, were in Greece; among the Twelve Labors of Hercules were victories over monsters inhabiting these places. The mountain Nysa (located in India, according to one tradition) was the boyhood home of Bacchus, the god of wine, whose chariot was drawn by tigers.

[58] Italian.

Near him is Tullus; he will rouse to arms
A race grown sluggish, little used to triumph.
Beyond him Ancus, even now too boastful,
Too fond of popular favor.[59] And then the Tarquins,
And the avenger Brutus, proud of spirit,   850
Restorer of the balance. He shall be
First holder of the consular power; his children
Will stir up wars again, and he, for freedom
And her sweet sake, will calm down judgment on them,
Unhappy, however future men may praise him,
In love of country and intense ambition.[60]
    "There are the Decii, and there the Drusi,
A little farther off, and stern Torquatus,
The man with the axe, and Camillus, the regainer
Of standards lost. And see those two, resplendent   860
In equal arms, harmonious friendly spirits
Now, in the shadow of night, but if they ever
Come to the world of light, alas, what warfare,
What battle-lines, what slaughter they will fashion,
Each for the other, one from Alpine ramparts
Descending, and the other ranged against him
With armies from the east, father and son
Through marriage, Pompey and Caesar.[61] O my children,
Cast out the thoughts of war, and do not murder
The flower of our country. O my son,   870
Whose line descends from heaven, let the sword
Fall from the hand, be leader in forbearing!
    "Yonder is one who, victor over Corinth,
Will ride in triumph home, famous for carnage
Inflicted on the Greeks; near him another,
Destroyer of old Argos and Mycenae
Where Agamemnon ruled; he will strike down
A king descended from Achilles; Pydna
Shall be revenge for Pallas' ruined temple,
For Trojan ancestors. Who would pass over,   880
Without a word, Cossus, or noble Cato,
The Gracchi, or those thunderbolts of warfare,
The Scipios, Libya's ruin, or Fabricius
Mighty with little, or Serranus, ploughing

---

[59] The religious and civic lawgiver Numa Pompilius, the warlike Tullus, and Ancus (according to Virgil, a demagogue) were, respectively, the second, third, and fourth kings of Rome (Romulus having been the first).

[60] Brutus (not to be confused with the Brutus who assassinated Julius Caesar centuries later) expelled the last (seventh) of the Roman kings, Tarquinius Superbus, and founded the Roman republic in 509 B.C. He had his sons executed for attempting to restore the old monarchical line.

[61] The Decii, Torquatus, and Camillus were military or civic heroes of the fourth and third centuries B.C. The Drusi were ancestors of Livia, wife of Caesar Augustus. The civil war (49–45 B.C.) between the forces of Julius Caesar and those of his son-in-law Pompey, in Virgil's own lifetime, had been part of the chain of events culminating in the accession of Augustus.

The humble furrow? My tale must hurry on:
I see the Fabii next, and their great Quintus
Who brought us back an empire by delaying.[62]
Others, no doubt, will better mould the bronze
To the semblance of soft breathing, draw, from marble,
The living countenance; and others plead   890
With greater eloquence, or learn to measure,
Better than we, the pathways of the heaven,
The risings of the stars; remember, Roman,
To rule the people under law, to establish
The way of peace, to battle down the haughty,
To spare the meek. Our fine arts, these, forever."[63]
    Anchises paused a moment, and they marvelled,
And he went on:—"See, how Marcellus[64] triumphs,
Glorious over all, with the great trophies
Won when he slew the captain of the Gauls,   900
Leader victorious over leading foeman.
When Rome is in great trouble and confusion
He will establish order, Gaul and Carthage
Go down before his sword, and triple trophies
Be given Romulus in dedication."
    There was a young man going with Marcellus,
Brilliant in shining armor, bright in beauty,
But sorrowful, with downcast eyes. Aeneas
Broke in, to ask his father: "Who is this youth[65]
Attendant on the hero? A son of his?   910
One of his children's children? How the crowd
Murmurs and hums around him! what distinction,
What presence, in his person! But dark night
Hovers around his head with mournful shadow.
Who is he, father?" And Anchises answered:—
"Great sorrow for our people! O my son,
Ask not to know it. This one fate will only
Show to the world; he will not be permitted
Any long sojourn. Rome would be too mighty,

---

[62] The "victor over Corinth" (line 873) was Mummius; the "another" of line 875 was probably Paullus (both second century B.C.). The latter, by defeating a Greek opponent, descended from Achilles, at the battle of Pydna, avenged Greek desecration of the Trojan temple of Pallas Athena during the Trojan War; see I.48–50, II.430–32 These two heroes, along with the other men named in lines 881–87, were among the greatest of the Roman military and political figures from the fifth through the second centuries B.C. The legacy of the episode with Dido is hinted at through the mention of the two Scipios and Quintus Fabius Maximus ("Cunctator," or "Delayer," famous for his drawn-out avoidance tactics), all three of whom won victories over Carthage in the Punic Wars (third and second centuries B.C.).

[63] In these memorable lines, one of the most famous passages in all of literature, the "Others" (line 888), with whose accomplishments Anchises is comparing those of the Romans, are primarily the Greeks. In oratory the Greeks were not in fact superior, but Anchises concedes even this area, so as to keep the distinction between the two peoples clean and emphatic.

[64] Roman general of the third century B.C.

[65] The Younger Marcellus—descendant of the Marcellus just described, nephew and son-in-law of Caesar Augustus, and presumed successor to him—died of malaria in 23 B.C. at the age of nineteen.

Too great in the gods' sight, were this gift hers. 920
What lamentation will the field of Mars[66]
Raise to the city! Tiber, gliding by
The new-built tomb, the funeral state, bear witness!
No youth from Trojan stock will ever raise
His ancestors so high in hope, no Roman
Be such a cause for pride. Alas for goodness,
Alas for old-time honor, and the arm
Invincible in war! Against him no one,
Whether on foot or foaming horse, would come
In battle and depart unscathed. Poor boy, 930
If you should break the cruel fates; if only—
You are to be Marcellus. Let me scatter
Lilies, or dark-red flowers, bringing honor
To my descendant's shade; let the gift be offered,
However vain the tribute."
    So through the whole wide realm they went together,
Anchises and his son, from fields of air
Learning and teaching of the fame and glory,
The wars to come, the toils to face, or flee from,
Latinus' city and the Latin peoples, 940
The love of what would be.
                    There are two portals,
Twin gates of Sleep, one made of horn, where easy
Release is given true shades, the other gleaming
White ivory, whereby the false dreams issue
To the upper air. Aeneas and the Sibyl
Part from Anchises at the second portal.[67]
He goes to the ships, again, rejoins his comrades,
Sails to Caieta's[68] harbor, and the vessels
Rest on their mooring-lines.

SUMMARY OF BOOKS VII–VIII

The Trojans continue their northward voyage along the western coast of Italy. They land and, while eating their meal off bread platters, suddenly realize that their acts fulfill the prophecy of hunger and that they are at the destined place. On the following day they reach the river Tiber and the city of King Latinus. He recognizes in Aeneas the realization of a prophecy that his daughter Lavinia would marry a stranger. At Juno's instigation, the Italian hero Turnus, a suitor of Lavinia who is jealous of Aeneas, stirs up opposition to the Trojans, and Aeneas prepares for war with him. Guided by a dream, Aeneas enlists the support of Evander, whose city lies on the future site of Rome. Aeneas' mother Venus presents him with a shield, made by the god Vulcan, on which important events in the future history of Rome have been carved, a history that culminates in the victory of Augustus over Antony and Cleopatra at Actium:

---

[66] The Campus Martius, site of Marcellus' tomb.

[67] Why Aeneas should emerge through the gate of falsehood is one of the most mystifying problems in the entire poem. Virgil may mean no more than that Aeneas ends his visit to the Lower World early in the night, since dreams dreamt at that time were considered deceiving. (The reliable dreams were those dreamt just before waking.) But the apparently deliberate effect of high-solemn mystery suggests some weightier meaning.

[68] A town about thirty-five miles up the coast from Cumae and the modern Naples.

from BOOK VIII: AENEAS AT THE SITE OF ROME

And the bright goddess through the clouds of heaven
Came bringing gifts, seeing her son alone
By the cold river in the quiet valley,
And spoke to him:—"Behold, the gifts made ready
By Vulcan's promised skill. Fear not, my son,
To face the wars with Turnus and the Latins!"
After the word, the embrace. She placed the armor,
All shining in his sight, against an oak-tree;   630
Rejoicing in the gift, the honor, he turned
His eyes to these, over and over again,
Could not be satisfied, took in his hands
The helmet with the terrible plumes and flame,
The fatal sword, the breastplate, made of bronze,
Fire-colored, huge, shining the way a cloud,
Dark-blue, turns crimson under the slanting sun,
The greaves of gold refined and smooth electrum,[1]
The spear, the final masterpiece, the shield.
    Hereon the great prophetic Lord of Fire   640
Had carved the story out, the stock to come,
The wars, each one in order, all the tale
Of Italy and Roman triumph.[2] Here
In Mars' green cave the she-wolf gives her udders
To the twin boys, turning half round to lick them,
And neither is afraid, and both are playing.[3]
Another scene presents the Circus-games,
When Romans took their Sabine brides, and war
Broke out between old Tatius and the sons
Of Romulus, and was ended, monarchs pledging   650
Peace at the altars over sacrifice.[4]
Mettus, the false, by the wild horses drawn
And quartered, sheds his life-blood over the brambles;[5]
Porsena, the besieger, rings the city
For Tarquin's sake, exile and tyrant; Romans

---

[1] Greaves were armor for the shins. Electrum was an alloy of gold and silver.

[2] The divinely made shield of Achilles in Homer's *Iliad*, Book XVIII, contains in pictures a synopsis of the ways of human life, in fairly universal terms. Virgil's equivalent, for Aeneas, is a vision of the glories of Roman history to come and of the Roman character.

[3] To make his usurped power secure, Amulius attempted to have his great-nephews, the infant Romulus and his twin brother, Remus, drowned in the Tiber, but they survived, being suckled by a she-wolf in the cave of the Lupercal on the site of Rome. Romulus grew up to found the city and establish its line of kings.

[4] The men of the newly founded city, having no women, seized them from Sabines who had come to watch the games in honor of Neptune being celebrated in the Circus, or amphitheater, of Rome. The seizing of the women caused war between the Romans and Sabines (ruled by Tatius), but it was halted through the intervention of the women, and the two peoples became allies.

[5] Mettus Fufetius was executed in the way described when, after having promised to fight for Rome during one of its early regional conflicts, he treacherously withdrew his troops from battle.

Rush on the steel for freedom; Clelia breaks
Her bonds to swim the river; and Horatius
Breaks down the bridge.[6] The guardian Manlius
Holds the high capitol and that crude palace
Fresh with the straw of Romulus; the goose   660
Flutters in silver through the colonnades
Shrieking alarm; the Gauls are near in darkness,
Golden their hair, their clothing, and their necks
Gleam white in collars of gold, and each one carries
Two Alpine javelins; they have long shields.
Near them, the Fire-god sets the priests with caps
Of wool, the miracle of the shields from heaven,
The Salii dancing, the Luperci naked,
And the chaste matrons riding through the city
In cushioned chariots.[7] Far off, he adds   670
The seats of Hell, the lofty gates of Pluto,
Penance for sin: Catiline, with the Furies
Making him cower; farther off, the good,
With Cato giving laws.[8] And all this scene
Bound with the likeness of the swelling ocean,
Blue water and whitecap, where the dolphins playing
Leap with a curve of silver. In the center
Actium,[9] the ships of bronze, Leucate[10] burning
Hot with the glow of war, and waves on fire
With molten gold. Augustus Caesar stands   680
High on the lofty stern; his temples flame
With double fire, and over his head there dawns

---

[6] After the Romans expelled their savage and tyrannical king Tarquinius Superbus, the Etrurian king Lars Porsena of Clusium attacked Rome in an attempt to restore Tarquinius to the throne. In the face of the enemy, Horatius held a bridge over the Tiber until it could be destroyed. This helped save the newborn (509 B.C.) Roman republic. Clelia was a young Roman woman who, having been taken hostage by Porsena, escaped by swimming the Tiber, was then returned to Porsena by the Romans, and finally was freed by Porsena, along with other prisoners, because he admired her courage.

[7] When Gauls from the Alps threatened the citadel of Rome in 390 B.C., the Roman consul Manlius was alerted to their night attack by the cackling of the sacred geese kept at the Capitol, where the early thatched hut of the founder Romulus was also preserved. Lines 666–70 describe religious celebrations of Roman victory and also acknowledge the Roman matrons, whose right to ride in luxury was earned by earlier contributions of their gold and jewels to the state.

[8] We see scenes of contrasted evil and good: Catiline, who in 63 B.C. plotted against the Roman government and is now punished in Hell by the Furies, and Cato the Younger (95–46 B.C.), the model of old-fashioned Roman virtue.

[9] The climactic scene, at the center of the shield, shows the naval victory by the forces of Octavian (later Caesar Augustus) over the combined forces of Mark Antony, his rival for power, and Cleopatra, the Egyptian queen who had become Antony's consort. The great battle took place at Actium, off western Greece, in 31 B.C.; it ended decades of Roman civil war. Virgil presents this battle as a conflict between Roman virtue and Eastern luxury, decadence, and religious barbarism. Antony's and Cleopatra's fleets returned to Egypt, after she panicked, and a year later both he and she died defeated, leaving Octavian in sole power and bringing peace to Rome.

[10] A promontory near Actium that served as base for Octavian's fleet.

His father's star.[11] Agrippa[12] leads a column
With favoring wind and god, the naval garland
Wreathing his temples. Antony assembles
Egypt and all the East; Antony, victor
Over the lands of dawn and the Red Sea,
Marshals the foes of Rome, himself a Roman,
With—horror!—an Egyptian wife. The surge
Boils under keel, the oar-blades churn the waters, 690
The triple-pointed beaks drive through the billows,
You would think that mountains swam and battled mountains,
That islands were uprooted in their anger.
Fireballs and shafts of steel are slanting showers,
The fields of Neptune redden with the slaughter.
The queen drives on her warriors, unseeing
The double snakes of death;[13] rattle and cymbals
Compete with bugle and trumpet. Monstrous gods,
Of every form and fashion, one, Anubis,
Shaped like a dog, wield their outrageous weapons 700
In wrath at Venus, Neptune, and Minerva.
Mars, all in steel, storms through the fray; the Furies
Swoop from the sky; Discord exults; Bellona,[14]
With bloody scourge, comes lashing; and Apollo
From Actium bends his bow. Egypt and India,
Sabaeans and Arabians, flee in terror.
And the contagion takes the queen, who loosens
The sheets to slackness, courts the wind, in terror,
Pale at the menace of death. And the Nile comes
To meet her, a protecting god, his mantle 710
Spread wide, to bring a beaten woman home.
And Caesar enters Rome triumphant, bringing
Immortal offerings, three times a hundred
New altars through the city. Streets are loud
With gladness, games, rejoicing; all the temples
Are filled with matrons praying at the altars,
Are heaped with solemn sacrifice. And Caesar,
Seated before Apollo's shining threshold,
Reviews the gifts, and hangs them on the portals.
In long array the conquered file, their garments, 720
Their speech, as various as their arms, the Nomads,
The naked Africans, Leleges, Carians,
Gelonians with quivers, the Morini,

---

[11] A comet representing the spirit of the late Julius Caesar was supposed to have appeared in 43 B.C. in honor of Octavian, his adopted son; thereafter Octavian wore a star on his helmet.

[12] War minister and commander of Octavian's forces at Actium.

[13] The ill-omened double snakes are especially appropriate to Cleopatra because she afterward committed suicide by allowing herself to be bitten by asps.

[14] Goddess of war.

Of mortals most remote, Euphrates moving
With humbler waves, the two-mouthed Rhine, Araxes,
Chafing beneath his bridge.[15]
            All this Aeneas
Sees on his mother's gift, the shield of Vulcan,
And, without understanding, is proud and happy
As he lifts to his shoulder all that fortune,
The fame and glory of his children's children.   730

SUMMARY OF BOOKS IX–XII

Turnus' army has been laying siege to the Trojan camp in Aeneas' absence. Aeneas returns to the battlefield with new allies, including Evander's forces under the command of his young son Pallas. A general battle ensues. Evander's troops are nearly defeated when Pallas rallies them, but Pallas is then killed by Turnus, who savagely exults over the defeated youth and callously strips him of his armor. Aeneas is enraged and grief-stricken, all the more because he had been entrusted by Evander with the care of his dear son. Aeneas seeks Turnus in order to avenge Pallas' death, but Juno lures Turnus away from the battlefield. With great ceremony, Aeneas sends Pallas' body back to his father, and a twelve-day truce is declared.

An agreement is reached under which Aeneas and Turnus will settle the war through single combat. But the agreement is violated by the Latins and general fighting breaks out again:

from BOOK XII: THE FINAL COMBAT

    And now his goddess-mother sent Aeneas
A change of purpose, to direct his column
More quickly toward the town, confuse the Latins   610
With sudden onslaught.[1] He was tracking Turnus
Here, there, all up and down the columns, watching,
Shifting his gaze, and so he saw that city
Immune from that fierce warfare, calm and peaceful.
The vision of a greater fight comes to him:
He calls Sergestus, Mnestheus, brave Serestus,
And takes position on a mound; the Trojans
Come massing toward him, shield and spear held ready.
And as he stands above them, he gives the orders:—
"Let there be no delay: great Jove is with us.   620
Let no man go more slackly, though this venture
Is new and unexpected. That city yonder,
The cause of war, the kingdom of Latinus,
Unless they own our mastery, acknowledge
Defeat, declare obedience, I will topple,

---

[15] The list of names is primarily geographic symbolism honoring Caesar Augustus and Rome. The wandering Nomads (Numidians) were from Africa, the Leleges and Carians from Asia, the Gelonians and Morini from eastern and northern Europe. The Araxes is the river Aras, in Armenia.

[1] Aeneas decides to assault Latinus' city directly rather than engage the enemy troops on the field outside the city.

Level its smoking roof-tops to the ground.
Or should I wait until it suits prince Turnus
To face the duel with me, and, once beaten,
Consent to fight again? This [2] is the head,
O citizens, this the evil crown of warfare.   630
Hurry, bring firebrands, win from fire the treaty!"
His words inflame their zeal, and, all together
They form a wedge; a great mass moves to the wall,
Ladders and sudden fire appear from nowhere;
The guards at the gate are butchered; steel is flying,
The sky is dark with arrows. Toward the city
Aeneas lifts his hand, rebukes Latinus,
Calling the gods to witness that his will
Was not for battle, it was forced upon him
By the Italians, double treaty-breakers,   640
His foes for now the second time. [3] The townsmen
Quarrel among themselves: "Open the town!",
Cry some, "Admit the Trojans!" and would drag
The king himself to the ramparts. Others hurry
With arms, man the defenses. When a shepherd
Trails bees to their hive in the cleft of a rock and fills it
With smarting smoke, there is fright and noise and fury
Within the waxen camp, and anger sharpened
With buzzing noises, and a black smell rises
With a blind sound, inside the rock, and rolling   650
Smoke lifts to empty air.
                        Now a new sorrow
Came to the weary Latins, shook the city
To its foundations, utterly. The queen
Had seen the Trojans coming and the walls
Under attack and fire along the gables
And no Rutulian column, nowhere Turnus
Coming to help. He had been killed, her hero,
She knew at last. [4] Her mind was gone; she cried
Over and over:—"I am the guilty one,
I am the cause, the source of all these evils!"   660
And other wilder words. And then she tore
Her crimson robes, and slung a noose and fastened
The knot of an ugly death to the high rafter.
The women learned it first, and then Lavinia:
The wide hall rings with grief and lamentation;
Nails scratch at lovely faces, beautiful hair
Is torn from the head. And Rumor spreads the story

---

[2] This city.

[3] The Italians, or Latins, had first violated a treaty of alliance with the Trojans, including a plan for Aeneas to marry Latinus' daughter Lavinia, then violated the single-combat treaty.

[4] Latinus' queen, Amata, had favored Turnus and bitterly opposed Aeneas as suitor for her daughter Lavinia's hand. The Rutulians were Turnus' people.

All up and down the town, and poor Latinus,
Rending his garments, comes and stares,—wife gone,
And city falling, an old man's hoary hair 670
Greyer with bloody dust.
               And meanwhile Turnus
Out on the plain pursues the stragglers, slower
And slower now, and less and less exultant
In his triumphant car. From the city comes
A wind that bears a cry confused with terror,
Half heard, but known,—confusion, darkness, sorrow,
An uproar in the town. He checks the horses,
Pauses and listens. And his sister prompts him:[5]—
"This way, this way! The Trojans run, we follow
Where victory shows the path. Let others guard 680
The houses with their valor. The Italians
Fall in the fight before Aeneas. Let us
Send death to the Trojans, in our turn. You will not
Come off the worse, in numbers or in honor."
Turnus replies:—"O sister, I have known,
A long while since, that you were no Metiscus,
Since first you broke the treaty and joined the battle.
No use pretending you are not a goddess.
But who, from high Olympus, sent you down
To bear such labors? Was it to see your brother 690
In pitiful cruel death? What am I doing,
What chance will fortune grant me? I have seen
A man I loved more than the rest, Murranus,
A big man, slain by a big wound, go down.
Ufens is fallen, lucky or unlucky,
In that he never saw our shame; the Trojans
Have won his body and arms. Our homes are burning,
The one thing lacking up to now,—and shall I
Endure this, not refute the words of Drances
With this right hand?[6] Shall I turn my back upon them? 700
Is it so grim to die? Be kind, O shadows,[7]
Since the high gods have turned their favor from me.
A decent spirit, undisgraced, no coward,
I shall descend to you, never unworthy
Of all my ancient line."
               He had hardly spoken
When a warrior, on foaming steed, came riding

---

[5] Turnus' sister Juturna, seduced by Jupiter and granted immortality as a water nymph in recompense, has disguised herself as Metiscus, her brother's charioteer, steering the chariot away from Aeneas in the hope of postponing Turnus' fated death.

[6] Drances, in an assembly of the Latins, had denounced Turnus and (unjustly) accused him of cowardice.

[7] The gods of the Lower World. They are contrasted with the "high gods," mentioned in the following line.

Through all the enemy. His name was Saces,
And his face was badly wounded by an arrow.
He called the name of Turnus, and implored him:—
"We have no other hope; pity your people!   710
Aeneas is a lightning-bolt; he threatens
Italy's topmost towers; he will bring them down
In ruins; even now the brands[8] are flying
Along the roof-tops. They look to you, the Latins,
They look for you; and king Latinus mumbles
In doubt—who are his sons, who are his allies?[9]
The queen, who trusted you the most, has perished
By her own hand, has fled the light in terror.
Alone before the gates the brave Atinas
And Messapus hold the line. Around them, squadrons   720
Crowd close on either side, and the steel harvest
Bristles with pointed swords. And here is Turnus
Wheeling his car across a plain deserted."
        Bewildered by disaster's shifting image,
Turnus is silent, staring; shame and sadness
Boil up in that great heart, and grief and love
Driven by frenzy. He shakes off the shadows;
The light comes back to his mind. His eyes turn, blazing,
From the wheels of the car to the walls of that great city
Where the flame billowed upward, the roaring blast   730
Catching a tower, one he himself had fashioned
With jointed beams and rollers and high gangways.
"Fate is the winner now; keep out of my way,
My sister: now I follow god and fortune.
I am ready for Aeneas, ready to bear
Whatever is bitter in death. No longer, sister,
Shall I be shamed, and you behold me. Let me,
Before the final madness, be a madman!"
He bounded from the chariot, came rushing
Through spears, through enemies; his grieving sister   740
He left behind, forgotten. As a boulder
Torn from a mountain-top rolls headlong downward,
Impelled by wind, or washed by storm, or loosened
By time's erosion, and comes down the hillside
A mass possessed of evil, leaping and bounding,
And rolling with it men and trees and cattle,
So, through the broken columns, Turnus rushes
On to the city, where the blood goes deepest
Into the muddy ground, and the air whistles
With flying spears. He makes a sudden gesture,   750
Crying aloud:—"No more, no more, Rutulians!

[8] Firebrands; flaming missiles.
[9] Latinus wonders whether the women among his people are to marry Trojans or Latins.

Hold back your weapons, Latins! Whatever fortune
There may be here is mine. I am the one,
Not you, to make the treaty good, to settle
The issue with the sword. That will be better."
They all made way and gave him room.
                                        Aeneas,
Hearing the name of Turnus, leaves the city,
Forsakes the lofty walls; he has no patience
With any more delay, breaks off all projects,
Exults, a terrible thunderer in armor,   760
As huge as Athos, or as huge as Eryx,
Or even father Apennine, that mountain
Roaring above the oaks, and lifting high
His crown of shimmering trees and snowy crest.[10]
Now all men turned their eyes, Rutulians, Trojans,
Italians, those who held the lofty ramparts,
Those battering at the wall below; their shoulders
Were eased of armor now. And king Latinus
Could hardly, in amazement, trust his senses
Seeing these two big men, born worlds apart,   770
Meeting to make decision with the sword.
The plain was cleared, and they came rushing forward,
Hurling, far off, their spears; the fight is on,
The bronze shields clang and ring. Earth gives a groan.
The swords strike hard and often; luck and courage
Are blent in one. And as on mighty Sila
Or on Taburnus' mountain,[11] when two bullocks
Charge into fight head-on, and trembling herdsmen
Fall back in fear, and the herd is dumb with terror,
And heifers, hardly lowing, stare and wonder   780
Which one will rule the woodland, which one the herd
Will follow meekly after, and all the time
They gore each other with savage horns, and shoulders
And necks and ribs run streams of blood, and bellowing
Fills all the woodland,—even so, Aeneas
And Daunus' son[12] clash shield on shield; the clamor
Fills heaven. And Jupiter holds the scales in balance
With each man's destiny as weight and counter,
And one the heavier under the doom of death.

    Confident, Turnus, rising to the sword   790
Full height, is a flash of light; he strikes. The Trojans,
The Latins, cry aloud and come up standing.
But the sword is treacherous; it is broken off

---

[10] Athos and Eryx were mountains in, respectively, northern Greece and Sicily. The Apennines were the mountains forming the geographic backbone of Italy.

[11] Sila was a mountain range and forest in southern Italy, Taburnus a mountain in central Italy.

[12] Turnus was the son of Daunus and the nymph Venilia.

With the blow half spent: the fire of Turnus finds
No help except in flight. Swift as the wind
He goes, and stares at a broken blade, a hand
Unarmed. The story is that in that hurry,
That rush of his, to arms, when the steeds were harnessed,
He took Metiscus' sword, not the one Daunus
Had left him.[13] For a while it served its purpose   800
While the Trojans ran away, but when it met
The armor Vulcan forged, the mortal blade
Split off, like brittle ice, with glittering splinters
Like ice on the yellow sand. So Turnus flies
Madly across the plain in devious circles:
The Trojans ring him round, and a swamp on one side,
High walls on the other.
                              Aeneas, the pursuer,
Is none too swift: the arrow has left him hurt;[14]
His knees give way, but he keeps on, keeps coming
After the panting enemy, as a hound,   810
Running a stag to bay, at the edge of the water
Or hedged by crimson plumes,[15] darts in, and barks,
And snaps his jaws, closes and grips, is shaken
Off from the flanks again, and once more closes,
And a great noise goes up the air; the waters
Resound, and the whole sky thunders with the clamor.
Turnus has time, even in flight, for calling
Loud to Rutulians, each by name, demanding,
In terrible rage, the sword, the sword, the good one,
The one he knows. Let anybody bring it,   820
Aeneas threatens, and death and doom await him,
And the town will be a ruin. Wounded, still
He presses on. They go in five great circles,
Around and back: no game, with silly prizes,
Are they playing now; the life and blood of Turnus
Go to the winner.
                     A wild olive-tree
Stood here, with bitter leaves, sacred to Faunus,[16]
Revered by rescued sailors, who used to offer
Ex-votos[17] to the native gods, their garments
In token of gratitude. For this the Trojans   830
Cared nothing, lopped the branches off to clear
The run of the field. Aeneas' spear had fastened
Deep in the trunk where the force of the cast had brought it,

---

[13] Like Aeneas' armor, the sword Turnus inherited from Daunus had been made by the god Vulcan.
   [14] Earlier in the day, Aeneas had been put temporarily out of action when he was wounded by an anonymous archer. His mother, Venus, had helped heal his wound.
   [15] In hunting, barriers made of colorful feathers were used to scare game animals and keep them inside the hunting precincts.
   [16] King Latinus' father, a rustic god.
   [17] Offerings made in fulfillment of a vow or in acknowledgment of a prayer answered.

Stuck in the grip of the root. Aeneas, stooping,
Yanks at the shaft; he cannot equal Turnus
In speed of foot, but the javelin is wingèd.
And Turnus, in a terrible moment of panic,
Cries:—"Faunus, pity me, and Earth, most kindly,
If ever I was reverent, as Aeneas
And those he leads have not been, hold the steel, 840
Do not let go!" He prayed, and he was answered.
Aeneas tugged and wrestled, pulled and hauled,
But the wood held on. And, while he strained, Juturna
Rushed forward, once again Metiscus' double,
With the good sword for her brother. Then Venus, angry
Over such wanton interference, enters
And the root yields. The warriors, towering high,
Each one renewed in spirit, one with sword,
One with the spear, both breathing hard, are ready
For what Mars[18] has to send.
       And Juno, gazing 850
From a golden cloud to earth, watching the duel,
Heard the all-powerful king of high Olympus:—
"What will the end be now, O wife? What else
Remains? You know, and you admit you know it,
Aeneas is heaven-destined, the native hero
Become a god,[19] raised by the fates, exalted.
What are you planning? with what hope lingering on
In the cold clouds? Was it proper that a mortal
Should wound a god?[20] that the sword, once lost, be given
Turnus again?—Juturna, of course, is nothing 860
Without your help—was it proper that the beaten
Increase in violence? Stop it now, I tell you;
Listen to my entreaties: I would not have you
Devoured by grief in silence; I would not have you
Bring me, again, anxiety and sorrow,
However sweet the voice. The end has come.
To harry the Trojans over land and ocean,
To light up war unspeakable, to defile
A home with grief, to mingle bridal and sorrow,—
All this you were permitted. Go no farther! 870
That is an absolute order." And Juno, downcast
In gaze, replied:—"Great Jove, I knew your pleasure:
And therefore, much against my will, left Turnus,
Left earth. Were it not so, you would not see me
Lonely upon my airy throne in heaven,
Enduring things both worthy and unworthy,

---

[18] The god of war.
[19] In the future, Aeneas will be deified and regarded as their own hero by the natives of Italy.
[20] The "god" is Aeneas; the "mortal" is the anonymous bowsman who wounded Aeneas earlier.

But I would be down there, by flame surrounded,
Fighting in the front ranks, and hauling Trojans
To battle with their enemies. Juturna,
I urged, I own, to help her wretched brother,   880
And I approved, I own, her greater daring
For his life's sake, but I did not approve,
And this I swear by Styx, that river whose name
Binds all the gods to truth, her taking weapons,
Aiming the bow.[21] I give up now, I leave
These battles, though I hate to. I ask one favor
For Latium, for the greatness of your people,
And this no law of fate forbids: when, later,
And be it so, they join in peace, and settle
Their laws, their treaties, in a blessèd marriage,   890
Do not command the Latins, native-born,
To change their language, to be known as Trojans,
To alter speech or garb; let them be Latium,
Let Alban kings endure through all the ages,[22]
Let Roman stock, strong in Italian valor,
Prevail: since Troy has fallen, let her name
Perish and be forgotten." Smiling on her,
The great creator answered:—"You are truly
True sister of Jove and child of Saturn, nursing
Such tides of anger in the heart![23] Forget it!   900
Abate the rise of passion. The wish is granted.
I yield, and more than that,—I share your purpose.
Ausonians[24] shall keep their old tradition,
Their fathers' speech and ways; their name shall be
Even as now it is. Their sacred laws,
Their ritual, I shall add, and make all Latins
Men of a common tongue. A race shall rise
All-powerful, of mingled blood; you will see them
By virtue of devotion rise to glories
Not men nor gods have known, and no race ever   910
Will pay you equal honor."[25] And the goddess
Gave her assent, was happy, changed her purpose,
Left heaven and quit the cloud.
                              This done, the father
Formed yet another purpose, that Juturna
Should leave her fighting brother. There are, men say,

---

[21] Juturna, in a different disguise, had been instrumental in the violation of the single-combat pact.

[22] Latium was the region in west-central Italy where the action of the second half of the poem has been taking place. The royal line of Alba Longa, the city Iulus/Ascanius will found, was prophetically described by Anchises in VI.787–808.

[23] The Greek god Cronus, identified by the Romans with Saturn, was notoriously violent, fiercely devouring almost all his children.

[24] Italians.

[25] Juno was one of the three deities worshiped in the great Roman temple at the Capitol (the other two being Jupiter and Minerva).

Twin fiends, or triple, sisters named the Furies,
Daughters of Night, with snaky coils, and pinions[26]
Like those of wind. They are attendant spirits
Before the throne of Jove and whet the fears
Of sickly mortals, when the king of heaven 920
Contrives disease or dreadful death, or frightens
The guilty towns in war. Now he dispatches
One of the three to earth, to meet Juturna,
An omen visible; and so from heaven
She flew with whirlwind swiftness, like an arrow
Through cloud from bowstring, armed with gall or poison,
Loosed from a Parthian quiver,[27] cleaving shadows
Swifter than man may know, a shaft no power
Has power of healing over:—so Night's daughter
Came down to earth, and when she saw the Trojans 930
And Turnus' columns, she dwindled, all of a sudden,
To the shape of that small bird, which, in the night-time,
Shrills its late song, ill-omened, on the roof-tops
Or over tombs, insistent through the darkness.
And so the fiend, the little screech-owl, flying
At Turnus, over and over, shrilled in warning,
Beating the wings against the shield, and Turnus
Felt a strange torpor seize his limbs, and terror
Made his hair rise, and his voice could find no utterance.

But when, far off, Juturna knew the Fury 940
By whir of those dread wings, she tore her tresses,
Clawed at her face, and beat her breast, all anguish
Over her brother:—"What can a sister do
To help you now, poor Turnus? What remains
For me to bear? I have borne so much already.
What skill of mine can make the daylight longer
In your dark hour? Can I face such a portent?[28]
Now, now, I leave the battle-line forever.
Foul birds, I fear enough; haunt me no further,
I know that beat of the wings, that deadly whirring; 950
I recognize, too well, Jove's arrogant orders,
His payment for my maidenhood. He gave me
Eternal life, but why? Why has he taken
The right of death away from me? I might have
Ended my anguish, surely, with my brother's,
Gone, at his side, among the fearful shadows,
But, no,—I am immortal. What is left me
Of any possible joy, without my brother?
What earth can open deep enough to take me,
A goddess, to the lowest shades?" The mantle, 960

[26] Wings.
[27] Parthia, in what is now Iran, was noted for skill in archery.
[28] Bad omen. The appearance here of one of the Furies, agents of retribution and punishing fate, gives the ending of the poem an effect like that of Greek tragedy.

Grey-colored, veiled her head, and the goddess, sighing,
Sank deep from sight to the greyness of the river.
    And on Aeneas presses: the flashing spear,
Brandished, is big as a tree; his anger cries:—
"Why put it off forever, Turnus, hang-dog?
We must fight with arms, not running. Take what shape
You will, gather your strength or craft; fly up
To the high stars, or bury yourself in earth!"
And Turnus shook his head and answered:—"Jove,
Being my enemy, scares me, and the gods,   970
Not your hot words, fierce fellow." And his vision,
Glancing about, beheld a mighty boulder,
A boundary-mark, in days of old, so huge
A dozen men in our degenerate era
Could hardly pry it loose from earth, but Turnus
Lifts it full height, hurls it full speed and, acting,
Seems not to recognize himself, in running,
Or moving, or lifting his hands, or letting the stone
Fly into space; he shakes at the knees, his blood
Runs chill in the veins, and the stone, through wide air going, 980
Falls short, falls spent. As in our dreams at night-time,
When sleep weighs down our eyes, we seem to be running,
Or trying to run, and cannot, and we falter,
Sick in our failure, and the tongue is thick
And the words we try to utter come to nothing,
No voice, no speech,—so Turnus finds the way
Blocked off, wherever he turns, however bravely.
All sorts of things go through his mind: he stares
At the Rutulians, at the town; he trembles,
Quails at the threat of the lance; he cannot see   990
Any way out, any way forward. Nothing.
The chariot is gone, and the charioteer,
Juturna or Metiscus, nowhere near him.
The spear, flung by Aeneas, comes with a whir
Louder than stone from any engine, louder
Than thunderbolt; like a black wind it flies,
Bringing destruction with it, through the shield-rim,
Its sevenfold strength, through armor, through the thigh.
Turnus is down, on hands and knees, huge Turnus
Struck to the earth. Groaning, the stunned Rutulians   1000
Rise to their feet, and the whole hill resounds,
The wooded heights give echo. A suppliant, beaten,
Humbled at last, his hands reach out, his voice
Is low in pleading:—"I have deserved it, surely,
And I do not beg off. Use the advantage.
But if a parent's grief has any power
To touch the spirit, I pray you, pity Daunus,
(I would Anchises), send him back my body.
You have won; I am beaten, and these hands go out
In supplication: everyone has seen it.   1010

No more. I have lost Lavinia. Let hatred
Proceed no further."
Fierce in his arms, with darting glance, Aeneas
Paused for a moment, and he might have weakened,
For the words had moved him, when, high on the shoulder,
He saw the belt of Pallas, slain by Turnus,
Saw Pallas on the ground, and Turnus wearing
That belt with the bright studs, of evil omen
Not only to Pallas now, a sad reminder,
A deadly provocation. Terrible   1020
In wrath, Aeneas cries:—"Clad in this treasure,
This trophy of a comrade, can you cherish
Hope that my hands would let you go? Now Pallas,
Pallas exacts his vengeance, and the blow
Is Pallas, making sacrifice!" He struck
Before he finished speaking: the blade went deep
And Turnus' limbs were cold in death; the spirit
Went with a moan indignant to the shadows.

Ovid

(43 B.C.–17 A.D.)

Ovid and Virgil have been the two most influential Latin narrative poets—
though for very different reasons. Ovid was born into an old established family
in the town now called Sulmona, about a hundred miles east of Rome, in
43 B.C.—one year after the assassination of Julius Caesar. He died in A.D. 17,
during the reign of Tiberius, Augustus's successor as emperor. Significantly,
even symbolically, the twelve-year-old Ovid was sent to Rome, to be educated
for the law, at very nearly the same time Augustus defeated Antony and
Cleopatra in the battle of Actium. The victory brought order and peace—
if also efficient autocracy—to the Roman state for the first time in generations. (See the Introduction to Virgil.) Virgil's values and sensibilities, shaped
and indeed scarred by the experience of civil war, were essentially conservative. Ovid was a decade too young to have known that trauma; his formative years were not shadowed by harrowing memories of iron, blood, and
strife. Like a Parisian boulevardier of the 1920s too young to have known
the trenches, Ovid frequented a somewhat younger set of artists less closely
associated than Virgil's circle was with the Augustan establishment.

   After a few routine assignments in the Roman civil service and some travel
in Greece, Ovid abandoned the law to become a professional poet. Although
the tradition that he was a dissipated playboy may or may not be true, there
is no doubt that, as poet, Ovid was witty, skeptical, and irreverent toward the
austere official Augustan values. For example, his *Ars Amatoria,* or *Art of Love*
(completed about 1 B.C.), a manual on how to conduct love affairs, is an
amusingly amoral, worldly, though also psychologically sensitive treatment
of men and women in love.

Predictably, the poem—and doubtless other poems treating love—got Ovid in serious trouble. In A.D. 8, though he was now the leading poet of Rome, he was summoned before Augustus, tried summarily, and banished to Tomis (in modern Romania), an outpost of the Roman Empire, and indeed of civilization. One reason for Ovid's exile is known: his authorship of *The Art of Love,* a work incompatible with Augustus's program for Roman piety. There was also a second reason, never explicitly identified by Ovid, that remains mysterious despite much detective work by scholars. Apparently it too was some personal or political offense against Augustus or his official code of values.

This most urban and urbane of men now had to endure not just the absence of metropolitan society and amenities but also real danger from hostile border tribes. From Tomis the poet wrote a number of poignant works in verse, directly or indirectly pleading for permission to return to the city and to the people he knew and loved. But Augustus did not relent, nor, after his death, did Tiberius. Ovid was still in exile when he died. All this is ironic; whatever real or imaginary excesses Ovid may have been guilty of, they can hardly have rivaled the enormities that Roman historians have attributed to Tiberius, Nero, and their ages.

Besides *The Art of Love* and a sequel to it, *Remedia Amoris* ("Cures for Love"), Ovid's love poetry includes the *Amores* ("Loves") and the *Heroides* ("Heroines' Letters").The *Amores* was his earliest major work, first published around 20 B.C. The version that has come down to us is not the one Ovid first published but, rather, a three-book revision of the original, five-book poem. Stylistically, therefore, what we have is not novice work. Even as revised, the poem retains a sassy impudence, aimed in several directions: toward official, puritanical sexual morality; toward traditional, stoic Roman values, and especially Augustus's version of them; toward a number of literary traditions; toward women, who are unabashedly treated as sexual prey, though also with affection and an almost cowed admiration. Not least, the irreverence is directed at the poet himself, who appears in various guises: as the smooth amatory expert; as the frustrated male, no match for women at the game of love; as the hardened cynic; as the helplessly enamored, bedazzled swain; as the vulnerable victim who ultimately pays a high price for playing with fire. It seems significant that the Ovid who, in the *Amores,* puts himself at the center of the erotic action will retreat from that personal, starring role in *The Art of Love,* where he becomes the disengaged coach instructing lovers and egging them on from the sidelines.

In the *Amores,* Ovid is particularly amusing, and intriguing, in his capacity as artist magnanimously bestowing poetic immortality on those women lucky enough to become his creative material by playing the game of love with him. This role—the lover as artist—is a key element in the *Amores.* Sometimes it is hilarious, as Ovid irritably tries to shoo away the high-serious Muse, swathed in the ceremonious garb of epic hexameters, so that he can have his frivolous fun, epitomized in the less dignified meter of elegiac couplets (the meter of almost all Ovid's poetry). But this is not mere fooling around. Implicit (and sometimes explicit) in the conflict between literary forms is a rejection by Ovid of the "hexameter values": all the stuffy and stoic "Roman" obsessions, including a high-serious, epic glorification of war. In the *Amores* I.9, Ovid elaborately compares the lover to the soldier in terms of their strategies, ways of life, and triumphs. The comparison is farcical but also makes a serious point and points a serious contrast: There are arenas of human challenge and fulfillment as important as the battlefield, and they have the advantage of giving pleasure rather than inflicting death. To be a poet and lover is to be soft in one sense but not in another.

Some experts construe the Ovid of the *Amores* as more interested in literature than in life, totally inventing the persona, the women, and the situations in the poem in order to satirize or otherwise comment on the literary conventions governing the traditions of love poetry. It is obvious that Ovid is, among other things, writing literary satire. But to see that as his whole, or even main, intent seems unconvincing. If we read the *Amores* as merely a literary game, for an audience of sophisticates in belles lettres, both the vividness of Ovid's comedy and the urgency of his ethical priorities are largely drained off. Ovid sounds like a man who means just what he says: that he likes to chase women and genuinely prefers that kind of campaign to its military alternative.

There is more, then, to Ovid's value system than the playboy philosophy. All the same, it remains true that most of his love poetry is emphatically male-centered. The *Heroides* is a major exception. The viewpoints in this work, written just before and after the turn of the century, are entirely feminine, except in the three sets where the women's letters are paired with those of their male correspondents, as with Paris and Helen. (That these paired sets are authentically by Ovid has sometimes been challenged, but the trend in recent years has been to reinstate them as his work.) All the women represented, drawn from legend and literature, have been abducted, abandoned, betrayed, or otherwise manipulated by men, though the women are not always blameless themselves.

One of the most interesting things about the *Heroides* is the counterpoint in the letters between standard legendary details and circumstances, as handed down from the traditional, heroic-age myths (to which Ovid is generally faithful) and the new tone imparted by Ovid, which can be banally modern. Because heroics are combined with soap opera, the psychological portraiture is often rich and suggestive. The mythic facts about Paris, for example, blend with modern modes of characterization (largely unconscious self-revelation on Paris's part) so as to develop and refine his ancient reputation as unheroic while also suggesting a commonplace, rather silly personal style of naivete and foppish vanity. Helen's ancient reputation for glamour is overlaid with a more modern, bourgeois concern on her part with respectability, reputation, "honor." I'm not that kind of girl, she suggests, though we know she is. The effect is ludicrous—both amusing and repellent.

The *Metamorphoses,* composed in the years immediately preceding Ovid's exile, belongs to his middle period, between the naughty early love poetry and the sad poetry of exile. The title suggests miraculous transformations, although this theme sometimes has only perfunctory importance in the tales. Few poems of any age or language have shaped so much later literature. There are many reasons for this influence. For one thing, the poem is an almost exhaustive handbook of the best-known classical myths; it is thus a treasury of good stories and indeed a reference work. It is also a rhetorical tour de force, a model illustrating a great variety of poetic, linguistic, and stylistic tricks. (Ovid's training in the law and public speaking did not go to waste.)

It is a wonderfully comic work. The characterizations of deities are sometimes amusingly casual, and both they and human beings are portrayed with complexity and sensitivity. It is also, in places, a tragic work, especially if one defines tragedy so as to include painful conflicts within individual persons independent of historical, public, and other grand consequences.

This interest in the idiosyncrasies, sometimes in the pathology, of feeling, especially of people in love, puts Ovid in somewhat the same relationship to Virgil that Euripides held to Aeschylus. Perhaps the nearest modern equivalent of the *Metamorphoses* is Byron's *Don Juan* (1818–23); defending his poem through a sneer at his brother Romantics' overintensity, Byron once wrote, "You have so many 'divine' poems; is it nothing to have written a human one?" Like *Don Juan*, the *Metamorphoses* is a seriocomic poem, simultaneously a spoof of the heroic tradition and a searching critique of it. In writing the poem, Ovid abandoned his usual poetic meter, the elegiac couplet, and chose instead the six-foot dactylic line used in the *Iliad*, the *Odyssey*, and the *Aeneid*. The meter is one of many indications that Ovid meant his poem to be compared with Virgil's epic. Sometimes the relationship is that of mock-epic diminution: Virgil's grand vision of origins, which finds the seeds of history and empire in the past, becomes for Ovid an account of the origin of such things as flowers and trees—rather like modern nursery tales about how the tiger got his stripes. Yet there is a saucy implication that Ovid can beat Virgil at his own game; if Virgil's epic could span a thousand years of legend and history, Ovid will outdo him by beginning, not with the fall of Troy, but with the aboriginal creation of the cosmos itself.

Ovid repeatedly undermines Virgil's moralism. And yet, as with Byron, his technique of deflation is itself a kind of moral statement. In treating the gods and goddesses not religiously but as recognizable human beings, Ovid satirizes Virgil's religious piety and his implication that the universe, though mysterious, is just.

From the late Middle Ages on, Ovid's poetry has never lost its appeal, for readers and for authors both minor and great. A number of attempts have been made to rehabilitate Ovid's moral values, mainly by treating him allegorically. And his strategies can be adapted to serious purposes, as Kafka demonstrates in our century in his novella *The Metamorphosis*. But the most typical attitude of later authors toward Ovid is not reverence but affection. His poetry is, above all, good entertainment, whether we define that term as diversion or as the deeper pleasure that comes from recognizing his wide range of sympathy and his understanding of human psychology.

FURTHER READING *(prepared by F.S.N.):* Concise introductory material can be found in the pertinent sections of the *Latin Literature* volume, ed. E. J. Kenney and W. V. Clausen, 1982, of *The Cambridge History of Classical Literature,* and in Michael Grant, *Greek and Latin Authors, 800 B.C.–A.D. 1000,* 1980. Sara Mack, *Ovid,* 1988, is a good comprehensive introduction to Ovid, his narrative methods, and other aspects of his work. In the influential book by Brooks Otis, *Ovid as an Epic Poet,* 1966, 2nd ed. 1970, a number of individual passages from Ovid are discussed, arranged according to topic. Ovid's life and literary art are treated by L. P. Wilkinson in *Ovid Recalled,* 1955, and in his shortened version *Ovid Surveyed,* 1962. Essays edited by J. W. Binns in *Ovid,* 1973, deal with a number of works by Ovid, and with the influence these works have had throughout the centuries. Peter Green's extensive introduction, very full notes, and detailed commentary in his translation *Ovid: The Erotic Poems,* 1982, are an excellent guide to the *Amores,* the *Ars Amatoria,* and the *Remedia Amoris.* The *Metamorphoses* is treated in Charles P. Segal, *Landscape in Ovid's Metamorphoses: A Study in the Transformations of a Literary Symbol,* 1969, which is useful on symbol, unity, tradition, and the motif of moral order; and in Otto Steen Due, *Changing Forms: Studies in the Metamorphoses of Ovid,* 1974. Frederick Ahl, *Metaformations,* 1985, is highly recommended for advanced undergraduates.

from *AMORES*

Translated by Peter Green

BOOK I

I

Arms, warfare, violence—I was winding up to produce a
  Regular epic, with verse-form to match—
Hexameters, naturally. But Cupid[1] (they say) with a snicker
  Lopped off one foot from each alternate line.[2]
"Nasty young brat," I told him, "who made *you* Inspector of Metres?
  We poets come under the Muses,[3] we're not in your mob.
What if Venus took over the weapons of blonde Minerva,
  While blonde Minerva began fanning passion's flame?[4]
Who'd stand for Our Lady of Wheatfields looking after rides and
    forests?
  Who'd trust the Virgin Huntress[5] to safeguard crops?   10
Imagine long-haired Apollo on parade with a pikestaff
  While the War-God fumbled tunes from Apollo's lyre![6]
Look, boy, you've got your own empire, and a sight too much
    influence
  As it is. Don't get ambitious, quit playing for more.
Or is your fief[7] universal? Is Helicon[8] yours? Can't even
  Apollo call his lyre his own these days?
I'd got off to a flying start, clean paper, one magnificent
  Opening line. Number two brought me down
With a bump. I haven't the theme to suit your frivolous metre:

---

[1] The child god Cupid is the son of Venus (the Greeks' Aphrodite), goddess of beauty, love, and sex.

[2] The hexameter line, used in high-serious poetry such as epic, consists of six feet, each foot either a dactyl (a long syllable followed by two short ones) or a spondee (two long syllables). The elegiac couplet, used in lightweight amatory poems such as the *Amores,* consists of one hexameter line followed by a five-foot line, broken into halves each having two and a half feet. *Arma,* the first word of this poem, is the first word also of Virgil's epic the *Aeneid.*

[3] Goddesses of inspiration.

[4] The virgin goddess Minerva (the Greeks' Athena) is the antithesis of Venus.

[5] Respectively, Ceres (the Greeks' Demeter), goddess of grain, harvest, and fertility; and Diana (the Greeks' Artemis), chaste goddess of the hunt.

[6] Apollo was god of (among other things) music; the War-God is Mars (the Greeks' Ares).

[7] Dominion; territory.

[8] The mountain of the Muses, source of the fountain of poetic inspiration.

  No boyfriend, no girl with a mane of coiffured hair—"   20
When I'd got so far, presto, he opened his quiver, selected
  An arrow to lay me low,
Then bent the springy bow in a crescent against his knee, and
  Let fly. "Hey, poet!" he called, "you want a theme? Take *that!*"
His shafts—worse luck for me—never miss their target:
  I'm on fire now, Love owns the freehold[9] of my heart.
So let my verse rise with six stresses, drop to five on the downbeat—
  Goodbye to martial epic, and epic metre too!
Come on then, my Muse, bind your blonde hair with a wreath of
  Sea-myrtle, and lead me off in the six-five groove!   30

2

What's wrong with me nowadays, how explain why my mattress
  Feels so hard, and the bedclothes will *never* stay in place?
Why am I kept awake all night by insomnia, thrashing around till
  Every weary bone in my body aches?
If Love were my assailant, surely I'd know it—unless he's
  Craftily gone under cover, slipped past my guard?
Yes, that must be it; heart skewered by shafts of desire, the raging
  Beast, passion, out at prowl in my breast.
Shall I give in? To resist might just bank up the furnace—
  All right, I give in. A well-squared load lies light.   10
Flourish a torch, it burns fiercer. I know, I've seen it. Stop the
  Motion, and pouf! it's out.
Yoke-shy rebellious oxen collect more blows and curses
  Than a team that's inured to the plough.
Your restive horse earns a wolf-curb, his mouth's all bruises;
  A harness-broken nag scarcely feels the reins.
It's the same with Love. Play stubborn, you get a far more thorough
  Going-over than those who admit they're hooked.
So I'm coming clean, Cupid: here I am, your latest victim,
  Hands raised in surrender. Do what you like with me.   20
No need for military action. I want terms, an armistice—
  You wouldn't look good defeating an unarmed foe.
Put on a wreath of myrtle, yoke up your mother's pigeons—[10]
  Your stepfather[11] himself will lend you a fine
Chariot: mount it, drive in triumph through the cheering
  Rabble, skilfully whipping your birds ahead,
With your train of prisoners behind you, besotted youths and maidens,
  Such pomp, such magnificence, your very own
Triumph: and I'll be there too, fresh-wounded, your latest
  Prisoner—displaying my captive mind—   30

---

[9] Permanent ownership.

[10] The myrtle was associated with Venus, as were doves.

[11] Probably Mars, who had an adulterous affair with Venus. The parade described in the following lines is based on the Roman "triumph," the procession through the city of a conquering hero, his chariot surrounded by defeated or enslaved captives.

With Conscience, hands bound behind her, and Modesty, and all
      Love's
   Other enemies, whipped into line.
You'll have them all scared cold, while the populace goes crazy,
   Waves to its conquering hero, splits its lungs.
And what an escort—the Blandishment Corps, the Illusion
   And Passion Brigade, your regular bodyguard:
These are the troops you employ to conquer men and immortals—
   Without them, why, you're nothing, a snail unshelled.
How proudly your mother will applaud your triumphal progress
   From high Olympus,[12] shower roses on your head; 40
Wings bright-bejewelled, jewels starring your hair, you'll
   Ride in a car of gold, all gold yourself.
What's more, if I know you, even on this occasion
   You'll burn the crowd up, break hearts galore all round:
With the best will in the world, dear, you can't keep your arrows
      idle—
   They're so hot, they scorch the crowd as you go by.
Your procession will match that of Bacchus, after he'd won the
      Ganges
   Basin (though *he* was drawn by tigers, not birds).[13]
So then, since I am doomed to be part of your—*sacré*[14] triumph,
   Why waste victorious troops on me now? 50
Take a hint from the campaign record of your cousin, Augustus
   Caesar[15]—*his* conquests became protectorates.

3

Fair's fair now, Venus. This girl's got me hooked. All I'm asking from
      her
   Is love—or at least some future hope for my own
Eternal devotion. No, even that's too much—hell, just let me love
      her!
   (*Listen*, Venus: I've asked you so often now.)
Say yes, pet. I'd be your slave for years, for a lifetime.
   Say yes—unswerving fidelity's my strong suit.
I may not have top-drawer connections, I can't produce blue-blooded
   Ancestors to impress you, my father's plain middle-class,
And there aren't any squads of ploughmen to deal with *my* broad
      acres—
   My parents are both pretty thrifty, and need to be. 10

---

[12] The mountain home of the gods.

[13] Bacchus, god of wine (the Greeks' Dionysus), was reared in India, the location of the river Ganges.

[14] Literally, *sacré* (French) means "sacred" but in effect means "damned" or "confounded."

[15] Augustus, Roman emperor in Ovid's day, tried to foster in his subjects an austere morality (though Augustus was far from exemplifying it himself). He later banished Ovid from Rome, partly because of the poet's irreverent writings.

What *have* I got on my side, then? Poetic genius, sweetheart,
    Divine inspiration. And love. I'm yours to command—
Unswerving faithfulness, morals above suspicion,
    Naked simplicity, a born-to-the-purple blush.
I don't chase thousands of girls, I'm no sexual circus-rider;[16]
    Honestly, all I want is to look after you
Till death do us part, have the two of us living together
    All my time, and know you'll cry for me when I'm gone.
Besides, when you give me yourself, what you'll be providing
    Is creative material. My art will rise to the theme   20
And immortalize *you*. Look, why do you think we remember
    The swan-upping of Leda, or Io's life as a cow,
Or poor virgin Europa whisked off overseas, clutching
    That so-called bull by the—horn?[17] Through poems, of course.
So you and I, love, will enjoy the same world-wide publicity,
    And our names will be linked, for ever, with the gods.

                                    4
"So your man's going to be present at this dinner-party?
    I hope he drops down dead before the dessert!
Does this mean no hands, just eyes (any chance guest's privilege)—
    Just to *look* at my darling, while *he*
Lies there with you beside him, in licensed embracement
    And paws your bosom or neck as he feels inclined?
I'm no longer surprised at those Centaurs for horsing around over
    Some cute little filly when they were full of wine[18]—
I may not live in the forest, or be semi-equipped as a stallion,
    But still *I* can hardly keep my hands to myself   10
When you're around. Now listen, I've got some instructions for you,
    And don't let the first breeze blow them out of your head!
Arrive before your escort. I don't see what can be managed
    If you do—but anyway, get there first.
When he pats the couch, put on your Respectable Wife expression,
    And take your place beside him—but nudge my foot
As you're passing by. Watch out for my nods and eye-talk,
    Pick up my stealthy messages, send replies.
I shall speak whole silent volumes with one raised eyebrow,
    Words will spring from my fingers, words traced in wine.   20
When you're thinking about the last time we made love together,
    Touch your rosy cheek with one elegant thumb.
If you're cross with me, and can't say so, then pinch the bottom
    Of your earlobe. But when I do or say

---

[16] Here, one who jumps from one running horse to another.

[17] Jove (the Greeks' Zeus), king of the gods, took many forms for his sexual adventures with human women, coming as a swan to Leda and to Europa as a bull. Jove changed Io into a heifer after Juno (the Greeks' Hera) became jealous of her.

[18] While attending the wedding feast of Perithous and Hippodamia, the Centaurs (who had horses' bodies and human heads) ran amok and tried to carry off the women.

Something that gives you especial pleasure, my darling,
  Keep turning the ring on your finger to and fro.
When you yearn for your man to suffer some well-merited misfortune
  Place your hands on the table as though in prayer.
If he mixes wine specially for you, watch out, make him drink it
  Himself. Ask the waiter for what *you* want   30
As you hand back the goblet. I'll be the first to seize it
  And drink from the place your lips have touched.
If *he* offers you tit-bits out of some dish he's tasted,
  Refuse what's been near his mouth.
Don't let him put his arms round your neck, and oh, don't lay that
  Darling head of yours on *his* coarse breast.
Don't let his fingers roam down your dress to touch up
  Those responsive nipples. Above all, don't you dare
Kiss him, not once. If you do, I'll proclaim myself your lover,
  Lay hand upon you, claim those kisses as mine.   40
So much for what I can see. But there's plenty goes on under
  A long evening wrap. The mere thought worries me stiff.
Don't start rubbing your thigh against his, don't go playing
  Footsy under the table, keep smooth from rough."
(I'm scared all right, and no wonder—I've been too successful
  An operator myself, it's my own
Example I find so unnerving. I've often petted to climax
  With my darling at a party, hand hidden under her cloak—)
"—Well, *you* won't do *that*. But still, to avoid the least suspicion,
  Remove such natural protection when you sit down.   50
Keep pressing fresh drinks—but no kisses—on your husband,
  Slip neat wine in his glass if you get the chance.
If he passes out comfortably, drowned in sleep and liquor,
  We must improvise as occasion dictates.
When we all (you too) get up and leave, remember
  To stick in the middle of the crowd—
That's where you'll find me, or I you: whenever
  There's a chance to touch me, please do!"
(Yet the most I can win myself is a few hours' respite:
  At nightfall my mistress and I must part.)   60
"At nightfall he'll lock you inside, and I'll be left weeping
  On that cold front doorstep—the nearest I can come
To your longed-for embraces, while *he's* enjoying, under license,
  The kisses, and more, that you give me on the sly.
What you *can* do is show unwilling, behave as though you're frigid,
  Begrudge him endearments, make sex a dead loss."
(Grant my prayer, Venus. Don't let either of them get pleasure
  Out of the act—*and certainly not her!*)
"But whatever the outcome tonight, when you see me tomorrow
  Just swear, through thick and thin, that you told him No."   70

8

There's a certain—well: any reader in need of a procuress? Listen,
  Try Dipsas. A certain bitch, snake, hag.

Dipsas, dipso, well-named. If *she* ever saw pink horses
  At sunrise, they weren't the Dawn's.[19]
She's a witch, mutters magical cantrips,[20] can make rivers
  Run uphill, knows the best aphrodisiacs—
When to use herbal brews, or the whirring bullroarer,[21]
  How to extract that stuff from a mare in heat.
She can control the weather, make a day overcast with
  Cloud at will, or brilliant and clear;   10
I've known times (believe it or not) when the moon turned bloody,
  And blood dripped from the stars.
It wouldn't surprise me if the old bitch grew feathers at nightfall
  And went flapping round like an owl—
I've heard rumours, it's possible. What's more, she's got double
  Pupils, a twin light glinting from each eye.
She conjures up long-dead souls from their crumbling sepulchres
  And has incantations to split the solid earth.
Well: this old hag undertook to suborn[22] *our* relationship,
  And a glibly poisonous tongue she had for the job.   20
By pure chance I overheard her. The big double doors stood open.
  Here, then, is what she said: "You know,
Dearie, you made a great hit with that rich young gentleman
  Yesterday. He'd got eyes for nobody else—
And why should he have? There's no girl more beautiful. Such a pity
  Your turn-out doesn't match your face.
I'd like to see you become as wealthy as you're good-looking—
  Once get you in the money, I shan't ever starve.
The stars were against you, dearie, Mars stood in opposition,
  But now Mars has wheeled off, and today   30
Venus is in the ascendant. Look how her rising favours
  Your lot: a rich suitor, and anxious to oblige!
Dead handsome, too, just about as pretty as you are—if he wasn't
  Bidding himself, why, people would bid for *him*.
Ah, that got a blush! Pale faces need colour, but Nature's method
  Is so unpredictable. Safer to stick to Art.[23]
Keep your eyes on your lap. Look demure, scale your responses
  To the size of each lover's gifts.
In the old days it was different. Those Sabine women stuck to
  One husband apiece. But then *they* didn't wash.[24]   40
Today Mars is so taken up with foreign campaigning
  That Venus has made a clean sweep of Rome,

[19] The reference is to the horse-drawn chariot of Aurora (the Greeks' Eos), goddess of the dawn.
[20] Spells.
[21] A wooden slat, attached to a string; when whirled, it made a roaring noise. It was part of a witch's stock in trade.
[22] Underhandedly corrupt.
[23] Cosmetics.
[24] The men of Rome in its primitive days got themselves wives by seizing the neighboring Sabine women, who had come to Rome to observe games being celebrated there. The women insisted on monogamy.

Her own Aeneas' city.[25] Pretty girls have a ball. No virgins
  Except the unasked—and a smart kid asks for herself.
Prissy-faced women are worth close scrutiny: you'll discover
  A frown can hide a multitude of sins.
Bending that bow made trial of Penelope's young wooers,
  A good stiff horn proved too much for them.[26]
Volatile time slips past us without our knowledge
  Like a swift-gliding river. Brass shines   50
With constant usage, a beautiful dress needs wearing,
  Leave a house empty, it rots.
Lack of exercise withers your beauty, you need to take lovers—
  And the treatment calls for more than one or two.
Run a string, take your pick. It's safer, less troublesome:
  Wolves that raid flocks eat best.
That poet of yours, now, what does he give you, except his latest
  Verses? Find the right lover, you'd scoop the pool.
Why isn't he richer? The patron god of poets[27]
  Wears gold, plays a gilded lyre.   60
Look, dear, stop worshipping genius, try generosity
  Just for a change. To give is a fine art.
And don't you look down your nose at some slave who's purchased
  His freedom. Chalked feet are no crime.[28]
Don't let yourself be fooled by ancestral portraits. Your lover's
  Broke? Then give him the boot, and his pedigree too.
When he asks for a night on the house because he's so handsome
  Tell him No. His boyfriend can foot the bill.
While you're spreading your net, go easy. Don't show too rapacious
  Or your bird may fly off. Once you've caught him, anything goes.   70
Some show of love does no harm: let him fancy himself your darling,
  But take good care you collect a *quid pro quo.*[29]
Don't say Yes every night. Pretend that you have a headache,
  Or make Isis your excuse, then you can plead
Religious abstention.[30] Enough's enough, though—he may get
    accustomed
  To going without, over-frequent rebuffs may cool
His passion off. Take gifts, but be deaf to entreaties—
  Let the lucky man hear his rival cursing outside.
You've hurt him? *He* started it. Throw a quick tantrum. This kind of
  Counter-attack will very soon choke him off.   80
But never stay angry too long. A festering quarrel
  Can make permanent enemies.

---

[25] Aeneas, legendary hero of Virgil's *Aeneid* and aboriginal forebear of the Romans, led the survivors of defeated Troy to Italy.

[26] In Homer's *Odyssey*, Book XXI, the suitors of Penelope, wife of the supposedly dead Odysseus, are unable to perform the feat she assigns them, of stringing Odysseus' bow.

[27] Apollo.

[28] The feet of newly imported slaves were marked with chalk.

[29] (Latin): something valuable in return.

[30] Ceremonial sexual abstinence in preparation for a feast of the goddess Isis.

Another trick you must learn is control of the tear-ducts,
    How to weep buckets at will—
And when you're deceiving someone, don't let perjury scare you:
    Venus ensures that her fellow-gods
Turn a deaf ear to such gambits. You must get yourself a houseboy
    And a well-trained maid, who can hint
What gifts will be welcome. Don't let them demand exorbitant
    Tips for themselves. Little presents soon add up.   90
Your sister and mother, your nurse, these can all help fleece a lover—
    Many hands make quick loot.
When you've run through all other excuses for getting presents
    Say it's your birthday, show him the cake.
Don't let him get cocksure, without any rivals:
    Love minus competition never wears well.
Leave the bed suspiciously rumpled, make sure he sees it,
    Flaunt a few sexy bruises on your neck—
Above all, show him his rival's presents (if none are forthcoming
    Order some yourself, from a good shop).   100
When you've dug enough gold, then protest he's being far too
        generous
    And ask him for a *loan*—which you'll never repay.
Beguile with sweet words, and blandish while you despoil him:
    A taste of honey will mask the nastiest dose.
These tactics are guaranteed by a lifetime's experience,
    So don't ignore them. Follow my advice.
And you'll never regret it. Ah, many's the time you'll bless me
    While I'm alive, and pray that my old bones
Lie easy after I'm gone—"
                            At this point my shadow
    Betrayed me. I was dying to get my hands   110
On those sparse white locks, to tear at the old hag's raddled[31]
    Cheeks and drink-bleary eyes.
May the gods strip the roof from her head, end her days in poverty,
    Send her horrible winters and an eternal thirst!

                                9

Every lover's on active service, my friend, active service, believe me,
    And Cupid has his headquarters in the field.
Fighting and love-making belong to the same age-group—
    In bed as in war, old men are out of place.
A commander looks to his troops for gallant conduct,
    A mistress expects no less.
Soldier and lover both keep night-long vigil,
    Lying rough outside their captain's (or lady's) door.
The military life brings long route-marches—but just let his mistress
    Be somewhere ahead, and the lover too   10

---

[31] Withered.

Will trudge on for ever, scale mountains, ford swollen rivers,
  Thrust his way through deep snow.
Come embarkation-time *he* won't talk of "strong north-easters",
  Or say it's "too late in the season" to put to sea.
Who but a soldier or lover would put up with freezing
  Nights—rain, snow, sleet? The first
Goes out on patrol to observe the enemy's movements,
  The other watches his rival, an equal foe.
A soldier lays siege to cities, a lover to girls' houses,
  The one assaults city gates, the other front doors.   20
Night attacks are a great thing. Catch your opponents sleeping
  And unarmed. Just slaughter them where they lie.
That's how the Greeks dealt with Rhesus and his wild Thracians
  While rustling those famous mares.[32]
Lovers, too, will take advantage of slumber (her husband's),
  Strike home while the enemy sleeps: getting past
Night patrols and eluding sentries are games both soldiers
  And lovers need to learn.
Love, like war, is a toss-up. The defeated can recover,
  While some you might think invincible collapse;   30
So if you've got love written off as an easy option
  You'd better think twice. Love calls
For guts and initiative. Great Achilles sulks for Briseis—
  Quick, Trojans, smash through the Argive wall!
Hector went into battle from Andromache's embraces
  Helmeted by his wife.
Agamemnon himself, the Supremo, was struck into raptures
  At the sight of Cassandra's tumbled hair;[33]
Even Mars was caught on the job, felt the blacksmith's meshes—
  Heaven's best scandal in years.[34] Then take   40
My own case. I was idle, born to leisure *en déshabillé*,[35]
  Mind softened by lazy scribbling in the shade.
But love for a pretty girl soon drove the sluggard
  To action, made him join up.
And just look at me now—fighting fit, dead keen on night exercises:
  If you want a cure for slackness, fall in love!

---

[32] In Homer's *Iliad,* Book X, the Greek heroes Odysseus and Diomedes raid the camp where the soldiers of Rhesus, newly arrived to support the Trojans, are sleeping. The two Greeks carry off Rhesus's fabulous horses.

[33] The references, again, are to the Trojan War. The Greeks' foremost warrior, Achilles, and the commander-in-chief, Agamemnon, quarreled over possession of Briseis, a woman Achilles had taken captive. The resentful Achilles remained for a time on the sidelines, allowing the Trojans some success in battle. After winning the war, Agamemnon took home with him the captive Trojan princess and prophet Cassandra. In Book VI of Homer's *Iliad,* the Trojan hero Hector takes his last farewell of his wife, after having temporarily removed his helmet because it frightened their infant son.

[34] Vulcan (the Greeks' Hephaestus), god of metalworking, having learned of the adulterous affair between his wife, Venus, and the god Mars, trapped them in bed together with a fine-meshed net that the cuckolded husband had crafted. See Homer's *Odyssey,* Book VIII.

[35] In semi-undress (French)—in a bathrobe, for example.

14

I *told* you to stop using rinses—and now just look at you!
    No hair worth mentioning left to dye.
Why couldn't you let well alone? It grew so luxuriantly,
    Right down to below your hips,
And fine—so fine you were scared to set it, like silken
    Threads in a vivid Chinese screen,
Or the filament spun by a spider, the subtle creation
    That she hangs beneath some deserted beam.
It was neither dark nor blonde, but a brindled[36] auburn,
    A mixture of both, like some tall cedar when   10
The outer bark's stripped off, in a dew-wet precipitous
    Valley of Ida.[37] Not to mention the fact
That it was so tractable, could be dressed in a hundred styles, and
    Never made you get cross. With no pins
Or curlers to make it go brittle, no bristling side-combs,
    Your maid could relax. I've been there
Often enough while she fixed it, but never once saw you
    Pick up a hairpin and stick it in her arm.
If it was early morning, you'd be propped up among lilac
    Pillows and coverlets, your hair   20
Not yet combed out. Yet even in tangled disorder
    It still became you. You looked like a wild
Exhausted Maenad, *al fresco.*[38]
                                    Poor down-fine tresses,
    What torture they had to endure!
You decided on corkscrew ringlets. The irons were heated,
    Your poor hair crimped and racked
Into spiralling curls "It's a crime," I told you, "a downright
    Crime to singe it like that. Why on earth
Can't you leave well alone? You'll *wreck* it, you obstinate creature,
    It's *not for burning.* Why, in its natural state   30
It'd make the best perm look silly—" No good. Her crowning
    Glory, that any mod god might well
Have envied, sleek tresses like those that sea-wet naked
    Dione holds up in the picture—gone, all gone.[39]
Why complain of the loss? You silly girl, you detested
    That waist-length tangle, so stop
Making sad *moues* [40] in your mirror. You must get accustomed
    To your own New Look, and forget
Yourself if you aim to attract. No rival's incantations
    Or tisanes[41] have harmed you, no witch   40

---

[36] Light with darker streaks.

[37] A mountainous region near Troy.

[38] The reference is to the streaming hair of the Maenads, frenzied worshipers of the wine god Bacchus. *Al fresco* (Italian) means out-of-doors.

[39] Dione is another name for Venus. The famous picture referred to, by the Greek artist Apelles (fourth century B.C.), shows Venus wringing out her wet hair.

[40] Pouts; grimaces.

[41] Medicinal broths (here, potions prepared by a witch).

Has hexed your rinse, you haven't—touch wood—had an illness;
　If your hair's fallen out, it's not
Any envious tongue that's to blame. You applied that concoction
　Yourself. It was you that did it. *All your fault.*
Still, after our German conquests a wig is easily come by—
　A captive Mädchen's tresses will see you through.
You'll blush, it's true, when your borrowed plumage elicits
　Admiration galore. You'll feel that the praise (like the hair)
Has been bought. Once you really deserved it. Now each compliment
　Belongs to some Rhine maiden, not to you.　　　　　　　50
Poor sweet—she's shielding her face to hide those ladylike
　Blushes, and making a brave effort not to cry
As she stares at the ruined hair in her lap, a keepsake
　Unhappily out of place. Don't worry, love,
Just put on your makeup. This loss is by no means irreparable—
　Give it time, and your hair will grow back as good as new.

15

Why, gnawing Envy, impute an idler's existence to me?
　Why dismiss the poet as a drone?
What's your complaint? That I've failed (though young and healthy)
　　to follow
　Tradition, or chase the dusty rewards
Of a soldier's career? That I haven't mugged up dull lawsuits,
　Or sold my eloquence like a whore
In the courts and Forum?[42] Such labours are soon forgotten.
　What *I* seek is perennial fame,
Undying world-wide remembrance. While Ida and Tenedos
　Still stand, while Simois still runs swift to the sea,[43]　　　10
Old Homer will live. While clustering grapes still ripen
　And wheat still falls to the scythe
Hesiod's works will be studied. The verse of Callimachus—
　Weak in imagination, strong on technique—
Has a worldwide readership. Sophoclean tragedy
　Is safe from Time's ravages. While sun and moon
Survive, so will Aratus. While the world holds one devious servant,
　Stern father, blandishing whore, or ponce[44] on the make
Menander's immortal. Rough Ennius, spirited Accius
　Have names time will never destroy. What age　　　　　　20
Will not cherish great Varro's epic of Argo's voyage,
　Jason's quest for the Golden Fleece?
The work of sublime Lucretius will prove immortal
　While the world itself endures;

---

[42] Ovid means that he has not gone into politics. The Forum was the Roman civic center.
[43] Places associated with the Trojan War, the subject of Homer's *Iliad*. The writers mentioned in lines 11–30 (all dead at the time when Ovid is writing) include both Greek (lines 11–19) and Latin (lines 19–30) poets. For some of them Ovid tries to capture briefly their typical subject matter or achievement.
[44] British slang for a pimp or a gaudily effeminate male.

And so long as Rome's empire holds sway over the nations,
   Virgil's country poems,[45] his *Aeneid*, will be read.
While Cupid's armoury still consists of torch and arrows
   Tibullus' elegant verse
Will always be quoted. From lands of sunset to sunrise, Gallus,
   Gallus and his Lycoris, will be renowned.   30
Though Time, in time, can consume the enduring ploughshare,
   Though flint itself will perish, poetry lives—
Deathless, unfading, triumphant over kings and their triumphs,
   Richer than Spanish river-gold. Let the crowd
Gape after baubles. To me may golden Apollo proffer
   A cup, brimming over, from the Castalian spring[46]
And a wreath of sun-loving myrtle.[47] May my audience always
   Consist of star-crossed lovers. Never forget
It's the living that Envy feeds on. After death the pressure
   Is taken off. All men get their due in the end.   40
So when the final flames have devoured my body, I shall
   Survive, and my better part live on.

BOOK 2

I

A second batch of verses by that naughty provincial poet,
   Naso,[1] the chronicler of his own
Wanton frivolities; another of Love's commissions (warning
   To puritans: *This volume is not for you*).
I want my works to be read by the far-from-frigid virgin
   On fire for her sweetheart, by the boy
In love for the very first time. May some fellow-sufferer,
   Perusing my anatomy of desire,
See his own passion reflected there, cry in amazement:
   "Who told this scribbler about my private affairs?"   10
One time, I recall, I got started on an inflated epic
   About War in Heaven, with all
Those hundred-handed monsters, and Earth's fell vengeance, and
     towering
   Ossa piled on Olympus (plus Pelion too).[2]
But while I was setting up Jove—stormclouds and thunderbolts
     gathered
   Ready to hand, a superb defensive barrage—

---

[45] Virgil's "country," or pastoral, poems are the *Eclogues* and *Georgics*.

[46] A spring on Mount Parnassus, which was sacred to Apollo and the Muses.

[47] Myrtle wreaths or garlands were used to honor poets.

[1] Ovid's full name was Publius Ovidius Naso. He was "provincial" in that he came from a region about a hundred miles east of Rome.

[2] A standard subject for high-serious poetry was the war of the Giants (sons of Earth) against the Olympian gods, during which the Giants assaulted Mount Olympus by piling mountains atop one another. The Giants were overcome by thunderbolts, invented by Minerva, made by Vulcan, and wielded by Jove.

My mistress staged a lock-out. I dropped Jupiter[3] and his lightnings
  That instant, didn't give him another thought.
Forgive me, good Lord, if I found your armoury useless—
  Her shut door ran to larger bolts   20
Than any *you* wielded. I went back to verses and compliments,
  My natural weapons. Soft words
Remove harsh door-chains. There's magic in poetry, its power
  Can pull down the bloody moon,
Turn back the sun, make serpents burst asunder
  Or rivers flow upstream.
Doors are no match for such spellbinding, the toughest
  Locks can be open-sesamed by its charms.[4]
But epic's a dead loss for me. I'll get nowhere with swift-footed
  Achilles, or with either of Atreus' sons.   30
Old what's-his-name wasting twenty years on war and travel,
  Poor Hector dragged in the dust —
No good.[5] But lavish fine words on some young girl's profile
  And sooner or later she'll tender herself as the fee,
An ample reward for your labours. So farewell, heroic
  Figures of legend—the *quid*
Pro quo[6] you offer won't tempt me. A bevy of beauties
  All swooning over my love-songs—that's what *I* want.

9B

If I heard a voice from heaven say "Live without loving,"
  I'd beg off. Girls are such exquisite hell.
When desire's slaked, when I'm sick of the whole business,
  Some kink in my wretched nature drives me back.
It's like riding a hard-mouthed horse, that bolts headlong, foam
    flying
  From his bit, and won't answer the rein—
Or being aboard a ship, on the point of docking, in harbour,
  When a sudden squall blows you back out to sea:
That's how the veering winds of desire so often catch me—
  Hot Love up to his lethal tricks again.   10
All right, boy,[7] skewer me. I've dropped my defences,
  I'm an easy victim. Why, by now
Your arrows practically know their own way to the target
  And feel less at home in their quiver than in me.

[3] Another name for Jove.
[4] Ovid puns on the Latin word *carmen,* which can mean both poem and magic spell. With the supernatural powers ascribed to poetry in lines 23–28 compare the powers attributed to the witch Dipsas in I.8.
[5] The heroes mentioned in lines 29–32 are all from Homer's epics: Achilles, Atreus' sons (Agamemnon and Menelaus, husband of the abducted Helen), and the Trojan leader Hector are in the *Iliad;* "old what's-his-name" is Odysseus, who is described in the *Odyssey* as taking ten years to return home after ten years of fighting at Troy.
[6] Return payment.
[7] Cupid (the Greeks' Eros, thus called "Love" in line 10).

I'm sorry for any fool who rates sleep a prime blessing
   And enjoys it from dusk to dawn
Night in, night out. What's sleep but cold death's reflection?
   Plenty of time for rest when you're in the grave.
My mistress deceives me—so what? I'd rather be lied to
   Than ignored. I can live on hope. Today   20
She'll be all endearments, tomorrow throw screaming tantrums,
   Envelop me one night, lock me out the next.
War, like love, is a toss-up. If Mars is inconstant, he gets that
   From you, his stepson.[8] You're quite
Unpredictable, Cupid, with your lucky-dip favours,
   And more volatile than your own wings.
Maybe you'll hear my appeal, though—your delectable mother[9]
   Might help there—and settle in as king of my heart?
Then admit the flighty sex *en masse* to your dominions
   And you'd have guaranteed popularity all round.   30

19

You may not feel any need (and more fool you) to guard that
   Girl of yours—but it sharpens *my* desire,
So would you oblige? What's allowed is a bore, it's what isn't
   That turns me on. What cold clod
Could woo with his rival's approval? We lovers need hope and
      despair in
   Alternate doses. An intermittent rebuff
Makes us promise the earth. Who wants a beautiful woman
   When she never deceives him? I can't
Love a girl who's not intermittently bitchy. Corinna[10] spotted
   My weakness (full marks!) and saw how   10
To use it against me. The times she invented a headache,
   And when I still hung around, just threw me out,
Or pretended she'd had an affair, looking horribly guilty
   When in fact she'd done nothing at all—
And having thus quickly rekindled my cooling ardour
   Would suddenly switch her mood
To the ultra-compliant. Her compliments, her sweet nothings,
   Her kisses—oh God, her kisses! So you too,
My latest eye-ravisher, must ensnare me at times by pretending
   To be frightened: must—on occasion—say No,   20
And leave me there, prostrate on your doorstep, to suffer
   Long hours of frosty cold, the whole night through.
Act thus, and my love will endure, grow stronger with each passing
   Year—that's the way I like it, that feeds the flame,
Love too indulged, too compliant, will turn your stomach
   Like a surfeit of sweet rich food.

---

[8] See I.2.24 and note.
[9] The goddess Venus.
[10] In most other poems in the *Amores*, Corinna is the name of the woman Ovid is in love with.

Had Danaë never been locked in that brazen turret, would Jupiter
    Ever have got her with child?
When Juno transmogrified Io into a horned heifer
    She increased the girl's sex-appeal.[11]   30
If you're after what's lawful and easy, then why not gather
    Leaves from the trees, or drink
Water out of the Tiber?[12] To prolong your dominion over
    Your lover calls for deception. (I hope I won't
Have cause to regret that statement.) Yet come what may, indulgence
    Irks me. I flee the eager, pursue the coy.
And as for *you*, man, so careless of your good lady,
    Why not start locking up at night?
Why not ask who it is comes tapping, ever so softly,
    On your front door—or why it is the dogs   40
Start barking at midnight? What about all those to-and-fro missives
    The maid delivers? How come your wife now sleeps
Alone so often? Why can't you get really worried just
    Once in a while, allow me to display
My skill at deception? To covet the wife of a dummy
    Is like stealing sand off the beach.
I'm warning you: put your foot down, play the heavy husband,
    Or I'll start going cold on your wife!
I've stood it quite long enough, always hoping you'd lock her
    Away out of sight, so that I   50
Could outwit you. But no. You clod, you put up with things no husband
    Should stand for a moment. Let me have the girl
And there's an end to my passion. Won't you *ever* deny me
    Entry, won't you beat me up one night?
Can't I ever feel scared? have insomnia? sigh in frustration?
    Won't you give me some good excuse
To wish you dead? I've no time for complaisant, pimping husbands—
    Their kinkiness spoils my fun.
Find someone else, who *likes* your easy-going habits, or if you
    Must have me as a rival, then *get tough!*   60

BOOK 3

I

There's this ancient wood—no axe has thinned it for ages,
    It might well be some spirit's home.
At its centre, a sacred spring, an arched limestone grotto,
    And sweet birdsong all around.
While I was strolling here, through an overwoven
    Dapple of shade, and wondering just what task

---

[11] Jupiter came to Danaê in a shower of gold, after her father had locked her in a tower lest she bear a son who, as had been prophesied, would slay him. In most versions of the Io myth, it is Jupiter who changes her into a heifer, in order to foil his jealous wife Juno.
[12] The river of Rome.

My Muse should embark on next, there appeared before me
    Elegy, perfumed hair caught up in a knot,
And short—I think—in one foot: good figure, nice dress, a loving
    Expression.[1] Even her lameness looked chic.   10
Behind her stalked barnstorming Tragedy, fraught brow hidden
    By flowing hair, mantle atrail in the dust,
Left hand waving a royal sceptre, high Lydian[2]
    Boots encasing her calves.
"Won't you *ever*," she asked me, "have done with love as a subject?
    Why get stuck in the same old poetic rut?
Your efforts to shock make gossip for drunken parties, a buzz at
    Every street-corner. As you walk by
Fingers point, people whisper: "Look, there goes that poet
    With the ultra-combustible heart."   20
All this shameless parade of your sexual activities makes you
    The talk of the whole town—and what do *you* care?
It's high time your inspiration chose a loftier model:
    You've idled enough. Start on some major work.
Your present theme cramps your style. Try the deeds of heroes—
    A subject (you'll find) more worthy of your art.
You've been playing at poetry—ballads for girl-adolescents,
    Juvenile stuff, the eternal *enfant terrible*.[3]
Now why not turn *my* way, make Roman tragedy famous,
    Give me the inspiration that I need?"   30
With that she nodded three or four times, her scarlet buskins[4]
    Holding her upright against the weight of her hair.
At this point, or so I recall, a mischievous expression
    Crept over Elegy's face. (Had she got
A myrtle-wand[5] In her hand? I think so.) "You posturing
    Windbag," she cried," do you *have* to be such a bore?
Can't you *ever* stop your pomposity? At least you condescended
    To attack me in elegiacs, you turned my own
Metre against me—not that I'd ever dream of comparing
    Your high palatial vein with my own   40
Minuscule talent. Besides, I'm frivolous, like my subject,
    And equally unheroic. All the same,
Without me Our Lady of Passion[6] would be plain vulgar—
    She needs my help as adviser and go-between.
The door your tough buskin can't break down flies open
    At one flattering word of mine;
Corinna took lessons from me, how to hoodwink porters
    Or spring the most foolproof lock,

---

[1] The elegiac couplet, the meter used in this and Ovid's other love poems, has a six-foot
line followed by a five-foot line. See the note to the *Amores*, I.i.4.
[2] Lydia was a region in Asia Minor.
[3] A shockingly unconventional person (literally, French for "terrible child").
[4] The heavy-soled laced boots worn by actors in ancient tragic drama.
[5] The myrtle was sacred to Venus, goddess of love.
[6] Venus.

How to slip out of bed in her nightdress and move with unerring
  Feet, like a cat, through the night.   50
Yet I've earned my advantage. I've beaten you by submitting
  To indignities which your pride
Would recoil from in horror. The times I've been nailed to indifferent
  Front doors, for any passer-by to read!
Why, I even remember lying snug in a maid's bosom
  Till some crusty chaperone took off—
Not to mention the time I was sent as a birthday present
  To that frightful girl who just tore me into shreds
And flushed me away. It was I who awakened your dormant
  Poetic genius. If *she's* after you now   60
It's me you should thank for it." "Ladies, please listen," I told them
  Nervously, "don't take offence—
One of you honours me with sceptre and buskins: high-flown
  Utterance springs to my lips at her touch.
But the other offers my passions undying glory: come then,
  Short foot and limping metre, it's you I choose!
I'm sorry, Tragedy. Just be patient awhile. Your service
  Demands a lifetime. *Her* needs are quickly met."
The goddess forgave me. I'd better get on with this little volume
  While I may—my subconscious is hatching a masterpiece.   70

3

Gods exist? Don't tell me. She went back on her sworn word—yet
  Her face looks no whit less pretty than before
That act of gross perfidy, her long hair has got no shorter
  Since she spat in divinity's eye. Her fair
Peaches-and-cream complexion is just as it was, the same delicate
  Flush warms her ivory cheek.
Those sweet little feet of hers are as tiny as ever; graceful
  And tall she was—graceful and tall she remains.
Bright eyes she had—they still shine like stars. Yet how many
  Times did the treacherous creature invoke   10
Them falsely to my deceit? Oh, I know the gods in heaven
  Forgive a girl's lies; true beauty enjoys divine
Status as such. Why, she swore an oath only the other
  Day, by the eyes of us both—but mine
Were the ones that suffered.[7] Come clean, Gods—if she bamboozled
  You with impunity, why should *I* have to pay
For another's offences? Isn't it bad enough that you ordered
  Andromeda to be sacrificed for her mama's
Crime of excessive beauty?[8] Worse still, that I find you puffball
  Witnesses, so that she fools   20

---

[7] She swore to the gods by both her own eyes and Ovid's, but only he came down with the eye ailment inflicted as divine punishment for the false oath.

[8] Cassiopeia incurred the wrath of the sea god Neptune when she boasted that she was more beautiful than the sea nymphs; as punishment, her daughter, Andromeda, was bound to a rock near the sea. (She was eventually rescued by Perseus.)

Us both with a laugh, unpunished. To redeem her perjury
  Must *I* pay the price, be stuck with a double con?
Either God is a word without substance, an empty bogey
  To play on the dumb credulity of the mob,
Or if he exists he's besotted by girls, allows them
  Exclusive rights, carte blanche.
We men aren't so lucky. Mars girds on his deadly broadsword
  Against us, Pallas Athene wields her spear
In unconquered might. Against us the bow of Apollo
  Is bent, and Jupiter poises his bolt,   30
Arm upflung—yet these same gods are scared of chastising
  A pretty blasphemer, they fear
Those who don't fear *them*. Then why bother to burn incense
  On their altars? We men should display
More courage. Jupiter's bolts blast his own high places and sacred
  Groves—but he's careful never to hit
A perjured lady. So many deserved it, yet only wretched
  Semele died, burnt up by her own zeal.
What, pray, would have happened if she'd resisted her lover's
  Advances? No motherly stint for divine Papa   40
Delivering Bacchus![9] Oh, what's the point of bombarding
  The sky with complaints? Gods have eyes, have hearts—
If *I* was divine, I'd legitimize ladies' barefaced
  Whoppers, let them take my godhead in vain.
Why, I'd even swear it was truth the little darlings were telling—
  I wouldn't be one of those mean old gods.
Still, darling, I'd be glad if you strained their forbearance
  A little less often—or left my eyes out of it.

                                    11A

I've stood enough, for too long. Heart and patience are both
      exhausted
  By this fickle obsession. So—*out!*
That's right, I've slipped the chain, achieved emancipation,
  Can blush—now—for what I once
Bore so unblushingly. Triumph: passion spurned and trodden
  Under my feet. A tardy access of horn-
Stiff will. Keep it up, stand firm. Such suffering's bound to
  Pay off in the end. Nasty medicine does you good.
How *could* I have swallowed such insults? The times I was driven
  Away from your door, to grovel on the bare   10
Pavement—*me*, a gentleman! The times I stood guard, slave-like,
  Outside your shuttered house (while you
Made love to God knows who) and was forced to watch your lover
  Lurch home exhausted, done in!

---

  [9] Semele, seduced by Jove and made pregnant with the god Bacchus, was maliciously persuaded by Juno to request a direct vision of Jove. Semele was destroyed by the sight as though
by lightning. Zeus rescued the fetal Bacchus from the dead Semele's womb and continued
the gestation in his thigh.

Yet even this hurt less than *him* seeing *me*—I could wish my
　　Bitterest enemy no worse a fate.
Was there ever a day when I failed to act as your personal
　　Watchdog, companion, shadow, lover, friend?
And wasn't it our relationship made you a public sweetheart,
　　One love-affair generating so many more? 20
Why remind you of all your sordid lies, those broken
　　Promises, worthless oaths
You swore to my undoing, the young men who gave you private
　　Signals at parties, coded exchanges? "She's sick,"
They told me: at once I hurried back like a madman, found you
　　The picture of health—and in my rival's arms.
Such incidents (there were others I'd sooner omit) have hardened
　　My heart at long last. So go find
Some other more willing victim. My vessel lies safe in harbour,
　　Garlanded,[10] indifferent to the swelling storm outside. 30
Leave off your blandishments. The old line's lost its magic
　　Hold on my senses. I'm not the fool I was.

11B

My capricious heart's a cockpit for conflicting emotions,
　　Love versus hate—but love, I think, will win.
I'll hate if I can. If not, I'll play the reluctant lover:
　　No ox loves the yoke—he's just stuck with what he hates.
A fugitive from your vices, I'm lured back by your beauty:
　　Your morals turn me off, your body on.
So I can live neither with nor without you, I don't seem
　　To know my own mind. I wish you were
Either less beautiful or more faithful: such a good figure
　　Doesn't go with your bad ways. 10
The facts demand censure, the face begs for love—and gets it,
　　Eclipsing (to my cost) its owner's crimes.
By the bed we shared, by all those gods who so often
　　Let you take their names in vain,
By your face, that image for me of high divinity,
　　By those eyes which captivated mine,
Spare me! And mine you'll always remain, whatever your nature;
　　Just choose—would you rather I loved
Freely or by constraint? Let me spread sail, cruise with a following
　　Breeze—make me want what I can't resist! 20

15

Mother of tender loves, you must find another poet:
　　My elegies are homing on their final lap.
Postscript concerning the author: of Paelignian extraction,
　　A man whose delights have never let him down,
Heir—for what that's worth—to an ancient family,
　　No brand-new knight jumped up

---

[10] Ships that reached port safely were draped with garlands.

Through the maelstrom fortunes of war.[11] Mantua boasts her Virgil,
  The Veronese their Catullus.[12] *I* shall become the pride
Of my fellow-Paelignians—a race who fought for freedom,
  Freedom with honour, in the Italian wars   10
That scared Rome witless. I can see some visitor to Sulmona
  Taking in its tiny scale, the streams and walls,
And saying: "Any township, however small, that could breed so
  Splendid a poet, I call great." Boy-god,
And you, Cyprian goddess,[13] his mother, remove your golden
  Standards from my terrain—
Horned Bacchus is goading me on to weightier efforts, bigger
  Horses, a really ambitious trip.[14]
So farewell, congenial Muse, unheroic elegiacs—
  Work born to live on when its maker's dead!   20

from *HEROIDES*

Translated by Daryl Hine

Ovid's *Heroides* ("Heroines") is a set of twenty-one fictional letters written either by legendary women or to them. Fifteen of the letters are freestanding solos; three others are paired with letters written to the women by their respective men. Among this latter set are an epistle from Paris to Helen and hers replying to him. On the upshot of these letters, we are to understand, will depend the eruption of the Trojan War.

Hecuba and Priam were king and queen of Troy, the enormously opulent city in Asia Minor. While pregnant with Paris, Hecuba dreamed that she would give birth to a firebrand. Frightened at the ill omen, the royal couple disowned Paris, who grew up as a simple shepherd. One day the young man was commanded by the gods to judge a divine beauty contest, the three contestants being Juno, queen of the gods (the Greeks' Hera); Minerva, or Pallas, goddess of wisdom (the Greeks' Athena); and Venus, goddess of love and beauty (the Greeks' Aphrodite). Each goddess tried to bribe the young judge, but the winning bribe was from Venus: In return for choosing her, Paris would be awarded Helen, the most beautiful of mortal women, wife of Menelaus of Sparta in Greece. Leaving behind the lovelorn wood nymph Oenone whose lover he had been in his days as a shepherd, Paris sailed for Greece with the intent of meeting and abducting Helen, his allotted prize.

In her early youth, Helen had been carried off by Theseus, ruler of Athens, but brought home again by her brothers, Castor and Pollux. When she became marriageable, and before she married Menelaus, the competition for Helen among her

[11] Ovid came originally from the town of Sulmona, in the Paelignian region, in east-central Italy (known today as the Abruzzi). The Paeligni had fought for freedom against Rome early in the first century B.C. but later were granted Roman citizenship. Ovid's family was an old, respected one, Roman citizens for generations, not one of the new-rich families spawned by the mid-century civil wars.

[12] The poets Virgil and Catullus (both first century B.C.) were also from the provinces—in their cases, northern Italy.

[13] Venus was especially venerated on the island of Cyprus.

[14] Bacchus was the patron god of drama. Ovid went on to write a tragedy, *Medea*, much admired in antiquity but now lost. He continued, though, to write much irreverent love poetry in the elegiac meter, including such works as *The Art of Love*.

countless suitors had been bitterly intense. A treaty, therefore, was made in advance: Helen's wooers agreed not only to respect her union with whoever won her but also to act in concert against any man who interfered with the resultant marriage. Their commitment to this pledge would, after Helen eloped with Paris, bring the Greeks together to fight the Trojans. The outcome of the divine beauty contest still rankling, Juno and Minerva would assist the Greeks in the war, Venus the Trojans.

Both Paris and Helen were descendants of Jupiter, Helen more directly, since she had been begotten by the god when, in the form of a swan, he ravished Leda, Helen's mother. [*Editors' headnote.*]

PARIS TO HELEN (XVI)

From Priam's son, whom nothing can avail
But Leda's daughter's salutation: hail!
Shall I speak out? Or is my love so well
Known that it would be tedious to tell?
Is my desire more obvious than I
Desire? You know that secrecy was my
Strong preference, until the day when we're
Free to enjoy each other without fear.
But I dissemble badly: who could hide
A fire whose brilliance cannot be denied?   10
If you insist that I articulate
The matter, *ardent* would describe my state.
Forgive my frankness, please, and read the rest
Not with a frowning face and lips compressed,
But with that air which suits your beauty best.
Your kind reception of this billet-doux[1]
Fills me with hopes you'll treat me kindly, too,
And that the queen of love made no mistake
About this quest she bade me undertake—
For, just in case you didn't know, divine   20
Protection of the highest kind is mine,
And I am brought here by a god's design.

The prize is great, but no more than my due.
Venus herself has promised me to you.
She aided me to trace the mazy way
Across the broad seas from the Trojan bay,
And furnished favorable winds, for she,
Born of the sea, is mistress of the sea.[2]
Just as she lulled the stormy waves to rest,
May she assuage the tumult in my breast   30
And give my hopes safe harbor as your guest.

---

[1] Love letter.
[2] By one account, Venus was born of sea foam gathering around the genitals of the ancient god Uranus, castrated by his usurping son, Cronus (the Romans' Saturn).

I brought with me what I did not discover
Here: my raison d'être as a lover.
Neither by storm nor error was I brought
Hither: this was the shore my vessel sought.
Don't think I sail the seas with goods for sale
(Heaven protect my tiny capital!)
Or that as a tourist I have come
(For we have bigger towns than yours at home!).
It's you I seek, whom Venus, don't forget,   40
Made mine. I yearned for you before we met;
Before I saw you, my soul recognized
The face that fame at first had advertised;
Nor is it strange if Cupid's arrows are
Equally fatal when shot from afar.
So fate decreed; don't try to topple fate.
Believe the tale I faithfully relate.

While in my mother's womb I lingered too
Late, my delivery long overdue,
She dreamt that from her swollen belly came   50
Forth an enormous firebrand all aflame.
Hecuba leapt up terrified, and told
Her nightmare to her husband, and the old
King asked his augurs what the dream foretold.
They prophesied that I'd set Troy on fire,
(Meaning, by this incendiary desire).
Exposed at birth, I was adopted by
Shepherds who raised me as a shepherd. My
Good looks seemed to belie my humble birth,
My spirit, too, proclaimed my hidden worth.   60
In Ida's[3] wooded vales there is a lone-
Some spot with oaks and pine trees overgrown,
Where neither placid sheep nor lazy cows
Nor goats that love a craggy landscape browse.
From there I glimpsed, when I had climbed a tree,
Beyond the walls and roofs of Troy, the sea.
Once, suddenly the earth was shaken by
Footsteps—it sounds incredible, but I
Speak truth: before my eyes on winged feet
Hermes[4] alighted. (Let me just repeat   70
The things I was permitted to behold.)
His godly fingers held a wand of gold.
Then on the greensward Juno, Pallas, and
Venus appeared with dainty feet to stand.
Sheer stupefaction and dumb terror made
My hair stand on end. "Don't be afraid,

[3] Ida was a mountain and mountainous region near Troy.
[4] Messenger god (the Romans' Mercury).

Just judge this beauty contest," Hermes said,
"Resolve these beauties' quarrel, and advise
Which of the three is worthy of first prize."
Then, Jove's command conveyed, without delay 80
Lest I refuse, he went his airy way.
Gradually I felt my nerve recover
Till I was not afraid to look them over.
They looked so lovely that I, to begin
With, wished that every one of them could win.
One nonetheless appealed to me above
The others—she, you know, who stirs both love
And rivalry. The bribes with which each tried
To influence the way I should decide!
Minerva courage, Juno power vaunted, 90
But I could not determine what I wanted,
Till Venus laughed, "Don't let such gifts affect
Your judgment, Paris. Dire is their effect.
I'll give you love. Though Leda's daughter's charms
Are unsurpassed, she'll fall into your arms."
Beauty's bribe proved irresistible,
And Venus returned to heaven invincible.

Meanwhile at last my fortunes had improved.
By certain signs my royal birth was proved;
Priam received his long-lost son with joy, 100
Decreeing a public holiday for Troy.
Girls yearned for me just as I yearn for you,
Thus you alone possess what not a few
Sighed for; not only dames of high degree
But dryads,[5] even, fell in love with me,
And if to Oenone I prefer
Yourself, no paramour is worthier.
I'm bound all other women to disparage
Now that I hope to win your hand in marriage.
My imagination used to keep 110
Your image before me, waking or asleep.
What will your presence do, whom I desire
Unseen? I burn before I touch the fire.

Not one to harbor hopes too long in vain,
I tried my luck upon the bounding main.
First to my hatchet Asian pine trees fell,
Or any kind of wood that floated well;
The slopes of Gargara[6] were stripped for timber,
And lofty Ida furnished me much lumber.

---

[5] Wood nymphs.
[6] A town and region on a bay south of Troy.

Curving hulls were built with oak keels, bent   120
And covered with a wooden tegument.
The rigging, masts and sails were added now,
And icons of the gods hung from the prow—
Venus on mine, who'd promised me a bride,
Full-length, with little Cupid at her side.
Soon all these preparations were complete,
And I could hardly wait to launch my fleet;
But, with my parents begging me to stay,
My undertaking suffered more delay.
Sister Cassandra[7] then began to wail   130
Just as the ships were ready to set sail,
"Why all this rush to fetch home fire and slaughter
Worse than you can guess across the water?"
True seer! the flames she prophesied are real,
For in my heart a raging fire I feel.

So I set out, and making use of most
Favorable winds, approached the Grecian coast.
Your husband made me welcome, not without
Discreet divine encouragement, no doubt;
Undoubtedly he showed me everything   140
In Sparta he deemed worth exhibiting.
So keen to see your famous charms was I
That nothing else at all could catch my eye;
And when I saw you, even as I held
My breath, my heart with new emotions swelled.
The face and form of Venus when she came
To judgment, I recall, looked much the same;
Had you competed in that contest, she
Might not have won the prize so easily.
Both far and wide extends your beauty's fame: 150
There is no land that does not praise your name;
Your loveliness has its equivalent
Nowhere from orient to occident.
Believe me, fame depreciates your true
Beauty, and rumour almost slanders you.
I find more here than hearsay promised me;
Legend falls short of your reality.

No wonder Theseus esteemed your charms
In toto worthy of a hero's arms!
You illustrated Spartan mores when   160
You wrestled nude in public with nude men.[8]
Well, who could blame him? Why return you, though?

---

[7] A Trojan princess and seer, whose prophecies always went unheeded.
[8] Spartans were noted for rigorous physical exercises (and an ascetic lifestyle).

A prize like you should never be let go.
I think that I would sooner lose my head
Than see somebody steal you from my bed;
Willingly these arms will never give
You up, or let you leave me while you live.
I'd not have sent you back before I got
Something venereal,[9] no matter what;
You would have given me your maidenhead, 170
Or that which may be sacrificed instead.
But simply give yourself, and you'll discover
In Paris a completely faithful lover,
For only in the ashes of my pyre[10]
Will my enflamed concupiscence[11] expire.

You I preferred to those great realms with which
Jove's wife and sister[12] promised to enrich
Me; if I could embrace you I'd despise
Minerva's promises to make me wise.
I don't regret my choice as foolish now; 180
My mind is made up once for all, I vow.
I beg you not to bring my hopes to nought,
Worthy of being with such trouble sought!
No base-born suitor for your noble hand
Am I; you shan't wed badly, understand.
You'll find a member of the Pleiades
And Jove himself among our family's
Forebears, and few mere mediocrities.[13]
My father rules the Asian continent,
Infinite in resources and extent; 190
There countless cities, gilded domes you'll see,
And temples worthy of their deity.
The towered walls of Troy you shall behold,
Walls which Apollo's music built of old.[14]
What can I tell you of the populace,
Who seem for earth almost too numerous?
Matrons of Troy will welcome you, for whom
The royal palace scarcely can find room.
You'll frequently exclaim, "How poor is Greece,
Whose cities have one wealthy house apiece!" 200

[9] Having to do with Venus, or sexual love.
[10] Cremating funeral fire.
[11] Carnal desire.
[12] Jove and Juno were son and daughter of Cronus.
[13] The Pleiades were seven daughters of Atlas, a primeval Titan. One of the daughters, Maia, was the mother of Hermes/Mercury by Jupiter. Dardanus, a son of Jupiter, was the aboriginal forebear of the Trojan line.
[14] Along with Neptune, Apollo had built the walls of Troy. (Both were defrauded of the wages due them for this work.)

I shouldn't sneer at Sparta, though in jest:
The land that bore you I consider blest.
Yet Sparta's stingy. You deserve to dress
Richly; that spot ill suits your loveliness.
With such a face you should spare no expense
On novel and exotic ornaments.
(Seeing the getup of our men of war,
You'll wonder what the Trojan women wore!)
Come, daughter of the Spartan countryside,
Do not disdain to be a Trojan's bride.   210
Trojan he was, and of our royal line,
Who now dilutes the gods' ambrosial wine;[15]
Trojan, Aurora's husband, snatched away
By the divine precursor of the day;[16]
Trojan, Anchises, whom the mother of
The wingèd Loves on Ida loved to love.[17]
You will not say your husband can compare
To me in youth and beauty, that I'll swear.
I do not have a relative, at least,
Who caused a blackout with his bloody feast.   220
Did Priam's father's bloody treachery
Give a bad name to the Myrtoan sea?
Among my ancestors, none vainly craves
For food and drink amid the Stygian waves.[18]
Yet, notwithstanding his descent, your spouse
Can boast of Jove's connection with his house.
And every night and all night long, this cad
Embraces you. It really is too bad!

I barely see you when we meat at meal-
Times—and then what agonies I feel!   230
I only wish that my worse enemies
Might all partake of banquets such as these!
Seeing that boor, his arm about your bare
Shoulders, I truly wish I weren't there.

---

[15] Ganymede, a beautiful young prince of early Trojan days, swept up into heaven by Jupiter to be the gods' cupbearer.

[16] Tithonus, another early Trojan prince, was so beautiful that Aurora, goddess of the dawn, took him for her lover and even granted him immortality (though, fatefully, she forget to exempt him from the process of aging).

[17] Anchises, beloved of Venus, was father by her of Aeneas, the Trojan hero of Virgil's *Aeneid*.

[18] The ancestors of Menelaus (and of his brother Agamemnon) perpetrated many atrocities. Atreus, their father, served his brother Thyestes' children to him as a dish at dinner. Their grandfather, Pelops, conspired with Myrtilus (for whom the Myrtoan Sea, part of the Aegean, was named) to kill a king by sabotaging his chariot, after which Pelops double-crossed Myrtilus and drowned him. Their great-grandfather, Tantalus, committed various crimes, for which he was punished in hell (the "Stygian" realm) by the "tantalizing" proximity of water and food he could not quite reach.

I burst with envy, watching him caress
Your lovely body underneath your dress.
In drink, when tenderly you kiss him right
In front of me, I drown the horrid sight,
Lowering my eyes if he holds you too tight.
In short, revolted by the things I saw, 240
The food I didn't want stuck in my craw.
Often I groaned aloud, and heard soon after
How my groans provoked your giddy laughter.
But when with wine I tried to quench desire,
Intoxication added fire to fire.
To see no more, I turned my head away,
But constantly my looks would stray your way.
The sight was painful, but what could I do?
My torment would be worse away from you.
I try to hide my state, I do my best, 250
But still my secret love is manifest,
Not just by word of mouth: my wounds are known
To you as well as if they were your own—
I wish that they were known to you alone!
How often tearfully I turned aside,
Lest Menelaus wonder why I cried.
Sometimes when drunk, recounting some romance,
I lent a personal significance
To every word, encountering your glance.
Who guessed that under a fictitious name 260
Myself and each true lover was the same?
At times, that I might speak more saucily,
I simulated inebriety.
Your dress, if it fell open, might lay bare
Your breasts, at which I could not help but stare:
Whiter than snow or milk they are, or than
Jove when he lay with Leda as a swan.
Astonished at this vision, I let slip
The goblet's twisted handle from my grip.
Each time you kissed your daughter, I would take 270
Your kisses from her lips for your sweet sake.
Singing old lays of love I'd sprawl supine,
Or with a nod send you a secret sign.
Your maids of honor recently I dared
Approach with winning words, but they declared
Only that they were scared, and left me there
Without an answer, halfway through my prayer.

I wish the gods would make you the reward
Of him who won your favors by the sword!
Like Atalanta, cunningly outrun, 280
Or Hippodameia once by Pelops won,
Like Deianira, carried off by force

By Hercules, who changed a river's course.[19]
In such case, my bravado might succeed,
And you would know that you'd been won indeed!
But now there's nothing else for me to do
But kiss your feet, if you'll allow me to,
And press my suit respectfully with you.
Sister of the Dioscuri,[20] your worth
Makes you their representative on earth.   290
Glorious beauty, who, had you not been
Jupiter's daughter, would have been his queen,
Either I'll take you home to be my wife
Or here in exile I shall end my life.
Love's arrow did not merely graze my heart
But penetrated to the deepest part;
Transfixed by that celestial dart, I guess
My sister[21] really was a prophetess!
Helen, this fateful love do not deride,
If you would have the gods upon your side.   300
So we may speak more privately, invite
Me to your bedroom at the dead of night.
Are you afraid to shame your marriage bed
And to betray the royal oaf you wed?
Poor, simpleminded Helen! To believe
Your looks innocuous—that *is* naive!
Alter your face, or else become more kind:
A modest loveliness is hard to find.
Venus and Jove enjoy the furtive act—
Like that in which he fathered you, in fact.   310
With parentage like yours, how could you be
Chaste? Is there nothing in heredity?
Behave yourself at Troy when we get there:
I want to be your only love affair!
Sin now, our wedding day will put it right—
If Venus' promises turn out alright!

So much your husband's actions seem to say:
To give me a free hand he stays away.

---

[19] Paris cites an odd assortment of examples to illustrate his point about winning brides
by the sword. The swift runner Atalanta, a determined virgin who would marry only a man
who defeated her in a foot race, was won when her suitor Hippomanes distracted her by throwing golden apples on the track. Hippodameia was the daughter of the king treacherously killed
by Pelops and Myrtilus (see the preceding note); she was to be given in marriage only to someone who defeated her father in a chariot race. To win his wife Deianira, Hercules had to out-
wrestle the river god Achelous; she later inadvertently caused Hercules' death.

[20] Castor and Pollux, Helen's heroic brothers, who were raised to the heavens as the constellation Gemini.

[21] Cassandra; see lines 130–135 and note.

No better time (he says) to visit Crete.
Oh, what a man! So prudent and discreet! 320
He left with this hospitable request:
"Take care for my sake of our Trojan guest."
But his commandment you neglect, I swear,
For of your guest you do not take good care.
If you think your god-given beauty can
Be rightly appreciated by that man,
You're wrong; for if he knew your value, would
He trust a stranger with his greatest good?
Even if you do not believe me, we
Should profit from such blind complicity, 330
Or we'd be stupider than he, to miss
A golden opportunity like this.
He all but ties the knot with his own hands,
So let's do what the simpleton demands.
Now all night long alone in bed you lie,
Night after endless night, and so do I.
Why not anticipate our honeymoon,
When night will be more radiant than noon?
I'll swear, in any formula that you
Suggest, and by your gods, that I'll be true. 340
If confidence is not misplaced, I hope
In person to persuade you to elope.
Afraid the deed will cover you with shame?
Well, don't be; I alone shall take the blame.
I'll merely follow Theseus' and your brothers'
Examples, as more pertinent than others';
For weren't you carried off by Theseus,
And weren't your brothers just as amorous?
The same old story will be told of us.
The Trojan fleet lies ready in the bay, 350
And wind and oar will speed our getaway.
You'll disembark at Troy like royalty;
The throng will hail a new divinity;
Along your route will clouds of incense rise
As at each step a sacred victim dies.
To every gift the house of Priam brings
You, Troy will add resplendent offerings.
But I can only hint at how much better
Your life will be in future, in this letter.

Don't worry, your abduction won't incite 360
Mayhem, with Greece arrayed in all its might.
How many women have been snatched before
Now, whose recovery provoked no war?
Believe me, Helen, there's no reason for
That fear. The Thracians were immune from slaughter
Although they took the king of Athens' daughter,

And Jason's homeland was not made to pay
When Jason with Medea ran away.
The very hero who abducted you
Once, abducted Ariadne too,
Yet Minos did not make a great to-do.[22]   370
Anxiety exceeds real danger here;
We fear what we should be ashamed to fear.
But say a great war does break out: I'm tough,
My weapons are injurious enough.[23]
The wealth of Asia, rich in men and horses,
Is more than equal to this land's resources.
Nor is your husband any braver than
Your lover, or a better fighting man.
Why, even as a lad I would attack   380
Our enemies to get our cattle back,
From which I got my nickname, Alexander,
Meaning "the best of men" or "the defender."
I beat the adolescent flower of Troy
In different competitions when a boy,
As an opponent formidable not
Only hand to hand, but a good shot.
You can't pretend that Menelaus ever
Struck you as precocious, skilled, and clever,
Nor can you give him what is worth another   390
Battalion, namely, Hector for a brother.[24]
Do you appreciate how brave and strong
This hero is to whom you will belong?
So, either the Greeks will not create a fuss
To get you back, or they will yield to us.
I don't mind taking arms for such a wife:
Magnificent prizes do promote some strife,
And if the whole world strove for you, your name
In times to come might gain undying fame.
Don't be afraid to hope. In recompense   400
The gods will favor your departure hence,
So claim your just deserts with confidence.

[22] Again, the examples Paris adduces are sinister. The first of these references may be to Procne (daughter of the legendary Athenian king Pandion), who married Tereus, king of Thrace. Tereus, Procne, and her sister Philomena suffered and committed several atrocities. Jason captured the Golden Fleece at Colchis, with the help of the king's daughter Medea, but she later committed several murders out of jealousy when Jason tired of her. Theseus, with the help of the princess Ariadne, killed the Minotaur, a predatory monster of Crete; Theseus later abandoned her, on the island of Naxos.

[23] Homer's *Iliad* shows Paris as a weakling in war, whom Helen treats with some contempt. According to tradition, though, he did kill the great Grecian warrior Achilles, with an arrow launched at long range.

[24] In the *Iliad*, Hector, the greatest of the Trojan warriors, treats Paris with forbearance but also expresses exasperation with his weakness. Helen will come to have something of a crush on Hector.

HELEN TO PARIS (XVII)

Now that your letter's thrust itself on my
Attention, politeness dictates a reply.
Profaning hospitality, you tried
To tempt your host's completely faithful bride.
Was it for this that our snug harbor gave
You shelter, tempest-tossed by wind and wave?
And though you were a total stranger, too,
Our palace portals opened wide to you?
O how could you repay our kindness so,
Intruding thus? And were you friend, or foe?   10
But you no doubt consider my complaint,
However justified, absurdly quaint:
Well, so be it! Better quaint than shameless,
Provided my behavior is blameless.
Although I don't affect a gloomy frown,
Sitting with knitted brows and eyes cast down,
My reputation and my pastimes are
Above reproach, and I do not, so far,
Condone adultery. I wonder at
Your confidence: what made you so sure that   20
I'd sleep with you? that, once a victim, I'm
Ripe for ravishment a second time?[1]
Had he seduced me, I might feel remorse,
But how was I to counter force with force?
Yet Theseus got no pleasure from his act;
I came back scared, virginity intact.
I struggled so, that if he snatched a kiss
Or two, he got no more from me than this,
With which your lust would not have been content.
Theseus—thank god!—was different,   30
His self-restraint diminished his offense,
Nor did his youth prevent his penitence,
And your success would add to his regret.
How notorious can a woman get!

Still, I might be kind enough to hear
Your suit—who can object if love's sincere?
Which I doubt, although I'm not suspicious.
I can't pretend my face is not delicious,
But trust has led so many girls astray,
And your sweet talk is insincere, they say.   40
"Chaste wives are not exactly numerous":
But why should my name not be cited thus?
Perhaps you think the precedent of my
Mother was one I could be ruined by?

---

[1] Helen is referring to her earlier abduction by Theseus. See the Headnote to the *Heroides*.

But Leda was deluded into sin:
A feathery seducer took her in.
If I succumb, it will be with my eyes
Open, my fall no "error" will disguise.
Her sin was blest, her partner was divine,
But where's the Jupiter to sanction mine?   50
Boast about your high descent, do you?
My family is quite distinguished too.
My father-in-law's remote forefather is
Jupiter, the grandfather of his
Father, Pelops, son of Tantalus—
But what has his descent to do with us?
Jove's my father; by a bird misled,
Credulous Leda took him to her bed.
Go tell the world about this tribe of yours,
And Priam, and your other ancestors,   60
Whom I respect—but you are fifth in line
From Jove, while my conception was divine.
Your empire is extensive, I admit,
But ours is not inferior to it,
Which, if more populous and richer than
Ours, is nonetheless barbarian.
Such promises your lavish letter made,
Even a goddess would, I'm sure, be swayed.
Your self is (were I tempted to transgress)
A better argument for wantonness.   70
If I don't keep my honor clear of stain,
It will be for your sake and not for gain.
And, though your gifts are precious to me, for
The giver's sake, your love means so much more
To me, and all the trouble that you take,
And all the miles you've voyaged for my sake.

I note your bold behavior, wretch, at table,
Dissembling just as far as I am able:
You look at me so naughtily that I
Find it difficult to meet your eye.   80
Sighing, you pick up the nearest cup
To me, and where I lately sipped you sup,
And neither your covert sign language nor
Your too expressive winks can I ignore,
Till, dreading lest my husband see the same,
Your blatant signals make me blush for shame.
"Nothing fazes him!" I whisper low,
And heaven only knows that this is so!
Scribbled on the tabletop in wine
I spotted your initials twined with mine;   90
Though I dismissed this then as poppycock,
I since have learned the meaning of such talk.

If I were going to sin, such blandishments
Might possibly exert some influence.
You have, I must admit, a pretty face,
And any girl might welcome your embrace.
Let others enjoy themselves in innocence!
My sense of married decency prevents
My sharing their amorous experience.
Learn from me how to dispense with beauty; 100
Abstinence from pleasure is a duty.
How many youths with your desires are wise,
Do you suppose? Do you alone have eyes?
The rest were less persistent, that is all.
You haven't got more heart: you've got more gall.

I wish you'd come in your swift vessel when
My maidenhood was sought by many men,
From whom I would have picked you at first sight—
My husband himself would overlook the slight.
Too late you've come to share preempted pleasures, 110
For what you hope to take, another treasures.
I might have liked to be your wife, but still
No husband holds me here against my will.
Stop using words to cause the downfall of
This tender heart which you affect to love.
Let me be faithful to my destiny—
You'll get no medal for seducing me.
Yet wasn't that the promise Venus made
When she and her sister goddesses displayed
Themselves before you in the Idaean glade? 120
One offered power, another martial pride,
But, "Helen," said the third, "will be your bride."
I can't believe those heavenly bodies lent
Their loveliness to your arbitrament,
But if they did, it surely is a lie
That your reward, and Venus' bribe, was I.
I am not so conceited I believe
Myself the greatest boon she could conceive.
Enough that men approve the way I look—
The praise of Venus only brings bad luck. 130
I shan't repudiate your homage, though:
How could I question what I wish were so?
If I was slow to credit you, I'm sorry:
In vital matters trust is dilatory.
I'm glad if what found favor in the eyes
Of Venus seems to you a worthy prize.
My beauty she had only to describe
And you rejected every other bribe,
So I'm your honor and your kingdom too.
I must be iron not to care for you. 140

Well, iron I'm not, and yet I think it wrong
To love someone to whom I can't belong.
Why should I try to till the seashore and
Pin false hopes upon the sterile sand?
Heaven knows that I am not so clever
As to deceive my doting husband ever!
In writing this clandestine letter, I'm
Abusing the alphabet for the first time.
Happy the skilled adulteress! I guess
How tricky are the paths of wickedness.   150
Confused, tormented by anxiety,
I think that every eye is fixed on me—
With reason: tittle-tattle I have heard,
Low talk, of which my handmaid brings me word.
Dissemble—or perhaps you'd rather go
Home? Why go, when you dissemble so?
In Menelaus' absence be discreet;
Our freedom is enlarged but not complete.
My husband was called suddenly away
On urgent business brooking no delay—   160
At least I thought it urgent anyway,
And when he stalled encouraged him to pack:
"The sooner you leave, the sooner you'll get back."
Reassured, he left with one request:
"Take care of Sparta—and our Trojan guest."
I had to laugh, and struggling to repress
My ribald giggles, answered merely, "Yes."
But now he's gone off on this Cretan jaunt
Don't think you can do anything you want,
For though he's absent I can feel his eyes   170
On us—have you forgotten kings have spies?
Rumor aggravating our position,
Your constant praise confirms his worst suspicion.
Renown, however pleasant, will be my
Ruin; better to give fame the lie.
You think it odd he leaves you with his wife?
He trusts my conduct and my blameless life.
He thinks that he can count, although my beauty
Makes him nervous, on my sense of duty.
"Do not overlook," you're telling me,   180
"This heaven-given opportunity
To profit by such dumb complacency."
Your opposition tempts me, but I'm scared;
I can't decide, my mind is unprepared.
My husband's gone, and you are lonely too,
Your looks please me as much as mine please you;
Long nights in the same house, and your discourse
Too sweet for purely verbal intercourse—
Everything is tempting me to stray,
Only some secret scruple blocks my way.   190

Where persuasion failed, may force succeed!
The only cure for backwardness indeed!
Victims sometimes don't find rape so bad:
I wish someone would force me to be glad.
It's easier to quell a new desire;
A little water quenches a fresh fire.
No stranger's love can be depended on;
Just when you think it's here to stay, it's gone.
Hypsipyle and Ariadne were
Each tricked into sleeping with a traveler,[2]   200
And did you not quite cavalierly wrong
Poor Oenone whom you liked so long?
You can't deny it! I have studied, so
To find out all about you, don't you know.
You could not, if you wanted, keep your word,
For your departure cannot be deferred.
Even as you're talking to me, and
While our night of bliss is being planned,
A western wind will waft you to your land;
Yes, in the midst of our debaucheries   210
You'll leave, and love will vanish on the breeze.
Shall I come too, as you are urging me
To do, your celebrated Troy to see
And marry into Priam's family?
No, am I so indifferent to fame
That I should fill the world with my bad name?
How will Sparta, how will Greece react?
And all of Asia—Troy itself, in fact?
What will Priam think, and Hecuba,
And all your brothers and your sisters-in-law?   220
How can you ever think me innocent
Again when you provide this precedent?
Every chance newcomer to appear
In Troy will fill you with dismay and fear;
Often in anger will you call me whore
While your own fault you're willing to ignore,
At once the scourge and prompter of my crime.
I pray that I'll be dead before that time!
And yet the splendid opulence of Troy,
Surpassing all you promised, I'd enjoy,   230
Purple and precious raiment, gold of which
There would be heaps enough to make me rich.

---

[2] During their voyage to seek the Golden Fleece, the Argonauts stopped for a time at Lemnos, where their leader, Jason, seduced Hypsipyle and then later abandoned her. On Ariadne, see the note to Paris's letter, lines 369–371.

Forgive me, but your gifts are not so grand.
Something still keeps me in my native land.
What help, if on your coast I should be wrecked,
From brother or father could I then expect?
Although false-hearted Jason promised all
She wanted to Medea, after all
Wasn't she driven from his father's hall?
How could she return, so much maligned,   240
To the family she left behind?[3]
I'm not afraid—nor was her ladyship,
But between cup and lip there's many a slip,
And many a ship with which the waves make sport,
You'll find, that had no trouble leaving port.
That bloody brand alarms me, which before
Your birth was due your mother dreamt she bore,
That prophecy as well, that Greece will come
And fire the topless towers of Ilium.[4]
Of course you're Venus' favorite, for she   250
Owes to you a twofold victory:
I fear the losing pair whom, if your boast
Is true, you robbed of what they wanted most.
No doubt if I eloped with you, a war
Would follow. Is our love worth fighting for?
Did not Hippodamia incite
The centaurs and the Lapiths once to fight?[5]
And do you think the justice of their cause
Will for a moment give my menfolk pause?
Although you vaunt your valor to the skies,   260
Such boastful words your countenance belies.
Your face and form are better fashioned for
Venus than Mars; her service suits you more;
Let strong men fight, while you make love not war.
Ask Hector, whom you laud, to fight for you:
Other fields deserve your derring-do,
And there I'd join you, were I not afraid,
And so would any knowledgeable maid.
Perhaps I shall, my honor laid aside,
And offer you my hands, which time has tied.   270
As for that tête-à-tête, I know what kind
Of private interview you have in mind!
Not so fast—your plans are immature
As yet—but time is on your side, I'm sure.

---

[3] On Medea, see Paris's letter, lines 367–368 and note. By helping Jason get the Golden
Fleece at Colchis, Medea alienated her people there. After fleeing with Jason to his home city,
Iolcus, Medea caused the death of that city's king, Pelias, so that she and Jason had to flee
once more, this time to Corinth, from Pelias' enraged subjects.

[4] Another name for Troy.

[5] At the feast celebrating the wedding of Hippodamia to Pirithous, one of the Lapiths, general violence broke out after a drunken Centaur assaulted the bride.

It's time that this clandestine letter, penned
With furtive, flagging fingers, had an end.
Further communication will be through
My maids, companions, and advisers too.

METAMORPHOSES

Translated by Rolfe Humphries

from BOOK I

My intention is to tell of bodies changed
To different forms; the gods, who made the changes,
Will help me—or I hope so—with a poem
That runs from the world's beginning to our own days.[1]

THE CREATION[2]

Before the ocean was, or earth, or heaven,
Nature was all alike, a shapelessness,
Chaos, so-called, all rude and lumpy matter,
Nothing but bulk, inert, in whose confusion
Discordant atoms warred: there was no sun
To light the universe; there was no moon   10
With slender silver crescents filling slowly;
No earth hung balanced in surrounding air;
No sea reached far along the fringe of shore.
Land, to be sure, there was, and air, and ocean,
But land on which no man could stand, and water
No man could swim in, air no man could breathe,
Air without light, substance forever changing,
Forever at war: within a single body
Heat fought with cold, wet fought with dry, the hard
Fought with the soft, things having weight contended   20
With weightless things.
                Till God, or kindlier Nature,[3]
Settled all argument, and separated
Heaven from earth, water from land, our air
From the high stratosphere, a liberation;

---

[1] The full fifteen-book poem ends with the transformations of Julius Caesar into a star and of Augustus, after his death (still in the future), into a god.

[2] The primordial transformation of chaos to order was itself a "metamorphosis." Compare the biblical account of creation in Genesis.

[3] The citing of two possible causes is a reflection of Ovid's wry religious skepticism.

So things evolved, and out of blind confusion
Found each its place, bound in eternal order.
The force of fire, that weightless element,
Leaped up and claimed the highest place in heaven;
Below it, air; and under them the earth
Sank with its grosser portions; and the water,   30
Lowest of all, held up, held in, the land.[4]

Whatever god it was, who out of chaos
Brought order to the universe, and gave it
Division, subdivision, he molded earth,
In the beginning, into a great globe,
Even on every side, and bade the waters
To spread and rise, under the rushing winds,
Surrounding earth; he added ponds and marshes,
He banked the river-channels, and the waters
Feed earth or run to sea, and that great flood   40
Washes on shores, not banks. He made the plains
Spread wide, the valleys settle, and the forest
Be dressed in leaves; he made the rocky mountains
Rise to full height, and as the vault of Heaven
Has two zones, left and right, and one between them
Hotter than these, the Lord of all Creation
Marked on the earth the same design and pattern.
The torrid zone too hot for men to live in,
The north and south too cold, but in the middle
Varying climate, temperature and season.   50
Above all things the air, lighter than earth,
Lighter than water, heavier than fire,
Towers and spreads; there mist and cloud assemble,
And fearful thunder and lightning and cold winds,
But these, by the Creator's order, held
No general dominion; even as it is,
These brothers brawl and quarrel; though each one
Has his own quarter, still, they come near tearing
The universe apart. Eurus is monarch
Of the lands of dawn, the realms of Araby,   60
The Persian ridges under the rays of morning.
Zephyrus holds the west that glows at sunset,
Boreas, who makes men shiver, holds the north,
Warm Auster governs in the misty southland,
And over them all presides the weightless ether,[5]
Pure without taint of earth.
                                These boundaries given,
Behold, the stars, long hidden under darkness,
Broke through and shone, all over the spangled heaven,

---

[4] The four primal elements were believed to be fire, air, earth, and water.
[5] The element of fire.

Their home forever, and the gods lived there,
And shining fish were given the waves for dwelling 70
And beasts the earth, and birds the moving air.

But something else was needed, a finer being,
More capable of mind, a sage, a ruler,
So Man was born, it may be, in God's image,
Or Earth, perhaps, so newly separated
From the old fire of Heaven, still retained
Some seed of the celestial force which fashioned
Gods out of living clay and running water.
All other animals look downward; Man,
Alone, erect, can raise his face toward Heaven. 80

THE FOUR AGES

The Golden Age was first, a time that cherished
Of its own will, justice and right; no law,
No punishment, was called for; fearfulness
Was quite unknown, and the bronze tablets[6] held
No legal threatening; no suppliant throng
Studied a judge's face; there were no judges,
There did not need to be. Trees had not yet
Been cut and hollowed, to visit other shores.
Men were content at home, and had no towns
With moats and walls around them; and no trumpets 90
Blared out alarums;[7] things like swords and helmets
Had not been heard of. No one needed soldiers.
People were unaggressive, and unanxious;
The years went by in peace. And Earth, untroubled,
Unharried by hoe or plowshare, brought forth all
That men had need for, and those men were happy,
Gathering berries from the mountain sides,
Cherries, or blackcaps, and the edible acorns.
Spring was forever, with a west wind blowing
Softly across the flowers no man had planted, 100
And Earth, unplowed, brought forth rich grain; the field,
Unfallowed, whitened with wheat, and there were rivers
Of milk, and rivers of honey, and golden nectar
Dripped from the dark-green oak-trees,
                                        After Saturn[8]
Was driven to the shadowy land of death,
And the world was under Jove, the Age of Silver
Came in, lower than gold, better than bronze.

---

[6] The Roman laws were written and publicly displayed on such tablets.
[7] Calls to battle.
[8] Chief of the gods in the older generation of divinities. He reigned during the Golden Age, until he was deposed by Jove and his dynasty.

Jove made the springtime shorter, added winter,
Summer, and autumn, the seasons as we know them.
That was the first time when the burnt air glowed   110
White-hot, or icicles hung down in winter.
And men built houses for themselves; the caverns,
The woodland thickets, and the bark-bound shelters
No longer served; and the seeds of grain were planted
In the long furrows, and the oxen struggled
Groaning and laboring under the heavy yoke.

Then came the Age of Bronze, and dispositions
Took on aggressive instincts, quick to arm,
Yet not entirely evil. And last of all
The Iron Age succeeded, whose base vein   120
Let loose all evil: modesty and truth
And righteousness fled earth, and in their place
Came trickery and slyness, plotting, swindling,
Violence and the damned desire of having.
Men spread their sails to winds unknown to sailors,
The pines came down their mountain-sides, to revel
And leap in the deep waters, and the ground,
Free, once, to everyone, like air and sunshine,
Was stepped off by surveyors. The rich earth,
Good giver of all the bounty of the harvest,   130
Was asked for more; they dug into her vitals,
Pried out the wealth a kinder lord had hidden
In Stygian[9] shadow, all that precious metal,
The root of evil. They found the guilt of iron,
And gold, more guilty still. And War came forth
That uses both to fight with; bloody hands
Brandished the clashing weapons. Men lived on plunder.
Guest was not safe from host, nor brother from brother,
A man would kill his wife, a wife her husband,
Stepmothers, dire and dreadful, stirred their brews   140
With poisonous aconite,[10] and sons would hustle
Fathers to death, and Piety lay vanquished,
And the maiden Justice, last of all immortals,
Fled from the bloody earth.
                                        Heaven was no safer.
Giants[11] attacked the very throne of Heaven,
Piled Pelion on Ossa, mountain on mountain
Up to the very stars. Jove struck them down
With thunderbolts, and the bulk of those huge bodies
Lay on the earth, and bled, and Mother Earth,

[9] Pertaining to the underground world.
[10] A plant related to monkshood, often poisonous.
[11] The Giants were offspring of Earth and Heaven; Ossa and Pelion are mountains in Thessaly, a region of Greece.

Made pregnant by that blood, brought forth new bodies, 150
And gave them, to recall her older offspring,
The forms of men. And this new stock was also
Contemptuous of gods, and murder-hungry
And violent. You would know they were sons of blood.

JOVE'S INTERVENTION

And Jove was witness from his lofty throne
Of all this evil, and groaned as he remembered
The wicked revels of Lycaon's table,
The latest guilt, a story still unknown
To the high gods. In awful indignation
He summoned them to council. No one dawdled. 160
Easily seen when the night skies are clear,
The Milky Way shines white. Along this road
The gods move toward the palace of the Thunderer,[12]
His royal halls, and, right and left, the dwellings
Of other gods are open, and guests come thronging.
The lesser gods live in a meaner section,
An area not reserved, as this one is,
For the illustrious Great Wheels of Heaven.
(Their Palatine Hill,[13] if I might call it so.)

They took their places in the marble chamber 170
Where high above them all their king was seated,
Holding his ivory sceptre, shaking out
Thrice, and again, his awful locks, the sign
That made the earth and stars and ocean tremble,
And then he spoke, in outrage: "I was troubled
Less for the sovereignty of all the world
In that old time when the snake-footed[14] giants
Laid each his hundred hands on captive Heaven.
Monstrous they were, and hostile, but their warfare
Sprung from one source, one body. Now, wherever 180
The sea-gods roar around the earth, a race
Must be destroyed, the race of men. I swear it!
I swear by all the Stygian rivers[15] gliding
Under the world, I have tried all other measures.
The knife must cut the cancer out, infection
Averted while it can be, from our numbers.
Those demigods, those rustic presences,
Nymphs, fauns, and satyrs, wood and mountain dwellers,
We have not yet honored with a place in Heaven,

---

[12] Jove.
[13] In the Rome of Ovid's time, the site of Caesar Augustus's dwelling.
[14] The lower part of the Giants' body was serpentine.
[15] To swear by the river Styx was the most solemn and binding oath a god could take.

But they should have some decent place to dwell in, 190
In peace and safety. Safety? Do you reckon
They will be safe, when I, who wield the thunder,
Who rule you all as subjects, am subjected
To the plottings of the barbarous Lycaon?"

They burned, they trembled. Who was this Lycaon,
Guilty of such rank infamy? They shuddered
In horror, with a fear of sudden ruin,
As the whole world did later, when assassins
Struck Julius Caesar down, and Prince Augustus [16]
Found satisfaction in the great devotion 200
That cried for vengeance, even as Jove took pleasure,
Then, in the gods' response. By word and gesture
He calmed them down, awed them again to silence,
And spoke once more:

THE STORY OF LYCAON

           "He has indeed been punished.
On that score have no worry. But what he did,
And how he paid, are things that I must tell you.
I had heard the age was desperately wicked,
I had heard, or so I hoped, a lie, a falsehood,
So I came down, as man, from high Olympus,
Wandered about the world. It would take too long 210
To tell you how widespread was all that evil.
All I had heard was grievous understatement!
I had crossed Maenala, a country bristling
With dens of animals, and crossed Cyllene,
And cold Lycaeus' [17] pine woods. Then I came
At evening, with the shadows growing longer,
To an Arcadian palace, where the tyrant
Was anything but royal in his welcome.
I gave a sign that a god had come, and people
Began to worship, and Lycaon mocked them, 220
Laughed at their prayers, and said: 'Watch me find out
Whether this fellow is a god or mortal,
I can tell quickly, and no doubt about it.'
He planned, that night, to kill me while I slumbered;
That was his way to test the truth. Moreover,
And not content with that, he took a hostage,
One sent by the Molossians,[18] cut his throat,
Boiled pieces of his flesh, still warm with life,

---

[16] A glance ahead to the very end of the poem, which celebrates the metamorphoses of these two Caesars.

[17] Maenala, Cyllene, Lycaeus are mountains in Arcadia, a rustic region in Greece.

[18] Inhabitants of Molossus, a city in Crete.

Broiled others, and set them before me on the table.
That was enough. I struck, and the bolt of lightning 230
Blasted the household of that guilty monarch.
He fled in terror, reached the silent fields,
And howled, and tried to speak. No use at all!
Foam dripped from his mouth; bloodthirsty still, he turned
Against the sheep, delighting still in slaughter,
And his arms were legs, and his robes were shaggy hair,
Yet he is still Lycaon, the same grayness,
The same fierce face, the same red eyes, a picture
Of bestial savagery. One house has fallen,
But more than one deserves to. Fury reigns 240
Over all the fields of Earth. They are sworn to evil,
Believe it. Let them pay for it, and quickly!
So stands my purpose."
              Part of them approved
With words and added fuel to his anger,
And part approved with silence, and yet all
Were grieving at the loss of humankind,
Were asking what the world would be, bereft
Of mortals: who would bring their altars incense?
Would earth be given the beasts, to spoil and ravage?
Jove told them not to worry; he would give them 250
Another race, unlike the first, created
Out of a miracle; he would see to it.

He was about to hurl his thunderbolts
At the whole world, but halted, fearing Heaven
Would burn from fire so vast, and pole to pole
Break out in flame and smoke, and he remembered
The fates had said that some day land and ocean,
The vault of Heaven, the whole world's mighty fortress,
Besieged by fire, would perish. He put aside
The bolts made in Cyclopean[19] workshops; better, 260
He thought, to drown the world by flooding water.

THE FLOOD

So, in the cave of Aeolus,[20] he prisoned
The North-wind, and the West-wind, and such others
As ever banish cloud, and he turned loose
The South-wind, and the South-wind came out streaming
With dripping wings, and pitch-black darkness veiling
His terrible countenance. His beard is heavy
With rain-cloud, and his hoary locks a torrent,

---

[19] The Cyclops were workers under Vulcan, the blacksmith god of fire.
[20] God of the winds; with the following lines compare the storm at the beginning of Virgil's *Aeneid*, Book I.

Mists are his chaplet,[21] and his wings and garments
Run with the rain. His broad hands squeeze together   270
Low-hanging clouds, and crash and rumble follow
Before the cloudburst, and the rainbow, Iris,
Draws water from the teeming earth, and feeds it
Into the clouds again. The crops are ruined,
The farmers' prayers all wasted, all the labor
Of a long year comes to nothing.
                                        And Jove's anger,
Unbounded by his own domain, was given
Help by his dark-blue brother. Neptune called
His rivers all, and told them, very briefly,
To loose their violence, open their houses,   280
Pour over embankments, let the river horses
Run wild as ever they would. And they obeyed him.
His trident[22] struck the shuddering earth; it opened
Way for the rush of waters. The leaping rivers
Flood over the great plains. Not only orchards
Are swept away, not only grain and cattle,
Not only men and houses, but altars, temples,
And shrines with holy fires. If any building
Stands firm, the waves keep rising over its roof-top,
Its towers are under water, and land and ocean   290
Are all alike, and everything is ocean,
An ocean with no shore-line.
                                        Some poor fellow
Seizes a hill-top; another, in a dinghy,
Rows where he used to plough, and one goes sailing
Over his fields of grain or over the chimney
Of what was once his cottage. Someone catches
Fish in the top of an elm-tree, or an anchor
Drags in green meadow-land, or the curved keel brushes
Grape-arbors under water. Ugly sea-cows
Float where the slender she-goats used to nibble   300
The tender grass, and the Nereids[23] come swimming
With curious wonder, looking, under water,
At houses, cities, parks, and groves. The dolphins
Invade the woods and brush against the oak-trees;
The wolf swims with the lamb; lion and tiger
Are borne along together; the wild boar
Finds all his strength is useless, and the deer
Cannot outspeed that torrent; wandering birds
Look long, in vain, for landing-place, and tumble,

---

[21] A garland for the head.
[22] The three-pronged spear wielded by the sea god Neptune.
[23] Sea nymphs.

Exhausted, into the sea. The deep's great license 310
Has buried all the hills, and new waves thunder
Against the mountain-tops. The flood has taken
All things, or nearly all, and those whom water,
By chance, has spared, starvation slowly conquers.

DEUCALION AND PYRRHA

Phocis,[24] a fertile land, while there was land,
Marked off Oetean from Boeotian fields.
It was ocean now, a plain of sudden waters.
There Mount Parnassus lifts its twin peaks skyward,
High, steep, cloud-piercing. And Deucalion came there
Rowing his wife. There was no other land, 320
The sea had drowned it all. And here they worshipped
First the Corycian[25] nymphs and native powers,
Then Themis, oracle and fate-revealer.
There was no better man than this Deucalion,
No one more fond of right; there was no woman
More scrupulously reverent than Pyrrha.
So, when Jove saw the world was one great ocean,
Only one woman left of all those thousands,
And only one man left of all those thousands,
Both innocent and worshipful, he parted 330
The clouds, turned loose the North-wind, swept them off,
Showed earth to heaven again, and sky to land,
And the sea's anger dwindled, and King Neptune
Put down his trident, calmed the waves, and Triton,[26]
Summoned from far down under, with his shoulders
Barnacle-strewn, loomed up above the waters,
The blue-green sea god, whose resounding horn
Is heard from shore to shore. Wet-bearded, Triton
Set lip to that great shell, as Neptune ordered,
Sounding retreat, and all the lands and waters 340
Heard and obeyed. The sea has shores; the rivers,
Still running high, have channels; the floods dwindle,
Hill-tops are seen again; the trees, long buried,
Rise with their leaves still muddy. The world returns.

Deucalion saw that world, all desolation,
All emptiness, all silence, and his tears
Rose as he spoke to Pyrrha: "O my wife,
The only woman, now, on all this earth,

---

[24]A mountainous region separating Boeotia from Oeta, a mountain range on the border of Thessaly.
[25]Of Corycus, a sacred grotto. Themis, in the next line, was a goddess of justice who controlled the oracle of Delphi before it became associated with Apollo.
[26]A merman, son of Neptune.

My consort and my cousin and my partner
In these immediate dangers, look! Of all the lands   350
To East or West, we two, we two alone,
Are all the population. Ocean holds
Everything else; our foothold, our assurance,
Are small as they can be, the clouds still frightful.
Poor woman—well, we are not all alone—
Suppose you had been, how would you bear your fear?
Who would console your grief? My wife, believe me,
Had the sea taken you, I would have followed.
If only I had the power, I would restore
The nations as my father[27] did, bring clay   360
To life with breathing. As it is, we two
Are all the human race, so Heaven has willed it,
Samples of men, mere specimens."
                                        They wept,
And prayed together, and having wept and prayed,
Resolved to make petition to the goddess
To seek her aid through oracles. Together
They went to the river-water, the stream Cephisus,
Still far from clear, but flowing down its channel,
And they took river-water, sprinkled foreheads,
Sprinkled their garments, and they turned their steps   370
To the temple of the goddess, where the altars
Stood with the fires gone dead, and ugly moss
Stained pediment and column. At the stairs
They both fell prone, kissed the chill stone in prayer:
"If the gods' anger ever listens
To righteous prayers, O Themis, we implore you,
Tell us by what device our wreck and ruin
May be repaired. Bring aid, most gentle goddess,
To sunken circumstance."
                                        And Themis heard them,
And gave this oracle: "Go from the temple,   380
Cover your heads, loosen your robes, and throw
Your mother's bones behind you!" Dumb, they stood
In blank amazement, a long silence, broken
By Pyrrha, finally: she would not do it!
With trembling lips she prays whatever pardon
Her disobedience might merit, but this outrage
She dare not risk, insult her mother's spirit
By throwing her bones around. In utter darkness
They voice the cryptic saying over and over,
What can it mean? They wonder. At last Deucalion   390
Finds the way out: "I might be wrong, but surely
The holy oracles would never counsel

---

[27] Prometheus, who made man from clay and also stole fire from heaven for human use.

A guilty act. The earth is our great mother,
And I suppose those bones the goddess mentions
Are the stones of earth; the order means to throw them,
The stones, behind us."
                              She was still uncertain,
And he by no means sure, and both distrustful
Of that command from Heaven; but what damage,
What harm, would there be in trying? They descended,
Covered their heads, loosened their garments, threw   400
The stones behind them as the goddess ordered.
The stones—who would believe it, had we not
The unimpeachable witness of Tradition?—
Began to lose their hardness, to soften, slowly,
To take on form, to grow in size, a little,
Become less rough, to look like human beings,
Or anyway as much like human beings
As statues do, when the sculptor is only starting,
Images half blocked out. The earthy portion,
Damp with some moisture, turned to flesh, the solid   410
Was bone, the veins were as they always had been.
The stones the man had thrown turned into men,
The stones the woman threw turned into women,
Such being the will of God. Hence we derive
The hardness that we have, and our endurance
Gives proof of what we have come from.
                                        Other forms
Of life came into being, generated
Out of the earth: the sun burnt off the dampness,
Heat made the slimy marshes swell; as seed
Swells in a mother's womb to shape and substance,   420
So new forms came to life. When the Nile river
Floods and recedes and the mud is warmed by sunshine,
Men, turning over the earth, find living things,
And some not living, but nearly so, imperfect,
On the verge of life, and often the same substance
Is part alive, part only clay. When moisture
Unites with heat, life is conceived; all things
Come from this union. Fire may fight with water,
But heat and moisture generate all things,
Their discord being productive. So when earth,   430
After that flood, still muddy, took the heat,
Felt the warm fire of sunlight, she conceived,
Brought forth, after their fashion, all the creatures,
Some old, some strange and monstrous.

*   *   *

The New Testament

(First and Second Centuries A.D.)

The name given to the distinctively Christian part of the Bible, the *New Testament,* can also be rendered as *New Covenant,* a term that has the advantage of underlining the intimate relationship, of kinship and separation, between it and what Christians call the Old Testament. The old covenant, sealed at Mount Sinai, was essentially a contract between God and the people of Israel. It was the culmination of a series of lesser covenants established between God and humanity, then between God and the Hebrew patriarchs. The contract spelled out the provisions by which God, on the occasion of the deliverance of the Hebrews from Egypt, revealed Himself to them and singled them out for special obligations and a special mission. Although the Exodus story, as told in the first six books of the Old Testament (the Hexateuch), has mythic content that links it to universal human religious insights, it nevertheless solemnizes a preeminently *historical* event, the establishment of the nation of Israel.

In later Old Testament times, written and popular traditions grew up stating that a divinely appointed Messiah would arise among the Jews to deliver them from their national tribulations and usher in a new era of triumph and glory. The Christians of the first century believed that this Messiah had in fact appeared, in the historical figure of Jesus of Nazareth. Through him God had established a new covenant, this time with a body of believers extending beyond the Jews. As the old covenant had been sealed with the ritual sprinkling of blood (Exodus 24:6–8), so had the new covenant, for this Messiah was—unexpectedly—a sacrificial victim. But he had risen from the dead as a pledge of an imminent second coming, or *Parousia,* that would vindicate God's newly adopted people. The doctrine of the Resurrection and the concomitant belief in the Parousia and final Judgment lay at the heart of Christian faith during the first century.

The canonical books of the New Testament, as finally defined several centuries after Jesus, number twenty-seven, all written in Greek: the four Gospels, some of unknown authorship but named Matthew, Mark, Luke, and John; a history of the early Church written by the author of Luke and called Acts of the Apostles; twenty-one letters, or Epistles, the most important of which are by St. Paul; and a visionary, allegorical work of prophecy named Revelation, or the Apocalypse. The earliest of these books are the Pauline letters, which were written mainly over the sixth decade of the first century; the other books were written at various dates extending through the end of the first century into the early part of the second century. Most of the New Testament books are statements of doctrine and church discipline; the more biographical ones are Acts and the four Gospels that center on the life and teaching of Jesus.

Although the four Gospels contain substantially similar accounts of the trial, sufferings, and execution of Jesus (the Passion), and all present an empty tomb that points to his resurrection, their portrayals of the earlier phases of Jesus' life are significantly different from one another. John, on the one hand, has its own distinctive material. Matthew, Mark, and Luke (the "synoptic" Gospels), on the other hand, contain a common fund of different material, and many passages have almost identical wording. In fact, approximately 99 percent of Mark, and much of its ordering of material, are paralleled (although sometimes recast) in Matthew and Luke. An enormous scholarly literature attempts to explain the significant overlap when these Gospels are "seen together" (the meaning of *synoptic*), and a consensus, called the two-document hypothesis, has dominated the field of interpretation during this century. The hypothesis proposes that Mark is the earliest Gospel (written around 65–70) and that Matthew and Luke, although written independently of each other (between about 80 and 95), are based partly on a direct knowledge of Mark. The shared but non-Markan material in Matthew and Luke is derived from a now lost collection, largely of sayings of Jesus, called Q (from German *Quelle,* "source"). Some authorities postulate that both Matthew and Luke also used other sources, called M and L, respectively. The synoptic problem is of course important in itself, but it has also intrigued scholars because it bears on the possibility of recovering facts about the historical Jesus from the earliest accounts. This search for the "real" Jesus, independent of later tendentious biases of the Gospel authors (the "evangelists"), was especially urgent in the nineteenth century. This search continues today, often from outside the distinctively Christian source materials—from archaeology, for example, or ancient history in general. The results, however, are often fanciful or farfetched. Scholars have attained some confidence concerning the typical teaching and activity of Jesus from the earliest form of sayings and stories, but they are doubtful that any of the evangelists, even the earliest, has provided an account either of Jesus' acts or of the sequence of his acts that is free from substantial interpretation.

That view may unsettle or puzzle readers accustomed to the goals of modern biography and historiography. But to the earliest Christians it was the overwhelming fact of the Messiah's death, resurrection, and imminent Parousia that was centrally important, not the circumstantial details of his life. (It is significant that the word translated as "gospel"—*good news*—did not originally refer as it usually does now to the formal genre represented by Matthew, Mark, Luke, and John but rather to the essential *message* just outlined.) Moreover, the tradition of both Jewish and pagan historiography assumed that the truth about any event or person could best be revealed by a respect for tradition and sources in the setting of the author's own creative intuition. This combination operates even in the author of Luke and Acts, the New Testament works governed most by the classical rules for writing history. The interest among Christians in what Jesus had said and done during his life as a whole arose only secondarily, and even then less from a modern need for historical accuracy in itself than from a sense of Jesus as an enduring, living presence and a desire to explore and authenticate the current doctrine and discipline of his living Church. The earliest Christians did not feel that the circumstantial data were of value apart from their significance.

It is important to recognize that each of the four Gospels has its own special intention and effect. They contain basic stories about Jesus' life and death that create an impression of coherence in the New Testament (some apocryphal Gospels written later do not cohere with these accounts), but the portraits differ unmistakably in their overtones: in Mark, Jesus is presented earthily, almost naturalistically; in Luke, beautifully and heroically; in John, with a supernal serenity; in Matthew, as compassionate but magisterial. More careful study reveals also differences between the Gospels in their doctrinal emphases, their views of the timing and nature of the coming apocalyptic Parousia, their definitions of ethical and communal duties of Christians, and their notions of worship. Each Gospel addresses the needs of a different group of early Christians in its own place and set of circumstances.

Matthew was probably written in Syria, as a manual of instruction for a well-established Christian community, containing both Jewish and Gentile converts, that was competing with Pharisaic Judaism after the destruction of the Jerusalem Temple in 70 A.D. The author is concerned to define the Church as the New Israel, replacing the old one by means of a way of righteousness surpassing the righteousness of the Pharisees (a difficult goal, because the Pharisees were the most fervently religious Jews within first-century Jewish society). Events of Jesus' life—especially healings, exorcisms, and other miraculous manifestations of messianic power—are integrated into a careful, five-fold structure culminating five times in authoritative, didactic discourses—a structure possibly designed deliberately to parallel the five books of Torah or Mosaic law. The first of these discourses is the Sermon on the Mount (chapters 5–7), which outlines Christian ethics and its spiritual premises. Much of the Sermon contrasts traditional teaching with the new Christian version of such teaching. The implication, it might seem, is that a new dispensation has replaced the old Law. At the same time, paradoxically, Jesus insists that the old Law remains in force: "Till heaven and earth pass, one jot or one tittle shall in no wise pass from the law, till all be fulfilled" (Matthew 5:18). The paradox can be partially resolved if we understand "fulfilled" to mean "brought to fruition" rather than "superseded": the Christian code is a living outgrowth of the Law, and it no more negates its origin than the fruit of a tree negates the tree's earlier history of bud and leaf. Accordingly, Matthew also has a strong sense of continuity with the Old Testament, including its iconography, symbolism, and settings. It is no coincidence that the Sermon in Matthew 5–7 takes place on a "mount" (actually, a hill), for this setting bears witness to its awesome earlier archetype, the Mount Sinai where God originally promulgated His teachings. In many ways, Matthew is the most "Jewish" of the gospels, despite the evident tensions between it and traditional Judaism.

FURTHER READING *(prepared by F.S.N.)*: *Harper's Bible Dictionary,* general ed. Paul J. Achtemeier, 1985, is scholarly but accessible to general readers and contains articles of manageable length on such topics as "Jesus" and "Jerusalem." The 1975 revision, by Allen C. Myers et al., of *The Eerdmans Bible Dictionary,* rep. 1987, is an excellent one-volume comprehensive reference work on the Bible, arranged alphabetically. Another excellent work of reference, containing general articles on the New Testament, introductions, exegesis, and expositions for individual books, is *The Interpreter's Bible,* ed. George A. Buttrick, 12 vols., 1952. Also very helpful is *The Interpreter's Dictionary of the Bible: An Illustrated Encyclopedia,* ed. George A. Buttrick, 4 vols., 1962, and its *Supplementary Volume,* ed. Keith Crim, 1976. For further useful articles, see John E. Steinmueller and Kathryn Sullivan, eds., *Catholic Biblical Encyclopedia: New Testament,* 1950. Werner Jaeger, *Early Christianity and Greek Paideia,* 1961, shows the influence of Greek civilization on Christianity; David Daube, *The New Testament and Rabbinic Judaism,* 1956, explores the relationship between Christianity and Judaism; and Howard Clark Kee, Franklin W. Young, and Karlfried Froehlich, *Understanding the New Testament,* 1957, 3rd ed. 1973, assembles excellent material on both the Hellenistic and the Jewish background to the Gospel narratives. Exegetical treatments of the individual books are given by A. E. Harvey, *The New English Bible: Companion to the New Testament,* 1970; and by Raymond E. Brown, Joseph A. Fitzmyer, and Roland E. Murphy, *The Jerome Biblical Commentary,* 1968. Early Christian beliefs, the expansion of the early Church, and its consolidation are discussed by James L. Price, *Interpreting the New Testament,* 1961. Anthony J. Tambasco, *In the Days of Jesus: The Jewish Background and Unique Teaching of Jesus,* 1983, is a short book capsulizing recent research on the Gospels and placing Jesus in the historical setting. Gerhard Lohfink, *Jesus and Community: The Social Dimension of Christian Faith,* trans. John P. Galvin, 1984, examines the life and mission of Jesus in the context of contemporary Judaism. David E. Aune, *Prophecy in Early Christianity and the Ancient Mediterranean World,* 1983, views the teaching of Jesus in the light of Jewish and Greco-Roman prophetic traditions. *The Literary Guide to the Bible,* eds. Robert Alter and Frank Kermode, 1987, includes introductions to both Testaments and essays on almost all the biblical books; Kermode writes on Matthew.

THE NEW TESTAMENT

King James Version (1611)

from THE GOSPEL ACCORDING TO SAINT MATTHEW

THE SERMON ON THE MOUNT

And seeing the multitudes, he went up into a mountain: and when he was set, his disciples came unto him: and he opened his mouth, and taught them, saying,[1]

Blessed are the poor in spirit: for theirs is the kingdom of heaven.
Blessed are they that mourn: for they shall be comforted.
Blessed are the meek: for they shall inherit the earth.
Blessed are they which do hunger and thirst after righteousness: for they shall be filled.
Blessed are the merciful: for they shall obtain mercy.
Blessed are the pure in heart: for they shall see God.
Blessed are the peacemakers: for they shall be called the children of God.
Blessed are they which are persecuted for righteousness' sake: for theirs is the kingdom of heaven.
Blessed are ye, when men shall revile you, and persecute you, and shall say all manner of evil against you falsely, for my sake. Rejoice, and be exceeding glad: for great is your reward in heaven: for so persecuted they the prophets which were before you. (5:1–12)

Ye are the salt of the earth: but if the salt have lost his savor, wherewith shall it be salted? it is thenceforth good for nothing, but to be cast out, and to be trodden under foot of men. Ye are the light of the world. A city that

---

[1] The Sermon on the Mount is often regarded as the quintessence of Christian ethical teaching. That it is given from a hill (or "mountain") underlines a basic theme in what follows: the relationship of the new teaching to the law of Moses, also delivered from a mountain (Sinai).

is set on an hill cannot be hid. Neither do men light a candle, and put it under a bushel,[2] but on a candlestick; and it giveth light unto all that are in the house. Let your light so shine before men, that they may see your good works, and glorify your Father which is in heaven. (5:13–16)

Think not that I am come to destroy the law, or the prophets: I am not come to destroy, but to fulfill. For verily I say unto you, Till heaven and earth pass, one jot or one tittle shall in no wise pass from the law, till all be fulfilled. Whosoever therefore shall break one of these least commandments, and shall teach men so, he shall be called the least in the kingdom of heaven: but whosoever shall do and teach them, the same shall be called great in the kingdom of heaven. For I say unto you, That except your righteousness shall exceed the righteousness of the scribes and Pharisees, ye shall in no case enter into the kingdom of heaven. (5:17–20)

Ye have heard that it was said by them of old time, 'Thou shalt not kill'; and 'whosoever shall kill shall be in danger of the judgment':[3] but I say unto you, That whosoever is angry with his brother without a cause shall be in danger of the judgment: and whosoever shall say to his brother, 'Raca,'[4] shall be in danger of the council:[5] but whosoever shall say, 'Thou fool,' shall be in danger of hell fire. Therefore if thou bring thy gift to the altar, and there rememberest that thy brother hath ought against thee; leave there thy gift before the altar, and go thy way; first be reconciled to thy brother, and then come and offer thy gift. Agree with thine adversary quickly, whiles thou art in the way with him;[6] lest at any time the adversary deliver thee to the judge, and the judge deliver thee to the officer, and thou be cast into prison. Verily I say unto thee, Thou shalt by no means come out thence, till thou hast paid the uttermost farthing.[7] (5:21–26)

Ye have heard that it was said by them of old time, 'Thou shalt not commit adultery': but I say unto you, That whosoever looketh on a woman to lust after her hath committed adultery with her already in his heart. And if thy right eye offend thee, pluck it out, and cast it from thee: for it is profitable for thee that one of thy members should perish, and not that thy whole body should be cast into hell. And if thy right hand offend thee, cut it off, and cast it from thee: for it is profitable for thee that one of thy members should perish, and not that thy whole body should be cast into hell. It hath been said, 'Whosoever shall put away his wife, let him give her a writing of divorcement': but I say unto you, That whosoever shall put away his wife, saving for the cause of fornication, causeth her to commit adultery: and whosoever shall marry her that is divorced committeth adultery. (5:27–32)

Again, ye have heard that it hath been said by them of old time, 'Thou shalt not forswear thyself, but shalt perform unto the Lord thine oaths': but I say unto you, Swear not at all; neither by heaven; for it is God's throne: nor by the earth; for it is his footstool: neither by Jerusalem; for it is the city of the great King. Neither shalt thou swear by thy head,[8] because thou canst

---

[2] A measuring tub for meal.

[3] Prosecutable in court. Jesus goes on to say that even anger should be similarly prosecutable, like actual murder.

[4] Blockhead or idiot.   [5] The Sanhedrin, the highest Jewish law court.

[6] On the way to court.

[7] The last penny of the money owed for which one is being sued.

[8] By one's self.

not make one hair white or black. But let your communication be, 'Yea, yea'; 'Nay, nay': for whatsoever is more than these cometh of evil. (5:33–37)

Ye have heard that it hath been said, 'An eye for an eye, and a tooth for a tooth': but I say unto you, That ye resist not evil: but whosoever shall smite thee on thy right cheek, turn to him the other also. And if any man will sue thee at the law, and take away thy coat, let him have thy cloak also. And whosoever shall compel thee to go a mile, go with him twain.[9] Give to him that asketh thee, and from him that would borrow of thee turn not thou away. (5:38–42)

Ye have heard that it hath been said, 'Thou shalt love thy neighbor, and hate thine enemy.'[10] But I say unto you, Love your enemies, bless them that curse you, do good to them that hate you, and pray for them which despitefully use you, and persecute you; that ye may be the children of your Father which is in heaven: for he maketh his sun to rise on the evil and on the good, and sendeth rain on the just and on the unjust. For if ye love them which love you, what reward have ye? do not even the publicans[11] the same? And if ye salute your brethren only, what do ye more than others? do not even the publicans so? Be ye therefore perfect, even as your Father which is in heaven is perfect. (5:43–48)

Take heed that ye do not your alms before men, to be seen of them: otherwise ye have no reward of your Father which is in heaven. Therefore when thou doest thine alms, do not sound a trumpet before thee, as the hypocrites do in the synagogues and in the streets, that they may have glory of men. Verily I say unto you, They have their reward. But when thou doest alms, let not thy left hand know what thy right hand doeth: that thine alms may be in secret: and thy Father which seeth in secret himself shall reward thee openly. (6:1–4)

And when thou prayest, thou shalt not be as the hypocrites are: for they love to pray standing in the synagogues and in the corners of the streets, that they may be seen of men. Verily I say unto you, They have their reward. But thou, when thou prayest, enter into thy closet,[12] and when thou hast shut thy door, pray to thy Father which is in secret; and thy Father which seeth in secret shall reward thee openly. But when ye pray, use not vain repetitions, as the heathen do: for they think that they shall be heard for their much speaking. Be not ye therefore like unto them: for your Father knoweth what things ye have need of, before ye ask him. After this manner therefore pray ye:

> Our Father which art in heaven,
> Hallowed be thy name.
> Thy kingdom come.
> Thy will be done
>   in earth as it is in heaven.

---

[9] Two.

[10] The Old Testament enjoins love of one's neighbor but not explicitly hatred of enemies. That was, however, a popular inference from the former.

[11] Tax collectors, a generally despised group; elsewhere in the Gospels they are usually mentioned more sympathetically.

[12] Private room. Jesus is not condemning, however, congregational prayer in the temple or synagogue.

Give us this day our daily bread.
And forgive us our debts,
  as we forgive our debtors.[13]
And lead us not into temptation,
  but deliver us from evil:[14]
For thine is the kingdom, and the power, and the glory, for ever.
  Amen.

For if ye forgive men their trespasses, your heavenly Father will also forgive you: but if ye forgive not men their trespasses, neither will your Father forgive your trespasses. (6:5–15)

Moreover when ye fast, be not, as the hypocrites, of a sad countenance: for they disfigure their faces, that they may appear unto men to fast. Verily I say unto you, They have their reward. But thou, when thou fastest, anoint thine head, and wash thy face;[15] that thou appear not unto men to fast, but unto thy Father which is in secret: and thy Father, which seeth in secret, shall reward thee openly. (6:16–18)

Lay not up for yourselves treasures upon earth, where moth and rust doth corrupt, and where thieves break through and steal: but lay up for yourselves treasures in heaven, where neither moth nor rust doth corrupt, and where thieves do not break through nor steal: for where your treasure is, there will your heart be also. The light of the body is the eye: if therefore thine eye be single,[16] thy whole body shall be full of light. But if thine eye be evil, thy whole body shall be full of darkness. If therefore the light that is in thee be darkness, how great is that darkness! (6:19–23)

No man can serve two masters: for either he will hate the one, and love the other; or else he will hold to the one, and despise the other. Ye cannot serve God and mammon.[17] Therefore I say unto you, Take no thought for your life, what ye shall eat, or what ye shall drink; nor yet for your body, what ye shall put on. Is not the life more than meat, and the body than raiment? Behold the fowls of the air: for they sow not, neither do they reap, nor gather into barns; yet your heavenly Father feedeth them. Are ye not much better than they? Which of you by taking thought can add one cubit[18] unto his stature? And why take ye thought for raiment? Consider the lilies of the field, how they grow; they toil not, neither do they spin: and yet I say unto you, That even Solomon in all his glory was not arrayed like one of these. Wherefore, if God so clothe the grass of the field, which today is, and tomorrow is cast into the oven,[19] shall he not much more clothe you, O ye of little faith? Therefore take no thought, saying, 'What shall we eat?' or, 'What shall we drink?' or, 'Wherewithal shall we be clothed?' (for after all these things do the Gentiles seek:) for your heavenly Father knoweth that ye have need of all these things. But seek ye first the kingdom of God, and

---

[13] The words *debts* and *debtors* can be rendered as, respectively, the wrongs we have committed and those that have been committed against us.

[14] In most of the earliest manuscripts, the Lord's Prayer ends here.

[15] Anointing and washing were part of preparing for a banquet.

[16] Healthy, as opposed to the "evil" (diseased) eye.

[17] Material possessions and money.   [18] About 20 inches.

[19] As fuel.

his righteousness; and all these things shall be added unto you. Take therefore no thought for the morrow: for the morrow shall take thought for the things of itself. Sufficient unto the day is the evil thereof.[20] (6:24–34)

Judge not, that ye be not judged. For with what judgment ye judge, ye shall be judged: and with what measure ye mete, it shall be measured to you again. And why beholdest thou the mote[21] that is in thy brother's eye, but considerest not the beam that is in thine own eye? Or how wilt thou say to thy brother, 'Let me pull out the mote out of thine eye'; and, behold, a beam is in thine own eye? Thou hypocrite, first cast out the beam out of thine own eye; and then shalt thou see clearly to cast out the mote out of thy brother's eye. (7:1–5)

Give not that which is holy unto the dogs, neither cast ye your pearls before swine, lest they trample them under their feet, and turn again and rend you. (7:6)

Ask, and it shall be given you; seek, and ye shall find; knock, and it shall be opened unto you: for every one that asketh receiveth; and he that seeketh findeth; and to him that knocketh it shall be opened. Or what man is there of you, whom if his son ask bread, will he give him a stone? Or if he ask a fish, will he give him a serpent? If ye then, being evil, know how to give good gifts unto your children, how much more shall your Father which is in heaven give good things to them that ask him? (7:7–11)

Therefore all things whatsoever ye would that men should do to you, do ye even so to them: for this is the law and the prophets. (7:12)

Enter ye in at the strait gate: for wide is the gate, and broad is the way, that leadeth to destruction, and many there be which go in thereat: because strait is the gate, and narrow is the way, which leadeth unto life, and few there be that find it. (7:13–14)

Beware of false prophets,[22] which come to you in sheep's clothing, but inwardly they are ravening wolves. Ye shall know them by their fruits. Do men gather grapes of thorns, or figs of thistles? Even so every good tree bringeth forth good fruit; but a corrupt tree bringeth forth evil fruit. A good tree cannot bring forth evil fruit, neither can a corrupt tree bring forth good fruit. Every tree that bringeth not forth good fruit is hewn down and cast into the fire. Wherefore by their fruits ye shall know them. (7:15–20)

Not every one that saith unto me, 'Lord, Lord,' shall enter into the kingdom of heaven; but he that doeth the will of my Father which is in heaven. Many will say to me in that day, 'Lord, Lord, have we not prophesied in thy name? and in thy name have cast out devils? and in thy name done many wonderful works?' And then will I profess unto them, 'I never knew you: depart from me, ye that work iniquity.' (7:21–23)

Therefore whosoever heareth these sayings of mine, and doeth them, I will liken him unto a wise man, which built his house upon a rock: and the rain descended, and the floods came, and the winds blew, and beat upon that house; and it fell not: for it was founded upon a rock. And every one

---

[20] Each day has anxieties enough of its own; one need not add to them worries about the future.

[21] A tiny speck of wood, as contrasted with a "beam," or large board.

[22] The caution against false prophets and that in the following passage against those who say "Lord, Lord" are less applicable to Jesus' own time than to the problems the early Church faced a half-century later (when Matthew was written).

that heareth these sayings of mine, and doeth them not, shall be likened unto a foolish man, which built his house upon the sand: and the rain descended, and the floods came, and the winds blew, and beat upon that house; and it fell: and great was the fall of it. (7:24–27)

And it came to pass, when Jesus had ended these sayings, the people were astonished at his doctrine: for he taught them as one having authority, and not as the scribes.[23] (7:28–29)

[23] He did not teach with a cautious conformity to tradition, like the scribes, but rather like the prophets.

The Middle Ages

*T*HE term *Middle Ages* as a description of the thousand-year period between the fifth and the fifteenth centuries—between the end of the Roman Empire and the Renaissance—is at once an oversimplification and a distortion of a long and complex period of European history. Coined by Renaissance and Enlightenment thinkers, the label *Middle Ages* (or its Latin form, the *Medieval* period) implies a mere transitional era, a long interruption in the continuity of Western history during which the classical culture of Greece and Rome, waiting to be revived in the Renaissance, lay dormant or dead.

From our perspective, we can see the Middle Ages in more positive terms, not as an interruption but as a fertile and dynamic period that produced a distinctive and permanently valuable culture of its own. It was more varied than a single, reductive label would imply. There is a certain unity in this long span of history that justifies our considering it as a single period, but within this unity is enormous diversity. Only the very early Middle Ages, from the sixth to the ninth centuries, were characterized by the cultural inertia often attributed to the whole period. The collapse of the Roman Empire left Europe for a time in chaos, with its economy, its social organization, and its culture brought almost to a halt. But even these "Dark Ages" were not without their rays of light, especially in areas where survivals of the Roman heritage or the Church preserved pockets of culture. In retrospect, we can see forces working during this fallow period that were to emerge later in a new and vital form of social organization. The new organization began to take shape in about the tenth century and led by the thirteenth century to a flowering of art and culture that anticipated and rivaled the Renaissance without forfeiting its own distinctively medieval character.

The formidable challenge to the early Middle Ages was to find a mode of social organization to replace the Roman Empire and to weave together the various threads of European culture: the remnants of Latin civilization, Christianity, and the northern, Germanic, "barbarian" tradition. The solution that gradually emerged over a period of several centuries lay in two institutions, the Roman Church and feudalism.

By the time of the Empire's final collapse, the Church had made great strides toward becoming a universal institution. Paul, the "Apostle of the Gentiles," was the chief architect in the conversion of Christianity from a parochial, nationalistic cult among dissident Jews to a universal religion. During the fourth century, Christianity gradually became the state religion of Rome; the emperor Theodosius at the end of the century formally proclaimed it as such, closed heathen temples, and forbade heathen sacrifices. Within a few years, pagans were actively persecuted as the Christians had been persecuted earlier.

At the beginning of the fifth century, the centralizing forces in Christianity culminated in the claim by Pope Innocent I to jurisdiction over all Christendom. The centrally organized Church was to a large extent modeled on the Empire. As the Empire gradually wasted away, the Church emerged more and more clearly as its spiritual heir and as a universal source of authority. It also became, for a thousand years, the heir and the chief custodian of Latin culture. It preserved much of the classic Roman literature and over the centuries fostered a rich body of medieval Latin writing, largely ecclesiastical in nature. This work included philosophy such as that of St. Augustine, St. Anselm, and St. Thomas Aquinas; rhetoric, such as Geoffrey of Vinsauf's; chronicles and compilations of legendary history, such as the *Gesta Romanorum* and the Venerable Bede's *Ecclesiastical History of the English Nation;* a rich body of Latin religious poetry, especially hymns; and many other works.

The power of the medieval church was based upon two propositions, which it inculcated almost universally: that the visible scene of human life was a perpetual conflict between the Kingdom of God and the Kingdom of the Devil, and that salvation for the individual was available only through the offices of the Church. This world was seen as secondary to the world to come, a testing ground determining whether the individual would spend eternity in Heaven or Hell. Because participation in the sacraments of the Church was a requirement for salvation, the Church vitally affected the individual's fate through all eternity, a fate that at its worst was regarded with a fearful literalness.

The elaborate bureaucracy of the Roman Empire was reflected in the detailed hierarchy through which the Church performed its functions and which, in its meticulous emphasis upon rank and degree, expressed one of the deepest and most pervasive habits of medieval thought. The individual was linked to God through an elaborate chain of hierarchical relationships. Above the individual believer was the priest; above the priest were, in succession, bishop, archbishop, cardinal, and pope. The ranks rose, beyond the earthly Church, above the pope through the intricate orders of angels to God Himself. The pope was thus, in this minutely detailed scheme of things, the direct representative of God on earth, with absolute power to "bind and loose."

Quite apart from its religious function, the medieval Church was a vitally important social institution in the Middle Ages. In an era full of political disorder and conflict, it provided a slight check upon secular warfare, by asserting an authority that transcended political boundaries. It tempered social oppression by opening Church offices to commoners and upholding the doctrine of the equality of all men before God. It also helped unify and stabilize European culture by defining a broadly accepted system of values and beliefs.

The fixed hierarchy of the medieval Church was mirrored in feudalism, the secular social and economic system that gradually emerged to replace the fallen Empire. Feudalism originated in the human need to band together for mutual protection in a lawless and chaotic age. Inhabitants of a particular region placed themselves under the protection of the most powerful local lord and in return for his military protection pledged certain services.

Like the Church, feudalism echoed certain aspects of the Roman Empire, notably the custom of clients gathering around wealthy patrons, but it also drew heavily upon the Germanic social organization, in which warriors gathered around a powerful chieftain, to whom they were bound by a complex system of obligations and rewards.

In its fully developed form, feudalism was, like the Church, a pyramidal structure encompassing all of society and organized by an intricate code of privileges and mutual commitments. The medieval king was the secular counterpart of the pope, subordinate to him only in matters of faith. The feudal system placed literal ownership of all the king's domain (except that controlled by the Church) in his hands. These lands, or "fiefs," were, in effect, leased and subleased down through hierarchical orders of nobility to the level of the individual manor, the basic social and economic unit of feudalism. Each nobleman became the "vassal" of his immediate superior and owed him, in return for the lands he was granted, money payments and, when demanded, military service. The exact terms of feudal obligations were never standardized across Europe. They depended on local custom, but they were quite precise and were ritualized in the ceremony of homage and investiture, in which the vassal knelt before his lord and, placing his hands between his lord's hands, vowed to fulfill the terms of his obligation. At the bottom of the feudal pyramid was the serf, bound to the land he worked and obliged to cultivate his lord's land as well, in a sort of peonage or sharecropper arrangement.

Feudal society thus consisted of only two classes, the people and the nobility, which included the orders of the Church as well as the secular feudal orders. There was no socially mobile middle class; such a class, outside the rigid ordering of rank, would have been incompatible with the idea of feudalism, and when it did begin to emerge late in the Middle Ages, it marked the beginning of the collapse of the whole system.

The first comparatively stable kingdom to be established after the fall of Rome was that of the Franks, founded by Clovis (465–511). Charlemagne (742–814), a descendant of Clovis, embarked upon a series of campaigns against the Saxons and Bavarians, the Moors of northeast Spain, and the Lombards in northern Italy, building an immense empire to rival that of the Caesars. He was crowned "Holy Roman Emperor" by Pope Leo III on Christmas Day, 800. Charlemagne's victories became the stuff of legend, and his deeds, along with those of his twelve "peers," were celebrated in a number of medieval works of which the *Song of Roland* is the most famous. The imperial court was also a great center of art and learning, the focal point of the "Carolingian renaissance." Charlemagne brought the learned monk Alcuin from England to found a palace school of theology and literature, imported architects from Italy to build a number of cathedrals, and encouraged the study of Latin literature as well as Germanic epics.

Another nucleus of culture in the early Middle Ages, the Benedictine monastic order, was founded in the late sixth century by St. Benedict of Nursia with the encouragement of the great medieval pope Gregory I (540–604), who launched a series of missions to Christianize the northern Germanic peoples. Within a century, the Benedictine monasteries had spread across Europe, succeeding the Roman schools as centers of learning. In these monasteries libraries were collected and copied, instruction was carried on, and medieval architecture was born, with many of the monks working as master masons in the construction of early cathedrals.

Charlemagne's empire was short-lived, crumbling under the impact of invasions from the north. The Vikings, seafaring warriors from Scandinavia, swept into England and northern France in the ninth century and established the kingdom of Normandy in 885. The result, however, was not a new age of barbarism. The Danish Vikings were gradually assimilated in England, where the reign of Alfred the Great of Wessex (871–899) accompanied a genuine revival of art and learning. The Vikings in Normandy were likewise assimilated with the Franks, and a similar revival of learning took place; when these Normans conquered England in 1066, they brought with them a culture superior to that of the Anglo-Saxons.

The eleventh and twelfth centuries were a time of explosive intellectual and cultural development. The Crusades, launched by Pope Urban II in 1095, were eventually a dismal failure as attempts to capture the Holy Lands from the "Saracens," but they had the unforeseen effect of bringing Europeans into contact with the riches of Muslim culture, literature, mathematics, and science. Industry and commerce began to revive across Europe, and a number of universities were founded: Oxford in 1167, Paris in 1170, Cambridge in 1209. Provence in southern France was a particularly fertile ground; a vigorous economic and cultural atmosphere brought the development of chivalry and a rich tradition of *troubadour* literature expressing chivalric values, a tradition paralleled in northern France by the poetry of the *trouvères*.

This rapid development culminated in the thirteenth century, the high point, in many ways, of medieval culture. Both the medieval papacy and the medieval monarchy reached the height of their power in the thirteenth century, the papacy under Innocent III, Gregory IX, and Nicholas III, the monarchy under such kings as Edward I of England, Louis IX of France, and Ferdinand III of Spain. The greatest of the Gothic cathedrals were built— Notre Dame de Paris, Mont-Saint-Michel, Rheims, Amiens, Chartres. The period also marked the golden age of Scholasticism, the philosophical project of reconciling the teachings of the Church with the logic of Aristotle, or faith with reason; St. Thomas Aquinas's *Summa Theologica,* the masterpiece of Scholasticism, was completed in 1273.

But already, at the peak of its triumph, the medieval system was beginning to show signs of its ultimate decline. The medieval monarchy received an ominous blow when the English barons forced King John to sign Magna Charta in 1215. The strains upon the medieval papacy surfaced in such conflicts as the prolonged struggles between the Guelphs (supporters of the Pope) and the Ghibellines (supporters of the Holy Roman Emperor) in the city-states of Italy. The rise in the thirteenth century of the guilds, organizations of skilled craftsmen, also heralded the rise of a middle class incompatible with the rigid categories of the feudal system and prophetic of its ultimate collapse.

These fragmenting tendencies gained momentum in the turbulent fourteenth century. The papacy was split, for most of the century, by the so-called Babylonian Captivity, 1305–1376, during which the papal see was removed to Avignon in France, and by the following Great Schism (1378–1417), when there were two, and sometimes even three, rival popes. The chaos that

1166

followed the Black Death in mid-century further weakened the feudal system. The second half of the century was shaken by people's revolutions: the French Jacquerie in 1358 and the English Peasants' Revolt in 1381. These and other uprisings were put down, with great cruelty, but they foreshadowed the end of economic serfdom.

The greatest imaginative writers of medieval Europe emerged during its decline. The medieval worldview is perhaps best expressed by such writers as Thomas Aquinas and John of Salisbury, but the masterpieces of medieval literature date from the fourteenth century: the *Divine Comedy*, the *Decameron*, the *Rhymes* of Petrarch, the *Canterbury Tales*. Paradoxically, none of these works is wholly medieval in spirit. The tension apparent in all of them between the passing medieval world and the emerging Renaissance world provides much of their energy.

That we can distinguish the "medieval" and the "modern" in such works, however tentatively, suggests that, despite the span and variety of the Middle Ages, there is a certain consistency in its worldview. At the risk of overgeneralizing, it is possible to point to three qualities pervasive enough to define the age: authoritarianism, comprehensiveness, and otherworldliness. The cathedral, often cited as the quintessential expression of the medieval spirit, illustrates all three tendencies. The system of communal engineering that made the building of cathedrals possible implies the subordination of individual creativity to collective authority. If one values the occasional evidences of individual personality, in the playful elaboration of a gargoyle carving, for instance, it is because such features are exceptions. Medieval literature, too, is often anonymous, and when we begin to hear, as in Petrarch, the sound of an individual voice, we know that a new element has entered the medieval literary world.

As for comprehensiveness, the cathedral was also a microcosm of an all-inclusive vision of life. Not only did it represent a synthesis of social values, art, and religion, but its art characteristically undertook to represent the whole Christian revelation, the divine plan from Creation to the Day of Judgment. The literary analogues were the compendiums, ambitious works that attempted a total view of human life, its individual parts placed in relation to a whole, as in Aquinas's *Summa Theologica* or Dante's *Divine Comedy*. And finally, the very shape of the cathedral, its great spires pointing away from the earth toward Heaven, suggests the pervasive otherworldliness of medieval life. This tendency made empirical science impossible but also, at its best, gave a hope and dignity to human life in an age when life was too often bleak and short. Medieval literature has its own distinctive form of earthiness, but it almost always provides a view of eternity too, whether in brief glimpses or in visionary panoramas.

The Middle Ages have a claim to the label the following age preempted; they were not merely a hiatus between the classic and modern worlds but in some ways themselves a renaissance, a rebirth after the collapse of Roman civilization. Much of the modern world has medieval origins: the modern state and the modern city, modern languages, and a large body of collective myth, including the idea of romantic love, are rooted in the Middle Ages. But the major medieval achievement was the welding together of the separate strands of Western culture—Hebrew, Greek, Roman, and Christian—

into a single culture. This culture has been greatly amplified and modified by succeeding ages, but it still retains the general shape the Middle Ages gave it.

The literature of the Middle Ages is as varied as the time that produced it. Its characteristic forms are the epic, the romance, the allegory, the folk-tale, the lyric, and the drama.

The Germanic and Celtic tribes had a body of heroic legend as rich as that which Homer drew upon for the *Iliad* and the *Odyssey*. There is good reason to believe that this material was in oral circulation for centuries before Christian monks, in about the eighth century, began to write it down. The earliest of the folk epics is the English *Beowulf,* which may have been based upon the exploits of a sixth-century Scandinavian warrior but acquired a heavy overlay of folklore before an eighth-century English monk put it in written form. (The poem as we know it dates from a tenth-century manuscript.) Although *Beowulf,* like the *Iliad* and the *Aeneid,* celebrates the virtues of its culture's heroic past, these virtues are not precisely the same as those of Greece and Rome. The poem provides a fascinating glimpse into an ancient Germanic courtly culture held together by the complex, ritualized mutual obligations of the *comitatus* relationship, the bond between Germanic warriors and their lord. Magnanimity, loyalty, and the willingness to fight to the death to ful-fill an obligation are the virtues celebrated, all against the background of a tragic belief in fate and eventual, inevitable defeat. This ethical system blends in *Beowulf* with other elements derived from Christianity and classical cul-ture. Beowulf has a Christian gentleness; his monstrous antagonists are iden-tified with Cain and the Devil himself, and in the end he, Christlike, lays down his life for his people. The *Beowulf* poet also apparently knew the *Aeneid.* Although he never alludes directly to Virgil's work, its influence is appar-ent in the poem's sophistication of organization and in the epic conception of Beowulf's character.

The other early medieval folk epics, in various ways, also depict the con-frontation of pagan heroic ethics with the ethics of classical culture and Christianity. The *Elder,* or *Poetic, Edda,* composed in the ninth century but writ-ten down in the twelfth century, preserves the heroic legends of Iceland; the *Hildebrandslied* (ninth century) and *Nibelungenlied* (early thirteenth century) record German heroic tales; the Irish sagas of Cu Chulainn and Conchubar (eighth to tenth centuries) and the Welsh *Mabinogion* (eleventh century) pre-serve the heroic tales of the Celts. In France, the epic spirit was expressed in the *chansons de geste;* the greatest of these was the *Song of Roland* (twelfth cen-tury), which, like most of the *chansons de geste,* deals with legends of Charlemagne and his knights. The *Poem of My Cid* (twelfth century) presents a Spanish hero to rival Roland and Cu Chulainn. The Icelandic sagas, dealing with events in Iceland between about 930 and 1030 but written down several centuries later, represent a late survival of the epic impulse, perhaps because of the relative cultural isolation of Iceland.

In general, however, epic yielded some ground to romance in the eleventh and twelfth centuries. The term *romance* was originally applied to the Old French language as distinguished from the parent language, Latin or "Roman." In time, however, it came to refer to any work in the French language and ultimately to the most common form of French works, the tale of chivalric

1168

adventure. France remained preeminent in the romance form throughout the Middle Ages. Romances were fundamentally epics in which the center of interest had shifted from warfare to love, especially the elaborately ritualized cult of "courtly love," which first developed among the *troubadours* of Provence and the *trouvères* of northern France. Originally half-facetious, it transferred the homage the epic hero owed to his lord to the romance hero's lady, developing an elaborate code to govern the relation between the sexes. The idealization inherent in courtly love was probably, in part, a sublimation of youthful ungratified fervor; it arose in castles where numbers of young, unmarried knights surrounded their lords and the lords' remote, unattainable ladies. The revival of interest in Greek romances and in Ovid's *Art of Love* was also a factor, as was the growing cult of the Virgin Mary beginning in the second half of the tenth century.

The favorite subjects of medieval romance derived from the Matter of Britain (the Celtic sagas, especially those of King Arthur), the Matter of France (the Charlemagne legends), and the Matter of Rome the Great (Greek and Roman stories). Popular and widely circulated romances included those of Chrétien de Troyes, who wrote the first extant French romance, *Eric and Enid* (twelfth century) and a number of other Arthurian romances; Gottfried von Strassburg's *Tristan* (c. 1200); Wolfram von Eschenbach's *Parzival* (c. 1200); *Floris and Blanchefleur* (c. 1250); *Amis and Amiloun* (before 1300); and *Ipomedon* (fourteenth century). Among the most readable of these romances today are the twelve short *lais* of the twelfth-century Marie de France, sophisticated probings into the psychology of love within magical, "Breton" settings.

By the thirteenth century, the worldliness and sensuality of the romances had led the Church to regard them as detrimental to faith. Following its regular policy of assimilation and incorporation, however, the Church did not ban romances but rather encouraged the writing of a new kind, the "moral romance," which advanced Christian ideals while staying within the narrative conventions of the genre. The romances of the Holy Grail, the thirteenth-century French *Romance of the Rose,* and the fourteenth-century English *Sir Gawain and the Green Knight* all belong to this second phase. By the fifteenth century, the romance had become stale and formulaic, and after a period of rambling, inflated prose romances, uneasy blends of chivalric and moral elements, the genre was transformed and blended with new emphases in the Renaissance.

The *Romance of the Rose* also illustrates another major genre of medieval literature, the allegory. One of the most influential works of the Middle Ages, the *Romance of the Rose* is a dream poem in which the poet visits the Garden of Delight, where he sees the Rose, which symbolizes his sweetheart. Major characters in the story are personified qualities: Idleness, Pleasure, Fair Welcome, Danger, Shame, and Evil Tongue. Primarily an allegory of courtly love, the poem is also a satire directed at a number of targets (including sexual infatuation, superstition, and the celibacy of the clergy) and a compendium of miscellaneous medieval lore. The work became immensely popular in France, England (where it was at least partly translated by Chaucer), and Italy (where it was translated into sonnet form, possibly by Dante). The use of a dream to introduce an allegorical narrative and of the dream-allegory structure to hold together a wide range of material was widely imitated for three hundred years. Chaucer's *Book of the Duchess, House of Fame,* and *Parliament of Fowls* are all dream allegories; even the *Canterbury Tales* exhibits some features of the genre, including the pilgrimage motif, the use of representative characters, and the inclusion of varied tales within a generally symbolic framework. The fourteenth-century *Confessio Amantis,* by Chaucer's contemporary John Gower, and *Piers Plowman,* by William Langland, both continue to use the form. Christine de Pizan's *Book of the City of Ladies* is a fascinating feminist dream allegory, a refutation of the misogynistic *Romance of the Rose* which uses its own techniques to confound it. The supreme masterpiece of the genre is Dante's *Divine Comedy.* Allegory was also an important element in medieval drama. It survived vigorously into later ages, in such works as Edmund Spenser's *Faerie Queene* (1596) and John Bunyan's *Pilgrim's Progress* (1675). In fact, allegory has never died out.

Epic, romance, and allegory were all aristocratic narrative forms, written and read (or listened to) by the medieval aristocracy and gentry. There was also throughout the Middle Ages a flourishing body of popular oral narrative: folktales, beast fables, bawdy anecdotes called *fabliaux,* and folk ballads. These popular works were occasionally collected and written down; there are several collections of versified *fabliaux;* beast fables are the basis of several beast epics, the most famous of which is the French *Romance of Reynard* (twelfth century); and many popular ballads survive, though in versions dating from long after the Middle Ages. The importance of the oral folk tradition lies less in directly surviving texts than in the pervasive influence it exerted upon written literature—as sources, for example, of the stories in the *Decameron* and the *Canterbury Tales.*

Among medieval literary forms, the lyric is second in importance only to romance. There was a rich tradition of Latin lyric poetry that included Latin hymns; praises of rulers or patrons; nature songs; and "Goliardic" poetry (light occasional secular poetry, often satiric, written mainly by clerics in pretended praise of the fictional "Bishop Golias"). Vernacular poetry flowered earliest in twelfth-century Provence in southern France among the *troubadours.* The *troubadours* (or "finders" of treasure) were courtly singers who composed and sang elaborate, highly wrought poems, transmitting them orally to professional minstrels called *jongleurs,* who in turn spread them from place to place. Their major form was the *canzone,* an expression of idealized love written in a complex and rigid rhyme scheme, although they developed a number of other forms as well. The Provençal lyric influenced the *trouvères* of northern France and the *Minnesingers* of Germany. (*Trouvère* also means "finder," and *Minnesinger* means "singer of romantic love.") But its most vigorous influence was in Italy, which traveling *troubadours* visited in the early thirteenth century. There they inspired a school of imitators some of whom wrote in Provençal themselves, as a tribute to their mentors. Florence became the birthplace of the *dolce stil novo*—a "sweet new style"—that combined the forms of the *troubadours* with a grave, philosophical content derived from Scholastic philosophy.

It is one of the more surprising facts about literary history that the very idea of drama had to be reinvented beginning in the tenth century. The plays of Plautus and Terence were read throughout the Middle Ages, and the tenth-century German nun Hroswitha of Gandersheim wrote several plays about saints' lives, imitating the form of Terence though not his ribald content.

Medieval readers seem to have thought that the Roman plays were merely monologues or dialogues to be declaimed, not acted, and Hroswitha apparently had no notion of actual performance. There was a live tradition of popular entertainment—mimes, jugglers, and clowns, as well as a body of pagan fertility plays—but no conception of the sustained acting of a dramatic text.

Drama was reborn out of the liturgy of the Church, beginning in the tenth century with brief dramatized episodes (tropes) inserted into the Mass and then developed over several centuries into increasingly elaborate plays. The plays were separated from the Church in the thirteenth century and came to be performed outdoors at the spring Corpus Christi festivals. The major forms (which overlap considerably) were the mystery play, based on scripture and performed at the festivals by "mysteries," or trade guilds; the miracle play, based on a saint's life and staged on his or her feast day; and the morality play, a moral allegory dramatizing the spiritual life of the typical man. Secular forms included the folk play, which was independent of the religious drama and dramatized the deeds of a popular hero such as Robin Hood or St. George; the farce, a genre derived from popular and classical rather than religious models; and the secular interlude, a short play for performance between the parts of a banquet or other celebration.

Medieval drama, like most medieval art, was an international phenomenon, flourishing in England, France, Germany, Spain, and Italy. Although it produced few masterpieces—*Everyman* is one—it made possible the flowering of drama in the Renaissance, which built not only upon the rediscovered drama of Greece and Rome but upon native traditions as well.

Medieval literature, like the age that produced it, was rich and diverse. And, again like the age itself, it was not merely a prelude to what followed but, in many respects, the matrix of the future. Fiction, poetry, and drama since the Renaissance have drawn heavily upon the classical heritage, but the forms in which they developed were established in the Middle Ages.

FURTHER READING *(prepared by J.H.):* C.W. Previté-Orton's *Shorter Cambridge Medieval History,* 2 vols., 1952, is a standard history of the Middle Ages. See also Denys Hay, *The Medieval Centuries,* 1965; Friedrich Heer, *The Medieval World,* 1962; Johan Huizinga, *The Waning of the Middle Ages,* 1924; and R. W. Southern, *The Making of the Middle Ages,* 1953. The rise of the individual is a key subject in Norman F. Cantor, *The Civilization of the Middle Ages,* 1993. An authoritative overview of medieval literature is J. A. Burrow's *Medieval Writers and Their Work,* 1982. *European Writers: The Middle Ages and the Renaissance,* ed. William T. H. Jackson and George Stade, 2 vols. (the second beginning with Petrarch), 1983, is a work of sound scholarship understandable by nonexperts. E. R. Curtius's *European Literature and the Latin Middle Ages,* trans. Willard Trask, 1953, is challenging but rewarding. C. S. Lewis's *The Discarded Image,* 1964, is a very readable description of the popular worldview that underlay medieval literature and culture. For aspects of medieval culture closely related to literature, see Henri Pirenne, *Mohammed and Charlemagne,* 1939; T. H. White, *The Book of Beasts,* 1956; Emile Male, *The Gothic Image,* trans. Dora Nussey, 1958; Erwin Panofsky, *Gothic Architecture and Scholasticism,* 1951; David C. Fowler, *The Bible in Early English Literature,* 1976 (a broader treatment of cultural contexts than the title would suggest); and John Cummins, *The Hound and the Hawk,* 1989 (on hunting). Two readable and fairly concise books on medieval philosophy are John Marenbon, *Early Medieval Philosophy, 480–1150: An Introduction,* 1983; and Michael Haren, *Medieval Thought: The Western Intellectual Tradition from Antiquity to the Thirteenth Century,* 1985; both address the relationship between philosophy and religion. Especially interesting, on the subject the title announces, are the essays collected in *Women in the Middle Ages and the Renaissance: Literary and Historical Perspectives,* ed. Mary Beth Rose, 1986. On particular genres, see, for lyric poetry, Maurice Valency's *In Praise of Love,* 1958 (on Provençal and Italian poetry); James J. Wilhelm, *Medieval Song,* 1971; and Frederick Goldin, *Lyrics of the Troubadours and Trouvères,* 1973. On epic and romance, W. P. Ker's *Epic and Romance,* 1897, is, despite its date, still valuable. See also *Arthurian Literature in the Middle Ages,* ed. R. S. Loomis, 1959, and Eugene Vinaver, *The Rise of Romance,* 1971. Various aspects of courtly life are discussed in Joachim Bumke, *Courtly Culture,* 1991. Good on medieval drama are V. A. Kolve, *The Play Called Corpus Christi,* 1966, and Rosemary Woolf, *The English Mystery Plays,* 1972.

The Koran (Qur'an)

(Seventh Century)

Sometime around the year 610, a forty-year-old Arab merchant named Muhammad, who lived in Mecca and who occasionally retreated to a hill cave for nights of meditation, had a vision of an angelic figure (later identified as the angel Gabriel) and heard a voice saying to him, "You are the Messenger of God. Recite!" Muhammad, who in some accounts was unlettered, replied, "I cannot recite." The angel repeated, "Recite in the name of the Lord!" Muhammad then recited spontaneously some lines of verse in praise of God. From this time until his death, twenty-two years later, Muhammad received periodic revelations. He committed the messages to memory and passed them on to followers, and they were sometimes written down. About 650, several years after Muhammad's death, they were gathered together to form the Koran, the sacred book of Islam, the religion that Muhammad founded. Islam is the youngest of the three great monotheistic world religions, the others being Judaism and Christianity. There are now about 935 million Muslims, many concentrated in North Africa, the Middle East, and Central Asia but others disseminated worldwide. There are about six million Muslims in the United States, for example.

Muhammad was born in Mecca in about 570. His father died before he was born, he lost his mother when he was six, and his grandfather, into whose care he had been placed, died when Muhammad was eight. He then came under the care of an uncle, who was a trader and the head of the Hashem clan in the tribe of Quraysh to which Muhammad belonged. When Muhammad was about twenty-five, Khadijah, a successful business woman for whom he worked, asked for his hand in marriage. She had four daughters and three sons from previous marriages, and she bore Muhammad six children, two sons who died young and four daughters, the best known of whom was Fatima. After Khadijah's death, Muhammad married several other women from other tribes.

The revelations began about 610, and Muhammad soon became regarded as a prophet and religious leader by a steadily increasing band of followers. The new religion came to be known as Islam, which means "surrender" in Arabic (that is, to the will of God), and adherents were known as Muslims ("those who have surrendered").

Opposition rose in Mecca to Muhammad and his teachings from those who resented his implicit criticism of the wealthy merchant class and feared his potential political power. There were rumors of plots to kill Muhammad, and in 622 he and about seventy followers in small groups slipped out of Mecca and moved to a town called Yathrib, subsequently renamed Medina ("city of the Prophet"). This journey is called the *hijrah* (Latin "hegira"), and the date on which it began is the beginning of the Islamic calendar; the first day of the Islamic Era (AH or Anno Hegirae) is July 16, 622 by Western reckoning. Muhammad spent the rest of his life in Medina, consolidating his rapidly increasing political and religious power. By 630, he had built a powerful federation of Arab tribes, destined as the Arab Muslim empire to spread across a large part of the globe, an area extending from Spain across Central Asia to India. Muhammad, however, did not live to see this great conquest; he died in 632.

The book that was derived from the revelations made to Muhammad is the Koran (Arabic: "recitation"). The texts of the revelations were preserved in oral traditions; followers memorized them and used them in ritual prayers. There is also a tradition that Muhammad had them written down soon after each revelation. They were not brought together into a book, though, until 651–52, when Uthman, the third caliph (successor to the Prophet), commissioned scholars to make an authoritative compilation.

The Koran is about the same length as the New Testament. It is divided into 114 chapters, or *suras*. *Sura* means "unit of revelation"; the more familiar term "chapter" is used in our selections here. Each chapter is divided into verses. The chapters, after the brief Opening (*Fatihah*), are arranged roughly in descending order of length. Each chapter has a traditional name derived from some characteristic word or phrase in the chapter ("The Cow," "The Bee," "The Night Journey"). In modern times, chapters and verses have been assigned numbers, and passages are often cited by number, as with the Bible. From the beginning of the Koran's history, chapters have been identified as Meccan or Medinan, depending on where they were revealed. Every chapter except the ninth begins with the invocation "In the name of God, the Merciful, the Compassionate." Twenty-nine of the chapters follow this invocation with one or more Arabic letters. (See the beginning of "Ya Sin," for example, in this book.) Muslim scholars insist that these mysterious letters are part of the original revelations, but there is no agreement on what they mean.

The arrangement of the Koranic chapters by length means that there is no chronological order to the collection. Nor is there any clear logical arrangement. Passages on similar topics are not discussed together but are scattered throughout the entire text, and there is no obvious sense of a gradually unfolding argument. These characteristics are perhaps inevitable in a book that originated in a series of separate revelations. The Koran is probably best read as a series of separate impassioned and prophetic utterances about how to construct an ideal, unified community.

Christians and Jews who approach the Koran for the first time are likely to be surprised by the amount of overlap with the Hebrew and Christian scriptures. As the Christian New Testament confirms the Hebrew Old Testament, so the Koran confirms them both. Muhammad did not see himself as negating the Hebrew and Christian revelations but as extending them, and he expected to be well received by Jews and Christians, the other "peoples of the book," an expectation that was, of course, not fulfilled. Muhammad appears in the Koran not as the Messiah but as the culminating figure in a series of prophets through whom God has communicated with humankind, including Abraham, Moses, David, and Jesus.

The teachings of the Koran form the core of Islam. Central among them is the doctrine of a single unified and unifying God. Islam has been compared to Judaism in its absolute insistence on monotheism and in its distrust of the Trinity as potentially polytheistic. More importantly, Islam is a worldly religion that insists on the unity of the sacred and the earthly, of faith and the practice of building a good society. Whereas Christianity originally defined itself by posing the church against the Roman state, Islam has no church and no priests. Muslims can pray in any place so long as they direct their prayers geographically toward Mecca, rather paradoxically, since that city where Muhammad grew up later rebelled, riven by clan and tribal warfare, against his revolutionary and egalitarian teachings.

In the early days of Islam, becoming a Muslim meant becoming part of a community ruled by social and divine laws of equality, justice, and fraternity to which the Muslim had to submit. The politics of Islam ("surrender") meant that Muslims would no longer be torn apart by clan and feudal rivalries and by hierarchies governed by the rich and powerful ruling class in Mecca.

Although the eschatology (the doctrine of last things, the Day of Judgement, and Hell and Heaven) of Islam and many of its narratives are similar to those of Christianity, Islam differs in its beginnings as a political rebellion against the existing social order. Historians who see it as a "revolutionary" religion do so because Muhammad's teachings required him to flee the anger of the rulers in Mecca in order to conduct guerrilla warfare against the old ways of running a society. The early struggles against social injustice continue in current fundamentalist justifications of *jihad* or "holy war." Koranic laws insisted on the defeat of the more than three hundred idols worshipped in Mecca in favor of one God and on the need to submit to new laws about such things as marriage, the spoils of war, slavery, inheritance, and the rights of women. The common practice of killing newborn girls was outlawed. The Koran also addresses matters of everyday life such as the disciplines of washing, eating, daily prayer, pilgrimage, fasting, and giving alms.

In Islam, as in Christianity, "in the beginning was the Word." Islamic history begins with Gabriel's command to "Recite!" and Islam's first mystery is how the untutored Muhammad produced the beautiful poetry and wisdom of the Koran. For Muslims even more than for Jews and Christians, God's presence is bound up in the words of their sacred book, since those words are literally God's, delivered to Muhammad through his intermediary Gabriel and taken from a parallel book in Heaven, a "guarded tablet" that is "the mother of the book." Muslims are therefore reluctant to have the Koran translated, and translators often refer to their work as interpretations or paraphrases rather than translations. Nevertheless, the book has been translated into different languages from the ninth century to the present. In the brief selections presented here, the emphasis has been placed on especially eloquent and poetic passages that play an important role in ordinary Muslim life, rather than on the central doctrinal passages.

FURTHER READING *(prepared by J.H.):* A comprehensive survey of Islam is the *Cambridge History of Islam,* ed. Peter Malcolm Holt et al., 1970. A more concise introduction is Fazlur Rahman, *Islam,* 2nd ed., 1979. *Islam and the Arab World,* ed. Bernard Lewis, 1976, is a useful collection of essays on various aspects of Islamic culture. A standard biography of Muhammad is W. Montgomery Watt, *Muhammad at Mecca,* 1953, and *Muhammad at Medina,* 1956, summarized in one volume, *Muhammad: Prophet and Statesman,* 1961. See also Maxime Rodinson, *Mohammad,* 1971. On the Koran, Abdullah Yusef Ali, *The Holy Qur'an: Text, Translation, Commentary,* 1978, is a comprehensive and valuable work. Other good introductions are Richard Bell, *Introduction to the Qur'an,* new ed., rev. and enl. W. Montgomery Watt, 1970; and Muhammad Abdel Haleem, *Understanding the Qur'an,* 1996. *The Essential Koran: The Heart of Islam: An Introductory Selection of Readings from the Qur'an,* translated and presented by Thomas Cleary, 1993, is helpful; "presented" in this case means offering quite poetic translations of selected passages, with a short but pithy introduction and ample notes directed toward the non-Muslim

from *THE KORAN*

Translated by Arthur J. Arberry

THE OPENING[1]

In the Name of God, the Merciful, the Compassionate[2]

Praise belongs to God, the Lord of all Being,
the All-merciful, the All-compassionate,
    the Master of the Day of Doom.

Thee only we serve; to Thee alone we pray for succour.   5
    Guide us in the straight path,
the path of those whom Thou hast blessed,
not of those against whom Thou art wrathful,
    nor of those who are astray.

from THE COW[3]

It is not piety, that you turn your faces[4]   177
    to the East and to the West.
        True piety is this:
to believe in God, and the Last Day,
the angels, the Book, and the Prophets,
to give of one's substance, however cherished,
    to kinsmen, and orphans,
    the needy, the traveller, beggars,
        and to ransom the slave,
    to perform the prayer, to pay the alms.
And they who fulfil their covenant
when they have engaged in a covenant,
    and endure with fortitude
    misfortune, hardship and peril,

---

[1] This short opening chapter (called the *Fatihah*) was revealed at Mecca. Perhaps the best-known passage in the Koran, it is used as a short, general prayer on any occasion. (The marginal numbers here and throughout the Koran refer not to line numbers but to the verse numbers in the Arabic original.)

[2] Each *surah*, or chapter, in the Koran (except for the ninth one, "Repentance") begins with this invocation, called the Basmalah, after the Arabic *Bismillah al-rahman al-rahim*.

[3] "The Cow," the second chapter of the Koran, is also the longest. It was revealed in Medina. As with most of the chapters, the traditional title is drawn from an identifying word or passage in the chapter, in this case a passage in which Moses commands his people to sacrifice a cow. Only two short, lyric sections are given here from this long chapter.

[4] Verse 177 beautifully summarizes Islamic beliefs.

these are they who are true in their faith,
these are the truly godfearing.

* * *

God 255
there is no god but He, the
Living, the Everlasting.[5]
Slumber seizes Him not, neither sleep;
to Him belongs
all that is in the heavens and the earth.
Who is there that shall intercede with Him
save by His leave?
He knows what lies before them
and what is after them,
and they comprehend not anything of His knowledge
save such as He wills.
His Throne comprises the heavens and earth;
the preserving of them oppresses Him not;
He is the All-high, the All-glorious.

LIGHT[6]

* * *

God is the Light of the heavens and the earth; 35
the likeness of His Light is as a niche
wherein is a lamp
(the lamp in a glass,
the glass as it were a glittering star)
kindled from a Blessed Tree,
an olive that is neither of the East nor of the West
whose oil wellnigh would shine, even if no fire touched it;
Light upon Light;
(God guides to His Light whom He will.)
(And God strikes similitudes for men,
and God has knowledge of everything.)
in temples God has allowed to be raised up,
and His Name to be commemorated therein;
therein glorifying Him, in the mornings and the evenings,
are men whom neither commerce nor trafficking

---

[5] Verse 255 is the famous "Throne Verse," a passage, like the *Fatihah* and "Sincere Religion" (Chapter 112), often recited by Muslims at moments of special reverence or crisis.

[6] "Light," the twenty-fourth chapter of the Koran, was revealed at Medina. The first verses of the chapter, omitted here, deal with chastity and gossip. Verse 35, called the Light Verse, is one of the most exalted and poetic sections of the Koran.

diverts from the remembrance of God
and to perform the prayer, and to pay the alms,
fearing a day when hearts and eyes shall be turned about,
that God may recompense them for their fairest works
and give them increase of His bounty;
and God provides whomsoever He will, without reckoning.

And as for the unbelievers,
their works are as a mirage in a spacious plain
which the man athirst supposes to be water,
till, when he comes to it, he finds it is nothing;
there indeed he finds God,
and He pays him his account in full; (and God is swift
at the reckoning.)
or they are as shadows upon a sea obscure   40
covered by a billow
above which is a billow
above which are clouds,
shadows piled one upon another;
when he puts forth his hand, wellnigh he cannot see it.
And to whomsoever God assigns no light,
no light has he.

Hast thou not seen how that whatsoever is in the heavens
and in the earth extols God,
and the birds spreading their wings?
Each—He knows its prayer and its extolling; and God knows
the things they do.
To God belongs the Kingdom of the heavens and the earth,
and to Him is the homecoming.
Hast thou not seen how God drives the clouds, then composes them,
then converts them into a mass,
then thou seest the rain issuing out of the midst of them?
And He sends down out of heaven mountains, wherein is hail,
so that He smites whom He will with it, and turns it aside
from whom He will;
wellnigh the gleam of His lightning snatches away the sight.
God turns about the day and the night;
surely in that is a lesson for those who have eyes.
God has created every beast of water,
and some of them go upon their bellies,
and some of them go upon two feet,
and some of them go upon four; God
creates whatever He will; God is powerful
over everything.

Now We have sent down signs making all   45
clear; God guides whomsoever He will
to a straight path.

They say, 'We believe in God and the
Messenger, and we obey.' Then after that
a party of them turn away; those—
    they are not believers.
When they are called to God and His Messenger
that he may judge between them, lo, a party of them
    are swerving aside;
but if they are in the right, they will come to
    him submissively.
What, is there sickness in their hearts,
or are they in doubt, or do they fear
that God may be unjust towards them
and His Messenger? Nay, but those—
    they are the evildoers.
All that the believers say, when they   50
are called to God and His Messenger, that he
may judge between them, is that they say,
'We hear, and we obey'; those—
    they are the prosperers.
Whoso obeys God and His Messenger,
and fears God and has awe of Him, those—
    they are the triumphant.
They have sworn by God the most earnest oaths,
if thou commandest them they will go forth.
Say: 'Do not swear; honourable obedience
is sufficient. Surely God is aware of
    the things you do.'
Say: 'Obey God, and obey the Messenger;
then, if you turn away, only upon
him rests what is laid on him, and
upon you rests what is laid on you.
If you obey him, you will be guided.
It is only for the Messenger to deliver
    the manifest Message.'

God has promised those of you who believe
and do righteous deeds that He will surely
make you successors in the land, even as He
made those who were before them successors,
and that He will surely establish their
religion for them that He has approved for them,
and will give them in exchange, after
their fear, security: 'They shall serve Me,
not associating with Me anything.'
Whoso disbelieves after that, those—
    they are the ungodly.
Perform the prayer, and pay the alms,   55
and obey the Messenger—haply so
    you will find mercy.

Think not the unbelievers able to frustrate
God in the earth; their refuge is the Fire—
        an evil homecoming.

O believers, let those your right hands own
and those of you who have not reached puberty[7]
ask leave of you three times—before
the prayer of dawn, and when you put off
your garments at the noon, and after
the evening prayer—three times of nakedness
for you. There is no fault in you or them, apart
from these, that you go about one to the other.
So God makes clear to you the signs; and God is
        All-knowing, All-wise.
When your children reach puberty, let them
ask leave, as those before them asked leave.
So God makes clear to you His signs; and God is
        All-knowing, All-wise.
Such women as are past child-bearing
and have no hope of marriage—there is no
fault in them that they put off their clothes,
so be it that they flaunt no ornament;
but to abstain is better for them; and God is
        All-hearing, All-knowing.

There is no fault in the blind, and there is   60
no fault in the lame, and there is no fault
in the sick, neither in yourselves, that you
eat of your houses, or your fathers' houses,
or your mothers' houses, or your brothers' houses,
or your sisters' houses, or the houses of
your uncles or your aunts paternal, or
the houses of your uncles or your aunts
maternal, or that whereof you own the keys,
or of your friend; there is no fault in you
that you eat all together, or in groups
        separately.
But when you enter houses, greet one another
with a greeting from God, blessed and good.
So God makes clear to you the signs; haply
        you will understand.

Those only are believers, who believe
in God and His Messenger and who, when they
are with him upon a common matter,
go not away until they ask his leave.
Surely those who ask thy leave—those are

---

[7]That is, slaves and children. This section of the chapter moves from exaltation of the power
and goodness of God to matters of proper conduct in domestic life, particularly of modesty
and privacy.

they that believe in God and His Messenger;
so, when they ask thy leave for some affair
of their own, give leave to whom thou wilt
of them, and ask God's forgiveness
for them; surely God is All-forgiving,
          All-compassionate.
Make not the calling of the Messenger
among yourselves like your calling
one of another. God knows those of you
who slip away surreptitiously; so let those
who go against His command beware, lest
a trial befall them, or there befall them
          a painful chastisement.

Why, surely to God belongs whatsoever is in the heavens
and the earth; He ever knows what state you are upon;
and the day when they shall be returned to Him, then He
will tell them of what they did; and God knows everything.

YA SIN [8]

In the Name of God, the Merciful, the Compassionate

Ya Sin

          By the Wise Koran,
     thou[9] art truly among the Envoys
          on a straight path;
the sending down of the All-mighty, the All-wise,
that thou mayest warn a people whose fathers were   5
     never warned, so they are heedless.
The Word has been realised against most of them,
     yet they do not believe.
     Surely We have put on their necks fetters
     up to the chin, so their heads are raised;
     and We have put before them a barrier and
     behind them a barrier; and We have covered
          them, so they do not see.
Alike it is to them whether thou hast warned them
or thou hast not warned them, they do not believe.
Thou only warnest him who follows the Remembrance   10
and who fears the All-merciful in the Unseen; so
     give him the good tidings of forgiveness
          and a generous wage.

---

[8] "Ya Sin," the thirty-sixth chapter of the Koran, revealed at Mecca, is named after the two mystical letters that precede it. Muhammed is said to have called it "the heart of the Koran." It has a special significance in Islam and is often recited to the dying and on ceremonial occasions.
[9] That is, Muhammed.

Surely it is We who bring the dead to life
and write down what they have forwarded
and what they have left behind; everything
We have numbered in a clear register.

Strike for them a similitude—
the inhabitants of the city,[10] when
    the Envoys came to it;
when We sent unto them two men,
but they cried them lies, so We
sent a third as reinforcement.
They said, 'We are assuredly
    Envoys unto you.'
They said, 'You are naught but
mortals like us; the All-merciful
has not sent down anything. You
    are speaking only lies.'
They said, 'Our Lord knows we are   15
    Envoys unto you;
and it is only for us to deliver
    the Manifest Message.'
They said, 'We augur ill of you. If
you give not over, we will stone you
and there shall visit you from us
    a painful chastisement.'
They said, 'Your augury is with you;
if you are reminded? But you are a
    prodigal people.'
Then came a man from the furthest part of
the city, running; he said, 'My people,
    follow the Envoys!
Follow such as ask no wage of you,   20
    that are right-guided.
And why should I not serve Him who
originated me, and unto whom
    you shall be returned?
What, shall I take, apart from Him, gods
whose intercession, if the All-merciful
desires affliction for me, shall not
avail me anything, and who will
    never deliver me?
Surely in that case I should be in
    manifest error.
Behold, I believe in your Lord;
    therefore hear me!'

---

[10] The city referred to in this exemplary story is generally held to be Antioch, to which Jesus sent first two disciples and then Simon Peter. The story is told in the Christian Bible in Acts 13.

It was said, 'Enter Paradise!' 25
He said, 'Ah, would that my people
    had knowledge
that my Lord has forgiven me
and that He has placed me
    among the honoured.'
And We sent not down upon his
people, after him, any host
out of heaven; neither would We
    send any down.
It was only one Cry and lo, they were
    silent and still.
Ah, woe for those servants! Never
comes unto them a Messenger, but
    they mock at him.
What, have they not seen how many 30
generations We have destroyed
    before them,
and that it is not unto them
    that they return?
They shall every one of them be arraigned
    before Us.

And a sign for them is the dead land, that We quickened
and brought forth from it grain, whereof they eat;
and We made therein gardens of palms and vines,
    and therein We caused fountains to gush forth,
that they might eat of its fruits and their hands' labour. 35
    What, will they not be thankful?
Glory be to Him, who created all the pairs
of what the earth produces, and of themselves,
    and of what they know not.
And a sign for them is the night; We strip it of the
    day and lo, they are in darkness.
And the sun—it runs to a fixed resting-place;
that is the ordaining of the All-mighty, the All-knowing.
And the moon—We have determined it by stations,
    till it returns like an aged palm-bough.
It behoves not the sun to overtake the moon, neither 40
    does the night outstrip the day,
        each swimming in a sky.
And a sign for them is that We carried their seed
        in the laden ship,
and We have created for them the like of it
        whereon they ride;
    and if We will, We drown them,
        then none have they to cry to,
        neither are they delivered,
    save as a mercy from Us, and enjoyment
        for a while.

And when it is said to them, 'Fear what is before you   45
and what is behind you; haply you will find mercy'—
yet never any sign of the signs of their Lord
comes to them, but they are turning away from it.
And when it is said to them, 'Expend of that God has
provided you,' the unbelievers say to the believers,
'What, shall we feed such a one whom, if God willed,
He would feed? You are only in manifest error!'

They also say, 'When shall this promise come to
          pass, if you speak truly?'
They are awaiting only for one Cry to seize them
          while they are yet disputing,
then they will not be able to make any testament,   50
          nor will they return to their people.
And the Trumpet shall be blown; then behold, they are sliding down
          from their tombs unto their Lord.
They say, 'Alas for us! Who roused us out of our sleeping place?
This is what the All-merciful promised, and the Envoys spoke truly.'
'It was only one Cry; then behold, they are all arraigned before Us.
So today no soul shall be wronged anything, and you shall not be
recompensed, except according to what you have been doing.
See, the inhabitants of Paradise today are busy in their rejoicing,   55
they and their spouses, reclining upon couches in the shade;
therein they have fruits, and they have all that they call for.
'Peace!'—such is the greeting, from a Lord All-compassionate.
'Now keep yourselves apart, you sinners, upon this day!
Made I not covenant with you, Children of Adam, that you   60
should not serve Satan—surely he is a manifest foe to you—
and that you should serve Me? This is a straight path.
He led astray many a throng of you; did you not understand?
This is Gehenna, then, the same that you were promised;
roast well in it today, for that you were unbelievers!'
Today We set a seal on their mouths, and their hands speak to Us,   65
and their feet bear witness as to what they have been earning.

          Did We will, We would have obliterated
          their eyes, then they would race to the path,
                    but how would they see?
          Did We will, We would have changed them
          where they were, then they could not go on,
                    nor could they return.
          And to whomsoever We give long life,
          We bend him over in His constitution; what,
                    do they not understand?

          We have not taught him poetry; it is not
          seemly for him. It is only a Remembrance
                    and a Clear Koran,
          that he may warn whosoever is living,   70

and that the Word may be realized against
    the unbelievers.

Have they not seen how that We have created for them
of that Our hands wrought cattle that they own?
We have subdued them to them, and some of them they ride,
        and some they eat;
other uses also they have in them, and beverages.
    What, will they not be thankful?
Yet they have taken, apart from God, gods;
    haply they might be helped.
They cannot help them, though they be hosts   75
    made ready for them.
So do not let their saying grieve thee;
assuredly We know what they keep secret
    and what they publish.

Has not man regarded how that We created him
        of a sperm-drop?
Then lo, he is a manifest adversary.
And he has struck for Us a similitude
    and forgotten his creation;
he says, 'Who shall quicken the bones
    when they are decayed?'
Say: 'He shall quicken them, who originated them
    the first time; He knows all creation,
who has made for you out of the green tree   80
    fire and lo, from it you kindle.'
Is not He, who created the heavens and earth,
able to create the like of them? Yes indeed;
    He is the All-creator, the All-knowing.
His command, when He desires a thing, is to say to it
        'Be,' and it is.
So glory be to Him, in whose hand is the dominion
        of everything,
    and unto whom you shall be returned.

SINCERE RELIGION[11]

In the Name of God, the Merciful, the Compassionate

Say: 'He is God, One,
God, the Everlasting Refuge,
who has not begotten, and has not been begotten,
and equal to Him is not any one.'

---

[11] "Sincere Religion," the one-hundred-and-twelfth chapter, holds, like the *Fatihah* and the Throne Verse, a special place in Islamic life. It is generally held to contain the essence of the Koran and of Islam, and Muhammed is said to have recommended reciting it a hundred times a day if possible. It was revealed at Mecca.

Beowulf

(Eighth Century?)

A recurring image in the great Old English epic *Beowulf* is a lonely island of light surrounded by vast and impenetrable darkness. The image is appropriate for the poem's own place in literary history. This earliest surviving example of the heroic poem in northern Europe rises up like a beacon across the intervening centuries. But it is shrouded in mysteries of the most basic kind. Scholars have succeeded in throwing some light on these mysteries, both from the evidence of the poem itself and from such external sources as archaeological discoveries. But much remains wrapped in darkness.

What is generally known about the poem can be quickly summed up. It is set in a half-historical, half-legendary past, perhaps in the sixth century A.D. (the historical King Hygelac was killed about 521) and among Germanic tribes in Scandinavia, in present-day Denmark and Sweden. The poem, most people agree, must have been composed between about 680 and 800, though minority views place it as late as the tenth century. It survives in a single manuscript, written in England about the year 1000. The poem was forgotten after its own day, and the manuscript lay buried, perhaps in a monastic library, until the sixteenth century, when it surfaced in the collection of an Elizabethan antiquarian. It eventually ended up in the British Museum, after being damaged in a fire in 1731. It was first printed in 1815.

So much for the external history of the poem (tentative as much of it is). For further light, we must look for the most part within the poem itself. The language and the versification of the poem need some explaining to modern readers. In the original Old English, *Beowulf* is written in alliterative verse. That is, instead of being built of poetic feet, each having the same number of syllables and the same pattern of accent, it has as its basic unit the line, which is divided into two half-lines separated by a caesura or short pause. Each half-line has two strong accents, with an indefinite number of syllables. The half-lines are tied together by alliteration; the same initial sound appears on at least one accented syllable in each of the half-lines. Kevin Crossley-Holland, in the excellent translation reprinted here, has used a rather loose modern adaptation of this system. Take the first three lines for example:

> Lísten!
>   The fáme   of Dánish kings
>   in <u>d</u>áys gone bý,   the <u>d</u>áring féats
> <u>w</u>órked by those héroes   are <u>w</u>éll kńown to us.

Here the caesuras have been indicated with spaces, the accents have been marked, and the alliterating sounds underlined. The pattern is clear, although Crossley-Holland does not adhere to it strictly. The first line, for example, has neither a clear caesura nor alliterating words. Elsewhere in the translation, he sometimes omits the caesura or lets it fall somewhere other than between the second and third stresses. He also uses alliteration much more lightly than the original does. Nevertheless, the effect of the translation is very close to the original. It is a strongly oral poetry, meant to be chanted rhythmically rather than read silently.

The other most striking feature of the language, again carried over from the original Old English by the translator, is its heavy use of stock phrases such as epithets. In the passage that introduces Grendel, for example, he is called within a few lines "the brutish demon," "the hellish fiend," "this gruesome creature," "notorious prowler of the borderland," "ranger of the moors," and "this cursed creature." Each of the major characters has a similar set of epithets, as do such things as the sea ("the whale's way," "the waves' domain," etc.).

Formulaic language of this sort is a basic device of oral poets, to whom it serves as a means of fitting together traditional verbal elements into a new composition. Like the rhythmic alliterative verse, its use suggests that *Beowulf* derives ultimately from oral verse. Some modern scholars have held that it was composed orally by an Old English *scop* or bard who was probably illiterate. The poem itself includes several references to such performances, not only the Creation song which maddens Grendel in lines 90–98, but even a song about Beowulf's exploits:

> And now and then one of Hrothgar's thanes
> who brimmed with poetry, and remembered lays,
> a man acquainted with ancient traditions
> of every kind, composed a new song
> in correct metre. Most skillfully that man
> began to sing of Beowulf's feat,
> to weave words together, and fluently
> to tell a fitting tale.
>
> (lines 858–865)

It is perhaps not too fanciful to see in such an account a description of how *Beowulf* itself came to be. In any case, the good reader of *Beowulf* will read it not as a modern poem designed mainly for the eye but as a "performance piece" intended primarily to be heard.

Beowulf's roots in orally transmitted, folk culture are also evident in its plot material, a curious mingling of circumstantial history and fairy-tale material. The poem is set in the historical past, and the poet places the central action against a background of historical events, sometimes presented rather elliptically and allusively, as in the story of the fight at Finnsburh (lines 1058ff.) or of the war between the Swedes and the Geats (lines 2902ff.). We can assume that the original readers (or hearers) of *Beowulf* would have had a good knowledge of this historical material and that a brief allusion would have called it to their minds. (We have tried to provide a substitute for this knowledge in the annotations to the historical passages.)

The *Beowulf* poet, though, keeps his history in the background; in the foreground is clearly fabulous material. Beowulf himself is part realistic Germanic warrior, part fairy-tale hero, with his supernatural strength and his ability to hold his breath under water for an entire day. Even his name betrays his folk-tale origins; he was originally part bear (*bee-wolf* means bear).

And Grendel and his mother and the dragon have nothing to do with history at all.

Why did the *Beowulf* poet, obviously a sophisticated artist, choose to center his epic upon three fairy-tale monsters? Nineteenth-century scholars, eager for historical information about the early Middle Ages, tended to be impatient with the monsters and wish that the poet had gone into more detail about the history of the Germanic tribes. The great Victorian scholar W. P. Ker complained in 1904, for example, that the plot was "preposterous" and that, by concentrating in the main plot on the monsters and confining the historical allusions to the background, the poem put "the irrelevances in the centre and the serious things on the outer edges." Ker was answered in 1936 by the critic and novelist J. R. R. Tolkien, author of *Lord of the Rings,* who argued that "the monsters are not an inexplicable blunder of taste; they are essential, fundamentally allied to the underlying ideas of the poem, which give it its lofty tone and high seriousness." For Tolkien, the monsters were symbolic of eternal forces of evil while remaining real monsters. The world of *Beowulf,* to him, is poised on the edge of the transition from pagan to Christian culture, and the monsters retain something of their pagan reality while anticipating also the allegorizing of the later Christian middle ages.

However one interprets the monsters (and Tolkien's interpretation has not won universal agreement), it is clear that the sequence of monster-fights provides the structure of the poem. Tolkien, and others, have seen the poem as falling into two parts: the youthful Beowulf's adventure against Grendel and his mother and the aged king's struggle with the dragon. Some have even found in the two-part, balanced structure of the narrative an echo, on a larger scale, of the balanced structure of the divided single lines of alliterative verse. Certainly the poet uses pairings frequently. The royal ship-burial of Scyld Scefing which opens the poem is balanced by Beowulf's burial which ends it. Character is often developed by contrasted pairs: Beowulf as a good king is unlike Heremod the bad one, and the generous Queen Higd is not like the tyrannical Queen Thryth. Sometimes the contrast is ironic: the fortunate Queen Wealhtheow seems unlike the tragic Queen Hildeburh, but if we know the later history of the Danish court, they seem more alike than different.

There are, however, after all, three monsters, and other critics have considered triple patterns to be at least as important in *Beowulf* as duple ones. In this poem of a little over three thousand lines, roughly a thousand lines are devoted to each of the three monsters, and it has been suggested that *Beowulf* was intended to be performed over three evenings, each devoted to a new monster. If the sequence of monsters is intended to suggest a progression, what is the point of the progression? There is an obvious contrast between Grendel and his mother, on the one hand, and the dragon on the other. Grendel and his mother are human, if horribly perverted, while the dragon seems to be evil itself. There is a similar progression from Grendel to his mother. The encounter with Grendel, dreadful as it is, at least takes place in a human habitation with other humans around; the fight with his mother takes place at the bottom of the fearful mere, in a psychologically suggestive setting that seems to move Beowulf closer to the heart of evil. On the other hand, the dragon does have some redeeming features; he has been wronged, as Grendel and his mother have not, and the poet treats him with some measure of respect.

The monster-fights, important as they are, are not all of the poem, however. One of the most striking features of the poem is its use of inset narratives or "digressions." In a sense the poem begins with a digression—the story of Scyld Scefing—and at least seven more times the poet turns aside to tell a loosely related story, in the episodes of the later burning of Heorot (lines 81–85 and 769–773), Sigemund (lines 865–890), Heremod (lines 891–905 and 1694–1709), the fight at Finnsburh (lines 1058–1149), Thryth (lines 1915–1946), the Danish-Heathobard feud (lines 2006–2054), and the Geatish-Swedish wars (lines 2460–2480, etc.). But this list does not suggest the pervasiveness of the use of allusion and analogy in the poem, sometimes only in a phrase or in the use of the same formula in different situations. A continuing challenge in reading *Beowulf* is exploring the relation of these inset stories to the main situation.

Taken as a whole, the allusiveness in *Beowulf* enriches the texture of the poem and gives it a curiously meditative, ruminative quality quite unlike the series of simple feats of strength it sometimes sounds like in summary. The three monster-fights are placed against a background of historical analogies and interwoven stories that some critics have seen as analogous to the complex, "interlaced" style of Old English art.

Certain themes run through the complex interweaving of narratives in *Beowulf,* and most of them center on the character of Beowulf himself as exemplar of a heroic code, first as a warrior and then as a king. The virtue that binds tribal society together is loyalty, both of a warrior to his king and of a king to his warriors. Wiglaf, in the dragon episode, is balanced as a good thane with the younger Beowulf, in one of the poem's many complex pairings, and the thanes who run away are implicitly compared with the loyal waiters by the lake in the episode with Grendel's mother. The emphasis upon heroic boasting and upon gift-giving may ring strange to modern ears. But pride and reward have different meanings in the world of *Beowulf.* In the last words of the poem, Beowulf is said to be, of all kings, the "most eager for fame," and the description seems to be wholly laudatory. The Germanic warrior's boasts and his jealousy over his reputation are regarded as virtues rather than vices, ways of reaffirming the values upon which the society depends. Rewards in *Beowulf* are similarly treated more as signs than for their material value. Hrothgar bestows great treasures upon Beowulf, but Beowulf surrenders them all to his king, Hygelac (receiving, to be sure, even greater ones). And the great treasure of the dragon is mostly buried with the hero. More than materialistic transactions, eagerness for reward and liberality in "ring-giving" are rituals confirming the heroic code.

The Germanic heroic code in *Beowulf* is, however, tempered with Christian values, although critics have been unable to agree upon their extent. Whoever put *Beowulf* in writing must have been a Christian, since at that time literacy was tied to a clerical vocation. Some critics have argued back from this fact and found *Beowulf* to be "profoundly Christian" or even an "allegory of salvation." The difficulty with such extreme positions is the absence of any specifically Christian references in the poem. The name "Christ" never appears, nor are there any references to the central doctrines of Christianity.

Such biblical references as there are are to the Old Testament, perhaps the part of the Bible easiest to assimilate to Germanic tribal culture. A number of pious sentiments are expressed, but none is specifically Christian. Hrothgar, for example, after Beowulf kills Grendel, says, "Let us give thanks at once to God Almighty for this sight," and goes on to assign the victory not only to Beowulf but also to "the Almighty's power." Such statements are monotheistic but not explicitly Christian. The question of the exact relationship between the Germanic heroic ethic and Christianity in *Beowulf* may never be precisely answered. Tolkien thought that the author was a Christian, "a learned man writing of old times, who looking back on the heroism and sorrow [felt] in them something permanent and something symbolical." Kenneth Sisam, on the other hand, surveyed the debates about the Christianity in the poem and rather iconoclastically concluded that the *Beowulf* poet was less concerned about Christianity and paganism than his critics have been.

The question of the Christianity of *Beowulf* or the lack of it is, in other words, one of the many shadowy areas that remain in our understanding of the poem. But such uncertainties should not stand in the way of reading and responding to a magnificent poem that is worthy of the place it occupies at the threshold of modern European literature.

FURTHER READING *(prepared by J.H.)*: For students interested in looking at *Beowulf* in Old English, the standard edition is *Beowulf and the Fight at Finnsburg*, ed. Friedrich Klaeber, 3rd ed., 1941. Somewhat less intimidating is *Beowulf: A Dual Language Edition*, ed. and trans. Howell D. Chickering, Jr., 2nd ed., 1982. Chickering prints a careful Anglo-Saxon text with a close, almost word-for-word modern English translation on facing pages. His hundred-page, section-by-section "Commentary" is an excellent starting point for the study of the poem. Frederick Rebsamen's *Beowulf: A Verse Translation*, 1992, includes a stimulating introduction to the poem. Among secondary works, Raymond W. Chambers' *Beowulf: An Introduction to the Study of the Poem*, 3rd ed., 1963, must be mentioned, although its voluminous presentation of background material is likely to tell the beginning reader more than he or she wants to know. Perhaps the best critical book on the poem is Arthur G. Brodeur's *The Art of Beowulf*, 1959. J. D. A. Ogilvy and Donald C. Baker's *Reading Beowulf: An Introduction to the Poem, Its Background, and Its Style*, 1983, provides the basic historical and critical background for a study of the poem. Fred C. Robinson, *Beowulf and the Appositive Style*, 1985, is a series of lectures on the style and structure of the poem which also argues for an interplay between Christian narrator and earlier, pagan subject. Among collections of important essays on *Beowulf* are *An Anthology of Beowulf Criticism*, ed. Lewis E. Nicholson, 1963, and *The Beowulf Poet*, ed. Donald K. Fry, 1968. Both include J. R. R. Tolkien's seminal *"Beowulf:* The Monsters and the Critics." *Beowulf* would seem to be the ultimate male poem, and one would not expect a study of its women to be very interesting. The reverse is proved by several recent studies, among them Alexandra Hennessey Olsen, "Women in *Beowulf,"* in *Approaches to Teaching Beowulf*, ed. Jess B. Bessinger, Jr., and Robert F. Yeager, 1984 and Jane Chance, "Grendel's Mother as Epic Anti-Type of the Virgin and Queen," in *Woman as Hero in Old English Literature*, 1986. A recording of *Beowulf* read in Old English helps one get a feel for the oral quality of the poem; an excellent one is Jess B. Bessinger, Jr., *Beowulf, Caedmon's Hymn, and Other Old English Poems Read in Old English*, 1962. Readers of *Beowulf* may also be interested in John Gardner's modern novel based on the poem: *Grendel*, 1971. Raymond Oliver et al., *Beowulf*, 1991, renders the story imaginatively in a modern verse form.

BEOWULF

Translated by Kevin Crossley-Holland

Listen!
    The fame of Danish kings
in days gone by, the daring feats
worked by those heroes are well known to us.
    Scyld Scefing often deprived his enemies,
many tribes of men, of their mead-benches.[1]
He terrified his foes; yet he, as a boy,
had been found a waif; fate made amends for that.
He prospered under heaven, won praise and honour,
until the men of every neighbouring tribe,
across the whale's way, were obliged to obey him   10
and pay him tribute. He was a noble king!
Then a son was born to him, a child
in the court, sent by God to comfort
the Danes; for He had seen their dire distress,
that once they suffered hardship for a long while,
lacking a lord; and the Lord of Life,
King of Heaven, granted this boy glory;
Beow was renowned—the name of Scyld's son
became known throughout the Norse lands.
By his own mettle, likewise by generous gifts   20
while he still enjoys his father's protection,
a young man must ensure that in later years
his companions will support him, serve
their prince in battle; a man who wins renown
will always prosper among any people.
    Then Scyld departed at the destined hour,
that powerful man sought the Lord's protection.
His own close companions carried him
down to the sea, as he, lord of the Danes,
had asked while he could still speak.   30
That well-loved man had ruled his land for many years.
There in harbour stood the ring-prowed ship,[2]
the prince's vessel, icy, eager to sail;
and then they laid their dear lord,
the giver of rings,[3] deep within the ship
by the mast in majesty; many treasures
and adornments from far and wide were gathered there.
I have never heard of a ship equipped
more handsomely with weapons and war-gear,

---

[1] The mead-bench—the high bench in a hall from which mead and gifts were distributed—was the symbol of the independence of a Germanic chieftain.

[2] A ship with a high, scrolled prow, perhaps with carvings in a ring pattern.

[3] Generous dispenser of treasure (in the form of gold rings).

swords and corslets; on his breast   40
lay countless treasures that were to travel far
with him into the waves' domain.
They gave him great ornaments, gifts
no less magnificent than those men had given him
who long before had sent him alone,
child as he was, across the stretch of the seas.
Then high above his head they placed
a golden banner and let the waves bear him,
bequeathed him to the sea; their hearts were grieving,
their minds mourning. Mighty men   50
beneath the heavens, rulers in the hall,
cannot say who received that cargo.
    When his royal father had travelled from the earth,
Beow of Denmark, a beloved king,
ruled long in the stronghold, famed
amongst men; in time Healfdene the brave
was born to him; who, so long as he lived,
grey-haired and redoubtable, ruled the noble Danes.
Beow's son Healfdene, leader of men,
was favoured by fortune with four children: 60
Heorogar and Hrothgar and Halga the good;
Yrse, the fourth, was Onela's queen,
the beloved wife of that warlike Swedish king.
    Hrothgar won honour in war,
glory in battle, and so ensured
his followers' support—young men
whose number multiplied into a mighty troop.
And he resolved to build a hall,
a large and noble feasting-hall
of whose splendours men would always speak,   70
and there to distribute as gifts to old and young
all the things that God had given him—
but not men's lives or the public land.
Then I heard that tribes without number, even
to the ends of the earth, were given orders
to decorate the hall. And in due course
(before very long) this greatest of halls
was completed. Hrothgar, whose very word was counted
far and wide as a command, called it Heorot.[4]
He kept his promise, gave presents of rings   80
and treasure at the feasting. The hall towered high,
lofty and wide-gabled—fierce tongues of loathsome fire
had not yet attacked it, nor was the time yet near
when a mortal feud should flare between father-
and son-in-law, sparked off by deeds of deadly enmity.

---

[4]The name means "hart," an animal symbolic of kingship to the Anglo-Saxons.

Then the brutish demon who lived in darkness
impatiently endured a time of frustration:
day after day he heard the din of merry-making
inside the hall, and the sound of the harp
and the bard's clear song. He who could tell   90
of the origin of men from far-off times lifted his voice,
sang that the Almighty made the earth,
this radiant plain encompassed by oceans;
and that God, all powerful, ordained
sun and moon to shine for mankind,
adorned all regions of the world
with trees and leaves; and sang that He gave life
to every kind of creature that walks about earth.
So those warrior Danes lived joyful lives,
in complete harmony, until the hellish fiend   100
began to perpetrate base crimes.
This gruesome creature was called Grendel,
notorious prowler of the borderland, ranger of the moors,
the fen and the fastness; this cursed creature
lived in a monster's lair for a time
after the Creator had condemned him
as one of the seed of Cain—the Everlasting Lord
avenged Abel's murder. Cain had
no satisfaction from that feud, but the Creator
sent him into exile, far from mankind,   110
because of his crime. He could no longer
approach the throne of grace, that precious place
in God's presence, nor did he feel God's love.
In him all evil-doers find their origin,
monsters and elves and spiteful spirits of the dead,
also the giants who grappled with God
for a long while; the Lord gave them their deserts.[5]
    Then, under cover of night, Grendel came
to Hrothgar's lofty hall to see how the Ring-Danes
were disposed after drinking ale all evening;   120
and he found there a band of brave warriors,
well-feasted, fast asleep, dead to worldly sorrow,
man's sad destiny. At once that hellish monster,
grim and greedy, brutally cruel,
started forward and seized thirty thanes
even as they slept; and then, gloating
over his plunder, he hurried from the hall,
made for his lair with all those slain warriors.
Then at dawn, as day first broke,
Grendel's power was at once revealed;   130

---

[5] The story of a race of evil giants descended from Cain comes from early interpretations of Genesis 6:4: "There were giants in the earth in those days, and also afterward, when the sons of God had relations with the daughters of men, who bore children to them."

a great lament was lifted, after the feast
an anguished cry at that daylight discovery.
The famous prince, best of all men, sat apart in mourning;
when he saw Grendel's gruesome footprints,
that great man grieved for his retainers.
This enmity was utterly one-sided, too repulsive,
too long-lasting. Nor were the Danes allowed respite,
but the very next day Grendel committed
violent assault, murders more atrocious than before,
and he had no qualms about it. He was caught up in his crimes.   140
Then it was not difficult to find the man
who preferred a more distant resting-place,
a bed in the outbuildings, for the hatred
of the hall-warden was quite unmistakable.
He who had escaped the clutches of the fiend
kept further off, at a safe distance.

Thus Grendel ruled, resisted justice,
one against all, until the best of halls
stood deserted. And so it remained:
for twelve long winters the lord of the Danes   150
was sorely afflicted with sorrows and cares;
then men were reminded in mournful songs
that the monster Grendel fought with Hrothgar
for a long time, fought with fierce hatred
committing crime and atrocity day after day
in continual strife. He had no wish for peace
with any of the Danes, would not desist
from his deadly malice or pay *wergild*[6]—
No! None of the counsellors could hold out hope
of handsome compensation at that slayer's hands.   160
But the cruel monster constantly terrified
young and old, the dark death-shadow
lurked in ambush; he prowled the misty moors
at the dead of night; men do not know
where such hell-whisperers shrithe[7] in their wanderings.
Such were the many and outrageous injuries
that the fearful solitary, foe of all men,
endlessly inflicted; he occupied Heorot,
that hall adorned with treasures, on cloudless nights.
This caused the lord of the Danes deep,   170
heart-breaking grief. Strong men often sat
in consultation, trying in vain to devise
a good plan as to how best valiant men
could safeguard themselves against sudden attack.

---

[6]"Man-gold," compensation, according to Germanic custom, for a murdered person, paid to his relatives.
[7]The translator's revival of an Anglo-Saxon word, *scrīpan:* to slip along smoothly but menacingly, like a snake.

At times they offered sacrifices to the idols
in their pagan tabernacles, and prayed aloud
to the soul-slayer[8] that he would assist them
in their dire distress. Such was the custom
and comfort of the heathen; they brooded in their hearts
on hellish things—for the Creator, Almighty God, 180
the judge of all actions, was neglected by them;
truly they did not know how to praise the Protector of Heaven,
the glorious Ruler. Woe to the man who,
in his wickedness, commits his soul to the fire's embrace;
he must expect neither comfort nor change.
He will be damned for ever. Joy shall be his
who, when he dies, may stand before the Lord,
seek peace in the embrace of our Father.
   Thus Healfdene's son endlessly brooded
over the afflictions of this time; that wise warrior 190
was altogether helpless, for the hardship upon them—
violent visitations, evil events in the night—
was too overwhelming, loathsome, and long-lasting.
   One of Hygelac's thanes, Beowulf by name,
renowned among the Geats[9] for his great bravery,
heard in his own country of Grendel's crimes;
he was the strongest man alive,
princely and powerful. He gave orders
that a good ship should be prepared, said he would sail
over the sea to assist the famous leader, 200
the warrior king, since he needed hardy men.
Wise men admired his spirit of adventure.
Dear to them though he was, they encouraged
the warrior and consulted the omens.
Beowulf searched out the bravest of the Geats,
asked them to go with him; that seasoned sailor
led fourteen thanes to the ship at the shore.
   Days went by; the boat was on the water,
moored under the cliff. The warriors, all prepared,
stepped onto the prow—the water streams eddied, 210
stirred up sand; the men stowed
gleaming armour, noble war-gear
deep within the ship; then those warriors launched
the well-built boat and so began their journey.
Foaming at the prow and most like a sea-bird,
the boat sped over the waves, urged on by the wind;
until next day, at the expected time,
so far had the curved prow come
that the travellers sighted land,
shining cliffs, steep hills, 220

---

[8]A Germanic god, probably Woden, seen as a "soul-slayer" from a Christian perspective.
[9]The Germanic tribe called the Geats lived in southwestern Sweden. They flourished in
the sixth century A.D.

broad headlands. So did they cross the sea;
their journey was at its end. Then the Geats
disembarked, lost no time in tying up
the boat—their corslets clanked;
the warriors gave thanks to God
for their safe passage over the sea.
    Then, on the cliff-top, the Danish watchman
(whose duty it was to stand guard by the shore)
saw that the Geats carried flashing shields
and gleaming war-gear down the gangway,   230
and his mind was riddled with curiosity.
Then Hrothgar's thane leapt onto his horse
and, brandishing a spear, galloped
down to the shore; there, he asked at once:
"Warriors! Who are you, in your coats of mail,
who have steered your tall ship over the sea-lanes
to these shores? I've been a coastguard here
for many years, kept watch by the sea,
so that no enemy band should encroach
upon this Danish land and do us injury.   240
Never have warriors, carrying their shields,
come to this country in a more open manner.
Nor were you assured of my leaders' approval,
my kinsmen's consent. I've never set eyes
on a more noble man, a warrior in armour,
than one among your band; he's no mere retainer,
so ennobled by his weapons. May his looks never belie him,
and his lordly bearing. But now, before you step
one foot further on Danish land
like faithless spies, I must know   250
your lineage. Bold seafarers,
strangers from afar, mark my words
carefully: you would be best advised
quickly to tell me the cause of your coming."
    The man of highest standing, leader of that troop,
unlocked his hoard of words, answered him:
"We are all Geats, hearth-companions of Hygelac;
my father was famed far and wide,
a noble lord, Ecgtheow by name—
he endured many winters before he,   260
in great old age, went on his way; every wise man
in this world readily recalls him.
We have sailed across the sea to seek your lord,
Healfdene's son, protector of the people,
with most honourable intentions; give us your guidance!
We have come on an errand of importance
to the great Danish prince; nor, I imagine, will the cause
of our coming long remain secret. You will know
whether it is true—as we have heard tell—
that here among the Danes a certain evil-doer,   270

a fearful solitary, on dark nights commits deeds
of unspeakable malice—damage
and slaughter. In all good conscience
I can counsel Hrothgar, that wise and good man,
how he shall overcome the fiend,
and how his anguish shall be assuaged—
if indeed his fate ordains that these foul deeds
should ever end, and be avenged;
he will suffer endless hardship otherwise,
dire distress, as long as Heorot, best of dwellings, 280
stands unshaken in its lofty place."
    Still mounted, the coastguard,
a courageous thane, gave him this reply:
"The discriminating warrior—one whose mind is keen—
must perceive the difference between words and deeds.
But I see you are a company well disposed
towards the Danish prince. Proceed, and bring
your weapons and armour! I shall direct you.
And I will command my companions, moreover,
to guard your ship with honour 290
against any foe—your beached vessel,
caulked so recently—until the day that timbered craft
with its curved prow shall carry back
the beloved man across the sea currents
to the shores of the storm-loving Geats:
he who dares deeds with such audacity and valour
shall be granted safety in the squall of battle."
    Then they hurried on. The ship lay still;
securely anchored, the spacious vessel
rode on its hawser. The boar crest, brightly gleaming, 300
stood over their helmets: superbly tempered,
plated with glowing gold, it guarded the lives
of those grim warriors. The thanes made haste,
marched along together until they could discern
the glorious, timbered hall, adorned with gold;
they saw there the best-known building
under heaven. The ruler lived in it;
its brilliance carried across countless lands.
Then the fearless watchman pointed out the path
leading to Heorot, bright home of brave men, 310
so that they should not miss the way;
that bold warrior turned his horse, then said:
"I must leave you here. May the Almighty Father,
of His grace, guard you in your enterprise.
I will go back to the sea again,
and there stand watch against marauding bands."
    The road was paved; it showed those warriors
the way. Their corslets were gleaming,
the strong links of shining chain-mail
clinked together. When the sea-stained travellers 320

had reached the hall itself in their fearsome armour,
they placed their broad shields
(worked so skilfully) against Heorot's wall.
Then they sat on a bench; the brave men's
armour sang. The seafarers' gear
stood all together, a grey-tipped forest
of ash spears; that armed troop was well equipped
with weapons.
            Then Wulfgar, a proud warrior,
asked the Geats about their ancestry:
"Where have you come from with these gold-plated shields,   330
these grey coats of mail, these visored helmets,
and this pile of spears? I am Hrothgar's
messenger, his herald. I have never seen
so large a band of strangers of such bold bearing.
You must have come to Hrothgar's court
not as exiles, but from audacity and high ambition."
Then he who feared no man, the proud leader
of the Geats, stern-faced beneath his helmet,
gave him this reply: "We are Hygelac's
companions at the bench: my name is Beowulf.   340
I wish to explain to Healfdene's son,
the famous prince, your lord,
why we have come if he, in his goodness,
will give us leave to speak with him."
Wulfgar replied—a prince of the Vandals,
his mettle, his wisdom and prowess in battle
were widely recognized: "I will ask
the lord of the Danes, ruler of the Scyldings,
renowned prince and ring-giver,
just as you request, regarding your journey,   350
and bring back to you at once whatever answer
that gracious man thinks fit to give me."
    Then Wulfgar hurried to the place where Hrothgar sat,
grizzled and old, surrounded by his thanes;
the brave man moved forward until he stood
immediately before the Danish lord;
he well knew the customs of warriors.
Wulfgar addressed his friend and leader:
"Geatish men have travelled to this land,
come from far, across the stretch of the seas.   360
These warriors call their leader Beowulf;
they ask, my lord, that they should be allowed
to speak with you. Gracious Hrothgar,
do not give them *no* for answer.
They, in their armour, seem altogether worthy
of the highest esteem. I have no doubt of their leader's
might, he who has brought these brave men to Heorot."
Hrothgar, defender of the Danes, answered:
"I knew him when he was a boy;

his illustrious father was called Ecgtheow; 370
Hrethel the Geat gave him his only daughter
in marriage; now his son, with daring spirit,
has voyaged here to visit a loyal friend.
And moreover, I have heard seafarers say—
men who have carried rich gifts to the Geats
as a mark of my esteem—that in the grasp
of his hand that man renowned in battle
has the might of thirty men. I am convinced
that Holy God, of His great mercy,
has directed him to us West-Danes 380
and that he means to come to grips with Grendel.
I will reward this brave man with treasures.
Hurry! Tell them to come in and meet
our band of kinsmen; and make it clear, too,
that they are most welcome to the Danes!"
Then Wulfgar went to the hall door with Hrothgar's reply:
"My conquering lord, the leader of the East-Danes[10]
commands me to tell you that he knows your lineage
and that you, so bold in mind, are welcome
to these shores from over the rolling sea. 390
You may see Hrothgar in your armour,
under your helmets, just as you are;
but leave your shields out here, and your deadly ashen spears,
let them await the outcome of your words."
    Then noble Beowulf rose from the bench,
flanked by his fearless followers; some stayed behind
at the brave man's bidding, to stand guard over their armour.
Guided by Wulfgar, the rest hurried into Heorot
together; there went that hardy man, stern-faced
beneath his helmet, until he was standing under Heorot's roof. 400
Beowulf spoke—his corslet, cunningly linked
by the smith, was shining: "Greetings, Hrothgar!
I am Hygelac's kinsman and retainer. In my youth
I achieved many daring exploits. Word of Grendel's deeds
has come to me in my own country;
seafarers say that this hall Heorot,
best of all buildings, stands empty and useless
as soon as the evening light is hidden under the sky.
So, Lord Hrothgar, men known by my people
to be noble and wise advised me to visit you 410
because they knew of my great strength:
they saw me themselves when, stained by my enemies' blood,
I returned from the fight when I destroyed five,
a family of giants, and by night slew monsters
on the waves; I suffered great hardship,

---

[10] The same as the "West-Danes" (1. 380). At various points in the poem, the Danes are called North-, South-, East-, and West-Danes, as well as Bright-Danes, Ring-Danes, and Spear-Danes. The variations are used for alliterative purposes.

avenged the affliction of the Storm-Geats and crushed
their fierce foes—they were asking for trouble.
And now, I shall crush the giant Grendel
in single combat. Lord of the mighty Danes,
guardian of the Scyldings, I ask one favour: 420
protector of warriors, lord beloved of your people,
now that I have sailed here from so far,
do not refuse my request—that I alone, with my band
of brave retainers, may cleanse Heorot.
I have also heard men say this monster
is so reckless he spurns the use of weapons.
Therefore (so that Hygelac, my lord,
may rest content over my conduct) I deny myself
the use of a sword and a broad yellow shield
in battle; but I shall grapple with this fiend   430
hand to hand; we shall fight for our lives,
foe against foe; and he whom death takes off
must resign himself to the judgement of God.
I know that Grendel, should he overcome me,
will without dread devour many Geats,
matchless warriors, in the battle-hall,
as he has often devoured Danes before. If death claims me
you will not have to cover my head,
for he already will have done so—
with a sheet of shining blood; he will carry off   440
the blood-stained corpse, meaning to savour it;
the solitary one will eat without sorrow
and stain his lair; no longer then
will you have to worry about burying my body.
But if battle should claim me, send this most excellent
coat of mail to Hygelac, this best of corslets
that protects my breast; it once belonged to Hrethel,
the work of Weland.[11] Fate goes ever as it must!"
   Hrothgar, protector of the Scyldings, replied:
"Beowulf, my friend! So you have come here,   450
because of past favours, to fight on our behalf!
Your father Ecgtheow, by striking a blow,
began the greatest of feuds. He slew Heatholaf of the Wylfings
with his own hand; after that, the Geats
dared not harbour him for fear of war.
So he sailed here, over the rolling waves,
to this land of the South-Danes, the honoured Scyldings;
I was young then, had just begun to reign
over the Danes in this glorious kingdom,
this treasure-stronghold of heroes; my elder brother,   460
Heorogar, Healfdene's son, had died
not long before; he was a better man than I!

---

[11] The blacksmith of the Scandinavian gods.

I settled your father's feud by payment;
I sent ancient treasures to the Wylfings
over the water's back; and Ecgtheow swore oaths to me.
It fills me with anguish to admit to all the evil
that Grendel, goaded on by his hatred,
has wreaked in Heorot with his sudden attacks
and infliction of injuries; my hall-troop is depleted,
my band of warriors; fate has swept them   470
into Grendel's ghastly clutches. Yet God can easily
prevent this reckless ravager from committing such crimes.
After quaffing beer, brave warriors of mine
have often boasted over the ale-cup
that they would wait in Heorot
and fight against Grendel with their fearsome swords.
Then, the next morning, when day dawned,
men could see that this great mead-hall was stained
by blood, that the floor by the benches
was spattered with gore; I had fewer followers,   480
dear warriors, for death had taken them off.
But first, sit down at our feast, and in due course,
as your inclination takes you, tell how warriors
have achieved greatness."
                    Then, in the feasting-hall,
a bench was cleared for the Geats all together,
and there those brave men went and sat,
delighting in their strength; a thane did his duty—
held between his hands the adorned ale-cup,
poured out gleaming liquor; now and then the poet sang,
raised his clear voice in Heorot; the warriors caroused,   490
no small company of Scyldings and Geats.
Ecglaf's son, Unferth, who sat at the feet
of the lord of the Scyldings, unlocked his thoughts
with these unfriendly words—for the journey of Beowulf,
the brave seafarer, much displeased him
in that he was unwilling for any man
in this wide world to gain more glory than himself:
"Are you the Beowulf who competed with Breca,
vied with him at swimming in the open sea
when, swollen with vanity, you both braved   500
the waves, risked your lives on deep waters
because of a foolish boast? No one,
neither friend nor foe, could keep you
from your sad journey, when you swam out to sea,
clasped in your arms the water-streams,
passed over the sea-paths, swiftly moved your hands
and sped over the ocean. The sea heaved,
the winter flood; for seven nights
you both toiled in the water; but Breca outstayed you,
he was the stronger; and then, on the eighth morning,   510
the sea washed him up on the shores of the Heathoreams.

From there he sought his own country,
the land of the Brondings who loved him well;
he went to his fair stronghold where he had a hall
and followers and treasures. In truth, Beanstan's son
fulfilled his boast that he could swim better than you.
So I am sure you will pay a heavy price—
although you have survived countless battle storms,
savage sword-play—if you dare
ambush Grendel in the watches of the night."   520
Beowulf, the son of Ecgtheow, replied:
"Truly, Unferth my friend, all this beer
has made you talkative: you have told us much
about Breca and his exploits. But I maintain
I showed the greater stamina, endured
hardship without equal in the heaving water.
Some years ago when we were young men,
still in our youth, Breca and I made a boast,
a solemn vow, to venture our lives
on the open sea; and we kept our word.   530
When we swam through the water, we each held
a naked sword with which to ward off
whales; by no means could Breca
swim faster than I, pull away from me
through the press of the waves—
I had no wish to be separated from him.
So for five nights we stayed together in the sea,
until the tides tore us apart,
the foaming water, the freezing cold,
day darkening into night—until the north wind,   540
that savage warrior, rounded against us.
Rough were the waves; fishes in the sea
were roused to great anger. Then my coat of mail,
hard and hand-linked, guarded me against my enemies;
the woven war-garment, adorned with gold,
covered my breast. A cruel ravager
dragged me down to the sea-bed, a fierce monster
held me tightly in its grasp; but it was given to me
to bury my sword, my battle weapon,
in its breast; the mighty sea-beast   550
was slain by my blow in the storm of battle.
In this manner, and many times, loathsome monsters
harassed me fiercely; with my fine sword
I served them fittingly.
I did not allow those evil destroyers to enjoy
a feast, to eat me limb by limb
seated at a banquet on the sea-bottom;
but the next morning they lay in the sand
along the shore, wounded by sword strokes,
slain by battle-blades, and from that day on   560
they could not hinder seafarers from sailing

over deep waters. Light came from the east,
God's bright beacon; the swell subsided,
and I saw then great headlands,
cliffs swept by the wind. Fate will often spare
an undoomed man, if his courage is good.
As it was I slew nine sea-beasts
with my sword. I have never heard
of a fiercer fight by night under heaven's vault
nor of a man who endured more on the ocean streams. 570
But I escaped with my life from the enemies' clutches,
worn out by my venture. Then the swift current,
the surging water, carried me
to the land of the Lapps. I have not heard tell
that you have taken part in any such contests,
in the peril of sword-play. Neither you nor Breca
have yet dared such a deed with shining sword
in battle—I do not boast because of this—
though of course it is true you slew your own brothers,
your own close kinsmen. For that deed, however clever 580
you may be, you will suffer damnation in hell.
I tell you truly, son of Ecglaf,
that if you were in fact as unflinching
as you claim, the fearsome monster Grendel
would never have committed so many crimes
against your lord, nor created such havoc in Heorot;
but he has found he need not fear unduly
your people's enmity, fearsome assault
with swords by the victorious Scyldings.
So he spares none but takes his toll 590
of the Danish people, does as he will,
kills and destroys, expects no fight
from the Spear-Danes. But soon, quite soon,
I shall show him the strength, the spirit and skill
of the Geats. And thereafter, when day dawns,
when the radiant sun shines from the south
over the sons of men, he who so wishes
may enter the mead-hall without terror."
    Then the grizzled warrior, giver of gold,
was filled with joy; the lord of the Danes, 600
shepherd of his people, listened to Beowulf's
brave resolution and relied on his help.
The warriors laughed, there was a hum
of contentment. Wealhtheow came forward,
mindful of ceremonial—she was Hrothgar's queen;
adorned with gold, that proud woman
greeted the men in the hall, then offered the cup
to the Danish king first of all.
She begged him, beloved of his people,
to enjoy the feast; the king, famed 610
for victory, ate and drank in happiness.

Then the lady of the Helmings walked about the hall,
offering the precious, ornamented cup
to old and young alike, until at last
the queen, excellent in mind, adorned with rings,
moved with the mead-cup towards Beowulf.
She welcomed the Geatish prince and with wise words
thanked God that her wish was granted
that she might depend on some warrior for help
against such attacks. The courageous warrior   620
took the cup from Wealhtheow's hands
and, eager for battle, made a speech:
Beowulf, the son of Ecgtheow, said:
"When I put to sea, sailed
through the breakers with my band of men,
I resolved to fulfil the desire
of your people, or suffer the pangs of death,
caught fast in Grendel's clutches.
Here, in Heorot, I shall either work a deed
of great daring, or lay down my life."   630
Beowulf's brave boast delighted Wealhtheow:
adorned with gold, the noble Danish queen
went to sit beside her lord.
    Then again, as of old, fine words were spoken
in the hall, the company rejoiced,
a conquering people, until in due course
the son of Healfdene wanted to retire
and take his rest. He realized the monster
meant to attack Heorot after the blue hour,
when black night has settled over all—   640
when shadowy shapes come shrithing
dark beneath the clouds. All the company rose.
Then the heroes Hrothgar and Beowulf saluted
one another; Hrothgar wished him luck
and control of Heorot, and confessed:
"Never since I could lift hand and shield,
have I entrusted this glorious Danish hall
to any man as I do now to you.
Take and guard this greatest of halls.
Make known your strength, remember your might,   650
stand watch against your enemy. You shall have
all you desire if you survive this enterprise."
    Then Hrothgar, defender of the Danes,
withdrew from the hall with his band of warriors.
The warlike leader wanted to sleep with Wealhtheow,
his queen. It was said the mighty king
had appointed a hall-guard—a man who undertook
a dangerous duty for the Danish king,
elected to stand watch against the monster.   660
Truly, the leader of the Geats fervently trusted
in his own great strength and in God's grace.

Then he took off his helmet and his corslet
of iron, and gave them to his servant,
with his superb, adorned sword,
telling him to guard them carefully.
And then, before he went to his bed,
the brave Geat, Beowulf, made his boast:
"I count myself no less active in battle,
no less brave than Grendel himself: 670
thus, I will not send him to sleep with my sword,
so deprive him of life, though certainly I could.
Despite his fame for deadly deeds,
he is ignorant of these noble arts, that he might strike
at me, and hew my shield; but we, this night,
shall forego the use of weapons, if he dares fight
without them; and then may wise God,
the holy Lord, give glory in battle
to whichever of us He should think fitting."
Then the brave prince leaned back, put his head 680
on the pillow while, around him,
many a proud seafarer lay back on his bed.
Not one of them believed he would see
day dawn, or ever return to his family
and friends, and the place where he was born;
they well knew that in recent days
far too many Danish men had come to bloody ends
in that hall. But the Lord wove the webs of destiny,
gave the Geats success in their struggle,
help and support, in such a way 690
that all were enabled to overcome their enemy
through the strength of one man. We cannot doubt
that mighty God has always ruled
over mankind.
          Then the night prowler
came shrithing through the shadows. All the Geats
guarding Heorot had fallen asleep—
all except one. Men well knew that the evil enemy
could not drag them down into the shadows
when it was against the Creator's wishes,
but Beowulf, watching grimly for his adversary Grendel, 700
awaited the ordeal with increasing anger.
Then, under night's shroud, Grendel walked down
from the moors; he shouldered God's anger.
The evil plunderer intended to ensnare
one of the race of men in the high hall.
He strode under the skies, until he stood
before the feasting-hall, in front of the gift-building
gleaming with gold. And this night was not the first
on which he had so honoured Hrothgar's home.
But never in his life did he find hall-wardens 710
more greatly to his detriment. Then the joyless warrior

journeyed to Heorot. The outer door, bolted
with iron bands, burst open at a touch from his hands:
with evil in his mind, and overriding anger,
Grendel swung open the hall's mouth itself. At once,
seething with fury, the fiend stepped onto
the tessellated floor; a horrible light,
like a lurid flame, flickered in his eyes.
He saw many men, a group of warriors,
a knot of kinsmen, sleeping in the hall. 720
His spirits leapt, his heart laughed;
the savage monster planned to sever,
before daybreak, the life of every warrior
from his body—he fully expected to eat
his fill at the feast. But after that night
fate decreed that he should no longer feed off
human flesh. Hygelac's kinsman,
the mighty man, watched the wicked ravager
to see how he would make his sudden attacks.
The monster was not disposed to delay; 730
but, for a start, he hungrily seized
a sleeping warrior, greedily wrenched him,
bit into his body, drank the blood
from his veins, devoured huge pieces;
until, in no time, he had swallowed the whole man,
even his feet and hands. Now Grendel stepped forward,
nearer and nearer, made to grasp the valiant Geat
stretched out on his bed—the fiend reached towards him
with his open hand; at once Beowulf perceived
his evil plan, sat up and stayed Grendel's outstretched arm. 740
Instantly that monster, hardened by crime,
realized that never had he met any man
in the regions of earth, in the whole world,
with so strong a grip. He was seized with terror.
But, for all that, he was unable to break away.
He was eager to escape to his lair, seek the company
of devils, but he was restrained as never before.
Then Hygelac's brave kinsman bore in mind
his boast: he rose from the bed and gripped
Grendel fiercely. The fiend tried to break free, 750
his fingers were bursting. Beowulf kept with him.
The evil giant was desperate to escape,
if indeed he could, and head for his lair
in the fens; he could feel his fingers cracking
in his adversary's grip; that was a bitter journey
that Grendel made to the ring-hall Heorot.
The great room boomed; all the proud warriors—
each and every Dane living in the stronghold—
were stricken with panic. The two hall-wardens 760
were enraged. The building rang with their blows.

It was a wonder the wine-hall withstood
two so fierce in battle, that the fair building
did not fall to earth; but it stood firm,
braced inside and out with hammered
iron bands. I have heard tell that there,
where they fought, many a mead-bench,
studded with gold, started from the floor.
Until that time, elders of the Scyldings
were of the opinion that no man could wreck   770
the great hall Heorot, adorned with horns,
nor by any means destroy it unless it were gutted
by greedy tongues of flame. Again and again
clang and clatter shattered the night's silence;
dread numbed the North-Danes, seized all
who heard the shrieking from the wall,
the enemy of God's grisly lay of terror,
his song of defeat, heard hell's captive
keening over his wound. Beowulf held him fast,
he who was the strongest of all men   780
ever to have seen the light of life on earth.
By no means did the defender of thanes
allow the murderous caller to escape with his life;
he reckoned that the rest of Grendel's days
were useless to anyone. Then, time and again,
Beowulf's band brandished their ancestral swords;
they longed to save the life, if they
so could, of their lord, the mighty leader.
When they did battle on Beowulf's behalf,
struck at the monster from every side,   790
eager for his end, those courageous warriors
were unaware that no war-sword,
not even the finest iron on earth,
could wound their evil enemy,
for he had woven a secret spell
against every kind of weapon, every battle blade.
Grendel's death, his departure from this world,
was destined to be wretched, his migrating spirit
was fated to travel far into the power of fiends.
Then he who for years had committed crimes   800
against mankind, murderous in mind,
and had warred with God, discovered
that the strength of his body could not save him,
that Hygelac's brave kinsman held his hand
in a vice-like grip; each was a mortal enemy
to the other. The horrible monster
suffered grievous pain; a gaping wound
opened on his shoulder; the sinews sprang apart,
the muscles were bursting. Glory in battle
was given to Beowulf; fatally wounded,   810

Grendel was obliged to make for the marshes,
head for his joyless lair. He was
well aware that his life's days were done,
come to an end. After that deadly encounter
the desire of every Dane was at last accomplished.
  In this way did the wise and fearless man
who had travelled from far cleanse Hrothgar's hall,
release it from affliction. He rejoiced in his night's work,
his glorious achievement. The leader of the Geats
made good his boast to the East-Danes;   820
he had removed the cause of their distress,
put an end to the sorrow every Dane had shared,
the bitter grief that they had been constrained
to suffer. When Beowulf, brave in battle,
placed hand, arm and shoulder—Grendel's
entire grasp—under Heorot's spacious roof,
that was evidence enough of victory.
  Then I have heard that next morning
many warriors gathered round the gift-hall;
leaders of men came from every region,   830
from remote parts, to look on the wonder,
the tracks of the monster. Grendel's death
seemed no grievous loss to any of the men
who set eyes on the spoor of the defeated one,
saw how he, weary in spirit, overcome in combat,
fated and put to flight, had made for the lake
of water-demons—leaving tracks of life-blood.
  There the water boiled because of the blood;
the fearful swirling waves reared up,
mingled with hot blood, battle gore;   840
fated, he hid himself, then joyless
laid aside his life, his heathen spirit,
in the fen lair; hell received him there.
  After this, the old retainers left the lake
and so did the company of young men too;
brave warriors rode back on their gleaming horses
from this joyful journey. Then Beowulf's exploit
was acclaimed; many a man asserted
time and again that there was no better
shield-bearer in the whole world, to north or south   850
between the two seas, under the sky's expanse,
no man more worthy of his own kingdom.
Yet they found no fault at all with their friendly lord,
gracious Hrothgar—he was a great king.
  At times the brave warriors spurred their bays,
horses renowned for their speed and stamina,
and raced each other where the track was suitable.
And now and then one of Hrothgar's thanes
who brimmed with poetry, and remembered lays,

a man acquainted with ancient traditions 860
of every kind, composed a new song
in correct metre. Most skilfully that man
began to sing of Beowulf's feat,
to weave words together, and fluently
to tell a fitting tale.
        He recounted all he knew
of Sigemund, the son of Waels;[12] many a strange story
about his exploits, his endurance, and his journeys
to earth's ends; many an episode
unknown or half-known to the sons of men, songs
of feud and treachery. Only Fitela knew of these things, 870
had heard them from Sigemund who liked to talk
of this and that, for he and his nephew
had been companions in countless battles—
they slew many monsters with their swords.
After his death, no little fame attached to Sigemund's name,
that courageous man who had killed the dragon,
guardian of the hoard. Under the grey rock
the son of the prince braved that dangerous deed
alone; Fitela was not with him;
for all that, as fate had it, he impaled 880
the wondrous serpent, pinned it to the rock face
with his patterned sword; the dragon was slain.
Through his own bravery, that warrior ensured
that he could enjoy the treasure hoard
at will; the son of Waels loaded it all
onto a boat, stowed the shining treasure
into the ship; the serpent burned in its own flames.
Because of all his exploits, Sigemund,
guardian of strong men, was the best known
warrior in the world—so greatly had he prospered— 890
after Heremod's prowess, strength and daring
had been brought to an end, when, battling with giants,
he fell into the power of fiends, and was at once
done to death.[13] He had long endured
surging sorrows, had become a source
of grief to his people, and to all his retainers.
And indeed, in those times now almost forgotten,
many wise men often mourned that great warrior,
for they had looked to him to remedy their miseries;
they thought that the prince's son would prosper 900
and attain his father's rank, would protect his people,

[12] The singer is paying Beowulf a high compliment in comparing him to Sigemund, one of the greatest Germanic heroes. Since Sigemund was renowned as a dragon-slayer (see ll. 875–882), the lines may also foreshadow the end of the poem.
[13] Heremod was the Danish king before the legendary Scyld (l. 4). Through the rest of the poem, he is the prototype of the bad king. (See, for example, ll. 1694ff.)

their heirlooms and their citadel, the heroes' kingdom,
land of the Scyldings. Beowulf, Hygelac's kinsman,
was much loved by all who knew him,
by his friends; but Heremod was stained by sin.
    Now and then the brave men raced their horses,
ate up the sandy tracks—and they were so absorbed
that the hours passed easily. Stout-hearted warriors
without number travelled to the high hall
to inspect that wonder; the king himself, too,   910
glorious Hrothgar, guardian of ring-hoards,
came from his quarters with a great company, escorted
his queen and her retinue of maidens into the mead-hall.
Hrothgar spoke—he approached Heorot,
stood on the steps, stared at the high roof
adorned with gold, and at Grendel's hand:
"Let us give thanks at once to God Almighty
for this sight. I have undergone many afflictions,
grievous outrages at Grendel's hands; but God,
Guardian of heaven, can work wonder upon wonder.   920
Until now, I had been resigned,
had no longer believed that my afflictions
would ever end: this finest of buildings
stood stained with battle blood,
a source of sorrow to my counsellors;
they all despaired of regaining this hall
for many years to come, of guarding it from foes,
from devils and demons. Yet now one warrior
alone, through the Almighty's power, has succeeded
where we failed for all our fine plans.   930
Indeed, if she is still alive,
that woman (whoever she was) who gave birth
to such a son, to be one of humankind,
may claim that the Creator was gracious to her
in her child-bearing. Now, Beowulf,
best of men, I will love you in my heart
like a son; keep to our new kinship
from this day on. You shall lack
no earthly riches I can offer you.
Most often I have honoured a man for less,   940
given treasure to a poorer warrior,
more sluggish in the fight. Through your deeds
you have ensured that your glorious name
will endure for ever. May the Almighty grant you
good fortune, as He has always done before!"
    Beowulf, the son of Ecgtheow, answered:
"We performed that dangerous deed
with good will; at peril we pitted ourselves
against the unknown. I wish so much
that you could have seen him for yourself,   950
that fiend in his trappings, in the throes of death.

I meant to throttle him on that bed of slaughter
as swiftly as possible, with savage grips,
to hear death rattle in his throat
because of my grasp, unless he should escape me.
But I could not detain him, the Lord
did not ordain it—I did not hold my deadly enemy
firm enough for that; the fiend jerked free
with immense power. Yet, so as to save
his life, he left behind his hand, 960
his arm and shoulder; but the wretched monster
has bought himself scant respite;
the evil marauder, tortured by his sins,
will not live the longer, but agony
embraces him in its deadly bonds,
squeezes life out of his lungs; and now this creature,
stained with crime, must await the day of judgement
and his just deserts from the glorious Creator."
　　After this, the son of Ecglaf boasted less
about his prowess in battle—when all the warriors, 970
through Beowulf's might, had been enabled
to examine that hand, the fiend's fingers,
nailed up on the gables. Seen from in front,
each nail, each claw of that warlike,
heathen monster looked like steel—
a terrifying spike. Everyone said
that no weapon whatsoever, no proven sword
could possibly harm it, could damage
that battle-hardened, blood-stained hand.
　　Then orders were quickly given for the inside of Heorot 980
to be decorated; many servants, both men and women,
bustled about that wine-hall, adorned that building
of retainers. Tapestries, worked in gold,
glittered on the walls, many a fine sight
for those who have eyes to see such things.
That beautiful building, braced within
by iron bands, was badly damaged;
the door's hinges were wrenched; when the monster,
damned by all his crimes, turned in flight,
despairing of his life, the hall roof only 990
remained untouched. Death is not easy
to escape, let him who will attempt it.
Man must go to the grave that awaits him—
fate has ordained this for all who have souls,
children of men, earth's inhabitants—
and his body, rigid on its clay bed,
will sleep there after the banquet.
　　　　　　　　　　　　Then it was time
for Healfdene's son to proceed to the hall,
the king himself was eager to attend the feast.
I have never heard of a greater band of kinsmen 1000

gathered with such dignity around their ring-giver.
Then the glorious warriors sat on the benches,
rejoicing in the feast. Courteously
their kinsmen, Hrothgar and Hrothulf,
quaffed many a mead-cup, confident warriors
in the high hall. Heorot was packed
with feasters who were friends; the time was not yet come
when the Scyldings practised wrongful deeds.[14]
Then Hrothgar gave Beowulf Healfdene's sword,
and a battle banner, woven with gold,   1010
and a helmet and a corslet, as rewards for victory;
many men watched while the priceless, renowned sword
was presented to the hero. Beowulf emptied
the ale-cup in the hall; he had no cause
to be ashamed at those precious gifts.
There are few men, as far as I have heard,
who have given four such treasures, gleaming with gold,
to another on the mead-bench with equal generosity.
A jutting ridge, wound about with metal wires,
ran over the helmet's crown, protecting the skull,   1020
so that well-ground swords, proven in battle,
could not injure the well-shielded warrior
when he advanced against his foes.
Then the guardian of thanes ordered
that eight horses with gold-plated bridles
be led into the courtyard; onto one was strapped
a saddle, inlaid with jewels, skilfully made.
That was the war-seat of the great king,
Healfdene's son, whenever he wanted
to join in the sword-play. That famous man   1030
never lacked bravery at the front in battle,
when men about him were cut down like corn.
Then the king of the Danes, Ing's descendants,[15]
presented the horses and weapons to Beowulf,
bade him use them well and enjoy them.
Thus the renowned prince, the retainers' gold-warden,
rewarded those fierce sallies in full measure,
with horses and treasure, so that no man
would ever find reason to reproach him fairly.
Furthermore, the guardian of warriors gave   1040
a treasure, an heirloom at the mead-bench,
to each of those men who had crossed the sea
with Beowulf; and he ordered that gold
be paid for that warrior Grendel slew
so wickedly—as he would have slain many another,
had not foreseeing God and the warrior's courage

---

[14] This vague foreshadowing may refer to a story that after Hrothgar died Hrothulf treacherously deposed and killed Hrothgar's son and successor Hrethric.
[15] An older name for the Danes. Ing was a legendary Danish king.

together forestalled him. The Creator ruled over
all humankind, even as He does today.
Wherefore a wise man will value forethought
and understanding. Whoever lives long 1050
on earth, endures the unrest of these times,
will be involved in much good and much evil.
 Then Hrothgar, leader in battle, was entertained
with music—harp and voice in harmony.
The strings were plucked, many a song rehearsed,
when it was the turn of Hrothgar's poet
to please men at the mead-bench, perform in the hall.
He sang of Finn's troop, victims of surprise attack,
and of how that Danish hero, Hnaef of the Scyldings,
was destined to die among the Frisian slain.[16] 1060
 Hildeburh, indeed, could hardly recommend
the honour of the Jutes; that innocent woman
lost her loved ones, son and brother,
in the shield-play; they fell, as fate ordained,
stricken by spears; and she was stricken with grief.
Not without cause did Hoc's daughter
mourn the shaft of fate, for in the light of morning
she saw that her kin lay slain under the sky,
the men who had been her endless pride
and joy. That encounter laid claim 1070
to all but a few of Finn's thanes,
and he was unable to finish that fight
with Hnaef's retainer, with Hengest in the hall,
unable to dislodge the miserable survivors;
indeed, terms for a truce were agreed:
that Finn should give up to them another hall,
with its high seat, in its entirety,
which the Danes should own in common with the Jutes;
and that at the treasure-giving the son of Folcwalda[17]
should honour the Danes day by day, 1080
should distribute rings and gold-adorned gifts
to Hengest's band and his own people in equal measure.
Both sides pledged themselves to this peaceful
settlement. Finn swore Hengest solemn oaths
that he would respect the sad survivors
as his counsellors ordained, and that no man there

---

[16] The story that the harpist tells is also the subject of a fragmentary Old English lay called *The Finnsburh Fragment.* Finn, king of the Jutes (Frisians), married Hildeburh, daughter of the Danish king Hoc. During a visit from Hildeburh's brother Hnaef, who has succeeded to the Danish throne, to Finnsburh (Finn's stronghold), a quarrel breaks out between the Jutes and the Danes of Hnaef's party, and many are killed, including Hnaef and Finn's and Hildeburh's son. Hengest succeeds Hnaef as king of the Danes, and an uneasy truce is arranged which requires the Danes to live at peace with Finn, who has slain their king. After a winter of resentment and tension, violence breaks out again; Hengest and the Danes kill Finn and take Hildeburh back to Denmark.
[17] Finn.

must violate the covenant with word or deed,
or complain about it, although they
would be serving the slayer of their lord
(as fate had forced those lordless men to do);   1090
and he warned the Frisians that if, in provocation,
they should mention the murderous feud,
the sword's edge should settle things.
The funeral fire was prepared, glorious gold
was brought up from the hoard: the best of Scyldings,[18]
that race of warriors, lay ready on the pyre.
Blood-stained corslets, and images of boars
(cast in iron and covered in gold)
were plentiful on that pyre, and likewise the bodies
of many retainers, ravaged by wounds;   1100
renowned men fell in that slaughter.
Then Hildeburh asked that her own son
be committed to the flames at her brother's funeral,
that his body be consumed on Hnaef's pyre.
That grief-stricken woman keened over his corpse,
sang doleful dirges. The warriors' voices
soared towards heaven. And so did the smoke
from the great funeral fire that roared
before the barrow; heads sizzled,
wounds split open, blood burst out   1110
from battle scars. The ravenous flames
swallowed those men whole, made no distinction
between Frisians and Danes; the finest men departed.
Then those warriors,[19] their friends lost to them,
went to view their homes, revisit the stronghold
and survey the Frisian land. But Hengest
stayed with Finn, in utter dejection, all through
that blood-stained winter. And he dreamed
of his own country, but he was unable to steer
his ship homeward, for the storm-beaten sea   1120
wrestled with the wind; winter sheathed the waves
in ice—until once again spring made its sign
(as still it does) among the houses of men:
clear days, warm weather, in accordance as always
with the law of the seasons. Then winter was over,
the face of the earth was fair; the exile
was anxious to leave that foreign people
and the Frisian land. And yet he brooded
more about vengeance than about a voyage,
and wondered whether he could bring about a clash   1130
so as to repay the sons of the Jutes.
Thus Hengest did not shrink from the duty of vengeance

---

[18] Hnaef.
[19] The Jutish survivors.

after Hunlafing had placed the flashing sword,
finest of all weapons, on his lap;[20]
this sword's edges had scarred many Jutes.
And so it was that cruel death by the sword later
cut down the brave warrior Finn in his own hall,
after Guthlaf and Oslaf, arrived from a sea-journey,
had fiercely complained of that first attack,
condemned the Frisians on many scores: 1140
the Scyldings' restless spirits could no longer
be restrained. Then the hall ran red with the blood
of the enemy—Finn himself was slain,
the king with his troop, and Hildeburh was taken.
The Scylding warriors carried that king's
heirlooms down to their ship,
all the jewels and necklaces they discovered
at Finn's hall. They sailed over the sea-paths,
brought that noble lady back to Denmark
and her own people.
            Thus was the lay sung,   1150
the song of the poet. The hall echoed with joy,
waves of noise broke out along the benches;
cup-bearers carried wine in glorious vessels.
Then Wealhtheow, wearing her golden collar, walked
to where Hrothgar and Hrothulf were sitting side by side,
uncle and nephew, still friends together, true to one another.
And the spokesman Unferth sat at the feet
of the Danish lord; all men admired
his spirit and audacity, although he had deceived
his own kinsmen in a feud. Then the lady of the Scyldings   1160
spoke these words: "Accept this cup, my loved lord,
treasure-giver; O gold-friend of men,
learn the meaning of joy again, and speak words
of gratitude to the Geats, for so one ought to do.
And be generous to them too, mindful of gifts
which you have now amassed from far and wide.
I am told you intend to adopt this warrior,
take him for your son. This resplendent ring-hall,
Heorot, has been cleansed; give many rewards
while you may, but leave this land and the Danish people   1170
to your own descendants when the day comes
for you to die. I am convinced
that gracious Hrothulf will guard our children
justly, should he outlive you, lord of the Scyldings,
in this world; I believe he will repay our sons
most generously if he remembers all we did
for his benefit and enjoyment when he was a boy."

[20]Hunlafing means "son of Hunlaf." Hunlaf was apparently one of the Danes killed in
Finnsburh and the brother of the Guthlaf and Oslaf mentioned in l. 1138. By placing his dead
father's sword in Hengest's lap, Hunlafing is calling for vengeance.

Then Wealhtheow walked to the bench where her sons,
Hrethric and Hrothmund, sat with the sons of thanes,
fledgling warriors; where also that brave man,   1180
Beowulf of the Geats, sat beside the brothers.
To him she carried the cup, and asked in gracious words
if he would care to drink; and to him she presented
twisted gold with courtly ceremonial—
two armlets, a corslet and many rings,
and the most handsome collar in the world.
I have never heard that any hero had a jewel
to equal that, not since Hama made off
for his fortress with the Brosings' necklace, that pendant
in its precious setting; he fled from the enmity   1190
of underhand Eormenric, he chose long-lasting gain.[21]
Hygelac the Geat, grandson of Swerting,
wore that necklace on his last raid
when he fought beneath his banner to defend his treasure,
his battle spoils; fate claimed him then,
when he, foolhardy, courted disaster,
a feud with the Frisians. On that occasion the famous prince
had carried the treasure, the priceless stones,
over the cup of the waves; he crumpled under his shield.
Then the king's body fell into the hands of Franks,   1200
his coat of mail and the collar also;
after that battle, weaker warriors picked at
and plundered the slain; many a Geat lay dead, guarding
that place of corpses.[22]
                              Applause echoed in the hall.
Wealhtheow spoke these words before the company:
"May you, Beowulf, beloved youth, enjoy
with all good fortune this necklace and corslet,
treasures of the people; may you always prosper;
win renown through courage, and be kind in your counsel
to these boys; for that, I will reward you further.   1210
You have ensured that men will always sing
your praises, even to the ends of the world,
as far as oceans still surround cliffs,
home of the winds. May you thrive, O prince,
all your life. I hope you will amass
a shining hoard of treasure. O happy Beowulf,
be gracious in your dealing with my sons.

[21] The Brosings' necklace had been worn by the goddess Freya. Nothing is known of its theft by Hama except what is given here. Eormenric was a famous king of the East Goths in the fourth century. To "choose long-lasting gain" is to become a Christian and give up worldly goods.

[22] The episode that is the subject of this digression is referred to three other times in the poem: ll. 2340ff., 2492ff., and 2902ff. Hygelac, Beowulf's king, rashly led a raid on the Frisians. He and his troop seized many Frisian treasures but on their way home by ship they were attacked by Franks. Hygelac was killed. Beowulf killed Daeghrefn, the Frankish champion and standard-bearer, and escaped by swimming back to Geatland. There he was first advisor to Heardred, Hygelac's young son and successor, and later king.

Here, each warrior is true to the others,
gentle of mind, loyal to his lord;
the thanes are as one, the people all alert, 1220
the warriors have drunk well. They will do as I ask."
    Then Wealhtheow retired to her seat
beside her lord. That was the best of banquets,
men drank their fill of wine; they had not tasted
bitter destiny, the fate that had come and claimed
many of the heroes at the end of dark evenings,
when Hrothgar the warrior had withdrawn
to take his rest. Countless retainers
defended Heorot as they had often done before;
benches were pushed back; the floor was padded 1230
with beds and pillows. But one of the feasters
lying on his bed was doomed, and soon to die.
They set their bright battle-shields
at their heads. Placed on the bench
above each retainer, his crested helmet,
his linked corslet and sturdy spear-shaft
were plainly to be seen. It was their habit,
both at home and in the field,
to be prepared for battle always,
for any occasion their lord might need 1240
assistance; that was a loyal band of retainers.
    And so they slept. One man paid a heavy price
for his night's rest, as often happened
after Grendel first held the gold-hall
and worked his evil in it, until he met his doom,
death for his crimes. For afterwards it became clear,
and well known to the Scyldings, that some avenger
had survived the evil-doer, still lived after
that grievous, mortal combat.
                            Grendel's mother
was a monster of a woman; she mourned her fate— 1250
she who had to live in the terrible lake,
the cold water streams, after Cain slew
his own brother, his father's son,
with a sword; he was outlawed after that;
a branded man, he abandoned human joys,
wandered in the wilderness. Many spirits, sent
by fate, issued from his seed; one of them, Grendel,
that hateful outcast, was surprised in the hall
by a vigilant warrior spoiling for a fight.
Grendel gripped and grabbed him there, 1260
but the Geat remembered his vast strength,
that glorious gift given him of God,
and put his trust for support and assistance
in the grace of the Lord; thus he overcame
the envoy of hell, humbled his evil adversary.
So the joyless enemy of mankind journeyed

to the house of the dead. And then Grendel's mother,
mournful and ravenous, resolved to go
on a grievous journey to avenge her son's death.
   Thus she reached Heorot; Ring-Danes, snoring, 1270
were sprawled about the floor. The thanes suffered
a serious reverse as soon as Grendel's mother
entered the hall. The terror she caused,
compared to her son, equalled the terror
an Amazon inspires as opposed to a man,
when the ornamented sword, forged on the anvil,
the razor-sharp blade stained with blood,
shears through the boar-crested helmets of the enemy.
Then swords were snatched from benches, blades
drawn from scabbards, many a broad shield 1280
was held firmly in the hall; none could don helmet
or spacious corslet—that horror caught them by surprise.
The monster wanted to make off for the moors,
fly for her life, as soon as she was found out.
Firmly she grasped one of the thanes
and made for the fens as fast as she could.
That man whom she murdered even as he slept
was a brave shield-warrior, a well-known thane,
most beloved by Hrothgar of all his hall retainers
between the two seas. Beowulf was not there; 1290
the noble Geat had been allotted another lodging
after the giving of treasure earlier that evening.
Heorot was in uproar; she seized her son's
blood-crusted hand; anguish once again
had returned to the hall. What kind of bargain
was that, in which both sides forfeited
the lives of friends?
                  Then the old king,
the grizzled warrior, was convulsed with grief
when he heard of the death of his dearest retainer.
   Immediately Beowulf, that man blessed with victory, 1300
was called to the chamber of the king. At dawn
the noble warrior and his friends, his followers,
hurried to the room where the wise man was waiting,
waiting and wondering whether the Almighty
would ever allow an end to their adversity.
Then Beowulf, brave in battle, crossed
the floor with his band—the timbers thundered—
and greeted the wise king, overlord of Ing's
descendants; he asked if the night had passed off
peacefully, since his summons was so urgent. 1310
   Hrothgar, guardian of the Scyldings, said:
"Do not speak of peace; grief once again
afflicts the Danish people. Yrmenlaf's
elder brother, Aeschere, is dead,
my closest counsellor and my comrade,

my shoulder-companion when we shielded
our heads in the fight, when soldiers clashed on foot,
slashed at boar-crests. Aeschere was all
that a noble man, a warrior should be.
The wandering, murderous monster slew him 1320
in Heorot; and I do not know where that ghoul,
drooling at her feast of flesh and blood,
made off afterwards. She has avenged her son
whom you savaged yesterday with vice-like holds
because he had impoverished and killed my people
for many long years. He fell in mortal combat,
forfeit of his life; and now another mighty
evil ravager has come to avenge her kinsman;
and many a thane, mournful in his mind
for his treasure-giver, may feel she has avenged 1330
that feud already, indeed more than amply;
now that hand lies still which once sustained you.
 I have heard my people say,
men of this country, counsellors in the hall,
that they have seen *two* such beings,
equally monstrous, rangers of the fell-country,
rulers of the moors; and these men assert
that so far as they can see one bears
a likeness to a woman; grotesque though he was,
the other who trod the paths of exile looked like a man, 1340
though greater in height and build than a goliath;
he was christened *Grendel* by my people
many years ago; men do not know if he
had a father, a fiend once begotten
by mysterious spirits. These two live
in a little-known country, wolf-slopes, windswept headlands,
perilous paths across the boggy moors, where a mountain stream
plunges under the mist-covered cliffs,
rushes through a fissure. It is not far from here,
if measured in miles, that the lake stands 1350
shadowed by trees stiff with hoar-frost.
A wood, firmly-rooted, frowns over the water.
There, night after night, a fearful wonder may be seen—
fire on the water; no man alive
is so wise as to know the nature of its depths.
Although the moor-stalker, the stag with strong horns,
when harried by hounds will make for the wood,
pursued from afar, he will succumb
to the hounds on the brink, rather than plunge in
and save his head. That is not a pleasant place. 1360
When the wind arouses the wrath of the storm,
whipped waves rear up black from the lake,
reach for the skies, until the air becomes misty,
the heavens weep. Now, once again, help may be had
from you alone. As yet, you have not seen the haunt,

the perilous place where you may meet this most evil monster
face to face. Do you dare set eyes on it?
If you return unscathed, I will reward you
for your audacity, as I did before,
with ancient treasures and twisted gold."   1370
    Beowulf, the son of Ecgtheow, answered:
"Do not grieve, wise Hrothgar! Better each man
should avenge his friend than deeply mourn.
The days on earth for every one of us
are numbered; he who may should win renown
before his death; that is a warrior's
best memorial when he has departed from this world.
Come, O guardian of the kingdom, let us lose
no time but track down Grendel's kinswoman.
I promise you that wherever she turns—   1380
to honeycomb caves, to mountain woods,
to the bottom of the lake—she shall find no refuge.
Shoulder your sorrows with patience
this day; this is what I expect of you."
    Then the old king leapt up, poured out his gratitude
to God Almighty for the Geat's words.
Hrothgar's horse, his stallion with plaited mane,
was saddled and bridled; the wise ruler
set out in full array; his troop of shield-bearers
fell into step. They followed the tracks   1390
along forest paths and over open hill-country
for mile after mile; the monster had made
for the dark moors directly, carrying the corpse
of the foremost thane of all those
who, with Hrothgar, had guarded the hall.
Then the man of noble lineage left Heorot far behind,
followed narrow tracks, string-thin paths
over steep, rocky slopes—remote parts
with beetling crags and many lakes
where water-demons lived. He went ahead   1400
with a handful of scouts to explore the place;
all at once he came upon a dismal wood,
mountain trees standing on the edge
of a grey precipice; the lake lay beneath,
blood-stained and turbulent. The Danish retainers
were utterly appalled when they came upon
the severed head of their comrade Aeschere
on the steep slope leading down to the lake;
all the thanes were deeply distressed.
    The water boiled with blood, with hot gore;   1410
the warriors gaped at it. At times the horn sang
an eager battle-song. The brave men all sat down;
then they saw many serpents in the water,
strange sea-dragons swimming in the lake,

and also water-demons, lying on cliff-ledges,
monsters and serpents of the same kind
as often, in the morning, molest ships
on the sail-road. They plunged to the lake bottom,
bitter and resentful, rather than listen
to the song of the horn. The leader of the Geats   1420
picked off one with his bow and arrow,
ended its life; the metal tip
stuck in its vitals; it swam more sluggishly
after that, as the life-blood ebbed from its body;
in no time this strange sea-dragon
bristled with barbed boar-spears, was subdued
and drawn up onto the cliff; men examined
that disgusting enemy.
                        Beowulf donned
his coat of mail, did not fear for his own life.
His massive corslet, linked by hand   1430
and skilfully adorned, was to essay the lake—
it knew how to guard the body, the bone-chamber,
so that his foe's grasp, in its malicious fury,
could not crush his chest, squeeze out his life;
and his head was guarded by the gleaming helmet
whlch was to explore the churning waters,
stir their very depths; gold decorated it,
and it was hung with chain-mail, as the weapon smith
had wrought it long before, wondrously shaped it
and beset it with boar-images, so that   1440
afterwards no battle-blade could do it damage.
Not least amongst his mighty aids was Hrunting,
the long-hilted sword Unferth lent him in his need;
it was one of the finest of heirlooms; the iron blade
was engraved with deadly, twig-like patterning,
tempered with battle blood. It had not failed
any of those men who had held it in their hands,
risked themselves on hazardous exploits,
pitted themselves against foes. That was not
the first time it had to do a hard day's work.   1450
Truly, when Ecglaf's son, himself so strong,
lent that weapon to his better as a swordsman,
he had forgotten all those taunts he flung
when tipsy with wine; he dared not chance
his own arm under the breakers, dared not
risk his life; at the lake he lost
his renown for bravery. It was not so with Beowulf
once he had armed himself for battle.
    The Geat, son of Ecgtheow, spoke:
"Great son of Healfdene, gracious ruler,   1460
gold-friend of men, remember now—
for I am now ready to go—

what we agreed if I, fighting on your behalf,
should fail to return: that you would always
be like a father to me after I had gone.
Guard my followers, my dear friends,
if I die in battle; and, beloved Hrothgar,
send to Hygelac the treasures you gave me.
When the lord of the Geats, Hrethel's son,
sees those gifts of gold, he will know   1470
that I found a noble giver of rings
and enjoyed his favour for as long as I lived.
And, O Hrothgar, let renowned Unferth
have the ancient treasure, the razor sharp
ornamented sword; and I will make my name
with Hrunting, or death will destroy me."
    After these words the leader of the Geats
dived bravely from the bank, did not even
wait for an answer; the seething water
received the warrior. A full day elapsed   1480
before he could perceive the bottom of the lake.
    She who had guarded the lake's length and breadth
for fifty years, vindictive, fiercely ravenous for blood,
soon realized that one of the race of men
was looking down into the monsters' lair.
Then she grasped him, clutched the Geat
in her ghastly claws; and yet she did not
so much as scratch his skin; his coat of mail
protected him; she could not penetrate
the linked metal rings with her loathsome fingers.   1490
Then the sea-wolf dived to the bottom-most depths,
swept the prince to the place where she lived,
so that he, for all his courage, could not
wield a weapon; too many wondrous creatures
harassed him as he swam; many sea-serpents
with savage tusks tried to bore through his corslet,
the monsters molested him. Then the hero saw
that he had entered some loathsome hall
in which there was no water to impede him,
a vaulted chamber where the floodrush   1500
could not touch him. A light caught his eye,
a lurid flame flickering brightly.
    Then the brave man saw the sea-monster,
fearsome, infernal; he whirled his blade,
swung his arm with all his strength,
and the ring-hilted sword sang a greedy war-song
on the monster's head. Then that guest realized
that his gleaming blade could not bite into her flesh,
break open her bone-chamber; its edge failed Beowulf
when he needed it; yet it had endured   1510
many a combat, sheared often through the helmet,

split the corslet of a fated man; for the first time
that precious sword failed to live up to its name.
　　Then, resolute, Hygelac's kinsman took his courage
in both hands, trusted in his own strength.
Angrily the warrior hurled Hrunting away,
the damascened sword with serpent patterns on its hilt;
tempered and steel-edged, it lay useless on the earth.
Beowulf trusted in his own strength,
the might of his hand. So must any man　　　　　　　　　　1520
who hopes to gain long-lasting fame
in battle; he must risk his life, regardless.
Then the prince of the Geats seized the shoulder
of Grendel's mother—he did not mourn their feud;
when they grappled, that brave man in his fury
flung his mortal foe to the ground.
Quickly she came back at him, locked him
in clinches and clutched at him fearsomely.
Then the greatest of warriors stumbled and fell.
She dropped on her hall-guest, drew her dagger,　　　　　1530
broad and gleaming; she wanted to avenge her son,
her only offspring. The woven corslet
that covered his shoulders saved Beowulf's life,
denied access to both point and edge.
Then Ecgtheow's son, leader of the Geats,
would have died far under the wide earth
had not his corslet, his mighty chain-mail,
guarded him, and had not holy God
granted him victory; the wise Lord,
Ruler of the Heavens, settled the issue　　　　　　　　　1540
easily after the hero had scrambled to his feet.
　　Then Beowulf saw among weapons an invincible sword
wrought by the giants, massive and double-edged,
the joy of many warriors; that sword was matchless,
well-tempered and adorned, forged in a finer age,
only it was so huge that no man but Beowulf
could hope to handle it in the quick of combat.
Ferocious in battle, the defender of the Scyldings
grasped the ringed hilt, swung the ornamented sword
despairing of his life—he struck such a savage blow　　　1550
that the sharp blade slashed through her neck,
smashed the vertebrae; it severed her head
from the fated body; she fell at his feet.
The sword was bloodstained; Beowulf rejoiced.
　　A light gleamed; the chamber was illumined
as if the sky's bright candle were shining
from heaven. Hygelac's thane inspected
the vaulted room, then walked round the walls,
fierce and resolute, holding the weapon firmly
by the hilt. The sword was not too large　　　　　　　　1560

for the hero's grasp, but he was eager to avenge
at once all Grendel's atrocities,
all the many visits the monster had inflicted
on the West-Danes—which began with the time
he slew Hrothgar's sleeping hearth-companions,
devoured fifteen of the Danish warriors
even as they slept, and carried off as many more,
a monstrous prize. But the resolute warrior
had already repaid him to such a degree
that he now saw Grendel lying on his death-bed,   1570
his life's-blood drained because of the wound
he had sustained in battle at Heorot. Then Grendel's corpse
received a savage blow at the hero's hands,
his body burst open: Beowulf lopped off his head.

    At once the wise men, anxiously gazing at
the lake with Hrothgar, saw that the water
had begun to chop and churn, that the waves
were stained with blood. The grey-haired Scyldings
discussed that bold man's fate, agreed
there was no hope of seeing that brave thane again—   1580
no chance that he would come, rejoicing in victory,
before their renowned king; it seemed certain
to all but a few that the sea-wolf had destroyed him.

    Then the ninth hour came. The noble Scyldings
left the headland; the gold-friend of men
returned to Heorot; the Geats, sick at heart,
sat down and stared at the lake.
Hopeless, they yet hoped to set eyes
on their dear lord.

              Then the battle-sword
began to melt like a gory icicle   1590
because of the monster's blood. Indeed,
it was a miracle to see it thaw entirely,
as does ice when the Father (He who ordains
all times and seasons) breaks the bonds of frost,
unwinds the flood fetters; He is the true Lord.
The leader of the Geats took none of the treasures
away from the chamber—though he saw many there—
except the monster's head and the gold-adorned
sword-hilt; the blade itself had melted,
the patterned sword had burnt, so hot was that blood,   1600
so poisonous the monster who had died in the cave.
He who had survived the onslaught of his enemies
was soon on his way, swimming up through the water;
when the evil monster ended his days on earth,
left this transitory life, the troubled water
and all the lake's expanse was purged of its impurity.

    Then the fearless leader of the seafarers
swam to the shore, exulting in his plunder,
the heavy burdens he had brought with him.

The intrepid band of thanes hurried towards him,   1610
giving thanks to God, rejoicing
to see their lord safe and sound of limb.
The brave man was quickly relieved of his helmet
and corslet.
            The angry water under the clouds,
the lake stained with battle-blood, at last became calm.
    Then they left the lake with songs on their lips,
retraced their steps along the winding paths
and narrow tracks; it was no easy matter
for those courageous men, bold as kings,
to carry the head away from the cliff   1620
overlooking the lake. With utmost difficulty
four of the thanes bore Grendel's head
to the gold-hall on a battle-pole;
thus the fourteen Geats, unbroken
in spirit and eager in battle, very soon
drew near to Heorot; with them, that bravest
of brave men crossed the plain towards the mead-hall.
Then the fearless leader of the thanes,
covered with glory, matchless in battle,
once more entered Heorot to greet Hrothgar.   1630
Grendel's head was carried by the hair
onto the floor where the warriors were drinking,
a ghastly thing paraded before the heroes and the queen.
Men stared at that wondrous spectacle.
    Beowulf, the son of Ecgtheow, said:
"So, son of Healfdene, lord of the Scyldings,
we proudly lay before you plunder from the lake;
this head you look at proves our success.
I barely escaped with my life from that combat
under the water, the risk was enormous;   1640
our encounter would have ended at once if God
had not guarded me. Mighty though it is,
Hrunting was no use at all in the battle;
but the Ruler of men—how often He guides
the friendless one—granted that I
should see a huge ancestral sword hanging,
shining, on the wall; I unsheathed it.
Then, at the time destiny decreed, I slew
the warden of the hall. And when the blood,
the boiling battle-blood burst from her body,   1650
that sword burnt, the damascened blade
was destroyed. I deprived my enemies
of that hilt; I repaid them as they deserved
for their outrages, murderous slaughter of the Danes.
I promise, then, O prince of the Scyldings,
that you can sleep in Heorot without anxiety,
rest with your retainers, with all the thanes
among your people—experienced warriors

and striplings together—without further fear
of death's shadow skulking near the hall." 1660
   Then the golden hilt, age-old work of giants,
was given to Hrothgar, the grizzled warrior,
the warlike lord; wrought by master-smiths,
it passed into the hands of the Danish prince
once the demons died; for that embittered fiend,
enemy of God, guilty of murder,
had abandoned this world—and so had his mother.
Thus the hilt was possessed by the best
of earthly kings between the two seas,
the best of those who bestowed gold on Norse men. 1670
   Hrothgar spoke, first examining the hilt,
the ancient heirloom. On it was engraved
the origins of strife in time immemorial,
when the tide of rising water drowned
the race of giants; their end was horrible;
they were opposed to the Eternal Lord,
and their reward was the downpour and the flood.
Also, on the sword-guards of pure gold,
it was recorded in runic letters, as is the custom,
for whom that sword, finest of blades, 1680
with twisted hilt and serpentine patterning
had first been made.
            Then Healfdene's wise son
lifted his voice—everyone listened:
"This land's grizzled guardian, who promotes truth
and justice amongst his people, and forgets nothing
though the years pass, can say for certain that this man
is much favoured by fate! Beowulf my friend,
your name is echoed in every country
to earth's end. You wear your enormous might
with wisdom and with dignity. I shall keep 1690
my promise made when last we spoke. You will
beyond doubt be the shield of the Geats
for days without number, and a source
of strength to warriors.
            Heremod was hardly that
to Ecgwala's sons, the glorious Scyldings;
he grew to spread slaughter and destruction
rather than happiness amongst the Danish people.
In mad rage he murdered his table-companions,
his most loyal followers; it came about
that the great prince cut himself off 1700
from all earthly pleasures, though God had endowed him
with strength and power above all other men,
and had sustained him. For all that, his heart
was filled with savage blood-lust. He never gave
gifts to the Danes, to gain glory. He lived joyless,

agony racked him; he was long an affliction
to his people. Be warned, Beowulf,
learn the nature of nobility. I who tell you
this story am many winters old.
                                        It is a miracle
how the mighty Lord in his generosity   1710
gives wisdom and land and high estate
to people on earth; all things are in His power.
At times he allows a noble man's mind to experience
happiness, grants he should rule over a pleasant,
prosperous country, a stronghold of men,
makes subject to him regions of earth,
a wide kingdom, until in his stupidity
there is no end to his ambition.
His life is unruffled—neither old age
nor illness afflict him, no unhappiness   1720
gnaws at his heart, in his land no hatred
flares up in mortal feuds, but all the world
bends to his will. He suffers no setbacks
until the seed of arrogance is sown and grows
within him, while still the watchman slumbers;
how deeply the soul's guardian sleeps
when a man is enmeshed in matters of this world;
the evil archer stands close with his drawn bow,
his bristling quiver. Then the poisoned shaft
pierces his mind under his helmet   1730
and he does not know how to resist
the devil's insidious, secret temptations.
What had long contented him now seems insufficient;
he becomes embittered, begins to hoard
his treasures, never parts with gold rings
in ceremonial splendour; he soon forgets
his destiny and disregards the honours
given him of God, the Ruler of Glory.
In time his transient body wizens and withers,
and dies as fate decrees; then another man   1740
succeeds to his throne who gives treasures and heirlooms
with great generosity; *he* is not obsessed with suspicions.
Arm yourself, dear Beowulf, best of men,
against such diseased thinking; always swallow pride;
remember, renowned warrior, what is more worthwhile—
gain everlasting. Today and tomorrow
you will be in your prime; but soon you will die,
in battle or in bed; either fire or water,
the fearsome elements, will embrace you,
or you will succumb to the sword's flashing edge,   1750
or to the arrow's flight, or to extreme old age;
then your eyes, once bright, will be clouded over;
all too soon, O warrior, death will destroy you.

I have ruled the Ring-Danes under the skies
for fifty years, shielded them in war
from many tribes of men in this world,
from swords and from ash-spears, and the time had come
when I thought I had no enemies left on earth.
All was changed utterly, gladness
became grief, after Grendel,   1760
my deadly adversary, invaded Heorot.
His visitations caused me continual pain.
Thus I thank the Creator, the Eternal Lord,
that after our afflictions I have lived to see,
to see with my own eyes this blood-stained head.
Now, Beowulf, brave in battle,
go to your seat and enjoy the feast;
tomorrow we shall share many treasures."
    The Geat, full of joy, straightway went
to find his seat as Hrothgar had suggested.   1770
Then, once again, as so often before,
a great feast was prepared for the brave warriors
sitting in the hall.
                        The shadows of night
settled over the retainers. The company arose;
the grey-haired man, the old Scylding,
wanted to retire. And the Geat, the shield-warrior,
was utterly exhausted, his bones ached for sleep.
At once the chamberlain—he who courteously
saw to all such needs as a thane,
a travelling warrior, had in those days—   1780
showed him, so limb-weary, to his lodging.
    Then Beowulf rested; the building soared,
spacious and adorned with gold; the guest
slept within until the black raven gaily
proclaimed sunrise. Bright light
chased away the shadows of night.
                            Then the warriors
hastened, the thanes were eager to return
to their own people; the brave seafarer
longed to see his ship, so far from that place.
Then the bold Geat ordered that Hrunting,   1790
that sword beyond price, be brought before Unferth;
he begged him to take it back and thanked him
for the loan of it; he spoke of it as an ally
in battle, and assured Unferth he did not
underrate it: what a brave man he was!
After this the warriors, wearing their chain-mail,
were eager to be off; their leader,
so dear to the Danes, walked to the daïs
where Hrothgar was sitting, and greeted him.
    Beowulf, the son of Ecgtheow, spoke: 1800
"Now we seafarers, who have sailed here from far,

beg to tell you we are eager
to return to Hygelac. We have been happy here,
hospitably entertained; you have treated us kindly.
If I can in any way win more of your affection,
O ruler of men, than I have done already,
I will come at once, eager for combat.
If news reaches me over the seas
that you are threatened by those around you
(just as before enemies endangered you) 1810
I will bring thousands of thanes,
all heroes, to help you. I know that Hygelac,
lord of the Geats, guardian of his people,
will advance me in word and deed
although he is young, so that I can back
these promises with spear shafts, and serve you
with all my strength where you need men.
Should Hrethric, Hrothgar's son, wish
to visit the court of the Geatish king,
he will be warmly welcomed. Strong men 1820
should seek fame in far-off lands."
   Hrothgar replied: "The wise Lord put these words
into your mind; I have never heard a warrior
speak more sagely while still so young.
You are very strong and very shrewd,
you speak with discerning. If your leader,
Hrethel's son, guardian of the people,
were to lose his life by illness or by iron,
by spear or grim swordplay, and if you survived him,
it seems to me that the Geats could not choose 1830
a better man for king, should you wish to rule
the land of your kinsmen. Beloved Beowulf,
the longer I know you, the more I like your spirit.
Because of your exploit, your act of friendship,
there will be an end to the gross outrages,
the old enmity between Geats and Danes;
they will learn to live in peace.
For as long as I rule this spacious land,
heirlooms will be exchanged; many men
will greet their friends with gifts, send them 1840
over the seas where gannets swoop and rise;
the ring-prowed ship will take tokens of esteem,
treasures across the waters. I know the Geats
are honourable to friend and foe alike,
always faithful to their ancient code."
   Then Healfdene's son, guardian of thanes,
gave him twelve treasures in the hall,
told him to go safely with those gifts
to his own dear kinsmen, and to come back soon.
That king, descendant of kings, 1850
leader of the Scyldings, kissed and embraced

the best of thanes; tears streamed down
the old man's face. The more that warrior thought,
wise and old, the more it seemed
improbable that they would meet again,
brave men in council. He so loved Beowulf
that he could not conceal his sense of loss;
but in his heart and in his head,
in his very blood, a deep love burned   1860
for that dear man.
                Then Beowulf the warrior,
proudly adorned with gold, crossed the plain,
exulting in his treasure. The ship
rode at anchor, waiting for its owner.
Then, as they walked, they often praised
Hrothgar's generosity. He was an altogether
faultless king, until old age deprived him
of his strength, as it does most men.
    Then that troop of brave young retainers
came to the water's edge; they wore ring-mail,   1870
woven corslets. And the same watchman
who had seen them arrive saw them now returning.
He did not insult them, ask for explanations,
but galloped from the cliff-top to greet the guests;
he said that those warriors in gleaming armour,
so eager to embark, would be welcomed home.
Then the spacious ship, with its curved prow,
standing ready on the shore, was laden with armour,
with horses and treasure. The mast towered
over Hrothgar's precious heirlooms.   1880
    Beowulf gave a sword bound round with gold
to the ship's watchman—a man who thereafter
was honoured on the mead-bench that much the more
on account of this heirloom.
                The ship surged forward,
butted the waves in deep waters;
it drew away from the shores of the Scyldings.
Then a sail, a great sea-garment, was fastened
with guys to the mast; the timbers groaned;
the boat was not blown off its course
by the stiff sea-breezes. The ship swept   1890
over the waves; foaming at the bows,
the boat with its well-wrought prow sped
over the waters, until at last the Geats
set eyes on the cliffs of their own country,
the familiar headlands; the vessel pressed forward,
pursued by the wind—it ran up onto dry land.
    The harbour guardian hurried down to the shore;
for many days he had scanned the horizon,
anxious to see those dear warriors once more.

He tethered the spacious sea-steed with ropes 1900
(it rode on its painter restlessly)
so that the rolling waves could not wrench it away.
Then Beowulf commanded that the peerless treasures,
the jewels and plated gold, be carried up from the shore.
He had not to go far to find the treasure-giver,
Hygelac son of Hrethel, for his house and the hall
for his companions stood quite close to the sea-wall.
That high hall was a handsome building;
it became the valiant king.
                 Hygd, his queen,
Haereth's daughter, was very young; but she 1910
was discerning, and versed in courtly customs,
though she had lived a short time only
in that citadel; and she was not too thrifty,
not ungenerous with gifts of precious treasures
to the Geatish thanes.
               Queen Thryth[23] was proud
and perverse, pernicious to her people.
No hero but her husband, however bold,
dared by day so much as turn his head
in her direction—that was far too dangerous;
but, if he did, he could bargain on being cruelly 1920
bound with hand-plaited ropes; soon
after his seizure, the blade was brought into play,
the damascened sword to settle the issue,
to inflict death. It is not right for a queen,
compelling though her beauty, to behave like this,
for a peace-weaver to deprive a dear man of his life
because she fancies she has been insulted.
But Offa, Hemming's kinsman, put an end to that.
Ale-drinking men in the hall have said
that she was no longer perfidious to her people, 1930
and committed no crimes, once she had been given,
adorned with gold, to that young warrior
of noble descent—once she had sailed,
at her father's command, to Offa's court
beyond the pale gold sea. After that,
reformed, she turned her life to good account;
renowned for virtue, she reigned with vision;
and she loved the lord of warriors in the high way
of love—he who was, as I have heard,
the best of all men, the mighty human race, 1940

---

[23] The story of Queen Thryth is introduced so abruptly as a contrast to Queen Hygd and seems so marginally relevant that many scholars suspect that a transitional passage has been lost. The difficulties of the vocabulary make it uncertain even that her name is Thryth; it may be Modthryth. Offa was a famous fourth-century king of the Continental Angles. The other characters in the story are otherwise unknown.

between the two seas. Offa the brave
was widely esteemed both for his gifts
and his skill in battle; he ruled his land
wisely. He fathered Eomer, guardian
of thanes, who was Hemming's kinsman,
grandson of Garmund, a goliath in battle.

Then Beowulf and his warrior band walked
across the sand, tramped over
the wide foreshore; the world's candle shone,
the sun hastening from the south. The men hurried too 1950
when they were told that the guardian of thanes,
Ongentheow's slayer,[24] the excellent young king,
held court in the hall, distributing rings.
Hygelac was informed at once of Beowulf's arrival—
that the shield of warriors, his comrade in battle,
had come back alive to the fortified enclosure,
was heading for the hall unscathed after combat.
Space on the benches for Beowulf and his band
was hastily arranged, as Hygelac ordered.

The guardian of thanes formally greeted 1960
that loyal man; then they sat down—
the unfated hero opposite the king,
kinsman facing kinsman. Haereth's daughter
carried mead-cups round the hall,
spoke kindly to the warriors, handed the stoups
of wine to the thanes. Hygelac began
to ask his companion courteous questions
in the high hall; he was anxious to hear
all that had happened to the seafaring Geats:
"Beloved Beowulf, tell me what became of you 1970
after the day you so hurriedly decided
to do battle far from here over the salt waters,
to fight at Heorot. And were you able
to assuage the grief, the well-known sorrow
of glorious Hrothgar? Your undertaking
deeply troubled me; I despaired, dear Beowulf,
of your return. I pleaded with you
not on any account to provoke that monster,
but to let the South-Danes settle their feud
with Grendel themselves. God be praised 1980
that I am permitted to see you safe and home."

Then Beowulf, the son of Ecgtheow, said:
"Half the world, lord Hygelac, has heard
of my encounter, my great combat
hand to hand with Grendel in that hall
where he had harrowed and long humiliated
the glorious Scyldings. I avenged it all;

---

[24] The story of the killing of Ongentheow, king of the Scylfings (Swedes), is told later in
the poem (ll. 2914–2992). Actually Hygelac did not kill Ongentheow himself, but led the raid
in which Ongentheow was killed.

none of Grendel's brood, however long
the last of that hateful race survives, 1990
steeped in crime, has any cause to boast about
that dawn combat.
                    First of all,
I went to the ring-hall to greet Hrothgar;
once Healfdene's great son knew of my intentions,
he assigned me a seat beside his own sons.
Then there was revelry; never in my life,
under heaven's vault, have I seen men
happier in the mead-hall. From time to time
the famous queen, the peace-weaver, walked across the floor,
exhorting the young warriors; often she gave 2000
some man a twisted ring before returning to her seat.
At times Hrothgar's daughter, whom I heard
men call Freawaru, carried the ale-horn
right round the hall in front of that brave company,
offered that vessel adorned with precious metals
to the thirsty warriors.
                        Young, and decorated
with gold ornaments, she is promised to Froda's noble son,
Ingeld of the Heathobards; that match was arranged
by the lord of the Scyldings, guardian of the kingdom;
he believes that it is an excellent plan 2010
to use her as a peace-weaver to bury old antagonisms,
mortal feuds. But the deadly spear rarely sleeps
for long after a prince lies dead in the dust,
however exceptional the bride may be!
    For Ingeld, leader of the Heathobards, and all
his retainers will later be displeased when he
and Freawaru walk on the floor—man and wife—
and when Danish warriors are being entertained.
For the guests will gleam with Heathobard heirlooms,
iron-hard, adorned with rings, 2020
precious possessions that had belonged
to their hosts' fathers for as long as they
could wield their weapons, until in the shield-play
they and their dear friends forfeited their lives.
Then, while men are drinking, an old
warrior will speak; a sword he has seen,
marvellously adorned, stirs his memory
of how Heathobards were slain by spears;
he seethes with fury; sad in his heart,
he begins to taunt a young Heathobard, 2030
incites him to action with these words:
    "Do you not recognize that sword, my friend,
the sword your father, fully armed, bore into battle
that last time, when he was slain by Danes,
killed by brave Scyldings who carried the field
when Withergyld fell and many warriors beside him?

See how the son of one of those
who slew him struts about the hall;
he sports the sword; he crows about that slaughter,
and carries that heirloom which is yours by right!"   2040
In this way, with acid words, he will endlessly
provoke him and rake up the past,
until the time will come when a Danish warrior,
Freawaru's thane, sleeps blood-stained,
slashed by the sword, punished by death
for the deeds of his father; and the Heathobard
will escape, well-acquainted with the country.
Then both sides will break the solemn oath
sworn by their leaders; and Ingeld will come
to hate the Scyldings, and his love for his wife   2050
will no longer be the same after such anguish and grief.
Thus I have little faith in friendship with Heathobards;
they will fail to keep their side of the promise,
friendship with the Danes.
                                         I have digressed;
Grendel is my subject. Now you must hear,
O treasure-giver, what the outcome was
of that hand-to-hand encounter. When the jewel of heaven
had journeyed over the earth, the angry one,
the terrible night-prowler paid us a visit—
unscathed warriors watching over Heorot.   2060
A fight awaited Hondscio, a horrible end
for that fated man; he was the first to fall;
Grendel tore that famous young retainer to bits
between his teeth, and swallowed the whole body
of that dear man, that girded warrior.
And even then that murderer, mindful of evil,
his mouth caked with blood, was not content
to leave the gold-hall empty-handed
but, famed for his strength, he tackled me,
gripped me with his outstretched hand.   2070
A huge unearthly glove swung at his side,
firmly secured with subtle straps;
it had been made with great ingenuity,
with devils' craft and dragons' skins.
Innocent as I was, the demon monster
meant to shove me in it, and many another
innocent besides; that was beyond him
after I leapt up, filled with fury.
It would take too long to tell you how I repaid
that enemy of men for all his outrages;   2080
but there, my prince, I ennobled your people
with my deeds. Grendel escaped,
and lived a little longer; but he left
behind at Heorot his right hand; and, in utter
wretchedness, sank to the bottom of the lake.

The sun rose; we sat down together
to feast, then the leader of the Scyldings
paid a good price for the bloody battle,
gave me many a gold-plated treasure.
There was talk and song; the grey-haired Scylding 2090
opened his immense hoard of memories;
now and then a happy warrior touched
the wooden harp, reciting some story,
mournful and true; at times the generous king
recalled in proper detail some strange incident;
and as the shadows lengthened, an aged thane,
cramped and rheumatic, raised his voice
time and again, lamenting his lost youth,
his prowess in battle; worn with winters,
his heart quickened to the call of the past. 2100
    In these ways we relaxed agreeably
throughout the long day until darkness closed in,
another night for men. Then, in her grief,
bent on vengeance, Grendel's mother
hastened to the hall where death had lain
in wait for her son—the battle-hatred
of the Geats. The horrible harridan avenged
her offspring, slew a warrior brazenly.
Aeschere, the wise old counsellor, lost
his life. And when morning came, 2110
the Danes were unable to cremate him,
to place the body of that dear man
on the funeral pyre; for Grendel's mother
had carried if off in her gruesome grasp,
taken it under the mountain lake.
Of all the grievous sorrows Hrothgar
long sustained, none was more terrible.
Then the king in his anger called upon your name
and entreated me to risk my life,
to accomplish deeds of utmost daring 2120
in the tumult of waves; he promised me rewards.
And so, as men now know all over the earth,
I found the grim guardian of the lake-bottom.
For a while we grappled; the water boiled
with blood; then in that battle-hall,
I lopped off Grendel's mother's head
with the mighty sword. I barely escaped
with my life; but I was not fated.
    And afterwards the guardian of thanes,
Healfdene's son, gave me many treasures. 2130
Thus the king observed excellent tradition:
in no wise did I feel unrewarded
for all my efforts, but Healfdene's son
offered me gifts of my own choosing;
gifts, O noble king, I wish now

to give to you in friendship. I still depend
entirely on your favours; I have few
close kinsmen but you, O Hygelac!"
　　Then Beowulf caused to be brought in
a standard bearing the image of a boar,   2140
together with a helmet towering in battle,
a grey corslet, and a noble sword; he said:
"Hrothgar, the wise king, gave me
these trappings and purposely asked me
to tell you their history: he said that Heorogar,[25]
lord of the Scyldings, long owned them.
Yet he has not endowed his own brave son,
Heoroweard, with this armour, much as
he loves him. Make good use of everything!"
　　I heard that four bays, apple-brown,   2150
were brought into the hall after the armour—
swift as the wind, identical. Beowulf gave them
as he gave the treasures. So should a kinsman do,
and never weave nets with underhand subtlety
to ensnare others, never have designs
on a close comrade's life. His nephew,
brave in battle, was loyal to Hygelac;
each man was mindful of the other's pleasure.
　　I heard that he gave Hygd the collar,
the wondrous ornament with which Wealhtheow,   2160
daughter of the prince, had presented him,
and gave her three horses also, graceful creatures
with brightly-coloured saddles; Hygd
wore that collar, her breast was adorned.
　　Thus Ecgtheow's son, feared in combat,
confirmed his courage with noble deeds;
he lived a life of honour, he never slew
companions at the feast; savagery was
alien to him, but he, so brave in battle,
made the best use of those ample talents   2170
with which God endowed him.
　　　　　　　　　　　　　He had been despised
for a long while, for the Geats saw no spark
of bravery in him, nor did their king deem him
worthy of much attention on the mead-bench;
people thought that he was a sluggard,
a feeble princeling. How fate changed,
changed completely for that glorious man!
　　Then the guardian of thanes, the famous king,
ordered that Hrethel's[26] gold-adorned heirloom
be brought in; no sword was so treasured   2180

---

[25] Heorogar was Hrothgar's elder brother, who preceded him on the Danish throne.
[26] Hygelac's father.

in all Geatland; he laid it in Beowulf's lap,
and gave him seven thousand hides of land,[27]
a hall and princely throne. Both men
had inherited land and possessions
in that country; but the more spacious kingdom
had fallen to Hygelac, who was of higher rank.

In later days, after much turmoil,
things happened in this way: when Hygelac lay dead
and murderous battle-blades had beaten down
the shield of his son Heardred,   2190
and when the warlike Swedes, savage warriors,
had hunted him down amongst his glorious people,
attacked Hereric's nephew with hatred,
the great kingdom of the Geats passed
into Beowulf's hands.[28] He had ruled it well
for fifty winters—he was a wise king,
a grizzled guardian of the land—when, on dark nights,
a dragon began to terrify the Geats:
he lived on a cliff, kept watch over a hoard
in a high stone barrow; below, there was   2200
a secret path; a man strayed
into this barrow by chance, seized
some of the pagan treasures, stole drinking vessels.
At first the sleeping dragon was deceived
by the thief's skill, but afterwards he avenged
this theft of gleaming gold; people far and wide,
bands of retainers, became aware of his wrath.
    That man did not intrude upon the hoard
deliberately, he who robbed the dragon;
but it was some slave, a wanderer in distress   2210
escaping from men's anger who entered there,
seeking refuge. He stood guilty of some sin.
As soon as he peered in, the outsider
stiffened with horror. Unhappy as he was,
he stole the vessel, the precious cup.
There were countless heirlooms in that earth-cave,
the enormous legacy of a noble people,
ancient treasures which some man or other
had cautiously concealed there many years
before. Death laid claim to all that people   2220
in days long past, and then that retainer
who outlived the rest, a gold-guardian
mourning his friends, expected the same fate—

---

[27]A hide was a unit of land measure, usually about 120 acres.
[28]Heardred succeeded his father Hygelac as king of the Geats. The story of the war with
the Swedes in which Heardred died is told more fully later (ll. 2366–2384).

thought he would enjoy those assembled heirlooms
a little while only. A newly-built barrow
stood ready on a headland which overlooked
the sea, protected by the hazards of access.
To this barrow the protector of rings brought the heirlooms,
the plated gold, all that part of the precious treasure
worthy of hoarding; then he spoke a few words: 2230
"Hold now, O earth, since heroes could not,
these treasures owned by nobles! Indeed, strong men
first quarried them from you. Death in battle,
ghastly carnage, has claimed all my people—
men who once made merry in the hall
have laid down their lives; I have no one
to carry the sword, to polish the plated vessel,
this precious drinking-cup; all the retainers
have hurried elsewhere. The iron helmet
adorned with gold shall lose its ornaments;   2240
men who should polish battle-masks are sleeping;
the coat of mail, too, that once withstood
the bite of swords in battle, after shields were shattered,
decays like the warriors; the linked mail may no longer
range far and wide with the warrior,
stand side by side with heroes. Gone is the pleasure
of plucking the harp, no fierce hawk
swoops about the hall, nor does the swift stallion
strike sparks in the courtyard. Cruel death
has claimed hundreds of this human race."   2250
     Thus the last survivor mourned time passing,
and roamed about by day and night,
sad and aimless, until death's lightning
struck at his heart.
                              The aged dragon of darkness
discovered that glorious hoard unguarded,
he who sought out barrows, smooth-scaled
and evil, and flew by night, breathing
fire; the Geats feared him greatly.
He was destined to find the hoard
in that cave and, old in winters, guard   2260
the heathen gold; much good it did him!
     Thus the huge serpent who harassed men
guarded that great stronghold under the earth
for three hundred winters, until
a man enraged him; the wanderer carried
the inlaid vessel to his lord, and begged him
for a bond of peace. Then the hoard was raided
and plundered, and that unhappy man
was granted his prayer. His lord examined
the ancient work of smiths for the first time.   2270
     There was conflict once more after the dragon
awoke; intrepid, he slid swiftly

along by the rock, and found the footprints
of the intruder; that man had skilfully
picked his way right past the dragon's head.
Thus he who is undoomed will easily survive
anguish and exile provided he enjoys
the grace of God. The warden of the hoard
prowled up and down, anxious to find
the man who had pillaged it while he slept.   2280
Breathing fire and filled with fury,
he circled the outside of the earth mound
again and again; but there was no one
in that barren place; yet he exulted at the thought
of battle, bloody conflict; at times he wheeled back
into the barrow, hunting for the priceless heirloom.
He realized at once that one of the race of men
had discovered the gold, the glorious treasure.
Restlessly the dragon waited for darkness;
the guardian of the hoard was bursting with rage,   2290
he meant to avenge the vessel's theft
with fire.
           Then daylight failed
as the dragon desired; he could no longer
confine himself to the cave but flew in a ball
of flame, burning for vengeance. The Geats
were filled with dread as he began his flight;
it swiftly ended in disaster for their lord.
    Then the dragon began to breathe forth fire,
to burn fine buildings; flame tongues flickered,
terrifying men; the loathsome winged creature   2300
meant to leave the whole place lifeless.
Everywhere the violence of the dragon, the venom
of that hostile one, was clearly to be seen—
how he had wrought havoc, hated and humiliated
the Geatish people. Then, before dawn he rushed back
to his hidden lair and the treasure hoard.
He had girdled the Geats with fire,
with ravening flames; he relied on his own strength,
and on the barrow and the cliff; his trust played him false.
    Then news of that terror was quickly brought   2310
to Beowulf, that flames enveloped
his own hall, best of buildings,
and the gift-throne of the Geats. That good man
was choked with intolerable grief.
Wise that he was, he imagined
he must have angered God, the Lord Eternal,
by ignoring some ancient law; he was seldom
dispirited, but now his heart was like lead.
    The fire dragon had destroyed the fortified hall,
the people's stronghold, and laid waste with flames   2320
the land by the sea. The warlike king,

prince of the Geats, planned to avenge this.
The protector of warriors, leader of men,
instructed the smith to forge a curious shield
made entirely of iron; he well knew
that a linden shield would not last long
against the flames. The eminent prince
was doomed to reach the end of his days on earth,
his life in this world. So too was the dragon,
though he had guarded the hoard for generations.   2330
    Then the giver of gold disdained
to track the dragon with a troop
of warlike men; he did not shrink
from single combat, nor did he set much store
by the fearless dragon's power, for had he not before
experienced danger, again and again
survived the storm of battle, beginning with that time
when, blessed with success, he cleansed
Hrothgar's hall, and crushed in battle
the monster and his vile mother?
                                        That grim combat   2340
in which Hygelac was slain—Hrethel's son,
leader of the Geats, dear lord of his people,
struck down by swords in the bloodbath
in Frisia—was far from the least
of his encounters. Beowulf escaped
because of his skill and stamina at swimming;
he waded into the water, bearing no fewer
than thirty corslets, a deadweight on his arms.
But the Frankish warriors who shouldered
their shields against him had no cause to boast   2350
about that combat; a handful only
eluded that hero and returned home.
Then the son of Ecgtheow, saddened and alone,
rode with the white horses[29] to his own people.
Hygd offered him heirlooms there, and even
the kingdom, the ancestral throne itself; for she feared
that her son would be unable to defend it
from foreign invaders now that Hygelac was gone.
But the Geats, for all their anguish, failed
to prevail upon the prince—he declined   2360
absolutely to become Heardred's lord,
or to taste the pleasures of royal power.
But he stood at his right hand,
ready with advice, always friendly,
and respectful, until the boy came of age
and could rule the Geats himself.

---

[29] That is, the waves.

Two exiles,[30]
Ohthere's sons, sailed to Heardred's court;
they had rebelled against the ruler of the Swedes,
a renowned man, the best of sea-kings,
gold-givers in Sweden. By receiving them, 2370
Heardred rationed the days of his life;
in return for his hospitality, Hygelac's son
was mortally wounded, slashed by swords.
Once Heardred lay lifeless in the dust,
Onela, son of Ongentheow, sailed home again;
he allowed Beowulf to inherit the throne
and rule the Geats; he was a noble king!
But Beowulf did not fail with help
after the death of the prince, although years passed;
he befriended unhappy Eadgils, Ohthere's son, 2380
and supplied him with weapons and warriors
beyond the wide seas. Eadgils afterwards
avenged Eanmund, he ravaged and savaged
the Swedes, and killed the king, Onela himself.
    Thus the son of Ecgtheow had survived
these feuds, these fearful battles, these acts
of single combat, up to that day
when he was destined to fight against the dragon.
Then in fury the leader of the Geats set out
with eleven to search for the winged serpent. 2390
By then Beowulf knew the cause of the feud,
bane of men; the famous cup
had come to him through the hands of its finder.
The unfortunate slave who first brought about
such strife made the thirteenth man
in that company—cowed and disconsolate,
he had to be their guide. Much against his will,
he conducted them to the entrance of the cave,
an earth-hall full of filigree work
and fine adornments close by the sea, 2400
the fretting waters. The vile guardian,
the serpent who had long lived under the earth,
watched over the gold, alert; he who hoped
to gain it bargained with his own life.
    Then the brave king sat on the headland,
the gold-friend of the Geats wished success
to his retainers. His mind was most mournful,

---

[30] The two exiles were Eanmund and Eadgils, sons of the Swedish king Ohthere, who had succeeded his father Ongentheow (see ll. 2914–2992). After Ohthere's death, his brother Onela usurped the throne. Eanmund and Eadgils fled to the Geatish court, where Heardred offered them protection. In retaliation, Onela attacked the Geats, killed both Eanmund and Heardred, and left Beowulf in charge of the conquered kingdom. Beowulf eventually helped the surviving son Eadgils overthrow Onela and regain the Swedish throne. (The poem tells this story so elliptically that many of the motivations and alliances remain obscure.)

angry, eager for slaughter; fate hovered
over him, so soon to fall on that old man,
to seek out his hidden spirit, to split   2410
life and body; flesh was to confine
the soul of the king only a little longer.
Beowulf, the son of Ecgtheow, spoke:
"Often and often in my youth I plunged
into the battle maelstrom; how well I remember it.
I was seven winters old when the treasure guardian,
ruler of men, received me from my father.
King Hrethel took me into his ward, reared me,
fed me, gave me gold, mindful of our kinship;
for as long as he lived, he loved me no less   2420
than his own three sons, warriors with me
in the citadel, Herebeald, Haethcyn, and my dear Hygelac.
A death-bed for the firstborn was unrolled
most undeservedly by the action of his kinsman—
Haethcyn drew his horn-tipped bow
and killed his lord-to-be; he missed his mark,
his arrow was stained with his brother's blood.
That deed was a dark sin, sickening
to think of, not to be settled by payment of *wergild;*
yet Herebeald's death could not be requited.   2430
    Thus the old king, Hrethel, is agonized
to see his son, so young, swing
from the gallows.³¹ He sings a dirge, a song
dark with sorrow, while his son hangs,
raven's carrion, and he cannot help him
in any way, wise and old as he is.
He wakes each dawn to the ache
of his son's death; he has no desire
for a second son, to be his heir
in the stronghold, now that his firstborn   2440
has finished his days and deeds on earth.
Grieving, he wanders through his son's dwelling,
sees the wine-hall now deserted, joyless,
home of the winds; the riders, the warriors,
sleep in their graves. No longer is the harp
plucked, no longer is there happiness in that place.
Then Hrethel takes to his bed, and intones
dirges for his dead son, Herebeald;
his house and his lands seem empty now,
and far too large. Thus the lord of the Geats   2450
endured in his heart the ebb and flow
of sorrow for his firstborn; but he could not
avenge that feud on the slayer—his own son;

³¹Since Haethcyn survives and inherits the throne, this hanging is apparently a ritual hanging of the dead Herebeald, dictated by the fact that he did not die in battle.

although Hrethel had no love for Haethcyn,
he could no more readily requite death
with death. Such was his sorrow that he lost
all joy in life, chose the light of God;
he bequeathed to his sons, as a wealthy man does,
his citadel and land, when he left this life.

Then there was strife, savage conflict 2460
between Swedes and Geats; after Hrethel's death
the feud we shared, the fierce hatred
flared up across the wide water.
The sons of Ongentheow, Onela and Ohthere,
were brave and battle-hungry; they had no wish
for peace over the sea but several times,
and wantonly, butchered the people of the Geats
on the slopes of Slaughter Hill. As is well known,
my kinsmen requited that hatred, those crimes;
but one of them paid with his own life— 2470
a bitter bargain; that fight was fatal
to Haethcyn, ruler of the Geats.
Then I heard that in the morning
one kinsman avenged another, repaid
Haethcyn's slayer with the battle-blade,
when Ongentheow attacked the Geat Eofor;
the helmet split, the old Swede fell,
pale in death; Eofor remembered
that feud well enough, his hand and sword
spared nothing in their death-swing. 2480

I repaid Hygelac for his gifts of heirlooms
with my gleaming blade, repaid him in battle,
as was granted to me; he gave me land
and property, a happy home. He had
no need to hunt out and hire mercenaries—
inferior warriors from the Gepidae,
from the Spear-Danes or from tribes in Sweden;
but I was always at the head of his host,
alone in the van; and I shall still fight
for as long as I live and this sword lasts, 2490
that has often served me early and late
since I became the daring slayer
of Daeghrefn, champion of the Franks.
He was unable to bring adornments,
breast-decorations to the Frisian king,
but fell in the fight bearing the standard,
a brave warrior; it was my battle-grip,
not the sharp blade, that shattered his bones,
silenced his heartbeat. Now the shining edge,
hand and tempered sword, shall engage in battle 2500
for the treasure hoard. I fought many battles
when I was young; yet I will fight again,

the old guardian of my people, and achieve
a mighty exploit if the evil dragon dares
confront me, dares come out of the earth-cave!"
    Then he addressed each of the warriors,
the brave heroes, his dear companions,
a last time: "I would not wield a sword
against the dragon if I could grasp this hideous being
with my hands (and thus make good my boast),   2510
as once I grasped the monster Grendel;
but I anticipate blistering battle-fire,
venomous breath; therefore I have with me
my shield and corslet. I will not give an inch
to the guardian of the mound, but at that barrow
it will befall us both as fate ordains,
every man's master. My spirit is bold,
I will not boast further against the fierce flier.
Watch from the barrow, warriors in armour,
guarded by corslets, which of us will better   2520
weather his wounds after the combat.
This is not your undertaking, nor is it
possible for any man but me alone
to pit his strength against the gruesome one,
and perform great deeds. I will gain the gold
by daring, or else battle, dread destroyer
of life, will lay claim to your lord."
    Then the bold warrior, stern-faced beneath his helmet,
stood up wlth his shield; sure of his own strength,
he walked in his corslet towards the cliff;   2530
the way of the coward is not thus!
Then that man endowed with noble qualities,
he who had braved countless battles, weathered
the thunder when warrior troops clashed together,
saw a stone arch set in the cliff
through which a stream spurted; steam rose
from the boiling water; he could not stay long
in the hollow near the hoard for fear
of being scorched by the dragon's flames.
Then, such was his fury, the leader of the Geats   2540
threw out his chest and gave a great roar,
the brave man bellowed; his voice, renowned
in battle, hammered the grey rock's anvil.
The guardian of the hoard knew the voice for human;
violent hatred stirred within him. Now no time
remained to entreat for peace. At once
the monster's breath, burning battle vapour,
issued from the barrow; the earth itself snarled.
The lord of the Geats, standing under the cliff,
raised his shield against the fearsome stranger;   2550
then that sinuous creature spoiled
for the fight. The brave and warlike king

had already drawn his keen-edged sword,
(it was an ancient heirloom); a terror of each other
lurked in the hearts of the two antagonists.
While the winged creature coiled himself up,
the friend and lord of men stood unflinching
by his shield; Beowulf waited ready armed.

    Then, fiery and twisted, the dragon swiftly
shrithed towards its fate. The shield protected 2560
the life and body of the famous prince
for far less time than he had looked for.
It was the first occasion in all his life
that fate did not decree triumph for him
in battle. The lord of the Geats raised
his arm, and struck the mottled monster
with his vast ancestral sword; but the bright blade's
edge was blunted by the bone, bit
less keenly than the desperate king required.
The defender of the barrow bristled with anger 2570
at the blow, spouted murderous fire, so that flames
leapt through the air. The gold-friend of the Geats
did not boast of famous victories; his proven sword,
the blade bared in battle, had failed him
as it ought not to have done. That great Ecgtheow's
greater son had to journey on from this world
was no pleasant matter; much against his will,
he was obliged to make his dwelling
elsewhere—sooner or later every man must leave
this transitory life. It was not long 2580
before the fearsome ones closed again.
The guardian of the hoard was filled with fresh hope,
his breast was heaving; he who had ruled a nation
suffered agony, surrounded by flame.
And Beowulf's companions, sons of nobles—
so far from protecting him in a troop together,
unflinching in the fight—shrank back into the forest
scared for their own lives. One man alone
obeyed his conscience. The claims of kinship
can never be ignored by a right-minded man. 2590

    His name was Wiglaf, a noble warrior,
Weohstan's son, kinsman of Aelfhere,
a leader of the Swedes;[32] he saw that his lord,
helmeted, was tormented by the intense heat.
Then he recalled the honours Beowulf had bestowed
on him—the wealthy citadel of the Waegmundings,

---

[32] Wiglaf's father, Weohstan, seems to have been by blood both Swedish and Geatish. He fought and killed Eanmund on behalf of the Swedish king Onela; perhaps he moved to Geatland after Eadgils, the brother of the man he killed, ascended the Swedish throne. As a member of the Waegmunding family, Wiglaf is a kinsman of Beowulf.

the rights to land his father owned before him.
He could not hold back then; he grasped the round,
yellow shield; he drew his ancient sword,
reputed to be the legacy of Eanmund,   2600
Ohthere's son.
                  Weohstan had slain him
in a skirmish while Eanmund was a wanderer,
a friendless man, and then had carried off
to his own kinsmen the gleaming helmet,
the linked corslet, the ancient sword
forged by giants. It was Onela,
Eanmund's uncle, who gave him that armour,
ready for use; but Onela did not refer to the feud,
though Weohstan had slain his brother's son.
For many years Weohstan owned that war-gear,   2610
sword and corslet, until his son was old enough
to achieve great feats as he himself had done.
Then, when Weohstan journeyed on from the earth,
an old man, he left Wiglaf—who was
with the Geats—a great legacy of armour
of every kind.
                  This was the first time
the young warrior had weathered the battle storm,
standing at the shoulder of his lord.
His courage did not melt, nor did his kinsman's sword
fail him in the fight. The dragon found that out   2620
when they met in mortal combat.
   Wiglaf spoke, constantly reminding
his companions of their duty—he was mournful.
"I think of that evening we emptied the mead-cup
in the feasting-hall, partook and pledged our lord,
who presented us with rings, that we would repay him
for his gifts of armour, helmets and hard swords,
if ever the need, need such as this, arose.
For this very reason he asked us
to join with him in this journey, deemed us   2630
worthy of renown, and gave me these treasures;
he looked on us as loyal warriors,
brave in battle; even so, our lord,
guardian of the Geats, intended to perform
this feat alone, because of all men
he had achieved the greatest exploits,
daring deeds. Now the day has come
when our lord needs support, the might
of strong men; let us hurry forward
and help our leader as long as fire remains,   2640
fearsome, searing flames. God knows
I would rather that fire embraced my body
beside the charred body of my gold-giver;

it seems wrong to me that we should shoulder
our shields, carry them home afterwards,
unless we can first kill the venomous foe,
guard the prince of the Geats. I know
in my heart his feats of old were such
that he should not now be the only Geat to suffer
and fall in combat; in common we shall share 2650
sword, helmet, corslet, the trappings of war."
 Then that man fought his way through the fumes,
went helmeted to help his lord. He shouted out:
"Brave Beowulf, may success attend you—
for in the days when you were young, you swore
that so long as you lived you would never allow
your fame to decay; now, O resolute king,
renowned for your exploits, you must guard your life
with all your skill. I shall assist you."
 At this the seething dragon attacked a second time; 2660
shimmering with fire the venomous visitor fell on his foes,
the men he loathed. With waves of flame, he burnt
the shield right up to its boss; Wiglaf's
corslet afforded him no protection whatsoever.
But the young warrior still fought bravely, sheltered
behind his kinsman's shield after his own
was consumed by flames. Still the battle-king
set his mind on deeds of glory; with prodigious strength
he struck a blow so violent that his sword stuck
in the dragon's skull. But Naegling snapped! 2670
Beowulf's old grey-hued sword
failed him in the fight. Fate did not ordain
that the iron edge should assist him
in that struggle; Beowulf's hand was too strong.
Indeed I have been told that he overtaxed
each and every weapon, hardened by blood, that he bore
into battle; his own great strength betrayed him.
 Then the dangerous dragon, scourge of the Geats,
was intent a third time upon attack; he rushed
at the renowned man when he saw an opening: 2680
fiery, battle-grim, he gripped the hero's neck
between his sharp teeth; Beowulf was bathed
in blood; it spurted out in streams.
Then, I have heard, the loyal thane
alongside the Geatish king displayed great courage,
strength and daring, as was his nature.
To assist his kinsman, that man in mail
aimed not for the head but lunged at the belly
of their vile enemy (in so doing his hand
was badly burnt); his sword, gleaming and adorned, 2690
sank in up to the hilt and at once the flames
began to abate. The king still had control then

over his senses; he drew the deadly knife,
keen-edged in battle, that he wore on his corslet;
then the lord of the Geats dispatched the dragon.
Thus they had killed their enemy—their courage
enabled them—the brave kinsmen together
had destroyed him. Such should a man,
a thane, be in time of necessity!
                                    That was the last
of all the king's achievements, his last   2700
exploit in the world. Then the wound
the earth-dragon had inflicted with his teeth
began to burn and swell; very soon he
was suffering intolerable pain as the poison
boiled within him. Then the wise leader
tottered forward and slumped on a seat
by the barrow; he gazed at the work of giants,
saw how the ancient earthwork contained
stone arches supported by columns.
Then, with his own hands, the best of thanes   2710
refreshed the renowned prince with water,
washed his friend and lord, blood-stained
and battle-weary, and unfastened his helmet.
    Beowulf began to speak, he defied
his mortal injury; he was well aware
that his life's course, with all its delights,
had come to an end; his days on earth
were exhausted, death drew very close:
"It would have made me happy, at this time,
to pass on war-gear to my son, had I   2720
been granted an heir to succeed me,
sprung of my seed. I have ruled the Geats
for fifty winters; no king of any
neighbouring tribe has dared to attack me
with swords, or sought to cow and subdue me.
But in my own home I have awaited
my destiny, cared well for my dependants,
and I have not sought trouble, or sworn
any oaths unjustly. Because of all these things
I can rejoice, drained now by death-wounds;   2730
for the Ruler of Men will have no cause to blame me
after I have died on the count that I deprived
other kinsmen of their lives. Now hurry,
dear Wiglaf; rummage the hoard
under the grey rock, for the dragon sleeps,
riddled with wounds, robbed of his treasure.
Be as quick as you can so that I may see
the age-old golden treasure, and examine
all the priceless, shimmering stones; once I
have set eyes on such a store, it will be   2740

more easy for me to die, to abandon
the life and land that have so long been mine."
   Then, I have been told, as soon as he heard
the words of his lord, wounded in battle,
Wiglaf hastened into the earth-cavern,
still wearing his corslet, his woven coat of mail.
After the fierce warrior, flushed with victory,
had walked past a daïs, he came upon
the hoard—a hillock of precious stones,
and gold treasure glowing on the ground;   2750
he saw wondrous wall-hangings; the lair
of the serpent, the aged twilight-flier;
and the stoups and vessels of a people
long dead, now lacking a polisher,
deprived of adornments. There were many old,
rusty helmets, and many an armlet
cunningly wrought. A treasure hoard,
gold in the ground, will survive its owner
easily, whosoever hides it!
And he saw also hanging high   2760
over the hoard a standard fashioned with gold strands,
a miracle of handiwork; a light shone from it,
by which he was able to distinguish the earth
and look at the adornments. There was no sign
of the serpent, the sword had savaged and slain him.
Then I heard that Wiglaf rifled the hoard
in the barrow, the antique work of giants—
he chose and carried off as many cups and salvers
as he could; and he also took the standard,
the incomparable banner; Beowulf's sword,   2770
iron-edged, had injured
the guardian of the hoard, he who had held it
through the ages and fought to defend it
with flames—terrifying, blistering,
ravening at midnight—until he was slain.
Wiglaf hurried on his errand, eager to return,
spurred on by the treasures; in his heart he was troubled
whether he would find the prince of the Geats,
so grievously wounded, still alive
in the place where he had left him.   2780
Then at last he came, carrying the treasures,
to the renowned king; his lord's life-blood
was ebbing; once more he splashed him
with water, until Beowulf revived a little,
began to frame his thoughts.
                Gazing at the gold,
the warrior, the sorrowing king, said:
"With these words I thank
the King of Glory, the Eternal Lord,

the Ruler, for all the treasures here before me,
that in my lifetime I have been able   2790
to gain them for the Geats.
And now that I have bartered my old life
for this treasure hoard, you must serve
and inspire our people. I will not long be with you.
Command the battle-warriors, after the funeral fire,
to build a fine barrow overlooking the sea;
let it tower high on Whaleness
as a reminder to my people.
And let it be known as *Beowulf's barrow*
to all seafarers, to men who steer their ships   2800
from far over the swell and the saltspray."

Then the prince, bold of mind, detached
his golden collar and gave it to Wiglaf,
the young spear-warrior, and also his helmet
adorned with gold, his ring and his corslet,
and enjoined him to use them well;
"You are the last survivor of our family,
the Waegmundings; fate has swept
all my kinsmen, those courageous warriors,
to their doom. I must follow them."   2810

Those were the warrior's last words
before he succumbed to the raging flames
on the pyre; his soul migrated from his breast
to meet the judgement of righteous men.

Then it was harrowing for the young hero
that he should have to see that beloved man
lying on the earth at his life's end,
wracked by pain. His slayer lay
there too, himself slain, the terrible
cave-dragon. That serpent, coiled evilly,   2820
could no longer guard the gold-hoard,
but blades of iron, beaten and tempered
by smiths, notched in battle, had taken him off;
his wings were clipped now, he lay
mortally wounded, motionless on the earth
at the mound's entrance. No more did he fly
through the night sky, or spread his wings,
proud of his possessions; but he lay prostrate
because of the power of Beowulf, their leader.
Truly, I have heard that no hero of the Geats,   2830
no fire-eater, however daring, could quell
the scorching blast of that venomous one
and lay his hands on the hoard in the lair,
should he find its sentinel waiting there,
watching over the barrow. Beowulf paid
the price of death for that mighty hoard;
both he and the dragon had travelled to the end

of this transitory life.
                              Not long after that
the lily-livered ones slunk out of the wood;
ten cowardly oath-breakers, who had lacked   2840
the courage to let fly with their spears
as their lord so needed, came forward together;
overcome with shame, they carried their shields
and weapons to where their leader lay;
they gazed at Wiglaf. That warrior, bone-weary,
knelt beside the shoulders of his lord; he tried
to rouse him with water; it was all in vain.
For all his efforts, his longing, he could not
detain the life of his leader on earth,
or alter anything the Ruler ordained.   2850
God in His wisdom governed the deeds
of all men, as He does now.
    Then the young warrior was not at a loss
for well-earned, angry words for those cowards.
Wiglaf, Weohstan's son, sick at heart,
eyed those faithless men and said:
"He who does not wish to disguise the truth
can indeed say that—when it was a question
not of words but war—our lord completely wasted
the treasures he gave you, the same war-gear   2860
you stand in over there, helmets and corslets
the prince presented often to his thanes on the ale-bench
in the feasting-hall, the very finest weapons
he could secure from far and wide.
The king of the Geats had no need to bother
with boasts about his battle-companions;
yet God, Giver of victories, granted
that he should avenge himself with his sword
single-handed, when all his courage was called for.
I could hardly begin to guard his life   2870
in the fight; but all the same I attempted
to help my kinsman beyond my power.
Each time I slashed at that deadly enemy,
he was a little weaker, the flames leaped
less fiercely from his jaws. Too few defenders
rallied round our prince when he was most pressed.
Now you and your dependants can no longer delight
in gifts of swords, or take pleasure in property,
a happy home; but, after thanes from far and wide
have heard of your flight, your shameful cowardice,   2880
each of your male kinsmen will be condemned
to become a wanderer, an exile deprived
of the land he owns. For every warrior
death is better than dark days of disgrace."
    Then Wiglaf ordered that Beowulf's great feat

be proclaimed in the stronghold, up along the cliff-edge,
where a troop of shield-warriors had waited all morning,
wondering sadly if their dear lord was dead,
or if he would return.
                The man who galloped
to the headland gave them the news at once;   2890
he kept back nothing but called out:
"The lord of the Geats, he who gave joy
to all our people, lies rigid on his death-bed;
slaughtered by the dragon, he now sleeps;
and his deadly enemy, slashed by the knife,
sleeps beside him; he was quite unable
to wound the serpent with a sword. Wiglaf,
son of Weohstan, sits by Beowulf,
the quick and the dead—both brave men—
side by side; weary in his heart   2900
he watches over friend and foe alike.
    Now the Geats must make ready for a time
of war, for the Franks and the Frisians,
in far-off regions, will hear soon
of the king's death. Our feud with the Franks
grew worse when Hygelac sailed with his fleet
to the shores of Frisia. Frankish warriors
attacked him there, and outfought him,
bravely forced the king in his corslet
to give ground; he fell, surrounded   2910
by his retainers; that prince presented
not one ornament to his followers. Since then,
the king of the Franks has been no friend of ours.
    Nor would I in the least rely on peace
or honesty from the Swedish people; everyone
remembers how Ongentheow slew Haethcyn,
Hrethel's son, in battle near Ravenswood
when, rashly, the Geats first attacked the Swedes.
At once Ongentheow, Ohthere's father,
old but formidable, retaliated; he killed   2920
Haethcyn, and released his wife from captivity,
set free the mother of Onela and Ohthere,
an aged woman bereft of all her ornaments;
and then he pursued his mortal enemies
until, lordless, with utmost difficulty,
they reached and found refuge in Ravenswood.
Then Ongentheow, with a huge army, penned in
those warriors, exhausted by wounds,
who had escaped the sword; all night long
he shouted fearsome threats at those shivering thanes,   2930
swore that in the morning he and his men would let
their blood in streams with sharp-edged swords,
and string some up on gallows-trees

as sport for birds. Just as day dawned
those despairing men were afforded relief;
they heard the joyful song of Hygelac's
horn and trumpet as that hero came,
hurrying to their rescue with a band of retainers.
After that savage, running battle, the soil
was blood-stained, scuffled—a sign of how 2940
the Swedes and the Geats fomented their feud.
Then Ongentheow, old and heavy-hearted,
headed for his stronghold with his retainers,
that resolute man retreated; he realized
how spirit and skill combined in the person
of proud Hygelac; he had no confidence
about the outcome of an open fight with the seafarers,
the Geatish warriors, in defence of his hoard,
his wife and children; the old man thus withdrew
behind an earth-wall. Then the Swedes were pursued, 2950
Hygelac's banner was hoisted over that earth-work
after the Geats, sons of Hrethel, had stormed
the stronghold. Then grey-haired Ongentheow
was cornered by swords, the king of the Swedes
was constrained to face and suffer his fate
as Eofor willed it. Wulf, the son
of Wonred, slashed angrily at Ongentheow
with his sword, so that blood spurted
from the veins under his hair. The old Swede,
king of his people, was not afraid 2960
but as soon as he had regained his balance
repaid that murderous blow with interest.
Then Wonred's daring son could no longer
lift his hand against the aged warrior
but, with that stroke, Ongentheow had sheared
right through his helmet so that Wulf, blood-stained,
was thrown to the ground; he was not yet doomed to die
but later recovered from that grievous wound.
When Wulf collapsed, his brother Eofor,
Hygelac's brave thane, swung his broad sword, 2970
made by giants, shattered the massive helmet
above the raised shield; Ongentheow fell,
the guardian of the people was fatally wounded.
Then many warriors quickly rescued Wulf,
and bandaged his wounds, once they had won control
(as fate decreed) of that field of corpses.
Meanwhile Eofor stripped Ongentheow's body
of its iron corslet, wrenched the helmet
from his head, the mighty sword from his hands;
he carried the old man's armour to Hygelac. 2980
He received those battle adornments, honourably
promised to reward Eofor above other men;

he kept his word; the king of the Geats,
Hrethel's son, repaid Eofor and Wulf
for all they had accomplished with outstanding gifts
when he had returned home; he gave each of them
land and interlocked rings to the value
of a hundred thousand pence—no man on earth
had cause to blame the brothers for accepting
such wealth, they had earned it by sheer audacity.   2990
Then, as a pledge of friendship, Hygelac gave
Eofor his only daughter to grace his home.

That is the history of hatred and feud
and deadly enmity; and because of it,
I expect the Swedes to attack us
as soon as they hear our lord is lifeless—
he who in earlier days defended a land
and its treasure against two monstrous enemies
after the death of its heroes, daring Scyldings,
he who protected the people, and achieved feats   3000
all but impossible.
                    Let us lose no time now
but go and gaze there upon our king
and carry him, who gave us rings,
to the funeral pyre. And let us not grudge gold
to melt with that bold man, for we have a mighty hoard,
a mint of precious metal, bought with pain;
and now, from this last exploit, a harvest
he paid for with his own life; these the fire
shall devour, the ravening flames embrace.
No thane shall wear or carry these treasures   3010
in his memory, no fair maiden shall hang
an ornament of interlinked rings at her throat,
but often and again, desolate, deprived of gold,
they must tread the paths of exile,
now that their lord has laid aside laughter,
festivity, happiness. Henceforth, fingers must grasp,
hands must hold, many a spear
chill with the cold of morning; no sound of the harp
shall rouse the warriors but, craving for carrion,
the dark raven shall have its say   3020
and tell the eagle how it fared at the feast
when, competing with the wolf, it laid bare the bones of corpses."

Thus the brave messenger told of and foretold
harrowing times; and he was not far wrong.
Those events were fated. Every man in the troop
stood up, stained with tears, and set out
for Eagleness to see that strange spectacle.
There they found him lifeless on the sand,
the soft bed where he slept, who often before
had given them rings; that good man's days   3030

on earth were ended; the warrior-king,
lord of the Geats, had died a wondrous death.
But first they saw a strange creature
there, a loathsome serpent lying
nearby; the fire-dragon, fierce
and mottled, was scorched by its own flames.
It measured fifty paces from head to tail;
sometimes it had soared at night
through the cool air, then dived
to its dark lair; now it lay rigid in death, 3040
no longer to haunt caverns under the earth.
Goblets and vessels stood by it,
salvers and valuable swords, eaten through
by rust, as if they had lain
for a thousand winters in the earth's embrace.
That mighty legacy, gold of men long dead,
lay under a curse; it was enchanted
so that no human might enter
the cavern save him to whom God,
the true Giver of Victories, Guardian of Men, 3050
granted permission to plunder the hoard—
whichever warrior seemed worthy to Him.
  Then it was clear that, whoever devised it,
the evil scheme of hiding the hoard under the rock
had come to nothing; the guardian had killed
a brave and famous man; that feud
was violently avenged. The day that a warrior,
renowned for his courage, will reach the end
(as fate ordains) of his life on earth,
that hour when a man may feast in the hall 3060
with his friends no longer, is always unpredictable.
It was thus with Beowulf when he tracked down
and attacked the barrow's guardian; he himself
was not aware how he would leave this world.
The glorious princes who first placed that gold there
had solemnly pronounced that until domesday
any man attempting to plunder the hoard
should be guilty of wickedness, confined,
tormented and tortured by the devil himself.
Never before had Beowulf been granted 3070
such a wealth of gold by the gracious Lord.
  Wiglaf, the son of Weohstan, said:
"Many thanes must often suffer
because of the will of one, as we do now.
We could not dissuade the king we loved,
or in any way restrain the lord of our land
from drawing his sword against the gold-warden,
from letting him lie where he had long lain
and remain in his lair until the world's end;

but he fulfilled his high destiny. The hoard,   3080
so grimly gained, is now easy of access;
our king was driven there by too harsh a fate.
I took the path under the earth-wall,
entered the hall and examined all
the treasures after the dragon deserted it;
I was hardly invited there. Hurriedly
I grasped as many treasures as I could,
a huge burden, and carried them here
to my king; he was still alive then,
conscious and aware of this world around him.   3090
He found words for his thronging thoughts,
born of sorrow, asked me to salute you,
said that as a monument to your lord's exploits
you should build a great and glorious barrow
over his pyre, for he of all men
was the most famous warrior on the wide earth
for as long as he lived, happy in his stronghold.
Now let us hurry once more together
and see the hoard of priceless stones,
that wonder under the wall; I will lead you   3100
so that you will come sufficiently close
to the rings, the solid gold. After we
get back, let us quickly build the bier,
and then let us carry our king,
the man we loved, to where he must
long remain in the Lord's protection."
    Then the brave warrior, Weohstan's son,
directed that orders be given to many men
(to all who owned houses, elders of the people)
to fetch wood from far to place beneath   3110
their prince on the funeral pyre:
                            "Now flames,
the blazing fire, must devour the lord of warriors
who often endured the iron-tipped arrow-shower,
when the dark cloud loosed by bow strings
broke above the shield-wall, quivering;
when the eager shaft, with its feather garb,
discharged its duty to the barb."
    I have heard that Weohstan's wise son
summoned from Beowulf's band his seven
best thanes, and went with those warriors   3120
into the evil grotto; the man leading
the way grasped a brand. Then those retainers
were not hesitant about rifling the hoard
as soon as they set eyes on any part of it,
lying unguarded, gradually rusting,
in that rock cavern; no man was conscience-stricken
about carrying out those priceless treasures
as quickly as he could. Also, they pushed the dragon,

the serpent over the precipice; they let the waves take him,
the dark waters embrace the warden of the hoard. 3130
Then the wagon was laden with twisted gold,
with treasures of every kind, and the king,
the old battle-warrior, was borne to Whaleness.

Then, on the headland, the Geats prepared a mighty pyre
for Beowulf, hung round with helmets and shields
and shining mail, in accordance with his wishes;
and then the mourning warriors laid
their dear lord, the famous prince, upon it.

And there on Whaleness, the heroes kindled
the most mighty of pyres; the dark wood-smoke 3140
soared over the fire, the roaring flames
mingled with weeping—the winds' tumult subsided—
until the body became ash, consumed even
to its core. The heart's cup overflowed;
they mourned their loss, the death of their lord.
And, likewise, a maiden of the Geats,
with her tresses swept up, intoned
a dirge for Beowulf time after time,
declared she lived in dread of days to come
dark with carnage and keening, terror of the enemy, 3150
humiliation and captivity.

Heaven swallowed the smoke.
Then the Geats built a barrow on the headland—
it was high and broad, visible from far
to all seafarers; in ten days they built the beacon
for that courageous man; and they constructed
as noble an enclosure as wise men
could devise, to enshrine the ashes.
They buried rings and brooches in the barrow,
all those adornments that brave men
had brought out from the hoard after Beowulf died. 3160
They bequeathed the gleaming gold, treasure of men,
to the earth, and there it still remains
as useless to men as it was before.

Then twelve brave warriors, sons of heroes,
rode round the barrow, sorrowing;
they mourned their king, chanted
an elegy, spoke about that great man:
they exalted his heroic life, lauded
his daring deeds; it is fitting for a man,
when his lord and friend must leave this life, 3170
to mouth words in his praise
and to cherish his memory.
Thus the Geats, his hearth-companions,
grieved over the death of their lord;
they said that of all kings on earth
he was the kindest, the most gentle,
the most just to his people, the most eager for fame.

The Song of Roland

(C. 1100 A.D.)

The name given to the Old French epics (written approximately between 1100 and 1500) is *chansons de geste,* or "songs of deeds." Those written during the first half of this period are heroic in spirit; thereafter they take on characteristics of the romance, assimilating love stories written in the spirit of "courtly love," a tradition that idealized women and turned the conventions of human love almost literally into a religion. The earlier *chansons de geste,* like the *Roland,* treat almost exclusively of men at war. The public matter of these poems is primarily the struggle of Christianity against the forces of evil as embodied in the Muslims, misrepresented as idolaters, partly out of ignorance and partly for propaganda purposes that sometimes were shaped by the Crusades against Islam waged in the eleventh, twelfth, and thirteenth centuries.

The central figures in most of the *chansons de geste* are Charlemagne (Charles the Great) and members of his court or dynasty. During his lifetime (742–814), the historical Charlemagne forged an empire extending from the Ebro River in Spain to the Elbe in middle Europe, spreading Christianity and centralizing rule. In 800 he was named by the Pope as Holy Roman Emperor, a title and office that, except for a break of a century or so soon after his death, continued to exist until 1806. A learned man himself, he patronized learning and the arts. The *chansons de geste* have, then, a basis in historical fact and are centered on a man who was a towering figure in the development of Western and Christian culture. In the interval between his lifetime and their composition, however, they took on overlays of poetic legend; in *The Song of Roland,* for example, Charlemagne is in intimate touch with the angels of God and is believed by the enemy to be two hundred years old.

The *Roland* is the earliest and best-known surviving specimen of *chanson de geste.* The poem was unknown until 1832, when the first of several manuscripts of the work was discovered. The best of these, located in the Bodleian Library at Oxford University, is a copy by an Anglo-Norman scribe of an earlier version. Scholarly interest in the poem has ever since been intense and widespread, and the *Roland* is now generally honored as the wellspring of French literature. Despite such interest and accolades, however, many basic facts about the poem remain mysteries, the subject of endless but inconclusive conjecture. The last line of the poem, ambiguous in almost every word, identifies the poet (or is it the scribe?) as a man named Turoldus, but nothing certain is known about him except that he was apparently a native of Normandy. The date of the poem is likewise uncertain, but the consensus, especially among those who regard the work as expressing the spirit of the First Crusade (1096–1108 in Palestine and Syria), points to a time near 1100. Moreover, opinion varies about the process of epic gestation that over the course of three centuries transformed the seed of historical fact into the existent poem. One theory is that the *Roland* is essentially a compilation of many separate folk compositions. A more recent, less romantic, hypothesis is that the poem is the work of a single masterful poet who drew on written works by traveling minstrels (*jongleurs*) who in turn drew on oral traditions kept alive along the pilgrimage routes between France and Spain. The controversy resembles closely the disputes about the identity of Homer, and as with Homer the case for a single great poet becomes stronger as readers and scholars come to recognize the distinctive artistry of *Roland* and the careful shaping that has been given the material.

The Song of Roland is an epic, not in the loose sense implying mere grandeur of effect but in very technical ways. It includes many of the marks of the classical epic, including the hyperbolic praise of the past and the heroes of old, the appearance of prophetic dreams and omens, the intervention at key moments of supernatural beings, councils held in the camps of the opposing armies, catalogs of the armies on both sides, the divine commissioning of a half-reluctant hero—Charles—to do the will of Heaven (the last lines show a weary but acquiescent Charles accepting again God's charge to defend Christendom). If we accept the theory that the poem is meant to inspirit the warriors of the First Crusade, we can detect the strategy by which the epic poet defines the characteristic virtues of his people as they were evinced in the past so that these virtues can be extrapolated through the crisis of the present into a hoped-for glorious future. These features are all prominent in the Virgilian epic, with which the *Roland* poet was probably acquainted. Also heroic or epic in manner are the poet's relish in descriptions of fierce individual combats, the defiances and boasts that frame the duels, the stylized epithets ("Charles whose flowing beard is white"). One notes too the resemblance between Homer's willful Achilles and Roland (up to a point—Roland has no touch of Achilles' sulkiness).

Like most epics, *The Song of Roland* is also a portrait of the social structure and values of its age. The basis of its society is feudalism and its system of vassalage. Although some important aspects of feudalism persisted all through the Middle Ages and, more vestigially, into modern times in such systems as the British peerage, true feudalism, with its hierarchical yet also decentralized structure, flourished mainly through the eleventh century. The trend thereafter moved slowly toward concentration of power in the sovereign and in the centralized modern national state. The idea of an absolutist monarch ruling by divine right does not emerge until the sixteenth and seventeenth centuries. It is significant that in the *Roland* Charles, although clearly a revered instrument of God's will, must abide by the decisions of his counselors and, in the trial of Ganelon, by the verdict of a jury of Ganelon's peers.

The essence of feudalism is the system of reciprocal bonds between a chief and the vassals who serve him. At the pinnacle is a sovereign, such as Charles, to whom his knights owe service, particularly in war, and who in return is pledged to defend them. Each of these vassal knights has the same relationship to his immediate followers, and so on down the scale to the humblest of common men. Some vassals were maintained as part of their lord's household and were brought up together, forming in the process a bond of close comradeship. Other vassals might be granted lands, or "fiefs," by their liege-lord. Whatever the arrangement, the feudal code of chivalry stressed courage, loyalty, and honor, both inherently and in the eyes of others; Roland, for example, is resolved never to behave in such a way as to inspire mocking songs about him and his men. This intimate system of ties, one man to another, is important in understanding even the narrative method of *The Song of Roland;* for example, one reason the poet dwells exclusively on the fights between prominent chiefs is that in the event of the leader's death his followers are entitled to quit the battle.

The values governing the action of the *Roland* are simply identified; they have to do almost exclusively with war and religion, which are intimately related to each other. (The union is epitomized with particular vividness in the archbishop Turpin, equally ready to perform priestly and martial service.) Success in battle is vital, not only for personal reasons but as a proof that God favors one's cause. The Christians are good. The Saracens are evil, although some of them may be attractive as persons and valiant as warriors. Philosophical subtleties are entirely absent from the poem, as are signs of inward conflict between inclination and duty. Even Ganelon, psychologically complex though he is, with no grudge against Charles, carries out his treacherous scheme without apparent misgivings. Complex ideas or sophistications of theology are foreign to the poem's ideological plainness of line. (In this respect the *Roland* is wholly unlike Virgil's *Aeneid*.) The poem's values are ultimately otherworldly and at the same time severely pragmatic.

The narrative method and linguistic style are in keeping with this directness. Few poems ever written are so "unpoetical" if by "poetry" we mean embellishment, richness of language, and rhetorical dazzle. The poet, like Homer, almost completely effaces himself; we know from his occasional expressions of exultation, grief, or partisanship that he sides wholeheartedly with the Christians, but of the distinctive personal cast of his mind there are few signs. Atmospheric descriptions—of scenery, for example—are rare and brief. The vocabulary is simple and limited, the syntax forthright. Figurative language such as similes is almost entirely absent. The versification is similarly square-hewn, the typical unit of statement coinciding with the individual line. But it would be a serious mistake to think of the poet as an artless primitive. His ability to create suspense is extraordinary, enhanced rather than spoiled by occasional glances at the action to come, a strategy that can create an almost Sophoclean dramatic irony. He is also psychologically acute, although recognition of this quality depends entirely on the reader, because, like Homer, the poet prefers to reveal nuances of behavior and motive objectively, through speeches and deeds, without commentary. The very spareness of description enhances its power when it does occur, as in the account of the storm that afflicts France in sympathy with Roland's death (laisse CX), or the memorably ominous lines about the mountain pass at Roncevaux: "High are the hills, deep valleys shun the light; / The cliffs rise grey, the gorges hold dark fear" (laisse LXVI). The effect of the narrative method and style is of absolute, unwavering honesty. One might go farther and find in the poem sublimity, a quality archetypically evoked by grandeur of theme rendered with simplicity.

We should also credit the poet with a sense of structural unity. Some scholars have found the Baligant episode extraneous—an anticlimax after the high drama of Roland's death, a distracting break between that scene and the final punishment of Ganelon, or both. Implicit in some of these interpretations is the assumption that the poem is exclusively centered on Roland personally, that he is an otherwise admirable hero tragically flawed in his pride so that he refuses to sound his horn for help, his eyes opened only when it is too late. But other interpretations are possible. For example, we can see Roland not as flawed but as justified in his lack of "prudence," uniquely clear-sighted in recognizing that the only way to encounter the forces of evil is all-out warfare to the death, not shaky and specious temporizing. The episode of Charles' battle against Baligant, embodying as Baligant and his army do the worldwide forces of evil rather than the limited threat of Spanish paganism, might thus be seen as the vindication of Roland's uncompromising views and a symbolic apocalyptic vindication of Christianity in itself.

The basic narrative unit in *The Song of Roland* is the verse paragraph, or laisse. Except in the *laisses similaires,* where the poet's repetitions serve to remove the action described from the flow of time and heighten its significance, each successive laisse moves the action at least slightly forward. Yet each is also a detached unit, making a new start and leading toward a focus of generalization or clarification in its last line. Thus the movement of the poem, from one laisse to another, has a fitful but compelling rhythm, like a series of short bursts of fire from a machine gun. The movement within each laisse has a similar staccato effect; each line is end-stopped and makes its own distinct statement in preparation for the final climax. Each line has ten syllables (not counting feminine endings), with a strong internal pause, or caesura, after the fourth (occasionally the sixth) syllable. Two stresses precede the caesura and two follow it. The ends of the lines throughout any one laisse are linked by assonance, the repetition of the same vowel sound. In the present translation by Patricia Terry, the caesura is indicated by a space in the middle of each line, and the climactic effect at the end of each laisse is suggested by assonance, which is sometimes also rhyme, in the last two lines. The following example, laisse CXXXVIII, is typical (in the Old French the caesuras are here represented by a space, as in the translation):

> Halt sont li pui   e tenebros e grant,
> Li val parfont   e les ewes coranz.
> Sonent cil graisle   e deriedre e devant,
> E tuit rachatent   encontre l'olifant.
> Li emperedre   chevalche iriedement,
> E li Françeis   coroços e dolent,
> Nen i at cel   n'i plort e se dement,
> E prient Deu   qu'il guarisset Rodlant
> Josqued il veignent   e'l champ comunement;
> Ensembl'od lui   i ferront veirement.
> De ço qui chalt?   car ne lor valt nient:
> Demorent trop,   n'i poedent estre a tens.   AOI.

> High are the hills,   and shadowy and vast,
> Deep the defiles,   and swift the mountain streams.
> The trumpets sound   ahead and to the rear,
> Blaring replies   to Roland's Oliphant.
> In bitter wrath   the Emperor rides on,
> The men of France   in sorrow and in rage;
> Not one but grieves   and bitterly laments,
> Praying that God   will keep Count Roland safe
> Until they come   and join him in the field—
> How they will fight   when they are at his side!
> What does it matter   how loyally they strive?
> They'll be too late   whenever they arrive.   AOI.

FURTHER READING *(prepared by W.J.R.):* Anyone interested in exploring *The Song of Roland* in detail should consult Gerald S. Brault's *The Song of Roland: An Analytical Edition,* 1978. Brault's work, in two volumes, is a monumental work of scholarship. Volume I contains an introduction and a commentary; Volume II contains the Oxford text and a facing-page English translation. Guides for the general reader include Robert Francis Cook, *The Sense of the Song of Roland,* 1987, and Eugene Vance, *Reading the Song of Roland,* 1970. A general discussion of *Roland* is available in John Fox's *A Literary History of France: The Middle Ages,* 1974. Also very helpful is Joseph J. Duggan, "The *Chanson de Roland* and the *Chansons de Geste,*" in *European Writers: Medieval and Renaissance,* Vol. I, ed. George Stade, 1984. Alain Renoir's "Roland's Lament: Its Meaning and Function in the *Chanson de Roland,*" *Speculum,* 35 (1960), 572–83, examines Roland's lament upon seeing his massacred army and relates the passage's tone and meaning to the structure of the first part of the work. On the social ethic in *Roland,* see John Halverson's "Ganelon's Trial," *Speculum,* 42 (1967), 661–69. Halverson discusses the poem's foundation in the Germanic feudal tradition and draws comparisons between *Roland* and *Beowulf* in order to illustrate the kinship-dominated social structure. Tony Hunt's "The Tragedy of Roland: An Aristotelian View," *Modern Language Review,* 74 (1979), 791–804, examines the poem's literary qualities and the reasons for its enduring appeal. John R. Allen's "Kinship in the *Chanson de Roland,*" in *Jean Misrahi Memorial Volume: Studies in Medieval Literature,* ed. Hans R. Runte and others, begins with a general discussion of the importance of blood ties in the poem and moves on to an investigation of a more complex type of kinship presented in *Roland.* The question of Roland's pride is considered in Jean Misrahi and William L. Hendrickson, "Roland and Oliver: Prowess and Wisdom, the Ideal of the Epic Hero," *Romance Philology,* 33 (1980), 357–72. The authors discuss what some have called Roland's "sinful" pride and make a defense of Roland's not calling for aid. Christian modifications of the Germanic ideal are also discussed.

from *THE SONG OF ROLAND*

Translated by Patricia Terry

I

The mighty Charles,[1]   our emperor and king,
Seven long years   has been at war in Spain;
That lofty land   lies conquered to the sea.
No fortress now   is standing in his way,
No walls, no towns   remain for him to break,
Except for Saragossa,   high on its hill,
Ruled by Marsile,   who has no love for God;
He serves Apollo,[2]   and to Mohammed prays—
But he will come,   and soon, to evil days!   AOI[3]

---

[1] Charlemagne, or Charles the Great (742–814), who from 771 to 814 ruled the Franks (a tribe inhabiting, approximately, the lands of modern France and Germany). As a matter of historical fact, he did not become emperor until 800, some 22 years later than the campaign (which lasted a few months, not seven years) upon which the poem seems to be based.

[2] According to the poet's distorted version of Islam, its three gods were Apollo, Mohammed, and Tervagant. In fact, the religion of Islam is emphatically monotheistic, worshiping Allah ("God") alone.

[3] These three letters, occurring usually at the end of sections ("laisses"), are one of the most puzzling mysteries about *Roland.* They may be some sort of exclamation.

II

In Saragossa,   the pagan king, Marsile,   10
Walks through an orchard   whose trees give cooling shade.
The king reclines   on a blue marble bench;
His host assembles,   some twenty thousand men.
He speaks these words   to all his dukes and counts:
"Now hear, my lords,   what evils weigh us down!
For Charles has come,   the ruler of sweet France,
To seize our lands,   and bring us to our knees.
I have no army[4]   to fight against his own;
No men of mine   will drive him to defeat—
Give me your counsel,   as you are true and wise,   20
Save me from death,   and from this bitter shame."
Mute are the pagans,   except for one alone:
Blancandrin speaks,   whose castle is Val-Fonde.

III

Among the pagans   Blancandrin was wise,
A trusted vassal,   a brave and loyal knight,
Clever enough   to think of good advice.
He tells the king,   "You need not be afraid.
Send word to Charles,   the arrogant, the proud,
That you in friendship   salute him as your lord,
Offer him gifts: bears and lions and dogs,   30
And seven hundred camels,   a thousand hawks,
Four hundred mule-loads   of silver and of gold,
And fifty carts   to form a wagon-train.
He'll have enough   to pay his hired men.
He has campaigned   so long here in this land,
He won't refuse   to go back home to Aix.[5]
Say you will meet him   in France, on Michael's Day,[6]
To be converted,   adopt the Christian law,
And do him homage   in friendship and good will.
If hostages are needed,   say you will send   40
Ten, even twenty,   to witness your good faith:
We'll have to yield   the sons our wives have borne—
The risk is death,   but I will send my own.
Better that they   should sacrifice their heads
Than that we lose   our honor and our pride,
And live as beggars   with all our rights denied!"   AOI

IV

Says Blancandrin,   "I swear by my right hand,
And by this beard   that ripples on my chest,
You'll see the French   disband their troops and go,

---

[4] This statement is inconsistent with the later information that Marsile's army numbers 400,000.
[5] Aix-la-Chapelle, now also called Aachen, a city in the Rhineland, was the capital of Charlemagne's realm.
[6] September 29.

The Franks[7] will soon   be on their way to France.   50
And when each one   has found his home again,
Charles, in the chapel   that he has built in Aix,
Will give a feast   in honor of the saint,
On Michael's Day,   when we'll have sworn to come—
But of our coming   the French will see no sign.
The king is proud,   and cruel is his heart;
He'll have the heads   of all our men cut off.
But better far   that they should lose their heads
Than that we lose   this shining land, fair Spain,
And be condemned   to hardship and disgrace."   60
The pagans say,   "That may well be the case!"

                                   VI

Then King Marsile   declares the council closed.
He tells his men,   "Thus you shall go, my lords:
Hold in your hands   the olive branch of peace,   80
And speak for me   to Charlemagne the king;
In his God's name,   ask him to grant me grace.
Say that before   a single month has passed,
I'll bring to France   a thousand of my men,
There be converted,   adopt the Christian law,
Become his vassal   in loyalty and love.
For this he'll have   what hostages he will."
Says Blancandrin,   "Our wishes he'll fulfill."   AOI

                                  VII

The ten white mules   are brought for them to ride;
Suatilie's king   had sent them to Marsile.   90
Their reins are gold,   their saddles silver-trimmed.
The envoys mount,   and as they ride away,
Each in his hand   holds high the olive branch.
They go to Charles,   who rules the Frankish land;
He will not see   the treachery they've planned.   AOI

                                 VIII

The Emperor Charles   is jubilant and gay:
The lofty walls   of Cordres are torn down,
His catapults   have laid its towers low;
His knights rejoice,   for great is their reward—
Silver and gold,   and costly gear for war.   100
In all the city   no pagan now remains
Who isn't dead   or one of the true Faith.
In a great orchard,   Charlemagne sits in state.

---

[7] "The 'Franks' (*Francs*) and 'French' (*Françeis*) are for the most part used as synonymous
terms. Occasionally, however, the Franks of France are distinguished from the Franks from
elsewhere in the Empire. It is stated that Charles prefers the men of France to all others (3031);
in 3976–77 the bishops of France are mentioned separately from those of Bavaria and Germany.
The boundaries of 'France' are also variable, sometimes including the whole of Charlemagne's
empire (larger than life), sometimes more restricted."—Translator's note.

With him are Roland,   and Oliver, his friend;
A duke called Samson,   and fiery Anseïs,
Geoffroy of Anjou,   flag-bearer for the king;
The two companions   Gerin and Gerier.
And with these barons   is no small group of men,
For fifteen thousand   came with them from sweet France.
The knights are seated   on carpets of white silk;   110
The older men,   or clever, pass the time
Playing backgammon,   or else they sit at chess;
The nimble youths   prefer to fence with swords.
Beneath a pine,   beside a briar-rose,
A throne is placed—   it's made of purest gold.
There sits the king,   the ruler of sweet France;
White is his beard,   and silver streaks his hair,[8]
Handsome his form,   his bearing very proud:
No stranger needs   to have him pointed out.
The Saracens[9]   dismount and come on foot   120
To greet the king,   as friendly envoys would.

                    IX
Then Blancandrin   begins to make his speech.
He says to Charles,   "May God grant you His grace,
That glorious Lord   to whom all men must pray!
We've come to you   at King Marsile's command;
He's learned about the law   that saves men's souls,
And of his wealth   he wants to offer you
Lions and bears,   and leash-trained hunting dogs,
And seven hundred camels,   a thousand hawks,
Silver and gold   four hundred mules will bear,   130
And fifty carts   to form a wagon-train.
These will be loaded   with silver coins and gold.
Enough for you   to well reward your men.
You have campaigned   so long here in this land,
It must be time   to go back home to Aix;
My lord Marsile   says he will follow you."
The Emperor Charles   holds both hands up toward God;
He bows his head,   and gives himself to thought.   AOI

                    X
The Emperor Charles   sits with his head bent low.
He was not known   for answering in haste: 140
Always he liked   to take his time to speak.
When he looked up,   his face was stern and proud.
Thus he replies: "You've spoken well indeed.
But King Marsile   has been no friend of mine;

---

[8] Charles is depicted as old, although historically he was only thirty-six at the time of the Spanish campaign.

[9] Arabs; Muslims.

Of what you say,   although your words are fair,
How shall I know   how much I can believe?"
"Take hostages,"   the Saracen replies,
"Ten or fifteen   or twenty you shall have;
Though he risks death,   I'll send a son of mine,
And there will be   some even nobler men.   150
When, in your palace   at Aix, you hold the feast
That celebrates   Saint Michael of the Sea,[10]
My lord Marsile   declares that he will come,
And, in those baths[11]   which were God's gift to you,
He will be baptized,   adopt the Christian faith."
Then answers Charles,   "It still is not too late."   AOI

XI

Fair was the evening,   the sun set pure of cloud.
By Charles' command   the mules were led to stalls.
In the great orchard   he had a tent set up,
And there he lodged   the envoys of Marsile;   160
Twelve of his servants   attended to their needs.
There they remained   until it was bright day.
When, in the morning,   the emperor arose,
He heard a mass   and matins[12] first of all,
And then the king   sat down beneath a pine,
And called his barons: for what he must decide
The men of France   would always be his guide.   AOI

XIII

"Barons, my lords,"   says Charles the Emperor,   180
"This I have heard   from envoys of Marsile:
Of his great wealth   he'll send me a good part,
Lions and bears,   and leash-trained hunting dogs,
Seven hundred camels,   a thousand hawks,
Four hundred mule-loads   of fine Arabian gold,
And with these gifts,   some fifty heavy carts.
But he requests   that I return to France,
And says that when   I'm home again in Aix,
He'll come and yield   to holy Christian law,
He'll take the Faith,   and hold his lands from me;   190
But I don't know   the secrets of his heart."
"We must think twice,"   they say, "before we start!"   AOI

XIV

The king has brought   his discourse to an end.
And now Count Roland   has risen to his feet;
He speaks his mind   against the Saracens,

[10] The reference is to Mont-Saint-Michel, the famous monastery on an island off the coast of Brittany (northwest France).
[11] Aix is famous for its hot mineral springs.
[12] An early-morning prayer service.

Saying to Charles, "You can't believe Marsile!
It's seven years since first we came to Spain;
For you I've conquered Noples and Commibles,
I took Val-Terre and all the land of Pine,
And Balaguer, Tudela, Sedilie. 200
There King Marsile displayed his treachery:
Of his vile pagans he sent to you fifteen;
Each in his hand held high the olive branch,
And when they spoke, we heard this very speech.
You let your Franks decide what should be done;
The plan they chose was foolishness indeed:
You sent two counts as envoys to the king,
Basant was one, the other was Basile—
They left their heads on a hill near Haltilies!
Finish the fight the way it was begun: 210
To Saragossa lead on your gathered host,
Though all your life at war here you remain,
Avenge those men so villainously slain!" AOI

XV

The Emperor Charles has kept his head bowed down;
He strokes his beard, arranges his moustache,
And to his nephew says neither yes nor no.
The French are silent, except for Ganelon;
He stands up straight and comes before the king,
With wrathful pride begins his argument,
Saying to Charles: "Believe no underling, 220
Not me, not Roland, who speaks against your good!
When King Marsile sends messengers to say
He'll place his hands in yours, and be your man,
He'll do you homage for all the lands of Spain,
And he'll observe our holy Christian law—
Whoever urges you to scorn this peace
Does not care, Sire, what kind of death we die.
A man too proud will recklessly advise;
Let's heed no fools, and keep to what is wise!" AOI

XVI

When he had stopped, Duke Naimon rose to speak; 230
In all the court there was no better man.
He said to Charles, "You've heard Count Ganelon;
I think the answer that he has given you
Contains good sense, if it be understood.
For King Marsile there's no hope in this war:
All of his castles have fallen to your hands,
Your catapults have broken down his walls,
His towns are burned, his men brought to defeat.
Now envoys ask your mercy for the king—
If we refuse, we're guilty of grave sin. 240
Since hostages will prove he did not lie,

In this great war   there's no one left to fight."
The Frenchmen say,   "The duke is in the right!"

                                    XVII
"Barons, my lords,   which one of you shall go
To Saragossa,   to talk with King Marsile?"
Duke Naimon says,   "I'll do it, by your leave.
Yield to me now   the envoy's staff and glove."
Answers the king,   "The wisest of my men!
By this white beard,   by my moustache I swear
So far from me   I'll never let you go.   250
Sit down; if you are wanted,   I'll let you know!"

                                    XVIII
"Barons, my lords,   what envoy can we send
To Saragossa,   held by the Saracen?"
Count Roland says,   "Let me talk to Marsile!"
"No, you shall not!"   Count Oliver replies,
"Your heart is fierce,   and you are quick to wrath—
If you are sent,   there's sure to be a fight.
By the king's leave,   I'll be the one to go."
Answers the king,   "Be quiet, both of you!
Not you nor he   will set foot in that town!   260
And by this beard   that you can see is white,
I'll tell you now   the twelve peers all must stay."
The French are silent;   they dare not disobey.

                                    XIX
Turpin of Reims   has risen from his place.
He says to Charles,   "Leave all your Franks in peace.
For seven years   you've been here in this land
Where you have suffered   great hardships and fatigue.
Give, Sire, to me   the envoy's staff and glove,
And I will seek   the Spanish Saracen;
I would be glad   to know what he is like."   270
But much displeased   the emperor replies,
"I'll hear no more—   go to your place and sit.
Keep your advice   until I ask for it!"   AOI

                                    XX
"My valiant knights,"   says Charles the Emperor,
"Choose for me now   the nobleman of France
Who is to take   my message to Marsile."
"I name," says Roland,   "Stepfather Ganelon."
The Franks reply,   "He'd do it very well;
We could not make   a wiser choice than this."
Count Ganelon   is furious indeed;   280
Casting aside   his cloak of marten furs,
He shows a tunic   made of the finest silk.

Steel-grey his eyes   and very proud his face,
His carriage noble,   his chest is large around;
He looks so handsome,   his peers all turn and stare.
He says, "You fool,   rash are your words, and wild.
Everyone knows   I'm stepfather to you,
Yet you name me   the envoy to Marsile!
If God should grant   that I come home again,
I won't forget—   and you'll face such a feud   290
That it will last   as long as you're alive!"
"I hear," says Roland,   "your foolishness and pride.
Everyone knows   I answer threats with scorn;
A man of wisdom   this embassy requires—
I'll take your place,   if the king so desires." AOI

XXI

Ganelon says,   "You shall not take my place!
You're not my man,   nor am I your liege-lord.[13]
But Charles commands me   to serve him in this way:
In Saragossa   I'll talk to King Marsile.
But I will find   some little trick to play,   300
Fit to relieve   my fury at this wrong."
Roland replies   with laughter loud and long. AOI

XXII

Count Ganelon,   when he hears Roland laugh,
Suffers such pain   he nearly splits with rage,
And he comes close   to falling in a faint.
He says to Roland,   "Now count me not your friend,
For you have swayed   this council to your will!
My rightful king,   you see me here at hand,
Ready to do   whatever you command. AOI

XXIII

"To Saragossa   I know that I must go.   310
And from that journey   no man comes to his home.
Remember this: your sister is my wife;
She bore my son—   there is no fairer youth—
His name is Baldwin;   he'll make a valiant man.
To him I leave   my fiefdoms, all my lands.
Grant him your care;   I'll see him not again."
Then answers Charles,   "You have too soft a heart.[14]
You know my will;   it's time for you to start." AOI

---

[13] Master to whom feudal loyalty is due.

[14] "Charles's irritated reply seems astonishing; one wonders if it does not conceal his embarrassed unwillingness to admit, once Ganelon has, to Charles's relief, been chosen, that the mission is indeed extremely dangerous."—Translator's note.

XXIV

Thus spoke the king,   "Come forward, Ganelon.
Take now from me   the envoy's staff and glove: 320
You've heard the Franks,   and they have chosen you."
Says Ganelon,   "Sire, this is Roland's work;
I'll have no love,   as long as I may live,
Either for him   or Oliver his friend.
All the twelve peers,   to whom he is so dear,
Sire, in your presence,   I challenge here and now!"
Then says the king,   "You yield too much to wrath.
Now you shall go,   since that is my command."
"I'll have the same   protection from Marsile
You gave Basant   and his brother Basile."   AOI   330

XXV

The Emperor Charles   holds out his right-hand glove,
But Ganelon,   who'd rather not be there,
Taking the gauntlet,[15]   lets it fall to the ground.
The Frenchmen say,   "Oh, God! What does this mean?
Surely this message   will bring us to our woe."
Says Ganelon,   "Your answer won't be slow."

XXVI

"Sire," says the count,   "now grant me leave to go;
Since go I must,   I care not for delay."
The king replies,   "In Jesu's name and mine!"
Then Charles' right hand   absolves the count from sin;   340
The staff and letter   are both given to him.

XXVII

Count Ganelon   returning to his tent,
Arrays himself   as if for waging war
With the best arms   his household can provide.
The spurs are gold   he fastens to his feet,
Murglais, his sword,   is hanging at his side,
And now he mounts   his war-horse Tachebrun,
The stirrup held   by his uncle Guinemer.
Then you could see   how many knights shed tears,
All of them saying,   "Alas! You go to die.   350
Long have you served   the great king at his court,
A noble vassal;   none fail to speak your praise.
The man who named you   the envoy to Marsile
Will not live long—   in spite of Charlemagne!
Roland was wrong   not to remember this:
Behind you stands   a mighty family."
And then they say,   "Let us go with you, lord."
The count replies,   "Almighty God forbid!
I'll die alone,   not sacrifice good knights.

---

[15] A glove worn as part of a suit of armor. That it is dropped is an ill omen.

But you must go,   my lords, back to sweet France   360
Where you will bring   my greetings to my wife,
To Pinabel,   my good friend and my peer,
And to my son,   Baldwin, whom you all know—
Give him your help,   and serve him as your lord."
Now toward Marsile   Ganelon sets his course.   AOI

                              XXVIII
Ganelon rides   under tall olive trees;
Now he has met   the envoys from Marsile,
And Blancandrin   is riding at his side;
Both of them talk   with great diplomacy.
Says Blancandrin,   "I marvel at your king—   370
For he has conquered   the whole of Italy,
And then to England   he crossed the salty sea
So that the Saxons   would pay Saint Peter's fee.[16]
And what of Spain   will Charlemagne require?"
The count replies,   "That's hidden in his mind.
A greater king   no man will ever find."   AOI

                              XXIX
Says Blancandrin,   "The Franks are noble men;
But they do wrong,   those warlike dukes and counts
When by the counsel   they give to Charlemagne
They wear him out,   and others suffer too."   380
Ganelon says,   "Of this I could accuse
Only Count Roland—   who'll pay for it some day.
Not long ago,   when Charles sat at his ease,
His nephew came   dressed in his battle gear—
He'd gone for plunder   somewhere near Carcasonne.
In Roland's hand   an apple shone, bright red;
He told his uncle,   'Accept it, my fair lord!
I bring you here   the crowns of every king.'
But his great pride   will lead him on too far,
For every day   we see him risk his life.   390
If he were killed,   there'd be an end to strife."   AOI

                              XXX
Says Blancandrin,   "Evil is Roland's heart.
He'd have the world   surrender to his will,
Proclaim his right   to every land on earth!
But by whose help   can he attempt so much?"
"The Franks of France!   He so commands their love,
They'll never fail him,   they're with him to a man.
He gives them gifts   of silver and much gold,
War-horses, mules,   brocades and costly arms;

[16] Monetary tribute to Rome. These lines exaggerate the actual historical achievements of Charlemagne.

The king himself   won't cross him in the least: 400
By Roland's sword   he'll rule to the far East!"   AOI

XXXI

So Ganelon   and Blancandrin ride on
Until they've made   a solemn pact: they vow
That they will seek   to have Count Roland slain.
They go their way,   and then dismount at last
In Saragossa   where a tall yew tree stands.
Under a pine   a throne has been set up,
Draped in brocade   of Alexandrian silk.
There sits the king,   the ruler of all Spain;
Around him wait   his twenty thousand men.   410
Not one of them   lets fall a single word;
They're all intent   on what they hope to hear
From those two men   who even now appear.

XXXII

Now Blancandrin   has come before Marsile,
And by the fist   he holds Count Ganelon.
He speaks these words: "Hail, in Mohammed's name,
Apollo's too,   whose Law we all obey!
We have delivered   your message to King Charles;
When he had heard us,   he raised his hands on high
To praise his God,   but gave us no reply.   420
Now he has sent you   one of his noble lords,
A count of France,   a man of power and wealth.
From him you'll learn   if there is hope for peace."
Marsile replies,   "We'll hear him; let him speak."

XXXIII

Count Ganelon   has taken careful thought,
Now he begins   in well-considered words,
Subtly contrived—[17]   the count knows how to talk.
He tells Marsile: "May God grant you His grace,
That glorious Lord   to whom all men must pray!
Now by the will   of Charlemagne the King,   430
You must accept   the holy Christian law,
And half of Spain   he'll let you hold in fief.
Should you refuse   agreement to these terms,
You'll find yourself   a captive and in chains,
Taken by force   to answer Charles at Aix.
There you'll be judged,   and you will be condemned
To die a death   of infamy and shame."

[17] "Ganelon is not only an accomplished liar but an enthusiastic one (see his description of the death of the Caliph, in laisse LIV). [In the speech that here follows] only the tone would seem to misrepresent Charlemagne, except that Marsile will be allowed to keep only half of Spain, in fief to Charles; the other half is to be ruled by Roland. Thus the latter is made, once again, the focal point of the pagans' anger."—Translator's note.

At that Marsile   in fear and fury raised
A throwing spear—   its feathering was gold;
He would have struck,   but that his men took hold.   AOI   440

XXXIV

In the king's face   they see the color change;
He stands there raging,   shaking his javelin.
Ganelon's hand   reaches to grasp his sword,
Out of the scabbard   draws it two finger lengths;
He tells the blade: "Shining you are, and fair!
Long have we served,   we two, at King Charles' court!
The Emperor of France   shall never say
I died alone   here in this foreign land
Before their best   have bought you at your price."
The pagans say,   "We must not let them fight!"   450

XXXV

The Saracens   prevail upon Marsile
Until the king   will take his seat again.
Said the Caliph,[18]   "You don't do any good
When you are ready   to strike the Frenchman down.
Just let him speak,   and listen to him well."
Ganelon says,   "My lord, I'll suffer that.
But I won't stop,   for all the gold God made,
For all the treasure   that's gathered in this land,
Before I give him,   if he will grant me time,
The message Charles   confided to my care,   460
The words he sends   his mortal enemy."
Ganelon wore   a cloak of sable furs
Covered in folds   of Alexandrian silk.
He throws it down—   it's caught by Blancandrin—
But has no thought   of letting go his sword:
His right hand grasps   the handle made of gold.
The pagans say,   "Noble he is, and bold!"   AOI

XXXVI

Count Ganelon   stands close beside the king,
And says to him,   "You have no cause for wrath
If Charlemagne   who rules the land of France   470
Says you must take   the holy Christian law:
One half of Spain   he'll let you hold in fief,
His nephew Roland   will rule the other part—
There you will have   a partner full of pride!
If you refuse   agreement to these terms,
In Saragossa   you soon will be besieged,
You'll find yourself   a prisoner in chains,
And straight away   you'll be led off to Aix.

---

[18] Successor of Mohammed; here, the Ethiopian ruler.

And then no palfrey,   no war-horse will you have,
Nor yet a mule   to ride with dignity,   480
But you'll be thrown   onto some pack-beast's back,
And lose your head   at that long journey's end.
Here is the message   I've brought at Charles' command."
He puts the letter   into Marsile's right hand.

XXXVII

Now King Marsile,   his face gone white with rage,
Breaks the seal open   and throws the wax away,
Looks at the letter   and sees what it contains.
"Thus writes King Charles   who rules the land of France:
He won't forget   his anger and his grief
About Basant   and his brother Basile   490
Whose heads I took   on a hill near Haltilie.
If I would make amends,   there's just one way:
I'll have to send him   my uncle, the Caliph;
If I refuse,   he'll have no love for me."
His son spoke up   and said to King Marsile,
"Wild empty words   we've had from Ganelon,
He's gone too far—   he well deserves to die.
Leave him to me,   and I'll do what is right."
Then Ganelon   prepared for the attack,
Brandished his sword,   the pine tree at his back.   500

XXXVIII

Into an orchard   the pagan king retired,
And with him went   the wisest of his men.
Blancandrin came   whose heavy beard was grey,
And Jurfaret,   Marsile's own son and heir,
And the Caliph,   his uncle and good friend.
Says Blancandrin,   "Summon the Frenchman here—
I have his word   that he will serve our cause."
Marsile replies,   "Then bring him to me now."
Blancandrin takes   the count by the right hand,
Walks through the orchard,   and leads him to Marsile.   510
They plot the treason   that cunning will conceal.   AOI

XXXIX

Thus speaks the king: "My fair lord Ganelon
I know I did   an ill-considered thing
When in my rage   I went to strike you down.
I pledge you now   by these fine sable furs—
The gold they're trimmed with   is worth five hundred pounds:
Tomorrow evening   I'll have made fair amends."
Says Ganelon,   "Your gift I won't refuse.
And if God please,   by this you shall not lose!"   AOI

XLI

The pagan says,   "Truly, I am amazed
By Charlemagne   whose hair is grey with age—

I know he's lived   more than two hundred years.[19]
He's dragged his body   through so many far lands,   540
Taken such blows   from lances and from spears,
So many kings   reduced to beggary,
It must be time   for him to look for peace."
"That will not happen   while Roland is alive;[20]
There's no such vassal   under the high-domed sky;
And very brave   is Oliver his friend.
While the twelve peers   whom Charlemagne so loves
Serve as his vanguard   with twenty thousand knights,
The king is safe;   he fears no man alive."   AOI

XLIII

"Fair Ganelon,"   then says the pagan king,
"You'll see no soldiers   better at war than mine,
And I can summon   four hundred thousand knights.
Can I not fight   King Charles and all his Franks?"
"If you should try it,"   Count Ganelon replies,
"I tell you this,   you'd massacre your men.
Forget that folly,   and hear what I advise:
To Charlemagne   send such a royal gift   570
As to amaze   and gratify the French.
Send twenty men   as hostages for you,
And then the king   will go home to sweet France.
Behind his army   the rear-guard will remain,
And with them Roland,   the nephew of the king,
And Oliver,   so gallant and so brave.
And there they die—   if you'll do as I say.
King Charles will see   the downfall of his pride;
He'll have no wish   to carry on the fight."   AOI

XLIV

Answers Marsile,   "My fair lord Ganelon,   580
Tell me the way   Count Roland can be killed."
Ganelon says,   "Here is the plan I've made:
The king will cross   the mountain pass at Cize,[21]
With a strong guard   remaining far behind.
He'll leave his nephew,   Count Roland, in the rear,
Oliver too,   in whom he has such faith,
With them a host   of twenty thousand Franks.

---

[19] An exaggeration typical of heroic poetry; the historical Charlemagne lived seventy-two years.

[20] "Here again Ganelon insists that only Roland is responsible for the pagans' misfortunes, and prepares the accomplishment of his own revenge, which depends on the separation of Roland and Charles. While the motive for this may be practical, as Marsile obviously could not hope to defeat the Emperor's entire army even with Ganelon's help, it seems that Ganelon really has no grudge against Charles in spite of the latter's obvious lack of enthusiasm for him. It should be remembered that Ganelon's wife is Charles's sister, and Roland's mother."— Translator's note.

[21] A valley in the northern Pyrenees, the mountains that separate France and Spain.

Then of your pagans,   a hundred thousand men
Must be sent out   to launch the first attack.
You'll see the Frenchmen   wounded and overcome—   590
Not that I say   your men won't suffer too.
If you attack   a second time that way,
You can be sure   that Roland won't escape.
Once you have done   this brave and knightly deed,
All your life long   from warfare you'll be freed.

XLV

"With that same blow   that struck Count Roland down,
You would cut off   the Emperor's right arm;
His mighty host   you'd scatter and destroy,
Nor would he find   so great a force again.
All of his Empire   would be restored to peace."   600
Marsile fell on his neck;   with joy he swore
That Ganelon   should loot his treasure-store.   AOI

XLVI

Then says Marsile,   "There's one thing more to do,
Since all good counsel   depends on perfect trust;
Give me your oath   that Roland is to die."
Ganelon says,   "That shall be as you wish."
He swore by relics[22]   he carried in his sword,
And so forever   turned from his rightful lord.   AOI

XLVII

A throne was there,   made all of ivory.
A book was brought   by King Marsile's command: 610
Laws of Mohammed   and Tervagant, his gods.
On this he swore,   the Spanish Saracen,
If he found Roland   was named to the rear-guard,
He would attack   with all his pagan knights,
And do his utmost   to see the Frenchman die.
"Amen to that!"   was Ganelon's reply.

LI

Then the king summons   his treasurer Malduit:
"Have they prepared   the tribute for King Charles?"
"The seven hundred camels,   by your command,
Have all been loaded   with silver and with gold,
And twenty men,   our noblest, set to go."   AOI

LII

King Marsile places   his arm around the count,
Saying to him,   "Valiant you are, and wise.
But as you keep   your God's most holy law,
I charge you never   to turn your heart from me!   650

---

[22] Remains of the bodies or of the personal effects of the saints.

Of all I own   I'll give you a good part:
Ten mules are loaded   with fine Arabian gold,
And every year   you'll have as much again.
Give Charles the keys   to this broad city's walls,
Tell him its treasures   will henceforth be his own,
And then name Roland   commander of the guard.
If I can find him   crossing some narrow pass,
There I'll attack   and fight him to the death."
Ganelon says,   "Then let us speed the day."
He mounts his horse,   and quickly rides away.   AOI   660

LIII

The Emperor Charles   has now retraced his steps
As far as Galne—   that was a captured town
Whose walls Count Roland   had leveled to the ground;
No one would live there   for the next hundred years.
He waits for news   of Ganelon's return,
And for the tribute   offered to him by Spain.
At dawn one morning,   just as the sky grows light,
Count Ganelon   comes back from his long ride.   AOI

LIV

The Emperor Charles   rose early on that day.
Now, having prayed   at matins and a mass,   670
He goes outside   and stands on the green grass.
Roland is with him,   the noble Oliver,
Naimon the Duke,   and many others too.
Ganelon comes,   treacherous and forsworn.
All of his cunning   he puts into his speech,
Saying to Charles,   "I greet you in God's name!
Here are the keys   to King Marsile's fair town;
From Saragossa,   treasures beyond all price,
And twenty nobles,   hostages—guard them well!
But King Marsile   has asked me to explain   680
Why you won't see   his uncle, the Caliph:
Before my eyes   a hundred thousand men
All armed in mail,   some with their helmets closed,
Swords at their belts,   the hilts inlaid with gold,
Sailed with that lord   out to the open sea.
They fled Marsile,   hating the Christian law
Which they refused   to honor and to keep.
They sailed away,   but had not gone four leagues
When they were caught   in such a frightful storm
They all were drowned.   So perished the Caliph.   690
Were he alive,   he'd be here with me now.
As for Marsile,   my lord, you can be sure
That well before   a single month has passed,
He'll follow you   when you return to France.
There he'll accept   the Faith that you uphold,
Both of his hands   he'll place between your own,

And do you homage   for all his lands in Spain."
Then said the king,   "For this may God be thanked!
You have done well,   and great shall be your prize."
Among the hosts,   a thousand trumpets sound;   700
The French break camp,   they load each mule and horse,
And toward sweet France   they gladly set their course.   AOI

LV
King Charles the Great   has conquered all of Spain,
Captured its forts,   its cities laid to waste;
His war, he says,   has now come to its end.
The emperor rides   once more toward his sweet France.
From Roland's spearhead   the flag of battle flies;
When, from a hilltop,   it waves against the sky,
The French make camp   throughout the countryside.
Pagans are riding   through valleys deep and dark,   710
Their coats of mail   are laced up to the chin,
Their helmets closed;   bright swords hang at their sides,
Shields at their necks,   a pennon on each lance;
Where trees grow thick   high on a hill they wait,
Four hundred thousand   watching for day's first light.
Alas! If only   the French could see that sight!   AOI

LVI
The day is over,   the night grows calm and still.
The Emperor Charles   goes to his bed and sleeps.
In dream he rides   through the great pass at Cize;
Clasped in his hands   he holds an ashwood spear: 720
Count Ganelon   wrenches it from his grasp,
With raging strength   shatters and breaks the wood,
And sends the splinters   flying against the sky.
King Charles sleeps on,   not opening his eyes.

LVIII
Darkness of night   gives way to shining dawn.
Throughout the host,   clarion trumpets sound.
Proud, on his horse,   the emperor appears.
"Barons, my lords,"   says Charlemagne the King,   740
"Narrow and dark   will be this mountain pass—
Who shall remain   to guard us from the rear?"
Ganelon says,   "Choose Roland, my stepson.
You have no baron   as valorous as he."
Fiercely the king   looks at the one who spoke,
And says to him: "Vile demon that you are!
You are insane,   possessed by deadly rage!
And in the vanguard—   who'll have the leader's place?"[23]
Ganelon says,   "Count Ogier the Dane.
None would do better,   and no one can complain."   750

---

[23] Charles asks who will assume Roland's usual position at the *head* of the army.

LIX

Count Roland heard   what Ganelon proposed,
And then he answered   with knightly courtesy:
"Noble stepfather,   now I must hold you dear,
For you have named me   commander of this guard.
The King of France   won't lose by my neglect
War-horse or palfrey,   that I can promise you;
He shall not lose   a single riding-mule,
Saddle-horse, pack-horse—   none shall give up its life
Until our swords   take payment for that prize."
Ganelon says,   "I know you tell no lies."   AOI   760

LX

When Roland heard   he'd stay with the rear-guard,
To his stepfather   he angrily replied:[24]
"Ignoble serf,   despicable foul wretch,
Do you suppose   I'll let the glove fall here
The way you dropped the staff [25]   at King Charles' feet?"   AOI

LXI

"My rightful lord,"   says Roland to the king,
"Give me the bow [26]   you're holding in your hand;
I promise you   that no man here will say
I let it fall,   like Ganelon that day
The envoy's staff   dropped out of his right hand."   770
The Emperor Charles   sits with his head bowed low,
Pulls his moustache,   and strokes his long white beard,
While in his eyes   unwilling tears appear.

LXII

At that Duke Naimon   stood up to speak his mind—[27]
The court could boast   no better man than he—
Saying to Charles,   "You have heard what's been said;
It's clear enough   that Roland is enraged.
He has been named   to go with the rear-guard;
You have no baron   who will dispute that now.
Give him the bow   that you yourself have bent;   780
Then choose good men   to fight at his command."
Charles puts the bow   in Roland's outstretched hand.

LXIII

The Emperor Charles   calls Roland to come forth.
"My noble nephew,   this is what I intend:
Half of my army   shall stay behind with you.

[24] Roland's sudden shift from "knightly courtesy" (line 752) to anger may indicate that laisse LX is not authentic; possibly, as Joseph Bédier and the translator suggest, the shift shows that Roland's words in LIX are ironic.
[25] Ganelon had dropped a glove, not a staff (laisse XXV).
[26] An emblem of command.
[27] "Duke Naimon's advice is always followed, usually to disaster."—Translator's note.

Accept their service,   and then you will be safe."
Count Roland answers,   "Never will I agree.
May God destroy me,   if I so shame my race!
Just twenty thousand   shall serve me, valiant Franks.
You'll cross the mountains,   safely in France arrive—   790
And fear no man   as long as I'm alive!"   AOI

                                LXIV
Roland has mounted   the horse he rides to war.
There comes to join him   his friend Count Oliver,
And Gerin comes,   the brave Count Gerier,
And Oton comes,   with him Count Bérengier,
And Astor comes,   and fiery Anseïs,
And old Gérard,   the Count of Roussillon,
The powerful and wealthy   Duke Gaïfier.
Says the Archbishop,   "My head on it, I'll go!"
"And I am with you,"   answers Count Gautier,   800
"I'm Roland's vassal—   my help is his by right."
Then they select   the twenty thousand knights.   AOI

                                LXV
Count Roland says   to Gautier de l'Hum:
"A thousand Franks,   men of our land, you'll take
To occupy   the hills and the ravines,
So that King Charles   may safely go his way."   AOI
Gautier answers,   "For you I'll do my best."
Leading away   a thousand Franks of France,
Gautier will guard   the mountains and ravines;
Whatever happens,   he won't come down again   810
Without a battle—   Almaris of Belferne
Gave them a fight;[28]   and seven hundred blades
Flashed from their scabbards   on that most evil day.

                                LXVI
High are the hills,   deep valleys shun the light;
The cliffs rise grey,   the gorges hold dark fear.
The French ride on   in misery and pain,
Their passing heard   some fifteen leagues around;
And when once more   they're back again in France,
In Gascony,   where Charlemagne is lord,
Then they remember   the lands they hold, their sons,   820
Their maiden daughters,   their fair and noble wives—
There is not one   who is not moved to weep
But of them all   none sorrows as does Charles,
For he has left   his nephew there in Spain;
And now his tears   the king cannot restrain.   AOI

_____

[28] The poet anticipates the fighting to come.

LXVII

All the twelve peers   have stayed behind in Spain;
They guard the pass   with twenty thousand Franks,
Courageous men   who do not fear to die.
And now King Charles   is riding home again;
He drapes his cloak   to hide his grieving face.   830
Duke Naimon rides   next to the emperor;
He says to Charles,   "What weighs your spirits down?"
The king replies,   "Who asks me that does wrong.
I can't keep silent   the sorrow that I feel,
For Ganelon   will be the doom of France.
Last night an angel   sent me a warning dream:
I held a spear—   he broke it from my grasp,
That count who named   my nephew to the guard.
And I left Roland   among that pagan race—
God! If I lose him   no one can take his place."   AOI   840

LXVIII

Charlemagne weeps;   he can't hold back his tears.
They grieve for him,   his hundred thousand Franks,
And for Count Roland   are suddenly afraid.
A traitor's lies   left him to die in Spain—
Rich gifts the pagan   bestowed on Ganelon:
Silver and gold,   brocades and silken cloaks,
Camels and lions,   fine horses, riding mules.
Now King Marsile   summons the lords of Spain,
His counts and viscounts,   his chieftains and his dukes,
His high emirs,[29]   and all their warrior sons: 850
Four hundred thousand   assemble in three days.
In Saragossa   the drums begin to sound;
They place Mohammed   high on the citadel—
No pagan fails   to worship him[30] and pray.
And then they ride   with all their might and main
Through Terre Certaine,[31]   through valleys, over hills,
Until they see   the battle-flags of France.
The twelve companions   are waiting with the guard;
When they are challenged,   the fighting will be hard.

LXIX

King Marsile's nephew   rides up before the host.   860
Laughing, he prods his mule   with a sharp goad,
And to his uncle   addresses this fair speech:
"For years, Lord King,   I've served you faithfully;
My only wages   were hardships, suffering,
And battles fought   and won on many fields.

---

[29] Arab chieftains.
[30] In fact, the use of graven images is forbidden in Islam.
[31] Possibly the term refers to Cerdagne, a valley in Catalonia, a region bordering on France, possibly to the southern slope of the Pyrenees.

I ask this boon: have Roland left to me!^{32}
I'll take his life   on my sharp-pointed spear,
And if Mohammed   protects me in the fight,
The land of Spain   once more shall be our own,
From the high passes   as far as Durestant!^{33} 870
Charles will be weary,   the Frenchmen will retreat;
In all your lifetime,   war will not touch your land."
King Marsile places   the gauntlet in his hand.^{34} AOI

[*Twelve pagan chieftains (including King Marsile's nephew Aelroth) vow to defeat
Roland, Oliver, and the other paladins (Charles's twelve peers). The pagans are
identified as Falsaron, Corsalis, Malprimis de Brigant, the emir (lord) of Balaguer,
the emir of Moriane, Torgis of Tortelose, Escrimiz of Valterne, Estorgant,
Estramariz, Margariz of Seville, and Chernuble de Munigre.*]

LXXIX
The pagans wear   Saracen coats of mail,
Most of them furnished   with triple-layered chains.
From Saragossa   come the good helms they lace;
They gird on swords   whose steel comes from Vienne;^{35}
Their shields are strong;   Valencia made their spears;
Their battle flags   are crimson, blue and white.
All mules and palfreys   must now be left behind;   1000
Each mounts his war-horse;   in close-knit ranks they ride.
Fair is the day,   the sun shines bright and clear,
Weapons and armor   glitter with fiery light,
A thousand trumpets   command more splendor still.
That great shrill clamor   reaches the Frenchmen's camp.
Oliver says,   "Companion, it would seem
That we will have   some Saracens to fight."
Roland replies,   "God grant that you be right!
Here we will stand,   defending our great king.
This is the service   a vassal owes his lord: 1010
To suffer hardships,   endure great heat and cold,
And in a battle   to lose both hair and hide.
Now every Frank   prepare to strike great blows—
Let's hear no songs   that mock us to our shame!^{36}
Pagans are wrong,   the Christian cause is right.
A bad example   I'll be in no man's sight."   AOI

---

^{32}Aelroth (we learn his name later, in XCIII) asks that he be the first to fight Roland.
^{33}Where this is located is uncertain; the line apparently means "from the Pyrenees to the southern border."
^{34}By placing the glove in his hand, Marsile grants his nephew's request.
^{35}A town on the Rhone River in France, noted for the manufacture of arms, as was Valencia in Spain.
^{36}That is, let no mocking songs be written about us.

LXXX

Count Oliver   has climbed up on a hill.
From there he searches   the valley to his right,
And sees that host   of pagan Saracens.
Then he calls out   to Roland, his sworn friend: 1020
"Coming from Spain   I see the fiery glow
Of shining hauberks,[37]   the blazing steel of helms.
For our brave Franks   this means great toil and pain.
And that foul traitor,   false-hearted Ganelon,
Knew this—that's why   he named us to the guard."
Count Roland answers,   "Stop, Oliver, be still!
Of my stepfather   I'll let no man speak ill."

LXXXI

Count Oliver   has climbed up on a hill;
From there he sees   the Spanish lands below,
And Saracens   assembled in great force.   1030
Their helmets gleam   with gold and precious stones,
Their shields are shining,   their hauberks burnished gold,
Their long sharp spears   with battle flags unfurled.
He tries to see   how many men there are:
Even battalions   are more than he can count.
And in his heart   Oliver is dismayed;
Quick as he can,   he comes down from the height,
And tells the Franks   what they will have to fight.

LXXXIII

Oliver says,   "The pagan might is great—
It seems to me,   our Franks are very few!   1050
Roland, my friend,   it's time to sound your horn;
King Charles will hear,   and bring his army back."
Roland replies,   "You must think I've gone mad!
In all sweet France   I'd forfeit my good name!
No! I will strike   great blows with Durendal,
Crimson the blade   up to the hilt of gold.
To those foul pagans   I promise bitter woe—
They all are doomed   to die at Roncevaux!"   AOI

LXXXIV

"Roland, my friend,   let the Oliphant[38] sound!
King Charles will hear it,   his host will all turn back,   1060
His valiant barons   will help us in this fight."
Roland replies,   "Almighty God forbid
That I bring shame   upon my family,
And cause sweet France   to fall into disgrace!
I'll strike that horde   with my good Durendal;
My sword is ready,   girded here at my side,
And soon you'll see   its keen blade dripping blood.

[37] Tunics of mail.   [38] Horn made of ivory.

The Saracens   will curse the evil day
They challenged us,   for we will make them pay."   AOI

LXXXV

"Roland, my friend,   I pray you, sound your horn!   1070
King Charlemagne,   crossing the mountain pass,
Won't fail, I swear it,   to bring back all his Franks."
"May God forbid!"   Count Roland answers then.
"No man on earth   shall have the right to say
That I for pagans   sounded the Oliphant!
I will not bring   my family to shame.
I'll fight this battle;   my Durendal shall strike
A thousand blows   and seven hundred more;
You'll see bright blood   flow from the blade's keen steel.
We have good men;   their prowess will prevail,   1080
And not one Spaniard   shall live to tell the tale."

LXXXVI

Oliver says,   "Never would you be blamed;
I've seen the pagans,   the Saracens of Spain.
They fill the valleys,   cover the mountain peaks;
On every hill,   and every wide-spread plain,
Vast hosts assemble   from that alien race;
Our company   numbers but very few."
Roland replies,   "The better, then, we'll fight!
If it please God   and His angelic host,
I won't betray   the glory of sweet France!   1090
Better to die   than learn to live with shame—
Charles loves us more   as our keen swords win fame."

LXXXVII

Roland's a hero,   and Oliver is wise;
Both are so brave   men marvel at their deeds.
When they mount chargers,   take up their swords and shields,
Not death itself   could drive them from the field.
They are good men;   their words are fierce and proud.
With wrathful speed   the pagans ride to war.
Oliver says,   "Roland, you see them now.
They're very close,   the king too far away.   1100
You were too proud   to sound the Oliphant:
If Charles were with us,   we would not come to grief.
Look up above us,   close to the Gate of Spain:[39]
There stands the guard—   who would not pity them!
To fight this battle   means not to fight again."
Roland replies,   "Don't speak so foolishly!
Cursed be the heart   that cowers in the breast!
We'll hold our ground;   if they will meet us here,
Our foes will find us   ready with sword and spear."   AOI

---

[39] The mountain pass.

LXXXIX

Archbishop Turpin　comes forward then to speak.
He spurs his horse　and gallops up a hill,
Summons the Franks,　and preaches in these words:
"My noble lords,　Charlemagne left us here,
And may our deaths　do honor to the king!
Now you must help　defend our holy Faith!
War is upon us—　I need not tell you that—　　　　　　1130
Before your eyes　you see the Saracens.
Confess your sins,　ask God to pardon you;
I'll grant you absolution　to save your souls.
Your deaths would be　a holy martyrdom,
And you'll have places　in highest Paradise."
The French dismount;　they kneel upon the ground.
Then the archbishop,　blessing them in God's name,
Told them, for penance,　to strike when battle came.[40]

XC

The kneeling Franks　have risen to their feet.
They are absolved,　and free from any sin;　　　　　　1140
Archbishop Turpin　has signed them with the cross.
Now they have mounted　swift horses bred for war;
They bear the weapons　befitting them as knights.
Thus they await　the Saracen attack.
Count Roland calls　Oliver to his side:
"My lord companion,　the words you spoke were true;
This is the work　of faithless Ganelon—
He sold us all　for treasure, gold and coins.
Now may he suffer　the emperor's revenge!
As for the bargain　that King Marsile has made,　　　1150
Without good swords　he'll forfeit what he paid."　AOI

XCI

At Roncevaux　Count Roland passes by,
Riding his charger,　swift-running Veillantif.
He's armed for battle,　splendid in shining mail.
As he parades,　he brandishes his lance,
Turning the point　straight up against the sky,
And from the spearhead　a banner flies, pure white,
With long gold fringes　that beat against his hands.
Fair to behold,　he laughs, serene and gay.
Now close behind him　comes Oliver, his friend,　　　1160
With all the Frenchmen　cheering their mighty lord.
Fiercely his eyes　confront the Saracens;
Humbly and gently　he gazes at the Franks,
Speaking to them　with gallant courtesy:

---

[40] The priest in confession administered absolution as God's agent, on condition that the sinner do penance; here fighting in battle is substituted for the usual forms of penance such as prayer, fasting, and almsgiving.

"Barons, my lords,   softly now, keep the pace!
Here come the pagans   looking for martyrdom.
We'll have such plunder   before the day is out,
As no French king   has ever won before!"
And at this moment   the armies join in war. AOI

XCII

Oliver says,   "I have no heart for words.   1170
You were too proud   to sound the Oliphant:
No help at all   you'll have from Charlemagne.
It's not his fault—   he doesn't know our plight,
Nor will the men   here with us be to blame.
But now, ride on,   to fight as you know how.
Barons, my lords,   in battle hold your ground!
And in God's name,   I charge you, be resolved
To strike great blows   for those you have to take.
Let's not forget   the war-cry of King Charles!"
He says these words,   and all the Franks cry out;   1180
No one who heard   that mighty shout, "Montjoie!" [41]
Would soon forget   the valor of these men.
And then, how fiercely,   God! they begin to ride,
Spurring their horses   to give their utmost speed,
They race to strike—   what else is there to do?
The Saracens stand firm;   they won't retreat.
Pagans and Christians,   behold! in battle meet.

XCIII

King Marsile's nephew,   Aelroth is his name,
First of the pagans,   rides out before the host,
Taunting our Franks   with loud malicious words: 1190
"Today, foul Frenchmen,   you'll break a lance with us;
You stand here now   abandoned and betrayed!
The king was mad   to leave you at the pass:
This day sweet France   will see its pride cast down.
The Emperor Charles   will lose his good right arm!"
Count Roland hears him,   God! with what pain and rage!
He spurs his horse   to run with all its might,
Levels his lance,   strikes Aelroth such a blow
His shield is shattered,   the hauberk split in two,
The pagan's bones   crack open in his chest,   1200
His broken spine   sticks out behind his back
So that the spear   drives out his very soul.
Under the thrust   the body starts to fall,
And Roland hurls him   a spear's length from his horse;
He falls down dead,   his neck broken in two.
But still Count Roland   gives him these parting words:

---

[41] Charles's battle cry. *Mont* means "hill" and *joie* means "joy." "Jenkins suggests also the pilgrims' cry of joy on seeing the end of their quest for Monte Gaudia or a similar hill near Jerusalem or Santiago, but no sure explanation exists."—Translator's note.

"Foul infidel,   King Charles is not a fool,
Nor was he ever   unfaithful to his trust.
Wisely he chose   that we should guard the pass;
Sweet France will lose   no glory here today.   1210
Strike on, you Franks!   First blood will win the fight!
Their cause is evil,   and we are in the right."   AOI

CX

Now fierce and grim   the battle rages on.
Oliver, Roland—   how valiantly they fight!
Turpin delivers   more than a thousand blows;
Among the peers   none dreams of holding back,
And all together,   the Franks, as one man, strike.
By hundreds, thousands,   the pagans fall and die;
There's no way out   except for those who flee:
Each one who stays   is living his last day.
But others die—   the best among the Franks—   1420
They'll never see   their families, their wives,
Or Charlemagne   who waits beyond the pass.
A fearful storm   that very day strikes France;
Through rushing winds   long peals of thunder roar,
And heavy rains,   enormous hailstones fall,
Great bolts of lightning   are striking everywhere.
Now the whole earth   is trembling dreadfully
From Saint Michel   all the way down to Seinz,
From Besançon   to Wissant on the sea;
There is no stronghold   without a shattered wall.   1430
At noontime shadows   darken the light of day;
The only brightness   comes when the black sky cracks,
And no man sees it   who isn't terrified.
Many declare,   "The world is at an end—
The Day of Wrath   has come upon us now!"
But they know nothing,   and they believe a lie.
The heavens grieve   that Roland is to die.

> [*Laisses XCIV–CXXVI: Meeting the first assault force of the pagans, Charles's pal-
> adins kill pagan chieftains in individual combat: Oliver kills Falsaron, Marsile's
> brother; Archbishop Turpin kills Corsalis; Gerin kills Malprimis de Brigant; Gerier
> kills the emir of Balaguer; Samson kills the emir of Moriane; Anseïs kills Torgis
> of Tortelose; Engelier kills Escrimiz of Valterne; Oton kills Estorgant; Bérengier kills
> Estramariz; Roland kills Chernuble de Munigre.*
>   *After Marsile's reinforcements join the battle, however, it becomes more even,
> and Charles's forces are gradually worn away by attrition. Most of the paladins are
> slain by pagans, though at the cost of their own lives at the hands of Roland, Oliver,
> and Archbishop Turpin.*]

CXXVII

Count Roland says   to Oliver his friend:
"My lord companion,   I'm sure you will agree
That our archbishop   makes a most valiant knight—

There is none better   on earth beneath the sky;
With lance in hand,   or spear, how he can fight!"
The count replies,   "Then let's go to his side!"
When he has spoken,   the Franks attack once more.
Hard are the blows,   the slaughter pitiless;
Many a Christian   is brought to grievous pain.
Then to behold   Roland and Oliver   1680
Wielding their swords   to cut the pagans down!
Beside them Turpin   thrusts with his mighty spear.
We know what happened   according to the *Geste,*
Chronicles, records   bear witness to the fact:
Four thousand pagans   by those few Franks were slain.
Through four assaults   the Frenchmen hold their ground.
But with the fifth   their strength comes to an end.
That final charge   kills all the knights of France
Except for sixty   who by God's will survive—
They'll make the pagans   pay dearly for their lives!   AOI   1690

CXXVIII

Count Roland sees   the slaughter of the Franks.
He says these words   to Oliver his friend:
"Noble companion,   what do you counsel now?
So many Franks   lie dead upon the field—
Well could we weep   for that fair land, sweet France,
Which will not see   these valiant lords again.
Oh! Charles, my friend,   if only you were here!
Oliver, brother,   how can we call him back?
Is there no way   to tell the king our plight?"
Oliver answers,   "Not if we save our fame.   1700
Better to die   than learn to live with shame."   AOI

CXXIX

Then Roland says,   "I'll sound the Oliphant.
King Charles will hear it   on the high mountain pass;
I promise you,   the Franks will all turn back."
Oliver answers,   "Then you would bring disgrace
And such dishonor   on your whole family
The shame of it   would last them all their lives.
Three times I asked,   and you would not agree;
You still can do it,   but not with my consent.
To sound the horn   denies your valor now.   1710
And both your arms   are red with blood of foes!"
The count replies,   "I've struck some pretty blows."   AOI

CXXX

Then Roland says,   "This has become a war.
I'll blow my horn,   and Charlemagne will hear."
Oliver says,   "Then you'll disgrace your name.
Each time I asked you,   companion, you refused.
If Charles were with us,   we would not come to grief.

No one can say   our Franks have been to blame.
I promise you—   I swear it by my beard—
If I should live   to see my sister's face,   1720
You'll never lie   in Alda's[42] sweet embrace!"   AOI

CXXXI

Then says the count,   "You're angry at me. Why?"
Oliver answers,   "Roland, you are to blame.
There is no madness   in courage for good cause,
But men should listen   to reason, not blind pride.
You were too reckless,   and so these Franks have died.
Never again   will we serve Charlemagne.
Had you believed me,   my lord would be here now,
We would have fought   and beat the Saracens,
Marsile would be   our prisoner, or dead.   1730
We are the victims   of your great prowess now!
We won't be there,   alas! to help King Charles,
A man whose peer   will not be seen on earth.
And you will die,   leaving sweet France to shame.
Brothers in arms   we've been until this day;
Now we have only   a last farewell to say."   AOI

CXXXII

Archbishop Turpin,   hearing their angry words,
Urges his horse   with spurs made of pure gold,
And riding up,   reproaches both of them:
"Roland, my lord,   and you, Lord Oliver,   1740
End your dispute,   I pray you, in God's name.
It's too late now   to blow the horn for help,
But just the same,   that's what you'd better do.
If the king comes   at least we'll be avenged—
Why should the Spaniards   go home safe to rejoice?
And then the Franks   will ride back to this place;
They'll find us dead,   our bodies hacked by swords,
Put us in coffins   carried on horses' backs,
And they will weep   for pity and for grief.
We will be buried   with honor in a church,   1750
And not be eaten   by wolves and pigs and dogs."
Then Roland answers: "Your words are wise, my lord."

CXXXIII

Count Roland presses   the horn against his mouth;
He grasps it hard,   and sounds a mighty blast.
High are the hills,   that great voice reaches far—
They hear it echo   full thirty leagues around.
Charlemagne hears,   and so do all his men.
The Emperor says,   "Our Franks are in a fight!"

---

[42] Roland's fiancee.

Count Ganelon   returns a swift reply:
"Except from you,   I'd take that for a lie!"   AOI   1760

CXXXIV

And now Count Roland,   in anguish and in pain,
With all his strength   sounds the great horn again.
Bright drops of blood   are springing from his mouth,
Veins in his forehead   are cracking with the strain.
That mighty voice   cries out a second time;
Charlemagne hears it,   high on the mountain pass,
Duke Naimon listens,   and so do all the Franks.
Then says the king,   "That is Count Roland's horn!
He'd never sound it,   except for an attack."
Ganelon says,   "What battle can there be?   1770
You have grown old,   your hair is streaked with white;
The words you speak   could well befit a child.
You ought to know   how great is Roland's pride—
The wonder is   God suffers it so long.
He captured Noples,   and not by your command,
And then flushed out   the Saracens inside;
He fought them all,   Roland, your loyal man,
And then took water   and washed the field of blood,
Hoping that you   would not detect the fight.
Just for a rabbit   he'll blow his horn all day!   1780
Now he is playing   some game to please his peers.
Who in the world   would dare make war on him!
Ride on, I tell you!   What are we waiting for?
We've far to go   to see our lands once more."   AOI

CXXXV

Count Roland's mouth   is crimson with his blood,
His temples broken   by the tremendous strain.
He sounds the horn   in anguish and in pain.
Charlemagne hears,   and so do all the Franks.
Then says the king,   "How long that horn resounds!"
Duke Naimon answers,   "Great valor swells the sound!   1790
Roland is fighting: he must have been betrayed—
And by that man   who tells you to hang back.
Take up your arms,   let your war-cry ring out!
Your household needs you,   now speed to its defense.
You've heard enough   how Roland's horn laments!"

CXXXVI

The Emperor Charles   orders his horns to sound.
The French dismount,   prepare themselves for war.
They put on hauberks,   helmets and golden swords;
Their shields are good,   heavy their spears and strong,
Their battle-flags   are crimson, blue and white.   1800
Riding their chargers,   the barons of the host
Spur on and gallop   back through the mountain pass.

Each to the other   pronounces this same vow:
"When we get there,   if Roland's still alive,
We'll fight beside him,   striking hard blows and straight."
What does it matter?   Their help will come too late.

                    CXXXVII
All afternoon   the sun shines bright and clear,
Armor and weapons   are gleaming in the light,
Hauberks and helmets   glitter as if on fire,
And all the shields,   brilliant with painted flowers,   1810
And all the spears   and gilded battle flags.
In bitter wrath   the Emperor rides on,
The men of France,   in sorrow and in rage.
There is not one   who can hold back his tears;
Because of Roland,   the Frenchmen are afraid.
King Charles commands   that Ganelon be seized;
Summoning forth   all of his household cooks,
He tells their chief,   Besgon, what should be done:
"Here is a felon   I'm leaving in your charge—
He has betrayed   the vassals of my house."   1820
The cook takes over;   a hundred kitchen boys,
The best and worst,   will guard Count Ganelon.
They pluck the hairs   from his moustache and beard,
Each with his fist   strikes him four mighty blows,
And then they beat him   with heavy sticks and clubs.
An iron collar   is put around his neck,
And then they chain him   as if he were a bear.
On a mule's back,   trussed up, he will remain.
They'll guard him well,   and wait for Charlemagne.   AOI

                    CXXXVIII
High are the hills,   and shadowy and vast,   1830
Deep the defiles,   and swift the mountain streams.
The trumpets sound   ahead and to the rear,
Blaring replies   to Roland's Oliphant.
In bitter wrath   the Emperor rides on,
The men of France   in sorrow and in rage;
Not one but grieves   and bitterly laments,
Praying that God   will keep Count Roland safe
Until they come   and join him in the field—
How they will fight   when they are at his side!
What does it matter   how loyally they strive?   1840
They'll be too late   whenever they arrive.   AOI

                    CXXXIX
Now Charlemagne   rides on in his great rage;
His beard, defiant,   outside his hauberk lies.
The lords of France   spur for the utmost speed,
There isn't one   but angrily laments
That they can't be   already on the field

Where Roland fights   against the Saracens.
I think his wound   won't let him long survive,
But God! the sixty   still fighting at his side—
No king or chieftain   has ever had their like.   AOI   1850

CXL

Count Roland sees   the mountains and the hills
Where all around him   the Franks are lying dead;
He weeps for them,   as a true knight would do.
"Barons, my lords,   may God forgive your sins,
And grant your souls   a place in Paradise,
On holy flowers   may you forever rest!
I've never seen   vassals better than you;
You followed me   so loyally and long,
For Charlemagne   we've won such mighty lands!
The king's own household,   alas! brings him to woe.   1860
And that fair country   where it is sweet to live
Today laid waste   and cruelly bereaved!
Barons of France,   because of me you die;
I can't protect you,   I cannot keep you safe:
Look now to God   who never failed a trust.
Oliver, brother,   I'll not break faith with you.
I'll die of grief,   if not by pagan spears.
My lord, companion,   there's still work for us here!"

CXLI

Roland has gone   back to the battlefield.
With Durendal   he strikes heroic blows: 1870
Faldrun de Pui   he cuts down first of all,
Then twenty-four   of the best pagan knights.
No man has ever   wanted revenge so much.
Just as the stag   runs to escape the hounds,
So do the pagans   before Count Roland flee.
Says the archbishop,   "Bravely you fight, and well!
Yours is the spirit   a chevalier must have,
If he bears arms   and has a horse to ride:
A man in battle   ought to be fierce and strong—
For one who isn't   I wouldn't give two cents.   1880
Instead of fighting   let him become a monk
And spend his days   praying for all our sins."
Roland replies,   "Strike on, and spare not one!"
With that the Franks   begin to fight once more.
Many a Christian   falls to the pagan swords.

CXLII

A man who knows   all captives will be slain
In such a battle   fights to the end of strength;
And so the Franks   like lions face their foes.
Behold Marsile: as a true knight would do,

He sits the horse   that he has named Gaignon,[43]   1890
Pricks with sharp spurs,   and rides against Bevon,
The lord of Beaune   and also of Dijon;
He breaks his shield,   the hauberk splits in two—
With that one blow   he fells the Frenchman dead.
Then Marsile kills   Ivoire and Ivon too,
And with them dies   Gérard of Roussillon.
Seeing that, Roland,   who isn't far away,
Says to the pagan,   "God smite you with His curse!
To you I owe   these good companions slain—
Nor shall we part   before that debt is paid!   1900
Now is the time   to teach you my sword's name."[44]
With that he charges   as a true knight would do;
The count's keen sword   cuts off Marsile's right hand,
Then Jurfaleu   surrenders his blond head—
He was a prince,   the son of King Marsile.
The pagans cry,   "Mohammed help us now!
Gods of our country,   give us revenge on Charles,
For he has sent   such felons here to fight
That death itself   can't drive them from the field."
They tell each other,   "Let's get away from here!"   1910
A hundred thousand   run from the French attack;
Whoever calls,   they won't be coming back.

                          CXLIII
What does it matter   that King Marsile has fled?
They must still fight   his uncle Marganice,[45]
The lord of Carthage,   Alfrere, and Garmalie,
That land accursed   called Ethiopia
Whose black men serve   as Marganice commands.
They have big noses,   their ears stick out too far;
Some fifty thousand   have come to fight the Franks.
They gallop boldly,   and in wild fury charge,   1920
Shouting the war-cry   dear to the pagan hosts.
Then Roland says,   "Here we'll win martyrdom.
Now I can see   how little time is left;
But cursed be he   who lets his life go cheap!
Strike them, my lords,   strike with your shining swords!
Give them a battle   whether you live or die,
That none may say   we brought sweet France to shame.
When Charlemagne   comes to this battlefield,
He'll see the hosts   of slaughtered Saracens—
For each of us   some fifteen pagans dead;   1930
Charles won't reproach us,   he'll bless us all instead." AOI

[43] The name means "watchdog."
[44] "Thus it is apparent that the name 'Durendal' has significance, but nothing further can be effectively said on the subject."—Translator's note.
[45] The caliph mentioned in laisses XXXV and LIV.

CXLIV

When Roland sees   this horde of infidels
Who all are darker   than is the blackest ink,
With nothing white   except their gleaming teeth,
He says aloud,   "There isn't any doubt,
Today we'll die—   I can believe it now.
Follow me, Frenchmen!   We'll give them one more charge!"
Oliver says,   "The devil take the last!"
The French attack;   their blows fall hard and fast.

CXLV

And when the pagans   see how few Franks are left,   1940
They take much pride   and comfort from the fact,
Telling each other,   "King Charles is in the wrong."
Then Marganice,   astride a sorrel[46] horse,
Pricks with gold spurs   and gallops from behind
To land his spear   deep in Oliver's back.
The gleaming hauberk   shatters and splits away,
The spear goes through   and opens up his chest.
Says Marganice,   "You've taken a hard blow!
Charlemagne left you   to wait here for your doom.
Let him not glory   in what he's done to Spain—   1950
Your death alone   avenges all our slain."

CXLVI

Oliver feels   how close he is to death.
He raises high   Halteclere's bright burnished blade,
Strikes Marganice,   and splits his tall gold helm,
Its jewels and flowers   fall shattered to the ground;
He cleaves his head   right down into the teeth,
Wrenching the sword,   he hurls the body down.
Then says the count,   "Be damned, you Saracen!
Whatever Charles   may have lost here today,
At least I'm sure   no wife or lady friend   1960
Will hear you boasting,   safe in your lands again,
Of how you captured   silver or gold from me:
Your triumphs here   will not be on parade."
He summons then   Count Roland to his aid.   AOI

CXLVII

Oliver knows   he has a fatal wound.
He'll never have his fill   of vengeance now.
In the melee   he fights on valiantly,
He cuts through spears,   the pagans' studded shields,
And feet and fists   and saddle-trees and spines.
Whoever watched him   cut pagans limb from limb,   1970
Bodies piled up   around him on the ground,
Would know that once   he'd seen a noble lord.

[46] Light brown or orange-brown.

The count remembers   the war-cry of King Charles,
And loud and clear   his voice rings out, "Montjoie!"
He calls to Roland,   summons his friend and peer,
"My lord, companion,   come fight beside me now!
We'll part in sorrow   before the sun goes down." AOI

CXLVIII
Roland is there;   he sees Oliver's face,
The skin is ashen,   so pallid it looks grey,
And from his wounds   bright blood is spurting out;   1980
Its heavy drops   flow down him to the ground.
"O God!" says Roland,   "I don't know what to do.
Was such great valor   destined to be cut down!
My noble friend,   you'll have no peer on earth.
Alas, sweet France!   You are bereft today
Of your good vassals,   laid waste and brought to shame;
The Emperor Charles   will sorely feel the lack."
With these words Roland   faints on his horse's back. AOI

CXLIX
Here is Count Roland   unconscious on his horse;
Oliver, wounded   and very close to death,   1990
Has bled so much   that both his eyes are dimmed:
Now far or near   he can't see well enough
To give a name   to any man alive.
When he encounters   Count Roland in the field,
Oliver strikes him,   cleaving his golden helm
Brilliant with jewels—   the nose-piece cracks in two—
And yet the blade   does not touch face or head.
Roland's eyes open,   and looking at his friend,
Softly and gently   he asks him only this:
"My lord, companion,   it's Roland—did you know?   2000
I've always loved you;   did you intend that blow?
You gave no challenge   before you charged at me."
Oliver says,   "I recognize your voice,
But I can't see you—   God keep you in His sight!
I struck at you!   I pray you, pardon me."
Roland replies,   "I am not hurt at all;
I do forgive you,   here and in front of God."
When he had spoken,   each leaned down toward his friend.
So, with great love,   they parted in the end.

CL
Oliver suffers   the agonies of death;   2010
He feels his eyes   turn back into his head,
He cannot hear,   he cannot see at all.
Now he dismounts,   and kneeling on the ground,
Aloud he asks   forgiveness for his sins;
He clasps his hands,   and holds them toward the sky,
Praying that God   will grant him Paradise,

And give His blessing   to Charles and to sweet France,
And to Count Roland   above all other men.
Then his heart fails him,   his shining helmet bows.
All of his body   sinks down against the ground;   2020
The count is dead—   no longer did he stay.
Lord Roland weeps,   lamenting bitterly;
Many have grieved,   but no man more than he.

                              CLI
When Roland sees   that Oliver is dead,
Lying face downward   stretched out against the ground,
With tender words   he bids his friend farewell:
"Alas, companion!   Your valor ends in woe.
We were together   so many years and days;
You never wronged me,   and I kept faith with you.
Now you are dead,   I grieve to be alive."   2030
The marquis faints   just as he says these words,
Still on his horse,   whose name is Veillantif;
The fine gold stirrups   will keep him sitting straight,
So he won't fall   however he may sway.

                              CLII
Before Count Roland   recovers from his faint,
While he still sits   unconscious on his horse,
The battle brings   disaster to his men:
The Franks are dead—   he's lost them, every one
Save the archbishop   and Gautier de l'Hum[47]
Who from the mountains   has now returned at last.   2040
He fought a battle   with Spanish Saracens.
His men are dead;   their enemies have won.
Down toward the valleys,   he flees now, all alone,
Searching for Roland,   calling to him for help:
"Ah, noble count!   Where are you, valiant lord?
When you were with me,   I never was afraid.
It's Gautier—   I conquered Maelgut!
Droon is my uncle,   his aged head is grey.
You used to love me,   because you knew me brave.
My spear is broken,   my shield has been pierced through,   2050
My hauberk's links   scattered and snapped apart,
Deep in my body   a pagan lance has thrust;
I'm dying now,   but they have bought me dear."
Roland wakes up   to hear his final words;
Turning his horse,   toward Gautier he spurs.   AOI

                              CLIII
Count Roland, grieving   and filled with bitter rage,
Rides once again   through the thick of the fight.

[47] For Gautier, see LXIV–LXV.

Twenty Spaniards   he throws dead to the ground,
Gautier kills six,   Archbishop Turpin five.
The pagans say,   "These men are monstrous fierce!   2060
Take care, my lords,   don't let them get away.
If you aren't traitors,   we'll rush upon them now—
If you aren't cowards,   they won't escape alive!"
Then riding onward   with a great hue and cry,
They charge the Franks   once more from every side.   AOI

CLIV

There is Count Roland,   a noble warrior,
Gautier de l'Hum,   a worthy chevalier,
Archbishop Turpin,   a veteran and brave:
None would be willing   to fail the other two.
In the melee   they strike the pagans down.   2070
A thousand Spaniards   dismount to fight on foot,
While forty thousand   stay on their horses' backs—
And even so   they don't dare come too near.
They throw their lances,   hurl their keen-bladed spears,
All sorts of weapons   come flying at the Franks;
With the first blows,   Count Gautier is killed,
Turpin of Reims   soon finds his shield pierced through,
His helmet breaks—   he's wounded in the head—
His chain-mail hauberk   is cracked and splits apart,
Four pagan spears   strike deep into his flesh,   2080
His war-horse, dying,   carries him to the ground.
O God! What sorrow   to see Turpin go down!   AOI

CLV

Turpin of Reims,   finding himself unhorsed,
With four deep wounds   where spears thrust through his flesh,
Leaps up again,   great fighter that he is,
Looks for Count Roland,   and hastens to his side,
Saying just this: "I am not beaten yet!
No man of courage   gives up while he's alive."
He draws Almace   whose blade is burnished steel,
Strikes in the throng   a thousand blows and more.   2090
Soon Charles will say   that Turpin spared no foe:
They found four hundred   around him in the field,
Some of them wounded,   some of them thrust clean through,
And there were others   who parted with their heads.
So says the *Geste,*   and someone who was there:
Saint Giles[48] for whom   Our Lord works miracles
Left an account   in Laon's church in France;
Everyone knows this,   or nothing understands.

---

[48] The meaning apparently is that the saint, about whom there were numerous legends, was present in spirit. No account of the battle written by him is known.

CLVI

Roland delivers   many a skillful blow,
But now his body   is fevered, drenched with sweat,   2100
His head is throbbing   under a dreadful pain,
His temples broken   from sounding his great horn.
Longing to know   if Charles is on his way,
Weakly, once more,   he blows the Oliphant.
King Charles stands still,   listening to that call;
"My lords," he says,   "now we have come to woe!
My nephew Roland   takes leave of us this day—
His horn's voice tells me   he won't be long alive.
Who wants to be there   had better speed his horse.
Let every trumpet   the host commands resound!"   2110
And sixty thousand   rang from the lofty peaks
Down through the valleys,   echoing loud and clear.
The pagans, listening,   think it no empty boast—
They say, "Here come   King Charles and all his host."   AOI

CLVII

The pagans say,   "Now Charles is coming back.
Those trumpet calls   rally the men of France;
We'll have great losses   if the Emperor comes,
And if Count Roland   lives to make war again,
We may as well   surrender all of Spain."
About four hundred   assemble, helmeted,   2120
The best who fought   among the Saracens;
With all their might   these men attack anew,
And then Count Roland   has work enough to do.   AOI

CLVIII

When Roland sees   the pagans closing in,
His heart grows stronger,   and prouder and more fierce.
He'll yield to none,   as long as he's alive.
Astride the horse   whose name is Veillantif,
He gallops toward them,   pricking with golden spurs;
Into the throng   he charges to attack.
Archbishop Turpin   is fighting at his side.   2130
The pagans say,   "Let's get away from here!
Those trumpet calls   mean that the Franks are near—
Their mighty king,   great Charles, will soon appear!"

CLIX

Count Roland's friendship   no coward ever knew,
Nor any man   false-hearted or too proud,
Nor any knight   who was not skilled at war.
To the archbishop   Roland addressed these words:
"I am on horseback,   my lord, and you're on foot;
For love of you,   here I shall take my stand—
We'll meet together   what good or evil comes,   2140
No mortal man   will make me leave your side.

We shall return   the Saracen attack.
What sword can equal   the blows of Durendal!
Turpin replies,   "Curse him whose arm grows slack!
We'll be avenged   when Charlemagne comes back."

CLX

The pagans say,   "Ours were unlucky stars!
Would that this evil day   had never dawned!
We've lost our peers,   our lords have all been slain,
The valiant Charles   is coming back again.
Now we can hear   the trumpets of his host,　　　2150
The mighty clamor   when the Franks shout 'Montjoie!'
And this Count Roland   is hideously fierce—
He can't be conquered   by men of flesh and blood.
Let's cast our lances   and then leave him alone."
The Saracens   throw many javelins,
Lances and darts,   and feathered throwing spears.
Count Roland's shield   is broken and pierced through,
His hauberk's mail   is cracked and split apart,
And still his body   has not been touched at all.
But Veillantif   has suffered thirty wounds;　　　2160
Beneath Count Roland   he falls dead to the ground.
Then all the pagans   yield to their fear and flee;
And Roland stands,   dismounted, on the field.　AOI

CLXI

The pagans flee,   furious and enraged,
Trying their best   to get away in Spain.
Count Roland lacks the means   to chase them now,
For he has lost   his war-horse Veillantif;
Against his will   he has to go on foot.
He went to give   Archbishop Turpin help,
Unlaced his helmet,   removed it from his head,　　　2170
And then took off   the hauberk of light mail;
The under-tunic   he cut into long strips
With which he stanched   the largest of his wounds,
Then lifting Turpin,   carried him in his arms
To soft green grass,   and gently laid him down.
In a low voice   Roland made this request:
"My noble lord,   I pray you, give me leave,
For our companions,   the men we held so dear,
Must not be left   abandoned now in death.
I want to go   and seek out every one,　　　2180
Carry them here,   and place them at your feet."
Said the archbishop,   "I grant it willingly.
The field belongs,   thank God, to you and me."

CLXII

Alone, Count Roland   walks through the battlefield,
Searching the valleys,   searching the mountain heights.

He found the bodies   of Ivon and Ivoire,
and then he found   the Gascon Engelier.
Gerin he found,   and Gerier his friend,
He found Aton   and then Count Bérengier,
Proud Anseïs he found,   and then Samson,   2190
Gérard the Old,   the Count of Roussillon.
He took these barons,   and carried every one
Back to the place   where the archbishop was,
And then he put them   in ranks at Turpin's knees.
Seeing them, Turpin   cannot restrain his tears;
Raising his hand,   he blesses all the dead.
And then he says,   "You've come to grief, my lords!
Now in His glory,   may God receive your souls,
Among bright flowers   set you in Paradise!
It's my turn now;   death keeps me in such pain,   2200
Never again   will I see Charlemagne."

CLXIII

Roland goes back   to search the field once more,
And his companion   he finds there, Oliver.
Lifting him in his arms,   he holds him close,
Brings him to Turpin   as quickly as he can,
Beside the others   places him on a shield;
Turpin absolves him,   signing him with the cross,
And then they yield   to pity and to grief.
Count Roland says,   "Brother in arms, fair friend,
You were the son   of Renier, the duke   2210
Who held the land   where Runers valley lies.
For breaking lances,   for shattering thick shields,
Bringing the proud   to terror and defeat,
For giving counsel,   defending what is right,
In all the world   there is no better knight."

CLXIV

When Roland sees   that all his peers are dead,
And Oliver   whom he so dearly loved,
He feels such sorrow   that he begins to weep;
Drained of all color,   his face turns ashen pale,
His grief is more   than any man could bear,
He falls down, fainting   whether he will or no.   2220
Says the archbishop,   "Baron, you've come to woe."

CLXV

When the archbishop   sees Roland on the ground,
He feels more sorrow   than he has ever known.
He reaches out   to grasp the Oliphant;
A swift stream waters   the plain at Roncevaux,
And there, for Roland,   he wants to fill the horn.
Taking short steps,   staggering, he sets out,
But in his weakness   he can't go very far—

He has no strength,   his wounds have bled too much;
He doesn't travel   even a hundred feet   2230
Before he falls—   his heart has given out.
Now death is trying   to put his soul to rout.

CLXVI

Meanwhile Count Roland   recovers from his faint,
He rises to his feet,   but with great pain.
He looks around him,   he searches up and down;
Beyond the place   where his companions lie,
Prone on the grass,   he sees the noble lord,
Archbishop Turpin,   God's delegate on earth.
Count Roland hears him   confessing he has sinned,
With his clasped hands   held upward toward the sky,   2240
Praying that God   will give him Paradise.
Turpin is dead   who fought for Charlemagne.
With mighty blows,   with wise and holy words,
Against the pagans   he championed the Faith.
May God in heaven   bless him and grant him grace.

CLXVII

Roland sees Turpin   lying there on the ground,
Entrails protruding   from his enormous wounds;
Above his forehead   his brains are bubbling out.
On Turpin's chest,   between his collarbones,
Roland has crossed   the beautiful white hands.   2250
Now he laments   as it is done in France:
"O nobly born,   illustrious chevalier,
To heaven's glory   I now commend your soul;
Our Lord will never   be served more willingly.
Since the Apostles,   there has been none like you
To keep the Law,   and bring men to the Faith.
From pain and sorrow   may your free soul arise;
May you find open   the gates of Paradise!"

CLXVIII

Now Roland knows   that death is very near.
His ears give way,   he feels his brain gush out.   2260
He prays that God   will summon all his peers;
Then, for himself,   he prays to Gabriel.[49]
Taking the horn,   to keep it from all shame,
With Durendal   clasped in his other hand,
He goes on, farther   than a good cross-bow shot,
West into Spain,   crossing a fallow field.
Up on a hilltop,   under two lofty trees,
Four marble blocks[50]   are standing on the grass.
But when he comes there,   Count Roland faints once more,
He falls down backward;   now he is at death's door.   2270

---

[49] The great archangel; like Michael, he is a leader of the heavenly hosts.
[50] Possibly boundary stones.

CLXIX

High are the hills   and very high the trees,
The four great blocks   of polished marble shine;
On the green grass   the count is lying still.
A Saracen   watches with steady eyes:
This man feigned death,   hiding among the slain;
His face and body   he had besmeared with blood.
Now he stands up   and dashes forward fast—
He's handsome, strong   and very valiant too,
But he won't live   to profit from his pride;
He falls on Roland,   seizing him and his arms   2280
And says these words: "Charles' nephew lost the fight!
When I go home,   his sword shall be my prize."
But as he pulls it,   Roland comes back to life.

CLXX

Count Roland feels   the pagan take his sword,
And opening his eyes,   he says just this:
"You look to me   like no one on our side!"
Raising the horn   he'd wanted to keep safe,
He strikes the helmet   shining with gold and jewels,
Shatters the steel,   smashes the skull and bones;
He puts both eyes   out of the pagan's head,   2290
And sends his body   crashing against the ground.
And then he asks him,   "How did you get so brave,
Dog, to attack me   with or without just cause?
Whoever heard this   would say you were insane!
But I have cracked   the Oliphant's broad bell;
Its gold and crystals   were shattered as it fell."

CLXXI

Count Roland feels   that he is going blind.
Now he stands upright,   using what strength remains;
All of the color   has vanished from his face.
In front of him   there is a dark grey stone.   2300
He strikes ten blows   in bitterness and grief;
The steel blade grates   but will not break or dent.
The count cries out,   "O Holy Mary, help!
O Durendal,   alas for your fair fame!
My life is over,   I'll care for you no more.
We've won such battles   together in the field.
So many lands   we've conquered, you and I,
For Charles to rule   whose beard is silver-grey.
No man must have you   who fights and runs away!
You have been long   in a good vassal's hands;   2310
You'll have no equal   in all of holy France."

CLXXIV

Count Roland feels   the very grip of death
Which from his head   is reaching for his heart.

He hurries then   to go beneath a pine;
In the green grass   he lies down on his face,
Placing beneath him   the sword and Oliphant;
He turns his head   to look toward pagan Spain.   2360
He does these things   in order to be sure
King Charles will say,   and with him all the Franks,
The noble count   conquered until he died.
He makes confession,   for all his sins laments,
Offers his glove to   God[51] in penitence.   AOI

CLXXVI

And now Count Roland,   lying beneath a pine,
Has turned his face   to look toward pagan Spain;
And he begins   remembering these things:
The many lands   his valor won the king,
Sweet France, his home,   the men of his own line,
And Charlemagne   who raised him in his house—   2380
The memories   make him shed tears and sigh.
But not forgetting   how close he is to death,
He prays that God   forgive him all his sins:
"O my true Father,   O Thou who never lied,
Thou who delivered   Lazarus from the grave,
Who rescued Daniel[52]   out of the lions' den,
Keep now my soul   from every peril safe,
Forgive the sins   that I have done in life."
Roland, in homage,   offers his glove to God.
Saint Gabriel comes   and takes it from his hand.   2390
His head sinks down   to rest upon his arm;
Hands clasped in prayer,   the count has met his end.
God sends from heaven   the angel Cherubin,[53]
Holy Saint Michael   who saves us from the sea,
And with these two   the Angel Gabriel flies.
Count Roland's soul   they bring to Paradise.

CLXXVII

Roland is dead;   his soul rests now with God.
The Emperor Charles   rides into Roncevaux;
On every road,   on every mountain path,
On every ell,   on every foot of land,   2400
They find a body   of Frank or Saracen.
King Charles cries out,   "Fair nephew, where are you?
Where's the archbishop?   Where is Count Oliver?
Where is Count Gerin,   and Gerier his friend?

---

[51] A symbolic gesture of dependence, as by a feudal vassal to his chief.

[52] For these two famous biblical miracles—the resurrection of Lazarus by Jesus and the divine protection of Daniel when the Persian king Darius had him imprisoned in the lions' den—see John, chapters 11 and 12, and Daniel, chapter 6.

[53] Here the reference is to a particular angel, not to the order of angels the word usually signifies.

Oton—where is he,   and noble Bérengier,
Ivoire and Ivon,   those two I held so dear?
Tell me what happened   to Gascon Engelier,
Where are Duke Samson,   the valiant Anseïs,
And Old Gérard,   the Count of Roussillon?
Where are the peers,   the twelve who stayed behind?"   2410
What good is asking   when no one can reply?
"God!" says the king,   "Now have I cause to grieve,
For where was I   when fighting here began!"
He pulls his beard   in anguish and in pain;
The lords of France   are weeping bitter tears,
And twenty thousand   faint in their grief and fall.
Duke Naimon feels   great sorrow for them all.

> [*Laisses CLXXVIII–CLXXXVI: Leaving an honor guard to watch over Roland
> and the other slain heroes, Charles pursues the retreating Saracens. A divine mira-
> cle arrests the sun in the sky, allowing Charles's army to slay part of the enemy and
> to drive the rest to panic and death by drowning in the river Ebro.*]

CLXXXVII

To Saragossa   the pagan king has fled.   2570
There he dismounts   beneath an olive tree,
Gives up his sword,   his hauberk and his helm;
On the green grass   the king lies down in shame.
Marsile's right hand   was cut completely off,
And he is fainting   from loss of blood and pain.
In front of him,   his wife Queen Bramimonde,
Weeping for grief,   cries out a loud lament.
The queen has with her   some twenty thousand men,
All of them cursing   Charlemagne and sweet France.
Now they attack   Apollo in his crypt,   2580
Reviling him,   disfiguring his form:
"Why, evil god,   have you brought us to shame?
Why have you suffered   the downfall of our king?
For faithful service   you give a poor reward!"
Then they take off   his scepter[54] and his crown,
And to a column   they tie him by the hands;
They knock him down,   stamping him with their feet,
And with great clubs   they smash him into bits.
They take the ruby   away from Tervagant,
And then Mohammed   they thrust into a ditch   2590
Where he'll be trampled   and gnawed by dogs and pigs.

> [*Laisses CLXXXVIII–CCLVII: On the following day, the great emir Baligant of
> "Babylon" (Cairo) arrives with his forces, too late for the battle but resolved to help
> Marsile and overcome Charles. He is told of the Saracens' defeat and of Roland's
> death.*]

---

[54] That is, the idol's.

Charles, after camping overnight, returns to Roncevaux. He finds Roland's body and utters a lovingly elegiac lament for him. The dead are buried. Roland, Oliver, and the archbishop Turpin—who will be buried in France—receive special honors.

The army of Baligant suddenly appears; Charles and his forces prepare for war again. The poet recites an epic catalog of Charles's armies, specifying what part of Europe each division comes from and who commands it. Charles prays for victory, he advances with his army, and they camp for the night.

The pagans too prepare for war. Baligant is described at some length, the poet expressing regret that so admirable a hero should not be a Christian. Baligant praises Charles. A catalog, corresponding to that of the Franks, shows that Baligant's army comes from many parts of the world.

The battle is joined on a broad plain, Roland's horn sounding to hearten the Franks. Many men, on both sides, die in the fierce fighting. Duke Naimon, after felling Baligant's son, is seriously wounded by the emir's brother but is rescued by Charles. Informed of his son's death, Baligant grieves. He rallies the pagans; the Franks fall back.]

CCLVIII

The day goes by;   darkness begins to fall;   3560
Pagans and Franks   are fighting with their swords.
Two men of courage   command these mighty hosts.
They don't forget   to sound their battle-calls,
The great emir   shouting his "Précieuse!"
And Charlemagne,   his famous cry "Montjoie!"
Each recognizes   the other's strong clear voice,
And then they meet   upon the battlefield.
They charge head on;   each one lands with his spear
So great a blow   upon the other's shield
It cracks wide open   below the heavy boss;   3570
The hauberk panels   are cracked and split apart,
And yet the spearheads   don't penetrate the flesh.
The girths give way,   throwing the saddles off,
With them both kings   come crashing to the ground.
Then, in an instant,   both have regained their feet
And drawn their swords,   ready to fight it out.
No way to end   this combat will be found
Till one of them   lies dead upon the ground.   AOI

CCLIX

A mighty hero   is Charlemagne of France,
And Baligant   will meet him unafraid.   3580
With swords unsheathed,   they come together now,
Their heavy shields   receiving mighty blows
Which split the leathers,   the double wooden frames;
The nails fall out,   the bosses break apart.
Then nothing shelters   the hauberks from the blades,
And fiery sparks   come flashing from their helms.
This is a combat   which has to last as long
As neither man   admits that he is wrong.   AOI

CCLX

Says the emir, "Charles, if you stop and think,
You will repent   of what you've done to me: 3590
You can't deny   that you have killed my son;
You do great wrong   when you invade my lands.
Become my vassal,   promise me fealty;
Come with me to the East   and serve me there."
King Charles replies,   "That would be vile disgrace.
I'll be no friend   to pagans, or make peace.
Receive the law   that is the gift of God,
Become a Christian,   and you shall know my love;
Serve Him, have faith   in that almighty King."
Says Baligant,   "Tediously you preach!"   3600
They draw their swords,   and there's an end to speech.

CCLXI

The great emir   is powerful and brave:
He strikes Charles' helmet   so terrible a blow
The burnished steel   is cracked and splits apart,
The sword blade cleaves   the emperor's thick hair
And slices off   a hand's breadth of his scalp,
Stripping the flesh   down to the naked bone.
Charlemagne staggers,   comes close to falling down,
But God won't have him   brought to defeat or slain:
Saint Gabriel   comes back to him once more,   3610
And says, "Great king,   what are you waiting for?"

CCLXII

Charlemagne hears   the angel's holy voice:
He's not afraid,   he knows he will not die.
His strength returns,   his mind is clear and calm.
And then he strikes   with the great sword of France;
The emir's helmet,   ablaze with jewels, cracks,
His head is broken   so that the brains spill out,
His face splits open   down to his long white beard:
He is stone dead   before he hits the ground.
Then Charles' "Montjoie!"   rings through the battlefield.   3620
Duke Naimon hears him   and hastens to his side
With Tencendur;[55]   the great king mounts his horse.
Now by God's will,   the pagans turn and flee;
The Frenchmen know   they've won their victory.

> [*Laisses CCLXIII–CCLXIX: In Saragossa, the king Marsile dies in anguish
> when he hears of the Saracens' defeat. Charles's forces occupy the city, destroying its
> idols, baptizing many of the pagans, and putting resisters to death. Marsile's queen,
> Bramimonde, who is to be converted by gentler means, is forcibly led away with the
> army, which returns to France. On reaching the border, Charles has Roland, Oliver,
> and Archbishop Turpin honorably entombed. Back in his capital, Aix, Charles*

---

[55] Charles's horse.

informs Roland's fiancee, Alda, of his death; rejecting Charles's compensatory offer of his own son and heir, she dies in grief.]

CCLXX

The Emperor Charles   has come back home to Aix.
There Ganelon,   the traitor, bound with chains,
In the high town,   before the palace stands.
To a great stake   the serfs have bound him fast,
Both of his hands   are tied with deerskin thongs,
They beat him well   with heavy sticks and rods:
That way he's treated   in the most proper style,   3740
And he must wait   in torment for his trial.

CCLXXI

As it is written   in the old chronicles,
Charlemagne summoned   vassals from many lands;[56]
And in the chapel   at Aix they're gathered now.
The day is solemn,   the feast they celebrate
Is Saint Silvester's—[57]   so many people say.
The trial begins   with speeches on both sides,
And Ganelon,   who did a traitor's deed,
Is dragged before   the emperor to plead.   AOI

CCLXXII

"Barons, my lords,"   says Charlemagne the king,   3750
"Give me your judgment   concerning Ganelon.
He was with me in Spain   among my host,
And there he robbed me   of twenty thousand Franks;
My nephew Roland   you'll never see again,
Nor Oliver,   so courteous and brave—
For gold and treasure   this man betrayed the peers."
"Sire," says the count,   "I won't conceal the truth:
Because of Roland   I lost both goods and gold.[58]
I wanted him   to suffer and to die;
But in that vengeance   there was no treachery."   3760
The Franks reply,   "We'll talk of this and see."

CCLXXIII

Before the king   behold Count Ganelon.
Stalwart he stands,   fair color in his face—
If he were loyal,   he'd look a noble lord.
He sees the French,   the judges who are there,
The thirty members   of his own family,

---

[56] Ganelon cannot be judged by Charlemagne himself; he must be tried by his peers.
[57] December 31.
[58] Ganelon may mean that Roland kept more than his proper share of the spoils of war in Spain. The basis of Ganelon's self-defense is that he opposed Roland openly, not in the secret manner that technically was necessary to the definition of treason.

And then he speaks,   his great voice ringing out:
"Barons of France,   for God's sake hear me now!
My lords, I fought   beside the emperor,
And served him well   in loyalty and love.   3770
His nephew Roland,   hating me in his heart,
Had me condemned   to torment and sure death:
I was to bring   Charles' message to Marsile—
I had the wit   and wisdom to survive.
I faced Count Roland   and challenged him aloud,
And Oliver,   and all the other peers.
Charlemagne heard me,   so did these noble lords:
I am avenged,   but not by treachery."
The Franks reply,   "We'll go and judge your plea."

CCLXXIV

Ganelon sees   his great trial has begun.   3780
Thirty kinsmen   the count has with him there,
Among them one   looked up to by the rest
Called Pinabel—   his castle is Sorence.
This man can argue   so that his views prevail,
And he's a hero   not easy to defeat.   AOI
Ganelon says,   "I place my trust in you—
Save me from death,   defend me in this trial!"
Says Pinabel,   "In no time you'll be free.
If any Frenchman   decides that you should hang,
The Emperor Charles   must have that judgment tried: 3790
My sword shall prove   these accusations lies."
Count Ganelon   with grateful thanks replies.

CCLXXV

Bavarians, Saxons,   have gone to judge the case,
Normans are with them,   Poitevins, men of France,
Germans are there,   and many Thiois too;
Those from Auvergne   show the most courtesy.
They speak more softly   because of Pinabel,
Telling each other,   "Let's bring this to an end,
Dismiss the trial,   and ask that Charles the King
For this one time   let Ganelon go free—   3800
He'll be his vassal   in loyalty and love.
Roland is dead;   you won't see him again.
No gold or treasure   will bring him back to life.
It would be madness   to fight for his sake now."
They all approve;   no one will disagree
But Geoffroy's[59] brother,   the chevalier Thierry.   AOI

CCLXXVI

And so the barons   return to Charlemagne,
Saying to him,   "Sire, we would ask for this:

---

[59] Geoffroy of Anjou, Charles' flag bearer (see VIII) and one of his right-hand men.

Acquit your captive,   let Ganelon go free,
Henceforth to serve you   loyally and with love.   3810
Grant him his life,   for he is nobly born;
And no man's death   will bring Count Roland back,
Nor any gold—   there's nothing to be done."
Then says the king,   "You're traitors, every one!"   AOI

CCLXXVII

When King Charles sees   they all have failed his cause,
He bows his head   so none can see his face;
His words and looks   proclaim his bitter woe.
And then before him   he sees a chevalier,
Thierry, whose brother   is Geoffroy of Anjou.
Not very stalwart,   he's lean and spare of build,[60]   3820
His hair is black,   his face is rather dark;
He isn't tall,   nor could you call him short.
With courtesy   he tells the emperor:
"Fair sire and king,   do not give way to grief!
You know I've served you   a long time faithfully.
Now all my forebears   through me protest this trial:
However Roland   may have wronged Ganelon,
No one may harm   a man who serves the king.
Count Ganelon   is thus a traitor proved;
His oath to you   was broken and betrayed.   3830
And so I judge   that he should hang and die,
And that his body   be treated as befits
A criminal   who's guilty of a crime.
If he has kinsmen   who'd argue this with me,
I'll use this sword   girded here at my side
To give my judgment   a prompt and sure defense."[61]
The Franks reply,   "Your argument makes sense."

CCLXXVIII

Now Pinabel   stands up before the king;
He's tall and strong,   valiant and very swift:
The man he strikes   won't see another day.   3840
He says to Charles,   "Sire, you convoked this trial;
Pray, then, keep order—   let's not have so much noise.
And as for Thierry,   his judgment has been heard.
I say he's wrong—   now let him come and fight."
His right-hand glove   he offers to the king.[62]

---

[60] "The point is that Thierry will really need God's help if he is to prevail against Pinabel; thus the case will be better proved. And when he does win, the Franks immediately shout, 'A holy miracle!' (3931)."—Translator's note.

[61] Technically, Thierry is defending a minority verdict of the jury; Pinabel, his opponent, will defend the majority verdict just rendered. In trials by combat, it was believed, the victory or defeat of the combatants demonstrated God's own judgment.

[62] The offering of the glove symbolizes the surrender to Charles of the combatant's feudal estate if he should be killed.

The emperor says,   "I ask for hostages."[63]
His thirty kinsmen   will sponsor Pinabel.
Says Charlemagne,   "He's free then, in your place."
They will be guarded   till justice ends the case.   AOI

CCLXXIX

When Thierry sees   that Pinabel will fight,   3850
He gives his glove,   the right one, to the king,
And Charlemagne,   his hostage, sets him free.
Charles has four benches   arranged to mark the field;
Those who will fight   go out to take their seats.
All think the challenge   well given, rightly met;
Ogier explains   how they are to proceed.
Horses and arms   are sent for with all speed.

CCLXXX

The knights are ready   to meet for their ordeal.   AOI
They've made confession,   have been absolved and blessed,
They've heard a mass,   taken communion too;   3860
Great offerings   they've given to the church.
Now when the champions   appear before the king,
They both are wearing   sharp spurs upon their feet,
They've put on hauberks,   shining and light and strong,
Their burnished helmets   are closed around their heads,
They gird on swords   whose hilts are of pure gold.
Around their necks   they hang their quartered shields,
Their right hands grasp   the long sharp-pointed spears.
Now they have mounted   war-horses bred for speed.
Seeing them go,   a hundred thousand knights   3870
Remember Roland   and weep for Thierry—
For God knows what   the end of this will be!

CCLXXXI

In a broad meadow   below Aix la Chapelle,
The barons meet;   their battle has begun.
Both are courageous,   both of them valiant lords,
And their war-horses   are spirited and swift.
They spur them hard,   and loosening the reins,
They charge each other   and strike with all their might.
Both shields are shattered—   they're broken into bits—
The hauberks break,   the girths are split apart,   3880
The saddles fall,   and with them both the knights.
A hundred thousand   are weeping at the sight.

CCLXXXII

Both chevaliers   have fallen to the ground.   AOI
Losing no time,   they're on their feet again.

---

[63] Hostages are kept to guarantee that the combatant will appear for the duel.

Agile and swift   is Pinabel, and strong;
They face each other—   they have no horses now—
And raise their swords   whose hilts are made of gold
To strike and hew   each other's shining helms;
Those heavy blows   can cut right through the steel.
The French lament,   thinking their man must fail.   3890
"O God," says Charles,   "now let the right prevail!"

                    CCLXXXIII
Says Pinabel,   "Thierry, admit you've lost!
I'll be your vassal   in loyalty and love,
All I possess   shall be at your command—
But reconcile   the king and Ganelon."
Then Thierry answers,   "That's easy to decide!
I'll take no offer   unworthy of a knight!
Let God determine   which one of us is right!"   AOI

                    CCLXXXIV
And Thierry says,   "Pinabel, you are brave;
You're tall and strong,   your body is well built,   3900
That you are valiant   is known to all your peers.
This is a battle   you can afford to lose!
I'll make your peace   with Charlemagne the king,
But Ganelon   must get what he deserves—
No day will pass   without his death retold."
Says Pinabel,   "Almighty God forbid!
I stand here now   for all my family—
I won't surrender   to any man on earth!
Better to die   than live to merit blame."
So once again   they slash with their great swords,   3910
Striking the helmets   brilliant with gold and jewels—
Great fiery sparks   fly out against the sky.
Now neither champion   will to the other yield
Until a dead man   is lying on the field.   AOI

                    CCLXXXV
He's a strong fighter,   Pinabel of Sorence,
The blow he strikes   on Thierry's burnished helm
Sends out such sparks   the grass is set on fire.
Then he springs forward,   the point of his steel blade
Cutting right through   from Thierry's forehead down;
Along his face   the sword point slashes deep,   3920
And blood springs out   all over his right cheek;
Down to his waist   the hauberk links all tear—
Without God's help,   he'd have died then and there!   AOI

                    CCLXXXVI
When Thierry sees   he's wounded in the face,
His bright blood falling   over the meadow grass,
Pinabel's helmet   of burnished steel he strikes:

Down through the nose-piece   it cracks and splits in two,
His skull is broken   and spills the brains inside;
With one last flourish   Thierry has felled him dead—
With that great blow   he's master of the field.   3930
The Frenchmen shout,   "A holy miracle!
Justice demands   that Ganelon must die,
With all the kinsmen   who came and took his side."   AOI

CCLXXXIX

They all agree: Bavarians, Alemans,   3960
Poitevins, Bretons,   and men from Normandy,
And first of all   the Franks who come from France,
That Ganelon   should die most horribly.
And so they order   four war-horses[64] brought out
To which they tie   Ganelon's feet and hands.
These are proud chargers,   spirited, bred for speed:
Four servants urge them   the way they ought to go.
There where a river   across a meadow flows,
Count Ganelon   is utterly destroyed:
His ligaments   are twisted and stretched out,   3970
His every limb   is cracked and splits apart;
On the green grass   the bright blood runs in streams.
So Ganelon   as a foul traitor died.
Let no man's treason   give comfort to his pride!

CCXC

The Emperor Charles,   his vengeance being done,
Summoned his bishops,   the ones who came from France,
Bavarians   and Alemans as well:
"A noble captive   is dwelling in this house;
She's heard such sermons   and edifying tales,
She trusts in God,   and wants to take the Faith.   3980
Baptize her now,   that God may have her soul."
The bishops answer,   "Let godmothers be found!"[65]

*   *   *

A great assembly   was gathered at the baths
To see the Queen of Spain   receive the Faith.
To Juliana   they now have changed her name.
She had true knowledge   when Christian she became.

CCXCI

The Emperor Charles,   once Justice has been done,
And his great anger   is finally appeased,   3990
Has Bramimonde   baptized into the Faith.
The day is over,   and in the dark of night
The king lies sleeping   in his high vaulted room.

---

[64] The execution by quartering contradicts earlier statements that Ganelon was to be hanged.
[65] The following line, indicated here by the spaced asterisks, is defective in the manuscript. It apparently described the godmothers.

Saint Gabriel is sent by God to say:
"Charlemagne, summon your empire's mighty hosts!
You'll march in force into the land of Bire;
You must relieve King Vivien at Imphe[66]
Where pagans hold his city under siege,
And Christian voices are crying for your help."
The Emperor Charles has no desire to go.
"God!" says the king, "how weary is my life!"   4000
He pulls his beard, the tears flow from his eyes.
Here ends the poem, for Turoldus declines.[67]

---

[66] "Nothing is known of Bire, Imphe, or Vivien except that they were all Christian."—Translator's note.

[67] "The ending of the poem, *Ci falt la geste que Turoldus declinet*, is very famous for being so enigmatic. *Que* may mean either 'which' or 'because' (Jenkins); *declinet* may mean 'to compose, sing, recite, or copy.' It may also mean to 'set,' as the sun sets, or to become infirm. While it is true that my version favors the idea of the poet's explaining why he does not continue his work with Charlemagne's new expedition, the reason for this disinclination is left as imprecise as possible. I hoped mainly to let the poem end with the same frustrating vagueness as does the original."—Translator's note.

Andreas Capellanus

(Late Twelfth Century)

Who invented romantic love, and when? The question is not as flippant as it sounds. It may seem absurd to claim that so elemental a part of human experience as romantic love—the "falling in love" experience depicted in countless thousands of novels, plays, movies, operas, and lyric poems—has existed for only eight centuries or so. But not a few people do believe just that, or something very close to it. No single person invented romantic love, the argument runs, but it evolved so rapidly from virtual nonexistence to full-blown human reality that, like the piano or automobile or airplane, it is better understood as an invention than as a product of long and gradual evolution. The phenomenon of romantic love, it is claimed, originated in the eleventh century and reached its first maturity in the latter half of the twelfth, in the form of "courtly love." (The term was coined by Gaston Paris in a landmark study he published in 1883.)

The argument we are considering does not merely credit courtly love with devising the *conventions* by which romantic love is expressed. We are talking not about manners of expressing romantic love but about the genesis of the thing itself. The enduring romantic conventions are better credited to the fourteenth-century poet Petrarch. Nor are we talking about sexual desire as such, which obviously goes back more than eight centuries. Courtly love is romantic and modern—as distinguished from classical and ancient—in its blending of physical desire with extravagant idealization. The upshot is a new kind of experience, of spiritual intoxication, a life-transforming conversion. It is analogous to religious conversion, in that one's very self seems remade, along with one's values and, often, one's response to the entire surrounding world. In his *Defence of Poetry* (1820), Percy Bysshe Shelley, the nineteenth-century Romantic poet, thus describes the revolution in values achieved by the medieval *troubadours* and their followers: "The freedom of women [compared, that is, with their status in antiquity] produced the poetry of sexual love. Love became a religion, the idols of whose worship were ever present. It was as if the statues of Apollo and the Muses had been endowed with life and motion, and had walked forth among their worshippers; so that earth became peopled by the inhabitants of a diviner world. The familiar appearance and proceedings of life became wonderful and heavenly, and a paradise was created as out of the wrecks of Eden." It would be hard to apply these sentiments and this tone to anything we know about antiquity or the early Middle Ages—except perhaps some passages of Plato and a poem or two by Sappho.

The work that best focuses this new model of romantic passion is *The Art of Courtly Love*, a Latin work by Andreas Capellanus ("Andreas the Chaplain"), written around 1185. Except what his book itself tells us (and that may not always be reliable), we know almost nothing about him. He was apparently a cleric, though hardly an ascetic or even a very pious one (he boasts at one point that the clergy are the best lovers and teases us about a near-affair of his with a nun). He was at best moderately learned. Indeed, if a great work is necessarily a product of genius, *The Art of Courtly Love* must fail the test, for Andreas was no genius. That fact, however, and our virtual ignorance of his life, are probably no great loss, since he is very probably writing up the ideas of the far more interesting people who commissioned his book and, in all likelihood, supplied its distinctive content. To see who they were, and what that distinctive content is, let us first drop back a century or so.

How courtly love developed is a controversial subject, but it apparently grew out of roots in eleventh-century Spain—a period when the bitter divisions between Islam and Christianity were in abeyance. Spanish Islamic literature of the period combined sensuality with a rather otherworldly Platonism. The mode spread to Provence in southeastern France, where it was further developed by the *troubadours,* wandering minstrels who specialized in love poetry, usually in the vernacular language rather than in Latin. One of the first of these *troubadour* poets was Duke William of Aquitaine, who in some of his later poems incorporated elements of the courtly love mode. But this mode had to wait for its full fruition until it became the credo of William's granddaughter, Eleanor of Aquitaine (1122–1204), one of the most spectacular and influential personalities of the medieval period. It was she, along with her daughters, who introduced courtly love to northern France and other parts of Europe.

Eleanor, Duchess of Aquitaine in her own right, and renowned for her beauty, intelligence, energy, and capacity for intrigue, was queen successively of both France and England. Married at the age of fifteen to Prince Louis (soon thereafter King Louis VII) of France, she came to play an active part in national affairs; among other things, she accompanied the king on the Second Crusade. Their marriage was annulled in 1152, officially because of an impediment of blood kinship but really because the royal spouses were incompatible. (For one thing, Louis doubted Eleanor's sexual fidelity.) Two years later, still only thirty-two years old, she married Henry of Anjou, another man who wasted no time in succeeding to a crown, as Henry II of England.

Once more, the marriage was a tempestuous one; indeed, Eleanor spent part of Henry's reign locked in a tower.

Eleanor's literary tastes and social ideas were passed on to her children, most notably to two daughters whom she had borne to Louis VII: Alix, who married Count Thibaut of Blois; and Marie, who married Count Henry of Champagne. Of the two, Marie was the more influential; the great French writer Chrétien de Troyes was one of her court poets and sometimes wrote works virtually at her dictate. It was also Marie, it would seem, who commissioned Andreas Capellanus to write *The Art of Courtly Love* and, very probably, she who provided him with many of the book's distinctive ideas about love.

These ideas emerge in Andreas's treatise as a complete system of love relationships, codified in sets of rules purportedly handed down by the god of love himself. The prime fact is the sovereignty of the lady, whose male lover stands in relation to her as a feudal vassal does to his master. Moreover, although Andreas organizes a key section of the book along lines specifying the relative social classes of the respective lovers, he presents love as essentially a leveling social force that can exist between any man and woman. Love is irresistible, or at any rate something it is perverse and dangerous to resist; the punishments suffered by the unloving in the hereafter anticipate the punishments in Dante's Hell. Jealousy is not only an inevitable side effect of love but almost its proper food. Love is enhanced by insecurity, elusiveness, difficulty, unattainability. Its spice is secrecy.

Love is also an ennobling experience, instilling every virtue into the lovers, especially the male one. The emotion is felt and expressed in heavily religious terms, which seem more than mere metaphor, as though to love were an imperative issued by God Himself, not just by a quasi-pagan god of love. This divine sanction is all the more startling in light of the firm and repeated assertion in Andreas's book that true love, properly defined, is never found in marriage, and his strong implication that adulterous love is the preferred norm. Like Ovid, who was especially popular in the twelfth century and strongly influenced him, Andreas envisages love as a fine art or craft that must be learned, under expert instruction such as one cannot get except from an adept—such as a lady who, being married, is no longer a mere novice herself. It goes without saying that, in Andreas, the Ovidian tone of flippant worldliness is entirely transformed, into devotional veneration.

That love and marriage are incompatible is the most lurid of the doctrines in *The Art of Courtly Love*. The notion may arise in part from the circumstances of a society wherein arranged marriages of pragmatic convenience were common, especially among the higher aristocracy. But the idea probably goes deeper, into the psychology that sees in romantic love something dangerous and adventurous (which seems true enough)—not to mention the recognized allure of the forbidden. And the fact remains that, however inoffensive their morality, hardly any love stories with a happy ending, from any era, follow the successful lovers across the bridge from successful wooing to the married state. Authors of love stories seem to recognize that romantic and married love, though both may be excellent, are not the same thing.

Even stranger to readers today will be the formality, even pedantry, of the dialogues between Andreas's maneuvering lovers. They split hairs, question definitions, assess the soundness of argumentative logic, make learned distinctions, and in other ways often sound more like members of debating teams than people buffeted by the winds of passion. They may claim to be so buffeted, even to be at the brink of death, but neither their logic nor their syntax seems the worse for that. But it is probably wrong to read these dialogues as realistic dialogue; rather, they are vehicles of instruction, aimed more at the reader than at the dramatic addressee. The methods are those of debating Schoolmen. We must remember too that courtly love amounts to a kind of pun. Its main meaning is "love conducted according to the manners of courtesy," but the idea of law courts is never far off. Briefs are drawn up; appeals are filed; precedents are set that govern by *stare decisis*. Much of the challenge for us in reading Andreas is to filter out these local, time-bound curiosities from the ideas that still govern in our culture and our lives.

FURTHER READING *(prepared by B. W.):* A classic, sometimes disputed, but still standard treatment of courtly love is C. S. Lewis, *The Allegory of Love: A Study In Medieval Tradition*, 1936. A parallel classic is Denis de Rougemont, *Love in the Western World*, rev. ed., trans. Montgomery Belgion, 1956. De Rougemont also includes a discussion of courtly love in his article "Love" in the *Dictionary of the History of Ideas*, 5 vols., ed. Philip P. Wiener, 1973. The introduction to John Jay Parry's translation *The Art of Courtly Love*, 1941, repr. 1990, conveys succinctly much general information about Andreas and about courtly love. Good scholarly treatments of Andreas include Barbara Marie Gaffney, *Andreas Capellanus and the Myth of Courtly Love*, 1977; and the section on Andreas in Peter L. Allen, *The Art of Love: Amatory Fiction from Ovid to the Romance of the Rose*, 1992. M. C. D'Arcy, *The Mind and Heart of Love*, 1947, is an excellent and readable study of the religious and philosophical implications of love. For illuminating treatments of Provençal and/or troubadour poetry, see Peter Dronke, *The Medieval Lyric*, 2nd ed., 1977; Frederick Goldin, *Lyrics of the Troubadours and Trouvères: An Anthology and History*, 1973; and L. T. Topsfield, *Troubadours and Love*, 1975. Good accounts of Eleanor of Aquitaine include Desmond Seward, *Eleanor of Aquitaine*, 1986; and William W. Kibler. *Eleanor of Aquitaine: Patron and Politician*, 1976. Other works on the subject of romantic love, though not on Andreas, are Dorothy Tennov, *Love and Limerence*, 1979, which provides a lively and incisive case-study approach (*limerence* being a coinage by the author designating romantic love); and Francesco Alberoni, *Falling In Love*, trans. Lawrence Venuti, 1983, which argues among other things that romantic love is, very literally, a revolutionary experience.

from *THE ART OF COURTLY LOVE*

Translated by John Jay Parry

from BOOK ONE

INTRODUCTION TO THE TREATISE ON LOVE

CHAPTER I. WHAT LOVE IS

Love is a certain inborn suffering derived from the sight of and excessive meditation upon the beauty of the opposite sex, which causes each one to wish above all things the embraces of the other and by common desire to carry out all of love's precepts in the other's embrace.

That love is suffering is easy to see, for before the love becomes equally balanced on both sides there is no torment greater, since the lover is always in fear that his love may not gain its desire and that he is wasting his efforts. He fears, too, that rumors of it may get abroad, and he fears everything that might harm it in any way, for before things are perfected a slight disturbance often spoils them. If he is a poor man, he also fears that the woman may scorn his poverty; if he is ugly, he fears that she may despise his lack of beauty or may give her love to a more handsome man; if he is rich, he fears that his parsimony in the past may stand in his way. To tell the truth, no one can number the fears of one single lover. This kind of love, then, is a suffering which is felt by only one of the persons and may be called "single love." But even after both are in love the fears that arise are just as great, for each of the lovers fears that what he has acquired with so much effort may be lost through the effort of someone else, which is certainly much worse for a man than if, having no hope, he sees that his efforts are accomplishing nothing, for it is worse to lose the things you are seeking than to be deprived of a gain you merely hope for. The lover fears, too, that he may offend his loved one in some way; indeed he fears so many things that it would be difficult to tell them.

That this suffering is inborn I shall show you clearly, because if you will look at the truth and distinguish carefully you will see that it does not arise out of any action; only from the reflection of the mind upon what it sees does this suffering come. For when a man sees some woman fit for love and shaped according to his taste, he begins at once to lust after her in his heart; then the more he thinks about her the more he burns with love, until he comes to a fuller meditation. Presently he begins to think about the fashioning of the woman and to differentiate her limbs, to think about what she does, and to pry into the secrets of her body, and he desires to put each part of it to the fullest use. Then after he has come to this complete meditation, love cannot hold the reins, but he proceeds at once to action; straightway he strives to get a helper and to find an intermediary. He begins to plan how he may find favor with her, and he begins to seek a place and a time opportune for talking; he looks upon a brief hour as a very long year, because he cannot do anything fast enough to suit his eager mind. It is well known that many things happen to him in this manner. This inborn suffering comes, therefore, from seeing and meditating. Not every kind of meditation can be the cause of love, an exessive one is required; for a restrained thought does not, as a rule, return to the mind, and so love cannot arise from it.

CHAPTER IV. WHAT THE EFFECT OF LOVE IS

Now it is the effect of love that a true lover cannot be degraded with any avarice. Love causes a rough and uncouth man to be distinguished for his handsomeness; it can endow a man even of the humblest birth with nobility of character; it blesses the proud with humility; and the man in love becomes accustomed to performing many services gracefully for everyone. O what a wonderful thing is love, which makes a man shine with so many virtues and teaches everyone, no matter who he is, so many good traits of character! There is another thing about love that we should not praise in few words: it adorns a man, so to speak, with the virtue of chastity, because he who shines with the light of one love can hardly think of embracing another woman, even a beautiful one. For when he thinks deeply of his beloved the sight of any other woman seems to his mind rough and rude. . . .

CHAPTER VI. IN WHAT MANNER LOVE MAY BE ACQUIRED, AND IN HOW MANY WAYS

FIFTH DIALOGUE
A nobleman speaks with a noblewoman

If any nobleman seeks the love of a noblewoman, let him try to attract her with these words. After he has got the conversation started, he should open his heart in this fashion:

"So much nobility is apparent in you, and you are distinguished by so much courtesy, that I believe in the presence of Your Prudence I may without fear of censure say all those things that are lying in my heart waiting to be said. For if men were not permitted to reveal to ladies, when they wished, the secrets of their hearts, then love, which men say is the fountain head and source of all good things, would already have perished utterly, and no man would be able to help another, and all works of courtesy would be unknown to mankind."

The woman says: "You are right, and it pleases me greatly to hear you say it."

The man says: "Although in the flesh I rarely come into your presence, in heart and in spirit I never depart from it, for the continual thought which I have of you makes me present with you very often and makes me see constantly with the eyes of the heart that treasure about which all my attention turns, and it brings me both pains and many solaces. For what a man desires with all his heart he is always afraid some unfavorable happening may interfere with. How faithful I am to you and with what devotion I am drawn to you no words of mine can tell. For it seems that if the fidelities of every living soul could be gathered together in a single person, the total would not be so great, by far, as the faith that prompts me to serve you, and there is nothing so unalterable in my heart as the intention of serving your glory; that would be glorious to me beyond all else, and I would consider it a great victory if I could do anything that would be pleasing to you and remain acceptable to Your Grace. Therefore, while I can see you no pain can touch me, nobody's plottings can disturb me, just the bare sight of the places which you seem to inhabit, when reflected in the air, provides me with powerful incentives for living and with many solaces for a lover. But when I cannot see you with my bodily eye or breathe the air about you, all the elements round about begin to rise up against me, and all kinds of torments begin to afflict me, and I can find no pleasure in any solaces except those deceitful visions that the drowsiness of slumber brings before me when I am asleep. But although sleep deceives me at times with a false gift, yet I am exceedingly grateful to him because he did see fit to deceive me with such a sweet and noble misrepresentation. For this drowsy gift furnishes me a way and a means for keeping alive and preserves me from the wrath of death; this seems to me a very great and special boon, for there is no use giving medicine to a dead man. But so long as I retain life, even though it may be a painful one, the light air can drench me with a shower of release or cover me with the waters of gladness. For I believe and have firm confidence that such a noble and worthy woman will not long permit me to endure such heavy pains, but will raise me up out of all my difficulties."

The woman says: "Truly in your person good sense has been ennobled and gentle words have found a home, since you can so thoughtfully and so prudently put forward your claims. I am properly grateful that you desire to think of me when I am absent and are determined to be of service to me in every way you can, and I, too, for my part will gladly think of you when you are absent, and I shall not refuse to accept your services at the proper time and place, since you are so great and so eminent a man of worth that it would be considered no honor to any woman to refuse them. Nay more, I do not wish you to be content with merely looking at the air, but you can have sight of me with your corporeal vision and look into my face. For I would rather exert myself to give you directions for keeping alive than offer you cause for death or incur the crime of homicide."

The man says: "Although in summertime the life of the crops may be prolonged by light showers, they are not saved from the danger of drying up unless they are drenched with rain. You can, in the way you mention, prolong the life of your lover, but cannot free him from serious danger of death. For a relapse seems more serious than the original disease and makes a man die a harder death, and it is worse to do without what we have been given some hope of attaining than that the wish alone prompts us to hope for. Therefore I would rather perish instantly than suffer the perils of death after many agonies. Therefore let Your Prudence consider and examine carefully which seems more to your credit—to give hope to a lover and so save him from the wrath of death and open up to him the road, which he does not know, to all good deeds, or by denying him this hope to close the road to all good deeds and open up the way of death."

The woman says: "Such aid as I can offer you—that is, that you may see me daily with your bodily eye—I have promised you freely, but what you are asking for you can never obtain by any amount of prayers or efforts, for I am firmly resolved with all my heart never to subject myself to the servitude of Venus or endure the torments of lovers. No one can know, unless he has experienced them, how many troubles lovers undergo, for they are exposed to so many pains and wearinesses that no one could learn them except from experience. But although I shall try by every means to avoid falling into Love's snares, I shall never refuse to you, or to any other man who wishes to serve me, the favor of doing so."

The man says: "My lady, God forbid that you should persist in this terrible error, for only those women who are known to have joined Love's army are considered worthy of true praise among men and deserve to be mentioned for their worth in the courts of all rulers. What good in the world it does to have anyone do any good deeds unless they take their origin from love I cannot see. Therefore let such beauty and such worth of character as yours tread the paths of love and try its fortunes, for neither the nature nor the character of a thing can be truthfully understood until it has been tried. Only after you have tried it is it proper for you to reject it."

The woman says: "Men find it easy enough to get into Love's court, but difficult to stay there, because of the pains that threaten lovers, while to get out is, because of the desirable acts of love, impossible or nearly so. For after a lover has really entered into the court of Love he has no will either to do or not to do anything except what Love's table sets before him or what may be pleasing to the other lover. Therefore we ought not seek a court of this kind, for one should by all means avoid entering a place which he cannot freely leave. Such a place may be compared to the court of hell, for although the door of hell stands open for all who wish to enter, there is no way of getting out after you are once in. I would rather, therefore, stay in France and be content with a few coppers and have freedom to go where I would, than to be subject to a foreign power, even though I were loaded down with Hungarian silver,[1] because to have so much is to have nothing. I have therefore good reason to hate the palace of Love, so you must look elsewhere for love, brother."

The man says: "No one can have a freer choice than not to wish to be separated from that which he desires with all his heart, for anybody ought to be pleased if he cannot help wishing what he desires with all his might, provided only that the thing is one that may be desired. But one can find nothing in the world more desirable than love, since from it comes the doing of every good thing and without it no one would do anything good in the world. It seems, therefore, that you ought to embrace Love's court with both arms, and his palace should not be at all hateful to you."

The woman says: "To fight under Love's protection may seem to anybody else liberty and a thing to lay hold of, but to me it seems the worst kind of servitude, a thing to be avoided at all costs. You are therefore laboring in vain, since the whole world could not move me from my position."

The man says: "If you choose to walk that path, unbearable torments will follow you, the like of which cannot be found and which it would be difficult to tell about."

The woman says. "I pray you tell me what these torments are which seem to threaten me because of this, so that if I foresee them they may hurt me less, since men say if you see an arrow commg, it doesn't strike so deep."

---

[1] This reference helps to date the present work; in 1185 or 1186 King Béla of Hungary married Marguerite, daughter of King Louis VII by his second wife and thus half-sister of the Countess Marie, who was Andreas's patron. Before the wedding King Béla had provided a detailed account of his annual revenues.

The man says: "If you saw these coming a long way off, they would strike you just as deep—unless you take care to rid yourself of this error we have been speaking of. Nevertheless, if you wish, you may hear about these torments. But first I wish to beg Your Grace to be so good as to tell me what place in Love's palace is reserved for you.

"Now men say, and it is true, that in the middle of the world there is built a palace with four very splendid façades, and in each of these is a marvellously beautiful door. The only people entitled to live in this palace are Love and certain communities of ladies. The eastern gate the God of Love has reserved for himself alone, but the other three are assigned to three definite classes of ladies. The ladies at the southern gate always linger around the open door, and you can always find them at the entrance. The ladies at the western gate do the same, except that you can always find them roaming around outside the entrance. But those who have been assigned to the care of the northern gate always keep the door shut and never look at anything outside the palace walls. With which of these groups do you say that you keep company?"

The woman says: "These things are too obscure for me, and your words are too allegorical; you will have to explain what you mean."

The man says: "Those who always linger around the open gate and are always to be found at the entrance are those women and ladies who, when anybody asks for admittance, learn by diligent inquiry what he deserves who seeks to come in by the open door and how good a character he has; and after they are fully convinced of a man's worth they admit the worthy ones with all honor, but drive the unworthy ones away from Love's palace. Those who claim the place at the western gate are those common women who never refuse any man, but admit everybody without distinction and are subject to the passions of everyone. But those who have the watch in the north and always keep their doors closed are those women who never open to anybody who knocks, but deny to everyone an entrance into Love's palace. Those at the south, then, are those women who wish to love and do not reject worthy lovers; this is proper since, being all in the south, they are worthy to be illumined by a ray from Love himself who lives in the east. Those of the west are loose women who seldom love anybody and are never loved by any good man; this is proper because, since their dwelling is in the west, the fiery ray of Love cannot reach to them from the east. Those of the north are those who refuse to love, although they may be loved by many; and this is proper, too, since the god has no consideration for those placed upon his left hand, because they are cursed.[2] Now from what I have said the arrangement of the palace of Love is clear."

The woman says: "Within the northern gate I maintain that I will be safe, not cursed."

---

[2] The allusion is to Matthew 25:41. Matthew 25:31–46 describes the Last Judgment, with the saved at God's right hand, the damned at His left.

The man says: "Listen, then, to the endless torments that are prepared for you.

"While I was attending as squire upon my lord, a certain very noble Robert,[3] on one very hot summer day I was riding with him and many other noble knights through the royal forest of France, and the woodland path led us to a most pleasant and delightful place. It was a grassy spot, surrounded on all sides by the trees of the forest. Here we all dismounted and turned our horses loose to graze; then after we had refreshed ourselves with a little nap we roused up and quickly saddled the wandering horses. But as my own horse had wandered a little farther in the pasture than the others, getting him ready took me so long that I found myself left alone in the glade. Not knowing the way, I was wandering around at a loss and looking carefully in all directions, when I spied an infinite number of mounted folk riding along at a walk near the edge of the wood. Believing firmly that my lord was riding among them, I was very glad and tried as hard as I could to ride up to them. But although I looked carefully I could not see him, since he was not among them. As I drew near and looked more carefully at the handsome throng, I saw a man riding in front of them, seated on a very beautiful horse, well worth looking at, and crowned with a golden diadem. Close after him followed a large and charming band of women, each of whom was mounted on a fair, fat horse with a gentle gait. Each woman was dressed in costly, many-colored garments with a gold-embroidered cloak and was accompanied by knights, one on the right hand and another on the left, while a third walked before her like a servant, holding her bridle in his hand all the time so that she rode gently forward on her horse without the least annoyance. Such was the dress and such the manner of riding of each woman in the first group. After them followed an unnumbered host of finely dressed knights who kept them from the clattering of those who followed them and from being annoyed by these people. Next to these there came a great multitude of women with various kinds of men, on foot and on horseback, pressing forward to serve them; but so great was the clatter of those who wished to be of service and so annoying was the crowd, that the women could not accept any services, nor could those who were ready to serve do so conveniently; and so the multitude of servants resulted in a great lack and deficiency of service, and the women would have considered it a great comfort, indeed, if they had been left to serve themselves.

"Then in the third group there followed a mean and abject troop of women. They were certainly very beautiful, but they were dressed in the most filthy clothes, wholly unsuited to the weather, for although they were in the burning heat of summer, they wore unwillingly garments of fox skins; besides that, they were very dirty and rode unbecomingly upon unsightly horses—that is, very lean ones that trotted heavily and had neither saddles nor bridles and went along with halting steps. No one tried to aid these women, who were without assistance from anyone, and besides, those on horseback and on foot who had gone ahead of them stirred up such a cloud of dust with their feet that the women could barely see each other, because the dust filled their eyes and clogged their lips.

---

[3] This could be any of several Roberts, including one who was uncle to Countess Marie and another, his son, who was her cousin.

"When I had carefully observed all these people and had commenced to wonder greatly what it all meant, a lady with a calm, dignified face, who after all the others had gone by followed them on a very thin and dirty horse that halted[4] on three feet, called me by name and bade me come to her. When I approached and saw her charming and beautiful face and that she was sitting on such a dirty horse, I at once offered her mine. But she declined it and said to me, 'You are looking for your lord, but you cannot find him here, because you have wandered rather far from his course.'

"I answered, 'My lady, I beg you, please deign to show me the right way,' to which she replied, 'Until you have seen these troops established in their own camps I cannot show you a safe road.' Then I replied, 'Then I ask you to explain to me, if you will, whose army this is that I see, and why so beautiful a woman has chosen to ride such a common horse and to wear such mean clothes.'

"To this the woman replied, 'This army which you see is that of the dead.' When I heard that, my soul was immediately troubled beyond measure, and my color changed, and all my bones began to loosen in their joints. Trembling and greatly terrified, I would gladly have left the company, but she began at once to speak comforting words to me and promised to keep me unharmed from every peril. She said, 'You will be safer and more secure here than in your father's house.' When I heard this I regained the quickening[5] spirit I had nearly lost, and, coming closer to her, I began to ask diligently about all these things. She answered all my questions in order, saying,

"'That knight whom you see crowned with a golden diadem, going before all the people, is the God of Love, who joins this army one day in every week, and in a marvellous fashion gives to each one his deserts, according as he has done good or evil in life. And those women, so beautiful and so honored, who follow after him in the first rank, are those most blessed of women who while they were alive knew how to conduct themselves wisely toward the soldiers of love, to show every favor to those who wished to love, and to give appropriate answers to those who under pretense of love sought love falsely; for this reason these women now have their full reward and are honored with inumerable gifts. Those women who follow in the second group and are so pestered by the services of so many men are those shameless women who while they lived did not fear to subject themselves to the pleasure of every man, but assented to the lust of any man who asked them and denied entrance within their gates to no man who sought it. And in this court they have earned this kind of reward. In return for their excessive giving of themselves and their indiscriminate acceptance of men they are unceasingly wearied by the indiscriminate services of innumerable people, and for them such services are converted into their harmful opposites and cause them great annoyance and shame. Then those women who follow in the last group, so meanly equipped, going along with downcast faces, without help from anybody and wearied by discomforts of all kinds, as you can plainly see with your own eyes (in which group I find a place), are those most wretched of all women who while they lived closed the palace of Love to all who wished to enter it and would not give a fitting answer to any man who did good deeds or who asked of them a cause and approval of well-doing; they rejected all who asked

---

[4]Limped.   [5]Life-giving.

to serve in Love's army and drove them away just as though they hated them, not at all considering what sort of person is this God of Love whom those who were asking for love sought to serve. So now we suffer these well-deserved punishments and receive from the King of Love, through whom the whole world is ruled and without whom no one does anything good in this world, payment appropriate to our sins. We are, besides these, subjected to so many other kinds of punishments which no one could know about unless he learned by experience, that it would be impossible for me to tell you about them and very difficult for you to listen to the account. Therefore let those women who are still living in the world take care lest they join us in these torments, since after they are dead no penance can be of any use to them.'

"I answered the woman, 'As I see and understand it, he who has chosen to do the things well pleasing to Love shall receive his reward a hundred-fold, while the god cannot pass over the sin of one who has dared offend him, but, it seems to me, will avenge more than a thousandfold the crime committed against him. It is unsafe, therefore, to offend such a god, and it is safest to serve in all things him who can reward his own with such gifts and afflict with such heavy torments those who scorn him. Therefore, my lady, I ask and beseech you with all my might to give me permission to leave, so that I may tell the ladies what I have seen.'

"She answered, 'You may not have leave to go until you have learned of the heavier and harder torments that we suffer and have seen the greater joy and beatitude of the other ladies.'

"While we were talking thus we had gone a good distance and had come to a most delightful spot, where the meadows were very beautiful and more finely laid out than mortal had ever seen. The place was closed in on all sides by every kind of fruitful and fragrant trees, each bearing marvellous fruits according to its kind. It was also divided concentrically into three distinct parts. The first of these, the central one, was separated from the next part and surrounded on all sides by it, while the third, on the outside, was completely walled off from the first by the intervening part. Now in the middle of the first and innermost part stood a marvellously tall tree, bearing abundantly all sorts of fruits, and its branches extended as far as the edge of the interior part. At the roots of the tree gushed forth a wonderful spring of the clearest water, which to those who drank of it tasted of the sweetest nectar, and in this spring one saw all sorts of little fishes. Beside the spring, on a throne made of gold and every sort of precious stones, sat the Queen of Love, wearing a gorgeous crown on her head, dressed in very costly robes, and holding a golden scepter in her hand. At her right hand was prepared a seat that glowed with everything costly and bright, but no one was sitting on it. This section, the inner one, was called 'Delightfulness,' because in it every sort of pleasant and delightful thing was to be found. And in this inner part were prepared a great many couches, marvellously decorated and completely covered with silken coverlets and purple decorations. From the spring I have mentioned many brooks and rivulets flowed out in all directions, watering the whole of Delightfulness, and every couch had a rivulet by it.

"The second part was called 'Humidity' and was arranged in this fashion: the brooks which stayed within their channels and watered Delightfulness, in this second part grew too large and overflowed all of Humidity so that you could see grass mixed with water just as you can in the fields in the rainy days of spring. And the water, after it flowed into this section, became so cold that no living being could bear to touch it, while from above the sun poured down an intolerable heat, for there wasn't a single tree to shade the place. But the water did not extend beyond the bounds of this part.

"The third and last part was called 'Aridity,' and with good reason, for water was completely lacking, the whole place was arid, and the heat of the sun's rays was intense, almost like fire, and the surface of the earth was like the bottom of a heated oven. All about the place were innumerable bundles of thorns, each with a pole through the middle which stuck out a distance of two cubits[6] at each end, and at either end of the pole stood a very strong man, holding the end of the pole in his hands. But there was a very beautiful road passing through Aridity and Humidity, leading to Delightfulness, and in it no one of these discomforts was felt in the least.

"When we came to this place, the King of Love entered first; and the Queen of Love received him with an embrace, and with her help he sat down on the throne prepared for him, holding a crystalline scepter in his hand, and after him, by the same road, followed all the first band of women and knights. For each of the women there was prepared a most beautiful couch on which to sit, and the knights chose for themselves the seats they preferred. No human tongue could tell how great was the blessedness and the glory of these people, for the whole place of Delightfulness was appointed for their pleasure, and before them jugglers of every kind sported and sang, and men played all kinds of musical instruments there.

"Next, through the same road came the whole crowd of common women who had been following them, and the crowd of men who had been trying to serve these women. They came as far as the edge of Delightfulness, and when they could not pass beyond they began to slacken rein in Humidity and to find what comfort they could there, since this was the place appointed for them by the court of Love. And what noises and lamentings there were would be most difficult to tell! And the torments of these women were greatly increased by the glory which they saw of those who were in Delightfulness. Then, at the same place entered the third and last throng of women—those who would not have pity on the soldiers of Love—and they came as far as the edge of Humidity; but when they found no entrance, they commenced to spread out all through Aridity, since that was the place prepared for them from of old. And there was a seat on a bundle of thorns prepared for each of the women, and the men assigned to each, as I mentioned, kept shaking the bundle so that the women were very severely torn by the sharp thorns; and their bare feet rested on the burning ground. So great was the grief and suffering there that I believe the like is scarcely to be found among the infernal powers themselves.

"When I had seen these things I asked for permission to depart, and she said, 'I cannot give you permission, but leave your horse here and go quickly to the King of Love, along the way by which he entered, and ask permission of him as though he were your lord and pay careful attention to what he bids you do. And do not forget to intercede for me.' As soon as I had heard

---

[6]A cubit is about 20 inches.

this I took the designated road and came before the King of Love and said to him, 'Mighty and glorious king, I render you all gratitude for deigning to reveal to me your mighty works and the wondrous secrets of your realm. Therefore I pray unceasingly to Your Grace to deign to bid me, your servant, do those things that are pleasing to you, and to indicate truly what are the chief rules in love, and at my intercession graciously to free from the heavier punishments that woman through whose beneficence I have been blessed with a sight like this, and in your mercy to give her a place here in Delightfulness with those women whom I see here in such honor, and finally, if you please, to give me leave to depart.'

"To my request he answered, 'You have been permitted to see our mighty works that through you our glory may be revealed to those who know it not, and that this sight which you now see may be a means of salvation for many ladies. We therefore command and firmly enjoin upon you that wherever you find a lady of any worth departing from our pathway by refusing to submit herself to love's engagements, you shall take care to relate to her what you have seen here and shall cause her to leave her erroneous ideas so that she may escape such very heavy torments and find a place here in glory. Know, then, that the chief rules in love are these twelve that follow:

    I. Thou shalt avoid avarice like the deadly pestilence and shalt embrace its opposite.

   II. Thou shalt keep thyself chaste for the sake of her whom thou lovest.

  III. Thou shalt not knowingly strive to break up a correct love affair that someone else is engaged in.

  IV. Thou shalt not choose for thy love anyone whom a natural sense of shame forbids thee to marry.

   V. Be mindful completely to avoid falsehood.

  VI. Thou shalt not have many who know of thy love affair.

 VII. Being obedient in all things to the commands of ladies, thou shalt ever strive to ally thyself to the service of Love.

VIII. In giving and receiving love's solaces let modesty be ever present.

  IX. Thou shalt speak no evil.

   X. Thou shalt not be a revealer of love affairs.

  XI. Thou shalt be in all things polite and courteous.

 XII. In practicing the solaces of love thou shalt not exceed the desires of thy lover.

There are also other lesser precepts of love which it would not profit you to hear, since you can find them in the book written to Walter.[7]

"'As for that woman for whom you pleaded, she may not find a place here within the bounds of Delightfulness, as you ask, because her own deeds have made it impossible for her to remain in so glorious an abode. However, in answer to your plea we grant her a fat and gentle horse with a saddle and bridle and that she may have no attendants to shake her bundle of thorns; and with our permission she may have a cold stone under her feet. Take

---

[7] That is, in the present work, which is addressed to a young man named Walter, of uncertain identity and perhaps imaginary. Walter is a novice being instructed by Andreas in the lore of love.

now this crystalline staff, and with our grace depart; but throw the staff into the first stream you find.'

"I took my way back and returned to the lady who had led me there, and I found her sitting on a bundle without any attendants, resting her feet very comfortably upon a stone newly placed there, having a fat horse with fine trappings by her side, and feeling very little pain. She thanked me effusively and added, 'Depart now with the favor of heaven, my friend, since you may not see more of the affairs of this court. For the others have a glory and we a torment twice as great as those you see, but it is not granted to any living person to behold them.' When she had finished speaking I mounted my own horse, and in the twinkling of an eye I was led through the waters that surrounded the place. Into them I threw the crystalline staff and returned unharmed to my own home.

"Behold then, my lady, how great is the affliction of those who will not love—to what torments they are subjected, and what glory and honor those have earned who did not close the gates of Love to those who desired to enter—so that you may lay aside your erroneous opinion and be worthy to receive the rewards and to escape the torments I have told you about. For it would be unseemly and a desperate evil were a woman so wise and so beautiful as you to be subjected to such heavy torments or to endure so many perils. Now so far as you are concerned I am free from the task appointed me by Love; but you must be attentive and harken to his precepts that you may be worthy to enter into the glory of his beatitude."

The woman says: "If those things which you say are true, it is a glorious thing to take part in the services of Love and very dangerous to reject his mandates. But whether what you say is true or false, the story of these terrible punishments frightens me so that I do not wish to be a stranger to Love's service; but I would be reckoned among his fellowship and would find myself a dwelling at the southern gate. I must therefore follow in every respect the custom of the ladies at the southern gate and neither reject everybody nor admit everybody who knocks at Love's gate. I shall try, therefore, to find out who is worthy to enter, and having tried him and known him I shall receive him in good faith."

The man says: "I give thanks to the most mighty King of Love who has seen fit to change your intention and to banish your dire error. But your statement that you wish to consider whether I should be admitted when I cry at the door of Love's palace seems to me a bitter thing, and your word seems rather harsh; for if you have decided about the worth of my character, you can have no real cause for further deliberation. Yet since it is not easy for all a man's good deeds to become known to everybody, it may be that mine are unknown to you, and so perhaps in view of the state of your knowledge this time for consideration for which you ask would be reasonable. But I have so much confidence in the worthy things I have done and in the justice of Your Nobility, that although the gift I ask for may be delayed, I do not believe that services can long be deprived of their rewards. Therefore may God wish me to feel that my hope is bearing fruit, and may the Divine Power make you think of me when I leave, just as I shall retain in my absence the constant thought of you."

SEVENTH DIALOGUE
A man of the higher nobility speaks with a woman of the simple nobility

When a man of the higher nobility addresses a woman of the simple nobility, let him use the same speeches that a nobleman and a man of the higher nobility use with a woman of the middle class,[8] except that part dealing with the commendation of birth, and he must not boast very much of the fact that he is noble. In addition he might begin with this formula:

"I ought to give God greater thanks than any other living man in the whole world because it is now granted me to see with my eyes what my soul has desired above all else to see, and I believe that God has granted it to me because of my great longing and because He has seen fit to hear the prayers of my importunate supplication. For not an hour of the day or night could pass that I did not earnestly pray God to grant me the boon of seeing you near me in the flesh. It is no wonder that I was driven by so great an impulse to see you and was tormented by so great a desire, since the whole world extols your virtue and your wisdom, and in the farthest parts of the world courts are fed upon the tale of your goodness just as though it were a sort of tangible food. And now I know in very truth that a human tongue is not able to tell the tale of your beauty and your prudence or a human mind to imagine it. And so the mighty desire, which I already had, of seeing you and serving you has greatly increased and will increase still more, because it is perfectly clear and manifest to me that merely to serve you is to reign over everything in this life and that without this no man in the world can do anything worthy of praise. Indeed I pray to God in heaven that of His grace He grant me only that I may always do what is wholly pleasing to Your Excellency, for if I do, no adversity can trouble me or evil chance of fortune embarrass me. And I wish ever to dedicate to your praise all the good deeds that I do and to serve your reputation in every way. For whatever good I may do, you may know that it is done with you in mind and with the constant thought of you."

The woman says: "I am bound to give you many thanks for lauding me with such commendations and exalting me with such high praise. You should know that because of all this your coming gives me joy and your presence is pleasing enough to me, since you tell me that being able to see me in the flesh is a sovereign remedy to you. I am happy, too, if I may be found worthy of such great blessedness as to be the cause or occasion of well-doing by you or any other men. But I want to warn you of one thing in particular: you must never praise anyone so highly that you may afterward be ashamed to qualify this praise by a word of disparagement, and you must not disparage anyone so much that you cannot afterward praise him without shame. Furthermore, you must never praise one woman so effusively that what you say detracts from the worth of any other woman. But saying that merely to be of service to me is to reign in this life seems to be an insult to all other ladies, to serve whom may perhaps be as praiseworthy as to serve me, or even more so. It would not be proper for you to refuse your services to any woman, because, it seems clear, you are a man of excellent character, famous for your

---

[8] These situations were covered earlier, in the Fourth and Sixth Dialogues of Chapter VI.

great courtesy and noted for your generosity. Therefore you do well if you strive to do the things that are in keeping with your birth and character. For men of the higher nobility are bound to have more noble manners than other men, and they do more harm to their reputations by a little boorishness or by refraining from doing good than men of low birth and common breeding do to theirs by comitting rather grave offenses. I am therefore glad if I am to you a cause and origin of good deeds, and so far as I am able I shall always and in all things give you my approval when you do well."

The man says: "I now see for myself very clearly that all the things that are told about you throughout the world are true. It is clear from your answer how wise you are and how fine your character. Your Prudence has therefore taken the pains to warn me to try to keep to moderation in praising or blaming anyone, and in this the fulness of your wisdom is manifest. God forbid that I should ever be so clearly taken in a falsehood as to say things that cast a shadow over what all men praise, for if we find anyone saying things in detraction of the fame of either bad men or good men, it can make no difference, among prudent men, in the reputation of the man about whom they are spoken; but we know that what the man says hurts his own reputation. Therefore whatever you may wish to say or do to me you may do safely without fear that I will tell evil tales about it. Yet you must be very careful in this affair because if you do good things nobody's mouth will refrain from praising your person; but if you do bad things, even though I may keep silent concerning the misdeeds you have done, since no man of character should relate bad things about anybody, I shall cease to sing your praises. Then the slanderers who know no moderation in their evil speaking, and whose meat and drink it is to ruin other people's reputations in their wicked fashion, will in their usual way never stop talking about the bad things you have done. As for my remark that merely to serve you is to reign in this life, I don't think there can be any harm to the other ladies in this, because I could not make my services more valuable to you were I to refuse them to the other ladies, while by obeying their wishes I believe I am continually doing what you want, especially when the services are done to other ladies for your sake. Moreover, your sweet and pleasing instruction has impressed upon me the fact that I should strive to do those things that are suitable to my birth and thoroughly in keeping with my character, advice which you know I am very eager to accept and wholly ready to follow, for no man who has any reputation for goodness should do things that depart from the way of good men, as what you have just said makes very clear. In the same way it seems to be in keeping with your character for you to be careful to act in accordance with the nature of the stock from which obviously you are descended. It is clear that nothing is more in keeping with your nobility than to attempt to act in such a way that those who look to you may always increase in their determination to do good and may be kept in the mood for it. But I know that if there is any man in the world who by the purity of his faith and his ready inclination to serve you is found worthy to be promised your solaces and by his merits to obtain your grace, I deserve to be honored by you before all the others and with greater rewards than anyone else. For by the best election I have chosen you from among all women to be my mighty lady, to whose services I wish ever to devote myself and to whose credit I wish to set down all my good deeds. From the bottom of my heart I ask your mercy, that you may look upon me as your particular man, just as I have devoted myself particularly to serve you, and that my deeds may obtain from you the reward I desire."

The woman says: "There is nothing in the world that my soul so eagerly desires as that men may know me to be one who does what is worthy of praise and reward, and I have full confidence in God the Father that so long as He preserves unharmed the disposition He has given me I shall never try to do anything that is not open to every criticism.[9] But it seems to me impossible wholly to escape the detractions of the wicked and difficult to curb them, for it would be much easier to take a stream that is flowing naturally down hill and lead it through the same channel swiftly back to its source than it would be to stop the mouths of slanderers or to keep them from plotting. Therefore I think we should leave them to their own devices instead of trying to correct those whose very nature makes it impossible for them to keep from speaking evil. We should merely despise their empty prattle and have no speech with them, because, no matter what good men may really do, if slanderers speak about them they always put an evil interpretation upon it. Therefore it is enough for any honest man to have a clear conscience and a good reputation among good men. As for the other matter, I admit it is true that by serving the desires of other ladies you seem to be serving me, but as for crediting me with all the good deeds done in the world, that seems to me unjustified and very unfair, since there may be many other women of as good or better character who are more worthy of the honor. Moreover it is my desire to use my nobility with such moderation that you, or any other man in the world who does good deeds for my sake, may always increase in the determination to do good and may be kept quite in the mood for it. Now you say that in everything you are devoted to my service and that you deserve greater rewards from me than any other man does, because of your great desire to serve me and because, as you say, you have chosen me as your particular lady. God forbid that any service done me, by you or anybody else, should long go unrewarded if it comes to my attention in any way. But your request that I should consider you as my particular man, just as you are particularly devoted to my service, and that I should give you the reward you hope for, I do not see how I can grant, since such partiality might be to the disadvantage of others who have as much desire to serve me as you have, or perhaps even more. Besides I am not perfectly clear as to what the reward is that you expect from me; you must explain yourself more clearly."

The man says: "What I said to you about evil speakers was not said with the idea of putting on you the burden of holding in check the inclinations of evil men, but that your well-considered deeds may show you to be of such a character that the envy of the wicked will always keep on increasing and the opinion of good men will guard you from their plots, as your judgment has already most prudently indicated, for among good men it is enough for anyone to have a clear conscience As for what you said about doing an

---

[9] That is, commendable, however close the scrutiny by potential critics.

injustice to other women if I credit all my good deeds to your praise, there seems to be nothing in that to wrong anybody or to give offense; although a woman ought to approve of a good deed done by anyone, every praise-worthy man should do all his good deeds to the special praise of one woman, and every woman of good sense, although she ought to be pleased by the good deeds of anyone, can laudably approve the acts of only one man, and she should consider them done to her special praise. No one is injured if I have devoted myself and my deeds, each and all, to your service and have acknowledged you as my special mistress. It is enough for the other women to be honored by the special services of other men; it wouldn't seem to do them any good for you to vex yourself with looking out for them, since my will is fixed on serving you in everything and the will cannot be controlled, as the teaching of the most learned Donatus[10] will show you, for the human will is so very free that no one's efforts can divert it from a purpose firmly formed. Therefore the other ladies can ask me nothing as their due except that, with an eye to your contemplation, I grant them such services as are acceptable to them and that I keep discreetly silent as to the source of these services; but by the obligation I owe you I am bound to be worthy of praise in all that I do and to avoid all stain of depravity. And you owe it to me, as you yourself have agreed, to see that the services I do for you shall not long go without their reward. You said too, that if Your Ladyship were to show me special good will it would be to the disadvantage of others who perhaps have a greater desire to serve you than I have, or as great a one. To this I answer that if any man has a greater determination to serve you than I have, or as great a one, I ask that I may get no aid from you, nor may any laws of reason protect me. You said also that you did not fully understand what the reward was that I was hoping for, toward which all my attention was directed. I desire Your Clemency to be informed that the reward I ask you to promise to give me is one which it is unbearable agony to be without, while to have it is to abound in all riches. It is that you should be pleasant to me unless your desire is opposed to me. It is your love which I seek, in order to restore my health, and which I desire to get by my hunting."

The woman says: "You seem to be wandering a long way from the straight path of love and to be violating the best custom of lovers, because you are in such haste to ask for love. For the wise and well-taught lover, when conversing for the first time with a lady whom he has not previously known, should not ask in specific words for the gifts of love, but he should try hard to give a hint to the lady he loves, and should show himself pleasant and courteous in all that he says; then he should be careful to act in such a way that his deeds praise him truly to his love, even when he is absent. Then as the third step he may with more assurance come to the request for love. But you have upset this order by a clear violation, and I believe you have done so because you think that I will be only too ready to grant what you ask, or because you are not experienced in the art of love. Therefore there is good cause to be suspicious of your love."

---

[10] Which Donatus is intended, and where this teaching appears in his work, are uncertain.

The man says: "If it is true that I have mixed up the order of love, it seems I have done so with your approval. For although my intention might have been guessed from what I said cautiously and in a roundabout way, you asked me to explain to you more clearly what I wanted, as though you did not understand. I did not, therefore, make my request with any idea that you would be too ready to grant it, nor was I asking for a too hasty gift of your love; I merely desired to make my intention clear to you as you asked me to. Besides, although the order you mention ought to be followed, it may be changed where there is sufficient reason for so doing. If my feelings are too strong to resist, and if I bear an inward wound of love, I may plead necessity as a defense against the charge of unworthiness, for urgent necessity can be bound by no rules of law. Besides, if I have any lack of judgment in love, I must necessarily seek the love of a woman of great wisdom and worth so that my inexperience may thereby be remedied and I may learn all the doctrine of love. If an inexperienced man should ask for the love of an inexperienced woman, their love could not develop properly or long endure in the proper condition. For even though a favorable breeze springs up after a ship has been exposed to unfavorable conditions at sea and has been subjected to tempests, if a moderate gust strikes it, it will sink and go to the bottom unless it has a trained steersman and rowers. Both of your arguments are therefore silenced by the best of answers and can in no way oppose my proposal."

The woman says: "Even though I found you in every respect worthy of love, still we are separated by too wide and too rough an expanse of country to be able to offer each other love's solaces or to find proper opportunities for meeting. Lovers who live near together can cure each other of the torments that come from love, can help each other in their common sufferings, and can nourish their love by mutual exchanges and efforts; those, however, who are far apart cannot perceive each other's pains, but each one has to relieve his own trouble and cure his own torments. So it seems that our love should go no further, because Love's rule teaches us that the daily sight of each other makes lovers love more ardently, while I can see on the other hand that by reason of distance love decreases and fails, and therefore everybody should try to find a lover who lives near by."

The man says: "You are troubling yourself to say what seems to be against all reason, for all men know that if one gets easily what he desires he holds it cheap and what formerly he longed for with his whole heart he now considers worthless. On the other hand, whenever the possession of some good thing is postponed by the difficulty of getting it, we desire it more eagerly and put forth a greater effort to keep it. Therefore if one has difficulty in obtaining the embraces of one's lover and obtains them rarely, the lovers are bound to each other in more ardent chains of love and their souls are linked together in heavier and closer bonds of affection. For constancy is made perfect amid the waves that buffet it, and perseverance is clearly seen in adversities. Rest seems sweeter to a man who is wearied by many labors than to one who lives in continual idleness, and a new-found shade seems to offer more to one who is burdened by the heat than to one who has been constantly in air of a moderate temperature. It is not one of Love's rules, as you said it was, that when lovers seldom meet the strength of their love is weakened, since we find it false and misleading. Therefore you cannot properly refuse me your love with the excuse of the long and difficult distance between us, but you should gratify me rather than someone who lives near by; besides it is easier to conceal a love affair when the lovers do not meet than when they converse frequently with each other."

The woman says: "So far as hiding one's love goes, I do not think there is any choice between a distant lover and one who is present. If the lover proves to be wise and clever it doesn't matter whether he is far from his beloved or near her, he will so govern his actions and his will that no one can guess the secrets of their love; on the other hand a foolish lover, whether far or near, can never conceal the secrets of his love. Your argument must therefore fall before this most obvious one on the other side. Besides there is another fact, by no means trivial, which keeps me from loving you. I have a husband who is greatly distinguished by his nobility, his good breeding, and his good character, and it would be wicked for me to violate his bed or submit to the embraces of any other man, since I know that he loves me with his whole heart and I am bound to him with all the devotion of mine. The laws themselves bid me refrain from loving another man when I am blessed with such a reward for my love."

The man says: "I admit it is true that your husband is a very worthy man and that he is more blest than any man in the world because he has been worthy to have the joy of embracing Your Highness. But I am greatly surprised that you wish to misapply the term 'love' to that marital affection which husband and wife are expected to feel for each other after marriage, since everybody knows that love can have no place between husband and wife. They may be bound to each other by a great and immoderate affection, but their feeling cannot take the place of love, because it cannot fit under the true definition of love. For what is love but an inordinate desire to receive passionately a furtive and hidden embrace? But what embrace between husband and wife can be furtive, I ask you, since they may be said to belong to each other and may satisfy all of each other's desires without fear that anybody will object? Besides, that most excellent doctrine of princes shows that nobody can make furtive use of what belongs to him. Do not let what I have said seem absurd to you, for husband and wife may be joined together by every sort of affection, but this feeling cannot take the place of love. In friendship we see the same thing. Father and son may feel every sort of affection for each other, but there is no true friendship between them, because, as Cicero tells us, the feeling that offspring of the blood have for each other is affection.[11] It is clear then that there is just as much difference between every kind of affection of husband and wife and the obligation of lovers as there is between the mutual affection of father and son and the strongest friendship between two men, so that in the one case we say there is no love, just as in the other we say friendship is lacking. So then you see clearly that love can by no means exercise its functions between husband and wife, but has wished to withdraw its privileges completely.

[11] The statement attributed to Cicero (Roman statesman, orator, and philosopher, 106–43 B.C.) is a somewhat inaccurate version of what he says in his *Friendship*, section 27.

"But there is another reason why husband and wife cannot love each other and that is that the very substance of love, without which true love cannot exist—I mean jealousy—is in such a case very much frowned upon and they should avoid it like the pestilence; but lovers should always welcome it as the mother and the nurse of love. From this you may see clearly that love cannot possibly flourish between you and your husband. Therefore, since every woman of character ought to love, prudently, you can without doing yourself any harm accept the prayers of a suppliant and endow your suitor with your love."

The woman says: "You are trying to take under your protection what all men from early times down have agreed to consider very reprehensible and to reject as hateful. For who can rightly commend envious jealousy or speak in favor of it, since jealousy is nothing but a shameful and evil suspicion of a woman? God forbid, therefore, that any worthy man should feel jealous about anyone, since this proves hostile to every prudent person and throughout the world is hated by everybody good. You are trying also, under cover of defining love, to condemn love between husband and wife, saying that their embraces cannot be furtive, since without fear that anyone may object they can fulfill each other's desires. But if you understood the definition correctly it could not interfere with love between husband and wife, for the expression 'hidden embraces' is simply an explanation in different words of the preceding one, and there seems to be no impossibililiy in husband and wife giving each other hidden embraces, even though they can do so without the least fear that anybody may raise an objection. Everyone should choose that love which may be fostered by security for continual embraces and, what is more, can be practiced every day without any sin. I ought therefore to choose a man to enjoy my embraces who can be to me both husband and lover, because, no matter what the definition of love may say, love seems to be nothing but a great desire to enjoy carnal pleasure with someone, and nothing prevents this feeling existing between husband and wife."

The man says: "If the theory of love were perfectly clear to you and Love's dart had ever touched you, your own feelings would have shown you that love cannot exist without jealousy, because, as I have already told you in more detail, jealousy between lovers is commended by every man who is experienced in love, while between husband and wife it is condemned throughout the world; the reason for this will be perfectly clear from a description of jealousy. Now jealousy is a true emotion whereby we greatly fear that the substance of our love may be weakened by some defect in serving the desires of our beloved, and it is an anxiety lest our love may not be returned, and it is a suspicion of the beloved, but without any shameful thought. From this it is clear that there are three aspects of jealousy. A truly jealous man is always afraid that his services may not be sufficient to retain the love of the woman he loves, and he is afraid that she may not love him as he loves her, and he is so tormented with anxiety that he wonders whether she doesn't have another lover, although he believes that this cannot possibly be. But that this last aspect of jealousy is not proper for a married man is clearly apparent, for a husband cannot suspect his wife without the thought that such conduct on her part is shameful. Pure jealousy, in the case of a husband, takes a stain from the defect of its subject and ceases to be what it was. Water likewise may be beautifully clear, but if it begins to run over a sandy bed it becomes cloudy from the sand and loses its natural clearness; so charity, although by nature it deserves the reward of eternal blessedness, if given to the poor by a hypocrite or out of desire for empty glory loses its efficacy and causes the man to forfeit both what he gives and his reward for giving it. It is therefore plain enough that we have clearly demonstrated that jealousy cannot have its natural place between husband and wife and that therefore love between them must necessarily cease, because these two things always go together. But between lovers this jealousy is said to be preservative of love, because all three aspects which we have attributed to it are necessary to a lover; therefore jealousy between lovers is not condemned. We find many, however, who are deceived in this matter and say falsely that a shameful suspicion is jealousy, just as many often make the mistake of saying that an alloy of silver and lead is the finest silver. Wherefore not a few, being ignorant of the origin and description of jealousy, are often deceived and led into the gravest error. For even between persons who are not married this false jealousy may find a place and then they are no longer called 'lovers' but 'gentleman friend' and 'lady friend.' As for what you tried to prove by your answer—that the love which can be practiced without sin is far preferable—that, apparently, cannot stand. For whatever solaces married people extend to each other beyond what are inspired by the desire for offspring or the payment of the marriage debt,[12] cannot be free from sin, and the punishment is always greater when the use of a holy thing is perverted by misuse than if we practice the ordinary abuses. It is a more serious offense in a wife than in another woman, for the too ardent lover, as we are taught by the apostolic law, is considered an adulterer with his own wife.[13] But it seems that no one should approve your interpretation, which you draw from the definition of love, for all the greater authors have told us that explanatory words must not be used in the actual definitions of things. From this everybody can see clearly that I have taken all the force out of your explanation, because that seems to be contrary to the meaning of the definition. But neither does your definition, which I admit you took from Love, have any reason back of it, for it includes the blind and the insane who, as the teaching of Andreas the Lover, chaplain of the royal court, shows us clearly, are to be completely banished from the court of Love.[14] Since, therefore, you cannot raise a reasonable objection to my application, no man will consider it to your credit if you make me languish for love of you and suffer so many torments on your account."

The woman says: "You haven't advanced any argurment, so far as I can see, that would weaken my opinion or properly compel me to assent to your desire. However, since those duties you impose on me look so very much as though they were real ones, in order to deprive you of any opportunity to make a charge against me I shall not refuse to have the decision given by any lady

---

[12]The Latin Vulgate Bible used by medieval Catholics describes the (presumably sexual) *debitum* ("debt") owed each other by spouses (I Corinthians 7:3).

[13]Many medieval Christian theologians and some earlier ones considered intensely sexual feelings between spouses to be sinfully lustful.

[14]*Andreas Capellanus* is Latin for "Andreas the Chaplain." The exclusion of the mentally unsound and of the blind had been asserted in Book I, Chapter 5.

or any man of character whom you may select, on the points at issue between us: namely, whether love can have any place between husband and wife and whether jealousy between lovers may properly be praised, for it seems to me that we can never settle this discussion or bring it a proper end."

The man says: "I do not care to seek the decision of anybody else in this case if you will only examine properly what you yourself have said."

The woman says: "The world never heard of anyone passing judgment on his own case, so I refuse to have anything to do with the matter, and I leave it to be entrusted to someone else."

The man says: "I give you full power to appoint the arbiter in this dispute; however, I want to be judged by a woman, not by a man."

The woman says: "If it suits you, it seems to me that the Countess of Champagne[15] ought to be honored in this affair and should settle the disagreement."

The man says: "I promise forever to abide by her decision in every respect and to keep it absolutely inviolate, because no one could ever have any reason to raise a question about her wisdom or the fairness of her decision. Let us then by common consent and desire write a letter showing the nature of our disagreement and the pledge we have made to abide by her deasion. Let us do it in this fashion:

The letter sent to the Countess of Champagne

To the illustrious and wise woman M., Countess of Champagne, the noble woman A. and Count G. send greeting and whatever in the world is more pleasing.

Ancient custom shows us plainly, and the way of life of the ancients demands, that if we are to have justice done we should seek first of all in the place where Wisdom is clearly known to have found a home for herself and that we should seek for the truth of reason at its source, where it is abundant, rather than beg for its decisions where it flows scantily in small streams. For a great poverty of possessions can scarcely offer to anyone a wealth of good things or distribute an abundance of fertility. Where the master is oppressed by great want it is wholly impossible for the vassal[16] to abound in wealth.

"Now on a certain day, as we sat under the shade of a pine tree of marvellous height and great breadth of spread, devoted wholly to love's idleness and striving to investigate Love's mandates in a good-tempered and spirited debate, we began to discern a twofold doubt, and we wearied ourselves with laborious arguments as to whether true love can find any place between husband and wife and whether jealousy flourishing between two lovers ought to be approved of. After we had argued the matter back and forth and each

---

[15]Marie, Countess of Champagne and Andreas's patron, was the daughter of King Louis VII by his first queen, Eleanor of Aquitaine. Marie, like her mother, was one of the principal exponents of the doctrines of "courtly love."

[16]Feudal dependent of a higher-ranking lord.

of us seemed to bolster up his position with reasonable arguments, neither one would give in to the other or agree with the arguments he brought forward. We ask you to settle this dispute, and we have sent you both sides of the question in detail, so that after you have carefully examined the truth of it our disagreement may be brought to a satisfactory end and settled by a fair decision. For knowing clearly and in manifest truth that you have a great abundance of wisdom and that you would not want to deprive anyone of justice, we believe that we will in no wise be deprived of it; we most urgently implore Your Excellency's decision, and we desire with all our hearts, begging you most humbly by our present address, that you will give continued attention to our case and that Your Prudence will render a fair decision in the matter without making any delay in giving the verdict."

The Letter sent back by the Countess of Champagne

"To the prudent and noble woman A. and the illustrious and famous Count G., M., Countess of Champagne, sends greeting.

"Since we are bound to hear the just petitions of everybody, and since it is not seemly to deny our help to those who ask what is proper, especially when those who go wrong on questions of love ask to be set right by our decision—which is what the tenor of your letter indicates—we have tried diligently and carefully to carry this out without any extended delay.

"Now your letter has shown that this is the doubt that has arisen between you: whether love can have any place between husband and wife and whether between lovers jealousy is blameworthy; in both questions each of you falls back on his own opinion and opposes that of the other, and you want us to give our opinion which side properly should get the decision. We have therefore examined carefully the statements of both sides and have in very truth inquired into the matter by every possible means, and we wish to end the case with this decision. We declare and we hold as firmly established that love cannot exert its powers between two people who are married to each other. For lovers give each other everything freely, under no compulsion of necessity, but married people are in duty bound to give in to each other's desires and deny themselves to each other in nothing. Besides, how does it increase a husband's honor if after the manner of lovers he enjoys the embraces of his wife, since the worth of character of neither can be increased thereby, and they seem to have nothing more than they already had a right to? And we say the same thing for still another reason, which is that a precept of love tells us that no woman, even if she is married, can be crowned with the reward of the King of Love unless she is seen to be enlisted in the service of Love himself outside the bonds of wedlock. But another rule of Love teaches that no one can be in love with two men. Rightly, therefore, Love cannot acknowledge any rights of his between husband and wife. But there is still another argument that seems to stand in the way of this, which is that between them there can be no true jealousy, and without it true love may not exist, according to the rule of Love himself, which says, 'He who is not jealous cannot love.'[17]

---

[17] This is the second in the list of thirty-one rules stated in Book Two, Chapter VIII.

"Therefore let this our verdict, pronounced with great moderation and supported by the opinion of a great many ladies, be to you firm and indubitable truth.

"The first day of May, in the year 1174, the seventh of the indiction."[18]

from BOOK TWO
HOW LOVE MAY BE RETAINED

CHAPTER VIII. THE RULES OF LOVE

Let us come now to the rules of love, and I shall try to present to you very briefly those rules which the King of Love is said to have proclaimed with his own mouth and to have given in writing to all lovers.

One of the knights of Britain was riding alone through the royal forest, going to see Arthur,[1] and when he had got well into the interior of this forest he came unexpectedly upon a young girl of marvellous beauty, sitting on a fine horse and binding up her hair. The knight lost no time in saluting her, and she answered him courteously and said, "Briton, no matter how hard you try you can't succeed in your quest unless you have our help." When he had heard these words he quickly asked the girl to tell him what he had come for, and then after that he would believe what she said to him. The young girl said to him, "When you asked for the love of a certain British lady, she told you that you could never obtain it unless you first brought back that victorious hawk which, men say, is on a golden perch in Arthur's court." The Briton admitted that all this was true, and the girl went on, "You can't get this hawk that you are seeking unless you prove, by a combat in Arthur's palace, that you enjoy the love of a more beautiful lady than any man at Arthur's court has; you can't even enter the palace until you show the guards the hawk's gauntlet,[2] and you can't get this gauntlet except by overcoming two mighty knights in a double combat."

The Briton answered, "I know that I cannot accomplish this task without your aid, and so I will submit myself to your direction, humbly beseeching you to give me your help in the matter and to permit me to claim, in view of the fact that you are directing me, that I enjoy the love of the more beautiful lady."

The young girl said to him, "If your heart is so stout that you are not afraid to carry out those things of which we have spoken, you may have from us what you ask." The Briton answered, "If you will grant my request, I know that I shall succeed in all that I hope for."

The young girl said to him, "Then let what you request be freely granted to you." Then she gave him the kiss of love and said, indicating the horse on which she was sitting, "This horse will take you everywhere you want to

---

[18]A fifteen-year period, used to date events.
[1]The legendary king of Britain; hero of the Round Table.
[2]Armored glove.

go; but you must go forward without any fear and oppose with the highest courage all those who try to stop you. But bear in mind that after you have gained the victory over the first two who defend the gauntlet you must not accept it from them, but must take it for yourself from the golden pillar where it hangs; otherwise you cannot prevail in the combat at the palace or accomplish what you desire."

When she finished speaking, the Briton put on his arms and, after she had given him leave to depart, began to go at a walk through the wood. At length, as he was passing through a wild and lonely place, he came to a certain river of marvellous breadth and depth, with great waves in it, and because of the great height of its banks it was impossible for anyone to reach it. But as he rode along the edge of the bank he came to a bridge which was of gold and had one end fastened to each bank; the middle of it, however, rested in the water, and he could see that it was so shaken that great waves often covered it. At that end of it which the Briton was approaching there was a knight of a ferocious aspect who was sitting on a horse. The Briton greeted him courteously enough, but the knight scorned to return the greeting and said, "Armed Briton, who come from such distant regions, what are you seeking?"

The Briton answered, "I am trying to cross the river by the bridge"; and the bridge keeper said, "Then you must be seeking death, which no stranger here has been able to escape. But if you want to go back home and leave all your arms here, I will take pity on your youth which has led you so rashly and so foolishly into other men's countries and into strange realms."

The Briton replied, "If I were to lay down my arms, you would gain little credit for the victory of a man in arms over an unarmed man; but if you can keep an armed man from going along the public way, then you may consider that your victory has won you glory. If you do not make way peaceably for me to go across the bridge, I shall simply try to force a passage with my sword."

When the bridge keeper heard that the young man was trying to force a passage with his sword, he began to gnash his teeth, and he fell into a great rage and said, "Young man, Britain sent you here in an evil hour, since you shall perish by the sword in this wilderness, and you will never be able to bring back news of the country to your lady. Woe to you, wretched Briton, who have not been afraid to seek the place of your death at the persuasion of a woman!" Then spurring his horse against the Briton he began to attack him with his sharp sword and to hammer him so cruelly that one stroke, glancing off his shield, cut through two folds of his hauberk[3] and into the flesh of his side so that the blood commenced to flow in abundance from the wound. The young man, stung by the pain of his wound, directed the point of his lance at the knight of the bridge, and with a mighty thrust pierced him through, bore him from his horse, and stretched him shamefully upon the ground. But when the Briton was about to smite off his head, the bridge keeper, by the most humble entreaties, sought and obtained mercy.

But on the other side of the river there stood a man of tremendous size, who, seeing the bridge keeper overcome by the Briton and this same Briton starting to cross the golden bridge, began to shake it so violently that much

---

[3]Coat of chain mail.

of the time it was hidden by the waves. But the Briton, having great confidence in the excellence of his horse, did not cease to press forward manfully over the bridge, and at length, after great difficulty and many duckings, he arrived at the farther end of it by virtue of his horse's efforts; there he drowned beneath the water the man who had been shaking the bridge and bound up the wound in his own side as well as he could.

After this the Briton began to ride through very beautiful fields, and after he had ridden for about a mile the path came out into a pleasant meadow, fragrant with all sorts of flowers. In this meadow was a palace, marvellously built in a circular form and very beautifully decorated. He could not find a door anywhere in the palace, nor could he see any inhabitants; but in the fields he found silver tables, and on them were all sorts of food and drink set among snow-white napkins. In the same pleasant meadow was a shell of the purest silver in which there was sufficient food and drink for a horse. He therefore drove his horse off to feed, and he himself walked completely around the palace; but finding no sign of any entrance to the dwelling or any evidence that the place was inhabited, he drew near to the table and, driven by his hunger, began ravenously to devour the food he found there. A very little while after he had begun to eat, a door of the palace opened quickly with such violence that the shock of it resounded like near-by thunder, and suddenly out of this door came a man of gigantic size, brandishing in his hands a copper club of immense weight, which he shook like a straw without the least effort. To the youth at the table he said, "What sort of man are you, so presumptuous that you were not afraid to come to this royal place and so coolly and disrespectfully to eat the food on the royal table of the knights?"

The Briton answered, "The royal table should be freely open to everybody, and it is not proper that anybody should be refused the royal food and drink. Moreover it is right for me to partake of the rations prepared for the knights, since knighthood is my sole care and a knightly task has brought me to this place. You are therefore doubly discourteous in trying to forbid me the royal table."

To this the doorkeeper replied, "Although this is the royal table, it is not proper for anyone to eat at it except those who are assigned to this palace, and they allow no one to go beyond this point unless he fights with the palace guards and defeats them. And if anyone is beaten by them, there is no hope for him. Therefore get up from the table and hurry back to where you belong, or tell me that you want to fight your way onward and why you have come this far."

The Briton said to him, "I am seeking the hawk's gauntlet; that is why I came. When I get it I shall try to go further and as victor in Arthur's court take the hawk. Where is this palace guard you mention who will keep me from going on?"

The doorkeeper replied, "You fool! What madness possesses you, Briton! It would be easier for you to die and come to life again ten times than to get those things you mention. I am the palace guard who will deprive you of your reputation and spoil Britain of your youth. I am so strong that when I am angry two hundred of the best knights of Britain can hardly withstand me."

The Briton answered, "Although you say you are very powerful, I would like to fight with you to show you what sort of men Britain produces; however, it isn't proper for a knight to fight with a footman."

The doorkeeper said to him, "I see that your bad luck has brought you to death in this place where my right hand has felled more than a thousand. And although I am not reckoned among the knights, I would like to fight with you while you are on horseback, because then if you yield to the valor of a footman you will have good reason to know what sort of person would be overcome by the boldness of a man like me if I were on horseback."

To this the Briton answered, "God forbid that I should ever fight on horseback against a man on foot, for against a foot soldier every man should fight on foot," and grasping his arms he rushed bravely at the enemy before him and with a blow of his sword slightly damaged the latter's shield. The guardian of the palace, greatly enraged at this and contemptuous of the Briton's small size, shook his brazen club so furiously that the Briton's shield was almost shattered by the concussion, and he himself was greatly terrified. Thinking that a second blow would finish the Briton, the guard raised his hand to strike again, but before the blow could fall the other quickly feinted and with his sword caught him on the arm, so that the right hand, still holding the club, fell to the ground. But as he was about to put an end to him, the guard cried out, "Are you the one discourteous knight that sweet Britain has produced, you who would slay a wounded man? If you will spare my life I can easily get for you what you want, but without me you can gain nothing."

The Briton said, "Porter, I will spare your life if you will do what you promise."

The guard said, "Wait a bit and I will quickly get you the hawk's gauntlet."

The Briton answered, "You robber and deceiver of men! Now I see plainly that you are trying to cheat me. If you want to save your life just show me the place where that gauntlet of yours is kept."

The guard then led the Briton into the innermost part of the palace where there was a very beautiful golden column that held up the whole weight of the palace, and on this column hung the gauntlet he was seeking. As he grasped it boldly and held it firmly in his left hand he heard a great noise, and although he saw nobody, a wailing began to resound throughout the palace, and a cry, "Woe! woe! in spite of us the victor enemy is carrying away the spoil."

He left the palace and, mounting his horse which was already saddled, continued his journey untll he came to a deligtful place where there were more of those beautiful fields filled with flowers, and in the fields was a palace finely built of gold. Its length was six hundred cubits, and its width two hundred. The roof and all the outer walls were of silver, and the inside was all of gold set with precious stones. The palace was divided into a great many rooms, and in the hall of state King Arthur was sitting on a golden throne surrounded by beautiful women, more than I could count, and before him stood many splendid knights. In this palace was a beautifully fashioned golden perch on which was the hawk he was seeking, and chained near by lay two hawking dogs. But before he could get to the palace his way was blocked by a heavily fortified barbican,[4] raised to protect the palace, and to the defense

---

[4]Defensive fortification at a gate or drawbridge.

of it were assigned twelve very strong knights who permitted no one to pass unless he showed them the gauntlet for the hawk or forced his way sword in hand.

When the Briton saw them, he quickly showed them the gauntlet and they fell back, saying, "Your life isn't safe if you go on this way; it will lead you to great trouble." But the Briton continued on to the interior of the palace and saluted King Arthur. When the knights pressed him to know why he had come there, he replied that he had come to carry off the hawk. One of the knights of the court asked him, "Why are you trying to get the hawk?" and he replied, "Because I enjoy the love of a more beautiful woman than any knight in this court has." The other answered him, "Before you can take away the hawk you will have to fight to prove that statement." "Gladly!" said the Briton. After a suitable shield had been given him both took their places armed within the lists;[5] setting spurs to their horses, they rushed together violently, shattering each other's shields and splintering their lances; then with their swords they smote each other and hewed to pieces the iron armor. After they had fought in this fashion for a long time, the vision of the knight of the palace, whom the Briton had struck on the head with two shrewd[6] blows in rapid succession, began to be so disturbed that he could see almost nothing. When the Briton perceived this, he leapt boldly upon him and quickly struck him, beaten, from his horse. Then he seized the hawk, and, glancing as he did so at the two dogs, he saw a written parchment, which was fastened to the perch with a little gold chain. When he inquired carefully concerning this, he was told, "This is the parchment on which are written the rules of love which the King of Love himself, with his own mouth, pronounced for lovers. You should take it with you and make these rules known to lovers if you want to take away the hawk peaceably." He took the parchment, and after he had been given courteous permission to depart, quickly returned, without any opposition, to the lady of the wood, whom he found in the same place in the grove where she was when he first came upon her as he was riding along. She rejoiced greatly over the victory he had gained and dismissed him with these words, "Dearest friend, go with my permission, since sweet Britain desires you. But, that your departure may not seem too grievous to you, I ask you to come here sometimes alone, and you can always have me with you." He kissed her thirteen times over and went joyfully back to Britain. Afterward he looked over the rules which he had found written in the parchment, and then, in accordance with the answer he had previously received, he made them known to all lovers. These are the rules.

I. Marriage is no real excuse for not loving.
II. He who is not jealous cannot love.
III. No one can be bound by a double love.
IV. It is well known that love is always increasing or decreasing.

---

[5]Arena for knightly combats.
[6]Sharp; penetrating.

V. That which a lover takes against the will of his beloved has no relish.

VI. Boys do not love until they arrive at the age of maturity.

VII. When one lover dies, a widowhood of two years is required of the survivor.

VIII. No one should be deprived of love without the very best of reasons.

IX. No one can love unless he is impelled by the persuasion of love.

X. Love is always a stranger in the home of avarice.

XI. It is not proper to love any woman whom one would be ashamed to seek to marry.

XII. A true lover does not desire to embrace in love anyone except his beloved.

XIII. When made public love rarely endures.

XIV. The easy attainment of love makes it of little value; difficulty of attainment makes it prized.

XV. Every lover regularly turns pale in the presence of his beloved.

XVI. When a lover suddenly catches sight of his beloved his heart palpitates.

XVII. A new love puts to flight an old one.

XVIII. Good character alone makes any man worthy of love.

XIX. If love diminishes, it quickly fails and rarely revives.

XX. A man in love is always apprehensive.

XXI. Real jealousy always increases the feeling of love.

XXII. Jealousy, and therefore love, are increased when one suspects his beloved.

XXIII. He whom the thought of love vexes eats and sleeps very little.

XXIV. Every act of a lover ends in the thought of his beloved.

XXV. A true lover considers nothing good except what he thinks will please his beloved.

XXVI. Love can deny nothing to love.

XXVII. A lover can never have enough of the solaces of his beloved.

XXVIII. A slight presumption causes a lover to suspect his beloved.

XXIX. A man who is vexed by too much passion usually does not love.

XXX. A true lover is constantly and without intermission possessed by the thought of his beloved.

XXXI. Nothing forbids one woman being loved by two men or one man by two women.

These rules, as I have said, the Briton brought back with him on behalf of the King of Love to the lady for whose sake he endured so many perils when he brought her back the hawk. When she was convinced of the complete faithfulness of this knight and understood better how boldly he had striven, she rewarded him with her love. Then she called together a court of a great many ladies and knights and laid before them these rules of Love, and bade every lover keep them faithfully under threat of punishment by the King of Love. These laws the whole court received in their entirety and promised forever to obey in order to avoid punishment by Love. Every person who had been summoned and had come to the court took home a written copy of the rules and gave them out to all lovers in all parts of the world.

Marie de France

(Late Twelfth Century)

"The first woman novelist of our era": that is the contemporary novelist John Fowles's description of Marie de France. The phrase is deliberately playful and paradoxical, especially in calling the author of twelve very brief verse romances a "novelist." Yet it is precise; Marie's gifts are those of a fiction writer rather than a poet. She excels in storytelling: in shaping often simple, apparently naive stories so as to make them powerfully evocative and anything but naive. Her characters are memorable, lightly sketched and yet psychologically convincing, even when they are engaged in fabulous actions. And she creates a highly distinctive fictional world, an imaginative "Brittany" that is simultaneously the world of fairy tales and a dreamlike version of her own courtly circle. Fowles's emphasis upon her femininity seems right, too. Marie works on a small scale—Fowles calls her "a laborer on two inches of ivory"—but within her miniature world she has a feminine eye for the nuances and often the absurdities of human emotions. After eight centuries, we can still recognize Marie's charming fictions as belonging to "our era."

The historical Marie is a shadowy figure. She is thought to be the author of three surviving works, the *Lais,* a collection of *Fables,* and a didactic, supernatural tale called *St. Patrick's Purgatory.* All three date from the second half of the twelfth century, and all three contain statements that they were written by someone named "Marie." At the end of the *Fables,* she also gives her nationality: "I shall name myself so that it will be remembered; / Marie is my name, I am of France." She also tells us in a Prologue to the *Lais* that she wrote them for a "noble king." Scholars have concluded that Marie must have been born in France but at some point went to England and wrote for the English court, heavily French in the years following the Norman Conquest. The noble king is probably Henry II, whose queen was Eleanor of Aquitaine, a sophisticated patron of literature. It is even possible that Marie was Henry II's half-sister. Henry's father, Geoffrey Plantagenet, had an illegitimate daughter named Marie, who became abbess of Shaftesbury about 1180, and some scholars have identified her with the evidently well-educated, apparently highly placed Frenchwoman who wrote under the name "Marie de France."

Whoever Marie was, her work is one of the finest literary expressions of the twelfth-century renaissance in European culture that marked the end of the so-called "dark ages." The preoccupation with military prowess that marked earlier medieval narrative gave way to an overwhelming interest in love as a literary subject, as the new class of courtly aristocrats who clustered around the great courts of England and France sought to define and mythologize their class values. Ovid's *Metamorphoses* and especially his *Art of Love* and *Remedy for Love* were translated and endlessly studied as a guide to the psychology of refined love. Classical stories were translated and adapted to emphasize their romantic elements, as in the *Romance of Aeneas* and the *Romance of Thebes.* Legendary histories such as William of Malmesbury's *Deeds of the English Kings* (about 1125) and Geoffrey of Monmouth's *History of the Kings of Britain* (about 1135) introduced Arthurian material soon to be worked into romances. During Marie's lifetime, Chrétien de Troyes, across the Channel, wrote the first account of the love of Lancelot and Guinevere.

Marie's special interest, in the *Lais,* was the "matter of Britain," Celtic or "Breton" stories. At the beginning of the first of the twelve *Lais,* "Guigemar," she writes, "The tales—and I know they're true— / from which the Bretons made their *lais* / I'll now recount for you briefly," and repeatedly through the collection, she refers to her "Breton" sources. Many of the stories do seem to be from Celtic folklore, but Marie perhaps reset even those from written French sources in a fairy-tale-like Wales or Brittany as a result of a literary vogue for Celtic material.

A certain amount of controversy centers around Marie's conception of a *lai.* Generally speaking, it is a short romance in rhyme that fuses super-natural elements, a fairy-tale "Celtic" setting, and a treatment of courtly love, originally performed by Breton minstrels to the accompaniment of a harp or a kind of lyre called a *rote.* Sometimes, Marie seems to use the term to refer to her sources, as in the prologue to "Guigemar"; at other times, she seems to use it to refer to her own work (although we are not sure that she gave her collection the title that the manuscript bears). Perhaps it is best to think of her poems as "literary *lais,*" sophisticated adaptations of folk *lais,* probably intended to be read rather than chanted or sung.

Marie's twelve *lais* are enormously varied in length, form, and subject mat-ter. But all of them center around the subject of love, like an elaborate set of variations on a single theme. The variations are so great that it is diffi-cult to generalize about her view of love. It is remarkably open-minded; adul-terous love is not ruled out, though generally she celebrates the possibilities for happiness within a loving marriage. She also celebrates sensuality, though she emphasizes the necessity for spiritual and emotional union as well. There is often tension in the *lais* between private ecstasy and public acknowledg-ment of love; love cannot survive the claustrophobia of secrecy and yet the world is often ranged against lovers who seek the endorsement of society. A recurring theme is what Marie calls *desmesure,* the passionate excess or loss of restraint characteristic of genuine love. This excess is one of the glories of love, but it carries within it the chief threat to continued love. Over and over in the stories, disaster ensues when one or the other of the lovers gives way to *desmesure* and oversteps the bounds of discretion and restraint.

The twelve stories in the *Lais* are so intricately interconnected by paral-lels, balances, and echoes that only a reading of the entire collection can convey the full range of Marie's variations on her theme. But *Bisclavret* and *Yonec* make a good pairing, partly because the first shows a false, disloyal love that is ultimately punished, while the other presents a genuine love that is ended by violence but is finally vindicated. Ironically, the false love is within marriage, the true one outside it. The two *lais* present a sharp contrast struc-turally as well. *Bisclavret,* like many of Marie's shorter *lais,* is centered around a single climactic scene, with the earlier part of the poem devoted to prepar-ing for that scene. *Yonec,* on the other hand, covers a long span of time, with the emphasis upon the earlier scenes and the final scene only a sort of coda to the main action. Both illustrate Marie's fondness for organizing her work around a central symbolic creature or object that suggests the nature of the love and its moral problems. Marie takes the primitive figure of the were-wolf in *Bisclavret* and turns it into an ironic and suggestive symbol of the central theme of the story, the conflict of bestiality and civilization in human nature. The bird-lover of *Yonec* is similarly suggestive as a representation of the story's themes of imprisonment and freedom, a symbol of love's power to enable us to liberate ourselves.

FURTHER READING *(prepared by J.H.):* The best introduction in English to the *Lais* is probably the present translators' *The Lais of Marie de France,* 1978. This volume contains a short appreciative foreword by John Fowles, a lengthy critical and historical introduction by the translators, translations of all the *lais,* and a short critical commentary on each. Marie's life, works, and milieu are well outlined in the Introduction to *The Fables of Marie de France,* trans. Mary Lou Martin, 1984. Paula Clifford's *Marie de France: Lais,* 1982, a volume in the Critical Guides to French Texts series, offers helpful critical analyses of the individual stories. Emanuel J. Mickel, Jr.'s *Marie de France,* 1974, in the Twayne's World Authors series, offers chapters on Marie's identity and intellectual background, as well as on the nature of the *lai,* Marie's plots and sources, her concept of love, and the narrative structure of the *lais.* In the title novella of *The Ebony Tower,* 1974, the novelist John Fowles gives a modern treatment to some of Marie's themes, followed by a short "Personal Note" on Marie and a translation of "Eliduc"—all of which makes for a dazzling "metafictional" improvisation and a provocative interpretation of Marie. Glyn S. Burgess's *Marie de France,* 1977, is an annotated bibliography of scholarship up to its date. Readers interested in women's writing in general during the Middle Ages can find fifteen authors, including Marie de France, excerpted and succinctly discussed in *Medieval Women Writers,* ed. and with Introduction by Katharina M. Wilson, 1984; the section on Marie is by Joan M. Ferrante. A helpful recent work is *In Quest of Marie de France, a Twelfth-Century Poet,* ed. Chantal A. Marechal, 1992.

BISCLAVRET (THE WEREWOLF)

Translated by Robert Hanning and Joan Ferrante

Since I am undertaking to compose *lais,*
I don't want to forget Bisclavret;
In Breton, the *lai's* name is *Bisclavret—*
the Normans call it *Garwaf [The Werewolf].*
In the old days, people used to say—
and it often actually happened—
that some men turned into werewolves
and lived in the woods.
A werewolf is a savage beast;
while his fury is on him   10
he eats men, does much harm,
goes deep in the forest to live.
But that's enough of this for now:
I want to tell you about the Bisclavret.

In Brittany there lived a nobleman
whom I've heard marvelously praised;
a fine, handsome knight
who behaved nobly.

He was close to his lord,
and loved by all his neighbors.   20
He had an estimable wife,
one of lovely appearance;
he loved her and she him,
but one thing was very vexing to her:
during the week he would be missing
for three whole days, and she didn't know
what happened to him or where he went.
Nor did any of his men know anything about it.
    One day he returned home
happy and delighted;   30
she asked him about it.
"My lord," she said, "and dear love,
I'd very much like to ask you one thing—
if I dared;
but I'm so afraid of your anger
that nothing frightens me more."
When he heard that, he embraced her,
drew her to him and kissed her.
"My lady," he said, "go ahead and ask!
There's nothing you could want to know,   40
that, if I knew the answer, I wouldn't tell you."
"By God," she replied, "now I'm cured!
My lord, on the days when you go away from me
I'm in such a state—
so sad at heart,
so afraid I'll lose you—
that if I don't get quick relief
I could die of this very soon.
Please, tell me where you go,
where you have been staying.   50
I think you must have a lover,
and if that's so, you're doing wrong."
"My dear," he said, "have mercy on me, for God's sake!
Harm will come to me if I tell you about this,
because I'd lose your love
and even my very self."
When the lady heard this
she didn't take it lightly;
she kept asking him,
coaxed and flattered him so much,   60
that he finally told her what happened to him—
he hid nothing from her.
"My dear, I become a werewolf:
I go off into the great forest,
in the thickest part of the woods,
and I live on the prey I hunt down."
When he had told her everything,
she asked further

whether he undressed or kept his clothes on [when he became a
    werewolf].
"Wife," he replied, "I go stark naked." 70
"Tell me, then, for God's sake, where your clothes are."
"That I won't tell you;
for if I were to lose them,
and then be discovered,
I'd stay a werewolf forever.
I'd be helpless
until I got them back.
That's why I don't want their hiding place to be known."
"My lord," the lady answered,
"I love you more than all the world; 80
you mustn't hide anything from me
or fear me in any way:
that doesn't seem like love to me.
What wrong have I done? For what sin of mine
do you mistrust me about anything?
Do the right thing and tell me!"
She harassed and bedeviled him so,
that he had no choice but to tell her.
"Lady," he said, "near the woods,
beside the road that I use to get there, 90
there's an old chapel
that has often done me good service;
under a bush there is a big stone,
hollowed out inside;
I hide my clothes right there
until I'm ready to come home."
    The lady heard this wonder
and turned scarlet from fear;
she was terrified of the whole adventure.
Over and over she considered 100
how she might get rid of him;
she never wanted to sleep with him again.
There was a knight of that region
who had loved her for a long time,
who begged for her love,
and dedicated himself to serving her.
She'd never loved him at all,
nor pledged her love to him,
but now she sent a messenger for him,
and told him her intention. 110
"My dear," she said, "cheer up!
I shall now grant you without delay
what you have suffered for;
you'll meet with no more refusals—
I offer you my love and my body;
make me your mistress!"

He thanked her graciously
and accepted her promise,
and she bound him to her by an oath.
Then she told him   120
how her husband went away and what happened to him;
she also taught him the precise path
her husband took into the forest,
and then she sent the knight to get her husband's clothes.
So Bisclavret[1] was betrayed,
ruined by his own wife.
Since people knew he was often away from home
they all thought
this time he'd gone away forever.
They searched for him and made inquiries   130
but could never find him,
so they had to let matters stand.
The wife later married the other knight,
who had loved her for so long.
    A whole year passed
until one day the king went hunting;
he headed right for the forest
where Bisclavret was.
When the hounds were unleashed,
they ran across Bisclavret;   140
the hunters and the dogs
chased him all day,
until they were just about to take him
and tear him apart,
at which point he saw the king
and ran to him, pleading for mercy.
He took hold of the king's stirrup,
kissed his leg and his foot.
The king saw this and was terrified;
he called his companions.   150
"My lords," he said, "come quickly!
Look at this marvel—
this beast is humbling itself to me.
It has the mind of a man, and it's begging me for mercy!
Chase the dogs away,
and make sure no one strikes it.
This beast is rational—he has a mind.
Hurry up: let's get out of here.
I'll extend my peace to the creature;
indeed, I'll hunt no more today!"   160
Thereupon the king turned away.
Bisclavret followed him;

---

[1] Until this point, "Bisclavret" is a common noun; hereafter it is used as the werewolf's name.

he stayed close to the king, and wouldn't go away;
he'd no intention of leaving him.
    The king led him to his castle;
he was delighted with this turn of events,
for he'd never seen anything like it.
He considered the beast a great wonder
and held him very dear.
He commanded all his followers,   170
for the sake of their love for him, to guard Bisclavret well,
and under no circumstances to do him harm;
none of them should strike him;
rather, he should be well fed and watered.
They willingly guarded the creature;
every day he went to sleep
among the knights, near the king.
Everyone was fond of him;
he was so noble and well behaved
that he never wished to do anything wrong.   180
Regardless of where the king might go,
Bisclavret never wanted to be separated from him;
he always accompanied the king.
The king became very much aware that the creature loved him.
    Now listen to what happened next.
The king held a court;
to help him celebrate his feast
and to serve him as handsomely as possible,
he summoned all the barons
who held fiefs from him.   190
Among the knights who went,
and all dressed up in his best attire,
was the one who had married Bisclavret's wife.
He neither knew nor suspected
that he would find Bisclavret so close by.
As soon as he came to the palace
Bisclavret saw him,
ran toward him at full speed,
sank his teeth into him, and started to drag him down.
He would have done him great damage   200
if the king hadn't called him off,
and threatened him with a stick.
Twice that day he tried to bite the knight.
Everyone was extremely surprised,
since the beast had never acted that way
toward any other man he had seen.
All over the palace people said
that he wouldn't act that way without a reason:
that somehow or other, the knight had mistreated Bisclavret,
and now he wanted his revenge.   210
And so the matter rested

until the feast was over
and until the barons took their leave of the king
and started home.
The very first to leave,
to the best of my knowledge,
was the knight whom Bisclavret had attacked.
It's no wonder the creature hated him.
    Not long afterward,
as the story leads me to believe,   220
the king, who was so wise and noble,
went back to the forest
where he had found Bisclavret,
and the creature went with him.
That night, when he finished hunting,
he sought lodging out in the countryside.
The wife of Bisclavret heard about it,
dressed herself elegantly,
and went the next day to speak with the king,
bringing rich presents for him.   230
When Bisclavret saw her coming,
no one could hold him back;
he ran toward her in a rage.
Now listen to how well he avenged himself!
He tore the nose off her face.
What worse thing could he have done to her?
Now men closed in on him from all sides;
they were about to tear him apart,
when a wise man said to the king,
"My lord, listen to me!   240
This beast has stayed with you,
and there's not one of us
who hasn't watched him closely,
hasn't traveled with him often.
He's never touched anyone,
or shown any wickedness,
except to this woman.
By the faith that I owe you,
he has some grudge against her,
and against her husband as well.   250
This is the wife of the knight
whom you used to like so much,
and who's been missing for so long—
we don't know what became of him.
Why not put this woman to torture
and see if she'll tell you
why the beast hates her?
Make her tell what she knows!
We've seen many strange things
happen in Brittany!"   260

The king took his advice;
he detained the knight.
At the same time he took the wife
and subjected her to torture;
out of fear and pain
she told all about her husband:
how she had betrayed him
and taken away his clothes;
the story he had told her
about what happened to him and where he went;   270
and how after she had taken his clothes
he'd never been seen in his land again.
She was quite certain
that this beast was Bisclavret.
The king demanded the clothes;
whether she wanted to or not
she sent home for them,
and had them brought to Bisclavret.
When they were put down in front of him
he didn't even seem to notice them;   280
the king's wise man—
the one who had advised him earlier—
said to him, "My lord, you're not doing it right.
This beast wouldn't, under any circumstances,
in order to get rid of his animal form,
put on his clothes in front of you;
you don't understand what this means:
he's just too ashamed to do it here.
Have him led to your chambers
and bring the clothes with him;   290
then we'll leave him alone for a while.
If he turns into a man, we'll know about it."
    The king himself led the way
and closed all the doors on him.
After a while he went back,
taking two barons with him;
all three entered the king's chamber.
On the king's royal bed
they found the knight asleep.
The king ran to embrace him.   300
He hugged and kissed him again and again.
As soon as he had the chance,
the king gave him back all his lands;
he gave him more than I can tell.
He banished his wife,
chased her out of the country.
She went into exile with the knight
with whom she had betrayed her lord.
She had several children
who were widely known   310

for their appearance:
several women of the family
were actually born without noses,
and lived out their lives noseless.

   The adventure that you have heard
really happened, no doubt about it.
The *lai* of Bisclavret was made
so it would be remembered forever.

YONEC

Translated by Robert Hanning and Joan Ferrante

Now that I've begun these *lais*
the effort will not stop me;
every adventure that I know
I shall relate in rhyme.
My intention and my desire
is to tell you next of Yonec,
how he was born and how his father
first came to his mother.
The man who fathered Yonec
was called Muldumarec.   10

There once lived in Brittany
a rich man, old and ancient.
At Caerwent, he was acknowledged
and accepted as lord of the land.
The city sits on the Duelas,
which at one time was open to boats.
The man was very far along in years
but because he possessed a large fortune
he took a wife in order to have children,
who would come after him and be his heirs.   20
The girl who was given to the rich man
came from a good family;
she was wise and gracious and very beautiful—
for her beauty he loved her very much.
Because she was beautiful and noble
he made every effort to guard her.
He locked her inside his tower
in a great paved chamber.
A sister of his,
who was also old and a widow, without her own lord,   30
he stationed with his lady
to guard her even more closely.
There were other women, I believe,

in another chamber by themselves,
but the lady never spoke to them
unless the old woman gave her permission.
So he kept her more than seven years—
they never had any children;
she never left that tower,
neither for family nor for friends.   40
When the lord came to sleep there
no chamberlain or porter
dared enter that room,
not even to carry a candle before the lord.
The lady lived in great sorrow,
with tears and sighs and weeping;
she lost her beauty,
as one does who cares nothing for it.
She would have preferred
death to take her quickly.   50

It was the beginning of April
when the birds begin their songs.
The lord arose in the morning
and made ready to go to the woods.
He had the old woman get up
and close the door behind him—
she followed his command.
The lord went off with his men.
The old woman carried a psalter
from which she intended to read the psalms.   60
The lady, awake and in tears,
saw the light of the sun.
She noticed that the old woman
had left the chamber.
She grieved and sighed
and wept and raged:
"I should never have been born!
My fate is very harsh.
I'm imprisoned in this tower
and I'll never leave it unless I die.   70
What is this jealous old man afraid of
that he keeps me so imprisoned?
He's mad, out of his senses;
always afraid of being deceived.
I can't even go to church
or hear God's service.
If I could speak to people
and enjoy myself with them
I'd be very gracious to my lord
even if I didn't want to be.   80
A curse on my family,

and on all the others
who gave me to this jealous man,
who married me to his body.
It's a rough rope that I pull and draw.
He'll never die—
when he should have been baptized
he was plunged instead in the river of hell;
his sinews are hard, his veins are hard,
filled with living blood.   90
I've often heard
that one could once find
adventures in this land
that brought relief to the unhappy.
Knights might find young girls
to their desire, noble and lovely;
and ladies find lovers
so handsome, courtly, brave, and valiant
that they could not be blamed,
and no one else would see them.   100
If that might be or ever was,
if that has ever happened to anyone,
God, who has power over everything,
grant me my wish in this."
When she'd finished her lament,
she saw, through a narrow window,
the shadow of a great bird.
She didn't know what it was.
It flew into the chamber;
its feet were banded; it looked like a hawk   110
of five or six moultings.
It alighted before the lady.
When it had been there awhile
and she'd stared hard at it,
it became a handsome and noble knight.
The lady was astonished;
her blood went cold, she trembled,
she was frightened—she covered her head.
The knight was very courteous,
he spoke first: 120
"Lady," he said, "don't be afraid.
The hawk is a noble bird,
although its secrets are unknown to you.
Be reassured
and accept me as your love.
That," he said, "is why I came here.
I have loved you for a long time,
I've desired you in my heart.
Never have I loved any woman but you
nor shall I ever love another,   130

yet I couldn't have come to you
or left my own land
had you not asked for me.
But now I can be your love."
The lady was reassured;
she uncovered her head and spoke.
She answered the knight,
saying she would take him as her lover
if he believed in God,
and if their love was really possible.   140
For he was of great beauty.
Never in her life
had she seen so handsome a knight—
nor would she ever.
"My lady," he said, "you are right.
I wouldn't want you to feel
guilt because of me,
or doubt or suspicion.
I do believe in the creator
who freed us from the grief   150
that Adam, our father, led us into
when he bit into the bitter apple.
He is, will be, and always was
the life and light of sinners.
If you don't believe me
send for your chaplain.
Say that you've suddenly been taken ill
and that you desire the service
that God established in this world
for the healing of sinners.   160
I shall take on your appearance
to receive the body of our lord God,
and I'll recite my whole credo for you.
You will never doubt my faith again."
She answered that she was satisfied.
He lay beside her on the bed
but he didn't try to touch her,
to embrace her or to kiss her.
Meanwhile, the old woman had returned.
She found the lady awake   170
and told her it was time to get up,
she would bring her clothes.
The lady said she was ill,
that the old woman should send for the chaplain
and bring him to her quickly—
she very much feared she was dying.
The old woman said, "Be patient,
my lord has gone to the woods.
No one may come in here but me."

The lady was very upset;   180
she pretended to faint.
When the other saw her, she was frightened;
she unlocked the door of the chamber
and sent for the priest.
He came as quickly as he could,
bringing the *corpus domini*.[1]
The knight received it,
drank the wine from the chalice.
Then the chaplain left
and the old woman closed the doors.   190
The lady lay beside her love—
there was never a more beautiful couple.
When they had laughed and played
and spoken intimately,
the knight took his leave
to return to his land.
She gently begged him
to come back often.
"Lady," he said, "whenever you please,
I will be here within the hour.   200
But you must make certain
that we're not discovered.
This old woman will betray us,
night and day she will spy on us.
She will perceive our love,
and tell her lord about it.
If that happens,
if we are betrayed,
I won't be able to escape.
I shall die."   210
With that the knight departed,
leaving his love in great joy.
In the morning she rose restored;
she was happy all week.
Her body had now become precious to her,
she completely recovered her beauty.
Now she would rather remain here
than look for pleasure elsewhere.
She wanted to see her love all the time
and enjoy herself with him.   220
As soon as her lord departed,
night or day, early or late,
she had him all to her pleasure.
God, let their joy endure!
Because of the great joy she felt,
because she could see her love so often,
her whole appearance changed.

---

[1] The "body of the Lord," bread for Communion.

But her lord was clever.
In his heart he sensed
that she was not what she had been.   230
He suspected his sister.
He questioned her one day,
saying he was astonished
that the lady now dressed with care.
He asked her what it meant.
The old woman said she didn't know—
no one could have spoken to her,
she had no lover or friend—
it was only that she was now more willing
to be alone than before.   240
His sister, too, had noticed the change.
Her lord answered:
"By my faith," he said, "I think that's so.
But you must do something for me.
In the morning, when I've gotten up
and you have shut the doors,
pretend you are going out
and leave her lying there alone.
Then hide yourself in a safe place,
watch her and find out   250
what it is, and where it comes from,
that gives her such great joy."
With that plan they separated.
Alas, how hard it is to protect yourself
from someone who wants to trap you,
to betray and deceive you!

Three days later, as I heard the story,
the lord pretended to go away.
He told his wife the story
that the king had sent for him by letter   260
but that he would return quickly.
He left the chamber and shut the door.
The old woman got up,
went behind a curtain;
from there she could hear and see
whatever she wanted to know.
The lady lay in bed but did not sleep,
she longed for her love.
He came without delay,
before any time had passed.   270
They gave each other great joy
with word and look
until it was time to rise—
he had to go.
But the old woman watched him,
saw how he came and went.

She was quite frightened
when she saw him first a man and then a bird.
When the lord returned—
he hadn't gone very far— 280
she told him and revealed
the truth about the knight
and the lord was troubled by it.
But he was quick to invent
a way to kill the knight.
He had great spikes of iron forged,
their tips sharpened—
no razor on earth could cut better.
When he had them all prepared
and pronged on all sides, 290
he set them in the window—
close together and firmly placed—
through which the knight passed
when he visited the lady.
God, he doesn't know what treachery
the villains are preparing.
The next day in the morning
the lord rose before dawn
and said he was going hunting.
The old woman saw him to the door 300
and then went back to bed
for day was not yet visible.
The lady awoke and waited
for the one she loved faithfully;
she said he might well come now
and be with her at leisure.
As soon as she asked,
he came without delay.
He flew into the window,
but the spikes were there. 310
One wounded him in his breast—
out rushed the red blood.
He knew he was fatally wounded;
he pulled himself free and entered the room.
He alighted on the bed, in front of the lady,
staining the bedclothes with blood.
She saw the blood and the wound
in anguish and horror.
He said, "My sweet love,
I lose my life for love of you. 320
I told you it would happen,
that your appearance would kill us."
When she heard that, she fainted;
for a short while she lay as if dead.
He comforted her gently,
said that grief would do no good,

but that she was pregnant with his child.
She would have a son, brave and strong,
who would comfort her;
she would call him Yonec.   330
He would avenge both of them
and kill their enemy.
But he could remain no longer
for his wound was bleeding badly.
He left in great sorrow.
She followed him with loud cries.
She leapt out a window—
it's a wonder that she wasn't killed,
for it was at least twenty feet high
where she made her leap,   340
naked beneath her gown.
She followed the traces of blood
that flowed from the knight
onto the road.
She followed that road and kept to it
until she came to a hill.
In the hill there was an opening,
red with his blood.
She couldn't see anything beyond it
but she was sure   350
that her love had gone in there.
She entered quickly.
She found no light
but she kept to the right road
until it emerged from the hill
into a beautiful meadow.
When she found the grass there wet with blood,
she was frightened.
She followed the traces through the meadow
and saw a city not far away.   360
The city was completely surrounded by walls.
There was no house, no hall or tower,
that didn't seem entirely of silver.
The buildings were very rich.
Going toward the town there were marshes,
forests, and enclosed fields.
On the other side, toward the castle,
a stream flowed all around,
where ships arrived—
there were more than three hundred sails.   370
The lower gate was open;
the lady entered the city,
still following the fresh blood
through the town to the castle.
No one spoke to her,
she met neither man nor woman.

When she came to the palace courtyard,
she found it covered with blood.
She entered a lovely chamber
where she found a knight sleeping.   380
She did not know him, so she went on
into another larger chamber.
There she found nothing but a bed
with a knight sleeping on it;
she kept going.
She entered the third chamber
and on that bed she found her love.
The feet of the bed were all of polished gold,
I couldn't guess the value of the bedclothes;
the candles and the chandeliers,   390
which were lit night and day,
were worth the gold of an entire city.
As soon as she saw him
she recognized the knight.
She approached, frightened,
and fell fainting over him.
He, who greatly loved her, embraced her,
lamenting his misfortune again and again.
When she recovered from her faint
he comforted her gently.   400
"Sweet friend, for God's sake, I beg you,
go away! Leave this place!
I shall die within the day,
there will be great sorrow here,
and if you are found
you will be hurt.
Among my people it will be well known
that they have lost me because of my love for you.
I am disturbed and troubled for you."
The lady answered: "Love,   410
I would rather die with you
than suffer with my lord.
If I go back to him he'll kill me."
The knight reassured her,
gave her a ring,
and explained to her
that, as long as she kept it,
her lord would not remember
anything that had happened—
he would imprison her no longer.   420
He gave her his sword
and then made her swear
no man would ever possess it,
that she'd keep it for their son.
When the son had grown and become
a brave and valiant knight,

she would go to a festival,
taking him and her lord with her.
They would come to an abbey.
There, beside a tomb,   430
they would hear the story of his death,
how he was wrongfully killed.
There she would give her son the sword.
The adventure would be recited to him,
how he was born and who his father was;
then they'd see what he would do.
When he'd told her and shown her everything,
he gave her a precious robe
and told her to put it on.
Then he sent her away.   440
She left carrying the ring
and the sword—they comforted her.
She had not gone half a mile
from the gate of the city
when she heard the bells ring
and the mourning begin in the castle,
and in her sorrow
she fainted four times.
When she recovered from the faints
she made her way to the hill.   450
She entered it, passed through it,
and returned to her country.
There with her lord
she lived many days and years.
He never accused her of that deed,
never insulted or abused her.
Her son was born and nourished,
protected and cherished.
They named him Yonec.
In all the kingdom you couldn't find   460
one so handsome, brave, or strong,
so generous, so munificent.
When he reached the proper age,
he was made a knight.
Hear now what happened
in that very year.

To the feast of St. Aaron,
celebrated in Caerleon
and in many other cities,
the lord had been summoned   470
to come with his friends,
according to the custom of the land,
and to bring his wife and his son,
all richly attired.
So it was; they went.

But they didn't know the way;
they had a boy with them
who guided them along the right road
until they came to a castle—
none more beautiful in all the world.   480
Inside, there was an abbey
of very religious people.
The boy who was guiding them to the festival
housed them there.
In the abbot's chamber
they were well served and honored.
Next day they went to hear Mass
before they departed,
but the abbot went to speak to them
to beg them to stay   490
so he could show them the dormitory,
the chapter house, and the refectory.
And since they were comfortable there,
the lord agreed to stay.
That day, after they had dined,
they went to the workshops.
On their way, they passed the chapter house,
where they found a huge tomb
covered with a cloth of embroidered silk,
a band of precious gold running from one side to the other.   500
At the head, the feet, and at the sides
burned twenty candles.
The chandeliers were pure gold,
the censers amethyst,
which through the day perfumed
that tomb, to its great honor.
They asked and inquired
of people from that land
whose tomb it was,
what man lay there.   510
The people began to weep
and, weeping, to recount
that it was the best knight,
the strongest, the most fierce,
the most handsome and the best loved,
that had ever lived.
"He was king of this land;
no one was ever so courtly.
At Caerwent he was discovered
and killed for the love of a lady.   520
Since then we have had no lord,
but have waited many days,
just as he told and commanded us,
for the son the lady bore him."
When the lady heard that news,

she called aloud to her son.
"Fair son," she said, "you hear
how God has led us to this spot.
Your father, whom this old man murdered,
lies here in this tomb. 530
Now I give and commend his sword to you.
I have kept it a long time for you."
Then she revealed, for all to hear,
that the man in the tomb was the father and this was his son,
and how he used to come to her,
how her lord had betrayed him—
she told the truth.
Then she fainted over the tomb
and, in her faint, she died.
She never spoke again. 540
When her son saw that she had died,
he cut off his stepfather's head.
Thus with his father's sword
he avenged his mother's sorrow.
When all this had happened,
when it became known through the city,
they took the lady with great honor
and placed her in the coffin.
Before they departed
they made Yonec their lord. 550

Long after, those who heard this adventure
composed a lay about it,
about the pain and the grief
that they suffered for love.

Anselm and Aquinas: The Existence of God

(Eleventh and Thirteenth Centuries)

Humanists and other cultural trailblazers of the Renaissance era—roughly, the fifteenth through the early seventeenth centuries—propagated a contemptuous caricature of medieval thinkers: as dry, pedantic hair-splitters, limited in their imaginative vision and confined within the suffocating limits of an excessively narrow and mechanical intellectual discipline. If, however, we measure the medieval and Renaissance eras by the canons of systematic, rigorous thinking in the sphere of formal philosophy, we could easily reverse this judgment and see the Renaissance as a falling-off. Doubtless the later caricature of the medieval Schoolmen, or scholastic philosophers, could apply to them at their worst (though the same charge might be brought against third-rate philosophers of any school or time). On the other hand, it is probably fair to say that Western philosophers since the seventeenth century have found more that is permanently worth chewing on in the formal philosophy produced between 1050 and 1350 than in that of the subsequent Renaissance period.

Nor are we talking about narrow technical matters. Medieval philosophy engages some of the broadest and most fundamental questions we can conceive of, including such problems in metaphysics as the nature of being, essence, existence, time, and infinity, along with such problems in epistemology as the role of the senses and their relationship to mind. Certain medieval thinkers also tried to prove, on rational grounds, the existence of God—not exactly what most people would call a narrow or trivial endeavor.

The two most famous medieval attempts to prove God's existence are those of St. Anselm (1033–1109) and St. Thomas Aquinas (1226–1274). Anselm's "ontological" proof is advanced in his *Proslogium,* or "Discourse." (The term *ontological,* which means "having to do with the nature of being and reality," was applied to Anselm's argument by the eighteenth-century philosopher Immanuel Kant.) Thomas Aquinas's "Five Ways" are included in his *Summa Theologica* (or *Summa Theologiae,* a title preferred by many scholars).

Anselm, a Benedictine monk, was born in the Piedmont town of Aosta and, during a particularly turbulent time, he served in England as a vigorous Archbishop of Canterbury. In effect, Anselm was the founder of the medieval scholastic tradition of philosophy. His best-known works include the *Proslogium,* the *Monologium* ("Soliloquy"), and *Cur Deus Homo* ("Why God Became Man"). Aquinas, a Dominican monk, was born in Roccasecca in southern Italy and devoted most of his career to teaching in Paris and various Italian cities. Among his voluminous writings are the two major treatises *Summa Contra Gentiles* ("Summation Against the Infidels"), c. 1259–64, and the magisterially comprehensive *Summa Theologica* ("Summation of Theology"), written over the last nine years or so of his life. Aquinas's thought represents the culmination of medieval scholastic thinking. It also brings together in a unique way various far-flung philosophical traditions: ancient (especially Aristotle's), Neoplatonic (especially St. Augustine's), Islamic (especially Avicenna's), and Jewish (especially Maimonides').

Both Anselm and Aquinas were devout Christian believers who wrote extensively, from devotional or theological viewpoints, about matters they considered accessible only through divine revelation. But both also wrote at times in a different, philosophical vein wherein the validity of arguments was to be tested by the rules of pure reason quite apart from revelation or religious faith. It is true that Anselm prefaces his ontological proof with the famous statement that he believes in order that he may understand (*credo ut intelligam*), not vice versa, but the proof is nonetheless advanced on its own rationalist terms. One could draw a rough analogy in this respect with a modern scientist who starts from an intuitive leap but then proceeds to a process of rigorous testing.

The first step in coming to grips with Anselm's ontological proof is to take it seriously. Many people encountering it for the first time react to it as a mere verbal trick, and not a very clever one at that. Further thought reveals that, valid or not, Anselm's reasoning is deep and substantial. Some of the greatest philosophers have spent considerable time examining it, either in Anselm's own form or in modified reformulations. The seventeenth-century French mathematician and philosopher René Descartes more or less accepted the proof. In the same century, Benedictus de Spinoza, the Dutch Jewish philosopher, and Gottfried Wilhelm Leibniz, the German polymath, put the proof to use for their purposes. Immanuel Kant, a century later, had to resort to elaborate reasoning to reject it, as did Bertrand Russell in the twentieth century. Indeed, Anselm's proof has probably gotten more attention in this century than ever before, as the revivals of the argument by Charles Hartshorne, Norman Malcolm, and other recent philosophers attest. About one thing commentators generally agree: that Anselm's way of defining and discussing God, whether or not he succeeded in proving God's existence, represents a major innovation by way of clarifying what believers understand God to be.

Aquinas's Five Ways represent a radically different intellectual method, generally much more empirical and rooted in observable phenomena. The first two of his "ways," having to do with motion and the physical operation of certain agents on objects, direct our attention to the world of observable events. The third "way" is a little more abstract, arguing from the existence of contingent things (which did not necessarily have to exist) to a being whose existence is absolutely necessary. The fourth "way" is what we may call "qualitative": gradations of goodness imply the existence of a supreme, defining Good. The fifth "way" is a variant of argument from design: the orderliness of the world necessitates the existence of a being that gives it order.

Anselm's and Aquinas's proofs are more than logical excursions; they are also challenges to imagination. Do both men understand God in the same way? Neither, it should be stressed, made any pretensions to understanding the ultimate nature or essence of God, though they believed that we can assign to Him certain meaningful attributes. But if God is unknowable, does systematic logic really have any proper role in religious experience? Is mystical religious experience a parallel alternative to logical thinking about God, or do the two approaches contradict each other? Is Aquinas on solid ground when he denies that chains of events can continue to infinity? Is any light thrown on this question by modern scientific cosmogonies, such as the big bang theory? Finally, does the severely logical bent of medieval philosophy throw any light on the medieval imagination? For example, does the fantastic quality present in much medieval literature and art—its science fiction aspect, as it were—contradict the logical bent of medieval philosophy, or are all these things ultimately cut from the same mental and imaginative cloth?

FURTHER READING *(prepared by M.C.):* Biographies of Anselm include Benedicta Ward, *Anselm of Canterbury: A Monastic Scholar,* 1990; and R. W. Southern, *St. Anselm: A Portrait in a Landscape,* 1990. Charles Hartshorne's introduction to the second edition, 1962, of *St. Anselm: Basic Writings,* trans. S. N. Deane, contains an incisive discussion of Anselm's proof; this volume preserves also the introduction to the first edition, 1903, 1948, where the responses to Anselm of several famous philosophers are excerpted. M. J. Charlesworth, trans., *St. Anselm's Proslogion,* 1965, contains a good introduction and a philosophical commentary. For a guide to Anselm's works, see Jasper Hopkins, *A Companion to the Study of St. Anselm,* 1972. Theological issues are discussed in Thomas V. Morris, *Anselmian Explorations,* 1987.

On the life of Aquinas, see James A. Weisheipl, *Friar Thomas d'Aquino: His Life, Thought and Works,* 1974; for a briefer summary, see Anthony John Patrick Kenney, *Aquinas,* 1980. Kenney discusses the natural theology of Aquinas in *The Five Ways,* 1969; he has also edited *Aquinas: A Collection of Critical Essays,* 1976. For a general discussion of Aquinas's work, see Étienne Gilson, *The Christian Philosophy of St. Thomas Aquinas,* 1956. Analogy in St. Thomas is discussed in David B. Burrell, *Aquinas: God and Action,* 1979; G. Klubertanz, *St. Thomas Aquinas on Analogy,* 1960; and Ralph M. McInerny, *The Logic of Analogy: An Interpretation of St. Thomas,* 1961. On its title subject, see Umberto Eco, *The Aesthetics of Thomas Aquinas,* 1989.

St. Anselm

(1033–1109)

from *PROSLOGIUM*[1]

Translated by S. N. Deane

from CHAPTER I.

Be it mine to look up to thy [God's] light, even from afar, even from the depths. Teach me to seek thee, and reveal thyself to me, when I seek thee, for I cannot seek thee, except thou teach me, nor find thee, except thou reveal thyself. Let me seek thee in longing, let me long for thee in seeking; let me find thee in love, and love thee in finding. Lord, I acknowledge and I thank thee that thou hast created me in this thine image, in order that I may be mindful of thee, may conceive of thee, and love thee; but that image has been so consumed and wasted away by vices, and obscured by the smoke of wrong-doing, that it cannot achieve that for which it was made, except thou renew it, and create it anew. I do not endeavor, O Lord, to penetrate thy sublimity, for in no wise do I compare my understanding with that; but I long to understand in some degree thy truth, which my heart believes and loves. For I do not seek to understand that I may believe, but I believe in order to understand. For this also I believe,—that unless I believed, I should not understand.

CHAPTER II.
Truly there is a God, although the fool hath said in his heart, There is no God.

And so, Lord, do thou, who dost give understanding to faith, give me, so far as thou knowest it to be profitable, to understand that thou art as we believe; and that thou art that which we believe. And, indeed, we believe that thou art a being than which nothing greater can be conceived. Or is there no such nature, since the fool hath said in his heart, there is no God? (Psalms xiv. I). But, at any rate, this very fool, when he hears of this being of which I speak—a being than which nothing greater can be conceived—understands what he hears, and what he understands is in his understanding; although he does not understand it to exist.

For, it is one thing for an object to be in the understanding, and another to understand that the object exists. When a painter first conceives of what

---

[1] *Proslogium* means "discourse."

he will afterwards perform, he has it in his understanding, but he does not yet understand it to be, because he has not yet performed it. But after he has made the painting, he both has it in his understanding, and he understands that it exists, because he has made it.

Hence, even the fool is convinced that something exists in the understanding, at least, than which nothing greater can be conceived. For, when he hears of this, he understands it. And whatever is understood, exists in the understanding. And assuredly that, than which nothing greater can be conceived, cannot exist in the understanding alone. For, suppose it exists in the understanding alone: then it can be conceived to exist in reality; which is greater.

Therefore, if that, than which nothing greater can be conceived, exists in the understanding alone, the very being, than which nothing greater can be conceived, is one, than which a greater can be conceived. But obviously this is impossible. Hence, there is no doubt that there exists a being, than which nothing greater can be conceived, and it exists both in the understanding and in reality.

CHAPTER III.

God cannot be conceived not to exist.—God is that, than which nothing greater can be conceived.—That which can be conceived not to exist is not God.

And it assuredly exists so truly, that it cannot be conceived not to exist. For, it is possible to conceive of a being which cannot be conceived not to exist; and this is greater than one which can be conceived not to exist. Hence, if that, than which nothing greater can be conceived, can be conceived not to exist, it is not that, than which nothing greater can be conceived. But this is an irreconcilable contradiction. There is, then, so truly a being than which nothing greater can be conceived to exist, that it cannot even be conceived not to exist; and this being thou art, O Lord, our God.

So truly, therefore, dost thou exist, O Lord, my God, that thou canst not be conceived not to exist; and rightly. For, if a mind could conceive of a being better than thee, the creature would rise above the Creator; and this is most absurd. And, indeed, whatever else there is, except thee alone, can be conceived not to exist. To thee alone, therefore, it belongs to exist more truly than all other beings, and hence in a higher degree than all others. For, whatever else exists does not exist so truly, and hence in a less degree it belongs to it to exist. Why, then, has the fool said in his heart, there is no God (Psalms xiv. i), since it is so evident, to a rational mind, that thou dost exist in the highest degree of all? Why, except that he is dull and a fool?

CHAPTER IV.

How the fool has said in his heart what cannot be conceived.—A thing may be conceived in two ways: (1) when the word signifying it is conceived; (2) when the thing itself is understood. As far as the word goes, God can be conceived not to exist; in reality he cannot.

But how has the fool said in his heart what he could not conceive; or how is it that he could not conceive what he said in his heart? since it is the same to say in the heart, and to conceive.

But, if really, nay, since really, he both conceived, because he said in his heart; and did not say in his heart, because he could not conceive; there is more than one way in which a thing is said in the heart or conceived. For, in one sense, an object is conceived, when the word signifying it is conceived; and in another, when the very entity, which the object is, is understood.

In the former sense, then, God can be conceived not to exist; but in the latter, not at all. For no one who understands what fire and water are can conceive fire to be water, in accordance with the nature of the facts themselves, although this is possible according to the words.[2] So, then, no one who understands what God is can conceive that God does not exist; although he says these words in his heart, either without any, or with some foreign, signification. For, God is that than which a greater cannot be conceived. And he who thoroughly understands this, assuredly understands that this being so truly exists, that not even in concept can it be non-existent. Therefore, he who understands that God so exists, cannot conceive that he does not exist.

I thank thee, gracious Lord, I thank thee; because what I formerly believed by thy bounty,[3] I now so understand by thine illumination, that if I were unwilling to believe that thou dost exist, I should not be able not to understand this to be true.

CHAPTER V.
God is whatever it is better to be than not to be; and he, as the only self-existent being, creates all things from nothing.

What art thou, then, Lord God, than whom nothing greater can be conceived? But what art thou, except that which, as the highest of all beings, alone exists through itself, and creates all other things from nothing? For, whatever is not this is less than a thing which can be conceived of. But this cannot be conceived of thee. What good, therefore, does the supreme Good lack, through which every good is? Therefore, thou art just, truthful, blessed, and whatever it is better to be than not to be. For it is better to be just than not just; better to be blessed than not blessed.

ANSELM'S APOLOGETIC

IN REPLY TO GAUNILON'S ANSWER IN BEHALF OF THE FOOL[4]

It was a fool against whom the argument of my Proslogium was directed. Seeing, however, that the author of these objections is by no means a fool, and is a Catholic speaking in behalf of the fool, I think it sufficient that I answer the Catholic.

---

[2] One can be acquainted with a word without understanding what the word means or the thing the word refers to.

[3] The gift of faith.

[4] As with Plato's *Apology*, "Apologetic" here means a defense of one's position, not an apology in the ordinary modern sense. Anselm is replying to objections by the monk Gaunilon of Marmoutier. Gaunilon contended that, if one reasoned as Anselm does in the *Proslogium*, there would have to be an island more perfect than any known island, since, if the former did not in fact exist, it would be less perfect than any known island—a contradiction.

CHAPTER I.

A general refutation of Gaunilon's argument. It is shown that a being than which a greater cannot be conceived exists in reality.

You say—whosoever you may be, who say that a fool is capable of making these statements—that a being than which a greater cannot be conceived is not in the understanding in any other sense than that in which a being that is altogether inconceivable in terms of reality, is in the understanding. You say that the inference that this being exists in reality, from the fact that it is in the understanding, is no more just than the inference that a lost island most certainly exists, from the fact that when it is described the hearer does not doubt that it is in his understanding.

But I say: if a being than which a greater is inconceivable is not understood or conceived, and is not in the understanding or in concept, certainly either God is not a being than which a greater is inconceivable, or else he is not understood or conceived, and is not in the understanding or in concept. But I call on your faith and conscience to attest that this is most false. Hence, that than which a greater cannot be conceived is truly understood and conceived, and is in the understanding and in concept. Therefore either the grounds on which you try to controvert me are not true, or else the inference which you think to base logically on those grounds is not justified.

But you hold, moreover, that supposing that a being than which a greater cannot be conceived is understood, it does not follow that this being is in the understanding; nor, if it is in the understanding, does it therefore exist in reality.

In answer to this, I maintain positively: if that being can be even conceived to be, it must exist in reality. For that than which a greater is inconceivable cannot be conceived except as without beginning. But whatever can be conceived to exist, and does not exist, can be conceived to exist through a beginning. Hence what can be conceived to exist, but does not exist, is not the being than which a greater cannot be conceived. Therefore, if such a being can be conceived to exist, necessarily it does exist.

Furthermore: if it can be conceived at all, it must exist. For no one who denies or doubts the existence of a being than which a greater is inconceivable, denies or doubts that if it did exist, its non-existence, either in reality or in the understanding, would be impossible. For otherwise it would not be a being than which a greater cannot be conceived. But as to whatever can be conceived, but does not exist—if there were such a being, its non-existence, either in reality or in the understanding, would be possible. Therefore if a being than which a greater is inconceivable can be even conceived, it cannot be non-existent.

But let us suppose that it does not exist, even if it can be conceived. Whatever can be conceived, but does not exist, if it existed, would not be a being than which a greater is inconceivable. If, then, there were a being a greater than which is inconceivable, it would not be a being than which a greater is inconceivable: which is most absurd. Hence, it is false to deny that a being than which a greater cannot be conceived exists, if it can be even conceived; much the more, therefore, if it can be understood or can be in the understanding.

Moreover, I will venture to make this assertion: without doubt, whatever at any place or at any time does not exist—even if it does exist at some place or at some time—can be conceived to exist nowhere and never, as at some place and at some time it does not exist. For what did not exist yesterday, and exists to-day, as it is understood not to have existed yesterday, so it can be apprehended by the intelligence that it never exists. And what is not here, and is elsewhere, can be conceived to be nowhere, just as it is not here. So with regard to an object of which the individual parts do not exist at the same places or times: all its parts and therefore its very whole can be conceived to exist nowhere or never.

For, although time is said to exist always, and the world everywhere, yet time does not as a whole exist always, nor the world as a whole everywhere. And as individual parts of time do not exist when others exist, so they can be conceived never to exist. And so it can be apprehended by the intelligence that individual parts of the world exist nowhere, as they do not exist where other parts exist. Moreover, what is composed of parts can be dissolved in concept, and be non-existent. Therefore, whatever at any place or at any time does not exist as a whole, even if it is existent, can be conceived not to exist.

But that than which a greater cannot be conceived, if it exists, cannot be conceived not to exist. Otherwise, it is not a being than which a greater cannot be conceived: which is inconsistent. By no means, then, does it at any place or at any time fail to exist as a whole: but it exists as a whole everywhere and always.

Do you believe that this being can in some way be conceived or understood, or that the being with regard to which these things are understood can be in concept or in the understanding? For if it cannot, these things cannot be understood with reference to it. But if you say that it is not understood and that it is not in the understanding, because it is not thoroughly understood; you should say that a man who cannot face the direct rays of the sun does not see the light of day, which is none other than the sunlight. Assuredly a being than which a greater cannot be conceived exists, and is in the understanding, at least to this extent—that these statements regarding it are understood.

CHAPTER IX.

The possibility of understanding and conceiving of the supremely great being. The argument advanced against the fool is confirmed.

But even if it were true that a being than which a greater is inconceivable cannot be conceived or understood; yet it would not be untrue that a being than which a greater cannot be conceived is conceivable and intelligible. There is nothing to prevent one's saying *ineffable*,[5] although what is said to be ineffable cannot be spoken of. *Inconceivable* is conceivable, although that to which the word *inconceivable* can be applied is not conceivable.[6] So,

---

[5] Incapable of being expressed or described.

[6] Thus, the nature of God is beyond human comprehension, though the statement that He is beyond comprehension can be understood.

when one says, *that than which nothing greater is conceivable,* undoubtedly what is heard is conceivable and intelligible, although that being itself, than which a greater is inconceivable, cannot be conceived or understood.

Or, though there is a man so foolish as to say that there is no being than which a greater is inconceivable, he will not be so shameless as to say that he cannot understand or conceive of what he says. Or, if such a man is found, not only ought his words to be rejected, but he himself should be contemned.

Whoever, then, denies the existence of a being than which a greater cannot be conceived, at least understands and conceives of the denial which he makes. But this denial he cannot understand or conceive of without its component terms; and a term of this statement is *a being than which a greater cannot be conceived.* Whoever, then, makes this denial, understands and conceives of that than which a greater is inconceivable.

Moreover, it is evident that in the same way it is possible to conceive of and understand a being whose non-existence is impossible; but he who conceives of this conceives of a greater being than one whose non-existence is possible. Hence, when a being than which a greater is inconceivable is conceived, if it is a being whose non-existence is possible that is conceived, it is not a being than which a greater cannot be conceived. But an object cannot be at once conceived and not conceived. Hence he who conceives of a being than which a greater is inconceivable, does not conceive of that whose non-existence is possible, but of that whose non-existence is impossible. Therefore, what he conceives of must exist; for anything whose non-existence is possible, is not that of which he conceives.

St. Thomas Aquinas
(1226–1274)

from *SUMMA THEOLOGICA**

QUESTION II

THE EXISTENCE OF GOD

FIRST ARTICLE

WHETHER THE EXISTENCE OF GOD IS SELF-EVIDENT?

We proceed thus to the First Article:—
Objection 1. It seems that the existence of God is self-evident. For those things are said to be self-evident to us the knowledge of which exists natu-

---

*Translator anonymous. Reprinted from *Introduction to Saint Thomas Aquinas,* ed. Anton C. Pegis, Modern Library, Random House, Inc. New York, 1948.

rally in us, as we can see in regard to first principles. But as Damascene says, *the knowledge of God is naturally implanted in all.*[1] Therefore the existence of God is self-evident.

Obj. 2. Further, those things are said to be self-evident which are known as soon as the terms are known, which the Philosopher says is true of the first principles of demonstration.[2] Thus, when the nature of a whole and of a part is known, it is at once recognized that every whole is greater than its part. But as soon as the signification of the name *God* is understood, it is at once seen that God exists. For by this name is signified that thing than which nothing greater can be conceived. But that which exists actually and mentally is greater than that which exists only mentally. Therefore, since as soon as the name *God* is understood it exists mentally, it also follows that it exists actually. Therefore the proposition *God exists* is self-evident.

Obj. 3. Further, the existence of truth is self-evident. For whoever denies the existence of truth grants that truth does not exist: and, if truth does not exist, then the proposition *Truth does not exist* is true: and if there is anything true, there must be truth. But God is truth itself: *I am the way, the truth, and the life* (*Jo.* xiv. 6). Therefore *God exists* is self-evident.

On the contrary, No one can mentally admit the opposite of what is self-evident, as the Philosopher states concerning the first principles of demonstration.[3] But the opposite of the proposition *God is* can be mentally admitted: *The fool said in his heart, There is no God* (*Ps.* lii. 1).[4] Therefore, that God exists is not self-evident.

I answer that, A thing can be self-evident in either of two ways: on the one hand, self-evident in itself, though not to us; on the other, self-evident in itself, and to us. A proposition is self-evident because the predicate[5] is included in the essence of the subject: *e.g., Man is an animal,* for animal is contained in the essence of man. If, therefore, the essence of the predicate and subject be known to all, the proposition will be self-evident to all; as is clear with regard to the first principles of demonstration, the terms of which are certain common notions that no one is ignorant of, such as being and non-being, whole and part, and the like. If, however, there are some to whom the essence of the predicate and subject is unknown, the proposition will be self-evident in itself, but not to those who do not know the meaning of the predicate and subject of the proposition. Therefore, it happens, as Boethius[6] says, that there are some notions of the mind which are common and self-evident only to the learned, as that incorporeal substances are not in space. Therefore I say that this proposition, *God exists,* of itself is self-evident, for the predicate is the same as the subject, because God is His own

---

[1] *Of Orthodox Faith,* I.i.3, by St. John Damascene, or John of Damascus (c. 676–c. 754), a theologian of the Eastern Church.

[2] By "the Philosopher," Aquinas invariably means Aristotle. The reference here is to his *Posterior Analytics,* I.3 (72b).

[3] Aristotle, *Metaphysics,* III.3 (1005b).

[4] Psalm 53 in Hebrew and Protestant bibles. Catholic versions traditionally number Psalms 10 through 147 as, respectively, 9 through 146.

[5] A predicate is whatever is stated, affirmed, or denied about a subject.

[6] Roman scholar and philosopher (c. 475–524 A.D.).

existence as will be hereafter shown.[7] Now because we do not know the essence of God, the proposition is not self-evident to us, but needs to be demonstrated by things that are more known to us, though less known in their nature—namely, by His effects.

Reply Obj. I. To know that God exists in a general and confused way is implanted in us by nature, inasmuch as God is man's beatitude. For man naturally desires happiness, and what is naturally desired by man is naturally known by him. This, however, is not to know absolutely that God exists; just as to know that someone is approaching is not the same as to know that Peter is approaching, even though it is Peter who is approaching; for there are many who imagine that man's perfect good, which is happiness, consists in riches, and others in pleasures, and others in something else.

Reply Obj. 2. Perhaps not everyone who hears this name *God* understands it to signify something than which nothing greater can be thought, seeing that some have believed God to be a body. Yet, granted that everyone understands that by this name *God* is signified something than which nothing greater can be thought, nevertheless, it does not therefore follow that he understands that what the name signifies exists actually, but only that it exists mentally. Nor can it be argued that it actually exists, unless it be admitted that there actually exists something than which nothing greater can be thought; and this precisely is not admitted by those who hold that God does not exist.

Reply Obj. 3. The existence of truth in general is self-evident, but the existence of a Primal Truth is not self-evident to us.

SECOND ARTICLE

WHETHER IT CAN BE DEMONSTRATED THAT GOD EXISTS?

We proceed thus to the Second Article:—

Objection I. It seems that the existence of God cannot be demonstrated. For it is an article of faith that God exists. But what is of faith cannot be demonstrated, because a demonstration produces scientific knowledge, whereas faith is of the unseen, as is clear from the Apostle (*Heb.* xi. I).[8] Therefore it cannot be demonstrated that God exists.

*   *   *   *   *   *

On the contrary, The Apostle says: *The invisible things of Him are clearly seen, being understood by the things that are made* (*Rom.* i. 20). But this would not be unless the existence of God could be demonstrated through the things that are made; for the first thing we must know of anything is, whether it exists.

I answer that, Demonstration can be made in two ways: One is through the cause, and is called *propter quid,* and this is to argue from what is prior absolutely. The other is through the effect, and is called a demonstration

---

[7] In a later section of the *Summa,* not included in this volume.

[8] For St. Thomas, "the Apostle" always means St. Paul. Tradition—as opposed to most modern biblical scholarship—often ascribed to Paul the Epistle to the Hebrews. The passage referred to reads, "Now faith is the substance of things hoped for, the evidence of things not seen."

quia;[9] this is to argue from what is prior relatively only to us. When an effect is better known to us than its cause, from the effect we proceed to the knowledge of the cause. And from every effect the existence of its proper cause can be demonstrated, so long as its effects are better known to us; because, since every effect depends upon its cause, if the effect exists, the cause must pre-exist. Hence the existence of God, in so far as it is not self-evident to us, can be demonstrated from those of His effects which are known to us.

Reply Obj. I. The existence of God and other like truths about God, which can be known by natural reason, are not articles of faith, but are preambles to the articles; for faith presupposes natural knowledge, even as grace presupposes nature and perfection the perfectible. Nevertheless, there is nothing to prevent a man, who cannot grasp a proof, from accepting, as a matter of faith, something which in itself is capable of being scientifically known and demonstrated.

THIRD ARTICLE

WHETHER GOD EXISTS?

We proceed thus to the Third Article:—

Objection I. It seems that God does not exist; because if one of two contraries be infinite, the other would be altogether destroyed. But the name *God* means that He is infinite goodness. If, therefore, God existed, there would be no evil discoverable; but there is evil in the world. Therefore God does not exist.

Obj. 2. Further, it is superfluous to suppose that what can be accounted for by a few principles has been produced by many. But it seems that everything we see in the world can be accounted for by other principles, supposing God did not exist. For all natural things can be reduced to one principle, which is nature; and all voluntary things can be reduced to one principle, which is human reason, or will. Therefore there is no need to suppose God's existence.

On the contrary, It is said in the person of God: *I am Who am* (*Exod.* iii. 14).

I answer that, The existence of God can be proved in five ways.

The first and more manifest way is the argument from motion. It is certain, and evident to our senses, that in the world some things are in motion. Now whatever is moved is moved by another, for nothing can be moved except it is in potentiality to that towards which it is moved; whereas a thing moves inasmuch as it is in act. For motion is nothing else than the reduction of something from potentiality to actuality. But nothing can be reduced from potentiality to actuality, except by something in a state of actuality. Thus that which is actually hot, as fire, makes wood, which is potentially hot, to be actually hot, and thereby moves and changes it. Now it is not possible that the same thing should be at once in actuality and potentiality in the same respect, but only in different respects. For what is actually hot cannot simultaneously be potentially hot; but it is simultaneously

---

[9] Latin *propter quid:* "on account of something"; *quia:* "because."

potentially cold. It is therefore impossible that in the same respect and in the same way a thing should be both mover and moved, *i.e.*, that it should move itself. Therefore, whatever is moved must be moved by another. If that by which it is moved be itself moved, then this also must needs be moved by another, and that by another again. But this cannot go on to infinity, because then there would be no first mover, and, consequently, no other mover, seeing that subsequent movers move only inasmuch as they are moved by the first mover; as the staff moves only because it is moved by the hand. Therefore it is necessary to arrive at a first mover, moved by no other; and this everyone understands to be God.

The second way is from the nature of efficient cause.[10] In the world of sensible things we find there is an order of efficient causes. There is no case known (neither is it, indeed, possible) in which a thing is found to be the efficient cause of itself; for so it would be prior to itself, which is impossible. Now in efficient causes it is not possible to go on to infinity, because in all efficient causes following in order, the first is the cause of the intermediate cause, and the intermediate is the cause of the ultimate cause, whether the intermediate cause be several, or one only. Now to take away the cause is to take away the effect. Therefore, if there be no first cause among efficient causes, there will be no ultimate, nor any intermediate, cause. But if in efficient causes it is possible to go on to infinity, there will be no first efficient cause, neither will there be an ultimate effect, nor any intermediate efficient causes; all of which is plainly false. Therefore it is necessary to admit a first efficient cause, to which everyone gives the name of God.

The third way is taken from possibility and necessity, and runs thus. We find in nature things that are possible to be and not to be, since they are found to be generated, and to be corrupted, and consequently, it is possible for them to be and not to be. But it is impossible for these always to exist, for that which can not-be at some time is not. Therefore, if everything can not-be, then at one time there was nothing in existence. Now if this were true, even now there would be nothing in existence, because that which does not exist begins to exist only through something already existing. Therefore, if at one time nothing was in existence, it would have been impossible for anything to have begun to exist; and thus even now nothing would be in existence—which is absurd. Therefore, not all beings are merely possible, but there must exist something the existence of which is necessary. But every necessary thing either has its necessity caused by another, or not. Now it is impossible to go on to infinity in necessary things which have their necessity caused by another, as has been already proved in regard to efficient causes. Therefore we cannot but admit the existence of some being having of itself its own necessity, and not receiving it from another, but rather causing in others their necessity. This all men speak of as God.

The fourth way is taken from the gradation to be found in things. Among beings there are some more and some less good, true, noble, and the like. But *more* and *less* are predicated of different things according as they resemble in their different ways something which is the maximum, as a thing is said to be hotter according as it more nearly resembles that which is hottest;

---

[10] In Aristotelian thought, an efficient cause is something that acts on something else; for example, a sculptor wielding a chisel would be the efficient cause of a statue.

so that there is something which is truest, something best, something noblest, and, consequently, something which is most being, for those things that are greatest in truth are greatest in being, as it is written in *Metaph.* ii.[11] Now the maximum in any genus is the cause of all in that genus, as fire, which is the maximum of heat, is the cause of all hot things, as is said in the same book. Therefore there must also be something which is to all beings the cause of their being, goodness, and every other perfection; and this we call God.

The fifth way is taken from the governance of the world. We see that things which lack knowledge, such as natural bodies, act for an end, and this is evident from their acting always, or nearly always, in the same way, so as to obtain the best result. Hence it is plain that they achieve their end, not fortuitously,[12] but designedly. Now whatever lacks knowledge cannot move towards an end, unless it be directed by some being endowed with knowledge and intelligence; as the arrow is directed by the archer. Therefore some intelligent being exists by whom all natural things are directed to their end; and this being we call God.

Reply Obj. I. As Augustine says: *Since God is the highest good, He would not allow any evil to exist in His works, unless His omnipotence and goodness were such as to bring good even out of evil.*[13] This is part of the infinite goodness of God, that He should allow evil to exist, and out of it produce good.

Reply Obj. 2. Since nature works for a determinate end under the direction of a higher agent, whatever is done by nature must be traced back to God as to its first cause. So likewise whatever is done voluntarily must be traced back to some higher cause other than human reason and will, since these can change and fail; for all things that are changeable and capable of defect must be traced back to an immovable and self-necessary first principle, as has been shown.

---

[11]Aristotle, *Metaphysics,* Ia.1 (993b).   [12]Accidentally.
[13]St. Augustine (354–430), Christian theologian and writer. The quotation is from his *Enchiridion,* XI.

Dante Alighieri

(1265–1321)

The reputation of Dante Alighieri, already high in the time immediately following his death, is today such as to rank him with Homer and Shakespeare at the summit of world literature and his *Divine Comedy* as perhaps the greatest single work of literary art. Dante's simple title was the *Commedia* (the epithet *Divina* was added on title pages beginning in the sixteenth century). The work was called a comedy because its style was a middle one beneath the high-serious tone of tragedy and because its movement was from sadness to joy. The *Comedy* is often described as the quintessence of the medieval worldview, a codification of the values of the high Middle Ages in art, science, theology, and philosophy. This view has considerable truth. It is not without its ironies, however; Dante felt nostalgia for the past and entertained hopes for the future, but he considered his own age vicious, corrupt, and benighted. The circumstances of his life and its public backdrop bear out his judgment in many respects.

Dante was born in 1265 in the independent, republican city-state of Florence, which in its commercial prosperity and its culture was beginning to rank with the leading cities of Europe. For decades before his birth an appallingly bloody feud had divided Florence into two factions: the Ghibellines, a feudal and military class allied with the Holy Roman Emperor, and the Guelfs, a middle-class party that tended to side with the papacy in its struggle against the empire. Dante's family were Guelfs. After an alternation of victories by one side over the other, the Guelfs triumphed decisively when Dante was a year old. But by the end of the century the Guelfs themselves had split into factions: the Blacks, who represented the nobility and were willing to tolerate papal political influence, and the Whites, who represented the commercial bourgeoisie and wanted political independence. Dante was a moderate White. After some military service, he held in his early thirties a succession of increasingly prominent political offices, becoming one of the chief magistrates of Florence in 1300, the year in which the events of the *Divine Comedy* are imagined to take place. Fighting broke out in the streets. Dante's solution was to help banish the leaders of both factions, including his brother-in-law and also Guido Cavalcanti, one of his best friends and a fellow poet. But the Blacks conspired with Dante's detested Pope Boniface VIII, who wished to establish his power in Florence and the surrounding region of Tuscany, and with the help of a foreign army the Whites were ousted, while Dante was absent on a diplomatic mission to Rome. In 1302 he was unjustly accused of barratry (graft), tried *in absentia*, fined the large sum of 5,000 florins, and banished for two years. When he refused to pay the fine and thus admit guilt, the banishment was ruled perpetual, under penalty of being burned alive. Dante never saw his beloved—and henceforth also hated—Florence again, or his wife, Gemma, whom he had married in his mid-twenties. The *Divine Comedy* refers often to this century-long saga of bloody and sleazy politics.

For a time Dante nourished the hope that the Whites would regain control of Florence, but these hopes remained unfulfilled, and gradually Dante became a party of one, disillusioned with all the factions. He was thereafter dependent on a series of patrons who gave him asylum in various Italian cities, mainly in the north. Tradition has it that he spent some time in France and possibly in England, at Oxford. In 1308 his hopes for the regeneration, reordering, and pacification of Italy, including Florence, were rekindled by the election of a new, idealistic Holy Roman Emperor, Henry VII. Dante believed that most of the political evils of his country, and some of the spiritual ones too, sprang from a lack of guidance by an enlightened emperor such as Rome had had in its best ancient days. But Henry's expedition to Italy failed, thwarted by party conflicts, the opposition of the Pope, and finally by Henry's death in 1313. Dante's hopes were once more disappointed. His very last years, however, were relatively serene; he had already circulated the first two parts of his *Comedy*, the *Inferno* and *Purgatory*, the fame of which helped sustain him, and his children were again with him. His last patron, in Ravenna, was a nephew of the Francesca da Rimini whose story Dante had told so movingly in *Inferno* canto V. Dante died in 1321, not long after he completed the *Paradise* and with it the entire *Comedy*.

As references in that work show, Dante's political vicissitudes are reflected in his art. Yet he lived another inner and creative life independent of public traumas. He seems to have had a happy childhood and a good education, probably under Dominican and Franciscan priests. He studied rhetoric under the philosopher-poet Brunetto Latini whom he honors in *Inferno* XV. He was early influenced by French Provençal poetry and by the Italian vernacular poetry that had only recently begun to flourish. A protégé of Guido Cavalcanti, Dante developed a *dolce stil nuovo* ("sweet new style"), rejecting elegant artifice for its own sake and emphasizing instead sincerity of feeling and substance in ideas. The central event of his earlier spiritual life is narrated in the *Vita Nuova* ("New Life"), an amatory and spiritual autobiography with allegorical overtones, which he composed in Italian in 1292. It records, in a mixture of lyric verse and prose commentary, Dante's first love, inspired in him at the age of nine by the sight of Beatrice Portinari, a girl one year younger. He immediately conceived for her a lifelong, intensely idealistic passion that owes much to the medieval tradition of worship of woman, to which Dante adds a moral and philosophical dimension. Nine years later Dante and Beatrice greeted each other. There followed episodes of alienation and psychological distress (apparently idealized, for Dante seems not to have had much close contact with Beatrice). After she died in 1290, he turned to a compassionate lady who later became an emblem of the philosophical pursuits that occupied him after Beatrice's death. The composition of the *Vita Nuova,* when Dante was twenty-seven, marks the end of the third nine-year period, the number symbolism foreshadowing an even more elaborate dependence in the *Divine Comedy* on threes and nines. In all this it is difficult to separate fact from idealization, but perhaps such a symbol-making mind as Dante's would reject the distinction. The *Vita Nuova* ends with the mention of a wondrous vision and with the determination by Dante that he will write no more of Beatrice until he can write of her "what has not before been written of any woman." This decision is one seed of the *Divine Comedy,* in which Beatrice ("giver of blessings") reappears, the Florentine girl transfigured as the heavenly lady who, having helped rescue Dante from his dark night, conducts him through the spheres of the celestial paradise. She becomes both a symbol and vehicle of God's love and revelation.

The study of philosophy and literature that Dante embarked on after the death of Beatrice was continued and deepened in later years until he had mastered most of the important ancient and medieval writers accessible in that time before the Renaissance revival of classical Greek. Indeed, he became one of the most learned men in Europe. He was indebted philosophically to Aristotle, by way of St. Thomas Aquinas. Poetically, he was immensely indebted to Virgil, whom he echoes again and again in the *Comedy* and chooses to represent as his guide through Hell and most of Purgatory, the realms that can be largely understood by the human reason that (among other things) Virgil represents. Dante claimed to know the *Aeneid* by heart. His erudition led him to attempt several ambitious works. Much of what he had learned by 1305 or so he tried to put into a philosophically encyclopedic work called the *Convivio* ("Banquet"), which was to contain fifteen treatises in alternating prose and verse, like the *Vita Nuova.* The *Convivio,* although abandoned by Dante in about 1308, is a landmark in its use of Italian prose instead of Latin for serious philosophical purposes, anticipating the choice of Italian for the *Comedy*. Conversely, Dante explored the general and practical principles involved in creating a worthy Italian language and literature in a Latin work of the same period, *De Vulgari Eloquentia* ("Of Eloquence in the Vernacular Tongue"), which he also left incomplete. Somewhat later, at the time Dante's hero Henry VII was in Italy, he wrote the Latin *De Monarchia,* in which, picking up a theme treated in the *Convivio,* Dante argued the bold thesis that the rightful powers of emperor and pope, respectively temporal and spiritual, were both derived directly from God. The implication was that in a Christian state the two should be separate but equal authorities and should limit themselves to their own mutually exclusive spheres. This idea influences not just the thematic content of the *Divine Comedy* but its very rationale and symbolism; for example, at the end of the *Inferno,* at the bottom and center of Hell, the place of supreme dishonor in the jaws of Satan, the author of all evil, is shared by the spiritual traitor Judas and imperial traitors Brutus and Cassius.

Dante wrote the *Comedy* between 1308 and 1321, completing the *Inferno* by 1312 and the *Purgatory* by 1315. Literally, it is an account of a privileged journey taken by Dante the character (who should be distinguished from the Dante who writes the poem after the fact) into the world of the afterlife. On this level the *Comedy* is a theological work. The damned are those who, each in his or her own way, have definitively rebelled against God's law and defied or ignored His mercy; these include pagans, Jews, and Christians. The saved are those who, having repented and been forgiven by God, dwell with Him in the celestial paradise. Also among the saved are those who, having died at peace with God, are still spiritually imperfect and must refine away their potential for evil in Purgatory, which Dante locates on a mountain in the southern ocean. The Christian faith is a prerequisite for beatitude, although the righteous Jews of the Old Testament period are saved by their implicit faith in Christ to come; moreover, Jewish infants and baptized Christian infants are also among the saved. The virtuous pagans of antiquity and of more modern times cannot enter Heaven; instead they dwell in Limbo, the uppermost circle of Hell, where their only suffering is to live without hope of redemption. These righteous pagans include even Virgil. Dante shows, especially in the *Paradise,* that he is troubled by the lot of these blameless persons, and in fact in *Paradise* XX he opens a loophole, revealing that at least some good pagans can finally be saved. But this is only a loophole, a faint gleam of mysterious hope, and much pathos arises in the *Inferno* and *Purgatory* from the assumption that the magisterial and fatherlike Virgil is inexorably excluded from eternal bliss.

Theologically, Purgatory is the most distinctively Catholic realm, reflecting one fundamental difference in belief between the Catholic and Protestant faiths. The basic Protestant position, as formulated two centuries later during the Reformation, is that human beings are saved by faith in God's mercy and grace; Catholics believe that we are saved by a combination of such faith and "works" (acts of goodness and remedial suffering). This latter view can make God seem a niggardly taskmaster, forgiving only grudgingly. But the Catholic view, if we can extrapolate from Dante's idea of the Redemption in *Paradise* VII, is that God is like a generous creditor who might have forgiven a debt outright but instead asks that part be repaid so as to salvage the self-respect and elevate the dignity of the sinner-debtor. Dante's purgatorians thus suffer, in a discipline of compensation, but joyfully and willingly. Because they can rise to a higher slope of the mountain as soon as they feel ready and worthy, their own wills are the essential ministers of the purgatorial process.

An awareness of such theological fundamentals is important for an understanding of the *Comedy*, but the modern appeal of the work, even for believers, is not primarily theological but rather ethical and artistic. The *Comedy* is intended to be a picture of the world we live in; the journey into the afterlife is also the struggle in this life of every person who confronts evil, conquers it, and rises above it. Dante most obviously makes us aware of the temporal life by portraying known persons, great and commonplace, antique and modern, dead and living, and by commenting frequently on immediate, local issues, especially politics. In describing the three great realms and making clear his own emotional states, he draws vivid comparisons with the scenes and landscapes of recognizable life—the breaking of a gambler's lucky streak, the shipyards at Venice, a tailor's squint, fireflies on a summer evening, windmills seen through mist.

Above all, Dante comments on earthly life through the descriptions of the punishments in Hell. These are not merely imposed from outside and after the fact; rather, they are symbols of the sins when they are truly understood and realized in imaginative fullness. Someone once said that the motto of the *Inferno* might well be "They got what they wanted." Or, in Gerard Manley Hopkins's words, "The lost are like this, and their scourge [is] to be . . . their sweating selves." Thus the adulterous lovers Francesca and Paolo will be united forever, airborne on the winds of passion; the suicides who separated soul from body will remain so divided even after the Last Judgment, when other creatures have reassumed their flesh; the heretics who denied the immortality of the soul lie forever in sarcophagi, which will be sealed at the Judgment just as, in effect, they predicted; the popes who desecrated their office for money are all crammed, upside down and head to foot, into a single hole, in a parody of the apostolic succession and the laying on of hands by which the episcopal office is transmitted; the grafters continue their life of concealment and trickery.

Moreover, the scheme of punishments in Hell reflects a theory of human nature and a rather complex scheme of ethics. (The divisions of Hell and of Purgatory are outlined by Virgil in *Inferno* XI and *Purgatory* XVII.) The merely sensual sinners are the least guilty, and of them the sexual sinners least of all, possibly because sex retains some touch of the love that, properly understood, is God. The next most guilty are the violent. But the worst sinners are those who pervert the divine plan of creation by misusing the specifically human power of reason—that is, the fraudulent. But even fraud has gradations, and it is worst when it is treacherous. And the worst form of treachery is that shown to lords and benefactors. God as understood by Dante is associated with motion and energy and it is therefore appropriate that the punishment for treacherous fraud is not the hellfire of popular imagination but complete entropy in the form of a lake of ice. The Limbo and the circle of the heretics are conceived in the light of distinctively Christian beliefs, but the remainder of the Inferno is defined in terms of nearly universal human insights and values.

Theologically, it may strike some people as arbitrary that in Dante salvation and damnation depend on the state of the human soul at the moment when, perhaps by sudden accident, death occurs, although in fact that notion is not uniquely Dantean or Christian. But from a moral rather than theological perspective, the idea suggests in the most powerful way possible that all actions in life are of incalculable consequence, each containing in itself the essence of utter good or utter evil. Perhaps it is Dante's sense of this urgency that makes him consign the contemptible trimmers, who were neither good nor evil, to the outer vestibule of Hell, lest their presence in Hell proper make "the wicked gain pride by comparison" (*Inferno* III.42).

Probably no great work of literature has a structure so precisely articulated as the *Divine Comedy*. It is governed, texturally and architecturally, by the numbers 3, 9, and 10. The entire *Comedy* has 100 cantos, the square of the perfect number 10. Each of the three great divisions has 33 cantos (the first of the 34 cantos in the *Inferno* serving as a prelude to the entire work). There are 9 (3 times 3) circles or spheres in each of the three realms, to which is added another region of a different order (the vestibule of Hell, the Garden of Eden, the empyrean Heaven), making a total of 10. The entire poem is written in tercets, three-line stanzas, and the Italian rhyme scheme is *terza rima* ("third rhyme"), a system of interlocking rhymes in the pattern *aba bcb cdc*, each end rhyme thus sounding three times. The tercet is the normal syntactical unit of statement, producing along with the rhyme scheme an effect of powerful but deliberate forward movement. The symbolism of threes is an ever-present acknowledgment of the divine Trinity. Dante's mind, like others in the Middle Ages, could imagine a God who is both love and mathematical order.

But the synthesizing imagination of Dante is best revealed not in such number symbolism but in the poem's total mode of understanding the structure of reality. Time is boldly conflated and twisted, sinners who have been in Hell for millennia coexist in an eternal now with those who have been dead for only a few years. The period of Dante's journey through Hell, from Good Friday to Easter Sunday, corresponds mythically to the time Jesus spent in the tomb. Cultures that were distinct on earth are homogenized in the hereafter, classical monsters and Christian demons reduced to a common denominator of allegorical and moral values. The boundaries between science, theology, philosophy, geography, history, and other branches of knowledge are virtually nonexistent; Dante hears lectures on politics and lunar astrophysics even in Paradise. Physical gravitation is closely identified with the spiritual operation of love, which is the motive power alike of the astronomical heavens and of every human act, good or bad. Evil and suffering, symbolized in *Inferno* XIV by the tears of a gigantic Cretan statue weeping for the sorrows and sins of human history, move ever downward, channeled by Hell's four rivers to the motionless center of the universe; in the meantime, from the mountain of Purgatory on the other side of the globe the river of Lethe flows down to join the others in the same place, carrying with it the dead memories of the vices of the saved. Conversely, as the repentant move up the slopes of Purgatory, the burden of their evil propensities is quite literally lightened, so that like modern astronauts they feel the ascent easier and easier until, made perfect again in Eden, they rise to Heaven as naturally as flames fly upward.

The ultimate goal of Dante the pilgrim and of the poem is the direct vision of God in the uncircumscribed empyrean heaven. In describing this experience, the last cantos of the *Paradise* achieve a sublimity unsurpassed in literature. There Dante must realize for us what is utterly suprasensory and beyond speech without relinquishing the poetic tools of language and sense imagery that are the poet's only means of communication. His imagistic media, as throughout the *Paradise,* are mainly light, color, and nearly abstract patterns. His subject is not only the Deity but the relationship of Deity to the immensely variegated, differentiated world of things, places, and people so much of which the *Comedy* has revealed:

In its depths I saw contained, bound with love
  in one volume, what is scattered
  on leaves throughout the world. . . . [*Paradise* XXXIII.85–87]

The paradox, fundamental to any theistic vision, is that a God who is one and changeless created and sustains the teeming variety of our world.

It is impossible for translation to capture the exquisite sound effects of Dante's Italian, particularly the incantatory echoing of consonant and vowel sounds in lines such as *Dei remi facemmo ali al folle volo* ("we made wings of our oars for the mad flight"—*Inferno* XXVI.125). But in many other respects Dante's style and manner are unusually translatable. Although convoluted passages do occur, the hallmarks of Dante's usual style are directness and economy. He prefers verbs and nouns, using adjectives sparingly, and then more for utilitarian description than for atmosphere or ornament. (As an example, see Ulysses' famous speech in *Inferno* XXVI.91–142.) Exactly because he is describing what none of us has seen, he is compelled, as a good technical writer is, to furnish lucid visual descriptions and analogies. His method is eminently dramatic, realized in the overt gestures and speech of his characters. The characterizations are masterful; the most memorable—Francesca, Farinata, Brunetto Latini, Ulysses, Ugolino—are accomplished in a few dozen lines. Much of this can be captured by a literal translator who, renouncing the hopeless effort to compete with Dante's versification, lets this most literal of poets speak directly to us in language as nearly unclouded as his own.

FURTHER READING *(prepared by W.J.R.):* A fine biography for the general reader is Monroe Stearns's *Dante: Poet of Love,* 1965, which is also a good introduction to *The Divine Comedy.* Carlo Golino's *Dante Alighieri,* 1979, which also provides both biographical information and criticism, has good discussions of works other than *The Divine Comedy.* Background material for the study of Dante's *Comedy,* a canto-by-canto summary, and critical analysis are combined in Aldo S. Bernardo and Anthony L. Pellegrini, *A Critical Study Guide to Dante's "Divine Comedy,"* 1968. The visual aids in this work are particularly useful. Especially accessible and helpful are Wallace Fowlie, *A Reading of Dante's "Inferno,"* 1981; and *Approaches to Teaching Dante's "Divine Comedy,"* ed. Carole Slande and Giovanni Cecchetti, 1982. The notes and running commentary in Mark Musa's translation of *The Divine Comedy,* completed in 1984, are extremely helpful. Uberto Limentani's *Dante's Comedy: Introductory Readings of Selected Cantos,* 1985, provides an excellent model of how to read the poem as a whole. Joan M. Ferrante's *The Political Vision of the Divine Comedy,* 1984, is another excellent study, even broader in its critical scope than the title implies. A general appreciation of the *Comedy* is offered in Thomas Goddard Bergin's *Dante's "Divine Comedy,"* 1971, which is also good on the cosmology. George Holmes's *Dante,* 1980, in the Past Masters series, is a good introductory overview, of manageable length. For a historical introduction to the *Comedy,* see Erich Auerbach's *Dante, Poet of the Secular World,* 1929, trans. Ralph Manheim, 1961. Auerbach's analysis of structure in the *Comedy* is also particularly readable and rewarding. *Dante: A Collection of Critical Essays,* ed. J. Freccero, 1965, contains thirteen articles by Auerbach, Pirandello, and others. Selected cantos are interpreted in Mark Musa's *Advent at the Gates,* 1974. Musa's discussion of ambiguity in the characterization of Francesca is especially interesting. Marianne Shapiro's *Woman, Earthly and Divine in the "Comedy" of Dante,* 1975, emphasizes the poet's relationship with Beatrice and offers a provocative discussion of Virgil's maternal and paternal aspects in the *Inferno.* Also valuable are David Nolan, ed., *Dante Commentaries: Eight Studies of "The Divine Comedy,"* 1977, and its companion volume, *Dante Soundings,* 1981. For clear explanations of Dante's Aristotelian ideas, see Patrick Boyde, *Perception and Passion in Dante's Comedy,* 1993.

THE DIVINE COMEDY

Translated, with interpolated summaries and
bracketed glosses, by H. R. Huse.

INFERNO

A SAMPLE OF THE ORIGINAL VERSE

*The opening tercets from Canto I will give readers an idea of the language and
form of the original work.*

Nel mezzo del cammin di nostra vita
  mi ritrovai per una selva oscura,
  chè la diritta via era smarrita.

Ah quanto a dir qual era è cosa dura
  esta selva selvaggia e aspra e forte
  che nel pensier rinnova la paura!

Tant'è amara che poco è più morte;
  ma per trattar del ben ch'io vi trovai,
  dirò dell'altre cose ch' i' v'ho scorte.

Io non so ben ridir com'io v'entrai,
  tant'era pieno di sonno a quel punto
  che la verace via abbandonai.   12

Ma poi ch'i' fui al piè d'un colle giunto,
  là dove terminava quella valle
  che m'avea di paura il cor compunto,

guardai in alto, e vidi le sue spalle
  vestite già de' raggi del pianeta
  che mena dritto altrui per ogni calle.

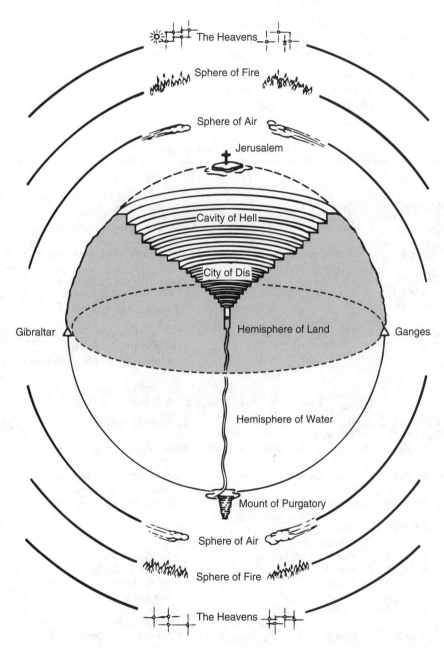

A diagram of the earth in the center of the universe.

Allor fu la paura un poco queta
  che nel lago del cor m'era durata
  la notte chi'i' passai con tanta pièta.

E come quei che con lena affannata
  uscito fuor del pelago alla riva
  si volge all'acqua perigliosa e guata,   24

così l'animo mio, ch'ancor fuggiva,
  si volse a retro a rimirar lo passo
  che non lasciò già mai persona viva.

OUTLINE OF THE INFERNO

Upper Hell, Incontinence

REGION	SINNERS	PUNISHMENTS
Vestibule	Trimmers, neutrals	Stung by insects, run after banners
Circle I	[Virtuous pagans, unbaptized infants]	Melancholy, desire without hope
Circle II	The lustful	Blown forever by storm winds
Circle III	The gluttons	Discomfort, all senses punished
Circle IV	The avaricious and the prodigal	Pushing rocks, useless labor
Circle V	The angry and the sullen	The angry thrashing about helplessly; the sullen submerged, emitting bubbles

Lower Hell, Malice (Violence and Fraud)

Circle VI	[Heretics]	In burning tombs
Circle VII	The violent	
Round 1	against neighbors, fellow men	Submerged in hot blood
Round 2	against self (suicides)	Enclosed in new bodies, as trees and bushes
Round 3	against God (blasphemers, sodomites, usurers)	On burning sand in rain of fire
Circle VIII	Fraud against those who have no special trust	
Bolgia 1	Panders and seducers	Whipped by devils
Bolgia 2	Flatterers	Covered with filth
Bolgia 3	Simonists	Upside down in holes, feet on fire
Bolgia 4	Soothsayers	Heads twisted, turned backward
Bolgia 5	Barrators	Covered by boiling pitch
Bolgia 6	Hypocrites	Wearing leaden mantles
Bolgia 7	Thieves	In snake pit, transformations
Bolgia 8	Evil counselors	Concealed in flames

OUTLINE OF THE INFERNO *(continued)*

Lower Hell, Malice (Violence and Fraud)

Bolgia 9	Sowers of discord	Wounds, mutilations
Bolgia 10	Falsifiers (alchemists, impersonators, counterfeiters, liars)	Diseases (leprosy, madness, dropsy, high fever)
Circle IX	Fraudulent against those who have special trust	
Caïna	Murderers of kindred	In ice to necks, heads bent forward
Antenora	Traitors to party or country	In ice to necks
Tolomea	Murderers of guests	In ice to necks, heads bent backward
Giudecca	Traitors to lords and benefactors	Completely submerged in ice

At the Center of the Earth (Universe)

Lucifer with Judas, Brutus, and Cassius in his three mouths, with three sets of wings sending forth a freezing blast of impotence, ignorance, and hatred.

NOTE: The souls in Circle I and Circle VI are outside of the classifications of Incontinence and Malice. They are guilty only from a Christian viewpoint, and Dante has to fit them as well as he can into the Aristotelian classification.

CANTO I

VIRGIL

The story begins on Thursday night, April 7, 1300. Dante, at the age of thirty-five, having completed half of man's traditional three-score years and ten, awakens to find himself in the forest of worldliness or sin. He cannot recall how he entered it: he had sunk, as men do, gradually and imperceptibly into sinful habits.

The night passes, and the sun (Divine Enlightenment or Righteous Choice) rises behind the Mount of Rectitude.

In the middle of the journey of our life
    I came to my senses in a dark forest,
    for I had lost the straight path.

Oh, how hard it is to tell
    what a dense, wild, and tangled wood this was,
    the thought of which renews my fear!

So terrible it is that death is hardly worse.
    But to reveal the good that I found there,
    I will speak first of other things.

I cannot tell how I entered it,
    so heavy with slumber was I at the moment
    when I abandoned the true way.

12

But when I had reached the foot of a hill,
    there where the valley ended
    which had filled my heart with fear,

I looked up, and saw its shoulders
    clothed already with the rays of the planet
    which leads men straight on every path.

Then the fear was somewhat quieted
    which had lasted in the lake of my heart
    during the night I had passed so piteously.

And as a seafarer, who has escaped from the storm
    to the shore, turns with wearied breath
    to the turbulent waters and gazes,   24

so I, still fleeing in my mind,
    turned back to look at the pass
    which no one before had ever left alive.

> *As Dante starts to climb the hill, a leopard, the symbol of luxury or lust, appears.*
> *It offers some opposition, but the early hour and the buoyant influence of Spring,*
> *the season when the universe was supposed to have been created, give him hope.*
> *Then a lion (Pride) assails him, rushing on with such fury that the very air*
> *around seems to tremble. And finally a she-wolf, the symbol of avarice or greed,*
> *the most widespread of vices. Dante (Mankind) feels that he could overcome*
> *the others, but at the sight of the wolf, he despairs.*[1]

After I had rested a little my weary body,
    I took my way over the lonely slope
    [climbing][2] so that the firm foot always was the lower.

And behold! almost at the beginning of the rise,
    a leopard, light, and very nimble,
    which was covered with a spotted hide!

It did not move from in front of me,
    but instead so blocked my way
    that several times I turned to go back.   36

The time was the beginning of the morning,
    and the sun was rising with those stars
    that were with it when Divine Love

first set those beautiful things in motion,
    so that I found cause for good hope
    concerning the beast with the gaily spotted hide

in the hour of the day and in the sweet season;
    but even so I feared again
    at the sight of a lion that confronted me.

---

[1] This is a traditional interpretation of the allegory of the three beasts. Other explanations
are possible—for example, that the leopard is Fraud, the lion Violence, and the wolf Incontinence.
These three evils would correspond to the tripartite classification of sins in Dante's Hell.

[2] The words within square brackets, here and later in *The Divine Comedy,* are explanations
inserted by the translator.

It appeared to be coming at me
  with head erect and with ravenous hunger,
  so that the air seemed afraid of it, 48

and a she-wolf came also, burdened
  in her leanness with all cravings,
  and which has indeed made many live in sorrow.

The sight of her brought such fear
  and such distress upon me
  that I lost hope of the ascent.

And as a gambler who gladly wins,
  but when the time comes for him to lose,
  weeps and is saddened in all his thoughts,

so I changed as the restless beast advanced
  against me, and little by little
  drove me down to where the sun is silent. 60

> *At this critical moment, Virgil (Reason, Philosophy), whose voice has long been*
> *unheard, appears. Dante forgets for a moment his despair, and bends reverently*
> *before his master. Then he mentions the wolf which has blocked his (and mankind's)*
> *reform. Virgil explains the nature of the greed for which the wolf stands: it is*
> *an element in nearly all the crimes men commit. But a "hound," a redeemer (var-*
> *iously identified), possibly from between the towns of Feltro and Montefeltro, will*
> *ultimately come.*

While I was falling back to a lower place
  someone appeared before me whose voice
  from long silence seemed faint.

When I saw him in that desolation,
  "Have pity on me!" I cried to him,
  "whoever you are, whether a shade or a real man."

He answered, "Not a man now,
  a man once I was, and both my parents
  were Lombards, Mantuans by city.

I was born *sub Julio*[3] although late,
  and I lived in Rome under the good Augustus
  at the time of the false and lying gods. 72

I was a poet and sang of [Aeneas] that just son
  of Anchises who came from Troy
  after proud Ilion had been burned.

But why do you return to such misery?
  Why not climb the delightful mountain
  which is the beginning and the source of all joy?"

---

[3] "Under Julius Caesar."

"Now are you that Virgil, that spring
    which pours forth so broad a stream of speech?"
    I answered him with bashful brow,

"Oh, honor and light of other poets,
    may the long study and great love help me
    which made me search through your volume!   84

You are my master and my author;
    you alone are the one from whom I took
    the style which has done me honor.

See the beast because of which I turned;
    save me from her, famous sage,
    for she makes my whole body tremble!"

"You must take another road," he answered
    after he had seen me weep,
    "if you want to escape from this wild place;

for the animal of which you complain
    lets no one pass along her way,
    but so hinders that she kills,   96

and she has a nature so vicious and perverse
    that she never satisfies her greedy desires,
    and after feeding is hungrier than before.

Many are the animals with which she mates,
    and there will be still more until the Hound comes
    that will make her die in pain.

He will not feed on earth or pelf,
    but on wisdom, love and virtue,
    and his nation will be between Feltro and Feltro.

He will be the savior of that humbled Italy
    for whom the virgin Camilla,
    Euryalus, Turnus, and Nisus[4] died of wounds.   108

He will hunt her through every town
    until he has driven her back to Hell,
    whence Envy [of man's happiness] first released her.

> *Now Virgil proposes to lead Dante through Hell and Purgatory, and outlines the course of the journey. In Heaven, Beatrice (Revelation, Theology) will be the guide.*
>
> *In his humble submission to the mystery of Divine Justice, Virgil accuses himself of "rebellion" against God's law. There is a note of sadness in his words, condemned as he is, for having lived before Christ, to an eternity of longing. Dante generously suggests his apology by a reference to the God the ancient poet did not and, of course, could not know.*

---

[4]Characters in the second half of Virgil's *Aeneid*, which describes war in Italy.

Therefore I think it best for you
  to follow me, and I will be your guide
  to take you through an eternal place [Hell]

where you will hear despairing cries
  and will see the tormented spirits
  each of whom proclaims the second death [damnation],

and you will see [in Purgatory] those who are contented
  in the fire, because they hope to come,
  whenever it may be, among the blessed,   120

to whom, then, if you wish to ascend,
  a guide worthier than I will take you:
  to her I will entrust you when I leave,

for that Emperor who reigns up there,
  because I was rebellious to His law,
  does not want me as a guide to His city.

Everywhere He reigns and there He rules;
  there is His seat and His high throne,
  O happy are those whom He chooses!"

And I to him, "Poet, I beg you
  by that God you did not know, in order
  that I may flee from this evil and worse,   132

take me where you have said,
  so that I may see St. Peter's gate
  and those you proclaim so sad."

Then he moved on, and I followed him.

CANTO II

BEATRICE

It is now the evening of Good Friday. The sun which had cheered Dante is going down, and the animals on earth (all workers in God's universe) are returning home from their labors of the day. In this dark moment, Dante's courage fails, and he wonders about the advisability of the journey. It is true, he reflects, that both Aeneas and St. Paul, the "Chosen Vessel," visited the future world; but Aeneas' visit led to the founding of the Roman Empire, divinely ordained to be the seat of the papacy, and St. Paul brought from Heaven a confirmation of the true faith. Dante disclaims any such mission.

The day was departing, and the darkening air
  was taking the creatures that are on earth
  from their daily toil, and I alone

was preparing to endure the hardship
  both of the journey and of the pity
  which unerring memory will relate.

O Muses, O lofty genius, aid me now!
   O mind which inscribed what I saw,
   here your worth will be revealed.

I began, "Poet, you who guide me,
   consider my strength, whether it is great enough
   before you commit me to the arduous journey.   12

You say that [Aeneas] the father of Sylvius,
   still subject to corruption,
   went bodily to the eternal world;

but that the Adversary of all Evil [God]
   should be gracious to him, thinking of the result
   and of who and what he was,

does not seem unreasonable to a thoughtful man;
   for he was chosen in the Empyrean heaven
   to be father of glorious Rome

and of her empire, both of which
   were established for the holy place
   where the successors of St. Peter sit.   24

On this journey through which you honor him,
   he heard things which led to his victory
   and to the papal mantle.

Afterward the Chosen Vessel [St. Paul] went there
   to bring comfort to the faith
   which is the beginning of the way of salvation.

But why should I go? Who grants it?
   I am not Aeneas, nor am I Paul;
   for that neither I nor others believe me worthy.

Therefore, if I allow myself to go,
   I fear the journey may be folly: you are wise
   and understand better than I can speak."   36

And, as a person unwills what he wills,
   and with new thoughts changes purpose,
   holding back from what he has started,

so I became on that dark slope,
   for, by thinking, I delayed the undertaking
   that I had begun so quickly.

> *Not deceived by this rationalizing, Virgil reproves Dante for being afraid. Then, to reassure him, he describes the occasion of his coming, a scene in the first circle of Hell where the souls of the virtuous pagans are "in suspense," longing for an understanding of God and of the mystery of life, with the realization that they can never attain it.*

"If I have understood your words rightly,"
    answered that magnanimous shade,
    "your resolution is dulled by cowardice

which often distracts a man
    and turns him away from honorable deeds,
    as imperfect sight causes an animal to shy.   48

To free you from this fear, I will tell
    why I came and what I heard
    when I first took pity on you.

I was among those who are in suspense,
    and a lady [Beatrice] called to me
    so blessed and beautiful that I asked her to command.

Her eyes shone more than the stars,
    and with an angelic voice,
    softly and sweetly she spoke to me,

'O courteous Mantuan soul whose fame
    still lasts on the earth, and will last
    as long as the world,   60

my friend, but not the friend of Fortune,
    is so impeded on the deserted slope
    that in fear he has turned back,

and, from what I have heard in Heaven,
    I am afraid he is already so lost
    that I have come too late for his relief.

Now go to him, and with your eloquent speech
    and with all else needful for his escape
    help him, so that I may be consoled.

I am Beatrice, bidding you to go;
    I come from a place to which I would return;
    Love moved me and makes me speak.   72

When I am in the presence of my Lord
    I will praise you often to Him.'
    She was silent then and I began,

'O lady of virtue [Revelation] through whom alone
    the human race excels all creatures contained
    within the heaven of the smallest orbit [all on earth],

your command so pleases me that complying
    if already begun would seem slow;
    you need only to reveal your desire;

but tell me why you do not shrink
    from descending to this depth from the broad expanse
    to which you are eager to return.'   84

Beatrice explains how, although pitying Dante, she can feel no distress at the working of Divine Justice.

The formal allegory of the scene in Heaven she then describes is as follows: Mary (Divine Mercy) sends Lucia (Illuminating Grace) to prepare the way for Beatrice (Revelation) whom Dante (Mankind) will perceive when Virgil (Reason) makes him ready to behold her.

'Since you wish to know so much
   I will tell you briefly,' she answered,
   'why I do not fear to come here.

We should be afraid only of things
   which can harm, not of others,
   since they are not fearful.

Through God's grace I am formed in such a way
   that your misery does not touch me,
   nor does a flame of this burning hurt me.

There is a gentle lady in Heaven [Mary]
   whose pity is aroused by the distress of him
   to whom I send you, and who tempers harsh judgment.   96

She called upon Lucia and said in her request,
   "Your faithful one now has need of you,
   and I recommend him to you."

Lucia, the enemy of all cruelty,
   arose and came to where I was
   seated by the ancient Rachel.

She said, "Beatrice, true praise of God,
   why do you not help him who loved you so much
   that through you he arose above the common crowd?

Do you not hear the pity of his cries?
   Do you not see Death struggling with him
   on the river [of evil] not less terrible than the sea?"   108

On earth men were never so swift
   to seek gain and flee from harm
   as I was after these words were spoken

to come here from my blessed seat,
   trusting in your noble speech
   which honors you and those who have heard it.'

After she said this to me
   she turned away her shining eyes in tears,
   which made me still readier to go,

and to you I came as she desired.
   I freed you from the beast
   which had cut off the short way up the fair mount.   120

So what is it? Why, why do you hold back?
Why keep such cowardice in your heart?
Why are you not bold and free,

since three such holy ladies
care for you in the court of Heaven,
and my words promise you so much good?"

As little flowers, bent down and closed by the frost of night,
stand up, all open on their stems,
when the sun comes back to warm and brighten them,

so I revived my failing strength,
and so much boldness rushed into my heart
that I began like one set free,   132

"O compassionate lady who gave aid to me!
O courteous shade who obeyed so quickly
the true words she spoke to you!

You have disposed my heart
with such desire for going by your account
that I have regained my first intent.

Now go, for one wish is in both of us,
you my leader [guide], my lord [superior], my master [teacher]!"
Thus I spoke to him, and when he started

I followed on the deep and wild way.

CANTO III

THE ENTRANCE

*In the faint light of the evening of Good Friday, the anniversary of the Crucifixion
when, according to the Creed, Christ "entered into Hell," the two travelers move
on to the gate over which appears a fearful inscription pointing out the woe within,
the eternal pain, the people lost even to hope. Divine Justice (incomprehensible
to reason alone) moved God in his three-fold attributes of Power, Wisdom, and
Love to create Hell. It was made when only eternal things (the elements, the heavens, and the angels) existed, and it also will last and function eternally.*

*On reading these words Dante begins again to doubt, but, ashamed to confess
his fear, he seeks delay or assurance by asking about their meaning which, incidentally, is painfully explicit. Virgil, undeceived, reproves Dante for his weakness.*

THROUGH ME YOU GO INTO THE CITY OF GRIEF,
THROUGH ME YOU GO INTO THE PAIN THAT IS ETERNAL,
THROUGH ME YOU GO AMONG PEOPLE LOST.

JUSTICE MOVED MY EXALTED CREATOR;
THE DIVINE POWER MADE ME,
THE SUPREME WISDOM, AND THE PRIMAL LOVE.

BEFORE ME ALL CREATED THINGS WERE ETERNAL,
AND ETERNAL I WILL LAST.
ABANDON EVERY HOPE, YOU WHO ENTER HERE.

These words of a dark coloring
 I saw written above a gate; whereupon I said,
 "Master, their meaning is hard for me."   12

Then he spoke like one who understands:
 "Here you must give up all distrust,
 here all cowardice must end.

We have come to the place where I said
 that you would see the woeful people
 who have lost the good of the intellect.

And after he had taken me by the hand,
 with a cheerful look which comforted me,
 he drew me within the secret place [the eternal world].

> *On entering, Dante sees little because of the darkness, but hears sounds which he distinguishes gradually as cries, languages, words, accents, voices, and finally as the dull noise of blows. Virgil contemptuously refuses to waste words on the souls here. They are the trimmers, the mediocre, the poor in spirit, the neutrals, joined with the angels who refused to take sides in the revolt against God. They are in a kind of vestibule, outside of Hell proper. Their punishment is slight compared to those which come later, yet they are envious of every other lot.*

There, sighs, lamentations, and deep wailings
 resounded through the starless air,
 so that at first I began to weep.   24

Diverse tongues, horrible languages,
 words of pain, accents of rage,
 voices loud and hoarse, and the sounds of blows

made a tumult which moved forever
 in that air unchanged by time,
 as sand eddies in a whirlwind.

And I said, my head girt with horror,
 "Master, what is it that I hear,
 and who are these people so overcome by pain?"

Then he to me, "This miserable fate
 afflicts the wretched souls of those
 who lived without infamy and without praise.   36

They are joined with that choir of wicked angels
 who were neither rebellious
 nor faithful to God, but for themselves.

The heavens, to remain beautiful, drove them out,
 nor would deep Hell receive them
 lest the wicked gain pride by comparison."

And I, "Master, what is so burdensome
 that it makes them lament loudly?"
 He answered, "Briefly I will tell you.

They have no hope of death,
    and their blind life is so debased
    that they are envious of every other lot.   48

The world does not grant them any fame;
    pity [of Heaven] and justice [of Hell] alike disdain them.
    Let us not speak of them, but look and pass on."

> *Some of these souls, neutral and perhaps sedentary in life, are condemned now to active partisanship. The poet recognizes one, but will not distinguish him with a name. Most commentators have identified him as Celestine V, a pope who, by his refusal to keep his office, allowed Dante's great enemy, Boniface VIII, to rise to power. There are less scandalous interpretations, however, notably as Pontius Pilate, who refused justice to Christ and who offers a better motivation for the extreme contempt shown here.*

And I, looking, saw a banner
    which, circling, moved so fast
    that it seemed to scorn all rest,

and behind it came such a throng of people
    that I never would have believed
    that death could have undone so many.

After I had recognized some of them,
    I saw and knew the shade of him
    who, through cowardice, made the great refusal.   60

At once I understood and was certain
    that this was the sect of the wicked
    displeasing both to God and to His enemies.

These wretches, who had never really lived,
    were naked and stung constantly
    by hornets and wasps that were there.

These made their faces stream with blood
    which, mixed with tears, was consumed
    by loathsome maggots at their feet.

> *When Dante asks about a crowd in the distance, Virgil tells him to wait and see. Taking this as a reproach, our poet remains silent for a long time.*
>
> *As the travelers move on, Charon appears, the ancient boatman of the Styx, who prophesies Dante's ultimate salvation and whom Virgil appeases with a kind of conjuring formula.*

When I began to look farther on
    I saw people on the shore of a great river;
    whereupon I said, "Master, now grant   72

that I should know who they are
    and what makes them so ready to pass over,
    as I discern through the faint light."

And he to me, "These things will be known to you
    when we stay our steps
    on the sad bank of the Acheron."

Then with eyes ashamed and lowered,
    fearing that my words might have offended him,
    I kept from speaking until we reached the stream.

And behold! coming toward us in a skiff
    an old man, white with ancient locks,
    shouting, "Woe to you, depraved spirits;   84

hope not ever to see Heaven.
    I come to take you to the other shore
    into eternal darkness, into heat and cold.

And you there, living soul,
    get away from these who are dead."
    But when he saw that I did not leave,

"By another way, at other ports," he said,
    "you will come ashore, not here;
    a lighter boat will carry you."

And my guide, "Charon, do not be disturbed;
    this is wished for where the power is
    to do what is wished; and ask no more."   96

Then were quieted the woolly cheeks
    of the boatman of the livid marsh
    who, around his eyes, had rings of flame.

> *The souls are impelled by a kind of instinct to seek their proper place, since sin
> leads inevitably to its own results, its own suffering.*
>
> *We are not told how Dante crosses the river. There is a flash, an earthquake,
> and he falls unconscious. On awakening he is on the other bank.*

But those weary and naked souls
    changed color and gnashed their teeth
    as soon as they heard the cruel words.

They cursed God and their parents,
    the human race, and the place, time, and seed
    of their begetting and of their birth.

Then, all together they withdrew,
    weeping loudly, to the accursed shore
    which awaits every man without fear of God.   108

Charon the demon, with eyes like glowing coals,
    beckoning to them, gathered them in,
    and hit with an oar any who delayed.

As in autumn the leaves fall
    one after the other, until the branch
    sees all its spoils upon the ground,

so, the evil seed of Adam
    fell to that shore, one by one, and at signals,
    as the falcon does at its recall.

Thus they go over the dark water,
    and before they have landed on the other shore,
    again on this side a new crowd assembles.   120

"My son," said the courteous master,
    "those who die in the wrath of God
    gather here from every country,

and they are ready to pass the river,
    for Divine Justice so spurs them
    that fear is changed into desire.

Along here no good spirit ever passes;
    therefore, if Charon complains of you,
    you can understand what his words imply."

When he had ended, the dark country
    trembled so that from fright
    my memory bathes me still with sweat.   132

The tearful land produced a blast
    which flashed a crimson light
    conquering all my senses;

and I fell, like one overcome by sleep.

CANTO IV

LIMBO

When Dante awakens from his swoon he is in Limbo, the first circle of Hell. He interprets Virgil's pallor as due to fear, but learns that it comes from pity for those in the ancient poet's own circle. Although Dante still refrains from questioning, Virgil is anxious to point out that the shades here committed no sin, but died unbaptized or lived before Christ. Their damnation is an article of faith, beyond man's understanding. Here there is no torment other than a sense of unfulfillment, a feeling that expresses itself in melancholy, in suspense, in a vague longing for knowledge of God and for a solution of the mystery of life without hope of ever having either.

The deep sleep into which I fell was broken
    by heavy thunder, so that I started,
    like one awakened by force,

and having risen, I glanced around
    and looked intently with rested eyes
    to discover where I was.

In truth, I found myself on the brink
   of the dolorous valley of the abyss
   which resounds with the sound of countless cries.

It was so dark, deep, and cloudy
   that in looking toward the bottom
   I could discern nothing.   12

"Now, let us go into the blind world,"
   the poet began all pale,
   "I will be first and you second."

And I, noticing his color, said,
   "How shall I come if you are afraid,
   you who always comfort me in my doubt?"

And he to me, "The anguish
   of the people down there paints on my face
   the pity which you mistake for fear.

Let us go, for the long way impels us."
   Thus he moved on and made me enter
   the first circle which girds the abyss.   24

Here, so far as one could tell by listening,
   there was no lament, but only sighs
   which made the eternal air tremble.

They came from the sadness without torment
   felt by the great crowd
   of children and of women and of men.

My good master said to me, "You do not ask
   what spirits these are. Now,
   I want you to know before you go farther

that they did not sin, but having merit
   was not enough, for they lacked baptism,
   which is a portal of the faith you hold;   36

and if they lived before Christianity
   they did not worship God rightly;
   among such as these am I myself.

For such defects, not for other faults,
   are we lost, and afflicted only
   in that we live in longing without hope."

Great grief gripped my heart when I heard this,
   for I knew that people of much worth
   were in that Limbo in suspense.

> *Dante now risks a timid question. He wants to know about the "Harrowing of
> Hell," when Christ was supposed to have gone to Limbo to release the ancient
> Hebrews who had believed in His coming. After the explanation the poets move
> on to a special region reserved for the great men of the past. Virgil (as Reason)
> approves the recognition of Dante as the sixth in rank of the world's poets.*

"Tell me, Master, tell me, sir," I began,
    wishing to be assured of the faith
    that destroys every error,   48

"did any ever through his own merit
    or another's leave here to be blessed?"
    And he, understanding my veiled speech, answered,

"I was new in this condition
    when I saw a Powerful One [Christ]
    crowned with the sign of victory [the cross as an aureole].

He took from here our first parent,
    Abel his son, and Noah,
    obedient Moses, the lawgiver,

the patriarch Abraham, and David, the king,
    Israel [Jacob] with his father and his sons,
    and Rachel for whom he [Jacob] did so much,   60

and many others, and he made them blessed,
    and I wish you to know that before then
    no human souls were ever saved."

We did not stop because of his remarks,
    but kept passing through the forest—
    the forest, I mean, of crowded spirits.

Our way had not yet taken us far
    after my slumber when I saw a light
    which dispelled a hemisphere of darkness.

We were still distant from the glow
    but not too far for me to discern
    that notable people occupied that place.   72

"O you who honor every science and art," I said,
    "who are these whose great merit
    separates them from the others?"

And he answered, "The deserved fame
    which still honors them in your life
    gains favor in Heaven, and thus promotes them."

Meanwhile a voice was heard, saying,
    "Honor the greatest poet;
    his shade which had left is returning."

When this voice was silent
    I saw four great figures come to us,
    their faces neither sad nor gay.   84

My good master began to speak:
    "See that one with sword in hand,
    coming ahead of the others as their lord.

He is Homer, the sovereign poet;
    the other. following, is Horace, the satirist;
    Ovid is the third, and Lucan the last.

Since each shares with me the title 'poet'
    which the single voice pronounced,
    they do me honor, and in doing this do well."

Thus I saw assembled the school
    of that lord of the lofty song who soars
    above the others like an eagle.   96

After they had talked together a little
    they turned to me with signs of greeting,
    and my master smiled at that.

And still more honor they showed me
    by making me one of their group,
    so that I was the sixth among such sages.

> *The poets now come to the Castle of Wisdom or Fame, surrounded by the walls
> of the cardinal and speculative virtues and defended by a moat which may rep-
> resent eloquence or desire for knowledge. They pass through the gates of the seven
> liberal arts. On a kind of enameled meadow within, the great spirits of the past
> appear: first the Trojans, Greeks, and legendary figures of early Rome; then philoso-
> phers, scientists, mathematicians, and doctors; and finally the Moorish scholar
> Averroës.*

Thus we continued toward the light,
    speaking of matters concerning which silence
    is as fitting now as speech was then,

and we arrived at the foot of a noble castle,
    seven times encircled by high walls,
    defended all around by a fair rivulet.   108

This we crossed as if on solid ground.
    Through seven gates I passed with these sages
    and we arrived on a meadow of fresh verdure.

There we saw people dignified and grave,
    of great authority in their semblance;
    they spoke seldom, and with soft voices.

Afterward we withdrew to one side
    to an open place, luminous and high,
    from which all could be seen.

There, standing on the green enamel,
    the great spirits were shown to me,
    to have seen whom I feel exalted.   120

I saw Electra[5] with many companions,
    among whom I recognized Hector and Aeneas,
    and Caesar clad in arms, with hawklike eyes.

---

[5] Not the daughter of Agamemnon and Clytemnestra but rather the mother of Dardanus,
founder of Troy.

I saw Camilla and Penthesilea
    on the other side, and I saw the Latian king,
    sitting with Lavinia, his daughter.

I saw that Brutus[6] who expelled the Tarquin,
    Lucretia, Julia, Marcia, and Cornelia;
    and alone, to one side, the Saladin.

When I had raised my eyes a little higher
    I saw the Master of the Knowing [Aristotle]
    sitting with his philosophic family.   132

All looked at him, all did him honor;
    there I saw Socrates and Plato
    who stood ahead of the others closest to him:

Democritus, who thought the world due to chance;
    Diogenes, Anaxagoras, and Thales,
    Empedocles, Heraclitus, and Zeno;

and I saw the good compiler of the qualities [of plants],
    Dioscorides, I mean; and Orpheus,
    Tully [Cicero], Linus, and Seneca, the moralist;

Euclid the geometer, and Ptolemy,
    Hippocrates, Avicenna, and Galen,
    and Averroës who made the great commentary [on Aristotle].   144

I cannot enumerate them all fully;
    my long theme so drives me on that many times
    my words fall short of the facts.

The sixfold company diminished to two [Virgil and Dante];
    by another way my wise guide took me,
    out of the quiet into the trembling air,

and I came to a place where no light shines.

CANTO V

FRANCESCA DA RIMINI
*Since Hell is like an inverted cone, the circumference of each succeeding circle
diminishes.*

*The guardian of the second ring is Minos, the ancient judge of the dead, rep-
resented by Dante as having some of the characteristics of a medieval demon.
Like Charon, Minos offers a slight opposition which is overcome by the conjur-
ing formula.*

Thus I descended from the first circle
    down to the second which encloses less space
    but so much more pain that it moves to tears.

---

[6] This is not the assassin of Julius Caesar; that Brutus appears at the center of Hell in Canto
XXXIV. The Brutus referred to here founded the ancient Roman republic.

There Minos stands, horrible and snarling,
    examining the offenses, judging,
    and sending down as he girds himself—

I mean that when an ill-born soul
    comes before him, it confesses wholly,
    and that discerner of sin,

seeing what place in Hell belongs to it,
    encircles himself with his tail as many times
    as the degrees he wants it to descend.   12

Always many stand in front of him;
    they come in turns to their judgment,
    confess and hear, and then are hurled below.

"O you who come to the painful refuge,"
    Minos said when he saw me,
    interrupting the work of his great office,

"consider how you entered and in whom you trust;
    do not let the breadth of the entrance deceive you."
    And my guide to him, "Why do you cry out?

Do not impede his fated going.
    It is wished for where the power is
    to do what is wished; so ask no more."   24

> *The poets hear and see the shades guilty of lust. A landslide caused by an earth-*
> *quake at the time of the Crucifixion perhaps reminds the restless souls as they*
> *pass of the impossibility of their redemption. Dante pities more than blames these*
> *victims of the flesh and of the imagination. They pass like birds in autumn flight.*

Now I begin to hear the sad notes of pain,
    now I have come to where
    loud cries beat upon my ears.

I have reached a place mute of all light
    which roars like the sea in a tempest
    when beaten by conflicting winds.

The infernal storm which never stops
    drives the spirits in its blast;
    whirling and beating, it torments them.

When they come in front of the landslide,
    they utter laments, moans, and shrieks;
    there they curse the Divine Power.   36

I learned that to such a torment
    carnal sinners are condemned
    who subject their reason to desire.

And, as starlings are borne by their wings
    in the cold season, in a broad and dense flock,
    so that blast carries the evil spirits.

Here, there, up, and down, it blows them;
    no hope ever comforts them
    of rest or even of less pain.

And as cranes go chanting their lays,
    making a long line of themselves in the air,
    so I saw coming, uttering laments,   48

shades born by that strife of winds.

> *Dante is eager to know who is punished here. No vulgar examples are cited but only glamorous figures of the ancient and medieval past whom love too completely mastered. Perhaps our poet suspects already that Francesca da Rimini and her lover are here. In any case he asks to speak to two who seem unusually light and is told to address them in the name of love, to which, in a nobler form, all his own life was a dedication. The real appeal, however, is in the sympathy expressed by the words, "O wearied souls!" Like doves borne on by desire, Francesca and Paolo leave their company, so responsive are they still to the slightest note of affection.*

I asked, "Master, who are these people
    whom the black air so punishes?"

"The first of those about whom
    you want to know," he said to me,
    "was an empress over many peoples,

by the vice of luxury so subdued
    that she made lust lawful in her decrees
    to take away the blame she had incurred.

She is Semiramis who, we read,
    succeeded Ninus, her spouse;
    she held the land that now the Sultan rules.   60

The other is she [Dido] who killed herself
    after breaking faith with the ashes of Sichaeus;
    next comes luxurious Cleopatra.

See Helen [of Troy] for whom
    so many bad years revolved, and the great Achilles
    whose last battle was with love.[7]

See Paris, Tristan,"—and he pointed out and named
    more than a thousand shades
    whom love had taken from our life.

After I had heard my teacher
    name the knights and ladies of olden times,
    pity overcame me, and I felt dismayed.   72

---

[7] Dante knew a medieval tradition according to which Achilles, as a result of love for a Trojan princess, was ambushed and killed.

I began, "Poet, willingly would I speak
    with those two who go together
    and seem so light upon the wind."

And he to me, "Wait until they come closer,
    then entreat them by the love
    which impels them and they will come."

As soon as the wind brought them to us,
    I raised my voice, "O wearied souls,
    come speak to us if it is not forbidden."

As doves summoned by their desire,
    with wings raised and firm, sail through the air,
    borne on to their sweet nest by their will alone,   84

so those spirits moved from the band where Dido is,
    coming to us through the malignant air,
    so responsive were they to my affectionate cry.

> *Now Francesca speaks, and her first words are an implied prayer to God whose*
> *mysterious justice has condemned her beyond remission, an unselfish prayer for*
> *this living soul who has shown them pity. It is a prayer for the "peace" which*
> *romantic and illicit love can never know. In her heart's response to Dante's sim-*
> *ple words, she treats him already as "gracious" and "benign" and exaggerates*
> *her own misdoing. Her story is a mere outline, told partly in terms of the max-*
> *ims of courtly love. With ladylike reticence she does not name herself or Paolo,*
> *her brother-in-law and lover, or even the city where she was born. Death itself*
> *would not have been so tragic: one moment for repentance might have permit-*
> *ted her to be saved; it was the suddenness of her and Paolo's death that was so*
> *cruel. Caïna, at the bottom of Hell, where traitors to kindred are punished, awaits*
> *her husband who surprised and killed them.*

"O living creature, gracious and benign,
    going through the dark air
    visiting us who stained the earth with blood,

if the King of the universe were friendly to us
    we would pray to Him for your peace,
    since you pity our perverse evil.

Whatever you are pleased to hear from us or say
    we will relate and listen to,
    while the wind, as now, is silent.   96

The city [Ravenna] where I was born
    lies on the shore where the Po descends
    with all its tributaries to find peace.

Love which flames quickly in noble hearts
    was kindled in this soul by the fair body
    taken from me; the manner [of that taking] still offends.

Love that exempts no one beloved from loving
   caught me so strongly with his charm
   that, as you see, it still does not leave me.

Love led us to one death together.
   Caïna waits for him who quenched our lives."
   These words were borne from them to us.   108

*On hearing this delicate outline of the tragedy, Dante bows his head, perhaps
recalling who the speaker is, and then naming Francesca, he asks, in words as
respectful and delicate as her own, about the immediate cause and occasion of
her sin. Although she dislikes to recall the intimate details, she speaks, unable
to refuse an affectionate appeal. There was no premeditation in her sin. She and
Paolo had been reading a love story without suspecting the effect it might have.
One moment of weakness overcame them, a moment which ended their reading
and their lives and which stands now in contrast to eternity.*

When I heard those afflicted souls
   I bent down my face, and held it low so long
   that the poet said, "Of what are you thinking?"

When I answered I began, "Alas!
   how many sweet thoughts, what desire
   led them to the woeful pass!"

Then I turned to them and said,
   "Francesca, your suffering
   makes me weep with sorrow and with pity,

But tell me, at the time of the sweet sighs,
   by what means and how love permitted you
   to know the dubious desires."   120

And she to me, "There is no greater pain
   than to recall a happy time in misery
   and this your teacher knows;

but if to learn the first root of our love
   you have such desire, I will answer
   like one who speaks and weeps.

One day for our delight we were reading
   about Lancelot, how love constrained him;
   alone we were and without any suspicion.

Several times that reading made our glances meet
   and changed the color of our faces;
   but one moment alone overcame us.   132

When we read how the fond smile [of Guinevere]
   was kissed by such a lover,
   he, who never will be separated from me,

kissed me, on my lips. all trembling.
A Gallehaut [pander] was the book and he who wrote it.
That day we read no farther."

While one spirit was saying this
the other wept, so that from pity
I fainted, as if I had been dying,

and I fell, as a dead body falls.

CANTO VI

THE GLUTTONS

On recovering my senses, which were stunned
by pity for the two kinsfolk
who overwhelmed me with sadness,

new torments and new tormented shades
I see around me, wherever I move
and wherever I turn to gaze.

> *The poets are now among the gluttons who are lying like pigs in a sty under a constant, unvarying rain. Although the punishments here are relatively mild, they are particularly distasteful to the luxury-loving. All the senses are afflicted: sight by the dismal setting, touch by the cold rain, smell and taste by the stench, and hearing by the loud barking of Cerberus, the three-headed dog, the bestial guardian of this circle. Cerberus is appeased, not by a honey cake, as in the* Aeneid, *but by dirt, to emphasize further the filthiness of gluttony.*

I am in the third circle of the rain,
eternal, accursed, cold, and heavy;
its amount and kind never change.

Large hailstones, dirty water, and snow
pour down through the dark air;
the ground that receives them stinks.   12

Cerberus, the fierce and cruel beast,
barks doglike with three throats
over those submerged there.

His eyes are red, his beard greasy and black,
his belly large, his paws armed with claws;
grasping the spirits, he flays and tears them.

The rain makes them howl like dogs;
they use one side to shelter the other;
often they turn, the profane wretches.

When Cerberus, the monster, saw us,
he opened his mouths and showed his teeth,
trembling in all his limbs.   24

And my leader, opening his hands,
    took some earth and threw handfuls
    into the ravenous gullets.

As a barking dog, longing for food,
    grows quiet after he has seized it,
    since he thinks only of eating,

so did those filthy heads of the demon Cerberus
    who thunders over the shades,
    making them wish they were deaf.

A soul nicknamed "Ciacco" (the pig) recognizes Dante but is himself unrecognizable since the bestial vice of gluttony disfigures. To spare the feelings of this shade Dante suggests that perhaps Ciacco's pain prevented the recognition.

We passed over the spirits subdued
    by the heavy rain, placing our feet
    on their nothingness which appears as flesh.   36

They were all lying on the ground
    except one who sat up quickly
    as soon as he saw us pass in front of him.

"O you, led through this Hell,"
    he said to me, "recognize me if you can;
    you were made [born] before I was unmade [died]."

And I to him, "The anguish that you feel
    perhaps takes you from my memory
    so that I do not seem ever to have seen you,

but tell me who you are, placed here
    in such punishment that, if others
    are greater, none is so displeasing."   48

And he to me, "Your city [Florence] so full of envy
    that it can hold no more
    kept me in the bright life.

The citizens called me Ciacco;
    for the damning sin of gluttony,
    as you see, I lie helpless in the rain.

And I, sad spirit, am not alone,
    for all of these are in similar pain
    for a like sin,"—and he said no more.

I answered, "Ciacco, your distress weighs upon me
    so that it moves to tears;
    but tell me, if you can, the fate   60

of the citizens of the divided city;
    if any one of them is just, and tell me
    why such discord has assailed it."

Then he to me, "After long dispute
    they will come to blows, and the rustic party [the Whites]
    Will drive out the other with much offense.

Afterward that faction will fall
    within three suns [years], and the other rise
    through one [Boniface VIII] who now is moving carefully.

For a long time it will hold high its head,
    keeping the other under heavy burdens,
    however much it may weep and be put to shame.   72

Two men are just, but are not listened to.
    Pride, envy, and avarice are the sparks
    which have enflamed all hearts."

Here he put an end to his sad words,
    and I said to him, "I wish to learn more,
    and beg you to grant me the gift of further speech.

Farinata and Tegghiaio, who were so worthy,
    Jacopo Rusticucci, Arrigo, and Mosca,
    and the others who set their minds to doing good,

tell me where they are, let me know about them,
    for a great desire urges me to find out
    if Heaven soothes or Hell embitters them."   84

And he, "They are among the blackest spirits;
    different sins weigh them to the bottom;
    if you go down so far, you will see them.

But when you are again in the sweet world,
    I beg you to recall me to the memory of others.
    More I will not say; this is all I answer."

He twisted his straight eyes asquint,
    looked at me a little, then bent his head,
    and fell to the level of the other blind ones.

My guide said to me, "No more will he awaken
    until the angelic trumpet sounds [on Judgment Day]
    when the hostile Power [hostile to sinners] will come.   96

Each then will find his sad tomb,
    will resume his flesh and form,
    and will hear what resounds to all eternity."

Thus we passed over the filthy mixture of the shades
    and of the rain, with slow steps,
    touching a little on the future life.

I asked, "Master, will these torments increase
    after the great judgment,
    or will they be less or equally painful?"

He answered, "Recall your science
  which maintains that the more perfect a thing is,
  the more bliss or pain it feels. 108

Although these accursed people
  never come to true perfection,
  they will be more complete after than before."

We bent our course along that way,
  saying much more than I relate,
  and came to a place for descending.

There we found Plutus, the great enemy.

CANTO VII

THE AVARICIOUS AND THE PRODIGAL

Plutus, the ancient god of wealth and here the guardian of the circle of the avaricious and the prodigal, is represented as an inflated monster. He speaks in a high voice, like certain fat men, and his words are not clearly comprehensible. A reference to the Power through which the archangel Michael defeated the revolt of Satan easily deflates this weak, unhealthy, and puffy creature, who collapses suddenly, without resistance.

"Papè Satàn, Papè Satàn, aleppe,"[8]
  Plutus began with a clucking voice,
  and that noble sage [Virgil], who understood,

said to comfort me, "Do not fear,
  for whatever power he may have,
  he cannot prevent our descending this rock."

Then he turned to that inflated visage
  and said, "Keep still, accursed wolf;
  consume yourself inwardly with your rage.

Not without reason is our going to the depth.
  It is decreed on high where Michael
  took vengeance for the proud revolt." 12

As sails swelled by the wind
  fall entangled when the mast breaks,
  so the cruel monster fell to the ground.

The avaricious on one side and the prodigal on the other push great weights around their respective semicircles. At the two points where they clash, like the waves between Scylla and Charybdis, they exchange insults and turn, going to the opposite point. Thus they work hard, like the avaricious on earth, but uselessly, missing the spiritual pleasures which make this life and the next worth while. All are alike, without distinction, and unrecognizable as individuals.

---

[8] These words are not clearly understandable; perhaps a threat and a warning to Satan. (Translator's note.)

Thus we descended into the fourth cavity,
    taking in more of the dismal bank
    which holds all the evil of the universe.

Ah, Justice of God! Who can combine
    so many new pains and torments,
    and why does our sin so waste us?

As the waves above Charybdis break
    against each other as they meet,
    so in this place the souls must clash.   24

Here I saw more people than elsewhere
    on one side and the other, shouting loudly
    and pushing weights with their chests.

They bump against each other and then all turn,
    pushing back the load and crying,
    "Why do you hoard?" or "Why do you squander?"

Thus they go on each side
    of the dark circle to the opposite point,
    shouting their insulting refrains.

When they reach that place, they turn again
    through their half circles to the other clash.
    And I, my heart oppressed, said,   36

"Master, now tell me who these are
    and if all the tonsured ones
    on the left are of the clergy?"

And he to me, "In the first life
    all were so twisted mentally
    that they could not spend with moderation.

Quite clearly their voices bark this out
    when they come to the two points of the circle
    where contrary faults divide them.

Those whose heads are tonsured, as you see,
    were clerics and popes and cardinals
    in whom avarice shows its strength."   48

And I, "Master, among such as these
    I must surely recognize some
    who were defiled by these vices."

And he to me, "You conceive a vain thought;
    the undiscerning life which made them sordid
    now leaves them too obscure for recognition.

Throughout eternity they will clash;
    some will arise from the grave with fists closed,
    and the others [the prodigal] with their hair shorn.

Bad giving and bad keeping have taken from them
    the fair world and placed them in this strife
    which words of mine will not glorify.   60

> *Wealth, according to Dante, is in the hands of a special divinity, Fortune, who performs her functions as the angels guide and direct the various heavens. No reason or moral order is discernible in the distribution of wealth among individuals, families, and nations.*

Now, my son, you can see how wealth,
    committed to Fortune, and for which
    the human race struggles, mocks us.

All the gold that is under the moon
    or ever was, could not give rest
    to one of these weary souls."

"Master," I asked, "now tell me,
    who is this Fortune
    with the world's riches in her hands?"

And he to me, "Oh foolish creatures,
    how deep is the ignorance that blinds you!
    Now I want you to hear my judgment.   72

He [God] whose understanding transcends all
    made the heavens and gave them guides,
    so that each part shines on all the others,

distributing the light equally.
    Likewise, for mundane splendors,
    He ordained a general minister and guide

to transfer vain wealth in due time
    from people to people, and from one to another family,
    beyond the intervention of human intelligence.

Thus one people rules and another languishes,
    according to her judgment, which is hidden from us,
    like a snake in the grass.   84

Your knowledge is of no avail against her;
    she foresees, judges, and rules her province
    as the other gods [angels] do theirs.

Her activity has no truce;
    necessity makes her quick to act,
    so that changes [in fortune] come often.

She is the one so reviled
    even by those who should praise her
    but who, instead, give her ill repute.

Yet she is blessed and does not hear;
    happy with the other primal [angelic] creatures
    she rules her sphere and rejoices in her bliss.   96

*It is now a little after midnight of Good Friday. In a swamp the poets see the
bemired souls of the angry and the bubbles made by the sullen beneath the surface. The travelers make a long detour to the left, which indicates an approach
to worse things.*

Now let us descend to greater misery;
    already each star that was rising when I started
    is falling, and staying too long is forbidden."

We crossed the circle to the inner bank
    along a stream which bubbled and flowed
    through a channel it had formed.

The water was darker than purplish-black;
    and, accompanying the murky waves,
    on a rough path, we reached the place below.

This dreary stream forms a marsh, the Styx,
    when it has reached the foot
    of the gray, malignant banks.   108

And I, who remained intent on looking,
    saw muddy people in that bog,
    naked, and with angry looks.

They struck each other not only with their hands,
    but with their heads, chests, and feet,
    and tore each other with their teeth, bit by bit.

My good master said, "Son, now see
    the souls of those whom anger overcame;
    I wish you to believe also

that under the water there are people sighing
    and making bubbles on the surface
    as your eyes tell you wherever you look.   120

Fixed in the slime they say, 'Sullen were we
    in the sweet air gladdened by the sun,
    keeping within us the fumes of spite;

now we are sullen in the black mire.'
    This hymn is gurgled in their throats,
    for they cannot speak in clear words."

Thus we covered a wide arc around the filthy slough
    between the dry bank and the swamp,
    with eyes turned to those swallowing the mire.

At last we came to the foot of a tower.

CANTO VIII

THE ANGRY AND THE SULLEN
Continuing the account of the fifth circle, Dante anxiously inquires about the meaning of certain signals. These are explained by the coming of a boat guided by Phlegyas,[9] the guardian of this round.

I say, continuing, that long before we reached
   the foot of the high tower
   our eyes were drawn to its top

by two little flames placed there;
   and another gave back a signal from so far
   that our eyes could hardly catch it.

Turning to the sea of all wisdom, I asked,
   "What does this mean? what does the other flame
   answer? and who are they who light it?"

And he to me, "Over the foul waters
   already you can see what is expected
   if the mist of the marsh does not hide it from you."   12

Never did a bowstring drive an arrow
   which sped so quickly through the air
   as a little boat I saw then

coming through the water toward us
   under the guidance of a single boatman
   who cried, "Now you are caught, fell spirit!"

"Phlegyas, Phlegyas, this time you cry out
   in vain," said my lord, "you will keep us
   only while crossing the slough."

As one who learns of a great trick
   played on him and who resents it,
   so Phlegyas became in his pent-up rage.   24

My guide stepped down into the boat,
   making me get in after him,
   and only then did it appear burdened.

As soon as my master and I had embarked,
   the ancient prow moved on,
   cleaving more of the water than it does with others.

> *Dante becomes angry at one of the shades, apparently incurring the very sin punished here, but is commended for it by Virgil. The episode is intended to show that righteous indignation is permissible. We cannot love gentleness and politeness intensely without disliking arrogance and incivility with equal intensity.*

---

[9]Enraged with Apollo for raping his daughter, Phlegyas set the god's temple on fire and was killed by him.

While we were going through the stagnant channel,
  a shade covered with mud rose up, saying [insolently],
  "Who are you, coming before your time?"

I answered, "If I come, I do not stay,
  but who are you, now so dirty?"
  And he, "You see I am one who weeps."   36

Then I to him, "With tears and grief
  stay here, damned spirit,
  for I recognize you for all your filth."

Then the shade stretched both hands toward the boat,
  but my wary master pushed him off, saying,
  "Get over there with the other dogs!"

And embracing me with both arms
  he kissed my face and said, "Indignant soul,
  may she be blessed who bore you!

In the world he was an arrogant person;
  no kindness adorned his memory,
  so his shade is furious here.   48

How many think themselves great kings
  who will lie like swine in the mire,
  leaving behind horrible censure."

And I, "Master, I would be glad
  to see him soused in this soup [muddy water]
  before we leave the pond."

He answered, "Before you see the shore
  you will be satisfied;
  it is proper that such a wish be granted."

In a little while I saw the muddy crowd
  wreak such havoc on him
  that I still praise and thank God for it.   60

All cried, "At Filippo Argenti!"
  and the raging Florentine spirit
  turned with his teeth upon himself.

Here we left him, and of him I say no more.
  A wailing now struck my ears,
  so that I looked ahead intently.

My good master said, "Now son,
  the City of Dis [Satan] draws near,
  with its grave citizens, its great garrison."

And I, "Master, already I discern its mosques
  clearly there within the valley,
  red, as if they had come out of fire."   72

He continued, "The eternal flames
   enkindling them make them glow
   as you see in this lower Hell."

We now arrived within the moats
   which surround the disconsolate city,
   the walls of which seemed of iron.

Not without making a wide circuit [to the left]
   did we come to where the boatman loudly cried,
   "Get out, here is the entrance!"

Above the gates more than a thousand [rebellious angels],
   rained down from Heaven, cried angrily,
   "Who is this one, without death,   84

going through the kingdom of the dead?"
   And my wise master signaled
   that he wished to speak with them secretly.

Then they held back their great anger
   and said, "You come alone and let him go
   who so boldly entered this kingdom.

Let him return by himself on the mad path;
   let him see if he can; for you will stay here,
   you who have led him through so dark a country."

> Threatened with the loss of Virgil (Reason), Dante begs not to be left alone. His
> guide tries to reassure him, but, as an intellectual rather than a suggestive force,
> he can do that only imperfectly. As Virgil leaves, Dante wonders whether the answer
> to a question about the success of the mission will be "yes," or "no." Virgil also
> is not sure, but, on returning, tries to comfort Dante by passing off his doubt
> and dismay as anger. He hopes, with the limited confidence reason gives, that
> an angel will bring divine aid.

Think, Reader, if I was frightened
   at the sound of the accursed words,
   for I did not believe I could ever return.   96

"O my dear guide, you who many times
   have made me safe and drawn me
   through deep peril confronting me,

do not leave me so undone," I said,
   "and if going farther is denied us,
   let us retrace our steps together rapidly."

Then that lord who had brought me there replied,
   "Do not fear, for no one can prevent our journey;
   by Such a One it has been granted.

Wait for me here, and with good hope
   comfort and feed your weary spirit,
   for I will not leave you in the lower world."   108

1418 — The Middle Ages

Thus my dear father went away
  and abandoned me, and I remained in doubt,
  for "yes" and "no" struggled within my mind.

I could not hear what he said to our adversaries,
  but he did not stay long with them
  before each of them raced back.

They closed the gates in the face
  of my lord, who remained outside
  and then came toward me with slow steps,

his eyes upon the ground and with a face
  shorn of all boldness. He asked, sighing,
  "Who has denied us the abode of woe?" 120

Then to me he said, "Although I may get angry,
  do not fear, for I will win the fight,
  whatever is contrived within.

This insolence of theirs is not new;
  they showed it once at a less secret gate
  which is now without a fastening.

Over it you saw the deadly inscription;[10]
  and already on this side of it,
  passing through the circles without escort,

someone descends who will open the city for us."

CANTO IX

THE CITY OF DIS

The hue that cowardice put on my face
  when I saw my guide come back
  made him repress more quickly his dismay.

He stopped, attentive, like a man listening;
  for sight could not go far
  through the dark air and thick mist.

"Still we must win the fight," he began,
  "if not . . . such help was offered us;
  oh, how I long for someone to come!"

I noticed how he covered up
  his first words with those that followed
  which expressed a different thought, 12

and his remark made me afraid
  because I drew the words cut off
  into a meaning perhaps worse than he intended.

[10] The words written over Hell's gate, III.1–9. Dante and Virgil are now about to enter the lower hell, where the sins of malice (violence and fraud) are punished.

Dante asks indirectly if Virgil really knows the way.

"To this depth of the dismal hole
  does any ever descend from the first circle
  where hope cut off is the only punishment?"

This question I asked, and he answered,
  "It seldom happens that one of us
  makes the journey on which I am going.

It is true that I was down here once before,
  conjured by that cruel Erichtho [a sorceress],
  who brought shades back to their bodies.   24

Not for long had my flesh been without me
  when she made me go within those walls
  to bring out a spirit from Judas' circle.[11]

That is the lowest and darkest place, the one
  farthest removed from the heaven that encircles all.
  I know the road well; therefore be reassured.

This swamp exhaling the great stench
  surrounds the woeful city
  which we cannot enter now peacefully."

> *Three Furies, handmaidens of Hecate, the ancient queen of Hell, symbols of madness or remorseful terror, rise up, citing their error in letting Theseus enter their region to rescue Persephone. Dante clings to Virgil with desperation. The Furies then call upon the Gorgon (Medusa, Despair) to turn the intruder to stone. Virgil warns his charge with great urgency not to look at her.*
>
> *The allegorical meaning is perhaps as follows: the reforming Christian (Dante), when confronted by remorseful terror (the Furies), may lose his reason (Virgil), but as long as hope remains, he can appeal for divine aid. Only despair (Medusa) cuts off irremediably the path to salvation.*

And more he said, but I do not recall it
  because my eyes drew all my thoughts
  to the glowing summit of the high tower   36

where suddenly three infernal Furies,
  with the shape and features of women,
  and stained with blood, stood upright.

They were girded with green hydras[12]
  and had serpents and horned snakes for hair
  with which their wild heads were bound.

And he who knew well the handmaidens
  of the Queen of eternal lamentation
  said to me, "Behold! the fierce Erinyes [Furies].

---

[11] The very lowest and innermost circle of Hell, described in Canto XXXIV.
[12] Monsters with several heads.

The one on the left is Megaera;
	she on the right, weeping, is Alecto;
	Tisiphone is in the middle,"—and with that he was silent. 48

They were tearing their breasts with their nails,
	beating themselves with their hands, and shouting
	so loudly that in fear I drew close to my master.

"Let Medusa come, and we will change him to stone,"
	they all said, looking down,
	"badly did we avenge the assault of Theseus."

"Turn back and keep your eyes closed,
	for if the Gorgon [Medusa] shows herself
	and you see her, there will be no returning."

Thus my master spoke, and he himself
	turned me around, not trusting my hands,
	but with his also covered my eyes. 60

O you who have sound understanding,
	observe the meaning hidden
	beneath the veil of the strange verses.

And now over the turbid waters
	came a crash full of terror
	at which both the shores trembled,

a sound like that of a whirlwind
	made violent by conflicting currents
	which hits the forest without restraint,

shatters, beats down, and sweeps away the boughs.
	Behind a cloud of dust it moves on fiercely,
	and makes the beasts and shepherds flee. 72

My master freed my eyes and said,
	"Now direct your sight over that ancient foam
	to where the mist is thickest."

As frogs before their enemy the snake
	scatter through the water
	until each squats on the bottom,

so I saw more than a thousand ruined spirits
	fleeing before one [an angel] who,
	with dry feet, passed over the Styx.

From his face he fanned that gross air,
	moving his left hand in front of it,
	and only with that effort seemed weary. 84

I saw at once that he was sent from Heaven,
	and I turned to my master, who made a sign
	that I should keep quiet and bow to him.

How full of scorn he seemed to me!
　　Coming to the gate, he opened it
　　with a wand, for there was no resistance.

"O outcasts from Heaven, despised creatures!"
　　he began, on the horrible threshold,
　　"why do you harbor this insolence?

Why do you oppose that will
　　whose purpose can never be hindered,
　　and which has several times increased your pain? 96

Of what use is it to butt against fate?
　　Your Cerberus [chained by Hercules] because of this
　　still has a chin and throat without hair."[13]

Then he turned back over the filthy road
　　and said no word to us, but seemed
　　like one intent on other cares

than those of the people near him;
　　and we moved on toward the city,
　　safe, after the holy words.

　　On entering, Dante sees open tombs, hotter than iron in a blacksmith's forge.
　　Each contains the leader of a heretical sect with his followers. Here, contrary to
　　their custom, the travelers turn to the right, perhaps to indicate that heresy can
　　be incurred honestly, although persistence in it is a sin of pride.

We entered without any strife,
　　and I, wanting to see what punishments
　　such a fortress enclosed, 108

as soon as within glanced around
　　and saw on every side a great plain
　　full of grief and torment.

As at Arles where the Rhone spreads out
　　or at Pola near [the bay of] Quarnero
　　which encloses Italy and bathes her boundaries,

the tombs make the land uneven,
　　so they did here, on all sides,
　　except that these graves were more terrible;

for among the tombs flames spread
　　by which they were so heated
　　that no trade needs iron hotter. 120

---

[13] Theseus of Athens (line 54) tried to carry off Persephone (Hecate), queen of the Underworld, but was himself held prisoner until he was rescued by Hercules, who in chaining the dog Cerberus tore the skin from its neck.

All their lids were open,
   and such harsh laments came from them
   as from the wretched and the suffering.

And I, "Master, who are the people
   buried within the tombs,
   making themselves heard by their painful sighs?"

And he to me, "Here are the archheretics[14]
   with their followers of every sect;
   and the tombs are laden much more than you think.

Like with like is buried,
   and the monuments are more and less hot."
   Then, after we had turned to the right,   132

we passed between the torments and the high battlements.

CANTO X

FARINATA DEGLI UBERTI

Now along a solitary path
   between the city wall and the torments,
   my master makes his way, and I behind him.

"O supreme genius, you who through the impious circles
   turn me [to the left or right] as you please," I began,
   "speak to me and satisfy my wishes.

The people lying in the sepulchres,
   might they be seen?—all the lids
   are raised and no one guards them."

And he to me, "All will be locked in
   when they return from Jehoshaphat [on Judgment Day]
   with the bodies they have left above.   12

> *Epicurus is with the heretics of Christian times since he, almost alone among*
> *ancient philosophers, denied the immortality of the soul.*
>
> *Still hesitant about asking questions, Dante represses his desire to see certain*
> *Florentines.*

On this side is the burial place
   of Epicurus and of all his followers
   who hold that the soul dies with the body.

---

[14]This circle of the heretics, like Limbo, is a special case, heresy being a mental or spiritual condition rather than one of the sins of behavior (Incontinence, Violence, Fraud) punished in the overall threefold scheme of Dante's Hell. Moreover, heresy, like failure to be baptized, is a fault defined not by universal ethics but from a specifically Christian point of view.

But concerning the question you ask
   you will soon be satisfied,
   and also as to the wish you keep silent."[15]

And I, "Good guide, I hide my thought
   only to speak little; not long ago
   you disposed me to do that."

> *A deep voice sounds amid the silence of the graves. It is that of Farinata degli Uberti, a Ghibelline leader who, in 1260, won the bloody battle of Montaperti over the Florentine Guelfs, to which party Dante's family belonged. In recalling the bloodshed, Farinata has a moment of spontaneous repentance. Dante timidly draws closer to his guide who then directs him toward this proud, towering figure.*

"O Tuscan, you who through the city of fire
   go alive, speaking thus modestly,
   may it please you to remain in this place.   24

Your speech shows you a native
   of that noble fatherland
   to which, perhaps, I was too harmful."

Suddenly this sound came
   from one of the tombs, so that, startled,
   I drew closer to my guide.

He said to me, "Turn around! what are you doing?
   See Farinata, who has stood erect;
   from the waist upward, wholly, you can see him!"

I had already fixed my eyes on his,
   and he lifted up his chest and head,
   as if he had scorn for Hell,   36

and the bold and ready hands of my guide
   pushed me among the sepulchres to him,
   saying, "Let your words be well chosen."

> *Disappointed in not seeing someone of his own generation, Farinata asks about Dante's ancestors. On hearing the names of these former enemies, he tells angrily how he had scattered them. Now Dante's partisan spirit is aroused. He points out that his party has been able to return to Florence, whereas Farinata's has not learned the art of getting back. Dante's remark is an unexpected blow for the Ghibelline captain, who is unaware of all the events and who remains silent, trying to recover and to collect his thoughts.*

When I was at the foot of his tomb
   he looked at me a little; then, almost disdainfully,
   he asked, "Who were your ancestors?"

---

[15] Possibly a wish to see Farinata.

I, desirous to obey, did not hide them,
  but revealed them all,
  whereupon he raised his brows a little

and said, "Fiercely were they adverse
  to me and to my ancestors and to my party,
  so that twice I scattered them."   48

"If they were driven out, they came back from every side,"
  I answered him, "both the first and the second time,
  but yours did not learn well that art!"

> *Now the shade of the father of Guido Cavalcanti, the latter a leading poet and
> Dante's best friend, rises beside the great Ghibelline leader. He too is not inter-
> ested in Dante. He assumes that our poet is allowed to visit Hell because of some
> peculiar merit, and since he cannot conceive of greater nobility of mind than
> that of his son, he wonders why Guido is not there also. Dante is perplexed, not
> knowing that the shades are ignorant of immediate happenings on earth, and
> replies ambiguously, implying lack of devotion on Guido's part to Virgil. The
> important point, however, is the past tense of the verb he uses. Cavalcante assumes
> from it that his son is dead, and from the embarrassed tone of Dante's remarks,
> suspects that Guido may have had a fate somewhat like his own. Dante's delay
> in answering confirms his fear, and he falls back into his tomb.*

Now beside him there arose to sight
  a shade visible down to his chin;
  I believe he had risen on his knees.

He looked around me as if anxious
  to see if someone else were with me,
  but when this expectation was wholly spent,

weeping he said, "If through this blind prison
  you go because of the greatness of your mind,
  where is my son? why is he not with you?"   60

And I to him, "By myself I do not come;
  Virgil, waiting there, guides me,
  whom perhaps your Guido held in disdain."

His words and the manner of his punishment
  had already revealed his name to me;
  therefore my reply was so complete.

Rising suddenly he cried, "What did you say?
  he *held*? Does he not live still?
  Does not the sweet light strike his eyes?"

When he was aware of some delay
  before I answered, he fell back supine
  and showed himself no more.   72

> *Meanwhile Farinata has been pondering over Dante's remark and, without tran-
> sition, oblivious to the drama enacted at his feet, he returns the verbal blow by
> predicting the poet's exile within four years. Relieved by this aggression, he asks*

in a more kindly tone why the Florentines have persecuted his family, and he points out proudly how, after the battle, when the Ghibelline leaders proposed razing Florence to the ground, he alone defended and saved her. Now Dante's partisan spirit is likewise softened, and in the conversation that follows he learns that the shades remember the past and can predict the future, but, like farsighted people, cannot see what is close at hand. This accounts for the misunderstanding between him and Cavalcante, and he asks to have his error corrected.

But that other magnanimous one, at whose instance
   I had stopped, did not change his expression,
   nor move his head, nor bend his body.

"And if," he said, continuing his first remark,
   "they have badly learned that art,
   it torments me more than this bed.

But not fifty times will be rekindled
   the face of her [Hecate, the moon] who rules here
   before you will know the hardness of that art!

And—so may you return sometime to the sweet world—
   tell me why the people are so fierce
   against my kindred in all their laws."   84

Then I to him, "The slaughter and havoc
   which dyed the [river] Arbia red
   cause such prayers to rise in our temple."

Sighing he shook his head and said,
   "In that I was not alone, nor certainly
   would I and the others have moved without cause,

but I was alone when all the rest
   agreed to wipe out Florence:
   I defended her openly before all."

"So may your descendants sometime have rest,"
   I replied, "please solve for me this puzzle
   which has now entangled my judgment.   96

It seems that you see, if I hear rightly,
   what the future brings,
   but for the present have a different vision."

"Like those with imperfect sight,
   we see things far from us," he said,
   "so much light the Supreme ruler still allows,

but when they come close, or exist, our minds
   do not perceive them, and, without news from others,
   we know nothing of your human state.

Therefore you can understand that our knowledge [gained from others]
   will be wholly dead after that moment [Judgment Day]
   when the gates of the future are closed."   108

Then, as if sorry for my fault,
   I said, "Now please tell that fallen one
   that his son is still joined with the living,

and if I was silent at his question,
   let him know it was because my thoughts
   were confused by the error you have corrected."

> *Before moving on, Virgil declares emphatically that Beatrice will reveal to Dante the course of his life. This is a mistake on Virgil's part: Cacciaguida, not Beatrice, makes the prophecy.[16]*
>
> *(The treatment of the heretics is a comedy of errors which illustrates the fallibility of human reason. The Epicureans, in their tombs, erred in thinking that the grave ended all; Farinata is deceived in several ways; Cavalcante makes a series of false assumptions; Dante likewise is bewildered. Finally Virgil [Reason itself] is emphatically wrong.)*

Already my master was calling me back,
   so that I begged the spirit more hastily
   to tell me who was with him.

He said, "With more than a thousand I lie:
   here is the second Frederick [of Sicily]
   and the Cardinal [Ubaldino]; of the others I am silent."   120

Then he hid himself, and toward the ancient poet
   I turned my steps, meditating
   about the prophecy hostile to me.

My guide moved on and, as we were going,
   he said to me, "Why are you so bewildered?"
   and I satisfied his request.

"Let your mind retain what you have heard
   against you," that sage commanded me,
   "and now listen to this," and he raised his finger:

"When you face the sweet light
   of her [Beatrice] whose fair eyes see everything
   you will learn from her the journey of your life."   132

Then he turned his steps to the left;
   we went from the wall toward the center
   along a path which goes into a valley

which even up there stifled us with its stench.

---

[16]This occurs in *Paradise,* Canto XVII, where the exile of Dante, separated from the places and people he cherished most, is poignantly outlined by Cacciaguida, Dante's great-great-grandfather.

CANTO XI

THE CLASSIFICATION OF SINS

As the poets proceed toward the inner edge of the sixth circle, they observe a tomb inscribed with the name of Anastasius. There was confusion in Dante's time between a pope and a heretical Byzantine emperor of that name.

While waiting to become accustomed to the smell which rises from a river of hot blood below, Virgil explains the various divisions of Hell.

To explain why usurers are classed with blasphemers and sodomites as doing violence to God, Virgil points out that Nature, which offers man its bounty, derives from God; that men's art (industry) gives further value to the products of Nature and, in a sense, derives also from God; that man was intended to earn his living through the bounty of Nature and by the sweat of his brow, and that usurers violate this divine plan.

At the end of the canto we learn by the position of the stars that it is about three hours after midnight, Saturday, April 9, 1300.

On the edge of a high bank
    formed by a circle of broken rocks
    we stood above a more cruel pack;

and here because of the horrible stench
    which the deep abyss exhales
    we approached behind the cover of a great tomb

on which I saw an inscription saying,
    "I hold Anastasius, the pope,
    whom Photinus drew from the straight path."

"Our descent must be slow, so that our sense of smell
    may get used to the foul breath,
    and then we will not heed it."   12

Thus my master spoke, and I, "Please find compensation,
    so that time will not be wasted."
    And he, "That is what I have been thinking of.

My son," he then continued,
    "below us are three smaller circles
    like those you are leaving,

full of accursed spirits. In order
    that sight alone may suffice henceforth,
    observe how and why they are confined.

The malice which Heaven reproves
    causes injury and grief to others
    either by violence or by fraud,   24

but because fraud is peculiar to man
    it displeases God more; therefore
    the fraudulent are placed lower and have more pain.

The next circle [seventh] is for the violent,
    and, since force can be used
    against God, oneself, and one's fellow men—

I mean against them or their property—
    it is divided into three bands
    as you will clearly hear.

Death and painful wounds may be inflicted
    on one's fellows, and plunder, arson,
    and extortion on their property.   36

Thus the first round torments, in various groups,
    assassins, plunderers, and robbers,
    and all who strike maliciously.

A man may commit violence against himself
    and against his property; therefore, in the second round,
    all who deprive themselves of your world

or gamble and dissipate their wealth
    must unavailingly repent
    and weep instead of being happy.

Violence is committed against the Deity
    by cursing Him and denying Him in one's heart;
    and by scorning Nature and her bounty;   48

therefore the smallest band stamps with its seal
    both Sodom [the sodomites] and Cahors [the usurers]
    and those [the blasphemers] who speak disdaining God.

Fraud which hurts man's conscience
    can be used against those who trust
    and against those who have no special confidence.

In the latter case, only the love that Nature makes
    [the natural brotherhood of man] is violated;
    thus, in the following [eighth] circle are nested

hypocrisy, flattery, sorcery,
    falsifying, theft, and simony,
    panders, barrators, and similar filth.   60

The other fraud violates
    both the love Nature creates and that
    which implies a special trust.

Therefore, in the smallest circle
    at the center of the universe where Dis [Satan] holds forth
    whoever betrays is eternally consumed."

And I, "Master, your account proceeds clearly
    and makes plain the division
    of this abyss and those who are in it,

but tell me, the souls [above] in the slimy bog,
    those whom the wind blows, and those the rain beats,
    and those who meet with such sharp tongues,   72

why are they not inside the ruddy city
    if God is angry with them,
    and if not, why are they in such a plight?"

He answered, "Why does your mind
    go astray more than usual?
    or are you thinking of something else?

Do you not remember those words
    with which your *Ethics* [of Aristotle] treats
    the three dispositions Heaven does not admit—

incontinence, malice, and mad bestiality—
    and how incontinence offends God less
    and incurs less blame?   84

If you consider this teaching
    and recall who is being punished
    outside of the city,

you will see why they are separated
    from these and why, less angrily,
    Divine Justice torments them."

"O Sun, you who heal every troubled vision,
    I am so glad to hear you explain
    that to question pleases me no less than knowing;

but go back a little," I said,
    "to where you say that usury offends
    divine goodness, and solve the puzzle."   96

"Philosophy," he said,
    "states in more than one place
    that Nature takes her course

from the Divine Intellect and from Its operation,
    and if you note well your *Physics,*
    you will find after not many pages

that your activity follows the divine plan,
    as the pupil does his master, so that your art [industry]
    is, as it were, a grandchild of God.

From these two [Nature and Industry], if you recall
    the early part of Genesis,
    man should earn his living and prosper.   108

And because the usurer takes another way,
    he scorns Nature in itself and in its follower [Industry],
    since he places his hope in something else.

But follow me now, for I wish to go.
    The Fishes [Pisces] are quivering on the horizon
    and the Chariot [Big Dipper] lies wholly over Caurus [the north-
        west],

and the cliff we descend is far over there.

CANTO XII

THE VIOLENT

*Near a break in the cliff, a landslide caused by the revulsion of the earth at the
Crucifixion, is the Minotaur, a creature with a man's body and a bull's head,
the bestial guardian of the circle of the violent. To get around this monster, Virgil
puts him in a blind rage by mentioning the circumstances of his death, how his
half sister, Ariadne, had guided Theseus through the labyrinth to him.*

The place where we came to descend the bank
    was craggy and, because of what was there [the Minotaur],
    such that every eye would shun it.

As the landslide which, on this side of Trento,
    struck the Adige, either because of an earthquake
    or from being undermined—

for, from the top of the mountain
    to the plain, the cliff has so fallen
    that it provides a path for one above—

such was the descent into this ravine;
    and on the edge of the broken chasm,
    the infamy of Crete [the Minotaur], conceived   12

in the false [wooden] cow,[17] was stretched out.
    On seeing us the monster bit himself
    like one subdued by anger.

My sage cried to him, "Perhaps you think
    the Duke of Athens [Theseus] is here
    who killed you in the world.

Get away, beast, for this man does not come
    instructed by your sister,
    but journeys on to see your punishments."

As a bull that breaks loose at the moment
    when it receives a mortal blow
    and cannot go straight, but plunges here and there,   24

so I saw the Minotaur stagger,
    and my wary guide shouted, "Run to the pass;
    while he is raging it is well for you to go down."

---

[17] The Minotaur was born of Pasiphae, wife of Minos, king of Crete, after she hid herself
inside a wooden cow in order to have intercourse with a bull.

Thus we made our way over the loose rocks
    which often moved under my feet
    because of the unusual burden.

As I went on, thinking, my guide said,
    "Perhaps you are wondering about this landslide
    guarded by the bestial wrath I outwitted.

Now I want you to know that the other time
    I went down here into deep Hell
    this cliff had not yet been broken,   36

but, if I discern correctly, shortly before
    He [Christ] came to the first circle
    to remove the great prey from Dis [at the "harrowing"]

the loathsome pit trembled on all sides
    so that I thought the universe felt love
    because of which some [philosophers] believed

the world has many times reverted to chaos [a fusion
    of the elements]; and at that moment these old rocks
    here and elsewhere fell down.

But look below, for the river of blood
    is near, in which are boiled
    those who through violence harm others."   48

     On the banks of the river are centaurs, creatures with horses' bodies, but whose
     heads (unlike that of the Minotaur) are human.

O blind greed, wicked and foolish,
    which so spurs us in the brief life,
    and in the eternal condemns to such pain!

I saw a wide moat making a bend
    surrounding the level ground [of the circle]
    like the one my escort had mentioned,

and between the foot of the bank and the ditch
    centaurs, armed with arrows, were running, in single file,
    as they used to go hunting in our world.

Seeing us descend all stopped,
    and three came from the band,
    having armed themselves with bows and arrows.   60

One shouted from afar, "To what punishment
    are you coming? Tell us from there;
    if not, I'll draw the bow!"

My master answered, "We will reply
    to Chiron over there; unfortunately,
    you were always quick to act."

Then he touched me and said, "That is Nessus
     who died for the beautiful Dejanira
     and by himself took vengeance for himself.[18]

The one in the middle, looking at his breast,
     is the great Chiron, the teacher of Achilles,
     and the other is Pholus, who was so full of rage.   72

Around the ditch they go by thousands
     shooting shades that rise from the blood
     farther than their sins allow."

As we drew near those rapid beasts
     Chiron took an arrow, and with the notch
     combed back the beard on his jaws,

and when he had uncovered his great mouth
     he said to his companions, "Did you notice
     that the one behind moves what he touches?

The feet of the dead do not do this."
     And my good guide, already close to the breast
     where the two natures were joined, answered,   84

"He is indeed alive, and thus alone
     I must show him the dark valley.
     Necessity brings him here, not pleasure.

A lady [Beatrice] who came from singing hallelujah
     entrusted this mission to me;
     he is no robber nor am I a thief.

Therefore, by that power through which
     I move my feet over so rough a road,
     give us one of your band to be with us,

to show us where the ford is, and to carry
     this man on his back, for he is not a spirit
     that can go through the air."   96

> *Chiron, turning to his better side, appoints Nessus as the leader. The party see
> first various Greek and Italian tyrants, sunk to their eyebrows in the blood; then
> assassins, among whom, shunned by the others, is the first Englishman men-
> tioned, Guy of Montfort who in a church at Viterbo killed Prince Henry. Henry's
> heart, it was said, was placed in a golden urn in Westminster Abbey.*

Chiron turned to his right
     and said to Nessus, "Go back and guide them,
     and if you meet another band, make it give way."

---

[18]While trying to abduct Dejanira, the centaur Nessus was killed by an arrow from her husband, Hercules. As he was dying, Nessus gave Dejanira a robe, stained with his blood, that
would supposedly preserve Hercules' love for her. But the robe killed Hercules, after which
she committed suicide.

We started with our trusted escort
    along the bank of the vermilion stream
    in which those boiled uttered loud cries.

I saw shades in it up to their eyebrows;
    and the great centaur said, "These are tyrants
    who engaged in bloodshed and in plunder.

Now they weep for their pitiless crimes.
    Here are Alexander and fierce Dionysius[19]
    who gave Italy years of woe,   108

and that head with such black hair
    is Azzolino; and the blond one,
    Opizzo da Este, who, in truth,

was killed by his stepson in the world above."
    Then I turned to the poet, who said,
    "Let him go first now and me second."

A little farther on the centaur stopped
    above a group who down to their throats
    appeared above the boiling stream.

Then he showed us a shade to one side, alone, saying,
    "That one, in God's bosom, pierced the heart
    that still is honored on the Thames."   120

Afterward I saw some who kept their heads
    and chests out of the stream,
    and of those I recognized many.

Thus, little by little, the blood grew shallow
    until it cooked only the feet,
    and there was our passage over the moat.

"As on this side you see the boiling river
    grow shallow," said the centaur,
    "so I wish you to believe

that on the other its bottom gets deeper
    until it reaches the place
    where tyrants must groan.   132

There Divine Justice torments
    that Attila who was a scourge on earth,
    and Pyrrhus and Sextus; and eternally it milks

the tears, which the boiling releases,
    from Rinieri da Corneto and Rinieri Pazzo
    who waged such warfare on the highways."

Then Nessus turned back and repassed the ford.

---

[19]Either Alexander the Great or another Alexander (of Pherae); Dionysius was tyrant of
Syracuse (fourth century B.C.).

CANTO XIII

PIER DELLE VIGNE

*The poets enter the wood of the Christian suicides. This wild forest represents
the world as it would be if all revolted against life. It is infested by the Harpies,
loathsome creatures, half human, half birds, which stand for the storm winds
of human passions.*

*In every way the suicides, now changed into trees or saplings, are frustrated.
They have used their power of movement to deprive themselves of what distinguished them from plants; but they have not found death. The Harpies they tried
to escape go with them, and the old agony is pent up in their new embodiments.*

Nessus had not yet reached the other side
    when we entered a wood
    that was marked by no path.

No green foliage was there, but of a dark color,
    no smooth branches, but knotty and twisted,
    no fruit, but poisonous thorns.

The wild beasts that shun cultivated places
    do not have such dense and tangled thickets
    [in the Maremma] between Cecina and Corneto.[20]

Here the ugly Harpies make their nests
    who with sad predictions of future harm
    drove the Trojans from the Strophades.[21]   12

They have wide wings and human necks and faces,
    feet with claws, and great feathered bellies;
    they utter laments on the strange trees.

My good master began to speak, saying,
    "Before you go any farther, know
    that you are in the second round and will be

until you come to the horrible sand.
    Therefore look closely and you will see
    what would seem incredible in my speech."

I heard moans on every side
    and saw no one to make them,
    so that I stopped, all bewildered.   24

I believe he believed that I believed
    that so many voices came from people
    hidden from us among the trees;

---

[20] Two towns, at the northern and southern edges of the Maremma, a swamp near Florence.
[21] Islands visited by Aeneas and the other Trojans in their wanderings after the fall of Troy.
This incident and one involving a bleeding shrub (referred to in line 48) occur in Virgil's
Aeneid, Book III.

therefore he said, "If you break
a twig of one of these woody plants
the thoughts you have will be corrected."

Then I stretched forth my hand
and plucked a small branch from a great thorn tree,
and its trunk cried, "Why do you break me?"

After it had grown dark with blood,
it began again to lament, "Why do you tear me?
have you no trace of pity?

36

We were men, and now are turned to wood;
your hand should have been more merciful
if we had been the souls of serpents."

As a green log, burning at one end,
drips from the other and hisses
with the steam that escapes,

so from the broken branch words and blood
came out together; and I let the twig fall
and stood like one afraid.

The tree whose branch Dante has broken is that of Pier delle Vigne, a famous statesman, scholar, and poet at the court of Frederick II of Sicily. (In several curious, repetitious lines Dante imitates the style of the Frederician poets.) Frederick accused him of treason, had him blinded and led in derision on an ass from town to town. To escape this dishonor, Pier is said to have beaten his head against the walls of his prison. Dante presents him as innocent, as the model of a devoted public servant. He is proud of the office he once held and still loyal to the king who could do no wrong. It was Envy, he says, the harlot at every court, who caused his death. And he swears by his new body that he was never unfaithful.

"If he [Dante] could have believed, offended soul,"
my master answered,
"what he has seen only in my verse,

48

he would not have raised his hand against you,
but the incredible thing made me prompt him
to do what grieves me.

Now tell him who you were, so that
to make amends, he may refresh your fame
in the world above to which he is permitted to return."

Then the tree, "You so allure me with kind words
that I cannot keep silent, and may you
not be wearied if I grow sticky talking.

I am the one who held both keys [of consent and denial]
to Frederick's heart, and who turned them,
locking and unlocking so softly

60

that I kept almost everyone from his secrets.
    Such trust I bore to the glorious office
    that I lost sleep and strength.

The harlot [Envy] who never from Caesar's dwelling
    has turned aside her shameless eyes,
    the common bane and vice of courts,

inflamed all minds against me,
    and the inflamed so inflamed Augustus [Frederick]
    that my joyous honors changed to dismal sorrow.

My soul with disgust and scorn,
    hoping to escape disdain,
    made me unjust to my just self.   72

By the new roots of this tree, I swear to you
    that I never broke faith with my lord
    who was so worthy of honor.

And if either of you return to the world,
    comfort my memory which still lies crushed
    by the blow that Envy gave it."

Pier tells how the souls fall and become trees and bushes.

After Judgment Day, the bodies the suicides could not endure for a few brief years will hang on their branches forever. This is the final frustration.

The poet waited a little and then said,
    "Since he is silent, do not lose the chance,
    but question him if you want to hear more."

And I answered, "*You* ask what you think
    will satisfy me, for I could not;
    such pity saddens me."   84

Then he began, "So may this man
    do freely for you what you ask,
    please tell us, imprisoned spirit,

how the soul becomes bound in these branches,
    and let us know if you can
    if any ever frees himself from them."

The tree blew loudly, and soon
    the wind changed into these sounds:
    "Briefly will you be answered.

When the fierce soul leaves the body
    from which it has torn itself,
    Minos sends it to the seventh depth.   96

It falls into the wood; no place is chosen for it,
    but where chance throws it
    it sprouts, like a grain of wheat.

It grows into a sapling and a wild tree;
　　the Harpies, feeding then upon its leaves,
　　give pain and to the pain an outlet.

Like the others we will come for our bodies,
　　but not to be clothed again with them,
　　for it is not right to get back what is rejected.

Here we will drag them, and
　　in the sad wood our bodies will be hung
　　on the branches of our injurious souls."　　　　　　　　108

> *Two spirits rush by, chased by the hounds of ruin and crying for a second death*
> *they can never have. These are souls of reckless squanderers, destroyers of their*
> *estates and indirectly of themselves. One, Lano, in desperate circumstances, allowed*
> *himself to be killed in the battle of Toppo.*

We were still attentive to the tree,
　　believing that it wished to say more,
　　when a loud sound startled us

as it does the hunter who sees the boar and chase
　　approach his post and who hears the beast
　　and the crash of the branches.

And behold! two on the left,
　　naked and scratched, fleeing so fast
　　that they broke the brambles of the wood.

The one in the front cried, "Now come, now come, O Death!"
　　and the other who saw himself outdistanced, called,
　　"Lano, your legs were not so nimble　　　　　　　　120

at the tournament of Toppo." And, perhaps
　　because his breath had failed, he plunged
　　into a bush, making a tangle of it and of himself.

Behind them the wood was full of black bitches,
　　ravenous and running fast,
　　like greyhounds just freed from the leash.

They fixed their teeth in the one who squatted
　　and tore him to pieces,
　　then carried off the suffering members.

My guide then took me by the hand
　　and led me to the bush, which lamented vainly
　　through its bleeding wounds.　　　　　　　　132

"O Giacomo da Sant'Andrea," it cried,
　　"what do you gain by making me a screen?
　　what blame have I for your wicked life?"

My master had stopped beside it and asked,
　　"Who were you, you who through so many breaks
　　blow forth your woeful blood and words?"

The soul in the bush deplores the situation in Florence where martial virtue has been sacrificed for money-making (represented by John the Baptist whose image was stamped on Florentine coins); then he identifies himself briefly, not by a name but by an act: he desecrated his own home by making a gallows in it.

And the bush to us, "O souls coming
  to see the shameful ravage
  that has so separated my leaves from me,

gather them together at the foot of the poor plant.
  I was of the city which changed its first patron [Mars]
  for the Baptist, because of which   144

that god will always sadden it with his art,
  and if, at the bridge over the Arno
  there did not remain a trace of him [the ruins of a statue],

those citizens who rebuilt the city
  on the ashes left by Attila[22]
  would have done their work in vain.

I made a gibbet for myself of my own house."

CANTO XIV

THE VIOLENT AGAINST GOD

The round of the violent against God or Nature is characterized by sterility. On the hot sand the blasphemers are lying supine, the sodomites are running, the usurers sitting. Over all is falling a rain of fire which, here and elsewhere, symbolizes the direct wrath of God.

Because love for my native city moved me,
  I gathered the scattered leaves and gave them back
  to him whose voice was already faint.

Then we came to where the second round [the wood]
  is divided from the third [the plain]
  and where is seen a fearful kind of justice.

To make the new place manifest,
  I say that we reached a desert
  which repels every plant from its bed.

The doleful wood forms a garland around it,
  just as the dismal moat does to the wood.
  Here, at the very edge, we stopped.   12

---

[22]Attila the Hun, fifth-century invader of Europe, was supposed to have sacked Florence. See also XII.134.

The ground was of dry, thick sand,
    not different from that [of the Libyan desert]
    once trod by Cato's feet.[23]

O how greatly the vengeance of God
    should be feared by everyone who reads
    what was apparent to my eyes!

I saw many groups of naked souls,
    all of whom wept miserably,
    but different positions were imposed on them.

Some were lying supine upon the ground,
    some were sitting, bent over,
    and others were running continually.   24

Those that kept moving were most numerous
    and those fewest who were lying in the torment,
    but their tongues were loosened by greater pain.

Over all the plain, falling slowly,
    dilated flakes of fire came down,
    like snow in Alps without a wind.

As Alexander in those hot parts
    of India saw flames fall on his host
    intact as far as to the ground,

and made his legions trample
    on the soil, since the fire
    could be extinguished better before it spread;   36

so fell the eternal heat
    by which the sand was kindled
    like tinder under flint, to double the pain.

Ever without rest was the dance
    of the miserable hands, now here, now there,
    brushing off the fresh burning.

> *Dante notices a shade still untamed, bold, indomitable, defying Jove and the thunderbolts which defeated the giants. Virgil has more contempt for this apparent superman than for anyone else in Hell. Flat on his back, feeling hour after hour eternally the power of the God he is defying, his attitude seems stupid rather than courageous, and is peculiarly disgusting to Reason.*

I began, "Master, you who have overcome everything
    except the fierce demons who rushed out against us
    at the entrance to the City,

---

[23] In 47 B.C., during the Roman civil war between Julius Caesar and Pompey, Cato led part of Pompey's army across Libya.

who is that great shade not heeding the fire,
    lying scornful and contorted,
    whom the rain does not seem to ripen?"   48

And he, aware that I was asking my guide
    about him, shouted loudly,
    "As I was alive, so am I dead.

Though Jove exhaust his smith from whom,
    angrily, he took the sharp thunderbolt
    by which I was struck on my last day,

and though he weary the others [the Cyclops] one by one
    in Mongibello [Mt. Etna] at the black forge,
    crying, 'Help, help, good Vulcan!'—

as he did in the battle of Phlegra [against the giants]—
    and hit me with all his strength,
    he could not have the joy of vengeance."   60

Then my guide spoke with such feeling
    that I had never heard his voice so loud,
    "O Capaneus, since your pride

remains untamed you are punished more.
    No torture except your rage itself
    would be adequate for your fury."

Then he turned to me with a better look, saying,
    "This was one of the seven kings
    who besieged Thebes; he held and still seems

to hold God in contempt, and to fear Him little;
    but, as I told him, his blasphemy
    is a fitting ornament for his breast.   72

The travelers come to where the overflow from Phlegethon, the river of blood, crosses the plain. The water of this little stream is like the Bulicame, a hot spring near Viterbo, where special bathhouses were provided for prostitutes. Its sterile banks offer a passageway, since over the blood-stained water the fire is quenched, a confirmation or symbol of atonement, the appeasing of God's wrath by human suffering.

Now follow me and be careful
    not to put your feet on the burning sand,
    but always keep them close to the wood."

In silence we came to where, out of
    the forest, a little rivulet gushes,
    the redness of which still makes me shudder.

As from the Bulicame a stream flows
    which sinful women share among themselves,
    so this one flowed across the sand.

Its bottom and both its sides
    were made of stone and also the banks
    on which I perceived that our way led.   84

"Among all the things I have shown you
    since we entered the gate
    whose threshold is denied to none,

nothing has been seen by your eyes
    as notable as the present stream
    which quenches all the flames above it."

These words were spoken by my guide,
    and I asked him to grant the food
    for which he had given me an appetite.

> *With elaborate symbolism, Virgil now tells of man's fall from grace and the consequences. On Mount Ida, in Crete, the center of the ancient world and the supposed cradle of the human race, there is a statue which represents the history of mankind. Its back is turned toward the East, its face in the direction of the course of empire. Its head, representing the Golden Age of the Ancients or the period of the Garden of Eden, is of gold; other parts, according to the various ages, are of different metals. One foot is of iron (the Roman Empire), the other of clay (the Papacy), and the weight of the statue bears too heavily on the latter, the cause, in Dante's view, of much of the anarchy and disorder in the world. The whole statue except the head has been cracked by man's sin. From this fissure tears drip. They flow down to Hell, form the waters of the Acheron, the Styx, the Phlegethon, and ultimately the frozen Cocytus. Thus, by a kind of conservation of sorrow, the tears shed through cruelty are not lost, but flow down to punish those who cause them.*
>
> *Another river, the Lethe, descends to Hell from Purgatory carrying with it the last trace, that is, the very memory, of sin.*

"In the middle of the sea," he said then,
    "lies a waste land, called Crete,
    under whose kings the world once was chaste.   96

A mountain there, named Ida,
    was joyous with water and with leaves;
    now it is deserted, like a thing worn out.

Rhea chose it for the safe cradle
    of her son [Jupiter]; and to hide him better
    when he cried, she had a clamor made.[24]

On the mountain stands a great old man [a statue]
    with back turned toward Damietta [in the East]
    and looking toward Rome as in a mirror.

His head is formed of fine gold,
    his arms and breast are of pure silver;
    then he is of brass as far as to the fork.   108

---

[24] Rhea was the wife of Saturn, who devoured most of his sons. To save their son Jupiter, she had his protectors, the Curetes, make loud noises to drown out the infant's crying.

From there down he is made of fine iron,
 except that the right foot is of baked clay,
 and he stands on that more than on the other.

Every part except the gold is broken
 by a fissure which drips tears
 and these, joining, cut through that bank,

flow down to this pit, and form the Acheron,
 the Styx, and the Phlegethon;
 then, moving on through this narrow channel,

go down to where there can be no further descent.
 They form Cocytus; and since you will see
 how that lake is, I do not describe it." 120

And I to him, "If the present stream
 comes thus from our world,
 why does it appear only here?"

And he, "You know that the place is round,
 and, although you have come far
 always descending to the left,

you have not yet completed the circle;
 therefore, if something new appears,
 it should not cause marveling."

Then I asked, "Master, where are the Phlegethon
 and Lethe, for you are silent about one [Lethe]
 and say that this rain forms the other." 132

"In all your questions you please me,"
 he replied, "but the boiling red water
 ought to answer one [about the Phlegethon].

You will see Lethe outside of this pit
 where souls go to wash themselves
 when guilt, repented, is removed.

Now it is time to leave the wood;
 see that you come behind me;
 the banks, not burned, offer a way,

and over them all fire is extinguished."

CANTO XV

BRUNETTO LATINI

The banks of the rivulet are like the dikes built by the Flemings or those made along the Brenta before the snow melts in the Chiarentana mountains. As the poets pass, they are eyed intently by a band of sodomites. Dante recognizes one as Brunetto Latini, a famous author and scholar, some of whose lectures Dante evidently heard. Dante extends his hand with reverence and, using the polite (voi) form of address, tells of his surprise at meeting him in this place.

Now one of the hard banks offers us a way,
  and the vapor of the stream makes a shelter
  which protects the shores and water from the fire.

As the Flemings between Wissant and Bruges,
  fearing the flood which rushes toward them,
  make a bulwark to repel the sea,

and as the Paduans do along the Brenta
  to defend their cities and their castles,
  before Chiarentana feels the heat,

in such a manner those banks were formed,
  although their builder, whoever he was,
  made them not so high nor so thick.   12

Already we were so far from the wood
  that I could not have seen where it was
  if I had turned back

when we met a band of spirits
  coming along the banks, and each gazed at us
  as, at dusk, under a new moon,

men are wont to look at each other,
  sharpening their eyes at us
  as an old tailor does at his needle's eye.

Thus gazed at by such a group,
  I was recognized by one who grasped my skirt
  and cried, "What a marvel!"   24

And as he held out his arm toward me
  I fixed my glance on his baked aspect
  so that his burned face did not prevent

the recognition of him by my memory.
  Lowering my hand toward his face,
  I asked, "Are *you* here, *ser* Brunetto?"

> *Brunetto proposes to accompany Dante by walking along below him. He must keep moving: restlessness is common to the punishment of all sexual sinners. Dante shows the greatest affection for his old master, a feeling reciprocated by Brunetto, who prophesies Dante's quarrel with the Florentines. They, according to legend, represent a fusion of the descendants of a Roman colony and of the rough hill people from Fiesole. Dante wishes that Brunetto had not been banished in a double sense from human nature, and pays him the supreme tribute to a teacher: he taught, not the minutiae of scholarship and pedantry, but the important things, how man, through fame, can make himself eternal.*

And he, "O my son, may it not displease you
  if Brunetto Latini goes back with you a little,
  letting his company move on."

I said to him, "As much as I can I beg you to,
    and if you want me to sit down with you,
    I will do so, if he with whom I go permits."   36

"O son," he said, "whoever of this flock
    stops one instant, lies afterward a hundred years
    without brushing off the fire that strikes him;

therefore, go on; I will follow at your skirts
    and then I will rejoin my band
    which goes lamenting its eternal punishment."

I did not dare go down from the path
    to be with him, but I held my head low
    like one who walks with reverence.

He began, "What chance or destiny
    brings you here before your last day,
    and who is this one showing you the road?"   48

"Up there in the serene life," I answered,
    "I went astray in a valley,
    before my allotted time was spent.

Yesterday morning I turned my back on it;
    then, as I was falling into it again, this shade appeared
    who is taking me home by this road."

And he to me, "If you follow your star
    you cannot fail to reach a glorious port
    if I discerned rightly in the fair life.

And if I had not died so early,
    seeing the heavens so gracious to you,
    I would have cheered you in your work.   60

That ungrateful, malignant people who of old
    came down from Fiesole and still keep
    the roughness of the mountains and the rocks

will become your enemies because of your good deeds.
    And that is right, for among the bitter sorb trees
    it is not fitting that the sweet fig bear fruit.

Old report in the world calls them blind,
    an avaricious, envious, haughty people:
    see that you cleanse yourself from their ways.

Your fate reserves such honor
    that both parties will be hungry for you;
    but far from the goat will be the grass!   72

Let the beasts of Fiesole make fodder
    of themselves and not touch the plant
    if one grows on their dung heap

in whom the holy virtues are revived
of those Romans who remained there
when it was made the nest of such wickedness."

"If my request could be fully granted,"
I answered him, "you would not yet
be exiled from human nature;

for in my mind is fixed and my heart knows
the dear and kindly image of you
as a father when, from hour to hour, 84

you taught how man makes himself eternal;
and while I am alive, it is fitting
that my tongue show how grateful I am.

What you say about my life I write down
and keep to be explained with another text
by a lady [Beatrice] who can do this if I see her.

This much I would have plain to you—
so may my conscience not chide me—
I am prepared for Fortune as she wills.

Such warnings are not new to my ears;
therefore, as they please, 'Let Fortune
turn her wheel, and the churl his mattock.'" 96

My master turned to the right
and looked at me, then said,
"He listens well who notes what is told."

> *Among the many famous and infamous men guilty of sodomy was Dante's bishop,
> whom Boniface VIII, instead of punishing severely, merely transferred to another
> see. Thus the two men whose duty was to teach Dante how to become eternal on
> earth and in Heaven are together.*
>
> *Brunetto hurriedly commends his work,* The Treasury, *to Dante and then leaves,
> running fast, his loss of dignity showing the effect of one vice on an otherwise
> venerable character.*

Nonetheless I continued talking
to *ser* Brunetto, and I asked
who were his most noted companions.

And he to me, "It is well to know of some;
of the others it is more laudable to keep silent,
for time would be short for so much speech.

Know briefly that all were clerks[25]
and scholars and of great fame,
by the same sin defiled on earth. 108

---

[25]Clerics.

Priscian goes with that wretched crowd,
    and Francesco d'Accorso; moreover,
    if you had a hankering for such filth,

you might see him who by the Servant of the Servants
    was transferred from the Arno to the Bacchiglione,
    where he left his ill-strained muscles.

I would say more, but my going and my speech
    must not continue longer, since I see new smoke
    rising over there from the sand.

People are coming with whom I must not be.
    Let my *Treasury*, in which I live
    be commended to you; more I do not ask."   120

Then he turned, and seemed like one of those
    who, at Verona, through the fields, run races
    for a green cloth; and of these he appeared to move

like the one who wins, and not like the one who loses.

CANTO XVI

THE WATERFALL

Already I had reached a place where the roar
    of the water falling into the next circle
    could be heard, like the hum of a beehive,

when three shades running together
    left a troop passing through the rain
    of the fiery torment.

They came toward us and each cried,
    "Stop, you who by your dress seem to us
    to come from our perverse city!"

Ah! what wounds I saw on their bodies,
    old and recent, burnt in by the flames!
    I still grieve whenever I recall it.   12

My teacher listened to their cries,
    then turned his face toward me and said,
    "Now wait, to these we must be courteous,

and if it were not for the fire
    which the nature of this place lets fall,
    I should say that haste befitted you more than them."

    Since the edge of the precipice is not far off, the shades propose to keep moving
    by circling around one spot.

As we stopped they began again their old lament,
    and when they had reached us
    all three made of themselves a circle,

as wrestlers, naked and oiled, are wont to do,
    watching for a hold and an advantage,
    before the tugs and blows begin.   24

Thus circling, all kept their eyes on me,
    so that their heads and necks,
    together with their feet, moved continually.

And one of them began, "If the misery of this sandy place
    and our scorched and burned faces
    cause scorn for us and for our prayers,

may our fame incline you to tell us
    who you are, you who move so securely
    your living feet through Hell.

The man in whose footsteps you see me tread,
    although he goes now bare and hairless,
    was of a higher rank than you might believe.   36

He was a grandson of the good Gualdrada;
    Guido Guerra was his name, and in his life
    he did much with counsel and with sword.

The other who treads the sand behind me
    is Tegghiaio Aldobrandi, whose voice
    should have been heeded in the world.

And I, placed on the cross with them,
    am Jacopo Rusticucci; and certainly my fierce wife
    troubles me more than anything else."

If I had been sheltered from the fire,
    I would have thrown myself down among them,
    and I believe my master would have permitted;   48

but since I would have been burned and cooked,
    fear overcame the good will
    which made me eager to embrace them.

Then I began, "Not contempt, but such grief
    as will not soon leave me,
    your condition caused in me

as soon as my lord spoke words
    through which I inferred
    that people like you were coming.

I am from your city; and always
    I have heard and told with affection
    of your honored deeds and names.   60

I leave the gall and go for the sweet fruit
    promised me by my truthful guide,
    but first I must descend to the center."

"So may your soul long guide your body,"
   he answered then,
   "and so may your fame shine after you,

tell us if courtesy and valor dwell
   in our city as they were wont
   or whether they have gone entirely,

for Guglielmo Borsiere who has suffered with us
   only a little while and is over there with his companions
   grieves us much with his remarks."   72

"New people and sudden gains, O Florence,
   have generated pride and excess in you
   so that already you are weeping!"

This I cried with my face raised, and the three
   who understood my words as a reply, glanced at each other
   as people do when the truth is spoken.

"If, at other times, it costs you so little
   to satisfy others," they all replied,
   "you are fortunate, speaking thus at will;

therefore, if you escape from this dark place
   and return to see the beautiful stars,
   when you can delight in saying 'I was there . . . '   84

see that you speak to others about us."
   Then they broke the wheel, and in their flight
   their nimble legs seemed wings.

An "amen" could not have been said
   so quickly as they disappeared;
   whereupon my master thought it best to go on.

I followed him, and we had not gone far
   before the waterfall was so near
   that we could hardly hear each other speak.

As the river which has its own channel at first
   from Monte Veso toward the east,
   on the left slope of the Apennines—   96

which is called Acquacheta up above
   before it flows to its lower bed,
   and at Forlì loses that name—

resounds there above San Benedetto dell'Alpe,
   because of falling in one single leap
   instead of being broken by a thousand,

so, down from a steep bank
   we found the colored water roaring so loudly
   that it soon would have hurt our ears.

A cord around Dante's waist probably stands for self-confidence, useful in combating incontinence, but worse than useless in dealing with the fraud ahead. He gives it to Virgil who throws it over the precipice as a signal. Dante waits anxiously to see what will happen.

I had a cord around my waist
   with which I had thought once
   to catch the leopard with the painted hide.   108

After I had loosened it from my body
   as my leader had ordered me,
   I handed it to him, coiled and knotted.

Then he turned to the right side,
   and threw it far from the bank
   down into that deep abyss.

"Surely," I said within myself, "something strange
   must respond to this new signal
   which my master so follows with his eyes."

Ah, how cautious we must be
   with those who see not only what we do
   but look also within our thoughts!   120

He said to me, "Soon what I am waiting for
   will come up, and what you are thinking about
   will be revealed to your eyes."

To the truth which appears to be a lie
   we should close our lips as long as we can,
   not to incur blamelessly a reproach;

but here I cannot keep silent and, Reader,
   by the notes of this Comedy, I swear to you—
   so may it not lack long favor—

that I saw, through that thick and dark air,
   a form marvelous to every steadfast heart
   come swimming up   132

as a swimmer rises after going down
   to loosen an anchor caught by a rock
   or something else hidden in the sea,

who stretches forth his arms and draws up his feet.

CANTO XVII

GERYON

The monster coming up is Geryon, a symbol of the fraud which is universal and more powerful than arms. His face has an honest look, but his body is reptile-like and covered with devious and intricate patterns, like oriental tapestries. He lies with his head on the bank as beavers were supposed to do when using their tails to throw their prey on the shore.

"Behold the beast with the pointed tail
 that can cross mountains and break through walls;
 behold the one that infects the whole world!"

Thus my guide began to speak to me
 and signaled to the beast to come ashore
 near the end of the stone banks we had walked on;

and that foul image of fraud came up
 and landed his head and breast,
 but did not put his tail upon the bank.

His face was that of an honest man,
 so kind an aspect it had outwardly,
 but all the rest was like a reptile.   12

He had two paws, hairy to the armpits;
 his back and breast and both sides
 were decorated with loops and circles;

never did Tartars nor Turks make cloth
 with more colors in groundwork and in pattern,
 nor did Arachne[26] ever put such webs on her loom.

As skiffs sometimes lie along the shore
 partly in the water and partly on land,
 and as up there among the gluttonous Germans

the beaver sits to carry on his war,
 so that worst of wild beasts lay
 on the edge which binds the sand with stone.   24

He darted his tail in the empty space,
 twisting up its venomous tip
 which was armed like that of a scorpion.

> The usurers (the remaining group of the violent against God) are crouching near
> the edge where it is easy to fall into the circle of fraud below. Dante treats them
> with the utmost contempt, as he does all mercenary souls. They are unrecogniz-
> able except by the coats of arms on their now empty purses.
>
> Virgil has warned Dante not to waste words on them: our poet does not speak
> at all. The usurers are still competing, quarreling, rivaling, and envying each
> other, without honor, courage, good manners, artistic or intellectual distinction.

My leader said, "We must now bend our course
 a little as far as to the wicked beast
 that is lying over there."

We descended to the right
 and took ten steps on the extreme edge
 in order to avoid the sand and the flames.

[26]A skilled weaver who challenged the goddess Minerva to a competition; Minerva later
changed her into a spider.

After we had reached the monster,
   I saw a little farther on some people on the sand
   sitting close to the empty space. 36

My master said, "So that you may take with you
   complete experience of this round,
   go and see their ways.

Let your talk with them be brief;
   until you return I will speak with this one
   so that he may lend us his strong shoulders."

Thus I advanced along the extreme edge
   of the seventh circle all alone
   to where the sad souls were sitting.

Through their eyes their grief burst forth;
   on this side and that they used their hands,
   brushing off the fire and lifting themselves from the hot ground; 48

not otherwise are dogs busy in summer,
   now with their muzzles and now with their paws,
   when bitten by gadflies or fleas.

In looking at the faces of some
   on whom the painful fire was falling,
   I could recognize none, but I noticed

that from the necks of each a purse hung
   which had a certain color and design
   and on which it seemed that their eyes feasted.

As I came looking at them,
   on a yellow purse I saw in azure
   the head and the form of a lion. 60

Then continuing the course of my glances,
   I saw another, red as blood,
   showing a goose whiter than butter.

And one who had a white sack marked
   with an azure pregnant sow,
   said to me, "What are you doing in this hole?

Now go away and, since you are still alive,
   know that my neighbor Vitaliano
   will sit here on my left side.

With these Florentines I am a Paduan;
   many times they deafen my ears,
   shouting, 'Let the sovereign knight come 72

who will bring the pouch marked by three goats.'"
   Then he twisted his mouth and stuck out his tongue
   as an ox does to lick its nose.

And I, fearing that to stay longer
  might annoy my master, who had admonished me
  to be brief, turned my back on those wearied souls.

  *When Dante climbs on Geryon's back over the immense void, he is so frightened
  he cannot speak.*

  *The transition from violence to deliberate, premeditated fraud is shown by the
  long and slow descent.*

I found my leader already mounted
  on the back of the fierce animal.
  He said to me, "Now be strong and bold;

we descend here by such stairs.
  Mount in front, for I wish to be placed
  so that the tail cannot hurt you."   84

As one who has the chill of the quartan fever
  so close that his nails are already blue,
  and who shivers merely at the sight of shade,

so I became on hearing these words,
  but Virgil's admonition caused the shame
  which, in sight of his master, makes a servant strong.

I placed myself on those big shoulders.
  "See that you hold me," I wished to say,
  but my voice did not come out as I thought.

And he who at other times helped me
  in other fears, as soon as I had mounted,
  embraced and held me with his arms;   96

then said, "Geryon, move now;
  let the circles be large and the descent slow;
  think of the new burden that you have."

As a little ship moves from its berth,
  back, back, thus Geryon moved off,
  and when he felt his whole body clear,

he turned his tail to where his breast had been,
  and stretching it out, moved it like an eel,
  and with his paws drew in the air.

I do not believe there was greater fear when Phaëthon[27]
  let loose the reins [of the sun's chariot] so that the sky
  as still appears [by the Milky Way] was scorched,   108

---

[27] Son of Apollo, the charioteer of the sun. Entrusted with his father's chariot, Phaëthon
lost control of it so that it burned the sky.

nor when poor Icarus[28] [while flying] felt his loins unfeathered
  because of the melting of the wax,
  his father shouting to him, "The wrong way you're taking!"

than was mine when I saw myself in the air
  on every side and with every view hidden
  except that of the beast.

It went on swimming slowly, slowly,
  circled and descended, but I was aware of the movement
  only by the wind blowing in my face and from below.

Already I heard the torrent on the right
  roaring horribly beneath us,
  so that I stretched out my head to look down.   120

Then I was still more afraid,
  for I saw fires and heard laments,
  at which I crouched back, all trembling.

I noticed then the descending and the circling
  which I had not seen before
  by the torments drawing near on every side.

As a falcon that has long been on the wing
  without seeing a bird or lure, and that makes the falconer cry,
  "Alas, you are coming down!"

descends wearily, after many circles,
  to where it had swiftly started out,
  and lands far from its master, sullen and angry,   132

so Geryon set us down on the bottom,
  at the foot of the jagged rock;
  then freed of the weight of our bodies,

he darted off, like an arrow-notch from the string.

CANTO XVIII

PANDERS, SEDUCERS, AND FLATTERERS

*The matter-of-fact description of Malebolge contrasts with the deviousness of the
fraud it harbors. The term means "evil pouches" or "purses," perhaps with some
reference to the greed which motivates most fraud. Those who sinned through
violence are in the open. The fraudulent, appropriately, are hidden in dark ditches.
Over the moats are "scogli," rocky bridges, which come together at the center like
spokes of a wheel.*

There is a place in Hell called Malebolge,
  all of stone and of an iron color
  like the bank which surrounds it.

---

[28] Icarus, for whom his father Daedalus made wings cemented with wax, flew too near the
sun and fell when it melted the wax.

Right in the middle of the baleful space
    a well, rather wide and deep, opens up
    whose features I will describe in their place.

The belt that remains, then,
    between the well and the high, hard bank,
    had its bottom divided into ten valleys.

As the ground appears
    where several moats surround a castle
    as a protection for the walls,   12

such was the design these made.
    And, as from the thresholds of fortresses
    little bridges extend to the outer banks,

so from the bottom of the wall, rough spans
    crossed the ditches and the banks down to the well
    which brings them all together and cuts them off.

In this place, shaken from the back of Geryon,
    we found ourselves, and the poet started
    to the left, and I moved on behind him.

> *The souls in the first bolgia or ditch are guided by traffic regulations as was the crowd at the jubilee in Rome in 1300, the panders on the outside going to the right, the seducers on the inside to the left.*
>
> *We now meet the first devils. These, appropriately, wear the horns associated with adultery. We find also the first shade who is ashamed. When recognized, he tells how he sold his sister to the Marquis of Este. He confesses also for the other Bolognese panders, more numerous than the little children learning the dialect word for "yes" within the boundaries of their province.*
>
> *Here, as elsewhere, movement characterizes punishments for sins related to sexuality. Where the activity was natural, the agent of punishment is wind, a natural force; where unnatural, as on the plain, a supernatural fire is falling. Here, among the fraudulent, a devil plies the whip.*

On the right I saw new misery,
    new torments, and new tormentors
    with which the first ditch was filled.   24

The sinners along the bottom of the ditch were naked,
    coming on this side facing us, on the other
    moving with us, but with longer steps.

Thus the Romans because of the great throng
    in the year of the jubilee, chose a way
    to divide the traffic on the bridge,

so that on one side all had their faces
    toward the Castle [of Sant' Angelo], and went to St. Peter's,
    on the other side they advanced toward the Mount [Giordano].

On both sides of the dark rock
   I saw horned demons with great whips
   beating the shades fiercely from behind. 36

Ah, how they made them lift their legs
   at the first stroke! Indeed,
   none waited for the second or for the third.

While I was going on, my eyes fell on one;
   whereupon immediately I said,
   "I am not fasting for the sight of him!"[29]

Therefore I delayed advancing to look;
   and my dear leader stopped with me
   and consented that I go back a little.

The whipped shade thought he could hide
   by lowering his face, but it availed him little,
   for I said, "You who cast your eyes on the ground, 48

if the features you wear are not false,
   are Venedico Caccianemico;
   but what brings you into such a pickle?"

And he to me, "Unwillingly I say it,
   but I am compelled by your clear speech
   which makes me recall the world.

I am the one who led Ghisolabella [his sister]
   to do the Marquis' [of Este's] will,
   however the vile tale may sound,

and I am not the only Bolognese weeping here;
   on the contrary the place is so full of them
   that as many tongues are not now being taught 60

to say 'sipa' between the Savena and the Reno;
   and if you want assurance of that,
   recall to your mind our avaricious hearts."

While he was speaking thus, a demon struck him
   with his whip, saying, "Away, pander!
   Here are no women to turn into cash!"

> *To see the seducers, who have been going to the left, the poets mount to the top of the bridge. They observe Jason, a dignified figure, but whipped, like the others. His principal crime, besides robbing the Colchians of the Golden Fleece and deserting Medea, was the seduction of Hypsipyle. The latter, according to the legend, had already shown her weakness by saving her father's life when the disgusted women of Lemnos tried to kill off all the men.*

---

[29] "I have seen this person before."

I rejoined my escort; then,
    after a few steps, we came
    to where a rough bridge projects from the bank.

Quite easily we climbed it,
    and turning to the right over its ridge
    we moved away from that eternal bank.   72

When we reached the point below which the bridge opens
    to give passage for those whipped,
    my leader said, "Stop, and let your sight

fall on these other ill-born souls
    whose faces you have not yet seen,
    since they have been going with us."

From the old bridge we looked at the file
    coming toward us on the other side
    and whom the whip likewise drove on.

And my good master, without my asking, said,
    "Look at that great one coming,
    who, for his pain, sheds no tears;   84

what a regal bearing he still has!
    That is Jason who through courage and slyness
    deprived the Colchians of their ram [Golden Fleece].

He passed through the island of Lemnos
    after the bold and pitiless women
    had given up to death all their men.

There, with gifts and fine words,
    he deceived Hypsipyle, the young girl
    who first had deceived all the others.[30]

He abandoned her pregnant and forlorn.
    Such guilt condemns him to this punishment;
    and vengeance is taken also for Medea.   96

With him go all those who deceive in this way:
    let this knowledge suffice for the first vale
    and for those it holds in its grip."

> *The poets proceed to where they can see the flatterers in the second ditch. Dante*
> *chooses the elegant Thaïs as his ancient example, perhaps to emphasize the essen-*
> *tial filthiness of these sinners who, like dogs, lick the sores of those they exploit.*
> *The contrast is all the more striking because the charge against her seems triv-*
> *ial. Moreover, Dante had misread the incident in Cicero; the guilty one was Gnatho,*
> *not Thaïs. But the lesson is clear: even Thaïs could not make flattery clean.*

---

[30] Hypsipyle spared her father and told the other women of Lemnos that he had been killed along with the other males. For a version of the Jason-Medea story, see Euripides' *Medea*.

We had already come to where the narrow road
　　crosses the second bank and makes of it
　　an abutment for another arch.

Here we heard people moaning in the next ditch
　　and puffing with their snouts
　　and hitting themselves with their hands.

The banks were encrusted with a mold
　　condensed from the vapor from below
　　which offends both the eyes and nose. 108

The bottom was so deep it could be seen
　　only by mounting to the summit of the arch
　　where the bridge stands highest.

We reached that place, and down in the ditch
　　I saw people plunged in excrement
　　which seemed to have come from human privies.

And while I was searching down there with my eyes,
　　I saw one with his head so smeared with filth
　　that you could not tell if he were a layman or a clerk.

He bawled to me, "Why are you so eager
　　to look at me more than at the other ugly ones?"
　　And I to him, "Because, if I remember well, 120

I saw you once with dry hair;
　　you are Alessio Interminei da Lucca;
　　therefore, I eye you more than all the rest."

Then beating on his pate, he said,
　　"The flatteries with which my tongue
　　was never cloyed have put me down here."

After that my guide said to me,
　　"See that you extend your gaze
　　so that your eyes may reach the face

of that filthy and disheveled wench
　　who is scratching herself with her dirty nails
　　and now squats and now is standing on her feet. 132

Thaïs,³¹ she is, the harlot
　　who answered her paramour when he said,
　　'Have I *great* favor with you?' 'No, *marvelous!*'

And with this let our sight be satisfied."

³¹ This is not the famous courtesan but a whore in a play by Terence, the Roman dramatist (second century B.C.).

CANTO XIX

THE SIMONISTS

Dante's objectivity ceases when we come to the simonists who by trafficking in church offices and enriching themselves tend to destroy the Church itself. Their fat feeds the fire which now punishes them.

O Simon Magus![32] O rapacious followers,
  you who should be wedded to righteousness
  and instead prostitute the things of God

for gold and silver, now for you
  it is necessary that the trumpet sound,
  since you are in the third ditch.

Already we had mounted to that part
  of the following bridge
  which hangs over the middle of the moat.

O Supreme Wisdom, how great is the art Thou showest
  in Heaven, on earth, and in the evil world,
  and how justly Thy power rewards!   12

I saw the livid stone covered with holes
  on the sides and on the bottom,
  all round, and of one breadth.

They appeared neither larger nor smaller
  than those in my beautiful San Giovanni
  made for the baptizers to stand in,

one of which, not many years ago, I broke
  to save a drowning child—and let this
  be my seal [on the truth] to undeceive all men.[33]

From the mouth of each a sinner's feet protruded
  and his legs up to the calf,
  and the rest remained within.   24

The soles of the feet of all were on fire,
  and their legs above the joints writhed so sharply
  that they would have broken withes or ropes.

As flames on oily things are wont
  to move only over the outer surface,
  so they did here from heel to toe.

"Who is that one, Master, who writhes so,
  twitching more than the others, his companions,
  and who feeds a ruddier flame?" I asked.

---

[32] Simon "the Magician," who, according to Acts of the Apostles 8, was rebuked by Peter for attempting to buy the powers of the apostles that only God could give. The word *simony* is derived from his name.

[33] Untrue rumors apparently had circulated about this incident, but what they were is not known.

And he to me, "If you want me to carry you down there
over the [inner] bank which slopes less steeply,
you will learn from him about himself and his misdeeds." 36

And I, "Whatever you want is good for me;
you are my lord, and you know that my will
is like your own, and you know also what I keep silent."

Then we came to the fourth bank
where we turned and descended on the left
down into the narrow and pitted bottom.

My kind master still did not put me down,
but carried me to the hole of the one
who was so lamenting with his shanks.

> *The inverted shade, Pope Nicholas III, mistakes Dante for Boniface VIII (still living in 1300) who, after outraging the Church (the "Bride of Christ"), is to follow him here. Nicholas belonged to the Orsini family (orso, bear), and used his office to advance the cubs. In this mockery of the apostolic succession, Boniface will be succeeded by Clement V, who, as the tool of Philip the Fair of France, transferred the papacy to Avignon. A certain vulgarity characterizes the speech of all mercenary sinners and the terms used to describe them.*

"O, whoever you are, sad spirit,
upside down, planted like a stake,"
I began to say, "if you can, speak." 48

I stood like the friar confessing a treacherous assassin
who, after being put in the hole [to be buried alive],
calls the confessor back to delay his death,

and he shouted, "Are you already standing there,
are you already there, O Boniface?—
The writing [Book of Fate] lied to me by several years.

Are you so quickly sated with the wealth
for which you were not afraid to seize the beautiful lady
through guile and then to outrage her?"

I became like those who wonder
if they are mocked, not understanding the words
said to them, and who are unable to reply. 60

Then Virgil said, "Tell him quickly
'I am not, I am not the one you think,'"
and I answered as I had been bidden.

At that the spirit twisted both his feet,
then sighing and with a tearful voice
he said, "What do you ask of me?

If you want so much to learn who I am
that you have come down the bank to hear,
know that I was clothed with the great mantle,

and truly I was a son of the she-bear
   so covetous to advance the cubs
   that on earth I put wealth, and here myself, in a sack.   72

Below, under my head, the others[34]
   who preceded me in simony are compressed,
   squeezed into the fissures of the rock.

Down there I also will be pressed
   when he comes for whom I took you
   when I asked the sudden question.

But I have already been roasted
   and have stood thus upside down longer
   than he will stay planted with reddened feet,

for after him, out of the West, will come
   a shepherd without law, of uglier deed,
   fit to cover both him and me.   84

He will be like the Jason[35] of whom we read in Maccabees,
   and as to Jason a king dealt gently,
   so will the ruler of France treat him."

> *Dante addresses Nicholas with intense feeling, restrained only by reverence for this sinner's past office. He mentions the Scarlet Woman, as the symbol of the corrupt Church.*
>
> *In this bolgia things are generally upside down. The clergy inverted their duties and are now inverted themselves; Dante, a layman, hears a confession, like a friar, and then preaches a sermon to an ex-pope.*

I do not know if I was now too bold,
   but I answered him in this strain:
   "Alas, now tell me, how much treasure

did our Lord ask of St. Peter
   before he put the keys in his hands?
   Surely he demanded only, 'Follow me!'

Nor did Peter and the others ask Matthias
   for gold or silver when he was chosen
   for the place the guilty soul [Judas] had lost.[36]   96

Therefore, stay there, for you are well punished,
   and keep securely the ill-got money
   which made you so bold against Charles [of Anjou].

---

[34] That is, the other simoniacal popes, all of whom are thrust into the same hole.

[35] In 2 Maccabees 4–5 (a book of the Roman Catholic Bible), the unworthy Jason obtains from the king of Syria by bribery the office of Jewish high priest.

[36] In Acts 1, Matthias is chosen by prayer and the casting of lots as successor to Judas as one of the twelve apostles.

And if I were still not prevented
  by reverence for the holy keys
  which you kept in the happy life,

I would use words still heavier;
  for your avarice afflicts the world,
  crushing the good and lifting up the bad.

The Evangelist [St. John] had shepherds like you in mind
  when she [the Scarlet Woman][37] that sitteth upon many waters
  was seen by him fornicating with kings,   108

she who was born with seven heads [virtues]
  and from ten horns [commandments] gained strength
  as long as virtue pleased the bridegroom [the papacy].

You have made a god of gold and silver,
  and how do you differ from the idolater,
  except that he worships one thing of gold, and you a hundred?

> *The papal claims to temporal power were based in part on the supposed gift of the Western Empire to St. Sylvester by Constantine. The document confirming this transfer was not recognized as a forgery until after Dante's time, but our poet held that the emperor had no power to make such a gift nor the pope to receive it.*
>
> *Virgil, as the representative of the Roman Empire in the political allegory, is so delighted with Dante's sermon that he carries his pupil out of the ditch and to the top of the next bridge.*

Ah, Constantine,[38] to how much ill gave birth
  not your conversion, but that dowry
  which the first rich father took from you!"

While I sang these notes to him,
  whether anger or conscience stung him,
  he kicked hard with both his feet.   120

I believe my leader was pleased,
  with such a contented look he listened
  to the true words I had expressed.

With both arms he took hold of me,
  and when he had me quite upon his breast,
  he remounted by the way we had come down,

nor did he tire of holding me tightly,
  but carried me to the top of the arch
  which crosses from the fourth to the fifth bank.

---

[37] The details Dante gives are from Revelation 17; the passage refers to Rome.
[38] Roman emperor from 306 to 337, a convert to Christianity who moved the capital of the empire to Constantinople.

.re, softly, he put down his burden—
   softly because of the rough and steep rocks
   which would have been a hard road even for goats.   132

From there another valley was disclosed.

CANTO XX

THE DIVINERS

*The sight of the soothsayers, diviners, and magicians, with their heads twisted
around and walking backward, makes Dante weep. He had previously shown
pity for the victims of our human defects, but now he is sorry for the punishment itself. This is a kind of protest against the divine order, and he is severely
rebuked by Virgil. The scolding is most striking since Virgil had been considered
a diviner, a master of magic art, and the sin punished here often tempted men
of learning like Dante himself.*

For new punishments I must make verses
   and provide matter for the twentieth canto
   of the first book, which is about the damned.

I was already placed where I could see
   into the uncovered depth
   which was bathed with tears of anguish,

and I saw people move silent and weeping
   through the circular valley, at the pace of those
   who chant litanies in this world.

When my eyes saw them more clearly
   each appeared to be twisted marvelously
   between the chin and the beginning of the chest,   12

for their faces were turned to the rear,
   and each was obliged to move backward,
   since seeing ahead was denied them.

Perhaps by the force of paralysis
   someone might be wholly twisted thus,
   but I have never seen the case nor believe it exists.

Reader, so may God let you profit
   by your reading, now think for yourself
   how I could keep my face dry

when I saw our [human] image, close at hand,
   so twisted that the tears from the eyes
   bathed the buttocks along the cleft.   24

Certainly I wept, leaning on a rock
   of the hard bridge, so that my escort said to me,
   "Are you, too, like the other fools?

Here pity lives when it is completely dead.
    Who is more impious than that one
    who feels sorrow for God's judgment?

> *Virgil now points out certain soothsayers of antiquity, characters chosen from*
> *various epic poems. The accounts of them are incorrect in some respects, perhaps*
> *to show once more the fallibility of men's minds. In discussing Manto, Virgil*
> *gives an account of the founding of Mantua different from one in the* Aeneid.
> *Moreover, in the* Purgatory, *Manto is mentioned as in a different circle. The*
> *digression interests even Dante only slightly.*

Lift up your head and see him [an augur] for whom
    the earth opened in the sight of the Thebans
    so that they cried, 'Where are you falling,

O Amphiaraus? why are you giving up the war?'
    and he did not stop rushing headlong
    down to Minos who seizes everyone;   36

observe how he has made a breast of his shoulders;
    because he wished to see too far ahead,
    he looks behind, and goes backward.

See Tiresias [a soothsayer] who changed his semblance
    when he became from man, a woman,
    transforming all his members,

and before he could regain his manly hair
    it was necessary for him to strike again
    the two entwined serpents with his wand.[39]

The one backing up to his belly
    is Aruns who, in the Luni mountains
    beneath which the Carrarese live and plow,   48

had a cave in the white marble for a dwelling
    from which no obstacle cut off
    a view of the sea or of the stars.

And she who covers her breasts
    which you do not see, with her loose tresses,
    and has on the other side all hairy skin,

was Manto, who sought through many lands
    before she settled where I was born
    and of her I would like for you to hear.

After her father had given up his life
    and Bacchus' city [Thebes] was enslaved
    she wandered a long time through the world.   60

---

[39] Tiresias had first been changed from a man into a woman when he struck two entwined
serpents with his wand; years later he saw and struck them again, whereupon he was changed
back into a man. Manto, mentioned later, was his daughter.

In beautiful Italy, above the Tyrol,
    at the foot of the Alps which enclose Germany,
    lies a lake named Benaco.

A thousand brooks and more bathe the Apennino
    from Guarda to Val Canonica
    whose waters come to rest in this lake.

In the middle is a point where the pastors
    of Trento, Brescia, and Verona
    could give a blessing if they went that way.

Peschiera lies as a fair and powerful rampart
    to face the Brescians and the Bergamese
    where the shore is lowest.   72

There, all that the lap of Benaco
    cannot hold must overflow
    through green pastures and make a river.

When the water begins to flow,
    it is no longer called Benaco, but Mincio
    as far as Governo, where it falls into the Po.

After a short course it finds a flat region
    over which it spreads and forms a marsh
    which in summer is wont to be noisome.

While passing there, the cruel virgin
    saw land in the middle of the fen
    uncultivated and devoid of inhabitants.   84

There, to shun all human intercourse,
    she, with her servants, stayed to practice her art,
    and lived, and left there her empty body.

Later the people scattered around
    gathered in that place which was strong
    because of the marsh on all sides.

They built the city on her bones
    and for her who first chose the place
    they called it Mantua, without other augury.

Once its people were more numerous
    before the madness of Casalodi [its ruler]
    was deceived by Pinamonte.   96

Therefore I warn you, that if you ever hear
    of another origin for my city,
    let no falsehood defraud the truth."

And I, "Master, your account is so certain
    and takes such hold on my belief
    that others would be like dead coals.

But tell me about the people passing by,
    whether you see any worthy of note,
    for to that alone my mind reverts."

The account of Eurypylus at the time of the Trojan wars differs also from its source in Virgil, a slip all the more striking since Dante implies that he knew the Aeneid *by heart.*

Among the modern soothsayers is Michael Scott who lived at the court of Frederick II of Sicily. His legend survived in Scotland down to modern times. Other minor figures include Guido Bonatti, an astrologer of Forlì, Asdente, the cobbler of Parma, and various fortune-tellers and witches.

In Italian folklore, the Man in the Moon is Cain. He is mentioned in indicating the time. It is about six o'clock on Saturday morning, April 9, 1300.

Then he said, "That one who from his cheeks
    lets his beard fall on his dark shoulders
    was an augur [during the Trojan War] when Greece was so empty
        of males   108

that scarcely any remained for the cradles,
    and in Aulis, together with Calchas,
    he set the time for setting sail for Troy.

Eurypylus was his name, and my lofty tragedy
    sings of him in one place,
    as you know well, since you know it all.

The other, so slender in the flanks,
    was Michael Scott, who really knew
    the game of magic frauds.

See also Guido Bonatti, see Asdente
    who now wishes he had attended
    to his leather and his thread, but too late repents.   120

See the poor women who left the needle,
    the shuttle, and the spindle, and became fortunetellers;
    they wrought magic with herbs and images.

But come now, for Cain with his thorns
    is already on the confines of both hemispheres
    and below Seville is sinking in the sea,

and last night the moon was round;
    you must remember, since it was not unwelcome
    at times in the deep wood."

Thus he spoke as we moved on.

CANTO XXI

THE BARRATORS (GRAFTERS)

Thus we went from bridge to bridge, talking of things
    my Comedy does not care to mention,
    and reached the top of the next arch

where we stopped to see the ditch
    and to hear the other vain laments;
    and I found it marvelously dark.

As in the shipyards of the Venetians,
    in winter, the tenacious pitch boils
    to calk their damaged ships,

since the sailors cannot navigate, and instead
    some build new boats, some strengthen the ribs
    of one that has made many voyages;   12

some hammer at the prow and some at the stern;
    some make oars, and some twist ropes;
    some mend the jib and mainsail,

so, not by fire, but through divine art
    a dense tar boils down there
    which coats the banks on each side.

I saw the pitch, but did not see in it
    anything except the bubbles which rise,
    swell up, and then collapse.

While I was looking fixedly down there
    my guide drew me from where I was,
    saying, "Look! look!"   24

Then I turned like one suddenly dismayed,
    striving to see something
    from which he must escape

and who, to see, does not delay his start;
    and I noticed behind us a black devil
    coming at a run over the bridge.

Ah, how fierce he was in aspect,
    and how ferocious he seemed in act,
    with wings open, and light upon his feet!

His shoulders which were high and sharp
    were burdened by the haunches of a sinner
    the sinews of whose feet he clutched.   36

From our bridge he cried, "O Malebranche [devils],
    here is one of the elders[40] of Santa Zita [Lucca],
    put him under while I go back for more

to that city I have so well furnished with them.
    Everyone is a barrator there, except Bonturo;[41]
    there, for money, a 'no' becomes a 'yes.'"

Down he hurled him, and turned back
    over the rough bridge, and never was a mastiff
    in such haste to follow a thief.

---

[40] Public officials of Lucca, of which Zita was the patron saint.
[41] This is ironic; Bonturo was an especially notorious grafter.

The sinner plunged in, then rose doubled up,
    but the demons hiding under the bridge shouted,
    "Here there is no Holy Face [as at Lucca] to pray to! 48

Here you do not swim as in the Serchio!
    So, unless you want to feel our hooks,
    don't show yourself above the pitch!"

Then they struck him with more than a hundred prongs,
    saying, "Here you must dance under cover
    and pilfer secretly if you can!"

Not otherwise do cooks have their scullions
    dip the meat in the middle of the boiler
    with forks, so that it will not float.

    Virgil holds a parley with the demons below the bridge. Then Dante rejoins his
    master, keeping as close to him (Reason) as he can, but using his eyes as well.
    The entire episode with the devils beginning here (a concession to the popular
    spirit of the Middle Ages) symbolizes incidentally Dante's narrow escape from
    Florence, where one of the false charges against him was barratry.

My good master said, "So that it may not appear
    that you are here, crouch down
    behind a rock and remain hidden, 60

and whatever outrage is done to me
    do not be afraid, for I know about this business;
    once before I was in a like affray."

Then he went to the head of the bridge,
    and as he arrived on the sixth bank
    he needed a steadfast heart.

With that fury and that uproar
    with which dogs run out at a beggar
    who suddenly stops and begs from where he is,

those devils rushed out from under the bridge,
    turning against him all their hooks.
    But he cried, "Let none of you be headstrong. 72

Before your grapples touch me,
    let one of you come forward to hear me
    and then decide about hooking me."

All shouted, "Let Malacoda go"; whereupon one
    stepped forward while the others stood firm,
    and came to him saying, "What good will it do him?"

"Do you think, Malacoda,
    that you see me here," my master said,
    "safe from all your opposition,

without divine will and propitious fate?
    Let me go on, for it is willed in Heaven
    that I should show another this wild way." 84

Then Malacoda's pride collapsed so suddenly
    that he let his hook fall at his feet
    and said to the others, "Do not strike him."

And my guide called to me, "O you, crouching quietly
    behind the rocks of the bridge,
    you may come now securely."

I started out and went quickly to him,
    and all the devils pressed forward,
    so that I feared they might not keep their pact.

Thus I once saw foot soldiers afraid
    on leaving Caprona under safe conduct,
    when they saw themselves among so many enemies.   96

I drew close to my guide with my whole body,
    but did not take my eyes
    from the devils' looks, which were not good.

They lowered their hooks, one saying to another,
    "Should I nick him on the rump?"
    and being answered, "Yes, let him have it!"

But the demon who had held the parley
    with my leader turned instantly,
    and said, "Quiet, quiet, Scarmiglione!"

> *Malacoda proposes that a squad accompany the travelers to the next "unbroken"*
> *bridge. Since all the bridges over the next bolgia are broken, the devils under-*
> *stand that a trick is to be played on Virgil. To be more convincing in his fraud,*
> *Malacoda cites some statistics to show how much time has passed since the*
> *Crucifixion and the resultant earthquake. Dante, using his senses and intuition,*
> *would prefer to go on alone, but Virgil (Reason), taken in, tries to reassure him;*
> *and the grotesque company moves on.*

Then he said to us, "You cannot go farther
    on this bridge, since the sixth arch
    lies all broken on the bottom,   108

but if you still want to go ahead,
    keep advancing along this bank;
    nearby is another bridge that provides a way.

Yesterday, five hours later than this hour
    a thousand two hundred and sixty-six years[42]
    were completed since the bridge here was broken.

I am sending some of my men over there
    to see if any are airing themselves;
    go with them, since they won't be harmful.

---

[42] Christ died at the age of thirty-three, and the present year is 1300, but Dante is presumably
dating from Christ's conception, not his birth.

Step forward, Alichino and Calcabrina,"
  he then began to say, "and Cagnazzo,
  and you, Barbariccia, guide the squad.   120

Let Libicocco come and Draghignazzo,
  Ciriatto with his tusks, and Graffiacane,
  and Farfarello, and mad Rubicante.

Look around the boiling glue;
  let these be safe as far as to the bridge
  which *all unbroken* passes over the dens."

"Oh, Master, what is this I see?"
  I exclaimed. "Ah, without escort, let us go alone
  if you know the way; as for me, I ask for none.

If you are as wary as usual,
  don't you see that they are gnashing their teeth,
  and with their frowns threaten grief to us?"   132

And he to me, "Do not be afraid,
  let them grind away as they like,
  because they do that for the wretches in the pitch."

The devils turned to the left on the bank,
  but first each pressed his tongue between his teeth,
  as a signal to their leader,

and he, for a trumpet, used his rump.[43]

CANTO XXII

CIAMPOLO OF NAVARRE

I have seen horsemen move camp
  and launch an attack, and hold their muster,
  and sometimes turn back to escape;

I have seen scouting parties in your land,
  O Aretines! and foragers start out,
  tournaments begin and races run,

sometimes at the sound of trumpets or of bells,
  with drums and with castle signals,
  and with familiar and strange devices,

but never yet did I see horse or footmen move
  to so strange a bugle call,
  or a ship at a sign on land or in the sky.   12

We went along with the ten demons;
  ah, fierce company! but "in church with saints,
  and in the tavern with the gluttons!"

[43] Farted.

I was attentive to the pitch to see
    what the bolgia contained
    and the people burning in it.

As dolphins make signs to sailors
    by the arching of their backs
    to prepare to save their ship,

so now and then, to relieve the pain,
    some of the sinners showed their backs
    and hid again as fast as lightning flashes;   24

and, as at the edge of the water of a ditch,
    frogs lie with just their muzzles out,
    hiding their feet and bodies,

so, on every side, the sinners lay;
    but when Barbariccia came near,
    they withdrew within the boiling.

I saw, and still my heart shudders at it,
    a soul waiting thus, just as it happens
    that one frog may remain when the others dart away,

and Graffiacane who was closest to him
    hooked his pitchy locks, and pulled him out
    so that he looked like an otter.   36

I already knew the names of all the demons
    so well did I note them when they were chosen,
    and as they called each other I noticed how.

"O Rubicante, see that you get your claws
    on him and skin him alive,"
    the accursed ones shouted all together,

and I, "Master, find out if you can
    who the unfortunate wretch is
    that has fallen into the hands of his enemies."

My guide went close to him and asked
    whence he came, and he replied,
    "I was born in the kingdom of Navarre.   48

My mother placed me as a servant to a lord,
    for she had borne me to a spendthrift,
    a destroyer of himself and of his property.

Then I was in the service of good King Thibault;
    there I began to commit barratry
    for which I give reckoning in this heat."

And Ciriatto from each side of whose mouth
    a tusk issued, as from a boar's,
    made him feel how one of them could rip.

The mouse had fallen among vicious cats;
    but Barbariccia took him in his arms
    and said, "Stand over there while I grip him."   60

And turning his face to my master,
    "Ask, if you want to hear more about him,"
    he said, "before the others mangle him."

My guide then said, "Now tell me, do you know
    any others under the pitch who are Italians?"
    And he answered, "A little while ago

I left one from a nearby island—
    (might I still be covered with him,
    for then I would fear neither claw nor hook!").

And Libicocco cried, "Too much have we endured,"
    and with his prong seized his arm
    and tearing it, carried off a sinew.   72

Draghignazzo also tried to lay hold
    of his legs, whereupon their corporal
    turned around with wicked looks.

When they were somewhat pacified
    my guide without delay addressed the sinner
    who was still looking at his wounds.

"Who is the one you say you left
    unluckily in order to come ashore?"
    and he replied, "It was Friar Gomita,

from Gallura, a vessel of every fraud
    who had his master's enemies in his hands
    and dealt with them so [gently] that all praise him.   84

Money he took, and let them off quietly
    as he says; and in other offices also
    he was not a little barrator, but a supreme one.

With him Don Michel Zanche of Logodoro
    keeps company, and their tongues
    are never tired of talking about Sardinia.

O me! see that one grinding his teeth;
    I would say more, but I am afraid
    he is getting ready to scratch my sticky coat!"

And their commander in chief, turning to Farfarello,
    who was rolling his eyes on the point of striking,
    said, "Get over there, vile bird!"   96

"If you wish to see or hear,"
    the frightened one [Ciampolo] then began,
    "some Tuscans or Lombards, I will have some come,

but let the Malebranche stand back a little
   so that their vengeance will not be feared,
   and I, sitting in this very place,

for one that I am, will make many come
   when I whistle, as it is our custom
   to do when any of us gets out."

Cagnazzo at these words raised his snout,
   shaking his head, and said, "Listen to the trick
   he has thought of to plunge down."   108

Then he [Ciampolo], who had a wealth of guile,
   answered, "I am too tricky indeed
   when I get greater sorrow for my friends!"

Alichino could hold back no longer
   and contrary to the others said,
   "If you plunge, I'll not gallop after you,

but will beat my wings above the pitch!
   Let the ridge be left and the bank made a screen
   to see if you can get the best of us."

O you who read will now hear new sport.
   All turned their eyes to the other side,
   and he first who had been most unwilling.   120

The Navarese chose well his time,
   steadied his feet upon the ground, and in an instant
   leaped, and from the marshal freed himself.

At that each was stung with guilt, and that one most
   who had been the cause of the mistake.
   He, swooping down, cried, "You're caught!"

but it availed little, for wings
   could not outstrip terror. The sinner went under,
   and his pursuer, flying, turned up his breast.

Not otherwise does the wild duck plunge
   when the falcon comes near
   which, defeated and angry, flies up again.   132

Calcabrina, furious at the trick,
   also went after him, eager for the sinner to escape
   so that he could start a quarrel.

And when the barrator had disappeared,
   he turned his claws on his companion
   and grappled with him above the ditch.

But Alichino was a full-grown hawk
   for clawing him back, and both fell
   into the middle of the boiling pond.

The heat at once broke their grip,
    but there was no way for them to rise,
    since their wings were so beglued.   144

Barbariccia, complaining with the rest,
    had four fly to the other bank
    with all their hooks, and quickly

on this side and that they went to their places
    and reached with their grapples to those stuck
    and already partly cooked within the crust;

and while they were embarrassed in this way we left them.

CANTO XXIII

THE HYPOCRITES

The devils' fight over the pitch has reminded Dante of a fable which tells how a frog offers to tow a mouse tied to himself over a stream, intending to pull the rodent under. A kite, seeing their struggle, swoops down and carries off both.

Silent, alone, and without company
    we went on, one in front of the other,
    as minor friars go along their way.

My thought was turned to Aesop's fable
    by the present quarrel, where he speaks
    of the frog and of the mouse;

for "mo" and "issa" [synonyms for "now"] are not more alike
    if one compares with close attention
    the beginning and the end of each case.

And, as one thought bursts from another,
    there arose from that one a second
    which caused my first fear to be doubled.   12

I reflected thus: "Those devils through us
    are mocked with such scorn and damage
    as, I believe, must enrage them.

If anger is added to ill will,
    they will rush after us more fiercely
    than a hound after the rabbit he snaps up."

Already I felt my hair stand on end from fear,
    and I looked back intently and said,
    "Master, if you do not quickly hide

yourself and me, I fear the Malebranche;
    we already have them right behind us,
    I so imagine it that I can feel them now."   24

And he, "If I were leaded glass [a mirror]
    I would not reflect your outer image
    more quickly than I do your inner feelings.

Just now your thoughts were coming among mine
    similar to them in force and in meaning,
    so that of them all I made one resolve.

If it happens that the right bank lies
    so that we can go into the next ditch,
    we will escape the dreaded chase."

He had not finished giving this counsel
    when I saw the demons not far away
    coming with wings extended to seize us.   36

My guide suddenly took hold of me and,
    as a mother who is awakened by a noise
    and sees close to her the burning flames,

who takes her son and flees, caring more for him
    than for herself, and who does not stop
    even long enough to put on any clothes,

so, down from the edge of the hard bank,
    lying on his back, my guide slid over the rock
    which walls one side of the ditch.

Water never ran so fast through a sluice
    to turn a millwheel, at the moment
    when it is closest to the paddles,   48

as my master went down over the bank,
    carrying me upon his breast,
    not as a companion, but as a son.

Scarcely had his feet touched the bottom
    when the devils reached the height above us,
    but there was nothing to fear,

for High Providence, which wished to put them
    as ministers of the fifth ditch,
    took from all of them the power to leave.

> *The hypocrites whom the travelers now see wear gowns brilliant outwardly but*
> *of lead, like those Frederick II was supposed to have had melted on the backs of*
> *offenders against the throne. Like all who affect a pose, they must carry the weight*
> *of it forever. They move slowly, watching their steps. A kind of whining reproach*
> *sounds in their affected reference to Dante's and Virgil's clothes and to their "run-*
> *ning." Not willing to commit themselves, they qualify the slightest promise with*
> *a "perhaps."*

Down there we found a painted people
    who moved around the circle with slow steps,
    weeping, and, in countenance, wearied and overcome.   60

They wore capes with low hoods coming down
   in front of their eyes, cut in the style
   of those worn by the monks of Cluny,

outwardly gilded, so that they dazzled,
   but within of lead, and so heavy
   that [in comparison] those Frederick used were of straw.

O mantle eternally tiring! We turned once more
   to the left, moving with the sinners
   and listening to their sad lament;

but, because of their loads, those weary people
   came so slowly that at every step we took
   we found ourselves in new company.   72

Therefore I said to my guide, "Try to find someone
   who by name or deed might be recognized,
   and look around as we move on."

And one who understood the Tuscan speech
   shouted from behind us, "Stay your steps,
   you who are running so through the dark air;

perhaps you will hear from me what you ask for."
   My guide turned around and said,
   "Wait, and then come on at his pace."

I stopped and saw two showing by their looks
   great eagerness to be with me,
   but their burden and the narrow way delayed them.   84

When they came up, with sidelong glances
   they looked at me, without saying a word,
   then turned to each other and remarked,

"This man, by the movement of his throat, seems alive,
   and if they are both dead, by what privilege
   do they go divested of the heavy gown?"

Then they addressed me, "O Tuscan, you who have come
   to the college of the sad hypocrites,
   do not disdain to tell us who you are."

And I to them, "I was born and grew up
   by the beautiful Arno river, in the great city,
   and I am in the body I have always had.   96

But who are you whose distilled grief
   drips down over your cheeks,
   and what punishment glitters so on you?"

*The two shades had been chosen as arbiters in the party strife of Florence instead
of the usual one man. Far from being neutral, they favored the Guelfs. As a
result certain houses of Ghibelline leaders near the old Gardingo fortress were
destroyed and the site was made into a public square.*

One shade, new to Virgil, naked, like Christ at the Crucifixion, is lying on the ground. This is Caiaphas, the high priest who, with others of the council of the Jews, favored sacrificing Christ.

And one answered, "The orange-colored mantles
    are of lead, so thick that their weight
    would make any scales creak.

We are Jolly Friars, and Bolognese,
    I Catalano, and he, Loderingo,
    appointed together by your city

(as a single man usually is taken)
    to preserve the peace, and what we did
    can still be seen around the Gardingo.   108

I began, "O Brothers, your evil . . ."
    but I said no more, for the sight of a shade on the ground,
    crucified with three stakes, caught my eye.

When he saw me he writhed all his body,
    breathing into his beard with sighs,
    and Friar Catalano who noticed that

said to me, "The transfixed one at whom you are looking
    counseled the Pharisees that it was fitting
    to torture one man for the people.[44]

Now he is lying crosswise and naked on the road,
    as you see; and he must feel
    the weight of each one who passes.   120

In a similar way his father-in-law is tortured
    in this ditch, and the others of the Council
    which was a seed of evil for the Jews."

Then I saw Virgil marveling
    over the one stretched out so basely,
    like a cross, in the eternal exile.

Virgil learns of the humiliating trick played on him by the devils of the fifth bolgia. The hypocrites are more expert in perceiving this deception than Reason itself. In his usual indirect manner, not committing himself, Catalano points out that the Devil tells lies. Virgil, angry at the trick and disgusted with Catalano, moves on contemptuously, without a word.

Afterward he addressed to the friar these words,
    "Please tell us, if you can,
    whether there is a gap on the right side

by which we two can get out of here
    without constraining the black angels
    to come and extricate us from this bottom."   132

---

[44]For the roles of Caiaphas and his father-in-law Annas in Jesus' passion, see John 11 and 18.

He answered, "Nearer than you expect
    is a bridge which begins at the outer circle
    and covers all the cruel valleys,

except that over this one it is broken.
    You will be able to climb up on its ruins
    which slope down the side and pile up on the bottom."

My guide stood a moment with his head lowered,
    then said, "Falsely did the one up there
    who hooks the sinners explain the matter."

And the friar added, "I once heard someone say at Bologna
    that the Devil has many vices, among which I heard
    that he is a liar and the father of lies." 144

Then with long steps my guide went on,
    a little disturbed in his looks by anger,
    and I also departed from the burdened ones,

following the imprints of the beloved feet.

CANTO XXIV

VANNI FUCCI

*A dainty comparison takes us for a moment into the fresh air of late winter when
the nights are beginning to get shorter and when the frost resembles for a while
the snow.*

The poets struggle laboriously to get out of the ditch of hypocrisy.

In that part of the young year
    when the sun warms his locks beneath Aquarius
    and the long nights are moving toward the south,

when the frost copies on the ground
    the image of her white sister
    although the point of her pen lasts but little,

the poor peasant whose fodder is getting low
    rises, looks out, and sees the fields all white;
    whereupon he strikes his thigh,

turns back and, lamenting, walks up and down
    like a wretch who does not know what to do.
    Later he looks out again and recovers hope 12

on seeing that the world, in a little while,
    has changed appearance; and he takes his crook
    and drives forth the lambs to feed.

Thus my master made me disheartened
    when I saw his face so troubled,
    and thus quickly to the sore the plaster came.

For, when we reached the ruins of the bridge
    my guide turned to me with that pleasant look
    which I saw first at the foot of the mountain.

He opened his arms, after having made a plan
    within his mind, and looking carefully
    at the rocks he took hold of me,   24

and like one who calculates while working,
    who always seems to provide ahead of time,
    on lifting me toward the top of one rock

examined another crag, saying,
    "Afterward catch hold of that,
    but see first if it will bear your weight."

It was not a way for one clothed in a leaden cloak,
    for we, he a shade and I pushed,
    could hardly mount from jag to jag.

And were it not that on this side
    the slope was shorter than on the other,
    I do not know about him, but I would have been exhausted;   36

but, since Malebolge slopes wholly
    toward the edge of the lowest well,
    the position of each ditch demands

that one side be higher than the other.
    We came finally to the place
    where the last stone is broken off.

The breath had been so pumped from my lungs
    as I went up that at the top
    I could go no farther, and sat down at once.

"Now you must free yourself from sloth,"
    my master said, "for, sitting on down
    or lying under covers, no one comes to fame,   48

without which whoever consumes his life
    leaves such vestige of himself on earth
    as smoke in air or foam on water.

Therefore get up, overcome your panting
    with the spirit which wins every battle
    if it does not sink with its heavy body.

A longer stairs must be climbed;
    it is not enough to have left this one;
    if you understand, act so that it may profit you."

I then got up showing myself better furnished
    with breath than I was, and I said,
    "Go on, for I am strong and bold."   60

The travelers now come to the ditch of the thieves.

We made our way up over the bridge
    which was rocky, narrow, and difficult,
    and much steeper than the previous ones.

I kept talking in order not to appear faint;
    whereupon from the next ditch a voice issued
    unsuited for forming words.

I do not know what it said, although I was already
    on top of the arch that crosses there,
    but whoever spoke seemed moved to anger.

I had turned to look down, but my living eyes
    could not penetrate to the bottom
    through the darkness; therefore I said,   72

"Master, let us try to reach the next bank,
    for, just as I hear, but do not understand,
    so I look, and can distinguish nothing."

"No reply do I make except by an act,"
    he said, "for a modest request
    should be followed silently by the deed."

We went down the bridge to the place
    where it joins the eighth bank,
    and then the ditch was revealed to me.

I saw in it a terrible pack of serpents
    of such diverse appearance
    that the memory of it still chills my blood.   84

Let Libya with its sands boast no longer,
    for if it produced chelydri, jaculi, and phareae,
    and cencri with amphisbaena [fabulous snakes],

it has never shown so many plagues
    or such bad ones, together with all of Ethiopia
    and the land [Arabia] which lies above the Red Sea.

Amid this cruel and dismal swarm, I saw people running,
    naked and terrified, without hope of hiding place
    or of heliotrope [to make themselves invisible].

Their hands were tied behind them by serpents
    which stuck their heads and tails through their backs,
    and were knotted together in front.   96

And behold! at one that was near our bank
    a serpent sprang and transfixed him
    right where the neck meets the shoulders.

Neither I nor O was ever written so quickly
    as he took fire and burned and fell
    like a cinder to the ground.

Then when he was thus destroyed
   the ashes came together of themselves
   and took on instantly the previous form.

Thus it is maintained by great sages
   that the Phoenix[45] dies and then is reborn
   when the five-hundredth year approaches.   108

During its life it feeds on neither grain
   nor herb, but on incense and amomum,
   and nard and myrrh make up its shroud.

And like one [an epileptic] who falls not knowing how,
   through the force of a demon pulling him to the ground
   or through some obstruction that paralyzes him,

and who, when he gets up, looks around, all bewildered
   by the great anguish he has suffered,
   and while looking sighs,

such was the sinner after he arose.
   O Power of God, how severe it is
   in showering down such blows of vengeance!   120

> *The stricken soul is Vanni Fucci, one of Dante's former political enemies, whom the poet had known, not as a thief, but only as hotheaded and violent. Vanni predicts obscurely and maliciously certain events which will lead to the defeat of the Florentine Whites.*

My guide then asked the sinner who he was;
   whereupon he answered, "I rained down from
   Tuscany into this gullet a little while ago.

A bestial, not human life, I liked,
   mule [of irregular birth] that I was; I am Vanni Fucci,
   a beast, and Pistoia was a den worthy of me."

I said to my guide, "Tell him not to slip away
   and ask what sin thrusts him down here,
   for I saw him once a man of blood and rage."

And the soul, having heard, did not dissemble,
   but directed toward me his face
   and his attention with a look of dismal shame.   132

Then he said, "It grieves me more
   that you have caught me in this misery
   than when I was taken from the other world.

I cannot deny what you ask for;
   I have been put down this far for the theft
   of the fine ornaments of the sacristy,

---

[45] The mythical bird that was consumed in fire every 500 years and then arose to new life from the ashes of its dead self.

for which another was falsely accused.
    But to keep you from enjoying this sight,
    if you ever get out of this dark place,

open your ears to my prophecy and hear:
    Pistoia first is thinned of Blacks,
    then Florence renews her masters and her ways;   144

Mars draws a fiery vapor [thunderbolt] from Val di Magra
    which is wrapped in turbid clouds,
    and in an impetuous and angry storm

a battle will be fought on the Piceno field;
    then the blast will pierce the mist
    so that every White will be wounded by it.

And I have told you this so that you may grieve."

CANTO XXV

THE METAMORPHOSIS OF THIEVES

At the end of his remarks the thief
    raised both hands, making the [obscene] sign of the fig,
    and shouting, "Take that, God, for at Thee I point them!"

From then on the serpents were my friends,
    for one coiled around his neck, as if saying,
    "I will not have you speak any more,"

and another encircled his arms and bound them,
    so clinching itself in front
    that he could not make a move with those members.

Ah, Pistoia, why do you not resolve to burn
    so that you will last no longer, since you surpass
    your own founders [followers of Catiline] in wickedness?   12

Through all the dark circles of Hell
    I saw no spirit so bold against God,
    not even him [Capaneus] who fell from the walls of Thebes.

The thief fled, saying nothing further.
    Then I saw a centaur, full of wrath, come calling,
    "Where is he? Where is the impious one?"

I do not believe Maremma has as many snakes
    as the centaur had on its back
    up to where our human form begins.

Upon his shoulders, behind his neck,
    a dragon was lying with open wings
    which set on fire all it met.   24

My master said, "That is Cacus [a fire-breathing monster]
    who, under the rocks of Mount Aventine,
    many times made a lake of blood.

He does not go on the same road as his brothers [the other centaurs]
    because of the theft he slyly made
    of the great herd [of cattle] kept near him,

which led to the end of his wicked life
    under the club of Hercules, who gave him
    perhaps a hundred blows, although hardly ten were felt."

While Virgil was saying this, the centaur ran off,
    and three spirits [Agnello, Buoso, and Puccio] came below us
    whom neither my master nor I had noticed   36

until they cried, "Who are you?"
    Whereupon our talking ceased,
    and we gave heed to them alone.

I did not recognize them, but it happened
    as sometimes occurs by chance
    that one needed to name the other,

saying, "Where can Cianfa [now a serpent] have remained?"
    In order to make my guide attentive,
    I held my finger against my mouth from chin to nose.

If you are slow, Reader, to believe
    what I am to relate, it will be no wonder,
    for I who saw it scarcely admit it to myself.   48

As I kept my eyes on them, a serpent [Cianfa]
    with six legs darted in front of one
    and fastened itself wholly to him.

With its middle feet it clasped his belly
    and with those in front seized his arms;
    then it set its fangs in both his cheeks.

It spread its hind feet over his thighs
    and thrust its tail between them
    drawing it up along his back.

Ivy never clung to a tree so tightly
    as the horrible beast
    entwined the other's members in its own;   60

then they grew together and exchanged their color
    as if they had been hot wax,
    nor did either one or the other appear as before.

Thus a dark hue moves ahead of a flame
    over a sheet of paper, as the whiteness
    dies away before it becomes black.

The other two [Buoso and Puccio] watched and shouted,
    "O me, Agnello, how you are changing!
    Behold! You are now neither two nor one."

The two heads had already fused into one,
    and the shapes of two faces appeared blended
    in the one in which the others had disappeared.   72

The two arms were formed of four strips;
    the thighs with the legs, the belly and the chest,
    became such members as were never seen.

All the former features were blotted out;
    the perverse image seemed two and none,
    and thus went away with slow steps.

As a lizard, under the great scourge
    of the dog days, passing from hedge to hedge,
    seems a flash as it crosses the path,

so appeared, making for the bellies
    of the remaining two, a small, fiery serpent,
    livid and black as a peppercorn,   84

and pierced that part in one of them
    where we first receive our nourishment;
    then fell, stretched out, in front of him.

The one transfixed [Buoso] looked at it, silently,
    and with feet motionless, yawned,
    as if sleep or a fever had come upon him.

He eyed the reptile, and the reptile him;
    from the wound of one and mouth of the other
    thick smoke issued and combined.

Let Lucan be silent now where he tells
    of poor Sabellus and of Nasidius [transformed by serpents],
    and wait to hear what is announced.   96

Let Ovid keep still concerning Cadmus and Arethusa,
    for if he changes one into a serpent in his verse
    and the other into a spring, I do not envy him,

since he never changed two natures
    face to face so that both forms
    were ready to exchange their substance.

The two responded to each other in such a way
    that the serpent made a fork of its tail,
    and the wounded shade drew its feet together.

The legs and the thighs united,
    so that in a little while there was no sign
    you could see of the joining.   108

The split tail took on the shape
    lost in the other; the skin of one became soft
    and that of the other hard.

I saw the arms withdraw through the armpits
    and the short legs of the reptile
    lengthen as much as the other's arms were shortened.

Then the hind feet, twisted together,
    became the member man hides,
    and the shade from his made two legs project.

As the smoke covered both with a new color
    it brought out hair on one
    and removed it from the other.   120

One got up and the other fell,
    neither, however, turning aside his gaze
    under which each had changed faces.

The one standing drew his snout toward his temples,
    and with the flesh left over
    ears were formed on the smooth cheeks.

What was not drawn back and remained
    in excess made a nose for the face
    and thickened the lips to a fit size.

The one on the ground stretched forth his nose,
    withdrew his ears within his head,
    as a snail does its horns,   132

and his tongue which had been undivided
    and apt for speech, split; and the forked tongue
    united; then the smoke stopped.

The soul that had become a brute
    fled hissing through the ditch,
    and after it the other, talking and sputtering.

Then he turned his new back to the reptile
    and said, "I want Buoso to run
    as I have, crawling over the way."

Thus I saw the seventh ballast change
    and interchange, and let the strangeness of it
    be my excuse if my pen has gone astray.   144

Although my eyes were somewhat confused
    and my mind bewildered, those shades
    could not slip away so secretly

that I did not recognize easily
    Puccio Sciancato, who was the only one
    of the three companions left unchanged.

> *The unidentified figure (originally the second snake) was Francesco de' Cavalcanti,
> killed by the people of Gaville. The town mourns because of the vengeance taken
> for him.*

The other was he because of whom you, Gaville, weep.

CANTO XXVI

ULYSSES

*The bitter tone of the beginning lines of an apostrophe to Florence ends quickly
when Dante thinks of the misfortune certain to come to his city, a disaster wished
for by neighboring towns, like Prato, not to mention enemies. Here, as elsewhere,
the invective expresses deep concern, a kind of inverted love.*

Rejoice, Florence, since you are so great
    that over land and over sea you beat your wings,
    and your name is famous in Hell!

Among the thieves I found five citizens of yours,
    such that shame comes over me;
    and you do not rise through them to great honor.

But if the truth is dreamed of near the morning,
    you will soon feel what Prato,
    not to mention others, craves for you.

And if that had already happened, it would not be
    too soon; so were it, since it has to be!
    for it will weigh heavier on me as I grow older.   12

*The poets reach the summit of the bridge over the bolgia where evil counseling
is punished. This sin, incurred mainly by those of superior intelligence, offered
constant temptations to Dante, an exile dependent upon patronage.*

*In the ditch below, lights appear, like fireflies at dusk on a summer evening. And
just as Elisha saw Elijah rise up, enveloped in a cloud of flame, so here the fire
concealed the spirits. Dante asks about a double flame, like that on the funeral
pyre of Eteocles and Polynices, two brothers who had killed each other.*

We departed, and over the steps
    which stones had made for our descent,
    my guide remounted, and drew me up,

and continuing our solitary way
    over the stones and rocks of the bridge,
    feet did not advance without help from hands.

I grieved then, and now I grieve again
    when I direct my thought to what I saw,
    and I control my mind more than usual

so that virtue alone may guide it.
    Thus, if a kindly star or something better [Divine Grace]
    has given an advantage, it may not be harmful through abuse.   24

As a peasant who is resting on a slope
    in the season when the sun that lights the world
    keeps his face least hidden from us—

at the hour when gnats take the place of flies—
    sees fireflies down below in the valley,
    perhaps where he gathers grapes or plows;

so, with as many flames the eighth bolgia
    was all resplendent, as I noticed
    when I came to where I could see the bottom.

And, as he [Elisha] who avenged himself with the bears
    saw the chariot of Elijah depart
    when the horses rose erect to Heaven[46]—   36

for he could not follow so closely with his eyes
    that he could see anything except the flame itself,
    like a little cloud rising upward—

so each light moved through the ditch,
    none revealing what it hid,
    and yet each concealed a sinner.

I was standing on the bridge leaning out to see,
    so that if I had not held to a rock,
    without being pushed I would have fallen,

and my guide, who saw me so attentive, said,
    "Within the fires are the spirits;
    each is wrapped in what is burning him."   48

"Master," I answered, "through hearing you
    I am more certain, but already I was aware
    that this was so, and wished to ask

who is in the fire which comes so divided at the top
    that it seems to rise from the pyre
    on which Eteocles was placed with his brother."

> *Ulysses and Diomed, in the double flame, are guilty on three counts: (1) the trick
> of the Trojan horse, which led to the destruction of Troy and the founding of
> Rome; (2) enticing Achilles to abandon Deidamia and to leave for the Trojan
> wars, and (3) the theft of the Palladium, a statue of Pallas on which the fate
> of Troy depended.*

He answered, "In that flame Ulysses and Diomed
    are tortured, and thus they go together
    in punishment as in their battles.

They groan within their flame for the ambush
    of the horse which was the portal
    through which came the noble ancestors of the Romans.[47]   60

Also they weep for the art on account of which
    Deidamia still grieves for Achilles,
    and they suffer too for the Palladium."

---

[46] For the ascent of Elijah to Heaven and the story of Elisha's revenge on some children
who taunted him for his baldness (they were attacked by bears), see 2 Kings 2.

[47] The story of the Trojan horse is told in Virgil's *Aeneid*, Book II. The Greeks besieging
Troy built a large wooden horse and concealed a band of troops inside it; the deluded Trojans
brought it into their city, which was then destroyed by the Greeks. The exiled Trojans wandered to Italy, where their descendants founded Rome.

"If they can speak within those fires," I said,
  "Master, I beg you earnestly, and beg again
  (and may my prayer be worth a thousand),

that you do not deny our waiting
  until the horned flame comes here;
  you see how my desire bends me toward it!"

And he to me, "Your request is worthy
  of praise; therefore I grant it,
  but see that your tongue keeps silent.   72

Let me speak, for I have conceived
  what you want to know. Since they were Greeks,
  they might shy away from your words."

> *When Virgil, who had celebrated Ulysses in the* Aeneid, *asks about his death,
> the latter, the representative of the spirit of adventure and of scientific discov-
> ery, answers with great dignity and relevance, pointing out how compelling was
> his desire for knowledge of the two worlds of things and of men. In the story
> Dante invents, instead of returning to Penelope and the comforts of home, Ulysses
> sails westward through the Mediterranean, then past Gibraltar, and out on the
> vast and terrifying Atlantic. His course, like that of Columbus almost two
> centuries after Dante, is west-southwest. Five months pass; the crew of old men
> see the constellations of the other hemisphere; then land (probably the island of
> Purgatory) appears. But a storm arises, and Ulysses ends his life in the glory
> of a last adventure.*

When the flame had come to where
  time and place seemed best to my guide,
  I heard him speak in these terms:

"O you two within one fire,
  if I merited thanks from you while I lived,
  if I deserved much or little

when in the world I wrote the lofty verses,[48]
  do not move, but let one of you tell
  where, lost, he went to die."   84

The greater horn of the ancient flame
  began to shake, murmuring like a fire
  struggling in the wind,

then moving the tip here and there,
  as if it were a tongue speaking,
  it formed words, and said:

"When I left Circe who detained me
  more than a year near Gaeta
  before Aeneas had named it thus,

---

[48] Dante had not read Homer's *Odyssey*. (Ulysses is the Latin name for Odysseus.)

neither fondness for my son, nor pity
    for an old father, nor the love for Penelope
    which should have made her happy,   96

could overcome in me the desire I had
    to gain experience of the world
    and of the vices and the worth of men.

I set out on the high, open sea,
    with only one ship, and with that little company
    by which I was not deserted.

Both coasts I saw as far as Spain,
    down to Morocco and the island of Sardinia
    and the others that are bathed in that sea.

I and my companions were old and slow
    when we came to that narrow pass [Gibraltar]
    where Hercules set up his landmarks   108

so that men should not venture beyond.
    On the right I left Seville,
    and on the other side had already passed Ceuta.

'O brothers,' I said, 'you who
    through a thousand perils have come to the West,
    to the brief vigil of our senses

which is left, do not deny
    experience of the unpeopled world
    to be discovered by following the sun.

Consider what origin you had;
    you were not created to live like brutes,
    but to seek virtue and knowledge.'   120

With this little speech I made my companions
    so eager for the journey
    that scarcely then could I have held them back,

and, having turned our stern to the morning,
    we made wings of our oars for the mad flight,
    always gaining on the left.

The night already saw the stars
    of the other pole, and ours [the North Star] so low
    it did not rise from the ocean floor.

Five times the light upon the moon
    had shone and been extinguished
    since we started on the deep way,   132

when a mount appeared to us,
    dim in the distance, and which seemed
    higher than any I had ever seen.

We rejoiced; but soon our joy changed to sorrow,
    for, from the new land a whirlwind arose
    which struck the prow of our ship.

Three times it made it whirl with all the water;
    the fourth time it lifted high the stern
    and made the prow go down as pleased Another [God],

until at last the sea closed over us."

CANTO XXVII

GUIDO DA MONTEFELTRO

A second flame roars like the brass statue of a bull in which prisoners were burned alive. This instrument of torture was made for a tyrant of Agrigentum and was tried out first on its inventor. The flame contains the soul of Guido da Montefeltro, a famous Ghibelline leader referred to in the Convivio *as "our most noble Italian." Guido enquires about Romagna, and Dante outlines briefly the conditions in that region, designating the various rulers by their armorial bearings.*

Already the flame was erect and quiet,
    having ended its speech, and was going from us
    with the leave of the dear Poet,

when another flame that came behind it
    made us turn our eyes to its tip
    because of a confused sound issuing from it.

As the Sicilian bull which roared first
    with the groans of the one who made it
    with his tools (and that was right)

bellowed with the voice of the tortured
    in such a way that, although it was of brass,
    it seemed transfixed with pain,   12

not having any opening or outlet
    from their source in the fire,
    the doleful words were transformed into its language.

After they had found their way
    up through the tip, giving it the vibration
    the tongue had imparted to them,

we heard it say, "O you to whom I direct my voice,
    and who were speaking Lombard just now,
    saying, 'Now go, further I do not urge you,'

although I have perhaps arrived somewhat late,
    do not be displeased to speak with me;
    you see it does not irk me, and I burn!   24

If you have just now fallen into this blind world
    from that sweet Latin land
    from which I bring all my sin,

tell me if the Romagnuols have peace or war,
    for I was from the mountains there
    between Urbino and the peak from which the Tiber comes."

I was still attentive and bent down
    when my leader nudged me, saying,
    "*You* speak, this is an Italian."

And I, having already prepared my reply,
    began without delay, "O soul,
    you who are hidden down there,   36

your Romagna is not and never was
    without strife in the hearts of its tyrants,
    but no open warfare did I leave there just now.

Ravenna stands as it has for many years,
    the eagle of Polenta brooding over it,
    and covering Cervia with its pinions.

The city [Forlì] which once bore the long siege,
    and made a bloody heap of the French,
    finds itself under the green claws [the Ordelaffi family].

The old and young mastiffs of Verrucchio [the Malatestas]
    who disposed badly of Mantagna [their prisoner],
    as usual, make an auger of their teeth.   48

The cities on the Lamone and the Santerno
    are ruled by the young lion in the white lair [Maghinardo da
        Susinana]
    who, from summer to winter, changes party.

And the city [Cesena] whose side the Savio bathes,
    as it lies between the mountain and the plain,
    lives [under party bosses] between tyranny and freedom.

Now I beg you to tell us who you are;
    do not be more reluctant than another has been;
    so may your name stay proudly in the world."

> *After a successful military career, Guido da Montefeltro withdrew from the world and joined the Franciscan order, hoping to make amends for the sins inseparable from military life and to prepare securely for the future world. His plan might have succeeded except for the pope, Boniface VIII, who asked him by what faithless stratagem he might defeat his enemies, offering absolution in advance for the evil counsel. Obliged either to comply or to disobey his superior, Guido chose what seemed (to a soldier) the lesser evil, and told how the pope might, through treachery, secure Palestrina, the stronghold of his enemies.*

After the flame had roared a while in its manner,
    the sharp tip moved to and fro,
    and breathed forth this sound: 60

"If I believed that my reply were to anyone
  who would ever return to the world,
  this flame would remain quiet,

but since no one from this ditch
  has ever returned alive, if I hear the truth,
  I will answer without fear of infamy.

I was a man of arms, and then a Cordelier,
  believing, thus girt, to make amends;
  and certainly my intent would have been realized

except for the Great Priest (may ill befall him!)
  who put me back into my former sins;
  and how and why I want you to hear.   72

While I had the form of the flesh and bones
  my mother gave me, my deeds
  were not lionlike, but those of a fox.

The tricks and the secret ways,
  I knew them all, and so carried on their art
  that my fame spread to the ends of the earth.

When I saw that I had reached
  that point in life when everyone
  should lower sail and coil his ropes,

what first had pleased me became repugnant
  and, having repented and confessed, I gave myself to God,
  and alas! that should have availed.   84

The Prince of the new Pharisees [Boniface VIII],
  waging war close to the Lateran—
  and not with Saracens or with Jews,

for every enemy of his was a Christian,
  and none had been a renegade at Acre
  or a merchant in the Sultan's land—

considered neither his high office
  and sacred orders, nor in me that cord I wore
  which used to make those bound with it thinner.

But, as Constantine called upon Sylvester[49]
  in Soracte to cure him of his leprosy,
  so he called me, as his physician,   96

to cure the fever of his pride.
  He asked advice of me, and I kept silent,
  because his words seemed drunken,

[49]For Constantine and Sylvester, see XIX.115–17, the translator's gloss, and the note. Sylvester, according to legend, cured Constantine by baptizing him, in return for which Constantine yielded up the western part of the Roman Empire.

and then he said, "Do not let your heart mistrust,
 right now I absolve you; let me know
 how to cast Palestrina to the ground.

I can open and close Heaven,
 as you know, since two are the keys
 that my predecessor [Celestine V] did not hold dear."[50]

The heavy arguments brought me to where
 silence seemed worse to me than complying,
 and I said, 'Father, since you wash away   108

the sin into which I now must fall,
 long promise with short fulfillment
 will make you triumph on your lofty seat.'

> *At Guido's death, St. Francis came for him, but a "black Cherub" from the eighth circle of Hell, the counterpart of those of the eighth heaven who likewise operate through intelligence, objected, and pointed out the impossibility of absolution in advance.*
>
> *Dante uses this extreme example to emphasize the point that salvation depends on the state of the soul at the moment of death. A similar contest, related in Purgatory, occurs in the case of Guido's son, but in almost exactly opposite circumstances.*

When I was dead, Francis came for me,
 but one of the black Cherubim said to him,
 'Don't take him, don't wrong me.

He must come down among my minions
 because he gave the fraudulent advice,
 since when I have been lurking to grasp his hair.

For one who does not repent cannot be absolved,
 nor can *repenting* and *willing* go together
 because the contradiction does not allow it.'   120

Ah, wretched me, how I shuddered
 when he seized me, saying,
 'Perhaps you did not think I was a logician!'

To Minos he brought me, who twisted his tail
 eight times around his stiff back,
 and after he had bitten it in his rage, he said,

'This is one for the thievish fire.'
 Therefore I am lost here as you see,
 and while moving, clothed in fire, I grieve."

When he had finished speaking
 the sorrowing spirit went on
 twisting and shaking his sharp flame.   132

---

[50]For Celestine V, see III.59–60 and translator's gloss.

My guide and I passed over the bridge
   to the top of the next arch
   which crosses the ditch in which a fee is paid

by those who get a burden by dividing [sowing discord].

CANTO XXVIII

THE SOWERS OF DISCORD

If it were possible to bring together the wounded on the battlegrounds of south-ern Italy in the long series of wars from ancient times down to the Norman inva-sions and the wars of Charles of Anjou against Manfred, the scene would be similar to that of the ninth bolgia.

Who even in unrhymed words [prose]
   could ever fully tell in many narrations
   of the blood and of the wounds I now saw?

Every tongue certainly would fail
   because our language and our memories
   are insufficient to contain so much.

If all the soldiers were assembled
   who, on the stormy fields of Apulia,
   have groaned for their blood

shed by Trojans, and in the long [Punic] war
   which made so vast a spoil of rings [from fingers of dead Romans],
   as Livy writes, who does not err,   12

together with those who suffered painful wounds
   by opposing Robert Guiscard [the Norman conqueror]
   and others whose bones are still piled up

at Ceperano, where every Apulian [allied with Manfred]
   was a traitor, and at Tagliacozzo
   where old Alardo conquered without arms [by strategy],

and were one to show his limbs pierced,
   another his cut off, the view would not equal
   the awful sight of the ninth ditch.

> *Mahomet, the first shade recognized, had been considered as originally a Christian and as the deliberate cause of the separation of the world into two monotheis-tic faiths. Mahomet mentions prophetically and with malicious pleasure Fra Dolcino, the leader of a heretical sect who, besieged in 1306, was forced by hunger to surrender.*

Indeed, a cask without a stave or endboard
   looks less mutilated than one I saw
   split from his chin down to where wind is broken.   24

His entrails hung between his legs,
   the vital parts appeared with the foul sack
   which makes excrement of what is swallowed.

While I was intently looking at him,
    he gazed at me, and with his hands opened his breast,
    saying, "Now see how I tear myself,

see how mangled Mahomet is!
    In front of me Ali [a son-in-law] goes weeping,
    his head split from chin to forelock;

and all the others you see here
    while alive were sowers of scandal and of schism
    and therefore are split like this.   36

A devil is here behind us who cuts us
    thus cruelly with the edge of his sword,
    reopening all the wounds

when we have gone around the doleful road,
    since they are healed
    before we come again before him.

But who are you, dallying on the bridge,
    perhaps to delay going to your punishment
    decreed upon your own confession?"

"Not yet has death come to him, nor does guilt
    bring him to torment," my master said,
    "but to give him complete experience,   48

I, who am dead, must take him
    down here from round to round, and this
    is as true as that I am speaking to you."

More than a hundred in the ditch,
    when they heard this, stopped to look at me,
    forgetting their pain in their marveling.

"Now tell Fra Dolcino, you who perhaps
    will soon see the sun again, that unless he wants
    to follow me he had better provide himself

with food, so that the snow
    will not bring victory to the Novarese,
    which otherwise would be hard for them to gain."   60

After he had lifted one foot to go
    Mahomet said these words to me,
    then placed it on the ground, moving on.

Pier da Medicina, another schismatic of whom little is known, adds the prophecy of the death of two citizens of Fano who will be called to a parley and treacherously thrown overboard. They will not need the usual protection from the squalls of Focara, since they will never reach that place. Then Curio is mentioned who from private motives urged Caesar to cross the Rubicon and begin the civil war. He wishes now he had never seen the town of Rimini near that river. Another sower of discord, Mosca, according to tradition advised the killing of an opponent to settle a feud rather than a milder punishment, since that, he thought, would end the matter. Instead, the murder led to the first conflict between the Guelfs and Ghibellines in Florence. On seeing Mosca, Dante's Florentine spirit flares up, and he tells him of the banishment of his family, the Lamberti, from the city.

Another who had his throat cut
    and his nose severed up to his eyebrows,
    and who had only a single ear,

having stopped to look with wonder,
    before the others cleared his windpipe
    which was all red outside, and said,

"O you whom sin does not condemn
    and whom I have seen in the Latin land,
    if too much resemblance does not deceive me,   72

recall to mind Pier da Medicina
    if ever you go back to see the sweet plain
    which from Vercelli slopes to Marcabò,

and make known to the two best men of Fano,
    to Messer Guido and to Angiolello,
    that, unless foresight here is vain,

they will be thrown from their ship
    and drowned near La Cattolica
    through the treachery of a base tyrant.

Between the islands of Cyprus and Majorca,
    Neptune has never seen so great a crime
    of pirates or of Argolic people [Greeks].   84

That traitor who sees with one eye only [Malatestino]
    and holds the city [Rimini] which someone here [Curio]
    would wish never to have seen,

will have them come for a parley with him,
    and will act so that to allay Focara's wind,
    they will need neither vow nor prayer."

And I to him, "Point out and tell me
    if you want me to take news of you above,
    who found the sight of that city bitter?"

Then he laid his hand on the jaw
    of one of his companions, and opened his mouth,
    saying, "This is he, and he does not speak.   96

While exiled, he quieted Caesar's fears,
    affirming that a man well prepared
    always loses by any delay."

Oh, how dismayed he seemed to me
    with his tongue cut in his throat,
    Curio, who before spoke so boldly!

And one who had both hands cut off,
    lifting the stumps in the dark air
    so that the blood dirtied his face,

cried, "Remember also Mosca
    who said, alas, 'A thing done has an end,'
    which was a seed of evil for the Tuscans."   108

And I added, "And death to your kindred,"
    whereupon he, heaping grief on grief,
    went off like one maddened by sorrow.

> *The last example is that of the Provençal poet Bertran de Born, who, Dante believed,
> had fomented a quarrel between Henry, the "young English king," and his father.*

But I remained to look at the throng,
    and I saw a thing I would fear
    to tell about without more proof,

except that conscience reassures me,
    the good companion which emboldens man
    under the breastplate of conscious innocence.

I saw certainly, and I still seem to see
    a body without a head, going on
    like the others of the sad troop.   120

It held by the hair its severed head
    dangling from its hand like a lantern,
    which looked at us and said, "Woe is me!"

Of itself it made a lamp for itself,
    and they were two in one and one in two;
    how this can be He knows who so ordains.

When it was at the foot of the bridge,
    it lifted the head high with its arm
    to bring the words closer to me,

which were, "Now see my terrible penalty,
    you who, breathing, are visiting the dead;
    judge if any is as great as this.   132

And, that you may take news of me,
    know that I am Bertran de Born, the one
    who gave the young king the evil encouragement.

I made father and son rebellious to each other;
    Ahithophel did not do worse to Absalom
    and to David with his wicked plots.[51]

---

[51] For Absalom's rebellion, incited by Ahithophel (or Achitophel), against his father King
David, see 2 Samuel 14–18.

Because I separated persons thus joined,
I now carry my brain, alas,
detached from its source in this body.

Thus retribution is observed in me."

CANTO XXIX

THE FALSIFIERS

Fascinated by the sight of the horrible wounds, Dante keeps looking at them and incurs a reproach. He excuses himself (he is growing up in his relationship with his master) by mentioning that he believed that a relative was there, Geri del Bello, whose violent death had not been avenged. Dante pities Geri, perhaps for the latter's obvious adherence even here to the code of family vengeance.

The time, as usual in Hell, is indicated by the position of the moon: it is now shortly after noon on Saturday.

The great crowd and the diverse wounds
had made my eyes so inebriated
that they were eager to remain and weep.

But Virgil said, "What are you looking at?
Why does your sight still rest down there
on the sad, mutilated shades?

You have not done so at the other ditches.
Consider, if you wish to count them,
that the valley circles for twenty-two miles;

already the moon is under our feet;
the time granted to us now is short,
and there is much more to see."   12

"If you had taken note," I answered then,
"of the cause that made me look,
perhaps you would have granted me a longer stay."

Meanwhile my guide kept going on
and I followed, making my reply
and adding, "Within that hollow

on which I kept my eyes fixed so closely
I believe a spirit of my own blood
laments the sin that costs so much down here."

Then my master said, "From now on
do not let your thoughts be distracted by him;
attend to something else and let him stay there,   24

for I saw him at the foot of the little bridge
pointing you out and threatening you with his finger,
and I heard him called Geri del Bello.

You were then so completely occupied
      with him [Bertran de Born] who once held Altaforte
      that you did not look over there, and he departed."

"O my guide, his death by violence
      which has not yet been avenged," I said,
      "by [relatives] the partners of his shame,

made him indignant; therefore he went off
      without speaking to me, as I judge,
      and by that he has made me pity him the more."   36

> *The shades in the tenth bolgia are divided into four groups: falsifiers (1) of met-*
> *als (alchemists), punished by leprosy and paralysis; (2) of persons (impersonators),*
> *punished by delirium or madness; (3) of coins (counterfeiters), afflicted with dropsy;*
> *and (4) of words (liars), suffering from high fever. Dante treats them with mild*
> *and amused contempt.*

Thus we talked as far as to the point
      which would have shown the next ditch
      to the bottom if there had been more light.

Then, when we were above
      the last cloister of Malebolge, so that
      its lay brothers could be observed by us,

diverse laments kept striking me
      which had their arrows barbed with such pity
      that I covered my ears with my hands.

Such suffering as there would be if the sick
      in the hospitals of Valdichiana, Maremma, and Sardinia
      [malarious regions] between July and September   48

were all together in one ditch,
      was here; and such stench issued
      as comes from festered limbs.

We descended to the last bank of the long bridge,
      still keeping to the left,
      and then my sight was clearer

down toward the bottom, where the minister
      of the Supreme Lord, Infallible Justice,
      punishes the falsifiers registered here.

I do not believe there was greater sadness
      to see all the people of Aegina sick
      when the air was so full of pestilence   60

that the animals, even to the little worm,
      fell dead—and then the ancient people,
      as the poets hold as true,

were restored by the seed of ants[52]—
  than it was to see in the dark ditch
  the spirits languish in diverse heaps.

One lay upon the belly and one upon the shoulders
  of another, and one on all fours
  was crawling along the dismal path.

Step by step we went without speaking,
  observing and listening to the sick,
  who could not lift their bodies.   72

I saw two sitting, leaning on each other
  as stewpan is propped against stewpan to warm,
  spotted with scabs from head to foot,

and never have I seen a currycomb handled so quickly
  by a stable boy whose master was waiting for him
  or by one staying up against his will

as each of these plied the clawing of his nails
  on himself, because of the great rage
  of itching that had no other help;

and the nails scraped off the scabs
  as a knife does the scales from bream
  or some other fish that has them larger.   84

"O you who disarm yourself with your fingers,
  at times making pincers of them,"
  my guide began to say to one of them,

"tell us if any Latin is among those
  who are here; so may your nails
  suffice eternally for this work!"

"We are both Latins whom you see
  so disfigured here," one answered, weeping,
  "but who are you, asking about us?"

My guide replied, "I am one descending
  with this *live* man from ledge to ledge,
  and I intend to show Hell to him."   96

Then the mutual support broke,
  and each of them, trembling, turned to me,
  with others who had overheard the words.

My good master drew close to me, saying,
  "Ask them what you want to know."
  And I began to speak as he desired:

---

[52]Juno inflicted on Aegina a plague that destroyed all living creatures except one man, Aeacus, at whose prayer Jupiter repopulated the island by changing ants into human beings. The story is told by Ovid.

"So may your memory not fade
    from human minds in the first world,
    but may it live on for many suns,

tell me who you are, and of what people;
    let not your ugly and annoying punishment
    make you afraid to reveal yourselves to me."   108

> Griffolino, a fraudulent alchemist, tells how he was burned by the presumptive
> father of the simple-minded Albero da Siena, who had taken seriously his remarks
> about flying. This prompts Dante to speak of the Sienese whose sometimes aris-
> tocratic folly was a standing joke in the bourgeois atmosphere of Florence. Dante
> is helped in his gibes by Capocchio, who mentions ironically the notorious spend-
> thrift Stricca and the "Spendthrifts' Club," a group of young Sienese who delib-
> erately ruined themselves by extravagance.

"I was of Arezzo," one answered,
    "and Albero da Siena had me burned at the stake;
    but what I died for does not bring me here.

It is true that I told him, speaking in jest,
    that I could rise in the air in flight,
    and he who had the desire but little sense

wanted me to show him the art, and because
    I did not make him a Daedalus [a flyer], he had me burned
    by one who considered him as a son.

But to the last ditch of the ten,
    Minos, who cannot err, condemned me
    for the alchemy that I practiced in the world."   120

And I said to the poet, "Now was there ever
    a people as silly as the Sienese?
    Certainly the French are not so by far."

Thereupon the other leper who heard me
    answered my question and said, "Except Stricca
    who knew how to spend with moderation,

and Niccolò who first discovered
    the expensive use of the clove
    in the garden[53] where such seed takes root,

and except the company in which
    Caccia d'Ascian squandered vineyard and forest
    and the Abbagliato displayed his wit.   132

But that you may know who seconds your remarks
    against the Sienese, sharpen your eyes toward me,
    so that my face may give the right response.

[53] The "garden" is Siena.

Then you will see that I am the shade of Capocchio
    who falsified the metals by alchemy,
    and you must recall, if I see you correctly,

how good an ape of nature I became."

CANTO XXX

MASTER ADAM AND THE FALSE GREEK

*Two terrible examples of insanity are cited at the beginning of this canto, the
hallucination of Athamas and the hysterical grief of Hecuba. Two impersonators
show a similar mania. One, Gianni Schicchi, had been engaged by Buoso Donati's
son to impersonate his father and dictate a more favorable will. The commission
was well performed except that the testator included himself in the legacy as the
heir of the "queen of the herd," a valuable mare. The other example is that of
Myrrha.*

At the time when Juno because of Semele
    was angry at the Theban royal family,
    as she had shown already more than once,

Athamas was stricken with such madness
    that on seeing his wife coming
    burdened with two sons, one on either hand,

he shouted, "Let us spread the net, so that I
    may catch the lioness and cubs as they pass";
    then he stretched out his pitiless claws,

and seizing one, whose name was Learchus,
    whirled him around and dashed him on a rock;
    and she, with her other burden, drowned herself.[54]   12

And when Fortune had brought low
    the bold pride of the Trojans
    so that both king and kingdom were blotted out,

sad Hecuba, miserable and captive,[55]
    after she had seen her [daughter] Polyxena slain
    and, forlorn, recognized the body of [her son] Polydorus

on the shore of the sea, in her madness
    barked like a dog, so greatly
    had grief wrenched her mind.

But neither Theban nor Trojan Furies
    were ever seen anywhere so cruel
    in goading beasts, much less human bodies,   24

---

[54]Juno, angered at her consort Jupiter's love for Semele, a Theban princess who bore his
son Bacchus, avenged herself on Semele's whole family. These included Semele's sister Ino,
Ino's husband Athamas, and their children.
[55]Hecuba, queen of Troy, was carried off by the Greeks after they destroyed the city.

as those I saw in two spirits, pale and naked,
   who ran biting as a hungry boar does
   when just released from the sty.

One rushed on Capocchio and seized him
   by the neck, then dragging him,
   made his belly scrape on the hard bottom.

And the Aretine [Griffolino], who remained trembling,
   said to me, "That mad one is Gianni Schicchi,
   and he goes thus tearing others."

"Oh," I said to him, "so may the other
   not bite you, please tell us
   who it is before it gets away."   36

And he to me, "That is the ancient spirit
   of wicked Myrrha;[56] who was devoted to her father
   beyond the bounds of lawful love.

She came thus to sin with him,
   changing herself into another's form,
   just as the other who is running off

undertook, to gain the mistress of the herd,
   to impersonate Buoso Donati,
   making a will and giving it a legal form."

After the two mad ones on whom
   I had kept my eyes had passed,
   I turned to look at the other ill-born shades.   48

> *The counterfeiters are swollen with dropsy. One, a master of the art, had served the counts of Romena in one of the coolest, best watered of mountain regions, and the image of the place where he had worked increases the torture of his thirst. Amused at the size of Master Adam's belly, Dante asks about two shades on his boundaries. One, Sinon, suffering now from high fever, had pretended to be a fugitive from the Greeks, and had persuaded the Trojans to take in the wooden horse. The other liar is Potiphar's wife. Sinon objects to being called a "Greek from Troy," and we have a quarrel, the pot calling the kettle black. Sinon, considering each counterfeit coin as a separate indictment, charges Master Adam with the commission of more sins than any other demon. His opponent, in rebuttal, mentions the infamous notoriety Sinon has gained through the works of Homer and Virgil. Dante is scolded for listening to the quarrel. He tries to reply, but is so ashamed that he cannot, and excuses himself by this embarrassment more effectively than if he had been able to speak.*

I saw one who would have looked like a lute
   if only he had had his legs cut off
   at the groin, where they join the body.

---

[56] The story of Myrrha's incestuous passion is told in Ovid's *Metamorphoses*, Book X.

The heavy dropsy, disproportioning him thus
    with humors badly absorbed,
    left his head too small for his belly,

and made him hold his lips apart
    as the hectic does who, for thirst,
    has one turned up, the other down.

"O you who are without any punishment
    in this wretched world, and I don't know why,"
    he said to us, "see and take note   60

of the misery of Master Adam!
    When alive I had enough of what I wanted,
    and now, alas! I long for a little drop of water.

The streams which from the green hills
    of Casentino flow down to the Arno,
    making their beds cool and soft,

always stand before my eyes and not in vain,
    for the vision of them dries me up
    more than the disease which wastes my features.

The rigid Justice which goads me
    takes advantage of the place where I sinned
    to put my sighs to quicker flight.   72

There is Romena where I counterfeited
    the [Florentine] currency sealed with the Baptist's image,
    for which I left my body burned above.

But if I could see the miserable soul
    of Guido or of Alessandro or their brother [his employers]
    I would not trade the sight for Fonte Branda [a spring].

One is already in, if the mad shades
    that move around tell the truth,
    but of what avail is it, if my limbs are tied?

Yet, if I were still nimble enough
    to make an inch in a hundred years,
    I would already have started out   84

to find them among these disgusting people,
    although the ditch circles for eleven miles,
    and is not less than half a mile across.

Because of them I am in such a household;
    they induced me to stamp the florins
    which had indeed *three* carats of alloy!"

And I to him, "Who are the two wretches,
    steaming like wet hands in winter,
    lying close to your right frontier?"

"Here I found them on raining down in this ditch,"
    he answered, "since when they have not turned over,
    nor will they, I believe, in eternity.   96

One is the lying woman who accused Joseph;[57]
    the other is false Sinon, the Greek from Troy;
    because of their fever they emit such stench."

And one of them [Sinon] who perhaps
    took badly being named thus darkly,
    with his fist struck the vile belly

which sounded like a drum, and Master Adam
    struck him back in the face with his arm
    which did not seem less hard,

saying to him, "Although locomotion is impossible
    because of my heavy limbs,
    I have an arm free for such business!"   108

Whereupon the other answered, "When you went
    to the fire, you were not so quick,
    but you were still quicker when you made the coins."

And he of the dropsy, "You tell the truth about this,
    but you were not so good a witness
    at Troy when the truth was asked of you."

"If I spoke falsely, you falsified the coins,"
    said Sinon, "and I am here for one fault,
    and you for more than any other demon."

"Remember, perjurer, the horse!" he of the swollen belly
    answered, "and let it be a plague to you
    that the whole world knows of it."   120

"And may the thirst that cracks your tongue
    be a curse to you," said the Greek, "and the foul water
    which makes a hedge before your eyes."

Then the counterfeiter, "Thus your mouth
    still opens to your harm, as usual,
    for, if I am thirsty and humor stuffs me up,

you have the burning and the headache,
    and to lick the mirror[58] of Narcissus
    you would not need a second invitation."

I was wholly intent on listening to them
    when my master said to me, "Now keep on gazing!
    a little more, and I will quarrel with you."   132

---

[57]After Joseph, son of Jacob, was sold into Egypt, the wife of Potiphar, an officer of Pharaoh, made sexual advances to Joseph. Rebuffed by him, she then accused him of making the advances. See Genesis 39.
    [58]Water. Narcissus fell in love with his own reflected image.

When I heard him speak to me with anger,
     I turned to him with such shame
     that the memory of it still haunts me.

As one who dreams of a misfortune
     and, while dreaming, hopes it is a dream,
     so that he longs for what is as if it were not,

so I became, not being able to speak
     although I wanted to excuse myself and did so,
     without knowing that I was doing it.

"Less shame washes away a greater fault,"
     said my master, "than yours has been;
     therefore, free yourself of all sadness   144

and take note that I am at your side
     if it happens again that chance catches you
     where people are in a similar wrangle,

for wishing to overhear it is a low desire."

CANTO XXXI

THE GIANTS

The same tongue first stung me
     so that it tinted both my cheeks,
     then offered me its cure.

Thus I hear that the lance of Achilles
     and of his father was wont first
     to wound and then to heal.

We turned our backs on the miserable ditch,
     going up without speaking
     over the bank which surrounds it.

Here it was less than night and less than day,
     so that my sight did not go far;
     but I heard a horn sound so loudly   12

that it would have made any thunder faint;
     and retracing the course the sound took
     I directed my eyes to one spot.

After the doleful rout,
     when Charlemagne lost his holy company,
     Roland did not blow so terribly.[59]

---

[59] See *The Song of Roland.* When Charlemagne's army returned from Spain toward France,
Roland commanded the elite rear guard. Set upon by the pagans and defeated, Roland refused
to blow his great horn to call for help until it was too late.

Only a short while did my eyes look toward the sound
 when I seemed to see many high towers,
 and I asked, "Master, tell me, what city is this?"

And he to me, "Since you are looking
 through the darkness from too far off
 your imagination leads you astray.   24

You will see when you arrive there
 how the senses are deceived by distance;
 therefore move a little faster."

Then he took me tenderly by the hand
 and said, "Before we go farther,
 to make the event seem less strange,

know that these are not towers, but giants,
 and they are in the well around the bank
 from the navel down, all of them."

As, when a mist has cleared somewhat,
 our eyes little by little make out
 what the vapor in the air had hidden,   36

so, piercing through the thick gloom
 on approaching closer and closer to the bank,
 my error fled, and my fear increased.

As, on the circle of its walls,
 Montereggione [a fortress] is crowned with towers,
 so, above the bank which surrounds the pit,

the horrible giants, whom Jove still threatens[60]
 when he thunders in the heavens,
 towered above us with half their bodies.

Already I saw the face, shoulders, and chest
 of one, and a large part of his belly,
 and both his arms down by his side.   48

Certainly when Nature gave up the art
 of producing these creatures she did well
 to deprive Mars of such agents;

and if she does not repent for elephants
 and whales, whoever looks closely
 will hold her more discreet and just,

for where the force of intellect [as in the giants]
 is added to ill will and strength,
 mankind can have no defense.

---

[60] Ovid's *Metamorphoses*, Book I, describes an attack on the gods by giants who piled mountains atop one another.

His face seemed to me as long and wide
   as the pine cone[61] at St. Peter's in Rome,
   and his other features were in proportion. 60

Thus the bank which was an apron
   from his middle down, showed so much of him
   that three Frieslanders [tall men] would have boasted

in vain to reach up to his hair.
   I saw, indeed, thirty great spans[62] of him
   down from [the neck] where a man buckles on his cloak.

> Nimrod, the builder of the Tower of Babel, a "mighty hunter before the Lord,"
> is with the giants who revolted against Jove. His words are meaningless. Virgil
> apostrophizes him for Dante's benefit. Then the travelers come to Antaeus, who
> was not present at the battle of the giants against the gods, and therefore is not
> bound like the others. Flattered by Virgil, who understands his fatuous charac-
> ter, Antaeus extends his hand and places the two poets on the bottom of the pit
> in the ninth and last circle.

"Raphèl maÿ amèch zabì almì"
   the savage mouth for which sweeter
   hymns were unfitting began to say.

And my guide to him, "Stupid soul,
   keep to your horn, and with it express yourself
   when anger or some other passion moves you. 72

Search around your neck and you will find the strap
   which holds it, O confused spirit;
   see it curving across your great chest."

Then he said to me, "He accuses himself.
   This is Nimrod, through whose evil thought
   a single tongue is not used in the world.[63]

Let us leave him and not speak in vain,
   for, as the language of others is to him,
   so is his to them, and is understood by none."

We kept on still to the left
   and at the distance of a crossbow shot
   we found another giant larger and fiercer. 84

Who the master was to bind him
   I cannot say, but his right arm
   at his back and the other in front

---

[61]A pine cone made of bronze, about ten feet high, is still visible in the Vatican.
[62]Hand spans.
[63]For the story of the Tower of Babel and the consequent confusion of tongues in the world, see Genesis 11.

were bound by a chain, which held him tied
    from the neck down, so that over his exposed part
    it encircled him five times.

"This haughty creature wished to make trial
    of his power against supreme Jove,"
    said my master; "therefore, he has such a reward.

Ephialtes is his name; he fought in the great battle
    when the giants frightened the gods:
    the arms he used once, he never moves."   96

Then I to my guide, "If possible
    I should like for my eyes
    to gain experience of the immense Briareus."

Whereupon he answered, "You will see Antaeus
    nearby, who speaks and is unbound
    and who will put us in the lowest depth of guilt.

The one you wish to see is farther on
    and is bound and built like this one
    except that he looks more ferocious."

Never did an earthquake jar
    so violently a massive tower
    as Ephialtes suddenly shook himself.   108

Then I feared death more than ever,
    and fright alone would have caused it,
    if I had not seen the chains.

We went on then and came to Antaeus
    who protruded above the bank
    fully five ells,[64] not counting his head.

"O you who in the fateful valley
    which made Scipio an heir of glory,
    when Hannibal and his army turned back,[65]

you who once brought a thousand lions as prey—
    and, if you had fought in the great war,
    with your brothers, it seems that some believe   120

the sons of Earth [the giants] might have conquered—
    put us down, do not disdain to do so,
    to where cold locks up Cocytus.

Do not make us go to Tityus or to Typhon;
    this man can give what is longed for here;
    therefore bend over and do not scornfully refuse.

---

[64] An ell is about four or five feet.
[65] Scipio and Hannibal were, respectively, Roman and Carthaginian generals.

He can revive your fame in the world,
    for he lives and expects a long life, if Divine Grace
    does not call him to herself ahead of time."

Thus my master spoke, and Antaeus
    hurriedly held out the hand whose grip
    Hercules once felt, and took hold of my master.   132

When Virgil felt himself grasped,
    he said to me, "Come, let me take hold of you."
    Then, of himself and me he made one bundle.

As the Garisenda tower seems to fall
    if looked at under its leaning side
    when a cloud passes over it in the opposite direction,

so Antaeus appeared to me as I watched
    while he bent over; and he was such
    that I would have wished to go by another way.

But lightly in the depth which swallows
    Lucifer with Judas he placed us,
    nor did he delay long bent over   144

but rose like a mast set in a ship.

CANTO XXXII

THE TRAITORS

The tone of the Comedy now becomes harsh, scornful, vindictive. Dante again calls upon the Muses, but this time on those who helped to build Thebes, "the ancient home of crime."

If I had rhymes rough and harsh enough
    to be fitting for the dismal hole
    on which all the other circles weigh,

I would press out the substance of my conception
    more fully; but since I do not have them,
    not without fear do I bring myself to speak.

For, to describe the bottom of the whole universe
    is not an enterprise to take up in jest,
    nor for a tongue that still cries "mamma" and "papa."

But may those ladies who helped Amphion
    to enclose Thebes aid my verse,
    so that words and facts will not differ.   12

O rabble, miscreated above all others,
    in this place to speak of which is hard,
    here [on earth] you would better have been sheep or goats!

When we were down in the dark well
    beyond the feet of the giant and much lower,
    and as I was still looking at the high wall,

I heard someone say, "Watch how you step!
   Move so you won't trample with your feet
   on the heads of the weary, miserable brothers."

Then I turned and saw a lake in front of me
   and under my feet which, frozen,
   had the appearance of glass and not of water.   24

The Danube in Austria never made in winter
   so thick a veil for its current,
   nor the Don up there under its cold skies,

as this did; for if Tambernicchi [a mountain]
   had fallen on it, or Pietrapana,
   it would not have given a creak even at the edge.

And as a frog lies croaking
   with just its muzzle out, in the season
   when the peasant woman thinks of gleaning,

so the shades were lying in the ice,
   livid up to where shame appears,
   their teeth chattering like storks' bills.   36

Each held his face down; their mouths
   gave evidence of the cold,
   and their eyes of their sad hearts.

*Caïna, the first division of the ninth circle, contains traitors to kindred, among
whom are the counts of Mangona, who killed each other in a quarrel over an
inheritance. Other minor figures also are mentioned.*

When I had looked around a little,
   I glanced at my feet and saw two so bound together
   that the hair on their heads was intermingled.

"Tell me, you who press your chests so close together,
   who you are," I asked, and they bent their necks,
   and after they had lifted their faces to me,

their eyes, which previously were wet only within,
   gushed through the lids, and the cold
   froze their tears and locked them up again.   48

A clamp never bound wood to wood so strongly.
   Then they, like two goats,
   butted each other, such anger overcame them.

And one who had lost both ears from the cold,
   with his face still downward, said,
   "Why do you look at us so much?

If you want to know who these two are,
   the valley from which the Bisenzio flows
   belonged to them and to their father, Albert.

They came from one body, and you might search
  through all Caïna[66] without finding a shade
  more worthy to be preserved in ice,   60

not him [Mordred] whose breast and shadow
  were laid open by a single blow from Arthur's hand,[67]
  not Focaccia; not this one who covers me

with his head, so that I cannot see beyond
  and whose name was Sassol Mascheroni,—
  if you are a Tuscan you know now who he was.

And, so that you will not put me to further speech,
  know that I was Camicion de' Pazzi, and am waiting
  for Carlino to make me [by comparison] seem innocent."

Afterward I saw a thousand faces made doglike
  by the cold; so that a shudder comes to me
  and always will at the sight of frozen pools.   72

> *Passing on to Antenora, the second division of the ninth circle, where traitors
> to party and country are kept, Dante accidentally kicks one shade who mentions
> Montaperti, the scene of a defeat of the Florentine Guelfs. Dante's suspicion is
> immediately aroused, and he tries by force to make the shade name himself. Another,
> however, treacherously gives him away as Bocca degli Abati who, at a critical
> moment in the battle, cut off the hand of the Florentine standardbearer, an act
> which was thought to have caused the defeat. Dante's violence incurs no reproach:
> the implication is that ordinary rules of conduct are inapplicable to the com-
> pletely depraved: one must keep away from them or act according to the code they
> establish. This is the realistic Gresham's law of competitive behavior. Bocca in
> turn mentions others, including Buoso da Duera, who had been bribed by Charles
> of Anjou, and Ganelon, the traitor in the* Song of Roland.

And while we were moving toward the center
  to which all weights are drawn
  and I was shivering in the eternal chill,

whether it was destiny or chance, I know not,
  but while walking among the heads
  my foot struck hard against the face of one.

Weeping it cried, "Why do you kick me?
  Unless you come to increase the vengeance
  for Montaperti, why do you molest me?"

And I, "Master, now wait for me here
  until this one relieves me of a doubt,
  then you can make me hurry as you wish."   84

---

[66] Named for Cain, who murdered his brother Abel (Genesis 4). All the treacherous sinners punished in this and the other three divisions of the ninth circle happen also to be involved
in murder.

[67] Mordred was the evil nephew of King Arthur and a would-be usurper. Arthur killed him
with a blow that penetrated his whole body.

My guide stood still, and I said to the shade
    who was still cursing loudly,
    "Who are you complaining thus of others?"

"Now who are you, going through Antenora[68]
    kicking others' cheeks," he answered,
    "harder than if you were alive?"

"I am alive," was my response,
    "and it may be dear to you, if you want fame,
    that I should include your name in my notes."

And he to me, "The contrary is what I want,
    get away from here; do not bother me,
    for you know badly how to flatter in this bottom."   96

Then I seized him by the scalp and said,
    "You will name yourself
    or not a hair will be left on your head."

And he to me, "Even if you tear it out
    and fall on my head a thousand times,
    I will not tell or show you who I am."

I had already twisted his hair in my hand
    and had pulled out more than one tuft,
    he howling with eyes cast down,

when another shouted, "What's the matter with you, Bocca?
    Isn't it enough to chatter with your jaws
    but you must bark?—What devil is after you?"   108

"Now," I said, "I do not want you to speak,
    damned traitor, for to your shame
    I will carry off true news of you."

"Go," he answered, "and tell what you want,
    but if you get out of here, don't keep silent
    about him who has his tongue so ready.

He is weeping here for the money of the French.
    'I saw,' you can say, 'him of Duera,
    down there where sinners are put to cool.'

If any one asks about the others here,
    you have beside you the one of Beccheria
    whose throat was cut by Florence.   120

Gianni de' Soldanier, I believe,
    is farther on, with Ganelon, and Tebaldello
    who opened Faenza while it was sleeping."

---

[68]Antenor was a Trojan who, according to medieval legend, betrayed his city to the Greeks. He is treated favorably in Homer's *Iliad*.

We now see a bestial example of hatred. One shade is gnawing the head of another, as Tydeus, after being mortally wounded by Menalippus whom he in turn killed, called for the head of his enemy and chewed on it. Aghast at such a sight, Dante wonders what could motivate such hatred and offers to help in the vengeance by making the reason for it known in case there is just cause.

We had already departed from him
  when I saw two frozen in one hole,
  so that the head of one was a hood for the other,

and as bread is chewed from hunger,
  so the one on top set his teeth in the other
  where the brain joins the neck.

Not otherwise did Tydeus gnaw
  in his rage the temples of Menalippus
  than he did this one's skull and flesh.   132

"O you who show by such bestial signs
  hatred of him whom you are chewing,
  tell me why," I said, "on this condition

that if you rightfully complain of him,
  knowing who you are and his sin,
  I may repay you up in the world

if that [tongue] with which I speak is not dried up [by death]."

CANTO XXXIII

COUNT UGOLINO

Count Ugolino, a Pisan, had allied himself with the Florentine Guelfs and in 1285 was in control of his city. Perhaps he is among the traitors because of this change of party and because of the transfer of certain castles. In that year the Ghibellines, led by the Archbishop Ruggieri, revolted. Ugolino was called treacherously to a parley, then imprisoned with two sons and two grandsons in what was later known as the "Tower of Hunger." After some months the door of the prison was nailed shut, and the five were left to die of starvation. The bodies, on their removal, appeared mutilated, perhaps rat-bitten. Ugolino recognizes Dante as a Florentine, therefore a Guelf, and explains why he is violating so terribly the obligations of a neighbor.

The sinner raised his mouth from his fierce repast,
  wiping it on the hair of the head
  the back of which he had despoiled,

and then began, "You wish that I renew
  desperate grief, which wrings my heart,
  merely in thinking of it, before I speak.

But if my words can be seeds to bear infamy
  to the traitor I am gnawing,
  you will see me both speak and weep.

I do not know who you are, nor by what means
　　you have come down here, but certainly
　　you seem a Florentine when I hear you.　　　　　　　　12

You must understand that I was Count Ugolino,
　　and this is the Archbishop Ruggieri;
　　now I will tell you why I am such a neighbor.

How, as the result of his evil thoughts,
　　I was seized, trusting in him,
　　and put to death, there is no need to tell,

but what you cannot have learned, that is,
　　how cruel my death was, you will hear
　　and know if he has offended me.

> *As in the Francesca episode, so here Dante reconstructs what could not be known,
> that is, the lonely, unwitnessed death of the five in prison. In the tower (com-
> pared to a "mew" in which falcons were kept while molting) several months had
> passed when a symbolic and prophetic dream revealed to the prisoners their fate.
> In describing it, Ugolino's fierce memory gets ahead of his words: the wolf becomes
> "a father" and the whelps "sons," and he turns on Dante, reproaching the poet
> for lack of feeling before he has told what happened.*

A little loophole in the mew which
　　because of me was called the 'Tower of Hunger'
　　and in which others will be imprisoned　　　　　　　24

had shown through its opening several moons already
　　when I had the evil dream
　　which tore away the veil of the future.

This one seemed the lord and master of the hunt,
　　chasing the wolf and whelps on the mountain
　　which prevents the Pisans from seeing Lucca.

With lean, eager, and well-trained hounds [the mob],
　　he had placed the Gualandi, Sismondi,
　　and Lanfranchi [as leaders] in front of him.

After a short course, the father and the sons
　　seemed to me weary, and I thought I saw
　　their bodies torn by the sharp teeth.　　　　　　　　36

When I had awakened before the dawn
　　I heard my children who were with me
　　weeping in their sleep and asking for bread.

You are cruel indeed not to grieve already
　　in thinking of what my heart foreboded;
　　and if you do not weep now, by what are you ever moved?

> *The drama passes in silence: almost nothing is said. On the first day Anselm,
> the smallest, showed concern for his father. On the second, Ugolino bit his hands
> from grief. That and the third day passed in complete silence. On the fourth,*

Gaddo weakened and died, and on the fifth and sixth, the others. On the seventh, Ugolino crawled over the bodies, and on the eighth, he succumbed, hunger having accomplished what grief could not do.

The hatred of Ugolino is communicated to Dante who bursts out in an invective against Pisa.

They were now awake, and the hour drew near
    when our food used to be brought to us,
    and each was afraid because of his dream;

and below I heard the door of the horrible tower
    nailed up; whereupon, without saying a word,
    I looked into the faces of my sons.   48

I did not weep, so stony did I become within.
    They cried, and my little Anselm said,
    'You look so [hard], father, what ails you?'

Still I shed no tears nor did I answer
    during all that day and the night after,
    until another sun came forth upon the world.

When a little light had entered
    the awful prison, and I saw
    on four faces my own aspect,

I bit both my hands from grief,
    and they, thinking I did it from hunger,
    suddenly got up and said,   60

'Father, it will be much less painful
    if you eat of us; you clothed us
    with this poor flesh; may you take it from us!'

I became quiet then not to make them more sad.
    That day and the next we all remained mute.
    Ah, hard earth, why did you not open!

After we had reached the fourth day,
    Gaddo fell stretched out at my feet, saying,
    'Father, why don't you help me?'

There he died; and as you see me
    I saw the three of them fall one by one
    between the fifth day and the sixth; then I began,   72

already blind, to crawl over each, and for two days
    I called them after they were dead.
    Then fasting did more than grief."[69]

When he had said this, with eyes awry,
    he seized again the wretched head with his teeth
    which gnawed upon the bone, like a dog's.

---

[69] This line can mean that hunger could make him die as grief could not or else that Ugolino was driven to cannibalism.

Ah, Pisa! shame of the people.
  of the beautiful land [Italy] where "si" ["yes"] is heard,
  since your neighbors are slow to punish you,

may the Capraia and Gorgona [islands] move
  and make a dam for the Arno at its mouth,[70]
  so that it may drown everyone in you;   84

for if Count Ugolino was reputed
  to have betrayed you of the castle,
  you should not have put his sons on such a cross.

Their young age made Uguccione
  and Brigata innocent, you modern Thebes![71]
  and the other two named by my song.

> *The poets move on to Tolomea, the third division, where traitors to guests are
> punished. The heads of these sinners are thrown back, so that the tears, freez-
> ing in the cups of their eyes, cause a painful pressure.*

We went farther on to where the frost
  roughly binds another people
  with faces thrown back, not turned down.

Weeping there prevents them from weeping:
  the tears which find a barrier in the eyes
  turn inward to increase the pain,   96

since they form a solid mass,
  and like visors of crystal fill
  the whole cavity beneath the eyebrows.

And, although, as in a callused spot,
  every feeling had gone from my face
  because of the intense cold,

already I seemed to notice a wind,
  so that I said, "Master, what causes this?
  Is not all vapor [atmospheric change] absent down here?"

And he to me, "Soon you will be
  where your eyes will see the cause
  of the blast and will give you the answer."   108

And one of the wretches in the cold crust
  shouted at us, "O souls so cruel
  that the last place is assigned to you,

take from my eyes the hard veils,
  so that I may relieve the pain a little
  that stuffs my heart before the tears freeze again."

> *To induce this soul to speak, Dante makes a promise with false intent, that is,
> he commits fraud, as previously in this circle he had committed violence. Our*

---

[70] Pisa is at the mouth of the river Arno.
[71] Thebes was considered the most wicked of the ancient cities.

poet is emphasizing again, in opposition to certain idealists, that golden rules and codes of honor presuppose a certain uniformity in the social group. To apply them without discrimination is merely to favor and give superior survival value to the fraudulent and dishonorable.

The soul whom Dante has tricked had had guests murdered at a banquet, the signal for the execution being, "Bring on the fruit." He is now getting expensive dates for cheap figs, that is, being repaid with interest. His soul, apparently, has descended "quick" into Hell, and is replaced in his body by a demon.

And I to him, "If you want me to help you,
    tell me who you are, and if I do not relieve you,
    may I go to the bottom of the ice!"[72]

He answered then, "I am Friar Alberigo,
    he of the fruit of the evil garden,
    and am getting here dates for my figs."   120

"Oh," I said to him, "are you dead already?"
    And he to me, "How my body fares
    in the world above, I have no knowledge.

Such an advantage this Tolomea[73] has
    that often a soul falls into it
    before Atropos [a Fate] has thrust it forth.

And—so may you remove more willingly
    the frozen tears from my face—
    know that when a soul betrays as I did,

its body is taken from it by a demon
    who afterward controls the flesh
    until its allotted years have passed.   132

It falls into such a cistern as this,
    and perhaps the body of the shade
    wintering behind me appears on earth.

You must know him if you have just come down;
    He is Ser Branca d'Oria [a Genoese], and many years
    have passed since he was thus locked up."

"I believe that you are deceiving me,"
    I said to him, "for Branca d'Oria has not died,
    but eats and sleeps and puts on clothes."

"In the ditch of the Malebranche above,"
    he said, "where the tenacious pitch is boiling,
    Michel Zanche [his victim] had not yet arrived   144

when a devil took over his body
    and that of a close relative
    who did the treacherous act with him.

[72] Dante must in any event go beneath the ice, because that is the way out of Hell; see the next canto.
[73] Probably named for Ptolemy, a soldier of Jericho who in 1 Maccabees 16 murders several of his relatives whom he invited to a banquet.

But reach out your hand, open my eyes";
    and I did not open them for him;
    and to be rude to him was fitting.

Ah, Genoese, men who are estranged
    from all good ways and full of all corruption,
    why are you not scattered from the earth,

for, with the worst spirit of Romagna [Alberigo],
    I found one of you whose soul
    for his deeds already bathes in Cocytus,   156

and in body seems still alive on earth!

CANTO XXXIV

Satan

To the first words of a Latin hymn to the cross, "The banners of the Lord come forth, . . ." Dante adds the word inferni, *applying them thus to Satan, the lord of Hell. Dante is now in Giudecca where traitors to benefactors are completely submerged in the ice.*

Satan is represented as the counterpart of the Trinity, with heads of three colors, yellow, black, and red, standing for impotence, ignorance, and hate, and corresponding to the divine power, wisdom, and love. His three pairs of wings send forth a threefold blast which freezes Cocytus. In the mouths of Lucifer are Judas, the traitor to Christ, and Brutus and Cassius, traitors to the Roman Empire. The poets reach Satan at six o'clock on Saturday evening, having spent twenty-four hours on the journey.

"*Vexilla Regis prodeunt inferni*
    toward us, therefore, look ahead,"
    my master said, "and try to discern him."

As, when a thick mist covers the land
    or when night darkens our hemisphere,
    a windmill, turning, appears from afar,

so now I seemed to see such a structure;
    then because of the wind, I drew back
    behind my guide, for there was no other protection.

Already—and with fear I put it into verse—
    I was where the shades are covered in the ice
    and show through like bits of straw in glass.   12

Some were lying, some standing erect,
    some on their heads, others on their feet,
    still others like a bow bent face to toes.

When we had gone so far ahead
    that my master was pleased to show me
    the creature [Lucifer] that once had been so fair,

he stood from in front of me, and made me stop,
   saying, "Behold, Dis![74] Here is the place
   where you must arm yourself with courage."

How faint and frozen I then became,
   do not ask, Reader, for I do not write it down,
   since all words would be inadequate.   24

I did not die and did not stay alive:
   think now for yourself, if you have the wit
   how I became, without life or death.

The emperor of the dolorous realm
   from mid-breast protruded from the ice,
   and I compare better in size

with the giants than they do with his arms.
   Consider how big the whole must be,
   proportioned as it is to such a part.

If he were once as handsome as he is ugly now,
   and still presumed to lift his hand against his Maker,
   all affliction must indeed come from him.   36

Oh, how great a marvel appeared to me
   when I saw three faces on his head!
   The one in front [hatred] was fiery red;

the two others which were joined to it
   over the middle of each shoulder
   were fused together at the top.

The right one [impotence] seemed between white and yellow;
   the left [ignorance] was in color like those
   who come from where the Nile rises.

Under each two great wings spread
   of a size fitting to such a bird;
   I have never seen such sails on the sea.   48

They had no feathers, and seemed
   like those of a bat, and they flapped,
   so that three blasts came from them.

Thence all Cocytus was frozen.
   With six eyes he wept, and over his three chins
   he let tears drip and bloody foam.

In each mouth he chewed a sinner with his teeth
   in the manner of a hemp brake,[75]
   so that he kept three in pain.

---

[74] Satan. (Dis, or Pluto, was the ancient god of the Underworld.)
[75] A machine for crushing stalks of hemp.

To the one in front the biting was nothing
    compared to the scratching, for at times,
    his back was stripped of skin.   60

"The soul up there with the greatest punishment,"
    said my master, "is Judas Iscariot. His head
    is inside the mouth, and he kicks with his legs.

Of the other two whose heads are down,
    the one hanging from the black face is Brutus;
    see how he twists and says nothing.

The other who seems so heavy set is Cassius.[76]
    But night is rising again now,
    and it is time to leave, for we have seen all."

> *At the center of the earth, also the center of gravity, the poets turn and begin
> climbing laboriously, the effort symbolizing the difficulty of getting rid of bad
> habits even when their ugliness is known. Lucifer now appears upside down,
> and the time changes to Saturday morning, since the travelers gain twelve hours
> in passing from Jerusalem time to that of Purgatory, directly opposite.*
>
> *Through the passage made by Lucifer as he fell, the poets reach the foot of Purgatory
> just before dawn on Easter Sunday.*
>
> *Each part of the Comedy ends with the word "stars," which stand for the goal
> of the journey, the objects farthest removed from Satan and the materialism of
> the earth, and whose beauty is most ethereal.*

When my guide was ready, I embraced his neck,
    and he took advantage of the time and place
    so that when the wings were wide open   72

he caught hold of the shaggy sides
    and descended from tuft to tuft
    between the tangled hair and the frozen crust.

When we were at the place where the thigh
    revolves on the swelling of the haunches,
    my guide, with effort and with difficulty,

turned his head to where he had had his feet,
    and grappled the hair, like one mounting,
    so that I thought he was returning into Hell.

"Hold fast, for by such stairs,"
    my master said, panting like one weary,
    "we must depart from so much evil."   84

Then he came through the opening in a rock
    and put me on its edge, sitting,
    and climbed toward me with wary steps.

---

[76] The place of Brutus and Cassius, the assassins of Julius Caesar, at the center of Hell is a
surprise to modern readers accustomed to think of them as heroic opponents of tyranny. But
to Dante they were traitors to the Roman Empire (in the person of Caesar), the agency of
earthly rule that properly counterweighs spiritual authority (Christ through the papacy).

I raised my eyes and thought
  that I would find Lucifer as I had left him,
  but saw him holding up his legs,

and if I then became perplexed,
  let dull people imagine who do not see
  what the point was that I had passed.

"Get up on your feet," said my master,
  "the road is long and the path rough, and already
  the sun has returned to mid-tierce [at 7:30 A.M.]." 96

The place where we were
  was no palace hall, but a natural dungeon,
  dark and with an uneven floor.

"Before I uproot myself from the abyss, Master,"
  I said when I was standing,
  "speak to me a little to dispel my error.

Where is the ice? and how is Satan planted
  so upside down? and how in such a short time
  has the sun made its way from evening to morning?"

And he to me, "You still imagine you are
  on the other side of the center where I grasped the hair
  of the wicked monster that pierces the world. 108

You were over there as long as I descended;
  when I turned, you passed the point
  to which all weights are drawn.

Now you have arrived in the hemisphere
  opposite that which dry land covers
  and at whose summit [Jerusalem] was consumed

the man [Christ] who was born and lived without sin.
  You have your feet on a little circle
  which forms the other face of Giudecca.[77]

Here it is morning when it is evening there,
  and Satan who made a ladder for us
  with his hair is still as he was before. 120

On this side he fell from Heaven, and the earth here,
  through fear, made a veil for itself
  of the sea, and came to our hemisphere,

and perhaps the land [Purgatory] which shows on this side,
  to flee from him, rushed up
  and left this passageway empty."[78]

---

[77] The innermost ring of the plain of ice; named for Judas.

[78] When Satan fell from Heaven into the southern hemisphere, the land there recoiled from him into the northern hemisphere; also, the land within the earth rushed back from him to form the island of Purgatory in the southern ocean, leaving empty the cavern through which Virgil and Dante emerge from Hell.

There is a place as remote
 from Beelzebub[79] as his tomb extends,
 not known by sight, but by the sound

of a little stream which descends in it
 along the hollow of a rock which it has eaten out
 with a slow and winding course."[80]   132

My guide and I started on that hidden way
 to return to the bright world,
 and, without caring for any rest,

we climbed, he first and I second,
 until I saw, through a round opening,
 the beautiful things that heaven bears,

and came forth to see again the stars.

OUTLINE OF PURGATORY

REGION	VICES	METHOD OF SUGGESTION	DISCIPLINES
Shore	[Excommunicated]		Waiting
Below gate	[Negligent]		Waiting
Ledge 1	Pride	Sculptures	Bending necks under heavy weights
Ledge 2	Envy	Voices	Practice in using other senses besides sight
Ledge 3	Anger	Visual and auditory imagery	Satiation with blindness of wrath
Ledge 4	Sloth	Recitation	Developing habit of speedy activity
Ledge 5	Avarice and Prodigality	Recitation	Satiation with living close to the ground
Ledge 6	Gluttony	Voices	Practice in abnegation
Ledge 7	Lust	Recitation	Purification by fire
The Earthly Paradise (Garden of Eden).			

NOTE: The suggestive treatment consists of constant contemplation of the "goads" and "checks," that is, beautiful examples of the opposite virtue and repulsive illustrations of the vice itself.

The first three vices are due to love of a bad object, the fourth to insufficient love, and the last three to disproportionate love.

[79] Here, another name for Satan.

[80] The stream is the river Lethe, which from Eden atop the mountain of Purgatory flows down to the center of the earth to join the four rivers of Hell, carrying with it the memory of the vices expiated in Purgatory. All evil, committed by the saved and the damned, thus comes to rest as dead weight, frozen and immobile, at the point of the universe farthest removed from God.

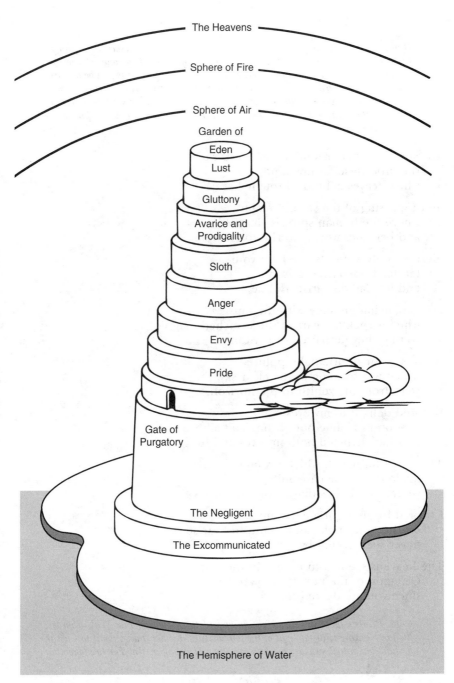

A diagram of Purgatory.

PURGATORY

CANTO I

CATO

*Dante indicates his new subject and invokes the "holy" Muses, especially Calliope,
the inspirer of epic poetry whom the daughters of King Pieros once challenged
in song, for which boldness they were changed into magpies. It is just before sunrise on Easter, April 10, 1300. The morning star, Venus, is obscuring with its
light the constellation of the Fishes. In the new sky are four stars representing
the cardinal virtues—Prudence, Temperance, Fortitude, and Justice[1]—previously
seen only by Adam and Eve.*

To move over better waters now hoists sail
   the little vessel of my mind
   which leaves behind so rough a sea;

and I will sing of the second realm
   where the human spirit is cleansed
   and becomes worthy to rise to Heaven.

Here, O holy Muses, since I am yours,
   let dead poetry be revived
   and let Calliope arise a while,

accompanying my song with the music
   which struck the ears of the wretched magpies
   so that they despaired of pardon.   12

A sweet color of oriental sapphire
   which was forming in the clear sky,
   pure from the zenith to the horizon,

restored delight to my eyes
   as soon as I came out of the dead air
   that had afflicted both my eyes and lungs.

The beautiful planet which prompts to love
   made the whole east smile,
   veiling the Fishes that escorted her.

I turned to the right and set my mind
   on the other pole, and I noticed four stars
   never seen except by the first people.   24

The heavens seemed to rejoice in their light.
   O region of the north, widowed!
   since you are denied that view.

*Cato, Dante's favorite hero of antiquity and the symbol of Free Will, appears,
his face shining with the light of the four virtues. Rather than submit to Caesar,
he had committed suicide, a Christian but not a pagan sin. For this devotion*

---

[1]Also called the "natural virtues" or "moral virtues."

*to freedom and for other merits he is made the guardian of Purgatory and will
be saved on Judgment Day.*[2]

When I had withdrawn my eyes from them,
    turning for a moment to the north
    where the Great Bear [Dipper] had already disappeared,

I saw a solitary old man near me,
    in semblance worthy of so much reverence
    than no son owes more to his father.

The beard he wore was long
    and streaked with white, like his hair
    of which two tresses fell upon his breast.   36

The rays of the four holy lights
    so brightened his face that he appeared
    as if the sun were shining on him.

"Who are you who, moving up the dark stream,
    have fled from the eternal prison?"
    he asked, shaking his plumelike beard.

"Who has guided you or given you a light
    to issue from the black night
    which darkens the infernal depth?

Are the laws of the abyss thus broken,
    or have decrees been changed in Heaven
    so that the damned may come to my cliffs?"   48

My guide then took hold of me,
    and with words and hands and gestures
    made reverent my knees and brow.

Then he answered, "By myself I do not come;
    a lady descended from Heaven, at whose prayers
    I helped this man with my companionship.

But, since it is your will that more
    of our present condition be explained,
    my will is not able to refuse you.

The man has not seen his last hour,
    but through his folly was so close to it
    that there was little time left.   60

I was sent to him, as I said,
    to rescue him, and there was no other way
    than this one on which I have started.

I have shown him all the wicked people
    and now propose to reveal those spirits
    who are purging themselves under your charge.

[2] There were two famous Romans named Cato. This one is Cato the Younger (95–46 B.C.).

How I have brought him here would take long to tell;
   a Power from above has helped me
   to bring him to see and to hear you.

May it please you to welcome his coming;
   he is seeking freedom, which is precious,
   as one who gives up life for it knows.   72

You understand, since death for you was not bitter
   in Utica where you left the clothing of your flesh
   which, on the great day, will be so bright.

The eternal laws are not broken by us,
   for this man lives, and Minos does not condemn me.
   I am from the circle where the chaste eyes

of your Marcia still seem to supplicate,
   O holy breast! that you hold her for your own.
   For love of her, then, incline toward us;

let us go through your seven kingdoms;
   I will tell her of your grace
   if you deign to be mentioned down there."   84

> *Cato states plainly his indifference to the fate of his wife, Marcia: the felicity of Heaven would be impaired if earthly relationships were not ended and if sorrow could be felt for the damned. He directs Virgil to gird Dante with a reed (Humility) and to wash his face, so that he can appear properly before the guardians of the ledges of Purgatory. The sun (Righteous Choice, Enlightenment) must be their guide henceforth.*
>
> *The two poets descend to the sea which Ulysses alone had sailed. There, the reed which Virgil plucks for Dante replaces itself. Humility cannot be defeated: the more it is crushed the more it grows.*

"Marcia pleased my eyes so much
   while I was yonder," he said then,
   "that I granted all the favors she asked.

Now that she dwells beyond the evil stream
   she cannot move me because of the law
   which was made when I came from there.

But if a lady from Heaven sends and commands you,
   as you say, there is no need for coaxing;
   it is enough that you ask me for her sake.

Go then and see that you gird this man
   with a slender rush, and that you bathe his face,
   so that all stains are washed from it,   96

for it would not be fitting that eyes
   darkened by any mist should meet
   the first minister of those in Paradise.

This little island, around its very base,
    where the waves beat upon it,
    bears reeds upon the soft mud.

No other plant which brings forth leaves
    or grows hard could exist there,
    since it would not yield to the waves.

Afterward do not return along here;
    the sun which is rising now will show you
    the easiest way to climb the mount."   108

Then he disappeared, and I got up
    without speaking and drew close
    to my guide, my eyes fixed on him.

He began, "My son, follow my steps,
    let us turn back, for from here
    the plain slopes down to its low bounds."

The dawn was dispelling the morning hour
    which fled before it, so that from afar
    I recognized the trembling of the sea.

We went over the solitary plain
    like men returning to the road they have lost
    who, until they get there, seem to walk in vain.   120

When we reached the place where the dew
    contends with the sun and
    in shaded spots had dried but little,

my master softly placed both hands
    spread out on the wet grass,
    and I, aware of his purpose,

held toward him my tear-stained cheeks
    on which he wholly restored the color
    which the smoke of Hell had hidden.

We came then to the deserted shore
    whose waters had never been sailed
    by anyone who afterward was able to return.   132

There he girded me, as another [Cato] wished.
    O marvel! for, as he plucked the humble plant,
    it was suddenly reborn as it was

in the place from which he had torn it.

CANTO II. *As a beautiful day dawns, a boat arrives at the island (the counterpart of Charon's boat at the border of Hell), bearing souls of the saved. One of the new arrivals is the musician Casella, an old friend of Dante's. Casella performs for Dante a song Dante himself had written, a fact that shows the survival among the saved of personal attributes they had in their former lives on earth. Cato rebukes the company for this delay, and they hasten toward the mountain of Purgatory.*

CANTO III. *At the foot of the mountain, unable to begin their ascent as yet, though they are eager to do so, are persons who died in the state of excommunication from the Church. This ecclesiastical penalty is observed in Purgatory but limited in its effect: the souls in question must delay their cleansing on the mount for a period thirty times as long as they lived excommunicated.*

CANTO IV. *Dante and Virgil pass through a fissure in the rock and make the arduous climb to the lowermost slope of the mountain. Dante is startled to see the sun to the north rather than (as in the northern hemisphere) to the south. Virgil comforts the exhausted Dante by telling him that the ascent becomes progressively easier as they climb the mountain. (This is because the burden of inclination to sin is progressively lightened.) They come upon another group of souls debarred as yet from Purgatory proper; these are the persons who repented only at the last minute, and they must delay their purgation for a period as long as they remained unrepentant in life.*

CANTO V. *Continuing up and around the mountain (which they must ascend counterclockwise), Dante and Virgil meet a group of late-repentant souls who were violently slain, including Jacopo del Cassero and a woman named Pia, who tells in a mere half-dozen lines a poignant story of death at her husband's hands. Here, as elsewhere in Purgatory, the souls are eager that the living pray for them, thus making their purgatorial process quicker and easier. Such mutual assistance and communication between the living and dead are part of the Dantean and Catholic understanding of the "communion of saints" mentioned in the Apostles' Creed.*

CANTO VI. *Virgil explains to Dante the nature of prayer—the fact, for example, that it does not deflect the divine will—but adds that a full explanation can come only from Christian revelation as embodied in Beatrice. At the mention of his beloved lady, Dante is excitedly eager to ascend. A cordial meeting between Virgil and Sordello, another man from Mantua, leads Dante to a sad comparison with the hatred and division that afflict the present cities of Italy, especially Florence.*

CANTO VII. *Virgil explains to Sordello, in a poignant passage, his own exclusion from salvation. Sordello explains to the two pilgrims that after sunset no one can ascend the mountain. He leads them to a peaceful valley where former monarchs who neglected the spiritual side of life must now delay their desired purgatorial discipline. In their fraternal amity, the rulers make a striking contrast with their former selves and many among the current generation of rulers.*

CANTO VIII. *Dante converses with some of the rulers, who, like other souls on the mountain, are astounded to learn that he still lives. The Valley, because it is outside Purgatory proper and therefore not immune to evil, is guarded by angels, who drive off an evil serpent that approaches. In the night sky are shining the three stars representing the "theological virtues" of faith, hope, and love. It is only during the day, however, when the four stars representing the moral virtues—prudence, justice, temperance, and fortitude—are above, that souls can ascend. This is a way of saying that the Purgatorial process leads essentially to natural rather than supernatural perfection.*

CANTO IX. *In sleep (his first since before the descent to Hell), Dante is borne upward by St. Lucia, to the outside of the gate of Purgatory proper. It is now morning, when ascent can take place. After ceremonially re-enacting the sacrament of Penance, or confession, Dante is admitted through the gate by the angel who guards it. On Dante's forehead the angel engraves seven P's standing for the seven capital sins (peccata). These will be erased, one by one, as Dante moves through the seven corresponding mountain ledges of Purgatory.*

CANTO X. *Being careful to observe the angel's command not to look back, Dante enters Purgatory proper and climbs upward with Virgil. They emerge on a terrace, some eighteen feet wide, its outer edge exposed dizzyingly to the sheer drop of the mountain wall. Here the vice of pride, which underlies all the others, is punished. The purgatorians must bend low under the weight of great stones they are carrying on their backs. On each terrace, "checks" and "goads" will appear, drawn from sacred and secular history. The checks are warnings about the vice punished; the goads are examples of the opposing virtue. On the terrace of pride, the goads consist of scenes, illustrating humility, carved on the inner wall.*

CANTO XI. *Dante must stoop down to converse with the proud souls. Thus, here as elsewhere in Purgatory, he participates in the discipline of suffering rather than simply observing it. Among the prideful is the painter Oderisi, who outlines the process by which new schools of painting and poetry (including Dante's own school) succeed one another. All will be superseded in turn, and therefore artists ought to feel no prideful sense of triumph. The same is true of military glory.*

CANTO XII. *On the ground the pilgrims walk upon are carved the checks: instances of proud behavior. The proud are thus brought low in contrast with the humble whose deeds are carved on the vertical inner wall. Before leaving the Terrace of Pride and climbing the stairs to the next terrace, Dante and Virgil meet an angel, who erases the first of the seven P's from Dante's brow, the incision of the other six P's thereby becoming shallower. The ascent will now become easier. A voice is heard quoting, from the gospel Beatitudes, the blessing on the poor in spirit. A corresponding angelic absolution and scriptural acclamation will recur on the other six terraces.*

CANTO XIII. *On the second terrace, of Envy, Dante meets souls whose eyelids are stitched shut, removing their perception of the beautiful and good things that they had once begrudged to others. They lean on one another in mutual dependency, and voices acclaim the virtue of generosity. Dante, in conversing with Sapia, one of the penitents, indicates that he too, after his death, will have to undergo this punishment, but only slightly compared with what he will have to suffer below, on the Terrace of Pride.*

CANTO XIV. *Another penitent, Guido del Duca, in response to Dante's apologetic reference to his birthplace on the Arno river, utters a scathing denunciation of the evil places the river passes through, notably Florence and Pisa. Voices sound in warning against the vice of envy.*

CANTO XV. *Guido had condemned humankind for fixing its attention on the things incompatible with partnership. Virgil explains to Dante the meaning of this cryptic statement: that, by being shared, material goods are diminished but spiritual goods are multiplied. The two reach the third terrace, of Wrath, where the souls are enveloped in smoke. In a vision that stuns him, Dante beholds instances of meekness.*

CANTO XVI. *As Virgil leads him, blinded, through the smoke, Dante hears the formerly wrathful souls singing harmoniously in praise of the Lamb of God. Dante meets Marco Lombardo, one of several purgatorians who condemn the degeneracy of the present world. In reply to Dante's question whether this degeneracy is due to stellar influence, or to the intrinsic degradation of life on earth, Marco indignantly rejects the determinism that those explanations would imply. He blames the evils of the times, rather, on the perversion of earthly rule caused by the Church's usurpation of temporal authority in addition to the spiritual authority that it rightfully exercises. Virgil and Dante approach the stair leading to the fourth terrace, of Sloth.*

CANTO XVII. *Dante and Virgil ascend the stairs to the circle of the Slothful, where silence reigns. Night falls, a time when ascent of the mountain is not allowed. Virgil takes this* opportunity to outline for Dante the scheme of Purgatory. Both the Creator and His creatures, Virgil explains, are moved by love. Sin arises when human reason distorts or misuses love. We cannot sin when we love what is inherently good, nor when we love secondary good in proper measure. When love takes the distorted form of rejoicing in our neighbor's ills, the results are pride, envy, and anger, the vices punished on the lower slopes of Purgatory. When we fail to pursue the highest good with sufficient zeal, the result is sloth, the vice punished on the fourth terrace. When we pursue in excessive or disproportionate ways the things that, while innocent, are not the supreme goods, the results are avarice (along with its twin opposite, prodigality), gluttony, and lust, which are purged on the three uppermost slopes. (This explanation takes place at the very midpoint of the poem, halfway through its middle section.)

CANTO XVIII.   In reply to Dante's further questioning, Virgil explains that love is the motive power of acts both good and evil. The mind is drawn toward a loved object, inclines toward it, and desires the fruition of desire through union with what is loved. No determinism is involved, since human reason has the power to reject specious good. Dante, about to fall asleep, is startled by a band of slothful spirits rushing by, eager to redeem their slothfulness even at night, when other creatures are at rest. Dante finally falls asleep.

CANTO XIX.   In the night Dante has another dream, this time of the Siren who represents the excessive indulgence in sensory pleasure. In accord with the scheme Virgil has outlined, the sensual vices will be cleansed on the next three terraces. Virgil, in the dream, strips the Siren, revealing the vileness that underlies her attractions. He and Dante climb to the fifth terrace, of the avaricious and prodigal. Penitents afflicted with these vices are lying face down, forced thus to confront their overattachment to the earth-bound senses. Dante now learns, from Pope Adrian V, that souls in Purgatory can skip terraces if they are free from the vices punished there. Dante kneels in reverence to the pope but is told by him not to do so; such earthly honors are no longer payable to individuals in the afterlife.

CANTO XX.   Dante hears praises of generosity and poverty from one of the souls lying prone, who proves to be the progenitor of the line of French kings. (The contrary warnings against avarice are recited at night.) The many evils perpetrated by this royal house are denounced. Dante is frightened into haste by a sudden violent tremor, as of an earthquake, and from the whole mountain rises a loud cry in praise of God.

CANTO XXI.   The explanation for the loud noise is provided by a spirit traveling upward whom the two pilgrims meet: it is a cry of exultation, given by the spirits on the mountain when one of their number has completed his or her penance and is ready to ascend to the earthly paradise atop the mountain. Each soul judges for itself, he explains, when it has sufficiently completed its purgation on the mount, that is, when impulse and desire coincide. The newcomer proves to be the ancient Roman poet Statius, who speaks with great admiration of Virgil, who had influenced him. He has not yet recognized that he is in the very presence of that Virgil, but the truth comes out when Dante's amusement prompts Statius's curiosity. When Statius learns the truth, he tries to kiss his poetic master's feet, spirits though they both are.

CANTO XXII.   As the three men leave the fifth terrace, Virgil expresses surprise that so noble a soul as Statius should have been guilty of avarice but is informed by Statius that he was guilty rather of prodigality, which is punished in the same circle. Statius adds that he owes his freedom from avarice, and indeed his very salvation, to his having read Virgil, who, through his eclogue prophesying the birth of a wondrous child, led Statius to the Christian faith. Virgil is compared to a man who walks in darkness, carrying a lantern that lights the way for those who follow but not for himself. Virgil, in turn, describes the position, in Limbo, of himself and of other ancient poets and worthies. Entering the Terrace of Gluttony, the travelers see a great fruit tree, sprayed with water from a fall nearby. From the tree comes a voice citing examples of abstinence.

CANTO XXIII. *Dante sees the formerly gluttonous purgatorians, now emaciated by the tantalizing prospect of the tree and of others like it around the ledge. Their penitential suffering brings them joy, however. Dante meets his old friend Forese Donati, who condemns the immoral dress of the Florentine women. Dante explains how he was delivered by Beatrice and Virgil from the worldliness in which he and Forese had formerly been immersed.*

CANTO XXIV. *Among the emaciated souls is Bonagiunta da Lucca, a poet from the old school superseded by that of Dante, with its* dolce stil nuovo, *"sweet new style." Dante explains its principle as stressing the truth in beautiful things rather than beautiful expression for its own sake. Bonagiunta approves this advance over the earlier poetic manner. From within another tree resembling the first one, a growth from the fatal tree in Eden, voices proclaim warnings against gluttony. Passing the angel of the circle, who emits a dazzling brightness and sweet odor, the three pilgrims leave the sixth terrace.*

CANTO XXV. *Dante is puzzled by the fact that bodily emaciation can be suffered by the souls they have just seen, although these souls have left their earthly bodies behind them. Virgil hints at an answer but must defer to Statius, who outlines to Dante the process of human embryology and God's inbreathing of the soul into the developing human being after it has passed the stages of lower plant and animal life. At death, this soul survives and renews its capacity for sense experience by projecting from itself an immaterial body. The travelers have now reached the seventh terrace, of the lustful; here fires burn around the terrace, forcing the three men to walk at its extreme outer edge. From within the flames are heard voices praising chastity.*

CANTO XXVI. *A group of purgatorians moving in the same direction as the pilgrims encounters another group, this one made up of former sodomites, moving in the other direction; both groups cry out warning examples of lust. All these sufferers remain within the flames, but Dante is able to talk with Guido Guinicelli, to whom he pays ardent tribute as the founder of his school of poetry. The troubador poet Arnaut Daniel, the foremost of the Provençal poets, is also honored and introduced. The implication is that poets, as singers of love, are especially prone to the vice of lust purged away on this terrace.*

CANTO XXVII. *Dante, Virgil, and Statius must now pass through a band of fire in the circle of the lustful. Dante is terrified, but Virgil gives him strength and courage by reminding Dante of his beloved, Beatrice. After they pass through the fire, night falls and takes away their power to move on. In his sleep Dante has a visionary dream, of Leah (symbol of the active life) and Rachel (symbol of contemplation). Virgil announces to Dante that he, Dante, has now reascended to the state of human perfection represented by Eden; his will is now purified and he has attained the condition of perfect freedom, no longer in need of direction from without. No longer subject to institutions, Dante is crowned and mitered, made his own king and bishop.*

CANTO XXVIII. *Dante now enters the fresh and fragrant Garden of Eden. On the other side of a stream he sees a beautiful young woman, Matilda, who embodies the spirit of the place. The dazzle of her laughing eyes as she looks at Dante are a voucher of the sweet and innocent love of Eden. She explains that Eden is above and free from earthly weather and that its two streams are derived directly from God, not from ordinary sources. One of the streams, Lethe, makes humans forget their past sins; the other stream, Eunoë, makes them remember their good deeds. Matilda suggests that the reality of Eden was the source of the pagan poets' half-true conceptions about a Golden Age. Virgil and Statius, themselves poets of antiquity, respond smilingly.*

CANTO XXIX. *Witnessing the landscape of Eden, Dante feels indignation at the sin that deprived humanity of so blissful a state. He sees approach a magnificent allegorical pageant, which Virgil is no longer capable of elucidating: seven candlesticks streaming colors (the gifts of the spirit); twenty-four elders (books of the Old Testament); four beasts (the Gospels); the Chariot of the Church, drawn by a griffon (Christ, with his two natures, human and divine); seven dancers (the three theological, or evangelical, virtues and the four cardinal, or moral, virtues); seven more elders (the remaining New Testament sources, namely Paul and the author of Acts; the four authors of other epistles; and the author of Revelation). The procession halts as a peal of thunder rings out.*

CANTO XXX

THE COMING OF BEATRICE (REVELATION)

The candlesticks are compared to the Septentrion, the constellation that contains the North Star. When they stop, all those in the procession turn expectantly toward the chariot of the Church which is to bring Beatrice (Revelation) to Dante (Mankind). At a call, angels hover over it, and within a rain of flowers that veil her, Beatrice appears, dressed in the colors of the three evangelical virtues. At this climactic moment, Latin phrases occur frequently, among them a line from the Aeneid *(Manibus o date lilia plenis!), spoken by an angel as the last and supreme compliment to Virgil, who must now disappear, eclipsed. Dante feels the effect of Beatrice's presence as he had on earth, and in his distress turns to Virgil. But his former guide, denied the sight of Revelation, has already disappeared, and Dante is left alone before the overwhelming spectacle to accomplish the painful but necessary rites of contrition, confession, and satisfaction (penance).*

When the Septentrion of the first heaven—
    which never knew rising or setting
    nor the veil of any mist except of sin

and which made everyone there aware
    of his duty, as the lower star does
    him who turns the helm to come to port—

had stopped, the true people who had come
    between it and the griffon[3]
    turned to the chariot as to their peace.

And one of them, as if sent from Heaven,
    cried three times in song *"Veni, sponsa, de Libano,"*[4]
    and all the others sang after him.   12

As the blessed, at the last trumpet call,
    will rise quickly from their graves,
    singing with regained voices "Hallelujah,"

so, above the divine vehicle
    a hundred [angels] rose *(ad vocem tanti senis)*[5]
    the ministers and messengers of eternal life.

---

[3]A beast with an eagle's head and wings and a lion's body.
[4]"Come with me from Lebanon, my spouse" (Song of Solomon 4:8). Allegorically, the line represents Christ's greeting to the Church.
[5]"At the voice of so great an elder."

All cried, *"Benedictus qui venis,"*[6]
  and scattering flowers above and around,
  "Manibus o date lilia plenis!"[7]

I have often seen at the beginning of the day
  the eastern sky all rosy, the rest
  of the heavens beautifully clear,   24

and the sun's face appear veiled,
  so that, through the tempering of the vapors,
  the eyes could look steadily at it.

Thus, within a cloud of flowers,
  thrown by angelic hands, which rose
  and fell on and around the chariot,

underneath a white veil, crowned with olive,
  a lady appeared to me, under a green mantle,
  dressed in the color of living flame.

And my spirit which already had spent
  so long a time without the trembling
  from awe which her presence caused,   36

without seeing her more clearly,
  through a hidden influence which came from her,
  felt the great power of its old love.

As soon as on my eyes the great virtue fell
  which already had pierced me
  before I was out of childhood,[8]

I turned to the left with the expectation
  which a child has who runs to its mother
  when afraid or afflicted,

to say to Virgil, "Not a drop of blood
  unmoved is left in me;
  I recognize the signs of the old love!"[9]   48

But Virgil had left me without his company,
  Virgil, my beloved father, Virgil,
  to whom I gave myself up for my salvation;

nor could all that our ancient mother lost [Eden]
  keep my cheeks, cleaned with dew,
  from being darkened again by tears.

---

[6]"Blessed are you who come" (cf. Matthew 21:9). This is a slight variation on the acclamation of Christ at his entrance into Jerusalem.
  [7]"Oh, give lilies with full hands!"
  [8]When Dante first saw the earthly Beatrice, he was less than nine years old. She died in 1290, when she was twenty-four, Dante twenty-five.
  [9]This line is translated from Virgil's *Aeneid*, Book IV, where Dido tells her sister Anna that Aeneas has reawakened in her the symptoms of love after she thought she had banished it from her life.

Now Beatrice speaks, not in her role as a tender friend, but severely, as a min-
ister of the sacraments, calling Dante by his name (which appears here only),
since the confession to follow must be personal and, in a manner, signed. Dante
is paralyzed by this reception, but when the angels show sympathy for him, his
awakened self-pity and his distress grow until he bursts into tears. Thus the first
stage of the sacrament is accomplished.

"Dante, although Virgil is leaving,
    do not weep yet, do not weep yet,
    for you must cry for another wound!"

As an admiral, at the prow or stern,
    looks at those who man the other ships,
    and heartens them to their work,   60

so—when I turned at the sound of my name,
    which is recorded here from necessity—
    at the left side of the chariot

I saw the lady who at first appeared
    veiled under the angelic shower
    directing her eyes at me from beyond the stream,

although the veil descending from her head,
    wreathed with Minerva's leaves [the olive],
    kept her from being completely manifest.

Queenlike, stern in her bearing,
    she continued, like one who speaks
    while holding back the sharpest words.   72

"Look at me! I am indeed, I am indeed Beatrice.
    How did you dare to approach the mount?
    Did you not know that here man is happy?"

My glances fell down to the clear stream;
    but seeing myself in it, I turned them
    to the grass, such shame burdened my face.

As a mother at times seems cruel
    to her son, so she appeared to me,
    since the taste of stern pity is bitter.

Then she was silent, and the angels sang
    at once, "*In te, Domine, speravi,*"[10]
    but did not go beyond *pedes meos.*[11]   84

As snow on the living rafters [trees]
    of the back of Italy [the Apennines] congeals
    when blown and packed by Slavic winds,

---

[10]"In thee, O Lord, do I put my trust" (Psalm 31:1).
[11]"My feet." These words occur in verse 8 of the psalm; after this verse the tone changes
from trust and assurance to despondency.

then, melted, trickles down, if a breath comes
 from the land [Africa] without shadows,
 like fire melting a candle,

so was I without tears or sighs
 before those [angels] whose song is accompanied
 by the melodies of the eternal spheres;

but when I heard in their sweet notes
 their pity for me, more than if they had said,
 "Lady, why do you shame him so?"   96

the frost which had gripped my heart
 became breath and water, and with anguish
 through mouth and eyes came from my breast.

> *To prepare for the next stage, Beatrice tells how Dante, after her death, had devoted himself to the* donna pietosa *of the* Vita Nuova[12] *(profane philosophy), and to worldliness.*

She, still standing at the side
 of the chariot, then turned to address
 the angels who had shown pity for me.

"You watch in the eternal day,
 so that neither night nor sleep hides from you
 a step taken on the ways of the world;

therefore, my answer takes greater care
 that he, weeping over there, should understand,
 and that his sin and sorrow should be equal.   108

Not only by the operation of the great spheres
 which direct each seed to some end,
 according as the stars are conjoined,

but through the bounty of Divine Grace
 which has such high vapors for its rain
 that our sight cannot come close to them,

this man was such, potentially, in his young life
 that every good disposition
 might have come to marvelous fruition;

but the more vigor there is in the soil
 the more malignant and rank it becomes
 if uncultivated or sown with bad seed.   120

For a while I sustained him with my countenance,
 and showing my youthful eyes to him,
 I led him with me in the right direction.

---

[12] The *New Life,* a quasi-allegorical work by Dante in which his spiritual autobiography is traced in terms of his various loves. *Donna pietosa* means "compassionate lady."

As soon as I was on the threshold
    of my second age, and changed life,
    he abandoned me, and gave himself to others.

When I had risen from flesh to spirit
    and beauty and virtue had increased in me,
    I was less dear to him and less esteemed,

and he turned his steps on an evil path,
    following false images of good
    which never fulfill their promise.   132

Nor did it avail me to invoke inspirations
    by which, in dreams and otherwise,
    I recalled him, so little did he care.

He fell so low that all means
    for his salvation would have been unavailing
    except to show him the lost people.

Therefore, I visited the portal of the dead,
    and to the one who brought him here,
    in sorrow I addressed my request.

The high decrees of God would be broken
    if Lethe were crossed and such a draught
    were tasted without any payment   144

of the penance that causes tears to flow."

CANTO XXXI

CONFESSION AND SATISFACTION
Beatrice now addresses Dante directly.

"O you beyond the sacred stream,"
    she continued without pausing,
    directing the point of her speech toward me

which even with the edge had seemed sharp,
    "say, say if this is true; to this accusation
    your confession must be joined."

My senses were so confused
    that my words began and were spent
    before released from their organs.

She waited a moment, then, "What are you thinking?"
    she questioned. "Answer me, for your sad memories
    are not yet impaired by the water [of Lethe]!"   12

Confusion and fear joined together
    sent forth such a "yes" from my mouth,
    that eyes were needed to hear it.

As a crossbow under too great a tension
    breaks both the string and the bow,
    so that the shaft hits its mark with less force,

so I burst under my heavy burden,
    pouring forth tears and sighs,
    and my voice died away on its passage.

Then she said, "In your desires for me [Revelation]
    which led you to love the good
    above which there is none to aspire to,   24

what chains or what hindering pitfalls
    did you find that you should lose
    the hope of going onward?

And what comforts or what advantages
    were displayed in the aspect of another good
    that you should seek it?"

After heaving a bitter sigh,
    scarcely had I voice for an answer,
    and my lips only with effort formed it.

Sobbing I said, "The present things,
    with their false pleasures, turned my steps away
    as soon as your face was hidden."   36

And she, "If you were silent or denied
    what you confess, your sin would not be concealed,
    known as it is by such a judge.

But when confession bursts
    from one's own mouth, the grindstone in our court
    turns back against the edge [of the sword of Justice].

Still to make you bear more shame
    for your error, and to make you stronger
    another time if you hear the sirens,

put aside your sowing of tears and listen,
    and you will hear how, when my flesh was buried,
    I should have led you in the opposite direction.   48

> *Beatrice refers again to the* pargoletta *(young girl). Then, by telling Dante to
> lift his "beard" instead of "chin," she points out indirectly that he is no child
> and should know better. Overcome by remorse, Dante falls in a faint, in this way
> giving "satisfaction," and accomplishing the last stage of the sacrament.*

Never did nature or art offer such delight
    as the fair members in which I was once enclosed
    and which are now in dust and scattered,

and if the supreme pleasure failed you
    at my death, what mortal thing
    should have drawn you with desire?

At the first shaft of fallacious things
 you should have lifted yourself up,
 following me, no longer [fallacious] like them.

No young girl or other vanity of such brief use
 should have weighed down your wings
 and exposed you to more blows. 60

A young bird takes two or three chances;
 but before the eyes of a full-grown one,
 the net is spread and the arrow shot in vain."

As children mute from shame stand listening,
 with their eyes on the ground,
 conscience-stricken and repentant,

so I stood; and she continued, "Since by hearing
 you suffer, lift up your beard,
 and you will have greater grief in looking."

With less effort a sturdy oak
 is uprooted by a wind of ours
 or by one from Iarbas' land [Libya] 72

than my chin was lifted at her command;
 and when by "beard" she meant my chin,
 I knew the venom of the argument.

Then when my face was raised,
 I saw the primal creatures [angels]
 resting from their scattering of flowers.

And my eyes, still insecure,
 saw Beatrice turned toward the beast
 which is one in two natures.

Under her veil and beyond the stream
 she seemed to surpass her former self
 more than she did others when on earth. 84

The thorn of repentance so pierced me then
 that of all things, those that had made me
 love them most now became most hateful to me.

Such remorse stung my heart
 that I fell, vanquished; and what became of me,
 she knows who caused this.

When my heart gave back a sense
 of outward things, I saw the lady [Matilda]
 above me, saying, "Hold to me, hold to me!"

She had drawn me into the river up to my throat,
 and pulling me behind her, moved on
 as lightly as a little boat over the water. 96

When I was near the sacred shore, *"Asperges me,"*[13]
    I heard so sweetly that I cannot keep the sound
    in mind, much less describe it.

The fair lady opened her arms,
    took my head, and held it down
    until I swallowed the water.

> *Matilda now takes Dante to the four nymphs (Prudence, Temperance, Fortitude, and Justice). These point out the deeper vision of the evangelical virtues (Faith, Hope, and Love) and bring Dante to the griffon (Christ), which he sees reflected in its twofold unity in the eyes of Revelation.*

Then she drew me forth, and led me, bathed,
    to the dance of the four nymphs,
    each of whom covered me with her arms.

"Here we are nymphs, and in Heaven stars.
    Before Beatrice came to the world
    we were ordained for her as handmaids.   108

We will lead you to her eyes; but the three
    over there who gaze more deeply
    will sharpen yours better for the light in them."

Thus they began to sing, and then took me
    with them to the breast of the griffon
    where Beatrice stood, turned toward us.

They said, "See that you do not spare your eyes;
    we have placed you before the jewels
    from which Love once shot his arrows."

A thousand desires hotter than flames
    bound my sight to the shining eyes
    which still were fixed upon the griffon.   120

As the sun in a mirror, not otherwise
    did the twofold creature shine in them,
    now with one, now with the other nature.

Think, Reader, if I marveled
    when I saw the object remain still
    and yet change in its image.

While full of joy and wonder, my soul
    tasted that [spiritual] food which,
    satisfying, gives hunger for itself;

showing themselves of a higher order
    by their actions, the other three [Virtues] advanced,
    dancing to their angelic measure.   132

---

[13]"Thou shalt sprinkle me" (King James Version "purge me") "with hyssop, and I shall be clean" (Psalm 51:7).

"Turn, Beatrice, turn your holy eyes,"
    was their song, "to your faithful one
    who, to see you, has taken so many steps!

Do us the favor of unveiling for him
    your smile, so that he may discern
    the second beauty which you conceal."

O splendor of the living, eternal light [of Beatrice]!
    who has become so pale in the shade of Parnassus,[14]
    or drunk so deeply at its well,

that he would not seem to have a clouded mind
    in trying to describe you as you appeared
    when the harmonious heavens alone veiled you,   144

and you disclosed yourself in the open air?

> CANTO XXXII. *Dante is temporarily blinded by the sight of Beatrice. When he recovers, he and Statius follow as the procession moves to the tree of the knowledge of good and evil, which represents civic obedience and the authority of the Empire, or civil state. The griffon pays tribute to the tree, and, in a gesture symbolic of the ideal fraternal equality of ecclesiastical and civil authority, the pole of the chariot of the Church is bound to the tree. Dante is overcome by sleep; when he awakens, the pageant has disappeared, leaving him with Beatrice and the representatives of the seven virtues. He is granted a vision of the tragic perversions that will afflict the church and the state.*

> CANTO XXXIII. *Beatrice hints at the coming of a political savior, but Dante fails to understand her. In consideration of his still-darkened mind, she promises to speak henceforth less enigmatically. Dante, with Statius, drinks from the fountain of Eunoè, which restores the memory of all good things as Lethe had obliterated the memory of evil ones. Now, in the full brightness of noonday, Dante is ready to leave Earth and ascend to the stars.*

OUTLINE OF PARADISE

The Correspondences

PLANETS, HEAVENS	LIGHT	POSITION	PHYSICAL CHARACTERISTICS	WEAKNESS OR STRENGTH
1. Moon	Pearly		Changing phases, spots	Weakness in Faith
2. Mercury	Veiled, eclipsed by sun	Within shadow of earth	Smallness	Weakness in Hope
3. Venus	Color of flame		Double center of motion	Weakness in Love
4. Sun	White		Brightness	Strength in Prudence
5. Mars	Red	Beyond shadow of earth	Redness	Strength in Fortitude
6. Jupiter	Silvery		Temperate quality	Strength in Justice

[14] The mountain sacred to Apollo and the Muses.

Outline of Paradise *(continued)*

The Correspondences

7. Saturn	Crystal (cold)	Along	Cold, ascetic	Strength in Temperance
8. Fixed Stars	Various	Golden Ladder	Variable	
9. Primum Mobile	Diaphanous		Diaphanous	
10. Empyrean				

The Correspondences

PLANETS, HEAVENS	SOULS REPRESENTED	SUBJECTS DISCUSSED	DENUNCIATIONS
1. Moon	Inconstant nuns	Vows	Ill-advised vows
2. Mercury	Lovers of earthly fame	Incarnation, atonement	Guelfs and Ghibellines
3. Venus	Sensual lovers	Heredity	Mercenary ecclesiastics
4. Sun	Theologians	God expounded in his creatures	Mendicant orders
5. Mars	Warriors of Faith	Decay of virility	Effeminacy of Florence
6. Jupiter	Just Rulers	Justice	Unjust rulers
7. Saturn	Monks	Predestination	Luxury and pomp of prelates
8. Fixed Stars	Apostles	Faith, Hope, Love	Unworthy popes
9. Primum Mobile		Angels	Popular preachers
10. Empyrean		[Beatific Vision]	Rejection of Henry VII

The Correspondences

PLANETS, HEAVENS	ANGELS	ANGELIC FUNCTION	HIERARCHIES	EARTHLY REPRESEN-ATIVES
1. Moon	Angels	Messengers to individuals		
2. Mercury	Archangels	Messengers to nations	Purifying	Deacons
3. Venus	Principalities	Guides of princes		
4. Sun	Powers	Subject to God		
5. Mars	Virtues	Divine motion	Illuminating	Priests
6. Jupiter	Dominations	Dominion		

OUTLINE OF PARADISE *(continued)*

The Correspondences

7. Saturn	Thrones	Stability			
8. Fixed Stars	Cherubim	Knowledge	}	Perfecting	Bishops
9. Primum Mobile	Seraphim	Love			
10. Empyrean					

Empyrean

Empyrean

Empyrean

Primum Mobile

Fixed Stars

Saturn

Jupiter

Mars

Sun

Venus

Mercury

Moon

Fire

Air · Water · Air

Earth

Fire

The Heavens.

PARADISE

CANTO I. *Dante prays for inspiration at the outset of his account of the third, celestial region. Following Beatrice's example, he gazes at the sun, so that his earthly nature is mystically transformed. Enrapt, he rises and hears the harmonies of heaven. Puzzled that he and Beatrice have left the earth and equally puzzled how they can ascend against gravity, Dante learns from his guide that they have now reached the point where ascent is the natural mode of motion, in accord with the proper affinity of perfected humanity with the divine.*

CANTO II. *Dante warns the reader of the immensity and profundity of the subject matter that is to follow. He and Beatrice reach the moon. Dante asks whether the dark patches on it are caused by their relatively low density. Beatrice demonstrates on scientific grounds that this explanation cannot be correct and then provides the true explanation: that the power of God, filtered through the guiding angelic intelligences, manifests itself more or less fully and brightly in the various parts of the material creation.*

CANTO III. *In the sphere of the moon, Dante becomes aware of faintly visible human features, so that at first he thinks they are mere reflections. They are in fact human souls, manifested in this lowest of heavens because they belong to the lowest order of the saved. But Dante learns from one of them, Piccarda, that "in His will is our peace"; every soul is perfectly happy to accept the lot accorded it by God.*

CANTO IV. *Dante is puzzled by two things: since the inconstant nuns were forced into inconstancy, why should this diminish their heavenly glory? and does their appearance in the sphere of the moon indicate that Plato was correct in saying that human souls come from and return to the planets? Beatrice answers the first question by explaining that acquiescence cannot be fully exonerated even when it is forced. To his second question she replies that the souls of the saved all reside with God in the Empyrean heaven and are revealed to Dante in the lower heavens simply to manifest their spiritual conditions.*

CANTO V. *In reply to a question about vows, Beatrice explains that they must always be kept but that in some cases substitutions can be made for the thing vowed. Vows can never be altered where, as in monastic vows, no equivalent can be substituted. As for vows that are wrong in themselves, to keep them would simply magnify the original evil of making them. Dante and Beatrice now reach the heaven of Mercury, where they encounter spirits once tainted with ambition. One of these is the sixth-century Roman emperor and lawgiver Justinian.*

CANTO VI. *Justinian tells of his conversion to Christian orthodoxy and outlines the history of the Roman empire, the political entity that Dante would like to see restored to its proper authority. The former emperor champions the values of peace, law, and self-sacrifice and condemns factional divisions.*

CANTO VII. *Beatrice outlines to Dante the dynamic of salvation. Fallen humanity, whose form the incarnate Jesus took on, was punished through his crucifixion for the sins of Eden. Dante is unsure why redemption had to take this form. Beatrice explains that humanity, after the Fall, could have been redeemed by God's free pardon but not by human efforts in themselves, since humanity was incapable of going down low enough to atone for the height to which it had sinfully aspired. Rather than forgive humanity outright, which would have been the way of mercy alone, God chose to fulfill both of his modes, "mercy and truth," forgiving but allowing humanity, through Jesus, to contribute something toward its own redemption. Beatrice further explains the difference between natural bodies, whose creation God entrusted to the angels, and the primal direct creations of God: the angels, the heavens, the bodies of Adam and Eve before they sinned.*

CANTO VIII. *In the heaven of Venus, Dante and Beatrice encounter souls who in life were especially given to amorous pursuits but have converted their carnal impulses to heavenly love. Carlo Martello, who was king of Hungary and whom Dante knew, speaks with him. Dante asks him why it is that noble family lines sometimes produce base offspring. Carlo replies that all human capacities are fitted for some valuable function in the world and that these capacities are not inherited but instilled by the heavens. Society brings out the worst in people by assigning roles according to hereditary station that ought to be assigned according to inherent merit.*

CANTO IX. *In other conversations with souls in the heaven of Venus, Dante hears further denunciations of corruption, especially in Florence and the Papacy. He learns too that after reaching Heaven the saved feel no repentance for past sins, which are now seen to have been occasions for God's saving forgiveness. But we are given to understand that the degree of bliss enjoyed by the souls in these lower heavens is limited owing to the vices that stained them on earth.*

CANTO X. *Dante and Beatrice rise to the fourth heaven, of the Sun, where the theologians are manifested. The sun being now near the equinox, Dante points out to the reader that the degree of tilt of the earth's axis in relation to the ecliptic is divinely ordained for the best effect. The theologians, rejoicing in the doctrine of the Trinity, stand out in their brightness even against the sun. Dante raptly contemplates the idea of God, but his trance is broken by his awareness of the enhanced beauty of Beatrice's smile (which becomes more and more dazzling as they ascend). From a circling crown of twelve theologians who surround Dante, St. Thomas Aquinas, the greatest of medieval theologians, emerges to talk with him and introduce the other souls.*

CANTO XI. *St. Thomas, who belonged to the Dominican religious order, recites the history of and praises St. Francis of Assisi, founder of the other great medieval order, dwelling especially on Francis' marriage with poverty. Thomas deplores the degeneracy of the monks.*

CANTO XII. *A second circle surrounds the first one, circling it in an effect like that of twin rainbows. From this second circle St. Bonaventure, a Franciscan, emerges to reciprocate St. Thomas' gesture and praise St. Dominic, upholder of truth and orthodoxy and founder of the Dominicans. Bonaventure too deplores the deterioration of monastic orders.*

CANTO XIII. *Thomas Aquinas solves a problem of interpretation for Dante, namely how to reconcile the attribution of supreme wisdom to Solomon with the attribution of perfect knowledge to the new-created Adam and to Christ. After outlining the way in which God's creative power is manifested diversely in His creatures, Thomas distinguishes royal wisdom—the kind Solomon possessed—from wisdom and knowledge in general. Thomas warns Dante, through this example, of the dangers of facile inferences, a danger to which philosophy and theology are all too prone.*

CANTO XIV. *Even before he puts it into words, Beatrice becomes aware of a problem puzzling Dante: will not the restoration of the body to the souls of the saved after the Last Judgment reimpose on them the burdens of flesh? The answer is given by Solomon: the complete human being includes body as well as soul, and when the two are ultimately united, the saved will both feel greater joy and be better able to love and serve God. The perfected body will not suffer from the limitations it now endures in earthly life. Dante and Beatrice pass into the sphere of Mars, where a white cross appears against the background of the red planet. Souls move rapidly along the surface of the cross, joyfully singing. These are the warriors of the faith.*

CANTO XV. *From the warriors appearing as lights on the cross in the heaven of Mars, one moves from it quickly and joyfully to accost Dante. He greets him with the joy Anchises, in the Sixth Book of Virgil's* Aeneid, *showed his son Aeneas when the latter visited Anchises in the realm of the dead. He identifies himself as Dante's great-great-grandfather, Cacciaguida, and describes the small town Florence was in earlier times. There he was born and lived before becoming a Crusader.*

CANTO XVI. *Dante is overcome both by humility toward his ancestor and by pride in his lineage. Cacciaguida contrasts the small and still-uncorrupted Florence of his day with what it has since become, describing in detail the vicissitudes of the old families and mourning the afflictions of the city.*

CANTO XVII. *On several occasions earlier in the* Comedy, *Dante had heard dire hints of calamity in his future. Cacciaguida, after explaining how his foreknowledge is consistent with free will, spells out plainly the sad future Dante has in store: his false indictment by Florence for the very acts of treachery that the city itself is guilty of; his impoverished and increasingly isolated exile; the hospitality that he will receive and be dependent on. But Cacciaguida bids Dante to have hopeful courage, to believe in his eventual vindication, and to publish his vision with unmitigated truthfulness.*

CANTO XVIII. *Dante, after musing on what his ancestor has told him, is recalled to awareness by Beatrice's beauty. Cacciaguida identifies some of the warriors appearing on the cross, after which Dante and his guide ascend to the heaven of Jupiter, the keynote of which is justice. Here spirits arrange themselves so as to spell out an appropriate biblical verse; the last letter re-forms as the eagle symbolic of Roman law. The perversion of law and justice in the world, especially by the Papacy, is lamented.*

CANTO XIX. *The souls that form the eagle are the just monarchs, who speak in unison. The heaven of justice seems the fitting place for Dante to explore his troubled doubts about the justice of excluding the righteous pagans from salvation. The kings answer by praising the justice of God, the Being who gives meaning to the very notion of justice, as beyond the comprehension and judgmental capacity of His creatures. They reaffirm that faith in Christ is necessary for salvation but then, intriguingly, declare that many heathens will be closer to God after the Last Judgment than some of those who are nominally Christians.*

CANTO XX. *The voice of the eagle names certain of the greatest souls there represented. Among those named are Ripheus the Trojan, a minor character whom Virgil, in the* Aeneid, *had praised as eminently just; and the pagan Roman emperor Trajan. That these pagans should have been saved, apparently in contravention of the doctrine that such is impossible, astonishes Dante and causes him to rejoice. Ripheus and Trajan, it is explained, were given visions of Christ to come or Christ having come in the past. The implication is that such revelations may have been made to others who are ordinarily considered outside the pale of salvation. Only God, it is revealed, knows which human beings are saved.*

CANTO XXI. *Beatrice and Dante rise to the heaven of Saturn, the realm of mystical contemplation. A replica of Jacob's ladder in Genesis extends down from above, and on it descend souls in light. Approached by one of them, the monk Peter Damiani, Dante inquires why Peter in particular has been singled out by God to address him. Peter replies that such individual particularities of Providence constitute a mystery even to the spirits in heaven. A former cardinal, Peter denounces the worldliness of high-ranking Church officials.*

CANTO XXII. *Dante has heard an outcry from the spirits, which, Beatrice explains to him, is a harbinger of divine vengeance. St. Benedict, the founder of Western monasticism, approaches Dante, who asks if he may see the saint in his full glory. Benedict replies that that will be accomplished in the Empyrean heaven beyond the realm of space and time. He too denounces the corruption of the monastic orders but holds out hope for their regeneration. The souls are swept up again out of sight, after which Dante and Beatrice rise to the heaven of the fixed stars. He gazes down at the heavens he has passed and at Earth, which appears tiny and insignificant.*

CANTO XXIII. *Dante experiences the stupendous vision of Christ amid the saved, a vision that stuns him into unconsciousness. When he comes to himself, however, his vision has been fortified by the sight, so that he is empowered to see the full beauty of Beatrice also, which is inexpressible in words. Christ having withdrawn in consideration of Dante's vulnerability, Dante gazes on the Virgin Mary and the Apostles. Mary is crowned by the angel Gabriel, and she too is lifted up beyond Dante's sight.*

CANTO XXIV. *As part of his preparation for the ultimate visions, Dante is examined, by St. Peter, on the nature and content of faith. As the foundation of faith, and of the existence of faith within him, Dante cites Scripture and the historical occurrence of miracles. He defines God first in terms of Aristotelian metaphysics and then in terms of the Trinity of which humankind learns by divine revelation.*

CANTO XXV. *Having passed the examination in faith, Dante is examined on hope, by St. James the Apostle. Beatrice vouches for the presence of hope in Dante, as the very virtue that has brought him to the vision of the heavens. To James' direct queries about the nature of hope Dante replies in terms of Scriptural definition; the content of his hope he centers on the resurrection of the body and the immortality of the soul. Dante having passed this second test, St. John appears in the midst of impenetrable light. Dante is told that he cannot see John's body, since only Jesus and his mother Mary have been bodily assumed into Heaven.*

CANTO XXVI. *Blinded by the glory of John, Dante is examined by him on the third of the theological virtues: love. After testifying to the power of love instilled in him by Beatrice, he declares God to be the comprehensive object of all love. Dante identifies the love of good with the love of God, citing both Aristotle and Scripture. He declares that God is to be loved both in Himself and because of His goodness to humankind. His sight restored after passing the third test, Dante converses with Adam, who lovingly answers his questions about the Garden of Eden and the Fall.*

CANTO XXVII. *St. Peter angrily denounces the corruption of the Papacy, the office he was the first to hold, and the corrupt Pope Boniface VIII, charging Dante to relay this message of indignation to those on Earth. The spirits soar above, beyond sight. Dante again looks down toward Earth, seeing it lighted like a gibbous moon. He and Beatrice rise to the Primum Mobile (First Mover), the outermost of the spherical heavens and the realm from which everything spatial and temporal takes its origin. Beyond the Primum Mobile exists the unlocalized, timeless abode of God and the saved in eternity.*

CANTO XXVIII. *Dante now sees a vision of the adoration of God by the nine orders of angels. The vision consists of a single point of intense light, surrounded by nine revolving concentric circles, of which the innermost is both the brightest and the swiftest—that is to say, a model directly opposed to that of the nine physical heavens, of which the outermost is the most excellent. The unsearchable relationship of God to His creations can, then, be understood and represented through either of these opposite models.*

CANTO XXIX. *Beatrice explains to Dante that God created other beings not so as to enhance Himself but so that joyful consciousness might exist outside of His own consciousness. She explains some metaphysical truths about Creation—for example, that the question what God did before Creation is meaningless, since time itself is meaningful only in connection with created reality. She narrates briefly the fall of the Satanic party and, among other truths about the angels, declares that each of these innumerable beings is wholly individualized.*

CANTO XXX. *The angelic spectacle fades away. Now, as Beatrice attains an indescribable new intensity of beauty, she and Dante leave behind the world of time and space and enter the Empyrean heaven, where they will behold the eternal forms of the angels and of the human saved. A great flash of light strengthens Dante to see the vision of the blessed who are gazing on God Himself.*

CANTO XXXI. *The saved are seated in a vast amphitheater, in the form of a rose, their gazes fixed on God. Angels fly in the space between them and God but without blocking divine or human vision. Dante is overwhelmed by the contrast with the troubled life of people on earth. Turning to look at the transfigured Beatrice, Dante finds that she has left him, as Virgil did earlier, and has been replaced by St. Bernard, the representative of contemplative, or immediately intuitive, vision. Bernard will help Dante attain the ultimate vision of God. Dante pours out his love and gratitude toward Beatrice, now in her place among the blessed; she smiles at him once more and then turns toward God. Dante is given a vision of the glory of the Virgin Mary.*

CANTO XXXII. *Bernard explains to Dante the arrangement here of the saved. Dividing the rose-amphitheater into two facing halves is a vertical line or plane separating the saved who lived before Christ (Hebrews) from the saved who lived after him (Christians). Mary has the highest place among the Hebrews. The two sides of the rose will have equal numbers when the half reserved for the Christian era is finally filled. The lower ranks, in each half, consist of saved infants who did not live long enough to help earn their own salvation. Dante is instructed to look toward Mary, to prepare himself for the final, divine vision.*

CANTO XXXIII

THE BEATIFIC VISION
A prayer to the Blessed Virgin, later copied in great part by Chaucer, opens the final canto.

The stages of the Beatific Vision are, in ascending order, a comprehension of the world, a vision of the Trinity, and, as a final revelation, a view of the Incarnation.

"Virgin mother, daughter of thy son,
    humble and exalted more than any creature,
    goal established by Eternal Counsel,

thou art the one by whom human nature
    was so ennobled that its Maker
    did not disdain to become its creature.

Within thy womb was rekindled the love
    through whose warmth this flower
    has blossomed in eternal peace.

Here thou art for us a noonday torch
    of charity, and down below, among mortals,
    a living fount of hope.   12

My lady, thou art so great and so triumphant
    that whoever wants and does not turn to thee
    would have his desire fly without wings.

Thy benignity succors not only those
    who ask, but many times
    freely anticipates the request.

In thee is mercy, in thee pity,
    in thee magnificence, in thee whatever goodness
    can be found in creatures is resumed.

Now, this man who from the deep well
    of the universe up to here
    has seen the spiritual lives, one after another,   24

begs thee of thy grace for strength,
    so that he may lift his eyes
    still higher toward the ultimate salvation.

And I who never for my own sight longed more
    than I do for his, offer thee all my prayers,
    and may they not be insufficient,

in order that thou, through thine, mayst dispel
    every cloud of his mortality, so that
    the Supreme Pleasure may reveal Itself to him.

I pray thee further, O Queen! thou who canst do
    what thou wilt, that thou keepest
    his affection sound after so great a vision.   36

May thy protection overcome his human impulses.
    Behold Beatrice with so many of the blessed
    clasping their hands to aid my prayer."

The eyes [of Mary] venerated and beloved
    by God, fixed on him who prayed, showed
    how gratefully devout prayers are heard.

Then they turned to the Eternal Light into which
    we must not think any mortal vision,
    however clear, can ever penetrate so deeply.

And I who drew near to the goal
    of all desires, ended, as I ought,
    within myself, the ardor of my longing.   48

Bernard signaled to me and smiled
    so that I might look up, but I
    already had made myself as he wished.

For my sight, growing pure, penetrated
    ever deeper into the rays
    of the Light which is true in Itself.

From then on my vision was greater
    than our speech which fails at such a sight,
    just as memory is overcome by the excess.

As one who in a dream sees clearly,
    and the feeling impressed remains afterward,
    although nothing else comes back to mind,   60

so am I; for my vision disappears
    almost wholly, and yet the sweetness
    caused by it is still distilled within my heart.

Thus, in sunlight, the snow melts away;
    thus the sayings of the Sibyl,[1] written
    on light leaves, were lost in the wind.

---

[1]A prophetess (Virgil, *Aeneid*, Books III, VI) who inscribed her prophecies on the leaves of trees which were then scattered by the wind.

O Supreme Light that risest so high
    above mortal concepts, give back to my mind
    a little of what Thou didst appear,

and make my tongue strong,
    so that it may leave to future peoples
    at least a spark of Thy glory!   72

For, by returning to my memory
    and by sounding a little in these verses
    more of Thy victory will be conceived.

By the keenness of the living ray I endured
    I believe I would have been dazed
    if my eyes had turned away from it;

and I remember that I was bolder
    because of that to sustain the view
    until my sight *attained* the Infinite Worth.

O abundant grace through which I presumed
    to fix my eyes on the Eternal Light
    so long that I consumed my vision on it!   84

In its depths I saw contained, bound with love
    in one volume, what is scattered
    on leaves throughout the world—

substances [things] and accidents [qualities] and their modes
    as if fused together in such a way
    that what I speak of is a single light.

The universal form [principle] of this unity
    I believe I saw, because more abundantly
    in saying this I feel that I rejoice.

One moment obscures more for me than twenty-five centuries
    have clouded since the adventure which made Neptune
    wonder at the shadow of the Argo [the first ship].[2]   96

Thus my mind with rapt attention
    gazed fixedly, motionless and attentive,
    continually enflamed by its very gazing.

In that light we become such
    that we can never consent
    to turn from it for another sight,

inasmuch as the good which is the object
    of the will is all in it, and outside of it
    whatever is perfect there is defective.

---

[2] The voyage of Jason and the Argonauts was considered to have taken place in the thirteenth century B.C. Dante means that the world has forgotten since then less than he has forgotten of the divine vision.

Now my speech, even for what I remember,
    will be shorter than that of an infant
    who still bathes his tongue at the breast.   108

Not that more than a single semblance
    was in the living light I gazed upon
    (for it is always as it was before),

but in my vision which gained strength
    as I looked the single appearance,
    through a change in me, was transformed.

Within the deep and clear subsistence
    of the great light three circles of three colors
    and of one dimension [the Trinity] appeared to me,

and one [the Son] seemed reflected from the other [the Father]
    as Iris by Iris,[3] and the third [the Holy Spirit]
    seemed fire emanating equally from both.   120

O how poor our speech is and how feeble
    for my conception! Compared to what I saw
    to say its power is "little" is to say too much.

O Eternal Light [Father], abiding in Thyself alone,
    Thou [Son] alone understanding Thyself, and Thou [Holy Spirit]
    understood only by Thee, Thou dost love and smile!

The circle which appeared in Thee
    as a reflected light [the Son]
    when contemplated a while

seemed depicted with our image within itself
    and of its own [the Circle's] color,
    so that my eyes were wholly fixed on it.   132

Like the geometer who strives
    to square the circle and cannot find
    by thinking the principle he needs

I was at that new sight. I wanted to see
    how the [human] image was conformed
    to the [divine] circle and has a place in it,

but my own wings were not enough for that—
    except that my mind was illumined by a flash
    [of Grace] through which its wish was realized.

For the great imagination here power failed;
    but already my desire and will [in harmony]
    were turning like a wheel moved evenly   144

by the Love which turns the sun and the other stars.

---

[3] Twin rainbows (Iris being the goddess of the rainbow).

Sir Gawain and the Green Knight

(Late Fourteenth Century)

Romance, as a literary term, refers today to a kind of formulaic fiction about love affairs, written quickly, sold cheaply, and consumed thoughtlessly, as a pleasantly erotic diversion. It originally referred to something considerably less humble. The word *romance* was coined in the early Middle Ages to mean anything written in the popular languages (that is, the *Romance* languages). It soon narrowed, however, to refer to a particular kind of work in a popular language: a long narrative in prose or verse telling of the adventures of chivalric heroes, usually involving courtly love affairs and fanciful or supernatural creatures and incidents. The form persisted in England through the Elizabethan period, but in the seventeenth century, rationalistic critics began to regard it as a survival of a barbarous past, and the term began a slow slide into disreputability. That slide has continued, despite a brief rehabilitation during the Romantic period, until today a "romance" is generally a vulgar, subliterary work. Gradually, through this long history, the word *romance* divided and came to refer to love affairs as well as the books that described them, and so today we can have romances as well as read them. This process is perhaps a case of life imitating art; undoubtedly people would have fallen in love even if romances had never been written, but they probably would not have understood and described their feelings in the same way without the model of the romance.

Sir Gawain and the Green Knight marks the highest achievement in the romance tradition in England, at least among the romances that have survived. It is preserved in a single manuscript, along with three religious poems, *Pearl, Patience,* and *Purity,* in the same style and probably by the same anonymous poet, generally referred to as the *Pearl* poet or the *Gawain* poet. The poem was forgotten for more than four centuries, until it was rediscovered in the 1830s in the British Library. It was in a tiny manuscript measuring five by seven inches in what had once been the library of an Elizabethan book collector named Sir Robert Cotton.

The author of *Gawain, Pearl, Patience,* and *Purity* (and possibly another poem, a life of St. Erkenwald) was, on the evidence of the language and content of his poems, a contemporary of Chaucer. But while Chaucer was living and writing in London, the *Gawain* poet was working in the West Midlands, perhaps in Cheshire, about a hundred and fifty miles northwest of London. He (or conceivably she) wrote in a style very different from Chaucer's comparatively simple, straightforward mode, a style that preserved, or perhaps revived, the old alliterative style of Old English poetry. The basic line of *Sir Gawain* has four stressed syllables and a variable number of unstressed ones, divided by a caesura between the second and third stresses and linked by three identical initial sounds (*alliterations*), either identical consonants or any vowels. These lines are grouped in stanzas with varying numbers of lines, and each stanza ends with a "bob and wheel": a word or phrase of two syllables (the "bob") and a quatrain (the "wheel") rhyming *abab* with the bob (which establishes the *b* rhyme).

Thus *Gawain* begins (in Banks's translation, which uses the same verse form as the original):

1551

When the <u>s</u>iege and assault / / <u>c</u>eased at Troy, and the <u>c</u>ity
Was <u>b</u>roken, and <u>b</u>urned / / all to <u>b</u>rands and to ashes,
The <u>w</u>arrior who <u>w</u>ove there / / the <u>w</u>eb of his treachery
<u>T</u>ried was for <u>t</u>reason, / / the <u>t</u>ruest on earth.

After fourteen lines of this kind, the stanza is brought to an end with a bob and wheel:

> Doth found.
> War, waste, and wonder there
> Have dwelt within its bound;
> And bliss has changed to care
> In quick and shifting round.

The effect of this highly wrought, old-fashioned verse form is a combination of primitive simplicity (the stresses and alliterations recalling songs chanted to the harp) and a sophisticated complexity (the combination of alliteration and rhyme creating a high level of self-consciousness).

The story of *Sir Gawain and the Green Knight* exhibits the same sort of successful blending of seemingly disparate elements. It is made up of a combination of three ancient and widespread folk motifs: the Beheading Game, the Temptation by the Hostess, and the Exchange of Winnings. No precedent has been discovered for the ingenious combination of these three elements into a single plot.

A further and even more complex blending is the combination of the simple folk elements with a sophisticated and courtly code of chivalric ethics. Gawain, and by extension Arthur's court, are being tested in the romance for the degree to which they exemplify the quality of *courtesy*. *Courtesy* (and its adjectival form *courteous*) chime like a bell throughout the poem, in dozens of repetitions, and evoke the basic moral code of the story. It is a complex word and concept in its fourteenth-century context, very far from its trivial modern sense of "politeness" or "manners." *Courtesy* derives from *court* and refers to the values of the court. These are not merely aristocratic "courtliness" but amount, as D. S. Brewer has explained in a fine essay on "Courtesy and the Gawain-Poet," to an inclusive ideal of personal integrity, realized in benevolent speech and actions toward other people. It refers not only to moral virtues such as self-control, bravery, and cleanliness (although those are certainly included) but also to such matters as physical beauty, eloquence, politeness, and wit. For the *Gawain* poet, such qualities are not "natural," no matter how gentle one's birth, but the result of education, and Gawain at one point is tellingly referred to as "nurture's fine father" (1. 919). *Courtesy*, then, is nearly synonymous with "civilization," what people can achieve given the leisure and the opportunity.

The action of *Sir Gawain and the Green Knight* is, in a sense, a testing of courtesy. Arthur's court is famed as the flower of chivalric courtesy, but we have a sense at the beginning of the romance that the knights have become complacent and self-indulgent. The emphasis is much more on the fifteen-day feast—"All meat and all mirth that a man might devise"—than on the sterner virtues, and there is something of a sneer in the Green Knight's voice when he announces that "here, I have heard, is the highest of courtesy" (1. 262). And indeed only Arthur responds to the giant's challenge until the youthful Gawain saves the honor of the court by stepping forth. The encounter with the Green Knight, which seems at first to test only Gawain's courage, turns out to test his courtesy in ways he could never have foreseen. (Gawain's version of courtesy, though, it should be noted, does not include the often associated codes of "courtly love." He, unlike courtly lovers, respects the marriage vows, a fact that, literally, saves his neck.)

Ranged against the power of Gawain's courtesy, the product of civilization, is that of the Green Knight, who seems allied to nature in its more sinister aspects. Descending upon Arthur's court in the dead of winter, on New Year's Day, all green and carrying a holly bush, the Knight seems to embody the fertile powers of nature, especially when we later learn that his chapel is a mere hole in the ground. But if the Knight embodies nature, he does not do so in any simple or obvious way. He himself can mimic "courtesy" and charm us as well as Gawain does. It is not until we realize the unequal bargain that he has made with the mortal Gawain and his apparent motives for doing so, in collaboration with the inimical Morgan le Fay, that we remember that, charming or not, he is a demon out to discredit the Round Table and destroy its principal hero.

Sir Gawain and the Green Knight, of course, makes no claim to present medieval England as it really was. But as a charming fantasy of a chivalric ideal that never was, akin in its polished artificiality to contemporary manuscript illumination, it is one of the most accomplished literary achievements of medieval England.

FURTHER READING *(prepared by J.H.):* For background on the author of *Gawain,* see the introduction to *The "Pearl"-Poet: His Complete Works,* ed. and trans. Margaret Williams, 1967; on genre, see Gillian Beer, *The Romance,* 1970; and for the historical context, see Thorlac Turville-Petre, *The Alliterative Revival,* 1977. Charles Moorman has a good critical analysis of *Gawain,* along with ones of *Pearl, Patience,* and *Purity,* in *The "Pearl"-Poet,* 1968. Useful book-length studies include Larry D. Benson, *Art and Tradition in "Sir Gawain and the Green Knight,"* 1965, and Marie Borroff, *"Sir Gawain and the Green Knight": A Stylistic and Metrical Study,* 1962. Collections of critical essays include *"Sir Gawain" and "Pearl": Critical Essays,* ed. Robert J. Blanch, 1966; *Critical Studies of "Sir Gawain and the Green Knight,"* ed. Donald R. Howard and Christian K. Zacher, 1968; and *Twentieth-Century Interpretations of "Sir Gawain and the Green Knight,"* ed. Denton Fox, 1968. A good guide to criticism is *"Sir Gawain and the Green Knight": A Reference Guide,* comp. Robert J. Blanch, 1984.

SIR GAWAIN AND THE GREEN KNIGHT

Translated by Theodore Howard Banks, Jr.

I

When the siege and assault ceased at Troy, and the city
Was broken, and burned all to brands and to ashes,
The warrior who wove there the web of his treachery

Tried was for treason, the truest on earth.[1]
'T was Æneas, who later with lords of his lineage
Provinces quelled, and became the possessors
Of well-nigh the whole of the wealth of the West Isles.[2]
Then swiftly to Rome rich Romulus[3] journeyed,
And soon with great splendor builded that city,
Named with his own name, as now we still know it.   10
Ticius to Tuscany turns for his dwellings;
In Lombardy Langobard lifts up his homes;[4]
And far o'er the French flood fortunate Brutus
With happiness Britain on hillsides full broad
                                    Doth found.[5]
             War, waste, and wonder there
             Have dwelt within its bound;
             And bliss has changed to care
             In quick and shifting round.

    And after this famous knight founded his Britain,   20
Bold lords were bred there, delighting in battle,
Who many times dealt in destruction. More marvels
Befell in those fields since the days of their finding
Than anywhere else upon earth that I know of.
Yet of all kings who came there was Arthur most comely;
My intention is, therefore, to tell an adventure
Strange and surprising, as some men consider,
A strange thing among all the marvels of Arthur.
And if you will list to the lay for a little,
Forthwith I shall tell it, as I in the town   30
                                    Heard it told
             As it doth fast endure
             In story brave and bold,
             Whose words are fixed and sure,
             Known in the land of old.

    In Camelot[6] Arthur the King lay at Christmas,
With many a peerless lord princely companioned,
The whole noble number of knights of the Round Table;[7]
Here right royally held his high revels,

---

[1] Aeneas, the prince of Troy who is the hero of the *Aeneid*. He is said to have been tried for treason because the Greeks tried him for refusing to hand over his sister Polyxena to them.

[2] The countries of Western Europe. The poet imagines descendants of Aeneas founding a series of European nations.

[3] Romulus, legendary founder of Rome, is not ordinarily said to be of Trojan ancestry.

[4] Ticius is apparently a descendant of Aeneas who founded Tuscany; he is not mentioned elsewhere. Langobard is the legendary founder of Lombardy.

[5] Brutus, the great-grandson of Aeneas, is the legendary founder of Britain, the westernmost of the European nations supposedly founded by Aeneas and the "lords of his lineage."

[6] The legendary seat of Arthur's kingdom, sometimes said to have been near Winchester or in Wales.

[7] The table Arthur had built to accommodate one hundred knights, made round to avoid a hierarchy among the knights. Oddly enough, the table described in the poem is not round.

Care-free and mirthful. Now much of the company, 40
Knightly born gentlemen, joyously jousted,
Now came to the court to make caroles; so kept they
For full fifteen days this fashion of feasting,
All meat and all mirth that a man might devise.
Glorious to hear was the glad-hearted gaiety,
Dancing at night, merry din in the daytime;
So found in the courts and the chambers the fortunate
Ladies and lords the delights they best loved.
In greatest well-being abode they together:
The knights whose renown was next to the Savior's, 50
The loveliest ladies who ever were living,
And he who held court, the most comely of kings.
For these fine folk were yet in their first flush of youth
                    Seated there,
        The happiest of their kind,
        With a king beyond compare.
        It would be hard to find
        A company so fair.

And now while the New Year was young were the nobles
Doubly served as they sat on the dais, 60
When Arthur had come to the hall with his court,
In the chapel had ceased the singing of mass;
Loud shouts were there uttered by priests and by others,
Anew praising Noel, naming it often.
Then hastened the lords to give handsel,[8] cried loudly
These gifts of the New Year, and gave them in person;
Debated about them busily, briskly.
Even though they were losers, the ladies laughed loudly,
Nor wroth was the winner, as well ye may know.[9]
All this manner of mirth they made till meat time, 70
Then when they had washed, they went to be seated,
Were placed in the way that appeared most proper,
The best men above. And Guinevere, beautiful,
Was in the midst of the merriment seated
Upon the rich dais, adorned all about:
Fine silks on all sides, and spread as a canopy
Tapestries treasured of Tars and Toulouse,[10]
Embroidered and set with stones most splendid—
They'd prove of great price if ye pence gave to buy them
                    Some day. 80
        The comeliest was the Queen,
        With dancing eyes of grey.
        That a fairer he had seen
        No man might truly say.

---

[8] Token gifts given for luck on New Year's.
[9] Handsels were accompanied by kisses.
[10] Tars (Turkestan) and Toulouse (in southern France) were famous for their weavings.

But Arthur would eat not till all were attended;
Youthfully mirthful and merry in manner,
He loved well his life, and little it pleased him
Or long to be seated, or long to lie down,
His young blood and wild brain were so busy and brisk.
Moreover, the King was moved by a custom   90
He once had assumed in a spirit of splendor:
Never to fall to his feast on a festival
Till a strange story of something eventful
Was told him, some marvel that merited credence
Of kings, or of arms, or all kinds of adventures;
Or some one besought him to send a true knight
To join him in proving the perils of jousting,
Life against life, each leaving the other
To have, as fortune would help him, the fairer lot.
This, when the King held his court, was his custom   100
At every fine feast 'mid his followers, freemen,
                              In hall.
                    And so with countenance clear
                    He stands there strong and tall,
                    Alert on that New Year,
                    And makes much mirth with all.

    At his place the strong King stands in person, full courtly
Talking of trifles before the high table.
There sat the good Gawain by Guinevere's side,
And Sir Agravain, he of the Hard Hand, also,   110
True knights, and sons of the sister of Arthur.
At the top, Bishop Baldwin the table begins,
And Ywain beside him ate, Urien's son.
On the dais these sat, and were served with distinction;
Then many a staunch, trusty man at the side tables.[11]
The first course was served to the sharp sound of trumpets,
With numerous banners beneath hanging brightly.
Then newly the kettledrums sounded and noble pipes;
Wild and loud warbles awakened such echoes
That many a heart leaped on high at their melody.   120
Came then the choice meats, cates rare and costly,
Of fair and fresh food such profusion of dishes
'T was hard to find place to put by the people
The silver that carried the various stews
                              On the cloth.
                    Each to his best loved fare
                    Himself helps, nothing loth;
                    Each two, twelve dishes share,
                    Good beer and bright wine both.

---

[11] The high table is on a raised platform at one end of the room, and the side tables are
on the main floor along the walls at right angles to the high table.

And now I will say nothing more of their service, 130
For well one may know that naught there was wanted.
Now another new noise drew nigh of a sudden,
To let all the folk take their fill of the feast.
And scarcely the music had ceased for a moment,
The first course been suitably served in the court,
When a being most dreadful burst through the hall door,
Among the most mighty of men in his measure.
From his throat to his thighs so thick were his sinews,
His loins and his limbs so large and so long,
That I hold him half-giant, the hugest of men, 140
And the handsomest, too, in his height, upon horseback.
Though stalwart in breast and in back was his body,
His waist and his belly were worthily small;
Fashioned fairly he was in his form, and in features
                              Cut clean.
              Men wondered at the hue
              That in his face was seen.
              A splendid man to view
              He came, entirely green.

    All green was the man, and green were garments: 150
A coat, straight and close, that clung to his sides,
A bright mantle on top of this, trimmed on the inside
With closely-cut fur, right fair, that showed clearly,
The lining with white fur most lovely, and hood too,
Caught back from his locks, and laid on his shoulders,
Neat stockings that clung to his calves, tightly stretched,
Of the same green, and under them spurs of gold shining
Brightly on bands of fine silk, richly barred;
And under his legs, where he rides, guards of leather.
His vesture was verily color of verdure: 160
Both bars of his belt and other stones, beautiful,
Richly arranged in his splendid array
On himself and his saddle, on silken designs.
'T would be truly too hard to tell half the trifles
Embroidered about it with birds and with flies
In gay, verdant green with gold in the middle;
The bit-studs, the crupper, the breast-trappings' pendants,
And everything metal enamelled in emerald.
The stirrups he stood on the same way were colored,
His saddle-bows too, and the studded nails splendid, 170
That all with green gems ever glimmered and glinted.
The horse he bestrode was in hue still the same,
                              Indeed;
              Green, thick, and of great height,
              And hard to curb, a steed
              In broidered bridle bright
              That such a man would need.

This hero in green was habited gaily,
And likewise the hair on the head of his good horse;
Fair, flowing tresses enfolded his shoulders,   180
And big as a bush a beard hung on his breast.
This, and the hair from his head hanging splendid,
Was clipped off evenly over his elbows,
In cut like a king's hood, covering the neck,
So that half of his arms were held underneath it.
The mane of the mighty horse much this resembled,
Well curled and combed, and with many knots covered,
Braided with gold threads about the fair green,
Now a strand made of hair, now a second of gold.
The forelock and tail were twined in this fashion,   190
And both of them bound with a band of bright green.
For the dock's length the tail was decked with stones dearly,
And then was tied with a thong in a tight knot,
Where many bright bells of burnished gold rang.
In the hall not one single man's seen before this
Such a horse here on earth, such a hero as on him
                              Goes.
                    That his look was lightning bright
                    Right certain were all those
                    Who saw. It seemed none might   200
                    Endure beneath his blows.

Yet the hero carried nor helmet nor hauberk,[12]
But bare was of armor, breastplate or gorget,[13]
Spear-shaft or shield, to thrust or to smite.
But in one hand he bore a bough of bright holly,
That grows most greenly when bare are the groves,
In the other an axe, gigantic, awful,
A terrible weapon, wondrous to tell of.
Large was the head, in length a whole ell-yard,[14]
The blade of green steel and beaten gold both;   210
The bit had a broad edge, and brightly was burnished,
As suitably shaped as sharp razors for shearing.
This steel by its strong shaft the stern hero gripped:
With iron it was wound to the end of the wood,
And in work green and graceful was everywhere graven.
About it a fair thong was folded, made fast
At the head, and oft looped down the length of the handle.
To this were attached many splendid tassels,
On buttons of bright green richly embroidered.
Thus into the hall came the hero, and hastened   220
Direct to the dais, fearing no danger.
He gave no one greeting, but haughtily gazed,

---

[12] A long tunic of chain mail.
[13] A piece of armor defending the throat.
[14] An English ell-yard was forty-five inches.

And his first words were, "Where can I find him who governs
This goodly assemblage? for gladly that man
I would see and have speech with." So saying, from toe
                      To crown
        On the knights his look he threw,
        And rolled it up and down;
        He stopped to take note who
        Had there the most renown.   230

    There sat all the lords, looking long at the stranger,
Each man of them marvelling what it might mean
For a horse and a hero to have such a hue.
It seemed to them green as the grown grass, or greener,
Gleaming more bright than on gold green enamel.
The nobles who stood there, astonished, drew nearer,
And deeply they wondered what deed he would do.
Since never a marvel they'd met with like this one,
The folk all felt it was magic or phantasy.
Many great lords then were loth to give answer,   240
And sat stone-still, at his speaking astounded,
In swooning silence that spread through the hall.
As their speech on a sudden was stilled, fast asleep
                      They did seem.
        They felt not only fright
        But courtesy, I deem.
        Let him address the knight,
        Him whom they all esteem.

    This happening the King, ever keen and courageous,
Saw from on high, and saluted the stranger   250
Suitably, saying, "Sir, you are welcome.
I, the head of this household, am Arthur;
In courtesy light,[15] and linger, I pray you,
And later, my lord, we shall learn your desire."
"Nay, so help me He seated on high," quoth the hero,
"My mission was not to remain here a moment;
But, sir, since thy name is so nobly renowned,
Since thy city the best is considered, thy barons
The stoutest in steel gear that ride upon steeds,
Of all men in the world the most worthy and brave,   260
Right valiant to play with in other pure pastimes,
Since here, I have heard, is the highest of courtesy—
Truly, all these things have brought me at this time.
Sure ye may be by this branch that I bear
That I pass as in peace, proposing no fight.
If I'd come with comrades, equipped for a quarrel,
I have at my home both hauberk and helmet,

[15] Alight.

Shield and sharp spear, brightly shining, and other
Weapons to wield, full well I know also.
Yet softer my weeds are, since warfare I wished not;   270
But art thou as bold as is bruited[16] by all,
Thou wilt graciously grant me the game that I ask for
                              By right."
                    Arthur good answer gave,
                    And said, "Sir courteous knight,
                    If battle here you crave,
                    You shall not lack a fight."

    "Nay, I ask for no fight; in faith, now I tell thee
But beardless babes are about on this bench.
Were I hasped in my armor, and high on a horse,   280
Here is no man to match me, your might is so feeble.
So I crave but a Christmas game in this court;
Yule and New Year are come, and here men have courage;
If one in this house himself holds so hardy,
So bold in his blood, in his brain so unbalanced
To dare stiffly strike one stroke for another,
I give this gisarme,[17] this rich axe, as a gift to him,
Heavy enough, to handle as pleases him;
Bare as I sit, I shall bide the first blow.
If a knight be so tough as to try what I tell,   290
Let him leap to me lightly; I leave him this weapon,
Quitclaim it forever, to keep as his own;
And his stroke here, firm on this floor, I shall suffer,
This boon if thou grant'st me, the blow with another
                              To pay;
                    Yet let his respite be
                    A twelvemonth and a day.
                    Come, let us quickly see
                    If one here aught dare say."

    If at first he had startled them, stiller then sat there   300
The whole of the court, low and high, in the hall.
The knight on his steed turned himself in his saddle,
And fiercely his red eyes he rolled all around,
Bent his bristling brows, with green gleaming brightly,
And waved his beard, waiting for one there to rise.
And when none of the knights spoke, he coughed right noisily,
Straightened up proudly, and started to speak:
"What!" quoth the hero, "Is this Arthur's household,
The fame of whose fellowship fills many kingdoms?
Now where is your vainglory? Where are your victories?   310
Where is your grimness, your great words, your anger?

---

[16] Rumored.
[17] A medieval weapon consisting of an axhead on a long shaft, carried by foot soldiers.

For now the Round Table's renown and its revel
Is worsted by one word of one person's speech,
For all shiver with fear before a stroke's shown."
Then so loudly he laughed that the lord was grieved greatly,
And into his fair face his blood shot up fiercely
                              For shame.
              As wroth as wind he grew,
              And all there did the same.
              The King that no fear knew   320
              Then to that stout man came.

    And said, "Sir, by heaven, strange thy request is;
As folly thou soughtest, so shouldest thou find it.
I know that not one of the knights is aghast
Of thy great words. Give me thy weapon, for God's sake,
And gladly the boon thou hast begged I shall grant thee."
He leaped to him quickly, caught at his hand,
And fiercely the other lord lights on his feet.
Now Arthur lays hold of the axe by the handle,
As if he would strike with it, swings it round sternly.   330
Before him the strong man stood, in stature
A head and more higher than all in the house.
Stroking his beard, he stood with stern bearing,
And with a calm countenance drew down his coat,
No more frightened or stunned by the axe Arthur flourished
Than if on the bench some one brought him a flagon
                              Of wine.
              Gawain by Guinevere
              Did to the King incline:
              "I pray in accents clear   340
              To let this fray be mine."

    "If you now, honored lord," said this knight to King Arthur,
"Would bid me to step from this bench, and to stand there
Beside you—so could I with courtesy quit then
The table, unless my liege lady disliked it—
I'd come to your aid before all your great court.
For truly I think it a thing most unseemly
So boldly to beg such a boon in your hall here,
Though you in person are pleased to fulfil it,
While here on the benches such brave ones are seated,   350
Than whom under heaven, I think, none are higher
In spirit, none better in body for battle.
I am weakest and feeblest in wit, I know well,
And my life, to say truth, would be least loss of any.
I only since you are my uncle have honor;
Your blood the sole virtue I bear in my body.
Unfit is this foolish affair for you. Give it
To me who soonest have sought it, and let
All this court if my speech is not seemly, decide

Without blame."   360
The nobles gather round,
And all advise the same:
To free the King that's crowned,
And Gawain give the game.

   The King then commanded his kinsman to rise,
And quickly he rose up and came to him courteously,
Kneeled by the King, and caught the weapon,
He left it graciously, lifted his hand,
And gave him God's blessing, and gladly bade him
Be sure that his heart and his hand both were hardy.   370
"Take care," quoth the King, "how you start, coz,[18] your cutting,
And truly, I think, if rightly you treat him,
That blow you'll endure that he deals you after."
Weapon in hand, Gawain goes to the hero,
Who boldly remains there, dismayed none the more.
Then the knight in the green thus greeted Sir Gawain,
"Let us state our agreement again ere proceeding.
And now first, sir knight, what your name is I beg
That you truly will tell, so in that I may trust."
"In truth," said the good knight, "I'm called Sir Gawain,   380
Who fetch you this blow, whatsoever befalls,
And another will take in return, this time twelvemonth,
From you, with what weapon you will; with no other
I'll go."
The other made reply:
"By my life here below,
Gawain, right glad am I
To have you strike this blow.

   By God," said the Green Knight, "Sir Gawain, it pleases me—
Here, at thy hand, I shall have what I sought.   390
Thou hast rightly rehearsed to me, truly and readily,
All of the covenant asked of King Arthur;
Except that thou shalt, by thy troth, sir, assure me
Thyself and none other shalt seek me, wherever
Thou thinkest to find me, and fetch thee what wages
Are due for the stroke that to-day thou dost deal me
Before all this splendid assembly." "Where should I,"
Said Gawain, "go look for the land where thou livest?
The realm where thy home is, by Him who hath wrought me,
I know not, nor thee, sir, thy court nor thy name.   400
Truly tell me thy title, and teach me the road,
And I'll use all my wit to win my way thither,
And so by my sure word truly I swear."
" 'T is enough; No more now at New Year is needed,"
The knight in the green said to Gawain the courteous:

---

[18] "Cousin," a term of endearment.

"If truly I tell when I've taken your tap
And softly you've struck me, if swiftly I tell you
My name and my house and my home, you may then
Of my conduct make trial, and your covenant keep;
And if no speech I speak, you speed all the better: 410
No longer need look, but may stay in your land.
                    But ho!
          Take your grim tool with speed,
          And let us see your blow."
          Stroking his axe, "Indeed,"
          Said Gawain, "gladly so."

    With speed then the Green Knight took up his stand,
Inclined his head forward, uncovering the flesh,
And laid o'er his crown his locks long and lovely,
And bare left the nape of his neck for the business.   420
His axe Gawain seized, and swung it on high;
On the floor his left foot he planted before him,
And swiftly the naked flesh smote with his weapon.
The sharp edge severed the bones of the stranger,
Cut through the clear flesh and cleft it in twain,
So the blade of the brown steel bit the ground deeply.
The fair head fell from the neck to the floor,
So that where it rolled forth with their feet many spurned it.
The blood on the green glistened, burst from the body;
And yet neither fell nor faltered the hero,   430
But stoutly he started forth, strong in his stride;
Fiercely he rushed 'mid the ranks of the Round Table,
Seized and uplifted his lovely head straightway;
Then back to his horse went, laid hold of the bridle,
Stepped into the stirrup and strode up aloft,
His head holding fast in his hand by the hair.
And the man as soberly sat in his saddle
As if he unharmed were, although now headless,
                    Instead.
          His trunk around he spun,   440
          That ugly body that bled.
          Frightened was many a one
          When he his words had said.

    For upright he holds the head in his hand,
And confronts with the face the fine folk on the dais.
It lifted its lids, and looked forth directly,
Speaking this much with its mouth, as ye hear:
"Gawain, look that to go as agreed you are ready,
And seek for me faithfully, sir, till you find me,
As, heard by these heroes, you vowed in this hall.   450
To the Green Chapel go you, I charge you, to get
Such a stroke as you struck. You are surely deserving,
Sir knight, to be promptly repaid at the New Year.

As Knight of the Green Chapel many men know me;
If therefore to find me you try, you will fail not;
Then come, or be recreant[19] called as befits thee."
With furious wrench of the reins he turned round,
And rushed from the hall-door, his head in his hands,
So the fire of the flint flew out from the foal's hoofs.
Not one of the lords knew the land where he went to,   460
No more than the realm whence he rushed in among them.
                    What then?
            The King and Gawain there
            At the Green Knight laughed again;
            Yet this the name did bear
            Of wonder among men.

    Though much in his mind did the courtly King marvel,
He let not a semblance be seen, but said loudly
With courteous speech to the Queen, most comely:
"To-day, my dear lady, be never alarmed;   470
Such affairs are for Christmas well fitted to sing of
And gaily to laugh at when giving an interlude,
'Mid all the company's caroles, most courtly.
None the less I may go now to get my meat;
For I needs must admit I have met with a marvel."
He glanced at Sir Gawain, and gladsomely said:
"Now sir, hang up thine axe; enough it has hewn."
O'er the dais 't was placed, to hang on the dosser,
That men might remark it there as a marvel,
And truly describing, might tell of the wonder.   480
Together these two then turned to the table,
The sovereign and good knight, and swiftly men served them
With dainties twofold, as indeed was most fitting,
All manner of meat and of minstrelsy both.
So the whole day in pleasure they passed till night fell
                    O'er the land.
            Now take heed Gawain lest,
            Fearing the Green Knight's brand,
            Thou shrinkest from the quest
            That thou hast ta'en in hand.   490

                            II
    This sample had Arthur of strange things right early,
When young was the year, for he yearned to hear boasts.
Though such words when they went to be seated were wanting,
Yet stocked are they now with hand-fulls of stern work.
In the hall glad was Gawain those games to begin,
But not strange it would seem if sad were the ending;
For though men having drunk much are merry in mind,
Full swift flies a year, never yielding the same,

---

[19] Coward or traitor.

The start and the close very seldom according.
So past went this Yule, and the year followed after, 500
Each season in turn succeeding the other.
There came after Christmas the crabbed Lenten,
With fish and with plainer food trying the flesh;
But then the world's weather with winter contends;
Down to earth shrinks the cold, the clouds are uplifted;
In showers full warm descends the bright rain,
And falls on the fair fields. Flowers unfold;
The ground and the groves are green in their garments;
Birds hasten to build, blithesomely singing
For soft summer's solace ensuing on slopes 510
Everywhere.
The blossoms swell and blow,
In hedge-rows rich and rare,
And notes most lovely flow
From out the forest fair.

After this comes the season of soft winds of summer,
When Zephyrus sighs on the seeds and the green plants.
The herb that then grows in the ground is right happy,
When down from the leaves drops the dampening dew
To abide the bright sun that is blissfully shining. 520
But autumn comes speeding, soon grows severe,
And warns it to wax full ripe for the winter.
With drought then the dust is driven to rise,
From the face of the fields to fly to the heaven.
With the sun the wild wind of the welkin[20] is struggling;
The leaves from the limbs drop, and light on the ground;
And withers the grass that grew once so greenly.
Then all ripens that formerly flourished, and rots;
And thus passes the year in yesterdays many,
And winter, in truth, as the way of the world is, 530
Draws near,
Till comes the Michaelmas[21] moon
With pledge of winter sere.
Then thinks Sir Gawain soon
Of his dread voyage drear.

Till the tide of Allhallows[22] with Arthur he tarried;
The King made ado on that day for his sake
With rich and rare revel of all of the Round Table,
Knights most courteous, comely ladies,
All of them heavy at heart for the hero. 540
Yet nothing but mirth was uttered, though many
Joyless made jests for that gentleman's sake.

[20] Sky.
[21] Feast of the archangel Michael, celebrated on September 29.
[22] All Saints' Day, November 1.

After meat, with sorrow he speaks to his uncle,
And openly talks of his travel, saying:
"Liege lord[23] of my life, now I ask of you leave.
You know my case and condition, nor care I
To tell of its troubles even a trifle.
I must, for the blow I am bound to, to-morrow
Go seek as God guides me the man in the green."
Then came there together the best in the castle: 550
Ywain, Eric, and others full many,
Sir Dodinel de Sauvage, the Duke of Clarence,
Lancelot, Lyonel, Lucan the good,
Sir Bors and Sir Bedevere, both of them big men,
Mador de la Port, and many more nobles.
All these knights of the court came near to the King
With care in their hearts to counsel the hero;
Heavy and deep was the dole in the hall
That one worthy as Gawain should go on that errand,
To suffer an onerous stroke, and his own sword   560
                         To stay.
              The knight was of good cheer:
              "Why should I shrink away
              From a fate stern and drear?
              A man can but essay."

He remained there that day; in the morning made ready.
Early he asked for his arms; all were brought him.
And first a fine carpet was laid on the floor,
And much was the gilt gear that glittered upon it.
Thereon stepped the strong man, and handled the steel,   570
Dressed in a doublet of Tars that cost dearly,
A hood made craftily, closed at the top,
And about on the lining bound with a bright fur.
Then they set on his feet shoes fashioned of steel,
And with fine greaves of steel encircled his legs.
Knee-pieces to these were connected, well polished,
Secured round his knees with knots of gold.
Then came goodly cuisses, with cunning enclosing
His thick, brawny thighs; with thongs they attached them.
Then the man was encased in a coat of fine mail,   580
With rings of bright steel on a rich stuff woven,
Braces well burnished on both of his arms,
Elbow-pieces gay, good, and gloves of plate,
All the goodliest gear that would give him most succor
                         That tide:
              Coat armor richly made,
              His gold spurs fixed with pride,
              Girt his unfailing blade
              By a silk sash to his side.

[23]A lord to whom one is bound to allegiance and service, under the feudal system.

When in arms he was clasped, his costume was costly; 590
The least of the lacings or loops gleamed with gold.
And armed in this manner, the man heard mass,
At the altar adored and made offering, and afterward
Came to the King and all of his courtiers,
Gently took leave of the ladies and lords;
Him they kissed and escorted, to Christ him commending.
Then was Gringolet ready, girt with a saddle
That gaily with many a gold fringe was gleaming,
With nails studded newly, prepared for the nonce.
The bridle was bound about, barred with bright gold; 600
With the bow of the saddle, the breastplate, the splendid skirts,
Crupper, and cloth in adornment accorded,
With gold nails arrayed on a groundwork of red,
That glittered and glinted like gleams of the sun.
Then he caught up his helm, and hastily kissed it;
It stoutly was stapled and stuffed well within,
High on his head, and hasped well behind,
With a light linen veil laid over the visor,
Embroidered and bound with the brightest of gems
On a silken border; with birds on the seams 610
Like painted parroquets preening; true love-knots
As thickly with turtle doves tangled as though
Many women had been at the work seven winters
      In town.
    Great was the circle's price
    Encompassing his crown;
    Of diamonds its device,
    That were both bright and brown.

Then they showed him his shield, sheer gules, whereon shone
The pentangle[24] painted in pure golden hue. 620
On his baldric he caught, and about his neck cast it;
And fairly the hero's form it befitted.
And why that great prince the pentangle suited
Intend I to tell, in my tale though I tarry.
'T is a sign that Solomon formerly set
As a token, for so it doth symbol, of truth.
A figure it is that with five points is furnished;
Each line overlaps and locks in another,
Nor comes to an end; and Englishmen call it
Everywhere, hear I, the endless knot. 630
It became then the knight and his noble arms also,
In five ways, and five times each way still faithful.
Sir Gawain was known as the good, refined gold,
Graced with virtues of castle, of villainy void,

[24] Pentacle, or five-pointed star, with magical or symbolic meaning.

       Made clean.
   So the pentangle new
   On shield and coat was seen,
   As man of speech most true,
   And gentlest knight of mien.

First, in his five wits he faultless was found;   640
In his five fingers too the man never failed;
And on earth all his faith was fixed on the five wounds
That Christ, as the creed tells, endured on the cross.
Wheresoever this man was midmost in battle,
His thought above everything else was in this,
To draw all his fire from the fivefold joys[25]
That the fair Queen of Heaven felt in her child.
And because of this fitly he carried her image
Displayed on his shield, on its larger part,
That whenever he saw it his spirit should sink not.   650
The fifth five the hero made use of, I find,
More than all were his liberalness, love of his fellows,
His courtesy, chasteness, unchangeable ever,
And pity, all further traits passing. These five
In this hero more surely were set than in any.
In truth now, fivefold they were fixed in the knight,
Linked each to the other without any end,
And all of them fastened on five points unfailing;
Each side they neither united nor sundered,
Evermore endless at every angle,   660
Where equally either they ended or started.
And so his fair shield was adorned with this symbol,
Thus richly with red gold wrought on red gules,
So by people the pentangle perfect 't was called,
        As it ought.
   Gawain in arms is gay;
   Right there his lance he caught,
   And gave them all good-day
   For ever, as he thought.

He set spurs to his steed, and sprang on his way   670
So swiftly that sparks from the stone flew behind him.
All who saw him, so seemly, sighed, sad at heart;
The same thing, in sooth, each said to the other,
Concerned for that comely man: "Christ, 't is a shame
Thou, sir knight, must be lost whose life is so noble!
To find, faith! his equal on earth is not easy.
'T would wiser have been to have acted more warily,
Dubbed yonder dear one a duke. He seems clearly
To be in the land here a brilliant leader:

---

[25] The "joys of Mary" were the Annunciation, Nativity, Resurrection, Ascension, and Assumption.

So better had been than brought thus to naught, 680
By an elf-man[26] beheaded for haughty boasting.
Who e'er knew any king such counsel to take,
As foolish as one in a Christmas frolic?"
Much was the warm water welling from eyes
When the seemly hero set out from the city
                              That day.
            Nowhere he abode,
            But swiftly went his way;
            By devious paths he rode,
            As I the book heard say. 690

      Through the realm of Logres[27] now rides this lord,
Sir Gawain, for God's sake, no game though he thought it.
Oft alone, uncompanioned he lodges at night
Where he finds not the fare that he likes set before him.
Save his foal, he 'd no fellow by forests and hills;
On the way, no soul but the Savior to speak to.
At length he drew nigh unto North Wales, and leaving
To left of him all of the islands of Anglesey,
Fared by the forelands and over the fords
Near the Holy Head; hastening hence to the mainland, 700
In Wyral he went through the wilderness.[28] There,
Lived but few who loved God or their fellows with good heart.
And always he asked of any he met,
As he journeyed, if nearby a giant they knew of,
A green knight, known as the Knight of the Green Chapel.
All denied it with nay, in their lives they had never
Once seen any hero who had such a hue
                              Of green.
            The knight takes roadways strange
            In many a wild terrene;[29] 710
            Often his feelings change
            Before that chapel 's seen.

      Over many cliffs climbed he in foreign countries;
From friends far sundered, he fared as a stranger;
And wondrous it were, at each water or shore
That he passed, if he found not before him a foe,
So foul too and fell that to fight he could fail not.
The marvels he met with amount to so many
Too tedious were it to tell of the tenth part.
For sometimes with serpents he struggled and wolves too, 720
With wood-trolls sometimes in stony steeps dwelling,

---

[26] Supernatural being.
[27] One of the names for Arthur's kingdom.
[28] Gawain's route may be followed on a map: north to the coast of north Wales, near the islands of Anglesey, then east across the River Dee to the forest of Wirral in Cheshire.
[29] Terrain.

And sometimes with bulls and with bears and with boars;
And giants from high fells hunted and harassed him.
If he'd been not enduring and doughty, and served God,
These doubtless would often have done him to death.
Though warfare was grievous, worse was the winter,
When cold, clear water was shed from the clouds
That froze ere it fell to the earth, all faded.
With sleet nearly slain, he slept in his armor
More nights than enough on the naked rocks,   730
Where splashing the cold stream sprang from the summit,
And hung in hard icicles high o'er his head.
Thus in peril and pain and desperate plights,
Till Christmas Eve wanders this wight through the country
                                    Alone.
                    Truly the knight that tide
                    To Mary made his moan,
                    That she direct his ride
                    To where some hearth-fire shone.

    By a mount on the morn he merrily rides   740
To a wood dense and deep that was wondrously wild;
High hills on each hand, with forests of hoar oaks
Beneath them most huge, a hundred together.
Thickly the hazel and hawthorn were tangled,
Everywhere mantled with moss rough and ragged,
With many a bird on the bare twigs, mournful,
That piteously piped for pain of the cold.
Sir Gawain on Gringolet goes underneath them
Through many a marsh and many a mire,
Unfriended, fearing to fail in devotion,   750
And see not His service, that Sire's, on that very night
Born of a Virgin to vanquish our pain.
And so sighing he said: "Lord, I beseech Thee,
And Mary, the mildest mother so dear,
For some lodging wherein to hear mass full lowly,
And matins, meekly I ask it, to-morrow;
So promptly I pray my pater and ave
                                    And creed."
                    Thus rode he as he prayed,
                    Lamenting each misdeed;   760
                    Often the sign he made,
                    And said, "Christ's cross me speed."

    He scarcely had signed himself thrice, ere he saw
In the wood on a mound a moated mansion,
Above a fair field, enfolded in branches
Of many a huge tree hard by the ditches:
The comeliest castle that knight ever kept.
In a meadow 't was placed, with a park all about,

And a palisade, spiked and pointed, set stoutly
Round many a tree for more than two miles. 770
The lord on that one side looked at the stronghold
That shimmered and shone through the shapely oak trees;
Then duly his helm doffed, and gave his thanks humbly
To Jesus and Julian,[30] both of them gentle,
For showing him courtesy, hearing his cry.
"Now good lodging," quoth Gawain, "I beg you to grant me."
Then with spurs in his gilt heels he Gringolet strikes,
Who chooses the chief path by chance that conducted
The man to the bridge-end ere many a minute
                        Had passed. 780
          The bridge secure was made,
          Upraised; the gates shut fast;
          The walls were well arrayed.
          It feared no tempest's blast.

    The hero abode on his horse by the bank
Of the deep, double ditch that surrounded the dwelling.
The wall stood wonderfully deep in the water,
And again to a huge height sprang overhead;
Of hard, hewn rock that reached to the cornices,
Built up with outworks under the battlements 790
Finely; at intervals, turrets fair fashioned,
With many good loopholes that shut tight; this lord
Had ne'er looked at a barbican[31] better than this one.
Further in he beheld the high hall; here and there
Towers were stationed set thickly with spires,
With finials wondrously long and fair fitting,
Whose points were cunningly carven, and craftily.
There numerous chalk-white chimneys he noticed
That bright from the tops of the towers were gleaming.
Such pinnacles painted, so placed about everywhere, 800
Clustering so thick 'mid the crenels, the castle
Surely appeared to be shaped to cut paper.[32]
The knight on his foal it fair enough fancies
If into the court he may manage to come,
In that lodging to live while the holiday lasts
                        With delight.
          A porter came at call,
          His mission learned, and right
          Civilly from the wall
          Greeted the errant knight. 810

[30] Patron saint of hospitality.
[31] A defensive tower built by the gate of a castle.
[32] That is, it looked as if it were made of cut paper. Paper constructions were often used as table decorations.

Quoth Gawain: "Good sir, will you go on my errand,
Harbor to crave of this house's high lord?"
"Yea, by Peter. I know well, sir knight," said the porter,
"You're welcome as long as you list here to tarry."
Then went the man quickly, and with him, to welcome
The knight to the castle, a courteous company.
Down the great drawbridge they dropped, and went eagerly
Forth; on the frozen earth fell on their knees
To welcome this knight in the way they thought worthy;
Threw wide the great gate for Gawain to enter.   820
He bid them rise promptly, and rode o'er the bridge.
His saddle several seized as he lighted,
And stout men in plenty stabled his steed.
And next there descended knights and esquires
To lead to the hall with delight this hero.
When he raised his helmet, many made haste
From his hand to catch it, to care for the courtly man.
Some of them took then his sword and his shield both.
Then Gawain graciously greeted each knight;
Many proud men pressing to honor that prince,   830
To the hall they led him, all hasped in his harness,
Where fiercely a fair fire flamed on the hearth.
Then came the lord of this land from his chamber
To fittingly meet the man on the floor,
And said: "You are welcome to do what your will is;
To hold as your own, you have all that is here
                          In this place."
          "Thank you," said Gawain then,
          "May Christ reward this grace."
          The two like joyful men   840
          Each other then embrace.

Gawain gazed at the man who so graciously greeted him;
Doughty he looked, the lord of that dwelling,
A hero indeed huge, hale, in his prime;
His beard broad and bright, its hue all of beaver;
Stern, and on stalwart shanks steadily standing;
Fell[33] faced as the fire, in speech fair and free.
In sooth, well suited he seemed, thought Gawain,
To govern as prince of a goodly people.
To his steward the lord turned, and strictly commanded   850
To send men to Gawain to give him good service;
And prompt at his bidding were people in plenty.
To a bright room they brought him, the bed nobly decked
With hangings of pure silk with clear golden hems.
And curious coverings with comely panels,
Embroidered with bright fur above at the edges;
On cords curtains running with rings of red gold;

[33] Fierce.

From Tars and Toulouse were the tapestries covering
The walls; under foot on the floor more to match.
There he soon, with mirthful speeches, was stripped 860
Of his coat of linked mail and his armor; and quickly
Men ran, and brought him rich robes, that the best
He might pick out and choose as his change of apparel.
When lapped was the lord in the one he selected,
That fitted him fairly with flowing skirts,
The fur by his face, in faith it seemed made,
To the company there, entirely of colors,
Glowing and lovely; beneath all his limbs were.
That never made Christ a comelier knight
                    They thought. 870
        On earth, or far or near,
        It seemed as if he ought
        To be a prince sans peer
        In fields where fierce men fought.

    A chair by the chimney where charcoal was burning
For Gawain was fitted most finely with cloths,
Both cushions and coverlets, cunningly made.
Then a comely mantle was cast on the man,
Of a brown, silken fabric bravely embroidered,
Within fairly furred with the finest of skins, 880
Made lovely with ermine, his hood fashioned likewise.
He sat on that settle in clothes rich and seemly;
His mood, when well he was warmed, quickly mended.
Soon was set up a table on trestles most fair;
With a clean cloth that showed a clear white it was covered,
With top-cloth and salt-cellar, spoons too of silver.
When he would the man washed, and went to his meat,
And seemly enough men served him with several
Excellent stews in the best manner seasoned,
Twofold as was fitting, and various fishes; 890
In bread some were baked, some broiled on the coals,
Some seethed, some in stews that were savored with spices;
And ever such subtly made sauces as pleased him.
He freely and frequently called it a feast,
Most courtly; the company there all acclaimed him
                    Well-bred.
        "But now this penance take,[34]
        And soon 't will mend," they said.
        That man much mirth did make,
        As wine went to his head. 900

    They enquired then and queried in guarded questions
Tactfully put to the prince himself,

[34] The lords and ladies jocularly say that Gawain has been doing penance because the elaborate meal has consisted only of fish dishes, as for a fast-day.

Till he courteously owned he came of the court
The lord Arthur, gracious and goodly, alone holds,
Who rich is and royal, the Round Table's King;
And that Gawain himself in that dwelling was seated,
For Christmas come, as the case had befallen.
When he learned that he had that hero, the lord
Laughed loudly thereat so delightful he thought it.
Much merriment made all the men in that castle   910
By promptly appearing then in his presence;
For all prowess and worth and pure polished manners
Pertain to his person. He ever is praised;
Of all heroes on earth his fame is the highest.
Each knight full softly said to his neighbor,
"We now shall see, happily, knightly behavior,
And faultless terms of talking most noble;
What profit 's in speech we may learn without seeking,
For nurture's fine father has found here a welcome;
In truth God has graciously given His grace   920
Who grants us to have such a guest as Gawain
When men for His birth's sake sit merry and sing.
                            To each
                    Of us this hero now
                    Will noble manners teach;
                    Who hear him will learn how
                    To utter loving speech."

  When at length the dinner was done, and the lords
Had risen, the night-time nearly was come.
The chaplains went their way to the chapels   930
And rang right joyfully, just as they should do,
For evensong solemn this festival season.
To this goes the lord, and the lady likewise;
She comes in with grace to the pew closed and comely,
And straightway Gawain goes thither right gaily;
The lord by his robe took him, led to a seat,
Acknowledged him kindly and called him by name,
Saying none in the world was as welcome as he was.
He heartily thanked him; the heroes embraced,
And together they soberly sat through the service.   940
Then longed the lady to look on the knight,
And emerged from her pew with many fair maidens;
In face she was fairest of all, and in figure,
In skin and in color, all bodily qualities;
Lovelier, Gawain thought, even than Guinevere.
He goes through the chancel[35] to greet her, so gracious.
By the left hand another was leading her, older
Than she, a lady who looked as if aged,
By heroes around her reverenced highly.

_____

[35] The portion of a church set off for the use of the clergy.

The ladies, however, unlike were to look on: 950
If fresh was the younger, the other was yellow;
Rich red on the one was rioting everywhere,
Rough wrinkled cheeks hung in rolls on the other;
One's kerchiefs, with clear pearls covered and many,
Displayed both her breast and her bright throat all bare,
Shining fairer than snow on the hillsides falling;
The second her neck in a neck-cloth enswathed,
That enveloped in chalk-white veils her black chin;
Her forehead in silk was wrapped and enfolded
Adorned and tricked with trifles about it 960
Till nothing was bare but the lady's black brows,
Her two eyes, her nose, and her lips, all naked,
And those were bleared strangely, and ugly to see.
A goodly lady, so men before God
                              Might decide!
            Her body thick and short,
            Her hips were round and wide;
            One of more pleasant sort
            She led there by her side.

When Gawain had gazed on that gay one so gracious 970
In look, he took leave of the lord and went toward them,
Saluted the elder, bowing full lowly,
The lovelier lapped in his two arms a little,
And knightly and comely greeted and kissed her.
They craved his acquaintance, and quickly he asked
To be truly their servant if so they desired it.
They took him between them, and led him with talk
To the sitting-room's hearth; then straightway for spices
They called, which men sped to unsparingly bring,
And with them as well pleasant wine at each coming. 980
Up leaped right often the courteous lord,
Urged many a time that the men should make merry,
Snatched off his hood, on a spear gaily hung it,
And waved it, that one for a prize might win it
Who caused the most mirth on that Christmas season.
"I shall try, by my faith, to contend with the finest
Ere hoodless I find myself, helped by my friends."
Thus with laughing speeches the lord makes merry
That night, to gladden Sir Gawain with games.
                              So they spent 990
            The evening in the hall.
            The king for lights then sent,
            And taking leave of all
            To bed Sir Gawain went.

On the morn when the Lord, as men all remember,
Was born, who would die for our doom, in each dwelling
On earth grows happiness greater for His sake;

So it did on that day there with many a dainty:
With dishes cunningly cooked at meal-times,
With doughty men dressed in their best on the dais.   1000
The old lady was seated the highest; beside her
Politely the lord took his place, I believe;
The gay lady and Gawain together sat, mid-most,
Where fitly the food came, and afterward fairly
Was served through the hall as beseemed them the best,
Of the company each in accord with his station.
There was meat and mirth, there was much joy, too troublous
To tell, though I tried in detail to describe it;
Yet I know both the lovely lady and Gawain
So sweet found each other's society (pleasant   1010
And polished their converse, courtly and private;
Unfailing their courtesy, free from offence)
That surpassing, in truth, any play of a prince was
                              Their game.
            There trumpets, drums and airs
            Of piping loudly came.
            Each minded his affairs,
            And those two did the same.

   Much mirth was that day and the day after made,
And the third followed fast, as full of delight.   1020
Sweet was the joy of St. John's day[36] to hear of,
The last, as the folk there believed, of the festival.
Guests were to go in the grey dawn, and therefore
They wondrously late were awake with their wine,
And danced delightful, long lasting caroles.
At length when 't was late they took their leave,
Each strong man among them to start on his way.
Gawain gave him good-day; then the good man laid hold of him,
Led to the hearth in his own room the hero;
There took him aside, and gave suitable thanks   1030
For the gracious distinction that Gawain had given
In honoring his house that holiday season,
And gracing his castle with courteous company.
"I'll truly as long as I live be the better
That Gawain at God's own feast was my guest."
"Gramercy,"[37] said Gawain, "by God, sir, not mine
Is the worth, but your own; may the high King reward you.
I am here at your will to work your behest,
As in high and low it behooves me to do
                              By right."   1040
            The lord intently tries
            Longer to hold the knight;
            Gawain to him replies
            That he in no way might.

[36] December 27.   [37] "Thank you."

Then the man with courteous question enquired
What dark deed that feast time had driven him forth,
From the King's court to journey alone with such courage,
Ere fully in homes was the festival finished.
"In sooth," said the knight, "sir, ye say but the truth;
From these hearths a high and a hasty task took me. 1050
Myself, I am summoned to seek such a place
As to find it I know not whither to fare.
I'd not fail to have reached it the first of the New Year,
So help me our Lord, for the whole land of Logres;
And therefore, I beg this boon of you here, sir;
Tell me, in truth, if you ever heard tale
Of the Chapel of Green, of the ground where it stands,
And the knight, green colored, who keeps it. By solemn
Agreement a tryst was established between us,
That man at that landmark to meet if I lived. 1060
And now there lacks of New Year but little;
I'd look at that lord, if God would but let me,
More gladly than own any good thing, by God's Son.
And hence, by your leave, it behooves me to go;
I now have but barely three days to be busy.
As fain would I fall dead as fail of my mission."
Then laughing the lord said: "You longer must stay,
For I'll point out the way to that place ere the time's end,
The ground of the Green Chapel. Grieve no further;
For, sir, you shall be in your bed at your ease 1070
Until late, and fare forth the first of the year,
To your meeting place come by mid-morning, to do there
                    Your pleasure.
          Tarry till New Year's day,
          Then rise and go at leisure.
          I'll set you on your way;
          Not two miles is the measure."

Then was Gawain right glad, and gleefully laughed.
"Now for this more than anything else, sir, I thank you.
I have come to the end of my quest; at your will 1080
I shall bide, and in all things act as you bid me."
The lord then seized him, and set him beside him,
And sent for the ladies to better delight him.
Seemly the pleasure among them in private.
So gay were the speeches he spoke, and so friendly,
The host seemed a man well-nigh mad in behavior.
He called to the knight there, crying aloud:
"Ye have bound you to do the deed that I bid you.
Here, and at once, will you hold to your word sir?"
"Yes, certainly sir," the true hero said; 1090
"While I bide in your house I obey your behest."
"You have toiled," said the lord; "from afar have travelled,
And here have caroused, nor are wholly recovered

In sleep or in nourishment, know I for certain.
In your room you shall linger, and lie at your ease
To-morrow till mass-time, and go to your meat
When you will, and with you my wife to amuse you
With company, till to the court I return.
      You stay
    And I shall early rise,   1100
    And hunting go my way."
    Bowing in courteous wise,
    Gawain grants all this play.

"And more," said the man, "let us make an agreement:
Whatever I win in the wood shall be yours;
And what chance you shall meet shall be mine in exchange.
Sir, let's so strike our bargain and swear to tell truly
Whate'er fortune brings, whether bad, sir, or better."
Quoth Gawain the good: "By God, I do grant it.
What pastime you please appears to me pleasant."   1110
"On the beverage brought us the bargain is made,"
So the lord of the land said. All of them laughed,
And drank, and light-heartedly revelled and dallied,
Those ladies and lords, as long as they liked.
Then they rose with elaborate politeness, and lingered,
With many fair speeches spoke softly together,
Right lovingly kissed, and took leave of each other.
Gay troops of attendants with glimmering torches
In comfort escorted each man to his couch
        To rest.   1120
    Yet ere they left the board
    Their promise they professed
    Often. That people's lord
    Could well maintain a jest.

        III
 Betimes rose the folk ere the first of the day;
The guests that were going then summoned their grooms,
Who hastily sprang up to saddle their horses,
Packed their bags and prepared all their gear.
The nobles made ready, to ride all arrayed;
 And quickly they leaped and caught up their bridles,   1130
And started, each wight on the way that well pleased him.
The land's beloved lord not last was equipped
For riding, with many a man too. A morsel
He hurriedly ate when mass he had heard,
And promptly with horn to the hunting field hastened.
And ere any daylight had dawned upon earth,
Both he and his knights were high on their horses.
The dog-grooms, accomplished, the hounds then coupled,
The door of the kennel unclosed, called them out,
On the bugle mightily blew three single notes;   1140

Whereupon bayed with a wild noise the brachets,[38]
And some they turned back that went straying, and punished.
The hunters, I heard, were a hundred. To station
                    They go,
        The keepers of the hounds,
        And off the leashes throw.
        With noise the wood resounds
        From the good blasts they blow.

    At the first sound of questing, the wild creatures quaked;
The deer fled, foolish from fright, in the dale,   1150
To the high ground hastened, but quickly were halted
By beaters, loud shouting, stationed about
In a circle. The harts were let pass with their high heads,
And also the bucks, broad-antlered and bold;
For the generous lord by law had forbidden
All men with the male deer to meddle in close season.
The hinds were hemmed in with hey! and ware!
The does to the deep valleys driven with great din.
You might see as they loosed them the shafts swiftly soar—
At each turn of the forest their feathers went flying—   1160
That deep into brown hides bit with their broad heads;
Lo! they brayed on the hill-sides, bled there, and died,
And hounds, fleet-footed, followed them headlong.
And hunters after them hastened with horns
So loud in their sharp burst of sound as to sunder
The cliffs. What creatures escaped from the shooters,
Hunted and harried from heights to the waters,
Were pulled down and rent at the places there ready;
Such skill the men showed at these low-lying stations,
So great were the greyhounds that quickly they got them   1170
And dragged them down, fast as the folk there might look
                    At the sight.
        Carried with bliss away,
        The lord did oft alight,
        Oft gallop; so that day
        He passed till the dark night.

    Thus frolicked the lord on the fringe of the forest,
And Gawain the good in his gay bed reposed,
Lying snugly, till sunlight shone on the walls,
'Neath a coverlet bright with curtains about it.   1180
As softly he slumbered, a slight sound he heard
At his door, made with caution, and quickly it opened.
The hero heaved up his head from the clothes;
By a corner he caught up the curtain a little,
And glanced out with heed to behold what had happened.

---

[38] Dogs that hunt by scent.

The lady it was, most lovely to look at,
Who shut the door after her stealthily, slyly,
And turned toward the bed. Then the brave man, embarrassed,
Lay down again subtly to seem as if sleeping;
And stilly she stepped, and stole to his bed,   1190
There cast up the curtain, and creeping within it,
Seated herself on the bedside right softly,
And waited a long while to watch when he woke.
And the lord too, lurking, lay there a long while,
Wondering at heart what might come of this happening,
Or what it might mean—a marvel he thought it.
Yet he said to himself, " 'T would be surely more seemly
By speaking at once to see what she wishes."
Then roused he from sleep, and stretching turned toward her,
His eyelids unlocked, made believe that he wondered,   1200
And signed himself so by his prayers to be safer
                         From fall.
        Right sweet in chin and cheek,
        Both white and red withal,
        Full fairly she did speak
        With laughing lips and small.

    "Good morrow, Sir Gawain," that gay lady said,
"You're a sleeper unwary, since so one may steal in.
In a trice you are ta'en! If we make not a truce,
In your bed, be you certain of this, I shall bind you."   1210
All laughing, the lady delivered those jests.
"Good morrow, fair lady," said Gawain the merry,
"You may do what you will, and well it doth please me,
For quickly I yield me, crying for mercy;
This method to me seems the best—for I must!"
So the lord in turn jested with laughter right joyous.
"But if, lovely lady, you would, give me leave,
Your prisoner release and pray him to rise,
And I'd come from this bed and clothe myself better;
So could I converse with you then with more comfort."   1220
"Indeed no, fair sir," that sweet lady said,
"You'll not move from your bed; I shall manage you better;
For here—and on that side too—I shall hold you,
And next I shall talk with the knight I have taken.
For well do I know that your name is Sir Gawain,
By everyone honored wherever you ride;
Most highly acclaimed is your courtly behavior
With lords and ladies and all who are living.
And now you're here, truly, and none but we two;
My lord and his followers far off have fared;   1230
Other men remain in their beds, and my maidens;
The door is closed, and secured with a strong hasp;
Since him who delights all I have in my house,
My time, as long as it lasts, I with talking

Shall fill.
My body's gladly yours;
Upon me work your will.
Your servant I, perforce,
Am now, and shall be still."

"In faith," quoth Sir Gawain, "a favor I think it,   1240
Although I am now not the knight you speak of;
To reach to such fame as here you set forth,
I am one, as I well know myself, most unworthy.
By God, should you think it were good, I'd be glad
If I could or in word or action accomplish
Your ladyship's pleasure—a pure joy 't would prove."
"In good faith, Sir Gawain," the gay lady said,
"Ill-bred I should be if I blamed or belittled
The worth and prowess that please all others.
There are ladies enough who'd be now more delighted   1250
To have you in thraldom, as here, sir, I have you,
To trifle gaily in talk most engaging,
To give themselves comfort and quiet their cares,
Than have much of the gold and the goods they command.
But to Him I give praise that ruleth the heavens,
That wholly I have in my hand what all wish."
So she
Gave him good cheer that day,
She who was fair to see.
To what she chanced to say   1260
With pure speech answered he.

Quoth the merry man, "Madam, Mary reward you,
For noble, in faith, I've found you, and generous.
People by others pattern their actions,
But more than I merit to me they give praise;
'T is your courteous self who can show naught but kindness."
"By Mary," said she, "to me it seems other!
Were I worth all the host of women now living,
And had I the wealth of the world in my hands,
Should I chaffer[39] and choose to get me a champion,   1270
Sir, from the signs I've seen in you here
Of courtesy, merry demeanor, and beauty,
From what I have heard, and hold to be true,
Before you no lord now alive would be chosen."
"A better choice, madam, you truly have made;
Yet I'm proud of the value you put now upon me.
Your servant as seemly, I hold you my sovereign,
Become your knight, and Christ give you quittance."
Thus of much they talked till mid-morning was past.

[39] Bargain; haggle.

The lady behaved as if greatly she loved him,   1280
But Gawain, on guard, right gracefully acted.
"Though I were the most lovely of ladies," she thought,
"The less would he take with him love." He was seeking,
                              With speed,
              Grief that must be: the stroke
              That him should stun indeed.
              She then of leaving spoke,
              And promptly he agreed.

    Then she gave him good-day, and glanced at him, laughing,
And startled him, speaking sharp words as she stood: 1290
"He who blesses all words reward this reception!
I doubt if indeed I may dub you Gawain."
"Wherefore?" he queried, quickly enquiring,
Afraid that he'd failed in his fashion of speech.
But the fair lady blessed him, speaking as follows:
"One as good as is Gawain the gracious considered,
(And courtly behavior's found wholly in him)
Not lightly so long could remain with a lady
Without, in courtesy, craving a kiss
At some slight subtle hint at the end of a story."   1300
"Let it be as you like, lovely lady," said Gawain;
"As a knight is so bound, I'll kiss at your bidding,
And lest he displease you, so plead no longer."
Then closer she comes, and catches the knight
In her arms, and salutes him, leaning down affably.
Kindly each other to Christ they commend.
She goes forth at the door without further ado,
And he quickly makes ready to rise, and hastens,
Calls to his chamberlain, chooses his clothes,
And merrily marches, when ready, to mass.   1310
Then he fared to his meat, and fitly he feasted,
Made merry all day with amusements till moonrise.
                              None knew
              A knight to better fare
              With dames so worthy, two:
              One old, one younger. There
              Much mirth did then ensue.

    Still was absent the lord of that land on his pleasure,
To hunt barren hinds in wood and in heath.
By the set of the sun he had slain such a number   1320
Of does and different deer that 't was wondrous.
Eagerly flocked in the folk at the finish,
And quickly made of the killed deer a quarry;
To this went the nobles with numerous men;
The game whose flesh was the fattest they gathered;
With care, as the case required, cut them open.

And some the deer searched at the spot of assay,[40]
And two fingers of fat they found in the poorest.
They slit at the base of the throat, seized the stomach,
Scraped it away with a sharp knife and sewed it; 1330
Next slit the four limbs and stripped off the hide;
Then opened the belly and took out the bowels
And flesh of the knot, quickly flinging them out.
They laid hold of the throat, made haste to divide, then,
The windpipe and gullet, and tossed out the guts;
With their sharp knives carved out the shoulders and carried them
Held through a small hole to have the sides perfect.
The breast they sliced, and split it in two;
And then they began once again at the throat,
And quickly as far as its fork they cut it; 1340
Pulled out the pluck,[41] and promptly thereafter
Beside the ribs swiftly severed the fillets,
Cleared them off readily right by the back-bone,
Straight down to the haunch, all hanging together.
They heaved it up whole, and hewed it off there,
And the rest by the name of the numbles[42]—and rightly—
                    They knew.
            Then where divide the thighs,
            The folds behind they hew,
            Hasten to cut the prize 1350
            Along the spine in two.

    And next both the head and the neck off they hewed;
The sides from the backbone swiftly they sundered;
The fee of the ravens[43] they flung in the branches.
They ran through each thick side a hole by the ribs,
And hung up both by the hocks of the haunches,
Each fellow to have the fee that was fitting.
On the fair beast's hide, they fed their hounds
With the liver and lights and the paunch's lining,
Among which bread steeped in blood was mingled. 1360
They blew boldly the blast for the prize; the hounds barked.
Then the venison took they and turned toward home,
And stoutly many a shrill note they sounded.
Ere close of the daylight, the company came
To the comely castle where Gawain in comfort
                    Sojourned.
            And when he met the knight
            As thither he returned,
            Joy had they and delight,
            Where the fire brightly burned. 1370

---

[40] Place to test the thickness of the fat.
[41] Tender meat taken from the throat.
[42] Edible organs.   [43] Bits of scrap meat flung to the birds.

In the hall the lord bade all his household to gather,
And both of the dames to come down with their damsels.
In the room there before all the folk he ordered
His followers, truly, to fetch him his venison.
Gawain he called with courteous gaiety,
Asked him to notice the number of nimble beasts,
Showed him the fairness of flesh on the ribs.
"Are you pleased with this play? Have I won your praise?
Have I thoroughly earned your thanks through my cunning?"
"In faith," said Sir Gawain, "this game is the fairest   1380
I've seen in the season of winter these seven years."
"The whole of it, Gawain, I give you," the host said;
"Because of our compact, as yours you may claim it."
"That is true," the knight said, "and I tell you the same:
That this I have worthily won within doors,
And surely to you with as good will I yield it."
With both of his arms his fair neck he embraced,
And the hero as courteously kissed as he could.
"I give you my gains. I got nothing further;
I freely would grant it, although it were greater."   1390
"It is good," said the good man; "I give you my thanks.
Yet things so may be that you'd think it better
To tell where you won this same wealth by your wit."
" 'T was no part of our pact," said he; "press me no more;
For trust entirely in this, that you've taken
                              Your due."
                    With laughing merriment
                    And knightly speech and true,
                    To supper soon they went
                    With store of dainties new,   1400

    In a chamber they sat, by the side of the chimney,
Where men right frequently fetched them mulled wine.
In their jesting, again they agreed on the morrow
To keep the same compact they came to before:
That whatever should chance, they'd exchange at evening,
When greeting again, the new things they had gotten.
Before all·the court they agreed to the covenant;
Then was the beverage brought forth in jest.
At last they politely took leave of each other,
And quickly each hero made haste to his couch.   1410
When the cock but three times had crowed and cackled,
The lord and his men had leaped from their beds.
So that duly their meal was dealt with, and mass,
And ere daylight they'd fared toward the forest, on hunting
                              Intent.
                    The huntsmen with loud horns
                    Through level fields soon went,
                    Uncoupling 'mid the thorns
                    The hounds swift on the scent.

Soon they cry for a search by the side of a swamp. 1420
The huntsmen encourage the hounds that first catch there
The scent, and sharp words they shout at them loudly;
And thither the hounds that heard them hastened,
And fast to the trail fell, forty at once.
Then such clamor and din from the dogs that had come there
Arose that the rocks all around them rang.
With horn and with mouth the hunters heartened them;
They gathered together then, all in a group,
'Twixt a pool in that copse and a crag most forbidding.
At a stone-heap, beside the swamp, by a cliff, 1430
Where the rough rock had fallen in rugged confusion,
They fared to the finding, the folk coming after.
Around both the crag and the rubble-heap searched
The hunters, sure that within them was hidden
The beast whose presence was bayed by the bloodhounds.
Then they beat on the bushes, and bade him rise up,
And wildly he made for the men in his way,
Rushing suddenly forth, of swine the most splendid.
Apart from the herd he'd grown hoary with age,
For fierce was the beast, the biggest of boars. 1440
Then many men grieved, full grim when he grunted,
For three at his first thrust he threw to the earth,
And then hurtled forth swiftly, no harm doing further.
They shrilly cried hi! and shouted hey! hey!
Put bugles to mouth, loudly blew the recall.
The men and dogs merry in voice were and many;
With outcry they all hurry after this boar
　　　　　　　　　　　　To slay.
　　　　　He maims the pack when, fell,
　　　　　He often stands at bay. 1450
　　　　　Loudly they howl and yell,
　　　　　Sore wounded in the fray.

Then to shoot at him came up the company quickly.
Arrows that hit him right often they aimed,
But their sharp points failed that fell on his shoulders'
Tough skin, and the barbs would not bite in his flesh;
But the smooth-shaven shafts were shivered in pieces,
The heads wherever they hit him rebounding.
But when hurt by the strength of the strokes they struck,
Then mad for the fray he falls on the men, 1460
And deeply he wounds them as forward he dashes.
Then many were frightened, and drew back in fear;
But the lord galloped off on a light horse after him,
Blew like a huntsman right bold the recall
On his bugle, and rode through the thick of the bushes,
Pursuing this swine till the sun shone clearly.
Thus the day they passed in doing these deeds,
While bides our gracious knight Gawain in bed,

With bed-clothes in color right rich, at the castle
                                            Behind.   1470
                              The dame did not forget
                              To give him greetings kind.
                              She soon upon him set,
                              To make him change his mind.

   Approaching the curtain, she peeps at the prince,
And at once Sir Gawain welcomes her worthily.
Promptly the lady makes her reply.
By his side she seats herself softly, heartily
Laughs, and with lovely look these words delivers:
"If you, sir, are Gawain, greatly I wonder   1480
That one so given at all times to goodness
Should be not well versed in social conventions,
Or, made once to know, should dismiss them from mind.
You have promptly forgotten what I in the plainest
Of talk that I knew of yesterday taught you."
"What is that?" said the knight. "For truly I know not;
If it be as you say, I am surely to blame."
"Yet I taught you," quoth the fair lady, "of kissing;
When clearly he's favored, quickly to claim one
Becomes each knight who practices courtesy."   1490
"Cease, dear lady, such speech," said the strong man;
"I dare not for fear of refusal do that.
'T would be wrong to proffer and then be repulsed."
"In faith, you may not be refused," said the fair one;
"Sir, if you pleased, you have strength to compel it,
Should one be so rude as to wish to deny you."
"By God, yes," said Gawain, "good is your speech;
But unlucky is force in the land I live in,
And every gift that with good will's not given.
Your word I await to embrace when you wish;   1500
You may start when you please, and stop at your pleasure."
                                            With grace
                              The lady, bending low,
                              Most sweetly kissed his face.
                              Of joy in love and woe
                              They talked for a long space.

   "I should like," said the lady, "from you, sir, to learn,
If I roused not your anger by asking, the reason
Why you, who are now so young and valiant,
So known far and wide as knightly and courteous   1510
(And principally, picked from all knighthood, is praised
The sport of true love and the science of arms;
For to tell of these true knights' toil, it is surely
The title inscribed and the text of their deeds,

How men their lives for their leal[44] love adventured,
Endured for their passion doleful days,
Then themselves with valor avenged, and their sorrow
Cast off, and brought bliss into bowers by their virtues),
Why you, thought the noblest knight of your time,
Whose renown and honor are everywhere noted, 1520
Have so let me sit on two separate occasions
Beside you, and hear proceed from your head
Not one word relating to love, less or more.
You so goodly in vowing your service and gracious
Ought gladly to give to a young thing your guidance,
And show me some sign of the sleights of true love.
What! know you nothing, and have all renown?
Or else do you deem me too dull, for your talking
                              Unfit?
                    For shame! Alone I come; 1530
                    To learn some sport I sit;
                    My lord is far from home;
                    Now, teach me by your wit."

    "In good faith," said Gawain, "God you reward;
For great is the happiness, huge the gladness
That one so worthy should want to come hither,
And pains for so poor a man take, as in play
With your knight with looks of regard; it delights me.
But to take up the task of telling of true love,
To touch on those themes, and on tales of arms 1540
To you who've more skill in that art, I am certain,
By half than a hundred men have such as I,
Or ever shall have while here upon earth,
By my faith, 't would be, madam, a manifold folly.
Your bidding I'll do, as in duty bound,
To the height of my power, and will hold myself ever
Your ladyship's servant, so save me the Lord."
Thus the fair lady tempted and tested him often
To make the man sin—what'er more she'd in mind;
But so fair his defence was, no fault was apparent, 1550
Nor evil on either side; each knew but joy
                              On that day.
                    At last she kissed him lightly,
                    After long mirth and play,
                    And took her leave politely,
                    And went upon her way.

    The man bestirs himself, springs up for mass.
Then made ready and splendidly served was their dinner;
In sport with the ladies he spent all the day.

___
[44] True.

But the lord through fields oft dashed as he followed   1560
The savage swine, that sped o'er the slopes,
And in two bit the backs of the best of his hounds
Where he stood at bay; till 't was broken by bowmen,
Who made him, despite himself, move to the open,
The shafts flew so thick when the throng had assembled.
Yet sometimes he forced the stoutest to flinch,
Till at last too weary he was to run longer,
But came with such haste as he could to a hole
In a mound, by a rock whence the rivulet runs out.
He started to scrape the soil, backed by the slope,   1570
While froth from his mouth's ugly corners came foaming.
White were the tushes he whetted, The bold men
Who stood round grew tired of trying from far
To annoy him, but dared not for danger draw nearer.
                                        Before,
                    So many he did pierce
                    That all were loth a boar
                    So frenzied and so fierce
                    Should tear with tusks once more,

      Till the hero himself came, spurring his horse,   1580
Saw him standing at bay, the hunters beside him.
He leaped down right lordly, leaving his courser,
Unsheathed a bright sword and strode forth stoutly,
Made haste through the ford where that fierce one was waiting.
Aware of the hero with weapon in hand,
So savagely, bristling his back up, he snorted
All feared for the wight lest the worst befall him.
Then rushed out the boar directly upon him,
And man was mingled with beast in the midst
Of the wildest water. The boar had the worse,   1590
For the man aimed a blow at the beast as he met him,
And surely with sharp blade struck o'er his breast bone,
That smote to the hilt, and his heart cleft asunder.
He squealing gave way, and swift through the water
                                        Went back.
                    By a hundred hounds he's caught,
                    Who fiercely him attack;
                    To open ground he's brought,
                    And killed there by the pack.

      The blast for the beast's death was blown on sharp horns,   1600
And the lords there loudly and clearly hallooed.
At the beast bayed the brachets, as bid by their masters,
The chief, in that hard, long chase, of the hunters.
Then one who was wise in woodcraft began
To slice up this swine in the seemliest manner.
First he hews off his head, and sets it on high;
Then along the back roughly rends him apart.

He hales out the bowels, and broils them on hot coals,
With these mixed with bread, rewarding his brachets.
Then slices the flesh in fine, broad slabs, 1610
And pulls out the edible entrails properly.
Whole, though, he gathers the halves together,
And proudly upon a stout pole he places them.
Homeward they now with this very swine hasten,
Bearing in front of the hero the boar's head,
Since him at the ford by the force of his strong hand
                        He slew.
          It seemed long till he met
          In hall Sir Gawain, who
          Hastened, when called, to get 1620
          The payment that was due.

   The lord called out loudly, merrily laughed
When Gawain he saw, and gladsomely spoke.
The good ladies were sent for, the household assembled;
He shows them the slices of flesh, and the story
He tells of his largeness and length, and how fierce
Was the war in the woods where the wild swine had fled.
Sir Gawain commended his deeds right graciously,
Praised them as giving a proof of great prowess.
Such brawn on a beast, the bold man declared, 1630
And such sides on a swine he had ne'er before seen.
Then they handled the huge head; the courteous hero
Praised it, horror-struck, honoring his host.
Quoth the good man, "Now Gawain yours is this game
By our covenant, fast and firm, you know truly."
"It is so," said the knight; "and as certain and sure
All I get I'll give you again as I pledged you."
He about the neck caught, with courtesy kissed him,
And soon a second time served him the same way.
Said Gawain, "We've fairly fulfilled the agreement 1640
This evening we entered on, each to the other
                    Most true."
          "I, by Saint Giles, have met
          None," said the lord, "like you.
          Riches you soon will get,
          If you such business do."

   And then the tables they raised upon trestles,
And laid on them cloths; the light leaped up clearly
Along by the walls, where the waxen torches
Were set by the henchmen who served in the hall. 1650
A great sound of sport and merriment sprang up
Close by the fire, and on frequent occasions
At supper and afterward, many a splendid song,
Conduits of Christmas, new carols, all kinds
Of mannerly mirth that a man may tell of.

Our seemly knight ever sat at the side
Of the lady, who made so agreeable her manner,
With sly, secret glances to glad him, so stalwart,
That greatly astonished was Gawain, and wroth
With himself; he in courtesy could not refuse her,   1660
But acted becomingly, courtly, whatever
The end, good or bad, of his action might be.
                                        When quite
                Done was their play at last,
                The host called to the knight,
                And to his room they passed
                To where the fire burned bright.

    The men there make merry and drink, and once more
The same pact for New Year's Eve is proposed;
But the knight craved permission to mount on the morrow: 1670
The appointment approached where he had to appear.
But the lord him persuaded to stay and linger,
And said, "On my word as a knight I assure you
You'll get to the Green Chapel, Gawain, on New Year's,
And far before prime,[45] to finish your business.
Remain in your room then, and take your rest.
I shall hunt in the wood and exchange with you winnings,
As bound by our bargain, when back I return,
For twice I've found you were faithful when tried:
In the morning 'best be the third time,' remember.   1680
Let's be mindful of mirth while we may, and make merry,
For care when one wants it is quickly encountered."
At once this was granted, and Gawain is stayed;
Drink blithely was brought him; to bed they were lighted.
                                        The guest
                In quiet and comfort spent
                The night, and took his rest.
                On his affairs intent,
                The host was early dressed.

    After mass a morsel he took with his men.   1690
The morning was merry; his mount he demanded.
The knights who'd ride in his train were in readiness,
Dressed and horsed at the door of the hall.
Wondrous fair were the fields, for the frost was clinging;
Bright red in the cloud-rack rises the sun,
And full clear sails close past the clouds in the sky.
The hunters unleashed all the hounds by a woodside:
The rocks with the blast of their bugles were ringing.
Some dogs there fall on the scent where the fox is,
And trail oft a traitoress using her tricks.   1700

---

[45] The canonical office for the first hour of the day, that is, 6:00 A.M.

A hound gives tongue at it; huntsmen call to him;
Hastens the pack to the hound sniffing hard,
And right on his track run off in a rabble,
He scampering before them. They started the fox soon;
When finally they saw him, they followed fast,
Denouncing him clearly with clamorous anger.
Through many a dense grove he dodges and twists,
Doubling back and harkening at hedges right often;
At last by a little ditch leaps o'er a thorn-hedge,
Steals out stealthily, skirting a thicket   1710
In thought from the wood to escape by his wiles
From the hounds; then, unknowing, drew near to a hunting-stand.
There hurled themselves, three at once, on him strong hounds,
                        All gray.
          With quick swerve he doth start
          Afresh without dismay.
          With great grief in his heart
          To the wood he goes away.

Huge was the joy then to hark to the hounds,
When the pack all met him, mingled together,   1720
Such curses they heaped on his head at the sight
That the clustering cliffs seemed to clatter down round them
In heaps. The men, when they met him, hailed him,
And loudly with chiding speeches hallooed him;
Threats were oft thrown at him, thief he was called;
At his tail were the greyhounds, that tarry he might not.
They rushed at him oft when he raced for the open,
And ran to the wood again, Reynard the wily.
Thus he led them, all muddied, the lord and his men,
In this manner along through the hills until midday.   1730
At home, the noble knight wholesomely slept
In the cold of the morn within comely curtains.
But the lady, for love, did not let herself sleep,
Or fail in the purpose fixed in her heart;
But quickly she roused herself, came there quickly,
Arrayed in a gay robe that reached to the ground,
The skins of the splendid fur skillfully trimmed close.
On her head no colors save jewels, well-cut,
That were twined in her hair-fret in clusters of twenty.
Her fair face was completely exposed, and her throat;   1740
In front her breast too was bare, and her back.
She comes through the chamber-door, closes it after her,
Swings wide a window, speaks to the wight,
And rallies him soon in speech full of sport
                    And good cheer.
          "Ah! man, how can you sleep?
          The morning is so clear."
          He was in sorrow deep,
          Yet her he then did hear.

In a dream muttered Gawain, deep in its gloom,   1750
Like a man by a throng of sad thoughts sorely moved
Of how fate was to deal out his destiny to him
That morn, when he met the man at the Green Chapel,
Bound to abide his blow, unresisting.
But as soon as that comely one came to his senses,
Started from slumber and speedily answered,
The lovely lady came near, sweetly laughing,
Bent down o'er his fair face and daintily kissed him.
And well, in a worthy manner, he welcomed her.
Seeing her glorious, gaily attired,   1760
Without fault in her features, most fine in her color,
Deep joy came welling up, warming his heart.
With sweet, gentle smiling they straightway grew merry;
So passed naught between them but pleasure, joy,
                                        And delight.
                    Goodly was their debate,
                    Nor was their gladness slight.
                    Their peril had been great
                    Had Mary quit her knight.

For that noble princess pressed him so closely,   1770
Brought him so near the last bound, that her love
He was forced to accept, or, offending, refuse her:
Concerned for his courtesy not to prove caitiff,[46]
And more for his ruin if wrong he committed,
Betraying the hero, the head of that house.
"God forbid," said the knight; "that never shall be";
And lovingly laughing a little, he parried
The words of fondness that fell from her mouth.
She said to him, "Sir, you are surely to blame
If you love not the lady beside whom you're lying,   1780
Of all the world's women most wounded in heart,
Unless you've one dearer, a lover you like more,
Your faith to her plighted, so firmly made fast
You desire not to loosen it—so I believe.
Now tell me truly I pray you; the truth,
By all of the loves that in life are, conceal not
                                Through guile."
                    The knight said, "By Saint John,"
                    And pleasantly to smile
                    Began, "In faith I've none,   1790
                    Nor will have for a while."

    "Such words," said the lady, "the worst are of all;
But in sooth I am answered, and sad it seems to me.
Kiss me now kindly, and quickly I'll go;

---

[46]A base, despicable person.

I on earth may but mourn, as a much loving mortal."
Sighing she stoops down, and kisses him seemly;
Then starting away from him, says as she stands,
"Now, my dear, at parting, do me this pleasure:
Give me some gift, thy glove if it might be,
To bring you to mind, sir, my mourning to lessen." 1800
"On my word," quoth the hero, "I would that I had here,
For thy sake, the thing that I think the dearest
I own, for in sooth you've deserved very often
A greater reward than one I could give.
But a pledge of love would profit but little;
'T would help not your honor to have at this time
For a keepsake a glove, as a gift of Gawain.
I've come on a mission to countries most strange;
I've no servants with splendid things filling their sacks:
That displeases me, lady, for love's sake, at present; 1810
Yet each man without murmur must do what he may
                              Nor repine."
            "Nay, lord of honors high,
            Though I have naught of thine,"
            Quoth the lovely lady, "I
            Shall give you gift of mine."

    She offered a rich ring, wrought in red gold,
With a blazing stone that stood out above it,
And shot forth brilliant rays bright as the sun;
Wit you well that wealth right huge it was worth. 1820
But promptly the hero replied, refusing it,
"Madam, I care not for gifts now to keep;
I have none to tender and naught will I take."
Thus he ever declined her offer right earnest,
And swore on his word that he would not accept it;
And, sad he declined, she thereupon said,
"If my ring you refuse, since it seems too rich,
If you would not so highly to me be beholden,
My girdle, that profits you less, I'll give you."
She swiftly removed the belt circling her sides, 1830
Round her tunic knotted, beneath her bright mantle;
'T was fashioned of green silk, and fair made with gold,
With gold, too, the borders embellished and beautiful.
To Gawain she gave it, and gaily besought him
To take it, although he thought it but trifling.
He swore by no manner of means he'd accept
Either gold or treasure ere God gave him grace
To attain the adventure he'd there undertaken.
"And, therefore, I pray, let it prove not displeasing,
But give up your suit, for to grant it I'll never 1840
                              Agree.
            I'm deeply in your debt
            For your kind ways to me.

                    In hot and cold I yet
                    Will your true servant be."

    "Refuse ye this silk," the lady then said,
"As slight in itself? Truly it seems so.
Lo! it is little, and less is its worth;
But one knowing the nature knit up within it,
Would give it a value more great, peradventure;   1850
For no man girt with this girdle of green,
And bearing it fairly made fast about him,
Might ever be cut down by any on earth,
For his life in no way in the world could be taken."
Then mused the man, and it came to his mind
In the peril appointed him precious 't would prove,
When he'd found the chapel, to face there his fortune.
The device, might he slaying evade, would be splendid.
Her suit then he suffered, and let her speak;
And the belt she offered him, earnestly urging it   1860
(And Gawain consented), and gave it with good will,
And prayed him for her sake ne'er to display it,
But, true, from her husband to hide it. The hero
Agreed that no one should know of it ever.
                              Then he
                    Thanked her with all his might
                    Of heart and thought; and she
                    By then to this stout knight
                    Had given kisses three.

    Then the lady departs, there leaving the lord,   1870
For more pleasure she could not procure from that prince.
When she's gone, then quickly Sir Gawain clothes himself,
Rises and dresses in noble array,
Lays by the love-lace the lady had left him,
Faithfully hides it where later he'd find it.
At once then went on his way to the chapel,
Approached in private a priest, and prayed him
To make his life purer, more plainly him teach
How his soul, when he had to go hence, should be saved.
He declared his faults, confessing them fully,   1880
The more and the less, and mercy besought,
And then of the priest implored absolution.
He surely absolved him, and made him as spotless,
Indeed, as if doomsday were due on the morrow.
Then among the fair ladies he made more merry
With lovely caroles, all kinds of delights,
That day than before, until darkness fell.
                              All there
                    Were treated courteously,
                    "And never," they declare,   1890

> "Has Gawain shown such glee
> Since hither he did fare."

In that nook where his lot may be love let him linger!
The lord's in the meadow still, leading his men.
He has slain this fox that he followed so long;
As he vaulted a hedge to get view of the villain,
Hearing the hounds that hastened hard after him,
Reynard from out a rough thicket came running,
And right at his heels in a rush all the rabble.
He, seeing that wild thing, wary, awaits him, 1900
Unsheaths his bright brand and strikes at the beast.
And he swerved from its sharpness and back would have started;
A hound, ere he could, came hurrying up to him;
All of them fell on him fast by the horse's feet,
Worried that sly one with wrathful sound.
And quickly the lord alights, and catches him,
Takes him in haste from the teeth of the hounds,
And over his head holds him high, loudly shouting,
Where brachets, many and fierce, at him barked.
Thither huntsmen made haste with many a horn, 1910
The recall, till they saw him, sounding right clearly.
As soon as his splendid troop had assembled,
All bearing a bugle blew them together,
The others having no horns all hallooed.
'T was the merriest baying that man ever heard
That was raised for the soul of Reynard with sounding
> Din.
> They fondle each dog's head
> Who his reward did win.
> Then take they Reynard dead 1920
> And strip him of his skin.

And now, since near was the night, they turned homeward,
Strongly and sturdily sounding their horns.
At last at his loved home the lord alighted,
A fire on the hearth found, the hero beside it,
Sir Gawain the good, who glad was withal,
For he had 'mong the ladies in love much delight.
A blue robe that fell to the floor he was wearing;
His surcoat, that softly was furred, well beseemed him;
A hood of the same hue hung on his shoulders, 1930
And both were bordered with white all about.
He, mid-most, met the good man in the hall,
And greeted him gladly, graciously saying:
"Now shall I first fulfil our agreement
We struck to good purpose, when drink was not spared."
Then Gawain embraced him, gave him three kisses,
The sweetest and soundest a man could bestow.

"By Christ, you'd great happiness," quoth then the host,
"In getting these wares, if good were your bargains."
"Take no care for the cost," the other said quickly,   1940
"Since plainly the debt that is due I have paid."
Said the other, "By Mary, mine's of less worth.
The whole of the day I have hunted, and gotten
The skin of this fox—the fiend take its foulness!—
Right poor to pay for things of such price
As you've pressed on me here so heartily, kisses
So good."
"Say no more," Gawain saith;
"I thank you, by the rood!"
How the fox met his death   1950
He told him as they stood.

With mirth and minstrelsy, meat at their pleasure
They made as merry as any men might
(With ladies' laughter, and launching of jests
Right glad were they both, the good man and Gawain)
Unless they had doted or else had been drunken.
Both the man and the company make many jokes,
Till the time is come when the two must be parted,
When finally the knights are forced to go bedward.
And first of the lord his respectful leave   1960
This goodly man took, and graciously thanked him:
"May God you reward for the welcome you gave me
This high feast, the splendid sojourn I've had here.
I give you myself, if you'd like it, to serve you.
I must, as you know, on the morrow move on;
Give me some one to show me the path, as you said,
To the Green Chapel, there, as God will allow me,
On New Year the fate that is fixed to perform."
"With a good will, indeed," said the good man; "whatever
I promised to do I deem myself ready."   1970
He a servant assigns on his way to set him,
To take him by hills that no trouble he'd have,
And through grove and wood by the way most direct
Might repair.
The lord he thanked again
For the honor done him there.
The knight his farewell then
Took of those ladies fair.

To them with sorrow and kissing he spoke,
And besought them his thanks most sincere to accept;   1980
And they, replying, promptly returned them,
With sighings full sore to the Savior commended him.
Then he with courtesy quitted the company,
Giving each man that he met his thanks

For kindness, for trouble he'd taken, for care
Whereby each had sought to serve him right eagerly.
Pained was each person to part with him then,
As if long they in honor had lived with that noble.
With people and lights he was led to his chamber,
To bed gaily brought there to be at his rest; 1990
Yet I dare not say whether soundly he slept,
For much, if he would, on the morn to remember
                    Had he.
          Let him lie stilly there
          Near what he sought to see.
          What happened I'll declare,
          If you will silent be.

                    IV
    The New Year draws near, and the nighttime now passes;
The day, as the Lord bids, drives on to darkness.
Outside, there sprang up wild storms in the world; 2000
The clouds cast keenly the cold to the earth
With enough of the north sting to trouble the naked;
Down shivered the snow, nipping sharply the wild beasts;
The wind from the heights, shrilly howling, came rushing,
And heaped up each dale full of drifts right huge.
Full well the man listened who lay in his bed.
Though he shut tight his lids, he slept but a little;
He knew by each cock that crowed 't was the tryst time,
And swiftly ere dawn of the day he arose,
For there shone then the light of a lamp in his room; 2010
To his chamberlain called, who answered him quickly,
And bade him his saddle to bring and his mailshirt.
The other man roused up and fetched him his raiment,
Arrayed then that knight in a fashion right noble.
First he clad him in clothes to ward off the cold,
Then his other equipment, carefully kept:
His pieces of plate armor, polished right cleanly,
The rings of his rich mail burnished from rust.
All was fresh as at first; he was fain to give thanks
                    To the men. 2020
          He had on every piece
          Full brightly burnished then.
          He, gayest from here to Greece,
          Ordered his steed again.

    He garbed himself there in the loveliest garments
(His coat had its blazon of beautiful needlework
Stitched upon velvet for show, its rich stones
Set about it and studded, its seams all embroidered,
Its lovely fur in the fairest of linings),
Yet he left not the lace, the gift of the lady: 2030

That, Gawain did not, for his own sake, forget.
When the brand[47] on his rounded thighs he had belted,
He twisted his love-token two times about him.
That lord round his waist with delight quickly wound
The girdle of green silk, that seemed very gay
Upon royal red cloth that was rich to behold.
But Gawain the girdle wore not for its great price,
Or pride in its pendants although they were polished,
Though glittering gold there gleamed on the ends,
But himself to save when he needs must suffer   2040
The death, nor could stroke then of sword or of knife
                      Him defend.
           Then was the bold man dressed;
           Quickly his way did wend;
           To all the court expressed
           His great thanks without end.

Then was Gringolet ready that great was and huge,
Who had safely, as seemed to him pleasant, been stabled;
That proud horse pranced, in the pink of condition.
The lord then comes to him, looks at his coat,   2050
And soberly says, and swears on his word,
"In this castle's a company mindful of courtesy,
Led by this hero. Delight may they have;
And may love the dear lady betide all her lifetime.
If they for charity cherish a guest,
And give so great welcome, may God reward them,
Who rules the heaven on high, and the rest of you.
Might I for long live my life on the earth,
Some repayment with pleasure I'd make, if 't were possible."
He steps in the stirrup, strides into the saddle,   2060
Receives on his shoulder the shield his man brings him,
And spurs into Gringolet strikes with his gilt heels;
Who leaps on the stones and lingers no longer
                    To prance.
           The knight on his horse sits,
           Who bears his spear and lance,
           The house to Christ commits,
           And wishes it good chance.

Then down the drawbridge they dropped, the broad gates
Unbarred, and on both sides bore them wide open.   2070
He blessed them quickly, and crossed o'er the planks there
(He praises the porter, who knelt by the prince
Begging God to save Gawain, and gave him goodday),
And went on his way with but one man attended

---

[47] Sword.

To show him the turns to that sorrowful spot
Where he must to that onerous onset submit.
By hillsides where branches were bare they both journeyed;
They climbed over cliffs where the cold was clinging.
The clouds hung aloft, but 't was lowering beneath them.
On the moor dripped the mist, on the mountains melted;   2080
Each hill had a hat, a mist-cloak right huge.
The brooks foamed and bubbled on hillsides about them,
And brightly broke on their banks as they rushed down.
Full wandering the way was they went through the wood,
Until soon it was time for the sun to be springing.
                             Then they
                Were on a hill full high;
                White snow beside them lay.
                The servant who rode nigh
                Then bade his master stay.   2090

   "I have led you hither, my lord, at this time,
And not far are you now from that famous place
You have sought for, and asked so especially after.
Yet, sir, to you surely I'll say, since I know you,
A man in this world whom I love right well,
If you'd follow my judgment, the better you'd fare.
You make haste to a place that is held full of peril;
One dwells, the worst in the world, in that waste,
For he's strong and stern, and takes pleasure in striking.
No man on the earth can equal his might;   2100
He is bigger in body than four of the best men
In Arthur's own household, Hector or others.
And thus he brings it about at the chapel:
That place no one passes so proud in his arms
That he smites him not dead with a stroke of his hand.
He's a man most immoderate, showing no mercy;
Be it chaplain or churl that rides by the chapel,
Monk or priest, any manner of man,
Him to slay seems as sweet as to still live himself.
So I say, as sure as you sit in your saddle   2110
You're killed, should the knight so choose, if you come here;
That take as the truth, though you twenty lives had
                         To spend.
                He's lived in this place long
                In battles without end.
                Against his strokes right strong
                You cannot you defend.

   "So let him alone, good Sir Gawain, and leave
By a different road, for God's sake, and ride
To some other country where Christ may reward you.   2120
And homeward again I will hie me, and promise

To swear by the Lord and all his good saints
(So help me the oaths on God's halidom[48] sworn)
That I'll guard well your secret, and give out no story
You hastened to flee any hero I've heard of."
"Thank you," said Gawain, and grudgingly added,
"Good fortune go with you for wishing me well.
And truly I think you'd not tell; yet though never
So surely you hid it, if hence I should hasten,
Fearful, to fly in the fashion you tell of,   2130
A coward I'd prove, and could not be pardoned.
The chapel I'll find whatsoever befalls,
And talk with that wight the way that I want to,
Let weal or woe follow as fate may wish.
                                    Though the knave,
                Hard to subdue and fell,
                Should stand there with a stave,
                Yet still the Lord knows well
                His servants how to save."

    Quoth the man, "By Mary, you've said now this much: 2140
That you wish to bring down your own doom on your head.
Since you'd lose your life, I will stay you no longer.
Put your helm on your head, take your spear in your hand,
And ride down this road by the side of that rock
Till it brings you down to the dale's rugged bottom;
Then look at the glade on the left hand a little:
You'll see in the valley that self-same chapel,
And near it the great-limbed knight who is guarding it.
Gawain the noble, farewell now, in God's name!
I would not go with thee for all the world's wealth,   2150
Nor in fellowship ride one more foot through the forest."
The man in the trees there then turns his bridle,
As hard as he can hits his horse with his heels,
And across the fields gallops, there leaving Sir Gawain
                            Alone.
                "By God," the knight said, "now
                I'll neither weep nor groan.
                Unto God's will I bow,
                And make myself his own."

    He strikes spurs into Gringolet, starts on the path;   2160
By a bank at the side of a small wood he pushes in,
Rides down the rugged slope right to the dale.
Then about him he looks, and the land seems wild,
And nowhere he sees any sign of a shelter,
But slopes on each side of him, high and steep,
And rocks, gnarled and rough, and stones right rugged.

[48] Holiness or holy relics.

The clouds there seemed to him scraped by the crags.
Then he halted and held back his horse at that time,
And spied on all sides in search of the chapel;
Such nowhere he saw, but soon, what seemed strange, 2170
In the midst of a glade a mound, as it might be,
A smooth, swelling knoll by the side of the water,
The falls of a rivulet running close by;
In its banks the brook bubbled as though it were boiling.
The knight urged on Gringolet, came to the glade,
There leaped down lightly and tied to the limb
Of a tree, right rugged, the reins of his noble steed,
Went to the mound, and walked all about it,
Debating what manner of thing it might be:
On the end and on each side an opening; everywhere 2180
Over it grass was growing in patches,
All hollow inside, it seemed an old cave
Or a crag's old cleft: which, he could not decide.
　　　　　　　　　　　　Said the knight,
　　　　　"Is this the chapel here?
　　　　　Alas, dear Lord! here might
　　　　　The fiend, when midnight's near,
　　　　　His matin prayers recite.

"Of a truth," said Gawain, "the glade here is gloomy;
The Green Chapel's ugly, with herbs overgrown. 2190
It greatly becomes here that hero, green-clad,
To perform in the devil's own fashion his worship.
I feel in my five senses this is the fiend
Who has made me come to this meeting to kill me.
Destruction fall on this church of ill-fortune!
The cursedest chapel that ever I came to!"
With helm on his head and lance in his hand
He went right to the rock of that rugged abode.
From that high hill he heard, from a hard rock over
The stream, on the hillside, a sound wondrous loud. 2200
Lo! it clattered on cliffs fit to cleave them, as though
A scythe on a grindstone some one were grinding.
It whirred, lo! and whizzed like a water-mill's wheel;
Lo! it ground and it grated, grievous to hear.
"By God, this thing, as I think," then said Gawain,
"Is done now for me, since my due turn to meet it
　　　　　　　　　　　　Is near.
　　　　　God's will be done! 'Ah woe!'
　　　　　No whit doth aid me here.
　　　　　Though I my life forego 2210
　　　　　No sound shall make me fear."

And then the man there commenced to call loudly,
"Who here is the master, with me to hold tryst?
For Gawain the good now is going right near.

He who craves aught of me let him come hither quickly;
'T is now or never; he needs to make haste."
Said somebody, "Stop," from the slope up above him,
"And promptly you'll get what I promised to give you."
Yet he kept up the whirring noise quickly a while,
Turned to finish his sharpening before he'd descend.   2220
Then he came by a crag, from a cavern emerging,
Whirled out of a den with a dreadful weapon,
A new Danish axe to answer the blow with;
Its blade right heavy, curved back to the handle,
Sharp filed with the filing tool, four feet in length,
'T was no less, by the reach of that lace gleaming brightly.
The fellow in green was garbed as at first,
Both his face and his legs, his locks and his beard,
Save that fast o'er the earth on his feet he went fairly,
The shaft on the stone set, and stalked on beside it.   2230
On reaching the water, he would not wade it;
On his axe he hopped over, and hastily strode,
Very fierce, through the broad field filled all about him
                              With snow.
            Sir Gawain met the man,
            And bowed by no means low,
            Who said, "Good sir, men can
            Trust you to tryst to go."

    Said the green man, "Gawain, may God you guard!
You are welcome indeed, sir knight, at my dwelling.   2240
Your travel you've timed as a true man should,
And you know the compact we came to between us;
A twelvemonth ago you took what chance gave,
And I promptly at New Year was pledged to repay you.
In truth, we are down in this dale all alone;
Though we fight as we please, here there's no one to part us.
Put your helm from your head, and have here your payment;
Debate no further than I did before,
When you slashed off my head with a single stroke."
"Nay," quoth Gawain, "by God who gave me my spirit,   2250
I'll harbor no grudge whatever harm happens.
Exceed not one stroke and still I shall stand;
You may do as you please, I'll in no way oppose
                              The blow."
            He left the flesh all bare,
            Bending his neck down low
            As if he feared naught there,
            For fear he would not show.

    Then the man in green raiment quickly made ready,
Uplifted his grim tool Sir Gawain to smite;   2260
With the whole of his strength he heaved it on high,
As threateningly swung it as though he would slay him.

Had it fallen again with the force he intended
That lord, ever-brave, from the blow had been lifeless.
But Gawain a side glance gave at the weapon
As down it came gliding to do him to death;
With his shoulders shrank from the sharp iron a little.
The other with sudden jerk stayed the bright axe,
And reproved then that prince with proud words in plenty:
"Not Gawain thou art who so good is considered,   2270
Ne'er daunted by host in hill or in dale;
Now in fear, ere thou feelest a hurt, thou art flinching;
Such cowardice never I knew of that knight.
When you swung at me, sir, I fled not nor started;
No cavil I offered in King Arthur's castle.
My head at my feet fell, yet never I flinched,
And thy heart is afraid ere a hurt thou feelest,
And therefore thy better I'm bound to be thought
                 On that score."
          "I shrank once," Gawain said,   2280
          "And I will shrink no more;
          Yet cannot I my head,
          If it fall down, restore.

    "But make ready, sir, quickly, and come to the point;
My destiny deal me, and do it forthwith;
For a stroke I will suffer, and start no further
Till hit with thy weapon; have here my pledged word."
Quoth the other, heaving it high, "Have at thee!"
As fierce in his manner as if he were mad,
He mightily swung but struck not the man,   2290
Withheld on a sudden his hand ere it hurt him.
And firmly he waited and flinched in no member,
But stood there as still as a stone or a stump
In rocky ground held by a hundred roots.
Then the Green Knight again began to speak gaily:
"It behooves me to hit, now that whole is thy heart.
Thy high hood that Arthur once gave you now hold back,
Take care that your neck at this cut may recover."
And Gawain full fiercely said in a fury,
"Come! lay on, thou dread man; too long thou art threatening.   2300
I think that afraid of your own self you feel."
"In sooth," said the other, "thy speech is so savage
No more will I hinder thy mission nor have it
                 Delayed."
          With puckered lips and brow
          He stands with ready blade.
          Not strange 't is hateful now
          To him past hope of aid.

    He lifts his axe lightly, and lets it down deftly,
The blade's edge next to the naked neck.   2310

Though he mightily hammered he hurt him no more
Than to give him a slight nick that severed the skin there.
Through fair skin the keen axe so cut to the flesh
That shining blood shot to the earth o'er his shoulders.
As soon as he saw his blood gleam on the snow
He sprang forth in one leap, for more than a spear length;
His helm fiercely caught up and clapped on his head;
With his shoulders his fair shield shot round in front of him,
Pulled out his bright sword, and said in a passion
(And since he was mortal man born of his mother   2320
The hero was never so happy by half),
"Cease thy violence, man; no more to me offer,
For here I've received, unresisting, a stroke.
If a second thou strikest I soon will requite thee,
And swiftly and fiercely, be certain of that,
                                        Will repay.
              One stroke on me might fall
              By bargain struck that way,
              Arranged in Arthur's hall;
              Therefore, sir knight, now stay!"   2330

    The man turned away, on his weapon rested,
The shaft on the ground set, leaned on the sharp edge,
And gazed at Sir Gawain there in the glade;
Saw that bold man, unblenching, standing right bravely,
Full-harnessed and gallant; at heart he was glad.
Then gaily the Green Knight spoke in a great voice,
And said to the man in speech that resounded,
"Now be not so savage, bold sir, for towards you
None here has acted unhandsomely, save
In accord with the compact arranged in the King's court.   2340
I promised the stroke you've received, so hold you
Well payed. I free you from all duties further.
If brisk I had been, peradventure a buffet
I'd harshly have dealt that harm would have done you.
In mirth, with a feint I menaced you first,
With no direful wound rent you; right was my deed,
By the bargain that bound us both on the first night,
When, faithful and true, you fulfilled our agreement,
And gave me your gain as a good man ought to.
The second I struck at you, sir, for the morning   2350
You kissed my fair wife and the kisses accorded me.
Two mere feints for both times I made at you, man,
                                        Without woe.
              True men restore by right,
              One fears no danger so;
              You failed the third time, knight,
              And therefore took that blow.

    " 'T is my garment you're wearing, that woven girdle,
Bestowed by my wife, as in truth I know well.

I know also your kisses and all of your acts 2360
And my wife's advances; myself, I devised them.
I sent her to try you, and truly you seem
The most faultless of men that e'er fared on his feet.
As a pearl compared to white peas is more precious,
So next to the other gay knights is Sir Gawain.
But a little you lacked, and loyalty wanted,
Yet truly 't was not for intrigue or for wooing,
But love of your life; the less do I blame you."
Sir Gawain stood in a study a great while,
So sunk in disgrace that in spirit he groaned; 2370
To his face all the blood in his body was flowing;
For shame, as the other was talking, he shrank.
And these were the first words that fell from his lips:
"Be cowardice cursed, and coveting! In you
Are vice and villainy, virtue destroying."
The lace he then seized, and loosened the strands,
And fiercely the girdle flung at the Green Knight.
"Lo! there is faith-breaking! evil befall it.
To coveting came I, for cowardice caused me
From fear of your stroke to forsake in myself 2380
What belongs to a knight: munificence, loyalty.
I'm faulty and false, who've been ever afraid
Of untruth and treachery; sorrow betide both
                    And care!
            Here I confess my sin;
            All faulty did I fare.
            Your good will let me win,
            And then I will beware."

    Then the Green Knight laughed, and right graciously said,
"I am sure that the harm is healed that I suffered. 2390
So clean you're confessed, so cleared of your faults,
Having had the point of my weapon's plain penance,
I hold you now purged of offence, and as perfectly
Spotless as though you'd ne'er sinned in your life.
And I give to you, sir, the golden-hemmed girdle,
As green as my gown. Sir Gawain, when going
Forth on your way among famous princes,
Think still of our strife and this token right splendid,
'Mid chivalrous knights, of the chapel's adventure.
This New Year you'll come to my castle again, 2400
And the rest of this feast in revel most pleasant
                    Will go."
            Then pressed him hard the lord:
            "My wife and you, I know
            We surely will accord,
            Who was your bitter foe."

    "No indeed," quoth the hero, his helm seized and doffed it
Graciously, thanking the Green Knight; "I've stayed

Long enough. May good fortune befall you; may He
Who all fame doth confer give it fully to you, sir. 2410
To your lady, gracious and lovely, commend me,
To her and that other, my honored ladies,
That so with their sleights deceived their knight subtly.
But no marvel it is for a fool to act madly,
Through woman's wiles to be brought to woe.
So for certain was Adam deceived by some woman,
By several Solomon, Samson besides;
Delilah dealt him his doom; and David
Was duped by Bath-sheba, enduring much sorrow.
Since these were grieved by their guile, 't would be great gain 2420
To love them yet never believe them, if knights could.
For formerly these were most noble and fortunate,
More than all others who lived on the earth;
                              And these few
          By women's wiles were caught
          With whom they had to do.
          Though I'm beguiled, I ought
          To be excused now too.

   "But your girdle," said Gawain, "may God you reward!
With a good will I'll use it, yet not for the gold, 2430
The sash or the silk, or the sweeping pendants,
Or fame, or its workmanship wondrous, or cost,
But in sign of my sin I shall see it oft.
When in glory I move, with remorse I'll remember
The frailty and fault of the stubborn flesh,
How soon 't is infected with stains of defilement;
And thus when I'm proud of my prowess in arms,
The sight of this sash shall humble my spirit.
But one thing I pray, if it prove not displeasing;
Because you are lord of the land where I stayed 2440
In your house with great worship (may He now reward you
Who sitteth on high and upholdeth the heavens),
What name do you bear? No more would I know."
And then "That truly I'll tell," said the other;
"Bercilak de Hautdesert here am I called.
Through her might who lives with me, Morgan le Fay,[49]
Well-versed in the crafts and cunning of magic
(Many of Merlin's[50] arts she has mastered,
For long since she dealt in the dalliance of love
With him whom your heroes at home know, that sage 2450
                              Without blame.
          'Morgan the goddess,' so
          She's rightly known by name.
          No one so proud doth go
          That him she cannot tame),

[49] King Arthur's half-sister.
[50] The magician of Arthur's court, who helped him become king.

"I was sent in this way to your splendid hall
To make trial of your pride, and to see if the people's
Tales were true of the Table's great glory.
This wonder she sent to unsettle your wits,
And to daunt so the Queen as to cause her to die   2460
From fear at the sight of that phantom speaker
Holding his head in his hand at the high table.
Lives she at home there, that ancient lady;
She's even thine aunt, King Arthur's half-sister,
Tyntagel's duchess's daughter, whom Uther
Made later the mother of mighty Lord Arthur.[51]
I beg thee, sir, therefore, come back to thine aunt;
In my castle make merry. My company love thee,
And I, sir, wish thee as well, on my word,
As any on earth for thy high sense of honor."   2470
He said to him, nay, this he'd never consent to.
The men kiss, embrace, and each other commend
To the Prince of Paradise; there they part
                    In the cold.
        Gawain on his fair horse
        To Arthur hastens bold;
        The bright Green Knight his course
        Doth at his pleasure hold.

Through the wood now goes Sir Gawain by wild ways
On Gringolet, given by God's grace his life.   2480
Oft in houses, and oft in the open he lodged,
Met many adventures, won many a victory:
These I intend not to tell in this tale.
Now whole was the hurt he had in his neck,
And about it the glimmering belt he was bearing,
Bound to his side like a baldric obliquely,
Tied under his left arm, that lace, with a knot
As a sign that with stain of sin he'd been found.
And thus to the court he comes all securely.
Delight in that dwelling arose when its lord knew   2490
That Gawain had come; a good thing he thought it.
The King kissed the lord, and the Queen did likewise,
And next many knights drew near him to greet him
And ask how he'd fared; and he wondrously answered,
Confessed all the hardships that him had befallen,
The happenings at chapel, the hero's behavior,
The lady's love, and lastly the lace.
He showed them the nick in his neck all naked
The blow that the Green Knight gave for deceit
                    Him to blame.   2500
        In torment this he owned;
        Blood in his face did flame;

---

[51] Igraine, duchess of Tintagel. Morgan le Fay was her daughter by her husband the duke.
King Arthur was her son by Uther, who slept with her under the magical influence of Merlin.

With wrath and grief he groaned,
When showing it with shame.

Laying hold of the lace, quoth the hero, "Lo! lord!
The band of this fault I bear on my neck;
And this is the scathe and damage I've suffered,
For cowardice caught there, and coveting also,
The badge of untruth in which I was taken.
And this for as long as I live I must wear,   2510
For his fault none may hide without meeting misfortune,
For once it is fixed, it can ne'er be unfastened."
To the knight then the King gave comfort; the court too
Laughed greatly, and made this gracious agreement:
That ladies and lords to the Table belonging,
All of the brotherhood, baldrics should bear
Obliquely about them, bands of bright green,
Thus following suit for the sake of the hero.
For the Round Table's glory was granted that lace,
And he held himself honored who had it thereafter,   2520
As told in the book, the best of romances,
In the days of King Arthur this deed was done
Whereof witness is borne by Brutus's book.
Since Brutus, that bold man, first came here to Britain,
When ceased, indeed, had the siege and assault
                                    At Troy's wall,
          Full many feats ere now
          Like this one did befall.
          May He with thorn-crowned brow
          To His bliss bring us all.   Amen.   2530

HONY SOYT QUI MAL PENCE.[52]

---

[52] "Shame be to him who evil thinks," the motto of the Order of the Garter, founded in the fourteenth century. Whoever added the motto to the end of *Sir Gawain* apparently associated the wearing of the green girdle to honor Gawain with the wearing of the Garter.

Geoffrey Chaucer
(1340?–1400)

One of the most versatile of English and of medieval poets, Chaucer was born in 1340 or a little later, the son of a London wine merchant. The comfortable middle-class family had been rising socially, and young Geoffrey served as a page in the household of the Countess of Ulster, where as an intimate of a noble family he was well educated and early acclimated to aristocratic values and manners. In 1359 he served on the Continent during one of the military campaigns of the Hundred Years' War, waged in the fourteenth and fifteenth centuries for control of disputed territories in France. He was captured and then ransomed with the help of King Edward III—an episode that marks the beginning of a series of favors, positions, and preferments (interrupted by some tribulations in the 1380s) that Chaucer received from English kings throughout his life. Besides serving again later in the army, he filled several high posts in the country's service: customs supervisor, director of public works, king's forester, and Member of Parliament. He undertook for the crown a number of important diplomatic missions to France, the Low Countries, Spain, and Italy. During his sojourns in Italy he was exposed to the work of the three fourteenth-century Italian masters, Dante, Boccaccio, and Petrarch; their influence on his later work is strong. Chaucer died in 1400, a year after the dethronement of Richard II by Henry IV, and was buried in what is now called the Poets' Corner of Westminster Abbey. That in a turbulent era he enjoyed the favor of three rulers says something about Chaucer as man and civil servant.

Chaucer's lifelong close association with public affairs and men of high station helps explain his urbanity and his wide-ranging knowledge of the world. The often mordant portraits of moral delinquents and, conversely, of saintly types in *The Canterbury Tales* testify that in his own way Chaucer is a social critic. But political matters do not play a large part in his works as they do in Dante's. Although he succeeded in portraying definitively the England of his time, Chaucer did so through the gifts he shares with the greatest storytellers: a sure and shrewd power of characterization, a keen eye for the quality of *things*, subtle and penetrating psychology, and an unfailing ear for good dialogue, which, like Shakespeare, he was able to accommodate naturally to a wide variety of verse forms, not to mention prose.

Chaucer's narrative genius is in many ways best exemplified in *Troilus and Criseyde* (1380s), one of his two supreme masterpieces. This poem of more than 8,000 lines, set during the Trojan War, allowed him to develop at book length a single story and to explore exhaustively the psychology of the characters, of whom the heroine Criseyde is the most complex. In *Troilus,* Chaucer also develops one of his favorite themes: the nature of love as it reveals the conflicting values of this world and the next.

The fullest range of Chaucer's powers emerges in his most popular work, *The Canterbury Tales,* which he wrote in the late 1380s and early 1390s. The work is unfinished; the plan outlined in the General Prologue calls for four stories from each of thirty or so travelers, but we have only one tale apiece from twenty-four of them. Moreover, the work exists in ten fragments, the order of which has had to be reconstructed by scholarly detective work. Nevertheless, enough was completed and joined together to give the impression of a whole, although not a fully assembled or finally polished one.

Like Boccaccio's *Decameron* (which Chaucer apparently did not know), *The Canterbury Tales* is framed by an agreement among the principals to tell stories to one another. Chaucer's scheme, in which the characters are drawn from all vocations and social classes and the tales usually are emphatically appropriate to the tellers and their stations in life, allows him to achieve a variety at least as wide as Boccaccio's and at the same time to join the tales organically to the basic story of the pilgrimage. That Chaucer's framework is a *religious* pilgrimage is not insignificant; the pilgrims and the characters in their stories are revealed in the light both of the world with which so many of them are preoccupied and also of eternity. The variety of the pilgrims and of their moral conditions has a similar effect; the depravity of characters such as the Pardoner, the integrity of the Knight and sanctity of the Parson, the more ambiguous status of such figures as the fastidious Prioress and the worldly Monk imply, taken together, a moral concern almost as profound as Dante's, if less insistent.

Chaucer is a distinctively English poet in many ways, but he also illustrates the characteristic internationalism of medieval culture and literature. Medieval authors were not expected to invent their own material, and Chaucer's tales, along with the frequent allusions and illustrations within them, are drawn mainly from non-English sources: French and Italian authors, classical legend and literature (notably Ovid), and the Bible (which Chaucer knew thoroughly). Chaucer reworks such materials in his own vein, infusing them with his distinctive qualities of drama, pathos, and wit. The media of the tales include an assortment of skillfully managed verse forms and genres. The Miller relates *a fabliau,* a comically bawdy tale of ordinary or "low" life; the Wife of Bath relates a folktale; the Pardoner delivers a sermon and a morally pointed "exemplum"; the Nun's Priest's tale is a mock-heroic beast fable. *The Canterbury Tales* includes also specimens of romance, saint's legend, "tragedy" (defined simply as an account of the downfall of an eminent personage), and other narrative genres.

Perhaps the most distinctive of Chaucer's gifts as storyteller is his ability to delineate characters and put them in realistic motion. They come most patently alive in the prologues to the individual tales and in the narrative links, but most of his people are realized three-dimensionally in the General Prologue as well. The pilgrims make up a human encyclopedia—comprehensive and universal but composed of unique individuals. Interpreting them can be problematical. The Wife of Bath, for example, projects to some readers an attractively earthy personality and to others a sinister moral obliquity. The Pardoner, unquestionably one of the most unsavory characters in world literature, raises questions too, most obviously about his motives in revealing his cynical duplicity so frankly to the company.

After the Normans conquered England in 1066, French became the language of polite society, while Latin continued to be the language of the learned. To a great extent this was still true in Chaucer's day. His decision to write in English at a time when the language was in a state of flux is a significant milestone in the development of English, like Dante's decision to write his *Divine Comedy* in Italian. But English continued to change radically for a long time after Chaucer, and it was not until the late seventeenth century that the evolution so slowed that the average modern reader can understand the language of the time without elaborate glossing. Chaucer's language, Middle English, is thus very different from the English of today. It is not so different, however, that modern readers should be discouraged from trying Chaucer in a good Middle English edition. The following is the beginning of the General Prologue:

> Whan that Aprille with his shoures soote
> The droghte of March hath perced to the rote,
> And bathed every veyne in swich licour

Of which vertu engendred is the flour;
Whan Zephirus eek with his swete breeth
Inspired hath in every holt and heeth
The tendre croppes, and the yonge sonne
Hath in the Ram his halve cours yronne,
And smale foweles maken melodye,
That slepen al the nyght with open ye   10
(So priketh hem nature in hir corages):
Than longen folk to goon on pilgrymages,
And palmers for to seken straunge strondes,
To ferne halwes, kouthe in sondry londes;
And specially from every shires ende
Of Engelond to Caunterbury they wende,
The holy blisful martir for to seke,
That hem hath holpen whan that they were seke.

FURTHER READING *(prepared by W.J.R. and M.C.):* George Kane's *Chaucer,* 1984, in the Past Masters series, is a short general introduction to the poet's life and work, particularly interesting on the division between the poet and narrator. Biographies of Chaucer that discuss his life and work in depth include Derek Pearsall, *The Life of Geoffrey Chaucer: A Critical Biography,* 1992; and Donald R. Howard, *Chaucer: His Life, His Works, His World,* 1987. Velma Bourgeois Richmond, *Geoffrey Chaucer,* 1992, treats incisively Chaucer's vision as a writer. Two works by Derek Stanley Brewer provide vivid sketches of Chaucer and his England: Brewer's *Chaucer,* 1953, is intended for the new student of Chaucer; his *Chaucer and His World,* 1978, contains a generous selection of illustrations. D. W. Robertson, Jr., *A Preface to Chaucer,* 1962, is an important work in Chaucer scholarship, taking a deductive approach to Chaucer's work through an extensive analysis of background material. Robertson's work is noted for its many unconventional interpretations. Muriel Bowden's *A Reader's Guide to Geoffrey Chaucer,* 1964, takes a more centrist approach. This book offers a biographical sketch and a long section on *The Canterbury Tales* that discusses various influences on Chaucer's writing. George Lyman Kittredge's *Chaucer and His Poetry,* 1915, reprinted in 1970, based on lectures delivered in 1914, remains fresh and instructive. Derek Albert Pearsall's *The Canterbury Tales,* 1985, includes a historical survey of the main critical issues raised by the work. David Aers, *Chaucer,* 1986, invites readers to examine the poet's work from modern perspectives, as does Stephen Thomas Knight, *Geoffrey Chaucer,* 1986, in the Rereading Literature series. Women and women's issues in Chaucer are treated in Jill Mann, *Geoffrey Chaucer,* 1991; Priscilla Martin, *Chaucer's Women: Nuns, Wives, and Amazons,* 1990; Margaret Hallissy, *Clean Maids, True Wives, Steadfast Widows: Chaucer's Women and Medieval Codes of Conduct,* 1993; and Elaine Tuttle Hansen, *Chaucer and the Fictions of Gender,* 1992. C. David Benson's *Chaucer's Drama of Style: Poetic Variety and Contrast in the "Canterbury Tales,"* 1986, discusses the topics mentioned in its title. One of the best essays on Chaucer's fabliaux can be found in Derek Brewer, *Chaucer: The Poet as Storyteller,* 1984, which also contains an essay on "The Nun's Priest's Tale" and another on Chaucer's place in European and English tradition. Critical perspectives from several centuries are represented in *Chaucer: "The Canterbury Tales": A Casebook,* ed. by J. J. Anderson, 1974. This volume includes Paul Ruggier's interesting "Irony in 'The Wife of Bath's Tale.'" Twenty-six essays, balanced between historical scholarship and literary criticism, are collected in *Chaucer: Modern Essays in Criticism,* ed. by Edward Wagenknecht, 1959. The emphasis is on *The Canterbury Tales,* including "The Pardoner's Tale" and "The Wife of Bath's Tale."

THE CANTERBURY TALES

Translated by Theodore Morrison

PROLOGUE

As soon as April pierces to the root
The drought of March, and bathes each bud and shoot
Through every vein of sap with gentle showers
From whose engendering liquor spring the flowers;
When zephyrs have breathed softly all about
Inspiring every wood and field to sprout,
And in the zodiac the youthful sun
His journey halfway through the Ram[1] has run;
When little birds are busy with their song
Who sleep with open eyes the whole night long   10
Life stirs their hearts and tingles in them so,
Then off as pilgrims people long to go,
And palmers[2] to set out for distant strands
And foreign shrines renowned in many lands.
And specially in England people ride
To Canterbury[3] from every countryside
To visit there the blessed martyred saint
Who gave them strength when they were sick and faint.
    In Southwark at the Tabard[4] one spring day
It happened, as I stopped there on my way,   20
Myself a pilgrim with a heart devout
Ready for Canterbury to set out,
At night came all of twenty-nine assorted
Travelers, and to that same inn resorted,
Who by a turn of fortune chanced to fall
In fellowship together, and they were all
Pilgrims who had it in their minds to ride
Toward Canterbury. The stable doors were wide,
The rooms were large, and we enjoyed the best,
And shortly, when the sun had gone to rest,   30
I had so talked with each that presently
I was a member of their company
And promised to rise early the next day
To start, as I shall show, upon our way.
    But none the less, while I have time and space,
Before this tale has gone a further pace,

---

[1] The sun is in Aries (the Ram) during late March and early April.
[2] Zealous pilgrims who traveled to far-distant places.
[3] A city about sixty miles southeast of London. In Canterbury Cathedral was located the shrine of St. Thomas à Becket, murdered there in 1170.
[4] An inn in Southwark, a suburb of London on the south bank of the Thames.

I should in reason tell you the condition
Of each of them, his rank and his position,
And also what array they all were in;
And so then, with a knight I will begin. 40
   A Knight was with us, and an excellent man,
Who from the earliest moment he began
To follow his career loved chivalry,
Truth, openhandedness, and courtesy.
He was a stout man in the king's campaigns
And in that cause had gripped his horse's reins
In Christian lands and pagan through the earth,
None farther, and always honored for his worth.
He was on hand at Alexandria's fall.[5]
He had often sat in precedence to all 50
The nations at the banquet board in Prussia.
He had fought in Lithuania and in Russia,
No Christian knight more often; he had been
In Moorish Africa at Benmarin,
At the siege of Algeciras in Granada,
And sailed in many a glorious armada
In the Mediterranean, and fought as well
At Ayas and Attalia when they fell
In Armenia and on Asia Minor's coast.
Of fifteen deadly battles he could boast, 60
And in Algeria, at Tremessen,
Fought for the faith and killed three separate men
In single combat. He had done good work
Joining against another pagan Turk
With the king of Palathia. And he was wise,
Despite his prowess, honored in men's eyes,
Meek as a girl and gentle in his ways.
He had never spoken ignobly all his days
To any man by even a rude inflection.
He was a knight in all things to perfection. 70
He rode a good horse, but his gear was plain,
For he had lately served on a campaign.
His tunic was still spattered by the rust
Left by his coat of mail, for he had just
Returned and set out on his pilgrimage.
   His son was with him, a young Squire, in age
Some twenty years as near as I could guess.
His hair curled as if taken from a press.[6]
He was a lover and would become a knight.
In stature he was of a moderate height 80
But powerful and wonderfully quick.

---

[5] The places mentioned in the following lines were sites of battles, mostly fought against Muslims and other so-called pagans.
   [6] Curlers.

He had been in Flanders, riding in the thick
Of forays in Artois and Picardy,
And bore up well for one so young as he,
Still hoping by his exploits in such places
To stand the better in his lady's graces.
He wore embroidered flowers, red and white,
And blazed like a spring meadow to the sight.
He sang or played his flute the livelong day.
He was as lusty as the month of May.   90
His coat was short, its sleeves were long and wide.
He sat his horse well, and knew how to ride,
And how to make a song and use his lance,
And he could write and draw well, too, and dance.
So hot his love that when the moon rose pale
He got no more sleep than a nightingale.
He was modest, and helped whomever he was able,
And carved as his father's squire at the table.
    But one more servant had the Knight beside,
Choosing thus simply for the time to ride: 100
A Yeoman, in a coat and hood of green.
His peacock-feathered arrows, bright and keen,
He carried under his belt in tidy fashion.
For well-kept gear he had a yeoman's passion.
No draggled feather might his arrows show,
And in his hand he held a mighty bow.
He kept his hair close-cropped, his face was brown.
He knew the lore of woodcraft up and down.
His arm was guarded from the bowstring's whip
By a bracer, gaily trimmed. He had at hip   110
A sword and buckler, and at his other side
A dagger whose fine mounting was his pride,
Sharp-pointed as a spear. His horn he bore
In a sling of green, and on his chest he wore
A silver image of St. Christopher,
His patron, since he was a forester.
    There was also a Nun, a Prioress,[7]
Whose smile was gentle and full of guilelessness.
"By St. Loy!"[8] was the worst oath she would say.
She sang mass well, in a becoming way,   120
Intoning through her nose the words divine,
And she was known as Madame Eglantine.
She spoke good French, as taught at Stratford-Bow,[9]
For the Parisian French she did not know.
She was schooled to eat so primly and so well
That from her lips no morsel ever fell.

---

[7] The head of a convent.
[8] A minor saint, popular with women at the royal court in Chaucer's day.
[9] A convent near London, where a dialect of French was spoken.

She wet her fingers lightly in the dish
Of sauce, for courtesy was her first wish.
With every bite she did her skillful best
To see that no drop fell upon her breast. 130
She always wiped her upper lip so clean
That in her cup was never to be seen
A hint of grease when she had drunk her share.
She reached out for her meat with comely air.
She was a great delight, and always tried
To imitate court ways, and had her pride,
Both amiable and gracious in her dealings.
As for her charity and tender feelings,
She melted at whatever was piteous.
She would weep if she but came upon a mouse 140
Caught in a trap, if it were dead or bleeding.
Some little dogs that she took pleasure feeding
On roasted meat or milk or good wheat bread
She had, but how she wept to find one dead
Or yelping from a blow that made it smart,
And all was sympathy and loving heart.
Neat was her wimple[10] in its every plait,
Her nose well formed, her eyes as gray as slate.
Her mouth was very small and soft and red.
She had so wide a brow I think her head 150
Was nearly a span[11] broad, for certainly
She was not undergrown, as all could see.
She wore her cloak with dignity and charm,
And had her rosary about her arm,
The small beads coral and the larger green,
And from them hung a brooch of golden sheen,
On it a large A and a crown above;
Beneath, "All things are subject unto love."
    A Priest accompanied her toward Canterbury,
And an attendant Nun, her secretary. 160
    There was a Monk, and nowhere was his peer,
A hunter, and a roving overseer.[12]
He was a manly man, and fully able
To be an abbot. He kept a hunting stable,
And when he rode the neighborhood could hear
His bridle jingling in the wind as clear
And loud as if it were a chapel bell.
Wherever he was master of a cell
The principles of good St. Benedict,[13]
For being a little old and somewhat strict, 170

---

[10]A cloth worn around the face; part of a nun's habit. [11]A hand span.
[12]An "outrider," a person who supervised monastic property at some distance from the monastery.
[13]Sixth-century author of a famous rule, or code, laying down strict regulations for monastic life.

Were honored in the breach, as past their prime.
He lived by the fashion of a newer time.
He would have swapped that text for a plucked hen
Which says that hunters are not holy men,
Or a monk outside his discipline and rule
Is too much like a fish outside his pool;
That is to say, a monk outside his cloister.
But such a text he deemed not worth an oyster.
I told him his opinion made me glad.
Why should he study always and go mad,   180
Mewed[14] in his cell with only a book for neighbor?
Or why, as Augustine commanded, labor
And sweat his hands? How shall the world be served?
To Augustine be all such toil reserved!
And so he hunted, as was only right.
He had greyhounds as swift as birds in flight.
His taste was all for tracking down the hare,
And what his sport might cost he did not care.
His sleeves I noticed, where they met his hand,
Trimmed with gray fur, the finest in the land.   190
His hood was fastened with a curious pin
Made of wrought gold and clasped beneath his chin,
A love knot at the tip. His head might pass,
Bald as it was, for a lump of shining glass,
And his face was glistening as if anointed.
Fat as a lord he was, and well appointed.
His eyes were large, and rolled inside his head
As if they gleamed from a furnace of hot lead.
His boots were supple, his horse superbly kept.
He was a prelate to dream of while you slept.   200
He was not pale nor peaked like a ghost.
He relished a plump swan as his favorite roast.
He rode a palfrey brown as a ripe berry.
    A Friar was with us, a gay dog and a merry,
Who begged his district[15] with a jolly air.
No friar in all four orders[16] could compare
With him for gallantry; his tongue was wooing.
Many a girl was married by his doing,
And at his own cost it was often done.
He was a pillar, and a noble one,   210
To his whole order. In his neighborhood
Rich franklins[17] knew him well, who served good food,
And worthy women welcomed him to town;
For the license that his order handed down,
He said himself, conferred on him possession

[14] Caged.
[15] The friar is a "limiter," assigned a territory (limits) within which he can beg.
[16] The Franciscans, Dominicans, Carmelites, and Augustinians.
[17] Country gentlemen.

Of more than a curate's[18] power of confession.
Sweetly the list of frailties he heard,
Assigning penance[19] with a pleasant word.
He was an easy man for absolution
Where he looked forward to a contribution,   220
For if to a poor order a man has given
It signifies that he has been well shriven,[20]
And if a sinner let his purse be dented
The Friar would stake his oath he had repented.
For many men become so hard of heart
They cannot weep, though conscience makes them smart.
Instead of tears and prayers, then, let the sinner
Supply the poor friars with the price of dinner.
For pretty women he had more than shrift.
His cape was stuffed with many a little gift,   230
As knives and pins and suchlike. He could sing
A merry note, and pluck a tender string,
And had no rival at all in balladry.
His neck was whiter than a fleur-de-lis,[21]
And yet he could have knocked a strong man down.
He knew the taverns well in every town.
The barmaids and innkeepers pleased his mind
Better than beggars and lepers and their kind.
In his position it was unbecoming
Among the wretched lepers to go slumming.   240
It mocks all decency, it sews no stitch
To deal with such riffraff; but with the rich,
With sellers of victuals, that's another thing.
Wherever he saw some hope of profiting,
None so polite, so humble. He was good,
The champion beggar of his brotherhood.
Should a woman have no shoes against the snow,
So pleasant was his "*In principio*"[22]
He would have her widow's mite[23] before he went.
He took in far more than he paid in rent   250
For his right of begging within certain bounds.
None of his brethren trespassed on his grounds!
He loved as freely as a half-grown whelp.
On arbitration-days[24] he gave great help,
For his cloak was never shiny nor threadbare
Like a poor cloistered scholar's. He had an air

---

[18] Parish priest.

[19] After a sinner confesses to the priest, he is granted absolution (forgiveness of his sins), provided he does the assigned penance.

[20] Given shrift (absolution) in the sacrament of confession.

[21] Lily.

[22] Latin for "in the beginning," the opening words of St. John's gospel. The friar uses Latin to show off.

[23] A tiny sum of money.

[24] "Love-days," when people settled their disputes, friars sometimes serving as judges.

As if he were a doctor or a pope.
It took stout wool to make his semicope[25]
That plumped out like a bell for portliness.
He lisped a little in his rakishness   260
To make his English sweeter on his tongue,
And twanging his harp to end some song he'd sung
His eyes would twinkle in his head as bright
As the stars twinkle on a frosty night.
Hubert this gallant Friar was by name.
     Among the rest a Merchant also came.
He wore a forked beard and a beaver hat
From Flanders. High up in the saddle he sat,
In figured cloth, his boots clasped handsomely,
Delivering his opinions pompously,   270
Always on how his gains might be increased.
At all costs he desired the sea policed[26]
From Middleburg in Holland to Orwell.
He knew the exchange rates, and the time to sell
French currency, and there was never yet
A man who could have told he was in debt
So grave he seemed and hid so well his feelings
With all his shrewd engagements and close dealings.
You'd find no better man at any turn;
But what his name was I could never learn.   280
     There was an Oxford Student too, it chanced,
Already in his logic well advanced.
He rode a mount as skinny as a rake,
And he was hardly fat. For learning's sake
He let himself look hollow and sober enough.
He wore an outer coat of threadbare stuff,
For he had no benefice[27] for his enjoyment
And was too unworldly for some lay[28] employment.
He much preferred to have beside his bed
His twenty volumes bound in black or red   290
All packed with Aristotle from end to middle
Than a sumptuous wardrobe or a merry fiddle.
For though he knew what learning had to offer
There was little coin to jingle in his coffer.
Whatever he got by touching up a friend
On books and learning he would promptly spend
And busily pray for the soul of anybody
Who furnished him the wherewithal for study.
His scholarship was what he truly heeded.
He never spoke a word more than was needed,   300
And that was said with dignity and force,
And quick and brief. He was of grave discourse,

---

[25] Jacket.   [26] That is, kept free of pirates.
[27] Position at a church.
[28] Secular. The student, or clerk, is preparing for a career in the Church.

Giving new weight to virtue by his speech,
And gladly would he learn and gladly teach.
  There was a Lawyer, cunning and discreet,
Who had often been to St. Paul's porch to meet
His clients. He was a Sergeant of the Law,
A man deserving to be held in awe,
Or so he seemed, his manner was so wise.
He had often served as Justice of Assize[29]   310
By the king's appointment, with a broad commission,
For his knowledge and his eminent position.
He had many a handsome gift by way of fee.
There was no buyer of land as shrewd as he.
All ownership to him became fee simple.[30]
His titles were never faulty by a pimple.
None was so busy as he with case and cause,
And yet he seemed much busier than he was.
In all cases and decisions he was schooled
That were of record since King William[31] ruled.   320
No one could pick a loophole or a flaw
In any lease or contract he might draw.
Each statute on the books he knew by rote.
He traveled in a plain, silk-belted coat.
  A Franklin[32] traveled in his company.
Whiter could never daisy petal be
Than was his beard. His ruddy face gave sign
He liked his morning sop of toast in wine.
He lived in comfort, as he would assure us,
For he was a true son of Epicurus[33]   330
Who held the opinion that the only measure
Of perfect happiness was simply pleasure.
Such hospitality did he provide,
He was St. Julian[34] to his countryside.
His bread and ale were always up to scratch.
He had a cellar[35] none on earth could match.
There was no lack of pasties in his house,
Both fish and flesh, and that so plenteous
That where he lived it snowed of meat and drink.
With every dish of which a man can think,   340
After the various seasons of the year,
He changed his diet for his better cheer.
He had coops of partridges as fat as cream,
He had a fishpond stocked with pike and bream.
Woe to his cook for an unready pot
Or a sauce that wasn't seasoned and spiced hot!

---

[29] Law court.   [30] Unqualified ownership.
[31] King William the Conqueror (ruled 1066–87).
[32] Country gentleman.
[33] Ancient Greek philosopher, often associated with love of pleasure, although this is an oversimplification of his teaching.
[34] Patron saint of hospitality.   [35] Wine cellar.

A table in his hall stood on display
Prepared and covered through the livelong day.
He presided at court sessions for his bounty
And sat in Parliament often for his county.   350
A well-wrought dagger and a purse of silk
Hung at his belt, as white as morning milk.
He had been a sheriff and county auditor.
On earth was no such rich proprietor!
       There were five Guildsmen, in the livery
Of one august and great fraternity,[36]
A Weaver, a Dyer, and a Carpenter,
A Tapestry-maker and a Haberdasher.
Their gear was furbished new and clean as glass.
The mountings of their knives were not of brass   360
But silver. Their pouches were well made and neat,
And each of them, it seemed, deserved a seat
On the platform at the Guildhall, for each one
Was likely timber to make an alderman.
They had goods enough, and money to be spent,
Also their wives would willingly consent
And would have been at fault if they had not.
For to be "Madamed" is a pleasant lot,
And to march in first at feasts for being well married,
And royally to have their mantles carried.   370
       For the pilgrimage these Guildsmen brought their own
Cook to boil their chicken and marrow bone
With seasoning powder and capers and sharp spice.
In judging London ale his taste was nice.
He well knew how to roast and broil and fry,
To mix a stew, and bake a good meat pie,
Or capon creamed with almond, rice, and egg.
Pity he had an ulcer on his leg!
       A Skipper was with us, his home far in the west.
He came from the port of Dartmouth, as I guessed.   380
He sat his carthorse pretty much at sea
In a coarse smock that joggled on his knee.
From his neck a dagger on a string hung down
Under his arm. His face was burnished brown
By the summer sun. He was a true good fellow.
Many a time he had tapped a wine cask mellow
Sailing from Bordeaux while the owner slept.
Too nice a point of honor he never kept.
In a sea fight, if he got the upper hand,
Drowned prisoners floated home to every land.   390
But in navigation, whether reckoning tides,
Currents, or what might threaten him besides,
Harborage, pilotage, or the moon's demeanor,
None was his like from Hull to Cartagena.

---

[36] Perhaps a religious lodge, since they all wear the same "livery," or uniform dress.

He knew each harbor and the anchorage there
From Gotland to the Cape of Finisterre
And every creek in Brittany and Spain,
And he had called his ship the *Madeleine.*
With us came also an astute Physician.
There was none like him for a disquisition 400
On the art of medicine or surgery,
For he was grounded in astrology.[37]
He kept his patient long in observation,
Choosing the proper hour for application
Of charms and images by intuition
Of magic, and the planets' best position.
For he was one who understood the laws
That rule the humors,[38] and could tell the cause
That brought on every human malady,
Whether of hot or cold, or moist or dry. 410
He was a perfect medico, for sure.
The cause once known, he would prescribe the cure,
For he had his druggists ready at a motion
To provide the sick man with some pill or potion—
A game of mutual aid, with each one winning.
Their partnership was hardly just beginning!
He was well versed in his authorities,
Old Aesculapius, Dioscorides,
Rufus, and old Hippocrates, and Galen,
Haly, and Rhazes, and Serapion, 420
Averroës, Bernard, Johannes Damascenus,
Avicenna, Gilbert, Gaddesden, Constantinus.[39]
He urged a moderate fare on principle,
But rich in nourishment, digestible;
Of nothing in excess would he admit.
He gave but little heed to Holy Writ.
His clothes were lined with taffeta; their hue
Was all of blood red and of Persian blue,
Yet he was far from careless of expense.
He saved his fees from times of pestilence, 430
For gold is a cordial,[40] as physicians hold,
And so he had a special love for gold.
  A worthy woman there was from near the city
Of Bath, but somewhat deaf, and more's the pity.
For weaving she possessed so great a bent
She outdid the people of Ypres and of Ghent.[41]

---

[37] It was common for physicians in Chaucer's day to be guided by the position of the heavenly bodies.

[38] The relative proportion in a person of the four "humors" (blood, black bile, phlegm, yellow bile) was believed to influence character as well as health.

[39] Famous ancient and medieval medical authorities.

[40] A medical stimulant. Gold was sometimes used as an ingredient.

[41] Centers of the weaving industry in Flanders.

No other woman dreamed of such a thing
As to precede her at the offering,[42]
Or if any did, she fell in such a wrath
She dried up all the charity in Bath.   440
She wore fine kerchiefs of old-fashioned air,
And on a Sunday morning, I could swear,
She had ten pounds of linen on her head.
Her stockings were of finest scarlet-red,
Laced tightly, and her shoes were soft and new.
Bold was her face, and fair, and red in hue.
She had been an excellent woman all her life.
Five men in turn had taken her to wife,
Omitting other youthful company—
But let that pass for now! Over the sea   450
She had traveled freely; many a distant stream
She crossed, and visited Jerusalem
Three times. She had been at Rome and at Boulogne,
At the shrine of Compostella, and at Cologne.
She had wandered by the way through many a scene.
Her teeth were set with little gaps between.[43]
Easily on her ambling horse she sat.
She was well wimpled, and she wore a hat
As wide in circuit as a shield or targe.[44]
A skirt swathed up her hips, and they were large.   460
Upon her feet she wore sharp-roweled spurs.
She was a good fellow; a ready tongue was hers.
All remedies of love she knew by name,
For she had all the tricks of that old game.
    There was a good man of the priest's vocation,
A poor town Parson of true consecration,
But he was rich in holy thought and work.
Learned he was, in the truest sense a clerk[45]
Who meant Christ's gospel faithfully to preach
And truly his parishioners to teach.   470
He was a kind man, fully of industry,
Many times tested by adversity
And always patient. If tithes[46] were in arrears,
He was loth to threaten any man with fears
Of excommunication;[47] past a doubt
He would rather spread his offering about
To his poor flock, or spend his property.
To him a little meant sufficiency.

[42] Offering at church.
[43] For a woman to be gap-toothed was considered a sign of being high sexed.
[44] A type of shield.
[45] A clergyman-scholar.
[46] One tenth of one's earnings, the sum due to the Church.
[47] Barring of a person from the church and sacraments—a serious penalty.

Wide was his parish, with houses far asunder,
But he would not be kept by rain or thunder, 480
If any had suffered a sickness or a blow,
From visiting the farthest, high or low,
Plodding his way on foot, his staff in hand.
He was a model his flock could understand,
For first he did and afterward he taught.
That precept from the Gospel he had caught,
And he added as a metaphor thereto,
"If the gold rusts, what will the iron do?"
For if a priest is foul, in whom we trust,
No wonder a layman shows a little rust. 490
A priest should take to heart the shameful scene
Of shepherds filthy while the sheep are clean.
By his own purity a priest should give
The example to his sheep, how they should live.
He did not rent his benefice[48] for hire,
Leaving his flock to flounder in the mire,
And run to London, happiest of goals,
To sing paid masses in St. Paul's for souls,
Or as chaplain from some rich guild take his keep,
But dwelt at home and guarded well his sheep 500
So that no wolf should make his flock miscarry.
He was a shepherd, and not a mercenary.
And though himself a man of strict vocation
He was not harsh to weak souls in temptation,
Not overbearing nor haughty in his speech,
But wise and kind in all he tried to teach.
By good example and just words to turn
Sinners to heaven was his whole concern.
But should a man in truth prove obstinate,
Whoever he was, of rich or mean estate, 510
The Parson would give him a snub to meet the case.
I doubt there was a priest in any place
His better. He did not stand on dignity
Nor affect in conscience too much nicety,
But Christ's and his disciples' word he sought
To teach, and first he followed what he taught.
    There was a Plowman with him on the road,
His brother, who had forked up many a load
Of good manure. A hearty worker he,
Living in peace and perfect charity. 520
Whether his fortune made him smart or smile,
He loved God with his whole heart all the while
And his neighbor as himself. He would undertake,
For every luckless poor man, for the sake
Of Christ to thresh and ditch and dig by the hour
And with no wage, if it was in his power.

[48] Hire out his position as pastor of his church.

His tithes on goods and earnings he paid fair.
He wore a coarse, rough coat and rode a mare.
　There also were a Manciple,[49] a Miller,
A Reeve, a Summoner, and a Pardoner,[50]   530
And I—this makes our company complete.
　As tough a yokel as you care to meet
The Miller was. His big-beefed arms and thighs
Took many a ram put up as wrestling prize.
He was a thick, squat-shouldered lump of sins.
No door but he could heave it off its pins
Or break it running at it with his head.
His beard was broader than a shovel, and red
As a fat sow or fox. A wart stood clear
Atop his nose, and red as a pig's ear   540
A tuft of bristles on it. Black and wide
His nostrils were. He carried at his side
A sword and buckler. His mouth would open out
Like a great furnace, and he would sing and shout
His ballads and jokes of harlotries and crimes.
He could steal corn[51] and charge for it three times,
And yet was honest enough, as millers come,
For a miller, as they say, has a golden thumb.
In white coat and blue hood this lusty clown,
Blowing his bagpipes, brought us out of town.   550
　The Manciple was of a lawyers' college,
And other buyers might have used his knowledge
How to be shrewd provisioners, for whether
He bought on cash or credit, altogether
He managed that the end should be the same:
He came out more than even with the game.
Now isn't it an instance of God's grace
How a man of little knowledge can keep pace
In wit with a whole school of learned men?
He had masters to the number of three times ten   560
Who knew each twist of equity and tort;
A dozen in that very Inn of Court
Were worthy to be steward of the estate
To any of England's lords, however great,
And keep him to his income well confined
And free from debt, unless he lost his mind,
Or let him scrimp, if he were mean in bounty;
They could have given help to a whole county
In any sort of case that might befall;
And yet this Manciple could cheat them all!   570

---

[49]A steward.
[50]A reeve was an overseer for an estate; a summoner summoned to the ecclesiastical court
persons charged with offenses against the Church; a pardoner distributed or sold pardons for
sins in the name of the Pope.
[51]Grain.

The Reeve was a slender, fiery-tempered man.
He shaved as closely as a razor can.
His hair was cropped about his ears, and shorn
Above his forehead as a priest's is worn.
His legs were very long and very lean.
No calf on his lank spindles could be seen.
But he knew how to keep a barn or bin,
He could play the game with auditors and win.
He knew well how to judge by drought and rain
The harvest of his seed and of his grain. 580
His master's cattle, swine, and poultry flock,
Horses and sheep and dairy, all his stock,
Were altogether in this Reeve's control.
And by agreement, he had given the sole
Accounting since his lord reached twenty years.
No man could ever catch him in arrears.
There wasn't a bailiff, shepherd, or farmer working
But the Reeve knew all his tricks of cheating and shirking.
He would not let him draw an easy breath.
They feared him as they feared the very death. 590
He lived in a good house on an open space,
Well shaded by green trees, a pleasant place.
He was shrewder in acquisition than his lord.
With private riches he was amply stored.
He had learned a good trade young by work and will.
He was a carpenter of first-rate skill.
On a fine mount, a stallion, dappled gray,
Whose name was Scot, he rode along the way.
He wore a long blue coat hitched up and tied
As if it were a friar's, and at his side 600
A sword with rusty blade was hanging down.
He came from Norfolk, from nearby the town
That men call Bawdswell. As we rode the while,
The Reeve kept always hindmost in our file.
  A Summoner in our company had his place.
Red as the fiery cherubim his face.
He was pocked and pimpled, and his eyes were narrow.
He was lecherous and hot as a cock sparrow.
His brows were scabby and black, and thin his beard.
His was a face that little children feared. 610
Brimstone or litharge bought in any quarter,
Quicksilver, ceruse, borax, oil of tartar,[52]
No salve nor ointment that will cleanse or bite
Could cure him of his blotches, livid white,
Or the nobs and nubbins sitting on his cheeks.
He loved his garlic, his onions, and his leeks.
He loved to drink the strong wine down blood-red.

---

[52] Remedies for skin diseases.

Then would he bellow as if he had lost his head,
And when he had drunk enough to parch his drouth,
Nothing but Latin issued from his mouth.   620
He had smattered up a few terms, two or three,
That he had gathered out of some decree—
No wonder; he heard law Latin all the day,
And everyone knows a parrot or a jay
Can cry out "Wat" or "Poll" as well as the pope;
But give him a strange term, he began to grope.
His little store of learning was paid out,
So "*Questio quod juris*"[53] he would shout.
He was a goodhearted bastard and a kind one.
If there were better, it was hard to find one.   630
He would let a good fellow, for a quart of wine,
The whole year round enjoy his concubine
Scot-free from summons, hearing, fine, or bail,
And on the sly he too could flush a quail.
If he liked a scoundrel, no matter for church law,
He would teach him that he need not stand in awe
If the archdeacon threatened with his curse—
That is, unless his soul was in his purse,
For in his purse he would be punished well.
"The purse," he said, "is the archdeacon's hell."   640
Of course I know he lied in what he said.
There is nothing a guilty man should so much dread
As the curse that damns his soul, when, without fail,
The church can save him, or send him off to jail.
He had the young men and girls in his control
Throughout the diocese; he knew the soul
Of youth, and heard their every last design.
A garland big enough to be the sign
Above an alehouse balanced on his head,
And he made a shield of a great round loaf of bread.   650
      There was a Pardoner of Rouncivalle[54]
With him, of the blessed Mary's hospital,
But now come straight from Rome (or so said he).
Loudly he sang, "Come hither, love, to me,"
While the Summoner's counterbass trolled out profound—
No trumpet blew with half so vast a sound.
This Pardoner had hair as yellow as wax,
But it hung as smoothly as a hank of flax.
His locks trailed down in bunches from his head,
And he let the ends about his shoulders spread,   660
But in thin clusters, lying one by one.
Of hood, for rakishness, he would have none,
For in his wallet[55] he kept it safely stowed.

---

[53] Latin for "What law governs this case?"—a phrase picked up in courtrooms.
[54] A hospital just outside London.   [55] Bag.

He traveled, as he thought, in the latest mode,
Disheveled. Save for his cap, his head was bare,
And in his eyes he glittered like a hare.
A Veronica[56] was stitched upon his cap,
His wallet lay before him in his lap
Brimful of pardons from the very seat
In Rome. He had a voice like a goat's bleat.   670
He was beardless and would never have a beard.
His cheek was always smooth as if just sheared.
I think he was a gelding or a mare;
But in his trade, from Berwick down to Ware,
No pardoner could beat him in the race,
For in his wallet he had a pillow case
Which he represented as Our Lady's veil;
He said he had a piece of the very sail
St. Peter, when he fished in Galilee
Before Christ caught him, used upon the sea.   680
He had a latten[57] cross embossed with stones
And in a glass he carried some pig's bones,
And with these holy relics, when he found
Some village parson grubbing his poor ground,
He would get more money in a single day
Than in two months would come the parson's way.
Thus with his flattery and his trumped-up stock
He made dupes of the parson and his flock.
But though his conscience was a little plastic
He was in church a noble ecclesiastic.   690
Well could he read the Scripture or saint's story,
But best of all he sang the offertory,[58]
For he understood that when this song was sung,
Then he must preach, and sharpen up his tongue
To rake in cash, as well he knew the art,
And so he sang out gaily, with full heart.
    Now I have set down briefly, as it was,
Our rank, our dress, our number, and the cause
That made our sundry fellowship begin
In Southwark, at this hospitable inn   700
Known as the Tabard, not far from the Bell.[59]
But what we did that night I ought to tell,
And after that our journey, stage by stage,
And the whole story of our pilgrimage.
But first, in justice, do not look askance
I plead, nor lay it to my ignorance
If in this matter I should use plain speech

---

[56]An image of Christ's features supposed to have been made on the veil of St. Veronica
after she let him wipe his face on it before the Crucifixion.
[57]Made of a brasslike metal.
[58]Part of the Catholic Mass.
[59]Another tavern.

And tell you just the words and style of each
Reporting all their language faithfully.
For it must be known to you as well as me   710
That whoever tells a story after a man
Must follow him as closely as he can.
If he takes the tale in charge, he must be true
To every word, unless he would find new
Or else invent a thing or falsify.
Better some breadth of language than a lie!
He may not spare the truth to save his brother.
He might as well use one word as another.
In Holy Writ Christ spoke in a broad sense,
And surely his word is without offense.   720
Plato, if his are pages you can read,
Says let the word be cousin to the deed.
So I petition your indulgence for it
If I have cut the cloth just as men wore it,
Here in this tale, and shown its very weave.
My wits are none too sharp, you must believe.
    Our Host gave each of us a cheerful greeting
And promptly of our supper had us eating.
The victuals that he served us were his best.
The wine was potent, and we drank with zest.   730
Our Host cut such a figure, all in all,
He might have been a marshal in a hall.[60]
He was a big man, and his eyes bulged wide.
No sturdier citizen lived in all Cheapside,[61]
Lacking no trace of manhood, bold in speech,
Prudent, and well versed in what life can teach,
And with all this he was a jovial man.
And so when supper ended he began
To jolly us, when all our debts were clear.
"Welcome," he said. "I have not seen this year   740
So merry a company in this tavern as now,
And I would give you pleasure if I knew how.
And just this very minute a plan has crossed
My mind that might amuse you at no cost.
    "You go to Canterbury—may the Lord
Speed you, and may the martyred saint reward
Your journey! And to while the time away
You mean to talk and pass the time of day,
For you would be as cheerful all alone
As riding on your journey dumb as stone.   750
Therefore, if you'll abide by what I say,
Tomorrow, when you ride off on your way,
Now, by my father's soul, and he is dead,

---

[60]Managing official in a great medieval house.
[61]A commercial street in London.

If you don't enjoy yourselves, cut off my head!
Hold up your hands, if you accept my speech."
　　Our counsel did not take us long to reach.
We bade him give his orders at his will.
"Well, sirs," he said, "then do not take it ill,
But hear me in good part, and for your sport,
Each one of you, to make our journey short, 760
Shall tell two stories, as we ride, I mean,
Toward Canterbury; and coming home again
Shall tell two other tales he may have heard
Of happenings that some time have occurred.
And the one of you whose stories please us most,
Here in this tavern, sitting by this post
Shall sup at our expense while we make merry
When we come riding home from Canterbury.
And to cheer you still the more, I too will ride
With you at my own cost, and be your guide. 770
And if anyone my judgment shall gainsay
He must pay for all we spend along the way.
If you agree, no need to stand and reason.
Tell me, and I'll be stirring in good season."
　　This thing was granted, and we swore our pledge
To take his judgment on our pilgrimage,
His verdict on our tales, and his advice.
He was to plan a supper at a price
Agreed upon: and so we all assented
To this command, and we were well contented. 780
The wine was fetched; we drank, and went to rest.
　　Next morning, when the dawn was in the east,
Up sprang our Host, who acted as our cock,
And gathered us together in a flock,
And off we rode, till presently our pace
Had brought us to St. Thomas' watering place.
And there our Host began to check his horse.
"Good sirs," he said, "you know your promise, of course.
Shall I remind you what it was about?
If evensong and matins don't fall out,[62] 790
We'll soon find who shall tell us the first tale.
But as I hope to drink my wine and ale,
Whoever won't accept what I decide
Pays everything we spend along the ride.
Draw lots, before we're farther from the Inn.
Whoever draws the shortest shall begin.
Sir Knight," said he, "my master, choose your straw.
Come here, my lady Prioress, and draw,
And you, Sir Scholar, don't look thoughtful, man!

---

[62] That is, if you feel this morning as you did last evening. Evensong and matins are evening and morning prayers.

Pitch in now, everyone!" So all began   800
To draw the lots, and as the luck would fall
The draw went to the Knight, which pleased us all.
And when this excellent man saw how it stood,
Ready to keep his promise, he said, "Good!
Since it appears that I must start the game,
Why then, the draw is welcome, in God's name.
Now let's ride on, and listen, what I say."
And with that word we rode forth on our way,
And he, with his courteous manner and good cheer,
Began to tell his tale, as you shall hear.   810

PROLOGUE TO THE MILLER'S TALE

When the Knight had finished,[1] no one, young or old,
In the whole company, but said he had told
A noble story, one that ought to be
Preserved and kept alive in memory,
Especially the gentlefolk, each one.
Our good Host laughed, and swore, "The game's begun,
The ball is rolling! This is going well.
Let's see who has another tale to tell.
Come, match the Knight's tale if you can, Sir Monk!"
    The Miller, who by this time was so drunk   10
He looked quite bloodless, and who hardly sat
His horse, he was never one to doff his hat
Or stand on courtesy for any man.
Like Pilate in the Church plays[2] he began
To bellow. "Arms and blood and bones," he swore,
"I know a yarn that will even up the score,
A noble one, I'll pay off the Knight's tale!"
    Our Host could see that he was drunk on ale.
"Robin," he said, "hold on a minute, brother.
Some better man shall come first with another.   20
Let's do this right. You tell yours by and by."
    "God's soul," the Miller told him, "that won't I!
Either I'll speak, or go on my own way."
    "The devil with you! Say what you have to say,"
Answered our Host. "You are a fool. Your head
Is overpowered."
                    "Now," the Miller said,
"Everyone listen! But first I will propound
That I am drunk, I know it by my sound.

---

[1] The Knight had led off the program of storytelling on the way to Canterbury; see the General Prologue, lines 745–810.
[2] The "mystery plays," based on the Bible, especially the Gospels.

If I can't get my words out, put the blame
On Southwark ale,[3] I ask you, in God's name!　　　　　　30
For I'll tell a golden legend[4] and a life
Both of a carpenter and of his wife,
How a student put horns on the fellow's head."
　"Shut up and stop your racket," the Reeve said.[5]
"Forget your ignorant drunken bawdiness.
It is a sin and a great foolishness
To injure any man by defamation
And to give women such a reputation.
Tell us of other things; you'll find no lack."
　Promptly this drunken Miller answered back:　　　　40
"Oswald, my brother, true as babes are suckled,
The man who has no wife, he is no cuckold.
I don't say for this reason that you are.
There are plenty of faithful wives, both near and far,
Always a thousand good for every bad,
And you know this yourself, unless you're mad.
I see you are angry with my tale, but why?
You have a wife; no less, by God, do I.
But I wouldn't, for the oxen in my plow,
Shoulder more than I need by thinking how　　　　　50
I may myself, for aught I know, be one.
I'll certainly believe that I am none.
A husband mustn't be curious, for his life,
About God's secrets or about his wife.
If she gives him plenty and he's in the clover,
No need to worry about what's left over."
　The Miller, to make the best of it I can,
Refused to hold his tongue for any man,
But told his tale like any low-born clown.
I am sorry that I have to set it down,　　　　　　60
And all you people, for God's love, I pray,
Whose taste is higher, do not think I say
A word with evil purpose; I must rehearse
Their stories one and all, both better and worse,
Or play false with my matter, that is clear.
Whoever, therefore, may not wish to hear,
Turn over the page and choose another tale;
For small and great, he'll find enough, no fail,
Of things from history, touching courtliness,
And virtue too, and also holiness.　　　　　　　70
If you choose wrong, don't lay it on my head.
You know the Miller couldn't be called well bred.

---

[3]Ale from the Host's inn, in the Southwark district of London, from which the pilgrimage had set out.
[4]A saint's life.
[5]The Reeve was a carpenter by trade; see the General Prologue, line 596.

So with the Reeve, and many more as well,
And both of them had bawdy tales to tell.
Reflect a little, and don't hold me to blame.
There's no sense making earnest out of game.

THE MILLER'S TALE

There used to be a rich old oaf who made
His home at Oxford, a carpenter by trade,
And took in boarders. With him used to dwell
A student who had done his studies well,
But he was poor; for all that he had learned,
It was toward astrology his fancy turned.
He knew a number of figures and constructions
By which he could supply men with deductions
If they should ask him at a given hour
Whether to look for sunshine or for shower,   10
Or want to know whatever might befall,
Events of all sorts, I can't count them all.
    He was known as handy[1] Nicholas, this student.
Well versed in love, he knew how to be prudent,
Going about unnoticed, sly, and sure.
In looks no girl was ever more demure.
Lodged at this carpenter's, he lived alone;
He had a room there that he made his own,
Festooned with herbs, and he was sweet himself
As licorice or ginger. On a shelf   20
Above his bed's head, neatly stowed apart,
He kept the trappings that went with his art,
His astrolabe,[2] his books—among the rest,
Thick ones and thin ones, lay his *Almagest*[3]—
And the counters for his abacus as well.
Over his cupboard a red curtain fell
And up above a pretty zither lay
On which at night so sweetly would he play
That with the music the whole room would ring.
"Angelus to the Virgin" he would sing   30
And then the song that's known as "The King's Note."[4]
Blessings were called down on his merry throat!
So this sweet scholar passed his time, his end
Being to eat and live upon his friend.

---

[1]"Chaucer's word is *hendë*, implying, I take it, both *ready to hand* and *ingratiating*. Nicholas was a Johnny-on-the-spot and also had a way with him."—Translator's note.
[2]An astronomical instrument, used to measure celestial altitudes.
[3]Handbook of the stars; from the treatise on astronomy by Ptolemy (2nd century A.D.).
[4]That is, both sacred and secular music.

This carpenter had newly wed a wife
And loved her better than he loved his life.
He was jealous, for she was eighteen in age;
He tried to keep her close as in a cage,
For she was wild and young, and old was he
And guessed that he might smack of cuckoldry. 40
His ignorant wits had never chanced to strike
On Cato's word, that man should wed his like;[5]
Men ought to wed where their conditions point,
For youth and age are often out of joint.
But now, since he had fallen in the snare,
He must, like other men, endure his care.
    Fair this young woman was, her body trim
As any mink, so graceful and so slim.
She wore a striped belt that was all of silk;
A piece-work apron, white as morning milk, 50
About her loins and down her lap she wore.
White was her smock, her collar both before
And on the back embroidered all about
In coal-black silk, inside as well as out.
And like her collar, her white-laundered bonnet
Had ribbons of the same embroidery on it.
Wide was her silken fillet,[6] worn up high,
And for a fact she had a willing eye.
She plucked each brow into a little bow,
And each one was as black as any sloe.[7] 60
She was a prettier sight to see by far
Than the blossoms of the early pear tree are,
And softer than the wool of an old wether.[8]
Down from her belt there hung a purse of leather
With silken tassels and with studs of brass.
No man so wise, wherever people pass,
Who could imagine in this world at all
A wench like her, the pretty little doll!
Far brighter was the dazzle of her hue
Than a coin struck in the Tower,[9] fresh and new. 70
As for her song, it twittered from her head
Sharp as a swallow perching on a shed.
And she could skip and sport as a young ram
Or calf will gambol, following his dam.
Her mouth was sweet as honey-ale or mead
Or apples in the hay, stored up for need.
She was as skittish as an untrained colt,
Slim as a mast and straighter than a bolt.

[5] The *Distichs*, a book of Latin maxims used in schools, was attributed to Dionysius Cato (4th century A.D.).
[6] Headband.
[7] A small black fruit resembling a plum.
[8] Sheep.
[9] The Tower of London, where coins were minted.

On her simple collar she wore a big brooch-pin
Wide as a shield's boss underneath her chin.   80
High up along her legs she laced her shoes.
She was a pigsney,[10] she was a primrose
For any lord to tumble in his bed
Or a good yeoman honestly to wed.
     Now sir, and again sir, this is how it was:
A day came round when handy Nicholas,
While her husband was at Oseney,[11] well away,
Began to fool with this young wife, and play.
These students always have a wily head.
He caught her in between the legs, and said,   90
"Sweetheart, unless I have my will with you
I'll die for stifled love, by all that's true,"
And held her by the haunches, hard. "I vow
I'll die unless you love me here and now,
Sure as my soul," he said, "is God's to save."
     She shied just as a colt does in the trave,[12]
And turned her head hard from him, this young wife,
And said, "I will not kiss you, on my life.
Why, stop it now," she said, "stop, Nicholas,
Or I will cry out 'Help, help,' and 'Alas!'   100
Be good enough to take your hands away."
     "Mercy," this Nicholas began to pray,
And spoke so well and poured it on so fast
She promised she would be his love at last,
And swore by Thomas à Becket, saint of Kent,[13]
That she would serve him when she could invent
Or spy out some good opportunity.
"My husband is so full of jealousy
You must be watchful and take care," she said,
"Or well I know I'll be as good as dead.   110
You must go secretly about this business."
     "Don't give a thought to that," said Nicholas.
"A student has been wasting time at school
If he can't make a carpenter a fool."
And so they were agreed, these two, and swore
To watch their chance, as I have said before.
When Nicholas had spanked her haunches neatly
And done all I have spoken of, he sweetly
Gave her a kiss, and then he took his zither
And loudly played, and sang his music with her.   120
     Now in her Christian duty, one saint's day,
To the parish church this good wife made her way,

---

[10] Cuckoo-flower; a term of endearment.
[11] A town near Oxford, site of an abbey where the carpenter performed jobs.
[12] A frame used by blacksmiths to immobilize horses being shod.
[13] The saint whose shrine at Canterbury was the goal of Chaucer's pilgrims.

And as she went her forehead cast a glow
As bright as noon, for she had washed it so
It glistened when she finished with her work.
　　Serving this church there was a parish clerk
Whose name was Absolom, a ruddy man
With goose-gray eyes and curls like a great fan
That shone like gold on his neatly parted head.
His tunic was light blue and his nose red,　　　　　　　130
And he had patterns that had been cut through
Like the windows of St. Paul's in either shoe.
He wore above his tunic, fresh and gay,
A surplice white as a blossom on a spray.
A merry devil, as true as God can save,
He knew how to let blood, trim hair, and shave,
Or write a deed of land in proper phrase,
And he could dance in twenty different ways
In the Oxford fashion, and sometimes he would sing
A loud falsetto to his fiddle string　　　　　　　　　140
Or his guitar. No tavern anywhere
But he had furnished entertainment there.
Yet his speech was delicate, and for his part
He was a little squeamish toward a fart.
　　This Absolom, so jolly and so gay,
With a censer[14] went about on the saint's day
Censing the parish women one and all.
Many the doting look that he let fall,
And specially on this carpenter's young wife.
To look at her, he thought, was a good life,　　　　　150
She was so trim, so sweetly lecherous.
I dare say that if she had been a mouse
And he a cat, he would have made short work
Of catching her. This jolly parish clerk
Had such a heartful of love-hankerings
He would not take the women's offerings;
No, no, he said, it would not be polite.
　　The moon, when darkness fell, shone full and bright,
And Absolom was ready for love's sake
With his guitar to be up and awake,　　　　　　　　160
And toward the carpenter's, brisk and amorous,
He made his way until he reached the house
A little after the cocks began to crow.
Under a casement he sang sweet and low,
"Dear lady, by your will, be kind to me,"
And strummed on his guitar in harmony.
This lovelorn singing woke the carpenter
Who said to his wife, "What, Alison, don't you hear
Absolom singing under our bedroom wall?"

[14] The vessel used in church to waft incense fumes.

"Yes, God knows, John," she answered, "I hear it all."   170
What would you like? In this way things went on
Till jolly Absolom was woebegone
For wooing her, awake all night and day.
He combed his curls and made himself look gay.
He swore to be her slave and used all means
To court her with his gifts and go-betweens.
He sang and quavered like a nightingale.
He sent her sweet spiced wine and seasoned ale,
Cakes that were piping hot, mead sweet with honey,
And since she was town-bred, he proffered money.   180
For some are won by wealth, and some no less
By blows, and others yet by gentleness.
    Sometimes, to keep his talents in her gaze,
He acted Herod in the mystery plays
High on the stage. But what can help his case?
For she so loves this handy Nicholas
That Absolom is living in a bubble.
He has nothing but a laugh for all his trouble.
She leaves his earnestness for scorn to cool
And makes this Absolom her proper fool.   190
For this is a true proverb, and no lie:
"It always happens that the nigh and sly
Will let the absent suffer." So 'tis said,
And Absolom may rage or lose his head
But just because he was farther from her sight
This nearby Nicholas got in his light.
    Now hold your chin up, handy Nicholas,
For Absolom may wail and sing "Alas!"
One Saturday when the carpenter had gone
To Oseney, Nicholas and Alison   200
Agreed that he should use his wit and guile
This simple jealous husband to beguile.
And if it happened that the game went right
She would sleep in his arms the livelong night,
For this was his desire and hers as well.
At once, with no more words, this Nicholas fell
To working out his plan. He would not tarry,
But quietly to his room began to carry
Both food and drink to last him out a day,
Or more than one, and told her what to say   210
If her husband asked her about Nicholas.
She must say she had no notion where he was;
She hadn't laid eyes on him all day long;
He must be sick, or something must be wrong;
No matter how her maid had called and cried
He wouldn't answer, whatever might betide.
    This was the plan, and Nicholas kept away,
Shut in his room, for that whole Saturday.

He ate and slept or did as he thought best
Till Sunday, when the sun was going to rest, 220
This carpenter began to wonder greatly
Where Nicholas was and what might ail him lately.
"Now, by St. Thomas, I begin to dread
All isn't right with Nicholas," he said.
"He hasn't, God forbid, died suddenly!
The world is ticklish these days, certainly.
Today I saw a corpse to church go past,
A man that I saw working Monday last!
Go up," he told his chore-boy, "call and shout,
Knock with a stone, find what it's all about 230
And let me know."
                The boy went up and pounded
And yelled as if his wits had been confounded.
"What, how, what's doing, Master Nicholas?
How can you sleep all day?" But all his fuss
Was wasted, for he could not hear a word.
He noticed at the bottom of a board
A hole the cat used when she wished to creep
Into the room, and through it looked in deep
And finally of Nicholas caught sight.
This Nicholas sat gaping there upright 240
As though his wits were addled by the moon
When it was new. The boy went down, and soon
Had told his master how he had seen the man.
    The carpenter, when he heard this news, began
To cross himself. "Help us, St. Frideswide![15]
Little can we foresee what may betide!
The man's astronomy has turned his wit,
Or else he's in some agonizing fit.
I always knew that it would turn out so.
What God has hidden is not for men to know. 250
Aye, blessed is the ignorant man indeed,
Blessed is he that only knows his creed!
So fared another scholar of the sky,
For walking in the meadows once to spy
Upon the stars and what they might foretell,
Down in a clay-pit suddenly he fell!
He overlooked that! By St. Thomas, though,
I'm sorry for handy Nicholas. I'll go
And scold him roundly for his studying
If so I may, by Jesus, heaven's king! 260
Give me a staff, I'll pry up from the floor
While you, Robin, are heaving at the door.
He'll quit his books, I think."

---

[15] Eighth-century saint; she was the patron of Oxford, both city and university.

                          He took his stand
Outside the room. The boy had a strong hand
And by the hasp he heaved it off at once.
The door fell flat. With gaping countenance
This Nicholas sat studying the air
As still as stone. He was in black despair,
The carpenter believed, and hard about
The shoulders caught and shook him, and cried out   270
Rudely, "What, how! What is it? Look down at us!
Wake up, think of Christ's passion, Nicholas!
I'll sign you with the cross to keep away
These elves and things!" And he began to say,
Facing the quarters of the house, each side,
And on the threshold of the door outside,
The night-spell: "Jesu and St. Benedict[16]
From every wicked thing this house protect . . ."
     Choosing his time, this handy Nicholas
Produced a dreadful sigh, and said, "Alas,   280
This world, must it be all destroyed straightway?"
     "What," asked the carpenter, "what's that you say?
Do as we do, we working men, and think
Of God."
                 Nicholas answered, "Get me a drink,
And afterwards I'll tell you privately
Of something that concerns us, you and me.
I'll tell you only, you among all men."
     This carpenter went down and came again
With a draught of mighty ale, a generous quart.
As soon as each of them had drunk his part   290
Nicholas shut the door and made it fast
And sat down by the carpenter at last
And spoke to him. "My host," he said, "John dear,
You must swear by all that you hold sacred here
That not to any man will you betray
My confidence. What I'm about to say
Is Christ's own secret. If you tell a soul
You are undone, and this will be the toll:
If you betray me, you shall go stark mad."
     "Now Christ forbid it, by His holy blood,"   300
Answered this simple man. "I don't go blabbing.
If I say it myself, I have no taste for gabbing.
Speak up just as you like, I'll never tell
Not wife nor child, by Him that harrowed hell."[17]
     "Now, John," said Nicholas, "this is no lie.
I have discovered through astrology
And studying the moon that shines so bright

---

[16]Italian monk; founder, c. 529, of the first Western monastic order.
[17]The Harrowing of Hell was Jesus' descent into Hell (more exactly, into Limbo) after the
Crucifixion, to liberate the souls of the pre-Christian just.

That Monday next, a quarter through the night,
A rain will fall, and such a mad, wild spate
That Noah's flood was never half so great. 310
This world," he said, "in less time than an hour
Shall drown entirely in that hideous shower.
Yes, every man shall drown and lose his life."
  "Alas," the carpenter answered, "for my wife!
Alas, my Alison! And shall she drown?"
For grief at this he nearly tumbled down,
And said, "But is there nothing to be done?"
  "Why, happily there is, for anyone
Who will take advice," this handy Nicholas said.
"You mustn't expect to follow your own head. 320
For what said Solomon, whose words were true?
'Proceed by counsel, and you'll never rue.'[18]
If you will act on good advice, no fail,
I'll promise, and without a mast or sail,
To see that she's preserved, and you and I.
Haven't you heard how Noah was kept dry
When, warned by Christ beforehand, he discovered
That the whole earth with water should be covered?"
  "Yes," said the carpenter, "long, long ago."
  "And then again," said Nicholas, "don't you know 330
The grief they all had trying to embark
Till Noah could get his wife into the Ark?[19]
That was a time when Noah, I dare say,
Would gladly have given his best black wethers away
If she could have had a ship herself alone.
And therefore do you know what must be done?
This demands haste, and with a hasty thing
People can't stop for talk and tarrying.
  "Start out and get into the house right off
For each of us a tub or kneading-trough,[20] 340
Above all making sure that they are large,
In which we'll float away as in a barge.
And put in food enough to last a day.
Beyond won't matter; the flood will fall away
Early next morning. Take care not to spill
A word to your boy Robin, nor to Jill
Your maid. I cannot save her, don't ask why.
I will not tell God's secrets, no, not I.
Let it be enough, unless your wits are mad,
To have as good a grace as Noah had. 350
I'll save your wife for certain, never doubt it.
Now go along, and make good time about it.

---

[18]Ecclesiasticus 32:19. This book of proverbs was canonical in the Roman Catholic Bible.
[19]"A stock comic scene in the mystery plays, of which the carpenter would have been an avid spectator."—Translator's note.
[20]A wooden tub for kneading dough.

"But when you have, for her and you and me,
Brought to the house these kneading-tubs, all three,
Then you must hang them under the roof, up high,
To keep our plans from any watchful eye.
When you have done exactly as I've said,
And put in snug our victuals and our bread,
Also an ax to cut the ropes apart
So when the rain comes we can make our start,   360
And when you've broken a hole high in the gable
Facing the garden plot, above the stable,
To give us a free passage out, each one,
Then, soon as the great fall of rain is done,
You'll swim as merrily, I undertake,
As the white duck paddles along behind her drake.
Then I shall call, 'How, Alison! How, John!
Be cheerful, for the flood will soon be gone.'
And 'Master Nicholas, what ho!' you'll say.
'Good morning, I see you clearly, for it's day.'   370
Then we shall lord it for the rest of life
Over the world, like Noah and his wife.
    "But one thing I must warn you of downright.
Use every care that on that selfsame night
When we have taken ship and climbed aboard,
No one of us must speak a single word,
Nor call, nor cry, but pray with all his heart.
It is God's will. You must hang far apart,
You and your wife, for there must be no sin
Between you, no more in a look than in   380
The very deed. Go now, the plans are drawn.
Go, set to work, and may God spur you on!
Tomorrow night when all men are asleep
Into our kneading-troughs we three shall creep
And sit there waiting, and abide God's grace.
Go along now, this isn't the time or place
For me to talk at length or sermonize.
The proverb says, 'Don't waste words on the wise.'
You are so wise there is no need to teach you.
Go, save our lives—that's all that I beseech you!"   390
    This simple carpenter went on his way.
Many a time he said, "Alack the day,"
And to his wife he laid the secret bare.
She knew it better than he; she was aware
What this quaint bargain was designed to buy.
She carried on as if about to die,
And said, "Alas, go get this business done.
Help us escape, or we are dead, each one.
I am your true, your faithful wedded wife.
Go, my dear husband, save us, limb and life!"   400
    Great things, in all truth, can the emotions be!
A man can perish through credulity

So deep the print imagination makes.
This simple carpenter, he quails and quakes.
He really sees, according to his notion,
Noah's flood come wallowing like an ocean
To drown his Alison, his pet, his dear.
He weeps and wails, and gone is his good cheer,
And wretchedly he sighs. But he goes off
And gets himself a tub, a kneading-trough, 410
Another tub, and has them on the sly
Sent home, and there in secret hangs them high
Beneath the roof. He made three ladders, these
With his own hands, and stowed in bread and cheese
And a jug of good ale, plenty for a day.
Before all this was done, he sent away
His chore-boy Robin and his wench likewise
To London on some trumped-up enterprise,
And so on Monday, when it drew toward night,
He shut the door without a candlelight 420
And saw that all was just as it should be,
And shortly they went clambering up, all three.
They sat there still, and let a moment pass.
    "Now then, 'Our Father,' mum!" said Nicholas,
And "Mum!" said John, and "Mum!" said Alison,
And piously this carpenter went on
Saying his prayers. He sat there still and straining,
Trying to make out whether he heard it raining.
    The dead of sleep, for very weariness,
Fell on this carpenter, as I should guess, 430
At about curfew time,[21] or little more.
His head was twisted, and that made him snore.
His spirit groaned in its uneasiness.
Down from his ladder slipped this Nicholas,
And Alison too, downward she softly sped
And without further word they went to bed
Where the carpenter himself slept other nights.
There were the revels, there were the delights!
And so this Alison and Nicholas lay
Busy about their solace and their play 440
Until the bell for lauds[22] began to ring
And in the chancel[23] friars began to sing.
    Now on this Monday, woebegone and glum
For love, this parish clerk, this Absolom
Was with some friends at Oseney, and while there
Inquired after John the carpenter.
A member of the cloister drew him away
Out of the church, and told him, "I can't say.

---

[21]About 8 or 9 P.M.
[22] The earliest of the canonical hours, celebrated in monasteries around 3 or 4 A.M.
[23] The railed-in area of a church near the altar.

I haven't seen him working hereabout
Since Saturday. The abbot sent him out   450
For timber, I suppose. He'll often go
And stay at the granary [24] a day or so.
Or else he's at his own house, possibly.
I can't for certain say where he may be."
    Absolom at once felt jolly and light,
And thought, "Time now to be awake all night,
For certainly I haven't seen him making
A stir about his door since day was breaking.
Don't call me a man if when I hear the cock
Begin to crow [25] I don't slip up and knock   460
On the low window by his bedroom wall.
To Alison at last I'll pour out all
My love-pangs, for at this point I can't miss,
Whatever happens, at the least a kiss.
Some comfort, by my word, will come my way.
I've felt my mouth itch the whole livelong day,
And that's a sign of kissing at the least.
I dreamed all night that I was at a feast.
So now I'll go and sleep an hour or two,
And then I'll wake and play the whole night through."   470
    When the first cockcrow through the dark had come
Up rose this jolly lover Absolom
And dressed up smartly. He was not remiss
About the least point. He chewed licorice
And cardamom to smell sweet, even before
He combed his hair. Beneath his tongue he bore
A sprig of Paris like a truelove knot. [26]
He strolled off to the carpenter's house, and got
Beneath the window. It came so near the ground
It reached his chest. Softly, with half a sound,   480
He coughed, "My honeycomb, sweet Alison,
What are you doing, my sweet cinnamon?
Awake, my sweetheart and my pretty bird,
Awake, and give me from your lips a word!
Little enough you care for all my woe,
How for your love I sweat wherever I go!
No wonder I sweat and faint and cannot eat
More than a girl; as a lamb does for the teat
I pine. Yes, truly, I so long for love
I mourn as if I were a turtledove."   490
    Said she, "You jack-fool, get away from here!
So help me God, I won't sing 'Kiss me, dear!'
I love another more than you. Get on,

---

[24] A barn, or perhaps farm, belonging to the abbey.
[25] The cock crowed around midnight and 3 A.M., and just before daybreak.
[26] A sprig of paris-herb, clover-shaped like a "truelove knot" and supposed to aid lovers.

For Christ's sake, Absolom, or I'll throw a stone.
The devil with you! Go and let me sleep."
    "Ah, that true love should ever have to reap
So evil a fortune," Absolom said. "A kiss,
At least, if it can be no more than this,
Give me, for love of Jesus and of me."
    "And will you go away for that?" said she.   500
    "Yes, truly, sweetheart," answered Absolom.
    "Get ready then," she said, "for here I come,"
And softly said to Nicholas, "Keep still,
And in a minute you can laugh your fill."
    This Absolom got down upon his knee
And said, "I am a lord of pure degree,[27]
For after this, I hope, comes more to savor.
Sweetheart, your grace, and pretty bird, your favor!"
    She undid the window quickly. "That will do,"
She said. "Be quick about it, and get through,   510
For fear the neighbors will look out and spy."
    Absolom wiped his mouth to make it dry.
The night was pitch dark, coal-black all about.
Her rear end through the window she thrust out.
He got no better or worse, did Absolom,
Than to kiss her with his mouth on the bare bum
Before he had caught on, a smacking kiss.
    He jumped back, thinking something was amiss.
A woman has no beard, he was well aware,
But what he felt was rough and had long hair.   520
    "Alas," he cried, "what have you made me do?"
    "Te-hee!" she said, and banged the window to.
    Absolom backed away a sorry pace.
    "You've bearded him!" said handy Nicholas.
"God's body, this is going fair and fit!"
    This luckless Absolom heard every bit,
And gnawed his mouth, so angry he became.
He said to himself, "I'll square you, all the same."
    But who now scrubs and rubs, who chafes his lips
With dust, with sand, with straw, with cloth and chips, 530
If not this Absolom? "The devil," says he,
"Welcome my soul if I wouldn't rather be
Revenged than have the whole town in a sack!
Alas," he cries, "if only I'd held back!"
His hot love had become all cold and ashen.
He didn't have a curse to spare for passion
From the moment when he kissed her on the ass.
That was the cure to make his sickness pass!
He cried as a child does after being whipped;
He railed at love. Then quietly he slipped   540

---

[27] In every way.

Across the street to a smith who was forging out
Parts that the farmers needed round about.
He was busy sharpening colter and plowshare[28]
When Absolom knocked as though without a care.
    "Undo the door, Jervice, and let me come."
    "What? Who are you?"
                        "It is I, Absolom."
    "Absolom, is it! By Christ's precious tree,[29]
Why are you up so early? Lord bless me,
What's ailing you? Some gay girl has the power
To bring you out, God knows, at such an hour!   550
Yes, by St. Neot,[30] you know well what I mean!"
    Absolom thought his jokes not worth a bean.
Without a word he let them all go by.
He had another kind of fish to fry
Than Jervice guessed. "Lend me this colter here
That's hot in the chimney, friend," he said. "Don't fear,
I'll bring it back right off when I am through.
I need it for a job I have to do."
    "Of course," said Jervice. "Why, if it were gold
Or coins in a sack, uncounted and untold,   560
As I'm a rightful smith, I wouldn't refuse it.
But, Christ's foot! how on earth do you mean to use it?"
    "Let that," said Absolom, "be as it may.
I'll let you know tomorrow or next day,"
And took the colter where the steel was cold
And slipped out with it safely in his hold
And softly over to the carpenter's wall.
He coughed and then he rapped the window, all
As he had done before.
                        "Who's knocking there?"
Said Alison. "It is a thief, I swear."   570
    "No, no," said he. "God knows, my sugarplum,
My bird, my darling, it's your Absolom.
I've brought a golden ring my mother gave me,
Fine and well cut, as I hope that God will save me.
It's yours, if you will let me have a kiss."
    Nicholas had got up to take a piss
And thought he would improve the whole affair.
This clerk, before he got away from there,
Should give *his* ass a smack; and hastily
He opened the window, and thrust out quietly,   580
Buttocks and haunches, all the way, his bum.
Up spoke this clerk, this jolly Absolom:
"Speak, for I don't know where you are, sweetheart."

---

[28] The colter was the vertical cutting blade of the plowshare. It was customary for black-smiths to begin work long before dawn.
[29] The Cross.
[30] Ninth-century saint.

Nicholas promptly let fly with a fart
As loud as if a clap of thunder broke,
So great he was nearly blinded by the stroke,
And ready with his hot iron to make a pass,
Absolom caught him fairly on the ass.
Off flew the skin, a good handbreadth of fat
Lay bare, the iron so scorched him where he sat.　　590
As for the pain, he thought that he would die,
And like a madman he began to cry,
"Help! Water! Water! Help, for God's own heart!"
At this the carpenter came to with a start.
He heard a man cry "Water!" as if mad.
"It's coming now," was the first thought he had.
"It's Noah's flood, alas, God be our hope!"
He sat up with his ax and chopped the rope
And down at once the whole contraption fell.
He didn't take time out to buy or sell　　600
Till he hit the floor and lay there in a swoon.
Then up jumped Nicholas and Alison
And in the street began to cry, "Help, ho!"
The neighbors all came running, high and low,
And poured into the house to see the sight.
The man still lay there, passed out cold and white,
For in his tumble he had broken an arm.
But he himself brought on his greatest harm,
For when he spoke he was at once outdone
By handy Nicholas and Alison　　610
Who told them one and all that he was mad.
So great a fear of Noah's flood he had,
By some delusion, that in his vanity[31]
He had bought himself these kneading-troughs, all three,
And hung them from the roof there, up above,
And he had pleaded with them, for God's love,
To sit there in the loft for company.
The neighbors laughed at such a fantasy,
And round the loft began to pry and poke
And turned his whole disaster to a joke.　　620
He found it was no use to say a word.
Whatever reason he offered, no one heard.
With oaths and curses people swore him down
Until he passed for mad in the whole town.
Wit, clerk, and student all stood by each other.
They said, "It's clear the man is crazy, brother."
Everyone had his laugh about this feud.
So Alison, the carpenter's wife, got screwed
For all the jealous watching he could try,
And Absolom, he kissed her nether eye,　　630
And Nicholas got his bottom roasted well.
God save this troop! That's all I have to tell.

[31] Folly.

PROLOGUE TO THE WIFE OF BATH'S TALE

"Experience,[1] though all authority
Was lacking in the world, confers on me
The right to speak of marriage, and unfold
Its woes. For, lords, since I was twelve years old
—Thanks to eternal God in heaven alive—
I have married at church door no less than five
Husbands, provided that I can have been
So often wed,[2] and all were worthy men.
But I was told, indeed, and not long since,
That Christ went to a wedding only once   10
At Cana, in the land of Galilee.[3]
By this example he instructed me
To wed once only—that's what I have heard!
Again, consider now what a sharp word,
Beside a well, Jesus, both God and man,
Spoke in reproving the Samaritan:
'Thou hast had five husbands'—this for a certainty
He said to her—'and the man that now hath thee
Is not thy husband.' True, he spoke this way,
But what he meant is more than I can say   20
Except that I would ask why the fifth man
Was not a husband to the Samaritan?
To just how many could she be a wife?
I have never heard this number all my life
Determined up to now. For round and round
Scholars may gloze, interpret, and expound,
But plainly, this I know without a lie,
God told us to increase and multiply.[4]
That noble text I can well understand.
My husband—this too I have well in hand—   30
Should leave both father and mother and cleave to me.[5]
Number God never mentioned, bigamy,
No, nor even octogamy; why do men
Talk of it as a sin and scandal, then?
        "Think of that monarch, wise King Solomon.[6]
It strikes me that *he* had more wives than one!

---

[1] The Wife's appeal to experience is somewhat unorthodox, since written works were supposed to have stronger authority. She shows, however, that she can cite them too (though not always accurately).

[2] The Wife is not sure that all her marriages were valid.

[3] For the wedding at Cana, where Christ changed water to wine, see the gospel of John, 2:1–11. For Jesus' meeting with the sinful Samaritan woman, mentioned a few lines later, see John 4:3–30.

[4] God's command to humankind at the creation; Genesis 1:28.

[5] Adam's words about Eve, Genesis 2:24: "Therefore shall a man leave his father and his mother, and shall cleave unto his wife: and they shall be one flesh."

[6] The Old Testament king had 700 wives and 300 concubines.

To be refreshed, God willing, would please me
If I got it half as many times as he!
What a gift he had, a gift of God's own giving,
For all his wives! There isn't a man now living 40
Who has the like. By all that I make out
This king had many a merry first-night bout
With each, he was so thoroughly alive.
Blessed be God that I have married five,
And always, for the money in his chest
And for his nether purse, I picked the best.
In divers[7] schools ripe scholarship is made,
And various practice in all kinds of trade
Makes perfect workmen, as the world can see.
Five husbands have had turns at schooling me. 50
Welcome the sixth, whenever I am faced
With yet another. I don't mean to be chaste
At all costs. When a spouse of mine is gone,
Some other Christian man shall take me on,
For then, says the Apostle, I'll be free
To wed, in God's name, where it pleases me.
To marry is no sin, as we can learn
From him; better to marry than to burn,[8]
He says. Why should I care what obloquy
Men heap on Lamech and his bigamy? 60
Abraham was, by all that I can tell,
A holy man; so Jacob was as well,
And each of them took more than two as brides,
And many another holy man besides.
Where, may I ask, in any period,
Can you show in plain words that Almighty God
Forbade us marriage? Point it out to me!
Or where did he command virginity?
The Apostle, when he speaks of maidenhood,
Lays down no law. This I have understood 70
As well as you, milords, for it is plain.
Men may advise a woman to abstain
From marriage, but mere counsels aren't commands.
He left it to our judgment, where it stands.
Had God enjoined us all to maidenhood
Then marriage would have been condemned for good.
But truth is, if no seed were ever sown,
In what soil could virginity be grown?
Paul did not dare command a thing at best
On which his Master left us no behest. 80

---

[7] Various.
[8] In 1 Corinthians 7:8–9, Paul recommends celibacy to the unmarried and widows, and then adds, "But if they cannot contain, let them marry: for it is better to marry than to burn."

"But now the prize goes to virginity.
Seize it whoever can, and let us see
What manner of man shall run best in the race!
But not all men receive this form of grace
Except where God bestows it by his will.
The Apostle was a maid, I know; but still,
Although he wished all men were such as he,
It was only *counsel* toward virginity.
To be a wife he gave me his permission,
And so it is no blot on my condition   90
Nor slander of bigamy upon my state
If when my husband dies I take a mate.
A man does virtuously, St. Paul has said,
To touch no woman—meaning in his bed.
For fire and fat are dangerous friends at best.
You know what this example should suggest.
Here is the nub: he held virginity
Superior to wedded frailty,
And frailty I call it unless man
And woman both are chaste for their whole span.   100
    "I am not jealous if maidenhood outweighs
My marriages; I grant it all the praise.
It pleases them, these virgins, flesh and soul
To be immaculate. I won't extol
My own condition. In a lord's household
You know that every vessel can't be gold.
Some are of wood, and serve their master still.
God calls us variously to do his will.
Each has his proper gift, of all who live,
Some this, some that, as it pleases God to give.   110
    "To be virgin is a high and perfect course,
And continence is holy. But the source
Of all perfection, Jesus, never bade
Each one of us to go sell all he had
And give it to the poor; he did not say
That all should follow him in this one way.
He spoke to those who would live perfectly,
And by your leave, lords, that is not for me!
The flower of my best years I find it suits
To spend on the acts of marriage and its fruits.   120
    "Tell me this also: why at our creation
Were organs given us for generation,
And for what profit were we creatures made?
Believe me, not for nothing! Ply his trade
Of twisting texts who will, and let him urge
That they were only given us to purge
Our urine; say without them we should fail
To tell a female rightly from a male
And that's their only object—say you so?
It won't work, as experience will show.   130

Without offense to scholars, I say this,
They were given us for both these purposes,
That we may both be cleansed, I mean, and eased
Through intercourse, where God is not displeased.
Why else in books is this opinion met,
That every man should pay his wife his debt?
Tell me with what a man should hope to pay
Unless he put his instrument in play?
They were supplied us, then, for our purgation,
But they were also meant for generation. 140
  "But none the less I do not mean to say
That all those who are furnished in this way
Are bound to go and practice intercourse.
The world would then grant chastity no force.
Christ was a maid, yet he was formed a man,
And many a saint, too, since the world began,
And yet they lived in perfect chastity.
I am not spiteful toward virginity.
Let virgins be white bread of pure wheat-seed.
Barley we wives are called, and yet I read 150
In Mark, and tell the tale in truth he can,
That Christ with barley bread cheered many a man.[9]
In the state that God assigned to each of us
I'll persevere. I'm not fastidious.
In wifehood I will use my instrument
As freely by my Maker it was lent.
If I hold back with it, God give me sorrow!
My husband shall enjoy it night and morrow
When it pleases him to come and pay his debt.
But a husband, and I've not been thwarted yet, 160
Shall always be my debtor and my slave.
From tribulation he shall never save
His flesh, not for as long as I'm his wife!
I have the power, during all my life,
Over his very body, and not he.
For so the Apostle has instructed me,[10]
Who bade men love their wives for better or worse.
It pleases me from end to end, that verse!"
  The Pardoner, before she could go on,
Jumped up and cried, "By God and by St. John, 170
Upon this topic you preach nobly, Dame!
I was about to wed, but now, for shame,
Why should my body pay a price so dear?
I'd rather not be married all this year!"

---

[9] The Wife alludes to the miracle in which Jesus fed 5,000 people with five barley loaves and two fishes.
[10] The Wife cites only the second half of the Apostle's (Paul's) statement (1 Corinthians 7:4): "The wife hath not power of her own body, but the husband: and likewise also the husband hath not power of his own body, but the wife."

"Hold on," she said. "I haven't yet begun.
You'll drink a keg of this before I'm done,
I promise you, and it won't taste like ale!
And after I have told you my whole tale
Of marriage, with its fund of tribulation—
And I'm the expert of my generation,   180
For I myself, I mean, have been the whip—
You can decide then if you want a sip
Out of the barrel that I mean to broach.
Before you come too close in your approach,
Think twice. I have examples, more than ten!
'The man who won't be warned by other men,
To other men a warning he shall be.'
These are the words we find in Ptolemy.
You can read them right there in his *Almagest*."[11]
        "Now, Madame, if you're willing, I suggest,"   190
Answered the Pardoner, "as you began,
Continue with your tale, and spare no man.
Teach us your practice—we young men need a guide."
        "Gladly, if it will please you," she replied.
"But first I ask you, if I speak my mind,
That all this company may be well inclined,
And will not take offense at what I say.
I only mean it, after all, in play.
        "Now, sirs, I will get onward with my tale.
If ever I hope to drink good wine or ale,   200
I'm speaking truth: the husbands I have had,
Three of them have been good, and two were bad.
The three were kindly men, and rich, and old.
But they were hardly able to uphold
The statute which had made them fast to me.
You know well what I mean by this, I see!
So help me God, I can't help laughing yet
When I think of how at night I made them sweat,
And I thought nothing of it, on my word!
Their land and wealth they had by then conferred   210
On me, and so I safely could neglect
Tending their love or showing them respect.
So well they loved me that by God above
I hardly set a value on their love.
A woman who is wise is never done
Busily winning love when she has none,
But since I had them wholly in my hand
And they had given me their wealth and land,
Why task myself to spoil them or to please
Unless for my own profit and my ease?   220
I set them working so that many a night

---

[11] The saying is not in the *Almagest*, although it was attributed to Ptolemy by a translator
of the work. The same is true of the Wife's later citation of Ptolemy.

They sang a dirge, so grievous was their plight!
They never got the bacon, well I know,
Offered as prize to couples at Dunmow[12]
Who live a year in peace, without repentance!
So well I ruled them, by my law and sentence,
They were glad to bring me fine things from the fair
And happy when I spoke with a mild air,
For God knows I could chide outrageously.
   "Now judge if I could do it properly!   230
You wives who understand and who are wise,
This is the way to throw dust in their eyes.
There isn't on the earth so bold a man
He can swear false or lie as a woman can.
I do not urge this course in every case,
Just when a prudent wife is caught off base;
Then she should swear the parrot's mad who tattled
Her indiscretions, and when she's once embattled
Should call her maid as witness, by collusion.
But listen, how I threw them in confusion: 240
   "'Sir dotard,[13] this is how you live?' I'd say.
'How can my neighbor's wife be dressed so gay?
She carries off the honors everywhere.
I sit at home. I've nothing fit to wear.
What were you doing at my neighbor's house?
Is she so handsome? Are you so amorous?
What do you whisper to our maid? God bless me,
Give up your jokes, old lecher. They depress me.
When I have a harmless friend myself, you balk
And scold me like a devil if I walk   250
For innocent amusement to his house.
You drink and come home reeling like a souse
And sit down on your bench, worse luck, and preach.
Taking a wife who's poor—this is the speech
That you regale me with—costs grievously,
And if she's rich and of good family,
It is a constant torment, you decide,
To suffer her ill humor and her pride.
And if she's fair, you scoundrel, you destroy her
By saying that every lecher will enjoy her;   260
For chastity at best has frail protections
If a woman is assailed from all directions.
   "'Some want us for our wealth, so you declare,
Some for our figure, some think we are fair,
Some want a woman who can dance or sing,
Some want kindness, and some philandering,
Some look for hands and arms well turned and small.

---

[12]A town in Essex, in southeastern England. Such a prize for peaceable couples was in fact given.
   [13]A senile person.

Thus, by your tale, the devil may take us all!
Men cannot keep a castle or redoubt[14]
Longer, you tell me, than it can hold out.   270
Or if a woman's plain, you say that she
Is one who covets each man she may see,
For at him like a spaniel she will fly
Until she finds some man that she can buy.
Down to the lake goes never a goose so gray
But it will have a mate, I've heard you say.
It's hard to fasten—this too I've been told—
A thing that no man willingly will hold.
Wise men, you tell me as you go to bed,
And those who hope for heaven should never wed.   280
I hope wild lightning and a thunderstroke
Will break your wizened neck! You say that smoke
And falling timbers and a railing wife
Drive a man from his house. Lord bless my life!
What ails an old man, so to make him chide?
We cover our vices till the knot is tied,
We wives, you say, and then we trot them out.
Here's a fit proverb for a doddering lout!
An ox or ass, you say, a hound or horse,
These we examine as a matter of course.   290
Basins and also bowls, before we buy them,
Spoons, spools, and such utensils, first we try them,
And so with pots and clothes, beyond denial;
But of their wives men never make a trial
Until they are married. After that, you say,
Old fool, we put our vices on display.
    "'I am in a pique if you forget your duty
And fail, you tell me, to praise me for my beauty,
Or unless you are always doting on my face
And calling me "fair dame" in every place,   300
Or unless you give a feast on my birthday
To keep me in good spirits, fresh and gay,
Or unless all proper courtesies are paid
To my nurse and also to my chambermaid,
And my father's kin with all their family ties—
You say so, you old barrelful of lies!
    "'Yet just because he has a head of hair
Like shining gold, and squires me everywhere,
You have a false suspicion in your heart
Of Jenkin, our apprentice. For my part   310
I wouldn't have him if you died tomorrow!
But tell me this, or go and live in sorrow:
That chest of yours, why do you hide the keys
Away from me? It's my wealth, if you please,

---

[14]A small fort or defensive hiding place.

As much as yours. Will you make a fool of me,
The mistress of our house? You shall not be
Lord of my body and my wealth at once!
No, by St. James himself, you must renounce
One or the other, if it drives you mad!
Does it help to spy on me? You would be glad   320
To lock me up, I think, inside your chest.
"Enjoy yourself, and go where you think best,"
You ought to say; "I won't hear tales of malice.
I know you for a faithful wife, Dame Alice."
A woman loves no man who keeps close charge
Of where she goes. We want to be at large.
Blessed above all other men was he,
The wise astrologer, Don Ptolemy,
Who has this proverb in his *Almagest:*
"Of all wise men his wisdom is the best   330
Who does not care who has the world in hand."
Now by this proverb you should understand,
Since you have plenty, it isn't yours to care
Or fret how richly other people fare,
For by your leave, old dotard, you for one
Can have all you can take when day is done.
The man's a niggard to the point of scandal
Who will not lend his lamp to light a candle;
His lamp won't lose although the candle gain.
If you have enough, you ought not to complain.   340
    "'You say, too, if we make ourselves look smart,
Put on expensive clothes and dress the part,
We lay our virtue open to disgrace.
And then you try to reinforce your case
By saying these words in the Apostle's name:
"In chaste apparel, with modesty and shame,
So shall you women clothe yourselves," said he,
"And not in rich coiffure or jewelry,
Pearls or the like, or gold, or costly wear."[15]
Now both your text and rubric, I declare,   350
I will not follow as I would a gnat!
    "'You told me once that I was like a cat,
For singe her skin and she will stay at home,
But if her skin is smooth, the cat will roam.
No dawn but finds her on the neighbors calling
To show her skin, and go off caterwauling.
If I am looking smart, you mean to say,
I'm off to put my finery on display.
    "'What do you gain, old fool, by setting spies?
Though you beg Argus[16] with his hundred eyes   360

---

[15] See St. Paul's First Epistle to Timothy 2:9.
[16] In mythology, a hundred-eyed giant who served as a guard.

To be my bodyguard, for all his skill
He'll keep me only by my own free will.
I know enough to blind him, as I live!
  "'There are three things,[17] you also say, that give
Vexation to this world both south and north,
And you add that no one can endure the fourth.
Of these catastrophes a hateful wife—
You precious wretch, may Christ cut short your life!—
Is always reckoned, as you say, for one.
Is this your whole stock of comparison,   370
And why in all your parables of contempt
Can a luckless helpmate never be exempt?
You also liken woman's love to hell,
To barren land where water will not dwell.
I've heard you call it an unruly fire;
The more it burns, the hotter its desire
To burn up everything that burned will be.
You say that just as worms destroy a tree
A wife destroys her spouse, as they have found
Who get themselves in holy wedlock bound.'   380
  "By these devices, lords, as you perceive,
I got my three old husbands to believe
That in their cups they said things of this sort,
And all of it was false; but for support
Jenkin bore witness, and my niece did too.
These innocents, Lord, what I put them through!
God's precious pains! And they had no recourse,
For I could bite and whinny like a horse.
Though in the wrong, I kept them well annoyed,
Or oftentimes I would have been destroyed!   390
First to the mill is first to grind his grain.
I was always the first one to complain,
And so our peace was made; they gladly bid
For terms to settle things they never did!
  "For wenching I would scold them out of hand
When they were hardly well enough to stand.
But this would tickle a man; it would restore him
To think I had so great a fondness for him!
I'd vow when darkness came and out I stepped,
It was to see the girls with whom he slept.   400
Under this pretext I had plenty of mirth!
Such wit as this is given us at our birth.
Lies, tears, and needlework the Lord will give
In kindness to us women while we live.
And thus in one point I can take just pride:
In the end I showed myself the stronger side.

  [17]Several of the examples of unpleasantness in the following lines are from Proverbs, chapter 30.

By sleight or strength I kept them in restraint,
And chiefly by continual complaint.
In bed they met their grief in fullest measure.
There I would scold; I would not do their pleasure. 410
Bed was a place where I would not abide
If I felt my husband's arm across my side
Till he agreed to square accounts and pay,
And after that I'd let him have his way.
To every man, therefore, I tell this tale:
Win where you're able, all is up for sale.
No falcon by an empty hand is lured.
For victory their cravings I endured
And even feigned a show of appetite.
And yet in old meat I have no delight; 420
It made me always rail at them and chide them,
For though the pope himself sat down beside them
I would not give them peace at their own board.
No, on my honor, I paid them word for word.
Almighty God so help me, if right now
I had to make my last will, I can vow
For every word they said to me, we're quits.
For I so handled the contest by my wits
That they gave up, and took it for the best,
Or otherwise we should have had no rest. 430
Like a mad lion let my husband glare,
In the end he got the worst of the affair.
  "Then I would say, 'My dear, you ought to keep
In mind how gentle Wilkin looks, our sheep.
Come here, my husband, let me kiss your cheek!
You should be patient, too; you should be meek.
Of Job and of his patience when you prate
Your conscience ought to show a cleaner slate.
He should be patient who so well can preach.
If not, then it will fall on me to teach 440
The beauty of a peaceful wedded life.
For one of us must give in, man or wife,
And since men are more reasonable creatures
Than women are, it follows that *your* features
Ought to exhibit patience. Why do you groan?
You want my body yours, and yours alone?
Why, take it all! Welcome to every bit!
But curse you, Peter, unless you cherish it!
Were I inclined to peddle my *belle chose,*[18]
I could go about dressed freshly as a rose. 450
But I will keep it for your own sweet tooth.
It's your fault if we fight. By God, that's truth!'

[18] Literally, "beautiful thing" (French).

"This was the way I talked when I had need.
But now to my fourth husband I'll proceed.
    "This fourth I married was a roisterer.
He had a mistress, and my passions were,
Although I say it, strong; and altogether
I was young and stubborn, pert in every feather.
If anyone took up his harp to play,
How I could dance! I sang as merry a lay   460
As any nightingale when of sweet wine
I had drunk my draft. Metellius,[19] the foul swine,
Who beat his spouse until he took her life
For drinking wine, had I only been his wife,
He'd never have frightened me away from drinking!
But after a drink, Venus gets in my thinking,
For just as true as cold engenders hail
A thirsty mouth goes with a thirsty tail.
Drinking destroys a woman's last defense
As lechers well know by experience.   470
    "But, Lord Christ, when it all comes back to me,
Remembering my youth and jollity,
It tickles me to the roots. It does me good
Down to this very day that while I could
I took my world, my time, and had my fling.
But age, alas, that poisons everything
Has robbed me of my beauty and my pith.
Well, let it go! Good-by! The devil with
What cannot last! There's only this to tell:
The flour is gone, I've only chaff to sell.   480
Yet I'll contrive to keep a merry cheek!
But now of my fourth husband I will speak.
    "My heart was, I can tell you, full of spite
That in another he should find delight.
I paid him for this debt; I made it good.
I furnished him a cross of the same wood,
By God and by St. Joce—in no foul fashion,
Not with my flesh; but I put on such passion
And rendered him so jealous, I'll engage
I made him fry in his own grease for rage!   490
On earth, God knows, I was his purgatory;
I only hope his soul is now in glory.
God knows it was a sad song that he sung
When the shoe pinched him; sorely was he wrung!
Only he knew, and God, the devious system
By which outrageously I used to twist him.
He died when I came home from Jerusalem.
He is buried near the chancel, under the beam

---

[19] The source of the story of Metellius is Valerius Maximus, one of Chaucer's favorite sources.

That holds the cross. His tomb is less ornate
Than the sepulcher where Darius[20] lies in state   500
And which the paintings of Appelles graced
With subtle work. It would have been a waste
To bury him lavishly. Farewell! God save
His soul and give him rest! He's in his grave.
    "And now of my fifth husband let me tell.
God never let his soul go down to hell
Though he of all five was my scourge and flail!
I feel it on my ribs, right down the scale,
And ever shall until my dying day.
And yet he was so full of life and gay   510
In bed, and could so melt me and cajole me
When on my back he had a mind to roll me,
What matter if on every bone he'd beaten me!
He'd have my love, so quickly he could sweeten me.
I loved him best, in fact; for as you see,
His love was a more arduous prize for me.
We women, if I'm not to tell a lie,
Are quaint in this regard. Put in our eye
A thing we cannot easily obtain,
All day we'll cry about it and complain.   520
Forbid a thing, we want it bitterly,
But urge it on us, then we turn and flee.
We are chary of what we hope that men will buy.
A throng at market makes the prices high;
Men set no value on cheap merchandise,
A truth all women know if they are wise.
    "My fifth, may God forgive his every sin,
I took for love, not money. He had been
An Oxford student once, but in our town
Was boarding with my good friend, Alison.   530
She knew each secret that I had to give
More than our parish priest did, as I live!
I told her my full mind, I shared it all.
For if my husband pissed against a wall
Or did a thing that might have cost his life,
To her, and to another neighbor's wife,
And to my niece, a girl whom I loved well,
His every thought I wouldn't blush to tell.
And often enough I told them, be it said.
God knows I made his face turn hot and red   540
For secrets he confided to his shame.
He knew he only had himself to blame.
    "And so it happened once that during Lent,
As I often did, to Alison's I went,

[20]According to legend, Darius, king of the ancient Persians, had a lavish tomb.

For I have loved my life long to be gay
And to walk out in April or in May
To hear the talk and seek a favorite haunt.
Jenkin the student, Alice, my confidante,
And I myself into the country went.
My husband was in London all that Lent.   550
I had the greater liberty to see
And to be seen by jolly company.
How could I tell beforehand in what place
Luck might be waiting with a stroke of grace?
And so I went to every merrymaking.
No pilgrimage was past my undertaking.
I was at festivals, and marriages,
Processions, preachings, and at miracle plays,[21]
And in my scarlet clothes I made a sight.
Upon that costume neither moth nor mite   560
Nor any worm with ravening hunger fell.
And why, you ask? It was kept in use too well.
    "Now for what happened. In the fields we walked,
The three of us, and gallantly we talked,
The student and I, until I told him he,
If I became a widow, should marry me.
For I can say, and not with empty pride,
I have never failed for marriage to provide
Or other things as well. Let mice be meek;
A mouse's heart I hold not worth a leek.   570
He has one hole to scurry to, just one,
And if that fails him, he is quite undone.
    "I let this student think he had bewitched me.
(My mother with this piece of guile enriched me!)
All night I dreamed of him—this too I said;
He was killing me as I lay flat in bed;
My very bed in fact was full of blood;
But still I hoped it would result in good,
For blood betokens gold, as I have heard.
It was a fiction, dream and every word,   580
But I was following my mother's lore
In all this matter, as in many more.
    "Sirs—let me see; what did I mean to say?
Aha! By God, I have it! When he lay,
My fourth, of whom I've spoken, on his bier,
I wept of course; I showed but little cheer,
As wives must do, since custom has its place,
And with my kerchief covered up my face.
But since I had provided for a mate,
I did not cry for long, I'll freely state.   590
And so to church my husband on the morrow
Was borne away by neighbors in their sorrow.

---

[21] Plays based on the lives of the saints.

Jenkin, the student, was among the crowd,
And when I saw him walk, so help me God,
Behind the bier, I thought he had a pair
Of legs and feet so cleanly turned and fair
I put my heart completely in his hold.
He was in fact some twenty winters old
And I was forty, to confess the truth;
But all my life I've still had a colt's tooth.
My teeth were spaced apart;[22] that was the seal   600
St. Venus printed, and became me well.
So help me God, I was a lusty one,
Pretty and young and rich, and full of fun.
And truly, as my husbands have all said,
I was the best thing there could be in bed.
For I belong to Venus in my feelings,
Though I bring the heart of Mars to all my dealings.
From Venus come my lust and appetite,
From Mars I get my courage and my might,   610
Born under Taurus, while Mars stood therein.
Alas, alas, that ever love was sin!
I yielded to my every inclination
Through the predominance of my constellation;
This made me so I never could withhold
My chamber of Venus, if the truth be told,
From a good fellow; yet upon my face
Mars left his mark, and in another place.
For never, so may Christ grant me intercession,
Have I yet loved a fellow with discretion,   620
But always I have followed appetite,
Let him be long or short or dark or light.
I never cared, as long as he liked me,
What his rank was or how poor he might be.
 "What should I say, but when the month ran out,
This jolly student, always much about,
This Jenkin married me in solemn state.
To him I gave land, titles, the whole slate
Of goods that had been given me before;
But my repentance afterward was sore!   630
He wouldn't endure the pleasures I held dear.
By God, he gave me a lick once on the ear,
When from a book of his I tore a leaf,
So hard that from the blow my ear grew deaf.
I was stubborn as a lioness with young,
And by the truth I had a rattling tongue,
And I would visit, as I'd done before,
No matter what forbidding oath he swore.
Against this habit he would sit and preach me
Sermons enough, and he would try to teach me   640

[22]A sign of lustiness.

Old Roman stories,[23] how for his whole life
The man Sulpicius Gallus left his wife
Only because he saw her look one day
Bareheaded down the street from his doorway.
   "Another Roman he told me of by name
Who, since his wife was at a summer's game
Without his knowledge, thereupon forsook
The woman. In his Bible he would look
And find that proverb of the Ecclesiast
Where he enjoins and makes the stricture fast   650
That men forbid their wives to rove about.
Then he would quote me this, you needn't doubt:
'Build a foundation over sands or shallows,
Or gallop a blind horse across the fallows,
Let a wife traipse to shrines that some saint hallows,
And you are fit to swing upon the gallows.'
Talk as he would, I didn't care two haws
For his proverbs or his venerable saws.
Set right by him I never meant to be.
I hate the man who tells my faults to me,   660
And more of us than I do, by your pleasure.
This made him mad with me beyond all measure.
Under his yoke in no case would I go.
   "Now, by St. Thomas, I will let you know
Why from that book of his I tore a leaf,
For which I got the blow that made me deaf.
   "He had a book, *Valerius,* he called it,
And Theophrastus, and he always hauled it
From where it lay to read both day and night
And laughed hard at it, such was his delight.   670
There was another scholar, too, at Rome
A cardinal, whose name was St. Jerome;
He wrote a book against Jovinian.
In the same book also were Tertullian,
Chrysippus, Trotula, Abbess Héloïse
Who lived near Paris; it contained all these,
Bound in a single volume, and many a one
Besides; the Parables of Solomon
And Ovid's *Art of Love.* On such vacation
As he could snatch from worldly occupation   680
He dredged this book for tales of wicked wives.[24]
He knew more stories of their wretched lives
Than are told about good women in the Bible.
No scholar ever lived who did not libel

---

[23] The following two stories are from Valerius Maximus.
[24] Jenkin's collection of anti-feminine literature is wide ranging, including the Bible; ancient classical authors such as Theophrastus and Ovid; early Christian authors such as Tertullian and Jerome; and medieval writers such as the twelfth-century Héloïse (loved by Abelard).

Women, believe me; to speak well of wives
Is quite beyond them, unless it be in lives
Of holy saints; no woman else will do.
Who was it painted the lion,[25] tell me who?
By God, if women had only written stories
Like wits and scholars in their oratories,[26]
They would have pinned on men more wickedness   690
Than the whole breed of Adam can redress.
Venus's children clash with Mercury's;
The two work evermore by contraries.
Knowledge and wisdom are of Mercury's giving,
Venus loves revelry and riotous living,
And with these clashing dispositions gifted
Each of them sinks when the other is uplifted.
Thus Mercury falls, God knows, in desolation
In the sign of Pisces, Venus's exaltation,   700
And Venus falls when Mercury is raised.
Thus by a scholar no woman can be praised.
The scholar, when he's old and cannot do
The work of Venus more than his old shoe,
Then sits he down, and in his dotage fond
Writes that no woman keeps her marriage bond!
   "But now for the story that I undertook—
To tell how I was beaten for a book.
   "Jenkin, one night, who never seemed to tire
Of reading in his book, sat by the fire   710
And first he read of Eve, whose wickedness
Delivered all mankind to wretchedness
For which in his own person Christ was slain
Who with his heart's blood bought us all again.
'By this,' he said, 'expressly you may find
That woman was the loss of all mankind.'
   "He read me next how Samson lost his hair.
Sleeping, his mistress clipped it off for fair;
Through this betrayal he lost both his eyes.[27]
He read me then—and I'm not telling lies—   720
How Deianeira, wife of Hercules,
Caused him to set himself on fire.[28] With these
He did not overlook the sad to-do
Of Socrates with *his* wives—he had two.
Xantippe emptied the pisspot on his head.
This good man sat as patient as if dead.

---

[25] In a fable of Aesop, a lion who sees a picture of a man killing a lion says that if lions could paint, the roles in the picture might be reversed.
[26] Private chapels.
[27] Judges, chapter 16. Samson confided to his beloved, Delilah, that his strength lay in his hair; she betrayed him by having it cut off while he was sleeping. Thus weakened, he was enslaved by the Philistines.
[28] In her jealousy she gave Hercules a poisoned robe, which caused him such agony that to escape the pain he had himself cremated.

He wiped his scalp; he did not dare complain
Except to say 'With thunder must come rain.'
"Pasiphaë,[29] who was the queen of Crete,
For wickedness he thought her story sweet. 730
Ugh! That's enough, it was a grisly thing,
About her lust and filthy hankering!
And Clytemnestra[30] in her lechery
Who took her husband's life feloniously,
He grew devout in reading of her treason.
And then he told me also for what reason
Unhappy Amphiaraus lost his life.
My husband had the story of *his* wife,
Eriphyle, who for a clasp of gold
Went to his Grecian enemies and told 740
The secret of her husband's hiding place,
For which at Thebes he met an evil grace.[31]
Livia and Lucilia, he went through
Their tale as well; they killed their husbands, too.
One killed for love, the other killed for hate.
At evening Livia, when the hour was late,
Poisoned her husband, for she was his foe.
Lucilia doted on her husband so
That in her lust, hoping to make him think
Ever of her, she gave him a love-drink 750
Of such a sort he died before the morrow.[32]
And so at all turns husbands come to sorrow!
"He told me then how one Latumius,
Complaining to a friend named Arrius,
Told him that in his garden grew a tree
On which his wives had hanged themselves, all three,
Merely for spite against their partnership.
'Brother,' said Arrius, 'let me have a slip
From this miraculous tree, for, begging pardon,
I want to go and plant it in my garden.' 760
"Then about wives in recent times he read,
How some had murdered husbands lying abed
And all night long had let a paramour
Enjoy them with the corpse flat on the floor;
Or driven a nail into a husband's brain
While he was sleeping, and thus he had been slain;
And some had given them poison in their drink.
He told more harm than anyone can think,

[29] She fell in love with a bull and gave birth to a monster, half bull and half human.

[30] Wife of Agamemnon, commander of the Greeks against Troy. On his return from the war, she and her paramour killed him.

[31] In mythology, Amphiaraus was tricked by his wife (who had been bribed) into joining an expedition against Thebes from which it was known that he would not return alive.

[32] In ancient Roman history there were two Livias, each of whom killed her husband. Lucilia was married to the great Roman poet Lucretius (first century B.C.); the story of the love potion is from St. Jerome.

And seasoned his wretched stories with proverbs
Outnumbering all the blades of grass and herbs
On earth. 'Better a dragon for a mate, 770
Better,' he said, 'on a lion's whims to wait
Than on a wife whose way it is to chide.
Better,' he said, 'high in the loft to bide
Than with a railing wife down in the house.
They always, they are so contrarious,
Hate what their husbands like,' so he would say.
'A woman,' he said, 'throws all her shame away
When she takes off her smock.' And on he'd go:
'A pretty woman, unless she's chaste also, 780
Is like a gold ring stuck in a sow's nose.'
Who could imagine, who would half suppose
The gall my heart drank, raging at each drop?
  "And when I saw that he would never stop
Reading all night from his accursed book,
Suddenly, in the midst of it, I took
Three leaves and tore them out in a great pique,
And with my fist I caught him on the cheek
So hard he tumbled backward in the fire.
And up he jumped, he was as mad for ire 790
As a mad lion, and caught me on the head
With such a blow I fell down as if dead.
And seeing me on the floor, how still I lay,
He was aghast, and would have fled away,
Till I came to at length, and gave a cry.
'Have you killed me for my lands? Before I die,
False thief,' I said, 'I'll give you a last kiss!'
  "He came to me and knelt down close at this,
And said, 'So help me God, dear Alison,
I'll never strike you. For this thing I have done 800
You are to blame. Forgive me, I implore.'
So then I hit him on the cheek once more
And said, 'Thus far I am avenged, you thief.
I cannot speak. Now I shall die for grief.'
But finally, with much care and ado,
We reconciled our differences, we two.
He let me have the bridle in my hand
For management of both our house and land.
To curb his tongue he also undertook,
And on the spot I made him burn his book. 810
And when I had secured in full degree
By right of triumph the whole sovereignty,
And he had said, 'My dear, my own true wife,
Do as you will as long as you have life;
Preserve your honor and keep my estate,'
From that day on we had settled our debate.
I was as kind, God help me, day and dark
As any wife from India to Denmark,

And also true, and so he was to me.
I pray the Lord who sits in majesty   820
To bless his soul for Christ's own mercy dear.
And now I'll tell my tale, if you will hear."
    "Dame," laughed the Friar, "as I hope for bliss,
It was a long preamble to a tale, all this!"
    "God's arms!" the Summoner said, "it is a sin,
Good people, how friars are always butting in!
A fly and a friar will fall in every dish
And every question, whatever people wish.
What do you know, with your talk about 'preambling'?
Amble or trot or keep still or go scrambling,   830
You interrupt our pleasure."
                              "You think so,
Sir Summoner?" said the Friar. "Before I go,
I'll give the people here a chance or two
For a laugh at summoners, I promise you."
    "Curse on your face," the Summoner said, "curse me,
If I don't tell some stories, two or three,
On friars, before I get to Sittingborne,[33]
With which I'll twist your heart and make it mourn,
For you have lost your temper, I can see."
    "Be quiet," cried our Host, "immediately,"   840
And ordered, "Let the woman tell her tale.
You act like people who've got drunk on ale.
Do, Madame, tell us. That is the best measure."
    "All ready, sir," she answered "at your pleasure,
With the license of this worthy Friar here."
    "Madame, tell on," he said. "You have my ear."

THE WIFE OF BATH'S TALE

In the old days when King Arthur ruled the nation,
Whom Welshmen speak of with such veneration,
This realm we live in was a fairy land.
The fairy queen danced with her jolly band
On the green meadows where they held dominion.
This was, as I have read, the old opinion;
I speak of many hundred years ago.
But no one sees an elf now, as you know,
For in our time the charity and prayers
And all the begging of these holy friars   10
Who swarm through every nook and every stream
Thicker than motes of dust in a sunbeam,
Blessing our chambers, kitchens, halls, and bowers,
Our cities, towns, and castles, our high towers,

[33]About forty miles from London.

Our villages, our stables, barns, and dairies,
They keep us all from seeing any fairies,
For where you might have come upon an elf
There now you find the holy friar himself
Working his district on industrious legs
And saying his devotions while he begs.　　　　　　　　　20
Women are safe now under every tree.
No incubus[1] is there unless it's he,
And all they have to fear from him is shame.
　　It chanced that Arthur had a knight who came
Lustily riding home one day from hawking,
And in his path he saw a maiden walking
Before him, stark alone, right in his course.
This young knight took her maidenhead by force,
A crime at which the outcry was so keen
It would have cost his neck, but that the queen,　　　　　30
With other ladies, begged the king so long
That Arthur spared his life, for right or wrong,
And gave him to the queen, at her own will,
According to her choice, to save or kill.
　　She thanked the king, and later told this knight,
Choosing her time, "You are still in such a plight
Your very life has no security.
I grant your life, if you can answer me
This question: what is the thing that most of all
Women desire? Think, or your neck will fall　　　　　40
Under the ax! If you cannot let me know
Immediately, I give you leave to go
A twelvemonth and a day, no more, in quest
Of such an answer as will meet the test.
But you must pledge your honor to return
And yield your body, whatever you may learn."
　　The knight sighed; he was rueful beyond measure.
But what! He could not follow his own pleasure.
He chose at last upon his way to ride
And with such answer as God might provide　　　　　50
To come back when the year was at the close.
And so he takes his leave, and off he goes.
　　He seeks out every house and every place
Where he has any hope, by luck or grace,
Of learning what thing women covet most.
But it seemed he could not light on any coast
Where on this point two people would agree,
For some said wealth and some said jollity,
Some said position, some said sport in bed
And often to be widowed, often wed.　　　　　60
Some said that to a woman's heart what mattered
Above all else was to be pleased and flattered.

---

[1] An evil spirit believed to have intercourse with women, in their sleep.

That shaft, to tell the truth, was a close hit.
Men win us best by flattery, I admit,
And by attention. Some say our greatest ease
Is to be free and do just as we please,
And not to have our faults thrown in our eyes,
But always to be praised for being wise.
And true enough, there's not one of us all
Who will not kick if you rub us on a gall.   70
Whatever vices we may have within,
We won't be taxed with any fault or sin.
    Some say that women are delighted well
If it is thought that they will never tell
A secret they are trusted with, or scandal.
But that tale isn't worth an old rake handle!
We women, for a fact, can never hold
A secret. Will you hear a story told?
Then witness Midas! For it can be read
In Ovid that he had upon his head   80
Two ass's ears that he kept out of sight
Beneath his long hair with such skill and sleight
That no one else besides his wife could guess.
He loved her well, and trusted her no less.
He begged her not to make his blemish known,
But keep her knowledge to herself alone.
She swore that never, though to save her skin,
Would she be guilty of so mean a sin,
And yet it seemed to her she nearly died
Keeping a secret locked so long inside.   90
It swelled about her heart so hard and deep
She was afraid some word was bound to leap
Out of her mouth, and since there was no man
She dared to tell, down to a swamp she ran—
Her heart, until she got there, all agog—
And like a bittern booming in the bog
She put her mouth close to the watery ground:
"Water, do not betray me with your sound!
I speak to you, and you alone," she said.
"Two ass's ears grow on my husband's head!   100
And now my heart is whole, now it is out.
I'd burst if I held it longer, past all doubt."
Safely, you see, awhile you may confide
In us, but it will out; we cannot hide
A secret. Look in Ovid if you care
To learn what followed; the whole tale is there.[2]
    This knight, when he perceived he could not find
What women covet most, was low in mind;

---

[2]See Ovid, *Metamorphoses*, Book XI. In Ovid, however, it is Midas's barber, not his wife, who reveals the secret.

But the day had come when homeward he must ride,
And as he crossed a wooded countryside 110
Some four and twenty ladies there by chance
He saw, all circling in a woodland dance,
And toward this dance he eagerly drew near
In hope of any counsel he might hear.
But the truth was, he had not reached the place
When dance and all, they vanished into space.
No living soul remained there to be seen
Save an old woman sitting on the green,
As ugly a witch as fancy could devise.
As he approached her she began to rise 120
And said, "Sir knight, here runs no thoroughfare.
What are you seeking with such anxious air?
Tell me! The better may your fortune be.
We old folk know a lot of things," said she.
    "Good mother," said the knight, "my life's to pay,
That's all too certain, if I cannot say
What women covet most. If you could tell
That secret to me, I'd requite you well."
    "Give me your hand," she answered. "Swear me true
That whatsoever I next ask of you, 130
You'll do it if it lies within your might
And I'll enlighten you before the night."
    "Granted, upon my honor," he replied.
    "Then I dare boast, and with no empty pride,
Your life is safe," she told him. "Let me die
If the queen herself won't say the same as I.
Let's learn if the haughtiest of all who wear
A net or coverchief upon their hair
Will be so forward as to answer 'no'
To what I'll teach you. No more; let us go." 140
With that she whispered something in his ear,
And told him to be glad and have no fear.
    When they had reached the court, the knight declared
That he had kept his day, and was prepared
To give his answer, standing for his life.
Many the wise widow, many the wife,
Many the maid who rallied to the scene,
And at the head as justice sat the queen.
Then silence was enjoined; the knight was told
In open court to say what women hold 150
Precious above all else. He did not stand
Dumb like a beast, but spoke up at command
And plainly offered them his answering word
In manly voice, so that the whole court heard.
    "My liege and lady, most of all," said he,
"Women desire to have the sovereignty
And sit in rule and government above
Their husbands, and to have their way in love.

That is what most you want. Spare me or kill
As you may like; I stand here by your will."   160
    No widow, wife, or maid gave any token
Of contradicting what the knight had spoken.
He should not die; he should be spared instead;
He was worthy of his life, the whole court said.
    The old woman whom the knight met on the green
Sprang up at this. "My sovereign lady queen,
Before your court has risen, do me right!
It was I who taught this answer to the knight,
For which he pledged his honor in my hand,
Solemnly, that the first thing I demand,   170
He would do it, if it lay within his might.
Before the court I ask you, then, sir knight,
To take me," said the woman, "as your wife,
For well you know that I have saved your life.
Deny me, on your honor, if you can."
    "Alas," replied this miserable man,
"That was my promise, it must be confessed.
For the love of God, though, choose a new request!
Take all my wealth, and let my body be."
    "If that's your tune, then curse both you and me,"   180
She said. "Though I am ugly, old, and poor,
I'll have, for all the metal and the ore
That under earth is hidden or lies above,
Nothing, except to be your wife and love."
    "My love? No, my damnation, if you can!
Alas," he said, "that any of my clan
Should be so miserably misallied!"
    All to no good; force overruled his pride,
And in the end he is constrained to wed,
And marries his old wife and goes to bed.   190
    Now some will charge me with an oversight
In failing to describe the day's delight,
The merriment, the food, the dress at least.
But I reply, there was no joy nor feast;
There was only sorrow and sharp misery.
He married her in private, secretly,
And all day after, such was his distress,
Hid like an owl from his wife's ugliness.
    Great was the woe this knight had in his head
When in due time they both were brought to bed.   200
He shuddered, tossed, and turned, and all the while
His old wife lay and waited with a smile.
"Is every knight so backward with a spouse?
Is it," she said, "a law in Arthur's house?
I am your love, your own, your wedded wife,
I am the woman who has saved your life.
I have never done you anything but right.
Why do you treat me this way the first night?

You must be mad, the way that you behave!
Tell me my fault, and as God's love can save, 210
I will amend it, truly, if I can."
    "Amend it?" answered this unhappy man.
"It can never be amended, truth to tell.
You are so loathsome and so old as well,
And your low birth besides is such a cross
It is no wonder that I turn and toss.
God take my woeful spirit from my breast!"
    "Is this," she said, "the cause of your unrest?"
"No wonder!" said the knight. "It truly is."
    "Now sir," she said, "I could amend all this 220
Within three days, if it should please me to,
And if you deal with me as you should do.
    "But since you speak of that nobility
That comes from ancient wealth and pedigree,
As if *that* constituted gentlemen,
I hold such arrogance not worth a hen!
The man whose virtue is pre-eminent,
In public and alone, always intent
On doing every generous act he can,
Take him—he is the greatest gentleman! 230
Christ wills that we should claim nobility
From him, not from old wealth or family.
Our elders left us all that they were worth
And through their wealth and blood we claim high birth,
But never, since it was beyond their giving,
Could they bequeath to us their virtuous living;
Although it first conferred on them the name
Of gentlemen, they could not leave that claim!
    "Dante the Florentine on this was wise:
'Frail is the branch on which man's virtues rise'— 240
Thus runs his rhyme—'God's goodness wills that we
Should claim from him alone nobility.'³
Thus from our elders we can only claim
Such temporal things as men may hurt and maim.
    "It is clear enough that true nobility
Is not bequeathed along with property,
For many a lord's son does a deed of shame
And yet, God knows, enjoys his noble name.
But though descended from a noble house
And elders who were wise and virtuous, 250
If he will not follow his elders, who are dead,
But leads, himself, a shameful life instead,
He is not noble, be he duke or earl.
It is the churlish deed that makes the churl.
And therefore, my dear husband, I conclude
That though my ancestors were rough and rude,

³*Purgatory,* Canto VII.

Yet may Almighty God confer on me
The grace to live, as I hope, virtuously.
Call me of noble blood when I begin
To live in virtue and to cast out sin.   260
    "As for my poverty, at which you grieve,
Almighty God in whom we all believe
In willful poverty chose to lead his life,
And surely every man and maid and wife
Can understand that Jesus, heaven's king,
Would never choose a low or vicious thing.
A poor and cheerful life is nobly led;
So Seneca and others have well said.
The man so poor he doesn't have a stitch,
If he thinks himself repaid, I count him rich.   270
He that is covetous, he is the poor man,
Pining to have the things he never can.
It is of cheerful mind, true poverty.
Juvenal[4] says about it happily:
'The poor man as he goes along his way
And passes thieves is free to sing and play.'
Poverty is a good we loathe, a great
Reliever of our busy worldly state,
A great amender also of our minds
As he that patiently will bear it finds.   280
And poverty, for all it seems distressed,
Is a possession no one will contest.
Poverty, too, by bringing a man low,
Helps him the better both God and self to know.
Poverty is a glass where we can see
Which are our true friends, as it seems to me.
So, sir, I do not wrong you on this score;
Reproach me with my poverty no more.
    "Now, sir, you tax me with my age; but, sir,
You gentlemen of breeding all aver   290
That men should not despise old age, but rather
Grant an old man respect, and call him 'father.'
    "If I am old and ugly, as you have said,
You have less fear of being cuckolded,
For ugliness and age, as all agree,
Are notable guardians of chastity.
But since I know in what you take delight,
I'll gratify your worldly appetite.
    "Choose now, which of two courses you will try:
To have me old and ugly till I die   300
But evermore your true and humble wife,
Never displeasing you in all my life,
Or will you have me rather young and fair
And take your chances on who may repair

---

[4]Roman poet (about 60–140 A.D.). The reference is to his *Satires,* X.

Either to your house on account of me
Or to some other place, it well may be.
Now make your choice, whichever you prefer."
  The knight took thought, and sighed, and said to her
At last, "My love and lady, my dear wife,
In your wise government I put my life. 310
Choose for yourself which course will best agree
With pleasure and honor, both for you and me.
I do not care, choose either of the two;
I am content, whatever pleases you."
  "Then have I won from you the sovereignty,
Since I may choose and rule at will?" said she.
  He answered, "That is best, I think, dear wife."
  "Kiss me," she said. "Now we are done with strife,
For on my word, I will be both to you,
That is to say, fair, yes, and faithful too. 320
May I die mad unless I am as true
As ever wife was since the world was new.
Unless I am as lovely to be seen
By morning as an empress or a queen
Or any lady between east and west,
Do with my life or death as you think best.
Lift up the curtain, see what you may see."
  And when the knight saw what had come to be
And knew her as she was, so young, so fair,
His joy was such that it was past compare. 330
He took her in his arms and gave her kisses
A thousand times on end; he bathed in blisses.
And she obeyed him also in full measure
In everything that tended to his pleasure.
  And so they lived in full joy to the end.
And now to all us women may Christ send
Submissive husbands, full of youth in bed,
And grace to outlive all the men we wed.
And I pray Jesus to cut short the lives
Of those who won't be governed by their wives; 340
And old, ill-tempered niggards who hate expense,
God promptly bring them down with pestilence!

WORDS OF THE HOST TO THE PARDONER

"Now my fine friend," he said, "you Pardoner,
Be quick, tell us a tale of mirth or fun."[1]
  "By St. Ninian," he said, "it shall be done,
But at this tavern here, before my tale,
I'll just go in and have some bread and ale."

---

[1] The Host, having heard a sad tale from the Physician, wants the Pardoner to tell a merrier one. The travelers are at a tavern.

The proper pilgrims in our company
Cried quickly, "Let him speak no ribaldry!
Tell us a moral tale, one to make clear
Some lesson to us, and we'll gladly hear."
   "Just as you wish," he said. "But I must think
Of something edifying while I drink."

PROLOGUE TO THE PARDONER'S TALE

"In churches," said the Pardoner, "when I preach,
I use, milords, a lofty style of speech
And ring it out as roundly as a bell,
Knowing by rote all that I have to tell.
My text is ever the same, and ever was:
Radix malorum est cupiditas.[2]
   "First I inform them whence I come; that done,
I then display my papal bulls,[3] each one.
I show my license first, my body's warrant,
Sealed by the bishop, for it would be abhorrent   10
If any man made bold, though priest or clerk,
To interrupt me in Christ's holy work.
And after that I give myself full scope.
Bulls in the name of cardinal and pope,
Of bishops and of patriarchs I show.
I say in Latin some few words or so
To spice my sermon; it flavors my appeal
And stirs my listeners to greater zeal.
Then I display my cases made of glass
Crammed to the top with rags and bones. They pass   20
For relics[4] with all the people in the place.
I have a shoulder bone in a metal case,
Part of a sheep owned by a holy Jew.
'Good men,' I say, 'heed what I'm telling you:
Just let this bone be dipped in any well
And if cow, calf, or sheep, or ox should swell
From eating a worm, or by a worm be stung,
Take water from this well and wash its tongue
And it is healed at once. And furthermore
Of scab and ulcers and of every sore   30
Shall every sheep be cured, and that straightway,
That drinks from the same well. Heed what I say:
If the good man who owns the beasts will go,
Fasting, each week, and drink before cockcrow
Out of this well, his cattle shall be brought
To multiply—that holy Jew so taught

---

[2] "Greed is the root of all evil," adapted from 1 Timothy 6:10.
[3] Documents.   [4] That is, of saints or biblical personages.

Our elders—and his property increase.
   "'Moreover, sirs, this bone cures jealousies.
Though into a jealous madness a man fell,
Let him cook his soup in water from this well, 40
He'll never, though for truth he knew her sin,
Suspect his wife again, though she took in
A priest, or even two of them or three.
   "'Now here's a mitten that you all can see.
Whoever puts his hand in it shall gain,
When he sows his land, increasing crops of grain,
Be it wheat or oats, provided that he bring
His penny or so to make his offering.
   "'There is one word of warning I must say,
Good men and women. If any here today 50
Has done a sin so horrible to name
He daren't be shriven[5] of it for the shame,
Or if any woman, young or old, is here
Who has cuckolded her husband, be it clear
They may not make an offering in that case
To these my relics; they have no power nor grace.
But any who is free of such dire blame,
Let him come up and offer in God's name
And I'll absolve him through the authority
That by the pope's bull has been granted me.' 60
   "By such hornswoggling I've won, year by year,
A hundred marks[6] since being a pardoner.
I stand in my pulpit like a true divine,
And when the people sit I preach my line
To ignorant souls, as you have heard before,
And tell skullduggeries by the hundred more.
Then I take care to stretch my neck well out
And over the people I nod and peer about
Just like a pigeon perching on a shed.
My hands fly and my tongue wags in my head 70
So busily that to watch me is a joy.
Avarice is the theme that I employ
In all my sermons, to make the people free
In giving pennies—especially to me.
My mind is fixed on what I stand to win
And not at all upon correcting sin.
I do not care, when they are in the grave,
If souls go berry-picking that I could save.
Truth is that evil purposes determine,
And many a time, the origin of a sermon: 80
Some to please people and by flattery
To gain advancement through hypocrisy,

[5] Absolved of sins in the confessional.
[6] The equivalent today of thousands of dollars.

Some for vainglory, some again for hate.
For when I daren't fight otherwise, I wait
And give him a tongue-lashing when I preach.
No man escapes or gets beyond the reach
Of my defaming tongue, supposing he
Has done a wrong to my brethren or to me.
For though I do not tell his proper name,
People will recognize him all the same.   90
By sign and circumstance I let them learn.
Thus I serve those who have done us an ill turn.
Thus I spit out my venom under hue
Of sanctity, and seem devout and true!
    "But to put my purpose briefly, I confess
I preach for nothing but for covetousness.
That's why my text is still and ever was
Radix malorum est cupiditas.
For by this text I can denounce, indeed,
The very vice I practice, which is greed.   100
But though that sin is lodged in my own heart,
I am able to make other people part
From avarice, and sorely to repent,
Though that is not my principal intent.
    "Then I bring in examples, many a one,
And tell them many a tale of days long done.
Plain folk love tales that come down from of old.
Such things their minds can well report and hold.
Do you think that while I have the power to preach
And take in silver and gold for what I teach   110
I shall ever live in willful poverty?
No, no, that never was my thought, certainly.
I mean to preach and beg in sundry lands.
I won't do any labor with my hands,
Nor live by making baskets. I don't intend
To beg for nothing; that is not my end.
I won't ape the apostles; I must eat,
I must have money, wool, and cheese, and wheat,
Though I took it from the meanest wretch's tillage
Or from the poorest widow in a village,   120
Yes, though her children starved for want. In fine,
I mean to drink the liquor of the vine
And have a jolly wench in every town.
But, in conclusion, lords, I will get down
To business: you would have me tell a tale.
Now that I've had a drink of corny ale,
By God, I hope the thing I'm going to tell
Is one that you'll have reason to like well.
For though myself a very sinful man,
I can tell a moral tale, indeed I can,   130
One that I use to bring the profits in
While preaching. Now be still, and I'll begin."

THE PARDONER'S TALE

There was a company of young folk living
One time in Flanders, who were bent on giving
Their lives to follies and extravagances,
Brothels and taverns, where they held their dances
With lutes, harps, and guitars, diced at all hours,
And also ate and drank beyond their powers,
Through which they paid the devil sacrifice
In the devil's temple with their drink and dice,
Their abominable excess and dissipation.
They swore oaths that were worthy of damnation;   10
It was grisly to be listening when they swore.
The blessed body of our Lord they tore—
The Jews, it seemed to them, had failed to rend
His body enough—and each laughed at his friend
And fellow in sin. To encourage their pursuits
Came comely dancing girls, peddlers of fruits,
Singers with harps, bawds and confectioners
Who are the very devil's officers
To kindle and blow the fire of lechery
That is the follower of gluttony.   20
    Witness the Bible, if licentiousness
Does not reside in wine and drunkenness!
Recall how drunken Lot, unnaturally,
With his two daughters lay unwittingly,
So drunk he had no notion what he did.[1]
    Herod, the stories tell us, God forbid,
When full of liquor at his banquet board
Right at his very table gave the word
To kill the Baptist, John, though guiltless he.[2]
    Seneca[3] says a good word, certainly.   30
He says there is no difference he can find
Between a man who has gone out of his mind
And one who carries drinking to excess,
Only that madness outlasts drunkenness.
O gluttony, first cause of mankind's fall,[4]
Of our damnation the cursed original
Until Christ bought us with his blood again!
How dearly paid for by the race of men
Was this detestable iniquity!
This whole world was destroyed through gluttony.   40
    Adam our father and his wife also
From paradise to labor and to woe

[1] See Genesis 19:30–36.
[2] See the versions of the story in the gospels of Matthew (chapter 14) and Mark (chapter 6).
[3] A Roman writer of the first century.
[4] Because Adam and Eve sinned by eating a forbidden fruit.

Were driven for that selfsame vice, indeed.
As long as Adam fasted—so I read—
He was in heaven; but as soon as he
Devoured the fruit of that forbidden tree
Then he was driven out in sorrow and pain.
Of gluttony well ought we to complain!
Could a man know how many maladies
Follow indulgences and gluttonies   50
He would keep his diet under stricter measure
And sit at table with more temperate pleasure.
The throat is short and tender is the mouth,
And hence men toil east, west, and north, and south,
In earth, and air, and water—alas to think—
Fetching a glutton dainty meat and drink.
　　This is a theme, O Paul, that you well treat:
"Meat unto belly, and belly unto meat,
God shall destroy them both," as Paul has said.[5]
When a man drinks the white wine and the red—   60
This is a foul word, by my soul, to say,
And fouler is the deed in every way—
He makes his throat his privy through excess.
　　The Apostle[6] says, weeping for piteousness,
"There are many of whom I told you—at a loss
I say it, weeping—enemies of Christ's cross,
Whose belly is their god; their end is death."
O cursed belly! Sack of stinking breath
In which corruption lodges, dung abounds!
At either end of you come forth foul sounds.   70
Great cost it is to fill you, and great pain!
These cooks, how they must grind and pound and strain
And transform substance into accident[7]
To please your cravings, though exorbitant!
From the hard bones they knock the marrow out.
They'll find a use for everything, past doubt,
That down the gullet sweet and soft will glide.
The spiceries of leaf and root provide
Sauces that are concocted for delight,
To give a man a second appetite.   80
But truly, he whom gluttonies entice
Is dead, while he continues in that vice.
　　O drunken man, disfigured is your face,
Sour is your breath, foul are you to embrace!
You seem to mutter through your drunken nose
The sound of "Samson, Samson," yet God knows

---

[5] See 1 Corinthians 6:13.
[6] St. Paul. See Philippians 3:18–19.
[7] Philosophical terms; "substance" is what a thing really is, "accident" is a nonessential quality or property of it.

That Samson[8] never indulged himself in wine.
Your tongue is lost, you fall like a stuck swine,
And all the self-respect that you possess
Is gone, for of man's judgment, drunkenness   90
Is the very sepulcher and annihilation.
A man whom drink has under domination
Can never keep a secret in his head.
Now steer away from both the white and red,
And most of all from that white wine keep wide
That comes from Lepe. They sell it in Cheapside
And Fish Street.[9] It's a Spanish wine, and sly
To creep in other wines[10] that grow nearby,
And such a vapor it has that with three drinks
It takes a man to Spain; although he thinks   100
He is home in Cheapside, he is far away
At Lepe. Then "Samson, Samson" will he say!
   By God himself, who is omnipotent,
All the great exploits in the Old Testament
Were done in abstinence, I say, and prayer.
Look in the Bible, you may learn it there.
   Attila,[11] conqueror of many a place,
Died in his sleep in shame and in disgrace
Bleeding out of his nose in drunkenness.
A captain ought to live in temperateness!   110
And more than this, I say, remember well
The injunction that was laid on Lemuel—
Not Samuel, but Lemuel, I say!
Read in the Bible; in the plainest way
Wine is forbidden to judges and to kings.[12]
This will suffice; no more upon these things.
   Now that I've shown what gluttony will do,
Now I will warn you against gambling, too;
Gambling, the very mother of low scheming,
Of lying and forswearing and blaspheming   120
Against Christ's name, of murder and waste as well
Alike of goods and time; and, truth to tell,
With honor and renown it cannot suit
To be held a common gambler by repute.
The higher a gambler stands in power and place,
The more his name is lowered in disgrace.
If a prince gambles, whatever his kingdom be,
In his whole government and policy
He is, in all the general estimation,
Considered so much less in reputation.   130

---

[8] The Old Testament hero. His story is told in Judges, chapters 13–16.
[9] Main streets in London.
[10] Be mixed with other wines.
[11] Attila the Hun, fifth-century invader of Europe.
[12] In Proverbs, 31:4, Lemuel's mother admonishes him, "It is not for kings to drink wine."
Not to be confused, the Pardoner insists, with Samuel, another Old Testament figure.

Stilbon,[13] who was a wise ambassador,
From Lacedaemon once to Corinth bore
A mission of alliance. When he came
It happened that he found there at a game
Of hazard all the great ones of the land,
And so, as quickly as it could be planned,
He stole back, saying, "I will not lose my name
Nor have my reputation put to shame
Allying you with gamblers. You may send
Other wise emissaries to gain your end,   140
For by my honor, rather than ally
My countrymen to gamblers, I will die.
For you that are so gloriously renowned
Shall never with this gambling race be bound
By will of mine or treaty I prepare."
Thus did this wise philosopher declare.
    Remember also how the Parthians'[14] lord
Sent King Demetrius, as the books record,
A pair of golden dice, by this proclaiming
His scorn, because that king was known for gaming,   150
And the king of Parthia therefore held his crown
Devoid of glory, value, or renown.
Lords can discover other means of play
More suitable to while the time away.
    Now about oaths I'll say a word or two,
Great oaths and false oaths, as the old books do.
Great swearing is a thing abominable,
And false oaths yet more reprehensible.
Almighty God forbade swearing at all,
Matthew be witness; but specially I call   160
The holy Jeremiah on this head.
"Swear thine oaths truly, do not lie," he said.
"Swear under judgment, and in righteousness."[15]
But idle swearing is a great wickedness.
Consult and see, and he that understands
In the first table of the Lord's commands
Will find the second of his commandments this:
"Take not the Lord's name idly or amiss."
If a man's oaths and curses are extreme,
Vengeance shall find his house, both roof and beam.   170
"By the precious heart of God," and "By his nails"—
"My chance is seven, by Christ's blood at Hailes,[16]

---

[13] This story and the following one about Demetrius are from a book by John of Salisbury,
a learned English scholar of the twelfth century. Lacedaemon (Sparta) and Corinth were city-
states of ancient Greece.

[14] Parthia was an ancient region in what is now Iran.

[15] In the gospel of Matthew, 5:34 (part of the Sermon on the Mount), Christ says, "Swear
not at all." See also Jeremiah 4:2.

[16] In the dice game of hazard, a player's "chance" was roughly the equivalent of his "point"
in modern craps. Hailes was an English abbey supposed to possess a relic of Christ's blood.

Yours five and three." "Cheat me, and if you do,
By God's arms, with this knife I'll run you through!"—
Such fruit comes from the bones, that pair of bitches:
Oaths broken, treachery, murder. For the riches
Of Christ's love, give up curses, without fail,
Both great and small!—Now, sirs, I'll tell my tale.
　　These three young roisterers of whom I tell
Long before prime[17] had rung from any bell　　　　　　　　180
Were seated in a tavern at their drinking,
And as they sat, they heard a bell go clinking
Before a corpse being carried to his grave.
One of these roisterers, when he heard it, gave
An order to his boy: "Go out and try
To learn whose corpse is being carried by.
Get me his name, and get it right. Take heed."
　　"Sir," said the boy, "there isn't any need.
I learned before you came here, by two hours.
He was, it happens, an old friend of yours,　　　　　　　　190
And all at once, there on his bench upright
As he was sitting drunk, he was killed last night.
A sly thief, Death men call him, who deprives
All the people in this country of their lives,
Came with his spear and smiting his heart in two
Went on his business with no more ado.
A thousand have been slaughtered by his hand
During this plague. And, sir, before you stand
Within his presence, it should be necessary,
It seems to me, to know your adversary.　　　　　　　　200
Be evermore prepared to meet this foe.
My mother taught me thus; that's all I know."
　　"Now by St. Mary," said the innkeeper,
"This child speaks truth. Man, woman, laborer,
Servant, and child the thief has slain this year
In a big village a mile or more from here.
I think it is his place of habitation.
It would be wise to make some preparation
Before he brought a man into disgrace."
　　"God's arms!" this roisterer said. "So that's the case!　　　　210
Is it so dangerous with this thief to meet?
I'll look for him by every path and street,
I vow it, by God's holy bones! Hear me,
Fellows of mine, we are all one, we three.
Let each of us hold up his hand to the other
And each of us become his fellow's brother.
We'll slay this Death, who slaughters and betrays.
He shall be slain whose hand so many slays,
By the dignity of God, before tonight!"
　　The three together set about to plight　　　　　　　　220

[17]An early morning hour, between seven and nine.

Their oaths to live and die each for the other
Just as though each had been to each born brother.
And in their drunken frenzy up they get
And toward the village off at once they set
Which the innkeeper had spoken of before,
And many were the grisly oaths they swore.
They rent Christ's precious body limb from limb—
Death shall be dead, if they lay hands on him!
　　When they had hardly gone the first half mile,
Just as they were about to cross a stile, 230
An old man, poor and humble, met them there.
The old man greeted them with a meek air
And said, "God bless you, lords, and be your guide."
　　"What's this?" the proudest of the three replied.
"Old beggar, I hope you meet with evil grace!
Why are you all wrapped up except your face?
What are you doing alive so many a year?"
　　The old man at these words began to peer
Into this gambler's face. "Because I can,
Though I should walk to India, find no man," 240
He said, "in any village or any town,
Who for my age is willing to lay down
His youth. So I must keep my old age still
For as long a time as it may be God's will.
Nor will Death take my life from me, alas!
Thus like a restless prisoner I pass
And on the ground, which is my mother's gate,
I walk and with my staff both early and late
I knock and say, 'Dear mother, let me in!
See how I vanish, flesh, and blood, and skin! 250
Alas, when shall my bones be laid to rest?
I would exchange with you my clothing chest,
Mother, that in my chamber long has been
For an old haircloth rag to wrap me in.'
And yet she still refuses me that grace.
All white, therefore, and withered is my face.
　　"But, sirs, you do yourselves no courtesy
To speak to an old man so churlishly
Unless he had wronged you either in word or deed.
As you yourselves in Holy Writ may read, 260
'Before an aged man whose head is hoar
Men ought to rise.'[18] I counsel you, therefore,
No harm nor wrong here to an old man do,
No more than you would have men do to you
In your old age, if you so long abide.
And God be with you, whether you walk or ride!
I must go yonder where I have to go."

[18] See Leviticus 19:32.

"No, you old beggar, by St. John, not so,"
Said another of these gamblers. "As for me,
By God, you won't get off so easily! 270
You spoke just now of that false traitor, Death,
Who in this land robs all our friends of breath.
Tell where he is, since you must be his spy,
Or you will suffer for it, so say I
By God and by the holy sacrament.
You are in league with him, false thief, and bent
On killing us young folk, that's clear to my mind."
    "If you are so impatient, sirs, to find
Death," he replied, "turn up this crooked way,
For in that grove I left him, truth to say, 280
Beneath a tree, and there he will abide.
No boast of yours will make him run and hide.
Do you see that oak tree? Just there you will find
This Death, and God, who bought again mankind,
Save and amend you!" So said this old man;
And promptly each of these three gamblers ran
Until he reached the tree, and there they found
Florins of fine gold, minted bright and round,
Nearly eight bushels of them, as they thought.
And after Death no longer then they sought. 290
Each of them was so ravished at the sight,
So fair the florins glittered and so bright,
That down they sat beside the precious hoard.
The worst of them, he uttered the first word.
    "Brothers," he told them, "listen to what I say.
My head is sharp, for all I joke and play.
Fortune has given us this pile of treasure
To set us up in lives of ease and pleasure.
Lightly it comes, lightly we'll make it go.
God's precious dignity! Who was to know 300
We'd ever tumble on such luck today?
If we could only carry this gold away,
Home to my house, or either one of yours—
For well you know that all this gold is ours—
We'd touch the summit of felicity.
But still, by daylight that can hardly be.
People would call us thieves, too bold for stealth,
And they would have us hanged for our own wealth.
It must be done by night, that's our best plan,
As prudently and slyly as we can. 310
Hence my proposal is that we should all
Draw lots, and let's see where the lot will fall,
And the one of us who draws the shortest stick
Shall run back to the town, and make it quick,
And bring us bread and wine here on the sly,
And two of us will keep a watchful eye

Over this gold; and if he doesn't stay
Too long in town, we'll carry this gold away
By night, wherever we all agree it's best."
    One of them held the cut out in his fist   320
And had them draw to see where it would fall,
And the cut fell on the youngest of them all.
At once he set off on his way to town,
And the very moment after he was gone
The one who urged this plan said to the other:
"You know that by sworn oath you are my brother.
I'll tell you something you can profit by.
Our friend has gone, that's clear to any eye,
And here is gold, abundant as can be,
That we propose to share alike, we three.   330
But if I worked it out, as I could do,
So that it could be shared between us two,
Wouldn't that be a favor, a friendly one?"
    The other answered, "How that can be done,
I don't quite see. He knows we have the gold.
What shall we do, or what shall he be told?"
    "Will you keep the secret tucked inside your head?
And in a few words," the first scoundrel said,
"I'll tell you how to bring this end about."
    "Granted," the other told him. "Never doubt,   340
I won't betray you, that you can believe."
    "Now," said the first, "we are two, as you perceive,
And two of us must have more strength than one.
When he sits down, get up as if in fun
And wrestle with him. While you play this game
I'll run him through the ribs. You do the same
With your dagger there, and then this gold shall be
Divided, dear friend, between you and me.
Then all that we desire we can fulfill,
And both of us can roll the dice at will."   350
Thus in agreement these two scoundrels fell
To slay the third, as you have heard me tell.
    The youngest, who had started off to town,
Within his heart kept rolling up and down
The beauty of these florins, new and bright.
"O Lord," he thought, "were there some way I might
Have all this treasure to myself alone,
There isn't a man who dwells beneath God's throne
Could live a life as merry as mine should be!"
And so at last the fiend, our enemy,   360
Put in his head that he could gain his ends
If he bought poison to kill off his friends.
Finding his life in such a sinful state,
The devil was allowed to seal his fate.
For it was altogether his intent
To kill his friends, and never to repent.

So off he set, no longer would he tarry,
Into the town, to an apothecary,
And begged for poison; he wanted it because
He meant to kill his rats; besides, there was   370
A polecat living in his hedge, he said,
Who killed his capons; and when he went to bed
He wanted to take vengeance, if he might,
On vermin that devoured him by night.
 The apothecary answered, "You shall have
A drug that as I hope the Lord will save
My soul, no living thing in all creation,
Eating or drinking of this preparation
A dose no bigger than a grain of wheat,
But promptly with his death-stroke he shall meet.   380
Die, that he will, and in a briefer while
Than you can walk the distance of a mile,
This poison is so strong and virulent."
 Taking the poison, off the scoundrel went,
Holding it in a box, and next he ran
To the neighboring street, and borrowed from a man
Three generous flagons. He emptied out his drug
In two of them, and kept the other jug
For his own drink; he let no poison lurk
In that! And so all night he meant to work   390
Carrying off the gold. Such was his plan,
And when he had filled them, this accursed man
Retraced his path, still following his design,
Back to his friends with his three jugs of wine.
 But why dilate upon it any more?
For just as they had planned his death before,
Just so they killed him, and with no delay.
When it was finished, one spoke up to say:
"Now let's sit down and drink, and we can bury
His body later on. First we'll be merry,"   400
And as he said the words, he took the jug
That, as it happened, held the poisonous drug,
And drank, and gave his friend a drink as well,
And promptly they both died. But truth to tell,
In all that Avicenna[19] ever wrote
He never described in chapter, rule, or note
More marvelous signs of poisoning, I suppose,
Than appeared in these two wretches at the close.
Thus they both perished for their homicide,
And thus the traitorous poisoner also died.   410
 O sin accursed above all cursedness,
O treacherous murder, O foul wickedness,

---

[19]Arab philosopher, physician, and author of a medical textbook of the early eleventh
century.

O gambling, lustfulness, and gluttony,
Traducer of Christ's name by blasphemy
And monstrous oaths, through habit and through pride!
Alas, mankind! Ah, how may it betide
That you to your Creator, he that wrought you
And even with his precious heart's blood bought you,
So falsely and ungratefully can live?
   And now, good men, your sins may God forgive   420
And keep you specially from avarice!
My holy pardon will avail in this,
For it can heal each one of you that brings
His pennies, silver brooches, spoons, or rings.
Come, bow your head under this holy bull!
You wives, come offer up your cloth or wool!
I write your names here in my roll, just so.
Into the bliss of heaven you shall go!
I will absolve you here by my high power,
You that will offer, as clean as in the hour   430
When you were born. —Sirs, thus I preach. And now
Christ Jesus, our souls' healer, show you how
Within his pardon evermore to rest,
For that, I will not lie to you, is best.
   But in my tale, sirs, I forgot one thing.
The relics and the pardons that I bring
Here in my pouch, no man in the whole land
Has finer, given me by the pope's own hand.
If any of you devoutly wants to offer
And have my absolution, come and proffer   440
Whatever you have to give. Kneel down right here,
Humbly, and take my pardon, full and clear,
Or have a new, fresh pardon if you like
At the end of every mile of road we strike,
As long as you keep offering ever newly
Good coins, not counterfeit, but minted truly.
Indeed it is an honor I confer
On each of you, an authentic pardoner
Going along to absolve you as you ride.
For in the country mishaps may betide—   450
One or another of you in due course
May break his neck by falling from his horse.
Think what security it gives you all
That in this company I chanced to fall
Who can absolve you each, both low and high,
When the soul, alas, shall from the body fly!
By my advice, our Host here shall begin,
For he's the man enveloped most by sin.
Come, offer first, Sir Host, and once that's done,
Then you shall kiss the relics, every one,   460
Yes, for a penny! Come, undo your purse!

"No, no," said he. "Then I should have Christ's curse!
I'll do nothing of the sort, for love or riches!
You'd make me kiss a piece of your old britches
And for a saintly relic make it pass
Although it had the tincture of your ass.
By the cross St. Helen[20] found in the Holy Land,
I wish I had your balls here in my hand
For relics! Cut'em off, and I'll be bound
If I don't help you carry them around.   470
I'll have the things enshrined in a hog's turd!"
   The Pardoner did not answer; not a word,
He was so angry, could he find to say.
   "Now," said our Host, "I will not try to play
With you, nor any other angry man."
   Immediately the worthy Knight began,
When he saw that all the people laughed, "No more,
This has gone far enough. Now as before,
Sir Pardoner, be gay, look cheerfully,
And you, Sir Host, who are so dear to me,   480
Come, kiss the Pardoner, I beg of you,
And Pardoner, draw near, and let us do
As we've been doing, let us laugh and play."
And so they kissed, and rode along their way.

THE KNIGHT'S INTERRUPTION
OF THE MONK'S TALE

"Stop!" cried the Knight.[1] "No more of this, good sir!
You have said plenty, and much more, for sure,
For only a little such lugubriousness
Is plenty for a lot of folk, I guess.
I say for me it is a great displeasure,
When men have wealth and comfort in good measure,
To hear how they have tumbled down the slope,
And the opposite is a solace and a hope,
As when a man begins in low estate
And climbs the ladder and grows fortunate,   10
And stands there firm in his prosperity.
That is a welcome thing, it seems to me,
And of such things it would be good to tell."
   "Well said," our Host declared. "By St. Paul's bell,
You speak the truth; this Monk's tongue is too loud.
He told how fortune covered with a cloud—
I don't know what-all; and of tragedy
You heard just now, and it's no remedy,

---

[20] She was believed to have discovered the cross of Jesus about 200 years after the Crucifixion.
[1] The Monk, whom the Knight interrupts, has been narrating a long series of "tragedies," tales about the fall of eminent personages.

When things are over and done with, to complain.
Besides, as you have said, it is a pain   20
To hear of misery; it is distressing.
Sir Monk, no more, as you would have God's blessing.
This company is all one weary sigh.
Such talking isn't worth a butterfly,
For where's the amusement in it, or the game?
And so, Sir Monk, or Don Pierce by your name,
I beg you heartily, tell us something else.
Truly, but for the jingling of your bells
That from your bridle hang on every side,
By Heaven's King, who was born for us and died,   30
I should long since have tumbled down in sleep,
Although the mud had never been so deep,
And then you would have told your tale in vain;
For certainly, as these learned men explain,
When his audience have turned their backs away,
It doesn't matter what a man may say.
I know well I shall have the essence of it
If anything is told here for our profit.
A tale of hunting, sir, pray share with us."
    "No," said the Monk, "I'll not be frivolous.   40
Let another tell a tale, as I have told."
    Then spoke our Host, with a rude voice and bold,
And said to the Nun's Priest, "Come over here,
You priest, come hither, you Sir John, draw near!
Tell us a thing to make our spirits glad.
Be cheerful, though the jade you ride is bad.
What if your horse is miserable and lean?
If he will carry you, don't care a bean!
Keep up a joyful heart, and look alive."
    "Yes, Host," he answered, "as I hope to thrive,   50
If I weren't merry, I know I'd be reproached."
And with no more ado his tale he broached,
And this is what he told us, every one,
This precious priest, this goodly man, Sir John.

THE NUN'S PRIEST'S TALE

Once a poor widow, aging year by year,
Lived in a tiny cottage that stood near
A clump of shade trees rising in a dale.
This widow, of whom I tell you in my tale,
Since the last day that she had been a wife
Had led a very patient, simple life.
She had but few possessions to content her.
By thrift and husbandry of what God sent her
She and two daughters found the means to dine.
She had no more than three well-fattened swine,   10

As many cows, and one sheep, Moll by name.
Her bower and hall were black from the hearth-flame
Where she had eaten many a slender meal.
No dainty morsel did her palate feel
And no sharp sauce was needed with her pottage.
Her table was in keeping with her cottage.
Excess had never given her disquiet.
Her only doctor was a moderate diet,
And exercise, and a heart that was contented.
If she did not dance, at least no gout prevented; 20
No apoplexy had destroyed her head.
She never drank wine, whether white or red.
She served brown bread and milk, loaves white or black,
Singed bacon, all this with no sense of lack,
And now and then an egg or two. In short,
She was a dairy woman of a sort.
　　She had a yard, on the inside fenced about
With hedges, and an empty ditch without,
In which she kept a cock, called Chanticleer.
In all the realm of crowing he had no peer. 30
His voice was merrier than the merry sound
Of the church organ grumbling out its ground
Upon a saint's day. Stouter was this cock
In crowing than the loudest abbey clock.
Of astronomy instinctively aware,
He kept the sun's hours with celestial care,
For when through each fifteen degrees it moved,
He crowed so that it couldn't be improved.
His comb, like a crenelated[1] castle wall,
Red as fine coral, stood up proud and tall. 40
His bill was black; like polished jet it glowed,
And he was azure-legged and azure-toed.
As lilies were his nails, they were so white;
Like burnished gold his hue, it shone so bright.
This cock had in his princely sway and measure
Seven hens to satisfy his every pleasure,
Who were his sisters and his sweethearts true,
Each wonderfully like him in her hue,
Of whom the fairest-feathered throat to see
Was fair Dame Partlet. Courteous was she, 50
Discreet, and always acted debonairly.
She was sociable, and bore herself so fairly,
Since the very time that she was seven nights old,
The heart of Chanticleer was in her hold
As if she had him locked up, every limb.
He loved her so that all was well with him.
It was a joy, when up the sun would spring,
To hear them both together sweetly sing,

[1]Having walls with notched openings at the top.

"My love has gone to the country, far away!"
For as I understand it, in that day 60
The animals and birds could sing and speak.
   Now as this cock, one morning at daybreak,
With each of the seven hens that he called spouse,
Sat on his perch inside the widow's house,
And next him fair Dame Partlet, in his throat
This Chanticleer produced a hideous note
And groaned like a man who is having a bad dream;
And Partlet, when she heard her husband scream,
Was all aghast, and said, "Soul of my passion,
What ails you that you groan in such a fashion? 70
You are always a sound sleeper. Fie, for shame!"
   And Chanticleer awoke and answered, "Dame,
Take no offense, I beg you, on this score.
I dreamt, by God, I was in a plight so sore
Just now, my heart still quivers from the fright.
Now God see that my dream turns out all right
And keep my flesh and body from foul seizure!
I dreamed I was strutting in our yard at leisure
When there I saw, among the weeds and vines,
A beast, he was like a hound, and had designs 80
Upon my person, and would have killed me dead.
His coat was not quite yellow, not quite red,
And both his ears and tail were tipped with black
Unlike the fur along his sides and back.
He had a small snout and a fiery eye.
His look for fear still makes me almost die.
This is what made me groan, I have no doubt."
   "For shame! Fie on you, faint heart!" she burst out.
"Alas," she said, "by the great God above,
Now you have lost my heart and all my love! 90
I cannot love a coward, as I'm blest!
Whatever any woman may protest,
We all want, could it be so, for our part,
Husbands who are wise and stout of heart,
No blabber, and no niggard, and no fool,
Nor afraid of every weapon or sharp tool,
No braggart either, by the God above!
How dare you say, for shame, to your true love
That there is anything you ever feared?
Have you no man's heart, when you have a beard? 100
Alas, and can a nightmare set you screaming?
God knows there's only vanity in dreaming!
Dreams are produced by such unseemly capers
As overeating; they come from stomach vapors
When a man's humors² aren't behaving right
From some excess. This dream you had tonight,

---

² The four substances in the body believed to determine personality types and states of health.
Dame Partlet discusses two: choler (bile) and melancholy (black bile).

It comes straight from the superfluity
Of your red choler, certain as can be,
That causes people terror in their dreams
Of darts and arrows, and fire in red streams, 110
And of red beasts, for fear that they will bite,
Of little dogs, or of being in a fight;
As in the humor of melancholy lies
The reason why so many a sleeper cries
For fear of a black bull or a black bear
Or that black devils have him by the hair.
Through other humors also I could go
That visit many a sleeping man with woe,
But I will finish as quickly as I can.
    "Cato, that has been thought so wise a man, 120
Didn't he tell us, 'Put no stock in dreams'?
Now, sir," she said, "when we fly down from our beams,
For God's sake, go and take a laxative!
On my salvation, as I hope to live,
I give you good advice, and no mere folly:
Purge both your choler and your melancholy!
You mustn't wait or let yourself bog down,
And since there is no druggist in this town
I shall myself prescribe for what disturbs
Your humors, and instruct you in the herbs 130
That will be good for you. For I shall find
Here in our yard herbs of the proper kind
For purging you both under and above.
Don't let this slip your mind, for God's own love!
Yours is a very choleric complexion.
When the sun is in the ascendant, my direction
Is to beware those humors that are hot.
Avoid excess of them; if you should not,
I'll bet a penny, as a true believer,
You'll die of ague, or a tertian fever. 140
A day or so, if you do as I am urging,
You shall have worm-digestives, before purging
With fumitory or with hellebore
Or other herbs that grow here by the score;
With caper-spurge, or with the goat-tree berry
Or the ground-ivy, found in our yard so merry.
Peck 'em up just as they grow, and eat 'em in!
Be cheerful, husband, by your father's kin!
Don't worry about a dream. I say no more."
    "Madame," he answered, "thanks for all your lore. 150
But still, to speak of Cato, though his name
For wisdom has enjoyed so great a fame,
And though he counseled us there was no need
To be afraid of dreams, by God, men read
Of many a man of more authority
Than this Don Cato could pretend to be

Who in old books declare the opposite,
And by experience they have settled it,
That dreams are omens and prefigurations
Both of good fortune and of tribulations   160
That life and its vicissitudes present.
This question leaves no room for argument.
The very upshot makes it plain, indeed.
    "One of the greatest authors that men read
Informs us that two fellow travelers went,
Once on a time, and with the best intent,
Upon a pilgrimage, and it fell out
They reached a town where there was such a rout
Of people, and so little lodging space,
They could not find even the smallest place   170
Where they could both put up. So, for that night,
These pilgrims had to do as best they might,
And since they must, they parted company.
Each of them went off to his hostelry
And took his lodging as his luck might fall.
Among plow oxen in a farmyard stall
One of them found a place, though it was rough.
His friend and fellow was lodged well enough
As his luck would have it, or his destiny
That governs all us creatures equally.   180
And so it happened, long before the day,
He had a dream as in his bed he lay.
He dreamed that his parted friend began to call
And said, 'Alas, for in an ox's stall
This night I shall be murdered where I lie.
Come to my aid, dear brother, or I die.
Come to me quickly, come in haste!' he said.
He started from his sleep, this man, for dread,
But when he had wakened, he rolled back once more
And on this dream of his he set no store.   190
As a vain thing he dismissed it, unconcerned.
Twice as he slept that night the dream returned,
And still another and third time his friend
Came in a dream and said, 'I have met my end!
Look on my wounds! They are bloody, deep, and wide.
Now rise up early in the morningtide
And at the west gate of the town,' said he,
'A wagon with a load of dung you'll see.
Have it arrested boldly. Do as bidden,
For underneath you'll find my body hidden.   200
My money caused my murder, truth to tell,'
And told him each detail of how he fell,
With piteous face, and with a bloodless hue.
And do not doubt it, he found the dream was true,
For on the morrow, as soon as it was day,
To the place where his friend had lodged he made his way,

And no sooner did he reach this ox's stall
Than for his fellow he began to call.
    "Promptly the stableman replied, and said,
'Your friend is gone, sir. He got out of bed   210
And left the town as soon as day began.'
    "At last suspicion overtook this man.
Remembering his dreams, he would not wait,
But quickly went and found at the west gate,
Being driven to manure a farmer's land
As it might seem, a dung cart close at hand
That answered the description every way,
As you yourself have heard the dead man say.
And he began to shout courageously
For law and vengeance on this felony.   220
'My friend was killed this very night! He lies
Flat in this load of dung, with staring eyes.
I call on those who should keep rule and head,
The magistrates and governors here,' he said.
'Alas! Here lies my fellow, done to death!'
    "Why on this tale should I waste further breath?
The people sprang and flung the cart to ground
And in the middle of the dung they found
The dead man, while his murder was still new.
    "O blessed God, thou art so just and true,   230
Murder, though secret, ever thou wilt betray!
Murder will out, we see it day by day.
Murder so loathsome and abominable
To God is, who is just and reasonable,
That he will never suffer it to be
Concealed, though it hide a year, or two, or three.
Murder will out; to this point it comes down.
    "Promptly the magistrates who ruled that town
Have seized the driver, and put him to such pain,
And the stableman as well, that under strain   240
Of torture they were both led to confess
And hanged by the neck-bone for their wickedness.
    "Here's proof enough that dreams are things to dread!
And in the same book I have also read,
In the very chapter that comes right after this—
I don't speak idly, by my hopes of bliss—
Two travelers who for some reason planned
To cross the ocean to a distant land
Found that the wind, by an opposing fate,
Blew contrary, and forced them both to wait   250
In a fair city by a harborside.
But one day the wind changed, toward eventide,
And blew just as it suited them instead.
Cheerfully these travelers went to bed
And planned to sail the first thing in the morning.
But to one of them befell a strange forewarning

And a great marvel. While asleep he lay,
He dreamed a curious dream along toward day.
He dreamed that a man appeared at his bedside
And told him not to sail, but wait and bide.   260
'Tomorrow,' he told the man, 'if you set sail,
You shall be drowned. I have told you my whole tale.'
He woke, and of this warning he had met
He told his friend, and begged him to forget
His voyage, and to wait that day and bide.
His friend, who was lying close at his bedside,
Began to laugh, and told him in derision,
'I am not so flabbergasted by a vision
As to put off my business for such cause.
I do not think your dream is worth two straws!   270
For dreams are but a vain absurdity.
Of apes and owls and many a mystery
People are always dreaming, in a maze
Of things that never were seen in all their days
And never shall be. But I see it's clear
You mean to waste your time by waiting here.
I'm sorry for that, God knows; and so good day.'
With this he took his leave and went his way.
But not the half his course had this man sailed—
I don't know why, nor what it was that failed—   280
When by an accident the hull was rent
And ship and man under the water went
In full view of the vessels alongside
That had put out with them on the same tide.
Now then, fair Partlet, whom I love so well,
From old examples such as these I tell
You may see that none should give too little heed
To dreams; for I say seriously, indeed,
That many a dream is too well worth our dread.
        "Yes, in St. Kenelm's life I have also read—   290
He was the son of Cynewulf, the king
Of Mercia—how this Kenelm dreamed a thing.
One day, as the time when he was killed drew near,
He saw his murder in a dream appear.
His nurse explained his dream in each detail,
And warned him to be wary without fail
Of treason; yet he was but seven years old,
And therefore any dream he could but hold
Of little weight, in heart he was so pure.
I'd give my shirt, by God, you may be sure,   300
If you had read his story through like me!
        "Moreover, Partlet, I tell you truthfully,
Macrobius[3] writes—and by his book we know
The African vision of great Scipio—
Confirming dreams, and holds that they may be

_____
[3]A fifth-century author of a commentary on Cicero's *Dream of Scipio*.

Forewarnings of events that men shall see.
Again, I beg, look well at what is meant
By the Book of Daniel in the Old Testament,
Whether *he* held that dreams are vanity!
Read also about Joseph. You shall see   310
That dreams, or some of them—I don't say all—
Warn us of things that afterward befall.
Think of the king of Egypt, Don Pharaoh;
Of his butler and his baker think also,
Whether they found that dreams have no result.[4]
Whoever will search through kingdoms and consult
Their histories reads many a wondrous thing
Of dreams. What about Croesus, Lydian king—
Didn't he dream he was sitting on a tree,
Which meant he would be hanged? Andromache,   320
The woman who was once great Hector's wife,
On the day that Hector was to lose his life,
The very night before his blood was spilled
She dreamed of how her husband would be killed
If he went out to battle on that day.
She warned him; but he would not heed nor stay.
In spite of her he rode out on the plain,
And by Achilles he was promptly slain.
But all that story is too long to tell,
And it is nearly day. I must not dwell   330
Upon this matter. Briefly, in conclusion,
I say this dream will bring me to confusion
And mischief of some sort. And furthermore,
On laxatives, I say, I set no store,
For they are poisonous, I'm sure of it.
I do not trust them! I like them not one bit!
    "Now let's talk cheerfully, and forget all this.
My pretty Partlet, by my hope of bliss,
In one thing God has sent me ample grace
For when I see the beauty of your face,   340
You are so scarlet-red about the eye,
It is enough to make my terrors die.
For just as true as *In principio*
Mulier est hominis confusio—[5]
And Madame, what this Latin means is this:
'Woman is man's whole comfort and true bliss'—
When I feel you soft at night, and I beside you,
Although it's true, alas, I cannot ride you
Because our perch is built so narrowly,
I am then so full of pure felicity   350
That I defy whatever sort of dream!"

---

[4] See Genesis, chapters 40–41. Joseph, imprisoned in Egypt, won his freedom by interpreting accurately the dreams of Pharaoh's butler and baker and later Pharaoh's own dreams.
[5] Literally, "In the beginning, woman is the ruin of man."

And day being come, he flew down from the beam,
And with him his hens fluttered, one and all;
And with a "cluck, cluck" he began to call
His wives to where a kernel had been tossed.
He was a prince, his fears entirely lost.
The morning had not passed the hour of prime
When he treaded Partlet for the twentieth time.
Grim as a lion he strolled to and fro,
And strutted only on his either toe. 360
He would not deign to set foot on the ground.
"Cluck, cluck," he said, whenever he had found
A kernel, and his wives came running all.
Thus royal as a monarch in his hall
I leave to his delights this Chanticleer,
And presently the sequel you shall hear.
　　After the month in which the world began,[6]
The month of March, when God created man,
Had passed, and when the season had run through
Since March began just thirty days and two, 370
It happened that Chanticleer, in all his pride,
While his seven hens were walking by his side,
Lifted his eyes, beholding the bright sun,
Which in the sign of Taurus had then run
Twenty and one degrees and somewhat more,
And knew by instinct, not by learned lore,
It was the hour of prime. He raised his head
And crowed with lordly voice. "The sun," he said,
"Forty and one degrees and more in height
Has climbed the sky. Partlet, my world's delight, 380
Hear all these birds, how happily they sing,
And see the pretty flowers, how they spring.
With solace and with joy my spirits dance!"
But suddenly he met a sore mischance,
For in the end joys ever turn to woes.
Quickly the joys of earth are gone, God knows,
And could a rhetorician's art indite it,
He would be on solid ground if he should write it,
In a chronicle, as true notoriously!
Now every wise man, listen well to me. 390
This story is as true, I undertake,
As the very book of Lancelot of the Lake
On which the women set so great a store.
Now to my matter I will turn once more.
　　A sly iniquitous fox, with black-tipped ears,
Who had lived in the neighboring wood for some three years,
His fated fancy swollen to a height,
Had broken through the hedges that same night
Into the yard where in his pride sublime

---

[6]According to tradition, the creation occurred at the beginning of spring.

Chanticleer with his seven wives passed the time. 400
Quietly in a bed of herbs he lay
Till it was past the middle of the day,
Waiting his hour on Chanticleer to fall
As gladly do these murderers, one and all,
Who lie in wait, concealed, to murder men.
O murderer, lurking traitorous in your den!
O new Iscariot, second Ganelon,
False hypocrite, Greek Sinon,[7] who brought on
The utter woe of Troy and all her sorrow!
O Chanticleer, accursed be that morrow 410
When to the yard you flew down from the beams!
That day, as you were well warned in your dreams,
Would threaten you with dire catastrophe.
But that which God foresees must come to be,
As there are certain scholars who aver.
Bear witness, any true philosopher,
That in the schools there has been great altercation
Upon this question, and much disputation
By a hundred thousand scholars, man for man.
I cannot sift it down to the pure bran 420
As can the sacred Doctor, Augustine,
Or Boëthius, or Bishop Bradwardine,[8]
Whether God's high foreknowledge so enchains me
I needs must do a thing as it constrains me—
"Needs must"—that is, by plain necessity;
Or whether a free choice is granted me
To do it or not do it, either one,
Though God must know all things before they are done;
Or whether his foresight nowise can constrain
Except contingently, as some explain; 430
I will not labor such a high concern.
My tale is of a cock, as you shall learn,
Who took his wife's advice, to his own sorrow,
And walked out in the yard that fatal morrow.
Women have many times, as wise men hold,
Offered advice that left men in the cold.
A woman's counsel brought us first to woe
And out of Paradise made Adam go
Where he lived a merry life and one of ease.
But since I don't know whom I may displease 440
By giving women's words an ill report,
Pass over it; I only spoke in sport.

---

[7] Judas Iscariot betrayed Jesus; Ganelon is the traitor in *The Song of Roland;* Sinon, by means of the Trojan horse, betrayed the Trojans to the besieging Greeks (see Virgil's *Aeneid,* Book II).

[8] All three had discussed the notoriously difficult matter of reconciling God's foreknowledge with man's free will. Augustine (353–430), author of the *Confessions,* was one of the greatest Christian theologians; Boëthius (about 475–524) was a Roman who wrote *The Consolation of Philosophy,* one of the most influential works in the Middle Ages; Bradwardine was a theologian of Chaucer's own century.

There are books about it you can read or skim in,
And you'll discover what they say of women.
I'm telling you the cock's words, and not mine.
Harm in no woman at all can I divine.
    Merrily bathing where the sand was dry
Lay Partlet, with her sisters all near by,
And Chanticleer, as regal as could be,
Sang merrily as the mermaid in the sea;   450
For the *Physiologus*[9] itself declares
That they know how to sing the merriest airs.
And so it happened that as he fixed his eye
Among the herbs upon a butterfly,
He caught sight of this fox who crouched there low.
He felt no impulse then to strut or crow,
But cried "cucock!" and gave a fearful start
Like a man who has been frightened to the heart.
For instinctively, if he should chance to see
His opposite, a beast desires to flee,   460
Even the first time that it meets his eye.
    This Chanticleer, no sooner did he spy
The fox than promptly enough he would have fled.
But "Where are you going, kind sir?" the fox said.
"Are you afraid of me, who am your friend?
Truly, I'd be a devil from end to end
If I meant you any harm or villainy.
I have not come to invade your privacy.
In truth, the only reason that could bring
This visit of mine was just to hear you sing.   470
Beyond a doubt, you have as fine a voice
As any angel who makes heaven rejoice.
Also you have more feeling in your note
Than Boëthius,[10] or any tuneful throat.
Milord your father once—and may God bless
His soul—your noble mother too, no less,
Have been inside my house, to my great ease.
And verily, sir, I should be glad to please
You also. But for singing, I declare,
As I enjoy my eyes, that precious pair,   480
Save you, I never heard a man so sing
As your father did when night was on the wing.
Straight from the heart, in truth, came all his song,
And to make his voice more resonant and strong
He would strain until he shut his either eye,
So loud and lordly would he make his cry,
And stand up on his tiptoes therewithal
And stretch his neck till it grew long and small.
He had such excellent discretion, too,
That whether his singing, all the region through,   490

---

[9]A book about animals, including legendary ones.
[10]Boëthius, along with his other works, wrote a treatise on music.

Or his wisdom, there was no one to surpass.
I read in that old book, *Don Burnel the Ass*,[11]
Among his verses once about a cock
Hit on the leg by a priest who threw a rock
When he was young and foolish; and for this
He caused the priest to lose his benefice.
But no comparison, in all truth, lies
Between your father, so prudent and so wise,
And this other cock, for all his subtlety.
Sing, sir! Show me, for holy charity,   500
Can you imitate your father, that wise man?"
　　Blind to all treachery, Chanticleer began
To beat his wings, like one who cannot see
The traitor, ravished by his flattery.
　　Alas, you lords, about your court there slips
Many a flatterer with deceiving lips
Who can please you more abundantly, I fear,
Than he who speaks the plain truth to your ear.
Read in Ecclesiastes,[12] you will see
What flatterers are. Lords, heed their treachery!   510
　　This Chanticleer stood tiptoe at full height.
He stretched his neck, he shut his eyelids tight,
And he began to crow a lordly note.
The fox, Don Russell, seized him by the throat
At once, and on his back bore Chanticleer
Off toward his den that in the grove stood near,
For no one yet had threatened to pursue.
　　O destiny, that no man may eschew!
Alas, that he left his safe perch on the beams!
Alas, that Partlet took no stock in dreams!   520
And on a Friday happened this mischance!
　　Venus, whose pleasures make the whole world dance,
Since Chanticleer was ever your true servant,
And of your rites will all his power observant
For pleasure rather than to multiply,
Would you on Friday[13] suffer him to die?
　　Geoffrey,[14] dear master of the poet's art,
Who when your Richard perished by a dart
Made for your king an elegy so burning,
Why have I not your eloquence and learning   530
To chide, as you did, with a heart so filled,
Fridays? For on a Friday he was killed.

---

[11] A twelfth-century poem by Nigel Wireker. The cock took his revenge by crowing late, thus causing the priest to oversleep on the day when he was to have been ordained.

[12] The intended reference is apparently not to Ecclesiastes but to Ecclesiasticus (a book of the Roman Catholic Bible), 12:10ff, 27:26.

[13] Friday is Venus's day. (Compare the French for *Friday, vendredi.*)

[14] Geoffrey of Vinsauf, a twelfth-century author of a book on poetry. It includes as an example a poem, written in an elaborate style, about the death of King Richard the Lion-Hearted (Richard I).

Then should I show you how I could complain
For Chanticleer in all his fright and pain!
    In truth, no lamentation ever rose,
No shriek of ladies when before its foes
Ilium fell, and Pyrrhus with drawn blade
Had seized King Priam by the beard and made
An end of him—the *Aeneid* tells the tale—[15]
Such as the hens made with their piteous wail   540
In their enclosure, seeing the dread sight
Of Chanticleer. But at the shrillest height
Shrieked Partlet. She shrieked louder than the wife
Of Hasdrubal, when her husband lost his life
And the Romans burned down Carthage; for her state
Of torment and of frenzy was so great
She willfully chose the fire for her part,
Leaped in, and burned herself with steadfast heart.
    Unhappy hens, you shrieked as when for pity,
While the tyrant Nero put to flames the city   550
Of Rome, rang out the shriek of senators' wives
Because their husbands had all lost their lives;
This Nero put to death these innocent men.
But I will come back to my tale again.
    Now this good widow and her two daughters heard
These woeful hens shriek when the crime occurred,
And sprang outdoors as quickly as they could
And saw the fox, who was making for the wood
Bearing this Chanticleer across his back.
"Help, help!" they cried. They cried, "Alas! Alack!   560
The fox, the fox!" and after him they ran,
And armed with clubs came running many a man.
Ran Coll the dog, and led a yelping band;
Ran Malkyn, with a distaff[16] in her hand;
Ran cow and calf, and even the very hogs,
By the yelping and the barking of the dogs
And men's and women's shouts so terrified
They ran till it seemed their hearts would burst inside;
They squealed like fiends in the pit, with none to still them.
The ducks quacked as if men were going to kill them.   570
The geese for very fear flew over the trees.
Out of the beehive came the swarm of bees.
Ah! Bless my soul, the noise, by all that's true,
So hideous was that Jack Straw's[17] retinue

[15] See Book II of Virgil's *Aeneid*. When the Greeks took Troy (Ilium), Pyrrhus, the son of Achilles, killed Priam, the Trojan king. The Nun's Priest goes on to compare the hens' lament over Chanticleer to the wailing when the Romans destroyed Carthage (second century B.C.) and when the emperor Nero supposedly burned Rome (A.D. 64).
[16] A long staff; part of a spinning wheel.
[17] In 1381, Jack Straw led into London a mob intent on killing foreigners.

Made never a hubbub that was half so shrill
Over a Fleming they were going to kill
As the clamor made that day over the fox.
They brought brass trumpets, and trumpets made of box,
Of horn, of bone, on which they blew and squeaked,
And those who were not blowing whooped and shrieked.
It seemed as if the very heavens would fall! 580
    Now hear me, you good people, one and all!
Fortune, I say, will suddenly override
Her enemy in his very hope and pride!
This cock, as on the fox's back he lay,
Plucked up his courage to speak to him and say,
"God be my help, sir, but I'd tell them all,
That is, if I were you, 'Plague on you fall!
Go back, proud fools! Now that I've reached the wood,
I'll eat the cock at once, for all the good 590
Your noise can do. Here Chanticleer shall stay.'"
    "Fine!" said the fox. "I'll do just what you say."
But the cock, as he was speaking, suddenly
Out of his jaws lurched expeditiously,
And flew at once high up into a tree.
And when the fox saw that the cock was free,
"Alas," he said, "alas, O Chanticleer!
Inasmuch as I have given you cause for fear
By seizing you and bearing you away,
I have done you wrong, I am prepared to say. 600
But, sir, I did it with no ill intent.
Come down, and I shall tell you what I meant.
So help me God, it's truth I'll offer you!"
    "No, no," said he. "We're both fools, through and through.
But curse my blood and bones for the chief dunce
If you deceive me oftener than once!
You shall never again by flattery persuade me
To sing and wink my eyes, by him that made me.
For he that willfully winks when he should see,
God never bless him with prosperity!" 610
    "Ah," said the fox, "with mischief may God greet
The man ungoverned, rash, and indiscreet
Who babbles when to hold his tongue were needful!"
    Such is it to be reckless and unheedful
And trust in flattery. But you who hold
That this is a mere trifle I have told,
Concerning only a fox, or a cock and hen,
Think twice, and take the moral, my good men!
For truly, of whatever is written, all
Is written for our doctrine, says St. Paul. 620
Then take the fruit, and let the chaff lie still.
Now, gracious God, if it should be your will,
As my Lord teaches, make us all good men
And bring us to your holy bliss! Amen.

Christine de Pizan

(1364–1430?)

"Who was it painted the lion, tell me who?" asks the Wife of Bath in Chaucer's *Canterbury Tales*. The Wife is thinking of an Aesopian fable in which a lion looks at a picture of a man killing a lion and remarks that if lions painted pictures, the roles might be reversed. Her point is that if books were written by women instead of elderly celibate clerics, the monotonous misogyny of medieval literature (of the sort that Jenkin, her fifth husband, infuriatingly read aloud) might be reversed. "By God," she goes on, "if women had only written stories / Like wits and scholars in their oratories, / They would have pinned on men more wickedness / Than the whole breed of Adam can redress."

It is a sentiment that Christine de Pizan, Chaucer's slightly younger contemporary, would have heartily endorsed. Only a few years after Chaucer wrote the Wife of Bath's Prologue, Christine was stung by her reading of a book by a dreary woman-hater named Mathéolus into breaking the long silence of medieval women and undertaking a sweeping universal history of women, defending her sex against the calumnies of the patriarchal tradition. *The Book of the City of Ladies* is an extraordinary production. It is both quintessentially of its age—in its allegorizing, cataloguing, and universalizing tendencies—and startlingly fresh in its tough, realistic treatment of feminist issues. After five centuries, it still has much to teach us.

Christine de Pizan was born in Venice. Both parents were from prominent Italian families. Her father was a noted physician and astrologer named Tommaso di Benvenuto da Pizzano (astrology was a respectable science in Christine's day, not very clearly differentiated from astronomy); her mother was a member of a well-known family named Mondino. When Christine was four, her family moved to Paris, where her father had accepted a position as court astrologer to King Charles V. Christine spent the rest of her life in France and thought of herself as a French writer.

Christine received some education from her father, against the wishes of her mother, apparently. When she was fifteen, she was married to a young man of her father's choosing, as was the custom. Her husband, about twenty-five years old, was Etienne de Castel, a young courtier who became secretary and notary to the king. The match was a happy one and produced three children. In 1390, however, after ten years of marriage, Castel suddenly died of a contagious disease. Pizzano had died three years before, after losing much of his fortune and suffering a long illness. The twenty-five-year-old widow was thus left with three children, a mother, and a niece to support. What money was left from her father's and husband's estates was tied up in litigation; it took fourteen years and large sums of money to settle her lawsuits.

Christine apparently resolved to earn her living by her pen. She launched into an intensive program of self-education, "like a child," she later wrote, "that one puts at first to studying his ABCs." She read ancient and then modern history, science, and finally poetry. During this period, in the early 1390s, she may also have worked in the book trade, as a manuscript copyist, according to a recent biographer. Throughout her life, she took an active interest in the physical format of her books, commissioning and overseeing their reproduction and illustration.

She had her first success as a writer around 1393, and by the end of the decade she was earning a dependable income from her work. She is thus often said to be the "first professional writer in Europe." Her writing falls into three periods. Between 1393 and 1400, she wrote mostly lyric poetry in the highly conventionalized forms popular at the time; these were eventually organized into three cycles of *ballades*. By 1400, she had turned her attention to longer, narrative poems. Several of these were fashionable "love debates," which described various lovers' dilemmas that were to be presented to a "court of love" for settlement. Others were more serious. *The Long Road of Learning* (1403) is a utopian dream-vision in which Christine visits the Court of Reason to learn who should rule a better world. *The Mutation of Fortune* (also 1403) traces the role of Fortune through universal history. Also around 1400, Christine began to turn more frequently to prose; the output of her last period consists almost exclusively of long prose works. These include a commissioned biography of King Charles V (1404), *The Book of the City of Ladies* (1405), *The Book of the Three Virtues* (1405), and a strange, semiautobiographical dream-vision called *Christine's Vision* (1405).

France was in turmoil during Christine's later years. Charles VI was mentally unstable, and several powerful nobles competed for control of the kingdom. War with England also threatened. Faced with such dangers, Christine entered a convent, apparently around 1418, and turned her attention to government and advice to princes: *The Book of the Body Politic* (1406–07), *Feats of Arms and of Chivalry* (1410), and *The Book of Peace* (1414). For her last work, she returned to poetry in *The Tale of Joan of Arc* to celebrate Joan's victory at Orléans in 1429. Joan's miraculous career seemed to vindicate not only Christine's faith in France but her faith in heroic women as well. Apparently, Christine died before Joan was captured by the English and burned at the stake in 1431.

Christine de Pizan's masterpiece, among her voluminous writings, is *The Book of the City of Ladies*. It perhaps had its origins in an interesting literary controversy she engaged in between 1399 and 1403 called the "Debate of *The Romance of the Rose*." *The Romance of the Rose* was an immensely long, immensely popular poem begun by Guillaume de Lorris around 1230 and completed by Jean de Meun in 1275–80. It tells the story of the attempt of Amant ("lover") to pick a beautiful Rose, guarded by various allegorical figures: Danger, Jealousy, and the like. Guillaume de Lorris's section is innocuous enough, but Jean de Meun's continuation is full of attacks on women. Christine had objected to Jean de Meun's slanders in *Cupid's Letter* (1399), but the debate really started in 1401, when one of the king's secretaries named Jean de Montreuil wrote an open letter to Christine praising Jean de Meun and rejecting her criticism. Christine replied, and before the debate ended more than twenty letters had been exchanged and several other people had entered the debate, including Jean Gerson, the chancellor of the University of Paris (on Christine's side) and Gontier Gol, another of the king's secretaries (on Jean de Montreuil's). The terms of the controversy were fairly complex, involving the literary merits of Jean de Meun's poem and its effect on public morality as well as its treatment of women, but it was the issue of misogyny that most interested Christine and that was to concern her two years later in *The Book of the City of Ladies.*

The Book of the City of Ladies is cast in one of the Middle Ages' favorite forms: the dream-vision. After a short prologue, in which Christine broods about an attack on women she has just read, a strange light appears in her room. Shuddering, "as if wakened from sleep," she lifts her head to see three crowned ladies standing before her: Reason, Rectitude, and Justice. The rest of the book is devoted to the building of the City of Ladies under the instruction of these three ladies. Or perhaps the book is an anti-dream-vision. Christine says that she felt "*as if* wakened from sleep," not that she *was* wakened. (In dream-visions, falling asleep is ordinarily described as "waking" into a dream.) She may thus be distinguishing her work from *The Romance of the Rose,* in which Amant does wake into his dream of the Rose, and suggesting that her book is truer than the *Romance.* The basic metaphor of the book—the building of a verbal, conceptual city—derives from St. Augustine's *City of God.* The City of Ladies is not meant to rival the City of God, of course, but the echo of Augustine's title and the personifications of virtue that preside over the building of the city are probably meant to place the whole enterprise within a Christian context. Christine echoes, too, the most famous dream-vision of the Middle Ages, the *Divine Comedy,* which she was among the first to introduce into France. The visionary experience, like Dante's, is presented as a response to confusion and discouragement, and the three feminine guides may owe something to the three ladies who watch over Dante's pilgrimage.

The most immediate source for *The Book of the City of Ladies,* however, is Boccaccio's *Concerning Famous Women,* a compendium of sketches of famous women, both good and bad, starting with Eve and ending with Boccaccio's contemporary, Johanna of Naples, Queen of Sicily, but principally drawn from mythology and antiquity. Christine draws about three-fourths of her examples from Boccaccio. Her treatment of them, however, is completely different. For one thing, she treats only good women; for another, she goes out of her way to present pagan and Christian, ancient and contemporary women together, whereas Boccaccio kept them sharply separate.

The third part of *The Book of the City of Ladies,* presided over by Justice, is given over to a series of lives of female saints, climaxed by the life of Christine's own name-saint. It is given here as an example of a very widespread and popular medieval literary form.

Christine, it hardly need be pointed out, is not a typical feminist in the modern sense. She never questions the medieval hierarchical social order; she merely wants women to hold an honored place within it. She also, as the climactic inclusion of the life of St. Christine demonstrates, remains firmly within a religious frame of reference. But she clearly is a feminist, if a medieval one. In her work, and preeminently in *The Book of the City of Ladies,* we hear a voice otherwise largely silenced in medieval literature: the voice of a woman.

FURTHER READING *(prepared by J.H.):* Much the fullest and best modern treatment in English of Christine de Pizan is Charity Cannon Willard's critical biography, *Christine de Pizan: Her Life and Works,* 1984. A more popularly written biography is Enid McLeod, *The Order of the Rose: The Life and Ideas of Christine de Pizan,* 1976. An excellent short critical overview is Earl Jeffrey Richards' introduction to his translation of *The Book of the City of Ladies,* 1982. A thoughtful treatment of Christine's feminism is F. Douglas

Kelly, "Reflections on the Role of Christine de Pisan as a Feminist Writer," *Sub-Stances* 2 (1972), 63–71. A good collection of essays on the same topic is *Ideals for Women in the Works of Christine de Pizan*, ed. Diane Bornstein, 1981. Bibliographies include Edith Yenal, *Christine de Pisan: A Bibliography of Writings by Her and About Her*, 1982; and Angus J. Kennedy, *Christine de Pizan: A Bibliographical Guide*, 1984. For a survey of fifteen women authors of the Middle Ages, including excerpts from their works and succinct discussions of them, see *Medieval Women Writers*, ed. with Introduction by Katharina M. Wilson, 1984; the section on Christine de Pizan is by Charity Cannon Willard. Also illuminating is Maureen Quilligan, *The Allegory of Female Authority: Christine de Pizan's Cité des Dames*, 1991.

from *THE BOOK OF THE CITY OF LADIES*

Translated by Earl Jeffrey Richards

HERE BEGINS THE BOOK OF THE CITY OF LADIES,
WHOSE FIRST CHAPTER TELLS WHY AND FOR WHAT
PURPOSE THIS BOOK WAS WRITTEN.

One day as I was sitting alone in my study surrounded by books on all kinds of subjects, devoting myself to literary studies, my usual habit, my mind dwelt at length on the weighty opinions of various authors whom I had studied for a long time. I looked up from my book, having decided to leave such subtle questions in peace and to relax by reading some light poetry. With this in mind, I searched for some small book. By chance a strange volume came into my hands, not one of my own, but one which had been given to me along with some others. When I held it open and saw from its title page that it was by Mathéolus,[1] I smiled, for though I had never seen it before, I had often heard that like other books it discussed respect for women. I thought I would browse through it to amuse myself. I had not been reading for very long when my good mother called me to refresh myself with some supper, for it was evening. Intending to look at it the next day, I put it down. The next morning, again seated in my study as was my habit, I remembered wanting to examine this book by Mathéolus. I started to read it and went on for a little while. Because the subject seemed to me not very pleasant for people who do not enjoy lies, and of no use in developing virtue or manners, given its lack of integrity in diction and theme, and after browsing here and there and reading the end, I put it down in order to turn my attention to more elevated and useful study. But just the sight of this book, even though it was of no authority, made me wonder how it happened that so many different men—and learned men among them—have been and are so inclined to express both in speaking and in their treatises and writings so many wicked insults about women and their behavior. Not only one or two and not even just this Mathéolus (for this book had a bad name anyway and was intended as a satire) but, more generally, judging from the treatises of all philosophers and poets and from all the orators—it would take too long to mention their

---

[1] The book is *The Book of the Lamentations of Mathéolus*, a long verse diatribe against women, written in Latin about 1300 and translated into French during Christine's lifetime.

names—it seems that they all speak from one and the same mouth. They all concur in one conclusion: that the behavior of women is inclined to and full of every vice. Thinking deeply about these matters, I began to examine my character and conduct as a natural woman[2] and, similarly, I considered other women whose company I frequently kept, princesses, great ladies, women of the middle and lower classes, who had graciously told me of their most private and intimate thoughts, hoping that I could judge impartially and in good conscience whether the testimony of so many notable men could be true. To the best of my knowledge, no matter how long I confronted or dissected the problem, I could not see or realize how their claims could be true when compared to the natural behavior and character of women. Yet I still argued vehemently against women, saying that it would be impossible that so many famous men—such solemn scholars, possessed of such deep and great understanding, so clear-sighted in all things, as it seemed—could have spoken falsely on so many occasions that I could hardly find a book on morals where, even before I had read it in its entirety, I did not find several chapters or certain sections attacking women, no matter who the author was. This reason alone, in short, made me conclude that, although my intellect did not perceive my own great faults and, likewise, those of other women because of its simpleness and ignorance, it was however truly fitting that such was the case. And so I relied more on the judgment of others than on what I myself felt and knew. I was so transfixed in this line of thinking for such a long time that it seemed as if I were in a stupor. Like a gushing fountain, a series of authorities, whom I recalled one after another, came to mind, along with their opinions on this topic. And I finally decided that God formed a vile creature when He made woman, and I wondered how such a worthy artisan could have deigned to make such an abominable work which, from what they say, is the vessel as well as the refuge and abode of every evil and vice. As I was thinking this, a great unhappiness and sadness welled up in my heart, for I detested myself and the entire feminine sex, as though we were monstrosities in nature. And in my lament I spoke these words:

"Oh, God, how can this be? For unless I stray from my faith, I must never doubt that Your infinite wisdom and most perfect goodness ever created anything which was not good. Did You yourself not create woman in a very special way and since that time did You not give her all those inclinations which it pleased You for her to have? And how could it be that You could go wrong in anything? Yet look at all these accusations which have been judged, decided, and concluded against women. I do not know how to understand this repugnance. If it is so, fair Lord God, that in fact so many abominations abound in the female sex, for You Yourself say that the testimony of two or three witnesses lends credence, why shall I not doubt that this is true? Alas, God, why did You not let me be born in the world as a man, so that all my inclinations would be to serve You better, and so that I would not stray in anything and would be as perfect as a man is said to be? But since Your kindness has not been extended to me, then forgive my negligence in Your service, most fair Lord God, and may it not displease You, for the servant who receives

---

[2]The phrase "natural woman" recalls *The Romance of the Rose*, in which the allegorical figure Nature argues that women are "naturally" unchaste.

fewer gifts from his lord is less obliged in his service." I spoke these words to God in my lament and a great deal more for a very long time in sad reflection, and in my folly I considered myself most unfortunate because God had made me inhabit a female body in this world.

HERE CHRISTINE DESCRIBES HOW THREE LADIES APPEARED TO HER AND HOW THE ONE WHO WAS IN FRONT SPOKE FIRST AND COMFORTED HER IN HER PAIN

So occupied with these painful thoughts, my head bowed in shame, my eyes filled with tears, leaning on the pommel of my chair's armrest, I suddenly saw a ray of light fall on my lap, as though it were the sun. I shuddered then, as if wakened from sleep, for I was sitting in a shadow where the sun could not have shone at that hour. And as I lifted my head to see where this light was coming from, I saw three crowned ladies standing before me, and the splendor of their bright faces shone on me and throughout the entire room. Now no one would ask whether I was surprised, for my doors were shut and they had still entered. Fearing that some phantom had come to tempt me and filled with great fright, I made the Sign of the Cross on my forehead.

Then she who was the first of the three smiled and began to speak, "Dear daughter, do not be afraid, for we have not come here to harm or trouble you but to console you, for we have taken pity on your distress, and we have come to bring you out of the ignorance which so blinds your own intellect that you shun what you know for a certainty and believe what you do not know or see or recognize except by virtue of many strange opinions. You resemble the fool in the prank who was dressed in women's clothes while he slept; because those who were making fun of him repeatedly told him he was a woman, he believed their false testimony more readily than the certainty of his own identity. Fair daughter, have you lost all sense? Have you forgotten that when fine gold is tested in the furnace, it does not change or vary in strength but becomes purer the more it is hammered and handled in different ways? Do you not know that the best things are the most debated and the most discussed? If you wish to consider the question of the highest form of reality, which consists in ideas or celestial substances, consider whether the greatest philosophers who have lived and whom you support against your own sex have ever resolved whether ideas are false and contrary to the truth. Notice how these same philosophers contradict and criticize one another, just as you have seen in the *Metaphysics* where Aristotle takes their opinions to task and speaks similarly of Plato and other philosophers. And note, moreover, how even Saint Augustine and the Doctors of the Church have criticized Aristotle in certain passages, although he is known as the prince of philosophers in whom both natural and moral philosophy attained their highest level. It also seems that you think that all the words of the philosophers are articles of faith, that they could never be wrong. As far as the poets of whom you speak are concerned, do you not know that they spoke on many subjects in a fictional way and that often they mean the contrary of what their words openly say? One can interpret them according to the grammatical figure of *antiphrasis*, which means, as you know, that if you call something bad, in fact, it is good, and also vice versa. Thus I advise you to profit from their works and to interpret them in the manner in which they are intended in those passages where they attack women. Perhaps this man, who called himself Mathéolus in his own book, intended it in such a way, for there are many things which, if taken literally, would be pure heresy. As for the attack against the estate of marriage—which is a holy estate, worthy and ordained by God—made not only by Mathéolus but also by others and even by the *Romance of the Rose* where greater credibility is averred because of the authority of its author, it is evident and proven by experience that the contrary of the evil which they posit and claim to be found in this estate through the obligation and fault of women is true. For where has the husband ever been found who would allow his wife to have authority to abuse and insult him as a matter of course, as these authorities maintain? I believe that, regardless of what you might have read, you will never see such a husband with your own eyes, so badly colored are these lies. Thus, in conclusion, I tell you, dear friend, that simplemindedness has prompted you to hold such an opinion. Come back to yourself, recover your senses, and do not trouble yourself anymore over such absurdities. For you know that any evil spoken of women so generally only hurts those who say it, not women themselves."

HERE CHRISTINE TELLS HOW THE LADY WHO HAD
SAID THIS SHOWED HER WHO SHE WAS AND WHAT HER
CHARACTER AND FUNCTION WERE AND TOLD HER
HOW SHE WOULD CONSTRUCT A CITY WITH THE HELP
OF THESE SAME THREE LADIES.

The famous lady spoke these words to me, in whose presence I do not know which one of my senses was more overwhelmed: my hearing from having listened to such worthy words or my sight from having seen her radiant beauty, her attire, her reverent comportment, and her most honored countenance. The same was true of the others, so that I did not know which one to look at, for the three ladies resembled each other so much that they could be told apart only with difficulty, except for the last one, for although she was of no less authority than the others, she had so fierce a visage that whoever, no matter how daring, looked in her eyes would be afraid to commit a crime, for it seemed that she threatened criminals unceasingly. Having stood up out of respect, I looked at them without saying a word, like someone too overwhelmed to utter a syllable. Reflecting on who these beings could be, I felt much admiration in my heart and, if I could have dared, I would have immediately asked their names and identities and what was the meaning of the different scepters which each one carried in her right hand, which were of fabulous richness, and why they had come here. But since I considered myself unworthy to address these questions to such high ladies as they appeared to me, I did not dare to, but continued to keep my gaze fixed on them, half-afraid and half-reassured by the words which I had heard, which had made me reject my first impression. But the most wise lady who had spoken to me and who knew in her mind what I was thinking, as one who has insight into everything, addressed my reflections, saying:

"Dear daughter, know that God's providence, which leaves nothing void or empty, has ordained that we, though celestial beings, remain and circulate among the people of the world here below, in order to bring order and maintain in balance those institutions we created according to the will of

God in the fulfillment of various offices, that God whose daughters we three all are and from whom we were born. Thus it is my duty to straighten out men and women when they go astray and to put them back on the right path. And when they stray, if they have enough understanding to see me, I come to them quietly in spirit and preach to them, showing them their error and how they have failed, I assign them the causes, and then I teach them what to do and what to avoid. Since I serve to demonstrate clearly and to show both in thought and deed to each man and woman his or her own special qualities and faults, you see me holding this shiny mirror which I carry in my right hand in place of a scepter. I would thus have you know truly that no one can look into this mirror, no matter what kind of creature, without achieving clear self-knowledge. My mirror has such great dignity that not without reason is it surrounded by rich and precious gems, so that you see, thanks to this mirror, the essences, qualities, proportions, and measures of all things are known, nor can anything be done well without it. And because, similarly, you wish to know what are the offices of my other sisters whom you see here, each will reply in her own person about her name and character, and this way our testimony will be all the more certain to you. But now I myself will declare the reason for our coming. I must assure you, as we do nothing without good cause, that our appearance here is not at all in vain. For, although we are not common to many places and our knowledge does not come to all people, nevertheless you, for your great love of investigating the truth through long and continual study, for which you come here, solitary and separated from the world, you have deserved and deserve, our devoted friend, to be visited and consoled by us in your agitation and sadness, so that you might also see clearly, in the midst of the darkness of your thoughts, those things which taint and trouble your heart.

"There is another greater and even more special reason for our coming which you will learn from our speeches: in fact we have come to vanquish from the world the same error into which you had fallen, so that from now on, ladies and all valiant women may have a refuge and defense against the various assailants, those ladies who have been abandoned for so long, exposed like a field without a surrounding hedge, without finding a champion to afford them an adequate defense, notwithstanding those noble men who are required by order of law to protect them, who by negligence and apathy have allowed them to be mistreated. It is no wonder then that their jealous enemies, those outrageous villains who have assailed them with various weapons, have been victorious in a war in which women have had no defense. Where is there a city so strong which could not be taken immediately if no resistance were forthcoming, or the law case, no matter how unjust, which was not won through the obstinance of someone pleading without opposition? And the simple, noble ladies, following the example of suffering which God commands, have cheerfully suffered the great attacks which, both in the spoken and the written word, have been wrongfully and sinfully perpetrated against women by men who all the while appealed to God for the right to do so. Now it is time for their just cause to be taken from Pharaoh's hands, and for this reason, we three ladies whom you see here, moved by pity, have come to you to announce a particular edifice built like a city wall, strongly constructed and well founded, which has been predestined and established by our aid and counsel for you to build, where no one will reside except all ladies of fame and women worthy of praise, for the walls of the city will be closed to those women who lack virtue."

HERE THE LADY EXPLAINS TO CHRISTINE THE CITY WHICH SHE HAS BEEN COMMISSIONED TO BUILD AND HOW SHE WAS CHARGED TO HELP CHRISTINE BUILD THE WALL AND ENCLOSURE, AND THEN GIVES HER NAME.

"Thus, fair daughter, the prerogative among women has been bestowed on you to establish and build the City of Ladies. For the foundation and completion of this City you will draw fresh waters from us as from clear fountains, and we will bring you sufficient building stone, stronger and more durable than any marble with cement could be. Thus your City will be extremely beautiful, without equal, and of perpetual duration in the world.

"Have you not read that King Tros founded the great city of Troy with the aid of Apollo, Minerva, and Neptune, whom the people of that time considered gods, and also how Cadmus founded the city of Thebes with the admonition of the gods?[3] And yet over time these cities fell and have fallen into ruin. But I prophesy to you, as a true sybil, that this City, which you will found with our help, will never be destroyed, nor will it ever fall, but will remain prosperous forever, regardless of all its jealous enemies. Although it will be stormed by numerous assaults, it will never be taken or conquered.

"Long ago the Amazon kingdom was begun through the arrangement and enterprise of several ladies of great courage who despised servitude, just as history books have testified.[4] For a long time afterward they maintained it under the rule of several queens, very noble ladies whom they elected themselves, who governed them well and maintained their dominion with great strength. Yet, although they were strong and powerful and had conquered a large part of the entire Orient in the course of their rule and terrified all the neighboring lands (even the Greeks, who were then the flower of all countries in the world, feared them), nevertheless, after a time, the power of this kingdom declined, so that as with all earthly kingdoms, nothing but its name has survived to the present. But the edifice erected by you in this City which you must construct will be far stronger, and for its founding I was commissioned, in the course of our common deliberation, to supply you with durable and pure mortar to lay the sturdy foundations and to raise the lofty walls all around, high and thick, with mighty towers and strong bastions, surrounded by moats with firm blockhouses, just as is fitting for a city with a strong and lasting defense. Following our plan, you will set the foundations deep to last all the longer, and then you will raise the walls so high that they will not fear anyone. Daughter, now that I have told you the reason for our coming and so that you will more certainly believe my words, I want you to learn my name, by whose sound alone you will be able to learn

---

[3] In connecting her City of Ladies with Thebes and Troy, Christine is following a commonplace of her time, which held that France was the natural heir to the culture of Greece and Rome. Legendary history held that the French kings were descended from Franco, the son of Hector of Troy.

[4] In Greek legend, the Amazons were a tribe of women who spent their time in hunting and warfare. In the Trojan War, they were supposed to have fought against the Greeks.

and know that, if you wish to follow my commands, you have in me an administrator so that you may do your work flawlessly. I am called Lady Reason; you see that you are in good hands. For the time being then, I will say no more."

HERE CHRISTINE TELLS HOW THE SECOND LADY TOLD HER NAME AND WHAT SHE SERVED AS AND HOW SHE WOULD AID HER IN BUILDING THE CITY OF LADIES

When the lady above finished her speech, before I could resume, the second lady began as follows: "I am called Rectitude and reside more in Heaven than on Earth, but as the radiance and splendor of God and messenger of His goodness, I often visit the just and exhort them to do what is right, to give to each person what is his according to his capacity, to say and uphold the truth, to defend the rights of the poor and the innocent, not to hurt anyone through usurpation, to uphold the reputation of those unjustly accused. I am the shield and defense of the servants of God. I resist the power and might of evil-doers. I give rest to workers and reward those who act well. Through me, God reveals to His friends His secrets; I am their advocate in Heaven. This shining ruler which you see me carry in my right hand instead of a scepter is the straight ruler which separates right from wrong and shows the difference between good and evil: who follows it does not go astray. It is the rod of peace which reconciles the good and where they find support and which beats and strikes down evil. What should I tell you about this? All things are measured by this ruler, for its powers are infinite. It will serve you to measure the edifice of the City which you have been commissioned to build, and you will need it for constructing the façade, for erecting the high temples, for measuring the palaces, houses, and all public buildings, the streets and squares, and all things proper to help populate the City. I have come as your assistant, and this will be my duty. Do not be uneasy about the breadth and long circuit of the walls, for with God's help and our assistance you will build fair and sturdy mansions and inns without leaving anything vague; and you will people the City with no trouble."

HERE CHRISTINE TELLS HOW THE THIRD LADY TOLD HER WHO SHE WAS AND HER FUNCTION AND HOW SHE WOULD HELP BUILD THE HIGH ROOFS OF THE TOWERS AND PALACES AND WOULD BRING TO HER THE QUEEN, ACCOMPANIED BY NOBLE LADIES.

Afterward, the third lady spoke and said, "My friend Christine, I am Justice, the most singular daughter of God, and my nature proceeds purely from His person. My residence is found in Heaven, on Earth, or in Hell: in Heaven, for the glory of the saints and blessed souls; on Earth, for the apportionment to each man of the good or evil which he has deserved; in Hell, for the punishment of the evil. I do not bend anywhere, for I have not friend nor enemy nor changeable will; pity cannot persuade me nor cruelty move me. My duty is only to judge, to decide, and to dispense according to each man's just deserts. I sustain all things in their condition, nothing could be stable without me. I am in God and God is in me, and we are as one and the same. Who follows me cannot fail, and my way is sure. I teach men and women of sound mind who want to believe in me to chastise, know, and correct themselves, and to do to others what they wish to have done to themselves, to distribute wealth without favor, to speak the truth, to flee and hate lies, to reject all viciousness. This vessel of fine gold which you see me hold in my right hand, made like a generous measure, God, my Father, gave me, and it serves to measure out to each his rightful portion. It carries the sign of the fleur-de-lis of the Trinity,[5] and in all portions it measures true, nor can any man complain about my measure. Yet the men of the Earth have other measures which they claim depend upon and derive from mine, but they are mistaken. Often they measure in my shadow, and their measure is not always true but sometimes too much for some and too little for others. I could give a rather long account of the duties of my office, but, put briefly, I have a special place among the Virtues, for they are all based on me. And of the three noble ladies whom you see here, we are as one and the same, we could not exist without one another; and what the first disposes, the second orders and initiates, and then I, the third, finish and terminate it. Thus I have been appointed by the will of us three ladies to perfect and complete your City, and my job will be to construct the high roofs of the towers and of the lofty mansions and inns which will all be made of fine shining gold. Then I will populate the City for you with worthy ladies and the mighty Queen whom I will bring to you. Hers will be the honor and prerogative among all other women, as well as among the most excellent women. And in this condition I will turn the City over to you, completed with your help, fortified and closed off with strong gates which I will search for in Heaven, and then I will place the keys in your hands."

HERE CHRISTINE TELLS HOW SHE
SPOKE TO THE THREE LADIES

When the speeches of all three ladies were over—to which I had listened intently and which had completely taken away the unhappiness which I had felt before their coming—I threw myself at their feet, not just on my knees but completely prostrate because of their great excellence. Kissing the earth around their feet, adoring them as goddesses of glory, I began my prayer to them:

"Oh ladies of supreme dignity, radiance of the heavens and light of the earth, fountains of Paradise and joy of the blessed, where did such humility come from to Your Highnesses that you have deigned to come down from your pontifical seats and shining thrones to visit the troubled and dark tabernacle of this simple and ignorant student? Who could give fitting thanks for such a boon? With the rain and dew of your sweet words, you have penetrated and moistened the dryness of my mind, so that it now feels ready to germinate and send forth new branches capable of bearing fruits of profitable virtue and sweet savor. How will such grace be bestowed on me that I will receive the boon, as you have said, to build and construct in the world from now on a new city? I am not Saint Thomas the Apostle, who through divine grace built a rich palace in Heaven for the king of India,[6] and my feeble sense does not know the craft, or the measures, or the study, or the

---

[5] The fleur-de-lis, or lily, the symbol of France, also symbolized the Trinity, because of its three petals in one flower.
[6] Thomas, one of the Twelve Apostles, was traditionally an apostle to Asia.

science, or the practice of construction. And if, thanks to learning, these things were within my ken, where would I find enough physical strength in my weak feminine body to realize such an enormous task? But nevertheless, my most respected ladies, although the awesomeness of this news seems strange to me, I know well that nothing is impossible for God. Nor do I doubt that anything undertaken with your counsel and help will not be completed well. Thus, with all my strength, I praise God and you, my ladies, who have so honored me by assigning me such a noble commission, which I most happily accept. Behold your handmaiden ready to serve. Command and I will obey, and may it be unto me according to your words."

HERE CHRISTINE TELLS HOW, UNDER REASON'S
COMMAND AND ASSISTANCE, SHE BEGAN TO EXCAVATE
THE EARTH AND LAY THE FOUNDATION.

Then Lady Reason responded and said, "Get up, daughter! Without waiting any longer, let us go to the Field of Letters. There the City of Ladies will be founded on a flat and fertile plain, where all fruits and freshwater rivers are found and where the earth abounds in all good things. Take the pick of your understanding and dig and clear out a great ditch wherever you see the marks of my ruler, and I will help you carry away the earth on my own shoulders."

I immediately stood up to obey her commands and, thanks to these three ladies, I felt stronger and lighter than before. She went ahead, and I followed behind, and after we had arrived at this field I began to excavate and dig, following her marks with the pick of cross-examination. . . .

CHRISTINE ASKS REASON WHETHER GOD HAS EVER
WISHED TO ENNOBLE THE MIND OF WOMAN WITH THE
LOFTINESS OF THE SCIENCES; AND REASON'S ANSWER.

[I, Christine, spoke: "I would like to know whether it has ever pleased God, who has bestowed so many favors] on women, to honor the feminine sex with the privilege of the virtue of high understanding and great learning, and whether women ever have a clever enough mind for this. I wish very much to know this because men maintain that the mind of women can learn only a little."

She answered, "My daughter, since I told you before, you know quite well that the opposite of their opinion is true, and to show you this even more clearly, I will give you proof through examples. I tell you again—and don't doubt the contrary—if it were customary to send daughters to school like sons, and if they were then taught the natural sciences, they would learn as thoroughly and understand the subtleties of all the arts and sciences as well as sons. And by chance there happen to be such women, for, as I touched on before, just as women have more delicate bodies than men, weaker and less able to perform many tasks, so do they have minds that are freer and sharper whenever they apply themselves."

"My lady, what are you saying? With all due respect, could you dwell longer on this point, please. Certainly men would never admit this answer is true, unless it is explained more plainly, for they believe that one normally sees that men know more than women do."

She answered, "Do you know why women know less?"

"Not unless you tell me, my lady."

"Without the slightest doubt, it is because they are not involved in many different things, but stay at home, where it is enough for them to run the household, and there is nothing which so instructs a reasonable creature as the exercise and experience of many different things."

"My lady, since they have minds skilled in conceptualizing and learning, just like men, why don't women learn more?"

She replied, "Because, my daughter, the public does not require them to get involved in the affairs which men are commissioned to execute, just as I told you before. It is enough for women to perform the usual duties to which they are ordained. As for judging from experience, since one sees that women usually know less than men, that therefore their capacity for understanding is less, look at men who farm the flatlands or who live in the mountains. You will find that in many countries they seem completely savage because they are so simpleminded. All the same, there is no doubt that Nature provided them with the qualities of body and mind found in the wisest and most learned men. All of this stems from a failure to learn, though, just as I told you, among men and women, some possess better minds than others. Let me tell you about women who have possessed great learning and profound understanding and treat the question of the similarity of women's minds to men's."

SHE BEGINS TO DISCUSS SEVERAL LADIES WHO WERE
ENLIGHTENED WITH GREAT LEARNING, AND FIRST
SPEAKS ABOUT THE NOBLE MAIDEN CORNIFICIA.

"Cornificia, the noble maiden, was sent to school by her parents along with her brother Cornificius when they were both children, thanks to deception and trickery.[7] This little girl so devoted herself to study and with such marvelous intelligence that she began to savor the sweet taste of knowledge acquired through study. Nor was it easy to take her away from this joy to which she more and more applied herself, neglecting all other feminine activities. She occupied herself with this for such a long period of time that she became a consummate poet, and she was not only extremely brilliant and expert in the learnedness and craft of poetry but also seemed to have been nourished with the very milk and teaching of perfect philosophy, for she wanted to hear and know about every branch of learning, which she then mastered so thoroughly that she surpassed her brother, who was also a very great poet, and excelled in every field of learning. Knowledge was not enough for her unless she could put her mind to work and her pen to paper in the compilation of several very famous books. These works, as well as her poems, were much prized during the time of Saint Gregory and he himself mentions them. The Italian, Boccaccio, who was a great poet,[8] discusses this fact in his work and at the same time praises this woman: 'O most great honor for a woman who abandoned all feminine activities and applied and devoted

---

[7] Cornificia, a first-century B.C. Roman aristocrat, was the sister of Cornificius, a Roman general. Both were poets.

[8] The book referred to is Boccaccio's *Concerning Famous Women* (1360–74), which was translated into French about 1401. It is Christine's principal source for *The Book of the City of Ladies*.

her mind to the study of the greatest scholars!' As further proof of what I am telling you, Boccaccio also talks about the attitude of women who despise themselves and their own minds, and who, as though they were born in the mountains totally ignorant of virtue and honor, turn disconsolate and say that they are good and useful only for embracing men and carrying and feeding children. God has given them such beautiful minds to apply themselves, if they want to, in any of the fields where glorious and excellent men are active, which are neither more nor less accessible to them as compared to men if they wished to study them, and they can thereby acquire a lasting name, whose possession is fitting for most excellent men. My dear daughter, you can see how this author Boccaccio testifies to what I have told you and how he praises and approves learning in women.". . .

HERE SHE SPEAKS OF SAPPHO, THAT MOST SUBTLE WOMAN, POET, AND PHILOSOPHER.

"The wise Sappho,[9] who was from the city of Mytilene, was no less learned. . . . This Sappho had a beautiful body and face and was agreeable and pleasant in appearance, conduct, and speech. But the charm of her profound understanding surpassed all the other charms with which she was endowed, for she was expert and learned in several arts and sciences, and she was not only well-educated in the works and writings composed by others but also discovered many new things herself and wrote many books and poems. Concerning her, Boccaccio has offered these fair words couched in the sweetness of poetic language: 'Sappho, possessed of sharp wit and burning desire for constant study in the midst of bestial and ignorant men, frequented the heights of Mount Parnassus, that is, of perfect study. Thanks to her fortunate boldness and daring, she kept company with the Muses, that is, the arts and sciences, without being turned away. She entered the forest of laurel trees filled with May boughs, greenery, and different colored flowers, soft fragrances and various aromatic spices, where Grammar, Logic, noble Rhetoric, Geometry, and Arithmetic live and take their leisure. She went on her way until she came to the deep grotto of Apollo, god of learning, and found the brook and conduit of the fountain of Castalia, and took up the plectrum and quill of the harp and played sweet melodies, with the nymphs all the while leading the dance, that is, following the rules of harmony and musical accord.' From what Boccaccio says about her, it should be inferred that the profundity of both her understanding and of her learned books can only be known and understood by men of great perception and learning, according to the testimony of the ancients. Her writings and poems have survived to this day, most remarkably constructed and composed, and they serve as illumination and models of consummate poetic craft and composition to those who have come afterward. She invented different genres of lyric and poetry, short narratives, tearful laments and strange lamentations about love and other emotions, and these were so well made and so well

---

[9] Sappho was a Greek poet of the seventh to sixth centuries B.C. Christine's semilegendary account of her is taken from Boccaccio. Christine could not have known Sappho's works directly, since by the fourteenth century, Sappho's ten volumes of collected works had long since been destroyed by clerical censors. A few of the poems were reconstructed, from scraps of papyrus and quotations by other authors, in the nineteenth century.

ordered that they were named 'Sapphic' after her. Horace recounts, concerning her poems, that when Plato, the great philosopher who was Aristotle's teacher, died, a book of Sappho's poems was found under his pillow.

"In brief this lady was so outstanding in learning that in the city where she resided a statue of bronze in her image was dedicated in her name and erected in a prominent place so that she would be honored by all and be remembered forever. This lady was placed and counted among the greatest and most famous poets, and, according to Boccaccio, the honors of the diadems and crowns of kings and the miters of bishops are not any greater, nor are the crowns of laurel and victor's palm.

"I could tell you a great deal about women of great learning. Leontium was a Greek woman and also such a great philosopher that she dared, for impartial and serious reasons, to correct and attack the philosopher Theophrastus,[10] who was quite famous in her time." . . .

Against Those Men Who Claim It Is Not Good for Women to Be Educated.

Following these remarks, I, Christine, spoke [to Lady Rectitude], "My lady, I realize that women have accomplished many good things and that even if evil women have done evil, it seems to me, nevertheless, that the benefits accrued and still accruing because of good women—particularly the wise and literary ones and those educated in the natural sciences whom I mentioned above—outweigh the evil. Therefore, I am amazed by the opinion of some men who claim that they do not want their daughters, wives, or kinswomen to be educated because their mores would be ruined as a result."

She responded, "Here you can clearly see that not all opinions of men are based on reason and that these men are wrong. For it must not be presumed that mores necessarily grow worse from knowing the moral sciences, which teach the virtues, indeed, there is not the slightest doubt that moral education amends and ennobles them. How could anyone think or believe that whoever follows good teaching or doctrine is the worse for it? Such an opinion cannot be expressed or maintained. I do not mean that it would be good for a man or a woman to study the art of divination or those fields of learning which are forbidden—for the holy Church did not remove them from common use without good reason—but it should not be believed that women are the worse for knowing what is good.

"Quintus Hortensius,[11] a great rhetorician and consumately skilled orator in Rome, did not share this opinion. He had a daughter, named Hortensia, whom he greatly loved for the subtlety of her wit. He had her learn letters and study the science of rhetoric, which she mastered so thoroughly that she resembled her father Hortensius not only in wit and lively memory but also in her excellent delivery and order of speech—in fact, he surpassed her in nothing. As for the subject discussed above, concerning the good which comes about through women, the benefits realized by this woman and her

---

[10] Theophrastus (third century B.C.) was a Greek Peripatetic philosopher and pupil of Aristotle. Leontium is known only in connection with this anecdote.

[11] Roman orator (114–50 B.C.). A leader of the aristocratic party, he was defeated (70 B.C.) by Cicero in the trial of Verres. His daughter Hortensia was as well educated and well known as Christine says she was.

learning were, among others, exceptionally remarkable. That is, during the time when Rome was governed by three men, this Hortensia began to support the cause of women and to undertake what no man dared to undertake. There was a question whether certain taxes should be levied on women and on their jewelry during a needy period in Rome. This woman's eloquence was so compelling that she was listened to, no less readily than her father would have been, and she won her case.

"Similarly, to speak of more recent times, without searching for examples in ancient history, Giovanni Andrea, a solemn law professor in Bologna not quite sixty years ago, was not of the opinion that it was bad for women to be educated. He had a fair and good daughter, named Novella, who was educated in the law to such an advanced degree that when he was occupied by some task and not at leisure to present his lectures to his students, he would send Novella, his daughter, in his place to lecture to the students from his chair. And to prevent her beauty from distracting the concentration of her audience, she had a little curtain drawn in front of her. In this manner she could on occasion supplement and lighten her father's occupation. He loved her so much that, to commemorate her name, he wrote a book of remarkable lectures on the law which he entitled *Novella super Decretalium,* after his daughter's name.[12]

"Thus, not all men (and especially the wisest) share the opinion that it is bad for women to be educated. But it is very true that many foolish men have claimed this because it displeased them that women knew more than they did. Your father, who was a great scientist and philosopher, did not believe that women were worth less by knowing science; rather, as you know, he took great pleasure from seeing your inclination to learning. The feminine opinion of your mother, however, who wished to keep you busy with spinning and silly girlishness, following the common custom of women, was the major obstacle to your being more involved in the sciences. But just as the proverb already mentioned above says, 'No one can take away what Nature has given,' your mother could not hinder in you the feeling for the sciences which you, through natural inclination, had nevertheless gathered together in little droplets. I am sure that, on account of these things, you do not think you are worth less but rather that you consider it a great treasure for yourself; and you doubtless have reason to."

And I, Christine, replied to all of this, "Indeed, my lady, what you say is as true as the Lord's Prayer."

HERE CHRISTINE SPEAKS TO RECTITUDE, WHO ARGUES AGAINST THOSE MEN WHO SAY THAT THERE ARE FEW CHASTE WOMEN, AND SHE TELLS OF SUSANNA.

"From what I see, my lady, all good and virtuous things are found in women. Where does the opinion that there are so few chaste women come from? Were this so, then all their other virtues would be nothing, since chastity is the supreme virtue in women. But from what I have heard you say, the complete opposite of what those men claim seems to be the case."

---

[12] Christine could have learned the story of Novella from her father, who was a colleague of Giovanni Andrea at the University of Bologna.

She replied, "From what I have already actually told you and from what you know about this, the contrary is quite obvious to you, and I could tell you more about this and then some. How many valiant and chaste ladies does Holy Scripture mention who chose death rather than transgress against the chastity and purity of their bodies and thoughts, just like the beautiful and good Susanna, wife of Joachim, a rich man of great authority among the Jews?[13] Once when this valiant lady Susanna was alone relaxing in her garden, two old men, false priests, entered the garden, approached her, and demanded that she sin with them. She refused them totally, whereupon, seeing their request denied, they threatened to denounce her to the authorities and to claim that they had discovered her with a young man. Hearing their threats and knowing that women in such a case were customarily stoned, she said, 'I am completely overwhelmed with anguish, for if I do not do what these men require of me, I risk the death of my body, and if I do it, I will sin before my Creator. However, it is far better for me, in my innocence, to die than to incur the wrath of my God because of sin.' So Susanna cried out, and the servants came out of the house, and, to put the matter briefly, with their disloyal testimony, these false priests managed to have Susanna condemned to death. Yet God who always provides for those dear to Him, opened the mouth of the prophet Daniel, who was a little child in his mother's arms and who, as Susanna was being led to her execution, with a great procession of people in tears following her, cried out that the innocent Susanna had been condemned because of a very grave mistake. So she was led back, and the false priests were thoroughly interrogated and found guilty by their own confessions. The innocent Susanna was freed and these men executed." . . .

REFUTING THOSE MEN WHO CLAIM WOMEN WANT
TO BE RAPED, RECTITUDE GIVES SEVERAL EXAMPLES,
AND FIRST OF ALL, LUCRETIA.[14]

Then I, Christine, spoke as follows, "My lady, I truly believe what you are saying, and I am certain that there are plenty of beautiful women who are virtuous and chaste and who know how to protect themselves well from the entrapments of deceitful men. I am therefore troubled and grieved when men argue that many women want to be raped and that it does not bother them at all to be raped by men even when they verbally protest. It would be hard to believe that such great villainy is actually pleasant for them."

She answered, "Rest assured, dear friend, chaste ladies who live honestly take absolutely no pleasure in being raped. Indeed, rape is the greatest possible sorrow for them. Many upright women have demonstrated that this is true with their own credible examples, just like Lucretia, the noblest Roman woman, supreme in chastity among Roman women, wife of a nobleman named Tarquin Collatinus. Now, when another man, Tarquin the Proud, son of King Tarquin, was greatly taken with love for this noble Lucretia, he did not dare to tell her because of the great chastity he saw in her, and, despairing of achieving his goal with presents or entreaties, he considered how he could

---

[13] The story of Susanna and the Elders is told in Daniel 13.
[14] The story of Lucretia and her rape by Tarquin the Proud is legendary history, set at the court of Tarquinius Superbus, traditionally the seventh and last king of Rome (sixth century B.C.).

have her through ruse. Claiming to be a close friend of her husband, he managed to gain entrance into her house whenever he wished, and once, knowing her husband was not at home, he went there and the noble lady received him with the honors due to someone whom she thought to be a close friend of her husband. However, Tarquin, who had something altogether different on his mind, succeeded in entering Lucretia's bedroom and frightened her terribly. Put briefly, after trying to coax her for a long time with promises, gifts, and favors, he saw that entreaties were getting him nowhere. He drew his sword and threatened to kill her if she made a sound and did not submit to his will. She answered that he should go ahead and kill her, for she would rather die than consent. Tarquin, realizing that nothing would help him, concocted a great malice, saying that he would publicly declare that he had found her with one of his sergeants. In brief, he so scared her with this threat (for she thought that people would believe him) that finally she suffered his rape. Lucretia, however, could not patiently endure this great pain, so that when daylight came she sent for her husband, her father, and her close relatives who were among the most powerful people in Rome, and, weeping and sobbing, confessed to them what had happened to her. Then, as her husband and relatives, who saw that she was overwhelmed with grief, were comforting her, she drew a knife from under her robe and said, 'This is how I absolve myself of sin and show my innocence. Yet I cannot free myself from the torment nor extricate myself from the pain. From now on no woman will ever live shamed and disgraced by Lucretia's example.' Having said this, she forcibly plunged the knife into her breast and collapsed dead before her husband and friends. They rushed like madmen to attack Tarquin. All Rome was moved to this cause, and they drove out the king and would have killed his son if they had found him. Never again was there a king in Rome. And because of this outrage perpetrated on Lucretia, so some claim, a law was enacted whereby a man would be executed for raping a woman, a law which is fitting, just, and holy." . . .

HERE [JUSTICE] SPEAKS OF SAINT CHRISTINE, VIRGIN.[15]

"If you want me to tell you about all the holy virgins who are in Heaven because of their constancy during martyrdom, it would require a long history, including Saint Cecilia, Saint Agnes, Saint Agatha, and countless others. If you want more examples, you need only look at the *Speculum historiale* of Vincent de Beauvais, and there you will find a great many.[16] However, I will tell you about Saint Christine, both because she is your patron and because she is a virgin of great dignity. Let me tell you at greater length about her beautiful and pious life.

"The blessed Saint Christine, virgin, was from the city of Tyre and was the daughter of Urban, master of the knights. Her father shut her up in a

[15] There were two Saint Christines in the medieval church: Saint Christine of Tyre, whose story Justice tells, and Saint Christine of Bolsena. The two became confused and came to share the same legendary history. Saint Christine of Tyre probably never existed; Saint Christine of Bolsena seems to have been a genuine martyr of the fourth century A.D. but was probably not named Christine. Her history, as Justice tells it, is of course purely legendary.

[16] Vincent of Beauvais was a thirteenth-century French Dominican friar whose *Mirror of History* was a compendium of knowledge, including many saints' lives.

tower because of her great beauty, and she had twelve maids with her. Her father also had a very beautiful chapel with idols built near Christine's chamber so that she could worship them. She, however, even as a twelve-year-old child, had already been inspired by the faith of Jesus Christ and did not pay any attention to the idols, so that her maids were astonished and repeatedly urged her to sacrifice. Yet when she took the incense, as if to sacrifice to the idols, she knelt at a window facing east, looked up to Heaven, and offered her incense to the immortal God. She spent the greater part of the night at this window, watching the stars, and sighing, piously praying to God to help her against her enemies. The maids, clearly aware her heart was in Jesus Christ, would often kneel before her, their hands clasped together, begging her not to place her trust in a strange God but to worship her parents' gods, for if she were discovered they would all be killed. Christine would answer that the Devil was deceiving them by urging them to worship so many gods and that there was but one God. When her father at last realized that his daughter refused to worship his idols, he was terribly grieved and upbraided her a great deal. She replied that she would gladly worship the God of Heaven. He thought she meant Jupiter and he was overjoyed and wanted to kiss her, but she cried out, 'Do not touch my mouth, for I wish to offer a pure offering to the celestial God.' The father was even happy with this. She returned to her chamber and nailed the door shut, then she knelt down and offered a holy prayer to God, weeping all the while. And the angel of the Lord descended and comforted her and brought her white bread and meat which she ate, for she had not tasted food for three days. Once, afterward, when Christine saw from her window several poor Christians begging at the foot of her tower, seeing that she had nothing to give them, she searched for her father's idols which were made of gold and silver, and she smashed them all and gave the fragments to the poor. When her father learned of this, he beat her cruelly. She openly declared he was deceived to worship these false images and that there was but a single God in the Trinity and that her father should worship Him whom she confessed, and she refused to worship any other in order to escape death. Thereupon her enraged father had her tied up with chains and led from square to square to be beaten and then thrown into prison. He himself wanted to be the judge of this dispute, so on the following day he had her brought before him and threatened her with every conceivable torture if she would not worship his idols. After he realized that he could not convince her with entreaties or threats, he had her sprawled completely nude and beaten so much that twelve men wearied at the task. And the father kept asking her what she thought and he said to her, 'Daughter, natural affection wrings my heart terribly to torment you who are my own flesh, but the reverence I have for my gods forces me to do this because you scorn them.' And the holy virgin replied, 'Tyrant who should not be called my father but rather enemy of my happiness, you boldly torture the flesh which you engendered, for you can easily do this, but as for my soul created by my Father in Heaven, you have no power to touch it with the slightest temptation, for it is protected by my Savior, Jesus Christ.' The cruel father, all the more enraged, had a wheel brought in, which he had ordered built, and ordered her tied to it and a fire built below it, and then he had rivers of boiling oil poured over her body. The wheel turned and completely crushed her. But God, the Father of all mercies, took pity on His servant and dispatched His angel to wreck the torture machines and to extinguish the fire, delivering the virgin, healthy and whole, and killing more than a thousand treacherous spectators who had been watching her without pity and who blasphemed the name of God. And her father asked her, 'Tell me who taught you these evil practices!' She replied, 'Pitiless despot, have I not told you that my Father, Jesus Christ, taught me this long-suffering as well as every right thing in the faith of the Living God? Because of this, I scorn your tortures and will repel all the Devil's assaults with God's strength!' Beaten and confounded, he ordered her thrown into a horrible, dark prison. While she was there, contemplating the extraordinary mysteries of God, three angels came to her in great radiance and brought her food and comforted her. Urban did not know what to do with her but could not stop devising new tortures for her. Finally, fed up completely and wishing to be free of her, he had a great stone tied around her neck and had her thrown into the sea. But as she was being thrown in, the angels took her, and she walked on the water with them. Then, raising her eyes to heaven, Christine prayed to Jesus Christ, that it please Him for her to receive in this water the holy sacrament of baptism which she greatly desired to have; whereupon Jesus Christ descended in His own person with a large company of angels and baptized her and named her Christine, from His own name, and He crowned her and placed a shining star on her forehead and set her on dry land. That night Urban was tortured by the Devil and died. The blessed Christine, whom God wanted to receive through martyrdom (which she also desired), was led back to prison by these criminals. The new judge, named Dyon, knowing what had been done to her, summoned her to appear before him, and he lusted after her because of her beauty. When he saw that his alluring words were of no use, he had her tortured again. He ordered that a large cauldron be filled with oil and that a roaring fire be built beneath it; he had her thrown in, upside down, and four men used iron hooks to rotate her. And the holy virgin sang melodiously to God, mocking her torturers and threatening them with the pains of Hell. When this enraged criminal of a judge realized that nothing was of any avail, he ordered her to be hanged by her long golden hair in the square, in front of all. The women rushed up to her, and, wailing out of pity that such a young girl be so cruelly tortured, they cried out to the judge, saying, 'Cruel felon, crueler than a savage beast, how could a man's heart conceive such monstrous cruelty against such a beautiful and tender maiden?' And all the women tried to mob him. Then the judge, who was afraid, said to her, 'Christine, friend, do not let yourself be tortured anymore, but come with me and we will go worship the supreme God who has upheld you.' He meant Jupiter, who was considered the supreme god, but she understood him in a completely different way and so she replied, 'You have spoken well, so I consent.' He had her taken down and brought up to the temple, and a large crowd followed them. Then he led her before the idols, thinking she would worship them, and she knelt down, looked up at Heaven, and prayed to God. Thereupon she stood up and, turning toward the idol, said, 'I command you in the name of Jesus Christ, oh evil spirit residing in this idol, to come out.' Whereupon the Devil immediately came out and made a loud and frightening din which scared all the spectators, who fell to the ground in fear. When the judge stood up again, he said, 'Christine, you have moved our omnipotent god, and, out of pity for you, he came out to see his creature.' This remark angered her, and she reproached him harshly for being too blind to recognize divine virtue, so she prayed to God to overturn the idol and reduce it to dust, which was done. And more than three thousand men were converted through the words and signs of this virgin. The terrified judge exclaimed, 'If the king finds out what this Christine has done against our god, he will utterly destroy me.' Thereupon, full of anguish, he went out of his mind and died. A third judge, named Julian, appeared, and he ordered Christine seized, boasting that he would make her worship the idols. In spite of all the force he could apply, he was unable physically to move her from the spot where she was standing, so he ordered a large fire built around her. She remained in the fire for three days, and from inside the flames were heard sweet melodies. Her tormentors were terrified by the amazing signs they saw. When the fire had burned out, she emerged fully healthy. The judge commanded that snakes be brought to him and had two asps (with their deadly poisonous bite) and two adders released upon her. But these snakes dropped down at her feet, their heads bowed, and did not harm her at all. Two horrible vipers were let loose, and they hung from her breasts and licked her. And Christine looked to Heaven and said, 'I give You thanks, Lord God, Jesus Christ, who have deigned to grant through Your holy virtues that these horrible serpents would come to know in me Your dignity.' The obstinate Julian, seeing these wonders, yelled at the snake-tender, 'Have you too been enchanted by Christine, so that you have no power to rouse the snakes against her?' Fearing the judge, he then tried to provoke the snakes into biting her, but they rushed at him and killed him. Since everyone was afraid of these serpents and no one dared approach, Christine commanded them in God's name to return to their cages without harming anyone, and they did so. She revived the dead man, who immediately threw himself at her feet and was converted. The judge, blinded by the Devil so that he was unable to perceive the divine mystery, said to Christine, 'You have sufficiently demonstrated your magic arts.' Infuriated, she replied, 'If your eyes would see the virtues of God, you would believe in them.' Then in his rage he ordered her breasts ripped off, whereupon milk rather than blood flowed out. And because she unceasingly pronounced the name of Jesus Christ, he had her tongue cut out, but then she spoke even better and more clearly than before of divine things and of the one blessed God, thanking Him for the bounties which He had given to her. She prayed that it please Him to receive her in His company and that the crown of her martyrdom be finally granted to her. Then a voice was heard from Heaven, saying, 'Christine, pure and radiant, the heavens are opened to you and the eternal kingdom waits, prepared for you, and the entire company of saints blesses God for your sake, for you have upheld the name of Your Christ from childhood on.' And she glorified God, turning her eyes to Heaven. The voice was heard saying, 'Come, Christine, my most beloved and elect daughter, receive the palm and everlasting crown and the reward for your life spent suffering to confess My name.' The treacherous Julian, who heard this voice, castigated the executioners and said they had not cut Christine's tongue short enough and ordered them to cut it so short that she could not speak to her Christ, whereupon they ripped out her tongue and cut it off at the root. She spat this cut-off piece of her tongue into the tyrant's face, putting out one of his eyes. She then said to him, speaking as clearly as ever, 'Tyrant, what does it profit you to have my tongue cut out so that it cannot bless God, when my soul will bless Him forever while yours languishes forever in eternal damnation? And because you did not heed my words, my tongue has blinded you, with good reason.' She ended her martyrdom then, having already seen Jesus Christ sitting on the right hand of His Father, when two arrows were shot at her, one in her side and the other in her heart. One of her relatives whom she had converted buried her body and wrote out her glorious legend."

O blessed Christine, worthy virgin favored of God, most elect and glorious martyr, in the holiness with which God has made you worthy, pray for me, a sinner, named with your name, and be my kind and merciful guardian. Behold my joy at being able to make use of your holy legend and to include it in my writings, which I have recorded here at such length out of reverence for you. May this be ever pleasing to you! Pray for all women, for whom your holy life may serve as an example for ending their lives well. Amen.

Everyman

(Late Fifteenth Century)

Everyman was written in England by an anonymous clerical playwright in about 1475. There is a similar Dutch play of the same period named *Elckerlyc. Everyman* may be a translation of the Dutch play, or both may be derived independently from a Latin work named *Homulus.* Current scholarly opinion tends to conclude, however, that the English play is the original. Nothing is known of the author, and although the play was apparently produced with some frequency in the seventy-five years following its composition, no production records survive.

Everyman is the best example of the medieval "morality play," characterized by an allegorical plot that deals with some archetypal action in human spiritual life and by characters who personify abstract ideas, such as Fellowship, Wealth, or Knowledge. Morality plays were only one genre in a rich body of drama that flourished in Europe from the tenth to the sixteenth century, fascinating both in its own right and as background to the flowering of an even richer and more varied drama in the Renaissance.

By the time of the fall of Rome, classical drama had already declined to the level of crude entertainment, and the collapse of the Roman Empire ended dramatic performance altogether for more than five centuries. When drama began to reemerge in the tenth century, it was again from religious roots. As classical drama had begun in the worship of Dionysus, so medieval drama was born in the Christian liturgy. The earliest bits of medieval drama were *tropes*, brief exchanges of dialogue introduced into the chanted liturgy. These tropes were gradually elaborated until by the twelfth century practically all the narrative portions of the Bible had been dramatized in short, often crude, but vivid plays presented in the churches at Christmas and Easter.

By the fourteenth century, these liturgical plays had attracted such large and unruly audiences that they were removed from the churches and presented in village streets, usually on Corpus Christi Day, in late May or early June. Production of the plays was taken over by the craft and trade guilds, although the clergy continued to play an active role, especially in writing the plays. By the end of the fourteenth century, every town of any size in England had its own cycle of religious plays. Some idea of the numbers of plays involved is suggested by the four cycles that survive: the York cycle of forty-eight plays, the Wakefield cycle of thirty-two plays, the Chester cycle of twenty-five plays, and the Coventry cycle of forty-two plays. The subject matter was quite varied, ranging from authentic biblical material to various folk accretions upon that material to saints' lives. (Scholars used to discriminate clearly between mystery plays, based on the Bible, and miracle plays dealing with the lives of saints, but the distinction is so blurry in practice that they are now sometimes grouped together as liturgical plays.)

The morality play was the last of the medieval dramatic genres to emerge, in the middle of the fourteenth century, although there were many precedents for such didactic, allegorical works in nondramatic literature. The recurring subjects of morality plays are suggested by the titles of some of those that preceded *Everyman: The Pride of Life, The Castle of Perseverance,* and *The Debate of the Body and the Soul.*

Medieval plays were produced in several different ways. When they were still performed inside churches, they were staged on platforms distributed around the church, with a different platform, or *mansion,* for each locale. When they moved outside the churches, they were performed on large, two-decker pageant wagons. A curtained-off lower level was used as a dressing room, and a platform on the second level, reached by a ladder, was used as a stage. Sometimes the action spilled off the wagon-stage and into an open area in front of the wagon, the *platea.* These pageant wagons moved from one stopping place in the town to another on performance days, the actors performing their play at each stop. Spectators could station themselves in one place and see the successive plays in the cycle performed in sequence.

By the time *Everyman* was performed, however, a somewhat different production method had been adopted for the longer morality plays. These were performed not as part of a cycle by members of a guild but independently by troupes of traveling players performing in town squares and on village greens. The original setting for *Everyman* was probably a stationary version of pageant-wagon staging: a two-story scaffold stage with an open space in front of it and probably two smaller sets, one on each side of the scaffold, for Goods and Good Deeds. This simple theater presented an elementary model of the medieval world view. God undoubtedly appeared on the "Heaven" of the top level, Death entered from the "Hell" of the covered lower level, and Everyman's main action was played on the "Earth" of the *platea.* In other respects as well, the theater and the conventions of staging allowed every element of the play to be translated into concrete, dramatic terms. The idea that earthly possessions weigh one down in the quest for salvation is vividly and amusingly presented by the immobilized Goods, unable to stir because of the chests and bags full of gold lying upon and around him. Similarly, the "scourge of penance" that Knowledge gives Everyman is no metaphor, but an actual whip.

The hasty reader of *Everyman* may dismiss it as crude and obvious, interesting only historically. It is true that the message of the play is presented with a crude directness and that its rhymed doggerel is naive, sometimes monotonous. But upon a closer reading, and especially after seeing a good performance, one's respect for the skill and artistry of the nameless playwright is likely to increase. The play presents a generalized, archetypal action, a sort of X ray of human experience, but this generalizing tendency is everywhere in tension with a robust and earthy specificity. Everyman is not only all men, but a very particular man, economically but tellingly characterized. He is a fundamentally good-hearted but superficial sensualist who, at the existential moment when he must confront the reality of his impending death, undergoes a radical and convincing psychological transformation. The secondary characters are handled with a similar economical skill and frequently with a mordant, ironic comic touch. Fellowship, Kindred and Cousin, Goods, and the rest are not mere walking abstractions but vivid embodiments of the qualities they represent. Fellowship, for example, within his short scene, is presented as hail-fellow-well-met, blustery, effusive, and full of reminiscences of drinking bouts, but quick to take his leave when he discovers that something more serious than a party is about to occur. The action, too, is poised on a delicate line between the general and the particular. The plot is often described as an archetypal journey through life, but it is actually not quite so general; it suggests the whole of life through focusing sharply upon its end. The story becomes not only a parable of all human lives but a moving and personal study in one man's experience. Even the jogtrot language, at first distracting, comes to have a crude, direct power that is very moving.

Paradoxically, *Everyman*, which seems so quintessentially of its age, has had a long and prominent history on the modern stage and has exercised a considerable influence upon modern drama. William Poel restaged the play in London in 1901 in the medieval manner; the revival attracted much favorable attention and was repeated a number of times during the following fifteen years. The great German director Max Reinhardt was inspired by Poel's production to present his own version, adapted by the poet and playwright Hugo von Hofmannsthal. Reinhardt's *Jedermann* (German for *Everyman*) was first performed in 1911 in an elaborate production in an old Berlin circus building. In 1920, Reinhardt restaged his version of the play in front of the Salzburg Cathedral as part of the Salzburg Festival. The play was enormously successful and has been repeated every year since then to enormous festival crowds, except for a nine-year dark period between 1937 and 1946, when Hitler banned it as "Jewish." The Dutch version of the play has a similar annual production at the Holland Festival in the city of Delft.

Everyman, along with other pre-realistic plays, has had a strong influence on the development of the postrealistic modern drama, especially as a model for dramatizing inner, psychological action. Its influence is especially clear in two modern plays that also deal with approaching death: Eugene Ionesco's *Exit the King* and Samuel Beckett's *Endgame*.

FURTHER READING *(prepared by W.J.R.):* A discussion of medieval drama, by Joseph A. Dane, is included in *European Writers: Medieval and Renaissance*, Vol. I, ed. George Stade, 1984. A thorough background study of miracle, mystery, and morality plays is Hardin Craig's *English Religious Drama of the Middle Ages*, 1955. In A. P. Rossiter's

English Drama from Early Times to the Elizabethans, 1950, morality plays are divided into two classes, those that view human life from cradle to grave and those that deal with a more specific situation. *The Castle of Perseverance* and *Everyman,* respectively, are discussed as representatives of these two classes, along with several other specimens. Glynne Wickham's *Shakespeare's Dramatic Hentage,* 1969, discusses the 1964 London production of *Everyman,* in which Everyman drifted onto stage wearing jeans and listening to music from the musical *Bye-bye Birdie.* Wickham discusses the persistence of the play's appeal and its ability to survive when transposed to a new setting. The first chapter of W. Roy MacKenzie's *The English Moralities from the Point of View of Allegory,* 1966, discusses the nature of the morality play, specifically considering *Everyman* as its best representative. Two complementary essays on the play's structure, a somewhat neglected topic, are Lawrence V. Ryan's "Doctrine and Dramatic Structure in *Everyman," Speculum,* 32 (1957), 722–35, and Thomas F. Van Laan's "*Everyman:* A Structural Analysis," *PMLA,* 78 (1963), 465–75. Ryan discusses the relationship between structure and doctrinal content, arguing that the play's moral lessons are a natural outgrowth of the action.

EVERYMAN

MESSENGER	KNOWLEDGE
GOD: *Adonai*[1]	CONFESSION
DEATH	BEAUTY
EVERYMAN	STRENGTH
FELLOWSHIP	DISCRETION
COUSIN	FIVE WITS
KINDRED	ANGEL
GOODS	DOCTOR
GOOD DEEDS	

Here beginneth a treatise how the High Father of Heaven sendeth Death to summon every creature to come and give account of their lives in this world, and is in manner of a moral play.

MESSENGER. I pray you all give your audience,
　　And hear this matter with reverence,
　　By figure[2] a moral play—
　　The *Summoning of Everyman* called it is,
　　That of our lives and ending shows   5
　　How transitory we be all our day.
　　This matter is wondrous precious,
　　But the intent of it is more gracious,[3]
　　And sweet to bear away.
　　The story saith:—Man, in the beginning,   10
　　Look well, and take good heed to the ending,
　　Be you never so gay!
　　Ye think sin in the beginning full sweet,

---

[1] Hebrew name for God.   [2] In form.   [3] Having to do with God's grace.

Which in the end causeth the soul to weep,
When the body lieth in clay. 15
Here shall you see how Fellowship and Jollity,
Both Strength, Pleasure, and Beauty,
Will fade from thee as flower in May.
For ye shall hear how our Heaven King
Calleth Everyman to a general reckoning. 20
Give audience, and hear what he doth say. [*Exit.*]

[GOD *speaketh from above.*]

GOD. I perceive, here in my majesty,
How that all creatures be to me unkind,
Living without dread in worldly prosperity.
Of ghostly sight[4] the people be so blind, 25
Drowned in sin, they know me not for their God.
In worldly riches is all their mind,
They fear not my rightwiseness,[5] the sharp rod;
My love that I showed when I for them died
They forget clean, and shedding of my blood red; 30
I hanged between two, it cannot be denied;
To get them life I suffered to be dead;
I healed their feet, with thorns hurt was my head.
I could do no more than I did, truly;
And now I see the people do clean forsake me. 35
They use the seven deadly sins damnable;
As pride, covetise, wrath, and lechery,
Now in the world be made commendable;
And thus they leave of angels the heavenly company.
Every man liveth so after his own pleasure, 40
And yet of their life they be nothing sure.
I see the more that I them forbear
The worse they be from year to year;
All that liveth appaireth[6] fast.
Therefore I will, in all the haste, 45
Have a reckoning of every man's person;
For, and[7] I leave the people thus alone
In their life and wicked tempests,
Verily they will become much worse than beasts;
For now one would by envy another up eat; 50
Charity they all do clean forget.
I hoped well that every man
In my glory should make his mansion,
And thereto I had them all elect;
But now I see, like traitors deject,[8] 55
They thank me not for the pleasure that I to them meant,
Nor yet for their being that I them have lent.

---

[4]Spiritual insight.   [5]Righteousness.   [6]Degenerates.
[7]If (frequently throughout the play).   [8]Abject.

I proffered the people great multitude of mercy,
And few there be that asketh it heartily;
They be so cumbered with worldly riches,   60
That needs on them I must do justice,
On every man living, without fear.
Where art thou, Death, thou mighty messenger?

[*Enter* DEATH.]

DEATH. Almighty God, I am here at your will,
   Your commandment to fulfil.   65
GOD. Go thou to Everyman,
   And show him, in my name,
   A pilgrimage he must on him take,
   Which he in no wise[9] may escape;
   And that he bring with him a sure reckoning   70
   Without delay or any tarrying.
DEATH. Lord, I will in the world go run over all,
   And cruelly out search both great and small.   [GOD *withdraws.*]
   Every man will I beset that liveth beastly
   Out of God's laws, and dreadeth not folly.   75
   He that loveth riches I will strike with my dart,
   His sight to blind, and from heaven to depart,
   Except that alms be his good friend,
   In hell for to dwell, world without end.
   Lo, yonder I see Everyman walking;   80
   Full little he thinketh on my coming;
   His mind is on fleshly lusts and his treasure;
   And great pain it shall cause him to endure
   Before the Lord, Heaven King.
   Everyman, stand still! Whither art thou going   85
   Thus gaily? Hast thou thy Maker forgot?
EVERYMAN. Why askest thou?
   Wouldst thou wete?[10]
DEATH. Yea, sir, I will show you;
   In great haste I am sent to thee   90
   From God out of his Majesty.
EVERYMAN. What, sent to me?
DEATH. Yea, certainly.
   Though thou have forgot him here,
   He thinketh on thee in the heavenly sphere,   95
   As, ere we depart, thou shalt know.
EVERYMAN. What desireth God of me?
DEATH. That shall I show thee;
   A reckoning he will needs have
   Without any longer respite.   100
EVERYMAN. To give a reckoning longer leisure I crave;
   This blind matter troubleth my wit.

[9]In no way (frequently throughout the play).   [10]Know.

DEATH. On thee thou must take a long journey;
  Therefore thy book of count[11] with thee thou bring;
  For turn again thou can not by no way. 105
  And look thou be sure of thy reckoning,
  For before God thou shalt answer and show
  Thy many bad deeds, and good but a few,
  How thou hast spent thy life, and in what wise,
  Before the Chief Lord of paradise. 110
  Have ado[12] that we were in that way,
  For, wete thou well, thou shalt make none attorney.[13]
EVERYMAN. Full unready I am such reckoning to give.
  I know thee not. What messenger art thou?
DEATH. I am Death, that no man dreadeth. 115
  For every man I 'rest, and no man spareth;
  For it is God's commandment
  That all to me should be obedient.
EVERYMAN. O Death! thou comest when I had thee least in mind!
  In thy power it lieth me to save,
  Yet of my goods will I give thee, if thou will be kind; 120
  Yea, a thousand pound shalt thou have,
  If thou defer this matter till another day.
DEATH. Everyman, it may not be, by no way!
  I set not by gold, silver, nor riches,
  Nor by pope, emperor, king, duke, nor princes. 125
  For, and I would receive gifts great,
  All the world I might get;
  But my custom is clean contrary.
  I give thee no respite. Come hence, and not tarry. 130
EVERYMAN. Alas! shall I have no longer respite?
  I may say Death giveth no warning.
  To think on thee, it maketh my heart sick,
  For all unready is my book of reckoning.
  But twelve year and I might have abiding, 135
  My counting-book I would make so clear,
  That my reckoning I should not need to fear.
  Wherefore, Death, I pray thee, for God's mercy,
  Spare me till I be provided of remedy.
DEATH. Thee availeth not to cry, weep, and pray; 140
  But haste thee lightly that thou were gone that journey,
  And prove thy friends if thou can.
  For wete thou well the tide abideth no man;
  And in the world each living creature
  For Adam's sin must die of nature. 145
EVERYMAN. Death, if I should this pilgrimage take,
  And my reckoning surely make,
  Show me, for saint charity,
  Should I not come again shortly?

---

[11]Accounts.   [12]Get ready.   [13]You cannot make anyone your representative.

DEATH. No, Everyman; and thou be once there,   150
    Thou mayst never more come here,
    Trust me verily.
EVERYMAN. O gracious God, in the high seat celestial,
    Have mercy on me in this most need!
    Shall I have no company from this vale terrestrial   155
    Of mine acquaintance that way me to lead?
DEATH. Yea, if any be so hardy,
    That would go with thee and bear thee company.
    Hie thee that thou were gone[14] to God's magnificence,
    Thy reckoning to give before his presence.   160
    What! weenest[15] thou thy life is given thee,
    And thy worldly goods also?
EVERYMAN. I had weened so, verily.
DEATH. Nay, nay; it was but lent thee;
    For, as soon as thou art gone,   165
    Another a while shall have it, and then go therefrom
    Even as thou hast done.
    Everyman, thou art mad! Thou hast thy wits[16] five,
    And here on earth will not amend thy life;
    For suddenly I do come.   170
EVERYMAN. O wretched caitiff![17] whither shall I flee,
    That I might 'scape endless sorrow?
    Now, gentle Death, spare me till tomorrow,
    That I may amend me
    With good advisement.   175
DEATH. Nay, thereto I will not consent,
    Nor no man will I respite,
    But to the heart suddenly I shall smite
    Without any advisement.
    And now out of thy sight I will me hie;   180
    See thou make thee ready shortly,
    For thou mayst say this is the day
    That no man living may 'scape away.   [*Exit* DEATH.]
EVERYMAN. Alas! I may well weep with sighs deep.
    Now have I no manner of company   185
    To help me in my journey and me to keep;
    And also my writing is full unready.
    How shall I do now for to excuse me?
    I would to God I had never been gete![18]
    To my soul a full great profit it had be;   190
    For now I fear pains huge and great.
    The time passeth; Lord, help, that all wrought.
    For though I mourn it availeth naught.
    The day passeth, and is almost a-go;[19]
    I wot[20] not well what for to do.   195

---

[14]Hasten to be gone.   [15]Thinkest.   [16]Senses.   [17]Knave.
[18]Born.   [19]Gone.   [20]Know.

To whom were I best my complaint to make?
What if I to Fellowship thereof spake,
And showed him of this sudden chance?
For in him is all mine affiance,[21]
We have in the world so many a day   200
Been good friends in sport and play.
I see him yonder, certainly;
I trust that he will bear me company;
Therefore to him will I speak to ease my sorrow.
Well met, good Fellowship, and good morrow!   205

[FELLOWSHIP *speaketh.*]

FELLOWSHIP. Everyman, good morrow, by this day!
 Sir, why lookest thou so piteously?
 If any thing be amiss, I pray thee me say,
 That I may help to remedy.
EVERYMAN. Yea, good Fellowship, yea,   210
 I am in great jeopardy.
FELLOWSHIP. My true friend, show to me your mind;
 I will not forsake thee to my life's end
 In the way of good company.
EVERYMAN. That was well spoken, and lovingly.   215
FELLOWSHIP. Sir, I must needs know your heaviness;
 I have pity to see you in any distress;
 If any have you wronged, ye shall revenged be,
 Though I on the ground be slain for thee,
 Though that I know before that I should die.   220
EVERYMAN. Verily, Fellowship, gramercy.[22]
FELLOWSHIP. Tush! by thy thanks I set not a straw!
 Show me your grief, and say no more.
EVERYMAN. If I my heart should to you break,
 And then you to turn your mind from me,   225
 And would not me comfort when you hear me speak,
 Then should I ten times sorrier be.
FELLOWSHIP. Sir, I say as I will do, indeed.
EVERYMAN. Then be you a good friend at need;
 I have found you true here before.   230
FELLOWSHIP. And so ye shall evermore;
 For, in faith, and thou go to hell,
 I will not forsake thee by the way!
EVERYMAN. Ye speak like a good friend. I believe you well;
 I shall deserve it, and I may.   235
FELLOWSHIP. I speak of no deserving, by this day!
 For he that will say and nothing do
 Is not worthy with good company to go;
 Therefore show me the grief of your mind,
 As to your friend most loving and kind.   240

[21] Trust.   [22] Thank you.

EVERYMAN. I shall show you how it is:
    Commanded I am to go a journey,
    A long way, hard and dangerous,
    And give a strict count without delay
    Before the high judge, Adonai. 245
    Wherefore, I pray you, bear me company,
    As ye have promised, in this journey.
FELLOWSHIP. That is matter indeed! Promise is duty;
    But, and I should take such a voyage on me,
    I know it well, it should be to my pain. 250
    Also it maketh me afeared, certain.
    But let us take counsel here as well as we can,
    For your words would fright a strong man.
EVERYMAN. Why, ye said if I had need,
    Ye would me never forsake, quick nor dead, 255
    Though it were to hell, truly.
FELLOWSHIP. So I said, certainly,
    But such pleasures be set aside, the sooth[23] to say.
    And also, if we took such a journey,
    When should we come again? 260
EVERYMAN. Nay, never again till the day of doom.
FELLOWSHIP. In faith, then will not I come there!
    Who hath you these tidings brought?
EVERYMAN. Indeed, Death was with me here.
FELLOWSHIP. Now, by God that all hath bought, 265
    If Death were the messenger,
    For no man that is living today
    I will not go that loath journey—
    Nor for the father that begat me!
EVERYMAN. Ye promised otherwise, pardie.[24] 270
FELLOWSHIP. I wot well I said so, truly;
    And yet if thou wilt eat, and drink, and make good cheer,
    Or haunt to women the lusty company,
    I would not forsake you while the day is clear,
    Trust me verily! 275
EVERYMAN. Yea, thereto ye would be ready;
    To go to mirth, solace, and play,
    Your mind will sooner apply
    Than to bear me company in my long journey.
FELLOWSHIP. Now, in good faith, I will not that way. 280
    But and thou wilt murder, or any man kill,
    In that I will help thee with a good will!
EVERYMAN. O, that is a simple advice indeed!
    Gentle fellow, help me in my necessity;
    We have loved long, and now I need, 285
    And now, gentle Fellowship, remember me!
FELLOWSHIP. Whether ye have loved me or no,
    By Saint John, I will not with thee go.

[23] Truth.   [24] *Par dieu:* indeed. (Literally, "by God.")s

EVERYMAN. Yet, I pray thee, take the labor, and do so much for me
   To bring me forward, for saint charity,   290
   And comfort me till I come without the town.
FELLOWSHIP. Nay, and thou would give me a new gown,
   I will not a foot with thee go;
   But, and thou had tarried, I would not have left thee so.
   And as now God speed thee in thy journey,   295
   For from thee I will depart as fast as I may.
EVERYMAN. Whither away, Fellowship? Will you forsake me?
FELLOWSHIP. Yea, by my fay,[25] to God I betake[26] thee.
EVERYMAN. Farewell, good Fellowship! For thee my heart is sore;
   Adieu for ever! I shall see thee no more.   300
FELLOWSHIP. In faith, Everyman, farewell now at the end!
   For you I will remember that parting is mourning.

                [*Exit* FELLOWSHIP.]

EVERYMAN. Alack! shall we thus depart indeed
   (Ah, Lady, help!) without any more comfort?
   Lo, Fellowship forsaketh me in my most need.   305
   For help in this world whither shall I resort?
   Fellowship here before with me would merry make,
   And now little sorrow for me doth he take.
   It is said, "In prosperity men friends may find,
   Which in adversity be full unkind."   310
   Now whither for succor shall I flee,
   Sith that[27] Fellowship hath forsaken me?
   To my kinsmen I will, truly,
   Praying them to help me in my necessity;
   I believe that they will do so,   315
   For "kind will creep where it may not go."[28]
   I will go say,[29] for yonder I see them go.
   Where be ye now, my friends and kinsmen?

             [*Enter* KINDRED *and* COUSIN.]

KINDRED. Here be we now, at your commandment.
   Cousin, I pray you show us your intent   320
   In any wise, and do not spare.
COUSIN. Yea, Everyman, and to us declare
   If ye be disposed to go any whither,
   For, wete you well, we will live and die together.
KINDRED. In wealth and woe we will with you hold,   325
   For over his kin a man may be bold.
EVERYMAN. Gramercy, my friends and kinsmen kind.
   Now shall I show you the grief of my mind.
   I was commanded by a messenger
   That is a high king's chief officer;   330
   He bade me go a pilgrimage, to my pain,

---

[25]Faith.   [26]Commit.   [27]Since.   [28]Walk.   [29]Try.

And I know well I shall never come again;
Also I must give a reckoning straight,
For I have a great enemy that hath me in wait,[30]
Which intendeth me for to hinder.   335
KINDRED. What account is that which ye must render?
  That would I know.
EVERYMAN. Of all my works I must show
  How I have lived, and my days spent;
  Also of ill deeds that I have used   340
  In my time, sith life was me lent;
  And of all virtues that I have refused.
  Therefore I pray you go thither with me,
  To help to make mine account, for saint charity.
COUSIN. What, to go thither? Is that the matter?   345
  Nay, Everyman, I had liefer fast bread and water
  All this five year and more.
EVERYMAN. Alas, that ever I was bore!
  For now shall I never be merry
  If that you forsake me.   350
KINDRED. Ah, sir, what! Ye be a merry man!
  Take good heart to you, and make no moan.
  But one thing I warn you, by Saint Anne,
  As for me, ye shall go alone.
EVERYMAN. My Cousin, will you not with me go?   355
COUSIN. No, by our Lady! I have the cramp in my toe.
  Trust not to me; for, so God me speed,
  I will deceive you in your most need.
KINDRED. It availeth not us to tice.[31]
  Ye shall have my maid with all my heart;   360
  She loveth to go to feasts, there to be nice,[32]
  And to dance, and abroad to start;
  I will give her leave to help you in that journey,
  If that you and she may agree.
EVERYMAN. Now show me the very effect of your mind.   365
  Will you go with me, or abide behind?
KINDRED. Abide behind? Yea, that will I, and I may!
  Therefore farewell till another day.   [*Exit* KINDRED.]
EVERYMAN. How should I be merry or glad?
  For fair promises men to me make,   370
  But when I have most need, they me forsake.
  I am deceived; that maketh me sad.
COUSIN. Cousin Everyman, farewell now,
  For verily I will not go with you;
  Also of mine own life an unready reckoning   375
  I have to account; therefore I make tarrying.
  Now, God keep thee, for now I go.   [*Exit* COUSIN.]
EVERYMAN. Ah, Jesus! is all come hereto?

---

[30] Lies in wait for me.   [31] Entice.   [32] Wanton.

Lo, fair words maketh fools fain;[33]
They promise and nothing will do certain. 380
My kinsmen promised me faithfully
For to abide with me steadfastly,
And now fast away do they flee.
Even so Fellowship promised me.
What friend were best me of to provide? 385
I lose my time here longer to abide.
Yet in my mind a thing there is:
All my life I have loved riches;
If that my Goods now help me might,
He would make my heart full light. 390
I will speak to him in this distress.
Where art thou, my Goods and riches?
GOODS [*from within*]. Who calleth me? Everyman? What, hast thou haste?
I lie here in corners, trussed and piled so high,
And in chests I am locked so fast, 395
Also sacked in bags—thou mayst see with thine eye—
I cannot stir; in packs low I lie.
What would ye have? Lightly me say.
EVERYMAN. Come hither, Goods, in all the haste thou may.
For of counsel I must desire thee. 400

[*Enter* GOODS.]

GOODS. Sir, and ye in the world have sorrow or adversity,
That can I help you to remedy shortly.
EVERYMAN. It is another disease that grieveth me;
In this world it is not, I tell thee so.
I am sent for another way to go, 405
To give a strict count general
Before the highest Jupiter of all;
And all my life I have had joy and pleasure in thee;
Therefore I pray thee go with me,
For, peradventure,[34] thou mayst before God Almighty 410
My reckoning help to clean and purify;
For it is said ever among,
That "money maketh all right that is wrong."
GOODS. Nay, Everyman; I sing another song,
I follow no man in such voyages; 415
For, and I went with thee,
Thou shouldst fare much the worse for me;
For because on me thou did set thy mind,
Thy reckoning I have made blotted and blind,
That thine account thou cannot make truly; 420
And that hast thou for the love of me.

---

[33]Glad.   [34]Perhaps.

EVERYMAN. That would grieve me full sore,
  When I should come to that fearful answer.
  Up, let us go thither together.
GOODS. Nay, not so! I am too brittle, I may not endure;   425
  I will follow no man one foot, be ye sure.
EVERYMAN. Alas! I have thee loved, and had great pleasure
  All my life-days on goods and treasure.
GOODS. That is to thy damnation, without lesing![35]
  For my love is contrary to the love everlasting.   430
  But if thou had me loved moderately during,
  As to the poor to give part of me,
  Then shouldst thou not in this dolor be,
  Nor in this great sorrow and care.
EVERYMAN. Lo, now was I deceived ere I was ware,   435
  And all I may wyte[36] my spending of time.
GOODS. What, weenest thou that I am thine?
EVERYMAN. I had weened so.
GOODS. Nay, Everyman, I say no;
  As for a while I was lent thee,   440
  A season thou hast had me in prosperity.
  My condition is man's soul to kill;
  If I save one, a thousand I do spill;[37]
  Weenest thou that I will follow thee
  From this world? Nay, verily.   445
EVERYMAN. I had weened otherwise.
GOODS. Therefore to thy soul Goods is a thief;
  For when thou art dead, this is my guise—[38]
  Another to deceive in the same wise
  As I have done thee, and all to his soul's reprief.[39]   450
EVERYMAN. O false Goods, curséd thou be!
  Thou traitor to God, that hast deceived me
  And caught me in thy snare.
GOODS. Marry! thou brought thyself in care,
  Whereof I am right glad.   455
  I must needs laugh, I cannot be sad.
EVERYMAN. Ah, Goods, thou hast had long my heartly love;
  I gave thee that which should be the Lord's above.
  But wilt thou not go with me indeed?
  I pray thee truth to say.   460
GOODS. No, so God me speed!
  Therefore farewell, and have good day.   [Exit GOODS.]
EVERYMAN. O, to whom shall I make my moan
  For to go with me in that heavy journey?
  First Fellowship said he would with me gone;   465
  His words were very pleasant and gay,
  But afterward he left me alone.
  Then spake I to my kinsmen, all in despair,
  And also they gave me words fair,

---

[35]Lying.   [36]Blame upon.   [37]Ruin.   [38]Practice; trick.   [39]Reproof.

They lacked no fair speaking, 470
But all forsook me in the ending.
Then went I to my Goods, that I loved best,
In hope to have comfort, but there had I least;
For my Goods sharply did me tell
That he bringeth many into hell. 475
Then of myself I was ashamed,
And so I am worthy to be blamed;
Thus may I well myself hate.
Of whom shall I now counsel take?
I think that I shall never speed 480
Till that I go to my Good Deeds.
But alas! she is so weak
That she can neither go nor speak.
Yet will I venture on her now.
My Good Deeds, where be you? 485

[GOOD DEEDS *speaks from the ground.*]

GOOD DEEDS. Here I lie, cold in the ground.
Thy sins hath me sore bound,
That I cannot stir.
EVERYMAN. O Good Deeds! I stand in fear;
I must you pray of counsel, 490
For help now should come right well.
GOOD DEEDS. Everyman, I have understanding
That ye be summoned account to make
Before Messias, of Jerusalem King;
And you do by me,[40] that journey with you will I take. 495
EVERYMAN. Therefore I come to you my moan to make;
I pray you that ye will go with me.
GOOD DEEDS. I would full fain, but I cannot stand, verily.
EVERYMAN. Why, is there anything on you fall?
GOOD DEEDS. Yea, sir, I may thank you of all; 500
If ye had perfectly cheered[41] me,
Your book of count full ready had be.
Look, the books of your works and deeds eke;[42]
Ah, see how they lie under the feet,
To your soul's heaviness. 505
EVERYMAN. Our Lord Jesus help me!
For one letter here I can not see.
GOOD DEEDS. There is a blind reckoning in time of distress!
EVERYMAN. Good Deeds, I pray you, help me in this need,
Or else I am for ever damned indeed; 510
Therefore help me to make my reckoning
Before the Redeemer of all thing,
That King is, and was, and ever shall.
GOOD DEEDS. Everyman, I am sorry of your fall,
And fain would I help you, and I were able. 515
EVERYMAN. Good Deeds, your counsel I pray you give me.

[40]If you take my advice.   [41]Cherished.   [42]Also.

GOOD DEEDS. That shall I do verily;
  Though that on my feet I may not go,
  I have a sister that shall with you also,
  Called Knowledge, which shall with you abide,   520
  To help you to make that dreadful reckoning.

                    [*Enter* KNOWLEDGE.]

KNOWLEDGE. Everyman, I will go with thee, and be thy guide
  In thy most need to go by thy side.
EVERYMAN. In good condition I am now in every thing,
  And am wholly content with this good thing;   525
  Thanked be God my Creator.
GOOD DEEDS. And when he hath brought thee there,
  Where thou shalt heal thee of thy smart,
  Then go you with your reckoning and your Good Deeds together
  For to make you joyful at heart   530
  Before the blesséd Trinity.
EVERYMAN. My Good Deeds, gramercy!
  I am well content, certainly,
  With your words sweet.
KNOWLEDGE. Now go we together lovingly   535
  To Confession, that cleansing river.
EVERYMAN. For joy I weep; I would we were there!
  But, I pray you, give my cognition
  Where dwelleth that holy man, Confession.
KNOWLEDGE. In the house of salvation;   540
  We shall find him in that place,
  That shall us comfort, by God's grace.

                [KNOWLEDGE *leads* EVERYMAN *to*
                CONFESSION.]

Lo, this is Confession. Kneel down and ask mercy,
  For he is in good conceit[43] with God almighty.
EVERYMAN [*kneeling*]. O glorious fountain, that all uncleanness doth
    clarify,   545
  Wash from me the spots of vice unclean,
  That on me no sin may be seen.
  I come, with Knowledge, for my redemption,
  Redempt with hearty and full contrition;
  For I am commanded a pilgrimage to take,   550
  And great accounts before God to make.
  Now, I pray you, Shrift,[44] mother of salvation.
  Help my Good Deeds for my piteous exclamation.
CONFESSION. I know your sorrow well, Everyman.
  Because with Knowledge ye come to me,   555
  I will you comfort as well as I can,
  And a precious jewel I will give thee,
  Called penance, voider of adversity;

---

[43] Esteem.   [44] The sacrament of confession.

Therewith shall your body chastised be,
With abstinence, and perseverance in God's service.   560
Here shall you receive that scourge of me.

[*Gives* EVERYMAN *a scourge.*]

Which is penance strong, that ye must endure
To remember thy Savior was scourged for thee
With sharp scourges, and suffered it patiently;
So must thou ere thou 'scape that painful pilgrimage.   565
Knowledge, keep him in this voyage,
And by that time Good Deeds will be with thee.
But in any wise be seeker of mercy,
For your time draweth fast, and ye will saved be;
Ask God mercy, and He will grant truly;   570
When with the scourge of penance man doth him bind,
The oil of forgiveness then shall he find.   [*Exit* CONFESSION.]
EVERYMAN. Thanked be God for his gracious work!
For now I will my penance begin;
This hath rejoiced and lighted my heart,   575
Though the knots be painful and hard within.
KNOWLEDGE. Everyman, look your penance that ye fulfil,
What pain that ever it to you be,
And Knowledge shall give you counsel at will
How your account ye shall make clearly.   580

[EVERYMAN *kneels.*]

EVERYMAN. O eternal God! O heavenly figure!
O way of rightwiseness! O goodly vision!
Which descended down in a virgin pure
Because he would Everyman redeem,
Which Adam forfeited by his disobedience.   585
O blesséd Godhead! elect and high divine,
Forgive me my grievous offence;
Here I cry thee mercy in this presence.
O ghostly treasure! O ransomer and redeemer!
Of all the world hope and conductor,   590
Mirror of joy, and founder of mercy,
Which illumineth heaven and earth thereby,
Hear my clamorous complaint, though it late be.
Receive my prayers; unworthy in this heavy life.
Though I be a sinner most abominable,   595
Yet let my name be written in Moses' table.
O Mary! pray to the Maker of all thing,
Me for to help at my ending,
And save me from the power of my enemy,
For Death assaileth me strongly.   600
And, Lady, that I may by means of thy prayer
Of your Son's glory to be partner,
By the means of his passion I it crave;
I beseech you, help my soul to save.   [*He rises.*]

Knowledge, give me the scourge of penance. 605
My flesh therewith shall give a quittance.
I will now begin, if God give me grace.
KNOWLEDGE. Everyman, God give you time and space.
Thus I bequeath you in the hands of our Savior,
Now may you make your reckoning sure. 610
EVERYMAN. In the name of the Holy Trinity,
My body sore punished shall be.   [*Scourges himself.*]
Take this, body, for the sin of the flesh;
Also thou delightest to go gay and fresh,
And in the way of damnation thou did me bring; 615
Therefore suffer now strokes of punishing.
Now of penance I will wade the water clear,
To save me from purgatory, that sharp fire.

                   [GOOD DEEDS *rises from floor.*]

GOOD DEEDS. I thank God, now I can walk and go,
And am delivered of my sickness and woe. 620
Therefore with Everyman I will go, and not spare;
His good works I will help him to declare.
KNOWLEDGE. Now, Everyman, be merry and glad!
Your Good Deeds cometh now, ye may not be sad;
Now is your Good Deeds whole and sound, 625
Going upright upon the ground.
EVERYMAN. My heart is light, and shall be evermore.
Now will I smite faster than I did before.
GOOD DEEDS. Everyman, pilgrim, my special friend,
Blesséd be thou without end. 630
For thee is prepared the eternal glory.
Ye have me made whole and sound,
Therefore I will bide by thee in every stound.[45]
EVERYMAN. Welcome, my Good Deeds; now I hear thy voice,
I weep for very sweetness of love. 635
KNOWLEDGE. Be no more sad, but ever rejoice;
God seeth thy living in his throne above.
Put on this garment to thy behoof,
Which is wet with your tears,
Or else before God you may it miss, 640
When you to your journey's end come shall.
EVERYMAN. Gentle Knowledge, what do ye it call?
KNOWLEDGE. It is the garment of sorrow;
From pain it will you borrow;
Contrition it is 645
That getteth forgiveness;
It pleaseth God passing well.
GOOD DEEDS. Everyman, will you wear it for your heal?

---

[45] In every situation; always.

[EVERYMAN *puts on garment of contrition.*]

EVERYMAN. Now blesséd be Jesu, Mary's Son,
For now have I on true contrition. 650
And let us go now without tarrying;
Good Deeds, have we clear our reckoning?
GOOD DEEDS. Yea, indeed I have it here.
EVERYMAN. Then I trust we need not fear.
Now, friends, let us not part in twain. 655
KNOWLEDGE. Nay, Everyman, that will we not, certain.
GOOD DEEDS. Yet must thou lead with thee
Three persons of great might.
EVERYMAN. Who should they be?
GOOD DEEDS. Discretion and Strength they hight,[46] 660
And thy Beauty may not abide behind.
KNOWLEDGE. Also ye must call to mind
Your Five Wits as for your counselors.
GOOD DEEDS. You must have them ready at all hours.
EVERYMAN. How shall I get them hither? 665
KNOWLEDGE. You must call them all together,
And they will hear you incontinent.[47]
EVERYMAN. My friends, come hither and be present;
Discretion, Strength, my Five Wits, and Beauty.

[*Enter* DISCRETION, STRENGTH, FIVE
WITS, *and* BEAUTY.]

BEAUTY. Here at your will we be all ready. 670
What will ye that we should do?
GOOD DEEDS. That ye would with Everyman go,
And help him in his pilgrimage.
Advise you, will ye with him or not in that voyage?
STRENGTH. We will bring him all thither, 675
To his help and comfort, ye may believe me.
DISCRETION. So will we go with him all together.
EVERYMAN. Almighty God, lovéd may thou be!
I give thee laud that I have hither brought
Strength, Discretion, Beauty, and Five Wits. Lack I naught; 680
And my Good Deeds, with Knowledge clear,
All be in company at my will here.
I desire no more to my business.
STRENGTH. And I, Strength, will by you stand in distress,
Though thou would in battle fight on the ground. 685
FIVE WITS. And though it were through the world round,
We will not depart for sweet nor sour.
BEAUTY. No more will I, unto death's hour,
Whatsoever thereof befall.

[46]Are called.   [47]At once.

DISCRETION. Everyman, advise you first of all;   690
    Go with a good advisement and deliberation.
    We all give you virtuous monition
    That all shall be well.
EVERYMAN. My friends, hearken what I will tell:
    I pray God reward you in his heavenly sphere.   695
    Now hearken, all that be here,
    For I will make my testament
    Here before you all present:
    In alms half my goods I will give with my hands twain
    In the way of charity, with good intent,   700
    And the other half still shall remain;
    I it bequeath to be returned there it ought to be.
    This I do in despite of the fiend of hell,
    To go quite out of his peril
    Ever after and this day.   705
KNOWLEDGE. Everyman, hearken what I say;
    Go to Priesthood, I you advise,
    And receive of him in any wise
    The holy sacrament and ointment together;
    Then shortly see ye turn again hither;   710
    We will all abide you here.
FIVE WITS. Yea, Everyman, hie you that ye ready were.
    There is no emperor, king, duke, nor baron,
    That of God hath commission
    As hath the least priest in the world being;   715
    For of the blesséd sacraments pure and benign
    He beareth the keys, and thereof hath the cure
    For man's redemption—it is ever sure—
    Which God for our soul's medicine
    Gave us out of his heart with great pain,   720
    Here in this transitory life, for thee and me.
    The blesséd sacraments seven there be:
    Baptism, confirmation, with priesthood good,
    And the sacrament of God's precious flesh and blood,
    Marriage, the holy extreme unction, and penance.   725
    These seven be good to have in remembrance,
    Gracious sacraments of high divinity.
EVERYMAN. Fain would I receive that holy body
    And meekly to my ghostly[48] father I will go.
FIVE WITS. Everyman, that is the best that ye can do.   730
    God will you to salvation bring,
    For priesthood exceedeth all other thing;
    To us Holy Scripture they do teach,
    And converteth man from sin, heaven to reach;
    God hath to them more power given,   735
    Than to any angel that is in heaven.

[48] Spiritual.

With five words[49] he may consecrate
God's body in flesh and blood to make,
And handleth his Maker between his hands.
The priest bindeth and unbindeth all bands,   740
Both in earth and in heaven;
Thou ministers all the sacraments seven;
Though we kissed thy feet, thou wert worthy;
Thou art the surgeon that cureth sin deadly:
No remedy we find under God   745
But all only priesthood.
Everyman, God gave priests that dignity,
And setteth them in his stead among us to be;
Thus be they above angels, in degree.

[*Exit* EVERYMAN.]

KNOWLEDGE. If priests be good, it is so, surely.   750
But when Jesus hanged on the cross with great smart,
There he gave out of his blessèd heart
The same sacrament in great torment.
He sold them not to us, that Lord omnipotent.
Therefore Saint Peter the Apostle doth say   755
That Jesus' curse hath all they
Which God their Savior do buy or sell,
Or they for any money do take or tell.
Sinful priests giveth the sinners example bad;
Their children sitteth by other men's fires, I have heard;   760
And some haunteth women's company
With unclean life, as lusts of lechery.
These be with sin made blind.
FIVE WITS. I trust to God no such may we find.
Therefore let us priesthood honor,   765
And follow their doctrine for our souls' succor.
We be their sheep, and they shepherds be
By whom we all be kept in surety.
Peace! for yonder I see Everyman come,
Which hath made true satisfaction.   770
GOOD DEEDS. Methinketh it is he indeed.

[*Re-enter* EVERYMAN.]

EVERYMAN. Now Jesu be your alder speed.[50]
I have received the sacrament for my redemption,
And then mine extreme unction.
Blessèd be all they that counseled me to take it!   775
And now, friends, let us go without longer respite.
I thank God that ye have tarried so long.

---

[49] The five words are *Hoc est enim corpus meum:* "For this is my body."
[50] Jesus be the succor of all of you.

Now set each of you on this rod[51] your hand,
And shortly follow me.
I go before, there I would be. God be our guide.   780
STRENGTH. Everyman, we will not from you go,
Till ye have done this voyage long.
DISCRETION. I, Discretion, will bide by you also.
KNOWLEDGE. And though this pilgrimage be never so strong,
I will never part you fro.   785
Everyman, I will be as sure by thee
As ever I did by Judas Maccabee.[52]

[*They go together to the grave.*]

EVERYMAN. Alas! I am so faint I may not stand,
My limbs under me do fold.
Friends, let us not turn again to this land,   790
Not for all the world's gold;
For into this cave must I creep
And turn to earth, and there to sleep.
BEAUTY. What, into this grave? Alas!
EVERYMAN. Yea, there shall you consume, more and less.   795
BEAUTY. And what, should I smother here?
EVERYMAN. Yea, by my faith, and never more appear.
In this world live no more we shall,
But in heaven before the highest Lord of all.
BEAUTY. I cross out all this; adieu, by Saint John!   800
I take my cap in my lap and am gone.
EVERYMAN. What, Beauty, whither will ye?
BEAUTY. Peace! I am deaf. I look not behind me,
Not and thou would give me all the gold in thy chest. [*Exit* BEAUTY.]
EVERYMAN. Alas, whereto may I trust?   805
Beauty goeth fast away from me;
She promised with me to live and die.
STRENGTH. Everyman, I will thee also forsake and deny.
Thy game liketh me not at all.[53]
EVERYMAN. Why, then ye will forsake me all?   810
Sweet Strength, tarry a little space.
STRENGTH. Nay, sir, by the rood[54] of grace,
I will hie me from thee fast,
Though thou weep till thy heart to-brast.[55]
EVERYMAN. Ye would ever bide by me, ye said.   815
STRENGTH. Yea, I have you far enough conveyed.
Ye be old enough, I understand,
Your pilgrimage to take on hand.
I repent me that I hither came.
EVERYMAN. Strength, you to displease I am to blame;   820
Yet promise is debt, this ye well wot.

---

[51]Cross.   [52]Jewish patriot, second century B.C.
[53]I do not like this game at all.   [54]Cross.   [55]Break into pieces.

STRENGTH. In faith, I care not!
  Thou are but a fool to complain.
  You spend your speech and waste your brain;
  Go, thrust thee into the ground.   [*Exit* STRENGTH.]   825
EVERYMAN. I had weened surer I should you have found.
  He that trusteth in his Strength
  She him deceiveth at the length.
  Both Strength and Beauty forsaketh me,
  Yet they promised me fair and lovingly.   830
DISCRETION. Everyman, I will after Strength be gone;
  As for me I will leave you alone.
EVERYMAN. Why, Discretion, will ye forsake me?
DISCRETION. Yea, in faith, I will go from thee;
  For when Strength goeth before   835
  I follow after evermore.
EVERYMAN. Yet, I pray thee, for the love of the Trinity,
  Look in my grave once piteously.
DISCRETION. Nay, so nigh will I not come.
  Farewell, every one!   [*Exit* DISCRETION.]   840
EVERYMAN. O all thing faileth, save God alone—
  Beauty, Strength, and Discretion;
  For when Death bloweth his blast,
  They all run from me full fast.
FIVE WITS. Everyman, my leave now of thee I take;   845
  I will follow the other, for here I thee forsake.
EVERYMAN. Alas! then may I wail and weep,
  For I took you for my best friend.
FIVE WITS. I will no longer thee keep;
  Now farewell, and there an end.   [*Exit* FIVE WITS.]   850
EVERYMAN. O Jesu, help! All hath forsaken me!
GOOD DEEDS. Nay, Everyman; I will bide with thee,
  I will not forsake thee indeed;
  Thou shalt find me a good friend at need.
EVERYMAN. Gramercy, Good Deeds! Now may I true friends see.   855
  They have forsaken me, every one;
  I loved them better than my Good Deeds alone.
  Knowledge, will ye forsake me also?
KNOWLEDGE. Yea, Everyman, when ye to death shall go;
  But not yet, for no manner of danger.   860
EVERYMAN. Gramercy, Knowledge, with all my heart.
KNOWLEDGE. Nay, yet I will not from hence depart
  Till I see where ye shall be come.
EVERYMAN. Methink, alas, that I must be gone
  To make my reckoning and my debts pay,   865
  For I see my time is nigh spent away.
  Take example, all ye that this do hear or see,
  How they that I loved best do forsake me,
  Except my Good Deeds that bideth truly.
GOOD DEEDS. All earthly things is but vanity.   870
  Beauty, Strength, and Discretion do man forsake,

Foolish friends and kinsmen, that fair spake,
All fleeth save Good Deeds, and that am I.
EVERYMAN. Have mercy on me, God most mighty;
And stand by me, thou Mother and Maid, holy Mary!   875
GOOD DEEDS. Fear not, I will speak for thee.
EVERYMAN. Here I cry God mercy!
GOOD DEEDS. Short our end, and 'minish our pain.
Let us go and never come again.
EVERYMAN. Into thy hands, Lord, my soul I commend.   880
Receive it, Lord, that it be not lost.
As thou me boughtest, so me defend,
And save me from the fiend's boast,
That I may appear with that blessèd host
That shall be saved at the day of doom.   885
In manus tuas—of might's most
For ever—*commendo spiritum meum.*[56]

[EVERYMAN *and* GOOD DEEDS *descend
into the grave.*]

KNOWLEDGE. Now hath he suffered that we all shall endure;
The Good Deeds shall make all sure.
Now hath he made ending.
Methinketh that I hear angels sing   890
And make great joy and melody
Where Everyman's soul received shall be.
ANGEL [*within*]. Come, excellent elect spouse to Jesu!
Here above thou shalt go   895
Because of thy singular virtue.
Now the soul is taken the body fro,
Thy reckoning is crystal clear.
Now shalt thou into the heavenly sphere,
Unto the which all ye shall come   900
That liveth well before the day of doom.

[*Exit* KNOWLEDGE. *Enter* DOCTOR[57]
for Epilogue.]

DOCTOR. This moral men may have in mind:
Ye hearers, take it of worth, old and young,
And forsake Pride, for he deceiveth you in the end,
And remember Beauty, Five Wits, Strength, and Discretion,   905
They all at the last do Everyman forsake,
Save his Good Deeds there doth he take.
But beware, and they be small
Before God he hath no help at all.
None excuse may be there for Everyman.   910
Alas, how shall he do then?

---

[56]"Into thy hands I commend my spirit."
[57]Theologian.

For, after death, amends may no man make,
For then mercy and pity doth him forsake.
If his reckoning be not clear when he doth come,
God will say, "*Ite, maledicti, in ignem aeternum.*"[58]   915
And he that hath his account whole and sound,
High in heaven he shall be crowned.
Unto which place God bring us all thither,
That we may live body and soul together.
Thereto help the Trinity!   920
Amen, say ye, for saint charity.

THUS ENDETH THIS MORAL PLAY OF EVERYMAN.

[58]"Go, cursed ones, into eternal fire."

The Renaissance

The word *renaissance* means *rebirth*. *Renaissance* purports to describe a movement in European intellectual, cultural, and political history that first flourished in Italy, mainly from the mid-fourteenth to the sixteenth centuries, and then in other parts of Europe during an overlapping but generally later period that ended in the mid-seventeenth century. The origin of the Renaissance, both the concept and the term, is of considerable interest in exploring the question, much debated in the twentieth century, whether there was any genuine rebirth in the Renaissance and whether the movement so labeled really had a distinctive existence.

To many people in the vanguard of Renaissance literature, art, and thought, the age did in fact seem new. The first major spokesman for this view was Petrarch (1304–1374), who believed that the thousand years separating his age from the fall of ancient Roman civilization had been a dark night and that the first priority of his contemporaries should be to restore ancient literature, for its own sake and in the interests of human virtue. His followers, the humanists of Italy and later of northern Europe, extended Petrarch's primarily literary emphasis to include important new directions in the fine arts, religious studies, philosophy, mathematics, and political theory. When the new heliocentric astronomy was developed (or rediscovered) by Copernicus (1473–1543), the new Protestant movement was launched in 1517 by Luther (1483–1546), and maritime exploration in the fifteenth and sixteenth centuries revealed to Europeans the existence of the western hemisphere, the age necessarily became aware that changes of awesome momentousness, for better or worse, were in process. But for the most part the consciousness by the age of its own novelty remained limited and was primarily a matter of high culture. The term *rebirth* was popularized during the Renaissance by the eminent art historian Giorgio Vasari in his *Lives of the Most Eminent Italian Painters, Sculptors, and Architects* (1550), in which Vasari acclaimed the new artists for having revived classical aesthetic values and recovered the faculty to see and depict nature.

The modern, much broader, concept of a Renaissance is largely the creation not of the age itself but of retrospect. To eighteenth-century Enlightenment thinkers the Renaissance was the age when medieval "superstition," especially revealed religion, was overthrown. But it was not until the nineteenth century that there emerged the model of the Renaissance familiar today, along with its mystique. The landmarks of this new model were Jules Michelet's volume on the Renaissance in his *History of France* (1855) and Jacob Burckhardt's *The Civilization of the Renaissance in Italy* (1860), in combination with the work of Burckhardt's followers who broadened his model of the early Italian Renaissance to include later periods, other parts of Europe, and fields such as economic life that Burckhardt had not treated in depth. For these scholars and their intellectual heirs the Renaissance was not only or even primarily a revival of learning and the arts but a period with its own organic coherence, a sudden and radical break with the Middle Ages, and the point of departure for the modern world. In Michelet's phrase, it marked "the discovery of the world and of man." Above all, the Renaissance was an age of individual personalities, liberated from the political constraints of Holy Roman Emperor and Pope, free to understand and express themselves for good or evil. The state, for Burckhardt, had become a "work of art," the product of events working through human personalities rather than something imposed by an external sanction such as tradition or the will of God. The age had a pagan vitality.

This view of the Renaissance has the obvious appeal of glamour, and it survives, as not only the popular model but also that of scholars, even when they feel they must reject or modify it as many of them have done. Medievalists especially have bridled. They insist that many of the supposedly new departures in the Renaissance—the revival of classical learning, the emergence of an urban culture that fostered the arts and a capitalist economy, exploration of distant lands, the development of the rationalist scientific mentality, the growth of a lay rather than clerical culture, and the rise of national states— were actually continuations of trends that began centuries before Petrarch. It is also highly questionable, according to champions of the Middle Ages, that the most typical Renaissance trends were advances for humankind. For the most skeptical among them, the Renaissance was not a rebirth but the twilight of the great medieval era.

The conviction remains that the concept of a Renaissance (whether that is the right word or not) is useful and represents something real. But it can no longer be argued easily that the discontinuity with the Middle Ages was radical or that a single spirit dominated all of southern and western Europe for three centuries or that the Renaissance is simply an early stage of modernism. The tendency in Renaissance studies today is to examine different places and stages of it closely, discriminating and qualifying conscientiously in accord with concrete evidence rather than broad formulas, however exhilarating. In this brief essay there is not enough space to record all the qualifications and exceptions that the complexity of the Renaissance age and culture calls for. Almost all the generalizations that follow are challengeable. Even so, they may be helpful, especially because many of them originate in the Renaissance view of itself. Moreover, they provide an index to the history of sensibility. In the last century or so readers have developed the habit, when reading Renaissance literature, of isolating and responding selectively to those qualities in it that have the expansiveness of spirit which, accurately or not, has been understood as distinctively Renaissance.

We can begin with humanism, an aspect of the Renaissance that touches on virtually all the others. In a broad sense, the term *humanism* can be defined as any view of the world that places humankind at the center of things. It is as old as Greek antiquity but also quite modern, numbering among its adherents a wide variety of groups ranging from Marxists to existentialists (religious, atheistic, and agnostic) to educators who insist on the primacy of the liberal arts and humanities. In a more restricted though still rather elastic sense, humanism refers to a distinctive habit of thought that pervades Renaissance art and philosophy. Beginning roughly in the latter fourteenth century, with such men as Petrarch, it spread over the following centuries throughout Europe; in the north it reached its zenith of creative expression in the first decades of the sixteenth century in the great Dutch scholar, theologian, and satirist Desiderius Erasmus (1466?–1536) and in his English colleague Thomas More (1478–1535), the author of *Utopia*.

The humanists tended to think of themselves as a new breed, and they do represent at least a striking shift in emphasis. They accorded human beings a high degree of autonomy, an extreme form of which was expressed by the Italian humanist Pico della Mirandola (1463–1494) in his *Oration on the Dignity of Man*. In a famous passage from that work God addresses man: "I have given you, Adam, neither a predetermined place nor a particular aspect nor any special prerogatives in order that you may take and possess these through your own decision and choice. The limitations on the nature of other creatures are contained within my prescribed laws. You shall determine your own nature without constraint from any barrier, by means of the freedom to whose power I have entrusted you. . . . I have made you neither heavenly nor earthly, neither mortal nor immortal so that, like a free and sovereign artificer, you might mold and fashion yourself into that form you yourself shall have chosen." Asceticism was no longer necessarily the hallmark of sanctity, and pleasure became more respectable, whether celebrated riotously as in Rabelais or in the more spiritualized form it usually took for the northern humanists. (It must be stated, however, that the stereotype of Italian humanists as pagan rather than Christian is a misleading caricature.) The world and the life of the body were to be accepted and rejoiced in, regarded not as signs that man is alienated from his higher self but as avenues that, in parallel with the soul, humanity can use for its fulfillment. In "The Godly Feast," one of Erasmus's *Colloquies*, the host Eusebius urges his dinner guests: "But while we feast our minds plenteously, let us not neglect their partners." Asked who these partners are, he replies, "Our bodies; aren't they partners of our minds? For I prefer 'partners' to 'instruments' or 'dwellings' or 'tombs.'" The honorific status given in the Middle Ages to clerical authority and to the ideal of celibacy was considerably modified.

The vehicle for realizing the humanists' ideals was to be reason—more concretely, education of the most comprehensive kind: physical, moral, literary, philosophical. The ancient classics became major and indispensable tools of this education; without them the truly good life could not be envisioned in its wholeness. The humanists were therefore earnestly committed to the recovery and editing of ancient texts (which were not so much discovered as unearthed from churches and monasteries). The texts included both the secular and (especially for the northern humanists) the religious; Erasmus, most notably, did a landmark Greek edition of the New Testament. Moreover, this philological scholarship was not regarded as fastidious purism or as intellectual escapism; quite the contrary, for the humanists had as prime goals both the perfection of individual human character and the reform of public evils, in church and state. They were activist social scientists. In their educational systems, they wished to substitute for the medieval concern with elaborate formal logic an ideal of practical and moral wisdom instilled through a curriculum dominated by poetry, history, moral philosophy, and—in lieu

1749

of medieval theology—the Bible itself. Although they were in one way elitists, aiming to train a special educated cadre of reforming leaders, they were also egalitarian to the extent that they prized feudal nobility of birth less than a moral and intellectual nobility, the signs of which were rhetorical eloquence, refined diction, and urbane wit, all these combined with rectitude of conduct.

Humanist thought, elusive and ambiguous though it sometimes seems, was fundamentally concerned with wholeness, of the human personality and of world view. The clearest example is in their religious thought. Most of them were firm believers in Christianity (such occasional puzzles as Rabelais and Montaigne notwithstanding), which they did not regard as a system in rivalry with pagan antiquity. Nor did they regard antiquity as a mere allegorizing of Christian revelation (as often in Dante); the achievement of a genuinely historical point of view, by which the events and ideas of classical times could be understood as they really were in themselves, was another of their prime goals, akin to their passion for rejecting spurious literary texts and traditions. Rather, they saw Christianity and paganism as organic parts of total truth. In "The Godly Feast," Eusebius says, "whatever is devout and contributes to good morals should not be called profane. Sacred Scripture is of course the basic authority in everything; yet I sometimes run across ancient sayings or pagan writings—even the poets'—so purely and reverently and admirably expressed that I can't help believing their authors' hearts were moved by some divine power. And perhaps the spirit of Christ is more widespread than we understand, and the company of saints includes many not in our calendar. Speaking frankly among friends, I can't read [certain of Cicero's works] without sometimes kissing the book and blessing that pure heart, divinely inspired as it was. . . . So that I would much rather let all of Scotus [the medieval philosopher] and others of his sort perish than the books of a single Cicero or Plutarch." Some of the humanists went so far as to envisage a primal religious revelation of which all the world's creeds are reflections.

The complexity of the Renaissance age is well illustrated in the ambiguous relationship between humanism and the religious currents of the time, especially the Protestant Reformation, customarily dated from Luther's definitive rebellion against the Catholic Church in 1517. The papacy had been in dire trouble in the fourteenth and fifteenth centuries, sorely tried by its "Babylonian captivity" when the seat of the papacy was moved to Avignon in France, then weakened by a period of schism when there were rival popes, and after that by a period when a council laid claim to ecclesiastical authority. In the meantime, skeptical and heretical movements that had grown out of the late Middle Ages were flourishing, and powerful movements stressing mystical experience and simple piety were spreading rapidly among both clergy and laity. The last half of the fifteenth century and the first two decades of the sixteenth, immediately before Luther's revolt, saw a reinvigorated papacy at its height of cultural glory: the renowned Vatican Library was created, and Popes Julius II and Leo X, reigning from 1503 to 1521, patronized the work of great artists, including Michelangelo and Raphael. But many of the popes of the time were concerned more with political and personal aggrandizement than with the spiritual welfare of the European church. Out of this background the Reformation emerged, claiming to reassert the values of

1750

authentic early Christianity, drawing for theological support on epistles by St. Paul and the writings of early Church Fathers like Augustine (and of course on the Gospels as the Reformers understood them), preaching that humanity was saved not by its own efforts ("works") but by faith. The Protestant opposition to indulgences (remissions of punishment in Purgatory) was therefore not merely a moral rebellion against the venal selling of them by Rome but a theological stance that rejected the whole idea of Purgatory, with its implication that human beings can satisfy divine justice through their own merits rather than exclusively in Christ.

The Reformation is in different ways an expression of humanist ideals and a contradiction of them. The Protestant attempt to recover the ancient text and meaning of the Bible and to spread them widely, free of medieval theological overlays, is akin to and indeed part of the humanist movement, which conservative Catholic churchmen distrusted. Both Protestants and humanists agreed also in their contempt for medieval scholasticism in general, in pressing for institutional reform in the church, and in encouraging the active role of the laity in intellectual and religious life. Both put a high value on simple piety in contrast with elaborate formal liturgy and complicated systems of devotion such as the veneration of saints and their relics and the earning of indulgences. On the other hand, the two movements differed in some fundamental ways. The humanists were essentially optimistic about human nature, asserting the crucial role of free will. This emphasis contradicted the view, held by John Calvin (1509–1564) and the Protestant radicals who followed him, that humanity is weak in its fallen state ("totally depraved," to use the technical term) and therefore dependent on God's free gift of grace rather than its own spiritual exertions. Humanists tended not to be interested in sectarian dogma as such, except—as with Erasmus and More—to resist divisive innovations that threatened Church unity. Moreover, though the humanists scorned most things medieval, their essential internationalism, typified in the insistence by Erasmus and More that the Church remain unified, is closer to the medieval model than to the new localism and nationalism that evolved in parallel with the Protestant churches. And the advocacy of religious tolerance by humanists like Erasmus is antithetical to the intense sectarian partisanship expressed both in Protestantism and in the Catholic Counter-Reformation. (The latter is best exemplified in the militant Society of Jesus, or Jesuits, founded on a military model in 1534 by the Spanish saint and former soldier Ignatius Loyola. In the literature of Protestant countries like England, the Jesuits generally appear not only as agents of "papist" religion but as unscrupulous, subversive machiavels working in the interest of foreign political powers. It is interesting, then, that Ignatius himself exhibited a kind of practical mysticism that owes something to the devotional trends, fostered by humanists, that had helped produce the Reformation.) Finally, the humanists' willingness to envisage the world in terms of classical models that might be compatible with Christianity but also existed independent of it did not square with the impulse in radical Protestantism to reject everything that was religiously neutral as pagan worldliness. The humanists were thus in a curious position after the Reformation, distrusted as sowers of heresy by many Catholics (despite his Catholicism, some of Erasmus's works were put on the *Index* of prohibited books) and rejected by many Protestants as fainthearted, worldly temporizers, the lukewarm whom God, in the biblical phrase, would spew out of His mouth.

The role of the Renaissance and of humanism in the evolution of modern science is also ambivalent. The discovery of the world and the discovery of the human that Michelet found in the Renaissance age are not necessarily parallel endeavors. It is true that the recovery of ancient authors made available to thinkers models of the cosmos not available in the Middle Ages, including the heliocentric astronomy with which Copernicus replaced the old Ptolemaic model, and some unknown works by ancient scientists like Archimedes were revived. Humanists encouraged the study of algebra and geometry, the latter overlapping with experiments by painters in visual perspective. Thus the way was prepared for the incomparable mathematical developments of the seventeenth century that provided the language of modern science. But the human-centeredness of the humanists, as is still true of some of their modern counterparts, sometimes took the form of an antagonism or at least indifference to science.

For modern science to develop, another radical change had also to occur: the medieval picture of the universe, with its beautiful model of correspondences between matter on one hand and theology and human psychology on the other, had to be replaced by a more objective view of nature as having its own autonomy independent of its roles of revealing God and reflecting the human. The medieval correlation between the four humors in the human body and their corresponding psychological dispositions, and between the humors and the four elements in material nature; the systematic linking of the heavenly spheres with the hierarchical orders of angels; the notion that an apple falls from a tree because it loves the earth—such ideas had to go. (E. M. W. Tillyard argues in *The Elizabethan World Picture*, 1946, that assumptions like these continued to dominate much of Renaissance thought and art.) The trend in the Renaissance to study nature more objectively appears, for example, in the concern for accurate anatomy—systematically in the work of Vesalius (1514–1564) and aesthetically in the proportions and musculature of painted or sculpted nudes. The dogmatic medieval reverence for Galen in medicine and for Aristotle in general was weakened.

The new empirical direction was, however, more an extrapolation of late medieval thought than a bold Renaissance innovation. Furthermore, although empiricism is fundamental to experimental method, it is probably less essential to pure science than the mental discipline of abstraction: one must learn, in accounting for the trajectory of the falling apple, to ignore certain quite objective facts about it—that it is a Winesap, is overripe, and has a worm in it—and concentrate exclusively on the abstract properties (mass, distance from other objects) it shares with all other gravitationally attracted bodies. It can be argued convincingly that this abstract habit of thinking is much closer than the humanists' practical wisdom to the medieval scholastic discipline.

In pure science, then, the Renaissance is probably best understood as a transition period. Technologically, however, there were some epochal advances. The most important by far was the invention in the late fifteenth century, by Johann Gutenberg (1400?–1468?) and others, of printing by movable type. In the last few decades of the century, several million books were printed, multiplying by an incalculable factor the impact of all the religious, intellectual, and literary trends in the later Renaissance. It is true that this invention too depended on earlier discoveries—in papermaking, for example—but the practical culmination of the technology of printing in the Renaissance itself marks one of the few unquestionable differences, not only from the Middle Ages but from all previous world history.

The new technology included also the navigational tools—again, drawing on pre-Renaissance and non-European cultures—that made possible the Renaissance age of geographic exploration. At the end of the fifteenth century Bartholomeu Dias and Vasco da Gama opened the route to India around the Cape of Good Hope and Columbus reached the New World; in the sixteenth century Magellan's crew and Francis Drake sailed around the globe. Such voyages had an enormous impact on the European imagination, influencing works like More's *Utopia* and Luiz Vaz de Camoëns' (1524–1580) Portuguese epic *The Lusiads,* which celebrates Vasco da Gama and vaunts his superiority to those mere Mediterranean sailors Odysseus and Aeneas. The new geographic discoveries also affected the politics and economics of Europe in important ways, accelerating the trends toward nationalism, middle-class power, economic capitalism, urbanization, and the shift of money and power from the Mediterranean to the countries on the Atlantic and the North Sea.

It is precisely in such sociological, political, and economic areas, however, that the nineteenth-century model of the Renaissance as a separate and distinct, organically whole age breaks down most seriously. It is beyond question that by the sixteenth century rulers such as Philip II in Spain and the Netherlands, Francis I in France, and Henry VIII in England had achieved unprecedented authority in their realms, built on their predecessors' consolidation of royal power, territory, and wealth in the fifteenth century. Because in many respects the feudal nobility was the greatest obstacle to royal authority, the monarchs' new power was wielded increasingly through complex bureaucracies staffed largely by a new kind of middle-class men distinguished less by birth than by talent or money. (Italy, with its city-states, was dominated by outside powers in the sixteenth century and was not unified as a nation until the nineteenth.) It is also true that these new national regimes, along with the Italian city-states, had begun to define themselves and their goals in increasingly secular and local terms, less dominated than in the past by the transnational authority of Pope or Holy Roman Emperor or by the model of European Christendom as a unity. Populations boomed; banking flourished as money came to replace payment in kind and services; cities grew dramatically in size and importance, along with the intellectual and artistic activity that urban centers help foster. But the roots of all these movements go back, in some cases several centuries, into the medieval period. Moreover, the Renaissance is ridden by a great political-cultural paradox: while medieval internationalism was losing ground to the more local autonomy of city-state and national monarchy, in accordance with an ideal of patriotic citizenship that the humanists encouraged, the different parts of Europe were at the same time becoming more intellectually and culturally interdependent—a trend, greatly reinforced by the printing press, that also owes much to the humanists. A roughly similar paradox exists in the twentieth century: the breakup of the international colonial systems into scores of autonomous new states has coincided with the internationalist movement represented politically in the United Nations and with developments in technology and communication that have helped transform the world into a "global village."

Just as the humanists reacted contemptuously against things medieval in the name of a revived antiquity, so their classicizing counterparts in the visual arts often rejected medieval art, in theory at least. The Italians coined for it the pejorative term *Gothic* with a glance at the barbarians who overran ancient Rome. Today that term survives, but the accompanying value judgment has changed vastly. The Gothic style, alive from the twelfth to the fifteenth centuries (in some parts of Europe into the sixteenth), is now regarded as the expression of one of the great ages of world art. Much of its painting has disappeared, although a good deal is known about how it used two-dimensional media from tapestries, stained glass, and glorious color illuminations in manuscripts. Above all, its public architecture survives in the great European cathedrals, which embody an organic unity and a fusion with sculpture and other arts scarcely to be paralleled since the age of the Parthenon in ancient Greece.

The transition from Gothic to Renaissance art is problematical, like so many other aspects of the period when it happened. Compared with the Gothic, Renaissance art is more concerned with classical forms and subjects, with secular themes directed to a more secular clientele, with landscape and other aspects of nature, with the illusion of depth, with individual portraiture, and generally with greater representational realism. All these trends are also observable, however, in late medieval Gothic art as it developed from the Romanesque style that prevailed between the tenth and twelfth centuries. Further complications arise when one distinguishes between different parts of Europe, different stages of the Renaissance, and different art media. There remains nevertheless an immense difference between the Gothic and Renaissance periods in degree and also in consciousness, for the new trends were pursued with a programmatic deliberateness in the Renaissance that one does not find in the earlier era.

The most comprehensive of these trends was the revival of antiquity. Architectural models still existed, especially in Italy, and could be imitated directly. The spirituality implicit in the vertical-line composition and pointed arches of the Gothic cathedral yielded to the essentially horizontal classical emphasis. (Another way of looking at this shift is to see the cutting edge of architectural innovation as having shifted south to Italy, since the great Gothic cathedrals, with their mystically soaring vertical lines and spaces and their walls opened up with stained glass, had been an almost exclusively northern phenomenon.) The dome was revived by Filippo Brunelleschi in his design for the Florence cathedral (1420), a landmark of the new style, and was used climactically by Michelangelo for St. Peter's in Rome. Classical columns, with their distinctive capitals marking the intersection of vertical with horizontal, took priority over the less clearly end-stopped Gothic pillars. In sculpture and painting, there were greater difficulties, since few antique models existed, especially in the early Renaissance before the discovery of statues such as the Apollo Belvedere. But artists in these media too did their enthusiastic best to classicize. Donatello (1386?–1466) pioneered in the revival of the freestanding nude and the equestrian statue. Painters, besides espousing the classical ideals of proportion and harmony, turned to ancient historical and mythological subjects—although the most frequent ones were still derived from the Bible and the lives of the saints.

The renewed interest in nature by Renaissance artists took many forms. The most obvious was an increased emphasis on landscape, though still almost always integrated with a human subject. The basic medieval worldview had regarded the physical creation as sacramental and symbolic, and the Renaissance did not by any means discard that view; Renaissance pictures continued to be expressions of ideas, often retaining a system of symbols and icons inherited from the Middle Ages, as myriad Renaissance "emblem books" attest. At the same time, Renaissance art suggests also that, apart from its human or divine analogies, the world "out there" can be reproduced for what it is in itself. The picture frame became a window through which one glimpsed the living world. (According to Vasari, Leonardo da Vinci once played a practical joke on his father by creating a terrifying picture so lifelike that it was mistaken for reality.) Anatomy became a formal study for artists; drawing from nude models became commonplace, and the nude as a subject became ubiquitous. Color effects were perfected, especially by Titian and other Venetians. Portraits of individuals became an important genre, as exemplified in the masterfully realistic ones done by Hans Holbein the Younger (1497?–1543) of Erasmus, More, and Henry VIII. This individualism of subject reinforces the general motif of individualism ascribed to the Renaissance in the nineteenth-century model.

Even more to the point is the new individualistic role of the artist. The greatest medieval works of art, the cathedrals, had been collective, indeed communal achievements, a union of large vision with the painstaking efforts of hundreds of skilled artists and craftsmen who remained anonymous. Many of the best medieval artists are identified today only by the word *Master* linked to the name of his city or one of his masterpieces. But in the Renaissance, artists, often working for individual patrons whom they glorified as individuals, came to think of themselves also as unique persons expressing their own unique visions and values. Some of them took to signing their canvases, a new practice, and even when they did not do so their works were figuratively signed by the unmistakable presence of their own personal styles. The medieval artist had been a maker and a servant of God; the Renaissance artist was a creator and, as such, God's rival.

Because it was essentially a literary movement, humanism naturally had its most direct impact on literature. Classical modes were revitalized—for example, the ode, the dialogue, and the pastoral, a form popular in Renaissance literary genres ranging from song to prose romance to drama. Besides serving as midwives of the revived classicism, some of the humanists created literary masterpieces themselves. They were at their best in the nonfictional or semifictional forms wherein inventiveness could be combined with the expression of ideas and opinions: letters, orations, dialogues, and treatises. Their admiration of Plato appears in the writings of Marsilio Ficino (1433–1499) and Pico della Mirandola, whose *Oration on the Dignity of Man* (1486) has already been mentioned. Dialogues included Erasmus's *Colloquies* (1519), More's *Utopia* (1516), and Baldassare Castiglione's *Book of the Courtier* (1514; published 1528), a vastly influential exposition of the ideal of the Renaissance gentleman. Erasmus's *Praise of Folly* (1509) is a many-sided ironic masterpiece that, like *Utopia,* shows the reformist side of humanism.

The most fundamental development in Renaissance literature was the growth of literary nationalism. All the important medieval vernacular languages of Europe had produced important literature, but it lived in the shadow of Latin, the international language, and the vernacular literatures themselves had typically reflected international rather than local traditions. In the Renaissance, political and personal allegiances to patrons, city-states, or national monarchies helped foster literary ambitions linked to the writers' own distinctive languages. Latin continued to thrive; among many other writers, More and Erasmus used it, in the works just mentioned, and into the seventeenth and eighteenth centuries it continued to be the normal vehicle for scientific discourse, including such monumental works as Isaac Newton's *Principia* (1687). It also remained the language of Roman Catholic liturgy and church government into the twentieth century. But the new Latin of the humanists was based on classical models such as Cicero's prose, and the concentration on such models helped to kill medieval Latin as a living language—a real loss, since in its spare directness medieval Latin had a beauty and functionality that the humanists did not properly appreciate. Their adulation for the classical tongues was also in some respects a roadblock to the development of the vernacular literatures; for example, humanism may have retarded for a time the development of Italian literature in the fifteenth century.

For the most part, though, the humanist impulse had the contrary effect: local patriotic feelings, reinforced by the humanist ideal of dedicated citizenship, inspired a desire to assert national identity while emulating in the national languages the achievements of antiquity. A notable example was the formation of the *Pléiade,* a group of sixteenth-century French writers that included Pierre de Ronsard (1524–1585), the greatest French poet of the Renaissance, and Joachim du Bellay (1522?–1560). Du Bellay, in his *Defense and Glorification of the French Language* (1549), produced the group's manifesto, calling for a French language and literature to rival that of Italy and antiquity in genres including tragedy, the ode, and the sonnet. The emergence of modern Italian vernacular literature had begun much earlier when Dante chose the Tuscan dialect for *The Divine Comedy,* supporting his program for Italian in a Latin treatise *On Eloquence in the Vernacular Tongue* (1304–1305), and later in the fourteenth century Petrarch and Boccaccio lent the weight of their prestige to Tuscan Italian. In Portugal, the achievements of Camoëns (1524–1580) in lyric and epic went a long way toward defining the Portuguese language. In the Protestant countries such as Germany, Holland, and England where the movement to translate the Bible into the vernacular could thrive, these translations were formative, especially Luther's German version (the New Testament in 1522, the Old Testament in 1534).

The most conscious and comprehensive assertions of Renaissance values appear in the long narrative works of the period, especially epics or works touched by the epic impulse. This is natural enough; the epic has always been a vehicle for communal ideas. If we did not know any of the great Renaissance epics and had to create a theoretical model for them on the basis of other tendencies of the time and clichés about it, we might arrive at something like this: a story of imposing events, written in a classical unrhymed verse, scornful of the outgrown medieval heritage, celebrating a modernist theme such as the recent achievements of the poet's own nation, and centered on a heroic but mentally elevated "Renaissance man" aglow with confidence and optimism. But, although virtually every Renaissance epic illustrates one or more of these motifs, what we most often find is a mixture, seemingly incongruous, of the modern, classical, and medieval, accompanied often by ambivalent value judgments. Some of these incongruities are attributable to the epic tradition itself, which since Virgil has tended to combine nationalist modernism with nostalgia, usually intimating a desire to keep alive what was best in the past and, on the other hand, a consciousness of having progressed beyond it.

Rabelais' *Gargantua and Pantagruel* (1532–52), Cervantes' *Don Quixote* (1605, 1615), and Shakespeare's English history plays (1591–1599) are not epics in a strict formal sense, but they have the scale, comprehensiveness, and national flavor of epic. Rabelais' work is perhaps the showcase example of worldly Renaissance exuberance; yet it also recalls the medieval "goliardic," a student tradition of wining and wenching. The searching complexities of *Don Quixote* build from a direct confrontation between an idealism symbolized by the medieval romances and a contrasting pragmatism, and which set of values Cervantes endorses is not a question to answer simply. The *Quixote* is among other things an examination of the Spanish national character, but in the spirit of a sensitive critique rather than of panegyric. Of Shakespeare's ten English history plays, eight span the period from the end of the fourteenth century to the emergence in 1485 of the Tudor dynasty still reigning in Shakespeare's time, and these plays have been taken sometimes to constitute Shakespeare's epic. In it he celebrates the emergence of peace and order from a fragmented, dying medieval feudalism, but he also portrays the noble beauty of the chivalric code. None of these three authors, then, is simply heralding the glories of a new civilization unrooted in the medieval past.

When we turn to works more strictly describable as epics (almost all of them, interestingly, written in rhymed rather than in classical verse forms), we find the same mixture of allegiances. Perhaps the closest thing to our hypothetical national and modernist model is Camoëns' *Lusiad* (1572), a poem that intricately imitates Virgil's *Aeneid* and acclaims triumphantly the unprecedented Portuguese voyages around the Cape to the Far East for the glory of the nation and of Catholic Christianity. Here the sense of a vast new world in contrast to the constricted Mediterranean world of epic memory accords well enough with the nineteenth-century vision of an expansive Renaissance spirit. Iberian interest in the new explorations is also reflected in several sixteenth-century Spanish epics by authors including Alonso de Ercilla y Zúñga (1534–1594) and the great dramatist Lope de Vega (1562–1635).

The definitive Italian Renaissance epics are quite another matter. They consist of a series of poems written in Ferrara under the patronage of the Este family: the *Orlando in Love* (1483) of Matteo Boiardo, the *Orlando Driven Mad* (1516) of Ludovico Ariosto, and the *Jerusalem Delivered* (1575) of Torquato Tasso. (Boiardo and Ariosto built from an earlier work, *Morgante the Giant*, written about 1480 by Luigi Pulci.) All these authors belong unmistakably to the Renaissance; Ariosto especially, with his gaiety, sophistication, and sensuousness, and his theme of the impossible quest, expresses something quintessential to his time and place. But, like Pulci and Boiardo, he treats medieval matter and heroes derived from the traditions of King Arthur, Charlemagne,

1757

and Roland, although the hero of the great, austere *chanson de geste* is scarcely recognizable in this new Orlando ("Roland," in Italian). These poems are much closer to the magical atmosphere and free form of medieval romance than to the classical epic. Tasso's poem conforms more nearly to the ancient models, but it too has a medieval subject (the first Crusade) and owes much to the romance genre and atmosphere; moreover, the ideal it celebrates is a united Christian Europe that in the days of the Counter-Reformation had become no more than a wistful memory.

Edmund Spenser (1552?–1599), although a fervent Renaissance Protestant, wrote in this tradition of Italianate medievalism. In *The Faerie Queene* (published 1590–1595) he attempted a portrait of the ideal human being based on a scheme of Aristotelian ethical virtues that medieval authors like Dante would probably have found congenial, and he chose for his vehicle a blend of romance, allegory, and archaic diction that also have strong medieval associations. On the other hand, Spenser's political allegory is modern and militantly Protestant, pitting Queen Elizabeth (Gloriana, the fairy queen) and her champions against evil popes and Catholic monarchs who serve as agents of the Satanic.

The culmination of Renaissance epic was achieved by Milton, who inherited many of Spenser's values but wrote an utterly different kind of poem. His *Paradise Lost,* influenced by *La Semaine* (*The Week,* 1578), an epic account of the creation by the French Protestant poet Guillaume du Bartas, treats the fall of humankind, a universal theme sanctioned by the divine truth of the Bible rather than the mere fictions of medieval legend or classic fable. In his close textural and structural use of Homer and Virgil, his antimedievalism (reflected in a scornful passage abusing the monastic orders), his contemptuous rejection of rhyme as medieval barbarism, his deliberate disavowal of medieval romance as an epic mode ("fabled knights / In battles feigned")—in all these respects Milton adopts the humanist stance. Even more fundamentally, *Paradise Lost* is humanist in its relative freedom from sectarian factionalism (the passage about the monks notwithstanding) and in its ultimate theme: freedom, more specifically human free will. In rising above the doctrinaire polemics for his nation and theology that he reserved for his Puritan prose tracts, Milton may well have achieved in *Paradise Lost,* more than any other major Renaissance epic poet and at the very end of the Renaissance, the humanist goals that in so many ways define the age.

Renaissance values appear in the epics as broad, comprehensive visions, but equally characteristic is a new kind of literary intimacy and particularity akin to the vogue of portrait painting and the new self-expressive role of the artist. The best literary portraits are the characters in Shakespeare's plays; although they often owe something to earlier literary and dramatic traditions such as the morality play, scores of them are fully realized individuals. It may seem paradoxical, then, that Shakespeare reveals very little of himself. For the epitome of Renaissance self-revelation we can go to Montaigne (1533–1592), whose *Essays* (1580–88) combine far-reaching speculation with the minutest factual details of his personal life and the quirks of his mind, all colored by his distinctive personality and voice.

But the principal medium for self-expression was the lyric. The prototype, once more, is Petrarch, whose lyrics focus so insistently on the poet himself. His Laura is clearly in the line of Dante's Beatrice, but, without denying that

Beatrice is a real woman or that Laura is idealized, one senses that the latter is far more fully a unique individual. In the sonnet especially, Petrarch started a Renaissance fashion taken up by almost all the lyric poets of Europe, including Camoëns, Ronsard, Spenser, Sir Philip Sidney (1554–1586), Shakespeare, and Milton. It became the confessional love poem *par excellence,* but even when the subject was not inherently private or amatory (Shakespeare on time, Donne on religious experience), the viewpoint on these more universal matters was still usually subjective. This is not to say that the sonnets were reliably autobiographical; in fact, the genre became one of the most artificial, convention-ridden of forms, full of stylized sighing lovers, cruel but idealized mistresses (sometimes quite fictional), and other stock devices of the courtly love apparatus whose roots extend back beyond Petrarch into the Middle Ages. But even the most conventional of the sonnets reflect the vogue of self-expression, since the sonneteer had at least to assume the guise of a man revealing his intimate thoughts or feelings. "Fool," says Sidney's muse to him, "look in thy heart and write." (Ultimately the Petrarchan tradition of courtly praise fell by its own weight of artificiality; Donne in his lyrics scrutinizes the conventions ironically, and Shakespeare could satirize them as he does in his Sonnet 130: "My mistress' eyes are nothing like the sun; / Coral is far more red than her lips' red . . . .") Often, too, the sonneteers' self-consciousness took the form of commentary on their own work; poetry and the poets' ability to give immortality to their addressees were frequent themes, and beneath the overlays of this convention is an authentic new sense of the power of art that is characteristic of the Renaissance.

The heightened interest during the Renaissance in objectifying the world, portraying individuals, and exploring the complexities of human psychology as it is reflected in behavior—all these were favorable conditions for a resurgent interest in drama, which, especially in England and Spain, flourished as it had not done since Greek antiquity. The exact origins of this new dramatic impulse are hard to untangle from one another. The classical revival was unquestionably important: the plays of Terence, Plautus, and Seneca known to the Middle Ages were now approached less exclusively as rhetorical models and more as literary theater; the Greek dramatists were rediscovered along with some plays by Plautus that had disappeared; at schools and universities plays were studied avidly, and scholars began to write classically inspired dramas of their own, in both Latin and the vernacular. The printing press helped immeasurably; in the half-century or so after it came into use, the plays of all the great ancient dramatists—Aeschylus, Sophocles, Euripides, Aristophanes, Plautus, Terence, and Seneca—were published. The same period saw the publication of Aristotle's *Poetics,* and with it came a new consciousness of classical "rules" such as the preservation of the unities. Tragedians learned from Seneca how to write a long play that held together; comic playwrights learned the intricacies of tight plotting from Plautus and Terence. When the public theaters of London began to thrive in the 1580s and 1590s, the first important plays were written by men who, like Thomas Kyd (1557?–1595) and Christopher Marlowe (1564–93), had learned their craft in the schools or universities.

Nevertheless, many of the greatest Renaissance plays are not in any obvious way classical. In both Spain and England, the most vital sources of the new drama were in native popular theatrical traditions which, in turn, had their ultimate roots in the medieval church. Shakespeare's friend and fellow playwright Ben Jonson (1572–1637), an aggressive advocate of classical form, felt himself to be in that role an enlightened exception among his formally footloose contemporaries. In Spain, the enormously prolific Lope de Vega (1562–1635) wrote a manifesto in 1609 rejecting classical rules; this anticlassical position was later modified by Calderón de la Barca (1600–1681), but he too in his more intellectual and theological vein was thoroughly Spanish in his religious preoccupations. Both Lope de Vega and Shakespeare blended the comic and the serious in a fashion closer to medievalism than to classicism. Even the staging of their plays, despite immense advances in professionalism and sophistication, recalls certain medieval features; for example, in the Elizabethan theater the areas below and above the main acting platform continued to be referred to as the "hell" and the "heaven," as in the three-level stage of the medieval period. (See the Introductions to *Everyman* and Shakespeare.)

The fact is that, although the Renaissance drama of England and Spain is unimaginable apart from either its medieval origins or the classical revival, it achieved expressive heights and explored human experience in ways not always clearly attributable to either strain. Religious themes continued to be immensely popular in Spain, but so were secular ones. In England these completely supplanted the overt devotional emphasis of the miracle, mystery, and morality plays. A Christian norm might be present, but, like the classicist goal of coherent unity, it was there organically and implicitly rather than texturally and explicitly. The history play perfected by Marlowe, Shakespeare, and Lope de Vega was an almost wholly new genre. Comedy owed something to medieval farce and to the stock characters of the Roman comedians (the "wily slave" transformed into the clowns and other clever "low" characters of playwrights such as Shakespeare), but in its highest reaches it became something new to the stage. In the Shakespearean comedies *Twelfth Night, As You Like It,* and *A Midsummer Night's Dream* (set, ludicrously, in ancient Athens but really in fairyland), laughter is combined with a warm and sympathetic insight into the romantic feelings of men and women, articulating a distinctive definition of love. Tragedy became both intimate and cosmic. The medieval notion of tragedy was simply the fall of a great personage from prosperous eminence (a strain vestigially recognizable in Shakespearean tragedies like *Macbeth*). The classical impulse in the Renaissance transformed this model radically—for example, Senecan models added a dimension of melodrama and a stoic sense of fatality, and from Aristotle came the notion of the hero's "tragic flaw." But no such formulas can define the great English tragedies of Marlowe, Shakespeare, or John Webster (1580?–1625). In Shakespeare's *Hamlet, King Lear, Othello,* and *Macbeth,* it is not only the hero's life and happiness but the entire vision of a morally ordered universe that is at stake, threatened by a demonic principle of evil that seems to have escaped human or divine control. Whether or not the principle of righteousness prevails in the end is a question that can be answered differently about different plays (opinion is notoriously divided about *King Lear*), but even when it does reassert itself, a terrible price has been paid in the suffering or destruction of precious, noble individuals. There is at the least a heartrending sense of human waste. But this sense is also mitigated by the very existence of human goodness, whether it triumphs or not. The integrity and love of Lear's daughter Cordelia are realities that in their nature cannot be denied or annulled, even by death. For dramatic visions so vast as these one must go back to Greek tragedy, and it might be argued that Shakespeare goes beyond the Greeks by combining with his cosmic themes a more intimate concern for the unique human person.

Italy, the original center of the humanist movement and the revival of antiquity, did not produce a great dramatic literature in the Renaissance, although some of its distinguished authors, including Ariosto and Tasso, produced notable plays, and there were occasional masterpieces such as Machiavelli's *Mandragola* (about 1518). Italy contributed influentially to post-Renaissance stagecraft, however; as in painting, it pioneered in the development of illusional perspective in stage settings, and it helped develop important architectural features like the proscenium arch. Such elements look past the Renaissance to the "picture-frame" stage that became the principal model for theater from the late seventeenth century until well into the twentieth. (Much of this new stagecraft reached other countries by way of Italian opera, a new art form developed around 1600 in rivalry with the integration of the arts in ancient Greek drama and crowned with immediate greatness in the works of Claudio Monteverdi [1567–1643].) The modern picture-frame stage, typically opening into someone's living room, is itself an emblem for the kind of realistically intimate drama often enacted on it, and the emblem represented by the physical theater is applicable to earlier dramatic traditions as well. The essentially public action of classical Greek drama took place before an unchanging background, the *skene* that typically represented a palace and concealed from the audience the merely domestic private scenes imagined to take place behind it. The medieval stage presented simultaneously to the audience three levels—heaven, earth, and hell—representing a constant awareness of the relationship between here and hereafter. The Renaissance stage of England and Spain was the vehicle for complete fluidity and variety, capable of representing, with the indispensable help of poetic language, any conceivable setting and of shifting from one to another instantaneously. The ceremonial and casual, the public and intimate, the lofty and low, the violent and serene, the realistic and romantic—all these manners and moods, in any combination, were at the service of the playwright and actors. It is therefore not surprising that Renaissance drama could encompass more of the world and of life than has been possible in the theater of any other age.

FURTHER READING *(prepared by W.J.R.):* One entry into the Renaissance is by way of Jacob Burckhardt's epoch-making and controversial study *The Civilization of the Renaissance in Italy,* first published in 1860 (discussed in the preceding Introduction), which emphasizes Renaissance individualism. More concise is J. H. Plumb's *The Italian Renaissance,* 1961, which in surveying the period refers often to Dante, Boccaccio, Petrarch, and Machiavelli. E. M. W. Tillyard's *The Elizabethan World Picture,* 1946, another historically influential study, identifies three models by which the cosmos was envisaged: as a chain, a set of correspondences, and a dance. Tillyard's *The English Renaissance: Fact or Fiction?,* 1952, identifies and discusses essential differences between medieval and Renaissance thought in order to answer the question posed by the title; see also the excellent discussions in *The Renaissance: A Reconsideration of the Theories and Interpretations of the Age,* ed. Tinsley Helton, 1961. Two of the essays in this volume warrant special mention: Harry Levin's "English Literature of the Renaissance" and

Paul Oskar Kristeller's "Changing Views of the Renaissance Since Jacob Burckhardt." The principles and attitudes reflected in Renaissance literature are treated in Douglas Bush's *Prefaces to Renaissance Literature,* 1965. Paul Oskar Kristeller's *Renaissance Thought and Its Sources,* ed. Michael Mooney, 1979, and Ernst Cassirer's *The Individual and the Cosmos in Renaissance Philosophy,* 1927, trans. Mario Domadi, 1963, are both careful and incisive; Kristeller begins with humanism and proceeds to study the classical fore-runners of Renaissance thought, Renaissance attitudes toward the individual, and other topics; Cassirer's classic examines the Renaissance as a systematic unity. Surveys of literature and literary history include *The Continental Renaissance, 1500–1600,* by W. A. Coupe, A. J. Krailsheimer, J. A. Scott, and R. W. Truman, 1971, 1978; and A. C. Spearing, *Medieval to Renaissance in English Poetry,* 1985. Recently, progress toward understanding the Renaissance has been made through the study of a number of specific topics. One of the most important of these has been the role of women in the period, addressed in *Women in the Middle Ages and the Renaissance,* ed. Mary Beth Rose, 1986; Margaret L. King, *Women of the Renaissance,* 1991; *The Women's Sharp Revenge: Five Women's Pamphlets from the Renaissance,* ed. Simon Shepherd, 1985; and Angeline Goreau, *The Whole Duty of a Woman: Female Writers in Seventeenth-Century England,* 1985. Unconventional sexuality in the era is treated in Bruce R. Smith, *Homosexual Desire in Shakespeare's England,* 1991. Other works with large social implications include the collection of essays *Science and the Arts in the Renaissance,* ed. John W. Shirley and F. David Hoeniger, 1985; and J. R. Hale, *War and Society in Renaissance Europe, 1450–1620,* 1985. Derrick Henry, *The Listener's Guide to Medieval and Renaissance Music,* 1983, is largely a discography, but it serves also as a brief musical history of the periods. Complementing older studies of the humanist movement such as Douglas Bush, *The Renaissance and English Humanism,* 1939, and Myron P. Gilmore, *The World of Humanism, 1453–1517,* 1952, are such works as Donald R. Kelley, *Renaissance Humanism,* 1991; Charles Trinkaus, *The Scope of Renaissance Humanism,* 1983; and Benjamin G. Kohl, *Renaissance Humanism, 1300–1550: A Bibliography of Materials in English,* 1985.

Francis Petrarch

(1304–1374)

Possibly the greatest love poet in Western literature was Francis Petrarch, the fourteenth-century Italian classicist, humanist, and literary arbiter. Born in Arezzo in 1304, Petrarch was set to the study of law, first at Montpellier and then at Bologna. When his father died, the twenty-two-year-old Petrarch renounced law and moved to the lively city of Avignon, the seat of the papacy during its "Babylonian captivity" from 1309 to 1378. After briefly considering the Church, he entered instead the service of the wealthy and powerful Colonna family, the first of a series of patrons who made it possible for Petrarch to devote his life exclusively to literature. He has thus been called the first modern man of letters. By 1341 his reputation was so high that he received a laurel crown as poet laureate from the Roman Senate, an honor Petrarch always treasured as symbolizing not only his own achievement but his spiritual links with the great poets of classical Rome. For the rest of his life, Petrarch continued to be a celebrated public man, an intimate and counselor of princes as well as an arbiter of literary taste. During his mature years, he moved from one residence to another, to Milan as guest of the Visconti, to Venice as guest of the Republic, and finally to Arqua, near Padua, where he spent the last four years of his life in a country retreat. He died in 1374, just before his seventieth birthday, his copy of Virgil open before him on his desk.

In his own day and his own estimation, Petrarch's major achievement was in his Latin works, which far outnumbered his Italian ones. In a letter to Boccaccio, written in his later years, he told of his decision, sometime in his thirties, to use Latin rather than Italian in his major literary work. He had, he said, already begun "a great work" in Italian but had given it up for fear that his words would be "mangled by the public." (Dante, who had visited Petrarch's family when Petrarch was seven, had completed *The Divine Comedy* in Italian in 1321, about fifteen years before Petrarch decided in favor of Latin.) The most important of Petrarch's many Latin works are *Africa*, an unfinished epic poem about Scipio Africanus, the third-century B.C. conqueror of Hannibal; the *Secretum Meum* (My Secret), a spiritual autobiography in the form of three imaginary dialogues between Petrarch and St. Augustine; and his *Letters*, both in verse and prose, which Petrarch himself carefully edited and collected into a number of volumes. The humane and liberal spirit of Petrarch's classical studies was to be a major influence in the development of Renaissance humanism throughout Europe.

Later ages have known Petrarch less as a classicist, however, than as the author of the collection of poems in Italian which he called the *Rerum vulgarium fragmenta* (Poetic Fragments in the Vernacular) and which is now generally known either as the *Canzoniere* (Lyric Poems) or simply the *Rhymes*. This collection of poems was gradually built up through Petrarch's mature life. At least three times Petrarch arranged them in systematic collections, and he was still polishing and rearranging them when he died; the final version of the sequence contains 366 poems, intended to be read, like the Breviary, over the course of a year.

The inspiration for the poems was Petrarch's crucial meeting, on April 6, 1327, with "Laura," in the church of St. Clare in Avignon. (Petrarch never revealed Laura's identity, but she is believed to have been Laurette de Noves, who had been married for two years when Petrarch met her and who had a number of children by the time of her death in 1348.) Petrarch adored her, hopelessly and from afar, until her death twenty-one years later and continued to cherish her memory in his poetry for another ten years, after which he professed to renounce earthly love and turn his thoughts only to God.

There is something faintly absurd to the modern reader about this protracted and self-conscious cultivation of a hopeless love (especially, perhaps, when one learns that Petrarch had two illegitimate children by different mothers during the time of his idealization of Laura). But there is more than a little of the conventional in Petrarch's adoration of Laura. By the time he wrote, there was already a long tradition of sequences of love poems addressed to an unattainable woman. Originating in the poems of the twelfth- and thirteenth-century *troubadours* of southern France, the tradition had found its most notable expression before Petrarch in Dante's *La Vita Nuova* (The New Life), devoted to the transformation of the real Beatrice Portinari into "Beatrice," a symbol of Christian salvation (Latin *beata*, "blessed"). A friend of Petrarch, Giacomo Colonna, even suggested that Laura was not a real person but an invented symbol of the poetic "laurel." Petrarch replied with some vehemence that Laura was indeed real and that no one could counterfeit the "weariness and pallor" that his hopeless love had given him. But real passion for a real woman does not preclude making her also into a conventional poetic figure.

What raised the *Rhymes* above the level of its predecessors and made it one of the most widely read and imitated collections of poems in literary history was the wealth of classical learning in the poems, their scope and variety, their arrangement into a developing structure, and their sheer beauty. The classicism of the *Rhymes* is not obtrusive, but it is the more powerful for being so thoroughly assimilated. Virgil, Horace, Catullus, and especially Ovid are echoed throughout the *Rhymes*. One realizes with something of a shock, for example, that the poem "Upon the breeze she spread her golden hair" (XC), personal as it seems, is a close reworking of a passage from the *Aeneid*. Ovid is a pervasive presence in the *Rhymes*, not the Ovid of the *Art of Love* or the moralized, allegorical Ovid of the medieval interpreters, but the Ovid of the *Metamorphoses;* Ovid's Daphne, who, pursued by Apollo, was changed into a laurel tree, is one of the most important classical analogues for the Laura in Petrarch's sequence. The *Rhymes* are quite varied both in form and content. Sonnets predominate; 317 of the 366 poems in the collection are in this form. But there are also a number of *canzoni* (poems made up of five or six stanzas of equal length, followed by a shorter *envoy*, such as CXXVI and CXXIX), and several other forms appear. Most of the poems are about Laura, but a significant number have nothing to do with her, dealing instead with politics, moral problems, friendship, and other topics. The sequence begins and ends with a renunciation of the poet's passion for Laura. The poems between fall most obviously into two groups: Part One, consisting of 265 poems that deal with the living Laura, and Part Two, consisting of 99 poems devoted to the memory of the dead Laura. The poems are arranged in loose chronology, but more important than chronology is the range of moods of the speaker, a range that includes every emotion from spiritual ecstasy to agonized self-laceration and melancholy resignation, every mood associated with love, perhaps, except the joy of physical consummation.

Laura comes to mean many things for Petrarch in the course of the poems; as Thomas G. Bergin has pointed out, they reveal at least four Lauras. One is the Laura of the poet's "laurel," his poetic ambitions which he pursues as Apollo pursued his Daphne. Another is Laura as a virtuous guide to Heaven, like Dante's Beatrice; this view of Laura comes to dominate the second part of the sequence, after Laura's death. A third Laura represents beauty itself, especially as a fascinating temptation that draws the poet away from his proper pursuit of salvation; this Laura appears most explicitly in the sonnets of recantation: I and CCCLXV. And finally, Laura is, of course, merely a young woman with whom the poet fell in love on a spring day in 1327; many of the poems do not emphasize any metaphoric meanings for Laura but present her as a real human presence.

It is not Laura, however, but the poet who is the protagonist of the *Rhymes*. His lady is described in loving detail, but always from outside, from the poet's point of view; Petrarch has no interest in the workings of Laura's mind or in her attitudes toward such subjects as, say, her husband or her children. The personality we remember after reading the poems is Petrarch's—nostalgic, melancholy, passionate and yet always curiously removed from life, an observer rather than a participant.

The deeply personal and introspective quality of the *Rhymes* and their brilliant technique established a vogue that endured for at least three centuries and left a permanent impression on Western poetry, especially love poetry. "Petrarchism" offered a way of portraying the loved one, as a fascinating combination of earthly and divine qualities; a characteristic stance for the lover; and a repertory of devices that could be endlessly imitated, sometimes well, sometimes clumsily and mechanically. These included a repertory of stock images—stormy seas, beautiful landscapes, marble tombs, battles—and a liberal use of antithesis (strong contrasts), oxymoron (contradictory terms), and hyperbole (exaggeration). (See Poem CXXXIV for examples of Petrarch's own use of such devices.) Exaggerated Petrarchan catalogues of the features of a stock, composite mistress had become so common by Shakespeare's time that he could parody them in his Sonnet 130:

> My mistress' eyes are nothing like the sun;
> Coral is far more red than her lips' red:
> If snow be white, why then her breasts are dun;
> If hairs be wires, black wires grow on her head.

But pervasive as Petrarch's literary influence was, his influence upon attitudes toward love was probably even greater; even today, lovers who never heard of Petrarch tend to adopt Petrarchan attitudes. "The amatory attitudes of the *Rhymes* have in fact been built into our culture," Thomas G. Bergin writes. "It is possible, of course, that some day there may be a revolution in human emotions, whether it be a new morality or a new erotic, but until that day comes we shall live by the code that Petrarch elaborated with such instinctive perception and such compelling sophistication." We may be somewhat more skeptical than Bergin about the desirability of some aspects of

Petrarchan love, such as the radical split between the physical and the spiritual; the "revolution in human emotions" he mentions may now be taking place. But until it is completed, we must agree that lovers' meetings "will take place in the kingdom that Petrarch has explored for them."

FURTHER READING *(prepared by W.J.R.)*: Thomas G. Bergin s *Petrarch*, 1970, is an excellent introduction to the study of Petrarch. Bergin provides a concise survey of Petrarch's life and a clear and substantial commentary on the *Triumphs* and the *Rhymes*. Ernest Hatch Wilkins's *Life of Petrarch*, 1961, is a more detailed biography of the poet. Morris Bishop's *Petrarch and His World*, 1963, analyzes Petrarch and his times in great detail, but it is nonetheless suited for the new student of the poet. Nicholas Mann, *Petrarch*, 1984, in the Past Masters series, is a short book on Petrarch's life and mind, emphasizing especially Petrarch's self-consciousness and image of himself. Kenelm Foster, *Petrarch, Poet and Humanist*, 1984, is a comprehensive biographical and critical study, especially valuable on the relationship between the classical and religious sides of Petrarch. Petrarch's Italian poetry is discussed with critical acumen and a sense of the historical context in Peter Hainsworth, *Petrarch the Poet; An Introduction to the Rerum Vulgarium Fragmenta*, 1988. Marjorie O'Rourke Boyle, *Petrarch's Genius: Pentimento and Prophecy*, 1991, is notably fresh and original. A Nobel Prize poet's thoughts on Petrarch are recorded in Salvatore Quasimodo's *The Poet and the Politician*, 1960, translated by Thomas G. Bergin, 1964. The second essay in this volume contains sections on both Petrarch's solitude and Dante's reputation. Stephen Minta's *Petrarch and Petrarchism: The English and French Traditions*, 1980, is an excellent anthology of poems by Petrarch and by English and French poets influenced by him. On the Renaissance humanists in general, see the Further Reading section of the Introduction to the Renaissance in the present book.

RHYMES

Translation and notes by Anthony Mortimer

I

All you that hear in scattered rhymes[1] the sound
of sighs on which I used to feed my heart
in my first youthful error when, in part,
I was another man, now left behind;

for the vain hopes, vain sorrows of my mind,   5
the tears and discourse of my varied art,
in any who have played a lover's part
pardon and pity too I hope to find.

---

[1] The poet regards his "scattered rhymes" as a collection of fragments *(Rerum vulgarium fragmenta)*, but there is also the possibility that they are scattered through the world. The whole sonnet is, indeed, indicative of Petrarch's ambiguous attitude towards the *Canzoniere*: he deplores it as evidence of a "youthful error," but he still hopes to find readers. (Notes, unless otherwise indicated, are by the translator.)

But now I see too well how I became
a tale for common gossip everywhere,   10
so that I grow ashamed of what I am;

and of my raving still the fruit is shame
and penitence, and last the knowledge clear
that all the world loves is a passing dream.

III

It was that very day on which the sun
in awe of his creator dimmed the ray,[1]
when I was captured, with my guard astray,
for your fine eyes, my lady, bound me then.

It hardly seemed the time for me to plan   5
defence against Love's stroke; I went my way
secure, unwary; so upon that day
of general sorrow all my pains began.

Love found me with no armour for the fight,
my eyes an open highway to the heart,   10
eyes that are now a vent for tears to flow.

And yet he played no honourable part,
wounding me with his shaft in such a state;
he saw you armed and dared not lift the bow.

XC

Upon the breeze she spread her golden hair[1]
that in a thousand gentle knots was turned,
and the sweet light beyond all measure burned
in eyes where now that radiance is rare;

and in her face there seemed to come an air   5
of pity, true or false, that I discerned:
I had love's tinder in my breast unburned,
was it a wonder if it kindled there?

---

[1] Petrarch first saw Laura at matins in the church of Saint Clare in Avignon on April 6, 1327. This was not the moveable feast of Good Friday, but, according to medieval calculations, the exact calendar anniversary of Christ's death.
[1] This sonnet is inspired by a description of Venus appearing to Aeneas in Virgil's *Aeneid*, Book I. (Editors' note.)

She moved not like a mortal, but as though
she bore an angel's form, her words had then   10
a sound that simple human voices lack;

a heavenly spirit, a living sun
was what I saw; now, if it is not so,
the wound's not healed because the bow grows slack.

CXXVI

Waters[1] fresh and sweet and clear
where the fair limbs reclined
of the one creature who to me seems woman;
and gentle tree-trunk where,
with sighs I call to mind,   5
the leaning side once loved to find a column;
flowers and grass that often
the light gown hid from sight
with the angelic breast;[2]
airs breathing holy rest   10
where Love with those fair eyes opened my heart:
come, and together grant
a hearing to my last lament.

If it be destiny,
and heaven works for this,   15
that Love should close these weeping eyes of mine,
then may some kindness lay
the body in your midst
and the soul naked to its home return;
death shall become less stern   20
if such a hope I bear
into that fearful pass,
for the soul's weariness
could find no calmer haven anywhere,
nor could it ever leave   25
the troubled flesh in a more quiet grave.

A time may come again
when she perhaps will stray
to the old haunt, untamed, yet fair and meek,

---

[1] The waters of the Sorgue in Vaucluse.
[2] Commentators have been unnecessarily puzzled here. The poet, in fact, recalls Laura in
a number of different attitudes: bathing in the river, leaning against a tree, and sitting on the
ground so that the gown which covers her breast also covers the grass and flowers.

and where she saw me then 30
upon that blessed day
will turn an eager and a happy look,
and there, O pity! seek
and find me turned to dust amid the stones:
at this may Love arise, 35
inspiring her with sighs
so sweet she forces heaven[3] and obtains
its mercy for my soul,
drying her eyes upon the lovely veil.

From the fair boughs there fell, 40
sweet in the memory,
upon her lap a rain of every flower,
and she sat there and still
was humble in such glory,
already covered by the loving shower; 45
upon the hem lay flowers,
and some the tresses crowned
which seemed that day to hold
both pearls and polished gold;
some rested on the waves, some on the ground; 50
some, sweetly turning through the air,
seemed in their drift to whisper: "Love reigns here."

How often I exclaimed,
seized by a sudden fear:
"For certain she was born in Paradise!" 55
Such deep oblivion came
from her celestial air,
the words, the gentle smiling, and the eyes,
so faintly did I seize
the image truth would show, 60
that I said sighing then:
"How came I here, or when?"
thinking myself in heaven, not here below.
And ever since I've loved this place
so much that elsewhere I can find no peace. 65

Song, had you beauty as you have desire,
intrepidly you could
go out among the crowd and leave this wood.

---

[3]Bosco [a modern Italian critic] points out that heaven will be impressed not by Laura's sorrow or piety, but by the sweetness of her sighs and the elegance of her gestures. Even the intercession of the living for the dead is seen in aesthetic terms.

CXXIX

From thought to thought, from mountainside to mountain
Love leads me on, since every beaten trail
I feel as hostile to my peace of mind.
If some deserted heath has stream or fountain,
or if two hills should hide a shadowed vale,   5
the spirit sees its suffering decline,
and there, as Love designs,
now laughs and weeps, now fears and learns to trust;
the face that follows where the spirit leads
grows clear and overclouds,   10
and no condition ever seems to last:
so, at the sight, a man who knew that life
would say: "He burns, and stands in doubtful strife."

Among high mountains and wild woods I find
some kind of rest; but each frequented place   15
becomes an enemy that my eyes abhor.
At every step a new thought comes to mind
of my dear lady, often bringing gladness
out of the torment that I feel for her;
and hardly would I prefer   20
to change the sweet and bitter life I bear
when I reflect: "Perhaps Love keeps in view
a better time for you;
you hate yourself, but she may hold you dear."
And with this thought sighing I change again: 25
"Can it be ever true? but how? and when?"

Where a tall pine-tree or a hill gives shade
sometimes I stop, and on the nearest stone
my mind will draw her face. At last I find,
on coming to myself, my breast is bathed   30
with that emotion; then "alas," I groan,
"where are you now? what have you left behind?"
But while my wandering mind
can be kept steadfastly on that first thought
and I forget myself and gaze on her,   35
then I feel Love so near
the soul is sated with its own deceit:
I see her in so many things, so fair,
that if the illusion lasts I ask no more.

Often I've seen (who will believe me now?)   40
on the green grass or in transparent water
her living self, in beech-trees or the face

of a white cloud, and ever fashioned so
that Leda[1] would have surely said her daughter
fades like a star outshone by the sun's rays; 45
and the more wild the place
I come upon, the lonelier the shore
the fairer does thought shadow forth[2] my love.
Then, when the truth removes
that sweet illusion, I sit as before, 50
cold and stone-dead upon the living stone,[3]
like one who thinks and weeps and writes alone.

To where the mountain shadows never lie,
towards the highest and best vantage-point,
a fierce desire often makes me start. 55
There I begin to measure with the eye
my sufferings, and tearfully give vent
to the sad mists that thicken in my heart,
when both my gaze and thought
span all that lies between me and the fair 60
face that is still so near and far away;
then, whispering to myself, I say:
"What can you know? this moment over there
perhaps your absence makes her sigh for you;"
and in this thought the spirit breathes anew. 65

My song, beyond this alp,
where skies are happier and clear above,
you'll find me sitting by a stream that flows
where gentle aura blows
in from a fresh and fragrant laurel-grove: 70
there is my heart and she that stole it from me;
and here my image all that you can see.[4]

[1] Leda, seduced by Zeus in the form of a swan, was the mother of Helen of Troy. (Editors' note.)

[2] The Italian word is *adombra*. More than "shadow forth" this suggests the conscious chiaroscuro of the painter, thus continuing the artist metaphor introduced in the previous stanza.

[3] The contrast is probably between the stone effigy on a tomb (*pietra morta*) and the natural stone (*pietra viva*) upon which the poet sits. Having transformed so many shapes into Laura's image, the poet now becomes an image himself. This reading is confirmed by the last line of the poem.

[4] The envoi sends the poem to join the poet's heart which is with Laura beyond the Alps. For once I have attempted to translate the pun on Laura's name.

CXXXIV

I find no peace, and have no arms for war,
and fear and hope, and burn and yet I freeze,
and fly to heaven, lying on earth's floor,
and nothing hold, and all the world I seize.

My jailer opens not, nor locks the door,   5
nor binds me to her, nor will loose my ties;
Love kills me not, nor breaks the chains I wear,
nor wants me living, nor will grant me ease.

I have no tongue, and shout; eyeless, I see;
I long to perish, and I beg for aid;   10
I love another, and myself I hate.

Weeping I laugh, I feed on misery,
by death and life so equally dismayed:
for you, my lady, am I in this state.

CCLXV

Fierce heart and bitter, and most cruel will,
sweet, humble, and angelic to the sight,
if this first rigor last throughout the fight,
the honour of their trophies will be small;

for when grass, leaf, and flower spring and fall,   5
when daylight comes, and in the dark of night,
always I weep. Indeed I have the right
on Love, my fate, my lady thus to call.

I live on hope alone, remembering
how I have seen a little moisture prove   10
to wear down marble and the solid stone:

there cannot be a heart so hard that weeping,
praying, and loving sometime will not move,
nor yet a will so cold it cannot burn.

CCXCII

The eyes I spoke of once in words that burn,
the arms and hands and feet and lovely face

that took me from myself for such a space
of time and marked me out from other men;

the waving hair of unmixed gold that shone,　　　　　5
the smile that flashed with the angelic rays
that used to make this earth a paradise,
are now a little dust, all feeling gone;

and yet I live, grief and disdain to me,
left where the light I cherished never shows,　　　　10
in fragile bark on the tempestuous sea.

Here let my loving song come to a close,
the vein of my accustomed art is dry,
and this, my lyre, turned at last to tears.[1]

CCCLXV[1]

I keep lamenting over days gone by,
the time I spent loving a mortal thing,
with no attempt to soar, although my wing
might give no mean example in the sky.[2]

You that my foul unworthy sins descry,　　　　　5
unseen and everlasting, heaven's King,
succour my soul, infirm and wandering,
and what is lacking let your grace supply;

so if I lived in tempest and in war,
I die in port and peace; however vain　　　　　10
the stay, at least the parting may be fair.

Now in the little life that still remains
and at my death may your quick hand be near:
in others, you well know, my hope is gone.

[1] See Job, 30:31, "My lyre is turned to mourning."
[1] The last sonnet, but not the last poem in the *Canzoniere,* which concludes with a canzone to the Virgin.
[2] The humility of the recantation is rendered more poignant by this lingering touch of human pride. Love for the "mortal thing" has been an obstacle to salvation, but there is also the explicit regret that it has prevented him from demonstrating his true worth in the eyes of the world.

Giovanni Boccaccio

(1313–1375)

The great triumvirate of Italian literature in the fourteenth century consists of Dante, Petrarch, and Boccaccio. Boccaccio, the youngest, was born in 1313, the illegitimate son of a merchant-banker who had family roots in or near Florence. The legend, nurtured by Boccaccio, that he was born in Paris of an aristocratic mother is now regarded skeptically. He spent his childhood, not very happily, in Florence, moving with his businessman father to Naples when Boccaccio was about fourteen. His father gave him twelve years of education, first in commerce and then in church law, but Boccaccio wanted above all else to be a poet. His contact with the aristocracy of Naples, who had banking connections with his father's firm, gave Boccaccio the opportunity to develop as both writer and gentleman, since the Neapolitan court was highly cultivated and intellectual in tone. At the same time, his connection with commerce, in Naples and later in Florence, taught him about the life of middle-class people. It was in Naples too that Boccaccio is supposed to have met "Fiammetta," the object of his passionate love—the equivalent for Boccaccio of Dante's Beatrice and Petrarch's Laura. The identity of Fiammetta in real life is uncertain, and her very existence has been questioned. Real or fictitious, however, she was the occasion or focus for much of Boccaccio's early work. In this period, he wrote mainly in Italian rather than in the traditional learned language, Latin.

In 1340, Boccaccio reluctantly left Naples, where he had been very happy, and returned to Florence, where his literary art reached its full flower, culminating in *The Decameron* (completed by 1353), or "Work of Ten Days." Boccaccio's earlier writing had been distinctly medieval in its concern with chivalric themes and its use of the genres of romance and allegory. Certain of his early works had revealed his gift of keen insight into human psychology, but nothing quite prepares us for *The Decameron,* with its brilliant dramatic and narrative styles and its rich variety of tones, from the wholly serious and tragic to the raucously farcical. Boccaccio had seen at first hand in Florence the ravages of the plague (the Black Death), and his vividly gruesome account of it at the beginning of *The Decameron* throws into relief the idyllic life led by the seven women and three men who tell the stories. The tone of their life in their country refuge is witty, refined, decorous, but relaxedly sensuous, in sharp contrast with the horrors they have escaped. The reader is aware, however, at some level of consciousness, of the terrible background. The most broadly comic parts of the work can be experienced as a reflex response to the plague, by characters and readers alike.

The Decameron served as a model for Italian prose writers and had an enormous influence on later European literature. But Boccaccio wrote no later works in the same vein. In 1350, he met Petrarch (of whom he had already written a biography), and the two men enjoyed a close friendship for the rest of their lives. Petrarch influenced Boccaccio in some important ways, turning him toward the Latin tongue and various scholarly projects (for example, compendia of ancient myths, of famous men and women, and of place names in classical literature). Petrarch seems also to have been one cause, though not the only one, of an increasingly moral and religious tone in Boccaccio's later years. On the other hand, it was Petrarch who, when Boccaccio contemplated burning his earlier works, persuaded him not to do so. Having proved himself, in *The Decameron,* to be a humanist in the modern, popular sense, the older Boccaccio proved himself a humanist in the more technical sense that has to do with the revival of ancient classical learning and literature. He was instrumental, for example, in encouraging the translation of the epics of Homer. He also wrote, in Italian, a treatise on Dante and a commentary on the first half of Dante's *Inferno.* Despite the honor of public offices and of several ambassadorships, the last decades of Boccaccio's life were unsettled, often overshadowed by poverty. He died in 1375, a year later than Petrarch.

The much discussed question whether Boccaccio belongs to the Middle Ages or to the Renaissance is for some scholars a pseudo-question, implying an overly simple view of the Middle Ages as piously ascetic and of the Renaissance as exclusively secular. Even if one allows for the distortions of stereotyping, however, it is difficult not to see in Boccaccio's work, or at least *The Decameron,* something distinctively modern. Much of his work looks backward to medieval chivalric values and beyond them to antiquity. But the worldly pragmatism of *The Decameron,* with its almost exclusive emphasis on human ingenuity and resourcefulness, is something genuinely new. Heaven and divine grace play almost no role in *The Decameron.* In the hundred tales, people are what the vicissitudes of life and their own characters make them, whether shrewd or gullible, high-minded or unscrupulous. Moreover, *The Decameron* also represents a transition to social realism; the ten storytellers have the manners of aristocrats, but many of the stories involve people of the lower and especially the middle classes. The essence of *The Decameron* is its variety—of subject matter, of tone, and of source (Boccaccio invented few, if any, of the tales *in toto*). The sense of a broad social and literary spectrum is one of the several parallels between Boccaccio and Chaucer, who was influenced by him.

Part of the worldliness of *The Decameron* is its notorious bawdiness, which is sometimes very explicit. Boccaccio's defensiveness on the matter shows that in his own time, and not only in later more prudish eras, some of the stories gave offense. Boccaccio tries to vindicate himself in his conclusion, advancing arguments that the reader may or may not find convincing. To them one may add the obvious: that the governing theme of *The Decameron* is love, and any comprehensive treatment of it must include the carnal as well as the psychological and spiritual. To many readers the main justification for the bawdiness will be the sparkling wit that characterizes many of the sexual episodes. It must be added too that the sexuality of *The Decameron* is intimately connected with its treatment of the sexes, particularly the very modern portrayal of women not as etherealized ideals but as realistic creatures of flesh and blood who are driven as much by desire as men are. The controversially patient Griselda is the exception that dramatizes the rule.

FURTHER READING *(prepared by W.J.R.):* Thomas Bergin's *Boccaccio,* 1982, is a comprehensive introduction to the author's life and writings. Valuable as a general introduction is Judith Powers Serafini-Sauli, *Giovanni Boccaccio,* 1982. Vittore Branca's *Boccaccio: The Man and His Works,* trans. Richard Monges, 1976, provides a brief biographical sketch. Book II is devoted to *The Decameron*, with discussions of the medieval tradition in Boccaccio's work, his narrative art, and other topics. Stephen A. McKnight, *Sacralizing the Secular*, 1989, throws light on the Renaissance understanding of the secular and Boccaccio's relation to it. On style, see *An Anatomy of Boccaccio's Style*, ed. Marga Cottino-Jones, 1968. Critical approaches in this volume range from linguistic to archetypal. The first essay offers an overview of Boccaccio criticism. Joan M. Ferrante's "Narrative Patterns in the *Decameron*," *Romance Philology*, 31 (1978), 585–604, looks at the entire *Decameron*, seeking to clarify the meaning of narrative themes. "The Worlds of the *Decameron*," Chapter Two in Yvonne Rodax's *The Real and the Ideal in the Novella of Italy, France and England*, 1968, discusses the achievement of vigorous reality in Boccaccio's tales, with a particular emphasis on medieval values. The first and third chapters in this work, on the novella and on *The Canterbury Tales*, are also of interest. Shirley S. Allen's "The Griselda Tale and the Portrayal of Women in the *Decameron*," *Philological Quarterly*, 56 (1977), 1–13, considers previous interpretations of the tale of "patient Griselda" and argues that viewing the tale as an ironic plea for women's rights is in accord with the overall unity of *The Decameron*. Marga Cottino-Jones' "Comic Modalities in the *Decameron*," in *Versions of Medieval Comedy*, ed. Paul G. Ruggiers, 1977, investigates the varying comic tones and makes some general observations on the nature of Boccaccio's comedy. Cormac Cuilleanáin's "Man and Beast in the *Decameron*," *Modern Language Review*, 75 (1980), 86–93, studies animal imagery and symbolism as it reveals Boccaccio's principal theme of man's existence in a social community. Demanding but exciting is Giuseppe Mazzotta, *The World at Play in Boccaccio's "Decameron*," 1986, which relates the work in incisive ways to the culture of its time.

THE DECAMERON

Translated by Richard Aldington

THE FIRST DAY

Here begins the first day of the Decameron, *wherein, after the author has showed the reasons why certain persons gathered to tell tales, they treat of any subject pleasing to them, under the rule of Pampinea.*

Most gracious ladies, knowing that you are all by nature pitiful, I know that in your judgment this work will seem to have a painful and sad origin. For it brings to mind the unhappy recollection of that late dreadful plague,[1] so pernicious to all who saw or heard of it. But I would not have this frighten you from reading further, as though you were to pass through nothing but sighs and tears in your reading. This dreary opening will be like climbing a steep mountain side to a most beautiful and delightful valley, which appears the more pleasant in proportion to the difficulty of the ascent. The end of happiness is pain, and in like manner misery ends in unexpected happiness.

This brief fatigue (I say brief, because it occupies only a few words) is quickly followed by pleasantness and delight, as I promised you above;

---

[1] The "Black Death," probably bubonic plague, killed millions in Europe and Asia in the mid-fourteenth century.

which, if I had not promised, you would not expect perhaps from this opening. Indeed, if I could have taken you by any other way than this, which I know to be rough, I would gladly have done so; but since I cannot otherwise tell you how the tales you are about to read came to be told, I am forced by necessity to write in this manner.

In the year 1348 after the fruitful incarnation of the Son of God, that most beautiful of Italian cities, noble Florence, was attacked by deadly plague. It started in the East either through the influence of the heavenly bodies or because God's just anger with our wicked deeds sent it as a punishment to mortal men; and in a few years killed an innumerable quantity of people. Ceaselessly passing from place to place, it extended its miserable length over the West. Against this plague all human wisdom and foresight were vain. Orders had been given to cleanse the city of filth, the entry of any sick person was forbidden, much advice was given for keeping healthy; at the same time humble supplications were made to God by pious persons in processions and otherwise. And yet, in the beginning of the spring of the year mentioned, its horrible results began to appear, and in a miraculous manner. The symptoms were not the same as in the East, where a gush of blood from the nose was the plain sign of inevitable death; but it began both in men and women with certain swellings in the groin or under the armpit. They grew to the size of a small apple or an egg, more or less, and were vulgarly called tumors. In a short space of time these tumors spread from the two parts named all over the body. Soon after this the symptoms changed and black or purple spots appeared on the arms or thighs or any other part of the body, sometimes a few large ones, sometimes many little ones. These spots were a certain sign of death, just as the original tumor had been and still remained.

No doctor's advice, no medicine could overcome or alleviate this disease. An enormous number of ignorant men and women set up as doctors in addition to those who were trained. Either the disease was such that no treatment was possible or the doctors were so ignorant that they did not know what caused it, and consequently could not administer the proper remedy. In any case very few recovered; most people died within about three days of the appearance of the tumors described above, most of them without any fever or other symptoms.

The violence of this disease was such that the sick communicated it to the healthy who came near them, just as a fire catches anything dry or oily near it. And it even went further. To speak to or go near the sick brought infection and a common death to the living; and moreover, to touch the clothes or anything else the sick had touched or worn gave the disease to the person touching.

What I am about to tell now is a marvelous thing to hear; and if I and others had not seen it with our own eyes I would not dare to write it, however much I was willing to believe and whatever the good faith of the person from whom I heard it. So violent was the malignancy of this plague that it was communicated, not only from one man to another, but from the garments of a sick or dead man to animals of another species, which caught the disease in that way and very quickly died of it. One day among other occasions I saw with my own eyes (as I said just now) the rags left lying in the street of a poor man who had died of the plague; two pigs came along and, as their habit is, turned the clothes over with their snouts and then munched at them, with the result that they both fell dead almost at once on the rags, as if they had been poisoned.

From these and similar or greater occurrences, such fear and fanciful notions took possession of the living that almost all of them adopted the same cruel policy, which was entirely to avoid the sick and everything belonging to them. By so doing, each one thought he would secure his own safety.

Some thought that moderate living and the avoidance of all superfluity would preserve them from the epidemic. They formed small communities, living entirely separate from everybody else. They shut themselves up in houses where there were no sick, eating the finest food and drinking the best wine very temperately, avoiding all excess, allowing no news or discussion of death and sickness, and passing the time in music and suchlike pleasures. Others thought just the opposite. They thought the sure cure for the plague was to drink and be merry, to go about singing and amusing themselves, satisfying every appetite they could, laughing and jesting at what happened. They put their words into practice, spent day and night going from tavern to tavern, drinking immoderately, or went into other people's houses, doing only those things which pleased them. This they could easily do because everyone felt doomed and had abandoned his property, so that most houses became common property and any stranger who went in made use of them as if he had owned them. And with all this bestial behavior, they avoided the sick as much as possible.

In this suffering and misery of our city, the authority of human and divine laws almost disappeared, for, like other men, the ministers and the executors of the laws were all dead or sick or shut up with their families, so that no duties were carried out. Every man was therefore able to do as he pleased.

Many others adopted a course of life midway between the two just described. They did not restrict their victuals so much as the former, nor allow themselves to be drunken and dissolute like the latter, but satisfied their appetites moderately. They did not shut themselves up, but went about, carrying flowers or scented herbs or perfumes in their hands, in the belief that it was an excellent thing to comfort the brain with such odors; for the whole air was infected with the smell of dead bodies, of sick persons and medicines.

Others again held a still more cruel opinion, which they thought would keep them safe. They said that the only medicine against the plague-stricken was to go right away from them. Men and women, convinced of this and caring about nothing but themselves, abandoned their own city, their own houses, their dwellings, their relatives, their property, and went abroad or at least to the country round Florence, as if God's wrath in punishing men's wickedness with this plague would not follow them but strike only those who remained within the walls of the city, or as if they thought nobody in the city would remain alive and that its last hour had come.

Not everyone who adopted any of these various opinions died, nor did all escape. Some when they were still healthy had set the example of avoiding the sick, and, falling ill themselves, died untended.

One citizen avoided another, hardly any neighbor troubled about others, relatives never or hardly ever visited each other. Moreover, such terror was struck into the hearts of men and women by this calamity, that brother abandoned brother, and the uncle his nephew, and the sister her brother, and very often the wife her husband. What is even worse and nearly incredible is that fathers and mothers refused to see and tend their children, as if they had not been theirs.

Thus, a multitude of sick men and women were left without any care except from the charity of friends (but these were few), or the greed of servants, though not many of these could be had even for high wages. Moreover, most of them were coarse-minded men and women, who did little more than bring the sick what they asked for or watch over them when they were dying. And very often these servants lost their lives and their earnings. Since the sick were thus abandoned by neighbors, relatives and friends, while servants were scarce, a habit sprang up which had never been heard of before. Beautiful and noble women, when they fell sick, did not scruple to take a young or old manservant, whoever he might be, and with no sort of shame, expose every part of their bodies to these men as if they had been women, for they were compelled by the necessity of their sickness to do so. This, perhaps, was a cause of looser morals in those women who survived.

In this way many people died who might have been saved if they had been looked after. Owing to the lack of attendants for the sick and the violence of the plague, such a multitude of people in the city died day and night that it was stupefying to hear of, let alone to see. From sheer necessity, then, several ancient customs were quite altered among the survivors.

The custom had been (as we still see it today) that women relatives and neighbors should gather at the house of the deceased, and there lament with the family. At the same time the men would gather at the door with the male neighbors and other citizens. Then came the clergy, few or many according to the dead person's rank; the coffin was placed on the shoulders of his friends and carried with funeral pomp of lighted candles and dirges to the church which the deceased had chosen before dying. But as the fury of the plague increased, this custom wholly or nearly disappeared, and new customs arose. Thus, people died, not only without having a number of women near them, but without a single witness. Very few indeed were honored with the piteous laments and bitter tears of their relatives, who, on the contrary, spent their time in mirth, feasting and jesting. Even the women abandoned womanly pity and adopted this custom for their own safety. Few were they whose bodies were accompanied to church by more than ten or a dozen neighbors. Nor were these grave and honorable citizens but grave-diggers from the lowest of the people who got themselves called sextons, and performed the task for money. They took up the bier and hurried it off, not to the church chosen by the deceased but the church nearest, preceded by four or six of the clergy with few candles and often none at all. With the aid of the grave-diggers, the clergy huddled the bodies away in any grave they could find, without giving themselves the trouble of a long or solemn burial service.

The plight of the lower and most of the middle classes was even more pitiful to behold. Most of them remained in their houses, either through poverty or in hopes of safety, and fell sick by thousands. Since they received no care and attention, almost all of them died. Many ended their lives in the streets both at night and during the day; and many others who died in their houses were only known to be dead because the neighbors smelled their decaying bodies. Dead bodies filled every corner. Most of them were treated in the same manner by the survivors, who were more concerned to get rid of their rotting bodies than moved by charity towards the dead. With the aid of porters, if they could get them, they carried the bodies out of the houses and laid them at the doors, where every morning quantities of the dead might be seen. They then were laid on biers, or, as these were often lacking, on tables.

Often a single bier carried two or three bodies, and it happened frequently that a husband and wife, two or three brothers, or father and son were taken off on the same bier. It frequently happened that two priests, each carrying a cross, would go out followed by three or four biers carried by porters; and where the priests thought there was one person to bury, there would be six or eight, and often, even more. Nor were these dead honored by tears and lighted candles and mourners, for things had reached such a pass that people cared no more for dead men than we care for dead goats. Thus it plainly appeared that what the wise had not learned to endure with patience through the few calamities of ordinary life, became a matter of indifference even to the most ignorant people through the greatness of this misfortune.

Such was the multitude of corpses brought to the churches every day and almost every hour that there was not enough consecrated ground to give them burial, especially since they wanted to bury each person in the family grave, according to the old custom. Although the cemeteries were full they were forced to dig huge trenches, where they buried the bodies by hundreds. Here they stowed them away like bales in the hold of a ship and covered them with a little earth, until the whole trench was full.

Not to pry any further into all the details of the miseries which afflicted our city, I shall add that the surrounding country was spared nothing of what befell Florence. The villages on a smaller scale were like the city; in the fields and isolated farms the poor wretched peasants and their families were without doctors and any assistance, and perished in the highways, in their fields and houses, night and day, more like beasts than men. Just as the townsmen became dissolute and indifferent to their work and property, so the peasants, when they saw that death was upon them, entirely neglected the future fruits of their past labors both from the earth and from cattle, and thought only of enjoying what they had. Thus it happened that cows, asses, sheep, goats, pigs, fowls and even dogs, those faithful companions of man, left the farms and wandered at their will through the fields, where the wheat crops stood abandoned, unreaped and ungarnered. Many of these animals seemed endowed with reason, for, after they had pastured all day, they returned to the farms for the night of their own free will, without being driven.

Returning from the country to the city, it may be said that such was the cruelty of Heaven, and perhaps in part of men, that between March and July more than one hundred thousand persons died within the walls of Florence, what between the violence of the plague and the abandonment in which the sick were left by the cowardice of the healthy. And before the plague it was not thought that the whole city held so many people.

Oh, what great palaces, how many fair houses and noble dwellings, once filled with attendants and nobles and ladies, were emptied to the meanest servant! How many famous names and vast possessions and renowned estates were left without an heir! How many gallant men and fair ladies and handsome youths, whom Galen, Hippocrates and Aesculapius[2] themselves would have said were in perfect health, at noon dined with their relatives and friends, and at night supped with their ancestors in the next world!

But it fills me with sorrow to go over so many miseries. Therefore, since I want to pass over all I can leave out, I shall go on to say that when our city was in this condition and almost emptied of inhabitants, one Tuesday morning the venerable church of Santa Maria Novella had scarcely any congregation for divine service except (as I have heard from a person worthy of belief) seven young women in the mourning garments suitable to the times, who were all related by ties of blood, friendship or neighborship. None of them was older than twenty-eight or younger than eighteen; all were educated and of noble blood, fair to look upon, well-mannered and of graceful modesty.

I should tell you their real names if I had not a good reason for not doing so, which is that I would not have any of them blush in the future for the things they say and hearken to in the following pages. The laws are now strict again, whereas then, for the reasons already shown, they were very lax, not only for persons of their age but for those much older. Nor would I give an opportunity to the envious (always ready to sneer at every praiseworthy life) to attack the virtue of these modest ladies with vulgar speech. But so that you may understand without confusion what each one says, I intend to give them names wholly or partly suitable to the qualities of each.

The first and eldest I shall call Pampinea, the second Fiammetta, the third Filomena, the fourth Emilia, the fifth Lauretta, the sixth Neifile, and the last Elisa[3] (or "the virgin") for a very good reason. They met, not by arrangement, but by chance, in the same part of the church, and sat down in a circle. After many sighs they ceased to pray and began to talk about the state of affairs and other things. After a short space of silence, Pampinea said:

"Dear ladies, you must often have heard, as I have, that to make a sensible use of one's reason harms nobody. It is natural for everybody to aid, preserve and defend his life as far as possible. And this is so far admitted that to save their own lives men often kill others who have done no harm. If this is permitted by the laws which are concerned with the general good, it must certainly be lawful for us to take any reasonable means for the preservation of our lives. When I think of what we have been doing this morning and still more on former days, when I remember what we have been saying, I perceive and you must perceive that each of us goes in fear of her life. I do not wonder at this, but, since each of us has a woman's judgment, I do wonder that we do not seek some remedy against what we dread.

"In my opinion we remain here for no other purpose than to witness how many bodies are buried, or listen whether the friars here (themselves reduced

---

[2] The first two were ancient Greek physicians; Aesculapius was a Greco-Roman god of medicine.

[3] Most of the names are derived from Greek and have something to do with love. The qualities or roles associated with the seven women are probably as follows: Pampinea (the eldest) is a leader and adviser; Fiammetta is loving and beloved; Filomena (related to "nightingale") is a lover of music; Emilia has pleasant manners; Lauretta (related to *laurel*) is learned; Neifile is young and naive; Elisa, who is also young, recalls *Elissa*, a name for Dido, the passionate Carthaginian queen in Virgil's *Aeneid*.

almost to nothing) sing their offices at the canonical hours,[4] or to display by our clothes the quantity and quality of our miseries to anyone who comes here. If we leave this church we see the bodies of the dead and the sick being carried about. Or we see those who had been exiled from the city by the authority of the laws for their crimes, deriding this authority because they know the guardians of the law are sick or dead, and running loose about the place. Or we see the dregs of the city battening on our blood and calling themselves sextons, riding about on horseback in every direction and insulting our calamities with vile songs. On every side we hear nothing but 'So-and-so is dead' or 'So-and-so is dying.' And if there were anyone left to weep we should hear nothing but piteous lamentations. I do not know if it is the same in your homes as in mine. But if I go home there is nobody left there but one of my maids, which fills me with such horror that the hair stands upon my head. Wherever I go or sit at home I seem to see the ghosts of the departed, not with the faces as I knew them but with dreadful looks which terrify me.

"I am ill at ease here and outside of here and at home; the more so since nobody who has the strength and ability to go away (as we have) now remains here, except ourselves. The few that remain (if there are any), according to what I see and hear, do anything which gives them pleasure or pleases their appetites, both by day and night, whether they are alone or in company, making no distinction between right and wrong. Not only laymen, but those cloistered in convents have broken their oaths and given themselves up to the delights of the flesh, and thus in trying to escape the plague by doing what they please, they have become lascivious and dissolute.

"If this is so (and we may plainly see it is) what are we doing here? What are we waiting for? What are we dreaming about? Are we less eager and active than other citizens in saving our lives? Are they less dear to us than to others? Or do we think that our lives are bound to our bodies with stronger chains than other people's, and so believe that we need fear nothing which might harm us? We were and are deceived. How stupid we should be to believe such a thing! We may see the plainest proofs from the number of young men and women who have died of this cruel plague.

"I do not know if you think as I do, but in my opinion if we, through carelessness, do not want to fall into this calamity when we can escape it, I think we should do well to leave this town, just as many others have done and are doing. Let us avoid the wicked examples of others like death itself, and go and live virtuously in our country houses, of which each of us possesses several. There let us take what happiness and pleasure we can, without ever breaking the rules of reason in any manner.

"There we shall hear the birds sing, we shall see the green hills and valleys, the wheat-fields rolling like a sea, and all kinds of trees. We shall see the open Heavens which, although now angered against man, do not withhold from us their eternal beauties that are so much fairer to look upon than the empty walls of our city. The air will be fresher there, we shall find a greater plenty of those things necessary to life at this time, and fewer troubles. Although the peasants are dying like the townsmen, still, since the houses

---

[4] Chant their prayers at the times of day specified by the Church.

and inhabitants are fewer, we shall see less of them and feel less misery. On the other hand I believe we are not abandoning anybody here. Indeed we can truthfully say that we are abandoned, since our relatives have either died or fled from death and have left us alone in this calamity as if we were nothing to them.

"If we do what I suggest, no blame can fall upon us; if we fail to do it, the result may be pain, trouble and perhaps death. Therefore I think that we should do well to take our servants and all things necessary, and go from one house to another, enjoying whatever merriment and pleasure these times allow. Let us live in this way (unless death comes upon us) until we see what end Heaven decrees to this plague. And remember that going away virtuously will not harm us so much as staying here in wickedness will harm others."

The other ladies listened to what Pampinea said, praised her advice, and in their eagerness to follow it began to discuss details, as if they were going to leave at once. But Filomena, who was a most prudent young woman, said:

"Ladies, although what Pampinea says is excellent advice, we must not rush off at once, as you seem to wish. Remember we are all women; and any girl can tell you how women behave together and conduct themselves without the direction of some man. We are fickle, wayward, suspicious, faint-hearted and cowardly. So if we have no guide but ourselves I greatly suspect that this company will very soon break up, without much honor to ourselves. Let us settle this matter before we start."

Elisa then broke in:

"Indeed men are a woman's head and we can rarely succeed in anything without their help; but how can we find any men? Each of us knows that most of her menfolk are dead, while the others are away, we know not where, flying with their companions from the end we wish to escape. To ask strangers would be unbecoming; for, if we mean to go away to save our lives we must take care that scandal and annoyance do not follow us where we are seeking rest and amusement."

While the ladies were thus arguing, three young men came into the church, the youngest of whom was not less than twenty-five. They were lovers whose love could not be quenched or even cooled by the horror of the times, the loss of relatives and friends, or even fear for themselves. The first was named Pamfilo, the second Filostrato, the third Dioneo.[5] They were pleasant, well-mannered men, and in this public calamity they sought the consolation of looking upon the ladies they loved. These ladies happened to be among our seven, while some of the others were related to one or other of the three men. They no sooner came into sight than the ladies saw them; whereupon Pampinea said with a smile:

"See how Fortune favors our plan at once by sending us these valiant and discreet young men, who will gladly act as our guides and servants if we do not refuse to accept them for such duties."

Neifile then became crimson, for she was one of the ladies beloved by one of the young men, and said:

---

[5] The name *Pamphilo* means "loving all"; *Filostrato* means "lover of strife" (perhaps the strife of being in love) and also "victim of love"; *Dioneo* is related to one of the names of Venus, goddess of sexual love.

"For God's sake, Pampinea, be careful what you are saying. I know quite well that nothing but good can be said of any of them and I am sure they could achieve greater things than this. I also think that their company would be fitting and pleasant, not only to us, but to ladies far more beautiful and charming than we are. But it is known to everyone that they are in love with some of us women here; and so, if we take them with us, I am afraid that blame and infamy will fall upon us, through no fault of ours or theirs."

Then said Filomena:

"What does that matter? If I live virtuously, my conscience never pricks me, whatever people may say. God and the truth will fight for me. If these men would come with us, then indeed, as Pampinea said, fortune would be favorable to our plan of going away."

The others not only refrained from censuring what she said, but agreed by common consent that the men should be spoken to, told their plan, and asked if they would accompany the ladies on their expedition. Without more ado, Pampinea, who was related to one of them, arose and went towards them where they stood looking at the ladies, saluted them cheerfully, told them the plan, and begged them in the name of all the ladies to accompany them out of pure and fraternal affection.

At first the young men thought this was a jest. But when they saw the lady was speaking seriously, they said they were willing to go. And in order to start without delay they at once gave the orders necessary for departure. Everything necessary was made ready, and word was sent on ahead to the place they were going. At dawn next morning, which was Wednesday, the ladies with some of their servants, and the young men with a man servant each, left the city and set out. They had not gone more than two miles when they came to the first place where they were to stay.

This estate was on slightly raised ground, at some distance from any main road, with many trees and plants, fair to look upon. At the top of the rise was a country mansion with a large inner courtyard. It had open colonnades, galleries and rooms, all beautiful in themselves and ornamented with gay paintings. Roundabout were lawns and marvelous gardens and wells of cool water. There were cellars of fine wines, more suitable to wine connoisseurs than to sober and virtuous ladies. The whole house had been cleaned, the beds were prepared in the rooms, and every corner was strewn with the flowers of the season and fresh rushes. All of which the company beheld with no little pleasure.

They all sat down to discuss plans, and Dioneo, who was a most amusing young man and full of witticisms, remarked:

"Ladies, your good sense, rather than our foresight, has brought us here. I do not know what you are thinking of doing with your troubles here, but I dropped mine inside the gates of the city when I left it with you a little time ago. Therefore, either you must make up your minds to laugh and sing and amuse yourselves with me (that is, to the extent your dignity allows), or you must let me go back to my troubles and stay in the afflicted city."

Pampinea, who had driven away her woes in the same way, cheerfully replied:

"Dioneo, you speak well, let us amuse ourselves, for that was the reason why we fled from our sorrows. But when things are not organized they cannot long continue. And, since I began the discussion which brought this fair company together and since I wish our happiness to continue, I think it necessary that one of us should be made chief, whom the others will honor and obey, and whose duty shall be to regulate our pleasures. Now, so that everyone—both man and woman—may experience the cares as well as the pleasures of ruling and no one feel any envy at not sharing them, I think the weight and honor should be given to each of us in turn for one day. The first shall be elected by all of us. At vespers[6] he or she shall choose the ruler for the next day, and so on. While their reigns last these rulers shall arrange where and how we are to spend our time."

These words pleased them all and they unanimously elected her for the first day. Filomena ran to a laurel bush, whose leaves she had always heard were most honorable in themselves and did great honor to anyone crowned with them, plucked off a few small branches and wove them into a fair garland of honor. When this was placed on the head of any one of them, it was a symbol of rule and authority over the rest so long as the party remained together.

Pampinea, thus elected queen, ordered silence. She then sent for the three servants of the young men and the four women servants the ladies had brought, and said:

"To set a first example to you all which may be bettered and thus allow our gathering to live pleasantly and orderly and without shame and to last as long as we desire, I appoint Dioneo's servant Parmeno as my steward, and hand over to him the care of the whole family and of everything connected with the dining hall. Pamfilo's servant Sirisco shall be our treasurer and buyer, and carry out Parmeno's instructions. Tindaro shall wait on Filostrato and Dioneo and Pamfilo in their rooms, when the other two servants are occupied with their new duties. Filomena's servant Licisca and my own servant Misia shall remain permanently in the kitchen and carefully prepare the food which Parmeno sends them. Lauretta's Chimera and Fiammetta's Stratilia shall take care of the ladies' rooms and see that the whole house is clean. Moreover we will and command that everyone who values our good grace shall bring back only cheerful news, wherever he may go or return from, and whatever he may hear or see."

Having given these orders, which were approved by everyone, she jumped gaily to her feet and said:

"Here are gardens and lawns and other delicious places, where each of us can wander and enjoy them at will. But let everyone be here at the hour of Tierce[7] so that we can eat together while it is still cool."

The company of gay young men and women, thus given the queen's permission, went off together slowly through the gardens, talking of pleasant matters, weaving garlands of different leaves, and singing love songs. After the time allotted by the queen had elapsed they returned to the house and found that Parmeno had carefully carried out the duties of his office. Entering a ground floor room decorated everywhere with broom[8] blossoms, they found tables covered with white cloths and set with glasses which shone like silver.

[6] One of the canonical hours; about 6 P.M.
[7] A canonical hour; 9 A.M.   [8] A shrub.

They washed their hands and, at the queen's command, all sat down in the places allotted them by Parmeno. Delicately cooked food was brought, exquisite wines were at hand, and the three men servants waited at table. Everyone was delighted to see things so handsome and well arranged, and they ate merrily with much happy talk.

All the ladies and young men could dance and many of them could play and sing; so, when the tables were cleared, the queen called for musical instruments. At her command Dioneo took a lute and Fiammetta a viol, and began to play a dance tune. The queen sent the servants to their meal, and then with slow steps danced with the two young men and the other ladies. After that, they began to sing gay and charming songs.

In this way they amused themselves until the queen thought it was time for the siesta. So, at the queen's bidding, the three young men went off to their rooms (which were separated from the ladies') and found them filled with flowers as the dining hall had been. And similarly with the women. So they all undressed and went to sleep.

Not long after the hour of Nones,[9] the queen arose and made the other women and the young men also get up, saying that it was harmful to sleep too long during the daytime. Then they went out to a lawn of thick green grass entirely shaded from the sun. A soft breeze came to them there. The queen made them sit down in a circle on the grass, and said:

"As you see, the sun is high and the heat great, and nothing can be heard but the cicadas in the olive trees. To walk about at this hour would be foolish. Here it is cool and lovely, and, as you see, there are games of chess and draughts which everyone can amuse himself with, as he chooses. But, if my opinion is followed, we shall not play games, because in games the mind of one of the players must necessarily be distressed without any great pleasure to the other player or the onlookers. Let us rather spend this hot part of the day in telling tales, for thus one person can give pleasure to the whole company. When each of us has told a story, the sun will be going down and the heat less, and we can then go walking anywhere we choose for our amusement. If this pleases you (for here I am ready to follow your pleasure) let us do it. If it does not please you, let everyone do as he likes until evening."

The women and men all favored the telling of stories.

"Then if it pleases you," said the queen, "on this first day I order that everyone shall tell his tale about any subject he likes."

She then turned to Pamfilo, who was seated on her right, and ordered him to begin with a tale. Hearing this command, Pamfilo at once began as follows, while all listened.[10]

THIRD DAY, TENTH TALE

Alibech becomes a hermit, and the monk Rustico teaches her how to put the devil in Hell. She is afterwards taken away and becomes the wife of Neerbale.

___

[9] A canonical hour; about 3 P.M.

[10] Here the series of a hundred tales, ten each day, begins. After the first day, when the choice of tales is unrestricted, each day has a prescribed theme.

Dioneo had listened closely to the queen's story, and, when it was over and only he remained to tell a story, he did not wait to be commanded, but smilingly began as follows:

Most gracious ladies, perhaps you have never heard how the devil is put into hell; and so, without departing far from the theme[1] upon which you have all spoken today, I shall tell you about it. Perhaps when you have learned it, you also will be able to save your souls, and you may also discover that although love prefers to dwell in gay palaces and lovely rooms rather than in poor huts, yet he sometimes makes his power felt among thick woods and rugged mountains and desert caves. Whereby we may well perceive that all of us are subject to his power.

Now, to come to my story—in the city of Capsa[2] in Barbery there lived a very rich man who possessed among other children a pretty and charming daughter, named Alibech. She was not a Christian, but she heard many Christians in her native town crying up the Christian Faith and service to God, and one day she asked one of them how a person could most effectively serve God. The reply was that those best serve God who fly furthest from the things of this world, like the hermits who had departed to the solitudes of the Thebaid[3] Desert.

The girl was about fourteen and very simple minded. Urged by a mere childish enthusiasm and not by a well ordered desire, she secretly set out next morning quite alone, without saying a word to anyone, to find the Thebaid Desert. Her enthusiasm lasted several days and enabled her with great fatigue to reach those solitudes. In the distance she saw a little hut with a holy man standing at its entrance. He was amazed to see her there, and asked her what she was seeking. She replied that by God's inspiration she was seeking to serve Him, and begged the hermit to show her the right way to do so. But the holy man saw she was young and pretty, and feared that if he kept her with him he might be tempted of the devil. So he praised her good intentions, gave her some roots and wild apples to eat and some water to drink, and said:

"Daughter, not far from here dwells a holy man who is a far greater master of what you are seeking than I am; go to him."

And so he put her on the way. When she reached him, she was received with much the same words, and passing further on came to the cell of a young hermit named Rustico, to whom she made the same request as to the others. To test his spiritual strength, Rustico did not send her away, but took her into his cell. And when night came, he made her a bed of palm leaves and told her to sleep there.

Almost immediately after this, temptation began the struggle with his spiritual strength, and the hermit found that he had greatly over-estimated his powers of resistance. After a few assaults of the demon he shrugged his shoulders and surrendered. Putting aside holy thoughts and prayers and macerations,[4] he began to think of her beauty and youth, and then pondered how he should proceed with her so that she should not perceive that he obtained

---

[1] The stories told on the third day (ruled by Neifile) concern people who by cleverness gained or regained something desirable.
[2] A city in Tunisia; Barbery is in northern Africa.
[3] Near Thebes, in Egypt.   [4] Starvation diets.

what he wanted from her like a dissolute man. First of all he sounded her by certain questions, and discovered that she had never lain with a man and appeared to be very simple minded. He then saw how he could bring her to his desire under pretext of serving God. He began by eloquently showing how the devil is the enemy of the Lord God, and then gave her to understand that the service most pleasing to God is to put the devil back into hell, to which the Lord God has condemned him. The girl asked how this was done, and Rustico replied:

"You shall soon know. Do what you see me do."

He then threw off the few clothes he had and remained stark naked, and the girl imitated him. He kneeled down as if to pray and made her kneel exactly opposite him. As he gazed at her beauty, Rustico's desire became so great that the resurrection of the flesh occurred. Alibech looked at it with amazement, and said:

"Rustico, what is that thing I see sticking out in front of you which I haven't got?"

"My daughter," said Rustico, "that is the devil I spoke of. Do you see? He gives me so much trouble at this moment that I can scarcely endure him."

Said the girl:

"Praised be God! I see I am better off than you are, since I haven't such a devil."

"You speak truly," said Rustico, "but instead of this devil you have something else which I haven't."

"What's that?" said Alibech.

"You've got hell," replied Rustico, "and I believe God sent you here for the salvation of my soul, because this devil gives me great trouble, and if you will take pity upon me and let me put him into hell, you will give me the greatest comfort and at the same time will serve God and please Him, since, as you say, you came here for that purpose."

In all good faith the girl replied: "Father, since I have hell in me, let it be whenever you please."

Said Rustico: "Blessings upon you, my daughter. Let us put him in now so that he will afterwards depart from me."

So saying, he took the girl to one of their beds, and showed her how to lie so as to imprison the thing accursed of God. The girl had never before put any devil into her hell and at first felt a little pain, and exclaimed to Rustico:

"O father! This devil must certainly be wicked and the enemy of God, for even when he is put back into hell he hurts it."

"Daughter," said Rustico, "it will not always be so."

To prevent this from happening, Rustico put it into hell six times, before he got off the bed, and so purged the devil's pride that he was glad to rest a little. Thereafter he returned often and the obedient girl was always glad to take him in; and then the game began to give her pleasure, and she said to Rustico:

"I see that the good men of Capsa spoke the truth when they told me how sweet a thing is the service of God. I certainly do not remember that I ever did anything which gave me so much delight and pleasure as I get from putting the devil into hell. I think that everyone is a fool who does anything but serve God."

Thus it happened that she would often go to Rustico, and say:

"Father, I came here to serve God and not to remain in idleness. Let us put the devil in hell."

And once as they were doing it, she said:

"Rustico, I don't know why the devil ever goes out of hell. If he liked to remain there as much as hell likes to receive and hold him, he would never leave it."

The girl's frequent invitations to Rustico and their mutual pleasures in the service of God so took the stuffing out of his doublet[5] that he now felt chilly where another man would have been in a sweat. So he told the girl that the devil must not be chastened or put into hell except when pride made him lift his head. "And we," he said, "have so quelled his rage that he prays God to be left in peace." And in this way he silenced the girl for a time. But when she found that Rustico no longer asked her to put the devil in hell, she said one day:

"Rustico, your devil may be chastened and give you no more trouble, but my hell is not. You should therefore quench the raging of my hell with your devil, as I helped you to quell the pride of your devil with my hell."

Rustico, who lived on nothing but roots and water, made a poor response to this invitation. He told her that many devils would be needed to soothe her hell, but that he would do what he could. In this way he satisfied her hell a few times, but so seldom that it was like throwing a bean in a lion's mouth. And the girl, who thought they were not serving God as much as she wanted, kept murmuring.

Now, while there was this debate between the excess of desire in Alibech's hell and the lack of potency in Rustico's devil, a fire broke out in Capsa, and burned Alibech's father with all his children and servants. So Alibech became heir to all his property. A young man named Neerbale, who had spent all his money in riotous living, heard that she was still alive and set out to find her, which he succeeded in doing before the Court took over her father's property as that of a man who had died without heirs. To Rustico's great relief, but against her will, Neerbale brought her back to Capsa and married her, and together they inherited her large patrimony. But before Neerbale had lain with her, certain ladies one day asked her how she had served God in the desert. She replied that her service was to put the devil in hell, and that Neerbale had committed a great sin by taking her away from such service. The ladies asked:

"And how do you put the devil in hell?"

Partly in words and partly by gestures, the girl told them. At this they laughed so much that they are still laughing, and said:

"Be not cast down, my child, they know how to do that here, and Neerbale will serve the Lord God with you in that way."

As they told it up and down the city, it passed into a proverb that the service most pleasing to God is to put the devil into hell. And this proverb crossed the seas and remains until this day.

Therefore, young ladies, when you seek God's favor, learn to put the devil in hell, because this is most pleasing to God and to all parties concerned, and much good may come of it.

---

[5] Jacket.

Dioneo's tale moved the chaste ladies to laughter hundreds of times, so apt and amusing did they find his words. When he had finished, the queen knew that the end of her reign had come, and therefore took the laurel wreath from her head and placed it upon Filostrato's, saying pleasantly:

"We shall soon find out if the wolf can guide the flock, as well as the flock has guided the wolves."

Filostrato laughingly replied:

"If my advice were followed, the wolves would have showed the flock how to put the devil in hell, as Rustico taught Alibech; and so they would not be called wolves, where you would not be the flock. However, since the rule now falls to me, I shall begin my reign."

Said Neifile:

"Filostrato, in trying to teach us, you might have learned wisdom, as Masetto da Lamporecchio learned it from the nuns,[6] and you might have regained your speech when your bones were rattling together from exhaustion!"

Filostrato, finding the ladies' sickles were as good as his shafts, ceased jesting, and occupied himself with the government of his kingdom. Calling the steward, he made enquiries into everything, and gave orders to ensure the well being and satisfaction of the band during his kingship. He then turned to the ladies and said:

"Amorous ladies, to my own misfortune—although I was quite aware of my disease—I have always been one of Love's subjects owing to the beauty of one of you. To be humble and obedient to her and to follow all her whims as closely as I could, was all of no avail to me, and I was soon abandoned for another. Thus I go from bad to worse, and believe I shall until I die. Tomorrow then it is my pleasure that we tell tales on a theme in conformity with my own fate—that is, about those persons whose love ended unhappily. In the long run I expect a most unhappy end for myself, and the person who gave me the nickname of Filostrato, or the Victim of Love, knew what she was doing."

So saying, he rose to his feet, and gave them all leave to depart until supper time.

The garden was so delightful and so beautiful that they all chose to remain there, since no greater pleasure could be found elsewhere. The sun was now not so hot, and therefore some of them began to chase the deer and rabbits and other animals which had annoyed them scores of times by leaping in among them while they were seated. Dioneo and Fiammetta began to sing the song of Messer Guglielmo and the Lady of Vergiu. Filomena and Pamfilo played chess. Thus, with one thing and another, time passed so quickly that supper time arrived long before they expected. The tables were set round the fountain, and there they ate their evening meal with the utmost pleasure.

When they rose from table, Filostrato would not depart from the path followed by the preceding queens, and so ordered Lauretta to dance and sing a song. And she said:

"My lord, I do not know any songs of other persons, and I do not remember any of my own which are fitting for this merry band. But if you wish to have one of those I remember, I will gladly sing it."

---

[6]A reference to another tale told earlier on the third day.

"Nothing of yours could be anything but fair and pleasing," said the king, "so sing it just as it is."

Then to the accompaniment of the others, Lauretta sang as follows in a sweet but rather plaintive voice:

No helpless lady has such cause to weep as I, who vainly sigh, alas, for love.

He who moves the heavens and all the stars[7] made me for His delight so fair, so sweet, so gracious and so lovely that I might show to every lofty mind some trace of that high Beauty which ever dwells within His presence. But a weak man, who knew not Beauty, found me undelightful and scorned me.

Once there was one who held me dear, and in my early years took me into his arms and to his thoughts, being quite conquered by my eyes. And time, that flies so swiftly, he spent in serving me; and I in courtesy made him worthy of me. But now, alas, he is taken from me.

Then came a proud presumptuous man, who thought himself both noble and valorous, and made me his, but through false belief became most jealous of me. And then, alas, I came near to despair, for I saw that I, who came into the world to pleasure many, was possessed by one alone.

I curse my luckless fate that ever I said "yes" to man, and changed to a wife's garb. I was so gay in my old plain maiden's dress! Now in these finer clothes I lead so sad a life, reputed less than chaste. O hapless wedding feast! Would I had died before I knew the fate it held for me!

O my first love, with whom I was so happy, who now in Heaven do stand before Him who created it, have pity on me. I cannot forget you for another. Let me feel that the flame wherewith you burned for me is not extinct, and pray that I may soon return to you.

Here ended Lauretta's song, which was noted carefully by them all, but interpreted differently. Some understood it in the Milanese sense—that it is better to be a good pig than a pretty girl.[8] Others were of a better, more sublime and truer understanding, but of this I shall not now speak.

After this the king had many torches brought and made them sing other songs as they sat on the grass and flowers, until the rising stars began to turn towards the west. Then, thinking it time for sleep, he said good night and sent each one to his room.

END OF THE THIRD DAY

---

[7] The mover is God; the line is a close paraphrase of the last line of Dante's *Divine Comedy.*
[8] That is, it is better to be an unhappy wife and alive than happily married and dead.

FOURTH DAY, SECOND TALE

Frate Alberto persuades a lady that the Angel Gabriel is in love with her and thus manages to lie with her several times. From fear of her relatives he flies from her house and takes refuge in the house of a poor man, who next day takes him to the Piazza as a wild man of the woods. He is recognized, arrested, and imprisoned.

The tale told by Fiammetta many times drew tears from her companions' eyes, but when it was ended the king said with a stern face:

"I should value my life little in comparison with half the joy Ghismonda had with Guiscardo.[1] Nor should you marvel at this, since while I am alive I suffer a thousand deaths hourly, and yet not one particle of delight is granted me. But, putting aside my life and its fate, it is my will that Pampinea should continue with a tale in part similar to my own fate. If she continues as Fiammetta has begun, doubtless some drops of dew will fall upon my amorous fire, and I shall feel them."

Pampinea felt the wishes of the company more through her own affection than through the king's words, and, being more willing to amuse them than to please the king, she determined to tell an amusing tale without departing from the subject given, and so began:

They say commonly in proverbial style: A wicked man who is thought to be good can do evil and yet not have it believed. This gives me ample material to speak on the subject proposed, and at the same time to show the hypocrisy of the monks. Their gowns are long and wide, their faces artificially pale, their voices humble and pleading when they ask something, loud and rude when they denounce their own vices in others, and when they declare how they obtain salvation of themselves and others by their gift. Not as men who seek Paradise, like ourselves, but as if they were its owners and lords, they allot a more or less eminent place there to everyone who dies, in accordance with the amount of money he leaves them; and thereby they first deceive themselves—if they really believe it—and then deceive those who put faith in their words. If I were permitted to do so, I could soon show many simple minded persons what is hidden in their ample gowns. Would to God that all their lies had the same fate as befell a minor friar,[2] who was no paltry fellow, but was considered one of the best casuists of Venice. It gives me the greatest pleasure to tell this tale, so that perhaps I may divert your minds with laughter and amusement from the pity you feel for Ghismonda's fate.

In Imola, most worthy ladies, there lived a man of wicked and corrupt life, named Berto della Massa. His evil deeds were so well known to many people of Imola that no one in Imola would believe him when he spoke truth, let alone when he lied. Seeing, then, that his tricks were useless there, he moved in despair to Venice, that welcomer of all wickedness, thinking that in that town he might make a different use of his vices than he had done before. As if conscience-stricken for his wicked deeds, he gave signs of the greatest humility. He became not only the most Catholic of men, but made

---

[1] Characters in the sad story with which Fiammetta had begun the fourth day's storytelling. The theme for the day, under Filostrato's rule, is love that ends unhappily.

[2] A member of the Franciscan religious order (Order of Friars Minor).

himself a minor friar, and took the name of Friar Alberto da Imola. In this guise he began to pretend to a severe life, praising penitence and abstinence, and never eating flesh or drinking wine when he could not get them good enough for him.

Never before had a thief, a ruffian, a forger, a murderer turned into a great preacher without having abandoned those vices, even when he had practiced them secretly. And after he had become a priest, whenever he was celebrating Mass at the altar in the presence of a large congregation, he always wept over the Saviour's Passion, for he was a man who could shed tears whenever he pleased. In short, what with his sermons and his tears, he so beguiled the Venetians that he was trustee and guardian of nearly everyone's will, the keeper of many people's money, the confessor and adviser of most men and women. Thus, from wolf he became shepherd, and in those parts the fame of his sanctity was greater than San Francesco's[3] ever was at Assisi.

Now, it happened that a silly stupid young woman, named Madonna Lisetta da ca Quirino, the wife of a merchant who was away in Flanders with the galleys, went with other women to confess to this holy friar. As she knelt at his feet like the Venetian she was—and they are all fools—he asked her half way through her confession if she had a lover. And she tartly replied:

"Why, messer friar, have you no eyes in your head? Do you think my beauties are no more than these other women's? I could have as many lovers as I wanted. But my beauty is not to be yielded to the love of anybody. How many beauties do you see like mine, for I should be beautiful in Paradise?"

And she went on to say so many things about her beauties that it was tedious to listen to her. Friar Alberto at once saw her weakness, and, feeling that she was ready made to his hand, he fell in love with her. But, reserving his flatteries for another time, he put on his saintly air and began to reprove her, and to say this was vain-glory and other things of the kind. So the lady told him he was a fool, and did not know how to distinguish one beauty from another. And Friar Alberto, not wanting to anger her too much, finished off the confession and let her go with the others.

A few days later he went with a trusted friend to Madonna Lisetta's house and took her aside into a room where they could not be seen. There he fell on his knees before her, and said:

"Madonna, I beseech you for God's sake to forgive me for what I said to you on Sunday when you spoke of your beauty, because I was so severely punished that night I have not been able to get up until today."

Then said Madonna Pot-stick: "And who punished you?"

"I will tell you," said Friar Alberto. "While I was praying that night, as I always do, I suddenly saw a bright light in my cell. Before I could turn to see what it was, I beheld a most beautiful young man with a large stick in his hand, who took me by the cowl, dragged me to my feet and beat me as if to break my bones. I asked him why he did this, and he replied: 'Because you presumed today to reprove the heavenly beauty of Madonna Lisetta whom I love more than anything except God himself.' And I asked: 'Who are you?' And he said he was the Angel Gabriel. 'O my lord,' said I, 'I beg you will

---

[3] Saint Francis of Assisi (1182?–1226), of whose piety many stories were told. He is eulogized in Dante's *Paradiso*, canto XI.

pardon me.' And he said: 'I will pardon you on condition that you go to her as soon as you can and obtain her forgiveness. And if she does not forgive you I shall return here, and so deal with you that you will be miserable for the rest of your days.' What he afterwards said to me I dare not tell you until you have pardoned me."

Donna Windy-noddle, who was as sweet as salt, was enchanted at these words, and thought them all true.

"I told you, Friar Alberto," said she, "that mine were heavenly beauties. But, so help me God, I am sorry for you, and to spare you any further trouble I forgive you, if only you will tell me truly what the Angel then said."

"Madonna," replied Friar Alberto, "since you have pardoned me, I will tell you willingly. But, you must not repeat a word of what I tell you to anyone in the world, if you do not want to destroy your happiness, you who are the luckiest woman in the world.

"The Angel Gabriel told me to tell you that he loves you so much he would often have come to spend the night with you, but for his fear of terrifying you. He now sends you a message through me to say that he wants to come to you one night and to spend part of it with you. But he is an Angel, and if he came to you in the form of an Angel you could not touch him; and so he says that for your delight he will come in a man's shape and bids you tell him when you want him to come and in whose shape, and he will come. And so you ought to think yourself more blessed than any other woman living."

Madonna Silly then said she was very glad to have the Angel Gabriel in love with her, because she loved him and always put up a fourpenny candle to him wherever she saw him painted. Whenever he liked to come to her he would be welcome and he would find her alone in her room, on one condition, which was that he would not abandon her for the Virgin Mary whom he was said to be very fond of; and she was inclined to believe this since whenever she saw his picture he was kneeling before the Virgin.[4] In addition, she said that the Angel should come in any shape he pleased—she would not be afraid.

Then said Friar Alberto:

"Madonna, you speak wisely, and I will arrange with him as you say. But you can do me a great favor, which will cost you nothing. The favor is that you will allow him to come in my body. This will be a very great favor because he will take the soul from my body and put it in Heaven, and he will enter into me, and my soul will be in Paradise as long as he remains with you."

Then said Madonna Littlewit:

"I am content. I want you to have this consolation for the stripes[5] you received on my account."

Said Friar Alberto:

"Tonight leave the door of your house open, so that he can come in. Since he is coming in a human body, he can only enter by the door."

The lady replied that this should be done. Friar Alberto departed, and she remained in such a state of delight that her chemise did not touch her

---

[4]The Annunciation, in which the angel Gabriel tells the Virgin Mary that she will be the mother of God, was a perennial subject of religious paintings.

[5]Blows.

backside, and the time she had to wait for the Angel Gabriel seemed like a thousand years.

Friar Alberto thought it better to be a good horseman than an Angel that night, so he fortified himself with all sorts of good cheer, in order not to be unhorsed too easily. He obtained permission to be out that night, and went with his trusted friend to the house of a woman friend, which he had made his starting point more than once before when he was going to ride the mare. From there he went in disguise to the lady's house, and having transformed himself into an Angel with the fripperies[6] he had brought with him, he went upstairs into the lady's bedroom. When she saw something white come in, she kneeled down. The Angel gave her his benediction, raised her to her feet, and signed to her to get into bed. She did so immediately in her willingness to obey, and the Angel got into bed with his devotee.

Friar Alberto was a robust and handsome man and in excellent health. Donna Lisetta was fresh and pretty and found him a very different person from her husband to lie with. That night he flew many times with her without wings, which made her call herself blessed; and in addition he told her a great many things about heavenly glory. Just before dawn, he collected his trappings and returned to his friend, who had kept friendly company with the other woman so that she should not feel afraid by sleeping alone.

After the lady had dined, she went with a woman friend to see Friar Alberto, and gave him news of the Angel Gabriel, telling him how the Angel looked and what he had said about the glory of eternal life, to which she added all sorts of marvelous fables.

"Madonna," said Friar Alberto, "I know not how you were with him, all I know is that last night he came to me, and when I had delivered him your message, he suddenly took my soul to a place where there were more flowers and roses than ever I saw, one of the most delicious places that ever existed, where my soul remained until dawn this morning. But what happened to my body I do not know."

"Didn't I tell you?" said the lady. "Your body lay all night in my arms with the Angel Gabriel. And if you don't believe me, look under your left breast, where I gave the Angel such a kiss that the mark will remain for several days."

Then said Friar Alberto:

"I will do something today which I have not done for a very long time. I shall undress myself to see if what you say is true."

After a lot more chatter, the lady returned home. And Friar Alberto thereafter visited her many times in the guise of an Angel, without the slightest difficulty. But one day Madonna Lisetta was with one of her gossips,[7] and as they were discussing their beauties, she said like the empty-pated fool she was, in order to show off:

"If you knew who was in love with my beauty you would not speak of anyone else's."

The gossip was anxious to hear about it, and knowing Lisetta well, said:

"Madonna, you may be right, but as I do not know whom you mean I shall not change my opinion so easily."

The lady, who had very little sense, then said:

---

[6] Gaudy costumes.   [7] Intimate friends.

"Gossip, he does not want it talked about, but the person I mean is the Angel Gabriel, who loves me more than himself, so he says, because I am the most beautiful person in the world or the Maremma."[8]

The gossip felt like laughing outright, but restrained herself to keep the conversation going, and said:

"God's faith, Madonna, if you mean the Angel Gabriel and say so, it must be true, but I did not think the angels did such things."

"Gossip," said the lady, "you are wrong. By God's favor, he does it better than my husband, and he tells me they do it up above. But, because he thinks me more beautiful than anyone in Heaven, he has fallen in love with me, and often spends a night with me. So you see!"

As soon as the gossip had left Madonna Lisetta, it seemed like a thousand years to her before she had got into a company where she could laugh at all this. She went to a gathering of women, and told them the whole tale. These women told their husbands and other women, and they told others, and so in less than two days the story was all over Venice. Among others who heard it were the lady's cousins, and, without saying anything to her, they made up their minds to find this Angel and see whether he could fly. So they watched for him every night.

Some rumors of all this came to the ears of Friar Alberto, who went to the lady one night to scold her for it. He was scarcely undressed when her cousins, who had seen him come in, were at the door. Friar Alberto heard them, and guessed what they were. He jumped up, and, having no other means of escape, opened a window overlooking the Grand Canal,[9] from which he threw himself into the water.

The water there was deep; he was a good swimmer, and so did himself no harm. He swam to the other side of the canal and immediately entered an open house there, begging the goodman[10] for the love of God to save his life, and told him all sorts of lies to explain why he was there naked at that hour of night.

The goodman, who was just setting off on his business, pitied Friar Alberto and put him into bed, telling him to stop there until he came back. He then locked the friar in, and went about his business.

When the lady's cousins entered her room, they found the Angel Gabriel had left his wings behind and flown away. They abused the lady indignantly, and, leaving her very disconsolate, returned home with the Angel's trappings.

Meanwhile, soon after dawn, the goodman was on the Rialto[11] and heard how the Angel Gabriel had gone to lie with Madonna Lisetta the night before, how he had been discovered by her relatives and had thrown himself into the canal, and nobody knew what had become of him. So he immediately realized that this was the man in his own house. He went home and after much discussion arranged that the Friar should pay him fifty ducats not to hand him over to the cousins; and this was done. Friar Alberto then wanted to leave, but the goodman said:

[8] A marshy region near Florence. The boast is ludicrous, since the Maremma is a mere local district.
[9] The famous canals of Venice serve in lieu of streets.
[10] A title of respect for a man below the rank of gentry.
[11] The commercial center of Venice.

"There is only one way of doing this. There is a festival today where one man leads another dressed like a bear or a wild man of the woods or one thing or another, and then there is a hunt in the Piazza di San Marco,[12] and when that is over the festival ends. Then everyone goes off where he pleases with the person he has brought in disguise. Now, you may be spied out here, and so, if you like, I will lead you along in some disguise and can take you wherever you like. Otherwise I don't see how you can leave here without being recognized. The lady's relatives know you must be in some house in the neighborhood, and have posted guards everywhere to catch you."

Friar Alberto did not at all like the idea, but he was so much afraid of the lady's relatives that he agreed to it, and told the man where he wanted to go, and how he should be led along. The goodman smeared him all over with honey and then covered him with feathers, put a chain round his neck and a mask on his face. In one hand he gave him a large stick and in the other two great dogs which he had brought from the butcher; and then he sent someone to the Rialto who announced that everyone who wanted to see the Angel Gabriel should go to the Piazza di San Marco. That was true Venetian good faith!

Having done this, he took the Friar out, and, walking before him, led him along on a chain; and everybody came round saying: "What's this? What's this?" And thus he took the Friar to the Piazza, where there was a great crowd of people, made up of those who had followed them and those who had come from the Rialto on hearing the announcement. He then led his wild man of the woods to a column in a conspicuous and elevated place, pretending that he was waiting for the hunt. The poor friar was greatly plagued by flies and gad-flies, because he was smeared all over with honey. And when the goodman saw that the Piazza was full of people, he pretended that he was going to unchain his wild man; but instead he took off Friar Alberto's mask, and shouted:

"Gentlemen, since the pig has not come to the hunt and since the hunt is off, I don't want you to have gathered here for nothing, and so I want you to see the Angel Gabriel who came down from Heaven to earth last night to console the ladies of Venice."

As soon as the mask was off, Friar Alberto was recognized by everybody, and there went up a great shout against him, everybody saying the most insulting things that ever were said to any scoundrel. And first one and then another threw all sorts of filth in his face. There he was kept a long time until the news reached the other friars of his convent. Six of them came down to the Piazza, threw a gown on his back and bound him, and then in the midst of a great tumult took him back to the monastery, where he was imprisoned. And it is believed that he soon died there after a life of misery.

Thus a man who was thought to be good and acted evilly without being suspected, tried to be the Angel Gabriel and was turned into a wild man of the woods; and, in the long run, was insulted as he deserved and came to weep in vain for the sins he had committed. Please God that this may happen to all like him.

---

[12] The principal public square of Venice; St. Mark is the city's patron saint.

FIFTH DAY, TENTH TALE

Pietro di Vinciolo goes out to sup. His wife brings a lover into the house; Pietro returns, and she hides the lover under a chicken coop. Pietro tells her how, while he was supping with Ercolano, a young man whom the wife had hidden was discovered. She blames Ercolano's wife, but an ass unhappily treads on the lover's finger as he is under the coop, and he gives a shriek; Pietro runs out, sees him, and perceives how his wife has tricked him; but in the end he pardons her fault.

The queen finished her tale, and they all praised God for having worthily rewarded Federigo; and then Dioneo began, without waiting to be ordered.[1]

I know not whether it be an accidental vice and the result of the corruption of men's manners, or whether it be a natural failing to laugh at bad things rather than at good deeds, especially when we are not directly concerned. Now since the task I undertook before and am about to carry out again, has no other object but to drive away melancholy from you and to raise mirth and merriment, I shall tell you this tale, enamored ladies, although its matter in part be less than chaste, because it may amuse you. While you listen to it, do as you do when you enter a garden and, stretching out your delicate hands, pluck the roses and avoid the thorns. In so doing, leave the bad man in his misfortune with his woes, and laugh at the amorous tricks of the wife, and feel compassion for the misfortunes of others, where it is needed.

Not long ago in Perugia there was a rich man named Pietro di Vinciolo, who took a wife, more to deceive others and to avoid the general opinion of himself among the Perugians, than for any desire he had of her. And Fortune was so far conformable to his wish that the wife he took was a robust wench with lively red hair, who would rather have had two husbands than one, whereas she had chanced upon a man who would rather have had to do with another man than with her.

In process of time she found this out. And since she was fresh and pretty, and felt herself friskish and robust, she got angry and often exchanged sharp words with her husband; and they led a miserable life together. But, seeing that this exhausted her without improving her husband, she said to herself:

"This man leaves me in sorrow and goes off in his vice in wooden shoes through the dry, while I am trying to carry someone else in a ship through the rain.[2] I took him as my husband and gave him a good large dowry, knowing him to be a man, and thinking he wanted what men do and ought to want; and if I had not thought he was a man, I would never have taken him. He knew I was a woman; why did he marry me if he didn't like women? This is unendurable. If I had not wanted to live the life of the world, I should have become a nun. If I wait for delight and pleasure from him, I might perhaps wait in vain until I am an old woman, and then vainly regret my lost youth. He himself is an example to me, that I should find some consolation, and some pleasure as he does. In me this pleasure will be commendable, whereas in him it is blameworthy; for I only offend the laws, whereas he offends the laws and Nature too."

---

[1] The theme of the stories on the fifth day, under Fiammetta's rule, is love transformed from grief to happiness.

[2] She means that sexually her husband goes against nature whereas she conforms to it.

Having thought this over a good many times, the good woman, with an idea of carrying out her plan secretly, became familiar with an old woman, who yet seemed more like a pious old thing than a bawd, always going to church services with beads in her hand and never talking about anything but the lives of the Fathers or the stigmata of St. Francis,[3] so that almost everybody thought she was a saint. And when she thought it a fitting time, the wife told her everything she intended.

"My child," said the old woman, "God, who knows everything, knows that in this you will do well. And if you did it for no other reason, yet you and every other young woman should do it, in order not to waste the time of your youth, because to those who have any understanding there is no grief like having wasted time. What the devil good are we when we are old, except to watch the supper on the hearth? If anyone knows it and can bear witness to it, I can. Now I am an old woman I realize with bitter soulprickings how I wasted my time. And although I did not lose it all (for I don't want you to think I was a simpleton), still I did not do what I could have done. When I remember it, and see what I now am, and think how nobody would kindle up a spark of desire for me, God knows what grief I feel.

"The same thing does not happen to men. They are born fitted for a thousand things and not for this only, while the larger number of them are much better old than young. But women are only born to do it and make children, and so are esteemed. And if you haven't noticed anything else, you ought to have noticed this—that we are always ready for it, which does not happen with men. Moreover, one woman would tire out many men, whereas many men cannot tire one woman. Now, since we are born for this, I say once more you will be doing well to give your husband tit for tat, so that in your old age your mind will not have any reproach to bring against your flesh.

"Everyone gets from this world what he takes from it, especially women, who have far more necessity to make use of time while they have it than men, because, as you can see for yourself, when we get old, neither husband nor anyone else wants to see us, so we're chased in the kitchen to tell tales to the cat, and scour the pots and pans. Worse than that even, they make songs about us, saying: 'The best morsels for the girls, and quinsies[4] to the old women'; and they say lots of other similar things.

"To keep you no longer in talk, I say now that you could not have spoken to anyone in the world who can be more useful to you than me; for however haughty a man may be I am not afraid to say what is necessary to him, and however harsh or boorish, I can smooth him down and bring him to the point I want. Tell me the one you want, and leave the rest to me. But remember, my child, that I am poor, and that you will be remembered in all my church-goings and all the paternosters I say; and I shall pray God for the souls of all your departed dead."

Thus ended the old woman. And the young woman came to an agreement with the old one that, if she saw him, she was to bring her a young man who often passed through the district; and she described him in such a way that the old woman knew who he was. Then she gave her a piece of salt meat, and sent her away.

---

[3] The Fathers were religious authorities in the ancient Christian church. St. Francis of Assisi was believed to have received in his own body the marks ("stigmata") of Christ's wounds.

[4] Inflammations of the throat; the literal meaning in the Italian is "things to choke on."

Not many days afterwards the old woman brought the young man described to her room, and soon afterwards another, according as the young woman wanted. And, although in fear of her husband, she did not miss the opportunity.

One evening her husband was going out to supper with a friend of his, named Ercolano, and so the girl arranged with the old woman to bring her a young man, who was one of the handsomest and pleasantest in Perugia. Which was quickly done. The young woman and the young man were just sitting down to supper, when they heard Pietro at the door, shouting to her to open it. When she heard it, the wife gave herself up for dead. Wanting to hide the young man if she could, and not having the cunning to get him out of the house or hide him elsewhere, she hid him under a chicken coop in a shed next to the room in which they were supping, and threw over it a piece of straw sacking she had emptied that day. After which, she quickly opened the door to her husband. When he came into the house, she said:

"You've guzzled up that supper pretty quickly."

"We never even tasted it," said Pietro.

"How did that happen?" asked his wife.

"I'll tell you," said Pietro. "Ercolano and his wife and I were sitting down to table when we heard somebody sneeze near us, to which we paid no attention the first and second times. But the person sneezed a third, a fourth, a fifth and many other times, which greatly surprised us. Ercolano was already a little annoyed with his wife because she had kept him waiting a long time at the door, and said to her in a rage: 'What does this mean? Who is it sneezing like this?' He got up from the table, and went to the staircase near at hand, under which was a cupboard to store things away, as we see arranged in houses every day.

"It seemed to him that the sound of the sneezing came from this cupboard, so he opened a little door in it, and as soon as this was opened there suddenly came out the worst stink of sulphur imaginable, which he had noticed before and had complained of, whereupon his wife had said: 'I am whitening my veils in there with sulphur, and the pots too, which I sprinkled with sulphur so that they would get the fumes, and put them under the staircase, and the smell still comes from them.' And after Ercolano had opened the door and the fumes had cleared off a little, he looked inside and saw the person who had sneezed and was still sneezing owing to the sulphur fumes. And as he sneezed, the sulphur had got such a hold on his chest, that he was not far from never sneezing or doing anything else again.

"As soon as Ercolano saw him, he shouted: 'Now I see, wife, the man for whose sake you kept us waiting at the door so long without opening when we came. But may I never have anything please me again, if I don't make you pay for this!' The wife, hearing this and seeing that her fault was discovered, fled from the table without attempting any excuse; and I don't know where she went. Ercolano, not noticing that his wife had fled, told the sneezing man to come out; but he was beyond all power of moving, and did not stir for anything Ercolano said.

"Thereupon Ercolano took him by one of his feet and dragged him out, and ran for a knife to kill him. But, fearing the police on my own account, I jumped up and prevented him from killing the man or doing him any harm. My shouting and defending him aroused the neighbors who came in and took the almost swooning young man, and carried him somewhere—I don't know where—out of the house. So our supper was quite spoiled by all this, and I not only haven't guzzled it but never even tasted it, as I said."

At this tale the wife perceived that there were others who knew as much as she did, although some had bad luck. She would have been glad to defend Ercolano's wife with words, but as blaming the faults of others seemed to her to make things easier for her own, she said:

"Here's fine doings! Here's a good and saintly woman! Here's the faith of a modest woman, who seemed to me so saintly that I would have confessed my sins to her. And, what's worse, she gives a mighty good example to the young, since she's getting old already. Cursed be the hour when she came into the world and the hour which allowed her to live, the wicked deceitful woman that she must be, the universal shame and scorn of all women on this earth! Curse her for leaving her chastity and the faith promised to her husband and the honor of the world, he that is such a good man and an honorable citizen and treated her so well, for another man, and not being ashamed to bring him to scorn and herself with him! So help me God, I'd have no pity on such women. They ought to be killed. They ought to be thrown into the fire and burned to ashes."

Then, recollecting that her lover was near at hand, hidden under the hen-coop, she began to urge Pietro to go to bed, as it was then bedtime. But Pietro was more anxious to have something to eat than to go to bed, and asked if there were not something for supper.

"Ah!" said the wife, "yes, indeed, there's supper! We're quite accustomed to have supper when you're not here! Yes, I'm Ercolano's wife, am I? Why don't you go to bed? Go to sleep this evening!"

Now, it happened that during the evening some of Pietro's workmen had brought certain things in from the country, and had stalled their asses without giving them any water to drink, in a little stable next to the shed. One of the asses was very thirsty indeed, and, managing to get his head out of the halter, walked out of the stable and went snuffing at everything, trying to find some water. And so he came up to the hen-coop where the young man was hidden.

He was on his hands and knees, and one of his fingers was outside the hen-coop. Now, as luck or ill luck would have it, the ass trod on his finger; whereupon, in his anguish, he uttered a yell. Pietro was astonished to hear it, and knew that someone must be in the house. He went out of the room and heard the young man moaning, for the ass had not yet taken its hoof off his finger and was still pressing heavily on it. Said Pietro: "Who's there?" He ran to the hen-coop, lifted it up, and saw the young man who, in addition to the pain he felt from the ass treading on his finger, was trembling with fear lest Pietro should do him an injury.

Pietro recognized him as a young man he had long been prowling after for his vicious pleasures, and asked him: "What are you doing here?" but the youth made no answer, and only begged him for the love of God to do him no harm.

"Get up," said Pietro, "I won't do you any harm; but tell me, how do you happen to be here, and why?"

The young man confessed everything. Pietro, no less joyous than his wife was distressed at the discovery, took him by the hand and led him into the room, where the wife was waiting in the greatest terror imaginable. Pietro made her sit down opposite and said:

"So you cursed so hard Ercolano's wife, and you said she ought to be burned and that she was the shame of you all—why didn't you say it of yourself? Or, if you didn't want to confess that, how could your conscience endure to say it of her, when you knew you had done the same thing as she had? Nothing, indeed, induced you to do it, except that all you women are alike, and you hope to hide your own sins under the failings of others. May fire come down from heaven and burn you all, vile generation that you are!"

The wife, seeing that at the first onslaught he had hurt her with nothing worse than words, and noticing that he was in high glee at holding such a handsome youth by the hand, plucked up heart and said:

"I am very sure that you would like fire to come from heaven and burn up all us women, since you are as fond of us as a dog is of sticks. But, God's Cross! You won't see it happen. I should like to have a little discussion with you, to find out what you complain of. It is indeed well to compare me with Ercolano's wife, a hypocritical, snivelling old woman, who gets what she wants out of him, and he treats her as well as a wife can be treated, which doesn't happen to me. For, granted that I am well clad and shod, you know how I fare in other matters and how long it is since you lay with me. I'd go with rags on my back and broken shoes and be well treated by you in bed, rather than have all these things and be treated as you treat me. Understand plainly, Pietro, I'm a woman like other women, and I want what they want. So, if I go seeking for what I can't get from you, there's no need to abuse me. At least I do you so much honor that I don't go with boys and scrubby fellows."

Pietro saw that she could go on talking all night, and so, as he cared nothing about her, he said:

"That's enough, wife. I'll be content with that. Will you be so gracious as to get us some supper, for I rather fancy this boy has had no more supper than I have."

"No, indeed," said the wife, "he has had no supper; for when you arrived in an ill hour, we were just sitting down to table to sup."

"Go along then," said Pietro, "and get us some supper, and afterwards I will arrange this affair in such a way that you will have nothing to complain of."

Finding her husband so agreeable, the wife jumped up and re-laid the table, brought out the supper she had prepared, and supped merrily with her bad husband and the young man. What Pietro arranged after supper to satisfy all three of them has entirely gone out of my head. But I know that next morning the young man found himself in the piazza, not quite knowing whether the night before he had been with the wife or the husband. And so, dear ladies, I want to tell you: "He who does it to you, you do it to him." And if you can't, keep it in mind while you can, so that the ass may receive what he gets at home.

Dioneo's tale was now ended, and the ladies' laughter was restrained less from lack of amusement than from shame. The queen, seeing that the end of her reign was at hand, stood up and took off her garland, and gracefully placed it on Elisa's head, saying:

"Madonna, it is now for you to give orders."

Having received the honor, Elisa followed the adopted routine and first arranged with the steward for what was needed during the period of her rule; after which she said to the satisfaction of the company:

"We have already heard how many people by means of good sayings and prompt retorts and quick wits have been able to turn the teeth of others on themselves with a sharp nip or have averted threatened dangers. And since this is a good topic and may be useful, my will is that tomorrow, with God's help, we tell tales within these limits—that is, of such persons who have retorted a witticism directed at them, or with a quick retort or piece of shrewdness have escaped destruction, danger or contempt."

This was highly commended by them all. Whereupon the queen rose to her feet, and gave them all to do as they chose until supper time. The merry company arose as the queen arose, and according to custom, each of them gave himself up to what pleased him most. But when the cicadas ceased their song, everyone was called, and they all went to supper. After this had been festively served, they went to singing and music. Emilia danced at the queen's command, and then Dioneo was ordered to sing a song. He immediately began: "Old mother Hale, lift up your tail, and see the good news I bring you." Whereat all the ladies burst out laughing, especially the queen, who ordered him to abandon that song and start another.

"Madonna," said Dioneo, "if I had cymbals, I would sing: 'Up with your petties, Monna Lapa,' or 'Under the olive tree springs the grass,' or would you like me to sing: 'The waves of the ocean make me ill with their motion'? But then I haven't any cymbals, so see which of these others you would like. Do you like: 'Out you go to be chopped to shreds, like a melon down in the garden beds'?"

"No," said the queen, "sing something else."

"Well," said Dioneo, "shall I sing: 'Monna Simona, put it up in the cask, it isn't the month of October'?"

"No, no," said the queen laughing, "sing a nice song, if you like, but not that one."

"Don't get angry, madonna," said Dioneo. "Which do you like best? I know over a thousand. Would you like: 'If I don't tickle my little prickle,' or 'Gently, gently, husband dear,' or 'I'll buy a cock for a hundred dollars'?"

"Dioneo," said the queen rather angrily, although all the others were laughing, "cease joking, and sing a pleasant song. If you don't, you will discover how angry I can be."

At this Dioneo left his jests, and began to sing as follows:

Love, the fair light that issues from her eyes has made me slave to thee and her.

The splendor of her lovely eyes, passing through mine, moved me before your flame was kindled in my heart. However great your worth, I learned it through her beauteous face; imagining which, I found my self gathering every virtue and yielding them to her—another cause of sighs in me.

Now, dear my Lord, I have become one among your followers, and in obedience await your grace; but yet I know not if the high desire which you have set within my breast and my unshaken faith are wholly known to her, who so possesses all my mind that save from her I would not and I do not hope for peace.

Therefore I pray you, sweet my love, to show them to her, and make her feel a little of your flame, in grace to me who, as you see, am all consumed with love, and bit by bit worn down with pain. And then, when it is time, commend me to her, as you should, and gladly would I come with you to do it.

When Dioneo by his silence showed that his song was ended, the queen, after having highly praised it, had others sung. And when part of the night was spent and the queen felt that the heat of day was quenched in night's coolness, she ordered everyone to rest as he chose until the following day.

HERE ENDS THE FIFTH DAY

TENTH DAY, TENTH TALE

The Marquess of Saluzzo is urged by his subjects to take a wife and, to choose in his own way, takes the daughter of a peasant. He has two children by her and pretends to her that he has killed them. He then pretends that he is tired of her and that he has taken another wife and so brings their own daughter to the house as if she were his new wife, after driving her away in her shift. She endures it all patiently. He brings her back home, more beloved by him than ever, shows her their grown children, honors her and makes others honor her as Marchioness.

When the king[1] had ended his long tale, which, to judge by their looks, had greatly pleased everyone, Dioneo said, laughing:

"The good man who was waiting to bring down the ghost's stiff tail that night would not have given two cents for all the praise you give Messer Torello![2]

Then, knowing that he was the only one left to tell a tale, he began:

Gracious ladies, as far as I can see, today has been given up to Kings, Sultans and such like persons; so, not to wander away too far from you, I shall tell you about a Marquess, but not of his munificence. It will be about his silly brutality, although good came of it in the end. I do not advise anyone to imitate him, for it was a great pity that good did come to him.

A long time ago the eldest son of the Marquess of Saluzzo was a young man named Gualtieri. He was wifeless and childless, spent his time hunting and hawking, and never thought about marrying or having children, wherein he was probably very wise. This displeased his subjects, who several times begged him to take a wife, so that he might not die without an heir and leave them without a ruler, offering to find him a wife born of such a father and mother as would give him good hopes of her and content him. To which Gualtieri replied:

"My friends, you urge me to do something I was determined never to do, seeing how hard it is to find a woman of suitable character, and how many of the opposite sort there are, and how wretched is the life of a man who takes a wife unsuitable to him. It is foolishness of you to think you can judge a girl by the characters of her father and mother (from which you

---

[1] Pamfilo, who rules over the tenth day. The theme of the day is liberal and munificent behavior.

[2] A reference to the immediately preceding story and to the first story of Day Seven.

argue that you can find me one to please me), for I do not see how you can really know the fathers' or the mothers' secrets. And even if you did know them, daughters are often quite different from their fathers and mothers.

"But you want me to take these chains, and I am content to do so. If it turns out badly I want to have no one to complain of but myself, and so I shall choose for myself. And I tell you that if you do not honor the wife I choose as your lady you will find out to your cost how serious a thing it is to have compelled me by your entreaties to take a wife against my will."

They replied that they were content, if only he would take a wife.

For some time Gualtieri had been pleased by the character of a poor girl in a hamlet near his house. He thought her beautiful, and that he might live comfortably enough with her. So he decided that he would marry her without seeking any further, and, having sent for her father, who was a very poor man, he arranged to marry her. Having done this, Gualtieri called together all his friends from the surrounding country, and said:

"My friends, it has pleased you to desire that I should marry, and I am ready to do so, more to please you than from any desire I have of taking a wife. You know you promised me that you would honor anyone I chose as your lady. The time has now come for me to keep my promise to you and you to keep yours to me. I have found a girl after my heart quite near here; I intend to marry her and to bring her home in a few days. So take thought to make a handsome marriage feast and how you can honorably receive her, so that I may consider myself content with your promise as you may be with mine."

The good men cheerfully replied that they were glad of it, and that they would consider her their lady and honor her as their lady in all things. After which, they all set about preparing a great and handsome wedding feast, and so did Gualtieri. He prepared a great and fine banquet, and invited many friends and relatives and noblemen and others. Moreover, he had rich and beautiful dresses cut out and fitted on a girl, who seemed to him about the same build as the girl he proposed to marry. And he also purchased girdles and rings and a rich and beautiful crown, and everything necessary to a bride.

When the day appointed for the wedding arrived, Gualtieri about the middle of Terce[3] mounted his horse, and so did those who had come to honor him. Everything being arranged, he said:

"Gentlemen, it is time to go for the bride."

Setting out with all his company he came to the hamlet and the house of the girl's father, where he found her drawing water in great haste, so that she could go with the other women to see Gualtieri's bride. And when Gualtieri saw her, he called her by her name, Griselda, and asked where her father was. She blushed and said:

"He is in the house, my lord."

Gualtieri dismounted, told everyone to wait for him, entered the poor little house where he found the girl's father (who was named Giannucole), and said to him:

"I have come to marry Griselda, but first I want to ask her a few things in your presence."

[3] 7:30 A.M.

He then asked her whether, if he married her, she would try to please him, and never be angry at anything he said or did, and if she would be obedient, and several other things, to all of which she said "Yes." Gualtieri then took her by the hand and led her forth. In the presence of all his company he had her stripped naked, and then the clothes he had prepared were brought, and she was immediately dressed and shod, and he had a crown put on her hair, all unkempt as it was. Everyone marveled at this, and he said:

"Gentlemen, I intend to take this girl as my wife, if she will take me as her husband."

He then turned to her, as she stood blushing and irresolute, and said:

"Griselda, will you take me as your husband?"

"Yes, my lord," she replied.

"And I will take you as my wife," said he.

Then in the presence of them all he pledged his faith to her; and they set her on a palfrey and honorably conducted her to his house. The wedding feast was great and handsome, and the rejoicing no less than if he had married the daughter of the King of France.

The girl seemed to have changed her soul and manners with her clothes. As I said, she was beautiful of face and body, and she became so agreeable, so pleasant, so well-behaved that she seemed like the daughter of a nobleman, and not Giannucole's child and a cattle herder; which surprised everyone who had known her before. Moreover, she was so obedient and so ready to serve her husband that he felt himself to be the happiest and best matched man in the world. And she was so gracious and kindly to her husband's subjects that there was not one of them but loved her and gladly honored her, while all prayed for her good and her prosperity and advancement. Whereas they had said that Gualtieri had showed little wisdom in marrying her, they now said that he was the wisest and shrewdest man in the world, because no one else would have known the lofty virtue hidden under her poor clothes and village garb.

In short, before long she acted so well that not only in the marquisate but everywhere people were talking of her virtues and good actions; and whatever had been said against her husband for having married her was now turned to the opposite. She had not long been with Gualtieri when she became pregnant, and in due time gave birth to a daughter, at which Gualtieri rejoiced greatly.

Soon after this the idea came to him to test her patience with a long trial and intolerable things. He said unkind things to her, seemed to be angry, and said that his subjects were most discontented with her on account of her low birth, and especially when they saw that she bore children. He said they were very angry at the birth of a daughter and did nothing but murmur. When the lady heard these words, she did not change countenance or cheerfulness, but said to him:

"My lord, you may do with me what you think most to your honor and satisfaction. I shall be content, for I know that I am less than they and unworthy of the honor to which you have raised me by your courtesy."

Gualtieri liked this reply and saw that no pride had risen up in her from the honor done her by him and others.

Soon after, he informed his wife in general terms that his subjects could not endure the daughter she had borne. He then gave orders to one of his servants whom he sent to her. The man, with a dolorous visage, said:

"Madonna, if I am to avoid death I must do what my lord bids me. He tells me I am to take your daughter and . . ."

He said no more, but the lady, hearing these words and seeing the servant's face, and remembering what had been said to her, guessed that he had been ordered to kill the child. She went straight to the cradle, kissed and blessed the child, and although she felt great anguish in her heart, put the child in the servant's arms without changing her countenance, and said:

"Do what my lord and yours has ordered you to do. But do not leave her for the birds and animals to devour her body, unless you were ordered to do so."

The servant took the child and told Gualtieri what the lady had said. He marveled at her constancy, and sent the servant with the child to a relative at Bologna, begging her to bring her up and educate her carefully, but without ever saying whose daughter she was.

After this the lady again became pregnant, and in due time brought forth a male child, which delighted Gualtieri. But what he had already done was not enough for him. He pierced the lady with a worse wound, and one day said to her in pretended anger:

"Since you have borne this male child, I cannot live at peace with my subjects, who complain bitterly that a grandson of Giannucole must be their lord after me. If I am not to be driven out, I fear I must do now as I did before, and in the end abandon you and take another wife."

The lady listened to him patiently, and her only reply was:

"My lord, content yourself and do what is pleasing to you. Do not think about me, for nothing pleases me except as it pleases you."

Not many days afterwards Gualtieri sent for his son in the same way that he had sent for his daughter, and while pretending in the same way to kill the child, sent it to be brought up in Bologna, as he had sent the girl. And his wife said no more and looked no worse than she had done about the daughter. Gualtieri marveled at this and said to himself that no other woman could have done what she did; and if he had not seen that she loved her children while she had them, he would have thought she did it to get rid of them, whereas he saw it was from obedience to him.

His subjects thought he had killed his children, blamed him severely and thought him a cruel man, while they felt great pity for his wife. And when the women condoled with her on the death of her children, she never said anything except that it was not her wish but the wish of him who begot them.

Several years after his daughter's birth, Gualtieri thought the time had come for the last test of his wife's patience. He kept saying that he could no longer endure to have Griselda as his wife, that he knew he had acted childishly and wrongly when he married her, that he therefore meant to solicit the Pope for a dispensation to marry another woman and abandon Griselda; for all of which he was reproved by many good men. But his only reply was that it was fitting this should be done.

Hearing of these things, the lady felt she must expect to return to her father's house and perhaps watch cattle as she had done in the past, and see another woman take the man she loved; at which she grieved deeply. But she prepared herself to endure this with a firm countenance, as she had endured the other wrongs of Fortune.

Not long afterwards Gualtieri received forged letters from Rome, which he showed to his subjects, pretending that the Pope by these letters gave him a dispensation to take another wife and leave Griselda. So, calling her before him, he said to her in the presence of many of his subjects:

"Wife, the Pope has granted me a dispensation to leave you and to take another wife. Now, since my ancestors were great gentlemen and lords of this country while yours were always laborers, I intend that you shall no longer be my wife, but return to Giannucole's house with the dowry you brought me, while I shall bring home another wife I have found more suitable for me."

At these words the lady could only restrain her tears by a great effort, beyond that of women's nature, and replied:

"My lord, I always knew that my lowly rank was in no wise suitable to your nobility; and the rank I have had with you I always recognized as coming from God and you, and never looked upon it as given to me, but only lent. You are pleased to take it back, and it must and does please me to return it to you. Here is the ring with which you wedded me; take it. You tell me to take the dowry I brought you; to do this there is no need for you to pay anything nor shall I need a purse or a sumpter horse,[4] for I have not forgotten that I came to you naked. If you think it right that the body which has borne your children should be seen by everyone, I will go away naked. But in exchange for my virginity, which I brought here and cannot carry away, I beg you will at least be pleased to let me take away one shift[5] over and above my dowry."

Gualtieri, who was nearer to tears than anyone else present, managed to keep his countenance stern, and said:

"You shall have a shift."

Those who were present urged him to give her a dress, so that she who had been his wife for thirteen years should not be seen to leave his house so poorly and insultingly as it would be for her to leave it in a shift. But their entreaties were vain. So the lady, clad only in her shift, unshod and with nothing on her head, commended him to God, left his house, and returned to her father accompanied by the tears and lamentation of all who saw her.

Giannucole (who had never believed it was true that Gualtieri would keep his daughter as a wife and had always expected this event), had kept the clothes she had taken off on the morning when Gualtieri married her. So she took them and put them on, and devoted herself to drudgery in her father's house, enduring the assaults of hostile Fortune with a brave spirit.

After Gualtieri had done this, he told his subjects that he was to marry the daughter of one of the Counts of Panago. He therefore made great preparations for the wedding, and sent for Griselda to come to him; and when she came, he said:

"I am bringing home the lady I have just married, and I intend to do her honor at her arrival. You know there is not a woman in the house who can prepare the rooms and do many other things needed for such a feast. You know everything connected with the house better than anyone, so you

---

[4] Packhorse.   [5] Loose undergarment; slip.

must arrange everything that is to be done, and invite all the women you think fit and receive them as if you were mistress of the house. Then, when the marriage feast is over, you can return home."

These words were a dagger in Griselda's heart, for she had not been able to dispense with the love she felt for him as she had her good fortune, but she said:

"My lord, I am ready."

So, in her coarse peasant dress, she entered the house she had left a little before in her shift, and had the rooms cleaned and arranged, put out hangings and carpets in the halls, looked to the kitchen, and set her hand to everything as if she had been a scullery wench of the house. And she never paused until everything was ready and properly arranged.

After this she invited all the ladies of the surrounding country in Gualtieri's name, and then awaited the feast. On the wedding day, dressed in her poor clothes, she received all the ladies with a cheerful visage and a womanly manner.

Gualtieri had had his children carefully brought up in Bologna by his relative, who was married into the family of the Counts of Panago. The daughter was now twelve years old, the most beautiful thing ever seen, and the boy was seven. He sent to her and asked her to come to Saluzzo with his son and daughter, to bring an honorable company with her, and to tell everyone that she was bringing the girl as his wife, and never to let anyone know that the girl was anything else. Her husband did what the Marquess asked, and set out. In a few days he reached Saluzzo about dinner time, with the girl and boy and his noble company; and all the peasants of the country were there to see Gualtieri's new wife.

The girl was received by the ladies and taken to the hall where the tables were spread, and Griselda went cheerfully to meet her, saying:

"Lady, you are welcome."

The ladies had begged Gualtieri, but in vain, to allow Griselda to stay in her room or to lend her one of her own dresses, so that she might not have to meet strangers in such a guise. They all sat down to table and began the meal. Every man looked at the girl and said that Gualtieri had made a good exchange, and Griselda above all praised her and her little brother.

Gualtieri now felt that he had tested his wife's patience as far as he desired. He saw that the strangeness of all this did not alter her and he was certain it was not the result of stupidity, for he knew her to be an intelligent woman. He thought it now time to take her from the bitterness which he felt she must be hiding behind a smiling face. So he called her to him, and in everyone's presence said to her smilingly:

"What do you think of my new wife?"

"My lord," replied Griselda, "I see nothing but good in her. If she is as virtuous as she is beautiful, as I well believe, I have no doubt that you will live with her the happiest lord in the world. But I beg you as earnestly as I can not to give her the wounds you gave the other woman who was your wife. I think she could hardly endure them, because she is younger and because she has been brought up delicately, whereas the other labored continually from her childhood."

Gualtieri saw that she really believed he was to marry the other, and yet spoke nothing but good of her. He made her sit down beside him, and said:

"Griselda, it is now time that you should reap the reward of your long patience, and that those who have thought me cruel and wicked and brutal should know that what I have done was directed towards a pre-determined end, which was to teach you to be a wife, then how to choose and keep a wife, and to procure me perpetual peace so long as I live with you. When I came and took you to wife, I greatly feared that this would not happen to me; and so, to test you, I have given you the trials and sufferings you know. I have never perceived that you thwarted my wishes by word or deed, and I think that in you I have the comfort I desire. I mean to give you back now what I deprived you of for a long time, and to heal the wounds I gave you with the greatest delight. Therefore, with a glad spirit, take her whom you think to be my wife and her brother as your children and mine. They are the children whom you and many others have long thought that I had cruelly murdered. And I am your husband, who loves you above all things, believing I can boast that no man exists who can so rejoice in his wife as I in you."

He then embraced and kissed her. She was weeping with happiness. They both arose and went to where their daughter was sitting, quite stupefied by what she had heard, and tenderly embraced her and her brother, thus undeceiving them and many of those present.

The ladies arose merrily from table and went with Griselda to her room. With better hopes they took off her old clothes and dressed her in one of her noble robes, and brought her back to the hall a lady, which she had looked even in her rags.

They rejoiced over their children, and everyone was glad at what had happened. The feasting and merrymaking were prolonged for several days, and Gualtieri was held to be a wise man, although they thought the testing of his wife harsh and intolerable. But above all they esteemed the virtue of Griselda.

The Count of Panago soon afterwards returned to Bologna. Gualtieri took Giannucole away from his labor and installed him as his father-in-law, so that he ended his days honorably and in great content. He afterwards married off his daughter to a nobleman of great wealth and distinction, and lived long and happily with Griselda, always honoring her as much as he could.

What more is to be said, save that divine souls are sometimes rained down from Heaven into poor houses, while in royal palaces are born those who are better fitted to herd swine than to rule over men? Who but Griselda could have endured with a face not only tearless but cheerful, the stern and unheard-of tests imposed on her by Gualtieri? It would perhaps not have been such a bad thing if he had chosen one of those women who, if she had been driven out of her home in a shift, would have let another man so shake her fur that a new dress would have come from it.

Dioneo's tale was over, and the ladies talked about it, taking first one part and then another, blaming some things and praising others. The king looked up at the sky and saw that the sun was already sinking towards the hour of Vespers,[6] and so, without rising, he spoke thus:

[6] 6 P.M.

"Beautiful ladies, as I think you know, human wisdom does not wholly consist in remembering past things and knowing the present; but grave men esteem it the highest wisdom to be able to foresee the future from a knowledge of both.

"As you know, it will be a fortnight tomorrow since we left Florence to find some amusement to support our health and vitality, and to escape the melancholy, agony and woes which have continued in our city since the beginning of the plague. In my opinion we have virtuously performed this. We have told merry tales, which perhaps might incline to concupiscence; we have eaten and drunk well, played and sung music, all of which things incite weak minds to things less than virtuous; but so far as I have seen there has not been one word or one act on your part or on ours which could be blamed. I have noticed only continual virtue, concord and fraternal familiarity; which is certainly most pleasing to me in your honor and in mine. Now, through too long a habit something might arise which would turn to annoyance, and if we stay away too long an opportunity for scandal might occur; and moreover each of us has now for one day exercised the honor which now dwells in me. I therefore think, if you agree, that it would be well for us to return to the place from which we set out. And, if you consider the matter, our being together is already known round about, and so our company might be increased in such a way as to destroy our pleasure. If you approve my advice, I shall retain the crown until we leave, which I think should be tomorrow. If you decide otherwise, I am quite ready to crown someone for tomorrow."

The discussion between the ladies and young men was long, but at last the king's advice was adopted as wise and virtuous, and they determined to do as he had said. So, having called the steward, he discussed with him what should be done next morning, and then, standing up, gave the company their freedom until supper time.

The ladies and the rest arose, and as usual amused themselves in different ways. They came to supper merrily, and after that began to sing and dance and play music. After Lauretta had danced, the king ordered Fiammetta to sing a song, and she began pleasantly as follows:

If Love came to us without jealousy, no woman living—whoever she might be—would
be so glad as I!

And if a woman should be pleased to find in her lover gay youth, the very pinnacle
of virtue, eagerness and prowess, wisdom, manners, eloquent speech and perfect
grace—I should be pleased, who love them all and see them in my hope.

But since I see that other ladies are as wise as I, I tremble with my fears and dread
the worst—which is that others may desire the man I love; and so my wondrous
fortune turns to woe and sighing, and all life seems ill.

If my lover were but as faithful as he is valiant, I should feel no jealousy. But now
so many ladies seek for lovers that I think all men are faithless. This stabs my heart
and makes me wish to die; I dread each woman who looks at him, and fear I may
be robbed of him.

Therefore in God's name I beg all ladies not to work this wrong on me; for should any seek to do me harm by word or sign or flattery, either I shall turn fool at learning it or she shall weep her bitter foolishness!

When Fiammetta had ended her song, Dioneo, who was sitting beside her, said laughingly:

"Madonna, you would be very courteous to let all women know this, so that no one in ignorance may deprive you of a possession, whose loss would make you so angry!"

After this, they sang several other songs, and when it was nearly midnight, the king commanded that they should all go to bed.

Next morning they arose after the steward had already sent off all their baggage, and returned to Florence under the guidance of their prudent king. The three young men left the seven ladies in Santa Maria Novella, where they had met; and after taking leave of them went about their business. And the ladies returned home.

END OF THE TENTH AND LAST DAY

from CONCLUSION

Most noble ladies, for whose delight I have given myself over to this long task, I believe that with the aid of divine grace it is more through your pious prayers than any merit of mine that I have carried out what I promised to do at the beginning of this work. So now, after giving thanks, first to God and then to you, I shall rest my pen and weary hand. I know that these tales can expect no more immunity than any others, as I think I showed in the beginning of the Fourth Day;[1] and so before I rest, I mean to reply to certain objections which might be made by you or others.

Some of you may say that in writing these tales I have taken too much license, by making ladies sometimes say and often listen to matters which are not proper to be said or heard by virtuous ladies. This I deny, for there is nothing so unchaste but may be said chastely if modest words are used; and this I think I have done.

But suppose it to be true—and I shall not strive with you, for you are certain to win—I reply that I have many arguments ready. First, if there is any license in some of them, the nature of the stories demanded it; and if any understanding person looks at them with a reasonable eye he will see that they could not be related otherwise, unless I had altered them entirely. And if there are a few words rather freer than suits the prudes, who weigh words more than deeds and take more pains to appear than to be good, I say that I should no more be reproved for having written them than

---

[1]At the beginning of Day Four, Boccaccio had defended himself against detractors who had charged him, among other things, with too great a fondness for women. He replied that love for them was almost irresistibly natural.

other men and women are reproved for daily saying "hole," "peg," "mortar," "pestle," "sausage," "Bologna sausage," and the like things.[2] My pen should be allowed no less power than is permitted the painter's brush; the painters are not censured for allowing Saint Michele to slay the serpent with a sword or lance and Saint Giorgio to kill the dragon as he pleases. They make Christ male and Eve female, and they fasten sometimes with one nail, sometimes with two, the feet of Him who died for the human race on the Cross.

In addition, anyone can see that these things were not told in church, where everything should be treated with reverent words and minds (although you will find plenty of license in the stories of the church); nor were they told in a school of philosophers, where virtue is as much required as anywhere else; nor among churchmen or other philosophers in any place; but they were told in gardens, in pleasure places, by young people who were old enough not to be led astray by stories, and at a time when everyone threw his cap over the mill and the most virtuous were not reproved for it.

But, such as they are, they may be amusing or harmful, like everything else, according to the persons who listen to them. Who does not know that wine is a most excellent thing, if we may believe Cinciglione and Scolaio,[3] while it is harmful to a man with a fever? Are we to say wine is wicked because it is bad for those who are feverish? Who does not know that fire is most useful and even necessary to mankind? And because it sometimes destroys houses, villages and towns, shall we say it is bad? Weapons defend the safety of those who wish to live in peace, but they also kill men, not through any wrong in them but through the wickedness of those who use them ill.

No corrupt mind ever understands words healthily. And just as such people do not enjoy virtuous words, so the well-disposed cannot be harmed by words which are somewhat less than virtuous, any more than mud can sully sunlight or earthy filth the beauty of the skies.

What books, what words, what letters are more holy, more worthy, more to be revered than those of the divine Scripture? Yet many people by perversely interpreting them have sent themselves and others to perdition. Everything in itself is good for something, and if wrongly used may be harmful in many ways; and I say the same of my tales. Whoever wants to turn them to bad counsel or bad ends will not be forbidden by the tales themselves, if by any chance they contain such things and are twisted and turned to produce them. Those who want utility and good fruits from them, will not find them denied; nor will the tales ever be thought anything but useful and virtuous if they are read at the times and to the persons for which they are intended. . . .

---

[2] Words that can be used literally and innocently or with sexual meanings. Boccaccio goes on to cite paintings in which images that might be considered phallic can be used for pious purposes.

[3] Names used to represent drinkers.

Niccolò Machiavelli

(1469–1527)

Niccolò Machiavelli—historian, theorist of history and of politics, and dramatist—was born in 1469 in Florence, a city he loved passionately and served or wished to serve throughout his life. His family had long been prominent in the city, but his father was impoverished, and Niccolò did not receive the best of formal educations; he learned Latin but not Greek, and he was in certain respects self-taught. Nevertheless, after a youth of which we know little, he achieved in 1498 an important post in the Florentine government, and from that time until 1512 he held several key offices having to do with the internal, foreign, and military affairs of the city (Florence was then a republic, as it had been on and off for centuries). His military interests and assignments helped foster in him one of his key ideas: the desirability of a native soldiery as contrasted with venal, undependable mercenaries. He also was entrusted with a good many important diplomatic missions that took him to France, Switzerland, Austria, southern Germany, and several parts of Italy.

During his travels he gained firsthand experience of the turbulence and disunited vulnerability of Italy, experience that he was to draw on in his writings. He also learned much about the realities of contemporary intrigue and power politics during an era of notorious violence and corruption, in Italy and throughout much of Europe. In 1502–1503 he observed at first hand the activities of Cesare Borgia, the unsavory political and military adventurer in whom Machiavelli, despite certain misgivings, found the boldness, acumen, and resourcefulness that he was to recommend in *The Prince*. Cesare's near-success in unifying central Italy provided in some respects a model for the larger unification of Italy that was one of Machiavelli's most cherished goals. The choice of such a model was to do Machiavelli's reputation no good when, later in the sixteenth century, gossip circulated about incestuous acts and murders by poison on the part of Cesare, his sister Lucrezia, and their father, Pope Alexander VI.

In 1512 the Medici family came to power in Florence, toppling the republic. Machiavelli was ousted from his posts and, suspected of disaffection as a member of the old government, was imprisoned and even tortured. Now in poverty, he retired to his modest patrimonial estate, where in 1513 he wrote *The Prince* and much of the *Discourses on the First Decade of Titus Livius*. The former work, on which Machiavelli's popular fame rests, was intended on a personal level to win favor with and office from the Medici rulers; Machiavelli dedicated the book first to Giuliano de' Medici and then, after his death in 1516, to his nephew Lorenzo. On a higher level the book was meant to serve the cause of Italian independence and unity by instructing and inspiring the leader who might deliver the country from its abject condition. In or around 1518 Machiavelli wrote the comedy *Mandragola,* or *The Mandrake Root,* a masterpiece of world drama. In 1520 he wrote *On the Art of War,* a milestone in the theory of military tactics. In his last years Machiavelli was given a few minor diplomatic assignments by the Medici and also won their patronage for certain written works, including a history of Florence. In 1527 the forces of the Holy Roman Emperor, Charles V, sacked Rome, an event that helped drive the Medici from power in Florence. Although the republic was restored, Machiavelli was not in favor with the new regime either, and his hope to return to public office was disappointed. He died in the same year.

Machiavelli's political writings, especially *The Prince,* present a difficult challenge to interpreters. In the later sixteenth century Machiavelli came to be regarded as the epitome of cold-blooded immorality; indeed, the "machiavel" became a stock character in Elizabethan drama, most notably in Christopher Marlowe's *Jew of Malta.* Marlowe's "Machiavelli" tells the audience, "I count religion but a childish toy, / And hold there is no sin but ignorance. . . . Might first made kings, and laws were then most sure / When . . . they were writ in blood." This myth about Machiavelli fed partly on itself, unbeholden to evidence from his writings, and it was reinforced in northern Europe by a stereotype of Italians as treacherous. What textual evidence there was came mainly from *The Prince;* the zealous republican Machiavelli of the *Discourses* seems a very different person. Certain passages in *The Prince,* and perhaps even its general tenor, do seem to support the traditional and popular view, which is by no means dead today even among informed readers of Machiavelli. At the very least, however, we owe it to Machiavelli to read what he actually wrote and to consider in what sense, if any, he really taught the doctrine often ascribed to him that "the end justifies the means."

But Machiavelli has many strong defenders. Besides appealing to the integrity of his private life and the evidence from works like the *Discourses,* his partisans urge a reappraisal of *The Prince* itself. Some of them praise Machiavelli as a political realist; they consider him one of the first thinkers to treat politics as a science rather than as a branch of ethics. Others have read *The Prince* as sustained, straight-faced irony, a devastating indictment of tyranny that for satiric purposes advises exactly the evils it seeks to expose. Others take *The Prince* more nearly at its word but subordinate the details of Machiavelli's practical advice to his main purpose, stated stirringly in Chapter 16, of uniting and liberating his country. In their view, Machiavelli thus becomes a precursor of the patriots of the Risorgimento, the century-long movement to unify and free Italy that culminated in 1870. Other admirers turn the emphasis from political science to literary art, emphasizing Machiavelli's creative side and the indisputable fact of his preeminence as a master of Italian prose.

In any case, there are many engrossing aspects of Machiavelli besides his morality. His prescriptions aside, his world view deserves attention in itself. In some ways he was a true Renaissance humanist, most clearly in his conviction that the classical past, which for Machiavelli meant primarily the Roman past, was directly relevant to the problems of modern times. This opinion is clearly not just sentimental nostalgia, for he finds in the ancients the same egocentric human nature he finds in his contemporaries. Yet out of selfishness and conflict, which for Machiavelli are givens in human nature and the state, the Romans created the greatest political entity the world has ever known. By the same token, since human nature does not change, he believes that the ancient glories can be revived, not by divine grace but by human skill and enterprise—within, admittedly, the limits of a fickle Fortune. The result is a unique and compelling vision, combining jaundiced caution with bracing self-assurance, unblinking realism with a peculiar brand of hope.

FURTHER READING *(prepared by W.J.R.)*: Roberto Ridolfi's *The Life of Niccolò Machiavelli,* 1954, trans. Cecil Grayson, 1963, is an excellent biography, as well as a comprehensive overview of Machiavelli's work. Ridolfi also provides an introductory account of the Italian Renaissance. The Past Masters series, which provides authoritative but fairly brief general introductions to great writers, includes Quentin Skinner's *Machiavelli,* 1981. Charles D. Tarlton's *Fortune's Circle,* 1970, uses Machiavelli's own writing to discover what it reveals about him. Machiavelli's literary art gets very good treatment in Peter Bondanella, *Machiavelli and the Art of Renaissance History,* 1974. Bondanella also has an essay on Machiavelli in *European Writers: Medieval and Renaissance,* Vol. 2, ed. George Stade, 1984. Silvia Ruffo-Fiore, *Niccolò Machiavelli,* 1982, attempts to draw together the political, historical, and literary aspects of Machiavelli. Proof that the image of him as an advocate of fraud and force is still alive is Mark Hulliung, *Citizen Machiavelli,* 1984. Sydney Anglo's *Machiavelli: A Dissection,* 1969, discusses each of Machiavelli's major works. For a sociological approach, see J. E. Siegel's "Violence and Order in Machiavelli," in *Violence and Aggression,* ed. Philip J. Wiener, 1974. Siegel examines Machiavelli's views on violence and attempts to reconcile Machiavelli's apparent brutality and his romantic idealism. Sebastian De Grazia, *Machiavelli in Hell,* 1989, analyzes the politics of *The Prince.* A feminist perspective is provided in Hanna Pitkin, *Fortune Is a Woman: Gender and Politics in the Thought of Niccolò Machiavelli,* 1984.

from *THE PRINCE*

Translated by Luigi Ricci, revised by E. R. P. Vincent

1

THE VARIOUS KINDS OF GOVERNMENT AND THE WAYS BY WHICH THEY ARE ESTABLISHED

All states and dominions which hold or have held sway over mankind are either republics or monarchies. Monarchies are either hereditary in which the rulers have been for many years of the same family, or else they are of recent foundation. The newly founded ones are either entirely new, as was Milan to Francesco Sforza,[1] or else they are, as it were, new members grafted on to the hereditary possessions of the prince that annexes them, as is the Kingdom of Naples to the King of Spain.[2] The dominions thus acquired have either been previously accustomed to the rule of another prince, or else have been free states, and they are annexed either by force of arms of the prince himself, or of others, or else fall to him by good fortune or special ability.[3]

---

[1]Milan had formerly been ruled by the Duke Filippo Maria Visconti; after his death, his son-in-law Sforza (1401–1466) betrayed the succeeding republic and assumed control as Duke of Milan in 1450.

[2]In 1500, King Louis XII of France and Ferdinand "the Catholic," King of Spain, agreed to share the rule of the much-disputed Kingdom of Naples, but in 1503 Ferdinand seized it by force for Spain.

[3]*Special ability* here translates the Italian *virtù.* A key word in Machiavelli, it can be variously interpreted as special ability, human ability, merit, ingenuity, worth, vigor, strength, or a number of related qualities. It almost never means "virtue."

2

OF HEREDITARY MONARCHIES

I will not here speak of republics, having already treated of them fully in another place.[4] I will deal only with monarchies, and will discuss how the various kinds described above can be governed and maintained. In the first place, the difficulty of maintaining hereditary states accustomed to a reigning family is far less than in new monarchies; for it is sufficient not to transgress ancestral usages, and to adapt one's self to unforeseen circumstances; in this way such a prince, if of ordinary assiduity, will always be able to maintain his position, unless some very exceptional and excessive force deprives him of it; and even if he be thus deprived, on the slightest mischance happening to the new occupier, he will be able to regain it.

We have in Italy the example of the Duke of Ferrara, who was able to withstand the assaults of the Venetians in 1484 and of Pope Julius in 1510,[5] for no other reason than because of the antiquity of his family in that dominion. In as much as the legitimate prince has less cause and less necessity to give offense, it is only natural that he should be more loved; and, if no extraordinary vices make him hated, it is only reasonable for his subjects to be naturally attached to him, the memories and causes of innovations being forgotten in the long period over which his rule has extended; whereas one change always leaves the way prepared for the introduction of another.

5

THE WAY TO GOVERN CITIES OR DOMINIONS
THAT, PREVIOUS TO BEING OCCUPIED,
LIVED UNDER THEIR OWN LAWS

When those states which have been acquired are accustomed to live at liberty under their own laws, there are three ways of holding them. The first is to despoil them; the second is to go and live there in person; the third is to allow them to live under their own laws, taking tribute of them, and creating within the country a government composed of a few who will keep it friendly to you. Because this government, being created by the prince, knows that it cannot exist without his friendship and protection, it will do all it can to keep them. What is more, a city used to liberty can be more easily held by means of its citizens than in any other way, if you wish to preserve it.

There is the example of the Spartans and the Romans. The Spartans held Athens and Thebes[6] by creating within them a government of a few; nevertheless they lost them. The Romans, in order to hold Capua, Carthage, and Numantia,[7] ravaged them, but did not lose them. They wanted to hold Greece in almost the same way as the Spartans held it, leaving it free and under its

---

[4] In the *Discourses on the First Decade of Titus Livius.* Livius, or Livy (59 B.C.–A.D. 17), wrote a history of ancient Rome from which Machiavelli believed much could be learned by the Italians of his own time. Livy's first ten books, or "decade," describe the early years of Rome, before it became an empire under the Caesars in the first century B.C.

[5] For more on the warlike Pope Julius II (reigned 1503–13), see chapters 16 and 25.

[6] Athens fell to Sparta in 404 B.C. The Spartans seized Thebes in 382 B.C.

[7] The Romans took Capua (in southwest Italy) in 211 B.C., Carthage (in north Africa, near modern Tunis) in 146 B.C., and Numantia (in Spain) in 133 B.C.

own laws, but they did not succeed; so that they were compelled to lay waste many cities in that province in order to keep it, because in truth there is no sure method of holding them except by despoiling them. And whoever becomes the ruler of a free city and does not destroy it, can expect to be destroyed by it, for it can always find a motive for rebellion in the name of liberty and of its ancient usages, which are forgotten neither by lapse of time nor by benefits received; and whatever one does or provides, so long as the inhabitants are not separated or dispersed, they do not forget that name and those usages, but appeal to them at once in every emergency, as did Pisa after so many years held in servitude by the Florentines.[8] But when cities or provinces have been accustomed to live under a prince, and the family of that prince is extinguished, being on the one hand used to obey, and on the other not having their old prince, they cannot unite in choosing one from among themselves, and they do not know how to live in freedom, so that they are slower to take arms, and a prince can win them over with greater facility and establish himself securely. But in republics there is greater life, greater hatred, and more desire for vengeance; they do not and cannot cast aside the memory of their ancient liberty, so that the surest way is either to lay them waste or reside in them.

15

OF THE THINGS FOR WHICH MEN, AND ESPECIALLY PRINCES, ARE PRAISED OR BLAMED

It now remains to be seen what are the methods and rules for a prince as regards his subjects and friends. And as I know that many have written of this, I fear that my writing about it may be deemed presumptuous, differing as I do, especially in this matter, from the opinions of others. But my intention being to write something of use to those who understand, it appears to be more proper to go to the real truth of the matter than to its imagination; and many have imagined republics and principalities which have never been seen or known to exist in reality;[9] for how we live is so far removed from how we ought to live, that he who abandons what is done for what ought to be done, will rather learn to bring about his own ruin than his preservation. A man who wishes to make a profession of goodness in everything must necessarily come to grief among so many who are not good. Therefore it is necessary for a prince who wishes to maintain himself to learn how not to be good, and to use this knowledge and not use it, according to the necessity of the case.

Leaving on one side, then, those things which concern only an imaginary prince, and speaking of those that are real, I state that all men, and especially princes, who are placed at a greater height, are reputed for certain qualities which bring them either praise or blame. Thus one is considered

---

[8] Pisa, a city west of Florence where the Arno, the river of Florence, flows into the sea, was controlled by Florence through most of the fifteenth century. When King Charles VIII of France swept through Italy in 1494, Pisa rebelled and was not subjugated by Florence again until 1509.

[9] For example, in Plato's *Republic*.

liberal,[10] another *misero* or miserly (using a Tuscan[11] term, seeing that *avaro* with us still means one who is rapaciously acquisitive and *misero* one who makes grudging use of his own); one a free giver, another rapacious; one cruel, another merciful; one a breaker of his word, another trustworthy; one effeminate and pusillanimous, another fierce and high-spirited; one humane, another haughty; one lascivious, another chaste; one frank, another astute; one hard, another easy; one serious, another frivolous; one religious, another an unbeliever, and so on. I know that every one will admit that it would be highly praiseworthy in a prince to possess all the above-named qualities that are reputed good, but as they cannot all be possessed or observed, human conditions not permitting of it, it is necessary that he should be prudent enough to avoid the scandal of those vices which would lose him the state, and guard himself if possible against those which will not lose it him, but if not able to, he can indulge them with less scruple. And yet he must not mind incurring the scandal of those vices without which it would be difficult to save the state, for if one considers well, it will be found that some things which seem virtues would, if followed, lead to one's ruin, and some others which appear vices result in one's greater security and well-being.

16

OF LIBERALITY AND NIGGARDLINESS

Beginning now with the first qualities above named, I say that it would be well to be considered liberal; nevertheless liberality such as the world understands it will injure you, because if used virtuously and in the proper way, it will not be known, and you will incur the disgrace of the contrary vice. But one who wishes to obtain the reputation of liberality among men must not omit every kind of sumptuous display, and to such an extent that a prince of this character will consume by such means all his resources, and will be at last compelled, if he wishes to maintain his name for liberality, to impose heavy taxes on his people, become extortionate, and do everything possible to obtain money. This will make his subjects begin to hate him, and he will be little esteemed being poor, so that having by this liberality injured many and benefited but few, he will feel the first little disturbance and be endangered by every peril. If he recognizes this and wishes to change his system, he incurs at once the charge of niggardliness.

A prince, therefore, not being able to exercise this virtue of liberality without risk if it be known, must not, if he be prudent, object to be called miserly. In course of time he will be thought more liberal, when it is seen that by his parsimony his revenue is sufficient, that he can defend himself against those who make war on him, and undertake enterprises without burdening his people, so that he is really liberal to all those from whom he does not take, who are infinite in number, and niggardly to all to whom he does not give, who are few. In our times we have seen nothing great done except by those who have been esteemed niggardly; the others have all been

---

[10] Free-giving; generous.
[11] Tuscany is Machiavelli's region, which includes Florence.

)e Julius II, although he had made use of a reputation for lib-
·der to attain the papacy, did not seek to retain it afterwards, so
that he might be able to wage war. The present King of France has carried
on so many wars without imposing an extraordinary tax, because his extra
expenses were covered by the parsimony he had so long practiced. The present King of Spain, if he had been thought liberal, would not have engaged
in and been successful in so many enterprises.

For these reasons a prince must care little for the reputation of being a
miser, if he wishes to avoid robbing his subjects, if he wishes to be able to
defend himself, to avoid becoming poor and contemptible, and not to be
forced to become rapacious; this niggardliness is one of those vices which
enable him to reign. If it is said that Cæsar attained the empire through liberality, and that many others have reached the highest positions through being
liberal or being thought so, I would reply that you are either a prince already
or else on the way to become one. In the first case, this liberality is harmful; in the second, it is certainly necessary to be considered liberal. Cæsar
was one of those who wished to attain the mastery over Rome, but if after
attaining it he had lived and had not moderated his expenses, he would have
destroyed that empire. And should any one reply that there have been many
princes, who have done great things with their armies, who have been thought
extremely liberal, I would answer by saying that the prince may either spend
his own wealth and that of his subjects or the wealth of others. In the first
case he must be sparing, but for the rest he must not neglect to be very liberal. The liberality is very necessary to a prince who marches with his armies,
and lives by plunder, sack, and ransom, and is dealing with the wealth of
others, for without it he would not be followed by his soldiers. And you may
be very generous indeed with what is not the property of yourself or your
subjects, as were Cyrus, Cæsar, and Alexander; for spending the wealth of
others will not diminish your reputation, but increase it, only spending your
own resources will injure you. There is nothing which destroys itself so much
as liberality, for by using it you lose the power of using it, and become either
poor and despicable, or, to escape poverty, rapacious and hated. And of all
things that a prince must guard against, the most important are being despicable or hated, and liberality will lead you to one or the other of these conditions. It is, therefore, wiser to have the name of a miser, which produces
disgrace without hatred, than to incur of necessity the name of being rapacious, which produces both disgrace and hatred.

17

OF CRUELTY AND CLEMENCY, AND WHETHER IT
IS BETTER TO BE LOVED OR FEARED

Proceeding to the other qualities before named, I say that every prince must
desire to be considered merciful and not cruel. He must, however, take care
not to misuse this mercifulness. Cesare Borgia was considered cruel, but
his cruelty had brought order to the Romagna, united it, and reduced it
to peace and fealty. If this is considered well, it will be seen that he was
really much more merciful than the Florentine people, who, to avoid the

name of cruelty, allowed Pistoia to be destroyed.[12] A prince, therefore, must not mind incurring the charge of cruelty for the purpose of keeping his subjects united and faithful; for, with a very few examples, he will be more merciful than those who, from excess of tenderness, allow disorders to arise, from whence spring bloodshed and rapine; for these as a rule injure the whole community, while the executions carried out by the prince injure only individuals. And of all princes, it is impossible for a new prince to escape the reputation of cruelty, new states being always full of dangers. Wherefore Virgil through the mouth of Dido says:

Res dura, et regni novitas me talia cogunt
Moliri, et late fines custode tueri.[13]

Nevertheless, he must be cautious in believing and acting, and must not be afraid of his own shadow, and must proceed in a temperate manner with prudence and humanity, so that too much confidence does not render him incautious, and too much diffidence[14] does not render him intolerant.

From this arises the question whether it is better to be loved more than feared, or feared more than loved. The reply is, that one ought to be both feared and loved, but as it is difficult for the two to go together, it is much safer to be feared than loved, if one of the two has to be wanting. For it may be said of men in general that they are ungrateful, voluble, dissemblers, anxious to avoid danger, and covetous of gain; as long as you benefit them, they are entirely yours; they offer you their blood, their goods, their life, and their children, as I have before said, when the necessity is remote; but when it approaches, they revolt. And the prince who has relied solely on their words, without making other preparations, is ruined; for the friendship which is gained by purchase and not through grandeur and nobility of spirit is bought but not secured, and at a pinch is not to be expended in your service. And men have less scruple in offending one who makes himself loved than one who makes himself feared; for love is held by a chain of obligation which, men being selfish, is broken whenever it serves their purpose; but fear is maintained by a dread of punishment which never fails.

Still, a prince should make himself feared in such a way that if he does not gain love, he at any rate avoids hatred; for fear and the absence of hatred may well go together, and will be always attained by one who abstains from interfering with the property of his citizens and subjects or with their women. And when he is obliged to take the life of any one, let him do so when there is a proper justification and manifest reason for it; but above all he must abstain from taking the property of others, for men forget more easily the death of their father than the loss of their patrimony. Then also pretexts for

[12] Pistoja was a city near Florence and under its control. Florence failed to assert its power and allowed a bloody civil war to continue.

[13] "The newness of the kingdom / And our strict need compel me to such measures— / Sentries on every border, far and wide"—*Aeneid,* Book I, Rolfe Humphries translation. Dido is explaining to the shipwrecked Trojans that, having only recently founded and settled Carthage, she and her people must take extreme security precautions.

[14] Lack of trust.

seizing property are never wanting, and one who begins to live by rapine will always find some reason for taking the goods of others, whereas causes for taking life are rarer and more fleeting.

But when the prince is with his army and has a large number of soldiers under his control, then it is extremely necessary that he should not mind being thought cruel; for without this reputation he could not keep an army united or disposed to any duty. Among the noteworthy actions of Hannibal[15] is numbered this, that although he had an enormous army, composed of men of all nations and fighting in foreign countries, there never arose any dissension either among them or against the prince, either in good fortune or in bad. This could not be due to anything but his inhuman cruelty, which together with his infinite other virtues, made him always venerated and terrible in the sight of his soldiers, and without it his other virtues would not have sufficed to produce that effect. Thoughtless writers admire on the one hand his actions, and on the other blame the principal cause of them.

And that it is true that his other virtues would not have sufficed may be seen from the case of Scipio (famous not only in regard to his own times, but all times of which memory remains), whose armies rebelled against him in Spain, which arose from nothing but his excessive kindness, which allowed more license to the soldiers than was consonant with military discipline. He was reproached with this in the senate by Fabius Maximus,[16] who called him a corrupter of the Roman militia. Locri having been destroyed by one of Scipio's officers was not revenged by him,[17] nor was the insolence of that officer punished, simply by reason of his easy nature; so much so, that some one wishing to excuse him in the senate, said that there were many men who knew rather how not to err, than how to correct the errors of others. This disposition would in time have tarnished the fame and glory of Scipio had he persevered in it under the empire, but living under the rule of the senate this harmful quality was not only concealed but became a glory to him.

I conclude, therefore, with regard to being feared and loved, that men love at their own free will, but fear at the will of the prince, and that a wise prince must rely on what is in his power and not on what is in the power of others, and he must only contrive to avoid incurring hatred, as has been explained.

18

IN WHAT WAY PRINCES MUST KEEP FAITH

How laudable it is for a prince to keep good faith and live with integrity, and not with astuteness,[18] every one knows. Still, the experience of our times shows those princes to have done great things who have had little regard

---

[15] Carthaginian general (247–182 B.C.), victorious against Rome for a time but finally defeated by Scipio. One of Hannibal's most spectacular feats was to lead his invading army across the Alps from Spain to Italy.

[16] Fabius Cunctator ("the Delayer"), noted for his tactic of harassing Hannibal's army without meeting it head-on. He became dictator of Rome in 217 B.C.

[17] Scipio took Locri, in southern Italy, in 205 B.C.

[18] The word as used here means craftiness or cunning.

for good faith, and have been able by astuteness to confuse men's brains, and who have ultimately overcome those who have made loyalty their foundation.

You must know, then, that there are two methods of fighting, the one by law, the other by force: the first method is that of men, the second of beasts; but as the first method is often insufficient, one must have recourse to the second. It is therefore necessary for a prince to know well how to use both the beast and the man. This was covertly taught to rulers by ancient writers, who relate how Achilles and many others of those ancient princes were given to Chiron the centaur to be brought up and educated under his discipline.[19] The parable of this semi-animal, semi-human teacher is meant to indicate that a prince must know how to use both natures, and that the one without the other is not durable.

A prince being thus obliged to know well how to act as a beast must imitate the fox and the lion, for the lion cannot protect himself from traps, and the fox cannot defend himself from wolves. One must therefore be a fox to recognise traps, and a lion to frighten wolves. Those that wish to be only lions do not understand this. Therefore, a prudent ruler ought not to keep faith when by so doing it would be against his interest, and when the reasons which made him bind himself no longer exist. If men were all good, this precept would not be a good one; but as they are bad, and would not observe their faith with you, so you are not bound to keep faith with them. Nor have legitimate grounds ever failed a prince who wished to show colorable excuse for the non-fulfilment of his promise. Of this one could furnish an infinite number of modern examples, and show how many times peace has been broken, and how many promises rendered worthless, by the faithlessness of princes, and those that have been best able to imitate the fox have succeeded best. But it is necessary to be able to disguise this character well, and to be a great feigner and dissembler; and men are so simple and so ready to obey present necessities, that one who deceives will always find those who allow themselves to be deceived.

I will only mention one modern instance. Alexander VI did nothing else but deceive men, he thought of nothing else, and found the occasion for it; no man was ever more able to give assurances, or affirmed things with stronger oaths, and no man observed them less; however, he always succeeded in his deceptions, as he well knew this aspect of things.

It is not, therefore, necessary for a prince to have all the above-named qualities, but it is very necessary to seem to have them. I would even be bold to say that to possess them and always to observe them is dangerous, but to appear to possess them is useful. Thus it is well to seem merciful, faithful, humane, sincere, religious, and also to be so; but you must have the mind so disposed that when it is needful to be otherwise you may be able to change to the opposite qualities. And it must be understood that a prince, and especially a new prince, cannot observe all those things which are considered good in men, being often obliged, in order to maintain the state, to act against faith, against charity, against humanity, and against religion. And, therefore, he must have a mind disposed to adapt itself according to the wind, and as

[19]Centaurs were half-man, half-horse.

variations of fortune dictate, and, as I said before, not deviate from what is good, if possible, but be able to do evil if constrained.

A prince must take great care that nothing goes out of his mouth which is not full of the above-named five qualities, and, to see and hear him, he should seem to be all mercy, faith, integrity, humanity, and religion. And nothing is more necessary than to seem to have this last quality, for men in general judge more by the eyes than by the hands, for every one can see, but very few have to feel. Everybody sees what you appear to be, few feel what you are, and those few will not dare to oppose themselves to the many, who have the majesty of the state to defend them; and in the actions of men, and especially of princes, from which there is no appeal, the end justifies the means. Let a prince therefore aim at conquering and maintaining the state, and the means will always be judged honorable and praised by every one, for the vulgar are always taken by appearances and the issue of the event; and the world consists only of the vulgar, and the few who are not vulgar are isolated when the many have a rallying point in the prince. A certain prince of the present time,[20] whom it is well not to name, never does anything but preach peace and good faith, but he is really a great enemy to both, and either of them, had he observed them, would have lost him state or reputation on many occasions.

23

HOW FLATTERERS MUST BE SHUNNED

I must not omit an important subject, and mention of a mistake which princes can with difficulty avoid, if they are not very prudent, or if they do not make a good choice. And this is with regard to flatterers, of which courts are full, because men take such pleasure in their own things and so deceive themselves about them that they can with difficulty guard against this plague; and by wishing to guard against it they run the risk of becoming contemptible. Because there is no other way of guarding one's self against flattery than by letting men understand that they will not offend you by speaking the truth; but when every one can tell you the truth, you lose their respect. A prudent prince must therefore take a third course, by choosing for his council wise men, and giving these alone full liberty to speak the truth to him, but only of those things that he asks and of nothing else; but he must ask them about everything and hear their opinion, and afterwards deliberate by himself in his own way, and in these councils and with each of these men comport himself so that every one may see that the more freely he speaks, the more he will be acceptable. Beyond these he should listen to no one, go about the matter deliberately, and be determined in his decisions. Whoever acts otherwise either acts precipitately through flattery or else changes often through the variety of opinions, from which it follows that he will be little esteemed.

I will give a modern instance of this. Pre' Luca,[21] a follower of Maximilian, the present emperor, speaking of this majesty said that he never took counsel with anybody, and yet that he never did anything as he wished; this arose from his following the contrary method to the aforesaid. As the emperor is

---

[20] King Ferdinand of Spain.
[21] Father Luke.

a secret man he does not communicate his designs to any one or take any advice, but as on putting them into effect they begin to be known and discovered, they begin to be opposed by those he has about him, and he is easily diverted from his purpose. Hence it comes to pass that what he does one day he undoes the next, no one ever understands what he wishes or intends to do, and no reliance is to be placed on his deliberations.

A prince, therefore, ought always to take counsel, but only when he wishes, not when others wish; on the contrary he ought to discourage absolutely attempts to advise him unless he asks it, but he ought to be a great asker, and a patient hearer of the truth about those things of which he has inquired; indeed, if he finds that anyone has scruples in telling him the truth he should be angry. And since some think that a prince who gains the reputation of being prudent is so considered, not by his nature but by the good counsellors he has about him, they are undoubtedly deceived. It is an infallible rule that a prince who is not wise himself cannot be well advised, unless by chance he leaves himself entirely in the hands of one man who rules him in everything, but happens to be a very prudent man. In this case he may doubtless be well governed, but it would not last long, for that governor would in a short time deprive him of the state; but by taking counsel with many, a prince who is not wise will never have united councils and will not be able to bring them to unanimity for himself. The counsellors will all think of their own interests, and he will be unable either to correct or to understand them. And it cannot be otherwise, for men will always be false to you unless they are compelled by necessity to be true. Therefore it must be concluded that wise counsels, from whoever they come, must necessarily be due to the prudence of the prince, and not the prudence of the prince to the good counsels received.

25

HOW MUCH FORTUNE CAN DO IN HUMAN AFFAIRS AND HOW IT MAY BE OPPOSED

It is not unknown to me how many have been and are of opinion that worldly events are so governed by fortune and by God, that men cannot by their prudence change them, and that on the contrary there is no remedy whatever, and for this they may judge it to be useless to toil much about them, but let things be ruled by chance. This opinion has been more held in our day, from the great changes that have been seen, and are daily seen, beyond every human conjecture. When I think about them, at times I am partly inclined to share this opinion. Nevertheless, that our free will may not be altogether extinguished, I think it may be true that fortune is the ruler of half our actions, but that she allows the other half or thereabouts to be governed by us. I would compare her to an impetuous river that, when turbulent, inundates the plains, casts down trees and buildings, removes earth from this side and places it on the other; every one flees before it, and everything yields to its fury without being able to oppose it; and yet though it is of such a kind, still when it is quiet, men can make provisions against it by dikes and banks, so that when it rises it will either go into a canal or its rush will not be so wild and dangerous. So it is with fortune, which shows her power where no measures have been taken to resist her, and directs her fury where she knows that no dikes or barriers have been made to hold her. And if you regard Italy, which has been the seat of these changes, and which has given the impulse to them, you will see her to be a country without dikes or banks of any kind. If she had been protected by proper measures, like Germany, Spain, and France, this inundation would not have caused the great changes that it has, or would not have happened at all.

This must suffice as regards opposition to fortune in general. But limiting myself more to particular cases, I would point out how one sees a certain prince to-day fortunate and to-morrow ruined, without seeing that he has changed in character or otherwise. I believe this arises in the first place from the causes that we have already discussed at length; that is to say, because the prince who bases himself entirely on fortune is ruined when fortune changes. I also believe that he is happy whose mode of procedure accords with the needs of the times, and similarly he is unfortunate whose mode of procedure is opposed to the times. For one sees that men in those things which lead them to the aim that each one has in view, namely, glory and riches, proceed in various ways; one with circumspection, another with impetuosity, one by violence, another by cunning, one with patience, another with the reverse; and each by these diverse ways may arrive at his aim. One sees also two cautious men, one of whom succeeds in his designs, and the other not, and in the same way two men succeed equally by different methods, one being cautious, the other impetuous, which arises only from the nature of the times, which does or does not conform to their method of procedure. From this it results, as I have said, that two men, acting differently, attain the same effect, and of two others acting in the same way, one attains his goal and not the other. On this depend also the changes in prosperity, for if it happens that time and circumstances are favorable to one who acts with caution and prudence he will be successful, but if time and circumstances change he will be ruined, because he does not change his mode of procedure. No man is found so prudent as to be able to adapt himself to this, either because he cannot deviate from that to which his nature disposes him, or else because having always prospered by walking in one path, he cannot persuade himself that it is well to leave it; and therefore the cautious man, when it is time to act suddenly, does not know how to do so and is consequently ruined; for if one could change one's nature with time and circumstances, fortune would never change.

Pope Julius II acted impetuously in everything he did and found the times and conditions so in conformity with that mode of procedure, that he always obtained a good result. Consider the first war that he made against Bologna while Messer Giovanni Bentivogli[22] was still living. The Venetians were not pleased with it, neither was the King of Spain, France was conferring with him over the enterprise, notwithstanding which, owing to his fierce and impetuous disposition, he engaged personally in the expedition. This move caused both Spain and the Venetians to halt and hesitate, the latter through fear, the former through the desire to recover the entire kingdom of Naples. On the other hand, he engaged with him the King of France, because seeing him make this move and desiring his friendship in order to put down the

---

[22] Member of a family of Bologna, attacked by Pope Julius II in 1506.

Venetians, that king judged that he could not refuse him his troops without manifest injury. Thus Julius by his impetuous move achieved what no other pontiff[23] with the utmost human prudence would have succeeded in doing, because, if he had waited till all arrangements had been made and everything settled before leaving Rome, as any other pontiff would have done, it would never have succeeded. For the king of France would have found a thousand excuses, and the others would have inspired him with a thousand fears. I will omit his other actions, which were all of this kind and which all succeeded well, and the shortness of his life did not suffer him to experience the contrary, for had times followed in which it was necessary to act with caution, his ruin would have resulted, for he would never have deviated from these methods to which his nature disposed him.

I conclude then that fortune varying and men remaining fixed in their ways, they are successful so long as these ways conform to circumstances, but when they are opposed then they are unsuccessful. I certainly think that it is better to be impetuous than cautious, for fortune is a woman, and it is necessary, if you wish to master her, to conquer her by force; and it can be seen that she lets herself be overcome by the bold rather than by those who proceed coldly. And therefore, like a woman, she is always a friend to the young, because they are less cautious, fiercer, and master her with greater audacity.

26

EXHORTATION TO LIBERATE ITALY
FROM THE BARBARIANS

Having now considered all the things we have spoken of, and thought within myself whether at present the time was not propitious in Italy for a new prince, and if there was not a state of things which offered an opportunity to a prudent and capable man to introduce a new system that would do honor to himself and good to the mass of the people, it seems to me that so many things concur to favor a new ruler that I do not know of any time more fitting for such an enterprise. And if, as I said, it was necessary in order that the power of Moses should be displayed, that the people of Israel should be slaves in Egypt, and to give scope for the greatness and courage of Cyrus that the Persians should be oppressed by the Medes,[24] and to illustrate the pre-eminence of Theseus[25] that the Athenians should be dispersed, so at the present time, in order that the might of an Italian genius might be recognised, it was necessary that Italy should be reduced to her present condition, and that she should be more enslaved than the Hebrews, more oppressed than the Persians, and more scattered than the Athenians; without a head, without order, beaten, despoiled, lacerated, and overrun, and that she should have suffered ruin of every kind.

---

[23]Pope.

[24]Inhabitants of Media, an ancient region in what is now northwestern Iran. Cyrus the Great (sixth century B.C.) founded the Persian Empire.

[25]A mythical king of Athens. The Athenians credited him with unifying the scattered communities of Attica, the region near Athens.

And although before now a gleam of hope has appeared which gave hope that some individual might be appointed by God for her redemption, yet at the highest summit of his career he was thrown aside by fortune, so that now, almost lifeless, she awaits one who may heal her wounds and put a stop to the pillaging of Lombardy,[26] to the rapacity and extortion in the Kingdom of Naples and in Tuscany, and cure her of those sores which have long been festering. Behold how she prays God to send some one to redeem her from this barbarous cruelty and insolence. Behold her ready and willing to follow any standard if only there be some one to raise it. There is nothing now she can hope for but that your illustrious house[27] may place itself at the head of this redemption, being by its power and fortune so exalted, and being favored by God and the Church, of which it is now the ruler. Nor will this be very difficult, if you call to mind the actions and lives of the men I have named. And although those men were rare and marvelous, they were none the less men, and each of them had less opportunity than the present, for their enterprise was not juster than this, nor easier, nor was God more their friend than He is yours. Here is a just cause; *iustum enim est bellum quibus necessarium, et pia arma ubi nulla nisi in armis spes est.*[28] Here is the greatest willingness, nor can there be great difficulty where there is great willingness, provided that the measures are adopted of those whom I have set before you as examples. Besides this, unexampled wonders have been seen here performed by God, the sea has been opened, a cloud has shown you the road, the rock has given forth water, manna has rained,[29] and everything has contributed to your greatness; the remainder must be done by you. God will not do everything, in order not to deprive us of free will and the portion of the glory that falls to our lot.

It is no marvel that none of the before-mentioned Italians have done that which it is to be hoped your illustrious house may do; and if in so many revolutions in Italy and so many war-like operations, it always seems as if military capacity were extinct, this is because the ancient methods were not good, and no one has arisen who knew how to discover new ones. Nothing does so much honor to a newly-risen man than the new laws and measures which he introduces. These things, when they are well based and have greatness in them, render him revered and admired, and there is not lacking scope in Italy for the introduction of every kind of new organization. Here there is a great virtue in the members, if it were not wanting in the heads. Look how in duels and in contests of a few the Italians are superior in strength, dexterity, and intelligence. But when it comes to armies they make a poor show; which proceeds entirely from the weakness of the leaders, for those that know are not obeyed, and every one thinks that he knows, there being hitherto nobody who has raised himself so high both by valor and fortune as to make the others yield. Hence it comes about that for so long a time, in all the wars waged during the last twenty years, whenever there has been

---

[26] By the Swiss and then the French. Lombardy is in northern Italy, surrounding Milan.

[27] The Medici family.

[28] Latin: "For a war that is necessary is a just one, and when arms are the only source of hope they are sacred."

[29] The divided sea, the guiding cloud, the water from the rock, and the manna were signs of divine favor when the Israelites escaped from bondage in Egypt; see Exodus 14, 13, 17, 16.

an entirely Italian army it has always been a failure, as witness Taro, then Alexandria, Capua, Genoa, Vailà, Bologna, and Mestri.[30]

If your illustrious house, therefore, wishes to follow those great men who redeemed their countries, it is before all things necessary, as the true foundation of every undertaking, to provide yourself with your own forces, for you cannot have more faithful, or truer and better soldiers. And although each one of them may be good, they will united become even better when they see themselves commanded by their prince, and honored and favored by him. It is therefore necessary to prepare such forces in order to be able with Italian prowess to defend the country from foreigners. And although both the Swiss and Spanish infantry are deemed terrible, none the less they each have their defects, so that a third method of array might not only oppose them, but be confident of overcoming them. For the Spaniards cannot sustain the attack of cavalry, and the Swiss have to fear infantry which meets them with resolution equal to their own. From which it has resulted, as will be seen by experience, that the Spaniards cannot sustain the attack of French cavalry, and the Swiss are overthrown by Spanish infantry. And although a complete example of the latter has not been seen, yet an instance was furnished in the battle of Ravenna,[31] where the Spanish infantry attacked the German battalions, which are organized in the same way as the Swiss. The Spaniards, through their bodily agility and aided by their bucklers,[32] had entered between and under their pikes[33] and were in a position to attack them safely without the Germans being able to defend themselves; and if the cavalry had not charged them they would have utterly destroyed them. Knowing therefore the defects of both these kinds of infantry, a third kind can be created which can resist cavalry and need not fear infantry, and this will be done by the choice of arms and a new organization. And these are the things which, when newly introduced, give reputation and grandeur to a new prince.

This opportunity must not, therefore, be allowed to pass, so that Italy may at length find her liberator. I cannot express the love with which he would be received in all those provinces which have suffered under these foreign invasions, with what thirst for vengeance, with what steadfast faith, with what love, with what grateful tears. What doors would be closed against him? What people would refuse him obedience? What envy could oppose him? What Italian would withhold allegiance? This barbarous domination stinks in the nostrils of every one. May your illustrious house therefore assume this task with that courage and those hopes which are inspired by a just cause, so that under its banner our fatherland may be raised up, and under its auspices be verified that saying of Petrarch:

> Valor against fell wrath
> Will take up arms; and be the combat quickly sped!
> For, sure, the ancient worth,
> That in Italians stirs the heart, is not yet dead.[34]

---

[30] These seven defeats occurred between 1495 and 1513   [31] In 1512.
[32] Small shields attached to the arm.
[33] Long spears used by infantry.
[34] An anti-German canzone by the Italian poet Petrarch (1304–1374), beginning "Italia mia" ("my Italy").

Marguerite de Navarre
(1492–1549)

A very few periods in history have witnessed a wholesale reexamination and redefinition of fundamental values. The twentieth century, it seems certain, will be remembered as one of these periods. Another such period was the sixteenth century in Europe. Whether the spiritual life demanded immersion in the world or withdrawal from it; whether society was best served by the principle of authority or the principle of independence; what it meant to be a Christian; what the distinctive roles (if there were distinctive roles) of men and women should be; how the institution of marriage could best promote individual happiness and social order—these questions are woven deep into sixteenth-century literature. The writings of Marguerite de Navarre are a good case in point. They are particularly instructive in that Marguerite combined firm convictions and the temperament of a believer with a profound openmindedness.

The marvel is that Marguerite, sister of the king of France and queen of a neighboring country, had time in her life for any such spiritual and psychological concerns, occupied as she was almost constantly with some of the key public events of an especially momentous period of European history. She was born in 1492, the daughter of Charles d'Orléans, Count of Angoulême, and his wife Louise de Savoie (often identified with Oisille in *The Heptameron*). The family was related to the reigning French royal house of Valois but lived on the outskirts of its favor and seemed unlikely to improve in fortunes. But the birth two years later of a son, François (Francis), kept dynastic hopes alive, and unexpected deaths among heirs to the throne made him king of France in 1515.

Meanwhile Marguerite had received a thorough education, as a by-product of her mother's attention to the rearing of the royal heir. (The father had died in 1496.) As a girl Marguerite read widely in the family's excellent library of ancient and modern writers. A stimulating life in her mother's cultivated circle ended for six years when in 1509 Marguerite entered into an arranged marriage with Charles, Duke of Alençon, a soldier with none of the mental or other attractions calculated to win his bride's love. This period of eclipse ended when her brother acceded to the throne, as King Francis I, and called Marguerite to share with him in the splendors of the royal court. The king and his sister proceeded, virtually, to introduce the Italian Renaissance into France, inaugurating a brilliant new era of art, literature, and social elegance. Marguerite, far more than Francis's queen, and almost as much as he, was the central figure in this vibrant new society.

She also exercised considerable administrative and diplomatic authority, as an adviser to her brother and in implementing plans of military preparedness throughout the country. When, in 1524, Francis led his army into Italy against the Spanish Holy Roman Emperor, Charles V, Marguerite and her mother governed France in the king's absence. In the following year they had to cope with a major crisis when, the king having been taken prisoner abroad, France witnessed widespread insurrection by local governments, nobles, and merchants. By traveling to Spain to bargain for her brother's freedom, Marguerite was instrumental in ending the war.

She also had to nurse her ailing husband through part of this period; he died in 1525. Two years later Marguerite was married again, to Henri d'Albret, King of Navarre, a coastal kingdom at the west end of the Pyrenees Mountains separating France from Spain. This time Marguerite gave her heart with her hand, though for his part Henri felt much less bound by the canons of marital fidelity. (The couple were later to appear, in *The Heptameron,* as Parlamente and Hircan.) For a time she continued to serve as a skilled diplomat on behalf of France. But increasingly her energies were occupied with the plight of her own new kingdom, largely under the control of Spain and, in its geographic position, symbolic of the new, ambiguous position she found herself in, as party to the complicated and not always edifying machinations of her husband, her brother, and the king of Spain. From that time on, until Francis died in 1547, Marguerite continued to act as a vitally important political agent for him, although the relationship was sometimes strained—notably by his high-handed treatment of her daughter Jeanne as an instrument, through marriage, of diplomatic policy. In her very last years Marguerite was able to spend a relatively (but only relatively) quiet life in Navarre. After two years of declining health, she died in 1549.

All this might sound like enough for one person, but there was in fact much more to Marguerite's life. In addition to her political and diplomatic activity, she invested enormous, and effective, energies in what today we would call social work. She reformed monasteries and convents; she established hospitals. Her artistic and intellectual patronage was likewise very widespread—in commissioning new works and in gathering under her protection advocates of all sorts of new ideas, sometimes dangerous ones. She never allied herself with the Protestants who broke with the Catholic Church, but she was strongly caught up in several movements that, to conservatives, seemed tarred with the same brush—the evangelical and humanist reform movements of the time—and she associated with suspect people such as Calvin and Rabelais. Like Rabelais, she got into serious trouble with the Sorbonne, the militantly conservative university in Paris that represented everything in the old scholastic intellectual culture that was repellent to both the new reformers and the humanist sponsors of the New Learning. In 1533, the Sorbonne condemned as heretical Marguerite's then-recent devotional poem *The Mirror of the Sinful Soul.* (It is ironic that, at exactly the same time, Thomas More, in many ways one of Marguerite's brothers in spirit, was adhering to the Roman church and thus digging his grave in Henry VIII's newly Protestant England.)

Thus far, a severely abridged account of Marguerite as a public figure has managed almost to avoid mentioning that she was an important writer. She is one of the very few authors to have distinguished themselves in all three of the major media of creative writing—prose fiction, in *The Heptameron;* drama, such as her late allegorical play *The Comedy of Mont-de-Marsan* (1548); and verse, notably her near-epic *Prisons* (of about the same date), concerning the ascent of the soul through the successive prisons of mundane love, ambition, and learning. Her works reveal a mind of considerable versatility, subtlety, tolerance, and complexity—in short, fineness of grain. This last quality is particularly striking, in light of the widespread assumption that immersion in political and other public affairs coarsens the sensibilities and fosters reductionist, simpleminded views. (Plato's Socrates came close to believing as much—another irony, in light of Marguerite's deep devotion to Plato.) Her mind illustrates a quality missing even in some of the best minds: an ability to rise above, or surprisingly invert, some of its own firmest convictions, in the interests of a more comprehensive view of reality. Jules Gelernt, in a book about Marguerite, shows how this operates in, for example, _The Comedy of Mont-de-Marsan._ In the play, the Wise Woman, a character who speaks for Marguerite's own cherished beliefs in the humanist New Learning and enlightened piety, is ultimately overshadowed by another character, the Woman Ravished with Love of God, who exists on a plane of spiritual experience that transcends both learning and piety.

In her last years Marguerite wrote (or so most scholars think) the work that became known, after its posthumous publication, as _The Heptameron._ Only seventy-odd of the projected hundred stories were completed (or have survived). It is modeled, as the Prologue indicates, on Boccaccio's _Decameron,_ and in some ways it clearly imitates that work—in the lush meadow setting, in the device of common flight from danger (a flood rather than the plague as in Boccaccio), in the conversational framework surrounding the ten tales told each day, in the recurrent themes (the wickedness of the friars, sexual plotting and trickery, and others), in the occasional bawdiness, and, not least, in the exploration of male-female relationships.

The Heptameron is, however, a very different kind of work, especially in its sustained concern with spiritual and ethical issues. Boccaccio's battle-of-the-sexes motif is much deepened and expanded, and the stakes are raised. (This may explain why Marguerite shapes her cast for a fair fight, with five men and five women instead of Boccaccio's three men and seven women.) The sexual sparring in Boccaccio is usually, by comparison, decorous and flirtatious, and feelings are seldom seriously ruffled. Marguerite's characters, however, often quarrel like undomesticated cats and dogs over the sex-related issues. The range of sensibilities and values is about as wide as it can possibly be. Among the women, Oisille is a model of otherworldliness; her male antithetical opposite is the brutally cynical Saffredent, who—for instance—sees rape as merely one method of seduction among others.

This milieu and atmosphere would seem likelier to produce a shouting match (which, in fact, does occur at times) than to foster searching moral explorations and bring out psychological fine points, and yet these are what _The Heptameron_ is all about. One reason is that the author is willing to entertain, and apparently sometimes empathize with, viewpoints that go against the fundamental grain of her temperament. It is clear, for example, that a kind of lofty Platonism (or Neoplatonism) is close to Marguerite's heart; Parlamente, her stand-in, delivers a memorable exposition of it at the end of Story Nineteen. It is also clear that the author, like other Renaissance humanists, connects Platonism with a Christian loftiness of vision, reflected—for example—by Simontaut's citation, in the same episode, of the First Epistle of John. But the spiritual "marriage" of the two lovers in Story Nineteen, with its subdued but lingering flavor of carnality, is likely to have disturbed some readers a little bit at least, and their misgivings are indeed expressed in the later postmortem, not decorously but in terms of the roundest ridicule.

As for the quotation from John, it too reappears, in a less reverent vein, after Story Thirty-six. Among the males, Dagoucin is the most uncompromising spokesman for platonic love (in the modern as well as the classic sense), an attitude for which he has to pay dearly by way of the quite raw, mocking incredulity expressed by certain of his hearers. The author is entirely capable of seeing the comedy in Dagoucin, a man so serenely determined to create a hermetic seal around his uncontaminated love that he would never risk revealing it even to his lady, who thus, for practical purposes, might as well not exist.

The fine grain of Marguerite's mind is reflected by the complexity of her vision, which in turn is reflected by the way in which different sets of values modify and interlock with one another. We get to appreciate this cumulatively, by reading various stories and noting more and more interconnections between matters that at first seem not to have much to do with one another. Take, for example, the very brief Story Fifty-five, about a Spanish widow commissioned to carry out her late husband's dying bequest of the proceeds from the sale of a fine horse. The point of the story might seem a simple one: the widow's amusing cleverness in adhering to the letter of the testator's instructions while also preserving his wealth for herself and her children. The ensuing discussion, however, explicitly raises a number of controversial issues and suggests some others implicitly. One of them is the greed of the Franciscan friars, whom Marguerite also treats in certain of the stories as lustful sexual predators. (P. A. Chilton, in the Introduction to the translation used in this anthology, provides an especially illuminating discussion of this sexual aggression.) The witheringly unfavorable attitude toward the Franciscans was not, in fact, something new in literature; one finds it also in Boccaccio and Chaucer. But in *The Heptameron* the friars are the focus for a whole complex of sociological, moral, and theological issues. For one thing, they stand for the old religious regime that the evangelical and humanist reformers found so benighted. They also stand for the monastic system, with its implicit hostility toward women and low valuation of marriage, which are central concerns in *The Heptameron* and were burning issues with the reformers and humanists, who fairly consistently attacked the enshrinement of the ideal of celibacy. As for deathbed bequests to the religious orders, the issue was not merely venal corruption in the Church but also the theological issue of belief in Purgatory, the concomitant belief in indulgences (remissions of punishment in Purgatory), and the notion that monetary gifts were one form of the "good works" that could earn indulgences. Behind that node of issues looms a still broader issue, the main theological battleground of the Reformation period: salvation by grace versus salvation by works. And even beyond that, at least for Marguerite, lies the problem of translating such theological concerns into a dynamic of love that can light up the heart with spiritual peace without ignoring the needs of a human society. Thus the feminist strands, for example, in Marguerite's work are part of a rich fabric of ideas and speculations. The intensity of the arguments that follow the stories is partly explained by the momentousness of such issues, far deeper-seated ones than those raised by, say, Boccaccio.

The discussions following the stories also have a bearing on the artistry of *The Heptameron*. Some of the stories—including the one about the horse—

are elegantly crafted in themselves, but many of them are not. Some of them simply trail off or are otherwise knocked askew. The key here is to take the ensuing discussion not just as commentary but as integral to the tale. The result is a new psychological complexity, reminding us that life is usually less tidy than invented art and epitomized in the discussion that, as often for Marguerite, is the climax of the narrative, not a mere appendage to it. The assertion made in the Prologue that the stories in *The Heptameron* are to be factual, not invented, may not always be literally true, but it is true at least in the sense that the barrier protecting the purity of literature from the unsettledness of life is often breached, in the interests of an urgent search, among many confusing options, for the most nearly comprehensive truth.

A NOTE ON THE TEXT

The Heptameron was first published some years after Marguerite's death, in printed editions significantly different from one another. Moreover, a large number of surviving manuscripts further complicate the problem of producing an authoritative text. The P. A. Chilton translation used in the present anthology prints certain manuscript variants in square brackets which, in the interests of smoother reading, have been removed in the pages that follow here. Readers interested in these textual discriminations should consult Chilton's volume in the Penguin Classics.

FURTHER READING *(prepared by B.W.):* One of the most useful general introductions to Marguerite's life and the general tendencies of her mind and work can be found in the opening chapter of Jules Gelernt's *World of Many Loves: The Heptameron of Marguerite de Navarre,* 1966. Samuel Putnam's *Marguerite of Navarre,* 1935, is a clear, accurate account of both life and works. P. A. Chilton's introduction to his translation of the complete *Heptameron,* 1984, lays out the basic critical issues economically and thoughtfully and touches on textual complications and the merits of earlier translations. Brief, stimulating discussions of several facets of Marguerite's work are included in I. D. McFarlane, *A Literary History of France: Renaissance France 1470–1589,* 1974. C. J. Blaisdell, "Marguerite de Navarre and Her Circle," in *Female Scholars: A Tradition of Learned Women Before 1800,* 1980, places Marguerite in the tradition so identified. Three book-length studies in English of *The Heptameron* are Jules Gelernt's book already cited; Marcel Tetel, *Marguerite de Navarre's "Heptameron": Themes, Language, and Structure,* 1973; and Betty J. Davis, *The Storytellers in Marguerite de Navarre's "Heptameron,"* 1978. Gelernt explores the versions of love in the stories and Marguerite's Neoplatonism, Tetel emphasizes figurative language and structure, and Davis looks at the characters in the frame-story and their interrelationships. Another good study of the framing is Glyn P. Norton, "Narrative Function in the *Heptameron* Frame-Story," in *La Nouvelle française à la Renaissance,* ed. Lionello Sozzi, 1981. On the relation to the Boccaccio model, see Donald Stone, "Boccaccio's *Decameron* and the *Heptameron,"* in his *From Tales to Truth: Essays on French Fiction in the Sixteenth Century,* 1973. Recent criticism has tended to concentrate on the feminist themes of the collection. Two good treatments of this subject are Paula Sommers, "Feminine Authority in the *Heptameron:* A Reading of Oysille," in *Modern Language Studies* 13 (1983), 52–59; and Robert W. Bernard, "Feminist Rhetoric for the Renaissance Woman in Marguerite de Navarre's *Heptameron,"* *Chimères* 15 (1982), 73–98. Patricia Francis Cholakian, *Rape and Writing in the Heptameron of Marguerite de Navarre,* 1991, provides a book-length feminist analysis.

THE HEPTAMERON

Translated by P. A. Chilton

The Heptameron is a series of tales told by ten persons of aristocratic birth who, owing to several misadventures, are marooned together at the abbey of Our Lady of Sarrance, in the Pyrenees Mountains in southern France. All of them have been cut off, while returning from the mineral-spring town of Cauterets, by torrential floods. Although they are thrown together mostly by chance, they have known one another for some time.

The sage among the group is Oisille, a pious elderly widow interested in seeing the abbey for its own sake. The others take shelter there out of necessity and a desire to spend their time with friends and acquaintances.

The group includes a subgroup made up of two women named Parlamente and Longarine and three men named Hircan, Dagoucin, and Saffredent. Parlamente and her husband, Hircan, along with young Longarine and her husband, had been traveling together, followed at a discreet distance by Dagoucin and Saffredent, two young devotees of Parlamente and Longarine. (Which man loves which woman is not explicitly stated.) The two married couples, while staying overnight as the unwitting guests of a bandit, became embroiled in a fight between their host and certain of his partners in crime. Dagoucin and Saffredent came to the rescue, but not before Longarine's husband was killed.

Two other young women, Nomerfide and Ennasuite, were driven to shelter while fleeing on horseback from a bear.

The two other men are Geburon, who narrowly escaped from a house where armed attackers had beset him, and Simontaut, who also narrowly escaped with his life, after rashly trying to ford the floodwaters on horseback. Simontaut is secretly devoted to Parlamente. (There is also a hint that Parlamente's husband, Hircan may be in love with an unidentified woman of the party.)

The travelers commission the building of a footbridge over a nearby river but find that the construction will take ten or twelve days. Anticipating boredom, they cast about for a way to pass the time. Oisille suggests scriptural readings and other pious exercises, but most of the travelers feel the need for more secular diversion also. Being informed by Parlamente that the French royal family have wanted a French equivalent of the hundred tales told in Boccaccio's *Decameron,* of which a translation from Italian has recently appeared, the travelers undertake to further the royal project by relating tales themselves, ten each day. Unlike those in Boccaccio, however, these tales are all to be based on actual fact. To tell their stories, the ten ladies and gentlemen assemble each afternoon in the lush grass and ample shade of a beautiful meadow adjoining the abbey.

(The work was completed only through the first seven days; it therefore never became a French Decameron but remained a "Heptameron" or "Work of Seven Days.") [*Editors' headnote.*]

"Since you speak so strongly in favor of women who get suspected wrongly, Longarine," said Hircan, "I choose you to tell us the eighth story, on condition that you don't make us all weep, like Madame Oisille did, with her excessive zeal for stories in praise of virtuous women."

Longarine broke into a hearty laugh, and said: "Since you want me to make you laugh, in my usual fashion, it won't be at the expense of women. Yet I *shall* tell you something to show how easy they are to deceive when they fill their heads with jealous thoughts, and pride themselves on their good sense for wanting to deceive their husbands."

STORY EIGHT

In the county of Alès[1] there was once a man by the name of Bornet, who had married a very decent and respectable woman. He held her honor and reputation very dear, as I am sure all husbands here hold the honor and reputation of *their* wives dear. He wanted her to be faithful to him, but was not so keen on having the rule applied to them both equally. He had become enamoured of his chambermaid, though the only benefit he got from transferring his affections in this way was the sort of pleasure one gets from varying one's diet. He had a neighbor called Sendras, who was of similar station and temperament to himself—he was a tailor and a drummer. These two were such close friends that, with the exception of the wife, there was nothing that they did not share between them. Naturally he told him that he had designs on the chambermaid.

Not only did his friend wholeheartedly approve of this, but did his best to help him, in the hope that he too might get a share in the spoils.

The chambermaid herself refused to have anything to do with him, although he was constantly pestering her, and in the end she went to tell her mistress about it. She told her that she could not stand being badgered by him any longer, and asked permission to go home to her parents. Now the good lady of the house, who was really very much in love with her husband, had often had occasion to suspect him, and was therefore rather pleased to be one up on him, and to be able to show him that she had found out what he was up to. So she said to her maid: "Be nice to him, dear, encourage him a little bit, and then make a date to go to bed with him in my dressing-room. Don't forget to tell me which night he's supposed to be coming, and make sure you don't tell anyone else."

The maid did exactly as her mistress had instructed. As for her master, he was so pleased with himself that he went off to tell his friend about his stroke of luck, whereupon the friend insisted on taking his share afterwards, since he had been in on the business from the beginning. When the appointed time came, off went the master, as had been agreed, to get into bed, as he thought, with his little chambermaid. But his wife, having abandoned her position of authority in order to serve in a more pleasurable one, had taken her maid's place in the bed. When he got in with her, she did not act like a wife, but like a bashful young girl, and he was not in the slightest suspicious. It would be impossible to say which of them enjoyed themselves more— the wife deceiving her husband, or the husband who thought he was deceiving his wife. He stayed in bed with her for some time, not as long as he might have wished (many years of marriage were beginning to tell on him), but as long as he could manage. Then he went out to rejoin his accomplice, and tell him what a good time he had had. The lustiest piece of goods he had ever come across, he declared. His friend who was younger and more active than he was, said: "Remember what you promised?"

"Hurry up, then," replied the master, "in case she gets up, or my wife wants her for something."

---

[1] A town in the Languedoc region of southern France. The theme of Stories 1–10, told on the first day, is dirty tricks played by women on men and vice versa.

Off he went and climbed into bed with the supposed chambermaid his friend had just failed to recognize as his wife. *She* thought it was her husband again, and did not refuse anything he asked for (I say "asked," but "took" would be nearer the mark, because he did not dare open his mouth). He made a much longer business of it than the husband, to the surprise of the wife, who was not used to these long nights of pleasure. However, she did not complain, and looked forward to what she was planning to say to him in the morning, and the fun she would have teasing him. When dawn came, the man got up, and fondling her as he got out of bed, pulled off a ring she wore on her finger, a ring that her husband had given her at their marriage. Now the women in this part of the world are very superstitious about such things. They have great respect for women who hang on to their wedding rings till the day they die, and if a woman loses her ring, she is dishonored, and is looked upon as having given her faith to another man. But she did not mind him taking it, because she thought it would be sure evidence against her husband of the way she had hoodwinked him.

The husband was waiting outside for his friend, and asked him how he had got on. The man said he shared the husband's opinion, and added that he would have stayed longer, had he not been afraid of getting caught by the daylight. The pair of them then went off to get as much sleep as they could. When morning came, and they were getting dressed together, the husband noticed that his friend had on his finger a ring that was identical to the one he had given his wife on their wedding day. He asked him where he had got it, and when he was told it had come from the chambermaid the night before, he was aghast. He began banging his head against the wall, and shouted: "Oh my God! Have I gone and made myself a cuckold without my wife even knowing about it?"

His friend tried to calm him down. "Perhaps your wife had given the ring to the girl to look after before going to bed?" he suggested. The husband made no reply, but marched straight out and went back to his house.

There he found his wife looking unusually gay and attractive. Had she not saved her chambermaid from staining her conscience, and had she not put her husband to the ultimate test, without any more cost to herself than a night's sleep? Seeing her in such good spirits, the husband thought to himself: "She wouldn't be greeting me so cheerfully if she knew what I'd been up to."

As they chatted, he took hold of her hand and saw that the ring, which normally never left her finger, had disappeared. Horrified, he stammered: "What have you done with your ring?"

She was pleased that he was giving her the opportunity to say what she had to say.

"Oh! You're the most dreadful man I ever met! Who do you think you got it from? You think you got it from the chambermaid, don't you? You think you got it from that girl you're so much in love with, the girl who gets more out of you than I've ever had! The first time you got into bed you were so passionate that I thought you must be about as madly in love with her as it was possible for any man to be! But when you came back the *second* time, after getting up, you were an absolute devil! Completely uncontrolled you were, didn't know when to stop! You miserable man! You must have been blinded by desire to pay such tribute to my body—after all you've had me long enough without showing much appreciation for my figure. So it wasn't because that young girl is so pretty and so shapely that you were enjoying yourself so much. Oh no! You enjoyed it so much because you were seething with some depraved pent-up lust—in short the sin of concupiscence was raging within you, and your senses were dulled as a result. In fact you'd worked yourself up into such a state that I think any old nanny-goat would have done for you, pretty or otherwise! Well, my dear, it's time you mended your ways. It's high time you were content with me for what I am—your own wife and an honest woman, and it's high time that you found *that* just as satisfying as when you thought I was a poor little erring chambermaid. I did what I did in order to save you from your wicked ways, so that when you get old, we can live happily and peacefully together without anything on our consciences. Because if you go on in the way you have been, I'd rather leave you altogether than see you destroying your soul day by day, and at the same time destroying your physical health and squandering everything you have before my very eyes! But if you will acknowledge that you've been in the wrong, and make up your mind to live according to the ways of God and His commandments, then I'll overlook all your past misbehavior, even as I hope God will forgive me *my* ingratitude to Him, and failure to love Him as I ought."

If there was ever a man who was dumbfounded and despairing, it was this poor husband. There was his wife, looking so pretty, and yet so sensible and so chaste, and he had gone and left her for a girl who did not love him. What was worse, he had had the misfortune to have gone and made her do something wicked without her even realizing what was happening. He had gone and let another man share pleasures which, rightly, were his alone to enjoy. He had gone and given himself cuckold's horns and made himself look ridiculous for evermore. But he could see she was already angry enough about the chambermaid, and he did not dare tell her about the other dirty trick he had played. So he promised that he would leave his wicked ways behind him, asked her to forgive him and gave her the ring back. He told his friend not to breathe a word to anybody, but secrets of this sort nearly always end up being proclaimed from the roof-tops, and it was not long before the facts became public knowledge. The husband was branded as a cuckold without his wife having done a single thing to disgrace herself.

*   *   *

"Ladies, it strikes me that if all the men who offend their wives like that got a punishment like that, then Hircan and Saffredent ought to be feeling a bit nervous."

"Come now, Longarine," said Saffredent, "Hircan and I aren't the only married men here, you know."

"True," she replied, "but you're the only two who'd play a trick like that."

"And just when have you heard of us chasing our wives' maids?" he retorted.

"If the ladies in question were to tell us the facts," Longarine said, "then you'd soon find plenty of maids who'd been dismissed before their payday!"

"Really," intervened Geburon, "a fine one you are! You promise to make us all laugh, and you end up making these two gentlemen annoyed."

"It comes to the same thing," said Longarine. "As long as they don't get their swords out, their getting angry makes it all the more amusing."

"But the fact remains," said Hircan, "that if our wives were to listen to what this lady here has to say, she'd make trouble for every married couple here!"

"I know what I'm saying, and who I'm saying it to," Longarine replied. "Your wives are so good, and they love you so much, that even if you gave them horns like a stag's, they'd still convince themselves, and everybody else, that they were garlands of roses!"

Everyone found this remark highly amusing, even the people it was aimed at, and the subject was brought to a close. Dagoucin, however, who had not yet said a word, could not resist saying: "When a man already has everything he needs in order to be contented, it is very unreasonable of him to go off and seek satisfaction elsewhere. It has often struck me that when people are not satisfied with what they already have, and think they can find something better, then they only make themselves worse off. And they do not get any sympathy, because inconstancy is one thing that is universally condemned."

"But what about people who have not yet found their 'other half'?" asked Simontaut. "Would you still say it was inconstancy if they seek her wherever she may be found?"

"No man can know," replied Dagoucin, "where his other half is to be found, this other half with whom he may find a union so equal that between the parts there is no difference; which being so, a man must hold fast where Love constrains him and, whatever may befall him, he must remain steadfast in heart and will. For if she whom you love is your true likeness, if she is of the same will, then it will be your own self that you love, and not her alone."[2]

"Dagoucin, I think you're adopting a position that is completely wrong," said Hircan. "You make it sound as if we ought to love women without being loved in return."

"What I mean, Hircan, is this. If love is based on a woman's beauty, charm and favors, and if our aim is merely pleasure, ambition or profit, then such love can never last. For if the whole foundation on which our love is based should collapse, then love will fly from us and there will be no love left in us. But I am utterly convinced that if a man loves with no other aim, no other desire, than to love truly, he will abandon his soul in death rather than allow his love to abandon his heart."

"Quite honestly, Dagoucin, I don't think you've ever really been in love," said Simontaut, "because if you had felt the fire of passion, as the rest of us have, you wouldn't have been doing what you've just been doing—describing Plato's republic,[3] which sounds all very fine in writing, but is hardly true to experience."

"If I have loved," he replied, "I love still, and shall love till the day I die. But my love is a perfect love, and I fear lest showing it openly should betray it. So greatly do I fear this, that I shrink to make it known to the lady whose love and friendship I cannot but desire to be equal to my own. I scarcely

---

[2] The allusion is to the fable related by Aristophanes in the *Symposium* of Plato, the ultimate ancient spokesman for the philosophy of idealism. According to the fable, each person is half of a primordial unified being, divided by the vindictive gods, and can find happiness only by being united with his or her separated soulmate.

[3] In another major dialogue, *The Republic,* Plato envisions the ideal society.

dare think my own thoughts, lest something should be revealed in my eyes, for the longer I conceal the fire of my love, the stronger grows the pleasure in knowing that it is indeed a perfect love."

"Ah, but all the same," said Geburon, "I don't think you'd be sorry if she did return your love!"

"I do not deny it. But even if I were loved as deeply as I myself love, my love could not possibly increase, just as it could not possibly decrease if I were loved less deeply than I love."

At this point, Parlamente, who was suspicious of these flights of fancy, said: "Watch your step, Dagoucin. I've seen plenty of men who've died rather than speak what's in their minds."

"Such men as those," he replied, "I would count happy indeed."

"Indeed," said Saffredent, "and worthy to be placed among the ranks of the Innocents—of whom the Church chants *'Non loquendo, sed moriendo confessi sunt'!*[4] I've heard a lot of talk about these languishing lovers, but I've never seen a single one actually die. I've suffered enough from such torture, but I got over it in the end, and that's why I've always assumed that nobody else ever really dies from it either."

"Ah! Saffredent, the trouble is that you desire your love to be returned," Dagoucin replied, "and men of your opinions never die for love. But I know of many who *have* died, and died for no other cause than that they have loved, and loved perfectly."

*   *   *

"I think," said Oisille, turning to Hircan, "that you are so fond of speaking ill of women, that you wouldn't have great difficulty in finding something good to say about men. So will you tell us the next story?"

"That's easy," he replied. "Not long ago I was told a tale that was very much to the credit of a certain gentleman. This was a man whose love, long-suffering and loyalty were so praiseworthy that I believe it my duty to prevent them sinking into oblivion."

STORY EIGHTEEN

My story is about a noble lord of excellent family.[1] He was living in one of the important towns in the kingdom of France, and was studying at the schools there. His desire was to attain that knowledge which is the key to honor and virtue among men of worth. At the age of seventeen or eighteen he was so knowledgeable that one would have thought him a shining example, fit to instruct his fellow-students. However, he was also to become a pupil in the School of Love. Now Love is a subtle teacher, and to ensure that his lessons would be heard and taken to heart, he concealed himself behind

---

[4] From the Collect for the mass on the feast of the Holy Innocents: "not by speaking, but by dying have they confessed." This feast, celebrated on December 28, honors the infants slaughtered by Herod in his attempt to kill the newborn Jesus.

[1] Stories 11–20, told on the second day, do not have a prescribed subject.

the fair eyes and face of a certain lady. She was the most beautiful lady in all the land, and as chance would have it, was in the town at that time for some lawsuit. But before setting about the conquest of the heart of the noble young lord, Love first vanquished the heart of the lady herself, by bringing all his manly perfections before her eyes. For he was indeed so fair of face, so fair of speech, so fair in all his ways that there was not a man in all the land, whatever his station, who could surpass him. Those of you who know how quickly the fire of love spreads when it starts to smoulder in the heart and in the imagination will understand that once Love enters two such perfect subjects, he never stops until he has rendered them obedient to his commands, until indeed he has filled them both so full of his clear light that all their thoughts, all their desires and all their speech are nothing but the blazing forth of his flame. With the timidity of youth, the young lord pursued his desires with the utmost caution. But already the lady was conquered. There was no need of force. Yet Modesty, that persistent companion of ladies, prevented her for a while from showing her feelings. But in the end, the fortress of the heart where Honor dwells was destroyed, and the poor lady gave herself up to that which she had never wished to resist.

In order to test the long-suffering, constancy and love of her servant, she acceded to his demands on one exceedingly difficult condition. If he was able to keep this condition, then she would love him perfectly for evermore. If, however, he were to fail, then he would not possess her for as long as he should live. The condition was this. She would be happy to go to bed with him and to talk with him there. But they were both to keep their nightshirts on, and he was to demand nothing more than her discourse and chaste kisses! The young man, who felt that there was no joy in the world to be compared with that which she was promising him, agreed. Evening came, and the promise was kept. However much she encouraged him, however much he was tempted, he refused to break his word. Purgatory itself could not, he felt, be worse than what he went through that night. Yet so great was his love, so firm was his hope, that he was happy to wait in patience, for he was sure that the eternal love which it had cost him so much to win would in the end be his. So he left her bed without once asking of her anything that would have gone against his promise. But the lady was, I think, more astonished than pleased by his upright behavior, and began to think that either he did not love her as much as he had said, or that he had found her less attractive than he had expected. Completely disregarding his demonstration of honor, chastity, patience and fidelity, she decided to put the young man's love to another test before keeping her own promise. To this end, she asked him to approach one of the girls in her entourage, a girl who was extremely attractive and somewhat younger than herself. The idea was that he should make amorous overtures to this young girl, so that people would think it was because of her that he came to the house so often. The young lord, quite certain that his lady loved him as much as he loved her, carried out to the letter everything she ordered him to do. He forced himself for her sake to pursue her young companion, who, seeing what a handsome, gently spoken young man he was, believed his lies rather than the truth, and promptly fell in love with him, thinking he loved her. When the lady realized things had gone as far as this, she decided at last to permit the young man, who was still pressing her to fulfil her promise, to come to her room at one hour after midnight.

She had, she told him, tried out his love and tested his obedience so thoroughly that it was only right that she should reward his long and patient wait. There can be no doubt about the joy which her loving and devoted servant experienced.

At the appointed hour he went to his lady's room. But she still wanted to test the strength of his love. So before he arrived, she took the young girl on one side, and said to her: "I know that there's a certain young gentleman who's in love with you, and I think you are no less passionately in love with him. Well, I feel so sorry for you both, that I've decided to give you the opportunity to talk on your own together for as long as you like."

The girl was so transported, that she could scarcely conceal the love she felt, and said that she could never refuse such a proposal. Following her mistress's advice, indeed her orders, she went to the appointed bedroom, undressed and lay down on the magnificent bed. The door was left half open, and all the candles lit, so that the girl and all her charms could be clearly seen. Then, pretending to go away, the lady herself hid near the bed in a spot where she could not be seen. It was not long before her poor devoted servant arrived, prompt at the appointed hour and fully expecting to find his beloved waiting for him as promised. In he crept, closed the door behind him, took off his gown and his fur-lined shoes, and went over to the bed, thinking to find there his heart's desire. No sooner did he stretch out his arms to embrace the recumbent figure he took to be his lady, than the poor girl, thinking he was all hers, flung her arms around his neck. The expression in her eyes and the passionate words she murmured would have been enough to put the holiest hermit off his paternosters![2] But prompted by his great love for his lady, the young man recognized both the voice and the face, and jumped out of the bed even faster than he had jumped in, when he realized that this was not the woman for whom he had suffered so long and so deeply!

Angry not only with the girl herself, but also with her mistress, he said: "I shall not be made other than I am either by your wild desires or by the wicked one who put you here! Seek to be an honest woman, for by no act of mine shall your good name be lost!"

Beside himself with rage, he marched out, and for a long time he did not come back to see his lady. However, Love, who never abandons hope, assured the young gentleman that the longer his constancy was tried and tested, the longer and pleasanter would be the enjoyment in the end. For her part, the lady, who had seen and heard everything, was surprised at the depth and constancy of his love, but it pleased her too, and she was anxious to see him again to ask his forgiveness for the pain she had inflicted in testing him. So at the earliest opportunity she addressed him in tones of such gracious tenderness that he not only forgot all his past torments, but even began to think of them with pleasure. For after all, it was through them that his constancy was honored at last, and through them that his lady was convinced of his love. From that hour on there were no more obstacles and no more trials, and from his lady he received all that his heart could desire.

*   *   *

[2] "Our Fathers"; recitations of the Lord's Prayer.

"Now, Ladies, can you tell me of a woman as constant, as patient and as faithful in love as the man in this story? Anyone who's been through such temptations will find the temptations we are shown in pictures of St. Anthony[3] as nothing by comparison. Anyone who can remain patient and chaste when beautiful women offer not only their beauty and their love, but also time, place and opportunity, will surely be virtuous enough to resist every single devil in Hell!"

"It is a great shame," said Oisille, "that he did not address himself to a woman who had the same resources of virtue as he. We should then have had the most perfect example of pure and perfect love that has ever been heard of."

"Tell me," said Geburon, "which of the two trials do you think was the most difficult for the young man to bear?"

"I think the second," Parlamente said, "because disappointment and resentment are the strongest temptations of all."

Longarine, however, felt that the first trial was the hardest, "since he had to overcome Love as well as overcome himself, in order to keep his promise."

"It is easy for you to talk," said Simontaut, "but those of us who know the truth in such matters ought to say what they think. As far as I'm concerned, he acted like an idiot the first time, and like a madman the second. You see, I think that by keeping his promise he only made his lady suffer as much as, or more than, he himself suffered. The only reason she made him make such a promise in the first place was so that she could make herself look more virtuous than she really was. She knew perfectly well that desperate love can't be held back by orders or oaths or by anything else in the whole world. But she wanted to make her vice look virtuous, and to make it appear that she could be won only by acts of virtue nothing less than heroic. The second time, he showed that he was mad to let the girl go, when she was so obviously in love with him and was certainly worth more than the woman he'd made his promise to. What is more, he had a good excuse, given the bitter disappointment he had just experienced."

Dagoucin objected to this, saying that his opinion was exactly the opposite, and that on the first occasion the young man had shown himself patient, constant and true to his word, while the second occasion showed that in his love he was perfect, true and faithful.

"And how do we know," said Saffredent, "that he wasn't one of those referred to in a certain chapter headed *De frigidis et maleficiatis?*[4] If Hircan had really wanted to sing this man's praises, he should have gone on to tell us how he acquitted himself once he got what he wanted. Then we could judge whether it was his virtue or his impotence that made him so well-behaved!"

"You may be quite sure," said Hircan, "that if he'd told me, I wouldn't have kept it back, any more than I have the rest of the story. But knowing him as well as I do, and knowing what his temperament is like, I shall always take the view that he acted the way he did because of the power of his love rather than because of frigidity or impotence."

---

[3] Egyptian saint (251–356) and ascetic, the first monk. His sexual temptations during a sojourn in the desert were proverbial and were frequently portrayed by painters.

[4] Latin: "On persons rendered frigid by magic spells," a papal document issued in the thirteenth century.

"Well," Simontaut replied, "if he was the kind of man you say, then he ought to have broken his oath. After all, even if she had got annoyed at a little thing like that, it wouldn't have been too difficult to calm her down again!"

"But perhaps she didn't want him to do it just then?" said Ennasuite.

"So what? Wasn't he strong enough to force her," Saffredent said, "seeing that she led him on?"

"Holy Mary!" exclaimed Nomerfide. "That's a fine way to talk! Do you think that's the way to win the favor of a lady you believe to be chaste and virtuous?"

"In my opinion," said Saffredent, "when a man desires that sort of thing from a woman, the greatest honor he can do her is to take her by force. Because, however humble a girl may be, she will want you to beg and beseech over and over again. There are others who have to be given a lot of presents before you can win them round. Others are so stupid that they let themselves go at the slightest trick or guile, and with them it's merely a matter of finding the right method. But when you're faced with one that's too sensible and good to be tricked, and too well-behaved to be won round by presents and talk, is one not justified in trying every possible means of conquering her? Whenever you hear that a man's taken a woman by force, you can take it from me that the woman in question must have deprived him of all hope of success by other means. You shouldn't think the worse of a man who risks his life like that in order to give vent to his love."

Geburon started to laugh. "I've often seen places besieged and taken by storm," he said, "because neither threats nor offers of money could persuade the defending forces to parley, for they say that once you engage in talks, you're already half defeated!"

"It would seem that all the love-affairs in the world are based on the kind of wicked passion that Simontaut and Saffredent have just been talking about!" said Ennasuite. "But there *are* people who have been in love, and loved long and constantly, without having those motives."

"If you know a story about somebody like that," said Hircan, "then I hand over to you for the next one."

"I do know such a story," she replied, "and shall be only too happy to tell it to you."

STORY NINETEEN

In the time of the Marquis of Mantua, who had married the sister of the Duke of Ferrara,[1] there was in the Duchess's household a lady-in-waiting by the name of Paulina. She was deeply beloved of a certain gentleman in the service of the Marquis. People marvelled at his attachment to Paulina, for, though poor, he was a man of valor, and one would have expected him, in view of his master's great liking for him, to have sought a match with a lady of means. But in his eyes Paulina was worth all the treasure in the world,

---

[1] This marriage took place in 1490. Mantua and Ferrara are in northern Italy.

and it was she alone whom he desired to marry and make his own. The Marchioness wanted to use her influence to bring about a better marriage for Paulina and did her best to deter her from marrying the gentleman who loved her so much, and often stopped them talking together. They would, she warned them, be the poorest and most miserable wretches in the whole of Italy if their marriage took place. But the gentleman could not be convinced by such arguments as these. For her part Paulina disguised her love as best she could—but dreamt about it none the less. Thus they continued in their love, living in the hope that one day their fortunes would improve.

During this time war broke out, and the gentleman was taken prisoner along with a Frenchman, who had left his love at home in France, just as he had left his in Italy. Finding that they were companions in the same misfortune, the two men began to tell one another their secrets. The Frenchman confessed that his heart too was captive, though he did not name its captor. He knew already that his comrade was in love with Paulina, for he too was in the service of the Marquis, and he urged him, as a friend concerned for his interests and well-being, to abandon this infatuation. The Italian gentleman of course swore that it was not within his power to do so. He said that if the Marchioness did not let him marry his beloved in recompense for his sufferings in captivity and all his other services, then he would become a Franciscan friar and serve no other master than God. His comrade could not believe this, for, apart from his devotion to Paulina, the Italian gentleman did not seem to him to show the slightest sign of monastic piety. Nine months later the Frenchman was set free, and succeeded in obtaining the subsequent release of his comrade, who then immediately approached the Marquis and Marchioness and pursued the matter of his marriage to Paulina for all he was worth. But he had no success. They constantly reminded him that if he and Paulina were to marry they would have to live in poverty. Moreover, neither his family nor hers were in favor of the match, and they forbade him to speak to her in the hope that his infatuation would vanish if he was deprived of all means of meeting her. He realized that he had no alternative but to obey. So he asked the Marchioness if he might say farewell to Paulina, promising that he would never thereafter speak to her again. Permission was granted, and he immediately went to Paulina and began the following speech:

"I can see, Paulina, that both Heaven and earth are against us and desire not only that we should not marry, but that we should not even see one another and talk together. The orders of our master and our mistress are harsh indeed. Well might they boast that by uttering one word they have wounded two hearts, two hearts in two bodies that cannot now but languish unto death, and thus do our cruel master and our cruel mistress show that neither Love nor Pity ever entered their breasts. Their wish, I know, is that we should make rich marriages elsewhere, for they do not know that true riches are to be found in happiness alone. So badly have they treated me, so much grief have they caused me, it is impossible that I should any more do them service with a cheerful heart. If I had not mentioned marriage, I believe they are not so scrupulous that they would have prevented me meeting and talking with you. But I would sooner die than demean my love and, after having loved you with a love that is noble and good, seek to have that which I would defend against all others. Therefore, since to continue to be able to see you would be a penance too hard to bear, and since not to see you would fill my heart, which can never stay empty, with a despair that would bring me to a miserable end, I have resolved, and my resolve has long been firm, that I shall enter the religious life. It is not that I do not know well enough that all men can be saved, whatever their condition, but my wish is to have leisure to contemplate the divine Goodness, who will I hope take pity on my youthful faults and change my heart, that I may come to love spiritual things as I have loved those which are temporal. If God grants me this grace, it shall be my continual occupation to pray for you. And I beg you, in the name of this true and faithful love that is ours, to remember me in your devotions and to pray to Our Lord that He will give me as much constancy when I cease to see you as He gave me contentment when I was able to look upon you. My whole life I have lived in the hope that one day I would through marriage to you have that which honor and conscience allow, but now that I give up that hope, now that I can never expect that you will treat me as a wife treats a husband, I beseech you that you treat me as a brother, and permit me to kiss you."

Perceiving how deeply he was suffering, and yet how honorably even in the midst of such despair he contented himself with such a modest request, poor Paulina, who had always been severe, answered nothing, but threw her arms about his neck, weeping bitterly. So violent were her tears, that her voice, her faculty of speech and all her strength left her, and she fell into a faint in his arms. He, filled as he was with love and sorrow, was so overcome that he too fell in a faint. One of Paulina's companions, seeing them both collapse on the ground, called for help, and they were given medicaments which revived them.

When Paulina realized that she had revealed the strength of her feelings, she was overcome with shame, for she had always sought to disguise her love. But she was able to excuse herself on the grounds that she had been overwhelmed by compassion for the gentleman's plight. He, unable to bear the pain of uttering his final adieu, hastily left the scene, his face set, as he fought back the emotion that welled in his heart. No sooner had he returned home than he collapsed on his bed, a lifeless corpse. Throughout that night he lamented aloud, and his cries were so heart-rending that his servants thought he must have lost parents, friends and everything he had. The next day he commended himself to Our Lord, and shared out among his servants what little he possessed, taking only a small sum of money for himself. Then, forbidding anyone to follow him, he wended his way alone to the convent of the Observant Friars,[2] where, in the firm resolve never again to leave those walls, he requested the friar's habit.[3] The Superior, who had seen him in the past, thought at first that he must be dreaming or that it must be some sort of a joke. Indeed there could hardly have been a man in the whole land who was less endowed with the qualities and gifts required of a friar, for his gifts were the solid virtues of a gentleman of honor. But once the good father had heard the words he had to speak, once he had seen the tears pouring in torrents down his face, though he did not know their cause, he had compassion on him and took him in. It was not long afterwards that he acknowledged the gentleman's perseverance and granted him the habit, which the gentleman received with due devotion.

---

[2] A reformed branch of the Franciscan order.
[3] The robe worn as the uniform of the order.

When the Marquis and Marchioness heard of this, they found it so strange that they could scarcely believe it. Paulina, desiring to show that she was not in any way subject to the dictates of love, covered up as best she was able the sorrow she felt at the gentleman's departure. So complete was her dissimulation that all those around her said that she had at last forgotten the feelings she had once had for her faithful and devoted servant. Five or six months passed by, and still she revealed nothing. One day during this time a monk visited her and showed her a song that had been composed by her faithful servant shortly after he had taken the habit. The tune was Italian and is quite well-known, but I have translated the words as closely as possible. They go like this:

> What will she say,
> My Lady, pray,
> What will she do, when her fair eyes
> See me thus dressed in monkish guise?

> Dear one, my own,
> Sweet one alone,
> Long speechless, wond'ring will she be,
> Troubled and torn
> Lady forlorn.
> Strange will it seem, then presently
> Her thoughts they will begin to dwell
> On convent close and holy cell,
> There to reside, eternally.
> *What will she say, etc.*

> What will they do,
> Who from us two
> Our love and joy did cause to go,
> Seeing that love
> Howe'er they strove
> They yet more perfect caused to grow?
> When they do look into our heart
> They surely will repent their part
> And bitter tears will surely flow.
> *What will she say, etc.*

> And if they say,
> Oh come away!
> And seek our souls so to divert,
> Then you and I
> Shall say, we'll die!
> Far rather that than ever part,
> For since we must their harshness bear,
> We two do now the long robe wear
> That we shall wear perpetually.
> *What will she say, etc.*

And if again
With marriage then
They seek our souls to taunt and tempt,
While they relate
That pleasant state
And how we should be thus content,
Our soul, we'll say, is at God's side,
His holy spouse, His heavenly bride,
So shall it be, eternally.
            What will she say, etc.

O love so great,
That through this gate
I have perforce for sorrow passed,
Ah! in this place
Grant me the grace
Without regret to pray and fast,
For this our love, our mutual love,
Shall rise so high, and dwell above
That God will be well pleased at last.
            What will she say, etc.

Then put behind
The joys that bind
In iron bonds so dire and fell!
Quit worldly fame
That leads in shame
Black souls through pride to depths of Hell!
Let us shun lust and vanity,
And take that love which in mercy
Lord Jesus gives, with Him to dwell.
            What will she say, etc.

Come then away,
Make no delay,
And with your best beloved go,
Fear not, I pray,
The habit gray,
Nor yet to flee this world below.
For with that love that's live and strong
From ashes must arise ere long
The phoenix true, enduringly.[4]
            What will she say, etc.

Just as on earth
Our love had birth,
Pure and perfect, noble, rare,

---

[4] In myth, the phoenix was a single beautiful bird that was consumed in fire after living
five hundred years in the desert but rose again to life from its own ashes.

It may appear,
Hidden here
In cloistered cell, beyond compare.
For loyal love that's true and sure
And endlessly shall e'er endure
Must lead to heav'n, eventually.
What will she say, etc.

She was sitting in a chapel as she read the song through, and when she had finished she wept bitterly, sprinkling the paper with the tears as they fell. Had it not been for her anxiety to avoid showing herself more moved than was becoming, she would even at that very moment have transported herself to some hermitage and shut herself away from all living creatures for evermore. But imbued as she was with the virtue of prudence, she was constrained to disguise her feelings for some little time longer. In her heart she was resolved to leave the world for ever, but in her outward appearance it was the very opposite she showed, for when in company she wore an expression that revealed nothing of her true self. For five or six months more she kept her intentions secret, appearing to the world gayer and happier even than she had used to be.

Then, one day, she went with her mistress to the Observant convent to hear high mass. As the priest, deacon and subdeacon came out of the sacristy[5] and made their way to the high altar, she beheld her poor suitor, who had still not completed his one year of novitiate.[6] He was serving as acolyte[7] and walked with eyes bent to the ground, bearing in his hands the altarcruets[8] covered in their white silk cloth. When she saw him attired thus in his vestments, his looks enhanced rather than diminished, she was so overcome with emotion that she made herself cough in order to cover up the color that had risen to her cheeks. Her poor servant could not fail to recognize the sound of her voice, a sound better known to him by far than the cloister bell. He dared not turn his head, yet as he passed by her, he could not prevent his eyes from turning in the direction that they had so long been accustomed to take. As he gazed sorrowfully upon her, he was so overwhelmed by the fire he believed almost extinct that in his desire to conceal it more than was in his power he fell to the ground at her feet. Fear lest the true cause be known led him to say that he had fallen over a broken pavingstone. But when Paulina realized that his change of habit could not change his heart, and that it was so long since he had entered the monastery that everyone would think she had forgotten him, she decided to carry out her long resolve. It was her desire that at the last their love should bring them together, that they should be alike in habit, condition and manner of life, just as at the beginning they had lived under the same roof, under the same master and under the same mistress. She had already more than four months previously made all the arrangements necessary for her entry into a convent, and one

---

[5] The deacon and subdeacon were the priest's assistants in celebrating mass. The sacristy was the room where the priest's vestments and the sacred vessels were stored.
[6] The trial period before becoming a full member of the order.
[7] Altar boy.
[8] The vessels containing the wine, water, and oil used by the priest in the mass.

morning she asked the Marchioness for permission to go and hear mass at the convent of Saint Clare.[9] Permission was granted, although the Marchioness was ignorant of the true reason for the request. As Paulina went past the Franciscan house, she stopped and asked the Father Superior to send her devoted servant, who, she said, was a relative, to speak to her. They met in a quiet chapel, and she addressed him thus:

"If my honor had allowed me to dare to enter the cloister as soon as you did, I should not have waited till now. But I have waited patiently, and now that my waiting has thwarted those who prefer to think ill of others than to think well, I am resolved to adopt the same condition of life and the same robes as you have adopted. I do not ask what people will say. For if your chosen way has brought you joy, I shall have my part therein. If it has brought you suffering, I have no wish to be spared. Whatever path you tread to Paradise, I wish to follow in your steps. For I believe that He who alone is worthy to be called true and perfect Love has drawn us to His service through a love that is reasonable and good, a love that through His Holy Spirit He will turn wholly unto Himself. And I beg you that we may put away the flesh of the old Adam that perisheth, and accept and put on that of Jesus Christ our Spouse."

Paulina's devoted servant, now a servant of God, was so filled with joy when he heard her express this sacred wish that, weeping tears of happiness, he strove to strengthen her resolve. Since he could have nothing of her but the enjoyment of the words she spoke, he held his lot happy indeed, for henceforth he would always be able to hear her, and her words would be such that both he and she would profit by them, living as they would in one love, one heart and one spirit, drawn and guided by the goodness of God. And he prayed that God would hold them in His hand, for in His hands no man can perish. As he spoke, he shed tears of love and joy. Then he bent to kiss her hand, but Paulina lowered her face to his, and in true charity they exchanged the holy kiss of love. Her soul thus filled with happiness, Paulina departed and went to the sister convent of Saint Clare, where after being received she took the veil.

Later she had the news conveyed to the Marchioness, who was so surprised she could not believe it, and went the very next day to try to make her change her mind. But Paulina's reply was firm. The Marchioness might have the power to remove her fleshly husband, the one in the world whom she had loved above all others, but that being so, she should now be satisfied and not seek to separate her from Him who was immortal and invisible, for neither the Marchioness nor any creature on earth had such power. Seeing that Paulina was resolute, the Marchioness kissed her, and filled with sorrow and regret, went on her way. From that time on Paulina and her servant lived devout and holy lives in their Observant houses. So devout and so holy were they, one cannot doubt that He whose law has its end in charity would tell them at their lives' end, even as He told Mary Magdalen, that their sins were forgiven, for they had loved much,[10] and that He would transport them in peace to the place whose recompenses surpass all human merits.

*   *   *

---

[9] St. Clare (1193–1253) founded the order of Franciscan nuns known as the Poor Clares.
[10] See Luke 7:47. Mary Magdalen was often interpreted to be a reformed harlot.

"Now you can't deny, Ladies, that the man's love was clearly the stronger. But it was so well repaid, that I only wish that everybody who fell in love had the same recompense."

"If that were the case," said Hircan, "there'd be more self-declared fools around than ever!"

"Do you call it folly if one loves with an honorable love in one's youth, and then converts this love entirely unto God?" asked Oisille.

"If melancholy and despair deserve praise," he replied laughing, "then Paulina and her devoted servant certainly deserve praise!"

"Yet God has many ways of drawing us to Him," said Geburon, "ways whose beginnings may seem bad, but whose end is good."

"Furthermore," said Parlamente, "I hold the view that no man will ever perfectly love God, unless he has perfectly loved some creature in this world."

"What do you mean by perfectly loved?" said Saffredent. "Is a perfect lover for you one of those paralytic individuals who adore their ladies from afar and never dare to bring their desires out into the open?"

"Those whom I call perfect lovers," replied Parlamente, "are those who seek in what they love some perfection, whether it be beauty, goodness or grace, those whose constant goal is virtue and whose hearts are so lofty and so pure that they would die rather than make their goal that which is low and condemned by honor and conscience. For the soul, which was created solely that it might return to its Sovereign Good, ceaselessly desires to achieve this end while it is still within the body. But the senses, by means of which the soul is able to have intelligence of its Sovereign Good, are dim and carnal because of the sins of our forefather Adam and consequently can reveal to the soul only those things which are visible and have some nearer approximation to perfection. The soul runs after these things, vainly thinking that in some external beauty, in some visible grace and in the moral virtues it will find the sovereign beauty, the sovereign grace and the sovereign virtue. But once the soul has searched out these things and tried and tested them, once it has failed to find in them Him whom it loves, it passes beyond. In the same way children, when they are small, like dolls and all manner of little things that are attractive to the eye and think that the pebbles they collect will make them rich; but then, as they grow up, the dolls they love are living people and the things they collect are the necessities of human life. Then, when they learn through experience that in earthly and transitory things there is neither perfection nor felicity, they desire to seek the source and maker of these things. Yet, if God does not open the eyes of faith, they will be in danger of leaving ignorance behind only to become infidel philosophers. For only faith can reveal and make the soul receive that Good which carnal and animal man cannot understand."

"Do you not see," said Longarine, "that uncultivated ground is desirable, although it bears nothing but useless trees and grasses, because it offers the hope that one day, when it is sown, it will bring forth good fruit? In the same way, if the heart of man feels no love for visible things, it will never attain the love of God when His word is sown therein. For the earth of his heart is sterile, cold and damned."

"So that's why most of your doctors of theology aren't spiritual doctors!" said Saffredent. "It's because all they'll ever like is good wine and ugly, sluttish chambermaids. They never try out what it's like to love ladies who are more refined!"

"If I could speak Latin properly," said Simontaut, "I'd quote St. John to you. He says 'he who loves not his brother whom he has seen, how can he love God whom he cannot see?'[11] For it is through things visible that one is drawn to the love of things invisible."

"But who is the man who is so perfect?" asked Ennasuite. *"Quis est ille, et laudabimus eum?"*[12]

To this Dagoucin replied: "There *are* men," he said, "who love so deeply and so perfectly that they would rather die than feel any desire that was contrary to the honor and conscience of their ladies, and yet they would not wish their ladies or anyone else to be aware of their feelings."

"Men like that," said Saffredent, "are chameleons—they live on nothing but air! The fact is that there's no such thing as a man who doesn't want to declare his love and know it's returned. What is more, if it *isn't* returned, I don't think there was ever a love fever that wasn't cured instantaneously. I've seen miracles enough to prove it!"

*   *   *

"But [said Parlamente] I don't think that these days there is a single man alive who is genuinely good with regard to ladies, and who can be trusted with a lady's honor and conscience. Women who believe it is otherwise, and accordingly act in complete confidence, end up by being deceived! They enter into such liaisons by way of God, and often get out of them by way of the Devil. I know many women who, under the guise of talking about God, embarked on a liaison which they later wanted to break but couldn't, because they were caught up in their own cloak of respectability. You see, vicious love disintegrates of its own accord, and is unable to survive in a heart that is pure. But 'virtuous' love has such subtle bonds that one gets caught before one notices them."

"From what you say," said Ennasuite, "no woman would ever want to be in love with a man. But your law is so harsh that it cannot endure."

"I know," said Parlamente, "but in spite of that, I still think it desirable that every woman should be content with her own husband, as I am with mine!"

Ennasuite felt that these words were aimed at her and colored: "I don't think you should assume the rest of us are any different at heart from yourself," she said, "unless you regard yourself as more perfect than we are."

"Well," said Parlamente, "so as not to get into an argument, let's see who Hircan will pick to speak next."

"I choose Ennasuite," he said, "to make up for what my wife has said."

"Well, since it's my turn," said Ennasuite, "I shall spare neither men nor women, in order to make everything equal. And seeing that you can't bring yourselves to admit that men can be good and virtuous, I'll take up the thread of the last story, and tell you one that is very similar."

---

[11] First Epistle of John 4:20.
[12] Latin: "Who is he, and we will praise him?"

STORY THIRTY-SIX

It is about a man who was president of the Parlement of Grenoble[1]— a man whose name I can't reveal, although I can tell you he wasn't a Frenchman. He was married to a very beautiful woman, and they lived a happy and harmonious life together. However, the President was getting on in years, and the wife began an affair with a young clerk who was called Nicolas. Every morning, when her husband went off to the Palais de Justice,[2] Nicolas would go to her bedroom to take his place. This was noticed by one of the President's servants, a man who had been in his household for thirty years, and who, being loyal to his master, could not do otherwise than tell him. The President was a prudent man, and was not prepared to believe the story without further evidence. He said that the servant was merely trying to sow discord between his wife and himself. If it was true, he said, then he ought to be able to show him the living proof. If he could not do so, then he would conclude that the man had been lying in order to destroy the love which he and his wife had for one another. The servant assured him that he should see with his own eyes what he had described.

One morning, as soon as the President had left for the courts and Nicolas had gone into the bedroom, the servant sent one of his fellow-servants to tell the master to come, while he stayed by the door to make sure Nicolas did not leave. When the President saw the servant give him the signal, he pretended he was feeling unwell, left the court, and hurried back home, where he found his other faithful old servant by the bedroom door assuring him that Nicolas was inside and that he had indeed only just gone in.

"Do not move from here," said the President. "As you know, there is no way in or out except through the small private room to which I alone have the key."

In went the President and found his wife and Nicolas in bed together. Nicolas, who had nothing on but his shirt, threw himself at the President's feet, begging forgiveness, while the wife started to weep.

"Your misdemeanor is a serious one, as you well know," said the President to his wife. "However, I do not wish to see my household dishonored or the daughters I have had by you disadvantaged. Therefore, I order you to cry no more and to listen to what I mean to do. And you, Nicolas, hide in my private room and make no noise."

Then he opened the door, called his old servant, and said:

"Did you not tell me that you would show me Nicolas and my wife in bed together? I came here on the strength of your word and might have killed my poor wife. I have found nothing to bear out what you have told me. I have looked all over the room and there is no one here, as I now desire to demonstrate to you."

---

[1] The Court of Justice of Grenoble, a city in southeastern France. The President, in this story, is modeled on a certain Geoffroy Carles, a northern Italian, who died in 1516. (His method of disposing of his wife was somewhat different, however, from what the story relates.) The theme of Stories 31–40, told on the fourth day, is the virtuous patience of wives in cementing their marriages and the prudence of men in preserving the honor of their houses.

[2] The law court building.

So saying, he made the servant look under the beds and everywhere else in the room. When he found nothing, the old man was amazed, and said to his master: "The Devil must have carried him off! I saw him come in, and he didn't come out through the door—yet I can see that he is not here!"

Then his master replied: "You are a miserable servant to try to sow discord between my wife and myself. Therefore I give you leave to depart. For the services that you have rendered I shall pay what I owe you and more. But leave quickly and take care not to be found in this town when twenty-four hours have passed!"

The President gave him five or six years' wages in advance, and knowing how loyal he was, said that he hoped to reward him further. So the servant went off in tears, and the President brought Nicolas out of his hiding-place. After telling his wife and her lover what he thought of their wicked behavior, he forbade them to give any hint of it to anyone. He then instructed his wife to dress more elegantly than usual and to take part in all the social gatherings, dances and festivities. He ordered Nicolas too to make merry more than before, but added that the moment he whispered in his ear the words "Leave this place!", he should take care to be out of town within three hours. So saying, he returned to the Palais de Justice without the slightest hint that anything had happened.

For the next fortnight he set about entertaining his friends and neighbors—something he had not at all been in the habit of doing. After the banquets which he gave, there were musicians with drums for the ladies to dance to. On one occasion he noticed that his wife wasn't dancing, and told Nicolas to be her partner. Nicolas, thinking the President had forgotten what had happened, danced with her quite gaily. But after the dance was over, the President, on the pretext of giving him some instructions about domestic duties, whispered into Nicolas's ear: "Leave this place and never return!"

Now Nicolas was sorry indeed to leave his lady, but none the less glad to escape with his life. The President impressed upon all his relatives, friends and neighbors how much he loved his wife. Then, one fine day in the month of May, he went into his garden and picked some herbs for a salad. After eating it, his wife did not live more than twenty-four hours, and the grief that the President showed was so great that nobody suspected that he was the agent of her death. And so he avenged himself on his enemy and saved the honor of his house.

$$*\qquad*\qquad*$$

"It is not my wish, Ladies, to praise the President's conscience, but rather to portray a woman's laxity, and the great patience and prudence of a man. And do not take offense, Ladies, I beg you, because the truth sometimes speaks just as much against you as against men. Both men and women have their share of vice as well as of virtue."

"If all those women who've had affairs with their domestics," said Parlamente, "were obliged to eat salads like that one, then I know a few who wouldn't be quite so fond of their gardens as they are, but would pull up all their herbs to avoid the ones that restore the honor of families by taking the lives of wanton mothers!"

Hircan, who guessed full well why she said this, replied angrily, "A woman of honor ought never to accuse another of doing things she herself would never do!"

"Knowing something is not the same as making foolish accusations," said Parlamente. "The fact remains that this poor woman paid a penalty which not a few deserve. And I think that the husband, considering that he was intent on revenge, conducted himself with remarkable prudence and good sense."

"And also with great malice," said Longarine, "as well as vindictiveness that was both protracted and cruel—which shows that he had neither God nor conscience in mind."

"And what would you have wanted him to do, then," asked Hircan, "to avenge himself for the worst outrage a woman can perpetrate against a man?"

"I would rather," she said, "that he had killed her out of anger, for the learned doctors say that such a sin is remissible,[3] because the first movements of the soul are not within man's powers. So if he had acted out of anger he might have received forgiveness."

"Yes," said Geburon, "but his daughters and his descendants would have borne the stigma for ever."

"He shouldn't have killed her," said Longarine, "for once rage had subsided, she could have lived with him as an honorable woman and the whole thing would have been forgotten."

"Do you really think," said Saffredent, "that he had really calmed down, just because he had managed to conceal his anger? I think that the day he made the salad he was just as angry as at first, because there are people whose first movements never subside till their passion is put into effect. And I'm glad to say the theologians regard this kind of sin as readily pardonable. I share their view on this."

"One needs to watch one's words with people as dangerous as you," said Parlamente, "but what I said was meant to apply to cases where the passion is so great that it suddenly overwhelms the senses, and does so to such an extent that reason cannot operate."

"Taking that point further," said Saffredent, "I would argue that a man who is deeply in love does not commit a sin, or only commits a venial sin, whatever he does. Because I'm certain that if he is in the grip of perfect love, he will not hear the voice of reason, either in his heart or in his understanding. And, if we're truthful about it, there's not one among us who's not experienced this wild passion, which, I believe, is readily pardonable. What is more, I believe that God is not even angered by sin of this kind, since it is one step in the ascend to perfect love of Him, to which one cannot ascend without passing up the ladder of worldly love. For St John says: 'How shall you love God, whom you see not, unless you love him whom you see?'"[4]

"There is not a single text in Holy Scripture, however beautiful," Oisille said, "that you would not turn to your own ends. But take care lest, like the

---

[3] Forgivable. The "doctors" are theologians.
[4] First Epistle of John 4:20. Compare the quotation of this text in the discussion following Story Nineteen.

spider, you turn wholesome meat into poison. Be you assured that it is indeed dangerous to draw on Scripture out of place and without necessity."

"Do you call telling the truth 'out of place' and 'without necessity'?" said Saffredent. "Do you mean to say, then, that when we're talking to you unbelieving ladies and call God to our aid, do you mean that we're taking His name in vain? But if there is any sin in *that*, it's you who should take the blame—because it's *your* unbelief that obliges us to look for all the oaths we can possibly think of. And even then we can't kindle the fire of charity in your icy hearts!"

"That just shows," said Longarine, "that you're all liars—for the truth is so mighty that we could do no other than believe you, were truth in the words you spoke. But the danger is that the daughters of Eve are too ready to believe this serpent."

"I can see, Parlamente, that women are invincible," replied Saffredent. "So I shall keep quiet, to see who Ennasuite will choose to speak next."

* * *

"You make me laugh when you mention conscience," said Simontaut. "Conscience is something I would rather a woman never troubled herself about."

"It would serve you right," said Nomerfide, "to have a wife like the one who, after her husband's death, turned out to be more concerned about his cash than his conscience."

"Then will you tell us the story," asked Saffredent, "if I invite you to be the next speaker?"

"I hadn't intended to tell such a short story," replied Nomerfide, "but since it is to the point, I will do so."

STORY FIFTY-FIVE

In the town of Saragossa[1] there was a rich merchant. Seeing that his death was near, and that he could not take his wealth with him—wealth which perhaps he had not acquired altogether honestly—he thought that he might make some amends for his sins by making some little donation or other to God. As if God grants his grace in return for money! Anyway, he made arrangements regarding his house, and gave instructions that a fine Spanish horse of his should be sold, and the proceeds distributed to the poor mendicants.[2] It was his wife whom he requested to carry out these instructions as soon as possible after his death. No sooner was the burial over and the first few tears shed, than the wife, who to say the least was no more stupid than Spanish women in general, approached her servant, who had also heard her husband's wishes.

---

[1] A city in northeastern Spain. Stories 51–60, told on the sixth day, concern deceptions motivated by greed, hatred, and vengeance.

[2] Beggars soliciting alms.

"I think I've lost enough," said she, "in losing my husband whom I loved so dearly, without losing his property as well. Not that I want to disobey his instructions. In fact, I want to carry out his wishes even better than he intended. You see, the poor man was so taken in by those greedy priests. He thought he would make a sacrifice to God after his death by giving away a sum of money, not a single écu[3] of which he would have given away during his lifetime, however great the need, as you know. So I've made up my mind that we shall do what he instructed us to do after his death—indeed we shall do better, and do what he *would* have done himself, had he lived a fortnight longer. Only not a soul must hear of it!"

The servant gave his word, and she went on: "You will go and sell his horse, and when they ask you how much you want, you will say one ducat.[4] But I also have an excellent cat that I want to sell, and you will sell it at the same time, for ninety-nine ducats. Together the horse and the cat will fetch a hundred ducats, which is what my husband wanted for the horse alone."

So the servant promptly went off to do as his mistress requested. As he was leading the horse across the square, carrying the cat in his arms, he was approached by a certain nobleman who had seen the horse before and was interested in acquiring it. Having asked the price, the nobleman received the answer: "One ducat!"

"I should be obliged if you would be serious," said the man.

"I assure you, Monsieur, that the price is one ducat. You have to buy the cat with it, of course. I can't let the cat go for less than ninety-nine ducats!"

The nobleman thought this was a fair enough bargain. On the spot he paid one ducat for the horse, and ninety-nine for the cat, as requested, and led his purchases away. The servant took the money back to his mistress, who was extremely pleased, and lost no time in giving away the proceeds from the sale of the horse to the poor mendicants. As for the rest, that went to provide for the wants of herself and her children.

* * *

"Well, what do you think of her? Wasn't she wiser than her husband, and wasn't she just as much concerned about his conscience as she was about doing well for her family?"

"I think she loved her husband," said Parlamente, "but realized that most men's minds wander when they're on their deathbeds, and knowing what his real intention was, she wanted to interpret his wishes for the benefit of their children, and I think it was very wise of her to do so."

"What!" exclaimed Geburon. "Do you not think it a grave error to fail to execute the last will and testament of deceased friends?"

"Indeed I do!" replied Parlamente. "Provided the testator is sound of mind and not deranged."

"Do you call it deranged," replied Geburon, "to give away one's goods to the Church and to the poor mendicants?"

"I do not call it deranged," she replied, "if a man distributes to the poor that which God has placed within his power. But to give away as alms what

---

[3]A coin worth three francs.
[4]A gold coin.

belongs to other people—I do not think that shows great wisdom. It's all too common to see the world's greatest usurers putting up ornate and impressive chapels, in the hope of appeasing God for hundreds of thousands of ducats' worth of sheer robbery by spending ten thousand ducats on a building! As if God didn't know how to count!"

"Indeed, I am frequently astonished," said Oisille, "that they presume to be able to appease God by means of the very things, which, when He came to earth, He condemned—things such as fine buildings, gilded ornaments, decorations and paintings. But, if they had rightly understood what God has said of human offerings in a certain passage—that 'the sacrifice of God is a troubled spirit: a broken and contrite heart, O God, shalt thou not despise'— and again, in another passage, what Saint Paul has said—that 'ye are the temple of the living God, in which He will dwell'—if they had rightly heard these words, I say, they would have taken pains to adorn their conscience while they were yet alive.[5] They would not have waited till a time when man can do neither good nor evil. Nor would they have done what is even worse and placed upon those who remain the burden of dispensing their alms to those upon whom, during their lifetime, they did not even deign to look. But He who reads men's hearts will not be deceived, and He will judge them not only according to their works, but according to the faith and charity that they have shown towards Him."

"Why is it, then," said Geburon, "that the Franciscans and Mendicants[6] talk of nothing else when a man's dying but of how we ought to make bequests to their monasteries, with the assurance that they will send us to Paradise whether we want or not?"

"What, Geburon!" broke in Hircan. "Have you forgotten your story about the Franciscans, that you're asking how men like that can possibly lie? I'll tell you, as far as I'm concerned, there's no one on this earth tells lies like they do. It may be that those who speak for the good of their community as a whole aren't to be criticized; but there are some who forget their vow of poverty in order to satisfy their own greed."

Michel de Montaigne
(1533–1592)

"I have no more made my book than my book has made me," Michel de Montaigne wrote, "'tis a book consubstantial with the author, of a peculiar design, a member of my life, and whose business is not designed for others, as that of all other books is." The book is his *Essays,* and perhaps no other work has ever coincided so precisely with the personality of its author, who was an extraordinarily complex, attractive, and in some ways baffling man.

Montaigne was born in 1533, the son of Pierre Eyquem, a wealthy merchant and mayor of Bordeaux. (Montaigne later discarded the name Eyquem and took instead the name of the family estate, the château de Montaigne

---

[5] The biblical quotations are from Psalms 51:17 and 2 Corinthians 6:16.
[6] Religious orders of begging friars.

in Périgord, in southwestern France.) Montaigne's father was deeply impressed with Renaissance ideas, and he attempted to give his son an experimental education that would fit him for the spirit of the new age. He sent his son to be nursed by a peasant woman in a village on his estate, so that the young Montaigne would develop a love and respect for common people. A Latin tutor came from Germany to oversee his first attempts at speech, to keep him from hearing French until he had mastered Latin, and thus to make Latin his native tongue.

When he was six, Montaigne was sent to school at the famous Collège de Guienne in Bordeaux, where he studied under a number of learned men destined to become key figures in Renaissance thought. After he had completed his course at Bordeaux, he went on to the study of law, probably at Toulouse, home of one of the famous law schools of France. When he was twenty-one, he became a member of a court and, three years later, a member of the Parlement of Bordeaux, where he was one of sixty magistrates whose duty it was to enforce the king's law. In his function as magistrate, Montaigne was an observer of, and sometimes a participant in, the religious conflicts between Catholics and Protestant Huguenots and in the brutal suppression of Huguenot "heretics." Here he seems to have developed the strong distaste for cruelty and brutal punishments that appears frequently in the *Essays*. The other notable influence upon Montaigne during these years was an intense friendship with another young member of the Parlement, Étienne de la Boétie, which lasted six years and ended only with the early death of La Boétie. La Boétie was a Humanist and a fine scholar who translated Xenophon and Plutarch and wrote poetry in both Latin and French.

In 1570, Montaigne resigned from the Parlement of Bordeaux and retired to his estate, "to the bosom of the learned Virgins" (the Muses), as he put it. For the rest of his life, his chief employment was the writing of his *Essays*, though there were many interruptions and temporary returns to active life: a year and a half of traveling in 1580–81, two terms as mayor of Bordeaux (during which the plague killed almost a third of the population of that city), and a period of exile from his château during the height of the plague and the Wars of Religion. The first two volumes of his *Essays* were published in 1580; in 1586–88, he thoroughly revised and expanded the earlier volumes and wrote a third one. Even after the publication of the edition of 1588, he continued to revise and expand the *Essays* through marginal annotations during the last four years of his life. He died of a severe inflammation of the throat on September 13, 1592.

Montaigne's *Essays* represent a new genre in Western literature. The nineteenth-century English critic Edmund Gosse wrote, "It is not often that we can date with any approach to accuracy the arrival of a new class of literature into the world. But it was in the month of March 1571 that the essay was invented." This exaggeration neglects the long process by which Montaigne developed his characteristic form, but it does suggest the orginality of his achievement. Montaigne began his work as a modest set of quotations from his readings, annotated with his own comments; a reminder of these origins remains in the many Latin quotations that punctuate the *Essays* in their final form. As he continued to write, however, his own comments began to outweigh the quotations and develop their own loose, rambling, almost free-associational structure. Frequently, the title of an essay serves only as the jumping-off place for a series of meditations that have little or no connection with the presumed subject. The style is easy and informal, though it can rise when appropriate to great eloquence; Montaigne's literary voice is distinctively witty, self-deprecating, and charming. Often long passages consist merely of a series of amusing and ingenious anecdotes, illustrations, and quotations spiraling around the subject. The nineteenth-century French critic Sainte-Beuve described Montaigne's style as "a continual epigram or a metaphor always renewing itself."

Montaigne's ideas have been the subject of almost continuous controversy since the *Essays* were first published. Some readers, noting that he regards human reason as powerless and the world as essentially unknowable, have concluded that his work implies indifference and resignation to ignorance. Others have found the essential spirit of modern science in his skeptical, inquiring spirit and his unwillingness to take anything merely on authority. His religious views are also variously interpreted. Few of his contemporaries found anything unorthodox in the *Essays,* but the Church later found their skeptical spirit questionable and in 1676 placed them on the *Index.* Some close students of Montaigne have found him profoundly Christian, while Ralph Waldo Emerson called his essay on Montaigne "The Skeptic," and Sainte-Beuve believed that he worked deliberately to undermine the teachings of Christianity. Equally controversial, across the centuries, has been the meaning of Montaigne's preoccupation with himself. In the seventeenth century, the French scientist and philosopher Pascal spoke of Montaigne's work as "the foolish project of painting himself." Others have seen this self-preoccupation as inspired both by the classical injunction to "know thyself" and the Renaissance emphasis on the importance of the individual mind, while modern readers have found in Montaigne a vivid anticipation of twentieth-century literature's intense interest in the inner world of the individual self.

The disagreements regarding Montaigne's work probably arise from attempts to impose a unity and consistency upon them that they do not have. Critics now usually divide his thought into three stages of development. In the first stage, he was deeply influenced by the philosophy of Seneca and by the personal model of Cato of Utica. During this period he held "Stoic" ideas of indifference to death, suffering, and misfortune. A second, "Skeptical" stage is marked by his writing of the long and important "Apology for Raymond Sebond." Skepticism had such a hold on Montaigne that in about 1576 he had a medal struck that depicted an evenly balanced scale above the personal motto, "*Que sçay-je?*" or "What do I know?" The third and last stage is often called the "Epicurean" stage; Montaigne's emphasis now shifts to the achievement of happiness through the exercise of the human faculties, physical as well as intellectual.

This tripartite scheme seems accurate as far as it goes, but even it may imply more consistency and order in Montaigne's work than actually exists. The real core of Montaigne's work is not a consistent set of ideas, but the continual presence of the man himself. He is constantly shifting and changing but is always vividly present at center stage. It is through Montaigne's constant attention to the details of his own life that he captures not only the quality of his own personality but also the rich variety and delight of life itself. The twentieth-century novelist and critic Virginia Woolf summed up this vitality in her essay on Montaigne: "It is life that emerges more and more clearly as these essays reach not their end, but their suspension in full career. It is life that becomes more and more absorbing as death draws near, one's self, one's soul, every part of existence: that one wears silk stockings summer and winter; puts water in one's wine; has one's hair cut after dinner; must have glass to drink from; has never worn spectacles; has a loud voice; carries a switch in one's hands; bites one's tongue, fidgets with one's feet; is apt to scratch one's ears; likes meat to be high; rubs one's teeth with a napkin (thank God, they are good!); must have curtains to one's bed; and, what is rather curious, began by liking radishes, then disliked them, and now likes them again. No fact is too little to let it slip through one's fingers."

Montaigne's spirit, as well as some of his recurring ideas and his characteristic style, are well illustrated in the two essays reprinted here. Montaigne's love of simplicity and "naturalness" is expressed vividly in the quaint but pointed essay "Of Cannibals." Montaigne, like most of his European contemporaries, was fascinated by reports of the New World; he had seen natives of Brazil at the court celebrations in Rouen in 1560 (celebrating the coming of age of Charles IX) and, as he tells us, had some Brazilian artifacts in his home. He delights in the curious details of cannibal life but, characteristically, lets his mind spiral around the implications of a comparison between the lives of these "noble savages" and his own life. "So we may well call these people barbarians," he writes, "in respect to the rules of reason, but not in respect to ourselves, who surpass them in every kind of barbarity." (This essay has an extrinsic interest in that Shakespeare adapted a passage from it, in John Florio's Elizabethan translation, and incorporated it into *The Tempest.*)

The most important fact to be noted about "Apology for Raymond Sebond," perhaps, is that it is not an apology for Raymond Sebond. Sebond, a fifteenth-century professor of medicine, theology, and philosophy at Toulouse, in Spain, had written a Latin work called *Liber Creaturarum,* or *Natural Theology* (1484), which Montaigne had translated into French for his father. In this book, Sebond had argued that human beings could arrive at a comprehensive knowledge of God through study of nature, God's creation. Montaigne apparently wrote his very long essay (only about 20 percent is represented in this excerpt) at the request of Princess Margaret of Valois, who asked him to defend the book he had translated. Montaigne's "apology" is halfhearted at best, and in the course of the essay, he comes close to defending a view precisely opposite to Sebond's: that the human mind is unable to know anything with certainty. The spine of his argument is simple: human beings are ill-equipped to know the world; knowledge can make us neither happy nor good, and anyway it is impossible to acquire; our senses are deceptive; the world is in such flux that knowledge is impossible; and so on. But in the course of developing his argument, Montaigne brings such curious and idiosyncratic detail to it that the essay is a delight to read.

Both "Of Cannibals" and the "Apology for Raymond Sebond" may be seen as expressions of the love of ordinary life that Woolf noted in Montaigne and his corresponding distrust of high-flying claims to power and knowledge. "The virtue of the soul," he wrote in "Of Repentance," "does not consist in flying high, but in walking orderly," and his ideal is not the grandeur of an Alexander but the modesty of a Socrates, who wanted not to conquer the world but to "carry on human life conformably with its natural condition."

FURTHER READING *(prepared by J.H.):* The standard biography is Donald M. Frame's *Montaigne: A Biography,* 1965. Frame's *Montaigne's "Essais": A Study,* 1969, is a lucid and thoughtful critical overview, as are Peter Burke's *Montaigne,* 1981, a volume in the Past Masters series, and Dorothy Coleman's *Montaigne's "Essais,"* 1987, in the Unwin Critical Library series. Erich Auerbach's chapter on Montaigne, "L'humaine condition," in *Mimesis: The Representation of Reality in Western Literature,* trans. Willard R. Trask, 1953, remains valuable and provocative. Of the many specialized studies that could be recommended, Barbara C. Bowen's *The Age of Bluff: Paradox and Ambiguity in Rabelais and Montaigne,* 1972, is especially readable and useful. Harold Bloom has edited two collections of essays on Montaigne: *Michel de Montaigne,* 1987, in the Modern Critical Views series, and *Montaigne's "Essays,"* 1987, in the Modern Critical Interpretations series. Both offer a good selection of recent criticism and guides to further reading. The former contains a fine essay by Catherine Demure: "The Paradox and the Miracle: Structure and Meaning in 'The Apology for Raymond Sebond.'" Two especially good advanced studies are Jean Starobinski's *Montaigne in Motion,* trans. Arthur Goldhammer, 1985, and Richard L. Regosin's *The Matter of My Book: Montaigne's "Essais" as the Book of the Self,* 1977. David Lewis Schaefer, *The Political Philosophy of Montaigne,* 1991, is valuable on its subject. Montaigne is among the authors discussed by the French feminist Christine Faure in *Democracy Without Women,* 1991.

ESSAYS

Translated by Donald M. Frame

OF CANNIBALS

When King Pyrrhus passed over into Italy, after he had reconnoitered the formation of the army that the Romans were sending to meet him, he said: "I do not know what barbarians these are" (for so the Greeks called all foreign nations), "but the formation of this army that I see is not at all barbarous."[1] The Greeks said as much of the army that Flamininus brought into their country,[2] and so did Philip, seeing from a knoll the order and distribution of the Roman camp, in his kingdom, under Publius Sulpicius Galba.[3] Thus we should beware of clinging to vulgar opinions, and judge things by reason's way, not by popular say.

I had with me for a long time a man who had lived for ten or twelve years in that other world which has been discovered in our century, in the place where Villegaignon landed, and which he called Antarctic France.[4] This discovery of a boundless country seems worthy of consideration. I don't know if I can guarantee that some other such discovery will not be made in the future, so many personages greater than ourselves having been mistaken about

---

[1] Pyrrhus (318–272 B.C.) was king of Epirus. This story is told in Plutarch's *Life of Pyrrhus.*
[2] T. Quintius Flamininus (230–144 B.C.) was a Roman general. See Plutarch's *Life of Flamininus* for this story.
[3] The reference is to Philip V, king of Macedon (221–179 B.C.). This story is told by the Roman historian Livy.
[4] The French explorer Villegaignon explored Brazil (Antarctic France) in 1557.

this one. I am afraid we have eyes bigger than our stomachs, and more curiosity than capacity. We embrace everything, but we clasp only wind.

Plato brings in Solon, telling how he had learned from the priests of the city of Saïs in Egypt that in days of old, before the Flood, there was a great island named Atlantis, right at the mouth of the Strait of Gibraltar, which contained more land than Africa and Asia put together, and that the kings of that country, who not only possessed that island but had stretched out so far on the mainland that they held the breadth of Africa as far as Egypt, and the length of Europe as far as Tuscany, undertook to step over into Asia and subjugate all the nations that border on the Mediterranean, as far as the Black Sea; and for this purpose crossed the Spains, Gaul, Italy, as far as Greece, where the Athenians checked them; but that some time after, both the Athenians and themselves and their island were swallowed up by the Flood.[5]

It is quite likely that that extreme devastation of waters made amazing changes in the habitations of the earth, as people maintain that the sea cut off Sicily from Italy—

> 'Tis said an earthquake once asunder tore
> These lands with dreadful havoc, which before
> Formed but one land, one coast
>
> VIRGIL

—Cyprus from Syria, the island of Euboea from the mainland of Boeotia; and elsewhere joined lands that were divided, filling the channels between them with sand and mud:

> A sterile marsh, long fit for rowing, now
> Feeds neighbor towns, and feels the heavy plow.
>
> HORACE

But there is no great likelihood that that island was the new world which we have just discovered; for it almost touched Spain, and it would be an incredible result of a flood to have forced it away as far as it is, more than twelve hundred leagues; besides, the travels of the moderns have already almost revealed that it is not an island, but a mainland connected with the East Indies on one side, and elsewhere with the lands under the two poles; or, if it is separated from them, it is by so narrow a strait and interval that it does not deserve to be called an island on that account.

It seems that there are movements, some natural, others feverish, in these great bodies, just as in our own. When I consider the inroads that my river, the Dordogne, is making in my lifetime into the right bank in its descent, and that in twenty years it has gained so much ground and stolen away the foundations of several buildings, I clearly see that this is an extraordinary disturbance; for if it had always gone at this rate, or was to do so in the future, the face of the world would be turned topsy-turvy. But rivers are subject to changes: now they overflow in one direction, now in another, now they keep to their course. I am not speaking of the sudden inundations whose causes

---

[5] The story of Atlantis appears in Plato's *Timaeus*.

are manifest. In Médoc,[6] along the seashore, my brother, the sieur d'Arsac, can see an estate of his buried under the sands that the sea spews forth; the tops of some buildings are still visible; his farms and domains have changed into very thin pasturage. The inhabitants say that for some time the sea has been pushing toward them so hard that they have lost four leagues of land. These sands are its harbingers; and we see great dunes of moving sand that march half a league ahead of it and keep conquering land.

The other testimony of antiquity with which some would connect this discovery is in Aristotle, at least if that little book *Of Unheard-of Wonders* is by him. He there relates that certain Carthaginians, after setting out upon the Atlantic Ocean from the Strait of Gibraltar and sailing a long time, at last discovered a great fertile island, all clothed in woods and watered by great deep rivers, far remote from any mainland; and that they, and others since, attracted by the goodness and fertility of the soil, went there with their wives and children, and began to settle there. The lords of Carthage, seeing that their country was gradually becoming depopulated, expressly forbade anyone to go there any more, on pain of death, and drove out these new inhabitants, fearing, it is said, that in course of time they might come to multiply so greatly as to supplant their former masters and ruin their state. This story of Aristotle does not fit our new lands any better than the other.

This man I had was a simple, crude fellow[7]—a character fit to bear true witness; for clever people observe more things and more curiously, but they interpret them; and to lend weight and conviction to their interpretation they cannot help altering history a little. They never show you things as they are, but bend and disguise them according to the way they have seen them; and to give credence to their judgment and attract you to it, they are prone to add something to their matter, to stretch it out and amplify it. We need a man either very honest, or so simple that he has not the stuff to build up false inventions and give them plausibility; and wedded to no theory. Such was my man; and besides this, he at various times brought sailors and merchants, whom he had known on that trip, to see me. So I content myself with his information, without inquiring what the cosmographers say about it.

We ought to have topographers who would give us an exact account of the places where they have been. But because they have over us the advantage of having seen Palestine, they want to enjoy the privilege of telling us news about all the rest of the world. I would like everyone to write what he knows, and as much as he knows, not only in this, but in all other subjects; for a man may have some special knowledge and experience of the nature of a river or a fountain, who in other matters knows only what everybody knows. However, to circulate this little scrap of knowledge, he will undertake to write the whole of physics. From this vice spring many great abuses.

Now, to return to my subject, I think there is nothing barbarous and savage in that nation, from what I have been told, except that each man calls barbarism whatever is not his own practice; for indeed it seems we have no other test of truth and reason than the example and pattern of the opinions

---

[6] Home of Montaigne's brother, Médoc is a district in southwestern France, northwest of Bordeaux.

[7] That is, the traveler referred to at the beginning of the essay.

and customs of the country we live in. *There* is always the perfect religion, the perfect government, the perfect and accomplished manners in all things. Those people are wild, just as we call wild the fruits that Nature has produced by herself and in her normal course; whereas really it is those that we have changed artificially and led astray from the common order, that we should rather call wild. The former retain alive and vigorous their genuine, their most useful and natural, virtues and properties, which we have debased in the latter in adapting them to gratify our corrupted taste. And yet for all that, the savor and delicacy of some uncultivated fruits of those countries is quite as excellent, even to our taste, as that of our own. It is not reasonable that art should win the place of honor over our great and powerful mother Nature. We have so overloaded the beauty and richness of her works by our inventions that we have quite smothered her. Yet wherever her purity shines forth, she wonderfully puts to shame our vain and frivolous attempts:

> Ivy comes readier without our care;
> In lonely caves the arbutus grows more fair;
> No art with artless bird song can compare.
> PROPERTIUS

All our efforts cannot even succeed in reproducing the nest of the tiniest little bird, its contexture, its beauty and convenience; or even the web of the puny spider. All things, says Plato, are produced by nature, by fortune, or by art; the greatest and most beautiful by one or the other of the first two, the least and most imperfect by the last.[8]

These nations, then, seem to me barbarous in this sense, that they have been fashioned very little by the human mind, and are still very close to their original naturalness. The laws of nature still rule them, very little corrupted by ours; and they are in such a state of purity that I am sometimes vexed that they were unknown earlier, in the days when there were men able to judge them better than we. I am sorry that Lycurgus and Plato did not know of them;[9] for it seems to me that what we actually see in these nations surpasses not only all the pictures in which poets have idealized the golden age and all their inventions in imagining a happy state of man, but also the conceptions and the very desire of philosophy. They could not imagine a naturalness so pure and simple as we see by experience; nor could they believe that our society could be maintained with so little artifice and human solder. This is a nation, I should say to Plato, in which there is no sort of traffic, no knowledge of letters, no science of numbers, no name for a magistrate or for political superiority, no custom of servitude, no riches or poverty, no contracts, no successions, no partitions, no occupations but leisure ones, no care for any but common kinship, no clothes, no agriculture, no metal, no use of wine or wheat. The very words that signify lying, treachery, dissimulation, avarice,

---

[8] Montaigne is paraphrasing a passage in Plato's *Laws*.
[9] Lycurgus was a Spartan lawgiver. Like Plato, he wrote of ideal societies, and, Montaigne suggests, both would have profited from knowing the culture of the New World cannibals.

envy, belittling, pardon—unheard of.[10] How far from this perfection would he find the republic that he imagined: *Men fresh sprung from the gods* [Seneca].

> These manners nature first ordained.
>
> VIRGIL

For the rest, they live in a country with a very pleasant and temperate climate, so that according to my witnesses it is rare to see a sick man there; and they have assured me that they never saw one palsied, bleary-eyed, toothless, or bent with age. They are settled along the sea and shut in on the land side by great high mountains, with a stretch about a hundred leagues wide in between. They have a great abundance of fish and flesh which bear no resemblance to ours, and they eat them with no other artifice than cooking. The first man who rode a horse there, though he had had dealings with them on several other trips, so horrified them in this posture that they shot him dead with arrows before they could recognize him.

The buildings are very long, with a capacity of two or three hundred souls; they are covered with the bark of great trees, the strips reaching to the ground at one end and supporting and leaning on one another at the top, in the manner of some of our barns, whose covering hangs down to the ground and acts as a side. They have wood so hard that they cut with it and make of it their swords and grills to cook their food. Their beds are of a cotton weave, hung from the roof like those in our ships, each man having his own; for the wives sleep apart from their husbands.

They get up with the sun, and eat immediately upon rising, to last them through the day; for they take no other meal than that one. Like some other Eastern peoples, of whom Suidas[11] tells us, who drank apart from meals, they do not drink then; but they drink several times a day, and to capacity. Their drink is made of some root, and is of the color of our claret wines. They drink it only lukewarm. This beverage keeps only two or three days; it has a slightly sharp taste, is not at all heady, is good for the stomach, and has a laxative effect upon those who are not used to it; it is a very pleasant drink for anyone who is accustomed to it. In place of bread they use a certain white substance like preserved coriander. I have tried it; it tastes sweet and a little flat.

The whole day is spent in dancing. The younger men go to hunt animals with bows. Some of the women busy themselves meanwhile with warming their drink, which is their chief duty. Some one of the old men, in the morning before they begin to eat, preaches to the whole barnful in common, walking from one end to the other, and repeating one single sentence several times until he has completed the circuit (for the buildings are fully a hundred paces long). He recommends to them only two things: valor against the enemy and love for their wives. And they never fail to point out this obligation, as their refrain, that it is their wives who keep their drink warm and seasoned.

There may be seen in several places, including my own house, specimens of their beds, of their ropes, of their wooden swords and the bracelets with

---

[10] The two sentences preceding are the famous passage adapted by Shakespeare in *The Tempest*, II.i.147.

[11] A tenth-century A.D. Greek lexicographer.

which they cover their wrists in combats, and of the big canes, open at one end, by whose sound they keep time in their dances. They are close shaven all over, and shave themselves much more cleanly than we, with nothing but a wooden or stone razor. They believe that souls are immortal, and that those who have deserved well of the gods are lodged in that part of heaven where the sun rises, and the damned in the west.

They have some sort of priests and prophets, but they rarely appear before the people, having their home in the mountains. On their arrival there is a great feast and solemn assembly of several villages—each barn, as I have described it, makes up a village, and they are about one French league from each other. The prophet speaks to them in public, exhorting them to virtue and their duty; but their whole ethical science contains only these two articles: resoluteness in war and affection for their wives. He prophesies to them things to come and the results they are to expect from their undertakings, and urges them to war or holds them back from it; but this is on the condition that when he fails to prophesy correctly, and if things turn out otherwise than he has predicted, he is cut into a thousand pieces if they catch him, and condemned as a false prophet. For this reason, the prophet who has once been mistaken is never seen again.

Divination is a gift of God; that is why its abuse should be punished as imposture. Among the Scythians, when the soothsayers failed to hit the mark, they were laid, chained hand and foot, on carts full of heather and drawn by oxen, on which they were burned.[12] Those who handle matters subject to the control of human capacity are excusable if they do the best they can. But these others, who come and trick us with assurances of an extraordinary faculty that is beyond our ken, should they not be punished for not making good their promise, and for the temerity of their imposture?

They have their wars with the nations beyond the mountains, further inland, to which they go quite naked, with no other arms than bows or wooden swords ending in a sharp point, in the manner of the tongues of our boar spears. It is astonishing what firmness they show in their combats, which never end but in slaughter and bloodshed; for as to routs and terror, they know nothing of either.

Each man brings back as his trophy the head of the enemy he has killed, and sets it up at the entrance to his dwelling. After they have treated their prisoners well for a long time with all the hospitality they can think of, each man who has a prisoner calls a great assembly of his acquaintances. He ties a rope to one of the prisoner's arms, by the end of which he holds him, a few steps away, for fear of being hurt, and gives his dearest friend the other arm to hold in the same way; and these two, in the presence of the whole assembly, kill him with their swords. This done, they roast him and eat him in common and send some pieces to their absent friends. This is not, as people think, for nourishment, as of old the Scythians used to do; it is to betoken an extreme revenge. And the proof of this came when they saw the Portuguese, who had joined forces with their adversaries, inflict a different kind of death on them when they took them prisoner, which was to bury them up to the waist, shoot the rest of their body full of arrows, and

---

[12] The Scythians were the inhabitants of a region in southeastern Europe and Asia, legendary for their barbarity. This story appears in the work of the Greek historian Herodotus.

afterward hang them. They thought that these people from the other world, being men who had sown the knowledge of many vices among their neighbors and were much greater masters than themselves in every sort of wickedness, did not adopt this sort of vengeance without some reason, and that it must be more painful than their own; so they began to give up their old method and to follow this one.

I am not sorry that we notice the barbarous horror of such acts, but I am heartily sorry that, judging their faults rightly, we should be so blind to our own. I think there is more barbarity in eating a man alive than in eating him dead; and in tearing by tortures and the rack a body still full of feeling, in roasting a man bit by bit,[13] in having him bitten and mangled by dogs and swine (as we have not only read but seen within fresh memory, not among ancient enemies, but among neighbors and fellow citizens, and what is worse, on the pretext of piety and religion), than in roasting and eating him after he is dead.

Indeed, Chrysippus and Zeno,[14] heads of the Stoic sect, thought there was nothing wrong in using our carcasses for any purpose in case of need, and getting nourishment from them; just as our ancestors, when besieged by Caesar in the city of Alésia, resolved to relieve their famine by eating old men, women, and other people useless for fighting.[15]

> The Gascons once, 'tis said, their life renewed
> By eating of such food.
>
> JUVENAL

And physicians do not fear to use human flesh in all sorts of ways for our health, applying it either inwardly or outwardly. But there never was any opinion so disordered as to excuse treachery, disloyalty, tyranny, and cruelty, which are our ordinary vices.

So we may well call these people barbarians, in respect to the rules of reason, but not in respect to ourselves, who surpass them in every kind of barbarity.

Their warfare is wholly noble and generous, and as excusable and beautiful as this human disease can be; its only basis among them is their rivalry in valor. They are not fighting for the conquest of new lands, for they still enjoy that natural abundance that provides them without toil and trouble with all necessary things in such profusion that they have no wish to enlarge their boundaries. They are still in that happy state of desiring only as much as their natural needs demand; anything beyond that is superfluous to them.

They generally call those of the same age, brothers; those who are younger, children; and the old men are fathers to all the others. These leave to their heirs in common the full possession of their property, without division or any other title at all than just the one that Nature gives to her creatures in bringing them into the world.

If their neighbors cross the mountains to attack them and win a victory, the gain of the victor is glory, and the advantage of having proved the

---

[13] These were accepted modes of execution in Montaigne's day.

[14] Chrysippus (291–208 B.C.) and Zeno (d. 264 B.C.) were, as noted, Stoic philosophers.

[15] This story of cannibalism appears in Caesar's *Gallic Wars*.

master in valor and virtue; for apart from this they have no use for the goods of the vanquished, and they return to their own country, where they lack neither anything necessary nor that great thing, the knowledge of how to enjoy their condition happily and be content with it. These men of ours do the same in their turn. They demand of their prisoners no other ransom than that they confess and acknowledge their defeat. But there is not one in a whole century who does not choose to die rather than to relax a single bit, by word or look, from the grandeur of an invincible courage; not one who would not rather be killed and eaten than so much as ask not to be. They treat them very freely, so that life may be all the dearer to them, and usually entertain them with threats of their coming death, of the torments they will have to suffer, the preparations that are being made for that purpose, the cutting up of their limbs, and the feast that will be made at their expense. All this is done for the sole purpose of extorting from their lips some weak or base word, or making them want to flee, so as to gain the advantage of having terrified them and broken down their firmness. For indeed, if you take it the right way, it is in this point alone that true victory lies:

> It is no victory
> Unless the vanquished foe admits your mastery.
>
> CLAUDIAN

The Hungarians, very bellicose fighters, did not in olden times pursue their advantage beyond putting the enemy at their mercy. For having wrung a confession from him to this effect, they let him go unharmed and unransomed, except, at most, for exacting his promise never again to take up arms against them.

We win enough advantages over our enemies that are borrowed advantages, not really our own. It is the quality of a porter, not of valor, to have sturdier arms and legs; agility is a dead and corporeal quality; it is a stroke of luck to make our enemy stumble, or dazzle his eyes by the sunlight; it is a trick of art and technique, which may be found in a worthless coward, to be an able fencer. The worth and value of a man is in his heart and his will; there lies his real honor. Valor is the strength, not of legs and arms, but of heart and soul; it consists not in the worth of our horse or our weapons, but in our own. He who falls obstinate in his courage, *if he has fallen, he fights on his knees* [Seneca]. He who relaxes none of his assurance, no matter how great the danger of imminent death; who, giving up his soul, still looks firmly and scornfully at his enemy—he is beaten not by us, but by fortune; he is killed, not conquered.

The most valiant are sometimes the most unfortunate. Thus there are triumphant defeats that rival victories. Nor did those four sister victories the fairest that the sun ever set eyes on—Salamis, Plataea, Mycale, and Sicily—ever dare match all their combined glory against the glory of the annihilation of King Leonidas and his men at the pass of Thermopylae.[16]

---

[16] Salamis, Plataea, Mycale, and Sicily were the sites of notable victories of the Greeks over the Persians and Carthaginians in the fifth century B.C. At Thermopylae, a narrow mountain pass in eastern Greece, a small band of Spartans held off the Persian army in 480 B.C.

Who ever hastened with more glorious and ambitious desire to win a battle than Captain Ischolas to lose one?[17] Who ever secured his safety more ingeniously and painstakingly than he did his destruction? He was charged to defend a certain pass in the Peloponnesus against the Arcadians. Finding himself wholly incapable of doing this, in view of the nature of the place and the inequality of the forces, he made up his mind that all who confronted the enemy would necessarily have to remain on the field. On the other hand, deeming it unworthy both of his own virtue and magnanimity and of the Lacedaemonian name to fail in his charge, he took a middle course between these two extremes, in this way. The youngest and fittest of his band he preserved for the defense and service of their country, and sent them home; and with those whose loss was less important, he determined to hold this pass, and by their death to make the enemy buy their entry as dearly as he could. And so it turned out. For he was presently surrounded on all sides by the Arcadians, and after slaughtering a large number of them, he and his men were all put to the sword. Is there a trophy dedicated to victors that would not be more due to these vanquished? The role of true victory is in fighting, not in coming off safely; and the honor of valor consists in combating, not in beating.

To return to our story. These prisoners are so far from giving in, in spite of all that is done to them, that on the contrary, during the two or three months that they are kept, they wear a gay expression; they urge their captors to hurry and put them to the test; they defy them, insult them, reproach them with their cowardice and the number of battles they have lost to the prisoners' own people.

I have a song composed by a prisoner which contains this challenge, that they should all come boldly and gather to dine off him, for they will be eating at the same time their own fathers and grandfathers, who have served to feed and nourish his body. "These muscles," he says, "this flesh and these veins are your own, poor fools that you are. You do not recognize that the substance of your ancestors' limbs is still contained in them. Savor them well; you will find in them the taste of your own flesh." An idea that certainly does not smack of barbarity. Those that paint these people dying, and who show the execution, portray the prisoner spitting in the face of his slayers and scowling at them. Indeed, to the last gasp they never stop braving and defying their enemies by word and look. Truly here are real savages by our standards; for either they must be thoroughly so, or we must be; there is an amazing distance between their character and ours.

The men there have several wives, and the higher their reputation for valor the more wives they have. It is a remarkably beautiful thing about their marriages that the same jealousy our wives have to keep us from the affection and kindness of other women, theirs have to win this for them. Being more concerned for their husbands' honor than for anything else, they strive and scheme to have as many companions as they can, since that is a sign of their husbands' valor.

Our wives will cry "Miracle!" but it is no miracle. It is a properly matrimonial virtue, but one of the highest order. In the Bible, Leah, Rachel, Sarah, and Jacob's wives gave their beautiful handmaids to their husbands; and Livia

---

[17] This story is told by the Greek historian Diodorus Siculus (first century B.C.).

seconded the appetites of Augustus, to her own disadvantage; and Stratonice, the wife of King Deiotarus, not only lent her husband for his use a very beautiful young chambermaid in her service, but carefully brought up her children, and backed them up to succeed to their father's estates.[18]

And lest it be thought that all this is done through a simple and servile bondage to usage and through the pressure of the authority of their ancient customs, without reasoning or judgment, and because their minds are so stupid that they cannot take any other course, I must cite some examples of their capacity. Besides the warlike song I have just quoted, I have another, a love song, which begins in this vein: "Adder, stay; stay, adder, that from the pattern of your coloring my sister may draw the fashion and the workmanship of a rich girdle that I may give to my love; so may your beauty and your pattern be forever preferred to all other serpents." This first couplet is the refrain of the song. Now I am familiar enough with poetry to be a judge of this: not only is there nothing barbarous in this fancy, but it is altogether Anacreontic.[19] Their language, moreover, is a soft language, with an agreeable sound, somewhat like Greek in its endings.

Three of these men, ignorant of the price they will pay some day, in loss of repose and happiness, for gaining knowledge of the corruptions of this side of the ocean; ignorant also of the fact that of this intercourse will come their ruin (which I suppose is already well advanced: poor wretches, to let themselves be tricked by the desire for new things, and to have left the serenity of their own sky to come and see ours!)—three of these men were at Rouen, at the time the late King Charles IX[20] was there. The king talked to them for a long time; they were shown our ways, our splendor, the aspect of a fine city. After that, someone asked their opinion, and wanted to know what they had found most amazing. They mentioned three things, of which I have forgotten the third, and I am very sorry for it; but I still remember two of them. They said that in the first place they thought it very strange that so many grown men, bearded, strong, and armed, who were around the king (it is likely that they were talking about the Swiss of his guard) should submit to obey a child, and that one of them was not chosen to command instead. Second (they have a way in their language of speaking of men as halves of one another), they had noticed that there were among us men full and gorged with all sorts of good things, and that their other halves were beggars at their doors, emaciated with hunger and poverty; and they thought it strange that these needy halves could endure such an injustice, and did not take the others by the throat, or set fire to their houses.

I had a very long talk with one of them; but I had an interpreter who followed my meaning so badly, and who was so hindered by his stupidity in taking in my ideas, that I could get hardly any satisfaction from the man. When I asked him what profit he gained from his superior position among his people (for he was a captain, and our sailors called him king), he told me that it was to march foremost in war. How many men followed him? He

---

[18] The story of Sarah and her maid Hagar appears in Genesis, chapter 16; that of Leah and Rachel in Genesis, chapter 30. The story of Livia is in Suetonius' *Life of Augustus* and that of Stratonice in Plutarch's *Bravery of Women*.

[19] Like the poetry of Anacreon (c. 563–c. 478 B.C.), a Greek poet known for his love poems.

[20] King Charles IX of France died in 1574.

pointed to a piece of ground, to signify as many as such a space could hold; it might have been four or five thousand men. Did all his authority expire with the war? He said that this much remained, that when he visited the villages dependent on him, they made paths for him through the underbrush by which he might pass quite comfortably.

All this is not too bad—but what's the use? They don't wear breeches.

APOLOGY FOR RAYMOND SEBOND

In truth, knowledge is a great and very useful quality; those who despise it give evidence enough of their stupidity. But yet I do not set its value at that extreme measure that some attribute to it, like Herillus the philosopher, who placed in it the sovereign good, and held that it was in its power to make us wise and content. That I do not believe, nor what others have said, that knowledge is the mother of all virtue, and that all vice is produced by ignorance. If that is true, it is subject to a long interpretation.

[RAYMOND SEBOND'S BOOK][1]

My house has long been open to men of learning, and is well known to them. For my father, who ruled it for fifty years and more, inflamed with that new ardor with which King Francis I embraced letters and brought them into credit, sought with great diligence and expense the acquaintance of learned men, receiving them at his house like holy persons having some particular inspiration of divine wisdom, collecting their sayings and discourses like oracles, and with all the more reverence and religion as he was less qualified to judge them; for he had no knowledge of letters, any more than his predecessors. Myself, I like them well enough, but I do not worship them.

Among others, Pierre Bunel, a man of great reputation for learning in his time, after staying a few days at Montaigne in the company of my father with other men of his sort, made him a present, on his departure, of a book entitled "Natural Theology, or Book of Creatures, by Master Raymond de Sabonde." And because the Italian and Spanish languages were familiar to my father, and this book was composed in a Spanish scrambled up with Latin endings, Bunel hoped that with a very little help he could make his profit of it, and recommended it to him as a very useful book and suited to the time in which he gave it to him; this was when the innovations of Luther were beginning to gain favor and to shake our old belief in many places.

In this he was very well advised, rightly foreseeing by rational inference that this incipient malady would easily degenerate into an execrable atheism. For the common herd, not having the faculty of judging things in themselves, let themselves be carried away by chance and by appearances, when once they have been given the temerity to despise and judge the opinions that they had held in extreme reverence, such as are those in which their salvation is concerned. And when some articles of their religion have been

---

[1] Bracketed subheadings are not in the original but have been supplied by the editors.

set in doubt and upon the balance, they will soon after cast easily into like uncertainty all the other parts of their belief, which had no more authority or foundation in them than those that have been shaken; and they shake off as a tyrannical yoke all the impressions they had once received from the authority of the laws or the reverence of ancient usage—

> For eagerly is trampled what once was too much feared
>
> LUCRETIUS

—determined from then on to accept nothing to which they have not applied their judgment and granted their personal consent.

Now some days before his death, my father, having by chance come across this book under a pile of other abandoned papers, commanded me to put it into French for him. It is nice to translate authors like this one, where there is hardly anything but the matter to reproduce; but those who have given much care to grace and elegance of language are dangerous to undertake, especially to render them into a weaker idiom.[2] It was a very strange and a new occupation for me; but being by chance at leisure at the time, and being unable to disobey any command of the best father there ever was, I got through it as best I could; at which he was singularly pleased, and ordered it to be printed; and this was done after his death.

I found the ideas of this author fine, the arrangement and sequence of his work good, and his plan full of piety. Because many people are busy reading it, and especially the ladies, to whom we owe additional help, I have often found myself in a position to help them by clearing their book of two principal objections that are made against it. His purpose is bold and courageous, for he undertakes by human and natural reasons to establish and prove against the atheists all the articles of the Christian religion; wherein, to tell the truth, I find him so firm and felicitous that I do not think it is possible to do better in that argument, and I think that no one has equaled him.

Since this work seemed to me too rich and splendid for an author whose name is so little known, and of whom all we know is that he was a Spaniard professing medicine at Toulouse about two hundred years ago, I once inquired of Adrianus Turnebus, who knew everything, what could be the truth about this book. He replied that he thought it was some quintessence extracted from Saint Thomas Aquinas; for in truth that mind, full of infinite erudition and admirable subtlety, was alone capable of such ideas. At all events, whoever is the author and inventor (and it is not reasonable, without greater occasion, to rob Sebond of that title), he was a very able man with many fine qualities.

[FIRST OBJECTION TO SEBOND AND DEFENSE]

The first criticism that they make of his work is that Christians do themselves harm in trying to support their belief by human reasons, since it is conceived only by faith and by a particular inspiration of divine grace. In this objection there seems to be a certain pious zeal, and for this reason we must try

---

[2] That is, French, which was considered "weaker" than Latin.

with all the more mildness and respect to satisfy those who advance it. This would be rather the task for a man versed in theology than for myself, who know nothing about it.

However, I think thus, that in a thing so divine and so lofty, and so far surpassing human intelligence, as is this truth with which it has pleased the goodness of God to enlighten us, it is very necessary that he still lend us his help, by extraordinary and privileged favor, so that we may conceive it and lodge it in us. And I do not think that purely human means are at all capable of this; if they were, so many rare and excellent souls, so abundantly furnished with natural powers, in ancient times, would not have failed to arrive at this knowledge through their reason. It is faith alone that embraces vividly and surely the high mysteries of our religion.

But this is not to say that it is not a very fine and very laudable enterprise to accommodate also to the service of our faith the natural and human tools that God has given us. There can be no doubt that this is the most honorable use that we could put them to, and that there is no occupation or design more worthy of a Christian man than to aim, by all his studies and thoughts, to embellish, extend, and amplify the truth of his belief. We do not content ourselves with serving God with mind and soul, we also owe and render him a bodily reverence; we apply even our limbs and movements and external things to honor him. We must do the same here, and accompany our faith with all the reason that is in us, but always with this reservation, not to think that it is on us that faith depends, or that our efforts and arguments can attain a knowledge so supernatural and divine. . . .

[SECOND OBJECTION TO SEBOND AND DEFENSE]

I have already, without thinking about it, half involved myself in the second objection which I had proposed to answer for Sebond.

Some say that his arguments are weak and unfit to prove what he proposes, and undertake to shatter them with ease. These must be shaken up a little more roughly, for they are more dangerous and malicious than the others. People are prone to apply the meaning of other men's writings to suit opinions that they have previously determined in their minds; and an atheist flatters himself by reducing all authors to atheism, infecting innocent matter with his own venom. These men have some prepossession in judgment that makes their taste jaded for Sebond's reasons. Furthermore, it seems to them that they are given an easy game when set at liberty to combat our religion by purely human weapons, which they would not dare attack in its authoritative and commanding majesty.

The means I take to beat down this frenzy, and which seems fittest to me, is to crush and trample underfoot human arrogance and pride; to make them feel the inanity, the vanity and nothingness, of man; to wrest from their hands the puny weapons of their reason; to make them bow their heads and bite the ground beneath the authority and reverence of divine majesty. It is to this alone that knowledge and wisdom belong; it alone that can have some self-esteem, and from which we steal what we account and prize ourselves for:

For God allows great thoughts to no one else.
HERODOTUS

Let us beat down this presumption, the first foundation of the tyranny of the evil spirit. *For God resisteth the proud, and giveth grace to the humble* [Saint Peter]. Intelligence is in all gods, says Plato, and in very few men.

Now it is nevertheless a great consolation to the Christian to see our frail mortal tools so properly suited to our holy and divine faith, that when they are used on subjects that are by their nature frail and mortal, they are no more completely and powerfully appropriate. Let us see then if man has within his power other reasons more powerful than those of Sebond, or indeed if it is in him to arrive at any certainty by argument and reason.

For Saint Augustine, arguing against these people, has good cause to reproach them for their injustice in that they hold those parts of our belief to be false which our reason fails to establish. And to show that there can be and can have been plenty of things whose nature and causes our reason cannot possibly establish, he puts before his adversaries certain known and indubitable experiences into which man confesses he has no insight; and this he does, like all other things, with careful and ingenious research. We must do more, and teach them that to convict our reason of weakness, there is no need to go sifting out rare examples, and that she is so lame and so blind that there is nothing so clear and easy as to be clear enough to her; that the easy and the hard are one to her; that all subjects alike, and nature in general, disavow her jurisdiction and mediation.

What does truth preach to us, when she exhorts us to flee worldly philosophy, when she so often inculcates in us that our wisdom is but folly before God; that of all vanities the vainest is man; that the man who is presumptuous of his knowledge does not yet know what knowledge is; and that man, who is nothing, if he thinks he is something, seduces and deceives himself? These statements of the Holy Spirit express so clearly and so vividly what I wish to maintain, that no other proof would be needed against men who would surrender with all submission and obedience to its authority. But these men insist on being whipped to their own cost and will not allow us to combat their reason except by itself.

Let us then consider for the moment man alone, without outside assistance, armed solely with his own weapons, and deprived of divine grace and knowledge, which is his whole honor, his strength, and the foundation of his being. Let us see how much presence he has in this fine array. Let him help me to understand, by the force of his reason, on what foundations he has built these great advantages that he thinks he has over other creatures. Who has persuaded him that that admirable motion of the celestial vault, the eternal light of those torches rolling so proudly above his head, the fearful movements of that infinite sea, were established and have lasted so many centuries for his convenience and his service? Is it possible to imagine anything so ridiculous as that this miserable and puny creature, who is not even master of himself, exposed to the attacks of all things, should call himself master and emperor of the universe, the least part of which it is not in his power to know, much less to command? And this privilege that he attributes to himself of being the only one in this great edifice who has the capacity to recognize its beauty and its parts, the only one who can give thanks for it to the architect and keep an account of the receipts and expenses of the world: who has sealed him this privilege? Let him show us his letters patent for this great and splendid charge.

Have they been granted in favor of the wise only? Then they do not touch many people. Are the fools and the wicked worthy of such extraordinary favor, and, being the worst part of the world, of being preferred to all the rest?

Shall we believe this man? *For whom then shall a man say that the world was made? Naturally, for those souls who have the use of reason. These are gods and men, to whom certainly nothing is superior* [Cicero, quoting Balbus]. We shall never have flouted enough the impudence of this coupling.

But, poor wight, what has he in himself worthy of such an advantage? When we consider the incorruptible life of the celestial bodies, their beauty, their greatness, their continual motion by so exact a rule;

> When the vaults of heaven meet our sight,
> Infinite worlds above, ether with stars alight;
> And when the course of sun and moon come to our mind;
> LUCRETIUS

when we consider the dominion and power that those bodies have, not only over our lives and the conditions of our fortune,

> For on the stars men's deeds and lives depend,
> MANILIUS

but over our very inclinations, our reasonings, our wills, which they govern, drive, and stir at the mercy of their influences, as our reason finds and teaches us;

> He learns that stars remotely seen
> Govern by silent laws, and intervene;
> To move the universe they alternate,
> And rule by certain signs the twists of fate;
> MANILIUS

when we see that not merely a man, nor a king, but kingdoms, empires, and all this world below move in step with the slightest movements of the heavens;

> How great a change the slightest motion brings:
> So great this kingdom is that governs kings;
> MANILIUS

if our virtue, our vices, our competence and knowledge, and this very dissertation that we are making about the power of the stars and this comparison of them to us, comes as our reason judges, by their medium and their favor;

> One, in love's delirium,
> Can cross the sea and conquer Ilium;
> Another man is destined laws to build;
> Fathers kill sons, fathers by sons are killed,
> And brother wounds armed brother in the fray.

This war is not of ours; Fate makes men stray,
Punish themselves, their members lacerate.

. . . .

This too is fated, that I write of fate;

MANILIUS

if we hold by the dispensation of heaven this portion of reason that we have, how can our reason make us equal to heaven? How subject its essence and conditions to our knowledge? All that we see in those bodies astonishes us. *What preparations, what instruments, what levers, what machines, what workmen performed so great a work?* [Cicero.]

Why do we deny them soul, and life, and reason? Have we recognized in them some inert, insensible stupidity, we who have no dealings with them except obedience? Shall we say that we have seen in no other creature than man the exercise of a rational soul? Well, have we seen anything like the sun? Does it fail to exist, because we have seen nothing like it, and its movements to exist, because there are none like them? If what we have not seen does not exist, our knowledge is marvelously shrunk: *How narrow are the limits of our mind!* [Cicero.]

Are these not dreams of human vanity, to make the moon a celestial earth, to imagine mountains and valleys there, like Anaxagoras; to plant habitations and human dwellings there, and set up colonies for our convenience, as Plato and Plutarch do; and to make our earth a bright star lighting the moon? *Among other human infirmities is this one also, mental fog, and not so much the need to err as the love of errors* [Seneca]. *The corruptible body weighs down the soul, and the earthy tabernacle oppresses the much pondering mind* [The Book of Wisdom, quoted by Saint Augustine].

[HUMAN BEINGS' PLACE IN CREATION]

Presumption is our natural and original malady. The most vulnerable and frail of all creatures is man, and at the same time the most arrogant. He feels and sees himself lodged here, amid the mire and dung of the world, nailed and riveted to the worst, the deadest, and the most stagnant part of the universe, on the lowest story of the house and the farthest from the vault of heaven, with the animals of the worst condition of the three;[3] and in his imagination he goes planting himself above the circle of the moon, and bringing the sky down beneath his feet. It is by the vanity of this same imagination that he equals himself to God, attributes to himself divine characteristics, picks himself out and separates himself from the horde of other creatures, carves out their shares to his fellows and companions the animals, and distributes among them such portions and faculties and powers as he sees fit. How does he know, by the force of his intelligence, the secret internal stirrings of animals? By what comparison between them and us does he infer the stupidity that he attributes to them?

When I play with my cat, who knows if I am not a pastime to her more than she is to me? Plato, in his picture of the golden age under Saturn, counts

---

[3]Animals were conventionally divided into those that walk, those that fly, and those that swim.

among the principal advantages of the man of that time the communication he had with the beasts; inquiring of them and learning from them, he knew the true qualities and differences of each one of them; whereby he acquired a very perfect intelligence and prudence, and conducted his life far more happily than we could possibly do. Do we need a better proof to judge man's impudence with regard to the beasts? That great author opined that in most of the bodily form that Nature gave them, she considered solely the use of prognostications that were derived from them in his time.

This defect that hinders communication between them and us, why is it not just as much ours as theirs? It is a matter of guesswork whose fault it is that we do not understand one another; for we do not understand them any more than they do us. By this same reasoning they may consider us beasts, as we consider them. It is no great wonder if we do not understand them; neither do we understand the Basques and the Troglodytes.[4] However, some have boasted of understanding them, like Apollonius of Tyana, Melampus, Tiresias, Thales, and others. And since it is a fact, as the cosmographers say, that there are nations that accept a dog as their king, they must give a definite interpretation to his voice and motions. We must notice the parity there is between us. We have some mediocre understanding of their meaning; so do they of ours, in about the same degree. They flatter us, threaten us, and implore us, and we them.

Furthermore, we discover very evidently that there is full and complete communication between them and that they understand each other, not only those of the same species, but also those of different species.

> Even dumb cattle and the savage beasts
> Varied and different noises do employ
> When they feel fear or pain, or thrill with joy.
>   LUCRETIUS

In a certain bark of the dog the horse knows there is anger; at a certain other sound of his he is not frightened. Even in the beasts that have no voice, from the mutual services we see between them we easily infer some other means of communication; their motions converse and discuss:

> Likewise in children, the tongue's speechlessness
> Leads them to gesture what they would express.
>   LUCRETIUS

Why not; just as well as our mutes dispute, argue, and tell stories by signs? I have seen some so supple and versed in this, that in truth they lacked nothing of perfection in being able to make themselves understood. Lovers grow angry, are reconciled, entreat, thank, make assignations, and in fine say everything, with their eyes:

> And silence too records
> Our prayers and our words.
>   TASSO

---

[4]Cave dwellers who lived on the western shore of the Red Sea.

What of the hands? We beg, we promise, call, dismiss, threaten, pray, entreat, deny, refuse, question, admire, count, confess, repent, fear, blush, doubt, instruct, command, incite, encourage, swear, testify, accuse, condemn, absolve, insult, despise, defy, vex, flatter, applaud, bless, humiliate, mock, reconcile, commend, exalt, entertain, rejoice, complain, grieve, mope, despair, wonder, exclaim, are silent, and what not, with a variation and multiplication that vie with the tongue. With the head: we invite, send away, avow, disavow, give the lie, welcome, honor, venerate, disdain, demand, show out, cheer, lament, caress, scold, submit, brave, exhort, menace, assure, inquire. What of the eyebrows? What of the shoulders? There is no movement that does not speak both a language intelligible without instruction, and a public language; which means, seeing the variety and particular use of other languages, that this one must rather be judged the one proper to human nature. I omit what necessity teaches privately and promptly to those who need it, and the finger alphabets, and the grammars in gestures, and the sciences which are practiced and expressed only by gestures, and the nations which Pliny says have no other language.

An ambassador of the city of Abdera, after speaking at length to King Agis of Sparta, asked him: "Well, Sire, what answer do you wish me to take back to our citizens?" "That I allowed you to say all you wanted, and as much as you wanted, without ever saying a word." Wasn't that an eloquent and thoroughly intelligible silence?

Moreover, what sort of faculty of ours do we not recognize in the actions of the animals? Is there a society regulated with more order, diversified into more charges and functions, and more consistently maintained, than that of the honeybees? Can we imagine so orderly an arrangement of actions and occupations as this to be conducted without reason and foresight?

> Some, by these signs and instances inclined,
> Have said that bees share in the divine mind
> And the ethereal spirit.
>
> VIRGIL

Do the swallows that we see on the return of spring ferreting in all the corners of our houses search without judgment, and choose without discrimination, out of a thousand places, the one which is most suitable for them to dwell in? And in that beautiful and admirable texture of their buildings, can birds use a square rather than a round figure, an obtuse rather than a right angle, without knowing their properties and their effects? Do they take now water, now clay, without judging that hardness is softened by moistening? Do they floor their palace with moss or with down, without foreseeing that the tender limbs of their little ones will lie softer and more comfortably on it? Do they shelter themselves from the rainy wind and face their dwelling toward the orient without knowing the different conditions of these winds and considering that one is more salutary to them than the other? Why does the spider thicken her web in one place and slacken it in another, use now this sort of knot, now that one, unless she has the power of reflection, and thought, and inference?

We recognize easily enough, in most of their works, how much superiority the animals have over us and how feeble is our skill to imitate them.

We see, however, in our cruder works, the faculties that we use, and that our soul applies itself with all its power; why do we not think the same thing of them? Why do we attribute to some sort of natural and servile inclination these works which surpass all that we can do by nature and by art? Wherein, without realizing it, we grant them a very great advantage over us, by making Nature, with maternal tenderness, accompany them and guide them as by the hand in all the actions and comforts of their life; while us she abandons to chance and to fortune, and to seek by art the things necessary for our preservation, and denies us at the same time the power to attain, by any education and mental straining, the natural resourcefulness of the animals: so that their brutish stupidity surpasses in all conveniences all that our divine intelligence can do.

Truly, by this reckoning, we should be quite right to call her a very unjust stepmother. But this is not so; our organization is not so deformed and disorderly. Nature has universally embraced all her creatures; and there is none that she has not very amply furnished with all powers necessary for the preservation of its being. For these vulgar complaints that I hear men make (as the license of their opinions now raises them above the clouds, and then sinks them to the antipodes) that we are the only animal abandoned naked on the naked earth, tied, bound, having nothing to arm and cover ourselves with except the spoils of others; whereas all other creatures Nature has clothed with shells, husks, bark, hair, wool, spikes, hide, down, feathers, scales, fleece, and silk, according to the need of their being; has armed them with claws, teeth, or horns for attack and defense; and has herself instructed them in what is fit for them—to swim, to run, to fly, to sing—whereas man can neither walk, nor speak, nor eat, nor do anything but cry, without apprenticeship—

> The infant, like a sailor tossed ashore
> By raging seas, lies naked on the earth,
> Speechless, helpless for life, when at his birth
> Nature from out the womb brings him to light.
> He fills the place with wailing, as is right
> For one who through so many woes must pass.
> Yet flocks, herds, savage beasts of every class
> Grow up without the need for any rattle,
> Or for a gentle nurse's soothing prattle;
> They seek no varied clothes against the sky;
> Lastly they need no arms, no ramparts high
> To guard their own—since earth itself and nature
> Amply bring forth all things for every creature
> LUCRETIUS

—those complaints are false, there is a greater equality and a more uniform relationship in the organization of the world. Our skin is provided as adequately as theirs with endurance against the assaults of the weather: witness so many nations who have not yet tried the use of any clothes. Our ancient Gauls wore hardly any clothes; nor do the Irish, our neighbors, under so cold a sky. But we may judge this better by ourselves; for all the parts of the body that we see fit to expose to the wind and air are found fit to endure it: face, feet, hands, legs, shoulders, head, according as custom invites us. For if there is a part of us that is tender and that seems as though it should fear the cold, it should be the stomach, where digestion takes place; our fathers left it uncovered, and our ladies, soft and delicate as they are, sometimes go half bare down to the navel. Nor are the bindings and swaddlings of infants necessary either; and the Lacedaemonian mothers raised their children in complete freedom to move their limbs, without wrapping or binding them. Our weeping is common to most of the other animals; and there are scarcely any who are not observed to complain and wail long after their birth, since it is a demeanor most appropriate to the helplessness that they feel. As for the habit of eating, it is, in us as in them, natural and needing no instruction:

> For each one feels his powers and his needs.
> LUCRETIUS

Who doubts that a child, having attained the strength to feed himself would be able to seek his food? And the earth produces and offers him enough of it for his need, with no other cultivation or artifice; and if not in all weather, neither does she for the beasts: witness the provisions we see the ants and others make for the sterile seasons of the year. These nations that we have just discovered to be so abundantly furnished with food and natural drink, without care or preparation, have now taught us that bread is not our only food, and that without plowing, our mother Nature had provided us in plenty with all we needed; indeed, as seems likely, more amply and richly than she does now that we have interpolated our artifice:

> At first and of her own accord the earth
> Brought forth sleek fruits and vintages of worth,
> Herself gave harvests sweet and pastures fair,
> Which now scarce grow, despite our toil and care,
> And we exhaust our oxen and our men;
> LUCRETIUS

the excess and unruliness of our appetite outstripping all the inventions with which we seek to satisfy it.

As for weapons, we have more that are natural than most other animals, and more varied movements of our limbs; and we get more service out of them, naturally and without lessons. Those who are trained to fight naked are seen to throw themselves into dangers like our own men. If some animals surpass us in this advantage, we surpass many others. And the skill to fortify and protect the body by acquired means, we possess by a natural instinct and precept. As proof that this is so, the elephant sharpens and whets the teeth which he uses in war (for he has special ones for this purpose, which he spares, and does not use at all for his other functions). When bulls go into combat, they spread and toss the dust around them; boars whet their tusks; and the ichneumon,[5] when he is to come to grips with the crocodile, arms his body, coats it, and crusts it all over with mud, well pressed and well

---

[5] A kind of African mongoose, said to be able to kill a crocodile.

kneaded, as with a cuirass. Why shall we not say that it is just as natural to arm ourselves with wood and iron?

As for speech, it is certain that if it is not natural, it is not necessary. Nevertheless, I believe that a child who had been brought up in complete solitude, remote from all association (which would be a hard experiment to make), would have some sort of speech to express his ideas. And it is not credible that Nature has denied us this resource that she has given to many other animals: for what is it but speech, this faculty we see in them of complaining, rejoicing, calling to each other for help, inviting each other to love, as they do by the use of their voice? How could they not speak to one another? They certainly speak to us, and we to them. In how many ways do we not speak to our dogs? And they answer us. We talk to them in another language, with other names, than to birds, hogs, oxen, horses; and we change the idiom according to the species:

> So ants amidst their sable-colored band
> Greet one another, and inquire perchance
> The road each follows, and the prize in hand.
>   DANTE

It seems to me that Lactantius attributes to beasts not only speech but also laughter. And the difference of language that is seen between us, according to the difference of countries, is found also in animals of the same species. Aristotle cites in this connection the various calls of partridges according to the place they are situated in,

> And various birds . . .
> Utter at different times far different cries . . .
> And some change with the changing of the skies
> Their raucous songs.
>   LUCRETIUS

But it is yet to be known what language this child would speak; and what is said about it by conjecture has not much appearance of truth. If they allege to me, against this opinion, that men naturally deaf do not speak at all, I reply that it is not only because they could not be taught speech by ear, but rather because the sense of hearing, of which they are deprived, is related to that of speech, and they hold together by a natural tie: so that what we speak we must speak first to ourselves, and make it ring on our own ears inwardly, before we send it to other ears.

I have said all this to maintain this resemblance that exists to human things, and to bring us back and join us to the majority. We are neither above nor below the rest: all that is under heaven, says the sage, incurs the same law and the same fortune,

> All things are bound by their own chains of fate.
>   LUCRETIUS

There is some difference, there are orders and degrees; but it is under the aspect of one and the same nature:

And all things go their own way, nor forget
Distinctions by the law of nature set.
LUCRETIUS

Man must be constrained and forced into line inside the barriers of this order. The poor wretch is in no position really to step outside them; he is fettered and bound, he is subjected to the same obligation as the other creatures of his class, and in a very ordinary condition, without any real and essential prerogative or preeminence. That which he accords himself in his mind and in his fancy has neither body nor taste. And if it is true that he alone of all the animals has this freedom of imagination and this unruliness in thought that represents to him what is, what is not, what he wants, the false and the true, it is an advantage that is sold him very dear, and in which he has little cause to glory, for from it springs the principal source of the ills that oppress him: sin, disease, irresolution, confusion, despair. . . .

[KNOWLEDGE CANNOT MAKE US HAPPY]

But to return to my subject, we have as our share inconstancy, irresolution, uncertainty, grief, superstition, worry over things to come, even after our life, ambition, avarice, jealousy, envy, unruly, frantic, and untamable appetites, war, falsehood, disloyalty, detraction, and curiosity. Indeed we have strangely overpaid for this fine reason that we glory in, and this capacity to judge and know, if we have bought it at the price of this infinite number of passions to which we are incessantly a prey. Unless we like to make much, as indeed Socrates does, of this notable prerogative over the other animals, that whereas Nature has prescribed to them certain seasons and limits to the pleasures of Venus, she has given us free rein at all hours and occasions.

As with wine for sick men, since it is rarely good and often bad, it is better not to use it at all, than in the hope of a doubtful benefit to incur a manifest risk; so I hardly know whether it would not have been better for the human race if this swift movement of thought, this acumen, this cleverness, which we call reason, had not been given to man at all, since it is a plague to many and salutary only to a few, rather than given so abundantly and so lavishly [Cicero].

What good can we suppose it did Varro and Aristotle to know so many things? Did it exempt them from human discomforts? Were they freed from the accidents that oppress a porter? Did they derive from logic some consolation for the gout? For knowing how this humor lodges in the joints, did they feel it less? Were they reconciled to death for knowing that some nations rejoice in it, and with cuckoldry for knowing that wives are held in common in some region? On the contrary, though they held the first rank in knowledge, one among the Romans, the other among the Greeks, and in the period when knowledge flourished most, we have not for all that heard that they had any particular excellence in their lives; in fact the Greek has a hard time to clear himself of some notable spots in his.

Have they found that sensual pleasure and health are more savory to him who knows astrology and grammar?

Does the illiterate's tool stand less erect?
HORACE

And are shame and poverty less troublesome?

> Disease and weakness you of course will miss,
> Escape both grief and pain, and possibly
> Win longer life, a better destiny.
>
> JUVENAL

I have seen in my time a hundred artisans, a hundred plowmen, wiser and happier than rectors of the university, and whom I would rather resemble. Learning, in my opinion, has a place among things necessary for life, like glory, nobility, dignity, or at best like beauty, riches, and such other qualities which are really useful for it, but remotely, and a little more in fancy than in nature.

We hardly need any more offices, rules, and laws of living, in our community than do the cranes and ants in theirs. And nevertheless we see that they conduct themselves in a very orderly manner without erudition. If man were wise, he would set the true price of each thing according as it was most useful and appropriate for his life.

If anyone will sum us up by our actions and conduct, a greater number of excellent men will be found among the ignorant than among the learned: I mean in every sort of virtue. The old Rome seems to me to have borne men of greater worth, both for peace and for war, than that learned Rome that ruined itself. Even if the rest were exactly equal, at least worth and innocence would remain on the side of the old, for they dwell singularly well with simplicity.

But I leave this subject, which would lead me farther than I would follow. I will add only this, that humility and submissiveness alone can make a good man. The knowledge of his duty should not be left to each man's judgment; it should be prescribed to him, not left to the choice of his reason. Otherwise, judging by the imbecility and infinite variety of our reasons and opinions, we would finally forge for ourselves duties that would set us to eating one another, as Epicurus says. . . .

[KNOWLEDGE CANNOT MAKE US GOOD]

As by simplicity life becomes pleasanter, so also does it become better and more innocent, as I was starting to say a while back. The simple and ignorant, says Saint Paul, raise themselves to heaven, and take possession of it; and we, with all our learning, plunge ourselves into the infernal abyss. I do not stop to consider either Valentinian, a declared enemy of knowledge and letters, or Licinius, Roman emperors both, who called them the poison and plague of any political state; or Mohammed, who, so I have heard, forbade learning to his followers. But the example of the great Lycurgus, and his authority, should certainly have great weight, and the reverence of that divine Lacedaemonian government, so great, so admirable, and so long flourishing in virtue and good fortune without any teaching or practice of letters. Those who return from that new world which was discovered in our fathers' time by the Spaniards can testify to us how much more lawfully and regulatedly these nations live, without magistrates and without law, than ours, where there are more officers and laws than there are other men and actions:

> Their hands are full of motions and petitions,
>   Their pockets stuffed with reams of briefs and writs,
> With powers of attorney, depositions,
>   Decisions, and opinions, and *op. cit.*'s,
> Designed to rob, with maximum efficience,
>   The simple folk of their remaining wits;
> Before, behind, no matter where they turn is
>   A host of lawyers, notaries, attorneys.
>
> ARIOSTO

It is what a Roman senator of the late period said, that their predecessors had a breath stinking of garlic, and a stomach perfumed with a good conscience; and that on the contrary those of his time smelled outwardly of nothing but perfume, though stinking within of every kind of vice. That is to say, so I think, that they had great learning and ability, and a great lack of integrity. Uncouthness, ignorance, simplicity, and crudity are prone to go with innocence; curiosity, subtlety, and learning bring malice in their train; humility, fear, obedience, and amenability (which are the principal qualities for the preservation of human society) require a soul that is open, docile, and with little presumption. . . .

[HUMAN BEINGS HAVE NO KNOWLEDGE]

Yet must I see at last whether it is in the power of man to find what he seeks, and whether that quest that he has been making for so many centuries has enriched him with any new power and any solid truth.

I think he will confess to me, if he speaks in all conscience, that all the profit he has gained from so long a pursuit is to have learned to acknowledge his weakness. The ignorance that was naturally in us we have by long study confirmed and verified.

To really learned men has happened what happens to ears of wheat: they rise high and lofty, heads erect and proud, as long as they are empty; but when they are full and swollen with grain in their ripeness, they begin to grow humble and lower their horns. Similarly, men who have tried everything and sounded everything, having found in that pile of knowledge and store of so many various things nothing solid and firm, and nothing but vanity, have renounced their presumption and recognized their natural condition.

It is what Velleius reproaches Cotta and Cicero for, that they learned from Philo that they had learned nothing.

Pherecydes, one of the Seven Sages, writing to Thales as he was dying, said: "I have ordered my friends, after they have buried me, to bring you my writings. If they satisfy you and the other sages, publish them; if not, suppress them: they contain no certainty that satisfies myself. Nor do I profess to know the truth and to attain it. I uncover things more than I discover them."

The wisest man that ever was,[6] when they asked him what he knew, answered that he knew this much, that he knew nothing. He was verifying

---

[6] Socrates.

what they say, that the greatest part of what we know is the least of those parts that we do not know; that is to say that the very thing we think we know is a part, and a very small part, of our ignorance.

We know things in a dream, says Plato, and we are ignorant of them in reality.

Almost all the ancients have said that nothing can be understood, nothing perceived, nothing known; that our senses are narrow, our minds weak, the course of our life short [Cicero].

As for Cicero himself, who owed all his worth to learning, Valerius says that in his old age he began to lose his esteem for letters. And while he practiced them, it was without obligation to any party, following what seemed probable to him now in one sect, now in another, keeping himself always in Academic doubt. *I must speak, but in such a way as to affirm nothing; I shall search into all things, doubting most of them and mistrusting myself* [Cicero].

I should have too easy a time if I wanted to consider man in his ordinary condition and in the mass; and yet I could do so according to his own rule, which judges the truth not by the weight of votes but by the number. Let us leave the people aside,

> Who waking snore . . .
> Whose life is dead, although they live and see,
>   LUCRETIUS

who are not conscious of themselves, who do not judge themselves, who leave most of their natural faculties idle.

I wish to take man in his highest estate. Let us consider him in that small number of excellent and select men who, having been endowed with fine and particular natural ability, have further strengthened and sharpened it by care, by study, and by art, and have raised it to the highest pitch of wisdom that it can attain. They have fashioned their soul to all directions and all angles, supported and propped it with all the outside assistance that was fit for it, and enriched and adorned it with all they could borrow, for its advantage, from the inside and the outside of the world; it is in them that the utmost height of human nature is found. They have regulated the world with governments and laws; they have instructed it with arts and sciences, and instructed it further by the example of their admirable conduct.

I shall take into account only these people, their testimony, and their experience. Let us see how far they have gone and where they have halted. The infirmities and defects that we shall find in this assembly the world may well boldly acknowledge as its own.

Whoever seeks anything comes to this point: he says either that he has found it, or that it cannot be found, or that he is still in quest of it. All philosophy is divided into these three types. Its purpose is to seek out truth, knowledge, and certainty.

The Peripatetics, Epicureans, Stoics, and others thought they had found it. These established the sciences that we have, and treated them as certain knowledge.

Clitomachus, Carneades, and the Academics despaired of their quest, and judged that truth could not be conceived by our powers. The conclusion of these men was man's weakness and ignorance. This school had the greatest following and the noblest adherents.

Pyrrho and other Skeptics or Epechists—whose doctrines, many of the ancients maintained, were derived from Homer, the Seven Sages, Archilochus, and Euripides, and were held by Zeno, Democritus, Xenophanes—say that they are still in search of the truth. These men judge that those who think they have found it are infinitely mistaken; and that there is also an overbold vanity in that second class that assures us that human powers are not capable of attaining it. For this matter of establishing the measure of our power, of knowing and judging the difficulty of things, is a great and supreme knowledge, of which they doubt that man is capable:

> Whoever thinks that we know nothing does not know
> Whether we know enough to say that this is so.
>
> LUCRETIUS

Ignorance that knows itself, that judges itself and condemns itself, is not complete ignorance: to be that, it must be ignorant of itself. So that the profession of the Pyrrhonians is to waver, doubt, and inquire, to be sure of nothing, to answer for nothing. Of the three functions of the soul, the imaginative, the appetitive, and the consenting, they accept the first two; the last they suspend and keep it ambiguous, without inclination or approbation, however slight, in one direction or the other. . . .

Our speech has its weaknesses and its defects, like all the rest. Most of the occasions for the troubles of the world are grammatical. Our lawsuits spring only from debate over the interpretation of the laws, and most of our wars from the inability to express clearly the conventions and treaties of agreement of princes. How many quarrels, and how important, have been produced in the world by doubt of the meaning of that syllable *Hoc!*[7]

Let us take the sentence that logic itself offers us as the clearest. If you say "It is fine weather," and if you are speaking the truth, then it is fine weather. Isn't that a sure way of speaking? Still it will deceive us. To show this let us continue the example. If you say "I lie," and if you are speaking the truth, then you lie. The art, the reason, the force, of the conclusion of this one are the same as in the other; yet there we are stuck in the mud.

I can see why the Pyrrhonian philosophers cannot express their general conception in any manner of speaking; for they would need a new language. Ours is wholly formed of affirmative propositions, which to them are utterly repugnant; so that when they say "I doubt," immediately you have them by the throat to make them admit that at least they know and are sure of this fact, that they doubt. Thus they have been constrained to take refuge in this comparison from medicine, without which their attitude would be inexplicable: when they declare "I do not know" or "I doubt," they say that this proposition carries itself away with the rest, no more nor less than rhubarb, which expels evil humors and carries itself off with them.

---

[7]Montaigne is referring to the controversy between Catholics and Protestants over transubstantiation, which centered on the meaning of Christ's words *Hoc est corpus meum* ("This is my body").

This idea is more firmly grasped in the form of interrogation: "What do I know?"[8]—the words I bear as a motto, inscribed over a pair of scales. . . .

[WE CANNOT RELY ON OUR SENSES]

This subject has brought me to the consideration of the senses, in which lies the greatest foundation and proof of our ignorance. All that is known, is doubtless known through the faculty of the knower; for since judgment comes from the operation of him who judges, it stands to reason that he performs this operation by his means and will, not by the constraint of others, as would happen if we knew things through the power and according to the law of their own essence.

Now all knowledge makes its way into us through the senses; they are our masters:

> No shorter pathway can persuasion find
> Into the human heart and human mind.
> LUCRETIUS

Knowledge begins through them and is resolved into them.

After all, we would know no more than a stone, if we did not know that there is sound, smell, light, taste, measure, weight, softness, hardness, roughness, color, smoothness, breadth, depth. There are the base and the principles of the whole edifice of our knowledge. And according to some, knowledge is nothing else but sensation. Whoever can force me to contradict the senses has me by the throat; he could not make me retreat any further. The senses are the beginning and the end of human knowledge:

> Our senses, you will find, did first provide
> The idea of truth; they cannot be denied.
> . . . .
> In what then should we place a greater trust
> Than in the senses?
> LUCRETIUS

Attribute to them as little as you can, still you must grant them this, that by way of them and by their mediation proceeds all our instruction. Cicero says that Chrysippus, having tried to disparage the power and strength of the senses, presented himself with arguments to the contrary, and such violent objections, that he could not satisfy them. Whereupon Carneades, who was upholding the opposite side, boasted that he would use the very weapons and words of Chrysippus to combat him, and therefore exclaimed against him: 'O wretched man, your strength has defeated you!"

We cannot conceive of an absurdity more extreme than to maintain that fire does not heat, that light does not illumine, that there is no weight or hardness in iron; these are items of knowledge brought to us by the senses;

---

[8]A reference to the medal Montaigne had struck, with the motto *Que sçay-je?* and an evenly balanced set of scales. See the Introduction to Montaigne.

and man has no belief or knowledge that can compare with this sort for certainty.

The first consideration that I offer on the subject of the senses is that I have my doubts whether man is provided with all the senses of nature. I see many animals that live a complete and perfect life, some without sight, others without hearing; who knows whether we too do not still lack one, two, three, or many other senses? For if any one is lacking, our reason cannot discover its absence. It is the privilege of the senses to be the extreme limit of our perception. There is nothing beyond them that can help us to discover them; no, nor can one sense discover the other:

> Can ears the errors of the eyes detect?
> Touch refute ears, or taste our touch correct?
> Nose confute touch, and eyes in turn prevail?
> LUCRETIUS

Together they all form the farthest limit of our faculties:

> Its function is defined
> To each apart, to each its power assigned.
> LUCRETIUS

It is impossible to make a man who was born blind conceive that he does not see; impossible to make him desire sight and regret its absence. Wherefore we should take no assurance from the fact that our soul is content and satisfied with those senses we have, seeing that it has no means of feeling its malady and imperfection therein, if any there be. It is impossible to say anything to this blind man, by reason, argument, or comparison, that will place in his imagination any apprehension of light, color, and sight. There is nothing further behind that can push that sense into evidence. When we see men blind from birth desire to see, it is not because they understand what they ask: they have learned from us that they lack something, that they have something to desire, which is in us; which they name perfectly well, and its effects and consequences; but nevertheless they do not know what it is, nor do they have a close or distant apprehension of it.

I have seen a gentleman of a good house, born blind, or at least blind from such an age that he does not know what sight is. He understands so little what he lacks, that he uses and employs as we do words appropriate to sight, and applies them in a manner all private and his own. He was presented with a boy, whose godfather he was; taking him in his arms, he said: "My, what a handsome boy! How good it is to see him! What a gay face he has!" He will say like one of us: "This room has a fine view; it is a clear day, the sun is shining bright." There is more; for because hunting, tennis, and shooting are our sports, and he has heard this, he is fond of them and keenly interested in them, and thinks he has the same share in them that we do; he finds excitement and pleasure in them, and yet he takes them in only through his ears. They call to him that there goes a hare when they are in a bit of fine open country where he can spur his horse; and then they tell him later that there is a hare caught; and he is as proud of his catch as he hears the others say they are. The tennis ball he takes in his left hand and strokes with his racket; with the harquebus[9] he shoots at random, and gets his fun by having his men tell him that he is either over or beside the mark.

What do we know about whether mankind is doing something equally foolish for lack of some sense, and whether by this lack the greater part of the face of things is hidden from us? What do we know about whether the difficulties we find in many works of nature come from that? And whether many actions of the animals that exceed our capacity are produced by the operation of some sense that we lack? And whether some of them have by this means a fuller and more complete life than ours?

We grasp an apple by almost all our senses; we find in it redness, smoothness, smell, and sweetness; besides these it may have other properties, like drying up or shrinking, to which we have no sense that corresponds. The properties that we call occult in many things, as that of the magnet to attract iron—is it not likely that there are sensory faculties in nature suitable to judge them and perceive them, and that the lack of such faculties causes our ignorance of the true essence of such things? Perhaps it is some particular sense that reveals to cocks the hours of morning and midnight, and moves them to crow; that teaches hens, before any practice and experience, to fear a sparrow hawk, and not a goose or a peacock, which are bigger creatures; which warns chickens of the quality in the cat that is hostile to them, and not to distrust the dog: to beware of mewing, a rather caressing sound, and not of barking, a harsh and quarrelsome sound; that teaches wasps, ants, and rats always to select the best cheese and the best pear, before having tasted them; and that guides the stag, the elephant, the snake, to the knowledge of a certain herb suitable for their cure.

There is no sense that does not have great dominion, and bring us by its means to know an infinite number of things. If we lacked the understanding of sounds, of harmony.and the voice, this lack would bring inconceivable confusion upon all the rest of our knowledge. For besides what is attached to the proper effect of each sense, how many arguments, consequences, and conclusions we draw in other things by the comparison of one sense with another! Let an intelligent man imagine human nature as produced originally without sight, and think how much ignorance and confusion such a lack would bring him, how much shadow and blindness in our soul: it will be seen from this how important to our knowledge of the truth is the privation of another such sense, or two, or three—if this privation is in us. We have formed a truth by the consultation and concurrence of our five senses, but perhaps we needed the agreement of eight or ten senses, and their contribution, to perceive it certainly and in its essence.

The schools that dispute man's knowledge dispute it principally because of the uncertainty and weakness of our senses; for since all knowledge comes to us by their means and mediation, if they err in the report they make to us, if they corrupt or alter what they carry to us from without, if the light that flows through them into our soul is obscured in passage, we have nothing left to go by. From this extreme difficulty have arisen all these fancies: that each object has in itself all that we find in it; that it has nothing of what

---

[9]A heavy musket, invented in the fifteenth century.

we think we find in it; and this of the Epicureans, that the sun is no bigger than it looks to us:

> Whate'er it is, it has no greater size
> Than what it seems to be, seen by our eyes;
> LUCRETIUS

that the appearances that show a body to be big to him who is near, and smaller to him who is far, are both true,

> Nor grant we therefore that our eyes are blind;
> . . . .
> Blame not on eyes the error of the mind;
> LUCRETIUS

and, boldly, that there is no deception in the senses, that we must submit to their mercy, and seek elsewhere reasons to excuse the difference and contradiction that we find in them, in fact invent any other falsehood or reverie (they go as far as that) rather than accuse the senses.

Timagoras swore that however much he pressed or turned his eyes, he had never seen the light of a candle doubled; and that that appearance came from a defect of the mind, not of the organ.

Of all absurdities the most absurd to the Epicureans is to disavow the power and effect of the senses.

> Hence what the senses see is always true.
> And if our reason cannot well expound
> Why what from near was square, from far is round,
> Although we lack the cause, 'tis better still
> Either appearance to interpret ill,
> Than from our hands to let the obvious go,
> To spurn our primal trust and overthrow
> The bases on which life and safety stay.
> For not alone would reason fail; straightway
> Our very life would fall, unless we dare
> To trust our senses, shun great heights, beware
> Of other similar dangers.
> LUCRETIUS

This desperate and most unphilosophical advice means nothing else than that human knowledge can maintain itself only by unreasonable, mad, and senseless reason; but that still it is better for man, in order to assert himself, to use it and any other remedy, however fantastic, than to admit his necessary stupidity: such a disadvantageous truth! He cannot escape the fact that the senses are the sovereign masters of his knowledge; but they are uncertain and deceivable in all circumstances. It is there that we must fight it out, and if just forces fail us, as they do, use stubbornness, heedlessness, impudence.

In case what the Epicureans say is true, to wit, that we have no knowledge if the appearances of the senses are false; and if what the Stoics say is also true, that the appearances of the senses are so false that they can produce no knowledge for us; we shall conclude, at the expense of these two great dogmatic sects, that there is no knowledge.

As for the error and uncertainty of the operation of the senses, each man can furnish himself with as many examples as he pleases, so ordinary are the mistakes and deceptions that they offer us. At the echo in a valley, the sound of a trumpet seems to come from in front of us, when it comes from a league behind:

> Two distant mountains like as one are seen,
> Though on the sea great distance lies between.
> .   .   .   .
> Astern the hills and meadows seem to fly,
> Which our ship skirts near by . . .
> .   .   .   .
> . . . When in midstream our steed stops short,
> Some power seems to bear his body athwart
> And force him up against the rushing stream.
>
> LUCRETIUS

When rolling a harquebus bullet under the forefinger, the middle finger being entwined over it, we have to force ourselves hard to admit that there is only one, so strongly does our sense represent two to us. For that the senses are many a time masters of reason, and constrain it to receive impressions that it knows and judges to be false, is seen at every turn. I leave aside the sense of touch, whose operations are closer, more vivid and substantial, which, so many times, by the effect of the pain it brings to the body, overthrows all those beautiful Stoical resolutions, and compels the man to cry out at his stomach who has established with all resoluteness this doctrine in his soul, that the colic, like every other malady and pain, is an indifferent thing, not having the power to reduce at all the supreme happiness and felicity in which the sage is lodged by his virtue.

There is no heart so faint that the sound of our drums and trumpets will not warm it, or so hard that the sweetness of music will not awaken it and caress it; no soul so crabbed as not to feel touched by some reverence on contemplating the somber vastness of our churches, the diversity of ornaments, and the order of our ceremonies, and on hearing the devotional sound of our organs and the harmony, so solemn and religious, of our voices. Even those who enter with disdain feel a certain shiver in their heart, and a certain awe, which makes them distrust their opinion.

As for me, I do not consider myself strong enough to listen sedately to verses of Horace or Catullus sung by an adequate voice from a young and beautiful mouth. And Zeno was right to say that the voice was the flower of beauty.

Someone tried to make me believe that a man whom all we Frenchmen know had overimpressed me by reciting to me some verses he had composed; that they were not the same on paper as in the air, and that my eyes would judge them contrary to my ears, so much influence utterance has in giving value and style to the works that come into its mercy. In which connection Philoxenus was not too choleric when, hearing someone giving a bad tone to some composition of his, he began to stamp on and break some tiles that belonged to the offender, saying: "I disrupt what is yours as you corrupt what is mine."

For what reason did even those who had themselves put to death by their own sure resolve turn away their face in order not to see the stroke that they were having dealt them? And why cannot those who for their health desire and order someone to cut into them and cauterize them endure the sight of the preparations, instruments, and operations of the surgeon, since sight is to have no participation in this pain? Are these not fit examples to prove the authority that the senses have over the reason?

No matter if we are aware that these tresses are borrowed from a page or a lackey, that this rosy complexion is a product of Spain, and that this whiteness and smoothness comes from the ocean sea; still sight must compel us to find the object more lovely and agreeable for it, against all reason. For in this there is nothing of the lady's own:

> Jewels and gold hide flaws; we are tricked by art;
> The girl is of herself the smallest part.
> Oft in all this you ask where your love lies:
> By this Gorgon shield rich love deceives the eyes.
> OVID

How much power the poets ascribe to the senses, who make Narcissus madly in love with his own reflection—

> All he admires for which he is admired;
> Unwitting, loves himself; yearned for, he yearns;
> Seeking, is sought; with flame self-kindled burns
> OVID

—and Pygmalion's understanding so troubled by the impression of the sight of his ivory statue, that he loves and serves it as though it were alive:

> Kisses he gives, and thinks they are returned;
> Pursues and holds, and thinks the flesh gives way
> Beneath his fingers, fears a mark will stay.
> OVID

Put a philosopher in a cage of thin iron wire in large meshes, and hang it from the top of the towers of Notre Dame of Paris: he will see by evident reason that it is impossible for him to fall, and yet (unless he is used to the trade of the steeplejacks) he cannot keep the sight of this extreme height from terrifying and paralyzing him. For we have trouble enough feeling secure in the galleries that are in our steeples, if they are wrought with openwork, even though they are of stone. There are some who cannot even bear the thought of them. Lay a beam between these two towers of such width as we need to walk on: there is no philosophical wisdom of such great firmness that it can give us courage to walk on it as we should if it were on the ground.

I have often experienced this in our mountains on this side of the border (and yet I am one of those who are only moderately frightened at such things): that I could not endure the sight of that infinite depth without a shiver and a trembling of the back of my legs and thighs, even though I was fully my own length away from the actual edge, and could not have fallen unless I had conveyed myself purposely into danger. I have also noticed there that whatever the height might be, provided that in the side some tree or jutting rock is present to support our sight a little and break it up, this relieves us and gives us assurance, as if it were a thing from which in case of a fall we could get help; but that sheer and unbroken precipices we cannot even look at without vertigo: *such that we cannot look down without dizziness both of eyes and of mind* [Livy]; which is an evident imposture of our sight.

That fine philosopher put out his eyes[10] to relieve his soul of the distractions that it received from them, and to be able to philosophize in greater freedom.

But on that score he should also have had his ears stopped up, which Theophrastus says are the most dangerous instrument we have for receiving violent impressions to disturb and alter us; and he should in short have deprived himself of all the other senses, that is to say of his life and his being. For they all have this power to command our reason and our soul. *Again it often happens that our mind is struck more vehemently by some sight, some depth of voice, some songs; often again by care and fear* [Cicero].

The doctors hold that there are certain temperaments that are stirred even to fury by some sounds and instruments. I have seen some who could not hear a bone gnawed under their table without losing patience; and there is hardly a man who is not disturbed by that harsh and piercing noise made by files scraping on iron; just as many, on hearing someone chewing nearby, or someone talking who has the passages of his nose or throat stopped up, are moved to the point of anger and hatred. That piping prompter of Gracchus, who softened, hardened, or directed his master's voice whenever he made a harangue at Rome, what use was he, if the movement and quality of the sound had not the power to move and alter the judgment of the audience? Truly there is good reason to make so much of the firmness of that fine faculty,[11] that lets itself be manipulated and altered by the accidental movements of so light a wind!

This same deception that the senses convey to our understanding they receive in their turn. Our soul at times takes a like revenge; they compete in lying and deceiving each other. What we see and hear when stirred with anger, we do not hear as it is:

> A double sun appears, and twin cities of Thebes.
> VIRGIL

The object that we love seems to us more beautiful than it is—

> Thus women oft we see, ugly and bent,
> Receive men's love, and honors eminent
> LUCRETIUS

---

[10] This story was told, probably falsely, of Democritus.
[11] The judgment.

—and uglier the one that we loathe. To a man vexed and afflicted the brightness of the day seems darkened and gloomy. Our senses are not only altered, but often completely stupefied by the passions of the soul. How many things we see which we do not notice if our mind is occupied elsewhere!

> Even in plain things you can plainly see,
> Unless you pay attention, they will be
> As though remote in time, or far away.
>   LUCRETIUS

It seems as though the soul draws the powers of the senses inward and occupies them. Thus both the inside and the outside of man is full of weakness and falsehood.

Those who have compared our life to a dream were perhaps more right than they thought. When we dream, our soul lives, acts, exercises all her faculties, neither more nor less than when she is awake; but if more loosely and obscurely, still surely not so much so that the difference is as between night and bright daylight; rather as between night and shade. There she sleeps, here she slumbers: more and less. It is always darkness, and Cimmerian darkness.

Sleeping we are awake, and waking asleep. I do not see so clearly in sleep; but my wakefulness I never find pure and cloudless enough. Moreover sleep in its depth sometimes puts dreams to sleep. But our wakefulness is never so awake as to purge and properly dissipate reveries, which are the dreams of the waking, and worse than dreams.

Since our reason and our soul accept the fancies and opinions which arise in it while sleeping, and authorize the actions of our dreams with the same approbation as they do those of the day, why do we not consider the possibility that our thinking, our acting, may be another sort of dreaming, and our waking another kind of sleep?

If the senses are our first judges, it is not ours alone that must be consulted, for in this faculty the animals have as much right as we have, or more. It is certain that some have hearing keener than man's, others sight, others smell, others touch or taste. Democritus said that the gods and the animals had much more perfect sensitive faculties than man.

Now between the effects of their senses and ours, the difference is extreme. Our saliva cleans and dries up our wounds; it kills a snake:

> So great the distance and the difference here,
> That one man's food others as poison fear.
> By man's saliva touched, snakes oft decay,
> And bite themselves to death.
>   LUCRETIUS

What property shall we attribute to saliva? According to us, or according to the snake? By which of the two points of view shall we prove its real essence, which we are seeking? Pliny says that there are in the Indies certain seahares which are poison to us and we to them, so that by a mere touch we kill them. Which is really poisonous, man or the fish? Which are we to believe, the fish about man, or man about the fish?

A certain quality of air infects man, which does not harm the ox; another infects the ox, which does not harm man. Which of the two, in truth and in nature, is the pestilential quality?

Those who have jaundice see all things as yellowish and paler than we do:

> Moreover, all that jaundiced people see
> Becomes pale yellow.
>   LUCRETIUS

Those who have that malady that the doctors call hyposphagma, which is a suffusion of blood under the skin, see everything as red and bloody. These humors which thus change the operations of our sight, how do we know but that they predominate in animals and are the ordinary thing with them? For we see some that have yellow eyes like our sufferers from jaundice, others that have them red and bloodshot. It is probable that to them the color of objects appears different than to us. Which of the two is the true judgment? For it is not said that the essence of things is referred to man alone. Hardness, whiteness, depth, and bitterness concern the service and knowledge of the animals as well as ours; nature has given to them the use of these as well as to us.

When we press our eye, we perceive the bodies that we are looking at as longer and more extended. Many animals have an eye thus pressed. So this lengthiness is perhaps the real shape of this body, not that which our eyes assign to it in their ordinary position. If we squeeze the eye from below, things seem double to us:

> Double the lights of lamps, flowering with flame,
> Double the face of man, his body twain.
>   LUCRETIUS

If our ears are stopped with anything, or our passages of hearing constricted, we receive the sound otherwise than we ordinarily do. The animals that have hairy ears, or that have only a very tiny hole in place of an ear consequently do not hear what we hear, and receive the sound differently.

We see at festivals and in theaters that when we hold up a pane tinted with some color against the light of the torches, everything in the place appears to us green, or yellow, or violet:

> In our great theaters this oft is done
> By veils of yellow, red, or rust, which run
> From poles and timbers, billowing but stretched tight.
> They dye the assembly with their tinted light,
> And on the stage, on statues row on row
> Of gods and parents, make their colors flow.
>   LUCRETIUS

It is likely that the eyes of animals, which we see are of different colors, make bodies appear to them as matching their eyes.

To judge the action of the senses, then, we should first of all be in agreement with the animals, and second, among ourselves. Which we are not in the least; and we get into disputes at every turn because one man hears, sees, or tastes something differently from someone else; and we dispute about the diversity of the images that the senses bring us as much as about anything else. By the ordinary rule of nature, a child hears, sees, and tastes otherwise than a man of thirty, and he otherwise than a sexagenarian.

The senses are in some people more obscure and dim, in others more open and acute. We receive things in one way and another, according to what we are and what they seem to us. Now since our seeming is so uncertain and controversial, it is no longer a miracle if we are told that we can admit that snow appears white to us, but that we cannot be responsible for proving that it is so of its essence and in truth; and, with this starting point shaken, all the knowledge in the world necessarily goes by the board.

What of the fact that our senses interfere with each other? A painting seems to the eye to be in relief, to the touch it seems flat. Shall we say that musk is agreeable or not, which rejoices our sense of smell and offends our taste? There are herbs and unguents suitable for one part of the body which injure another. Honey is pleasant to the taste, unpleasant to the sight. As for those rings which are cut in the form of feathers and are called in heraldry feathers without ends, there is no eye that can discern their width and that can defend itself against this illusion, that on one side they grow wider, and narrower and tapering on the other, even when you roll them around your finger; however, to the touch they seem equal in width and everywhere alike.

Those persons who, to enhance their voluptuousness, in ancient times used mirrors made to enlarge and magnify the object they reflect, so that the members which they were to put to work should please them the more by this ocular growth: to which of the two senses did they give the victory, to the sight which showed them these members stout and long as they liked, or to the touch which showed them small and contemptible?

Is it our senses that lend the object these differing qualities, and do the objects nevertheless have only one? As we see in the bread we eat: it is only bread, but our use makes of it bones, blood, flesh, hair, and nails:

> As food, dispersed through all our members, dies,
> And other substance of itself supplies.
>
> LUCRETIUS

The moisture that the root of a tree sucks up becomes trunk, leaf, and fruit; and the air, being but one, by being applied to a trumpet is diversified into a thousand kinds of sounds. Is it our senses, I say, which likewise fashion these objects out of various qualities, or do they really have them so? And in the face of this doubt, what can we decide about their real essence?

Moreover, since the accidents of illnesses, madness, or sleep make things appear to us otherwise than they appear to healthy people, wise men, and waking people, is it not likely that our normal state and our natural disposition can also assign to things an essence corresponding to our condition, and accommodate them to us, as our disordered states do? And that our health is as capable of giving them its own appearance as sickness? Why should the temperate man not have some vision of things related to himself, like the intemperate man, and likewise imprint his own character on them?

The jaded man assigns the insipidity to the wine; the healthy man, the savor; the thirsty man, the relish.

Now, since our condition accommodates things to itself and transforms them according to itself, we no longer know what things are in truth; for nothing comes to us except falsified and altered by our senses. When the compass, the square, and the ruler are off, all the proportions drawn from them, all the buildings erected by their measure, are also necessarily imperfect and defective. The uncertainty of our senses makes everything they produce uncertain:

> As in a building, if the rule is false,
> If a bent square gives verticals untrue,
> And if the level is at all askew,
> Then all must be defective and at fault,
> Forward or backward leaning, lame and halt;
> Some part already seems about to fall;
> Then, from those first mistakes, down tumbles all.
> Thus any reasoning of yours on things
> Must needs be false, that from false senses springs.
>   LUCRETIUS

Furthermore, who shall be fit to judge these differences? As we say in disputes about religion that we need a judge not attached to either party, free from preference and passion, which is impossible among Christians, so it is in this. For if he is old, he cannot judge the sense perception of old age, being himself a party in this dispute; if he is young, likewise; healthy, likewise; likewise sick, asleep, or awake. We would need someone exempt from all these qualities, so that with an unprejudiced judgment he might judge of these propositions as of things indifferent to him; and by that score we would need a judge that never was.

To judge the appearances that we receive of objects, we would need a judicatory instrument; to verify this instrument, we need a demonstration; to verify the demonstration, an instrument: there we are in a circle.

Since the senses cannot decide our dispute, being themselves full of uncertainty, it must be reason that does so. No reason can be established without another reason: there we go retreating back to infinity.

Our conception is not itself applied to foreign objects, but is conceived through the mediation of the senses; and the senses do not comprehend the foreign object, but only their own impressions. And thus the conception and semblance we form is not of the object, but only of the impression and effect made on the sense; which impression and the object are different things. Wherefore whoever judges by appearances judges by something other than the object.

And as for saying that the impressions of the senses convey to the soul the quality of the foreign objects by resemblance, how can the soul and understanding make sure of this resemblance, having of itself no communication with foreign objects? Just as a man who does not know Socrates, seeing his portrait, cannot say that it resembles him.

Now if anyone should want to judge by appearances anyway, to judge by all appearances is impossible, for they clash with one another by their contradictions and discrepancies, as we see by experience. Shall some selected appearances rule the others? We shall have to verify this selection by another selection, the second by a third; and thus it will never be finished.

[EVERYTHING, EXCEPT GOD, IS IN CONSTANT CHANGE]

Finally, there is no existence that is constant, either of our being or of that of objects. And we, and our judgment, and all mortal things go on flowing and rolling unceasingly. Thus nothing certain can be established about one thing by another, both the judging and the judged being in continual change and motion.

We have no communication with being, because every human nature is always midway between birth and death, offering only a dim semblance and shadow of itself, and an uncertain and feeble opinion. And if by chance you fix your thought on trying to grasp its essence, it will be neither more nor less than if someone tried to grasp water: for the more he squeezes and presses what by its nature flows all over, the more he will lose what he was trying to hold and grasp. Thus, all things being subject to pass from one change to another, reason, seeking a real stability in them, is baffled, being unable to apprehend anything stable and permanent; because everything is either coming into being and not yet fully existent, or beginning to die before it is born.

Plato said that bodies never had existence, but did have birth; thinking that Homer had made the Ocean father of the gods, and Thetis mother, to show us that all things are in perpetual flux, change, and variation—an opinion common to all the philosophers before his time, as he says, except Parmenides alone, who denied things movement, on whose power he sets great store. Pythagoras thought that all matter is flowing and sliding. The Stoics, that there is no present time, and that what we call present is only the juncture and meeting of the future and the past. Heraclitus, that never had a man entered the same river twice.

Epicharmus, that he who once borrowed money does not owe it now; and that he who last night was invited to come to dine this morning, today comes uninvited, seeing that he and his hosts are no longer themselves: they have become others. And that no mortal substance can be found twice in the same state; for by the suddenness and nimbleness of its change, it is now dissipated, now reassembled; it comes, and then goes. So that what is beginning to be born never arrives at the perfection of being; forasmuch as this birth is never completed, and never stops as being at an end, but from the seed onward goes on ever changing and shifting from one thing into another. As from human seed is made first in the mother's womb a formless fruit, then a fully formed infant; then, outside the womb, an infant at the breast; afterward it becomes a boy; then in turn a youth; then a grown man; then an older man; finally a decrepit old man. So that the subsequent age and generation is always undoing and destroying the preceding one:

> Time alters all the nature of the world;
> From one state to another all must change;
> Nothing remains itself, but all things range;
> Nature modifies all and changes all.
>
>   LUCRETIUS

And then we stupidly fear one kind of death, when we have already passed and are still passing through so many others. For not only, as Heraclitus used to say, is the death of fire the generation of air, and the death of air the generation of water; but even more obviously we can see it in ourselves. Our prime dies and passes when old age comes along, and youth ends in the prime of the grown man, childhood in youth, and infancy in childhood. And yesterday dies in today, and today will die in tomorrow, and there is nothing that abides and is always the same.

For, to prove that this is so, if we always remain one and the same, how is it that we rejoice now in one thing, and now in another? How is it that we love opposite things or hate them, praise them or blame them? How do we have different affections, no longer retaining the same feeling within the same thought? For it is not plausible that we take up different passions without changing; and what suffers change does not remain one and the same, and if it is not one and the same, it also *is* not; but together with its *being the same*, it also changes its simple *being*, from one thing always becoming another. And consequently the senses of nature are mistaken and lie, taking what appears for what is, for want of really knowing what it is that *is*.

But then what really is? That which is eternal: that is to say, what never had birth, nor will ever have an end; to which time never brings any change. For time is a mobile thing, which appears as in a shadow, together with matter, which is ever running and flowing, without ever remaining stable or permanent. To which belong the words *before* and *after,* and *has been* or *will be,* which at the very first sight show very evidently that time is not a thing that *is;* for it would be a great stupidity and a perfectly apparent falsehood to say that that *is* which is not yet in being, or which already has ceased to be. And as for these words, *present, immediate, now,* on which it seems that we chiefly found and support our understanding of time, reason discovering this immediately destroys it; for she at once splits and divides it into future and past, as though wanting to see it necessarily divided in two.

The same thing happens to nature that is measured, as to time that measures it. For there is nothing in it either that abides or is stable; but all things in it are either born, or being born, or dying. For which reason it would be a sin to say of God, who is the only one that *is,* that he *was* or *will be.* For those terms represent declinings, transitions, or vicissitudes of what cannot endure or remain in being. Wherefore we must conclude that God alone *is*—not at all according to any measure of time, but according to an eternity immutable and immobile, not measured by time or subject to any decline; before whom there is nothing, nor will there be after, nor is there anything more new or more recent; but one who really is—who by one single *now* fills the *ever;* and there is nothing that really is but he alone—nor can we say "He has been," or "He will be"—without beginning and without end.

To this most religious conclusion of a pagan I want to add only this remark of a witness of the same condition,[12] for an ending to this long and boring discourse, which would give me material without end: "O what a vile and abject thing is man," he says, "if he does not raise himself above humanity!" That is a good statement and a useful desire, but equally absurd. For to make the handful bigger than the hand, the armful bigger than the arm, and to hope to straddle more than the reach of our legs, is impossible and unnatural. Nor can man raise himself above himself and humanity; for he can see only with his own eyes, and seize only with his own grasp.

He will rise, if God by exception lends him a hand; he will rise by abandoning and renouncing his own means, and letting himself be raised and uplifted by purely celestial means.

It is for our Christian faith, not for his Stoical virtue, to aspire to that divine and miraculous metamorphosis.

Miguel de Cervantes Saavedra
(1547–1616)

Don Quixote is one of the greatest works of art in Western literature, but in a sense it is surprising that it should have been a work of art at all. It began its life as a humble parody of contemporary popular literature, written by an elderly failed playwright in a more or less desperate attempt to make money, possibly even as he lay in prison for shortages in his accounts as a petty government official. Cervantes may have conceived of the total work in all its complexity and grandeur from the very beginning, but it seems more likely that even he was surprised at the way the work developed, from an unpretentious extended joke to an almost mythic narrative. Growing from roots deep in the popular culture of his time, it reached the loftiest heights of speculation about human nature.

Miguel de Cervantes Saavedra was born in 1547, the fourth of seven children of an impoverished physician. During Miguel's childhood the family moved from one village to another to flee from creditors. By 1564, when he was sixteen, the family had settled in Seville, where Miguel was enrolled in a Jesuit school; he seems later to have studied for a time at the University of Salamanca. Any hopes he may have had for an academic career, however, were blasted when he got involved, at the age of twenty-one, in a duel within the precincts of the royal palace in Madrid. The royal court sentenced him to lose his right hand and be exiled for ten years; Cervantes fled to Italy to escape the execution of the sentence.

He was not to return to Spain for twelve years, and those years were filled with hardships and adventures more spectacular than any in the romances he was to parody in *Don Quixote*. After a brief period of service in Rome in the retinue of the cardinal-elect Giulio Acquaviva, he enlisted in the Spanish forces of the Holy League opposing Turkish control of the Mediterranean. His first engagement was the famous Battle of Lepanto. Cervantes was on

---

[12] The Stoic philosopher Seneca (4 B.C.–A.D. 65).

board a ship called the *Marquesa* when the battle began, sick with a fever and confined to his bunk. Despite his condition, he immediately asked to be placed in the most dangerous position and fought gallantly throughout the battle. In the action, he received two shots in the chest and his left hand was shattered; he was never to recover full use of it. Cervantes received an increase in pay for his bravery and a letter of commendation from his commander, Don John of Austria, brother of King Philip II. After his convalescence, he spent four more years in the army, campaigning in Sardinia, Naples, and southern Italy.

Finally, in 1575, Cervantes set sail for Spain again in the company of his brother Rodrigo, who had joined the colors at the same time as Cervantes. Off the coast of southern France, the ship was attacked by pirates and captured, and everyone on board was carried off to Algiers to be sold as slaves. Cervantes remained in slavery for five years, conducting himself with the utmost gallantry. Four times he attempted to organize a general rising among the 24,000 Christian slaves in Algiers. All these attempts failed, and each time Cervantes took full responsibility, in spite of the potential penalty of death by torture. The Dey of Algiers, Hassan Pacha, each time pardoned him, however, since he privately admired Cervantes' courage. Rodrigo was ransomed comparatively early by his family back in Spain, but Cervantes' ransom price was much higher because of the letter of commendation to the Spanish king his captors found in his possession. He was not ransomed until 1580, half of the money coming from his hardpressed family and the other half from sympathetic Spanish residents of Algiers.

Cervantes was thirty-three when he finally returned to Spain. He was crippled and without a job; his family was deeply in debt. Don John was by now dead, and since his memory was hated by the king, Cervantes could not use his commendation to get preferment. He spent the next twenty-five years trying desperately to earn a meager living. He wrote a number of plays, none notably successful. During his theatrical days he fell in love with an actress, Ana Franca de Rojas. They had a child, Isabel, whom Cervantes was left to rear when Ana deserted him. In 1584, at the age of thirty-seven, he married a nineteen-year-old girl, Catalina de Palacios y Salazar Vozmediano; he then had to support a household consisting of his wife, Isabel, his mother, his two sisters, and his widowed mother-in-law. He finally succeeded in getting a government post as a traveling agent charged with requisitioning supplies for the Invincible Armada, the massive fleet that Philip was preparing to launch against England in 1588. As a "commissary," he not only had to face angry mobs of villagers who resented the army's appropriation of their goods but had to deal also with a government bureaucracy that at one point was two years behind with his salary. Cervantes was twice imprisoned for shortages in his accounts, owing to a combination of his superiors' own chaotic records, an untimely bank failure, and doubtless his own inadequacies as a bookkeeper. There is a tradition, based on an ambiguous passage in the Prologue to Book I of *Don Quixote* (the story was "just what might be begotten in a prison, where every discomfort is lodged and every dismal noise has its dwelling"), that he began his great novel in the prison at Seville in 1597.

However this may be, soon after his release Cervantes was hard at work on *Don Quixote,* which was first published in 1605, the year in which his contemporary Shakespeare produced *King Lear.* Cervantes' book was an immediate best-seller; it went through a number of printings the first year and was very promptly translated into French, Italian, and other European languages. Its success brought Cervantes little except the satisfaction of fame; he received no royalties beyond the small initial sum paid him by the publisher.

From the time the first part was published, Cervantes had planned a continuation, but it did not appear for ten years. In 1614, he had written fifty-nine chapters of the sequel when he learned that a pirated continuation had been published by one Alonso Fernandez de Avellaneda. Furious he rushed through the ending of Part II, incorporating in the part he had already finished an attack upon the "false Quixote." Part II was also successful, but again it did little to relieve the author's chronic poverty. Aged and ill, he spent the last two years of his life finishing *Persiles and Sigismunda*, an episodic romance he had begun in 1609. (It was published posthumously.) In the dedication to this work, written on his deathbed to his patron the Conde de Lemos, he wrote the famous lines, adapted from an old ballad, "With one foot in the stirrup, and in the anguish of death, My Lord, I write to thee." He died on April 23, 1616; ten days later in England, Shakespeare died, also on April 23 (since the English calendar was still unreformed).

Don Quixote is a long novel, one of the longest ever written, but it is not a word too long. An abridgment can only suggest the cumulative effect of the book's movement from primitive burlesque to the mysteriously moving climax. At the heart of the novel are the mad knight himself, his common-sensical squire Sancho, and their gradually unfolding relationship. Quixote and Sancho are inseparable, bound together like spirit and flesh as are their fictional descendants Sherlock Holmes and Dr. Watson, Stephen Dedalus and Leopold Bloom in Joyce's *Ulysses,* and Didi and Gogo in Beckett's *Waiting for Godot.* The division is not absolute: Quixote has his earthy side, and it is Sancho who clings to a dream of being governor of an island. It is not Sancho, finally, who represents the claims of unimaginative reality, but the barber and the curate, guardians of flesh and spirit in the everyday world in their respective roles as bleeder and spiritual advisor. Similarly, it is not Don Quixote himself who represents dreams kicked loose from all contact with the earth, but the romances with which he has addled himself. Quixote and Sancho are not allegorical figures but real human beings, each torn between dream and reality. The novel traces their profound, moving, and richly comic negotiation with each other. This negotiation consists of the gradual "Sanchification" of Quixote and the "Quixotification" of Sancho; the Knight moves from a world of pure delusion to a vision of real life ennobled by idealism, while Sancho begins to see the substantial world through the eyes of his master, as touched by the dream. By the end of the novel, all hope of his island gone, Sancho still longs for the quest: "Up with you this instant, out of your bed! . . . Who knows but we may find Lady Dulcinea behind a hedge, disenchanted and as fresh as a daisy!"

As, for his protagonists, Cervantes draws upon the most fundamental of human relationships, so for his plot he turns to the most basic of narratives, the journey. The key to all the great quest stories is the goal of the quest. Odysseus, on his journey home, is in quest of Ithaca and Penelope, the world of ordinary life after the heroic but distorted world of military action. Dante, in his dream journey through the afterlife, seeks to leave the Dark Wood of worldly confusion and find the security of God's holy order. Quixote's quest remains in the Dark Wood on this earth: the dusty and sterile landscape of La Mancha, the emblem of a modern world from which it seems all glory has fled. His quest, literally for chivalric adventure, is more fundamentally for the spark of imagination that redeems ordinary life. And ultimately he finds this spark, not in absurd romances but within himself.

FURTHER READING *(prepared by W.J.R.):* Melveena McKendrick s biography *Cervantes,* 1980, is a good introduction for the general reader. Manuel Duran's *Cervantes,* 1974, a somewhat more succinct biography, contains a good introductory chapter on Spanish culture in Cervantes' time and includes a long discussion of *Don Quixote.* An excellent evaluation of Cervantes as a critical theorist can be found in E. C. Riley's *Cervantes' Theory of the Novel,* 1962, which places Cervantes' ideas in the literary context of his time and discusses such topics as structural unity, verisimilitude, and the function of history. Riley's later, more comprehensive study, *Don Quixote,* 1986, is an excellent historical and critical analysis of the work. Cervantes' role in the development of the novel is addressed in Michael McKeon, *The Origins of the English Novel, 1600 to 1740,* 1987, and in Stephen Gilman, *The Novel According to Cervantes,* 1989. Diverse critical approaches are represented in *Cervantes: A Collection of Critical Essays,* ed. Lowry Nelson, Jr., 1969. This volume includes Erich Auerbach's "The Enchanted Dulcinea" and Thomas Mann's "Voyage with Don Quixote." The essays on *Don Quixote* gathered in the Norton Critical Edition, ed. Joseph R. Jones and Kenneth Douglas, 1981, are also well selected. Ruth El Saffar's *Distance and Control in "Don Quixote,"* 1975, explores a wide variety of narrative techniques employed by Cervantes, concentrating on the dynamics of role switching by the characters. John C. Weiger's *The Individuated Self,* 1979, distinguishes "individuation" from individualism in an examination of personal freedom in *Don Quixote* and is interesting on the emergence of self-knowledge in the novel. John J. Allen's *Don Quixote: Hero or Fool?: A Study in Narrative Techniques,* 1969, discusses stylistic devices, levels of fiction, and the relationship between author, reader, and character. The subject of chivalry is the starting point for a provocative study in Howard Mancing's *The Chivalric World of Don Quijote: Style, Structure, and Narrative Technique,* 1982.

DON QUIXOTE

Translated by Walter Starkie

from PART I

CHAPTER I

Which tells of the quality and manner of life of the famous gentleman Don Quixote of La Mancha

At a village of La Mancha, whose name I do not wish to remember,[1] there lived a little while ago one of those gentlemen who are wont to keep a lance in the rack, an old buckler, a lean horse, and a swift greyhound. His stew

---

[1] Cervantes was purposely vague in describing Don Quixote's birthplace. An old Spanish ballad begins "At a village in La Mancha." (Notes are adapted and expanded from those of the translator.)

had more beef than mutton in it and most nights he ate a hodgepodge, pickled and cold. Lentil soup on Fridays, "tripe and trouble" on Saturdays,[2] and an occasional pigeon as an extra delicacy on Sundays consumed three quarters of his income. The remainder was spent on a jerkin of fine puce, velvet breeches, and slippers of the same stuff for holidays, and a suit of good, honest homespun for weekdays. His family consisted of a housekeeper about forty, a niece not yet twenty, and a lad who served him both in the field and at home and could saddle the horse or use the pruning knife. Our gentleman was about fifty years of age, of a sturdy constitution, but wizened and gaunt-featured, an early riser and a devotee of the chase. They say that his surname was Quixada or Quesada (for on this point the authors who have written on this subject differ), but we may reasonably conjecture that his name was Quixana. This, however, has very little to do with our story; enough that in its telling we swerve not a jot from the truth. You must know that the abovementioned gentleman in his leisure moments (which was most of the year) gave himself up with so much delight and gusto to reading books of chivalry that he almost entirely neglected the exercise of the chase and even the management of his domestic affairs. Indeed his craze for this kind of literature became so extravagant that he sold many acres of arable land to purchase books of knight-errantry, and he carried off to his house as many as he could possibly find. Above all, he preferred those written by the famous Feliciano de Silva[3] because of the clarity of his writing and his intricate style, which made him value those books more than pearls, especially when he read of those courtships and letters of challenge that knights sent to ladies, often containing expressions such as: "The reason for your unreasonable treatment of my reason so enfeebles my reason that I have reason to complain of your beauty." And again: "The high heavens, which with your divinity divinely fortify you with stars, make you the deserver of the desert that is deserved by your greatness." These and similar rhapsodies bewildered the poor gentleman's understanding, for he racked his brain day and night to unbowel their meaning, which not even Aristotle himself could have done if he had been raised from the dead for that very purpose. He was not quite convinced of the number of wounds that Don Belianís gave and received in battle, for he considered that however skillful the surgeons that cured him may have been, the worthy knight's face and body must have been bedizened with scars and scabs. Nevertheless he praised the author for concluding his book with the promise of endless adventure, and many times he felt inclined to take up his pen and finish it off himself, as it is there promised. He doubtless would have done so, and successfully too, had he not been diverted by other plans and purposes of greater moment. He often debated with the curate of the village—a man of learning, a graduate of Sigüenza—on the relative merits of Palmerin of England and Amadis of Gaul. But Master Nicholas, the village barber, affirmed that no one could be compared with the Knight of the Sun and that if, indeed, any could be matched with him, it was Don Galaor, the brother of Amadis of Gaul, for he had a nature adapted to every whim

---

[2] Spaniards ate meagerly on Saturdays, in commemoration of a victory over the Moors in 1212.

[3] A sixteenth-century writer of romances, famous for *Don Florisel de Niquea* (1532), from which the following quotation is taken.

of fortune; he was not so namby-pamby and whimpering a knight as his brother, and as for valor, he was in every respect his equal.

In short, he so immersed himself in those romances that he spent whole days and nights over his books; and thus with little sleeping and much reading, his brains dried up to such a degree that he lost the use of his reason. His imagination became filled with a host of fancies he had read in his books— enchantments, quarrels, battles, challenges, wounds, courtships, loves, tortures, and many other absurdities. So true did all this phantasmagoria from books appear to him that in his mind he accounted no history in the world more authentic. He would say that the Cid Ruiz Díaz was a very gallant knight, but not to be compared with the Knight of the Burning Sword, who with a single thwart blow cleft asunder a brace of hulking, blustering giants. He was better pleased with Bernardo del Carpio, because at Roncesvalles he had slain Roland the Enchanted by availing himself of the stratagem Hercules had employed on Antaeus, the son of the Earth, whom he squeezed to death in his arms. He praised the giant Morgante, for he alone was courteous and well bred among that monstrous brood puffed up with arrogance and insolence. Above all, he admired Rinaldo of Montalbán,[4] especially when he saw him sallying out of his castle to plunder everyone who came his way, and when beyond the seas he made off with the idol of Mohammed which, as history says, was of solid gold. But he would have parted with his housekeeper and his niece into the bargain for the pleasure of rib roasting the traitor Galalón.[5]

At last, having lost his wits completely, he stumbled upon the oddest fancy that ever entered a madman's brain. He believed that it was necessary, both for his own honor and for service of the state, that he should become a knight-errant, roaming through the world with his horse and armor in quest of adventures and practicing all that had been performed by the knights-errant of whom he had read. He would follow their life, redressing all manner of wrongs and exposing himself to continual dangers, and at last, after concluding his enterprises, he would win everlasting honor and renown. The poor gentleman fancied himself already crowned emperor of Trebizond for the valor of his arm. And thus excited by these agreeable delusions, he hastened to put his plans into operation.

The first thing he did was to refurbish some rusty armor that had belonged to his great grandfather and had lain moldering in a corner. He cleaned it and repaired it as best he could, but he found one great defect: instead of a complete helmet there was just the simple morion.[6] This want he ingeniously remedied by making a kind of visor out of pasteboard, and when it was fitted to the morion, it looked like an entire helmet. It is true that in order to test its strength and see if it was swordproof, he drew his sword and gave it two strokes, the first of which instantly destroyed the result of a week's labor. It troubled him to see with what ease he had broken the helmet in

---

[4] One of Charlemagne's knights and the hero of Boiardo's romance *Orlando Innamorato (Roland in Love)*. Palmerin of England, Amadis of Gaul, The Knight of the Sun, The Cid Ruiz Diaz, The Knight of the Burning Sword, Bernardo del Carpio, and Morgante are all characters in actual romances.

[5] Galalón, or Ganelon of Mayence, was another of Charlemagne's knights who betrayed him at Rouncevalles. See *The Song of Roland*.

[6] Headpiece of a helmet, without the visor.

pieces, so to protect it from such an accident, he remade it and fenced the inside with a few bars of iron in such a manner that he felt assured of its strength, and without caring to make a second trial, he held it to be a most excellent helmet. Then he went to see his steed, and although it had more cracks in its hoof than there are quarters in a Spanish real[7] and more faults than Gonella's jade, which was all skin and bone,[8] he thought that neither the Bucephalus of Alexander nor the Cid's Babieca could be compared with it.[9] He spent four days deliberating over what name he would give the horse, for (as he said to himself) it was not right that the horse of so famous a knight should remain without a name. So he endeavored to find one that would express what the animal had been before he had been the mount of a knight-errant, and what he now was. It was indeed reasonable that when the master changed his state, the horse should change his name too and assume one pompous and high-sounding, as suited the new order he was about to profess. So after having devised, erased, and blotted out many other names, he finally decided to call the horse Rozinante—a name, in his opinion, lofty, sonorous, and significant, for it explained that he had been only an ordinary hack before he had been raised to his present status of first of all the hacks in the world.[10]

Now that he had given his horse a name so much to his satisfaction, he resolved to choose one for himself, and after seriously considering the matter for eight whole days, he finally determined to call himself Don Quixote. For that reason the authors who have related this most true story have deduced that his name must undoubtedly have been Quixada and not Quesada, as others would have it. Then, remembering that the valiant Amadis had not been content to call himself simply Amadis, but added thereto the name of his kingdom and native country to render it more illustrious, calling himself Amadis of Gaul, so he, like a good knight, also added the name of his province and called himself Don Quixote of La Mancha. In this way he openly proclaimed his lineage and country, and at the same time he honored it by taking its name.

Now that his armor was scoured, his morion made into a helmet, his horse and himself newly named, he felt that nothing was wanting but a lady of whom to be enamored, for a knight-errant who was loveless was a tree without leaves and fruit, a body without soul. "If," said he, "for my sins or through my good fortune I encounter some giant—a usual occurrence to knights-errant—and bowling him over at the first onset or cleaving him in twain, I finally vanquish and force him to surrender, would not it be better to have some lady to whom I may send him as a trophy? Then, when he comes into her presence, he may kneel before her and humbly say: 'Madam, I am the giant Caraculiambro, Lord of the Island of Malindrania, whom the never-adequately-praised Don Quixote of La Mancha has overcome in single combat. He has commanded me to present myself before you so that your highness may dispose of me as you wish.'" How glad was our knight

---

[7] A *real* was a silver coin. There were eight *cuartos*, or "cracks," in a real.

[8] Pedro Gonella was the clown of the Duke of Ferrara in the fifteenth century; his horse, all skin and bones, was the theme of many of his jokes.

[9] Bucephalus was Alexander the Great's horse, Babieca that of Ruy Diaz, hero of the twelfth-century Spanish epic *The Cid.*

[10] *Rozin,* or *rocin,* means an ordinary horse; *ante,* before.

when he had made these discourses to himself, but chiefly when he had found one whom he might call his lady! It happened that in a neighboring village there lived a good-looking country lass with whom he had been in love, although it is understood that she never knew or was aware of it. She was called Aldonza Lorenzo, and it was to her that he thought fit to entrust the sovereignty of his heart. He sought a name for her that would not vary too much from her own and yet would approach that of a princess or a lady of quality. At last he resolved to call her Dulcinea of El Toboso (she was a native of that town), a name in his opinion musical, uncommon, and expressive, like the others he had devised.

CHAPTER II

Which deals with our imaginative hero's first sally from his home

Once these preparations were made he was anxious to put his designs into operation without delay, for he was spurred on by the conviction that the world needed his immediate presence; so many were the grievances he intended to rectify, the wrongs he resolved to set right, the harms he meant to redress, the abuses he would reform, and the debts he would discharge. And so, without acquainting a living soul with his intentions, and wholly unobserved, one morning before daybreak (it was one of the hottest in the month of July), he armed himself cap-a-pie, mounted Rozinante, placed his ill-constructed helmet on his head, braced on his buckler, grasped his lance, and through the door of his back yard sallied forth into the open country, mightily pleased to note the ease with which he had begun his worthy enterprise. But scarcely had he issued forth when he was suddenly struck by so terrible a thought that he almost gave up his whole undertaking, for he just then remembered that he had not yet been dubbed a knight, and therefore, in accordance with the laws of chivalry, he neither could nor ought to enter the lists against any knight. Moreover, even if he had been dubbed, he should, as a novice, have worn white armor without any device on his shield until he had won it by force of arms. These thoughts made him stagger in his purpose; but as his madness prevailed over every reason, he determined to have himself knighted by the first person he should meet, like many others of whom he had read in the books that distracted him. As to white armor, he intended at the first opportunity to scour his own so that it would be whiter than ermine. In this way he calmed himself and continued his journey, letting his horse choose the way, believing that in this consisted the true spirit of adventure.

As our brand-new adventurer proceeded, he kept conversing with himself in this manner: "Who doubts but that in future ages, when the true story of my famous deeds is brought to light, the wise man who writes it will describe my first sally in the morning as follows: 'Scarcely had the rubicund Apollo spread over the face of the vast and spacious earth the golden tresses of his beautiful hair, and scarcely had the little painted birds with their tuneful tongues saluted in sweet and melodious harmony the coming of rosy Aurora, who, leaving the soft couch of her jealous husband, revealed herself to mortals through the gates and balconies of the Manchegan horizon, when the famous knight Don Quixote of La Mancha, quitting his downy bed of ease, mounted his renowned steed, Rozinante, and began to ride over the ancient and memorable plain of Montiel.'"[11] (And indeed he was doing so.) Continuing his discourse, he added: "O happy era, O happy age, wherein my famous deeds shall be revealed to the world, deeds worthy to be engraved in bronze, sculptured in marble, and painted in pictures for future record! O thou wise enchanter, whosoever thou mayest be, whose duty it will be to chronicle this strange history, do not, I beseech thee, forget my good horse, Rozinante, the everlasting companion of my wanderings." Then, as if really enamored, he cried: "O Dulcinea, my princess! Sovereign of this captive heart! Grievous wrong hast thou done me by dismissing me and by cruelly forbidding me by decree to appear in thy beauteous presence. I pray thee, sweet lady, to remember this poor, enslaved heart, which for love of thee suffers so many pangs."

To such words he added a sequence of other foolish notions all in the manner of those that his books had taught him, imitating their language as nearly as he could. And all the while he rode slowly on while the sun rose with such intense heat that it would have been enough to dissolve his brains, if he had had any left. He traveled almost the whole of that day without meeting any adventure worthy of note, wherefore he was much troubled, for he was eager to encounter someone upon whom he could try the strength of his doughty arm. Some authors say his first adventure was that of the Pass of Lápice; others hold it was that of the windmills, but according to my investigations and according to what is written in the annals of La Mancha, he traveled all that day, and at dusk both he and his horse were tired and nearly dead with hunger. He looked around him on every side to see whether he could discover any castle or shepherd's hut where he might rest and find nourishment. He then saw, not far from the road, an inn, which was as welcome to him as a star leading him not to the portals but to the very palace itself of his redemption. So he hastened on and reached it before dark.

Now there chanced to be standing at the door two young wenches who belonged to the category of women of the town, as they say. They were on their way to Seville in the company of certain carriers who halted for the night in that inn. As all our adventurer saw, thought, or imagined seemed to happen in accordance with what he had read in his books of chivalry, no sooner did he see the inn than it assumed in his eyes the semblance of a castle with four turrets, the pinnacles of which were of glittering silver including drawbridge, deep moat, and all the appurtenances with which such castles are depicted. And so he drew near to the inn (which he thought was a castle), and at a short distance from it, he halted Rozinante, expecting that some dwarf would mount the battlements to announce by trumpet blast the arrival of a knight-errant at the castle. But when he saw that they tarried, and as Rozinante was pawing the ground impatiently in eagerness to reach the stable, he approached the inn door and there saw the two young doxies, who appeared to him to be two beautiful damsels or graceful ladies

---

[11] Memorable because it was the scene of a famous battle in 1369.

enjoying the fresh air at the castle gate. It happened also at this very moment that a swineherd, as he gathered his hogs (I ask no pardon,[12] for so they are called) from the stubblefield, blew a horn that assembled them, and instantly Don Quixote imagined it was what he expected, namely, that some dwarf was giving notice of his arrival. Therefore, with extraordinary satisfaction he went up to the inn and the ladies. But when they saw a man armed in that manner draw near with lance and buckler, they started to take to their heels, full of fear. Don Quixote, perceiving their alarm, raised his pasteboard visor, and displaying his withered and dusty countenance, accosted them gently and gravely: "I beseech your ladyships, do not flee, nor fear the least offense. The order of chivalry that I profess does not permit me to do injury to anyone, and least of all to such noble maidens as your presences denote you to be."

The wenches kept gazing earnestly, endeavoring to catch a glimpse of his face, which its ill-fashioned visor concealed; but when they heard themselves called maidens, a thing so out of the way of their profession, they could not restrain their laughter, which was so boisterous that Don Quixote exclaimed in anger: "Remember that modesty is becoming in beautiful ladies, whereas laughter without cause denotes much folly. However," added he, "I do not say this to offend you or to incur your displeasure, for my one desire is to do you honor and service." The strange language of the knight was not understood by the ladies, and this, added to his uncouth appearance, increased their laughter and his annoyance, and he would have proceeded further but for the timely appearance of the innkeeper, a man who by reason of his extreme corpulence was of very peaceable disposition. As soon as he saw that uncomely figure all armed, in accouterments so ill sorted as were the bridle, lance, buckler, and corselet, he felt inclined to join the damsels in their mirth. But out of fear of such a medley of warlike gear, he resolved to be civil, and so he said: "Sir knight, if you are seeking a lodging, you will find all in abundance here, with the exception of a bed for there are none in this inn." Don Quixote, observing the humility of the governor of the fortress (for such the landlord and the inn appeared to him), answered: "Anything, sir castellan, suffices me:

> My ornaments are arms,
> My pastime is in war."

The host thought he called him a castellan because he took him to be one of the Simple-Simon Castilians,[13] whereas he was an Andalusian, one of those from the Sanlúcar shore, no less a thief than Cacus[14] and not less mischievous than a truant scholar or court page. And so he made the following reply: "If so, your worship's beds must be hard rocks and your sleep an everlasting watching;[15] wherefore you may boldly dismount and I can assure you that you can hardly miss being kept awake all year long in this house,

---

[12] Spanish peasants still beg one's pardon when mentioning pigs, a custom picked up from the neighboring Muslims, who abhor pork.

[13] *Castellano* means both "castellan" (a governor of a castle) and "Castilian" (a native of Castile).

[14] Cacus, in Roman mythology, stole some of Hercules' cattle.

[15] The innkeeper quotes the same ballad Quixote quotes above.

much less one single night." Saying this, he went and held Don Quixote's stirrup, who forthwith dismounted, though with much difficulty, for he had not broken his fast all that day. He then told the host to take great care of his horse, saying that he was one of the finest pieces of horseflesh that ever ate bread. The innkeeper looked him over but thought him not so good by half as his master had said. After stabling him, he returned to receive his guest's orders and found the damsels (who had now become reconciled to him) disarming him, but though they were able to take off the back- and breast-plates, they did not know how to undo his gorget[16] or remove his counterfeit helmet, which he had tied on with green ribbons in such a way that they could not be untied. It was necessary to cut them because the knots were so intricate, but he would not allow this to be done, and so remained all that night with his helmet on, and was the strangest and pleasantest sight imaginable.

And while he was being disarmed by those lights-o'-love whom he imagined to be ladies of quality of that castle, he said to them with great charm:

> "There never was on earth a knight
> So waited on by ladies fair
> As once was he, Don Quixote hight,
> When first he left his village dear:
> Damsels to serve him ran with speed
> And princesses to dress his steed.[17]

"Rozinante, ladies, is the name of my horse, and Don Quixote of La Mancha my own. I never intended to discover myself until deeds performed in your service should have proclaimed me, but the need of adapting to my present purpose the old ballad of Sir Lancelot has made my right name known to you prematurely. But the day will come when your ladyships shall command and I obey, and the valor of my arm make plain my desire to serve you."

The girls, unaccustomed to such flourishes of rhetoric, made no reply but asked whether he would eat anything. "Fain would I break my fast," answered Don Quixote, "for I think that a little food would be of great service to me." That day happened to be a Friday and there was nothing in the inn but some pieces of fish, called in Castile pollack, in Andalusia codfish, in some parts ling, and in others troutlets, or Poor Jack. They asked him if he would eat some troutlets, for they had no other fish to offer him. "Provided there are many little trout," answered Don Quixote, "they will supply the place of one salmon trout, for it is the same to me whether I receive eight single reals or one piece of eight. Moreover, those troutlets may turn out to be like unto veal, which is better than beef, and kid, which is superior to goat. Be that as it may, let it come in quickly, for the toil and weight of arms cannot be sustained without the good government of the guts." As the air was cool, they placed the table at the door of the inn, and the landlord brought a portion of ill-soaked and worse-cooked codfish and a piece of bread as black and moldy as the knight's arms. It was a laughable sight to see him eat, for as he had his helmet and his visor up, he could not feed himself, and so

---

[16] Throatpiece.

[17] Quixote is quoting, and altering, a ballad about Sir Lancelot, as he acknowledges below.

one of the ladies performed that service for him. But it would have been impossible for him to drink had not the innkeeper bored a cane, and placing one end in his mouth, poured in the wine at the other end. All this he endured patiently rather than cut the ribbons of his helmet.

While he was at his meal, a hog-gelder happened to sound his reed flageolet four or five times as he came near the inn. This was a still more convincing proof to Don Quixote that he was in a famous castle where they were entertaining him with music, that the codfish was salmon trout, the bread of the purest white, the whores ladies, and the innkeeper the governor of the fortress. All this made him applaud his own resolution and his enterprising sally. There was only one thing that vexed him: he regretted that he was not dubbed a knight, for he thought that he could not lawfully undertake any adventure until he had received the order of knighthood.

CHAPTER III

Which relates the pleasant method by which Don Quixote had himself dubbed knight

As he was tormented by that thought, he made short work of his meager, pothouse supper. Then he called for his host, shut himself up with him in the stable, and fell upon his knees, saying: "I will never rise from this place, valorous knight, until your courtesy grants me the boon I seek, one that will redound to your glory and to the advantage of the human race." The innkeeper, seeing his guest at his feet and hearing such words, stared at him in bewilderment, without knowing what to do or say. He tried to make him get up, but in vain, for the latter would not consent to do so until the boon he demanded was granted. "I expected no less from your magnificence," answered Don Quixote, "and so I say unto you that the boon I have demanded and that you, out of your liberality, have granted unto me is that tomorrow morning you will dub me knight. This night I shall watch over my arms in the chapel of your castle,[18] and tomorrow, as I have said, you will fulfill my earnest desires so that I may sally forth through the four parts of the world in quest of adventures on behalf of the distressed, as is the duty of knighthood and knights-errant who, like myself, are devoted to such achievements."

The host, who was, as we said before, a bit of a wag and already had some doubts about his guest's sanity, now found all his suspicions confirmed, but he resolved to humor him so that he might have sport that night. He told the knight that his wishes were very reasonable, for such pursuits were natural to knights so illustrious as he seemed and his gallant bearing showed him to be. He added that he himself in the days of his youth had devoted himself to the same honorable profession and had wandered over various parts of the world in search of adventures; and, moreover, he had not failed to visit the curing grounds of Málaga, the Isles of Riarán, the Precinct of Seville, the Quicksilver Square of Segovia, the Olive field of Valencia, the Circle of Granada, the Strand of Sanlúcar, the Colt Fountain of Córdoba, the Taverns of Toledo, and divers other haunts where he had proved the

---

[18] In chivalric romances, the "vigil" (watching over one's arms overnight) was an important part of the ceremony of knighthood.

nimbleness of his feet and the lightness of his fingers, committing wrongs in plenty, accosting many widows, deflowering sundry maidens, tricking some minors, and finally making himself known and famous to all the tribunals and courts over the length and breadth of Spain.[19] At last he had retired to this castle, where he lived on his own and on other men's revenues, entertaining therein knights-errant of every quality, solely for the great affection he bore them, and that they might share their goods with him in return for his benevolence. He further told him that in his castle there was no chapel where he could watch over his arms, for he had knocked it down to build it anew. However, in case of necessity, he might watch over the arms wherever he pleased, and therefore, he might watch that night in the castle courtyard. Then, the following morning, with God's help, the required ceremonies would be carried out in such a way that he would be dubbed a knight so effectively that nowhere in the world could one more perfect be found. He asked if Don Quixote had brought any money. "Not a farthing," answered the knight, "for I have never read in the stories of knights-errant that they ever carried money with them."

"You are mistaken," answered the landlord, "for although the stories are silent on this matter, seeing that the authors did not think it necessary to specify such obvious requirements as money and clean shirts, yet there is no reason to believe that the knights had none. On the contrary, it was an established fact that all knights-errant (whose deeds fill many a volume) carried their purses well lined against accidents, and moreover, they carried, in addition to shirts, a small chest of ointments to heal their wounds, for in the plains and deserts where they fought and were wounded, there was no one to cure them unless they were lucky enough to have some wise enchanter for friend who straightaway would send through the air in a cloud some damsel or dwarf with a vial of water possessed of such power that upon tasting a single drop of it, they would instantly find their wounds as perfectly cured as if they had never received any. But when the knights had no such friend, they always insisted that their squires should be provided with money and such necessities as lint and ointments; and when they had no squires (which was very seldom), they themselves carried those things on the crupper of their horse in saddlebags so small that they were scarcely visible, for except in such a case, the custom of carrying saddlebags was not allowed among knights-errant. I must, therefore, advise you," he continued, "nay, I might even command you, seeing that you are shortly to become my godson in chivalry, never from this day forward to travel without money or without the aforesaid necessities, and you will see how serviceable you will find them when least you expect it."

Don Quixote promised to follow his injunctions carefully, and an order was given for him to watch over his armor in a large yard adjoining the inn. When the knight had collected all his arms together, he laid them on a stone trough that was close by the side of a wall. Then embracing his buckler and grasping his lance, he began with stately air to pace up and down in front of the trough, and as he began his parade, night began to close in.

---

[19] The places the innkeeper names were all associated with robbers and thieves.

The landlord, meanwhile, told all who were in the inn of the madness of his guest, the arms vigil, and the knighthood dubbing that was to come. They were astonished at such a strange kind of madness and flocked to observe him from a distance. They saw that sometimes he paced to and fro and at other times he leaned on his lance and gazed fixedly at his arms for a considerable time. It was now night, but the moon shone so clearly that she might have almost vied with the luminary that lent her splendor, and thus every action of our new knight could be seen by the spectators.

Just at this moment one of the carriers in the inn took it into his head to water his team of mules, to do which would necessitate removing Don Quixote's arms from the trough. But the knight, as he saw him approach, cried out in a loud voice: "O thou, whosoever thou art, rash knight that dost prepare to lay hands upon the arms of the most valiant knight-errant who ever girded sword, take heed and touch them not if thou wouldst not leave thy life in guerdon[20] for thy temerity." The carrier paid no heed to this warning (it would have been better for him if he had), but seizing hold of the armor by the straps, he threw it a good way from him. No sooner did Don Quixote perceive this than, raising his eyes to heaven and fixing his thoughts (as it seemed) upon his lady, Dulcinea, he said: "Assist me, O lady, in this first affront that is offered to thy vassal's heart. Let not thy favor and protection fail me in this first encounter." Uttering these and similar words, he let slip his buckler, and raising the lance in both hands, he gave the carrier such a hefty blow on the pate that he felled him to the ground in so grievous a plight that if he had followed it with a second, there would have been no need of a surgeon to cure him. This done, he put back his arms and began to pace to and fro as peacefully as before.

Soon after, another carrier, not knowing what had happened (for the first still lay unconscious), came out with the same intention of watering his mules and began to take away the arms that were encumbering the trough, when Don Quixote, not saying a word or imploring assistance from a soul, once more dropped his buckler, lifted up his lance, and without breaking it to pieces, opened the second muleteer's head in four places. All the people in the inn rushed out when they heard the noise, and the landlord among them. As soon as Don Quixote saw them, he braced on his buckler and laid his hands upon his sword, saying: "O lady of beauty, strength and vigor of my enfeebled heart! Now is the time for thee to turn the eyes of thy greatness upon this thy captive knight, who stands awaiting so great an adventure." These words, it seemed to him, filled him with such courage that if all the muleteers in the world had attacked him he would not have retreated one step. The wounded men's companions, seeing them in such an evil plight, began from afar to rain a shower of stones upon Don Quixote, who defended himself as best he could with his buckler, but he did not dare to leave the trough for fear of leaving his arms unprotected. The landlord shouted at them to let him alone, for he had told them the man was mad, and as such, he would be acquitted even if he killed every one of them. Don Quixote shouted still louder, called them caitiffs and traitors, and the lord of the castle a cowardly, baseborn knight for allowing knights-errant to be treated in such a manner. "I would make thee understand," cried he, "what a traitorous scoundrel thou

[20] Recompense.

art had I but been dubbed a knight. But as for you, ye vile and base rabble, I care not a fig for you; fire on, advance, draw near, and hurt me as much as you dare. Soon ye shall receive the reward for your folly and presumption." Such was the undaunted boldness with which he uttered these words that his attackers were struck with terror. And so, partly through fear and partly through the persuasive words of the landlord, they ceased to fling stones at him, and he allowed them to carry off their wounded, after which he returned to the guard of his arms with as much calm gravity as before.

The landlord did not relish the mad pranks of his guest, so he determined to make an end of them and give him his accursed order of chivalry before any further misfortune occurred. And so, going up to him, he excused himself for the insolent way those low fellows had treated him, without his knowledge or consent, adding that they had been well chastised for their rashness. He repeated what he had said before: that there was no chapel in that castle, nor was one necessary for what remained to be done; that the chief point of the knighting ceremony consisted in the accolade and the tap on the shoulders, according to the ceremonial of the order,[21] and that might be administered in the middle of a field; that he had performed the duty of watching over his armor, for he had watched more than four hours, whereas only two were required. All this Don Quixote believed and said that he was then ready to obey him, but yet begged him to conclude with all the brevity possible, for if he should be attacked again when he was armed a knight, he was determined not to leave one person alive in the castle, except those whom, out of respect for the governor of the fortress and at his request, he would spare. The governor, being warned and alarmed at possible consequences, brought out forthwith a book in which he kept his account of the straw and barley supplied to the carriers, and with a stump of candle, which a boy held lighted in his hands, and accompanied by the two above-mentioned damsels, he went over to Don Quixote and ordered him to kneel. He then read in his manual as if he had been repeating some pious oration. In the midst of the prayer he raised his hand and gave him a good blow on the neck, and after that gave a royal thwack on the shoulders, all the time mumbling between his teeth as if praying. After this he commanded one of the ladies to gird on his sword, which she did with much discretion and aplomb, plenty of which was needed to prevent them all from bursting with laughter at every stage of the ceremonies; but the prowess they had beheld in the new knight made them restrain their laughter. As she girded on his sword, the good lady said: "God make you fortunate, knight, and give you success in your contests." Don Quixote demanded then how she was called that he might henceforward know to whom he was beholden for the favor received, for he was resolved to give her a share of the honor that his valor should merit. And she answered with great humility that she was called La Tolosa and was a cobbler's daughter from Toledo, who lived near Sancho Bienaya Square, and that she would always serve him and consider him her lord wherever she happened to be. Don Quixote replied, requesting her for his sake to call herself henceforth Lady Tolosa, which she promised to do. Then the other lady buckled on his spur and he addressed her in very nearly the same terms as the lady of the sword. He asked her name,

---

[21] The "accolade" (a ceremonial embrace) and a ceremonial tap on the shoulders with a sword were part of the ceremony conferring knighthood.

and she said she was called La Molinera and was daughter of an honest miller of Antequera. He begged her to take a title and call herself Lady Molinera, at the same time making new offers of service.

Don Quixote could not rest until he found himself mounted on horseback and sallying forth in quest of adventures, and after saddling Rozinante, he mounted, but not before he had embraced his host and said so many extravagant words in thanking him for having dubbed him knight that it is impossible to tell them. The landlord, that he might speed the parting guest, answered him in no less rhetorical flourishes but in briefer words, and without asking him to pay for his lodging, he let him go with a godspeed.

CHAPTER IV

What happened to our knight when he sallied from the inn

It was about daybreak when Don Quixote sallied forth from the inn, so happy, so lively, and so excited at finding himself knighted that his very horse girths were ready to burst for joy. But calling to mind the advice of his host concerning the necessary accouterments for his travels, especially the money and the clean shirts, he resolved to return home to provide himself with them and with a squire. He had in view a certain laboring man of the neighborhood who was poor and had children but was otherwise very well fitted for the office of squire to a knight. With this thought in mind he turned Rozinante toward his village, and the horse, knowing full well the way to his stable, began to trot so briskly that his hoofs seemed hardly to strike the ground. The knight had not traveled far when he thought he heard the faint cries of someone in distress from a thicket on his right hand. No sooner had he heard them than he said: "I render thanks to heaven for such a favor. Already I have an opportunity of performing the duty of my profession and of reaping the harvest of my good ambition. Those cries must surely come from some distressed man or woman who needs my protection." Then turning his reins, he guided Rozinante toward the place from which he thought the cries came. A short distance within the wood he saw a mare tied to an oak and to another a youth of about fifteen years of age naked from the waist up. It was he who was crying out, and not without reason, for a lusty countryman was flogging him with a leather strap, and every blow he accompanied with a word of warning and advice, saying, "Keep your mouth shut and your eyes skinned." The boy answered: "I'll never do it again, master. By God's passion, I won't do it again and I promise in future to be more careful of your flock."

When Don Quixote saw what was happening, he said in an angry voice: "Discourteous knight, it is a caitiff's deed to attack one who cannot defend himself. Get up on your horse and take your lance" (for the farmer, too, had a lance leaning against the oak tree to which the mare was tied) "I will show you that you have been acting a coward's part." The countryman, at the sight of the strange apparition in armor brandishing a lance over him, gave himself up for lost and so replied submissively: "Sir knight, this youth I am chastising is a servant of mine, whom I employ to look after a flock of sheep in the neighborhood, but he is so careless that every day he loses one, and when I punish him for his negligence or rascality, he says I do it because I am a skinflint and will not pay him his wages. Upon my life and soul, he lies."

"Have you the impudence to lie in my presence, vile serf?" said Don Quixote. "By the sun that shines on us I will pierce you through and through with this lance of mine. Pay him instantly and none of your denials. If not, by almighty God who rules us all, I will annihilate you this very moment. Untie him at once."

The countryman lowered his head and without a word untied his servant. Don Quixote then asked the boy how much his master owed him. He replied nine months' wages at seven reals a month. Don Quixote, having calculated the sum, found that it came to sixty-three reals and told the farmer to pay up the money unless he wished to die. The farmer, who was shaking with fear, then answered that on the word of one in a tight corner and also upon his oath (yet he had sworn nothing), he did not owe so much, for they must deduct three pairs of shoes that he had given the boy and a real for two bloodlettings that he had when he was sick.

"That is all very well," answered Don Quixote, "but let the shoes and the bloodletting stand for the blows that you have given him for no fault of his own; if he wore out the leather of the shoes you gave him, you wore out his skin, and if the barber drew blood from him when he was sick,[22] you drew blood from him when he was in good health; so in this matter he owes you nothing."

"The trouble is, sir knight," said the countryman, "that I have no money on me. If Andrés comes home with me, I'll pay him ready money down."

"I go home with him?" said the boy. "Not on your life, sir! I would not think of doing such a thing; the moment he gets me alone he'll flay me like a Saint Bartholomew."[23]

"He will not do so," answered Don Quixote. "I have only to command and he will respect me and do my behest. So I shall let him go free and guarantee payment to you, provided he swears by the order of knighthood that he has received."

"Take heed, sir, of what you are saying," said the boy. "My master is no knight; he has not received any order of knighthood. He is Juan Haldudo the wealthy, a native of Quintanar."

"That matters little," answered Don Quixote, "there may be Haldudos who are knights, especially as every man is the son of his own works."

"That's true," said Andrés, "but what kind of works is my master the son of? Isn't he denying me the wages of my sweat and toil?"

"I'm not denying them, brother Andrés," answered the countryman. "Do, please, come with me and I swear by all the orders of knighthood there are in the world to pay you, as I said before, every real down and even perfumed into the bargain."

"I'll spare you the perfume," said Don Quixote. "Give them to him in good, honest reals and I shall be satisfied; but see to it that you carry out your oath. If not, I swear by the same oath to return and chastise you, and I am sure to find you, even if you hide away from me more successfully than a lizard. And if you want to know who it is who gives you this command, learn that I am the valiant Don Quixote of La Mancha, the undoer of wrongs

---

[22] Barbers also functioned as surgeons.

[23] Saint Bartholomew, one of the twelve apostles and martyrs, was said to have been flayed to death.

and injuries. So, God be with you, and do not forget what you have promised and sworn, on pain of the penalty I have stated." With these words he spurred Rozinante and in a moment he was far away.

The countryman gazed after him, and when he saw that he had gone through the wood and was out of sight, he turned to his servant, Andrés, saying: "Come here, my boy; I want to pay you what I owe you in accordance with the commands of that undoer of wrongs."

"So you will, I swear," said Andrés; "and you had better obey the orders of that good knight—may he live a thousand years. He is such a courageous man and such a fair judge that by Saint Roch, if you don't pay me, he'll be back and he'll do what he threatened."

"And I'll swear I will too," answered the countryman, "and to show you my goodwill, I'll double the debt so that I can double the pay." Catching the boy by the arm, he tied him again to the oak and gave him such a drubbing that he left him for dead. "Now, master Andrés," said he, "call out to that undoer of wrongs and you'll find that he won't undo this one. Indeed I don't think I'm finished with you yet, for I've a mind to flay you alive as you feared a moment ago." At last he untied him and gave him leave to go off and fetch his judge to carry out the threatened sentence. As for Andrés, he went off sorely fretful, swearing that he would seek out the valiant Don Quixote of La Mancha and tell him all that happened, and he would make his tormentor pay sevenfold. However, he departed in tears, while his master stayed behind laughing.

Such was the manner in which the valiant Don Quixote undid that wrong.

Meanwhile the knight was quite pleased with himself, for he believed that he had begun his feats of arms in a most successful and dignified manner, and he went on riding toward his village, saying to himself in a low voice: "Well mayest thou call thyself the happiest of all women on earth, O Dulcinea of El Toboso, peerless among beauties, for it was thy fortune to have subject to thy will so valiant and celebrated a knight as is and shall be Don Quixote of La Mancha, who, as all the world knows, received only yesterday the order of knighthood and today has undone the greatest wrong that ever ignorance designed or cruelty committed. Today from the hand of that pitiless foe he seized the lash with which he so unjustly scourged that tender child."

Just then he came to a road that branched into four directions, and forthwith he was reminded of the crossroads where knights-errant would halt to consider which road they should follow. To imitate their example he paused for a moment's meditation, and then he slackened the reins, leaving Rozinante to choose the way. The horse followed his original intention, which was to make straight in the direction of his stable.

When Don Quixote had ridden about two miles, he saw a big company of people who, as it appeared later, were traders of Toledo on their way to buy silk in Murcia. There were six of them and they carried sunshades. They were accompanied by four servants on horseback and three muleteers on foot. No sooner had Don Quixote perceived them than he fancied a new adventure was at hand. So, imitating as closely as possible the exploits he had read about in his books, he resolved now to perform one that was admirably molded to the present circumstances. So, with a lofty bearing he fixed himself firmly in his stirrups, grasped his lance, covered himself with his buckler, and stood in the middle of the road waiting for those knights-errant to approach (for such he supposed them to be). As soon as they came within earshot, Don Quixote, raising his voice, cried out in an arrogant tone: "Let all the world stand still if all the world does not confess that there is not in all the world a fairer damsel than the Empress of La Mancha, the peerless Dulcinea of El Toboso."

At the sound of those words the traders pulled up and gazed in amazement at the grotesque being who uttered them. Both the tone and the appearance of the horseman gave clear proof of his insanity, but they wished to consider in more leisurely fashion the meaning of this confession that he insisted upon. So one of them, who was a trifle waggish in humor and had plenty of wit, addressed him as follows: "Sir knight, we do not know this lady you speak of. Show her to us, and if she is as beautiful as you say, we shall willingly and universally acknowledge the truth of your claim."

"If I were to show her to you," answered Don Quixote, "what merit would there be in acknowledging a truth so manifest to all? The important point is that you should believe, confess, affirm, swear, and defend it without setting eyes on her. If you do not, I challenge you to try battle with me, ye presumptuous and overweening band. Come on now, one by one as the traditions of chivalry declare, or else all together according to the foul custom of your breed. Here I stand waiting for you, trusting in the justice of my cause."

"Sir knight," answered the trader, "I beseech you in the name of all the princes here present not to force us to burden our consciences by confessing something we have never seen or heard, especially when it is so prejudicial to the empresses and queens of Alcarria and Extremadura.[24] Please show us some picture of that lady, even if it is no bigger than a grain of wheat, for a thread will enable us to judge the whole skein and we shall be satisfied and you yourself happy and content. I believe that we already are so much on your side that even if your lady's picture shows that one eye squints and the other drips vermilion and sulphur, yet in spite of all, to gratify you, we shall say all that you please in her favor."

"Drip indeed, you infamous scoundrels!" cried Don Quixote in a towering rage. "Nothing of the kind drips from her eyes, but only ambergris and civet in cotton wool. She is not squint-eyed nor hunchbacked, but straighter than a Guadarrama spindle. But you shall pay the penalty for the great blasphemy you have uttered against so peerless a beauty as my lady." With those words he attacked the man who had spoken to him, so fiercely with couched lance that if good fortune had not caused Rozinante to stumble and fall midway, the merchant would have paid dearly for his rashness. Rozinante fell and his master rolled a good distance over the ground. Although he tried to rise, he could not, for he was so impeded by the lance, the buckler, the spurs, the helmet, and the weight of the ancient armor. However, as he was struggling to arise, he kept on crying: "Flee not, cowardly rabble! Wait, slavish herd! It is not my fault, but the fault of my horse, that I am stretched here."

One of the muleteers of the company, who indeed was not very good-natured, when he heard the poor fallen knight say such arrogant words, could not resist the temptation to give him the answer on his ribs. So he went up

---

[24] Both backward, primitive regions.

to him, took the lance, broke it into pieces, and with one of them he so bela-bored our poor Don Quixote that in spite of his armor he thrashed him like a measure of wheat. His masters shouted to him not to beat him so much and to leave off; but the fellow was angry and would not stop the game until he had spent what remained of his rage. Then, running to get the rest of the pieces of the lance, he splintered them all on the wretched knight, who, in the midst of all this tempest of blows that rained on him, did not for a moment close his mouth, but bellowed out threats to heaven and earth and those villainous cutthroats (for so they appeared to him). At last the mule-teer became wearied and the traders pursued their journey, carrying with them plenty of matter for conversation at the expense of the poor drubbed knight. And when he was alone, he tried to see if he could get up, but if he could not do so when he was hale and hearty, how could he do it when he was bruised and battered? And yet he counted himself lucky, for he thought that his misfortune was peculiar to knights-errant and he attributed the whole accident to the fault of his horse. But so bruised was his whole body that it was impossible for him to get up.

CHAPTER V

In which is continued the account of our knight's mishap

Seeing that he couldn't stir, he resolved to have recourse to his usual rem-edy, which was to think of some incident from one of his books. His mad-ness made him remember that of the Marquess of Mantua and Baldwin, whom Carloto left wounded on the mountainside[25]—a story familiar to children, not unknown to youths, celebrated and even believed by old men, yet for all that, no more authentic than the miracles of Mohammed. Now this story, so he thought, exactly fitted his present circumstances, so with great display of affliction he began to roll about on the ground and to repeat in a faint voice the words that the wounded knight in the wood was supposed to have said:

> "Where art thou, lady of my heart,
> That for my woe thou dost not grieve?
> Alas, thou do know'st not my distress,
> Or thou art false and pitiless."

In this manner he repeated the ballad until he came to those verses that say: "O noble Marquess of Mantua, my uncle and liege lord." By chance there happened to pass by at that very moment a peasant of his own village, a neigh-bor, who was returning from bringing a load of wheat to the mill. And he, seeing a man lying stretched out on the ground, came over and asked him who he was and what was the cause of his sorrowful lamentation. Don Quixote, firmly believing that the man was the Marquess of Mantua, his uncle, would not answer but continued reciting his ballad, which told of his misfortunes and of the loves of the Emperor's son with his wife, just as the book relates

---

[25] Carloto, son of Charlemagne, was the hero of a well-known ballad, which Quixote quotes below.

it. The peasant was amazed to hear those extravagant words. Then taking off his visor, which had been broken to pieces in the drubbing, he wiped the dust off his face. No sooner had he done so than he recognized him and said: "Master Quixana" (for that must have been how people called him when he had his wits and had not been transformed from a staid gentleman into a knight-errant) "who left you in such a state?" But he kept on reciting his ballad and made no answer to what he was asked. The good man then, as best as he could, took off his breast- and back-plate to see if he was wounded, but he saw no blood or scar upon him. He managed to lift him up from the ground and with the greatest difficulty hoisted him on to his ass, thinking that beast an easier mount. Then he gathered together all his arms, not omitting even the splinters of the lance, tied them into a bundle, and laid them upon Rozinante's back. Then taking the horse by the bridle and the ass by the halter, he set off toward his village, meditating all the while on the foolish words that Don Quixote kept saying. And Don Quixote on his part was no less pensive, for he was so beaten and bruised that he could hardly hold himself onto the ass, and from time to time he uttered such melancholy sighs that seemed to pierce the skies that the peasant felt again moved to ask him what was the cause of his sorrow. But it must have been the Devil himself who supplied him with stories so similiar to his circumstances, for at that instant, forgetting Baldwin, he remembered the Moor Abindarráez whom the governor of Antequera, Rodrigo de Narváez, took prisoner to his castle.[26] So when the peasant asked him again how he was, he answered word for word as the captive Abindarráez answered Rodrigo de Narváez, just as he had read in Montemayor's *Diana,* where the story is told. And he applied it so artfully to his own case that the peasant wished he were in Hell rather than to have to listen to such a hodgepodge of foolishness. This convinced him that his neighbor was mad, so he made haste to reach the village and thereby escape being further plagued by Don Quixote's long discourse. The latter ended by saying: "I would have you know, Master Rodrigo de Narváez, that the beauteous Jarifa I have mentioned is now the fair Dulcinea of El Toboso, for whom I have done, still do, and shall do the most famous deeds of chivalry that ever have been, are, or ever shall be seen in the world." To this the peasant answered: "Take heed, sir, that I am neither Don Rodrigo de Narváez nor the Marquess of Mantua, but Pedro Alonso, your neighbor, and you are neither Baldwin nor Abindarráez, but the honorable gentleman Master Quixana."

"I know who I am," answered Don Quixote, "and I know that I can be not only those I have mentioned but also the Twelve Peers of France and even the Nine Worthies, for my exploits will surpass all they have ever jointly or separately achieved."[27]

With this and sundry topics of conversation they reached the village at sunset, but the peasant waited until it was dark so that no one would see the belabored knight so sorrily mounted. When he thought the time had come,

---

[26] There were a number of romance tales about the love of the captive Moor Abindarráez for the beautiful Jarifa. One version of the story is in Jorge de Montemayor's romance *Diana* (1561), which Quixote mentions.

[27] The Twelve Peers were Charlemagne's chief knights, all equal in rank. The Nine Worthies, in medieval lore, were nine famous men, three Jewish, three pagan, and three Christian, subjects of a number of tales and chronicles.

he entered the village and went to Don Quixote's house, which he found in an uproar. The curate and the village barber, great friends of Don Quixote, happened to be there and the housekeeper was addressing them in a loud voice: "What do you think, Master Licentiate Pedro Pérez" (that was the curate's name) "of my master's misfortune? For the past six days neither he, nor his horse, nor his buckler, nor his lance, nor his armor has appeared. Woe is me! I'm now beginning to understand, and I'm as sure of it as I am of death that those accursed books of chivalry that he continually reads have turned his brain topsy-turvy. Now that I think of it I remember hearing him say to himself many a time that he wished to become a knight-errant and go through the world in search of adventures. The Devil and Barabbas[28] take such books, for they have ruined the finest mind in all La Mancha!" The niece said the same and a little more: "You must know, Master Nicholas" (this was the name of the barber) "that it was a frequent occurrence for my uncle to read these soulless books of misadventures for days and nights on end. At the end of that time he would cast the book from his hands, clutch his sword, and begin to slash the walls. Then, when he was grown very weary, he would say that he had killed four giants as big as towers and that the sweat that dripped off him after his great exertions, he would say, was blood from the wounds he had received in battle. Then he would drink a great jugful of water and become calm and peaceable, saying that the water was a most precious liquor that his friend the great enchanter Esquife had given him. I, however, blame myself for all, for not having warned you of my uncle's extravagant behavior. You might have cured him before things reached such a state, and you would have burned all those excommunicated books (he has many, mind you), for they all deserve to be burned as heretics."

"I agree with that," said the curate, "and I hold that tomorrow must not pass without a public inquiry being made into them. They should be condemned to the fire to prevent them from tempting those who read them to do what my poor master must have done."

All this Don Quixote and the peasant heard. The latter finally understood the infirmity of his neighbor and began to shout: "Open your doors, all of you, to Sir Baldwin and the Marquess of Mantua, who is grievously wounded, and to the Moor Abindarráez, who is led captive by the valiant Rodrigo de Narváez, governor of Antequera."

Hearing these cries, they all rushed out and straightaway recognized their friend. They ran to embrace him, but he had not yet dismounted from the ass, for he was not able to do so. He said: "Stand back, all of you. I have been sorely wounded through the fault of my horse; carry me to my bed and, if possible, call the wise Urganda to examine and cure my wounds."

"A thousand curses," said the housekeeper then. "My heart told me clearly on which foot my master limped. Come on upstairs, sir; we'll know how to look after you here without that Urganda woman. Curses, aye, a hundred curses on those books of chivalry that have driven you to this!"

They carried him to his bed and searched his body for wounds, but could find none. He said he was all bruised after a great fall he had with his horse, Rozinante, when he was fighting ten giants, the fiercest and most overweening in the world.

[28] The robber whom Pilate pardoned instead of Christ; see, for example, Matthew 27:15–26.

"Aha!" said the curate. "So there are giants too in the dance. By the sign of the Cross I swear I'll burn the lot of them before tomorrow night."

They questioned Don Quixote a thousand times, but he would give no answer. He only asked them to give him food and allow him to sleep, for rest was what he needed most. . . .

[*In a chapter omitted here, the curate and the barber examine the contents of Don Quixote's library and burn all the books on knight-errantry. They examine the title pages and comment critically on the absurd contents.*]

CHAPTER VII

Of the second sally of our good knight Don Quixote of La Mancha

. . . . That same night the housekeeper burned all the books she could find in the courtyard and in the house, and some that perished in the flames deserved to be preserved forever in the archives, but fate and the laziness of the inquisitor did not allow it, and thus in their case the saying was fulfilled that the saint sometimes pays for the sinner. One of the remedies that the curate and the barber then prescribed for their friend's infirmity was to wall up the room where the books had been stored so that when he rose he should not find them, for once the cause had been removed, the effect might cease. And they agreed to tell him that an enchanter had whisked books, room, and all away. The plan was carried out with great speed.

Two days later Don Quixote got up, and the first thing he did was to go and see his books, and as he could not find the room in which he had left them, he went up and down and all over the house looking for it. He came to the place where the door used to be and felt the wall with his hands, staring around him on all sides without saying a word. At last he asked the housekeeper where was the study in which he kept his books. The housekeeper, who knew exactly what she had to answer, said: "What manner of study is your worship looking for? There are no studies or books in this house now, for the Devil in person took all away."

"It was not the Devil," said the niece, "but an enchanter who arrived on a cloud one night after you went away from here. He got down off the serpent on which he was riding and went into the room. I don't know what he did in there, but soon after he went flying out through the roof, leaving the house full of smoke. When we looked to see what he had done, we could see no books or room, but we remember very well, myself and the housekeeper, that when the wicked old man was about to depart, he said in a loud voice that owing to the secret enmity he bore against the owner of those books and of the room, he had done damage that would soon be clear. He also said that he was called Muñatón the wizard."

"Frestón was the name he wished to say," answered Don Quixote.

"I don't know," said the housekeeper, "whether he was called Frestón or Fritón; I only know that his name ended in *-tón*."

"That is true," said Don Quixote. "He is a wise enchanter, a great enemy of mine, and looks upon me with a malicious eye, for he knows by his skill and wisdom that in the course of time I shall fight in single combat with a knight whom he favors, and I shall win, in spite of all his machinations; so, he tries to do me all the hurt he can. But I affirm that he will never prevail over what has been ordained by Heaven."

"Who has any doubts on that score?" said the niece. "But, dear uncle, what have you to do with such quarrels? Is it not better to stay peacefully at home instead of roaming the world in search of better bread than is made of wheat, not to mention that many who go for wool come home shorn?"

"My dear niece," answered Don Quixote, "how far you are off the mark! Before they ever shear me, I'll have plucked and lopped off the beards of all who think they can touch the tip of a single hair of mine."

The two would not make any further reply, for they saw that his anger was rising. As a matter of fact, he remained a fortnight peacefully at home without showing any signs of wanting to repeat his former vagaries. During those days he held many pleasant arguments with his two old friends the curate and the barber. He would maintain that what the world needed most of all was plenty of knights-errant and that he himself would revive knight-errantry. The curate sometimes contradicted him; at other times he would give in to him, for had he not adopted this procedure, he could never have dealt with him.

During this interval Don Quixote made overtures to a certain laboring man, a neighbor of his and an honest fellow (if such a term can be applied to one who is poor), but with very little wit in his pate. In effect, he said so much to him and made so many promises that the poor wight resolved to set out with him and serve him as squire. Among other things Don Quixote told him that he should be most willing to go with him because some time or another he might meet with an adventure that would earn for him, in the twinkling of an eye, some island, and he would find himself governor of it. With those and other promises, Sancho Panza (for that was the fellow's name) left his wife and children and engaged himself as squire to his neighbor. Don Quixote then set about raising money, and by selling one thing, pawning another, and throwing away the lot for a mere song, he gathered a respectable sum. He furnished himself likewise with a buckler borrowed from a friend, repaired his broken helmet as best he could, and informed his squire, Sancho, of the day and hour when he intended to sally forth so that the latter might supply himself with all that was needed. He charged him particularly to carry saddlebags. Sancho said he would do so and added that he was thinking of bringing an ass with him, for he had a good one and he was not used to travel on foot. At the mention of the ass Don Quixote hesitated a little, racking his brains to remember any case of a knight-errant who was attended by a squire mounted on ass-back, but he could not remember any such case. Nevertheless, he resolved to let him take his ass, for he intended to present him with a more dignified mount when he got the opportunity, by unhorsing the first discourteous knight he came across. He also provided himself with shirts and other necessities, thus following the advice the innkeeper had given him.

After all these preparations had been made, Don Quixote, without saying farewell to his housekeeper and niece, Panza to his wife and children, set out one night from the village without being seen. They traveled so far that night that at daybreak they were sure that no one would find them, even if they were pursued.

Sancho Panza rode along on his ass like a patriarch, with his saddlebags and wineskin, full of a huge longing to see himself governor of the island his master had promised to him. Don Quixote happened to take the same road as on his first journey, that is, across the Plain of Montiel, which he now traveled with less discomfort than the last time, for as it was early in the morning, the rays of the sun did not beat down directly upon them, but slantwise, and so did not trouble them. Presently Sancho Panza said to his master: "Mind, your worship, sir knight-errant, you don't let slip from your memory the island you've promised me; I'll be able to rule it well, no matter how big it is."

To which Don Quixote replied: "I would have you know, my friend Sancho, that knights-errant of long ago were accustomed to make their squires governors of the islands or kingdoms they won, and I have resolved not to neglect so praiseworthy a custom. Nay, I wish to surpass them in it, for they sometimes, perhaps even on the majority of occasions, waited till their squires were grown old, and then when they were cloyed with service after enduring bad days and worse nights, they conferred upon them some title, such as count or at least marquess, of some valley of more or less account. But if you live and I live, I may, before six days have passed, even conquer a kingdom with a string of dependencies, which would fall in exactly with my plan of crowning you king of one of them. Do not, however, think this strange, for knights-errant of my kind meet with such extraordinary and unexpected chances that I might easily give you still more than I am promising."

"And so," answered Sancho Panza, "by that token, if I became king by one of those miracles you mention, at least my chuck[29] Juana Gutiérrez would become queen and my children princes."

"Who doubts it?" answered Don Quixote.

"I doubt it," replied Sancho Panza, "for I truly believe that even if God were to rain kingdoms down upon earth, none would sit well on the head of Mari Gutiérrez.[30] Believe me, sir, she's not worth two farthings as queen; countess would suit her better, and even then, God help her."

"Leave all in God's hands, Sancho," answered Don Quixote. "He will do what is best for her, but do not humble yourself so far as to be satisfied with anything less than the title of lord-lieutenant."

"I'll not indeed, sir," replied Sancho, "for a famous master like yourself will know what is fit for me and what I can carry."

CHAPTER VIII

Of the valiant Don Quixote's success in the terrifying and never-before-imagined adventure of the windmills, with other events worthy of happy remembrance

Just then they came in sight of thirty or forty windmills that rise from that plain, and no sooner did Don Quixote see them than he said to his squire: "Fortune is guiding our affairs better than we ourselves could have wished. Do you see over yonder, friend Sancho, thirty or forty hulking giants? I intend

---

[29] A term of endearment. Juana is Sancho's wife.
[30] Gutiérrez is Juana's (or Mari's) maiden name; elsewhere she is called Juana Panza.

to do battle with them and slay them. With their spoils we shall begin to be rich, for this is a righteous war and the removal of so foul a brood from off the face of the earth is a service God will bless."

"What giants?" asked Sancho Panza.

"Those you see over there," replied his master, "with their long arms; some of them have them well-nigh two leagues in length."

"Take care, sir," cried Sancho. "Those over there are not giants but windmills, and those things that seem to be arms are their sails, which when they are whirled around by the wind turn the millstone."

"It is clear," replied Don Quixote, "that you are not experienced in adventures. Those are giants, and if you are afraid, turn aside and pray whilst I enter into fierce and unequal battle with them."

Uttering these words, he clapped spurs to Rozinante, his steed, without heeding the cries of his squire, Sancho, who warned him that he was not going to attack giants but windmills. But so convinced was he that they were giants that he neither heard his squire's shouts nor did he notice what they were, though he was very near them. Instead, he rushed on, shouting in a loud voice: "Fly not, cowards and vile caitiffs; one knight alone attacks you!" At that moment a slight breeze arose and the great sails began to move. When Don Quixote saw this, he shouted again: "Although you flourish more arms than the giant Briareus, you shall pay for it!"[31]

Saying this and commending himself most devoutly to his lady, Dulcinea, whom he begged to help him in this peril, he covered himself with his buckler, couched his lance, charged at Rozinante's full gallop, and rammed the first mill in his way. He ran his lance into the sail, but the wind twisted it with such violence that it shivered the lance in pieces and dragged both rider and horse after it, rolling them over and over on the ground, sorely damaged.

Sancho Panza rushed up to his assistance as fast as his ass could gallop, and when he reached the knight, he found that he was unable to move, such was the blow that Rozinante had given him in the fall.

"God help us!" cried Sancho. "Did I not tell you, sir, to mind what you were doing, for those were only windmills? Nobody could have mistaken them unless he had windmills in his brain."

"Hold your peace, good Sancho," replied Don Quixote. "The affairs of war are, above all others, subject to continual change. Moreover, I am convinced, and that is the truth, that the magician Frestón, the one who robbed me of my study and books, has changed those giants into windmills to deprive me of the glory of victory; such is the enmity he bears against me. But in the end his evil arts will be of little avail against my doughty sword."

"God settle it in His own way," cried Sancho as he helped his master to rise and remount Rozinante, who was well-nigh disjointed by his fall.

They conversed about the recent adventure as they followed the road toward the Pass of Lápice, for there, Don Quixote said, they could not fail to find many and various adventures, seeing that it was a much frequented spot. Nevertheless he was very downcast at the loss of his lance, and in mentioning it to his squire, he said: "I remember having read of a Spanish knight

---

[31]Briareus was a hundred-armed, fifty-headed giant in Greek mythology. He helped Zeus to overthrow the Titans.

called Diego Pérez de Vargas, who, when he broke his sword in a battle, tore off a huge branch from an oak and with it did such deeds of prowess that day and pounded so many Moors that he earned the surname of Machuca,[32] and so he and his descendants were called from that day onwards Vargas y Machuca. I mention this because I intend to tear from the first oak tree we meet such a branch, with which I am resolved to perform such deeds that you will consider yourself fortunate to witness, exploits that men will scarcely credit."

"God's will be done," said Sancho. "I'll believe all your worship says; but straighten yourself a bit in the saddle, for you seem to be leaning over on one side, which must be from the bruises you received in your fall."

"That is true," replied Don Quixote, "and if I do not complain, it is because knights-errant must never complain of any wound, even though their guts are protruding from them."

"If that be so, I've no more to say," answered Sancho, "but God knows I'd be glad to hear you complain when anything hurts you. As for myself, I'll never fail to complain at the smallest twinge, unless this business of not complaining applies also to squires."

Don Quixote could not help laughing at the simplicity of his squire and told him that he might complain whenever he pleased and to his heart's content, for he had never read anything to the contrary in the order of chivalry. Sancho then bade his master consider that it was now time to eat, but the latter told him to eat whenever he fancied. As for himself, he had no appetite at the moment. Sancho no sooner had obtained leave than he settled himself as comfortably as he could upon his ass, and taking out of his saddle-bags some of the contents, he jogged behind his master, munching deliberately; and every now and then he would take a stiff pull at the wineskin with such gusto that the ruddiest tapster in Málaga would have envied him. While he rode on, swilling away in that manner, he did not remember any promise his master might have made to him, and so far from thinking it a labor, he thought it a life of ease to go roaming in quest of adventures, no matter how perilous they might be.

They spent that night under some trees, and from one of them Don Quixote tore a withered branch that might, at a pinch, serve him as a lance, and he fixed to it the iron head of the one he had broken. All that night he did not sleep, for he kept thinking of his lady, Dulcinea. In this way he imitated what he had read in his books, where knights spent many sleepless nights in forests and wastes, reveling in memories of their fair ladies. Not so Sancho Panza, whose belly was full of something more substantial than chicory water. He made one long sleep of it, and if his master had not roused him, not even the rays of the sun beating on his face nor the joyful warbling of the hosts of birds would have awakened him. When he got up he tested the wineskin once more and found it somewhat flabbier than the night before. This saddened him, for he thought that they were not in the way to remedy that loss as soon as would satisfy him. Don Quixote would not break his fast, for as we have said before, he was resolved to nurture himself on savory remembrances. . . .

---

[32] The verb *machucar* means "to pound." The story of Diego Pérez de Vargas, a sort of Spanish Hercules, is told in another old ballad.

[In the following chapters, Don Quixote attacks two monks and some muleteers who he thinks are necromancers carrying off a princess; he encounters a beautiful maiden, Marcella, who is as independent and idealistic as Quixote himself; he is beaten by herdsmen who object to Rozinante's amorous attentions to their mares; and he becomes embroiled in a dispute in an inn when he mistakenly thinks a servant girl is a beautiful princess who has fallen in love with him. This incident ends with Sancho being tossed in a blanket.]

CHAPTER XVIII

In which an account is given of the conversation that took place between Sancho Panza and his master, Don Quixote, with other adventures worth recording

. . . . Suddenly Don Quixote saw a large, dense cloud of dust rolling toward them. Turning to Sancho, he said: "This is the day, Sancho, on which shall be clearly seen the good that fate has in store for us; this is the day, I say, on which I shall show the might of my arm and on which I intend to do deeds that shall be written in the books of fame for succeeding ages. Do you see that dust cloud, Sancho? Know then that it is churned up by a mighty army composed of sundry and innumerable people who are marching this way."

"If so, there must be two armies," said Sancho, "for here on this side there is as great a cloud of dust."

Don Quixote turned around to look at it, and seeing it was so, he rejoiced, for he fancied that there were indeed two armies coming to fight each other in the midst of that spacious plain. For his imagination at all hours of the day and night was full of battles, enchantments, adventures, follies, loves, and challenges as are related in the books of chivalry, and all his words, thoughts, and actions were turned to such things. As for the clouds of dust he had seen, they were raised by two large flocks of ewes and rams that were being driven along the same road from opposite directions, which, because of the dust, could not be seen until they came near.

So earnest was Don Quixote in calling them armies that Sancho came to believe it and asked: "Well, what are we to do?"

"What?" said Don Quixote. "Why, favor and help the distressed and needy. You must know, Sancho, that the army marching toward us in front is led by the mighty emperor Alifanfarón, lord of the great island of Trapobana;[33] the other, which is marching at our back, is the army of his foe, the king of the Garamantans, Pentapolín of the Naked Arm, for he always goes into battle with his right arm bare."

"Why do these two gentlemen hate each other so much?" asked Sancho.

"They are enemies," replied Don Quixote, "because Alifanfarón is a furious pagan and is in love with the daughter of Pentapolín, a beautiful, graceful lady and a Christian. Her father refuses to give her to the pagan king unless he abandon first the false religion of Mohammed and turn Christian."

"By my beard," said Sancho, "Pentapolín does right, and I'll help as best I can."

---

[33] Most of the high-sounding names in this passage are imaginary. Trapobana, or Taprobana, is the ancient name given the island of Sri Lanka.

"Then you will do your duty," said Don Quixote, "for it is not necessary to be dubbed a knight to engage in battles such as these."

"I understand," replied Sancho, "but where shall we tie this ass that we may be sure of finding him after the scuffle is over? I think it was never customary to go into battle mounted on such a beast."

"That is true," said Don Quixote. "What you must do is to leave the ass to his own devices. Let him take his chance whether he get lost or not, for after winning this battle we shall have so many horses that even Rozinante runs the risk of being exchanged for another. Now listen to me carefully while I give you an account of the principal knights in the two approaching armies. Let us withdraw to that hillock over there to get a better view of the two armies."

They did so, and standing on the top of the hill, they could have discerned the two flocks that Don Quixote had converted into armies had their eyes not been blinded by the clouds of dust. But seeing in his imagination what did not exist, he began to say in a loud voice: "The knight you see yonder with the yellow armor, who bears on his shield a crowned lion couchant at a damsel's feet, is the valiant Laurcalco, lord of the Silver Bridge. The other with armor flowered with gold, who bears on his shield three crowns argent on an azure field, is the fearsome Micocolembo, grand duke of Quirotia. The other, with gigantic limbs, who marches on his right, is the undaunted Brandabarbarán of Boliche, lord of the Three Arabias. He is wearing a serpent's skin and bears a gate as a shield, which, fame says, was one of those belonging to the temple that Samson pulled down when by his death he took revenge on his enemies.[34] Now turn your eyes to this other side, and there you will see, in front of this other army, the victorious and never vanquished Timonel of Carcajona, prince of New Biscay, who comes clad in armor quartered azure, vert, argent, and or. He bears on his shield a cat or on a field gules with a scroll inscribed *Miau*, which is the beginning of his mistress' name—according to report—the peerless Miaulina, daughter of Alfeñiquén, duke of Algarbe. The other, who weighs down and oppresses the back of that powerful and spirited charger, with armor as white as snow and a white shield without a device, is a novice knight of the French nation called Pierre Papin, lord of the baronies of Utrique. The other pricking with iron heel the flanks of that nimble zebra and carrying for arms the azure cups is the doughty duke of Nerbia, Espartafilardo of the Wood, who bears on his shield the device of an asparagus plant, with a motto in Castilian which says: *My fortune trails.*"

So he went on, naming many imaginary knights in each squadron as his fancy dictated and giving extemporaneously to each his armor, colors, devices, and mottoes, for he was completely carried away by his strangely deluded imagination. He continued without a pause: "That squadron in the front is composed of men of various nations: Here are they who drink of the sweet waters of the famous Xanthus; mountaineers who tread the Massilian fields; those who sift the pure and fine gold of Arabia; dwellers on the celebrated cool shores of clear Thermodon; those who drain in various ways the golden Pactolus; the Numidians, unreliable in their promises; Persians, famous for

---

[34] See Judges 16.

their bows and arrows; Parthians; Medes, who fight as they flee; Arabs, with their movable houses; Scythians as cruel as they are fair; Ethiopians with pierced lips; and countless other nations, whose faces I recognize and behold, although their names I do not recollect. In that other squadron come drinkers of the crystal waters of the olive-bearing Betis; men who burnish and polish their faces with the liquor of the ever-rich and golden Tagus; men who enjoy the health-giving waters of the divine Genil; dwellers in the Tartessian plain with their abundant pastures; men who enjoy the Elysian fields of Jérez; men of La Mancha rich and crowned with golden corn; men clad in iron, survivors of the ancient Gothic race; bathers in the Pisuerga, famous for its mild current; men who graze their flock on the broad pastures of the winding Guadiana, famous for its hidden current;[35] men who shiver with the cold of the wooded Pyrenees and among the white snows of the lofty Apennines; as many as all Europe contains and encloses."

By God! How many provinces did he name! How many nations did he enumerate, giving to each, with wonderful speed, its peculiar attributes, so absorbed and wrapped up was he in all that he had read in his lying books! Sancho Panza hung on his words without uttering one. Now and then he turned his head to see whether he could perceive the knights and giants his master named. Seeing none, he said at last: "Master, I'll commend to the Devil any man, giant, or knight of all those you mentioned who is actually here. At least I do not see them. Perhaps all may be enchantment like last night's specters."

"Why do you say that?" said Don Quixote. "Do you not hear the neighing of the horses, the blaring of the trumpets, and the rattle of the drums?"

"I hear nothing," answered Sancho, "but the bleating of sheep and lambs." And so it was, for now the two flocks were close at hand.

"The fear you are in," said Don Quixote, "allows you neither to see nor to hear correctly, for one of the effects of fear is to disturb the senses and make things seem different from what they are. If you are so afraid, stand to one side and leave me alone, for I alone am sufficient to give the victory to the side that I shall assist." With these words he clapped spurs to Rozinante, and with lance couched, rode down the hillside like a thunderbolt.

Sancho shouted at him: "Come back, master, come back! I swear to God that those you are going to charge are only sheep and lambs. Come back! Woe to the father who begat me! What madness is this? Look! There is neither giant, nor knight, nor cats, nor arms, nor shield quartered or entire, nor azures true or bedeviled. Sinner that I am, what are you doing?"

Don Quixote, however, did not turn back, but charged on, shouting as he went: "Ho! You knights who fight under the banners of the valiant emperor Pentapolín of the Naked Arm! Follow me, all of you, and you will see how easily I will take vengeance for him on his enemy, Alifanfarón of Trapobana."

With these words he dashed into the midst of the flock of sheep and began to spear them with as much courage and fury as if he were fighting his mortal enemies. The shepherds and herdsmen who came with the flock shouted to him to stop, but seeing that words were of no avail, they unloosed their slings and began to salute his ears with stones as big as one's fist. Don Quixote

[35] The Guadiana River runs underground through part of La Mancha.

took no notice of their stones but galloped to and fro, crying out: "Where are you, proud Alifanfarón? Where are you? Come to me, for I am but one knight and wish to try my strength with you, man to man, and take away your life for the wrong you do to the valiant Pentapolín." At that instant a smooth pebble hit him in the side and buried two ribs in his entrails. Finding himself in such a bad way, he thought for certain that he was killed or sorely wounded, and remembering his balsam, he took out his cruse[36] and raised it to his mouth to drink. But before he could swallow what he wanted, another pebble struck him full on the hand, broke the cruse to pieces, carried away with it three or four teeth and grinders out of his mouth, and badly crushed two fingers of his hand. And such was the force of those two blows that the poor knight fell off his horse onto the ground. The shepherds ran up to him, and believing that they had killed him, they collected their flocks in great haste, carried away their dead sheep, which were more than seven, and departed without further inquiry.

All this time Sancho stood on the hillock watching his master's mad escapade and tearing his beard and cursing the unlucky hour and moment when he first met him. But seeing him lying on the ground and the shepherds out of sight, he came down the hill, went up to his master, and found him in a very bad way, although not quite unconscious. So he said to him: "Did I not tell you, sir, to come back, for those you went to attack were not armies, but flocks of sheep?"

"That rascal of an enchanter, my enemy, can counterfeit and make men vanish. Know, Sancho, that it is a very easy matter for such men to make us see what they please, and this malignant persecutor of mine, envious of the glory that I was to reap in this battle, has changed the squadrons of enemy into flocks of sheep. Now, for my sake, Sancho, do one thing to undeceive yourself and see the truth of what I am telling you. Get up on your ass and follow them softly, and you will see that when they have gone a little distance away, they will return to their original shapes, and ceasing to be sheep, will become grown-up, mature men as when I described them to you at first. But do not go now, for I need your assistance. Come and see how many of my teeth are missing, for I do not think I have a single one left in my mouth."

Sancho went so close that he almost thrust his eyes into his mouth, and it was precisely at the fatal moment when the balsam that had been fretting in Don Quixote's stomach came up to the surface; and with the same violence that a bullet is fired out of a gun, all that he had in his stomach discharged itself upon the beard of the compassionate squire.

"Holy Mary!" cried Sancho. "What has happened to me? The poor sinner must be at death's door, for he's puking blood at the mouth." But reflecting a little, he was soon convinced by the color, smell, and taste that it was not blood, but the balsam that he had seen him drink; and so great was the loathing he felt that his own stomach turned, and he emptied its full cargo upon his master, and both were in a precious pickle. Sancho rushed to his ass to take something out of his saddlebags to clean himself and his master, and when he did not find them, he was on the verge of losing his mind. He cursed himself again and vowed in his heart to leave his master and return

---

[36] An earthen pot. "Balsam" is any soothing medicine.

to his home, although he would lose his wages for service and his hopes of becoming governor of the promised island.

Don Quixote had now risen, and keeping his left hand to his mouth lest the rest of his teeth fall out, with the other he took hold of Rozinante's bridle (who had not stirred from his master's side, such was his well-bred loyalty) and went over to his squire, who stood leaning against his ass with his cheek upon his hand, looking like the picture of a man lost in thought.

The knight, seeing him in that mood and so full of melancholy, said to him: "Learn, Sancho, that one man is not more than another unless he achieves more than another. All those storms that fall upon us are signs that soon the weather will be fair and that things will go smoothly, for it is not possible for evil or good to last forever. Hence we may infer that as our misfortunes have lasted so long, good fortunes must be near. So, you must not vex yourself about my mischances, for you have no share in them."

"How not?" replied Sancho. "I suppose him they tossed in a blanket yesterday was not my father's son? And the saddlebags that are missing today with all my chattels is someone else's misfortune?"

"What, are the saddlebags missing, Sancho?" asked Don Quixote.

"Yes, they are missing," answered Sancho.

"In that case, we have nothing to eat today," said Don Quixote.

"Very true," said Sancho, "if these fields are barren of the herbs that your worship says he knows all about and with which unfortunate knights-errant like yourself generally supply their wants."

"Nevertheless," answered Don Quixote, "at the present moment I would rather have a quarter-loaf of bread or a cottage loaf and a couple of heads of salted pilchards than all the herbs that Dioscorides describes, though his book be illustrated by Doctor Laguna.[37] But, good Sancho, get up on your ass and follow me, for God, who provides for all, will not desert us, especially being engaged, as we are, in His service. He does not abandon the gnats of the air, nor the worms of the earth, nor the tadpoles of the water, and He is so merciful that He maketh His sun shine on the good and the evil and He causeth the rain to fall upon the just and the unjust."

"Your worship," said Sancho, "were fitter to be a preacher than a knight-errant."

"Knights-errant, Sancho," said Don Quixote, "knew, and ought to know, somewhat of all things, for there have been knights-errant in past ages who were as ready to make a sermon or a speech on the king's highway as though they had taken their degrees at the University of Paris; whence it may be inferred that the lance never blunted the pen, nor the pen the lance."

"Well, may it turn out as you say," answered Sancho. "But let us be gone and endeavor to get a lodging tonight; and I pray to God we may find a place where there are no blankets, blanketeers, specters, or enchanted Moors; and if there are, may the Devil keep the lot of them."

"Ask that of God, my son," said Don Quixote, "and lead me where you please, for on this occasion I will leave the choice of lodging to you. But give me your hand and feel with your finger how many teeth and grinders I have lost on this right side of my upper jaw, for there I feel the pain."

---

[37]Andrés de Laguna, a famous sixteenth-century physician, translated the work of Dioscorides, a first-century A.D. Greek physician and pharmacologist.

Sancho put in his finger, and feeling about, asked: "How many grinders did your worship have before on this side?"

"Four," answered Don Quixote, "besides the wisdom tooth, all of them whole and sound."

"Mind well, master, what you say," answered Sancho.

"I say four, if not five," said Don Quixote, "for in all my life I have never had a tooth or grinder pulled from my mouth, nor has any fallen out or been destroyed by decay."

"Well then, on this lower side," said Sancho, "you have only two grinders and a half, but on the upper, not even half a one, for it is as smooth as the palm of my hand."

"Woe is me," cried Don Quixote, hearing these sad tidings from his squire. "I would rather they lopped off an arm, provided it were not my sword arm; for you must know, Sancho, that a mouth without grinders is like a mill without grindstone, and a tooth is far more to be prized than a diamond. But all this must be suffered by those who profess the stern order of chivalry. Mount, friend, and lead the way, for I will follow you at what pace you please. . . ."

[*In the succeeding sections, Don Quixote attacks a funeral party, mistakes a cloth mill for a supernatural danger, and deprives a barber of his basin, which he takes to be the "golden helmet of Mambrino," referred to in Ariosto's* Orlando Furioso.]

CHAPTER XXII

Of the liberty Don Quixote gave to a number of unfortunates who were being borne, much against their will, where they had no wish to go

Cide Hamete Benengeli, the Arabian and Manchegan author,[38] relates in this most grave, high-sounding, precise, pleasant, and imaginative history that after the conversation between the famous Don Quixote of La Mancha and Sancho Panza, his squire, which is reported at the end of the twenty-first chapter, Don Quixote raised his eyes and saw coming, along the road he was taking, about a dozen men on foot strung together like beads on a great iron chain. The chain was fastened around their necks and they were handcuffed. With them were two men on horseback, and two others followed on foot. The horsemen had firelocks, and those on foot pikes and swords.

As soon as Sancho Panza saw them he said: "Here's a chain of galley slaves, men forced by the king, going to serve in the galleys."

"How! Men forced?" answered Don Quixote. "Is it possible that the king forces anybody?"

"I don't say that," answered Sancho, "but they are people condemned for their offenses to serve the king in the galleys."

"Then it is a fact," replied Don Quixote, "however you put it, that these men are being taken to their destination by force and not by their own free will."

[38] Cide Hamete Benengeli is the imaginary author Cervantes has earlier introduced as the writer of an old manuscript, in Arabic, containing the history of Don Quixote. This device allows the narrator to step in and out of the story, commenting on the presentation as well as on the content of the narrative.

"That is so," said Sancho.

"Then," said his master, "here is the opportunity for me to carry out my duty: to redress grievances and give help to the poor and the afflicted."

"I beg you, sir," said Sancho, "to consider that justice, which is the king himself, does no violence to these men, but only punishes those who have committed crime."

By this time the chain gang came up, and Don Quixote in very courteous words asked those in charge to be good enough to inform him why they conducted people away in that manner. One of the guardians on horseback replied that they were slaves condemned by His Majesty to the galleys and that there was no more to be said, nor ought Don Quixote to desire any further information.

"Nevertheless," answered Don Quixote, "I would like to hear from each one of them individually the cause of his disgrace." To this the guardian on horseback answered: "Though we have here the register of the crimes of all these unlucky fellows, this is no time to produce and read them. Draw near, sir, and ask it from themselves. No doubt they'll tell you their tales, for men of their sort take delight in boasting of their rascalities."

With this leave, which Don Quixote would have taken for himself if they had not given it, he went up to the gang and asked the first man for what crimes he found himself in such straits. The man answered that it was for being in love.

"For that and no more?" cried Don Quixote. "If men are sent to the galleys for being in love, I should have been pulling an oar there long ago."

"My love was not of the kind your worship imagines," replied the galley slave. "Mine was that I loved too much a basket of fine linen, which I embraced so lovingly that if the law had not taken it from me by violence, I should not of my own free will have forsaken it even to this present day. I was caught in the act, so there was no need for torture. The case was a short one. They gave my shoulders a hundred lashes and in addition three years' hard labor in the *gurapas,* and that's an end of it."

"What are *gurapas?*" said Don Quixote.

"*Gurapas* are galleys," answered the convict, who was a young man of about twenty-four, born, as he said, at Piedrahita.

Don Quixote put the same question to the second, who returned no answer, for he seemed too downcast and melancholy to speak. But the first one spoke for him and said: "Sir, this gentleman goes for being a canary bird—I mean a musician or singer."

"Is it possible," said Don Quixote, "that musicians and singers are sent to galleys?"

"I should say so, sir," replied the galley slave. "There's nothing worse than to sing under torture."

"Well," said Don Quixote, "I, on the contrary, have heard it said: 'Who sings in grief, procures relief.'"

"Down here it's the exact opposite," said the slave, "for he who sings once, weeps the rest of his life."

"I do not understand it," said Don Quixote. One of the guards then said to him: "You know, sir, among these unsanctified folk 'to sing under torture' means to confess on the rack. They put this poor sinner to the torture and he confessed his crime of being a rustler, which means that he was a cattle thief; and because he confessed, he was condemned to the galleys for six years, with the addition of two hundred lashes that he carries on his shoulders. He's always sad and pensive, for the other thieves bully, abuse, and despise him because he confessed and hadn't the courage to say a couple of *nos*. For as they say, 'A *nay* has as many letters as a *yea*,' and it is good luck for a criminal when there are no witnesses and proofs and his fate depends on his own tongue. In my opinion there's much truth in that."

"I think so also," said Don Quixote, and he passed on to where the third slave stood, and put to him the same question as to the others. The man replied quickly and coolly, saying: "I'm off to their ladyship the galleys because I wanted ten ducats."

"I will give you twenty with all my heart to free you from that misfortune," said Don Quixote.

"That," replied the slave, "would be like one who has money in the middle of the sea and yet is perishing of hunger because he has nowhere to buy what he needs. I say this because, if I'd had the twenty ducats your worship offers me at the right time, I would have greased the lawyer's palm with them and so sharpened my advocate's wit that I would now be strolling about in the marketplace at Toledo instead of being trailed along here like a greyhound. But God is great; patience is enough."

Don Quixote passed on to the fourth, who was a man of venerable appearance, with a white beard reaching below his chest. No sooner was he asked the reason for his being there than he began to weep and would not answer a word; but the fifth convict lent him a tongue and said: "This honest gentleman is off for four years to the galleys after having appeared in the usual procession dressed in full pomp and mounted."[39]

"That means, I suppose," said Sancho, "carried to shame in view of the whole people."

"You have said it," answered the galley slave, "and the offense for which they gave him this punishment was for having been an ear broker, and a body broker too. What I mean to say is that this gentleman goes for pimping and for fancying himself as a bit of a wizard."

"If it had been merely for pimping," said Don Quixote, "he certainly did not deserve to go rowing in the galleys, but rather to command them and be their captain. For the profession of pimp is no ordinary office, but one requiring wisdom and most necessary in any well-governed state. None but wellborn persons should practice it. In fact, it should have its overseers and inspectors, as there are of other offices, limited to a certain appointed number, like exchange brokers.[40] If this were done, many evils would be prevented, which now take place because this profession is practiced only by foolish and ignorant persons such as silly women, page boys, and mountebanks of few years' standing and less experience, who, in moments of difficulty, when the utmost skill is needed, allow the tidbit to freeze between their fingers and their mouth and scarcely know which is their right hand. I should like to

---

[39] Those condemned for witchcraft or wizardry were dealt with by the Holy Office. They were mounted on mules with face to the tail and led in procession through the streets accompanied by a noisy crowd. They wore a *coroza* or paper miter, carried a lighted candle, and were flogged through the streets.

[40] Don Quixote's ironic praise of pimps echoes a stock joke in sixteenth-century Spanish literature.

go on and give reasons why it is right to make special choice of those who have to fill such an important office in the state, but this is not the place to do it. Some day I will tell my views to those who may provide a remedy; at present I only wish to say that the sorrow I felt at seeing your gray hairs and venerable countenance in so much distress for pimping has entirely vanished when I learn that you are a wizard; though I know well that there are no sorceries in the world that can affect and force the will, as some simple people imagine. Our will is free and no herb nor charm can compel it. What such gullible wenches and lying rascals do is to mix some potion or poison that drives men crazy, claiming that it has the power to rouse love; whereas I maintain that it is impossible to force a man's will."

"That is true, sir," said the worthy old man; "and indeed I was not guilty of witchcraft; as for being a pimp, I couldn't deny it, but I never thought there was any harm in it, for all my intention was that the whole world should enjoy themselves and live together in peace and quiet without quarrels or troubles. But my good intentions could not save me from going to a place from which I have no hope of return, laden as I am with years and so worried with a bladder trouble that does not give me a moment's rest." He now began to weep as before, and Sancho felt so sorry for him that he drew from his purse a four-real piece and gave it to him as alms.

Don Quixote passed on and asked another what his offense was. He answered with much more pleasantness than the former: "I am here because I played a little too much of a game with two cousins of mine and with two other sisters who were not mine. In short, I carried the game so far with them all that the result of it was the increasing of my kindred so intricately that no devil could make it out. It was all proved against me, I hadn't a friend, and I hadn't a groat; my neck was in the utmost danger; they gave me six years in the galleys; I concurred: it's fair punishment for my guilt; I'm young; if only my life lasts, all will turn out for the best. If you, sir, have anything about you to relieve us poor devils, God will repay you in Heaven and we will have care on earth to ask God in our daily prayers to give you as long and prosperous a life and health as your kind presence deserves."

This convict was dressed in a student's habit, and one of the guards told Don Quixote that he was a great talker and a fine Latin scholar.

Behind all these came a man about thirty years of age, of very comely looks, except that he had a slight squint. He was differently tied from the rest, for he wore a chain to his leg so long that it wound around his whole body. He had, besides, around his neck two iron rings, one of which was fastened to the chain, and the other, called a keep friend or friend's foot, had two irons that came down from it to his waist, at the ends of which were fixed two manacles. These held his hands locked with a great padlock so that he could neither put his hands to his mouth nor bend down his head to his hands.

Don Quixote asked why this man was loaded with more fetters than the rest. The guard answered that it was because he had committed more crimes than all the rest put together and that he was such a desperate rascal that, though they carried him fettered in that way, they were not sure of him but feared that he might give them the slip.

"What crimes did he commit," said Don Quixote, "that have deserved no greater penalty than being sent to the galleys?"

"He is going for ten years," said the guard, "which is the same as civil death. I need only tell you that this man is the famous Ginés de Pasamonte, alias Ginesillo de Parapilla."

"Master commissary," said the galley slave, "don't go so fast and don't let us start defining names and surnames. Ginés is my name, not Ginesillo, and Pasamonte is my family name, not Parapilla as you say. Let every man first look to himself and he'll do a good deal."

"Keep a civil tongue, mister out-and-out robber," answered the commissary. "Otherwise we'll shut you up, whether you like it or not."

"I know," answered the galley slave, "that man goes as God pleases; but one day someone will know whether my name is Ginesillo de Parapilla or not."

"Don't they call you that, you lying trickster?"

"They do," answered Ginés, "but I'll make them stop calling me by that name or I'll shear them where I don't care to mention in company. And now, sir, if you have something to give us, hand it out and good-bye, for you tire us with your inquiries about other men's lives. If you want to know mine, I am Ginés de Pasamonte, whose life has been written by these very fingers of mine."

"He speaks the truth," said the commissary. "He himself has written his own history—as good a one as you could wish, and he pawned the book in jail for two hundred reals."

"Aye, and I intend to redeem it," said Ginés, "even if it stood at two hundred ducats."

"Is it good?" said Don Quixote.

"It is so good," answered Ginés, "that it means trouble for *Lazarillo de Tormes*[41] and for all that has been written or ever shall be written in that style. I assure you it deals with truths and truths so attractive and entertaining that no fiction could compare with them."

"What is the title of the book?" asked Don Quixote.

"*The Life of Ginés de Pasamonte*," answered Gines himself.

"Is it finished yet?" asked Don Quixote.

"How can it be finished," answered Gines, "when my life isn't finished yet? What is written tells everything from my birth down to this last time I was packed off to the galleys."

"Then you have been there before?" said Don Quixote.

"To serve God and the king," answered Ginés; "on the last occasion I was there for four years, and I know already the taste of hard tack and the lash. I'm not too sorry to return there, for I'll have an opportunity to finish my book. I've still many things to say, and in the galleys of Spain there's more than enough leisure, though I don't need much for what I have to write because I know it by heart."

"You seem to be a clever fellow," said Don Quixote.

"Aye. And an unlucky one," replied Ginés, "for bad luck always pursues genius."

"It pursues knaves," interrupted the commissary.

"I've already told you, sir commissary," answered Pasamonte, "not to go so fast. The lords of the land didn't give you that rod to mistreat us but to

---

[41] An anonymous "rogue novel" published in 1554.

guide us and take us where His Majesty has ordered. If not, by Heaven—But enough! Perhaps one day the dirty work that was done in the inn may come out in the wash; in the meantime mum's the word, and let every man live well and speak better. Now let us move on, for we've had too much of this diversion."

The commissary raised his rod to strike Pasamonte in answer to his threats, but Don Quixote intervened, asking him not to ill-treat the convict since it was only fair that one who had his hands so tied should be somewhat free with his tongue. Then, turning toward the gang, he said: "I have gathered from all you have said, dearest brethren, that although they punish you for your faults, yet the pains you suffer do not please you, and that you go to them with ill will and against your inclination. I realize, moreover, that perhaps it was the lack of courage of one fellow on the rack, the want of money of another, the want of friends of a third, and finally the biased sentence of the judge that have been the cause of your not receiving the justice to which you were entitled. Now all this prompts and even compels me to perform on your behalf the task for which I was sent into the world, and for which I became a knight-errant, and to which end I vowed to succor the needy and help those who are oppressed by the powerful. But as it is prudent not to do by evil means what can be done by fair, I wish to entreat these gentlemen, your guardians and the commissary, to be kind enough to loose you and let you go in peace, for there will be plenty of men to serve the king on worthier occasions; it seems to me a harsh thing to make slaves of those whom God and nature made free. What is more, gentlemen of the guard," added Don Quixote, "these unfortunate creatures have done nothing against you yourselves. Let each man be answerable for his own sins; there is a God in Heaven who does not fail to punish the wicked nor to reward the good. It is not right that honest men should be executioners of others when they have nothing to do with the case. I ask this boon of you in a peaceable and quiet manner, and if you grant it, I shall give you my thanks. If, on the other hand, you will not grant it willingly, then shall this lance and sword of mine, wielded by my invincible arm, force you to do my bidding."

"This is a pleasant jest," answered the commissary. "You have ended your ranting with a fine joke. Do you want us to hand over to you those the king has imprisoned, as if we had the authority to let them go or you to order us to do it? Go your way, good sir, and a pleasant journey. Settle the basin straight on your pate, and don't go looking for a cat with three legs."[42]

"You are a cat, a rat, and a knave," answered Don Quixote. Without another word he ran at him so fiercely that, not giving him time to defend himself, he struck him to the ground badly wounded by his lance. It was lucky for the knight that this was the one who carried the firelock. The guards were astounded at this unexpected event. But they recovered themselves, and the horsemen drew their swords, the footmen clutched their pikes, and all of them threw themselves upon Don Quixote, who quietly waited for their attack. No doubt he would have been in great danger if the slaves, seeing a chance of liberty, had not broken the chain by which they were tied together. The confusion was such that the guards, first trying to prevent the galley slaves from getting loose, then defending themselves against Don Quixote, who

---

[42]A proverbial expression that means "Don't go looking for the impossible."

attacked them, did nothing to any purpose. Sancho, for his part, helped to release Ginés de Pasamonte, who was the first that leaped free and unfettered upon the plain. The latter then set upon the fallen commissary and relieved him of his sword and firelock, with which, aiming first at one and then at another, although he never fired it, he cleared the plain of guards, for they all fled no less from Pasamonte's firelock than from the showers of stones that the liberated slaves flung at them.

Sancho was much worried by all that had happened, for he had a shrewd suspicion that the guards who had fled would report the matter to the Holy Brotherhood,[43] who would raise the alarm and sally out in pursuit of the criminals, and he said so to his master, begging him to leave that place at once and hide themselves in the neighboring sierra.

"That is all very well," answered Don Quixote, "but I know what we should do now." Then he called all the galley slaves, who were now running hither and thither in a riotous mood and had stripped the commissary to the skin, and when they had gathered around him in a circle, he addressed them as follows: "It is the duty of well-bred people to be grateful for benefits received, and ingratitude is one of the most hateful sins in the eyes of God. I say this, sirs, because you know what favor you have received from me, and the only return I wish and demand is that you all go from here, laden with the chains from which I have just freed your necks, to the city of El Toboso. There you are to present yourselves before Lady Dulcinea of El Toboso and tell her that her Knight of the Rueful Figure sent you there to commend his service to her. You are to tell her, point by point, the details of this famous adventure, and when you have done this, you may then go whichever way you please and good luck be with you."

Ginés de Pasamonte answered for all the rest, saying: "That which you demand, sir, is impossible to perform, because we must not travel the roads together, but go alone and separate so that we may not be found by the men of the Holy Brotherhood, who will be sure to come out to search for us. What you can do, and ought to do, is to change this service and duty to the Lady Dulcinea of El Toboso into a certain number of Ave Marias and credos that we shall say for your worship's intention. And this we may do by night or by day, resting or on the run, at peace or at work; but if you think that we are now going to return to the fleshpots of Egypt—to our chains, I mean—and start off on the road to El Toboso, you might as well imagine that it's already nighttime, whereas it is not yet ten o'clock in the morning. To expect this from us is like expecting pears off an elm tree."

"I vow then," said Don Quixote in a rage, "sir whoreson, Don Ginesillo de Parapilla, or whatever you call yourself, that you will go alone, with your tail between your legs and the whole length of chain on your back."

Pasamonte, who was a truculent fellow (he now understood that Don Quixote was not very sane, seeing the foolish thing he had done by setting them free), would not stand being abused in this manner; so he winked at his companions, and they from a distance began to rain a shower of stones on Don Quixote, whose buckler gave him scant cover; and poor Rozinante paid no more attention to the spur than if his flanks were made of bronze. Sancho took cover behind his ass and thus sheltered himself against the squall

---

[43] A tribunal organized to punish highway robbers.

of stones that burst about them. Don Quixote was less able to shield himself against the countless stones that hit him with such force that at last they stretched him on the ground. Scarcely had he fallen when the student Ginés jumped upon him, and taking the basin from his head, gave him three or four blows with it on the shoulders and then struck it repeatedly on the ground, almost breaking it into pieces. They then stripped him of a tunic he wore over his armor, and they would have seized his hose too had they not been hindered by his greaves.[44] They took Sancho's cloak, leaving him in his underclothes, and after dividing among themselves the rest of the spoils, each went his own way, with more thought of escaping the Holy Brotherhood than of dragging their chains to Lady Dulcinea of El Toboso.

All that remained were the ass, Rozinante, Sancho, and Don Quixote. The ass pensively hanging his head, shaking his ears every now and then as if he thought the storm of stones was not yet over; Rozinante prostrate lying beside his master on the ground; Sancho in his underclothes, trembling at the thought of the Holy Brotherhood; and Don Quixote, in the dumps at finding himself so ill-treated by those for whom he had done so much.

[*Don Quixote decides to do penance in the wilderness of the Sierra Morena as other knights-errant do who have been absent too long from their mistresses. He sends Sancho to deliver a letter to Dulcinea. Quixote then meets a young man, Cardenio (whom Quixote calls the "Knight of the Wood"), who has lost his love to a false friend, Ferdinand. Meanwhile Sancho meets the curate and the barber, and they persuade him to join in a strategem to get Don Quixote to return to his village. They and Cardenio meet Dorothea, a woman deceived and abandoned by Cardenio's betrayer Ferdinand; she agrees to help them deceive the knight by playing the role of a princess, "Micomicona." They return to Quixote, and charmed by "Micomicona," he agrees to help her regain her "kingdom." The party stops at an inn on the way back to the village— the same inn where Sancho was tossed in a blanket. Here the curate reads them a manuscript called* A Tale of Ill-Advised Curiosity, *in which a husband comes to grief through testing his wife's fidelity. The story raises some of the same questions of reality and illusion explored in the novel itself. At the inn, Cardenio is reunited with his Lucinda, and Ferdinand claims Dorothea as his true wife. A returned captive of the Turks arrives at the inn and tells the party of his experiences and his escape (experiences reminiscent of Cervantes' own). Other guests arrive, including a judge with a beautiful young daughter who is pursued by a lovesick boy posing as a muleteer. After the ugly servant woman Maritornes plays a cruel trick on Quixote, the curate and the barber place him in a barred oxcart to take him back to his village. On the journey, Sancho manages to free his master from the cart. Quixote meets a goatherd and offers to rescue his lover from a nunnery; the goatherd, however, becomes angry and beats Quixote.*]

CHAPTER LII

*Of the quarrel that Don Quixote had with the goatherd, with the rare adventure
of the disciplinants, which he successfully achieved with the sweat of his brow*

. . . . It so happened that year that the clouds had denied the earth their moisture; so, throughout the valleys of that region, processions, public prayers, and penances were ordered to beseech Heaven to open the flood gates of its mercy and send them rain. It was for this purpose, therefore, that the people of a neighboring village were coming in procession to a holy shrine that stood on a hill at the edge of the valley. Don Quixote, as soon as he

---

[44]Armor for the lower legs.

saw the strange attire of the disciplinants, did not pause to recall the many occasions on which he had seen a similar sight before but immediately imagined that it was some kind of adventure that was reserved for him alone as knight-errant. He was all the more confirmed in his opinion by mistaking an image that they carried all swathed in mourning for some noble lady whom those ruffians and unmannerly churls were carrying away against her will.

No sooner did this thought flash through his mind than he rushed over to Rozinante, who was grazing nearby, and taking off the bridle and buckler that hung from the pommel of the saddle, he bridled him in an instant. Then, asking Sancho for his sword, he mounted Rozinante, and bracing his buckler, he cried in a loud voice to all those present: "Now, valiant company, ye shall see how necessary it is that there be in the world knights who profess the order of knight-errantry; now, I say, shall ye see, in the restoration of that captive lady to liberty, whether knights-errant ought to be valued!"

Saying this, he clapped his heels to Rozinante (for spurs he had none), and at a half gallop (for nowhere in all this truthful history can one read that Rozinante ever went at full speed) he advanced to encounter the disciplinants, though the curate and the barber tried to stop him. But all their efforts were in vain, nor could he be stopped by the screams of Sancho, who shouted: "Master, where are you going? What devils in your heart are driving you on to attack our Catholic faith? Mind, sir! Bad 'cess to it! That is a procession of disciplinants and the lady they're carrying on the bier is the most blessed image of the Immaculate Virgin. Take heed, sir, what you're doing; this time I can assure you that it's not what you think."

Sancho wasted his breath, for his master was so set upon encountering the sheeted ones and upon freeing the lady in black that he heard not a word, and even if he had, he would not have turned back though the king himself had commanded him. When he reached the procession, he stopped Rozinante, who already wanted to rest a little, and in a hoarse, angry voice he cried out: "You there, who cover up your faces probably because you are evil, halt and pay heed to my words!"

The first to halt were those who were carrying the image. Then, one of the four priests who chanted the litanies, noticing the strange appearance of Don Quixote, the leanness of Rozinante, and other ludicrous details, answered him, saying: "Brother, if you have anything to say, say it quickly, for these brethren are scourging their flesh, and we cannot, nor is it right that we should, stop to listen to anything that may not be said in two words."

"I will say it in one," replied Don Quixote. "You must instantly free that beauteous lady whose tears and sad appearance show clearly that you are bearing her away against her will and that you have done her some grievous wrong. But I, who came into the world to redress such injuries, will not allow you to move one single step forward till you have restored to her the liberty she desires and deserves."

From these words all who heard them concluded that Don Quixote must be some madman, and they began to laugh heartily. But their laughter only served to add gunpowder to the knight's fury, for without another word he drew his sword and attacked the litter. One of those who carried it, leaving the burden to his comrades, stepped forward to encounter Don Quixote, brandishing a forked pole on which they propped the litter while resting, and with it he parried the heavy stroke that the knight aimed at him. The force of the stroke snapped the pole in two, but with the remaining stump that was left in his hand he dealt the knight such a thwack on the shoulder of his sword-arm that his buckler was unable to shield him against the rustic onslaught, and down came poor Don Quixote to the ground in a bad way. Sancho, who came panting after him, seeing him fall, called out to his assailant not to strike him again, for he was a poor enchanted knight who had done nobody any harm all his life. The peasant stopped, not, however, on account of Sancho's appeal, but because he saw that Don Quixote stirred neither hand nor foot. And, believing that he had killed him, he hastily tucked up his habit to his girdle and set off, racing like a deer across the country.

By that time everyone in Don Quixote's company had reached where he lay, but when the men in the procession saw them running in their direction and with them troopers of the Holy Brotherhood with their crossbows, they feared some trouble. So, they clustered in a circle about the image: the penitents lifted their hoods and grasped their lashes; the priests brandished their tapers, and all waited for the attack with the firm resolve to defend themselves, and if they could, to take the offensive against their aggressors. But Fortune arranged matters better than they expected, for Sancho did nothing but cast himself upon the body of his master, making over him the most sorrowful and drollest lament in the world, for he truly believed that Don Quixote was dead. Our curate was recognized by one of the priests in the procession, and this calmed the apprehension of both sides. Our curate in a few words told the second curate of Don Quixote's condition; then, he and the whole crowd of disciplinants went to see whether or not the poor knight was dead, and heard Sancho Panza proclaim with tears in his eyes: "O flower of chivalry, one single blow of a cudgel has finished the course of your well-spent years! O glory of your race, honor and credit to all La Mancha, and even to the whole world, which, now that you are gone, will be overrun with evildoers, who will no longer fear punishment for their iniquities! O liberal above all the Alexanders, since for a mere eight months' service you have given me the best island that the sea surrounds! O humble to the haughty and arrogant to the humble! Resister of perils, sufferer of affronts, lover without cause, imitator of the good, scourge of the wicked, enemy of the base! In a word, knight-errant, which is the highest thing anyone could say!"

At the cries and groans of Sancho, Don Quixote revived, and the first words he said were: "He who lives absent from thee, sweet Dulcinea, endures far greater sufferings than these. Help me, friend Sancho, to lift myself into the enchanted cart, for I am no longer in a condition to press the saddle of Rozinante; this shoulder of mine is broken to pieces."

"That I'll do with all my heart, dear master," replied Sancho, "and let us go back to our village in the company of these gentlemen, and there we will make schemes for another sally that may be more profitable to us."

"You speak well, Sancho," answered the knight. "It is prudent for us to wait until the evil influence of the stars that now reigns passes away."

The canon, the curate, and the barber approved this resolution, and after they had enjoyed Sancho Panza's fooleries to the full, they placed Don Quixote on the cart as before. The procession resumed its former order and went on its way. The goatherd took his leave of them all, and as the troopers refused to go any further, the curate paid them what he owed them. The canon then begged the curate to let him know what might happen to Don Quixote (whether he recovered from his madness or remained in it), and with this he took his leave. Thus they all parted and went their several ways.

The party now consisted only of the curate, the barber, Don Quixote, Sancho, and good Rozinante, who bore all the ups and downs as patiently as his master. The wagoner yoked his oxen, and having laid Don Quixote on a bundle of hay, plodded his way at his usual calm, deliberate pace, following the directions of the curate; and at the end of six days they reached Don Quixote's village. They made their entrance at noon, and as it happened to be Sunday, all the people were in the marketplace when the wagon passed through. Everyone rushed to see who was in it, and when they recognized their townsman, they were amazed. A boy ran off at full speed to give the news to his housekeeper and his niece that their master and uncle was coming home lean and yellow, stretched out on a bundle of hay in an oxcart. It was a pathetic thing to hear the cries of the two ladies, the blows they gave themselves, the execrations they uttered afresh against the books of chivalry, all of which were repeated when they saw Don Quixote enter the door of his house.

As soon as she received news of Don Quixote's arrival, Sancho Panza's wife ran there, and as soon as she saw Sancho, her first inquiry was whether the ass had come home in good condition. Sancho replied that he was in better health than his master.

"Thanks be to God," said she, "for this great favor. Now tell me, husband, what good have you got from your squireship? What petticoat have you brought for me? What dainty shoes for your children?"

"I've brought you nothing of the kind, dear wife," said Sancho, "But I've other things of more consequence."

"I'm glad to hear so," answered the wife. "Show me those things of more consequence. I'm dying to see them to gladden my heart, for I've been mournful and down in the mouth all those ages you've been away."

"I'll show them to you at home, wife," said Sancho. "For the present, hold your soul in patience. Please God we may sally out another time in search of adventures and you'll soon see me count or governor of an island, and not one of those around here, but the finest that can be found."

"May the Lord be pleased to grant it, husband, for we're in sore need of it. Tell me now; what's all this about islands? I don't catch your meaning."

"Honey is not for an ass's mouth," answered Sancho. "You'll see in good time, wife, aye, and you'll be all agape at hearing yourself called ladyship by all your vassals."

"What are you prating about ladyships, islands, and vassals?" cried Juana Panza, for that was the name of Sancho's wife, not because they were relatives, but because in La Mancha it is customary for wives to take their husbands' last name.

"Don't fret yourself, Juana, and be in such a hurry to know everything at once; it's enough for you to know that I'm telling the truth, so mum's the word; but I can tell you one thing by the way, namely, that there's nothing in this world so pleasant as for an honest man to be squire to a knight-errant on the prowl for adventures. It's true that most of those we encountered were not as comfortable as a body would wish, for out of a hundred adventures, ninety-nine usually turned out cross and crooked. I know by experience, for from some I came off blanketed and from others bruised and battered, but when all's said and done, it's a fine thing to be gadding about spying for chances, crossing mountains, exploring woods, climbing rocks, visiting castles, lodging in inns at our own sweet will, with devil a maravedi to pay."

While this conversation was passing between Sancho Panza and Juana Panza, his wife, Don Quixote's housekeeper and niece received the knight, undressed him, and put him into his old bed. He looked at them with squinting eyes, for he could not make out where he was. The curate told the niece to take very good care of her uncle and to be very watchful lest he should make another sally, telling her the trouble it had cost to get him home. The two women began their lamentations once more, again execrating the books of chivalry and imploring Heaven to plunge the authors of so many lies and absurdities into the bottomless abyss. In fact, they were at their wits' end, for they were afraid they might lose their master and uncle the moment he felt a little better. And events turned out as they feared.

But though the author of this history has eagerly and diligently inquired after Don Quixote's exploits on his third sally, he has not been able to discover any account of them, at least from any authentic documents. Only tradition has preserved in the memory of La Mancha that the third time Don Quixote left his home he went to Saragossa, where he took part in some famous jousts in that city, and that he had adventures there worthy of his valor and of his sound intelligence. Nor would our author have been able to discover any details of his death, nor would he even have heard of it, if Fortune had not thrown in his path an aged physician who had in his possession a leaden box that he said he had discovered among the ruined foundations of an ancient hermitage that was being rebuilt. In this box he had found certain parchments written in the Gothic script, but in Castilian verse, which contained many of his exploits and emphasized the beauty of Dulcinea of El Toboso, the shape of Rozinante, the fidelity of Sancho Panza, and the burial of Don Quixote himself, with various epitaphs and eulogies on his life and character. Such as could be deciphered and interpreted the trustworthy author of this original and matchless history has set down here, and he asks no recompense from his readers for the immense pains it has cost him to ransack all the archives of La Mancha to drag it into light. All he asks is that they should give it as much credit as sensible men are wont to give to the books of chivalry, which are held in such high esteem in the world. With this he will reckon himself well paid and satisfied, and he will be encouraged to go in search of other histories, perhaps less truthful than this one, but at least as inventive and entertaining. . . .

from PART II

CHAPTER I

What passed between the curate, the barber, and Don Quixote regarding the knight's infirmity

Cide Hamete Benengeli in the second part of this history concerning Don Quixote's third sally relates that the curate and the barber remained nearly a month without seeing him, in order not to revive past events and bring them back to his memory. But this did not prevent them from visiting his niece and his housekeeper, whom they charged to be careful to treat him well and give him to eat such food as was comforting and good for heart and brain, for they had every reason to believe that all his misfortunes proceeded from that quarter. The two women declared that they were doing so and that they would continue to lavish care and affection on their master, for they had noticed that he gave signs at times of being in his right mind. This news gave the curate and the barber great satisfaction, for it seemed to prove that they had done right in bringing him back enchanted in the ox wagon, as has been related in the last chapter of the first part of this great and accurate history. So, they resolved to visit him and test his recovery, though they thought that was scarcely possible, and they agreed not to touch in any way on knight-errantry, so as not to run the risk of ripping open wounds that were still so tender.

They paid him a visit at last and found him sitting up in his bed, dressed in a green-baize jacket and a red Toledo cap and so lean and shriveled that he looked as if he had been turned into a mummy. He welcomed them cordially and to their questions about his health he replied intelligently in very well-chosen words. In the course of conversation they discoursed on so-called affairs of state and systems of government, correcting this abuse and condemning that, reforming one practice and abolishing another, each one of the three setting himself up as a new lawgiver, a modern Lycurgus, or a brand-new Solon.[1] And to such a degree did they remodel the state that they might as well have cast it into a furnace and forged a new one. And Don Quixote spoke with such good sense on all the subjects they treated that the two examiners believed, without shadow of doubt, that he was quite recovered and in full possession of his wits. The niece and the housekeeper were present at the conversation and could not find adequate words to thank God when they saw that their master was so clear in his mind. The curate, however, changed his original plan, which was not to touch on the subject of chivalry, and resolved to test Don Quixote's recovery thoroughly to see whether it was genuine or not; so, changing from one subject to another, he came at last to talk of some news that had come from the capital. Among other things he said that they had it for certain that the Turk was descending with a powerful fleet, but no one knew what his designs were or where the mighty storm would burst. And owing to this fear, which almost every year rouses men to arms, all Christendom was on the alert, and His Majesty had made provision for the defense of the coast of Naples, Sicily, and island of Malta.

"His Majesty has acted like a most prudent warrior," replied Don Quixote, "in fortifying his realms in time, so that the enemy may not find him unprepared; but if he would take my advice, I would counsel him to take one precaution of which His Majesty is not aware at the present moment."

No sooner did the curate hear this than he said to himself: "God protect you, my poor Don Quixote, for it looks to me as if you are tumbling from the pinnacle of your madness into the deep abyss of your simple-mindedness."

---

[1] The legendary Lycurgus (seventh century B.C.) reformed the Spartan constitution; Solon reformed the Athenian government in 594 B.C.

But the barber, who already had the same suspicions as the curate, asked Don Quixote what kind of measures he thought they should adopt, for perhaps they might be added to the long list of unpractical projects usually offered to princes.

"Mine, Mr. Scrapebeard," said Don Quixote, "are not unpractical but highly practical."

"No harm meant," replied the barber, "but experience has shown that all or most of the projects presented to His Majesty are either impossible, absurd, or damaging to the king and the country."

"But mine," rejoined Don Quixote, "is neither impossible nor ridiculous, but the easiest, the justest, the readiest, and the simplest that could enter the mind of any thinking man."

"Your worship is slow in telling us about it, Don Quixote," said the curate.

"I do not wish to tell it now," said Don Quixote, "and have it reach by tomorrow morning the ears of the lords of the Council, and for someone else to get the thanks and the reward for my pains."

"As for me," said the barber, "I give my word here and before God that I'll not repeat what you say to king, or rook, or earthly man,[2] an oath I learned from the ballad of the priest, who in the prologue warns the king against the thief who had robbed him of a hundred doubloons and his ambling mule."

"I do not know the story," said Don Quixote, "but I know that the oath is a good one, because I believe that the barber is an honest man."

"Even if he were not," said the curate, "I will go bail for him and vouch that he'll speak as much as a dumb man, under pain of any penalty imposed by the court."

"And who will go bail for your reverence?" said Don Quixote.

"My profession," replied the curate, "which is to keep secrets."

"Bless my heart!" exclaimed Don Quixote. "What else has His Majesty to do but to order by public crier all the knights-errant who are wandering about Spain to assemble at the capital on a certain day, and even if no more than half a dozen came, might there not be one among them who alone would be strong enough to annihilate the whole army of the Turk? Let your worships give me your attention and follow me. Is it, mark you, an unheard-of exploit for a single knight-errant to cut to bits an army of two hundred thousand men as if all together had but one throat or were made of almond paste? Now tell me, how many histories are there full of such marvels? If there were living today—to my misfortune, though I shall not say to anyone else's—the famous Don Belianís or any one of those of the innumerable offspring of Amadis of Gaul![3] If any of them were living today and were to face the Turk, I would not be in the latter's shoes. But God will take care of his people and will provide someone who, if not as resolute as the knights-errant of old, will at least not be behind them in spirit. God understands me, and I say no more."

"Alas!" cried the niece, at this point. "Strike me dead if my master doesn't want to turn knight-errant again."

---

[2] A metaphor from chess; kings and rooks are chess pieces.

[3] Heroes of Fernández' *Don Belianio of Greece* (1547) and the anonymous Spanish romance *Amadis of Gaul* (thirteenth or fourteenth century).

To which Don Quixote replied: "A knight-errant I shall die, and let the Turk make his descent or ascent whenever he will and with whatever power he can. I say once more that God understands, and I say no more."

At this the barber chimed in: "Allow me, your worships, to tell you a short tale about something that took place at Seville, for as it fits this situation like a glove, I'm dying to tell it."

Don Quixote and the curate gave him leave, and the others pricked up their ears; so, the barber began as follows: "In the madhouse at Seville was a certain man whose relations had put him there because he had lost his wits. He had graduated in common law at Osuna, but even if it had been at Salamanca, many think he would have been just as mad. This graduate, at the end of some years of confinement, convinced himself that he was sane and in his right mind, and in this frame of mind he wrote to the archbishop, imploring him earnestly and in convincing terms to order his release from the misery in which he lived, for his relatives kept him there in order to enjoy his share of the estate, and in spite of the clearest evidence they wished to have him stay mad till his death. The archbishop, impressed by his many sensible and well-reasoned letters, ordered one of his chaplains to ascertain from the governor of the madhouse whether what the licentiate wrote was true. He asked him to speak to the madman, and if he seemed to be in his senses, to set him at liberty. The chaplain did so, and the governor informed him that the man was still mad, and that though he often talked like a person of great intelligence, in the end he would break out into wild tirades as crazy and exaggerated as his previous talk had been sensible, as he would find out by speaking to him. The chaplain wished to do so, and when he visited the madman, he talked with him for an hour and more, and in all that time he never said a queer or crazy word but spoke so sensibly that the chaplain was obliged to believe him sane. Among other things that the madman said was that the governor had an edge against him because he did not want to lose the bribes his relations paid him for declaring that he was still mad, though with lucid intervals. The greatest obstacle he had to deal with in his misfortunes, he said, was his great wealth, for in order to enjoy it his enemies misjudged him and cast doubts upon the mercy that Our Lord had done him by turning him from a beast into a man. In short, he spoke so convincingly as to throw suspicion on the governor and to make his relatives appear covetous and inhuman and himself so sane that the chaplain resolved to take him away with him, so that the archbishop might see him and verify the truth for himself. In all good faith, then, the worthy chaplain begged the governor to give orders for the licentiate to be given back the clothes in which he had arrived. But the governor once more bade him mind what he was doing, for the licentiate undoubtedly was still mad. However, the governor's warning could not prevail upon the chaplain to leave the madman behind; so, seeing that the archbishop had given the order, the governor obeyed, and the madman was given back his clothes, which were new and decent. When he found himself stripped of his lunatic's dress and clothed in the garb of sanity, he begged the chaplain out of charity to allow him to bid farewell to his mad companions. The chaplain told him he would like to accompany him and see the inmates who were lodged there. So they went upstairs, accompanied by some other people who were present, and the madman went up to a cage in which was a raging maniac who happened to be calm and quiet at the time, and said to him: 'My brother, see if you have any commands for me. I am going home, for God in His infinite mercy and goodness has been pleased to restore me to my senses, though I don't deserve it. Now I am sane and in my right mind, for to God's power nothing is impossible. Put great hope and trust in Him; since He has restored me to my former state, He will restore you too, if you have faith in Him. I will send you some dainties to eat, and be sure you eat them, for I must tell you that I am convinced, as one who has gone through it, that all our madness proceeds from our having our bellies empty and our brains full of wind. Take heart! Have courage! For despondency in our misfortunes weakens our health and hastens death.'

"Another madman in another cage opposite the raging lunatic's overheard all that the graduate said, and rising from an old mat on which he was lying stark naked, he asked in a loud voice who this man was who was going away cured and sane. The graduate replied: 'It is I, brother, who am going. I have no need to stay here any longer, for which I give infinite thanks to Heaven, which has done me this great favor.'

"'Mind what you say, graduate, and don't let the Devil deceive you,' answered the madman. 'Rest your feet and stay snugly and quietly at home, and you'll spare yourself the return journey.'

"'I know that I am well,' rejoined the graduate, 'and shall not have to go the rounds again.'

"'You well?' cried the madman. 'Good! We shall see. God be with you, but I vow to Jupiter, whose majesty I represent on earth, that for the sin that Seville is committing today in releasing you from this house and treating you as a sane man, I shall inflict such punishment on her as shall be remembered for centuries and centuries to come, amen. Do you not know, you mean little graduate, that I have the power to do so? For let me tell you, I am Jupiter the thunderer and hold in my hands the flaming thunderbolts with which I can and do threaten to destroy the world. But with one punishment alone I mean to chastise this ignorant city. For three whole years I will not rain on it and on all the surrounding districts, and the time is to be reckoned from the instant I utter this threat. You free, you sane, you in your right senses? And I mad and sick and in chains? I would as soon think of raining as hang myself.'

"The madman's loud burst of oratory attracted the attention of the bystanders, but our graduate, turning to our chaplain and seizing him by the hands, cried: 'Don't be concerned, my dear sir; take no notice of what this lunatic says, for if he is Jupiter and will not rain, I am Neptune, the father and god of the waters, and I will rain as often as I please and whenever it is necessary.'

"To which the chaplain replied: 'All the same, Lord Neptune, it would not be right to annoy Lord Jupiter. Your worship may remain at home, and we will come back for you another day when we have more time.'

"The governor and the bystanders burst out laughing, and the chaplain was half ashamed at their jeering. The graduate was stripped and clapped in his cage, and that is the end of my story."

"So that, Master Barber, is the story," said Don Quixote, "that suited our situation so well that you had to tell it? O Master Scrapebeard! How blind is he who cannot see through a sieve! Is it possible that your worship does not know that comparisons between wit and wit, valor and valor, beauty and beauty, birth and birth, are always hateful and cause resentment? I, Master Barber, am not Neptune, the god of the waters, and I am not setting myself up as a wise man when I am not. I only strive to convince the world of its errors in not reviving that most fortunate age in which the order of chivalry flourished. But our depraved age does not deserve to enjoy so great a blessing as did those in which knights-errant undertook and burdened their shoulders with the defense of kingdoms, the protection of damsels, the relief of children and orphans, the chastisement of the proud, and the rewarding of the humble. Most of our knights nowadays prefer to nestle in the damasks, brocades, and other rich silks they wear than in armored coats of mail. There are now no knights who sleep in the fields, exposed to the rigor of the heavens in full armor from head to foot. There is no one now who snatches a nap, as they say, resting on his lance and with his feet on the stirrups as knights-errant did of old. There is no one now to sally forth from this wood and enter that mountain, and from there to go to a wasted and deserted shore of the sea, most often stormy and tempestuous, and to find there on the beach a little boat without oars, sail, mast, or tackle, and with undaunted heart to fling himself in and entrust himself to the implacable waves of the deep sea, which at one moment toss him up to the sky, and at another engulf him in the abyss. Then, exposing his chest to the irresistible tempest, he finds himself, when he least expects it, more than nine thousand miles from the place where he embarked; and leaping on to a remote and unknown shore, he undergoes experiences worthy to be inscribed not on parchment, but on brass. Today sloth triumphs over industry, idleness over labor, vice over virtue, arrogance over bravery, and theory over the practice of arms, which only lived and flourished in the Golden Age and among knights-errant. If I am not right, tell me, who was more virtuous and valiant than the renowned Amadis of Gaul? Who was wiser than Palmerin of England? Who more pleasant and dexterous than Tirante the White? Who more gallant than Lisuarte of Greece? Who a greater slasher or more slashed than Don Belianís? Who more undaunted than Perión of Gaul, or more eager to face peril than Felixmarte of Hyrcania? Or more sincere than Esplandian? Who more impetuous than Cirongilio of Thrace? Who more fearless than Rodamante? Who more prudent than King Sobrino? Who bolder than Rinaldo? Who more invincible than Orlando? And who more high-spirited and courteous than Ruggiero, from whom are descended today the dukes of Ferrara, according to Turpin's cosmography? [4] All these knights and many more I could mention, Master Priest, were knights-errant, the light and glory of chivalry. These, and such as these, I should wish to take part in my project, and if they did, His Majesty would find himself well served at great saving of expense, and the Turk would be left tearing his beard. Therefore I wish to remain at home, since the chaplain is not taking me out, and if Jupiter, as the barber has said, will not rain, here am I who will rain whenever I please. This I say so that Master Basin may see that I understand him."

[4] The heroes mentioned are all characters in Spanish romances or in romances by Ariosto and Boiardo. Turpin's cosmography is a fictitious work.

"Really, Don Quixote," said the barber, "that wasn't why I told you the tale. I meant well by it, so help me God, and your worship shouldn't take offense."

"I know best whether I took offense or not," replied Don Quixote.

The curate then remarked: "Although I've hardly said a word up to now, I should like to relieve myself of a scruple that is gnawing and scraping at my conscience upon hearing Don Quixote's last remarks."

"The curate has license for other more solemn matters," answered Don Quixote, "so he can declare his scruple, for it is unpleasant to go about with scruples on one's conscience."

"Well, with your leave," replied the curate, "I shall reveal my scruple. It is that I am unable to convince myself in any way, Don Quixote, that all this crew of knights-errant your worship has mentioned have really and truly been people of flesh and blood living in this world. On the contrary, I think that it is all fiction, fable, and lies, dreams told by men awake, or rather half asleep."

"That is another mistake," replied Don Quixote, "into which many have fallen who do not believe that such knights have ever existed. Often with different people and at different times I have tried to expose this almost universal error to the light of truth. On some occasions I have not succeeded in my purpose; on others I have, supporting my argument with evidence so infallible that I might say I have seen Amadis of Gaul with my own eyes. He was a man tall of stature and fair of face, with a well-trimmed black beard, and his looks were half mild and half severe. He was short of speech, slow to anger, and quickly appeased. Now in the same manner in which I have portrayed Amadis, I could, I believe, paint and describe all the knights-errant who wander in the histories, for I have absolute faith that they were exactly as the histories tell us, and my knowledge of their deeds and their characters makes it possible for me by sound philosophy to make out their features, their complexions, and their statures."

"How big then, my dear Don Quixote," inquired the barber, "would the giant Morgante have been in your worship's opinion?"

"As to the existence of giants," replied Don Quixote, "there are various opinions. But Holy Scripture, which cannot depart from the truth by so much as an inch, proves that they existed by telling us the story of that great Philistine, Goliath, who was seven cubits and a half tall, which is a prodigious height.[5] There have been also found in the island of Sicily shinbones and shoulder blades of a size that shows that their owners were giants and as tall as great towers; geometry proves this beyond a doubt. Nevertheless, I am unable to say with certainty what was the size of Morgante, although I imagine he could not have been so very tall, and I am inclined to this opinion by discovering in the history where special emphasis is laid upon his deeds that he often slept under a roof, and since he found houses to contain him, it is clear that his size was not excessive."

"That is true," said the curate, who, delighted to hear him talk such nonsense, then asked him what he felt about the features of Rinaldo of Montalbán

---

[5] The story of Goliath is told in I Samuel 17, where his height is given as six and a half cubits, about nine feet nine inches. The giant Morgante appears in a sixteenth-century romance by Pulci.

and of Orlando and the other Peers of France, for they all were knights-errant.

"Of Rinaldo," replied Don Quixote, "I make bold to say that he was broad in face, red-complexioned, with rolling and rather prominent eyes, very thin-skinned and choleric, friendly to robbers and to vagabonds. About Roland, or Rotolando, or Orlando—for histories give him all these names—I am positively convinced that he was of middle stature, broad-shouldered, rather bowlegged, dark-complexioned, and red-bearded, with a hairy body and a threatening appearance, abrupt in speech, but very polite and well bred."

"If Orlando was no more of a gentleman than your worship has made out," said the curate, "it was no wonder that the lady Angélica the Fair rejected him for the gaiety, the dash, and the charm of the downy-cheeked Moorling to whom she gave herself. She showed good sense in falling in love with Medoro's gentleness rather than with the roughness of Orlando."[6]

"That Angélica, sir priest," answered Don Quixote, "was a giddy, wanton damsel, and a trifle flighty, and she left the world as full of her indiscretions as of her famous beauty. She scorned a thousand lords—a thousand valiant and a thousand wise lords—and contented herself with a smooth-faced little chit of a page with no other fortune than the reputation he gained by his loyalty to his friend. The great singer of her beauty, the celebrated Ariosto, did not dare, or perhaps did not care, to relate what happened to this lady after her base surrender—for no doubt her conduct was not too chaste—and left her with these lines:

> 'And how she won the scepter of Cathay,
> Another bard will sing to a mellower lay.'

"This, no doubt, was a kind of prophecy, for poets are also called *vates*, which means diviners. This truth can be plainly seen, for since then a famous Andalusian poet has wept and sung about her tears, and another celebrated and unique Castilian poet has sung her beauty."[7]

"Tell me, Don Quixote," interposed the barber, "has there been no poet who has made some satire on this lady Angélica, among all those who have praised her?"

"I truly believe," replied Don Quixote, "that if Sacripante or Orlando had been poets, they would have given the damsel a trouncing, for it is right and natural for poets who have been scorned or not accepted by their ladies, either fictitious or modeled on those they have chosen as mistresses of their thoughts, to revenge themselves in satires and lampoons, a vengeance assuredly unworthy of generous hearts. But up to now there has come to my notice no defamatory verse against the lady Angélica, who turned the whole world topsy-turvy."

"A miracle," exclaimed the curate.

---

[6] Quixote and the curate are referring to the Italian comic romance *Orlando Furioso (Roland Driven Mad)*, 1532, by Ludovico Ariosto. Quixote misquotes a couplet from this work below.

[7] The Andalusian poet is Luis Barahona de Soto, and the Castilian is Lope de Vega, both of whom wrote poems about the romance heroine Angélica.

But at this point they heard the housekeeper and the niece, who had withdrawn from their conversation, making an outcry in the yard, and they all ran out to see what the noise was about.

CHAPTER II

Which deals with the notable quarrel between Sancho Panza and Don Quixote's niece and housekeeper, with other amusing incidents

The story tells that the noise Don Quixote, the curate, and the barber heard were the niece and the housekeeper screaming indignantly at Sancho Panza, who was struggling to get in and see Don Quixote, while they were holding the door against him.

"What does that feckless gadabout want in this house? Off with you to your own haunts, brother, for it's you and none other who deludes my master and leads him gallivanting over hill and dale."

To which Sancho replied: "Housekeeper of Satan! I'm the one who is deluded and led gallivanting over hill and dale, and not your master; it is he who led me on a jaunt all over the world, and you are wide off the mark. It was he who tricked me away from home, with his colloguing, promising me an island, and I'm still waiting for it."

"May those foul islands choke you," replied the niece, "damn you, Sancho. And what are those isles of yours? Are they something to eat, you glutton and gormandizer?"

"They are not anything to eat," answered Sancho, "but to govern and rule, and better than any four cities and richer than four judgeships at court."

"You shan't come in here, all the same," said the housekeeper, "you bag of mischief, you sack of villainies! Go and govern your house, till your plot, and rid your empty pate of isles and islands."

The curate and the barber were greatly amused to hear this conversation of the three, but Don Quixote was afraid Sancho would blurt out a whole heap of mischievous nonsense and touch upon points that might not be wholly to his credit. So, he called to him and bade the two women to hold their tongues and let him enter. Sancho went in, and the curate and the barber took their leave of the knight. They despaired of his cure, for they saw how fixed he was in his crazy notions and how deeply absorbed by his accursed nonsensical knight-errantry. And so the curate said to the barber: "You will see, my friend; when we least expect it, our knight will be off bush-ranging."

"I've no doubt of that," replied the barber, "but I'm less surprised at the knight's madness than at the squire's foolishness in believing the story of the isle, for I'm sure that all the disappointments imaginable will not drive it out of his head."

"May God help them," said the curate, "and let us keep our eyes open and see what comes of this crazy alliance of knight and squire. Both of them seem to be cast in the same mold, and the master's eccentricities would not be worth a farthing without the squire's foolishness."

"That's true," said the barber, "and I should be very glad to know what the two of them are talking about this moment."

"I dare wager," replied the curate, "that the niece or the housekeeper will tell us by and by, for they are not the kind to refrain from listening."

In the meantime Don Quixote had shut himself in his room with Sancho, and when they were alone, he said: "I am deeply grieved, Sancho, that you have said and still say that it was I took you from your cottage, when you know that I myself did not stay at home. We set out together, together we lived, together we wandered. One and the same fortune, one and the same destiny has fallen upon us both; if they tossed you in a blanket once, they have beaten me a hundred times, and this is the one advantage I have over you."

"That is quite right," answered Sancho, "for as your worship says, disasters belong rather to knights-errant than to their squires."

"You are mistaken, Sancho," said Don Quixote. "Remember the saying: *quando caput dolet,* etc."[8]

"I understand no language but my own," replied Sancho.

"I mean," said Don Quixote, "that when the head aches, all the limbs feel pain; and so, as I am your lord and master, I am your head, and you are a part of me because you are my servant; and for that reason the evil that touches me, or shall touch me, should hurt you, and yours should hurt me."

"So it should be," said Sancho, "but when they tossed me, the limb, in the blanket, my head was outside the wall, watching me fly through the air and not feeling any pain. But since the limbs have to suffer the head's pain, the head should also be made to suffer for the limbs."

"Do you mean to suggest, Sancho," replied Don Quixote, "that I felt no pain when they were tossing you? If that is what you say, you are wrong. You should not even think such a thing, for I felt more pain then in my spirit than you did in your body. But let us put that aside for the present, for there will be a time when we can consider the matter and come to a proper conclusion. Now tell me, Sancho, my friend, what do they say about me in the village? What opinion of me have the common people and the gentry and the knights? What do they say of my valor, of my deeds, and of my courtesy? How do they speak of the enterprise I have undertaken to revive and restore to the world the forgotten order of chivalry? In short, Sancho, I want you to tell me all that has come to your ears. You must answer me without exaggerating praise or mitigating blame. For it is the duty of loyal vassals to speak the truth to their lords without exaggerating it through flattery or lessening it through vain deference. And I would have you know, Sancho, that if the naked truth reached the ears of princes without the trappings of flattery, these times would be different, and other ages would more fitly be reputed iron than ours, which I reckon to be of gold. Take this warning, Sancho, and discreetly and faithfully give me the true answer to the questions I have asked you."

"I'll do so with all my heart, sir," replied Sancho, "on condition that your worship does not get angry at what I say, for you want me to tell you the naked truth and not to dress it in any clothes, except those I found it in."

"On no account shall I be angry," answered Don Quixote. "You can speak freely, Sancho, without beating about the bush."

---

[8] *Quando caput dolet, caetera membra dolent* is the complete proverb. Quixote translates it below: "When the head aches, all the limbs feel pain."

"Then the first thing I'll say is that the common people take your worship for a mighty great madman, and they think I'm no less of a simpleton. The gentry say that you're not content with being a country gentleman and that you have turned yourself into a don and thrust yourself into knighthood with no more than a few miserable vinestocks and two acres of land, with a tatter behind and another in front to bless your name. The knights say they don't relish seeing the petty gentry setting themselves up against them, especially those squireens who black their shoes and darn their black stockings with green silk."

"That," said Don Quixote, "has nothing to do with me, for I am always well dressed and never patched. Ragged I may be, but ragged more from the wear and tear of my armor than from time."

"As to your worship's valor, courtesy, and exploits," continued Sancho, "there are different opinions. Some say, 'mad but droll'; others, 'valiant but unfortunate'; others, 'courteous but saucy'; and so they go sticking their noses into this and that until they don't leave a whole bone either in your body or in mine."

"Observe, Sancho," said Don Quixote, "that whenever virtue is found in an eminent degree, it is persecuted. Few or none of the famous heroes of old have escaped being slandered by malicious tongues. Julius Caesar, a most high-spirited, most prudent, and most valiant captain, was branded as ambitious and not too clean either in his garments or in his morals. Alexander, whose exploits achieved for him the name of Great, was said to have been somewhat of a drunkard. And Hercules, the hero of the many labors, according to gossips was lascivious and effeminate. Don Galaor, the brother of Amadis of Gaul, is rumored to have been over-lecherous and his brother to have been a sniveler. So, Sancho, seeing that there is so much slander against good men, what they say about me may pass if it is no more than what you have told me."

"Ah, but there's the rub, body of my father!" replied Sancho.

"Is there anything more then?" asked Don Quixote.

"Faith an' we still have to skin the tail,' said Sancho. "Why, up to now it has been tarts and fancy bread, but if your worship wants to know all about the calumnies they fling at you, I'll bring you here presently one who will tell you the lot of them without missing an atom, for last night Bartolome Carrasco's son arrived from studying at Salamanca, where he was made a bachelor. And when I went up to welcome him, he told me that the history of your worship is already told in a book by the name of *The Ingenious Gentleman Don Quixote of La Mancha.* And he says that they also mention me in it by my own very name of Sancho Panza, and Lady Dulcinea of El Toboso, too, and many a thing that happened to us in private, which made me cross myself in amazement to think how the history writer could have got wind of what he wrote."

"You may be sure, Sancho," said Don Quixote, "that the author of our history is some wise enchanter, for nothing can be hidden from them."

"But if the author of this history was a wise enchanter," replied Sancho, "how comes it about that according to the bachelor Sansón Carrasco—for that's the man's name—the author of our history is called Cide Hamete Berengena?"

"That is a Moor's name," rejoined Don Quixote.

"So it may be," answered Sancho, "for I have heard that Moors for the most part are very fond of eggplants."[9]

"You must be mistaken, Sancho," said Don Quixote, "in the name of this Cide, which in Arabic means lord."

"Very likely," replied Sancho, "but if you would like to have me bring the bachelor here, I'll go for him like a shot."

"You will do me a great favor, my friend," said Don Quixote. "What you have told me makes me anxious, and I shall not eat a mouthful that will do me good until I am informed of everything."

"Then I'll go to fetch him," answered Sancho.

So, leaving his master, he went off to find the bachelor, with whom he returned in a short while. And between these three a most entertaining conversation took place.

CHAPTER III

Of the ridiculous conversation that passed between Don Quixote, Sancho Panza, and the bachelor Sansón Carrasco

Don Quixote remained very pensive, waiting for the bachelor Sansón Carrasco, from whom he expected to hear how he had been put into a book, as Sancho had told him. He could not convince himself that such a history could exist, for the blood of the enemies he had slain was hardly dry on the blade of his sword, yet they were already saying that his high deeds of chivalry were in print. Nevertheless, he imagined that some sage, either friend or enemy, by his magic art had given them to the press; if a friend, to magnify and exalt them above the most renowned feats of any knight-errant; if an enemy, to annihilate them and place them below the meanest ever written of some base squire, although, he said to himself, the deeds of squires were never written of. If, however, it were true that such history was in existence, seeing that it was about a knight-errant, it must of necessity be grandiloquent, lofty, distinguished, and true. This thought consoled him somewhat, but he was worried to think that its author was a Moor, as the name Cide suggested, for he could expect no truth from the Moors, since they are all impostors, forgers, and schemers. He also dreaded that his love affairs might be treated indelicately, which might lead to the disparagement and prejudice of Lady Dulcinea of El Toboso's good name. For he was anxious that it should be made quite clear that he had always been faithful to her and had always shown her respect, turning a blind eye to all queens, empresses, and damsels of every degree for her sake. And so, Sancho, when he returned with Carrasco, found him rapt and absorbed in these and countless other fancies, but the knight received the new guest with courtesy.

The bachelor, though his name was Sansón, was no giant in stature, but was a very great wag. He was of sallow complexion, very sharp witted, about twenty-four years of age, with a round face, a flat nose, and a large mouth—all signs of a mischievous disposition and of one who is fond of joking and making fun, as he showed straightaway, for no sooner did he see Don Quixote

---

[9] The "Arabic manuscript" is supposed to have been found at Toledo, where the inhabitants were jokingly called *berengeneros* (the egg-planters).

than he dropped to his knees before him, saying: "Let your mightiness give me your hands to kiss, Sir Don Quixote of La Mancha. By the habit of St. Peter[10] that I wear—though I've taken no more than the first four orders—your worship is one of the most famous knights-errant there has ever been or ever shall be in all the rotundity of the earth. Blessings on Cide Hamete Benengeli, who has written the history of your doughty deeds, and double blessings on the connoisseur who took the trouble to have it translated from Arabic into our Castilian vulgar tongue for the universal entertainment of mankind."

Don Quixote made him rise and said: "So it is true that there is a history of me and that it was a Moor and a wise man who wrote it."

"So true is it," said Sansón, "that I believe there are today in print more than twelve thousand volumes of the said history. For proof you have only to ask Portugal, Barcelona, and Valencia, where they have been printed, and it is rumored that it is being printed at Antwerp, and I am convinced that there is not a country or language in the world in which it will not be translated."[11]

"One of the things," said Don Quixote in reply, "which shall give the greatest pleasure to a virtuous and eminent man is to see himself in his lifetime printed and in the press, and with a good name on people's tongues, a good name, I repeat, for were it the contrary, no death could be so bad."

"If it is a question of a good reputation and a good name," said the bachelor, "your worship singly carries off the palm from all knights-errant, for the Moor in his language and the Christian in his have taken great pains to portray for us, quite realistically, your worship's gallantry, your great courage in facing perils, your patience in adversity and in sufferings, whether because of misfortunes or because of wounds, and the chastity and continence in the platonic loves of your worship and my lady. Doña Dulcinea of El Toboso."

"Never," butted in Sancho at this point, "have I heard Lady Dulcinea called doña, but plain Lady Dulcinea of El Toboso. So, history has gone astray."

"That's not an important objection," replied Carrasco.

"No, surely," replied Don Quixote, "but tell me, Master Bachelor, which of my deeds are most highly praised in this history?"

"About that point," answered the bachelor, "opinions vary as tastes vary. Some favor the adventure of the windmills, which seemed to your worship to be Briareuses and giants; others, the adventure of the fulling mills.[12] One is all for the description of the two armies, which afterward turned out to be two flocks of sheep; another praises the one of the corpse they were carrying to Segovia for burial. This one declares that the best of all is the freeing of the galley slaves, that one says that none equals that of the Benedictine giants and the combat with the valiant Biscayan."

"Tell me, Master Bachelor," cried Sancho, "does the adventure with the Yanguesans come in, when our good Rozinante had the notion of looking for mushrooms at the bottom of the sea?"[13]

---

[10] The ecclesiastical dress worn by university students.

[11] Ten editions had already been published of the first part of *Don Quixote* by 1612–13, when Cervantes is thought to have written this chapter.

[12] Cloth mills. (The episode is omitted in this selection.)

[13] The adventures of the funeral party, the Benedictine "giants," the valiant Biscayan, and the Yanguesans are all omitted here.

"The sage left nothing in the inkhorn," answered Sansón. "He tells everything and touches on every point, even the capers that the worthy Sancho cut on the blanket."

"I cut no capers on the blanket," answered Sancho, "but in the air I did, and more than I would have liked."

"In my opinion," said Don Quixote, "there is no human history in the world which has not its ups and downs, especially those that deal with knight-errantry. They can never be full of lucky incidents alone."

"For all that," replied the bachelor, "some who have read your history say that they would have been glad if the author had omitted some of the countless drubbings that were given Don Quixote in his various encounters."

"Ah! There's where the truth of the story comes in," rejoined Sancho.

"Yet, they might in all fairness have kept quiet about them," said Don Quixote, "for there is no point in writing about actions that do not change or affect the truth of the story, if they tend to diminish the stature of the hero. Aeneas, I am sure, was not as pious as Virgil made him out to be, nor Ulysses as prudent as he is described in Homer." [14]

"That is true," replied Sansón, "but it is one thing to write as a poet, and another as a historian. The poet can tell or sing of things, not as they were, but as they ought to have been; the historian must relate them not as they should have been, but as they were, without adding to or subtracting from the truth."

"Well, if this Moor is out for truth," said Sancho, "then my beatings will be found there as well as my master's, for they never took measure of his worship's shoulders without measuring my whole body. But there's no wonder in that, for that same master of mine says that the limbs must take their fair share of the head's pain."

"You're a cunning rogue, Sancho," answered Don Quixote, "I swear your memory never fails you when you want to remember something."

"Even if I wanted to forget the cudgelings I got," said Sancho, "devil a bit would the bruises let me, for they're still as plain as paint on my ribs."

"Be quiet, Sancho," said Don Quixote, "and don't interrupt the bachelor, who, I hope, will now tell me what they say of me in this history he has referred to."

"And of me," said Sancho, "for I'm told that I am one of the principal presonages in it."

"*Personage,* not *presonages,* Sancho, my friend," said Sansón.

"So, here we have another word corrector!" rejoined Sancho. "If it goes on like this, we'll never come to the end of it in this life."

"May I be blowed, Sancho," replied the bachelor, "if you're not the second person in the history! Why, there are some who prefer to hear you talk than the best parts in the whole book, though, to be sure, there are others who say you were much too credulous in taking as Gospel truth that island Don Quixote has promised you."

"The sun is still shining on the thatch," [15] said Don Quixote, "and in the meantime, as Sancho is growing older and riper in experience, wit, and years,

---

[14] The references are to Virgil's *Aeneid* and Homer's *Odyssey*. Ulysses is Odysseus.

[15] A proverbial expression, meaning "the day is not over yet" or "there is still time."

he will become fitter and more able for the post of governor than he is at present."

"By God, sir," said Sancho, "any island I can't govern at my age, I'll never govern, even if I live to be as old as Methuselah.[16] The worst of it is that this isle of yours keeps itself hidden away the Lord knows where, and not that I haven't brains enough to govern it."

"Commend it to God, Sancho," said Don Quixote, "and all will be well, perhaps better than you think, for not a leaf stirs on a tree without God's will."

"That is true," said Sansón, "for if God is willing, Sancho will not lack a thousand isles, much less one."

"I have seen governors about here," said Sancho, "who, in my opinion, don't come up to the sole of my shoe. Yet, for all that they're called lordship and served on silver."

"Those are not governors of isles," answered Sansón, "but of other governments that are easier handled. Governors of isles must at least be grammarians."

"I'll deal with the *gram*," said Sancho, "but as to the *marians*, I'll let them be, for I don't understand them. But leaving this matter of a governorship in God's hands—may He put me where I can serve Him best—let me say, Master Bachelor, that I'm mighty glad the author of this history has spoken of me in such a way that the things told of me don't give offense, for as I'm a good squire, if he'd said any derogatory things about me, not becoming the old Christian I am, our quarrel would reach the ears of the deaf."

"That would be to work miracles," said Sansón.

"Miracles or no miracles," said Sancho, "let everyone mind how he speaks or writes about persons, and not jot down helter-skelter the first thing that comes into his noddle."

"One of the blemishes they find in this history," said the bachelor, "is that the author has inserted in it a novel called 'The Tale of Ill-Advised Curiosity'—not that it is bad or badly told, but that it is out of place and has nothing to do with the history of his worship, Don Quixote."[17]

"I'll bet," rejoined Sancho, "that the son of a dog has made a pretty kettle of fish of everything."

"Now I am sure," said Don Quixote, "that the author of my story is no sage but some ignorant prater who set himself blindly and aimlessly to write it down and let it turn out anyhow, like Orbaneja, the painter of Ubeda, who, when they asked him what he was painting, used to answer: 'Whatever it turns out.' Sometimes he would paint a cock in such a way and so little like one that it was necessary to write beside it in Gothic characters: 'This is a cock.' And so it must be with my history, which will need a commentary to be understood."

"No," replied Sansón, "for it's so plain that there is nothing in it to cause any difficulty. Children finger it, young people read it, grown men know it by heart, and old men praise it. It is so thumbed and read and so familiar to all kinds of people that no sooner do they catch sight of a lean hack than

---

[16] Nine hundred and sixty-nine years old, according to Genesis 5:25.

[17] This episode is omitted in this selection. Here and below, Cervantes is citing actual criticisms of Part I.

they cry out: 'There goes Rozinante.' Those who are most given to reading it are pages, for there's no lord's antechamber in which you will not find a *Don Quixote*. When one lays it down, another picks it up; some grab at it, others beg for it. This story, in fact, is the most delightful and least harmful entertainment ever seen to this day, for nowhere in it can one detect even the shadow of an indelicate expression or an uncatholic thought."

"To write in any other way," said Don Quixote, "would be to write not truths but lies, and historians who resort to lying ought to be burned like coiners of false money. But I do not know what induced the author to make use of novels and irrelevant tales when he had so much to write of in mine. No doubt he felt bound by the proverb: 'With straw or with hay, what odds we say!' For really if he had confined himself to my thoughts, my sighs, my tears, my righteous desires, and my enterprises, he could have compiled a volume greater than all the works of El Tostado, or at least as big.[18] So, my conclusion is, Master Bachelor, that one needs good judgment and ripe understanding to write histories or books of any sort whatsoever. To be witty and write humorously requires great genius. The most cunning part in a comedy is the clown's, for a man who wants to be taken for a simpleton must never be one. History is like a sacred text, for it has to be truthful, and where the truth is, there is God. But in spite of this, there are some who write books and toss them off into the world as though they were pancakes."

"There is no book so bad," said the bachelor, "that there is not something good in it."[19]

"No doubt of that," replied Don Quixote, "but it often happens that authors who have deservedly reaped and won great fame by their books have lost it all, or at least lessened it, when they have given them to the press."

"The reason of that is," answered Sansón, "that printed books are viewed at leisure, and so their faults are easily noticed, and the greater the fame of their authors, the more closely they are examined. Celebrated men of genius, great poets, and famous historians are always, or as a rule, envied by those who make it their pleasure and special pastime to judge the writings of others, without having published anything of their own."

"That is no wonder," said Don Quixote, "for there are many theologians who are no good in the pulpit, but excellent at recognizing the faults or excesses of those who preach."

"All that is so, Don Quixote," said Carrasco, "but I would be happy if those censors would be more merciful and less scrupulous and if they refrained from pitilessly stressing the specks on the bright sun of the work they are crabbing. For if *aliquando bonus dormitat Homerus*,[20] let them reflect how long he stayed awake to give us the light of his work with the least possible shadow. And it is possible that what seem to be faults to them are moles, which at times heighten the beauty of the face that has them. And so, I say that he who prints a book runs a very great risk, for it is absolutely impossible to write one that will satisfy and please every reader."

---

[18] Alonso de Madrigal, bishop of Ávila, who wrote under the pen name "El Tostado," was so prolific a writer of devotional works that there was a proverb, "He writes more than El Tostado."

[19] Carrasco is quoting the Roman naturalist Pliny the Elder.

[20] "Worthy Homer sometimes nods." (Horace, *Art of Poetry*, line 359.)

"The one that treats of me," said Don Quixote, "must have pleased but few."

"Rather the opposite, for as there are an infinite number of fools in the world, an infinite number of people have enjoyed that history. But there are some who have found fault and assailed the author's memory for forgetting who it was who robbed Sancho of his ass, for it is not then stated and it is only from the context that we infer that it was stolen. Yet, a little later on we find Sancho riding on this same ass, and we are never told how he turned up again. They also say that he forgot to put down what Sancho did with the hundred crowns he found in the leather bag in the Sierra Morena, for they were never mentioned again. Many people want to know what he did with them and how did he spend them, for it is one of the major omissions in the work."

"I'm not prepared now, Master Sansón," replied Sancho, "to go into details or accounts, for I feel faint in the stomach and if I don't cure it with a few swigs of the old stuff, it will put me on St. Lucy's thorn.[21] I have a drop at home, and my old woman is waiting for me. When I've had my dinner, I'll come back and answer all your worship's questions, and all the world's whether it's about my losing the ass or spending the hundred crowns."

Then, without waiting for an answer or saying another word, he went home.

Don Quixote begged and prayed the bachelor to stay and take potluck with him. He accepted the invitation and stayed for the meal, and a pair of pigeons were added to the usual fare. Knight-errantry was discussed at table, and Carrasco was careful to humor the knight. When the meal was over, they took their siesta until Sancho returned. . . .

[*In the following chapters, Sancho supplies Sansón Carrasco with certain details of his and Quixote's adventures and reassures his wife Teresa that his quest with Quixote will result in his being governor of an island. Quixote's niece Antonia tries to dissuade him from further adventures, but he resolves to embark on a "third sally." He and Sancho ride out, bound first for Toboso, to see Dulcinea. There Sancho tricks Quixote by telling him that Dulcinea has been changed by enchantment into a country wench; he introduces him to three such wenches. Quixote, discouraged, rides on with Sancho; they encounter a band of strolling players. The actors have just performed a morality play called* The Parliament of Death *and are costumed as Death, an angel, and a knight. The Fool of the company frightens Rozinante and Sancho's ass Dapple, who throw their riders, but Quixote yields to Sancho's advice not to do battle with these false Kings, Princes, and Emperors.*]

CHAPTER XII

Of the strange adventure that befell the gallant Don Quixote with the brave Knight of the Mirrors

Don Quixote and his squire spent the night following their encounter with Death beneath some tall and shady trees, and the former, at Sancho's persuasion, partook of the food from the store carried by Dapple. While they were at supper, Sancho said to his master: "Sir, what a fool I should have

---

[21] Make me weak with hunger (proverbial).

been if I had chosen for my reward the spoils of the first adventure accomplished by your worship, instead of the foals of the three mares![22] Well, well, a sparrow in the hand is better than a vulture on the wing."

"Nevertheless, Sancho," replied Don Quixote, "if you had let me attack as I wished, the Empress' gold crown and Cupid's painted wings would have fallen to you as spoils, for I would have seized them by force and put them into your hands."

"The scepters and crowns of stage emperors," answered Sancho Panza, "are never made of real gold, but only of brass or tinfoil."

"That is true," said Don Quixote, "the ornaments of the drama should not be real, but only make-believe and fiction like the drama itself. Indeed, Sancho, I want you to turn a kindly eye upon the play and in consequence upon those who represent and compose it, for they are all productive of much good to the state, placing before us at every step a mirror in which we may see vividly portrayed the action of human life. Nothing, in fact, more truly portrays us as we are and as we would be than the play and the players. Now tell me, have you never seen a play acted in which kings, emperors, pontiffs, knights, ladies, and divers other characters are introduced? One plays the bully, another the rogue; this one the merchant, that the soldier; one the wise fool, another the foolish lover. When the play is over and they have divested themselves of the dresses they wore in it, the actors are all again upon the same level."

"Yes, I've seen it," answered Sancho.

"Well, then," said Don Quixote, "the same happens in the comedy and life of this world, where some play emperors, others popes, and in short, all the parts that can be brought into a play; but when it is over, that is to say, when life ends, death strips them all of the robes that distinguished one from the other, and all are equal in the grave."

"A brave comparison!" said Sancho. "Though not so new, for I've heard it many a time, as well as that one about the game of chess: so long as the game lasts, each piece has its special office, and when the game is finished, they are all mixed, shuffled, and jumbled together and stored away in the bag, which is much like ending life in the grave."

"Each day, Sancho," said Don Quixote, "you are becoming less doltish and more wise."

"Yes, master, for some of your wisdom must stick to me," said Sancho, "just as land that is of itself barren and dry will eventually, by dint of dunging and tilling, come to yield a goodly crop. What I mean to say is that your worship's talk has been the dung that has fallen upon the barren soil of my poor wit and that the time during which I have served you and enjoyed your company has been the tillage. With the help of this I hope to yield fruit that are like blessings and such that will not slide away from the paths of good breeding that you have made in my shallow understanding."

Don Quixote laughed at Sancho's affected style of speech and perceived that what he said about his improvement was true, for from time to time he spoke in a way that astonished him; though on most occasions when Sancho tried to talk in argument and in a lofty style, his speech would end by toppling down from the peak of his simplicity into the abyss of his ignorance.

---

[22] The reward Quixote has promised Sancho for news of Dulcinea.

And where he showed his culture and his memory best was in his use of proverbs, no matter whether they came pat to the subject or not, as must have been seen already and noted in the course of this history.

In such a conversation they spent a great part of the night, but Sancho felt a wish to let down the hatches of his eyes, as he used to say when he wanted to sleep. So, having unharnessed Dapple, he left him free to crop the abundant pasture. He did not take the saddle off Rozinante, as his master's express orders were that as long as they were in the field or not sleeping under a roof, Rozinante was not to be unsaddled; it was, by the way, an ancient custom, established and observed by knights-errant, to take off the bridle and hang it on the saddlebow; but to remove the saddle from the horse—never on your life! Sancho observed this rule and gave him the same liberty he had given Dapple, whose friendship for Rozinante was so unequaled and so close that a tradition handed down from father to son says that the author of this true history wrote some chapters on the subject that, in order to preserve the propriety and decorum due to so heroic a history, he did not include. At times, however, he forgets this resolve and describes how, as soon as the two beasts were together, they would scratch one another, and how, when they were tired or satisfied, Rozinante would lay his neck across Dapple's more than half a yard beyond, and the pair would stand in that position, gazing thoughtfully at the ground, for three days, or at least, as long as they were left alone and hunger did not compel them to look for food.

It is said that the author left on record a comparison between their friendship and that of Nisus and Euryalus, and of Pylades and Orestes, and if this is true, it can be understood how steadfast must the friendship of these two animals have been to the wonder of the world and to the shame of humankind, who fail so lamentably to preserve friendship for one another.[23] Because of this it has been said:

> Friend to friend no more draws near,
> And the jouster's cane has become a spear.[24]

And that other song that goes:

> Says friend to friend: "Here's mud in your eye!"

But let no one imagine that the author went off the tracks when he compared the friendship of these animals to that of men, for men have received many lessons from dumb beasts and learned many things of value, as for example: from storks the enema, from dogs vomiting and gratitude, from cranes watchfulness, from ants thrift, from elephants chastity, and loyalty from the horse.

At last, Sancho fell asleep at the foot of a cork tree, and Don Quixote dozed under a robust oak. But a short time had elapsed when a noise he heard behind awoke the latter, and standing up, he gazed in the direction

---

[23] Nisus and Euryalus were two friends who accompanied Aeneas to Italy, in Virgil's *Aeneid.* Pylades, son of the king of Phocis, accompanied Orestes back to Argos to avenge his father Agamemnon's death; see Aeschylus' *The Libation Bearers,* in the *Oresteia.*

[24] A line from a popular ballad.

the noise came from, and spied two men on horseback, one of whom, letting himself slip from the saddle, said to the other: "Dismount, friend and take the bridles off the horses, for this spot seems to me both rich in grass for them and in silence and solitude for my love-sick thoughts."

Saying this, he stretched himself upon the ground, and as he flung himself down, the armor he wore clattered—a manifest proof by which Don Quixote knew him to be a knight-errant—and going over to Sancho, who was fast asleep, he pulled him by the arm, and after rousing him with no small difficulty, he said to him in a low voice: "Brother Sancho, we have an adventure."

"God send us a good one," said Sancho, "and where, master, may Mistress Adventure be?"

"Where, Sancho?" answered Don Quixote. "Turn your eyes and there you will see stretched a knight-errant, who, I believe, is not too happy, for I saw him fling himself off his horse and throw himself on the ground with signs of dejection, and as he fell, his armor clattered."

"But how does your worship make out that this is an adventure?" said Sancho.

"I do not insist," answered Don Quixote, "that this is a full adventure, but it is the beginning of one, for this is the way adventures begin. But listen, for he seems to be tuning a viol or lute, and by the way he is spitting and clearing his throat, he must be preparing to sing something."

"Faith and so he is," answered Sancho. "He must be a lovesick knight."

"There is no knight-errant who is not," said Don Quixote. "Let us listen to him, for if he sings, by that thread we shall gain a clue to his thoughts, for the tongue speaks out of the abundance of the heart."

Sancho was about to reply to his master, but the voice of the Knight of the Wood, which was neither very bad nor very good, prevented him, and the two, listening attentively, heard the following sonnet:[25]

> O cruel one, bestow on me
> Some token of your sovereign sway,
> Which I may follow earnestly,
> And never from its precepts stray.
> If you would have me fade away
> In silence, then account me dead,
> But if you'd hear my ancient lay,
> Then Love himself my cause shall plead.
> My soul to contraries inured
> Is made of wax and adamant,
> And well prepared for Cupid's law.
> Whether soft or hard my heart is yours,
> To grave it leave to you I'll grant,
> And to your will I'll bow with awe.

With a sigh that seemed to spring from the depths of his heart, the Knight of the Wood ended his song, and after a short pause he exclaimed in a sad and sorrowful voice: "O most beautiful and ungrateful woman in all the world! Is it possible, most serene Casildea of Vandalia, for thee to allow thy captive

[25] Cervantes is parodying conventional love poetry of his time.

knight to be consumed and to perish in perpetual wandering and in harsh and unkind labors? Is it not enough that I have compelled all the knights of Navarra, of León, of Tartessus, Castile, and all the knights of La Mancha as well, to acknowledge thee to be the most beautiful lady in the world?"

"Not so," cried Don Quixote at this, "for I am of La Mancha, and I have acknowledged no such thing, nor could I, nor ought I, acknowledge anything so prejudicial to the beauty of my mistress. This knight, as you can see, Sancho, is raving. But let us listen; perhaps he will give himself away still more."

"That he will surely," answered Sancho, "for he seems the kind who'll go on mourning and groaning for a month on end."

This was not so, however, for the Knight of the Wood, overhearing voices nearby, proceeded no further with his lamentations, but sprang to his feet and called out in a loud but courteous voice: "Who goes there? Who are you? Are you by any chance one of the band of the happy or of the afflicted?"

"Of the afflicted," answered Don Quixote.

"Then come to me," replied the Knight of the Wood, "and you will come to the very fountainhead of sorrow and affliction."

Don Quixote, when he heard such gentle and courteous words, went over to him, and Sancho likewise. The melancholy knight then took Don Quixote by the arm and said: "Sit down here, sir knight. Now that I know that I have found you in this place, where solitude and the night dews, the natural couch and proper dwelling of knights-errant, keep you company, I need no further proof that you belong to their number."

To which Don Quixote answered: "I am a knight, and of the order you mention; and although sorrows, misfortunes, and disasters keep their abode in my soul, they have not scored away my compassion for the misfortunes of others. From what you were singing a moment ago I gathered that yours are amorous woes—I mean, of the love you have for that ungrateful beauty whom you named in your lament."

While this conversation was proceeding, they were seated side by side upon the hard sward, in peace and good company, not in the manner of men who at break of day would have to break one another's heads.

"Are you, sir knight, perchance, in love?" inquired the Knight of the Wood.

"To my woe, I am," answered Don Quixote, "though the sorrows arising from well-placed affections should be accounted blessings rather than calamities."

"That is true," replied he of the Wood, "provided disdain does not unbalance our reason and understanding, for if exaggerated, it resembles vengeance."

"I was never disdained by my lady," said Don Quixote.

"No, surely not," said Sancho, who stood close by, "my lady is as meek as a yearling ewe and softer than butter."

"Is this your squire?" asked he of the Wood.

"Yes, he is," said Don Quixote.

"This is the first time I have ever seen a squire," said he of the Wood, "who dared to speak while his master was speaking. Anyhow, there is mine over there, who is as tall as his father, and it cannot be proved that he has ever opened his lips when I was speaking."

"By my faith," said Sancho, "I have spoken and am fit to speak before one as great, and even—But let it be, it'll be worse to stir it about."

The squire of the Wood then took Sancho by the arm, saying: "Let us two go where we can talk squirelike together, and leave these gentlemen, our masters, to butt at each other, telling the story of their loves. I wager the day will find them at it without having settled anything."

"With all my heart," said Sancho, "and I'll tell your worship who I am so that you may judge whether I deserve to be counted among the number of most talkative squires."

The two squires then withdrew to one side, and a dialogue passed between them as droll as that of their masters was serious.

CHAPTER XIII

In which the adventure of the Knight of the Wood is continued, with the wise, novel, and agreeable conversation between the two squires

The knights and squires were separated, the latter telling the stories of their lives, the former of their loves; but the history tells first of the conversation between the servants, and then follows with that between their masters. And so, it relates that he of the Wood, when they had drawn a little aside, said to Sancho: "It's a wearisome life we lead, sir, those of us who are squires to knights-errant. We certainly eat our bread in the sweat of our brows, which is one of the curses God laid on our first parents."[26]

"It may be said, too," added Sancho, "that we eat it in the chill of our bodies, for who suffers the heat and the cold worse than the wretched squires of knight-errantry? It wouldn't be so bad if we had something to eat, for sorrows are lighter when there's bread to eat, but there are times when we go a day or two without breaking our fast, unless it be on the wind that blows."

"All that can be put up with," said he of the Wood, "when we have hopes of a reward, for unless he serves an especially unlucky knight-errant, a squire is sure after a little time to find himself at least rewarded with a handsome government of some island or a tidy countship."

"I have told my master already," said Sancho, "that I'll be content with the government of some island, and he's so noble and generous that he has promised it to me many a time."

"As for me," said he of the Wood, "I'll be content with a canonry[27] for my services, and my master has already assigned me one."

"Your master," said Sancho, "must then be a knight in the ecclesiastical line and can grant such favors to his good squire, but mine is only a layman, though I do remember some wise, but in my opinion, intriguing folks who tried to persuade him to have himself made archbishop. He, however, would be nothing but an emperor, and I was trembling all the time lest he should become bitten with the fancy of going into the Church, for I didn't consider myself suitable to hold offices in it. In fact, I may as well tell you that, though I look like a man, I'm just a beast as far as the Church is concerned."

"Ah! That's where you are wrong," said he of the Wood. "Those insular governorships are not all plain sailing. Some are twisted, some poor, some dreary, and in short, the loftiest and best regulated brings with it a heavy

---

[26] See Genesis 3:1.
[27] A minor ecclesiastical appointment.

load of worry and trouble, which the unlucky wight to whose lot it has fallen bears upon his shoulders. Far better would it be for us who profess this plague-stricken service to return to our homes and there spend our days in more pleasant occupations, such as hunting and fishing, for where in the world would you find a squire so poor as not to have a hack, a couple of greyhounds, and a fishing rod with which to while away the time in his own village?"

"I'm not short of any of these things," said Sancho. "It's true I've no hack, but I've an ass that is worth twice as much as my master's horse. God send me a bad Easter, and may it be the next one, if I would swap him, even if I got four bushels of barley to boot. You'll laugh at the value I'm putting on my Dapple, for dapple is the color of my ass. As for greyhounds, I'm in no want, for there are plenty of them in my home town, and surely the finest sport of all is where it's at other people's expense."

"Truly and earnestly, sir squire," said he of the Wood, "I've made up my mind to give up the drunken frolics of these knights of ours and go back to my village and bring up my children, for I've three like three oriental pearls."

"I've two," said Sancho, "fit to be presented to the Pope in person, especially a girl whom I'm rearing to be a countess, please God, though against her mother's wishes."

"And how old is this lady who is being brought up to be a countess?" inquired he of the Wood.

"Fifteen years, more or less," replied Sancho, "but she's as tall as a lance and as fresh as an April morning and as strong as a porter."

"Those qualities," said he of the Wood, "make her fit to be not only a countess but a nymph of the greenwood. Ah, the frisky whore! What spunk the jade must have!"

To this Sancho replied somewhat sulkily: "She's no whore, nor was her mother, nor will either of them be, please God, so long as I'm alive. And do keep a civiller tongue on you. Considering that you've been reared among knights-errant, who are the last word in courtesy, I don't think your language is becoming."

"Oh, how little you understand the language of compliments, sir squire," answered he of the Wood. "Do you mean to tell me that you don't know that when a horseman lands a good lance thrust at a bull in the square, or when anyone does anything very well, the people are accustomed to say: 'How well the whoreson rogue has done it!' and what seems to be insulting in the phrase is high praise? Come, sir, let you disown the sons or daughters whose actions don't earn their parents such compliments."

"Yes, I do disown them," answered Sancho, "and in the same way you may heap the whole of whoredom straightaway on me, my wife, and my children, for all they do and say is over and above deserving of like praise. And that I may see them again, I pray God deliver me from mortal sin, which is the same as delivering me from this dangerous squire business into which I've fallen for the second time, baited and bribed by a purse with a hundred ducats in it that I found one day in the heart of the Sierra Morena.[28] And I tell you the Devil is always putting before my eyes, here, there, and everywhere, a bag full of doubloons, which I'm forever turning over with my hand and hugging it and carrying it home with me to make investments and

[28] Sancho is referring to an incident in Part I, omitted here.

settle rents and live like a prince. So long as I think of this, I don't care a fig for all the toils I endure with this fool of a master of mine, whom I know to be more of a madman than a knight."

"Hence the common saying that 'covetousness bursts the bag,'" said he of the Wood; "but if you mean to talk of such men, let me tell you that there is no greater in the world than my master, for he is one of those of whom it is said: 'Care for his neighbor kills the ass,' for he makes a madman of himself in order that another knight may recover the wits he has lost,[29] and he goes about looking for what, were he to find it, may, for all I know, hit him in the snout."

"Is he by any chance in love?" asked Sancho.

"He is," said he of the Wood, "with a certain Casildea of Vandalia, the rawest[30] and most hard-boiled lady in the world, but it is not on the score of rawness that he limps, for he has other greater plans rumbling in his belly; you'll hear him speak of them before long."

"No matter how smooth the road, there's sure to be some rut or hollow in it," said Sancho. "In other houses they cook beans, but in mine it is by the potful;[31] madness has always more followers and hangers-on than wisdom; but if the common saying is true, that 'to have a friend in grief gives some relief,' I may draw consolation from you, for your master is as crazy as mine."

"Crazy but valiant," answered he of the Wood, "and more roguish than crazy or valiant."

"Mine is not like that," replied Sancho. "I mean, he has nothing of the rogue in him. On the contrary, he has a soul as simple as a pitcher; he could do no harm to anyone, but good to all, nor has he any malice in him; why, a child would convince him it is night at noonday, and it is on account of this simplicity that I love him as I love the cockles of my heart, and I can't invent a way of leaving him, no matter what piece of foolishness he does."

"Nevertheless, brother and sir," said he of the Wood, "if the blind lead the blind, both are in danger of falling into the ditch. It is better for us to retire quickly and get back to our dens, for those who seek adventures don't always find good ones."

Sancho kept spitting from time to time, and as the charitable Squire of the Wood noticed that his spittle was gluey and somewhat dry, he said: "It seems to me that all this talk of ours has made our tongues stick to our palates, but I have a loosener, hanging from the saddlebow of my horse, which is quite good." And getting up, he came back a moment later with a large skin of wine and a pasty half a yard long, which is no exaggeration, for it was composed of a domestic rabbit so big that Sancho, as he held it, took it to be a goat, not to say a kid, and gazing at it, he said: "Is this what you carry along with you, sir?"

"What were you thinking then?" said the other. "Am I perchance some homespun, water-drinking squire? I carry better food supplies on my horse's crupper than a general does when he is on the march."

---

[29] In the incident in the Sierra Morena, Don Quixote has tried to imitate such romance heroes as Ariosto's Orlando by going mad with love.

[30] The Spanish puns here on *crudo*, which means both "raw" and "cruel."

[31] Sancho means his bad luck comes in quantity. This paragraph is a good example of Sancho's "proverbial" style; he quotes four proverbs.

Sancho fell to, without any need of pressing. In the dark he gobbled lumps as large as knots on a tether, observing as he ate: "You are indeed a trusty and a loyal squire, round and sound, grand and gorgeous, as is proved by this feast, which, if it has not come here by magic, seems like it at least; and not like me, poor devil, who am only carrying in my saddlebags a scrap of cheese so hard that you could brain a giant with it, and to keep it company, a few dozen carob pods and as many filberts and walnuts. Thanks to the poverty of my master and the idea he has and the rule he follows that knights-errant must not feed on anything except dried fruits and the herbs of the field."

"By my faith," replied he of the Wood, "my stomach is not made for thistles or wild pears from the woods. Let our masters keep to their opinions and laws of chivalry, and eat what is prescribed. As for me, I carry my meat baskets and this wineskin slung from my saddlebow, whether they like it or not, and I'm so devoted to her, aye, and so arrantly fond of her, that hardly a minute passes without my giving her a thousand kisses and hugs."

Saying this, he put the skin into Sancho's hands, who, raising it up, pressed it to his mouth and remained gazing at the stars for a quarter of an hour. When he had finished his drink, he let his head fall on one side, and heaving a deep sigh, he exclaimed: "Whoreson rogue, what a tip-top liquor it is!"

"There you are," said he of the Wood when he heard Sancho's exclamation. "See how you have praised my wine by calling it 'whoreson.'"

"Well," said Sancho, "I confess that I'm aware it's no dishonor to call somebody whoreson when we mean to praise him. Now tell me, sir, by the life you love best, is this Ciudad Real wine?"

"O peerless wine taster!" said he of the Wood, "From there and from nowhere else has it come, and it is a few years old, too."

"Trust me in that," said Sancho. "I knew I'd make a successful guess as to where it came from. Would you believe me, sir, when I tell you that I've such a great natural instinct in testing wines that no sooner do I smell one of them than I tell its country, its kind, its flavor and age, the changes it will undergo, and every detail concerning the wine. But you needn't wonder, for I've had in my family, on my father's side, the two finest wine tasters La Mancha has known for many a long year, and to prove what I'm saying, I'll tell you what happened to them. They were both given wine from a cask to try, and they were asked their opinion about its condition, quality, goodness or badness. One of them tested it with the tip of his tongue, the other did no more than hold it to his nose. The first said that the wine tasted of iron; the second that it had a flavor of cordovan leather. The owner declared that the cask was clean, and that the wine had no blending that could have imparted a taste of iron or leather. Notwithstanding this, the two famous wine tasters stuck to their point. Time went by, the wine was sold, and when the cask was cleaned, a small key was found in it hanging to a cordovan thong. Consider now whether one who comes of such a stock is able to give an opinion in such matters."

"Since that is so," said he of the Wood, "let us give up going in search of adventures; and since we have loaves, don't let us go looking for tarts, but return to our cots, for there God will find us if it be His will."

"I'll serve my master till he gets to Saragossa," said Sancho, "then maybe we'll come to an understanding."

Finally, the two worthy squires talked so much and drank so much that they had need of sleep to tie up their tongues and allay their thirst, for to quench it was impossible. And so the pair of them, clinging to the now nearly empty wineskin and with half-chewed morsels in their mouths, fell fast asleep; and there we will leave them for the present to relate what took place between the Knight of the Wood and him of the Rueful Figure.

CHAPTER XIV

In which the adventure of the Knight of the Wood is continued

Among the many speeches that passed between Don Quixote and the Knight of the Wood, our history tells us that the latter said to Don Quixote: "In a word, sir knight, I wish you to know that my destiny, or rather my choice, led me to become enamored of a certain lady, the peerless Casildea of Vandalia. I call her peerless, because she has no peer in bodily stature, rank, or beauty. This Lady Casildea repaid my honorable desires by forcing me, as his step-mother did Hercules,[32] to engage in many perilous exploits, promising me at the end of each that, with the end of the next, I should obtain the object of all my hopes. But my labors have gone increasing link by link until they are past counting, nor do I know which is to be the one that will finally announce the accomplishment of my honorable wishes. On one occasion she ordered me to go and challenge that famous giantess of Seville known as the Giralda,[33] who is as valiant and strong as if made of brass, and though never stirring from one spot, is the most changeable and volatile woman in the world. I came, I saw, I conquered, and I made her keep still and on one point, for none but north winds blew for more than a week. On another occasion she made me go and weigh the mighty Bulls of Guisando,[34] an enter-prise that should have been recommended to porters rather than to knights. Another time she commanded me to fling myself into the pit of Cabra,[35] an unheard-of peril, and bring her back a detailed account of what is hidden in its abyss. I stopped the motion of the Giralda; I weighed the Bulls of Guisando; I descended into the pit and drew to the light of day the secrets of its abyss; yet my hopes are as dead as dead can be, and her orders and disdains as much alive as ever. And now her last command is for me to go through all provinces of Spain and compel all the knights-errant wandering about to confess that she is the most beautiful woman alive today and that I am the most valiant and the most enamored knight on earth. In accordance with her demand I have already traveled over the greater part of Spain and have vanquished many knights who have had the presumption to gain-say me. But my greatest pride and boast is that I have conquered in single combat that so famous knight Don Quixote of La Mancha, and made him confess that my Casildea is more beautiful than his Dulcinea. By this victory

[32] Hercules' "stepmother" was Hera, since he was the son of Zeus by the mortal Alcmena. Hera imposed the labors of Hercules.
[33] The Giralda is actually a fourteen-foot brass statue of Faith on the top of the great tower of the Cathedral of Seville.
[34] The Bulls of Guisando are four rough granite figures of animals in the district of Ávila.
[35] The pit of Cabra in the district of Córdoba is traditionally supposed to be the shaft of an ancient mine.

alone I consider that I have conquered all the knights in the world, for the said Don Quixote has vanquished them all, and since I have vanquished him, his glory, his fame, and his honor are forthwith transferred to my person, and his innumerable exploits are now set down to my account and have become mine."

Don Quixote was astounded to hear such words from the Knight of the Wood, and he was a thousand times on the point of telling him he lied and had the *you lie!* on the tip of his tongue, but he restrained himself as best he could in order to make him confess the lie out of his own mouth. So, he said to him calmly: "I say nothing about your worship, sir knight, having vanquished most of the knights of Spain, and even of the world, but I doubt that you have conquered Don Quixote of La Mancha. Perhaps it may have been some other knight who resembled him, though, indeed, there are few like him."

"How! Not vanquished him?" said he of the Wood. "By Heaven above us, I fought Don Quixote and vanquished him and overcame him. He is a man of tall stature, gaunt features, lanky shriveled limbs; his hair is turning gray, his nose is aquiline and a little hooked, and his moustaches are long, black, and drooping. He goes into battle under the name of the Knight of the Rueful Figure, and he has for squire a peasant called Sancho Panza. He presses the back and curbs the reins of a famous horse called Rozinante, and finally, he has for mistress of his will a certain Dulcinea of El Toboso, once upon a time known as Aldonza Lorenzo, just as mine, whose name is Casildea and who comes from Andalusia, I call Casildea of Vandalia. If all these tokens do not suffice to vindicate the truth of my words, here is my sword, which will compel incredulity itself to give credence to it."

"Softly, sir knight," said Don Quixote, "and listen to what I am about to say. You must know that this Don Quixote you speak about is the greatest friend I have in the world; in fact, I may say that I regard him as I would my very self, and by the precise tokens you have given of him I am sure that he must be the same whom you vanquished. On the other hand, I see with my eyes and feel with my hands that it is impossible for him to be the same, unless, perhaps, that particular enemy of his, who is an enchanter, may have taken his shape in order to allow himself to be vanquished so as to cheat him of the fame that his noble exploits as a knight have won him throughout the world. To confirm this I must tell you that only two days ago these said enchanters, his enemies, changed the shape and person of the fair Dulcinea of El Toboso into a vulgar and mean village lass,[36] and in the same manner they must have transformed Don Quixote. If all this does not suffice to convince you of the truth of my words, here stands Don Quixote himself: he will maintain it by arms, on foot or on horseback or in any way you wish."

With these words he stood up and grabbed his sword, waiting for the decision of the Knight of the Wood, who in a voice equally calm replied: "A good prayer needs no sureties. He who managed to vanquish you once when transformed, Señor Don Quixote, may well hope to conquer you in your person. But since it is not right for knights to perform their deeds in the dark like highwaymen and bullies, let us wait till daylight, that the sun may look down

---

[36] An episode omitted here, in which Sancho plays a thoughtless trick on Quixote.

on our achievements. And it must be a condition of our battle that the vanquished shall remain entirely at the mercy of the conqueror, provided that what is imposed shall be becoming a knight."

"I am more than satisfied with these conditions," answered Don Quixote.

And so saying, they went to seek their squires, whom they found snoring in the same posture as when sleep first waylaid them. They roused them and ordered them to prepare the steeds, for at sunrise the two knights would engage in bloody single combat. When Sancho heard the news, he was thunderstruck, fearing for the safety of his master, because of the tales that he had heard the Squire of the Wood tell of his knight's powers. Without saying a word, however, the two squires went off in search of their beasts, for the three horses and the dapple had smelled each other and were by this time all together.

On the way, he of the Wood said to Sancho: "You must know, brother, that fighting men from Andalusia are accustomed, when they are seconds in any combat, not to stand idle with their hands folded while their champions are engaged. I'm saying this to remind you that while our masters are fighting, we, too, must have a fight and knock one another to splinters."

"That custom, sir squire," replied Sancho, "may be current among the bullies and fighting men you mention, but never in any circumstances among the squires of knights-errant. At least I have never heard my master speak of such a custom, and he knows all the rules of knight-errantry by heart. But even if it is an express rule that squires should fight while their masters are fighting, I don't intend to follow it, but to pay the penalty that might be imposed on peacefully minded squires like myself, for I'm sure it will not be more than a couple of pounds of wax.[37] I would prefer to pay that, for I know it will cost me less than the plasters I'll need to heal my head, which I already reckon to be smashed in two pieces. Furthermore, I cannot fight, for I've no sword and never in my life carried one."

"I know a good remedy for that," said he of the Wood. "I've here two linen bags of the same size; you take one and I'll take the other, and we'll have a bout of bag-blows on equal terms."

"If that's the way it goes," answered Sancho, "I'm game, for such a fight will beat the dust off us rather than hurt us."

"That mustn't happen," replied the other, "for we'll put in the bags, to keep the wind from blowing them away, half a dozen fine smooth stones, all of the same weight. In this way we'll be able to pound one another without doing much damage."

"Body of my father," said Sancho, "what a nice kind of sable skins and pads of cotton wool he's putting into the bags to save breaking our heads and mashing our bones to powder! But even if they were filled with pads of raw silk, I tell you, my dear sir, there's to be no fighting for me. Let our masters fight and take their medicine, but let us eat, drink, and be merry, for Time is anxious enough to snatch away our lives from us without our going out in search of appetizers to finish them off before they reach their season and drop off the tree for very ripeness."

"Still," said he of the Wood, "we must fight, if only for half an hour."

---

[37] Fines payable in wax were imposed for trifling offenses; the wax was used to make church candles.

"Not on your life," replied Sancho; "I'm not going to be so churlish or ungrateful as to pick any quarrel, no matter how trifling, with one whom I have eaten and drunk with; besides, who the devil could manage to fight in cold blood, without anger or annoyance?"

"I'll provide a remedy for that," said he of the Wood. "Before we start fighting I'll walk nicely and gently up to your worship and give you three or four buffets that will land you at my feet. By this means I'll rouse your choler though it be sleeping sounder than a dormouse."

"I've a trick against yours that's just as good," replied Sancho. "I'll take up a stout cudgel, and before your worship gets near enough to raise my choler, I'll send yours to sleep with such sound whacks that it will not awake unless it be in the next world, where all know that I am not the kind of man to let my face be messed about by anyone. Let each man watch out for his own arrow, though, mind you, the better way would be for everyone to let his choler sleep in peace, for no one knows the heart of his neighbor, and many a man comes for wool and goes back shorn; and God always blessed the peacemakers and cursed the peace-breakers; for if a baited cat who's shut in turns into a lion, God knows what I, who am a man, shall turn into. So, from now on I warn you, Mister Squire, that I'll put down to your account all the harm and damage that may come of our quarrel."

"I agree," said he of the Wood; "God will send the dawn and all will be as right as rain."

And now a thousand kinds of little painted birds began to warble in the trees, and with their blithe and jocund notes they seemed to welcome and salute the fresh Aurora, who already was showing her beautiful countenance through the gates and balconies of the East, shaking from her tresses countless liquid pearls. The plants, bathing in that fragrant moisture, seemed likewise to shed a spray of tiny white gems, the willow trees distilled sweet manna, the fountains laughed, the brooks murmured, and the meadows clad themselves in all their glory at her coming. But hardly had the light of the day allowed things to be seen and distinguished, when the first object that Sancho Panza caught sight of was the Squire of the Wood's nose, which was so big that it almost overshadowed his whole body. It is said, indeed, that it was of huge size, hooked in the middle, all covered with warts, and of a mulberry color like an eggplant, and that it hung down two fingers' length below his mouth. The size, the color, the warts, and the hook of the aforesaid nose made its owner's face so hideous that Sancho, as he gazed at it, began to shudder hand and foot like a child in a fit of epilepsy, and he resolved in his heart to let himself be given two hundred buffets rather than to allow his choler to provoke him into attacking that monster.

Don Quixote looked at his adversary and found that he already had his helmet on, with the visor down, so that he could not see his face, but he noticed that he was a muscular man, though not very tall in stature. Over his armor he wore a surcoat or cassock of a cloth that seemed to be of the finest gold, all bedizened with many little moons of glittering mirrors, which gave him a most gallant and showy appearance. Above his helmet fluttered a great cluster of green, yellow, and white plumes, and his lance, which was leaning against a tree, was very long and thick and had a steel point more than a palm in length.

Don Quixote noticed everything, and from what he saw he inferred that the said knight must be very powerful; but for all that he did not fear as Sancho did, but with noble courage he addressed the Knight of the Mirrors, saying: "If your great longing to fight, sir knight, has not exhausted your courtesy, I would beg you earnestly to raise your visor a little that I may see if the gallantry of your countenance corresponds with that of your accouterment."

"Whether you are vanquished or victor in this enterprise, sir knight," answered he of the Mirrors, "you will have more than enough time and opportunity to see me. If I do not now satisfy your request, it is because, in my opinion, I should wrong the beauteous Casildea of Vandalia by wasting time in raising my visor before forcing you to confess what you know I demand."

"Well," said Don Quixote, "while we are mounting our steeds you can surely tell me if I am the Don Quixote whom you said you vanquished."

"To that we answer," said he of the Mirrors, "that you are as like the knight whom I vanquished as one egg is like another, but as you say that enchanters persecute you, I dare not say whether you are the aforesaid or not."

"That is enough," said Don Quixote, "to convince me of your deception; however, to relieve you of your misapprehensions, let our horses be brought, and in less time than you would take in raising your visor, if God, my lady, and my arm prevail, I shall see your face, and you shall see that I am not the vanquished Don Quixote you consider me to be."

Therefore, cutting short further words, they mounted their horses, and Don Quixote turned Rozinante's reins in order to take up the requisite ground for charging back upon his rival, while he of the Mirrors did the same; but Don Quixote had hardly gone twenty paces when he heard himself called by the Knight of the Mirrors, who said, when each had returned halfway: "Remember, sir knight, that the condition of our battle is that the vanquished, as I said before, shall be at the disposal of the victor."

"I know it already," answered Don Quixote, "but there is a proviso that what is commanded and imposed upon the vanquished must not transgress the bounds of chivalry."

"That is understood," replied he of the Mirrors.

Just at this moment the amazing nose of the squire presented itself to Don Quixote's view, and he was no less astonished to see it than Sancho had been, so much so that he took him for some monster or else for a human being of some new species that is rarely seen on the face of the earth. Sancho, seeing his master go off to take his ground, did not want to remain alone with the nosy individual, for he was afraid that one flick of that nose on his own would end the battle as far as he was concerned and leave him stretched on the ground either because of the blow or because of fright; so, he ran after his master, holding on to one of Rozinante's stirrups, and when he thought it was time to turn about, he said: "I beg your worship, master, before you turn to charge, to help me climb up on that cork tree, from where I may witness your gallant encounter with this knight at better ease and comfort than from the ground."

"I am rather of the opinion, Sancho," said Don Quixote, "that you would even mount a scaffold to see the bulls without danger."

"To tell you the truth," replied Sancho, "the fearsome nose of that squire has me all in a dither and full of terror, so that I dare not stay near him."

"It is, indeed, such a one," said Don Quixote, "that were I not what I am, it would strike fear in me, too. So, come, I will help you to climb up where you will."

While Don Quixote stopped to let Sancho climb into the cork tree, he of the Mirrors took as much ground as he considered necessary, and thinking that Don Quixote had done likewise, without waiting for any sound of trumpet or other signal to direct them, he wheeled his horse, which was no swifter or better-looking than Rozinante, and at his top speed, which was no more than an easy trot, advanced to meet his foe, but noticing that he was busy hoisting Sancho up into the tree, he drew reins and halted midway, for which his steed was profoundly grateful, for it was unable to move. Don Quixote, imagining that his rival was careering down on top of him, drove his spurs vigorously into the lean flanks of Rozinante and made him dash along in such a way that, as the history relates, this was the one occasion when he was seen to make an attempt to gallop, for on all others he did no more than plain easy trotting; and with this unheard-of fury he charged at him of the Mirrors, who was digging the spurs into his horse up to the buttons, without being able to make him stir an inch from the spot where he had halted in his career. At this critical moment did Don Quixote bear down upon his adversary, who was in difficulties with his horse and embarrassed with his lance, for he could neither manage it nor was there time to put it into the rest. Don Quixote, however, paid scant heed to such embarrassments, but in perfect safety and without taking any risk crashed into him of the Mirrors with such force that in spite of himself, he threw him to the ground over the horse's rump and so great was the fall that he lay apparently dead, not stirring hand or foot. No sooner did Sancho see him fall than he slid down the cork tree and ran at top speed to where his master was, who, after dismounting from Rozinante, stood over the Knight of the Mirrors. Unlacing his helmet to see if he was dead and to give him air if haply he were alive, he saw—Who can say what he saw without arousing the wonder, astonishment, and awe of all who hear it? He saw, the history says, the very face, the very figure, the very aspect, the very physiognomy, the very effigy, the very image of the bachelor Sansón Carrasco. As soon as he saw him, he cried out in a loud voice: "Come, Sancho, and behold what you have to see but not to believe; make haste, my son, and learn what wizards and enchanters are able to accomplish."

Sancho came up, and when he saw the face of the bachelor Carrasco, he began to cross himself a thousand times and bless himself as many more. All this time the prostrate knight showed no signs of life, and Sancho said to Don Quixote: "In my opinion, master, you should stick your sword into the mouth of this one who looks like the bachelor Carrasco, and perhaps in him you will kill one of your enemies, the enchanters."

"That is good advice," said Don Quixote, "for the fewer enemies, the better."

Then, drawing his sword, he was about to put into operation Sancho's advice, when the Squire of the Mirrors came up, now minus the nose that had made him so hideous, and cried out in a loud voice: "Mind what you are doing, Señor Don Quixote, for that man lying at your feet is your friend the bachelor Sansón Carrasco, and I am his squire."

"And what about the nose?" said Sancho, seeing him without his former hideous appendage.

"I have it here in my pocket," said the latter, and sticking his hand into his right pocket, he drew out a clownish nose of varnished pasteboard of the kind we have already described.

Sancho, then, after peering at him more and more closely, exclaimed in a loud voice of amazement: "Holy Mary, protect us! Isn't it Tomé Cecial, my neighbor and comrade?"

"Who else would I be?" replied the unnosed squire. "Tomé Cecial I am, comrade and friend, Sancho Panza, and I'll tell you presently of the means, the vagaries, the schemings, that brought me here; but in the meantime, beg and beseech your master not to touch, maltreat, wound, or kill the Knight of the Mirrors, whom he has lying at his feet, for without doubt he is the bold and ill-advised bachelor Sansón Carrasco, our compatriot."

At this moment he of the Mirrors came to his senses, and Don Quixote no sooner saw it than he held the naked point of his sword to his face, saying: "You are a dead man, knight, unless you confess that the peerless Dulcinea of El Toboso surpasses your Casildea of Vandalia in beauty; besides, you have to promise that if you survive this combat and fall, you will go to the city of El Toboso and present yourself before her on my behalf, letting her do with you what she pleases. And if she leaves you to your own devices, you must return and look for me (the trail of my deeds will guide you in my direction) and tell me all that has taken place between her and you. These are conditions that do not depart from the terms of knight-errantry."

"I confess," said the fallen knight, "that the torn and dirty shoe of Lady Dulcinea of El Toboso is better than the ill-combed though clean beard of Calsildea, and I promise to go and return from her presence to yours and give you a complete and detailed account of what you ask me."

"You have also to confess and believe," added Don Quixote, "that the knight you vanquished was not, nor could be, Don Quixote of La Mancha, but somebody else who resembles him, just as I confess and believe that you, though you appear to be the bachelor Sansón Carrasco, are not he, but another like him, and that my enemies have conjured you up before me in his shape that I may restrain and moderate my impetuous wrath and make humane use of my glorious victory."

"I confess, judge, and consider everything to be as you confess, judge, and consider it," answered the crippled knight. "Let me rise, I pray you, if the shock of my fall will allow it, for I am indeed in a very bad way."

Don Quixote helped him to rise, with his squire Tomé Cecial, off whom Sancho never for an instant took his eyes and whom he questioned incessantly, proving thereby to his own satisfaction that the latter was truly the Tomé Cecial he said he was. But Sancho was so impressed by what his master had said about the enchanters having changed the figure of the Knight of the Mirrors into that of the bachelor Sansón Carrasco that he was unable to believe the truth of what he saw with his own eyes. In the end, both master and man remained under their delusion; and so he of the Mirrors and his squire, feeling down in the dumps and out of tune with the world, took their departure from Don Quixote and Sancho, intending to look for some place where the knight's ribs might be plastered and strapped.

Don Quixote and Sancho continued to make their way toward Saragossa, and the history leaves them at this point in order to give an account of who were the Knight of the Mirrors and his nosy squire.

CHAPTER XV

In which is told who the Knight of the Mirrors and his squire were

Don Quixote rode onward in great spirits. He was extremely pleased, elated, and vainglorious at having won a victory over such a valiant knight as he imagined him of the Mirrors to be, and from his knightly word he expected to learn whether his lady still continued to be enchanted, for the said vanquished knight was bound, on pain of ceasing to be one, to return and give him a report of what took place between himself and her. But if Don Quixote was thinking of one thing, he of the Mirrors was certainly thinking of another. In fact, the latter had no other thought at the moment than to find some place where he might get poulticed, as we have said before.

The history then says that when the bachelor Sansón Carrasco counseled Don Quixote to resume his relinquished knight-errantry, he did so in consequence of a conference he had previously held with the curate and the barber upon the measures to be taken to induce Don Quixote to stay at home in peace and quiet, without exciting himself over his accursed adventures. At that conclave it was decided by the unanimous vote of all, and at the special instance of Carrasco, that Don Quixote should be allowed to set out, as it was impossible to restrain him, that Sansón should sally forth as a knight-errant, join battle with him, for which a pretext could readily be found, and vanquish him—an easy matter they thought—and that it should be agreed and regulated that the one conquered should remain at the mercy of his conqueror. And once Don Quixote was vanquished, the knight-bachelor would order him to go back to his village and home and not leave it for two years or until some other command was imposed upon him, all of which conditions Don Quixote would carry out without fail rather than break the laws of chivalry. During the period of his seclusion, he might possibly forget his foolish notions, or else an opportunity might be found of discovering a sure remedy for his madness.

Carrasco undertook the task, and Tomé Cecial, Sancho's comrade and neighbor, a merry, scatterbrained fellow, offered his services as squire. Sansón armed himself as has been described, and Tomé Cecial, to avoid being recognized by his comrade when they met, fitted on over his natural nose the false one already mentioned. And so they followed the same road as Don Quixote and very nearly reached him in time to be present at the adventure of the cart of Death, and at last they met in the wood, where everything that the wise reader has read took place. And if it had not been for the extraordinary fancies of Don Quixote, who took it into his head that the bachelor was not the bachelor, Master Bachelor would be forever incapacitated from taking his degree as licentiate, because he did not find nests where he expected to find birds. Tomé Cecial, seeing how badly their plans had turned out and what a wretched end their expedition had come to, said to the bachelor: "For sure, Master Sansón Carrasco, we've met with our deserts. It's easy to plan and start an enterprise, but most times it's hard to get out of it safe and sound. Don Quixote is mad, and we are sane, but he comes off safe and in high spirits, while you, master, are left drubbed and downcast. Tell us, now, who is the greater madman, he who is so because he can't help it, or he who is so of his own free will?"

To which Sansón replied: "The difference between these two madmen is that he who is so perforce will be one forever, but he who is so of his own accord can leave off being one whenever he likes."

"That being so," said Tomé Cecial, "I was mad of my own accord when I agreed to become your squire, and of my own accord, I wish to leave off being one and go back home."

"You may please yourself," replied Sansón, "but to imagine that I am going home before I have given Don Quixote a beating is an absurdity, and it is not my wish to make him recover his wits that will drive me to hunt him now, but a lust for revenge, for the aching of my ribs will not let me form a more charitable resolve."

The two conversed in such a manner until they reached a town where by good fortune they found a bone-setter who cured the hapless Sansón. Then, Tomé Cecial went home, leaving the bachelor behind nursing his revenge. Our history will return to him at the proper time, but now it must frolic along with Don Quixote.

CHAPTER XVI

Of what happened when Don Quixote met a wise gentleman of La Mancha

Don Quixote continued his journey full of the joy, satisfaction, and high spirits we have described, fancying himself, owing to his late victory, the most valiant knight-errant in the world. All the adventures that might happen to him from that day on he reckoned as already successfully accomplished; he despised enchanters and enchantments; he gave no thought to the innumerable beatings he had received in the course of his knight-errantry, nor to the stoning that had knocked out half his teeth, nor to the ingratitude of the galley slaves, nor to the bold insolence of the Yanguesans who had belabored him with their staves. Finally he said to himself that if he could only discover a method of disenchanting his Lady Dulcinea, he would not envy the highest good fortune that the most fortunate knight-errant of past ages ever achieved or could achieve.

He was riding along entirely absorbed in these fancies when Sancho said to him: "Isn't it strange, master, that I've still before my eyes that monstrous and hugeous nose of my comrade Tomé Cecial?"

"Can it be, Sancho, that you really believe that the Knight of the Mirrors was the bachelor Sansón Carrasco, and his squire, Tomé Cecial, your comrade?"

"I don't know what I'm to say to that," answered Sancho. "I only know that the details he gave me about my house, my wife, and my children, no one but himself could have given me; and as for his face, once he had removed the nose, it was the very face of Tomé Cecial, for I've often seen him in my village—there was but a wall between my house and his—and the tone of his voice was just the same."

"Let us be reasonable, Sancho," replied Don Quixote. "Now tell me, how it can be argued that the bachelor Sansón Carrasco would come as a knight-errant, armed with arms offensive and defensive, to do battle with me? Have I, perchance, ever been his enemy? Have I ever given him cause to have a grudge against me? Am I his rival, or does he make profession of arms that he should envy the fame I have earned in them?"

"But what shall we say, master," replied Sancho, "about that knight, whoever he was, being the very image of the bachelor Carrasco, and his squire the dead spit of my comrade Tomé Cecial? And if that is enchantment, as your worship says, was there no other form in the world for them to take the likeness of?"

"It is all," said Don Quixote, "an artifice and trick of the malignant magicians who persecute me and who, guessing that I was to be victorious in the conflict, settled that the vanquished knight should display the face of my friend the bachelor in order that my affection for him might intervene to halt my sharp blade and restrain my mighty arm and moderate the righteous indignation of my heart, so that he who sought to rob me of my life by trickery should save his own. And in proof, you know already, Sancho, through experience, which cannot lie or deceive, how easy it is for enchanters to change some countenances into others, making the beautiful ugly and the ugly beautiful, for not two days ago you saw with your own eyes the beauty and elegance of the peerless Dulcinea in all its perfection and natural grace, while I saw her in the ugly and mean form of a coarse country wench, with cataracts in her eyes and a stinking breath from her mouth. Seeing that the perverse enchanter caused such a wicked transformation, it is no wonder that he effected that of Sansón Carrasco and of your comrade in order to snatch away my victory. Nevertheless, I console myself, because when all is said and done, I have been victorious over my enemy, no matter what shape he took."

"God knows the truth of it all," answered Sancho. Knowing as he did that the transformation of Dulcinea had been a device and trick of his own, he was not at all pleased by his master's wild fancies; but he did not like to reply, for fear of saying anything that would reveal his trickery.

While they were conversing, they were overtaken by a man who was riding on the same road behind them, mounted on a very handsome gray mare and dressed in an overcoat of fine green cloth slashed with tawny velvet and a hunting cap of the same to match. His mare's trappings were rustic and for riding with short stirrups, and were also of purple and green. He wore a Moorish scimitar hanging from a broad baldric[38] of green and gold, and his leggings were of the same make. His spurs were not gilt but covered with green lacquer and so glossy and burnished that, because they matched the rest of his apparel, they looked better than if they had been made of pure gold. When the stranger overtook them, he greeted them courteously and would have pressed on ahead, had not Don Quixote accosted him, saying: "Gallant sir, if your worship is taking the same road as ourselves and if haste is not your object, I should be grateful if we could ride together."

"Indeed," replied the man on the mare, "I should not have passed on ahead of you if I had not been afraid that your horse would be disturbed by my mare's company."

"You may, sir," answered Sancho, "in all safety rein in your mare, for our horse is the most modest and well behaved in the world. He has never misconducted himself on such an occasion as this, and the only time he didn't

---

[38] Shoulder strap.

behave, my master and I paid for it seven times over. Your worship, I repeat, may pull up, if you wish; why, if they served your mare to him between two courses, our horse wouldn't even look her in the face, I assure you."

The traveler drew rein and gazed with amazement at the figure and face of Don Quixote, who was riding without his helmet, which Sancho carried like a wallet on the pommel of Dapple's saddle. And the more the man in green stared at Don Quixote, the more did Don Quixote stare at the man in green, who seemed to him a man of substance. He appeared to be about fifty years of age; his gray hairs were few, his face aquiline, his expression between cheerful and grave—in short, his dress and general appearance stamped him as a man of fine endowments. What the man in green thought of Don Quixote was that he had never seen a man of that kind or physiognomy; he was amazed at his long scrawny neck, his tall body, his gaunt sallow face, his armor, his gestures and his carriage, a figure and image not seen in those parts for many a year.

Don Quixote observed how attentively the traveler was staring at him and assumed that his astonishment was due to his curiosity. So, being courteous and eager to oblige everybody, he anticipated the latter's questions and said to him: "I should not wonder if your worship were surprised at my appearance, which is both strange and out of the ordinary. But you will cease to do so when I tell you, as I do now, that I am a knight

'Of those, as people say, who ride
In quest of valiant enterprise.'

I have left my native country; I have pledged my estate; I have forsaken my comfort and delivered myself into the arms of Fortune to lead where she will. I have sought to revive the now extinct order of knight-errantry, and for many a day, stumbling here, falling there, flung down in one place and rising up in another, I have been accomplishing a great part of my design, succoring widows, protecting maidens, and relieving wives, orphans, and young children, the proper and natural office of knights-errant; and so, by my many valiant and Christian deeds I have been found worthy to appear in print in almost all, or at least most, of the nations of the earth. Thirty thousand volumes of my history have been printed, and it is on the way to be printed thirty thousand times more, if Heaven does not prevent it. In fact, to sum up all in a few words, or in one word, I must tell you that I am Don Quixote of La Mancha, otherwise called the Knight of the Rueful Figure. And though to praise oneself is degrading, I am compelled at times to sound my own, though naturally only when there is no one present to sound them. So, gentle sir, neither this horse, nor this lance, nor this shield, nor this squire, nor all these arms together, nor the sallowness of my face, nor my lanky limbs, should henceforth astonish you, now that I have informed you who I am and what profession I follow."

After saying this Don Quixote remained silent, and the man in green delayed so long in answering that he seemed unable to find words, but after a while he said: "You rightly guessed my thoughts, sir knight, when you noted my amazement, but you have not managed to dispel the wonder the sight of you causes in me. Though you say that it should be removed once I know who you are, it has not done so. On the contrary, now that I know, I am all the more perplexed and astounded. What! Is it possible that there are knights-errant in the world today and that histories are printed about real knight-errantries? I cannot persuade myself that there is anyone on earth today who favors widows, protects maidens, honors wives, and succors orphans, and I would not have believed it had I not seen it in your worship with my own eyes. Blessed be Heaven for that history of your noble and authentic chivalries, which your worship says is in print, for it will cast into oblivion the innumerable books of counterfeit knights-errant with which the world is filled, that do such harm to good morals and such damage and discredit to genuine history."

"There is much to be said," answered Don Quixote, "on this point of whether the stories of knights-errant are fictions or not."

"But is there anyone who doubts their falsity?" asked the man in green.

"I doubt it," replied Don Quixote, "but there let the matter rest. If our journey lasts, I hope, with God's help, to convince your worship that you have done wrong in going along with the stream of those who declare that they are not true."

From this last remark of Don Quixote the traveler began to suspect that he must be some crazy fellow, but he waited for further evidence to confirm his suspicions. But before they could broach any other subject, Don Quixote begged him to say who he was, since he had told him already something about his way of life.

To which the man in green replied: "I, Knight of the Rueful Figure, am a gentleman and native of a village where, please God, we shall go to dine today. I am more than moderately rich, and my name is Don Diego de Miranda. I spend my life with my wife, my children, and my friends. My pursuits are hunting and fishing, but I keep neither hawk nor hounds, but only a quiet pointer and a saucy ferret or two. I have about six dozen books, some in Spanish and some in Latin, some historical and some devotional, but books of chivalry have never even crossed my threshold. I read profane books more than devotional, provided they give me honest entertainment, delight me by their language, and startle and keep me in suspense by their plots, though there are very few of this kind in Spain. Sometimes I dine with my neighbors and friends, and very often they are my guests. My table is clean, well appointed, and never stinted. I take no pleasure in scandal and allow none in my presence; I do not pry into my neighbors' lives, nor do I spy on other men's actions. I hear Mass every day; I share my goods with the poor, without boasting of my good works, lest hypocrisy and vainglory worm themselves into my heart, for they are foes that subtly waylay even the wariest. I try to make peace between those I know to be at loggerheads. I am devoted to Our Lady and always put my trust in the infinite mercy of Our Lord."

Sancho listened most attentively to the account of the gentleman's life and occupation, and he said to himself that it was a good and holy life and that the man who led it must be able to work miracles. So, flinging himself off Dapple and hastily seizing the gentleman's right stirrup, devoutly and almost in tears he kissed his feet again and again.

At this the gentleman exclaimed: "What are you doing, brother? Why these kisses?"

"Let me kiss you," answered Sancho, "for I do believe your worship's the first saint I've seen riding with short stirrups in all the days of my life."

"I am no saint," replied the gentleman, "but a great sinner. But you, brother, must be good; your simplicity proves it."

Sancho regained his saddle, after having succeeded in extracting a laugh out of his melancholy master and causing fresh amazement in Don Diego. Don Quixote then asked the gentleman how many children he had and said that the ancient philosophers, who were devoid of the true knowledge of God, held that the highest good lay in the gifts bestowed by Nature and Fortune, and in the number of friends and good children.

"I, Don Quixote," rejoined the gentleman, "have one son, and if he did not exist, perhaps I might count myself more fortunate than I do at present, not because he is wicked, but because he is not as good as I would wish. He is eighteen years old; he has been for six years in Salamanca studying Latin and Greek, and when I wished him to proceed to the study of other sciences, I found him so steeped in the one of Poetry—if it can be called a science— that there was no way of getting him to take cheerfully to Law, which I would like him to study, or to the queen of all the sciences, Theology. I wish him to be a credit to his family, for we live in an age when our princes highly reward virtuous and deserving learning, for learning without virtue is like pearls on a dunghill. All his day he spends in discussing whether Homer expressed himself well or ill in such and such verse of the *Iliad;* whether Martial was indecent or not in some epigram; whether such and such verses of Virgil are to be understood in this way or in that. In short, all his conversation concerns the books of those poets, and those of Horace, Persius, Juvenal, and Tibullus, for he has no high opinion of modern writers in Spanish. Yet, in spite of his dislike for poetry in the vernacular, his thoughts are now absorbed in making a gloss on four verses they have sent him from Salamanca, which, I believe, refer to some literary competition."

To all this Don Quixote replied: "Children, sir, are part of their parents' bowels, and so we must love them, whether they are good or bad, as we love the souls that give us life. It is the duty of their parents to guide them from infancy along the paths of virtue, good breeding, and Christian behavior, so that, grown up, they may be the staff of their parents' old age and the glory of their posterity. But when it comes to forcing them to study this or that science, I consider it unwise, although there may be no harm in persuading them; and seeing that they are in no need of studying to earn their daily bread, as the student is lucky enough to be endowed by Heaven with parents who spare him that, my advice is that they should be permitted to pursue the branch of learning to which they are most inclined. And although that of Poetry is less useful than it is pleasurable, it is certainly not one of those that dishonor their votary. Poetry, my dear sir, I would compare to a tender, young, and ravishingly beautiful maiden, whom many other maidens, namely, all the other sciences, strive to enrich, to polish, and to adorn. And she has to exact service from all, and all of them can only become exalted through her. But this maiden refuses to be manhandled, or dragged through the streets, or exposed to the public at the market corners or in the antechambers of palaces, for she is fashioned of an alchemy of such power that anyone who knows how to treat her will transmute her into purest gold of inestimable price. He who possesses her must keep her within bounds, not letting her descend to base lampoons or impious sonnets; she must not be displayed for sale, unless in heroic poems, in mournful tragedies, or in merry and artificial comedies. She must not suffer herself to be handled by buffoons, nor by the vulgar mob, who are incapable of recognizing or valuing the treasures she enshrines. Do not imagine, sir, that by vulgar I mean only the common and humble people, for everyone who is ignorant, be he a prince or a lord, can and should be included in the category of the vulgar; so anyone with the qualifications I have mentioned who takes up and treats Poetry will become famous and his name will be held in esteem among all the civilized nations of the world. As to what you say, sir, of your son not appreciating the poetry in our Spanish tongue, I am convinced that he is wrong there, and the reason in this: the great Homer did not write in Latin because he was a Greek, nor Virgil in Greek because he was a Latin. In short, all the ancient poets wrote in the tongues they sucked with their mother's milk, and they did not go out in quest of strange ones to express the greatness of their conceptions; and this being so, it is only reasonable that the fashion should extend to all nations, and the German poet should not be undervalued because he writes in his language, nor the Castilian, nor even the Biscayan, who writes in his. But your son, sir, as I believe, does not dislike the poetry in the vulgar tongue, but only the poets who are merely vernacular and know no other tongues or other sciences to adorn, jog, and stimulate their natural inspiration. And yet, even in this we may be mistaken, for according to true belief, the poet is born—that is to say, the natural poet sallies forth from his mother's womb a poet, and with that impulse that Heaven has given him, without further study or art, he composes things that prove the truth of the saying: *est Deus in nobis*,[39] etc. Let me also say that the natural poet who makes use of art will improve himself and be much greater than the poet who relies only on his knowledge of the art. The reason is clear, for art is not better than nature, but merely perfects her. So, nature combined with art and art with nature will produce a most perfect poet. To conclude my speech, noble sir, your worship should allow your son to go where his star calls him, for if he is as good a student as he should be and if he has successfully mounted the first step of learning, which is that of the languages, he will ascend of his own accord to the summit of humane letters, which so well become a gentleman of leisure, and adorn, honor, and exalt him as miters do bishops or robes learned doctors of law. But your worship should chide your son if he writes lampoons to the prejudice of the characters of others, and punish him and tear them up; but if he writes satires after the manner of Horace, reproving vice in general terms and as elegantly as the Roman did, praise him, for a poet may lawfully castigate envy and upbraid the envious in his verses and flagellate other vices, too, provided he does not single out any particular person, though there are poets who run the risk of banishment to the Isles of Pontus for the sake of uttering one malicious jibe.[40] If the poet, however, is chaste in his morals, he will be chaste also in his verses.

---

[39] The complete quotation is "There is a god in us; he stirs and lo! we feel his fire." (Ovid, *Festivals*, VI.5.)

[40] Ovid was banished thus by the Emperor Augustus, presumably for writing *The Art of Love*.

The pen is the tongue of the soul, and the thoughts begotten there will burgeon in whatever he writes. And when kings and princes behold the miraculous science of Poetry in subjects who are wise, virtuous, and grave, they honor, esteem, and reward them, and even crown them with the leaves of the tree that lightning never strikes, as a warning that no one should attack men whose temples are honored and adorned by such crowns." [41]

The man in green was lost in amazement at Don Quixote's reasoning, so much so that he began to alter the opinion he had formed of the knight's craziness. But in the middle of the conversation, which was not much to his taste, Sancho had strayed from the road to beg a little milk from some shepherds who were milking their ewes close by; and just as the gentleman was about to renew the conversation, highly delighted with Don Quixote's wisdom and good sense, the latter, lifting his head, saw a cart decorated with the king's colors coming along the road by which they were traveling. Imagining that this must be some new adventure, he shouted to Sancho to come and bring him his helmet. Sancho, hearing himself called, left the shepherds, and spurring on Dapple, hastened toward his master, to whom befell a stupendous and fearful adventure.

CHAPTER XVII

In which is set forth the highest point that Don Quixote's unheard-of courage ever reached, with the happily terminated adventure of the lions

Our history relates that when Don Quixote called Sancho to bring him his helmet, the latter was buying some curds from the shepherds, and being flustered by his master's pressing call, he did not know what to do with them nor how to carry them. So, in order not to lose them, as he had already paid for them, he thought it best to pour them into his master's helmet, and using this clever shift, he turned back to see what his master needed. Don Quixote cried out to him: "Give me that helmet, my friend, for either I know precious little of adventures, or what I see yonder is one that should, and does, require me to arm myself."

The man in green heard this and gazed around in all directions without seeing anything but a cart coming toward them with two or three small flags, which made him think that it was carrying the king's treasure, and so he told Don Quixote. But the knight did not believe it, for he always firmly imagined that everything that befell him must be adventures and still more adventures. So, he replied: "Forewarned is forearmed. Nothing is lost by taking precautions, for I know by experience that I have enemies visible and invisible, and I never know when or where, nor in what moment, nor in what shape they may attack me."

And turning to Sancho, he asked him for his helmet, and as the squire had no time to take out the curds, he had to give it to him as it was. Don Quixote took it, and without noticing what was in it, he clapped it on his head hastily, and as the curds were pressed and squeezed, the whey began to pour down over Don Quixote's face and beard, which gave him such a

---

[41] This refers to the laurel tree.

start that he exclaimed to Sancho: "What's this, Sancho? I think my head is softening, or my brains are melting, or else I am sweating from head to foot. But if I am sweating, it is certainly not from fear, though I am truly sure the adventure I have to face is a terrible one. Give me something to wipe myself with, for this copious sweat is blinding my eyes."

Sancho held his tongue and handed him a cloth, thanking God that his master had not found out the truth.

Don Quixote wiped himself and took off the helmet to see what it was that made his head feel cool, and seeing the white mess inside the helmet, he put it up to his nose, and sniffing he said: "By my Lady Dulcinea of El Toboso, these are curds you have put here, you treacherous, impudent, ill-favored squire!"

To which with calm composure Sancho replied: "If they are curds, master, give them to me, and I'll eat them; but let the Devil eat them, for it must be he who put them there! How could you ever imagine that I would have the impudence to soil your worship's helmet? Indeed, you must already know the culprit! In faith, master, from the understanding which God has given me, I am convinced that I, too, must have enchanters who persecute me as a creature and limb of your worship, and they must have put that nasty mess there in order to rouse your patience to anger and make you drub my ribs as you are wont to do. But this time they have missed their mark, for I put my trust in my master's good sense; he must have considered that I have no curds or milk, or anything of the kind, and if I had, it is in my belly I would put them and not in the helmet."

"That may be," replied Don Quixote.

The gentleman had observed all with amazement, especially when Don Quixote, after wiping clean his head, face, beard, and helmet, put it on again, stood up in his stirrups, and feeling for his sword and grasping his lance, cried: "Now, come what may, I stand ready to face Satan himself in battle."

At this moment the cart with the flags approached. In it was nobody but the carter, who rode one of the mules, and a man who was seated in front. Don Quixote stood in front of it and said: "Whither are you going, brothers? What cart is this? What have you got in it? What flags are those?"

To this the carter replied: "The cart is mine, but in it is a fine pair of caged lions that the general is sending from Oran as a present to His Majesty, and the flags are of the king, our master, which signify that what is inside the cart is his property."

"Are the lions big?" asked Don Quixote.

"So big," said the man at the door of the cart, "that none bigger, or even as big, have ever crossed from Africa into Spain. I am the keeper and I've carried many, but never a pair like these. They are male and female; the male is in the front cage, and the female in the one behind. They are now very hungry, for they've eaten nothing today; so it would be best for your worship to stand aside, for we must make haste to reach the place where we may give them their feed."

To this Don Quixote answered, smiling slightly: "Lion cubs to me? To me lion cubs? At such a time, too? Then, by God, those gentlemen who send them here will soon see whether I am the man to be frightened by lions. Dismount, my good man, and since you are the keeper, open the cages and drive out these beasts. In the midst of this open field I will let them know who Don Quixote of La Mancha is, in spite of the enchanters who have sent them to me."

"Goodness gracious!" muttered the gentleman in green at this. "Our good knight is giving me proof of his nature. The curds, no doubt, have softened his skull and mellowed his brains."

At this point Sancho came up to him and exclaimed: "Sir, for God's sake, try and stop my master fighting with these lions; if he fights them, they'll tear us all to pieces."

"Is your master so crazy," the gentleman replied, "that you actually fear and believe he will really fight those furious beasts?"

"He's not crazy," replied Sancho, "but foolhardy."

"I'll make him stop," said the gentleman. And going up to Don Quixote, who was pressing the keeper to open the cages, he said: "Sir knight, knights-errant should engage in enterprises that hold out some prospect of success, but not in those that are entirely devoid of it, for valor that verges on temerity has more of madness about it than bravery. Moreover, these lions have not come against you, nor do they dream of doing so. They are going to be presented to His Majesty, and it is not right to detain them or hinder their journey."

"Get you gone, my dear sir," answered Don Quixote, "and look to your tame partridge and your spry ferret, and let every man look to his own duty; this is mine, and I know whether these gentlemen, the lions, are coming against me or not." Then turning to the keeper, he said sharply: "I swear, sir rascal, that if you don't open the cage at once, I'll stitch you to the cart with this lance."

The carter saw the armed phantom's grim determination and said to him: "Please, sir, for charity's sake, let me unhitch the mules and place myself in safety along with them before the lions are unleashed, for if they kill my beasts, I'm ruined for life, seeing that all I possess is this cart and the mules."

"O man of little faith!" replied Don Quixote. "Get down and unyoke, and do what you will; soon you will see that your toils were in vain and that you might have spared yourself the trouble."

The carter got down and in haste unyoked, and the keeper called out in a loud voice: "Bear witness, all who are here, how against my will and under compulsion I open the cages and let loose the lions. And I protest to this gentleman that all the harm and mischief these beasts shall do will be put to his account, together with my wages and dues as well. You, sir, take cover before I open; as for myself, I am sure they will do me no harm."

Once more the gentleman in green entreated the knight not to commit such an act of madness, for to engage in such freakish folly was to tempt Providence, but Don Quixote answered that he knew what he was up to. The gentleman warned him once more to mind what he was doing, for he was surely mistaken.

"Well, sir," replied Don Quixote, "if your worship does not wish to witness what you believe is about to be a tragedy, clap spurs to your gray mare and retire to safety."

Hearing this, Sancho besought his master with tears in his eyes to give up such an enterprise, compared with which the adventure of the windmills and the fearsome one of the fulling mills and, in fact, all the deeds his master had attempted in the whole course of his life were nothing but cakes and fancy bread. "Look sir," said he, "here there is no enchantment nor anything of the kind, for through the chinks and bars of the cage I have seen the claw of a live lion, and I'm sure that a lion with such a claw must be bigger than a mountain."

"Fear, at any rate," answered Don Quixote, "will make it seem bigger to you than half the earth. Retire, Sancho, and leave me. If I die here, you know our old compact. You will go straight to Dulcinea; I say no more."

Other words he added to those declarations that took away all hope that he would give up his insane purpose. The man in green would have resisted him, but not being so well armed, he thought it would be imprudent to fight with a madman, for he now was convinced that the knight was stark, staring mad. Don Quixote then went on pressing the keeper and repeating his threats, which gave the gentleman a chance to spur his mare, Sancho to prod Dapple, and the carter his mules—all trying to get away from the cart as far as possible before the lions erupted from their cages. Sancho wept for his master's death, for this time he truly believed he would perish at the claws of the lions, He cursed his luck and the unlucky hour when he took it into his head to return to his service. Nevertheless, in spite of all his tears and groans, he took good care to flog up Dapple so as to drive him farther away from the cart. Then, when the keeper saw that those who had fled were far enough away, he again entreated and warned Don Quixote as he had done before, but the knight replied that he heard him but would listen to no more warnings or entreaties and bade him make haste. While the keeper was opening the first cage, Don Quixote was considering whether it would be better to do battle on foot or on horseback, and in the end he decided to fight on foot, for he was afraid Rozinante would take fright at the lions. He, therefore, sprang off his horse, flung his lance aside, and braced his buckler on his arm. Then, unsheathing his sword with marvelous valor and undaunted heart, he advanced at a leisurely pace and posted himself in front of the cart, commending his soul to God and then to his lady, Dulcinea.

We now must observe that when the author of our true history came to this point, he exclaimed: "O brave and incomparably courageous Don Quixote of La Mancha! Mirror wherein all the valiant may behold themselves! You second Don Manuel of León,[42] who was the honor and glory of Spanish knights! With what words shall I describe this most fearful exploit, or how make it credible to future ages? What praises can be unfitting and unmeet for you, though hyperbole be piled on hyperbole? You on foot, you alone, you bold and undaunted with only a simple sword and no trenchant Toledo blades of the little dog make,[43] with a shield of not very bright and shining steel, you stand watchful and ready for the two fiercest lions ever bred in African forests! Let your deeds themselves, valiant Manchegan, extol you; here I leave them in all their glamor, for I lack words to glorify them."

Here the author broke off his apostrophe and proceeded to take up the thread of his history, saying:

The keeper, seeing that Don Quixote had taken up his position and that it was impossible to avoid letting loose the male lion without falling under the rage of the wrathful and undaunted knight, opened wide the doors of

---

[42] A famous knight of the time of Ferdinand and Isabella.
[43] A little dog was the trademark of Julián del Rey, a famous armorer of Toledo.

the first cage, containing, as we have said, the male lion. The beast was now seen to be of extraordinary size and of grim and awful aspect. The first thing he did was to turn around in the cage in which he lay and to extend his claws and stretch himself out to his full length. Then, he opened his mouth and yawned very leisurely, and with about two palms' lengths of tongue, which he put out, he licked the dust from his eyes and washed his face. When this was done, he put his head out of the cage and gazed all around with eyes like blazing coals, a sight that would have struck terror in temerity itself. Don Quixote alone stood looking at him intently, longing for him to leap out of the cart and come to close grips with him, when he hoped to hack him to pieces. Up to such a point did his unheard-of madness raise him. The noble lion, however, more courteous than arrogant, took scant notice of such childish bravado, and after looking around about him, as we have said, he turned his back and showed Don Quixote his hind parts, after which coolly and calmly he flung himself down in the cage. Seeing this, Don Quixote ordered the keeper to prod him and tease him to make him come out.

"I will not do so," replied the keeper, "for if I excite him, the first he will tear to pieces will be myself. Be content, sir, with what you have done, which leaves no more to be said on the score of courage, and don't try to tempt Fortune a second time. The lion has the door open; he's free to come out or not; since he hasn't come out up to now, he won't come out all day. Your worship's sturdy heart has been already shown to the world; no gallant champion, to my way of thinking, is bound to do more than to challenge his enemy and wait for him in the field. If his rival doesn't come, to him sticks the disgrace, and the man who waits his ground carries off the crown of victory."

"That is true," replied Don Quixote; "so, shut the door, my friend, and give me a sworn statement of what you have seen me do here, in the best form you can; to wit, that you did open for the lion, that I waited for him, that he did not come out, that still I waited for him, that still he did not come out, and that he lay down again. I am not bound to do more. Away with enchantments and God protect right, truth, and true chivalry! Shut the door, friend, while I signal to the fugitive and absent to return that they may learn of this exploit from your lips."

The keeper did so, and Don Quixote, sticking on the point of his lance the cloth with which he had wiped the shower of curds off his face, began to signal to those who were still continuing to flee, though looking around at every step, urged on by the gentleman in green. Sancho, happening to notice the signal of the white cloth, exclaimed: "May I be blowed if my master has not conquered the wild beasts, for he's calling us!"

They all stopped, and seeing that it was Don Quixote who was making the signals, losing some of their fear, they approached little by little until they clearly heard the voice of Don Quixote calling to them. At length they reached the cart, and as they came up, Don Quixote said to the carter: "Yoke your mules once more, my friend, and continue your journey, and you, Sancho, give him two gold crowns for himself and for the keeper as a compensation for the delay they have had through me."

"I'll give them with a heart and a half," said Sancho; "but what has happened to the lions? Are they alive or dead?"

Then the keeper gave a detailed account of the encounter, praising to the skies the power and valor of Don Quixote, at whose sight the cowed lion dared not to come out of his cage, though he had held the door open a good while, and that it was only because he had told the knight that it was tempting Providence to excite the lion and force him to come out, as he wanted him to do, that the knight had, against his will, allowed him to close the door.

"What do you think of this, Sancho?" said Don Quixote. "Are any enchantments able to prevail against true valor? The enchanters may be able to rob me of good luck, but of courage they cannot."

Sancho gave them the gold crowns, the carter yoked up, the keeper kissed Don Quixote's hands for the guerdon received and promised him to give an account of the brave exploit to the king himself as soon as he saw him at court.

"Then," said Don Quixote, "if His Majesty should happen to ask who performed it, you must say that it was the Knight of the Lions, for it is my wish that from this day on there may be changed, altered, and transformed the name that till now I have borne of the Knight of the Rueful Figure. In this I follow the ancient custom of knights-errant, who changed their names when they pleased or when it suited them."

The cart went on its way and Don Quixote, Sancho, and the gentleman in the green coat continued theirs.

All this while Don Diego de Miranda had not opened his mouth, so carefully was he watching and noting every word and action of Don Quixote, who appeared to him to be at once a sane man turned mad and a madman who had glimmers of sanity. The first part of this history had not yet come to his notice, for if he had read it, he would have ceased to wonder at the knight's deeds, since he would have ascertained the nature of his madness. But as he did not know it, he sometimes took him for sane, sometimes for mad. For what Don Quixote said was consistent, elegant, and well expressed, but what he did was eccentric, rash, and absurd. "What could be madder," he reflected, "than to put on a helmet full of curds and believe that enchanters had melted one's brains? And what could be rasher and more absurd than to insist on fighting with lions?"

Don Quixote interrupted his soliloquy by saying: "No doubt, Don Diego de Miranda, your worship regards me as both foolish and mad. And it would be no wonder if you did, for my actions can have no other interpretation. Nevertheless, I wish your worship to note that I am not so mad or foolish as I must have appeared to you. It is a fine sight to see a gallant knight under the eyes of his king give effective lance thrusts at a brave bull in the midst of a great square; it is a fine sight to see a knight, all armed in burnished armor, pace the lists in merry jousts before the ladies; and it is a fine sight to see all those knights who in military exercises or the like entertain, cheer, and if one may say so, honor the courts of their princes. But finer than all these is to see a knight-errant roaming through deserts and solitudes, by crossroads and forests and mountains, in quest of perilous adventures, in order to bring them to a happy and fortunate conclusion only for the sake of glory and lasting renown. It is a finer sight, I say, to see a knight-errant succoring a widow in some lonely waste than a courtier knight dallying with a maiden in the cities. All knights have their particular offices; let the courtier serve the ladies, lend pomp and circumstance to the royal court by his gay liveries, support poor knights at his beautiful table, arrange jousts, maintain tourneys, and show himself generous, liberal and lavish, and a good Christian above everything, for in this way he will fulfill his precise obligations. But let the knight-errant explore the corners of the world, penetrate the most intricate labyrinths, encounter at every step the impossible, brave the scorching rays of the sun in midsummer on high and unpeopled deserts, and in winter the grim inclemency of the winds and frosts; let no lions daunt him, nor hobgoblins scare him, nor dragons terrify him, for to seek them, attack them, and conquer them all are his principal duties. And as the lot has fallen on me to be of the number of knights-errant, I cannot then fail to attempt everything that seems to me to fall within the bounds of my duty. So, it was strictly my right to attack these lions whom I attacked just now, although I knew it to be rash temerity, for I know well what valor is, namely, a virtue that is situated between the two vicious extremes, which are cowardice and rashness. But it is far better for the brave man to mount to the height of rashness than to sink into the depths of cowardice, for just as it is easier for the generous than for the miser to be prodigal, so it is easier for the daring than for the cowardly to become truly valiant. And in the matter of encountering adventures, let your worship, Don Diego, believe me that it is better to lose the game by a card too much than by one too little, for 'this knight is rash and foolhardy' sounds better in the hearer's ears than 'such a knight is timid and cowardly.'"

"Let me admit, Don Quixote," replied Don Diego, "that all that your worship has said and done is adjusted by the balance of reason itself, and I believe that if the laws and ordinances of knight-errantry had been lost, they would be found in your worship's heart, as in their right repository and archive. . . .

[*Quixote and Sancho remain four days at the home of the "Knight of the Green Coat," Don Diego de Miranda; Quixote converses with Don Lorenzo, his host's son. Riding on, they attend a village wedding. The bride, Quiteria, is marrying the wealthy Comacho rather than her real lover, the impoverished Basilio. At the wedding, Basilio appears, stabs himself, and as a dying wish, asks to be married to Quiteria, who can then marry Comacho within a few minutes as a widow. She consents, but after the ceremony Basilio jumps up, unhurt, and claims the bride. A riot almost breaks out, but Quixote defends the newlyweds. He spends three days with them and lectures Basilio on marriage.*]

CHAPTER XXII

In which is given an account of the great adventure of the cave of Montesinos, in the heart of La Mancha, which our gallant Don Quixote brought to a happy conclusion

. . . . "Remember, O wise Basilio," added Don Quixote, "that a certain sage, I know not who, held that there was not more than one good woman in all the world, and he advised everyone to think and believe that this one good woman was his own wife, and so he would live happy. I myself am not married, nor, so far, has it even come into my mind to be so; nevertheless, I would dare to give advice to anyone who might ask it, as to the mode in which he should seek a wife to marry. The first thing I would advise him is to pay more attention to reputation than to fortune, for the good woman does not win a good name solely by being good, but by appearing so, for looseness and public frivolity do greater injury to a woman's honor than secret misdeeds. If you bring a good woman to your house, it will be an easy matter to keep her good, and even improve her in that goodness. But if you bring home a bad one, you will find it a hard task to mend her ways, for it is not easy to pass from one extreme to another. I do not say it is impossible, but I consider it difficult."

Sancho, who had been listening to all this, said to himself: "Whenever I say a word that has a bit of marrow and substance about it, this master of mine straightaway says that I ought to take a pulpit in my hand and roam the world preaching fine sermons; but I say of him that when he starts stringing sentences and giving counsels, not only might he take a pulpit in his hand, but two on each finger, and go into the marketplaces with the cry, 'Who'll buy my wares?' on his lips. Devil take him for a knight-errant, what a number of things he knows! I used to think to myself that the only things he knew had to do with chivalry, but there's not a thing he doesn't peck at nor dip his spoon into."

Sancho kept mumbling to himself so loud that his master overheard him and asked: "What are you muttering about, Sancho?"

"I'm not saying or murmuring anything," said Sancho, "only saying to myself that I wish I had heard what your worship has just said before I got married. Perhaps I'd say now: 'The ox that's loose licks himself well!'"

"Is Teresa[44] so bad then, Sancho?" said Don Quixote.

"She's not too bad," replied Sancho, "but she's not very good; at least, she's not as good as I would like her to be."

"You do wrong, Sancho," said Don Quixote, "to speak ill of your wife, for she is the mother of your children."

"We don't owe each other a thing," answered Sancho, "for she speaks ill of me when she's got the whim, especially when she's jealous; then Satan himself couldn't stomach her."

They remained three days with the newlyweds by whom they were treated and served as royalty. Don Quixote asked the nimble licentiate to get them a guide to conduct them to the cave of Montesinos, of which so many wonderful things were related in those parts, for he had a great wish to explore it and to see with his own eyes if the wonders reported were true. The licentiate replied that he would get him a cousin of his own, a famous scholar, one much given to reading books of chivalry, who would be very glad to guide him to the mouth of the cave and would show him the lagoons of Ruidera, which were also famous all over La Mancha, and even all over Spain. He also said that Don Quixote would enjoy his kinsman's company, who was well versed in writing books and in dedicating them to princes.

The cousin arrived later on, with a she-ass in foal, whose packsaddle was covered with a many-colored rug or sackcloth. Sancho saddled Rozinante, harnessed Dapple, and stocked his saddlebags, to which we should add those of

---

[44] In Part I, Sancho's wife's name is given as Juana (or Mari) Gutiérrez; in Part II, Cervantes calls her Teresa Cascajo, apparently by mistake.

the cousin, which likewise were well supplied. And so, commending themselves to God and taking leave of all, they set out on the road leading to the famous cave of Montesinos.[45]

On the way Don Quixote asked the cousin of what kind were his pursuits, his profession, and studies. To which he replied that his profession was that of a humanist, and his pursuits and studies were to write books for publication, all of great profit and no less entertainment to the state; that one of them was entitled *The Book of Liveries,* in which he described seven hundred and three devices, with their colors, mottoes, and ciphers, from which the gentlemen at court could select and use whichever they pleased on the occasion of festivals and revels, without having to beg them from anybody or rack their brains, as they say, to invent them to suit their wishes and purposes.

"For," he said, "I give appropriate devices to the jealous, the scorned, the forgotten, and the absent, which fit them like a glove. I have another book as well, which I mean to call *Metamorphoses,* or *The Spanish Ovid,* a new and most original work in which, while parodying Ovid, I describe the Giralda of Seville, the Angel of the Magdalen, the Gutter of Vecinguerra at Còrdoba, and the Bulls of Guisando, the Sierra Morena, the fountains of Leganitos and Lavapiés in Madrid, not forgetting that of the Piojo, that of the Golden Gutter, and that of the Priora; and all these with such allegories, metaphors, and transformations that they will entertain, astonish, and instruct at the same time.[46] I also have another book that I call the *Supplement to Polydore Virgil,*[47] which deals with the invention of things. It is a work of deep learning and research, because I clarify and verify in most elegant style the subjects of great importance that Polydore omitted. He forgot to tell us who was the first man who ever had catarrh and who was the first to use ointments to cure himself of the French pox.[48] All this I explain with the utmost precision on the testimony of twenty-five authorities. So your worship may judge whether I have not worked well, and whether this book will not be indispensable to the whole world."

Sancho, who had been listening carefully to the cousin's narrative, said to him: "Tell me, sir, and best of luck with the printing of your books, but can you inform me—of course you can, as you know everything—who was the first man who scratched his head? I'm of the opinion that it must have been our father Adam."

"Yes, it must have been," answered the cousin, "for there is no doubt Adam had a head and hair; and that being so, and as he was the first man in the world, he must sometimes have scratched himself."

---

[45] There is an actual cave of Montesinos in La Mancha. It is very deep and is said to end in the feudal castle of Rochefrías.

[46] The Giralda of Seville and the Angel of the Magdalen were statues on the tops of churches in Seville and Salamanca. The Gutter of Vecinguerra was a sewer in Córdoba. The Bulls of Guisando (referred to, like the Giralda of Seville, earlier) were rough stone statues in Ávila, reportedly marking the site of one of Caesar's victories. The Sierra Morena is a range of mountains. The other wonders are fountains in Madrid. The cousin wants to imitate the Roman poet Ovid (43 B.C.–A.D. 18), whose *Metamorphoses* is a collection of mythological stories of transformations.

[47] Polydore Virgil (c. 1470–1550) was an Italian historian who wrote a book named *On the Invention of Things.* The cousin's projects parody those of the Renaissance humanists.

[48] A reference to the use of mercury ointments to cure syphilis.

"So I believe," answered Sancho; "tell me now, who was the first tumbler in the world?"

"Frankly, brother," replied the cousin, "I am not able to solve that at present, until I have gone further in my studies. I shall look into the matter when I get back to my books, and I'll answer you when we meet again, for this must not be the last time."

"Look here, sir," answered Sancho, "don't go to any trouble about it, for I've hit upon the answer to my question. The first tumbler in the world, let me tell you, was Lucifer, for when they threw or pitched him out of Heaven, he went tumbling into the pit of hell."

"You are right, my friend," said the cousin.

"That question and answer," said Don Quixote, "are not yours, Sancho. You have heard them from someone else."

"Whist, sir," answered Sancho, "for if I start questioning and answering, I shan't be done till tomorrow morning. Yes, for if it's just a matter of asking idiotic questions and giving silly replies, I needn't go begging help from the neighbors."

"You have said more than you know, Sancho," said Don Quixote, "for there are some people who tire themselves out learning and proving things that, once learned and proved, don't matter a straw as far as the mind or memory is concerned."

That day was spent in such pleasant discussions, and at night they put up in a little village that the cousin told Don Quixote was no more than six miles from the cave of Montesinos. He added that if he was determined to enter it, he would need to provide himself with ropes so that he might be tied up and lowered into its depths.

Don Quixote said that even if it reached to the abyss, he was determined to see where it ended. So, they bought about a hundred fathoms of rope, and next day at two o'clock in the afternoon they arrived at the cave. Its mouth is wide and spacious, but full of thorns and wild fig bushes and brambles and briars, so thick and intertwined that they completely close it up.

When they caught sight of it, the cousin, Sancho, and Don Quixote dismounted, and the first two straightaway tied up the latter very firmly with the ropes, and while they were binding him and winding them around him, Sancho said: "Mind what you're doing, master; don't bury yourself alive, or put yourself where you'll be like a flask lowered down into a well to cool. Surely it's no affair of yours to be exploring this place, which must be worse than an underground dungeon."

"Tie me up and hold your peace," replied Don Quixote. "Such an enterprise as this has been reserved for me."

The guide then said: "I pray you, Señor Don Quixote, to note and examine with a hundred eyes all that is inside the cave. Perhaps there may be things that I may include in one of my books."

"The drum is in hands that will know well how to beat it," said Sancho.

When Don Quixote's binding was complete, which went over his doublet but not over his armor, he said: "It was remiss of us not to have provided ourselves of a little bell to be tied on the rope close to me. By the sound you would know that I was still descending and was alive. However, since that is impossible, let God's hand guide me."

Saying this, he fell upon his knees, and in a low voice he offered up a prayer to Heaven, beseeching God to help him and give him success in his new perilous adventure. Then, in a loud voice he cried: "O mistress of my actions and movements, most illustrious and peerless Dulcinea of El Toboso, if it is possible for the prayers and the supplications of thy venturesome lover to reach thy ears, by thy incomparable beauty I beseech thee to listen to them, for they do but beg thee not to refuse me thy favor and protection at this moment when I need them so urgently. I am about to plunge, to engulf, and to sink myself in the abyss that yawns at my feet, only to make the world recognize that if thou dost favor me, there is no impossible feat that I may not accomplish."

With those words he approached the cavern, and finding that it was not possible to let himself down or make an entrance unless by force of arm or by cutting a passage, he drew his sword and began to cut away the brambles at the mouth of the cave. At the noise he made, a great number of crows and jackdaws fluttered out so thickly and with such a rush that they knocked Don Quixote down, and if he had been as superstitious as he was a good Catholic, he would have taken it for an evil omen and would have refused to bury himself in such a place. At last, he rose to his feet, and seeing that no more crows came out, or night birds such as bats, which had flown out at the same time as the crows, he let the cousin and Sancho give him rope, and he began to lower himself into the depths of the dreaded cave. As he entered it, Sancho gave him his blessing and made a thousand signs of the Cross over him, saying: "May God and the Rock of France and the Trinity of Gaeta[49] guide you, O flower, cream, and skimming of knights-errant! There you go, you bully of the world, heart of steel, and of arm of bronze. Once more, may God guide you and bring you back safe and sound to the light of this world of ours you are leaving to bury yourself in darkness."

The cousin likewise offered up similar prayers and supplications.

Don Quixote, as he descended, called out for more and more rope, and they gave it to him little by little. When his shouts, which sounded from the cave as through a funnel, could not be heard, they had already uncoiled the hundred fathoms of rope. They were of the opinion that they should pull up Don Quixote, for they had no more rope to give him. They waited, however, for about half an hour and then began to gather in the rope with great ease and without any weight, a sign that made them believe that Don Quixote had remained inside. Sancho, when he realized this, wept bitterly and pulled away in great haste in order to learn the worst. But when they came to about eighty fathoms, they felt a weight, which cheered them up considerably. At last, at ten fathoms they saw Don Quixote clearly, and Sancho shouted to him, saying: "Welcome back, master, we fancied you were staying down there to found a family."

Don Quixote answered not a word, and when they had pulled him all the way up, they saw that his eyes were shut and that he appeared to be fast asleep.

---

[49] The Rock of France is a statue of the Virgin discovered in the fifteenth century, on the road between Salamanca and Cuidad Rodrigo. The chapel of the Holy Trinity of Gaeta was north of Naples.

They laid him on the ground and untied him, but still he did not awake. Then, they turned him over this way and that, and so shook him and rolled him about that at last he came to himself and stretched himself as if he had just awakened from a deep sleep. Looking around him from one side to another like one who had great fear on him, he cried: "God forgive you, friends; you have snatched me from the most delightful vision that any human being has ever beheld. Now indeed I know that all the pleasant things of this life pass away like a shadow and a dream, or wither like the flowers of the field.[50] O hapless Montesinos! O sorely wounded Durandarte! O unlucky Belerma! O tearful Guadiana, and ye luckless daughters of Ruidera, who show by your waters the tears your eyes did shed!"[51]

The cousin and Sancho listened with great attention to the words of Don Quixote, who uttered them as though they were torn from his very bowels. They besought him to explain what he meant and to tell them what he had seen in the hell below.

"Hell do you call it?" said Don Quixote. "Do not call it thus, for it does not deserve such a name, as you will see presently."

He then begged them to give him something to eat, for he was very hungry. They spread the cousin's saddlecloth on the grass, visited their saddlebags, and seated together in good brotherly fellowship, they lunched and supped at the same time.

Then, when the saddlecloth was removed, Don Quixote said: "Let no one stir. Now, my sons, give me all your attention."

CHAPTER XXIII

Of the wonderful things that the consummate Don Quixote said he had seen in the deep cave of Montesinos, whose impossibility and immensity have caused this adventure to be considered apocryphal

It was then about four o'clock in the afternoon when the sun veiled itself behind clouds and shone with subdued light, so that Don Quixote was enabled to relate without heat and discomfort what he had seen in the cave of Montesinos to his two illustrious auditors. He began as follows: "About twelve or fourteen fathoms down in the depth of this dungeon, on the right hand, there is a recess big enough to contain a large cart with its mules. A tiny ray of light enters through some chinks or crevices that are open to the earth's surface. This recess I saw when I was weary and downcast at finding myself dangling in the air by the rope and traveling down through that dark region below without any clear idea of where I was going; so, I determined to enter it and rest for a moment. I shouted to you not to let out more rope until I should ask for it, but you must not have heard me. I then gathered in the rope you were letting down, and after making a coil of it, I sat down upon it, meditating all the while on what I ought to do in order to lower myself to the bottom of the cavern, seeing that I had no one to hold me up. While

---

[50] The idea and the language are biblical. See, for example, Psalm 102:11: "My days are like an evening shadow; I wither away like grass." For the idea that "life is a dream," see Calderón's play of that title.

[51] These are all characters in chivalric romances.

I was thus perplexed, suddenly and without warning a deep sleep fell upon me, and without knowing the why or the wherefore, I awoke and found myself in the midst of the most delightful meadow that Nature could create or the most vivid imagination visualize. I opened my eyes, I rubbed them, and I found that I was not asleep but wide awake. Nevertheless, I felt my head and my heart to make sure that I myself was there and not some vain specter, but the touch, the feeling, the discourse I held with myself, proved to me that I was the same then as I am here at this moment. Then I saw before me a sumptuous royal palace or castle, with walls that seemed to be made of clear, transparent crystal, and through two great doors that opened I saw a venerable old man come toward me, clad in a long cloak of purple-colored serge that trailed on the ground. He wore over his shoulders and breast a scholar's green-satin hood, and his head was covered with a black Milanese cap, and his snow-white beard fell below his waist. He carried no arms at all, only a rosary of beads that were bigger than fair-sized walnuts—indeed, each tenth bead was like a moderate-sized ostrich egg. His bearing, his gait, his gravity, and his imposing presence, each thing by itself and all of them together, held me spellbound with admiration. He came up to me, and the first thing he did was to embrace me closely. Then he said: 'For many an age, valiant knight Don Quixote of La Mancha, we who inhabit these enchanted solitudes have waited to see you, that you may announce to the world what lies buried in the deep cavern that you have entered, called the cave of Montesinos, an exploit reserved for your invincible heart and spirit. Come with me, illustrious sir, for I wish to show you the wonders that this transparent palace contains, whereof I am the governor and perpetual chief warden, for I am Montesinos himself, after whom the cave is named.'

"No sooner had he said that he was Montesinos than I asked him if the story told in the world above was true, that he had cut the heart of his great friend Durandarte out of his breast with a little dagger and carried it to Lady Belerma, in accordance with Durandarte's instructions at the point of death.[52] He replied that the story was correct in all particulars save in the matter of the dagger, for it was not a dagger, nor little, but a burnished poniard sharper than an awl."

"That same poniard," said Sancho, "must be one of those made by Ramón de Hoces, the Sevillian."[53]

"I do not know," said Don Quixote, "but it could not have been made by that poniard maker, for Ramón de Hoces lived yesterday, whereas the affair of Roncesvalles, where this misfortune took place, was many years ago. But this matter is not of importance; it does not disturb or alter the truth of the story."

"You are right," said the cousin. "Pray proceed, Señor Don Quixote, for I am listening to you with the greatest pleasure in the world."

"And I am no less pleased to tell the story," said Don Quixote. "Well, to continue, the venerable Montesinos led me into the palace of crystal, where in a lower hall, all made of alabaster and extremely cool, there stood an elaborately carved marble tomb, on top of which I saw a knight stretched out

---

[52] This story is told in the chivalric "Ballads of Montesinos." Through this whole section, the story of the heart is told with an absurd literalness.

[53] Unidentified. Presumably a contemporary knife maker.

full length, not of bronze or marble, but of actual flesh and bone. He had his right hand (which to my eyes appeared somewhat hairy and sinewy, a sign that its owner was of great muscular strength) placed over his heart, but before I could question Montesinos, he, seeing me gaze in amazement at the tomb, said: 'This is my friend Durandarte, flower and mirror of the true lovers and valiant knights of his time. He is kept enchanted here, as I am myself and many other men and women, by that Gallic enchanter Merlin,[54] who, they say, was the Devil's son; but, in my opinion, he is no Devil's son, for he knows, as the saying goes, a deal more than the Devil. How or why he enchanted us, no one knows, but time will reveal the reason at no distant date. What amazes me is that I know as surely as that it is now day that Durandarte ended his life in my arms and that after his death I extracted his heart with my own hands; indeed, it must have weighed a couple of pounds, for according to scientists, he who has a large heart is endowed with greater valor than he who has a small one. Now since the knight did really die, how comes it that he moans and complains from time to time as if he were alive?'

"As he said these words that wretched Durandarte cried aloud:

> " 'O my cousin Montesinos!
> Heed, I pray, my last request:
> When thou seest me lying dead
> And my soul from my corpse has fled,
> With thy poniard or thy dagger
> Pluck the heart from out my breast,
> And hie thee with it to Belerma.' "[55]

"On hearing these words the venerable Montesinos sank upon his knees before the hapless knight, and with tears in his eyes, he exclaimed: 'Long since, Sir Durandarte, my dearest cousin, have I done what you bade me on the rueful day when I lost you. I took out your heart as best I could, without leaving the slightest piece of it in your breast; I wiped it with a lace handkerchief; I went off with it by the road to France, after having first laid you in the bosom of the earth with tears so plentiful that they suffced to wash and cleanse my hands of the blood that stained them when I groped in your bowels. Then, O cousin of my soul, as further proof, at the first place I reached after leaving Roncesvalles, I sprinkled a few pinches of salt on your heart that it might not smell badly and that I might bring it, if not fresh, at least pickled, into the presence of Lady Belerma, whom, along with you and me, and Guadiana, your squire, and the duenna Ruidera and her seven daughters and two nieces, and other friends, Merlin the Wizard keeps here enchanted these many years. And though five hundred years have passed, not one of us has died. Ruidera and her daughters and nieces alone are missing, for Merlin, pitying them for the tears they had shed, changed them into so many lagoons, which now in the world of the living and in the province of La Mancha

---

[54] The wizard in the Arthurian legends. He was Welsh, not "Gallic," though he was claimed by the Bretons.
[55] Cervantes is quoting, and combining, two actual ballads.

the people call the lagoons of Ruidera.[56] The seven daughters belong to the kings of Spain and the two nieces to the knights of a very holy order, called the Order of St. John.[57] Guadiana, your squire, who also was bewailing your fate, was changed into a river of his own name, but when he reached the surface of the earth and saw the sun of another Heaven, so great was his sorrow at finding that he was leaving you that he plunged into the bowels of the earth.[58] Nevertheless, as he cannot avoid following his natural course, from time to time he comes forth and shows himself to the sun and the world. The lagoons I have mentioned supply him with their waters, and with their help and the help of many others he enters Portugal in all his pomp and glory. But wherever he goes he shows his sadness and melancholy and takes no pride in breeding choice and tasty fish, but only coarse and tasteless kinds, very different from those of the golden Tagus.[59] All this, my cousin, I have told you many times before, but since you make me no answer, I am afraid you do not believe me, or do not hear me, which greatly distresses me, as God knows. Now I have news to give you, which, while it may not alleviate your sorrows, will by no means increase them. Learn that you have here before you (open your eyes and you will see him) that great knight about whom the magician Merlin has prophesied so many things; that Don Quixote of La Mancha, I say, who once again and to better purpose than in the past has revived in the present the already forgotten order of knight-errantry. By his aid and favor we may be disenchanted, for great deeds are reserved for great men.'

" 'And if this does not take place,' replied the hapless Durandarte in a swooning voice; 'if this may not be, then, O cousin, I say: patience and shuffle the cards.'[60] And turning over on his side, he relapsed into his former silence without speaking another word.

"And now a great outcry and lamentations arose, accompanied by deep groans and pitiful sobbings. I turned around and saw through the walls of crystal in another hall a procession of two lines of fair damsels all clad in mourning, with white turbans of Turkish fashion on their heads. Behind, in the rear of the procession, walked a lady, for so her dignity proclaimed her to be, also clothed in black, with a white veil so long and ample that it kissed the ground. Her turban was twice as large as the largest of any of the others; she had eyebrows that met, and her nose was rather flat; her mouth was large, but her lips were red; her teeth, which at times she showed, were few and not well set, though as white as peeled almonds. She carried in her hands a fine handkerchief, and in it, as well as I could make out, a mummified heart, for it was all dried up and pickled. Montesinos said that all those in the procession were servants of Durandarte and Belerma, who were enchanted there with their master and mistress, and that the last one, she who bore the heart wrapped up in the handkerchief, was the Lady Belerma,

[56] The "lagoons of Ruidera" were a series of lakes in the vicinity of the ancient Muslim castle of Ruidera.

[57] Two of the lakes (the "nieces") were in the domain of the Order of St. John.

[58] The fact that the Guadiana River in La Mancha flows underground for some distance has already been mentioned in Part I.

[59] A river in central Spain.

[60] A proverb among cardplayers.

who with her damsels, four days a week, walked in that procession and sang, or rather wept, her sorrowful dirges over the body and wretched heart of his cousin. He added that if she appeared to me somewhat ugly, or at least, not as beautiful as fame reported, it was because of the bad nights and the worse days she spent in that enchantment, as I could see by the great dark circles around her eyes and her sickly complexion. 'And,' said he, 'her sallowness and the rings around her eyes do not come from the periodical ailment common to women, for it is many months, and even years, since it has appeared at her gates, but from the grief her own heart suffers for that object that she continually holds in her hands; it brings back to her memory the misfortune of her luckless lover. If it were not for this, scarcely would the great Dulcinea of El Toboso, so renowned in all these parts, and even in all the world, equal her in beauty, charm, and wit.'

" 'Go slow, Don Montesinos,' said I. 'Tell your story rightly, for you are aware that all comparisons are odious, and there is no reason to compare one person with another. The peerless Dulcinea of El Toboso is what she is, and Doña Belerma is what she is and has been, and there let the matter rest.'

"To which he answered: 'Forgive me, Don Quixote, for I confess that I was wrong in saying that Lady Dulcinea could scarcely equal Lady Belerma, for it was enough for me to learn, I know not by what indications, that you are her knight, to make me bite my tongue rather than compare her to anything but Heaven itself.' After this satisfaction that the great Montesinos gave me, my heart recovered from the shock it had received at hearing my lady compared to Belerma."

"And yet I'm amazed," cried Sancho, "that your worship did not jump upon the old fellow and kick every bone in his body and tear out his beard, without leaving a hair in it."

"No, Sancho, my friend," said Don Quixote, "it would not have been right for me to do so, for we are all bound to show respect to the aged, even though they be not knights, but especially to those who are and who become enchanted. I am certain that I owed him nothing in the matter of the many questions and answers that passed between us."

At this point the cousin remarked: "I cannot understand, Don Quixote, how in so short a space of time as you were down below you were able to see so many things and to say and answer so much."

"How long is it since I went down?" asked Don Quixote.

"A little more than an hour," replied Sancho.

"That cannot be," answered Don Quixote, "for night came when I was down there, and then morning, and again a night and a morning three times, so that, by my reckoning, I have been three days in these remote regions hidden from the upper world."

"My master must be right," said Sancho, "for since everything that has happened to him is by enchantment, perhaps what seems an hour to us would seem three days and nights down there."

"That must be so," said Don Quixote.

"Did you, dear sir, eat anything all that time?" asked the cousin.

"I have not broken my fast," answered Don Quixote, "nor did I feel hunger, even in my imagination."

"Do the enchanted eat?" inquired the cousin.

"They do not eat," answered Don Quixote, "nor do they void excrement, but it is thought that their nails, hair, and beard grow."

"And do the enchanted ones sleep, master?" asked Sancho.

"Certainly not," replied Don Quixote, "at any rate, during the three days I spent with them no one closed an eye; neither did I."

"This is a point," said Sancho, "where the proverb comes pat: 'Tell me the company you keep and I'll tell you what you are.' You, master, kept company with enchanted fellows who were fasting and watching. What wonder, then, that you neither ate nor slept while you were with them? But forgive me, master, if I tell you that of all you've said up to the present, God seize me—I was just going to say the devil—if I believe a single word."

"What!" cried the cousin. "Could Don Quixote tell a lie? Why, even if he wished to do so, this was no time for him to invent such a load of lies."

"I don't believe my master tells lies," answered Sancho.

"If not, what do you believe?" asked Don Quixote.

"I believe," said Sancho, "that this fellow Merlin, or these enchanters who bewitched the whole crew your worship says you saw and talked to down below, has piled your imagination with all that hodgepodge you have been telling and with everything else that you still have to tell."

"That might be, Sancho," replied Don Quixote, "but as a matter of fact, it is not so, for all that I have told you I saw with my own eyes and touched with my own hands. Now, what will you say when I tell you that among the countless marvelous things Montesinos showed me, he pointed out three peasant girls who were capering and frisking like she-goats over those delightful fields, and no sooner had I caught sight of them than I recognized one as the peerless Dulcinea of El Toboso and the other two as the same country wenches that were with her and to whom we spoke on the road from El Toboso? I asked Montesinos if he knew them. He answered that he did not, but that he thought they must be some enchanted ladies of quality, for it was but a few days since they had made their appearance in those meadows. He added that I should not be surprised at that, because many ladies of past and present times were enchanted there in various strange shapes, and among them he recognized Queen Guinevere and her duenna, Quintañona, who poured out the wine for Lancelot 'When from Brittany he came.'"[61]

As soon as Sancho Panza heard his master say this, he thought he would lose his wits, or else die with laughter, for since he knew the truth about the pretended enchanting of Dulcinea and had been himself the enchanter and the concocter of all the evidence, he made up his mind, beyond all shadow of a doubt, that his master was out of his wits and mad as a March hare. So, he said to him: "It was a bitter day, dear master, when you went below to the other world, and it was an unlucky moment when you met Señor Montesinos, who has so transmogrified you for us. Up here, master, you were in your full senses, just as God has given you, uttering your maxims and giving counsels at every turn, and not as you are now, blabbing the greatest balderdash that ever was known."

---

[61] From the ballad on Lancelot that Don Quixote quoted in the first adventure in the inn in Part I.

"I know you, Sancho," replied Don Quixote, "so, I pay no heed to your words."

"No more do I to yours," said Sancho, "even though you beat me or kill me for those I've spoken or mean to speak if you don't correct and mend your own. But tell me, now that we're at peace, what made you recognize the lady our mistress? If you did speak to her, what did you say, and what did she say in reply?"

"I recognized her," said Don Quixote, "because she wore the same clothes as when you showed her to me. I spoke to her, but she did not answer a word, but only turned her back on me and fled, and she ran at such a pace that an arrow would not have overtaken her. I wanted to follow her and would have done so if Montesinos had not advised me not to weary myself in doing so, for it would be vain, especially as the hour was approaching when it would be necessary for me to leave the cave. He told me, moreover, that in time he would tell me how he, Belerma, Durandarte, and all who were there were to be disenchanted. What pained me most of all was that while Montesinos was speaking to me, one of the two attendants of the hapless Dulcinea came up to me without my having seen her coming, and with tears in her eyes, she said to me in a low agitated voice: 'My Lady Dulcinea of El Toboso kisses your worship's hand and beseeches you to let her know how you are; because she is in great need, she also entreats your worship as earnestly as she can to be so good as to lend her, upon this new dimity petticoat I have here, half a dozen reals, or as many as you have, which she promises to repay in a very short time.' Such a message amazed me; so, turning to Montesinos, I said: 'Is it possible, Señor Montesinos, that persons of quality who are enchanted can suffer need?' He replied: 'Believe me, Don Quixote of La Mancha, what is called want is the fashion all over the world; it extends throughout, touches everyone, and doesn't even spare the enchanted. And since Lady Dulcinea of El Toboso sends to borrow the six reals, and the security is apparently good, there is nothing to do but to give them to her, for she must no doubt be in sore straits.'

" 'I will not take a pledge for her,' I replied, 'nor can I yet give her what she asks, for all I have is four reals,' which I gave her (they were those that you, Sancho, gave me the other day to hand as alms to the poor I met on the road), and I said: 'Tell your mistress, my dear friend, that I am distressed to hear of her troubles and that I wish I were a Fúcar[62] to relieve them; I would have her know that I cannot be, and ought not to be, in good health, seeing that I lack her pleasant company and witty conversation. So, I beseech her as earnestly as I can to allow herself to be seen and greeted by this her captive and foot-weary cavalier. You must tell her also that when she least expects it, she will hear that I have made a vow, like the one that the Marquess of Mantua made to avenge his nephew Baldwin when he found him dying on the mountainside, which was not to eat bread off a tablecloth, with some other trifles he added, until he had avenged him.[63] And I will do the same:

---

[62] "Fúcar" is the Spanish form of "Fugger," the name of a famous family of Bavarian bankers and financiers in the Middle Ages.

[63] The story of Carloto and Baldwin has already been told in Part I.

not to rest, and to wander over the seven regions of the earth more diligently than the Infante Don Pedro of Portugal,[64] until I have freed her from her enchantment.'

" 'All that and more, your worship should do for my lady,' said the damsel in answer, and taking the four reals, instead of making me a curtsy she cut a caper that lifted her two yards up into the air."

"Holy God!" shouted Sancho at this point. "Is it possible that such things can happen in the world and that enchanters and enchantments can have the power to change the good sense of my master into such crazy folly? O master, master, for God's sake, mind yourself, consider your honor and give no credit to this empty balderdash that has destroyed your senses."

"You talk this way, Sancho, because you love me," said Don Quixote, "and because you are inexperienced in the affairs of the world. Everything that presents points of difficulty appears to you impossible. But after time has passed I shall tell you about some of the things I saw below that will make you believe what I have related, for its truth admits no reply or question."

CHAPTER XXIV

In which a thousand trifles are recounted, as nonsensical as they are necessary to the true understanding of this great history

The translator of this great history from the original written by its first author, Cide Hamete Benengeli, says that when he came to the adventure of the cave of Montesinos, he found written in the margin, in the hand of Hamete, these words: "I am unable to understand or to persuade myself that all that is written in the previous chapter literally happened to the valiant Don Quixote. The reason is that all the adventures until now have been feasible and probable, but this one of the cave I can find no way of accepting it as true, seeing that it exceeds all reasonable bounds. Nevertheless, I cannot possibly believe that Don Quixote, who was the most truthful gentleman and the noblest knight of the times, could tell a lie; why, he could not lie, even if they riddled him with arrows. On the other hand, when I consider the minute and detailed manner in which he has spoken, I find it still more impossible to believe that he could have fashioned such a tissue of absurdities in so short time.

"So, if this adventure seems apocryphal, it is not I who am to blame, for I write it down without vouching its truth or falsity. You, cautious reader, as you are wise, must judge for yourself, for I cannot, and should not, do more. One thing, however, is certain, that finally he retracted it on his deathbed and confessed that he had invented it, since he believed that it fitted in well with the adventures he had read of in his histories.". . .

[*In a long section which follows, Don Quixote and Sancho, among other adventures, are entertained in the home of a duke and duchess who have read the First Part of their history and who play an elaborate series of practical jokes on them. The duke pretends to make Sancho the*

---

[64]A celebrated traveler. His account of his travels in the East was published in 1554.

governor of an island, where he surprises everyone by the wisdom of his decisions. Meanwhile at the castle, Quixote is the victim of a series of jests, but he maintains his dignity; both he and Sancho grow in stature as the duke and duchess appear progressively more foolish. Leaving the palace, Quixote and Sancho encounter a group setting up a pastoral Arcadia, who treat them kindly. They then meet a Robin Hood-like highwayman, Roque Guinart, who befriends them. They go to Barcelona, where they are the guests of Don Antonio Moreno, who plays tricks on Quixote even more cruel than those in the castle of the duke and duchess.]

CHAPTER LXIV

Of the adventure that gave Don Quixote more sorrow than any that had ever befallen him

. . . . One morning when Don Quixote was riding out for an airing on the strand, armed cap-a-pie—for, as he often said, "my ornaments are arms, my rest the battle fray," and he was never a moment without them—he spied a knight riding toward him, armed like himself from head to foot, with a shining moon painted on his shield, who, when he came within hearing, called out to him: "Illustrious knight and never-enough-renowned Don Quixote of La Mancha, I am the Knight of the White Moon, whose unheard-of exploits perchance may have reached your ears. I come to enter into combat with you and to compel you by sword to own and confess that my mistress, whoever she may be, is incomparably more beautiful than your Dulcinea of El Toboso. If you will fairly confess this truth, you will spare your own life and me the trouble of taking it. If you are resolved to fight and if victory be mine, my terms require that you relinquish arms and the quest of adventures and retire to your home for the space of one year, where you shall live quietly and peaceably, without laying hand to your sword, for thus you will improve your temporal and spiritual welfare. But should you vanquish me, my head shall be at your mercy, my arms and my steed shall be yours, and the fame of my deeds shall be added to yours. Consider what is best for you and give me your answer without delay, for this day must decide the issue of this affair."

Don Quixote was surprised, not to say dumbfounded, as much by the arrogance of the Knight of the White Moon's challenge, as at the subject of it; so, with solemn gravity and composure he replied: "Knight of the White Moon, whose exploits have not yet come to my ears, I will make you swear that you have never set eyes upon the illustrious Dulcinea, for if you had done so, I am confident that you would never have made this claim, since the sight of her perfections must have convinced you that there never was, or ever can be, beauty comparable to hers. And so, without calling you a liar, I declare that you are mistaken and accept your challenge upon the spot, this very day. Furthermore, I accept all your conditions, with the exception of the transfer of your exploits, for they are unknown to me; I must remain contented with my own, such as they are. Choose, then, your ground and I shall do the same, and may St. Peter bless him whom God favors."

Meanwhile the viceroy, who had been informed of the arrival of the Knight of the White Moon and of the conversation that he was holding with Don Quixote, hastened to the scene of action accompanied by Don Antonio and others, firmly convinced that this must be some new jest invented by Don Antonio Moreno or by some other gentleman of the city. They arrived just as Don Quixote was wheeling Rozinante about to take his ground, and perceiving that they were on the point of attacking one another, the viceroy intervened and asked what was the reason for such a sudden encounter. The Knight of the White Moon replied that it was a question of preeminence in beauty, and then he briefly told what he had said to Don Quixote concerning the conditions of the duel. The viceroy then went up to Don Antonio and asked him in a whisper if he knew who the Knight of the White Moon was, or whether it was some trick they wished to play upon Don Quixote. Don Antonio answered that he did not know who he was, or whether the challenge was in earnest or not. The viceroy was troubled by that answer and wondered whether he ought or ought not to let the battle continue. At length, by dint of persuading himself that it was some jest, he withdrew, saying: "Gentlemen, if there be no other remedy than confession or death, and if Don Quixote is stubborn in his resolve, and you, Knight of the White Moon, are obstinate likewise, then in God's name go to it."

The Knight of the White Moon in courteous and well-chosen words thanked the viceroy for what he had done, and Don Quixote did likewise. And after recommending himself to Heaven and to his Dulcinea, he retired to take a longer compass of the ground, for he saw his opponent do the same; then, without any flourish of trumpets or any other martial instrument to give the signal for the outset, they both turned their horses around at the same instant. But he of the White Moon, who was mounted on the fleeter steed, met Don Quixote two-thirds down the course and hurtled into him with such a fierce onslaught that, without touching him with his lance, which he seemed purposely to hold aloof, he brought both horse and rider to the ground. He then sprang upon him and said as he clapped his lance to his opponent's visor: "Knight, you are vanquished and a dead man if you don't confess in accordance with the conditions of our challenge."

Don Quixote, who was bruised and stunned, without lifting his visor and as though speaking from the tomb, said in a faint low voice: "Dulcinea of El Toboso is the most beautiful woman in the world, and I am the most unfortunate knight on earth, and it isn't just that my weakness should discredit this truth. Go on, knight, press on with your lance and take away my life, since you have robbed me of my honor."

"That I shall certainly never do," said he of the White Moon. "Long may the fame of Lady Dulcinea of El Toboso's beauty live and flourish! All I demand is that the great Don Quixote should retire to his village for one year, or for a period to be fixed by me, in accordance with the agreement drawn up before this battle."

The viceroy, Don Antonio, and many others witnessed all that passed, and they heard Don Quixote promise that he would fulfill all the terms of their engagement like a genuine and punctilious knight, provided nothing was required to the prejudice of Lady Dulcinea. When this declaration was made, he of the White Moon turned about his horse, and after bowing to the viceroy, he rode at a half gallop into the city.

The viceroy commanded Don Antonio to go after him and to ascertain by all possible means who he was. Then, they raised Don Quixote from the ground, and uncovering his face, they found him pale and bathed in sweat. Rozinante was in such a plight that he was unable to stir for some time. As for Sancho, he was so sorrowful and cast down that he knew not what to say or do; he fancied that all had taken place in dreams and that the whole business was the result of enchantment. He saw his master overthrown and bound to lay aside his arms for a whole year. He imagined that his master's glory had been finally eclipsed and his own hopes from the latter's recent promises vanished like smoke in the wind. He was afraid that Rozinante might be crippled forever and his master's bones be permanently knocked out of joint, though it would be no small blessing if his madness were knocked out of him. In the end they carried the knight into the city on a hand-chair that the viceroy had sent for. The viceroy himself returned, eager to ascertain who was this Knight of the White Moon who had left Don Quixote in such a piteous state.

CHAPTER LXV

Which reveals who the Knight of the White Moon was, with the liberation of Don Gregorio and other incidents

Don Antonio Moreno rode after the Knight of the White Moon, and a great number of boys also followed, pestering him until he took refuge in an inn inside the city. Don Antonio entered there, too, as he was eager to make his acquaintance. A squire came forward to receive him and take off his armor, and he shut himself up in a lower room, where he was followed by Don Antonio, who was on tenterhooks to know who he was. Then, when the Knight of the White Moon found that the gentleman would not leave him, he said: "I know very well, sir, what you have come here for: to find out who I am. As it happens, there is no reason for me to conceal myself; so, while my servant is taking off my armor, I shall tell you the whole truth of my story, without omitting a single detail. You must know sir, that I am called the bachelor Sansón Carrasco; I come from the same town as Don Quixote of La Mancha, whose madness and folly have been the cause of deep sorrow to his friends and neighbors. I myself felt particular sympathy for his sad case, and as I believed his recovery to depend upon his remaining quietly at home, I earnestly endeavored to accomplish that end. And so, about three months ago I sallied forth myself as a knight-errant, calling myself the Knight of the Mirrors and intending to fight and vanquish him without doing him any harm and to impose as the condition of our combat that the vanquished should be at the mercy of the conqueror. Feeling certain of my success, I expected to send him home for twelve months, hoping that during that time he might be restored to health. But Fortune willed otherwise, for it was he who vanquished me; he unhorsed me, and my scheme was of no avail. He continued his journey, and I returned home vanquished, ashamed, and injured by my fall. Nevertheless, I did not abandon my scheme, as you have seen this day, and as he is so punctilious and so particular in observing the laws of knight-errantry, he is sure to perform his promise. This, sir, is my whole story, and I beseech you not to reveal me to Don Quixote, in order that my good intentions may produce their fruit and that the worthy gentleman may recover his sense, for when he is freed from the follies of chivalry, he is a man of excellent understanding."

"O sir!" replied Don Antonio. "May God forgive you for the wrong you have done in robbing the world of the most diverting madman who was ever seen. Is it not plain, sir, that his cure can never benefit mankind half as much as the pleasure he affords by his eccentricities? But I feel sure, sir, that all your art will not cure such deep-rooted madness; were it not uncharitable, I would express the hope that he may never recover, for by his cure we would lose not only the knight's good company, but also the drollery of his squire, Sancho Panza, which is enough to transform melancholy itself into mirth. All the same, I shall hold my peace and not breathe a word to him, to see whether I am right in suspecting that all Mister Carrasco's efforts will have no effect."

The bachelor answered that the business in any case was far advanced and that he was confident there would be a favorable result. And so, after Don Antonio had offered to follow the latter's instructions, the bachelor took his leave that same day. He had his armor tied on a mule; he mounted the charger on which he had done battle and left the city for home, meeting no adventure on the way worthy of mention in this true history.

Don Antonio told the viceroy everything that Carrasco had said. The viceroy was not too pleased by it, for Don Quixote's retirement would mean a loss to all those who were entertained by the tales of his mad adventures.

For six days Don Quixote was confined to his bed, dejected, melancholy, thoughtful, out of humor, and full of bleak reflections on his luckless overthrow. Sancho strove hard to comfort him, saying: "Raise your head, master, cheer up and thank your stars that you've come off without even a broken rib. Remember, sir, that 'They that give must take'; and that 'Where there are hooks there aren't always flitches.' Come now, sir, a fig for the doctor! You've no need of him. Let us be off for home, and give up this gallivanting up and down in search of adventures in lands and places, God knows where. And when you come to think of it, I'm the one who's the greater loser by this, though it's your worship who is in a worse pickle. Though with my government I gave up all desire of being a governor again, I've never lost the hankering to be a count. But I may as well say good-bye to all that if your worship gives up trying to be a king and resigns your profession of chivalry! So all my hopes end in smoke."

"Be quiet, Sancho. Do you not see that my seclusion and retirement need only last a year? After that I shall return to my honored calling, and I am bound to win a kingdom, and some countship or other for you."

"God grant you may," said Sancho, "and let sin be deaf, for I've always heard that good hopes are better than poor holdings. . . ."

[*On the journey home, Quixote considers becoming a pastoral shepherd; he and Sancho meet several people from their past adventures, including the duke and duchess, who play one last trick on them. Sancho continues the self-flagellation the duke claimed was necessary to free Dulcinea from her enchantment, though he whips trees instead of himself whenever possible. Without realizing it, they arrive at their village.*]

CHAPTER LXXIII

Of the omens that Don Quixote met at the entrance to his village, with other incidents that embellish and accredit this great history

As they entered the village, Cide Hamete informs us, Don Quixote noticed two boys pummeling one another on the threshing floor, and heard one say to the other: "Don't fash[65] yourself, Periquillo, for you'll never see her in all the days of your life."

Don Quixote, overhearing this, said to Sancho: "Did you catch what the boy said, 'You'll never see her in all the days of your life?'"

"Well," rejoined Sancho, "what does it matter what the boy said?"

"What?" retorted his master. "Don't you realize that such words, when applied to my affairs, clearly portend that I shall never see my Dulcinea?"

Sancho was about to answer again, but was hindered from so doing by a great hue and cry of hounds and huntsmen in full pursuit of a hare, which was so hard pressed that she came and squatted for shelter just between Dapple's feet. Immediately Sancho laid hold of her and presented her to Don Quixote, but the knight kept muttering to himself: *"Malum signum! Malum signum!*[66] A hare runs away, hounds pursue her, and Dulcinea does not appear."

"You are a strange man, sir," said Sancho. "Let us suppose that poor bunny here is Mistress Dulcinea, the greyhounds that followed her are the wicked enchanters who transmogrified her into a country lass; she races away, I catch her and hand her safe and sound to your worship, and you hold her in your arms and pet her: what harm is there in this, and what bad omen is this?"

By this time the two boys who had been fighting came up to see the hare, and when Sancho inquired why they had been fighting, he was answered by the boy who had uttered the ominous words, that he had snatched from his playmate a cage full of crickets, which he would not give back to him again. Sancho pulled a threepenny piece out of his pocket and gave it to the boy for his cage; and giving it to Don Quixote, he said: "There you are, sir; all the tokens of bad luck have been brought to nothing, and though I am a blockhead, I'm convinced all these things have no more to do with our affairs than the clouds of yesteryear. And if I remember right, I've heard the curate of our village say that no decent self-respecting Christian should give ear to such foolishness; and I've heard you yourself, master, say not many days ago that all those Christians who troubled their heads with fortune-telling rubbish were no better than nincompoops. So without more ado let us make straight for our homes."

By now the huntsmen had come up and asked for their hare, which Don Quixote delivered up to them. They passed on, and just as they were entering the town, they perceived the curate and the bachelor Sansón Carrasco at their devotions in a small field. We must add that Sancho had thrown over Dapple and the bundle of arms, as a cover, the buckram robe painted with

---

[65] Worry.

[66] "A bad sign."

flames of fire that they had put on him in the duke's castle on the night when Altisidora rose from the dead.[67] He had also fitted the miter on Dapple's head, and this ornament transformed him as strangely as ever an ass was transformed in all the world. The curate and the bachelor recognized them at once and hastened toward them with open arms. Don Quixote dismounted and embraced them affectionately. Meanwhile the boys, who are as sharp-eyed as lynxes and miss no detail, sighted the ass's miter and rushed up to look at it, saying: "Have a look, boys! Here is Sancho's ass gaudier than Mingo, and Don Quixote's hack leaner than ever."[68]

Surrounded by the boys of the town and attended by the curate and the bachelor, they moved toward the house of Don Quixote, where they found the housekeeper and his niece, who had heard of their arrival, waiting for them on the doorstep. News had also reached Teresa, the wife of Sancho Panza, and she came running half-naked and with her hair all tousled, leading by the hand her daughter, Sanchica. But when she found that her husband was not quite dressed up to her notions of what a governor should wear, she said: "What's all this, husband? You look as if you'd plodded all the way on shanks' mare! You look more misgoverned than governor, I'm thinking."

"Whisht, Teresa!" said Sancho. "Many a time there's a hook but devil a flitch on it.[69] First of all, let us go home, and then I'll tell you wonders. I've money, and after all, that is what counts, and I made it by my own labors without harming a soul."

"Bring home the money, my dear," said Teresa, "no matter how or where you've earned it; after all there's nothing new in that."

Sanchica then hugged her father and asked what he had brought her, for she longed for his return as the flowers do for the dew in May. So, she caught hold of her father's waistband with one hand and pulled Dapple after her by the halter with the other, and her mother took Sancho by the arm on the other side, and away they all went to his cottage, leaving Don Quixote in his own house under the care of his niece and housekeeper with the curate and the bachelor to keep him company.

Don Quixote drew the last two aside, and without observing time or season, he gave them a short account of his defeat and the obligation he lay under of remaining in his village for a year, which, like a true knight-errant, he was determined to observe most faithfully. He added that he intended to become a shepherd and spend that year in the solitude of the fields and woods, giving rein to his amorous thoughts and practising the virtues of the pastoral life. Furthermore, he begged them, if more important duties were not a hindrance, to become his companions, and he assured them that he would furnish them with sufficient sheep and cattle to enable them to belong to such a profession. He let them know that the principal part of the business was already done, for he had planned names that would fit them exactly. The curate asked him what they were, and Don Quixote replied that he was

---

[67] The story of this practical joke in the duke's castle is omitted here.

[68] A reference to a popular fifteenth-century poem named *Mingo Revulgo*, in which Mingo is dressed in a blue smock and red doublet.

[69] A proverb: "Sometimes there's a hook, but no bacon on it."

to call himself the shepherd Quixotiz, the bachelor the shepherd Carrascón, the curate the shepherd Curiambro, and Sancho Panza the shepherd Panzino. They were all astonished at Don Quixote's new strain of madness, but considering that this might be a means of preventing him from wandering from home and hoping at the same time that within the year he might be cured of his mad knight-errantry, they applauded his pastoral folly as a wise idea and offered to become his companions in carrying it out.

"Better still," said Sansón Carrasco, "as all the world is now aware that I am a very celebrated poet, I shall compose pastoral or courtly verses at every turn, or such as may best assist our cause, so that we may entertain ourselves in the lonely wastes where we may have to wander. But what is most important, gentlemen, is for each one of us to choose the name of the shepherdess he intends to celebrate in his verses, and not to have a single tree, no matter how tough its bark, on which her name is not inscribed and cut on it, as is the custom of love-sick shepherds."

"That is quite right," answered Don Quixote, "though for myself I have no need to seek for the name of any imaginary shepherdess, for I have the peerless Dulcinea of El Toboso, glory of these banks, ornament of these meadows, the prop of beauty, the cream of grace, and in short, the cynosure of all praise, however exaggerated it may be."

"That is true," said the curate, "but we must look around for indulgent shepherdesses who are easy to manage, and we may have to trim their angles if they don't square with us."

"And if they should fail," added Sansón Carrasco, "we'll give them the names in print that are known to all the world: Phyllidas, Amaryllises, Dianas, Fleridas, Galateas, and Belisardas;[70] since they're for sale in the markets, we can easily buy them and keep them for our own. If my lady—my shepherdess, I should say—by chance be called Ana, I'll celebrate her under the name of Anarda; if Francisca, I'll call her Francenia; and if Lucía, Lucinda: that is all it will come to. And if Sancho Panza is to enter our confraternity, he can celebrate his wife, Teresa Panza, under the name Teresaina."

Don Quixote smiled at the application of the name and the curate extolled his chaste and honorable resolution, repeating his offer to bear him company for as long as he could spare from compulsory duties. With this they took leave of him, advising him to take care of his health and to adopt a healthy diet.

As luck would have it, the housekeeper and the niece heard the conversation between the three on the subject of the pastoral life, and no sooner had the priest and the bachelor gone than they both burst into Don Quixote's room, and the niece cried: "Mercy on us, uncle! What does this mean? We thought that you had come to stay at home and live here like a quiet, honest gentleman, and here you are longing to wander off into fresh labyrinths, becoming a 'gentle shepherd, come and go.' In truth, uncle, the straw is too old to make pipes of."

"Heaven help us, sir!" added the housekeeper. "How will your worship be able to stand the summer's heat, the winter's frost, and the howling of the wolves in the open country? Pray, sir, you mustn't think of it; it's a business

---

[70] Common names in pastoral poetry.

for strong men who are born and bred to it from the days when they were babes in arms. And if it comes to worst, better to be a knight-errant than a shepherd. Mark my words, master, and heed my counsel; I'm not full of food and drink, but fasting, and I'm no chicken, but fifty years of age, and I say to you: Stay at home, look after your property, go to confession often, do good to the poor, and let me take the blame if you go wrong."

"My dear girls, do cease your prating," Don Quixote answered. "I know best what I have to do; only help me to my bed, for I do not feel very well. Remember that whether I be a knight-errant or an errant shepherd, you will always find me ready to provide for you, and you may rely on my good faith."

And his affectionate daughters—for so the niece and the housekeeper undoubtedly were—undressed him, put him to bed, where they brought him something to eat, and made him as comfortable as possible.

CHAPTER LXXIV

Of how Don Quixote fell ill, of the will he made, and of his death

As all human things, especially the lives of men, are not eternal, and even their beginnings are but steps to their end, and as Don Quixote was under no special dispensation of Heaven, he was snatched away by death when he least expected it. Whether his sickness was caused by his melancholic reflections on his defeat, or whether it was so preordained by Providence, he was stricken down by a violent fever that confined him to his bed for six days. All that time his good friends, the priest, the bachelor, and the barber, often visited him, and his trusty squire, Sancho Panza, never left his bedside. They were convinced that his sickness was due to his sorrow at having been defeated and his disappointment in the matter of Dulcinea's disenchantment; and so, they tried in every way to cheer him up. The bachelor begged him to pluck up his spirits and get up from his bed so that they might begin their pastoral life, adding that he had already written an eclogue that would put Sannazaro's[71] nose out of joint, and that he had bought with his own money from a shepherd of Quintanar two pedigreed dogs to watch the flock, one called Barcino and the other Butrón. But this had no effect, for Don Quixote continued to mope as before. A physician was sent for, who, after feeling his pulse, took a rather gloomy view of the case and told him that he should provide for his soul's health, for that of his body was in dangerous condition. Don Quixote received the news calmly and serenely, but his niece, his housekeeper, and his squire began to weep as bitterly as if he had been laid out already. The physician was of the opinion that melancholy and mortification had brought him to death's door. Don Quixote then asked them to leave him for a little while, as he wished to sleep. They retired, and he slept at a stretch, as they say, for more than six hours, and the housekeeper and the niece were afraid that he might not waken from it. At length he did awaken and cried out in a loud voice: "Blessed be the Almighty for this

---

[71] Jacapo Sannazaro (1456–1533) was famous for his pastoral novel *Arcadia.*

great benefit He has granted me! Infinite are His mercies, and undiminished even by the sins of men."

The niece, who was listening very attentively to these words of her uncle, found more sense in them than there was in his usual talk, at least since he had fallen ill, and she questioned him: "What do you mean, uncle? Has any thing strange taken place? What mercies and what sins of men are you talking about?"

"Mercies," answered Don Quixote, "that God has just this moment granted to me in spite of all my sins. My judgment is now clear and unfettered, and that dark cloud of ignorance has disappeared, which the continual reading of those detestable books of knight-errantry had cast over my understanding. Now I see their folly and fraud, and my sole regret is that the discovery comes too late to allow me to amend my ways by reading others that would enlighten my soul. I find, dear niece, that my end approaches, but I would have it remembered that though in my life I was reputed a madman, yet in my death this opinion was not confirmed. Therefore, my dear child, call my good friends, the priest, the bachelor Sansón Carrasco, and Master Nicholas, the barber, for I wish to make my confession and my will."

There was no need for the niece to go to the trouble, for presently all three arrived at the house, and Don Quixote no sooner saw them than he said: "My dear friends, welcome the happy news! I am no longer Don Quixote of La Mancha, but Alonso Quixano, the man whom the world formerly called the Good, owing to his virtuous life. I am now the sworn enemy of Amadis of Gaul and his innumerable brood; I now abhor all profane stories of knight-errantry, for I know only too well, through Heaven's mercy and through my own personal experience, the great danger of reading them."

When his three friends heard him talk thus, they concluded that he was stricken with some new madness. Sansón then said to him: "What does all this mean, Don Quixote? Now that we have just received news that Lady Dulcinea is disenchanted, and now that we are just about to become shepherds and spend our days singing and living like princes, you talk about turning yourself into a hermit. No more foolish tales, I beg you, and come back to your senses."

"Those foolish tales," replied Don Quixote, "that up to now have been my bane may with Heaven's help turn to my advantage at my death. Dear friends, I feel that I am rapidly sinking; therefore, let us put aside all jesting. I want a priest to hear my confession, and a notary to draw up my will. At such a moment a man must not deceive his soul; therefore, I beg you to send for the notary while the priest hears my confession."

Don Quixote's words amazed his hearers, but though they were at first skeptical about the return of his sanity, they were forced to take him at his word. One of the symptoms that made them fear he was near the point of death was the suddenness with which he had recovered his intellect, for after what he had already said, he conversed with such good sense and displayed such true Christian resignation that they believed his wits had been restored at last. The curate, therefore, told the company to leave the room, and he confessed Don Quixote. In the meantime the bachelor hastened to fetch the notary, and presently he returned with him and with Sancho Panza. The latter (who had already heard from the bachelor the news of his master's plight), finding the niece and the housekeeper in tears, began to make wry faces and finally burst out crying. After the priest had heard the sick man's confession, he came out saying: "There is no doubt that Alonso Quixano is at the point of death, and there is also no doubt that he is in his entire right mind; so, we should go in and enable him to make his will."

These sad tidings burst open the floodgates of the housekeeper's, the niece's, and the good squire's swollen eyes; their tears flowed fast and furious, and a thousand sighs rose from their breasts, for, indeed, as it has been noted, the sick gentleman, whether as Alonso Quixano the Good or as Don Quixote of La Mancha, had always been so good-natured and so agreeable that he was beloved not only by his family, but by all who knew him.

The notary, with the rest of the company, then went into the sick man's chamber, and Don Quixote stated the preamble to the will, commending his soul to Heaven and including the customary Christian declarations. When he came to the legacies he said:

"Item, I give and bequeath to Sancho Panza, whom in my madness I made my squire, whatever money he has of mine in his possession; and whereas there are accounts and reckonings to be settled between us for what he has received and disbursed, my will and pleasure is that he should not be required to furnish any account of such sums, and whatever may remain due to me, which must be but little, be enjoyed by him as my free gift, and may he prosper with it. And as when I was mad, he was through my means made governor of an island, I would now, in my right senses, give him the government of a kingdom, were it in my power, for his honesty and his faithfulness deserve it.

"And now, my friend," said he, turning to Sancho, "forgive me for making you appear as mad as I was myself, and for drawing you into my errors and persuading you that there have been and still are knights-errant in the world."

"Woe is me!" cried Sancho all in tears. "Don't die on me; but take my advice and live on for many a year; the maddest trick a man can play in his life is to yield up the ghost without more ado, and without being knocked on the head or stabbed through the belly to mope away and die of the doldrums. Shame on you, master; don't let the grass grow under your feet. Up with you this instant, out of your bed, and let us put on our shepherd's clothing and off with us to the fields as we had resolved a while back. Who knows but we may find Lady Dulcinea behind a hedge, disenchanted and as fresh as a daisy. If it's your defeat that is tearing your heart, lay the blame on me and say that it was my fault in not tightening Rozinante's girths enough, and that was why you were unhorsed. You must remember, too, sir, from your books on knight-errantry how common it was for knights to jostle one another out of the saddle, and he who's lying low today may be crowning his victory tomorrow."

"Just so," said Sansón; "there is good sense in what honest Sancho says."

"Go softly, I pray you, gentlemen," replied Don Quixote; "one should never look for birds of this year in the nests of yesteryear. I was mad, but I am now in my senses; I was once Don Quixote of La Mancha, but I am now, as I said before, Alonso Quixano the Good, and I hope that my repentance and my sincere words may restore me to the same esteem as you had for me before. So now proceed, Mr. Notary.

"Item, I declare and appoint Antonia Quixano, my niece, here present, sole heiress of all my estate, both real and personal, after all my just debts and legacies have been paid and deducted out of my goods and chattels; and the first charges on the estate shall be salaries due to my housekeeper, together with twenty ducats over and above her salary wages, which I leave and bequeath her to buy a gown.

"Item, I appoint the curate and the bachelor Sansón Carrasco, here present, to be the executors of this my last will and testament.

"Item, it is my will that if my niece Antonia Quixano should wish to marry, it will be with none but a person who, upon strict investigation, shall be found never to have read a book of knight-errantry in his life; but if it should be ascertained that he is acquainted with such books and she still insists on marrying him, she is then to lose all rights to my bequest, which my executors may then distribute in charity as they think fit.

"Item, I entreat the said executors that if at any time they happen to meet with the author of a certain book entitled *The Second Part of the Exploits of Don Quixote of La Mancha,* they will in my name most heartily beg his pardon for my having been unwittingly the cause of his writing such an amount of folly and triviality as he has done. Indeed, as I depart from this life my conscience troubles me that ever I was the cause of his publishing such a book."

After finishing the will, he swooned away and stretched his body to its full length in the bed. The company were alarmed and ran to his assistance; but these fainting attacks were repeated with great frequency during the three days that he lived after he had made his will. The household was in grief and confusion; and yet, after all, the niece continued to eat her meals, the housekeeper drowned her sorrows in wine, and Sancho Panza puffed himself up with satisfaction, for the thought of a legacy possesses a magic power to remove, or at least to soothe, the pangs that the heir should otherwise feel for the death of his friend.

At length Don Quixote's last day came, after he had received all the sacraments and expressed his abhorrence of books of knight-errantry. The notary, who was present, said that he had never read of any knight who ever died in his bed so peacefully and like a good Christian as Don Quixote. And so, amid the tears and lamentations of his friends, who knelt by his bedside, he gave up the ghost, that is to say, he died. And when the priest saw that he had passed away, he bade the notary give him a certificate stating that Alonso Quixano the Good, commonly known as Don Quixote of La Mancha, had died a natural death. This he desired lest any other author, except Cide Hamete Benengeli, take the opportunity of raising him from the dead and presume to write endless histories of his pretended adventures.

Such was the death of that imaginative gentleman Don Quixote of La Mancha, whose native place Cide Hamete did not wish to ascertain, with the intention that all the towns and villages in La Mancha should vie with one another for the honor of having given him birth, as the seven cities of Greece did for Homer. We shall omit the lamentations of Sancho and those of the niece and the housekeeper, as well as the epitaphs that were composed for his tomb, and we shall only quote the following, which the bachelor Sansón Carrasco inscribed on it:

Here lies the noble fearless knight,
Whose valor rose to such a height;

> When Death at last did strike him down,
> His was the victory and renown.
> He reck'd the world of little prize,
> And was a bugbear in men's eyes;
> But had the fortune in his age
> To live a fool and die a sage.[72]

And said the most prudent Cide Hamete to his pen: "Here you shall rest, hanging from this rack by this copper wire, my quill. Whether you are well cut or badly pointed here you shall live long ages, unless presumptuous and unworthy historians take you down to profane you. But before they touch you, warn them in as strong terms as you are able:

> Beware, beware, all petty knaves
> I may be touched by none:
> This enterprise, my worthy king,
> Is kept for me alone.[73]

For me alone Don Quixote was born, and I for him. He knew how to act, and I knew how to write. We two alone are as one, despite that fictitious and Tordesillescan scribe who has dared, and may dare again with his coarse and ill-trimmed ostrich quill, to write the exploits of my valorous knight.[74] This is no burden for his shoulders, no subject for his frostbound muse; and should you by chance get to know him, do warn him to let Don Quixote's weary and moldering bones rest in the grave, and not seek, against all canons of death, to carry him off to Old Castile, compelling him to leave the tomb where he really and truly lies stretched out full length, powerless to make a third expedition[75] and new sally. Surely his two, which have met with approval and have delighted all the people who knew about them, both here and abroad, are enough to make a mockery of all the innumerable sallies undertaken by all the countless knights-errant. Thus you will comply with your Christian profession by offering good advice to one who wishes you ill, and I shall be proud to be the first author who ever enjoyed witnessing the full effect of his writing. For my sole aim has been to arouse men's scorn for the false and absurd stories of knight-errantry, whose prestige has been shaken by this tale of my true Don Quixote, and which will, without any doubt, soon crumble in ruin. Vale."[76]

---

[72] Samuel Putnam points out that these lines are "a doggerel imitation of the epitaphs composed by village poets."

[73] A quotation from an old ballad.

[74] Another attack on the "false Quixote," whose author was reputedly from Tordesillas.

[75] This should be "fourth expedition." Don Quixote had three expeditions, one alone and two with Sancho.

[76] Farewell.

William Shakespeare
(1564–1616)

Shakespeare's plays and poems, taken together, have a quality of impersonality, or suprapersonality, transcending the limitations and biases that one normally finds in a single author. If we try to understand Shakespeare through his works, he is everything and everyone. Each of his plays is its own place, with a distinctive mood, method, and thematic emphasis; collectively, they define a mind and a sensibility that seem nearly as inclusive as the world itself. It is appropriate, then, if also tantalizing, that we know so little about the inner workings of the mind of Shakespeare as an individual and artist. Nineteenth-century critical tradition tended to find autobiographical revelations in the plays and some of the poems (especially the *Sonnets*), and modern psychoanalytic criticism purports to find in them revelations of Shakespeare's unconscious mind, but all the hard facts we have about him are impersonal or external: records of law and vital statistics, annals of the Elizabethan and Jacobean stage, and references to him by contemporary authors and playgoers.

Shakespeare was born in the town of Stratford, in the geographic heart of England, in April 1564. His father was a tradesman and prominent member of the town government, his mother a descendant of a very old family. Although he did not go to a university, he got a good education at the Stratford grammar school, especially in the Latin classics. (Ovid seems to have been one of his favorite authors.) In 1582 he married Anne Hathaway, by whom he had two daughters and a son who died in boyhood. How and where Shakespeare spent his early twenties is obscure; by 1590 or so, however, he was active in the London theater. During the next decade he became highly popular as a playwright and poet (among his nondramatic works are *Venus and Adonis, The Rape of Lucrece,* and the famous *Sonnets*), apparently making a good living and also acquiring influential friends. In 1596, almost certainly through Shakespeare's efforts, his family was granted a coat of arms. By 1612 or so, when he stopped writing, he had composed more than three dozen plays. He died on April 23, 1616—very nearly on the same day Cervantes died.

Shakespeare wrote his plays for performance; he had little or no interest in having them printed and published. A reading audience for plays did exist, however, and many of Shakespeare's were in fact published during his lifetime—some in good versions, others in very poor ones. In 1623, seven years after Shakespeare died, the "First Folio," a comprehensive collection of almost all his plays, was issued under the supervision of two members of Shakespeare's old company. The Folio contains, among other tributes, a famous one by the eminent contemporary poet and playwright Ben Jonson. Not a man to bestow praise lightly, Jonson rated Shakespeare above all his contemporary dramatists. His true peers, according to Jonson, were Aeschylus, Sophocles, and Euripides; in comedy, Jonson asserted, Shakespeare was peerless. This tribute has proved to be an accurate prophecy of Shakespeare's reputation in later ages.

Beginning with the First Folio, it has been customary to divide Shakespeare's plays into three categories: tragedies, comedies, and histories. But these labels are inadequate; Shakespeare's plays are typically blends of different tones and genres. Certain of the histories (*Richard the Second*, for example) can accurately be called tragedies. The comedies are of several different kinds; the early *Comedy of Errors* and *Taming of the Shrew* are mainly farcical; *A Midsummer Night's Dream* combines farce with lyrical fantasy; the "romantic" comedies of Shakespeare's middle period (including *As You Like It* and *Twelfth Night*) are warmly exuberant works that place fairly realistic characters in never-never-land settings; the "dark" comedies like *Measure for Measure* include some disturbing, uncomic elements; the late *Winter's Tale* and *Tempest* treat serious themes but with a disregard for realism that has earned for them the name romances. Some of the tragedies mingle comic episodes with their prevalent high seriousness (as in *Romeo and Juliet* and *Macbeth*), and several are based on history, especially that of ancient Rome (*Julius Caesar, Antony and Cleopatra, Coriolanus*).

To enumerate briefly the qualities that make Shakespeare great is impossible, since the individual plays and poems are so different from one another. Every age from Shakespeare's time to the present has found something different in him to admire. All ages, however, have recognized his supreme skill in inventing sharply etched characters; it frequently happens that long after one has forgotten the exact story of a play one remembers its people with absolute vividness. It is true, paradoxically, that many of Shakespeare's characters represent universal types; Romeo's name has become a synonym for the fervent young lover, and the adjective *Falstaffian* has entered the common vocabulary of English as an epithet for robust, expansive heartiness. But none of Shakespeare's characters is merely a type. Scores of them are fully realized persons, absolutely individualized new creations even when they are adapted from earlier sources. (Few of Shakespeare's stories were wholly invented by him.) More than anything else, it is his power to create such characters that has prompted extravagant praise of Shakespeare's "godlike" genius. Some critics, in fact, have speculated about the characters, even those Shakespeare wholly invented, almost as though they had a real existence outside of the plays. Such excesses, odd as they may seem, are understandable, for the characters do seem to speak and act as of their own volition, with the combination of inevitability and unpredictability that one finds in living human beings.

The power to create characters and tell compelling stories underlies one traditional view of Shakespeare: that his plays are children of "nature" rather than of "art." That view of him no longer has much currency. Both in their total conception and in their craftsmanship, most Shakespearean plays are both powerful and skillfully controlled. He is expert in managing plot lines and is particularly fond of double plotting.

Perhaps the ultimate reason for Shakespeare's power is simply his mastery of language as an expressive and poetic medium. The many pages given to Shakespeare in dictionaries of quotations attest the beauty and memorability of his words. But such excerpting, which removes Shakespeare's lines from their dramatic context, also does him a disservice, suggesting as it does that he was a gnomic philosopher at large. The well known lines from *Hamlet* "To thine own self be true, / And it must follow, as the night the day, / Thou canst not then be false to any man" have been quoted countless times without an awareness that in the play they illustrate a pompous old man's self-importance. The true measure of Shakespeare's language is its effectiveness in the play where it occurs; much of Shakespeare's artistry lies in his skill in giving different characters different poetic imaginations and voices. Moreover, the quality of a play's language—plain or ornate, ceremonial or colloquial, quiet or declamatory, direct or fraught with images and figures of speech—is intimately wedded to the governing themes and distinctive atmospheres. Whether the plays generated their linguistic texture or the other way around is a difficult question. Whatever the answer, it remains true that language—prose or verse—is the principal shaping force of Shakespearean drama.

When people refer to Shakespeare's history plays, of which there are ten, they mean plays about English history; the plays he based on Roman history are all considered tragedies. Eight of the English histories fall into two groups, each made up of four plays. One tetralogy, consisting of some of Shakespeare's earliest plays, deals with the reigns of Henry VI and Richard III, in the latter fifteenth century. They culminate with Richard's defeat and the accession of the Tudor monarchs from which Shakespeare's queen, Elizabeth, descended. The other tetralogy, written in the latter 1590s, when Shakespeare's skills had matured considerably, deals with the years 1399–1415. These plays include *Richard II*, the two parts of *Henry IV*, and *Henry V*.

The first three of the plays just mentioned have a close continuity with one another, with frequent backglances in the sequels at their predecessors. On the other hand, each—including each part of *Henry IV*—is shaped as a unified whole that can stand on its own. There is an almost exact analogy with modern films, where a hit movie spawns follow-ups that are enriched by an understanding of their predecessors but can be understood and appreciated as separate works. *Richard II* had told the story of Richard's deposition by the politically skillful Henry Bolingbroke, who assumed the throne in 1399 as Henry IV, with powerful help from the Percy family, of Northumberland in northern England. Richard (in Shakespeare's version of the story) was murdered in 1400, at the instigation of the new king. The action of *Henry the Fourth, Part One*, takes place about three years later. The guilt-ridden Henry IV has been planning an expiatory pilgrimage to the Holy Land, but his attention is turned instead to a series of rebellions. The Percy family, including the excitable and impetuous young Harry Hotspur, have come to resent King Henry because of his alleged neglect of them and his failure to properly recognize their crucial role in putting him on the throne. Meanwhile, the king's young son, Prince Henry, or Hal, has taken to frequenting a low-life circle of carousing companions who include the fat and dissipated knight Sir John Falstaff. The play alternates between these two levels of action, a "high" level of grave national issues and a "low" level of tavern comedy. As the play progresses, the two levels gradually merge.

Mark Van Doren began his essay on *Henry IV, Part One*, by declaring flatly, "No play of Shakespeare is better than *Henry IV*." It probably comes closer to revealing the full range of Shakespeare's genius than any other single play. Moreover, it encapsulates all three of the traditional categories of Shakespearean drama: it is a history, but it includes what are probably the best comic scenes Shakespeare ever wrote, and its last act is tragedy as much as anything else. Structurally, it is one of Shakespeare's most brilliant achievements, a good example of his skill in double plotting, changes of pace and tone, and the preparation for a climactic denouement.

Even if the play had none of these virtues, it would be cherished for its characters. Of these the most memorable of all is Falstaff, whom one famous critic classes among Shakespeare's four most wonderful creations, along with Hamlet, Cleopatra, and Iago (the villain in *Othello*). It is probably no coincidence that each of these four characters, and Falstaff probably even more than the others, is a consummate actor. He is himself a mercurial master of change of pace, of poses (rake, swashbuckling good fellow, ladies' man, pious innocent ruined by bad company), and of wit ranging the full gamut from high to low comedy. The two other principal characters—Hotspur, the quixotic hothead, and Prince Hal, the wayward but level-headed pragmatist—make a fascinating study in contrasts. Each is parodied in turn, and their relative claims on our sympathy are an urgent challenge to interpretation and response. Minor characters are memorable too—the magisterial but touchy self-proclaimed magician, Glendower, for example, and Hotspur's winsome wife, Kate. The characters, especially Hotspur, Hal, and Falstaff, come together not just as ingredients in a story but as exponents of key themes: honor, for example, and the relative claims of public and private life.

(New readers of Shakespeare may wish to glance at certain passages in other plays that throw light on the principals of *Henry IV, Part One:* the moving elegy for Hotspur by his wife in Act II, scene iii of the *Second Part;* the final parting between Hal and Falstaff, shown in Act V, scene v, of the same play; and the description of Falstaff's death by the tavern Hostess in *Henry V,* Act II, scene iii).

NOTE ON SHAKESPEARE'S STAGE

The public theaters of Shakespeare's day were modeled architecturally on inn-yards, where, a generation or so earlier, plays had commonly been presented by itinerant troupes of actors. The theaters were large three-story structures, round, square, or multisided in shape, surrounding an open-air arena. Three sides of the theater consisted of galleries, facing inward toward the arena. From the fourth side, a large platform stage, about five feet high, perhaps forty feet deep and twenty-five feet wide, projected into the arena; around it stood those spectators ("groundlings") who paid the lowest price of admission. At the back of this stage were two doors and a curtained alcove used for "discovery" scenes. There was some sort of acting space on the second level, as well, perhaps another curtained alcove and perhaps a projecting balcony, supported by posts rising from the main stage. There may have been a third level as well, occasionally used by actors but intended primarily for musicians. To avoid harassment by the Puritanically minded London government, the theaters were built outside the city limits, especially on the south bank of the Thames. A theater could accommodate about two thousand people, drawn from every social level from the laboring class through the titled aristocracy.

As in ancient Greek drama, spectacle was important on Shakespeare's stage. Costumes were elaborate, and the style of acting was emphatic and declamatory. All the actors were male; the female roles were played by boys. There was little or no scenery, and action flowed continuously without scene or act divisions. Because the plays were performed in the afternoon, under the sky, settings such as storms or night scenes had to be evoked by the play's language; the imagination of the audience thus played a crucial part, as in modern radio drama.

A reconstruction of the Fortune Theater by Walter H. Godfrey. (From Shakespeare's Theatre *by Ashley H. Thorndike.)*

Shakespeare's theater was literally what a modern director and critic has called "the empty space," to be filled by the playwright's, the actors', and the audience's imaginations. The Greek *skene* building and *orchestra* were well suited for plays that took place "before the palace" and dramatized the public lives of scapegoat-kings. The neutral, fluid space of the Elizabethan stage was ideally suited to drama calling for the free movement of the imagination. The line between illusion and reality, nebulous in any kind of theater, was especially so in Shakespeare's, and his plays are full of scenes that question what is "real," as in *King Lear,* Act IV, scene vi, in which the blind Gloucester thinks he is on the top of a cliff. Edgar knows that Gloucester is "really" in a flat field, while we see that the field is as imaginary as the cliff and that the characters are really on a wooden stage.

FURTHER READING *(prepared by W.J.R.):* S. Schoenbaum s *William Shakespeare: A Compact Documentary Life,* 1977, a revision of an earlier biography, discusses the major stages of Shakespeare's life and the contemporary theatrical world. For a handsome biography, full of color photographs, see Anthony Burgess's *Shakespeare,* 1970. A stimulating introductory overview, treating Shakespeare topically and discussing the metaphysics of *King Lear,* is Germaine Greer's *Shakespeare,* 1986. Other good introductions to Shakespearean criticism are *The New Century Shakespeare Handbook,* ed. Sandra Clark, 1974, and Stanley Wells's *Shakespeare: The Writer and His Work,* 1978. Clark's work contains a brief biographical sketch, notes on productions of Shakespeare's work in his own time, and numerous photographs of modern productions. Wells discusses Shakespeare's England and his theater and provides an overview of Shakespearean criticism. For a clearly written discussion of Shakespeare's organizing principles in each play, see Maynard Mack, *Everybody's Shakespeare,* 1993. Charles

Boyce, *Shakespeare A to Z*, 1991, summarizes many Shakespearean discussions for the general reader. Comprehensive discussions of Shakespeare, in lectures by two of the century's great critics, are printed in Mark Van Doren, *Shakespeare*, 1939, 1953; and Northrop Frye, *Northrop Frye on Shakespeare*, 1986. On Shakespeare's great tragedies, A. C. Bradley's *Shakespearean Tragedy*, 1904, is still valuable and readable. This work, which greatly influenced interpretations of the tragedies, studies *Hamlet, Othello, King Lear*, and *Macbeth*. An overview of criticism is provided in *Shakespeare and His Critics*, ed. F. E. Halliday, 1947, rev. 1957, which contains commentary on all the first folio plays and the minor poems. Two fine works on staging and related topics are Cécile de Banke's *Shakespearean Stage Production, Then and Now*, 1953, and S. Schoenbaum's *Shakespeare: The Globe and the World*, 1979. Banke's work is a detailed study of staging, acting, costuming, and other aspects of production relevant for the modern amateur producer of Shakespeare. Schoenbaum's work is filled with color photographs, drawings, and diagrams; modern productions of Shakespeare, including film adaptations, are also treated. John Russell Brown, *Discovering Shakespeare: A New Guide to the Plays*, 1981, invites new readers to consider the plays as performance rather than through traditional methods of literary analysis. E. M. W. Tillyard, *Shakespeare's History Plays*, 1947, remains a classic. The Norton Critical Edition of *Henry the Fourth, Part I*, ed. James L. Sanderson, 1962, includes a well-annotated text and critical essays on the play. A more recent collection is David Bevington, ed., *Henry the Fourth, Parts I and II: Critical Essays*, 1986. For a comprehensive guide, see *Henry IV, Parts 1 and 2: An Annotated Bibliography*, comp. Catherine Gira and Adele Seeff, 1994.

HENRY IV, PART I

Footnotes by G. B. Harrison

DRAMATIS PERSONAE

KING HENRY *the Fourth*
HENRY, *Prince of Wales* ⎱ *sons to*
JOHN *of Lancaster* ⎰ *the King*
EARL OF WESTMORELAND
SIR WALTER BLUNT
THOMAS PERCY, *Earl of Worcester*
HENRY PERCY, *Earl of Northumberland*
HENRY PERCY, *surnamed* HOTSPUR, *his son*
EDMUND MORTIMER, *Earl of March*
RICHARD SCROOP, *Archbishop of York*
ARCHIBALD, *Earl of Douglas*
OWEN GLENDOWER
SIR RICHARD VERNON
SIR JOHN FALSTAFF
SIR MICHAEL, *a friend to the Archbishop of York*

POINS
GADSHILL
PETO
BARDOLPH

LADY PERCY, *wife to Hotspur and sister to Mortimer*
LADY MORTIMER, *daughter to Glendower and wife to Mortimer*
MISTRESS QUICKLY, *hostess of a tavern in Eastcheap*

LORDS, OFFICERS, SHERIFF, VINTNER, CHAMBERLAIN, DRAWERS, *two* CARRIERS, TRAVELERS, *and* ATTENDANTS

SCENE—England and Wales.

ACT I

SCENE I. London. The palace.

[*Enter* KING HENRY, LORD JOHN OF LANCASTER,
the EARL OF WESTMORELAND, SIR WALTER BLUNT, *and others.*]
KING. So shaken as we are, so wan with care,
Find we[1] a time for frighted peace to pant,
And breathe short-winded accents of new broils
To be commenced in stronds[2] afar remote.
No more the thirsty entrance of this soil
Shall daub her lips with her own children's blood.
No more shall trenching war[3] channel her fields,
Nor bruise her flowerets[4] with the armèd hoofs
Of hostile paces. Those opposèd eyes,
Which, like the meteors[5] of a troubled heaven,   10
All of one nature, of one substance bred,
Did lately meet in the intestine shock[6]
And furious close[7] of civil butchery,
Shall now, in mutual well-beseeming[8] ranks,
March all one way, and be no more opposed
Against acquaintance, kindred, and allies.
The edge of war, like an ill-sheathèd knife,
No more shall cut his master. Therefore, friends,
As far as to the sepulcher of Christ,
Whose soldier now, under whose blessèd cross   20
We are impressèd[9] and engaged to fight,
Forthwith a power of English shall we levy,
Whose arms were molded in their mothers' womb
To chase these pagans in those holy fields
Over whose acres walked those blessed feet
Which fourteen hundred years ago were nailed
For our advantage on the bitter cross.
But this our purpose now is twelvemonth old,
And bootless 'tis to tell you we will go.
Therefore we meet not now.[10] Then let me hear   30
Of you, my gentle cousin[11] Westmoreland,
What yesternight our Council did decree
In forwarding this dear expedience.[12]

---

[1]**Find we,** let us find.   [2]Strands, shores.   [3]**trenching war,** trench warfare.
[4]Little flowers.   [5]Comets or shooting stars, regarded as terrifying omens.
[6]**intestine shock,** clash of civil war.   [7]Hand-to-hand battle.
[8]**well-beseeming,** seemly.   [9]Enlisted.
[10]**bootless . . . now,** i.e., there is no need to tell you of my decision, which has long been
made. Our present meeting is to consider the details. **bootless,** vain.
[11]Kinsman, used of any near relation.
[12]**dear expedience,** urgent enterprise, dear to me.

WEST. My liege, this haste was hot in question,[13]
    And many limits of the charge[14] set down
    But yesternight, when all athwart[15] there came
    A post[16] from Wales loaden[17] with heavy news,
    Whose worst was that the noble Mortimer,[18]
    Leading the men of Herefordshire to fight
    Against the irregular[19] and wild Glendower,   40
    Was by the rude hands of that Welshman taken,
    A thousand of his people butchered.
    Upon whose dead corpse there was such misuse,
    Such beastly shameless transformation,
    By those Welshwomen done as may not be
    Without much shame retold or spoken of.
KING. It seems then that the tidings of this broil
    Brake off our business for the Holy Land.
WEST. This matched with other did, my gracious lord;
    For more uneven[20] and unwelcome news   50
    Came from the north and thus it did import:
    On Holyrood Day,[21] the gallant Hotspur there,
    Young Harry Percy, and brave Archibald,
    That ever valiant and approvèd[22] Scot,
    At Holmedon[23] met,
    Where they did spend a sad and bloody hour,
    As by discharge of their artillery,
    And shape of likelihood,[24] the news was told.
    For he that brought them, in the very heat
    And pride of their contention[25] did take horse,   60
    Uncertain of the issue[26] any way.
KING. Here is a dear, a true industrious friend,
    Sir Walter Blunt, new-lighted from his horse,
    Stained with the variation of each soil
    Betwixt that Holmedon and this seat of ours,
    And he hath brought us smooth and welcome news.
    The Earl of Douglas is discomfited.
    Ten thousand bold Scots, two and twenty knights,
    Balked[27] in their own blood did Sir Walter see
    On Holmedon's plains. Of prisoners, Hotspur took   70
    Mordake the Earl of Fife, and eldest son
    To beaten Douglas; and the Earl of Athol,
    Of Murray, Angus, and Menteith.

---

[13]**hot in question,** under eager discussion.
[14]**limits . . . charge,** estimates of the cost.
[15]Cutting across.   [16]Messenger.   [17]Laden.
[18]Mortimer had a substantive claim to the throne.
[19]Unruly.   [20]Rough.   [21]**Holyrood Day,** September 14.
[22]Tried.   [23]In Northumberland, near the Scottish border.
[24]**shape of likelihood,** what was likely to happen.
[25]**pride . . . contention,** height of battle.
[26]Result.   [27]Laid in ridges.

And is not this an honorable spoil?
A gallant prize? Ha, Cousin, is it not?
WEST. In faith,
   It is a conquest for a prince to boast of.
KING. Yea, there thou makest me sad and makest me sin
   In envy that my Lord Northumberland
   Should be the father to so blest a son—   80
   A son who is the theme of honor's tongue,
   Amongst a grove, the very straightest plant,
   Who is sweet Fortune's minion[28] and her pride—
   Whilst I, by looking on the praise of him,
   See riot and dishonor stain the brow
   Of my young Harry. Oh, that it could be proved
   That some night-tripping fairy[29] had exchanged
   In cradle clothes our children where they lay,
   And called mine Percy, his Plantagenet!
   Then would I have his Harry, and he mine.   90
   But let him from my thoughts. What think you, Coz,[30]
   Of this young Percy's[31] pride? The prisoners
   Which he in this adventure hath surprised
   To his own use he keeps, and sends me word
   I shall have none but Mordake Earl of Fife.
WEST. This is his uncle's teaching. This is Worcester,
   Malevolent[32] to you in all aspécts,
   Which makes him prune[33] himself, and bristle up
   The crest of youth against your dignity.
KING. But I have sent for him to answer this,   100
   And for this cause awhile we must neglect
   Our holy purpose to Jerusalem.
   Cousin, on Wednesday next our Council we
   Will hold at Windsor. So inform the lords,
   But come yourself with speed to us again,
   For more is to be said and to be done
   Than out of anger[34] can be uttered.
WEST. I will, my liege.   [*Exeunt.*]

---

[28]Darling.
[29]**night-tripping fairy,** a fairy coming by night. The fairies, so some believed, used sometimes to steal a beautiful child and to leave a changeling in its place.
[30]Cousin.
[31]**young Percy,** Shakespeare depicts Hotspur as a rash youth of about the same age as Prince Hal. Actually at the battle of Shrewsbury (1403) the Prince was barely 14 years old and Percy was 39.
[32]Boding evil, like a planet that brings disaster.
[33]Preen, like a hawk in good condition trimming its feathers.
[34]**out of anger,** from an angry heart.

SCENE II. London. An apartment of the Prince's.

[*Enter the* PRINCE OF WALES *and* FALSTAFF.]

FAL. Now, Hal, what time of day is it, lad?

PRINCE. Thou art so fat-witted, with drinking of old sack[1] and unbut-
toning thee after supper and sleeping upon benches after noon,
that thou hast forgotten to demand that truly which thou wouldst
truly know. What a devil hast thou to do with the time of the day?
Unless hours were cups of sack, and minutes capons, and clocks
the tongues of bawds, and dials the signs of leaping houses,[2] and
the blessed sun himself a fair hot wench in flame-colored taffeta,[3]
I see no reason why thou shouldst be so superfluous to demand
the time of the day.   10

FAL. Indeed, you come near me now, Hal; for we that take purses go
by the moon and the seven stars, and not by Phoebus,[4] he, "that
wandering knight so fair." And I prithee, sweet wag, when thou art
King, as, God save thy Grace—Majesty I should say, for grace thou
wilt have none——

PRINCE. What, none?

FAL. No, by my troth,[5] not so much as will serve to be prologue to an
egg and butter.

PRINCE. Well, how then? Come, roundly, roundly.

FAL. Marry, then, sweet wag, when thou art King, let not us that are   20
squires of the night's body be called thieves of the day's beauty.[6]
Let us be Diana's foresters,[7] gentlemen of the shade, minions of
the moon. And let men say we be men of good government,[8] being
governed, as the sea is, by our noble and chaste mistress the moon,
under whose countenance we steal.

PRINCE. Thou sayest well, and it holds well too; for the fortune of us
that are the moon's men doth ebb and flow like the sea, being governed, as the sea is, by the moon. As for proof, now—a purse of
gold most resolutely snatched on Monday night and most dissolutely
spent on Tuesday morning; got with swearing "Lay by"[9] and spent   30
with crying "Bring in"[10]—now in as low an ebb as the foot of
the ladder,[11] and by and by in as high a flow as the ridge of the
gallows.

FAL. By the Lord, thou sayest true, lad. And is not my hostess of the
tavern a most sweet wench?

[1] Spanish dry white wine.   [2] **leaping houses,** brothels.
[3] **flame-colored taffeta,** bright red silk—the color flaunted by harlots.
[4] The sun, with a pun on the Knight of the Sun, hero of a chivalric romance.
[5] Truth.
[6] **let . . . beauty,** i.e., do not let us who are gentlemen of the dark (i.e., highwaymen) be
called *thieves of the day's beauty* (i.e., loafers)—with a pun on "beauty" and "booty."
[7] **Diana's foresters,** thieves who rob by night. **Diana,** the moon.
[8] **good government,** well-behaved.   [9] **Lay by,** i.e., "stick 'em up."
[10] **Bring in,** i.e., the drink.
[11] From which a condemned man was thrust off the gallows into space.

PRINCE. As the honey of Hybla,[12] my old lad of the castle.[13] And is not a buff jerkin [14] a most sweet robe of durance?[15]

FAL. How now, how now, mad wag! What, in thy quips [16] and thy quiddities? [17] What a plague have I to do with a buff jerkin?

PRINCE. Why, what a pox have I to do with my hostess of the tavern?   40

FAL. Well, thou hast called her to a reckoning many a time and oft.

PRINCE. Did I ever call for thee to pay thy part?

FAL. No. I'll give thee thy due, thou hast paid all there.

PRINCE. Yea, and elsewhere, so far as my coin would stretch. And where it would not, I have used my credit.

FAL. Yea, and so used it that, were it not here apparent that thou art heir [18] apparent——But I prithee, sweet wag, shall there be gallows standing in England when thou art King? And resolution[19] thus fobbed [20] as it is with the rusty curb of old Father Antic [21] the law? Do not thou, when thou art King, hang a thief.   50

PRINCE. No, thou shalt.

FAL. Shall I? Oh, rare! By the Lord, I'll be a brave judge.

PRINCE. Thou judgest false already. I mean thou shalt have the hanging of the thieves and so become a rare hangman.

FAL. Well, Hal, well, and in some sort it jumps [22] with my humor [23] as well as waiting in the court, I can tell you.

PRINCE. For obtaining of suits?

FAL. Yea, for obtaining of suits,[24] whereof the hangman [25] hath no lean wardrobe. 'Sblood,[26] I am as melancholy as a gib-cat [27] or a lugged bear.[28]   60

PRINCE. Or an old lion, or a lover's lute.

FAL. Yea, or the drone of a Lincolnshire bagpipe.

PRINCE. What sayest thou to a hare,[29] or the melancholy of Moorditch?[30]

FAL. Thou hast the most unsavory similes, and art indeed the most comparative,[31] rascaliest, sweet young Prince. But, Hal, I prithee trouble me no more with vanity. I would to God thou and I knew where a commodity[32] of good names were to be bought. An old lord of the Council rated [33] me the other day in the street about you, sir, but I marked him not; and yet he talked very wisely, but I regarded him not; and yet he talked wisely, and in the street too.   70

---

[12] In Sicily, famous for its honey.

[13] **old . . . castle,** roisterer, with a pun on Falstaff's original name of Oldcastle.

[14] **buff jerkin,** leather coat worn by the sheriff's sergeant.

[15] **robe of durance,** coat that endures (wears well) and that takes you to *durance* (prison).

[16] Wisecracks.   [17] Quibbles.

[18] **here . . . heir,** a pun, *heir* being pronounced as "hair."

[19] A stout heart.   [20] Fubbed, cheated.

[21] **Father Antic,** i.e., Daddy Buffoon.   [22] Agrees.   [23] Whim.

[24] **obtaining of suits,** with a pun on *suit*—"petitions to the sovereign for favor" and "clothes."

[25] The clothes of the executed were the hangman's perquisite.

[26] By God's blood.   [27] Tom-cat.

[28] **lugged bear,** bear torn by the dogs.

[29] Regarded as a melancholy creature.

[30] **melancholy of Moorditch,** Moorditch was one of the open sewers of the City of London, proverbial for its stink.

[31] Quick at making comparisons.   [32] Parcel.   [33] Rebuked.

PRINCE. Thou didst well, for wisdom cries out in the streets, and no man regards it.[34]

FAL. Oh, thou hast damnable iteration,[35] and art indeed able to corrupt a saint. Thou hast done much harm upon me, Hal. God forgive thee for it! Before I knew thee, Hal, I knew nothing; and now am I, if a man should speak truly, little better than one of the wicked. I must give over this life, and I will give it over. By the Lord, an[36] I do not, I am a villain. I'll be damned for never a king's son in Christendom.

PRINCE. Where shall we take a purse tomorrow, Jack? 80

FAL. 'Zounds,[37] where thou wilt, lad. I'll make one. An I do not, call me villain and baffle[38] me.

PRINCE. I see a good amendment of life in thee—from praying to purse-taking.

FAL. Why, Hal, 'tis my vocation, Hal. 'Tis no sin for a man to labor in his vocation.

[*Enter* POINS.] Poins! Now shall we know if Gadshill have set a match.[39] Oh, if men were to be saved by merit, what hole in Hell were hot enough for him? This is the most omnipotent villain that ever cried "Stand" to a true man. 90

PRINCE. Good morrow, Ned.

POINS. Good morrow, sweet Hal. What says Monsieur Remorse? What says Sir John Sack and Sugar? Jack! How agrees the Devil and thee about thy soul, that thou soldest him on Good Friday last for a cup of Madeira and a cold capon's leg?[40]

PRINCE. Sir John stands to his word, the Devil shall have his bargain, for he was never yet a breaker of proverbs.[41] He will give the Devil his due.

POINS. Then art thou damned for keeping thy word with the Devil.

PRINCE. Else he had been damned for cozening[42] the Devil. 100

POINS. But, my lads, my lads, tomorrow morning, by four o'clock, early at Gadshill![43] There are pilgrims going to Canterbury with rich offerings,[44] and traders riding to London with fat purses. I have vizards[45] for you all, you have horses for yourselves. Gadshill lies tonight in Rochester. I have bespoke[46] supper tomorrow night in Eastcheap. We may do it as secure as sleep. If you will go, I will stuff your purses full of crowns. If you will not, tarry at home and be hanged.

FAL. Hear ye, Yedward,[47] if I tarry at home and go not, I'll hang you for going.

---

[34] **wisdom . . . it,** quoted loosely from Proverbs I:20–24.
[35] Ability to quote.   [36] If.   [37] By God's Wounds.   [38] Disgrace.
[39] **set a match,** "framed a holdup."
[40] **Good . . . leg,** Good Friday being the Church's most solemn fast day, to drink Madeira and eat chicken was a damnable sin.
[41] **breaker of proverbs,** one to prove proverbs false.
[42] Cheating.
[43] Near Rochester in Kent. Some slight confusion is caused as the same name is used by one of the gang.
[44] **rich offerings,** i.e., for the shrine of Saint Thomas à Becket at Canterbury.
[45] Masks.   [46] Ordered.   [47] A form of Edward, Poins's first name.

POINS. You will, chops? [110]

FAL. Hal, wilt thou make one?

PRINCE. Who, I rob? I a thief? Not I, by my faith.

FAL. There's neither honesty, manhood, nor good fellowship in thee, nor thou camest not of the blood royal, if thou darest not stand for ten shillings.[48]

PRINCE. Well then, once in my days I'll be a madcap.

FAL. Why, that's well said.

PRINCE. Well, come what will, I'll tarry at home.

FAL. By the Lord, I'll be a traitor then, when thou art King.

PRINCE. I care not. [120]

POINS. Sir John, I prithee, leave the Prince and me alone. I will lay him down such reasons for this adventure that he shall go.

FAL. Well, God give thee the spirit of persuasion and him the ears of profiting, that what thou speakest may move and what he hears may be believed,[49] that the true Prince may, for recreation sake, prove a false thief; for the poor abuses of the time want countenance.[50] Farewell. You shall find me in Eastcheap.

PRINCE. Farewell, thou latter spring![51] Farewell, Allhallow summer![52]

[*Exit* FALSTAFF.]

POINS. Now, my good sweet honey lord, ride with us tomorrow. I have a jest to execute that I cannot manage alone. Falstaff, Bardolph, [130] Peto, and Gadshill shall rob those men that we have already waylaid. Yourself and I will not be there, and when they have the booty, if you and I do not rob them, cut this head off from my shoulders.

PRINCE. How shall we part with them in setting forth?

POINS. Why, we will set forth before or after them, and appoint them a place of meeting, wherein it is at our pleasure to fail, and then will they adventure upon the exploit themselves; which they shall have no sooner achieved but we'll set upon them.

PRINCE. Yea, but 'tis like that they will know us by our horses, by our habits,[53] and by every other appointment,[54] to be ourselves. [140]

POINS. Tut! Our horses they shall not see, I'll tie them in the wood. Our vizards we will change after we leave them. And, sirrah, I have cases of buckram[55] for the nonce,[56] to immask our noted outward garments.

PRINCE. Yea, but I doubt they will be too hard for us.

POINS. Well, for two of them, I know them to be as true-bred cowards as ever turned back; and for the third, if he fight longer than he sees reason,[57] I'll forswear arms. The virtue of this jest will be the

---

[48] **blood . . . shillings,** pun on *royal*, a coin worth 10s.

[49] **God . . . believed,** Falstaff constantly drops into the pious jargon of professional preachers.

[50] **want countenance,** need encouragement.

[51] **latter spring,** late spring; i.e., green autumn.

[52] **Allhallow summer,** Indian summer. Allhallow (All Saints' Day) is on November 1.

[53] Clothes.   [54] Accouterment.

[55] **cases of buckram,** overalls of coarse linen.

[56] Occasion.

[57] **fight . . . reason,** This is Falstaff's avowed rule of life; see, for example, Act V, scene iv.

incomprehensible lies that this same fat rogue will tell us when we
meet at supper—how thirty, at least, he fought with; what wards,[58] 150
what blows, what extremities he endured. And in the reproof[59] of
this lies the jest.

PRINCE. Well, I'll go with thee. Provide us all things necessary and meet
me tomorrow night in Eastcheap. There I'll sup. Farewell.

POINS. Farewell my lord.   [*Exit.*]

PRINCE. I know you all,[60] and will a while uphold[61]
The unyoked humor[62] of your idleness.
Yet herein will I imitate the sun,
Who doth permit the base contagious[63] clouds
To smother up his beauty from the world,   160
That, when he please again to be himself,
Being wanted, he may be more wondered at
By breaking through the foul and ugly mists
Of vapors that did seem to strangle him.
If all the year were playing holidays,
To sport would be as tedious as to work.
But when they seldom come, they wished-for come,
And nothing pleaseth but rare accidents.
So, when this loose behavior I throw off
And pay the debt I never promisèd,   170
By how much better than my word I am,
By so much shall I falsify men's hopes.
And like bright metal on a sullen[64] ground,
My reformation, glittering o'er my fault,
Shall show more goodly and attract more eyes
Than that which hath no foil[65] to set it off.
I'll so offend, to make offense a skill,[66]
Redeeming time[67] when men think least I will.

                                                    [*Exit.*]

SCENE III. *London. The palace.*

[*Enter the* KING, NORTHUMBERLAND, WORCESTER,
HOTSPUR, SIR WALTER BLUNT, *with others.*]

KING. My blood hath been too cold and temperate,
Unapt to stir at these indignities,
And you have found me;[1] for accordingly
You tread upon my patience. But be sure
I will from henceforth rather be myself,[2]

---

[58] Defense; fencing stances.   [59] Rebuttal.

[60] **I . . . all,** This soliloquy is important for the understanding of the Prince's later treatment of Falstaff and the gang.

[61] Tolerate.   [62] **unyoked humor,** unrestrained behavior.

[63] Poisonous.   [64] Dull.

[65] Sheet of metal placed behind a jewel to set off its brilliance by contrast.

[66] Art.   [67] **Redeeming time,** making up for the time I have lost.

[1] **found me,** found me out.   [2] I.e., King.

Mighty and to be feared, than my condition,[3]
Which hath been smooth as oil, soft as young down,
And therefore lost that title of respect[4]
Which the proud soul ne'er pays but to the proud.
WOR. Our house, my sovereign liege, little deserves   10
  The scourge of greatness to be used on it,
  And that same greatness too which our own hands
  Have holp[5] to make so portly.[6]
NORTH. My lord——
KING. Worcester, get thee gone, for I do see
  Danger and disobedience in thine eye.
  O sir, your presence is too bold and peremptory,
  And Majesty might never yet endure
  The moody frontier of a servant brow.[7]
  You have good leave to leave us.[8] When we need   20
  Your use and counsel, we shall send for you.
                                          [*Exit* WORCESTER.]
  [*To* NORTHUMBERLAND] You were about to speak.
NORTH.   Yea, my good lord.
  Those prisoners in your Highness' name demanded,[9]
  Which Harry Percy here at Holmedon took,
  Were, as he says, not with such strength denied
  As is delivered to your Majesty.
  Either envy,[10] therefore, or misprision[11]
  Is guilty of this fault, and not my son.
HOT. My liege, I did deny no prisoners.
  But I remember, when the fight was done,   30
  When I was dry with rage and éxtreme toil,
  Breathless and faint, leaning upon my sword,
  Came there a certain lord, neat, and trimly dressed,
  Fresh as a bridegroom, and his chin new-reaped[12]
  Showed like a stubble land at harvest home.
  He was perfumèd like a milliner,
  And 'twixt his finger and his thumb he held
  A pouncet box,[13] which ever and anon
  He gave his nose and took 't away again;
  Who therewith angry, when it next came there,   40
  Took it in snuff.[14] And still he smiled and talked,
  And as the soldiers bore dead bodies by,

[3]**than my condition,** than my naturally mild disposition.
[4]**title of respect,** claim to be respected.
[5]Helped.   [6]Magnificent.
[7]**moody . . . brow,** frowning look on a servant's brow.
[8]**leave . . . us,** a polite phrase of dismissal.
[9]**prisoners . . . demanded,** In earlier times a prisoner became the property of his captor, who released him on payment of a ransom according to his rank and wealth.
[10]Malice—of Hotspur's enemies.   [11]Misunderstanding.
[12]**chin new-reaped,** beard closely cut.
[13]**pouncet box,** small box containing perfume, which the fastidious sniffed to counteract foul smells.
[14]**Took . . . snuff,** sniffed, with a pun on the idiomatic meaning "resented."

He called them untaught knaves, unmannerly,
To bring a slovenly unhandsome corse[15]
Betwixt the wind and his nobility.
With many holiday and lady terms[16]
He questioned me, amongst the rest, demanded
My prisoners in your Majesty's behalf.
I then, all smarting with my wounds being cold,
To be so pestered with a popinjay,[17]   50
Out of my grief[18] and my impatience
Answered neglectingly I know not what,
He should, or he should not; for he made me mad
To see him shine so brisk, and smell so sweet,
And talk so like a waiting gentlewoman[19]
Of guns and drums and wounds—God save the mark!—[20]
And telling me the sovereign'st[21] thing on earth
Was parmaceti[22] for an inward bruise;
And that it was great pity, so it was,
This villainous saltpeter should be digged   60
Out of the bowels of the harmless earth,
Which many a good tall[23] fellow had destroyed
So cowardly; and but for these vile guns,
He would himself have been a soldier.
This bald unjointed chat[24] of his, my lord,
I answered indirectly, as I said.
And I beseech you, let not his report
Come current[25] for an accusation
Betwixt my love and your high Majesty.
BLUNT. The circumstance considered, good my lord,   70
   Whate'er Lord Harry Percy then had said
   To such a person and in such a place,
   At such a time, with all the rest retold,
   May reasonably die and never rise
   To do him wrong, or any way impeach[26]
   What then he said, so he unsay it now.
KING. Why, yet[27] he doth deny his prisoners,
   But with proviso[28] and exception,
   That we at our own charge shall ransom straight
   His brother-in-law, the foolish Mortimer,   80
   Who, on my soul, hath willfully betrayed

---

[15]Corpse.
[16]**holiday . . . terms,** fancy phrases, as opposed to "working-day" or plain English.
[17]Parrot.   [18]Smart (of my wounds).
[19]**waiting gentlewoman,** lady in waiting, the essence of fancy femininity.
[20]**God . . . mark,** an impatient apology for a coarse remark.
[21]Most excellent.
[22]Spermaceti, a fatty substance found in the whale and used as an ointment.
[23]Brave.
[24]**bald . . . chat,** slight disconnected chatter.
[25]**Come current,** be regarded as valid.
[26]Accuse, call in question.   [27]Still, after all.   [28]Stipulation.

The lives of those that he did lead to fight
Against that great magician,[29] damned Glendower,
Whose daughter, as we hear, the Earl of March
Hath lately married. Shall our coffers, then,
Be emptied to redeem a traitor home?
Shall we buy treason, and indent[30] with fears,
When they have lost and forfeited themselves?
No, on the barren mountains let him starve.
For I shall never hold that man my friend   90
Whose tongue shall ask me for one penny cost
To ransom home revolted Mortimer.
HOT. Revolted Mortimer!
He never did fall off,[31] my sovereign liege,
But by the chance of war. To prove that true
Needs no more but one tongue for all those wounds,
Those mouthèd[32] wounds, which valiantly he took
When on the gentle Severn's sedgy[33] bank,
In single opposition, hand to hand,
He did confound[34] the best part of an hour   100
In changing hardiment[35] with great Glendower.
Three times they breathed and three times did they drink,
Upon agreement, of swift Severn's flood;
Who then, affrighted with their bloody looks,
Ran fearfully among the trembling reeds,
And hid his crisp head in the hollow bank
Bloodstainèd with these valiant combatants.
Never did base and rotten policy[36]
Color her working[37] with such deadly wounds;
Nor never could the noble Mortimer   110
Receive so many, and all willingly.
Then let not him be slandered with revolt.
KING. Thou dost belie him,[38] Percy, thou dost belie him.
He never did encounter with Glendower.
I tell thee,
He durst as well have met the Devil alone
As Owen Glendower for an enemy.
Art thou not ashamed? But, sirrah,[39] henceforth
Let me not hear you speak of Mortimer.
Send me your prisoners with the speediest means,   120
Or you shall hear in such a kind from me
As will displease you. My Lord Northumberland,
We license your departure with your son.
Send us your prisoners, or you will hear it.

---

[29] For Glendower's supposed supernatural powers, see Act III, scene i.
[30] Make an agreement.   [31] **fall off,** desert.   [32] Looking like a mouth.
[33] Reedy.   [34] Consume.
[35] **changing hardiment,** exchanging blows.
[36] Cunning.   [37] **Color . . . working,** disguise its real intention.
[38] **belie him,** lie about him.
[39] A form of address used to an inferior, here deliberately insulting.

[*Exeunt* KING HENRY, BLUNT, *and train.*]

HOT. An if the Devil come and roar for them,
I will not send them. I will after straight
And tell him so, for I will ease my heart,
Albeit I make a hazard [40] of my head.

NORTH. What, drunk with choler? [41] Stay and pause awhile.
Here comes your uncle.

[*Re-enter* WORCESTER.]

HOT.   Speak of Mortimer!   130
'Zounds, I will speak of him, and let my soul
Want mercy if I do not join with him.
Yea, on his part I'll empty all these veins,
And shed my dear blood drop by drop in the dust,
But I will lift the downtrod Mortimer
As high in the air as this unthankful King,
As this ingrate and cankered [42] Bolingbroke.

NORTH. Brother, the King hath made your nephew mad.

WOR. Who struck this heat up after I was gone?

HOT. He will, forsooth, have all my prisoners.   140
And when I urged the ransom once again
Of my wife's brother, then his cheek looked pale,
And on my face he turned an eye of death,
Trembling even at the name of Mortimer.

WOR. I cannot blame him. Was not he proclaimed
By Richard that dead is the next of blood?

NORTH. He was, I heard the proclamation.
And then it was when the unhappy King—
Whose wrongs in us God pardon! [43]—did set forth
Upon his Irish expedition,   150
From whence he intercepted [44] did return
To be deposed and shortly [45] murderèd.

WOR. And for whose death we in the world's wide mouth
Live scandalized and foully spoken of.

HOT. But, soft, I pray you. Did King Richard then
Proclaim my brother [46] Edmund Mortimer
Heir to the crown?

NORTH.   He did, myself did hear it.

HOT. Nay, then I cannot blame his cousin King,
That wished him on the barren mountains starve.
But shall it be that you, that set the crown   160
Upon the head of this forgetful man,
And for his sake wear the detested blot
Of murderous subornation, [47] shall it be
That you a world of curses undergo,

---

[40] Risk.   [41] Wrath.   [42] Malignant.
[43] **Whose . . . pardon,** may God forgive the wrongs committed by us against him.
[44] Being hindered.   [45] In a short time.   [46] Brother-in-law.
[47] **wear . . . subornation,** wear the mark of shame as accessories to murder. **subornation,** procuring someone to commit a crime.

Being the agents, or base second means,[48]
The cords, the ladder, or the hangman rather?
Oh, pardon me that I descend so low,
To show the line[49] and the predicament[50]
Wherein you range[51] under this subtle King.
Shall it for shame be spoken in these days,   170
Or fill up chronicles in time to come,
That men of your nobility and power
Did gage[52] them both in an unjust behalf,
As both of you—God pardon it!—have done,
To put down Richard, that sweet lovely rose,
And plant this thorn, this canker,[53] Bolingbroke?
And shall it in more shame be further spoken,
That you are fooled, discarded, and shook off
By him for whom these shames ye underwent?
No, yet time serves wherein you may redeem   180
Your banished honors, and restore yourselves
Into the good thoughts of the world again,
Revenge the jeering and disdained[54] contempt
Of this proud King, who studies day and night
To answer all the debt he owes to you
Even with the bloody payment of your deaths.
Therefore, I say——
WOR.   Peace, Cousin, say no more.
And now I will unclasp a secret book,
And to your quick-conceiving[55] discontents
I'll read you matter deep and dangerous,   190
As full of peril and adventurous spirit
As to o'erwalk a current roaring loud
On the unsteadfast footing of a spear.[56]
HOT. If he fall in, good night! Or sink or swim.
Send danger from the east unto the west,
So honor cross it from the north to south,
And let them grapple. Oh, the blood more stirs
To rouse a lion than to start a hare!
NORTH. Imagination of some great exploit
Drives him beyond the bounds of patience.[57]   200
HOT. By Heaven, methinks it were an easy leap,
To pluck bright honor from the pale-faced moon,
Or dive into the bottom of the deep,
Where fathom line could never touch the ground,
And pluck up drownèd honor by the locks,
So he that doth redeem her thence might wear

---

[48]**second means,** assistants.   [49]Disgrace.   [50]Class, category.   [51]Rank.
[52]Pledge, engage.   [53]Wild rose, contrasted with the garden rose.
[54]Disdainful.   [55]**quick-conceiving,** quick-witted.
[56]**unsteadfast . . . spear,** with a spear as unsteady bridge.
[57]Self-control.

Without corrival[58] all her dignities.
But out upon this half-faced fellowship![59]
WOR. He apprehends a world of figures[60] here,[61]
But not the form of what he should attend. 210
Good Cousin, give me audience for a while.
HOT. I cry you mercy.
WOR.   Those same noble Scots
That are your prisoners——
HOT.   I'll keep them all.
By God, he shall not have a Scot of them.
No, if a Scot would save his soul, he shall not.
I'll keep them, by this hand.
WOR.   You start away
And lend no ear unto my purposes.
Those prisoners you shall keep.
HOT.   Nay, I will, that's flat.
He said he would not ransom Mortimer,
Forbade my tongue to speak of Mortimer. 220
But I will find him when he lies asleep,
And in his ear I'll holloa "Mortimer!"
Nay, I'll have a starling[62] shall be taught to speak
Nothing but "Mortimer," and give it him,
To keep his anger still in motion.
WOR. Hear you, Cousin, a word.
HOT. All studies here I solemnly defy,
Save how to gall[63] and pinch this Bolingbroke.
And that same sword-and-buckler[64] Prince of Wales, 230
But that I think his father loves him not
And would be glad he met with some mischance,
I would have him poisoned with a pot of ale.
WOR. Farewell, kinsman. I'll talk to you
When you are better tempered to attend.
NORTH. Why, what a wasp-stung and impatient fool
Art thou to break into this woman's mood,
Tying thine ear to no tongue but thine own!
HOT. Why, look you, I am whipped and scourged with rods,
Nettled,[65] and stung with pismires,[66] when I hear 240
Of this vile politician,[67] Bolingbroke.
In Richard's time—what do you call the place?—
A plague upon it, it is in Gloucestershire,

---

[58]Partner.
[59]**half-faced fellowship,** starving partnership, i.e., sharing of honor which is insufficient for two to share.
[60]Shapes, fantasies.
[61]**apprehends . . . here,** i.e., he is entirely carried away by his imagination.
[62]The starling, like the jackdaw and the parrot, can be taught to mimic sound.
[63]Make sore.   [64]**sword-and-buckler,** swashbuckler.
[65]Whipped with nettles.   [66]Ants.   [67]Schemer.

'Twas where the madcap Duke his uncle kept,
His uncle York, where I first bowed my knee
Unto this king of smiles, this Bolingbroke—
'Sblood!—When you and he came back from Ravenspurgh.
NORTH. At Berkeley Castle.[68]
HOT. You say true.   250
Why, what a candy deal[69] of courtesy
This fawning greyhound then did proffer me!
Look, "when his infant fortune came to age,"
And "gentle Harry Percy," and "kind Cousin."
Oh, the devil take such cozeners! God forgive me!
Good Uncle, tell your tale, I have done.
WOR. Nay, if you have not, to it again.
We will stay[70] your leisure.
HOT.   I have done, i' faith.
WOR. Then once more to your Scottish prisoners.
Deliver them up without their ransom straight,   260
And make the Douglas' son your only mean[71]
For powers[72] in Scotland; which, for divers reasons
Which I shall send you written, be assured
Will easily be granted. [*To* NORTHUMBERLAND] You, my lord,
Your son in Scotland being thus employed,
Shall secretly into the bosom creep
Of that same noble prelate, well beloved,
The Archbishop.
HOT.   Of York, is it not?
WOR. True, who bears hard[73]   270
His brother's death at Bristol, the Lord Scroop.
I speak not this in estimation,[74]
As what I think might be, but what I know
Is ruminated,[75] plotted, and set down,
And only stays but to behold the face
Of that occasion that shall bring it on.
HOT. I smell it. Upon my life, it will do well.
NORTH. Before the game is afoot, thou still[76] let'st slip.[77]
HOT. Why, it cannot choose but be a noble plot.
And then the power of Scotland and of York,   280
To join with Mortimer, ha?
WOR.   And so they shall.
HOT. In faith, it is exceedingly well aimed.
WOR. And 'tis no little reason bids us speed,
To save our heads by raising of a head;[78]

---

[68]**Berkeley Castle,** site of an encounter between the future king Henry IV, backed by the Percys, and the supporters of his predecessor, Richard II. Shakespeare treats the episode in *Richard II,* II.iii.
[69]**candy deal,** deal of candy, i.e., hypocritical.
[70]Await.   [71]Means.   [72]Forces, armies.   [73]**bears hard,** takes hardly.
[74]**in estimation,** as a guess.   [75]Considered.   [76]Continuously.
[77]**let'st slip,** let loose the greyhound.   [78]Armed force.

For, bear ourselves as even as we can,[79]
The King will always think him in our debt,
And think we think ourselves unsatisfied,
Till he hath found a time to pay us home.
And see already how he doth begin
To make us strangers to his looks of love. 290
HOT. He does, he does. We'll be revenged on him.
WOR. Cousin, farewell. No further go in this
Than I by letters shall direct your course.
When time is ripe, which will be suddenly,
I'll steal to Glendower and Lord Mortimer,
Where you and Douglas and our powers at once,
As I will fashion[80] it, shall happily meet,
To bear our fortunes in our own strong arms,
Which now we hold at much uncertainty.
NORTH. Farewell, good Brother. We shall thrive, I trust. 300
HOT. Uncle, adieu. Oh, let the hours be short
Till fields and blows and groans applaud our sport!

[*Exeunt.*]

ACT II

SCENE I. Rochester. An innyard.

[*Enter a* CARRIER *with a lantern in his hand.*]
1. CAR. Heigh-ho! An it be not four by the day, I'll be hanged. Charles's
Wain[1] is over the new chimney, and yet our horse not packed.[2] What,
ostler!
OSTLER. [*Within*] Anon, anon.
1. CAR. I prithee, Tom, beat[3] Cut's[4] saddle, put a few flocks[5] in the
point.[6] Poor jade,[7] is wrung[8] in the withers[9] out of all cess.[10]
[*Enter another* CARRIER.]
2. CAR. Peas and beans are as dank here as a dog, and that is the next
way to give poor jades the bots.[11] This house is turned upside down
since Robin Ostler died.
1. CAR. Poor fellow, never joyed since the price of oats rose. It was 10
the death of him.
2. CAR. I think this be the most villainous house in all London road
for fleas. I am stung like a tench.[12]

---

[79]**bear . . . can,** however discreetly we may behave.   [80]Contrive.
[1]**Charles's Wain,** Charles's Wagon, the constellation of the Great Bear, called also the Great
Dipper.
[2]**horse . . . packed,** Carriers at this time used pack horses for transport.
[3]I.e., to make the padding more even.
[4]Name of a horse with a docked tail.
[5]Tufts of wool.   [6]Pommel.   [7]Horse in poor condition.   [8]Galled.
[9]Point of the shoulder.   [10]**out . . . cess,** excessively.   [11]Worms.
[12]The tench and the loach (fresh-water fish) are sometimes infested with a form of louse.

1. CAR. Like a tench! By the mass, there is ne'er a king Christen[13] could be better bit than I have been since the first cock.
2. CAR. Why, they will allow us ne'er a jordan,[14] and then we leak in your chimney, and your chamber lye[15] breeds fleas like a loach.
1. CAR. What, ostler! Come away and be hanged! Come away.
2. CAR. I have a gammon of bacon[16] and two razes[17] of ginger, to be delivered as far as Charing Cross.
1. CAR. God's body! The turkeys in my pannier[18] are quite starved. What, ostler! A plague on thee! Hast thou never an eye in thy head? Canst not hear? An 'twere not as good deed as drink to break the pate on thee, I am a very villain. Come, and be hanged! Hast no faith in thee?

[*Enter* GADSHILL.]

GADS. Good morrow, carriers. What's o'clock?
1. CAR. I think it be two o'clock.
GADS. I prithee lend me thy lantern, to see my gelding in the stable.
1. CAR. Nay, by God, soft,[19] I know a trick worth two of that, i' faith.
GADS. I pray thee, lend me thine.
2. CAR. Aye, when? Canst tell?[20] Lend me thy lantern, quoth he? Marry, I'll see thee hanged first.
GADS. Sirrah carrier, what time do you mean to come to London?
2. CAR. Time enough to go to bed with a candle, I warrant thee. Come, Neighbor Mugs, we'll call up the gentlemen. They will along with company, for they have great charge.[21]   [*Exeunt* CARRIERS.]
GADS. What ho! Chamberlain![22]
CHAM. [*Within*] At hand, quoth pickpurse.
GADS. That's even as fair as—at hand, quoth the chamberlain; for thou variest no more from picking of purses than giving direction doth from laboring. Thou layest the plot[23] how.

[*Enter* CHAMBERLAIN.]

CHAM. Good morrow, Master Gadshill. It holds current that I told you yesternight. There's a franklin[24] in the wild[25] of Kent hath brought three hundred marks[26] with him in gold. I heard him tell it to one of his company last night at supper—a kind of auditor, one that hath abundance of charge too, God knows what. They are up already, and call for eggs and butter. They will away presently.
GADS. Sirrah, if they meet not with Saint Nicholas' clerks,[27] I'll give thee this neck.

---

[13] Christian.   [14] Chamber pot.
[15] **chamber lye,** urine. Elizabethan sanitary arrangements and domestic habits were crude.
[16] **gammon of bacon,** cured ham.
[17] Roots.   [18] Basket.   [19] Go easy.
[20] **canst tell,** i.e., "Do you think I'm a fool?"   [21] **great charge,** much money.
[22] Man in charge of the bedrooms at an inn.
[23] **layest . . . plot,** It was a common complaint that the chamberlains of inns were in league with highwaymen.
[24] Rich farmer.
[25] Weald; the hilly district in Kent and adjoining counties.
[26] 13s 4d (two-thirds of a pound).
[27] **Saint Nicholas' clerks,** thieves, Saint Nicholas being their patron saint.

CHAM. No, I'll none of it. I pray thee, keep that for the hangman, for 50
I know thou worshipest Saint Nicholas as truly as a man of falsehood may.

GADS. What talkest thou to me of the hangman? If I hang, I'll make
a fat pair of gallows; for if I hang, old Sir John hangs with me, and
thou knowest he is no starveling. Tut! There are other Trojans[28]
that thou dreamest not of, the which for sport sake are content to
do the profession some grace; that would, if matters should be looked
into, for their own credit sake, make all whole. I am joined with
no foot landrakers,[29] no long-staff sixpenny strikers,[30] none of these
mad mustachio purple-hued maltworms;[31] but with nobility and tran- 60
quility, burgomasters and great oneyers,[32] such as can hold in,[33]
such as will strike sooner than speak, and speak sooner than drink,
and drink sooner than pray. And yet, 'zounds, I lie; for they pray
continually to their saint, the commonwealth; or rather, not pray
to her, but prey on her, for they ride up and down on her and make
her their boots.[34]

CHAM. What, the commonwealth their boots? Will she hold out water
in foul way?

GADS. She will, she will—justice hath liquored[35] her. We steal as in
a castle, cocksure. We have the receipt[36] of fern seed,[37] we walk 70
invisible.

CHAM. Nay, by my faith, I think you are more beholding to the night
than to fern seed for your walking invisible.

GADS. Give me thy hand. Thou shalt have a share in our purchase,[38]
as I am a true man.

CHAM. Nay, rather let me have it, as you are a false thief.

GADS. Go to. "Homo" is a common name to all men. Bid the ostler bring
my.gelding out of the stable. Farewell, you muddy[39] knave.

[*Exeunt.*]

SCENE II. The highway, near Gadshill.

[*Enter* PRINCE HENRY *and* POINS.]

POINS. Come, shelter, shelter. I have removed Falstaff's horse, and he
frets like a gummed velvet.[1]

PRINCE. Stand close.

[*Enter* FALSTAFF.]

---

[28] Good lads.

[29] **foot landrakers,** roving foot pads; i.e., thieves so poor that they go on foot.

[30] **long-staff . . . strikers,** robbers who use a long staff and will hold a man up for a pittance.

[31] **mustachio . . . maltworms,** red-faced tipplers with great mustaches.

[32] Ones.   [33] **hold in,** keep their mouths shut.

[34] Booty. The chamberlain caps his remark with a pun on leather boots.

[35] Greased.   [36] Directions for using, recipe.

[37] **fern seed,** The seed of the fern is so small that it was said to be invisible, and if found
on Saint John's Day, to confer invisibility on the finder.

[38] In thieves' language, plunder.   [39] Muddleheaded.

[1] **gummed velvet,** Cheap velvet (as well as taffeta) was sometimes treated with gum to give
it stiffening, but it frayed sooner.

FAL. Poins! Poins, and be hanged! Poins!

PRINCE. Peace, ye fat-kidneyed rascal! What a brawling dost thou keep!

FAL. Where's Poins, Hal?

PRINCE. He is walked up to the top of the hill. I'll go seek him.

FAL. I am accursed to rob in that thief's company. The rascal hath removed my horse, and tied him I know not where. If I travel but four foot by the squier[2] further afoot, I shall break my wind. Well, I doubt not but to die a fair death for all this, if I 'scape hanging for killing that rogue. I have forsworn[3] his company hourly any time this two and twenty years, and yet I am bewitched with the rogue's company. If the rascal have not given me medicines[4] to make me love him, I'll be hanged; it could not be else, I have drunk medicines. Poins! Hal! A plague upon you both! Bardolph! Peto! I'll starve ere I'll rob a foot further. An 'twere not as good a deed as drink, to turn true man and to leave these rogues, I am the veriest varlet[5] that ever chewed with a tooth. Eight yards of uneven ground is threescore and ten miles afoot with me, and the stony-hearted villains know it well enough. A plague upon it when thieves cannot be true one to another! [*They whistle.*] Whew! A plague upon you all! Give me my horse, you rogues, give me my horse, and be hanged! 10 20

PRINCE. Peace, ye fat-guts! Lie down, lay thine ear close to the ground and list if thou canst hear the tread of travelers.

FAL. Have you any levers to lift me up again, being down? 'Sblood, I'll not bear mine own flesh so far afoot again for all the coin in thy father's exchequer. What a plague mean ye to colt[6] me thus?

PRINCE. Thou liest. Thou art not colted, thou art uncolted. 30

FAL. I prithee, good Prince Hal, help me to my horse, good king's son.

PRINCE. Out, ye rogue! Shall I be your ostler?

FAL. Go hang thyself in thine own heir-apparent garters! If I be ta'en, I'll peach for this. An I have not ballads made on you all and sung to filthy tunes, let a cup of sack be my poison. When a jest is so forward, and afoot too! I hate it.

[*Enter* GADSHILL, BARDOLPH *and* PETO *with him.*]

GADS. Stand.

FAL. So I do, against my will.

POINS. Oh, 'tis our setter.[7] I know his voice. Bardolph, what news?

BARD. Case[8] ye, case ye, on with your vizards. There's money of the King's coming down the hill, 'tis going to the King's exchequer. 40

FAL. You lie, ye rogue, 'tis going to the King's tavern.

GADS. There's enough to make us all.

FAL. To be hanged.

PRINCE. Sirs, you four shall front them in the narrow lane, Ned Poins and I will walk lower. If they 'scape from your encounter, then they light on us.

PETO. How many be there of them?

GADS. Some eight or ten.

---

[2]Square, rule. [3]Sworn off. [4]Love potions. [5]Knave. [6]Trick.
[7]The accomplice who brings the victim in. [8]Mask.

FAL. 'Zounds, will they not rob us? 50
PRINCE. What, a coward, Sir John Paunch?
FAL. Indeed I am not John of Gaunt, your grandfather, but yet no coward, Hal.
PRINCE. Well, we leave that to the proof.
POINS. Sirrah Jack, thy horse stands behind the hedge. When thou needest him, there thou shalt find him. Farewell, and stand fast.
FAL. Now cannot I strike him, if I should be hanged.
PRINCE. Ned, where are our disguises?
POINS. Here, hard by. Stand close.

[Exeunt PRINCE *and* POINS.]

FAL. Now, my masters, happy man be his dole,[9] say I. Every man to 60
his business.

[Enter the TRAVELERS.]

1. TRAV. Come, neighbor. The boy shall lead our horses down the hill.
We'll walk afoot awhile, and ease our legs.
THIEVES. Stand!
TRAVS. Jesus bless us!
FAL. Strike, down with them, cut the villains' throats! Ah, whoreson[10]
caterpillars,[11] bacon-fed knaves! They hate us youth. Down with them,
fleece them.
TRAVS. Oh, we are undone, both we and ours forever!
FAL. Hang ye, gorbellied[12] knaves, are ye undone? No, ye fat chuffs,[13] 70
I would your store were here![14] On, bacons,[15] on! What, ye knaves!
Young men must live. You are grand jurors,[16] are ye? We'll jure ye,
'faith.

[Here they rob them and bind them. Exeunt.]
[Re-enter PRINCE HENRY *and* POINS *disguised.]*

PRINCE. The thieves have bound the true men. Now could thou and
I rob the thieves and go merrily to London, it would be argument[17]
for a week, laughter for a month, and a good jest forever.
POINS. Stand close. I hear them coming.

[Enter the THIEVES *again.]*

FAL. Come, my masters, let us share, and then to horse before day.
An the Prince and Poins be not two arrant[18] cowards, there's no
equity stirring.[19] There's no more valor in that Poins than in a wild 80
duck.
PRINCE. Your money!
POINS. Villains! *[As they are sharing, the* PRINCE *and* POINS *set upon them;
they all run away; and* FALSTAFF, *after a blow or two, runs away too, leaving the booty behind them.]*
PRINCE. Got with much ease. Now merrily to horse.
The thieves are all scattered and possessed with fear
So strongly that they dare not meet each other.

---

[9]**happy . . . dole,** i.e., here's luck; lit., may the lucky man have his reward.
[10]Bastard.   [11]Parasites.   [12]Big-bellied.   [13]Mean misers.
[14]**were here,** i.e., in your bellies.   [15]Fat pigs.
[16]**grand jurors,** i.e., men of highest respectability.
[17]Matter for talk.   [18]Complete.
[19]**no . . . stirring,** no sound judgment in the world.

Each takes his fellow for an officer.
Away, good Ned. Falstaff sweats to death,
And lards the lean earth as he walks along.
Were't not for laughing, I should pity him.   90
POINS. How the rogue roared!   [*Exeunt.*]

SCENE III. Warkworth Castle.

[*Enter* HOTSPUR *alone, reading a letter.*]
HOT. "But, for mine own part, my lord, I could be well contented to
be there, in respect of the love I bear your house." He could be
contented. Why is he not, then? In respect of the love he bears our
house. He shows in this he loves his own barn better than he loves
our house. Let me see some more. "The purpose you undertake
is dangerous"—why, that's certain. 'Tis dangerous to take a cold,
to sleep, to drink; but I tell you, my lord fool, out of this nettle
danger we pluck this flower safety. "The purpose you undertake
is dangerous; the friends you have named uncertain; the time itself
unsorted;[1] and your whole plot too light for the counterpoise of   10
so great an opposition." Say you so, say you so? I say unto you again,
you are a shallow cowardly hind,[2] and you lie. What a lackbrain is
this! By the Lord, our plot is a good plot as ever was laid, our friends
true and constant—a good plot, good friends, and full of expectation. An excellent plot, very good friends. What a frosty-spirited
rogue is this! Why, my Lord of York[3] commends the plot and the
general course of the action. 'Zounds, an I were now by this rascal, I could brain him with his lady's fan. Is there not my father,
my uncle, and myself? Lord Edmund Mortimer, my Lord of York,
and Owen Glendower? Is there not besides the Douglas? Have I   20
not all their letters to meet me in arms by the ninth of the next
month? And are they not some of them set forward already? What
a pagan rascal is this, an infidel! Ha! You shall see now in very sincerity of fear and cold heart, will he to the King, and lay open all
our proceedings. Oh, I could divide myself, and go to buffets,[4] for
moving[5] such a dish of skim milk with so honorable an action! Hang
him! Let him tell the King. We are prepared. I will set forward tonight.
[*Enter* LADY PERCY.] How now, Kate! I must leave you within these
two hours.
LADY P. O my good lord, why are you thus alone?   30
For what offense have I this fortnight been
A banished woman from my Harry's bed?
Tell me, sweet lord, what is't that takes from thee
Thy stomach,[6] pleasure, and thy golden sleep?
Why dost thou bend thine eyes upon the earth,
And start so often when thou sit'st alone?

[1] Ill-chosen.   [2] Female deer, the essence of timidity.
[3] **Lord of York,** Richard Scroop, Archbishop of York.
[4] **go to buffets,** come to blows.   [5] Trying to move.   [6] Appetite.

Why hast thou lost the fresh blood in thy cheeks,
And given my treasures[7] and my rights of thee
To thick-eyed[8] musing and cursed melancholy?
In thy faint slumbers I by thee have watched,   40
And heard thee murmur tales of iron wars,
Speak terms of manage[9] to thy bounding steed,
Cry "Courage! To the field!" And thou hast talked
Of sallies and retires,[10] of trenches, tents,
Of palisadoes,[11] frontiers,[12] parapets,
Of basilisks, of cannon, culverin,[13]
Of prisoners' ransom, and of soldiers slain,
And all the currents[14] of a heady[15] fight.
Thy spirit within thee hath been so at war
And thus hath so bestirred thee in thy sleep   50
That beads of sweat have stood upon thy brow,
Like bubbles in a late-disturbèd stream.
And in thy face strange motions have appeared,
Such as we see when men restrain their breath
On some great sudden hest.[16] Oh, what portènts are these?
Some heavy business hath my lord in hand,
And I must know it, else he loves me not.

HOT. What ho! [*Enter* SERVANT.] Is Gilliams with the packet gone?
SERV. He is, my lord, an hour ago.
HOT. Hath Butler brought those horses from the sheriff?   60
SERV. One horse, my lord, he brought even now.
HOT. What horse? A roan, a crop-ear,[17] is it not?
SERV. It is, my lord.
HOT.   That roan shall be my throne.
Well, I will back him straight. Oh, Esperance![18]
Bid Butler lead him forth into the park.

                                     [*Exit* SERVANT.]

LADY P. But hear you, my lord.
HOT. What say'st thou, my lady?
LADY P. What is it carries you away?
HOT. Why, my horse, my love, my horse.
LADY P. Out, you mad-headed ape!   70
A weasel hath not such a deal of spleen[19]
As you are tossed with. In faith,
I'll know your business, Harry, that I will.

---

[7] I.e., that ought to be mine.
[8] **thick-eyed,** dull-sighted, because he sees nothing.
[9] Horsemanship.   [10] **sallies . . . retires,** raids and retreats.
[11] Defensive protection of pointed stakes.   [12] Barricades.
[13] **basilisks . . . culverin,** the heavier pieces of artillery. The basilisk was of 5-inch caliber and fired a shot of 15.5 lbs., the cannon of 8-inch caliber with a 60-lb. shot, the culverin of 5.5 inch caliber with a 17-lb. shot. Shakespeare is thinking of Elizabethan ordnance rather than the cannon used in 1400.
[14] Courses, rapid movement.   [15] Fierce.   [16] Command, action.
[17] **crop-ear,** with short ears.   [18] Hope—the battle cry of the Percys.
[19] Anger, passion.

I fear my brother Mortimer doth stir
About his title, and hath sent for you
To line[20] his enterprise. But if you go——
HOT. So far afoot, I shall be weary, love.
LADY P. Come, come, you paraquito,[21] answer me
   Directly unto this question that I ask.
   In faith, I'll break thy little finger, Harry,   80
   An if thou wilt not tell me all things true.
HOT. Away, Away, you trifler! Love! I love thee not,
   I care not for thee, Kate. This is no world
   To play with mammets[22] and to tilt with lips.[23]
   We must have bloody noses and cracked crowns,
   And pass them current[24] too. God's me, my horse!
   What say'st thou, Kate? What wouldst thou have with me?
LADY P. Do you not love me? Do you not, indeed?
   Well, do not, then, for since you love me not,
   I will not love myself. Do you not love me?   90
   Nay, tell me if you speak in jest or no.
HOT. Come, wilt thou see me ride?
   And when I am o' horseback, I will swear
   I love thee infinitely. But hark you, Kate,
   I must not have you henceforth question me
   Whither I go, nor reason whereabout.
   Whither I must, I must. And, to conclude,
   This evening must I leave you, gentle Kate.
   I know you wise, but yet no farther wise
   Than Harry Percy's wife. Constant you are,   100
   But yet a woman. And for secrecy,
   No lady closer, for I well believe
   Thou wilt not utter what thou dost not know,
   And so far will I trust thee, gentle Kate.
LADY P. How! So far?
HOT. Not an inch further. But hark you, Kate,
   Whither I go, thither shall you go too;
   Today will I set forth, tomorrow you.
   Will this content you, Kate?
LADY P.   It must of force.   [*Exeunt.*]

SCENE IV. The Boar's Head Tavern in Eastcheap.

[*Enter the* PRINCE, *and* POINS.]
PRINCE. Ned, prithee come out of that fat[1] room, and lend me thy
   hand to laugh a little.
POINS. Where hast been, Hal?

---

[20] Strengthen.   [21] Parrot.   [22] Dolls.   [23] **tilt . . . lips,** kiss.
[24] With a pun on *"cracked crowns"*; i.e., broken heads, and crown pieces, cracked and so not
current.
[1] Stuffy.

PRINCE. With three or four loggerheads[2] amongst three or fourscore hogsheads.[3] I have sounded the very base string of humility.[4] Sirrah, I am sworn brother to a leash[5] of drawers, and can call them all by their Christen names, as Tom, Dick, and Francis. They take it already upon their salvation that though I be but Prince of Wales, yet I am the king of courtesy; and tell me flatly I am no proud Jack, like Falstaff, but a Corinthian,[6] a lad of mettle, a good boy, by the Lord, so they call me, and when I am King of England, I shall command all the good lads in Eastcheap. They call drinking deep, dyeing scarlet, and when you breathe in your watering,[7] they cry "hem!"[8] and bid you play it off.[9] To conclude, I am so good a proficient in one quarter of an hour that I can drink with any tinker in his own language during my life. I tell thee, Ned, thou hast lost much honor that thou wert not with me in this action. But, sweet Ned—to sweeten which name of Ned, I give thee this pennyworth of sugar, clapped even now into my hand by an underskinker,[10] one that never spake other English in his life than "Eight shillings and sixpence," and "You are welcome," with this shrill addition, "Anon,[11] anon, sir! Score[12] a pint of bastard[13] in the Half-Moon,"[14] or so. But, Ned, to drive away the time till Falstaff come, I prithee do thou stand in some by-room while I question my puny[15] drawer to what end he gave me the sugar. And do thou never leave calling "Francis," that his tale to me may be nothing but "Anon." Step aside, and I'll show thee a precedent.[16]

POINS. Francis!

PRINCE. Thou art perfect.

POINS. Francis! [*Exit* POINS.]

[*Enter* FRANCIS.]

FRAN. Anon, anon, sir. Look down into the Pomgarnet,[17] Ralph.

PRINCE. Come hither, Francis.

FRAN. My lord?

PRINCE. How long hast thou to serve, Francis?[18]

FRAN. Forsooth, five years, and as much as to——

POINS. [*Within*] Francis!

FRAN. Anon, anon, sir.

PRINCE. Five year! By'r Lady, a long lease for the clinking of pewter. But, Francis, darest thou be so valiant as to play the coward with thy indenture[19] and show it a fair pair of heels and run from it?

---

[2]Blockheads.   [3]Casks.
[4]**sounded . . . humility,** i.e., have sunk to the lowest depth.
[5]Set of three, properly used of a *leash* of greyhounds.
[6]A gay lad.   [7]Drinking.
[8]**cry "hem",** one of those exclamations made by topers, like "Here's how."
[9]**play it off,** get it down.   [10]Assistant bartender.
[11]At once or by and by, the drawer's cry, "Coming, sir."
[12]Chalk up, the method of recording a debt for drink still used in English public houses.
[13]A sweet white wine.
[14]**Half-Moon:** Each room in an inn or a tavern had its own name.
[15]Freshman.   [16]Specimen.   [17]Pomegranate—another room.
[18]**How . . . Francis,** i.e., how many years of your apprenticeship still remain. As Francis has only served two of his seven years, he is sixteen.
[19]Agreement of apprenticeship.

FRAN. Oh, Lord, sir, I'll be sworn upon all the books in England I could   40
find in my heart.[20]
POINS. [*Within*] Francis!
FRAN. Anon, sir.
PRINCE. How old art thou, Francis?
FRAN. Let me see—about Michaelmas next I shall be——
POINS. [*Within*] Francis!
FRAN. Anon, sir. Pray stay a little, my lord.
PRINCE. Nay, but hark you, Francis. For the sugar thou gavest me, 'twas
a pennyworth, was't not?
FRAN. Oh, Lord, I would it had been two!   50
PRINCE. I will give thee for it a thousand pound. Ask me when thou
wilt, and thou shalt have it.
POINS. [*Within*] Francis!
FRAN. Anon, anon.
PRINCE. Anon, Francis? No, Francis, but tomorrow, Francis; or, Francis,
o' Thursday; or indeed, Francis, when thou wilt. But Francis!
FRAN. My lord?
PRINCE. Wilt thou rob this leathern-jerkin, crystal-button, not-pated,
agate-ring, puke-stocking, caddis-garter, smooth-tongue, Spanish-
pouch——[21]   60
FRAN. Oh, Lord, sir, who do you mean?
PRINCE. Why, then, your brown bastard is your only drink, for look you,
Francis, your white canvas doublet will sully. In Barbary,[22] sir, it can-
not come to so much.
FRAN. What, sir?
POINS. [*Within*] Francis!
PRINCE. Away, you rogue! Dost thou not hear them call? [*Here they both
call him; the* DRAWER *stands amazed, not knowing which way to go.*]
                    [*Enter* VINTNER.]
VINT. What, standest thou still, and hearest such a calling? Look to
the guests within. [*Exit* FRANCIS.] My lord, old Sir John, with half-
a-dozen more, are at the door. Shall I let them in?   70
PRINCE. Let them alone awhile, and then open the door. [*Exit* VINTNER.]
Poins!
                    [*Re-enter* POINS.]
POINS. Anon, anon, sir.
PRINCE. Sirrah, Falstaff and the rest of the thieves are at the door. Shall
we be merry?
POINS. As merry as crickets, my lad. But hark ye, what cunning match[23]
have you made with this jest of the drawer? Come, what's the issue?[24]

---

[20]**could . . . heart,** i.e., very willing.
[21]**leathern-jerkin . . . Spanish-pouch,** This list gives the outward characteristics of a prosperous innkeeper: leather coat (*jerkin*) with crystal buttons, close-cropped head (*not-pated*),
large ring, gray (*puke*) stockings, worsted (*caddis*) garters, a *smooth tongue,* and a *pouch* of *Spanish*
leather.
[22]**In Barbary,** in North Africa—but the Prince's words have passed beyond location.
[23]**what . . . match,** what is the game.   [24]Result.

PRINCE. I am now of all humors[25] that have showed themselves humors since the old days of Goodman Adam to the pupilage[26] of this present twelve o'clock at midnight.   80
[*Re-enter* FRANCIS.] What's o'clock, Francis?
FRAN. Anon, anon, sir.   [*Exit.*]
PRINCE. That ever this fellow should have fewer words than a parrot, and yet the son of a woman! His industry is upstairs and downstairs, his eloquence the parcel[27] of a reckoning. I am not yet of Percy's mind, the Hotspur of the North, he that kills me some six or seven dozen of Scots at a breakfast, washes his hands, and says to his wife, "Fie upon this quiet life! I want work." "O my sweet Harry," says she, "how many hast thou killed today?" "Give my roan horse a drench,"[28] says he, and answers "Some fourteen" an hour after—   90
"a trifle, a trifle." I prithee call in Falstaff. I'll play Percy, and that damned brawn[29] shall play Dame Mortimer his wife. "Rivo!"[30] says the drunkard. Call in ribs, call in tallow.
                    [*Enter* FALSTAFF, GADSHILL, BARDOLPH, *and* PETO;
                    FRANCIS *following with wine.*]
POINS. Welcome, Jack. Where hast thou been?
FAL. A plague of all cowards, I say, and a vengeance too! Marry, and amen! Give me a cup of sack, boy. Ere I lead this life long, I'll sew netherstocks[31] and mend them and foot them too. A plague of all cowards! Give me a cup of sack, rogue. Is there no virtue extant?[32]
                                                      [*He drinks.*]
PRINCE. Didst thou never see Titan[33] kiss a dish of butter? Pitiful-hearted Titan, that melted[34] at the sweet tale of the sun's! If thou didst,   100
then behold that compound.
FAL. You rogue, here's lime[35] in this sack too. There is nothing but roguery to be found in villainous man. Yet a coward is worse than a cup of sack with lime in it. A villainous coward! Go thy ways, old Jack, die when thou wilt. If manhood, good manhood, be not forgot upon the face of the earth, then am I a shotten[36] herring. There live not three good men unhanged in England, and one of them is fat, and grows old. God help the while![37] A bad world, I say. I would I were a weaver, I could sing psalms[38] or anything. A plague of all cowards, I say still.   110
PRINCE. How now, woolsack! What mutter you?

---

[25]**of . . . humors,** i.e., will match my mood with any man's.
[26]Boyhood.   [27]Items.   [28]Purge.   [29]Fat pig.
[30]Another drinker's exclamation.
[31]Stockings, at this time cut out of material and sewed, not knitted.
[32]**virtue extant,** manhood in existence.
[33]The sun.   [34]**that melted,** i.e., the butter.
[35]Used to adulterate wine by giving it a better color and taste.
[36]Without its roe.   [37]**God . . . while,** God help these times.
[38]**weaver . . . psalms,** Weavers were often psalm-singing Puritans.

FAL. A king's son! If I do not beat thee out of thy kingdom with a dagger of lath,[39] and drive all thy subjects afore thee like a flock of wild geese, I'll never wear hair on my face more. You Prince of Wales!

PRINCE. Why, you whoreson round man, what's the matter?

FAL. Are not you a coward? Answer me to that. And Poins there?

POINS. 'Zounds, ye fat paunch, an ye call me coward, by the Lord, I'll stab thee.

FAL. I call thee coward! I'll see thee damned ere I call thee coward. But I would give a thousand pound I could run as fast as thou canst. You are straight enough in the shoulders, you care not who sees your back. Call you that backing of your friends? A plague upon such backing! Give me them that will face me. Give me a cup of sack. I am a rogue if I drunk today. 120

PRINCE. O villain! Thy lips are scarce wiped since thou drunkest last.

FAL. All's one for that. [*He drinks.*] A plague of all cowards, still say I.

PRINCE. What's the matter?

FAL. What's the matter! There be four of us here have ta'en a thousand pound this day morning. 130

PRINCE. Where is it, Jack? Where is it?

FAL. Where is it! Taken from us it is—a hundred upon poor four of us.

PRINCE. What, a hundred, man?

FAL. I am a rogue if I were not at half-sword[40] with a dozen of them two hours together. I have 'scaped by miracle. I am eight times thrust through the doublet,[41] four through the hose;[42] my buckler[43] cut through and through; my sword hacked like a handsaw—*ecce signum!*[44] I never dealt[45] better since I was a man. All would not do. A plague of all cowards! Let them speak. If they speak more or less than truth, they are villains and the sons of darkness. 140

PRINCE. Speak, sirs, how was it?

GADS. We four set upon some dozen——

FAL. Sixteen at least, my lord.

GADS. And bound them.

PETO. No, no, they were not bound.

FAL. You rogue, they were bound, every man of them, or I am a Jew else, an Ebrew[46] Jew.

GADS. As we were sharing, some six or seven fresh men set upon us——

FAL. And unbound the rest, and then come in the other. 150

PRINCE. What, fought you with them all?

FAL. All! I know not what you call all, but if I fought not with fifty of them, I am a bunch of radish. If there were not two or three and fifty upon poor old Jack, then am I no two-legged creature.

PRINCE. Pray God you have not murdered some of them.

---

[39] **dagger of lath,** wooden dagger.
[40] **at half-sword,** within half a sword's length. A cautious fighter kept at greater distance.
[41] Coat. [42] Breeches. [43] Small shield.
[44] **ecce signum,** behold the sign. [45] Fought. [46] Hebrew.

FAL. Nay, that's past praying for. I have peppered two of them—two I am sure I have paid,[47] two rogues in buckram suits. I tell thee what, Hal, if I tell thee a lie, spit in my face, call me horse.[48] Thou knowest my old ward.[49] Here I lay, and thus I bore my point. Four rogues in buckram let drive at me—— 160

PRINCE. What, four? Thou saidst but two even now.

FAL. Four, Hal, I told thee four.

POINS. Aye, aye, he said four.

FAL. These four came all afront, and mainly[50] thrust at me. I made me no more ado, but took all their seven points in my target, thus.

PRINCE. Seven! Why, there were but four even now.

FAL. In buckram?

POINS. Aye, four, in buckram suits.

FAL. Seven, by these hilts,[51] or I am a villain else.

PRINCE. Prithee let him alone. We shall have more anon. 170

FAL. Dost thou hear me, Hal?

PRINCE. Aye, and mark thee too, Jack.

FAL. Do so, for it is worth the listening to. These nine in buckram that I told thee of——

PRINCE. So, two more already.

FAL. Their points being broken——

POINS. Down fell their hose.[52]

FAL. Began to give me ground. But I followed me close, came in foot and hand, and with a thought seven of the eleven I paid.

PRINCE. Oh, monstrous! Eleven buckram men grown out of two! 180

FAL. But, as the Devil would have it, three misbegotten knaves in Kendal green[53] came at my back and let drive at me; for it was so dark, Hal, that thou couldst not see thy hand.

PRINCE. These lies are like their father that begets them—gross as a mountain, open, palpable. Why, thou clay-brained guts, thou knotty-pated[54] fool, thou whoreson, obscene, greasy tallow catch——[55]

FAL. What, art thou mad? Art thou mad? Is not the truth the truth?

PRINCE. Why, how couldst thou know these men in Kendal green when it was so dark thou couldst not see thy hand? Come, tell us your reason. What sayest thou to this? 190

POINS. Come, your reason, Jack, your reason.

---

[47] Paid home, done for. [48] Like the ass, the horse was regarded as stupid.

[49] Stance, position of guard. Here Falstaff reenacts his heroic exploit.

[50] Violently. [51] Sword hilt.

[52] **Their . . . hose,** Poins puns on the other meaning of *points,* laces tying the hose to the doublet.

[53] **Kendal green,** cloth made (originally at Kendal in Westmoreland) of the poorest quality wool, and used by woodmen and servants.

[54] **knotty-pated,** blockhead.

[55] **tallow catch,** the word is variously emended and interpreted. Johnson suggested "keech"—a lump of fat prepared by the butcher for the candlemaker. A *tallow catch* would naturally be a "thing for catching tallow"; i.e., the rim on the candlestick which, when piled up with the drippings of wax, is no bad image for Falstaff.

FAL. What, upon compulsion? 'Zounds, an I were at the strappado, or all the racks[56] in the world, I would not tell you on compulsion. Give you a reason on compulsion! If reasons were as plentiful as blackberries, I would give no man a reason upon compulsion, I.

PRINCE. I'll be no longer guilty of this sin—this sanguine[57] coward, this bed-presser, this horseback-breaker, this huge hill of flesh——

FAL. 'Sblood, you starveling,[58] you elf skin,[59] you dried neat's tongue,[60] you bull's pizzle,[61] you stock-fish![62] Oh, for breath to utter what is like thee! You tailor's yard, you sheath, you bow case, you vile standing tuck——[63]   200

PRINCE. Well, breathe a while, and then to it again, and when thou hast tired thyself in base comparisons, hear me speak but this.

POINS. Mark, Jack.

PRINCE. We two saw you four set on four and bound them, and were masters of their wealth. Mark now, how a plain tale shall put you down. Then did we two set on you four; and, with a word, outfaced you from your prize, and have it, yea, and can show it you here in the house. And, Falstaff, you carried your guts away as nimbly, with as quick dexterity, and roared for mercy, and still run and roared,   210 as ever I heard bull calf. What a slave art thou, to hack thy sword as thou hast done, and then say it was in fight! What trick, what device, what starting hole,[64] canst thou now find out to hide thee from this open and apparent shame?

POINS. Come, let's hear, Jack. What trick hast thou now?

FAL. By the Lord, I knew ye as well as he that made ye. Why, hear you, my masters. Was it for me to kill the heir apparent? Should I turn upon the true Prince? Why, thou knowest I am as valiant as Hercules. But beware instinct, the lion will not touch the true prince.[65] Instinct is a great matter, I was now a coward on instinct. I shall think the   220 better of myself and thee during my life, I for a valiant lion, and thou for a true Prince. But, by the Lord, lads, I am glad you have the money. Hostess, clap to the doors. Watch tonight, pray tomorrow. Gallants, lads, boys, hearts of gold, all the titles of good fellowship come to you! What, shall we be merry? Shall we have a play extempore?

PRINCE. Content, and the argument[66] shall be thy running away.

FAL. Ah, no more of that, Hal, an thou lovest me!

[*Enter* HOSTESS.]

HOSTESS. O Jesu, my lord the Prince!

---

[56]**strappado . . . racks,** forms of torture.

[57]One suffering from an excess of the sanguine humor, which produced a ruddy complexion.

[58]**you starveling,** Falstaff, being thoroughly roused, retorts with a string of images expressing the thinness of the Prince.

[59]**elf skin,** sometimes emended to eelskin, but probably it meant snakeskin.

[60]**neat's tongue,** ox tongue.

[61]**bull's pizzle,** A bull's penis was often dried and used as a whip.

[62]Dried codfish.   [63]**standing tuck,** a rapier stuck in the ground.

[64]**starting hole,** a hole into which a rabbit bolts for safety.

[65]**lion . . . prince,** This was very generally believed.

[66]Plot.

PRINCE. How now, my lady the hostess! What sayest thou to me? 230

HOSTESS. Marry, my lord, there is a nobleman of the Court at door would speak with you. He says he comes from your father.

PRINCE. Give him as much as will make him a royal man,[67] and send him back again to my mother.

FAL. What manner of man is he?

HOSTESS. An old man.

FAL. What doth gravity out of his bed at midnight? Shall I give him his answer?

PRINCE. Prithee do, Jack.

FAL. Faith, and I'll send him packing. [*Exit.*] 240

PRINCE. Now, sirs. By'r Lady, you fought fair; so did you, Peto; so did you, Bardolph. You are lions too, you ran away upon instinct, you will not touch the true prince—no, fie!

BARD. Faith, I ran when I saw others run.

PRINCE. Faith, tell me now in earnest, how came Falstaff's sword so hacked?

PETO. Why, he hacked it with his dagger, and said he would swear truth out of England but he would make you believe it was done in fight, and persuaded us to do the like.

BARD. Yes, and to tickle our noses with speargrass to make them bleed, 250 and then to beslubber[68] our garments with it and swear it was the blood of true men. I did that I did not this seven year before, I blushed to hear his monstrous devices.

PRINCE. O villain, thou stolest a cup of sack eighteen years ago, and wert taken with the manner,[69] and ever since thou hast blushed extempore. Thou hadst fire and sword on thy side, and yet thou rannest away. What instinct hadst thou for it?

BARD. My lord, do you see these meteors? Do you behold these exhalations?[70,71]

PRINCE. I do. 260

BARD. What think you they portend?

PRINCE. Hot livers and cold purses.

BARD. Choler,[72] my lord, if rightly taken.

PRINCE. No, if rightly taken, halter.

[*Re-enter* FALSTAFF.] Here comes lean Jack, here comes barebone. How now, my sweet creature of bombast![73] How long is't ago, Jack, since thou sawest thine own knee?

FAL. My own knee! When I was about thy years, Hal, I was not an eagle's talon in the waist, I could have crept into any alderman's thumb

---

[67] **as . . . man,** i.e., 3 shillings, 4 pence, which in the old British coinage was the difference between a *royal* (10 shillings) and a noble (6 shillings, 8 pence). It is a sign of Prince Hal's low behavior that he should make such jokes about a nobleman of the Court.

[68] Smear. [69] **with . . . manner,** in the act.

[70] Meteors.

[71] **meteors . . . exhalations,** Bardolph indicates his own fiery face which, he claims, is proof that he is a man of wrath.

[72] Anger; pronounced in the same way as "collar," and so puns on the two words are common.

[73] Cotton batting, used to stuff garments to make them appear baggy.

ring.[74] A plague of sighing and grief! It blows a man up like a blad- 270
der. There's villainous news abroad. Here was Sir John Bracy from
your father; you must to the Court in the morning. That same mad
fellow of the North, Percy, and he of Wales, that gave Amamon[75]
the bastinado[76] and made Lucifer cuckold,[77] and swore the Devil
his true liegeman[78] upon the cross of a Welsh hook—what a plague
call you him?

POINS. O, Glendower.[79]

FAL. Owen, Owen, the same. And his son-in-law Mortimer, and old
   Northumberland, and that sprightly Scot of Scots, Douglas, that runs
   o' horseback up a hill perpendicular—— 280

PRINCE. He that rides at high speed and with his pistol kills a sparrow
   flying.

FAL. You have hit it.

PRINCE. So did he never the sparrow.

FAL. Well, that rascal hath good mettle[80] in him. He will not run.

PRINCE. Why, what a rascal art thou then, to praise him so for running!

FAL. O' horseback, ye cuckoo, but afoot he will not budge a foot.

PRINCE. Yes, Jack, upon instinct.

FAL. I grant ye, upon instinct. Well, he is there too, and one Mordake,
   and a thousand bluecaps[81] more. Worcester is stolen away tonight; 290
   thy father's beard is turned white with the news. You may buy land
   now as cheap as stinking mackerel.

PRINCE. Why, then, it is like, if there come a hot June and this civil
   buffeting hold, we shall buy maidenheads as they buy hobnails, by
   the hundreds.

FAL. By the mass, lad, thou sayest true; it is like we shall have good
   trading that way. But tell me, Hal, art not thou horrible afeard?
   Thou being heir apparent, could the world pick thee out three such
   enemies again as that fiend Douglas, that spirit Percy, and that devil
   Glendower? Art thou not horribly afraid? Doth not thy blood thrill 300
   at it?

PRINCE. Not a whit, i' faith. I lack some of thy instinct.

FAL. Well, thou wilt be horribly chid tomorrow when thou comest to
   thy father. If thou love me, practice an answer.

PRINCE. Do thou stand for[82] my father, and examine me upon the particulars of my life.

FAL. Shall I? Content. This chair shall be my state,[83] this dagger my
   scepter, and this cushion my crown.

PRINCE. Thy state is taken for a joined stool,[84] thy golden scepter for
   a leaden[85] dagger, and thy precious rich crown for a pitiful bald 310
   crown!

---

[74] **thumb ring,** large seal ring, especially common on the thumbs of businessmen.
[75] The name of a fiend.   [76] Thrashing.
[77] A man deceived by his wife.   [78] Subject.
[79] **O, Glendower,** probably Shakespeare wrote *O* in his manuscript as abbreviation for Owen,
which the printer mistook for an exclamation.
[80] Matter, material.   [81] Scots.   [82] Represent.   [83] Throne.
[84] **joined stool,** wooden stool made by a joiner.   [85] Blunt.

FAL. Well, an the fire of grace be not quite out of thee, now shalt thou
    be moved. Give me a cup of sack to make my eyes look red, that it
    may be thought I have wept; for I must speak in passion, and I will
    do it in King Cambyses'[86] vein.
PRINCE. Well, here is my leg.[87]
FAL. And here is my speech. Stand aside, nobility.
HOSTESS. Oh Jesu, this is excellent sport, i' faith!
FAL. Weep[88] not, sweet queen, for trickling tears are vain.
HOSTESS. Oh, the father,[89] how he holds his countenance![90]   320
FAL. For God's sake, lords, convey my tristful[91] queen,
    For tears do stop the floodgates of her eyes.
HOSTESS. Oh Jesu, he doth it as like one of these harlotry players[92]
    as ever I see!
FAL. Peace, good pint pot; peace, good ticklebrain. Harry, I do not
    only marvel where thou spendest thy time, but also how thou art
    accompanied.[93] For though the camomile,[94] the more it is trod-
    den on, the faster it grows, yet youth, the more it is wasted, the
    sooner it wears. That thou art my son, I have partly thy mother's
    word, partly my own opinion, but chiefly a villainous trick[95] of thine   330
    eye, and a foolish hanging of thy nether[96] lip, that doth warrant[97]
    me. If then thou be son to me, here lies the point; why, being son
    to me, art thou so pointed at? Shall the blessed sun of heaven prove
    a micher[98] and eat blackberries? A question not to be asked. Shall
    the son of England prove a thief and take purses? A question to
    be asked. There is a thing, Harry, which thou hast often heard of,
    and it is known to many in our land by the name of pitch. This
    pitch, as ancient writers do report, doth defile; so doth the com-
    pany thou keepest. For, Harry, now I do not speak to thee in drink
    but in tears, not in pleasure but in passion, not in words only, but   340
    in woes also. And yet there is a virtuous man whom I have often
    noted in thy company, but I know not his name.
PRINCE. What manner of man, an it like your Majesty?
FAL. A goodly portly[99] man, i' faith, and a corpulent; of a cheerful
    look, a pleasing eye, and a most noble carriage. And, as I think,
    his age some fifty, or, by'r Lady, inclining to threescore. And now
    I remember me, his name is Falstaff. If that man should be lewdly
    given, he deceiveth me, for, Harry, I see virtue in his looks. If then

[86] **King Cambyses',** the chief character in an early drama which still survives; it is a marvelous specimen of ridiculous rant.
[87] **my leg,** my curtsy.
[88] **Weep . . . eyes,** Falstaff begins in the artificial style of earlier plays, of the kind still being
acted by a rival company at the Rose theater.
[89] **Oh . . . father,** by God the Father.
[90] **holds . . . countenance,** keeps a straight face.
[91] Sad, a poetical word.
[92] **harlotry players,** worthless players. As the Admiral's Men were the only other company
then playing in London, the parody of their heavy style was obvious.
[93] **how . . . accompanied,** what company you keep.
[94] **For . . . camomile,** The whole of this passage is a parody of the elaborate style of Lyly's
Euphues. The *camomile* is a small creeping aromatic plant with a flower like a daisy.
[95] Habit.   [96] Lower.   [97] Guarantee.   [98] A truant.   [99] Dignified.

the tree may be known by the fruit, as the fruit by the tree, then, peremptorily[1] I speak it, there is virtue in that Falstaff. Him keep with, the rest banish. And tell me now, thou naughty varlet, tell me, where hast thou been this month? 350

PRINCE. Dost thou speak like a king? Do thou stand for me, and I'll play my father.

FAL. Depose me? If thou dost it half so gravely, so majestically, both in word and matter, hang me up by the heels for a rabbit-sucker[2] or a poulter's[3] hare.

PRINCE. Well, here I am set.

FAL. And here I stand. Judge, my masters.

PRINCE. Now, Harry, whence come you? 360

FAL. My noble lord, from Eastcheap.

PRINCE. The complaints I hear of thee are grievous.

FAL. 'Sblood, my lord, they are false. Nay, I'll tickle ye[4] for a young Prince, i' faith.

PRINCE. Swearest thou, ungracious[5] boy? Henceforth ne'er look on me. Thou art violently carried away from grace. There is a devil haunts thee in the likeness of an old fat man, a tun[6] of man is thy companion. Why dost thou converse with that trunk of humors,[7] that bolting hutch[8] of beastliness, that swollen parcel of dropsies, that huge bombard[9] of sack, that stuffed cloak bag[10] of guts, that roasted Manningtree[11] ox with the pudding in his belly, that reverend vice,[12] that gray iniquity, that father ruffian, that vanity in years? Wherein is he good, but to taste sack and drink it? Wherein neat and cleanly,[13] but to carve a capon and eat it? Wherein cunning,[14] but in craft? Wherein crafty,[15] but in villainy? Wherein villainous, but in all things? Wherein worthy, but in nothing? 370

FAL. I would your Grace would take me with you.[16] Whom means your Grace?

PRINCE. That villainous abominable misleader of youth, Falstaff, that old white-bearded Satan. 380

FAL. My lord, the man I know.

PRINCE. I know thou dost.

FAL. But to say I know more harm in him than in myself were to say more than I know. That he is old, the more the pity, his white hairs do witness it; but that he is, saving your reverence, a whoremaster, that I utterly deny. If sack and sugar be a fault, God help the wicked! If to be old and merry be a sin, then many an old host that I know is damned. If to be fat be to be hated, then Pharaoh's lean kine are to be loved. No, my good lord. Banish Peto, banish Bardolph,

---

[1] Conclusively.   [2] **rabbit-sucker,** young rabbit.   [3] Poulterer.
[4] **I'll . . . ye,** I'll show you how to do it.   [5] Graceless.   [6] Large barrel.
[7] **trunk of humors,** great collection of diseases.
[8] **bolting hutch,** round bin into which flour was sifted.
[9] Large leather jug.
[10] **cloak bag,** for carrying cloaks, "kit bag."
[11] A town in Essex where there was a famous cattle market. At fairs it was often a custom to roast an ox whole.
[12] The Devil in the old Morality Plays.   [13] Clever.
[14] Skillful.   [15] A craftsman.   [16] **take . . . you,** explain yourself.

banish Poins. But for sweet Jack Falstaff, kind Jack Falstaff, true Jack 390
Falstaff, valiant Jack Falstaff, and therefore more valiant, being, as
he is, old Jack Falstaff, banish not him thy Harry's company, banish not him thy Harry's company. Banish plump Jack, and banish
all the world.

PRINCE. I do, I will. [*A knocking heard. Exeunt* HOSTESS, FRANCIS, *and*
BARDOLPH.]

[*Re-enter* BARDOLPH, *running.*]

BARD. Oh, my lord, my lord! The sheriff with a most monstrous watch[17]
is at the door.

FAL. Out, ye rogue! Play out the play. I have much to say in the behalf
of that Falstaff.

[*Re-enter the* HOSTESS.]

HOSTESS. Oh Jesu, my lord, my lord!— 400

PRINCE. Heigh, heigh! The Devil rides upon a fiddlestick.[18] What's the
matter?

HOSTESS. The sheriff and all the watch are at the door. They are come
to search the house. Shall I let them in?

FAL. Dost thou hear, Hal? Never call a true piece of gold a counterfeit. Thou art essentially mad, without seeming so.

PRINCE. And thou a natural coward, without instinct.

FAL. I deny your major,[19] If you will deny the sheriff, so; if not, let him
enter. If I become not a cart[20] as well as another man, a plague
on my bringing up! I hope I shall as soon be strangled with a hal- 410
ter as another.

PRINCE. Go, hide thee behind the arras,[21] the rest walk up above. Now,
my masters, for a true face and good conscience.

FAL. Both which I have had; but their date is out,[22] and therefore I'll
hide me.

PRINCE. Call in the sheriff.

[*Exeunt all except the* PRINCE *and* PETO.]
[*Enter the* SHERIFF *and the* CARRIER.]

Now, Master Sheriff, what is your will with me?

SHER. First, pardon me, my lord. A hue and cry[23]
Hath followed certain men unto this house.

PRINCE. What men? 420

SHER. One of them is well known, my gracious lord,
A gross fat man.

CAR.   As fat as butter.

PRINCE. The man, I do assure you, is not here,
For I myself at this time have employed him.
And, sheriff, I will engage my word to thee

---

[17] Body of police officers.
[18] **Devil . . . fiddlestick,** what's all the fuss about?
[19] **I . . . major,** I deny your major premise, i.e., the main argument on which your conclusion is based; a phrase used in academic arguments. Falstaff puns also on "mayor." "Major"
and "mayor" were pronounced alike.
[20] Which will take him to execution.   [21] Curtain.
[22] **date is out,** time is expired.
[23] **hue . . . cry,** an alarm setting the entire populace on the track of a criminal.

That I will, by tomorrow dinnertime,
Send him to answer thee, or any man,
For anything he shall be charged withal.
And so let me entreat you leave the house.
SHER. I will, my lord. There are two gentlemen   430
Have in this robbery lost three hundred marks.
PRINCE. It may be so, If he have robbed these men,
He shall be answerable. And so farewell.
SHER. Good night, my noble lord.
PRINCE. I think it is good morrow, it is not?
SHER. Indeed, my lord, I think it be two o'clock.
                            [*Exeunt* SHERIFF *and* CARRIER.]
PRINCE. This oily rascal is known as well as Paul's.[24] Go, call him forth.
PETO. Falstaff!—Fast asleep behind the arras, and snorting like a horse.
PRINCE. Hark how hard he fetches breath. Search his pockets. [*He
   searcheth his pockets, and findeth certain papers.*] What hast thou found?   440
PETO. Nothing but papers, my lord.
PRINCE. Let's see what they be. Read them.
PETO. [*Reads.*]
   "Item, A capon, ... 2s.2d.
   Item, Sauce, ... 4d.
   Item, Sack, two gallons, ... 5s.8d.
   Item, Anchovies and sack after supper, ... 2s.6d.
   Item, Bread, ... ob.[25]"
PRINCE. Oh, monstrous! But one halfpennyworth of bread to this intol-
   erable deal of sack! What there is else, keep close, we'll read it at
   more advantage. There let him sleep till day. I'll to the Court in   450
   the morning. We must all to the wars, and thy place shall be honorable. I'll procure this fat rogue a charge of foot,[26] and I know
   his death will be a march of twelvescore.[27] The money shall be paid
   back again with advantage.[28] Be with me betimes in the morning.
   And so good morrow, Peto.
PETO. Good morrow, good my lord.   [*Exeunt.*]

ACT III

SCENE I. Bangor. The ARCHDEACON'*s house.*

[*Enter* HOTSPUR, WORCESTER, MORTIMER, *and* GLENDOWER.]
MORT. These promises are fair, the parties sure,
   And our induction[1] full of prosperous hope.
HOT. Lord Mortimer, and Cousin Glendower,
   Will you sit down?

---

[24] The old St. Paul's Cathedral in London, a towering Gothic edifice.
[25] One half-penny.
[26] **charge of foot,** commission as commander of a company of infantry.
[27] I.e., paces. The pace was 60 inches.   [28] Interest.
[1] Opening.

And Uncle Worcester. A plague upon it!
I have forgot the map.
GLEND.   No, here it is.
   Sit, Cousin Percy. Sit, good Cousin Hotspur,
   For by that name as oft as Lancaster
   Doth speak of you, his cheek looks pale, and with
   A rising sigh he wisheth you in Heaven.   10
HOT. And you in Hell, as oft as he hears Owen
   Glendower spoke of.
GLEND. I cannot blame him. At my nativity[2]
   The front[3] of heaven was full of fiery shapes,
   Or burning cressets;[4] and at my birth
   The frame and huge foundation of the earth
   Shaked like a coward.
HOT. Why, so it would have done at the same season if your mother's
   cat had but kittened, though yourself had never been born.
GLEND. I say the earth did shake when I was born.   20
HOT. And I say the earth was not of my mind
   If you suppose as fearing you it shook.
GLEND. The heavens were all on fire, the earth did tremble.
HOT. Oh, then the earth shook to see the heavens on fire,
   And not in fear of your nativity.
   Diseasèd nature oftentimes breaks forth
   In strange eruptions; oft the teeming[5] earth
   Is with a kind of colic pinched and vexed
   By the imprisoning of unruly wind
   Within her womb; which, for enlargement striving,   30
   Shakes the old beldam[6] earth and topples down
   Steeples and moss-grown towers. At your birth
   Our grandam earth, having this distemperature,[7]
   In passion[8] shook.
GLEND.   Cousin,[9] of many men
   I do not bear these crossing.[10] Give me leave
   To tell you once again that at my birth
   The front of heaven was full of fiery shapes,
   The goats ran from the mountains, and the herds
   Were strangely clamorous to the frighted fields.
   These signs have marked me extraordinary,   40
   And all the courses of my life do show
   I am not in the roll of common men.
   Where is he living, clipped in[11] with the sea
   That chides[12] the banks of England, Scotland, Wales,

---

[2] Moment of birth.   [3] Forehead.   [4] **burning cressets,** stars blazing like beacons.
[5] Pregnant. This theory of earthquakes—that they were caused by the expulsion of wind from within the earth—was generally believed.
[6] Grandmother.   [7] Disorder.   [8] Agitation.
[9] Kinsman; used of any relation. Hotspur is remotely related to Glendower through Lady Percy, whose brother Edmund was married to Glendower's daughter.
[10] Opposition.   [11] **clipped in,** encircled.   [12] Roars against.

Which calls me pupil,[13] or hath read to me?[14]
And bring him out that is but woman's son
Can trace[15] me in the tedious ways of art,[16]
And hold me pace[17] in deep experiments.

HOT. I think there's no man speaks better Welsh. I'll to dinner.

MORT. Peace, Cousin Percy, you will make him mad. 50

GLEND. I can call spirits from the vasty deep.

HOT. Why, so can I, or so can any man;
But will they come when you do call for them?

GLEND. Why, I can teach you, Cousin, to command
The Devil.

HOT. And I can teach thee, Coz, to shame the Devil[18]
By telling truth. Tell truth, and shame the Devil.
If thou have power to raise him, bring him hither,
And I'll be sworn I have power to shame him hence.
Oh, while you live, tell truth, and shame the Devil! 60

MORT. Come, come, no more of this unprofitable chat.

GLEND. Three times hath Henry Bolingbroke made head[19]
Against my power. Thrice from the banks of Wye
And sandy-bottomed Severn have I sent him
Bootless[20] home and weather-beaten back.

HOT. Home without boots, and in foul weather too!
How 'scapes he agues,[21] in the Devil's name?

GLEND. Come, here's the map. Shall we divide our right
According to our threefold order[22] ta'en?

MORT. The Archdeacon hath divided it 70
Into three limits[23] very equally.
England, from Trent and Severn hitherto,
By south and east is to my part assigned.
All westward, Wales beyond the Severn shore,
And all the fertile land within that bound,
To Owen Glendower. And, dear Coz, to you
The remnant northward, lying off from Trent.
And our indentures tripartite[24] are drawn;
Which being sealed interchangeably,[25]
A business that this night may execute, 80
Tomorrow, Cousin Percy, you and I
And my good Lord of Worcester will set forth
To meet your father and the Scottish power,
As is appointed us, at Shrewsbury.
My father[26] Glendower is not ready yet,

---

[13]**calls me pupil,** i.e., is my master.   [14]**hath . . . me,** has been my tutor.
[15]Follow.   [16]**tedious . . . art,** difficult course of magic.
[17]**hold me pace,** keep pace with me.
[18]**shame . . . Devil,** because he is the father of lies.
[19]**made head,** advanced.   [20]Profitless.   [21]Fever.
[22]**our . . . order,** agreement made between us three.   [23]Divisions.
[24]**indentures tripartite,** documents drawn up in triplicate.
[25]**sealed interchangeably,** each party sealing each copy of the agreement.
[26]I.e., father-in-law.

Nor shall we need his help these fourteen days.
Within that space you may have drawn together
Your tenants, friends, and neighboring gentlemen.
GLEND. A shorter time shall send me to you, lords.
And in my conduct shall your ladies come, 90
From whom you now must steal and take no leave;
For there will be a world of water shed
Upon the parting of your wives and you.
HOT. Methinks my moiety,[27] north from Burton here,
In quantity equals not one of yours.
See how this river comes me cranking in,[28]
And cuts me from the best of all my land
A huge half-moon, a monstrous cantle[29] out.
I'll have the current in this place dammed up,
And here the smug[30] and silver Trent shall run 100
In a new channel, fair and evenly.
It shall not wind with such a deep indent,[31]
To rob me of so rich a bottom[32] here.
GLEND. Not wind? It shall, it must. You see it doth.
MORT. Yea, but
Mark how he bears his course, and runs me up
With like advantage on the other side,
Gelding the oppos'd continent[33] as much
As on the other side it takes from you.
WOR. Yea, but a little charge[34] will trench him here 110
And on this north side win this cape of land,
And then he runs straight and even.
HOT. I'll have it so. A little charge will do it.
GLEND. I'll not have it altered.
HOT.   Will not you?
GLEND. No, nor you shall not.
HOT.   Who shall say me nay?
GLEND. Why, that will I.
HOT. Let me not understand you, then. Speak it in Welsh.
GLEND. I can speak English, lord, as well as you;
For I was trained up in the English Court,
Where, being but young, I fram'd to the harp 120
Many an English ditty lovely well,
And gave the tongue a helpful ornament,[35]
A virtue that was never seen in you.
HOT. Marry,[36]
And I am glad of it with all my heart.
I had rather be a kitten and cry mew
Than one of these same meter balladmongers.[37]

---

[27] Share.   [28] **me . . . in,** comes winding into my part.
[29] Slice.   [30] Smooth.   [31] Indentation.   [32] Valley.
[33] **opposed continent,** opposite bank.   [34] Cost.
[35] **helpful ornament,** i.e., musical accompaniment.
[36] Mary, by the virgin.
[37] **meter balladmongers,** doggerel rhymesters.

I had rather hear a brazen canstick turned,[38]
Or a dry wheel grate on the axletree;
And that would set my teeth nothing on edge,   130
Nothing so much as mincing poetry.
'Tis like the forced gait of a shuffling nag.
GLEND. Come, you shall have Trent turned.
HOT. I do not care. I'll give thrice so much land
    To any well-deserving friend.
    But in the way of bargain, mark ye me,
    I'll cavil on the ninth part of a hair.
    Are the indentures drawn? Shall we be gone?
GLEND. The moons shines fair, you may away by night.
    I'll haste the writer, and withal   140
    Break with[39] your wives of your departure hence.
    I am afraid my daughter will run mad,
    So much she doteth on her Mortimer.   [*Exit.*]
MORT. Fie, Cousin Percy! How you cross my father!
HOT. I cannot choose. Sometime he angers me
    With telling me of the moldwarp[40] and the ant,
    Of the dreamer Merlin[41] and his prophecies,
    And[42] of a dragon and a finless fish,
    A clip-winged griffin[43] and a molten raven,
    A couching lion and a ramping[44] cat,   150
    And such a deal of skimble-skamble[45] stuff
    As puts me from my faith. I tell you what—
    He held me last night at least nine hours
    In reckoning up the several[46] devils' names
    That were his lackeys. I cried "hum," and "well, go to,"
    But marked him not a word. Oh, he is as tedious
    As a tired horse, a railing wife,
    Worse than a smoky house. I had rather live
    With cheese and garlic in a windmill, far,
    Than feed on cates[47] and have him talk to me   160
    In any summerhouse[48] in Christendom.
MORT. In faith, he is a worthy gentleman,
    Exceedingly well read, and profited
    In strange concealments;[49] valiant as a lion,
    And wondrous affable, and as bountiful
    As mines of India. Shall I tell you, Cousin?
    He holds your temper[50] in a high respect,
    And curbs himself even of his natural scope

---

[38]**brazen . . . turned,** brass candlestick being cut out on the lathe.
[39]**Break with,** break the news to.   [40]Mole.
[41] The old magician at King Arthur's Court. As the Welsh were (more or less) descendants of Arthur's British countrymen, Merlin's prophecies would appeal to Glendower.
[42]**And . . . cat,** These beasts occur as symbols in ancient prophecies.
[43]Fabulous beast—half lion, half eagle.   [44]On its hind legs.
[45]**skimble-skamble,** rambling.   [46]Separate, different.
[47]Delicacies.   [48]Country house.
[49]**profited . . . concealments,** expert in strange mysteries.   [50]Character.

When you come 'cross his humor; faith, he does.
I warrant you that man is not alive 170
Might so have tempted him as you have done
Without the taste of danger and reproof.
But do not use it oft, let me entreat you.
WOR. In faith, my lord, you are too willful-blame;[51]
And since your coming hither have done enough
To put him quite beside his patience.
You must needs learn, lord, to amend this fault.
Though sometimes it show greatness, courage, blood—
And that's the dearest[52] grace it renders you—
Yet oftentimes it doth present harsh rage, 180
Defect of manners, want of government,[53]
Pride, haughtiness, opinion,[54] and disdain;
The least of which haunting a nobleman
Loseth men's hearts, and leaves behind a stain
Upon the beauty of all parts besides,
Beguiling[55] them of commendation.
HOT. Well, I am schooled. Good manners be your speed![56]
Here come our wives, and let us take our leave.
              [*Re-enter* GLENDOWER *with the* LADIES.]
MORT. This is the deadly spite[57] that angers me—
My wife can speak no English, I no Welsh. 190
GLEND. My daughter weeps. She will not part with you.
She'll be a soldier too, she'll to the wars.
MORT. Good Father, tell her that she and my aunt Percy
Shall follow in your conduct speedily.
            [GLENDOWER *speaks to* LADY MORTIMER *in Welsh,*
                      and she answers him in the same.]
GLEND. She is desperate here, a peevish self-willed harlotry,[58] one that
no persuasion can do good upon.
                [LADY MORTIMER *speaks in Welsh.*]
MORT. I understand thy looks. That pretty Welsh[59]
Which thou pour'st down from these swelling heavens[60]
I am too perfect in; and but for shame,
In such a parley[61] should I answer thee. 200
              [LADY MORTIMER *speaks again in Welsh.*]
I understand thy kisses and thou mine,
And that's a feeling disputation.[62]
But I will never be a truant, love,
Till I have learned thy language; for thy tongue
Makes Welsh as sweet as ditties highly penned,
Sung by a fair queen in a summer's bower,
With ravishing division,[63] to her lute.

---

[51]**willful-blame,** to be blamed for willfulness.   [52]Most valuable.
[53]Self-control.   [54]Conceit.   [55]Causing to lose.
[56]**Good . . . speed,** may good manners bring you luck.
[57]Vexation.   [58]Silly girl.   [59]**pretty Welsh,** i.e., tears.
[60]**swelling heavens,** i.e., eyes full of tears.   [61]Manner of speech.
[62]**feeling disputation,** conversation by touch.   [63]Melody.

GLEND. Nay, if you melt, then will she run mad.
                              [LADY MORTIMER *speaks again in Welsh.*]
MORT. Oh, I am ignorance itself in this!
GLEND. She bids you on the wanton[64] rushes[65] lay you down   210
     And rest your gentle head upon her lap,
     And she will sing the song that pleaseth you
     And on your eyelids crown the god of sleep,
     Charming your blood with pleasing heaviness,[66]
     Making such difference 'twixt wake and sleep
     As is the difference betwixt day and night
     The hour before the heavenly-harnessed team[67]
     Begins his golden progress in the east.
MORT. With all my heart I'll sit and hear her sing.
     By that time will our book,[68] I think, be drawn.   220
GLEND. Do so,
     And those musicians that shall play to you
     Hang in the air a thousand leagues from hence,
     And straight they shall be here. Sit, and attend.
HOT. Come, Kate, thou art perfect in lying down. Come quick, quick,
     that I may lay my head in thy lap.
LADY P. Go, ye giddy goose.   [*The music plays.*]
HOT. Now I perceive the Devil understands Welsh,
     And 'tis no marvel he is so humorous.[69]
     By'r Lady, he is a good musician.   230
LADY P. Then should you be nothing but musical, for you are altogether
     governed by humors. Lie still, ye thief, and hear the lady sing in
     Welsh.
HOT. I had rather hear Lady, my brach,[70] howl in Irish.
LADY P. Wouldst thou have thy head broken?
HOT. No.
LADY P. Then be still.
HOT. Neither—'tis a woman's fault.
LADY P. Now God help thee!
HOT. To the Welsh lady's bed.   240
LADY P. What's that?
HOT. Peace! She sings.
                    [*Here* LADY MORTIMER *sings a Welsh song.*]
     Come Kate, I'll have your song too.
LADY P. Not mine, in good sooth.[71]
HOT. Not yours, in good sooth! Heart! You swear like a comfit-maker's[72]
     wife. "Not you, in good sooth," and "as true as I live," and "as God
     shall mend me," and "as sure as day,"
     And givest such sarcenet surety for thy oaths[73]

---

[64] Luxuriant.   [65] Used to cover floors.   [66] Drowsiness.
[67] I.e., the horses of the sun.   [68] Agreement.
[69] Full of whims.   [70] Bitch.
[71] Truth.   [72] Candymaker.
[73] **sarcenet . . . oaths,** You swear by such soft things. **sarcenet,** fine silk.

As if thou never walk'st further than Finsbury.[74]
Swear me, Kate, like a lady as thou art,   250
A good mouth-filling oath, and leave "in sooth"
And such protest of pepper gingerbread[75]
To velvet guards[76] and Sunday citizens.[77]
Come, sing.
LADY P.   I will not sing.
HOT. 'Tis the next way to turn tailor,[78] or be red-breast teacher.[79] An
the indentures be drawn, I'll away within these two hours, and so
come in when ye will.   [*Exit.*]
GLEND. Come, come, Lord Mortimer, you are as slow
As hot Lord Percy is on fire to go.
By this our book is drawn. We'll but seal,   260
And then to horse immediately.
MORT.   With all my heart.   [*Exeunt.*]

SCENE II. *London. The palace.*

[*Enter the* KING, PRINCE OF WALES, *and others.*]
KING. Lords, give us leave. The Prince of Wales and I
Must have some private conference. But be near at hand,
For we shall presently have need of you.
                                        [*Exeunt* LORDS.]
I know not whether God will have it so,
For some displeasing service I have done,
That, in his secret doom,[1] out of my blood[2]
He'll breed revengement and a scourge for me;
But thou dost in thy passages of life
Make me believe that thou art only marked
For the hot vengeance and the rod of Heaven   10
To punish my mistreadings. Tell me else,
Could such inordinate[3] and low desires,
Such poor, such bare, such lewd,[4] such mean attempts,
Such barren pleasures, rude society,
As thou art matched withal and grafted to,
Accompany the greatness of thy blood,
And hold their level with thy princely heart?
PRINCE. So please your Majesty, I would I could

---

[74] Finsbury fields, where London citizens took their Sunday-afternoon walk.
[75] **pepper gingerbread,** a very mild form of heat.
[76] **velvet guards,** literally bands of velvet used to ornament a gown (and still used on the gown of a Ph.D.).
[77] **Sunday citizens,** citizens in their Sunday best.
[78] **turn tailor,** Tailors (before the invention of the sewing machine) used to sing at their work as they sat cross-legged.
[79] **redbreast teacher,** one who teaches caged birds to sing. The little English robin was highly valued as a songbird.
[1] Judgment.   [2] **out . . . blood,** through one of my children.
[3] Intemperate.   [4] Low.

Quit[5] all offenses with as clear excuse
As well as I am doubtless I can purge   20
Myself of many I am charged withal.
Yet such extenuation let me beg
As, in reproof[6] of many tales devised,
Which oft the ear of greatness needs must hear,
By smiling pickthanks[7] and base newsmongers,
I may for some things true wherein my youth
Hath faulty wandered and irregular
Find pardon on my true submission.
KING. God pardon thee! Yet let me wonder, Harry,
At thy affections, which do hold a wing   30
Quite from the flight[8] of all thy ancestors.
Thy place in Council thou hast rudely lost,
Which by thy younger brother is supplied,
And art almost an alien to the hearts
Of all the Court and princes of my blood.
The hope and expectation of thy time[9]
Is ruined, and the soul of every man
Prophetically doth forethink thy fall.
Had I so lavish of my presence been,
So common-hackneyed[10] in the eyes of men,   40
So stale and cheap to vulgar company,
Opinion,[11] that did help me to the crown,
Had still kept loyal to possession,[12]
And left me in reputeless banishment,
A fellow of no mark nor likelihood.
By being seldom seen, I could not stir
But like a comet I was wondered at,
That men would tell their children "This is he."
Others would say, "Where, which is Bolingbroke?"
And then I stole all courtesy from Heaven,   50
And dressed myself in such humility
That I did pluck allegiance from men's hearts,
Loud shouts and salutations from their mouths,
Even in the presence of the crownèd King.
Thus did I keep my person fresh and new,
My presence, like a robe pontifical,[13]
Ne'er seen but wondered at. And so my state,
Seldom but sumptuous, showed like a feast,
And won by rareness such solemnity.
The skipping[14] King, he ambled up and down,   60

---

[5]Acquit myself of.   [6]Rebuttal.
[7]Men who curry favor by telling tales.
[8]**affections . . . flight,** desires, natural inclinations . . . fly a different course.
[9]Lifetime.
[10]**common-hackneyed,** at every man's call. A hackney is a hired horse.
[11]Popular opinion.
[12]**loyal to possession,** loyal to the possessor, i.e., Richard II.
[13]**robe pontifical,** a bishop's robe.   [14]Frivolous.

With shallow jesters and rash bavin[15] wits,
Soon kindled and soon burnt; carded[16] his state,
Mingled his royalty with capering fools,
Had his great name profanèd with their scorns,
And gave his countenance, against his name,[17]
To laugh at gibing[18] boys and stand the push[19]
Of every beardless vain comparative,[20]
Grew a companion to the common streets,
Enfeoffed[21] himself to popularity,[22]
That, being daily swallowed by men's eyes,   70
They surfeited with honey and began
To loathe the taste of sweetness, whereof a little
More than a little is by much too much.
So when he had occasion to be seen,
He was but as the cuckoo is in June,[23]
Heard, not regarded; seen, but with such eyes
As, sick and blunted with community,[24]
Afford no extraordinary gaze,
Such as is bent on sunlike majesty
When it shines seldom in admiring eyes;   80
But rather drowsed and hung their eyelids down,
Slept in his face[25] and rendered such aspèct[26]
As cloudy[27] men use to their adversaries,
Being with his presence glutted, gorged, and full.
And in that very line,[28] Harry, standest thou;
For thou hast lost thy princely privilege
With vile participation.[29] Not an eye
But is aweary of thy common sight,
Save mine, which hath desired to see thee more,
Which now doth that I would not have it do—   90
Make blind itself with foolish tenderness.
PRINCE. I shall hereafter, my thrice gracious lord,
    Be more myself.
KING.   For all the world
    As thou art to this hour[30] was Richard then
    When I from France set foot at Ravenspurgh,
    And even as I was then is Percy now.
    Now, by my scepter and my soul to boot,

---

[15] Brushwood for kindling, worthless and easily broken.
[16] Adulterated.   [17] **against . . . name,** contrary to the interest of his reputation.
[18] Mocking.   [19] **stand . . . push,** endure the sallies of.
[20] **beardless . . . comparative,** every boy who cared to make jokes at his expense.
[21] Conveyed, made himself over to.   [22] Low company, common people.
[23] **cuckoo . . . June,** The cry of the cuckoo, a bird regarded as foolish and disorderly, was a novelty in early spring but a familiar, monotonous irritant by June.
[24] That which is common.
[25] **in . . . face,** in his presence—a gross insult.
[26] Look.   [27] Sullen.   [28] Class.
[29] **vile participation,** mixing with low company.
[30] **to . . . hour,** up to now.

He hath more worthy interest to the state
Than thou the shadow of succession;[31]
For of no right,[32] nor color like to right,   100
He doth fill fields with harness[33] in the realm,
Turns head against the lion's armèd jaws,
And being no more in debt to years than thou,[34]
Leads ancient lords and reverend bishops on
To bloody battles and to bruising arms.
What never-dying honor hath he got
Against renownèd Douglas!—whose high deeds,
Whose hot incursions[35] and great name in arms
Holds from all soldiers chief majority
And military title capital[36]   110
Through all the kingdoms that acknowledge Christ.
Thrice hath this Hotspur, Mars in swathling[37] clothes,
This infant warrior, in his enterprises
Discomfited great Douglas, ta'en him once,
Enlarged him, and made a friend of him,
To fill the mouth of deep defiance up[38]
And shake the peace and safety of our throne.
And what say you to this? Percy, Northumberland,
The Archbishop's Grace of York, Douglas, Mortimer,
Capitulate[39] against us and are up.   120
But wherefore do I tell these news to thee?
Why, Harry, do I tell thee of my foes,
Which art my near'st and dearest enemy?
Thou that art like enough through vassal[40] fear,
Base inclination, and the start of spleen[41]
To fight against me under Percy's pay,
To dog his heels and curtsy at his frowns,
To show how much thou art degenerate,
PRINCE. Do not think so, you shall not find it so.
And God forgive them that so much have swayed   130
Your Majesty's good thoughts away from me!
I will redeem all this on Percy's head,
And in the closing of some glorious day
Be bold to tell you that I am your son;
When I will wear a garment all of blood,
And stain my favors[42] in a bloody mask
Which, washed away, shall scour my shame with it.
And that shall be the day, whene'er it lights,

---

[31] **shadow of succession,** shadowy right of succession.
[32] **of no right,** with no right.   [33] Armor.
[34] **no . . . thou,** see I, i., note 31.   [35] Raids.
[36] **Holds . . . capital,** keeps from all other soldiers the claim to be considered the greatest.
[37] Swaddling.
[38] **To . . . up,** so that defiance may speak with a loud mouth.
[39] Make agreement.   [40] Slavish.
[41] **start of spleen,** impulse of bad temper.
[42] Features, face.

That this same child of honor and renown,
This gallant Hotspur, this all-praisèd knight,   140
And your unthought-of Harry chance to meet.
For every honor sitting on his helm,
Would they were multitudes, and on my head
My shames redoubled! For the time will come
That I shall make this Northern youth exchange
His glorious deeds for my indignities.
Percy is but my factor,[43] good my lord,
To engross[44] up glorious deeds on my behalf.
And I will call him to so strict account
That he shall render every glory up—   150
Yea, even the slightest worship[45] of his time—
Or I will tear the reckoning from his heart.
This, in the name of God, I promise here.
The which if He be pleased I shall perform,
I do beseech your majesty may salve[46]
The long-grown wounds of my intemperance.
If not, the end of life cancels all bands,[47]
And I will die a hundred thousand deaths
Ere break the smallest parcel[48] of this vow.
KING. A hundred thousand rebels die in this.   160
   Thou shalt have charge and sovereign trust herein. [*Enter* BLUNT.]
   How now, good Blunt? Thy looks are full of speed.
BLUNT. So hath the business that I come to speak of.
   Lord Mortimer of Scotland hath sent word
   That Douglas and the English rebels met
   The eleventh of this month at Shrewsbury.
   A mighty and a fearful head[49] they are,
   If promises be kept on every hand,
   As ever offered foul play in a state.
KING. The Earl of Westmoreland set forth today,   170
   With him my son, Lord John of Lancaster;
   For this advértisement is five days old.
   On Wednesday next, Harry, you shall set forward,
   On Thursday we ourselves will march. Our meeting
   Is Bridgenorth. And, Harry, you shall march
   Through Gloucestershire, by which account,
   Our business valued,[50] some twelve days hence
   Our general forces at Bridgenorth shall meet.
   Our hands are full of business. Let's away.
   Advantage feeds him fat[51] while men delay.   180

                                        [*Exeunt.*]

---

[43]Agent, buyer.   [44]Buy up wholesale.   [45]Honor.   [46]Heal.
[47]Bonds, debts.   [48]Portion.   [49]Force.
[50]**Our . . . valued,** considering how much we have to do.
[51]**Advantage . . . fat,** advantage makes the most of his opportunities.

SCENE III. *Boar's Head Tavern in Eastcheap.*

[*Enter* FALSTAFF *and* BARDOLPH.]

FAL. Bardolph, am I not fallen away vilely since this last action?[1] Do
I not bate?[2] Do I not dwindle? Why, my skin hangs about me like
an old lady's loose gown, I am withered like an old applejohn.[3] Well,
I'll repent, and that suddenly, while I am in some liking.[4] I shall
be out of heart[5] shortly, and then I shall have no strength to repent.
An I have not forgotten what the inside of a church is made of, I
am a peppercorn, a brewer's horse[6]—the inside of a church!
Company, villainous company, hath been the spoil of me.

BARD. Sir John, you are so fretful you cannot live long.

FAL. Why, there is it. Come sing me a bawdy song, make me merry. I   10
was as virtuously given as a gentleman need to be—virtuous enough;
swore little; diced not above seven times a week; went to a bawdyhouse not above once in a quarter—of an hour; paid money that
I borrowed, three of four times; lived well, and in good compass.[7]
And now I live out of all order, out of all compass.

BARD. Why, you are so fat, Sir John, that you must needs be out of all
compass, out of all reasonable compass, Sir John.

FAL. Do thou amend thy face, and I'll amend my life. Thou art our
admiral,[8] thou bearest the lantern in the poop,[9] but 'tis in the nose
of thee. Thou art the Knight of the Burning Lamp.   20

BARD. Why, Sir John, my face does you no harm.

FAL. No, I'll be sworn, I make as good use of it as many a man doth
of a deaths-head[10] or a memento mori.[11] I never see thy face but
I think upon Hell-fire and Dives[12] that lived in purple, for there
he is in his robes, burning, burning. If thou wert anyway given to
virtue, I would swear by thy face; my oath should be "By this fire,
that's God's angel."[13] But thou art altogether given over, and wert
indeed, but for the light in thy face, the son of utter darkness. When
thou rannest up Gadshill in the night to catch my horse, if I did
not think thou hadst been an ignis fatuus[14] or a ball of wildfire,[15]   30
there's no purchase in money. Oh, thou art a perpetual triumph,[16]
an everlasting bonfire light! Thou hast saved me a thousand marks
in links[17] and torches, walking with thee in the night betwixt tavern and tavern. But the sack that thou hast drunk me would have

---

[1] **last action,** i.e., the Gadshill affair.   [2] Grow thin.   [3] Withered apple, long kept.
[4] **in . . . liking,** in good condition.   [5] **out of heart,** have no heart for it.
[6] **brewer's horse,** old and decrepit.
[7] (Lit., circumference) limits, with a pun on Falstaff's girth.
[8] The admiral's ship, which led the way and carried a lighted lantern by night so that the
fleet should keep together.
[9] Stern.   [10] **death's-head,** skull.   [11] **memento mori,** reminder of death.
[12] The rich man in the parable of Dives and Lazarus. See Luke 16:19–31.
[13] **By . . . angel,** a parody of a line in Chapman's *Blind Beggar of Alexandria,* a recent and
popular play at the Rose Theater.
[14] **ignis fatuus,** will-o'-the-wisp.   [15] Firework.
[16] Rejoicing, celebrated with torches and bonfires.
[17] Torches used to light the way on a dark night.

bought me lights as good cheap at the dearest chandler's[18] in Europe. I have maintained that salamander[19] of yours with fire any time this two and thirty years, God reward me for it!

BARD. 'Sblood, I would my face were in your belly!

FAL. God-a-mercy! So should I be sure to be heart-burned. [*Enter* HOSTESS.] How now, Dame Partlet the hen![20] Have you inquired yet who picked my pocket? 40

HOSTESS. Why, Sir John, what do you think, Sir John? Do you think I keep thieves in my house? I have searched, I have inquired, so has my husband, man by man, boy by boy, servant by servant. The tithe[21] of a hair was never lost in my house before.

FAL. Ye lie, hostess. Bardolph was shaved[22] and lost many a hair, and I'll be sworn my pocket was picked. Go to, you are a woman, go.

HOSTESS. Who I? No, I defy thee. God's light, I was never called so in mine own house before!

FAL. Go to, I know you well enough. 50

HOSTESS. No, Sir John, you do not know me, Sir John. I know you, Sir John. You owe me money, Sir John, and now you pick a quarrel to beguile me of it. I bought you a dozen of shirts to your back.

FAL. Dowlas,[23] filthy dowlas. I have given them away to baker's wives, and they have made bolters[24] of them.

HOSTESS. Now, as I am a true woman, holland[25] of eight shillings an ell.[26] You owe money here besides, Sir John, for your diet and by-drinkings,[27] and money lent you, four and twenty pound.

FAL. He had his part of it. Let him pay.

HOSTESS. He? Alas, he is poor, he hath nothing. 60

FAL. How! Poor? Look upon his face—what call you rich? Let them coin his nose, let them coin his cheeks. I'll not pay a denier.[28] What, will you make a younker[29] of me? Shall I not take mine ease in mine inn but I shall have my pocket picked? I have lost a seal ring of my grandfather's worth forty mark.

HOSTESS. Oh Jesu, I have heard the Prince tell him, I know not how oft, that that ring was copper![30]

FAL. How! The Prince is a Jack,[31] a sneak-cup.[32] 'Sblood, an he were here, I would cudgel him like a dog if he would say so.

[*Enter the* PRINCE *and* PETO, *marching, and* FALSTAFF *meets them playing on his truncheon like a fife.*]

How now, lad! Is the wind in that door, i' faith? Must we all march? 70

BARD. Yea, two and two, Newgate fashion.[33]

HOSTESS. My lord, I pray you hear me.

---

[18] Seller of candles.   [19] A kind of lizard, believed to enjoy fire.
[20] **Dame . . . hen,** the wife of Chanticleer the cock in the story of Reynard the Fox.
[21] Tenth part.   [22] Caught venereal disease.   [23] Coarse linen.
[24] Sieves for sifting flour from bran.   [25] Fine linen.   [26] 45 inches.
[27] **by-drinkings,** drinks between meals.
[28] The smallest English coin, worth one-tenth of a penny.   [29] "Sucker."
[30] Copper-gilt was the cheapest kind of imitation gold.   [31] Knave.
[32] **sneak-cup,** one who steals cups from taverns, the lowest kind of theft.
[33] **Newgate fashion,** i.e., like the chain gang. **Newgate,** the London prison for felons.

PRINCE. What sayest thou, Mistress Quickly? How doth thy husband?
I love him well, he is an honest man.
HOSTESS. Good my lord, hear me.
FAL. Prithee let her alone, and list to me.
PRINCE. What sayest thou, Jack?
FAL. The other night I fell asleep here behind the arras, and had my
pocket picked. This house is turned bawdyhouse; they pick pockets.
PRINCE. What didst thou lose, Jack?   80
FAL. Wilt thou believe me, Hal? Three or four bonds of forty pound
apiece, and a seal ring of my grandfather's.
PRINCE. A trifle, some eightpenny matter.
HOSTESS. So I told him, my lord, and I said I heard your Grace say so.
And, my lord, he speaks most vilely of you, like a foul-mouthed man
as he is, and said he would cudgel[34] you.
PRINCE. What! He did not?
HOSTESS. There's neither faith, truth, nor womanhood in me else.
FAL. There's no more faith in thee than in a stewed prune, nor
no more truth in thee than in a drawn fox,[35] and for womanhood,   90
Maid Marian may be the deputy's wife of the ward to thee.[36] Go,
you thing, go.
HOSTESS. Say, what thing? What thing?
FAL. What thing! Why, a thing to thank God on.
HOSTESS. I am no thing to thank God on, I would thou shouldst know
it. I am an honest man's wife. And, setting thy knighthood aside,
thou art a knave to call me so.
FAL. Setting thy womanhood aside, thou art a beast to say otherwise.
HOSTESS. Say, what beast, thou knave, thou?
FAL. What beast! Why, an otter.   100
PRINCE. An otter, Sir John! Why an otter?
FAL. Why, she's neither fish nor flesh. A man knows not where to have
her.
HOSTESS. Thou art an unjust man in saying so. Thou or any man knows
where to have me, thou knave, thou!
PRINCE. Thou sayest true, hostess, and he slanders thee most grossly.
HOSTESS. So he doth you, my lord, and said this other day you ought[37]
him a thousand pound.
PRINCE. Sirrah, do I owe you a thousand pound?
FAL. A thousand pound, Hal! A million! Thy love is worth a million.   110
Thou owest me thy love.
HOSTESS. Nay, my lord, he called you Jack, and said he would cudgel
you.
FAL. Did I, Bardolph?
BARD. Indeed, Sir John, you said so.

---

[34]Beat.   [35]**drawn fox,** fox driven from cover, and so cunning.
[36]**Maid . . . thee,** Maid Marian, the woman in Robin Hood's gang, was a character in a
morris dance, an English folk dance in which a story was acted by costumed dancers. She was
played by a man as lumpish and awkward. The wife of the deputy of the ward was likely to
give herself airs of dignity. Falstaff means "you are more lumpish than Maid Marian compared
with a most stately matron."
[37]Owed.

FAL. Yea, if he said[38] my ring was copper.

PRINCE. I say 'tis copper.[39] Darest thou be as good as thy word now?

FAL. Why, Hal, thou knowest, as thou art but man, I dare; but as thou art Prince, I fear thee as I fear the roaring of the lion's whelp.

PRINCE. And why not as the lion? 120

FAL. The King himself is to be feared as the lion. Dost thou think I'll fear thee as I fear thy father? Nay, an I do, I pray God my girdle break.

PRINCE. Oh, if it should, how would thy guts fall about thy knees! But, sirrah, there's no room for faith, truth, nor honesty in this bosom of thine; it is all filled up with guts and midriff. Charge an honest woman with picking thy pocket! Why, thou whoreson, impudent, embossed[40] rascal, if there were anything in thy pocket but tavern reckonings, memorandums of bawdyhouses, and one poor penny-worth of sugar candy to make thee long-winded, if thy pocket were 130 enriched with any other injuries[41] but these, I am a villain. And yet you will stand to it, you will not pocket up wrong. Art thou not ashamed?

FAL. Dost thou hear, Hal? Thou knowest in the state of innocency Adam fell, and what should poor Jack Falstaff do in the days of villainy?[42] Thou seest I have more flesh than another man, and therefore more frailty. You confess, then, you picked my pocket?

PRINCE. It appears so by the story.

FAL. Hostess, I forgive thee. Go, make ready breakfast. Love thy husband, look to thy servants, cherish thy guests. Thou shalt find me 140 tractable[43] to any honest reason. Thou seest I am pacified still.[44] Nay, prithee be gone. [*Exit* HOSTESS.] Now, Hal, to the news at Court. For the robbery, lad, how is that answered?

PRINCE. Oh, my sweet beef,[45] I must still be good angel to thee. The money is paid back again.

FAL. Oh, I do not like that paying back. 'Tis a double labor.

PRINCE. I am good friends with my father, and may do anything.

FAL. Rob me the exchequer the first thing thou doest, and do it with unwashed hands[46] too.

BARD. Do, my lord. 150

PRINCE. I have procured thee, Jack, a charge of foot.

FAL. I would it had been of horse. Where shall I find one that can steal well? Oh for a fine thief, of the age of two and twenty or there-abouts! I am heinously[47] unprovided. Well, God be thanked for these rebels, they offend none but the virtuous. I laud them, I praise them.

PRINCE. Bardolph!

BARD. My lord?

PRINCE. Go bear this letter to Lord John of Lancaster, to my brother John; this to my Lord of Westmoreland. [*Exit* BARDOLPH.] Go, Peto,

---

[38] **if he said,** The word "if" allowed one to make a threat while leaving room to retreat.
[39] **I . . . copper,** Here Falstaff gets the "lie direct."   [40] Swollen.
[41] **pocket . . . injuries,** a pun on the phrase "to pocket up injuries."
[42] **days of villainy,** these wicked times.   [43] Agreeable.   [44] Always.
[45] Ox.   [46] **unwashed hands,** without stopping to wash your hands.
[47] Atrociously.

to horse, to horse, for thou and I have thirty miles to ride yet ere   160
dinnertime. [*Exit* PETO.] Jack, meet me tomorrow in the Temple
Hall at two o'clock in the afternoon.
There shalt thou know thy charge, and there receive
Money and order for their furniture.[48]
The land is burning, Percy stands on high,
And either we or they must lower lie.   [*Exit.*]
FAL. Rare words! Brave world! Hostess, my breakfast, come!
Oh, I could wish this tavern were my drum!   [*Exit.*]

ACT IV

SCENE I. *The rebel camp near Shrewsbury.*

[*Enter* HOTSPUR, WORCESTER, *and* DOUGLAS.]

HOT. Well said, my noble Scot. If speaking truth
In this fine age were not thought flattery,
Such attribution[1] should the Douglas have
As not a soldier of this season's stamp[2]
Should go so general current through the world.
By God, I cannot flatter, I do defy
The tongues of soothers;[3] but a braver place
In my heart's love hath no man than yourself.
Nay, task me to my word.[4] Approve[5] me, lord.
DOUG. Thou art the king of honor.   10
No man so potent breathes upon the ground
But I will beard[6] him.
HOT.   Do so, and 'tis well.
[*Enter a* MESSENGER *with letters.*]
What letters hast thou there?—I can but thank you.
MESS. These letters come from your father.
HOT. Letters from him! Why comes he not himself?
MESS. He cannot come, my lord, he is grievous sick.
HOT. 'Zounds! How has he the leisure to be sick
In such a justling[7] time? Who leads his power?
Under whose government come they along?
MESS. His letters bear his mind, not I, my lord.   20
WOR. I prithee tell me, doth he keep his bed?
MESS. He did, my lord, four days ere I set forth,
And at the time of my departure thence
He was much feared by his physicians.

---

[48] Equipment.
[1] Citation of merits.
[2] **season's stamp,** of this year's minting. The idea is that Douglas is like a new coin, acceptable (*current*) everywhere as valuable.
[3] Flatterers.
[4] **task . . . word,** cause me to make my word good.   [5] Put to the proof.
[6] Dare; lit., pull by the beard.   [7] Jostling, disturbed.

WOR. I would the state of time had first been whole[8]
    Ere he by sickness had been visited.
    His health was never better worth[9] than now.
HOT. Sick now! Droop now! This sickness doth infect
    The very lifeblood of our enterprise.
    'Tis catching hither, even to our camp.   30
    He writes me here that inward sickness—
    And that his friends by deputation[10] could not
    So soon be drawn,[11] nor did he think it meet
    To lay so dangerous and dear[12] a trust
    On any soul removed but on his own.
    Yet doth he give us bold advértisement[13]
    That with our small conjunction[14] we should on,
    To see how fortune is disposed to us;
    For, as he writes, there is no quailing now,
    Because the King is certainly possessed[15]   40
    Of all our purposes. What say you to it?
WOR. Your father's sickness is a maim to us.
HOT. A perilous gash, a very limb lopped off.
    And yet, in faith, it is not; his present want[16]
    Seems more than we shall find it. Were it good
    To set[17] the exact[18] wealth of all our states
    All at one cast?[19] To set so rich a main[20]
    On the nice hazard[21] of one doubtful hour?
    It were not good, for therein should we read
    The very bottom and the soul of hope,
    The very list,[22] the very utmost bound[23]   50
    Of all our fortunes.
DOUG.   Faith, and so we should,
    Where now remains a sweet reversion.[24]
    We may boldly spend upon the hope of what
    Is to come in.
    A comfort of retirement[25] lives in this.
HOT. A rendezvous, a home to fly unto,
    If that the Devil and mischance look big[26]
    Upon the maidenhead of our affairs.
WOR. But yet I would your father had been here.   60
    The quality and hair[27] of our attempt
    Brooks no division. It will be thought
    By some, that know not why he is away,

---

[8] **I . . . whole,** I wish the times themselves had first been healthy.
[9] **better worth,** worth more.   [10] Deputy; i.e., he could not send anyone else.
[11] Drawn together.   [12] Important.   [13] Advice.
[14] Forces that have joined.   [15] Informed.
[16] **his . . . want,** the need of him at this present time.
[17] Hazard.   [18] Entire.   [19] Throw of the dice.   [20] Stake.
[21] **nice hazard,** delicate chance.   [22] Limit.   [23] Boundary.
[24] Portion yet to come.
[25] **comfort of retirement,** a place to which we can retire for comfort.
[26] **look big,** threaten.   [27] Nature.

That wisdom, loyalty, and mere dislike
Of our proceedings kept the Earl from hence.
And think how such an apprehension
May turn the tide of fearful faction,[28]
And breed a kind of question in our cause;
For well you know we of the offering[29] side
Must keep aloof from strict arbitrament,[30]   70
And stop all sight holes, every loop from whence
The eye of reason may pry in upon us.
This absence of your father's draws[31] a curtain
That shows the ignorant a kind of fear
Before not dreamed of.
HOT.   You strain too far.
I rather of his absence make this use.
It lends a luster and more great opinion,
A larger dare to our great enterprise,
Than if the Earl were here; for men must think
If we without his help can make a head[32]   80
To push against a kingdom, with his help
We shall o'erturn it topsy-turvy down.
Yet all goes well, yet all our joints are whole.
DOUG. As heart can think. There is not such a word
Spoke of in Scotland as this term of fear.
                    [*Enter* SIR RICHARD VERNON.]
HOT. My cousin Vernon! Welcome, by my soul.
VER. Pray God my news be worth a welcome, lord.
The Earl of Westmoreland, seven thousand strong,
Is marching hitherward; with him Prince John.
HOT. No harm. What more?
VER.   And further, I have learned,   90
The King himself in person is set forth,
Or hitherward intended speedily,
With strong and mighty preparation.
HOT. He shall be welcome too. Where is his son,
The nimble-footed madcap Prince of Wales,
And his comrades, that daffed[33] the world aside
And bid it pass?
VER.   All furnished,[34] all in arms;
All plumed like estridges that with the wind
Bated like eagles having lately bathed;[35]

---

[28]**fearful faction,** timid rebellion.   [29]Challenging.
[30]**strict arbitrament,** exact judgment.   [31]Draws back.
[32]**make a head,** raise an army.   [33]Waved.
[34]**bid it pass,** cried "let the world pass"; i.e., "who cares a damn?" **furnished,** in full armor.
[35]**All . . . bathed,** These lines are much annotated. As they stand they mean: "All wearing plumes like ostriches that flap their wings (*bate*) in the wind like eagles that have lately bathed." But the comparison seems hardly apt. Either a line has been omitted after *wind,* or *with* is a misprint of some such verb as *wing.*

Glittering in golden coats, like images;[36]   100
As full of spirit as the month of May,
And gorgeous as the sun at midsummer;
Wanton[37] as youthful goats, wild as young bulls.
I saw young Harry, with his beaver[38] on,
His cuisses[39] on his thighs, gallantly armed,
Rise from the ground like feathered Mercury,[40]
And vaulted with such ease into his seat
As if an angel dropped down from the clouds
To turn and wind a fiery Pegasus,[41]
And witch[42] the world with noble horsemanship.   110
HOT. No more, no more. Worse than the sun in March,
  This praise doth nourish agues. Let them come.
  They come like sacrifices in their trim,[43]
  And to the fire-eyed maid of smoky war
  All hot and bleeding will we offer them.
  The mailèd Mars[44] shall on his altar sit
  Up to the ears in blood. I am on fire
  To hear this rich reprisal[45] is so nigh
  And yet not ours. Come, let me taste my horse,
  Who is to bear me like a thunderbolt   120
  Against the bosom of the Prince of Wales.
  Harry to Harry shall, hot horse to horse,
  Meet and ne'er part till one drop down a corse.
  Oh that Glendower were come!
VER.   There is more news.
  I learned in Worcester, as I rode along,
  He cannot draw his power this fourteen days.
DOUG. That's the worst tidings that I hear of yet.
WOR. Aye, by my faith, that bears a frosty sound.
HOT. What may the King's whole battle[46] reach unto?
VER. To thirty thousand.
HOT.   Forty let it be.   130
  My father and Glendower being both away,
  The powers of us may serve so great a day.
  Come, let us take a muster speedily.
  Doomsday is near. Die all, die merrily.
DOUG. Talk not of dying. I am out of[47] fear
  Of death or death's hand for this one half-year.

                                   [*Exeunt.*]

---

[36] I.e., of the saints in a Catholic church.
[37] Lusty.   [38] Visor of a helmet.   [39] Thigh pieces.
[40] **feathered Mercury,** Mercury, the messenger of the gods, wore winged sandals.
[41] Perseus's winged horse.   [42] Bewitch.
[43] **in . . . trim,** dressed up.
[44] **mailed Mars,** the god of war in his armor.
[45] Prize.
[46] Main army.
[47] **out of,** free from.

SCENE II. A public road near Coventry.

[*Enter* FALSTAFF *and* BARDOLPH.]

FAL. Bardolph, get thee before to Coventry, fill me a bottle of sack. Our soldiers shall march through, we'll to Sutton Co'fil'[1] tonight.

BARD. Will you give me money, Captain?

FAL. Lay out,[2] lay out.

BARD. This bottle makes an angel.[3]

FAL. An if it do, take it for thy labor. And if it make twenty, take them all, I'll answer the coinage.[4] Bid my Lieutenant Peto meet me at town's end.

BARD. I will, Captain. Farewell.   [*Exit.*]

FAL. If I be not ashamed of my soldiers,[5] I am a soused gurnet.[6] I have misued the King's press[7] damnably. I have got, in exchange of a hundred and fifty soldiers, three hundred and odd pounds. I press me none but good householders, yeomen's[8] sons; inquire me out contracted bachelors,[9] such as had been asked twice on the banns; such a commodity[10] of warm slaves as had as lieve[11] hear the Devil as a drum; such as fear the report of a caliver[12] worse than a struck fowl or a hurt wild duck. I pressed me none but such toasts-and-butter, with hearts in their bellies no bigger than pins' heads, and they have bought out their services. And now my whole charge consists of ancients, corporals, lieutenants, gentlemen of companies,[13] slaves as ragged as Lazarus in the painted cloth[14] where the glutton's dogs licked his sores; and such as indeed were never soldiers, but discarded unjust servingmen,[15] younger sons to younger brothers,[16] revolted tapsters, and ostlers trade-fallen;[17] the cankers of a calm world and a long peace, ten times more dishonorable ragged than an old-faced ancient. And such have I to fill up the rooms of them that have bought out their services that you would

10

20

---

[1] **Sutton Co'fil',** Sutton Coldfield, a town in Warwickshire.

[2] **Lay out,** pay for it.

[3] **makes an angel,** comes to an angel (10s), which you owe me.

[4] **take . . . coinage,** Falstaff deliberately misunderstands Bardolph's "make"—"if the bottle will make angels, I'll guarantee the coins."

[5] **If . . . soldiers,** Falstaff was typical of many dishonest captains in the 1590's—here, by accepting bribes to exempt from conscription men who could afford to pay.

[6] **soused gurnet,** pickled gurnet (sea fish with a large head).

[7] **King's press,** the right to conscript soldiers granted by the King's commission.

[8] Wealthy farmers.

[9] **contracted bachelors,** bachelors engaged to be married in a short time.

[10] Parcel.   [11] Soon.

[12] Lighter form of musket or harquebus, used by the infantry.

[13] **charge . . . companies,** Falstaff has picked up a selection of veterans of various ranks. **ancients,** ensigns, second lieutenants. **gentlemen of companies,** gentlemen of good family who served in the ranks of the companies of noblemen.

[14] **Lazarus . . . cloth,** In taverns and less wealthy houses painted cloths showing scenes from the Scripture and classical legend were hung on the walls instead of the more costly tapestry.

[15] Servants from some great household.

[16] **younger . . . brothers,** young gentlemen who had no hope of an allowance or a legacy.

[17] **ostlers trade-fallen,** unemployed grooms.

think that I had a hundred and fifty tattered prodigals lately come
from swine-keeping, from eating draff and husks.[18] A mad fellow[19]
met me on the way and told me I had unloaded all the gibbets[20] 30
and pressed the dead bodies. No eye hath seen such scarecrows.
I'll not march through Coventry with them, that's flat. Nay, and
the villains march wide betwixt the legs, as if they had gyves[21] on,
for indeed I had the most of them out of prison. There's but a shirt
and a half in all my company; and the half-shirt is two napkins tacked
together and thrown over the shoulders like a herald's coat[22] without sleeves; and the shirt, to say the truth, stolen from my host at
St. Alban's, or the red-nose innkeeper of Daventry. But that's all
one. They'll find linen enough on every hedge.[23]

[*Enter the* PRINCE *and* WESTMORELAND.]

PRINCE. How now, blown[24] Jack! How now, quilt! 40

FAL. What, Hal! How now, mad wag! What a devil dost thou in Warwickshire? My good Lord of Westmoreland, I cry you mercy. I thought
your honor had already been at Shrewsbury.

WEST. Faith, Sir John, 'tis more than time that I were there, and you
too; but my powers are there already. The King, I can tell you, looks
for us all. We must away all night.

FAL. Tut, never fear me. I am as vigilant as a cat to steal cream.

PRINCE. I think to steal cream indeed, for thy theft hath already made
thee butter. But tell me, Jack, whose fellows are these that come
after? 50

FAL. Mine, Hal, mine.

PRINCE. I did never see such pitiful rascals.

FAL. Tut, tut, good enough to toss,[25] food for powder, food for powder. They'll fill a pit as well as better. Tush, man, mortal men, mortal men.

WEST. Aye, but, Sir John, methinks they are exceeding poor and bare,
too beggarly.

FAL. Faith, for their poverty, I know not where they had that; and for
their bareness, I am sure they never learned that of me.

PRINCE. No, I'll be sworn, unless you call three fingers[26] on the ribs 60
bare. But, sirrah, make haste. Percy is already in the field.

FAL. What, is the King encamped?

WEST. He is, Sir John. I fear we shall stay too long.

FAL. Well,
To the latter end of a fray and the beginning of a feast
Fits a dull fighter and a keen guest.   [*Exeunt.*]

---

[18] **draff . . . husks,** offal and husks, like the Prodigal Son in the parable who "would fain
have filled his belly with the husks that the swine did eat" (Luke, 15:11–32).
[19] **mad fellow,** wit.
[20] **unloaded . . . gibbets,** The bodies of executed felons were often hung up in iron cages
near the scene of the crime until they rotted.
[21] Fetters on the legs.
[22] **herald's coat,** a sleeveless coat embroidered with the royal coat of arms.
[23] **linen . . . hedge,** The washing was laid on the hedges to dry and air.
[24] Inflated.
[25] **good . . . toss,** i.e., on pikes; "good enough for cannon fodder."
[26] **three fingers,** i.e., three fingers' thickness of fat.

SCENE III. The rebel camp near Shrewsbury.

[*Enter* HOTSPUR, WORCESTER, DOUGLAS, *and* VERNON.]

HOT. We'll fight with him tonight.

WOR.   It may not be.

DOUG. You give him then advantage.

VER.   Not a whit.

HOT. Why say you so? Looks he not for supply?[1]

VER. So do we.

HOT.   His is certain, ours is doubtful.

WOR. Good Cousin, be advised, stir not tonight.

VER. Do not, my lord.

DOUG.   You do not counsel well.
    You speak it out of fear and cold heart.

VER. Do me no slander, Douglas. By my life,
    And I dare well maintain it with my life,
    If well-respected[2] honor bid me on,   10
    I hold as little counsel with weak fear
    As you, my lord, or any Scot that this day lives.
    Let it be seen tomorrow in the battle
    Which of us fears.

DOUG.   Yea, or tonight.

VER.   Content.

HOT. Tonight, say I.

VER. Come, come, it may not be. I wonder much,
    Being men of such great leading[3] as you are,
    That you foresee not what impediments
    Drag back our expedition.[4] Certain horse[5]
    Of my cousin Vernon's are not yet come up.   20
    Your uncle Worcester's horse came but today,
    And now their pride and mettle[6] is asleep,
    Their courage with hard labor tame and dull,
    That not a horse is half the half of himself.

HOT. So are the horses of the enemy
    In general, journey-bated[7] and brought low.
    The better part of ours are full of rest.

WOR. The number of the King exceedeth ours.
    For God's sake, Cousin, stay till all come in.

                    [*The trumpet sounds a parley.*]
                [*Enter* SIR WALTER BLUNT.]

BLUNT. I come with gracious offers from the King,   30
    If you vouchsafe me hearing and respect.

HOT. Welcome, Sir Walter Blunt, and would to God
    You were of our determination![8]
    Some of us love you well, and even those some
    Envy your great deservings and good name

---

[1]Reinforcements.   [2]**well-respected,** well-considered (not foolhardy).
[3]Experience in leadership.   [4]Haste.   [5]Cavalry.   [6]Ardor.
[7]**journey-bated,** tired by the journey.   [8]Mind.

Because you are not of our quality,[9]
But stand against us like an enemy.
BLUNT. And God defend[10] but still I should stand so
So long as out of limit and true rule
You stand against anointed Majesty.
But to my charge.[11] The King hath sent to know 40
The nature of your griefs, and whereupon
You conjure from the breast of civil peace
Such bold hostility, teaching his duteous land
Audacious cruelty. If that the King
Have any way your good deserts forgot,
Which he confesseth to be manifold,
He bids you name your griefs, and with all speed
You shall have your desires with interest,
And pardon absolute for yourself and these 50
Herein misled by your suggestion.[12]
HOT. The King is kind, and well we know the King
Knows at what time to promise, when to pay.
My father and my uncle and myself
Did give him that same royalty he wears.
And when he was not six and twenty strong,
Sick in the world's regard,[13] wretched and low,
A poor unminded outlaw sneaking home,
My father gave him welcome to the shore.
And when he heard him swear and vow to God 60
He came but to be Duke of Lancaster,
To sue his livery[14] and beg his peace
With tears of innocency and terms of zeal,[15]
My father, in kind heart and pity moved,
Swore him assistance, and performed it too.
Now when the lords and barons of the realm
Perceived Northumberland did lean to him,
The more and less came in with cap and knee—
Met him in boroughs, cities, villages,
Attended him on bridges, stood in lanes, 70
Laid gifts before him, proffered him their oaths,
Gave him their heirs as pages, followed him
Even at the heels in golden[16] multitudes.
He presently, as greatness knows itself,
Steps me a little higher than his vow
Made to my father while his blood was poor,
Upon the naked shore at Ravenspurgh;
And now, forsooth, takes on him to reform
Some certain edicts and some strait[17] decrees

[9] Fellowship, party.   [10] Forbid.
[11] **my charge,** what I have been instructed (*charged*) to say.
[12] Temptation.   [13] **Sick . . . regard,** poorly regarded by the world.
[14] **sue . . . livery,** claim his inheritance.   [15] **terms of zeal,** protestations of loyalty.
[16] Wearing their richest clothes.   [17] Strict.

That lie too heavy on the commonwealth, 80
Cries out upon abuses, seems to weep
Over his country's wrongs. And by this face,
This seeming brow of justice, did he win
The hearts of all that he did angle for—
Proceeded further, cut me off the heads
Of all the favorites that the absent King
In deputation[18] left behind him here
When he was personal[19] in the Irish war.
BLUNT. Tut, I came not to hear this.
HOT.   Then to the point.
In short time after, he deposed the King, 90
Soon after that, deprived him of his life.
And in the neck[20] of that, tasked[21] the whole state.
To make that worse, suffered his kinsman March,
Who is, if every owner were well placed,
Indeed his king, to be engaged[22] in Wales,
There without ransom to lie forfeited;
Disgraced me in my happy victories,
Sought to entrap me by intelligence;[23]
Rated[24] mine uncle from the Council board,
In rage dismissed my father from the Court; 100
Broke oath on oath, committed wrong on wrong;
And in conclusion drove us to seek out
This head of safety,[25] and withal to pry
Into his title, the which we find
Too indirect[26] for long continuance.
BLUNT. Shall I return this answer to the King?
HOT. Not so, Sir Walter. We'll withdraw a while.
Go to the King, and let there be impawned[27]
Some surety for a safe return again,
And in the morning early shall mine uncle 110
Bring him our purposes. And so farewell.
BLUNT. I would you would accept of grace and love.
HOT. And maybe so we shall.
BLUNT.   Pray God you do.   [*Exeunt.*]

SCENE IV. York. The ARCHBISHOP'S *palace.*

[*Enter the* ARCHBISHOP OF YORK *and* SIR MICHAEL.[1]]
ARCH. Hie, good Sir Michael, bear this sealèd brief[2]
With wingèd haste to the Lord Marshal,

---

[18] **In deputation,** as his deputies.   [19] **was personal,** went in person.
[20] **in . . . neck,** on top of.   [21] Taxed.   [22] Held as pledge, hostage.   [23] Spies.
[24] Dismissed with abuse.   [25] **head of safety,** armed force to keep us safe.
[26] Not in the straight line of descent.   [27] Kept as hostage.
  [1] **Sir Michael,** He has not been identified, presumably a priest or knight in the Archbishop's service.
  [2] Letter.

This to my cousin Scroop, and all the rest
To whom they are directed. If you knew
How much they do import, you would make haste.
SIR M. My good lord.
I guess their tenor.[3]
ARCH.   Like enough you do.
Tomorrow, good Sir Michael, is a day
Wherein the fortune of ten thousand men
Must bide the touch;[4] for, sir, at Shrewsbury,   10
As I am truly given to understand,
The King with mighty and quick-raisèd power
Meets with Lord Harry. And I fear, Sir Michael—
What with the sickness of Northumberland,
Whose power was in the first proportion,[5]
And what with Owen Glendower's absence thence,
Who with them was a rated sinew[6] too
And comes not in, o'er-ruled by prophecies—
I fear the power of Percy is too weak
To wage an instant[7] trial with the King.   20
SIR M. Why, my good lord, you need not fear.
There is Douglas and Lord Mortimer.
ARCH. No, Mortimer is not there.
SIR M. But there is Mordake, Vernon, Lord Harry Percy,
And there is my Lord of Worcester and a head
Of gallant warriors, noble gentlemen.
ARCH. And so there is. But yet the King hath drawn
The special head[8] of all the land together—
The Prince of Wales, Lord John of Lancaster,
The noble Westmoreland and warlike Blunt,   30
And many mo[9] corrivals[10] and dear men
Of estimation[11] and command in arms.
SIR M. Doubt not, my lord, they shall be well opposed.
ARCH. I hope no less, yet needful 'tis to fear,
And, to prevent[12] the worst, Sir Michael, speed.
For if Lord Percy thrive not ere the King
Dismiss his power, he means to visit us,[13]
For he hath heard of our confederacy,[14]
And 'tis but wisdom to make strong against him.
Therefore make haste. I must go write again   40
To other friends. And so farewell, Sir Michael.

                                    [*Exeunt.*]

---

[3] Import.   [4] **bide . . . touch,** be put to the test.
[5] **in . . . proportion,** the largest part.
[6] **rated sinew,** strength highly valued.
[7] Immediate.
[8] **special head,** crack troops, "shock troops."
[9] More.   [10] Supporters
[11] **dear . . . estimation,** men highly regarded.
[12] Forestall.   [13] **visit us,** come our way.
[14] Conspiracy.

ACT V

SCENE I. The KING*'s camp near Shrewsbury.*

[*Enter the* KING, PRINCE OF WALES, LORD JOHN OF
LANCASTER, SIR WALTER BLUNT, *and* FALSTAFF.[1]]
KING. How bloodily the sun begins to peer
  Above yon busky[2] hill! The day looks pale
  At his distemperature.[3]
PRINCE.   The southern wind
  Doth play the trumpet[4] to his purposes,
  And by his hollow whistling in the leaves
  Foretells a tempest and a blustering day.
KING. Then with the losers let it sympathize,
  For nothing can seem foul to those that win.
      [*The trumpet sounds. Enter* WORCESTER *and* VERNON.]
  How now, my Lord of Worcester! 'Tis not well
  That you and I should meet upon such terms   10
  As now we meet. You have deceived our trust,
  And made us doff our easy robes of peace
  To crush our old limbs in ungentle steel.
  This is not well, my lord, this is not well.
  What say you to it? Will you again unknit
  This churlish knot[5] of all-abhorrèd war?
  And move in that obedient orb[6] again
  Where you did give a fair and natural light,
  And be no more an exhaled meteor,[7]
  A prodigy of fear,[8] and a portent   20
  Of broachèd[9] mischief to the unborn times?
WOR. Hear me my liege.
  For mine own part, I could be well content
  To entertain the lag end of my life
  With quiet hours, for I do protest
  I have not sought the day of this dislike.
KING. You have not sought it! How comes it, then?
FAL. Rebellion lay in his way, and he found it.
PRINCE. Peace, chewet,[10] peace!
WOR. It pleased your Majesty to turn your looks   30
  Of favor from myself and all our house.
  And yet I must remember[11] you, my lord,
  We were the first and dearest of your friends.

---

[1] It is worth noting that Shakespeare places Falstaff in immediate attendance on the King.
[2] Bushy.   [3] Sickness.
[4] **play . . . trumpet,** like the trumpeter blowing an introductory flourish.
[5] **churlish knot,** knot which unites men for a brutal purpose.
[6] **obedient orb,** sphere of obedience, like a planet taking its natural course in orbit.
[7] **exhaled meteor,** meteor created of vapor drawn up by the sun.
[8] **prodigy of fear,** a fearful sign of disaster.
[9] Set loose; lit., tapped (like a cask).
[10] Jackdaw.   [11] Remind.

For you my staff of office[12] did I break
In Richard's time, and posted[13] day and night
To meet you on the way, and kiss your hand,
When yet you were in place and in account
Nothing so strong and fortunate as I.
It was myself, my brother, and his son
That brought you home, and boldly did outdare 40
The dangers of the time. You swore to us,
And you did swear that oath at Doncaster,
That you did nothing purpose 'gainst the state,
Nor claim no further than your new-fall'n right,[14]
The seat of Gaunt, Dukedom of Lancaster.
To this we swore our aid. But in short space
It rained down fortune showering on your head;
And such a flood of greatness fell on you,
What with our help, what with the absent King,
What with the injuries of a wanton[15] time, 50
The seeming sufferances[16] that you had borne,
And the contrarious winds that held the King
So long in his unlucky Irish wars
That all in England did repute him dead.
And from this swarm of fair advantages
You took occasion to be quickly wooed
To gripe[17] the general sway[18] into your hand;
Forgot your oath to us at Doncaster;
And being fed by us you used us so
As that ungentle gull,[19] the cuckoo's bird,[20] 60
Useth the sparrow—did oppress our nest;
Grew by our feeding to so great a bulk
That even our love durst not come near your sight
For fear of swallowing, but with nimble wing
We were enforced, for safety sake, to fly
Out of your sight and raise this present head.
Whereby we stand opposèd by such means
As you yourself have forged against yourself,
By unkind usage, dangerous countenance,[21]
And violation of all faith and troth[22] 70
Sworn to us in your younger enterprise.
KING. These things indeed you have articulate,[23]
Proclaimed at market crosses, read in churches.

---

[12] **staff of office,** ceremonial staff of authority; Worcester is recalling the time when he withdrew his allegiance from the former, deposed king Richard II in favor of Henry IV.
[13] Rode hastily.
[14] **new-fall'n right,** inheritance which had recently come.
[15] Wild.   [16] Injuries.   [17] Grip.
[18] **general sway,** rule of the whole state.
[19] Nestling.
[20] **cuckoo's bird,** The cuckoo appropriated the nests of other birds.
[21] **dangerous countenance,** threatening looks.
[22] Truth.   [23] Drawn up in schedules.

To face[24] the garment of rebellion
With some fine color that may please the eye
Of fickle changelings[25] and poor discontents,
Which gape and rub the elbow at the news
Of hurly-burly innovation.[26]
And never yet did insurrection want
Such water colors to impaint his cause,   80
Nor moody beggars, starving for a time
Of pell-mell havoc[27] and confusion.

PRINCE. In both your armies there is many a soul
    Shall pay full dearly for this encounter
    If once they join in trial. Tell your nephew,
    The Prince of Wales doth join with all the world
    In praise of Henry Percy. By my hopes,
    This present enterprise set off his head,[28]
    I do not think a braver gentleman,
    More active-valiant or more valiant-young,   90
    More daring or more bold, is now alive
    To grace this latter age with noble deeds.
    For my part, I may speak it to my shame,
    I have a truant been to chivalry,[29]
    And so I hear he doth account me too.
    Yet this before my father's majesty—
    I am content that he shall take the odds[30]
    Of his great name and estimation,
    And will, to save the blood on either side,
    Try fortune with him in a single fight.   100

KING. And, Prince of Wales, so dare we venture thee,
    Albeit considerations infinite
    Do make against it. No, good Worcester, no,
    We love our people well, even those we love
    That are misled upon your cousin's part.
    And, will they take the offer of our grace,
    Both he and they and you—yea, every man—
    Shall be my friend again and I'll be his.
    So tell your cousin, and bring me word
    What he will do. But if he will not yield,   110
    Rebuke and dread correction wait on us[31]
    And they shall do their office. So, be gone.
    We will not now be troubled with reply.
    We offer fair, take it advisedly.

                                        [*Exeunt* WORCESTER *and* VERNON.]

PRINCE. It will not be accepted, on my life.
    The Douglas and the Hotspur both together
    Are confident against the world in arms.

---

[24] Trim.   [25] Turncoats.
[26] **hurly-burly innovation,** confusion and revolution.   [27] Slaughter.
[28] **set . . . head,** being excepted.   [29] Knightly deeds.
[30] **take . . . odds,** have the advantage.   [31] **wait on us,** are our servants.

KING. Hence, therefore, every leader to his charge,[32]
　For on their answer will we set on them.
　And God befriend us as our cause is just! 120
　　　　[*Exeunt all but the* PRINCE OF WALES *and* FALSTAFF.]
FAL. Hal, if thou see me down in the battle, and bestride me so, 'tis
　a point of friendship.
PRINCE. Nothing but a colossus[33] can do thee that friendship. Say thy
　prayers, and farewell.
FAL. I would 'twere bedtime, Hal, and all well.
PRINCE. Why, thou owest God a death. [*Exit.*]
FAL. 'Tis not due yet, I would be loath to pay Him before his day. What
　need I be so forward with him that calls not on me? Well, 'tis no
　matter. Honor pricks me on.[34] Yea, but how if honor prick me off[35]
　when I come on? How then? Can honor set to[36] a leg? No. Or an 130
　arm? No. Or take away the grief of a wound? No. Honor hath no
　skill in surgery, then? No. What is honor? A word. What is in that
　word honor? What is that honor? Air. A trim[37] reckoning! Who hath
　it? He that died o' Wednesday. Doth he feel it? No. Doth he hear
　it? No. 'Tis insensible, then? Yea, to the dead. But will it not live
　with the living? No. Why? Detraction[38] will not suffer it. Therefore
　I'll none of it. Honor is a mere scutcheon.[39] And so ends my
　catechism.
　　　　　　　　　　　　　　　　　　　　　　　[*Exit.*]

SCENE II. *The rebel camp.*

　　　　　[*Enter* WORCESTER *and* VERNON.]
WOR. Oh, no, my nephew must not know, Sir Richard,
　The liberal and kind offer of the King.
VER. 'Twere best he did.
WOR. 　　　　　　　　　　Then are we all undone.
　It is not possible, it cannot be
　The King should keep his word in loving us.
　He will suspect us still, and find a time
　To punish this offense in other faults.
　Suspicion all our lives shall be stuck full of eyes;
　For treason is but trusted like the fox,
　Who, ne'er so tame, so cherished and locked up, 10
　Will have a wild trick[1] of his ancestors.

---

[32] Command.
[33] The Colossus of the Aegean island of Rhodes—one of the Seven Wonders of the Ancient
World—was a gigantic statue straddling the harbor entrance.
[34] **Honor . . . on,** honor spurs me forward to heroism.
[35] **prick me off,** mark me down on the casualty list.
[36] **set to,** mend. [37] Neat. [38] Slander.
[39] Coat of arms, painted on boards or cloth, carried in the funeral of a gentleman and afterward hung up in the church.
[1] **wild trick,** wild habits.

Look how we can, or[2] sad or merrily,
Interpretation will misquote[3] our looks,
And we shall feed like oxen at a stall,
The better cherished, still the nearer death.
My nephew's trespass may be well forgot.
It hath the excuse of youth and heat of blood,
And an adopted name of privilege,[4]
A harebrained Hotspur, governed by a spleen.[5]
All his offenses live upon my head   20
And on his father's. We did train[6] him on,
And, his corruption being ta'en from us,
We, as the spring of all, shall pay for all.
Therefore, good Cousin, let not Harry know,
In any case, the offer of the King.
VER. Deliver[7] what you will, I'll say 'tis so.
    Here comes your cousin.
                    [*Enter* HOTSPUR *and* DOUGLAS.]
HOT.   My uncle is returned.
    Deliver up[8] my Lord of Westmoreland.
    Uncle, what news?   30
WOR. The King will bid you battle presently.[9]
DOUG. Defy him by the Lord of Westmoreland.
HOT. Lord Douglas, go you and tell him so.
DOUG. Marry, and shall, and very willingly.
                                                              [*Exit.*]

WOR. There is no seeming mercy in the King.
HOT. Did you beg any? God forbid!
WOR. I told him gently of our grievances,
    Of his oath-breaking, which he mended thus,
    By now forswearing[10] that he is forsworn.
    He calls us rebels, traitors, and will scourge   40
    With haughty arms this hateful name in us.
                    [*Re-enter* DOUGLAS.]
DOUG. Arm, gentlemen, to arms! For I have thrown
    A brave defiance in King Henry's teeth—
    And Westmoreland, that was engaged,[11] did bear it—
    Which cannot choose but bring him quickly on.
WOR. The Prince of Wales stepped forth before the King
    And, Nephew, challenged you to single fight.
HOT. Oh, would the quarrel lay upon our heads,
    And that no man might draw short breath[12] today
    But I and Harry Monmouth! Tell me, tell me,   50
    How showed his tasking?[13] Seem'd it in contempt?

---

[2]Either.
[3]**Interpretation . . . misquote,** men will deliberately misinterpret.
[4]**adopted . . . privilege,** His nickname Hotspur will be his excuse.
[5]Impetuosity.   [6]Lure.   [7]Report.
[8]**Deliver up,** release. Westmoreland had been hostage for Worcester's safe return.
[9]Immediately.   [10]Falsely denying on oath.   [11]Pledged as hostage.
[12]**draw . . . breath,** i.e., in fighting.   [13]Challenge.

VER. No, by my soul. I never in my life
   Did hear a challenge urged[14] more modestly,
   Unless a brother should a brother dare
   To gentle exercise and proof of arms.
   He gave you all the duties of[15] a man,
   Trimmed up your praises with a princely tongue,
   Spoke your deservings like a chronicle,
   Making you ever better than his praise
   By still dispraising praise valued with you.[16]   60
   And, which became him like a prince indeed,
   He made a blushing cital[17] of himself,
   And chid his truant youth with such a grace
   As if he mastered there a double spirit
   Of teaching and of learning instantly.
   There did he pause. But let me tell the world,
   If he outlive the envy[18] of this day,
   England did never owe[19] so sweet a hope,
   So much miscónstrued in his wantonness.
HOT. Cousin, I think thou art enamored   70
   On his follies. Never did I hear
   Of any prince so wild a libertine.
   But be he as he will, yet once ere night
   I will embrace him with a soldier's arm,
   That he shall shrink under my courtesy.
   Arm, arm with speed. And, fellows, soldiers, friends,
   Better consider what you have to do
   Than I, that have not well the gift of tongue,
   Can lift your blood up with persuasion.
                 [*Enter a* MESSENGER.]
MESS. My lord, here are letters for you.   80
HOT. I cannot read them now.
   O gentlemen, the time of life is short!
   To spend that shortness basely were too long
   If life did ride upon a dial's point,[20]
   Still[21] ending at the arrival of an hour.
   An if we live, we live to tread on kings;
   If die, brave death when princes die with us!
   Now, for our consciences, the arms are fair
   When the intent[22] of bearing them is just.
                 [*Enter another* MESSENGER.]
MESS. My lord, prepare. The King comes on apace.   90
HOT. I thank him, that he cuts me from my tale,
   For I profess not talking, only this—
   Let each man do his best. And here draw I
   A sword whose temper[23] I intend to stain

[14] Put forward.   [15] **duties of,** respect due to.
[16] **By . . . you,** by continuously saying that your praise was undervalued.
[17] Recital.   [18] Malice.   [19] Own.
[20] **dial's point,** hand of a clock.   [21] Always.
[22] Cause.   [23] Lit., hardness, quality.

With the best blood that I can meet withal
In the adventure of this perilous day.
Now, Esperance! Percy! and set on.
Sound all the lofty instruments of war,
And by that music let us all embrace;
For, heaven to earth, some of us never shall   100
A second time do such a courtesy.
                    [*The trumpets sound. They embrace, and exeunt.*]

                    SCENE III. Plain between the camps.

            [*The* KING *enters with his power. Alarum to the battle.*[1]
              Then enter DOUGLAS *and* SIR WALTER BLUNT.]
BLUNT. What is thy name, that in the battle thus
    Thou crossest me? What honor dost thou seek
    Upon my head?
DOUG.   Know then, my name is Douglas,
    And I do haunt thee in the battle thus
    Because some tell me that thou art a King.
BLUNT. They tell thee true.
DOUG. The Lord of Stafford dear today hath bought
    Thy likeness; for instead of thee, King Harry,[2]
    This sword hath ended him. So shall it thee
    Unless thou yield thee as my prisoner.   10
BLUNT. I was not born a yielder, thou proud Scot,
    And thou shalt find a King that will revenge
    Lord Stafford's death.
            [*They fight.* DOUGLAS *kills* BLUNT. *Enter* HOTSPUR.]
HOT. O Douglas, hadst thou fought at Holmedon thus,
    I never had triumphed upon a Scot.
DOUG. All's done, all's won. Here breathless lies the King.
HOT. Where?
DOUG. Here.
HOT. This, Douglas? No. I know this face full well.
    A gallant knight he was, his name was Blunt,   20
    Semblably furnished[3] like the King himself.
DOUG. A fool go with thy soul[4] whither it goes!
    A borrowed title hast thou bought too dear.
    Why didst thou tell me that thou wert a king?
HOT. The King hath many marching in his coats.[5]

---

[1]**Alarum . . . battle,** battle noises.
[2]**thee . . . Harry,** Blunt is wearing the King's coat of arms and not his own, and so is mistaken by Douglas for the King.
[3]**Semblably furnished,** wearing similar armor.
[4]**A . . . soul,** a proverbial phrase, "you foolish soul."
[5]Coats of arms.

DOUG. Now, by my sword, I will kill all his coats.
I'll murder all his wardrobe, piece by piece,
Until I meet the King.
HOT. Up, and away!
Our soldiers stand full fairly for the day.[6] [*Exeunt.*]
[*Alarum. Enter* FALSTAFF, *alone.*]
FAL. Though I could 'scape shot-free[7] at London, I fear the shot here. 30
Here's no scoring but upon the pate. Soft! Who are you? Sir Walter
Blunt. There's honor for you! Here's no vanity![8] I am as hot as molten
lead, and as heavy too. God keep lead out of me! I need no more
weight than mine own bowels. I have led my ragamuffins where
they are peppered.[9] There's not three of my hundred and fifty left
alive, and they are for the town's end, to beg during life. But who
comes here?
[*Enter the* PRINCE.]
PRINCE. What, stand'st thou idle here? Lend me thy sword.
Many a nobleman lies stark and stiff
Under the hoofs of vaunting enemies 40
Whose deaths are yet unrevenged. I prithee lend me thy sword.
FAL. O Hal, I prithee give me leave to breathe a while. Turk
Gregory[10] never did such deeds in arms as I have done this day. I
have paid Percy, I have made him sure.
PRINCE. He is, indeed, and living to kill thee. I prithee lend me thy
sword.
FAL. Nay, before God, Hal, if Percy be alive, thou get'st not my sword.
But take my pistol, if thou wilt.
PRINCE. Give it me. What, is it in the case?
FAL. Aye, Hal, 'tis hot, 'tis hot. There's that will sack a city. 50
[*The* PRINCE *draws it out, and finds it
to be a bottle of sack.*]
PRINCE. What, is it a time to jest and dally now?
[*He throws the bottle at him. Exit.*]
FAL. Well, if Percy be alive, I'll pierce[11] him. If he do come in my
way, so. If he do not, if I come in his willingly, let him make a car-
bonado[12] of me. I like not such grinning honor as Sir Walter hath.
Give me life, which if I can save, so; if not, honor comes unlooked-
for, and there's an end. [*Exit.*]

---

[6]**full . . . day,** i.e., are full of fight.
[7]**shot-free,** without paying the *shot* (the tavern bill) which had been scored up against him.
[8]**no vanity,** spoken ironically. "Who said honor was not a vain thing?"
[9]**where . . . peppered,** Falstaff's heroism has a base motive. Until the army is remustered
he will pocket the pay of his dead soldiers.
[10]**Turk Gregory,** Pope Gregory VII, who had a reputation for ferocity. The Turk was proverbial for cruelty.
[11]Pronounced "perse," a pun on "Percy."
[12]Piece of meat slashed for broiling.

SCENE IV. Another part of the field.

[*Alarum. Excursions.*[1] *Enter the* KING, *the* PRINCE, LORD
JOHN OF LANCASTER, *and* EARL OF WESTMORELAND.]

KING. I prithee
   Harry, withdraw thyself, thou bleed'st too much.
   Lord John of Lancaster, go you with him.
LANC. Not I, my lord, unless I did bleed too.
PRINCE. I beseech your Majesty, make up,[2]
   Lest your retirement do amaze[3] your friends.
KING. I will do so.
   My Lord of Westmoreland, lead him to his tent.
WEST. Come, my lord, I'll lead you to your tent.
PRINCE. Lead me, my lord? I do not need your help.   10
   And God forbid a shallow scratch should drive
   The Prince of Wales from such a field as this,
   Where stained[4] nobility lies trodden on
   And rebels' arms triumph in massacres!
LANC. We breathe[5] too long. Come, Cousin Westmoreland,
   Our duty this way lies. For God's sake, come.
                      [*Exeunt* PRINCE JOHN *and* WESTMORELAND.]
PRINCE. By God, thou hast deceived me, Lancaster,
   I did not think thee lord of such a spirit.
   Before, I loved thee as a brother, John,
   But now I do respect thee as my soul.   20
KING. I saw him hold Lord Percy at the point
   With lustier maintenance than I did look for
   Of such an ungrown warrior.
PRINCE.   Oh, this boy
   Lends mettle[6] to us all!   [*Exit.*]
                      [*Enter* DOUGLAS.]
DOUG. Another King! They grow like Hydra's heads.[7]
   I am the Douglas, fatal to all those
   That wear those colors on them. What art thou,
   That counterfeit'st the person of a king?
KING. The king himself, who, Douglas, grieves at heart
   So many of his shadows[8] thou hast met   30
   And not the very King. I have two boys
   Seek Percy and thyself about the field.
   But, seeing thou fall'st on me so luckily,
   I will assay[9] thee. So defend thyself.
DOUG. I fear thou art another counterfeit,
   And yet, in faith, thou bear'st thee like a king.

---

[1] Noises to indicate rapid movements in battle.
[2] **make up,** go up to the front line.   [3] Fill with dismay.
[4] Bloodstained.   [5] Rest.   [6] Courage.
[7] **Hydra's heads,** Hydra was a many-headed monster slain by Hercules. As soon as one head was cut off, two others grew in its place.
[8] Imitations.   [9] Challenge.

But mine I am sure thou art, whoe'er thou be,
And thus I win thee.
    [*They fight; the* KING *being in danger, re-enter* PRINCE OF WALES.]
PRINCE. Hold up thy head, vile Scot, or thou art like
  Never to hold it up again! The spirits   40
  Of valiant Shirley, Stafford, Blunt,[10] are in my arms.
  It is the Prince of Wales that threatens thee,
  Who never promiseth but he means to pay.
                        [*They fight:* DOUGLAS *flies.*]
  Cheerly, my lord. How fares your Grace?
  Sir Nicholas Gawsey hath for succor sent,
  And so hath Clifton. I'll to Clifton straight.
KING. Stay, and breathe a while.
  Thou hast redeemed thy lost opinion,[11]
  And showed thou makest some tender[12] of my life,
  In this fair rescue thou hast brought to me.   50
PRINCE. Oh God! They did me too much injury
  That ever said I hearkened for[13] your death.
  If it were so, I might have let alone
  The insulting[14] hand of Douglas over you,
  Which would have been as speedy in your end
  As all the poisonous potions in the world,
  And saved the treacherous labor of your son.
KING. Make up to Clifton. I'll to Sir Nicholas Gawsey.   [*Exit.*]
              [*Enter* HOTSPUR.]
HOT. If I mistake not, thou art Harry Monmouth.
PRINCE. Thou speak'st as if I would deny my name.   60
HOT. My name is Harry Percy.
PRINCE.   Why, then I see
  A very valiant rebel of the name.
  I am the Prince of Wales. And think not, Percy,
  To share with me in glory any more.
  Two stars keep not their motion in one sphere,
  Nor can one England brook a double reign
  Of Harry Percy and the Prince of Wales.
HOT. Nor shall it, Harry, for the hour is come
  To end the one of us. And would to God
  Thy name in arms were now as great as mine!   70
PRINCE. I'll make it greater ere I part from thee,
  And all the budding honors on thy crest
  I'll crop, to make a garland for my head.
HOT. I can no longer brook thy vanities.
                        [*They fight.*]
              [*Enter* FALSTAFF.]
FAL. Well said, Hal! To it, Hal! Nay, you shall find no boy's play here,
  I can tell you.

---

[10] **Shirley . . . Blunt,** who have all fallen in the battle.   [11] Reputation.
[12] **makest . . . tender,** hast some regard for.
[13] **hearkened for,** desired.   [14] Triumphing.

[*Re-enter* DOUGLAS; *he fights with* FALSTAFF, *who falls down as if he were
    dead, and exit* DOUGLAS. HOTSPUR *is wounded, and falls.*]

HOT. O Harry, thou hast robbed me of my youth!
    I better brook the loss of brittle life
    Than those proud titles thou hast won of me.
    They wound my thoughts worse than thy sword my flesh.   80
    But thought's the slave of life, and life Time's fool,
    And Time, that takes survèy of all the world,
    Must have a stop.[15] Oh, I could prophesy,
    But that the earthy and cold hand of death
    Lies on my tongue. No, Percy, thou art dust,
    And food for——   [*Dies.*]
PRINCE. For worms, brave Percy, Fare thee well, great heart!
    Ill-weaved ambition, how much art thou shrunk!
    When that this body did contain a spirit,
    A kingdom for it was too small a bound,[16]   90
    But now two paces of the vilest earth
    Is room enough. This earth that bears thee dead
    Bears not alive so stout a gentleman.
    If thou wert sensible[17] of courtesy,
    I should not make so dear a show of zeal.[18]
    But let my favors[19] hide thy mangled face,
    And, even in thy behalf, I'll thank myself
    For doing these fair rites of tenderness.
    Adieu, and take thy praise with thee to Heaven!
    Thy ignominy sleep with thee in the grave,   100
    But not remembered in thy epitaph!
                             [*He spieth* FALSTAFF *on the ground.*]
    What, old acquaintance! Could not all this flesh
    Keep in a little life? Poor Jack, farewell!
    I could have better spared a better man.
    Oh, I should have a heavy miss of thee
    If I were much in love with vanity![20]
    Death hath not struck so fat a deer today,
    Though many dearer, in this bloody fray.
    Emboweled[21] will I see thee by and by.
    Till then in blood by noble Percy lie.   [*Exit.*]   110
FAL. [*Rising up*] Emboweled! If thou embowel me today, I'll give you
    leave to powder[22] me and eat me too tomorrow. 'Sblood, 'twas time
    to counterfeit, or that hot termagant[23] Scot had paid me scot and
    lot[24] too. Counterfeit? I lie, I am no counterfeit. To die is to be a

---

[15] **thought's . . . stop,** thought can only exist while there is life, but life is treated like a fool
by Time, and Time itself will end—a thought in one form or another constantly recurring in
Shakespeare's plays.
    [16] Boundary.   [17] Able to feel.   [18] **show of zeal,** mark of respect.
    [19] Scarf or handkerchief given to a knight by his lady.   [20] Folly.
    [21] Disemboweled. He carries on the metaphor and pun of deer, for the last act in the hunt
was the disemboweling of the slain deer.
    [22] Pickle.   [23] Ferocious.   [24] **paid . . . lot,** paid all dues.

counterfeit, for he is but the counterfeit of a man who hath not the life of a man. But to counterfeit dying when a man thereby liveth is to be no counterfeit, but the true and perfect image of life indeed. The better part of valor is discretion, in the which better part I have saved my life. 'Zounds, I am afraid of this gunpowder Percy, though he be dead. How if he should counterfeit too, and rise? By my faith, I am afraid he would prove the better counterfeit. Therefore I'll make him sure. Yea, and I'll swear I killed him. Why may he not rise as well as I? Nothing confutes me but eyes, and nobody sees me. Therefore, sirrah [*Stabbing him*], with a new wound in your thigh, come you along with me.

[*Takes up* HOTSPUR *on his back.*]

[*Re-enter the* PRINCE OF WALES *and* LORD JOHN OF LANCASTER.]

PRINCE. Come, Brother John, full bravely hast thou fleshed
Thy maiden sword.[25]

LANC.   But, soft! Whom have we here?
Did you not tell me this fat man was dead?

PRINCE. I did, I saw him dead,
Breathless and bleeding on the ground. Art thou alive?
Or is it fantasy[26] that plays upon our eyesight?
I prithee, speak, we will not trust our eyes
Without our ears. Thou art not what thou seem'st.

FAL. No, that's certain, I am not a double[27] man. But if I be not Jack Falstaff, then am I a Jack. There is Percy [*Throwing the body down*]. If your father will do me any honor, so; if not, let him kill the next Percy himself. I look to be either earl or duke, I can assure you.

PRINCE. Why, Percy I killed myself, and saw thee dead.

FAL. Didst thou? Lord, Lord, how this world is given to lying! I grant you I was down and out of breath, and so was he. But we rose both at an instant, and fought a long hour by Shrewsbury clock. If I may be believed, so; if not, let them that should reward valor bear the sin upon their own heads. I'll take it upon my death, I gave him this wound in the thigh. If the man were alive, and would deny it, 'zounds, I would make him eat a piece of my sword.

LANC. This is the strangest tale that ever I heard.

PRINCE. This is the strangest fellow, Brother John.
Come, bring your luggage nobly on your back.
For my part, if a lie may do thee grace,
I'll gild it with the happiest terms[28] I have.

[*A retreat is sounded.*]

The trumpet sounds retreat,[29] the day is ours.
Come, Brother, let us to the highest[30] of the field,
To see what friends are living, who are dead.

[*Exeunt* PRINCE OF WALES *and* LANCASTER.]

---

[25]**fleshed . . . sword,** you have fought bravely in your first action.
[26]Imagination, illusion.   [27]I.e., a double of myself.
[28]**happiest terms,** best phrases.
[29]**trumpet . . . retreat,** i.e., to recall the troops from the pursuit.
[30]I.e., ground.

FAL. I'll follow, as they say, for reward. He that rewards me, God reward
    him! If I do grow great, I'll grow less; for I'll purge, and leave sack,
    and live cleanly as a nobleman should do.   [*Exit.*]

SCENE V. *Another part of the field.*

[*The trumpets sound. Enter the* KING, PRINCE OF WALES,
LORD JOHN OF LANCASTER, EARL OF WESTMORELAND,
    with WORCESTER *and* VERNON *prisoners.*]

KING. Thus ever did rebellion find rebuke.
    Ill-spirited[1] Worcester! Did not we send grace,
    Pardon, and terms of love to all of you?
    And wouldst thou turn our offers contrary,
    Misuse the tenor of thy kinsman's trust?
    Three knights upon our party slain today,
    A noble Earl and many a creature else
    Had been alive this hour
    If like a Christian thou hadst truly borne
    Betwixt our armies true intelligence.   10
WOR. What I have done my safety urged me to.
    And I embrace this fortune patiently,
    Since not to be avoided it falls on me.
KING. Bear Worcester to the death, and Vernon too.
    Other offenders we will pause upon.
                    [*Exeunt* WORCESTER *and* VERNON, *guarded.*]
    How goes the field?
PRINCE. The noble Scot, Lord Douglas, when he saw
    The fortune of the day quite turned from him,
    The noble Percy slain, and all his men
    Upon the foot of fear, fled with the rest;   20
    And falling from a hill, he was so bruised
    That the pursuers took him. At my tent
    The Douglas is, and I beseech your Grace
    I may dispose of him.
KING.   With all my heart.
PRINCE. Then, Brother John of Lancaster, to you
    This honorable bounty shall belong.
    Go to the Douglas, and deliver him
    Up to his pleasure, ransomless and free.
    His valor shown upon our crests today
    Hath taught us how to cherish such high deeds   30
    Even in the bosom of our adversaries.
LANC. I thank your Grace for this high courtesy,
    Which I shall give away immediately.
KING. Then this remains, that we divide our power.
    You, Son John, and my cousin Westmoreland
    Toward York shall bend you with your dearest[2] speed,

_____
[1] **Ill-spirited,** evil-spirited.   [2] Best.

To meet Northumberland and the prelate Scroop,
Who, as we hear, are busily in arms.
Myself and you, Son Harry, will toward Wales,
To fight with Glendower and the Earl of March.   40
Rebellion in this land shall lose his sway,
Meeting the check[3] of such another day.
And since this business so fair is done,
Let us not leave till all our own be won.   [*Exeunt.*]

[3] **Meeting . . . check,** incurring such a disaster.

John Donne
(1572–1631)

The first thing the reader of John Donne's poems is likely to be struck by is their tone of voice. We read "For God's sake hold your tongue, and let me love," and we are suddenly hearing an extraordinary voice: vital, energetic, flashing mercurially from the abrupt and colloquial to the gnarled and difficult, thirsty to drink all experience and all learning, from the earthiest to the most sublime, tirelessly histrionic, whipping dramatic masks on and off with dazzling speed, simultaneously attentive to the brain, the soul, and the genitals. It is, in short, a Renaissance voice. If Hamlet had been a poet, we feel that he would not have written the piece of doggerel to the "beautified Ophelia" that Polonius quotes; he is more likely to have written John Donne's poems.

Donne was born in 1572, during an intensely anti-Catholic age in England, into a devoutly Roman Catholic family in London. His father was a prosperous dealer in iron and hardware; his mother was the daughter of John Heywood, the Elizabethan satirist and playwright. Many details of Donne's early life are missing, but it appears that he spent his youth to the age of twenty-five in a variety of pursuits, all directed toward finding some way to make a place for himself as a Catholic in a fervently Protestant world. He enrolled at Oxford when he was twelve and remained there until he was almost sixteen. (Catholic parents often sent their children to the university at a very early age in order to avoid their having to take the Oath of Supremacy, required of university students at the age of sixteen, acknowledging Queen Elizabeth as "Supreme Governor" of the church. In any case, Donne would not have been allowed, as a Catholic, to take a degree at either Oxford or Cambridge.) Upon leaving Oxford, he seems to have traveled for as much as four years in Italy and Spain. When he was nineteen, he returned to London and became a law student at the Inns of Court. If contemporary reports are to be trusted, he made the most of the life of a London law student; he was said to be "not dissolute, but very neat [witty and fashionable], a great visitor of ladies, a great frequenter of plays, a great writer of conceited verses." He seems to have combined his life as a fashionable man about town, however, with that of a serious student, not only of the law but also of theology. He surveyed, as he later wrote, "the body of divinity, as it was then controverted betwixt the Reformed and the Roman Church"; the result was that he ceased to be a practicing Catholic, although he did not become an Anglican until some years later. Leaving the Inns of Court in 1596, Donne got a taste of war, sailing under Sir Walter Raleigh to attack the Spanish shipping in Cadiz harbor and under the Earl of Essex to engage Spanish treasure ships off the Azores. Upon his return, since he was no longer a Catholic, he was able to obtain a position as secretary to Sir Thomas Egerton, Keeper of the Great Seal. The way to success seemed open; in 1601, Donne served as Member of Parliament for one of several constituencies controlled by Egerton.

These great expectations ended abruptly, however, when Donne, after three years in Egerton's service, secretly married Ann More, the seventeen-year-old niece of Egerton's wife. Egerton himself had no particular objection to the marriage, but Ann's father, Sir George More, was infuriated: he forced Egerton to dismiss Donne immediately; he had Donne, along with two friends who had abetted him, committed to prison; and he appealed the marriage to the Court of High Commission. Donne, in his letter to Ann telling her of his dismissal, concluded: "John Donne, Ann Donne, undone."

Donne was released from prison after two months and his marriage was ratified by the Archbishop of Canterbury, but his career was in ruins. For the next dozen years, between the ages of twenty-nine and forty-one, he was hard put to earn a living for his growing family. (He and Ann had twelve children, seven of whom survived childhood.) Much of his time during these years was spent in seeking preferment at Court, trying to get the secretaryship or ambassadorship for which his service with Egerton was to have prepared him, and in assisting Thomas Morton, one of King James's chaplains, in the preparation of Protestant propaganda intended to convert Catholics "by weight of reason" rather than by law.

Finally, in 1615, at the age of forty-three, Donne yielded to pressure from Morton and from King James and took Anglican Holy Orders. Almost immediately he was appointed Reader in Divinity at Lincoln's Inn, where he preached to a fashionable and intelligent congregation of lawyers and courtiers. Donne's wit, eloquence, and histrionic flair served him well in the pulpit, and he soon became famous for his sermons. He became Dean of St. Paul's in 1621, and during the remaining ten years of his life he continued to preach his eloquent and dramatic sermons, one hundred and sixty of which survive. Obsessed with death, he preached his own funeral sermon a few weeks before he died and had his portrait painted in his shroud. He wrote "Hymn to God, My God, in My Sickness" on his deathbed. Death came in 1631.

Donne's witty and highly wrought poems have often tested the poetic sensibilities of succeeding ages. In his own time, his works were prized by followers who found in them an alternative to the content and language of Elizabethan lyricism, which had grown somewhat mechanical and facile with age. But the "Metaphysical" style went out of fashion about thirty years after Donne's death, and neither the eighteenth nor the nineteenth century had much use for him. Though intellectual, he lacked the clarity and universality the Neoclassicists sought; though passionate, he lacked the un-ironic directness that pleased Romantic tastes. In the early twentieth century he was rediscovered by readers dissatisfied with the exhausted poetic rhetoric of the late nineteenth century, as his original readers had been with the fag end of sixteenth-century poetry. In Donne these moderns found the toughness of mind, the passionate intensity, and the openness to a wide range of experience that they sought in their new poetry. The result has been the elevation of Donne to a major place among English poets, a position he continued to hold long after the struggle for a modern poetry was won.

Donne is an intensely dramatic poet—most of his poems present a particular speaker addressing a particular listener in a specific place—and what he dramatizes is himself. His is a voice that can move dazzlingly from a harsh, colloquial line to a singingly beautiful one, or from a moment of cynical, shallow wit to one of intense and simple feeling. When his poems are read dramatically, their wit often seems a defense against despair; death is never far from Donne's mind, even in his lightest moods. There is always the bone beneath the "subtle wreath of hair," and even to make love is to "die." Donne's distinctive voice, even after the witty paradoxes and the intellectual fireworks have ceased to startle, is likely to continue to ring in the reader's ear.

FURTHER READING *(prepared by W.J.R.):* Good studies described by their titles are George A. E. Parfitt, *John Donne: A Literary Life,* 1989; John Carey, *John Donne: Life, Mind, and Art,* 1981; and R. C. Bald, *John Donne: A Life,* ed. Wesley Milgate, 1970. Robert H. Ray, *A John Donne Companion,* 1990, is a handy reference guide. Frank J. Warnke, *John Donne,* 1987, is an excellent introduction to Donne's life and works. Arnold Stein, *John Donne's Lyrics: The Eloquence of Action,* 1962, is a good comprehensive critical study of the poetry. James Winny's *A Preface to Donne,* 1970, contains excellent introductory material on Donne's religious, intellectual, and literary backgrounds. Several poems are also studied individually, including "The Sun Rising" and "Batter my Heart." *Donne, Songs and Sonnets: A Casebook,* ed. Julian Lovelock, 1973, provides a biographical introduction, a sampling of early criticism of Donne's poetry, and selections from twentieth-century criticism by C. S. Lewis, Arnold Stein, and others. For an overview of the decline and rise of Donne's reputation, see Murray Roston's *The Soul of Wit,* 1974, which also discusses the divine poems, considering at length the paradox of Donne as rake and religious writer. J. B. Leishman's *The Monarch of Wit,* 1951, 6th ed. 1962, begins with a general discussion of Donne's place in seventeenth-century poetry and then treats the epigrams and satires, songs and sonnets, and the divine poems in detail in separate sections. The tercentenary year of Donne's death—1931—was celebrated with *A Garland for John Donne,* ed. Theodore Spencer, 1931, rpt. 1958. Eight essays on fairly general topics are collected in this volume, the lead essay being T. S. Eliot's "Donne in Our Time." More recent critical perspectives are represented in *Essential Articles for the Study of John Donne's Poetry,* ed. John R. Roberts, 1975, which discusses Donne's reputation, his prosody, his love poetry, and other topics.

THE GOOD-MORROW

I wonder by my troth, what thou and I
Did, till we lov'd? were we not wean'd till then?
But suck'd on country pleasures,[1] childishly?
Or snorted we in the seven sleepers' den?[2]

---

[1] Rural pleasures, but also a sexual pun.
[2] The seven sleepers were seven Christian youths of Ephesus who were said to have taken refuge in a cave during the persecution of the emperor Decius and slept for two centuries.

'Twas so; but this,[3] all pleasures fancies be.   5
If ever any beauty I did see,
Which I desir'd, and got, 'twas but a dream of thee.

And now good-morrow to our waking souls,
Which watch not one another out of fear;
For love all love of other sights controls,   10
And makes one little room[4] an everywhere.
Let sea-discoverers to new worlds have gone,
Let maps to other, worlds on worlds have shown,
Let us possess one world, each hath one, and is one.[5]

My face in thine eye, thine in mine appears,   15
And true plain hearts do in the faces rest;
Where can we find two better hemispheres[6]
Without sharp North, without declining West?
What ever dies, was not mixt equally;[7]
If our two loves be one, or thou and I   20
Love so alike that none do slacken, none can die.

SONG

Go, and catch a falling star,
    Get with child a mandrake root,[1]
Tell me, where all past years are,
    Or who cleft the Devil's foot,[2]
Teach me to hear Mermaids singing,   5
    Or to keep off envy's stinging,
            And find
            What wind
Serves to advance an honest mind.

If thou be'st born to strange sights,   10
    Things invisible to see,
Ride ten thousand days and nights,
    Till age snow white hairs on thee,
Thou, when thou return'st, wilt tell me
All strange wonders that befell thee,   15
            And swear
            No where
Lives a woman true, and fair.

---

[3]Compared to this love.   [4]Their bedroom.
[5]That is, each has the world of the other, and each is a world to the other.
[6]Donne may have been thinking of "cordiform" maps which depicted each hemisphere as a heart.
[7]An axiom in alchemy. *Equally* here means "uniformly."
[1]The forked root of the mandrake looks like the lower half of a human body.
[2]The devil is said to be recognizable by his cloven hoof.

If thou find'st one, let me know,
Such a Pilgrimage were sweet; 20
Yet do not, I would not go,
Though at next door we might meet,
Though she were true, when you met her,
And last, till you write your letter,
Yet she 25
Will be
False, ere I come, to two, or three.

THE CANONIZATION

For God's sake hold your tongue, and let me love;
Or chide my palsy, or my gout,
My five grey hairs, or ruin'd fortune flout;
With wealth your state, your mind with arts improve,
Take you a course,[1] get you a place,[2] 5
Observe his Honour, or his Grace,[3]
Or the King's real, or his stamped face[4]
Contemplate; what you will, approve,[5]
So you will let me love.

Alas, alas, who's injur'd by my love? 10
What merchant's ships have my sighs drown'd?
Who says my tears have overflow'd his ground?
When did my colds a forward spring remove?
When did the heats which my veins fill
Add one more to the plaguy bill?[6] 15
Soldiers find wars, and lawyers find out still
Litigious men, which quarrels move,[7]
Though she and I do love.

Call us what you will, we are made such by love;
Call her one, me another fly,[8] 20
We're tapers too, and at our own cost die,[9]
And we in us find the Eagle and the Dove.[10]

---

[1] That is, a course of action leading to worldly success.
[2] A job.
[3] 1) A judge or a nobleman, 2) the qualities of honor and grace.
[4] Stamped on a coin.   [5] Try out, test.
[6] The list of deaths from the plague.   [7] Who start quarrels.
[8] The taper-fly, which was attracted to flame and burned itself in it, was said to be hermaphroditic and resurrectable.
[9] Sexual intercourse was thought to shorten life. Therefore lovers are like candles, which get shorter as they burn. *Die* is a slang term for having sexual intercourse.
[10] Symbols, in medieval literature, of righteousness and mercy.

The Phoenix riddle[11] hath more wit
By us; we two being one, are it.
So to one neutral thing both sexes fit,   25
We die and rise the same,[12] and prove
Mysterious by this love.

We can die by it, if not live by love,
And if unfit for tombs and hearse[13]
Our legend be, it will be fit for verse;   30
And if no piece of Chronicle we prove,[14]
We'll build in sonnets pretty rooms;[15]
As well a well-wrought urn becomes
The greatest ashes, as half-acre tombs,
And by these hymns, all shall approve   35
Us canonized for Love:

And thus invoke us; You whom reverend love
Made one another's hermitage;
You, to whom love was peace, that now is rage;
Who did the whole world's soul contract, and drove   40
Into the glasses of your eyes[16]
(So made such mirrors, and such spies,
That they did all to you epitomize,)
Countries, Towns, Courts: beg from above
A pattern of your love![17]

THE FUNERAL

Whoever comes to shroud me, do not harm
Nor question much
That subtle wreath of hair, which crowns my arm;[1]
The mystery, the sign you must not touch,
For 'tis my outward Soul,   5
Viceroy to that, which then to heaven being gone,
Will leave this to control,
And keep these limbs, her Provinces, from dissolution.

---

[11] The Phoenix bird, which was resurrected from its own ashes, was also said to be hermaphroditic.

[12] In sexual intercourse, we become sexless (*neutral*), because one sex cancels out the other. But after intercourse, we mysteriously are two different sexes again. *Die* and *rise* also have sexual meanings.

[13] Funereal poems were pinned to hearses.

[14] If we are not recorded in history, or if we do not beget children as described in I Chronicles 1–9.

[15] Mausoleum rooms and stanzas (in Italian).

[16] That is, drove the whole world into each other's eyes by gazing at each other.

[17] Ask the god of love for a pattern of your love.

[1] Such bracelets found on corpses are described by several medieval writers, including Giraldus Cambrensis.

For if the sinewy thread my brain lets fall
    Through every part,[2]   10
Can tie those parts, and make me one of all;
These hairs which upward grew, and strength and art
    Have from a better brain,
Can better do 't;[3] except[4] she meant that I
    By this should know my pain,   15
As prisoners then are manacled, when they're condemn'd to die.

Whate'er she meant by it, bury it with me,
    For since I am
Love's martyr, it might breed idolatry,
If into others' hands these Reliques came;   20
    As 'twas humility
To afford to it all that a Soul can do,[5]
    So, 'tis some bravery,
That since you would save none of me, I bury some of you.

THE FLEA

Mark but this flea, and mark in this,
How little that which thou deny'st me is;
It suck'd me first, and now sucks thee,
And in this flea, our two bloods mingled be;[1]
Thou know'st that this cannot be said   5
A sin, nor shame, nor loss of maidenhead,
    Yet this enjoys before it woo,
    And pamper'd swells with one blood made of two,
    And this, alas, is more than we would do.

Oh stay, three lives in one flea spare,   10
Where we almost, yea more than married are.
This flea is you and I, and this
Our marriage bed, and marriage temple is;
Though parents grudge, and you, we're met,
And cloistered in these living walls of jet.   15
    Though use make you apt to kill me,
    Let not to that, self murder added be,
    And sacrilege,[2] three sins in killing three.

---

[2] The nervous system which makes him one being.
[3] That is, tie the parts of the body together.
[4] Unless.
[5] It was submission to give to it all that a soul can do.
[1] The three united in the flea—the flea himself, the lover, and the mistress—thus echo the Trinity, an idea that recurs throughout the poem.
[2] Sacrilege because the flea is a "marriage temple."

Cruel and sudden, hast thou since
Purpled thy nail, in blood of innocence?   20
Wherein could this flea guilty be,
Except in that drop which it suck'd from thee?
Yet thou triumph'st, and say'st that thou
Find'st not thyself, nor me the weaker now;
    'Tis true, then learn how false, fears be;   25
Just so much honour, when thou yield'st to me,
Will waste, as this flea's death took life from thee.

A VALEDICTION: FORBIDDING MOURNING[1]

As virtuous men pass mildly away,
    And whisper to their souls, to go,
Whilst some of their sad friends do say,
    The breath goes now, and some say, no:

So let us melt, and make no noise,   5
    No tear-floods, nor sigh-tempests move,
'Twere profanation of our joys
    To tell the laity our love.

Moving of th' earth brings harms and fears,
    Men reckon what it did and meant,   10
But trepidation of the spheres,[2]
    Though greater far, is innocent.

Dull sublunary[3] lovers' love
    (Whose soul is sense[4]) cannot admit
Absence, because it doth remove   15
    Those things which elemented[5] it.

But we by a love, so much refin'd,
    That ourselves know not what it is,
Inter-assurèd of the mind,
    Care less eyes, lips, and hands to miss.   20

Our two souls therefore, which are one,
    Though I must go, endure not yet[6]
A breach, but an expansion,
    Like gold to aery thinness beat.

---

[1] Donne wrote this poem to his wife when he went to the Continent with Sir Robert Drury in 1611.

[2] *Trepidation* was the term used for the trembling of the outermost sphere (the *primum mobile*) in the Ptolemaic universe; this gave movement to the other spheres. The word also means "fear" of heavenly disturbances.

[3] Beneath the moon; earthly.   [4] Dependent upon sensual gratification.

[5] Created or composed.   [6] Nevertheless do not allow.

If they be two, they are two so 25
    As stiff twin compasses[7] are two,
Thy soul the fixed foot, makes no show
To move, but doth, if th' other do.

And though it in the centre sit,
    Yet when the other far doth roam, 30
It leans, and hearkens after it,
    And grows erect, as that comes home.

Such wilt thou be to me, who must
    Like th' other foot, obliquely[8] run;
Thy firmness makes my circle just, 35
    And makes me end, where I begun.

LOVE'S DIET

To what a cumbersome unwieldiness
And burdenous corpulence my love had grown,
    But that I did, to make it less,
    And keep it in proportion,
Give it a diet, made it feed upon 5
That which love worst endures, *discretion.*

Above one sigh a day I allow'd him not,
Of which my fortune, and my faults had part;
    And if sometimes by stealth he got
    A she sigh from my mistress' heart, 10
And thought to feast on that, I let him see
'Twas neither very sound, nor meant to me.[1]

If he wrung from me a tear, I brined[2] it so
With scorn or shame, that him it nourish'd not;
    If he suck'd hers, I let him know 15
    'Twas not a tear, which he had got,
His drink was counterfeit, as was his meat;
For, eyes which roll towards all, weep not, but sweat.

Whatever he would dictate, I writ that,
But burnt my letters; when she writ to me, 20
    And that that favour made him fat,
    I said, if any title be

[7] That is, the two legs of a compass.
[8] Not in a straight line. The lover travels in a circle, and then, when the compass is closed, returns to his starting place.
[1] This is a difficult line. It probably means either, "The *she sigh* was neither a true ("very") sound, nor meant *for* me," or "The *she sigh* was to me neither a true sound nor sincerely intended."
[2] Salted.

Convey'd by this, Ah, what doth it avail,
To be the fortieth name in an entail?[3]

Thus I reclaim'd my buzzard[4] love, to fly   25
At what, and when, and how, and where I choose;
   Now negligent of sport I lie,
   And now as other falconers use,
I spring[5] a mistress, swear, write, sigh and weep:
And the game kill'd, or lost, go talk, and sleep.   30

ELEGY XIX
TO HIS MISTRESS GOING TO BED

Come, Madam, come, all rest my powers defy,
Until I labour, I in labour lie.[1]
The foe oft-times having the foe in sight,
Is tired with standing though he never fight.[2]
Off with that girdle, like heaven's Zone glistering,   5
But a far fairer world encompassing.
Unpin that spangled breastplate which you wear,
That th' eyes of busy fools may be stopt there.
Unlace yourself, for that harmonious chime
Tells me from you, that now it is bed time.   10
Off with that happy busk,[3] which I envy,
That still can be, and still can stand so nigh.
Your gown going off, such beauteous state reveals,
As when from flowry meads th' hill's shadow steals.
Off with that wiry Coronet and show   15
The hairy Diadem which on you doth grow:
Now off with those shoes, and then safely tread
In this love's hallow'd temple, this soft bed.
In such white robes, heaven's Angels used to be
Receiv'd by men; thou Angel bring'st with thee   20
A heaven like Mahomet's Paradise;[4] and though
Ill spirits walk in white, we easily know,
By this these Angels from an evil sprite,
Those set our hairs, but these our flesh upright.
   Licence my roving hands, and let them go,   25
Before, behind, between, above, below.

---

[3]An *entail* is a paper documenting a line of descent of ownership or inheritance. The lover doubts that he will win the mistress, since he is so far down on the list.

[4]That is, rapacious but slow.

[5]Rouse from hiding, as in hunting with falcons.

[1]Until I get to work at sexual intercourse, I lie in agony waiting.

[2]Note sexual double meanings.

[3]Corset.

[4]The paradise of Islam was supposed to be full of fleshly pleasure.

O my America! my new-found-land
My kingdom, safeliest when with one man mann'd,
My Mine of precious stones, My Empery,
How blest am I in this discovering thee! 30
To enter in these bonds, is to be free;
Then where my hand is set, my seal[5] shall be.
　　Full nakedness! All joys are due to thee,
As souls unbodied, bodies uncloth'd must be,
To taste whole joys. Gems which you women use 35
Are like Atlanta's balls,[6] cast in men's views,
That when a fool's eye lighteth on a Gem,
His earthly soul may covet theirs, not them.
Like pictures, or like books' gay coverings made
For lay-men, are all women thus array'd; 40
Themselves are mystic books, which only we
(Whom their imputed grace will dignify)
Must see reveal'd. Then since that I may know,[7]
As liberally,[8] as to a Midwife, show
Thyself: cast all, yea, this white linen hence, 45
There is no penance due to innocence.
　　To teach thee, I am naked first; why then
What needst thou have more covering than a man.

HOLY SONNETS

X

Death be not proud, though some have called thee
Mighty and dreadful, for, thou art not so,
For, those, whom thou think'st, thou dost overthrow,
Die not, poor death, nor yet canst thou kill me.
From rest and sleep, which but thy pictures be, 5
Much pleasure, then from thee, much more must flow,
And soonest our best men with thee do go,
Rest of their bones, and soul's delivery.
Thou art slave to Fate, Chance, kings, and desperate men,
And dost with poison, war, and sickness dwell, 10
And poppy, or charms can make us sleep as well,
And better than thy stroke; why swell'st thou then?
One short sleep past, we wake eternally,
And death shall be no more; death, thou shalt die.

---

[5]Both "impression" and "sign of ownership."
[6]Atalanta (usually so spelled) lost a race to Hippomenes because she paused three times to pick up three golden apples which Venus had given him and which he threw in her path.
[7]Both "have knowledge" and "have intercourse."
[8]Both "freely" and "lewdly."

XIV

Batter my heart, three-person'd God; for, you
As yet but knock, breathe, shine, and seek to mend;
That I may rise, and stand, o'erthrow me, and bend
Your force, to break, blow, burn and make me new.
I, like an usurp'd town, to another due,   5
Labour to admit you, but Oh, to no end,
Reason your viceroy in me, me should defend,
But is captiv'd, and proves weak or untrue.
Yet dearly I love you, and would be loved fain,
But am betroth'd unto your enemy: 10
Divorce me, untie, or break that knot again,
Take me to you, imprison me, for I
Except you enthral me, never shall be free,
Nor ever chaste, except you ravish me.

A HYMN TO GOD THE FATHER

I

Wilt Thou forgive that sin where I begun,[1]
  Which is my sin, though it were done before?[2]
Wilt Thou forgive that sin, through which I run,
  And do run still: though still I do deplore?
    When Thou hast done, Thou hast not done,   5
      For I have more.

II

Wilt Thou forgive that sin by which I have won
  Others to sin? and, made my sin their door?
Wilt Thou forgive that sin which I did shun
  A year, or two: but wallowed in, a score?   10
    When Thou hast done, Thou hast not done,
      For I have more.

III

I have a sin of fear, that when I have spun
  My last thread, I shall perish on the shore;[3]
Swear by Thyself, that at my death Thy son   15
  Shall shine as He shines now, and heretofore;
    And, having done that, Thou hast done,
      I fear no more.

---

[1] Original sin.
[2] Note the pun on Donne's name, here and below.
[3] As opposed to going to heaven.

John Milton

(1608–1674)

John Milton was one of the world's greatest and most influential poets, the author of the definitive English epic, the last towering figure of the European Renaissance, and a prominent partisan, on the Puritan and Republican side, in the momentous English Civil War, fought in the seventeenth century over issues of church and civil government. The issues of his day in certain ways mark the beginning of the modern political era.

Milton was born in London in 1608; his father, disinherited for converting from Roman Catholicism to Protestantism, was a successful businessman (and a gifted musician) who found it proper, the family having risen in the world, to give his son John the best of humanist educations, through private tutors and at St. Paul's School. The precocious evidence John gave of intellectual and poetic ability made the church, rather than a more worldly profession, seem his natural calling, and, although Milton later in his life chose not to be ordained, he remained grateful that his education had not been narrow and merely pragmatic. In 1625 he entered Cambridge University; there, after problems with his first tutor, he achieved distinction, though he chafed at what he considered the university's intellectual conservatism. At Cambridge he earned the nickname "The Lady" because of his delicate good looks, his religious seriousness, and the ascetic tendencies that (as his later life would reveal) coexisted with a passionate and even sensuous side of his character. In 1629 he wrote his first great poem in English (he composed in Latin and Italian also), the *Ode on the Morning of Christ's Nativity,* which anticipates *Paradise Lost* by its references to the overcoming of the heathen gods at the coming of Christ. After taking his B.A. in 1629 and his M.A. in 1632, he retired to his father's estate, where he studied intensively, preparing himself, as he felt, for some great enterprise in literature or public life. Before the age of thirty, when this period of retirement ended, Milton had also written *L'Allegro* and *Il Penseroso* (twin poems praising, respectively, the cheerful and contemplative characters), the brief masque *Arcades,* the longer masque *Comus* (a platonic celebration of the triumph of virtue and chastity over evil and sensuality), and *Lycidas,* a pastoral elegy that some critics consider the greatest lyric poem in English. Written to commemorate the premature death of an acquaintance, *Lycidas* dramatizes Milton's concern over the mystery and injustice of death, the possible unfulfillment of his own hopes in life, and the assurance of spiritual victory through submission to divine Providence—all this in the context of an almost unbelievably rich pattern of classical allusion and creative imitation.

In 1638 Milton left England to spend fifteen months on the Continent, mainly in Florence, Rome, and Naples. During this "grand tour," he met a number of eminent men of learning and culture, including Hugo Grotius, the Dutch expositor of international law, and Galileo, who at the time was in trouble with the Church because of his speculations in astronomy. Milton was for the most part gratified by his reception, which gave him increased confidence in his powers. It is both characteristic and prophetic that, as Milton later put it, he "openly defended . . . the reformed religion in the very metropolis of popery" despite plots said to have been hatched against him by the Jesuits. He aborted a trip to Sicily and Greece when he learned of the outbreak of civil disturbances in England, and some months later he was back there. Around the time of his return, King Charles I was forced to convene a hostile Parliament; over the next two decades, during which many battles were fought between the Royalists/Episcopalians and their Republican/Puritan antagonists, the Presbyterian party first rose to power, being succeeded later by an even more radical party of Independents; Charles I was beheaded in 1649; a republic (the "Commonwealth") was declared; Oliver Cromwell was named Lord Protector (dictator, virtually) between 1653 and his death in 1658; his ineffectual son Richard succeeded him but abdicated; and finally, to Milton's dismay, the monarchy was restored in 1660 in the person of the heretofore exiled Charles II.

After returning from his Italian tour, Milton pondered an ambitious literary work, particularly a drama on an English or scriptural subject, and it is possible that he did begin a play on his favorite topic, the fall of humankind, which he later chose for his epic. But his sense of commitment to the cause of religious and civil freedom as he understood it made him put aside his ambitious literary plans for the greater part of two decades, during which he composed many treatises and pamphlets directed against his personal and political enemies and those of the revolutionary government. His first efforts dealt with the evils of the episcopal system (rule by bishops) in the Church of England, an issue that Milton conceived to be part of the larger issue of general human freedom. An ill-considered marriage, which for a time was broken off, prompted a series of tracts boldly arguing for the legality of divorce on grounds of incompatibility, a position that in its alleged libertinism alienated not only the Royalists but the Presbyterians as well. In 1644, in opposition to a parliamentary censorship law, he wrote *Areopagitica,* a classic rationale for freedom of the press and individual responsibility that, curiously, uses arguments against an artificially sheltered, untested virtue that seem at least to be similar to those Satan and Eve use in Book IX of *Paradise Lost* to justify eating the fruit of the Tree of Knowledge of Good and Evil. He also wrote on education, history, and theology. In 1649, the year Charles was beheaded, he wrote *The Tenure of Kings and Magistrates,* a tract that earned him the favor of the regicide regime by arguing that a king's tenure and very life were subject to the will of the people. Milton was made Latin Secretary in the government, a post that involved foreign correspondence and official defenses of the regime against its opponents at home and abroad. But his eyesight, which for some time had been failing, deteriorated until total blindness came in 1652, after which time he was gradually relieved of official duties and was able (especially after 1654) to turn his energies again to literature. Milton was sustained in part by his belief that loss of literal vision was compensated by a strengthened inner light and vision—a hope that was later expressed movingly in the hymn to light that opens Book III of *Paradise Lost.* In the latter 1650s he began his epic *Paradise Lost,* which he completed by 1665; it was published in 1667, in a ten-book version that he later altered to twelve. Meanwhile, the restoration of the Royalists brought Milton's life into peril, though for reasons not entirely clear he was released, after being arrested, with just a fine. Thereafter, despite reduced financial circumstances and some friction with his relatives, he lived a fairly regular and outwardly uneventful life, composing verse (the inspiration for which is said to have come mainly in the winter during the hours before dawn), singing and playing music, walking in his garden, meditating and being read to, receiving admiring visitors. In 1671 were published the "short epic" *Paradise Regained* (a sequel to *Paradise Lost* that centers on Christ's resistance to Satan's temptations in the wilderness as narrated, for example, in the fourth chapter of Matthew's gospel) and the drama *Samson Agonistes*. The latter, based on the story of Samson in Judges 13–16, has irresistible autobiographical relevance as the story of a blinded hero, living his last days in captivity, who undergoes a spiritual renewal and finally triumphs over his wicked captors. *Samson Agonistes* has been praised as the nearest English equivalent of ancient Greek drama and as a work on the same level of greatness as *Paradise Lost*. Thus Milton's stature as a poet is attested in all three traditional poetic modes: lyric (his sonnets must be mentioned along with works already named), epic, and drama. After a final pamphlet in 1673 warning against resurgent "popery" under Charles II, Milton died, in 1674, of gout.

In *Paradise Lost* Milton aimed at grandeur, comprehensiveness, and universal relevance. This is most clearly true in the choice of subject itself, for to Christians no theme could be more awesome than that of the fall of our first parents, which "Brought death into the world, and all our woe" (I.3) and the counterpoised Redemption that is outlined theologically in Book III and historically in Book XII. It was a theme, Milton tells us, that he was "long choosing and beginning late" (IX.26). The question to what extent the poem transcends the interests of Christian theology has been much debated. Milton's approach can be cited on both sides: on one hand, he is careful to integrate into his poem the whole fabric of pagan antiquity, thus achieving something like mythic universality; on the other hand, he takes pains to distinguish the distorted versions of truth expressed by the pagans from the literal and naked truth of biblical revelation on which his epic is based. The pagan gods, for example, are the true devils in disguise. Aiming at universality, Milton subordinates in *Paradise Lost* the notes of political and religious partisanship he sounds in his tracts. His political opposition to the restored monarchy appears chiefly by innuendo, and although there is in the poem some peculiarly Miltonic theology (his apparently unorthodox view of the Trinity, for example), and some direct sectarian invective, his treatment of the Son's redeeming self-sacrifice is essentially in the mainstream of Christian tradition.

Whatever limitations Milton's theology, idiosyncratic or more broadly Christian, may imply for the persuasiveness of his *answers*, it is hardly questionable that he defines compellingly the ultimate *issues* explored in all theodicies (attempts to "justify God's ways")—questions of cosmic justice, the origin of physical suffering and of moral evil, and the relationship of these to human free will. Indeed, the motif of liberty is at the heart of *Paradise Lost* and is perhaps the most vital link between the values of the poem and those Milton cherished in his personal and public life. Moreover, his treatment of liberty is complex. His belief that we stand or fall essentially on our own, without either the compulsion or the effective help of earthly authority, is part both of radical Protestantism and of modern libertarianism. Yet it is also true that the Son's obedient submission to the Father is for Milton the prototype of all true liberty. *Paradise Lost* thus raises some questions about the relationship between absolute human autonomy and acquiescence in the cosmic order that assert themselves in any age, under any system.

Milton's claim to have raised the subject matter of epic to a new level of grandeur and truth is itself part of the epic tradition. In this claim he is following the precedent of Virgil, who (to apply a phrase of Milton's) also tried to be "doctrinal and exemplary to a nation" by implicitly substituting for Homeric objectivity and concern with war a set of values that, while still communal, are more inward, ethical, philosophical. Like Virgil, Milton tells a story whose historical, and not merely mythical, dimension is important to him. The matter is of the greatest possible public import. Yet Milton, while insisting on the literal existence of hell, heaven, and the earthly paradise, gives them also an extended spiritual dimension. Hell is a state of mind, one that Satan creates for himself and carries with him everywhere he goes. Paradise is lost by Adam and Eve, but Book XII assures them that, through faith in and imitation of the redeeming Son of God, they can achieve "A Paradise within thee, happier far" (XII.587) than the one they forfeited. In a passage where he both acknowledges and repudiates his epic ancestry, Milton substitutes for "Wars, hitherto the only argument / Heroic deemed" the "better fortitude / Of patience and heroic martyrdom" (IX.28–32). It is enormously significant that in *Paradise Regained* he balances against the "disobedience" (*Paradise Lost,* I.1) of the fallen Adam not the climax of Jesus' public life in the Passion and Resurrection but the most private incident in his career, the obedience to his Father manifested in the Temptation in the Wilderness.

Much of the power of *Paradise Lost* comes from qualities that might seem alien to the opinionated Milton: a kind of evenhandedness or at least intellectual and imaginative empathy that he extends to ideas and characters opposed to what he is championing. Easily the best example is Satan, one of the supreme triumphs of literary characterization. Shelley and other interpreters in the Romantic tradition went so far as to consider him the real hero of the poem. That was surely not Milton's intent, yet it remains true that Satan is given dramatic autonomy. He is treated with grandeur, in, for example, Books I and II, and sometimes with touches of pathos as in the soliloquy that opens Book IV. (Ironically, as it has seemed to some readers, the Milton who in life defended rebellion against monarchy identifies the insubordinate Satan in the epic poem as the origin of evil.) Belial, whom Milton calls "lewd," "gross," and one who could "make the worse appear / The better reason" (I.490–491; II.113–114), is endowed with breathtaking imagination and made to utter a noble encomium on the human mind, "this intellectual being, / Those thoughts that wander through eternity" (II.147–148). And, as mentioned earlier, Satan and Eve sound somewhat like *Areopagitica.* Such anomalies can suggest a failure by Milton to control the tone of the poem or else, as William Blake's *Marriage of Heaven and Hell* charges, a lapse in self-knowledge by Milton. Against which it might be argued that in true epics heroes and heroism have worthy, however evil, adversaries. If the temptations and errors of Satan and humankind had no plausibility and seductive power, their fall would seem not tragic but fatuous.

Paradise Lost is a consummate work of art, in architecture and surface. The sublime hymn to light in Book III, for example, serves structurally to emphasize the emergence of Satan, and the poem, from the sulfurous horror of hell and darkness to the ambrosial brightness of heaven. These same transitional lines also mark the elaborate parallelism between the council scenes of Books II and III, including the antithetical offers by Satan and the Son of God, respectively, to destroy and to save humanity. Figures of speech are powerful; the modulation of the metaphysical praise of light into Milton's mourning for his personal blindness is capped by a sublime metaphor in which the outward-radiating natural sun that fertilizes the world and dispels darkness becomes the emblem of a fertilizing spiritual sun that shines toward a center:

> So much the rather thou celestial Light
> Shine inward, and the mind through all her powers
> Irradiate, there plant eyes, all mist from thence
> Purge and disperse, that I may see and tell
> Of things invisible to mortal sight. (III.51–55)

The grand style in *Paradise Lost,* the style generally called "Miltonic," is the high ceremonial one that Milton recognized as appropriate to epic. Vowel sounds are often sonorous ("To bellow through the vast and boundless deep"— I.177). Half-repetitions (the "Miltonic turn") have an effect that can be both epigrammatic and swelling ("Thus high uplifted beyond hope, aspires / Beyond thus high"—II.7–8). Exotic, evocative proper names are heaped on one another (IV.268–83). Long-extended similes are used as in Homer and Virgil (I.302–13, 768–92), often with even greater psychological suggestiveness. Sentences are prolonged through whole "verse paragraphs," the sense drawn out inexorably from one line to the next—sustaining elevation of tone or creating suspense or introducing bold imaginative surprises that one is not allowed to linger over as climaxes.

In fact, however, the poem has many voices. The speeches in the infernal council in Book II are not just magniloquent; they are specifically modeled on parliamentary oratory. Moreover, even this section is varied within itself, the headlong Moloch sounding not at all like the subtle, intellectually speculative Belial. Satan's soliloquy in Book IV is in itself a mixture of tones, from subdued remorse to anguish to desperate recklessness. Adam and Eve can address each other like royal consorts in their unfallen state but with colloquial acrimony at the end of Book IX after their fall. Milton abandoned the dramatic genre for the epic, but he retained the variety of speech one finds in the best dramas.

Although Shakespeare may have been rated as highly, Milton's influence on English literature in the 150 years following his death in 1674 was much greater, indeed incalculable. To imitate Shakespeare, who created in his plays and poems a score of different worlds, is nearly equivalent to imitating the whole variety of human experience. But Milton's work, despite its wide variety of genre and tone, has a kind of finished architectural coherence that, blending with the events of his life and his forcefully expressed ideas, has the effect of a single massive literary and personal presence. He dominated the eighteenth-century imagination as Newton dominated its science, partly because of his grandeur of manner, partly because of the fascination of his theological argument, partly because he synthesized while he transformed a vast body of ancient and Renaissance culture. The English Romantic poets, especially Blake, Wordsworth, Shelley, and Keats, all took Milton, in one way or another, as a touchstone for their most considered statements about human values and the place of humanity in the cosmic order.

FURTHER READING *(prepared by W.J.R.):* William Riley Parker's *Milton: A Biography,* 2 vols., 1968, is a standard modern biography; as an introduction, Douglas Bush's *John Milton: A Sketch of His Life and Writings,* 1964, is recommended. Also very good, especially for new readers of Milton, is A. N. Wilson, *The Life of John Milton,* 1983. The subject identified in his book's title is treated topically in James Thorpe, *John Milton: The Inner Life,* 1983. An admirable introduction to *Paradise Lost,* discussing the poem as psychology, doctrine, drama, and from several other perspectives, is G. K. Hunter, *Paradise Lost,* 1980. Arnold Stein's *Answerable Style: Essays on "Paradise Lost,"* 1953, is an excellent study of the poem. C. S. Lewis's *A Preface to "Paradise Lost,"* 1942, rev. 1960, discusses the poem's ideas and style in a lively, rigorous fashion, in the contexts of classical and Christian tradition. An excellent introduction is David M. Miller's *John Milton: Poetry,* 1978, which includes a biographical introduction and discussions of *Paradise Lost, Paradise Regained,* and *Samson Agonistes,* in a manner suitable for general readers. Northrop Frye's *The Return of Eden,* 1965, contains excellent essays, including Frye's celebrated analysis of foreground and background action in *Paradise Lost.* Douglas Bush's *"Paradise Lost" in Our Time,* 1945, discusses the negative reaction to Milton's epic in the twentieth century, Milton's religion and ethics, methods of characterization, and other topics. Helen Gardner's *A Reading of "Paradise Lost,"* 1965, contains a helpful discussion of the modern meaning of *Paradise Lost;* an appendix contains Gardner's earlier (1948) and important essay on Satan and his appeal as a heroic figure. Joan Webber's *Milton and His Epic Tradition,* 1979, surveys early epics beginning with Homer and relates this tradition to *Paradise Lost* and *Paradise Regained. New Essays on "Paradise Lost,"* ed. Thomas Kranidas, 1971, contains good essays on the theme of Book III, innocence and experience in *Paradise Lost,* the Fall, and other topics. Don Cameron Allen's *The Harmonious Vision,* 1954, deals with nearly all of Milton's poetry in an attempt to define the overall unity of Milton's thought. Gender issues are addressed by Phillip Gallagher in *Milton, the Bible, and Misogyny,* 1990; and by John T. Shawcross in his biography *John Milton,* 1993. The classic attack on Milton as a sexist is Mary Wollstonecraft's in *A Vindication of the Rights of Woman,* 1792. Diane Kelsey McColley, *Milton's Eve,* 1983, asserts Eve's positive role in the scheme of *Paradise Lost,* taking issue with the idea that the portrayal of her is antifeminist. Catherine Belsey's *John Milton,* 1988, in the Rereading Literature series, reconsiders critical issues from a contemporary theoretical perspective. On Milton's status as humanist and his political background, see Joan S. Bennett, *Reviving Liberty,* 1989.

PARADISE LOST

Selected Notes by James Holly Hanford

THE VERSE: The measure is English heroic verse without rime, as that of Homer in Greek, and of Virgil in Latin; rime being no necessary adjunct or true ornament of poem or good verse, in longer works especially, but the invention of a barbarous age, to set off wretched matter and lame metre; graced indeed since by the use of some famous modern poets, carried away by custom, but much to their own vexation, hindrance, and constraint to express many things otherwise, and for the most part worse than else they would have expressed them. Not without cause, therefore, some both Italian and Spanish poets of prime note have rejected rime both in longer and shorter works, as have also, long since, our best English tragedies, as a thing of itself, to all judicious ears, trivial and of no true musical delight; which consists only in apt numbers, fit quantity of syllables, and the sense variously drawn out from one verse into another, not in the jingling sound of like endings, a fault avoided by the learned ancients both in poetry and all good oratory. This neglect then of rime so little is to be taken for a defect, though it may seem so perhaps to vulgar readers, that it rather is to be esteemed an example set, the first in English, of ancient liberty recovered to heroic poem from the troublesome and modern bondage of riming.

from BOOK I

THE ARGUMENT

This first book proposes first in brief the whole subject, Man's disobedience, and the loss thereupon of Paradise wherein he was placed: then touches the prime cause of his fall, the Serpent, or rather Satan in the Serpent; who revolting from God, and drawing to his side many legions of angels, was by the command of God driven out of Heaven with all his crew into the great Deep. Which action passed over, the poem hastes into the midst of things, presenting Satan with his angels now fallen into Hell, described here, not in the center (for Heaven and Earth may be supposed as yet not made, certainly not yet accursed) but in a place of utter darkness, fitliest called Chaos. Here Satan with his angels lying on the burning lake, thunderstruck and astonished, after a certain space recovers, as from confusion, calls up him who next in order and dignity lay by him; they confer of their miserable fall. Satan awakens all his legions, who lay till then in the same manner confounded; they rise: their numbers, array of battle, their chief leaders named, according to the idols known afterwards in Canaan and the countries adjoining. To these Satan directs his speech, comforts them with hope yet of regaining Heaven, but tells them lastly of a new world and new kind of creature to be created, according to an ancient prophecy or report in Heaven; for that angels were long before this visible creation, was the opinion of many ancient Fathers. To find out the truth of this prophecy, and what to determine thereon, he refers to a full council. What his associates thence attempt. Pandemonium the palace of Satan rises, suddenly built out of the Deep; the infernal peers there sit in council.

Of Man's first disobedience, and the fruit*
Of that forbidden tree, whose mortal taste
Brought death into the world, and all our woe,
With loss of Eden, till one greater Man
Restore us, and regain the blissful seat,

---

*All footnotes are by Hanford unless otherwise stated. Some notes are abridged. The Arguments are by Milton.
1 ff. Milton follows the conventional epic procedure in his opening. For the various elements or steps in this procedure, cf. *Iliad* i. 1 ff., *Aeneid* i. 1 ff.
2. mortal, deadly.

Sing Heavenly Muse, that on the secret top
Of Oreb, or of Sinai, didst inspire
That shepherd, who first taught the chosen seed,
In the beginning how the Heavens and Earth
Rose out of Chaos; or if Sion hill   10
Delight thee more, and Siloa's brook that flowed
Fast by the oracle of God, I thence
Invoke thy aid to my adventurous song,
That with no middle flight intends to soar
Above the Aonian mount, while it pursues
Things unattempted yet in prose or rhyme.
And chiefly thou O Spirit, that dost prefer
Before all temples the upright heart and pure,
Instruct me, for thou knowest; thou from the first
Wast present, and with mighty wings outspread   20
Dove-like sat'st brooding on the vast Abyss
And madest it pregnant: what in me is dark
Illumine, what is low raise and support;
That to the height of this great argument
I may assert Eternal Providence,
And justify the ways of God to men.
    Say first, for Heaven hides nothing from thy view,
Nor the deep tract of Hell, say first what cause
Moved our grand parents in that happy state,
Favored of Heaven so highly, to fall off   30
From their Creator, and transgress his will
For one restraint, lords of the world besides?
Who first seduced them to that foul revolt?
The infernal Serpent; he it was, whose guile,
Stirred up with envy and revenge, deceived
The Mother of Mankind; what time his pride

    6. Heavenly Muse. The Christian poets adopted the classical muse of Astronomy, whose name (Urania, the Heavenly) qualified her for the new office, as the patroness of their divine inspiration. Milton identifies her with the Holy Spirit of Scripture and so turns his invocation into a prayer.
    7. of Oreb or of Sinai. Cf. Exod. 19:20 and Deut. 4:10. Milton carefully follows Scripture even in its apparent contradiction.
    8. That shepherd, Moses.
    10. Sion hill, Mount Zion, one of the hills on which the city of Jerusalem is built.
    11. Siloa's brook, "the waters of Shiloah that go softly" (Isa. 8:6).
    12. Fast by the oracle of God, i.e., close to the Temple of Jerusalem.
    15. Above the Aonian mount. Milton means that his theme is loftier than any that the Pagan poets could sing. The **Aonian mount** is Helicon, sacred to the muses.
    21. Gen. 1:1, 2. The Hebrew word translated in the Authorized Version "moved" can also be rendered "brooded." The Holy Spirit takes the form of a dove in Luke 3:22.
    24. argument, subject.
    25. assert, maintain the cause of.
    26. justify, make apparent the justice of. The real issue in Milton's mind is whether an intelligent and righteous will rules man's destiny, or a blind or capricious or malicious one. The justification hinges on (1) the affirmation of man's freedom and responsibility, and (2) the scheme of salvation through Christ which is set forth in the poem as a whole.
    29. our grand parents, i.e., our original ancestors, Adam and Eve.
    32. for, because of.

Had cast him out from Heaven, with all his host
Of rebel angels, by whose aid aspiring
To set himself in glory above his peers,
He trusted to have equalled the Most High, 40
If he opposed; and with ambitious aim
Against the throne and monarchy of God,
Raised impious war in Heaven and battle proud
With vain attempt. Him the Almighty Power
Hurled headlong flaming from the ethereal sky
With hideous ruin and combustion down
To bottomless perdition, there to dwell
In adamantine chains and penal fire,
Who durst defy the Omnipotent to arms.
    Nine times the space that measures day and night 50
To mortal men, he with his horrid crew
Lay vanquished, rolling in the fiery gulf
Confounded though immortal. But his doom
Reserved him to more wrath; for now the thought
Both of lost happiness and lasting pain
Torments him; round he throws his baleful eyes,
That witnessed huge affliction and dismay
Mixed with obdurate pride and steadfast hate.
At once as far as angel's ken he views
The dismal situation waste and wild: 60
A dungeon horrible, on all sides round
As one great furnace flamed, yet from those flames
No light, but rather darkness visible
Served only to discover sights of woe,
Regions of sorrow, doleful shades, where peace
And rest can never dwell, hope never comes
That comes to all; but torture without end
Still urges, and a fiery deluge, fed
With ever-burning sulphur unconsumed:
Such place Eternal Justice had prepared 70
For those rebellious, here their prison ordained
In utter darkness, and their portion set
As far removed from God and light of Heaven
As from the center thrice to the utmost pole.
Oh how unlike the place from whence they fell!

---

53. Confounded, defeated and ruined.   **57. witnessed,** bore witness to, expressed.
59. angel's ken, an angel's range of vision.
63. darkness visible, darkness not quite absolute. The words perhaps express also the idea of the darkness having a positive quality.
64. discover, reveal.
66. Cf. Dante, *Inferno*, iii: "All hope abandon, ye who enter here."
68. urges, afflicts.
72. utter, outer—as in Scripture. But there is also a suggestion of the modern sense.
74. from the center thrice to the utmost pole. The center is the center of the earth; the **utmost pole** is the pole of the outermost sphere of the visible heavens. The distance from hell to the empyrean (the supreme heaven) is ordinarily felt by Milton to be much greater than this exact calculation makes it.

There the companions of his fall, o'erwhelmed
With floods and whirlwinds of tempestuous fire,
He soon discerns, and weltering by his side
One next himself in power, and next in crime,
Long after known in Palestine, and named   80
Beëlzebub. To whom the Arch-Enemy,
And thence in Heaven called Satan, with bold words
Breaking the horrid silence thus began.
    "If thou beest he; but Oh how fallen! how changed
From him, who in the happy realms of light
Clothed with transcendent brightness didst outshine
Myriads, though bright: if he whom mutual league,
United thoughts and counsels, equal hope
And hazard in the glorious enterprise,
Joined with me once, now misery hath joined   90
In equal ruin: into what pit thou seest
From what height fallen, so much the stronger proved
He with his thunder, and till then who knew
The force of those dire arms? Yet not for those,
Nor what the potent victor in his rage
Can else inflict, do I repent or change,
Though changed in outward luster, that fixed mind
And high disdain, from sense of injured merit,
That with the Mightiest raised me to contend,
And to the fierce contention brought along   100
Innumerable force of spirits armed
That durst dislike his reign, and, me preferring,
His utmost power with adverse power opposed
In dubious battle on the plains of Heaven,
And shook his throne. What though the field be lost?
All is not lost; the unconquerable will,
And study of revenge, immortal hate,
And courage never to submit or yield:
And what is else not to be overcome?
That glory never shall his wrath or might   110
Extort from me. To bow and sue for grace
With suppliant knee, and deify his power
Who from the terror of this arm so late
Doubted his empire, that were low indeed,
That were an ignominy and shame beneath
This downfall; since by fate the strength of gods
And this empyreal substance cannot fail,
Since through experience of this great event,

---

    81. Beëlzebub. Cf. Matt. 12:24. **Arch-Enemy.** Satan in Hebrew means "adversary."
    84 ff. If thou beest he, etc. The sentence is not completed. The entire speech is made dis-
jointed to indicate Satan's emotional stress.
    110. That glory, i.e., the glory of subduing Satan's will.
    114. Doubted, feared for.
    116 ff. since by fate, etc. Satan denies that he was created by and is therefore subordinate
to God. His egotism makes him a polytheist or more specifically a Manichee.

In arms not worse, in foresight much advanced,
We may with more successful hope resolve
To wage by force or guile eternal war,
Irreconcilable to our grand foe,
Who now triumphs, and in the excess of joy
Sole reigning holds the tyranny of Heaven."
  So spake the apostate Angel, though in pain,
Vaunting aloud, but racked with deep despair;
And him thus answered soon his bold compeer.
  "O Prince, O Chief of many thronèd Powers,
That led the embattled Seraphim to war
Under thy conduct, and in dreadful deeds
Fearless, endangered Heaven's perpetual King,
And put to proof his high supremacy,
Whether upheld by strength, or chance, or fate;
Too well I see and rue the dire event,
That with sad overthrow and foul defeat
Hath lost us Heaven, and all this mighty host
In horrible destruction laid thus low,
As far as gods and heavenly essences
Can perish: for the mind and spirit remains
Invincible, and vigor soon returns,
Though all our glory extinct, and happy state
Here swallowed up in endless misery.
But what if he our conqueror (whom I now
Of force believe almighty, since no less
Than such could have o'erpowered such force as ours)
Have left us this our spirit and strength entire,
Strongly to suffer and support our pains,
That we may so suffice his vengeful ire,
Or do him mightier service as his thralls
By right of war, whate'er his business be,
Here in the heart of Hell to work in fire,
Or do his errands in the gloomy deep;
What can it then avail, though yet we feel
Strength undiminished, or eternal being
To undergo eternal punishment?"
  Whereto with speedy words the Arch-Fiend replied.
"Fallen Cherub, to be weak is miserable,
Doing or suffering: but of this be sure,
To do aught good never will be our task,
But ever to do ill our sole delight,
As being the contrary to his high will
Whom we resist. If then his providence
Out of our evil seek to bring forth good,

120. **successful hope,** hope of success.
128–29. **throned Powers, Seraphim.** The angelic orders in Dante and the Catholic theologians are, from lowest to highest, as follows: Angels, Archangels, Principalities, Powers, Virtues, Dominions, Thrones, Cherubim, Seraphim. Milton uses many of these names interchangeably.
148. **suffice,** satisfy.

Our labor must be to pervert that end,
And out of good still to find means of evil;
Which oft-times may succeed, so as perhaps
Shall grieve him, if I fail not, and disturb
His inmost counsels from their destined aim.
But see the angry victor hath recalled
His ministers of vengeance and pursuit   170
Back to the gates of Heaven; the sulphurous hail
Shot after us in storm, o'erblown hath laid
The fiery surge, that from the precipice
Of Heaven received us falling, and the thunder,
Winged with red lightning and impetuous rage,
Perhaps hath spent his shafts, and ceases now
To bellow through the vast and boundless deep.
Let us not slip the occasion, whether scorn,
Or satiate fury yield it from our foe.
Seest thou yon dreary plain, forlorn and wild,   180
The seat of desolation, void of light,
Save what the glimmering of these livid flames
Casts pale and dreadful? Thither let us tend
From off the tossing of these fiery waves,
There rest, if any rest can harbor there,
And re-assembling our afflicted powers,
Consult how we may henceforth most offend
Our enemy, our own loss how repair,
How overcome this dire calamity,
What reinforcement we may gain from hope;   190
If not, what resolution from despair."
    Thus Satan talking to his nearest mate
With head uplift above the wave, and eyes
That sparkling blazed; his other parts besides,
Prone on the flood, extended long and large,
Lay floating many a rood, in bulk as huge
As whom the fables name of monstrous size,
Titanian or Earth-born, that warred on Jove,
Briareos or Typhon, whom the den
By ancient Tarsus held, or that sea-beast   200
Leviathan, which God of all his works
Created hugest that swim the ocean stream:
Him haply slumbering on the Norway foam,

---

   167. if I fail not, unless I mistake.   **178. Let us not slip,** Let us not let slip.
   186. afflicted powers, routed forces.   **197. as whom,** as those whom.
   198. Titanian, or Earth-born. The Titans and Giants in classical mythology were sons of
Heaven (Uranus) and Earth (Ge).
   199. Briareos or Typhon. The former was a Titan, the latter a Giant.
   201. Leviathan. Cf. Psalms 104:26, and Job 41. The monster was often associated with the
whale or the crocodile. Milton does not specifically identify it with either, although he suggests characteristics of both.
   203 ff. This is an old traveller's story, the most familiar version being in the *Arabian Nights.*
night-foundered, i.e., lost in the darkness as completely as a sunken ship is lost in the ocean.

The pilot of some small night-foundered skiff,
Deeming some island, oft, as seamen tell,
With fixëd anchor in his scaly rind,
Moors by his side under the lee, while night
Invests the sea, and wishëd morn delays:
So stretched out huge in length the Arch-Fiend lay
Chained on the burning lake; nor ever thence 210
Had risen or heaved his head, but that the will
And high permission of all-ruling Heaven
Left him at large to his own dark designs,
That with reiterated crimes he might
Heap on himself damnation, while he sought
Evil to others, and enraged might see
How all his malice served but to bring forth
Infinite goodness, grace and mercy shown
On Man by him seduced, but on himself
Treble confusion, wrath and vengeance poured. 220
    Forthwith upright he rears from off the pool
His mighty stature; on each hand the flames
Driven backward slope their pointing spires, and rolled
In billows, leave in the midst a horrid vale.
Then with expanded wings he steers his flight
Aloft, incumbent on the dusky air
That felt unusual weight, till on dry land
He lights, if it were land that ever burned
With solid, as the lake with liquid fire,
And such appeared in hue; as when the force 230
Of subterranean wind transports a hill
Torn from Pelorus, or the shattered side
Of thundering Ætna, whose combustible
And fuellëd entrails thence conceiving fire,
Sublimed with mineral fury, aid the winds,
And leave a singëd bottom all involved
With stench and smoke: such resting found the sole
Of unblest feet. Him followed his next mate,
Both glorying to have scaped the Stygian flood
As gods, and by their own recovered strength, 240
Not by the sufferance of supernal power.
    "Is this the region, this the soil, the clime,"
Said then the lost Archangel, "this the seat
That we must change for Heaven, this mournful gloom

208. **invests,** covers as with a garment.
226. **incumbent,** leaning on.
232. **Pelorus,** Cape Faro in Sicily, near Mt. Aetna.
235. **sublimed,** sublimated, converted to gaseous form, but also with the original sense of lifted up; **the winds,** i.e., the winds or gases within the earth which were supposed to be the cause of earthquakes.
236. **involved,** wrapped in.
244. **change for,** take in exchange for.

For that celestial light? Be it so, since he
Who now is sovran can dispose and bid
What shall be right. Farthest from him is best,
Whom reason hath equalled, force hath made supreme
Above his equals. Farewell happy fields
Where joy for ever dwells: Hail horrors, hail   250
Infernal world, and thou profoundest Hell
Receive thy new possessor: one who brings
A mind not to be changed by place or time.
The mind is its own place, and in itself
Can make a Heaven of Hell, a Hell of Heaven.
What matter where, if I be still the same,
And what I should be, all but less than he
Whom thunder hath made greater? Here at least
We shall be free; the Almighty hath not built
Here for his envy, will not drive us hence: 260
Here we may reign secure, and in my choice
To reign is worth ambition, though in Hell:
Better to reign in Hell than serve in Heaven.
But wherefore let we then our faithful friends,
The associates and co-partners of our loss,
Lie thus astonished on the oblivious pool,
And call them not to share with us their part
In this unhappy mansion; or once more
With rallied arms to try what may be yet
Regained in Heaven, or what more lost in Hell?"   270
    So Satan spake, and him Beëlzebub
Thus answered. "Leader of those armies bright,
Which but the Omnipotent none could have foiled,
If once they hear that voice, their liveliest pledge
Of hope in fears and dangers, heard so oft
In worst extremes, and on the perilous edge
Of battle when it raged, in all assaults
Their surest signal, they will soon resume
New courage and revive, though now they lie
Grovelling and prostrate on yon lake of fire,   280
As we erewhile, astounded and amazed;
No wonder, fallen such a pernicious height!"
    He scarce had ceased when the superior Fiend
Was moving toward the shore; his ponderous shield,

---

246. sovran, sovereign, supreme in power.

254–55. The supremacy of the mind is one of Milton's favorite ideas. The corollary of this utterance of Satan's is to be found in IV, 20–23.

257–58. all but less than, etc. Usually interpreted as "all but equal to" or "less only than," but other or additional meanings are possible. "What I should be" is, in Satan's mind, God's equal. He would rather be anything but inferior and, since the mind is its own place, he *can* be equal in everything but power. The confusion of grammar is no greater than the confusion of frustrated human emotion.

266. oblivious, causing forgetfulness. Milton is thinking of the classical Lethe.

276. edge. Latin *acies*, edge, means also battle line.

Ethereal temper, massy, large, and round,
Behind him cast; the broad circumference
Hung on his shoulders like the moon, whose orb
Through optic glass the Tuscan artist views
At evening from the top of Fesolë,
Or in Valdarno, to descry new lands, 290
Rivers or mountains in her spotty globe.
His spear, to equal which the tallest pine
Hewn on Norwegian hills, to be the mast
Of some great ammiral, were but a wand,
He walked with, to support uneasy steps
Over the burning marle, not like those steps
On Heaven's azure; and the torrid clime
Smote on him sore besides, vaulted with fire.
Nathless he so endured, till on the beach
Of that inflamëd sea, he stood and called 300
His legions, angel forms, who lay entranced,
Thick as autumnal leaves that strew the brooks
In Vallombrosa, where the Etrurian shades
High over-arched embower; or scattered sedge
Afloat, when with fierce winds Orion armed
Hath vexed the Red-Sea coast, whose waves o'erthrew
Busiris and his Memphian chivalry
While with perfidious hatred they pursued
The sojourners of Goshen, who beheld
From the safe shore their floating carcasses 310
And broken chariot wheels; so thick bestrewn
Abject and lost lay these, covering the flood,
Under amazement of their hideous change.
He called so loud, that all the hollow deep
Of Hell resounded. "Princes, Potentates,
Warriors, the flower of Heaven, once yours, now lost,

288. **the Tuscan artist,** Galileo, whom Milton had visited during his stay in Italy.
289. **Fesolë,** Fiesole, a small town located on a hill just outside Florence.
290. **Valdarno,** the valley of the Arno, in which Florence is located. Galileo's last residence was at Arcetri, west of the main part of the city. He was blind or almost so when Milton visited him and lamented that he could no longer look at the universe which his discoveries had made more wonderful.
294. **ammiral,** admiral, flagship.
296. **marle,** soil.
299. **Nathless,** nevertheless.
302 ff. Note the series of brilliant Homeric similes used to emphasize the numbers of the fallen angels. They are compared (1) when lying on the lake, to fallen leaves and floating seaweed; (2) when flying, to a cloud of locusts; (3) when alighted, to a huge invading army.
303. **Vallombrosa,** a district about eighteen miles from Florence, containing a famous monastery which Milton is said to have visited. The name is Italian for "shady valley."
305. **Orion,** a constellation proverbially associated with storms.
307 ff. Cf. Exod. 14. **Busiris** was an ancient Egyptian king, whom Milton for some reason identifies with the Pharaoh whose hosts were drowned in the Red Sea. **Memphian** is here equivalent to Egyptian, Memphis being the ancient capital of Egypt. **The sojourners of Goshen** are, of course, the Israelites.
312. **Abject,** cast down (Latin *abjectus*).

If such astonishment as this can seize
Eternal spirits; or have ye chosen this place
After the toil of battle to repose
Your wearied virtue, for the ease you find   320
To slumber here, as in the vales of Heaven?
Or in this abject posture have ye sworn
To adore the conqueror, who now beholds
Cherub and Seraph rolling in the flood
With scattered arms and ensigns, till anon
His swift pursuers from Heaven gates discern
The advantage, and descending tread us down
Thus drooping, or with linkèd thunderbolts
Transfix us to the bottom of this gulf.
Awake, arise, or be for ever fallen!"   330
    They heard and were abashed, and up they sprung
Upon the wing, as when men wont to watch
On duty, sleeping found by whom they dread,
Rouse and bestir themselves ere well awake.
Nor did they not perceive the evil plight
In which they were, or the fierce pains not feel;
Yet to their general's voice they soon obeyed
Innumerable. As when the potent rod
Of Amram's son in Egypt's evil day
Waved round the coast, up called a pitchy cloud   340
Of locusts, warping on the eastern wind,
That o'er the realm of impious Pharaoh hung
Like night, and darkened all the land of Nile:
So numberless were those bad angels seen
Hovering on wing under the cope of Hell
'Twixt upper, nether, and surrounding fires;
Till, as a signal given, the uplifted spear
Of their great Sultan waving to direct
Their course, in even balance down they light
On the firm brimstone, and fill all the plain;   350
A multitude, like which the populous North
Poured never from her frozen loins, to pass
Rhene or the Danaw, when her barbarous sons
Came like a deluge on the South, and spread

320. virtue, valor, strength (Latin *virtus*).
328. linkèd thunderbolts. The thunderbolts are compared to linked cannon balls.
335. Nor did they not, i.e., they did.
338 ff. As when the potent rod, etc. Cf. Exod. 10:12–15. Moses was Amram's son.
340. pitchy, dark as pitch.
341. warping, working slowly forward with a bending or swerving motion. The term is primarily nautical.
345. cope, vault or canopy.
351. A multitude, etc. Milton concentrates in a simile the history of the barbarian invasions of the Roman Empire. Successive inroads were made by the Goths, the Vandals, and the Huns.
353. Rhene, the Rhine (from Latin *Rhenus*). **Danaw,** the Danube (from German *Donau*).

Beneath Gibraltar to the Libyan sands.
Forthwith from every squadron and each band
The heads and leaders thither haste where stood
Their great commander; godlike shapes and forms
Excelling human, Princely Dignities,
And Powers that erst in Heaven sat on thrones; 360
Though of their names in heavenly records now
Be no memorial, blotted out and rased
By their rebellion from the Books of Life.
Nor had they yet among the sons of Eve
Got them new names, till wandering o'er the Earth,
Through God's high sufferance for the trial of Man,
By falsities and lies the greatest part
Of mankind they corrupted to forsake
God their Creator, and the invisible
Glory of him that made them to transform 370
Oft to the image of a brute, adorned
With gay religions full of pomp and gold,
And devils to adore for deities:
Then were they known to men by various names,
And various idols through the heathen world.

*   *   *

Meanwhile the wingèd heralds by command
Of sovran power, with awful ceremony
And trumpet's sound, throughout the host proclaim
A solemn council forthwith to be held
At Pandemonium, the high capitol
Of Satan and his peers; their summons called
From every band and squarèd regiment
By place or choice the worthiest; they anon
With hundreds and with thousands trooping came 760
Attended. All access was thronged, the gates
And porches wide, but chief the spacious hall
(Though like a covered field, where champions bold
Wont ride in armed, and at the Soldan's chair
Defied the best of Paynim chivalry
To mortal combat or career with lance)

355. **Beneath Gibraltar,** i.e., south of Gibraltar. The Vandals crossed from Spain into North Africa.
364 ff. **Nor had they yet,** etc. The idea that the fallen angels become the pagan divinities goes back to early Patristic sources. The identification furnishes Milton with abundant biblical and mythological data regarding the inhabitants of hell.
753. **awful,** awe-inspiring.
756. **Pandemonium,** the abode of all the demons. The name, which is a Miltonic coinage, may have been suggested by *Pantheon,* the abode of all the gods.
757 ff. **their summons,** etc. The council is in reality a sort of military Parliament.
763–66. The allusion is to the single combats between Pagans and Crusaders described in the Italian romances of chivalry. **Soldan** is a variant of Sultan.

Thick swarmed, both on the ground and in the air,
Brushed with the hiss of rustling wings. As bees
In spring time, when the sun with Taurus rides,
Pour forth their populous youth about the hive 770
In clusters; they among fresh dews and flowers
Fly to and fro, or on the smoothèd plank,
The suburb of their straw-built citadel,
New rubbed with balm, expatiate and confer
Their state affairs. So thick the airy crowd
Swarmed and were straitened; till the signal given,
Behold a wonder! they but now who seemed
In bigness to surpass Earth's giant sons,
Now less than smallest dwarfs, in narrow room
Throng numberless, like that Pygmean race 780
Beyond the Indian mount, or fairy elves,
Whose midnight revels, by a forest side
Or fountain, some belated peasant sees
Or dreams he sees, while overhead the Moon
Sits arbitress, and nearer to the Earth
Wheels her pale course; they on their mirth and dance
Intent, with jocund music charm his ear;
At once with joy and fear his heart rebounds.
Thus incorporeal spirits to smallest forms
Reduced their shapes immense, and were at large, 790
Though without number still, amidst the hall
Of that infernal court. But far within,
And in their own dimensions like themselves,
The great Seraphic Lords and Cherubim
In close recess and secret conclave sat,
A thousand demi-gods on golden seats,
Frequent and full. After short silence then
And summons read, the great consult began.

from BOOK II

THE ARGUMENT

*The consultation begun, Satan debates whether another battle is to be hazarded
for the recovery of Heaven: some advise it, others dissuade. A third proposal is*

---

769. when the Sun with Taurus rides, i.e., when the sun is in the zodiacal sign of the Bull
(between April 19 and May 20).
774. excpatiate and confer, walk abroad and discuss.
776. straitened, crowded.
780 ff. The **Indian mount** is probably Imaus in the Himalayas.
781 ff. Milton is here drawing on the traditions of English fairy poetry.
785. arbitress, spectator.   **790. were at large,** had ample room.
793. like themselves, i.e., in their own shapes.   **795. recess,** retirement.
797. frequent, crowded.

*preferred, mentioned before by Satan, to search the truth of that prophecy or tra-
dition in Heaven concerning another world, and another kind of creature, equal,
or not much inferior, to themselves, about this time to be created. Their doubt
who shall be sent on this difficult search; Satan, their chief, undertakes alone
the voyage; is honoured and applauded. The council thus ended, the rest betake
them several ways and to several employments, as their inclinations lead them,
to entertain the time till Satan return. He passes on his journey to Hell gates,
finds them shut, and who sat there to guard them; by whom at length they are
opened, and discover to him the great gulf between Hell and Heaven; with what
difficulty he passes through, directed by Chaos, the Power of that place, to the
sight of this new world which he sought.*

High on a throne of royal state, which far
Outshone the wealth of Ormus and of Ind,
Or where the gorgeous East with richest hand
Showers on her kings barbaric pearl and gold,
Satan exalted sat, by merit raised
To that bad eminence; and from despair
Thus high uplifted beyond hope, aspires
Beyond thus high, insatiate to pursue
Vain war with Heaven, and by success untaught,
His proud imaginations thus displayed. 10
    "Powers and Dominions, Deities of Heaven,
For since no deep within her gulf can hold
Immortal vigor, though oppressed and fallen,
I give not Heaven for lost. From this descent
Celestial Virtues rising, will appear
More glorious and more dread than from no fall,
And trust themselves to fear no second fate.
Me though just right, and the fixed laws of Heaven
Did first create your leader, next, free choice,
With what besides, in counsel or in fight, 20
Hath been achieved of merit, yet this loss
Thus far at least recovered, hath much more
Established in a safe unenvied throne
Yielded with full consent. The happier state
In Heaven, which follows dignity, might draw
Envy from each inferior; but who here
Will envy whom the highest place exposes
Foremost to stand against the Thunderer's aim
Your bulwark, and condemns to greatest share
Of endless pain? Where there is then no good 30
For which to strive, no strife can grow up there

2. **Ormus,** a city on the Persian Gulf, famous as a market for precious stones. It is often
mentioned by Renaissance travelers. **Ind,** India.
4. **barbaric pearl and gold.** The sprinkling of powdered pearls and gold dust on a monarch
at his coronation was an Oriental custom.
9. **success,** i.e., ill-success, the outcome of his former attempt.
17. **trust themselves,** etc., i.e., their experience has given them such confidence that they
will not fear to fall again.
24 ff. Satan, like Belial (112 ff.), knows how to "make the worse appear the better reason."

From faction; for none sure will claim in Hell
Precedence, none whose portion is so small
Of present pain, that with ambitious mind
Will covet more. With this advantage then
To union, and firm faith, and firm accord,
More than can be in Heaven, we now return
To claim our just inheritance of old,
Surer to prosper than prosperity
Could have assured us; and by what best way,   40
Whether of open war or covert guile,
We now debate; who can advise, may speak."
    He ceased, and next him Moloch, sceptred king,
Stood up, the strongest and the fiercest spirit
That fought in Heaven; now fiercer by despair.
His trust was with the Eternal to be deemed
Equal in strength, and rather than be less
Cared not to be at all; with that care lost
Went all his fear: of God, or Hell, or worse
He recked not, and these words thereafter spake.   50
    "My sentence is for open war. Of wiles,
More unexpert, I boast not; them let those
Contrive who need, or when they need, not now.
For while they sit contriving, shall the rest,
Millions that stand in arms, and longing wait
The signal to ascend, sit lingering here
Heaven's fugitives, and for their dwelling-place
Accept this dark opprobrious den of shame,
The prison of his tyranny who reigns
By our delay? No, let us rather choose,   60
Armed with Hell flames and fury, all at once
O'er Heaven's high towers to force resistless way,
Turning our tortures into horrid arms
Against the Torturer; when to meet the noise
Of his almighty engine he shall hear
Infernal thunder, and for lightning see
Black fire and horror shot with equal rage
Among his angels, and his throne itself
Mixed with Tartarean sulphur and strange fire,
His own invented torments. But perhaps   70
The way seems difficult and steep to scale
With upright wing against a higher foe.

    50. **thereafter spake,** spoke accordingly.
    51. **sentence,** judgment, opinion (Latin *sententia*). Moloch is the type of blunt warrior who
knows no other method of winning an object than to fight for it. Milton must have known
such among the leaders of the Commonwealth.
    63. **tortures,** i.e., the flames which torture.
    65. **engine,** instrument—referring to the thunderbolt.
    69. **Tartarean,** infernal (from Tartarus, a classical name for hell).

Let such bethink them, if the sleepy drench
Of that forgetful lake benumb not still,
That in our proper motion we ascend
Up to our native seat; descent and fall
To us is adverse. Who but felt of late
When the fierce foe hung on our broken rear
Insulting, and pursued us through the deep,
With what compulsion and laborious flight 80
We sunk thus low? The ascent is easy then;
The event is feared; should we again provoke
Our stronger, some worse way his wrath may find
To our destruction; if there be in Hell
Fear to be worse destroyed; what can be worse
Than to dwell here, driven out from bliss, condemned
In this abhorrèd deep to utter woe;
Where pain of unextinguishable fire
Must exercise us without hope of end
The vassals of his anger, when the scourge 90
Inexorably, and the torturing hour
Calls us to penance? More destroyed than thus
We should be quite abolished and expire.
What fear we then? what doubt we to incense
His utmost ire? which to the height enraged,
Will either quite consume us, and reduce
To nothing this essential, happier far
Than miserable to have eternal being;
Or if our substance be indeed divine,
And cannot cease to be, we are at worst 100
On this side nothing; and by proof we feel
Our power sufficient to disturb his Heaven,
And with perpetual inroads to alarm,
Though inaccessible, his fatal throne;
Which if not victory is yet revenge."
He ended frowning, and his look denounced
Desperate revenge, and battle dangerous

---

73. such, i.e., those who reason thus. **sleepy drench,** sleep-producing drink. The word **drench** suggests contempt.

74. forgetful, causing forgetfulness. Cf. I, 266 and note.

75–77. The natural (**proper**) motion of Spirits, as of fire, is upward. For them to fall is therefore unnatural (**adverse**).

79. Insulting. The original Latin meaning (*insultans,* leaping upon) is implied.

82. event, outcome.

89. exercise, torment.

94. what doubt we, i.e., why do we hesitate.

97. essential, essence, spiritual being.

104. fatal, upheld by fate. Admitting that the throne is so upheld, Moloch is forced to grant its inaccessibility.

106. denounced, proclaimed.

To less than gods. On the other side up rose
Belial, in act more graceful and humane;
A fairer person lost not Heaven; he seemed   110
For dignity composed and high exploit;
But all was false and hollow; though his tongue
Dropped manna, and could make the worse appear
The better reason, to perplex and dash
Maturest counsels: for his thoughts were low;
To vice industrious, but to nobler deeds
Timorous and slothful: yet he pleased the ear,
And with persuasive accent thus began.
    "I should be much for open war, O Peers,
As not behind in hate, if what was urged   120
Main reason to persuade immediate war,
Did not dissuade me most, and seem to cast
Ominous conjecture on the whole success:
When he who most excels in fact of arms,
In what he counsels and in what excels
Mistrustful, grounds his courage on despair
And utter dissolution, as the scope
Of all his aim, after some dire revenge.
First, what revenge? The towers of Heaven are filled
With armèd watch, that render all access   130
Impregnable; oft on the bordering deep
Encamp their legions, or with óbscure wing
Scout far and wide into the realm of Night
Scorning surprise. Or could we break our way
By force, and at our heels all Hell should rise
With blackest insurrection, to confound
Heaven's purest light, yet our great enemy
All incorruptible would on his throne
Sit unpolluted, and the ethereal mould
Incapable of stain would soon expel   140
Her mischief, and purge off the baser fire,
Victorious. Thus repulsed, our final hope
Is flat despair; we must exasperate
The almighty victor to spend all his rage,
And that must end us, that must be our cure,
To be no more; sad cure; for who would lose,
Though full of pain, this intellectual being,
Those thoughts that wander through eternity,

---

109. act, bearing.
113. manna. Cf. Exod. 16:31: "the taste of it was like wafers made with honey."
119 ff. Cf. with the abrupt beginning of Moloch's speech the insinuating oratory of Belial.
Like a skilled debater, he turns his opponent's own argument against him.
    124. fact of arms, feat of arms (Latin *factum,* deed).
    136. blackest insurrection. Cf. 65–70. Belial answers Moloch point by point.
    139. mould, substance.
    141. Her mischief, i.e., the damage or pollution caused by hell-fire.

To perish rather, swallowed up and lost
In the wide womb of uncreated Night, 150
Devoid of sense and motion? And who knows,
Let this be good, whether our angry foe
Can give it, or will ever? How he can
Is doubtful; that he never will is sure.
Will he, so wise, let loose at once his ire,
Belike through impotence, or unaware,
To give his enemies their wish, and end
Them in his anger, whom his anger saves
To punish endless? 'Wherefore cease we then?'
Say they who counsel war; 'we are decreed, 160
Reserved, and destined to eternal woe;
Whatever doing, what can we suffer more,
What can we suffer worse?' Is this then worst,
Thus sitting, thus consulting, thus in arms?
What when we fled amain, pursued and struck
With Heaven's afflicting thunder, and besought
The Deep to shelter us? this Hell then seemed
A refuge from those wounds. Or when we lay
Chained on the burning lake? that sure was worse.
What if the breath that kindled those grim fires 170
Awaked should blow them into sevenfold rage
And plunge us in the flames? or from above
Should intermitted vengeance arm again
His red right hand to plague us? What if all
Her stores were opened, and this firmament
Of Hell should spout her cataracts of fire,
Impendent horrors, threatening hideous fall
One day upon our heads; while we perhaps
Designing or exhorting glorious war,
Caught in a fiery tempest shall be hurled 180
Each on his rock transfixed, the sport and prey
Of racking whirlwinds, or for ever sunk
Under yon boiling ocean, wrapped in chains;
There to converse with everlasting groans,
Unrespited, unpitied, unreprieved,
Ages of hopeless end; this would be worse.
War therefore, open or concealed, alike
My voice dissuades; for what can force or guile
With him, or who deceive his mind, whose eye

152. **Let this be good,** i.e., granting that this (annihilation) is desirable.
156. **Belike,** no doubt. As frequently in Shakespeare, the word implies irony. **impotence,** lack of self-control.
165. **What when,** i.e., how was it when. **amain,** with all haste, precipitately.
177. **Impendent,** overhanging.
182. **racking,** twisting, torturing.
185. Note how the repetition of the prefix intensifies the effect of utter hopelessness.
186. **of hopeless end,** without hope of end.

Views all things at one view? He from Heaven's height   190
All these our motions vain, sees and derides;
Not more almighty to resist our might
Than wise to frustrate all our plots and wiles.
Shall we then live thus vile, the race of Heaven
Thus trampled, thus expelled to suffer here
Chains and these torments? Better these than worse,
By my advice; since fate inevitable
Subdues us, and omnipotent decree,
The victor's will. To suffer, as to do,
Our strength is equal, nor the law unjust   200
That so ordains: this was at first resolved,
If we were wise, against so great a foe
Contending, and so doubtful what might fall.
I laugh when those who at the spear are bold
And venturous, if that fail them, shrink and fear
What yet they know must follow, to endure
Exile, or ignominy, or bonds, or pain,
The sentence of their conqueror: this is now
Our doom; which if we can sustain and bear,
Our súpreme foe in time may much remit   210
His anger, and perhaps, thus far removed,
Not mind us not offending, satisfied
With what is punished; whence these raging fires
Will slacken, if his breath stir not their flames.
Our purer essence then will overcome
Their noxious vapor, or inured not feel,
Or changed at length, and to the place conformed
In temper and in nature, will receive
Familiar the fierce heat, and void of pain;
This horror will grow mild, this darkness light,   220
Besides what hope the never-ending flight
Of future days may bring, what chance, what change
Worth waiting, since our present lot appears
For happy though but ill, for ill not worst,
If we procure not to ourselves more woe."
   Thus Belial with words clothed in reason's garb,
Counselled ignoble ease, and peaceful sloth,
Not peace; and after him thus Mammon spake.
   "Either to disenthrone the King of Heaven
We war, if war be best, or to regain   230

---

   191. motions, proposals, plots.
   213. With what is punished, i.e., with the punishment already inflicted.
   219. Familiar the fierce heat, etc., i.e., the fierce heat, by becoming familiar, will be no longer painful. The considerations which move Belial are in complete accordance with his character and philosophy.
   224. For happy, etc., i.e., viewed as a happy situation the present one is bad, but it is not so bad as it might be.

Our own right lost. Him to unthrone we then
May hope, when everlasting Fate shall yield
To fickle Chance, and Chaos judge the strife:
The former, vain to hope, argues as vain
The latter; for what place can be for us
Within Heaven's bound, unless Heaven's Lord supreme
We overpower? Suppose he should relent
And publish grace to all, on promise made
Of new subjection; with what eyes could we
Stand in his presence humble, and receive   240
Strict laws imposed, to celebrate his throne
With warbled hymns, and to his Godhead sing
Forced halleluiahs; while he lordly sits
Our envied Sovran, and his altar breathes
Ambrosial odors and ambrosial flowers,
Our servile offerings. This must be our task
In Heaven, this our delight; how wearisome
Eternity so spent in worship paid
To whom we hate. Let us not then pursue,
By force impossible, by leave obtained   250
Unacceptable, though in Heaven, our state
Of splendid vassalage, but rather seek
Our own good from ourselves, and from our own
Live to ourselves, though in this vast recess,
Free, and to none accountable, preferring
Hard liberty before the easy yoke
Of servile pomp. Our greatness will appear
Then most conspicuous, when great things of small,
Useful of hurtful, prosperous of adverse
We can create, and in what place soe'er   260
Thrive under evil, and work ease out of pain
Through labor and endurance. This deep world
Of darkness do we dread? How oft amidst
Thick clouds and dark doth Heaven's all-ruling Sire
Choose to reside, his glory unobscured,
And with the majesty of darkness round
Covers his throne; from whence deep thunders roar,
Mustering their rage, and Heaven resembles Hell!
As he our darkness, cannot we his light
Imitate when we please? This desert soil   270
Wants not her hidden luster, gems and gold;
Nor want we skill or art, from whence to raise
Magnificence; and what can Heaven show more?

234. **argues,** proves.
249. **pursue,** seek to regain.
271. **Wants not,** is not without.

Our torments also may in length of time
Become our elements, these piercing fires
As soft as now severe, our temper changed
Into their temper; which must needs remove
The sensible of pain. All things invite
To peaceful counsels, and the settled state
Of order, how in safety best we may   280
Compose our present evils, with regard
Of what we are and where, dismissing quite
All thoughts of war: ye have what I advise."
  He scarce had finished, when such murmur filled
The assembly, as when hollow rocks retain
The sound of blustering winds, which all night long
Had roused the sea, now with hoarse cadence lull
Seafaring men o'erwatched, whose bark by chance
Or pinnace anchors in a craggy bay
After the tempest: such applause was heard   290
As Mammon ended, and his sentence pleased,
Advising peace; for such another field
They dreaded worse than Hell: so much the fear
Of thunder and the sword of Michaël
Wrought still within them; and no less desire
To found this nether empire, which might rise
By policy and long process of time,
In emulation opposite to Heaven.
Which when Beëlzebub perceived, than whom,
Satan except, none higher sat, with grave   300
Aspéct he rose, and in his rising seemed
A pillar of state; deep on his front engraven
Deliberation sat and public care;
And princely counsel in his face yet shone,
Majestic though in ruin: sage he stood,
With Atlantean shoulders fit to bear
The weight of mightiest monarchies; his look
Drew audience and attention still as night
Or summer's noontide air, while thus he spake.

    278. sensible, sense. The use of an adjective for a noun is a Latinism which Milton frequently adopts.
    281. Compose, adjust.
    290 ff. such applause, etc. Mammon's proposal is an improvement on Belial's in that it supplies an activity consistent with the abandonment of a futile renewal of the attempt on Heaven. But the desire for revenge expressed by Moloch and felt by all the demons remains to be satisfied.
    299. Beëlzebub. Cf. I, 79–81 and note. In the Old Testament the name is applied to the sun-god of the Philistines.
    302. front, forehead.
    306. Atlantean shoulders, shoulders like those of Atlas, who in Greek mythology supported the heavens.

"Thrones and imperial Powers, Offspring of Heaven, 310
Ethereal Virtues; or these titles now
Must we renounce, and changing style, be called
Princes of Hell? for so the popular vote
Inclines, here to continue, and build up here
A growing empire; doubtless; while we dream,
And know not that the King of Heaven hath doomed
This place our dungeon, not our safe retreat
Beyond his potent arm, to live exempt
From Heaven's high jurisdiction, in new league
Banded against his throne, but to remain 320
In strictest bondage, though thus far removed,
Under the inevitable curb, reserved
His captive multitude. For he, be sure,
In height or depth, still first and last will reign
Sole king, and of his kingdom lose no part
By our revolt, but over Hell extend
His empire, and with iron scepter rule
Us here, as with his golden those in Heaven.
What sit we then projecting peace and war?
War hath determined us, and foiled with loss 330
Irreparable; terms of peace yet none
Vouchsafed or sought; for what peace will be given
To us enslaved, but custody severe,
And stripes, and arbitrary punishment
Inflicted? and what peace can we return,
But to our power hostility and hate,
Untamed reluctance, and revenge though slow,
Yet ever plotting how the conqueror least
May reap his conquest, and may least rejoice
In doing what we must in suffering feel? 340
Nor will occasion want, nor shall we need
With dangerous expedition to invade
Heaven, whose high walls fear no assault or siege
Or ambush from the Deep. What if we find
Some easier enterprise? There is a place
(If ancient and prophetic fame in Heaven
Err not), another world, the happy seat
Of some new race called Man, about this time
To be created like to us, though less
In power and excellence, but favored more 350
Of him who rules above; so was his will

313. **the popular vote,** i.e., the state of opinion indicated by the applause given Mammon.
315. **doubtless.** The word is used sarcastically.
330. **determined us,** ended us or perhaps determined our future.
336. **to our power,** up to the limits of our power.
337. **Untamed reluctance,** untamable resistance.
346. **fame,** rumor.

Pronounced among the gods, and by an oath,
That shook Heaven's whole circumference, confirmed.
Thither let us bend all our thoughts, to learn
What creatures there inhabit, of what mould
Or substance, how endued, and what their power,
And where their weakness, how attempted best,
By force or subtlety. Though Heaven be shut,
And Heaven's high Arbitrator sit secure
In his own strength, this place may lie exposed,   360
The utmost border of his kingdom, left
To their defence who hold it; here perhaps
Some advantageous act may be achieved
By sudden onset, either with Hell fire
To waste his whole creation, or possess
All as our own, and drive as we were driven,
The puny habitants; or if not drive,
Seduce them to our party, that their God
May prove their foe, and with repenting hand
Abolish his own works. This would surpass   370
Common revenge, and interrupt his joy
In our confusion, and our joy upraise
In his disturbance; when his darling sons
Hurled headlong to partake with us, shall curse
Their frail original, and faded bliss,
Faded so soon. Advise if this be worth
Attempting, or to sit in darkness here
Hatching vain empires." Thus Beëlzebub
Pleaded his devilish counsel, first devised
By Satan, and in part proposed; for whence,   380
But from the author of all ill, could spring
So deep a malice, to confound the race
Of Mankind in one root, and Earth with Hell
To mingle and involve, done all to spite
The great Creator? But their spite still serves
His glory to augment. The bold design
Pleased highly those infernal States, and joy
Sparkled in all their eyes; with full assent

---

354. Thither let us, etc. Beëlzebub's proposal does not exclude Mammon's, which had itself appropriated Belial's; but it goes beyond both in supplying a rational project of revenge. The whole movement of the discussion has been constructively forward toward the formation of a policy satisfactory to all, and Beëlzebub, who is Satan's mouthpiece, has been simply waiting the opportune moment to introduce Satan's own scheme. His intelligence is far more comprehensive than that of the preceding speakers. It is easy to believe that Milton had been present at deliberations of the Council of State, and that he had noted with care the play of mind in them.
356. endued, equipped.
375. original, originator, i.e., Adam.
380. in part proposed, i.e., in an earlier speech, I, 645 ff.
382. confound, destroy completely.
387. States, princes or representatives.

They vote: whereat his speech he thus renews.
"Well have ye judged, well ended long debate,   390
Synod of gods, and like to what ye are,
Great things resolved; which from the lowest deep
Will once more lift us up, in spite of Fate,
Nearer our ancient seat; perhaps in view
Of those bright confines, whence with neighboring arms
And opportune excursion we may chance
Re-enter Heaven; or else in some mild zone
Dwell not unvisited of Heaven's fair light
Secure, and at the brightening orient beam
Purge off this gloom; the soft delicious air,   400
To heal the scar of these corrosive fires
Shall breathe her balm. But first whom shall we send
In search of this new world? whom shall we find
Sufficient? who shall tempt with wandering feet
The dark unbottomed infinite Abyss
And through the palpable obscure find out
His uncouth way, or spread his airy flight
Upborne with indefatigable wings
Over the vast abrupt, ere he arrive
The happy isle; what strength, what art can then   410
Suffice, or what evasion bear him safe
Through the strict senteries and stations thick
Of angels watching round? Here he had need
All circumspection, and we now no less
Choice in our suffrage; for on whom we send,
The weight of all and our last hope relies."
    This said, he sat; and expectation held
His look suspense, awaiting who appeared
To second, or oppose, or undertake
The perilous attempt; but all sat mute,   420
Pondering the danger with deep thoughts; and each
In other's countenance read his own dismay
Astonished; none among the choice and prime
Of those Heaven-warring champions could be found
So hardy as to proffer or accept
Alone the dreadful voyage; till at last
Satan, whom now transcendent glory raised
Above his fellows, with monarchal pride
Conscious of highest worth, unmoved thus spake.

404. tempt, attempt, try.
406. palpable obscure, tangible darkness.
407. uncouth, unknown, strange.
409. the vast abrupt, the region of Chaos, which is a gulf or breach (Lat. *abruptum*), an emptiness.
412. stations, outposts, guards.
415. Choice in our suffrage, care in our selection.
418. suspense, suspended.

"O Progeny of Heaven, empyreal Thrones,   430
With reason hath deep silence and demur
Seized us, though undismayed. Long is the way
And hard, that out of Hell leads up to light;
Our prison strong, this huge convex of fire,
Outrageous to devour, immures us round
Ninefold, and gates of burning adamant
Barred over us prohibit all egress.
These passed, if any pass, the void profound
Of unessential Night receives him next
Wide gaping, and with utter loss of being   440
Threatens him, plunged in that abortive gulf.
If thence he scape into whatever world,
Or unknown region, what remains him less
Than unknown dangers and as hard escape.
But I should ill become this throne, O Peers,
And this imperial sovranty, adorned
With splendor, armed with power, if aught proposed
And judged of public moment, in the shape
Of difficulty or danger, could deter
Me from attempting. Wherefore do I assume   450
These royalties, and not refuse to reign,
Refusing to accept as great a share
Of hazard as of honor, due alike
To him who reigns, and so much to him due
Of hazard more, as he above the rest
High honored sits? Go therefore mighty Powers,
Terror of Heaven, though fallen; intend at home,
While here shall be our home, what best may ease
The present misery, and render Hell
More tolerable; if there be cure or charm   460
To respite or deceive, or slack the pain
Of this ill mansion; intermit no watch
Against a wakeful foe, while I abroad
Through all the coasts of dark destruction seek
Deliverance for us all: this enterprise
None shall partake with me." Thus saying rose
The Monarch, and prevented all reply;
Prudent, lest from his resolution raised
Others among the chief might offer now

---

431. demur, hesitation.
439. unessential, having no real being. Night and Chaos are thought of by Milton as merely negative, not really created.
441. abortive, prematurely brought forth and therefore unformed.
445 ff. But I should ill, etc. Satan's offer is parallel to that of Christ in III, 217 ff.
450. Me. Note the emphasis given by the meter.
457. intend, plan, consider.   **461. deceive,** beguile.
467. prevented, anticipated (a good example of the transition from the older, literal meaning of the word to the modern).
468. from his resolution raised, encouraged by his bravery.

(Certain to be refused) what erst they feared; 470
And so refused might in opinion stand
His rivals, winning cheap the high repute
Which he through hazard huge must earn. But they
Dreaded not more the adventure than his voice
Forbidding; and at once with him they rose;
Their rising all at once was as the sound
Of thunder heard remote. Towards him they bend
With awful reverence prone; and as a god
Extol him equal to the Highest in Heaven.
Nor failed they to express how much they praised, 480
That for the general safety he despised
His own: for neither do the spirits damned
Lose all their virtue; lest bad men should boast
Their specious deeds on Earth, which glory excites,
Or close ambition varnished o'er with zeal.
    Thus they their doubtful consultations dark
Ended rejoicing in their matchless chief:
As when from mountain tops the dusky clouds
Ascending, while the North wind sleeps, o'erspread
Heaven's cheerful face, the louring element 490
Scowls o'er the darkened landscape snow or shower;
If chance the radiant sun with farewell sweet
Extend his evening beam, the fields revive,
The birds their notes renew, and bleating herds
Attest their joy, that hill and valley rings.
O shame to men! Devil with devil damned
Firm concord holds, men only disagree
Of creatures rational, though under hope
Of heavenly grace; and God proclaiming peace,
Yet live in hatred, enmity, and strife 500
Among themselves, and levy cruel wars,
Wasting the Earth, each other to destroy:
As if (which might induce us to accord)
Man had not hellish foes enow besides,
That day and night for his destruction wait!

*   *   *

477–79. This deification of Satan is a precedent for the idolatries of men.
    483. **virtue,** merit—but not moral goodness, for that, Milton would hold, is inconsistent
with disobedience to God.
    484. **specious deeds,** deeds which, though having all the appearance of being public-
spirited and self-sacrificing, are really the fruit of personal ambition masquerading as zeal for
the common good. Under Milton's theory the demons can furnish a precedent for all that is
great and magnanimous in men except the one essential of a righteous will. He never forgets
that Satan and the rest are angels fallen.
    490. **element,** sky.
    492. **If chance,** if it chances that.

from BOOK III

THE ARGUMENT

God, sitting on his throne, sees Satan flying towards this World, then newly cre-
ated; shows him to the Son, who sat at his right hand; foretells the success of
Satan in perverting mankind; clears his own justice and wisdom from all impu-
tation, having created Man free and able enough to have withstood his tempter;
yet declares his purpose of grace towards him, in regard he fell not of his own
malice, as did Satan, but by him seduced. The Son of God renders praises to his
Father for the manifestation of his gracious purpose towards Man; but God again
declares that grace cannot be extended towards Man without the satisfaction of
Divine Justice: Man hath offended the majesty of God by aspiring to Godhead,
and therefore, with all his progeny, devoted to death, must die, unless some one
can be found sufficient to answer for his offence, and undergo his punishment.
The Son of God freely offers himself a ransom for Man: the Father accepts him,
ordains his incarnation, pronounces his exaltation above all names in Heaven
and Earth; commands all the angels to adore him: they obey, and hymning to
their harps in full choir, celebrate the Father and the Son. Meanwhile Satan alights
upon the bare convex of this World's outermost orb; where wandering he first
finds a place since called the Limbo of Vanity; what persons and things fly up
thither; thence comes to the gate of Heaven, described ascending by stairs, and
the waters above the firmament that flow about it. His passage thence to the orb
of the sun: he finds there Uriel, the regent of that orb, but first changes himself
into the shape of a meaner angel, and pretending a zealous desire to behold the
new creation, and Man whom God had placed here, inquires of him the place
of his habitation, and is directed; alights first on Mount Niphates.

Hail holy Light, offspring of Heaven first-born,
Or of the Eternal coeternal beam
May I express thee unblamed? since God is light,
And never but in unapproachèd light,
Dwelt from eternity, dwelt then in thee,
Bright effluence of bright essence increate.
Or hear'st thou rather pure ethereal stream,
Whose fountain who shall tell? Before the sun,
Before the Heavens thou wert, and at the voice
Of God, as with a mantle didst invest   10
The rising world of waters dark and deep,
Won from the void and formless infinite.
Thee I revisit now with bolder wing,
Escaped the Stygian pool, though long detained
In that obscure sojourn, while in my flight
Through utter and through middle darkness borne

2–3. May I, without blame, call thee coeternal with God?
6. Light is God's essence and as such is uncreated; but it is also what flows from him (effluence) and was the first created thing.
7–8. Or hear'st. Milton now says that the relation of the effluence to the essence is a mystery.
16. utter, outer, i.e., Hell.

With other notes than to the Orphean lyre
I sung of Chaos and eternal Night,
Taught by the heavenly Muse to venture down
The dark descent, and up to re-ascend, 20
Though hard and rare: thee I revisit safe,
And feel thy sovran vital lamp; but thou
Revisit'st not these eyes, that roll in vain
To find thy piercing ray, and find no dawn;
So thick a drop serene hath quenched their orbs,
Or dim suffusion veiled. Yet not the more
Cease I to wander where the Muses haunt
Clear spring, or shady grove, or sunny hill,
Smit with the love of sacred song; but chief
Thee Sion, and the flowery brooks beneath 30
That wash thy hallowed feet, and warbling flow,
Nightly I visit; nor sometimes forget
Those other two equalled with me in fate,
So were I equalled with them in renown,
Blind Thamyris and blind Mæonides,
And Tiresias and Phineus prophets old:
Then feed on thoughts, that voluntary move
Harmonious numbers; as the wakeful bird
Sings darkling, and in shadiest covert hid
Tunes her nocturnal note. Thus with the year 40
Seasons return; but not to me returns
Day, or the sweet approach of even or morn,
Or sight of vernal bloom, or summer's rose,
Or flocks, or herds, or human face divine;
But cloud instead, and ever-during dark
Surrounds me, from the cheerful ways of men
Cut off, and for the book of knowledge fair
Presented with a universal blank
Of Nature's works to me expunged and razed,
And wisdom at one entrance quite shut out. 50
So much the rather thou celestial Light
Shine inward, and the mind through all her powers
Irradiate, there plant eyes, all mist from thence
Purge and disperse, that I may see and tell
Of things invisible to mortal sight.
　　Now had the Almighty Father from above,
From the pure Empyrean where he sits

17. Orphean lyre. There was an Orphic hymn to night. Milton means that his poem is of higher inspiration, being based on Scripture.
　　25. drop serene, a translation of the medical term *gutta serena,* used of blindness in which the eye is not clouded. The "clear drop" is a humor which blocks the optic nerve.
　　26. dim suffusion, cataract.
　　29. sacred song, poetry, which is divine as coming from the muses.
　　30. To visit the brooks by Sion is to read Scripture.
　　35. Mæonides, Homer.

High throned above all height, bent down his eye,
His own works and their works at once to view.
About him all the sanctities of Heaven   60
Stood thick as stars, and from his sight received
Beatitude past utterance; on his right
The radiant image of his glory sat,
His only Son; on Earth he first beheld
Our two first parents, yet the only two
Of mankind, in the happy garden placed,
Reaping immortal fruits of joy and love,
Uninterrupted joy, unrivalled love
In blissful solitude. He then surveyed
Hell and the gulf between, and Satan there   70
Coasting the wall of Heaven on this side Night
In the dun air sublime, and ready now
To stoop with wearied wings and willing feet
On the bare outside of this World, that seemed
Firm land imbosomed without firmament,
Uncertain which, in ocean or in air.
Him God beholding from his prospect high,
Wherein past, present, future he beholds,
Thus to his only Son foreseeing spake.
    "Only begotten Son, seest thou what rage   80
Transports our Adversary, whom no bounds
Prescribed, no bars of Hell, nor all the chains
Heaped on him there, nor yet the main Abyss
Wide interrupt can hold; so bent he seems
On desperate revenge, that shall redound
Upon his own rebellious head. And now
Through all restraint broke loose he wings his way
Not far off Heaven, in the precincts of light,
Directly towards the new-created World,
And Man there placed, with purpose to assay   90
If him by force he can destroy, or worse,
By some false guile pervert; and shall pervert;
For Man will hearken to his glozing lies,
And easily transgress the sole command,

---

72. sublime, elevated.

74–76. Satan is ready to light on the *primum mobile,* the outer shell of the created universe,
not on the earth itself. The substance of this shell is indeterminate. The "firmament" is the
visible sky, which separates the waters above from the waters beneath the earth. The shell is
"without," i.e., outside of this firmament, or perhaps rather not composed of it, as the other
spheres must be. The "waters above" constitute the crystalline sphere, inside the *primum mobile,*
but also make a sea on top of it. Milton is not only adjusting the biblical account of creation
to the Ptolemaic idea of the spheres but making the conception philosophic as well. The *primum mobile* is a link between God and his universe.

76. Uncertain which, it being uncertain whether the shell hung in water or in air. Milton
suggests that the business about the firmament and the waters is obscure, as indeed it is.

Sole pledge of his obedience; so will fall
He and his faithless progeny. Whose fault?
Whose but his own? Ingrate, he had of me
All he could have; I made him just and right,
Sufficient to have stood, though free to fall.
Such I created all the Ethereal Powers   100
And spirits, both them who stood and them who failed;
Freely they stood who stood, and fell who fell.
Not free, what proof could they have given sincere
Of true allegiance, constant faith, or love,
Where only what they needs must do, appeared,
Not what they would? what praise could they receive?
What pleasure I from such obedience paid,
When will and reason (reason also is choice)
Useless and vain, of freedom both despoiled,
Made passive both, had served necessity,   110
Not me. They therefore as to right belonged,
So were created, nor can justly accuse
Their Maker, or their making, or their fate,
As if predestination overruled
Their will, disposed by absolute decree
Or high foreknowledge; they themselves decreed
Their own revolt, not I. If I foreknew,
Foreknowledge had no influence on their fault,
Which had no less proved certain unforeknown.
So without least impulse or shadow of fate,   120
Or aught by me immutably foreseen,
They trespass, authors to themselves in all,
Both what they judge and what they choose; for so
I formed them free, and free they must remain,
Till they enthrall themselves: I else must change
Their nature, and revoke the high decree
Unchangeable, eternal, which ordained
Their freedom; they themselves ordained their fall.
The first sort by their own suggestion fell,
Self-tempted, self-depraved; Man falls, deceived   130
By the other first; Man therefore shall find grace,
The other none. In mercy and justice both,
Through Heaven and Earth, so shall my glory excel,
But mercy first and last shall brightest shine."
    Thus while God spake, ambrosial fragrance filled
All Heaven, and in the blessed spirits elect
Sense of new joy ineffable diffused.
Beyond compare the Son of God was seen

---

114 ff. Predestination, in Milton's theology, was a conditional decree of God, not an absolute one, as in strict Calvinism. Milton is not the first or the last thinker to maintain the paradox that God foresees but not immutably.

Most glorious; in him all his Father shone
Substantially expressed; and in his face   140
Divine compassion visibly appeared,
Love without end, and without measure grace,
Which uttering thus he to his Father spake.
    "O Father, gracious was that word which closed
Thy sovran sentence, that Man should find grace;
For which both Heaven and Earth shall high extol
Thy praises with the innumerable sound
Of hymns and sacred songs, wherewith thy throne
Encompassed shall resound thee ever blest.
For should Man finally be lost, should Man   150
Thy creature late so loved, thy youngest son
Fall circumvented thus by fraud, though joined
With his own folly? that be from thee far,
That far be from thee, Father, who art judge
Of all things made, and judgest only right.
Or shall the Adversary thus obtain
His end, and frustrate thine, shall he fulfil
His malice, and thy goodness bring to nought,
Or proud return though to his heavier doom,
Yet with revenge accomplished, and to Hell   160
Draw after him the whole race of mankind,
By him corrupted? or wilt thou thyself
Abolish thy creation, and unmake,
For him, what for thy glory thou hast made?
So should thy goodness and thy greatness both
Be questioned and blasphemed without defence."
    To whom the great Creator thus replied.
"O Son, in whom my soul hath chief delight,
Son of my bosom, Son who art alone
My word, my wisdom, and effectual might,   170
All hast thou spoken as my thoughts are, all
As my eternal purpose hath decreed:
Man shall not quite be lost, but saved who will,
Yet not of will in him, but grace in me
Freely vouchsafed; once more I will renew
His lapsèd powers, though forfeit and enthralled
By sin to foul exorbitant desires;
Upheld by me, yet once more he shall stand
On even ground against his mortal foe,
By me upheld, that he may know how frail   180
His fallen condition is, and to me owe
All his deliverance, and to none but me.
Some I have chosen of peculiar grace

175–76. Man's free will, like Satan's, has lapsed with his disobedience. Because his sin came
from an outside suggestion his power to choose good is renewed by an act of Grace, as Satan's
is not.

Elect above the rest; so is my will.
The rest shall hear me call, and oft be warned
Their sinful state, and to appease betimes
The incensèd Deity, while offered grace
Invites; for I will clear their senses dark,
What may suffice, and soften stony hearts
To pray, repent, and bring obedience due. 190
To prayer, repentance, and obedience due,
Though but endeavored with sincere intent,
Mine ear shall not be slow, mine eye not shut.
And I will place within them as a guide
My umpire Conscience, whom if they will hear,
Light after light well used they shall attain,
And to the end persisting, safe arrive.
This my long sufferance and my day of grace
They who neglect and scorn shall never taste;
But hard be hardened, blind be blinded more, 200
That they may stumble on, and deeper fall;
And none but such from mercy I exclude.
But yet all is not done; Man disobeying,
Disloyal breaks his fealty, and sins
Against the high supremacy of Heaven,
Affecting Godhead, and so losing all,
To expiate his treason hath nought left,
But to destruction sacred and devote,
He with his whole posterity must die;
Die he or justice must; unless for him 210
Some other able, and as willing, pay
The rigid satisfaction, death for death.
Say Heavenly Powers, where shall we find such love?
Which of ye will be mortal to redeem
Man's mortal crime, and just the unjust to save?
Dwells in all Heaven charity so dear?"
   He asked, but all the heavenly choir stood mute,
And silence was in Heaven; on Man's behalf
Patron or intercessor none appeared,
Much less that durst upon his own head draw 220
The deadly forfeiture, and ransom set.
And now without redemption all mankind
Must have been lost, adjudged to Death and Hell
By doom severe, had not the Son of God,
In whom the fulness dwells of love divine,
His dearest mediation thus renewed.

---

184. Elect. In Calvinistic thought the elect include all who are to be saved, in contrast to the "reprobate," who are predestined before their birth to be damned; with Milton, on the other hand, the elect are only a special group of saints to whom goodness and salvation come easily. The rest of mankind are prone to sin but capable of repentance.
   203 ff. God's immutable decree cannot be evaded. If justice is to be satisfied there must be death for sin. The solution is the sacrifice of Christ, who, like Adam, is the representative of mankind.

"Father, thy word is passed, Man shall find grace;
And shall grace not find means, that finds her way,
The speediest of thy wingéd messengers,
To visit all thy creatures, and to all   230
Comes unprevented, unimplored, unsought?
Happy for Man, so coming; he her aid
Can never seek, once dead in sins and lost;
Atonement for himself or offering meet
Indebted and undone, hath none to bring.
Behold me then, me for him, life for life
I offer; on me let thine anger fall;
Account me Man; I for his sake will leave
Thy bosom, and this glory next to thee
Freely put off, and for him lastly die   240
Well pleased; on me let Death wreak all his rage;
Under his gloomy power I shall not long
Lie vanquished; thou hast given me to possess
Life in myself for ever; by thee I live;
Though now to Death I yield, and am his due
All that of me can die, yet that debt paid,
Thou wilt not leave me in the loathsome grave
His prey, nor suffer my unspotted soul
For ever with corruption there to dwell;
But I shall rise victorious, and subdue   250
My vanquisher, spoiled of his vaunted spoil;
Death his death's wound shall then receive, and stoop
Inglorious, of his mortal sting disarmed.
I through the ample air in triumph high
Shall lead Hell captive maugre Hell, and show
The powers of darkness bound. Thou at the sight
Pleased, out of Heaven shalt look down and smile,
While by thee raised I ruin all my foes,
Death last, and with his carcass glut the grave:
Then with the multitude of my redeemed,   260
Shall enter Heaven long absent, and return,
Father, to see thy face, wherein no cloud
Of anger shall remain, but peace assured
And reconcilement; wrath shall be no more
Thenceforth, but in thy presence joy entire."
   His words here ended, but his meek aspéct
Silent yet spake, and breathed immortal love
To mortal men, above which only shone
Filial obedience. As a sacrifice
Glad to be offered, he attends the will   270
Of his great Father. Admiration seized
All Heaven, what this might mean, and whither tend
Wondering; but soon the Almighty thus replied.

---

236 ff. Christ's highly dramatic offer, with its reception, is in studied contrast to Satan's
in Book II, 430 ff.

"O thou in Heaven and Earth the only peace
Found out for mankind under wrath, O thou
My sole complacence! well thou know'st how dear
To me are all my works, nor Man the least
Though last created, that for him I spare
Thee from my bosom and right hand, to save,
By losing thee a while, the whole race lost! 280
Thou therefore whom thou only canst redeem,
Their nature also to thy nature join;
And be thyself Man among men on Earth,
Made flesh, when time shall be, of virgin seed,
By wondrous birth; be thou in Adam's room
The head of all mankind, though Adam's son.
As in him perish all men, so in thee
As from a second root shall be restored,
As many as are restored; without thee, none.
His crime makes guilty all his sons; thy merit 290
Imputed shall absolve them who renounce
Their own both righteous and unrighteous deeds,
And live in thee transplanted, and from thee
Receive new life. So Man, as is most just,
Shall satisfy for Man, be judged and die,
And dying rise, and rising with him raise
His brethren, ransomed with his own dear life.
So heavenly love shall outdo hellish hate,
Giving to death, and dying to redeem,
So dearly to redeem what hellish hate 300
So easily destroyed, and still destroys
In those who, when they may, accept not grace. . . ."

*   *   *

from BOOK IV

THE ARGUMENT

*Satan, now in prospect of Eden, and nigh the place where he must now attempt
the bold enterprise which he undertook alone against God and Man, falls into
many doubts with himself, and many passions, fear, envy, and despair; but at
length confirms himself in evil, journeys on to Paradise, whose outward prospect
and situation is described, overleaps the bounds, sits in the shape of a cormorant
on the Tree of Life, as highest in the Garden, to look about him. The Garden
described; Satan's first sight of Adam and Eve; his wonder at their excellent form
and happy state, but with resolution to work their fall; overhears their discourse;
thence gathers that the Tree of Knowledge was forbidden them to eat of under
penalty of death, and thereon intends to found his temptation by seducing them
to transgress; then leaves them a while, to know further of their state by some
other means. Meanwhile Uriel, descending on a sunbeam, warns Gabriel, who
had in charge the gate of Paradise, that some evil spirit had escaped the Deep,*

and passed at noon by his sphere, in the shape of a good angel, down to Paradise; discovered after by his furious gestures in the mount. Gabriel promises to find him ere morning. Night coming on, Adam and Eve discourse of going to their rest: their bower described; their evening worship. Gabriel, drawing forth his bands of night-watch to walk the round of Paradise, appoints two strong angels to Adam's bower, lest the evil spirit should be there doing some harm to Adam or Eve sleeping; there they find him at the ear of Eve, tempting her in a dream, and bring him, though unwilling, to Gabriel; by whom questioned, he scornfully answers, prepares resistance, but hindered by a sign from Heaven, flies out of Paradise.

O for that warning voice, which he who saw
The Apocalypse heard cry in Heaven aloud,
Then when the Dragon, put to second rout,
Came furious down to be revenged on men,
"Woe to the inhabitants on Earth!" that now,
While time was, our first parents had been warned
The coming of their secret foe, and scaped,
Haply so scaped, his mortal snare; for now
Satan, now first inflamed with rage, came down,
The tempter ere the accuser of mankind,   10
To wreak on innocent frail Man his loss
Of that first battle, and his flight to Hell.
Yet not rejoicing in his speed, though bold,
Far off and fearless, nor with cause to boast,
Begins his dire attempt, which nigh the birth
Now rolling, boils in his tumultuous breast,
And like a devilish engine back recoils
Upon himself; horror and doubt distract
His troubled thoughts, and from the bottom stir
The Hell within him, for within him Hell   20
He brings, and round about him, nor from Hell
One step no more than from himself can fly
By change of place. Now conscience wakes despair
That slumbered, wakes the bitter memory
Of what he was, what is, and what must be
Worse; of worse deeds worse sufferings must ensue.
Sometimes towards Eden which now in his view
Lay pleasant, his grievèd look he fixes sad,
Sometimes towards Heaven and the full-blazing sun,
Which now sat high in his meridian tower.   30
Then much revolving, thus in sighs began.
    "O thou that with surpassing glory crowned,
Look'st from thy sole dominion like the god

1 ff. This opening passage is based on the vision of St. John recorded in Rev. 12.
    10. The tempter ere the accuser. In St. John's vision, Satan, routed from heaven for the second time, comes down to earth as "the accuser of our brethren" (Rev. 12:10). But, as Milton points out, he first came to earth in the role of tempter. The word "devil" is a corruption of the Greek *diabolos*, meaning literally "slanderer" or "accuser."
    11. wreak, avenge.
    27. The literal meaning of **Eden** is "delight."
    31. much revolving, pondering many things.

Of this new world; at whose sight all the stars
Hide their diminished heads; to thee I call,
But with no friendly voice, and add thy name
O Sun, to tell thee how I hate thy beams
That bring to my remembrance from what state
I fell, how glorious once above thy sphere;
Till pride and worse ambition threw me down 40
Warring in Heaven against Heaven's matchless King.
Ah wherefore! He deserved no such return
From me, whom he created what I was
In that bright eminence, and with his good
Upbraided none; nor was his service hard.
What could be less than to afford him praise,
The easiest recompense, and pay him thanks,
How due! Yet all his good proved ill in me,
And wrought but malice; lifted up so high
I 'sdeined subjection, and thought one step higher 50
Would set me highest, and in a moment quit
The debt immense of endless gratitude,
So burdensome still paying, still to owe;
Forgetful what from him I still received,
And understood not that a grateful mind
By owing owes not, but still pays, at once
Indebted and discharged; what burden then?
Oh had his powerful destiny ordained
Me some inferior angel, I had stood
Then happy; no unbounded hope had raised 60
Ambition. Yet why not? some other Power
As great might have aspired, and me though mean
Drawn to his part; but other Powers as great
Fell not, but stand unshaken, from within
Or from without, to all temptations armed.
Hadst thou the same free will and power to stand?
Thou hadst. Whom hast thou then or what to accuse,
But Heaven's free love dealt equally to all?
Be then his love accurst, since love or hate,
To me alike it deals eternal woe. 70
Nay cursed be thou; since against his thy will
Chose freely what it now so justly rues.
Me miserable! which way shall I fly
Infinite wrath and infinite despair?
Which way I fly is Hell; myself am Hell;
And in the lowest deep a lower deep
Still threatening to devour me opens wide,

41. Cf. I, 116, 117 and note. The uncompromising egotism of Satan's public utterances now gives way to a secret admission of God's supremacy.
50. 'sdeined, disdained.
51. quit, requite, pay.
52–57. Satan means that gratitude is in itself payment, whereas payment alone does not release from a debt of gratitude.

To which the Hell I suffer seems a Heaven.
O then at last relent: is there no place
Left for repentance, none for pardon left?   80
None left but by submission; and that word
Disdain forbids me, and my dread of shame
Among the spirits beneath, whom I seduced
With other promises and other vaunts
Than to submit, boasting I could subdue
The Omnipotent. Ay me, they little know
How dearly I abide that boast so vain,
Under what torments inwardly I groan;
While they adore me on the throne of Hell,
With diadem and scepter high advanced   90
The lower still I fall, only supreme
In misery; such joy ambition finds.
But say I could repent, and could obtain
By act of grace my former state; how soon
Would height recall high thoughts, how soon unsay
What feigned submission swore: ease would recant
Vows made in pain, as violent and void.
For never can true reconcilement grow
Where wounds of deadly hate have pierced so deep;
Which would but lead me to a worse relapse   100
And heavier fall: so should I purchase dear
Short intermission bought with double smart.
This knows my Punisher; therefore as far
From granting he, as I from begging peace.
All hope excluded thus, behold instead
Of us, outcast, exiled, his new delight,
Mankind created, and for him this World.
So farewell hope, and with hope farewell fear,
Farewell remorse! All good to me is lost;
Evil be thou my good; by thee at least   110
Divided empire with Heaven's King I hold
By thee, and more than half perhaps will reign;
As Man ere long, and this new World shall know."
    Thus while he spake, each passion dimmed his face
Thrice changed with pale, ire, envy, and despair,
Which marred his borrowed visage, and betrayed
Him counterfeit, if any eye beheld.
For heavenly minds from such distempers foul
Are ever clear. Whereof he soon aware,
Each perturbation smoothed with outward calm,   120
Artificer of fraud; and was the first

---

87. abide, suffer for.
90. advanced, elevated. **Me** (89) is the word modified.
115. Thrice changed with pale, i.e., each of the passions (**ire, envy, and despair**) dims the natural luster of his countenance. **Pale** is of course used as a noun.

That practised falsehood under saintly show,
Deep malice to conceal, couched with revenge.
Yet not enough had practised to deceive
Uriel once warned; whose eye pursued him down
The way he went, and on the Assyrian mount
Saw him disfigured, more than could befall
Spirit of happy sort. His gestures fierce
He marked and mad demeanor, then alone,
As he supposed, all unobserved, unseen. 130
So on he fares, and to the border comes
Of Eden, where delicious Paradise,
Now nearer, crowns with her enclosure green,
As with a rural mound the champaign head
Of a steep wilderness, whose hairy sides
With thicket overgrown, grotesque and wild,
Access denied; and overhead up grew
Insuperable height of loftiest shade,
Cedar, and pine, and fir, and branching palm,
A sylvan scene, and as the ranks ascend 140
Shade above shade, a woody theater
Of stateliest view. Yet higher than their tops
The verdurous wall of Paradise up sprung;
Which to our general sire gave prospect large
Into his nether empire neighboring round.
And higher than that wall a circling row
Of goodliest trees loaden with fairest fruit,
Blossoms and fruits at once of golden hue
Appeared, with gay enamelled colors mixed;
On which the sun more glad impressed his beams 150
Than in fair evening cloud, or humid bow,
When God hath showered the earth; so lovely seemed
That landscape. And of pure now purer air
Meets his approach, and to the heart inspires
Vernal delight and joy, able to drive
All sadness but despair; now gentle gales
Fanning their odoriferous wings dispense
Native perfumes, and whisper whence they stole
Those balmy spoils. As when to them who sail
Beyond the Cape of Hope, and now are past 160
Mozambic, off at sea north-east winds blow
Sabæan odors from the spicy shore
Of Araby the Blest, with such delay

123. couched with, lying hidden with.
126. the Assyrian mount, Niphates.
132 ff. Eden is apparently thought of as embracing the greater part of the Tigris and Euphrates region. Paradise is a garden in the east of Eden.
134. champaign head, level summit.
145. nether empire, i.e., the outlying territories of Eden.
149. enamelled, bright and variegated.

Well pleased they slack their course, and many a league
Cheered with the grateful smell old Ocean smiles.
So entertained those odorous sweets the Fiend
Who came their bane, though with them better pleased
Than Asmodëus with the fishy fume,
That drove him, though enamored, from the spouse
Of Tobit's son, and with a vengeance sent   170
From Media post to Egypt, there fast bound.
   Now to the ascent of that steep savage hill
Satan had journeyed on, pensive and slow;
But further way found none, so thick entwined,
As one continued brake, the undergrowth
Of shrubs and tangling bushes had perplexed
All path of man or beast that passed that way.
One gate there only was, and that looked east
On the other side; which when the Arch-Felon saw,
Due entrance he disdained, and in contempt,   180
At one slight bound high overleaped all bound
Of hill or highest wall, and sheer within
Lights on his feet. As when a prowling wolf,
Whom hunger drives to seek new haunt for prey,
Watching where shepherds pen their flocks at eve
In hurdled cotes amid the field secure,
Leaps o'er the fence with ease into the fold;
Or as a thief bent to unhoard the cash
Of some rich burgher, whose substantial doors,
Cross-barred and bolted fast, fear no assault,   190
In at the window climbs, or o'er the tiles:
So clomb this first grand thief into God's fold;
So since into his Church lewd hirelings climb.
Thence up he flew, and on the Tree of Life,
The middle tree and highest there that grew,
Sat like a cormorant; yet not true life
Thereby regained, but sat devising death
To them who lived; nor on the virtue thought
Of that life-giving plant, but only used
For prospect, what well used had been the pledge   200
Of immortality. So little knows
Any, but God alone, to value right
The good before him, but perverts best things
To worst abuse, or to their meanest use.

---

   167 ff. The allusion is to an episode related in the apocryphal Book of Tobit, 8. Tobit's
son is married to a maiden of Media, who is beloved by the evil spirit Asmodeus; to get rid
of this spirit he is instructed by the angel Raphael to burn the heart and liver of a fish. The
odor drives Asmodeus into Egypt, where the angel binds him.
   172. savage, woody.
   176. perplexed, made difficult.
   181. bound . . . bound. Note the play on words.
   194. Tree of Life. Cf. Gen.
   196. like a cormorant, i.e., in the shape of a ravenous bird of prey.

Beneath him with new wonder now he views
To all delight of human sense exposed
In narrow room Nature's whole wealth, yea more,
A Heaven on Earth, for blissful Paradise
Of God the garden was, by him in the east
Of Eden planted; Eden stretched her line 210
From Auran eastward to the royal towers
Of great Seleucia, built by Grecian kings,
Or where the sons of Eden long before
Dwelt in Telassar. In this pleasant soil
His far more pleasant garden God ordained;
Out of the fertile ground he caused to grow
All trees of noblest kind for sight, smell, taste;
And all amid them stood the Tree of Life,
High-eminent, blooming ambrosial fruit
Of vegetable gold; and next to life 220
Our death the Tree of Knowledge grew fast by,
Knowledge of good bought dear by knowing ill.
Southward through Eden went a river large,
Nor changed his course, but through the shaggy hill
Passed underneath ingulfed, for God had thrown
That mountain as his garden mould, high raised
Upon the rapid current, which through veins
Of porous earth with kindly thirst up drawn,
Rose a fresh fountain, and with many a rill
Watered the garden; thence united fell 230
Down the steep glade, and met the nether flood,
Which from his darksome passage now appears,
And now divided into four main streams,
Runs diverse, wandering many a famous realm
And country whereof here needs no account;
But rather to tell how, if art could tell,
How from that sapphire fount the crispëd brooks,
Rolling on orient pearl and sands of gold,
With mazy error under pendent shades
Ran nectar, visiting each plant, and fed 240
Flowers worthy of Paradise, which not nice art
In beds and curious knots, but Nature boon
Poured forth profuse on hill and dale and plain,

211. **Auran,** a district of Syria, about fifty miles south of Damascus.
212. **Seleucia,** a city on the Tigris, about twenty miles southeast of modern Bagdad.
214. **Telassar,** an ancient site in Mesopotamia.
219. **blooming,** bearing.
223 ff. **Southward . . . no account.** Cf. Gen. 2:10. In IX, 71–73 Milton identifies this river with the Tigris.
233. **four main streams.** Cf. Gen. 2:10–14.
238. **orient,** lustrous.
239. **error,** wandering (the literal meaning of Latin *error*).
241–42. The natural profusion of Paradise is contrasted with the artificial arrangement of an Italian garden. **nice,** fastidious. **boon,** bounteous. This passage played a part in supporting later preference for the so-called English garden and for the love of natural scenery generally.

Both where the morning sun first warmly smote
The open field, and where the unpierced shade
Imbrowned the noon-tide bowers. Thus was this place,
A happy rural seat of various view;
Groves whose rich trees wept odorous gums and balm,
Others whose fruit burnished with golden rind
Hung amiable, Hesperian fables true,   250
If true, here only, and of delicious taste.
Betwixt them lawns, or level downs, and flocks
Grazing the tender herb, were interposed,
Or palmy hillock, or the flowery lap
Of some irriguous valley spread her store,
Flowers of all hue, and without thorn the rose.
Another side, umbrageous grots and caves
Of cool recess, o'er which the mantling vine
Lays forth her purple grape, and gently creeps
Luxuriant; meanwhile murmuring waters fall   260
Down the slope hills, dispersed, or in a lake,
That to the fringèd bank with myrtle crowned
Her crystal mirror holds, unite their streams.
The birds their choir apply; airs, vernal airs,
Breathing the smell of field and grove, attune
The trembling leaves, while universal Pan,
Knit with the Graces and the Hours in dance,
Led on the eternal Spring. Not that fair field
Of Enna, where Proserpine gathering flowers
Herself a fairer flower by gloomy Dis   270
Was gathered, which cost Ceres all that pain
To seek her through the world; nor that sweet grove
Of Daphne by Orontes, and the inspired
Castalian spring, might with this Paradise
Of Eden strive; nor that Nyseian isle,
Girt with the river Triton, where old Cham
Whom Gentiles Ammon call and Lybian Jove,

247. various view, varied aspect.
250–51. Milton means that here, if anywhere, was to be found such fruit as classical myth attributed to the Garden of the Hesperides. **amiable,** lovely.
255. irriguous, well-watered.
266 ff. Classical writers often made "the dance of the Hours" symbolic of the orderly succession of the seasons.
269 ff. Enna, etc. Proserpine (Greek Persephone), the daughter of Ceres, goddess of agriculture (Greek Demeter), was abducted by Dis, god of the Underworld, from her garden in Enna (in Sicily). After a long search, Ceres found her daughter in the Underworld and arranged that she should spend part of her time there and part on the earth. The myth obviously describes the alternation of the seasons. (Editors' note.)
273. Daphne, a town situated on the river **Orontes,** about five miles from Antioch. It contained a grove and fountain sacred to Apollo, the fountain being named after the more famous **Castalian spring** at Delphi.
275. that Nyseian isle, the island of Nysa, situated in the midst of the river **Triton** in northern Africa. The identification of Jupiter Ammon with Noah's son Ham (**Cham**) is an interesting Miltonic touch.

Hid Amalthea and her florid son
Young Bacchus from his stepdame Rhea's eye;
Nor where Abassin kings their issue guard, 280
Mount Amara, though this by some supposed
True Paradise, under the Ethiop line
By Nilus' head, enclosed with shining rock,
A whole day's journey high, but wide remote
From this Assyrian garden, where the Fiend
Saw undelighted all delight, all kind
Of living creatures new to sight and strange.
Two of far nobler shape erect and tall,
God-like erect, with native honor clad
In naked majesty seemed lords of all, 290
And worthy seemed, for in their looks divine
The image of their glorious Maker shone,
Truth, wisdom, sanctitude severe and pure,
Severe but in true filial freedom placed;
Whence true authority in men; though both
Not equal, as their sex not equal seemed;
For contemplation he and valor formed,
For softness she and sweet attractive grace;
He for God only, she for God in him.
His fair large front and eye sublime declared 300
Absolute rule; and hyacinthine locks
Round from his parted forelock manly hung
Clustering, but not beneath his shoulders broad:
She as a veil down to the slender waist
Her unadornèd golden tresses wore
Dishevelled, but in wanton ringlets waved
As the vine curls her tendrils, which implied
Subjection, but required with gentle sway,
And by her yielded, by him best received,
Yielded with coy submission, modest pride, 310
And sweet reluctant amorous delay.
Nor those mysterious parts were then concealed;
Then was not guilty shame; dishonest shame
Of Nature's works, honor dishonorable,

---

281. Mount Amara, a high hill on the Abyssinian plateau, the place of seclusion where, according to tradition, the Abyssinian princes were sent to be educated.
282. Ethiop line, the equator.
289. God-like erect. Milton makes man's upright stature a symbol of his superiority to the brutes and of his instinctive aspiration.
295 ff. Throughout the poem Milton carefully distinguishes between the relative endowments and obligations of man and woman. The sexes are not equal, he insists, and authority quite properly belongs to the male. But the position which he accords woman, when considered in the light of theological tradition, is exceedingly high.
300. front, brow.
301. hyacinthine, i.e., dark in color.
306. wanton, loose, unbound.
313. dishonest, unchaste.

Sin-bred, how have ye troubled all mankind
With shows instead, mere shows of seeming pure,
And banished from man's life his happiest life,
Simplicity and spotless innocence.
So passed they naked on, nor shunned the sight
Of God or angel, for they thought no ill;   320
So hand in hand they passed, the loveliest pair
That ever since in love's embraces met:
Adam the goodliest man of men since born
His sons, the fairest of her daughters Eve.
Under a tuft of shade that on a green
Stood whispering soft, by a fresh fountain side
They sat them down; and after no more toil
Of their sweet gardening labor than sufficed
To recommend cool Zephyr, and made ease
More easy, wholesome thirst and appetite   330
More grateful, to their supper-fruits they fell,
Nectarine fruits which the compliant boughs
Yielded them, sidelong as they sat recline
On the soft downy bank damasked with flowers.
The savory pulp they chew, and in the rind
Still as they thirsted scoop the brimming stream;
Nor gentle purpose, nor endearing smiles
Wanted, nor youthful dalliance, as beseems
Fair couple linked in happy nuptial league,
Alone as they. About them frisking played   340
All beasts of the earth, since wild, and of all chase
In wood or wilderness, forest or den;
Sporting the lion ramped, and in his paw
Dandled the kid; bears, tigers, ounces, pards,
Gambolled before them; the unwieldy elephant
To make them mirth used all his might, and wreathed
His lithe proboscis; close the serpent sly
Insinuating, wove with Gordian twine
His braided train, and of his fatal guile
Gave proof unheeded; others on the grass   350
Couched, and now filled with pasture gazing sat,
Or bedward ruminating; for the sun
Declined was hasting now with prone career

---

323. the goodliest man of men since born, etc. The idiom is obviously illogical, but it has
ample precedent in Elizabethan English as well as in Greek and Latin.
333. recline, i.e., reclining.
334. damasked, ornamented with a variegated pattern.
337. purpose, conversation.
343. ramped, reared on his hind legs.
348. Gordian twine, intricate tangle. The reference is to the famous Gordian knot, which
no one could untie but which Alexander the Great finally cut with his sword.
352. ruminating, chewing the cud.

To the Ocean Isles, and in the ascending scale
Of Heaven the stars that usher evening rose:
When Satan still in gaze, as first he stood,
Scarce thus at length failed speech recovered sad.
"Oh Hell! what do mine eyes with grief behold!
Into our room of bliss thus high advanced
Creatures of other mould, earth-born perhaps,   360
Not spirits, yet to heavenly spirits bright
Little inferior; whom my thoughts pursue
With wonder, and could love, so lively shines
In them divine resemblance, and such grace
The hand that formed them on their shape hath poured.
Ah gentle pair, ye little think how nigh
Your change approaches, when all these delights
Will vanish and deliver ye to woe,
More woe, the more your taste is now of joy;
Happy, but for so happy ill secured   370
Long to continue, and this high seat your Heaven
Ill fenced for Heaven to keep out such a foe
As now is entered; yet no purposed foe
To you whom I could pity thus forlorn
Though I unpitied. League with you I seek,
And mutual amity so strait so close,
That I with you must dwell, or you with me
Henceforth; my dwelling haply may not please
Like this fair Paradise, your sense, yet such
Accept your Maker's work; he gave it me,   380
Which I as freely give; Hell shall unfold,
To entertain you two, her widest gates,
And send forth all her kings; there will be room,
Not like these narrow limits, to receive
Your numerous offspring; if no better place,
Thank him who puts me loath to this revenge
On you who wrong me not, for him who wronged.
And should I at your harmless innocence
Melt, as I do, yet public reason just,
Honor and empire with revenge enlarged,   390
By conquering this new World, compels me now
To do what else though damned I should abhor."
    So spake the Fiend, and with necessity,
The tyrant's plea, excused his devilish deeds.
Then from his lofty stand on that high tree
Down he alights among the sportful herd
Of those four-footed kinds, himself now one,

354. **the Ocean Isles,** i.e., the extreme west. Milton may here have in mind the Azores, but
the figure is used by classical writers without definite geographical reference.

389. By excusing his crime on the ground of political expediency, Satan once more demonstrates his proficiency in Machiavellian statecraft. That he can feel human pity is a survival of
the divine endowment which he has perverted.

Now other, as their shape served best his end
Nearer to view his prey, and unespied
To mark what of their state he more might learn 400
By word or action marked. About them round
A lion now he stalks with fiery glare;
Then as a tiger, who by chance hath spied
In some purlieu two gentle fawns at play,
Straight couches close, then rising changes oft
His couchant watch, as one who chose his ground
Whence rushing he might surest seize them both
Griped in each paw; when Adam first of men
To first of women Eve thus moving speech,
Turned him all ear to hear new utterance flow. 410
    "Sole partner and sole part of all these joys,
Dearer thyself than all, needs must the Power
That made us, and for us this ample World,
Be infinitely good, and of his good
As liberal and free as infinite,
That raised us from the dust and placed us here
In all this happiness, who at his hand
Have nothing merited, nor can perform
Aught whereof he hath need, he who requires
From us no other service than to keep 420
This one, this easy charge, of all the trees
In Paradise that bear delicious fruit
So various, not to taste that only Tree
Of Knowledge, planted by the Tree of Life,
So near grows death to life, whate'er death is,
Some dreadful thing no doubt; for well thou know'st
God hath pronounced it death to taste that Tree;
The only sign of our obedience left
Among so many signs of power and rule
Conferred upon us, and dominion given 430
Over all other creatures that possess
Earth, air, and sea. Then let us not think hard
One easy prohibition, who enjoy
Free leave so large to all things else, and choice
Unlimited of manifold delights;
But let us ever praise him, and extol
His bounty, following our delightful task
To prune these growing plants, and tend these flowers,
Which were it toilsome, yet with thee were sweet."
    To whom thus Eve replied. "O thou for whom 440
And from whom I was formed flesh of thy flesh,
And without whom am to no end, my guide
And head, what thou hast said is just and right.

411. Note the double play on words: **partner . . . part; sole . . . sole.** The first *sole* is used in the ordinary sense of "only," the second in the sense of "unrivaled," or "chief."

For we to him indeed all praises owe,
And daily thanks, I chiefly who enjoy
So far the happier lot, enjoying thee
Pre-eminent by so much odds, while thou
Like consort to thyself canst nowhere find.
That day I oft remember, when from sleep
I first awaked, and found myself reposed 450
Under a shade on flowers, much wondering where
And what I was, whence thither brought, and how.
Not distant far from thence a murmuring sound
Of waters issued from a cave and spread
Into a liquid plain, then stood unmoved
Pure as the expanse of Heaven; I thither went
With unexperienced thought, and laid me down
On the green bank, to look into the clear
Smooth lake, that to me seemed another sky.
As I bent down to look, just opposite 460
A shape within the watery gleam appeared
Bending to look on me: I started back,
It started back, but pleased I soon returned,
Pleased it returned as soon with answering looks
Of sympathy and love; there I had fixed
Mine eyes till now, and pined with vain desire,
Had not a voice thus warned me. 'What thou seest,
What there thou seest, fair creature, is thyself,
With thee it came and goes; but follow me,
And I will bring thee where no shadow stays 470
Thy coming, and thy soft embraces, he
Whose image thou art, him thou shalt enjoy
Inseparably thine; to him shalt bear
Multitudes like thyself, and thence be called
Mother of human race.' What could I do
But follow straight, invisibly thus led?
Till I espied thee, fair indeed and tall,
Under a platane; yet methought less fair,
Less winning soft, less amiably mild,
Than that smooth watery image; back I turned, 480
Thou following cried'st aloud, 'Return fair Eve,
Whom fliest thou? whom thou fliest, of him thou art,
His flesh, his bone; to give thee being I lent
Out of my side to thee, nearest my heart,
Substantial life, to have thee by my side
Henceforth an individual solace dear.
Part of my soul I seek thee, and thee claim
My other half.' With that thy gentle hand

470. **stays,** awaits.
479. **less amiably mild,** i.e., less fitted to inspire love.
486. **individual,** inseparable.

Seized mine, I yielded, and from that time see
How beauty is excelled by manly grace   490
And wisdom, which alone is truly fair."
   So spake our general mother, and with eyes
Of conjugal attraction unreproved,
And meek surrender, half embracing leaned
On our first father; half her swelling breast
Naked met his under the flowing gold
Of her loose tresses hid. He in delight
Both of her beauty and submissive charms
Smiled with superior love, as Jupiter
On Juno smiles, when he impregns the clouds   500
That shed May flowers; and pressed her matron lip
With kisses pure. Aside the Devil turned
For envy, yet with jealous leer malign
Eyed them askance, and to himself thus plained.
   "Sight hateful, sight tormenting! thus these two
Imparadised in one another's arms,
The happier Eden, shall enjoy their fill
Of bliss on bliss, while I to Hell am thrust,
Where neither joy nor love, but fierce desire,
Among our other torments not the least,   510
Still unfulfilled with pain of longing pines;
Yet let me not forget what I have gained
From their own mouths. All is not theirs, it seems;
One fatal tree there stands, of Knowledge called,
Forbidden them to taste. Knowledge forbidden?
Suspicious, reasonless. Why should their Lord
Envy them that? can it be sin to know,
Can it be death? and do they only stand
By ignorance, is that their happy state,
The proof of their obedience and their faith?   520
O fair foundation laid whereon to build
Their ruin! Hence I will excite their minds
With more desire to know, and to reject
Envious commands, invented with design
To keep them low whom knowledge might exalt
Equal with gods. Aspiring to be such,
They taste and die; what likelier can ensue?
But first with narrow search I must walk round
This garden, and no corner leave unspied;

---

   493. unreproved, unreprovable.
   500. impregns, impregnates. Hera typifies the lower air or haze which surrounds the earth,
Zeus the upper air (aether). The mingling of the two produces the spring with its flowers.
   504. plained, complained, murmured.
   521 ff. Satan's own experience has taught him the allurement of godlike power, and the
outcome of any attempt to gain it. He therefore has little difficulty in determining the most
effective temptation. Cf. IX, 705 ff.

A chance but chance may lead where I may meet 530
Some wandering spirit of Heaven, by fountain side,
Or in thick shade retired, from him to draw
What further would be learned. Live while ye may,
Yet happy pair; enjoy, till I return,
Short pleasures, for long woes are to succeed."
    So saying, his proud step he scornful turned,
But with sly circumspection, and began
Through wood, through waste, o'er hill, o'er dale, his roam.

                    *   *   *

    Now came still Evening on, and Twilight gray
Had in her sober livery all things clad;
Silence accompanied, for beast and bird, 600
They to their grassy couch, these to their nests
Were slunk, all but the wakeful nightingale;
She all night long her amorous descant sung;
Silence was pleased. Now glowed the firmament
With living sapphires; Hesperus that led
The starry host, rode brightest, till the Moon
Rising in clouded majesty, at length
Apparent queen unveiled her peerless light,
And o'er the dark her silver mantle threw.
When Adam thus to Eve. "Fair consort, the hour 610
Of night, and all things now retired to rest
Mind us of like repose, since God hath set
Labor and rest, as day and night to men
Successive, and the timely dew of sleep
Now falling with soft slumberous weight inclines
Our eye-lids; other creatures all day long
Rove idle, unemployed, and less need rest;
Man hath his daily work of body or mind
Appointed, which declares his dignity,
And the regard of Heaven on all his ways; 620
While other animals unactive range,
And of their doings God takes no account.
To-morrow ere fresh morning streak the east
With first approach of light, we must be risen,
And at our pleasant labor, to reform
Yon flowery arbors, yonder alleys green,
Our walks at noon, with branches overgrown,
That mock our scant manuring, and require
More hands than ours to lop their wanton growth.
Those blossoms also, and those dropping gums, 630
That lie bestrown unsightly and unsmooth,

530. **A chance but,** there is a chance that.
603. **descant,** a song, or rather a soprano part.   605. **Hesperus,** the evening star.
608. **Apparent,** manifest.   628. **manuring,** cultivating.

Ask riddance, if we mean to tread with ease;
Meanwhile, as Nature wills, night bids us rest."
　To whom thus Eve with perfect beauty adorned.
"My author and disposer, what thou bidd'st
Unargued I obey; so God ordains.
God is thy law, thou mine; to know no more
Is woman's happiest knowledge and her praise.
With thee conversing I forget all time,
All seasons and their change, all please alike.　　　　　　　　　640
Sweet is the breath of Morn, her rising sweet,
With charm of earliest birds; pleasant the Sun
When first on this delightful land he spreads
His orient beams, on herb, tree, fruit, and flower,
Glistering with dew; fragrant the fertile Earth
After soft showers; and sweet the coming on
Of grateful Evening mild, then silent Night
With this her solemn bird and this fair Moon,
And these the gems of Heaven, her starry train:
But neither breath of Morn when she ascends　　　　　　　　650
With charm of earliest birds, nor rising Sun
On this delightful land, nor herb, fruit, flower,
Glistering with dew, nor fragrance after showers,
Nor grateful Evening mild, nor silent Night,
With this her solemn bird, nor walk by moon,
Or glittering star-light, without thee is sweet.
But wherefore all night long shine these? for whom
This glorious sight, when sleep hath shut all eyes?"
　To whom our general ancestor replied.
"Daughter of God and Man, accomplished Eve,　　　　　　　660
Those have their course to finish, round the Earth
By morrow evening, and from land to land
In order, though to nations yet unborn,
Ministering light prepared, they set and rise;
Lest total Darkness should by night regain
Her old possession, and extinguish life
In nature and all things; which these soft fires
Not only enlighten, but with kindly heat
Of various influence foment and warm,
Temper or nourish, or in part shed down　　　　　　　　　670
Their stellar virtue on all kinds that grow

640. All seasons, i.e., all times of the day. Spring is the only season of the year that Eve has yet experienced.
642. charm, song.
650 ff. Note how the imagery of the preceding nine lines is repeated with subtle variations in phrasing. Milton frequently makes effective use of repetition, but nowhere else does he work it into so elaborate a pattern. He is adorning or sophisticating a Homeric device, as he does in his use of similes, and in his structural adaptation of the epic throwback.
665. total Darkness, i.e., the darkness of Chaos.
667 ff. The doctrine of stellar influence, which formed the basis of astrology, was still widely current in the seventeenth century. Milton seems to take its validity for granted.

On Earth, made hereby apter to receive
Perfection from the sun's more potent ray.
These then, though unbeheld in deep of night,
Shine not in vain, nor think, though men were none,
That Heaven would want spectators, God want praise;
Millions of spiritual creatures walk the Earth
Unseen, both when we wake, and when we sleep.
All these with ceaseless praise his works behold
Both day and night. How often from the steep   680
Of echoing hill or thicket have we heard
Celestial voices to the midnight air,
Sole, or responsive each to other's note,
Singing their great Creator; oft in bands
While they keep watch, or nightly rounding walk,
With heavenly touch of instrumental sounds
In full harmonic number joined, their songs
Divide the night, and lift our thoughts to Heaven."
    Thus talking, hand in hand alone they passed
On to their blissful bower; it was a place   690
Chosen by the sovran Planter, when he framed
All things to Man's delightful use; the roof
Of thickest covert was inwoven shade,
Laurel and myrtle, and what higher grew
Of firm and fragrant leaf; on either side
Acanthus, and each odorous bushy shrub
Fenced up the verdant wall; each beauteous flower,
Iris all hues, roses, and jessamine
Reared high their flourished heads between, and wrought
Mosaic; underfoot the violet,   700
Crocus, and hyacinth with rich inlay
Broidered the ground, more colored than with stone
Of costliest emblem. Other creature here,
Beast, bird, insect, or worm durst enter none;
Such was their awe of Man. In shadier bower
More sacred and sequestered, though but feigned,
Pan or Sylvanus never slept, nor Nymph
Nor Faunus haunted. Here in close recess
With flowers, garlands, and sweet-smelling herbs
Espousèd Eve decked first her nuptial bed,   710
And heavenly choirs the hymenæan sung,
What day the genial angel to our sire
Brought her in naked beauty more adorned,

688. **Divide the night,** i.e., into watches.
703. **emblem,** embossed or inlaid ornamentation.
707. **Pan, Sylvanus, and Faunus** were classical deities of the fields and woods. The qualifying **though but feigned** phrase, used with reference to their haunts, implies a judgment on much of the subject matter of pagan poetry. Milton frequently asserts the superior truth of his own materials. Cf. 250, 251, and note.
712. **genial,** nuptial, instrumental to marriage.

More lovely than Pandora, whom the gods
Endowed with all their gifts, and O too like
In sad event, when to the unwiser son
Of Japhet brought by Hermes, she ensnared
Mankind with her fair looks, to be avenged
On him who had stole Jove's authentic fire.
   Thus at their shady lodge arrived, both stood,   720
Both turned, and under open sky adored
The God that made both sky, air, Earth, and Heaven,
Which they beheld, the moon's resplendent globe
And starry pole: "Thou also mad'st the night,
Maker Omnipotent, and thou the day,
Which we in our appointed work employed
Have finished happy in our mutual help
And mutual love, the crown of all our bliss
Ordained by thee, and this delicious place
For us too large, where thy abundance wants   730
Partakers, and uncropped falls to the ground.
But thou hast promised from us two a race
To fill the Earth, who shall with us extol
Thy goodness infinite, both when we wake,
And when we seek, as now, thy gift of sleep."
   This said unanimous, and other rites
Observing none, but adoration pure
Which God likes best, into their inmost bower
Handed they went; and eased the putting off
These troublesome disguises which we wear,   740
Straight side by side were laid, nor turned, I ween,
Adam from his fair spouse, nor Eve the rites
Mysterious of connubial love refused;
Whatever hypocrites austerely talk
Of purity and place and innocence,
Defaming as impure what God declares
Pure, and commands to some, leaves free to all.
Our Maker bids increase; who bids abstain
But our destroyer, foe to God and Man?
Hail wedded Love, mysterious law, true source   750
Of human offspring, sole propriety
In Paradise of all things common else.

714 ff. The allusion is to a myth related by Hesiod. To be avenged on Prometheus, who
had stolen fire from heaven for the use of mortals, Jove sent to earth **Pandora** ("the all-gifted"),
on whom each of the gods had bestowed some fatal charm. Hermes conducted her to Epimetheus,
the **unwiser son of Japhet,** who married her, despite the warning of his brother. Thereupon
all the ills which she had brought from heaven were released to afflict humanity.
   719. authentic, original.
   739. Handed, hand in hand.
   744 ff. Whatever hypocrites, etc. Throughout this passage, Milton is quite obviously taking issue with the advocates of monasticism and celibacy.
   751. sole propriety, sole property. Their love for each other is the one thing in Paradise
which Adam and Eve have as their exclusive possession.

By thee adulterous lust was driven from men
Among the bestial herds to range; by thee,
Founded in reason, loyal, just, and pure,
Relations dear, and all the charities
Of father, son, and brother first were known.
Far be it, that I should write thee sin or blame,
Or think thee unbefitting holiest place,
Perpetual fountain of domestic sweets, 760
Whose bed is undefiled and chaste pronounced,
Present or past, as saints and patriarchs used.
Here Love his golden shafts employs, here lights
His constant lamp, and waves his purple wings,
Reigns here and revels; not in the bought smile
Of harlots, loveless, joyless, unendeared,
Casual fruition; nor in court-amours,
Mixed dance, or wanton mask, or midnight ball,
Or serenate, which the starved lover sings
To his proud fair, best quitted with disdain. 770
These lulled by nightingales, embracing slept,
And on their naked limbs the flowery roof
Showered roses, which the morn repaired. Sleep on
Blest pair; and O yet happiest if ye seek
No happier state, and know to know no more.

* * *

BOOK V: THE ARGUMENT

Morning approached, Eve relates to Adam her troublesome dream; he likes it not, yet comforts her; they come forth to their day labors; their morning hymn at the door of their bower. God, to render Man inexcusable, sends Raphael to admonish him of his obedience, of his free estate, of his enemy near at hand—who he is, and why his enemy, and whatever else may avail Adam to know. Raphael comes down to Paradise; his appearance described; his coming discerned by Adam afar off, sitting at the door of his bower; he goes out to meet him, brings him to his lodge, entertains him with the choicest fruits of Paradise got together by Eve; their discourse at table. Raphael performs his message, minds Adam of his state and of his enemy; relates, at Adam's request, who that enemy is, and how he came to be so, beginning from his first revolt in Heaven, and the occasion thereof; how he drew his legions after him to the parts of the North, and there incited them to rebel with him, persuading all but only Abdiel, a Seraph, who in argument dissuades and opposes him, then forsakes him.

756. **charities,** affections.
767. **nor in court-amours,** etc. Milton may be thinking specifically of the court of Charles II; but he is also thinking of the general chivalric tradition, the artificial conventions of which he believes to be irreconcilable with the ideal domestic relationship.
769. **serenate,** serenade. **starved,** i.e., suffering from cold.
775. **know to know no more,** i.e., are wise enough not to seek further knowledge.

BOOK VI: THE ARGUMENT

Raphael continues to relate how Michael and Gabriel were sent forth to battle against Satan and his angels. The first fight described; Satan and his Powers retire under night. He calls a council; invents devilish engines, which, in the second day's fight, put Michael and his angels to some disorder; but they at length, pulling up mountains, overwhelmed both the force and machines of Satan. Yet, the tumult not so ending, God, on the third day, sends Messiah his Son, for whom he had reserved the glory of that victory. He, in the power of his Father, coming to the place, and causing all his legions to stand still on either side, with his chariot and thunder driving into the midst of his enemies, pursues them, unable to resist, towards the wall of Heaven; which opening, they leap down with horror and confusion into the place of punishment prepared for them in the deep. Messiah returns with triumph to his Father.

BOOK VII: THE ARGUMENT

Raphael, at the request of Adam, relates how and wherefore this World was first created: that God, after the expelling of Satan and his angels out of Heaven, declared his pleasure to create another World, and other creatures to dwell therein; sends his Son with glory, and attendance of angels, to perform the work of creation in six days: the angels celebrate with hymns the performance thereof, and his reascension into Heaven.

BOOK VIII: THE ARGUMENT

Adam inquires concerning celestial motions; is doubtfully answered, and exhorted to search rather things more worthy of knowledge. Adam assents, and still desirous to detain Raphael, relates to him what he remembered since his own creation: his placing in Paradise, his talk with God concerning solitude and fit society, his first meeting and nuptials with Eve. His discourse with the angel thereupon; who, after admonitions repeated, departs.

BOOK IX

THE ARGUMENT

Satan, having compassed the Earth, with meditated guile returns as a mist by night into Paradise; enters into the serpent sleeping. Adam and Eve in the morning go forth to their labors, which Eve proposes to divide in several places, each laboring apart: Adam consents not, alleging the danger, lest that enemy, of whom they were forewarned, should attempt her found alone. Eve, loth to be thought not circumspect or firm enough, urges her going apart, the rather desirous to make trial of her strength; Adam at last yields. The Serpent finds her alone: his subtle approach, first gazing, then speaking, with much flattery extolling Eve above all other creatures. Eve, wondering to hear the Serpent speak, asks how he attained to human speech and such understanding, not till now; the Serpent answers, that by tasting of a certain tree in the garden he attained both to speech and reason, till then void of both. Eve requires him to bring her to that tree, and finds it to be the Tree of Knowledge forbidden. The Serpent, now grown bolder, with many wiles and arguments induces her at length to eat; she, pleased with the taste, deliberates a while whether to impart thereof to Adam or not; at last brings him of the fruit; relates what persuaded her to eat thereof. Adam, at first amazed, but perceiving her lost, resolves through vehemence of love to perish with her, and, extenuating the trespass, eats also of the fruit. The effects thereof in them both; they seek to cover their nakedness; then fall to variance and accusation of one another.

No more of talk where God or angel guest
With Man, as with his friend, familiar used
To sit indulgent, and with him partake
Rural repast, permitting him the while
Venial discourse unblamed. I now must change
Those notes to tragic; foul distrust and breach
Disloyal on the part of man, revolt
And disobedience; on the part of Heaven
Now alienated, distance and distaste,
Anger and just rebuke, and judgment given,   10
That brought into this World a world of woe,
Sin and her shadow Death, and Misery
Death's harbinger. Sad task, yet argument
Not less but more heroic than the wrath
Of stern Achilles on his foe pursued
Thrice fugitive about Troy wall; or rage
Of Turnus for Lavinia disespoused;
Or Neptune's ire or Juno's, that so long
Perplexed the Greek and Cytherea's son;
If answerable style I can obtain   20
Of my celestial patroness, who deigns
Her nightly visitation unimplored,
And dictates to me slumbering, or inspires
Easy my unpremeditated verse;
Since first this subject for heroic song
Pleased me long choosing and beginning late;
Not sedulous by nature to indite

1 ff. The long conversation between Raphael and Adam, forming the substance of Books V–VIII, has introduced the antecedent action and illuminated more fully the existing situation. Now before entering upon the climax of his narrative, Milton pauses for a brief meditative interlude. The personal allusions in the opening lines of this book are of exceptional interest.

6–12. Cf. I, 3. The theme announced at the beginning of the poem is repeated in expanded form.

13 ff. Having restated his theme, Milton here asserts its superiority to the themes of the three great classical epics: (1) the *Iliad,* which deals with **the wrath of stern Achilles;** (2) the *Odyssey,* which relates the outcome of **Neptune's ire** against the Greek Odysseus; (3) the *Aeneid,* the first part of which is motivated by the hostility of **Juno** toward Aeneas (**Cytherea's son**), and the second part by the anger of **Turnus** at the loss of **Lavinia.**

20. answerable style, i.e., a style commensurate with the dignity of the theme.

21–23. Cf. III, 29–40. The implication is that with Milton composition was a spontaneous process, based on a passive reception of impressions and ideas.

25 ff. From the Cambridge MS. it is evident that the subject of *Paradise Lost* (together with various other subjects drawn from biblical and British history) was in Milton's mind by 1640 or soon after. The actual composition of the epic could not have been begun much before 1658.

Wars, hitherto the only argument
Heroic deemed, chief mastery to dissect
With long and tedious havoc fabled knights 30
In battles feigned; the better fortitude
Of patience and heroic martyrdom
Unsung; or to describe races and games,
Or tilting furniture, imblazoned shields,
Impresses quaint, caparisons and steeds,
Bases and tinsel trappings, gorgeous knights
At joust and tournament; then marshalled feast
Served up in hall with sewers and seneshals,
The skill of artifice or office mean,
Not that which justly gives heroic name 40
To person or to poem. Me of these
Nor skilled nor studious, higher argument
Remains, sufficient of itself to raise
That name, unless an age too late, or cold
Climate, or years damp my intended wing
Depressed, and much they may, if all be mine,
Not hers who brings it nightly to my ear.
   The sun was sunk, and after him the star
Of Hesperus, whose office is to bring
Twilight upon the Earth, short arbiter 50
'Twixt day and night, and now from end to end
Night's hemisphere had veiled the horizon round;
When Satan who late fled before the threats
Of Gabriel out of Eden, now improved
In meditated fraud and malice, bent
On Man's destruction, maugre what might hap
Of heavier on himself, fearless returned.
By night he fled, and at midnight returned
From compassing the Earth, cautious of day,
Since Uriel, regent of the sun, descried 60
His entrance, and forewarned the Cherubim
That kept their watch; thence full of anguish driven,
The space of seven continued nights he rode
With darkness, thrice the equinoctial line
He circled, four times crossed the car of Night

33. races and games. Milton is thinking of the detailed accounts in *Iliad* xxiii, and *Aeneid* v.
34. tilting furniture, etc., i.e., the trappings of chivalry.
35. impresses, devices on shields.
36. bases, kilt-like garments worn by knights on horseback.
41–43. Me . . . remains. To me, who am, etc., there remains.
44–45. an age too late, i.e., too late a period in the world's history. The notion of universal retrogression was fairly common in the seventeenth century. Though Milton had argued against the theory, he here shows that he is not unaffected by fear that it may be true. **or cold Climate.** The idea that a northern climate is unfavorable to works of the mind goes back to Aristotle.
56. maugre, in spite of.

From pole to pole, traversing each colure;
On the eighth returned, and on the coast averse
From entrance or cherubic watch, by stealth
Found unsuspected way. There was a place,
Now not, though sin, not time, first wrought the change,   70
Where Tigris at the foot of Paradise
Into a gulf shot under ground, till part
Rose up a fountain by the Tree of Life;
In with the river sunk, and with it rose
Satan involved in rising mist, then sought
Where to lie hid; sea he had searched and land
From Eden over Pontus, and the pool
Mæotis, up beyond the river Ob;
Downward as far antarctic; and in length
West from Orontes to the ocean barred   80
At Darien, thence to the land where flows
Ganges and Indus. Thus the orb he roamed
With narrow search, and with inspection deep
Considered every creature, which of all
Most opportune might serve his wiles, and found
The serpent subtlest beast of all the field.
Him after long debate, irresolute
Of thoughts revolved, his final sentence chose
Fit vessel, fittest imp of fraud, in whom
To enter, and his dark suggestions hide   90
From sharpest sight; for in the wily snake,
Whatever sleights none would suspicious mark,
As from his wit and native subtlety
Proceeding, which in other beasts observed,
Doubt might beget of diabolic power
Active within beyond the sense of brute.
Thus he resolved, but first from inward grief
His bursting passion into plaints thus poured.
    "O Earth, how like to Heaven, if not preferred
More justly, seat worthier of Gods, as built   100
With second thoughts, reforming what was old!
For what God after better worse would build?

---

66. traversing each colure. The colures are two great circles intersecting at the poles, one passing through the equinoxes, the other (at right angles to it) through the solstices. Satan follows each of these lines from south to north and back, keeping always within the earth's shadow.

69 ff. Cf. IV, 223–30. Satan makes his entrance from the north side. Satan's wanderings, first described astronomically, are here described geographically. Northward he had gone over the Black Sea (**Pontus**) and the Sea of Azof (**the pool Mæotis**), beyond the Siberian river **Ob** to the pole; thence southward to the Antarctic. Westward he had gone along the Syrian river **Orontes,** over the Mediterranean and Atlantic to the Isthmus of Panama (**Darien**), and from there across the Pacific to India (the land of **Ganges and Indus**).

82. orb, the world.   **88. sentence,** decision.   **89. imp,** offspring.

99 ff. "O Earth," etc. Cf. Satan's soliloquy on first gaining sight of Eden, IV, 32 ff. As then, he is torn by passion, but now there is less of remorse, more of bitterness and despair.

Terrestrial Heaven, danced round by other Heavens
That shine, yet bear their bright officious lamps,
Light above light, for thee alone, as seems,
In thee concentring all their precious beams
Of sacred influence. As God in Heaven
Is center, yet extends to all, so thou
Centring receivest from all those orbs; in thee,
Not in themselves, all their known virtue appears   110
Productive in herb, plant, and nobler birth
Of creatures animate with gradual life
Of growth, sense, reason, all summed up in Man.
With what delight could I have walked thee round,
If I could joy in aught, sweet interchange
Of hill and valley, rivers, woods, and plains,
Now land, now sea, and shores with forest crowned,
Rocks, dens, and caves; but I in none of these
Find place or refuge; and the more I see
Pleasures about me, so much more I feel   120
Torment within me, as from the hateful siege
Of contraries; all good to me becomes
Bane, and in Heaven much worse would be my state.
But neither here seek I, no nor in Heaven
To dwell, unless by mastering Heaven's Supreme;
Nor hope to be myself less miserable
By what I seek, but others to make such
As I, though thereby worse to me redound:
For only in destroying I find ease
To my relentless thoughts; and him destroyed,   130
Or won to what may work his utter loss,
For whom all this was made, all this will soon
Follow, as to him linked in weal or woe;
In woe then, that destruction wide may range.
To me shall be the glory sole among
The infernal Powers, in one day to have marred
What he Almighty styled, six nights and days
Continued making, and who knows how long
Before had been contriving, though perhaps
Not longer than since I in one night freed   140
From servitude inglorious well nigh half
The angelic name, and thinner left the throng
Of his adorers. He to be avenged,
And to repair his numbers thus impaired,
Whether such virtue spent of old now failed
More angels to create, if they at least
Are his created, or to spite us more,
Determined to advance into our room

---

103. danced round by other Heavens. Milton frequently compares the motion of the heavenly bodies to a dance.
142. name, race, stock.

A creature formed of earth, and him endow,
Exalted from so base original,
With heavenly spoils, our spoils. What he decreed 150
He effected; Man he made, and for him built
Magnificent this World, and Earth his seat,
Him lord pronounced, and, O indignity!
Subjected to his service angel wings,
And flaming ministers to watch and tend
Their earthy charge. Of these the vigilance
I dread, and to elude, thus wrapped in mist
Of midnight vapor glide obscure, and pry
In every bush and brake, where hap may find 160
The serpent sleeping, in whose mazy folds
To hide me, and the dark intent I bring.
O foul descent! that I who erst contended
With Gods to sit the highest, am now constrained
Into a beast, and, mixed with bestial slime,
This essence to incarnate and imbrute,
That to the height of deity aspired;
But what will not ambition and revenge
Descend to? Who aspires must down as low
As high he soared, obnoxious first or last 170
To basest things. Revenge, at first though sweet,
Bitter ere long back on itself recoils;
Let it; I reck not, so it light well aimed,
Since higher I fall short, on him who next
Provokes my envy, this new favorite
Of Heaven, this man of clay, son of despite,
Whom us the more to spite his Maker raised
From dust: spite then with spite is best repaid."
  So saying, through each thicket dank or dry,
Like a black mist low creeping, he held on 180
His midnight search, where soonest he might find
The serpent. Him fast sleeping soon he found
In labyrinth of many a round self-rolled,
His head the midst, well stored with subtle wiles;
Not yet in horrid shade or dismal den,
Nor nocent yet, but on the grassy herb
Fearless unfeared he slept. In at his mouth
The Devil entered, and his brutal sense,
In heart or head, possessing soon inspired
With act intelligential, but his sleep 190
Disturbed not, waiting close the approach of morn.
  Now whenas sacred light began to dawn
In Eden on the humid flowers, that breathed
Their morning incense, when all things that breathe,

---

163 ff. Satan's imbruting himself within the serpent is the final step in his progressive degeneration. His own words explain the symbolism.
170. obnoxious, liable, subject.

From the Earth's great altar send up silent praise
To the Creator, and his nostrils fill
With grateful smell, forth came the human pair
And joined their vocal worship to the choir
Of creatures wanting voice; that done, partake
The season, prime for sweetest scents and airs;   200
Then commune how that day they best may ply
Their growing work; for much their work outgrew
The hands' dispatch of two gardening so wide.
And Eve first to her husband thus began.
    "Adam, well may we labor still to dress
This garden, still to tend plant, herb, and flower,
Our pleasant task enjoined, but till more hands
Aid us, the work under our labor grows,
Luxurious by restraint; what we by day
Lop overgrown, or prune, or prop, or bind,   210
One night or two with wanton growth derides
Tending to wild. Thou therefore now advise
Or hear what to my mind first thoughts present:
Let us divide our labors, thou where choice
Leads thee, or where most needs, whether to wind
The woodbine round this arbor, or direct
The clasping ivy where to climb, while I
In yonder spring of roses intermixed
With myrtle, find what to redress till noon.
For while so near each other thus all day   220
Our task we choose, what wonder if so near
Looks intervene and smiles, or object new
Casual discourse draw on, which intermits
Our day's work, brought to little, though begun
Early, and the hour of supper comes unearned."
    To whom mild answer Adam thus returned.
"Sole Eve, associate sole, to me beyond
Compare above all living creatures dear,
Well hast thou motioned, well thy thoughts employed
How we might best fulfil the work which here   230
God hath assigned us, nor of me shalt pass
Unpraised; for nothing lovelier can be found
In woman, than to study household good,
And good works in her husband to promote.
Yet not so strictly hath our Lord imposed
Labor, as to debar us when we need
Refreshment, whether food, or talk between,
Food of the mind, or this sweet intercourse
Of looks and smiles, for smiles from reason flow,

199–200. partake The season, i.e., share the beauties of the morning. As in IV, 640, **season** refers to the time of day.
218. spring, clump, thicket.
229. motioned, proposed.

To brute denied, and are of love the food, 240
Love not the lowest end of human life.
For not to irksome toil, but to delight
He made us, and delight to reason joined.
These paths and bowers doubt not but our joint hands
Will keep from wilderness with ease, as wide
As we need walk, till younger hands ere long
Assist us. But if much converse perhaps
Thee satiate, to short absence I could yield;
For solitude sometimes is best society,
And short retirement urges sweet return. 250
But other doubt possesses me, lest harm
Befall thee severed from me; for thou know'st
What hath been warned us, what malicious foe
Envying our happiness, and of his own
Despairing, seeks to work us woe and shame
By sly assault; and somewhere nigh at hand
Watches, no doubt, with greedy hope to find
His wish and best advantage, us asunder,
Hopeless to circumvent us joined, where each
To other speedy aid might lend at need; 260
Whether his first design be to withdraw
Our feälty from God, or to disturb
Conjugal love, than which perhaps no bliss
Enjoyed by us excites his envy more;
Or this, or worse, leave not the faithful side
That gave thee being, still shades thee and protects.
The wife, where danger or dishonor lurks,
Safest and seemliest by her husband stays,
Who guards her, or with her the worst endures."
    To whom the virgin majesty of Eve, 270
As one who loves, and some unkindness meets,
With sweet austere composure thus replied.
    "Offspring of Heaven and Earth, and all Earth's lord,
That such an enemy we have, who seeks
Our ruin, both by thee informed I learn,
And from the parting angel overheard
As in a shady nook I stood behind,
Just then returned at shut of evening flowers.
But that thou shouldst my firmness therefore doubt
To God or thee, because we have a foe 280
May tempt it, I expected not to hear.
His violence thou fear'st not, being such,
As we, not capable of death or pain,
Can either not receive, or can repel.
His fraud is then thy fear, which plain infers

---

245. **wilderness,** wildness (i.e., too luxuriant growth of vegetation).
265. **Or this, or worse,** i.e., whether his design (261) be this or worse.
276. **from the parting angel,** i.e., from Raphael as he was parting from Adam.

Thy equal fear that my firm faith and love
Can by his fraud be shaken or seduced;
Thoughts, which how found they harbor in thy breast,
Adam, misthought of her to thee so dear?"
    To whom with healing words Adam replied.   290
"Daughter of God and Man, immortal Eve,
For such thou art, from sin and blame entire;
Not diffident of thee do I dissuade
Thy absence from my sight, but to avoid
The attempt itself, intended by our foe.
For he who tempts, though in vain, at least asperses
The tempted with dishonor foul, supposed
Not incorruptible of faith, not proof
Against temptation. Thou thyself with scorn
And anger wouldst resent the offered wrong,   300
Though ineffectual found. Misdeem not then,
If such affront I labor to avert
From thee alone, which on us both at once
The enemy, though bold, will hardly dare,
Or daring, first on me the assault shall light.
Nor thou his malice and false guile contemn;
Subtle he needs must be, who could seduce
Angels, nor think superfluous others' aid.
I from the influence of thy looks receive
Access in every virtue, in thy sight   310
More wise, more watchful, stronger, if need were
Of outward strength; while shame, thou looking on,
Shame to be overcome or overreached,
Would utmost vigor raise, and raised unite.
Why shouldst not thou like sense within thee feel
When I am present, and thy trial choose
With me, best witness of thy virtue tried."
So spake domestic Adam in his care
And matrimonial love; but Eve, who thought
Less attributed to her faith sincere,   320
Thus her reply with accent sweet renewed.
    "If this be our condition, thus to dwell
In narrow circuit straitened by a foe,
Subtle or violent, we not endued
Single with like defence, wherever met,
How are we happy, still in fear of harm?
But harm precedes not sin: only our foe
Tempting affronts us with his foul esteem
Of our integrity; his foul esteem
Sticks no dishonor on our front, but turns   330

    292. entire, untouched.   **310. access,** growth, increase.
    318. domestic, devoted to home life and its duties.
    320. less, too little.
    328. affronts. The literal meaning "strikes on the forehead" is implied (Latin *ad + frons*).
Note how the image is expanded in the two lines following.

Foul on himself; then wherefore shunned or feared
By us? who rather double honor gain
From his surmise proved false, find peace within,
Favor from Heaven, our witness, from the event.
And what is faith, love, virtue, unassayed
Alone, without exterior help sustained?
Let us not then suspect our happy state
Left so imperfect by the Maker wise,
As not secure to single or combined.
Frail is our happiness, if this be so,   340
And Eden were no Eden thus exposed."
  To whom thus Adam fervently replied.
"O Woman, best are all things as the will
Of God ordained them; his creating hand
Nothing imperfect or deficient left
Of all that he created, much less Man,
Or aught that might his happy state secure,
Secure from outward force: within himself
The danger lies, yet lies within his power;
Against his will he can receive no harm.   350
But God left free the will, for what obeys
Reason is free, and Reason he made right,
But bid her well be ware, and still erect,
Lest by some fair appearing good surprised
She dictate false, and misinform the will
To do what God expressly hath forbid.
Not then mistrust, but tender love enjoins,
That I should mind thee oft, and mind thou me.
Firm we subsist, yet possible to swerve,
Since Reason not impossibly may meet   360
Some specious object by the foe suborned,
And fall into deception unaware,
Not keeping strictest watch, as she was warned.
Seek not temptation then, which to avoid
Were better, and most likely if from me
Thou sever not; trial will come unsought.
Wouldst thou approve thy constancy, approve
First thy obedience; the other who can know,
Not seeing thee attempted, who attest?
But if thou think trial unsought may find   370

335. **And what is faith, love, virtue,** etc., i.e., what value have these qualities unless they
have been tested and found able to stand by their own merits. Milton here puts in the mouth
of Eve an argument which he himself used in *Areopagitica.* Cf. the famous passage: "I cannot
praise a fugitive and cloistered virtue," etc.
  339. **to single or combined,** i.e., to us singly or together.
  341. **no Eden,** no place of delight. Cf. note on IV, 27, 28.
  348 ff. **within himself . . . no harm.** The principle of human responsibility is fundamental
to Milton's whole philosophy.
  353. **still erect,** ever alert.
  367. **approve,** give proof of, confirm.

Us both securer than thus warned thou seem'st,
Go; for thy stay, not free, absents thee more;
Go in thy native innocence, rely
On what thou hast of virtue, summon all,
For God towards thee hath done his part, do thine."
　So spake the patriarch of mankind, but Eve
Persisted; yet submiss, though last, replied.
　"With thy permission then, and thus forewarned,
Chiefly by what thy own last reasoning words
Touched only, that our trial, when least sought,　　　　380
May find us both perhaps far less prepared,
The willinger I go, nor much expect
A foe so proud will first the weaker seek;
So bent, the more shall shame him his repulse."
　Thus saying, from her husband's hand her hand
Soft she withdrew, and like a wood-nymph light,
Oread or Dryad, or of Delia's train,
Betook her to the groves, but Delia's self
In gait surpassed and goddess-like deport,
Though not as she with bow and quiver armed,　　　　390
But with such gardening tools as art yet rude,
Guiltless of fire had formed, or angels brought.
To Pales, or Pomona, thus adorned,
Likest she seemed, Pomona when she fled
Vertumnus, or to Ceres in her prime,
Yet virgin of Proserpina from Jove.
Her long with ardent look his eye pursued
Delighted, but desiring more her stay.
Oft he to her his charge of quick return
Repeated, she to him as oft engaged　　　　400
To be returned by noon amid the bower,
And all things in best order to invite
Noontide repast, or afternoon's repose.
O much deceived, much failing, hapless Eve,
Of thy presumed return! event perverse!
Thou never from that hour in Paradise
Found'st either sweet repast or sound repose;
Such ambush, hid among sweet flowers and shades,
Waited with hellish rancor imminent
To intercept thy way, or send thee back　　　　410
Despoiled of innocence, of faith, of bliss.

371. securer, i.e., "less prepared" (381).
　387. Oread or Dryad, a nymph of the mountains or of the trees. **Delia,** the goddess Diana, born on the island of Delos.
　392. Guiltless of fire. The uses of fire are not discovered until after the fall.
　393 ff. Pales was a Roman goddess of flocks, **Pomona** of fruits, **Ceres** of agriculture; **Vertumnus** was god of the changing seasons.
　396. Yet virgin of, not yet the mother of.
　402. And all things in best order, i.e., to have all things in best order.

For now, and since first break of dawn the Fiend,
Mere serpent in appearance, forth was come,
And on his quest, where likeliest he might find
The only two of mankind, but in them
The whole included race, his purposed prey.
In bower and field he sought, where any tuft
Of grove or garden-plot more pleasant lay,
Their tendance or plantation for delight,
By fountain or by shady rivulet. 420
He sought them both, but wished his hap might find
Eve separate; he wished, but not with hope
Of what so seldom chanced; when to his wish,
Beyond his hope, Eve separate he spies,
Veiled in a cloud of fragrance, where she stood,
Half spied, so thick the roses bushing round
About her glowed, oft stooping to support
Each flower of slender stalk, whose head though gay
Carnation, purple, azure, or specked with gold,
Hung drooping unsustained; them she upstays 430
Gently with myrtle band, mindless the while
Herself, though fairest unsupported flower,
From her best prop so far, and storm so nigh.
Nearer he drew, and many a walk traversed
Of stateliest covert, cedar, pine, or palm,
Then voluble and bold, now hid, now seen
Among thick-woven arborets and flowers
Imbordered on each bank, the hand of Eve:
Spot more delicious than those gardens feigned
Or of revived Adonis, or renowned 440
Alcinous, host of old Laertes' son,
Or that, not mystic, where the sapient king
Held dalliance with his fair Egyptian spouse.
Much he the place admired, the person more.
As one who long in populous city pent,
Where houses thick and sewers annoy the air,
Forth issuing on a summer's morn to breathe
Among the pleasant villages and farms
Adjoined, from each thing met conceives delight,

432. **Herself . . . flower.** The metaphor is repeated from IV, 270.
436. **voluble,** rolling (Latin *volubilis*).
437. **arborets,** small trees, shrubs.
438. **hand,** handiwork.
439 ff. The gardens of Alcinous, the Phaeacian ruler who entertained Odysseus (**old Laertes'
son**), are described in *Odyssey* vii. The garden of Solomon (**the sapient king**) is mentioned in
Scripture; hence, from Milton's point of view, it is not **feigned** or **mystic** (i.e., mythical) like
the others. Cf. Song of Sol. 7:2, and I Kings 3:1.
440, 442. **Or . . . or,** either . . . or.
445 ff. The attitude toward nature revealed in this simile anticipates Wordsworth's. Note
especially the idea that natural objects, lovely in themselves, are enhanced in meaning by their
human associations. Milton's treatment is ordinarily more impersonal.
446. **annoy,** pollute, render noisome.

The smell of grain, or tedded grass, or kine,   450
Or dairy, each rural sight, each rural sound;
If chance with nymph-like step fair virgin pass,
What pleasing seemed, for her now pleases more,
She most, and in her look sums all delight.
Such pleasure took the Serpent to behold
This flowery plat, the sweet recess of Eve
Thus early, thus alone; her heavenly form
Angelic, but more soft and feminine,
Her graceful innocence, her every air
Of gesture or least action overawed   460
His malice, and with rapine sweet bereaved
His fierceness of the fierce intent it brought.
That space the Evil One abstracted stood
From his own evil, and for the time remained
Stupidly good, of enmity disarmed,
Of guile, of hate, of envy, of revenge;
But the hot hell that always in him burns,
Though in mid Heaven, soon ended his delight,
And tortures him now more, the more he sees
Of pleasure not for him ordained; then soon   470
Fierce hate he recollects, and all his thoughts
Of mischief, gratulating, thus excites.
    "Thoughts, whither have ye led me, with what sweet
Compulsion thus transported to forget
What hither brought us, hate, not love, nor hope
Of Paradise for Hell, hope here to taste
Of pleasure, but all pleasure to destroy,
Save what is in destroying; other joy
To me is lost. Then let me not let pass
Occasion which now smiles, behold alone   480
The woman, opportune to all attempts,
Her husband, for I view far round, not nigh,
Whose higher intellectual more I shun,
And strength, of courage haughty, and of limb
Heroic built, though of terrestrial mould,
Foe not informidable, exempt from wound,
I not; so much hath Hell debased, and pain
Enfeebled me, to what I was in Heaven.
She fair, divinely fair, fit love for Gods,
Not terrible, though terror be in love   490
And beauty, not approached by stronger hate,
Hate stronger, under shew of love well feigned,
The way which to her ruin now I tend."
    So spake the Enemy of mankind, enclosed
In serpent, inmate bad, and toward Eve

---

450. tedded grass, grass just mown and spread out for drying.
465. Stupidly good, i.e., stupefied into goodness.
485. of terrestrial mould, of earthly substance.

Addressed his way, not with indented wave,
Prone on the ground as since, but on his rear,
Circular base of rising folds, that towered
Fold above fold a surging maze; his head
Crested aloft, and carbuncle his eyes; 500
With burnished neck of verdant gold, erect
Amidst his circling spires, that on the grass
Floated redundant. Pleasing was his shape,
And lovely, never since of serpent kind
Lovelier; not those that in Illyria changed
Hermione and Cadmus, or the god
In Epidaurus; nor to which transformed
Ammonian Jove, or Capitoline was seen,
He with Olympias, this with her who bore
Scipio the height of Rome. With tract oblique 510
At first, as one who sought access, but feared
To interrupt, sidelong he works his way.
As when a ship by skilful steersman wrought
Nigh river's mouth or foreland, where the wind
Veers oft, as oft so steers, and shifts her sail;
So varied he, and of his tortuous train
Curled many a wanton wreath in sight of Eve,
To lure her eye; she busied heard the sound
Of rustling leaves, but minded not, as used
To such disport before her through the field, 520
From every beast, more duteous at her call,
Than at Circean call the herd disguised.
He bolder now, uncalled before her stood,
But as in gaze admiring. Oft he bowed
His turret crest, and sleek enamelled neck,
Fawning, and licked the ground whereon she trod.
His gentle dumb expression turned at length
The eye of Eve to mark his play; he glad
Of her attention gained, with serpent tongue
Organic, or impulse of vocal air, 530
His fraudulent temptation thus began:

500. **carbuncle,** i.e., deep red, suggesting passion.
502. **spires,** coils.   505. **changed,** took the place of.
506. **Hermione** and her husband **Cadmus,** king of Thebes, were changed into serpents at their own request, in order to escape the miseries of human life. The god of medicine, Aesculapius, took the form of a serpent when going from **Epidaurus** to Rome for the purpose of staying a pestilence.
507. **nor to which transformed,** etc., i.e., nor those serpents into which Jove was seen transformed. According to a myth told by Plutarch, Jupiter Ammon (**Ammonian Jove**) was the father of Alexander the Great, having been observed in the shape of a serpent with **Olympias,** Alexander's mother. A similar myth portrayed Jupiter Capitolinus as the father of Scipio Africanus.
517. **wanton,** playful.
522. **Circean call.** The allusion is to the well-known myth of Circe, an enchantress who changed men into beasts and kept them in complete subjection to her will.
529. **with serpent tongue,** etc. Satan either uses the serpent's vocal organs directly or causes his words seemingly to come from them.

"Wonder not, sovran mistress, if perhaps
Thou canst, who art sole wonder, much less arm
Thy looks, the heaven of mildness, with disdain,
Displeased that I approach thee thus, and gaze
Insatiate, I thus single, nor have feared
Thy awful brow, more awful thus retired.
Fairest resemblance of thy Maker fair,
Thee all things living gaze on, all things thine
By gift, and thy celestial beauty adore,   540
With ravishment beheld, there best beheld
Where universally admired; but here
In this enclosure wild, these beasts among,
Beholders rude, and shallow to discern
Half what in thee is fair, one man except,
Who sees thee? (and what is one?) who shouldst be seen
A Goddess among Gods, adored and served
By angels numberless, thy daily train."
    So glozed the Tempter, and his proem tuned;
Into the heart of Eve his words made way,   550
Though at the voice much marvelling; at length
Not unamazed she thus in answer spake.
    "What may this mean? Language of man pronounced
By tongue of brute, and human sense expressed?
The first at least of these I thought denied
To beasts, whom God on their creation-day
Created mute to all articulate sound;
The latter I demur, for in their looks
Much reason, and in their actions, oft appears.
Thee, Serpent, subtlest beast of all the field   560
I knew, but not with human voice endued;
Redouble then this miracle, and say,
How cam'st thou speakable of mute, and how
To me so friendly grown above the rest
Of brutal kind, that daily are in sight?
Say, for such wonder claims attention due."
    To whom the guileful Tempter thus replied.
"Empress of this fair World, resplendent Eve,
Easy to me it is to tell thee all
What thou command'st, and right thou shouldst be obeyed.   570
I was at first as other beasts that graze
The trodden herb, of abject thoughts and low,
As was my food, nor aught but food discerned
Or sex, and apprehended nothing high:
Till on a day roving the field, I chanced
A goodly tree far distant to behold

544. **shallow,** i.e., too shallow.
549. **glozed,** smoothed over his real motive with flattery.
558. **demur,** remain in doubt about.
563. **How cam'st thou speakable of mute,** i.e., how did you, being mute, become capable of speech.

Loaden with fruit of fairest colors mixed,
Ruddy and gold. I nearer drew to gaze;
When from the boughs a savory odor blown,
Grateful to appetite, more pleased my sense 580
Than smell of sweetest fennel or the teats
Of ewe or goat dropping with milk at even,
Unsucked of lamb or kid, that tend their play.
To satisfy the sharp desire I had
Of tasting those fair apples, I resolved
Not to defer; hunger and thirst at once,
Powerful persuaders, quickened at the scent
Of that alluring fruit, urged me so keen.
About the mossy trunk I wound me soon,
For high from ground the branches would require 590
Thy utmost reach or Adam's: round the tree
All other beasts that saw, with like desire
Longing and envying stood, but could not reach.
Amid the tree now got, where plenty hung
Tempting so nigh, to pluck and eat my fill
I spared not, for such pleasure till that hour
At feed or fountain never had I found.
Sated at length, ere long I might perceive
Strange alteration in me, to degree
Of reason in my inward powers, and speech 600
Wanted not long, though to this shape retained.
Thenceforth to speculations high or deep
I turned my thoughts, and with capacious mind
Considered all things visible in Heaven,
Or Earth, or middle, all things fair and good;
But all that fair and good in thy divine
Semblance, and in thy beauty's heavenly ray
United I beheld; no fair to thine
Equivalent or second, which compelled
Me thus, though importune perhaps, to come 610
And gaze, and worship thee of right declared
Sovran of creatures, universal Dame."
    So talked the spirited sly Snake; and Eve
Yet more amazed unwary thus replied.
    "Serpent, thy overpraising leaves in doubt
The virtue of that fruit, in thee first proved.
But say, where grows the tree, from hence how far?
For many are the trees of God that grow
In Paradise, and various, yet unknown
To us; in such abundance lies our choice, 620
As leaves a greater store of fruit untouched,

---

581. According to popular belief, serpents were especially fond of fennel and were in the habit of sucking milk from sheep and goats.
    605. middle, i.e., the air.
    612. universal Dame, mistress of the universe.
    613. spirited, i.e., inspired by Satan.

Still hanging incorruptible, till men
Grow up to their provision, and more hands
Help to disburden Nature of her birth."
    To whom the wily Adder, blithe and glad.
"Empress, the way is ready, and not long;
Beyond a row of myrtles, on a flat,
Fast by a fountain, one small thicket past
Of blowing myrrh and balm; if thou accept
My conduct, I can bring thee thither soon."   630
    "Lead then," said Eve. He leading swiftly rolled
In tangles, and made intricate seem straight,
To mischief swift. Hope elevates, and joy
Brightens his crest, as when a wandering fire,
Compact of unctuous vapor, which the night
Condenses, and the cold environs round,
Kindled through agitation to a flame,
Which oft, they say, some evil spirit attends,
Hovering and blazing with delusive light,
Misleads the amazed night-wanderer from his way   640
To bogs and mires, and oft through pond or pool,
There swallowed up and lost, from succor far.
So glistered the dire Snake, and into fraud
Led Eve our credulous mother, to the tree
Of prohibition, root of all our woe;
Which when she saw, thus to her guide she spake.
    "Serpent, we might have spared our coming hither,
Fruitless to me, though fruit be here to excess,
The credit of whose virtue rest with thee,
Wondrous indeed, if cause of such effects.   650
But of this tree we may not taste nor touch;
God so commanded, and left that command
Sole daughter of his voice; the rest, we live
Law to ourselves, our reason is our law."
    To whom the Tempter guilefully replied.
"Indeed? Hath God then said that of the fruit
Of all these garden trees ye shall not eat,
Yet lords declared of all in Earth or air?"
    To whom thus Eve yet sinless. "Of the fruit
Of each tree in the garden we may eat,   660
But of the fruit of this fair tree amidst
The garden, God hath said, 'Ye shall not eat
Thereof, nor shall ye touch it, lest ye die.'"

---

    622. incorruptible, incapable of decay.
    624. birth, i.e., the products to which she has given birth.
    629. blowing, blossoming.
    634 ff. This description of the ignis fatuus combines a semiscientific explanation with a
popular superstition. Whether Milton actually believed the phenomenon the work of an evil
spirit he does not say.
    643. fraud, offense, harm.   **653. the rest,** as for the rest.
    661–63. Milton here follows very closely the phraseology of Gen. 3:1–3.

She scarce had said, though brief, when now more bold
The Tempter, but with show of zeal and love
To Man, and indignation at his wrong,
New part puts on, and as to passion moved,
Fluctuates disturbed, yet comely and in act
Raised, as of some great matter to begin.
As when of old some orator renowned 670
In Athens or free Rome, where eloquence
Flourished, since mute, to some great cause addressed,
Stood in himself collected, while each part,
Motion, each act won audience ere the tongue,
Sometimes in height began, as no delay
Of preface brooking through his zeal of right.
So standing, moving, or to height upgrown,
The Tempter all impassioned thus began.
"O sacred, wise, and wisdom-giving Plant,
Mother of science, now I feel thy power 680
Within me clear, not only to discern
Things in their causes, but to trace the ways
Of highest agents, deemed however wise.
Queen of this Universe, do not believe
Those rigid threats of death; ye shall not die:
How should ye? by the fruit? it gives you life
To knowledge; by the threatener? look on me,
Me who have touched and tasted, yet both live,
And life more perfect have attained than fate
Meant me, by venturing higher than my lot. 690
Shall that be shut to Man, which to the beast
Is open? or will God incense his ire
For such a petty trespass, and not praise
Rather your dauntless virtue, whom the pain
Of death denounced, whatever thing death be,
Deterred not from achieving what might lead
To happier life, knowledge of good and evil;
Of good, how just? of evil, if what is evil
Be real, why not known, since easier shunned?
God therefore cannot hurt ye, and be just; 700
Not just, not God; not feared then, nor obeyed:
Your fear itself of death removes the fear.
Why then was this forbid? Why but to awe,
Why but to keep ye low and ignorant,
His worshippers; he knows that in the day
Ye eat thereof, your eyes that seem so clear,

668. **Fluctuates.** The word is used literally. Milton means that the serpent moves his body to and fro, in order to give visible expression to his assumed emotion.

679 ff. **"O sacred, wise . . ."** The serpent's speech is a masterpiece of persuasion, uniting intense emotional fervor with closely packed and seemingly irrefutable arguments. Milton does not wish to make Eve too easy a victim.

680. **science,** knowledge (Latin *scientia*).

687. **To,** in addition to.

Yet are but dim, shall perfectly be then
Opened and cleared, and ye shall be as Gods,
Knowing both good and evil as they know.
That ye should be as Gods, since I as Man,   710
Internal Man, is but proportion meet,
I of brute human, ye of human Gods.
So ye shall die perhaps, by putting off
Human, to put on Gods, death to be wished,
Though threatened, which no worse than this can bring.
And what are Gods, that Man may not become
As they, participating godlike food?
The Gods are first, and that advantage use
On our belief, that all from them proceeds;
I question it, for this fair Earth I see,   720
Warmed by the sun, producing every kind,
Them nothing. If they all things, who enclosed
Knowledge of good and evil in this tree,
That whoso eats thereof, forthwith attains
Wisdom without their leave? and wherein lies
The offence, that Man should thus attain to know?
What can your knowledge hurt him, or this tree
Impart against his will, if all be his?
Or is it envy, and can envy dwell
In heavenly breasts? These, these and many more   730
Causes import your need of this fair fruit.
Goddess humane, reach then, and freely taste!"
    He ended, and his words replete with guile
Into her heart too easy entrance won.
Fixed on the fruit she gazed, which to behold
Might tempt alone, and in her ears the sound
Yet rung of his persuasive words, impregned
With reason, to her seeming, and with truth;
Meanwhile the hour of noon drew on, and waked
An eager appetite, raised by the smell   740
So savory of that fruit, which with desire,
Inclinable now grown to touch or taste,
Solicited her longing eye; yet first
Pausing a while, thus to herself she mused.
    "Great are thy virtues, doubtless, best of fruits,
Though kept from Man, and worthy to be admired,
Whose taste, too long forborne, at first assay
Gave elocution to the mute, and taught
The tongue not made for speech to speak thy praise.
Thy praise he also who forbids thy use   750
Conceals not from us, naming thee the Tree

732. **humane,** gracious, gentle in demeanor.
737. **impregned,** impregnated.
739–43. Physical appetite is an important factor in Eve's decision, but she does not admit
it to herself.

Of Knowledge, knowledge both of good and evil;
Forbids us then to taste, but his forbidding
Commends thee more, while it infers the good
By thee communicated, and our want;
For good unknown sure is not had, or had
And yet unknown, is as not had at all.
In plain then, what forbids he but to know,
Forbids us good, forbids us to be wise?
Such prohibitions bind not. But if Death   760
Bind us with after-bands, what profits then
Our inward freedom? In the day we eat
Of this fair fruit, our doom is, we shall die.
How dies the Serpent? He hath eaten and lives,
And knows, and speaks, and reasons, and discerns,
Irrational till then. For us alone
Was death invented? or to us denied
This intellectual food, for beasts reserved?
For beasts it seems; yet that one beast which first
Hath tasted, envies not, but brings with joy   770
That good befallen him, author unsuspect,
Friendly to man, far from deceit or guile.
What fear I then, rather what know to fear
Under this ignorance of good and evil,
Of God or death, of law or penalty?
Here grows the cure of all, this fruit divine,
Fair to the eye, inviting to the taste,
Of virtue to make wise; what hinders then
To reach, and feed at once both body and mind?"
  So saying, her rash hand in evil hour   780
Forth reaching to the fruit, she plucked, she eat.
Earth felt the wound, and Nature from her seat
Sighing through all her works gave signs of woe,
That all was lost. Back to the thicket slunk
The guilty Serpent, and well might, for Eve
Intent now only on her taste, nought else
Regarded; such delight till then, as seemed,
In fruit she never tasted, whether true
Or fancied so, through expectation high
Of knowledge, nor was Godhead from her thought.   790
Greedily she ingorged without restraint,

758. **In plain,** frankly (i.e., in plain terms).
771. **author unsuspect,** informant not to be suspected.
778. **Of virtue,** i.e., having the power.
781. **eat.** Milton regularly uses this form of the preterite. Since the pronunciation corresponds to the spelling, lines 781 and 782 form a rhymed couplet, giving effective emphasis to a crucial point in the action.
791. **Greedily she ingorged without restraint.** In terms of human ethics as opposed to theology, Milton interprets the sin of Adam and Eve as a sin of excess, a violation of temperance. Eve's initial greed is therefore a symbol of all the other forms of excess in which she and Adam afterwards indulge.

And knew not eating death. Satiate at length,
And heightened as with wine, jocund and boon,
Thus to herself she pleasingly began.
  "O sovran, virtuous, precious of all trees
In Paradise, of operation blest
To sapience, hitherto obscured, infamed,
And thy fair fruit let hang, as to no end
Created; but henceforth my early care,
Not without song, each morning, and due praise,   800
Shall tend thee, and the fertile burden ease
Of thy full branches offered free to all;
Till dieted by thee I grow mature
In knowledge, as the Gods who all things know;
Though others envy what they cannot give;
For had the gift been theirs, it had not here
Thus grown. Experience, next to thee I owe,
Best guide; not following thee, I had remained
In ignorance, thou open'st Wisdom's way,
And givest access, though secret she retire.   810
And I perhaps am secret; Heaven is high,
High and remote to see from thence distinct
Each thing on Earth; and other care perhaps
May have diverted from continual watch
Our great Forbidder, safe with all his spies
About him. But to Adam in what sort
Shall I appear? Shall I to him make known
As yet my change, and give him to partake
Full happiness with me, or rather not,
But keep the odds of knowledge in my power   820
Without copartner? so to add what wants
In female sex, the more to draw his love,
And render me more equal, and perhaps,
A thing not undesirable, sometime
Superior; for inferior who is free?
This may be well. But what if God have seen
And death ensue? then I shall be no more,
And Adam wedded to another Eve,
Shall live with her enjoying, I extinct;
A death to think. Confirmed then I resolve   830
Adam shall share with me in bliss or woe.

  792. knew not eating, i.e., knew not that she was eating.
  793. boon, gay.
  795. virtuous, precious of all trees, i.e., most virtuous, most precious, etc. The idiom is
classical.
  796-97. of operation blest To sapience, i.e., so blest as to have the power of conferring
wisdom.
  797. infamed, not known.
  815. safe, not likely to do harm.
  817 ff. Shall I to him, etc. The first fruits of Eve's sin are selfishness and jealousy—the
negation of her original qualities.

So dear I love him, that with him all deaths
I could endure, without him live no life."
    So saying, from the tree her step she turned,
But first low reverence done, as to the power
That dwelt within, whose presence had infused
Into the plant sciential sap, derived
From nectar, drink of Gods. Adam the while
Waiting desirous her return, had wove
Of choicest flowers a garland to adorn   840
Her tresses, and her rural labors crown,
As reapers oft are wont their harvest queen.
Great joy he promised to his thoughts, and new
Solace in her return, so long delayed;
Yet oft his heart, divine of something ill,
Misgave him; he the faltering measure felt;
And forth to meet her went, the way she took
That morn when first they parted. By the Tree
Of Knowledge he must pass; there he her met,
Scarce from the tree returning; in her hand   850
A bough of fairest fruit that downy smiled,
New gathered, and ambrosial smell diffused.
To him she hasted; in her face excuse
Came prologue, and apology to prompt,
Which with bland words at will she thus addressed.
    "Hast thou not wondered, Adam, at my stay?
Thee I have missed, and thought it long, deprived
Thy presence, agony of love till now
Not felt, nor shall be twice, for never more
Mean I to try what rash untried I sought,   860
The pain of absence from thy sight. But strange
Hath been the cause, and wonderful to hear:
This tree is not as we are told, a tree
Of danger tasted, nor to evil unknown
Opening the way, but of divine effect
To open eyes, and make them Gods who taste;
And hath been tasted such. The Serpent wise,
Or not restrained as we, or not obeying,
Hath eaten of the fruit, and is become
Not dead as we are threatened, but thenceforth   870

835–36. Eve's perverted conception of God quickly manifests itself in idolatry.
837. sciential, capable of bestowing knowledge.
838–44. Adam the while . . . delayed. The situation closely parallels that in *Iliad* xxii, where Andromache is described making preparations for Hector's return, not knowing that he is already slain.
845. divine of, foreboding.
846. faltering measure, i.e., the uneven beating of his heart.
853–54. in her face . . . prompt. Milton means that the appearance of Eve's face served as a fitting introduction to her verbal apology. The stage imagery is perhaps intended to suggest her insincerity; she approaches Adam in an assumed character.

Endued with human voice and human sense,
Reasoning to admiration, and with me
Persuasively hath so prevailed, that I
Have also tasted, and have also found
The effects to correspond, opener mine eyes,
Dim erst, dilated spirits, ampler heart,
And growing up to Godhead; which for thee
Chiefly I sought, without thee can despise.
For bliss, as thou hast part, to me is bliss;
Tedious, unshared with thee, and odious soon.   880
Thou therefore also taste, that equal lot
May join us, equal joy, as equal love;
Lest thou not tasting, different degree
Disjoin us, and I then too late renounce
Deity for thee, when fate will not permit."
    Thus Eve with countenance blithe her story told;
But in her cheek distemper flushing glowed.
On the other side, Adam, soon as he heard
The fatal trespass done by Eve, amazed,
Astonied stood and blank, while horror chill   890
Ran through his veins, and all his joints relaxed;
From his slack hand the garland wreathed for Eve
Down dropped, and all the faded roses shed.
Speechless he stood and pale, till thus at length
First to himself he inward silence broke.
    "O fairest of creation, last and best
Of all God's works, creature in whom excelled
Whatever can to sight or thought be formed,
Holy, divine, good, amiable, or sweet!
How art thou lost, how on a sudden lost,   900
Defaced, deflowered, and now to death devote!
Rather how hast thou yielded to transgress
The strict forbiddance, how to violate
The sacred fruit forbidden! Some cursèd fraud
Of enemy hath beguiled thee, yet unknown,
And me with thee hath ruined, for with thee
Certain my resolution is to die;
How can I live without thee, how forgo
Thy sweet converse and love so dearly joined,
To live again in these wild woods forlorn?   910
Should God create another Eve, and I
Another rib afford, yet loss of thee
Would never from my heart; no, no! I feel
The link of nature draw me: flesh of flesh,
Bone of my bone thou art, and from thy state

---

872. to admiration, in a way to be admired.
    877–78. which for . . . Chiefly I sought. Eve ends her plea with an open falsehood.
Cf. 816–25.
    901. devote, doomed, accursed.
    914 ff. flesh of flesh, etc. Cf. Gen. 2:23.

Mine never shall be parted, bliss or woe."
    So having said, as one from sad dismay
Recomforted, and after thoughts disturbed
Submitting to what seemed remediless,
Thus in calm mood his words to Eve he turned. 920
    "Bold deed thou hast presumed, adventurous Eve,
And peril great provoked, who thus hast dared,
Had it been only coveting to eye
That sacred fruit, sacred to abstinence
Much more to taste it under ban to touch.
But past who can recall, or done undo?
Not God Omnipotent, nor Fate. Yet so
Perhaps thou shalt not die; perhaps the fact
Is not so heinous now, foretasted fruit,
Profaned first by the Serpent, by him first 930
Made common and unhallowed ere our taste,
Nor yet on him found deadly; he yet lives,
Lives, as thou saidst, and gains to live as Man
Higher degree of life, inducement strong
To us, as likely tasting to attain
Proportional ascent, which cannot be
But to be Gods, or angels, demi-gods.
Nor can I think that God, Creator wise,
Though threatening, will in earnest so destroy
Us his prime creatures, dignified so high, 940
Set over all his works, which in our fall,
For us created, needs with us must fail,
Dependent made; so God shall uncreate
Be frustrate, do, undo, and labor lose,
Not well conceived of God, who though his power
Creation could repeat, yet would be loth
Us to abolish, lest the Adversary
Triumph and say: 'Fickle their state whom God
Most favors, who can please him long? Me first
He ruined, now mankind; whom will he next?' 950
Matter of scorn not to be given the Foe;
However, I with thee have fixed my lot,
Certain to undergo like doom: if death
Consort with thee, death is to me as life;
So forcible within my heart I feel
The bond of nature draw me to my own,
My own in thee, for what thou art is mine;
Our state cannot be severed; we are one,
One flesh; to lose thee were to lose myself."

---

928. fact, deed (Latin *factum*).
    932. he yet lives, etc. Having determined his course on nonrational grounds, Adam proceeds to rationalize just as Eve had done.
    953. Certain, resolved.

So Adam, and thus Eve to him replied.   960
"O glorious trial of exceeding love,
Illustrious evidence, example high!
Engaging me to emulate, but short
Of thy perfection, how shall I attain,
Adam, from whose dear side I boast me sprung,
And gladly of our union hear thee speak,
One heart, one soul in both; whereof good proof
This day affords, declaring thee resolved,
Rather than death or aught than death more dread
Shall separate us, linked in love so dear,   970
To undergo with me one guilt, one crime,
If any be, of tasting this fair fruit,
Whose virtue (for of good still good proceeds,
Direct, or by occasion) hath presented
This happy trial of thy love, which else
So eminently never had been known.
Were it I thought death menaced would ensue
This my attempt, I would sustain alone
The worst, and not persuade thee, rather die
Deserted, than oblige thee with a fact   980
Pernicious to thy peace, chiefly assured
Remarkably so late of thy so true,
So faithful love unequalled; but I feel
Far otherwise the event, not death, but life
Augmented, opened eyes, new hopes, new joys,
Taste so divine, that what of sweet before
Hath touched my sense, flat seems to this and harsh.
On my experience, Adam, freely taste,
And fear of death deliver to the winds."
    So saying, she embraced him, and for joy   990
Tenderly wept, much won that he his love
Had so ennobled, as of choice to incur
Divine displeasure for her sake, or death.
In recompense (for such compliance bad
Such recompense best merits) from the bough
She gave him of that fair enticing fruit
With liberal hand; he scrupled not to eat
Against his better knowledge, not deceived,
But fondly overcome with female charm.
Earth trembled from her entrails, as again   1000
In pangs, and Nature gave a second groan;
Sky loured, and muttering thunder, some sad drops

977–83. Were it I thought . . . unequalled. Cf. 826–33. **oblige,** render liable to punishment.
    1000 ff. Earth trembled, etc. The idea that the fall was marked by convulsions of the earth and other signs of nature's grief is a literary and theological tradition. While it has no direct scriptural authority, it may have been suggested by the analogous portents accompanying the crucifixion of Christ (Matt. 27:51).

Wept at completing of the mortal sin
Original; while Adam took no thought,
Eating his fill, nor Eve to iterate
Her former trespass feared, the more to soothe
Him with her loved society, that now
As with new wine intoxicated both
They swim in mirth, and fancy that they feel
Divinity within them breeding wings   1010
Wherewith to scorn the Earth. But that false fruit
Far other operation first displayed,
Carnal desire inflaming: he on Eve
Began to cast lascivious eyes, she him
As wantonly repaid; in lust they burn,
Till Adam thus 'gan Eve to dalliance move.
  "Eve, now I see thou art exact of taste
And elegant, of sapience no small part,
Since to each meaning savor we apply,
And palate call judicious; I the praise   1020
Yield thee, so well this day thou hast purveyed.
Much pleasure we have lost, while we abstained
From this delightful fruit, nor known till now
True relish, tasting; if such pleasure be
In things to us forbidden, it might be wished
For this one tree had been forbidden ten.
But come; so well refreshed, now let us play,
As meet is, after such delicious fare;
For never did thy beauty since the day
I saw thee first and wedded thee, adorned   1030
With all perfections, so inflame my sense
With ardor to enjoy thee, fairer now
Than ever, bounty of this virtuous tree."
  So said he, and forbore not glance or toy
Of amorous intent, well understood
Of Eve, whose eye darted contagious fire.
Her hand he seized, and to a shady bank,
Thick overhead with verdant roof embowered,
He led her nothing loth; flowers were the couch,
Pansies, and violets, and asphodel,   1040
And hyacinth, Earth's freshest softest lap.
There they their fill of love and love's disport
Took largely, of their mutual guilt the seal,
The solace of their sin, till dewy sleep
Oppressed them, wearied with their amorous play.

1003–4. the mortal sin Original. This is Milton's only use in the poem of the theological
term "original sin."
  1019. The word savor is derived from Latin *sapere*, which means both "to taste" and "to be
wise." Milton represents Adam as playing on this double meaning in explaining why Eve's *taste*
can properly be called judicious.
  1034. toy, caress.

Soon as the force of that fallacious fruit,
That with exhilarating vapor bland
About their spirits had played, and inmost powers
Made err, was now exhaled, and grosser sleep,
Bred of unkindly fumes, with conscious dreams   1050
Encumbered, now had left them, up they rose
As from unrest, and each the other viewing,
Soon found their eyes how opened, and their minds
How darkened; innocence, that as a veil
Had shadowed them from knowing ill, was gone,
Just confidence, and native righteousness,
And honor from about them, naked left
To guilty Shame. He covered, but his robe
Uncovered more. So rose the Danite strong,
Herculean Samson, from the harlot-lap   1060
Of Philistean Delilah, and waked
Shorn of his strength, they destitute and bare
Of all their virtue. Silent, and in face
Confounded, long they sat, as strucken mute,
Till Adam, though not less than Eve abashed,
At length gave utterance to these words constrained.
    "O Eve, in evil hour thou didst give ear
To that false worm, of whomsoever taught
To counterfeit Man's voice, true in our fall,
False in our promised rising; since our eyes   1070
Opened we find indeed, and find we know
Both good and evil, good lost and evil got,
Bad fruit of knowledge, if this be to know,
Which leaves us naked thus, of honor void,
Of innocence, of faith, of purity,
Our wonted ornaments now soiled and stained,
And in our faces evident the signs
Of foul concupiscence; whence evil store,
Even shame, the last of evils; of the first
Be sure then. How shall I behold the face   1080
Henceforth of God or angel, erst with joy
And rapture so oft beheld? those heavenly shapes
Will dazzle now this earthly, with their blaze
Insufferably bright. Oh might I here
In solitude live savage, in some glade
Obscured, where highest woods impenetrable
To star or sunlight, spread their umbrage broad
And brown as evening! Cover me ye pines,
Ye cedars, with innumerable boughs

    1050. unkindly, contrary to nature.
    1058. He covered, etc. i.e., shame covered them with his robe, but in so doing revealed to
them their nakedness.
    1059. So rose the Danite strong, etc. Cf. Judg. 16:4–20.
    1068. worm, serpent.
    1079. the last of evils, i.e., the greatest (Latin *extremus*). **the first,** i.e., the lesser.

Hide me, where I may never see them more. 1090
But let us now, as in bad plight, devise
What best may for the present serve to hide
The parts of each from other that seem most
To shame obnoxious, and unseemliest seen,
Some tree whose broad smooth leaves together sewed,
And girded on our loins, may cover round
Those middle parts, that this new comer, Shame,
There sit not, and reproach us as unclean."
　So counselled he, and both together went
Into the thickest wood; there soon they chose 1100
The fig-tree, not that kind for fruit renowned,
But such as at this day to Indians known
In Malabar or Decan spreads her arms
Branching so broad and long, that in the ground
The bended twigs take root, and daughters grow
About the mother tree, a pillared shade
High overarched, and echoing walks between;
There oft the Indian herdsman shunning heat
Shelters in cool, and tends his pasturing herds
At loop-holes cut through thickest shade. Those leaves 1110
They gathered, broad as Amazonian targe,
And with what skill they had, together sewed,
To gird their waist, vain covering if to hide
Their guilt and dreaded shame; Oh how unlike
To that first naked glory. Such of late
Columbus found the American so girt
With feathered cincture, naked else and wild
Among the trees on isles and woody shores.
Thus fenced, and as they thought, their shame in part
Covered, but not at rest or ease of mind, 1120
They sat them down to weep, nor only tears
Rained at their eyes, but high winds worse within
Began to rise, high passions, anger, hate,
Mistrust, suspicion, discord, and shook sore
Their inward state of mind, calm region once
And full of peace, now tossed and turbulent;
For Understanding ruled not, and the Will
Heard not her lore, both in subjection now
To sensual Appetite, who from beneath
Usurping over sovran Reason claimed 1130
Superior sway. From thus distempered breast,
Adam, estranged in look and altered style,
Speech intermitted thus to Eve renewed.

1094. obnoxious. Cf. note on 170.
1103. Malabar refers to the western coast of Hindustan, especially the southern part. Decan, or Deccan, is a name applied to the entire peninsula.
1111. Amazonian targe, shield of the Amazons.
1127 ff. For Understanding . . . sway. The tripartite division of the soul, which underlies this passage, is Platonic. Cf. 351–56.

"Would thou hadst hearkened to my words, and stayed
With me, as I besought thee, when that strange
Desire of wandering this unhappy morn,
I know not whence possessed thee; we had then
Remained still happy, not as now, despoiled
Of all our good, shamed, naked, miserable.
Let none henceforth seek needless cause to approve   1140
The faith they owe; when earnestly they seek
Such proof, conclude, they then begin to fail."
  To whom soon moved with touch of blame thus Eve.
"What words have passed thy lips, Adam severe!
Imputest thou that to my default, or will
Of wandering, as thou call'st it, which who knows
But might as ill have happened thou being by,
Or to thyself perhaps? Hadst thou been there,
Or here the attempt, thou couldst not have discerned
Fraud in the Serpent, speaking as he spake;   1150
No ground of enmity between us known,
Why he should mean me ill, or seek to harm.
Was I to have never parted from thy side?
As good have grown there still a lifeless rib.
Being as I am, why didst not thou the head
Command me absolutely not to go,
Going into such danger as thou saidst?
Too facile then, thou didst not much gainsay,
Nay didst permit, approve, and fair dismiss.
Hadst thou been firm and fixed in thy dissent,   1160
Neither had I transgressed, nor thou with me."
  To whom then first incensed Adam replied.
"Is this the love, is this the recompense
Of mine to thee, ingrateful Eve, expressed
Immutable when thou wert lost, not I,
Who might have lived and joyed immortal bliss,
Yet willingly chose rather death with thee?
And am I now upbraided, as the cause
Of thy transgressing? not enough severe,
It seems, in thy restraint. What could I more?   1170
I warned thee, I admonished thee, foretold
The danger, and the lurking enemy

1141. owe, possess.
1163 ff. Adam's statement is a fascinating mixture of right and wrong judgment, self-knowledge, and self-deception. In Milton's theory he is the superior being, but his reasoning is flawed by passion: "Understanding ruled not." Lines 1166–67 are certainly not a fair representation of the facts, being inconsistent with what he said in lines 908–10, above: "How can I live without thee?" On the other hand, he has come to the point of partly recognizing his own weakness: "And perhaps I also erred." How detached Milton himself is in all this it is really very difficult to say.
1164. expressed, demonstrated.

That lay in wait; beyond this had been force,
And force upon free will hath here no place.
But confidence then bore thee on, secure
Either to meet no danger or to find
Matter of glorious trial; and perhaps
I also erred in overmuch admiring
What seemed in thee so perfect, that I thought
No evil durst attempt thee, but I rue 1180
That error now, which is become my crime,
And thou the accuser. Thus it shall befall
Him who to worth in women overtrusting
Lets her will rule; restraint she will not brook,
And left to herself, if evil thence ensue,
She first his weak indulgence will accuse."
Thus they in mutual accusation spent
The fruitless hours, but neither self-condemning,
And of their vain contest appeared no end.

from BOOK X

THE ARGUMENT

Man's transgression known, the guardian angels forsake Paradise, and return up to Heaven to approve their vigilance, and are approved; God declaring that the entrance of Satan could not be by them prevented. He sends his Son to judge the transgressors; who descends, and gives sentence accordingly; then in pity clothes them both, and reascends. Sin and Death, sitting till then at the gates of Hell, by wondrous sympathy feeling the success of Satan in this new world, and the sin by Man there committed, resolve to sit no longer confined in Hell, but to follow Satan, their sire, up to the place of Man. To make the way easier from Hell to this world to and fro, they pave a broad highway or bridge over Chaos, according to the track that Satan first made; then, preparing for Earth, they meet him, proud of his success, returning to Hell; their mutual gratulation. Satan arrives at Pandemonium; in full assembly relates, with boasting, his success against Man; instead of applause is entertained with a general hiss by all his audience, transformed, with himself also, suddenly into serpents, according to his doom given in Paradise; then, deluded with a show of the Forbidden Tree springing up before them, they greedily reaching to take of the fruit chew dust and bitter ashes. The proceedings of Sin and Death; God foretells the final victory of his Son over them, and the renewing of all things; but for the present commands his angels to make several alterations in the heavens and elements. Adam, more and more perceiving his fallen condition, heavily bewails, rejects the condolement of Eve; she persists, and at length appeases him: then, to evade the curse likely to fall on their offspring, proposes to Adam violent ways, which he approves not, but, conceiving better hope, puts her in mind of the late promise made them, that her seed should be revenged on the Serpent, and exhorts her with him to seek peace of the offended Deity by repentance and supplication.

                                          Thus began
Outrage from lifeless things; but Discord first,
Daughter of Sin, among the irrational,
Death introduced through fierce antipathy.
Beast now with beast 'gan war, and fowl with fowl,   710
And fish with fish; to graze the herb all leaving,
Devoured each other; nor stood much in awe
Of Man, but fled him, or with countenance grim
Glared on him passing. These were from without
The growing miseries, which Adam saw
Already in part, though hid in gloomiest shade,
To sorrow abandoned, but worse felt within,
And in a troubled sea of passion tossed,
Thus to disburden sought with sad complaint.
    "O miserable of happy! is this the end   720
Of this new glorious World, and me so late
The glory of that glory, who now, become
Accurst of blessed, hide me from the face
Of God, whom to behold was then my height
Of happiness. Yet well, if here would end
The misery; I deserved it, and would bear
My own deservings; but this will not serve:
All that I eat or drink, or shall beget,
Is propagated curse. O voice once heard
Delightfully, 'Increase and multiply,'   730
Now death to hear! for what can I increase
Or multiply, but curses on my head?
Who of all ages to succeed, but feeling
The evil on him brought by me, will curse
My head: 'Ill fare our Ancestor impure,
For this we may thank Adam'; but his thanks
Shall be the execration; so besides
Mine own that bide upon me, all from me
Shall with a fierce reflux on me redound,
On me as on their natural center light   740
Heavy, though in their place. O fleeting joys
Of Paradise, dear bought with lasting woes!
Did I request thee, Maker, from my clay
To mould me Man, did I solicit thee
From darkness to promote me, or here place
In this delicious garden? As my will
Concurred not to my being, it were but right
And equal to reduce me to my dust,
Desirous to resign and render back
All I received, unable to perform   750
Thy terms too hard, by which I was to hold
The good I sought not. To the loss of that,
Sufficient penalty, why hast thou added
The sense of endless woes? inexplicable

Thy justice seems; yet to say truth, too late
I thus contest; then should have been refused
Those terms whatever, when they were proposed.
Thou didst accept them; wilt thou enjoy the good,
Then cavil the conditions? And though God
Made thee without thy leave, what if thy son   760
Prove disobedient, and reproved, retort,
'Wherefore didst thou beget me? I sought it not.'
Wouldst thou admit for his contempt of thee
That proud excuse? yet him not thy election,
But natural necessity begot.
God made thee of choice his own, and of his own
To serve him, thy reward was of his grace,
Thy punishment then justly is at his will.
Be it so, for I submit, his doom is fair,
That dust I am, and shall to dust return.   770
O welcome hour whenever! Why delays
His hand to execute what his decree
Fixed on this day? Why do I overlive,
Why am I mocked with death, and lengthened out
To deathless pain? How gladly would I meet
Mortality my sentence, and be earth
Insensible, how glad would lay me down
As in my mother's lap! There I should rest
And sleep secure; his dreadful voice no more
Would thunder in my ears, no fear of worse   780
To me and to my offspring would torment me
With cruel expectation. Yet one doubt
Pursues me still, lest all I cannot die,
Lest that pure breath of life, the spirit of Man
Which God inspired, cannot together perish
With this corporeal clod; then in the grave
Or in some other dismal place, who knows
But I shall die a living death? O thought
Horrid, if true! Yet why? It was but breath
Of life that sinned; what dies but what had life   790
And sin? the body properly hath neither.
All of me then shall die: let this appease
The doubt, since human reach no further knows.
For though the Lord of all be infinite,
Is his wrath also? Be it, Man is not so,
But mortal doomed. How can he exercise
Wrath without end on Man whom death must end?
Can he make deathless death? That were to make
Strange contradiction, which to God himself
Impossible is held, as argument   800
Of weakness, not of power. Will he draw out,
For anger's sake, finite to infinite
In punished Man, to satisfy his rigor

Satisfied never? That were to extend
His sentence beyond dust and Nature's law,
By which all causes else according still
To the reception of their matter act,
Not to the extent of their own sphere. But say
That death be not one stroke, as I supposed,
Bereaving sense, but endless misery   810
From this day onward, which I feel begun
Both in me and without me, and so last
To perpetuity: Ay me, that fear
Comes thundering back with dreadful revolution
On my defenceless head; both Death and I
Am found eternal, and incorporate both,
Nor I on my part single, in me all
Posterity stands cursed. Fair patrimony
That I must leave ye, sons; oh were I able
To waste it all myself, and leave ye none!   820
So disinherited how would ye bless
Me now your curse! Ah, why should all mankind
For one man's fault thus guiltless be condemned,
If guiltless? But from me what can proceed
But all corrupt, both mind and will depraved,
Not to do only, but to will the same
With me? How can they then acquitted stand
In sight of God? Him after all disputes
Forced I absolve; all my evasions vain
And reasonings, though through mazes, lead me still   830
But to my own conviction: first and last
On me, me only, as the source and spring
Of all corruption, all the blame lights due;
So might the wrath. Fond wish! couldst thou support
That burden heavier than the Earth to bear,
Than all the World much heavier, though divided
With that bad woman? Thus what thou desirest
And what thou fearst, alike destroys all hope
Of refuge, and concludes thee miserable
Beyond all past example and future,   840
To Satan only like, both crime and doom.
O Conscience, into what abyss of fears
And horrors hast thou driven me; out of which
I find no way, from deep to deeper plunged!"
    Thus Adam to himself lamented loud
Through the still night, not now, as ere Man fell,
Wholesome and cool and mild, but with black air
Accompanied, with damps and dreadful gloom,
Which to his evil conscience represented

805–8. In all other matters where causes produce effects, the effect is in accordance with
the nature and properties of the thing being acted on. (Editors' note.)

All things with double terror. On the ground 850
Outstretched he lay, on the cold ground, and oft
Cursed his creation, Death as oft accused
Of tardy execution, since denounced
The day of his offence. "Why comes not Death,"
Said he, "with one thrice-acceptable stroke
To end me? Shall Truth fail to keep her word,
Justice divine not hasten to be just?
But Death comes not at call, Justice divine
Mends not her slowest pace for prayers or cries.
O woods, O fountains, hillocks, dales, and bowers, 860
With other echo late I taught your shades
To answer, and resound far other song."
Whom thus afflicted when sad Eve beheld,
Desolate where she sat, approaching nigh,
Soft words to his fierce passion she assayed;
But her with stern regard he thus repelled.
   "Out of my sight, thou serpent, that name best
Befits thee with him leagued, thyself as false
And hateful; nothing wants, but that thy shape,
Like his, and color serpentine, may show 870
Thy inward fraud, to warn all creatures from thee
Henceforth; lest that too heavenly form, pretended
To hellish falsehood, snare them. But for thee
I had persisted happy, had not thy pride
And wandering vanity, when least was safe,
Rejected my forewarning, and disdained
Not to be trusted, longing to be seen
Though by the Devil himself, him overweening
To overreach, but with the Serpent meeting
Fooled and beguiled, by him thou, I by thee, 880
To trust thee from my side, imagined wise,
Constant, mature, proof against all assaults,
And understood not all was but a show
Rather than solid virtue, all but a rib
Crooked by nature, bent, as now appears,
More to the part sinister from me drawn;
Well if thrown out, as supernumerary
To my just number found. Oh why did God,
Creator wise, that peopled highest Heaven
With spirits masculine, create at last 890
This novelty on Earth, this fair defect
Of Nature, and not fill the World at once
With men as angels without feminine,
Or find some other way to generate
Mankind? This mischief had not then befallen,
And more that shall befall, innumerable
Disturbances on Earth through female snares,
And strait conjunction with this sex. For either
He never shall find out fit mate, but such

As some misfortune brings him, or mistake,   900
Or whom he wishes most shall seldom gain,
Through her perverseness, but shall see her gained
By a far worse, or if she love, withheld
By parents, or his happiest choice too late
Shall meet, already linked and wedlock-bound
To a fell adversary, his hate or shame;
Which infinite calamity shall cause
To human life, and household peace confound."
   He added not, and from her turned, but Eve
Not so repulsed, with tears that ceased not flowing,   910
And tresses all disordered, at his feet
Fell humble, and embracing them, besought
His peace, and thus proceeded in her plaint:
   "Forsake me not thus, Adam, witness Heaven
What love sincere and reverence in my heart
I bear thee, and unweeting have offended,
Unhappily deceived; thy suppliant
I beg, and clasp thy knees; bereave me not,
Whereon I live, thy gentle looks, thy aid,
Thy counsel in this uttermost distress,   920
My only strength and stay. Forlorn of thee,
Whither shall I betake me, where subsist?
While yet we live, scarce one short hour perhaps,
Between us two let there be peace, both joining,
As joined in injuries, one enmity
Against a foe by doom express assigned us,
That cruel Serpent. On me exercise not
Thy hatred for this misery befallen,
On me already lost, me than thyself
More miserable. Both have sinned, but thou   930
Against God only, I against God and thee,
And to the place of judgment will return,
There with my cries importune Heaven, that all
The sentence from thy head removed may light
On me, sole cause to thee of all this woe,
Me, me only, just object of his ire."
   She ended weeping, and her lowly plight,
Immovable till peace obtained from fault
Acknowledged and deplored, in Adam wrought
Commiseration; soon his heart relented   940
Towards her, his life so late and sole delight,
Now at his feet submissive in distress,
Creature so fair his reconcilement seeking,
His counsel whom she had displeased, his aid;
As one disarmed, his anger all he lost,
And thus with peaceful words upraised her soon:
   "Unwary, and too desirous, as before,
So now, of what thou knowst not, who desirest
The punishment all on thyself; alas,

Bear thine own first, ill able to sustain
His full wrath whose thou feel'st as yet least part, 950
And my displeasure bear'st so ill. If prayers
Could alter high decrees, I to that place
Would speed before thee, and be louder heard,
That on my head all might be visited,
Thy frailty and infirmer sex forgiven,
To me committed and by me exposed.
But rise, let us no more contend, nor blame
Each other, blamed enough elsewhere, but strive
In offices of love, how we may lighten 960
Each other's burden in our share of woe;
Since this day's death denounced, if aught I see,
Will prove no sudden, but a slow-paced evil,
A long day's dying to augment our pain,
And to our seed (O hapless seed!) derived."
    To whom thus Eve, recovering heart, replied.
"Adam, by sad experiment I know
How little weight my words with thee can find,
Found so erroneous, thence by just event
Found so unfortunate; nevertheless, 970
Restored by thee, vile as I am, to place
Of new acceptance, hopeful to regain
Thy love, the sole contentment of my heart
Living or dying, from thee I will not hide
What thoughts in my unquiet breast are risen,
Tending to some relief of our extremes,
Or end, though sharp and sad, yet tolerable,
As in our evils, and of easier choice.
If care of our descent perplex us most,
Which must be born to certain woe, devoured 980
By Death at last, (and miserable it is
To be to others cause of misery,
Our own begotten, and of our loins to bring
Into this cursëd World a woeful race,
That after wretched life must be at last
Food for so foul a monster), in thy power
It lies, yet ere conception, to prevent
The race unblest, to being yet unbegot.
Childless thou art, childless remain; so Death
Shall be deceived his glut, and with us two 990
Be forced to satisfy his ravenous maw.
But if thou judge it hard and difficult,
Conversing, looking, loving, to abstain
From love's due rites, nuptial embraces sweet,
And with desire to languish without hope,
Before the present object languishing
With like desire, which would be misery
And torment less than none of what we dread,
Then both our selves and seed at once to free

From what we fear for both, let us make short,   1000
Let us seek Death, or he not found, supply
With our own hands his office on ourselves;
Why stand we longer shivering under fears
That show no end but death, and have the power,
Of many ways to die the shortest choosing,
Destruction with destruction to destroy."
    She ended here, or vehement despair
Broke off the rest; so much of death her thoughts
Had entertained as dyed her cheeks with pale.
But Adam with such counsel nothing swayed,   1010
To better hopes his more attentive mind
Laboring had raised, and thus to Eve replied.
    "Eve, thy contempt of life and pleasure seems
To argue in thee something more sublime
And excellent than what thy mind contemns;
But self-destruction therefore sought, refutes
That excellence thought in thee, and implies,
Not thy contempt, but anguish and regret
For loss of life and pleasure overloved.
Or if thou covet death, as utmost end   1020
Of misery, so thinking to evade
The penalty pronounced, doubt not but God
Hath wiselier armed his vengeful ire than so
To be forestalled; much more I fear lest death
So snatched will not exempt us from the pain
We are by doom to pay; rather such acts
Of contumacy will provoke the Highest
To make death in us live. Then let us seek
Some safer resolution, which methinks
I have in view, calling to mind with heed   1030
Part of our sentence, that thy seed shall bruise
The Serpent's head; piteous amends, unless
Be meant, whom I conjecture, our grand foe
Satan, who in the serpent hath contrived
Against us this deceit. To crush his head
Would be revenge indeed; which will be lost
By death brought on ourselves, or childless days
Resolved, as thou proposest; so our foe
Shall scape his punishment ordained, and we
Instead shall double ours upon our heads.   1040
No more be mentioned then of violence
Against ourselves, and wilful barrenness,
That cuts us off from hope, and savors only
Rancor and pride, impatience and despite,
Reluctance against God and his just yoke
Laid on our necks. Remember with what mild

    1015. what thy mind contemns, the life and pleasure your mind shows contempt for. (Editors'
note.)

And gracious temper he both heard and judged,
Without wrath or reviling; we expected
Immediate dissolution, which we thought
Was meant by death that day, when lo, to thee 1050
Pains only in child-bearing were foretold,
And bringing forth, soon recompensed with joy,
Fruit of thy womb; on me the curse aslope
Glanced on the ground: with labor I must earn
My bread; what harm? Idleness had been worse;
My labor will sustain me; and lest cold
Or heat should injure us, his timely care
Hath unbesought provided, and his hands
Clothed us unworthy, pitying while he judged;
How much more, if we pray him, will his ear 1060
Be open, and his heart to pity incline,
And teach us further by what means to shun
The inclement seasons, rain, ice, hail, and snow,
Which now the sky with various face begins
To show us in this mountain, while the winds
Blow moist and keen, shattering the graceful locks
Of these fair spreading trees; which bids us seek
Some better shroud, some better warmth to cherish
Our limbs benumbed, ere this diurnal star
Leave cold the night, how we his gathered beams 1070
Reflected, may with matter sere foment,
Or by collision of two bodies grind
The air attrite to fire, as late the clouds
Justling or pushed with winds rude in their shock
Tine the slant lightning, whose thwart flame driven down
Kindles the gummy bark of fir or pine,
And sends a comfortable heat from far,
Which might supply the sun. Such fire to use,
And what may else be remedy or cure
To evils which our own misdeeds have wrought, 1080
He will instruct us praying, and of grace
Beseeching him, so as we need not fear
To pass commodiously this life, sustained
By him with many comforts, till we end
In dust, our final rest and native home.
What better can we do, than to the place
Repairing where he judged us, prostrate fall
Before him reverent, and there confess
Humbly our faults, and pardon beg, with tears
Watering the ground, and with our sighs the air 1090

1070–78. Various means of inventing or producing fire.
1071. matter sere, dry materials. **foment,** increase the heat of.
1073. attrite, rubbed together.
1075. Tine, kindle. **thwart,** slanting.
1078. supply the sun, replace the heat of the sun. (Notes to lines 1070–1078 are by the anthology editors.)

Frequenting, sent from hearts contrite, in sign
Of sorrow unfeigned, and humiliation meek.
Undoubtedly he will relent and turn
From his displeasure; in whose look serene,
When angry most he seemed and most severe,
What else but favor, grace, and mercy shone?"
    So spake our father penitent, nor Eve
Felt less remorse. They forthwith to the place
Repairing where he judged them, prostrate fell
Before him reverent, and both confessed   1100
Humbly their faults, and pardon begged, with tears
Watering the ground, and with their sighs the air
Frequenting, sent from hearts contrite, in sign
Of sorrow unfeigned, and humiliation meek.

BOOK XI: THE ARGUMENT

The Son of God presents to his Father the prayers of our first parents now repent-
ing, and intercedes for them. God accepts them, but declares that they must no
longer abide in Paradise; sends Michael with a band of Cherubim to dispossess
them, but first to reveal to Adam future things; Michael's coming down. Adam
shows to Eve certain ominous signs; he discerns Michael's approach; goes out
to meet him; the Angel denounces their departure. Eve's lamentation. Adam pleads,
but submits; the Angel leads him up to a high hill; sets before him in vision
what shall happen till the Flood.

from BOOK XII

THE ARGUMENT

The Angel Michael continues from the Flood to relate what shall succeed; then,
in the mention of Abraham, comes by degrees to explain, who that Seed of the
Woman shall be which was promised Adam and Eve in the Fall; his incarna-
tion, death, resurrection, and ascension; the state of the Church till his second
coming. Adam greatly satisfied and recomforted by these relations and promises
descends the hill with Michael; wakens Eve, who all this while had slept, but
with gentle dreams composed to quietness of mind and submission. Michael in
either hand leads them out of Paradise, the fiery sword waving behind them,
and the Cherubim taking their stations to guard the place.

    Here Adam interposed. "O sent from Heaven,   270
Enlightener of my darkness, gracious things
Thou hast revealed, those chiefly which concern
Just Abraham and his seed. Now first I find
Mine eyes true opening, and my heart much eased,
Erewhile perplexed with thoughts what would become
Of me and all mankind; but now I see
His day, in whom all nations shall be blest,
Favor unmerited by me, who sought
Forbidden knowledge by forbidden means.

This yet I apprehend not, why to those 280
Among whom God will deign to dwell on Earth
So many and so various laws are given;
So many laws argue so many sins
Among them; how can God with such reside?"
　To whom thus Michael. "Doubt not but that sin
Will reign among them, as of thee begot;
And therefore was law given them to evince
Their natural pravity, by stirring up
Sin against law to fight; that when they see
Law can discover sin, but not remove, 290
Save by those shadowy expiations weak,
The blood of bulls and goats, they may conclude
Some blood more precious must be paid for Man,
Just for unjust, that in such righteousness
To them by faith imputed, they may find
Justification towards God, and peace
Of conscience, which the law by ceremonies
Cannot appease, nor man the moral part
Perform, and not performing cannot live.
So law appears imperfect, and but given 300
With purpose to resign them in full time
Up to a better covenant, disciplined
From shadowy types to truth, from flesh to spirit,
From imposition of strict laws, to free
Acceptance of large grace, from servile fear
To filial, works of law to works of faith.
And therefore shall not Moses, though of God
Highly beloved, being but the minister
Of law, his people into Canaan lead;
But Joshua whom the Gentiles Jesus call, 310
His name and office bearing, who shall quell
The adversary Serpent, and bring back
Through the world's wilderness long-wandered Man
Safe to eternal Paradise of rest.
Meanwhile they in their earthly Canaan placed
Long time shall dwell and prosper, but when sins
National interrupt their public peace,
Provoking God to raise them enemies,
From whom as oft he saves them penitent
By judges first, then under kings; of whom 320
The second, both for piety renowned

---

287. evince, to demonstrate. In Milton's theology the Mosaic law was given "for the hardness of men's hearts." It was abrogated by the new testament of love in Christ, the "better covenant" of line 302.
　303. shadowy types. Christian interpretation found allegorical illustrations of the truth everywhere in Old Testament history. Thus the burnt offerings are a symbol of the true sacrifice of a contrite heart; Moses is a mediator and foreshadows the office of the Redeemer; Joshua, leading his people into the promised land, is again Christ making possible salvation for the elect.

And puissant deeds, a promise shall receive
Irrevocable, that his regal throne
For ever shall endure; the like shall sing
All prophecy: that of the royal stock
Of David (so I name this king) shall rise
A Son, the Woman's Seed to thee foretold,
Foretold to Abraham, as in whom shall trust
All nations, and to kings foretold, of kings
The last, for of his reign shall be no end.   330
But first a long succession must ensue,
And his next son for wealth and wisdom famed,
The clouded ark of God till then in tents
Wandering, shall in a glorious temple enshrine.
Such follow him, as shall be registered
Part good, part bad, of bad the longer scroll,
Whose foul idolatries and other faults
Heaped to the popular sum, will so incense
God, as to leave them, and expose their land,
Their city, his temple, and his holy ark   340
With all his sacred things, a scorn and prey
To that proud city, whose high walls thou saw'st
Left in confusion, Babylon thence called.
There in captivity he lets them dwell
The space of seventy years, then brings them back,
Remembering mercy, and his covenant sworn
To David, stablished as the days of Heaven.
Returned from Babylon by leave of kings
Their lords, whom God disposed, the house of God
They first re-edify, and for a while   350
In mean estate live moderate, till grown
In wealth and multitude, factious they grow;
But first among the priests dissension springs,
Men who attend the altar, and should most
Endeavor peace; their strife pollution brings
Upon the temple itself; at last they seize
The scepter and regard not David's sons,
Then lose it to a stranger, that the true
Anointed King Messiah might be born
Barred of his right; yet at his birth a star   360
Unseen before in Heaven proclaims him come,
And guides the eastern sages, who inquire
His place, to offer incense, myrrh, and gold;
His place of birth a solemn angel tells
To simple shepherds, keeping watch by night;
They gladly thither haste, and by a choir
Of squadroned angels hear his carol sung.
A Virgin is his mother, but his Sire
The Power of the Most High; he shall ascend

---

332. **his next son.** Solomon. See I Kings 6–7 and II Chron. 3–4.

The throne hereditary, and bound his reign 370
With Earth's wide bounds, his glory with the Heavens."
  He ceased, discerning Adam with such joy
Surcharged, as had like grief been dewed in tears,
Without the vent of words, which these he breathed.
  "O prophet of glad tidings, finisher
Of utmost hope! now clear I understand
What oft my steadiest thoughts have searched in vain,
Why our great Expectation should be called
The Seed of Woman: Virgin Mother, hail,
High in the love of Heaven, yet from my loins 380
Thou shalt proceed, and from thy womb the Son
Of God Most High; so God with Man unites.
Needs must the Serpent now his capital bruise
Expect with mortal pain: say where and when
Their fight, what stroke shall bruise the Victor's heel."
  To whom thus Michael. "Dream not of their fight
As of a duel, or the local wounds
Of head or heel: not therefore joins the Son
Manhood to Godhead, with more strength to foil
Thy enemy; nor so is overcome 390
Satan, whose fall from Heaven, a deadlier bruise,
Disabled not to give thee thy death's wound;
Which he, who comes thy Savior, shall recure,
Not by destroying Satan, but his works
In thee and in thy seed. Nor can this be,
But by fulfilling that which thou didst want,
Obedience to the law of God, imposed
On penalty of death, and suffering death,
The penalty to thy transgression due,
And due to theirs which out of thine will grow: 400
So only can high justice rest appaid.
The law of God exact he shall fulfil
Both by obedience and by love, though love
Alone fulfil the law; thy punishment
He shall endure by coming in the flesh
To a reproachful life and cursèd death,
Proclaiming life to all who shall believe
In his redemption, and that his obedience
Imputed becomes theirs by faith, his merits
To save them, not their own, though legal works. 410
For this he shall live hated, be blasphemed,
Seized on by force, judged, and to death condemned
A shameful and accursed, nailed to the cross
By his own nation, slain for bringing life;
But to the cross he nails thy enemies,
The law that is against thee, and the sins
Of all mankind, with him there crucified,

---

373. **had,** would have.   383. **capital,** of the head, but with the idea also of "chief."

Never to hurt them more who rightly trust
In this his satisfaction; so he dies,
But soon revives, Death over him no power   420
Shall long usurp; ere the third dawning light
Return, the stars of morn shall see him rise
Out of his grave, fresh as the dawning light,
Thy ransom paid, which Man from Death redeems,
His death for Man, as many as offered life
Neglect not, and the benefit embrace
By faith not void of works. This godlike act
Annuls thy doom, the death thou shouldst have died,
In sin for ever lost from life; this act
Shall bruise the head of Satan, crush his strength   430
Defeating Sin and Death, his two main arms,
And fix far deeper in his head their stings
Than temporal death shall bruise the Victor's heel,
Or theirs whom he redeems, a death like sleep,
A gentle wafting to immortal life.
Nor after resurrection shall he stay
Longer on Earth than certain times to appear
To his disciples, men who in his life
Still followed him; to them shall leave in charge
To teach all nations what of him they learned   440
And his salvation, them who shall believe
Baptizing in the profluent stream, the sign
Of washing them from guilt of sin to life
Pure, and in mind prepared, if so befall,
For death, like that which the Redeemer died.
All nations they shall teach; for from that day
Not only to the sons of Abraham's loins
Salvation shall be preached, but to the sons
Of Abraham's faith wherever through the world;
So in his seed all nations shall be blest.   450
Then to the Heaven of Heavens he shall ascend
With victory, triumphing through the air
Over his foes and thine; there shall surprise
The Serpent, Prince of air, and drag in chains
Through all his realm, and there confounded leave;
Then enter into glory, and resume
His seat at God's right hand, exalted high
Above all names in Heaven; and thence shall come,
When this world's dissolution shall be ripe,
With glory and power to judge both quick and dead,   460
To judge the unfaithful dead, but to reward
His faithful, and receive them into bliss,
Whether in Heaven or Earth, for then the Earth
Shall all be Paradise, far happier place
Than this of Eden, and far happier days."
    So spake the Archangel Michael, then paused,
As at the world's great period; and our Sire

Replete with joy and wonder thus replied.
"O goodness infinite, goodness immense!
That all this good of evil shall produce,   470
And evil turn to good; more wonderful
Than that which by creation first brought forth
Light out of darkness! full of doubt I stand,
Whether I should repent me now of sin
By me done and occasioned, or rejoice
Much more, that much more good thereof shall spring,
To God more glory, more good will to men
From God, and over wrath grace shall abound.
But say, if our Deliverer up to Heaven
Must reascend, what will betide the few   480
His faithful, left among the unfaithful herd,
The enemies of truth; who then shall guide
His people, who defend? will they not deal
Worse with his followers than with him they dealt?"
     "Be sure they will," said the Angel; "but from Heaven
He to his own a Comforter will send,
The promise of the Father, who shall dwell
His Spirit within them, and the law of faith
Working through love, upon their hearts shall write,
To guide them in all truth, and also arm   490
With spiritual armor, able to resist
Satan's assaults, and quench his fiery darts,
What man can do against them, not afraid,
Though to the death, against such cruelties
With inward consolations recompensed,
And oft supported so as shall amaze
Their proudest persecutors. For the Spirit
Poured first on his Apostles, whom he sends
To evangelize the nations, then on all
Baptized, shall them with wondrous gifts endue   500
To speak all tongues, and do all miracles,
As did their Lord before them. Thus they win
Great numbers of each nation to receive
With joy the tidings brought from Heaven: at length
Their ministry performed, and race well run,
Their doctrine and their story written left,
They die; but in their room, as they forewarn,
Wolves shall succeed for teachers, grievous wolves,

473 ff. The paradox which makes the Fall of Man at once the greatest of human calamities and the occasion of man's highest experience of good is a commonplace of Christian thinking.
     508 ff. Wolves shall succeed for teachers. In this review of the perversion of the Church Milton touches on every essential point in the attack of Protestant against Catholic, of Puritan against Anglican. The clergy have substituted "man-made tradition" for the "plain truth of Scripture"; they have sought rank and title instead of imitating the simplicity of the early church; they have invoked secular power for the suppression of dissent; they have taught that authority and not inner conviction should rule the individual in matters of belief, and that salvation may be obtained by ritualistic observance rather than by repentance. Milton had been saying these things more or less all his life.

Who all the sacred mysteries of Heaven
To their own vile advantages shall turn   510
Of lucre and ambition, and the truth
With superstitions and traditions taint,
Left only in those written records pure,
Though not but by the Spirit understood.
Then shall they seek to avail themselves of names,
Places and titles, and with these to join
Secular power, though feigning still to act
By spiritual, to themselves appropriating
The Spirit of God, promised alike and given
To all believers; and from that pretence,   520
Spiritual laws by carnal power shall force
On every conscience; laws which none shall find
Left them enrolled, or what the Spirit within
Shall on the heart engrave. What will they then
But force the Spirit of Grace itself, and bind
His consort Liberty; what but unbuild
His living temples, built by faith to stand,
Their own faith, not another's: for on earth
Who against faith and conscience can be heard
Infallible? yet many will presume: 530
Whence heavy persecution shall arise
On all who in the worship persevere
Of Spirit and Truth; the rest, far greater part,
Will deem in outward rites and specious forms
Religion satisfied; Truth shall retire
Bestuck with slanderous darts, and works of faith
Rarely be found. So shall the world go on,
To good malignant, to bad men benign,
Under her own weight groaning till the day
Appear of respiration to the just,   540
And vengeance to the wicked, at return
Of Him so lately promised to thy aid,
The Woman's Seed, obscurely then foretold,
Now amplier known thy Savior and thy Lord,
Last in the clouds from Heaven to be revealed
In glory of the Father, to dissolve
Satan with his perverted world, then raise
From the conflagrant mass, purged and refined,
New Heavens, new Earth, ages of endless date
Founded in righteousness and peace and love,   550
To bring forth fruits joy and eternal bliss."
    He ended; and thus Adam last replied.
"How soon hath thy prediction, Seer blest,
Measured this transient world, the race of time,
Till time stand fixed: beyond is all abyss,
Eternity, whose end no eye can reach.
Greatly instructed I shall hence depart,
Greatly in peace of thought, and have my fill

Of knowledge, what this vessel can contain;
Beyond which was my folly to aspire. 560
Henceforth I learn, that to obey is best,
And love with fear the only God, to walk
As in his presence, ever to observe
His providence, and on him sole depend,
Merciful over all his works, with good
Still overcoming evil, and by small
Accomplishing great things, by things deemed weak
Subverting worldly strong, and worldly wise
By simply meek; that suffering for truth's sake
Is fortitude to highest victory, 570
And to the faithful death the gate of life;
Taught this by his example whom I now
Acknowledge my Redeemer ever blest."
    To whom thus also the Angel last replied.
"This having learned, thou hast attained the sum
Of wisdom; hope no higher, though all the stars
Thou knew'st by name, and all the ethereal powers,
All secrets of the deep, all Nature's works,
Or works of God in heaven, air, earth, or sea,
And all the riches of this world enjoy'dst, 580
And all the rule, one empire; only add
Deeds to thy knowledge answerable, add faith,
Add virtue, patience, temperance, add love,
By name to come called charity, the soul
Of all the rest: then wilt thou not be loth
To leave this Paradise, but shalt possess
A Paradise within thee, happier far.
Let us descend now therefore from this top
Of speculation; for the hour precise
Exacts our parting hence; and see the guards, 590
By me encamped on yonder hill, expect
Their motion, at whose front a flaming sword,
In signal of remove, waves fiercely round;
We may no longer stay: go, waken Eve;
Her also I with gentle dreams have calmed
Portending good, and all her spirits composed
To meek submission: thou at season fit
Let her with thee partake what thou hast heard,
Chiefly what may concern her faith to know,
The great deliverance by her seed to come 600
(For by the Woman's Seed) on all mankind.
That ye may live, which will be many days,
Both in one faith unanimous though sad,
With cause for evils past, yet much more cheered
With meditation on the happy end."

591–92. expect Their motion, await the moment of moving.

He ended, and they both descend the hill;
Descended, Adam to the bower where Eve
Lay sleeping ran before, but found her waked;
And thus with words not sad she him received.
    "Whence thou return'st, and whither went'st, I know;   610
For God is also in sleep, and dreams advise,
Which he hath sent propitious, some great good
Presaging, since with sorrow and heart's distress
Wearied I fell asleep. But now lead on;
In me is no delay; with thee to go,
Is to stay here; without thee here to stay,
Is to go hence unwilling; thou to me
Art all things under Heaven, all places thou,
Who for my wilful crime art banished hence.
This further consolation yet secure   620
I carry hence; though all by me is lost,
Such favor I unworthy am vouchsafed,
By me the Promised Seed shall all restore."
    So spake our mother Eve, and Adam heard
Well pleased, but answered not; for now too nigh
The Archangel stood, and from the other hill
To their fixed station, all in bright array
The Cherubim descended; on the ground
Gliding meteorous, as evening mist
Risen from a river o'er the marish glides,   630
And gathers ground fast at the laborer's heel
Homeward returning. High in front advanced,
The brandished sword of God before them blazed
Fierce as a comet; which with torrid heat,
And vapor as the Libyan air adust,
Began to parch that temperate clime; whereat
In either hand the hastening angel caught
Our lingering parents, and to the eastern gate
Led them direct, and down the cliff as fast
To the subjected plain; then disappeared.   640
They looking back, all the eastern side beheld
Of Paradise, so late their happy seat,
Waved over by that flaming brand, the gate
With dreadful faces thronged and fiery arms.
Some natural tears they dropped, but wiped them soon;
The world was all before them, where to choose
Their place of rest, and Providence their guide.
They hand in hand with wandering steps and slow,
Through Eden took their solitary way.

    614 ff. Eve's words suggest those of Ruth, "Whither thou goest I will go," but also Andromache's
to Hector in the *Iliad*.

Chronology

❈ THE ANCIENT WORLD

Political and Social Events	*Intellectual and Cultural Events*

B.C.

ca. 2750 Date of possibly historical Gilgamesh
ca. 2100–2000 Empire of Ur
ca. 1830 First dynasty of Babylonian kings begins
13th *c.* Hebrew Exodus from Egypt into Canaan
1193–1184 Trojan War
ca. 1100 Dorians migrate into Peloponnesus
953 Dedication of Temple at Jerusalem

931 Jews split into the Northern Kingdom of Israel and the Southern Kingdom of Judah
826 Founding of Carthage
776 First Olympic games in Greece
753 Traditional date of founding of Rome by Romulus and Remus
750–500 Era of Greek colonization

597 Babylonian captivity of the Jews
6th *c.* Ascendancy of the Persian Empire

538 The Persians under Cyrus capture Babylon and free the Jews

509 Traditional date of the founding of the Roman Republic
490 Athenians defeat Persians at the Battle of Marathon
480 The Greek fleet defeats the Persians at the Battle of Salamis
461–429 The Periclean Age in Athens

431-404 Peloponnesian War and the fall of Athens

336–323 Conquests of Alexander

264–146 Punic Wars
146 Roman conquest of Greece

---

ca. 3000 Bricks first used by Egyptians and Assyrians. Invention of the wheel.
ca. 2700 Egyptian ruler Cheops builds Great Pyramid at Giza
ca. 2500 Early Minoan civilization in Crete
ca. 1860 Construction of Stonehenge begins in Britain
10th *c.* Oral traditions of Jews attain first written form (the J strand); oral epics in circulation among the Greeks

6th *c.* Rise of free statuary and Doric and Ionic temple architecture
586 The piper Sakadas wins the pipe contest at the Greek Pythian games with a piece representing Apollo's fight with a dragon
585 Thales makes the first prediction of a solar eclipse
534 Thespis' dramatic performances in Athens

432 The Parthenon completed
429 The Acropolis completed

399 The death of Socrates

334 Founding of the Library at Alexandria

ca. 150 Frieze from the Altar of Zeus at Pergamon

- *Gilgamesh (ca.* 2000 B.C.)

Old Testament (10th–2nd *c.*)

Homer (8th *c.*)

Sappho (7th–6th *c.*)

Aeschylus (*ca.* 525–456)

Sophocles (496–406)

Euripides (*ca.* 480–406)

Aristophanes (*ca.* 450–*ca.* 386)

Plato (*ca.* 427–*ca.* 348)

Aristotle (384–322)

Political and Social Events	*Intellectual and Cultural Events*
60 First Triumvirate (Pompey, Julius Caesar, Crassus)	
58–50 Caesar's Gallic Wars	
44 Assassination of Caesar	
43 Second Triumvirate (Antony, Octavian, Lepidus)	
27–A.D.14 Augustus Caesar Emperor of Rome	
ca. 4 Birth of Christ	
A.D.	
ca. 29 Crucifixion of Christ	
64 Burning of Rome and first Christian persecutions	
70 Titus, son of Emperor Vespasian, suppresses a Jewish revolt, destroys the Temple at Jerusalem, and massacres and exiles Jews (the *Diaspora,* or Scattering)	70 Colosseum begun at Rome
	81 Arch of Titus completed at Rome
84 Roman conquest of Britain	
	118–126 Construction of the Pantheon at Rome
132 Jews rebel again, recapture Jerusalem, and set up a state of Israel	
135 Jewish revolt crushed; the Final Diaspora	
	211–217 Construction of Roman Baths of Caracalla
250 Decius, Emperor of Rome, makes emperor-worship compulsory and orders persecution of Christians	
286 Emperor Diocletian divides the Empire into Eastern and Western Empires	
323–337 Constantine Emperor in the East. He moves the capital to Constantinople and allows Christianity in the empire	
351 Emperor Julian attempts to reintroduce paganism in place of Christianity	
395 Emperor Theodosius makes Christianity the official religion of Rome	

Catullus (*ca.* 84–*ca.* 54)

Virgil (70–19)

Ovid (43 B.C.–A.D. 17)

New Testament (1st and 2nd *c.*)

Political and Social Events	*Intellectual and Cultural Events*
401 Pope Innocent I claims universal jurisdiction over the Roman Church	
	413 St. Augustine, *The City of God*
	ca. 450 Establishment of the seven liberal arts as regular course of study
476 The end of the Roman Empire	

❦ THE MIDDLE AGES

	527–565 Construction of the Hagia Sophia, Constantinople
622–624 Beginning of Mohammedan Era and Holy War	622 Hegira of Mohammed
711 Conquest of Spain by Arabs	
	ca. 750 Arabic science brought to Europe
768–814 Charlemagne ruler of Franks and Holy Roman Emperor	
9th *c.* Feudal system develops among the Franks and spreads across Europe	9th *c.* Music cultivated in monasteries; development of "sequences" (elaborated passages) in liturgical music
856–875 Vikings overrun England	
	ca. 925 The *Quem Quaeritis* trope, earliest surviving example of the staged sections of the Mass which were to form the basis of medieval drama
	ca. 1025 Guido of Arezzo's earliest writings on the theory of music
1066 Norman conquest of England	
	ca. 1080 The Bayeux Tapestry
	1086 The Domesday Book compiled in England
	1094 Construction begins on St. Mark's Cathedral, Venice
1095–1291 Period of the Crusades	
	1145 Chartres Cathedral begun
	ca. 1150 Troubadours flourish in Provence; rise of universities in Europe; flourishing of scholasticism
	1163 Cornerstone laid for Notre Dame in Paris

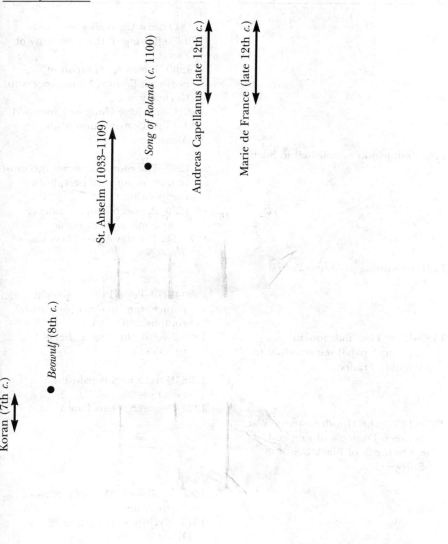

Koran (7th *c.*)

● *Beowulf* (8th *c.*)

St. Anselm (1033–1109)

● *Song of Roland* (*c.* 1100)

Andreas Capellanus (late 12th *c.*)

Marie de France (late 12th *c.*)

Political and Social Events	*Intellectual and Cultural Events*
	1167 Oxford University founded
	1170 Beginning of the University of Paris
	ca. 1200 Trouvères flourish in northern France, Minnesingers in Germany
	1209 Cambridge University founded
	1213–1380 Construction of the Alhambra
1233 Inquisition established in Spain	
	ca. 1240 The motet becomes the most important form of polyphonic composition
	ca. 1250 Period of the *ars antiqua* polyphonic style in music
	1270 St. Thomas Aquinas, *Summa Theologica*
1271 Beginning of Marco Polo's travels	
	1300–1370 Period of *ars nova* in France, the "new art" of musical composition
1309–1378 The "Babylonian Captivity": papal see removed to Avignon, France	1305 Giotto, the Arena chapel frescoes
	1308 Duccio begins painting the Siena panels
	1327 Petrarch meets Laura
1337–1453 The Hundred Years' War between France and England	
1348 Outbreak of Black Death in Europe	
	1360 Guillaume Machaut, Mass of Notre Dame
	1376 Wycliffe's translation of the Bible
	1426 Jan and Hubert Van Eyck begin the Ghent Altarpiece
1431 Joan of Arc burned as a witch	1436 Guillaume Dufay, *Nuper rosarum flores*
	ca. 1450 Ascendancy of humanism in Italy
1453 Fall of Constantinople to Ottoman Turks ends the Byzantine Empire and marks the end of the Middle Ages	

Lives of Authors

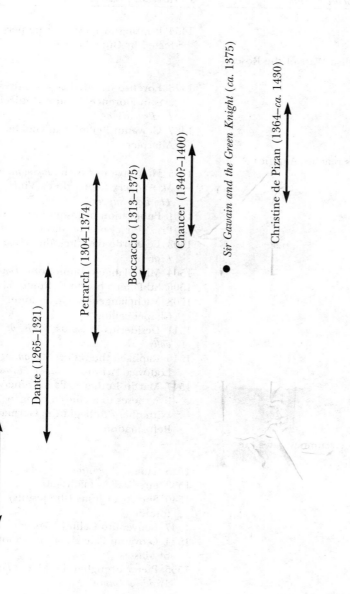

Thomas Aquinas (ca. 1225–1274)

Dante (1265–1321)

Petrarch (1304–1374)

Boccaccio (1313–1375)

Chaucer (1340?–1400)

Sir Gawain and the Green Knight (ca. 1375)

Christine de Pizan (1364–ca. 1430)

❋ THE RENAISSANCE

Political and Social Events	*Intellectual and Cultural Events*
	1454 Printing by movable type perfected by Gutenberg
1455–1485 English Wars of the Roses	
	1478 Lorenzo de' Medici patronizes arts in Florence; Sandro Botticelli, *La Primavera*
	1487 Giovanni Bellini, San Giobbe Altarpiece
1492 Columbus reaches America	
	1495 Hieronymus Bosch, *Temptation of St. Anthony;* Leonardo da Vinci, *The Last Supper*
	1501 Publication of Josquin des Prez's first book of Masses
	1503 Leonardo da Vinci, the *Mona Lisa*
	1504 Michelangelo Buonarotti, *David*
	1506 St. Peter's begun in Rome
	1508 Michelangelo begins Sistine Chapel ceiling
	1511 Desiderius Erasmus, *Praise of Folly*
	1516 Raphael, the *Sistine Madonna;* Lodovico Ariosto, *Orlando Furioso*
	1517 Martin Luther nails his ninety-five theses to a church door in Wittenberg to begin the German Reformation
1522 Magellan circumnavigates the globe	
	1525 Titian, *Deposition*
	1533 First Italian madrigals
	1540 Society of Jesus (the Jesuits) founded
	1547 Benvenuto Cellini, *Perseus*
	1554 Giovanni Palestrina, first book of Masses
	1555 Pieter Breughel the Elder, *The Wedding Dance*
1572 Saint Bartholomew's Day massacre: French Protestants massacred	
	1575–1625 The school of "English virginalist" composers, including William Byrd, Thomas Morley, and Orlando Gibbons
1588 England defeats the invading Spanish Armada	

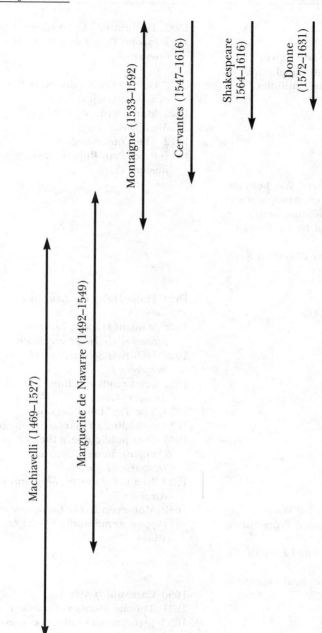

- *Everyman* (late 15th c.)

Machiavelli (1469–1527)

Marguerite de Navarre (1492–1549)

Montaigne (1533–1592)

Cervantes (1547–1616)

Shakespeare 1564–1616

Donne (1572–1631)

Political and Social Events	_Intellectual and Cultural Events_
	1592 Tintoretto, _The Last Supper_
	1597 Jacopo Peri, _Dafne_ (the first
1598 The Edict of Nantes gives	opera)
French Protestants equal political	
rights with Roman Catholics	1602 Galileo Galilei discovers the law
	of falling bodies
	1605 Monteverdi, _Fifth Book of_
	Madrigals
	1612 The Louvre begun
	1614 Peter Paul Rubens, _The Descent_
	from the Cross
1618–1648 Thirty Years' War between	
Catholics and Protestants over suc-	
cession of Holy Roman Empire	
1619 Introduction of Negro slavery	
into America	
1620 Pilgrims land at Plymouth Rock	
	1624 Franz Hals, _The Laughing_
	Cavalier
	1628 William Harvey, _Essay on the_
	Motion of the Heart and Blood
	1629 Heinrich Schütz, _Sacred_
	Symphony I
	1631 Rembrandt van Rijn, _The_
	Anatomy Lesson
	1634 The Taj Mahal begun
	1636 Founding of Harvard College
	1637 First public opera theater
	(Venice); René Descartes,
	Discourse on Method
	1639 Nicholas Poussin, _Shepherds in_
	Arcadia
1642–1660 English Civil War,	1642 Monteverdi, _The Coronation of_
Commonwealth, and Protectorate	_Poppea;_ Rembrandt, _The Night_
	Watch
1643 Louis XIV crowned King of	
France	
1649 Charles I of England executed	
	1650 Carissimi, _Jephta_
	1651 Thomas Hobbes, _Leviathan_
	1653 Jean-Baptiste Lully becomes
	court composer at Paris
1665 Great Plague in London	
1666 Great Fire in London	

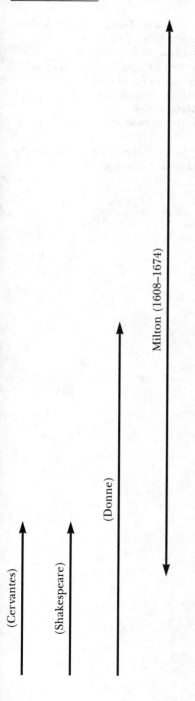

(Cervantes)

(Shakespeare)

(Donne)

Milton (1608–1674)

Political and Social Events	*Intellectual and Cultural Events*
	1667 Giovanni Lorenzo Bernini, colonnade of St. Peter's
	1670 Blaise Pascal, *Pensées*
	1675 Sir Christopher Wren begins St. Paul's Cathedral
	1687 Isaac Newton, *Principia Mathematica*
1689 Peter the Great begins reform and modernization of Russia	1689 Henry Purcell, *Dido and Aeneas*
	1690 John Locke, *An Essay Concerning Human Understanding*
1692 Witchcraft trials at Salem, Massachusetts	

Acknowledgments

Index

Note: First lines of short poems and titles of books of the Bible are in roman type. Titles of long works are in italics. Titles of short works are in italics in the general alphabetical listing but in roman type when listed as sub-entries under their authors' names.

A

The Aeneid, from, 997
AESCHYLUS, 606
  The Oresteia, 609
    Agamemnon, 610
    The Eumenides, 663
    The Libation Bearers, 699
Agamemnon, 610
ALIGHIERI, DANTE. *See* DANTE
    ALIGHERI
All you that hear in scattered
    rhymes the sound, 1766
Amores, from, 1107
The Ancient World,
    Introduction, 1
ANDREAS CAPELLANUS, 1313
  The Art of Courtly Love,
    from, 1316
ANSELM, SAINT, 1364, 1367
  Proslogium, from, 1367
Antigone, 785
The Apology, 942
Apology for Raymond Sebond,
    from, 1872
AQUINAS, SAINT THOMAS, 1364,
    1372
  Summa Theologica, from, 1372
ARISTOPHANES, 869
  Lysistrata, 872
ARISTOTLE, 962

  Poetics, from, 965
Army wife in Sardis, To an, 603
The Art of Courtly Love, from, 1316
As virtuous men pass mildly away,
    2100

B

Batter my heart, three-person'd
    God; for, you, 2104
Beowulf, 1186, 1191
The Bible. *See* THE OLD
    TESTAMENT; THE NEW
    TESTAMENT
Bisclavret (The Werewolf), 1346
Bless the Lord, O my soul, 125
BOCCACCIO, GIOVANNI, 1774
  The Decameron, from, 1776
    The First Day, 1776
    Third Day, Tenth Tale, 1786
    Fourth Day, Second Tale,
      1792
    Fifth Day, Tenth Tale, 1798
    Tenth Day, Tenth Tale, 1804
    Conclusion, from, 1812
The Book of the City of Ladies,
    from, 1703
By the rivers of Babylon, there we
    sat down, 127